The Sexual Exploitation
of Children

The Sexual Exploitation of Children

Michael T. Flannery
Associate Dean for Faculty Development
Judge George Howard, Jr. Distinguished Professor of Law
University of Arkansas at Little Rock
William H. Bowen School of Law

Raymond C. O'Brien
Professor of Law
The Catholic University of America
Columbus School of Law

Carolina Academic Press
Durham, North Carolina

ISBN: 978-1-61163-540-9
LCCN: 2015953055

Carolina Academic Press, LLC
700 Kent Street
Durham, North Carolina 27701
Telephone (919) 489-7486
Fax (919) 493-5668
www.cap-press.com

Printed in the United States of America

The weak can never forgive. Forgiveness is the attribute of the strong.
—Mahatma Gandhi

To: John Doe
I forgive you.

MTF

To: Francis Xavier O'Neil
Faithful in constancy, a witness

ROB

Summary of Contents

Contents

Table of Cases

Principal cases are in **bold** type. Non-principal cases are in roman type. References are to pages.

Table of Web-Based Resources

Acquaintance Exploiters

United States Department of Justice, The National Strategy for Child Exploitation Prevention and Interdiction Report to Congress, Aug. 2010, http://www.justice.gov/psc/docs/nat strategyreport.pdf

Charitable Immunity

Stephen J. Riccardulli, Michael D. Dillon, and Amy S. Beard, *Tort Liability of Religious Organizations*, available at http://www.americanbar.org/newsletter/publications/law_trends_news_practice_area_e_newsletter_home/litigation_runquist.html (2009)

Child Sex Trafficking

Polaris Project, *2014 State Ratings on Human Trafficking Laws*, available at http://www.polarisproject.org/what-we-do/policy-advocacy/national-policy/state-ratings-on-human-trafficking-laws

Polaris Project, *Trafficking Victims' Protection Act (TVPA) — Fact Sheet*, available at http://www.rescue.org/sites/default/files/resource-file/trafficking%20victims%20protection%20act%20fact%20sheet_0.pdf

The Optional Protocol to the United Nations Convention on the Rights of the Child on the Sale of Children, Child Prostitution, and Child Pornography, available at http://www.ohchr.org/Documents/ProfessionalInterest/crc-sale.pdf (2002)

The White House, Coordination, Collaboration, Capacity: Federal Strategic Plan on Service for Victims of Human Trafficking in the United States 2013-2017 (2013), available at http://www.ovc.gov/pubs/FederalHuman TraffickingStrategicPlan.pdf

Civil Commitment

National Conference of State Legislatures, *Sex Offender Enactments Database*, available at http://www.ncsl.org/research/civil-and-criminal-justice/sex-offender-enactments-database.aspx (last updated Dec. 2014) (including current legislative updates since 2008)

National District Attorneys Association, Civil Commitment of Sex Offenders, available at http://www.ndaa.org/pdf/Sex%20Offender%20Civil%20Commitment-April%20 2012.pdf

Commercial Market for Children

National Center for Missing & Exploited Children, *Commercial Sexual Exploitation of Children: A Fact Sheet*, available at http://www.missingkids.com/en_US/documents/ CCSE_Fact_Sheet.pdf

Congresswoman Ann Wagner, 2nd District of Missouri, *Human Trafficking & Online Prostitution Advertising*, available at http://wagner.house.gov/Human%20Trafficking %20%26%20Online%20Prostitution%20Advertising

Dating Exploitation

Guttmacher Institute, *American Teens' Sexual and Reproductive Health, Fact Sheet*, at 1 (May 2014), available at www.guttmacher.org

Geoffrey Simpson, *19-Year-Old Jailed, Put on Sex Offender List for Having Consensual Sex With Girl Who Lied About Age on 'Hook-Up App'*, available at http://latest.com/ 2015/06/19-year-old-jailed-put-on-sex-offender-list-for-having-consensual-sex-with-girl-who-lied-about-age-on-hook-up-app/ (June 18, 2015)

Educational Institutions

Report of the Special Investigative Counsel Regarding the Actions of the Pennsylvania State University Related to the Child Sexual Abuse Committed by Gerald A. Sandusky, available at http://www.nytimes.com/interactive/2012/07/12/sports/ncaafootball/13pennstate-document.html?_r=0

Sandusky Grand Jury Presentment, available at http://www.washingtonpost.com/wp-srv/sports/documents/sandusky-grand-jury-report11052011.html

Female Exploiters

Helena Andrews, *Molly Shattuck pleads guilty to the rape of a 15-year-old*, available at http://www.washingtonpost.com/blogs/reliable-source/wp/2015/06/16/molly-shattuck-pleads-guilty-to-the-rape-of-a-15-year-old/

Helen Freund, *Destrehan High School teacher Shelley Dufresne had 'prior sexual encounters' with student, police say*, available at http://www.nola.com/crime/index.ssf/2014/10/ destrehan_high_school_teacher_1.html

Josh Gardner, *'She doesn't deserve to be here': Teacher 'who had sex with three students' is defended by VICTIM in court as judge says she'll stand trial for continuing relations with 17-year-old while she was on bail*, available at http://www.dailymail.co.uk/news/ article-2912771/She-doesn-t-deserve-Teacher-sex-three-students-defended-victim-judge-says-ll-stand-trial-continued-relations-17-year-old.html

Rebecca A. Geddes, Graham A. Tyson & Scott McGreal, *Gender Bias in the Education System: Perceptions of Teacher-Student Sexual Relationships*, Psychiatry, Psychology and Law, available at http://dx.doi.org/10.1080/13218719.2012.728428

Jeffrey Kofman, *Double Standard in LaFave Case?*, available at http://abcnews.go.com/ GMA/LegalCenter/story?id=1752245&page=1

Kevin Troy Reneau, *Framing the Catholic Church: The New York Times Coverage of the Catholic Church 2006–2011*, available at https://mospace.umsystem.edu/xmlui/handle/10355/14565

Punitive Damages

American Tort Reform Association, *Punitive Damages Reform*, available at http://www.atra .org/issues/punitive-damages-reform

Aimee Green, *Portland jury awards $18.5 million in punitive damages in Boy Scout sexual-abuse case*, THE OREGONIAN, Apr. 23, 2010, available at http://www.oregonlive.com/portland/index.ssf/2010/04/jury_awards_millions_in_punati.html

Sexual Abuse Civil Lawsuits That Have Gone to Trial, available at http://www.bishop-ac countability.org/legal/civil_trials.htm

Religious Institutions

Amy Julia Harris, The Center for Investigative Reporting, *Catholic diocese declare bankruptcy on eve of sexual abuse trials*, available at http://www.revealnews.org/article/catholic-dioceses-declare-bankruptcy-on-eve-of-sexual-abuse-trials/ (Feb. 2, 2015)

Michael Paulson, *World doesn't share US view of scandal*, BOST. GLOBE, Apr. 8, 2002, at A1, available at http://www.pulitzer.org/archives/6741

Sexual Abuse by U.S. Catholic Clergy Settlements and Monetary Awards in Civil Suits, available at http://www.bishop-accountability.org/settlements/

Mitch Smith, *Catholic Archdiocese in Minnesota Charged Over Sex Abuse by Priest*, N.Y. TIMES, June 5, 2015, available at http://www.nytimes.com/2015/06/06/us/catholic-archdiocese-in-minnesota-charged-over-sex-abuse-by-priest.html

Mitch Smith and Laurie Goodstein, *2 Bishops Resign in Minnesota Over Sexual Abuse Scandal*, N.Y. TIMES, June 15, 2015, available at http://www.nytimes.com/2015/06/15/us/archbishop-nienstedt-and-aide-resign-in-minnesota-over-sex-abuse-scandal.html?_r=0

United States Conference of Catholic Bishops, *Charter for the Protection of Children and Young People*, available at http://www.usccb.org/issues-and-action/child-and-youth-protection/charter.cfm (June 2002)

United States Conference of Catholic Bishops and The John Jay College of Criminal Justice, *The Nature and Scope of Sexual Abuse of Minors by Catholic Priests and Deacons in the United States 1950-2002*, available at http://www.bishop-accountability .org/reports/2004_02_27_JohnJay_revised/2004_02_27_John_Jay_Main_Report_ Optimized.pdf

Pat Wingert, *Priests Commit No More Abuse Than Other Males*, NEWSWEEK, Apr. 7, 2010, available at http://www.newsweek.com/priests-commit-no-more-abuse-other-males-70625

Reporting Requirements

Child Welfare Information Gateway, *Mandatory Reporters of Child Abuse and Neglect*, available at https://www.childwelfare.gov/pubpdfs/manda.pdf (current through Nov. 2013)

Child Welfare Information Gateway, *Penalties for Failure to Report and False Reporting of Child Abuse and Neglect*, available at https://www.childwelfare.gov/pubPDFs/report.pdf (current through Nov. 2013)

Sentencing

United States Sentencing Commission, *2014 USSC Guidelines Manual*, available at http://www.ussc.gov/guidelines-manual/2014/2014-ussc-guidelines-manual
United States Sentencing Commission, *Report to the Congress: Federal Child Pornography Offenses*, available at http://www.ussc.gov/news/congressional-testimony-and-reports/sex-offense-topics/report-congress-federal-child-pornography-offenses (Dec. 2012)

Sexting

Kimberly J. Mitchell, David Finkelhor, Lisa M. Jones, and Janis Wolak, *Prevalence and Characteristics of Youth Sexting: A National Study*, available at http://pediatrics.aap publications.org/content/early/2011/11/30/peds.2011-1730
Mobile Media Guard, U.S. Sexting Laws, available at http://mobilemediaguard.com/state_main.html
Janis Wolak, David Finkelhor and Kimberly Mitchell, *How Often Are Teens Arrested for Sexting? Data From a National Sample of Police Cases*, available at http://pediatrics.aap publications.org/content/early/2011/11/30/peds.2011-2242

Sextortion

Alabama predator sentenced to 18 years for Facebook extortion attempts: How he got access, available at http://blog.al.com/spotnews/2009/04/auburn_alabama_predator_senten.html (Apr. 17, 2009)
The Amanda Todd Story, available at http://nobullying.com/amanda-todd-story/
College Student is Sentenced for 'Sextortion', available at http://www.thedailybeast.com/articles/2014/03/18/college-student-is-sentenced-for-sextortion.html (Mar. 18, 2014)
Experts increasingly worried about 'sextortion' of minors online, available at http://www.nbc-news.com/news/other/experts-increasingly-worried-about-sextortion-minors-on line-f6C10645107 (July 16, 2013)
FBI Report, A Case of 'Sextortion,' available at http://www.fbi.gov/news/stories/2013/february/sextortion-cons-like-bieber-ruse-targeted-minor-girls/sextortion-cons-like-bieber-ruse-targeted-minor-girls
Police break up global webcam 'sextortion' ring, available at http://www.theverge.com/2014/5/2/5674294/police-break-up-global-webcam-sextortion-ring-philippines (May 2, 2014)
Richard Finkbiner, Indiana 'Sextortionist,' Sentenced To 40 Years For Webcam Sex Offenses, available at http://www.huffingtonpost.com/2013/06/26/richard-finkbiner-indiana-sentenced-sextortionist_n_3504094.html (June 26, 2013)
'Sextortion' is an online 'epidemic' against children, available at http://www.usatoday .com/story/news/nation/2014/07/01/sextortion-teens-online/11580633/ (July 2, 2014)
Suffolk boy, 13, charged in alleged "sextortion" case, available at http://hampton roads.com/2014/05/suffolk-boy-13-charged-alleged-sextortion-case (May 28, 2014)

Update on Sextortion at Eisenhower High, available at http://www.gq.com/news-politics/big-issues/201002/wisconsin-high-school-sex-scandal-update (Feb. 26, 2010)

Social Institutions

Patrick Boyle, *Scouting's sex abuse trail leads to 50 states*, WASH. TIMES, May 20, 1991, available at http://www.newsline.umd.edu/Boyle/shonor1.htm

Calif. attorney seeks to use 'perversion' files in Boy scout sex abuse trial, available at http://www.chicagotribune.com/news/nationworld/chi-perversion-files-boy-scout-sex-abuse-trial-20150108-story.html (Jan. 8, 2015)

Tracking decades of allegations in the boy scouts, available at http://spreadsheets.latimes.com/boyscouts-cases/

U.S. Department of Health and Human Services, Centers for Disease Control and Prevention, National Center for Injury Prevention and Control, Janet Saul and Natalie C. Audage, *Preventing Child Sexual Abuse Within Youth-Serving Organizations: Getting Started on Policies and Procedures* (2007), available at http://www.cdc.gov/violenceprevention/pdf/PreventingChildSexualAbuse-a.pdf

Statute of Limitations

Professor Marci A. Hamilton, www.sol-reform.com

National Conference of State Legislatures, *State Civil Statutes of Limitations in Child Sexual Abuse Cases*, available at http://www.ncsl.org/research/human-services/state-civil-statutes-of-limitations-in-child-sexua.aspx

National District Attorneys Association, *Statutes of Limitation for Civil Action for Offenses Against Children Compilation*, available at http://www.ndaa.org/pdf/Statutes%20of%20Limitations%20for%20Civil%20Actions%20for%20Offenses%20Against%20Children%20(2013%20Update).pdf

National District Attorneys Association, *Statutes of Limitation for Prosecution of Offenses Against Children*, available at http://www.ndaa.org/pdf/Statute%20of%20Limitations%20for%20Prosecution%20of%20Offenses%20Against%20Children%202012.pdf (Aug. 2012)

Rape, Abuse & Incest National Network, *Statutes of Limitations*, available at https://apps.rainn.org/CrimeDef/landing-page-statutes.cfm

Statutes of Limitations for Sexual Assault: A State-by-State Comparison, available at http://victimsofcrime.org/docs/DNA%20Resource%20Center/sol-for-sexual-assault-check-chart---final---copy.pdf?sfvrsn=2

Stranger Exploiters

National Sex Offender Public Website, *Facts and Statistics*, available at http://www.nsopw.gov/(X(1)S(4nlx2gubapqca532iei00ueq))/en/Education/FactsStatistics?AspxAutoDetectCookieSupport=1

Preface

The sexual exploitation of a child is distinct from neglect, abandonment, or physical and emotional abuse of a child. Nonetheless, because of the elusive definition of sexual exploitation, these other types of abuse may exist concomitantly, often masking the sexual motivation of the perpetrator. State and federal legislatures struggle with defining sexual exploitation in a manner sufficient to safeguard the due process rights of a child, as well as an alleged perpetrator, and enforce the state's obligation to provide for the liberty interests of its citizens. Commentators and drafters of legislation have fashioned more precise and usable definitions of child sexual exploitation that increasingly look to the interaction between the alleged perpetrator and the child. But the character and nature of sexual exploitation of children continues to change, heightened by Internet technology. The reason for this casebook is to provide current resources to permit classroom discussion, thus permitting a measure of consensus and a basis for response in the future.

Chapter One explores the unique dynamics of the relationship between the exploiter and the exploited. Although more than a quarter of all child sexual exploitation supposedly occurs in the child's home at the hands of a parent or someone known to the parent, the familial setting is merely one context in which sexual exploitation of a child is commonly facilitated. But those who exploit in other contexts demonstrate common characteristics that identify one as an exploiter — most commonly these are the characteristics of a "pedophile." Chapter One demonstrates that pedophilic tendencies may be exhibited not just by common stereotypes, but by family members, acquaintances, strangers, females, authority figures, and even other children. All of these relationships, as they bear on the exploitation of children, are explored in Chapter One. Information about the developmental effect of sexual exploitation of children has altered the portrayal of pedophiles within these roles and has changed public perception of the state's response to the issue. The result has been the development and expansion of sex offender registries, mandatory reporting requirements, and increased criminal and civil penalties.

Chapter Two explores more specifically the nature of sexual exploitation and the variety of forms in which it may be perpetrated. Drawing a distinction between sexual abuse and sexual exploitation, Chapter Two explores the specific conduct that may qualify one's actions as sexually abusive or exploitative. Often, common activities that typically do not introduce criminal or civil liability, such as dating between two persons, or mutual bonding and nurturing between two consenting individuals, may qualify as sexually culpable behavior when occurring within a relationship involving a minor. Even without sexual contact, the mere "grooming" of a child with sexual intent may be exploitative. Likewise, liability may be introduced without any physical contact at all, such as for those who permit a child to be exploited by others, entice a child to engage in sexually explicit conduct, or engage in their own sexual activity using a child as an object of their sexual intent, such as by a voyeur or an exhibitionist. Additionally, Internet technology allows for greater and more private sexual access to children, thereby obfuscating the parameters of what conduct qualifies as sexually exploitative. Legislative efforts to clarify the definition of sexual exploitation in the face of modern technology have spawned new crimes, such as "sexting" and "sextortion." These also will be explored in Chapter Two.

Chapters Three and Four more fully explore the commercial aspects of child sexual exploitation. Chapter Three addresses the Internet as a resource for fulfilling sexually exploitative tendencies, specifically those involving the production, receipt, possession, and distribution of child pornography. Federal and state efforts to combat child pornography, historically, have been merely responsive to the ever-increasing accessibility, affordability, and anonymity of a global Internet. The existing jurisdictional rules of commerce have expanded significantly to accommodate the global reach of the Internet, as legislatures and courts continue to define the parameters of Internet child pornography. Chapter Four explores the more specific commercial markets that foster the exploitation of children—sex trafficking and prostitution, both of which have taken on local, national, and international aspects.

Chapter Five provides material pertinent to the mandated reporting of suspected child sexual exploitation. Commentary on sexual exploitation has shifted from conceptualizing the abuser as ill and in need of treatment to concluding that the exploiter is a criminal who warrants punishment. The developmental effect of sexual exploitation upon children has changed public perception, and with the change in public perception has come the expansion of mandated reporting requirements, balanced with issues of immunity for reporting in good faith and the application of professional privileges. Often, the success of reporting requirements is judged not by the criminal prosecution of those who fail to report, but by the civil liability for damages that result from such a failure. All of these issues are tempered by the applicable statute of limitations in any given jurisdiction. Nevertheless, reasonable suspicion—reported or not—is the first step. The attendant publicity of civil negligence suits brought against persons or organizations who knew or should have known of existing abuse and then failed to stop the abuse, serve to educate and motivate reporting of suspected abuse. Compensation to victims has been significant; this is a recent development in the law applicable to the sexual exploitation of children.

Chapter Six explores the evidentiary issues related to the sexual exploitation of children. Proof of sexual exploitation is as elusive as defining the conduct precipitating the report. Corroboration by an adult is often lacking, and physical evidence of the abuse is often absent as well. Legislatures and courts struggle with the constitutional limits of investigation and prosecution, particularly as related to the due process interests involving the search of one's home and computers for evidence of child pornography or other evidence of sexual exploitation. Likewise, testimony from the child can be influenced by fear and intimidation, and testimony by adults many years after the alleged incidents can be barred by statutes of limitations or faulty recollections. Because the majority of abuse occurs in the home by relatives of persons known to the parents, issues of privacy, immunity, and coercion abound. Courts and legislatures have sought to arrive at the truth of the allegations by accommodating constitutional safeguards, permitting testimony by minors to be obtained in a manner less than public, or by employing syndrome evidence suggesting that exploitation may have occurred. An example would be the Child Sexual Abuse Accommodation Syndrome (CSAAS).

Investigative and evidentiary issues lay the foundation for Chapter Seven, which governs the criminal and civil liability for the sexual exploitation of children. The changing public perception of sexual abuse has led to reformation of the applicable statute of limitations for raising both criminal and civil claims. Criminal liability for sexual exploitation culminates in an expansive patchwork of sentencing variables, grounded in a predetermined window of incarceration designated for each crime. Considerations of proportionate sentencing, special circumstances, and volitional enhancements are determinative of outcomes and serve to shape public perceptions. In turn, public perceptions serve to introduce expansive sentencing conditions, such as limitations on computer use, satellite monitoring, and public registration requirements. Public perception has equally influenced civil liability, especially with respect to expansive terms of commitment beyond incarceration and restitution for victims of sexual exploitation.

Chapter Eight addresses the institutional exploitation of children and the liability that accompanies the fiduciary obligations of institutional authorities to report abuse. The multiple instances of sexual exploitation of a child are horrific—shockingly so. Then too, the emotional and physical consequences are long-lasting and often insurmountable. Organizations that became implicated in failure to report suspicions of sexual exploitation have been handicapped by ongoing judgments, both in monetary terms and in the courts of public opinion. There has been a massive shift in attitude towards the sexual exploitation of minors, just as there was with gender equality, personal privacy, and domestic violence.

This casebook seeks to assemble the law pertaining to the sexual exploitation of children as it exists today. This is a pivotal time. Undoubtedly, the influence of attorneys, judges, and legislators will formulate future responses to exploitative conduct. Certainly, if more is known about the issues, those responsible for the protection of children may be better equipped to manifest a more comprehensive response.

Note on Editing

Some text, footnotes, and citations have been edited to make the cases we have included more manageable and relevant to the teaching tool applicable to a three- or four-credit course. The footnotes that are included contain the original footnote numbers from the original source. All omissions are indicated with an appropriate ellipses symbol to indicate that material has been omitted.

The Sexual Exploitation
of Children

Chapter One

The Exploiter and the Exploited

I. Defining the Parameters of Child Sexual Exploitation

Adair v. State of Texas

Court of Appeals of Texas, 2013
2013 WL 6665033

BOB PEMBERTON, Justice.

A jury convicted appellant Thomas H. Adair, Sr., of two counts of the offense of aggravated sexual assault of a child. *See* Tex. Penal Code § 22.021. For each count, punishment was assessed at ten years' imprisonment and a $10,000 fine, but the district court suspended imposition of each sentence and placed Adair on community supervision for five years....

The jury heard evidence that Adair had sexually assaulted his granddaughter, G.T., who was 15 years old at the time of trial. G.T. testified that, when she was approximately five years old, Adair began touching her "in not so public places." G.T. explained that "it started one day when we were in the pool and he was going to throw me, like, into the water, and when he was picking me up he put his hand underneath my bathing suit bottoms and started touching me." G.T. specified that Adair touched the inside of her sexual organ using his fingers. After that, G.T. testified, "it happened almost every time we went swimming together." According to G.T., the "touching" was not limited to digital penetration. She explained that, one day, while Adair was babysitting G.T. at his house, he entered the room where she was playing video games, closed the door, got lubricant out of a cabinet, and then, in G.T.'s words, "[H]e got on the bed and knelt at my feet and pulled my pants down, and I think he just unzipped his, and then he put the lube on my vagina and he put his penis in my vagina." Afterwards, G.T. testified, Adair made her promise not to tell her grandmother, telling her, "This is our little secret." G.T. explained that this was the only time that Adair "put [his] penis in [her] vagina," but she also described other incidents when Adair had either attempted to engage or actually did engage in sexual conduct with her. G.T. eventually told her eight-year-old brother what was happening to her, but "He just kind of waved me off and didn't believe me." G.T. further testified that when she was nine years old, during another incident at the swimming pool, she told Adair to stop or else she would tell her grandmother. After that, G.T. recounted, Adair stopped, and the abuse ended.

3

Approximately two years after the abuse ended, G.T. made an outcry to her mother, Shelli Miller. Miller testified that during an argument with her daughter, G.T. had told her, "You've never been raped by your grandfather." Miller asked G.T. to specify the grandfather to which she was referring, and G.T. told her that it was Adair, who was also Miller's father. Miller then proceeded to call her mother, Paula Adair, told Paula what G.T. had said, and then listened as Paula told Adair what Miller had told her. Miller did not know what Adair said in response but "heard him get upset." Miller then ended the call with Paula and called the Bastrop County Sheriff's Department, who told her to have G.T. write a statement describing the abuse. Miller asked G.T. to do so, and G .T. complied. The handwritten statement, which was admitted into evidence, contained the following: "From the age of 5 to 9. In the pool, in the music room, in the barn, in [Adair's] room. I told him no and I told him to stop. I snuck out one time so he couldn't do it."

While waiting for the police to arrive, Miller called Paula again and had a second conversation with her. Paula told Miller to ask G.T. questions about what had happened, and Miller proceeded to do so. Miller asked G.T. if it was "a full blown rape," to which G.T. responded, "Yes, it was a full blown rape." When this response was conveyed to Paula, Miller could hear Adair reply, in the background, "I never full blown raped that child." Shortly thereafter, Miller told Paula that she was "going to press charges" against Adair, and the conversation ended.... The case was investigated by Detective Joel Wade of the Bastrop County Sheriff's Department. Wade arranged for G.T. to be interviewed at the Children's Advocacy Center, and he observed the interview. Wade also interviewed Miller, obtained information from her regarding G.T.'s outcry, and then arranged for a sexual-assault examination to be performed on G.T. After that, Wade arranged a non-custodial interview with Adair, which we discuss in more detail as it becomes relevant to Adair's first and fourth issues on appeal, and an interview with Paula.... The interview of G.T. at the Children's Advocacy Center was conducted by forensic interviewer Mindy Graber. Graber testified that G.T. described the abuse to her (again using the word "rape" to describe what had happened), identified on a diagram the body parts that were involved, identified "Tom Adair" as the perpetrator, and indicated that the abuse had started when G.T. was five and continued until she was nine. G.T. also described Adair's body position during the rape as "lying on top of her" and further specified that Adair had taken off his clothes and her clothes. G.T. added that "sometimes it hurt when he did it and sometimes it didn't hurt, and that it burned when she peed but usually a couple of hours after that it would stop."

The physical exam of G.T. was performed by Kassy Havel, a sexual assault nurse examiner. Havel testified that G.T. described the alleged abuse to her in detail, including identifying Adair as the perpetrator, the manner in which he had abused her, and the time period during which the abuse had occurred. During the exam, Havel observed no trauma to G.T.'s genitals. Dr. Beth Nauert, a pediatrician and expert in the area of child sexual abuse, reviewed Havel's report. Dr. Nauert testified that there was nothing in Havel's report that she found to be unusual and that she agreed with Havel's findings. Nauert further testified that when a physical examination is not performed until two years after penetration has occurred, "most likely ... the examination of the child is going to be normal," with no signs of injury or trauma to the child's sexual organ.... The State also called Dr. William Carter, a psychologist in private practice with expertise in the area of child sexual abuse, whose testimony we discuss in more detail as it becomes relevant to Adair's third issue on appeal. During his testimony, Carter answered a series of hypothetical questions concerning the psychological and behavioral patterns often observed in the victims and perpetrators of child sexual abuse. The hypothetical questions closely mirrored the allegations in this case.... The defense called two witnesses. Patricia Crane, a sexual assault nurse examiner, testified that she had reviewed Havel's report and concluded that there was "no physical evidence of sexual assault." The other witness, J.S., a former childhood friend of G.T., testified without elaboration that G.T. "was a liar."

The jury found Adair guilty as charged and assessed punishment as noted above. The district court sentenced Adair in accordance with the jury's verdict. Adair subsequently filed a motion for new trial in which he alleged, among other grounds, that the jury verdict had not been unanimous. Following a hearing, the district court denied the motion for new trial. This appeal followed.... [Discussion of issues of jury unanimity and admissibility of evidence related to pre-arrest interview with police is omitted].

Adair first asserts that trial counsel should have objected to testimony by Dr. Carter relating to the characteristics of child victims of sexual abuse. Carter testified that "about 80 to 90 percent of the time" in child-sex-abuse cases, there is "a pre-existing relationship" between the perpetrator and the child. This relationship, Carter explained, makes it difficult for the child to tell others about the abuse, particularly when the perpetrator is a close family member such as a grandfather. Carter also testified that if the victim first reports the abuse to a child sibling, and if the sibling does not believe the victim or refuses to say anything to adults, this causes the victim to feel helpless and discourages her from telling others. Carter further opined that if the victim eventually told her grandfather to stop, and if he stopped, the victim might think that the abuse is over, try to move on with her life, and not talk about the abuse again until years later. When the victim does decide to talk about the abuse, Carter added, she might have difficulty remembering the details of what had happened and might also experience difficulty in testifying about the abuse in court. Carter also testified that when the victim first reports the abuse to another child, it is less likely that the child is lying on behalf of an adult. Finally, the State asked Carter the following question: "Is it possible to conclude from the research that you have familiarized yourself with that when a child says that she's been abused that there is a distinct possibility that she has been abused?" Carter answered, "Yes, that's certainly a very real possibility." In Adair's view, the above testimony was tantamount to testifying that the victim was telling the truth.... –

Carter was asked to describe how a hypothetical perpetrator would behave in response to the victim not reporting the abuse. Carter testified that such an abuser would "feel emboldened," think that he was "getting away with it," and would be encouraged to continue the abuse. Counsel did not object to this testimony, and Adair asserts that counsel should have objected that Carter was not qualified to render an opinion on the matter. Carter was later asked to opine on the meaning of a statement by a hypothetical perpetrator, in response to being confronted regarding the abuse, that he "didn't full blown rape the child." Carter testified that he would find such a statement "to be interesting" and "would question the acknowledgment of at least something happening on the part of the accused." Counsel objected to this testimony on the basis that it misstated the evidence (which the district court overruled), but Adair asserts on appeal that counsel should have further objected on the basis that Carter was not qualified to "read Thomas Adair's mind and render a conclusion as [to] what Mr. Adair meant if he in fact made the statement." ...

During jury selection, the prosecutor showed the venire a photograph of an unnamed individual. The prosecutor then identified the individual as serial killer Ted Bundy and proceeded to question the panel as to whether they could tell "from looking at the picture that he was a serial killer." The prosecutor subsequently asked the panel questions regarding what "child molesters" look like, concluding with the following: "Is there anyone here who believes that people of a certain category, certain occupation, certain gender, certain sociable status, certain religious beliefs, that they could never sexually assault a child?

Can you think of any examples? Policemen would never do that. Priests never would do that." Adair characterizes the prosecutor's use of the photograph and questioning of the venire as "comparing Adair to Ted Bundy" and claims that trial counsel was ineffective in failing to object to that characterization.

We disagree. In contending that the prosecutor's conduct was impermissible, Adair cites to cases in which courts have held that it is improper, during closing argument, for the State to compare the defendant to notorious criminals. *See, e.g., Gonzalez v. State*, 115 S.W.3d 278, 284–85 (Tex.App.–Corpus Christi 2003, pet. ref'd) (comparing defendant to Osama bin Laden); *Brown v. State*, 978 S.W.2d 708, 714 (Tex.App.–Amarillo 1998, pet. ref'd) (comparing defendant to Jeffrey Dahmer, John Wayne Gacy, and Ted Bundy); *Stell v. State*, 711 S.W.2d 746, 748–49 (Tex.App.–Corpus Christi 1986, no pet.) (comparing defendant to Lee Harvey Oswald). The rationale is that such arguments are based on evidence outside the record. *See Gonzalez*, 115 S.W.3d at 284. "The purpose of closing argument is to facilitate the jury in properly analyzing the evidence presented at trial so that it may 'arrive at a just and reasonable conclusion based on the evidence alone, and not on any fact not admitted in evidence.'" *Campbell v. State*, 610 S.W.2d 754, 756 (Tex.Crim.App.1980) (quoting *Stearn v. State*, 487 S.W.2d 734, 736 (Tex.Crim.App.1972)). Thus, if the prosecutor had compared Adair to Ted Bundy during closing argument, that might have been the basis for a legitimate objection by counsel.

In this case, however, we are dealing with jury selection, not jury argument. The purpose of voir dire is different than the purpose of argument. Voir dire encompasses at least three objectives: (1) to elicit information that would establish a basis for a challenge for cause because the venireman is legally disqualified from serving or is biased or prejudiced for or against one of the parties or some aspect of the relevant law; (2) to facilitate the intelligent use of peremptory challenges that may be "exercised without a reason stated, without inquiry and without being subject to the court's control"; and (3) to indoctrinate the jurors on the party's theory of the case and to establish rapport with the prospective jury members. *See Sanchez v. State*, 165 S.W.3d 707, 710–11 (Tex.Crim.App.2005). Here, part of the State's theory of the case was that Adair, the victim's grandfather, was capable of sexually assaulting his granddaughter, despite his appearance and familial status. Thus, it would not fall below an objective standard of reasonableness for counsel to conclude that the prosecutor's questioning was a permissible attempt to use a photograph of Bundy to illustrate that appearances can be deceiving, and to attempt to discern the panel's views on that and other issues applicable to the case. *See Wingo v. State*, 189 S.W.3d 270, 271 (Tex.Crim.App.2006) ("A question may be proper if it seeks to discover a juror's views on an issue applicable to the case."). Additionally, counsel could have had a strategic reason for not objecting. Specifically, counsel, too, might have wanted to know how the venire would respond to the prosecutor's reference to Bundy so that counsel could intelligently exercise her peremptory challenges. Accordingly, we cannot conclude that counsel was ineffective in declining to object to the prosecutor's questioning. We overrule Adair's third issue....

We affirm the judgments of the district court.

Notes

The *Adair* case presents a common factual scenario that will be presented throughout this casebook—the sexual exploitation of a child. As evidenced by the issues raised in *Adair*, and the broad spectrum of legal issues presented throughout this casebook, the sexual exploitation of children may be perpetrated by anyone, against any child, and in a variety of contexts. The legal context addressed by the *Adair* court is the ineffective assistance of counsel. But within that context, the court grapples with the fact that experts are now able to identify common characteristics of both victims and perpetrators of child sexual exploitation. For victims—the exploited—this may include typical disclosure behaviors, responsive defense mechanisms, and other behavioral cues. For perpetrators—the exploiters—this may include common responses to the exploited and their families, decisions to continue or discontinue perpetrating the abuse, and other defensive behavioral posturing. The *Adair* case and the related commentaries in this section present some of these common characteristics shared by the exploited and the exploiters. The legal issue of whether such evidence may be admitted in court in the prosecutorial process is addressed more specifically in Chapter Six, Evidence of Sexual Exploitation. However, identifying and understanding some of the common characteristics of the exploited and the exploiters will help define the broad parameters within which the sexual exploitation of children takes place.

A. The Exploited

Ryan C. W. Hall and Richard C. W. Hall

A Profile of Pedophilia: Definition, Characteristics of Offenders,
Recidivism, Treatment Outcomes, and Forensic Issues

82 Mayo Clin. Proc. 457 (2007)

Pedophiles may target certain types of families when looking for children to abuse. [One] study ... noted that the parents of children who had been abused by pedophiles had notable characteristics, such as a lower overall education and a higher rate of absenteeism from home. The mothers of abused children had less education than control group mothers and were more likely to be single parents. A significant number of fathers in the molested group were absent for at least 3 years before the child turned 16 years old. The fathers themselves tended to be of lower socioeconomic and educational levels than controls, but this finding was not statistically significant probably because a substantial amount of data were missing concerning the absentee fathers.... Similar findings occurred in [another] study ... in which pedophiles were interviewed about how they selected the children they abused. The pedophiles stated they would choose vulnerable individuals (eg, children living in a divorced home, emotionally needy or unhappy children) and/or children who were receptive to their advances, even if that child did not meet the pedophile's usual physical pattern of attraction....

Generally, abused children experience the greatest psychological damage when the abuse occurs from father figures (close neighbors, priests or ministers, coaches) or involves force and/or genital contact.... The specific long-term effects on abused children as they grow into adulthood are difficult to predict. Some individuals adapt and have a higher degree of resilience, whereas others are profoundly and negatively changed. Studies have found that the children abused by pedophiles have higher measures of trauma, depression, and neurosis on standardized psychometric testing.... Individuals who experience long-term abuse are significantly more likely to have affective illness (eg, depression), anxiety disorders (eg, generalized anxiety disorders, posttraumatic stress disorder, panic attacks), eating disorders (anorexia in females), substance abuse, personality disorders, and/or adjustment disorders and to make suicidal gestures or actually engage in serious suicide attempts than those who are not abused.... These children often have problems with long-term intimacy and feelings of guilt and shame over their role in the incident.... In addition, sexually abused children have lower levels of education and a higher frequency of unemployment.... It is difficult to determine whether the higher frequency of unemployment is because of the sexual abuse or whether the unemployment as an adult is a marker for a trait that led the abused child to be seen as vulnerable as a child....

[In clinical treatment of] 10 adult men who were molested by a priest or minister ... [m]any of these men reported initially liking the relationship with the clergyman because of the attention they received and having a special relationship with a person of power and respect. Later, these men reported feeling rejected, abandoned, and betrayed. They all reported multiple sexual acts. Five were "passed around" to other pedophilic clergy, who also engaged in multiple sexual acts with them. Common features seen in the abused men included guilt, anger, and confusion about the abuse. Eight of the abused men had either treatment-refractory or recurrent depression, ... had divorced at least twice, ... had made serious suicide attempts, and 4 had alcohol or drug dependency issues. All reported fear of isolation from others, shame, and a fear of emotional dependency on others. Five reported they were gay or bisexual, whereas 3 of the remaining 5 had difficulty with both emotional and physical intimacy with their spouses....

Treatment of sexually abused individuals varies on the basis of the type of abuse experienced, the duration of abuse, the degree of interpersonal support available, the personality of the individual, and the resulting psychiatric condition that arose. Most of these conditions respond well to pharmacologic treatment with medications such as selective serotonin reuptake inhibitors (SSRIs), individual therapy (insight oriented, cognitive behavioral, or supportive psychotherapy), and group or family therapy. It is important that survivors of abuse at any age (children or adults) who show signs of having serious psychiatric problems such as anxiety, panic attacks, depression, a loss or fear of normal adult sexual desire, suicidal ideation, chronic irritability, demoralization, avoidance of intimacy behaviors, or social delay or problems be referred for psychiatric help.

B. The Exploiter

It is common in legal literature to refer to child sexual "exploitation" as a narrow category of child sexual offenses that involve the use of children for commercial advantage, such as in the context of prostitution or human trafficking, both of which will be addressed in detail in Chapter Four, Commercial Exploitation of Children. However, throughout this casebook, we refer to child sexual "exploitation" as including any form of child sexual abuse or other child sexual offense, including those that are performed not just for commercial gain, but for the offender's own sexual gratification. This broader scope of offense is consistent with the generally accepted definition of "exploitation" and is necessary in light of the expanding scope of protection that Congress, courts, and legislatures seek to cloak over sexually vulnerable children. The broad scope of sexual exploitation, as defined throughout this casebook, will be addressed in Chapter Two (Defining Exploitation). *See, e.g., United States v. Bach*, 400 F.3d 622 (8th Cir. 2005); *State v. Chester*, 133 Wash. 2d 15, 940 P.2d 1374 (1997) (included in Chapter Two, *infra*).

Within the broad scope of "exploitation," the concept of a "sexual exploiter" often conjures images of deviant old men dressed in trench coats, lurking for children in dark alleys or from *[handwritten margin notes: "3 types of Offenders; 1.) pedo 2.) predator 3.) molester"]*

behind bushes. Such stereotypical offenders are often generalized as "pedophiles." But in fact, the term "pedophile" identifies a very specific category of sexual offender: one who, for a period of at least six months, fantasizes or is sexually aroused by children under 13 years of age. The deviant offender described above, who lurks after children older than 13 years old, may be more accurately defined as a child "molester," which is an offender who does not necessarily demonstrate an ongoing pattern of sexual abuse. Yet a third category of offender may be defined as a "sexually violent predator," which is an offender who satisfies three specific criteria: (1) an underlying conviction for a sexually violent crime or history of such conduct; (2) a mental abnormality or personality disorder (often pedophilia); and (3) a likelihood to reoffend unless confined in a secure facility. Thus, what identifies any offender within any of these categories is not necessarily the nature of the sexual offense that is committed, but rather the personal characteristics of the offender that identify him or her as manifesting predictable sexually offensive behavior. Thus, not all sexual exploiters are necessarily pedophiles, and not all pedophiles are necessarily sexually violent predators, although one could, in fact, qualify as all three. Likewise, not all sexual exploiters are deviant old men. Although most sexual offenses are committed by pedophiles, a sexual exploiter may be a parent, guardian, or other family member; an exploiter may be male or female—an adult or a minor—a stranger or an acquaintance. Each category may include exploiters. The following material describes the various characteristics that identify an offender as a specific type of exploiter and presents some of the legal issues that are unique to each category of exploiter.

1. Exploiter as Pedophile

Ryan C. W. Hall and Richard C. W. Hall

A Profile of Pedophilia: Definition, Characteristics of Offenders, Recidivism, Treatment Outcomes, and Forensic Issues

82 MAYO CLIN. PROC. 457 (2007)

Pedophilia is a clinical diagnosis usually made by a psychiatrist or psychologist.... By diagnostic criteria of the *Diagnostic and Statistical Manual of Mental Disorders, Fourth Edition*, a pedophile is an individual who fantasizes about, is sexually aroused by, or experiences sexual urges toward prepubescent children (generally <13 years) for a period of at least 6 months. Pedophiles are either severely distressed by these sexual urges, experience interpersonal difficulties because of them, or act on them.... Pedophiles usually come to medical or legal attention by committing an act against a child because most do not find their sexual fantasies distressing or ego-dystonic enough to voluntarily seek treatment....

Generally, the individual must be at least 16 years of age and at least 5 years older than the juvenile of interest to meet criteria for pedophilia. In cases that involve adolescent offenders, factors such as emotional and sexual maturity may be taken into account before a diagnosis of pedophilia is made.... Pedophiles usually report that their attraction to children begins around the time of their puberty or adolescence, but this sexual attraction to children can also develop later in life.... If the clinical diagnosis of pedophilia is based on a specific act, it usually is not solely the result of intoxication or caused by another state or condition that may affect judgment, such as mania.... These cases are distinguished from pedophilia by the act being contrary to the individual's usual sexual behaviors and fantasies.... Some studies have found that as many as 50% to 60% of pedophiles also have a substance abuse or dependence diagnosis, but what is important is that their attraction to children is present in both the sober and the intoxicated state....

The course of pedophilia is usually long term.... In a study that examined the relationship between age and types of sexual crimes, ... up to 44% of pedophiles ... were in the older adult age range (age, 40–70 years). When compared with rapists and sexual sadists, pedophiles comprise 60% of all older offenders, indicating that pedophiles offend in their later years at a greater rate than other sexual offenders....

Technically, individuals who engage in sexual activities with pubescent teenagers under the legal age of consent (ages 13–16 years) are known as hebophiles (attracted to females) or ephebophiles (attracted to males).... The term *hebophilia* (also spelled as *hebephilia*) is becoming a generic term to describe sexual interest in either male or female pubescent children.... Distinctions noted in the literature between hebophiles and pedophiles are that hebophiles tend to be more interested in having reciprocal sexual affairs or relationships with children, are more opportunistic when engaging in sexual acts, have better social functioning, and have a better posttreatment prognosis than pedophiles.... The term *teleiophile* applies to an adult who prefers physically mature partners.... There is also a subclassification of pedophilia known as *infantophilia*, which describes individuals interested in children younger than 5 years.... These distinctions are important in understanding current research about paraphilias, selection criteria for studies of sexual behavior, and tests that gauge sexual interest (eg, plethysmography)....

Pedophiles are approximately 2.5 times more likely to engage in physical contact with a child than simply voyeuristic or exhibitionistic activities.... Typically, pedophiles engage in fondling and genital manipulation more than intercourse, with the exceptions occurring in cases of incest, of pedophiles with a preference for older children or adolescents, and when children are physically coerced....

Child molestation is not a medical diagnosis and is not necessarily a term synonymous with pedophilia.... A child molester is loosely defined as any individual who touches a child to obtain sexual gratification with the specifier that the offender is at least 4 to 5 years older than the child.... The age qualifier is added to eliminate developmentally normal childhood sex play (e.g., two 8-year-olds "playing doctor").... By this definition, a 13-year-old who touches an 8-year-old would be considered a child molester but would not meet criteria to be a pedophile. The NIBRS [National Incident-Based Reporting System] data on juvenile sexual assaults found that 40% of assaults against children younger than 12 years were committed by juveniles, with the most frequent age of the offenders being 14 years old.... Data from [one] study ... showed that 40% of child molesters, who were later diagnosed as having pedophilia, had molested a child by the time they were 15 years old. An estimated 88% of child molesters and 95% of molestations (one person, multiple acts) are committed by individuals who now or in the future will also meet criteria for pedophilia.... Pedophilic child molesters on average commit 10 times more sexual acts against children than nonpedophilic child molesters....

Pedophiles are subdivided into several classifications. One of the first distinctions made when classifying pedophiles is to determine whether they are "exclusively" attracted to children (exclusive pedophile) or attracted to adults as well as children (nonexclusive pedophile). In a study ... of 2429 adult male pedophiles, only 7% identified themselves as exclusively sexually attracted to children, which confirms the general view that most pedophiles are part of the nonexclusive group. Pedophiles are usually attracted to a particular age range and/or sex of child. Research categorizes male pedophiles by whether they are attracted to only male children (homosexual pedophilia), female children (heterosexual pedophilia), or children from both sexes (bisexual pedophilia).... The percentage of homosexual pedophiles ranges from 9% to 40%, which is approximately 4 to 20 times higher than the rate of adult men attracted to other adult men (using a prevalence rate of adult homosexuality of 2%–4%).... This finding does not imply that homosexuals are more likely to molest children, just that a larger percentage of pedophiles are homosexual or bisexual in orientation to children.... Individuals attracted to females usually prefer children between the ages of 8 and 10 years.... Individuals attracted to males usually prefer slightly older boys between the ages of 10 and 13 years.... Heterosexual pedophiles, in self-report studies, have on average abused 5.2 children and committed an average of 34 sexual acts vs. homosexual pedophiles who have on average abused 10.7 children and committed an average of 52 acts.... Bisexual offenders have on average abused 27.3 children and committed more than 120 acts.... A study ... of 377 nonincarcerated, non-incest-related pedophiles, whose legal situations had been resolved and who were surveyed using an anonymous self-report questionnaire, found that heterosexual pedophiles on average reported abusing 19.8 children and committing 23.2 acts, whereas homosexual pedophiles had abused 150.2 children and committed 281.7 acts. These studies confirm law enforcement reports about the serial nature of the crime, the large number of children abused by each pedophile, and the underreporting of assaults.... Studies that used self-reports and polygraphs show that pedophiles currently in treatment underreport their current interest in children and past behaviors....

It is difficult to estimate the true prevalence of pedophilia because few pedophiles voluntarily seek treatment and because most of the available data are based on individuals who have become involved with the legal system.... It is unknown how many individuals have pedophilic fantasies and never act on them or who do act but are never caught.... An estimated 1 in 20 cases of child sexual abuse is reported or identified....

It is difficult to present a classic personality pattern for pedophilia because of the various subgroups that exist.... Some individuals who have pedophilia are able to present themselves as psychologically normal during examination or superficial encounters, even though they have severe underlying personality disorders.... Studies have shown that people with pedophilia generally experience feelings of inferiority, isolation or loneliness, low self-esteem, internal dysphoria, and emotional immaturity. They have difficulty with mature age-appropriate interpersonal interactions, particularly because of their reduced assertiveness, elevated levels of passive-aggressivity, and increased anger or hostility.... These traits lead to difficulty dealing with painful affect, which results in the excessive use of the major defense mechanisms of intellectualization, denial, cognitive distortion (eg, manipulation of fact), and rationalization.... Even though pedophiles often have difficulty with interpersonal relationships, 50% or more will marry at some point in their lives....

It is common for people who are diagnosed as having pedophilia to also experience another major psychiatric disorder ... at some time in their life.... [R]esults suggest that pedophiles are more socially alienated and less emotionally stable than most other people.... Many pedophiles also demonstrate narcissistic,

sociopathic, and antisocial personality traits. They lack remorse and an understanding of the harm their actions cause....

The notion of impulsivity as a personality factor in pedophiles is often debated.
Pedophiles frequently report trouble controlling their behavior, although it is
rare for them to spontaneously molest a child. The fact that 70% to 85% of
offenses against children are premeditated speaks against a lack of perpetrator
control.... [Researchers] suggest that, instead of viewing pedophilia as the result
of an impulse-aggressive trait (e.g., unplanned with no consideration for consequences), it should be viewed as the result of a compulsive-aggressive trait
(planned with the intention of relieving internal pressures or urges)....

A substantial amount of research has been performed on what leads one to
be attracted to children. Pedophilia, especially the exclusive type, may be best
thought of as its own category of sexual orientation, not something that is superimposed on an existing heterosexual or homosexual identity.... This theory
then raises the questions, "Do people choose to be pedophiles or are they born
that way? If they are born that way, can any type of treatment convert them into
a normal adult sexual orientation?" These questions remain an area of medical
controversy.... [Researchers have theorized that there are a variety of neuropsychiatric and neurodevelopmental factors that may contribute to this dilemma,
such as intelligence level, the prominence of left-handedness, impaired cognitive
abilities, neuroendocrine differences, and brain abnormalities, as well as a high
comorbidity of impulse control disorders (e.g., explosive personality disorder,
kleptomania, pyromania, pathological gambling). Researchers have also studied
certain medical conditions of the temporal lobe that can lead to hypersexual or
hyposexual behavior that are predominant in pedophiles versus controls.]

A question this raises is whether some of the changes noted in pedophiles are
related to problems of brain development and maturation or represent brain
changes that have resulted from life experiences, such as being physically abused
and sexual victimized themselves as children.... Studies of neurochemical
differences in pedophiles vs controls have also been performed.... [Researchers]
interpreted ... findings to indicate that pedophiles had a serotonergic disturbance,
most likely caused by [dysfunctional neurons].... [Other studies that assess the
relevance of head trauma as a predisposing risk factor for being diagnosed as
having pedophilia, concluding that] "injuries in early childhood may result in
one being sexually oriented toward children. A secondary finding of the study
was that individuals who were pedophiles were more likely to have mothers who
received psychiatric treatment than controls. The authors postulated that this
finding might indicate a genetic linkage or predisposition to pedophilia but
associated environmental factors could not be ruled out....

Environmental factors may predispose individuals to become pedophiles. Pedophiles often report environmental stress as a factor that increases their urges
or desire to offend against children.... One of the most obvious examples of an
environmental factor that increases the chances of an individual becoming an
offender is if he or she were sexually abused as a child. This relationship is known
as the "victim-to-abuser cycle" or "abused-abusers phenomena." ... The numbers
reported for pedophiles who were abused as children range from 28% to 93%
vs approximately 15% for random controls.... Studies that examined females
who committed sexual acts against children reported that 47% to 100% of them
had experienced sexual assault as children.... Individuals who engage in

homosexual pedophilia were more likely to have been abused than individuals who engage in heterosexual pedophilia.... Some studies have also found that pedophiles and hebophiles who were abused tend to have an age preference for children that is similar to the age at which they were abused....

Many theories have speculated on why the "abused-abusers phenomena" occurs: identification with the aggressor, in which the abused child is trying to gain a new identity by becoming the abuser; an imprinted sexual arousal pattern established by early abuse; early abuse leading to hypersexual behavior; or a form of social learning took place.... Of note, although abused individuals are more likely to abuse others, most individuals who are abused do not perpetuate the cycle.... There is also legitimate concern regarding the validity of many of the self-reports of pedophiles who claim to have been abused as children themselves. These statements are often made in a legal or group treatment setting, in which pedophiles may be trying to mitigate their sentence or gain sympathy for their behavior.

Historically, pedophiles are likely to have repeated a grade in school (approximately 61%) or required special education classes.... Academic difficulties occur in both pedophiles and hebophiles at twice the odds ratio seen for perpetrators of sexual offenses against adults.... Some studies have also found that pedophiles have lower levels of education and employment than the general population, but this may be a prison sampling artifact.... [Several studies] found that nonviolent pedophiles were educationally similar to, or better educated than, samples of sociopaths, sexual murderers, and controls, but these studies excluded cognitively impaired individuals.

A study ... that compared 260 pedophiles with 260 matched controls found a correlation between fraternal birth order (having more older male siblings) and the pedophile having a homosexual orientation. Similar findings exist linking birth order and adult homosexuality.... Other studies have found correlations for older maternal age and pedophilia, which may also be a marker for birth order.... Whether these correlations are due to social or biologic factors is unclear. One theory to explain how male birth order affects sexual orientation is the presence of antimale maternal antibodies in multiparous women, which affect neuropathway development in the fetus....

Pedophilia is a complex, often compulsive, psychosexual disorder with profound implications for the abused child, perpetrator, and community. It is important for physicians to understand the various types of pedophiles, the profile of the abused children, and the offenders' responses to treatment and their risk for repeated offense. The combination of pharmacologic and behavioral treatment coupled with close legal supervision appears to help reduce the risk of repeated offense. However, the interventions do not change the pedophile's basic sexual orientation toward children. Further research is needed to better identify clinically significant differences among the different types of pedophiles. Such knowledge, it is hoped, will result in better treatments, improved allocation of medical and legal resources, and a reduction in the number of abused children.

Notes

Identifying specific factors that qualify one as a pedophile is relevant to the determination of one's status as a sexually violent predator (SVP). Sexually violent predator laws— applicable in 20 states and the District of Columbia, as of 2014—allow states or the federal government to impose requirements or restrictions on sex offenders after their sentence has been completed. A more detailed discussion of these laws is presented in Chapter Seven, Criminal and Civil Liability, as well as at the end of this chapter, with respect to civil restrictions for registration on sex offender registries for both adult and juvenile sexual offenders. For an international perspective on this subject, see Mark D. Kielsgard and Jack Burke, *Post-Incarceration Supervision of Pedophile Offenders: An International Comparative Study*, 51 CRIM. L. BULL. 1 (Jan./Feb. 2015); Mark Kielsgard, *Myth-Driven State Policy: An International Perspective of Recidivism and Incurability of Pedophile Offenders*, 47 CREIGHTON L. REV. 247 (2014). In the following case, note the factors that the court considers in determining whether the defendant qualifies as a sexually violent predator and the significance of the defendant's diagnosis as a pedophile in that determination. Note the factor on which the experts disagree with respect to the defendant's diagnosis as a pedophile. What constitutional issues are implicated by the court's holding? How does a diagnosis as a pedophile affect the application of SVP laws and the constitutional analysis?

People v. Smith

California Court of Appeal, First District, 2011
2011 WL 2434040

KLINE, P.J....

Psychologist Christopher North, testifying as an expert for the prosecution, stated his opinion that appellant, 52 years old, met the criteria for [a] [sexually violent predator (SVP)]. He explained that to meet the criteria, a person has to have been convicted of raping or molesting at least one victim; has to have a diagnosed mental disorder that makes him likely to commit sex crimes in the future; and has to present a serious risk of committing a new sexually violent predatory crime if not treated in a secure setting.

North interviewed appellant on December 2, 2008, and reviewed pertinent records, including the records of conviction and police or probation reports concerning appellant's 1981 conviction for oral copulation of his nephew Harold and his 1989 conviction for lewd and lascivious acts upon his nephew Gerald. In 1976, when appellant was 19 years old, he invited his seven-year-old step-nephew, Harold, into his bedroom to listen to records. Harold emerged from the room looking "pale and sick," and told his mother that appellant had "played with his penis" and orally copulated him. Harold's father walked into the bedroom, saw appellant's pants down and his penis exposed and then called the authorities. Harold said that appellant had molested him once before and he had told his mother, but she did not believe him. Appellant was convicted of oral copulation of a minor, which North testified qualifies as a sexually violent offense because of the sexual activity and victim's age. He admitted to North that he had molested Harold twice.

In 1989, appellant was convicted of another sexually violent offense, molesting then eight-year-old Gerald. This offense, North testified, also qualified as a sexually violent offense. Two 17-year-old boys saw Gerald's older brother Michael "humping" Gerald with appellant watching. They told the parents, who called the police. Appellant said that the boys' mother had asked him to watch them, but the mother told the police she had told appellant to leave because she did not want him with the boys. Gerald told the police that appellant had also molested him, with the two engaging in fondling and mutual oral copulation, and appellant ejaculating. Michael also said appellant had orally copulated him and appellant was charged with this offense, but the charge was dropped when appellant pled guilty to molesting Gerald. Appellant was sentenced to 11 years in prison.

In 1979, while on probation for molesting Harold, appellant was questioned about molesting six-year-old Marty, the son of his step-brother and step-brother's girlfriend, whom he had been babysitting. Marty had spent the night in appellant's bed with him every other Friday night for about six months, and Marty told his mother he and appellant had engaged in mutual oral copulation on two different occasions. Appellant's probation was revoked and he was sent to Atascadero State Hospital for treatment as a mentally disordered sex offender. Appellant admitted to North that he had molested Marty twice.... In 1989, while being questioned about molesting Gerald, appellant admitted having sodomized a boy named David in the early 1980's. North asked appellant about this and appellant denied it; when North showed him the police report documenting his admission, appellant said he did not recall it. In 1995, appellant was taken into custody on a parole violation when he was found sleeping in the same bed with his seven- and 10-year-old nephews.

North diagnosed appellant with pedophilia, which he defined as involving "recurrent, intense, sexually-arousing fantasies, urges or behaviors involving sexual activity with pre-pubescent children," generally children under age 13, by a person at least 16 years old and at least five years older than the children. The fantasies, urges or behaviors must persist for a minimum of six months and the individual must act on the urges or suffer significant distress or impaired functioning as a result of them. Appellant's offenses spanned 13 years and were all committed against children under the required age when appellant was over age 16 and at least five years older than the children. On cross-examination, North testified that a child molester, as opposed to a pedophile, would engage in sexual activity with a child but not necessarily on an ongoing basis; the distinction is that a pedophile has a "repeated pattern or history of sexual activity with children."

North opined that appellant's pedophilia affected his ability to control his emotions and behavior and predisposed him to commit criminal sexual acts to an extent that made him a menace to the health and safety of others. He explained that appellant did not take the problem seriously and was not cooperative with probation and parole. On probation, after molesting Harold, appellant resisted going to sex offender treatment and, when he did go, was so unmotivated that the psychologist concluded there was no point in treating his pedophilia and instead focused on the drinking problem from which appellant also suffered. Appellant molested Marty while on probation and was sent to Atascadero State Hospital for treatment, but grew increasingly less cooperative over 20 months, until he was sent back to court as not amenable to treatment. After serving his prison sentence for the conviction based on his molestation of Gerald, appellant violated his parole by sleeping in a bed with his nephews. North believed appellant had difficulty controlling his behavior as evidenced by the fact that incarceration did not deter him from committing further offenses. North also felt appellant's pedophilia impaired his empathy, noting appellant had told another doctor that his offenses did not have negative effects on the victims and, when asked if the boys enjoyed the sexual activity, said "'[t]hey didn't look at me like they disliked it.'" A treatment program for pedophilia was available at Coalinga State Hospital, where appellant was residing, but appellant had not chosen to participate in it, despite having admitted in 1989 that he needed help for his sexual problems.

North also diagnosed appellant with alcohol dependence. Appellant started drinking in his teens and was drinking heavily by about age 21. He had four convictions for driving under the influence, was drinking heavily around the time he molested Harold, and was reluctant to participate in the alcohol treatment that was ordered as part of his probation. After his parole in 1994, he was returned to prison at least twice for problems with drinking. Appellant had told three doctors that he had thoughts of and impulses to have sex with boys after he drank alcohol, including one he told he only had these thoughts when he drank, but in fact some of appellant's offenses were committed at times he was not drinking, including his molestation of Marty. North testified that alcohol use is a risk factor for appellant, lessening his self-control and increasing the likelihood of him molesting a child.

The fact appellant had not been convicted of a sex offense since 1989 did not affect North's opinion that appellant currently suffers from pedophilia. North testified it is generally accepted in the mental health field that pedophilia is a disorder that does not heal itself over time and cannot be cured, but can be managed. Nor did the fact that appellant had not been caught "acting out sexually" while at the state hospital change North's opinion that he currently suffered from pedophilia, because appellant was strongly motivated not to appear interested in children so that he would be released and he did not have contact with children. In his experience, having performed some 600 to 800 sexually violent predator evaluations, North stated that it was "pretty rare" for such an individual to act out sexually while in a confined environment. North testified that appellant's problems arose when he was out in the community and, since he had only been in the community for about three years since his 1989 conviction, his opportunity to molest had been "fairly limited." North acknowledged that he did not know what degree of access appellant had to his nephews during this period.

North opined that as a result of his pedophilia, appellant presented a substantial, serious and well-founded risk of engaging in sexually violent predatory criminal behavior without appropriate treatment and custody. This opinion was based on actuarial tools, tests and risk factors used by psychologists to determine this likelihood. Appellant scored six on the Static-99, putting him in the "high risk" category and indicating a 13 to 28 percent probability of him reoffending within five years, and a 17 to 37 percent probability of reoffending within 10 years. His score on the Static-2002 was seven, in the moderate to high risk category, and his score on the Minnesota Sex Offender Screening Tool Revised was five, in the moderate risk category. These instruments assessed fixed factors based on appellant's history and North testified they were considered "moderate predictors." North also considered five dynamic factors research had identified as important in assessing recidivism: significant social influences, intimacy deficits, sexual self-regulation, general self-regulation, and cooperation with supervision. North testified that appellant appeared to be largely a loner, associated primarily with family members, and did not appear to have had close friendships, to be attracted to women or to have had committed relationships with adults; there was little information bearing on appellant's sexual self-regulation because he had not been participating in treatment; and his general self-control seemed "pretty good" in a custodial setting, but not very good in the community.

North testified that the definition of "predatory" used by Department evaluators asks whether the subject targets strangers or casual acquaintances or establishes relationships with children for the purpose of victimization. North believed appellant was likely to promote a relationship with a child through babysitting, which North considered predatory, as he had done in the offenses against his nephews. North noted that appellant had engaged in "grooming" behavior—ingratiating himself to a child or parents to set up a situation in which to molest the child—with Marty, acting as a "big brother," and that almost all of appellant's victims were developmentally disabled or hyperactive, making them vulnerable and particularly prone to predation. North estimated a 30 to 40 percent probability that appellant would be arrested for a new sex offense within 10 years of release, stating this was a conservative estimate because it focused on actual arrest and many sex offenses are not detected or reported. He acknowledged this estimate was based on his own clinical judgment rather than a "scientific-approved tool" or empirical evidence.... North did not consider appellant an incest offender, viewing incest as limited to immediate family within a household. He was not an "extrafamilial molester" either, but somewhere in between the two. Incest offenders have a lower recidivism rate than extrafamilial offenders.

Clinical psychologist George Grosso also testified for the prosecution as an expert in the area of SVP evaluations and opined that appellant met the criteria for an SVP. Grosso interviewed appellant on December 3, 2008, after reviewing his records. He diagnosed appellant with pedophilia nonexclusive, sexually attracted to males, and with personality disorder, not otherwise specified, with borderline antisocial traits.... Although appellant's sexual self-regulation while in custody had been satisfactory, the fact that appellant's pedophilia involved attraction to males was significant because research showed that individuals attracted to prepubescent boys tend to have a chronic condition and to recidivate under stress and at approximately twice the rate of those who offend against prepubescent girls.... Grosso testified that appellant's offenses were predatory in that he established or promoted relationships with his victims for the purpose of victimization.... Grosso also noted that appellant did not have certain "protective" factors that research showed could reduce an individual's likelihood of reoffending: He had not been successful in the community for more than 10 years without offending, he was not of sufficiently advanced age to reduce his likelihood of offending, and he did not have health issues that seriously impeded his functioning....

The prosecution's third expert witness, psychologist Jack Vognsen, also testified that appellant met the criteria for an SVP. Vognsen had interviewed appellant three times, in 2002, 2006 and 2008, and appellant had given differing accounts of his offenses. His diagnosis for appellant was pedophilia with a sexual attraction to boys. He believed appellant's pedophilia affected his ability to control his behavior and predisposed him to commit criminal sexual acts so as to make him a menace to others' health and safety, as shown by his history of continuing to offend despite criminal sanctions, and that appellant's alcohol use allowed him to disregard the consequences of his behavior. His opinion was not affected by the fact that appellant had not suffered a conviction since 1989, because he viewed pedophilia as "something like a sexual orientation" which, in adults, tends to be "pretty fixed." ... Vognsen believed there was a substantial, serious and well-founded likelihood appellant would reoffend in a sexually violent and predatory manner if released. The three actuarial instruments Vognsen used yielded results that were "very close to each other" and put appellant's risk of reoffending between moderate and high. Appellant's score on the Static-99 Revised was 6, with a 16.7 to 37.3 percent risk of reoffending within 10 years, and his score on the Static-2002 was 7, with a risk of 13.3 to 32.1 percent within 10 years. Vognsen estimated appellant was at the halfway point in the range, possibly toward the high end, explaining that appellant was not like a high risk offender because he was not a generally antisocial person, but not like the low end because he had not participated in treatment. Vognsen estimated appellant's risk of being charged or convicted of a new sexual offense within 10 years to be about 25 percent.... Vognsen viewed appellant as having a "strong deviant sexual preference," indicated by the young age of his victims and lack of evidence of adult sexual relations, and saw his alcohol dependence as reflecting an impaired ability to control his behavior. Vognsen viewed the statutory definition of predatory as intended to exclude incest offenders, who he said reoffend at about half the rate of non-incest sexual offenders. Appellant's offenses were predatory rather than incestuous because he promoted or enhanced his relationships with the children in order to engage in sexual conduct with them. Vognsen believed appellant should remain in custody with treatment because there was no evidence he would voluntarily undergo treatment in the community.

Clinical psychologist Lisa Jeko testified as an expert for appellant.... Although Jeko recognized that there could be predatory sexual offenses even within a family, she did not view appellant's conduct as "pronounced, prolonged seeking out of victims" or going outside the family for a victim, and concluded appellant's offenses were incestuous and not predatory....

Clinical psychologist Theodore Donaldson evaluated appellant in August 2006, and had since reviewed the newer evaluations by Dr. Vognsen, Dr. North, Dr. Grosso and Dr. Jeko.... [footnote omitted]. He did not speak with appellant again because he had the new evaluations and "nothing ha[d] changed" in that appellant had not done anything consistent with a diagnosis of pedophilia.... Donaldson thought there was insufficient evidence to conclude appellant was a pedophile. He testified that it was very difficult to distinguish between a person suffering from pedophilia, a mental illness involving a sexual preference for children or "persistent fantasy preoccupation," from an opportunistic child molester who "has sex with children because they're convenient." A pedophilia diagnosis would require current signs and symptoms of the mental disorder and current difficulty controlling offending conduct. Donaldson did not see evidence of pedophilia because appellant's offenses involved someone related to him and available, and he had no history of seeking out children; he went for eight years while out of custody, from 1981 to 1989, without any known pedophilic behaviors, indicating he either did not have the urges or was able to control them; he displayed no signs of pedophilia while incarcerated (such as interest in pornography or suggestive pictures of children); and while he had parole violations after his release in 1994, none involved sexual offenses. Donaldson noted that mental illness does not go into remission when a person is incarcerated, so that if one is mentally ill, some signs and symptoms will be revealed. Additionally, there was no evidence appellant was unable rather than unwilling to control his conduct. Donaldson criticized the risk assessment tools used to establish a probability of recidivism for not sufficiently taking into account the base rate (percentage of offenders released who reoffend within a specified amount of time) and factors such as age and nature of the population studied. He believed these instruments resulted in estimates that were too high because the base rates used in the instruments were higher than the base rates in California. Donaldson felt too much attention was paid to risk estimates because if a person is currently a pedophile with serious difficulty controlling the behavior, the person necessarily is currently likely to reoffend. He also believed that dynamic risk factors had "no place" in SVPA evaluations, as studies had shown adding these factors decreased the accuracy of prediction. Studies also showed that coerced treatment had no effect on recidivism.

Appellant testified that Harold, Marty, Gerald and Michael were his nephews. He acknowledged that he molested Harold twice and spent five years at Atascadero State Hospital as a result. He completed the two-and-one-half-year sexual offender treatment program twice, but when asked to do it a third time, he refused and asked to be returned to state prison. Within two to three weeks of returning to prison, he was released on parole.... Appellant testified that he molested Marty while on probation for the offense against Harold. He knew Marty was his brother's son before he molested the boy. He had been drinking when he molested both Marty and Harold, about 12 beers on each occasion; he was drinking every day at that time.... After being released from prison in 1980 or 1981, appellant testified, he did not molest anyone until 1989, when he molested Gerald twice. He had been drinking both times. Appellant testified that he never molested Gerald's brother Michael, but "played with his private area" when Michael asked him to. Michael was 17 years old and appellant considered him an adult.

Appellant went to prison for his offenses against Gerald and was released in 1994. One of the conditions of his parole was that he not have unsupervised contact with children. Having nowhere to live while waiting to move into an apartment that was being remodeled, appellant obtained permission from his parole agent to live with his brother for a couple of weeks. The parole officer knew there were children in the house. Appellant slept in the dining room and never shared a bed with, touched or molested his nephews, but after about a week the parole officer found appellant had violated parole. Appellant testified that he took and passed a polygraph test regarding this incident, but the polygraph was never given to his parole officer and could not be found.

Appellant testified that he had not sexually molested anyone after he was released in 1994. He explained that he had had a lot of time for thinking and realized how what he had done was wrong, was ruining his nephews' lives and causing him to lose the respect of his nephews and family. He had written to his nephews, apologizing and asking for forgiveness; they had forgiven him and wanted him to join them in Nebraska. Appellant acknowledged that his criminal record included alcohol related violations, among them three convictions for driving under the influence, the last in 1986, and that his offenses against his nephews all involved alcohol. He considered himself an alcoholic and testified that he had participated in several sobriety programs and had been sober for nine years. Appellant had been aware of alcohol and illegal drugs at Atascadero and at Coalinga State Prison, but did not partake of either. He was aware of pornographic material at both institutions, but did not look at it and did not want to ever again "do what I've done before."

Appellant testified that at Atascadero he attended substance abuse programs and training classes in mechanics, plumbing, carpentry and computer skills, and had obtained his GED, hoping he would be able to go home and have a trade to make a living. In prison, in addition to Alcoholics Anonymous, he participated in an program teaching skills such as "when to appropriately and inappropriately act" and took college classes for several months, but was dropped when he missed class due to having to be in court.

Appellant testified that he had attended Phase One of the sex offender treatment program at Atascadero, and again at Coalinga, but did not participate further because he did not feel it was relevant to him; friends who had completed the program told him it was a waste of time and remained in custody years after completing it. Also, his prior attorney advised him not to take the program. Appellant felt he needed help, but wanted to get it from a treatment program on the outside such as the one he had attended while on parole. He wanted to move to Nebraska, where his siblings, nephews and nieces lived. He was welcome to stay with them until he found a place of his own, and they had found a program for him in the community. Appellant testified that he thought he was a pedophile before but not currently, as he had shown no signs of reoffending in 20 years. He testified that he did not plan to have sexual contact with anyone in the future, noting that he was 52 years old and dealing with repeated cancer surgeries. He acknowledged that he had pled guilty to a charge of failing to register as a sex offender in 1999, but insisted that he did so only on the advice of his attorney and, in fact, he had not failed to register....

The [Sexually Violent Predator Act (SVPA)] defines a "sexually violent predator" as "a person who has been convicted of a sexually violent offense against one or more victims and who has a diagnosed mental disorder that makes the person a danger to the health and safety of others in that it is likely that he or she will engage in sexually violent criminal behavior." ([Welfare and Institutions Code] § 6600, subd. (a)(1).) "Under the [SVPA], a person is 'likely' to engage in sexually violent criminal behavior (i.e., reoffend) if he or she 'presents a substantial danger, that is, a serious and well-founded risk, that he or she will commit such crimes if free in the community.' (*People v. Superior Court (Ghilotti)*

(2002) 27 Cal.4th 888, 922, italics omitted.)" ([*People v. McKee* (2010) 47 Cal.4th 1172, 1186].) ... As originally enacted, the SVPA "provided for the involuntary civil commitment for a two-year term of confinement and treatment of persons who, by a unanimous jury verdict after trial ... [citations omitted] are found beyond a reasonable doubt to be an SVP (former § 6604). (*People v. Williams* (2003) 31 Cal.4th 757, 764; *Hubbart v. Superior Court* (1999) 19 Cal.4th 1138, 1143, 1147 (*Hubbart*).) A person's commitment could not be extended beyond that two-year term unless a new petition was filed requesting a successive two-year commitment. (Former §§ 6604, 6604.1; *Cooley v. Superior Court* (2002) 29 Cal .4th 228, 243, fn. 5.) On filing of a recommitment petition, a new jury trial would be conducted at which the People again had the burden to prove beyond a reasonable doubt that the person was currently an SVP. (Former §§ 6604, 6605, subds. (d), (e).)" (*McKee, supra*, 47 Cal.4th at p. 1185.)

In 2006, the SVPA was amended by Proposition 83, which, among other things, changed an SVP commitment from a two-year term to an indefinite commitment. (*McKee, supra*, 47 Cal.4th at p. 1186.) Under the current law, if a court or jury determines beyond a reasonable doubt that an individual is an SVP, the individual is committed to the custody of the Department for an indeterminate term. (*Id.* at pp. 1186–1187.) "An SVP can only be released conditionally or unconditionally if the [Department] authorizes a petition for release and the state does not oppose it or fails to prove beyond a reasonable doubt that the individual still meets the definition of an SVP, or if the individual, petitioning the court on his own, is able to bear the burden of proving by a preponderance of the evidence that he is no longer an SVP." (*Id.* at p. 1187.) ...

Noting Dr. North's testimony that the definition of pedophilia requires "recurrent, intense, sexually-arousing fantasies, urges or behaviors involving sexual activity with pre-pubescent children," which "persist for a minimum of six months" and "cause the individual significant distress or impairment in functioning," appellant urges that there was no evidence of such factors for at least 20 years. He points out that the most recent information North cited for concluding appellant lacked the ability to control his behavior was the 1995 parole violation involving sharing a bed with his nephews, and that North agreed appellant had shown "a high level of control" in that he had not been charged with a sexual offense since 1989. Dr. Grosso also testified there was no current evidence that appellant's volitional control was impaired, noting that because appellant was currently not around children, the only available evidence was from when he was last around them. Appellant suggests the prosecution's experts did not even agree on the distinction between pedophilia and child molestation: Dr. North testified that a pedophile has a repeated pattern of sexual activity with children, whereas a child molester might act on only one occasion and for "other reasons"....

The prosecution witnesses testified that pedophilia is a lifelong condition and appellant's history of reoffending after periods of incarceration demonstrated his inability to control his behavior. The experts discussed appellant's failure to participate meaningfully in sex offender treatment and the fact that his opportunities to reoffend had been limited by his incarceration; found his scores on actuarial tests used to predict recidivism to be in the moderate to high categories; and found deficiencies in the dynamic factors used to assess risk of recidivism. They were not persuaded by the fact that appellant had not been found to act out sexually while at the state hospital or to have committed a recent sex offense because his opportunities to reoffend had been limited by his incarceration and lack of contact with children.... As appellant stresses, his expert witness Dr. Donaldson was highly critical of the tests used and factors considered by the prosecution witnesses in formulating their opinions on appellant's risk of future offense, and testified that there was no current evidence that appellant was unable to control his behavior. Through this testimony and the arguments of counsel, the jury was fully presented with the differing expert opinions and offered reasons to discredit the prosecution witnesses' conclusions. The jury chose to accept the prosecution's evidence.

Appellant is correct that the jury could find him to be a sexually violent predator only upon evidence that he currently suffered from a diagnosed mental disorder that prevents him from controlling his sexually violent behavior. (*Hubbart, supra*, 19 Cal.4th 1138, 1162; see *People v. Rasmuson* (2006) 145 Cal.App.4th 1487, 1509 (*Rasmuson*).) Appellant relies upon a caution expressed in *Rasmuson*, which reversed a trial court's denial of an SVP's petition for conditional release. (*Rasmuson*, at p. 1491.) *Rasmuson* stated: "A person's history should not be determinative of whether he or she is a danger to reoffend.... That history is static and will never change. As substantial time has passed, its reliability as a predictor of a defendant's future behavior becomes more equivocal. If such static factors predominated in the assessment of whether an SVP should be given conditional release, a serious offender would never be released regardless of what events subsequent to his offenses revealed...." (*Id.* at p. 1509.)

In *Rasmuson*, eight mental health professionals, including staff members from the institution where the defendant was being treated, Department evaluators and a psychologist who worked for the program that would supervise the defendant on conditional release all agreed that the defendant would not present a significant danger to the community if he was conditionally released due to factors including that he was taking medication that virtually eliminated his sexual arousal and deviant fantasies, he had completed all phases of treatment at Atascadero and worked hard on relapse prevention, and he would be supervised by a program that was "virtually 'failsafe.'" (*Rasmuson, supra*, 145 Cal.App.4th at p. 1508.) There was no evidence to the contrary, and the prosecution's opposition to conditional release was based on the heinous nature of the defendant's past offense and the fact that he had reoffended shortly after a release almost two decades earlier.... [citation omitted].

The point appellant derives from *Rasmuson*, that history alone cannot be the basis of a current SVP finding, is perfectly valid. Unlike that case, however, here there was evidence in addition to appellant's history of offending that he currently posed a danger to the community due to his pedophilia. As the prosecution experts explained, evaluation of appellant's current situation necessarily depended on his history, as he had not been at liberty in the community in recent years. (See *People v. Sumahit, supra*, 128 Cal.App.4th at p. 353 ["Because he currently lacks access to children, [defendant's] lack of outward signs of sexual deviance is not dispositive of whether he is likely to reoffend if released into society at large. Such an assessment must include consideration of his past behavior, his attitude toward treatment and other risk factors applicable to the facts of his case"].) The prosecution experts' conclusion that appellant was currently unable to control his conduct due to his pedophilia was supported by their testimony concerning the chronic nature of the mental illness, appellant's history of reoffending when released into the community, appellant's failure to participate meaningfully in therapy, and their evaluation of appellant's performance on actuarial instruments and other factors used in the field as a basis for estimating risk of reoffense. Indeed, even Dr. Jeko, one of appellant's expert witnesses, agreed that appellant currently suffered from pedophilia and posed a moderate to moderately high risk of sexually reoffending, concluding that appellant did not meet the statutory definition of an SVP only because she viewed his offenses as incestuous rather than predatory.

Appellant also urges that the SVPA approach to commitment is "the near equivalent of using inadmissible 'profile evidence.'" *People v. Robbie* (2001) 92 Cal.App.4th 1075, upon which appellant relies, reversed a criminal conviction for sex offenses where the trial court improperly permitted a prosecution witness to testify, in response to hypothetical questions, that the conduct the victim described was characteristic of a certain type of sex offender. *Robbie* explained that the problem with profile evidence is that it begins with a faulty major premise — that criminals and only criminals act in a given way — and asks the jury to conclude from that premise that because the defendant acted that way, the defendant is a criminal. (*Id.* at p. 1085.) Appellant asserts that in the SVPA context, the predicate crimes plus diagnosis amount to a fixed historical profile that cannot change over time. This argument ignores the role of the SVPA's requirement of proof of current dangerousness as well as predicate offenses and a diagnosed mental disorder. As *Rasmuson* illustrates, an individual may have committed qualifying offenses in the past and currently suffer from a continuing mental disorder, yet lack the required current dangerousness because of progress in treatment or other factors....

Appellant next contends that the statutory definition of "predatory" as including an act directed toward "an individual with whom a relationship has been established or promoted for the primary purpose of victimization" is void for vagueness. He argues that the term "promoted" is overly vague, does not provide adequate notice of what is prohibited and, as applied in this case, violates his right to due process of law.... Appellant contends that the expert witnesses "never defined what they meant" when they testified that appellant "promoted" the relationship with his nephews, "leaving that term to innuendo and inference." Since his victims were nephews with whom he had a preexisting relationship, he questions how it could be possible to determine that he "promoted" his relationship with them. He further argues that the SVPA does not say whether a family relationship, as opposed to one with a stranger, "qualifies." ..."In common usage, 'promote' means to contribute to the progress or growth of...." (*People v. Ngoun* (2001) 88 Cal.App.4th 432, 436, citing Webster's New College Dict. (1995) p. 885.) Contrary to appellant's assertion, all of the prosecution experts explained what they meant by testifying that appellant promoted the relationship with his nephews within the meaning of the SVPA. As explained above, all described the behavior by which they believed appellant groomed his victims, fostered relationships and created situations in which he could molest them. The experts testified that, although appellant had a preexisting relationship with the boys by virtue of their family ties, appellant actively engaged in conduct designed to facilitate the molestation. We fail to see how this testimony left uncertain what they meant by testifying that appellant promoted the relationships for the primary purpose of victimization.

Nor is the statute ambiguous as to whether the "promoted" relationship can be with a family member. Section 6600, subdivision (e), defines "predatory" as an act "directed toward a stranger, a person of casual acquaintance with whom no substantial relationship exists, *or* an individual with whom a relationship has been established or promoted for the primary purpose of victimization." The use of the disjunctive in the definition creates different categories of victims: An act can be predatory if it is committed against a stranger or casual acquaintance without proof that the offender "established or promoted" a relationship with the victim *or* an act can be predatory if committed against someone with whom the offender has more than a casual relationship *if* the offender "established or promoted" a relationship with the victim for the "primary purpose of victimization." The statute cannot be read as requiring that the victim be a stranger. It does not refer to intrafamily relationships one way or another. By failing to exclude family relationships, the statutory definition includes them if the offender "promoted" the relationship for the requisite purpose.

Appellant asks what an uncle with a preexisting relationship with his nephews would have to do to "promote" the family tie. The issue is not simply promoting the family tie; it is promoting the family tie "for the primary purpose of victimization." The prosecution witnesses answered appellant's question: The evidence that appellant promoted his relationship with his victims for the primary purpose of molesting them, as the experts described, is that he engaged in grooming behavior by developing a big brother type relationship with one nephew, brought another into a private space, and used babysitting to create the opportunity for molestation. It was the jury's task to determine whether appellant in fact acted to develop relationships with the boys for the primary purpose of molesting the boys, or only acted within the preexisting contours of his familial relationship with them. That the evidence might be susceptible of more than one interpretation does not render the statutory definition unconstitutionally vague....

[T]he judgment is affirmed [in part].

We concur: LAMBDEN and RICHMAN, JJ.

Notes

According to the definition of "pedophile" applied in *Smith*, a pedophile is one who is at least 16 years old and who, for a period of at least six months, is urged to act upon, or suffers distress or impairment from, intense sexual fantasies involving prepubescent children who are at least five years younger than the offender. In cases like *Smith*, we see the relevant effect of a diagnosis of pedophilia with respect to the offender's status as a sexually violent predator. For a discussion of the effect of a defendant's diagnosis as a pedophile within the context of sentencing, see *United States v. Garthus*, 652 F.3d 715 (7th Cir. 2011) (defendant's characteristics as a pedophile "suggest that he is more dangerous than the average consumer of child pornography"). In addressing the various categories of exploiters that are discussed below, consider what, if any, effect the distinct characteristics of each category have on the outcomes of the cases. Are cases involving female exploiters analyzed differently that those involving males? Do cases in which minors exploit other minors warrant special analysis? Are defendants diagnosed as pedophiles viewed differently than defendants diagnosed with other forms of sexual deviation? Does the relationship between the exploiter and the exploited affect the determination of one's dangerousness or likelihood for recidivism? How does public perception play a role in treatment outcomes? The cases and materials that follow address these questions.

2. Female Exploiters

Ryan C. W. Hall and Richard C. W. Hall

A Profile of Pedophilia: Definition, Characteristics of Offenders, Recidivism, Treatment Outcomes, and Forensic Issues

82 Mayo Clin. Proc. 457 (2007)

In general, most individuals who engage in pedophilia or paraphilias are male.... There was a time when it was believed that females could not be pedophiles because of their lack of long-term sexual urges unless they had a primary psychotic disorder.... When women were studied for sexually inappropriate behavior directed toward children, these behaviors were classified as "sexual abuse" or "molestation" but not pedophilia.... From federal data on sexual crimes, females were reported to be the "molester" in 6% of all juvenile cases.... [A] study ... of 4007 "child molesters" found 1% to be female, but the authors believed this number was low because of the systematic underreporting of women for molestation.... One reason why acts of pedophilia committed by women are underreported is that many acts are not recognized because they occur during the course of regular "nurturing or caregiving activities," such as when bathing and dressing children.... Another reason is that when adult women engage in sexual acts with adolescent boys, others do not perceive this activity as abuse but rather a fortunate rite of passage.... The law sees it otherwise.

Pedophilic women tend to be young (22–33 years old); have poor coping skills; may meet criteria for the presence of a psychiatric disorder, particularly depression or substance abuse; and frequently also meet criteria for being personality disordered (antisocial, borderline, narcissistic, dependent).... In incidents in which women are identified as being involved in sexually inappropriate acts with children, there is an increased chance of a male pedophile being involved as well.... When a male co-offender is involved, usually more than 1 child is involved. Molested children tend to be both male and female and are more likely to be related to the offender. In these cases, the female offender is also likely to have committed a nonsexual offense and a sexual offense.... Cases that involve a male codefendant rightfully or wrongfully often do not result in the woman being charged.... [M]ost studies are based on male offenders.

State v. Hardie

Court of Appeals of Ohio, Fourth District, 2001
141 Ohio App. 3d 1, 749 N.E.2d 792

KLINE, Presiding Judge....

On January 14, 2000, [Mary J.] Hardie pled guilty to two counts of corruption of a minor, a violation of R.C. 2907.04(A). In March 2000, the trial court held a hearing to determine if Hardie is a sexual predator. At the hearing, the only witness was Dr. James Michael Harding. Dr. Harding interviewed Hardie for about an hour and administered testing for another hour and forty minutes. Dr. Harding testified that there is very little research or statistical information available about female sexual offenders. He opined that offenses by females are underreported. He explained that he did not use the tests ordinarily used to assess the likelihood that a male sex offender will reoffend because they have not been "normed as to a female." Instead, he administered a MMPI-2 test, which provides objective measures for some of the factors that have been shown to predict recidivism. The results of this test indicate that Hardie is "anxious, tense, fearful, lacking self-confidence, lacking insight into [herself], lacking insight into how others perceive [her], and * * * [has] an extreme need for affection." People with this profile tend to have poor treatment prognosis for psychological problems unless they can be motivated to participate in treatment. Dr. Harding stated that if such a person is motivated, long-term treatment is required for any benefit.

Dr. Harding then testified about the statutory risk factors for recidivism. He explained that the following characteristics of Hardie and her offenses are associated with high risk: (1) Hardie had multiple victims; (2) Hardie committed multiple offenses against each victim; (3) Hardie provided alcohol to the victims, although it was not clear whether she did so in order to impair the victims; (4) Hardie attempted to minimize the offenses and attempted to place responsibility for the offenses on her poor relationship with her husband, which caused her to have low self-esteem and be depressed; (5) Hardie stopped offending only after being caught with one of the victims; (6) Hardie's chronic low self-esteem and tolerance of treatment by the victims that she perceived to be inappropriate indicate social skills deficits, especially with intimacy; and (7) Hardie experienced cognitive distortions regarding the victims (she knew her offenses were wrong, but attempted to minimalize them because the victims were "experienced" and she complained about the victims' treatment of her).

Dr. Harding next explained that the following characteristics of Hardie and her offenses are associated with a low risk of recidivism: (1) Hardie has no prior juvenile or adult offenses; (2) the offenses did not occur in a public place; (3) the victims were older than thirteen; (4) Hardie has no history of substance abuse; (5) there was no allegation of force or threats of force against the victims; (6) no history of violent, disruptive, or paranoid behavior on the part of Hardie; (7) no history of unstable employment; and (8) the victims were not strangers.

The trial court also considered a presentence investigation report prepared by the Ohio Adult Parole Authority. The report indicates that Hardie engaged in vaginal intercourse and oral sex with two fourteen-year-old twin brothers who were family friends. She purchased alcohol and cigarettes for the victims and her own children. She admitted that she knew that what she was doing was wrong. The victims told investigators that the sexual conduct was consensual and that Hardie did not use force.... The trial court found that Hardie is likely to engage in the future in one or more sexually oriented offenses and determined that she is a sexual predator. The trial court sentenced Hardie to a sentence of eighteen months on each count, to be served concurrently....

In her only assignment of error, Hardie asserts that the trial court erred in determining that she is a sexual predator. A sexual predator is defined as a person who has been convicted of or has pled guilty to committing a sexually oriented offense and is likely to engage in the future in one or more sexually oriented offenses. R.C. 2950.01(E). Sexual predator classification proceedings under R.C. 2950.09 are civil in nature and require the prosecution to prove by clear and convincing evidence that an offender is a sexual predator. R.C. 2950.09(B); *State v. Cook* (1998), 83 Ohio St.3d 404, 408, 700 N.E.2d 570, 575. We will not reverse a trial court's determination that an offender is a sexual predator if some competent credible evidence supports it.... [citations omitted]. This deferential standard of review applies even though the state must prove that the offender is a sexual predator by clear and convincing evidence.... [citations omitted].

In order to determine if the offender is likely to engage in future sexually oriented offenses, the trial court must consider all relevant factors, including those listed in R.C. 2950.09(B)(2). These factors are:

"(a) The offender's age;

"(b) The offender's prior criminal record regarding all offenses, including, but not limited to, all sexual offenses;

"(c) The age of the victim of the sexually oriented offense for which sentence is to be imposed;

"(d) Whether the sexually oriented offense for which sentence is to be imposed involved multiple victims;

"(e) Whether the offender used drugs or alcohol to impair the victim of the sexually oriented offense or to prevent the victim from resisting;

"(f) If the offender previously has been convicted of or pleaded guilty to any criminal offense, whether the offender completed any sentence imposed for the prior offense and, if the prior offense was a sex offense or a sexually oriented offense, whether the offender participated in available programs for sexual offenders;

"(g) Any mental illness or mental disability of the offender;

"(h) The nature of the offender's sexual conduct, sexual contact, or interaction in a sexual context with the victim of the sexually oriented offense and whether the sexual conduct, sexual contact, or interaction in a sexual context was part of a demonstrated pattern of abuse;

"(i) Whether the offender, during the commission of the sexually oriented offense for which sentence is to be imposed, displayed cruelty or made one or more threats of cruelty;

"(j) Any additional behavioral characteristics that contribute to the offender's conduct."

We note that the statute requires a court to consider all relevant factors. The statute does not, however, require a trial court to make explicit findings regarding relevant factors.... [citations omitted]. Furthermore, a trier of fact may look at past behavior in determining future propensity because past behavior is often an important indicator for future propensity.... [citations omitted]. For that very reason, a court may designate a first-time offender as a sexual predator.... [citations omitted].... A court is under no obligation to "tally up" the R.C. 2950.09(B)(2) factors in any particular fashion.... [citations omitted]. A court may classify an offender as a "sexual predator" even if only one or two statutory factors are present, so long as the totality of the relevant circumstances provides clear and convincing evidence that the offender is likely to commit a future sexually oriented offense.... A court may properly designate an offender as a sexual predator even in the absence of expert testimony from the state.... [citations omitted]....

Neither party disputes that Hardie pled guilty to committing a sexually oriented offense. Therefore, the only issue in this case is whether there is some competent, credible evidence that she is likely to engage in the future in one or more sexually oriented offenses. We find that there is some competent, credible evidence to support the trial court's finding that Hardie is likely to engage in one or more sexually oriented offenses in the future. Dr. Harding outlined many characteristics of Hardie and her offenses that indicate that she is likely to reoffend. Among these were the multiple offenses against the multiple victims, the provision of alcohol to the victims, Hardie's chronic low self-esteem and tendency to place responsibility for her offenses on other persons, and Hardie's continuation of the offense until she was caught. Accordingly, we find that the trial court's decision that Hardie is a sexual predator is not against the manifest weight of the evidence and affirm the judgment of the trial court.

Judgment affirmed.

EVANS and HARSHA, JJ., concur.

Notes

In the *Hardie* decision, the court determined the female defendant to be a sexual predator based on the report of an expert who considered objective factors that have been shown to predict recidivism but that were not the factors normally applied to male sexual offenders and were not specifically weighted for application to female offenders. In fact, most sexual offenses against children are committed by males. Sexual offenses against children that are committed by females tend to garner significant media attention precisely because they are unique and prompt significant social interest. For example, consider the following three cases:

Case One: The most prominent case involving a female sexual offender was that of Mary Kay Letourneau—a 35-year-old sixth grade teacher and mother of four children—who had sexual intercourse with Vili Fualaau—a 13-year-old student who attended the school where Letourneau taught. *See State v. Letourneau*, 100 Wash. App. 424, 997 P.2d 436 (2000). Letourneau plead guilty to two counts of second degree rape of a child and was sentenced to 89 months in jail. She would serve only 180 days in jail if she complied with specific sentence conditions, including three years of specialized sexual deviancy treatment. Another of her sentence conditions was that she was to have no contact with Fualaau for the remainder of her life. However, less than two weeks after her release from prison, police discovered Letourneau having sexual relations with Fualaau in her car, and she was resentenced to serve seven years in prison. During her re-incarceration, Letourneau gave birth to two more children, each of whom was fathered by her victim, Fualaau. While in prison, Letourneau and Fualaau published a book in France titled, *"Only One Crime, Love."* Her financial gain from the book, as a violation of her sentence conditions, prompted further litigation. Upon Letourneau's release from prison in 2004, she registered as a Level 2 sex offender. The court revoked the no-contact order at the request of Fualaau, who had since turned 18 years old. Letourneau and Fualaau married in 2005 and gained celebrity status. Letourneau's story was recounted in a made-for-TV movie, called *"All-American Girl: The Mary Kay Letourneau Story."* Letourneau's name has become synonymous with females who exploit male minors.

Case Two: In another infamous female sex offender case, similar to that of Letourneau, Pamela Rogers Turner—a 27-year-old Tennessee teacher—had sex with her 13-year-old student and, in 2005, was charged with four counts of sexual battery by an authority figure. *See* Bill Poovey, *Ex-Teacher Goes to Jail for Nude Photos*, available at http://www.washingtonpost.com/wp-dyn/content/article/2006/07/14/AR2006071401111.html (last visited Jan. 22, 2015). Turner was sentenced to nine months in jail and eight years of probation. However, like Letourneau, she violated her probation by sending nude photos and sexual videos of herself to the same boy and was sentenced to serve the remainder of her eight-year sentence in prison, plus two more years for sexual exploitation of a minor for sending the additional photos of herself to the boy. *Id. See also* Josh Gardner, *'She doesn't deserve to be here': Teacher 'who had sex with three students' is defended by VICTIM in court as judge says she'll stand trial for continuing relations with 17-year-old while she was on bail*, available at http://www.dailymail.co.uk/news/article-2912771/She-doesn-t-deserve-Teacher-sex-three-students-defended-victim-judge-says-ll-stand-trial-continued-relations-17-year-old.html (last visited Jan. 22, 2015) (describing case of 35-year-old Utah high school teacher Brianne Altice, who faces dozens of felony charges, including rape and unlawful sexual activity, but nevertheless is supported by one of her victims).

Case Three: Another female sex offender, Debra Lafave, was a 24-year-old Florida teacher who had sex on several occasions with a 14-year-old student. Lafave faced at least 15 years in prison for her offenses. Instead, Lafave agreed to a sentence of three years of house arrest and seven years of probation. But the court rejected the plea agreement, stating that any sentence that did not require jail time would "undermine the credibility of [the] court, and the criminal justice system as a whole, and would erode public confidence in our schools." *See* Jeffrey Kofman, *Double Standard in LaFave Case?*, available at http://abcnews.go.com/GMA/LegalCenter/story?id=1752245&page=1 (last viewed Jan. 22, 2015). When psychologists testified that a trial would severely traumatize the minor victim, Lafave retained her probation and avoided prison. Her sentence prompted a social media firestorm over the "implicit belief among Americans that Lafave is 'too pretty for prison,'" *see* Suzanne Goldenberg, *Too Pretty for Prison*, THE GUARDIAN, MAR. 23, 2006. Subsequently, Lafave petitioned the court to terminate her probation four years early, in 2011. Her petition was granted, and the victim's family appealed. The District Court of Appeal quashed the probation termination in 2012, *see State v. Lafave*, 113 So.3d 31 (Fla. App. 2 Dist. 2012) (enforcing "no early termination" of probation provision in negotiated plea agreement), and in 2013, Lafave was ordered to continue her probation until the Florida Supreme Court resolved the case. In October 2014, the Florida Supreme Court held that the state lacked jurisdiction to seek the District Court's review of the probation termination and quashed the decision of the District Court of Appeal which reinstated Lafave's probation, *see Lafave v. State*, 149 So.3d 662 (2014).

For other notorious cases, see the cases of Shelley Dufresne — a 32-year-old Louisiana teacher and mother of three, who had "threesome" sex with a 16-year-old student and another 24-year-old teacher, Rachel Respess. *See* Helen Freund, *Destrehan High School teacher Shelley Dufresne had 'prior sexual encounters' with student, police say*, available at http://www.nola.com/crime/index.ssf/2014/10/destrehan_high_school_teacher_1.html (last visited Jan. 22, 2015). Also, former NFL Cheerleader Molly Shattuck — a 47-year-old mother of three and, at the time, wife of Mayo Shattuck, the former CEO of Constellation Energy — was charged with several counts of rape and unlawful sexual contact with a 15-year-old boy. *See* Terri Sanginiti and James Fisher, *Cops: Ex-Ravens cheerleader had sex with boy in Delaware*, available at http://www.delawareonline.com/story/news/crime/2014/11/05/cops-ravens-cheerleader-sex-delaware-boy/18527125/ (last visited Jan. 22, 2015). Shattuck pled guilty to a single count of rape in the fourth degree in June 2015 and faces up to 15 years in prison. Helena Andrews, *Molly Shattuck pleads guilty to the rape of a 15-year-old*, available at http://www.washingtonpost.com/blogs/reliable-source/wp/2015/06/16/molly-shattuck-pleads-guilty-to-the-rape-of-a-15-year-old/ (last visited June 28, 2015).

In all of these cases, like the exploitation committed in *State v. Hardie*, the exploitation committed by the female offenders consisted of consensual sexual activity with an adolescent minor with whom the female exploiter had an ongoing or previously-existing relationship. Often, this involves a "student-teacher" relationship. Nevertheless, the offense is no less exploitative of the minor involved. For a discussion of whether teachers who engage in sexual relationships with their students should be held to a higher standard, see Katelyn Burch Busby, Student Author, *EDUCATION — Student-Teacher Relationships — Should Teachers Be Held to a Higher Standard? Understanding the Laws Governing Sexual Relationships Between Students and Teachers in Primary and Secondary Schools. Paschal v. State, 2012 Ark. 127, 388 S.W.3d 429*, 36 UALR L. REV. 103 (2013) (calling for bright-line rule prohibiting teachers from engaging in sexual contact with students, regardless of age, until the student graduates from high school). All of these cases demonstrate the difficulty of identifying, prosecuting, and appropriately responding to female exploiters, especially those who tend to recidivate.

Despite a relatively recent rise in reporting of female sex offenses — mostly due to state and federal legislation, such as "Megan's Law" (N.J. Stat. Ann. § 2C:7-1-7-11 (1994)) and the "Wetterling Act" (codified at 42 U.S.C. § 14071 (2006)), the question remains whether there should be a difference in the risk assessment protocol applicable to male and female sexual offenders. Is such a difference constitutionally sufficient? If so, should it be statutorily required? The *Sex Offender Registry Board* case raises these considerations.

Doe v. Sex Offender Registry Board

Supreme Court of Massachusetts, 2013
466 Mass. 594, 999 N.E.2d 478

LENK, J....

The requirement to register as a sex offender is governed by a set of statutes enacted in 1999, which were designed "to protect ... the vulnerable members of our communities from sexual offenders." St. 1999, c. 74, preamble. In enacting the sex offender registration statute, the Legislature was concerned primarily with "the danger of recidivism posed by sex offenders, especially sexually violent offenders who commit predatory acts characterized by repetitive and compulsive behavior." St. 1999, c. 74, § 1. To address this problem, the Legislature created a regime of registration and "classification of such offenders on an individualized basis according to their risk of reoffense and degree of dangerousness." ... An offender may be classified into one of three categories of dangerousness, with differing attendant duties and implications for the public dissemination of the offender's information....

The statute requires that [the Sex Offender Registry Board (SORB)] transmit registration information on all offenders to the "police departments in the municipalities where such sex offender lives, has a secondary address and works and attends an institution of higher learning or, if in custody, intends to live and work and attend an institution of higher learning upon release and where the offense was committed and to the Federal Bureau of Investigation." ... Information pertaining to level one sex offenders is not disseminated to the general public.... The duty to comply with registration requirements persists for twenty years, at a minimum, from the date of conviction of the underlying offense or release from custody....

As we have emphasized, the sex offender registration law implicates constitutionally protected liberty and privacy interests. See, e.g., *Doe v. Attorney Gen.*, 426 Mass. 136, 144, 686 N.E.2d 1007 (1997). Because of the breadth of the statute, and to safeguard these interests, "careful and individualized due process is necessary to sort sexual predators likely to repeat their crimes from large numbers of offenders who pose no danger to the public, but who are nonetheless caught in the statute's far-flung net of registration." *Doe, Sex Offender Registry Bd. No. 972 v. Sex Offender Registry Bd.*, 428 Mass. 90, 105, 697 N.E.2d 512 (1998) (Marshall, J., concurring in part and dissenting in part).

To facilitate individualized determinations of the likelihood of recidivism, and to serve the public's interest in the accurate identification of potential risk, the statute directs SORB to promulgate regulations for classifying sex offenders into one of the three categories of dangerousness. See G.L. c. 6, § 178K (1)–(2). The statute sets forth a nonexhaustive list of factors to consider, G.L. c. 6, § 178K (1) *(a)–(l)*, which the regulations augment by formulating specific guidelines for the application of each factor. See 803 Code Mass. Regs. § 1.40 (2002) (guidelines). The guidelines list twenty-four factors to consider in making a determination of potential risk.... Each factor includes a discussion of the reasons it is germane to predicting recidivism; almost all of the factors are supported by citations to relevant scientific studies.... This grounding in "the available literature," ... ensures that an offender's ultimate classification is the product of reasoned application of validated empirical studies. The guidelines provide that "the definitions, explanations, principles, and authorities contained in these Factors shall guide the Hearing Examiner in reaching a Final Classification decision." ... SORB bears the burden of justifying the appropriateness of its classification determination by a preponderance of the evidence. 803 Code Mass. Regs. § 1.10(1) (2002). See *Doe, Sex Offender Registry Bd. No. 8725 v. Sex Offender Registry Bd.*, 450 Mass. 780, 782 n. 4, 882 N.E.2d 298 (2008).

Here, Doe argues that SORB did not meet this burden, particularly in light of compelling scientific evidence that female offenders generally pose a much lower risk of reoffense. Doe argues that the hearing examiner arbitrarily ignored this evidence on female recidivism and reached a classification determination without having considered the effect of Doe's gender on her risk of dangerousness and likelihood of reoffense. She contends further that the hearing examiner abused his discretion in denying her motion for funds for an expert who would have testified to current knowledge on females' risk of sexually reoffending and to the application of the guidelines to one in Doe's circumstances....

In 2006, Doe pleaded guilty in the United States District Court for the District of Massachusetts to two counts of conspiracy, 18 U.S.C. § 371 (2006); one count of transporting a minor to engage in prostitution, 18 U.S.C. § 2423 (2006); one count of transporting an individual to engage in prostitution, 18 U.S.C. § 2421 (2006); and one count of sex trafficking of children, 18 U.S.C. § 1591 (2006). The convictions arose from Doe's management of an escort service in New England from approximately 2000 to 2002.... [footnote omitted].... Doe started the escort service after ceasing to work as a prostitute for various "pimps," at whose hands she had suffered a number of serious physical assaults.... [footnote omitted]. The service, which employed up to twenty individuals at any given time, primarily offered erotic full-body massages; Doe instructed her employees that they had the "option" of having sexual relations with clients if the employees were so inclined and if they felt they could do so safely. Doe collected a fixed dollar amount from each payment that an employee received, and the employee kept the remainder, whatever the nature of the services performed.

Although she asked potential employees for identification documents before hiring them, Doe employed four minors in her escort service between 2001 and 2002. One of the minors, Minor A, began working for Doe when she was fourteen years old, using a false New York identification card that listed her age as nineteen. Doe sent Minor A on multiple client calls, in Massachusetts, New Hampshire, and Rhode Island, and sometimes drove her to these calls. In July of 2001, Doe saw Minor A's picture on a National Center for Missing and Exploited Children poster and learned the girl's actual age. Shortly thereafter, she directed another employee to telephone the center to report Minor A's location.

The resulting criminal investigation by the Federal Bureau of Investigation revealed the employment of Minors B, C, and D in Doe's escort service. Approximately three years after she ceased operation of the service, Doe was arrested; she was indicted for and pleaded guilty to sexually offending only against Minor A.... [footnote omitted]. Doe was sentenced to a term of incarceration for the crime of transporting a minor to engage in prostitution, deemed served while she spent seventeen months incarcerated awaiting trial, prior to entry of her plea. She was sentenced to a three-year period of supervised release for the other offenses....

In April, 2008, SORB notified Doe of its preliminary recommendation that she be classified as a level two sex offender, pursuant to G.L. c. 6, § 178K (2) *(b)*. Doe timely requested a hearing to challenge that recommendation, pursuant to G.L. c. 6, § 178L (1) *(a)*. She submitted several prehearing motions addressing the applicability of SORB's guidelines to female sex offenders. A hearing was held on October 8, 2008. After the hearing, but before rendering a decision, the hearing examiner recused himself with the agreement of the parties. A second hearing examiner was appointed to assume the case and issue a decision on the basis of the record and the previous examiner's findings.

Prior to the hearing, Doe moved for funds for an expert witness, pursuant to G.L. c. 6, § 178L (1) *(a)*, to testify concerning research on female sexual recidivism. She argued that SORB's guidelines did not encompass scientific research regarding rates of reoffense among female sex offenders. In support of this argument, Doe submitted nearly all of the scientific studies cited by the guidelines' twenty-four risk factors, demonstrating that the studies were based almost exclusively on male subjects. She also offered two additional articles, not referenced in the guidelines, that specifically studied female sex offenders. One of the authors of those articles has published extensive research on other aspects of male sex offender recidivism, relied upon throughout the guidelines' discussion of the various risk factors. See 803 Code Mass. Regs. § 1.40.

Stating that research into female sex offender recidivism is "a work in progress" that "does not rise to the level of a breakthrough as to warrant restructuring the SORB classification guidelines," the first hearing examiner denied Doe's motion and subsequently denied her motion for reconsideration, made at the hearing. The second hearing examiner affirmed this decision, stating that there was "no reason to exercise discretion" to grant Doe's motion, where the regulations provide that females are to be classified in the same manner as males and the statute uses gender-neutral language, and where Doe "offered only an unpersuasive generic need for an expert witness." ...

Doe denied recruiting individual employees to work for her escort service. Rather, she testified that candidates approached her seeking work after seeing advertisements that she ran in local newspapers. The individuals that Doe hired often had worked previously as prostitutes for what Doe termed local "pimps"; Doe stated that she encouraged people to leave their pimps and to work for her instead because she offered a safer working environment.[5] ... Doe eventually became romantically involved with a man who helped her to stop her drug abuse, and by the time she became pregnant with their child in 2002, she was no longer using drugs. She has not done so since that time. After the birth of her daughter, Doe let the escort service advertisements lapse and began attending community college in order to obtain a general educational development certificate (GED). She now lives with her daughter and a friend of her mother, and she has been employed as a waitress, bartender, and manager at a restaurant since 2006.

In rendering a decision, the second hearing examiner determined that Doe's Federal convictions of transporting a minor to engage in prostitution and sex trafficking of children were "like violations" matching the Massachusetts offense of inducing a minor into prostitution, G.L. c. 272, § 4A. He determined that Doe posed a low risk of reoffense and should be classified as a level one sex offender, rather than the level two classification SORB initially recommended. He based his conclusion on the application of certain factors indicating heightened risk, including "repetitive and compulsive" behavior and "sex offenses involving children." See 803 Code Mass. Regs. § 1.40(2), (9)(c)(12). He also noted that Doe's "significant criminal record" contributed to an "elevated concern regarding [her] risk to reoffend and degree of dangerousness." Citing the test for compulsiveness that looks to whether, "in the interval between acts of sexual misconduct, the offender had sufficient opportunity to reflect on the wrongfulness of [her] conduct and take remedial measures by avoidance, counseling or otherwise, to stop [her]self from committing

---

5. Doe and her friend both testified that she earned a reputation among prostitutes as someone who would take them in and provide safe shelter after the pimps they worked for became too abusive. Sometimes Doe provided a rental automobile or a cellular telephone to assist them in leaving abusive pimps. She became known among these women as the "ho savior."

This testimony, while uncontested, was not viewed by the hearing examiner as mitigating in any way. He characterized it as overly "altruistic" and stated, "That [Doe] provided these women *and minors* with a safer place to work does not excuse her behavior" (emphasis in original).

subsequent acts of sexual misconduct," the hearing examiner determined that Doe's conduct was "compulsive" as that term is used in the regulations. See 803 Code Mass. Regs. § 1.40(2)(c). The examiner also considered factors that tend to reduce risk, such as Doe's "acceptance of responsibility" and "current home situation." See 803 Code Mass. Regs. § 1.40(9)(c)(13), 1.40(12).... Doe sought judicial review of SORB's decision in the Superior Court, pursuant to G.L. c. 6, § 178M, and G.L. c. 30A, § 14. A Superior Court judge held that the classification decision was supported by substantial evidence and affirmed SORB's recommended classification level.... [footnote omitted]. Doe appealed, and we granted her application for direct appellate review....

Pursuant to G.L. c. 6, § 178M, a sex offender may seek judicial review of SORB's final classification determination in accordance with G.L. c. 30A, § 14. A reviewing court will set aside or modify SORB's decision if it was "*(a)* [i]n violation of constitutional provisions"; "*(b)* [i]n excess of the statutory authority or jurisdiction" of SORB; "*(c)* [b]ased upon an error of law"; "*(d)* [m]ade upon unlawful procedure"; "*(e)* [u]nsupported by substantial evidence"; "*(f)* [u]nwarranted by facts found by the court ... where the court is constitutionally required to make independent findings of fact"; or "*(g)* [a]rbitrary or capricious, an abuse of discretion, or otherwise not in accordance with law." G.L. c. 30A, § 14(7)....

Contrary to SORB's characterization of Doe's claim, Doe does not challenge the overall validity of the guidelines. Rather, she argues that SORB did not meet its burden of proving her risk of sexual reoffense, particularly in light of the hearing examiner's arbitrary failure to consider the relevance of gender as an additional factor alongside the other risk factors outlined in the guidelines. She argues further that the hearing examiner abused his discretion by denying her motion for funds for an expert who would have testified to female sexual recidivism, where Doe showed that the hearing examiner otherwise would not have competent evidence before him to assess Doe's risk of reoffense.

SORB "bears the burden of justifying [its] classification [determination] by a preponderance of the evidence at an evidentiary hearing at which an offender has the right to present evidence and cross-examine witnesses, and after which the hearing examiner must make 'specific, written, detailed, and individualized findings' supporting the board's final classification." *Doe, Sex Offender Registry Bd. No. 941 v. Sex Offender Registry Bd.*, 460 Mass. 336, 338, 951 N.E.2d 344 (2011), quoting *Doe, Sex Offender Registry Bd. No. 972 v. Sex Offender Registry Bd.*, 428 Mass. 90, 91, 697 N.E.2d 512 (1998). The guidelines that SORB uses to make these findings were last updated in 2002; the "available literature" cited is largely between fifteen and twenty years old, see 803 Mass Code. Regs. § 1.40, and is based almost exclusively on observation of male sex offenders. Such emphasis on males is not necessarily surprising, given that the sex offender population is overwhelmingly male. See Cortoni, Hanson, & Coache, The Recidivism Rates of Female Sexual Offenders Are Low: A Meta-Analysis, 22 Sexual Abuse 387, 388 (2010) (Cortoni, Hanson, & Coache) (meta-analysis of ten studies carried out in Australia, Canada, New Zealand, United Kingdom, and United States).[7]

There is a growing body of research, however, on that portion of the sex offender population that is female, approximately five per cent of all offenders.... As we noted in *Doe [, Sex Offender Registry Bd. No. 151564 v. Sex Offender Registry Bd.*, 456 Mass. 612, 621 n. 5, 925 N.E.2d 533 (2010)], a case examining the importance of consideration of a sex

---

7. SORB argues that this article, from 2010, should not be considered on appeal, as it was not part of the 2008 hearing record. This argument is without merit, as we often consider scientific studies in rendering decisions with broad societal implications. See, e.g., *Commonwealth v. Walker*, 460 Mass. 590, 601–602, 953 N.E.2d 195 (2011) (citing articles on eyewitness identification issues); *Commonwealth*

offender's current age in reaching a classification determination, "[k]nowledge concerning sexual offender recidivism risk has advanced considerably during the past [eleven] years." *Id.*, quoting Public Safety and Emergency Preparedness Canada, Predictors of Sexual Recidivism: An Updated Meta-Analysis, at 1 (2004). Since 2002, an increasing amount of research has focused on female sexual recidivism, suggesting that different pathways lead females to offend,[8] and that females have weaker impulses to reoffend; research has found that females have a much lower rate of sexually reoffending than do males, with some studies showing a one per cent recidivism rate as compared to 13.4 per cent among males. F. Cortoni & R.K. Hanson, Correctional Service of Canada, A Review of the Recidivism Rates of Adult Female Sexual Offenders, at 1, 7, 12 (2005) (Cortoni & Hanson)....

Although the guidelines do not take into account the gender of the sex offender, SORB is empowered by both the statute and the regulations to consider "any information useful," G.L. c. 6, §178L (1), and 803 Mass.Code Regs. §1.38(2) (2002), "including information introduced by the plaintiff," *Doe, Sex Offender Registry Bd. No. 3844 v. Sex Offender Registry Bd.*, 447 Mass. 768, 777, 857 N.E.2d 485 (2006), in arriving at a classification decision. The ability to consider other useful information not specifically contemplated by the guidelines is an important safety valve protecting a sex offender's due process rights.... To that effect, we held in *Doe No. 151564, supra* at 622–623, 925 N.E.2d 533, that it was error not to consider as other useful information the effect of age on recidivism, notwithstanding the lack of explicit reference to age as a factor in the guidelines, where substantial evidence regarding this effect was presented at the hearing. See *Doe, Sex Offender Registry Bd. No. 136652 v. Sex Offender Registry Bd.*, 81 Mass.App.Ct. 639, 656, 966 N.E.2d 826 (2012) (holding that it was arbitrary and capricious for SORB to fail to consider "studies referenced in the record showing the differences between the psychological development and outlook of children and mature adults" when classifying sex offender who was ten years old at time of offense).

Here, both the first and second hearing examiners accepted in evidence the studies on female sexual recidivism that Doe offered, but concluded that they did not present new information to be taken into account in making a classification determination. Neither hearing examiner questioned the accuracy or the reliability of the studies, or cited countervailing studies. Rather, the first hearing examiner characterized research into female recidivism as a "work in progress" that did not "rise to the level of a breakthrough as to warrant restructuring of the SORB classification guidelines." The second hearing examiner, in rendering a decision, agreed, stating that "[SORB]'s regulations and mission need not be halted until a greater consensus on the predictors of female sex offender recidivism is reached in the scientific community, nor should [SORB] amend its regulations each time a new study contradicts its factors." He thus concluded that "classification may be determined generically" based on "common sense factors."

SORB argues that the hearing examiners properly declined to give weight to the studies that Doe submitted, because "being a 'female offender' is neither an additional nor mitigating risk factor to be considered by the Hearing Examiner," and the regulations specifically provide that the risk factors are to apply with equal force to both males and

---

v. Pytou Heang, 458 Mass. 827, 836–837, 942 N.E.2d 927 (2011) (citing articles on accuracy of ballistics testing).

8. For example, research indicates that female sex offenders are more likely than male sex offenders to have a history of sexual victimization; females are more likely to commit a sex offense with a co-offending male, often as a result of coercion by the male; and offending by females is more likely to occur within caregiving situations. Center for Sex Offender Management, United States Department of Justice, Female Sex Offenders, at 7 (2007).

females. See 803 Code Mass. Regs. § 1.39(4) (2002). SORB contends further that the studies Doe offered do not prove beyond a reasonable doubt that SORB's risk factors are inapplicable to female sex offenders. This stance misses the mark for several reasons.

First, in sex offender classification proceedings, the offender bears no burden of proof, let alone one beyond a reasonable doubt. Rather, the burden is on SORB to undertake a "sound application of [the risk-classification] factors to derive a true and accurate assessment of an offender's potential for reoffending," *Doe, Sex Offender Registry Bd. No. 136652 v. Sex Offender Registry Bd., supra* at 656, 966 N.E.2d 826. Second, Doe does not argue that all of the guidelines' risk factors are inapplicable to females, but rather that recent research on females' lower rates of sexual recidivism also should be weighed. As the second hearing examiner noted, SORB need not update its guidelines every time a new study is published. However, the development of evolving research is among the reasons that a hearing examiner is empowered to consider "any information useful" beyond the enumerated risk factors. G.L. c. 6, § 178L (1); 803 Code Mass. Regs. § 1.38(2). The ability to consider other information provides the flexibility to respond to authoritative research as it is published, where it is relevant in a given case. There is a circularity, and an irony, in SORB's argument that the guidelines apply with equal force to males and females simply because SORB has declared that to be the case in promulgating its regulations, which are themselves based on research conducted almost exclusively on male subjects. SORB's argument thus amounts to the equivalent of the claim that we rejected in *Doe No. 151564, supra* at 622, 925 N.E.2d 533, where "it justifie [d] its decision not to consider age solely on the basis that age is not considered as a factor in its regulations."

Here, authoritative evidence was introduced suggesting that the guidelines, developed as they were from studies of male offenders, could not predict accurately the recidivism risk of a female offender, and that such risk could not be evaluated without examining the effect of gender. One study, from 2005, found that female sex offenders exhibited a one per cent sexual recidivism rate, as compared to a 13.4 per cent sexual recidivism rate in males. Cortoni & Hanson, *supra* at 1, 7, 12. That study cautioned that "risk tools developed on male sexual offenders are unlikely to apply to females. Simply extrapolating from the male sexual offender literature to assess risk in female sexual offenders is likely to lead to invalid risk appraisal and unintended consequences." *Id.* at 12–13. The other study, from 2007, corroborated this finding, concluding that because "most tools that assess sex offense-specific issues have been developed for and normed on male sex offenders, their use with female sex offenders [is] questionable, at best." Center for Sex Offender Management, United States Department of Justice, Female Sex Offenders, at 8 (2007).

The 2005 study called for further research to establish empirically validated risk factors for female sexual recidivism, but suggested that, until such research occurs, "an evaluation of risk take[ ] into consideration dynamic risk factors related to general recidivism in women. These risk factors include antisocial attitudes and associates, substance abuse as precursor to offending, problematic relationships, and emotional dyscontrol." Cortoni & Hanson, *supra* at 13. Thus, while it is not necessarily the case that all risk factors contained in the guidelines are categorically inapplicable to females,[9] the proffered research strongly indicates that the factors have a weaker predictive value for females, whose sexual recidivism rates are substantially lower than their general recidivism rates (i.e., commission of any offense, sexual or otherwise). See Cortoni & Hanson, *supra* at 7 (finding female general recidivism rate of 20.2 per cent). See also Cortoni, Hanson, & Coache, *supra* at 396

---

9. The guidelines contain a number of risk factors roughly analogous to those identified in the 2005 study. For example, factor 9(b) considers an offender's antisocial behavior, 803 Code Mass.

(finding female sexual recidivism rate of between one and three per cent and general recidivism rate of between nineteen and twenty-four per cent).[10] Moreover, insofar as the proffered research reveals a substantially lower recidivism rate for females as a group, it appears that gender itself has meaningful predictive value as a distinct risk factor.

These studies thus constituted current, validated evidence demonstrating the relevance of gender in assessing the risk of reoffense that Doe posed to the general public. The hearing examiner ultimately rejected this evidence without "cit[ing] any studies to the contrary." *Doe No. 151564, supra* at 622, 925 N.E.2d 533. See *Cohen v. Board of Registration in Pharmacy*, 350 Mass. 246, 251–252, 214 N.E.2d 63 (1966) (rejection of evidence does not create substantial evidence to contrary). Just as in *Doe No. 151564, supra* at 622– 623, 925 N.E.2d 533, where "it was arbitrary and capricious for [SORB] to classify Doe's 'risk of reoffense and degree of dangerousness' " without considering the "substantial evidence presented at the hearing concerning the effect of age on recidivism," so, too, here SORB arbitrarily and capriciously failed to evaluate evidence of the effect of gender, both on the potency of existing risk factors in predicting reoffense, and as a risk factor in its own right, in arriving at a classification determination.[11]

More broadly, notwithstanding the safety valve of the "any useful information" provision, it is incumbent upon SORB to ensure that its guidelines are, in fact, based on "the available literature." 803 Code Mass. Regs. § 1.40. We do not purport to suggest a frequency with which the guidelines must be updated, but caution that guidelines that fail to heed growing scientific consensus in an area may undercut the individualized nature of the hearing to which a sex offender is entitled, an important due process right. See *Doe, Sex Offender Registry Bd. No. 10800 v. Sex Offender Registry Bd.*, 459 Mass. 603, 626, 947 N.E.2d 9 (2011), and cases cited. See also *Doe No. 151564, supra* at 623 n. 6, 925 N.E.2d 533, citing *Commonwealth v. Lanigan*, 419 Mass. 15, 27, 641 N.E.2d 1342 (1994) ("Where, as here, scientific knowledge in a field is rapidly evolving ... the applicable standards may require more frequent modification in order to reflect accurately the current state of knowledge" [citation omitted]). This potential for the frustration of individualized risk assessment is particularly conspicuous where the growing scientific

---

Regs. § 1.40(9)(b) (2002); factor 12 considers the nature of an offender's relationships with family, friends, and acquaintances, 803 Code Mass. Regs. § 1.40(12) (2002); and factor 16 considers an offender's substance or alcohol abuse, 803 Code Mass. Regs. § 1.40(16) (2002).

10. Indeed, other States also have recognized the limitations of using risk-assessment tools based on males to determine female sexual recidivism. See, e.g., *Matter of Risk Level Determination of S.S.*, 726 N.W.2d 121, 125–126 (Minn.Ct.App.2007) (department of corrections erred in "fail[ing] to implement a statutorily sound procedure for the comparably few female offenders it must also assess," where tool it relied on was "statistically valid only as applied to male sex offenders, and ... [had] never been used for female offenders"); *Matter of Coffel*, 117 S.W.3d 116, 128–129 (Mo.Ct.App.2003) (determination of female sex offender as sexually violent predator not based on substantial evidence where experts had experience with male sex offenders only; "the research that has been performed on the factors that cause males to sexually reoffend cannot be applied to female sex offenders"). California appears to be the only State to have enacted statutory provisions requiring the use of different risk-assessment tools for female sex offenders. See Cal.Penal Code § 290.04(c) (Deering 2008). However, while California's statute directs a review committee to research risk-assessment tools for female sex offenders, it appears that, to date, such a tool has yet to be developed.

11. Because we decide Doe's claims under the Administrative Procedure Act, G.L. c. 30A, § 14(7), we do not reach the constitutional arguments, put forth in the amicus brief, that the hearing examiner's failure to evaluate scientific evidence on female sexual recidivism, and its denial of expert-witness funds, violated Doe's right to equal protection pursuant to the Fourteenth Amendment to the United States Constitution and art. 12 of the Massachusetts Declaration of Rights. See *Commonwealth v. Vega*, 449 Mass. 227, 234, 866 N.E.2d 892 (2007).

consensus suggests specific factors that have quantifiable effects on recidivism rates, such as age and gender. The sex offender registration statute delegates authority to SORB to implement its statutory provisions and to make classification determinations for individual offenders. See G.L. c. 6, § 178K. SORB, as a body with specialized knowledge, is authorized to make decisions and promulgate regulations with all relevant information before it; indeed, "[i]t is in everyone's best interests — including the best interests of sex offenders themselves — that [SORB] work from accurate, up to date, and thorough information." *Doe, Sex Offender Registry Bd. No. 89230 v. Sex Offender Registry Bd.*, 452 Mass. 764, 774, 897 N.E.2d 1001 (2008) (*Doe No. 89230*), quoting *Roe v. Attorney Gen.*, 434 Mass. 418, 430, 750 N.E.2d 897 (2001). The application of accurate and up-to-date information, including all known and empirically validated risk factors, thereby ensures that hearing examiners have the tools they need to arrive at individualized classification determinations. Such determinations must be grounded in a corpus of objective facts and data, necessarily dynamic and evolving to revise collective understanding of the risk that various individuals pose to the public. Given that "[t]he sex offender registry law mandates that the board promulgate guidelines to determine accurately 'the level of [an offender's] risk of reoffense and the degree of dangerousness to the public,'" *Doe No. 151564, supra* at 623 n. 6, 925 N.E.2d 533, quoting G.L. c. 6, § 178K (1), and that eleven years have passed since SORB last updated those guidelines, during which time knowledge and understanding of sexual recidivism has expanded considerably, compliance with this statutory charge requires incorporation of current information.

Particularly in light of the length of time that has elapsed since the guidelines were last revised, and the research published in the intervening years on female sexual recidivism, "the accuracy of the classification decision [would have been] enhanced by the addition to the evidentiary record of additional expert evidence in the form of testimony or reports."[12] *Doe No. 89230, supra* at 773, 897 N.E.2d 1001. At the very least, an expert could have offered assistance as to the possible limitations of applying SORB's risk factors to Doe.

"[I]n moving for expert witness funds, the burden [is] on the sex offender to identify and articulate the reason or reasons, connected to a condition or circumstance special to [her], that [she] needs to retain a particular type of expert. A general motion for funds to retain an expert to provide an opinion on the sex offender's risk of reoffense, without more, would appear to be insufficient." *Id.* at 775, 897 N.E.2d 1001. Here, Doe supported her motion for expert funds with significant evidence that the research undergirding SORB's guidelines was limited almost exclusively to male sexual recidivism, in addition to evidence indicating that females have lower over-all rates of sexual recidivism. Doe's request did not demonstrate simply a "generic need for an expert witness," as the second hearing examiner determined, but instead identified a particular characteristic or condition peculiar to her that the guidelines do not appear to contemplate, and that an available expert is qualified to address. It was therefore an abuse of discretion to deny Doe's motion for expert-witness funds, where Doe established that the hearing examiner

---

12. Pursuant to G.L. c. 6, § 178L (1) *(a)*, an "indigent offender may … apply for and [SORB] may grant payment of fees for an expert witness in any case where [SORB] in its classification proceeding intends to rely on the testimony or report of an expert witness prepared specifically for the purposes of the classification proceeding." The hearing examiner has discretion to grant funds for an expert even where SORB does not intend to use expert evidence. *Doe, Sex Offender Registry Bd. No. 89230 v. Sex Offender Registry Bd.*, 452 Mass. 764, 773–774, 897 N.E.2d 1001 (2008).

would not otherwise have competent evidence before him to assess fully Doe's risk of reoffense.[13] ...

The judgment of the Superior Court, affirming SORB's classification determination of Doe as a level one sex offender, is vacated and set aside. The matter is remanded to SORB for further proceedings consistent with this opinion.

So ordered.

CORDY, J. (concurring).

I concur completely in the court's holding and rationale, and write separately only to object to the inclusion of footnote 13. The issue discussed in that footnote, whether sex

---

13. An expert also might have been useful in shedding light on the application of the guidelines' risk factors to economically motivated, noncontact offenses like Doe's; in particular, an expert could have explained whether the underlying behavior was "repetitive" and "compulsive" within the meaning of the guidelines. See 803 Code Mass. Regs. § 1.40(2). The second hearing examiner acknowledged the financial motivation underlying Doe's crimes, but concluded that "[n]othing in the regulations or statute require[s] an independent determination regarding the sexual motivation behind the commission of a sex offense, the sexual motivation being presumed by the offense itself." While we do not suggest that financially driven offenses cannot also be sexually motivated, the sexual impetus behind a crime should not be so assumed, especially where, as here, there is "no overt evidence" that an individual was motivated "by her own sexual desires and gratification." See *Doe, Sex Offender Registry Bd. No. 151564 v. Sex Offender Registry Bd.*, 456 Mass. 612, 619, 925 N.E.2d 533 (2010), citing G.L. c. 6, § 178K (1)(b)(iii) ("The board is permitted to consider the underlying facts of the prior conviction"). Furthermore, although the Legislature's inclusion of offenses such as living off of or sharing earnings of a minor prostitute, G.L. c. 272, § 4B, and the dissemination of child pornography, G.L. c. 272, § 29B, within the ambit of the sex offender registration statute, see G.L. c. 6, § 178C, reflects an acknowledgment that people exploit children for a variety of reasons, sexual or otherwise, it does not follow that the underlying conduct of these crimes is necessarily repetitive or compulsive.

The hearing examiner recognized that Doe's "sexual misconduct [was] not prompted by sexual desire or compulsion," but nevertheless concluded that Doe's offending was repetitive and compulsive, a factor that the guidelines identify as establishing a high risk of reoffense. See 803 Code Mass. Regs. § 1.40(2). It is not clear, however, that running an escort service is the kind of "compulsive" sexually deviant conduct anticipated by either the statute or the regulations. The sex offender registration statute does not evince a specific concern with those who are driven to crime by financial need but, in several places, contemplates that a sex offender may have a "mental abnormality," a condition that "predisposes that person to the commission of criminal sexual acts to a degree that makes such person a menace to the health and safety of other persons." See G.L. c. 6, §§ 178C, 178E, 178K (1) *(a)* (i). Accordingly, the statute envisions the need for "counseling, therapy or treatment" to address issues such as "repetitive and compulsive behavior." See, e.g., G.L. c. 6, § 178K(1)*(a)*(ii), *(c)*.

As discussed *supra*, in enacting the sex offender registration statute, the Legislature was concerned primarily with protecting vulnerable members of the community from the violent and predatory acts of certain sex offenders. See, e.g., St. 1999, c. 74, § 1 (noting "the danger of recidivism posed by sex offenders, especially sexually violent offenders who commit predatory acts characterized by repetitive and compulsive behavior"); Norton, Haley "Not Optimistic" on Meeting Court's Sex Offender Concerns, State House News Service, Aug. 25, 1999 (statement of Governor Paul Cellucci to criminal justice committee) ("It seems like every time we turn around, there is another terrible instance of one of these monsters molesting a child, raping a woman or spreading terror throughout a community"). See also 42 U.S.C. § 16901 (2006) (Federal analog of Commonwealth's sex offender registration statute, Adam Walsh Child Protection and Safety Act of 2006, enacted to prevent "vicious attacks by violent predators"). Nothing contained in the legislative history or the guidelines of which we are aware, or to which SORB points, suggests that individuals may be predisposed to running escort services, or that doing so may present an irrepressible compulsion akin to a recognized condition such as paraphilia, "characterized by 'recurrent, intense sexually arousing fantasies, sexual urges, or [certain] behaviors.'" *Doe, Sex Offender Registry Bd. No. 1211 v. Sex Offender Registry Bd.*, 447 Mass. 750, 766 n. 15, 857 N.E.2d 473 (2006), quoting American Psychiatric Association, Diagnostic and Statistical Manual of Mental Disorders 566 (4th ed. 2000).

offenses motivated by impulses other than those that are sexual in nature, such as financial gain, are a proper basis on which to find a risk of reoffense and a corresponding classification by the Sex Offender Registry Board (SORB), is not before the court. To the extent that one might infer from the footnote that only sexually motivated offenses enumerated in the SORB statute are appropriately considered in the risk analysis, I disagree.

In enacting the SORB statute, the Legislature was concerned with protecting vulnerable members of the community, especially children, from sexual predators of all types. Accordingly, the offenses enumerated in that statute include not only violent sexual acts, but also the crimes of inducing or aiding in the inducement of minors into a life of prostitution (G.L. c. 272, §4A); living off or sharing the earnings of prostitution committed by minors (G.L. c. 272, §4B); posing or exhibiting children in a state of nudity (G.L. c. 272, §29A); and disseminating child pornography (G.L. c. 272, §29B). Persons engaging in such conduct, and posing a risk of doing so in the future, regardless of the motivation of their conduct, are as much a danger to children in the community as other forms of sexual predators. In my view, such persons and the risks they pose are plainly encompassed within the SORB statute, and I would not suggest otherwise.

Notes

Female sex offenders seldom fit the stereotype of male sex offenders — they rarely offend against strangers or serialize their victims, and they rarely exhibit an exclusive preference for children. *See* Julia Hislop, *Law Overlooks Female Offenders*, N.Y. Times, Feb. 21, 2013. The court in *Doe v. Sex Offender Registry Bd.* recognized many differentiating risk factors between male and female sexual offenders, specifically those regarding recidivism. Likewise, in *In re Coffel*, 117 S.W.3d 116 (Mo. App. E.D. 2003), which is referenced in *Doe v. Sex Offender Registry Bd.*, the court held that "the use of clinical judgment to assess the risk of reoffense [for female sex offenders] has been shown to be no more reliable than flipping a coin." *See also United States v. Miller*, 601 F.3d 734, 739–40 (7th Cir. 2010) ("district court's comments about the likelihood of recidivism and the inefficacy of sex offender treatment, though perhaps consistent with commonly held views, are subject to debate"). *But see Olsen v. State*, 2012 WL 1438475 (reversible error not to admit expert testimony regarding female sex offenders and grooming in sentencing phase); *In re Detention of Bergen*, 121 Wash. App. 1078 (2004) (issue of cross-validation goes to weight and not admissibility); *State v. Thomas*, 1998 WL 401838 (rejecting argument that Ohio sexual registry statute, as applied to females, is not rationally related to the state's interest absent evidence showing high recidivism rates among female sex offenders). *See also In re Care and Treatment of Norton*, 123 S.W.3d 170, 171 (Mo. 2004) (Wolff, concurring) (recognizing inapplicability of studies regarding male offenders to female offenders because "the reasons men and women commit sex offenses are fundamentally different.").

In light of such differences between male and female offenders, and inconsistency over the use of expert opinions on the effect such differences, some courts require that the procedural requirements for assessing the future risk of male sex offenders be weighted to accommodate application to the assessment of female offenders. *See, e.g., In re Risk Level Determination of S.S.*, 726 N.W.2d 121 (Minn. Ct. App. 2007). In light of the risk factors discussed in *Doe v. Sex Offender Registry Bd.*, how should an assessment of female sexual offenders be weighted? How would more statistical data on female sex offenders affect the development of appropriate risk assessment and treatment for females?

For additional discussion of the differential treatment of female sex offenders, see Connie Hassett-Walker, Thomas Lateano and Michael Di Benedetto, *Do Female Sex Offenders Receive Preferential Treatment in Criminal Charging and Sentencing?*, 35 Justice System

J. 62 (2014) (concluding in study that "[w]hile female sex offenders were charged less harshly than the males, it was not due to the relationship with their victims.... Instead ... female sex offenders who victimized adolescents were charged less severely, possibly because of the assumption that the (male) victims were consenting participants...."); Christos Tsopelas, Spyridoula Tsetsou, Petros Ntounas, and Athanassios Douzenis, *Female Perpetrators of Sexual Abuse of Minors: What Are the Consequences for the Victims?*, 35 INT'L J. L. & PSY-CHIATRY 305 (2012) (concluding that sexual abuse by female perpetrators is sometimes considered more acceptable than sexual abuse by males, and that psychological interventions may be helpful in reducing female sexual abuse and its consequences on the victims); Rebecca A. Geddes, Graham A. Tyson & Scott McGreal, *Gender Bias in the Education System: Perceptions of Teacher-Student Sexual Relationships*, PSYCHIATRY, PSYCHOLOGY AND LAW, available at http://dx.doi.org/10.1080/13218719.2012.728428 (last viewed Jan. 29, 2015) (finding gender bias in favor of female teachers on emotional reactions of anger and desire for consequences); Christos Tsopelas, Tsetsou Spyridoula, and Douzenis Athanasios, *Review on Female Sexual Offenders: Findings About Profile and Personality*, 34 INT'L J. L & PSYCHIATRY 122 (2011) (concluding that female sex offenders are usually young, are often friends or relatives of the victim, and use more persuasion and psychological coercion than male sex offenders, however, the psychological consequences for the victim can be more severe); Sara G. West, Susan Hatters Firedman, and Ki Dan Kim, *Women Accused of Sex Offenses: A Gender-Based Comparison*, 29 BEHAVIORAL SCIENCES & THE L. 728 (2011) (finding many psychiatric similarities between male and female sex offenders, but finding that female offenders more frequently had victims of both genders); Alisa Graham, *Simply Sexual: The Discrepancy in Treatment Between Male and Female Sex Offenders*, 7 WHITTIER J. CHILD & FAM. ADVOC. 145 (2007) (comparing sentencing between male and female offenders under statutory rape laws); Donna M. Vandiver and Jeffery T. Walker, *Female Sex Offenders: An Overview and Analysis of 40 Cases*, 27 CRIM. JUSTICE REV. 284 (2002) (observing differences between male and female Arkansas sex offenders and indicating a need for new sex offender typology).

3. Minor Exploiters

Although offenders who sexually exploit children are often adult pedophiles, a growing number of sexual offenses against children are committed by other minors who do not necessarily fit the pedophile or sexual predator characteristics and whose acts are not always compulsive, but may be the product of impulsive or curious child-play or, often, may be consensual. How courts and legislatures define the scope of child sexual exploitation under these circumstances has a significant impact on outcomes for both juvenile offenders and minor victims. Consider the scope of what constitutes abuse or exploitation in the following cases.

B.B. v. State

Supreme Court of Florida, 1995
659 So. 2d 256

WELLS, Justice....

[Sixteen-year-old] B.B. was charged on January 21, 1993, with sexual battery. The victim was also sixteen years of age. After B.B. was deposed, the state attorney amended the petition from sexual battery to unlawful carnal intercourse pursuant to section 794.05, Florida Statutes (1991). Section 794.05 provides that:

(1) Any person who has unlawful carnal intercourse with any unmarried person, of previous chaste character, who at the time of such intercourse is under the age of 18 years, shall be guilty of a felony of the second degree, punishable as provided in s. 775.082, s. 775.083, or s. 775.084.

(2) It shall not be a defense to a prosecution under this section that the prosecuting witness was not of previous chaste character at the time of the act when the lack of previous chaste character in the prosecuting witness was caused solely by previous intercourse between the defendant and the prosecuting witness.

B.B. filed a motion to declare the statute unconstitutional as violative of his right to privacy and to dismiss the petition. The circuit court, relying on *In re T.W.*, 551 So.2d 1186 (Fla.1989), found section 794.05 unconstitutional and granted the motion. Specifically, the trial court found that petitioner had a right to privacy guaranteed by article I, section 23 of the Florida Constitution and that the right outweighed the State's interest in protecting minors from the conduct of others.... The State appealed, and the district court reversed the circuit court's findings, relying on *Jones v. State*, 619 So.2d 418 (Fla. 5th DCA 1993), *approved*, 640 So.2d 1084 (Fla.1994). The district court certified the above question to this Court.

Initially, we note that section 794.05 is materially different from section 800.04, Florida Statutes (1991),[1] which we upheld in *Jones v. State*, 640 So.2d 1084 (Fla.1994), against an attack as to its constitutionality. We do not recede in any way from the holding or reasoning in *Jones*.... Unlike the *Jones* case, our focus is not upon whether a minor's consent to sexual intercourse is a defense to a prosecution under a statute prohibiting sexual activity with a minor. Likewise, we do not view the issue presented in this case as being whether it is for the legislature or the courts to determine "Florida's age of consent." If our decision were based upon whether minors could consent to sexual activity as though they were adults, our decision would be "no" for the reasons stated in Justice Kogan's concurring opinion in *Jones v. State*, 640 So.2d 1084, 1087 (Fla.1994). The issue here, however, is whether a minor who engages in "unlawful" carnal intercourse with an unmarried minor of previous chaste character can be adjudicated delinquent of a felony of the second degree in light of the minor's right to privacy guaranteed by the Florida Constitution.

In *In re T.W.*, 551 So.2d 1186 (Fla.1989), the majority of this Court recognized that based upon the unambiguous language of article I, section 23 of the Florida Constitution,

---

1. Section 800.04, Florida Statutes (1991):

Any person who:

(1) Handles, fondles or makes an assault upon any child under the age of 16 years in a lewd, lascivious, or indecent manner;

(2) Commits actual or simulated sexual intercourse, deviate sexual intercourse, sexual bestiality, masturbation, sadomasochistic abuse, actual lewd exhibition of the genitals, or any act or conduct which simulates that sexual battery is being or will be committed upon any child under the age of 16 years or forces or entices the child to commit any such act;

(3) Commits an act defined as sexual battery under s. 794.011(1)(h) upon any child under the age of 16 years; or

(4) Knowingly commits any lewd or lascivious act in the presence of any child under the age of 16 years, without committing the crime of sexual battery, commits a felony of the second degree, punishable as provided in s. 775.082, s. 775.083, or s. 775.084. Neither the victim's lack of chastity nor the victim's consent is a defense to the crime proscribed by this section.

"[t]he right to privacy extends to '[e]very natural person.' Minors are natural persons in the eyes of the law and '[c]onstitutional rights do not mature and come into being magically only when one attains the state-defined age of majority.'" *Id.* at 1193. Our analysis, therefore, begins with the recognition that the right to privacy extends to B.B.

Our decision in *Winfield v. Division of Pari-Mutuel Wagering*, 477 So.2d 544 (Fla.1985), instructs that we next determine whether this minor had a legitimate expectation of privacy in carnal intercourse. Carnal intercourse is by express definition an intimate act. In *Shevin v. Byron, Harless, Schaffer, Reid and Associates, Inc.*, 379 So.2d 633, 636 (Fla.1980), we recognized that various intimate personal activities such as marriage, procreation, contraception, and family relationships fall within the privacy interest recognized by the Federal Constitution. Following the 1980 adoption of article I, section 23 of the Florida Constitution, this Court held that Florida's privacy amendment, which provides "an explicit textual foundation for those privacy interests inherent in the concept of liberty" extends to minors with respect to abortion. *In re T.W.*, 551 So.2d at 1192 (quoting *Rasmussen v. South Fla. Blood Serv., Inc.*, 500 So.2d 533, 536 (Fla.1987)). Consistent with these decisions, we conclude that Florida's clear constitutional mandate in favor of privacy is implicated in B.B., a sixteen-year-old, engaging in carnal intercourse.

Having determined that this statute does implicate B.B.'s right to privacy, the "stringent test" enunciated in *Winfield* must be applied to the statute. Again, our analysis is in accord with the opinion concurred in by the majority in *In re T.W.*, holding that "[c]ommon sense dictates that a minor's rights are not absolute; in order to overcome these constitutional rights, a statute must survive the stringent test announced in *Winfield*: The state must prove that the statute furthers a compelling state interest through the least intrusive means." 551 So.2d at 1193. Thus, once it is determined that a citizens's privacy interest is implicated, this test shifts the burden to the State to justify the intrusion of privacy. We find that the State failed to meet its burden in applying section 794.05 to adjudicate a minor as a delinquent second-degree felon.

The State contends that the compelling state interest furthered by this statute is the same as the state interest which we found to be compelling in *Jones*. However, in *Jones* we were dealing with a situation where section 800.04 was applied to charge an adult engaged in sexual activity with a minor under the age of sixteen years. We there held, and reiterate here, that the rights of privacy that have been granted to minors do not vitiate the legislature's efforts to protect minors from the conduct of others. "'[S]exual exploitation of children is a particularly pernicious evil that sometimes may be concealed behind the zone of privacy.... The state unquestionably has a very compelling interest in preventing such conduct.'" 640 So.2d at 1086 (quoting *Schmitt v. State*, 590 So.2d 404 (Fla.1991), *cert. denied*, 503 U.S. 964, 112 S.Ct. 1572, 118 L.Ed.2d 216 (1992)).

While we do recognize that Florida does have an obligation and a compelling interest in protecting children from sexual activity before their minds and bodies have sufficiently matured to make it appropriate, safe, and healthy for them and that this interest pertains to one minor engaging in carnal intercourse with another, the crux of the State's interest in an adult-minor situation is the prevention of exploitation of the minor by the adult. Whereas in this minor-minor situation, the crux of the State's interest is in protecting the minor from the sexual activity itself for reasons of health and quality of life. Having distinguished between the State's interest in the adult-minor situation and in the minor-minor situation, we conclude that the State has failed to demonstrate in this minor-minor situation that the adjudication of B.B. as a delinquent through the application of section 794.05 is the least intrusive means of furthering what we have determined to be the State's compelling interest.

The history of this particular statute is rooted in a law created before 1892. *See* § 2598, Revised Statutes of Fla. (1892); 22 Fla.Stat.Ann. 727 (1992) (Historical and Statutory Notes). The law was enacted originally for the purpose of "protecting the virginity of young maidens," *Simmons v. State*, 151 Fla. 778, 783–84, 10 So.2d 436, 438 (1942), and to "protect virtuous young women … within the specific age from defilement." *State v. Bowden*, 154 Fla. 511, 516, 18 So.2d 478, 481 (1944). In 1921, the law was changed to protect both males and females. See Ch. 8596, Laws of Fla. (1921). In 1935, this Court expressed the view that the statute was "designed to protect the youth of this State of both sexes from the initial violation of their actual condition of sexual chastity, rather than from the consequences of their subsequent voluntary indulgence in unmorality." *Deas v. State*, 119 Fla. 839, 842, 161 So. 729, 730 (1935). It was on this basis that the Court explained why the statute protected only unmarried minors who were chaste.

We agree with the opinion of the Fourth District Court of Appeal in *Victor v. State*, 566 So.2d 354 (Fla. 4th DCA 1990), that the purpose of section 794.05(1), Florida Statutes, is "to protect minors from sex acts imposed by adults." *Victor*, 566 at 356. Here, though, section 794.05 is not being applied in furtherance of the purpose delineated by the district court in *Victor*. Section 794.05 is not being utilized as a shield to protect a minor, but rather, it is being used as a weapon to adjudicate a minor delinquent. Thus, we do not hold that section 794.05 is facially unconstitutional but only that it is unconstitutional as applied to this 16-year-old as a basis for a delinquency proceeding.

At present, we will not debate morality in respect to the statute or debate whether this century-old statute fits within the contemporary "facts of life." We do say that if our decision was what should be taught and reasoned to minors, the unequivocal text of our message would be abstinence. We are all too aware of the real-life crisis of children having children. The impact is evidenced daily in delinquency and dependency proceedings in the juvenile divisions of our circuit courts. We recognize the plague of AIDS and the evidence that this epidemic and the rampant spread of serious communicative disease are the sad product of sexual promiscuity. However, our decision is not about what should be taught but about what can be adjudicated to be delinquency as a second-degree felony.

For the reasons stated herein, we quash the decision of the district court, hold section 794.05, Florida Statutes (1991), to be unconstitutional as applied to a minor who is sought to be prosecuted pursuant to the statute, and remand for proceedings consistent with this opinion.

It is so ordered.

OVERTON and ANSTEAD, JJ., concur.

KOGAN, J., concurs with an opinion, in which ANSTEAD, J., concurs.

GRIMES, C.J., dissents with an opinion, in which SHAW, J., concurs.

HARDING, J., dissents with an opinion.

KOGAN, Justice, concurring.

Our law has held that, with respect to unmarried persons, "chaste" means possessing virginity. *Williams v. State*, 92 Fla. 125, 109 So. 305 (1926). Thus, by its own terms the statute at issue here does not protect unmarried minors who had lost their virginity through a liaison with a third party prior to the act in question. This singularly odd state of affairs indicates that the real objective of this statute is not to protect children as a class, but to prevent the loss of chastity of those not already "despoiled." Any person — child or adult—thus does not violate this particular statute by a sexual liaison with an unchaste minor.[2]

I frankly find the assumptions underlying this result appalling. As I stated in *Jones*, the state does have a compelling interest in preventing the sexual exploitation of children as a class and can do so by establishing a minimum age of consent. The problems of pregnancy, sexually transmitted disease, and psychological injury are of special concern with the very young, as a body of well documented research now shows. *Jones*, 640 So.2d at 1087–92 (Kogan, J., concurring). But I am utterly at a loss to explain how the state can justify a statute such as this one, that seems to regard unchaste minors as being somehow less deserving of the state's protection than those who are otherwise. This view is a painfully short-sighted relic of a bygone era that was willing to punish nonmarital sexual acts severely, even to the point of regarding the innocent offspring of those unions as "children of no one" not even entitled to an inheritance. Any statute that purports to grant special status to a favored group of children over all others, to my mind at least, must be regarded as inherently questionable. On its face this statute suggests discrimination and most likely grants special status to an elite group of children.

Laws should protect everyone, not merely a favored subgroup. All children deserve the state's protection, subject only to the rights our Constitution invests in those children and their parents or guardians. I agree with the majority that privacy is implicated here. However, the statute's application only to "chaste" children renders the state's interest less than compelling, in the context of sex between two minors. There is no sound reason why only the chaste ones should be protected from the dangers of premature and repeated sexual acts if the state genuinely purports to be protecting children as a class. Indeed, one of the assumptions of this statute—that children engaging in serial promiscuity are less deserving—strikes me as patently absurd and self-defeating. If anything, such children are all the more in danger and thus all the more in need of assistance.

I also am highly puzzled about who should be regarded as the "aggressor" and who the "victim" when both partners are minors. If both are "chaste," then a fair reading of the statute would indicate that both have committed a felony. Yet, this effectively means each child was both aggressor and victim in a single act, which stretches credence to the breaking point. Attempting to brand one as the aggressor and the other as the victim raises very serious questions of equal protection, especially where prosecutors always assume that one type of child—such as "the boy," or the one who is "unchaste"—must be the aggressor.

Moreover, still other problems arise in this last situation. Identifying the male or "unchaste" partner as the aggressor will not always be borne out by the facts. The studies I cited in *Jones* indicate that some children—even boys—fall into a tragic cycle of sexual exploitation by others, which robs them of virginity but certainly does not indicate they

---

2. A variety of other criminal statutes might apply, however, depending on the facts of the case. I also must note that, while Chief Justice Grimes correctly quotes my concurrence in *Jones*, the two statutes he compares differ in a crucial respect: Section 794.05 requires that the child be chaste whereas section 800.04 does not. Indeed, the latter statute states in pertinent part:

> Neither the victim's lack of chastity nor the victim's consent is a defense to the crime proscribed [statutory rape].

§ 800.04, Fla.Stat. (1991). Thus, I do not agree with his assessment that my concurrence in *Jones* compels the result he advocates. In *Jones*, the state in fact had a compelling interest because it was trying to protect all children, whereas in the present case the state has selected a privileged few for favored protection. The question in the instant case thus is whether the state can select a subgroup of children for special protections not afforded to others.

are aggressors. And I am utterly unwilling to say that repeat victims of sexual exploitation must be considered aggressors merely because of prior victimization by third parties. This would be little better than blaming the true victim and coddling the actual aggressor, directly contrary to the very interests the state is trying to serve.

In so saying, I stress that this case does not involve the separate problem of *adults* engaging in sexual acts with a minor, nor does the certified question raise issues of due process or equal protection. This opinion accordingly rests solely on a privacy analysis. Art. I, § 23, Fla. Const. Finally, I would suggest that the legislature revisit this statute and either modernize it or decide if it is genuinely necessary in light of the variety of other statutes more than adequately protecting children from sexual predation. Absent revision, application of this statute in other situations is likely to be a fertile source of expensive litigation in the years ahead. The legislature might wish to consider whether the cost of defending an archaically worded statute such as this one is worthwhile.

ANSTEAD, J., concurs.

GRIMES, Chief Justice, dissenting.

In *Jones v. State*, 640 So.2d 1084 (Fla.1994), this Court upheld section 800.04, Florida Statutes (1991), which prohibited sexual intercourse with a person under the age of sixteen. Section 794.05, Florida Statutes (1991), prohibits sexual intercourse with an unmarried person of previous chaste character under the age of eighteen. Neither statute refers to the age of the person against whom the prohibition is directed. For purposes of our discussion, the only material difference between the statutes is the age limit of the persons sought to be protected. Persons under the age of eighteen are still considered minors, and as this Court held in *Jones*, the legislature has a strong policy interest in protecting minors from harmful sexual conduct. I cannot see how *In re T.W.*, 551 So.2d 1186 (Fla.1989), can be read to support the proposition that a sixteen-year-old child has a privacy right to have sex.

In holding section 794.05 unconstitutional as applied, the majority appears to be saying that a sixteen-year-old child has a constitutional right to engage in sex with another sixteen-year-old child, though an older person would not have such a right. However, section 794.05 reflects a legislative determination to protect chaste and unmarried children under the age of eighteen from the dangers of having sex with anyone, regardless of age. While the prevention of exploitation of children by older persons is certainly one objective of the statute, the statute does not make this distinction and it is clearly not the only objective. As noted by Justice Kogan in his concurring opinion in *Jones*, the State has a right to prevent children and young adolescents from being exposed to the wide-ranging risks associated with premature sexual activity.

If B.B. is adjudicated delinquent of a second-degree felony, he may have an argument that the particular sanction imposed upon him for having sex with another sixteen-year-old is cruel and unusual punishment. *See Hale v. State*, 630 So.2d 521 (Fla.1993), *cert. denied*, 513 U.S. 909, 115 S.Ct. 278, 130 L.Ed.2d 195 (1994). However, this question is not before us. Despite the majority's effort to restate the issue, the question before us is whether it is for the legislature or the courts to determine the age of consent for minors to engage in sex. Referring again to Justice Kogan's opinion in *Jones*:

> The legislature, I believe, can choose any age within a range that bears a clear relationship to the objectives the legislature is advancing. Some reasonable age of consent must be established because of the obvious vulnerabilities of most youngsters and the impossibility of legally defining "maturity" for allegedly precocious teens in this context.

640 So.2d at 1090 (Kogan, J., concurring). The legislature has established the cutoff as being at the age of eighteen. The fact that in contemporary society many couples may be engaging in sex below the age of eighteen makes it neither legal nor right....

Clark v. Roccanova

E.D. Ky., 2011
772 F. Supp. 2d 844

JENNIFER B. COFFMAN, Chief Judge....

The instant lawsuit arises out of a civil claim under Chapter 110 of Title 18 of the United States Code regarding the sexual exploitation of a minor child. In 2006, Roccanova, Rudy and Lynch coerced, enticed and persuaded Clark to produce a sexually explicit video, in violation of 18 U.S.C. § 2251. That same year, all three defendants transmitted the video in interstate commerce on the internet, in violation of 18 U.S.C. § 2252. All parties were 14 years old at the time of these actions. Prior to filing an answer to Clark's complaint, all three defendants have filed motions to dismiss and Rudy has filed a motion to strike....

The defendants are covered by the law, even if they are not adults. Nothing in the plain language of the statutes or their legislative history indicates that Congress intended 18 U.S.C. § 2251 and § 2252 to apply only to the conduct of adults. Both statutes prohibit creation, possession and transmission of child pornography by any "person." While "person" is not defined in 18 U.S.C. § 2256, the statute's definition of "identifiable minor" begins by stating that a minor is a "person." 18 U.S.C. § 2256(9)(A). This indicates that "person" is meant to refer to an individual of any age, not just an adult. Neither statute at issue contains language which would narrow the definition of "person" to mean only adults.... Additionally, there is nothing in the legislative history which would indicate Congress intended "person" to mean an adult. 18 U.S.C. § 2251 and § 2252 were first enacted as part of the Protection of Children Against Sexual Exploitation Act of 1997, Pub.L. No. 95-225, 92 Stat. 7 (1978). In all legislative records regarding the statutes at issue, Congress refers only to "persons" and does not narrow the term to adults.... Rather, the legislative history of the Act states that the "Committee on Human Resources has a deep and abiding concern for the health and welfare of the *children* and the *youth of America*," and therefore "condemns such base and sordid activities which may permanently traumatize and warp the minds of the *children* involved." S.Rep. No. 95-438, at 3–4 (1977), U.S. Code Cong. & Admin.News 1978, pp. 40, 40–42 (emphasis added). Encounters which produce child pornography "cannot help but have a deep psychological, humiliating impact on these youngsters and jeopardize the possibility of healthy, affectionate relationships in the future." *Id.* at 6. Nothing in the record indicates that a child would be less traumatized if that pornography is created or transmitted by a child rather than an adult. Lynch argues that the phrase "use of a minor" in the definition of "child pornography" demonstrates that Congress intended to target adults.... However, nothing in the phrase, the rest of the definition or the congressional record indicates that only an adult can "use" a minor.

Child pornography has no First Amendment protection because of its negative impact on the child involved, *Ashcroft v. Free Speech Coalition*, 535 U.S. 234, 122 S.Ct. 1389, 152 L.Ed.2d 403 (2002), even if it depicts a work of value. *New York v. Ferber*, 458 U.S. 747, 102 S.Ct. 3348, 73 L.Ed.2d 1113 (1982). Child pornography is limited to depictions of actual children, because protection of children is the purpose of the legislation. *Ashcroft,*

535 U.S. at 250, 122 S.Ct. 1389. Nothing in the jurisprudence indicates that such harm could be done only by adult perpetrators.... It is not surprising that no federal precedent exists for a suit against a minor under these statutes, given the relatively recent rapid emergence of "sexting" by minors. However, prosecutors have begun to charge minors under child pornography statutes. *See* Sarah Wastler, *The Harm in "Sexting"?: Analyzing the Constitutionality of Child Pornography Statutes that Prohibit the Voluntary Production, Possession, and Dissemination of Sexually Explicit Images by Teenagers*, 33 Harv. J.L. & Gender 687 (2010).... Thus, based on the plain language of the statutes, legislative history and case law, Clark has a claim under the statutes, and the court will deny the defendants' motion to dismiss on this basis....

Clark's first cause of action, that the defendants solicited the production of sexually explicit visual depictions in violation of 18 U.S.C. § 2251(a), alleges sufficient facts to state a plausible claim against Roccanova, Rudy and Lynch. In her complaint, Clark asserts many facts which support her allegation against Roccanova. She specifies several conversations with Roccanova, detailing his actions in convincing Clark to send him the video.... Regarding Lynch and Rudy's involvement in persuading Clark to create and send the video, Clark's complaint is less detailed but sufficient. Clark states, "Defendants Rudy and Lynch were also present and aided and abetted Defendant Roccanova's efforts to coerce, entice and persuade Plaintiff Clark to produce a sexually explicit video." ... These facts are sufficient to make Clark's claim of relief plausible. Therefore, the court will deny the motions to dismiss for all defendants as to count one.

Clark's second and third causes of action, asserting that all three defendants possessed and caused to be distributed in interstate commerce the sexually explicit visual depictions in violation of 18 U.S.C. § 2252(a), contain sufficient factual assertions to state a plausible claim as to Roccanova and Rudy but not as to Lynch. With regard to Roccanova and Rudy, Clark's complaint contains numerous factual assertions with regard to their behavior in possession, manipulation and transmission of the video to other persons via the internet.... However, Clark gives no facts with regard to Lynch's involvement in the transmitting of this video. She asserts only that "Defendants acted in concert with each other" in possessing and transmitting the video.... This is no more than an unadorned accusation and is not sufficient to survive a motion for dismissal. Therefore, the court will deny the motion for dismissal as to Roccanova and Rudy but will grant the motion as to Lynch on counts two and three....

Clark has asserted sufficient facts in her complaint to survive a motion to dismiss for failure to establish an element of 18 U.S.C. § 2251, notwithstanding the *in pari delicto* doctrine. In her complaint, Clark alleges that she received several telephone calls from Roccanova asking for the video in question and threatening to withhold his friendship if the video was not produced.... Roccanova asserts that this behavior was not enough to satisfy 18 U.S.C. § 2251 to "employ[ ], use[ ], persuade [ ], induce[ ], entice[ ], or coerce[ ]." However, "induce" is defined as "[t]o lead (a person), by persuasion or some influence or motive that acts upon the will...." Oxford English Dictionary (2nd ed. 1989). Roccanova's actions, in concert with those of Rudy and Lynch, meet the definition of "induce." Clark has stated a cause of action, as the defendants' alleged actions fall under 18 U.S.C. § 2251.

The doctrine of *in pari delicto* does not apply, since Clark was induced into sending the video. 18 U.S.C. § 2251 states that "any person who ... induces ... any minor to engage in ... sexually explicit conduct ... shall be punished as provided under subsection (e)." This implies that the minor who is induced to engage in this conduct is not the person to be punished. Rather, Clark is the victim specifically protected, rather than the initial perpetrator. The doctrine of *in pari delicto* does not compel the court to grant the defendants' motion to dismiss....

Accordingly,

IT IS ORDERED that Lynch's motion to dismiss ... is DENIED as to count 1 and GRANTED as to counts 2 and 3.

IT IS FURTHER ORDERED that Roccanova's motion to dismiss ... is DENIED....

A.H. v. State

Fla. App. 1 Dist., 2007
949 So. 2d 234

WOLF, J....

By Amended Petition of Delinquency, 16-year-old appellant, A.H., and her 17-year-old boyfriend, J.G.W., were charged as juveniles under the child pornography laws. The charges were based on digital photos A.H. and J.G.W. took on March 25, 2004, of themselves naked and engaged in sexual behavior. The State alleged that, while the photos were never shown to a third party, A.H. and J.G.W. emailed the photos to another computer from A.H.'s home. A.H. and J.G.W. were each charged with one count of producing, directing or promoting a photograph or representation that they knew to include the sexual conduct of a child, in violation of section 827.071(3), Florida Statutes.[1]

A.H. filed a motion to dismiss on October 24, 2005, arguing that section 827.071(3), Florida Statutes, was unconstitutional as applied to her. She contended that her privacy interests were implicated in the charges, that she was actually younger than her alleged victim, J.G.W., and that criminal prosecution was not the least intrusive means of furthering a compelling state interest. A hearing was held on the motion to dismiss on November 30, 2005, after which the trial court issued an order denying the motion. The order included the following conclusions:

> Assuming that the child's right to privacy is implicated, the standard for evaluating whether the State may regulate the sexual conduct of minors, articulated in *B.B. v. State*, 659 So.2d 256, 258–59 (Fla.1995), requires the State to show both that it has a compelling interest and that it is furthering this interest in the least intrusive manner.

> As to the first prong of the test, whether the State has a compelling interest in regulating the sexual behavior of minors, this Court recognizes a compelling state interest in protecting children from sexual exploitation, particularly the form of sexual exploitation involved in this case. This compelling interest exists whether the person sexually exploiting the child is an adult or a minor and is certainly triggered by the production of 117 photographs of minors engaging in graphic sexual acts. *State v. A.R.S.*, 684 So.2d 1383, 1387 (Fla. 1st DCA 1996).

> The Court further finds that prosecuting the child under the statute in question is the least intrusive means of furthering the State's compelling interest. Not prosecuting the child would do nothing to further the State's interest. Prosecution enables the State to prevent future illegal, exploitative acts by supervising and providing any necessary counseling to the child. The Court finds that the State has shown that Section 827.071(3), Florida Statutes, as applied to the child, is

---

1. J.G.W. was also charged with one count of possession of child pornography under section 827.071(5), Florida Statutes (2005).

the least intrusive means of furthering the State's compelling interest in preventing the sexual exploitation of children, rendering the statute constitutional.

Three weeks later, A.H. entered a nolo contendere plea to the charge and was placed on probation. Based on the supplemental record that has been filed, we find appellant specifically reserved her right to appeal the issue raised on the motion to dismiss.

A.H. argues that the trial court erred in denying her motion to dismiss below because the statute is unconstitutional as applied to her. She relies, in part, on the 1995 Florida Supreme Court decision in *B.B. v. State*, 659 So.2d 256 (Fla.1995), in which she alleges the court held that a child's privacy interests under article I, section 23 of the Florida Constitution are triggered by engaging in sexual conduct.... According to A.H., given the lack of a significant age difference or of any allegation that the pictures were shown to a third party, the only compelling state interest that could be involved here was the protection of the co-defendants from engaging in sexual behavior until their minds and bodies had matured. A.H. argues that prosecuting her for the second-degree felony of promoting a sexual performance by a child was not the least intrusive means of furthering this interest. Therefore, she maintains that section 827.071(3), Florida Statutes, is unconstitutional as applied to her, and the trial court's ruling to the contrary must be reversed.

Implicit in A.H.'s argument is that article I, section 23 protects a minor's right to have sexual intercourse and that this right of privacy extends to situations where the minor memorializes the act through pictures or video. We cannot accept this argument.... In *State v. A.R.S.*, 684 So.2d 1383 (Fla. 1st DCA 1996), we addressed the constitutionality of section 827.071(3), Florida Statutes, the same statute at issue in this case. In that case, the court assumed "that a minor's privacy interests were implicated." *Id.* The court went on to hold that the State had a compelling interest "to protect minors from exploitation by anyone who induces them to appear in a sexual performance and shows that performance to other people." *Id.* at 1387.... As Judge Allen noted in his concurrence in *A.R.S.*, the law relating to a minor's right of privacy to have sex with another minor is anything but clear. *See also State v. Raleigh*, 686 So.2d 621 (Fla. 5th DCA 1996). It is unnecessary, however, for us to enter that quagmire. The question before us is, even assuming that the privacy provision of article I, section 23 of the Florida Constitution extends to minors having sexual intercourse, whether that right extends to them memorializing that activity through photographs.

"Florida's right to privacy is a fundamental right that requires evaluation under a compelling state interest standard. However, before the right to privacy attaches and the standard is applied, a reasonable expectation of privacy must exist." *Bd. of County Comm'rs of Palm Beach County v. D.B.*, 784 So.2d 585, 588 (Fla. 4th DCA 2001). Whether an individual has a legitimate expectation of privacy is determined by considering all the circumstances, especially objective manifestations of that expectation. *City of N. Miami v. Kurtz*, 653 So.2d 1025, 1028 (Fla.1995).... A number of factors lead us to conclude that there is no reasonable expectation of privacy under these circumstances.

First, the decision to take photographs and to keep a record that may be shown to people in the future weighs against a reasonable expectation of privacy. *See Four Navy Seals v. Associated Press*, 413 F.Supp.2d 1136 (S.D.Cal.2005) (holding active duty military members who allowed photographs to be taken of prisoner abuse did not have reasonable expectation of privacy under state constitution).... Second, the photographs which were taken were shared by the two minors who were involved in the sexual activities. Neither had a reasonable expectation that the other would not show the photos to a third party. Minors who are involved in a sexual relationship, unlike adults who may be involved in a mature committed relationship, have no reasonable expectation that their relationship will continue and that the photographs will not be shared with others intentionally or unintentionally. One motive for revealing the photos is profit. Unfortunately, the market for child pornography in this country, according to news reports, appears to be flourishing. *See, e.g.,* "Child porn ring busted, 27 face charges," March 15, 2006, http://www.msnbc. msn.com/id/11839832; Jeremy W. Peters, *Another Arrest in Webcam Pornography Case,* N.Y. Times, May 16, 2006, available at http://www. nytimes.com (search the NYT Archive since 1981 for "Webcam Pornography Case," then click on title). These 117 sexually explicit photographs would undoubtedly have market value.... In addition, a number of teenagers want to let their friends know of their sexual prowess. Pictures are excellent evidence of an individual's exploits. A reasonably prudent person would believe that if you put this type of material in a teenager's hands that, at some point either for profit or bragging rights, the material will be disseminated to other members of the public.

Distribution of these types of photos is likely, especially after the relationship has ended. It is not unreasonable to assume that the immature relationship between the co-defendants would eventually end. The relationship has neither the sanctity of law nor the stability of maturity or length. The subjective belief of these co-defendants that the photos might not be shared is not dispositive. In fact, the defendant in this case expressed her concern to law enforcement that her co-defendant might do something disagreeable with the photographs.... The mere fact that the defendant may have subjectively believed that the pictures would remain private does not control; it is whether society is willing to recognize an objective expectation.... The fact that these photographs may have or may not have been shown in no way affects the minor's reasonable expectation that there was a distinct and real possibility that the other teenager involved would at some point make these photos public.

Even assuming, arguendo, that a reasonable expectation of privacy existed, the statute in the instant case serves a compelling state interest. In *A.R.S.,* 684 So.2d at 1387, this court addressed the statute in question where a minor had videotaped himself involved in sexual conduct with a female minor and played the videotape for a third party.

> Assuming that a minor's privacy interests are implicated in the instant case, we recognize that the state's compelling interest in section 827.071 is different. The statute is not limited to protecting children only from sexual exploitation by adults, nor is it intended to protect minors from engaging in sexual intercourse. The state's purpose in this statute is to protect minors from exploitation by anyone who induces them to appear in a sexual performance and shows that performance to other people. *See Schmitt v. State,* 590 So.2d 404, 412 (Fla.1991) (stating that the "obvious purpose" of section 827.071 "is to prohibit certain forms of child exploitation"), *cert. denied,* 503 U.S. 964, 112 S.Ct. 1572, 118 L.Ed.2d 216 (1992). The State's interest in protecting children from exploitation in this statute is the same regardless of whether the person inducing the child to appear in a sexual performance and then promoting that performance is an adult or a minor.

Id.

Appellant asserts that the State only has a compelling interest when the photograph or video is shown to a third party. The Legislature has, however, recognized a compelling interest in seeing that the videotape or picture including "sexual conduct by a child of less than 18 years of age" is never produced. §827.071(3), Fla. Stat.... As previously stated, the reasonable expectation that the material will ultimately be disseminated is by itself a compelling state interest for preventing the production of this material. In addition, the statute was intended to protect minors like appellant and her co-defendant from their own lack of judgment.

Without either foresight or maturity, appellant engaged in the conduct at issue, then expressed concern to law enforcement personnel that her co-defendant may do something inappropriate, i.e., disseminate sexually explicit photos that were lodged on his computer. Appellant was simply too young to make an intelligent decision about engaging in sexual conduct and memorializing it. Mere production of these videos or pictures may also result in psychological trauma to the teenagers involved.... Further, if these pictures are ultimately released, future damage may be done to these minors' careers or personal lives. These children are not mature enough to make rational decisions concerning all the possible negative implications of producing these videos.

In addition, the two defendants placed the photos on a computer and then, using the internet, transferred them to another computer. Not only can the two computers be hacked, but by transferring the photos using the net, the photos may have been and perhaps still are accessible to the provider and/or other individuals. Computers also allow for long-term storage of information which may then be disseminated at some later date. The State has a compelling interest in seeing that material which will have such negative consequences is never produced.

The decision of the trial court is affirmed.

THOMAS, J., concurs; PADOVANO, J., dissents with opinion.

PADOVANO, J. dissenting.

Section 827.071(3) Florida Statutes was designed to protect children from abuse by others, but it was used in this case to punish a child for her own mistake. In my view, the application of this criminal statute to the conduct at issue violates the child's right to privacy under Article 1, Section 23 of the Florida Constitution. For this reason, I would reverse.

The supreme court held in *B.B. v. State*, 659 So.2d 256 (Fla.1995), that a statute prohibiting unlawful carnal intercourse is unconstitutional as applied to a minor. In support of this holding, the court reasoned that the citizens of Florida had issued a "clear constitutional mandate in favor of privacy" by adopting Article 1, Section 23 of the Florida Constitution. *B.B.* 659 So.2d at 259. The court went on to say that the right of privacy is not limited to adults, but that it applies to children, as well.... I am not able to reconcile the supreme court's holding in *B.B.* with the court's decision in this case. The majority points out that the child in *B.B.* was charged with unlawful sexual intercourse while the child in this case was charged with photographing an act of sexual intercourse, but I think this a distinction without a difference. As in *B.B.*, the child in this case had sex with another minor. The only additional fact is that, in this case, the two took photographs of themselves and shared the photos with each other. There is no indication that the photos were intended to be any less private than the act itself. Consequently, I am unable to conclude that Article 1, Section 23 is inapplicable or that it somehow offers the child in this case less protection.

The majority is correct to say that *B.B.* involved a prosecution under a different statute. However, the principle of constitutional law articulated in the opinion is not one that applies only to a particular statute. To the contrary, it is a principle that would apply to any statute that is used in a way that violates the right of privacy. If a minor cannot be criminally prosecuted for having sex with another minor, as the court held in *B.B.*, it follows that a minor cannot be criminally prosecuted for taking a picture of herself having sex with another minor. Although I do not condone the child's conduct in this case, I cannot deny that it is private conduct. Because there is no evidence that the child intended to show the photographs to third parties, they are as private as the act they depict.

The majority relies on the decision of this court in *State v. A.R.S.*, 684 So.2d 1383 (Fla. 1st DCA 1996), but that case does not support the decision the court has made here. In *A.R.S.*, the child made a videotape of himself and a younger female child engaging in a sexual activity and then played the videotape to a third person at a time when the female was not present. The act of displaying the videotape was the main reason the court gave for its decision. As the court explained, "The state's purpose in [section 827.071] is to protect minors from exploitation by anyone who induces them to appear in a sexual performance *and shows that performance to other people.*" *A.R.S.*, 684 So.2d at 1387. In contrast, the child in this case did not show the photographs to anyone. Nor has she been charged with doing so. She stands accused of nothing more than taking photographs of herself and her boyfriend.

The fact that the delinquent child in *A.R.S.* showed the videotape to a third party is significant for the reasons given by the court and for another reason not mentioned in the opinion. The voluntary publication of the videotape to a third party completely undermined the delinquent child's claim of privacy. Unlike the accused child in this case, *A.R.S.* was not in a good position to claim that his actions were protected by the constitutional right of privacy. Whatever privacy rights he had in the videotape he made of himself and another child engaging in an intimate act, he gave up entirely when she showed the tape to another person.

The majority concludes that the child in this case did not have a reasonable expectation that the photographs would remain private. To support this conclusion, the majority speculates about the many ways in which the photographs might have been revealed to others. The e-mail transmission might have been intercepted. The relationship might have ended badly. The boyfriend might have wanted to show the photo to someone else to brag about his sexual conquest. With all due respect, I think these arguments are beside the point. Certainly there are circumstances in which the photos might have been revealed unintentionally to third parties, but that would always be the case.... That the Internet is easily hacked, as the majority says, is not material. The issue is whether the child intended to keep the photos private, not whether it would be possible for someone to obtain the photos against her will and thereby to invade her privacy. The majority states that the child "placed the photos on a computer and then, using the internet, transferred them to another computer," as if to suggest that she left them out carelessly for anyone to find. That is not what happened. She sent the photos to her boyfriend at his personal e-mail address, intending to share them only with him.

The method the child used to transmit the photos to her boyfriend carries some danger of disclosure, but so do others. If the child had taken a printed photograph and placed it in her purse, it might have been disclosed to third parties if her purse had been lost or stolen. If she had mailed it to her boyfriend in an envelope, it might have been revealed if the envelope had been delivered to the wrong address and mistakenly opened. As these examples illustrate, there is always a possibility that something a person intends to keep private will eventually be disclosed to others. But we cannot gauge the reasonableness of a person's expectation of privacy merely by speculating about the many ways in which it might be violated.

The critical point in this case is that the child intended to keep the photographs private. She did not attempt to exploit anyone or to embarrass anyone. I think her expectation of privacy in the photographs was reasonable. Certainly, an argument could be made that she was foolish to expect that, but the expectation of a sixteen year old cannot be measured by the collective wisdom of appellate judges who have no emotional connection to the event. Perhaps if the child had as much time to reflect on these events, she would have eventually concluded, as the majority did, that there were ways in which these photos might have been unintentionally disclosed. That does not make her expectation of privacy unreasonable.

For these reasons, I believe the court has committed a serious error. The statute at issue was designed to protect children, but in this case the court has allowed the state to use it against a child in a way that criminalizes conduct that is protected by constitutional right of privacy. In the process, the court has rendered a decision that expressly and directly conflicts with the decision of the Florida Supreme Court in *B.B.* on the same point of law. The child in that case was prosecuted under a different statute, but the constitutional principles are the same and they should be applied in the same way in this case.

Note

In *B.B.*, the court found that privacy rights extend to minors (in that case, a 16-year-old) and that the state must demonstrate a compelling reason to interfere with the privacy right of a minor to engage in sexual intercourse. The court recognized preventing sexual exploitation of children as a compelling reason but found that, as applied to that particular 16-year-old, delinquency proceedings were not the least restrictive means of achieving that goal. In *B.B.*, the court drew a distinction between protecting children from the exploitation of adults and protecting children from the sexual act itself. In *Clark*, the purpose of the statute was preventing the act that was performed, and the court found that criminal prosecution furthered this compelling interest. In *A.H.*, despite a strong dissent on the point, the court recognized the privacy interests of the children involved, but balanced those interests against the state's interest in protecting children from the sexual acts involved. Not only does the court recognize the unique vulnerability and immaturity of children and their inability to appreciate the consequences of their actions, but the court recognizes the state's compelling interest in protecting children from the sexual activity in which they engage, even when the activity— in this case, pornography—is not engaged in with an adult or shared with any third party.

Like the case of *A.R.S.*, on which the majority in *A.H.* relied, in *In re C.S.*, 84 A.3d 698 (Pa. 2014), the Pennsylvania Supreme Court reversed the Court of Common Pleas and reinstated a delinquency petition against a teenager, C.S., in a case in which two consenting teens produced a video tape of their sexual activity, and one of the teens shared the video with C.S., who then posted the video on Facebook. C.S. was charged with child pornography, but the lower court, *sua sponte*, held the Pennsylvania statute to be unconstitutionally vague and dismissed C.S.'s delinquency determination. The Pennsylvania Supreme Court reversed, holding that the court erred by acting as an advocate for C.S. and that C.S.'s constitutional challenge could not be raised for the first time on appeal. The consenting teen who shared the video with C.S. also shared the video with several other youths and posted the video on the internet, but he was not charged. The cases beg the question of where poor judgment by consenting teen-agers ends and exploitation by child pornographers begins. This issue is discussed in further in Chapter Two, Section II.E (Sexting), *infra*. For additional discussion of the legal issues involving juvenile sex offenders, see Charles A. Phipps, *Misdirected Reform: On Regulating Consensual Sexual Activity Between Teenagers*, 12 Cornell J.L. & Pub. Pol'y 373 (2003) (critiquing arguments regarding statutory rape law reforms). For discussion of the First Amendment constitutional issues involved when teens engage in consensual sex and record their activity, see Chapter Three, Section II.B (Defining Child Pornography).

Juvenile sexual offenders comprise a diverse group that defies normative sexual offender stereotypes. According to the National Incident-Based Reporting System, juveniles account for more than one-third of those known to police to have committed sex offenses against minors (approximately 89,000 in 2004) and are more likely than adult offenders to offend in groups and at schools, to have more male and younger (under age 11) victims, and to offend against acquaintances. *See* David Finkelhor, Richard Ormrod and Mark Chaffin, *Juveniles Who Commit Sex Offenses Against Minors*, Juv. Justice Bulletin, 1–2 (Dec. 2009). Juvenile offenders are much more likely than adult offenders to have victims who are under age 12. One out of 8 juvenile offenders is under age 12 (31 percent of female offenders are under age 12, compared to 14 percent of male offenders), and 1 out of 20 juvenile offenders is under age 9. *Id.* Half of all juvenile offenders are age 15–17. Female offenders make up 7 percent of juvenile offenders and are more likely to involve multiple-victim and multiple-perpetrator offenses. *Id.* at 6. Female juvenile offenders also are more likely to have victims who are family members or males. Juvenile offenders are less likely than adult offenders to rape their victims, but are more likely to sodomize or fondle their victims, and are more likely to commit their offenses in the afternoon and at school, rather than in the evening or at night, in the home. *Id.* at 3. Pre-teen offenders, who often are referred to as "children with sexual behavior problems," demonstrate a prevalence of a history of sexual abuse. *Id.* Yet a high percentage of sex-offending youth (85–95 percent) demonstrate a low risk of sex crime recidivism. *Id.* Actuarial risk assessment tools are used to predict the small percentage of juvenile sex offenders who do recidivate.

All of these statistics demonstrate the need for preventive and treatment efforts to focus on the unique relationship between minor exploiters and their minor victims. Florida, for example, has employed specific regulations addressing the investigation of "child-on-child" sexual abuse that are designed to reduce the stigma associated with child sexual abuse, especially in cases that are not derived from repetitive and pervasive sexual behaviors, but also to address the harm to child victims. *See* Fla. Admin. Code r. 65C-29.007 (Child-on-Child Sexual Abuse) (as amended Dec. 31, 2014). The difficulty, however, is determining the scope of exploitative behaviors and the treatment needs of both the exploiter and the exploited. Even more complicated are the cases in which the sexual behaviors of the minors are committed within a "consensual" sexual relationship, raising the question of the applicability of statutory rape laws to juvenile offenders. *See, e.g.*, Jake Tover, *"For Never Was a Story of More Woe Than This of Juliet and Her Romeo"—An Analysis of the Unexpected Consequences of Florida's Statutory Rape Law and Its Flawed "Romeo and Juliet" Exception*, 38 Nova L. Rev. 145 (2013); Danielle Flynn, *All the Kids Are Doing It: The Unconstitutionality of Enforcing Statutory Rape Laws Against Children & Teenagers*, 47 New Eng. L. Rev. 681 (2013); Jordan Franklin, *Where Art Thou, Privacy?: Expanding Privacy Rights of Minors in Regard to Consensual Sex: Statutory Rape Laws and the Need for a "Romeo and Juliet" Exception in Illinois*, 46 John Marshall L. Rev. 309 (2012); Michael H. Meidinger, *Peeking Under the Covers: Taking a Closer Look at Prosecutorial Decision-Making Involving Queer Youth and Statutory Rape*, 32 B. C. J.L. & Soc. Just. 421 (2012); Lisa Pearlstein, Note, *Walking the Tightrope of Statutory Rape Laws: Using International Legal Standards to Serve the Best Interests of Juvenile Offenders and Victims*, 47 Am. Crim. L. Rev. 109 (2010); Lewis Bossing, Note, *Now Sixteen Could Get You Life: Statutory Rape, Meaningful Consent, and the Implications for Federal Sentence Enhancement*, 73 N.Y.U. L. Rev. 1205 (1998); Britton Guerrina, Comment, *Mitigating Punishment for Statutory Rape*, 65 U. Chi. L. Rev. 1251 (1998) (discussing enforcement of statutory rape laws); Heidi Kitrosser, *Meaningful Consent: Toward a New Generation of Statutory Rape Laws*, 4 Va. J. Soc. Pol'y & L. 287 (1997). Controversy also surrounds any requirements for inclusion of juveniles on sex offender registries. For further discussion on this issue, see Chapter One, Section II.B.2 (Registration of Juveniles), *infra*.

4. *Acquaintance Exploiters*

Ryan C. W. Hall and Richard C. W. Hall

A Profile of Pedophilia: Definition, Characteristics of Offenders,
Recidivism, Treatment Outcomes, and Forensic Issues

82 Mayo Clin. Proc. 457 (2007)

Another common pedophilic specifier is whether the abused children are limited to family members (ie, incest).... Federal data show that 27% of all sexual offenders assaulted family members. Fifty percent of offenses committed against children younger than 6 years were committed by a family member, as were 42% of acts committed against children 6 to 11 years old and 24% against children 12 to 17 years old.... [One] study ... found that 68% of "child molesters" had molested a family member; 30% had molested a stepchild, a foster child, or an adopted child; 19% had molested 1 or more of their bio-logic children; 18% had molested a niece or nephew; and 5% had molested a grandchild. In [another] study ... of anonymous nonincarcerated offenders, heterosexual incest pedophiles had abused 1.8 children and committed 81.3 acts, whereas homosexual incest pedophiles had abused 1.7 children and committed 62.3 acts....

For nonparental incest and nonviolent incidences of pedophilia, the child knows the offender (eg, neighbor, relative, family friend, or local individual with authority) an estimated 60% to 70% of the time.... Pedophiles often intentionally try to place themselves in a position where they can meet children and have the opportunity to interact with children in an unsupervised way, such as when babysitting, doing volunteer work, doing hobbies, or coaching sports.... Pedophiles usually obtain access to children through means of persuasion, friendship, and behavior designed to gain the trust of the child and parent.... Individuals in [one] study ... who experienced long-term abuse, reported abuse starting at an earlier age (8.2 years on average compared with 11.5 years for single abuse) and were more likely to be abused by a parental figure such as a stepfather or neighbor. Female and younger children are often molested in their own home or the residence of the offender, whereas male and older children are most likely to be molested outside their home in locations such as roadways, fields or woods, schools, or motels or hotels.... In cases of violent assaults (ie, requiring force), approximately 70% of the time the child does not know the pedophile....

United States Department of Justice

The National Strategy for Child Exploitation Prevention and
Interdiction Report to Congress, Aug. 2010

http://www.justice.gov/psc/docs/natstrategyreport.pdf

National Center for Missing & Exploited Children (NCMEC) data indicates that the vast majority of identified child pornography victims (69% of their data set) were abused/exploited by people familiar to the children. In the NCMEC data set these people included parents, other relatives, neighbors, family, friends, babysitters, coaches, and guardians' partners; only a small fraction of victims (4% of the NCMEC data set) were victimized by individuals with whom the child had no relationship. The abuse typically happens in the privacy of a home—

away from prying eyes—and the victim is easily manipulated and shamed or scared into submission and silence.

United States v. Batton

Tenth Circuit, 2010
602 F.3d 1191

TYMKOVICH, Circuit Judge....

Trial testimony shows Batton's interaction with the victim began several years before the crime occurred. In 2000, the victim's parents moved to Douglas, Wyoming, with their two sons. They purchased a townhouse, and their neighbors were William Batton, his wife, Liz, and Liz's son. The two families formed a solid friendship, and over the next two years, they spent a great deal of time together, including holidays. The victim's mother often spoke with both Batton and his wife about day-to-day life, as well as more personal matters.

Some time in 2002, the victim's parents moved 30 miles west of Douglas to Glenrock, Wyoming. The parents then went through a divorce. During and after the divorce, the Battons continued to have a close friendship with the victim's mother and her children. In particular, the Battons maintained regular contact with the mother's eight-year-old son, J.D., who seemed especially troubled by his parents' separation. Batton suggested to J.D.'s mother that it might benefit J.D. to get away on occasion from the circumstances surrounding his parents' divorce, and he asked for permission to spend time with J.D. every once in a while. The mother agreed.... Over the course of several years, Batton and his wife took J.D. to the movies, the state fair, dinner, and their places of employment. J.D. also spent the night at the Battons' house on several occasions. During the summer of 2006, Batton told J.D.'s mother that he wanted to reward J.D. for earning good grades by taking him on a trip to the Black Hills in South Dakota. The mother consented, and J.D. traveled with Batton and his wife to South Dakota, where they visited monuments and explored various sights.

From 2006 to 2007, J.D.'s mother and her children regularly met with the Battons. J.D. continued to do well in school, and Batton once again offered to take J.D. on a congratulatory trip, this time to Chicago. Batton's wife and her business partner would be attending a conference, and Batton wanted to bring J.D. along, hoping to take him to various sights in the city while his wife attended her meetings. J.D.'s mother again agreed, feeling J.D. would enjoy the trip, especially since he had never been to Chicago.... In late July, 2007, Batton, his wife, her business partner, and J.D. traveled to Chicago, returning a week later. J.D.'s mother thought nothing of the trip until January, 2008, when Batton called her and informed her, for reasons that are not clear, that he had been in prison the previous weekend for failing to register as a sex offender. Although Batton tried to convince J.D.'s mother that it was nothing of consequence and that a family in Ohio was merely trying to extort money from him because of something that had happened long before, J.D.'s mother decided not to allow Batton to visit with J.D. in the future unless she or her fiancé were present.

Several days later, her worries still lingering, J.D.'s mother searched on-line for information relating to Batton and his Ohio offenses. What she found disturbed her: a number of newspaper articles detailing Batton's 1995 conviction for sexual assault on a 14-year-old boy. She immediately left work and drove to J.D.'s school, where she pulled him from class. She drove J.D. home, explained that Batton had been in trouble, and asked J.D. if Batton had ever touched him in a sexual way. J.D. answered in the affirmative.... After conferring with her fiancé, J.D.'s mother phoned the Converse County Sheriff's Office to report what J.D. had told her. That phone call resulted in an investigation, which eventually led to Batton's prosecution.... At trial, J.D. testified that Batton had touched his genitalia on a number of occasions from the time J.D. was in second grade until he finished sixth grade. He also testified that on the second and third days of the Chicago trip, Batton had engaged in sexual contact with him.

Over Batton's objections, the trial court allowed the jury to hear (1) evidence of Batton's 1995 Ohio conviction, including testimony from the victim in that case; (2) Instruction 36, which read, in part, that the government "offered [the evidence regarding the 1995 conviction] for its bearing on any matter to which it is relevant, including ... the improbability that the Defendant has been falsely or mistakenly accused of these crimes," ... and (3) testimony from Dr. Heineke, the government's expert who testified regarding the general methods of sex offenders.... [W]e agree with the district court that the evidence of Batton's 1995 conviction is relevant. Despite the passage of time, the similarities between the victims and the conduct in each of the cases is striking—they fully support a pattern of grooming[3] and assaulting young male victims....

Batton contends the district court erred in allowing the testimony of Dr. William Heineke, the government's expert witness. We review "de novo the question of whether the district court employed the proper legal standard and performed its gatekeeper role in admitting expert testimony." *United States v. Rodriguez-Felix*, 450 F.3d 1117, 1122 (10th Cir.2006) (citations omitted). We review for abuse of discretion the district court's actual "application of this standard in deciding whether to admit or exclude an expert's testimony." *Id.* The district court retains broad discretion in assessing an expert's reliability, and we reverse only if the district court's conclusion is "arbitrary, capricious, whimsical or manifestly unreasonable or when we are convinced that the district court made a clear error of judgment or exceeded the bounds of permissible choice in the circumstances." *Dodge v. Cotter Corp.*, 328 F.3d 1212, 1223 (10th Cir.2003) (quotations omitted).

Prior to allowing the testimony of Dr. Heineke, the trial court held a *Daubert* hearing to determine his qualifications and the reliability of his proposed testimony. *See Daubert v. Merrell Dow Pharm., Inc.*, 509 U.S. 579, 113 S.Ct. 2786, 125 L.Ed.2d 469 (1993) (requiring district courts to determine whether experts are qualified and reliable). After hearing arguments from both Batton and the government and after considering testimony on Dr. Heineke's experience and qualifications, the trial court ruled that Dr. Heineke had extensive expertise regarding sex offenders and their victims because of his long clinical career in treating both and by virtue of his research in the area.... The district court concluded it would allow Dr. Heineke to testify, but only about the characteristics of sex offenders and their victims to dispel any of the jurors' misconceptions that the only people who commit sexual offenses are strangers, not trusted family members or friends.... The trial court emphasized that Dr. Heineke was not to offer any opinions about how his testimony might relate to the facts of Batton's case, nor was he to offer any opinions about the credibility of witnesses.... Batton argues that even with those limitations in place, Dr. Heineke's testimony was nothing more than improper "profile" evidence. Batton contends the testimony did nothing but frame the way the jury saw the evidence that followed and how it perceived Batton.

We disagree. We have previously allowed testimony regarding criminal methods that are beyond the common knowledge of lay jurors. "Expert testimony is properly admitted if the subject matter is closely related to a particular profession, business or science and

---

3. The term "grooming" is the process whereby a sex offender earns the trust and confidence of a victim before engaging in a sexual act. Sana Loue, *Legal and Epidemiological Aspects of Child Maltreatment*, 19 J. Legal Med. 471, 479 (1998).

is not within the common knowledge of the average layperson." *United States v. Kunzman*, 54 F.3d 1522, 1530 (10th Cir.1995). *See United States v. McDonald*, 933 F.2d 1519, 1522 (10th Cir.1991) (allowing an expert to testify regarding the specific practices of the drug trade, about which lay jurors might have misconceptions). Our reasoning for this is rooted in Federal Rule of Evidence 702:

> If scientific, technical, or other specialized knowledge will assist the trier of fact to understand the evidence or to determine a fact in issue, a witness qualified as an expert by knowledge, skill, experience, training or education may testify thereto in the form on an opinion or otherwise.

Thus, we have declined in the past to classify "evidence into categories of profile or non-profile." *McDonald*, 933 F.2d at 1522. Rather, we have focused our inquiry on whether the "specialized knowledge ... will assist the trier of fact in <u>understanding the evidence</u>." *Id.*

Dr. Heineke testified that sex offenders are generally not strangers to their victims and their families but are more often than not close family members, friends, or well-respected individuals in a community who often use their positions to groom their victims into trusting them. He also informed the trial court that many lay persons carry a common misconception that sex offenders are only strangers or fit some misconceived criminal caricature. This specialized information may very well be beyond the knowledge of many jurors. *See* Robin Fretwell Wilson, *Undeserved Trust: Reflections on the ALI's Treatment of De Facto Parents, in* Reconceiving the Family: Critique of the American Law Institute's Principles of the Law of Family Dissolution, 90, 117–118 (Robin Fretwell Wilson, ed., 2006) (showing that many of the behaviors legal doctrines equate with good parenting are the same behaviors used by child molesters to groom their victims, including reading to children and bathing, dressing, disciplining, and showering children with attention and gifts); Jon R. Conte, *The Nature of Sexual Offenses Against Children, in* Clinical Approaches to Sex Offenders and Their Victims (Clive R. Hollin & Kevin Howells eds., 1991) (explaining many of the techniques sex offenders use to groom their victims).

Other circuits have reached a similar conclusion. For example, in *United States v. Romero*, 189 F.3d 576 (7th Cir.1999), the Seventh Circuit held that contemporary expert testimony regarding the modus operandi of child molesters was admissible. ... In *Romero*, the defendant was charged with kidnapping and transporting a minor with the intent to engage in criminal sexual activity. The trial court allowed expert testimony regarding the practices of child sex abusers to dispel "from the jurors' minds the widely held stereotype of a child molester as a 'dirty old man in a wrinkled raincoat' who snatches children off the street." ... The Seventh Circuit approved the trial court's decision, noting that the expert testimony showed the sex abusers' grooming techniques.... Most notably, the testimony "illuminated how seemingly innocent conduct such as [the defendant's] extensive discussions ... [with his victim] ... could be part of a seduction technique." ...

Similarly, the Fifth Circuit in *United States v. Hitt*, 473 F.3d 146 (5th Cir.2006), held that the admission of expert testimony regarding the modus operandi of child molesters, including grooming, was not an abuse of discretion.... As in other cases we have discussed, in *Hitt*, the defendants were charged with transporting a minor across state lines for the purpose of engaging in illicit sexual activity.... The defendants argued that such expert testimony was inappropriate character evidence and should not have been admitted.... The Fifth Circuit rejected that argument, noting that several other circuits also allowed testimony regarding the grooming methods of sex offenders. *Id.* (citing *United States v. Hayward*, 359 F.3d 631, 636–37 (3d Cir.2004) (holding that expert testimony regarding the grooming techniques of child molesters was admissible)).

We do not find the trial court abused its discretion in concluding the jurors would benefit from learning of the modus operandi of sex offenders. The methods sex offenders use are not necessarily common knowledge. The trial court held a thorough *Daubert* hearing, where the parties discussed at length Dr. Heineke's qualifications. The record supports the trial court's determination that Dr. Heineke had sufficient expertise to discuss how sex offenders prepare their victims. Further, the trial court was careful to limit Dr. Heineke's testimony to only the correction of possible juror misconceptions regarding how sex offenders behave and what they look like. With those limitations in place, the trial court was well within its discretion to allow Dr. Heineke's testimony....

Because we find the district court did not err in admitting evidence of the 1995 conviction, in instructing the jury, or in allowing Dr. Heineke's testimony, we AFFIRM Batton's conviction.

Notes

The *Batton* case involves expert testimony about acquaintance exploitation and discusses the stereotypical misconceptions about the relationships between perpetrators and children and the common characteristics of compliant child victims that are affected by the nature of the relationship. The legal issue of whether a court should admit or exclude expert testimony about this and other evidentiary topics, such as the "grooming" behaviors that are so commonly demonstrated, varies and is discussed in more detail in Chapter Six, Section II.C (Grooming), *infra*. Likewise, "grooming," as a key component of the sexually exploitative process, is discussed more fully in Chapter Two (Defining Exploitation), *infra*. However, we will see the "grooming" aspect of the relationship between the exploiter and the exploited throughout this casebook. As we address the variety of other relationships in which the sexual abuse and sexual exploitation of children arise, note the prevalence of the grooming aspects within each of the relationships. Specifically, in the following section, note that grooming does not occur only within the home, between family members. Rather, such typical behavior is a quintessential aspect of child sexual exploitation that occurs on a national and international level.

5. Exploiters as Travelers

a. Interstate Travel

United States v. McGuire

Seventh Circuit, 2010

627 F.3d 622

POSNER, Circuit Judge.

The defendant was convicted by a jury of traveling in interstate and foreign commerce for the purpose of having sex with a minor, and was sentenced to 25 years in prison. His appeal argues that while he indeed had sex with minors on trips that crossed state and national boundaries, sex was not the purpose of the travel. He further argues that the judge should have excluded the testimony of other minors, besides the one whom he was charged with molesting, under Rule 403 of the Federal Rules of Evidence, on the ground that the additional testimony was unduly prejudicial. He does not challenge his sentence.

McGuire was a prominent Jesuit priest who in 1983 had begun serving as the spiritual director of Mother Teresa's order of nuns—the Missionaries of Charity—and as her confessor. A resident of Canisius House, in Evanston, Illinois, a dwelling for Jesuit priests, he led retreats all over the world modeled on the spiritual exercises of Saint Ignatius of

Loyola, the founder of the Jesuit order. In 1997, when his molestation of a boy named Dominick began, he was elderly — 67 — and suffering from a long list of diseases, including diabetes and asthma, and disabilities resulting from frequent surgeries. He recruited boys such as Dominick to accompany him on his travels to the retreats, explaining that he needed the boys to carry his bags, to provide him with medications, physical therapy, and massages, and to wash his feet.

He used the boys for sex as well. Dominick was a fatherless child of 13 who became the defendant's ward. From 1997 to 2001 the defendant engaged in frequent sexual activity with Dominick, often on trips to retreats; the details of the activity need not detain us. He engaged in similar acts with the four other boys who testified, and indeed with many more. His sexual predation (which had begun long before — perhaps decades before — his molestation of Dominick began) involved the following *modus operandi*: sleeping in the same bed with the boys; receiving massages from them that began innocently but evolved into sexual fondling of him that he commanded them to perform; displaying pornographic movies and magazines to "educate" the boys about sex and the "beauty of the human form"; eliciting confessions that they had masturbated and threatening to expose as a masturbator any boy who complained about molestation; and insisting that complaint would be futile because no one would believe that a priest of the defendant's prominence was a pedophile.

The defendant's religious superiors began to be suspicious of him as early as 1991, though he was not defrocked until 2008. In 1991 they ordered him not to travel with anyone under the age of 18. In 1995 the threshold was raised to 21 and in 2001 to 30. In 2000 they forbade his having his young assistants stay with him at Canisius House. He continued to travel with boys after being forbidden to do so. His defense at trial was that Dominick had concocted a false claim of sexual molestation in the hope of obtaining money.

The defendant was charged with violating 18 U.S.C. § 2423(b), which is one of four closely related provisions of the federal criminal code. The four are as follows:

18 U.S.C. § 2421: Whoever knowingly transports any individual in interstate or foreign commerce, or in any Territory or Possession of the United States, with intent that such individual engage in prostitution, or in any sexual activity for which any person can be charged with a criminal offense, or attempts to do so, shall be fined under this title or imprisoned not more than 10 years, or both.

18 U.S.C. § 2423(a): Transportation with intent to engage in criminal sexual activity. — A person who knowingly transports an individual who has not attained the age of 18 years in interstate or foreign commerce, or in any commonwealth, territory or possession of the United States, with intent that the individual engage in prostitution, or in any sexual activity for which any person can be charged with a criminal offense, shall be fined under this title and imprisoned not less than 10 years or for life.

18 U.S.C. § 2423(b): Travel with intent to engage in illicit sexual conduct. — A person who travels in interstate commerce or travels into the United States, or a United States citizen or an alien admitted for permanent residence in the United States who travels in foreign commerce, for the purpose of engaging in any illicit sexual conduct with another person shall be fined under this title or imprisoned not more than 30 years, or both.

18 U.S.C. § 2423(c): Engaging in illicit sexual conduct in foreign places. — Any United States citizen or alien admitted for permanent residence who travels in foreign commerce, and engages in any illicit sexual conduct with another person shall be fined under this title or imprisoned not more than 30 years, or both.

Section 2421 is the original Mann Act, as amended in minor respects. Section 2423(a), intended to protect minors from sexual predation, mirrors the Mann Act but imposes more severe penalties. Section 2423(b), the provision under which the defendant was prosecuted, was added to expand the protection of minors still further; it punishes travel in interstate commerce even if no minor is transported, if the purpose of the travel is sex with a minor. (Prosecutors frequently use this section to prosecute persons who cross state lines to rendezvous with minors whom they meet in online chat rooms. See, e.g., *United States v. Buttrick*, 432 F.3d 373 (1st Cir.2005).) Section 2423(c) was added to punish persons who travel in foreign commerce and have sex with a minor in the course of the trip regardless of what the defendant intended when he set out on it.

It is apparent that if, as the jury found, the defendant had molested Dominick on their travels, he violated sections 2421, 2423(a), and 2423(c). E.g., *United States v. Bonty*, 383 F.3d 575, 578 (7th Cir.2004); *United States v. Snow*, 507 F.2d 22, 23 (7th Cir.1974); *United States v. Hitt*, 473 F.3d 146, 150 (5th Cir.2006). But inexplicably the government charged the defendant only with violating section 2423(b), which requires that the travel be for the purpose of engaging in illegal sexual activity. This charging decision (which the government's lawyer was unable to explain to us at the oral argument) enabled the defendant to argue that the purpose of his trips was merely to conduct retreats; sex was not the purpose but a welcome byproduct (if the government's evidence was believed) of the opportunities that the retreats created, as the boys were more vulnerable when far from home and the defendant's molestation of them was less likely to be detected by his religious superiors, who as we know had suspected him for many years of being a child molester yet had taken no effective steps to protect young boys from him.

The courts have had trouble dealing with cases in which the travel prosecuted under section 2423(b) may have had dual purposes, only one of which was to have sex with minors. The statute says "the" purpose must be sex rather than "a" purpose, but in *United States v. Vang*, 128 F.3d 1065, 1068 (7th Cir.1997), we approved a jury instruction which said that sex didn't have to be "the sole purpose" of the travel, though it did have to be "a dominant purpose, as opposed to an incidental one. A person may have more than one dominant purpose for traveling across a state line." To speak of multiple dominant purposes is not idiomatic, but given the evidence in *Vang* the precise wording of the instruction hardly mattered. Other cases, too, fasten on "dominant," but then define it down to mean "significant," "efficient and compelling," "predominat[ing]," "motivating," not "incidental," or not "an incident" to the defendant's purpose in traveling. E.g., *United States v. Julian*, 427 F.3d 471, 485 (7th Cir.2005); *United States v. Hitt, supra*, 473 F.3d at 152; *United States v. Hayward*, 359 F.3d 631, 637–38 (3d Cir.2004); *United States v. Meacham*, 115 F.3d 1488, 1495–96 (10th Cir.1997); *United States v. Campbell*, 49 F.3d 1079, 1083–84 (5th Cir.1995); *United States v. Ellis*, 935 F.2d 385, 390 (1st Cir.1991); *United States v. Bennett*, 364 F.2d 77, 79 (4th Cir.1966).

These verbal formulas are strained; the courts turn handsprings trying to define "dominant" as if it were a statutory term, see, e.g., *United States v. Miller*, 148 F.3d 207, 212–13 (2d Cir.1998), which it is not. It would be better to ask whether, had a sex motive not been present, the trip would not have taken place or would have differed substantially. See, e.g., *United States v. Snow, supra*, 507 F.2d at 24; *United States v. Farley*, 607 F.3d 1294, 1335 (11th Cir.2010); *United States v. Meacham, supra*, 115 F.3d at 1495–96.

We can place the blame for judicial preoccupation with the word "dominant" on the Supreme Court, which in *Mortensen v. United States*, 322 U.S. 369, 374, 64 S.Ct. 1037, 88 L.Ed. 1331 (1944), a Mann Act case, said that engaging in forbidden sexual activity "must be the dominant purpose of such interstate movement." That was dictum, because the sole purpose of the movement in question was to give several prostitutes an innocent vacation—that is, one in which they would *not* be plying their trade. There were not multiple purposes, of which one was sexual, so there was no occasion to identify a dominant purpose. But later cases, ignoring Justice Holmes's admonition to think things not words, have tended to treat "dominant purpose" as if it were the language of the Mann Act itself, and, later still, as if it were the language of the statutes, including 18 U.S.C. §2423(b), that restate and extend the Act; and from the cases the term entered jury instructions. (The evolution of "dominant purpose" is considered at length in our opinion in *United States v. Vang, supra*, 128 F.3d at 1070–72.) The Fourth Circuit stated sensibly in *United States v. Bennett, supra*, 364 F.2d at 77, 78 n. 4, that "the 'dominant motive' test seems completely inappropriate in any case involving multiple purposes, some of which were legitimate but one of which is proscribed by [section] 2421," and equally by section 2423(b). But the defendant does not challenge the jury instructions, so the only question is whether the jury was unreasonable in convicting him.

To answer the question we need to be clear about the meaning of the statutory term "travels"; that will get us further than worrying the word "dominant." To say that a sexual predator "travels" in interstate or foreign commerce to a retreat is not a full description of the travel in this case. He travels in interstate or foreign commerce to a retreat in the company of a boy he intends to molest—that is the full description. The purpose of the travel so understood is to engage in illegal sexual conduct. See *United States v. Meacham, supra*, 115 F.3d at 1495–96; *United States v. Ellis, supra*, 935 F.2d at 390–91.

At the oral argument we put the following hypothetical case to the defendant's lawyer. A man who travels frequently abroad on business has two assistants. One is an older woman. The other is young and beautiful. He needs only one of the assistants to accompany him; they are equally competent; but he chooses to take the young woman because he hopes to have sex with her. The purpose of his travel is business; but the purpose of his travel with this assistant rather than the other one is sex—legal sex, in the example, but that's not the point; the point is that the purpose of his choosing this particular way to travel is sex rather than business. Cf. *United States v. Snow, supra*, 507 F.2d at 24; *United States v. Meacham, supra*, 115 F.3d at 1495–96. The defendant's lawyer was unable to distinguish the present case from our hypothetical case.

It would be different if in that case the traveling businessman had only one assistant, the beautiful young woman. He hopes that he might have sex with her on the trip, yet he would have made the same trip, taking her with him, even if he had had no such designs. In that event sex would not have been the purpose of the trip with her, but a possible bonus that could however have played no part in his decision to take the trip—he was ordered to take it and needed, for purely business reasons, to take the assistant with him. Compare *Hansen v. Haff*, 291 U.S. 559, 563, 54 S.Ct. 494, 78 L.Ed. 968 (1934) ("if the purpose of the journey was not sexual intercourse, though that be contemplated, the statute is not violated"), with *Ghadiali v. United States*, 17 F.2d 236, 237 (9th Cir.1927) (the defendant "had a right to cause [his secretary] to be transported in interstate commerce in the discharge of her secretarial duties without transgressing the provisions of the law; but if, in addition to the secretarial duties, it was also his purpose to have sexual intercourse with her, and, entertaining such purpose, transported her in interstate commerce, he would be guilty").

After 1991 the defendant was forbidden to travel with minors to his retreats—and all the trips with Dominick took place after that. If a trip has dual purposes, one licit but intended to bolster an illicit sexual purpose, the sexual purpose is "the" purpose, in a reasonable sense of the word. Suppose a salesman employed by Sears Roebuck is directed by Sears to travel to Singapore to sell clothes dryers there. Instead he travels to Bangkok because he wants to patronize child prostitutes. He sells some clothes dryers in Bangkok in the intervals between his visits to the child prostitutes and alters the invoices to make it seem that the sales occurred in Singapore. The purpose of his travel would be sex rather than business, though business would be transacted during the trip. See *United States v. Snow, supra,* 507 F.2d at 24; *United States v. Meacham, supra,* 115 F.3d at 1495–96; *United States v. Farley, supra,* 607 F.3d at 1335; *United States v. Bredimus,* 234 F.Supp.2d 639, 646 (N.D.Tex.2002), affirmed, 352 F.3d 200 (5th Cir.2003). The defendant in our case had, so far as appears, broad latitude concerning the number and location of the retreats he led, and he configured his travels to optimize his sexual activity....

Affirmed.

Note

Participating in interstate or foreign travel for the purpose of engaging in sexual activity with a minor is governed by federal statute within the Mann Act, specifically 18 U.S.C. §§ 2421 and 2423(b), as is discussed in the *McGuire* decision. Sections 2421 and 2423(a) involve the travel of the exploited victim and criminalizes the transportation of a minor in interstate or foreign commerce "with the intent that the minor engage in prostitution, or in any sexual activity for which the person could be prosecuted for a criminal offense." Conviction under this section imposes a mandatory minimum sentence of 10 years and a statutory maximum sentence of life. As opposed to other statutes, § 2423(a) requires the existence of an actual child. The most notorious conviction under this provision was in 2010, when Brian David Mitchell was sentenced to life in prison for famously kidnapping then 14-year-old Elizabeth Smart, in 2002. See *United States v. Mitchell,* 2010 WL 4782980 (regarding purpose of Mitchell's travel with Smart); *United States v. Mitchell,* 706 F. Supp.2d 1148 (D. Utah 2010) (regarding Mitchell's competency to stand trial). However, § 2423(b) involves the travel of the exploiter and criminalizes traveling in interstate or foreign travel "for the purpose of engaging in illicit sexual conduct with another person." Under § 2423(b), there is no mandatory minimum sentence and there is a statutory maximum sentence of 30 years. The term "illicit sexual conduct" is defined, in part, within the statute as "any commercial sex act (as defined in [18 U.S.C. § 1591]) with a person under 18 years of age." 18 U.S.C. § 2423(f)(2). Under either provision, the focus of the court must be upon the statute; § 2423(a) and (b) serve to protect children from sexual predators who travel with the intent of committing illicit sex acts with a child, whereas § 2423(c) addresses circumstances under which the purpose of the travel has nothing to do with an intent to sexually abuse or exploit a child, but such abuse occurs during travel with an otherwise innocent purpose.

In this light, consider the following cases, which involve the application of the same federal statutes but involve foreign travel that is less clearly motivated by sexual activity since there are multiple purposes for the foreign travel. In *United States v. Pendleton* and *United States v. Schneider,* no sexual activity occurred during the trip to foreign lands. Compared to the court in *McGuire,* how does the court in *Schneider* deal with the difficulties created by the holding in *Mortensen,* which is discussed in both cases?

b. Foreign Travel

United States v. Pendleton

Third Circuit, 2011

658 F.3d 299

HARDIMAN, Circuit Judge.....

On November 25, 2005, Thomas Pendleton boarded a plane in New York City and flew to Hamburg, Germany. Six months after his arrival in Germany, Pendleton sexually molested a fifteen-year-old boy. German authorities arrested Pendleton, and a jury in Hamburg found him guilty of "engaging in sexual acts with a person incapable of resistance." After serving nineteen months in a German prison, Pendleton returned to the United States, where he was arrested and indicted by a federal grand jury in the District of Delaware on one count of engaging in noncommercial illicit sexual conduct in a foreign place, in violation of 18 U.S.C. § 2423(c) and (f)(1).... Adopted in 2003 as part of the Prosecutorial Remedies and Other Tools to End the Exploitation of Children Today Act (the PROTECT Act), § 2423(c) provides: "Any United States citizen or alien admitted for permanent residence who travels in foreign commerce, and engages in any illicit sexual conduct with another person shall be fined under this title or imprisoned not more than 30 years, or both." The statute defines "illicit sexual conduct" in two ways: (1) "a sexual act (as defined in section 2246) with a person under 18 years of age that would be in violation of chapter 109A if the sexual act occurred in the special maritime and territorial jurisdiction of the United States;" or (2) "any commercial sex act (as defined in section 1591) with a person under 18 years of age." 18 U.S.C. § 2423(f). Pendleton was indicted under the first subpart of § 2423(f), which criminalizes noncommercial sex with a minor.

Pendleton moved to dismiss the indictment, challenging Congress's authority to regulate noncommercial activity outside the United States under the Foreign Commerce Clause and the Due Process Clause of the Fifth Amendment. The District Court denied Pendleton's motion, holding that 18 U.S.C. § 2423(c) was a valid exercise of Congress's power to regulate the "channels" of foreign commerce.[1] See United States v. Clark, 435 F.3d 1100, 1114 (9th Cir.2006) ("[T]he phrase 'travels in foreign commerce' unequivocally establishes that Congress specifically invoked the Foreign Commerce Clause."). The District Court also held that Pendleton's due process claim was foreclosed by our decision in United States v. Martinez-Hidalgo, 993 F.2d 1052, 1056 (3d Cir.1993).[2] ... Following a two-day jury trial, Pendleton was convicted of engaging in illicit sexual conduct in Germany in violation of 18 U.S.C. § 2423(c), and he was sentenced to thirty years in prison.[3]

---

1. The legislative history of the PROTECT Act does not include a statement regarding the source of Congress's authority to enact § 2423(c). See generally H.R. Rep. No. 108-66, at 51, reprinted in 2003 U.S.C.C.A.N. 683, 686 (Apr. 9, 2003). However, the language of § 2423(c) was adopted verbatim from an earlier bill—the Sex Tourism Prohibition Improvement Act of 2002—which relied on the Foreign Commerce Clause as the basis for its constitutional authority. See H.R. Rep. No. 525, at 5, 2002 WL 1376220, at *5 (June 24, 2002).

2. Pendleton asks us to reexamine Martinez-Hidalgo's holding that no due process violation occurs when Congress criminalizes conduct abroad that is "condemned universally by law-abiding nations." Id. at 1056. We will not do so because a panel of this Court has no authority to overrule a precedential opinion of the Court. See Mariana v. Fisher, 338 F.3d 189, 201 (3d Cir.2003).

3. Pendleton also was sentenced to a concurrent term of ten years in prison for failing to register as a sex offender, in violation of the Adam Walsh Child Protection and Safety Act of 2006. See United States v. Pendleton, 636 F.3d 78 (3d Cir.2011). Pendleton was first convicted of sexually abusing children in Michigan in 1981 and was sentenced to 24 months probation. In 1993, a New Jersey jury found

Pendleton timely appealed the District Court's judgment of sentence and seeks reversal [because] the "noncommercial" prong of 18 U.S.C. §2423(c) is facially unconstitutional.... Pendleton's constitutional claim is subject to plenary review. *United States v. Singletary*, 268 F.3d 196, 199 (3d Cir.2001). Because Pendleton raises a facial challenge, we will invalidate the statute only if we find "that no set of circumstances exists under which the Act would be valid, i.e., that the law is unconstitutional in all of its applications." *Wash. State Grange v. Wash. State Republican Party*, 552 U.S. 442, 449, 128 S.Ct. 1184, 170 L.Ed.2d 151 (2008) (citations and internal quotation marks omitted). The Supreme Court has noted that a facial challenge is the "most difficult challenge to mount successfully." *United States v. Salerno*, 481 U.S. 739, 745, 107 S.Ct. 2095, 95 L.Ed.2d 697 (1987)....

The Constitution authorizes Congress "to regulate Commerce with foreign Nations, and among the several States, and with the Indian Tribes." U.S. Const. art. I, §8, cl. 3. In the early days of the Republic, the Supreme Court defined "commerce" broadly to include "every species of commercial intercourse" between two parties. *Gibbons v. Ogden*, 22 U.S. 1, 193–94, 9 Wheat. 1, 6 L.Ed. 23 (1824). More recently, the Supreme Court has recognized "three general categories of regulation in which Congress is authorized to engage under its commerce power." *Gonzales v. Raich*, 545 U.S. 1, 5, 125 S.Ct. 2195, 162 L.Ed.2d 1 (2005). These include: (1) the use of the channels of interstate commerce; (2) the instrumentalities of interstate commerce, or persons or things in interstate commerce; and (3) activities that substantially affect interstate commerce. *Lopez*, 514 U.S. [549,] 558–59, 115 S.Ct. 1624 [(1995)]. In its pathmarking decision in *Lopez*, the Supreme Court held unconstitutional a statute criminalizing the possession of a firearm in a school zone because it did not fall within one of the three aforementioned categories. Five years later, in *United States v. Morrison*, the Court struck down portions of the Violence Against Women Act on similar grounds. 529 U.S. 598, 617, 120 S.Ct. 1740, 146 L.Ed.2d 658 (2000) ("The concern ... that Congress might use the Commerce Clause to completely obliterate the Constitution's distinction between national and local authority seems well founded.")....

Although jurisprudence on the so-called "dormant" Foreign Commerce Clause is well-developed, "[c]ases involving the reach of ... congressional authority to regulate our citizens' conduct abroad are few and far between." *Clark*, 435 F.3d at 1102. Courts have consistently held that the Foreign Commerce Clause requires a jurisdictional nexus "with" the United States, *see, e.g., U.S. v. Weingarten*, 632 F.3d 60 (2d Cir.2011) (stating that a person who travels from one foreign nation to another to commit an illicit sex act may not be punished pursuant to Congress's foreign commerce power); *Cheng v. Boeing Co.*, 708 F.2d 1406, 1412 (9th Cir.1983) ("The Federal Aviation Act does not apply to the activities of a foreign carrier operating between two foreign points without contact in the United States."), but there is precious little case law on how to establish the requisite link to commercial interests in the United States. In the absence of Supreme Court precedent on the issue, the Court of Appeals for the Ninth Circuit determined that the *Lopez* framework—which developed to "reconcile[ ] ... the conflicting claims of state and national power"—has little analytical value in the Foreign Commerce Clause context. *Clark*, 435 F.3d at 1118. Rather than applying *Lopez*'s three-part framework to determine whether a

---

Pendleton guilty of various sex crimes against a 12-year-old boy and he was sentenced to seven years in prison. About three years after his release from prison, Pendleton traveled to Latvia and was convicted there for sex crimes against two children, ages 9 and 13. A little over a year after Pendleton was released from a Latvian prison he committed the offense at issue in this case.

statute has a "constitutionally tenable nexus with foreign commerce," the Ninth Circuit proposed a "global, commonsense approach," which considers "whether the statute bears a rational relationship to Congress's authority under the Foreign Commerce Clause."[5] *Id.*

The Government urges us to adopt the Ninth Circuit's approach to the Foreign Commerce Clause. Although we agree with *Clark* that the Interstate Commerce Clause developed to address "unique federalism concerns" that are absent in the foreign commerce context, we are hesitant to dispose of *Lopez*'s "time-tested" framework without further guidance from the Supreme Court. *See id.* at 1119 (Ferguson, J., dissenting). The Supreme Court has not yet held that Congress has greater authority to regulate activity outside the United States than it does within its borders; in fact, the language used to describe its extraterritorial jurisdiction is quite similar to that used in *Lopez. See, e.g., Hartford Fire Ins. Co. v. California*, 509 U.S. 764, 795, 113 S.Ct. 2891, 125 L.Ed.2d 612 (1993) (recognizing that the Sherman Antitrust Act applies extraterritorially, and stating that a jurisdictional nexus exists when "foreign conduct was meant to produce and did in fact produce some substantial effect in the United States"). In any case, we need not reach the fundamental question of whether the Supreme Court will adopt the Ninth Circuit's broad articulation of the Foreign Commerce Clause because, as we shall explain, §2423(c) is a valid congressional enactment under the narrower standard articulated in *Lopez....*

"[T]he authority of Congress to keep the channels of interstate commerce free from immoral and injurious uses has been frequently sustained, and is no longer open to question." *Heart of Atlanta Motel, Inc. v. United States*, 379 U.S. 241, 256, 85 S.Ct. 348, 13 L.Ed.2d 258 (1964) (quoting *Caminetti v. United States*, 242 U.S. 470, 491, 37 S.Ct. 192, 61 L.Ed. 442 (1917)); *see also Morrison*, 529 U.S. at 612, 120 S.Ct. 1740 (describing the Court's holding in *Lopez*, and noting that although 18 U.S.C. §922(g) contains "no express jurisdictional element which might limit its reach to a discrete set of firearm possessions that additionally have an explicit connection with or effect on interstate commerce, ... [s]uch a jurisdictional element [would have] establish[ed] that the enactment is in pursuance of Congress's regulation of interstate commerce") (citations and internal quotation marks omitted). Unlike Congressional authority to regulate activities affecting interstate commerce under the third category in *Lopez*, Congress's authority to regulate the *channels* of commerce is not confined to regulations with an economic purpose or impact. *See, e.g., Caminetti*, 242 U.S. at 491, 37 S.Ct. 192 (criminalizing the interstate transportation of a woman or girl for prostitution); *Perez v. United States*, 402 U.S. 146,

---

5. The Ninth Circuit in *Clark* claims to borrow this "rational basis" test from the Supreme Court's holding in *Gonzales v. Raich. See* 545 U.S. at 5, 125 S.Ct. 2195 (holding that Congress had a "rational basis" for believing that intrastate possession and manufacture of marijuana had a substantial effect on interstate commerce). As the dissent in *Clark* rightly notes, however, the "rational basis" analysis in *Raich* went to Congress's "substantial effects" determination. The Supreme Court has articulated several factors to be weighed in determining whether an activity "substantially affects" interstate commerce: (1) whether the regulated activity is economic in nature; (2) whether the statute contains an "express jurisdictional element" linking its scope in some way to interstate commerce; (3) whether Congress made express findings regarding the effects of the regulated activity on interstate commerce; and (4) attenuation of the link between the regulated activity and interstate commerce. *See Morrison*, 529 U.S. at 611–12, 120 S.Ct. 1740.

The "rational basis" standard articulated by the Ninth Circuit in *Clark* does not consider any of these factors. Rather, its open-ended inquiry seems to borrow more heavily from the Supreme Court's pre-*Lopez* jurisprudence, which held that a court's "investigation ... end[s]" once it determines that "legislators ... have a rational basis for finding a chosen regulatory scheme necessary to the protection of commerce." *Katzenbach v. McClung*, 379 U.S. 294, 303–04, 85 S.Ct. 377, 13 L.Ed.2d 290 (1964).

150, 91 S.Ct. 1357, 28 L.Ed.2d 686 (1971) (banning the interstate shipment of kidnapped persons); *United States v. Cummings*, 281 F.3d 1046, 1049–51 (9th Cir.2002) (holding that the International Parental Kidnapping Crime Act regulates the channels of foreign commerce by prohibiting the removal or retention of a child outside the United States "with intent to obstruct the lawful exercise of parental rights").

In *United States v. Tykarsky*, we held that 18 U.S.C. §2423(b), which criminalizes interstate travel with intent to engage in illicit sexual conduct with a minor, is a valid exercise of Congress's power to regulate the channels of commerce. 446 F.3d 458, 470 (3d Cir.2006); *accord United States v. Hawkins*, 513 F.3d 59, 61 (2d Cir.2008) (per curiam); *United States v. Buttrick*, 432 F.3d 373, 374 (1st Cir.2005); *Bredimus*, 352 F.3d at 205–207. Pendleton attempts to distinguish *Tykarsky* by noting that unlike §2423(b), §2423(c) includes no intent requirement. Citing *United States v. Rodia* for the proposition that "[t]he mere presence of a jurisdictional element ... does not in and of itself insulate a statute from judicial scrutiny under the Commerce Clause," Pendleton claims the District Court should have inquired whether "the jurisdictional component in this case limits the statute to items that have an explicit connection with, or effect upon, [foreign] commerce." 194 F.3d 465, 472 (3d Cir.1999) (finding that 18 U.S.C. §2252(a)(4)(B)'s jurisdictional requirement that materials like film and cameras move in interstate commerce "is only tenuously related to the ultimate activity regulated: intrastate possession of child pornography"). No such connection exists here, Pendleton argues, because his conviction under §2423(c) would stand even if he traveled through the channels of commerce for an entirely lawful purpose and only later formed the intent to engage in illicit sex with a minor. Contrary to Pendleton's assertions, however, a statute need not include an element of *mens rea* to trigger the first prong of *Lopez*.

In *United States v. Shenandoah*, we upheld portions of the Sex Offender Registration and Notification Act (SORNA), 18 U.S.C. §2250(a)(1) and (2) and 42 U.S.C. §14072(i)(1), making it illegal for a sex offender to fail to properly register after traveling in interstate commerce. 595 F.3d 151, 161 (3d Cir.2010); *accord United States v. Ambert*, 561 F.3d 1202, 1211 (11th Cir.2009); *United States v. May*, 535 F.3d 912, 921 (8th Cir.2008). Like the provision at issue here (§2423(c)), SORNA does not require that a sex offender intend, at the time of travel, to later violate federal registration requirements. Nor does SORNA require the Government to demonstrate a temporal connection between the time of travel and a sex offender's failure to register. *United States v. Husted*, 2007 U.S. Dist. LEXIS 56662, at *9 (W.D. Okla. June 29, 2007) (citing H.R.Rep. No. 109-218 (Sept. 7, 2005)) ("[T]he legislative history of the statute shows Congress chose not to incorporate a temporal requirement but, instead, intended to encompass all sex offenders."). For instance, a "tier I sex offender" who moves from one state to another and, years later, violates SORNA's provisions by failing to update his information on an annual basis can be convicted under the statute. 18 U.S.C. §2250(a)(1); *see Carr v. United States*, ___ U.S. ___, ___, 130 S.Ct. 2229, 2235, 176 L.Ed.2d 1152 (2010) (observing in dicta that "[a] sequential reading [of the statute] ... helps to assure a nexus between a defendant's interstate travel and his failure to register as a sex offender").[6]

---

6. In this respect, SORNA's "failure to register" provision is similar to the federal felon-in-possession law, 18 U.S.C. §922(g), enacted pursuant to Congress's authority under the Commerce Clause. Section 922(g) makes it unlawful for a felon to "possess in or affecting commerce, any firearm or ammunition ... which has been shipped or transported in interstate or foreign commerce." In *United States v. Singletary*, we held that the transport of a weapon through the channels of interstate commerce—however remote in the distant past—provides a sufficient jurisdictional nexus to satisfy *Lopez*'s first prong. 268 F.3d 196, 200 (3d Cir.2001) (citing *Scarborough v. United States*, 431 U.S. 563, 564, 97 S.Ct. 1963, 52

Nevertheless, SORNA was specifically enacted to address "one of the biggest problems in our current sex offender registry," 152 Cong. Rec. S8012-14 (daily ed. July 20, 2006), 2005 WL 2034118, namely, sex offenders who go "missing" from the national registry by moving from one state to another, H.R. Rep. No. 109-218(1) (2005), 2005 WL 2210642. Finding that "over 10,000 sex offenders, or nearly one-fifth in the Nation ... are 'missing,'" *id.*, Congress chose to regulate the behavior of all sex offenders who cross state lines. Because Congress invoked its authority to regulate "the use of interstate commerce to facilitate forms of immorality," *Shenandoah*, 595 F.3d at 161 (citing *Brooks v. United States*, 267 U.S. 432, 436, 45 S.Ct. 345, 69 L.Ed. 699 (1925)), it was not obliged to include an express intent or temporal element in its definition of the offense. *Accord United States v. Dixon*, 551 F.3d 578 (7th Cir.2008) (summarily rejecting defendant's Commerce Clause argument, noting that the defendant "must in the heat of argument have forgotten the Mann Act"); *United States v. Hann*, 574 F.Supp.2d 827, 833 (M.D.Tenn.2008) ("[*Lopez*] encompasses § 2250(a) because the statute regulates sex offenders who travel in interstate commerce even though the threat Congress was attempting to address—failure to register as a sex offender—is an intrastate activity.") (citations omitted).

The same rationale applies to Pendleton's case. Just as SORNA's "failure to report" provision was intended to prevent convicted sex offenders from "us[ing] the channels of interstate commerce in evading a State's reach," *Carr*, 130 S.Ct. at 2238, Congress enacted § 2423(c) to close "significant loopholes in the law that persons who travel to foreign countries seeking sex with children are currently using to their advantage in order to avoid prosecution," H.R. Rep. No. 107-525, at 3 (summarizing the purpose of adopting language similar to § 2423(c) in the Sex Tourism Prohibition Improvement Act). Specifically, Congress found that American citizens were using the channels of foreign commerce to travel to countries where "dire poverty and ... lax enforcement" would allow them to "escape prosecution" for their crimes of child sexual abuse. 148 Cong. Rec. 3884; *id.* at 3885 ("Sadly, we know that many Americans go abroad to prey on young girls in other countries because laws protecting women are very weak, non-existent, or not enforced."); H.R. Rep. No. 107-525, at 4 ("According to the National Center for Missing and Exploited Children, child-sex tourism is a major component of the worldwide sexual exploitation of children and is increasing. There are more than 100 web sites devoted to promoting teenage commercial sex in Asia alone."); *see also* 109 H.R. 2012, 109th Cong. § 2 (2005) ("The United Nations estimates that sex trafficking, including sex tourism, generates approximately $5,000,000,000 a year in revenues. There are a number of United States-based companies that overtly and explicitly facilitate sex tours, often involving the sexual exploitation of children. According to some estimates, up to 1/4 of international sex tourists are American.").

Members of Congress also expressed concern that § 2423(b) would not adequately deter child-sex tourists because prosecutors were having an "extremely difficult" time "proving intent in such cases." 148 Cong. Rec. 3884 (stating that intent is particularly "difficult to prove without direct arrangement booked through obvious child sex-tour networks."). This, in turn, "creat[ed] a loophole in the law for men who go abroad to have sex with minors, which in the United States is considered statutory rape." *Id.* Section 2423(c) was enacted to close the enforcement gap and to "send a message to those who go to foreign countries to exploit children that no one can abuse a child with impunity." *Id.* Thus, as it did with SORNA, Congress enacted § 2423(c) to regulate persons who use

---

L.Ed.2d 582 (1977)). Similarly, under § 2423(c), a person's travel through foreign commerce continues to provide a link to his illicit sexual conduct long after his travel is complete.

the channels of commerce to circumvent local laws that criminalize child abuse and molestation. And just as Congress may cast a wide net to stop sex offenders from traveling in interstate commerce to evade state registration requirements, so too may it attempt to prevent sex tourists from using the channels of foreign commerce to abuse children. *Id.*; *Clark*, 435 F.3d at 1116 ("Congress legitimately exercises its authority to regulate the channels of commerce where a crime committed on foreign soil is necessarily tied to travel in foreign commerce, even where the actual use of the channels has ceased."); *N. Am. Co. v. SEC*, 327 U.S. 686, 705, 66 S.Ct. 785, 90 L.Ed. 945 (1946) ("Congress may impose relevant conditions and requirements on those who use the channels of interstate commerce in order that those channels will not become the means of promoting or spreading evil, whether of a physical, moral or economic nature.").

In sum, because the jurisdictional element in § 2423(c) has an "express connection" to the channels of foreign commerce, *Morrison*, 529 U.S. at 612, 120 S.Ct. 1740, we hold that it is a valid exercise of Congress's power under the Foreign Commerce Clause.... [footnote omitted].... For the foregoing reasons, we will affirm the District Court's judgment of conviction and sentence.

United States v. Schneider

United States District Court, Eastern District, Pennsylvania, 2011
817 F. Supp. 2d 586

JUAN R. SÁNCHEZ, District Judge....

The charges against Schneider, an American citizen who, in 2001, was 36 years old, stem from his travel on August 22, 2001, from the United States to Russia in the company of Roman Zavarov, a 15-year-old Russian boy. At the time of his travel, Schneider had housed Zavarov in his Moscow apartment for three years and, during the year immediately preceding the flight, had engaged in regular sexual activity with him.[2]

Schneider first met Zavarov in 1998 when Zavarov was 12 years old. Zavarov had recently been forced to leave a prestigious ballet training program in Russia at the Moscow Academy of Ballet (the Academy) — also known as the Bolshoi Academy — after his parents became unable to pay his dormitory fees. Zavarov's parents wanted their son to continue his ballet training and considered sending him to a ballet school in St. Petersburg, where he had a scholarship. In the summer of 1998, however, two of Zavarov's former Academy instructors, Nikolai Dokukin and Tatiana Dokukina, raised the possibility of securing payment for Zavarov's education at the Academy from Schneider, a ballet afficionado, who had told the Dokukins he was interested in creating a charitable organization to provide scholarships to talented arts students in Russia.

At the time, Schneider was working in Moscow as an attorney and had become acquainted with the Dokukins because of his interest in ballet. After meeting the Dokukins, Schneider became involved at the Academy, donating furniture to the Academy, paying for ballet footwear for the students, and providing grants to the instructors. He also visited ballet classes at the Academy and videotaped the students, telling Dokukina he planned to send the videos to his friend, Olga Kostritzky, an instructor at the School of American

---

2. Although the Government asserted Schneider sexually molested Zavarov for the entire three-year period preceding their travel to the United States, this Court limited evidence of such illicit sexual conduct to the period between August 22, 2000, and November 22, 2001, pursuant to Federal Rule of Evidence 403.... [citation omitted].

Ballet. Within a month of meeting Schneider, Dokukina told him about Zavarov's financial troubles and asked if he would be willing to sponsor Zavarov's ballet education. Schneider indicated he might be interested, but told Dokukina he wished to meet Zavarov and see a demonstration of his ballet ability before agreeing to sponsor him.... Schneider and the Dokukins went to Zavarov's house and asked him to perform a number of ballet exercises. Schneider videotaped this demonstration, during which Zavarov was dressed in only a pair of black underpants.[3] During the demonstration, Dokukina told the Zavarovs, "if you show this recording, they will grab him for ballet and throw you into the bargain. They'll be asking where did you dig up this treasure?"... Dokukina testified that having such a tape would provide Zavarov a "huge chance to be admitted to [a ballet] school."... Zavarov's parents were interested in having Schneider finance their son's education and agreed to additional meetings with Schneider. During one of these meetings, Zavarov's father asked Schneider for a loan so that he could repay the debt he owed to the Academy for Zavarov's delinquent dorm fees. Schneider agreed, loaning Zavarov's father 4,300 rubles, approximately $470 at the time. A notary public in Russia drafted a loan agreement, which was signed by Schneider and Zavarov's parents, requiring the Zavarovs to repay the loan over four months, with the final payment due December 31, 1998.[4]

At another meeting, Schneider told Zavarov's father that after Zavarov re-enrolled at the Academy he would not live in the dormitory, but would instead live with Schneider. Schneider explained he could provide better accommodations because Zavarov would have his own room in Schneider's apartment, would get better rest and better food, and would have access to a personal ballet instructor. Although this arrangement made Zavarov's father uncomfortable, he felt he had to agree to it to ensure his son was able to re-enroll at the Academy. Before Zavarov moved in, the Zavarov family visited Schneider's apartment, a two-room apartment with one small bedroom and a larger main room. Schneider told the Zavarovs he would sleep in the bedroom and Zavarov would sleep on a pull-out couch in the main room. The Zavarovs were satisfied that this was an appropriate sleeping arrangement for their son.

When the new school term started, Zavarov began living with Schneider from Monday to Friday, returning to his parents' home on weekends, holidays, and in the summer. Schneider discouraged Zavarov's father from visiting him during the week, telling him Zavarov had everything he needed. While at Schneider's apartment, Zavarov was primarily taken care of by a woman who lived across the hall from Schneider, Ludmila Kozyreva. Kozyreva woke Zavarov up, prepared his breakfast, helped him get ready for school in the morning, watched him after school, and prepared his dinner. Because the Zavarovs did not know Schneider well, Zavarov's father advised his son to tell Kozyreva if he was sexually molested by Schneider.[5] During the time Zavarov lived with Schneider, Schneider paid for his food and some of his clothing and purchased other items for Zavarov, including a Playstation video game console and a bicycle. Schneider also paid for Dokukin to provide private dance lessons to Zavarov in Schneider's apartment, and bought Zavarov a cellular phone.

---

3. Zavarov's mother testified that, although she felt uncomfortable that Zavarov was not fully dressed, such limited dress is necessary for ballet demonstrations as it enables a viewer to see all of the dancer's movements.

4. Although the final loan payment was due at the end of 1998, the Zavarovs did not fully repay the debt until August 5, 2000.

5. Zavarov never told Kozyreva that Schneider was molesting him, though he sought her help on one occasion when Schneider became angry after Zavarov's father appeared at the apartment unannounced.

In 2001, when Zavarov was 15 years old, Schneider encouraged Zavarov to apply to summer ballet programs in the United States and elsewhere, and offered to take Zavarov to Philadelphia so he could study at the Rock School. Zavarov testified that in the year before he and Schneider traveled to the United States, Schneider had been engaging in oral and anal sex with him approximately three to four times a week, with the encounters typically taking place at night in Schneider's bedroom.[6] Schneider told Zavarov to keep these encounters secret because people would not understand their relationship, and Schneider would go to jail.[7] Schneider also told Zavarov that if Schneider was gone, Zavarov "[wouldn't] be able to fulfill [his] dreams as a ballet dancer and [would] stay in Russia." ...

Zavarov also testified that Schneider had previously told him their relationship was similar to the relationship of the famous Russian ballet dancer, Vaslav Nijinsky, and his mentor and director, Sergei Diaghilev. When Zavarov was 13, Schneider showed him *Nijinsky*, a film that depicts Diaghilev and Nijinsky as lovers, and suggests that Nijinsky was emotionally destroyed after he ended his relationship with Diaghilev to pursue a heterosexual marriage.[8] After the film, Schneider told Zavarov that Nijinsky made a mistake by leaving Diaghilev, and warned him not to make the same mistake. Schneider also told Zavarov relationships with girls were disgusting, and Zavarov should avoid girls because they would take advantage of him. That same year, Schneider gave Zavarov a birthday card inscribed with the message, "Romanicov, until trillion thirty years, your friend, Ken," and told Zavarov they should be together "until trillion thirteen years." ... Before they traveled to the United States, Zavarov thought of Schneider as his friend and role model. In an essay he wrote as part of a school application, Zavarov said Schneider had made him very happy by re-enrolling him in the Academy and by helping him with any problems he had, and described Schneider as a "friend" and "second father." ...

Schneider helped Zavarov complete his application for the Rock School, which admitted Zavarov to its summer program and awarded him a scholarship, which paid for Zavarov's travel to and from Philadelphia. After his acceptance to the summer program, Zavarov and his parents went to the United States Embassy in Moscow to apply for a travel visa. In the application, Zavarov's parents authorized Schneider to take Zavarov to the United States from July 4, 2001, until August 31, 2001. When Schneider and Zavarov traveled to Philadelphia, Zavarov stayed with Schneider's parents at their home in Berwyn, a suburb of Philadelphia. Schneider did not stay at the Berwyn home for the summer because he was traveling for work, although he visited Zavarov there occasionally. While Schneider and Zavarov were in United States, they did not engage in any sexual activity, though Schneider held Zavarov's hand, hugged him, and kissed him once.... On August 22, 2001, Schneider and Zavarov flew from Philadelphia to Moscow. After arriving in Moscow, Zavarov went to his parents' house and stayed with them for a week before he returned to school. When Zavarov returned to school and moved back into Schneider's apartment, the sexual activity between Schneider and Zavarov resumed, and continued to occur two to three times per week.... Zavarov never told his parents that he had been sexually abused by Schneider. After he began living with Schneider, however, his personality

---

6. Schneider denied ever having had any sexual contact with Zavarov.

7. Schneider also worried the effects of his contact with Zavarov would be discovered by a nurse at the Bolshoi Academy, and told Zavarov if the nurse asked about any injuries to his rectum, he should say he was using a hemorrhoid stick. When the nurse attempted to examine Zavarov, Schneider called the school to complain about her, and she was eventually fired.

8. At trial, the Government played portions of this movie to the jury, including a portion in which Nijinsky's character simulated masturbation during a ballet performance.

changed. His father noticed he was more withdrawn and silent, and seemed to be keeping something to himself. Zavarov eventually moved to the United States and, in 2008, Zavarov told his girlfriend, Gina D'Amico—whom he has since married—about Schneider's sexual molestation, revealing that Schneider had sexually abused him while he lived with Schneider in Russia.

On August 12, 2008, Zavarov filed a civil lawsuit against Schneider and others, bringing claims stemming from Schneider's sexual abuse. After Zavarov filed his lawsuit, he was contacted by the Federal Bureau of Investigation, which thereafter launched a criminal investigation into Schneider's conduct with Zavarov. On January 14, 2010, Schneider was charged in a two-count indictment with (1) traveling in foreign commerce for the purpose of engaging in sex with a minor, in violation of 18 U.S.C. § 2423(b) (Count I), and (2) transporting a person in foreign commerce with the intent that such person engage in criminal sexual conduct, in violation of 18 U.S.C. § 2421 (Count II). Schneider was convicted of both charges on October 1, 2010, following a jury trial....

To secure a conviction pursuant to § 2423(b), the Government is not required to prove criminal activity was "*the* dominant purpose of interstate travel." *See United States v. Hayward*, 359 F.3d 631, 638 (3d Cir.2004). Instead, when multiple motives for interstate travel exist, the Government must prove illegal sexual activity was "a dominant purpose" of the defendant's travel. *Id.*; *see also United States v. Vang*, 128 F.3d 1065, 1072 (7th Cir.1997) (explaining "[d]espite the contrary implication suggested by the word 'dominant,' an immoral purpose need not be the most important of defendant's reasons when multiple purposes are present") (quoting *United States v. Snow*, 507 F.2d 22, 23 (7th Cir.1974)); *United States v. Campbell*, 49 F.3d 1079, 1082–83 (5th Cir.1995) (holding, with regard to a § 2421 conviction, a jury may find a "dominant purpose" to engage in illegal activity existed when such activity is " 'one of the efficient and compelling purposes' " or "one motivating purpose" of the defendant's travel (citation omitted)).[10] In evaluating whether trial evidence proved an illicit travel purpose in "cases in which the travel prosecuted under [§] 2423(b) may have had dual purposes, only one of which was to have sex with minors," a court must consider whether a rational juror could have found illicit intentions were the but-for cause of the travel, asking "whether, had a sex motive not been present, the trip would not have taken place or would have differed substantially." *United States v. McGuire*, 627 F.3d 622, 624–25 (7th Cir.2010).

At trial, the Government presented evidence showing Schneider engaged in frequent sexual activity with Zavarov from August 2000 until sometime in July 2001. That same month, Schneider flew with Zavarov and then accompanied him to Schneider's parents' house in Berwyn. For the next two months, Schneider was traveling elsewhere and only occasionally spent time at the Berwyn home. At the end of August, following the conclusion of Zavarov's summer ballet program, Schneider returned to Berwyn, picked up Zavarov, traveled to the airport with him, and boarded a plane to Moscow with him. Schneider argues because he lived and worked in Moscow, and thus had a need to return there independent of any sexual relationship with Zavarov, the jury could not reasonably have found the desire to resume sexual activity with Zavarov was a dominant purpose of his return travel to Moscow. However, because Schneider flew from Pennsylvania with Zavarov at the conclusion of Zavarov's summer program, the jury could have reasonably inferred that Schneider did not choose the location or date of his travel to Moscow for business

---

10. As the Seventh Circuit explained, "[j]udicial interpretations of the Mann Act (§ 2421) necessarily color [courts'] reading of § 2423(b)" because they are "part of the same general legislative framework" and "employ[ ] the same 'for the purpose of' phrase." *Vang*, 128 F.3d at 1069.

or personal reasons, but rather flew on that day and from that location to further his intent to resume his sexual activity with Zavarov. The evidence was therefore sufficient to permit a rational juror to find a dominant purpose of Schneider's August 22, 2001, travel to Moscow was to engage in sex with Zavarov. *See id.* at 626 (holding a priest who traveled internationally to hold spiritual retreats also traveled for the purpose of engaging in illicit sex because he "configured his travels to optimize his [illicit] sexual activity").

Schneider similarly argues the evidence presented at trial was insufficient to sustain his conviction for a violation of §2421. Count II of the Indictment charged

> [o]n or about August 22, 2001, in the Eastern District of Pennsylvania, and elsewhere, defendant KENNETH SCHNEIDER transported a person in foreign commerce with the intent that such person engage in any sexual activity for which any person can be charged with a criminal offense, to wit, defendant SCHNEIDER transported [Zavarov], ... from Philadelphia, Pennsylvania to Moscow, Russia with the intent that [Zavarov], under compulsion based on [Zavarov's] dependence on Schneider, engage in anal intercourse, which would be a violation of Article 133 of the Russian Criminal Code. All in violation of Title 18, United States Code, Section 2421....

[citation to record omitted]. At the close of trial, this Court instructed the jury that in order to prove Schneider was guilty of Count II, the Government must prove beyond a reasonable doubt that (1) Schneider knowingly transported Zavarov in foreign commerce, (2) with the intent that Zavarov engage in criminal sexual activity with Schneider, and (3) Schneider specifically intended to compel Zavarov to engage in sodomy by taking advantage of Zavarov's material or other dependence on Schneider.... The jury was further instructed, "the Government need not prove that a criminal sexual act was the sole purpose for Schneider transporting Zavarov to Russia, but the Government must prove that it was a dominant purpose as opposed to an incidental one." ...

Schneider asserts the evidence was insufficient to show his primary purpose in transporting Zavarov from Philadelphia to Moscow was to engage in illegal sexual activity, arguing because he did not pay for Zavarov's transportation, and because Zavarov's flight to Moscow was necessary to return him to his parents' home and the Bolshoi Academy, no reasonable jury could conclude Zavarov was transported by Schneider for the purpose of engaging in criminal sexual activity. Alternatively, Schneider argues even if the evidence was sufficient to prove his intent in transporting Zavarov to Moscow on August 22, 2001, was to engage in criminal sexual activity, such illicit motivations on that date cannot have been his dominant purpose as a matter of law because no illegal sexual activity took place during Zavarov's time in Philadelphia, and it is inappropriate to examine Schneider's intent only with regard to Zavarov's return trip to Moscow. Schneider argues that, viewing the trip as a whole, no reasonable jury could conclude the dominant purpose of the trip was to engage in criminal sexual activity.[11]

In support of his argument, Schneider relies on *Mortensen v. United States*, 322 U.S. 369, 64 S.Ct. 1037, 88 L.Ed. 1331 (1944), a case in which the Supreme Court overturned a Mann Act conviction, holding two owners of a Nebraska house of prostitution who vacationed in Utah with two of their prostitute-employees did not transport the women back to Nebraska "for the purpose of" furthering illegal sexual activity because the entirety

---

11. Because the Court finds this alternative argument has merit, the Court need not address the sufficiency of the evidence regarding Schneider's purpose in transporting Zavarov on August 22, 2001. This Court notes, however, the Government introduced no evidence that Schneider paid for or scheduled Zavarov's transportation.

of the trip was recreational and included no acts of prostitution or immorality. Although the transported women resumed their activities as prostitutes within ten days of returning from the vacation, the Court ruled the women's resumption of prostitution was unrelated to the Mortensens' transportation of the women from Utah to Nebraska. *Id.* at 376, 64 S.Ct. 1037.

In *Mortensen*, the Court explained the jury could have "assumed [the Mortensens] anticipated that the two girls would resume their activities as prostitutes upon their return to [Nebraska]," but held such anticipation, without more, does not "operate to inject a retroactive illegal purpose into the return trip[,] ... [n]or does it justify an arbitrary splitting of the round trip into two parts so as to permit an inference that the [outbound] trip was innocent while the purpose of the homeward journey [ ] was criminal." *Id.* at 375, 64 S.Ct. 1037. The Court further explained, "[t]he return journey under the circumstances of this case cannot be considered apart from its integral relation with the innocent round trip as a whole. There is no evidence of any change in the purpose of the trip during its course. If innocent when it began it remained so until it ended. Guilt or innocence does not turn merely on the direction of travel during part of a trip not undertaken for immoral ends." *Id.*

In the years since *Mortensen* was decided, courts have infrequently applied its holding to prosecutions under § 2421, perhaps because it is uncommon for defendants operating houses of prostitution or sexually abusing minors to take their prostitutes or sexual abuse victims on vacations or other innocent journeys. A review of cases that have discussed *Mortensen*, however, is instructive. In the year after the decision was issued, the Third Circuit considered a case in which a defendant who employed a woman as a prostitute in Philadelphia took her on an innocent day trip to Atlantic City, after which she resumed her prostitution activities in Philadelphia. *United States v. Oriolo*, 146 F.2d 152 (3d Cir.1944). Although there was no evidence any illegal activity took place during the Atlantic City trip, the court distinguished the case from *Mortensen* because, on the return trip, the defendant told the woman she would have to resume her prostitution once back in Philadelphia, and the court held this statement constituted evidence of a change in the purpose of the trip during its course. *Id.* at 154. The Supreme Court summarily reversed the court's judgment, citing *Mortensen*. *Oriolo v. United States*, 324 U.S. 824, 65 S.Ct. 683, 89 L.Ed. 1393 (1945).

Ten years later, the Supreme Court again summarily reversed a case in reliance on *Mortensen*. *See Becker v. United States*, 348 U.S. 957, 75 S.Ct. 449, 99 L.Ed. 747 (1955). In *Becker*, the Eighth Circuit reviewed the Mann Act conviction of a defendant who encouraged a woman employed as an exotic dancer—a profession viewed at the time as falling within the Mann Act's prohibition on sexual immorality—to travel across interstate lines. *Becker v. United States*, 217 F.2d 555 (8th Cir.1954). The woman worked in Wisconsin, and traveled to Minneapolis to spend Thanksgiving with her mother and daughter. When she embarked on her trip, she intended to return to Wisconsin, though she had not determined the date of her return or purchased a round trip ticket. After Thanksgiving, the woman became uncertain whether she still wished to return to Wisconsin. Learning of her uncertainty, the defendant begged her to come back, then paid the cost of her return trip. *Id.* at 556–57. The Eighth Circuit held, because of this inducement, the jury could have concluded the woman did not return to Wisconsin because of her original intention to return, but was induced by the defendant to return and engage in illicit sexual activity. The Supreme Court reversed, citing *Mortensen*. *Becker*, 348 U.S. at 957, 75 S.Ct. 449.

Other courts have relied on *Mortensen*'s innocent round trip analysis to reverse Mann Act convictions after finding the purpose of a round trip journey was wholly lawful, even when the return trip delivered the transported person back to resume illicit sexual behavior. *See, e.g., Smart v. United States*, 202 F.2d 874, 875 (5th Cir.1953) (reversing Mann Act conviction where defendant's interstate transportation of two women who worked for her as prostitutes was for the sole purpose of resolving legal matters and where no act of prostitution took place during the trip); *United States v. Ross*, 257 F.2d 292 (2d Cir.1958) (reversing conviction of defendant who took prostitute on weekend trips from New York to New Jersey upon finding it "clear beyond peradventure of doubt that [the defendant] and [the prostitute] considered these weekends as devoted to recreation and refreshment" apart from any illegal purpose); *cf. United States v. Hon*, 306 F.2d 52 (7th Cir.1962) (reversing conviction of defendant who traveled with a female companion from Nevada to Maryland to visit the companion's mother, despite that the companion engaged in prostitution during the course of the trip, after holding there was insufficient evidence the defendant was involved in or encouraged the prostitution, making the illegal sexual acts merely incidental to the journey), *abrogated on other grounds by United States v. Snow*, 507 F.2d 22, 26 (7th Cir.1974).

The Third Circuit recently reviewed a defendant's Mann Act conviction for transporting a minor among multiple states as part of a prostitution ring. *United States v. Williams*, 428 Fed.Appx. 134 (3d Cir.2011). In affirming the conviction, the court distinguished the defendant's actions from the actions of the defendants in *Mortensen*, stating "[i]n no sense was [the defendant's] transport of [the minor] a vacation, à la *Mortensen*, and more than sufficient evidence permitted the jury to conclude that he possessed the requisite intent for conviction — i.e., the 'calculated means for effectuating' [the minor's] prostitution." *Id.* at 139 (quoting *Mortensen*, 322 U.S. at 375, 64 S.Ct. 1037).

The facts of the instant case are on point with *Mortensen*. Here, Zavarov applied to a number of ballet programs for the summer of 2001, and eventually decided to enroll at the Rock School in Philadelphia, which awarded Zavarov with a scholarship covering his tuition and transportation costs. Zavarov's parents applied for a travel visa with the American Embassy and authorized Zavarov to travel to and from the United States escorted by Schneider. Zavarov traveled to Philadelphia in July 2001, and returned a little over a month later, on August 22, 2001, after the conclusion of his summer program. Although Schneider accompanied Zavarov on his flight to Philadelphia, and delivered Zavarov to Schneider's parents' house, he visited the house sporadically throughout the summer. From July until August, Zavarov attended ballet classes. The Government concedes Schneider and Zavarov did not engage in sexual activity while Zavarov was in Pennsylvania. Viewing the round trip as a whole, it is apparent Zavarov's travel to Pennsylvania was solely for the purpose of continuing his ballet education. There is no evidence of any change in the purpose of his trip during its course, and his time in Pennsylvania constituted a complete interlude from Schneider's sexual activity with him insofar as no such activity took place in Pennsylvania.

Upon consideration of the record, the outcome in this case is controlled by *Mortensen*. Even if the evidence introduced at trial was sufficient for a jury to infer Schneider transported Zavarov on August 22, 2001, with the intent to engage in criminal sexual activity, such a conclusion can only be drawn if Zavarov's return trip to Moscow is examined in isolation, without consideration of the purpose of Zavarov's round trip journey to Philadelphia. Viewing the evidence in this manner is expressly prohibited by *Mortensen*, which denounced an "arbitrary splitting of [a] round trip into two parts so as to permit an inference that the purpose of the [outbound trip] was innocent while the purpose of the homeward journey [ ] was criminal." 322 U.S. at 375, 64 S.Ct. 1037. Because the sole purpose of Zavarov's journey from beginning to end was to receive ballet instruction in the United

States, and Schneider's transport of Zavarov to Philadelphia was therefore innocent as well, this Court cannot hold that Schneider's guilt "turn[s] merely on the direction of travel during part of a trip not undertaken for immoral ends." *Id.* Schneider's conviction for a violation of § 2421 must therefore be reversed. *See id.* at 376, 64 S.Ct. 1037 ("People of not good moral character, like others, travel from place to place and change their residence. But to say that because they indulge in illegal or immoral acts they travel for that purpose, is to emphasize that which is incidental and ignore what is of primary significance.") (quoting *Hansen v. Haff*, 291 U.S. 559, 562–63, 54 S.Ct. 494, 78 L.Ed. 968 (1934)).

The Government concedes *Mortensen* remains good law, but argues this case is distinguishable because the purpose of Zavarov's trip to Philadelphia was not wholly innocent. Although conceding no criminal sexual activity took place during Zavarov's trip, the Government asserts the travel was still tainted by improper purpose because it was organized by Schneider to coerce Zavarov to continue submitting to his sexual abuse. The Government points to no evidence, however, justifying the inference Zavarov would have refused to continue engaging in sexual activity with Schneider if he had not traveled to Philadelphia. *See Van Pelt v. United States*, 240 F. 346, 348 (4th Cir.1917) (explaining a defendant cannot be seen to have used transportation to induce a woman to engage in illicit sexual activity where their sexual activity had been ongoing and there was no evidence the transportation served the purpose of "more surely, more readily, or more safely induc[ing] her to yield to his wishes"); *cf. Langford v. United States*, 178 F.2d 48, 52 (9th Cir.1949) (holding a defendant used interstate transport to induce a woman to continue engaging in prostitution where the woman had twice left him, but was persuaded to return by the promise of the journey).

The Government also contends the instant case is distinguishable from *Mortensen* because, unlike the prostitutes in *Mortensen*, who were "under no obligation or compulsion of any kind to return to [Nebraska] to work [as prostitutes]," 322 U.S. at 372, 64 S.Ct. 1037, Zavarov was being psychologically manipulated by Schneider insofar as he was not free to travel in the manner he would have preferred. The Government, however, points to no evidence suggesting Schneider compelled or coerced Zavarov to travel to Philadelphia or to later return to Moscow. Rather, Zavarov wanted to study ballet in the United States.

Schneider argues, if this Court determines his Count II conviction should be reversed pursuant to *Mortensen*, then his conviction under Count I should also be reversed on the same basis because the innocent round trip rationale should apply not only to Zavarov's transport but also to Schneider's travel. Schneider, however, points to no case in which a court has extended the rationale of *Mortensen* to a § 2423(b) violation. Moreover, Schneider's August 22, 2001, travel is distinct from Zavarov's August 22, 2001, travel. While Zavarov's trip was the return portion of a pre-planned, round trip journey from Moscow to Philadelphia, Schneider's August 22, 2001, flight did not constitute the conclusion of an innocent round trip to Philadelphia. Instead, Schneider's journey occurred that day so he could escort Zavarov back to Russia after several weeks apart. As previously discussed, Schneider embarked on such travel to return in Zavarov's company to Moscow, where he could more readily resume his sexual abuse and run a reduced risk of detection. Because the Government presented evidence Schneider's travel to Moscow was not part of an innocent round trip, but was a flight made after he had traveled throughout the United States and elsewhere, the rationale of *Mortensen* does not apply, and it is not improper to focus only on Schneider's intent in making the trip from Philadelphia to Russia. As previously discussed, the evidence was sufficient to convict Schneider of violating § 2423(b)....

Schneider first argues Count I of the Indictment should be dismissed because it is facially unconstitutional as an undue restriction on his right to travel internationally. "While the right to travel is well-established, no federal court has ever held that an individual has a fundamental right to travel for an illicit purpose." *United States v. Bredimus*, 352 F.3d 200, 210 (5th Cir.2003). Instead, the Third Circuit has explicitly rejected the argument that § 2423(b) impermissibly burdens the fundamental right to travel. *United States v. Tykarsky*, 446 F.3d 458, 472 (3d Cir.2006) ("Congress clearly has a compelling interest in punishing individuals who travel interstate to engage in illicit sexual activities with minors, and § 2423(b) is narrowly tailored to serve that interest."); *accord United States v. Hornaday*, 392 F.3d 1306 (11th Cir.2004) (holding Congress did not exceed its Commerce Clause authority in enacting § 2423(b)); *United States v. Han*, 230 F.3d 560, 565 (2d Cir.2000) (same). Because the Third Circuit has held § 2423(b) does not unconstitutionally burden the right to travel, Count I of the Indictment will not be dismissed on this ground....

Schneider next challenges the constitutionality of § 2421 as applied to him. First, he asserts it is void for vagueness because his prosecution incorporated an offense under Russian law which includes terms with uncertain meanings, has no official English translation, and is so ill-defined as to permit arbitrary enforcement thereof. Section 2421 criminalizes "knowingly transport[ing] any individual in interstate or foreign commerce ... with intent that such individual engage in ... any sexual activity for which any person can be charged with a criminal offense." The Indictment charged the sexual activity in which Schneider intended to engage was a violation of Article 133 of the Russian Criminal Code, which criminalizes compelling a person to engage in a sexual act "by means of blackmail, threat of destruction, damaging, or seizure of property or by taking advantage of the material or other dependence of the victim." William E. Butler, trans., *Criminal Code of the Russian Federation*, 86, 4th ed. (2004) (translating *Ugolovnyi Kodeks Rossiiskoi Federatsii* [UK RF] (Criminal Code) art. 133 (Russ.) (hereinafter Butler translation)).[15] In mounting his vagueness challenge, Schneider does not challenge the language of § 2421 itself, but challenges the Russian statute and the jury instruction regarding the statute.

The jury instruction regarding Article 133 was considered by this Court before trial, after Schneider filed a Notice of Issues of Foreign Law. *See* Fed.R.Crim.P. 26.1 ("A party intending to raise an issue of foreign law must provide the court and all parties with reasonable written notice."). In his Notice, Schneider proffered a translation of Article 133, an expert analysis of this provision, and an explication of the rules of Russian criminal procedure, to the extent such rules were applicable to this case. Thereafter, this Court held a hearing at which defense witness Professor William Butler, Ph.D., a law professor who has authored a Russian/English legal dictionary and has translated the Russian Criminal Code into English, testified as to the meaning of the terms in Article 133. In forming his opinion on the meaning of Article 133, Butler consulted between eight and ten commentaries on the Russian Criminal Code. Butler prefaced his opinion by stating the meaning of Russian law is difficult to ascertain because there is no official English translation of the Criminal Code, the Russian Criminal Code does not provide definitions for terms used in its criminal offenses, and there is no case law interpreting the Russian Criminal Code because there is no concept of precedent under Russian law.

---

15. Although it is now a crime in Russia to have sex with a person under 16 years of age, in 2001 the age of consent in Russia was 15, so the Government could not have charged Schneider with intending to violate Russian criminal prohibitions on engaging in sexual acts with a minor because Zavarov was 15 in August 2001.

Butler first provided his translation of Article 133 as, "[t]he compelling of a person to perform sexual intercourse, sodomy, lesbian act, or other actions of a sexual character by means of blackmail, threat of destruction, damaging, or seizure of property or by taking advantage of the material or other dependence of the victim." ... Based on his translation of the RCC and his consultation of RCC commentaries, Butler analyzed the terms "compelling," "material dependence," and "other dependence" because the Indictment charged Schneider with transporting Zavarov with the intent that Zavarov, "under compulsion based on [his] dependence on Schneider, engage in anal intercourse" with Schneider.... Butler stated the term "compelling" under Russian law is distinct from the use of force or threat of force. Instead, compelling is an objective, real pressure affecting the will of the victim and is weightier than allurements or promises of future benefit. He also stated "material dependence" in Russia means financial dependence, and indicated a person is financially dependent under Russian law if that person would effectively be left out in the cold without any means of sustenance if such dependence was interrupted. Next, he explained the term "other dependence" under Russian law is a catch-all phrase which he believes was included in Article 133 to allow for consideration of other kinds of dependence, but he found no examples of what such other dependence may be.

The Government agreed with Butler's translation of the language in Article 133, but argued this Court should simply read the translated provision to the jury, without providing specific guidance as to the meaning of the terms used therein. Schneider objected, arguing this Court should instruct the jury on the meaning of the terms "compelling" and "material dependence" under Russian law, based on Butler's analysis. Agreeing with Schneider's position, this Court fashioned its jury instruction on Article 133 based on a transcription of Butler's testimony, including his testimony regarding the term "other dependence." With regard to "other dependence," this Court charged the jury as follows: "Russian law also allows you to find a person was otherwise dependent. The Russian Criminal Code does not give an example of what other dependence is, so you, as the jury, may at your discretion decide whether a person was otherwise dependent." Schneider argues this instruction was too vague to be constitutional and impermissibly permitted the jury to imbue "otherwise dependent" with any meaning it chose.[16] ...

In the instant case, the reference to Russian law in the Indictment placed this Court in the difficult position of both ascertaining the meaning of a provision of the Russian Criminal Code and charging the jury in accordance with the provision in a manner that was both legally correct and consistent with due process. Upon review, this Court finds, although the jury charge on the meaning of Article 133 was consistent with Butler's expert testimony, and was a correct statement of Russian law, this law does not comply with the requirements of the due process clause because it is too vague. As Butler testified, the statute allows for a conviction under Article 133 based on a finding the person compelled to engage in sexual intercourse was not materially dependent on the defendant, but was "otherwise dependent."

It is unclear whether such "other dependence" must be objective or subjective, whether it must be reasonable for the person to feel such dependence, or whether an unreasonable dependence upon another may suffice. There is no indication whether "other dependence" must be fostered by the defendant or if it could arise through no effort on the defendant's

---

16. Schneider also argues the jury instruction regarding the terms "compelling" and "material dependence" were too vague. Because this Court found the evidence was insufficient to prove Zavarov was "materially dependent" on Schneider, this Court need not address whether these terms are too vague to withstand constitutional scrutiny.

part. The statute also does not specify the extent of such dependence or the import such dependence must have on the victim's livelihood and well-being. A law is void for vagueness "if it leaves judges and jurors free to decide, without any legally fixed standards, what is prohibited and what is not in each particular case." [*Giaccio v. Pennsylvania*, 382 U.S. 399, 403, 86 S. Ct. 518, 518 (1966)]. This is the precise problem with the disputed instruction in this case. Based on Butler's testimony, this Court instructed the jurors they could use their discretion to decide whether a person was otherwise dependent, because the Russian Criminal Code did not define the term. This is similar to the Pennsylvania law found unconstitutional in *Giaccio*, which "contain[ed] no standards at all." 382 U.S. at 402, 86 S.Ct. 518. Here, the Russian statute provided no guidance by which the jury could evaluate "other dependence." As translated, this statute does not "give adequate warning of the boundary between the permissible and the impermissible applications of the law." ... [citation omitted]. Accordingly, this law is too vague to satisfy American standards of due process and Schneider's conviction on Count II is reversed on this alternative basis as well.[17]

Schneider next argues § 2421 is unconstitutional as applied because it is based on a violation of a foreign country's law "that was not and would not be prosecuted in [America] and is based on a stretched interpretation or application of the foreign statute." ... Schneider contends the language of § 2421 does not suggest that, by penalizing transporting a person "with intent that such person engage in prostitution, or in any sexual offense for which any person can be charged with a criminal offense...," Congress intended to include criminal offenses which arise under foreign laws.[18] Schneider further argues such an interpretation of Congressional intent would be absurd, and potentially unconstitutional, insofar as many other countries outlaw sexual conduct which is legal in the United States, including nonmarital sexual activity and sexual activity between two people of the same sex.

The Government asserts, in enacting § 2421, Congress intended to include a violation of the law in a foreign jurisdiction, noting the language of the statute does not limit prosecution to those crimes where a person transports another with the intent to engage in an act which would be a crime in the United States. The Government further asserts it is inconsistent with Congressional intent to construe the statute to mean a defendant who takes a victim to another country to sexually abuse him could only be prosecuted for a violation of the other country's laws if there was an identical American state or federal law criminalizing the same conduct.

While the Third Circuit has held "no due process violation occurs when Congress criminalizes conduct abroad that is 'condemned universally by law-abiding nations,'" [*United States v. Pendleton*, 658 F.3d 299, 302, n. 2, 2011 WL 3907120 at *1 n. 2] (summarizing

---

17. That Schneider was charged with transporting Zavarov with intent to violate Article 133, rather than an actual violation of Article 133, does not affect the vagueness analysis. The same concerns of fair notice apply to a charge of intent to violate the law, and it similarly offends notions of justice to sustain a conviction for intending to commit an act prohibited in a statute containing language too broad and vague to enable a person of ordinary intelligence to conform his behavior to the law.

18. Schneider argues the absence of specific intent is clear when this statute is compared to the Lacey Act, 16 U.S.C. § 3372, in which Congress explicitly prohibited conduct that would constitute a violation of "any State, or any foreign law" related to the importation of fish, wildlife, or plants. *See United States v. McNab*, 331 F.3d 1228 (11th Cir.2003) (upholding conviction for importing lobster parts in violation of Honduran fishing regulations); *see also* 18 U.S.C. § 846 (prohibiting smuggling in foreign nations in violation of that nation's laws, provided the nation reciprocally enforces American smuggling laws within its borders).

the holding in *United States v. Martinez-Hidalgo*, 993 F.2d 1052, 1056 (3d Cir.1993)), the Supreme Court recently held an American's prior felony conviction in Japan could not serve as the predicate offense for a prosecution under the felon-in-possession statute, even though the statute forbids possession of a gun by any person "who has been convicted in any court," because inclusion of a defendant's foreign conviction record "may include a conviction for conduct that domestic laws would permit." *Small v. United States*, 544 U.S. 385, 389, 125 S.Ct. 1752, 161 L.Ed.2d 651 (2005). *But see McNab*, 331 F.3d at 1239 (upholding Lacey Act conviction of a defendant who transported lobster parts packaged in violation of Honduran fishing regulations, holding regulations promulgated by foreign governments to protect wildlife are encompassed by the phrase "any foreign law" in the Lacey Act); *United States v. Lee*, 937 F.2d 1388, 1393 (9th Cir.1991) (upholding Lacey Act conviction for violation of Taiwanese fishing regulations and stating "the Act does not impermissibly delegate any legislative power to foreign governments" nor does it " 'call for the assimilation of foreign law into federal law' " (citation omitted)). This Court, however, need not determine whether § 2421 is unconstitutional to the extent it incorporates the law of a foreign country which criminalizes actions that are not prohibited here because this Court will reverse Schneider's § 2421 conviction under *Mortensen*, pursuant to his as-applied constitutional challenge, and for insufficiency of the evidence....

Schneider's challenge to evidence regarding the *Nijinsky* film is two-fold. He first argues any evidence he showed the film to Zavarov was improper prior bad acts evidence introduced in violation of Federal Rule of Evidence 404(b). Rule 404(b) provides evidence of "other crimes, wrongs, or acts" is not admissible "to prove the character of a person in order to show action in conformity therewith." Such evidence, however, may be admissible to show "motive, opportunity, intent, preparation, plan, knowledge, identity or absence of mistake or accident." *Id.* Schneider argues evidence he showed *Nijinsky* to Zavarov could constitute the crime of corrupting the morals of a minor[19] and suggest to the jury that Schneider has the propensity to commit crimes involving children. *See United States v. Sampson*, 980 F.2d 883, 887 (3d Cir.1992) (stating the government "must clearly articulate how [other bad acts] evidence fits into a chain of logical inferences, no link of which can be the inference that because the defendant committed [similar] offenses before, he therefore is more likely to have committed this one"). The Government contends the film was "intrinsic to the charged offenses" insofar as the film shows Schneider's "psychosexual entanglement with the child victim," and his intent when he traveled with Zavarov in 2001.... Here, testimony about the film *Nijinsky* was introduced for a proper purpose. The Government has shown a chain of logical inferences between this film and Schneider's offense; because Schneider showed Zavarov the film and warned Zavarov not to leave him the way Nijinsky left his older patron lover, Diaghilev, it was more likely Schneider intended to have a sexual relationship with Zavarov, and this evidence revealed his motive and intent, proper exceptions to Rule 404(b).

Schneider next argues, even if testimony regarding *Nijinsky* did not violate Rule 404(b), the Government violated Rule 403 by showing excerpts of the film to the jury, including scenes which depicted two men kissing and showed a young man simulating masturbation. This Court agrees excerpts of the film were unduly prejudicial inasmuch as they included sexual content unrelated to the charges in this case. However, although this evidence was unduly prejudicial and not particularly probative, introduction of this evidence was

---

19. *See* 18 Pa.C.S. § 6301 ("[W]hoever, being of the age of 18 years and upwards, by any act corrupts or tends to corrupt the morals of any minor less than 18 years of age, ... commits a misdemeanor of the first degree.").

harmless because it does "not appear the evidence had a substantial impact on the jury's verdict." *United States v. Ali*, 493 F.3d 387, 392–93 n. 3 (3d Cir.2007). The film was introduced pursuant to the Government's theory showing Zavarov the film revealed Schneider's intent to engage in sexual acts with Zavarov. However, if these excerpts from the film had not been played for the jury, it would not have affected the jury's verdict because the evidence Schneider had engaged in sexual acts with Zavarov—and intended to do so again at the time of his travel on August 22, 2001—was overwhelming.

Zavarov testified Schneider performed oral sex on him and directed Zavarov to perform oral sex on Schneider, and eventually had anal sex with Zavarov at least three times per week. Although Zavarov's parents did not know about these sexual encounters, his parents testified that after Zavarov began living with Schneider, his demeanor changed and he became sullen and withdrawn. Zavarov explained how Schneider grew close to him and became like a second father, telling Zavarov he hoped they would be together for "trillion thirteen years" and warning Zavarov not to leave him or his ballet career would end. Zavarov's wife, D'Amico, testified that, years later, Zavarov still has issues with intimacy and struggles with depression because of Schneider's prior sexual assaults. Defense witness Christina Bates, who served as Zavarov's therapist, testified when he came to see her he felt angry, hostile, anxious, and depressed, and reported issues related to his childhood. Zavarov also told Bates he became agitated and upset when people approached him or hugged him from behind. Another defense witness, Simon Gronic, a 14-year-old boy from Moldova, testified that although Schneider never had oral or anal sex with him, Schneider also sponsored his arts education, traveled with him to the United States, and touched him in ways that made him feel uncomfortable.

In light of this overwhelming evidence showing Schneider sexually assaulted Zavarov, and traveled with the intent to continue engaging in such assaults, the Government's introduction at trial of excerpts of *Nijinsky* was harmless error. Accordingly, Schneider's motion for a new trial is denied.... For the foregoing reasons, this Court will enter a judgment of acquittal on Count II of the Indictment, and will otherwise affirm the jury's verdict. An appropriate order follows.

Notes

Distinguish the scenario in *Schneider* from "sex trafficking," which involves the commercial exploitation of children and which is discussed in more detail in Chapter Four, Section II.A (Sex Trafficking), *infra*. Note, too, in *Schneider*, the typical characteristics that exemplify the dynamics between the exploiter and the exploited—there is not a surprising abduction of the child or a violent sexual conflict; rather, the abuse is premised on a nurturing relationship built upon trust, the offering of gifts, and the systematic psychological dependency that accompanies the exploitation. Such typical dynamics are qualified as "grooming" behaviors and will be discussed more comprehensively in Chapter Two, Section I.D ("Grooming"), *infra*. Note, however, how important these behaviors are for the court's application of the relevant federal statutes criminalizing foreign travel for the purpose of sexual exploitation of a child and the purposes that motivate the travel.

As the *Schneider* court notes, the rule applied in the *Mortensen* case requires that the court consider the purpose for the trip as a whole; the "innocent round trip" rule of *Mortensen* does not allow an individual assessment of an isolated portion of the trip. However, in *Schneider*, the *Mortensen* rationale is only applicable to the child victim's travel. Under § 2423(b), which involves the foreign travel of the exploiter—in this case, Schneider—the court held that Schneider's purpose in traveling with Zavarov on a return trip to Russia, on that specific date and flight, was to "more readily resume his sexual abuse and run a reduced risk of detection." Is this reasoning consistent with the application of the rule in the *McGuire* case, *supra*? Although the court deems much of the evidence presented to be prejudicial but harmless error, insightful lawyering by the prosecuting attorney and a broad perspective of the relationship dynamics between the exploiter and the exploited are critical factors in *Schneider*. In September 2015, the United States Court of Appeals for the Third Circuit affirmed the decision. *See United States v. Schneider*, 801 F.3d 186 (3d Cir. 2015).

6. *Stranger Exploiters*

People v. Hunter

Supreme Court of Colorado, 2013
2013 Colo. 48, 307 P.3d 1083

JUSTICE RICE delivered the Opinion of the Court.

This case involves Respondent James Henry Hunter's designation as a sexually violent predator ("SVP") and requires we interpret the word "stranger" in the relationship criterion of the SVP statute. § 18-3-414.5(1)(a)(III), C.R.S. (2012). We hold that "stranger" in this statute means either the victim is not known by the offender or the offender is not known by the victim at the time of the offense.... After applying our interpretation of the word "stranger" in the relationship criterion of the SVP statute to the record in this case, we hold that the court of appeals erred when it reversed the trial court's ruling designating Hunter as an SVP. We therefore reverse the judgment of the court of appeals....

A jury convicted Hunter of second-degree burglary, sexual assault, sexual assault on a child, and a crime of violence. The evidence at trial showed that Hunter—who was wearing a mask during the assault and was otherwise unidentifiable by the victims— broke into his neighbor's home and sexually assaulted her and her five-year-old daughter. The trial court designated Hunter as an SVP under section 18-3-414.5(1)(a). Hunter appealed and the court of appeals affirmed his conviction, but reversed the trial court's SVP designation. *People v. Hunter*, No. 04CA699, slip op. at 15, 2007 WL 611882 (Colo.App. Mar. 1, 2007) (not selected for official publication) (*Hunter I*). The court of appeals remanded the case to allow the trial court to make specific findings as to whether either victim was a stranger to Hunter or whether he had established or promoted a relationship with either victim primarily for the purpose of sexual victimization, as required under the "relationship" criterion of the SVP statute, section 18-3-414.5(1)(a)(III).... [citation omitted].... On remand, Hunter argued that he was not a stranger to the victims. The trial court disagreed and designated Hunter as an SVP. The trial court found that Hunter's victims were strangers as neither knew Hunter during the assault.

Hunter appealed and the court of appeals reversed the trial court's SVP designation. See *People v. Hunter*, 240 P.3d 424, ___ (Colo.App.2009) (selected for official publication) (*Hunter II*). It held that "nothing in the statute indicates that the [relationship] criterion is met when the victim knows the offender, but is unable to identify him, as was the case here." *Id.* Judge Casebolt dissented and opined that the "majority's interpretation yields an anomalous, if not absurd, result"; he posited that the better interpretation "requires that we read 'stranger to the offender' as meaning either the victim is a stranger to the offender or the offender is a stranger to the victim, when analyzed at the time the offense was committed." *Id.* at 427–28 (Casebolt, J., dissenting). Judge Casebolt reasoned—based on the purpose of the SVP designation—that "[t]he danger to the public that the perpetrator may reoffend exists in both settings, and [his] interpretation [therefore] gives effect to the entire statute." *Id.* at 428 (Casebolt, J., dissenting).... We granted certiorari to determine whether the court of appeals erred in holding that Hunter's victims were not strangers based on the circumstances of this case.[1] We reverse the judgment of the court of appeals and hold that Hunter met the relationship criterion of the SVP statute because his victims were "strangers" at the time of the offense....

The trial court ultimately determines whether an offender satisfies the four criteria of section 18-3-414.5(1)(a) and therefore qualifies for SVP designation. *Allen v. People*, 2013 CO 44, ¶ 1, ___P.3d ___, 2013 WL 3323904 (released concurrently). In this case, we interpret the term "stranger" in the relationship criterion of the SVP statute to determine whether the court of appeals erred in designating Hunter as an SVP. We defer to the trial court's factual determinations, but review de novo whether the trial court's factual findings support an SVP designation. *See People v. Tixier*, 207 P.3d 844, 849 (Colo.App.2008).

Under the relationship criterion of the SVP statute, an offender is an SVP if the "victim was a *stranger* to the offender." § 18-3-414.5(1)(a)(III) (emphasis added). Accordingly, we must determine the meaning of "stranger" in the SVP statute.... Because the word "stranger" is not ambiguous, we begin and end our analysis by considering the term's plain meaning. In common parlance a stranger is an individual who is "a person not known or familiar to one." *Webster's New College Dictionary* 1415 (2005). Similarly, Black's Law Dictionary defines the word stranger as "[o]ne not standing toward another in some relation implied in the context." *Black's Law Dictionary* 1556 (9th ed. 2004). Given the importance of the context of any given interaction to the definition of "stranger," we agree with Judge Casebolt's dissent and understand "stranger" to mean the relationship criterion is satisfied where either the victim is not known by the offender or the offender is not known by the victim, at the time of the offense. Moreover, defining "stranger" by considering the context of the parties' relationship at the time of the offense is consistent with the community safety and notice purpose of the SVP designation because it ensures a proper designation for offenders likely to reoffend in both situations: where the victim is not known by the offender or the offender is not known by the victim. *See People v. Tuffo*, 209 P.3d 1226, 1230 (Colo.App.2009) (noting that "the registration and notification requirements established in the SVP statute are intended to protect the community"); *see also Allen*, ¶ 7 (noting that the SVP designation's stated purpose is to protect the community (citation omitted)).

Similarly, the Sex Offense Management Board's ("SOMB's") risk assessment screening instrument (the "Screening Instrument")[2] defines "stranger" by considering the context of the victim and offender's relationship at the time of the assault. Specifically, the Screening Instrument notes, "the victim is a stranger to the offender when [the victim has] ... little or no familiar or personal knowledge of said offender." SOMB Handbook: Sexually Violent

---

1. Specifically, we granted certiorari on two issues: 1. Whether the court of appeals erred in its conclusion that, under section 18-3-414.5(1)(a), C.R.S. (2009), the victims and the defendant were not "strangers" based on the circumstances of this case.

   2. Whether the court of appeals should have made sexually violent predator findings on the alternate grounds that the defendant "established or promoted a relationship" with the victim primarily for the purpose of sexual victimization. Alternatively, whether the appropriate remedy is to remand the case to the trial court for further findings.

Because of our resolution of the first issue, we need not reach the alternative grounds posited by Hunter. Moreover, our interpretation of the "stranger" criterion does not require we remand this proceeding to the trial court.

2. Because the SOMB is not tasked with promulgating a definition of stranger we need not defer to the Screening Instrument's definition of "stranger." *See Allen*, ¶ 9. Nonetheless, in this instance, because of the SOMB's familiarity with the SVP designation, we find its definition in the Screening Instrument persuasive. *See Sullivan v. Indus. Claim Appeals Office*, 22 P.3d 535, 538 (Colo.App.2000) ("A court may also look outside the statute to related sources for the definition of an applicable term.").

Predator Assessment Screening Instrument (SVPASI) Background and Instructions 68 (August 2010) http://dcj.state.co.us/odvsom/sex_offender/SO_Pdfs/SVPASI?ANDBOOK 2010.pdf. Accordingly, our interpretation of "stranger" is consistent with the Screening Instrument's definition because, like the Screening Instrument, we determine that a "stranger" includes the situation where the offender is not known by the victim at the time of the offense.... We hold that "stranger" in the relationship criterion of the SVP statute means either the victim is not known to the offender or the offender is not known to the victim, at the time of the offense.[3] We now apply our interpretation of "stranger" in the relationship criterion of the SVP statute to the facts of this case....

The court of appeals erred when it reversed the trial court's decision designating Hunter as an SVP. Record evidence supports the trial court's finding that Hunter was a stranger to both victims at the time of the assault. Considering the mother's perspective first, she testified that her only meaningful interaction with Hunter occurred six months prior to the sexual assault when she joined Hunter and his wife for dinner. Besides the mother's limited interaction with Hunter, the sexual assault occurred in the mother's trailer, during the dead of night, and while the mother was "half-asleep." And, immediately upon entering her trailer, Hunter struck the mother in her lip and then "bashed her in the eye," further disorienting his victim. The mother also testified that Hunter obscured her vision during the assault by placing a blanket over her head at various intervals.... Moreover, during the assault Hunter often asked about "Carl." The mother did not know any man named Carl. Hunter also expressed frustration about the lack of cash in the trailer because he claimed the mother "worked in a bank," which she did not. These confusing statements likely undermined the mother's ability to identify her assailant. Though the mother testified at trial that she might have recognized Hunter's voice during the assault, on cross-examination Hunter's counsel introduced evidence of an earlier interview where the victim admitted "there was something about his voice that just really didn't sound like [Hunter]."... Additionally, the trial court found that Hunter—who was wearing a mask during the assault—"was not known to [the victims,] so he was there as a stranger when the assault started and throughout the assault." The trial court also observed that Hunter's identification in this case was based on DNA evidence because neither victim affirmatively identified Hunter as the perpetrator. Deferring to the trial court's factual findings, we agree that, in the *context* of the assault, Hunter was a stranger to the mother.

The facts in the record supporting the trial court's finding that Hunter was a stranger to the mother also support the trial court's finding that Hunter was a stranger to the daughter. In addition to the facts described above, the daughter was only five years old at the time of the assault, and had previously interacted with Hunter less than her mother. The daughter also never indicated that she recognized Hunter's voice during the assault. Moreover, at the start of the assault, Hunter forced alcohol down the daughter's throat and, as a result, she was likely unconscious during most of the assault. Given her age, limited previous interaction with Hunter, and drugged state, the *context* of this crime supports the trial court's determination that Hunter was a stranger to the daughter at the

---

3. Notably, our definition conflicts with dicta from a division of the court of appeals addressing the meaning of "stranger" in the SVP statute. *See Tixier*, 207 P.3d at 847. That division suggested "stranger" meant a victim "with whom the offender has no definable relationship." *Id.* The *Tixier* court's definition of stranger fails to give proper effect to the SVP designation because it does not consider the importance of context to the plain meaning of "stranger." *Id.* Rather, it considers the term "stranger" more generally. Its interpretation, moreover, is deficient as it fails to recognize the community notice purpose of the statute: protecting individuals from offenders who commit crimes against strangers.

time of the assault.... In sum, neither victim knew Hunter was the person committing the assault. Thus, Hunter's victims were strangers at the time of the assault and he therefore meets the relationship criterion of the SVP designation. We reverse the court of appeals and reinstate the trial court's designation of Hunter as an SVP....

We hold that the term "stranger" in the relationship criterion of the SVP statute is satisfied where the victim does not know the offender or the offender does not know the victim at the time of the offense. In light of our interpretation of the word "stranger" in the relationship criterion, we also hold that the court of appeals erred when it reversed the trial court's decision to designate Hunter as an SVP. We therefore reverse the court of appeals' judgment and reinstate the trial court's SVP designation.

JUSTICE COATS concurs in the judgment.... [Justice Coats's concurring opinion is omitted].

JUSTICE MÁRQUEZ dissents, and JUSTICE BOATRIGHT joins in the dissent....

I respectfully dissent. The majority concludes in this case that the "context" of the interaction between an offender and victim during an assault is not only relevant, but dispositive to determining whether the offender was a "stranger" for purposes of designating the offender a sexually violent predator ("SVP"). I disagree. The term "stranger" in section 18-3-414.5(1)(a)(III), C.R.S. (2012), looks strictly to the existing relationship (or lack thereof) between the offender and victim. Importantly, the nature of this relationship does not vary with a victim's ability to identify the offender during an assault. In my view, the majority's context-driven approach misconstrues the purpose of the relationship criterion of the SVP designation under section 18-3-414.5(1)(a)(III) and leads to absurd results....

As I note in my concurrence in *Allen v. People*, the relationship criterion of the SVP designation focuses on the "predatory" nature of the offense. *Allen v. People*, 2013 CO 44, ¶ 30, ___ P.3d ___ (Márquez, J., concurring in the judgment). Given that the SVP designation seeks to identify that subset of high risk predators who warrant community notification, see § 16-13-901, C.R.S. (2012), the relationship criterion in section 18-3-414.5(1)(a)(III) looks to the pool of victims targeted by sexually violent offenders. The criteria in section 18-3-414.5(1)(a)(III) represent a legislative judgment that an offender poses a higher risk to the broader community where the offender targets "stranger[s]" or seeks to "establish[ ] or promote[ ] a relationship" with individuals "primarily for the purpose of sexual victimization." The general assembly has concluded that the risk posed by such a predatory offender (that is, an offender who demonstrates a propensity to target a broader pool of potential victims) justifies alerting the greater community to the presence of that offender. Thus, the focal point of the relationship criterion is the type of victim targeted; accordingly, section 18-3-414.5(1)(a)(III) is concerned with the existing relationship (or lack thereof) between the offender and the victim. Importantly, the egregiousness of the offender's conduct during the commission of the sexual assault (although highly relevant to sentencing) has no bearing on this particular aspect of the SVP designation.

A "stranger" is "a person not known or familiar to one," ... [citation to record omitted], or "a person or thing that is unknown or with whom one is unacquainted," *Webster's Third New International Dictionary* 2256 (2002). Thus, a person is a "stranger" if one lacks a general familiarity or acquaintance with that person. Importantly, whether a person is a "stranger" does not depend on the circumstances of a particular interaction; rather, the term reflects the general lack of a relationship between two people. An existing relationship is not altered simply because a person's perception is impaired in some way during an encounter. In other words, a person's temporary inability to recognize a friend or relative under certain circumstances (because it is dark, or the person's vision is obscured, for example) does not render that friend or relative a "stranger." ...

The majority holds that "stranger" in the relationship criterion of the SVP statute means "either the victim is not known to the offender or the offender is not known to the victim." ... I have no quarrel with this narrow definition per se; it is consistent with my view that section 18-3-414.5(1)(a)(III) is focused on the existing relationship between the offender and the victim. My disagreement stems from the majority's application of this definition in this case — in particular, the majority's reliance on the circumstances of the assault to conclude that a "stranger" relationship existed between the offender and his victims; specifically, circumstances that impaired the victims' ability to identify their attacker. For example, the majority emphasizes that the assault occurred in the "dead of night," while the mother was "half-asleep"; that Hunter further disoriented the mother and "obscured her vision" by placing a blanket over her head and making "confusing statements"; and that he "was wearing a mask," and forced alcohol down the daughter's throat such that she was "likely unconscious" during most of the assault.... These circumstances unquestionably depict the terror Hunter caused his victims during this horrific assault. And, to the extent that the circumstances of an assault are evidence of whether the offender and victim had an existing relationship, they may be relevant.[4] However, to the extent such circumstances merely reflect the victim's inability to identify an otherwise known assailant, they are irrelevant to the determination of the relationship criterion in section 18-3-414.5(1)(a)(III).

An offender who hinders his victim's efforts to identify him is not necessarily the equivalent of an offender who targets actual strangers or seeks to establish or promote a relationship primarily for the purpose of sexual victimization. The SVP designation contemplates only the latter category of high risk offenders. For example, a jealous ex-boyfriend might attack his former girlfriend in the dark or blindfold her during an assault to avoid being identified. Or, an uncle might drug his niece before sexually assaulting her so that she is too disoriented to resist or recognize her attacker. In these scenarios, the offender has targeted a victim with whom he has a known relationship — indeed, a victim within his family or circle of known friends. But under the majority's approach, the victim's inability to identify the offender during the assault becomes dispositive — rendering these hypothetical victims "strangers" for purposes of the relationship criterion of the SVP designation. In my view, this approach leads to absurd results and contravenes clear legislative intent to designate as sexually violent predators only those offenders who present a sufficiently high risk to the broader community to warrant affirmative notification. Finally, as I noted in my concurrence in *Allen*, the majority's reliance on circumstances suggesting that Hunter conducted his attack to avoid being identified illustrates my concern that courts "may be tempted to allow the horrific circumstances of a particular crime (appropriately considered for purposes of sentencing) to influence their determination of the separate, statutory SVP designation." *Allen*, ¶ 38 (Márquez, J., concurring in the judgment).

I agree with the court of appeals' conclusion that the trial court applied the wrong legal standard to determine whether Allen qualified as an SVP; however, I would remand the case for further proceedings to determine whether Hunter and the victims were "strangers" within the meaning of section 18-3-414.5(1)(a)(III). Regardless, I cannot join the majority in reversing the court of appeals and affirming the trial court's order. Therefore, I respectfully dissent....

---

4. Indeed, the court of appeals noted that the prosecution argued in closing that Hunter wore a mask during the assault precisely because the victims knew him. *People v. Hunter*, 240 P.3d 424, 426 (Colo.App.2009).

Notes

According to the United States Department of Justice, child sexual exploitation by strangers (persons not family members or known to the child victim) occurs in approximately 10% of all child sexual exploitation cases. *See* National Sex Offender Public Website, *Facts and Statistics*, available at http://www.nsopw.gov/(X(1)S(4nlx2gubapqca532iei00ueq))/en/Education/FactsStatistics?AspxAutoDetectCookieSupport=1 (last visited Jan. 27, 2015). Under the relevant SVP law, the focus of which is to protect the public through a notification requirement, offenders who are "strangers" with their victims subject the general community to greater risk of sexual violence by their inclination to act against anyone with whom they are not acquainted. But observe the varied interpretations of the term "stranger" that were applied in the *Hunter* decision: the majority opinion applies a definition that considers the context within which an individual attack takes place, whereas Justice Márquez's opinion offers an interpretation devoid of any consideration of the details of the attack, but which, rather, considers only the pre-existing nature of the relationship between the exploiter and the exploited. In light of the purpose of the SVP law — to protect the public through no-tification — which is the more appropriate interpretation and application of "stranger"?

II. Responses to Criminals or Patients

Ryan C. W. Hall and Richard C. W. Hall

A Profile of Pedophilia: Definition, Characteristics of Offenders, Recidivism, Treatment Outcomes, and Forensic Issues

82 Mayo Clin. Proc. 457 (2007)

No treatment for pedophilia is effective unless the pedophile is willing to engage in the treatment. Individuals can offend again while in active psychotherapy, while receiving pharmacologic treatment, and even after castration.... Currently, much of the focus of pedophilic treatment is on stopping further offenses against children rather than altering the pedophile's sexual orientation toward children. [One study] found that individuals still showed sexual interest in children, as measured by the AASI [Abel Assessment for Sexual Interest], even after a year of combined psy-chotherapy and pharmacotherapy, whereas the pedophiles' self-reported frequency of urges and masturbation had decreased. These findings indicate that the urges can be managed, but the core attraction does not change.... Other interventions designed to manage these pedophilic urges include careful forensic and therapeutic monitoring and reporting, use of testosterone-lowering medications, use of [selective serotonin reuptake inhibitors] (SSRIs), and surgical castration....

A popular treatment option is testosterone suppression by pharmacologic means (eg, antiandrogenic therapy or chemical castration).... Although physical castration seems definitive in preventing repeated sexual offenses, some physically castrated pedophiles have restored their potency by taking exogenous testosterone and then abused again.... Chemical castration has many advantages over physical castration. It requires follow-up visits, continuous monitoring, and psychiatric reevaluation to continue the medication and is reversible for health reasons.... Depending on the mechanism of action of the agent used, it can take from 3 to 10 months before one sees a decrease in sexual desire.... Reduced libido also seems to make some offenders more responsive to psychotherapy.... A drawback to hormone therapy vs castration is its annual cost, which can range from $5000 to $20,000 a year....

Selective serotonin reuptake inhibitors represent a nonhormonal treatment that has been suggested for paraphilias in general and specifically for pedophilia.... Currently, no blinded placebo-controlled trials have shown that SSRIs are effective for the treatment of pedophilia; however, open-label trials and case reports suggest that SSRIs may be helpful for treating pedophilia.... These medications can provide a helpful adjunct to structured regulated surveillance, psychotherapy, and hormonal treatment. Part of the basis for the use of an SSRI is the neuropsychiatric data that show serotonin abnormalities and impulse control problems in some pedophiles. These findings are similar to those found in patients with OCD, who respond to SSRIs.... Selective serotonin reuptake inhibitors seem to lessen the sexual ruminations and increased sexual urges that pedophiles report related to situational stress and internal discord.... The diminished sexual drive produced by SSRIs, which is usually perceived as an adverse effect of the medication, may be beneficial for pedophiles....

Medications that may be used in the future to treat pedophiles include topiramate and other medications ... Topiramate has been shown to be useful in treating addictions such as gambling, kleptomania, binge eating, and substance use.... Although no prospective clinical trials have documented its effectiveness in pedophiles, several case reports have recently described topiramate's effectiveness in reducing or stopping unwanted sexual behaviors in paraphilic and nonparaphilic (eg, prostitutes, compulsive viewers of general pornography, patients with compulsive masturbation) patients....

Psychotherapy is an important aspect of treatment, although debate exists concerning its overall effectiveness for long-term prevention of new offenses.... Psychotherapy can be individual, group based, or, most commonly, a combination of the two. The general strategy toward psychotherapy with pedophiles is a cognitive behavioral approach (addressing their distortions and denial) combined with empathy training, sexual impulse control training, relapse prevention, and biofeedback.... Several studies have demonstrated that the best outcomes in preventing repeat offenses against children occur when pharmacological agents and psychotherapy are used together.... A controversial approach is the use of aversion conditioning and masturbatory reconditioning to change the individual's sexual orientation away from children. Similar techniques were used with homosexual adults in the middle to late 20th century. Although some clinicians claimed to be able to reorient homosexual people to heterosexuality and to decrease the pleasure reward cycle of pedophiles with these techniques, such methods are no longer used at reputable treatment centers....

Just as the prevalence of pedophilia is not accurately known, the rate of recidivism against a child is also unknown. Recidivism is a term with many definitions, which affect reported rates of repeated offenses. For example, some studies look at additional arrests for any offense, others only look at arrests for sexual crimes, and some only look at convictions, whereas others analyze self-reported reoffenses.... The data on recidivism underestimate its rate because many treatment studies do not include treatment dropout figures, cannot calculate the number of repeated offenses that are not reported, and do not use polygraphs to confirm self-reports.... Another complicating factor is the period during which the data are collected. Some studies report low recidivism rates, but these numbers apply to individuals followed up during periods of active treatment only or for short periods after treatment is terminated (e.g., 1–5 years)....

The published rates of recidivism are in the range of 10% to 50% for pedophiles depending on their grouping.... Some studies have reported that certain classes of pedophiles (eg, homosexual, nonrelated) have the highest rate for repeated offending compared with other sex offenders.... Generally, homosexual and bisexual pedophiles have higher recidivism rates than heterosexual pedophiles.... Incest pedophiles generally have the lowest rate of reoffense.... The more deviant the sexual practices of the offender, the younger the abused child; the more sociopathic or antisocial personality traits displayed, the greater the treatment noncompliance; and the greater the number of paraphilic interests reported by the offender, the higher the likelihood of reoffense.... Several actuarial and self-report tests have been designed to help physicians and law enforcement officers predict which individuals are at higher risk for repeated offense, but currently no single test or combination of tests can accurately identify the future activity of an individual....

In a study of the characteristics of individuals who repeatedly offend, [researchers] found that one fourth of heterosexual pedophiles ... and half of homosexual and bisexual pedophiles ... repeated offenses (as evidenced by repeated arrests for a sexual violation or a self-reported violation) during a 25- to 32-year period.... [T]he characteristics that predict repeated offenses for homosexual and bisexual pedophiles were (1) being exclusive pedophiles, (2) being of average to above average intelligence, (3) being middle-aged at the time of the primary offense, (4) abusing children aged 12 to 14 years, (5) engaging in coitus at an earlier age than non-repeat offenders, and (6) having a diagnosed personality disorder.... Repeat offending heterosexual pedophiles were characterized as (1) having poor family relationships and support, (2) having engaged in intercourse before the age of 19 years, (3) being middle-aged or older at the time of the index case, and (4) having initially abused young children (3– 5 years old) who were unknown to them.... Most of the repeated offenses occurred 10 years after the initial offense. Whether this delay was initially due to successful treatment, incarceration, or other factors is unknown....

A. Paraphilia

A primary factor in the legal qualification of sexual exploitation is the sexual gratification of the exploiter. For many exploiters, sexual gratification is derived from the fixation on, and often employment of, extreme or atypical behavior, which may include sexual activity with children. In fact, the sexual gratification of the exploiter may depend on the specific behavior. This condition may be referred to as a paraphilia. A paraphilia can include a focus on a particular object, such as children, animals, or undergarments, or may involve engaging in a particular act, such as, for example, sadism, voyeurism, exhibitionism, or any of a variety of not otherwise specified atypical paraphilias, referred to as NOS paraphilias, which are categorized as atypical behaviors, but not mental disorders. Paraphilias are far more common in men than in women.

Paraphilias typically include sexual behaviors that society views as distasteful or abnormal. Pedophilia—sexual activity with a pre-pubescent child under a determined age—is the most common form of paraphilia. Hebephilia (the sexual preference for pubescent, or early adolescent, children) is addressed in the case that follows—*United States v. Carta*. Other common paraphilias include exhibitionism (gaining sexual gratification by exposing one's genitals to strangers), voyeurism (gaining sexual gratification by observing unsuspecting victims), both of which are discussed in Chapter Two, Section II (Sexual Exploitation Through Non-Physical Conduct), *infra*, and frotteurism (touching or rubbing against a nonconsenting person). Less common paraphilias may include fetishism (gaining sexual pleasure from use of inanimate objects), sexual masochism (gaining sexual gratification by being humiliated or tortured), sexual sadism (inflicting humiliation or suffering on others) and transvestic fetishism (cross-dressing). There may be more than 500 qualified sub-forms of paraphilias that are not otherwise specified (paraphilias NOS). There is much debate over which paraphilias should be included in the Diagnostic and Statistical Manual of Mental Disorders (DSM), which, prior to 1980, referred to this condition as "sexual deviation." The current version of the DSM (DSM-V) includes eight specific paraphilic conditions: exhibitionistic disorder, fetishistic disorder, frotteuristic disorder, pedophilic disorder, sexual masochism disorder, sexual sadism disorder, transvestic disorder, and voyeuristic disorder, in addition to the residual category of paraphilia NOS.

Although the DSM-V draft attempts to draw a clearer distinction between non-normative but non-pathological sexual behavior and paraphilic disorders, like pedophilia, many paraphilias are nevertheless qualified as illegal; these include hebephilia, voyeurism, and exhibitionism. As you read the following case, consider the role that the paraphilia diagnosis plays in determining the outcome. In considering this, note that until 1974, the American Psychiatric Association included homosexually in the DSM at the top of the deviant classifications. By modern standards, homosexuality is now viewed as an entirely separate construct than common paraphilias. *See generally* James M. Cantor, *Is Homosexuality a Paraphilia? The Evidence For and Against*, 41 Arch. Sex. Behav. 237 (2012) (concluding that "homosexuality is a characteristic distinct from the paraphilias."). Analogistically, consider in Chapter One, Section II.B (Public Perceptions), *infra*, the outlying perspective that sexual activity with consenting children is a form of normative adult sexual behavior. What is the difference in the social and legal perspectives of homosexuality, sexual activity with consenting children, and any of the other categories of paraphilia? By what basis should courts distinguish categories or assess relative deviance? What role does the DSM play for the courts in making these determinations? To what extent is any rubric affected by social and cultural values? *See generally* Michael B. First & Robert L. Halon, *Use of DSM Paraphilia Diagnoses in Sexually Violent Predator Commitment Cases*, 36 J. Am. Acad. Psychiatry L. 443 (2008) (describing valid means of making DSM-IV-TR paraphilic diagnosis relevant to triers of fact with regard to application of SVP commitment statutes).

United States v. Carta

First Circuit, 2012

690 F.3d 1

HOWARD, Circuit Judge....

Carta pled guilty to federal child pornography charges in 2002 and was sentenced to five years in prison and three years of supervised release. Prior to his scheduled release in 2007, the Bureau of Prisons certified that Carta was a "sexually dangerous person" and commenced proceedings pursuant to the [Adam Walsh Child Protection and Safety Act ("ACT")], which authorizes civil commitment of a person in federal custody. 18 U.S.C. § 4248(a). A "sexually dangerous person" is one "who has engaged or attempted to engage in sexually violent conduct or child molestation and is sexually dangerous to others." 18 U.S.C. § 4247(a)(5). A determination that an individual is a "sexually dangerous person" requires the government to prove by clear and convincing evidence that he "suffers from a serious mental illness, abnormality, or disorder as a result of which he would have serious difficulty in refraining from sexually violent conduct or child molestation if released." *Id.* § 4247(a)(6).[2] ... After a district judge ruled that the government had failed to establish that Carta's diagnosis of "paraphilia not otherwise specified characterized by hebephilia" was a "serious mental illness, abnormality or disorder" within the meaning of the Act, *United States v. Carta*, 620 F.Supp.2d 210 (D.Mass.2009) (*"Carta I"*), a panel of this court reversed, holding that the district court erred in ruling that the government had failed to establish the serious mental illness element. *United States v. Carta*, 592 F.3d 34, 44 (1st Cir.2010) (*"Carta II"*). The case was remanded for consideration of "whether the requisite dangerousness exists." *Id.* A different district court judge subsequently conducted a seven-day trial, ultimately ruling in the government's favor. *See United States v. Carta*, No. 07-12064-PBS, 2011 WL 2680734 (D.Mass. July 7, 2011) (*"Carta III"*). This timely appeal followed. ...

We begin by observing that Carta, who was 42 years old when he pled guilty to the child pornography charges for which he was incarcerated, does not deny that the Act's first element—that he has engaged in child molestation in the past—is satisfied. His lengthy history of committing sexual abuse, beginning when he was 11 years old and including many such acts over the course of three decades, is detailed in both district court orders. *See Carta III*, 2011 WL 2680734 at *3–7; *Carta I*, 620 F.Supp.2d at 212–14. We eschew repeating the details of his history here. In addition to his prior abusive conduct, Carta also displayed troubling behavior while in a sex offender treatment program in federal prison. After being transferred at his request to a prison in North Carolina that offered the program, Carta dropped out in part because of his inappropriate interest in the program's younger members. *Carta II*, 592 F.3d at 37.

Given Carta's concession as to the first element, the remaining issues before us are whether he suffers from a serious mental illness, abnormality or disorder and, if so, whether such condition would result in his having serious difficulty refraining from sexually violent conduct or child molestation. ... At the heart of the first issue is the diagnosis proffered by the government expert, Dr. Amy Phenix, who testified that Carta was afflicted with a mental disorder known as "paraphilia not otherwise specified ("NOS") characterized by hebephilia." The Diagnostic and Statistical Manual of Mental Disorders ("DSM IV" or "DSM") describes the "essential features" of paraphilia as follows:

> [R]ecurrent, intense sexually arousing fantasies, sexual urges, or behaviors generally involving 1) nonhuman objects, 2) the suffering or humiliation of oneself or one's partner, or 3) children or other nonconsenting persons, that occur over a period of at least 6 months ... [and that] cause clinically significant distress or impairment in social, occupational, or other important areas of functioning.

Carta II, 592 F.3d at 38 (quoting Am. Psychiatric Ass'n, DSM 522–23 (4th ed. 2000)). The "not otherwise specified" portion of the diagnosis stems from the fact that hebephilia is not one of the specific conditions listed in the DSM IV, either separately or as an example of paraphilia. *Id.* While the precise contours of hebephilia are the subject of debate, it

---

2. If the government meets its burden, the inmate is committed to the custody of the United States Attorney General. 18 U.S.C. § 4248(d). If the state in which he is currently domiciled or was tried will accept him, he will be transferred to the state for "care, custody and treatment." *Id.* If not, the Attorney General must place him in a "suitable facility" for treatment until such time as the state accepts custody or he is no longer sexually dangerous. *Id.* § 4248(e). A committed individual is also permitted to file a motion seeking discharge with the court that ordered his commitment. *Id.* § 4247(h). If denied, there is a 180-day waiting period before he can again seek relief. *Id.*

suffices to say that the disorder consists of a sexual attraction to adolescents, as opposed to, for example, a specified paraphilia such as pedophilia, a sexual attraction to pre-pubescent children. *Id.* (citing DSM at 527–28).

The parties dispute whether our determination in *Carta II* that the government had established the mental disorder element is binding as law of the case. It is.... The only issue before us in *Carta II* was whether the district court in *Carta I* had correctly ruled that the diagnosis of paraphilia NOS characterized by hebephilia was not a serious mental illness, abnormality or disorder. We determined that the statutory definition of "serious mental illness" is not limited to either the consensus of the medical community or to maladies identified in the DSM. *Carta II*, 592 F.3d at 39–40. Additionally, we noted that even if hebephilia lacks sufficient indicia to fit it within the statutory praxis, paraphilia itself is listed in the DSM, as is the category "paraphilia not otherwise specified." *Id.* at 40. Thus, we discounted the testimony of defense expert Dr. Leonard Bard that hebephilia is not a generally accepted diagnosis and does not fit within the DSM definition of paraphilia. In the end, we concluded that "Dr. Phenix's report, Carta's past history of sexually abusing minors, his in-prison behavior and his expressed attitudes justify classifying him as suffering from paraphilia: he has a decades-long sexual fixation on minors that plainly has 'caused significant distress or impairment' in his life." *Id.* at 40.[3]

On remand to determine whether Carta would have serious difficulty in refraining from sexually violent conduct or child molestation, the district court nevertheless acceded to Carta's request to accept additional evidence on the mental condition issue. *Carta III*, 2011 WL 2680734 at *2. The court need not have done so.... In *Carta II*, we explicitly decided the serious mental illness question.... Carta, however, argues that new evidence compels re-examination of the issue. Indeed, the district court allowed him to introduce an article written after *Carta II*, in which two drafters of the DSM IV express their doubts about the propriety of a forensic diagnosis of paraphilia NOS with a hebephilia descriptor. The court also appointed, at Carta's request, Dr. Robert Prentky, who interviewed Carta for six hours and reviewed his records. Although Dr. Prentky testified that Carta did not suffer from a serious mental illness, he agreed with Dr. Phenix that paraphilia NOS with a descriptor of hebephilia can be an appropriate diagnosis. But this additional disagreement among experts does nothing to alter the scenario that we analyzed in *Carta II*, and therefore our determination that Carta fits within the "serious mental illness" prong of the Act was (and remains) binding.... That said, however, nothing about our law of the case analysis should be read to suggest that we have cause to doubt the district court's conclusion that the proof provided during the court's supplemental inquiry satisfied the second element of the Act. The judge's analysis of the serious mental condition issue, taking into account the additional evidence, does not come close to qualifying as clear error. *See* Fed.R.Civ.P. 52(a)(6)....

Turning to the third element, we note that the Act does not define "serious difficulty in refraining" from sexually violent conduct or child molestation. Nevertheless, sufficient guidance comes from the Supreme Court's pre-Act review of a Kansas civil commitment statute in *Kansas v. Crane*, 534 U.S. 407, 122 S.Ct. 867, 151 L.Ed.2d 856 (2002). In *Crane*, the Court held that a showing of "serious difficulty in controlling behavior" was a prerequisite to civil commitment of a sexually dangerous person. *Id.* at 413, 122 S.Ct. 867. Such lack of control need not be "demonstrable with mathematical precision," but the defendant's lack of control "must be sufficient to distinguish the dangerous sexual offender whose

---

3. One example of the impact of Carta's fixation on his life is his report that he spent between twelve and fourteen hours per day on the internet searching for and viewing child pornography and masturbating to images two to three times daily.

serious mental illness, abnormality, or disorder subjects him to civil commitment from the dangerous but typical recidivist convicted in an ordinary criminal case." *Id.*

In ruling in the government's favor, the district court relied on transcripts from *Carta I*, testimony from Drs. Phenix, Prentky and Bard, and Carta's own testimony and history. As for the experts, Dr. Phenix concluded that Carta would have serious difficulty refraining from sexually molesting children if released; Dr. Prentky and Dr. Bard disagreed.... Although Carta refused to allow her to interview him, Dr. Phenix based her opinion on her review of Carta's records, as well as her use of three different risk-assessment actuarial tools to yield a re-offense rate. *Carta III*, 2011 WL 2680734 at *14–16, *23. The district court did not entirely accept Dr. Phenix's actuarial conclusions, however, because her analysis included a subjective step that contributed to the finding of a higher re-offense rate, but which has not been empirically validated. *Id.* at *14 n. 1.... In addition to applying the actuarial tools, Dr. Phenix observed other risk factors present in Carta's life, including the absence of social support, the presence of significant intimacy deficits and poor sexual and non-sexual self-regulation, and a demonstrated lack of cooperation with supervision. In sum, Dr. Phenix testified that Carta was the same person that he was when he entered treatment — still believing that sexual relationships with thirteen year-old boys were permissible.

Dr. Prentky, who did meet with Carta, used a diagnostic tool (known as the SVR-20) that excluded from consideration sex crimes that had not been legally adjudicated. *Id.* at *20. Dr. Prentky combined the score from this model with other factors, including, *e.g.*, the lack of documented sexual offenses and significant sanctions, as well as Carta's infraction-free presence in the community pending sentencing and the fact that he neither had re-offended after a criminal sanction nor had a sex-related disciplinary problem in prison. *Id.* Ultimately, although Dr. Prentky believed that Carta would have serious difficulty refraining from general anti-social behavior, he did not think that such difficulty would carry over into sexually violent conduct or child molestation. *Id.*

Dr. Bard relied on an actuarial test that assessed Carta's likelihood of recidivism at seven to fifteen percent. He acknowledged, however, that the tool did not account for Carta's then-current situation, but instead combined factors from his past and compared them to others with similar data points. *Id.* at *18. To overcome this limitation, Dr. Bard created a "dynamic risk assessment" that combined the test with other factors. He placed considerable weight on the fact that Carta had not engaged in any sexual misconduct while in prison. He placed little significance, however, on Carta's actions during his time in the federal prison treatment program. Essentially, Dr. Bard took the position that since there is nothing illegal or deviant about having a relationship with a twenty-five year-old, Carta's actions did not point to a likelihood of re-offense. To the contrary, Dr. Bard suggested that these actions demonstrated that Carta was "mov[ing] his level of attraction from teenagers to twenty-somethings." *Id.* Moreover, Dr. Bard accepted Carta's explanation for having dropped out of the treatment program — it resulted from his stubbornness about admitting that he had made a mistake, rather than from inappropriate contact with other program members. *Id.*... Ultimately, Dr. Bard testified that Carta is "a very different person" and that his likelihood of re-offense would be tempered by the presence of a support system in the form of therapists, family members and a probation officer. *Id.* at *19. He testified that Carta's attraction, impulsivity and anger "are not the same now as [they were] in the past" and that "[he] is able to control his behavior as evidenced by his nine plus years in prison without any serious violence." *Id.*

The district court concluded that none of the experts' testimony could be given full weight, noting that Dr. Bard believed that paraphilia NOS (hebephilia) is not a valid diagnosis under any circumstances, that Dr. Phenix's methodology included a subjective step, and that Dr. Prentky's analysis did not include Carta's self-reported crimes. *Id.* at *23. Additionally, the court was less convinced than Dr. Prentky that Carta had undergone "considerable self-transformation" while in custody awaiting the hearing in this case.... The court also considered numerous other factors. In Carta's favor were the lack of sexual misconduct either during the interval between his guilty plea and his incarceration or while he was in prison, the fact that he was seeking treatment during the pendency of the hearing, and his advancing age. *Id.* at *24. At the same time, however, the court observed that Carta's history of sexual crimes and anti-social behavior was deeply troubling, and his impulsive actions and volatility when faced with adversity were highly concerning. *Id.* Additionally, the court found that Carta continued to engage in distorted thinking, exemplified by his attempt to rationalize his behavior by stating that both a thirteen year old boy and his daughter's boyfriend had initiated sexual contact with him. *Id.*[4] Finally, the court noted that Carta's inability to refrain from engaging with younger participants while in the federal sex offender treatment program, and his departure from the program, demonstrated a disturbing degree of impulsiveness. *Id.* at *25.

Carta targets the weight that the district court assigned to the many strands of evidence in the mix. Two specific points stand out. First, Carta places great significance on the fact that he committed no sexual offenses or violations while incarcerated. The relevance of that behavior, however, is limited by the fact that the main targets of his attraction—adolescent boys—are inaccessible in prison. Next, he says that the district court placed insufficient weight on his lack of sexual misconduct while he was in the community pending sentencing, as well as on his lack of re-offense after being sanctioned. Compared to these relatively short time frames on which Carta focuses, however, he has a lengthy pre-sanction history of sexual misbehavior involving children. We have no difficulty accepting the premise that multiple instances of post-sanction recidivism can buttress a commitment decision. *See, e.g. United States v. Shields*, 649 F.3d 78, 89 (1st Cir.2011); *United States v. Hunt*, 643 F.Supp.2d 161, 181 (D.Mass.2009). But we do not read the Act as *requiring* previous post-sanction misconduct.

Aside from those two assertions, the essence of Carta's argument is that more weight should have been given to the testimony of the experts who testified in his favor, with correspondingly less placed on Dr. Phenix's testimony, his own past conduct, and his departure from the federal prison treatment program. After reviewing the district court's factfinding for clear error, we have no warrant to upset that court's assessment of the evidence. *Carta II*, 592 F.3d at 39.[5] As the district court acknowledged, the "serious difficulty refraining" assessment presented the most vexing issue. *Id.* at *22. But it is abundantly clear that the court carefully weighed the evidence and the competing views espoused by each of the experts.... Our task is not to re-weigh the evidence or to make credibility assessments.... The district court, in its role as factfinder, was free to "decide among reasonable interpretations of the evidence," *Shields*, 649 F.3d at 89, and the factfinder's choice between two permissible views of the evidence cannot be clearly erroneous....

---

4. Carta takes issue with this finding, arguing on appeal that there is no evidence that he was lying about the encounters, and that the other individuals *did* initiate them. We read the district court's concern as, even assuming that Carta was truthful, the encounters nevertheless were inappropriate no matter who initiated them.

5. We summarily reject Carta's argument that the district court committed legal error—subject to de novo review—by saddling him with the burden of proving that he was not dangerous. Contrary to Carta's claim, the district court's conclusion that Carta lacked the tools to control his behavior was a finding of fact that the court used to buttress its ultimate conclusion.

As we have observed before, "there is no crystal ball that an examining expert or court might consult to predict conclusively whether a past offender will recidivate." *Shields*, 649 F.3d at 87. Ultimately, we can find clear error only if "we are left with the definite and firm conviction that a mistake has been committed." *United States v. D'Andrea*, 648 F.3d 1, 14 (1st Cir.2011) (citation and quotation marks omitted). No such error was committed here.... The judgment of the district court is affirmed.

Notes

Much controversy surrounds the inclusion of hebephilia in the DSM classification of mental disorders. Many view sexual attraction to pubescent adolescents as a normative behavior that should not be categorized as a mental disorder and misused to civilly commit, as sexually violent predators, offenders who commit illegal, but psychologically normative, offenses. *See* John Mathew Fabian, *Diagnosing and Litigating Hebephilia in Sexually Violent Predator Civil Commitment Proceedings*, 39 J. AM. ACAD. PSYCHIATRY L. 496 (2011). Although hebephilia was not included as a deviate disorder in the most recent version of the DSM (DSM-V), the *Carta* decision makes clear that despite its clinical categorization, its legal significance lies in its relevance to future sexual offenses and dangerousness, thus delineating the conflict between treatment and prosecution as an appropriate response. For further discussion of the controversy surrounding the relevance of hebephilia as a mental disorder, see Janina Neutze, Dorit Grundmann, Gerold Scherner and Klaus Michael Beier, *Undetected and Detected Child Sexual Abuse and Child Pornography Offenders*, 35 INTERNATIONAL J. L. & PSYCHIATRY 168 (2012); Karen Franklin, *Hebephilia: Quintessence of Diagnostic Pretextuality*, 28 BEHAVIORAL SCIENCES & L. 751 (2010).

B. Public Perceptions

Society's intolerance of, and response to, the sexual exploitation of children, particularly with respect to its perception of the pedophile as either a deviant criminal or, in some way, a helpless victim of his or her uncontrollable (but not necessarily untreatable) impulses, is disclosed in the cultural narratives told through public media outlets and political and legal discourse. In 2011, the Public Health Institute released a study finding that, nationally, between 2007 and 2009, fewer than one news story per week focused on the topic of child sexual abuse, with even fewer covering the issue in detail. *See* Berkeley Media Studies Group, *Case by Case: News Coverage of Child Sexual Abuse* (May 24, 2011), available at bmsg.org/pdfs/bmsg_issue19.pdf. *But see* Kathryn J. Fox, *Incurable Sex Offenders, Lousy Judges & The Media: Moral Panic Sustenance in the Age of New Media*, 38 AM. J. CRIM. JUST. 160, 166 (2013) (stating that coverage of the topic of sex offenders, particularly with respect to sentencing, in English-language newspapers has increased over time). The report reveals that 73 percent of the stories emphasized the criminal components of the cases related to the perpetrators and after-the-fact interventions, rather than the impact of the abuse on the victims and their families, and preventing exploitation before it occurs. *Id.* at 7. The report concludes that such episodic reporting makes it easier for the public to blame the victim and reinforces ideas that the problem is too complicated to understand or address. Conversely, more thematic reporting of the broader context of child sexual abuse makes it easier for the public to see the problem as more of a shared government and institutional responsibility. *Id.* at 14. *See also* Larissa Smage, *Framing Effects on Attitudes Toward Pedophiles*, University of Wisconsin–Platteville Undergraduate Research and Creative Endeavors, OnLine Journal, Vol. IV (concluding that organizing information and framing issues influences peoples' attitudes about pedophiles, including empathy, attribution of responsibility, and attitudes toward treatment). For a discussion of how the New York Times framed the issue of sexual abuse within the Catholic Church, see Kevin Troy Reneau, *Framing the Catholic Church: The New York Times Coverage of the Catholic Church 2006–2011*, available at https://mospace.umsystem.edu/xmlui/handle/ 10355/14565 (last visited June 28, 2015). For a discussion of the news coverage specific to the Penn State University scandal, see Berkeley Media Studies Group, *Breaking News on Child Sexual Abuse: Early Coverage of Penn State* (Jan. 2012), available at http:// www.bmsg.org/sites/default/files/bmsg_report_breaking_news_on_child_sexual_abuse.pdf (last visited June 28, 2015).

Social science research indicates a "moral panic" connected to pedophiles in contemporary society. *See* Kieran McCartan, *'Here There Be Monsters': the Public's Perception of Paedophiles with Particular Reference to Belfast and Leicester*, 44 MED. SCI. LAW. 327 (2004). *See generally* Kieran McCartan, *Media Constructions of, and Reactions to, Paedophilia in Modern Society*, *in* Managing High-Risk Sex Offenders in the Community: Risk Management, Treatment and Social Responsibilities (K. Harrison, eds. 2010) (concluding that a more realistic representation of pedophilia in the media could affect public perception and social construction and assist in child protection); Jane Divita Woody, *Media Coverage of Child Sexual Abuse: An Opportunity for Family Therapists to Help Families and Communities*, 30 AM. J. FAM. THERAPY 417 (2002) (discussing sexual education in therapy in response to widespread media attention). Although, historically, panic over sex offenders has tended to be cyclical, *see* Philip Jenkins, MORAL PANIC: CHANGING CONCEPTS OF THE CHILD MOLESTER IN MODERN AMERICA, 215 (1998), a variety of cultural factors, such as the child welfare movement, health and mental health services, and political pressures, have shaped the discourse of sexual exploitation and have made the modern panic more permanent. *See* Fox, *supra*, at 165. The media's failure to differentiate the various types of sex offenders in its reporting contributes to the public's moral panic. As local reports of specific incidences reach the broader national market and distort the issues through television, cable news programs, and internet blogs, the focus of the problem often shifts from the individual perpetrators to a failed legal system that encourages expansive judicial discretion. *See* Kathryn J. Fox, *Incurable Sex Offenders, Lousy Judges & The Media: Moral Panic Sustenance in the Age of New Media*, 38 AM. J. CRIM. JUST. 160 (2012). As judicial discretion broadens and public panic increases, broader and more punitive legislation is constructed that focuses on public protection and is suspicious of rehabilitation.

An example of social responses prompted by heightened media attention occurred in November 2010, when the on-line retailer Amazon.com offered in its "Kindle" bookstore the e-book *"The Pedophile's Guide to Love and Pleasure: A Child-Lover's Code of Conduct,"* by Phillip R. Greaves. Faced with objections, Amazon.com initially defended the book, but subsequently removed it after readers threatened to boycott the retailer. Amazon.com later reinstated the book, only to remove it for a second time when again confronted with public objections. Greaves was arrested on December 20, 2010, when detectives ordered a signed copy of Greaves' book and had it shipped to the agency's jurisdiction, whereupon Greaves violated local laws prohibiting the distribution of "obscene material depicting minors engaged in harmful conduct." Greaves pleaded no contest to the charges and was later released on probation. Similar books taking a positive view of child sexuality and challenging widespread anxiety about pedophilia have received similar responses. *See, e.g.*, Judith Levine, HARMFUL TO MINORS: THE PERILS OF PROTECTING CHILDREN FROM SEX (2002) (published by University of Minnesota Press). In response to heightened public perception, several airline carriers have gone so far as to adopt policies prohibiting male adults from sitting next to unaccompanied minors. *See Pedophilia Panic: Barring Single*

Men from Sitting Next to Kids on Planes, available at http://theweek.com/article/index/231954/pedophilia-panic-barring-single-men-from-sitting-next-to-kids-on-planes# (last visited Jan. 17, 2014). And many agree that the sexual abuse scandal within the Catholic Church is exacerbated by how the media has framed the issue to the public. *See* Carol Glatz, *Media 'Panic' Over Pedophilia Mars Prevention*, Nat'l Cath. Reporter (May 14, 2010), available at http://ncronline.org (last visited Jan. 15, 2014) (observing a lack of expert opinion in media coverage on issue); Mark Silk, *Panic Attack*, N.Y. TIMES, Jan. 28, 1996 (concluding that the social construction of the sexual abuse crisis in the Catholic Church arose from within Roman Catholicism itself).

Just as the public's perception of harm to children may be influenced by the media's coverage of notorious acts of exploitation and the "devilization" of the sexual predator, research suggests that the public's perception of recidivism and the efficacy of psychiatric rehabilitation also may be influenced by inaccurate media presentations that ignore treatment success. *See* F.S. Berlin and H.M. Malin, *Media Distortion of the Public's Perception of Recidivism and Psychiatric Rehabilitation*, 148 AM. J. PSYCHIATRY 1572 (1991); *see also* Kathryn J. Fox, *Incurable Sex Offenders, Lousy Judges & The Media: Moral Panic Sustenance in the Age of New Media*, 38 AM. J. CRIM. JUST. 160 (2012). Research shows that treating low-risk sex offenders can actually exacerbate the risk of reoffending, *see* P. Gendreau, T. Little & C. Goggin, *A Meta-Analysis of the Predictors of Adult Offender Recidivism: What Works!*, 34 CRIMINOLOGY 575 (1996), yet popular opinion reveals that a majority of people view sex offenders as untreatable. Such media distortion perpetuates moral indignation and punitive regulation. *See* S.S. Beale, *The News Media's Influence on Criminal Justice Policy: How Market-Driven News Promotes Punitiveness*, 48 WILL. & MARY L. REV. 397 (2006).

Nevertheless, some who advocate a more lenient perspective to adult-child sexuality view the issue, culturally, as simply the next category of relationship in a line of learned acceptance, following premarital sex and homosexual sex. The American Psychiatric Association's diagnostic manual has not included homosexuality in its list of mental disorders since 1973, but pedophilia remains included. The objective of what social conservatives call the "pro-pedophilia" movement is to find support in the scientific and academic forums. Strategically, normalizing pedophilia begins by framing "child sexual abuse" within the limited scope of cases in which actual harm to children is demonstrated, rather than assumed. A landmark study supporting this view, in which the authors recommended that sexual encounters in which children are willing participants and have positive reactions should be termed "adult-child sex" rather than "abuse," was published in a 1998 issue of Psychological Bulletin. *See* Bruce Rind, Robert Bauserman and Philip Tromovitch, *A Meta-Analytic Examination of Assumed Properties of Child Sexual Abuse Using College Samples*, 124 PSYCHOLOGICAL BULL. 22 (July 1998). The U.S. House of Representatives unanimously passed a resolution to reject the study, and numerous other studies refute its findings. The American Psychological Association, which first published the article, also subsequently passed a resolution stating that "sexual relations between children and adults are abusive, exploitive, reprehensible and properly punishable by law." *See* Mark O'Keefe, *Values and Philanthropy: Controversial Studies Push Change in Society's View of Pedophilia*, available at http://come-and-hear.com/editor/ca-newhouse/index.html (Last visited June 28, 2015). Responsive to, and affected by, this strategy, however, is the developing body of law addressing many of the issues covered in this casebook, such as non-physical interaction between adult and child, *see* Chapter 2, Section II (Sexual Abuse Through Non-Physical Conduct), *infra*; consensual conduct by children, including sexting, *see* Chapter 2, Section II.E.2 (Sexting by Minors), *infra*; and conduct involving mere depictions of minors, *see* Chapter 3, Section II.A (Scope of Child Pornography Regulation), *infra*.

The law regarding the civil commitment of sexually violent predators also is directly affected by how these issues are framed and with what perspective society views the various categories of offenders—whether it be the view of the pedophile as either a criminal to be punished or a patient to be treated, or the view of sexually active teenagers as either curious, consenting partners exercising poor judgment or unwitting victims of child pornography or other forms of sexual exploitation. Although the issue of civil commitment of sexually violent predators will be addressed more comprehensively in Chapter Seven, Criminal and Civil Liability, *infra*, note the dichotomous perspective of the pedophile in the following case. Which perspective does the court adopt? What is the basis of the court's decision? By what criterion does the court consider whether civil commitment is an appropriate response? What objective is the court seeking to accomplish?

People v. Allman

Court of Appeal, Fourth District, California, 2003
Not Reported in Cal. Rptr. 2d, 2003 WL 1558186

HUFFMAN, Acting P.J....

In 1974 Allman, then 32 and a fixated female pedophile since the age of 10, took a six-year-old girl into a bathroom, locked the door, disrobed both of them, and rubbed his erect penis in the child's vaginal area with force sufficient to cause later-noticed bruising. Charged with lewd acts with a child but allowed to plead guilty to a related misdemeanor, Allman was granted probation. In 1976 probation for the offense was terminated and his conviction set aside and dismissed. In 1980 Allman pleaded guilty to committing lewd and lascivious acts upon a 13-year-old baby sitter and an 11-year-old friend of Allman's daughter, then 12. Allman was committed to Patton State Hospital as a mentally disordered sex offender (MDSO).

Released from Patton in 1983 and placed on five years' probation, Allman was placed in a local treatment program and eventually discharged from probation in 1988. While he had been on probation, however, Allman was continuing a long series of sexual offenses against five girls ranging in age from five to 15, including multiple penis-vagina contacts. In 1989 Allman pled guilty to five of 15 charged offenses and later was committed to Atascadero State Hospital as an SVP. In a written statement to the probation officer before his sentencing in 1989, Allman wrote that "I committed this crime by having to [sic] much trust in my self thought I had my self under control, I began to put my self alone with young girls."... In support of his conditional release petition, Allman presented the testimony of two medical personnel from Atascadero State Hospital: Mary Flavan and Jay Seastrunk, both staff psychiatrists at the hospital.... [footnote omitted]. Dr. Flavan is Allman's treating psychiatrist at Atascadero, and Dr. Seastrunk has examined Allman....

Dr. Flavan explained the five phase program at Atascadero for conditional release candidates which involves (1) an understanding of the mental disorders involved in sexually predatory offenders; (2) an undertaking by the offender to examine his own past by constructing an autobiography while also learning more about human sexuality and personal interactions; (3) consolidating and reviewing the matters and documentation prepared in phase 2; (4) preparation for and meeting with conditional release program personnel and community treatment personnel; leading to (5) conditional release into a community treatment program.

The phased program includes encouragement of the use of anti-androgens, which reduce testosterone levels so that the offender is not subject to sexual urges, and in point of fact, while it is not a written hospital policy that only those using anti-androgens may be considered for release, both of the two patients at Atascadero who are in phase 4 are on anti-androgens.[4] Allman has refused on the advice of his counsel to participate in the phased treatment program, which resulted in the most recent staff evaluation recommending against his release because of his rejection of other treatment programs apart from the anti-androgen drug Lupron. (Dr. Flavan also doubted Allman's ability to participate in the phased relapse prevention program because of Allman's generally impaired learning ability, possibly due to an earlier stroke[,] and difficulty in following extensive directions.)

Allman has been receiving Lupron, an effective anti-androgen, for eight months, and his testosterone level is well below that of a normal male. Testosterone can be readily replaced in a variety of ways, however, and Allman would have to be subject to regular blood testing to ensure he was not evading the effects of Lupron by replacement testosterone ingestion. Dr. Flavan believed Allman would present a risk of reoffending of less than five percent were he to remain on Lupron and not either take replacement testosterone or abscond from supervision. Allman, who has been fixated on very young girls since the age of 10 and has no interest in changing, would otherwise be "100 percent [likely] to reoffend."...

Dr. Seastrunk believed Allman could only be safely conditionally released if he were on Lupron therapy "that was appropriately monitored and followed through." As Dr. Flavan had also stated, this would require thrice-monthly testing of Allman's blood to ensure he was not replacing the testosterone from other sources. Dr. Seastrunk also believed cognitive therapy (as noted, often refused on the advice of counsel) was medically useful in reducing recidivism, although not achieving the degree of reduction that use of Lupron produced.... As did Dr. Flavan, Dr. Seastrunk agreed Allman was almost certain to reoffend if not subject to the effects of Lupron.[5] It would be "very easy" for Allman to obtain testosterone supplements in San Diego, which would render him again a danger to the community within a period of about three days....

The program director for the conditional release program in San Diego County testified she believed Allman, because of his refusal to participate in the phased treatment program, would "pose[ ] quite a high risk of reoffending if he were to come back into the community." Some participants in conditional release programs simply walk away from supervision, and the supervision provided would not preclude someone like Allman from obtaining testosterone supplements.

Dr. Robert Knapp, the medical director of Atascadero State Hospital, testified that Allman had the ability to complete the phased cognitive behavioral therapy program, and the use of anti-androgen drugs alone was not sufficient to preclude reoffense.[6] As Dr. Knapp

---

4. In fact, out of a population of about 400 at Atascadero, only a quarter actively participate in the phased relapse prevention program, with 10 in phase 1, 79 in phase 2, 10 in phase 3 and only two in phase 4.

5. At one point Dr. Seastrunk agreed with Dr. Flavan's estimate Allman would be 100 percent likely to reoffend. It was this testimony to which the trial judge apparently alluded when he observed, in granting the People's petition to recommit Allman as an SVP, that Allman's own witnesses "said he has a 110 percent chance — they almost said that — one of them might have said that he has a 110 percent chance of reoffending. Mr. Allman can't help himself. He will reoffend, there's no question about it."

6. Dr. Knapp also testified that in the five years of the five phase cognitive training program, only one person had gotten so far as to be "on the verge of entering stage five." Dr. Knapp also confirmed Dr. Flavan's earlier estimate that three-quarters of the population of committed SVP's at Atascadero were not taking part in the five phase treatment program.

put it "particularly, in our setting, within a few miles of here … I can get all the testosterone injectable you want. A person doesn't have to be suffering from lack of testosterone. All it takes is one shot. One shot away from a rape or molestation. If the drive is there, a person will find a way to fulfill it." … Dr. Gabrielle Paladino also testified that Allman has the ability to successfully complete the phase program, that he was in denial about his problems, and even though Allman cooperated in taking his medication, Dr. Paladino testified anti-androgens alone would not adequately reduce the risk and Allman was a high risk to reoffend if he were released to the community without completing the phase program.[7] …

By written decision filed November 19, 2001, the court denied the petition for conditional release because it found that Allman "has not proven by a preponderance of the evidence that he will not be a danger to the community by re-offending were his request [for conditional release] granted." In denying the petition, the court noted that even were the failure rate for recidivism while on Lupron as low as 2.4 percent, there was no way of knowing whether or not Allman could be in the treatment-resistant group because Allman had refused to participate in the available behavioral therapy programs, and there was no way to prevent Allman if he were released to the community from simply disappearing, obtaining testosterone and reoffending….

[O]n December 4, 2001, the court found Allman to be an SVP….

Section 6608, subdivision (d) provides in pertinent part: "The court shall hold a hearing to determine whether the person committed would be a danger to the health and safety of others in that it is likely he … will engage in sexually violent criminal behavior due to his … diagnosed mental disorder if under supervision and treatment in the community." The heart of Allman's appellate argument is that the trial judge by omitting reference to the word "likely"[11] in his decision effectively placed a burden on Allman to prove *beyond a reasonable doubt*, rather than merely to prove by a preponderance of the evidence, that he would not be likely to reoffend were he released to "supervision and treatment in the community." We do not so read the record…. As the trial judge expressly observed in his statement of decision, Allman "ha[d] not proven *by a preponderance of the evidence* that he will not be a danger to the community by re-offending…." That is, Allman had not persuaded the judge he was not a "a danger to the community" in that he had failed to persuade the judge the weight of the evidence was against his reoffending.

---

7. Dr. Paladino, who had at one point had Charles Manson as her patient, testified Allman was not an unamenable-to-treatment "psychopath" like Manson, but was instead a person who could, if he chose to do so, benefit from cognitive therapy.

11. The meaning of *likely* in the context of other provisions of the Sexually Violent Predator Act has been set out: "We agree with the People that '*likely* to engage in acts of sexual violence' (italics added), as used in section 6601, subdivision (d), does not mean the risk of reoffense must be higher than 50 percent. Instead, the phrase requires a determination that, as the result of a current mental disorder which predisposes the person to commit violent sex offenses, he or she presents a *substantial danger*—that is, a *serious and well-founded risk*—of reoffending in this way if free. If an evaluator finds such a serious and well-founded risk, but nonetheless recommends against commitment or recommitment solely because the evaluator cannot conclude the person is *more likely than not* to reoffend, the evaluator has applied the statute erroneously." *People v. Superior Court (Ghilotti)* (2002) 27 Cal.4th 888, 916, 119 Cal.Rptr.2d 1, 44 P.3d 949 (*Ghilotti*). The same definition of "likely" has been applied in two other instances of cases under the Act, *People v. Roberge* (2003) 29 Cal.4th 979, 980, 129 Cal.Rptr.2d 861, 62 P.3d 97 [§ 6600, subd. (a)] and *Cooley v. Superior Court* (2002) 29 Cal.4th 228, 254–255, 127 Cal.Rptr.2d 177, 57 P.3d 654 [§ 6602, subd. (a)]. While appellate counsel at oral argument urged we define "likely" in this case, with respect to section 6608, subdivision (d), differently than the consistent definition approved by our Supreme Court in other parts of the Act, we see no reason to do so, even were such within our power.

Omission of the term "likely" from the statement of decision does not at all mean the judge must now be deemed to have applied a burden of proof other than the one he articulated. In fact, given the definition of "likely" as set out by our Supreme Court in footnote 11, *ante*, inclusion of the term "likely" into the decisional standard might be deemed to have itself raised, rather than lowered, Allman's burden of proof. The judge herein was entrusted with determining whether Allman had shown by a preponderance of the evidence he would not be a danger if conditionally released; our task is only to determine whether any substantial evidence supports the determination made....

Allman's appellate argument assumes that the trier of fact must assume that a petitioner will in fact avail himself of community support, will in fact take his medicine, will in fact not counteract the medicine with drugs which are readily available particularly in this community, and will not abscond from supervision. In this case, when the dubious quality of all the above factors are considered, together with the additional factors that (1) Allman may be among that small percentage of persons who commit sexually violent offenses even while on anti-androgens, and (2) Allman's refusal to participate in any of the available cognitive therapies and his half century as a fixated pedophile largely in denial make his compliance with supervision and medication very *un* likely, there was abundant (indeed, overwhelming) evidence to support a finding Allman did not met [sic] his burden of showing by a preponderance of the evidence he was not a danger if released.

As our Supreme Court has observed in an analogous matter:

> "Particularly when one ... has previously been committed as an SVP, and thus has already been subject, while in hospital confinement, to the SVPA's mandated treatment program (§ 6606, subds. (a), (c)), the evaluators may obviously assess his or her progress, if any, as a factor in determining whether he or she represents a substantial danger if unconditionally released at the end of a commitment term.... There appears no statutory reason why the evaluators may not consider these factors as bearing on the overall assessment of the person's risk of reoffending if free of custody.... Such a conclusion is consistent with the SVPA's ... provisions for determining whether a person is, is not, remains, or is no longer an SVP, or whether he or she meets the requirements of conditional release during a term of commitment. In each instance, the issue is the degree of danger the person presents under the circumstances contemplated, i.e., either conditional release or complete freedom without conditions. (See, e.g., §§ 6605, subds.(c), (d) [after annual mental exam, committed person must be released before expiration of term unless state proves person remains disordered and dangerous 'if discharged'], 6608, subds. (a), (d) [person may be conditionally released during commitment term if court finds he or she is not dangerous if placed 'under supervision and treatment in the community'].)"[12] (*Ghilotti, supra,* 27 Cal.4th at pp. 927–928, 119 Cal.Rptr.2d 1, 44 P.3d 949.)

---

12. As our Supreme Court also noted, "Our conclusion also conforms with available authority. Decisions addressing similar schemes for the civil commitment of mentally disordered and dangerous persons have held that the person's amenability to voluntary treatment is a factor in determining whether commitment is necessary. (*People v. Bolden* (1990) 217 Cal.App.3d 1591, 1600, 266 Cal.Rptr. 724 [in proceeding for extended commitment of person found not guilty by reason of insanity, defendant may present evidence that medication is effective and he will take medication]; *People v. Williams* (1988) 198 Cal.App.3d 1476, 1482–1483, 244 Cal.Rptr. 429 [in restoration to sanity proceeding for person found not guilty by reason of insanity, trial court erred by instructing that person could not be restored to sanity unless it was shown he needed no medication]; *Conservatorship of Davis* (1981) 124 Cal.App.3d 313, 319–321, 177 Cal.Rptr. 369 [in conservatorship proceeding under

This is not to say that nonparticipation in therapy programs is the only or even the most important factor to be resolved. As noted in *Ghilotti*:

> "Of course, given the compelling protective purposes of the SVPA, the evaluators must weigh the possibility of voluntary treatment with requisite care and caution. Common sense suggests that the pertinent factors should include (1) the availability, effectiveness, safety, and practicality of community treatment for the particular disorder the person harbors, (2) whether the person's mental disorder leaves him or her with volitional power to pursue such treatment voluntarily; (3) the intended and collateral effects of such treatment, and the influence of such effects on a reasonable expectation that one would voluntarily pursue it; (4) the person's progress, if any, in any mandatory SVPA treatment program he or she has already undergone; (5) the person's expressed intent, if any, to seek out and submit to any necessary treatment, whatever its effects; and (6) any other indicia bearing on the credibility and sincerity of such an expression of intent." (*Ghilotti, supra,* 27 Cal.4th at p. 929, 119 Cal.Rptr.2d 1, 44 P.3d 949.)

In this case the evidence uniformly supported the conclusion Allman was almost certain to reoffend if released, and indeed the fact the evidence supported a beyond a reasonable doubt determination Allman was likely to reoffend mandates affirming of the order now challenged, as not only did Allman fail to carry his "preponderance" burden, he failed to raise even a reasonable doubt as to the propriety of denying his petition.[13] ... As earlier noted, Allman's appellate counsel directs our attention to a variety of testimonial and documentary evidence generally supporting efficacy of anti-androgen therapy with respect to pedophiles, but the resolution of these issues was a matter for the trial court, not this one. "The credibility of the experts and their conclusions were matters resolved against defendant by the [judge]. We are not free to reweigh or reinterpret the evidence. (*People v. Perry* (1972) 7 Cal.3d 756, 785, fn. 17, 103 Cal.Rptr. 161, 499 P.2d 129.) Moreover, we must draw all reasonable inferences in favor of the judgment. (*People v. McCleod* (1997) 55 Cal.App.4th 1205, 1220–1221, 64 Cal.Rptr.2d 545.) Here, the [trier of fact] could reasonably believe the evidence of the prosecution witnesses and reject that of the defense

---

Lanterman-Petris-Short Act, jury may be instructed that person is not gravely disabled if he or she understands the need for treatment and has made a meaningful commitment to pursue it].)" (*Ghilotti, supra,* 27 Cal.4th at p. 928, 119 Cal.Rptr.2d 1, 44 P.3d 949.)

13. The fact two witnesses testified Allman *might* succeed on outpatient status is not controlling, as the decision in this case could be supported even without reference to any of the testimony supporting release. As another court held with respect to an analogous proceeding, wherein a murderer committed by reason of insanity was seeking outpatient status: "Having found no constitutional infirmity in requiring defendant to prove that he is not dangerous, we consider whether the trial court abused its discretion in rejecting the conclusions of the doctors and other experts that he would not be dangerous on outpatient status.... In both hearings, the prosecution did not put on any expert witnesses to support its argument of dangerousness. Defendant therefore urges that he met his burden of proof by uncontradicted evidence that far exceeded the preponderance of the evidence burden placed on him. He also argues that the trial court abused its discretion in failing to decide the case in accordance with the overwhelming weight of the evidence.... There was certainly ample evidence of lack of dangerousness presented in both hearings. The issue, therefore, becomes whether the trial court abused its discretion in deciding the case contrary to the weight of the evidence...." (*People v. Sword, supra,* 29 Cal.App.4th at pp. 625–626, 34 Cal.Rptr.2d 810.) The court went on to say: "Is it an abuse of discretion to deny outpatient status without any current expert testimony supporting the conclusion that defendant is dangerous? In our view it is not, because the trial court is entitled to consider the validity of the opinions presented to it in determining whether defendant met his burden of proving that he was not dangerous. Having failed to convince the trial court that the opinions were valid, defendant failed to carry his burden of persuasion." (*Id.* at p. 630, 34 Cal.Rptr.2d 810.)

witness. We therefore conclude that sufficient evidence existed from which a rational fact finder could determine that defendant could not control his sexually violent behavior and would likely reoffend if released." (*People v. Mercer, supra,* 70 Cal.App.4th at pp. 466–467, 82 Cal.Rptr.2d 723.) That holding applies to this case also....

The judgment (order denying conditional release) is affirmed.

WE CONCUR: NARES and McDONALD, JJ.

Notes

In addition to judicial responses, many commentators advocate a variety of legislative responses ranging from monitoring sexual offenders with GPS tracking systems, *see* Marisa L. Mortensen, Comment, *GPS Monitoring: An Ingenious Solution to the Threat Pedophiles Pose to California's Children,* 27 J. Juv. L. 17 (2006), to castration, *see* Laura S. Chism, *The Case for Castration: A "Shot" Towards Rehabilitation of Sexual Offenders,* 37 L. & Psychol. Rev. 193 (2013). Any restrictions targeting sex offenders must pass constitutional muster. *See Doe v. Prosecutor, Marion County, Indiana,* 705 F.3d 694 (7th Cir. 2013) (law prohibiting registered sex offenders from using social networking websites, instant messaging services, and chat programs held unconstitutional as not narrowly tailored to serve significant governmental interest); *Doe v. Jindal,* 853 F.2d 596 (M.D. La. 2012) (Louisiana statute precluding registered sex offenders from using or accessing social networking websites, chat rooms, and peer-to-peer networks held to be facially overbroad); *People v. Godinez,* 2012 WL 5954580 (Cal. Super. A.D.) (local ordinance criminalizing any person required to register as a sex offender who enters into or upon any "[c]ounty park where children regularly gather," without written permission of the county Sherriff preempted by State law); *Doe v. City of Lafayette,* 377 F.3d 757 (7th Cir. 2004) (permanent ban of convicted sex offenders from city parks did not violate offender's First Amendment or due process rights). For discussion of prohibitions on internet use, see Eva Conner, Comment, *Why Don't You Take a Seat Away from that Computer: Why Louisiana Revised Statute 14:91.5 Is Unconstitutional,* 73 La. L. Rev. 883 (2013) (arguing that narrowly tailored social-networking-website restrictions on sex offenders may be constitutional). The most prevalent legislative response to sexual offenders has been the use of mandatory sexual offender registries, more commonly known as "Megan's Law." In the following cases, consider the perspective of the courts in assessing whether the imposition of sex offender registration requirements are punitive or remedial in nature.

C. Registry of Sexual Offenders

1. Generally

Smith v. Doe

United States Supreme Court, 2003
538 U.S. 84, 123 S. Ct. 1140

Justice KENNEDY delivered the opinion of the Court.

The Alaska Sex Offender Registration Act requires convicted sex offenders to register with law enforcement authorities, and much of the information is made public. We must decide whether the registration requirement is a retroactive punishment prohibited by the *Ex Post Facto* Clause....

The State of Alaska enacted the Alaska Sex Offender Registration Act (Act) on May 12, 1994. 1994 Alaska Sess. Laws ch. 41. Like its counterparts in other States, the Act is termed a "Megan's Law." Megan Kanka was a 7-year-old New Jersey girl who was sexually assaulted and murdered in 1994 by a neighbor who, unknown to the victim's family, had prior convictions for sex offenses against children. The crime gave impetus to laws for mandatory registration of sex offenders and corresponding community notification. In 1994, Congress passed the Jacob Wetterling Crimes Against Children and Sexually Violent Offender Registration Act, title 17, 108 Stat.2038, as amended, 42 U.S.C. § 14071, which conditions certain federal law enforcement funding on the States' adoption of sex offender registration laws and sets minimum standards for state programs. By 1996, every State, the District of Columbia, and the Federal Government had enacted some variation of Megan's Law.

The Alaska law, which is our concern in this case, contains two components: a registration requirement and a notification system. Both are retroactive. 1994 Alaska Sess. Laws ch. 41, § 12(a). The Act requires any "sex offender or child kidnapper who is physically present in the state" to register, either with the Department of Corrections (if the individual is incarcerated) or with the local law enforcement authorities (if the individual is at liberty). Alaska Stat. §§ 12.63.010(a), (b) (2000). Prompt registration is mandated. If still in prison, a covered sex offender must register within 30 days before release; otherwise he must do so within a working day of his conviction or of entering the State. § 12.63.010(a). The sex offender must provide his name, aliases, identifying features, address, place of employment, date of birth, conviction information, driver's license number, information about vehicles to which he has access, and postconviction treatment history. § 12.63.010(b)(1). He must permit the authorities to photograph and fingerprint him. § 12.63.010(b)(2).

If the offender was convicted of a single, nonaggravated sex crime, he must provide annual verification of the submitted information for 15 years. §§ 12.63.010(d)(1), 12.63.020(a)(2). If he was convicted of an aggravated sex offense or of two or more sex offenses, he must register for life and verify the information quarterly. §§ 12.63.010(d)(2), 12.63.020(a)(1). The offender must notify his local police department if he moves. § 12.63.010(c). A sex offender who knowingly fails to comply with the Act is subject to criminal prosecution. §§ 11.56.835, 11.56.840.

The information is forwarded to the Alaska Department of Public Safety, which maintains a central registry of sex offenders. § 18.65.087(a). Some of the data, such as fingerprints, driver's license number, anticipated change of address, and whether the offender has had medical treatment afterwards, are kept confidential. §§ 12.63.010(b), 18.65.087(b). The following information is made available to the public: "the sex offender's or child kidnapper's name, aliases, address, photograph, physical description, description[,] license [and] identification numbers of motor vehicles, place of employment, date of birth, crime for which convicted, date of conviction, place and court of conviction, length and conditions of sentence, and a statement as to whether the offender or kidnapper is in compliance with [the update] requirements ... or cannot be located." § 18.65.087(b). The Act does not specify the means by which the registry information must be made public. Alaska has chosen to make most of the nonconfidential information available on the Internet....

Respondents John Doe I and John Doe II were convicted of sexual abuse of a minor, an aggravated sex offense. John Doe I pleaded *nolo contendere* after a court determination that he had sexually abused his daughter for two years, when she was between the ages of 9 and 11; John Doe II entered a *nolo contendere* plea to sexual abuse of a 14-year-old child. Both were released from prison in 1990 and completed rehabilitative programs for sex offenders. Although convicted before the passage of the Act, respondents are covered by it. After the initial registration, they are required to submit quarterly verifications and notify the authorities of any changes. Both respondents, along with respondent Jane Doe, wife of John Doe I, brought an action under Rev. Stat. § 1979, 42 U.S.C. § 1983, seeking to declare the Act void as to them under the *Ex Post Facto* Clause of Article I, § 10, cl. 1, of the Constitution and the Due Process Clause of § 1 of the Fourteenth Amendment. The United States District Court for the District of Alaska granted summary judgment for petitioners. In agreement with the District Court, the Court of Appeals for the Ninth Circuit determined the state legislature had intended the Act to be a nonpunitive, civil regulatory scheme; but, in disagreement with the District Court, it held the effects of the Act were punitive despite the legislature's intent. In consequence, it held the Act violates the *Ex Post Facto Clause. Doe I v. Otte*, 259 F.3d 979 (C.A.9 2001). We granted certiorari. 534 U.S. 1126, 122 S.Ct. 1062, 151 L.Ed.2d 966 (2002)....

This is the first time we have considered a claim that a sex offender registration and notification law constitutes retroactive punishment forbidden by the *Ex Post Facto Clause*. The framework for our inquiry, however, is well established. We must "ascertain whether the legislature meant the statute to establish 'civil' proceedings." *Kansas v. Hendricks*, 521 U.S. 346, 361, 117 S.Ct. 2072, 138 L.Ed.2d 501 (1997). If the intention of the legislature was to impose punishment, that ends the inquiry. If, however, the intention was to enact a regulatory scheme that is civil and nonpunitive, we must further examine whether the statutory scheme is " 'so punitive either in purpose or effect as to negate [the State's] intention' to deem it 'civil.' " *Ibid.* (quoting *United States v. Ward*, 448 U.S. 242, 248–249, 100 S.Ct. 2636, 65 L.Ed.2d 742 (1980)). Because we "ordinarily defer to the legislature's stated intent," *Hendricks, supra*, at 361, 117 S.Ct. 2072, " 'only the clearest proof' will suffice to override legislative intent and transform what has been denominated a civil remedy into a criminal penalty," *Hudson v. United States*, 522 U.S. 93, 100, 118 S.Ct. 488, 139 L.Ed.2d 450 (1997) (quoting *Ward, supra*, at 249, 100 S.Ct. 2636); see also *Hendricks, supra*, at 361, 117 S.Ct. 2072; *United States v. Ursery*, 518 U.S. 267, 290, 116 S.Ct. 2135, 135 L.Ed.2d 549 (1996); *United States v. One Assortment of 89 Firearms*, 465 U.S. 354, 365, 104 S.Ct. 1099, 79 L.Ed.2d 361 (1984)....

Whether a statutory scheme is civil or criminal "is first of all a question of statutory construction." *Hendricks, supra*, at 361, 117 S.Ct. 2072 (internal quotation marks omitted); see also *Hudson, supra*, at 99, 118 S.Ct. 488. We consider the statute's text and its structure to determine the legislative objective. *Flemming v. Nestor*, 363 U.S. 603, 617, 80 S.Ct. 1367, 4 L.Ed.2d 1435 (1960). A conclusion that the legislature intended to punish would satisfy an *ex post facto* challenge without further inquiry into its effects, so considerable deference must be accorded to the intent as the legislature has stated it.

The courts "must first ask whether the legislature, in establishing the penalizing mechanism, indicated either expressly or impliedly a preference for one label or the other." *Hudson, supra*, at 99, 118 S.Ct. 488 (internal quotation marks omitted). Here, the Alaska Legislature expressed the objective of the law in the statutory text itself. The legislature found that "sex offenders pose a high risk of reoffending," and identified "protecting the public from sex offenders" as the "primary governmental interest" of the law. 1994 Alaska Sess. Laws ch. 41, § 1. The legislature further determined that "release of certain information about sex offenders to public agencies and the general public will assist in protecting the public safety." *Ibid.* As we observed in *Hendricks*, where we examined an *ex post facto* challenge to a postincarceration confinement of sex offenders, an imposition of restrictive measures on sex offenders adjudged to be dangerous is "a legitimate nonpunitive governmental objective and has been historically so regarded." 521 U.S., at 363, 117 S.Ct. 2072. In this case, as in *Hendricks*, "[n]othing on the face of the statute suggests that the legislature sought to create anything other than a civil ... scheme designed to protect the public from harm." *Id.*, at 361, 117 S.Ct. 2072.

Respondents seek to cast doubt upon the nonpunitive nature of the law's declared objective by pointing out that the Alaska Constitution lists the need for protecting the public as one of the purposes of criminal administration.... As the Court stated in *Flemming v. Nestor*, rejecting an *ex post facto* challenge to a law terminating benefits to deported aliens, where a legislative restriction "is an incident of the State's power to protect the health and safety of its citizens," it will be considered "as evidencing an intent to exercise that regulatory power, and not a purpose to add to the punishment." 363 U.S., at 616, 80 S.Ct. 1367 (citing *Hawker v. New York*, 170 U.S. 189, 18 S.Ct. 573, 42 L.Ed. 1002 (1898)). The Court repeated this principle in *89 Firearms*, upholding a statute requiring forfeiture of unlicensed firearms against a double jeopardy challenge. The Court observed that, in enacting the provision, Congress "'was concerned with the widespread traffic in firearms and with their general availability to those whose possession thereof was contrary to the public interest.'" 465 U.S., at 364, 104 S.Ct. 1099 (quoting *Huddleston v. United States*, 415 U.S. 814, 824, 94 S.Ct. 1262, 39 L.Ed.2d 782 (1974)). This goal was "plainly more remedial than punitive." 465 U.S., at 364, 104 S.Ct. 1099. These precedents instruct us that even if the objective of the Act is consistent with the purposes of the Alaska criminal justice system, the State's pursuit of it in a regulatory scheme does not make the objective punitive.

Other formal attributes of a legislative enactment, such as the manner of its codification or the enforcement procedures it establishes, are probative of the legislature's intent. See *Hendricks, supra*, at 361, 117 S.Ct. 2072; *Hudson, supra*, at 103, 118 S.Ct. 488; *89 Firearms, supra*, at 363, 104 S.Ct. 1099. In this case these factors are open to debate. The notification provisions of the Act are codified in the State's "Health, Safety, and Housing Code," § 18, confirming our conclusion that the statute was intended as a nonpunitive regulatory measure. Cf. *Hendricks, supra*, at 361, 117 S.Ct. 2072 (the State's "objective to create a civil proceeding is evidenced by its placement of the Act within the [State's] probate code, instead of the criminal code" (citations omitted)). The Act's registration provisions, however, are codified in the State's criminal procedure code, and so might seem to point in the opposite direction. These factors, though, are not dispositive. The location and labels of a statutory provision do not by themselves transform a civil remedy into a criminal one. In *89 Firearms*, the Court held a forfeiture provision to be a civil sanction even though the authorizing statute was in the criminal code. 465 U.S., at 364–365, 104 S.Ct. 1099. The Court rejected the argument that the placement demonstrated Congress' "intention to create an additional criminal sanction," observing that "both criminal and civil sanctions may be labeled 'penalties.'" *Id.*, at 364, n. 6, 104 S.Ct. 1099.

The same rationale applies here. Title 12 of Alaska's Code of Criminal Procedure (where the Act's registration provisions are located) contains many provisions that do not involve criminal punishment, such as civil procedures for disposing of recovered and seized property, Alaska Stat. § 12.36.010 *et seq.* (2000); laws protecting the confidentiality of victims and witnesses, § 12.61.010 *et seq.*; laws governing the security and accuracy of criminal justice information, § 12.62.110 *et seq.*; laws governing civil postconviction actions, § 12.72.010 *et seq.*; and laws governing actions for writs of habeas corpus, § 12.75.010 *et seq.*, which under Alaska law are "independent civil proceeding[s]," *State v. Hannagan*, 559 P.2d 1059, 1063 (Alaska 1977). Although some of these provisions relate to criminal administration, they are not in themselves punitive. The partial codification of the Act in the State's criminal procedure code is not sufficient to support a conclusion that the legislative intent was punitive.

The procedural mechanisms to implement the Act do not alter our conclusion. After the Act's adoption Alaska amended its Rules of Criminal Procedure concerning the acceptance of pleas and the entering of criminal judgments. The rule on pleas now requires the court to "infor[m] the defendant in writing of the requirements of [the Act] and, if it can be determined by the court, the period of registration required." Alaska Rule Crim. Proc. 11(c)(4) (2002). Similarly, the written judgments for sex offenses and child kidnapings "must set out the requirements of [the Act] and, if it can be determined by the court, whether that conviction will require the offender or kidnapper to register for life or a lesser period." Alaska Stat. § 12.55.148(a) (2000).

The policy to alert convicted offenders to the civil consequences of their criminal conduct does not render the consequences themselves punitive. When a State sets up a regulatory scheme, it is logical to provide those persons subject to it with clear and un-ambiguous notice of the requirements and the penalties for noncompliance. The Act requires registration either before the offender's release from confinement or within a day of his conviction (if the offender is not imprisoned). Timely and adequate notice serves to apprise individuals of their responsibilities and to ensure compliance with the regulatory scheme. Notice is important, for the scheme is enforced by criminal penalties. See §§ 11.56.835, 11.56.840. Although other methods of notification may be available, it is effective to make it part of the plea colloquy or the judgment of conviction. Invoking the criminal process in aid of a statutory regime does not render the statutory scheme itself punitive.

Our conclusion is strengthened by the fact that, aside from the duty to register, the statute itself mandates no procedures. Instead, it vests the authority to promulgate im-plementing regulations with the Alaska Department of Public Safety, §§ 12.63.020(b), 18.65.087(d) — an agency charged with enforcement of both criminal *and* civil regulatory laws. See, *e.g.*, § 17.30.100 (enforcement of drug laws); § 18.70.010 (fire protection); § 28.05.011 (motor vehicles and road safety); § 44.41.020 (protection of life and property). The Act itself does not require the procedures adopted to contain any safeguards associated with the criminal process. That leads us to infer that the legislature envisioned the Act's implementation to be civil and administrative. By contemplating "distinctly civil procedures," the legislature "indicate[d] clearly that it intended a civil, not a criminal sanction." *Ursery*, 518 U.S., at 289, 116 S.Ct. 2135 (internal quotation marks omitted; alteration in original)....
We conclude, as did the District Court and the Court of Appeals, that the intent of the Alaska Legislature was to create a civil, nonpunitive regime....

In analyzing the effects of the Act we refer to the seven factors noted in *Kennedy v. Mendoza-Martinez*, 372 U.S. 144, 168–169, 83 S.Ct. 554, 9 L.Ed.2d 644 (1963), as a useful framework. These factors, which migrated into our *ex post facto* case law from double jeopardy jurisprudence, have their earlier origins in cases under the Sixth and Eighth Amendments, as well as the Bill of Attainder and the *Ex Post Facto* Clauses. See *id.*, at 168–169, and nn. 22–28, 83 S.Ct. 554. Because the *Mendoza-Martinez* factors are designed to apply in various constitutional contexts, we have said they are "neither exhaustive nor dis-positive," *United States v. Ward*, 448 U.S., at 249, 100 S.Ct. 2636; *89 Firearms*, 465 U.S., at 365, n. 7, 104 S.Ct. 1099, but are "useful guideposts," *Hudson*, 522 U.S., at 99, 118 S.Ct. 488. The factors most relevant to our analysis are whether, in its necessary operation, the regulatory scheme: has been regarded in our history and traditions as a punishment; imposes an affirmative disability or restraint; promotes the traditional aims of punishment; has a rational connection to a nonpunitive purpose; or is excessive with respect to this purpose....

The fact that Alaska posts the information on the Internet does not alter our conclusion. It must be acknowledged that notice of a criminal conviction subjects the offender to public shame, the humiliation increasing in proportion to the extent of the publicity. And the ge-ographic reach of the Internet is greater than anything which could have been designed in colonial times. These facts do not render Internet notification punitive. The purpose and the principal effect of notification are to inform the public for its own safety, not to humiliate the offender. Widespread public access is necessary for the efficacy of the scheme, and the attendant humiliation is but a collateral consequence of a valid regulation.... The State's Web site does not provide the public with means to shame the offender by, say, posting comments underneath his record. An individual seeking the information must take the initial step of going to the Department of Public Safety's Web site, proceed to the sex offender registry, and then look up the desired information. The process is more analogous to a visit to an official archive of criminal records than it is to a scheme forcing an offender to appear in public with some visible badge of past criminality. The Internet makes the document search more efficient, cost effective, and convenient for Alaska's citizenry.

We next consider whether the Act subjects respondents to an "affirmative disability or restraint." *Mendoza-Martinez, supra,* at 168, 83 S.Ct. 554. Here, we inquire how the effects of the Act are felt by those subject to it. If the disability or restraint is minor and indirect, its effects are unlikely to be punitive.... The Act imposes no physical restraint, and so does not resemble the punishment of imprisonment, which is the paradigmatic affirmative disability or restraint. *Hudson,* 522 U.S., at 104, 118 S.Ct. 488. The Act's obligations are less harsh than the sanctions of occupational debarment, which we have held to be non-punitive. See *ibid.* (forbidding further participation in the banking industry); *De Veau v. Braisted,* 363 U.S. 144, 80 S.Ct. 1146, 4 L.Ed.2d 1109 (1960) (forbidding work as a union official); *Hawker v. New York,* 170 U.S. 189, 18 S.Ct. 573, 42 L.Ed. 1002 (1898) (revocation of a medical license). The Act does not restrain activities sex offenders may pursue but leaves them free to change jobs or residences.

The Court of Appeals sought to distinguish *Hawker* and cases which have followed it on the grounds that the disability at issue there was specific and "narrow," confined to particular professions, whereas "the procedures employed under the Alaska statute are likely to make [respondents] *completely unemployable*" because "employers will not want to risk loss of business when the public learns that they have hired sex offenders." 259 F.3d, at 988. This is conjecture. Landlords and employers could conduct background checks on the criminal records of prospective employees or tenants even with the Act not in force. The record in this case contains no evidence that the Act has led to substantial occupational or housing disadvantages for former sex offenders that would not have otherwise occurred through the use of routine background checks by employers and landlords. The Court of Appeals identified only one incident from the 7-year history of Alaska's law where a sex offender suffered community hostility and damage to his business after the information he submitted to the registry became public. *Id.,* at 987–988. This could have occurred in any event, because the information about the individual's conviction was already in the public domain.... Although the public availability of the information may have a lasting and painful impact on the convicted sex offender, these consequences flow not from the Act's registration and dissemination provisions, but from the fact of conviction, already a matter of public record. The State makes the facts underlying the offenses and the resulting convictions accessible so members of the public can take the precautions they deem necessary before dealing with the registrant.... The Court of Appeals reasoned that the requirement of periodic updates imposed an affirmative disability. In reaching this conclusion, the Court of Appeals was under a misapprehension, albeit one created by the State itself during the argument below, that the offender had to update the registry in person. *Id.,* at 984, n. 4. The State's representation was erroneous. The Alaska statute, on its face, does not require these updates to be made in person. And, as respondents conceded at the oral argument before us, the record contains no indication that an in-person appearance requirement has been imposed on any sex offender subject to the Act....

The Court of Appeals held that the registration system is parallel to probation or supervised release in terms of the restraint imposed. 259 F.3d, at 987. This argument has some force, but, after due consideration, we reject it. Probation and supervised release entail a series of mandatory conditions and allow the supervising officer to seek the revocation of probation or release in case of infraction. See generally *Johnson v. United States*, 529 U.S. 694, 120 S.Ct. 1795, 146 L.Ed.2d 727 (2000); *Griffin v. Wisconsin*, 483 U.S. 868, 107 S.Ct. 3164, 97 L.Ed.2d 709 (1987). By contrast, offenders subject to the Alaska statute are free to move where they wish and to live and work as other citizens, with no supervision. Although registrants must inform the authorities after they change their facial features (such as growing a beard), borrow a car, or seek psychiatric treatment, they are not required to seek permission to do so. A sex offender who fails to comply with the reporting requirement may be subjected to a criminal prosecution for that failure, but any prosecution is a proceeding separate from the individual's original offense. Whether other constitutional objections can be raised to a mandatory reporting requirement, and how those questions might be resolved, are concerns beyond the scope of this opinion. It suffices to say the registration requirements make a valid regulatory program effective and do not impose punitive restraints in violation of the *Ex Post Facto* Clause.

The State concedes that the statute might deter future crimes. Respondents seize on this proposition to argue that the law is punitive, because deterrence is one purpose of punishment.... This proves too much. Any number of governmental programs might deter crime without imposing punishment. "To hold that the mere presence of a deterrent purpose renders such sanctions 'criminal'... would severely undermine the Government's ability to engage in effective regulation." *Hudson, supra*, at 105, 118 S.Ct. 488; see also *Ursery*, 518 U.S., at 292, 116 S.Ct. 2135; *89 Firearms*, 465 U.S., at 364, 104 S.Ct. 1099.... The Court of Appeals was incorrect to conclude that the Act's registration obligations were retributive because "the length of the reporting requirement appears to be measured by the extent of the wrongdoing, not by the extent of the risk posed." 259 F.3d, at 990. The Act, it is true, differentiates between individuals convicted of aggravated or multiple offenses and those convicted of a single nonaggravated offense. Alaska Stat. § 12.63.020(a)(1) (2000). The broad categories, however, and the corresponding length of the reporting requirement, are reasonably related to the danger of recidivism, and this is consistent with the regulatory objective.

The Act's rational connection to a nonpunitive purpose is a "[m]ost significant" factor in our determination that the statute's effects are not punitive. *Ursery, supra*, at 290, 116 S.Ct. 2135. As the Court of Appeals acknowledged, the Act has a legitimate nonpunitive purpose of "public safety, which is advanced by alerting the public to the risk of sex offenders in their communit[y]." 259 F.3d, at 991. Respondents concede, in turn, that "this alternative purpose is valid, and rational." ... They contend, however, that the Act lacks the necessary regulatory connection because it is not "narrowly drawn to accomplish the stated purpose." ... A statute is not deemed punitive simply because it lacks a close or perfect fit with the nonpunitive aims it seeks to advance. The imprecision respondents rely upon does not suggest that the Act's nonpunitive purpose is a "sham or mere pretext." *Hendricks*, 521 U.S., at 371, 117 S.Ct. 2072 (KENNEDY, J., concurring).... In concluding the Act was excessive in relation to its regulatory purpose, the Court of Appeals relied in large part on two propositions: first, that the statute applies to all convicted sex offenders without regard to their future dangerousness; and, second, that it places no limits on the number of persons who have access to the information. 259 F.3d, at 991–992. Neither argument is persuasive.

Alaska could conclude that a conviction for a sex offense provides evidence of substantial risk of recidivism. The legislature's findings are consistent with grave concerns over the high rate of recidivism among convicted sex offenders and their dangerousness as a class. The risk of recidivism posed by sex offenders is "frightening and high." *McKune v. Lile*, 536 U.S. 24, 34, 122 S.Ct. 2017, 153 L.Ed.2d 47 (2002); see also *id.*, at 33, 122 S.Ct. 2017 ("When convicted sex offenders reenter society, they are much more likely than any other type of offender to be rearrested for a new rape or sexual assault" (citing U.S. Dept. of Justice, Bureau of Justice Statistics, Sex Offenses and Offenders 27 (1997); U.S. Dept. of Justice, Bureau of Justice Statistics, Recidivism of Prisoners Released in 1983, p. 6 (1997))).

The *Ex Post Facto* Clause does not preclude a State from making reasonable categorical judgments that conviction of specified crimes should entail particular regulatory consequences. We have upheld against *ex post facto* challenges laws imposing regulatory burdens on individuals convicted of crimes without any corresponding risk assessment. See *De Veau*, 363 U.S., at 160, 80 S.Ct. 1146; *Hawker*, 170 U.S., at 197, 18 S.Ct. 573. As stated in *Hawker*: "Doubtless, one who has violated the criminal law may thereafter reform and become in fact possessed of a good moral character. But the legislature has power in cases of this kind to make a rule of universal application...." *Ibid.* The State's determination to legislate with respect to convicted sex offenders as a class, rather than require individual determination of their dangerousness, does not make the statute a punishment under the *Ex Post Facto* Clause.

Our decision in *Hendricks*, on which respondents rely, ... is not to the contrary. The State's objective in *Hendricks* was involuntary (and potentially indefinite) confinement of "particularly dangerous individuals." 521 U.S., at 357–358, 364, 117 S.Ct. 2072. The magnitude of the restraint made individual assessment appropriate. The Act, by contrast, imposes the more minor condition of registration. In the context of the regulatory scheme the State can dispense with individual predictions of future dangerousness and allow the public to assess the risk on the basis of accurate, nonprivate information about the registrants' convictions without violating the prohibitions of the *Ex Post Facto* Clause.

The duration of the reporting requirements is not excessive. Empirical research on child molesters, for instance, has shown that, "[c]ontrary to conventional wisdom, most reoffenses do not occur within the first several years after release," but may occur "as late as 20 years following release." National Institute of Justice, R. Prentky, R. Knight, & A. Lee, U.S. Dept. of Justice, Child Sexual Molestation: Research Issues 14 (1997).

The Court of Appeals' reliance on the wide dissemination of the information is also unavailing. The Ninth Circuit highlighted that the information was available "world-wide" and "[b]roadcas[t]" in an indiscriminate manner. 259 F.3d, at 992. As we have explained, however, the notification system is a passive one: An individual must seek access to the information. The Web site warns that the use of displayed information "to commit a criminal act against another person is subject to criminal prosecution." http:// www.dps.state.ak.us/ nSorcr/asp/ (as visited Jan. 17, 2003) (available in the Clerk of Court's case file). Given the general mobility of our population, for Alaska to make its registry system available and easily accessible throughout the State was not so excessive a regulatory requirement as to become a punishment. See D. Schram & C. Milloy, Community Notification: A Study of Offender Characteristics and Recidivism 13 (1995) (38% of recidivist sex offenses in the State of Washington took place in jurisdictions other than where the previous offense was committed).... The excessiveness inquiry of our *ex post facto* jurisprudence is not an exercise in determining whether the legislature has made the best choice possible to address the problem it seeks to remedy. The question is whether the regulatory means chosen are reasonable in light of the nonpunitive objective. The Act meets this standard.

The two remaining *Mendoza-Martinez* factors—whether the regulation comes into play only on a finding of scienter and whether the behavior to which it applies is already a crime—are of little weight in this case. The regulatory scheme applies only to past conduct, which was, and is, a crime. This is a necessary beginning point, for recidivism is the statutory concern. The obligations the statute imposes are the responsibility of registration, a duty not predicated upon some present or repeated violation.... Our examination of the Act's effects leads to the determination that respondents cannot show, much less by the clearest proof, that the effects of the law negate Alaska's intention to establish a civil regulatory scheme. The Act is nonpunitive, and its retroactive application does not violate the *Ex Post Facto* Clause. The judgment of the Court of Appeals for the Ninth Circuit is reversed, and the case is remanded for further proceedings consistent with this opinion.

It is so ordered....

[Concurring opinions by Justices Thomas and Souter, and dissenting opinions by Justice Stevens and Ginsburg, with whom Justice Breyer joins, are omitted].

Notes

In *Smith*, the United States Supreme Court rejected an *ex post facto* challenge to Alaska's sex offender registration law, finding Alaska's scheme to be remedial rather than punitive. However, in his dissenting opinion, Justice Stevens determined that widespread public access to such personal and constantly updated information would have a severe stigmatizing effect on the personal liberty interests of the convicted. *Smith v. Doe*, 538 U.S. 84, 111 (2003) (Stevens, dissenting). Justice Stevens held the sanctions to be punitive because they: "(1) constitute a severe deprivation of the offender's liberty, (2) are imposed on everyone who is convicted of a relevant criminal offense, and (3) are imposed only on those criminals," none of which are present within any civil sanctions. *Id.* at 112. Justice Stevens held that these punitive aspects are adequately justified by two of the traditional aims of punishment—retribution and deterrence—but only for post-enactment offenses. *Id.* at 114. Justice Ginsburg, with whom Justice Breyer joined, also dissented, finding that the Alaska Act "imposes onerous and intrusive obligations on convicted sex offenders; and it exposes registrants, through aggressive public notification of their crimes, to profound humiliation and community-wide ostracism...." *Id.* at 115 (Ginsburg, dissenting). In Justice Ginsburg's view,

> [i]ts registration and reporting provisions are comparable to conditions of supervised release or parole; its public notification regimen, which permits placement of the registrant's face on a webpage under the label "Registered Sex Offender," calls to mind shaming punishments once used to mark an offender as someone to be shunned....

Id. at 115–16. Justice Ginsburg determined that by applying to all convicted sex offenders, without regard to their future dangerousness or risk of reoffending, the Act exceeded its legitimate civil purpose: "to promote public safety by alerting the public to potentially recidivist sex offenders in the community...." *Id.* at 116–17. Most importantly for Justice Ginsburg, the Act made no provision for the possibility of rehabilitation. "However plain it may be that a former sex offender currently poses no threat of recidivism, he will remain subject to long-term monitoring and inescapable humiliation...." *Id.* at 117.

Some State Supreme Courts have determined that other state registration schemes that categorically impose sanctions are punitive. For example, in *State v. Williams*, 952 N.E.2d 1108 (Ohio 2011), the Ohio Supreme Court declared Ohio's registration scheme to be punitive in nature. *See also, e.g., Wallace v. State*, 905 N.E.2d 371, 384 (Ind. 2009) ("[T]he non-punitive purpose of the Act, although of unquestioned importance, does not serve to render as non-punitive a statute that is so broad and sweeping."); *State v. Letalien*, 985 A.2d 4, 26 (Me. 2009) ("[W]e hold that the retroactive application of the lifelong registration requirement and quarterly in-person verification procedures of SORNA of 1999 ... is punitive."). Consider the effect of such a holding in the following case, in which the Supreme Court of Ohio addressed the application of mandatory registration requirements to juvenile sex offenders.

2. Registration of Juveniles

In re C.P.

Supreme Court of Ohio, 2012
967 N.E.2d 729

PFEIFER, J....

On June 26, 2009, a multicount complaint was filed in Athens County Juvenile Court against appellant, C.P., who was 15 years old at the time. The complaint alleged that C.P. was a delinquent child and charged him with two counts of rape and one count of kidnapping with sexual motivation, each count a first-degree felony if committed by an adult. The victim was a six-year-old boy, a relative of C.P.... The state immediately moved the juvenile court to transfer jurisdiction to the Athens County Court of Common Pleas, General Division. On July 29, 2009, the juvenile court held a hearing pursuant to R.C. 2152.12(B) to determine whether to retain jurisdiction over C.P.'s case. The parties stipulated that there was probable cause to believe that C.P. had committed the alleged offenses. The court learned that at age 11, C.P. had been adjudicated delinquent in Utah for sexually abusing his half-sister, who was two years younger than C.P., and that C.P. had undergone over two years of sex-offender treatment there as a result of his adjudication.

At a hearing held on August 24, 2009, the court denied the state's motion to transfer jurisdiction over C.P. to the general division to be tried as an adult. The judge stated,

> I think we can have our best chance of working with [C.P.] in the juvenile system and I don't think everything has been exhaustively tried there. It doesn't mean that there won't be consequences and it doesn't mean that there won't be loss of freedom there certainly will be if convicted of this offense [sic], but I think we have time within the juvenile system and we have resources within the juvenile system to work with this boy. So, I deny the state's motion for transfer and we'll continue to work with this within the juvenile system.

In ruling against transfer, the judge cited the factors in R.C. 2152.12(E)(6) ("[t]he child is not emotionally, physically, or psychologically mature enough for the transfer") and (E)(7) ("[t]he child has a mental illness or is a mentally retarded person").

C.P. thus remained under the jurisdiction of the juvenile court. The state sought to have C.P. sentenced as a serious youthful offender ("SYO") pursuant to R.C. 2152.13(A)(4)(b), and on September 14, 2009, the grand jury returned an indictment against him with an SYO specification attached to each of the three counts.... On September 23, 2009, C.P. entered an admission to each charge in the indictment; because of the nature of his offenses, he was eligible for a discretionary SYO dispositional sentence pursuant to R.C. 2152.11(D)(2)(b). At a subsequent hearing, the court found C.P. to be a delinquent child and designated him an SYO in relation to each offense, imposing a three-year minimum commitment to the Ohio Department of Youth Services on each count, to run concurrently. As part of the SYO disposition, the court imposed three concurrent five-year prison terms, which were stayed pending C.P.'s successful completion of his juvenile dispositions.... Further, the court advised C.P. of the duties and classification automatically imposed upon him by R.C. 2152.86. Pursuant to R.C. 2152.86(A)(1), the court classified C.P. a juvenile-offender registrant and informed him of his duty to abide by the registration and notification requirements of R.C. Chapter 2950. The court also classified C.P. a public-registry-qualified juvenile-offender registrant ("PRQJOR"). Pursuant to R.C. 2152.86(B)(1), C.P. was automatically classified as a Tier III sex-offender/child-victim offender. The judge further informed C.P. of his registration requirements:

> You are required to register in person with the sheriff of the county in which you establish residency within three days of coming into that county, or if temporarily domiciled for more than three days. If you change residence address you shall provide written notice of that residence change to the sheriff with whom you are most recently registered and to the sheriff in the county in which you intend to reside at least 20-days prior to any change of residence address. * * * You are required to provide to the sheriff temporary lodging information including address and length of stay if your absence will be for seven days or more. Since you are a public registry qualified juvenile offender registrant you are also required to register in person with the sheriff of the county in which you establish a place of education immediately upon coming to that county. * * * You are also required to register in person with the sheriff of the county in which you establish a place of employment if you have been employed for more than three days or for an aggregate of 14 days in a calendar year. * * * Employment includes voluntary services. As a public registry qualified juvenile offender registrant, you * * * also shall provide written notice of a change of address or your place of employment or your place of education at least 20 days prior to any change and no later than three days after the change of employment. * * * [Y]ou shall provide written notice within three days of any change in vehicle information, e-mail addresses, internet identifiers or telephone numbers registered to or used by you to the sheriff with whom you are most recently registered.* * * [Y]ou are required to abide by all of the above described requirements * * * for your lifetime as a Tier III offender with in person verification every 90-days. That means for the rest of your life * * * every three months you're going to be checking in with [the] sheriff where you live or work or both. * * * Failure to register, failure to verify on the specific notice and times as outlined here will result in criminal prosecution.

C.P. appealed his automatic classification as a Tier III juvenile-offender registrant and PRQJOR to the Fourth District Court of Appeals, arguing that R.C. 2152.86 violated his rights to due process and equal protection and his right against cruel and unusual punishment. The court of appeals affirmed the judgment of the trial court.... The cause is before this court upon the acceptance of a discretionary appeal....

This court has recently held, in a case involving an adult offender, that the enhanced sex-offender reporting and notification requirements contained in R.C. Chapter 2950 enacted by Am.Sub.S.B. No. 10 ("S.B. 10") are punitive in nature, making their retroactive application unconstitutional: "Following the enactment of S.B. 10, all doubt has been removed: R.C. Chapter 2950 is punitive." *State v. Williams*, 129 Ohio St.3d 344, 2011-Ohio-3374, 952 N.E.2d 1108, ¶ 16. In this case we consider the constitutionality of the prospective, automatic application of those reporting and notification requirements to certain juvenile offenders.... Pursuant to changes brought about by S.B. 10, R.C. 2152.86 creates a new class of juvenile sex-offender registrants: public-registry-qualified juvenile-offender registrants. PRQJORs are subject to more stringent registration and notification requirements than other juvenile-offender registrants. Moreover, the requirements are imposed automatically rather than at the discretion of a juvenile judge.

Pursuant to R.C. 2152.86, PRQJOR status is assigned to juveniles who (1) were 14 through 17 years old when the offense was committed, (2) have been adjudicated a delinquent child for committing certain specified sexually oriented offenses, including rape, gross sexual imposition when the victim is under 12, sexual battery of a child under age 12, and aggravated murder, murder, or kidnapping with a purpose to gratify the sexual needs or desires of the offender, and (3) have had a court impose on them a serious youthful offender ("SYO") dispositional sentence under R.C. 2152.13....

As we explained in *State v. D.H.*, 120 Ohio St.3d 540, 2009-Ohio-9, 901 N.E.2d 209, the nature of an SYO disposition requires that the juvenile remain under the continuing jurisdiction of a juvenile judge:

> A juvenile charged as a potential serious youthful offender does not face bindover to an adult court; the case remains in the juvenile court. Under R.C. 2152.11(A), a juvenile defendant who commits certain acts is eligible for "a more restrictive disposition." That "more restricted disposition" is a "serious youthful offender" disposition and includes what is known as a blended sentence—a traditional juvenile disposition coupled with the imposition of a stayed adult sentence. R.C. 2152.13. The adult sentence remains stayed unless the juvenile fails to successfully complete his or her traditional juvenile disposition. R.C. 2152.13(D)(2)(a)(iii). Theoretically, the threat of the imposition of an adult sentence encourages a juvenile's cooperation in his own rehabilitation, functioning as both carrot and stick.

Id. at ¶ 18.

Only further bad acts by the juvenile as he is rehabilitated in the juvenile system can cause the stayed adult penalty to be invoked:

> Any adult sentence that the trial court imposes through R.C. 2152.13(D)(2)(a)(i) is only a potential sentence—it is stayed pursuant to R.C. 2152.13(D)(2)(a)(iii) "pending the successful completion of the traditional juvenile dispositions imposed." R.C. 2152.13(D)(2)(a)(ii) requires the court to impose a juvenile disposition when it imposes an adult sentence; how the juvenile responds to that disposition will determine whether the stay is lifted on the adult sentence.

Id. at ¶ 30.

R.C. 2152.86 changes the very nature of an SYO disposition, imposing an adult penalty immediately upon the adjudication. The juvenile is not given the opportunity to avoid the adult portion of his punishment by successfully completing his juvenile rehabilitation. Instead, he must comply with all of S.B. 10's reporting and notification requirements for Tier III sexual offenders contained in R.C. Chapter 2950.... A PRQJOR must personally register with the sheriff within three days of coming into a county in which he resides or temporarily is domiciled for more than three days. R.C. 2950.04(A)(3)(a). He must also register with the sheriff of any county he enters to attend school or any county in which he is employed for more than three days. R.C. 2950.04(A)(3)(b)(i), (ii), and (iii). PRQJORs must personally verify that information with the sheriff every 90 days. R.C. 2950.06(B)(3) and (C)(1). Any time that information changes, the PRQJOR must notify the sheriff within three days. R.C. 2950.05(A).

At the time of registration, PRQJORs must provide information such as license-plate numbers of vehicles available to them and e-mail addresses, Internet identifiers, and telephone numbers registered to or used by them. R.C. 2950.04(C)(6) and (10). Any changes in that information must be reported to the sheriff within three days. R.C. 2950.05(D).... PRQJORs must comply with the community-notification requirements of R.C. 2950.11(A) and (B). As part of the notification requirements, local sheriffs disseminate the offender's picture and personal information to neighbors, local children services agencies, school officials, day-care centers, local universities, and volunteer organizations in contact with minors. R.C. 2950.11(A). The persons notified receive information regarding the youth's residence, place of employment, and school, as well as information about the adjudicated offense and a photograph. R.C. 2950.11(B). As a further requirement, PRQJORs must be included on the Ohio attorney general's electronic sex-offender registration and notification database ("eSORN"). R.C. 2950.13(A)(11)....

Both the method of assignment and the obligations of PRQJORs assigned to Tier III differ from those juveniles placed in Tier III as juvenile-offender registrants ("JORs"). For juveniles adjudicated delinquent through a traditional juvenile disposition and who were age 14 or older at the time of their delinquent act, an assignment to Tier III is not automatic. Instead, if the juvenile court finds that the child is a JOR under R.C. 2152.82(A), the court holds a hearing to determine the JOR's tier classification. R.C. 2152.82(B). (Juveniles under 14 are not subject to registration requirements, regardless of the offense.) Which tier such an offender is placed in rests within the juvenile court's discretion. *Id.* If the court finds that the JOR is a Tier III sex-offender/child-victim offender, then the court may impose certain notification requirements contained in R.C. 2950.10 and 2950.11. R.C. 2152.82(B).

Though all JORs must register personally with the sheriff within three days of entering into a county where they will reside or be temporarily domiciled, R.C. 2950.04(A)(3)(a), a PRQJOR must comply with additional registration requirements. PRQJORs must personally register with the sheriff of any county in which they attend school or in which they are employed for more than three days or for 14 or more days in a calendar year, regardless of whether the juvenile resides in or has a temporary domicile in that county. R.C. 2950.04(A)(3)(b). They must report within three days any change of vehicle information, e-mail addresses, Internet identifiers, and telephone numbers. R.C. 2950.05(D).

Notification requirements also differ significantly. JORs assigned to Tier III are subject to community notification only if the juvenile court orders it, R.C. 2152.82(B), and to victim notification only if the victim requests it. R.C. 2950.10. The registration information of JORs is not disseminated on the Internet. For PRQJORs, on the other hand, the community- and victim-notification requirements are automatic. R.C. 2950.11(F)(1)(a); 2950.10(B)(2). Further, the state must place PRQJORs on its public Internet database. R.C. 2950.13(A)(11).

The potential for reclassification varies greatly between PRQJORs and JORs. For JORs, the juvenile court must conduct a hearing "upon completion of the disposition of that child" to determine whether the child should be reclassified. R.C. 2152.84(A)(1). Additionally, a JOR may file a petition for reclassification three years after the court issues its order pursuant to that mandatory hearing, a second petition three years later, and further petitions every five years thereafter. R.C. 2152.85(B). PRQJORs, in contrast, do not receive a reclassification hearing upon the completion of their juvenile disposition. Instead, they are placed on a reclassification track similar to that of adult Tier III offenders. They are not eligible for a reclassification hearing until 25 years after their statutory registration duties begin. R.C. 2950.15(C)(2) and 2152.85(G).... In sum, for PRQJORs, Tier III classification imposes a lifetime penalty that extends well beyond the age at which the juvenile court loses jurisdiction. It is a consequence that attaches immediately and leaves a juvenile with no means of avoiding the penalty by demonstrating that he will benefit from rehabilitative opportunities....

The Eighth Amendment to the United States Constitution states, "Excessive bail shall not be required, nor excessive fines imposed, nor cruel and unusual punishments inflicted." That the Eighth Amendment prohibits torture is elemental. *Wilkerson v. Utah*, 99 U.S. 130, 136, 25 L.Ed. 345 (1878). But the bulk of Eighth Amendment jurisprudence concerns not whether a particular punishment is barbaric, but whether it is disproportionate to the crime. Central to the Constitution's prohibition against cruel and unusual punishment is the "precept of justice that punishment for crime should be graduated and proportioned to [the] offense." *Weems v. United States*, 217 U.S. 349, 367, 30 S.Ct. 544, 54 L.Ed. 793 (1910).... Proportionality review falls within two general classifications: the first involves "challenges to the length of term-of-years sentences given all the circumstances in a particular case." The second, which until recently was applied only in capital cases, involves "cases in which the Court implements the proportionality standard by certain categorical restrictions." *Graham v. Florida*, 560 U.S. 48, 130 S.Ct. 2011, 2021, 176 L.Ed.2d 825 (2010).... In this case, we address the second classification of cases. Within that classification, there are two subsets, "one considering the nature of the offense, the other considering the characteristics of the offender." *Id.* at 2022, 176 L.Ed.2d 825. In regard to the nature of the offense, for instance, the court has held that capital punishment is impermissible for nonhomicide crimes against individuals. *Kennedy v. Louisiana*, 554 U.S. 407, 437, 128 S.Ct. 2641, 171 L.Ed.2d 525 (2008). In this juvenile case, we are dealing with the second subset, the characteristics of the offender.

In recent years, the court has established categorical rules prohibiting certain punishments for juveniles. In *Roper v. Simmons*, 543 U.S. 551, 125 S.Ct. 1183, 161 L.Ed.2d 1 (2005), the court prohibited the death penalty for defendants who committed their crimes before the age of 18. In *Graham*, the court held that the Eighth Amendment prohibits imposition of a life-without-parole sentence on a juvenile offender who did not commit homicide. It is important to note that in both *Roper* and *Graham*, the court addressed the cases of juveniles who had been tried as adults. Here, we address the imposition of a sentence upon a child who remains under the jurisdiction of the juvenile court.

The court engages in a two-step process in adopting categorical rules in regard to punishment: first, the court considers whether there is a national consensus against the sentencing practice at issue, and second, the court determines "in the exercise of its own independent judgment whether the punishment in question violates the Constitution." *Graham*, 560 U.S. at ___, 130 S.Ct. at 2022, 176 L.Ed.2d 825....

In 2006, Congress passed the Adam Walsh Child Protection and Safety Act ("Adam Walsh Act"), P.L. No. 109-248, 120 Stat. 587, codified at 42 U.S.C. 16901 et seq. Section 16912(a) of the Adam Walsh Act "directs every jurisdiction to maintain a sex-offender registry conforming to the requirements of the Act. And to ensure compliance, Congress directed that states that did not adopt the Adam Walsh Act risked losing ten percent of certain federal crime-control funds that would otherwise be allocated to them. Section 16925(a)." *State v. Bodyke*, 126 Ohio St.3d 266, 2010-Ohio-2424, 933 N.E.2d 753, ¶ 19. These registry requirements are contained in the Sex Offender Registration and Notification Act ("SORNA"), Title I of the Adam Walsh Act.

Ohio was the first state to implement SORNA. *Id.* at ¶ 20. By the start of 2011, only three other states were in substantial compliance with SORNA. http:// www.ojp.usdoj. gov/newsroom/pressreleases/2011/SMART11054.htm. Then, on January 11, 2011, the United States attorney general issued Supplemental Guidelines for Sex Offender Registration and Notification, 76 Fed.Reg. 1630 ("Supplemental Guidelines"). These guidelines made significant changes to the National Guidelines for Sex Offender Registration and Notification issued on July 2, 2008. 73 Fed.Reg. 38030. The attorney general promulgated the Supplemental Guidelines in furtherance of his key role in the implementation of SORNA; SORNA "charges the Attorney General with responsibility for issuing guidelines and regulations to interpret and implement SORNA and for determining whether jurisdictions have substantially implemented SORNA in their programs. See 42 U.S.C. 16912(b), 16925." 76 Fed.Reg. at 1631.... In releasing the Supplemental Guidelines, the attorney general noted that one of the largest barriers to compliance by states was the fact that "SORNA includes as covered 'sex offender[s]' juveniles at least 14 years old who are adjudicated delinquent for particularly serious sex offenses." 76 Fed.Reg. at 1636. An April 2009 50-state survey on SORNA conducted by the National Consortium for Justice Information and Statistics stated that "[t]he most commonly cited barrier to SORNA compliance was the act's juvenile registration and reporting requirements, cited by 23 states." National Consortium for Justice Information and Statistics, Survey on State Compliance with the Sex Offender Registration and Notification Act (SORNA) (2009) 2. In 2008, the Council of State Governments promulgated a resolution against the application of SORNA to juveniles, stating that "[t]he Council of State Governments strongly opposes SORNA's application to juvenile sex offenders and urges Congress to revise the law to more accurately address the needs of juvenile offenders." http://www.csg.org/knowledge center/docs/CSG%20Resolution%20Opposing%20SORNA%20Application%20to%20Juvenile %20Offenders.pdf.... In January 2011, because of that resistance by the states, the attorney general exercised his authority under 42 U.S.C. 16918(c)(4) "to provide that jurisdictions need not publicly disclose information concerning persons required to register on the basis of juvenile delinquency adjudications." 76 Fed.Reg. at 1632.

The change created a new discretionary exemption from public disclosure on the Internet. Moreover, the attorney general announced that jurisdictions are also no longer required to provide registration information to "certain school, public housing, social service, and volunteer entities, and other organizations, companies, or individuals who request notification. * * * Accordingly, if a jurisdiction decides not to include information on a juvenile delinquent sex offender on its public Web site, as is allowed by these supplemental guidelines, information on the sex offender does not have to be disclosed to these entities." 76 Fed.Reg. at 1637.

Thus, in response to the national foot-dragging on SORNA compliance, the attorney general completely lifted the requirement that juveniles be placed on eSORN and that certain entities be notified of their status: "[F]ollowing the issuance of these supplemental guidelines, there is no remaining requirement under SORNA that jurisdictions publicly disclose information about sex offenders whose predicate sex offense 'convictions' are juvenile delinquency adjudications." 76 Fed.Reg. at 1632.... Thus, the attorney general acknowledged that to be SORNA compliant in January 2011 required less in the area of publication of a juvenile's status than it had previously:

> Given this change, the effect of the remaining registration requirements under SORNA for certain juvenile delinquent sex offenders is, in essence, to enable registration authorities to track such offenders following their release and to make information about them available to law enforcement agencies. * * * There is no remaining requirement under SORNA that jurisdictions engage in any form of public disclosure or notification regarding juvenile delinquent sex offenders. Jurisdictions are free to do so, but need not do so to any greater extent than they may wish.

76 Fed.Reg. at 1632.

This declaration is a major shift in policy, reflective of a national consensus against the very policy that Ohio imposed as part of its attempt to comply with SORNA. In short, outside of three other states, the rest of the nation dealt with an entirely different landscape vis-à-vis SORNA. The goalposts had been moved—after Ohio and other states had already instituted a system that the rest of the nation resisted. The assumption that a national consensus favored publication of juvenile sex offenders' personal information had collapsed. Even after the Supplemental Guidelines, as of December 2011, the United States Justice Department has reported that only 15 states are in substantial compliance with SORNA. National Conference of State Legislatures, Adam Walsh Child Protection and Safety Act Compliance News, http://www.ncsl.org/?tabid=12696 (updated Dec. 14, 2011); http://www.governing.com/blogs/fedwatch/States-Find-SORNA-Non-Compliance-Cheaper.html (Nov. 11, 2011)....

Although national consensus is an important factor in the determination of whether a punishment is cruel or unusual, this court must also conduct an independent review of the sentencing practice in question to determine whether it fits within the constraints of the Eighth Amendment. *Graham*, 560 U.S. at ___, 130 S.Ct. at 2026, 176 L.Ed.2d 825, citing Roper, 543 U.S. at 575, 125 S.Ct. 1183, 161 L.Ed.2d 1. "The judicial exercise of independent judgment requires consideration of the culpability of the offenders at issue in light of their crimes and characteristics, along with the severity of the punishment in question, * * * [and] whether the challenged sentencing practice serves legitimate penological goals." *Graham* at 2026, 176 L.Ed.2d 825....

In regard to the culpability of the offenders, we note that Ohio has developed a system for juveniles that assumes that children are not as culpable for their acts as adults. The court's decision in *Graham* supports this self-evident principle:

> *Roper* established that because juveniles have lessened culpability they are less deserving of the most severe punishments. 543 U.S., at 569, 125 S.Ct. 1183. As compared to adults, juveniles have a " 'lack of maturity and an underdeveloped sense of responsibility' "; they "are more vulnerable or susceptible to negative influences and outside pressures, including peer pressure"; and their characters are "not as well formed." *Id.*, at 569–570, 125 S.Ct. 1183. These salient characteristics mean that "[i]t is difficult even for expert psychologists to differentiate between the juvenile offender whose crime reflects unfortunate yet transient immaturity, and the rare juvenile offender whose crime reflects irreparable corruption." *Id.*, at 573, 125 S.Ct. 1183. Accordingly, "juvenile offenders cannot with reliability be classified among the worst offenders." *Id.*, at 569, 125 S.Ct. 1183. A juvenile is not absolved of responsibility for his actions, but his transgression "is not as morally reprehensible as that of an adult." *Thompson* [*v. Oklahoma*, 487 U.S. 815] at 835, 108 S.Ct. 2687, [101 L.Ed.2d 702 (1988)] (plurality opinion).

Graham, 560 U.S. 48, 130 S.Ct. at 2026, 176 L.Ed.2d 825.

Not only are juveniles less culpable than adults, their bad acts are less likely to reveal an unredeemable corruptness:

> Juveniles are more capable of change than are adults, and their actions are less likely to be evidence of "irretrievably depraved character" than are the actions of adults. *Roper*, 543 U.S., at 570, 125 S.Ct. 1183, 161 L.Ed.2d 1. It remains true that "[f]rom a moral standpoint it would be misguided to equate the failings of a minor with those of an adult, for a greater possibility exists that a minor's character deficiencies will be reformed." *Ibid.*

Graham at 2026–2027, 176 L.Ed.2d 825.

In this case we address a lifetime penalty—albeit open to review after 25 years—making the offender's potential for redemption particularly relevant. Juvenile offenders are more capable of change than adult offenders. And again, we are dealing in this case with juveniles who remain under the jurisdiction of the juvenile court. Based on the review of a juvenile judge, juveniles deemed serious youthful offenders have been determined to be amenable to the rehabilitative aims of the juvenile system. They are in a category of offenders that does not include the worst of those who commit crimes as juveniles....

An important consideration in addressing culpability in an independent review of a punishment for Eighth Amendment purposes is the nature of the offenses to which the penalty may apply. In this case, R.C. 2152.86 applies to sex offenses, including rape. R.C. 2152.86(A)(1)(a). In *Graham*, the court stated that "defendants who do not kill, intend to kill, or foresee that life will be taken are categorically less deserving of the most serious forms of punishment than are murderers." *Graham* at 2027, 176 L.Ed.2d 825. The court bluntly noted, "Although an offense like robbery or rape is 'a serious crime deserving serious punishment,' *Enmund [v. Florida*, 458 U.S. 782] at 797, 102 S.Ct. 3368, [73 L.Ed.2d 1140 (1982)], those crimes differ from homicide crimes in a moral sense." *Graham*, 560 U.S. at ____, 130 S.Ct. at 2027, 176 L.Ed.2d 825.... Thus, as the court pointed out in *Graham*, a juvenile who did not kill or intend to kill has "twice diminished moral culpability" on account of his age and the nature of his crime. *Id.* Thus, when we address the constitutionality of the penalties resulting from an application of R.C. 2152.86, we first recognize that those punishments apply to juveniles with a reduced degree of moral culpability....

The next step in the Eighth Amendment analysis is a consideration of the punishment. In this case, as opposed to *Roper* and *Graham*, we are not dealing with the harshest and next-harshest possible sentences, death and life without possibility of parole. Indeed, in this case, if C.P.'s behavior does not warrant the imposition of the adult portion of his SYO sentence, he will not spend time in an adult prison cell. When his juvenile commitment is complete, he will no longer be confined. However, his punishment will continue. Registration and notification requirements for life, with the possibility of having them lifted only after 25 years, are especially harsh punishments for a juvenile. In *Graham*, the court wrote that a life sentence for a juvenile is different from such a sentence for an adult; the juvenile will spend a greater percentage of his life in jail than the adult. *Graham*, 560 U.S. 48, 130 S.Ct. at 2028, 176 L.Ed.2d 825.... Here, too, the registration and notification requirements are different from such a penalty for adults. For juveniles, the length of the punishment is extraordinary, and it is imposed at an age at which the character of the offender is not yet fixed. Registration and notification necessarily involve stigmatization. For a juvenile offender, the stigma of the label of sex offender attaches at the start of his adult life and cannot be shaken. With no other offense is the juvenile's wrongdoing announced to the world. Before a juvenile can even begin his adult life, before he has a chance to live on his own, the world will know of his offense. He will never have a chance to establish a good character in the community. He will be hampered in his education, in his relationships, and in his work life. His potential will be squelched before it has a chance to show itself. A juvenile—one who remains under the authority of the juvenile court and has thus been adjudged redeemable—who is subject to sex-offender notification will have his entire life evaluated through the prism of his juvenile adjudication. It will be a constant cloud, a once-every-three-month reminder to himself and the world that he cannot escape the mistakes of his youth. A youth released at 18 would have to wait until age 43 at the earliest to gain a fresh start. While not a harsh penalty to a career criminal used to serving time in a penitentiary, a lifetime or even 25-year requirement of community notification means everything to a juvenile. It will define his adult life before it has a chance to truly begin....

Finally, in an Eighth Amendment analysis, we must consider the penological justifications for the sentencing practice. *Graham*, 560 U.S. at ___, 130 S.Ct. at 2028, 176 L.Ed.2d 825. Since we are deciding a case involving a juvenile who has not been bound over to adult court, the goals of juvenile disposition are relevant to our analysis. R.C. 2152.01 establishes the purposes of any juvenile disposition:

> (A) The overriding purposes for dispositions under this chapter are to provide for the care, protection, and mental and physical development of children subject to this chapter, protect the public interest and safety, hold the offender accountable for the offender's actions, restore the victim, and rehabilitate the offender. These purposes shall be achieved by a system of graduated sanctions and services.

Lifetime registration and notification requirements run contrary to R.C. 2152.01's goals of rehabilitating the offender and aiding his mental and physical development. Instead, lifetime registration and notification ensure that PRQJORs will encounter continued difficulties, because of their offenses, long into adulthood. Notification and registration anchor the juvenile offender to his crime.... As for protecting the public interest and safety, some might argue that the registration and notification requirements further those aims. However, it is difficult to say how much the public interest and safety are served in individual cases, because the PRQJOR statutory scheme gives the juvenile judge no role in determining how dangerous a child offender might be or what level of registration or notification would be adequate to preserve the safety of the public.... The PRQJOR penalties do meet the statutory objective of accountability. However, a major issue in this case is whether the depth and duration of the accountability that R.C. 2152.86 requires of a juvenile offender are excessive. Another statutory goal, restoring the victim, is advanced only minimally by the requirements of R.C. 2152.86.

In addition to the penological considerations laid out by Ohio's legislature, *Graham* set forth "the goals of penal sanctions that have been recognized as legitimate—retribution, deterrence, incapacitation, and rehabilitation" and considered whether any of those goals justified a sentence of life without parole for juveniles committing nonhomicide crimes. *Id.*, 560 U.S. at ___, 130 S.Ct. at 2028, 176 L.Ed.2d 825.... The court held that retribution could not support the sentence in that case, because "'[t]he heart of the retribution rationale is that a criminal sentence must be directly related to the personal culpability of the criminal offender,' *Tison [v. Arizona*, 481 U.S. 137, 149, 107 S.Ct. 1676, 95 L.Ed.2d 127 (1987)]," and because "'[w]hether viewed as an attempt to express the community's moral outrage or as an attempt to right the balance for the wrong to the victim, the case for retribution is not as strong with a minor as with an adult.' [*Roper*,] 543 U.S., at 571, 125 S.Ct. 1183 [161 L.Ed.2d 1]." *Graham* at 2028, 176 L.Ed.2d 825. As the court recognized in *Graham*, retribution does not justify imposing the same serious penalty on a less culpable defendant.

The court in *Graham* also discounted the penological goal of deterrence for the same reason we do in this case:

> Because juveniles' "lack of maturity and underdeveloped sense of responsibility * * * often result in impetuous and ill-considered actions and decisions," *Johnson v. Texas*, 509 U.S. 350, 367, 113 S.Ct. 2658, 125 L.Ed.2d 290 (1993), they are less likely to take a possible punishment into consideration when making decisions.

Graham, 560 U.S. at ___, 130 S.Ct. at 2028–2029, 176 L.Ed.2d 825. Further, in this case, the significance of the particular punishment and its effects are less likely to be understood by the juvenile than the threat of time in a jail cell. Juveniles are less likely to appreciate the concept of loss of future reputation....

Finally, as to the final penological goal—rehabilitation—we have already discussed the effect of forcing a juvenile to wear a statutorily imposed scarlet letter as he embarks on his adult life. "Community notification may particularly hamper the rehabilitation of juvenile offenders because the public stigma and rejection they suffer will prevent them from developing normal social and interpersonal skills—the lack of those traits [has] been found to contribute to future sexual offenses." Michele L. Earl-Hubbard, *The Child Sex Offender Registration Laws: The Punishment, Liberty Deprivation, and Unintended Results Associated with the Scarlet Letter Laws of the 1990s*, 90 Nw.U.L.Rev. 788, 855–856 (1996).

In addition to increasing the likelihood of reoffense, publication of a juvenile's offense makes reintegration into society more difficult, due in part to the personal economic impact:

> Sex offender registration constitutes an additional form of punishment for juvenile sex offenders, perhaps more substantial than that experienced by adult sex offenders. Many juvenile sex offenders are released back into society after completion of their court-imposed disposition at an age when they would ordinarily first be entering the workforce and find themselves unable to obtain employment due to their publicized "sex offender" label. Any job in education, health care, or the military is virtually impossible to get.

Phoebe Geer, *Justice Served? The High Cost of Juvenile Sex Offender Registration*, 27 Developments in Mental Health Law 33, 48–49 (2008). Any job that requires a background check is placed virtually out of reach. *Id.* And although a PRQJOR's employer's name is not made public under R.C. 2950.11(B)(2), the employer's address is. That fact can only harm a juvenile offender's employment prospects.

The social response to publication of a juvenile's sexual offenses also affects rehabilitation:

> When a sex offender registration and notification law requires door-to-door neighborhood notification, public announcements, or listing on a sex offender website, the likelihood that a juvenile offender's peers and community will discover the offense is very high. Public disclosure may inspire "vigilantism, public shame, social ostracism, and various types of adverse legal action, including loss of employment and eviction."

Id. at 47, quoting Stacey Hiller, *The Problem with Juvenile Sex Offender Registration: The Detrimental Effects of Public Disclosure*, 7 B.U.Pub.Int.L.J. 271, 287 (1998).

We conclude that the social and economic effects of automatic, lifetime registration and notification, coupled with an increased chance of reoffense, do violence to the rehabilitative goals of the juvenile court process. As the court decided in *Graham* in regard to a life sentence without parole for juvenile offenders, we find that penological theory "is not adequate to justify" the imposition of the lifetime registration and notification requirements of R.C. 2152.86 for juveniles. *Graham*, 560 U.S. at ___, 130 S.Ct. at 2030, 176 L.Ed.2d 825.... In sum, the limited culpability of juvenile nonhomicide offenders who remain within the jurisdiction of the juvenile court, the severity of lifetime registration and notification requirements of PRQJOR status, and the inadequacy of penological theory to justify the punishment all lead to the conclusion that the lifetime registration and notification requirements in R.C. 2152.86 are cruel and unusual. We thus hold that for a juvenile offender who remains under the jurisdiction of the juvenile court, the Eighth Amendment forbids the automatic imposition of lifetime sex-offender registration and notification requirements....

R.C. 2152.86 eliminates the discretion of the juvenile judge, this essential element of the juvenile process, at the most consequential part of the dispositional process. R.C. 2152.86 requires the automatic imposition of a lifetime punishment—with no chance of reconsideration for 25 years—without benefit of a juvenile judge weighing its appropriateness. An automatic longterm punishment is contrary to the juvenile system's core emphasis on individual, corrective treatment and rehabilitation. As we held in *In re Caldwell*, 76 Ohio St.3d 156, 157, 666 N.E.2d 1367 (1996),

> [t]he legislative purpose regarding [juveniles] has been laid out in R.C. 2151.01: to provide for the care, protection, and mental and physical development of children, to protect the public from the wrongful acts committed by juvenile delinquents, and to rehabilitate errant children and bring them back to productive citizenship, or, as the statute states, to supervise, care for and rehabilitate those children. Punishment is not the goal of the juvenile system, except as necessary to direct the child toward the goal of rehabilitation.

R.C. 2152.86(B)(1) requires the imposition of an adult penalty for juvenile acts without input from a juvenile judge. Under R.C. 2152.86, the court cannot consider individual factors about a child or his background, cannot have a say in how often a child must register or where he must register, or determine how publication of the offense might affect rehabilitation. An SYO offender remains within the jurisdiction of the juvenile court, but R.C. 2152.86 removes the juvenile court's ability to exercise its most important role in rehabilitation. Fundamental fairness requires that the judge decide the appropriateness of any such penalty.

R.C. 2152.86's automatic imposition of an adult punishment—lifetime reporting and notification—stands in contrast to the R.C. 2152.14 process for invoking the adult portion of the sentence in an SYO disposition. R.C. 2152.14 installs procedural protections for juveniles before the adult portion of their disposition can be invoked. For instance, the juvenile must commit a *further* bad act while in custody before the invocation process can begin. A request must be filed showing that there is reasonable cause to believe that the "person committed an act that is a violation of the rules of the institution and that could be charged as any felony or as a first degree misdemeanor offense of violence if committed by an adult" or that the person "has engaged in conduct that creates a substantial risk to the safety or security of the institution, the community, or the victim." R.C. 2152.14(A)(2)(a) and (b).

Once the request is filed, the adult portion of the sentence cannot be invoked without a public hearing. R.C. 2152.14(D). The juvenile has a right to counsel that may not be waived and the right to present evidence on his own behalf, "including evidence that [he] has a mental illness or is a mentally retarded person." *Id.* If the person submits evidence that he has a mental illness or is mentally retarded, the court must consider that evidence in determining whether to invoke the adult portion of the SYO dispositional sentence.

Further, pursuant to R.C. 2152.14(E)(1), the court must find by clear and convincing evidence not only that the person serving the juvenile portion of an SYO dispositional sentence engaged in the conduct—the additional bad act—he is accused of, but also that the conduct "demonstrates that [he] is unlikely to be rehabilitated during the remaining period of juvenile jurisdiction." And under R.C. 2152.14(E)(2), the juvenile court has the discretion to "modify the adult sentence the court invokes to consist of any lesser prison term that could be imposed for the offense." ... Thus, for the bulk of Ohio's SYO scheme, the juvenile court retains discretion to deal individually with juvenile offenders, and procedural protections are in place before adult punishment can be invoked. Even after additional bad acts by a juvenile, the judge has the discretion not to invoke the adult sentence, or to lessen the one imposed at the time of the juvenile disposition. On the other hand, even for a juvenile who is amenable to rehabilitation and commits no further bad acts during his juvenile disposition, the adult consequences of registration and notification attach immediately. PRQJORs have no right to present evidence or even be heard on the issue of their classification.

Once the juvenile court makes its SYO determination, the juvenile judge never gets an opportunity to determine whether the juvenile offender has responded to rehabilitation or whether he remains a threat to society. Even if the adult portion of his sentence is not invoked, the sex-offender classification is irrevocable. The timing of the classification—immediately upon the imposition of SYO status—leaves no room for the judge to determine whether the juvenile offender has been rehabilitated. And the automatically imposed punishment lasts far longer than the jurisdiction of the juvenile court.... Again, we are dealing with juveniles who remain in the juvenile system through the decision of a juvenile judge—a decision made through the balancing of the factors set forth in R.C. 2152.12(B)—that the juvenile at issue is amenable to the rehabilitative purpose of the juvenile system. The protections and rehabilitative aims of the juvenile process must remain paramount; we must recognize that juvenile offenders are less culpable and more amenable to reform than adult offenders....

We conclude that R.C. 2152.86 is unconstitutional because the penalty it imposes violates the prohibitions against cruel and unusual punishment contained in the Eighth Amendment to the United States Constitution and the Ohio Constitution, Article I, Section 9. Further, we hold that R.C. 2152.86 is unconstitutional because the procedure involved in imposing the punishments violates the Due Process Clause of the Fourteenth Amendment to the United States Constitution and the Ohio Constitution, Article I, Section 16....

Judgment reversed and cause remanded.

O'CONNOR, C.J., and LUNDBERG STRATTON, LANZINGER, and McGEE BROWN, JJ., concur.

O'DONNELL and CUPP, JJ., dissent.... [the opinions are omitted].

Notes

As applied to juveniles, some courts have rejected the argument that public registration is punitive in nature. In *United States v. Juvenile Male*, for example, the Ninth Circuit Court of Appeal determined that application of the federal Sex Offender Registration and Notification Act ("SORNA") to juveniles did not constitute cruel and unusual punishment. 670 F.3d 999, 1010–11 (2012). The court held that although the Act may expose juvenile defendants and their families to potential shame and humiliation for acts committed while still an adolescent, 25 years of registration in a sex offender database is not a disproportionate punishment since the juveniles do not face any risk of incarceration or threat of physical harm. *Id.* Other courts have held that not only do SORNA registration requirements not constitute cruel and unusual punishment, they are not even punitive. *See United States v. May*, 535 F.3d 912, 920 (8th Cir.2008) ("SORNA's registration requirement demonstrates no congressional intent to punish sex offenders"); *see also United States v. Young*, 585 F.3d 199, 204–05 (5th Cir. 2009); *In re Z.B.*, 2008 S.D. 108, 757 N.W.2d 595, ¶ 24 (although striking down state's public-registration statute on equal protection grounds, holding such measures to be regulatory, not penal."); *In re Ronnie A.*, 355 S.C. 407, 409, 585 S.E.2d 311 (2003) ("sex offender registration, regardless of the length of time, is non-punitive"). In the case of *C.P.*, however, the Ohio Supreme Court reversed the Court of Appeals and held that "[t]o the extent that it imposes automatic, lifelong registration and notification requirements on juvenile sex offenders tried within the juvenile system, R.C. 2152.86 violates the constitutional prohibition against cruel and unusual punishment ... and the due process clause...." *In re C.P.*, 131 Ohio St. 3d 513. The court then remanded the case to the trial court. However, the holding in *In re C.P.* left some doubt as to the parameters of punishment that may be imposed on juvenile sex offenders.

Only several months after the decision in *In re C.P.*, the United States Supreme Court decided *Miller v. Alabama*, 132 S. Ct. 2455 (2012), in which the Supreme Court considered the sentences of two defendants—one from Arkansas and the other from Alabama—who were sentenced to mandatory life in prison without the possibility of parole for crimes they committed when they were 14 years old. The Court held that juveniles may not *automatically* be sentenced to life without the possibility of parole under the Eighth Amendment, but may be subject to individualized consideration and punishment. Within the confines of this framework established in *Miller*, upon remand, the trial court in *In re C.P.* vacated its prior order that automatically classified C.P. as a PRQJOR. After a hearing on the matter, the court imposed the same classifications upon C.P., but in a discretionary manner. Following the remand, C.P. appealed the trial court's determination that classified him as a juvenile offender registrant and as a Tier III sex offender and, thereby, subject to the imposition of statutory notification provisions. C.P. argued, first, that the community notification scheme was unconstitutional because it was contrary to the rehabilitative purpose of the juvenile sanctions. He also argued that the scheme violates due process by allowing sanctions that extend beyond the age limitation for juvenile court jurisdiction. However, the trial court refused to consider these claims because C.P. had raised them for the first time on appeal, thereby forfeiting those arguments. *See In re C.P.*, 2013 WL 967898 (Ohio App. 4 Dist), 2013-Ohio-899 (Feb. 22, 2013). For further discussion about *In re C.P.*, see Ben Blumenthal, *In re C.P.: The Ohio Supreme Court's Expansion of* Roper v. Simmons *and* Graham v. Florida *to the Realm of Juvenile Sex Offender Registration*, 41 Hastings Const. L.Q. 457 (2014) (arguing that "*In re C.P.'s* implicit categorical ban on lifetime registration for juveniles is unsustainable under Eighth Amendment jurisprudence."). For further discussion on the application of registration requirements to juvenile offenders, see Carole J. Petersen and Susan M. Chandler, *Sex Offender Registration and the Convention on the Rights of the Child: Legal and Policy Implications of Registering Juvenile Sex Offenders*, 3 William & Mary Policy Rev. 1, 5 (2011) (arguing that "no child should be required to register as a sex offender unless an individualized assessment determines that the juvenile poses a significant risk to the community.").

Chapter Two

Defining Exploitation

I. Sexual Exploitation Through Physical Conduct

A. Sexual Abuse of a Minor

United States v. Ramirez-Garcia

Eleventh Circuit, 2011

646 F.3d 778

HUCK, District Judge: ...

The facts material to this appeal are undisputed. Ramirez-Garcia, a Mexican citizen, illegally entered the United States in May 2000. In 2002, Ramirez-Garcia was arrested in North Carolina and charged with two counts of statutory rape and two counts of taking indecent liberties with a child. The latter charges were brought pursuant to N.C. Gen.Stat. § 14-202.1, which states:

> (a) A person is guilty of taking indecent liberties with children if, being 16 years of age or more and at least five years older than the child in question, he either:
>
> (1) Willfully takes or attempts to take any immoral, improper, or indecent liberties with any child of either sex under the age of 16 years for the purpose of arousing or gratifying sexual desire; or
>
> (2) Willfully commits or attempts to commit any lewd or lascivious act upon or with the body or any part or member of the body of any child of either sex under the age of 16 years.

Ramirez-Garcia pled guilty to the two counts of taking indecent liberties with a child, receiving a sentence of two consecutive terms of 20–24 months. The record does not reveal how Ramirez-Garcia violated § 14-202.1.... The Transcript of Plea—which is a form, not an actual transcript—and the Judgment and Commitment forms indicate that Ramirez-Garcia pled guilty to taking indecent liberties with a child, without specifying whether Ramirez-Garcia's actions violated the first or second prong of N.C. Gen.Stat. § 14-202.1(a). The Transcript of Plea reveals that the State dismissed the statutory rape charges in exchange for Ramirez-Garcia's guilty pleas to taking indecent liberties with a child. In 2005, upon his release from prison, immigration authorities deported Ramirez-Garcia to Mexico....

Prior to the sentencing hearing, the United States Probation Office determined that Ramirez-Garcia's base level offense score under the guidelines was 8, pursuant to USSG

§ 2L1.2. Ramirez-Garcia did not contest that calculation. He did, however, object to the Probation Office's recommendation that the court impose a 16-level enhancement pursuant to USSG § 2L1.2(b)(1)(A). The Probation Office reasoned that Ramirez-Garcia's prior convictions for taking indecent liberties with a child were "crimes of violence" pursuant to the Sentencing Guidelines because they involved "sexual abuse of a minor." ... [footnote omitted]. Combined with reductions for acceptance of responsibility, the Probation Office calculated that Ramirez-Garcia's total offense level was 21.... Ramirez-Garcia objected to the Probation Office's recommendation, arguing that the North Carolina offense of taking indecent liberties with a child encompassed acts not included in the definition of "sexual abuse of a minor." The Probation Office rejected that argument and submitted its findings and recommendations to the district court. The district court held a sentencing hearing, at which Ramirez-Garcia repeated his assertion that the North Carolina convictions were not "crimes of violence" because they did not constitute "sexual abuse of a minor." ... The district court concluded that the North Carolina offense was "a similar crime" to sexual abuse of a minor.... Thus, the district [court] found that the 16-level sentencing enhancement was appropriate....

The Court has held that "sexual abuse of a minor," as referenced in § 2L1.2 of the Sentencing Guidelines, is "a perpetrator's physical or nonphysical misuse or maltreatment of a minor for a purpose associated with sexual gratification." *United States v. Padilla-Reyes*, 247 F.3d 1158, 1163 (11th Cir.2001). In *Padilla-Reyes*, the Eleventh Circuit defined "sexual abuse of a minor" using *Webster's Third New International Dictionary* and *Black's Law Dictionary* in order to give the words their plain meaning that comports with common usage. The Court focused on "the perpetrator's intent in committing the abuse[,] ... to seek libidinal gratification." 247 F.3d at 1163. The Court noted that the plain meaning of "abuse" includes "acts that involve physical contact between the perpetrator and the victim and acts that do not." *Id.*

Ramirez-Garcia urges the Court to reconsider the definition of "sexual abuse of a minor" that it formulated in *Padilla-Reyes*. Ramirez-Garcia asserts that, in *Padilla-Reyes*, the Court failed to derive a generic, contemporary definition of "sexual abuse of a minor," as required by the Supreme Court in *Taylor v. United States*, 495 U.S. 575, 110 S.Ct. 2143, 109 L.Ed.2d 607 (1990). Ramirez-Garcia contends we must look to "definitions of the [enumerated offense] adopted in the various states, criminal law treatises, and the Model Penal Code to formulate a generic, contemporary definition of the crime." *See Palomino Garcia*, 606 F.3d at 1327–28 (describing the Supreme Court's process in *Taylor* for deriving a generic definition of the traditional, common-law offense of burglary)....

Ramirez-Garcia's assertion that the *Padilla-Reyes* court failed to properly formulate a generic definition of "sexual abuse of a minor" is incorrect. While courts should consult state definitions, treatises, and the Model Penal Code when deriving a generic definition of traditional, common law offenses like burglary and aggravated assault, the present case involves "sexual abuse of a minor," which is a non-traditional offense. *United States v. Baza-Martinez*, 464 F.3d 1010, 1015 (9th Cir.2006). For offenses not developed in the common law, courts define a generic offense based on " 'the ordinary, contemporary, and common meaning' of the statutory words [,]" which involves "coupl[ing] the dictionary definition of 'abuse' with the common understanding of 'sexual' and 'minor.' " *Id.* (internal citations omitted); *United States v. Lopez-Solis*, 447 F.3d 1201, 1206–07 (9th Cir.2006). Other circuits have taken this approach when defining the phrase "sexual abuse of a minor" as used in the Sentencing Guidelines. *See, e.g., United States v. Sonnenberg*, 556 F.3d 667, 670 (8th Cir.2009); *United States v. Diaz-Ibarra*, 522 F.3d 343, 349 (4th Cir.2008); *United States v. Izaguirre-Flores*, 405 F.3d 270, 275 (5th Cir.2005). In *Padilla-Reyes*, our Court implemented this same approach, relying on dictionary definitions to give the words in "sexual abuse of a minor" a plain meaning that comports with common usage. 247 F.3d at 1163.... [footnote omitted]. Ramirez-Garcia cites no authority indicating that this Court may reexamine *Padilla-Reyes* and redefine "sexual abuse of a minor" utilizing the analysis employed for traditional, common law offenses such as assault and burglary. Importantly, Ramirez-Garcia cannot cite any authority that enables this Court to overturn *Padilla-Reyes*, which is binding precedent, except upon en banc review or reversal by the Supreme Court. *See United States v. Vega-Castillo*, 540 F.3d 1235, 1236 (11th Cir.2008).

Having determined in *Padilla-Reyes* that "sexual abuse of a minor" is "a perpetrator's physical or nonphysical misuse or maltreatment of a minor for a purpose associated with sexual gratification," the Court need only ensure that the scope of this definition is no narrower than the scope of the North Carolina offense of taking indecent liberties with a child. 247 F.3d at 1163. The Court previously has held that the term "sexual abuse of a minor," as used in 8 U.S.C. § 1101(a)(43)(A), includes the conduct proscribed by § 14-202.1, the North Carolina offense of taking liberties with a child. *Bahar v. Ashcroft*, 264 F.3d 1309, 1311 (11th Cir.2001). It is clear that the North Carolina statute is no broader than *Padilla-Reyes'* definition of "sexual abuse of a minor" for the purpose of USSG § 2L1.2.

"Misuse" or "maltreatment" are expansive words that include many different acts. The *Padilla-Reyes* definition does not limit "sexual abuse of a minor" to instances where the perpetrator is present in front of the minor, where the minor is aware of the abuse, or where the perpetrator makes contact with the minor. The North Carolina statute is similarly broad, but no broader. North Carolina courts have found that the following persons violated § 14-202.1: (1) a high school basketball coach who covertly video-taped a student changing clothes, *State v. McClees*, 108 N.C.App. 648, 424 S.E.2d 687 (1993); (2) a karate instructor who had sexually explicit and graphic phone conversations with a pupil, *State v. Every*, 157 N.C.App. 200, 578 S.E.2d 642 (2003); (3) a man who gave a sexually graphic note to his minor neighbor, which included requests that she participate in sexual activity with him, *State v. McClary*, 198 N.C.App. 169, 679 S.E.2d 414 (2009); and (4) a man who masturbated in a bed next to a young girl, *State v. Hammett*, 182 N.C.App. 316, 642 S.E.2d 454 (2007). Although none of these offenses involved contact with a minor, and some even did not involve the perpetrator's presence in front of the minor, North Carolina state courts determined that all involved taking indecent liberties with a child. It is clear that all these acts also are encompassed within the *Padilla-Reyes* generic, federal definition — they all involve either misuse or maltreatment of a minor for the perpetrator's sexual gratification.[10] Ramirez-Garcia points to no North Carolina cases involving facts that do not fit within the contours of the broad *Padilla-Reyes* definition, nor any hypothetical situation that would violate N.C. Gen.Stat. § 14-202.1 while avoiding *Padilla-Reyes'* definition. Thus, the Court finds that the *Padilla-Reyes* definition of "sexual abuse of a minor" is at least as broad and inclusive as § 14-202.1.

For the reasons given, the Court affirms the judgment of the district court.

AFFIRMED.

---

10. Both definitions focus on the abuser's purpose, rather than any apparent harm to the minor. *Compare Diaz-Ibarra*, 522 F.3d at 350 ("[O]nce a defendant misuses the minor with the intent to achieve sexual gratification, the act of abuse is complete, irrespective of whether the minor suffered some physical or psychological injury."), *with State v. Hartness*, 326 N.C. 561, 391 S.E.2d 177, 180 (1990) (noting a "[d]efendant's purpose for committing such act is the gravamen of this offense; the particular act performed is immaterial"), *and State v. McClary*, 198 N.C.App. 169, 679 S.E.2d 414, 418 (2009) ("Neither a completed sex act nor an offensive touching of the victim are required to violate the statute.").

Notes

As stated by the court in *Ramirez-Garcia*, and supported by the cases discussed therein, sexual abuse of a minor may be determined, not by the harmful consequences for the child or the specific conduct of the abuser, but by the intent of the abuser to gain sexual gratification through his or her conduct. There does not need to be specific physical contact by the abuser or a threshold level of resulting harm to the child for sexual abuse to have occurred. *See, e.g., Arkansas Department of Human Services v. R.F.,* 2013 Ark. App. 694 (2013) (defendant father guilty of sexual abuse of a minor where father forced seven-year-old autistic son, who suffered with cerebral palsy and was restricted to wheel chair, to watch pornography on television). The purposeful use of the child to gain sexual gratification is determinative in *Ramirez-Garcia.* Compare this approach with the qualification employed in the following case — *In re A.B.* — in which the abuser has no intent to gain sexual gratification through his conduct. Why is the conduct, nevertheless, qualified as sexual abuse?

In re A.B.

Court of Appeal, Fourth District, California, 2011
Not Reported in Cal. 3d, 2011 WL 193402 Rptr.

ARONSON, J....

On the morning of December 4, 2008, 14-year-old M.R. stood on the track at her Santa Ana intermediate school with two other girls. She wore gym shorts and a T-shirt, and had just completed a run with her second period physical education (PE) class. While the girls chatted about weekend plans, M.R. had her back turned to other students, who continued to run around the track. She felt someone poke her bottom. She described it as quick, hard poke with a finger to the center of her buttocks, penetrating about an inch. She turned and saw 13-year-old A.B. standing with other boys about a foot away. She did not know A.B. well, but their PE classes ran together weekly.... Angry, she asked him why he jabbed her. A.B. walked away laughing with his companions. She followed, said something she did not recall, and A.B. responded by her calling her a "bitch." She responded with another comment, and walked away. A.B. then exclaimed he "fucked [her] mother." She replied, " 'What you say?' " ... and took a step toward him. He pushed her, and she pushed him back. A.B. spit at her. She walked toward him, and he grabbed her arms and spit at her again. She pulled away and then tripped him to the ground. M.R. also fell and began hitting A.B. in the face. He pulled her hair and slapped her. They rolled on the ground and grappled until a teacher separated them. During the fracas, M.R. scratched A.B.'s face and bit his shoulder....

A.B. told the school police officer he "accidentally" touched M.R. in the "butt area." He testified he accidentally bumped into M.R. and her friend while racing around the track. He apologized and kept running, but M.R. came after him and started hitting him. He grabbed her hands, she bit him on the shoulder, and they fell to the ground. He denied laughing, making the statements about her and her mother, pulling her hair or hitting her. After serving a five-day school suspension, he returned to class, he testified, and M.R. apologized to him for lying. A.B. explained he did not tell the school police officer "everything" because he was nervous and scared.

Following a jurisdictional hearing concluding in February 2010, the juvenile court found A.B. committed sexual battery. The court declared him to be a ward and placed him on probation subject to various terms and conditions including counseling, 40 hours of community service and preparation of a written apology letter to M.R.... A.B. challenges the sufficiency of the evidence to support the finding he committed sexual battery. Specifically, he asserts the evidence shows he touched the victim only to annoy or irritate her and not for the purposes of sexual abuse. We agree with A.B. the evidence does not show he touched the victim for sexual arousal or gratification. The issue therefore is whether his conduct constituted sexual abuse under section 243.4. Section 243.4 provides: "(e)(1) Any person who touches an intimate part of another person, if the touching is against the will of the person touched, and is for the specific purpose of sexual arousal, sexual gratification, or sexual abuse, is guilty of misdemeanor sexual battery...." A "touch" is defined as "physical contact with another person, whether accomplished directly, through the clothing of the person committing the offense, or through the clothing of the victim." (§ 243.4, subd. (f).) " 'Intimate part' means the sexual organ, anus, groin, or buttocks of any person, and the breast of a female." (§ 243.4, subd. (g)(1).)

In re Shannon T. (2006) 144 Cal.App.4th 618 (Shannon T.) supports the juvenile court's finding. There, the appellate court concluded the term "sexual abuse" in section 243.4 encompassed "a purpose of insulting, humiliating, intimidating, or physically harming a person sexually by touching an 'intimate part' of the person...." (Shannon T., supra, 144 Cal.App.4th at p. 621.) In Shannon T., a 14-year-old boy approached a 16-year-old girl at school and said, " 'Get off the phone. You're my "ho." ' " The girl responded " 'whatever,' " and continued to talk on her cell phone, but the minor pursued her, complaining, " 'Don't talk to me like that.' " He slapped her face, grabbed her arm, and pinched her breast, causing her to cry. The pinch resulted in a small bruise above her left nipple. The victim acknowledged she and the minor had been friends and had previously engaged in playful hitting.... The minor challenged the finding he committed sexual battery, arguing the evidence showed he did not touch the victim's breast for the purpose of "sexual arousal, sexual gratification, or sexual abuse." The appellate court disagreed, concluding the term "sexual abuse" was "not limited to causing physical injury to the person; it includes causing emotional harm by the use of offensive conduct.... [C]onduct intended to insult or humiliate a person is the 'abuse' of that person. [Citation.]" (Shannon T., supra, 144 Cal.App.4th at p. 622.) The court stated, "The lesson learned is that, in a civilized society, mature people ordinarily do not touch the intimate parts of other people without consent, and that a person who does so acts at his or her peril of being found to have committed sexual battery." (Id. at p. 623.)

A.B. contends Shannon T. was wrongly decided. He complains the court "cherry-pick[ed]" definitions of "abuse," erred by defining the term "abuse" rather than interpreting the statute's reference to "sexual abuse," and ignored other definitions of "sexual abuse." He also asserts "abuse" has several meanings, and Shannon T. should have applied the rule of lenity and narrowly construed the term to require an intent to cause pain, injury or physical discomfort.

In construing section 243.4's proscription against unconsented touching of a person's intimate parts "for the specific purpose of sexual arousal, sexual gratification, or sexual abuse," we must, if possible, give significance to all the words in a statute; therefore, we must avoid constructions that would render some words surplusage.... [citation omitted]. Accordingly, the Legislature must have intended the term "sexual abuse" in section 243.4 to cover conduct other than an unconsented touching solely for sexual arousal or gratification.

Relying on People v. White (1986) 179 Cal.App.3d 193 (White), A.B. contends the Legislature inserted the word "sexual" before the words "gratification" and "abuse" to proscribe conduct intended to cause injury or pain. In White, the defendant physically injured an infant when he inserted his finger in the child's anus. The defendant was convicted of violating section 289, which prohibited sexual penetration "for the purpose of sexual arousal, gratification or abuse." The appellate court rejected the defendant's argument that the term "sexual abuse" in section 289 required the perpetrator to act with a lewd or sexual motive, explaining that "[t]he term 'abuse' imports an intent to injure or hurt badly, not lewdness." (*White, supra,* 179 Cal.App.3d at p. 205.) Following *White,* A.B. concludes the evidence is insufficient to support his conviction because his touching annoyed but did not injure the victim.

As the Attorney General notes, there is a significant difference between section 289, the statute considered in *White,* and sexual battery. With sexual penetration, the act must be accomplished against the victim's will "by means of force, violence, duress, menace, or fear of immediate and unlawful bodily injury...." (§ 289.) But a battery is committed by any touching of an intimate part of another person against the person's will. (§ 243.4, subd. (e)(1).) Considering the different evils each statute addresses, it is not incongruous to define sexual abuse under section 289 as conduct intended to cause pain or injury, while broadly defining sexual abuse to establish sexual battery. Indeed, *Shannon T.* discussed *White* in comparing the two statutes and concluded the sexual battery statute did not require the perpetrator to inflict the same type of harm that must be shown under the statute prohibiting sexual penetration....

Finally, A.B. argues *Shannon T.* failed to consider the serious consequences flowing from its holding. Correctly noting that an adult convicted under section 243.4 must register as a sex offender for life (§ 290, subd. (c)), and may not reside within 2000 feet of schools and parks (§ 3003.5, subd. (b)), he argues, "[i]t is difficult to believe the Legislature intended that sexual harassment become a sex registerable offense."... [footnote omitted]. We may not assume *Shannon T.* failed to consider these consequences. In any event, A.B.'s argument is more appropriately addressed to the Legislature. We are in no position to say these consequences are inappropriate for an adult who touches intimate portions of another's body for the purpose of insult or humiliation. Moreover, A.B.'s argument appears to assume sex offender registration applies only to crimes committed with a sexual motivation. *White,* which A.B. does not criticize, did not involve a sexual intent.

A.B. does not dispute sufficient evidence supports the juvenile court's finding he touched an intimate part of M.R.'s body for the purpose of insulting or humiliating her.... [citation omitted]. The purpose may be inferred from his conduct in laughing with his companions after he touched her, as well as his derogatory language after she confronted him. Substantial evidence supports the finding A.B. committed sexual battery....

The judgment is affirmed.

WE CONCUR: RYLAARSDAM, Acting P.J., and FYBEL, J.

Notes

The offensive conduct in *In re A.B.* is held to constitute sexual abuse, not because the abuser obtained sexual gratification from the conduct, but because he touched an intimate body part of his victim, without her consent, for the purpose of insulting or humiliating her. Note that for this specific sexual abuse provision (sexual battery), the abuser need not inflict any injury or pain. The mere touching of an intimate body part, without consent, is sufficient. And, as the court in *A.B.* notes, the consequences for the abuser with respect to registering as a sex offender are the same as for any other sex offender.

Congress has defined sexual abuse as "caus[ing] another person to engage in a sexual act by threatening or placing that other person in fear" or engaging in a sexual act with another person who is "incapable of appraising the nature of the conduct or [is] physically incapable of declining participation in, or communicating unwillingness to engage in, that sexual act...." 18 U.S.C. § 2242. When such conduct is committed, or is attempted to be committed, by force or by threat of death, serious bodily injury, or kidnapping, such conduct is defined as "aggravated sexual abuse." *See* 18 U.S.C. § 2241 (also includes engaging in, or attempting to engage in, a sexual act with another person who is rendered unconscious or qualifiedly impaired). If such conduct is knowingly committed, or attempted, with someone between the ages of 12 and 16 who is at least 4 years younger than the offender, then the offender shall be imprisoned for not less than 30 years or for life. *Id.* If the victim is under 12 years old, then the offender need only intend to commit such conduct to be convicted. *Id.* Where such acts are committed, or attempted, on a minor without force, the prison sentence will be not more than 15 years. *See* 18 U.S.C. § 2243(a).

Under state law, typically the abuser must be older than the victim. *See, e.g.,* ALASKA STAT. §§ 11.41.434 (sexual abuse of a minor in the first degree) and 11.41.436 (sexual abuse of a minor in the second degree, requiring various age parameters for different qualifying acts); ARK. CODE § 5-14-124(c) (affirmative defense to sexual assault in the first degree that "actor was not more than three (3) years older than the victim); TEX. PENAL CODE § 21.11 (affirmative defense to "indecency with a child" that the actor "was not more than three years older than the victim and of the opposite sex). For certain offenses, some states require only that the victim be a specific age. *See, e.g.,* 18 PA. CONSOL. STAT. ANN. § 3121 ("A person commits the offense of rape of a child, a felony in the first degree, when the person engages in sexual intercourse with a complainant who is less than 13 years of age."); R.I. GEN. LAWS § 11-37-8.1 ("A person is guilty of first degree child molestation sexual assault if he or she engages in sexual penetration with a person fourteen (14) years of age or under."). Other states may require that the perpetrator be a specific number of years older than the victim to constitute the named offense. *See, e.g.,* N.Y. PENAL LAW § 130.65 ("A person is guilty of sexual abuse in the first degree when he or she subjects another person to sexual contact ... [w][hen the other person is less than eleven years old; or ... [w]hen the other person is less than thirteen years old and the actor is twenty-one years old or older."); N.C. GEN. STAT. § 14-27.7A (varying felony classes for defendant who engages in a sexual act with a victim who is 13, 14, or 15 years old and "the defendant is at least six years older than the person" or "more than four but less than six years older than the person."); TENN. CODE ANN. § 39-13-506 (defining various classes of statutory rape depending on various age differences between the victim and the offender).

B. Sexual Exploitation of a Minor

United States v. Bach

Eighth Circuit, 2005
400 F.3d 622

MURPHY, Circuit Judge....

In October 2000 Sergeant Brook Schaub of the St. Paul Police Department was contacted by a mother concerned about a document on her family computer. It contained a partial log of a communication between her minor son (AM) ... [footnote omitted] and someone using the name "dlbch15," asking if AM wanted to see dlbch15 again and to suggest a place where he could hide something for AM. Dlbch15 added that he would like to see AM if he were going to drive to St. Paul to deliver it. When the police questioned AM about this message, he said it had been received in a chat room on the website www.yahoo.com and that dlbch15 planned to hide Playboy magazines for him in the bushes near a business on Ford Parkway. AM admitted that he had met dlbch15 on Ford Parkway, but he denied any sexual contact with him. Police showed AM a photo of [the defendant, Dale Robert] Bach, but he did not identify him as dlbch15.

When Sergeant Schaub accessed the user profile … [footnote omitted] for dlbch15 at Yahoo!, he found it listed a male named Dale, age 26, from Minneapolis. Schaub also discovered that the nickname dlbch15 was linked to the email address dlbch15@prodigy.com, and he sent an administrative subpoena to Prodigy seeking subscriber information. Prodigy identified Dale Bach as the subscriber and listed his address and telephone number. Further investigation revealed that Bach was a registered sex offender because of a 1995 state conviction for criminal sexual conduct in the third degree, involving sex with a fourteen year old boy…. Schaub sent a letter to Yahoo!, requesting that it retain on its server any incoming or outgoing email messages associated with the account dlbch15@yahoo.com. He then obtained a Ramsey County search warrant on January 3, 2001, seeking Yahoo! emails between dlbch15 and possible victims of criminal sexual conduct, including but not limited to AM. The warrant also sought internet protocol addresses (IPs)[4] linking dlbch15 to possible victims of criminal sexual conduct or of online enticement for sexual purposes. The warrant was faxed from Minnesota to Yahoo! in Santa Clara, California…. Five days later Schaub received a package from Yahoo!. Inside was a zip disk containing all of the emails preserved in the accounts belonging to AM and Bach (dlbch15@yahoo.com). Yahoo! also sent printed copies of six emails retrieved from Bach's account. Among them was one dated August 1, 2000, apparently a reply to a message from dlbch15@yahoo.com about meeting the next day and exchanging pictures. Other email messages concerned dlbch15's meeting and exchanging pictures with various individuals.

One email in Bach's account had been received from Fabio Marco in Italy; that transmission is the basis for Bach's conviction for receiving child pornography. Marco's email to Bach had an attached photograph which showed a young nude boy sitting in a tree, grinning, with his pelvis tilted upward, his legs opened wide, and a full erection. Below the image was the name of AC, a well known child entertainer. Evidence at trial showed that a photograph of AC's head had been skillfully inserted onto the photograph of the nude boy so that the resulting image appeared to be a nude picture of AC posing in the tree.

In some of his email messages, dlbch15 directed the recipient to visit a particular site to view a picture of himself. The individual pictured at that site looks like Bach's driver license photo. The Yahoo! files also revealed that dlbch15 used other screen names, including "seeknboyz" and one incorporating Bach's telephone number. The registration material associated with the Yahoo! account listed Minneapolis as dlbch15's residence and December 27, 1958 as his birthdate, the same day as Bach's. Since Yahoo! was not Bach's internet service provider, it was unable to generate and provide IPs linking him to other addresses.

---

4. An IP is generated when one computer connects with another through the internet; each IP is unique to a particular computer at the time of the connection and can be used to identify the source of the connection.

Officers obtained a search warrant to search Bach's residence near the end of January 2001. The warrant authorized seizure of computer hard drives, storage devices, and other evidence tending "to show the possession or distribution of child pornography or the enticement of children online." The warrant was executed on January 29, and officers seized various items, including Bach's computer, his disks, and a digital camera. Among the effects seized were seven digital camera images which Bach had taken in August 2000 of a boy engaging in sexually explicit conduct. These pictures were of RH, who testified at trial that he was the boy in the photos and that he had been sixteen at the time they were made. The trial evidence also showed that one photograph of RH had been sent on the internet from Bach's computer to another minor with whom he corresponded.... [T]he case was presented to the jury on four counts.... Count 7 charged Bach with employing a minor to produce visual depictions of the minor involved in sexually explicit conduct in interstate or foreign commerce (pictures of RH), in violation of 18 U.S.C. § 2251(a). Bach was convicted on all four counts, and the district court imposed concurrent sentences of 121 months for counts 1, 4, and 6 and 180 months for count 7....

Bach's final argument relates to his sentence on count 7. The district court sentenced him to 15 years on his conviction on that count under 18 U.S.C. § 2251(a), for employing a minor to produce a visual depiction of the minor involved in sexually explicit conduct. At the time of Bach's offense there was a mandatory minimum punishment of 15 years for a § 2251(a) conviction, if the defendant had been previously convicted under state law for an offense "relating to the sexual exploitation of children." 18 U.S.C. § 2251(d) (2001). Although Congress amended the statute in 2003 to increase the mandatory minimum punishment to 25 years by adding § 2251(e), Bach was appropriately sentenced under the lower mandatory term rather than the one in effect at the time of sentencing.... Bach contends that the district court erred in imposing the mandatory minimum sentence, arguing that his prior state conviction did not relate to the sexual exploitation of children but to child abuse, and so his conviction did not fit within the federal statute's triggering definition. He asserts that his 1995 Minnesota conviction for third degree criminal sexual conduct did not involve the production of child pornography and that due process and the rule of lenity require that the term "sexual exploitation of children" be strictly construed against the government and in his favor.

Bach argues that the legislative history of the Protection of Children Against Sexual Exploitation Act of 1977 under which § 2251 was initially enacted, supports his interpretation in that its purpose was to curtail the production and widespread trafficking of child pornography. *See* S.Rep. No. 95-438 (1977). His conviction for criminal sexual conduct had nothing to do with this activity he asserts. Congress was aware of the distinction between "sexual exploitation of children" and "child abuse" he says, because it distinguished the two terms in other federal statutes. He mentions as an example 18 U.S.C. § 3509, which defines exploitation as "child pornography or child prostitution" and child abuse as "the physical or mental injury, sexual abuse or exploitation, or negligent treatment of a child." He points out that the title of Chapter 110, 18 U.S.C. §§ 2251–2260, is "Sexual Exploitation and Other Abuse of Children" while § 2251, which criminalizes the manufacture of child pornography, is entitled "Sexual exploitation of children."

The government argues that Bach's argument is misplaced, pointing out that this court specifically held in *United States v. Smith*, 367 F.3d 748, 751 (8th Cir.2004), that the term "[sexual exploitation of children] unambiguously refers to any criminal sexual conduct with a child." The Minnesota statute on criminal sexual conduct in the third degree covers sexual penetration of a child between 13 and 16. Minn.Stat. § 609.344 subd. 1(b). The government asserts that this Minnesota statutory definition of criminal sexual conduct covers the exact type of conduct Congress had in mind when it created the § 2251(d) enhancement, citing *United States v. Galo*, 239 F.3d 572, 581–82 (3d Cir.2001) (in applying the § 2251(d) enhancement, court should look to statutory definition of prior offense rather than to the conduct giving rise to the conviction).

Bach responds that even though we held in *Smith* that "sexual exploitation of children" includes any criminal sexual conduct with a child, we should now apply the rule of lenity because *Smith* did not involve a due process challenge to the interpretation of § 2251(d). We reject this contention. The defendant in *Smith* had also argued that "sexual exploitation of children" is limited to pornography or criminal sexual conduct captured in visual depictions, but the argument was rejected. Although the federal statute does not define the term sexual exploitation of children, it covers "any criminal sexual conduct with a child [which by its very nature] takes advantage of, or exploits, a child sexually." *Smith*, 367 F.3d at 751. We also observed that the federal crimes listed in § 2251(d) as triggering the mandatory minimum penalty were not limited to offenses involving pornography or visual depictions. *Id.* In *Smith* we held that the term "sexual exploitation of children" unambiguously refers to any criminal sexual conduct with a child, and the rule of lenity does not apply where a statute is unambiguous. *Moskal v. United States*, 498 U.S. 103, 107–08, 111 S.Ct. 461, 112 L.Ed.2d 449 (1990). We conclude that the district court did not err by imposing a mandatory minimum sentence under § 2251(d) based on Bach's state court conviction for engaging in criminal sexual conduct with a child....

We therefore affirm the judgment of the district court....

Notes

Under federal and state law, there may be distinct definitions of child sexual abuse and child sexual exploitation. *See, e.g., State v. Bishop*, 753 P.2d 439 (Utah 1988) (where defendant took nude photographs of child, court distinguished between "sexual abuse of a child" statute and "sexual exploitation of a minor" statute on the basis that the sexual abuse statute "proscribes conduct involving the touching of children and the taking of indecent liberties with children," whereas the purpose of the sexual exploitation statute was to criminalize the commercial production of child pornography and eliminate the market for such materials). For relevant federal statutes, see 18 U.S.C. §§ 2251 (Sexual exploitation of children), 2252 (Certain activities relating to material involving the sexual exploitation of minors), and 2256 (definitions). However some definitions of child abuse include sexual exploitation, which typically is more narrowly defined to include conduct related to the commercial use of child pornography. *See, e.g.*, 18 U.S.C. § 3509(a) (for purposes of "Child victims' and child witnesses' rights," "the term 'sexual abuse' includes the employment, use, persuasion, inducement, enticement, or coercion of a child to engage in, or assist another person to engage in sexually explicit conduct or the rape, molestation, prostitution, or other form of sexual exploitation of children, or incest with children.").

As demonstrated in the *Bach* decision, child sexual exploitation may be broadly construed to involve any criminal sexual conduct that exploits children. In *Brackins v. State*, 84 Md. App. 157, 578 A.2d 300 (1990), for example, the defendant stepfather partially disrobed his 12-year-old stepdaughter and took a seminude Polaroid snapshot of her. He then discarded the photograph within seconds of taking it; he made no commercial use of the photograph. The court held that he exploited the child when he disrobed her for his own pleasure and that the Polaroid snapshot was not a necessary element of the exploitation. The court held that this exploitation was sufficient to satisfy the child abuse statute. In *State v. Oliver*, 2008 WL 5226649 (Mo. App. S.D.), the defendant possessed digital photographs of young boys "touching their own buttocks to reveal their anuses for the purpose of the 'apparent sexual stimulation or gratification ...' of the viewer of the photograph...." The defendant argued that the legislature could not have intended to prohibit photographing nude children under the statute prohibiting sexual exploitation of a minor because that conduct was already prohibited under the statute prohibiting abuse of a child. However, the court held that the conduct may be prohibited under both statutes and that the State has the discretion to decide under which statutory scheme to charge the defendant. *Id.* at *10. As other categories of child sexual exploitation are discussed, note the expansive application of statutory definitions.

State v. Chester

Supreme Court of Washington, 1997
133 Wash. 2d 15, 940 P.2d 1374

GUY, Justice....

Defendant Gary Chester was convicted of sexual exploitation of a minor based on his secret filming of his 14-year-old stepdaughter, while the stepdaughter was in her bedroom dressing for school.... On the morning of January 12, 1994, while the stepdaughter was in the shower, the Defendant placed a video camera under the child's bed, aiming it toward a mirror on the closet door. The beginning of the videotape, ... shows the Defendant setting up the camera, covering a portion of the camera with clothing or bedding, and then leaving the room. The videotape then shows Defendant's stepdaughter walking into the room, wrapped in a towel. The tape goes on to show the stepdaughter walking in and out of the picture as she dressed. The videotape shows the stepdaughter from the front and back, both unclothed and partially clothed.

Testimony showed that the Defendant initially explained his actions as a "dumb joke" and that he was playing "Candid Camera." According to the State's evidence, he eventually admitted that he expected to see his stepdaughter in some state of undress because she would be coming out of the shower. He reportedly said he did not give much thought to whether she would be naked or wearing some type of underwear or bra. Police testified that he also said he thought he might see her in a pose bending over in her underwear.... A jury found Defendant Chester guilty of sexual exploitation of a minor, with a special finding that he acted with sexual motivation.... [footnote omitted]. The Court of Appeals reversed his conviction, holding there was insufficient evidence under the statute to convict. *State v. Chester*, 82 Wash.App. 422, 918 P.2d 514, *review granted*, 130 Wash.2d 1016, 928 P.2d 412 (1996). We granted the State's petition for review....

The provisions of the sexual exploitation of children statute which are pertinent to this case are the following:

RCW 9.68A.040. Sexual exploitation of a minor—Elements of crime—Penalty.

(1) A person is guilty of sexual exploitation of a minor if the person:

(a) Compels a minor by threat or force to engage in sexually explicit conduct, knowing that such conduct will be photographed or part of a live performance;

(b) Aids, invites, employs, authorizes, or causes a minor to engage in sexually explicit conduct, knowing that such conduct will be photographed or part of a live performance; or

(c) Being a parent, legal guardian, or person having custody or control of a minor, permits the minor to engage in sexually explicit conduct, knowing that the conduct will be photographed or part of a live performance.

(2) Sexual exploitation of a minor is a class B felony punishable under chapter 9A.20 RCW.

RCW 9.68A.011. Definitions.

....

(3) "Sexually explicit conduct" means actual or simulated:

....

(e) Exhibition of the genitals or unclothed pubic or rectal areas of any minor, or the unclothed breast of a female minor, for the purpose of sexual stimulation of the viewer....

The Court of Appeals held that, under subsection (b) of the statute, the State was required to prove that the Defendant initiated, influenced or otherwise caused the child to exhibit her breasts or pubic area and that the exhibition was initiated for the purpose of sexually stimulating the viewer. The Court of Appeals then held that, under the facts of this case, there was insufficient evidence to support the conviction under this subsection....

The State argues that the Court of Appeals' interpretation of the statute as requiring influence or communication with the child adds an element to the crime which the Legislature did not contemplate. The State argues that the statute prohibits all photographs of children that are taken for the purpose of sexually stimulating the viewer. Defendant Chester challenges this interpretation of the statute as unconstitutionally vague or overbroad. This statute has previously withstood constitutional challenges in this court and in the Court of Appeals. *See State v. Farmer*, 116 Wash.2d 414, 805 P.2d 200, 13 A.L.R.5th 1070 (1991); *State v. Bohannon*, 62 Wash.App. 462, 814 P.2d 694 (1991). We also have held that it does not prohibit all nude photographs of children. *Farmer*, 116 Wash.2d at 421, 805 P.2d 200. *See also* RCW 9.68A.001. The question before us is whether the statute prohibits a person from filming a nude child, without the child's knowledge and where the exhibition of nudity is accomplished without the involvement of the defendant....

On its face, RCW 9.68A.040(1)(b) is not ambiguous. *See State v. Knutson*, 64 Wash.App. 76, 81 n. 4, 823 P.2d 513 (1991) (holding RCW 9.68A.040 is not ambiguous). It becomes ambiguous, and subject to constitutional challenges for vagueness, only if its language is stretched and twisted to fit facts not clearly within its scope.... The statute sets out the elements of the offense, making it a crime to (1) aid, invite, employ, authorize or cause a minor to (2) engage in sexually explicit conduct (3) knowing that the conduct will be photographed.... The words "aids, invites, employs, authorizes or causes" are not defined in the statute. In the absence of a specific statutory definition, words in a statute are given their common law or ordinary meaning.... [citations omitted]. A nontechnical word may be given its dictionary definition.... [citation omitted].... Each of these words is an active verb. Each requires some affirmative act of assistance, interaction, influence or communication on the part of a defendant which initiates and results in a child's display of sexually explicit conduct.

In this case, the Defendant placed a camera under his stepdaughter's bed, hoping and expecting to catch her on film in a state of undress. Although he intended to observe her, he did not communicate with her in any way and he did not assist her in any way. There is no evidence in the record that the Defendant aided (supported or helped), invited (requested or induced), employed (hired or used), authorized (empowered or gave a right) or caused (brought about, induced or compelled) his stepdaughter to engage in sexually explicit conduct. If it had intended to criminalize the secret filming of a nude child who is unaware of the filming, the Legislature could have included the kind of conduct that occurred here within the prohibitions of the statute. As it exists, however, it does not appear that the Legislature intended, under the current provisions of the sexual exploitation of minors statute, to criminalize the photographing of a child, where there is no influence by the defendant which results in the child's sexually explicit conduct.... [footnote omitted].

Defendant Chester was alternatively charged under RCW 9.68A.040(1)(c), which prohibits a parent from permitting the minor to engage in sexually explicit conduct knowing that the conduct will be photographed. "Permit" is not defined in the statute. Its dictionary definition is to expressly or formally consent, to allow, or to acquiesce by failure to prevent. BLACK's, *supra*, at 1140; WEBSTER's, *supra*, at 1683. While "permit" may suggest passive conduct, it appears that *the aim of subsection (c) of the sexual exploitation statute is to prohibit a parent from allowing a child to be exploited under subsection (a) or (b) of the statute.* The language of the statute does not support a contrary interpretation. If a parent, or stepparent, were actively involved in causing the exhibition or other sexually explicit conduct, then the parent would be subject to the terms of subsection (a) or (b). *We interpret RCW 9.68A.040(1)(c) to prohibit the parent's knowing failure or refusal to protect his or her child from sexual exploitation by another....*

We hold that the Defendant's conduct, although contemptible, does not fall within the prohibitions of the sexual exploitation of minors statute.

Affirmed.

DURHAM, C.J., and SMITH, JOHNSON, MADSEN and SANDERS, JJ., concur.

ALEXANDER, Justice, dissenting.

I dissent. In my view the evidence produced at trial was sufficient to support Chester's conviction. Clearly, there was evidence from which a jury could find beyond a reasonable doubt all of the elements of the crime of sexual exploitation of a minor, as defined in RCW 9.68A.040(1)(c). Reading that subsection in conjunction with the definition in RCW 9.68A.011(3)(e), a parent, legal guardian, or person having custody or control of a child, is guilty of sexual exploitation of a minor if he or she "permits" the minor in his or her control to engage in "[e]xhibition of the genitals ... for the purpose of sexual stimulation of the viewer," knowing that the child's conduct will be photographed. The evidence here showed that Chester secretly videotaped his stepdaughter while she was undressing. The jury found that he did so with sexual motivation.... Nothing more is required.

The majority reasons that the "aim of subsection (c) of the sexual exploitation statute is to prohibit a parent from allowing a child to be exploited under subsection (a) or (b) of the statute." ... On that basis, it concludes that subsection (c) prohibits a parent only from participating in sexually exploitative conduct by *another*.... That view of subsection (c) is inexplicable. By requiring the participation of a third party, the majority reads an extra element into the offense and controverts rules of construction that it professes to endorse—the court "may not add language to a clear statute" and should give the words of a statute their "ordinary meaning." ...

The majority concedes that the term "permit" includes acquiescence or "failure to prevent." ... By knowingly videotaping his stepchild while she was undressed, Chester failed to prevent her from exhibiting herself, and thus permitted the conduct that RCW 9.68A.040(1)(c) proscribes. Neither that subsection nor any other part of the statute says anything about the involvement of a third party. Under the majority's reasoning, Chester would be guilty of violating subsection (c) had he allowed a neighbor to secretly videotape his stepdaughter, yet is not guilty when he engages in that same act. This distinction makes no sense. It makes no difference to the child whether a third person or the parent engages in the "viewing"; in either case, the child is being exploited, which is precisely the evil that the statute seeks to prevent. *See, e.g.*, RCW 9.68A.001 ("The care of children is a sacred trust....").

That does not end the inquiry, however. I agree with the majority that Chester's conviction cannot be upheld unless the evidence is sufficient to convict Chester under both RCW 9.68A.040(1)(b) and (c) because the verdict form does not indicate which subsection of the statute the jury found he violated. *See State v. Ortega-Martinez*, 124 Wash.2d 702, 708, 881 P.2d 231 (1994). Reading RCW 9.68A.040(1)(b) also in conjunction with the definition in RCW 9.68A.011(3)(e), a person is guilty of sexual exploitation of a minor if he or she "[a]ids, invites, employs, authorizes, or causes a minor" to exhibit his or her genitals for the purpose of sexually stimulating the viewer, "knowing that such conduct will be photographed." Although Chester did not aid, invite, employ, authorize', or cause his stepdaughter to *undress*, in my view, he caused her to exhibit herself *in a sexual nature*; by knowingly filming her when she was undressed, Chester converted what otherwise would have been an innocent act into an "exhibition ... *for the purpose of sexual stimulation*." RCW 9.68A.011(3)(e) (emphasis added). This conduct runs afoul of subsection (b) of RCW 9.68A.040(1).

The majority concludes that subsection (b) does not prohibit a parent or stepparent from filming a child nude without the child's consent, albeit for the purpose of sexual stimulation of the viewing stepparent, as long as the exhibition of the nudity is without the child's knowledge. Again, the majority reads an element in to the statute that is not there. The statute says nothing about the child being aware that he or she is being exploited. I fail to see how a defendant's conduct is any less culpable because the child victim is sexually exploited in a surreptitious fashion.

In my judgment, there is sufficient evidence to support the jury's finding that Chester violated subsections (b) and (c) of RCW 9.68A.040(1). I would therefore uphold the conviction.

DOLLIVER and TALMADGE, JJ., concur.

Notes

In *Chester*, the issue is whether the defendant's conduct of secretly videotaping his partially nude 14-year-old stepdaughter constitutes sexual exploitation. The court held that it does not because the defendant did not communicate with his daughter in any way or assist her in any way to engage in sexual activity. Note that the determining factor must be the statute, which seeks to distinguish between nostalgically photographing a naked infant playing in a bath and filming a naked adolescent exiting the shower. The difficulty of this distinction is illustrated in the disagreement between the majority and dissenting opinions. Also relevant is the court's consideration of whether the defendant sexually exploited his stepdaughter by permitting her to be videotaped in this manner. Despite a strong dissent on this issue, the court held that the scope of the relevant exploitation statute is limited to a parent's knowing failure or refusal to protect his or her child from sexual exploitation *by others*. Therefore, the defendant's conduct in *Chester* is not included under the sexual exploitation provision. The court notes that if the legislature intended to criminalize the secret filming of a nude child who is unaware of the filming, it must include that conduct within the prohibitions of the statute. For a discussion of what *does* constitute "permitting" sexual exploitation of children, see Chapter Two, Section II.A (Permitting Exploitation), *infra*.

C. Dating Exploitation

Children may engage in sexual relationships with other children as part of an intimate, voluntary dating relationship between themselves. Statistics indicate that 61% of minors have had sex by the time of their 18th birthday; 48% have had sex by their 17th birthday; 33% have had sex by their 16th birthday; and 16% have had sex by their 15th birthday. Fewer than 2% of children have had sex before their 12th birthday. Guttmacher Institute, *American Teens' Sexual and Reproductive Health, Fact Sheet*, at 1 (May 2014), available at www.guttmacher.org (accessed June 13, 2014). Although many of these sexual experiences may have involved sexual activity with an adult (a partner over the age of 18), 70% of sexually experienced female adolescents and 50% of sexually experienced male adolescents report that their first sexual experience was with a steady partner; 16% of females and 28% of males report that their first sexual experience was with someone they just met or who was just a friend. *Id.* Regardless of the nature of the relationship, however, sexual activity between two minors still qualifies as abuse or exploitation under most statutory definitions. *See* Chapter One, Section I.B.3 (Minor Exploiters), *supra*. Should legislatures draw exceptions or limitations when the sexual activity involves two minors who voluntarily engage in sexual activity, rather than an adult who takes liberties with a minor? What if the minor lies about his or her age? *See* Geoffrey Simpson, *19-Year-Old Jailed, Put on Sex Offender List for having Consensual Sex With Girl Who Lied About Age on 'Hook-Up App'*, available at http://latest.com/2015/06/19-year-old-jailed-put-on-sex-offender-list-for-having-consensual-sex-with-girl-who-lied-about-age-on-hook-up-app/ (June 18, 2015) (19-year-old must register for 25 years as a sex offender and is banned from internet for five years for consensual sex with 14-year-old who represented herself as 17) (last accessed June 29, 2015). Do the normal rules of consent apply to voluntary sexual relationships involving minors? The following case addresses these questions.

Smith v. Jones

Mass. App. Ct., 2006
67 Mass. App. Ct. 129, 852 N.E.2d 670

COWIN, J. ...

The plaintiff and the defendant met in the sixth grade and, in July, 2002, when each was thirteen, began a dating relationship. In March, 2003, their relationship became intimate, the intimacy continuing when they entered a new school in September, 2003. The sexual aspect of the relationship was voluntary, although at least some of it came about because the plaintiff desired to accommodate the defendant. In January, 2004, the couple broke up, but continued periodic sexual activity until the defendant left school in March, 2004. The night before the defendant left school, he sent the plaintiff an electronic mail message (e-mail) that he wished he could "stab [her] in the heart." However, the plaintiff never took the threat seriously, and never experienced concern that the defendant would actually do her physical harm.

During the dating relationship, the plaintiff suffered from depression and was treated for the condition by psychologists. In December, 2003, the plaintiff wrote an English paper describing her condition and referring to the support she received from the defendant. Nevertheless, after the relationship ended, the plaintiff reflected in her journal that the sexual activity had been "painful" and "wrong," and that the defendant's convincing her that the activity was the right thing to do was rape. In August, 2004, by which time the parties' sexual relationship had been over for five months, the plaintiff heard from a friend that the defendant would be attending a school located in the same community as her own school. She discussed this with her psychologist, decided to tell her mother of the sexual nature of the previous relationship, ... [footnote omitted] and did so on August 18, 2004.

On August 23, 2004, the plaintiff's mother filed, on behalf of the plaintiff, a "Complaint for Protection From Abuse" pursuant to G.L. c. 209A. An ex parte hearing, at which the plaintiff testified, was held on the complaint that same day. Although much of the tape of the hearing is inaudible, the record does contain testimony by the plaintiff that the defendant had sent the e-mail stating that he wished he could stab her in the heart. She testified also that she feared that the defendant would embarrass her at her school. On the strength of this testimony, a judge issued a temporary abuse prevention order.

On September 3, 2004, a hearing was conducted before a second judge to determine whether the order should be extended. The plaintiff's English paper and the journal entry referred to above were introduced in evidence. In addition, she testified that she feared that the defendant might come to her school, and that being around him caused her to become so nervous that she physically shook. She expanded on this by explaining that, while the defendant had not harmed her or threatened to do so, she was afraid that he could "humiliate" her, say "terrible things" to her, tell others "terrible" and "humiliating" things about her, and thus upset her and "put [her] into a bad mental state." She admitted that she did not fear physical harm at the hands of the defendant as a result of his e-mail. There was no evidence either that the couple had had contact since March, 2004, or that the defendant had given any indication that he would contact the plaintiff in the future.... The judge found that the plaintiff had a reasonable fear that the defendant, once he entered the nearby school, would attempt to resume their sexual relationship, and concluded that this would constitute "abuse" as defined in G.L. c. 209A, § 1, because, given the plaintiff's age, the sexual activity would be nonconsensual. See G.L. c. 265, § 23.... Accordingly, the judge extended the order for one year, a period that ended on September 3, 2005....

At the outset, the statute applies only to acts "between family or household members," a class that includes individuals who "are or have been engaged in a substantive dating or engagement relationship." G.L. c. 209A, § 1(e), as inserted by St.1990, c. 403, § 2. The defendant acknowledges that he and the plaintiff had a substantive dating relationship. Once that is established, the question is whether "abuse" has been demonstrated. "Abuse" is a defined term that further restricts the statute's reach. It consists of "the occurrence of one or more of the following acts between family or household members: (a) attempting to cause or causing physical harm; (b) placing another in fear of imminent serious physical harm; (c) causing another to engage involuntarily in sexual relations by force, threat or duress." While only G.L. c. 209A, § 1(b), requires explicitly that the harm feared be "imminent," we have interpreted §§ 1(a) and 1(c) to require imminent physical or sexual harm as well. See *Dollan v. Dollan*, 55 Mass.App.Ct. 905, 906, 771 N.E.2d 825 (2002) ("We also read the Legislature's language in § 1 ['attempting,' 'placing,' and 'causing'] as revealing an intent to limit the definition of abuse to the present tense"). A determination whether harm is imminent, however, may involve an inquiry whether the defendant has engaged in abusive behavior in the past, and whether such behavior is likely to resume. See, e.g., *Litchfield v. Litchfield*, 55 Mass.App.Ct. 354, 356, 770 N.E.2d 554 (2002); *Dollan v. Dollan, supra* at 906, 771 N.E.2d 825; *Corrado v. Hedrick*, 65 Mass.App.Ct. 477, 483, 841 N.E.2d 723 (2006).

We turn to the record before us to decide whether the plaintiff satisfied her burden of proof under the precise statutory definitions at either the ex parte or the extension hearing. Notwithstanding that both the ex parte and the extension orders have expired, the appeal is not moot. The defendant "could be adversely affected by [the orders] in the event of future applications for an order under G.L. c. 209A or in bail proceedings ... [and] has a surviving interest in establishing that the orders were not lawfully issued, thereby, to a limited extent, removing a stigma from his name and record." *Wooldridge v. Hickey*, 45 Mass.App.Ct. 637, 638, 700 N.E.2d 296 (1998) (citation omitted).... [footnote omitted].... In order to obtain an ex parte order, the plaintiff must demonstrate a "substantial likelihood of immediate danger of abuse." ... [citation omitted]. To extend an ex parte order, the plaintiff must show that he or she is suffering from abuse, or that a protective order is "necessary to protect her from the likelihood of 'abuse.'" *Iamele v. Asselin*, 444 Mass. at 739, 831 N.E.2d 324. See G.L. c. 209A, § 3; *Frizado v. Frizado*, 420 Mass. at 596, 651 N.E.2d 1206. No presumption arises from the fact that a prior order has issued; it is the plaintiff's burden to establish that the facts that exist at the time extension of the order is sought justify relief. See *Jones v. Gallagher*, 54 Mass.App.Ct. at 889–890, 768 N.E.2d 1088.

At the ex parte hearing, evidence of the defendant's e-mail statement that he wished he could stab the plaintiff in the heart was introduced.... [T]he transcript does not contain the plaintiff's statement that she did not believe that the defendant would actually harm her. In addition, when the judge asked the plaintiff whether she was afraid that the defendant would "come after her," the plaintiff's response was ambiguous at best.... [footnote omitted]. Given what could have been a threat, together with the plaintiff's uncertain response thereto, the judge permissibly concluded that there was a substantial likelihood of abuse as defined in G.L. c. 209A, § 1(*b*) ("placing another in fear of imminent serious physical harm"), and justifiably issued an ex parte order.

We acknowledge the implicit concern of the judge who presided at the hearing on the application to extend the order that, given their history, the renewed proximity of the parties presaged possible future unpleasantness or worse. That, however, does not translate by itself into a basis for G.L. c. 209A relief, and we are not persuaded by the evidence that the plaintiff sustained her burden under the statute.... There has been no showing that the defendant attempted to cause or caused the plaintiff physical harm. See G.L. c. 209A, § 1(*a*). The closest that the testimony comes to such a proposition is the plaintiff's statement that, when the parties engaged in anal intercourse, she experienced pain. We do not believe that pain associated with sexual activities in which the parties voluntarily engaged (see *infra*) constitutes "physical harm" as contemplated by the Legislature in the statutory definition of "abuse." ... Furthermore, neither the judge nor the plaintiff appears to have treated the case as one embraced by § 1(*a*).

Nor was there evidence that the defendant placed the plaintiff in fear of imminent serious physical harm. See G.L. c. 209A, § 1(*b*). In contrast to the evidence at the ex parte hearing, the plaintiff admitted that she did not interpret the defendant's stated desire to stab her in the heart as a threat to be taken literally. She testified instead that the defendant had not physically harmed her, nor had he threatened to do so. Accordingly, there was no basis for a finding of actual apprehension on the part of the plaintiff, a prerequisite for relief under § 1(*b*). See *Iamele v. Asselin*, 444 Mass. at 737, 831 N.E.2d 324. While inquiry in these cases often focuses on whether a given plaintiff's fear is reasonable, see *Vittone v. Clairmont*, 64 Mass.App.Ct. 479, 486, 834 N.E.2d 258 (2005), there must be at least fear or apprehension of some sort to begin with, or the definition set forth in § 1(*b*) is not satisfied.

Instead, what the plaintiff described was a fear that the defendant would embarrass or humiliate her, thereby causing her mental or emotional harm. She testified also that the defendant's presence caused her to shake out of nervousness. However, "[g]eneralized apprehension, nervousness, feeling aggravated or hassled, i.e., psychological distress from vexing but nonphysical intercourse, when there is no threat of imminent serious physical harm, does not rise to the level of fear of imminent serious physical harm." *Wooldridge v. Hickey*, 45 Mass.App.Ct. at 639, 700 N.E.2d 296. While "physical manifestations of emotional harm resulting in the aggravation of preexisting medical conditions" might in some circumstances constitute "physical harm," see *Larkin v. Ayer Div. of the Dist. Ct. Dept.*, 425 Mass. 1020, 1020, 681 N.E.2d 817 (1997), the physical manifestation of emotional distress to which the plaintiff testified here is not the physical harm to which the statute is addressed.

The principal legal foundation of the judge's decision is found in G.L. c. 209A, § 1(*c*), and is embraced by his determination that there is "ample basis to conclude that the plaintiff currently and reasonably fears [the] defendant may attempt to resume their sexual relationship. Given her age, that would be involuntary, and so abuse." General Laws c. 209A, § 1(*c*), as amended by St.1990, c. 403, § 2, defines "abuse" as "causing another to engage involuntarily in sexual relations by force, threat or duress." The judge appears to have equated the term "involuntary" with "nonconsensual."

Of course the plaintiff, then less than sixteen, was legally incapable of "consenting" to sexual intercourse.... [citation omitted]. That does not mean, however, that the plaintiff necessarily participated in the sexual activities involuntarily. The plaintiff's testimony, together with her adolescence, make the question whether sex with the defendant was in fact voluntary difficult to answer. She testified that she did not enjoy certain aspects of the sexual activity, and in retrospect should not have permitted herself to become so involved. On the other hand, she also testified that she continued to participate in order to please the defendant. Considering peer and other pressures to engage in sexual experiences to which young people are often subjected, the concept of voluntariness can become considerably ambiguous.

It is unnecessary, however, to resolve the question on this record. In our view, the outcome does not turn on an absence of voluntariness per se, but rather on the reason for arguably involuntary sexual relations. General Laws c. 209A, § 1(*c*), is explicit that "abuse" in this context is causing engagement in sexual relations "by force, threat or duress." The record, even construed in the light most favorable to the plaintiff, contains no basis for a finding that this occurred. There is no evidence that the defendant physically forced the plaintiff, or that he threatened her, or that he left her with no reasonable choice but to engage in sexual relations. See *Commonwealth v. Perl*, 50 Mass.App.Ct. 445, 446–450, 737 N.E.2d 937 (2000) (duress requires immediate threat, no reasonable opportunity to escape, and no other choice in the circumstances). In the absence of involuntary sex induced by force, threat or duress, the relationship cannot be regulated under G.L. c. 209A.

The distinction is not arbitrary. The statute is devoted to the curbing of domestic violence, of which compelled sexual relations is one aspect. Apart from the e-mail discussed above, there is no evidence of violence or proposed violence in the parties' past relationship. Nor is there evidence that the defendant might attempt to force involuntary sex on the plaintiff in the future. In fact, there was no evidence that he had contacted her in any way between March, 2004, and the continuance hearing in September, 2004. The defendant's past acts may be punishable under the criminal law; they do not, for the reasons stated, justify application of the narrowly defined provisions of G.L. c. 209A....

The ex parte abuse prevention order is affirmed. The extension order is vacated. The District Court shall notify the appropriate law enforcement agency of this decision in accordance with G.L. c. 209A, § 7, third par., and shall direct that agency to destroy all record of the vacated order.

So ordered.

Notes

In *Smith*, the court noted the concern over the stigma that attaches to minors convicted of criminal offenses involving sexual relationships with other minors. Many states qualify these relationships under their criminal statutory rape or "Romeo and Juliet" laws, which generally include provisions that negate the sex offender registration requirement for qualified teenage offenders. *See, e.g.*, FLA. STAT. § 943.04354 (2013) ("[A] person shall be considered for removal of the requirement to register as a sexual offender or sexual predator only if the person: … [i]s not more than 4 years older than the victim of this violation who was 13 years of age or older but younger than 18 years of age at the time the person committed this violation.") (amendment to ages effective Oct. 1, 2014); *but see State v. Samuels*, 76 So. 3d 1109 (Fla. App. 5 Dist. 2011) (defendant convicted of committing lewd and lascivious battery on child not eligible, under Romeo and Juliet law, for removal from registration requirement because difference in age was more than four years); *State v. Marcel*, 67 So.3d 1223 (Fla. App. 3 Dist. 2011) (18-year-old defendant who pleaded nolo contendere to unlawful and intentional touching of a person under 16 years of age in a lewd or lascivious manner not excepted from lifetime registration and reporting requirements for consensual conduct by young people where victim was 4 years, 3 months, and 8 days younger than defendant); *Courson v. State*, 24 So.3d 1249 (Fla. App. 1 Dist. 2009) (offenders with multiple sex crime convictions held ineligible for exemption from sexual offender registration requirement); *In the Matter of E.R.*, 40 Kan. App.2d 986, 197 P.3d 870 (2008) (12-year-old defendant who sexually fondled 14-year-old girl not excepted from registration requirement under Romeo and Juliet exception because statutory language required offender to be older than victim). *See also Crooks v. State*, 125 P.3d 1090 (Kan. App. 2006) (statutory rape law that criminalized sexual intercourse with child under 14 only if adult and child were not married did not violate equal protection). For further discussion of Romeo and Juliet laws and related issues, see Jake Tover, *"For Never Was A Story of More Woe Than This of Juliet and Her Romeo"—An Analysis of the Unexpected Consequences of Florida's Statutory Rape Law and Its Flawed "Romeo and Juliet" Exception*, 38 NOVA L. REV. 145 (2013) (arguing that Florida's statutory rape law is too harsh on otherwise consenting teenagers); Jordan Franklin, *Where Art Thou, Privacy?: Expanding Privacy Rights of Minors in Regard to Consensual Sex: Statutory Rape Laws and the Need for a "Romeo and Juliet" Exception in Illinois*, 46 JOHN MARSHALL L. REV. 309 (2012) (arguing that shifting cultural norms of minors' sexuality supports expansive privacy rights of minors and calling for reform of Illinois' statutory rape laws); Caitlyn Silhan, *The Present Case Does Involve Minors: An Overview of the Discriminatory Effects of Romeo and Juliet Provisions and Sentencing Practices on Lesbian, Gay, Bisexual, and Transgendered Youth*, 20 LAW & SEXUALITY REV. LESBIAN, GAY, BISEXUAL & LEGAL ISSUES 97 (2011) (arguing unconstitutionality of "Romeo and Juliet" laws that discriminate against LGBT minors); Steve James, *Romeo and Juliet Were Sex Offenders: An Analysis of the Age of Consent and a Call for Reform*, 78 UMKC L. REV. 241 (2009) (calling for reform of age of consent laws); Nancy Bourke, *Heeding the Equal Protection Clause in the Case of* State v. Limon *and in Other Instances of Discriminatory Romeo and Juliet Statutes*, 12 WIDENER L. REV. 613 (2006) (discussing equal protection aspects of Romeo and Juliet laws as applied between heterosexual and homosexual teens).

D. "Grooming"

Kenneth Lanning

Child Molesters: A Behavioral Analysis

National Center for Missing & Exploited Children, 27–28 (5th ed., 2010)

[G]rooming/seduction is defined as a variety of techniques used by a sex offender to access and control potential and actual child victims. This process takes access, time, and interpersonal skill. How much time depends on the needs of the child and skills of the adult. If done well the process not only gains the victim's initial cooperation, but also decreases the likelihood of disclosure by the victim and increases the likelihood of ongoing, repeated access. The greater the skill of the offender in selecting and seducing vulnerable victims, the more successful the acquaintance molester is and the longer he avoids discovery. How long such offenders get away with this type of victimization is usually determined by how well they select their victims, how good they are at identifying and filling their victims' needs, how much time they have to invest in the process, how proficient they are at seducing and controlling their victims, and how proficient others who might observe the process are at recognizing and responding to it. Although it is possible to manipulate and control child victims through the infliction of nonviolent stress, pressure, and pain, these techniques will generally not be considered grooming....

Acquaintance child molesters typically groom and seduce their child victims with the most effective combination of attention, affection, kindness, privileges, recognition, gifts, alcohol, drugs, or money until they have lowered the victims' inhibitions and gained their cooperation and "consent." The exact nature of this seduction depends in part on the developmental stages, needs, and vulnerabilities of the targeted child victims and nature of the relationship with the offender. The skilled offender adjusts his methods to fit the targeted child. Offenders who prefer younger child victims are more likely to first "seduce" the victim's parents/guardians to gain their trust and obtain increased access to the potential victim. The offender then relies more on techniques involving fun, games, and play to manipulate younger children into sex. Those who prefer older child victims are more likely to take advantage of normal time away from their family and then rely more on techniques involving ease of sexual arousal, rebelliousness, inexperience, and curiosity to manipulate the children into sex. Some offenders simultaneously befriend their victim's parents/guardians (*e.g.*, telling parents/guardians they want to mentor or help their child) and work to alienate the child from the parents/guardians (*e.g.*, telling children their parents/guardians don't want them to have fun).

The grooming or seduction process usually consists of identifying preferred or acceptable child targets; gathering information about interests and vulnerabilities; gaining access (*i.e.*, sports, religion, education, online computer); filling emotional and physical needs; lowering inhibitions; and gaining and maintaining control (*i.e.*, bonding, competition, [challenges], peer pressure, sympathy, threats). Although the vulnerability may be greater when a troubled child from a dysfunctional family is groomed by an adult authority figure, the fact is any child can be groomed by any reasonably nice adult with interpersonal skills.

Many children have only a vague or inaccurate concept of "sex." They are seduced and manipulated by more experienced adult offenders and often, depending in part on their age and intellect, do not fully understand or recognize what they were getting into. As previously stated some "inappropriate" activity that is part of this "grooming" or seduction process can also provide sexual gratification for the adult. Victims who are seduced or engaged in compliant behavior are less likely to disclose their victimization and more likely to voluntarily return to be victimized again and again. Younger children may believe they did something "wrong" or "bad" and are afraid of getting into trouble. Older children may be more ashamed and embarrassed. Some victims not only do not disclose what happened, but they often strongly deny it happened when confronted.

Recognition and understanding of the concepts of grooming and compliance must be applied to all child victims and not just those who fit some preconceived stereotype of innocence. Whether children come from a "good" or dysfunctional home and do or do not get attention and affection at home should not be the determining factors in accepting their vulnerability to grooming and seduction. Child victims cannot be held to idealistic and superhuman standards of behavior. Their frequent cooperation in their victimization must be viewed as an understandable human characteristic and must be addressed when developing investigative and prevention strategy (Lanning, 2005).

Morris v. State

Court of Criminal Appeals of Texas, 2011
361 S.W.3d 649

KELLER, P.J., delivered the opinion of the Court in which JOHNSON, KEASLER, HERVEY, COCHRAN, and ALCALA, JJ., joined....

When the victim in this case was eleven years old, his mother began dating appellant. Appellant and the victim would go to the park, rollerblade, and ride mountain bikes. They would discuss sexual matters, including sex and masturbation. Appellant told the victim that this was "guy talk" and not to mention it to his mother. Later, appellant gave the victim back rubs, and these back rubs continued after appellant married the victim's mother.

Once, after seeing a movie, appellant asked the victim if he had masturbated yet. Appellant was persistent in this questioning until the victim gave him an answer. At some point, the victim got a full-sized bed, and appellant would tuck him into bed. At this time, he would talk to the victim about masturbation and sex and would rub the victim's back. While rubbing the victim's back, appellant was wearing only briefs. And sometimes appellant would take those off, and take the victim's underwear off, so they could have skin-to-skin contact. Appellant would also rub the victim's buttocks and sometimes rub his chest and thighs. Occasionally, appellant's hands would brush against the victim's testicles. At first, appellant stayed in the victim's room for thirty minutes to an hour, but eventually he stayed the entire night.

A couple of times, appellant measured the victim's penis. By the time the victim was fifteen years old, appellant wanted to cuddle with the victim every night for the entire night. During that time, appellant would take him on trips to haul hay. On the way back from two of those trips, appellant stopped at an adult bookstore to buy adult magazines or a pornographic video for the victim. One time, appellant also showed the victim how to find free pornography on the internet. On the trips, appellant touched the victim's penis through the victim's clothing two or three times. Each time, it was part of a "game." ... At night, appellant would also play a "game" where the victim would have to guess whether it was appellant's finger or penis that was poking the victim's back. Appellant also touched the victim's penis a number of times under the victim's underwear for four to five seconds. ...

The State sought to offer the testimony of Special Texas Ranger David Hullum regarding the conduct of child molesters. Ranger Hullum had been in law enforcement for over twenty-nine years and had over 3500 hours of law-enforcement training. He had been a Texas Ranger in Eastland for approximately nine years and had played a major role in the investigation of several hundred sexual offenses, approximately seventy-five of which involved child victims. In these cases, Ranger Hullum interviewed both child victims and suspects. Ranger Hullum was also a member of a "cold case" committee that met quarterly to discuss unsolved murders and sexual offenses. ... In response to questioning from the State, Ranger Hullum affirmed that he had been recognized as an expert in the trial court and other courts in connection with sexual offenses against children. He explained that he had experience in his investigations with determining the existence of grooming techniques. He testified that he had specialized experience and training in the techniques or ploys used by child molesters against children.

On cross-examination, Ranger Hullum acknowledged that he had no education in psychology or psychiatry. When asked about his specialized training, Ranger Hullum responded that he had quite a few classroom hours at the Department of Public Safety (DPS). The teachers included DPS employees, officers from other law-enforcement agencies, and employees of Child Protective Services. At least one of the teachers was a psychiatrist. However, Ranger Hullum could not name any of the individual instructors or where they received their education or training. When asked by the defense whether he had ever read a book or article on "grooming," Ranger Hullum responded, "Yes," but he could not recite any authors or titles. ...

Before the jury, Ranger Hullum described "grooming" as "an attempt by the offender to get the victim compliant with what he wants to happen." He explained that grooming typically occurs over an extended time period and involves spending intimate time alone with the child. Ranger Hullum further explained that grooming involves an element of trust, created by an emotional tie between the offender and the victim. Ranger Hullum cited specific examples of grooming such as supplying the child with alcohol or pornography, engaging in sexual banter, giving or withholding gifts, or telling the child about the adult's own prior sexual experiences. The prosecutor framed a hypothetical that involved a gradual increase in the amount of time an adult stayed each night in a child's bedroom, until the adult spent the entire night there, and asked if that would be an example of grooming. ... [footnote omitted]. Ranger Hullum responded that it would be a "perfect example."

Ranger Hullum elaborated that grooming was really no different from behavior that occurs in high school dating. He explained that a boy on a date might put his "arm around the young lady to see how she would react to that, if she would object." Likewise, Ranger Hullum explained, an adult offender "wants to see how that child's going to react to that first touching," with the object of the offender's behavior being to "desensitize" the child. When asked about whether back rubs can sometimes be grooming, Ranger Hullum responded affirmatively, saying, "It's also a way to desensitize the child of having those hands placed on that back. And you start off in a neutral area where the child doesn't believe that there is anything wrong with this touching, and then you progress to other areas, more sensitive areas."

Further, he explained that grooming can involve joking about or minimizing the offender's conduct—which communicates to the child, "Hey, look, there's nothing serious happening here." When asked whether it would be "unusual for a defendant to fool the victim with games ... to obtain sexual contact," Ranger Hullum replied that what is being described is "just disguised foreplay," which can take the form of a game or horseplay.... When asked whether pornography had anything to do with grooming, Ranger Hullum said, "It's critical in this aspect. Pornography overstimulates—sexually overstimulates the child." He also explained that it was fairly common for pornography to be involved in sex offenses against children....

Appellant was convicted of indecency with a child. On appeal, appellant contended that the trial court erred in allowing Ranger Hullum to testify as an expert about "methodology" ... [footnote omitted] and "grooming." Appellant complained that the State had presented no evidence that the theory had been accepted by the scientific, psychiatric, or psychological community. He noted that Ranger Hullum could not recall the title or author of a single book or article he had read and could not identify the lone psychiatrist involved in his training. He also pointed out that Ranger Hullum was not himself a psychiatrist or psychologist.

Appellant then cited *Nenno v. State*[3] for the test for determining the admissibility of evidence from fields of expertise outside the hard sciences. Relying upon *Perez v. State*,[4] appellant claimed that the State had failed to satisfy the first *Nenno* prong, "whether the field of expertise is a legitimate one," ... [footnote omitted] because the record is silent concerning the existence of literature that supports or reflects the underlying theory. Appellant stated that he could find no reported Texas case holding that an expert may testify as to "grooming." Finally, appellant asserted that experience alone cannot establish reliability, or else "twenty years of reading tea leaves would make fortune-telling a legitimate field of expertise."

The court of appeals rejected these claims.... [footnote omitted]. Characterizing Ranger Hullum's testimony as involving a "soft science," the appellate court employed the *Nenno* test.... [footnote omitted]. It found that Ranger Hullum's qualifications "were not only based upon the writings or experiences of others but were also based upon his own considerable experience." ... [footnote omitted]. The court noted Ranger Hullum's 3500 hours of law-enforcement training and the numerous cases that he investigated that related to sexual offenses against children.... [footnote omitted]. The court of appeals found Ranger Hullum's training, background, and experience to differ significantly from the witness that was found insufficiently qualified in *Perez*.... [footnote omitted].

In his ground for review, appellant contends: "The court of appeals erred in holding that testimony about 'grooming' was admissible where there was no showing that the study of 'grooming' was a legitimate field of expertise." In support of this ground, appellant argues that the State had "the burden to introduce some sort of research or other evidence to support the expert's opinion." He equates the situation here with what occurred in *Coble v. State*,[11] where the psychiatrist, Dr. Coons, "cited no books, articles, journals, or even other forensic psychiatrists" for the validity of his methodology.[12] Appellant complains

---

3. 970 S.W.2d 549 (Tex.Crim.App.1998).

4. 25 S.W.3d 830, 837 (Tex.App.–Houston [1st Dist.] 2000, no pet.).

11. 330 S.W.3d 253 (Tex.Crim.App.2010).

12. *See id.* at 277. In *Coble*, the defendant did not "quarrel with the first prong—the legitimacy of the field of forensic psychiatry, nor, apparently, with the second prong—[that] Dr. Coon's testimony is within the scope of forensic psychiatry, but he contend[ed] that Dr. Coon's testimony did not properly rely upon the accepted principles of forensic psychiatry, at least as far as those principles

that Ranger Hullum's "methodology appears to have been nothing more than his own observations as a law enforcement officer, without testing from *any* source as to the validity of his conclusions." Appellant further states that there is nothing "to show that anyone has undertaken a scientific study of 'grooming.'" "Perhaps offenders who prey on children do act as Ranger Hullum testified," appellant says, "but there is only his word for it." Appellant contends that Ranger Hullum's testimony should not have been admitted absent empirical data in the record showing, "for example, how many men who give back rubs to their children turn out to be 'grooming' them?" Appellant argues that the court of appeals erroneously "equate[d] the experience of an expert witness with the reliability of his testimony." ...

When the subject of an expert's testimony is "scientific knowledge," then the basis of that testimony must be grounded in the accepted methods and procedures of science.... [footnote omitted]. For expert testimony based upon "hard" science, we employ the *Kelly*[16] test for reliability: (1) the underlying scientific theory must be valid, (2) the technique applying the theory must be valid, and (3) the technique must have been properly applied on the occasion in question.... [footnote omitted]. Although the inquiry is somewhat more flexible for soft sciences than for Newtonian and medical science, "'soft' science does not mean soft standards." ... [footnote omitted]. But expert testimony does not have to be based upon science at all; by its terms, Rule 702, by applying to "technical or other specialized knowledge," permits even nonscientific expert testimony.[19]

Recognizing the flexible nature of a Rule 702 inquiry, in *Nenno*, we set forth a framework for evaluating the reliability of expert testimony in fields of study outside the hard sciences.... [footnote omitted]. This framework consisted of three questions: (1) whether the field of expertise is a legitimate one, (2) whether the subject matter of the expert's testimony is within the scope of that field, and (3) whether the expert's testimony properly relies upon and/or utilizes the principles involved in the field.... [footnote omitted]. We explained that this was simply a translation of the *Kelly* test appropriately tailored to areas outside of hard science.... [footnote omitted]. In employing the *Nenno* framework, we also explicitly refrained from developing rigid distinctions between "hard" science, "soft" sciences, and nonscientific testimony because we recognized that the distinction between various types of testimony may often be blurred.... [footnote omitted].

In addressing "hard" science under the *Kelly* test, we have observed that trial courts do not necessarily have to relitigate what is valid science in every case: "It is only at the dawn of judicial consideration of a particular type of forensic scientific evidence that trial courts must conduct full-blown 'gatekeeping' hearings under *Kelly*." ... [footnote omitted]. "Trial courts are not required to re-invent the scientific wheel in every trial." ... [footnote omitted]. This observation with respect to the hard sciences logically applies to all types of expert testimony.... [footnote omitted]. Whether a field of study is legitimate and whether the subject matter is within the scope of that field are questions that are capable of being resolved as a general matter, so that courts can take judicial notice of the reliability

---

apply to the prediction of long-term future dangerousness." *Id.* at 274. Our conclusion in *Coble* concerned the third prong, that "the prosecution did not satisfy its burden of showing the scientific reliability of Dr. Coon's methodology for predicting future dangerousness." *Id.* at 279. In contrast, appellant's petition challenges whether "the study of 'grooming' was a legitimate field of expertise," which he argues is an attack on the first prong (the legitimacy of the field of study), and which we later consider as an attack on the second prong (whether the subject matter is within the scope of the field).... Because it concerned the third prong only, *Coble* is of limited assistance to our inquiry today.

16. *Kelly v. State*, 824 S.W.2d 568 (Tex.Crim.App.1992).

19. *See* R. 702; *see also Nenno*, 970 S.W.2d at 560–61.

(or unreliability) of the type of evidence at issue.... [footnote omitted]. Taking judicial notice of reliability usually requires that a trial court somewhere has examined and assessed the reliability of the evidence.[28] ...

We believe that appellant's claim that "grooming" has not been shown to be a legitimate field of expertise misapprehends where the concept of "grooming" fits into the *Nenno* framework. In *Nenno* we recognized the experience-based study of "the behavior of offenders who sexually victimize children" as a legitimate field of expertise.[29] "Grooming" is a subject matter that may fall within the scope of that field....

Because we have already held that the behavior of people who sexually victimize children is, under *Nenno*'s first prong, a legitimate field of expertise, we will construe appellant's claim as an attack under *Nenno*'s second prong. We address, then, whether the subject matter of "grooming" is within the scope of the field of studying the behavior of people who sexually victimize children. In answering that question, we must ascertain whether "grooming" has been established as a phenomenon and what kind of expertise is required to recognize that phenomenon.... Although the record in this case may be sparse, an examination of court decisions establishes rather clearly that we are not at the "dawn of judicial consideration" for this type of testimony. Cases that refer to "grooming" in one way or another are legion. The number of published cases is significant, but once one considers unpublished cases as well, the number is overwhelming. We cite the unpublished cases, not as authority, ... [footnote omitted] but simply as an indication that the concept of grooming has gained widespread recognition.

References to the concept of grooming can be found in at least twenty-nine Texas court-of-appeals cases from eleven courts of appeals. In eleven of those cases, from six

---

28. *Id.; but see id.* at 34–35, 37 (Keller, P.J., concurring) (matters of common knowledge can be recognized without a prior determination of reliability and a "less exacting inquiry" may be required if "a large number of jurisdictions recognize the validity or reliability of a scientific theory or technique").

In his dissent, Judge Price claims that we run afoul of the statement in *Hernandez* that "judicial notice on appeal cannot serve as the sole source of support for a bare trial court record concerning scientific reliability." Dissent by Price, J. at 678 (quoting *Hernandez*, 116 S.W.3d at 31–32). At oral argument, appellant's counsel also relied upon this portion of *Hernandez* to argue that the federal cases cited by the State were irrelevant because they had not been presented to the trial court. But *Hernandez* was speaking specifically about *scientific* evidence. In general, judges are not scientists and lack expertise to assess the reliability of scientific principles on their own. *See GE v. Joiner*, 522 U.S. 136, 148, 118 S.Ct. 512, 139 L.Ed.2d 508 (1997) (Breyer, J., concurring) ("judges are not scientists and do not have the scientific training that can facilitate the making of such decisions").

But, first, as Judges Meyers, Womack, and Keasler suggested in questioning at oral argument, the evidence at issue in this case was not scientific; rather, it was testimony based upon experience. Such evidence is akin to the beekeeper example referred to in Judge Cochran's questioning: a beekeeper may testify from experience that bumblebees always fly into the wind, because, even though he is not a scientist with an understanding of aerodynamics, he has seen a lot more bumblebees than the jurors have. *See Gammill v. Jack Williams Chevrolet*, 972 S.W.2d 713, 724–25 (Tex.1998) (quoting from *Berry v. City of Detroit*, 25 F.3d 1342, 1349–50 (6th Cir.1994)). And the experience-based testimony at issue in the present case involved a topic with which courts are familiar: behaviors engaged in by criminals. Courts are far better qualified to assess the reliability of this type of evidence than scientific evidence. We will not extend *Hernandez*'s rule with respect to scientific evidence to the dissimilar situation before us.

And second, contrary to Judge Price's belief, this case does not present a "bare trial court record" concerning the reliability of grooming. "Reliability" in this context depends upon the accuracy of the notion that grooming is a common phenomenon. Ranger Hullum's testimony concerning his experience regarding grooming behaviors is some evidence that grooming behaviors are common.

29. *See Nenno*, 970 S.W.2d at 562.

courts of appeals, the appellate courts upheld the admission of expert testimony on grooming against various challenges, including some based upon Rule 702.... [footnote omitted]. In another case, a court of appeals found one witness to be unqualified and held that another witness improperly addressed the facts of the case, but the court nevertheless recognized testimony about what constitutes grooming to be legitimate.... [footnote omitted]. At least one court relied upon expert testimony on grooming in a sufficiency-of-the-evidence analysis, ... [footnote omitted] and numerous other Texas court-of-appeals cases have referred to expert testimony on grooming.... [footnote omitted]. A review of all of these cases makes clear that "grooming" is not something that Ranger Hullum made up; the cases reveal a number of witnesses, including those in law enforcement, speaking about the matter.... [footnote omitted]. Expert testimony about grooming has also been discussed in at least a few decisions from federal district courts in Texas.... [footnote omitted]. And one federal district-court decision even involved a Texas venireman who explained the concept of grooming during voir dire.[41]

But recognition of the concept of grooming extends far beyond Texas. The concept has become well known in the federal system. The Fifth and Tenth Circuits have expressly held that expert testimony on "grooming" is admissible under Federal Rule of Evidence 702.[42] Earlier cases from the Third and Seventh Circuits have held such evidence to be admissible under Rule 702, but have referred to this kind of evidence as "seduction" rather than "grooming."[43] Similarly, an earlier case from the DC Circuit upheld the admission of such "seduction" evidence against a challenge under Federal Rule of Evidence 403.[44] The Second and Ninth Circuits have expressly recognized the concept of "grooming,"[45] and the Seventh Circuit has done so in later cases.[46] Opinions from the Fourth, Sixth, and Eighth Circuits contain definitions of, or other references to, grooming.[47] The Court

---

41. *McClellan v. Cockrell*, 2003 WL 22119501, 11, 2003 U.S. Dist. LEXIS 17385, 29 (N.D., Dallas Div. Tex. September 3), *adopted by*, 2003 WL 22251419, 2003 U.S. Dist. LEXIS 17372 (N.D.Tex., Dallas Div. Sept. 29) (opinions not designated for publication) (When asked by prosecutor about "grooming," the venireman explained: "It's when an adult will befriend a child and start taking them places and doing things just like a buddy system, and it progresses from there to petting on the head to petting them in other places." Defendant did not show that prosecutor's question was improper).

42. *United States v. Hitt*, 473 F.3d 146, 152 & n. 4, 158 (5th Cir.2006); *United States v. Batton*, 602 F.3d 1191, 1198, 1198 n. 3, 1200–02 (10th Cir.2010).

43. *United States v. Hayward*, 359 F.3d 631, 636 (3rd Cir.2004) (discussing testimony by Kenneth Lanning regarding the "seduction process"); *United States v. Romero*, 189 F.3d 576, 583–85 (7th Cir.1999) (discussing Lanning's testimony about "sophisticated psychological techniques" child molesters use to "'seduce' their victims"). *See also Hitt*, 473 F.3d at 158 (citing *Romero* and *Hayward* in connection with admissibility of "grooming" evidence); *Batton*, 602 F.3d at 1202 (discussing *Romero* and *Hitt* and mentioning *Hitt*'s citation to *Hayward*); *Jones v. United States*, 990 A.2d 970, 978 (D.C.App.2010) (Kenneth Lanning referred to seduction techniques as "grooming").

44. *United States v. Long*, 328 F.3d 655, 665–68 (D.C.Cir.2003) (Lanning's testimony about the "seduction process").

45. *United States v. Brand*, 467 F.3d 179, 203 (2nd Cir.2006); *United States v. Goetzke*, 494 F.3d 1231, 1235 (9th Cir.2007); *United States v. Johnson*, 132 F.3d 1279, 1283 & n. 2 (9th Cir.1997).

46. *United States v. Chambers*, 642 F.3d 588, 593–94 (7th Cir.2011); *United States v. Gladish*, 536 F.3d 646, 649 (7th Cir.2008). The Third Circuit has also used the term "grooming." *Coley v. County of Essex*, 462 Fed.Appx. 157, 159–61, 2011 WL 2065065, 2–3, 2011 U.S.App. LEXIS 10690, 7–8 (3rd Cir. May 26) (not designated for publication) (referring to "grooming" process in which abuse escalates over time).

47. *United States v. Fancher*, 513 F.3d 424, 431 (4th Cir.2008) (finding by trial judge that defendant "grooms or grows" his victims and could not stop grooming victims even from jail); *United States v. Shafer*, 573 F.3d 267, 271 (6th Cir.2009) (reference by trial judge to "grooming conduct"); *United States v. Young*, 613 F.3d 735, 739 & n. 3 (8th Cir.2010), *cert. denied*, ___ U.S. ___, 131 S.Ct. 962, 178 L.Ed.2d 793 (2011) (reference to Internet Crimes Against Children Task Force's definition of

of Appeals for the Armed Forces has upheld the admission of expert testimony about grooming to show the psychological impact of the defendant's offenses on the victim.[48] And the District of Columbia Court of Appeals has upheld the admission of expert testimony about grooming under its standard for the admissibility of expert testimony.[49] ... A number of federal district courts, in published and unpublished opinions or orders, have also discussed or referred to "grooming." ... [O]thers expressly determined that such evidence was admissible.... [51] ... Other federal district courts ... referred to evidence of the defendant's extraneous conduct as admissible to show grooming,[57] or made their own determinations that grooming had occurred.[58]

Further, the concept of grooming has been discussed or at least referred to in opinions from state appellate courts in at least thirty-eight other states. A few of these opinions have specifically upheld the admission of expert testimony on the subject,[59] but many more have referred to the concept of grooming in a way that contributes to the conclusion that it is a well-recognized phenomenon. Many of these courts have defined or recognized the concept of grooming in the abstract,[60] while others have relied upon the concept of

---

grooming); *United States v. Mikowski*, 332 Fed.Appx. 250, 251 n. 2 (6th Cir.2009) (not designated for publication) (setting out a definition of grooming); *United States v. Blum*, 404 Fed.Appx. 89, 92 & n. 3 (8th Cir.2010) (not designated for publication) (setting forth a definition of grooming found in the record).

48. *United States v. Patterson*, 54 M.J. 74, 75, 78 (C.A.A.F.2000).

49. *Jones*, 990 A.2d at 978.

51. *Light v. Martel*, 2009 WL 4456385, 3–4, 6–10, 2009 U.S. Dist. LEXIS 115715, 8–9, 17–26 (N.D.Cal. November 30) (not designated for publication); *Simonton v. Evans*, 2009 WL 482362, 5– 6, 2009 U.S. Dist. LEXIS 13599, 15–16 (S.D.Cal. February 23) (not designated for publication).

57. *Sullivan v. Schriro*, 2005 WL 5966149, 11, 2005 U.S. Dist. LEXIS 26339, 31 (D.Ariz. August 15) (not designated for publication); *Kittle v. Vasbinder*, 2010 WL 890208, 2–3, 2010 U.S. Dist. LEXIS 21788, 6–7 (E.D.Mich. March 10) (not designated for publication); *Clark v. Bock*, 2002 WL 31772023, 3–4, 2002 U.S. Dist. LEXIS 23577, 9–10 (E.D.Mich. October 28) (not designated for publication).

58. *United States v. Wetmore*, 766 F.Supp.2d 319, 321–22 (D.Mass.2011); *United States v. Blake*, 2010 WL 702958, 2, 6, 2010 U.S. Dist. LEXIS 23014, 4–5, 16 (E.D.Cal. February 24) (not designated for publication) (characterizing allegations that provided probable cause for a search warrant as "grooming"); *United States v. Hansel*, 2006 U.S. Dist. LEXIS 54725, 2 (N.D.Iowa August 4) (not designated for publication); *United States v. Gleich*, 2005 WL 741921, 1–2, 3–4, 2005 U.S. Dist. LEXIS 5149, 4–6, 9–10 (D.N.D. March 30) (not designated for publication).

59. *State v. Sorabella*, 277 Conn. 155, 213–14, 891 A.2d 897, 932–33 (2006) (rejecting complaints about Kenneth Lanning's testimony); *Haycraft v. State*, 760 N.E.2d 203, 210–11 (Ind.App. 1st Dist.2001), *transfer denied*, 774 N.E.2d 514 (Ind.2002) (holding the testimony admissible as that of a "skilled witness" under Indiana's R. 701); *People v. Petri*, 279 Mich.App. 407, 415–16, 760 N.W.2d 882, 888, *appeal denied*, 482 Mich. 1186, 758 N.W.2d 562 (2008) (Detective could give definition of "grooming" without being an expert but even assuming expert testimony was required, he would have qualified); *State v. Berosik*, 352 Mont. 16, 23, 214 P.3d 776, 782–83 (2009) (upholding admissibility of expert testimony on grooming against relevance and R. 403 objections and explaining, "In Montana, expert testimony explaining the complexities of child sexual abuse for the purpose of assisting jurors in understanding and evaluating a child's testimony is admissible."); *State v. Horton*, 200 N.C.App. 74, 80– 81, 682 S.E.2d 754, 758–59 (2009) (upholding admission of expert testimony about grooming techniques against objection that it did not corroborate the testimony of the child).

60. *State v. Grainge*, 186 Ariz. 55, 58, 918 P.2d 1073, 1076 (Ariz.App.1996) (stating that "grooming can be a continuing process that fosters continued acquiescence to [the defendant's] sexual crimes"); *Cannon v. State*, 296 Ga.App. 687, 688, 675 S.E.2d 560, 562–63 (2009) (observing that state had presented evidence of a pattern of "grooming"); *Doe v. Sex Offender Registry Bd.*, 459 Mass. 603, 606, 947 N.E.2d 9, 16 (2011) (reference to "extended periods of 'grooming'"); *People v. Steele*, 283 Mich.App. 472, 491– 92, 769 N.W.2d 256, 269–70, *appeal denied*, 485 Mich. 996, 775 N.W.2d 146 (2009) (definition of "grooming"); *State v. Sage*, 357 Mont. 99, 103–04, 103 n. 3, 235 P.3d 1284, 1287 & n. 3 (2010) (definition of "grooming"); *State Farm Ins. Co. v. Bruns*, 156 N.H. 708, 713, 942 A.2d 1275, 1280 (2008) (citing *State v. McIntyre*, 151 N.H. 465, 468, 861 A.2d 767, 770 (2004) ("describing 'grooming' as a progression in the

grooming as a basis for admitting other evidence,[61] and still others have relied upon the concept of grooming in deciding to take protective action.[62] In acting to protect the welfare of a child, a Louisiana appellate court pointedly stated: "[W]e find nothing in the law that would require the courts to ignore such behavior and leave a child at the mercy of the perpetrator until more harm is done."[63] ...

Some courts have recognized the targeting of grooming as one of the purposes of a particular criminal statute,[83] and the term "grooming" has been used by trial courts[84] and

---

level of abuse"); *Commonwealth v. Meals*, 590 Pa. 110, 117–18, 912 A.2d 213, 217 (2006) (defining "grooming behavior"); *In re Application of Nash*, 317 Or. 354, 359 n. 3, 855 P.2d 1112, 1114 n. 3 (1993) (defining grooming); *State v. Warren*, 165 Wash.2d 17, 35 195 P.3d 940, 949 (2008) (citing *State v. DeVincentis*, 150 Wash.2d 11, 22, 74 P.3d 119 (2003) as discussing evidence of grooming behaviors in child sexual abuse case); *Wease v. State*, 170 P.3d 94, 114, 116 (Wyo.2007) (referring to "grooming" process).

61. *State v. Jacobson*, 283 Conn. 618, 628–29, 633–38, 930 A.2d 628, 635–36, 638–40 (2007); *State v. Truman*, 150 Idaho 714, 249 P.3d 1169, 1177–78 (Idaho App.2010) (Evidence of prior acts by defendant with the victim was admissible to show his "continuing criminal design to cultivate a relationship with [the victim] such that she would concede to his sexual demands, also known as 'grooming.'"); *State v. Reid*, 2011 Ida.App. Unpub. LEXIS 261, 11–13 (July 22) (not designated for publication) (extraneous conduct evidenced a common methodology and technique in grooming, controlling, and abusing step-daughters); *Piercefield v. State*, 877 N.E.2d 1213, 1216 & n. 1 (Ind.App.2007), *transfer denied*, 891 N.E.2d 34 (Ind.2008) (defining grooming and holding that evidence of defendant's prior acts was admissible to show "preparation or plan" because the evidence showed the defendant's "grooming of the children to familiarize them with touching and create more physical relationship with them"); *State v. Query*, 594 N.W.2d 438, 443–44 (Iowa App.1999) (prior bad acts could be reasonably interpreted as grooming, showing defendant's motive, intent, plan knowledge, or absence of mistake); *State v. Sena*, 144 N.M. 821, 827, 192 P.3d 1198, 1204 (2008) (upholding the admission of evidence of defendant's prior behavior as "grooming evidence"); *State v. Christensen*, 561 N.W.2d 631, 632–33 (N.D.1997) (trial court did not abuse discretion in admitting evidence of prior non-criminal acts of touching to show "grooming"); *State v. Borck*, 230 Or.App. 619, 630–31, 633–35, 635 n. 10, 216 P.3d 915, 920–21, 922–23, 923 n. 10, *modified on other grounds*, 232 Or.App. 266, 221 P.3d 749 (2009), *review denied*, 348 Or. 291, 231 P.3d 795 (2010) (letters from defendant admissible to show grooming, which in turn tended to show that the defendant's touching was not benign or incidental); *State v. Pottebaum*, 2008 WL 5397848, 9–10, 2008 Tenn.Crim.App. LEXIS 1005, 25–28 (Tenn.Crim.App.2008, appeal denied) (not designated for publication) (trial court did not err in admitting evidence of defendant's prior behavior toward victim under Rule 404(b) because, in part, it showed "grooming").

62. *People in the Interest of C.L.S.*, 934 P.2d 851, 856 (Colo.App.1996, cert. denied) (juvenile court found sufficient evidence of behaviors that might be a grooming procedure to justify requiring child's father to submit to a sexual-aggression evaluation and possible treatment); *In the Interest of D.D.*, 653 N.W.2d 359, 362 (Iowa 2002) (expressing concern about child protection worker's characterization of father's behavior as "part of a grooming process" for more serious sexual abuse in upholding juvenile-court intervention on behalf of children); *Newton v. Berry*, 15 So.3d 262, 263–64, 266–67 (La.App. 2nd Cir.2009) (upholding protective order under Domestic Abuse Assistance statute after recognizing that the stepfather had engaged in grooming behavior); *Matter of Mudge v. Huxley*, 79 A.D.3d 1395, 1396–97, 914 N.Y.S.2d 339, 340–41 (A.D. 3rd Dept.2010) (upholding suspension of teacher certification because rational basis supported conclusion that teacher was engaged in grooming students); *Grosinger v. M.D. (In re M.D.)*, 598 N.W.2d 799, 807–08 (N.D.1999) (upholding order committing subject as a sexually dangerous individual in part on evidence that subject was engaging in "grooming" conduct).

63. *Newton*, 15 So.3d at 267.

83. *United States v. Berg*, 640 F.3d 239, 252 (7th Cir.2011) (federal criminal enticement statute "targets the sexual grooming of minors as well as the actual sexual exploitation of them"); *Powell's Books v. Kroger*, 622 F.3d 1202, 1206, 1215 (9th Cir.2010) (recognizing that Oregon criminal statutes were aimed at practices of "luring" and "grooming" that expose minors to sexually explicit materials in the hopes of lowering their inhibitions against engaging in sexual conduct but finding the statutes unconstitutional because they reach a significant amount of material that is not obscene as to minors); *Am. Booksellers Found.*, 202 F.Supp.2d at 316–17 (Vermont statute, *see* this opinion, footnote 52).

84. *See* this opinion, footnotes 58 and 65; *United States v. Dorvee*, 616 F.3d 174, 180 (2nd Cir.2010); *Fancher*, 513 F.3d at 431; *Shafer*, 573 F.3d at 271; *United States v. Beith*, 407 F.3d 881, 885 (7th Cir.2005);

sex-offender treatment programs,[85] and by at least one state hospital,[86] criminal task force,[87] and probation and parole department.[88] Some courts have used the word "classic" in connection with the term "grooming"—e.g., "classic grooming behavior"—which suggests that these courts view the existence of such a phenomenon as well established.[89] At a military court martial, the expert witness—the Chief of Child Adolescent Family Psychiatry at the Eisenhower Medical Center—testified that grooming was "a fairly well documented phenomena of what certain individuals do to seduce children."[90]

As can be seen from the above discussion, grooming evidence has been received by courts from numerous types of experts—which include psychiatrists, psychologists, therapists, and social workers—but, of importance here, also includes some people who work in law enforcement.[91] In *Coble*, we explained, "Although *Nenno* dealt with the admission of expert testimony concerning future dangerousness, it dealt with the testimony by a layman whose analysis was based on his experience studying sexual victimization of children." ... [footnote omitted]. In characterizing Lanning as a "layman," we did not mean to suggest that he was not an "expert"—we had just finished saying that *Nenno* dealt with the admission of expert testimony.... [footnote omitted]. Rather, we meant that Lanning was not a psychiatrist or psychologist. But because of his research, "Lanning possessed superior knowledge concerning the behavior of offenders who sexually victimized children." ... [footnote omitted]. Grooming evidence is, at its most basic level, testimony describing the common behaviors of child molesters and whether a type of evidence is consistent with grooming.[95] A person can, through his experience with child-sex-abuse cases gain superior knowledge regarding the grooming phenomenon.

United States v. Holt, 510 F.3d 1007, 1010–11 (9th Cir.2007); *Sullivan*, 2005 WL 5966149 at 11, 2005 U.S. Dist. LEXIS 26339 at 31.

85. *See Penley*, 52 Fed.Appx. at 202; *Schnitzler*, 518 F.Supp.2d at 1101.

86. *Force*, 2009 WL 2407838 at 2–3, 4, 2009 U.S. Dist. LEXIS 68497 at 6–7, 10[.]

87. *Young*, 613 F.3d at 739 n. 3 (Internet Crimes Against Children Task Force).

88. *Munguia*, 253 P.3d at 1085.

89. *Brand*, 467 F.3d at 203 (referring to "classic 'grooming' behavior in preparation for a future sexual encounter"); *United States v. Abston*, 304 Fed.Appx. 701, 704 n. 4 (10th Cir.2008) (referring to "a classic progression-type grooming process used by pedophiles or child molesters"); *Gleich*, 2005 WL 741921 at 2, 2005 U.S. Dist. LEXIS 5149 at 6 (concluding that defendant "fits the classic profile of a pedophile who was engaged in a clever and calculated scheme to 'groom' a new victim"); *United States v. Garner*, 67 M.J. 734, 735–36, 738–39 (N.M.C.C.A.2009), *aff'd*, 69 M.J. 31 (C.A.A.F.2010) (quoting, with approval, from *Brand*); *State v. Garcia*, 200 Ariz. 471, 476, 28 P.3d 327, 332 (Ariz.App.2001) (referring to "classic 'grooming' activity in molestation cases"); *See also Lopez*, 2008 WL 2487244, 2008 U.S. Dist. LEXIS 113464 (prosecutor's argument that defendant "engaged in classic grooming"); *John Y.*, cited in this opinion, footnote 68.

90. *Patterson*, 54 M.J. at 76.

91. *See* this opinion, footnotes 39 and 64; *United States v. Jordan*, 435 F.3d 693, 696 (7th Cir.2006) (Special Agent Eric Szatkowski); *Am. Booksellers Found.*, 202 F.Supp.2d at 316–17 (police officer); *Light*, 2009 WL 4456385, 3–4, 6–10, 2009 U.S. Dist. LEXIS 115715 at 8–9, 17–26 (Carl Lewis, *see Rot*, cited in this opinion, footnote 64); *Lopez*, 2008 WL 2487244, 4–5, 13–18, 18–20, 2008 U.S. Dist. LEXIS 113464 at 12, 37–47, 50–54 (police detective); *Christy*, 2010 WL 2977610 at 4 & n. 5, 8, 2010 U.S. Dist. LEXIS 71300 at 11–12 & n. 5, 23–24 (Special Victims Detective with sheriff's office); *Haycraft*, 760 N.E.2d 203 at 210–11 (police detective).

95. The court of appeals in the present case also addressed claims that Ranger Hullum and another witness were improperly allowed to express an opinion on appellant's guilt. *Morris*, 2010 WL 2224651 at 1–9. Assuming that the questions were improper, *id.* at 2, the court conducted a harm analysis and found any error to be harmless. *Id.* at 9. We did not grant review of the harmless error question.

Because it is beyond the scope of our review in this case, we do not address whether an expert can express an opinion on a defendant's probable guilt based on grooming theory and, if so, what qualifications would be required to do so.

Virtually all of Ranger Hullum's testimony about the phenomenon of grooming finds support in the cases: that it is an attempt by the offender to create a compliant victim;[96] that it involves an escalation of conduct over a (sometimes extended) period of time;[97] that it can involve spending intimate time alone with the child;[98] that it involves having the child's trust;[99] that it is like dating;[100] that it is designed to desensitize the child;[101] that it often begins with innocuous touches that progress to more sensitive areas or with minor touching that progresses to more blatant sexual acts;[102] and that it can involve supplying the child with alcohol[103] or pornography,[104] giving gifts,[105] giving back rubs or massages,[106] engaging in "games" or horseplay,[107] or talking about the adult's own prior sexual experiences.[108] ... From our discussion, we conclude that grooming as a phenomenon exists and that a law enforcement-official with a significant amount of experience with child sex abuse cases may be qualified to talk about it.[109] ...

---

96. *See e.g.*, B.W., 909 N.E.2d at 474; *Cook*, 2010 WL 3910585 at 1–2, 2010 Tex.App. LEXIS 8095 at 4; *Mitchell*, 2008 WL 4899195 at 1–2, 2008 Tex.App. LEXIS 8594 at 3; *Light*, 2009 WL 4456385 at 3–4, 2009 U.S. Dist. LEXIS 115715 at 8–9[.]

97. *See e.g.*, *Weatherly*, 283 S.W.3d at 491–92; *United States v. Hofus*, 598 F.3d 1171, 1177 & n. 4 (9th Cir.), *cert. denied*, ___ U.S. ___, 131 S.Ct. 364, 178 L.Ed.2d 235 (2010); *Patterson*, 54 M.J. at 76; *Sorabella*, 277 Conn. at 213–14, 891 A.2d at 932–33; *Garcia*, 126 Idaho at 1043, 895 P.2d at 1236; *Piercefield v. State*, 877 N.E.2d at 1216 & n. 1.

98. *See e.g.*, *Liberatore*, 478 F.Supp.2d at 750; *Lopez*, 2008 WL 2487244 at 14–15, 2008 U.S. Dist. LEXIS 113464 at 39–40.

99. *See e.g.*, *Weatherly*, 283 S.W.3d at 491–92; *Smith*, 470 F.3d at 335 n. 3; *Young*, 613 F.3d at 739 n. 3; *Hofus*, 598 F.3d at 1177 & n. 4; *Batton*, 602 F.3d at 1198 n. 3; *Wetmore*, 766 F.Supp.2d at 321–22; *Jacobson*, 283 Conn. at 628–29, 930 A.2d at 635–36; *Piercefield*, 877 N.E.2d at 1216 n. 1; *Coates v. State*, 175 Md.App. at 607, 930 A.2d at 1151; *Martineau v. State*, 242 S.W.3d at 459; *Sage*, 357 Mont. at 103 n. 3, 235 P.3d at 1287 n. 3.

100. *See Van Houten*, 2009 WL 481883 at 4, 2009 Tex.App. LEXIS 1301 at 11; *Raymond*, 700 F.Supp.2d at 151.

101. *See e.g.*, *Hitt*, 473 F.3d at 152; *State Farm Fire & Casualty Co.*, 183 Ariz. at 519 n. 4, 905 P.2d at 528 n. 4; *Steele*, 283 Mich.App. at 491–92, 769 N.W.2d at 269–70; *Berosik*, 352 Mont. at 23, 214 P.3d at 782–83; *Borck*, 230 Or.App. at 630–31, 633–35, 216 P.3d at 920–21, 922–23.

102. *See e.g.*, *Steele*, 283 Mich.App. at 491–92, 769 N.W.2d at 269–70; *Petri*, 279 Mich.App. at 415, 760 N.W.2d at 888; *State v. Horton*, 200 N.C.App. at 80, 682 S.E.2d at 759; *C.C.*, 187 Ohio App.3d at 372, 932 N.E.2d 360, 365; *Borck*, 230 Or.App. at 630–31, 633–35, 216 P.3d at 920–21, 922–23.

103. *See e.g.*, *Berg*, 640 F.3d at 249; *Long*, 328 F.3d at 665; *Garcia*, 200 Ariz. at 476–77, 28 P.3d at 332–33; *Jones*, 990 A.2d at 976.

104. *See e.g.*, *Dorvee*, 616 F.3d at 180; *Powell's Books*, 622 F.3d at 1206; *Long*, 328 F.3d at 665; *Am. Booksellers Found.*, 202 F.Supp.2d at 316; *United States v. Banker*, 63 M.J. 657, 660(A.F.C.C.A.2006), *aff'd*, 64 M.J. 437 (C.A.A.F.2007); *Jones*, 990 A.2d 970, 976.

105. *See e.g.*, *Hernandez*, 973 S.W.2d at 790; *Hitt*, 473 F.3d at 152; *Long*, 328 F.3d at 665; *Liberatore*, 478 F.Supp.2d at 750; *Morris*, 246 F.Supp.2d at 1132; *Nash*, 317 Or. at 359 n. 3, 855 P.2d at 1114 n. 3.

106. *See e.g.*, *Light*, 2009 WL 4456385 at 3–4, 2009 U.S. Dist. LEXIS 115715 at 8–9 ("back rubs"); *Piercefield v. State*, 877 N.E.2d at 1216 (massages); *Warren*, 165 Wash.2d at 35, 195 P.3d at 949, *citing DeVincentis*, 150 Wash.2d at 22, 74 P.3d at 125–26 (massages).

107. *See Hernandez*, 973 S.W.2d at 790 (tag game involving pressing penis against victim's backside while both were clothed); *Wagner*, 2010 WL 2163845 at 2, 2010 Tex.App. LEXIS 4087 at 4 ("pony ride" game); *Light*, 2009 WL 4456385 at 3–4, 2009 U.S. Dist. LEXIS 115715 at 8–9 (may include play such as wrestling and "slapping of the butt"); *Miller*, 273 Va. at 544, 643 S.E.2d at 210 (using games and other methods to engage the victims' interests).

108. *Jordan*, 435 F.3d at 696 (expert testified that reference to previous relationship with a much younger girl was a grooming technique).

109. Judge Price misunderstands *Nenno*, or at least which prong of *Nenno* is at issue. He contends that "[u]biquity does not begin to prove reliability" because "the world is full of psychics, horoscopes, tarot card readers, and fortune cookies." ... All of these are examples of fields that have not been recognized by courts as legitimate. If a field is not legitimate, then the prevalence of a practice or

Now we consider the inverse question. Is the grooming phenomenon just common knowledge? Does expert testimony add anything to what the jury already knows? ... [footnote omitted]. We recognize that social awareness of child sex abuse has grown through the years. One of the original justifications for grooming testimony was to dispel what was thought to be "a widely held stereotype of a child molester as 'a dirty old man in a wrinkled raincoat' who snatches children off the street as they wait for the school bus."[111] Some courts have suggested that the stereotype is no longer widely held and that jurors today no longer need to be informed by experts about the grooming techniques of child molesters.[112] Other courts have suggested that the factfinder or the appellate court can infer grooming from the defendant's conduct without the assistance of an expert.[113]

Nevertheless, we find the weightier and more persuasive authority to be that expert grooming testimony is useful to the jury. Recent appellate cases suggest that grooming testimony still involves matters beyond the understanding of the jury.[114] The District of Columbia Court of Appeals has explained that, "[w]hile the continuing vitality of such stereotypes may be debatable, we cannot conclude that the trial judge in this case abused

---

subject within the field would not demonstrate anything. Assessing personality based upon one's zodiac sign may be a common occurrence in astrology, for example, but astrology itself has not been held to be a legitimate field of study. As we explained above, the relevant field of study has already been recognized as legitimate in *Nenno*: the experience-based study of "the behavior of offenders who sexually victimize children." *See Nenno*, 970 S.W.2d at 562. How often "grooming" as a subject is addressed by practitioners within this field is clearly relevant to the reliability of grooming testimony as a whole.

Moreover, saying that a field of study or a subject within a field occurs frequently in the world around us is not the same as saying that the matter is addressed frequently in the court system. Judge Price has offered nothing to suggest that one can find frequent references in court decisions to psychics or astrology in anything other than a pejorative sense; he has not cited a single case in which a court admitted such matters into evidence, relied upon such matters in assessing the sufficiency of the evidence, or relied upon such matters in assessing punishment or evaluating a defendant's future dangerousness for various purposes (e.g. civil commitment, pretrial detention, child custody).

Judge Price also faults this Court for not showing "indisputable acceptance in the psychological community," ... but the psychological community is not the relevant field of study in the present case. Ranger Hullum did not testify as a psychologist but as an experience-based expert, like Kenneth Lanning, the expert in *Nenno*.

111. *Jones*, 990 A.2d at 978. *See also Romero*, 189 F.3d at 584; *Long*, 328 F.3d at 667; *Batton*, 602 F.3d at 1201.

112. *Raymond*, 700 F.Supp.2d at 151 ("Those observations are hardly rocket science. A jury in 2010 does not need expert testimony to help it understand that not every child abuser is 'a dirty old man in a wrinkled raincoat' who snatches children off the street as they wait for the school bus."); *Schneider*, 83 Fed. R. Evid. Serv. (Callaghan) 820, 2010 WL 3734055 at 7, 2010 U.S. Dist. LEXIS 99662 at 20 ("While such evidence may have been helpful to juries in the past, this Court agrees with the conclusion that a jury in 2010 does not need expert testimony to show that child sexual abusers can often be ostensibly responsible and well-meaning adults who occupy positions of trust in society.")

113. *Banker*, 63 M.J. at 660 ("This Court's finding of a pattern of grooming is merely a conclusion we reached after careful review of the evidence in this case."); *Sena*, 144 N.M. at 827, 192 P.3d at 1204 ("[W]e do not agree that the grooming evidence in the instant case needed an expert witness to explain to the jury how Defendant's behavior showed his sexual intent or his lack of mistake or accident.... Lay persons are well-aware of what it means to act with a sexual intent, and therefore can identify behavior as exhibiting that trait without the aid of an expert witness.").

114. *Batton*, 602 F.3d at 1202 ("The methods sex offenders use are not necessarily common knowledge."); *Berosik*, 352 Mont. at 23, 214 P.3d at 782 ("[The expert's] testimony concerned a subject about which lay persons would have little or no experience."); *Jones*, 990 A.2d at 978. *See also Van Houten*, 2009 WL 481883 at 5, 2009 Tex.App. LEXIS 1301 at 15 ("[The expert] stated the concept of grooming is information that is not generally known by the common lay person and that testimony about grooming would aid lay persons in understanding a child molestation situation.").

her discretion in ruling that Lanning's grooming testimony 'was beyond the ken of a lay trier of fact and would be helpful to the jurors in their consideration of the evidence.' "[115] We think the D.C. court put the issue in proper perspective when it said, "*Modus operandi* testimony may be helpful ... even though it may be familiar to 'the average reader of the daily press.' " ... [footnote omitted]. Although it may be true that many jurors will be aware of the concept of grooming (in practice if not necessarily by name), that does not mean that all jurors will be aware of the concept or that the jurors will have the depth of understanding needed to resolve the issues before them....

We reject appellant's claim that the record failed to show the legitimacy of "grooming" as a subject of expert testimony because the legitimacy of "grooming" as a subject of expert testimony has been established sufficiently to be judicially noticed.[117] We affirm the judgment of the court of appeals....

COCHRAN, J., concurring in which JOHNSON, J., joined.

Given the ground for review that we granted in this case, I agree with the majority's resolution. This is the ground that we granted:

> The court of appeals erred in holding that purportedly expert testimony about "grooming" was admissible where there was no showing that the study of "grooming" was a legitimate field of expertise.

---

115. *Jones*, 990 A.2d at 978.

117. Judge Price concedes that "it may sometimes be appropriate for an appellate court to take judicial notice ... for the first time on direct appeal" but contends that "judicial notice of an adjudicative fact should never be taken for the first time by a discretionary review court." ... He cites no authority for this proposition, and his reasoning is not persuasive. He argues that this Court's job is to "shepherd the jurisprudence," *id.* at 676, but that is exactly what we are doing in determining the general reliability of grooming testimony, an important issue that this Court has the ultimate responsibility to resolve. He criticizes us for "doing the vast bulk of the research for the State," *id.* at 676, but the thoroughness of our analysis of this important issue should not depend upon the thoroughness of the briefs.

Judge Price also misapprehends the significance of the procedural posture of this case. He complains that the State did not ask the court of appeals to take judicial notice of the reliability of grooming testimony. *Id.* at 675. But as the prevailing party at trial, the State "was not required to raise any allegations before the court of appeals." *Volosen v. State*, 227 S.W.3d 77, 79, 80 (Tex.Crim.App.2007) (State appellee may raise for the first time in a petition for discretionary review the argument that a statutory defense was inapplicable to the county in which the conduct occurred). *See also Rhodes v. State*, 240 S.W.3d 882, 886 ns. 8, 9 (Tex.Crim.App.2007) (State appellee may raise for the first time in a petition for discretionary review an estoppel argument that was not raised on original submission in the court of appeals or addressed by that court).

Judge Price also accuses this Court of taking judicial notice "without alerting the appellant beforehand to allow him to marshal some argument in this Court ... why judicial notice ... may not be appropriate." ... He suggests that appellant's "only opportunity ... to challenge the propriety of our action is via a motion for rehearing." ... But, as the Judge Price himself acknowledges, the State advanced the judicial notice argument in its brief on discretionary review, ... and the State cited relevant federal cases on the matter.... The State cited *Hitt, Hayward,* and *Romero* on the legitimacy of grooming testimony and *Batton* on the methods of sex offenders not being common knowledge. On the day of oral argument, the State filed a supplemental list of authorities, which included citations to the Texas courts of appeals cases of *Davenport* and *Van Houten*.

At oral argument the State reiterated its position that judicial notice could be taken and it discussed *Bryant*, another Texas court of appeals case. As we noted earlier, appellant's counsel contended at oral argument that the federal cases were not relevant, under *Hernandez*, because they were not presented to the trial court. He did not make the argument that Judge Price now makes on his behalf regarding the absence of a request for judicial notice before the court of appeals. Appellant had the opportunity to respond and did respond at oral argument to the State's judicial notice contention. That the defense was not blind-sided by this contention is suggested by the fact that he did not request permission to file a supplemental brief. *See* Tex.R.App. P. 70.4.

The only question that we need address is the legitimacy of a phenomenon known as "grooming" behavior by those who use a particular method to get a person to comply with what the groomer wants. This is not rocket science. It does not depend upon any scientific, technical, or psychological principles or methodology. This type of testimony does not depend upon educational expertise, any calculable rate of error, learned treatises, peer review, or any other esoteric skill. This is not even "soft science."[2] It is just "horse sense" expertise developed over many years of personal experience and observation. It is "modus operandi" evidence that may or may not be relevant in a particular case. We may take judicial notice of the *legitimacy* of such a behavioral phenomenon by, *inter alia*, looking to decisions from other courts that have addressed that issue. What our decision in *Hernandez* forbids is taking judicial notice, for the first time on appeal, of *the scientific reliability* of a particular machine, such as the Adx machine in that case, or of an intoxilyzer machine, or DNA or blood lab technology, or a particular scientific methodology for which there has not been some showing, in a trial court hearing, of its scientific reliability.[3]

Texas law has long allowed such experiential "horse sense" expertise. For example, in one 1929 case, the court of civil appeals held that an experienced cowman was qualified to give his opinion on how many men were needed to handle a herd of cattle.[4] Just as Texas has long recognized that farmers may be expert witnesses in matters peculiarly within their knowledge, ... [footnote omitted] so may police officers. We, along with federal courts and other state courts have recognized that police officers, based solely on their years of experience and training, may qualify as experts to testify about a wide variety of "modus operandi" techniques of illegal enterprises or conduct.... [footnote omitted]. Their expert "modus operandi" testimony may be admissible when it is both relevant to a disputed issue and when that "modus operandi" testimony is of appreciable assistance to the jury ... [footnote omitted] because it is outside the average juror's experience or full understanding.... [footnote omitted]....

Appellant argued in the trial court, and on appeal, that "the State had presented no evidence that 'the theory under which he's going to express these opinions [is] accepted by the scientific community or the psychiatric community or the psychological community[.]'" ... [footnote omitted]. He is absolutely correct. This Court need not take judicial notice of the scientific, psychological, or psychiatric "reliability" of expertise concerning the "modus operandi" of grooming. Indeed we should not. As the dissent appropriately notes, the concept of scientific "reliability" has no application to such testimony. "Grooming" is simply a behavioral phenomenon that may or may not apply in a given scenario. One cannot, for example, determine the scientific reliability of a police officer's testimony that when Dan sidled up to Simon, looked around to make sure no one else was watching, then quickly gave Simon a $10 bill and took something from Simon's hand, that this was a drug transaction. There is no determinable "error rate" for how many times this type of interaction is a drug transaction versus something else. There are probably few treatises, research studies, or peer review articles written on the topic of the reliability of a drug transaction "modus operandi." There is no psychological principle involved in such experiential "modus operandi" expertise; it is simply that the police officer, like Justice

---

2. *See Nenno v. State*, 970 S.W.2d 549, 560–61 (Tex.Crim.App.1998).

3. *Hernandez v. State*, 116 S.W.3d 26, 30–32 (Tex.Crim.App.2003).

4. *Texas & P. Ry. Co. v. Edwards*, 21 S.W.2d 754, 757 (Tex.Civ.App.–El Paso 1929), *rev'd on other grounds*, 36 S.W.2d 477 (Tex. Comm'n App.1931).

Stewart on seeing pornography, "knows it when he sees it,"[12] or at least he has an expert opinion, based on his experience and training, concerning the significance of the particular circumstances. What the witness must be able to do is explain how his experience and training qualifies him to make assessments of a certain type of behavior and precisely why, based on that experience and training, he has formed an opinion of this particular set of circumstances.

The witness may be wrong, of course, in the particular case. Not every street corner encounter such as described above is a drug transaction. Not every developing close relationship between a young boy and an older man that involves lollipops, back-rubs, or trips to the ice-cream store is an instance of "grooming." But the relative likelihood of these particular circumstances involving that particular "modus operandi" are generally matters for cross-examination.[13] ... Nor is this an example of a scientific expert, such as a psychiatrist like Dr. Coons, testifying to unscientific "horse sense" dressed up in a doctor's white robe. As we stated in *Coble v. State*,[14] the danger with unscientific expertise posing as science is that the jury will accept it uncritically.[15] There is no such danger when evaluating a police officer's testimony concerning a "modus operandi" such as "grooming." It is "horse sense" in plain clothes; the jury can immediately grasp the concept and use it or reject as they see fit.... Because the only question before us is whether the behavioral phenomenon of "grooming" is a legitimate one that may a suitable subject for expert testimony, I join the majority opinion.

MEYERS, J., dissenting in which PRICE and WOMACK, JJ., joined.

The court of appeals said that under the record in this case, the trial court did not abuse its discretion in admitting testimony regarding Appellant's "grooming" of the victim. Appellant contends that the court of appeals based this determination on the purported expert's experience, rather than whether "grooming" is a legitimate field of scientific examination. The majority disagrees and takes judicial notice that "grooming" is sufficiently established as a subject of expert testimony. Judge Cochran concurs that "grooming" is a legitimate issue for expert testimony, but says that this type of expertise is experiential and is not related to scientific reliability.

Irrespective of whether the study of "grooming" behavior is a legitimate field of expertise, I do not think Hullum was qualified to be an expert on this issue. He had no degree in any field of study involving human behavior, no specialized training in "grooming" behavior, and he did not show that the training and experience he did have enabled him to distinguish such behavior. His testimony that he believed Appellant engaged in

---

12. *Jacobellis v. Ohio*, 378 U.S. 184, 197, 84 S.Ct. 1676, 12 L.Ed.2d 793 (1964) (Stewart, J., concurring).

13. Appellant argues that there must be empirical data to support the phenomenon of "grooming" behavior before it can be the subject for expert testimony: "Where, however, in the record before the Court is there any empirical data showing, for example, how many men who give back rubs to their children turn out to be 'grooming' them?".... But that is not a necessary requirement under Rule 702, nor is it a requirement of any purely experiential expertise. It is, of course, a proper topic for vigorous cross-examination.

14. 330 S.W.3d 253 (Tex.Crim.App.2010).

15. *Id.* at 279 n. 68 (noting that, if Dr. Coons's methodology were unscientific, the intuitive appeal of his opinions would be doubly dangerous as the jury might accept his testimony uncritically) (citing *Flores v. Johnson*, 210 F.3d 456, 465–66 (5th Cir.2000) (Garza, J., concurring) ("[T]he problem here (as with all expert testimony) is not the introduction of one man's opinion on another's future dangerousness, but the fact that the opinion is introduced by one whose title and education (not to mention designation as an 'expert') gives him significant credibility in the eyes of the jury as one whose opinion comes with the imprimatur of scientific fact.")).

"grooming" behaviors expressed to the jury his opinion as to Appellant's guilt. Allowing him to testify was error and, although we did not grant Appellant's ground for review regarding harm, I would say that the error was harmful. I respectfully dissent.

PRICE, J., dissenting in which MEYERS and WOMACK, JJ., joined....

After doing the vast bulk of the research for the State, the Court now essentially holds (despite the absence of any actual litigation on the subject below) that case law from other jurisdictions demonstrates that grooming is such a well-established psychological concept that the State, as proponent of the grooming-based testimony here, need not have been required to prove it at all. The Court proceeds to take this judicial notice in the absence of any request from the State at either the trial or appellate level and without alerting the appellant beforehand to allow him to marshal some argument in this Court (having not been called upon to do so in either of the lower courts, since judicial notice was not sought there) why judicial notice of the particular adjudicative fact at issue in this case may not be appropriate. I cannot bring myself to go along with this....

When this Court takes judicial notice of an adjudicative fact for the first time on discretionary review, we become involved as petty fact-finders, to the detriment of our proper role as ultimate arbiters of the law. Inserting ourselves in the adjudicative fact-finding function exposes us to accusations of judicial activism, even favoritism. We risk distorting the jurisprudence to fit a desired result in the particular case rather than accepting the case in the posture that it comes to us and using it dispassionately to shape the law, hopefully for the better. I want no part of that.

This is not to say that I doubt that, at a certain point, a principle of the soft sciences may become so well accepted that a trial or appellate court could appropriately take judicial notice of the reliability of expert testimony deriving from that principle. Far from it. Once the proponents of expert testimony have satisfied their burden to establish reliability with sufficient regularity in the course of Rule 705 hearings,[8] it makes perfect sense at some point to ask the next trial court, or even an appellate court, to take judicial notice of that reliability.... [footnote omitted]. This effectively relieves the proponent of the onus, each and every time he subsequently offers such testimony, of having to re-prove the first prong of the *Nenno* soft-science standard—whether the field of expertise is legitimate.... [footnote omitted]. From that point on, the proponent need only prove that his expert is qualified and has appropriately utilized the reliable principle in arriving at his expert opinion. This Court may then decide, if called upon to do so in a petition for discretionary review, whether judicial notice in the lower court was appropriate—as a jurisprudential question, after comprehensive briefing from the affected parties. I agree that this approach well serves the interest of judicial economy. But today the Court skips far too many steps.... [footnote omitted].

In the instant case, the State failed to demonstrate at the Rule 705 hearing *either* that the psychological principle behind its proffered grooming testimony was reliable *or* that it has been found to be reliable, after full ventilation of the issue, in a sufficient number of other cases to justify asking the trial court to take judicial notice of that adjudicative fact. Nor did the State even ask the court of appeals in this case to judicially notice reliability. Still, the Court today takes it upon itself to hold Ranger Hullum's testimony admissible, and does so without even affording the appellant an opportunity to dispute whether the psychology behind grooming-based expert testimony is so universally ac-

---

8. *See* TEX. R. EVID. 705 (providing opponent of expert testimony to conduct *voir dire* examination, outside jury's presence, to test factual basis for expert's opinion testimony).

knowledged that it ought properly to be deemed the subject of judicial notice. It seems to me that the appellant could muster a pretty stout argument. In taking judicial notice today, the Court does not rely upon the frequency with which trial courts have admitted such testimony after full-blown Rule 705 hearings, in Texas or anywhere else. Nor does the Court identify an abundance of psychological literature that confirms beyond cavil the abiding reliability of grooming-based expert testimony.... [footnote omitted]. Instead, the Court invokes case law from other jurisdictions, much of which does not even address the question of reliability, *per se*. It is almost as if the Court regards the sheer number of cases in which proponents have simply *offered* expert testimony with respect to grooming as inviolable empirical proof of the provenance of the psychological principle behind it. But the world is also full of psychics, horoscopes, tarot card readers, and fortune cookies. Ubiquity does not begin to prove reliability—much less does it prove it definitively, as is required for judicial notice.

In our per curiam opinion in *Hernandez v. State*, we observed that "appellate courts may take judicial notice of other appellate opinions concerning a specific scientific theory or methodology in evaluating a trial judge's *Daubert/Kelly* 'gatekeeping' decision[.]" ... [footnote omitted]. But in the next breath we insisted that "judicial notice on appeal cannot serve as the sole source of support for a bare trial court record concerning scientific reliability." ... [footnote omitted]. If judicial notice cannot serve this function on direct appeal, I do not see how the Court can permit it to serve that function for the first time on discretionary review on a similarly bare trial court record. Where is the legal consistency that discretionary review is meant to foster? ... [footnote omitted]. To relieving the State of its burden to demonstrate the reliability of grooming-based expert testimony, or to at least demonstrate the propriety of taking judicial notice of that adjudicative fact by showing indisputable acceptance in the psychological community, I dissent....

In her concurring opinion, Judge Cochran argues that the reliability of Hullum's expert testimony need not be evaluated under the guise of "soft science" at all because it is based, not upon scientific or quasi-scientific principles, but on his experience and training. She makes a valid point. I do not doubt that a police officer may appropriately testify from his training and experience about such matters as modus operandi. A single police officer's many years of experience, and/or any training he may have that stems from the collective experience of other police officers over time, may well provide a sufficient empirical basis to establish the reliability of expert testimony of this kind—what Judge Cochran calls "experiential 'horse sense' expertise." ... [footnote omitted]. Even so, as Judge Cochran acknowledges, "What the witness must be able to do is explain how his experience and training qualifies him to make assessments of a certain type of behavior and precisely why, based on that experience and training, he has formed an opinion of this particular set of circumstances." ... [footnote omitted].

The record in this case shows no such thing. The best that can be said is that Hullum had personally investigated approximately seventy-five cases involving sexual assaults on children, and that he had an unspecified amount of training with respect to the investigation of such offenses, including what he called "methodology." He was not asked, and he did not say, whether that training embraced the concept of grooming. He simply acknowledged that he had "experience" "in the investigation" of "grooming techniques," without explaining what that was. At no time did the prosecutor elicit from Hullum during the Rule 705 hearing, nor did Hullum ever volunteer, any information about exactly what it was he had learned in all of his training and experience to equip him to testify with respect to grooming. I cannot tell from his testimony, or from any other testimony that the State proffered at the Rule 705 hearing, what the "behavioral phenomenon" of grooming is at all, ... [footnote omitted] much less how Hullum's experience and training have taught him to recognize it.

The prosecutor, the trial court, and Hullum himself, all seem to have taken the attitude that, because Hullum had been allowed to testify about grooming on prior occasions, his testimony must likewise be admissible here. But, as the court of appeals observed, appellate courts "must review the trial court's ruling in light of what was before the trial court at the time of its ruling." ... [footnote omitted]. The State was the proponent of Hullum's expert testimony and, as such, it was required to carry the burden of making a record to show that, from his experience and/or training, Hullum is able to say that grooming is indeed a verifiable behavioral phenomenon that he can identify and explain. I do not know whether Hullum could have said that at this Rule 705 hearing, had he been asked. But he did not, and he was not. Failing to appreciate this deficiency in the record, Judge Cochran ultimately relieves the proponent of the evidence of its burden to show reliability no less than the majority does.

Notes

The issue of the admissibility of evidence in child sexual exploitation cases, including within the specific context of grooming, will be addressed more comprehensively in Chapter Six, Section II.C (Grooming), *infra*. For an institutional perspective of grooming behavior, *see generally* Chapter Eight (Institutional Exploitation of Children), *infra*. What is important in *Morris*, however, is the recognition of the exploitive dynamic of the grooming conduct and how it affects not only the nature of the relationship between the child and the abuser, but how children, parents, law enforcement officials, courts, and the public perceive and respond to this systematic behavior and the motives behind it. In addressing the variety of forms of exploitation that are discussed in this casebook — particularly within Chapter Two (Defining Exploitation), Chapter Three (Internet Sexual Exploitation of Children), and Chapter Eight (Institutional Exploitation of Children) — consider how grooming behavior may play a factor in each form of exploitation. For further discussion of the concept of grooming, see generally Samantha Craven, Sarah Brown and Elizabeth Gilchrist, *Current Responses to Sexual Grooming: Implications for Prevention*, 46 Howard J. Crim. Just. 60, 60–71 (2007) (outlining current responses to sexual grooming); Anne-Marie McAlinden, *'Setting 'Em Up': Personal, Familial and Institutional Grooming in the Sexual Abuse of Children*, 15 Soc. & Leg. Stud. 339, 339–62 (2006) (arguing that discourses on grooming have created ambiguities about child sexual abuse and that the law is limited in its response to grooming behavior).

One of the common variables of grooming behavior is the use of pornography (not necessarily child pornography) to either stimulate a child to sexual activity or to desensitize a child to accept other, more direct forms of sexual contact. The Adam Walsh Child Protection and Safety Act of 2006, specifically 18 U.S.C. § 2252A(a)(6), criminalizes the use of child pornography "for purposes of inducing or persuading a minor to participate in any activity that is illegal...." Violation of this provision authorizes a sentence of 5 to 20 years. 18 U.S.C. § 2252A(b). If the offender has a prior sexual abuse or child pornography conviction, the sentence is increased to 15 to 40 years. *Id.* In 2010, Jerry Alan Penton became the first person to be sentenced under this federal law for grooming a minor for sexual exploitation by providing the child with child pornography.

United States v. Penton

Eleventh Circuit, 2010
380 Fed. Appx. 818

PER CURIAM:

Jerry Alan Penton appeals his conviction [...] for providing child pornography to a minor for the purpose of inducing her to participate in illegal activity (Count 1), possession of child pornography (Count 2), and receipt or distribution of child pornography (Count 3). On appeal, Penton challenges the sufficiency of the evidence..., arguing that ... as to Count 1, the evidence was insufficient for the jury to find that the child pornography was used for the purpose of persuading a minor to engage in illegal conduct....

[T]he Government's evidence was sufficient to sustain Penton's conviction for showing child pornography to a minor for the purpose of inducing her to participate in illegal activity in violation of 18 U.S.C. § 2252A(a)(6). Specifically, the child victim (A.K.) testified that Penton showed her a movie on his computer that depicted a minor girl touching herself sexually and included an older man and another minor girl in a sexual situation. A.K. further testified that immediately after showing her the child pornography, Penton removed A.K.'s clothing and sexually molested her, while also touching himself sexually. Given the temporal proximity of Penton's showing A.K. the pornographic movie and his sexual touching of both A.K. and himself, the jury was entitled to infer that he had showed her the movie for the purpose of persuading her to engage in sexual conduct. That Penton denied the occurrence of these events does not change the outcome, as the jury's credibility determinations must be accepted on review. *See Wright*, 392 F.3d at 1273.

As such, the Government's evidence was sufficient to show that Penton showed child pornography to A.K., a minor, for the purpose of persuading A.K. to engage in sexual contact with him, which, given her age, was illegal. Thus, the evidence was sufficient to establish the elements of a § 2252A(a)(6) violation....

AFFIRMED.

Notes

Penton received a 40-year sentence for his grooming conviction, which included convictions for knowingly distributing and possessing thousands of images of child pornography. *See Child Molester Nets 40-Year Sentence Under New Federal Anti-Grooming Law*, Federal Bureau of Investigation Press Release, July 15, 2009, available at http://www.fbi.gov/mobile/press-releases/2009/mo071509a.htm (last visited June 19, 2014). As a result of the investigation and conviction of Penton, the National Center for Missing and Exploited Children was able to identify many of the children depicted in the images as known child victims from other states and countries. *Id.* As part of his sentence, when released from prison, Penton will spend the rest of his life on supervised release, with restrictions on his ability to use a computer or to have contact with anyone under the age of 18. For discussion of conditions of sentencing, see Chapter Seven, Section I.C.5 (Conditions Imposed in Sentencing), *infra*.

II. Sexual Exploitation Through Non-Physical Conduct

A. Permitting Exploitation

In *State v. Chester, supra,* the court held that a step-father who secretly videotaped, for his own gratification, his step-daughter undressing in her room did not sexually exploit the child and that the step-father did not "permit" the minor to engage in sexually explicit conduct because he did not "permit" the sexual exploitation of the child *by another*. Consider how the court interprets the relevant statute in the following case, in which the sexual exploitation is perpetrated "*by another*," but the issue is whether it must be a parent who permits the exploitation to occur.

State v. Porter
Court of Appeals of Oregon, 2011
241 Or. App. 26, 249 P.3d 139

BREWER, C.J....

In 2006, defendant, his wife Leblanc-Porter, and two men, Davies and Clements, rented a house in Oregon. They had previously lived together in Arizona. Defendant, who had received money from an inheritance, paid the rent and the household expenses. Various members of the household engaged in sadomasochistic sexual practices with one another, and there were pornographic materials and sexual devices throughout the house.

In early 2007, Leblanc-Porter's 15-year-old daughter, D, came from Arizona to live in the household. D initially was enrolled in a public school, but was soon taken out of school and enrolled in a home-schooling course. At approximately the same time, Leblanc-Porter decided that D should be trained to be sexually submissive to Davies. During the course of more than a month, Leblanc-Porter and Davies sexually abused D in numerous ways. Some of the abuse involved using sexual devices on D, posing D in sexual positions in the common areas of the house, and requiring D to remain in those positions while others observed her. All of the adults in the household were in the common areas at times when D was being abused there, although the physical acts perpetrated against D were committed by Leblanc-Porter and Davies. The charges in the present case stem from three occasions when defendant was present in a room while D was being abused there. It is undisputed that defendant did not actively participate in that sexual abuse. However, D testified that defendant appeared at times to enjoy watching her being abused.

ORS 163.670(1) provides:

> "A person commits the crime of using a child in a display of sexually explicit conduct if the person employs, authorizes, permits, compels or induces a child to participate or engage in sexually explicit conduct for any person to observe or to record in a photograph, motion picture, videotape or other visual recording."

Although the crimes at issue here were alleged in the terms of the statute, the parties tried the case as one that involves "permit[ting]." Defendant argued in his motion for a judgment of acquittal, and repeats in this court, that he did not "permit" D to be used in a display of sexually explicit conduct because, although D is his wife's daughter, he had no legal relationship to her. Defendant argues that, "[b]efore one can be said to 'permit' something, one must have authority to forbid it." (Quoting *State v. Pyritz*, 90 Or.App. 601, 605, 752

P.2d 1310 (1988)). According to defendant, therefore, only a person with "legal power to authorize a child to engage in sexual conduct" may be guilty of the crime because only such legal power could forbid the child from engaging in the conduct. Taken to its logical extreme, defendant's argument is difficult to follow, because, given the strictures of ORS 163.670(1), *nobody* has "legal power" to authorize the use of a child in a display of sexually explicit conduct, as that is precisely the harm the statute seeks to prevent. *See generally State v. Stoneman*, 323 Or. 536, 547, 920 P.2d 535 (1996) (noting that ORS 163.670 describes "the most serious kind of harm covered by this part of the criminal code" and the purpose of this part of the criminal code is to prevent "the underlying harm caused by child sexual abuse"). To the extent that defendant simply means that, to be criminally liable under the statute for "permit[ting]" a child to engage in sexually explicit conduct for another person to observe, a person must have legal responsibility for, or legal authority over, the victim, we disagree.

The word "permits" is not defined in the pertinent statutory scheme. Defendant suggests that its ordinary meaning in this context is "to consent to expressly or formally." *Webster's Third New Int'l Dictionary* 1163 (unabridged ed. 2002). The ordinary meaning of the word, however, is not so restrictive:

> "1: to consent to expressly or formally: grant leave for or the privilege of: ALLOW, TOLERATE <~smoking> <~an appeal> <~access to records> 2: to give (a person) leave: AUTHORIZE <obliged to ~ others to use his patent—Tris Coffin> <~me to offer my congratulations> * * * 4: to make possible Amer. Guide Series: Conn.>"

Thus, "permit" can be used to denote a narrow concept, such as express consent, but it also can mean something less than express consent, such as "tolerate" or "make possible." We also note that "permit" is not a statutory synonym of "authorize," because the latter term is listed separately in ORS 163.670(1). So, the question is whether "permit" is meant to convey a meaning equally or more restrictive than express consent, as defendant suggests, or whether it is meant to convey a somewhat less restrictive meaning, such as "tolerate" or "make possible." ... Both parties cite appellate decisions that have examined the meaning of the word "permit" in the context of various criminal statutes, and both assert that the case law construing those statutes supports their respective positions. As explained below, to the extent that the case law concerning different statutes is helpful in understanding the meaning of ORS 163.670, we conclude that, on balance, it supports the state's position.

In *State v. Reiland*, 153 Or.App. 601, 958 P.2d 900 (1998), we considered the meaning of the word "permit" as used in ORS 163.575, concerning endangering the welfare of a minor. That statute provides in pertinent part that a person commits the crime of endangering the welfare of a minor if the person knowingly "[p]ermits a person under 18 years of age to enter or remain in a place where unlawful activity involving controlled substances is maintained or conducted[.]" *Id.* at 604, 958 P.2d 900. In *Reiland*, the defendant had been convicted under both ORS 163.575 and another statute that criminalized "allow[ing] the child to stay * * * on premises and in the immediate proximity where controlled substances are criminally delivered or manufactured for consideration or profit." ORS 163.547(1). In addressing whether those offenses merged, we stated:

> "Here, we do not agree that proof that defendant 'allowed children to stay' and 'permitted children to remain' require proof of different elements. We note at the outset that 'allow' and 'permit' are synonyms. *Webster's Third New Int'l Dictionary* 58, 1683 (unabridged ed. 1993), as are 'stay' and 'remain,' Id. at 2231, 1919. We have previously construed the word 'permit' and required that '[b]efore one can be said to "permit" something, one must have authority to forbid it.'

State v. Pyritz, 90 Or.App. 601, 605, 752 P.2d 1310 (1988) (construing ORS 167.222(1)). The state argues that the child neglect prohibition against allowing a child to stay in a place where drugs are sold or used requires proof that the person has authority over the child, while the child endangerment prohibition against permitting a child to remain requires proof that the person has authority over the place. That is a distinction without a difference. *The owner of the place where drugs are being sold or used has authority over the child by virtue of the person's ownership of the place, just as others have authority over the child by virtue of their positions as parent, guardian, teacher, or public official."*

153 Or.App. at 604–05, 958 P.2d 900 (emphasis added). In short, we concluded that, at least for purposes of the statutes at issue there, "permit" and "allow" were synonymous, and that the notion from *Pyritz* that in order to permit something, "one must have the authority to forbid it," 90 Or.App. at 605, 752 P.2d 1310, encompassed a defendant's authority to forbid a crime from being carried out on his or her property, and not merely his or her legal authority over the child victim involved in the crimes. Thus, *Reiland* lends some support to the state's position that, in the context of statutes aimed at preventing harm to child victims, words such as "permit" and "allow" need not necessarily relate to one's authority over the child.

On the other hand, both of the statutes at issue in *Reiland* referred not only to the child victim, but also specifically referred to "a place," ORS 163.575, or "on premises," ORS 163.547, where the offense occurred. ORS 163.670, by contrast, contains no reference to the location where the crime of "using a child in a display of sexually explicit conduct" occurs. Thus, although *Reiland* undercuts defendant's suggestion that "permits" necessarily refers only to authority over a child victim, it is not dispositive here, given the dissimilarity of the statutes involved.

We turn to *Pyritz*, on which we relied in *Reiland*, for further guidance. That case, like *Reiland*, is of limited utility here, because it concerned "keep[ing], maintain[ing], frequent[ing], or remain[ing]" at a place while knowingly *"permitting* persons to use controlled substances in such place [.]" 90 Or.App. at 604, 752 P.2d 1310 (emphasis added). The defendant in *Pyritz* argued that the statute at issue was unconstitutionally vague. In that context, we concluded that "permitting" meant that a person "who, (1) having legal authority over persons who use, keep, or sell illegal controlled substances, at the specified place where the defendant frequents or remains, (2) authorizes or consents to such use, possession, or sale." *Id.* at 605, 752 P.2d 1310 (omitted). Defendant asserts that this case is like *Pyritz* and that "permitting" in this context, as in that one, requires legal authority over the victim. Again, however, the parallels between the statutes involved are not strong. The court in *Pyritz* began its discussion by acknowledging the rather broad definition of the word "permit," when it quoted from *Lemery v. Leonard*, 99 Or. 670, 678, 196 P. 376 (1921):

> "[O]ne cannot be said to have permitted a thing of which he has no knowledge or means of knowledge, so, that, if his animals escape from his enclosure without his knowledge or negligence, he does not come within the prohibitions of the statute against 'permitting' his stock to be at large. To 'permit' means to allow by tacit consent or by not hindering, taking no steps to prevent, or to grant leave by express consent or authorization."

(Quoting *Holly & Co. v. Simmons*, 38 Tex.Civ.App. 124, 85 S.W. 325, rev'd, 99 Tex. 230, 89 S.W. 776 (1905)). In *Lemery*—which concerned a statute that prohibited an owner from permitting sheep to run "at large"—the court focused primarily on the meaning of the term "at large." *Lemery*, 99 Or. at 673, 196 P. 376. That issue is so far afield from the question here that further discussion of that line of cases would be unhelpful, except to reinforce that, in some contexts, "permitting" carries a rather broad meaning, and in others, a narrower meaning.

Here, the legislature's intent is more apparent when ORS 163.670 is examined in context. As noted, the purpose of ORS 163.665 through 163.693 is to prevent "the underlying harm caused by child sexual abuse." *Stoneman*, 323 Or. at 547, 920 P.2d 535. Using a child in a display of sexually explicit conduct, ORS 163.670, is a Class A felony, and it is the most serious offense in the pertinent group of offenses. ORS 163.670 proscribes live presentations of sexually explicit conduct involving a child as well as the creation of visual recordings of sexually explicit conduct involving a child.

This group of statutes also includes two Class B felonies. Encouraging child sexual abuse in the first degree, ORS 163.684, applies where a person imports into the state visual depictions of sexually explicit conduct involving a child, or "develops, duplicates, publishes, prints, disseminates, exchanges, displays, finances, attempts to finance or sells" such materials. Possession of materials depicting sexually explicit conduct of a child in the first degree, ORS 163.688, involves using such materials "to induce a child to participate or engage in sexually explicit conduct."

There are also two Class C felonies in the pertinent group of statutes. ORS 163.686, which proscribes encouraging child sexual abuse in the second degree, prohibits various types of possession or purchase of recorded images of sexually explicit conduct involving a child, as well as paying to observe, or observing, sexually explicit conduct by a child, "for the purpose of arousing or gratifying the sexual desires of the person or another person," knowing that the use of the child in a sexual display constituted child abuse. Possession of materials depicting sexually explicit conduct of a child in the second degree, ORS 163.689, involves possession of the materials depicting sexually explicit conduct with the intent to use them to induce a child to engage in sexually explicit conduct.

Finally, the group also includes several Class A misdemeanors. Encouraging child sexual abuse in the third degree, ORS 163.687, generally prohibits the possession of depictions of sexually explicit conduct involving a child for purposes of arousing or satisfying sexual desire, while knowing or failing to be aware of a substantial and unjustifiable risk that the use of the child in a sexual display involved child abuse. Failure to report child pornography, ORS 163.693, applies when a person processes or produces a photograph depicting sexually explicit conduct involving a child but fails to report it to law enforcement agencies. Defenses to the various offenses include an exception for certain medical procedures, educational purposes, and law enforcement purposes, as well as an affirmative defense for each of the offenses, except ORS 163.670, based on lack of knowledge of the victim's age.

Thus, the statutory scheme begins with the most serious offense, which involves the actual creation of child pornography or the use of a child in a sexual display for a live audience. The next level of seriousness concerns distributing child pornography or using child pornography to induce children to engage in sexual conduct. The third descending level of seriousness generally concerns possession or observation of child pornography with the knowledge that a child was abused to create it, or intending to use such materials to induce a child to engage in sexually explicit conduct. Finally, the lowest level of crimes in the group generally involves possession or observation of child pornography while failing to be aware of a substantial and unjustifiable risk that a child was being abused, or, if a person is involved in processing images, failing to report the existence of child pornography. To summarize, the statutory scheme punishes most harshly the creation of child pornography, next, its distribution, beyond that, its use to promote further abuse of children, and finally, its use in general.

If defendant were correct that the phrase "permits * * * a child to participate or engage in sexually explicit conduct" can refer only to a person with legal authority over the child, then the statute—which, as noted, provides the most serious penalties among child pornography crimes—would *not criminalize* a significant amount of conduct that occurs in the making or presentation of child pornography. For example, the photographers who record a child engaging in sexually explicit conduct, as well as persons who provide the equipment and the venue for the use of the child in a display of sexually explicit conduct, would commit no crime when they participate in the creation of child pornography. Yet, as the statutory context demonstrates, the conduct of the distributors and consumers of child pornography is criminalized. It is unfathomable that the legislature would have chosen to insulate from prosecution the people who are instrumental in the production of live or recorded displays of sexually explicit conduct by children, while criminalizing the distribution and viewing of such conduct.

Accordingly, we conclude that, when it used in ORS 163.670 the phrase "permits * * * a child to participate or engage in sexually explicit conduct," the legislature did not intend to limit liability to those with a legal relationship to the child; rather, we conclude that the legislature intended "permit" to convey the broader meaning of "allow" or "make possible." In this case, viewing the evidence in the light most favorable to the state, there was sufficient evidence that defendant permitted his stepdaughter to be used in displays of sexually explicit conduct in his home. Accordingly, the trial court properly denied defendant's motion for judgment of acquittal.

Affirmed.

Notes

The court in *Porter* employs a broad application of statutory terms because of the context in which the conduct occurs. This practice has constitutional implications, and this is discussed in the following decision.

People v. Maness

Supreme Court of Illinois, 2000
191 Ill. 2d 478, 247 Ill. Dec. 490, 732 N.E.2d 545

Justice BILANDIC delivered the opinion of the court: ...

Section 5.1 of the Wrongs to Children Act (Act) (720 ILCS 150/1 *et seq.* (West 1992)) prohibits the offense of "permitting the sexual abuse of a child." For purposes of this case, section 5.1 provides:

> "A. A parent or step-parent who knowingly allows or permits an act of criminal sexual abuse or criminal sexual assault as defined in Section 12-13, 12-14, 12-15 or 12-16 of the 'Criminal Code of 1961,' [720 ILCS 5/12-13, 12-14, 12-15, 12-16 (West 1992)], upon his or her child and fails to take reasonable steps to prevent its commission or future occurrences of such acts commits the offense of permitting the sexual abuse of a child. For purposes of this Section, 'child' means a minor under the age of 17 years....

Relevant to the facts of this case is the underlying provision of the criminal sexual abuse statute, section 12-15 of the Criminal Code of 1961, which provides that "[t]he accused commits criminal sexual abuse if he or she commits an act of sexual penetration or sexual conduct with a victim who was at least 13 years of age but under 17 years of age and the accused was less than 5 years older than the victim." 720 ILCS 5/12-15(c) (West 1998). Criminal sexual abuse is a Class A misdemeanor. 720 ILCS 5/12-15(d) (West 1998)....

On November 19, 1997, defendant, Kathy Maness, was charged in the circuit court of Randolph County with the offense of permitting the sexual abuse of a child. See 720 ILCS 150/5.1 (West 1992). The charging instrument alleged that defendant, the mother of Lynlee Jo Otten, a minor under the age of 17 years, knowingly allowed or permitted Leonard A. Owens, Jr. to commit an act of criminal sexual abuse upon Lynlee, "in that Leonard A. Owens, Jr. committed an act of sexual penetration with Lynlee Jo Otten, who was at least 13 years of age, but under 17 years of age when the act was committed, in that Leonard A. Owens, Jr. placed his penis in the vagina of Lynlee Jo Otten, and Leonard A. Owens, Jr. was less than five years older than Lynlee Jo Otten, and the defendant did fail to take reasonable steps to prevent its commission." Defendant was alleged to have committed this offense in Randolph County, Illinois, where she and Lynlee lived, between the months of January and August of 1997.

Lynlee Otten was born on October 28, 1983. Leonard Owens was born on February 25, 1979. They started dating each other in August 1996, and began having sexual intercourse in December 1996. Between December 1996, and approximately April 1997, when the pair terminated their relationship, Lynlee and Leonard had sexual intercourse 15 to 20 times.... At some point after the sexual relationship began, Lynlee told defendant, her mother, that she and Leonard were having sexual intercourse. Defendant confronted both Lynlee and Leonard about the sexual relationship, expressed her disapproval, and discussed the implications of sexual intercourse.... Defendant obtained birth control pills for Lynlee and allowed Leonard on numerous occasions to spend the night at the family home. Defendant was aware that, on some of these occasions, Leonard slept in Lynlee's bedroom and had sexual intercourse with Lynlee. Defendant was also aware that, during the relevant time period, Leonard was 17 years old, and Lynlee was 13 years old. The record shows that Leonard pled guilty to criminal sexual abuse in connection with the facts of this case. See 720 ILCS 5/12-15 (West 1998).

According to an investigative report from the Department of Children and Family Services (DCFS), defendant stated that she did not know what steps to take to prevent the sexual relationship between Lynlee and Leonard. Defendant further stated that Leonard "was a nice boy and was better than most of the younger boys Lynlee was hanging around with," and that "it was safer for Lynlee to be having sex with [Leonard] at home than [with] somebody else out of the home environment." The DCFS report discloses that defendant "feels she has some control of the daughter's sexual activities if it occurs in the home." ... Defendant filed a motion to dismiss the charge, arguing that section 5.1 is unconstitutionally vague as to what constitutes "reasonable steps" to prevent the commission of future acts of sexual abuse. According to defendant, the statute exposes any parent to prosecution if a child "becomes pregnant, sires a child, asks for birth control devices, or seeks any counsel from the teenager's parents regarding sexual activity." Defendant also argued that section 5.1 of the Act, both on its face and as applied in this case, violates defendant's fundamental liberty right to raise her child free from undue state influence as guaranteed by the fourteenth amendment to the United States Constitution and article I, section 2, of the Illinois Constitution of 1970.

Following a hearing, the circuit court, in a verbal order, granted defendant's motion to dismiss the charge. The transcript of the order reveals that the circuit court found that section 5.1 "may implicate first amendment concerns of the defendant or of a parent or guardian to effectively address the problem of underage teenage sex in their particular family situation." The circuit court also held that section 5.1 is unconstitutionally vague as to what constitutes "reasonable steps" to prevent the commission of future acts of sexual abuse.... The State appealed directly to this court. Because the circuit court declared section 5.1 of the Act unconstitutional on its face, this court has jurisdiction over this appeal pursuant to Supreme Court Rule 603 (134 Ill.2d R. 603)....

We review *de novo* a circuit court's holding with respect to the constitutionality of a statute. *Russell v. Department of Natural Resources*, 183 Ill.2d 434, 441, 233 Ill.Dec. 782, 701 N.E.2d 1056 (1998). Statutes carry a strong presumption of constitutionality, and the party challenging the constitutionality of a statute bears the burden of rebutting this presumption. *Russell*, 183 Ill.2d at 441, 233 Ill.Dec. 782, 701 N.E.2d 1056. Here, that party is defendant, who for the reasons set forth below has met this burden.

A cornerstone of our jurisprudence is that no person shall be deprived of life, liberty, or property without due process of law. U.S. Const., amends. V, XIV; Ill. Const.1970, art. I, § 2. Due process of law requires that the proscriptions of a criminal statute be clearly defined. *City of Chicago v. Morales*, 177 Ill.2d 440, 448, 227 Ill.Dec. 130, 687 N.E.2d 53 (1997), *aff'd*, 527 U.S. 41, 119 S.Ct. 1849, 144 L.Ed.2d 67 (1999). To satisfy the vagueness doctrine, a criminal statute must meet two requirements. First, the statute must provide a person of ordinary intelligence a reasonable opportunity to distinguish between lawful and unlawful conduct so that he or she may act accordingly. *Russell*, 183 Ill.2d at 442, 233 Ill.Dec. 782, 701 N.E.2d 1056; *Morales*, 177 Ill.2d at 449, 227 Ill.Dec. 130, 687 N.E.2d 53. "'No one may be required at peril of life, liberty or property to speculate as to the meaning of penal statutes. All are entitled to be informed as to what the State commands or forbids.'" *Morales*, 177 Ill.2d at 450, 227 Ill.Dec. 130, 687 N.E.2d 53, quoting *Lanzetta v. New Jersey*, 306 U.S. 451, 453, 59 S.Ct. 618, 619, 83 L.Ed. 888, 890 (1939). Thus, a statute is unconstitutionally vague "if its terms are so indefinite that 'persons of common intelligence must necessarily guess at its meaning and differ as to its application.'" *Fagiano v. Police Board*, 98 Ill.2d 277, 282, 74 Ill.Dec. 525, 456 N.E.2d 27 (1983), quoting *Polyvend, Inc. v. Puckorius*, 77 Ill.2d 287, 299–300, 32 Ill.Dec. 872, 395 N.E.2d 1376 (1979).

Second, the statute must adequately define the offense in order to prevent arbitrary and discriminatory enforcement. *Russell*, 183 Ill.2d at 442, 233 Ill.Dec. 782, 701 N.E.2d 1056; *Morales*, 177 Ill.2d at 449, 227 Ill.Dec. 130, 687 N.E.2d 53. The statute must provide explicit standards to regulate the discretion of governmental authorities who apply the law. *Russell*, 183 Ill.2d at 442, 233 Ill.Dec. 782, 701 N.E.2d 1056; *Morales*, 177 Ill.2d at 456, 227 Ill.Dec. 130, 687 N.E.2d 53. If the legislature fails to provide minimal guidelines to govern law enforcement, a criminal law "may permit 'a standardless sweep [that] allows policemen, prosecutors, and juries to pursue their personal predilections.'" *Kolender v. Lawson*, 461 U.S. 352, 358, 103 S.Ct. 1855, 1858, 75 L.Ed.2d 903, 909 (1983), quoting *Smith v. Goguen*, 415 U.S. 566, 575, 94 S.Ct. 1242, 1248, 39 L.Ed.2d 605, 613 (1974).

Section 5.1 does not satisfy these requirements. To be charged under section 5.1, a parent must knowingly allow or permit an enumerated act of criminal sexual abuse or sexual assault to be committed upon his or her child, and fail to take "reasonable steps" to prevent its commission or future occurrences. 720 ILCS 150/5.1 (West 1992). It is unclear what the "reasonable steps" are that a parent must take in order to comply with the statute. The facts of this case demonstrate this uncertainty. As the record reveals, defendant's 13-year-old daughter confided in defendant that she was having sexual intercourse with her 17-year-old boyfriend. At this point, defendant, as a parent, took steps. She confronted her daughter and her daughter's boyfriend about the sexual relationship, expressed her disapproval, and discussed the implications of sexual intercourse. The statute does not set forth what more the statute commands.

We recognize that defendant obtained birth control pills for her daughter and allowed her daughter's boyfriend to spend the night at the family home. Defendant was aware that at times her daughter and her daughter's boyfriend slept together in her daughter's bedroom and had sexual intercourse with each other. Defendant, however, stated that she did not know what steps to take to prevent the sexual relationship between her daughter and her daughter's boyfriend, and that she felt she had more control over her daughter's sexual activities if they occurred in the home. We are in no position to determine whether defendant's actions constituted "reasonable steps" under the statute. We find that section 5.1 leaves a parent to speculate as to what the statute commands.

Furthermore, section 5.1 risks arbitrary and discriminatory enforcement. As we have discussed, the statute does not set forth standards to regulate what constitute "reasonable steps." There are no guidelines for authorities to follow in evaluating what "reasonable steps" are from case to case. This is certainly not a decision that should be left to the "personal predilections" of the governmental authorities who must apply section 5.1. Section 5.1 enumerates several underlying offenses. Regardless of the underlying offense, it is unclear what a parent must do to take "reasonable steps" under the statute, and authorities remain without standards to guide their enforcement of section 5.1.

We note that, in reviewing whether a statute is vague, a court may also consider the legislative purpose and the evil that the statute is designed to remedy. *People v. R.G.*, 131 Ill.2d 328, 361, 137 Ill.Dec. 588, 546 N.E.2d 533 (1989). The legislative history is silent as to the purposes underlying the need for section 5.1. The legislative debates concerning the bill that created the offense of permitting the sexual abuse of a child contain only general references to the name of the offense. We therefore have no information to help define what the statute commands. A person of ordinary intelligence is left to guess at its meaning and disagree as to its application. Due process of law requires that the proscriptions of a criminal statute be clearly defined. Section 5.1 fails to satisfy this requirement.

The dissent states that the "majority has not cited any authority for the proposition that a 'reasonableness' standard renders a criminal statute unconstitutionally vague, and I see no basis for reaching that conclusion with respect to section 5.1." 191 Ill.2d at 490, 247 Ill.Dec. at 497, 732 N.E.2d at 552 (Harrison, C.J., dissenting, joined by Miller and McMorrow, JJ.). The dissent then proceeds to discuss several areas of law where a reasonableness standard is used. We, of course, do not suggest that a reasonableness standard renders a statute unconstitutionally vague. Rather, we hold that the statute at issue in this case, section 5.1, is unconstitutionally vague because it is not clear what the "reasonable steps" are that a parent must take in order to avoid criminal prosecution thereunder.

The dissent further contends that there "are numerous instances in which application of the statute would be proper," and then purports to give an example. 191 Ill.2d at 490, 247 Ill.Dec. at 497, 732 N.E.2d at 552 (Harrison, C.J., dissenting, joined by Miller and McMorrow, JJ.). The dissent's reasoning is flawed. The legal test for whether a statute withstands a vagueness challenge is well settled. To satisfy the vagueness doctrine, a criminal statute must provide both fair warning of the prohibited conduct and explicit guidelines for those who must apply the law. See, *e.g.*, *Morales*, 177 Ill.2d at 449, 227 Ill.Dec. 130, 687 N.E.2d 53. Section 5.1 fails to meet this test. Section 5.1 requires a parent who knowingly allows an enumerated act to be committed upon his or her child to take "reasonable steps" to prevent the commission of the enumerated act. However, it is not clear what the "reasonable steps" are that a parent must take in order to comply with the statute and avoid criminal prosecution. The dissent's answer, that "a mother who gave express permission to one of her adult male friends to have sex with her 12-year-old daughter would clearly fall within the statute's prohibitions" (191 Ill.2d at 490, 247 Ill.Dec. at 497, 732 N.E.2d at 552 (Harrison, C.J., dissenting, joined by Miller and McMorrow, JJ.)), begs the question of what a parent must in fact do in the first instance to comply with section 5.1's requirement of taking "reasonable steps" to prevent the enumerated act. The statute criminally punishes all parents who knowingly permit an enumerated act to occur and fail to take "reasonable steps" to prevent the act. Do "reasonable steps" mean that the parent must call the police, ban the offender from the home, send the child away, speak with the offender? The point is that, regardless of the underlying conduct, section 5.1 leaves a parent to speculate as to what the statute commands.

The dissent also concludes that defendant took "no steps" to prevent the abuse. 191 Ill.2d at 491, 247 Ill.Dec. at 497, 732 N.E.2d at 552 (Harrison, C.J., dissenting, joined by Miller and McMorrow, JJ.). The record reveals otherwise. Defendant confronted her daughter and her daughter's boyfriend about the sexual relationship, expressed her disapproval, and discussed the implications of sexual intercourse. What the dissent really appears to be saying is that defendant did not do enough. However, neither section 5.1, nor the dissent for that matter, specifies what more defendant must have done to avoid criminal prosecution.

We hold that section 5.1 is unconstitutionally vague. We therefore affirm the circuit court's order dismissing the charge against defendant. Consequently, we need not determine whether section 5.1 unconstitutionally infringes upon defendant's fundamental right to raise her child. We also note that, because the offense of permitting the sexual abuse of a child is no longer a Class 1 felony (see *People v. Cervantes*, 189 Ill.2d 80, 243 Ill.Dec. 233, 723 N.E.2d 265 (1999)), we need not address defendant's argument raised in this court that applying section 5.1 to her conduct violates the constitutional prohibition against disproportionate penalties.

Affirmed.

Chief Justice HARRISON, dissenting:

Section 5.1 of the Wrongs to Children Act (720 ILCS 150/5.1 (West 1992)) imposes on parents a duty to take "reasonable steps" to prevent the commission or future occurrence of criminal sexual abuse of their children. Although my colleagues find this standard problematic, I do not believe that it renders the statute unconstitutionally vague. A penal statute comports with due process so long as the statute's prohibitions are sufficiently definite, when measured by common understanding and practices, to give a person of ordinary intelligence fair warning as to what conduct is prohibited, and the statute marks boundaries sufficiently distinct for judges and juries fairly to administer the law in accordance with the intent of the legislature. *People v. Hickman*, 163 Ill.2d 250, 256–57, 206 Ill.Dec. 94, 644 N.E.2d 1147 (1994).

Section 5.1 satisfies these requirements. While the statute does not specifically enumerate what constitute "reasonable steps" to prevent the commission or future occurrence of criminal sexual abuse, it is not alone in this regard. A similar standard has been employed successfully in many other areas of the law. For example, section 1(D)(m) of the Adoption Act (750 ILCS 50/1(D)(m) (West 1998)) provides that where a child has been removed from a parent by the State, the parent's failure to make "reasonable efforts" to correct the conditions that were the basis for removal of the child is grounds for finding the parent unfit. As a matter of common law, hospitals and physicians must take "reasonable steps" to avoid a foreseeable tragedy in their facility. See *Winger v. Franciscan Medical Center*,

299 Ill.App.3d 364, 375, 233 Ill.Dec. 748, 701 N.E.2d 813 (1998). Under the Domestic Violence Act of 1986 (750 ILCS 60/101 *et seq.* (West 1998)), law enforcement officials have a duty to promptly undertake "all reasonable steps" to assist persons protected by the Act. *Calloway v. Kinkelaar*, 168 Ill.2d 312, 326, 213 Ill.Dec. 675, 659 N.E.2d 1322 (1995). Tort law dictates that if an accident is reasonably foreseeable, a party is charged with responsibility to take "reasonable steps" to avoid it. See *Cannon v. Commonwealth Edison Co.*, 250 Ill.App.3d 379, 384–85, 190 Ill.Dec. 183, 621 N.E.2d 52 (1993).

Whether a party has acted reasonably will necessarily depend on the facts and circumstances of each particular case. What action is reasonable under the circumstances is not always easy to assess. Experience has shown, however, that when dealing with diverse and unpredictable situations, a " reasonableness" standard is the best measure for judging human conduct. Accordingly, the "reasonable man" standard has become a fundamental part of our jurisprudence. We constantly call upon citizens and law enforcement officials to follow and apply this standard. Again, examples are easy to summon. "Reasonableness" plays a pivotal role in assessing the legality of police stops. *People v. Gonzalez*, 184 Ill.2d 402, 422–24, 235 Ill.Dec. 26, 704 N.E.2d 375 (1998). It is integral to the law of self-defense (*People v. Morgan*, 187 Ill.2d 500, 533, 241 Ill.Dec. 552, 719 N.E.2d 681 (1999)) and the law governing trade secrets (765 ILCS 1065/2(d) (West 1998); *Jackson v. Hammer*, 274 Ill.App.3d 59, 66–67, 210 Ill.Dec. 614, 653 N.E.2d 809 (1995)).

The majority has not cited any authority for the proposition that a "reasonableness" standard renders a criminal statute unconstitutionally vague, and I see no basis for reaching that conclusion with respect to section 5.1. Even if one could hypothesize circumstances in which application of the statute would be uncertain, that is not the test. A statute is unconstitutionally vague on its face only if it is incapable of any valid application (*People v. Wawczak*, 109 Ill.2d 244, 249, 93 Ill.Dec. 378, 486 N.E.2d 911 (1985)), *i.e.*, where " 'no set of circumstances exists under which the [statute] would be valid.' " *In re C.E.*, 161 Ill.2d 200, 211, 204 Ill.Dec. 121, 641 N.E.2d 345 (1994), quoting *United States v. Salerno*, 481 U.S. 739, 745, 107 S.Ct. 2095, 2100, 95 L.Ed.2d 697, 707 (1987).

Section 5.1 is not infirm under this standard. There are numerous instances in which application of the statute would be proper. For example, a mother who gave express permission to one of her adult male friends to have sex with her 12-year-old daughter would clearly fall within the statute's prohibitions.... Because there are valid applications for the statute and because the law does not involve first amendment rights, the determination as to whether the statute is constitutionally infirm must be made in the factual context of this particular case. *Russell v. Department of Natural Resources*, 183 Ill.2d 434, 442, 233 Ill.Dec. 782, 701 N.E.2d 1056 (1998). Maness does not have standing to argue that the statute might be vague as applied to someone else. See *People v. Jihan*, 127 Ill.2d 379, 385, 130 Ill.Dec. 422, 537 N.E.2d 751 (1989). A defendant may be prosecuted under a statute without violating her due process rights if her conduct clearly falls within the statutory proscription even though the statute may be vague as to other conduct. *People v. Anderson*, 148 Ill.2d 15, 28, 169 Ill.Dec. 288, 591 N.E.2d 461 (1992).

What Maness is alleged to have done in this case clearly falls within the prohibitions of section 5.1 of the Wrongs to Children Act. Maness knowingly permitted Leonard Owens, Jr., a 17-year-old boy, to repeatedly commit criminal sexual abuse of her 13-year-old daughter. Although Maness confronted the couple about their activities, counseled them and expressed her disapproval, the record also shows that she facilitated the criminal sexual abuse by allowing Owens to sleep with her daughter in her daughter's bedroom. When Owens had sex with Maness' daughter, it was usually in the bedroom and usually while Maness and her husband were at home. Maness was aware of this sexual activity and took no steps to stop it. Her view was that if her daughter was going to have sex with Owens, it was safer if she did so at home where Maness had some control.

Maness' contention that she was uncertain as to the law's application is unpersuasive. While persons of ordinary intelligence may sometimes be left to speculate as to what constitute "reasonable steps" to prevent the commission of criminal sexual abuse, this is not one of those situations. Maness is not being prosecuted because of how she counseled her daughter regarding her sexuality or because she obtained birth control medication and prophylactics for her daughter to use. Maness' problem is that the law in Illinois prohibits 17-year-olds from having sex with 13-year-olds, and Maness repeatedly and expressly allowed a 17-year-old to have sex with her daughter in her house. Any person of ordinary intelligence would understand that such conduct constitutes a failure to take "reasonable steps" to prevent criminal sexual abuse within the meaning of the law.

There is likewise no merit to Maness' contention that the statute is invalid because it unduly infringes on a parent's right to raise her child. Under the fourteenth amendment, parents have a "fundamental liberty interest * * * in the care, custody, and management of their child[ren,]" with which the government may not interfere unduly. *Santosky v. Kramer*, 455 U.S. 745, 753–54, 102 S.Ct. 1388, 1394–95, 71 L.Ed.2d 599, 606 (1982). Parental autonomy, however, is not absolute. See *Lehman v. Stephens*, 148 Ill.App.3d 538, 547, 101 Ill.Dec. 736, 499 N.E.2d 103 (1986). In matters concerning child abuse and neglect, a parent's rights yield to the state's interest in protecting its children. *American Federation of State, County & Municipal Employees v. Department of Central Management Services*, 173 Ill.2d 299, 319, 219 Ill.Dec. 501, 671 N.E.2d 668 (1996).... The right to be a parent does not encompass the right to abuse one's child or to allow one's child to be abused. If Maness had knowingly allowed Owens to inject her daughter with heroin and provided the couple with a place in her home where the drugs could be injected, there would be no question that Maness could be prosecuted for child endangerment (720 ILCS 5/12-21.6 (West 1998)) or worse, without offending the constitution. The result should not be different because the abuse involves illegal sex rather than illegal drugs.

For the foregoing reasons, the judgment of the circuit court should be reversed and the cause should be remanded for further proceedings. I therefore dissent.

Justices MILLER and McMORROW join in this dissent.

Note

In *Maness*, the issue involved a mother's failure to prevent her minor daughter from engaging in consensual sexual intercourse. The court struck down the Illinois statute as unconstitutionally vague, but the legislative effort to impose parental liability for the acts of one's child has expanded to other areas of responsibility, such as failing to providing adequate supervision and contributing to delinquent behavior. See Susan S. Huo, *A Little Privacy, Please: Should We Punish Parents for Teenage Sex?*, 89 Ky. L.J. 135 (2001) (advocating against parental liability for childrens' sexual activity based on family privacy concerns). With respect to permitting exploitation, more typical, perhaps, are situations in which one parent becomes aware or suspects that a child is being sexually abused or exploited by the other parent but fails to believe the child or takes no measures to protect the child from continued abuse or exploitation. Would such behavior satisfy a criminal provision similar to the applicable statute in *Porter*? Would such conduct constitute child abuse or exploitation? If not, may it still qualify under a civil standard of child neglect sufficient for the state to intervene? *See, e.g.*, ARK. CODE ANN. §9-27-303(18)(A)(iii), (iv) (2014) (child deemed "dependent-neglected juvenile" if at substantial risk of serious harm for parent's act or omission involving sexual abuse or sexual exploitation).

In considering this question, the court in *In the Matter of Glenn*, 154 Misc.2d 677, 587 N.Y.S.2d 464 (1992), perceived a range of conduct that fell within a scale of liability between abuse and neglect, with abuse consisting of active participation in the conduct against the children, and neglect consisting of careless, negligent, or inattentive passivity by failing to exercise a minimum degree of care to protect the children, i.e., conduct that is not deliberate. *See Glenn*, 154 Misc. 2d at 682–83; 587 N.Y.S.2d at 467. In *Glenn*, the father had sexually abused the children by improper touching, which the mother observed. When she confronted the father, he threatened to kill her. The mother failed to report the sexual abuse or to protect the children. In *Glenn*, the court accepted evidence that the mother was a victim of "Battered Woman's Syndrome" and held that the mother knew of the sexual abuse of the children but was powerless to stop it, or to protect the children, because she was a victim of the syndrome. Thus, the court deemed her passive behavior as neglect, but not abuse. *See also State v. Stewart*, 228 W. Va. 406, 719 S.E.2d 876, 885 (2011) (admitting expert testimony of evidence of battered woman syndrome in murder trial to negate intent element); *Pickle v. State*, 280 Ga. App. 821, 635 S.E.2d 197, 201, 203–04 (2006) (evidence of battered person syndrome admissible to rebut intent for aggravated assault of child); *Mott v. Stewart*, No. 98-CV-239, 2002 WL 31017646, at *6 (D. Ariz. Aug. 30, 2002) (court erred by excluding expert testimony of character traits of battered women, offered to negate intent in felony child abuse); *Porter v. State*, 243 Ga. App. 498, 532 S.E.2d 407, 416 (2000) (expert testimony on battered woman syndrome admissible to show whether defendant knew of husband's actions related to child abuse charge against her). *But see Brewington v. State*, 98 So.3d 628 (Fla. App. 2 Dist. 2012) (in case of aggravated manslaughter of a child, defendant failed to establish that the theory that battered woman syndrome could negate mens rea for failing to protect a child had been sufficiently tested and generally accepted by the relevant scientific or psychological community, such as to satisfy the requirements under *Frye* test). For further discussion of this subject, see Kathy Luttrell Garcia, *Battered Women and Battered Children: Admissibility of Evidence of Battering and its Effects to Determine the Mens Rea of a Battered Woman Facing Criminal Charges for Failing to Protect a Child From Abuse*, 24 J. Juv. L. 101, 104 (2003–04). *See also* Emily Winograd Leonard, *Expecting the Unattainable: Caseworker Use of the "Ideal" Mother Stereotype Against the Nonoffending Mother for Failure to Protect From Child Sexual Abuse Cases*, 69 N.Y.U. Annual Survey of Am. L. 311 (2013) (discussing issue within emergency removal proceeding process).

Nevertheless, many states expressly impose liability on parents who fail to prevent the sexual exploitation of children in their care. *See, e.g.*, Ark. Code § 5-27-221 (2014) ("Permitting abuse of a minor" includes recklessly failing to prevent "sexual intercourse, deviate sexual activity, sexual contact, or ... physical injury...."); Iowa Code § 726.6 (2013) (parent guilty of child endangerment when he or she "knowingly permits the continuing physical or sexual abuse of a child or minor."); N.J. Stat. Ann. § 2A:61B-1 (2014) ("parent ... who knowingly permits or acquiesces in sexual abuse by any other person also commits sexual abuse...."). *See also Sullivan v. State*, 378 S.W.3d 921, 2011 Ark. App. 576, vacated 386 S.W.3d 507, 2012 Ark. 74 (2011) (trial court within authority to require defendant convicted of "permitting the abuse of a minor," to register as a sex offender). Consider, also, that if the person aware of the abuse is not expressly criminally liable, such a person still may be subject to state reporting requirements for failure to report the abuse to authorities. State statutory reporting requirements are discussed in Chapter Five (Reporting Child Sexual Exploitation), *infra*.

B. Enticement

United States v. Taylor

Seventh Circuit, 2011
640 F.3d 255

POSNER, Circuit Judge.

The defendant was charged with violating 18 U.S.C. § 2422(b), which provides that anyone who, "using the mail or any facility or means of interstate or foreign commerce, or within the special maritime and territorial jurisdiction of the United States[,] knowingly persuades, induces, entices, or coerces any individual who has not attained the age of 18 years, to engage in prostitution or any sexual activity for which any person can be charged with a criminal offense, or attempts to do so, shall be fined under this title and imprisoned not less than 10 years or for life." He was convicted by a jury and sentenced to the statutory minimum of 10 years in prison. The appeal requires us to construe the statutory term "sexual activity" — surprisingly an issue on which there is very little law....

The government relied on two Indiana offenses to convict the defendant: "touch[ing] or fondl[ing] the person's own body ... in the presence of a child less than fourteen (14) years of age with the intent to arouse or satisfy the sexual desires of the child or the older person," Ind.Code § 35-42-4-5(c)(3) ("fondling in the presence of a minor" is the name of this crime), and "knowingly or intentionally solicit[ing] a child under fourteen (14) years of age [or believed to be so] ... to engage in ... any fondling or touching intended to arouse or satisfy the sexual desires of either the child or the older person." § 35-42-4-6(b)(3) ("child solicitation"). The defendant does not contend in this appeal that the conduct that he was accused of engaging in did not violate the Indiana statutes. He contends rather that such conduct is not "sexual activity" within the meaning of the federal statute, and therefore that his conviction — which was solely for violating federal law — should be quashed....

A police officer entered an online chat room, where she "met" the defendant and identified herself as a 13-year-old girl. (It's because she was actually an adult that the defendant was charged with and convicted of an attempt rather than of a completed crime; section 2422(b) explicitly punishes an attempt just as severely.) After making a number of sexual comments to her that she pretended to welcome, the defendant masturbated in front of his webcam, thus attempting to violate the "fondling in the presence of a minor" statute; and, in addition, by inviting the "girl" to masturbate, he attempted to violate the "child solicitation" statute as well. If an adult's masturbating in front of a child in an effort to arouse the child's sexual desires, and a child's fondling herself in a sexually suggestive way, as by masturbating, are forms of "sexual activity" within the meaning of the federal statute, then the defendant's violations of the two Indiana statutes violated section 2422(b) as well.

"Sexual activity" is not a defined term in the federal criminal code (Title 18). Chapter 117 of the code, which contains section 2422, doesn't have a definition section. The next section after section 2422 states that as used in that next section "the term 'illicit sexual conduct' means ... a sexual act (as defined in section 2246) with a person under 18 years of age." 18 U.S.C. § 2423(f). The relevant part of section 2246, which appears in Chapter 109A of Title 18, defines "sexual act" as "the intentional touching, not through the clothing, of the genitalia of another person who has not attained the age of 16 years." 18 U.S.C. § 2246(2)(D). The defendant was not charged with attempting to touch the supposed girl, and of course that would be impossible in an online chat room. So if section 2422(b) criminalized a "sexual act" rather than "sexual activity," it would be reasonably clear that he could not be convicted, unless the definition of "sexual act" elsewhere in Title 18 were thought to cast no light on its meaning in section 2422(b). On the contrary, we have previously used definitions found in Chapter 109A (the chapter in which section 2246, defining "sexual act," appears) to assist in interpreting provisions in other chapters of Title 18 that punish sexual crimes. *United States v. Osborne*, 551 F.3d 718, 720 (7th Cir.2009). Section 2422(b) is one of those provisions.

We need to decide whether "sexual activity" encompasses a broader range of acts than "sexual act." If it did, one would expect the term to be defined in the statute, to indicate just how broad that range was. Is watching a pornographic movie, or a pole dancer, or a striptease artist, or Balthus's erotic paintings, or Aubrey Beardsley's pornographic sketches, or Titian's "Rape of Europa," or "Last Tango in Paris" a "sexual activity"? How about inducing someone to watch one of these shows? Wikipedia defines "sexual activity" very broadly; the Wikipedia entry for "Human Sexual Activity" says that "sexual activity … includes conduct and activities which are intended to arouse the sexual interest of another, such as strategies to find or attract partners (mating and display behavior), and personal interactions between individuals, such as flirting and foreplay." "Human Sexual Activity," http://en.wikipedia.org/wiki/Human_sexual_activity (visited April 1, 2011). Does the government think that the term "sexual activity" in 18 U.S.C. § 2242(b) includes flirting? Well, how about "flashing"? That is "sexual activity" in the literal sense, though it does not involve physical contact and so is not a "sexual act." It is generally considered a rather minor sex crime, certainly not the sort of crime for which a minimum of 10 years in prison is a proper sentence. In Indiana, for example, "a person at least eighteen (18) years of age who knowingly or intentionally, in a public place, appears in a state of nudity with the intent to be seen by a child less than sixteen (16) years of age commits public indecency, a Class A misdemeanor." Ind.Code § 35-45-4-1(b). And the maximum prison sentence for a Class A misdemeanor is only one year. § 35-50-3-2. Yet if the government's broad conception of "sexual activity" were accepted, then by virtue of that misdemeanor law a flasher in the lobby of the federal courthouse in South Bend, if charged under 18 U.S.C. § 2422(b), would be courting a prison sentence of at least 10 years.

One possible inference from the absence of a statutory definition of "sexual activity" is that the members of Congress (those who thought about the matter, at any rate) considered the terms "sexual act" and "sexual activity" interchangeable. This inference is reinforced by the fact that until 1998 section 2422(b) used the term "sexual act," while the preceding subsection, 2422(a), used "sexual activity," even though the two subsections were otherwise very similar, except that (a) concerns transporting minors across state lines rather than interstate solicitation and specifies a considerably lighter punishment (no minimum and a maximum of 20 years, versus a 10-year minimum and a maximum of life in (b)). In 1998, "sexual act" in (b) was changed to "sexual activity," but the committee report uses the terms "sexual activity" and "sexual act" interchangeably, indicating that the terms have the same meaning—that the purpose of the wording change from "sexual act" to "sexual activity" was merely to achieve semantic uniformity of substantively identical prohibitions, rather than to broaden the offense in (b). H.R.Rep. No. 105-557, at 10, 20 (1998), reprinted in 1998 U.S.C.C.A.N. 678, 679, 688. The implication that Congress regards "sexual activity" as a synonym for "sexual act" is further supported by the fact that the statute brackets "sexual activity" with "prostitution," which involves physical contact. We find nothing in the 1998 amendment or its discussion by members of Congress to suggest a legislative purpose of subjecting less serious sexual misconduct (misconduct involving no physical contact) to the draconian penalties in subsection (b).

Elsewhere in the vast body of federal statutory law we find scattered references to "sexual conduct," "sexual act," and "sexual activity" or "sexual activities," but the terms seem to be regarded as synonymous, as in 42 U.S.C. § 608(a)(7)(C)(iii)(IV), which defines "battered or subjected to extreme cruelty" to include "being forced as the caretaker relative of a dependent child to engage in nonconsensual sexual acts or activities." It would be unrealistic to suppose that Congress never uses synonyms—that every word or phrase in a statute has a unique meaning, shared by no other word or phrase elsewhere in the vast federal code.... One might think that "sexual activity" connoted a series of acts rather than a single act: for example, being a sexual predator rather than committing a single act of sexual predation, or being a prostitute. But that is not argued (it would make the express reference to prostitution in the statute redundant, though many statutes are littered with redundancies), and anyway there is a separate provision for enhanced punishment of sex-crime recidivists. 18 U.S.C. § 2426.

The government argues that as a matter of ordinary usage, "sexual activity" includes masturbation. True—but so does "sexual act." Yet Congress as we know defined "sexual act" as excluding sex acts that do not involve physical contact between two people. If "sexual activity" is no broader than "sexual act," it doesn't include solitary sex acts either. Congress elsewhere has defined "sexually explicit conduct" to include masturbation, but that's in a statute (18 U.S.C. § 2256(2)(A)) that criminalizes films and videos of children masturbating. (Maybe the defendant in this case could have been charged with attempting to produce child pornography because he asked the supposed minor to masturbate for him on her webcam. See 18 U.S.C. § 2252(a)(1), (b)(1). She said she had no webcam.) ... The government acknowledges that "sexual activity for which a person can be charged with a criminal offense" is explicitly defined to include producing child pornography. 18 U.S.C. § 2427. Explicitly defining sexual activity to include producing child pornography was needed only if the term "sexual activity" requires contact, since the creation of pornography doesn't involve contact between the pornographer and another person; this is further evidence that "sexual activity" as used in the federal criminal code does require contact.

Last the government cites cases in which courts have referred to masturbation as a form of sexual activity. In none was the question that this appeal presents raised. In one the court treated "sexual activity" as a synonym for "sexual acts." *United States v. Lee*, 502 F.3d 447, 448 (6th Cir.2007). In two others, *United States v. Root*, 296 F.3d 1222, 1235–36 (11th Cir.2002), and *United States v. Tello*, 600 F.3d 1161, 1163 (9th Cir.2010), the defendant intended to have sexual intercourse with the (supposed) girl that he met in the chat room, and he actually traveled to meet her. *United States v. Holt*, 510 F.3d 1007, 1009 (9th Cir.2007), a case not cited by the government, is similar to *Root* and *Tello*: the defendant traveled in order to meet and have sex with the supposed minor. The unreported decision in *United States v. Wales*, 127 Fed.Appx. 424 (10th Cir.2005), involved facts similar to those of this case, but again masturbation was merely assumed to be sexual activity within the meaning of section 2422(b). In our case of *United States v. Cochran*, 534 F.3d 631, 634 n. 3 (7th Cir.2008)—another case factually similar to the present one—the question of the meaning of the term "sexual activity" in section 2422(b) was neither raised by the appellant nor answered by the court. Finally, *United States v. Womack*, 509 F.2d 368, 372 n. 4 (D.C.Cir.1972), was a pornography case; it had nothing to do with section 2422(b), and merely illustrates (as do the other cases cited by the government) that masturbation is a form of "sexual activity" in the ordinary-language sense of the term, which judges use on occasion just as laypersons do. Masturbation is also a "sexual act" in that sense, but not in the statutory sense.

To repeat our basic point: if "sexual activity" and "sexual act" are synonymous in Title 18, as they appear to be, then "sexual activity" requires contact because "sexual act," we know, does. We cannot be certain that they are synonyms. Maybe our interpretation of section 2422(b) is no more plausible than the government's. But when there are two equally plausible interpretations of a criminal statute, the defendant is entitled to the benefit of the more lenient one. "[T]he tie must go to the defendant." *United States v. Santos*, 553 U.S. 507, 514, 128 S.Ct. 2020, 170 L.Ed.2d 912 (2008); see also *Bell v. United States*, 349 U.S. 81, 83–84, 75 S.Ct. 620, 99 L.Ed. 905 (1955) (Frankfurter, J.). "This venerable rule [the 'rule of lenity,' as it is called] not only vindicates the fundamental principle that no citizen should be held accountable for a violation of a statute whose commands are uncertain, or subjected to punishment that is not clearly prescribed. It also places the weight of inertia upon the party that can best induce Congress to speak more clearly and keeps courts from making criminal law in Congress's stead." *United States v. Santos, supra*, 553 U.S. at 514, 128 S.Ct. 2020.

Congress will have to define "sexual activity" more broadly than "sexual act" if it wants to bring the kind of behavior engaged in by the defendant in this case within the prohibition of section 2422(b) via the fondling and child-solicitation offenses found in the Indiana criminal code, when the defendant neither made nor, so far as appears, attempted or intended physical contact with the victim. In the meantime, however, assuming the defendant's conception of the breadth of the Indiana statutes is correct, our interpretation of the federal statute will not allow the likes of the defendant to elude just punishment. For his more serious Indiana offense (child solicitation involving use of the Internet, which Indiana law treats as an aggravating circumstance), he could be sentenced to eight years in prison by an Indiana court. See Ind.Code §§ 35-42-4-6(b)(3), 35-50-2-6(a).

The judgment is reversed with instructions to enter a judgment of acquittal.

Reversed and Remanded.

MANION, Circuit Judge, concurring.

The court has presented a thorough comparative analysis of federal law and precedent to conclude that "sexual activity" and "sexual act" mean the same thing—under either label, any such act that does not involve physical contact between two people is excluded. I would not go so far and equate the term "sexual activity" with "sexual act." Sexual activity is a broader term that includes things sexual that do not involve the actual physical encounter.... I do, however, agree that there are serious problems with this case: I do not believe that Jeffrey P. Taylor could be successfully prosecuted for either of the Indiana crimes that the government alleged he committed, and for that reason, I respectfully concur with the court's judgment.

Under § 2422(b), the government must establish that Taylor "induced" a minor "to engage in ... any sexual activity for which any person can be charged with a criminal offense." 18 U.S.C. § 2422(b). The government alleged that Taylor could be charged with fondling in the presence of a minor and solicitation. Ind.Code § 35-42-4-5(c)(3) ("fondling"); *Id.* § 34-42-4-6 ("solicitation"). The fondling statute provides, in relevant part, that it is a crime when an adult "touches or fondles the person's own body; in the presence of a child less than fourteen years of age with the intent to arouse or satisfy the sexual desires" of either the child or adult. Ind.Code 35-42-4-5(c). At trial, Taylor's defense was that he thought the person "elliegirl1234" with whom he was having these online conversations was an adult, and the idea that he was engaging with [a] minor was a fantasy. He did not argue that using a webcam did not place him in the presence of a minor, and thus he could not be convicted under § 35-42-4-5(c). Although Taylor failed to argue that his actions did not violate Indiana law, I would still address the argument on plain-error review.

The Indiana statute does not qualify the term "presence" with words like "actual" or "constructive"; it simply states the adult must fondle himself "in the presence of" a minor. And Indiana has not defined the term presence in the statute. *Black's*, however, defines presence as:

> 1. The state or fact of being in a particular place and time [his presence at the scene saved two lives]. 2. Close physical proximity coupled with awareness [the agent was in the presence of the principal].

Black's Law Dictionary 1302 (9th ed.2009). The *Oxford English Dictionary* provides much the same definition: "The place or space in front of or around a person; the immediate vicinity of a person." 12 *Oxford English Dictionary* 392–93 (2d ed.1989). Both definitions are spatial; they refer to a person being in a particular place with another individual. As a term in legal usage, "presence" comes up most often in the crime of robbery. In that context, a perpetrator must steal something from the other person's presence. Ind.Code § 35-42-5-1 (defining robbery as the taking of "property from another person or from the presence of another person"). Meaning: The property must be taken when the person and the robber are in the same physical place — presence cannot be divorced from physical proximity. *Coates v. State*, 534 N.E.2d 1087, 1096 (Ind.1989). Not surprisingly, the concept of physical proximity has arisen in cases under the Indiana fondling statute at issue here. One Indiana court has stressed that the element of presence does not mean the minor has to know about the fondling; all it requires is that the child "*be at the place* where the defendant's conduct occurs." *Baumgartner v. State*, 891 N.E.2d 1131, 1138 (Ind.App.Ct.2008) (emphasis added). In the dictionary and as illustrated in the robbery context and *Baumgartner*, presence is defined by physical proximity.

Although Indiana courts have not addressed whether the element of "presence" is satisfied by something other than actual physical presence, other courts have.[1] Georgia has a statute that is worded similarly to the Indiana statute; it requires that the adult be "in the presence of" the child. Ga.Code § 16-6-4(a)(1). And Georgia courts have held that conversations over phones and webcams do not put the adult in the presence of the child.[2] Likewise, the Court of Appeals for the Armed Forces has held that neither a phone call nor a webcam constitutes being in the presence of another person.[3] ... As a matter of common sense, most would agree with those courts: electronic communications do not place one person in another's presence. When Taylor and "elliegirl1234" communicated over Instant Messenger they were not in one another's presence. The same would be said if they had that conversation over the phone. The fact that a webcam is used does not change the analysis. Taylor's visual

---

1. Concerning this statute, the only case discussing whether a webcam puts the adult in the minor's presence is a federal district court case where the defendant conceded that he was in the presence of the minor. *United State v. Cochran*, 510 F.Supp.2d 470 (N.D.Ind.2007). And on appeal we specifically noted that Cochran's argument did not concern whether he violated Indiana law. *United States v. Cochran*, 534 F.3d 631, 635 n. 3 (7th Cir.2008). So, *Cochran* is of no precedential or persuasive value.

2. *Vines v. State*, 269 Ga. 438, 499 S.E.2d 630, 632 (1998) (telephone); *Selfe v. State*, 290 Ga.App. 857, 660 S.E.2d 727 (2008) (webcam).

3. *United States v. Knowles*, 15 U.S.C.M.A. 404, 405, 35 C.M.R. 376 (C.M.A.1965) (telephone); *United States v. Miller*, 67 M.J. 87, 89 (Army Ct.Crim.App.2008) (webcam). After the *Knowles* case the military code was amended, and presence was clarified to only include physical presence. A thorough review of this development of the law on the issue of presence and technology is presented in Maj. Patrick D. Pflaum, *Shocking and Embarrassing Displays On-Line: Recent Developments in Military Crimes Involving Indecent Conduct Via Webcam*, Army Lawyer (March 2010)

image on the computer doesn't make him anymore physically present than his voice does— it just enhances the effect. *See Selfe*, 660 S.E.2d at 730 (noting "[b]ecause both telephone and computer communications are by electronic transmissions, we are unable to distinguish the two modes as it relates to the necessity of 'presence' "). And there is no reason to unsettle or expand the accepted definition of "presence" to fit conversations over webcams when it wouldn't fit a conversation over the phone.

That's not to say there isn't a strong argument to be made that webcams and other similar technologies put two people in the constructive presence of one another.[4] Many, many courts have held this.[5] But in those cases, the courts have interpreted statutes that did not concern "presence"; instead some other term is used, usually the word "with."[6] In those states, presence is not an element of the offense; the prosecution only has to prove that the adult's actions would impair the health and morals of the child.[7] Indiana's legislature has, however, made "presence" an element of the offense. It has not qualified the term with "actual or constructive," and if the term "presence" is expanded to include constructive and actual presence, that development should not come from the courts, especially the federal courts.... In sum, for Taylor to be convicted of fondling under § 35-42-4-5, the government had to prove that he was in the presence of a child. Since a webcam did not place him in the presence of "elliegirl1234," Taylor could not have been convicted of that offense.

The next issue is whether Taylor could have been convicted under Indiana law for solicitation. While masturbating over the webcam, Taylor also had a conversation with "elliegirl1234" over Instant Messenger, in which he told her to touch and caress her vagina. It was also during this typed conversation that "elliegirl1234" twice asked whether she and Taylor would meet, and twice Taylor told her that they could not—in his words, their relationship would remain a "fantasy." ... Here, Taylor did not want to meet and have sex with "elliegirl1234," nor did he seek to meet "elliegirl1234" so he could fondle her. The only fondling that Taylor solicited was for "elliegirl1234" to touch herself, apart from him. That takes the case out of the typical solicitation scenario where an adult solicits a minor to meet and engage in sexual conduct, *Laughner v. State*, 769 N.E.2d 1147, 1156

---

4. *E.g., State v. McClees*, 108 N.C.App. 648, 424 S.E.2d 687, 689 (1993) ("Through the forces of modern electronic technology, namely the video camcorder, one can constructively place himself in the 'presence' of another."); *State v. Whitmore*, 58 So.3d 583, 590 (La.App.Ct.2010); *State v. Every*, 157 N.C.App. 200, 578 S.E.2d 642, 649 (2003) (finding that use of a telephone, "albeit arguably less than modern, renders *defendant constructively present* under these circumstances." (emphasis added)).

5. *E.g., Brooker v. Commonwealth*, 41 Va.App. 609, 587 S.E.2d 732, 735–36 (2003) (webcam); *McClees*, 424 S.E.2d at 689 (refusing "to hold that the words 'with any child' " require a defendant to be "within a certain distance of, or in close proximity to the child"); *see also United States v. Izaguirre-Flores*, 405 F.3d 270, 275 (5th Cir.2005) (noting that for purpose of the sentencing guidelines "[g]ratifying or arousing one's sexual desires in the actual or constructive presence of a child is sexual abuse of a minor"); *Rabuck v. State*, 129 P.3d 861, 867 (Wyo.2006) (finding a video camera constitutes constructive presence); *People v. Lopez*, 185 Cal.App.4th 1220, 111 Cal.Rptr.3d 232, 238–39 (2010) (finding a video camera constitutes constructive touching).

6. *E.g.,* N.C. Stat. § 14-202.1 (criminalizing taking "any immoral, improper, or indecent liberties *with any child* " (emphasis added)); Va.Code 18.2 § 18.2-370 (punishing indecent exposure when done "*with any child* " (emphasis added)); Wyo. Stat. § 14-3-105(a) (providing, in pertinent part, "any person knowingly taking immodest, immoral or indecent liberties with any child ... is guilty of a felony." (emphasis added)).

7. Conn. Gen.Stat. § 53-21(a)(1); *State v. Elliott*, 127 Conn.App. 464, 14 A.3d 439, 445–46 (2011) (finding that masturbating over a webcam so a child can see would injure the child's morals).

(Ind.Ct.App.2002); *Kuypers v. State,* 878 N.E.2d 896, 898–99 (Ind.Ct.App.2008), and makes Taylor's case unusual.

Under Indiana law, a person is guilty of soliciting a minor if the person "solicits" the child "to engage in (1) sexual intercourse; (2) deviate sexual conduct; or (3) any fondling or touching intended to arouse or satisfy the sexual desires of either the child or the older person." Ind.Code § 35-42-4-6. There are two ways to read the statute: does the solicitation have to be for "fondling" or "touching" with the other person, or does simply instructing a person to do so apart from the adult qualify. The first way would proscribe any solicitation of a child to fondle herself, even if it is at a location and time apart from the adult. So, under that reading, a salacious letter that directed the minor to masturbate would be a crime. The other construction would mean that the solicitation would have to be for fondling with the adult. These legitimate and competing readings render the final element ambiguous.

As a matter of statutory construction, when we have terms that are open to competing definitions, we usually define them in reference to the terms they appear with. As the Supreme Court has cautioned, the rule that "a word is known by the company it keeps, while not an inescapable rule, is often wisely applied where a word is capable of many meanings to avoid the giving of unintended breadth of the [legislature]." *National Muffler Dealers Ass'n, Inc. v. United States,* 440 U.S. 472, 486 n. 20, 99 S.Ct. 1304, 59 L.Ed.2d 519 (1979) (quoting *Jarecki v. G.D. Searle & Co.,* 367 U.S. 303, 307, 81 S.Ct. 1579, 6 L.Ed.2d 859 (1961)). A related rule of construction dictates that when specific words of limited meaning and application are followed by words of a more general meaning, "the general words are to be construed as including only those things that are like those designated by the specific words." *Salter v. State,* 906 N.E.2d 212, 220 (Ind.Ct.App.2009).

Here, the statute proscribes soliciting a child to engage in sex, deviate sex, and fondling. When someone solicits sex and presumably deviate sex, it requires another person — those acts cannot be done alone. Generally, when someone solicits a child for sex it means that the adult is soliciting the child to have sex with him, not that the adult is encouraging the child to have sex apart from the person doing the soliciting, or have sex as a general matter. If we read the terms fondling and touching in the same manner as sex and deviate sex, only fondling and touching that is done with the other person would be included, and not simply touching that occurs at a person's request but apart from the other person. This would confine the statute to the typical scenario where the adult seeks to meet the child to have sex with or to fondle her. And it would not reach the situation of the salacious letter. Indeed, adopting this sensible way of reading the statute keeps us from giving it unintended breadth. *National Muffler Dealers Ass'n, Inc.,* 440 U.S. at 486, 99 S.Ct. 1304. Additionally, this reading is reinforced by the rule of lenity, which instructs that "ambiguity in the meaning of a statutory provision should be resolved in favor of the defendant." *United States v. Turcotte,* 405 F.3d 515, 535 (7th Cir.2005). If the Indiana legislature wants to expand the definition to include Taylor's conduct, it can easily do so without the ambiguity. And if the Indiana courts face a similar case and interpret the statute expansively, then it would be binding on us. But since there is no similar Indiana case on this issue, I do not believe the statute covers Taylor's conduct.

Of course, the government is not obliged to wait for Indiana to have a case on point before it can charge Taylor with a crime under § 2422, but when Congress chooses to define a crime by state law, federal prosecutors cannot exceed the scope of the state law and seek to punish conduct that is not illegal under the statutes listed in the indictment — even though the conduct is extremely disturbing. Here, the prosecutor was free to charge Taylor with many other crimes; in addition to the offenses pointed out by the court's opinion, the prosecutor could have charged Taylor with at least two federal offenses. 18 U.S.C. § 1470 (attempting to transfer obscene matter to a minor); 47 U.S.C. § 223(d)(1) (sending obscene images to a minor).

It bears noting one final reason for giving the solicitation statute a limited reading. When this statute was passed in 1984, Taylor's conduct was unimaginable. While law constantly trails crime, in the context of sexual behavior and technology the problem is particularly clear — the old laws will not do. The legislature has to specifically address this lamentable behavior and determine what the law truly proscribes. Under our current laws, with the advent and prevalence of "sexting" and virtual sexual behavior, many, many citizens are engaging in behavior that could make them felons. *See* Jordan J. Szymialis, *Sexting: A Response To Prosecuting Those Growing Up with a Growing Trend*, 44 Ind. L.Rev. 301 (2010) (a thorough article surveying the problem and offering suggestions for the legislature).[8] It is not enough to let the courts figure it out and to try to see if old definitions fit this new and troubling behavior.

In sum, although Taylor's conduct was inappropriate and extremely troubling, I do not believe it would constitute a crime under either of the Indiana statutes listed in the indictment. For that reason, I concur with the court's judgment.

Notes

Upon remand, Taylor was charged with two counts of using the Internet in an attempt to transfer obscene material to a minor, in violation of 18 U.S.C. § 1470 — a different crime related to his 2006 activities in the online chat room. *See United States v. Taylor*, 2011 WL 5025222 (N.D. Indiana) (denying Taylor's constitutional challenge to Congress's power to regulate the transmission of obscene material over the Internet, holding that "the internet is a worldwide communications system [and] has widely been accepted as both a channel of interstate commerce and an instrumentality of interstate commerce ... even if none of the communications were transferred over state lines."). Taylor then appealed that decision on a variety of other grounds, but the Seventh Circuit Court of Appeals affirmed his convictions for those crimes. *See United States v. Taylor*, 2015 WL 328654 (7th Circuit).

United States v. Fugit
Fourth Circuit, 2012
703 F.3d 248

WILKINSON, Circuit Judge: ...

A grand jury in the Eastern District of Virginia returned a two-count indictment against Fugit on May 24, 2007. Count One charged him with distributing child pornography, in violation of 18 U.S.C. § 2252A(a)(2) and (b)(1). Count Two charged him with violating 18 U.S.C. § 2422(b), which provides, in pertinent part:

> Whoever, using the mail or any facility or means of interstate or foreign commerce, ... knowingly persuades, induces, entices, or coerces any individual who

---

8. *See also* Terri Day, *The New Digital Dating Behavior — Sexting*, 33 Hastings Comm. & Ent. L.J. 69 (2010); Robin Fretwell Wilson, *Sex Play in Virtual Worlds*, 66 Wash. & Lee L.Rev. 1127 (2009) (outlining how pedophiles use virtual worlds to solicit children, and the rise of virtual sex); Federal Trade Commission Report to Congress, *Virtual Worlds and Kids: Mapping the Risks*, 2009 WL 4755418 (F.T.C.) (giving recommendations to Congress on how to combat the threat to children in virtual worlds).

has not attained the age of 18 years, to engage in prostitution or any sexual activity for which any person can be charged with a criminal offense, or attempts to do so, shall be fined under this title and imprisoned not less than 10 years or for life.

Count Two alone is at issue here....

On November 28, 2005, while claiming to be a young girl named "Kimberly," Fugit held a conversation in an internet chat room with an eleven-year-old girl, "Jane Doe # 2." He asked her questions regarding her breasts and genitals, her underwear, slumber parties, and whether she had ever appeared naked in front of men. He also obtained her telephone number. Pretending to be Kimberly's father, Fugit telephoned Jane Doe # 2 shortly thereafter and engaged her "in an inappropriate sexual conversation." He asked whether she had "seen a grown man naked," whether "she minded if he came in to check on her while she was naked," whether "she would mind seeing him naked," and whether she would "get naked for him." Tracking the text of 18 U.S.C. § 2422(b), the Statement of Facts concluded its discussion of this incident by noting that Fugit "admits that he knowingly persuaded, induced, enticed or coerced Jane Doe # 2 to engage in a sexual activity, to wit; Taking Indecent Liberties with Children, in violation of § 18.2-370 of the Code of Virginia 1950, as amended, for which he could be charged."

Likewise, on December 12, 2005, once more posing as "Kimberly," Fugit chatted online with a ten-year-old girl, "Jane Doe # 1," and obtained her telephone number. Approximately five minutes later, he telephoned her, pretended to be Kimberly's father, and engaged her "in an inappropriate sexual conversation." The Statement of Facts further described how this latter incident precipitated an extensive police investigation. During the execution of a search warrant at his residence, Fugit told police that he had "attempted to contact children on the computer and telephone" and that an internet account of his had been "bumped" several times because of inappropriate contact with minors. Law enforcement discovered, "among other things" on Fugit's computer, that he had once distributed a child pornography image over e-mail....

Apparently referencing the incidents discussed above, the [pre-sentence report (PSR)] described how Fugit, in claiming to be Kimberly's father, asked Jane Doe # 2 "to masturbate and take her shirt off" and repeatedly demanded that she remove her pants. And with regard to Jane Doe # 1, among other statements, Fugit "informed her of the rules he would impose" if she spent the night at his house, "instructed her to call him 'Daddy,' " and stated that he "would perform a 'finger test' on [her] by rubbing her all over with his finger." Additionally, he said "that he would allow her to touch his penis" and asked her "to take her clothes off." ... Moreover, the PSR made clear that the incidents involving Jane Does # 1 and # 2 were anything but isolated occurrences. Investigation revealed that Fugit had participated in internet chats with 129 individuals who appeared to be children, twelve of whom police confirmed were indeed minors between nine and twelve years old. During these dozen conversations, which occurred between March 2005 and January 2006, Fugit "always represented himself to be a child and often asked inappropriate questions," including

> the child's breast size, whether or not the child had pubic hair, whether or not the child slept in the nude, whether or not the child engaged in masturbation, what type of underwear the child wore, and whether or not the child had been naked in front of a member of the opposite sex.

As with Jane Does # 1 and # 2, Fugit often proceeded to engage these children in telephone conversations involving "inappropriate sexual comments."

Finally, the PSR disclosed that 289 still images and twenty-four videos of child pornography—at least some of which were extremely graphic—were found on Fugit's computers. In addition to the single occasion described in the Statement of Facts, the PSR revealed that law enforcement identified forty-three instances of child pornography distribution between September 2004 and January 2006, some involving multiple images.

Following a hearing on December 19, 2007, the district court sentenced Fugit to ... 310 months.... Fugit appealed only his sentence, and this court affirmed the judgment of the district court. *United States v. Fugit*, 296 Fed.Appx. 311 (4th Cir.2008) (per curiam).... On October 1, 2009, Fugit filed a motion for post-conviction relief pursuant to 28 U.S.C. § 2255. He contested his convictions on ten grounds. The district court denied the motion in its entirety, rejecting each of Fugit's claims on the merits and also seeming to find that several were procedurally defaulted. This court granted a certificate of appealability on the following issue[ ], which relate[s] to Count Two only: (1) "whether Fugit's stipulated conduct constituted attempted inducement of 'sexual activity' of a minor within the meaning of 18 U.S.C. § 2422(b)"....

Fugit's primary contention is that the district court erred in interpreting 18 U.S.C. § 2422(b), the statute underlying his conviction on Count Two.... As outlined above, 18 U.S.C. § 2422(b) comprises four elements: "(1) use of a facility of interstate commerce; (2) to knowingly persuade, induce, entice, or coerce; (3) a person who is younger than eighteen; (4) to engage in an illegal sexual activity." *United States v. Kaye*, 451 F.Supp.2d 775, 782 (E.D.Va.2006). Fugit's claim of actual innocence focuses exclusively on the "sexual activity" component of the fourth element. He contests neither the other three elements nor the illegality component of the fourth, effectively conceding that his behavior violated § 18.2-370 of the Code of Virginia, which prohibits taking indecent liberties with children. Fugit acknowledges that his behavior was—to put it mildly—"reprehensible." Nevertheless, he argues that the phrase "sexual activity" in § 2422(b) incorporates an irreducible minimum of interpersonal physical contact—and that, because the relevant interactions with his victims neither included nor referenced such contact, he cannot have been guilty of violating the statute....

"Statutory interpretation necessarily begins with an analysis of the language of the statute." *Chris v. Tenet*, 221 F.3d 648, 651 (4th Cir.2000). As far as the text of § 2422(b) is concerned, Fugit appears to have pulled his proposed interpersonal physical contact requirement out of a hat. The statute is simply not framed in the terms for which he contends: it mentions nothing about physical contact. In fact, it does not expressly demarcate the meaning of "sexual activity" in any way, instead leaving the term undefined. By contrast, where similar statutory terms were meant to encompass only a specific subset of conduct, Congress took care to define them explicitly for purposes of the sections or chapters in which they are found. *See, e.g.*, 18 U.S.C. § 2246(2) (defining "sexual act"); *id.* § 2246(3) (defining "sexual contact"); *id.* § 2256(2) (defining "sexually explicit conduct"); *id.* § 2423(f) (defining "illicit sexual conduct").

When analyzing the meaning of an undefined statutory term, "we must first 'determine whether the language at issue has a plain and unambiguous meaning.'" *Chris*, 221 F.3d at 651 (quoting *Robinson v. Shell Oil Co.*, 519 U.S. 337, 340, 117 S.Ct. 843, 136 L.Ed.2d 808 (1997)). We think the meaning of "sexual activity" in § 2422(b) is indeed plain and that this meaning extends beyond interpersonal physical contact.... In determining the meaning of "sexual," we find instructive a definition from Webster's: "of or relating to the sphere of behavior associated with libidinal gratification." *Webster's New International Dictionary* 2082 (3d ed. 1993). This court has previously relied on this very definition in a related context. *See United States v. Diaz-Ibarra*, 522 F.3d 343, 349 (4th Cir.2008) (interpreting the phrase "sexual abuse of a minor" for purposes of sentencing enhancement in U.S. Sentencing Guidelines Manual § 2L1.2). Likewise, we find the most pertinent definition of "activity" to be "an occupation, pursuit, or recreation in which a person is active." *Webster's, supra*, at 22.

Thus, as a matter of plain meaning, the phrase "sexual activity" as used in § 2422(b) comprises conduct connected with the "active pursuit of libidinal gratification" on the part of any individual. The fact that such conduct need not involve interpersonal physical contact is self-evident. *See Diaz-Ibarra*, 522 F.3d at 351–52 (concluding that "'sexual abuse of a minor' means the 'perpetrator's physical *or nonphysical* misuse or maltreatment of a minor for a purpose associated with sexual gratification'" (emphasis added))…. This meaning of the "sexual activity" element is not only plain; it also renders the statutory scheme coherent as a whole. This court has made clear that § 2422(b) "was designed to protect children from the act of solicitation itself." *United States v. Engle*, 676 F.3d 405, 419 (4th Cir.2012) (quoting *United States v. Hughes*, 632 F.3d 956, 961 (6th Cir.2011), cert. denied, ___ U.S. ___, 131 S.Ct. 2975, 180 L.Ed.2d 257 (2011)). Consequently, by forbidding the knowing persuasion, inducement, enticement, or coercion of a minor, the statute "criminalizes an intentional attempt to achieve a *mental* state—a minor's assent—regardless of the accused's intentions concerning the actual consummation of sexual activities with the minor." *Id.* (quoting *United States v. Berk*, 652 F.3d 132, 140 (1st Cir.2011)). The primary evil that Congress meant to avert by enacting § 2422(b) was the psychological sexualization of children, and this evil can surely obtain in situations where the contemplated conduct does not involve interpersonal physical contact.

We cannot accept Fugit's contention that absent an interpersonal physical contact requirement, § 2422(b) becomes a trap capable of snaring all sorts of innocent behavior. For several reasons, our interpretation of the term "sexual activity" is hardly open-ended. First, wide swaths of behavior simply cannot be described as "sexual activity": indeed, the overwhelming preponderance of human interaction does not involve the "active pursuit of libidinal gratification" in any minimally tenable way…. Second, § 2422(b) concerns only conduct that is already criminally prohibited. That is, § 2422(b) does not criminalize enticement of "sexual activity," full stop; instead, it forbids enticement of "sexual activity *for which any person can be charged with a criminal offense.*" The latter category is considerably narrower than the former. As a general matter, conduct that is innocuous, ambiguous, or merely flirtatious is not criminal and thus not subject to prosecution under § 2422(b)…. Third, § 2422(b) addresses only behavior involving children. And there exists, of course, a vast range of everyday adult-child interactions that are neither remotely erotic nor independently illegal—from the salutary mentoring of teachers, coaches, and counselors to the unintentional jostling between strangers traversing a crowded city sidewalk…. Finally, we believe that the Seventh Circuit's decision in *United States v. Taylor*, 640 F.3d 255 (7th Cir.2011), upon which Fugit places great weight, was mistaken. The *Taylor* court held that the phrase "sexual activity" in § 2422(b) is synonymous with the phrase "sexual act," as defined in 18 U.S.C. § 2246(2). *Id.* at 259–60. That complex provision defines "sexual act" to require not only interpersonal physical contact but interpersonal physical contact involving the genitalia or anus—and, for persons who are sixteen or older, requires either oral sex or actual penetration of the genital or anal opening.

We decline *Taylor's* invitation to cut and paste this restrictive definition into § 2422(b) because doing so would contravene express statutory text. Section 2246 explicitly limits the definitions provided therein to the chapter in which it resides. Specifically, the very first words of the section are "[a]s used in this chapter" (with the various definitions following), and the section's title is "[d]efinitions for chapter." Whereas § 2246 appears in

Chapter 109A of Title 18, § 2422(b) is situated in an entirely different location, Chapter 117. Simply put, we find "no indication that Congress intended to import the definitions of chapter 109A to [another] chapter." *United States v. Sonnenberg*, 556 F.3d 667, 670 (8th Cir.2009).... For the foregoing reasons, we hold that the phrase "sexual activity" in § 2422(b) denotes conduct connected with the "active pursuit of libidinal gratification" on the part of any individual—nothing more, nothing less—and, therefore, does not incorporate an invariable requirement of interpersonal physical contact....

Count Two appears to have been based on Fugit's behavior toward Jane Doe # 2. The conduct described in the PSR with respect to this victim is condemnatory. Fugit tricked this eleven-year-old child into providing her telephone number during an online chat in which he pretended to befriend her as a girl named "Kimberly." During that chat, Fugit "inquired as to the child's breast size, her underwear, and whether or not she had been nude in front of boys." When he telephoned her, "[t]he victim asked to speak to Kimberly, however, the defendant refused and stated that he was Kimberly's father and needed to ask the victim some questions first." Later in the conversation, he "inquired as to where the victim's parents were and told her he wanted her to go to another room." Fugit thus attempted to lure this young girl away from her protectors in hopes of exploiting her undisturbed. The PSR further describes Fugit's telephone inquiries to Jane Doe # 2 "about her underwear and bras" and whether she "had seen other girls naked," had been "in a hot tub with other girls and boys," had "seen a grown man naked," and "would mind seeing him naked." Following these questions, Fugit requested that she remove her shirt and, on more than one occasion, demanded that she take off her pants as well. He also asked her to masturbate. That such conduct qualifies as involving the "active pursuit of libidinal gratification" on Fugit's part is beyond question.

Nor is the conduct disclosed in the Statement of Facts at all exonerative. To the contrary, that document described how Fugit baited two children into participating in "inappropriate sexual conversation[s]" and asked at least one a barrage of questions regarding her anatomy, underwear, and experiences, as well as whether the two of them could be naked in front of each other. Engaging young girls in the kind of discussions described above plainly involves them in "sexual activity"—that is, the "active pursuit of libidinal gratification." The idea of an adult man behaving in such a manner is utterly unpersuasive of "actual innocence," and Fugit's procedural default of his statutory claim cannot be excused on this ground.... There are cases where the most learned doctrines of law match the most untutored lessons of common experience. This is one of those. There is no innocence here, save that of the child victims. Collateral review has nothing to correct.

The judgment is affirmed....

Notes

Many states have adopted statutes similar to 18 U.S.C. § 2422(a) that criminalize the use of the Internet to entice or coerce minors to engage in sexual activity. *See, e.g.,* Conn. Gen. Stat. Ann. § 53A-90 (2007) (Enticing a minor); *State v. Shah*, 39 A.3d 1165, 1171 (Conn. App. 2012) (traveling to the prearranged meeting place constitutes a substantial step toward the commission of enticing a minor and supports conviction of attempting to entice); *see also, e.g.,* Ala. Code § 13A-6-69 (Child molestation; luring child someplace in order to perform or to propose sexual acts); Alaska Stat. § 11.41.452 (Online enticement of a minor); Colo. Rev. Stat. §§ 18-3-305 (Enticement of a child) and 18-3-306 (Internet luring of a child); Neb. Rev. Stat. § 28-311 (Criminal child enticement; attempt; penalties). Under either the federal or various state versions, note that for a conviction of enticement, the defendant need not intend to engage in sexual activity with the child, but must merely intend to entice the child to do so and take a substantial step toward the commission of the crime. There remains a circuit split created by the Seventh Circuit (*Taylor*) and the Fourth Circuit (*Fugit*) regarding the scope of the term "sexual activity."

A defendant may be convicted of enticement of a minor under 18 U.S.C. § 2422(b) for communicating with an actual child. However, as expressly noted in *Taylor*, involvement of an actual minor is not required to sustain a conviction for *attempted* enticement under 18 U.S.C. § 2422. *Taylor*, 640 F.3d at 257. *See, e.g., United States v. Rothenberg*, 610 F.3d 621 (11th Cir. 2010) (defendant convicted without dealing directly with real or fictitious minor, but rather by chatting online with two consenting adults and actively coaching and encouraging intermediary adults about how to sexually exploit minors under their influence). *See also United States v. Gagliardi*, 506 F.3d 140, 147 (2d Cir. 2007) ("Section 2422(b) explicitly proscribes *attempts* to entice a minor, which suggests that actual success is not required for a conviction and that a defendant may thus be found guilty if he fails to entice an actual minor because the target whom he believes to be underage is in fact an adult." (emphasis in original)); *United States v. Tykarsky*, 446 F.3d 458, 466 (3d Cir. 2006) ("Congress did not intend to allow the use of an adult decoy, rather than an actual minor, to be asserted as a defense to § 2422(b)."); *United States v. Hicks*, 457 F.3d 838, 841 (8th Cir.2006) ("[A] defendant may be convicted of attempting to violate § 2422(b) even if the attempt is made towards someone the defendant believes is a minor but who is actually not a minor."); *United States v. Helder*, 452 F.3d 751 (8th Cir. 2006) ("impossibility" unavailable as defense); *United States v. Sims*, 428 F.3d 945, 960 (10th Cir. 2005); *United States v. Meek*, 366 F.3d 705, 717–20 (9th Cir. 2004); *United States v. Root*, 296 F.3d 1222, 1227–29 (11th Cir. 2002); *United States v. Farner*, 251 F.3d 510, 513 (5th Cir. 2001). *But see United States v. Nitschke*, 843 F. Supp.2d 4 (D.C. 2011) (defendant cannot be charged with attempted enticement where he merely tells adult in online chat that he would like to join him in sex that adult has already pre-arranged with minor). In addition, the defendant may still be convicted for attempted enticement, even when the minor is a willing participant. *See United States v. Herbst*, 666 F.3d 504 (8th Cir. 2012) (fictitious 13-year-old indicated in online chat that she welcomed defendant's enticing communications).

Convictions for attempted enticement often arise through internet sting operations in which law enforcement officials pose as minors, such as those in *Dateline NBC*'s popular investigative television series *To Catch a Predator*. For further discussion of *attempted* enticement of a minor, see Korey J. Christensen, *Reforming Attempt Liability Under 18 U.S.C. § 2422(b): An Insubstantial Step Back from* United States v. Rothenberg, 61 DUKE L.J. 693 (2011) (discussing problematic expansion of threshold level of conduct to satisfy substantial step toward commission of crime under § 2422(b)); Andriy Pazuniak, *A Better Way to Stop Online Predators: Encouraging a More Appealing Approach to § 2422(b)*, 40 SETON HALL L. REV. 691 (2010) (drawing distinction between an attempt to persuade a minor to engage in illegal sexual activity from an attempt to engage in sexual activity with a minor); Bridget M. Boggess, *Attempted Enticement of a Minor: No Place for Pedophiles to Hide Under 18 U.S.C. § 2422(b)*, 72 Mo. L. REV. 909 (2007) (discussing attempted enticement and possible defenses).

C. Voyeurism

State v. Wilson

Court of Appeals of Ohio, 2011
192 Ohio App. 3d 189, 948 N.E.2d 515

DIANE V. GRENDELL, Judge....

On March 18, 2008, Wilson was indicted by the Portage County Grand Jury on one count of attempted voyeurism, a misdemeanor of the first degree in violation of R.C. 2923.02, for conduct that, if successful, would have constituted a violation of R.C. 2907.08(D)(1) and (E)(4), and one count of voyeurism, a misdemeanor of the third degree in violation of R.C. 2907.08(A) and (E)(2).... V.B. (a minor at the time of the offenses) testified that in January 2008, she was living at 4805 Wayne Road, in Mantua Township, Ohio, with Wilson (her stepfather), Ellen Mary Wilson (her mother), and three younger siblings. At this time, V.B. was a senior at Crestwood High School.

In August 2007, Ellen Mary Wilson began employment in Pennsylvania, which required her to be away from home during the work week. V.B. testified that her relationship with Wilson had always been awkward. After her mother began staying in Pennsylvania during the week days, Wilson's demeanor toward her became friendlier, while his discipline became stricter.... In September or October 2007, V.B. testified that Wilson hung her underwear on a wall tapestry in their living room and later asked her if she had received his present. She thought this conduct was "weird" but put her underwear away without doing anything more.... After this, V.B. testified that she found a pornographic VHS tape on her bed. Since she had seen Wilson watch pornography, she returned the tape to him. V.B. testified that the tape reappeared on her bed, and again, she returned it to Wilson. According to V.B., this scenario happened regularly for about three weeks, until she put the tape away in her desk drawer.... About a week after Christmas 2007, V.B. found a vibrator in blue wrapping paper on her desk. A day or two later, Wilson asked her whether she had received the present. She responded, "yes," and the matter was not discussed further. V.B. showed the vibrator to her friend, Kristi Levanduski, and told the students at her school lunch table about it.... V.B. also testified that throughout this period, she would regularly hear Wilson going down into the basement while she showered, as the wooden steps leading to the basement were next to the shower. V.B. testified she knew the footsteps were Wilson's because they were heavy and he wore work boots, while her next-youngest sibling would have been only ten years old at the time.... Wilson's conduct made V.B. suspicious that he might be watching her.

On January 28, 2008, V.B. returned home with her friend, Levanduski, and they searched her bedroom. In an air vent, about a foot from the ceiling, they found a camera. V.B. testified that the flutes of this vent faced downward, whereas the flutes of other vents were turned upward. They next investigated the shower. Levanduski went in the shower with a flashlight and V.B. went to the basement, only five steps below the main floor of the house. Wilson has a work bench in the basement, which stands next to a wall shared with the shower upstairs. A piece of material was hanging on the wall, but V.B. could see a light behind it. When she removed the material she found a hole, just below eye level, that allowed her to see Levanduski in the shower.... V.B. called her paternal grandmother, and Levanduski took pictures of the camera and the hole in the shower with her cell phone. The women packed a bag of clothes for V.B., and they went to Levanduski's house. Sheriff's deputies arrived at the Levanduski residence, and V.B. and Levanduski made written statements.

V.B. testified that she had been grounded recently for excessive cell-phone usage and for receiving poor grades on her interim report. V.B. admitted that by Christmas 2007, she knew the family would be moving to Pennsylvania. V.B. was vocal in expressing her unwillingness to move and said she would do whatever it takes not to move.... Levanduski testified and corroborated V.B.'s testimony regarding the discovery of the camera in the bedroom vent and the hole in the shower. Levanduski's testimony differed in certain particulars. According to Levanduski, she was in the basement looking at V.B. through the hole. Levanduski confirmed that V.B. had told her about Wilson's behavior and showed her the vibrator prior to the discovery of the camera and hole on January 28, 2008.

Matthew L. Skilton, a deputy sheriff with the Portage County Sheriff's Department, testified that on January 28, 2008, he responded to a call of "suspicious activity" by visiting V.B. at the Levanduski residence. Skilton took written statements from V.B. and Levanduski and met with Detective DJ Walker, also of the Portage County Sheriff's Department. Skilton and Walker obtained a search warrant before proceeding to the Wilson residence.... Deputy Skilton testified that Wilson did not appear surprised when he and Detective Walker arrived to execute the warrant. Wilson had already dismantled the camera and had it lying on the table with various power cords. At the officers' request, Wilson went into the attic and dismantled a converter box, which was part of the system that allowed Wilson to view what the camera was transmitting from the television set. Wilson explained that he installed the camera because V.B.'s grades were dropping and he thought something was going on with her. Wilson also claimed V.B. would arrive home late from work. According to Skilton, Wilson said he did not suspect drug or alcohol abuse, but could not say exactly what he suspected V.B. of doing.

Initially, Deputy Skilton was unable to locate the hole in the shower. After speaking with V.B. by cell phone, he went to the basement and found the piece of cloth on the wall, covering the hole. Skilton testified that the hole had recently been covered by caulk, which was still wet and tacky. Skilton wiped the caulk away and was able to see into the shower. In particular, he could view Detective Walker in the shower from his knees to his head. Skilton described the hole as being at least one-eighth of an inch thick, about the size of a pencil, and perfectly round as if it had been drilled.... Deputy Skilton testified that Wilson explained the caulk by claiming that there had been problems with the shower leaking water. Wilson denied using the hole to watch V.B. while showering. Wilson denied ever seeing V.B. in a state of undress in her bedroom, claiming that he would turn the camera off if he thought she might be naked. Wilson also claimed that giving V.B. the vibrator was a mistake, and that it had been intended for his wife.... Detective Walker corroborated Deputy Skilton's testimony regarding the hole in the shower and Wilson's explanation of the camera and vibrator. Walker testified that Wilson denied making any recordings using the camera because he did not know how to record and/or because the recording device was not hooked up to the television. Walker also testified that he and Skilton took photographs of V.B.'s bedroom, the shower, and the basement.

Ellen Mary Wilson, V.B.'s mother, testified for the defense. She testified that Wilson had helped raise V.B. since infancy and treated her as his own daughter. In the months prior to the January 28, 2008 incident, there were problems with V.B. regarding her grades, cell-phone and computer usage, behavior, and curfew violations. V.B. would not willingly move to Pennsylvania. A few days before January 28, 2008, Ellen and V.B. argued about moving to Pennsylvania, and Ellen decided to move V.B. there before the end of the school year because she did not trust her at home with the other children.... Ellen Wilson testified that there had been a problem with the shower's leaking water for many months and that she and Wilson had both tried, unsuccessfully, to stop the leaks by caulking.... Ellen admitted that Wilson did not tell her that he had installed the camera in V.B.'s bedroom until after its presence was discovered....

Wilson testified that the police arrived at his house to execute the search warrant after 1:00 a.m. on January 29, 2008. He said he removed the camera before their arrival because he wanted to be "perfectly honest" with them and allow them to inspect the camera. Wilson confirmed that he and Ellen Wilson had serious concerns about V.B.'s grades and behavior during the fall and winter of 2007. Wilson did not have an explanation as to why he did not inform Ellen that he was installing the camera, but claimed that they had discussed doing so. He placed the camera in V.B.'s room because she was isolating herself there. Wilson testified that the camera, although directly connected to its power source, could transmit images wirelessly to the television. He testified that the camera was installed about three days before its discovery. Wilson denied that he had ever viewed V.B. undressed or undressing.... Wilson denied viewing V.B. in the shower. He testified that the shower leaked chronically, and he was caulking it every two or three days to correct the problem. He had placed a rag over the hole to "hold the caulk in place so it didn't get washed out by the water." Wilson denied applying fresh caulk to the shower on the evening of January 28, 2008.... Wilson denied hanging V.B.'s underwear in the living room, giving her a pornographic video, and giving her a vibrator.

At the close of all the evidence, counsel for Wilson moved for a dismissal of both charges pursuant to Criminal Rule 29.... On December 14, 2009, at the conclusion of the trial, the municipal court found Wilson guilty of voyeurism and attempted voyeurism.... On January 15, 2010, a sentencing hearing was held. The municipal court sentenced Wilson to 180 days in jail for attempted voyeurism (a first-degree misdemeanor), with 90 days suspended, and 60 days in jail for voyeurism (a third-degree misdemeanor), with 30 days suspended. The court ordered the sentences to be served consecutively for an aggregate jail sentence of 120 days. Additionally, the court imposed a fine of $1,000, with $750 suspended, and designated Wilson a Tier I sex offender.... In order to convict Wilson of third-degree voyeurism, the state was required to prove, beyond a reasonable doubt, that between January 21 and January 28, 2008, "for the purpose of sexually arousing or gratifying the person's self," he "surreptitiously invade[d] the privacy of [V.B.], to spy or eavesdrop upon [her]." R.C. 2907.08(A).... In order to convict Wilson of first-degree attempted voyeurism, the state was required to prove, beyond a reasonable doubt, that between January 21 and January 28, 2008, he attempted to "secretly or surreptitiously videotape, film, photograph, or otherwise record [V.B.] under or through the clothing being worn by [her] for the purpose of viewing the body of, or the undergarments worn by, [V.B.]." R.C. 2907.08(D).... Wilson maintains that the state failed to prove the reason he had placed the camera in V.B.'s room, i.e., that he had done so for the purpose of sexually arousing or gratifying himself. The purpose element of voyeurism "is typically proved by evidence that the accused was in a state of undress and/or had engaged in masturbation while peering into a home or other building at people inside." *State v. Haldeman* (Nov. 22, 2000), 2nd Dist. No. 18199, 2000 WL 1726858, at *3. Neither circumstance was demonstrated with respect to Wilson.

Initially, we note that the purpose of sexually arousing or gratifying oneself is only an element of third-degree voyeurism, i.e., the charge that Wilson observed V.B. while showering. With respect to first-degree voyeurism, i.e., the attempted recording of V.B., the state need only prove a purpose of viewing her body and/or undergarments.... Although there was no evidence that Wilson was in a state of undress and/or masturbating at the time he viewed V.B. showering, a purpose of sexual arousal or gratification may be inferred from other circumstances. If pornography is part of the circumstances surrounding the invasion of the victim's privacy, then a purpose of sexual arousal or gratification may be inferred. See, e.g., *State v. Nunez*, 6th Dist. No. H-09-019, 2010-Ohio-3435, 2010 WL 2891495, at ¶ 66 (video of the offender's daughter in the bathroom also contained commercial pornography); *Haldeman*, 2000 WL 1726858 (an offender, caught looking in the window of another's home, had a vibrator and pornographic materials in his vehicle).... In the present case, V.B. testified that Wilson had given her a pornographic video and a vibrator several weeks prior to the time he was charged with viewing her in the shower. This evidence suggests that Wilson had a sexual interest in V.B., and in that context, his viewing her in the shower was for the purpose of sexual arousal and gratification.

The courts have also held that the sexual-arousal and/or gratification element may be inferred where there is no innocent, i.e., nonsexual, explanation for the offender's conduct. See, e.g., *Huron v. Holsapple* (Aug. 8, 1997), 6th Dist. No. E-96-063, 1997 WL 457971, at *3 (offender was caught "looking at the victim through her window during a time in the morning when the victim, a fourteen-year-old girl, was dressing for school"); *State v. Million* (1989), 63 Ohio App.3d 349, 351, 578 N.E.2d 869 (evidence that the offender used a hand-held mirror to look into an adjacent bathroom stall would support an inference of a purpose of sexual arousal or gratification "since innocent explanations for his behavior do not readily come to mind").... In the present case, Wilson provided no innocent explanation for viewing V.B. in the shower, inasmuch as he denied doing so. No innocent explanation for such behavior is readily apparent. Moreover, Wilson's explanation for the hole itself is less than credible. The officers of the Portage County Sheriff's Department described a hole, perfectly round as if it had been drilled, that allowed one to view another in the shower. At the time officers viewed the hole, caulking had recently been applied to cover the hole. The hole was also covered by a rag, which Wilson claimed was to keep moisture off the caulk, although any moisture would have come from inside the shower rather than from the basement. The rag and caulking suggest that Wilson was trying to conceal the hole.

Wilson further argues there was no evidence that he actually saw V.B. nude. We note that it was not necessary that Wilson actually saw V.B. naked in order to be convicted of either third-degree voyeurism or first-degree attempted voyeurism.

Finally, Wilson argues that V.B.'s and Levanduski's testimony is self-contradictory and incredible. V.B. testified that she was in the basement and viewed Levanduski in the shower, while Levanduski testified that she was in the basement and viewed V.B. in the shower. This inconsistency in their testimony raises some concern as to their credibility, but it is the prerogative of the trier of fact to resolve such discrepancies. *State v. Antill* (1964), 176 Ohio St. 61, 67, 26 O.O.2d 366, 197 N.E.2d 548. What is material to the charges against Wilson is that the physical evidence establishes that a person's whole body could be viewed from the basement through a hole in the shower. This fact was corroborated by the testimony of Deputy Skilton and Detective Walker.... Wilson claims that it is incredible that V.B. would tell Levanduski and her friends at school about the pornography and the vibrator but not a responsible adult. V.B. testified that she did not tell an adult because she was embarrassed and/or mistrustful of the adults, while she was more comfortable confiding in her friends. Wilson does not explain why V.B.'s decision to confide in her friends rather than an adult renders her testimony less credible, particularly when her suspicions about him were confirmed by the physical evidence....

For the forgoing reasons, the judgment of the Portage County Municipal Court, Ravenna Division, finding Wilson guilty of attempted voyeurism and voyeurism, is affirmed. Costs are to be taxed against appellant.

Judgment affirmed.

RICE and TRAPP, JJ., concur.

Notes

In *Wilson*, the court applies the Ohio state statute governing "voyeurism." The federal statute addressing "video voyeurism" is 18 U.S.C. § 1801, which governs anyone who "has the intent to capture an image of a private area of an individual without their consent, and knowingly does so under circumstances in which the individual has a reasonable expectation of privacy...." 18 U.S.C. § 1801(a) (video voyeurism). Under the federal statute, "circumstances in which that individual has a reasonable expectation of privacy" includes both private and public settings. *See* 18 U.S.C. § 1801(b)(5). However, in *State v. Glas*, 147 Wash.2d 410, 54 P.3d 147 (2002), the Supreme Court of Washington held that the state voyeurism statute did not cover intrusions of privacy in public places and, thus, did not prohibit "upskirt" photography in a public location. Other courts have held similarly where the respective state statutes focused on the location of the intrusion rather than the nature of the intrusion upon a person's private interests. *See generally* Lance E. Rothenberg, *Re-Thinking Privacy: Peeping Toms, Video Voyeurs, and the Failure of Criminal Law to Recognize a Reasonable Expectation of Privacy in the Public Space*, 49 Am. U.L. Rev. 1127 (2000). In the following decision, note that the defendant's state conviction for voyeurism is overturned based on the limited scope of the applicable state statute, but his actions are still sufficient to convict him of felony attempted child exploitation.

Delagrange v. State of Indiana

Supreme Court of Indiana, 2014
5 N.E.3d 354
[superseded by statute, as stated in *Sandleben v. State*,
22 N.E.3d 782 (Ind. App. 2014)]

MASSA, Justice....

On February 27, 2010, Delagrange left his home in Fort Wayne and drove approximately one hundred miles to the Castleton Square Mall in Indianapolis. He then wandered around for nearly eight hours trying to take "upskirt" photographs of women and girls as they were shopping. After he selected a particular victim, he would approach her from behind and try to inveigle his foot between her legs. Once in position, he would reach into his pocket and pull on a piece of fishing line attached to the cuff of his pants leg, thereby exposing a video camera attached to his shoe. By means of this procedure, Delagrange collected approximately seven minutes of actual images.

Unsurprisingly, Delagrange's unusual behavior attracted attention, and a store employee contacted police. After a brief confrontation, an officer arrested Delagrange and discovered his camera system. Detectives later identified four girls from the recorded images: K.V., T.G., and C.B., all aged seventeen, and A.K., aged 15. Those images depicted "the area under the skirt and between the legs" of the victims, but did not depict any "uncovered genitals."... The State charged Delagrange with four counts of Class C felony attempted child exploitation [and] ten counts of Class D felony voyeurism.... By agreement of the parties, the trial court dismissed the voyeurism charges, but it denied Delagrange's motion to dismiss the attempted child exploitation charges. Delagrange successfully sought interlocutory appeal of that ruling, but the Court of Appeals affirmed the trial court and remanded the case. *Delagrange v. State*, 951 N.E.2d 593, 596 (Ind.Ct.App.2011), *trans. denied* 962 N.E.2d 649 (Ind.2011)....

After trial, the jury convicted Delagrange of the remaining five counts. He appealed, arguing the evidence was insufficient to support his convictions for attempted child exploitation. A divided panel of the Court of Appeals reasoned the child exploitation statute

> demands the child be performing the sexual conduct, which herein required the child be exhibiting her uncovered genitals with the intent to satisfy someone's sexual desires. Therefore, in order for Delagrange's attempt to commit child exploitation, each child must have been exhibiting her uncovered genitals with the intent to satisfy sexual desires.

Delagrange v. State, 981 N.E.2d 1227, 1232 (Ind.Ct.App.2013). As the State had presented no evidence of that, the panel reversed Delagrange's four convictions for attempted child exploitation.... .[footnote omitted]. Judge Najam dissented, in part because he believed the majority's interpretation "undermines the goal of the statute, which is to criminalize the exploitation of child victims." *Id.* at 1235 (Najam, J., dissenting)....

Delagrange argues the evidence was insufficient to support his convictions for attempted child exploitation.... [footnote omitted]. First, he argues "the State failed to prove all the factual elements enumerated in the child exploitation statute by direct evidence" because none of the images depicted "sexual conduct" as that term is used in the child exploitation statute.... Second, he argues that in the absence of such depictions, "it was wholly unreasonable for the jury to infer that Mr. Delagrange had attempted to make such proscribed images" because his victims were fully clothed and it was wintertime.... Each of the attempted child exploitation charges stated, in pertinent part:

> On or about February 27, 2010 David Delagrange did attempt to commit the felony of Child Exploitation that is to knowingly or intentionally produce and/ or create and/or film and/or videotape and/or [sic] a digitized image of a performance or incident that includes *sexual conduct* by a child under eighteen (18) years of age ... by engaging in conduct that constituted a substantial step toward the commission of said offense that is; attach a camera to his shoe and recorded video of the area under the skirt or dress of the child.

[Citation to pleadings omitted] [Emphasis in original]. At the time of the charged acts, the relevant portion of the child exploitation statute provided: " 'Sexual conduct' means ... exhibition of the uncovered genitals intended to satisfy or arouse the sexual desires of any person." Ind.Code § 35-42-4-4(a) (2008). Delagrange argues that because the State presented no evidence that any of the images he captured depict uncovered genitals, it failed to prove an element of the charged offense.... We disagree. Had Delagrange been charged with child exploitation, his argument might have merit, but he was charged with *attempted* child exploitation. Under Indiana law, "a person attempts to commit a crime when, acting with the culpability required for commission of the crime, he engages in conduct that constitutes a substantial step toward commission of the crime." Ind.Code § 35-41-5-1(a) (2008).[3] Thus, the State need not show Delagrange actually succeeded in capturing images of uncovered genitals; rather, it must show that he took a "substantial step" toward doing so.... And whether Delagrange took such a "substantial step" is a question for the fact-finder, which brings us to Delagrange's second argument: that it was unreasonable for the jury to infer he intended to capture images of uncovered genitals, rather than—as he testified—pictures of "high heels, boots, pantyhose, panty shots, [and] nylons."....
[citation to pleadings omitted]. In the context of child exploitation, as in other crimes,

---

3. This statute was cosmetically amended in 2013, but the substance of this section remains unchanged. *See* Ind.Code § 35-41-5-1(a) (2013) (replacing "he" with "the person").

the intent element "may be established by circumstantial evidence and may be inferred from the actor's conduct and the natural and usual sequence to which such conduct usually points." *Bowles v. State*, 737 N.E.2d 1150, 1152 (Ind.2000).

On this point, we find *Saxton v. State*, 790 N.E.2d 98 (Ind.2003) instructive. In *Saxton*, the defendant probationer was caught standing outside a woman's home and staring into her bathroom window at five o'clock in the morning. *Id.* at 98. He was arrested and charged with voyeurism, and the trial court revoked his probation. *Id.* He appealed, arguing that because the victim never testified, the State failed to prove he did not have her permission to be there. *Id.* We found sufficient circumstantial evidence of lack of permission:

> Put in terms of sufficiency of the evidence, the question becomes: can a trial court infer that someone caught standing on an air conditioner staring into a woman's bathroom at 5 a.m. who runs off rather forcefully when challenged was a person peeping without the permission of the target? We say yes, and affirm the judgment of the trial court.

Id. at 99–100.... And just so here: can a jury infer that someone taking "upskirt" photographs of women and girls by means of a concealed shoe camera does so in the hope that some of them will not be wearing undergarments? We say yes. Delagrange testified he intended "to get fetish photography, which is high heels, boots, pantyhose, panty shots, nylons," ... but the jurors were not required to credit that testimony. After all, one victim testified she was not wearing leggings. And on cross-examination, Delagrange's answers suggested his interest was not limited to his victim's clothing. When the prosecutor asked whether Delagrange intended to "videotape what was under their skirt [sic]," Delagrange admitted he did.... When the prosecutor asked "what else" Delagrange had a fetish for, he answered: "I love the female form.".... In light of that circumstantial evidence, the jury could reasonably infer that Delagrange intended to capture not just images of undergarments but also—or instead—images of uncovered genitals.

Finally, we note that Delagrange's trial counsel repeatedly drew a parallel between the images Delagrange captured with his ersatz equipment and a famous photograph of Marilyn Monroe standing over an air vent. This analogy was unpersuasive for a lack of similarity between a photograph of a knowing and consenting adult and a video of an unknowing and unconsenting child. The former is legal;[4] the latter is not....

We hereby affirm the trial court.

DICKSON, C.J., RUCKER, DAVID, and RUSH, JJ., concur.

Notes

The voyeuristic behavior of Delagrange was sufficient to satisfy the state definition of attempted child exploitation. *See also State v. Myers*, 146 N.M. 128, 207 P.3d 1105 (2009) (voyeuristic images of adolescent female victims taken before or after they used unisex

---

4. A near-identical photograph of an *unconsenting* adult was found to be a civil tort—invasion of privacy. *See Daily Times Democrat v. Graham*, 276 Ala. 380, 162 So.2d 474, 478 (1964) ("To hold that one who is involuntarily and instantaneously enmeshed in an embarrassing pose forfeits her right of privacy merely because she happened at the moment to be part of a public scene would be illogical, wrong, and unjust."). But scholars have opined "civil law is an inadequate vehicle to redress the anti-social behavior manifest in video voyeurism" because it is so often clandestine; thus, "the majority of victims are never likely to realize that they, in fact, have been victimized ... and consequently may never initiate a civil suit." Lance E. Rothenberg, *Re-Thinking Privacy: Peeping Toms, Video Voyeurs, and the Failure of Criminal Law to Recognize a Reasonable Expectation of Privacy in the Public Space*, 49 Am. U.L.Rev. 1127, 1149 (2000) (internal citations omitted)....

bathroom sufficiently "lewd" to satisfied crime of sexual exploitation of children). The State originally charged Delagrange with ten counts of felony voyeurism, however, at the time, the voyeurism statute did not encompass the specific behavior that Delagrange committed. Instead, it criminalized only traditional "peeping Tom" behavior, in which one "peeps" into protected areas that offer traditional expectations of privacy: the home, restrooms, baths, showers, and dressing rooms. *See* IND. CODE § 35-45-4-5(a)(1) to (2) (2010). To cover such intrusions in a public place, state legislatures must expressly address the nature of the intrusion into the private interest, rather than merely the forum in which the intrusion takes place. *See, e.g.*, CAL. PENAL CODE § 647(k)(1) (West) (adding subsection to voyeurism statute to cover intrusions in public places where privacy is reasonably expected). Subsequent to the decision in *Delagrange*, the Indiana legislature amended the voyeurism statute to include public voyeurism by criminalizing non-consensual "upskirt" photography, regardless of the victim's age:

> "A person who (1) without the consent of the individual; and (2) with intent to peep at the private area of an individual; peeps at the private area of an individual and records an image by means of a camera commits public voyeurism ..." P.L. 75-2011, § 1, 2011 Ind. Acts 696, 696–98 (codified at Ind.Code § 35-45-4-5(d) (Supp. 2013)); *see also id.* (codified at Ind.Code § 35-45-4-5(a) (Supp.2013) (defining "private area" as "the naked or undergarment clad genitals, pubic area, or buttocks of an individual.")).

Delagrange v. State, 5 N.E.3d at 358, n.4.

> The crime of public voyeurism recognizes expectations of privacy in the digital age without criminalizing mere looking within a public space. Thus, whereas peeping into an area with a traditional expectation of privacy is, standing alone, an act sufficient to support a conviction for voyeurism, *see* I.C. § 35-45-4-5(b)(1)(A), (b)(2) (2012), in a public space, one must peep and record an image by means of a camera. *See* I.C. § 35-45-4-5(d)(2) (2012).

Sandleben v. State, 22 N.E.3d 782 (Ind. Ct. App. 2014) (defendant guilty of public voyeurism by using underwater camera to attempt to peep at naked genitals, pubic area, and buttocks of two 12-year-old girls swimming in local pool).

Most state voyeurism statutes apply to offenses committed against any person. *See, e.g.*, ARK. CODE § 5-16-101 (Crime of video voyeurism); WYO. STAT. § 6-4-304 (Voyeurism; penalties); LA. REV. STAT. ANN. § 14:283(A) ("[W]hoever commits the crime of video voyeurism shall, upon a first conviction thereof, be fined not more than two thousand dollars or imprisoned, with or without hard labor, for not more than two years, or both."). But the statutes may increase the penalties for the crime when it is committed against a child. *See* LA. REV. STAT. ANN. § 14:283(B)(4) (imposing fine not more than ten thousand dollars and imprisonment at hard labor for not less than two years or more than ten years, without benefit of probation, parole, or suspension of sentence, when victim is child under the age of seventeen). *See also State v. Holmes*, 130 So. 3d 999 (La. App. 2 Cir. 2014) (sentence to ten years hard labor not excessive for deacon who installed hidden video cameras in church bathroom to record female juveniles who used bathroom at church function); *but see State v. Boudreaux*, 945 So. 2d 898 (La. App. 2 Cir. 2006) (total sentence of 56 years imprisonment at hard labor for 14 counts of video voyeurism was constitutionally excessive under circumstances). Some states provide that any evidence resulting from the commission of video voyeurism crimes shall be deemed contraband. *See* LA. REV. STAT. ANN. § 14:283(E); *see also* KY. REV. STAT. § 531.110 (all photographs, film, videotapes, or other images that become in the possession of law enforcement, the prosecution, or the courts, as a result of video voyeurism litigation shall be sealed and, upon the conclusion of the case, destroyed).

D. Exhibitionism / Indecent Exposure

Kentucky Statutes

§ 510.148 Indecent exposure in the first degree

(1) A person is guilty of indecent exposure in the first degree when he intentionally exposes his genitals under circumstances in which he knows or should know that his conduct is likely to cause affront or alarm to a person under the age of eighteen (18) years....

State v. Beine

Supreme Court of Missouri, 2005
162 S.W.3d 483

CHARLES B. BLACKMAR, Senior Judge....

James Beine was employed as a counselor at the Patrick Henry Elementary School in St. Louis City. During the 2000–2001 school year one of Mr. Beine's duties was to prevent disruptive behavior by students in the school's halls and restrooms. To perform this duty, Mr. Beine often had to enter the restrooms designated for males.... During the 2000–2001 school year, all restrooms in the school were designated only as being for males, females, or unisex. No restrooms were expressly designated for students only, and adults sometimes used the large public restrooms frequented by the students.

K.L., C.M., and J.M., three male students at Patrick Henry under the age of 14, asserted that in the spring of 2001, Mr. Beine exposed himself to them while they were using the restroom near the school gym.... K.L. and C.M. testified that sometime in the spring of 2001 Mr. Beine entered the restroom while they were using it. Mr. Beine proceeded to use a urinal next to the boys. C.M. and K.L. further allege that Mr. Beine stood 3 or 4 feet from the urinal and urinated into it in an arc. K.L. and C.M. claimed that they could see Mr. Beine's "private part." ... J.M., C.M.'s younger brother, testified that on another occasion in the spring of 2001, he entered the restroom while Mr. Beine was using a urinal. J.M. proceeded also to use a urinal and then wash his hands at the sink while Mr. Beine continued to use the urinal. As J.M. was washing his hands, a group of boys entered the restroom and began causing a ruckus. J.M. claimed that Mr. Beine turned from the urinal and told the boys to "shut up." Mr. Beine's pants were allegedly unzipped and his penis exposed when he turned to discipline the boys. Mr. Beine quickly turned back and zipped up his pants before proceeding to prevent the restroom disturbance.

Mr. Beine was initially indicted on three counts of sexual misconduct involving a child by indecent exposure, in violation of section 566.083.1(1) ... [footnote omitted] , reading as follows:

> A person commits the crime of sexual misconduct involving a child if the person:
>
> (1) Knowingly exposes the person's genitals to a child less than fourteen years of age in a manner that would cause a reasonable adult to believe that the conduct is likely to cause affront or alarm to a child less than fourteen years of age.

A fourth count, involving K.L., was added later. The jury found Mr. Beine guilty on all four counts. The trial court accepted the jury's recommendation and sentenced Mr. Beine to four years on each count. It ordered three of the sentences to be served consecutively and one to be served concurrent with the consecutive sentences for a total of twelve years imprisonment. Mr. Beine appealed. Because he challenges the validity of a state statute, this Court has jurisdiction. Mo. Const. art. V, sec. 3....

There is no question that the appellant knowingly exposed his genitals to persons under the age of fourteen. This is often necessary in a men's restroom. There is serious question, however, about the sufficiency of the evidence to support the charges "that the defendant [exposed his genitals] in a manner that would cause a reasonable adult to believe that such conduct was likely to cause affront or alarm to a child less than fourteen years of age." ... The state is not required to show that any child was actually affronted or alarmed. There was no direct evidence as to how a reasonable adult might react to the appellant's behavior, and there is no citation that sheds any light on how that proposition might be established by evidence.... The state puts strong reliance on the testimony of a fellow inmate of an Illinois jail as to a conversation he said he had with the appellant, after he was arrested on the present charges. Conceding the jury's right to believe this testimony, and overlooking the notorious unreliability of jailhouse snitches, the testimony still manifestly lacks substance. It does not show anything about the appellant's state of mind when he committed the acts shown by the evidence. What it shows, rather, is a realization after the fact that something about the restroom encounter, or any other encounter for that matter, bothered some boys. The testimony proves nothing about how the appellant's conduct might appear to a reasonable adult at the time it occurred.

One of the appellant's duties at the school was to monitor the restroom. Anybody who has attended a public grade school knows that boisterous behavior is not unusual in restrooms, especially when students are released in substantial numbers for recess. Thus, the appellant was in a place where his duties required him to be. When no boys are present, there is no need for a monitor. There was no prohibition on his using the restroom for his personal needs while he was properly there. It is quite common for men and boys to use a common facility at sporting events, Boy Scout camps, horse shows, and other public events. In so doing, it is necessary for the users to expose their private parts. Fathers regularly take their pre-K sons into public restrooms. The evidence that on two occasions the appellant stood at a distance from the urinal and urinated in an arc in the presence of the boys cannot reasonably be construed as likely to cause affront or alarm. The boys used such phrases as "embarrassed" and "funny" when talking about their reaction to the incident, but these hardly equate to "affront" or "alarm." The argument that the children were not accustomed to any adults being in the restroom when they were present is at war with the admitted evidence that the appellant had the duty of monitoring the restroom.

State v. Moore, 90 S.W.3d 64, 67–69 (Mo. banc 2002), a case on which the state places strongly reliance, approves the dictionary definition of "affront" as "a deliberately offensive act or utterance; an offense to one's self respect," and of "alarm" as "apprehension of an unfavorable outcome, of failure, or dangerous consequences; an occasion of excitement or apprehension." *Moore* goes on to say, "To be impolite is not enough. To be annoying is insufficient." "Affront" might connote an exhibition by a man of his genitalia to a woman or girl. "Alarm" would indicate a suggestion of physical encounter to either a male or a female. The record shows no indication of anything that would properly come within these definitions. The state simply has not proved criminal conduct under the applicable statute. For this reason, the judgment on all counts must be reversed.... While this conviction cannot stand because the evidence was insufficient to convict Mr. Beine, this conviction also cannot stand because the portion of the statute upon which Mr. Beine was charged and convicted is patently unconstitutional.... [footnote omitted].

The appellant essentially claims that section 566.083.1(1) is unconstitutional because it punishes innocent conduct, contains no requirement of criminal intent (mens rea), and does not advise a person in the position of the appellant as to what he must do to avoid violation of the statute when his conduct is otherwise lawful. The only express statutory requirement of knowing conduct is that of knowingly exposing one's genitals to a child less than 14 years of age. The act of a man in exposing his genitals in the process of urinating in a public restroom is not only innocent but often necessary. The statute contains two essential elements: first, the act of exposing one's genitals and, second, exposure in a manner that would cause a reasonable adult to believe that the conduct is likely to cause affront or alarm to a child less than 14 years of age. The appellant argues that this last portion of the subsection is completely lacking in any explicit requirement of a mental state.... In essence, Mr. Beine contends that the statute is overbroad—it prohibits conduct to which a person is constitutionally entitled along with conduct that a person has no right to engage in. Mr. Beine is correct. A person necessarily must knowingly expose himself in a great many situations. One of those situations is when a man uses a public restroom. Even if a reasonable person might think that in some of these restroom situations a child is likely to suffer affront or alarm from witnessing such exposure, that alone cannot make the exposure criminal. If that were the case, no person would ever be able to use a public restroom without risking a criminal charge. As such, the statute prohibits two types of conduct: some of which a person has no right to engage in and the other of which a person has a right to engage in. When a statute prohibits conduct a person has no right to engage in and conduct a person has a right to engage in, the statute is unconstitutionally overbroad. *See City of St. Louis v. Burton*, 478 S.W.2d 320, 323 (Mo.1972); *Christian v. Kansas City*, 710 S.W.2d 11, 12–14 (Mo.App.1986)....

The purpose of the overbreadth doctrine is to ensure that a statute does not punish innocent conduct. The Court may take judicial notice that all persons have to relieve themselves regularly, that the need for such relief may arise suddenly, that public facilities are regularly provided, and that males of all ages regularly use the facilities provided for them, necessarily exposing their genitals in the process. Section 566.083.1(1) leaves adults in a state of uncertainty about how they may take care of their biological needs without danger of prosecution when a child is present in the same public restroom. Because a person's right to use public restrooms is about as fundamental a right as one can imagine, probably equal to or more fundamental than speech rights, the overbreadth doctrine should extend to this case and permit Mr. Beine to contest section 566.083.1(1) even if he had no right to engage in the conduct he engaged in.

But it is not clear that Mr. Beine had no right to do what he did. The evidence that the state introduced at trial essentially showed only that Mr. Beine used a public restroom while boys were present and stood at a little further distance from the urinal than men usually do, and that Mr. Beine accidentally turned around without zipping his pants zipper up to discipline some boys that were causing a disturbance in the restroom. This is constitutionally protected conduct, so even if the overbreadth doctrine did not apply to this case, Mr. Beine can still contest the constitutionality of the statute by arguing that it prohibits conduct to which he is constitutionally entitled to engage in. So the aspect of the overbreadth doctrine as applied in [*State v.*] *Carpenter*, [736 S.W.2d 406 (Mo. Banc 1987)], that of allowing an appellant to take advantage of the doctrine because of the effect of the statute on others, even though the appellant's conduct may not represent protected speech, has no application here, because this appellant was engaging in lawful, and necessary, conduct.

The state also seeks to hold that section 566.083.1(1) is constitutional by applying the "knowingly" mens rea requirement to both the exposure and to the manner of exposure requirements enumerated in the statute. Specifically, the state argued that 566.083.1(1) requires the state to present evidence not only that the appellant knowingly exposed his genitals to a child less than 14 years old, but also that he knowingly did so in a manner that would cause a reasonable adult to believe that the conduct was likely to cause affront or alarm to a child of less than 14 years. The state thereby adds a word that the legislature did not see fit to include, suggesting that the addition is appropriate pursuant to the Court's duty to sustain a statute as against a constitutional challenge if at all possible.

The only authority relied upon by the state to rewrite section 566.083.1(1) is *State v. Moore*, 90 S.W.3d 64, 67 (Mo. banc 2002), but *Moore* involved section 566.095, a sexual solicitation statute. That statute makes criminal a defendant's conduct when the defendant "solicits ... another person to engage in sexual conduct under circumstances in which he knows that his requests or solicitation is likely to cause affront or alarm." That statute implies knowing conduct in the act of solicitation because knowledge is inherent in the word "solicitation." The statute also specifically enumerates a knowing mens rea to the "likely to cause affront or alarm" requirement. As such, the statute governing *Moore* contains the explicit language of scienter that section 586.083.1(1) lacks.... *Moore* also provides little if any instruction for this case because *Moore's* facts are very different from the facts in this case. There a 61-year-old man solicited a 13-year-old virgin to perform an act of fellatio on him. The Court had no problem in finding that Moore's conduct was within "a core of unprotected expression" that could be punished, even by a statute that is rather broadly drawn.... Section 566.083.1(1) differs from the statute involved in *Moore* by referring to exposure in "a manner that would cause a reasonable adult to believe that the conduct is likely to cause affront or alarm to a child less than fourteen years of age," rather than focusing on the effect of the exposure on the child or children witnessing the exposure. The accused is required to guess what a hypothetical reasonable adult might believe as to the effect on the children witnessing the event. No precedent for this kind of requirement has been cited. It is a slim reed to support a 12-year sentence. The *Moore* statute requires a direct and knowing address to the child, who presumably would be the person affronted or alarmed. It is clearly distinguishable....

The judgment on all counts is reversed. Inasmuch as the state has had an opportunity of proving its case, and has failed to do so, double jeopardy prohibits a retrial. The case, then, should be remanded with directions to enter judgment of acquittal on all counts. *State v. Self*, 155 S.W.3d 756 (Mo. banc 2005).

WHITE, C.J., WOLFF and TEITELMAN, JJ., concur.

STITH J., concurs in part and dissents in part in separate opinion filed.

PRICE and LIMBAUGH, JJ., concur in opinion of STITH, J.

RUSSELL, J., not participating.

LAURA DENVIR STITH, Judge, concurring in part and dissenting in part.

I concur in the principal opinion's determination that there was insufficient evidence to support the submission as to J.M. I dissent from the principal opinion's determination that there was insufficient evidence to support the submissions as to C.M. or K.L. and from its finding that section 566.083.1, RSMo 2000, ... [footnote omitted] is unconstitutional based on its erroneous conclusion that the statute solely requires proof that defendant knowingly exposed his genitals to a child under 14. On its face, the statute requires proof that defendant knowingly exposed his genitals to a child under 14 in a manner that would cause a reasonable adult to believe that the conduct is likely to cause affront or alarm to a child less than 14. This is not unduly vague or overbroad. Because the evidence of such conduct was sufficient to support the guilty verdicts as to the incidents involving K.L. and C.M., I would affirm those convictions....

A more detailed factual statement is appropriate here than that set out in the principal opinion as a basis for addressing Mr. Beine's sufficiency claims.... James Beine was employed as a counselor at Patrick Henry Elementary School in St. Louis for the 2000–2001 school year. One of his duties was to monitor the hall and restrooms to prevent disruptive behavior. School policy and practice sometimes required male staff members to enter the boys' restrooms in their roles as "bathroom monitors." ... K.L., C.M., and J.M. were students at Patrick Henry during the 2000–2001 school year. At that time, the school did not have a restroom solely designated for the male faculty and staff, although there were unisex restrooms available for faculty and staff throughout the building. Mr. Washington, the school's principal, testified that there was no written policy forbidding use of the boys' restrooms by adult staff, but that it would not have been considered appropriate for the adult staff members to have used the children's restrooms when the children were using them, although adult staff might use these restrooms on occasion if no children were present....

Challenges to the constitutionality of a statute are legal issues that are reviewed *de novo*. *Baldwin v. Dir. of Revenue*, 38 S.W.3d 401, 405 (Mo. banc 2001). "A statute is presumed to be constitutional and will not be invalidated unless it clearly and undoubtedly violates some constitutional provision and palpably affronts fundamental law embodied in the constitution." *Bd. of Educ. of St. Louis v. State*, 47 S.W.3d 366, 368–369 (Mo. banc 2001). Any doubt concerning a statute's constitutionality must be resolved in favor of its validity. *State v. Mahurin*, 799 S.W.2d 840, 842 (Mo. banc 1990). "[W]hen a constitutional and unconstitutional reading of a statute are equally possible," the court must choose the constitutional one. *Spradlin v. City of Fulton*, 924 S.W.2d 259, 263 (Mo. banc 1996). In addition, the rule of lenity requires that ambiguity in a penal statute be construed against the government and in favor of persons on whom the penalties will be imposed. *J.S. v. Beaird*, 28 S.W.3d 875, 877 (Mo. banc 2000). *See also State v. Rowe*, 63 S.W.3d 647, 650 (Mo. banc 2002).

These principles require rejection of Mr. Beine's argument that section 566.083.1 does not require that a defendant act "knowingly" as to the conduct that forms the basis for violation of that statute. As noted above, the paragraph in question states:

> A person commits the crime of sexual misconduct involving a child if the person:
>
> 1. *Knowingly exposes the person's genitals* to a child less than 14 years of age *in a manner that would cause a reasonable adult to believe that the conduct is likely to cause affront or alarm to a child less than 14 years of age.*

Sec. 566.083.1 (emphasis added). The meaning of the italicized portion of the statute has been addressed previously by this Court, albeit in *dicta*, in *State v. Moore*, 90 S.W.3d 64, 67 (Mo. banc 2002). *Moore* rejected an argument that another statute, section 566.095.1, was unconstitutionally vague because it made solicitation of sexual conduct a crime if done "under circumstances in which he knows that his requests or solicitation is likely to cause affront or alarm." *Id.* In discussing why section 566.095.1 was constitutional as to child victims, this Court compared it to section 566.083.1, the statute at issue in the instant case, and to another statute using similar language. *Moore* noted that both of the latter statutes "prohibit conduct *that is known or believed* 'likely to cause affront or alarm', presumably to distinguish a criminal act of exposing oneself from conduct that is accidental, inadvertent, or otherwise done without an intent to do harm." *Id.* at n. 8 (emphasis added). It said this was sufficiently specific to avoid constitutional challenge.

Moore was correct in its reading of section 566.083.1. The word "knowingly" as used in section 566.083.1 applies to the entire sentence in which it appears; nothing limits its application to only the first portion of that sentence. The statute does not merely require the State to present evidence that the defendant knowingly exposed his genitals to a child less than 14 years old. To the contrary, this single sentence requires the State to show that defendant knowingly exposed his genitals to a person under 14 in a manner that would cause a reasonable adult to believe that the conduct was likely to cause affront or alarm to a child of less than 14 years. If the person does not knowingly act in this manner, he has not violated the statute.

As so construed, section 566.083.1 is not unconstitutionally vague. As this Court has previously recognized, "impossible standards of specificity are not required." *State v. Brown*, 660 S.W.2d 694, 697 (Mo. banc 1983):

> If the terms or words used in the statute are of common usage and are understandable by persons of ordinary intelligence, they satisfy the constitutional requirements as to definiteness and certainty.

Id. Mr. Beine suggests that even if the statute requires that he act knowingly, the word "knowingly" is itself vague. But:

> A person acts knowingly '(1) With respect to his conduct or to attendant circumstances when he is aware of the nature of his conduct or that those circumstances exist; or (2) With respect to a result of his conduct when he is aware that his conduct is practically certain to cause that result.'

Mahurin, 799 S.W.2d at 844, *quoting*, sec. 562.016.3. *Moore* applied this definition, holding that in determining whether a defendant acted "knowingly", a court looks at how the person would expect the recipient of the sexual solicitation to feel as a result of the comment. *Moore*, 90 S.W.3d at 68. *Moore* held that the adult in that case could be held to know that solicitation of a child to perform a criminal sexual act was likely to cause affront or alarm. *Id.*

Moore also rejected a contention, similar to the one now made by Mr. Beine, that the phrase "likely to cause affront or alarm" is vague, stating:

> In the context in which 'affront' and 'alarm' are used in section 566.095, what is prohibited are sexual requests or solicitations that the defendant knows are likely to cause such a reaction. To be impolite is not enough. To be annoying is insufficient. The words 'affront or alarm' convey, respectively, a deliberate offense or a feeling of danger. At the least, real emotional turmoil must result.

90 S.W.3d at 67. *Moore* further described the conduct of exposing one's genitals to a child as "inherently criminal behavior." *Id.* at 68 at n. 8.

Applying these principles here, the statute is not unconstitutionally vague in making it criminal for a defendant to knowingly expose his genitals to a child less than 14 in a manner that would cause a reasonable adult to believe that the conduct is likely to cause affront or alarm to a child less than 14 years of age. The statute informed Mr. Beine that he cannot expose himself in a manner that he knows is likely to cause deliberate offense or a feeling of danger. Mr. Beine's vagueness challenge is rejected.

Mr. Beine also argues that the statute is overbroad. As the principal opinion concedes, an overbreadth argument is normally cognizable only where a person claims First

Amendment free speech rights are infringed or chilled. *See, e.g., Artman v. State Bd. Of Registration for the Healing Arts*, 918 S.W.2d 247, 251 (Mo. banc 1996). Here, unlike in *Moore*, 90 S.W.3d at 66–67, the statute at issue criminalizes conduct, not speech, and Mr. Beine admits he was not attempting to communicate to the boys when acting in the manner alleged; to the contrary, he denied any intent to cause them affront or alarm or knowledge that his conduct might do so. The principal opinion nonetheless finds constitutional concerns in the statute because it construes the statute to criminalize unknowing behavior based solely on the reactions of others. As discussed in detail above, this construction of the statute is incorrect. The statute criminalizes only knowingly exposing ones genitals to a child in a manner that the defendant knows a reasonable adult would believe was likely to cause affront or alarm to the child. It does not chill protected conduct....

Mr. Beine also argues that, even if this Court rejects his constitutional challenge, the evidence was not sufficient to support his convictions. He did not contest that he knowingly exposed his genitals in the course of urinating or that he knew the children were less than 14 years of age. But, he argues the record does not support a finding that he knew his conduct would affront or alarm the boys or that a reasonable person would believe that his conduct would do so, and there was no evidence that it did.... It should be noted preliminarily that the statute does not require the State to show that these particular boys were actually affronted or alarmed, only that a defendant knowingly acted in a manner that he knew would cause a reasonable adult to believe his conduct was likely to affront or alarm a child of less than 14 years of age. *See* sec. 566.083.1. Of course, this does not make proof whether a particular child showed affront or alarm irrelevant; it merely is not dispositive....

This evidence, when considered in combination with Mr. Longwell's testimony, was sufficient for a reasonable juror to find that Mr. Beine knowingly exposed his genitals to children under 14 years of age in a manner that would cause a reasonable adult to believe that the conduct was likely to cause the children affront or alarm. Mr. Beine was in a position of authority, and the children were not accustomed to any adult being in the bathroom when they were present. A reasonable person would believe that an adult with authority over children, who entered the bathroom while the children were using it, and who urinated in the fashion Mr. Beine did in front of children, showing his penis to them, would find that conduct likely to cause affront or alarm to a child less than 14 years of age. That is sufficient to support a conviction under the statute....

The evidence is not sufficient to affirm the judgment as to the count involving J.M. That count alleged that on another occasion in the spring of 2001, Mr. Beine went into the boys' bathroom near the gymnasium and began using the urinal. So far as the record shows, no child was in the room when Mr. Beine was first there. However, J.M., who was in the third grade and is the younger brother of C.M., entered the boys' bathroom as Mr. Beine was urinating. J.M. used a urinal and finished before Mr. Beine and went to wash his hands at the sinks. As J.M. was washing his hands, some other boys entered the room and began to argue loudly. Mr. Beine, who had still been using the urinal, turned around and told the disruptive boys to "shut up." His pants were still unzipped as he did so, and J.M. says he saw Mr. Beine's penis.... While J.M.'s testimony is sufficient to show that Mr. Beine exposed his penis to J.M., it is not sufficient to show that he knowingly did so in a manner that a reasonable adult would believe would more likely than not cause affront or alarm to a child of less than 14. As *Moore* stated, "To be impolite is not enough. To be annoying is insufficient. The words 'affront or alarm' convey, respectively, a deliberate offense or a feeling of danger. At the least, real emotional turmoil must result." 90 S.W.3d at 67.

Here, there is no showing of deliberate offense, a feeling of danger, or real emotional turmoil. The evidence shows that the whole incident occurred very quickly. Mr. Beine was already in the bathroom when J.M. and the other boys entered. The principal said that on occasion an adult might use one of the boys' rooms if no one was in it at the time. He did not flaunt himself as he had on the other occasions involved in this appeal, and J.M. did not see his penis while he was urinating. While J.M. did see Mr. Beine's penis, he did so only briefly as Mr. Beine was hurriedly zipping up his pants after turning around from the urinal and yelling at the other boys to "shut up." Nothing suggests that he particularly focused on J.M. or purposely exposed himself to J.M. or to any of the other boys. J.M. said he was disgusted, but from the testimony this appears in large part to be because he had been told to shut up. J.M. did not indicate whether any of the other boys saw Mr. Beine's penis or complained about it. No charges were brought based on alleged exposure by Mr. Beine to the other boys, although a large group of them were in the bathroom at the time. While Mr. Beine's admissions to Mr. Longwell could support a finding that he exposed himself to J.M. on some occasion, it does not support knowingly doing so on this occasion....

Note

The relevant statute in *Beine* was held to be unconstitutional because it criminalized otherwise innocent, legal conduct—in this case, using a urinal in the same bathroom with children. *See also Jenkins v. Commonwealth*, 308 S.W.3d 704 (Ky. 2010) (defendant not guilty of indecent exposure after showering nude with boys at public swim club with no intent to cause alarm). Note the difference between the majority and dissenting opinions with respect to the *mens rea* requirement. Which interpretation of the "knowing" requirement better fulfills the purpose of the statute?

Note that state requirements for criminal exposure may vary with respect to the body parts that must be exposed, *see State v. Fly*, 348 N.C. 556, 501 S.E.2d 656, 659 (1998) (defendant who displays only his buttocks but not his anus or his genitals does not commit indecent exposure), whether exposure must occur with someone else present, and whether someone else present must actually see the exposed body part, *see State v. Vars*, 157 Wash. App. 482, 237 P.3d 378, 382 (2010) ("witness's observation of the offender's genitalia is immaterial"); *People v. Carbajal*, 114 Cal. App. 4th 978, 8 Cal. Rptr. 3d 206, 211 (2003) (California law requires presence of another person, but other person does not have to see defendant's genitals); *Young v. State*, 109 Nev. 205, 215, 849 P.2d 336, 343 (1993) (offense does not require visual observation by others). As demonstrated in *Beine*, the outcome may depend on the reasonably anticipated reaction of the person who witnessed the exposure. *See also Jenkins*, 308 S.W.3d at 714 (no evidence that defendant's removal of swimming trunks in shower had any effect on boys sharing shower).

Because exhibitionism is a noncontact offense, alone, it may not qualify under state law standards as a "sex offense." *See, e.g., State v. P.H.*, 22 Misc.3d 689, 874 N.Y.S.2d 733 (2008) (exhibitionism, standing alone, is not a "sex offense" under New York Mental Hygiene Law). However, when exhibitionism is determined, even though it is a noncontact offense, it may still satisfy the mental illness component of the requirements for civil commitment as a sexually violent predator when there has been a history of other contact offenses associated with the act of exhibitionism. *See, e.g., Commonwealth v. Fay*, 467 Mass. 574, 5 N.E.3d 1216, *cert. denied* 135 S.Ct. 150 (2014) (defendant determined to be a menace to health and safety of others in future); *Commonwealth v. Walker*, 83 Mass. App. Ct. 901, 983 N.E.2d 711 (2013) (exhibitionists who also engaged in contact offending more likely to be associated with contact sexual offenses in future); *State v. Peter Y.*, 99 A.D.3d 1059, 952 N.Y.S.2d 651 (3 Dept. 2012) (prisoner diagnosed with pedophilia and paraphilia, including urophilia—sexual arousal from urine—and sexual arousal from making obscene phone calls, was a dangerous sex offender requiring civil confinement;

prisoner's wide range of sexual interests, including bestiality, exhibitionism, bondage, and sadomasochism, determined that disorders predisposed him to committing sex offenses, as he was unable to control his sexual urges); *In re Williams*, 292 Kan. 96, 253 P.3d 327 (2011) (diagnosis of sex offender as having antisocial personality disorder, alcohol dependence, substance abuse, exhibitionism, and paraphilia "not otherwise specified" was sufficient to establish, as element in establishing that offender was a sexually violent predator (SVP), that he suffered from a mental abnormality or personality disorder); *State v. Andre L.*, 84 A.D.3d 1248, 924 N.Y.S.2d 467 (2 Dept. 2011) (in proceeding seeking civil management of alleged sex offender, first-degree robbery determined to be sexually motivated where offender left home dressed in women's undergarments with intention of exposing himself, and robbery was part of offender's thrill involving sexual arousal; offender suffered from exhibitionism and fetishism disorders that made it unlikely he could control impulses to expose himself and have sexual contact with unknown women); *In re Commitment of Bohannan*, 379 S.W.3d 293 (Tex. App. 9 Dist.), *review granted*, *affirmed* 388 S.W.3d 296, *rehearing denied*, *cert. denied* 133 S.Ct. 2746 (2010) (civil commitment warranted under SVP law where defendant diagnosed with paraphilia not otherwise specified with features of pedophilia, sadism, and exhibitionism).

E. Sexting

1. Sexting By Adults

State v. Stuckey

Court of Appeals of Wisconsin, 2013
349 Wis. 2d 654, 837 N.W.2d 160

REILLY, J.

Wisconsin Stat. § 948.10(1)(a) (2011–12)[1] establishes that it is a Class I felony when one exposes genitals to a child "for purposes of sexual arousal or sexual gratification." An example of the type of actor targeted by this statute is the sexual pervert who exposes himself to a child in a park. The twist in this case is that the State charged Zachary Stuckey with violating this statute by taking a picture of his penis and then sending the picture via the internet (colloquially known as "sexting") to a fourteen-year-old girl. Stuckey moved to dismiss this charge, arguing that § 948.10 requires an in-person exposure. The circuit court agreed and reasoned that the proper charge, given the facts presented, was a charge of exposing a child to harmful material contrary to Wis. Stat. § 948.11.

The State appeals on the ground that while it could have charged Stuckey under Wis. Stat. § 948.11, it is also proper to charge him under Wis. Stat. § 948.10. We disagree as § 948.10 lacks the scienter element of age of the victim that is necessary in a variable obscenity statute. Section 948.11, also a variable obscenity statute, was amended by the legislature to include such a scienter element following *State v. Weidner*, 2000 WI 52, 235 Wis.2d 306, 611 N.W.2d 684. *Weidner* is on point with the facts present in this case, and *Weidner* concluded that because the State did not bear the burden to prove scienter under § 948.11(2), the statute was unconstitutional in the context of the internet and other situations that do not involve face-to-face contact. *Weidner*, 235 Wis.2d 306, ¶ 37. As *Weidner* requires a scienter element in a variable obscenity statute, we affirm.... As this appeal involves an

---

1. All references to the Wisconsin Statutes are to the 2011–12 version unless otherwise noted.

order granting a motion to dismiss for failure to state a crime in the criminal complaint, we accept the following facts set forth in the criminal complaint as true.

Stuckey was eighteen years old when he "met" fourteen-year-old Jane Doe ... [footnote omitted] on Facebook[3] on November 12, 2011. After he turned nineteen, Stuckey texted a photo of his penis from his cell phone to Doe's cell phone. Stuckey and Doe later met in person at a movie theater. During the movie, Stuckey kissed Doe and touched her breast on the outside of her shirt. Based on the above facts, the State charged Stuckey with three crimes: Count 1—use of a computer to facilitate a child sex crime contrary to Wis. Stat. § 948.075(1r); Count 2—exposing genitals or pubic area to a child contrary to Wis. Stat. § 948.10(1)(a); and Count 3—second-degree sexual assault of a child contrary to Wis. Stat. § 948.02(2). Pursuant to Stuckey's motion, the circuit court dismissed Count 2....

We start our discussion with the language of the statute.... [citation omitted]. Wisconsin Stat. § 948.10 states in full,

(1) Whoever, for purposes of sexual arousal or sexual gratification, causes a child to expose genitals or pubic area or exposes genitals or pubic area to a child is guilty of the following:

(a) Except as provided in par. (b), a Class I felony.

(b) A Class A misdemeanor if any of the following applies:

1. The actor is a child when the violation occurs.

2. At the time of the violation, the actor had not attained the age of 19 years and was not more than 4 years older than the child.

(2) Subsection (1) does not apply under any of the following circumstances:

(a) The child is the defendant's spouse.

(b) A mother's breast-feeding of her child.

The State argues that the legislature intended for the statute to be read expansively so as to encompass both in-person exposures and remote exposures such as Stuckey's "sexting" of his penis to Doe. The problem with such an expansive reading is that Wis. Stat. § 948.10 does not expressly require that the actor know or reasonably know the age of the child-victim or have face-to-face contact prior to the exposure such as is present in other crimes involving crimes against children. Cf. Wis. Stat. §§ 948.055(2), 948.075(1r), 948.11(2), 948.12(1m). In adherence to Weidner, we find this last point dispositive and hold that § 948.10, as it reads today, may only be applied in settings in which the exposure occurs where there is face-to-face contact....

The fact situation from Weidner is strikingly similar to the facts of this case. Lane R. Weidner began communicating with sixteen-year-old Samantha B. over an internet chat room known as "Teenage Romance." Weidner, 235 Wis.2d 306, ¶¶ 2–3. Weidner used the internet to send a naked picture of himself to Samantha B. Id. Weidner was charged with violating Wis. Stat. § 948.11(2) (1997–98), which prohibited the dissemination of harmful material to minors.... [citation omitted]. Weidner argued that § 948.11(2) (1997–98) was unconstitutional under the First Amendment for failing to require that the State prove Weidner's knowledge of the victim's minority status.... At the time of the Weidner decision,

---

3. Facebook is an online social networking service. Facebook allows anyone who declares himself or herself to be at least thirteen years old to become a registered user of the site. See Facebook Statement of Rights and Responsibilities, https://www.facebook.com/legal/terms (last updated Dec. 11, 2012).

scienter was an affirmative defense that the defendant had to prove to avoid criminal liability and not an element to be proved by the State. *See* § 948.11(2)(c) (1997–98).

The *Weidner* court concluded that because age represented the critical element separating illegal conduct under Wis. Stat. § 948.11 from that conduct protected under the First Amendment, some form of scienter was required to avert significant constitutional dilemmas.... [citation omitted]. The court concluded that because the State did not bear the burden to prove scienter under § 948.11(2), the statute was unconstitutional in the context of the internet and other situations that do not involve face-to-face contact.... [citation omitted].... In response to *Weidner*, the legislature amended Wis. Stat. § 948.11 to ensure the State was required to prove beyond a reasonable doubt that the defendant reasonably knew that the child was under the age of eighteen or that the defendant had face-to-face contact with the child before or during the sale, rental, exhibition, playing, distribution, or loan of the harmful material. *See* 2001 Wis. Act 16, §§ 3976, 3977, 3979, 3981....

The *Weidner* court noted that Wis. Stat. § 948.11(2) prohibits a person from exhibiting to children those materials deemed obscene to minors but not obscene to adults, which is known as a variable obscenity statute.... [citation omitted]. Variable obscenity distinguishes between obscene and non-obscene offenses based on the audience to which the content is directed and the nature of the content's appeal or impact on the targeted audience. *See* William B. Lockhart & Robert C. McClure, *Censorship of Obscenity: The Developing Constitutional Standards*, 45 Minn. L.Rev. 5, 78 (1960). Thus, while exhibiting hard-core pornography might be criminalized regardless of the audience, exhibiting soft-core pornography might be criminalized under a variable obscenity statute when it is targeted at children. Variable obscenity statutes are premised on established tenets recognizing the significance of age in First Amendment jurisprudence.... [citation omitted]. Sexual expression that is appropriate for adults may not be suitable for children.... [citation omitted]. Accordingly, the government may regulate the exposure of minors to sexually explicit content in promoting the government's compelling interest to safeguard the physical and psychological well-being of children....

A variable obscenity statute such as Wis. Stat. § 948.11 requires a "knowing and affirmative" violation. *State v. Thiel*, 183 Wis.2d 505, 535, 515 N.W.2d 847 (1994). An individual violates § 948.11 if he or she, aware of the nature of the material, knowingly offers or presents for inspection to a specific minor or minors material defined as harmful to children in § 948.11(1)(b). *Thiel*, 183 Wis.2d at 535. The *Thiel* court and the Jury Instruction Committee thought it important and necessary to define the verb "exhibit" to explicitly explain that that word represents a knowing, affirmative act in the context of a conviction under § 948.11. *State v. Gonzalez*, 2011 WI 63, ¶ 42, 335 Wis.2d 270, 802 N.W.2d 454....

Like Wis. Stat. § 948.11, Wis. Stat. § 948.10 is a variable obscenity statute. The legislature created § 948.10 in 1987 by altering some of the elements of the crime of lewd and lascivious behavior from Wis. Stat. § 944.20(1)(b), which criminalizes the act of "publicly and indecently" exposing genitals or pubic area. Legis. Council Staff, Wisconsin Legislative Council Report No. 7 to the 1987 Legislature, Legislation on Crimes Against Children, at 17 (Apr. 21, 1987) [hereinafter "Report No. 7"]. The lewd and lascivious statute is contained within Wis. Stat. ch. 944's subch. IV applicable to crimes of obscenity and has been construed by courts to apply to obscene conduct when children or unwilling adults are present. *See Reichenberger v. Warren*, 319 F.Supp. 1237, 1239 (W.D.Wis.1970).

The first element of Wis. Stat. § 944.20(1)(b) is that "[t]he defendant exposed genitals," which tracks the first element of Wis. Stat. § 948.10, "[t]he defendant exposed genitals to (name of child)." ... [citation omitted]. With the modification of the lewd and lascivious statute as applicable to child-victims, however, the legislature eliminated the requirement that the exposure be done "publicly" or "indecently." ... [citation omitted]. Instead, the legislature substituted a requirement that the exposure be done "for the purpose of sexual arousal or gratification." ... We discern the legislative intent was to protect children in both private and public settings and to criminalize the exposure of genitalia to children whether the exposure is "indecent" (i.e. obscene) or not. As §948.10 criminalizes certain activity directed toward children that could be considered legal when directed toward adults, it can be considered a variable obscenity statute.[4] *See Weidner*, 235 Wis.2d 306, ¶9.

Even though Wis. Stat. §948.10 is a variable obscenity statute, neither the language of the statute nor the related jury instructions require the State to prove scienter (i.e., knowledge) of the age of the person receiving the transmission. Although the exposure must be done "for purposes of sexual arousal or sexual gratification," the exposure does not need to be knowingly and affirmatively directed toward a specific minor or minors. *Cf. Thiel*, 183 Wis.2d at 535. The jury instructions for §948.10 expressly instruct that knowledge of the child's age is not required and mistake is not a defense.... [citations omitted]. Section 948.10 essentially sets forth a strict liability offense that deprives an individual of the opportunity to prove lack of knowledge or mistake. *See State v. Robins*, 2002 WI 65, ¶30, 253 Wis.2d 298, 646 N.W.2d 287. As it relates to Stuckey's conduct over the internet as alleged by the State, §948.10 thus lacks a scienter element as to the age of the person receiving the digital image of genitals or even a requirement that a child was the intended recipient. Under the reasoning set forth in *Weidner*, §948.10 cannot be applied in the context of the internet or similar situations that do not involve face-to-face contact. Presented with almost the same fact situation as in *Weidner*, in which the supreme court found that the State could not constitutionally rely on a variable obscenity statute that lacked a scienter element, the State cannot now rely on another variable obscenity statute lacking a scienter element to criminalize Stuckey's "sexting" behavior.

We conclude that Wis. Stat. §948.10, like other statutes within Wis. Stat. ch. 948 that create strict liability for crimes against children, can only be employed in situations involving face-to-face contact at the time of the crime, i.e., in-person exposures. *See State v. Trochinski*, 2002 WI 56, ¶39, 253 Wis.2d 38, 644 N.W.2d 891 ("[P]ersonal contact between the perpetrator and the child-victim is what allows the State to impose on the defendant the risk that the victim is a minor.").... We affirm the circuit court's dismissal of Count 2 charging Stuckey with exposing genitals to a child as Wis. Stat. §948.10 is a crime only in those situations involving face-to-face contact at the time of the crime. As the State acknowledges, Stuckey can be charged under Wis. Stat. §948.11 for sending harmful material to a child via the internet.

Order affirmed....

---

4. We recognize that, unlike Wis. Stat. §948.11, Wis. Stat. §948.10 does not consider the effect of the "nature of the materials" on the child-victim, but rather the purpose of the exposure by the actor. As United States Supreme Court Chief Justice Warren stated in a concurring opinion where he endorsed the variable concept of obscenity, "The conduct of the defendant is the central issue, not the obscenity of a book or picture. The nature of the materials is, of course, relevant as an attribute of the defendant's conduct, but the materials are thus placed in context from which they draw color and character." *Roth v. United States*, 354 U.S. 476, 495 (1957) (Warren, C.J., concurring). Section 948.10 targets the "color and character" of the defendant's conduct in carrying out the exposure "for purposes of sexual arousal or sexual gratification." The legislature has determined that there is harm in a defendant who exposes himself or herself to a blind child for the purpose of sexual arousal just as surely as in one who exposes himself or herself to a seeing child for the same purpose.

GUNDRUM, J. (concurring).

I write separately to express that I do not believe constitutional application of Wis. Stat. § 948.10 is limited to only situations involving "in-person" exposures.... I believe it also can be constitutionally utilized in situations involving live face-to-face interaction which is not necessarily "in person."

In *State v. Weidner*, 2000 WI 52, 235 Wis.2d 306, 611 N.W.2d 684, our supreme court found Wis. Stat. § 948.11, as then written, constitutionally deficient because it permitted the prosecution of persons for distributing harmful materials to minors without requiring face-to-face contact, which would allow such persons to reliably and conveniently ascertain the age of the person receiving the materials.... [citation omitted]. As the majority points out, the defendant in *Weidner* communicated with his victim through an internet chat room and subsequently sent her a picture of himself naked.... [citations omitted]. The communication between the two did not involve any face-to-face contact.... [citation omitted].... In deciding *Weidner*, before the widespread use of live face-to-face interactive internet capabilities, such as Skype,[5] the court went out of its way to indicate that face-to-face interaction over the internet would present a different constitutional question than the non-face-to-face internet communication at issue in the case before it.

We note at the outset that our constitutional inquiry is premised on internet communication that does not involve face-to-face contact. However, we are cognizant of the evolving nature of technology and that future communication over the internet may entail face-to-face contact. Our present analysis is essentially based on the distinction we draw between face-to-face interaction and interaction that does not involve face-to-face contact.... [citation omitted]. The court concluded that "[t]he lack of face-to-face interaction" impeded the ability of a person to "ascertain reliably the age of the recipient," and, because of this, effectively chilled speech between adults.... [citation omitted].

The type of live face-to-face interactive technology the supreme court referenced in 2000 is now readily available and frequently utilized. Whether through the internet or another medium, such technology provides a means by which individuals can directly and immediately harm children by exposing themselves and/or persuading children to do the same. Significantly, live face-to-face interaction also presents a would-be offender a means by which to directly and immediately assess the age of the person on the other end of the video communication nearly as effectively as in an in-person scenario. In my opinion, and as alluded to in *Weidner*, such technology affords sufficient reliability for determining the age of the person on the other end of the communication and makes constitutional the application of Wis. Stat. § 948.10 in such cases.

Note

Face-to-face interaction is an evolving factor in life and in law. In *Stuckey*, the court grapples with an older statute and its inapplicability to modern technology. For further discussion on this issue, see Reid McEllrath, *Keeping Up With Technology: Why A Flexible Juvenile Sexting Statute Is Needed to Prevent Overly Severe Punishment in Washington State*, 89 WASH. L. REV. 1009 (2014); Sonia Livingstone and Peter K. Smith, *Annual Research Review: Harms Experienced by Child Users of Online and Mobile Technologies: the Nature, Prevalence and Management of Sexual and Aggressive Risks in the Digital Age*, 55 J. CHILD PSYCHOL. & PSYCHIAT. 635 (2014); Carrie L. M. Thompson, *Let's Talk About Sex: Illinois'*

---

5. Skype is a "software application and online service that enables voice and video phone calls over the Internet," http://dictionary.com (last visited June 24, 2013).

Legislative Response to Sexting, 24 DCBA BRIEF 22 (Oct. 2011). However, even modern "sexting" laws often apply only to teens. When an adult texts sexually explicit material to a minor, courts must often rely on other criminal offenses involving obscenity and other forms of photographic exploitation, such as the *Stuckey* court recognized. *See also State v. Brown*, 2015 WL 326450 (Kan. Ct. App.) (18-year-old convicted of sexual exploitation of a child after 15-year-old girlfriend texted sexually explicit picture of herself, at his request); *State v. Canal*, 773 N.W.2d 528 (Iowa 2009) (18-year-old texted picture of erect penis to minor, charged with knowingly disseminating obscene material to a minor). In the following case, in which the adult defendant exchanged sexually explicit images with a minor, consider whether the laws applicable to child pornography are sufficient to address the offense involved.

United States v. Nash

United States District Court, Northern District, Alabama, 2014
1 F. Supp. 3d 1240

KARON OWEN BOWDRE, Chief Judge.

An odd day arises when a young man, who could legally have consensual sex with his sixteen-year-old girlfriend, will forever be labeled a sex offender for receiving provocative pictures of her that she sent him via text message. Such is the day of modern technology; a day when we not only combat the despicable perversion of child pornography, but also must account for the rampant proliferation of "sexting"[1] among teenagers and young adults. This court, and other district courts across the nation, bear the burden of taking into account these realities of this age of technology, while still imposing a sentence that is "sufficient, but not greater than necessary" to meet the purposes of sentencing. 18 U.S.C. § 3553(a).

This matter came before the court for the sentencing of twenty-two-year-old Defendant John Bradley Nash, who has pled guilty to one count of possession of child pornography. This memorandum opinion supplements findings made on the record at the sentencing hearing on November 7, 2013.... For the reasons stated on the Record and further explained below, the court sentences the Defendant John Bradley Nash to 60 months probation with special conditions. The court imposes this unusual sentence because of unusual circumstances....

As a result of the execution of a sealed warrant and the review of the Defendant's computer and cell phone, investigators found images of 16-year-old female E.L. on Nash's cell phone. These four images showed E.L. involved in lewd and lascivious behavior that qualifies as child pornography.[2] During an initial interview, E.L. admitted that she was in a consensual sexual relationship with Nash and that she took the pictures of herself and sent them to Nash. During a subsequent interview, E.L. stated that Nash persuaded her to take the pictures of herself but Nash denies that he persuaded E.L. to take the pictures....

The court is particularly troubled by the application of the Sentencing Guidelines to "sexting" cases involving a consensual and legal relationship. Sexting is a widespread phenomena among teenagers and young adults. Regardless of the appropriateness of engaging in such virtual conversations, the court doubts that this behavior is the kind that Congress

---

1. Merriam-Webster defines "sexting" as "the sending of sexually explicit messages or images by cell phone." m-w.com, "sexting."

2. A total of ten images were found on Nash's phone, but six of those images were duplicates of the four different images.

was targeting when it passed child pornography laws. While Mr. Nash's relationship with E.L. may be inappropriate, it was perfectly *legal* in the state of Alabama where the age of consent is sixteen. *See* Ala.Code § 13A-6-70(c)(1). The difference in age between Mr. Nash and E.L. was six years, and the difference in maturity levels was likely less than that. Based on the forensic psychosexual evaluation and Dr. Preston's testimony, Mr. Nash was an emotionally immature twenty-two-year-old young man with untreated ADHD who entered into an ill-advised—but perfectly legal—relationship and received four lascivious picture messages from his sixteen-year-old girlfriend....

A 2008 study from The National Campaign to Prevent Teen and Unplanned Pregnancy (NCPTUP) suggested that 22% of teen girls and 18% of teen boys ("teens" are defined as ages 13 to 19) and 36% of young adult women and 31% of young adult men ("young adults" are defined as ages 20–26) are sending or posting nude or semi-nude images of themselves.[9] In contrast, a survey from the Pew Research Center's Internet & American Life Project found that only "4% of cell-owning teens ages 12–17 say they have sent sexually suggestive nude or nearly nude images of themselves to someone else via text messaging" and 15% say they have received such images of someone they know.[10] Although the article *Stemming Sexting: Sensible Legal Approaches to Teenagers' Exchange of Self-Produced Pornography* aptly notes that the numbers from either study should be viewed with skepticism given both the questionable survey methods—particularly with the NCPTUP study—and the amount of social disapproval associated with the topic, no one disputes that sexting is a significant phenomenon among teenagers and young adults today.[11] ... The article continues to point out: "The concern that sexted images can be easily distributed over peer-to-peer networks or otherwise fall in to the hands of sexual predators ... is not a risk most teens recognize. Nor do most teens realize that their actions are illegal and could qualify them for a decades-long sex offender registration requirement." *Id.* at 562.

In recent years, many young people—like Mr. Nash—have come face-to-face with these unintended consequences. For example, an eighteen-year-old Florida man was convicted of distributing child pornography after sending nude pictures of his sixteen-year-old ex-girlfriend to her friends and family in a fit of anger over their breakup (the girl had taken the photos of herself).[12] An eighteen-year-old Cincinnati woman committed suicide after nude pictures she had sent her boyfriend were circulated around her high school. *Id.* at 152. A sixty-year-old high school assistant principal was prosecuted for having semi-nude photographs of a young girl on his work computer; he had recently confiscated the photos from a sixteen-year old boy and was preserving them as evidence. The boy's own mother reported the incident to the police. *Id.* at 153.... Based on these stories, statistics, and commentaries, the court takes into account the proliferation of sexting among young people today and its unintended consequences as a factor in determining Mr. Nash's sentence.

The court also takes into account the number and type of images that were on Mr. Nash's cell phone. The four pictures, as despicable as they were, were not photographs

---

9. *See* The National Campaign to Prevent Teen and Unplanned Pregnancy, *Sex and Tech: Results from a Survey of Teens and Young Adults* (2008) http://www.thenationalcampaign.org/sextech/pdf/sextech_summary.pdf.

10. Amanda Lenhart, *Teens and Sexting: How and why minor teens are sending sexually suggestive nude or nearly nude images via text messaging*, Pew Internet & American Life Project (December 2009), *http://www. pewinternet.org/Reports/2009/Teens-and-Sexting.aspx.*

11. *See* Elizabeth C. Eraker, *Stemming Sexting: Sensible Legal Approaches to Teenagers' Exchange of Self-Produced Pornography*, 25 Berkely Tech. L.J. 555, 559–60 (2010).

12. Robert H. Wood, *The Failure of Sexting Criminalization: A Plea for the Exercise of Prosecutorial Restraint*, 10 Mich. Telecomm. & Tech L.Rev. 151, 153 (2009).

of a prepubescent minor, were not masochistic, were not torture or bondage, and were not the totally-beyond-human-consideration photographs that are present in so many cases involving child pornography. No evidence exists that Mr. Nash shared these images with others—they were not uploaded on any file sharing device to be disseminated across the country and did not appear on his computer, only on his cell phone where E.L. had sent them by text. These four images were the only child pornography found on his phone or his computer. The court does not minimize the wrongness of Mr. Nash's conduct, but notes that it is not as horrific as the conduct that the court must frequently address in the most common kinds of child pornography cases.

The court must also balance the history and characteristics of Mr. Nash. His age plays a significant role in his conduct and his sentence. Studies show that until age 25, the part of the brain that governs judgment, decision-making and impulse control is still in the developmental process.... [footnote omitted]. Male brains specifically develop even more slowly than female brains; female brains develop an average of two years earlier than male brains.... [footnote omitted]. In an NPR interview, Dr. Sandra Aamodt specifically noted that "[m]any of ... what we think of as the costs of adolescence ... are actually more issues with young adults, people in the 18 to 25 range, largely because they have more opportunities to get into these kinds of trouble...." ... [footnote omitted].... Furthermore, Dr. Preston, who completed the forensic psychosexual evaluation of Mr. Nash, testified regarding these trends. After affirming that Mr. Nash suffered from untreated ADHD at the time of his relationship with E.L., Dr. Preston stated:

> "Well, there's a—a lot of recent research that says the brain doesn't fully mature until about the age of twenty-five, so we're seeing people with attention deficit hyperactivity disorder tend to be a little bit later on that curve, as well as exhibit some symptoms or signs of immaturity." He continued to explain that he thought "it would be more likely than not [Mr. Nash] would be below average on immaturity and the ability to do some of the socialization that most people his age would be able to do," and answered affirmatively when asked whether Mr. Nash's immaturity could have contributed to the conduct at issue in the hearing....

Based on the court's research and Dr. Preston's testimony, Mr. Nash's inappropriate relationship with E.L. occurred during a time when he was still incapable of fully adult decision-making. Although his age requires that he be treated as an adult, his immaturity is a factor that the court considers in sentencing.

The court finds that Mr. Nash was a very immature, troubled twenty-two-year-old man at the time of the offense. He was in a consensual relationship with a sixteen-year-old girl—a relationship that was not wise, but was not in-and-of-itself illegal. Mr. Nash's ADHD was not medicated at the time, and he suffered from depression—factors that likely contributed to his unwise choices, although not excusing it.... The court also takes into account the steps he has taken since that time for therapy and treatment. Immediately after being arrested in July 2012, Mr. Nash voluntarily began intense counseling and treatment. He began seeing Dr. Preston on a monthly basis in July 2012 and then began seeing Lonnie Jones, a licensed therapist in November 2012. In March 2013 he also began seeing Dr. Scariya Kumaramangalam, a psychiatrist, who treated him and prescribed medications for Mood Disorder. Dr. Preston determined that "Mr. Nash is does [sic] not qualify as per the diagnostic criteria as a pedophile." ...

This extremely immature young man differs from the typical child pornography defendant who generally has a cache of hundreds of images obtained from peer-to-peer exchanges or from his own creation; instead Mr. Nash had four separate images sent to him by his *girlfriend*. Because of his young age and immaturity, the court questions whether the Bureau of Prisons can adequately accommodate and protect Mr. Nash—another reason why incarceration is not appropriate in this case.... The court must craft a sentence that reflects the seriousness of the offense and promotes the respect for the law. In doing so, the court specifically finds that a Guideline sentence would be excessive and would not provide respect for the law *in this particular case*. The court also considers the need to afford adequate deterrence to criminal conduct. Based at least in part on Dr. Preston's testimony, the court believes that Mr. Nash will not repeat his conduct or engage in any other similar conduct. The court finds no need for incarceration to protect the public from further crimes by him. The court will, however, impose terms and conditions that include treatment to make sure that Mr. Nash continues along the path of recovery that he is now on, and to ensure that deterrence and protection will not be an issue in the future.[16] This sentence will allow for the needed correctional treatment in the most effective manner and will avoid unwarranted similarities in sentencing among *dissimilar* defendants.

Pursuant to the court's authority under *United States v. Booker* to impose a sentence outside the Guideline range, and following the guidance of *Gall*, 552 U.S. at 38, 128 S.Ct. 586, the court takes the extraordinary but not unprecedented step of placing Mr. Nash on probation for a term of sixty months. In making this determination, the court relies on several cases in which appellate courts have affirmed the imposition of probation in similar cases with similar or higher Guideline ranges.... By imposing probation, the court imposes much more than a slap on Mr. Nash's hand. He will forever be a convicted felon and will forever be labeled a "sex offender" in the state of Alabama. Although Mr. Nash's father pleaded with the court not to brand his son as such for the rest of his life, the court has no authority to avoid this overly-harsh, life-long result. Although Mr. Nash is a Tier I sex offender under federal law, requiring registration for only 15 years pursuant to 42 U.S.C. § 16915(a)(1), under the Alabama law bringing the state into compliance with the requirements of the Adam Walsh Child Protection and Safety Act, *all* adult sex offenders must register *for life*. Ala.Code § 15-20A-3(b).[17] The sex offender label that Mr. Nash's father pleaded with the court to avoid is statutorily mandated, and the court has no power to change this unwarranted life sentence unless Congress and/or the Alabama legislature

---

16. Those conditions include the standard conditions of supervised release, the standard sex offender conditions, and particularized conditions including specific sex offender/mental health treatment, six months home confinement, and community service that may include warning young people of the dangers of sexting. Those conditions are set out in the Judgment and Commitment Order filed simultaneously with this Memorandum Opinion.

17. Specifically, in Alabama, sex offender registration involves many collateral consequences; for example,

- Publishing on a public website of the offender's personal information, including name, address, employer, school attendance, photo, license plate number, and criminal history of any sex offense, Ala.Code § 15-20A-8;
- Requiring the offender to appear in person every three months to verify registration information, Ala.Code § 15-20A-10;
- Prohibiting the offender from residing or staying more than three consecutive days in a living accommodation within 2,000 feet of any school or childcare facility, Ala.Code § 15-20A-11;
- Prohibiting the offender from working or volunteering in a school or other facility or business that provides services primarily to children, Ala.Code § 15-20A-13; and
- Requiring the offender to report in person and procure a travel permit before leaving his or her residence for three or more consecutive days and procure a permit at least 21 days in advance before traveling outside of the country, Ala.Code § 15-20A-15.

change the law. The court considers the harshness of this "life sentence" in imposing probation in this case.

In an article addressing a similar law in Missouri,[18] the author noted: "The registry is today's ultimate 'scarlet letter.' Long after they've served their time, sex offenders remain barred from parks and schools and limited in their employment and housing options. Their names and faces are posted on the Internet, easily accessible to friends and neighbors." ... [footnote omitted]. Such a "scarlet letter" seems particularly harsh for a young man who possessed four photos sent to him by his girlfriend with whom he had a legal and consensual sexual relationship—certainly an unintended consequence of sexting.... According to a 2012 survey by the National Center for Missing and Exploited Children, over 736,000 sex offenders were registered in the United States at that time.[20] When that registry includes the full range of sex offenders—from those like Mr. Nash who engaged in sexting with his girlfriend to the hard core child predators—the effectiveness of the registry wanes. The court does not criticize the implementation of these restrictions in many circumstances, but simply notes that even Mr. Nash's probationary sentence involves serious, tangible consequences that will follow him for the rest of his life.

As part of his conditions of probation, after completion of some treatment, the court requires Mr. Nash to participate in five hours of community service under the supervision of the probation officer. The court is convinced that Mr. Nash has many positive gifts to give back to the community, but first needs to benefit from further treatment. In a few years, when Mr. Nash and his probation officer, in consultation with his treatment provider, believe the time is right, the court urges that Mr. Nash consider speaking out against sexting and the problems that it has caused. Although young people may not listen to this court, they need to know that sexting is a very real problem that can have very real, unexpected consequences. Mr. Nash, as someone who is facing those consequences, is in an ideal position to tell them. The court does not require this of Mr. Nash—it only requires the five hours of community service—but desires that Mr. Nash consider this request in a few years.... The message of the damages of sexting and the egregious consequences it can bring is one that needs to be shared with teenagers and young people, legislative bodies, and members of the justice system.

2. Sexting by Minors

Miller v. Skumanick

United States District Court, Middle District of Pennsylvania, 2009
605 F. Supp. 2d 634

JAMES M. MUNLEY, District Judge....

At issue in this case is the practice of "sexting," which has become popular among teenagers in recent years.... According to the plaintiffs, this is "the practice of sending or posting sexually suggestive text messages and images, including nude or semi-nude photographs, via cellular telephones or over the Internet." ... Typically, the subject takes a picture of him- or herself with a digital camera or cell phone camera, or asks someone else to take that picture.... That picture is stored as a digitized image and then sent via the text-message or photo-send function on a cell phone, transmitted by computer through

---

18. The Alabama law, unlike the Missouri law, does not require lifetime registry of *juvenile* sex offenders.

20. 2012 Annual Report, National Center for Missing and Exploited Children, pg. 5, available at www.missingkids.com/en_US/publications/NC171.pdf.

electronic mail, or posted to an internet website like Facebook or MySpace.... This practice is widespread among American teenagers; studies show approximately 20% of Americans age 13–19 have done it....

In October 2008, Tunkhannock, Pennsylvania School District officials confiscated several students' cell phones, examined them and discovered photographs of "scantily clad, semi-nude and nude teenage girls." ... Many of these girls were enrolled in the district.... The School District reported that male students had been trading these images over their cell phones.... The School District turned the phones over to Defendant Skumanick, the District Attorney of Wyoming County, Pennsylvania.... Skumanick began a criminal investigation.... In November 2008, Skumanick stated publically to local newspaper reporters and a district assembly at Tunkhannock High School that students who possess inappropriate images of minors could be prosecuted under Pennsylvania law for possessing or distributing child pornography, 18 Penn.Stat. § 6312, or criminal use of a communication facility, 18 Penn. Stat..§ 7512.... Skumanick pointed out that these charges were felonies that could result in long prison terms and would give even juveniles a permanent record.... Defendant contends that if found guilty of these crimes, the three minor plaintiffs would probably be subject to registration as sex offenders under Pennsylvania's Registration of Sexual Offenders Act ("Meghan's Law"), 42 P.S. § 9791, for at least ten years and have their names and pictures displayed on the state's sex-offender website....

On February 5, 2009, Skumanick sent letters to the parents of approximately twenty Tunkhannock students, including the adult plaintiffs in this case.... Skumanick sent this letter to the students on whose cell phones the pictures were stored and to the girls shown in the photos.... According to the plaintiffs, he did not send the letter to those who had disseminated the images.... The letter informed the parents that their child had been "identified in a police investigation involving the possession and/or dissemination of child pornography." ... The letter also promised that the charges would be dropped if the child successfully completed a six- to nine-month program focused on education and counseling.... The children and parents were invited to a meeting on February 12, 2009 to discuss the issue.... The letter warned that "charges will be filed against those that do not participate or those that do not successfully complete the program." ...

Skumanick held the meeting on February 12, 2009 at the Wyoming County Courthouse.... At that meeting, Skumanick reiterated his threat to prosecute unless the children submitted to probation, paid a $100 program fee and completed the program successfully.... When asked by a parent at the meeting why his daughter—who had been depicted in a photograph wearing a bathing suit—could be charged with child pornography, Skumanick replied that the girl was posed "provocatively," which made her subject to the child pornography charge.... When the father of Marissa Miller asked Skumanick who got to decide what "provocative" meant, the District Attorney replied that he refused to argue the question and reminded the crowd that he could charge all the minors that night.... Instead, Skumanick asserted, he had offered them a plea deal.... He told Mr. Miller that "these are the rules. If you don't like them, too bad." ...

The proposed program—which the plaintiffs call a "re-education program"—is divided between girls' and boys' programs.... [footnote omitted]. The program is designed to teach the girls to "gain an understanding of how their actions were wrong," "gain an understanding of what it means to be a girl in today's society, both advantages and disadvantages," and "identify nontraditional societal and job roles." ... Included in the "homework" for the program is an assignment including "[w]hat you did" and "[w]hy it was wrong." ... The program was initially purported to last six to nine months, but was eventually reduced to two hours per week over five weeks....

At the February 12 meeting, Skumanick asked all those present to sign an agreement assigning the minors to probation and to participation in the program.... Only one parent agreed to sign the form for her child.... Skumanick gave the parents forty-eight hours to agree to the offer or the minors would be charged.... After parents objected, Skumanick extended the time frame for agreeing to his program to a week.... Skumanick told parents he would show them the photographs in question at the end of the meeting....

Plaintiff MaryJo Miller and her ex-husband met with Skumanick at his invitation on February 10, 2009.... Skumanick showed them the photograph that involved their daughter Marissa.... The photograph in question was approximately two years old, and showed Plaintiffs Marissa Miller and Grace Kelly from the waist up, each wearing a white, opaque bra.... Marissa was speaking on the phone and Grace using her hand to make the peace sign.... The girls were thirteen years old at the time the picture was taken.... Despite Ms. Miller's protests to the contrary, Skumanick claimed that this image met the definition of child pornography because the girls were posed "provocatively." ... The Millers objected to Skumanick's legal claims, insisting that their daughter had a right to a jury trial if charged.... Skumanick informed them that no jury trials exists in Juvenile Court.... He also promised to prosecute both girls on felony child-pornography charges if they did not agree to his conditions.... After the February 12 meeting, Skumanick showed Jane Doe the photograph of her daughter Nancy.[2] ... The photograph, more than a year old, showed Nancy Doe wrapped in a white, opaque towel.... The towel was wrapped around her body, just below her breasts.... It looked as if she had just emerged from the shower....

The plaintiffs emphasize that neither of these two photographs depicted any sexual activity.... Neither showed the girls' genitalia or pubic area.... Skumanick said the pictures were among those on the confiscated cell phones, but he would not divulge who owned the phones.... At the time that plaintiffs filed their complaint, Skumanick had refused repeated requests to provide plaintiffs' counsel with copies of the pictures.... He asserted that he could be charged with a child pornography crime for sharing a copy.... The minors insist that they did not disseminate the photographs to anyone else, but that another person sent those pictures "to a large group of people" without their permission.... According to the complaint, Skumanick's only basis for the threatened prosecution of the three girls is that they allowed themselves to be photographed.... In early March, he asserted to plaintiffs' counsel that the three were accomplices in the production of child pornography.... During the hearing on the TRO conducted by this court on March 26, 2009, the defendant reiterated that he intends to charge the girls if they refuse to participate in the education program....

On February 25, 2009, plaintiffs received a letter dated February 23, 2009.... This letter advised parents that they were scheduled for a February 28, 2009 appointment at the Wyoming County Courthouse to "finalize the paperwork for the informal adjustment." ... Plaintiffs contend that an "informal adjustment" amounts to a guilty plea in the juvenile context, since it allows for probation before judgment.... Parents who attended the February 28, 2009 meeting informed plaintiffs that agreeing to the informal adjustment would subject plaintiffs to the "re-education" course, six months of probation and drug testing during those six months.... All of the parents and minors except the three here involved agreed to the conditions.... Defendant has temporarily deferred prosecution to the three minors here to allow plaintiffs' counsel to research the issues in this case.... During the hearing on the TRO, defendant gave his word as an officer of the court that he would not bring charges against the minor plaintiffs before this court renders a decision....

---

2. Plaintiff Jane Doe filed her complaint under a pseudonym, seeking to protect her identity and that of her daughter. She also filed a motion for leave of court to do so....

Plaintiffs' complaint raises three causes of action all filed pursuant to 42 U.S.C. § 1983 for violation of constitutional rights. Count I alleges retaliation in violation of plaintiffs' First Amendment right to free expression. Plaintiffs contend that the photographs in question are not in violation of any obscenity law and are thus expression protected by the First Amendment. Skumanick therefore threatens charges against them without a legitimate basis in an attempt to force the girls to abandon their constitutional rights and submit to the "re-education program," probation and drug testing. Count II alleges retaliation in violation of plaintiffs' First Amendment right to be free from compelled expression. The program in which the minor plaintiffs would be compelled to participate requires them to write a paper about "how their actions were wrong." Since minor plaintiffs did not violate any law, plaintiffs contend that this requirement is compelled speech. Count III, brought by the minor plaintiffs' parents, alleges retaliation against the parents for exercising their Fourteenth Amendment substantive due process right as parents to direct their children's upbringing. Plaintiffs allege that Skumanick's attempt to force their children to attend the class and participate in programs designed to let them "gain an understanding of how their actions were wrong," "gain an understanding of what it means to be a girl in today's society," and "identify non-traditional societal and job roles" infringes on their right to control the upbringing of their children. ...

Plaintiffs filed a motion for a TRO ... on March 25, 2009. The motion seeks an order from the court enjoining Defendant Skumanick and his officials, employees agents and assigns from initiating criminal charges against plaintiffs Marissa Miller, Grace Kelly and Nancy Doe for the two photographs at issue, or for any other photographs of the girls unless the images depict sexual activity or exhibit the genitals in a lascivious way. ... The court held a hearing on plaintiffs' motion for a TRO on March 26, 2009. At the hearing, the defendant agreed that Plaintiffs Jane and Nancy Doe should be allowed to proceed under pseudonyms, and that the court record be sealed to protect the identities of these individuals and to prevent the release of sensitive information.[3] The defendant also agreed to turn over to the plaintiffs' counsel copies of the photographs that are at issue in this case. Plaintiff MaryJo Miller testified during the hearing, as did Defendant Skumanick. After hearing this testimony, the court entertained argument from both sides. The court also ordered the defendant to file a brief in response to plaintiffs' motion. Defendant did so on March 27, 2009. Plaintiffs then filed a reply brief, bringing the case to its present posture. ...

An injunction is an "extraordinary remedy" that is never awarded as of right. *Winter v. Natural Resources Defense Council*, 555 U.S. 7, 129 S.Ct. 365, 375, 172 L.Ed.2d 249 (2008). The Third Circuit Court of Appeals has outlined four factors that a court ruling on a motion for a preliminary injunction must consider: (1) whether the movant has shown a reasonable probability of success on the merits; (2) whether the movant will be irreparably injured by denial of the relief; (3) whether granting preliminary relief will result in even greater harm to the nonmoving party; and (4) whether granting the preliminary relief will be in the public interest. *Crissman v. Dover Downs Entertainment Inc.*, 239 F.3d 357, 364 (3d Cir.2001). These same factors are used to determine a motion for a temporary restraining order. *Bieros v. Nicola*, 857 F.Supp. 445, 446 (E.D.Pa.1994). ... The above factors merely "structure the inquiry" and no one element will necessarily determine the outcome. The court must engage in a delicate balancing of all the elements, and attempt to minimize the probable harm to legally protected interests between the time of the preliminary injunction to the final hearing on the merits. *Constructors Association*

---

3. In any case, the court finds that the minor plaintiff's interest in having her identity protected in this sensitive matter outweighs the public's interest in knowing who brought the claim.

of Western Pa. v. Kreps, 573 F.2d 811, 815 (3d Cir.1978). The movant bears the burden of establishing these elements. *Adams v. Freedom Forge Corp.*, 204 F.3d 475, 486 (3d Cir.2000)....

As a preliminary matter, all three of plaintiffs' claims are retaliation claims which allege that defendant's threatened prosecution is retaliation for the exercise of their First and Fourteenth Amendment rights for refusing to participate in the education program at issue here. To prevail on a retaliation claim, a plaintiff must prove "(1) that he engaged in constitutionally-protected activity; (2) that the government responded with retaliation; and (3) that the protected activity caused the retaliation." *Eichenlaub v. Twp. of Indiana*, 385 F.3d 274, 282 (3d Cir.2004).... The plaintiffs' complaint is largely that they are being compelled—through threat of a prosecution that clearly lacks any basis—to participate in a "reeducation" program with which they disagree. Plaintiffs insist that retaliation exists here because (1) minor plaintiffs have a constitutional right to avoid the courses and their parents have a constitutional right to direct their education; (2) prosecution of the girls would be retaliation (an adverse action); and (3) because the girls' pictures were not illegal, the only reason to prosecute them would be in retaliation for exercising their constitutional right not to participate in the program. The court will examine each of the three elements of the retaliation claim to determine whether plaintiffs have established a reasonable likelihood of success on the merits....

The parents in this case have a Fourteenth Amendment right substantive due process right "to be free from state interference with family relations." *Gruenke v. Seip*, 225 F.3d 290, 303 (3d Cir.2000). "Choices about marriage, family life, and the upbringing of children are among associational rights this Court has ranked as 'of basic importance in our society,' rights sheltered by the Fourteenth Amendment against the State's unwarranted usurpation, disregard, or disrespect." *M.L.B. v. S.L.J.*, 519 U.S. 102, 117, 117 S.Ct. 555, 136 L.Ed.2d 473 (1996) (quoting *Boddie v. Connecticut*, 401 U.S. 371, 376, 91 S.Ct. 780, 28 L.Ed.2d 113 (1971)). Indeed, "the interest of parents in the care, custody, and control of their children ... is perhaps the oldest of the fundamental liberty interests recognized by" the Supreme Court. *Troxel v. Granville*, 530 U.S. 57, 65, 120 S.Ct. 2054, 147 L.Ed.2d 49 (2000). As early as 1923, the Supreme Court found that "the 'liberty' protected by the Due Process Clause includes the right of parents to 'establish a home and bring up children' and 'to control the education of their own.'" *Id.* (quoting *Meyer v. Nebraska*, 262 U.S. 390, 399, 43 S.Ct. 625, 67 L.Ed. 1042 (1923)).... Plaintiff MaryJo Miller testified at the TRO hearing that she did not want her child to attend the program.... She objected to a requirement that her daughter write an essay describing "what she did wrong and how it affected the victim in the case." ... From Ms. Miller's perspective, her daughter "was the victim" of whoever sent out the photographs.... Since her daughter had done "nothing wrong," she should not have to write such an essay.... In their complaint, all of the parents allege that this program violates this right to direct their children's education....

The minors contend that they have asserted their right to be free from compelled speech. "'Since *all* speech inherently involves choices of what to say and what to leave unsaid,' one important manifestation of the principle of free speech is that one who chooses to speak may also decide 'what not to say.'" *Hurley v. Irish-American Gay, Lesbian & Bisexual Group of Boston*, 515 U.S. 557, 573, 115 S.Ct. 2338, 132 L.Ed.2d 487 (1995) (quoting *Pacific Gas & Electric Co. v. Public Utilities Comm'n of Cal.*, 475 U.S. 1, 11, 106 S.Ct. 903, 89 L.Ed.2d 1 (1986)). Thus, "[t]he Supreme Court has long recognized that, in addition to restricting suppression of speech, 'the First Amendment may prevent the government from ... compelling individuals to express certain views.'" *Forum for Academic and Institutional Rights v. Rumsfeld*, 390 F.3d 219, 235 (3d Cir.2004) (quoting *United States v. United Foods, Inc.*, 533 U.S. 405, 410, 121 S.Ct. 2334, 150 L.Ed.2d 438 (2001)). This view exists because "'[a]t the heart of the First Amendment lies the principle that each person should decide for himself or herself the ideas and beliefs deserving of expression, consideration and adherence.'" *Id.* at 236 (quoting *Turner Broad. Sys., Inc. v. FCC*, 512 U.S. 622, 641, 114 S.Ct. 2445, 129 L.Ed.2d 497 (1994)). Among the categories of compelled speech found impermissible by the supreme court "is government action that forces a private speaker to propagate a particular message chosen by the government." *Id.* Here, the minor plaintiffs contend that they will be compelled to write an essay that explains what they did wrong. Because they contend that they in no way violated the law, they further contend that being compelled to describe their behavior as wrong on threat of a felony conviction forces them to express a belief they do not hold and thus violates their right to be free of compelled speech.... We find that both the parents and the children have asserted constitutionally protected activity sufficient to meet the standard that they are reasonably likely to succeed on the merits on this issue....

The Third Circuit Court of Appeals has held that an adverse action by the government sufficient to support a retaliation claim has occurred if "'the alleged retaliatory conduct was sufficient 'to deter a person of ordinary firmness' from exercising his First Amendment Rights.'" *Allah v. Seiverling*, 229 F.3d 220, 225 (3d Cir.2000) (quoting *Suppan v. Dadonna*, 203 F.3d 228, 235 (3d Cir.2000)). "[A]s a general matter the First Amendment prohibits government officials from subjecting an individual to retaliatory actions, including criminal prosecutions, for speaking out." *Hartman v. Moore*, 547 U.S. 250, 256, 126 S.Ct. 1695, 164 L.Ed.2d 441 (2006). The court finds here plaintiffs' claim that the threat of a felony prosecution would deter an ordinary person from exercising her constitutional rights meets the "reasonable likelihood of success on the merits" standard....

In support of this prong of a retaliation claim, plaintiffs argue that the images in question here could not possibly support a charge of child pornography under Pennsylvania law. As such, the defendant's threat to charge the minor plaintiffs with a felony is not a genuine attempt to enforce the law, but instead an attempt to force the minor plaintiffs to participate in the education program. The fact that the defendant continues to promise prosecution if the girls refuse to participate indicates that the charges are retaliation for their refusal to engage in compelled speech. In the case of the parents, this threat is an attempt to compel them to abandon their Fourteenth Amendment right to control their child's upbringing.... [footnote omitted].

Plaintiffs assert that the defendant has no basis in Pennsylvania law for prosecuting the girls. Defendant has asserted that the photographs are "provocative," but "provocative photos," plaintiffs contend, are not illegal under Pennsylvania law even when they involve minors. The statute in question, 18 Penn. Stat. §6312, prohibits the distribution of images depicting a prohibited sexual act, and defines "prohibited sexual act" to mean "sexual intercourse ... masturbation, sadism, masochism, bestiality, fellatio, cunnilingus, lewd exhibition of the genitals or nudity if such nudity is depicted for the purpose of sexual stimulation or gratification of any person who might view such depiction." 18 Penn. Stat. §6312(a). The plaintiff contends that the images here do not even remotely meet this definition....

The court here offers no final conclusion on the merits of plaintiffs' position. Testimony and evidence at the TRO hearing, as well as allegations in the verified complaint, however, indicate a reasonable likelihood that the plaintiffs could prevail on this aspect. While the court emphasizes that its view is preliminary and not intended to absolve the plaintiffs of any potential criminal liability, plaintiffs make a reasonable argument that the images presented to the court do not appear to qualify in any way as depictions of prohibited sexual acts. Even if they were such depictions, the plaintiffs argument that the evidence to this point indicates that the minor plaintiffs were not involved in disseminating the images is also a reasonable one. Thus, a reasonable likelihood exists that plaintiffs will succeed on the merits, and this factor weighs in favor of granting a TRO....

The next factor for us to examine is whether the plaintiffs will suffer irreparable harm if a TRO does not issue. *Crissman*, 239 F.3d at 364. Plaintiffs argue that even a temporary violation of First Amendment rights constitutes irreparable harm. Indeed, threat of prosecution has a chilling effect on plaintiffs expressing themselves by appearing in photographs, even such innocent photographs as those in bathing suits. Irreparable harm also exists because plaintiffs could not sue Skumanick if they were found not guilty after a prosecution, since he would be immune as prosecutor. Defendant contends that plaintiffs have adequate remedies other than an equitable one, and therefore they do not face any irreparable harm. Since the minors have not yet been prosecuted, they still have the opportunity to dispute any charges brought against them through a defense in court and appeal following any finding of delinquency.

Plaintiffs do not seek monetary damages from the defendant. If they did, they would have an adequate remedy at law and the court would normally decline to provide equitable relief. *See Frank's GMC Truck Center, Inc. v. General Motors Corp.*, 847 F.2d 100, 102 (3d Cir.1988) (finding that "[t]he availability of adequate monetary damages belies a claim of irreparable injury [and a] purely economic injury, compensable in money, cannot satisfy the irreparable injury requirement."). Here, plaintiffs seek the extraordinary remedy of injunctive relief because they allege that defendant's actions abrogate their First Amendment rights. The United States Supreme Court and the Third Circuit Court of Appeals have held that "'[t]he loss of First Amendment freedoms, for even minimal periods of time, unquestionably constitutes irreparable injury.'" *Swartzwelder v. McNeilly*, 297 F.3d 228, 241 (3d Cir.2002) (quoting *Elrod v. Burns*, 427 U.S. 347, 373, 96 S.Ct. 2673, 49 L.Ed.2d 547 (1976)). The plaintiffs here have demonstrated a reasonable likelihood of success on the merits of their First Amendment claims, and have therefore demonstrated that they face irreparable harm from defendant's threatened actions. This factor too weighs in favor of issuing a TRO....

The third factor we must examine is harm to the non-moving party. *Crissman*, 239 F.3d at 364. The court finds that no harm would come to the non-moving party by delaying prosecution on this matter. The defendant himself has to this point refrained from filing charges, and thus does not appear to feel immediate prosecution is necessary to protect the public from the crimes that the girls here allegedly committed. Indeed, his brief in opposition to the motion for a TRO does not address the issue of harm to the non-moving party. The court finds, therefore, that the harm to the non-moving party is clearly insignificant and outweighed by the harm faced by the plaintiffs from not granting the injunctive relief. If defendant insists that charges be filed at a later date, the twelve-year statute of limitations under Pennsylvania law means that he could bring appropriate prosecutions at the close of the litigation in this case. 42 Penn. Cons. Stat. § 5552(B.1). The court is confident that the matter will be resolved before that statute of limitations runs. Thus, this factor as well weighs towards granting the TRO.

The final factor for us to examine is the public interest. *Crissman*, 239 F.3d at 364. "As a practical matter, if a plaintiff demonstrates both a likelihood of success on the merits and irreparable injury, it almost always will be the case that the public interest will favor the plaintiff. Nonetheless, district courts should award preliminary injunctive relief only upon weighing all four factors." *AT & T v. Winback & Conserve Program*, 42 F.3d 1421, 1427 n. 8 (3d Cir.1994). The plaintiffs argue that the public interest would be protected by issuing the TRO since the public interest is served by enjoining a baseless prosecution brought in retaliation for the exercise of constitutional rights.... The court agrees with the plaintiffs that the public interest would be served by issuing a TRO in this matter as the public interest is on the side of protecting constitutional rights. This factor too supports issuing a TRO....

Upon balancing the TRO factors, we find that each factor weighs in favor of granting the TRO. Accordingly, we will grant the plaintiffs' motion for a temporary restraining order. An appropriate order follows....

Notes

The injunction not to prosecute was subsequently made permanent. *Miller v. Mitchell*, 2010 WL 1779925 (M.D. Pa. 2010). For another case involving a school district's response to the issue of sexting, see *S.N.B. v. Pearland Independent School District*, 2014 WL 2207864 (U.S. Dist. S.D. Tex) (student transferred to disciplinary alternative education program after violating school's prohibition of sexting not deprived of liberty or property interest).

As recognized by the courts in the preceeding cases and by many commentators, "sexting" has become epidemic among teens. *See* Kimberly J. Mitchell, David Finkelhor, Lisa M. Jones, and Janis Wolak, *Prevalence and Characteristics of Youth Sexting: A National Study*, available at http://pediatrics.aappublications.org/content/early/2011/11/30/peds.2011-1730 (last accessed Nov. 9, 2014); Janis Wolak, David Finkelhor and Kimberly Mitchell, *How Often Are Teens Arrested for Sexting? Data From a National Sample of Police Cases*, available at http://pediatrics.aappublications.org/content/early/2011/11/30/peds.2011-2242 (last accessed Nov. 9, 2014). In response to this emerging epidemic, many states have adopted legislation that criminalizes "sexting" by minors. Since 2009, at least 20 states have enacted bills to address the problem of teen sexting. For an excellent survey of state sexting laws and media focus on the issue, see Mobile Media Guard, U.S. Sexting Laws, available at http://mobilemediaguard.com/state_main.html (last visited Feb. 10, 2015). In 2013, at least nine states introduced bills or resolutions aimed at sexting; Arkansas, Georgia, and West Virginia enacted legislation in 2013. For Arkansas, see Ark. Code § 5-27-609 (Possession of sexually explicit digital material); *see also*, Sidney L. Leasure, *Criminal Law — Teenage Sexting in Arkansas: How Special Legislation Addressing Sexting Behavior in Minors Can Salvage Arkansas's Teens' Futures*, 35 UALR L. Rev. 141 (2012). For Georgia, see Ga. Code Ann. §§ 16-12-100 (Sexual exploitation of children), 16-12-100.1 (Electronically furnishing obscene material to minors), 16-12-100.2 (Computer or Electronic Pornography and Child Exploitation Prevention Act of 2007), and 16-12-100.3 (Obscene telephone contact with child). For West Virginia, see W. Va. Code § 49-5-13g (Sexting educational diversion program). For examples of other sexting laws, see Fla. Stat. Ann. § 847.0141 (Sexting; prohibited acts; penalties); Hawaii Rev. Stat. §§ 712-1215.5 (Promoting minor-produced sexual images in the first degree) and 712-1215.6 (Promoting minor-produced sexual images in the second degree); R.I. Gen. Laws § 11-9-1.4 (Minor electronically disseminating indecent material to another person — "Sexting" prohibited).

This trend in sexting legislation has led to extensive debate over the propriety of criminalizing sexting behavior for teens, expecially in light of the sex offender registration requirements that result and other constitutional considerations. For comments on this debate, see JoAnne Sweeny, *Sexting and Freedom of Expression: A Comparative Approach*, 102 Ky. L.J. 103 (2013/2014); John Kip Cornwell, *Sexting: 21st-Century Statutory Rape*, 66 S.M.U. L. Rev. 111 (2013); Joanna R. Lampe, *A Victimless Sex Crime: The Case for Decriminalizing Consensual Teen Sexting*, 46 U. Mich. J. L. Reform 703 (2013) (calling for criminalization of non-consensual or exploitative sexting, but not consensual teen sexting); Mallory N. Myers, *Texas Legislative Implications for Minors Accused of Sexting*, 45 St.

Mary's L.J. 73 (2013); Nicole A. Poltash, *Snapchat and Sexting: A Snapshot of Baring Your Bare Essentials*, 19 Richmond J. L. & Technology 1 (2013); Matthew H. Birkhold, *Freud on the Court: Re-interpreting Sexting & Child Pornography Laws*, 23 Fordham Intellectual Prop., Media & Ent. L.J. 897 (2013); Julia Halloran McLaughlin, *Exploring the First Amendment Rights of Teens in Relationship to Sexting and Censorship*, 45 U. Mich. J. L. Reform 315 (2012); Lijia Gong and Alina Hoffman, *Sexting and Slut-Shaming: Why Prosecution of Teen Self-Sexters Harms Women*, 13 Georgetown J. Gender & L. 577 (2012); Jamie L. Williams, *Teens, Sexts, & Cyberspace: the Constitutional Implications of Current Sexting & Cyberbullying Laws*, 20 William & Mary Bill of Rights J. 1017 (2012); Antonio M. Haynes, *The Age of Consent: When Is Sexting No Longer "Speech Integral to Criminal Conduct"?*, 97 Cornell L. Rev. 369 (2012); John M. Krattiger, *Sex-Cells: Evaluating Punishments for Teen "Sexting" in Oklahoma and Beyond*, 63 Ok. L. Rev. 317 (2011); Maryam F. Mujahid, *Romeo and Juliet—A Tragedy of Love by Text: Why Targeted Penalties That Offer Front-End Severity and Back-End Leniency Are Necessary to Remedy the Teenage Mass-Sexting Dilemma*, 55 Howard L.J. 173 (2011); Todd A. Fichtenberg, *Sexting Juveniles: Neither Felons Nor Innocents*, 6 I/S: J. L. & Pol'y for Info. Soc'y 695 (2011); Amanda M. Hiffa, *OMG TXT PIX PLZ: The Phenomenon of Sexting and the Constitutional Battle of Protecting Minors From Their Own Devices*, 61 Syracuse L. Rev. 499 (2011); Susan Hanley Duncan, *A Legal Response Is Necessary for Self-Produced Child Pornography: A Legislator's Checklist for Drafting the Bill*, 89 Or. L. Rev. 645 (2010).

Epitomizing the difficulty of enacting balanced legislation that criminalizes indecent and harmful activity involving minors but also accommodates other constitutional, criminal, and civil considerations for minors who exercise poor judgment, is the legislative predicament confronted by the court in *State of Florida v. C.M.*, 2015 WL 71949, in which the legislature essentially legalized sexting among teens. In *C.M.*, the state brought delinquency charges against a juvenile who texted a photograph of her vagina to a 13-year-old classmate because she was bored. The applicable sexting statute in Florida provided that a minor's first offense of sexting is a noncriminal violation that does not constitute a delinquent act and, thus, is not subject to prosecution under a petition for delinquency, but is punishable by community service or fine. *See C.M.*, 2015 WL 71949 at *1–2 (citing Fla. Stat. § 847.0141(1)(a) (2013)). It is only a second or third offense that qualifies as a criminal misdemeanor, and a fourth offense as a felony. Therefore, the court was forced to dismiss the charges, recognizing that Florida law provides no court with jurisdiction to determine civil infractions committed by juveniles. Accordingly, no juvenile can ever be criminally charged with a first (or any subsequent) offense for sexting. The court in *C.M.* called for the legislature to correct this procedural debacle.

F. Sextortion

In April 2014, Jared James Abrahams—a college computer science major—was sentenced to 18 months in federal prison after he used malware to hack into the webcams of more than 150 young girls and remotely operated their webcams to capture nude photos and videos of the girls, then blackmailed them to send more sexually explicit photos and videos of themselves. This behavior is termed "sextortion." He even coerced two teenage victims from Ireland and Canada to engage in sexual acts with him during "Skype" sessions. *See U.S. v. Abrahams*, No. SA13-422M (C.D. Cal., Santa Ana, Mar. 17, 2014). One of the young girls he blackmailed was former Miss Teen USA, Cassidy Wolf, with whom he attended high school. Abrahams included many other victims in several countries. *See College Student is Sentenced for 'Sextortion'*, available at http://www.thedailybeast.com/

articles/2014/03/18/college-student-is-sentenced-for-sextortion.html (Mar. 18, 2014) (accessed Nov. 7, 2014).

One sextortionist in Indiana—Richard Finkbiner—was sentenced to 40 years in prison after blackmailing more than a dozen teenage boys and girls, from 9 different states, ranging in ages from 12 to 16, to perform lewd sexual acts on video webcam and then threatening to upload the videos onto the web if the minors did not provide more explicit videos of themselves. Authorities discovered on Finkbiner's computers more than 22,000 videos from more than 150 victims collected over a period of two years. *See Richard Finkbiner, Indiana 'Sextortionist,' Sentenced To 40 Years For Webcam Sex Offenses*, available at http://www.huffingtonpost.com/2013/06/26/richard-finkbiner-indiana-sentenced-sextortionist_n_3504094.html (June 26, 2013) (accessed July 15, 2014); *Experts increasingly worried about 'sextortion' of minors online*, available at http://www.nbcnews.com/news/other/experts-increasingly-worried-about-sextortion-minors-online-f6C10645107 (July 16, 2013) (accessed July 15, 2014).... For other examples of sextortion plots, see *Alabama predator sentenced to 18 years for Facebook extortion attempts: How he got access*, available at http://blog.al.com/spotnews/2009/04/auburn_alabama_predator_senten.html (Apr. 17, 2009) (accessed July 15, 2014) (describing case of Jonathan Vance, sentenced to 18 years in prison after attempt to extort nude photographs from at least 50 teenagers by hacking into their Yahoo, Hotmail, Facebook, and MySpace accounts, locking out the victims from their accounts, and then demanding explicit photographs to relinquish control of their accounts); *FBI Report, A Case of 'Sextortion,'* available at http://www.fbi.gov/news/stories/2013/february/sextortion-cons-like-bieber-ruse-targeted-minor-girls/sextortion-cons-like-bieber-ruse-targeted-minor-girls (last accessed Nov. 8, 2014) (describing case of Alabama man sentenced to 35 years in prison for posing online as Justin Bieber to gain trust of victims); *Update on Sextortion at Eisenhower High*, available at http://www.gq.com/news-politics/big-issues/201002/wisconsin-high-school-sex-scandal-update (Feb. 26, 2010) (accessed July 15, 2014) (describing case of 18-year-old Anthony Stancl, sentenced to 15 years in prison for posing as a girl on Facebook and enticing at least 31 boys to send him naked pictures of themselves and using pictures to blackmail at least 7 of the boys, ranging in ages from 15 to 18, to have sex with him; six years earlier, Stancl had been convicted as a juvenile of sexual assault of a 3-year-old boy); *Suffolk boy, 13, charged in alleged "sextortion" case*, available at http://hamptonroads.com/2014/05/suffolk-boy-13-charged-alleged-sextortion-case (May 28, 2014) (accessed July 15, 2014) (describing 13-year-old perpetrator who blackmailed at least six girls into performing sex acts, including performing oral sex on a school bus).

As authorities more strictly address the crimes of sexual predators, more and more cases of sextortion are revealed. The Internet Crimes Against Children Task Force reports that it received 5,300 sextortion complaints in 2010, and 7,000 complaints in 2013. *See 'Sextortion' is an online 'epidemic' against children*, available at http://www.usatoday.com/story/news/nation/2014/07/01/sextortion-teens-online/11580633/ (July 2, 2014) (accessed July 15, 2014). Many children lured into the extortion have committed suicide. In a case that drew international attention to the issue, 15-year-old Amanda Todd committed suicide just hours after disclosing, in an online social media video, her experience of being blackmailed into an online sextortion scheme. *See The Amanda Todd Story*, available at http://nobullying.com/amanda-todd-story/ (last accessed Nov. 8, 2014).

Responses to the problem have been global in scale. The Department of Homeland Security has implemented an education platform in elementary and high schools through its Homeland Security Investigations unit, and has dismantled an international sextortion network run out of the Philippines (referred to as the "sextortion capital of the world"), resulting in the arrest of nearly 60 suspects, who collected thousands of dollars from hundreds of victims from Asia, Europe, and the United States. *See Police break up global webcam 'sextortion' ring,* available at http://www.theverge.com/2014/5/2/5674294/police-break-up-global-webcam-sextortion-ring-philippines (May 2, 2014) (accessed July 15, 2014). The following case involves claims of "sextortion," but the context of the claims is a Strategic Lawsuit Against Public Participation (SLAPP), brought by the alleged "sextortionist."

Backlund v. Stone

Court of Appeal, Second District, California, 2012
2012 WL 3800883

BOREN, P.J.

An aspiring lawyer in his 30's named Christopher Stone operated a website for teenagers on which he posted lewd photographs and other scandalous and salacious material. Stone presented himself in the mainstream media as an expert on the topic of "sextortion," a form of blackmail characterized by threats to humiliate a person by posting nude photographs on the Internet. In February 2010, Stone tweeted a threat to "spam" a seminude photograph of a teenage girl; she was subsequently interviewed by an investigative reporter for an article about Stone's threat to publicly humiliate her. Stone has now sued the girl for defamation. Following de novo review, we direct the trial court to strike Stone's pleading as a Strategic Lawsuit Against Public Participation (SLAPP). (Code Civ. Proc., § 425.16.)[1] ...

Alyssa Backlund filed suit against Christopher Stone and Stone's website "StickyDrama.com" in November 2010. In November 2009, Stone posted a lewd image of a minor female, with commentary that the image "appears to depict Alyssa Marie Robertson masturbating next to an infant. Such an act, in addition to being morally repugnant, probably violates several statutes pertaining to exposing children to obscenity." Stone published plaintiff's personal contact information with the image, which was viewed by thousands of people. Viewers posted comments of outrage and disgust, referred to plaintiff as a "whore," and contacted plaintiff directly via the link provided by Stone. Plaintiff is not the person depicted in the lewd image.... Stone's publication of an image falsely purporting to depict her in a lewd act exposed plaintiff to hatred, contempt, ridicule and disgrace. Backlund asserts causes of action for defamation and false light. Stone *admits* that he posted an image of a masturbating girl on StickyDrama, with plaintiff's contact information.

In February 2010, Stone obtained a topless photograph of plaintiff and sent her a publicly viewable "tweet" stating, "Message him again, and your floppy titties are spammed all over the place. Last warning."[2] Stone's threat and the seminude photo of plaintiff were accessible to anyone on the Internet. Plaintiff did not consent to disclose the photo, and found the threat of public humiliation highly offensive. Plaintiff asserts a cause of action for public disclosure of private facts based on Stone's threat to spam the compromising photo of her. Stone *admits* that he threatened to publicly expose the indecent photo of Backlund unless she stopped contacting his houseguest Tammen.... Backlund's complaint asserts that Stone filed a small claims action for defamation against her, but never served it. Stone urged his website followers to contact a television company to ask that he appear on the *Judge Judy* show, so that Stone could participate in a segment involving his small claims case against Backlund. Backlund alleges that Stone filed the small claims action for the purpose of harassing her.

---

1. All undesignated statutory references in this opinion are to the Code of Civil Procedure.
2. "Him" refers to a friend of Stone's named Parker Tammen.

Stone moved to strike Backlund's complaint as a SLAPP. He argued that his publication of Backlund's name, residential address, and a map to her home (in connection with the publication of the lewd photograph) was not a public disclosure of private facts. At the same time, Stone conceded that a search of public records does not show plaintiff's residential address. Stone believed the lewd photograph depicted Backlund, so he included plaintiff's name and contact information in his posting. Stone subsequently realized that he was mistaken: the photograph actually depicts an underage girl in Ohio, not plaintiff. He removed plaintiff's personal contact link from the photograph, and offered to post on StickyDrama the heading, "Alyssa Marie Buckland [sic] is Not the Most Vile Camwhore Alive."

The trial court denied defendant's motion to strike Backlund's complaint. It found that Stone's Internet posting of child pornography is not protected free speech: section 425.16 "does not apply to indisputably illegal communications that are inherently criminal." Posting a link to plaintiff's personal webpage with comments attributing the wrongful child obscenity to plaintiff also does not implicate the anti-SLAPP statute. Stone did not appeal from the trial court's denial of his anti-SLAPP motion.... After defendant's anti-SLAPP motion was denied, he filed a cross-complaint against Backlund for defamation and intentional infliction of emotional distress. Despite being a purveyor of child pornography (by posting on the Internet images of an underage girl masturbating next to an infant), Stone paints himself as a noble crusader who protects "naïve and unsuspecting [Internet] users [who] are easy prey to sex offenders." Stone trumpets that he "gained a reputation among mainstream media," leading to features about him in the New York Times, CNN, and Fox News about "sextortion"—the use of compromising nude photographs to blackmail the people in the photo.

Stone socializes with "Internet celebrities and online entertainers" who have "cult status" on StickyDrama and like-minded websites. Backlund was a fan of StickyDrama and wanted to join Stone's "milieu of 'stars.'" After Backlund sent repeated messages to one of Stone's houseguests, Parker Tammen, Stone admits sending Backlund a threatening "tweet" in February 2010, "telling her that an indecent picture she sent to Mr. Tammen would be exposed if she contacted Mr. Tammen again." Stone claims that his threat is not "sextortion" because he did not demand money, property, or additional nude photos from Backlund. At the time, Stone was 31 years old and Backlund was 19.

After Stone publicly threatened Backlund, she was interviewed by online journalist Adrian Chen for an article that appeared on Gawker.com in July 2010. The article initially stated that Stone committed "sextortion" by threatening to expose a seminude photo of Backlund taken when she was underage, but was corrected at Backlund's request to show that the photo was taken the week of her 18th birthday. Stone's threatening tweet to Backlund was shown in the Gawker article, which was entitled "StickyDrama's Christopher Stone Is a 'Sextortion' Expert in More Ways Than One." Chen quoted a Fox News report featuring Stone, which stated, "'A new type of blackmail is trapping teenagers, especially those who have sent provocative pictures to friends. Hackers are stealing those photos and threatening their senders.'" Chen noted that Stone appeared on television ostensibly to warn teens about the dangers of sextortion, but neglected to mention that he is a expert on the subject because sextortion is something that Stone engages in himself. Gawker quotes Backlund (identified as "Sarah") expressing fear of Stone because of his threats to spam her topless image, saying, "He scares me shitless ... he'll take anything he can to smash you."

Stone asserts a defamation per se claim against Backlund, alleging that her statements to Gawker journalist Chen are false, unprivileged, expose him to hatred, contempt and ridicule, and tend to injure his business. The statements are defamatory because they charge him with the immoral and criminal activity of exposing a topless photo of an underage girl on the Internet, and by regularly threatening to expose compromising pictures of young girls. Stone also seeks damages for emotional distress....

An issue of public interest is " any issue in which the public is interested. In other words, the issue need not be 'significant' to be protected by the anti-SLAPP statute." (*Nygard, Inc. v. Uusi-Kerttula* (2008) 159 Cal.App.4th 1027, 1042.) We have no difficulty concluding that the topics of cyber-bullying and "sextortion" are matters of public interest. Stone himself provides the proof in his moving papers: he attaches documents showing that the danger to children posed by sextortion has been a topic of widespread media coverage and has resulted in federal investigations and prosecutions. The FBI addresses the topic on its webpage, to alert people how to avoid becoming victims of sextortion. Stone was interviewed on a television program regarding sextortion. If a newsletter sent to a handful of homeowners in a residential community qualifies as constitutionally protected commentary on a matter of public interest (*Damon v. Ocean Hills Journalism Club* (2000) 85 Cal.App.4th 468), then a topic like sextortion that commands the attention of a nationwide audience on Fox News and CNN—as well as the attention of the FBI—certainly qualifies as a matter of public interest....

The article on Gawker takes aim at Stone's credibility as a television news commentator on sextortion. The article includes the tweet from Stone to Backlund, threatening to spam "your floppy titties ... all over the place." Stone admits making this threat. The article begins by saying that five months after Stone made the threat, "he appeared in a news report calmly warning teens about the dangers of 'sextortion.'" Gawker takes Fox News to task for featuring Stone, whose expertise in sextortion "comes from his own attempts at bullying a teenaged girl into silence by threatening to release topless photos of her."[3]

Backlund's comments printed on Gawker.com are afforded protection by the anti-SLAPP statue. When Stone chose to be featured in the print and television media as an expert on the topic of cyber-harassment, he "voluntarily subjected [himself] to inevitable scrutiny and potential ridicule by the public and the media." (*Seeling v. Infinity Broadcasting Corp.* (2002) 97 Cal.App.4th 798, 807–808.) Because Stone markets his expertise on sextortion, Backlund was within her rights to share Stone's threatening tweet, and to comment about her fear of Stone, who possesses nude photos of her "and if I talk to anyone about it or stick my nose into anything then he'll release them." The Gawker article contributes to the ongoing public discussion about sextortion, and about Stone's role as a media commentator in that debate. As such, Backlund's statements were not private at all: they were a public comment about a publicly disseminated threat against her made by public figure Stone. Publicity about Stone's threats and Backlund's resulting fear of Stone provide a cautionary lesson to the youthful readers of Gawker, who might read Chen's article and decide not to upload nude images of themselves, lest the images fall into the wrong hands and pose the risk of public humiliation in front of countless people. The published article about Backlund's chilling personal experience with Christopher Stone addresses a matter of grave public concern.[4] ...

---

3. The author of the Gawker article sees sextortion as a type of cyber-bullying, which occurs when the Internet is used to hurt or embarrass others. "'Children have killed each other and committed suicide after having been involved in a cyberbullying incident,'" and it is a growing problem. (*D.C. v. R.R., supra*, 182 Cal.App.4th at p. 1218.) The topic has provoked numerous scholarly discussions, including one from the National Crime Prevention Council.... Cyber-bullying is a matter of public interest.

4. After the Gawker article appeared, Stone publicly posted Backlund's private address, a photo of her family home, and a new threat: "Lying to @ Adrian Chen will prove to be a costly and embarrassing mistake. And he will not help you." This underscores the insidious ease and pernicious aspect of cyber-

The trial court did not reach the second prong of the anti-SLAPP analysis, having erroneously concluded that this involved a "private" matter. We review the case de novo, so we discuss the second prong. Once the first prong of an anti-SLAPP motion is satisfied, the burden shifts to the party asserting the cause of action to establish a probability of prevailing. (*HMS Capital, Inc. v. Lawyers Title Co.* (2004) 118 Cal.App.4th 204, 213.) If the claim stated in the pleading is supported by sufficient prima facie evidence, it is not subject to being stricken as a SLAPP.... [citations omitted].

Stone is a limited public figure. A limited public figure "is an individual who voluntarily injects him or herself or is drawn into a specific public controversy, thereby becoming a public figure on a limited range of issues" regarding the controversy giving rise to the alleged defamation. (*Ampex Corp. v. Cargle, supra*, 128 Cal.App.4th at p. 1577; *Gertz v. Robert Welch, Inc.* (1974) 418 U.S. 323, 351.) It is sufficient that the person "attempts to thrust him or herself into the public eye." (*Gilbert v. Sykes* (2007) 147 Cal.App.4th 13, 24.) Stone voluntarily thrust himself into a public controversy concerning the publication of lewd or compromising photographs of teenagers on the Internet. In November 2009, by his own admission, Stone published an image of an underage masturbating girl on StickyDrama, along with plaintiff's contact information, on a notorious website he operated. In February 2010, Stone admittedly tweeted a threat to spam a topless photograph of plaintiff. In July 2010, Stone appeared on Fox News to discuss "the scary new phenomenon" of publishing compromising photographs of teenagers. He has also been featured in the New York Times and on CNN.

Stone became a limited public figure by operating a publicly accessible website that published lewd photos of minors, and by seeking the public eye when he appeared on television and in print media to discuss the topic of sextortion. "Once he places himself in the spotlight on a topic of public interest, his private words and conduct relating to that topic become fair game." (*Gilbert v. Sykes, supra*, 147 Cal.App.4th at p. 25 [defendant thrust himself into the public debate on the merits of plastic surgery by appearing on a television show].) Public figures must prove by clear and convincing evidence that an alleged defamatory statement was made with actual malice. (*New York Times Co. v. Sullivan* (1964) 376 U.S. 254, 279–280.)

Stone fails to carry his burden of showing a probability that he will prevail on the merits of his claim. At the outset, we observe that Stone forfeited or conceded the second prong because he "offered no evidence in the trial court and makes no argument on appeal to establish that he is likely to succeed on the merits of his claim." (*Neville v. Chudacoff* (2008) 160 Cal.App.4th 1255, 1263, fn. 7.) ... There is no proof that any of Backlund's statements during her interview were made with actual malice. Stone offers only the inadmissible allegations of his unverified cross-complaint, along with his equally inadmissible declaration. Neither of those documents provide any proof of malice, let alone clear and convincing proof. Stone's claims for emotional distress and injunctive relief fall along with his defamation claim, because Backlund was exercising her right to free speech. (See *Molko v. Holy Spirit Assn.* (1988) 46 Cal.3d 1092, 1120 [threats of divine retribution from church members was protected religious speech and could not form the basis of a claim for intentional infliction of emotional distress]; *Brunette v. Humane Society of Ventura County* (2002) 40 Fed.Appx. 594, 598 [while emotional distress may be considered an element of damage in a properly stated defamation action, it cannot form the basis of an independent claim on the same facts].)

---

threats, and explains why it is a topic of public concern. Stone's new post can be perceived as a threat to physically harm Backlund and her family by displaying the location of their home.

We note that this was the third article about Stone that appeared on Gawker.com: the first two were "StickyDrama: The Teen Gossip Site Run by a 31-Year-Old Pornographer" and "StickyDrama's Owner Recorded a Live-Streamed Rape and Blogged About It — But Didn't Report It." Despite repeated features damning his reputation, Stone did not sue Gawker.com or Adrien Chen for defamation. Instead, he focused on a teenager to whom he admittedly sent a threatening message, when she expressed her concerns and fears to the public about that threat. This follows Stone's admitted publication of a lewd photograph of an underage girl, whom he falsely identified as plaintiff. Given Stone's scurrilous and outrageous behavior toward young women, he cannot be heard to complain when confronted by one of his victims.[5] ...

The judgment is reversed. Backlund is entitled to recover her attorney fees and costs on appeal. The case is remanded with directions to the trial court to enter an order (1) dismissing Stone's cross-complaint and (2) awarding attorney fees and costs to Backlund incurred in both the trial court proceedings and on appeal.

We concur:

ASHMANN-GERST, J.

CHAVEZ, J.

---

5. Stone attends ... Law School. An applicant to the California Bar has the burden of establishing "good moral character," which includes "qualities of honesty, fairness, candor, trustworthiness, observance of fiduciary responsibility, respect for and obedience to the law, and respect for the rights of others and the judicial process." (State Bar Rules, rule 4.40.) Stone's Internet activities are abusive, unethical, demonstrate a manifest lack of maturity, discretion and good judgment, and mandate a thorough investigation into his fitness for State Bar membership. Stone must provide a copy of this opinion to the State Bar if he applies for admission to practice law in California.

Chapter Three

Internet Sexual Exploitation of Children

I. Internet Parameters: Accessibility and Anonymity

In *United States v. Robertson*, 350 F.3d 1109 (10th Cir. 2003), the court noted the following:

> Some of the great virtues of the internet—its flexibility, universal accessibility, and privacy—also make it an especially potent venue for sexual predators to communicate with minors regarding illicit sexual encounters. The anonymity of these communications, in particular, serves both to ensnare the child and to thwart the protective efforts of law enforcement.... Children commonly make wide use of the internet, often with little parental supervision, and sometimes with a dangerous degree of naivete. Behind the anonymous veil of the internet, predators can locate young people in teen chat rooms or other child-friendly sites, assume false identities, establish relationships, deploy pornographic images and other sexual enticements, and arrange for meetings—all shielded from the eyes of parents, police, or other protectors. As Representative Hutchinson explained shortly before the passage of the [Child Protection and Sexual Predator Punishment Act of 1998] ... :
>
>> [B]y the year 2002, 45 million children will use the Internet to talk with friends, do homework assignments and explore the vast world around them. Computer technologies and Internet innovations have unveiled a world of information that is literally just a mouse click away....

Id. at 1110, 1113–14. *See also United States v. Reaves*, 253 F.3d 1201, 1203–05 (10th Cir. 2001) (discussing the role of the Internet in the sexual exploitation of children).

United States v. C.R.

United States District Court, Eastern District of New York, 2011
792 F. Supp. 2d 343
[Vacated and Remanded by *United States v. Reingold*, 731 F.3d 204
(2nd Cir.(N.Y.) 2013), *infra*, Chapter Seven]

JACK B. WEINSTEIN, Senior District Judge: …

Defendant, C.R., pled guilty to "distribution" of child pornography he had obtained using a computer. Others shared his still and video images through a networking program. Access to the pictures he acquired were alleged to constitute electronic "distribution" of child pornography. See 18 U.S.C. § 2252(a)(2)…. Defendant was nineteen years old at the time of the offense. He started using computers to view this material when he was fifteen…. C.R. is subject to a statutory minimum prison sentence of five-years, with a maximum of twenty years, and a Guidelines range of 63–78 months. There also must be imposed what may amount to lifetime control on defendant as a sex offender. *See* 42 U.S.C. §§ 16911, 16915(a)(1) (fifteen years for lowest risk federal offenders); § 16915(b) (possibility of early termination for federal offenders after ten years); N.Y. Corr. Law § 168-h(1) (twenty years for lowest risk offender).

As applied to this defendant and this case, the statutory minimum five-year sentence of imprisonment is unconstitutional. It is cruel and unusual…. The Guidelines sentence is excessive…. Imposed is a thirty-month sentence for intensive medical treatment in prison. This will be followed by long-term post-prison curative therapy and strict control for many years under supervised release by the court's probation service…. Society will be best protected by this regimen rather than by a longer term of imprisonment; C.R. should be prepared to assume a useful law-abiding life rather than one of a broken and dangerous, ex-prisoner deviant. Were it not for Congress's strongly expressed preference for incarceration in these cases, the court would have imposed a long … term of supervised release with medical treatment outside of prison…. Further general or specific deterrence is not required. The adult who abused the child in one of the abhorrent known victim child pornography video series found on defendant's computer was sentenced to fifty years in prison. Another adult who stalked and harassed this child with pictures of her abuse was sentenced to twenty years in prison…. This case illustrates some of the troubling problems in sentencing adolescents who download child pornography on a file-sharing computer service. Posed is the question: To protect the public and the abused children who are shown in a sexually explicit manner in computer images, do we need to destroy defendants like C.R.? … Widely shown video images are involved. While "[a]ny social problem that exists at the intersection of adolescence, sex, technology, and criminal law compels strong reactions from all sides … it often results in sensationalism and oversimplification of complex and multifaceted issues making it more difficult to discuss the problem rationally and productively." Mary G. Leary, *Sexting or Self-Produced Child Pornography? The Dialogue Continues—Structured Prosecutorial Discretion within a Multidisciplinary Response*. 17 Va. J. Soc. Pol'y. & L. 486, 487–88 (2010). Sexual development is complex and subtle. It varies widely with the individual. The law will cause serious and unnecessary harm to adolescent defendants by applying a mechanical and unnecessarily harsh sentencing scheme to address the broad range of culpability and circumstances involved in child pornography crimes….

The offense for which C.R. is being prosecuted occurred when he was living for a short time with his biological mother while attending community college in Queens, New

York.... She had met a man thirteen years' her junior at an addiction recovery program; they married.... The couple had a daughter, now six years old.... Household dynamics were turbulent.... The biological mother and C.R. had a difficult relationship, and he never developed a closeness with his stepfather.... To avoid confrontations, C.R. would return home from school late at night after everyone was asleep.... High on marijuana and, occasionally, other drugs, he would download and view child pornography on a computer in the living room where he slept.... During this period an undercover Federal Bureau of Investigation agent selected and transferred a child pornography file from defendant's computer, at the agent's initiative, through a peer-to-peer electronic file sharing program named "Gigatribe." ... It provides for sharing of images and videos among a closed network of "buddies." ... *United States v. Griffin*, 510 F.3d 354, 356 (2d Cir.2007) (describing mechanics of a similar program called "KaZaa"); *United States v. Ladeau*, No. 09-CR-40021, at *1, 2010 WL 1427523 (D.Mass., Apr. 7, 2010) (describing mechanics of Gigatribe)....

The FBI agent observed a user, later identified as C.R., with the username "Boysuck0416." C.R. had created a "mini-profile" on the site listing his true gender and date of birth.... After joining the defendant's "buddy list," the FBI agent viewed and downloaded ten videos and one still image of child pornography from the "added music" folder of the defendant's computer.... It is this downloading by the FBI from defendants' files that is the basis for the present prosecution.... Based on the information obtained by the FBI, the government executed a search warrant of defendant's stepfather's and biological mother's home.... Seized by the agents were two computers used exclusively by defendant.... C.R. admitted to downloading and viewing child pornography videos on both computers through the Gigatribe website, and to trading videos and digital images via Limewire, another peer-to-peer program.... C.R. had accessed files from between five and eight fellow Gigatribe users and shared his materials with ten to twenty other users.... The defendant never paid or charged for any child pornography.... Nor is there any indication that he used the Internet or any sort of pornography to meet or engage with any child, sexually or otherwise. "There appeared to be no child pornography material involving either very young (under 5 or 6) children, or scenes of bondage, sadism or violence." ...

Defendant does not raise constitutional or other challenges to the procedures by which evidence was obtained against him. On September 16, 2009, the defendant, then twenty years old, appeared before a magistrate judge and pled guilty to Count One of a five-count indictment.... Charged in the count was that on November 17, 2008, the defendant distributed a video that contained child pornography in violation of 18 U.S.C. §2252(a)(2).... It was explained to defendant that a mandatory minimum five-year sentence was applicable, with a possible supervised release term of life and registration as a sex offender.... Although the government considered pursuing only possession charges—which would not have triggered the minimum—that option was abandoned after defendant voluntarily revealed his sexual history during plea negotiations....

[T]he effect on one victim, "Vicky," of continued use of pictures of her abuse by many viewers was seriously adverse.... C.R. was one of the many thousands who viewed the Vicky series. Whether a sentence of many years imprisonment for passive viewers will improve the victim's life is dubious. *See generally* Aya Gruber, *A Distributive Theory of Criminal Law*, 52 Wm. of Mary L. Rev 1, 73 (2010).... This was not a victimless crime. As revealed by testimony and other information, the child victims suffer not only from the initial physical sexual abuse of their tormentors, but also from the knowledge that their degradation will be repeatedly viewed electronically into near perpetuity by a large audience....

[At this part of the opinion, but omitted here, the court includes the testimony of Special F.B.I. Agent Thomas Thompson, who described the scope of the defendant's computer files contained on two computers seized during the execution of the search warrant. Agent Thompson testified that he had discovered at least two hundred images and at least one hundred video files containing child pornography, the majority of which involved boys between the ages of ten and twelve (and some even younger) engaged in sexual acts, including oral sex, anal sex, and regular penetration. One video depicted an adult male anal penetrating a boy approximately eight years old. The files that were obtained were sent to the National Center of Exploited and Missing Children, where they are compared to a base of images and video files containing known victims of child pornography. From this, it was determined that the defendant's files contained images and videos of at least fourteen known victim series. With this information, authorities are able to record the series name, the description of the child abuse in the series, the number of known victims in the series, the age of the victims at the time of the abuse, the time frame of the abuse, where the abuse occurred, and how many reports regarding the series were submitted. One of the series contained on the defendant's files was "Sponge Bob," which occurred between 2003 and 2009 and depicted prepubescent boys (the youngest was six years old) engaged in sexual acts including oral sex, masturbation and anal penetration of the child. Another series—TARA—occurred between 2003 and 2008 and contained video files on eleven prepubescent male children (the youngest was five years old) engaged in sexual acts with each other and male offenders, including oral sex and anal penetration. Another series—the "Vicky" series—contained images and video files of prepubescent children engaged in a series of extreme sexual acts, including oral sex, masturbation, genital penetration, foreign object genital contact, and bondage. The "Helen" series, which included a four-year-old child, depicted prepubescent female children engaged in graphic sexual acts, oral sex, sexual intercourse, and anal penetration. Three of the series— Dalmation, TARA, and Vicky—have victim impact statements associated with them.]

The Court of Appeals for the Second Circuit has recognized a dearth of data on critical issues affecting risks, dangers, and appropriate sentences in these cases. *See, e.g., United States v. Dorvee*, 604 F.3d 84, 94 (2d Cir.2010) (finding error in sentencing court's "apparent assumption" about link between possession of child pornography and risk of acting out); *United States v. Falso*, 544 F.3d 110, 122 (2d Cir.2008) (finding error in district court's reliance on defendant's history of sexual abuse of minor and "general proclivities" of child pornographers in finding probable cause to issue a search warrant in child pornography investigation). See also *United States v. Stern*, 590 F.Supp.2d 945 (N.D.Ohio 2008) (recognizing the difference in culpability between viewing and producing child pornography as well as the wide variation of sentences in child pornography cases)....

Changing over the years and within societies has been the view of what was malign adult or child pornography; appropriate sexual relationships of gender, age and class; social mores; and criminal or other legal inhibitions. No one in authority now defends on any generally accepted moral or legal ground the sexual abuse of children for public viewing and commercial advantage. Much of the public seemingly approves congressionally adopted strong criminal sanctions against child pornography, subject to constitutional limitations. *See United States v. Polizzi*, 549 F.Supp.2d 308, 378–86 (E.D.N.Y.2008) (historical discussion).

By contrast with concern about sexual abuse is the acknowledged necessity of excluding from the circle of condemnation proud parents' photos and home videos of their naked infants held over their "kitchen sink" bath or of toddlers sans clothes in sunlight on the lawn (or even of not uncommon diapering scenes). Sent by mail or electronically to grandparents (or shown on wide screen or television), such images would lack the essential scienter required for criminal condemnation—libidinal, erotic, carnal, erogenous, lustful, prurient, concupiscent, malicious, etc.—even though they might conceivably be misused for malign purposes. *See, e.g.*, Karen R. Long, *Lynn Powell's 'Framing Innocence' shows Oberlin rising up for an accused mother*, http://www.cleveland.com/books/index.ssf/2010/09/lynn_powells_framing_innocence.html, Sept. 6, 2010, (discussing prosecution and ultimate settlement of felony child pornography charges against mother for taking photographs of her eight-year-old daughter in the shower); Thomas Korosec, *1-Hour Arrest: When does a snapshot of a mother breastfeeding her child become kiddie porn? Ask the Richardson Police.*, Dallas Observer, April 17, 2003, *available at* http://www.dallas observer.com/2003-04-17/news/1-hour-arrest. *See also* Kate Taylor, *Artist's Daughter Wants Video Back*, N.Y. Times, Jul. 7, 2010 (discussing New York University's consideration, later abandoned, of acquiring films created by well-known artist Larry Rivers, depicting his two adolescent daughters, naked or topless, being interviewed by him about their developing breasts); *see also United States v. Szymanski*, 631 F.3d 794 (6th Cir.2011) (rejecting defendant's guilty plea because district court failed to adequately explain the rigorous scienter requirement necessary for a conviction under the receipt of child pornography statute). "[T]he Supreme Court interpreted § 2252(a) to mean that defendant convicted of receiving child pornography must have known, not just that he was receiving *something*, but that what he was receiving was child pornography." *Id.* at 799; *see also United States v. X-Citement Video, Inc.*, 513 U.S. 64, 68, 70–73, 78, 115 S.Ct. 464, 130 L.Ed.2d 372 (1994). To avoid a Comstockian crisis of over-prosecution, good sense of prosecutors (however dangerous such reliance is in a democracy) must be assumed.... Characterizations of a defendant viewer as an adult in child pornography cases tend to cluster around age fourteen. *See ...* State Statutes on Juvenile Child Pornography, ... (age twelve (one state), age thirteen (two states). Age fourteen (fifteen states), age sixteen (nine states), age seventeen (two states), age eighteen (twelve states), age twenty (one state), unclear (eight states))....

The digital revolution of the 1980s and 1990s enormously increased the ways that child pornography can be created, accessed, and distributed. New technologies abound for sending and receiving such materials over the Internet, including email, websites, social networking programs, chatrooms, and peer-to-peer file sharing programs.... Although it is impossible to quantify with precision the size of the child pornography market, there is a consensus that technological advances have led to its proliferation over the past twenty years. *See, e.g.*, Tim McGlone, *As child porn activity grows, efforts to trap offenders do, too*, The Virginian-Pilot (Jan. 16, 2011), available at, http://hamptonroads.com/2011/01/child-porn-activity-grows-efforts-trap-offenders-do-too ("[C]hild pornography was a dying industry until the Internet and peer-to-peer networks developed. 'It went from almost dead to now a growing epidemic.'") (quoting Neil MacBride, United States Attorney for the Eastern District of Virginia); U.S. Dep't of Justice, *The National Strategy for Child Exploitation Prevention and Interdiction: A Report to Congress* 11–16 (2010) [hereinafter, DOJ, National Strategy] (noting view of law enforcement and prosecutors); Taylor & Quayle, *supra*, at 9 (indicating view among academics); Nat'l Center for Missing and Exploited Children, *Press Release: Child Porn Among Fastest Growing Internet Business* (Nov. 9, 2005), *available at* http://www.missingkids.com (reporting view of children's advocacy group). *But cf.* Jenkins, *supra*, at 32–34 ("News media [have] used extravagantly inflated statistics to present child porn as pressing social menace."); William A. Fisher & Azy Barak, *Internet Pornography: A Social Psychological Perspective on Internet Sexuality*, 38 J. of Sex Res. 4, 312, 313–14 (2001) (noting "inconsistencies and *prima facia* questionable claims in research on the prevalence of sexually explicit materials, on and off the Internet").

Child pornography was widely accessible even in the 1960s and 1970s, owing in part to changes in general views of sexuality in the United States and Europe. The late 1960s marked the beginning of a commercial boom in the production of such materials, particularly in the Netherlands and Scandinavian countries. Jenkins, *supra*, at 30–32. Magazines produced in this era, some of which established powerful "brand identities," depicted children of varying ages—from toddlers to teenagers—in various states of undress and engaged in explicit sexual activities with each other and with adults. *Id.* at 31. As a result of the commercial importation and domestic production of magazines and films, it was "easy to walk into a store in New York, Los Angeles, or London to purchase what was frankly advertised as child porn." *Id.* at 32. The commercial child pornography market garnered an audience beyond the "child porn world strictly defined" as magazines notionally devoted to rock music and radical politics in the 1970s would, on occasion, utilize pictures of pubescent nudes. *Id.*. . . The existence of easily available subscription-based child pornography websites confirms the continued production and distribution of child pornography as a vast profit-making enterprise. Much of the material is sent electronically from Eastern European and Asian countries, with constantly changing sources and shifts in computer centers that makes prosecution of producers and vendors difficult. . . .

There is no universal definition of child pornography. Legal proscriptions vary widely by jurisdiction, both in terms of the age of the children and the nature of content proscribed. *See* DOJ, Child Pornography on the Internet, *supra* at 7; Taylor & Quayle, *supra* at 28–30; Second World Congress, Theme Paper on Child Pornography, *supra* at 9–13. . . . Section 2256 of Title 18 of the United States Code stresses—but is not limited to—"sexually explicit conduct." It provides that:

> (8) "Child pornography" is any visual depiction, including any photograph, film, video, picture, or computer or computer-generated image or picture … of sexually explicit conduct, where—
> (A) the production of such visual depiction involves the use of a minor engaging in sexually explicit conduct;
> (B) such visual depiction is a digital image, computer image, or computer-generated image that is, or is indistinguishable from, that of a minor engaging in sexually explicit conduct; or
> (C) such visual depiction has been created, adapted, or modified to appear that an identifiable minor is engaging in sexually explicit conduct.

18 U.S.C. § 2256. It further states that:

> [S]exually explicit conduct" means actual or simulated—
> (i) sexual intercourse, including genital-genital, oral-genital, anal-genital, or oral-anal, whether between persons of the same or opposite sex; (ii) bestiality; (iii) masturbation; (iv) sadistic or masochistic abuse; or (v) lascivious exhibition of the genitals or pubic area of any person[.]

18 U.S.C. § 2256(2)(A); *accord* § 2256(2)(B). Although the statute as originally enacted defined a "minor" as an individual under the age of sixteen; it was amended in 1984 to cover persons up to age eighteen. *See* Pub.L. No. 98-292, § 5(a)(1) (codified as amended at 18 U.S.C. § 2256(1)).

Depictions need not portray sexual contact with children to fall within the scope of the federal prohibition. Neither nakedness nor physical contact is required. "Lascivious exhibition of genitals or pubic area," 18 U.S.C. § 2256(2)(A)(v), has been interpreted broadly to include pictures focused on a child's pubic region, even where the subject is alone and clothed. *See, e.g., United States v. Knox*, 32 F.3d 733, 744–45 (3d Cir.1994); *United States v. Musumeci*, 307 Fed. Appx. 471, 473 (2d Cir.2008) (approving *Knox*, 32 F.3d at 744–45).... Researchers investigating the nature of child pornography in the contemporary market have identified ten levels of image severity: (1) indicative; (2) nudist; (3) erotica; (4) posing; (5) erotic posing; (6) explicit erotic posing; (7) explicit sexual activity; (8) assault; (9) gross assault; and (10) sadistic/bestiality. *See* Taylor & Quayle, *supra*, at 31–36. The characteristics of depictions span a wide spectrum—from seemingly innocuous beach pictures to vile depictions of sexual assaults. Although not completely consonant with legal definitions, the categories are helpful in understanding the contemporary child pornography market and its impact on victims and others. *See* DOJ, Child Pornography on the Internet, *supra*, at 7 (utilizing taxonomy set forth in Taylor & Quayle, *supra*, at 31–36)....

A congressionally funded survey of Internet-related crimes indicates that many individuals arrested for child pornography possession had images falling on the severe end of the spectrum—both in terms of the age of children depicted and the content. *See generally* Janis Wolak, David Finkelhor, and Kimberly Mitchell, *Child-Pornography Possessors Arrested in Internet-Related Crimes: Findings from the National Juvenile Victimization Study* (2005) [hereinafter Wolak et al., *Child Pornography Possessors*]. The majority of individuals surveyed were found to have pictures of prepubescent children engaged in sexually explicit activity: 83 percent had images of children below the ages of six and twelve; 92 percent had images of minors focusing on the genitals or showing explicit sexual activity; 80 percent had pictures showing sexual penetration of a child; and 71 percent had images showing sexual contact between an adult and a child. *Id.* at 4–5....

There is no single "profile" of the child pornography viewer. A report by law enforcement officials indicates that he "may come from all walks of life and show few warning signs." ... Perusal of newspaper headlines reveals that child pornography arrests, indictments, and convictions span socioeconomic and professional boundaries.... Less diversity apparently exists among federal offenders prosecuted, in terms of age, race, and sex. It has been said that: "[a]mong the few distinguishing features of offenders are that they are likely to be white, male, and between the ages of twenty-six and forty, and may be heavy Internet users." DOJ, Child Pornography on the Internet, *supra*, at 14 (citing research). Younger offenders appear to be a rarity, but this may be due to a reluctance of some authorities to charge persons in this age group. *See, e.g.,* Wolak et al., *Varieties of Child Pornography Production, supra*, at 34–36 (noting that 89 percent of a sample of individuals arrested for child pornography production in 2000 were older than twenty-eight years old); *cf.* U.S. Sentencing Commission, *Annual Report* 35 (2009) (4.1 percent of federal offenders, for all federal offenses combined, were under the age of twenty-one). *But cf.* Taylor & Quayle, *supra*, at 5 (observing that individuals as young as thirteen are involved in distribution of child pornography).... Analyses by law enforcement agencies imply that individuals who obtain and view child pornography over the Internet are diverse— not only in the nature of images viewed but also in their motivations for doing so.... Interviews with offenders confirm that child pornography is sought for a variety of reasons. Key themes include the use of child pornography: (1) for sexual arousal; (2) for collecting; (3) as a way of facilitating social relationships; (4) as a way of avoiding real life; and (5) for other "recreational" purposes, including out of impulse, curiosity, or short-term entertainment. Sexual arousal has been identified as a dominant motivating factor, often functioning in combination with the others. *See* Sheldon & Howitt, *supra*, at 109–121; DOJ, Child Pornography on the Internet, *supra*, at 14; Taylor & Quayle, *supra*, at 80, 83.

Factors other than a desire for sexual gratification hold particular salience in the context of Internet pornography. With respect to collecting, computer-related technologies permit users to amass vast and unique "libraries" of child pornography. *See* DOJ, National Strategy, *supra*, at 11–12; Howitt & Sheldon, *supra*, at 117–119; Jenkins, *supra*, at 101. Whereas in decades past, individuals might have obtained a limited number of "French pictures," magazines, or videotapes in stores or through mail-order catalogues, today, many thousands of child pornographic images and videos can be obtained by clicking a button. *See, e.g.*, DOJ, National Strategy, *supra*, at 12 (citing example of offender who amassed one million images and many videos, some running an hour in length). "There is an Internet subculture of child pornography aficionados whose main interest seems to be not only enjoying viewing child pornography, but collecting it." Ferraro & Casey, *supra*, at 73.

Social dimensions are substantial in the accessing, viewing, and trading of child pornography on the Internet. While some Internet users may view and download child pornography with limited or no online interaction, *see* Sheldon & Howitt, *supra*, at 119–120, others are drawn to a sense of "belonging" that comes with participating in online networks or communities of like-minded individuals. Statements of offenders are illustrative. *See, e.g., id.* at 119 ("[The Internet] offered a kind of place to meet people and talk about similar fantasies … I'm getting an element of feeling that I'm wanted … I got a thrill of being … accepted …"); *id.* ("I was more interested in the conversations I was getting, the friendship I was getting.… I was very lonely.… [T]o prove that they were genuine they sent me the indecent stuff … I had to prove … that I [was] genuine by doing the same to them."); Taylor & Quayle, *supra*, at 139 ("I got almost … more satisfaction from actually just interacting with my fellow paedoph[iles] … [than] I did actually looking at the pictures."); *id.* ("I wanted people to like me. I've always been like that[.]").

A perceived sense of community may serve to normalize and reinforce deviant behavior of child pornographers, in some instances leading to a cycle of viewing increasingly graphic images, or even prompting the seeking out of individuals for illicit sexual encounters. Such a cycle has been acknowledged by some offenders. *See, e.g.*, Taylor & Quayle, *supra*, at 111–112 (discussing "downloading spiral," where user said he was "getting so much from something that wasn't real … you go back to reality and reality feels even worse than it was before"); *id.* at 186 ("I was finding more and more explicit stuff on the computer and I was looking at the computer thinking oh … they're doing it … it can't be that bad … it's there you know … I'm not doing any harm and she doesn't seem to mind.…"); *id.* ("I'd look at those [images] and all I wanted to do was abuse her.… [I'd] make sure she was asleep and then I'd abuse."); *id.* at 188 ("I was actually getting quite bored as it were … with the sort of child pornography … I was becoming sort of much more obsessed with bondage … and sort of torture … imagery. So … I'd kind of exhausted … the potential that it had for sexual arousal."). *But see id.* at 183 ("[T]he big thing I kept saying and I believed it … with every inch of my body … was that this was OK because … I'm not touching anybody … it's better for me to sit here fantasizing and looking at pictures … and … not doing anything else.").

A sizeable number of offenders appear to join the online world of child pornography precisely because it is disconnected from face-to-face interactions in the real world. *See generally* Taylor & Quayle, *supra*, at 97–119; Sherry Turkle, *Life on the Screen* (1995). To some, online pornography appears to be a coping mechanism, a way to avoid troubles of real life. *See, e.g.*, Sheldon & Howitt, *supra*, at 113 ("It's just coping with life.… [I]t was a form of escapism … to get out of my dilemma.… [W]hen I went on the net … [I] was swept away … I was in … m[y] own little world."). To others, it is a way of anonymous self-exploration or a way to satisfy curiosities. *See, e.g.*, Michele Ybarra, Kimberly J. Mitchell, *Exposure to Internet Pornography Among Child and Adolescents: A National Survey*,

8 CyberPsychology & Behav. 473, 474, 483 (2005) (discussing prevalence of older youths accessing pornography at a time when it is "developmentally appropriate to be sexually curious"). Some research indicates that involvement in Internet child pornography may be particularly appealing to individuals who "embrace ... risk taking" or seek "immediate stimulus," whether sexual or otherwise. *See* Taylor & Quayle, *supra*, at 18, 175....

Child pornography can, and often does, depict serious sexual and physical abuse of children.... A persistent concern is that observing child pornography might lead viewers to themselves sexually abuse children in the future. Reliable empirical evidence on this issue is lacking. A few statistically unreliable studies of convicted child pornography offenders indicate that a considerable percentage have abused children in the past. *See, e.g.*, Michael L. Bourke & Andres E. Hernandez, *The "Butner Study" Redux: A Report of the Incidence of Hands-on Child Victimization by Child Pornography Offenders*, 24 J. Fam. Violence 183, 187 (2009) (observing that 85 percent of 155 prisoners participating in 18-month intensive residential sexual offender treatment program reported having committed acts of sexual abuse against minors); DOJ, *National Strategy, supra*, at 19 ("The National Juvenile Online Victimization (NJOV) study revealed contact offenses in one of every six cases that began as a child pornography investigation."); *see also, e.g.*, Kenneth Lanning, *National Center for Missing and Exploited Children, Child Molesters: A Behavioral Analysis* (5th ed.2010) (reporting anecdotal information based on interviews with convicted offenders). These investigations have been widely cited as evidence of the risk of future dangerousness posed by individuals who view child pornography. *See, e.g.*, Audrey Rogers, *Child Pornography's Forgotten Victims*, 28 Pace L.Rev. 847, 852–54 (2008) (citing The Butner Study and NJOV survey); *Enhancing Child Protection Laws After the April 16, 2002 Supreme Court Decision*, Ashcroft v. Free Speech Coalition: *Hearing Before the Subcomm. on Terrorism, and Homeland Security of the H. Comm. on the Judiciary*, 107th Cong. 17 (2002) (statement of Michael J. Heimbach, Crimes Against Children Unit, Criminal Division, FBI) (citing Lanning, *supra*)....

Scientifically acceptable empirical analyses have thus far failed to establish a causal link between the mere passive viewing of child pornography—particularly by male adolescents—and the likelihood of future contact offenses. *See, e.g.*, L. Webb, et al., *Characteristics of Internet Child Pornography Offenders: A Comparison with Child Molesters*, 19 Sexual Abuse 449, 464 (2007) (finding Internet-only offenders "significantly less likely to fail in the community than child molesters," and concluding that "by far the largest subgroup of internet offenders would appear to pose a very low risk of sexual recidivism"), *available at* http://sax.sagepub.com/content/19/4/449.full.pdf+html; Jerome Endrass et al., *The Consumption of Internet Child Pornography and Violent Sex Offending*, 9 BMC Psychiatry 43 (2009) ("[T]he consumption of child pornography alone does not seem to represent a risk factor for committing hands-on sex offenses ... at least not in those subjects without prior convictions for hands-on sex offenses"), *available at* http://www.ncbi.nlm.nih.gov/pmc/articles/PMC2716325/pdf/1471-244X-9-43.pdf; Rettinger, *supra*, at 11 ("[T]he majority of studies in this area have been done in the context of adult, rather than child, pornography. There are also methodological and ethical difficulties in examining such relationships."); Taylor & Quayle, *supra* at 72 ("Overall, there appears to be little support for the allegation of a direct causal link between viewing pornography and subsequent offending behavior."); *id.* at 93–94 ("The relationship between contact offenses and pornography remains unclear.... [F]or some respondents, pornography was used as a substitute for actual offending, whereas for others, it acted as a blueprint and stimulus for a contact offense."); Michael C. Seto & Angela W. Eke, *The Criminal Histories and Later Offending of Child Pornography Offenders*, 17 Sexual Abuse 201, 201 (2005) (noting, at the time of publication, that there were "no published data on the future offending of child pornography offenders"); Jenkins, *supra*, at 173 ("[T]he statistics establish no causal link between child porn materials and actual behavior."); Sheldon & Howitt, *supra*, at 203–204 ("There is a common assumption that Internet child pornography offenses constitute stepping-stones that finally lead to direct sex offending against children. This idea is common but ... the evidence is not strong in its favor."); *cf.* Stephen T. Holmes & Ronald M. Holmes, *Sex Crimes: Patterns and Behavior* 157 (3d ed.2009) ("Exposure to [adult] pornography may play a positive role in the maturational process of non-offenders. The most important finding is that [contact] sex criminals, not only as adolescents but also as adults, see less pornography than [non-offenders].")....

Varying interactions of unquantifiable forces pushing in a variety of directions determine the appropriate sentence in child pornography cases. The assessment of whether an offender will act out in the future requires a prosecutor's and judge's careful, informed and somewhat experiential judgment—like other sentencing factors—on a case by case basis rather than by a rigid *a priori* scheme applicable to all cases. Ultimately, the judgment is based on rough calculations of nonquantifiable risks and benefits, cruelties and compassions; statute and precedent provide limited guidance in the individual prosecution. *Cf.* Justice David H. Souter, Harvard Commencement Remarks, Harvard Gazette Online (May 27, 2010), http://news.harvard.edu/gazette/story/2010/05/text-of-justice-david-souters-speech ("I don't forget my own longings for certainty, which heartily resisted the pronouncement of Justice Holmes, that certainty generally is illusion and repose is not our destiny.... [We] can still address the constitutional uncertainties the way they must have been envisioned, by relying on reason, by respecting all the words the Framers wrote, by facing facts, and by seeking to understand their meaning for living people."); William J. Brennan, *The Constitution of the United States: Contemporary Ratification*, 27 S. Tex. L.Rev. 433 (1986) (exploring the obligation of Article III judges to speak for the current community in interpreting the Constitution); Stephen Breyer, *Judicial Review: A Practicing Judge's Perspective*, 78 Tex. L.Rev. 761 (2000) (discussing the "set of cases ... in which there is an inevitable tension between the will of the elected legislature and the work of the unelected judge," noting that "every legal decision interacts ... with other decisions, principles, standards, practices, and institutional understandings, always modifying the 'web' of the law; and every decision affects ... the way in which that web, in turn, affects the world.... [I]n respect to constitutional matters, estimates of vertical effects—that is, the real world consequences of horizontal interactions—have a particularly important role to play."); Justice Samuel A. Alito, Jr., *Learned Hand: Undeniably Great Judge*, New York Law Journal, June 14, 2010, at 2; *Spector Motor Service v. Walsh, Inc.*, 139 F.2d 809, 814 (2d Cir.1944) ("In addition to the general course of decisions ... we shall examine certain specific trends ... more directly applicable to the present issue."); *id.* at 823 (Hand, J., dissenting) ("It is always embarrassing for a lower court to say whether the time has come to disregard a decision of a higher court, not yet explicitly overruled, because they parallel others in which the higher court has expressed a contrary view. I agree that one should not wait for formal retraction in the face of charges plainly foreshadowed; the higher court may not entertain an appeal in the case before the lower court, or the parties may not choose to appeal."); Essay, *The Roles of a Federal District Court Judge*, 76 Brook. L.Rev. 2, 454 (2011) ("Ultimately, it is the trial judge's conscience, exercised under the constraints of our rule of law, that guides the pen writing an opinion justifying a judgment.")....

The production of child pornography can severely harm children. In the most extreme instances, they suffer not only physical and mental abuse, but death. A well-publicized example is Thea Pumbroek. When six years old she died of a cocaine overdose in the bathroom of an Amsterdam hotel in the mid-1980s, while being filmed for a pornographic video. *See* Taylor & Quayle, *supra*, at x–xi, 42–43. The killing of children in the production of child pornography may not be accidental. *Cf.* Comment, *Sentencing "Cybersex Offender": Individual Offenders Require Individualized Conditions when Courts Restrict Their Computer Use and Internet Access*, 58 Cath. U.L.Rev. 779, 789 n. 67 (2009) (discussing defendant who "expressed interest in chatroom message that advertised 'snuff films of little children'").... Many children who are not physically injured in the making of child pornography grow up knowing, or learning later, that their abuse has been frozen in time — sold, circulated, and traded long after physical trauma ended, often for use in masturbation. *See, e.g., New York v. Ferber*, 458 U.S. 747, 759, 102 S.Ct. 3348, 73 L.Ed.2d 1113 (1982) (noting harm suffered by child victims from circulation of images); *accord Osborne v. Ohio*, 495 U.S. 103, 110–111, 110 S.Ct. 1691, 109 L.Ed.2d 98 (1990). The following example is not atypical:

> When Amy was a little girl, her uncle made her famous in the worst way: as a star in the netherworld of child pornography. Photographs and videos known as 'the Misty series' depicting her abuse have circulated on the internet for more than 10 years, and often turn up in the collections of those arrested for possession of illegal images.... Amy's uncle is now in prison, but she is regularly reminded of his abuse whenever the government notifies her that her photos have turned up in yet another prosecution. More than 800 of the notices ... have arrived at Amy's home ...

See John Schwartz, *Child Pornography, and an Issue of Restitution*, N.Y. Times, Feb. 3, 2010. Analysis of messages posted by participants in "Wonderland" — a well-known and now defunct electronic bulletin board frequented by child pornographers — illustrates that demand for such images persists, and may even increase, over time:

> [R]emember the case of 'Helena,' probably a British girl, who tragically, may be one of the best-known sex stars on the Web. In the late 1980s, as a little girl of seven or eight, Helena became the subject of a photo series that depicted her not only in all the familiar nude poses of hardcore pornography but also showed her in numerous sex acts with Gavin, a boy of about the same age. Both are shown having sex with an adult man, presumably Helena's father. The images are collectively known by various names but the commonest is "hel-lo," that is, "Helena/Lolita." Since their first appearance they have had an astonishing afterlife; probably not a day has passed without the hel-lo images appearing anew on some electronic server somewhere in the world, and they are cherished by thousands of collectors worldwide. They seem to be the standard starter kit for the child porn novice....
>
> Or we might consider the more recent KG and KX series, the 'kindergarten' photos, which together represent perhaps the most prized collections currently available on the Net. KG is a series of hundreds (maybe thousands) of nude images of several very young girls, mainly between the ages of three and six years old, with each item including the girls' name — Helga, Inga, and so on. The photographs date from the mid-1990s, and they likely derive from Germany or Scandinavia.... The KG collection exists alongside a still more sought-after version, KX, which depicts the same children in hard-core sexual situations with one or more men. Put simply, most are pictures of four- and five-year old girls performing oral sex and masturbation on adult men. The immense popularity of the KG images ensured an enthusiastic market for KX, which entered general circulation in early 2000.

See Jenkins, *supra*, at 2–3; *see generally* Taylor & Quayle, *supra*, at 8 ("Child pornography ... represents and preserves that abuse or sexualized image for as long as that photograph [or video] remains."); Ferraro & Casey, *supra*, at 5 ("Child pornography is a permanent record of a child's sexual assault that exploits the victim each time it is viewed for pleasure."). The harm to the victims, families, and communities arising from the production and continued circulation of such images is great, but impossible to quantify. Ferraro & Casey, *supra*, at 5. *But cf.* Schwartz, *supra* (describing one child pornography victim's attempt to obtain restitution from possessors of images depicting the abuse she suffered years prior)....

[At this part of the opinion, but omitted here, the court includes the testimony of qualified psychologist, Dr. Mary Anne Layden, who described the effects of child pornography on both the viewers and viewed. Dr. Layden described that, at the time of the trauma, victims start with physical harms, such as anal and vaginal ripping, and often sexually transmitted diseases of the vagina, mouth, and eyes, which may take decades to heal. In addition, there are psychological consequences that present in childhood and stay through adult life, such as depression, suicidality, and post traumatic stress disorder; others, such as flashbacks, "reexperiencing," arousal, hypervigilance, avoidance problems, and other cognitive symptoms, may not occur until adulthood. Additionally, realization in adult life that images of their childhood sexual abuse are permanently circulating on the Internet impacts the victims and deepens the pathologies from which they are already suffering. Dr. Layden also discussed the effect of child pornography on the "Market For Child Pornography" and how it factors in to the practice of "grooming" other children who are not depicted in the child pornography, as well as the correlation between the consumption of child pornography for sexual pleasure and acting out what may be depicted in the child pornography. Dr. Layden concluded that the consumption of "child pornography was actually a better predictor of pedophilia diagnosis than actually even hav[ing] raped a child."]

[A significant portion of the court opinion dealing with psychological testimony, including that regarding the abuse of the child victims portrayed in the various child pornography series, as well as the psychological reports and risk assessments regarding the defendant, is omitted. Also omitted here is the court's lengthy discussion of the statutory history of the federal sentencing scheme, the history of child pornography legislation, and various public policy concerns related to child pornography legislation.]

C.R.'s crimes are serious and warrant punishment. Children were abused to produce the material he collected. They will experience continued—often heightened—harm from knowledge of the widely accessible visualization of their abuse on video.... Defendant's "distribution" in this case involved creating a screen name on two peer-to-peer file sharing programs, Gigatribe and Limewire, using known child pornography search terms with his user name to advertise his interest in child pornography, and creating an electronic folder on his computer's hard drive where he saved one image of child pornography and 100 child pornography videos that he downloaded from the programs. The forensic analysis of the two Dell computers C.R. utilized to view and distribute child pornography revealed 100 images and 200 videos of child pornography. While even a relatively small participation in the viewing of child pornography may help fuel the market for this material, a distinction must be made between a minor sharer at C.R.'s level and an extensive commercial distributer....

Another weighty consideration is the nature of the images depicted on defendant's computer.... [T]he majority of images on defendant's computers involved boys between the ages of ten and twelve.... These files, while seriously troubling, were not of the brutal type found on the computers of many other defendants the courts have encountered in such cases. *Cf. United States v. Reiner*, 468 F.Supp.2d 393, 398 (E.D.N.Y.2006) (cataloging violent images, movies and stories found on defendant's computer). C.R. did not have images of bondage, sadism, or violence.... The government disputes this contention arguing "all child pornography is inherently violent, in that it depicts the rape of non-consenting children. Indeed, every image of child pornography represents a victim who has been abused, exploited and raped." ... Any sexual assault of a child is a violent act that causes tremendous harm to the victim. The Sentencing Commission has chosen to distinguish between sexual content and sexual content involving violent conduct.

In this case, C.R., appropriately and with the government's concurrence, did not receive a four-point enhancement for possessing images containing "sadistic or masochistic conduct or other depictions of violence." *See* § 2G2.2(b)(4). The absence of such images is significant because it probably decreases (the court assumes in the absence of good scientific studies) the likelihood that C.R. would act out to harm a child. "Though the empirical evidence of a correlation between pornography and sexual assault is equivocal ... studies relatively consistently indicate that any aggressive behavior that may be observed is not because the violent images contained a sexual theme, but that it is the violence that is relevant." Hamilton, *supra* ... (discussing study showing a correlation between sexually aggressive behavior and sexually violent pornography, but not with nonviolent pornography)....

There are several mitigating factors when considering the individual characteristics of this defendant. C.R. began viewing pornographic images when he was about 15 years old — well below the 18 year statutory "juvenile" line. The majority of the images he viewed involved young boys between the ages of 10 and 12, not far from his own age group when he started viewing the material. The Supreme Court has authorized consideration of a defendant's age and maturity in two recent decisions. *See ... Roper*, 543 U.S. 551, 125 S.Ct. 1183 (relying on scientific research documenting lack of maturity in young people and continued brain development to find death penalty unconstitutional when imposed on an individual whose crime was committed before age 18) and *Graham*, 130 S.Ct. at 2048 (relying on research to find imposition of life without parole for non-homicide crimes unconstitutional when applied to individuals under 18).

Federal courts have emphasized the fundamental difference between the conduct of an immature defendant whose child pornography habit began in adolescence and others whose conduct began as an adult. *See United States v. Polito*, 215 Fed.Appx. 354, 357 (5th Cir.2007) (per curiam) (upholding a sentence of probation when use began during adolescence) *contra United States v. McElheney*, 524 F.Supp.2d 983, 997 (E.D.Tenn.2007) (affirming guideline sentence for adult offender) ("Typically, defendants in [child pornography] cases are first offenders, highly educated, middle aged, with solid work histories."). "[Y]outh is more than a chronological fact. It is a time and condition of life when a person may be most susceptible to influence and to psychological damage." *Gall v. United States*, 552 U.S. 38, 58, 128 S.Ct. 586, 169 L.Ed.2d 445 (2007) (internal citation omitted) (below guidelines sentence for college student who withdrew from drug conspiracy and reformed behavior).

> The need to protect this crime's victims is not lessened by the perpetrator's age. That being said, the courts have a radically different statutory scheme in place to punish 14 year olds who are looking at pictures of other 14-year olds, as this behavior is fundamentally different in kind than a 40-year old who looks at 14-year olds. The 14-year old is acting on normal impulses in an unacceptable manner (and may well be unaware of the impact of his crime), whereas the 40-year old is acting on deviant impulses and is expected to understand the terror that this crime inflicts upon its victims.

United States v. Stern, 590 F.Supp.2d 945, 954, n. 6 (N.D.Oh.2008) (below guidelines sentence for young man who began looking at child pornography at the age of 14 but stopped following his arrest at age 22).

Because C.R. was only 15 when he started viewing child pornography and the entirety of his offense conduct occurred during his teenage years, consideration must be given to the defendant's impressionable age, sexual exploration, and potential lack of awareness regarding the potential harms of his crime. Defendant's continued use of child pornography until his arrest at age nineteen, four years after his conduct first began, must be considered; as C.R. matured chronologically, his activities did not cease. C.R. had continued difficulty controlling his behavior and was not receiving any treatment to address his inappropriate sexual desires. His continued viewing of child pornography on file sharing networks during his teenage years must be balanced against mental health evaluations that indicate C.R. is "grossly naïve and immature;" scientific research explaining that pre-frontal lobe development, the part of his brain that manages impulse control, judgment, and decision making, persists until the mid-twenties; lack of any effective steps by his parents to control or have C.R. treated for his emotional problems; and creation by his adult custodians of an unhealthy sexual atmosphere bound to exacerbate the sexual problems of this adolescent....

The defendant is immature, but is bright and capable of a useful productive life, and a future without violation of sexual offense laws, given adequate treatment, supervision and control. This will be provided under the sentence imposed.... The punishment imposed is substantial, reflecting the seriousness of the offense. It will promote respect for the law.... General deterrence is satisfied. The sentence will send a clear message that child pornography is condemned and that even a defendant with compelling personal characteristics such as youth, mental immaturity, motivation for treatment, and positive educational and employment history should not be excused.... Sharing child pornography through a computer network program is not a victim-less crime. Recognition of the harm this crime causes to innocent children who are abused to produce this heinous material is necessary....

Were there no five-year mandatory minimum sentence the court would have imposed a probationary sentence with supervised release and outpatient treatment.... The testimony strongly supported the therapeutic value of an intensive outpatient course of treatment for this defendant. Given the strong public policy support for some incarceration to deter future like conduct, the punishment imposed is appropriate.

Following a full analysis of the constitutional issues and statutory criteria for sentencing defendant under 18 U.S.C. § 2252(a)(2) for distribution of child pornography; and a careful consideration of the need to protect the public and to avoid unnecessary harm to the defendant, a sentence of thirty months incarceration is imposed. Credit is to be given for the time spent at FMC Devens while defendant was being evaluated on order of the court.... Five years of supervised release and a special assessment of $100 is mandated. No fine is assessed since defendant has no substantial monetary assets and is unlikely to have any in the foreseeable future.

The recommendation of Probation and the policy statement at U.S.S.G § 5D1.2(c) that the maximum sentence of lifetime supervised release be imposed, ... is rejected as too severe and inhibitory of the total rehabilitation possible while defendant is still in his early twenties. *See also United States v. Apodaca*, No. 09-50372, 641 F.3d 1077, 1085–88, 2011 WL 1365794, *7–10 (April 12, 2011 9th Cir.) (Fletcher. J concurring) (critiquing application of U.S.S.G. § 5D1.2(c) on Internet-only child pornography offenders because it "grossly overestimate[s] the risk that [such defendants] will commit contact sex offenses against children"); *United States v. Albertson*, No. 09-1049, 645 F.3d 191, 200, 2011 WL 1662786, *7 (3d Cir. May 4, 2011) (considering appropriate computer-related supervised release conditions for child pornography offenders and concluding "in a time where the daily necessities of life and work demand not only internet access but internet fluency, sentencing courts need to select the least restrictive alternative for achieving their sentencing purposes"). Defendant will, in any event, be subject to long-time supervision under the state and federal sex offender registration and notification laws. *See* 42 U.S.C. §§ 16911, 16915(a)(1); § 16915(b); N.Y. Corr. Law § 168-h(1) (twenty years for lowest risk offender)…. Forfeited to the government shall be all equipment, photos, videos, and any other material used by defendant in obtaining, viewing, collecting or distributing child or adult pornography. Forfeiture to the government of this material is ordered.

A part, and condition, of the sentence is service of the term of imprisonment at the Federal Medical Center Devens with treatment in the residential Sex Offender Treatment Program. The defendant has requested, is prepared for, and intends to cooperate in this program. Conversations with officials at Devens have assured the court that this treatment will be available to C.R.… Defendant shall self-surrender at Devens as soon as he is directed to do so by the Bureau of Prisons or the United States Attorney. Until then, bail is continued. *See United States v. Polouizzi. See* 760 F.Supp.2d 284, 287–88 (E.D.N.Y.2011); *United States v. Polouizzi*, 697 F.Supp.2d 381 (E.D.N.Y.2010) (unconstitutionality of limits on bail in sex cases).

SO ORDERED.

[Omitted here is a series of Appendices, one of which includes a chart of the various state statutes on juvenile sentencing for child pornography.]

Notes

In a 401-page opinion, Judge Weinstein held that the five-year minimum sentence for child pornography was unconstitutional as applied to the defendant, C.R., and, instead, sentenced him to thirty months. In September 2013, referring to C.R. by his full name — Cory Reingold — the United States Court of Appeals for the Second Circuit vacated Judge Weinstein's order and remanded the case for C.R. to be resentenced in accordance with the minimum requirements. *See United States v. Reingold*, 731 F.3d 204 (2nd Cir. (N.Y.) 2013), *infra*, Chapter Seven, Section I.C.2 (Sentencing Variables, Proportionality). Judge Weinstein responded the same day, writing in a nine-page Memorandum to the Court of Appeals that "[t]he effect of harsh minimum sentences in cases such as C.R.'s is, effectively, to destroy young lives unnecessarily." *United States v. C.R.*, 972 F. Supp. 2d 457, 457 (E.D.N.Y. 2013). He stated that the mandatory five-year minimum is "unjust," and that the case "exemplifies the sometimes unnecessary cruelty of our federal law." *Id.*

> In imposing a sentence on … the passive adolescent who saves or automatically passes on what he observed through automatic file sharing, with no *mens rea* as to possible harm … — with no danger of acting out — a statutorily mandated five, ten, or fifteen year sentence plus post-prison lifetime restraints on where the defendant can live or work and with whom he can associate, is so unnecessarily destructive as to evoke the dread that the sentence itself constitutes a grave injustice — a sentence shockingly divergent from the American criteria for defensible penology.

Id. at 459. However, in determining the proportionality of C.R.'s sentence in relation to the crime, the United States Court of Appeals for the Second Circuit commented on the role that advanced Internet technology plays in such cases:

[no] mitigation [can] be located in the fact that Reingold's crimes were facilitated by a recent "digital revolution" that has "enormously increased the ways that child pornography can be created, accessed, and distributed." *United States v. C.R.*, 792 F. Supp. 2d at 367. The ease with which a person can access and distribute child pornography from his home—often with no more effort than a few clicks on a computer—may make it easier for perpetrators to delude themselves that their conduct is not deviant or harmful. But technological advances that facilitate child pornography crimes no more mitigate the real harm caused by these crimes than do technological advances making it easier to perpetrate fraud, traffic drugs, or even engage in acts of terrorism—all at a distance from victims—mitigate those crimes. If anything, the noted digital revolution may actually aggravate child pornography crimes insofar as an expanding market for child pornography fuels greater demand for perverse sexual depictions of children, making it more difficult for authorities to prevent their sexual exploitation and abuse. *See generally United States v. Lewis*, 605 F.3d 395, 403 (6th Cir. 2010) (noting that distribution through computers "is particularly harmful because it can reach an almost limitless audience" (internal quotation marks omitted).... But precisely because the prevention of such exploitation and abuse is "a government objective of surpassing importance," *New York v. Ferber*, 458 U.S. at 757..., we cannot view the distribution of child pornography, however accomplished, as anything but a serious crime that threatens real, and frequently violent, harm to vulnerable victims, *cf. Harmelin v. Michigan*, 501 U.S. at 1002–03 (Kennedy, J., concurring) (observing that characterization of drug possession with intent to distribute as "nonviolent and victimless" crime "is false to the point of absurdity" given "pernicious effects" of drug use).

Reingold, 731 F.3d at 217. In November 2013, Judge Weinstein reluctantly resentenced Reingold to five years. Reingold stated: "Even though it's unfair I have to hold my head up and just do this and live my life.... I just think it's unfair that a judge isn't allowed to sentence how he wants to." Selim Algar, *Judge forced to re-sentence child porn perv to five years*, N.Y. Post, Nov. 6, 2013.

United States v. Kramer

Eighth Circuit, 2011
631 F.3d 900

WOLLMAN, Circuit Judge.

Steve Wozniak, co-founder of Apple Computer, recently mused: "Everything has a computer in it nowadays." ... [footnote omitted]. But is an ordinary cellular phone—used only to place calls and send text messages—a computer? The district court, ... [footnote omitted] relying on the definition of "computer" found in 18 U.S.C. § 1030(e)(1), concluded that Neil Kramer's was, and imposed an enhanced prison sentence for its use in committing an offense. We affirm....

Neil Kramer pleaded guilty to transporting a minor in interstate commerce with the intent to engage in criminal sexual activity with her, a violation of 18 U.S.C. § 2423(a). He also acknowledged that he used his cellular telephone—a Motorola Motorazr V3—to make voice calls and send text messages to the victim for a six-month period leading up to the offense.... The district court—over Kramer's objection—concluded that the phone was a "computer," *see* 18 U.S.C. § 1030(e)(1), applied a two-level enhancement for its use to facilitate the offense, *see* U.S. Sentencing Guidelines Manual § 2G1.3(b)(3)

(2009), and sentenced Kramer to 168 months' imprisonment. Although this sentence is within both the original and enhanced guidelines ranges, the district court acknowledged that without the enhancement it would have sentenced Kramer to 140 months' imprisonment.... Kramer argues (1) that application of the enhancement was procedural error because a cellular telephone, when used only to make voice calls and send text messages, cannot be a "computer" as defined in 18 U.S.C. § 1030(e)(1), and (2) that even if a phone could be a computer, the government's evidence was insufficient to show that his phone met that definition....

U.S. Sentencing Guidelines Manual § 2G1.3(b)(3) provides a two-level enhancement for "the use of a computer ... to ... persuade, induce, entice, coerce, or facilitate the travel of, the minor to engage in prohibited sexual conduct...." "'Computer' has the meaning given that term in 18 U.S.C. § 1030(e)(1)," U.S. Sentencing Guidelines Manual § 2G1.3(b)(3) cmt. n.1 (2009), that is, it "means an electronic, magnetic, optical, electrochemical, or other high speed data processing device performing logical, arithmetic, or storage functions, and includes any data storage facility or communications facility directly related to or operating in conjunction with such device," 18 U.S.C. § 1030(e)(1). It does not, however, "include an automated typewriter or typesetter, a portable hand held calculator, or other similar device." 18 U.S.C. § 1030(e)(1).... Kramer first argues that the district court incorrectly interpreted the term "computer" to include a "basic cell phone" being used only to call and text message the victim. In his view, the enhancement should apply only when a device is used to access the Internet. We disagree.

The language of 18 U.S.C. § 1030(e)(1) is exceedingly broad. If a device is "an electronic ... or other high speed data processing device performing logical, arithmetic, or storage functions,"[3] it is a computer. This definition captures any device that makes use of a electronic data processor, examples of which are legion. *Accord* Orin S. Kerr, *Vagueness Challenges to the Computer Fraud and Abuse Act*, 94 Minn. L.Rev. 1561, 1577 (2010) ("Just think of the common household items that include microchips and electronic storage devices, and thus will satisfy the statutory definition of 'computer.' That category can include coffeemakers, microwave ovens, watches, telephones, children's toys, MP3 players, refrigerators, heating and air-conditioning units, radios, alarm clocks, televisions, and DVD players, in addition to more traditional computers like laptops or desktop computers." (footnote omitted)). Additionally, each time an electronic processor performs any task—from powering on, to receiving keypad input, to displaying information—it performs logical, arithmetic, or storage functions. These functions are the essence of its operation. *See* The New Oxford American Dictionary 277 (2d ed. 2005) (defining "central processing unit" as "the part of a computer in which operations are controlled and executed").

Furthermore, there is nothing in the statutory definition that purports to exclude devices because they lack a connection to the Internet. To be sure, the term computer "does not include an automated typewriter or typesetter, a portable hand held calculator, or other similar device." 18 U.S.C. § 1030(e)(1). But this hardly excludes all non-Internet-

---

3. The parties disagree over the meaning of this language. Kramer argues that the word "electronic" modifies "high speed data processing device" and therefore the device must be both "electronic" and "high speed." The government argues that "electronic, magnetic, optical, [and] electrochemical" data processing devices are, by their nature, "high speed," and the language "other high speed" was included to expand the statute to cover additional types of high-speed devices that were not, or could not be, enumerated. We need not resolve this dispute because even if Kramer's reading of the statute is correct, a modern cellular phone can be a "high speed" electronic device. Indeed, modern cellular phones process data at comparable or faster rates than the desktop computers that existed when § 1030(e)(1) was enacted.

enabled devices from the definition of "computer"—indeed, this phrasing would be an odd way to do it. Whatever makes an automated typewriter "similar" to a hand held calculator—the statute provides no further illumination—we find few similarities between those items and a modern cellular phone containing an electronic processor. Therefore we conclude that cellular phones are not excluded by this language.[4]

Of course, the enhancement does not apply to every offender who happens to use a computer-controlled microwave or coffeemaker. Application note 4 to § 2G1.3(b)(3) limits application of the enhancement to those offenders who use a computer "to communicate directly with a minor or with a person who exercises custody, care, or supervisory control of the minor." U.S. Sentencing Guidelines Manual § 2G1.3(b)(3) cmt. n.4 (2009). Therefore, the note continues, the enhancement "would not apply to the use of a computer or an interactive computer service to obtain airline tickets for the minor from an airline's Internet site." *Id.* This is a meaningful limitation on the applicability of the enhancement, but it is no help to Kramer.

We acknowledge that a "basic" cellular phone might not easily fit within the colloquial definition of "computer." We are bound, however, not by the common understanding of that word, but by the specific—if broad—definition set forth in § 1030(e)(1). Now it may be that neither the Sentencing Commission nor Congress anticipated that a cellular phone would be included in that definition.[5] As technology continues to develop, § 1030(e)(1) may come to capture still additional devices that few industry experts, much less the Commission or Congress, could foresee.[6] But to the extent that such a sweeping definition was unintended or is now inappropriate, it is a matter for the Commission or Congress to correct. We cannot provide relief from plain statutory text. *See United States v. Mitra*, 405 F.3d 492, 495 (7th Cir.2005) ("As more devices come to have built-in intelligence, the effective scope of [§ 1030(e)(1)] grows. This might prompt Congress to amend the statute but does not authorize the judiciary to give the existing version less coverage than its language portends.").....

Kramer's second contention—that the government's evidence was insufficient to demonstrate that *his* cellular phone was a computer—also fails. "The government must

---

4. Kramer's reliance on *United States v. Lay*, 583 F.3d 436 (6th Cir.2009), is misplaced. In *Lay*, the Sixth Circuit affirmed a § 2G1.3(b)(3) enhancement on the ground that the defendant used a computer to develop a relationship with the victim, even though future communications were exclusively by mobile phone and other "offline" modes. The court said that "[t]o allow a predator to use a computer to develop relationships with minor victims, so long as the ultimate consummation is first proposed through offline communication, would not serve the purpose of the enhancement." 583 F.3d at 447. As Kramer sees it, *Lay* "implicitly distinguishes use of a cellular telephone from use of a traditional computer when applying the enhancement." ... That may be so. But in that case the government never argued that the mobile phone itself was a computer, nor did the court ever consider or decide that issue. Whether the court in *Lay* would have expressly adopted this implicit distinction we do not know, because the issue was never squarely presented to it. *Lay*, therefore, does not help us decide this case.

5. Indeed the Commission, explaining its reasons for "expand[ing] the enhancement" found in guidelines § 2G2.2(b)(5) to include the use of an "interactive computer service," expressed its view that "the term 'computer' did not capture all types of Internet devices." U.S. Sentencing Guidelines Manual supp. to app. C, amend. 664, at 59 (2009). Therefore, it continued, "the amendment expands the definition of 'computer' to include other devices that involve interactive computer services (*e.g.*, Web-Tv)." ...

6. In a now-famous understatement, Popular Mechanics once predicted: "Where a calculator like the ENIAC today is equipped with 18,000 vacuum tubes and weighs 30 tons, computers in the future may have only 1000 vacuum tubes and perhaps weigh only 1.5 tons." Andrew Hamilton, *Brains that Click*, Popular Mechanics, Mar. 1949, at 162, 258.

prove the facts needed to support a sentencing enhancement by a preponderance of the evidence, and we review the district court's fact findings for clear error." *United States v. Kain*, 589 F.3d 945, 952 (8th Cir.2009).... The government introduced the phone's user's manual and a printout from Motorola's website describing the phone's features.... The government did not, however, offer any expert testimony regarding the phone's capabilities. Although doing so might have aided our review, the materials presented to the district court were sufficient to show by a preponderance of the evidence that Kramer's phone was an "electronic ... or other high speed data processing device" that "perform[ed] logical, arithmetic, or storage functions" when Kramer used it to call and text message the victim.

The printout reveals that the phone is powered by a "680 mAh Li-ion" battery, ... has "5MB" of memory, ... is capable of running software, ... makes use of a "Graphic Accelerator" to run its color display screens, ... has a "User-customizable" main menu, ... and comes with "Preloaded" text messages, ... Also, the user's manual contains a "Software Copyright Notice" which warns that the phone "may include copyrighted Motorola and third-party software stored in semiconductor memories or other media." ... Together, these are sufficient to show that the phone makes use of an electronic data processor.

Furthermore, that processor performs arithmetic, logical, and storage functions when the phone is used to place a call. The user's manual notes that the phone "keeps lists of incoming and outgoing calls, even for calls that did not connect," ... and "displays the phone number for incoming calls in [the] phone's external and internal displays." ... Additionally, the phone keeps track of the "Network connection time," which is "the elapsed time from the moment [the user] connect[s] to [the] service provider's network to the moment [the user] end[s] the call by pressing [the end key]." ... This counting function alone is sufficient to support a finding that the phone is performing logical and arithmetic operations when used to place calls.

The same is true when the phone is used to send text messages. Most fundamentally, the phone stores sets of characters that are available to a user when typing a message.... As the user types, the phone keeps track of the user's past inputs and displays the "entered text," ... i.e., the message being composed. The user may also delete characters previously entered, either "one letter at a time" or all at once.... In addition, the phone allows the users to "set different primary and secondary text entry modes, and easily switch between modes as needed when [they] enter data or compose a message," including "iTAP" mode which uses "software" to "predict[ ] each word" as it is entered.... These capabilities all support the district court's finding that the phone performed arithmetic, logical, and storage functions when Kramer used it to send text messages to the victim....

For these reasons, we affirm Kramer's sentence.

II. Defining Internet Exploitation of Minors: Child Pornography

A. The Scope of Child Pornography Regulation

Ashcroft v. Free Speech Coalition
United States Supreme Court, 2002
535 U.S. 234, 122 S. Ct. 1389

Justice KENNEDY delivered the opinion of the Court.

We consider in this case whether the Child Pornography Prevention Act of 1996 (CPPA), 18 U.S.C. §2251 *et seq.*, abridges the freedom of speech. The CPPA extends the federal prohibition against child pornography to sexually explicit images that appear to depict minors but were produced without using any real children. The statute prohibits, in specific circumstances, possessing or distributing these images, which may be created by using adults who look like minors or by using computer imaging. The new technology, according to Congress, makes it possible to create realistic images of children who do not exist. See Congressional Findings, notes following 18 U.S.C. §2251.

By prohibiting child pornography that does not depict an actual child, the statute goes beyond *New York v. Ferber*, 458 U.S. 747, 102 S.Ct. 3348, 73 L.Ed.2d 1113 (1982), which distinguished child pornography from other sexually explicit speech because of the State's interest in protecting the children exploited by the production process. See *id.*, at 758, 102 S.Ct. 3348. As a general rule, pornography can be banned only if obscene, but under *Ferber*, pornography showing minors can be proscribed whether or not the images are obscene under the definition set forth in *Miller v. California*, 413 U.S. 15, 93 S.Ct. 2607, 37 L.Ed.2d 419 (1973). *Ferber* recognized that "[t]he *Miller* standard, like all general definitions of what may be banned as obscene, does not reflect the State's particular and more compelling interest in prosecuting those who promote the sexual exploitation of children." 458 U.S., at 761, 102 S.Ct. 3348.

While we have not had occasion to consider the question, we may assume that the apparent age of persons engaged in sexual conduct is relevant to whether a depiction offends community standards. Pictures of young children engaged in certain acts might be obscene where similar depictions of adults, or perhaps even older adolescents, would not. The CPPA, however, is not directed at speech that is obscene; Congress has proscribed those materials through a separate statute. 18 U.S.C. §§1460–1466. Like the law in *Ferber*, the CPPA seeks to reach beyond obscenity, and it makes no attempt to conform to the *Miller* standard. For instance, the statute would reach visual depictions, such as movies, even if they have redeeming social value.

The principal question to be resolved, then, is whether the CPPA is constitutional where it proscribes a significant universe of speech that is neither obscene under *Miller* nor child pornography under *Ferber*.... Before 1996, Congress defined child pornography as the type of depictions at issue in *Ferber*, images made using actual minors. 18 U.S.C. §2252 (1994 ed.). The CPPA retains that prohibition at 18 U.S.C. §2256(8)(A) and adds three other prohibited categories of speech, of which the first, §2256(8)(B), and the third, §2256(8)(D), are at issue in this case. Section 2256(8)(B) prohibits "any visual depiction, including any photograph, film, video, picture, or computer or computer-generated image or picture," that "is, or appears to be, of a minor engaging in sexually explicit conduct." The prohibition on "any visual depiction" does not depend at all on how the image is produced. The section captures a range of depictions, sometimes called "virtual child pornography," which include computer-generated images, as well as images produced by more traditional means. For instance, the literal terms of the statute embrace a Renaissance painting depicting a scene from classical mythology, a "picture" that "appears to be, of a minor engaging in sexually explicit conduct." The statute also prohibits Hollywood movies, filmed without any child actors, if a jury believes an actor "appears to be" a minor engaging in "actual or simulated ... sexual intercourse." § 2256(2).

These images do not involve, let alone harm, any children in the production process; but Congress decided the materials threaten children in other, less direct, ways. Pedophiles might use the materials to encourage children to participate in sexual activity. "[A] child who is reluctant to engage in sexual activity with an adult, or to pose for sexually explicit photographs, can sometimes be convinced by viewing depictions of other children 'having fun' participating in such activity." Congressional Finding (3), notes following § 2251. Furthermore, pedophiles might "whet their own sexual appetites" with the pornographic images, "thereby increasing the creation and distribution of child pornography and the sexual abuse and exploitation of actual children." *Id.*, Findings (4), (10)(B). Under these rationales, harm flows from the content of the images, not from the means of their production. In addition, Congress identified another problem created by computer-generated images: Their existence can make it harder to prosecute pornographers who do use real minors. See *id.*, Finding (6)(A). As imaging technology improves, Congress found, it becomes more difficult to prove that a particular picture was produced using actual children. To ensure that defendants possessing child pornography using real minors cannot evade prosecution, Congress extended the ban to virtual child pornography.

Section 2256(8)(C) prohibits a more common and lower tech means of creating virtual images, known as computer morphing. Rather than creating original images, pornographers can alter innocent pictures of real children so that the children appear to be engaged in sexual activity. Although morphed images may fall within the definition of virtual child pornography, they implicate the interests of real children and are in that sense closer to the images in *Ferber*. Respondents do not challenge this provision, and we do not consider it.

Respondents do challenge § 2256(8)(D). Like the text of the "appears to be" provision, the sweep of this provision is quite broad. Section 2256(8)(D) defines child pornography to include any sexually explicit image that was "advertised, promoted, presented, described, or distributed in such a manner that conveys the impression" it depicts "a minor engaging in sexually explicit conduct." One Committee Report identified the provision as directed at sexually explicit images pandered as child pornography. See S.Rep. No. 104-358, p. 22 (1996) ("This provision prevents child pornographers and pedophiles from exploiting prurient interests in child sexuality and sexual activity through the production or distribution of pornographic material which is intentionally pandered as child pornography"). The statute is not so limited in its reach, however, as it punishes even those possessors who took no part in pandering. Once a work has been described as child pornography, the taint remains on the speech in the hands of subsequent possessors, making possession unlawful even though the content otherwise would not be objectionable.

Fearing that the CPPA threatened the activities of its members, respondent Free Speech Coalition and others challenged the statute in the United States District Court for the Northern District of California. The Coalition, a California trade association for the adult-entertainment industry, alleged that its members did not use minors in their sexually explicit works, but they believed some of these materials might fall within the CPPA's expanded definition of child pornography. The other respondents are Bold Type, Inc., the publisher of a book advocating the nudist lifestyle; Jim Gingerich, a painter of nudes; and Ron Raffaelli, a photographer specializing in erotic images. Respondents alleged that the "appears to be" and "conveys the impression" provisions are overbroad and vague, chilling them from producing works protected by the First Amendment. The District Court disagreed and granted summary judgment to the Government. The court dismissed the overbreadth claim because it was "highly unlikely" that any "adaptations of sexual works like 'Romeo and Juliet,'... will be treated as 'criminal contraband.'"...

The Court of Appeals for the Ninth Circuit reversed. See 198 F.3d 1083 (1999). The court reasoned that the Government could not prohibit speech because of its tendency to persuade viewers to commit illegal acts. The court held the CPPA to be substantially overbroad because it bans materials that are neither obscene nor produced by the exploitation of real children as in *New York v. Ferber*, 458 U.S. 747, 102 S.Ct. 3348, 73 L.Ed.2d 1113 (1982). Judge Ferguson dissented on the ground that virtual images, like obscenity and real child pornography, should be treated as a category of speech unprotected by the First Amendment. 198 F.3d, at 1097. The Court of Appeals voted to deny the petition for rehearing en banc, over the dissent of three judges. See 220 F.3d 1113 (2000)....
While the Ninth Circuit found the CPPA invalid on its face, four other Courts of Appeals have sustained it. See *United States v. Fox*, 248 F.3d 394 (C.A.5 2001); *United States v. Mento*, 231 F.3d 912 (C.A.4 2000); *United States v. Acheson*, 195 F.3d 645 (C.A.11 1999); *United States v. Hilton*, 167 F.3d 61(C.A.1), cert. denied, 528 U.S. 844, 120 S.Ct. 115, 145 L.Ed.2d 98 (1999). We granted certiorari. 531 U.S. 1124, 121 S.Ct. 876, 148 L.Ed.2d 788 (2001)....

The First Amendment commands, "Congress shall make no law ... abridging the freedom of speech." The government may violate this mandate in many ways, *e.g.*, *Rosenberger v. Rector and Visitors of Univ. of Va.*, 515 U.S. 819, 115 S.Ct. 2510, 132 L.Ed.2d 700 (1995); *Keller v. State Bar of Cal.*, 496 U.S. 1, 110 S.Ct. 2228, 110 L.Ed.2d 1 (1990), but a law imposing criminal penalties on protected speech is a stark example of speech suppression. The CPPA's penalties are indeed severe. A first offender may be imprisoned for 15 years. § 2252A(b)(1). A repeat offender faces a prison sentence of not less than 5 years and not more than 30 years in prison. *Ibid.* While even minor punishments can chill protected speech, see *Wooley v. Maynard*, 430 U.S. 705, 97 S.Ct. 1428, 51 L.Ed.2d 752 (1977), this case provides a textbook example of why we permit facial challenges to statutes that burden expression. With these severe penalties in force, few legitimate movie producers or book publishers, or few other speakers in any capacity, would risk distributing images in or near the uncertain reach of this law. The Constitution gives significant protection from overbroad laws that chill speech within the First Amendment's vast and privileged sphere. Under this principle, the CPPA is unconstitutional on its face if it prohibits a substantial amount of protected expression. See *Broadrick v. Oklahoma*, 413 U.S. 601, 612, 93 S.Ct. 2908, 37 L.Ed.2d 830 (1973).

The sexual abuse of a child is a most serious crime and an act repugnant to the moral instincts of a decent people. In its legislative findings, Congress recognized that there are subcultures of persons who harbor illicit desires for children and commit criminal acts to gratify the impulses. See Congressional Findings, notes following § 2251; see also U.S. Dept. of Health and Human Services, Administration on Children, Youth and Families, Child Maltreatment 1999 (estimating that 93,000 children were victims of sexual abuse in 1999). Congress also found that surrounding the serious offenders are those who flirt with these impulses and trade pictures and written accounts of sexual activity with young children....

As a general principle, the First Amendment bars the government from dictating what we see or read or speak or hear. The freedom of speech has its limits; it does not embrace certain categories of speech, including defamation, incitement, obscenity, and pornography produced with real children. See *Simon & Schuster, Inc. v. Members of N.Y. State Crime Victims Bd.*, 502 U.S. 105, 127, 112 S.Ct. 501, 116 L.Ed.2d 476 (1991) (KENNEDY, J., concurring). While these categories may be prohibited without violating the First Amendment, none of them includes the speech prohibited by the CPPA. In his dissent from the opinion of the Court of Appeals, Judge Ferguson recognized this to be the law and proposed that virtual child pornography should be regarded as an additional category of unprotected speech. See 198 F.3d, at 1101. It would be necessary for us to take this step to uphold the statute.

As we have noted, the CPPA is much more than a supplement to the existing federal prohibition on obscenity. Under *Miller v. California*, 413 U.S. 15, 93 S.Ct. 2607, 37 L.Ed.2d 419 (1973), the Government must prove that the work, taken as a whole, appeals to the prurient interest, is patently offensive in light of community standards, and lacks serious literary, artistic, political, or scientific value. *Id.*, at 24, 93 S.Ct. 2607. The CPPA, however, extends to images that appear to depict a minor engaging in sexually explicit activity without regard to the *Miller* requirements. The materials need not appeal to the prurient interest. Any depiction of sexually explicit activity, no matter how it is presented, is proscribed. The CPPA applies to a picture in a psychology manual, as well as a movie depicting the horrors of sexual abuse. It is not necessary, moreover, that the image be patently offensive. Pictures of what appear to be 17-year-olds engaging in sexually explicit activity do not in every case contravene community standards.

The CPPA prohibits speech despite its serious literary, artistic, political, or scientific value. The statute proscribes the visual depiction of an idea — that of teenagers engaging in sexual activity — that is a fact of modern society and has been a theme in art and literature throughout the ages. Under the CPPA, images are prohibited so long as the persons appear to be under 18 years of age. 18 U.S.C. §2256(1). This is higher than the legal age for marriage in many States, as well as the age at which persons may consent to sexual relations. See §2243(a) (age of consent in the federal maritime and territorial jurisdiction is 16); U.S. National Survey of State Laws 384–388 (R. Leiter ed., 3d ed. 1999) (48 States permit 16-year-olds to marry with parental consent); W. Eskridge & N. Hunter, Sexuality, Gender, and the Law 1021–1022 (1997) (in 39 States and the District of Columbia, the age of consent is 16 or younger). It is, of course, undeniable that some youths engage in sexual activity before the legal age, either on their own inclination or because they are victims of sexual abuse.

Both themes — teenage sexual activity and the sexual abuse of children — have inspired countless literary works. William Shakespeare created the most famous pair of teenage lovers, one of whom is just 13 years of age. See Romeo and Juliet, act I, sc. 2, l. 9 ("She hath not seen the change of fourteen years"). In the drama, Shakespeare portrays the relationship as something splendid and innocent, but not juvenile. The work has inspired no less than 40 motion pictures, some of which suggest that the teenagers consummated their relationship. *E.g.*, Romeo and Juliet (B. Luhrmann director, 1996). Shakespeare may not have written sexually explicit scenes for the Elizabethan audience, but were modern directors to adopt a less conventional approach, that fact alone would not compel the conclusion that the work was obscene.

Contemporary movies pursue similar themes. Last year's Academy Awards featured the movie, Traffic, which was nominated for Best Picture. See Predictable and Less So, the Academy Award Contenders, N.Y. Times, Feb. 14, 2001, p. E11. The film portrays a teenager, identified as a 16-year-old, who becomes addicted to drugs. The viewer sees the degradation of her addiction, which in the end leads her to a filthy room to trade sex for drugs. The year before, American Beauty won the Academy Award for Best Picture. See "American Beauty" Tops the Oscars, N.Y. Times, Mar. 27, 2000, p. E1. In the course of the movie, a teenage girl engages in sexual relations with her teenage boyfriend, and another yields herself to the gratification of a middle-aged man. The film also contains a scene where, although the movie audience understands the act is not taking place, one character believes he is watching a teenage boy performing a sexual act on an older man.

Our society, like other cultures, has empathy and enduring fascination with the lives and destinies of the young. Art and literature express the vital interest we all have in the formative years we ourselves once knew, when wounds can be so grievous, disappointment so profound, and mistaken choices so tragic, but when moral acts and self-fulfillment are still in reach. Whether or not the films we mention violate the CPPA, they explore themes within the wide sweep of the statute's prohibitions. If these films, or hundreds of others of lesser note that explore those subjects, contain a single graphic depiction of sexual activity within the statutory definition, the possessor of the film would be subject to severe punishment without inquiry into the work's redeeming value. This is inconsistent with an essential First Amendment rule: The artistic merit of a work does not depend on the presence of a single explicit scene. See Book Named "John Cleland's Memoirs of a Woman of Pleasure" v. Attorney General of Mass., 383 U.S. 413, 419, 86 S.Ct. 975, 16 L.Ed.2d 1 (1966) (plurality opinion) ("[T]he social value of the book can neither be weighed against nor canceled by its prurient appeal or patent offensiveness"). Under Miller, the First Amendment requires that redeeming value be judged by considering the work as a whole. Where the scene is part of the narrative, the work itself does not for this reason become obscene, even though the scene in isolation might be offensive. See Kois v. Wisconsin, 408 U.S. 229, 231, 92 S.Ct. 2245, 33 L.Ed.2d 312 (1972) (per curiam). For this reason, and the others we have noted, the CPPA cannot be read to prohibit obscenity, because it lacks the required link between its prohibitions and the affront to community standards prohibited by the definition of obscenity.

The Government seeks to address this deficiency by arguing that speech prohibited by the CPPA is virtually indistinguishable from child pornography, which may be banned without regard to whether it depicts works of value. See New York v. Ferber, 458 U.S., at 761, 102 S.Ct. 3348. Where the images are themselves the product of child sexual abuse, Ferber recognized that the State had an interest in stamping it out without regard to any judgment about its content. Id., at 761, n. 12, 102 S.Ct. 3348; see also id., at 775, 102 S.Ct. 3348 (O'CONNOR, J., concurring) ("As drafted, New York's statute does not attempt to suppress the communication of particular ideas"). The production of the work, not its content, was the target of the statute. The fact that a work contained serious literary, artistic, or other value did not excuse the harm it caused to its child participants. It was simply "unrealistic to equate a community's toleration for sexually oriented materials with the permissible scope of legislation aimed at protecting children from sexual exploitation." Id., at 761, n. 12, 102 S.Ct. 3348.

Ferber upheld a prohibition on the distribution and sale of child pornography, as well as its production, because these acts were "intrinsically related" to the sexual abuse of children in two ways. Id., at 759, 102 S.Ct. 3348. First, as a permanent record of a child's abuse, the continued circulation itself would harm the child who had participated. Like a defamatory statement, each new publication of the speech would cause new injury to the child's reputation and emotional well-being. See id., at 759, and n. 10, 102 S.Ct. 3348. Second, because the traffic in child pornography was an economic motive for its production, the State had an interest in closing the distribution network. "The most expeditious if not the only practical method of law enforcement may be to dry up the market for this material by imposing severe criminal penalties on persons selling, advertising, or otherwise promoting the product." *Id.*, at 760, 102 S.Ct. 3348. Under either rationale, the speech had what the Court in effect held was a proximate link to the crime from which it came.

Later, in *Osborne v. Ohio*, 495 U.S. 103, 110 S.Ct. 1691, 109 L.Ed.2d 98 (1990), the Court ruled that these same interests justified a ban on the possession of pornography produced by using children. "Given the importance of the State's interest in protecting the victims of child pornography," the State was justified in "attempting to stamp out this vice at all levels in the distribution chain." *Id.*, at 110. *Osborne* also noted the State's interest in preventing child pornography from being used as an aid in the solicitation of minors. *Id.*, at 111, 110 S.Ct. 1691. The Court, however, anchored its holding in the concern for the participants, those whom it called the "victims of child pornography." *Id.*, at 110, 110 S.Ct. 1691. It did not suggest that, absent this concern, other governmental interests would suffice....

In contrast to the speech in *Ferber*, speech that itself is the record of sexual abuse, the CPPA prohibits speech that records no crime and creates no victims by its production. Virtual child pornography is not "intrinsically related" to the sexual abuse of children, as were the materials in *Ferber*. 458 U.S., at 759, 102 S.Ct. 3348. While the Government asserts that the images can lead to actual instances of child abuse, ... the causal link is contingent and indirect. The harm does not necessarily follow from the speech, but depends upon some unquantified potential for subsequent criminal acts.... The Government says these indirect harms are sufficient because, as *Ferber* acknowledged, child pornography rarely can be valuable speech. See 458 U.S., at 762, 102 S.Ct. 3348 ("The value of permitting live performances and photographic reproductions of children engaged in lewd sexual conduct is exceedingly modest, if not *de minimis*"). This argument, however, suffers from two flaws. First, *Ferber's* judgment about child pornography was based upon how it was made, not on what it communicated. The case reaffirmed that where the speech is neither obscene nor the product of sexual abuse, it does not fall outside the protection of the First Amendment. See *id.*, at 764–765, 102 S.Ct. 3348 ("[T]he distribution of descriptions or other depictions of sexual conduct, not otherwise obscene, which do not involve live performance or photographic or other visual reproduction of live performances, retains First Amendment protection").

The second flaw in the Government's position is that *Ferber* did not hold that child pornography is by definition without value. On the contrary, the Court recognized some works in this category might have significant value, see *id.*, at 761, 102 S.Ct. 3348, but relied on virtual images — the very images prohibited by the CPPA — as an alternative and permissible means of expression: "[I]f it were necessary for literary or artistic value, a person over the statutory age who perhaps looked younger could be utilized. Simulation outside of the prohibition of the statute could provide another alternative." *Id.*, at 763, 102 S.Ct. 3348. *Ferber*, then, not only referred to the distinction between actual and virtual child pornography, it relied on it as a reason supporting its holding. *Ferber* provides no support for a statute that eliminates the distinction and makes the alternative mode criminal as well....

The CPPA, for reasons we have explored, is inconsistent with *Miller* and finds no support in *Ferber*. The Government seeks to justify its prohibitions in other ways. It argues that the CPPA is necessary because pedophiles may use virtual child pornography to seduce children. There are many things innocent in themselves, however, such as cartoons, video games, and candy, that might be used for immoral purposes, yet we would not expect those to be prohibited because they can be misused. The Government, of course, may punish adults who provide unsuitable materials to children, see *Ginsberg v. New York*,

390 U.S. 629, 88 S.Ct. 1274, 20 L.Ed.2d 195 (1968), and it may enforce criminal penalties for unlawful solicitation. The precedents establish, however, that speech within the rights of adults to hear may not be silenced completely in an attempt to shield children from it. See *Sable Communications of Cal., Inc. v. FCC*, 492 U.S. 115, 109 S.Ct. 2829, 106 L.Ed.2d 93 (1989). In *Butler v. Michigan*, 352 U.S. 380, 381, 77 S.Ct. 524, 1 L.Ed.2d 412 (1957), the Court invalidated a statute prohibiting distribution of an indecent publication because of its tendency to "'incite minors to violent or depraved or immoral acts.'" A unanimous Court agreed upon the important First Amendment principle that the State could not "reduce the adult population ... to reading only what is fit for children." *Id.*, at 383, 77 S.Ct. 524. We have reaffirmed this holding. See *United States v. Playboy Entertainment Group, Inc.*, 529 U.S. 803, 814, 120 S.Ct. 1878, 146 L.Ed.2d 865 (2000) ("[T]he objective of shielding children does not suffice to support a blanket ban if the protection can be accomplished by a less restrictive alternative"); *Reno v. American Civil Liberties Union*, 521 U.S., at 875, 117 S.Ct. 2329 (The "governmental interest in protecting children from harmful materials ... does not justify an unnecessarily broad suppression of speech addressed to adults"); *Sable Communications v. FCC*, *supra*, at 130–131, 109 S.Ct. 2829 (striking down a ban on "dial-a-porn" messages that had "the invalid effect of limiting the content of adult telephone conversations to that which is suitable for children to hear").

Here, the Government wants to keep speech from children not to protect them from its content but to protect them from those who would commit other crimes. The principle, however, remains the same: The Government cannot ban speech fit for adults simply because it may fall into the hands of children. The evil in question depends upon the actor's unlawful conduct, conduct defined as criminal quite apart from any link to the speech in question. This establishes that the speech ban is not narrowly drawn. The objective is to prohibit illegal conduct, but this restriction goes well beyond that interest by restricting the speech available to law-abiding adults.

The Government submits further that virtual child pornography whets the appetites of pedophiles and encourages them to engage in illegal conduct. This rationale cannot sustain the provision in question. The mere tendency of speech to encourage unlawful acts is not a sufficient reason for banning it. The government "cannot constitutionally premise legislation on the desirability of controlling a person's private thoughts." *Stanley v. Georgia*, 394 U.S. 557, 566, 89 S.Ct. 1243, 22 L.Ed.2d 542 (1969). First Amendment freedoms are most in danger when the government seeks to control thought or to justify its laws for that impermissible end. The right to think is the beginning of freedom, and speech must be protected from the government because speech is the beginning of thought.

To preserve these freedoms, and to protect speech for its own sake, the Court's First Amendment cases draw vital distinctions between words and deeds, between ideas and conduct. See *Kingsley Int'l Pictures Corp.*, 360 U.S., at 689, 79 S.Ct. 1362; see also *Bartnicki v. Vopper*, 532 U.S. 514, 529, 121 S.Ct. 1753, 149 L.Ed.2d 787 (2001) ("The normal method of deterring unlawful conduct is to impose an appropriate punishment on the person who engages in it"). The government may not prohibit speech because it increases the chance an unlawful act will be committed "at some indefinite future time." *Hess v. Indiana*, 414 U.S. 105, 108, 94 S.Ct. 326, 38 L.Ed.2d 303 (1973) (*per curiam*). The government may suppress speech for advocating the use of force or a violation of law only if "such advocacy is directed to inciting or producing imminent lawless action and is likely to incite or produce such action." *Brandenburg v. Ohio*, 395 U.S. 444, 447, 89 S.Ct. 1827, 23 L.Ed.2d 430 (1969) (*per curiam*). There is here no attempt, incitement, solicitation, or conspiracy. The Government has shown no more than a remote connection between speech that might encourage thoughts or impulses and any resulting child abuse. Without a significantly stronger, more direct connection, the Government may not prohibit speech on the ground that it may encourage pedophiles to engage in illegal conduct.

The Government next argues that its objective of eliminating the market for pornography produced using real children necessitates a prohibition on virtual images as well. Virtual images, the Government contends, are indistinguishable from real ones; they are part of the same market and are often exchanged. In this way, it is said, virtual images promote the trafficking in works produced through the exploitation of real children. The hypothesis is somewhat implausible. If virtual images were identical to illegal child pornography, the illegal images would be driven from the market by the indistinguishable substitutes. Few pornographers would risk prosecution by abusing real children if fictional, computerized images would suffice.

In the case of the material covered by *Ferber*, the creation of the speech is itself the crime of child abuse; the prohibition deters the crime by removing the profit motive. See *Osborne*, 495 U.S., at 109–110, 110 S.Ct. 1691. Even where there is an underlying crime, however, the Court has not allowed the suppression of speech in all cases. *E.g., Bartnicki, supra*, at 529, 121 S.Ct. 1753 (market deterrence would not justify law prohibiting a radio commentator from distributing speech that had been unlawfully intercepted). We need not consider where to strike the balance in this case, because here, there is no underlying crime at all. Even if the Government's market deterrence theory were persuasive in some contexts, it would not justify this statute.

Finally, the Government says that the possibility of producing images by using computer imaging makes it very difficult for it to prosecute those who produce pornography by using real children. Experts, we are told, may have difficulty in saying whether the pictures were made by using real children or by using computer imaging. The necessary solution, the argument runs, is to prohibit both kinds of images. The argument, in essence, is that protected speech may be banned as a means to ban unprotected speech. This analysis turns the First Amendment upside down.... The Government may not suppress lawful speech as the means to suppress unlawful speech. Protected speech does not become unprotected merely because it resembles the latter. The Constitution requires the reverse. "[T]he possible harm to society in permitting some unprotected speech to go unpunished is outweighed by the possibility that protected speech of others may be muted...." *Broadrick v. Oklahoma*, 413 U.S., at 612, 93 S.Ct. 2908. The overbreadth doctrine prohibits the Government from banning unprotected speech if a substantial amount of protected speech is prohibited or chilled in the process.

To avoid the force of this objection, the Government would have us read the CPPA not as a measure suppressing speech but as a law shifting the burden to the accused to prove the speech is lawful. In this connection, the Government relies on an affirmative defense under the statute, which allows a defendant to avoid conviction for nonpossession offenses by showing that the materials were produced using only adults and were not otherwise distributed in a manner conveying the impression that they depicted real children. See 18 U.S.C. §2252A(c).

The Government raises serious constitutional difficulties by seeking to impose on the defendant the burden of proving his speech is not unlawful. An affirmative defense applies only after prosecution has begun, and the speaker must himself prove, on pain of a felony conviction, that his conduct falls within the affirmative defense. In cases under the CPPA, the evidentiary burden is not trivial. Where the defendant is not the producer of the work, he may have no way of establishing the identity, or even the existence, of the actors. If the evidentiary issue is a serious problem for the Government, as it asserts, it will be at least as difficult for the innocent possessor. The statute, moreover, applies to work created before 1996, and the producers themselves may not have preserved the records necessary to meet the burden of proof. Failure to establish the defense can lead to a felony conviction.

We need not decide, however, whether the Government could impose this burden on a speaker. Even if an affirmative defense can save a statute from First Amendment challenge, here the defense is incomplete and insufficient, even on its own terms. It allows persons to be convicted in some instances where they can prove children were not exploited in the production. A defendant charged with possessing, as opposed to distributing, proscribed works may not defend on the ground that the film depicts only adult actors. See *ibid.* So while the affirmative defense may protect a movie producer from prosecution for the act of distribution, that same producer, and all other persons in the subsequent distribution chain, could be liable for possessing the prohibited work. Furthermore, the affirmative defense provides no protection to persons who produce speech by using computer imaging, or through other means that do not involve the use of adult actors who appear to be minors. See *ibid.* In these cases, the defendant can demonstrate no children were harmed in producing the images, yet the affirmative defense would not bar the prosecution. For this reason, the affirmative defense cannot save the statute, for it leaves unprotected a substantial amount of speech not tied to the Government's interest in distinguishing images produced using real children from virtual ones.

In sum, § 2256(8)(B) covers materials beyond the categories recognized in *Ferber* and *Miller*, and the reasons the Government offers in support of limiting the freedom of speech have no justification in our precedents or in the law of the First Amendment. The provision abridges the freedom to engage in a substantial amount of lawful speech. For this reason, it is overbroad and unconstitutional....

Respondents challenge § 2256(8)(D) as well. This provision bans depictions of sexually explicit conduct that are "advertised, promoted, presented, described, or distributed in such a manner that conveys the impression that the material is or contains a visual depiction of a minor engaging in sexually explicit conduct." The parties treat the section as nearly identical to the provision prohibiting materials that appear to be child pornography. In the Government's view, the difference between the two is that "the 'conveys the impression' provision requires the jury to assess the material at issue in light of the manner in which it is promoted." ... The Government's assumption, however, is that the determination would still depend principally upon the content of the prohibited work.... We disagree with this view. The CPPA prohibits sexually explicit materials that "conve[y] the impression" they depict minors. While that phrase may sound like the "appears to be" prohibition in § 2256(8)(B), it requires little judgment about the content of the image. Under § 2256(8)(D), the work must be sexually explicit, but otherwise the content is irrelevant. Even if a film contains no sexually explicit scenes involving minors, it could be treated as child pornography if the title and trailers convey the impression that the scenes would be found in the movie. The determination turns on how the speech is presented, not on what is depicted. While the legislative findings address at length the problems posed by materials that look like child pornography, they are silent on the evils posed by images simply pandered that way.

The Government does not offer a serious defense of this provision, and the other arguments it makes in support of the CPPA do not bear on § 2256(8)(D). The materials, for instance, are not likely to be confused for child pornography in a criminal trial. The Court has recognized that pandering may be relevant, as an evidentiary matter, to the question whether particular materials are obscene. See *Ginzburg v. United States*, 383 U.S.

463, 474, 86 S.Ct. 942, 16 L.Ed.2d 31 (1966) ("[I]n close cases evidence of pandering may be probative with respect to the nature of the material in question and thus satisfy the [obscenity] test"). Where a defendant engages in the "commercial exploitation of erotica solely for the sake of their prurient appeal," *id.*, at 466, 86 S.Ct. 942, the context he or she creates may itself be relevant to the evaluation of the materials.

Section 2256(8)(D), however, prohibits a substantial amount of speech that falls outside *Ginzburg's* rationale. Materials falling within the proscription are tainted and unlawful in the hands of all who receive it, though they bear no responsibility for how it was marketed, sold, or described. The statute, furthermore, does not require that the context be part of an effort at "commercial exploitation." *Ibid.* As a consequence, the CPPA does more than prohibit pandering. It prohibits possession of material described, or pandered, as child pornography by someone earlier in the distribution chain. The provision prohibits a sexually explicit film containing no youthful actors, just because it is placed in a box suggesting a prohibited movie. Possession is a crime even when the possessor knows the movie was mislabeled. The First Amendment requires a more precise restriction. For this reason, § 2256(8)(D) is substantially overbroad and in violation of the First Amendment....

For the reasons we have set forth, the prohibitions of §§ 2256(8)(B) and 2256(8)(D) are overbroad and unconstitutional. Having reached this conclusion, we need not address respondents' further contention that the provisions are unconstitutional because of vague statutory language.

The judgment of the Court of Appeals is affirmed.

It is so ordered.

Justice THOMAS, concurring in the judgment.

In my view, the Government's most persuasive asserted interest in support of the Child Pornography Prevention Act of 1996 (CPPA), 18 U.S.C. § 2251 *et seq.*, is the prosecution rationale—that persons who possess and disseminate pornographic images of real children may escape conviction by claiming that the images are computer generated, thereby raising a reasonable doubt as to their guilt.... At this time, however, the Government asserts only that defendants *raise* such defenses, not that they have done so successfully. In fact, the Government points to no case in which a defendant has been acquitted based on a "computer-generated images" defense.... While this speculative interest cannot support the broad reach of the CPPA, technology may evolve to the point where it becomes impossible to enforce actual child pornography laws because the Government cannot prove that certain pornographic images are of real children. In the event this occurs, the Government should not be foreclosed from enacting a regulation of virtual child pornography that contains an appropriate affirmative defense or some other narrowly drawn restriction.

The Court suggests that the Government's interest in enforcing prohibitions against real child pornography cannot justify prohibitions on virtual child pornography, because "[t]his analysis turns the First Amendment upside down. The Government may not suppress lawful speech as the means to suppress unlawful speech." ... But if technological advances thwart prosecution of "unlawful speech," the Government may well have a compelling interest in barring or otherwise regulating some narrow category of "lawful speech" in order to enforce effectively laws against pornography made through the abuse of real children. The Court does leave open the possibility that a more complete affirmative defense could save a statute's constitutionality, ... implicitly accepting that some regulation of virtual child pornography might be constitutional. I would not prejudge, however, whether a more complete affirmative defense is the only way to narrowly tailor a criminal statute that prohibits the possession and dissemination of virtual child pornography. Thus, I concur in the judgment of the Court.

Justice O'CONNOR, with whom THE CHIEF JUSTICE and Justice SCALIA join as to Part II, concurring in the judgment in part and dissenting in part.

The Child Pornography Prevention Act of 1996 (CPPA), 18 U.S.C. § 2251 *et seq.*, proscribes the "knowin[g]" reproduction, distribution, sale, reception, or possession of images that fall under the statute's definition of child pornography, § 2252A(a). Possession is punishable by up to 5 years in prison for a first offense, § 2252A(b), and all other transgressions are punishable by up to 15 years in prison for a first offense, § 2252A(a). The CPPA defines child pornography to include "any visual depiction ... of sexually explicit conduct" where "such visual depiction is, or *appears to be*, of a minor engaging in sexually explicit conduct," § 2256(8)(B) (emphasis added), or "such visual depiction is advertised, promoted, presented, described, or distributed in such a manner that *conveys the impression* that the material is or contains a visual depiction of a minor engaging in sexually explicit conduct," § 2256(8)(D) (emphasis added). The statute defines "sexually explicit conduct" as "actual or simulated— ... sexual intercourse ... ; ... bestiality; ... masturbation; ... sadistic or masochistic abuse; or ... lascivious exhibition of the genitals or pubic area of any person." § 2256(2).

The CPPA provides for two affirmative defenses. First, a defendant is not liable for possession if the defendant possesses less than three proscribed images and promptly destroys such images or reports the matter to law enforcement. § 2252A(d). Second, a defendant is not liable for the remaining acts proscribed in § 2252A(a) if the images involved were produced using only adult subjects and are not presented in such a manner as to "convey the impression" they contain depictions of minors engaging in sexually explicit conduct. § 2252A(c).

This litigation involves a facial challenge to the CPPA's prohibitions of pornographic images that "appea[r] to be ... of a minor" and of material that "conveys the impression" that it contains pornographic images of minors. While I agree with the Court's judgment that the First Amendment requires that the latter prohibition be struck down, I disagree with its decision to strike down the former prohibition in its entirety. The "appears to be ... of a minor" language in § 2256(8)(B) covers two categories of speech: pornographic images of adults that look like children ("youthful adult pornography") and pornographic images of children created wholly on a computer, without using any actual children ("virtual child pornography"). The Court concludes, correctly, that the CPPA's ban on youthful adult pornography is overbroad. In my view, however, respondents fail to present sufficient evidence to demonstrate that the ban on virtual child pornography is overbroad. Because invalidation due to overbreadth is such "strong medicine," *Broadrick v. Oklahoma*, 413 U.S. 601, 613, 93 S.Ct. 2908, 37 L.Ed.2d 830 (1973), I would strike down the prohibition of pornography that "appears to be" of minors only insofar as it is applied to the class of youthful adult pornography....

I disagree with the Court, however, that the CPPA's prohibition of virtual child pornography is overbroad. Before I reach that issue, there are two preliminary questions: whether the ban on virtual child pornography fails strict scrutiny and whether that ban is unconstitutionally vague. I would answer both in the negative.

The Court has long recognized that the Government has a compelling interest in protecting our Nation's children. See *Ferber, supra*, at 756–757, 102 S.Ct. 3348 (citing cases). This interest is promoted by efforts directed against sexual offenders and actual child pornography. These efforts, in turn, are supported by the CPPA's ban on virtual child pornography. Such images whet the appetites of child molesters, ... who may use the images to seduce young children,.... Of even more serious concern is the prospect that defendants indicted for the production, distribution, or possession of actual child pornography may evade liability by claiming that the images attributed to them are in fact computer-generated.... Respondents may be correct that no defendant has successfully employed this tactic. See, *e.g.*, *United States v. Fox*, 248 F.3d 394 (C.A.5 2001); *United States v. Vig*, 167 F.3d 443 (C.A.8 1999); *United States v. Kimbrough*, 69 F.3d 723 (C.A.5 1995); *United States v. Coleman*, 54 M.J. 869 (Army Ct.Crim.App.2001). But, given the rapid pace of advances in computer-graphics technology, the Government's concern is reasonable. Computer-generated images lodged with the Court by *amici curiae* National Law Center for Children and Families et al. bear a remarkable likeness to actual human beings. Anyone who has seen, for example, the film Final Fantasy: The Spirits Within (H. Sakaguchi and M. Sakakibara directors, 2001) can understand the Government's concern. Moreover, this Court's cases do not require Congress to wait for harm to occur before it can legislate against it. See *Turner Broadcasting System, Inc. v. FCC*, 520 U.S. 180, 212, 117 S.Ct. 1174, 137 L.Ed.2d 369 (1997).

Respondents argue that, even if the Government has a compelling interest to justify banning virtual child pornography, the "appears to be ... of a minor" language is not narrowly tailored to serve that interest. See *Sable Communications of Cal., Inc. v. FCC*, 492 U.S. 115, 126, 109 S.Ct. 2829, 106 L.Ed.2d 93 (1989). They assert that the CPPA would capture even cartoon sketches or statues of children that were sexually suggestive. Such images surely could not be used, for instance, to seduce children. I agree. A better interpretation of "appears to be ... of" is "virtually indistinguishable from"—an interpretation that would not cover the examples respondents provide. Not only does the text of the statute comfortably bear this narrowing interpretation, the interpretation comports with the language that Congress repeatedly used in its findings of fact ... See, *e.g.*, Congressional Finding (8), notes following 18 U.S.C. §2251 (discussing how "visual depictions produced wholly or in part by electronic, mechanical, or other means, including by computer, which are virtually indistinguishable to the unsuspecting viewer from photographic images of actual children" may whet the appetites of child molesters). See also *id.*, Findings (5), (12). Finally, to the extent that the phrase "appears to be ... of" is ambiguous, the narrowing interpretation avoids constitutional problems such as overbreadth and lack of narrow tailoring. See *Crowell v. Benson*, 285 U.S. 22, 62, 52 S.Ct. 285, 76 L.Ed. 598 (1932).

Reading the statute only to bar images that are virtually indistinguishable from actual children would not only assure that the ban on virtual child pornography is narrowly tailored, but would also assuage any fears that the "appears to be ... of a minor" language is vague. The narrow reading greatly limits any risks from "'discriminatory enforcement.'" *Reno v. American Civil Liberties Union*, 521 U.S. 844, 872, 117 S.Ct. 2329, 138 L.Ed.2d 874 (1997). Respondents maintain that the "virtually indistinguishable from" language is also vague because it begs the question: from whose perspective? This problem is exaggerated. This Court has never required "mathematical certainty" or "'meticulous specificity'" from the language of a statute. *Grayned v. City of Rockford*, 408 U.S. 104, 110, 92 S.Ct. 2294, 33 L.Ed.2d 222 (1972).

The Court concludes that the CPPA's ban on virtual child pornography is overbroad. The basis for this holding is unclear. Although a content-based regulation may serve a compelling state interest, and be as narrowly tailored as possible while substantially serving that interest, the regulation may unintentionally ensnare speech that has serious literary, artistic, political, or scientific value or that does not threaten the harms sought to be combated by the Government. If so, litigants may challenge the regulation on its face as overbroad, but in doing so they bear the heavy burden of demonstrating that the regulation forbids a substantial amount of valuable or harmless speech. See *Reno, supra,* at 896, 117 S.Ct. 2329 (O'CONNOR, J., concurring in judgment in part and dissenting in part) (citing *Broadrick,* 413 U.S., at 615, 93 S.Ct. 2908). Respondents have not made such a demonstration. Respondents provide no examples of films or other materials that are wholly computer generated and contain images that "appea[r] to be ... of minors" engaging in indecent conduct, but that have serious value or do not facilitate child abuse. Their overbreadth challenge therefore fails....

Although in my view the CPPA's ban on youthful adult pornography appears to violate the First Amendment, the ban on virtual child pornography does not. It is true that both bans are authorized by the same text: The statute's definition of child pornography to include depictions that "appea[r] to be" of children in sexually explicit poses. 18 U.S.C. § 2256(8)(B). Invalidating a statute due to overbreadth, however, is an extreme remedy, one that should be employed "sparingly and only as a last resort." *Broadrick, supra,* at 613, 93 S.Ct. 2908. We have observed that "[i]t is not the usual judicial practice, ... nor do we consider it generally desirable, to proceed to an overbreadth issue unnecessarily." *Board of Trustees of State Univ. of N.Y. v. Fox,* 492 U.S. 469, 484–485, 109 S.Ct. 3028, 106 L.Ed.2d 388 (1989).... Heeding this caution, I would strike the "appears to be" provision only insofar as it is applied to the subset of cases involving youthful adult pornography. This approach is similar to that taken in *United States v. Grace,* 461 U.S. 171, 103 S.Ct. 1702, 75 L.Ed.2d 736 (1983), which considered the constitutionality of a federal statute that makes it unlawful to "parade, stand, or move in processions or assemblages in the Supreme Court Building or grounds, or to display therein any flag, banner, or device designed or adapted to bring into public notice any party, organization, or movement." 40 U.S.C. § 13k (1994 ed.). The term "Supreme Court ... grounds" technically includes the sidewalks surrounding the Court, but because sidewalks have traditionally been considered a public forum, the Court held the statute unconstitutional only when applied to sidewalks.

Although 18 U.S.C. § 2256(8)(B) does not distinguish between youthful adult and virtual child pornography, the CPPA elsewhere draws a line between these two classes of speech. The statute provides an affirmative defense for those who produce, distribute, or receive pornographic images of individuals who are actually adults, § 2252A(c), but not for those with pornographic images that are wholly computer generated. This is not surprising given that the legislative findings enacted by Congress contain no mention of youthful adult pornography. Those findings focus explicitly only on actual child pornography and virtual child pornography. See, *e.g.,* Finding (9), notes following § 2251 ("[T]he danger to children who are seduced and molested with the aid of child sex pictures is just as great when the child pornographer or child molester uses visual depictions of child sexual activity produced wholly or in part by electronic, mechanical, or other means, including by computer, as when the material consists of unretouched photographic images of actual children engaging in sexually explicit conduct"). Drawing a line around, and striking just, the CPPA's ban on youthful adult pornography not only is consistent with Congress' understanding of the categories of speech encompassed by § 2256(8)(B), but also preserves the CPPA's prohibition of the material that Congress found most dangerous to children.

In sum, I would strike down the CPPA's ban on material that "conveys the impression" that it contains actual child pornography, but uphold the ban on pornographic depictions that "appea[r] to be" of minors so long as it is not applied to youthful adult pornography.

Chief Justice REHNQUIST, with whom Justice SCALIA joins in part, dissenting.

I agree with Part II of Justice O'CONNOR's opinion concurring in the judgment in part and dissenting in part. Congress has a compelling interest in ensuring the ability to enforce prohibitions of actual child pornography, and we should defer to its findings that rapidly advancing technology soon will make it all but impossible to do so. *Turner Broadcasting System, Inc. v. FCC*, 520 U.S. 180, 195, 117 S.Ct. 1174, 137 L.Ed.2d 369 (1997) (we "'accord substantial deference to the predictive judgments of Congress'" in First Amendment cases).

I also agree with Justice O'CONNOR that serious First Amendment concerns would arise were the Government ever to prosecute someone for simple distribution or possession of a film with literary or artistic value, such as Traffic or American Beauty.... I write separately, however, because the Child Pornography Prevention Act of 1996 (CPPA), 18 U.S.C. § 2251 *et seq.*, need not be construed to reach such materials.

We normally do not strike down a statute on First Amendment grounds "when a limiting construction has been or could be placed on the challenged statute." *Broadrick v. Oklahoma*, 413 U.S. 601, 613, 93 S.Ct. 2908, 37 L.Ed.2d 830 (1973). See, *e.g.*, *New York v. Ferber*, 458 U.S. 747, 769, 102 S.Ct. 3348, 73 L.Ed.2d 1113 (1982) (appreciating "the wide-reaching effects of striking down a statute on its face"); *Parker v. Levy*, 417 U.S. 733, 760, 94 S.Ct. 2547, 41 L.Ed.2d 439 (1974) ("This Court has ... repeatedly expressed its reluctance to strike down a statute on its face where there were a substantial number of situations to which it might be validly applied"). This case should be treated no differently.

Other than computer-generated images that are virtually indistinguishable from real children engaged in sexually explicit conduct, the CPPA can be limited so as not to reach any material that was not already unprotected before the CPPA. The CPPA's definition of "sexually explicit conduct" is quite explicit in this regard. It makes clear that the statute only reaches "visual depictions" of:

> "[A]ctual or simulated ... sexual intercourse, including genital-genital, oral-genital, anal-genital, or oral-anal, whether between persons of the same or opposite sex; ... bestiality; ... masturbation; ... sadistic or masochistic abuse; or ... lascivious exhibition of the genitals or pubic area of any person." 18 U.S.C. § 2256(2).

The Court and Justice O'CONNOR suggest that this very graphic definition reaches the depiction of youthful looking adult actors engaged in suggestive sexual activity, presumably because the definition extends to "simulated" intercourse.... Read as a whole, however, I think the definition reaches only the sort of "hard core of child pornography" that we found without protection in *Ferber, supra,* at 773–774, 102 S.Ct. 3348. So construed, the CPPA bans visual depictions of youthful looking adult actors engaged in *actual* sexual activity; mere *suggestions* of sexual activity, such as youthful looking adult actors squirming under a blanket, are more akin to written descriptions than visual depictions, and thus fall outside the purview of the statute.[1]

The reference to "simulated" has been part of the definition of "sexually explicit conduct" since the statute was first passed.... See Protection of Children Against Sexual Exploitation Act of 1977, Pub.L. 95-225, 92 Stat. 7. But the inclusion of "simulated" conduct, alongside "actual" conduct, does not change the "hard core" nature of the image banned. The

---

1. Of course, even the narrow class of youthful looking adult images prohibited under the CPPA is subject to an affirmative defense so long as materials containing such images are not advertised or promoted as child pornography. 18 U.S.C. § 2252A(c).

reference to "simulated" conduct simply brings within the statute's reach depictions of hardcore pornography that are "made to look genuine," Webster's Ninth New Collegiate Dictionary 1099 (1983)—including the main target of the CPPA, computer-generated images virtually indistinguishable from real children engaged in sexually explicit conduct. Neither actual conduct nor simulated conduct, however, is properly construed to reach depictions such as those in a film portrayal of Romeo and Juliet, ... which are far removed from the hardcore pornographic depictions that Congress intended to reach.

Indeed, we should be loath to construe a statute as banning film portrayals of Shakespearian tragedies, without some indication—from text or legislative history—that such a result was intended. In fact, Congress explicitly instructed that such a reading of the CPPA would be wholly unwarranted. As the Court of Appeals for the First Circuit has observed:

> "[T]he legislative record, which makes plain that the [CPPA] was intended to target only a narrow class of images—visual depictions 'which are virtually indistinguishable to unsuspecting viewers from unretouched photographs of actual children engaging in identical sexual conduct.'" *United States v. Hilton*, 167 F.3d 61, 72 (1999) (quoting S.Rep. No. 104-358, pt. I, p. 7 (1996)).

Judge Ferguson similarly observed in his dissent in the Court of Appeals in this case:

> "From reading the legislative history, it becomes clear that the CPPA merely extends the existing prohibitions on 'real' child pornography to a narrow class of computer-generated pictures easily mistaken for real photographs of real children." *Free Speech Coalition v. Reno*, 198 F.3d 1083, 1102 (C.A.9 1999).

See also S.Rep. No. 104-358, pt. IV(C), at 21 ("[The CPPA] does not, and is not intended to, apply to a depiction produced using *adults* engaging i[n] sexually explicit conduct, even where a depicted individual may appear to be a minor" (emphasis in original)); *id.*, pt. I, at 7 ("[The CPPA] addresses the problem of 'high-tech kiddie porn'"). We have looked to legislative history to limit the scope of child pornography statutes in the past, *United States v. X-Citement Video, Inc.*, 513 U.S. 64, 73–77, 115 S.Ct. 464, 130 L.Ed.2d 372 (1994), and we should do so here as well.[2]

This narrow reading of "sexually explicit conduct" not only accords with the text of the CPPA and the intentions of Congress; it is exactly how the phrase was understood prior to the broadening gloss the Court gives it today. Indeed, had "sexually explicit conduct" been thought to reach the sort of material the Court says it does, then films such as Traffic and American Beauty would not have been made the way they were.... (discussing these films' portrayals of youthful looking adult actors engaged in sexually suggestive conduct). Traffic won its Academy Award in 2001. American Beauty won its Academy Award in 2000. But the CPPA has been on the books, and has been enforced, since 1996. The chill felt by the Court, ... ("[F]ew legitimate movie producers ... would risk distributing images in or near the uncertain reach of this law"), has apparently never been felt by those who actually make movies.

To the extent the CPPA prohibits possession or distribution of materials that "convey the impression" of a child engaged in sexually explicit conduct, that prohibition can and should be limited to reach "the sordid business of pandering" which lies outside the bounds of First Amendment protection. *Ginzburg v. United States*, 383 U.S. 463, 467, 86 S.Ct. 942, 16 L.Ed.2d 31 (1966); *e.g., id.*, at 472, 86 S.Ct. 942 (conduct that "deliberately

---

2. Justice SCALIA does not join this paragraph discussing the statute's legislative record.

emphasized the sexually provocative aspects of the work, in order to catch the salaciously disposed," may lose First Amendment protection); *United States v. Playboy Entertainment Group, Inc.*, 529 U.S. 803, 831–832, 120 S.Ct. 1878, 146 L.Ed.2d 865 (2000) (SCALIA, J., dissenting) (collecting cases). This is how the Government asks us to construe the statute, ... and it is the most plausible reading of the text, which prohibits only materials "*advertised, promoted, presented, described, or distributed in such a manner* that conveys the impression that the material is or contains a visual depiction of a minor engaging in sexually explicit conduct." 18 U.S.C. § 2256(8)(D) (emphasis added).

The First Amendment may protect the video shopowner or film distributor who promotes material as "entertaining" or "acclaimed" regardless of whether the material contains depictions of youthful looking adult actors engaged in nonobscene but sexually suggestive conduct. The First Amendment does not, however, protect the panderer. Thus, materials promoted as conveying the impression that they depict actual minors engaged in sexually explicit conduct do not escape regulation merely because they might warrant First Amendment protection if promoted in a different manner. See *Ginzburg, supra*, at 474–476, 86 S.Ct. 942; cf. *Jacobellis v. Ohio*, 378 U.S. 184, 201, 84 S.Ct. 1676, 12 L.Ed.2d 793 (1964) (Warren, C. J., dissenting) ("In my opinion, the use to which various materials are put—not just the words and pictures themselves—must be considered in determining whether or not the materials are obscene"). I would construe "conveys the impression" as limited to the panderer, which makes the statute entirely consistent with *Ginzburg* and other cases.

The Court says that "conveys the impression" goes well beyond *Ginzburg* to "prohibi[t][the] possession of material described, or pandered, as child pornography by someone earlier in the distribution chain." ... The Court's concern is that an individual who merely possesses protected materials (such as videocassettes of Traffic or American Beauty) might offend the CPPA regardless of whether the individual actually intended to possess materials containing unprotected images....

This concern is a legitimate one, but there is, again, no need or reason to construe the statute this way. In *X-Citement Video, supra*, we faced a provision of the Protection of Children Against Sexual Exploitation Act of 1977, the precursor to the CPPA, which lent itself much less than the present statute to attributing a "knowingly" requirement to the contents of the possessed visual depictions. We held that such a requirement nonetheless applied, so that the Government would have to prove that a person charged with possessing child pornography actually knew that the materials contained depictions of real minors engaged in sexually explicit conduct. 513 U.S., at 77–78, 115 S.Ct. 464. In light of this holding, and consistent with the narrow class of images the CPPA is intended to prohibit, the CPPA can be construed to prohibit only the knowing possession of materials actually containing visual depictions of real minors engaged in sexually explicit conduct, or computer-generated images virtually indistinguishable from real minors engaged in sexually explicit conduct. The mere possession of materials containing only suggestive depictions of youthful looking adult actors need not be so included.

In sum, while potentially impermissible applications of the CPPA may exist, I doubt that they would be "substantial ... in relation to the statute's plainly legitimate sweep." *Broadrick*, 413 U.S., at 615, 93 S.Ct. 2908. The aim of ensuring the enforceability of our Nation's child pornography laws is a compelling one. The CPPA is targeted to this aim by extending the definition of child pornography to reach computer-generated images that are virtually indistinguishable from real children engaged in sexually explicit conduct. The statute need not be read to do any more than precisely this, which is not offensive to the First Amendment.

For these reasons, I would construe the CPPA in a manner consistent with the First Amendment, reverse the Court of Appeals' judgment, and uphold the statute in its entirety.

People v. Hollins

Supreme Court of Illinois, 2012
361 Ill. Dec. 402, 971 N.E.2d 504

Justice GARMAN delivered the judgment of the court, with opinion....

On March 19, 2009, defendant was charged by information in the circuit court of Stephenson County with three counts of child pornography: (1) between January 1, 2008, and December 1, 2008, defendant knowingly photographed A.V., a child whom defendant knew to be under the age of 18 years, while actually engaged in an act of sexual penetration with defendant, in violation of section 11-20.1(a)(1)(i); (2) between January 1, 2008, and December 1, 2008, defendant knowingly photographed A.V., a child whom defendant knew to be under the age of 18 years, while actually engaged in an act of sexual penetration involving the sex organs of the child, in violation of section 11-20.1(a)(1)(ii); and (3) between January 1, 2008, and December 1, 2008, defendant knowingly used A.V., a child whom defendant knew to be under the age of 18 years, to appear in a photograph in which A.V. would be depicted as actually engaging in an act of sexual penetration with defendant, in violation of section 11-20.1(a)(4)....

[D]efendant admitted that, at the time of the offenses, he was 32 years old and A.V. was 17.... He also argued that because portions of the statute criminalize and punish legal activity, those portions are in violation of the proportionate penalties clause and therefore unconstitutional. A hearing was held on the motion on July 21, 2009, at which the trial court denied the motion.... On August 24, 2009, defendant waived his right to a jury trial and elected to proceed with a bench trial. On September 22, 2009, a stipulated bench trial was held. The first stipulation was from Detective Sergeant Jim Drehoble of the Freeport police department, who would testify that he investigated a complaint made by A.V.'s mother involving A.V. and defendant. She reported to police that her daughter had been having sex with defendant, a 32-year-old registered sex offender. She showed Drehoble four or five pictures depicting sexual penetration that had been sent to A.V.'s e-mail from an e-mail address she knew belonged to defendant. The mother was able to identify A.V. in the pictures because A.V.'s pubic area was shaved. When the interview was completed, Drehoble had the mother e-mail a copy of the photos to his department e-mail.

On January 20, 2009, Drehoble and another detective went to defendant's home and later interviewed him at the Freeport police department. Defendant advised his date of birth was September 13, 1976, and acknowledged he knew A.V. was 17 years old when they had sex. He also knew her birth date. The interview was recorded and attached to the stipulation as part of the record. Also entered as exhibits attached to the stipulation were pictures of defendant and A.V. having sex. Defendant admitted to taking the pictures of himself having sex with A.V. with his cell phone. He acknowledged that he knew A.V. was under age 18 when he had sex with her and took the pictures. Defendant acknowledged that they were in Freeport, Stephenson County, Illinois, when he took pictures of himself and A.V. having sex.

The second stipulation stated that A.V. would testify her birth date is February 8, 1991. She lived with her mother in Freeport. She turned 17 on February 8, 2008, and 18 on February 8, 2009. She met defendant at her home in January 2008 when she was 16. At that time they only talked with each other. She later saw defendant again at Highland College, where they were in some of the same classes together. She and defendant became reacquainted and became friends. She was 17 years old when she went to Highland and had a consensual sexual relationship with defendant. She would testify that during one of the times she had sex with defendant he took a photo or photos of them during the act of sexual intercourse. She, along with her mother, reported this relationship to Drehoble on December 1, 2008. On that date, A.V. was still 17 years old. There was no further sexual relationship between herself and defendant after December 1, 2008. She would identify defendant in court as the person with whom she had a sexual relationship and who had taken the picture or pictures of her during an act of sexual intercourse as defendant had placed his penis inside her vagina.

The third stipulation was that A.V.'s mother would testify that she gave birth to A.V. on February 8, 1991, and her daughter went to Highland College in Freeport. The mother had known defendant, as he was at one time a foster child in her mother's (A.V.'s grand-mother's) household. She brought the pictures to Drehoble after retrieving them from her daughter's e-mail. She noticed the pictures had been sent from an e-mail address she recognized as defendant's. She knew the pictures were of A.V.'s vaginal area because her daughter's pubic area was shaved. After she discussed the matter with Drehoble, the police determined there was no crime for sexual assault or abuse offenses due to the age of her daughter. On January 20, 2009, she again made a complaint to Drehoble in relation to the pictures taken and e-mailed copies of the photos to Drehoble upon his request.... The trial court found defendant guilty of three counts of child pornography and sentenced him to concurrent terms of eight years' imprisonment for each count. Defendant appealed, arguing that the child pornography statute is unconstitutional as applied to him and that his convictions violated the one-act, one-crime doctrine. The appellate court rejected both of defendant's arguments and affirmed his convictions....

At the time defendant was charged and convicted of his offense, the child pornography statute defined "child" as follows:

> "'Child' includes a film, videotape, photograph, or other similar visual medium or reproduction or depiction by computer that is, or appears to be, that of a person, either in part, or in total, under the age of 18, regardless of the method by which the film, videotape, photograph, or other similar visual medium or reproduction or depiction by computer is created, adopted, or modified to appear as such. 'Child' also includes a film, videotape, photograph, or other similar visual medium or reproduction or depiction by computer that is advertised, promoted, presented, described, or distributed in such a manner that conveys the impression that the film, videotape, photograph, or other similar visual medium or reproduction or depiction by computer is of a person under the age of 18." 720 ILCS 5/1y1-20.1(f)(7) (West 2008).[1] ...

---

1. The text of the statute was changed effective July 1, 2011, as follows: "For the purposes of this Section, 'child pornography' includes a film, videotape, photograph, or other similar visual medium or reproduction or depiction by computer that is, or appears to be, that of a person, either in part, or in total, under the age of 18 and at least 13 years of age or a severely or profoundly mentally retarded person, regardless of the method by which the film, videotape, photograph, or other similar visual medium or reproduction or depiction by computer is created, adopted, or modified to appear as such. 'Child pornography' also includes a film, videotape, photograph, or other similar visual medium or reproduction or depiction by computer that is advertised, promoted, presented, described, or distributed in such a manner that conveys the impression that the film, videotape, photograph, or other similar visual medium or reproduction or depiction by computer is of a person under the age

Defendant contends that this statute, as applied, violates the due process clause of both the United States and Illinois constitutions. Defendant concedes that, as this case does not implicate a fundamental right, the test for determining whether the statute complies with substantive due process is the rational basis test. *People v. Dabbs*, 239 Ill.2d 277, 292, 346 Ill.Dec. 484, 940 N.E.2d 1088 (2010). A statute will be upheld under the rational basis test so long as it bears a rational relationship to a legitimate legislative purpose and is neither arbitrary nor unreasonable. *Dabbs*, 239 Ill.2d at 292, 346 Ill.Dec. 484, 940 N.E.2d 1088....

Defendant first argues that the application of the child pornography statute to persons old enough to legally consent to the private sexual activity they have chosen to photograph does nothing to accomplish the legislative purpose of protecting children from sexual exploitation and abuse. Defendant claims that here, no child was being exploited or abused. Rather, the "child" in question was a 17-year-old who, under Illinois law, could legally consent to sex and who was involved in a legal, consensual sexual relationship with her boyfriend. 720 ILCS 5/12-16(d) (West 2008).

In applying the rational basis test, the court must first ascertain the statute's public purpose in order to test whether its provisions reasonably implement that purpose. *People v. Marin*, 342 Ill.App.3d 716, 722–23, 277 Ill.Dec. 285, 795 N.E.2d 953 (2003). The purpose of the child pornography statute is to prevent the sexual abuse and exploitation of children. *People v. Geever*, 122 Ill.2d 313, 326, 119 Ill.Dec. 341, 522 N.E.2d 1200 (1988). This court, citing the United States Supreme Court's decision in *New York v. Ferber*, 458 U.S. 747, 756–59, 102 S.Ct. 3348, 73 L.Ed.2d 1113 (1982), has noted that child pornography is intrinsically related to child sexual abuse and states have a compelling interest in safeguarding the physical and psychological health of children. *People v. Alexander*, 204 Ill.2d 472, 477, 274 Ill.Dec. 414, 791 N.E.2d 506 (2003). "[C]hild pornography is an offense against the child and causes harm 'to the physiological, emotional, and mental health' of the child." *People v. Lamborn*, 185 Ill.2d 585, 588, 236 Ill.Dec. 764, 708 N.E.2d 350 (1999) (quoting *Ferber*, 458 U.S. at 758, 102 S.Ct. 3348). "Child pornography is particularly harmful because the child's actions are reduced to a recording which could haunt the child in future years, especially in light of the mass distribution system for child pornography." *Lamborn*, 185 Ill.2d at 589, 236 Ill.Dec. 764, 708 N.E.2d 350 (citing *Ferber*, 458 U.S. at 759, 102 S.Ct. 3348). The United States Supreme Court has also found that child pornography impacts a child's reputational interest and emotional well-being. *Ashcroft v. Free Speech Coalition*, 535 U.S. 234, 249, 122 S.Ct. 1389, 152 L.Ed.2d 403 (2002).

Thus, the State contends that the statute, as applied, is rationally related to the state's legitimate interest in protecting the psychological welfare of children. Defendant counters that this interest is frustrated when the victim depicted in the photograph is a 17-year-old involved in a legal, consensual relationship. An identical argument was taken up by the Nebraska Supreme Court in *State v. Senters*, 270 Neb. 19, 699 N.W.2d 810 (2005).

In *Senters*, the defendant was charged with making child pornography for videotaping himself having sex with his 17-year-old girlfriend. In Nebraska, while it was legal in most situations for someone over the age of 16 to consent to sex, it was still "unlawful for 'a person to knowingly make, publish, direct, create, provide, or in any manner generate any visual depiction of sexually explicit conduct'" with a person under the age of 18 as one of its participants or portrayed observers. *Senters*, 699 N.W.2d at 813 (quoting

---

of 18 and at least 13 years of age or a severely or profoundly mentally retarded person." 720 ILCS 5/ 11–20.1(f)(7) (West 2010).

Neb.Rev.Stat. § 28-1463.02(1) (Reissue 1995)). "Thus, while the 17-year-old student could legally consent to having sexual relations with Senters, videotaping the act was illegal." *Senters*, 699 N.W.2d at 813–14.

On appeal to the Nebraska Supreme Court, the defendant challenged the statute both on its face and as applied to himself as violative of both the United States and Nebraska constitutions' due process clauses. *Senters*, 699 N.W.2d at 814. The court rejected the defendant's argument that the United States Supreme Court decision in *Lawrence v. Texas*, 539 U.S. 558, 123 S.Ct. 2472, 156 L.Ed.2d 508 (2003), gave him a fundamental right to sexual privacy, and applied the rational basis test. *Senters*, 699 N.W.2d at 817. The court found that "[t]he State undoubtedly has a legitimate reason to ban the creation of child pornography," as it "is often associated with child abuse and exploitation, resulting in physical and psychological harm to the child." *Senters*, 699 N.W.2d at 817. The court was not persuaded by the defendant's argument that the law, at least as it applied to him, was not rationally related to the state's legitimate interest because it also prohibited a person from videotaping lawful sexual conduct for private, noncommercial purposes. The court found that even if the intimate act is intended "to remain secret, a danger exists that the recording may find its way into the public sphere, haunting the child participant for the rest of his or her life. It is reasonable to conclude that persons 16 and 17 years old, although old enough to consent to sexual relations, may not fully appreciate that today's recording of a private, intimate moment may be the Internet's biggest hit next week." *Senters*, 699 N.W.2d at 817.

The court further rejected the defendant's argument that, if the legislature were concerned about reputational harm, it should punish distribution rather than production of the videotape. The court held that "[i]f sexually explicit conduct is not recorded, it cannot be distributed," and thus it was reasonable to find that "criminalizing the making of recordings depicting persons under 18 years of age engaged in sexually explicit conduct furthers the goal of protecting those persons from the reputational harm that would occur if the recordings were distributed." *Senters*, 699 N.W.2d at 818.

A federal court addressing this issue reached a similar conclusion. In *United States v. Bach*, 400 F.3d 622 (8th Cir.2005), cited by the *Senters* court, the defendant was charged with possessing visual depictions which had been produced by using a minor engaged in sexually explicit conduct, transmitting such visual depictions, and using a minor to produce visual depictions of the minor engaged in sexually explicit conduct. *Bach*, 400 F.3d at 628. The defendant, on appeal, argued that, even though a person under 18 constituted a minor for the purposes of the federal child pornography statutes, the images were protected by the liberty and privacy components of the due process clause of the fifth amendment because the photos portrayed noncriminal sexual conduct, as the minor was 16 and the age of consent under Minnesota (the state where the offenses took place) and federal law was 16. The *Bach* court rejected the defendant's *Lawrence*-based argument, finding *Lawrence* not applicable to the defendant's situation. The court noted that Congress changed the definition of a minor in the child pornography laws in 1984 to apply to anyone under 18 because it found that the previous ceiling of 16 had hampered enforcement of child pornography laws since, with the 16-year-old ceiling, there was sometimes confusion about whether a subject was a minor since children enter puberty at different ages. *Bach*, 400 F.3d at 629. The court concluded that the congressional choice to regulate child pornography by defining "minor" as an individual under 18 was rationally related to the government's legitimate interest in enforcing child pornography laws. *Bach*, 400 F.3d at 629.

We find the reasoning employed by the Nebraska Supreme Court in *Senters* and the United States Court of Appeals for the Eighth Circuit in *Bach* persuasive. Under the rational basis analysis, a statute will be upheld so long as it bears a rational relationship to a legitimate legislative purpose, and it is neither arbitrary nor unreasonable. *Dabbs*, 239 Ill.2d at 292, 346 Ill.Dec. 484, 940 N.E.2d 1088. Here, as discussed above, the legitimate government purpose is protecting children from sexual abuse and exploitation, and the prohibition of photographing or videotaping minors engaged in sexual activity bears a rational relationship to protecting them from such abuse. Raising the age to 18, even though the age of consent for sexual activity is 17, is a reasonable means of accomplishing this legitimate government purpose as it aids the State in enforcing child pornography laws. See *Bach*, 400 F.3d at 629; *Dabbs*, 239 Ill.2d at 293–94, 346 Ill.Dec. 484, 940 N.E.2d 1088.

Further, as argued by the State, there are rational, reasonable arguments in support of having a higher age threshold for appearance in pornography than for consent to sexual activity. The consequences of sexual activity are concrete, and for the most part, readily apparent to teenagers: possible pregnancy, sexually transmitted diseases, and emotional issues. Many, if not most, teenagers who are 16 and 17 will have been apprised of these consequences by parents or sexual education classes in school. The dangers of appearing in pornographic photographs or videos are not as readily apparent and can be much more subtle. Memorialization of the sexual act makes permanent an intimate encounter that can then be distributed to third parties. These concerns are exacerbated in the modern digital age, where once a picture or video is uploaded to the Internet, it can never be completely erased or eradicated. It will always be out there, hanging over the head of the person depicted performing the sexual act. Defendant argues that these photographs were meant to be kept private between himself and A.V. and were never intended for distribution to any third party; thus there was no danger of impugning A.V.'s reputational interest. However, despite the best intentions of the parties involved in such a situation, there is no guarantee private photographic images will always remain private. For a variety of reasons, once-private material can someday be made public, whether by accident, theft, or the actions of a scorned former partner. Setting the age of consent at 18 for appearance in pornographic materials is a reasonable, rational approach to protecting children from sexual exploitation or abuse.

In his reply brief, defendant cites to our recent decision in *People v. Madrigal*, 241 Ill.2d 463, 350 Ill.Dec. 311, 948 N.E.2d 591 (2011), in support of his argument that the statute unconstitutionally punishes innocent behavior. The situation in the present case is distinguishable from that which confronted this court in *Madrigal*, where we considered the constitutionality of section 16G-5(a)(7) of the identity theft statute (720 ILCS 5/16G-15(a)(7) (West 2008)). In *Madrigal*, we found the subsection at issue unconstitutional under the rational relationship test because it violated due process. The purpose of the statute was to protect the economy and people of Illinois from the ill-effects of identity theft. *Madrigal*, 241 Ill.2d at 467, 350 Ill.Dec. 311, 948 N.E.2d 591. This court noted that it has repeatedly held that a statute violates substantive due process of both the United States and Illinois constitutions when a statute subjects wholly innocent conduct to criminal penalty without requiring a culpable mental state beyond mere knowledge. *Madrigal*, 241 Ill.2d at 467, 350 Ill.Dec. 311, 948 N.E.2d 591. Such a method is not a reasonable means of preventing the targeted conduct. *Madrigal*, 241 Ill.2d at 468, 350 Ill.Dec. 311, 948 N.E.2d 591.

The subsection at issue in *Madrigal* did not require criminal intent, criminal knowledge, or a criminal purpose in order to subject a person to a felony conviction and punishment. *Madrigal*, 241 Ill.2d at 470–71, 350 Ill.Dec. 311, 948 N.E.2d 591. Rather, the subsection "require[d] only that a person knowingly use any 'personal identification information or personal identification document of another for the purpose of gaining access to any record of the actions taken, communications made or received, or other activities or transactions of that person, without the prior express permission of that person.'" *Madrigal*, 241 Ill.2d at 471, 350 Ill.Dec. 311, 948 N.E.2d 591 (quoting 720 ILCS 5/16G-15(a)(7) (West 2008)). Personal identifying information ranged from readily accessible public information such as a person's name or address to confidential information like a social security or bank account number. The net result was that section 16G-15(a)(7) would potentially punish as a felony a wide array of wholly innocent conduct, such as doing a Google search by entering someone's name, which could uncover numerous records of actions taken, communications made or received, or other activities or transactions of that person. *Madrigal*, 241 Ill.2d at 471–72, 350 Ill.Dec. 311, 948 N.E.2d 591. Thus, because the subsection potentially punished a significant amount of wholly innocent conduct not related to the statute's purpose, the court found it was not a rational way of addressing the issue of identity theft. *Madrigal*, 241 Ill.2d at 473, 350 Ill.Dec. 311, 948 N.E.2d 591.

Unlike the hypothetical situation discussed in *Madrigal*, the conduct at issue here is not "wholly innocent." In *Madrigal*, the term "innocent conduct" meant conduct not germane to the harm identified by the legislature, in that the conduct was wholly unrelated to the legislature's purpose in enacting the law. *Madrigal*, 241 Ill.2d at 473, 350 Ill.Dec. 311, 948 N.E.2d 591. Here, while it is true that the underlying conduct being recorded is legal, it is the actual recording of that conduct, and the consequences to the child that flow therefrom, that is the interest being protected by the statute as applied. The legislature's purpose in enacting the statute was not necessarily to protect from the harm in the sexual act itself, but the memorialization of that act, for the reasons discussed above....

Here, defendant does not make any argument or claim that government agents or action invaded his privacy. Rather, he claims the existence of the law itself criminalizing the recording of a consensual, legal sexual encounter violates the privacy clause. The act itself is not at issue. The issue is the recording of that act. The legislature has determined that those who are under the age of 18 may not legally consent to be recorded or photographed in pornographic material, and has made it illegal to record such material in order to protect those who are under 18 from sexual abuse and exploitation. The mere fact that the illegal recording of the sexual act in question took place in private, rather than in public, does not implicate the privacy clause.... We find the reasoning of the *Senters* court to be both persuasive and applicable in this case. The statute is clear that persons under age 18 may not be represented in visual depictions of sexual activity. Defendant's only real argument here seems to be that, because he knew he could have sex with a 17-year-old, he did not know, and it is not fair, that it was illegal to record that sexual encounter with the same 17-year-old. As stated above, the statute is clear and definite, and ignorance of the statute is no defense. *People v. Izzo*, 195 Ill.2d 109, 115, 253 Ill.Dec. 425, 745 N.E.2d 548 (2001) ("A principle deeply embedded in our system of jurisprudence is that one's ignorance of the law does not excuse unlawful conduct.")....

Defendant next argues that the application of the statute to him violates the equal protection clauses of the United States and Illinois constitutions. Defendant claims that he belongs to a class of people (such as the defendants in *Senters* and *Bach*) who engage in legal sexual activities with consensual partners and choose to photograph their private interactions, thereby violating child pornography statutes that define child so as to include such otherwise legal sex partners. Defendant was not in the same position as a person who photographs a child not old enough to engage in sexual activity, but rather defendant argues he was in the same position as anyone who photographs his or her legal, consenting sex partner. According to defendant, it is not reasonable or fair for the legislature to prohibit the sex partners of such people from photographing such otherwise lawful, private, sexual activity.

"The court applies the same equal protection analysis under both the United States and Illinois Constitutions." [*People v.*] *Donoho*, 204 Ill.2d [159,] 176, 273 Ill.Dec. 116, 788 N.E.2d 707 [(2003)]. Equal protection challenges generally require the government to treat similarly situated people in a similar manner. *Donoho*, 204 Ill.2d at 176–77, 273 Ill.Dec. 116, 788 N.E.2d 707. In evaluating challenges under equal protection, the court must first determine whether the statute implicates a fundamental right or whether it discriminates against a suspect class. *Donoho*, 204 Ill.2d at 177, 273 Ill.Dec. 116, 788 N.E.2d 707. Defendant concedes that his equal protection claim is subject to a rational basis analysis, thereby implicitly acknowledging he is not a member of a suspect class and no fundamental right is at issue. *Donoho*, 204 Ill.2d at 177, 273 Ill.Dec. 116, 788 N.E.2d 707 ("[w]here no suspect class or fundamental right is involved, the court evaluates the statute using the rational basis test"). Under the rational basis test, we will uphold the statute if it has a rational relationship to a legitimate purpose and is neither arbitrary nor discriminatory. *Donoho*, 204 Ill.2d at 177, 273 Ill.Dec. 116, 788 N.E.2d 707.

Here, the *Senters* decision is again instructive. The defendant in *Senters* challenged the law under equal protection, arguing that he had a fundamental right to sexual privacy under the *Lawrence* case and claimed that the age classification used in the Nebraska law was overinclusive because it prohibited recording sex acts that were legal. *Senters*, 699 N.W.2d at 818. The *Senters* court disagreed and applied the rational basis test, concluding that the law survived rational basis review for the same reasons set out in the court's discussion of substantive due process. *Senters*, 699 N.W.2d at 818.

Similarly, for reasons discussed above in the due process section of this opinion, application of the statute to defendant does not violate equal protection. Defendant is not a member of a suspect class and no fundamental right is implicated. The statute's requirement that a person be 18 or older to engage in the memorialization of a sexual act has a rational relationship to the legitimate purpose of preventing the sexual abuse or exploitation of children. Further, the statute's age requirement is neither arbitrary nor discriminatory, for reasons also discussed in the previous section....

For the foregoing reasons, we find no violation of either the United States or the Illinois constitution in the application of the child pornography statute to defendant. The judgments of the circuit and appellate courts are affirmed.

Affirmed.

Chief Justice KILBRIDE and Justices THOMAS, KARMEIER, and THEIS concurred in the judgment and opinion.

Justice BURKE dissented, with opinion, joined by Justice FREEMAN.

Justice BURKE, dissenting:

I write separately because the majority has overlooked *United States v. Stevens*, 559 U.S. [460], 130 S.Ct. 1577, 176 L.Ed.2d 435 (2010), an important decision from the United States Supreme Court that fundamentally affects the way the present case must be analyzed....

On one occasion while they were engaged in sexual intercourse, defendant used his cellphone camera to take five photographs of himself and A.V. All five photographs are extreme closeups of the couples' genitals. Neither defendant's nor A.V.'s face appears in any of the photographs and there are no visible identifying marks such as scars or tattoos.... At the request of A.V., defendant sent the photographs to A.V.'s e-mail account. Neither defendant nor A.V. had any intent to distribute the photographs to third parties and no attempt was made to do so. The photographs were discovered, however, when A.V.'s mother accessed A.V.'s e-mail account. A.V.'s mother contacted the Freeport police, who then spoke to defendant....

While the age of consent in Illinois is generally 17, Illinois' child pornography statute sets the age at which a person may legally be photographed engaging in sexually explicit conduct at 18. Thus, while defendant did not violate any law when he had sexual intercourse with A.V., he did violate the law when he took a picture of the act.... Defendant challenges this statutory scheme on constitutional grounds. In essence, defendant alleges that the State violated his right to substantive due process when it applied the child pornography statute to him because the photographs that he took of himself and A.V. depict private, lawful conduct.

The majority addresses defendant's constitutional claim under rational basis review. The majority does so based on defendant's concession that no fundamental constitutional rights, including first amendment rights, are implicated by criminally prohibiting the photographs taken by defendant. See, *e.g.*, *In re D.W.*, 214 Ill.2d 289, 310, 292 Ill.Dec. 937, 827 N.E.2d 466 (2005) ("Unless a fundamental constitutional right is implicated, the rational basis test applies, and the statute will be upheld so long as it bears a rational relationship to a legitimate state interest."). The proposition that the photographs are not entitled to first amendment protection stems, in turn, from the United States Supreme Court's decision in *New York v. Ferber*, 458 U.S. 747, 102 S.Ct. 3348, 73 L.Ed.2d 1113 (1982).

In *Ferber*, the Court considered a first amendment challenge to a statute which prohibited persons from "knowingly promoting sexual performances by children under the age of 16 by distributing material which depicts such performances." *Id.* at 749, 102 S.Ct. 3348. The defendant in the case had sold two films that showed young boys masturbating. *Id.* at 752, 102 S.Ct. 3348.... The Court upheld the statute and, in so doing, recognized a "category of child pornography which * * * is unprotected by the First Amendment." *Id.* at 764, 102 S.Ct. 3348. The Court identified several policy justifications for excluding child pornography from first amendment protection: (1) it is a governmental objective of "surpassing importance" to prevent the "sexual exploitation and abuse of children" that occurs in the creation of the material (*id.* at 756–57, 102 S.Ct. 3348); (2) the distribution of the material is "intrinsically related to the sexual abuse of children," both because the materials produced are a "permanent record" of the children's participation and the harm to the child is exacerbated by their circulation, and because prohibiting distribution of the material is the only effective way to stop "the production of material which requires the sexual exploitation of children" (*id.* at 759, 102 S.Ct. 3348); (3) it is a crime "throughout the Nation" to employ children in the creation of pornography, and thus the advertising and selling of child pornography provide an "economic motive" for and are "an integral part of" that criminal activity (*id.* at 761–62, 102 S.Ct. 3348); (4) "[t]he value of permitting live performances and photographic reproductions of children engaged in lewd sexual conduct is exceedingly modest, if not *de minimis*" (*id.* at 762, 102 S.Ct. 3348). For these reasons, the Court concluded that "the evil to be restricted * * * overwhelmingly outweighs the expressive interests, if any, at stake" and "it is permissible to consider these materials as without the protection of the First Amendment." *Id.* at 763–64, 102 S.Ct. 3348. Subsequently, in *Osborne v. Ohio*, 495 U.S. 103, 110 S.Ct. 1691, 109 L.Ed.2d 98 (1990), the Court relied on the rationales discussed in *Ferber* to extend the categorical exclusion for child pornography to include not only distribution but also possession of the material.

Ferber was read by courts, including this one, as having defined a broad category of unprotected expressive content — visual depictions of sexual conduct, "suitably" defined by statute, of children under "a specified age." *People v. Lamborn*, 185 Ill.2d 585, 590, 236 Ill.Dec. 764, 708 N.E.2d 350 (1999) (citing *Ferber*, 458 U.S. at 764–65, 102 S.Ct. 3348). This categorical exclusion was justified by the harms of child pornography discussed in *Ferber*, but it was widely assumed that those harms did not have to be present in an individual case for the material to be unprotected. That is, *Ferber* appeared to hold that the scope of the child pornography category was "not limited to materials whose production would generate the harms that the categorical exclusion was based on." John A. Humbach, *'Sexting' and the First Amendment*, 37 Hastings Const. L.Q. 433, 458 (2010). Rather, the category of constitutionally unprotected content was simply visual depictions of sexual conduct by children under a specified age.

This broad reading of *Ferber* was called into question by the Supreme Court's decision in *Ashcroft v. Free Speech Coalition*, 535 U.S. 234, 122 S.Ct. 1389, 152 L.Ed.2d 403 (2002). In that case, the Court struck down on first amendment grounds a federal law that criminalized sexually explicit images that appear to depict minors but that were produced without using any real children, *i.e.*, "virtual" child pornography. In reaching this result, the Court distinguished *Ferber* in language that seemed to suggest that the category of child pornography exempted from first amendment protection was "not merely justified but also shaped by reference to the particular harms that motivated its creation." Humbach, *supra*, at 461.... The Court, stated, for example, that "*Ferber's* judgment about child pornography was based upon how it was made, not on what it communicated" (*Free Speech Coalition*, 535 U.S. at 250–51, 122 S.Ct. 1389), and that the "production of the work, not its content, was the target of the statute" (*id.* at 249, 122 S.Ct. 1389). The Court distinguished "virtual" child pornography from unprotected child pornography by stating that, "[i]n the case of the material covered by *Ferber*, the creation of the speech is itself the crime of child abuse" whereas with virtual child pornography "there is no underlying crime at all." *Id.* at 254, 122 S.Ct. 1389. The Court also observed that "[i]n contrast to the speech in *Ferber*, speech that itself is the record of sexual abuse, [virtual pornography] records no crime and creates no victims by its production." *Id.* at 250, 122 S.Ct. 1389.

In short, *Free Speech Coalition* seemed "to view crime prevention as the core reason why the Court should deny constitutional protection to child-pornography materials." Humbach, *supra*, at 462; see also, *e.g.*, Sarah Wastler, *The Harm in "Sexting"?: Analyzing the Constitutionality of Child Pornography Statutes That Prohibit the Voluntary Production, Possession, and Dissemination of Sexually Explicit Images by Teenagers*, 33 Harv. J.L. & Gender 687, 697 (2010) ("*Free Speech Coalition* clarified that child pornography was limited to those images that are the 'record of sexual abuse' and that sexually explicit images of minors that are 'neither obscene nor the product of sexual abuse' retain the protection of the First Amendment.").... Nevertheless, the facts of *Free Speech Coalition* were limited to virtual images, not images of real people. Arguably, therefore, the broad categorical exclusion from first amendment protection of sexually explicit images of children under a specified age remained unchanged, even after *Free Speech Coalition*.

The broad categorical exclusion underlies the majority opinion here. Because the category of child pornography exempted from first amendment protection is presumed by the majority to include any sexually explicit pictures of persons under a specified age, it does not matter that A.V.'s sexual conduct with defendant was legal and consensual. Nor does it matter, as a general proposition, that there are significant differences between criminally, sexually abusing a 9- or 10-year-old child in order to create and distribute commercial child pornography, and taking private photographs of legal, consensual sexual activity. All that matters under this approach is that the person who was photographed engaged in sexual conduct is under a specified age, in this case 18. So long as this criteria is met, as it was in this case, then the photographs receive no first amendment protection and the state's decision to criminalize their creation is subject only to rational basis review.

But this analysis is no longer valid after *United States v. Stevens*, 559 U.S. [460], 130 S.Ct. 1577, 176 L.Ed.2d 435 (2010). In *Stevens*, the Court considered a first amendment challenge to a federal statute that criminalized the creation, sale, or possession of certain depictions of animal cruelty. The government, arguing in support of the statute, pointed to *Ferber* and argued that, as in that case, the Court should recognize a category of speech exempted from first amendment protection. The Court described the government's argument as "a free-floating" balancing test for first amendment coverage and rejected it as both "startling and dangerous." *Stevens*, 559 U.S. at [460], 130 S.Ct. at 1585. The Court then explained how *Ferber* should be understood:

> "When we have identified categories of speech as fully outside the protection of the First Amendment, it has not been on the basis of a simple cost-benefit analysis. In *Ferber*, for example, we classified child pornography as such a category, 458 U.S., at 763 [102 S.Ct. 3348]. We noted that the State of New York had a compelling interest in protecting children from abuse, and that the value of using children in these works (as opposed to simulated conduct or adult actors) was *de minimis*. *Id.*, at 756–757, 762 [102 S.Ct. 3348]. But our decision did not rest on this 'balance of competing interests' alone. *Id.*, at 764 [102 S.Ct. 3348]. We made clear that *Ferber* presented a special case: The market for child pornography was 'intrinsically related' to the underlying abuse, and was therefore 'an integral part of the production of such materials, an activity illegal throughout the Nation.' *Id.*, at 759, 761 [102 S.Ct. 3348]. As we noted, ' "[i]t rarely has been suggested that the constitutional freedom for speech and press extends its immunity to speech or writing used as an integral part of conduct in violation of a valid criminal statute." ' *Id.*, at 761–762 [102 S.Ct. 3348] (quoting *Giboney [v. Empire Storage & Ice Co.*, 336 U.S. 490, 498, 69 S.Ct. 684, 93 L.Ed. 834 (1949)]). Ferber thus grounded its analysis in a previously recognized, long-established category of unprotected speech, and our subsequent decisions have shared this understanding. See *Osborne v. Ohio*, 495 U.S. 103, 110 [110 S.Ct. 1691, 109 L.Ed.2d 98] (1990) (describing *Ferber* as finding 'persuasive' the argument that the advertising and sale of child pornography was 'an integral part' of its unlawful production (internal quotation marks omitted)); *Ashcroft v. Free Speech Coalition*, 535 U.S. 234, 249–250, 122 S.Ct. 1389, 152 L.Ed.2d 403 (2002) (noting that distribution and sale 'were intrinsically related to the sexual abuse of children,' giving the speech at issue 'a proximate link to the crime from which it came' (internal quotation marks omitted))." *Stevens*, 559 U.S. at ___, 130 S.Ct. at 1586.

After rejecting the government's reliance on *Ferber*, the Court went on to strike down the statute at issue on overbreadth grounds.

Following *Stevens* it is clear that there is no first amendment exception for child pornography, *per se*. Rather, child pornography is simply one example of an historical category of speech that is exempted from first amendment protection: speech that is an "integral part of conduct in violation of a valid criminal statute." Or, to put it another way, for a photograph to be child pornography in the federal constitutional sense, and thus be exempted from first amendment protection, the photograph must be "an integral part of conduct in violation of a valid criminal statute."

Stevens was one of [the] "most doctrinally significant constitutional opinions of the Supreme Court's October 2009 Term" (Charles W. "Rocky" Rhodes, *The Historical Approach to Unprotected Speech and the Quantitative Analysis of Overbreadth in United States v. Stevens,* 559 U.S. ___, 130 S.Ct. 1577, 176 L.Ed.2d 435 (2010), 2010 Emerging Issues 5227 (LexisNexis July 30, 2010)), and its effect on the constitutional definition of child pornography has been widely recognized:

> "[W]hereas before *Stevens* many believed—perhaps erroneously—that any sexually explicit image of a minor was child pornography, this belief is now fatally flawed. Instead, in determining whether a particular nonobscene image constitutes child pornography, the initial question must be whether there is specific illegal conduct to which the speech is integral." Antonio Haynes, *The Age of Consent: When is Sexting No Longer 'Speech Integral to Criminal Conduct'?,* 97 Cornell L. Rev. 369, 394–95 (2012).

> "The *Stevens* Court reconciles *Ferber, Osborne,* and *Free Speech Coalition* to the conclusion that the creation of child pornography is a criminal act and the depiction thereof is the subject of a previously recognized and long-standing category of unprotected speech. Absent this connection between the image and the crime, First Amendment protection is presumed." Carmen Naso, *Sext Appeals: Re-assessing the Exclusion of Self-Created Images From First Amendment Protection,* 7 Crim. L. Brief 4, 11 (2011).

> "[I]n *Stevens* the Supreme Court recast its *Ferber* decision as having been squarely grounded in the longstanding categorical First Amendment exclusion of expression that is 'an integral part of conduct in violation of a valid criminal statute.' In the *Ferber* case, the particular 'integral' relationship between the expressive material at issue—child pornography—and the underlying criminal conduct—sexual abuse of children—was the fact that the criminal conduct was carried out in order to generate the expressive material * * *." Nadine Strossen, *A Big Year For the First Amendment: United States v. Stevens: Restricting Two Major Rationales for Content-Based Speech Restrictions,* 2009–10 Cato Sup.Ct. Rev. 67, 90.

> "[*Stevens*] explained *Ferber* as a special case because the child pornography market is 'intrinsically related' to the underlying abuse. According to *Stevens, Ferber* did not affirm a new exception to the First Amendment, but was a special example of the historically unprotected category of speech integral to the commission of a crime." Harvard Law Review Association, *The Supreme Court 2009 Term, Leading Cases, I. Constitutional Law, D. Freedom of Speech and Expression,* 124 Harv. L. Rev. 239, 247 (2010).

> "Any doubts as to the limits of *Ferber* and *Osborne,* pertaining to the policy justifications for child pornography prohibitions, were laid to rest by the recent Supreme Court decision in *U.S. v. Stevens,* where the Court made it clear that child pornography laws cannot be constitutionally applied in circumstances where no actual minor is sexually abused during the production of the material. Accordingly, child pornography can only be stripped of its constitutional protection if it records actual sexual abuse of child victims." Lawrence Walters, *Symposium, Sexually Explicit Speech, How to Fix the Sexting Problem: An Analysis of the Legal and Policy Considerations for Sexting Legislation,* 9 First Amend. L. Rev. 98, 113–14 (2010).

Stevens' importance to this case is clear. There was nothing unlawful about the production of the photographs taken by defendant in this case because the sexual conduct between defendant and A.V. was entirely legal. The photographs are therefore not child pornography as defined by the Supreme Court for purposes of the first amendment. And, because the photographs taken by defendant are not child pornography for purposes of the first amendment, we cannot simply presume that rational basis review is appropriate in this case.... [footnote omitted].

Stevens was decided in April of 2010, well before defendant filed his appeal in this court. Nevertheless, despite the availability of *Stevens*, and despite its clear relevance, defendant's appellate counsel has not cited the case. To the contrary, as noted above, defendant's counsel has expressly conceded that the photographs at issue here are not entitled to first amendment protection and that the State's application of the child pornography statute in this case is subject only to rational basis review.

A court of review is not required to accept a concession by a party on an issue of law. See, *e.g.*, *United States v. Vega-Ortiz*, 425 F.3d 20, 22 (1st Cir.2005); *Deen v. Darosa*, 414 F.3d 731, 734 (7th Cir.2005). *Stevens* is binding authority on this court, and the decision goes to a core issue in this case—the level of scrutiny to apply to defendant's constitutional challenge. Moreover, because *Stevens* was decided after *State v. Senters*, 270 Neb. 19, 699 N.W.2d 810 (2005), and *United States v. Bach*, 400 F.3d 622 (8th Cir.2005), the two principal cases relied upon by the majority, it was not discussed in those cases. Further, this is a criminal case with a substantial liberty interest at stake. Given these circumstances, I would reject defense counsel's concession. I would order the parties to brief the effect of *Stevens*' holding—that child pornography, for purposes of the first amendment, exists only if it is "an integral part of conduct in violation of a valid criminal statute"—on our disposition of this case.

For the foregoing reasons, I respectfully dissent.

Justice FREEMAN joins in this dissent.

Notes

Because of the exponential growth of the pornography industry, especially as a result of the global accessibility of the Internet, the constitutional balance shifts in favor of expansive restrictions within the child pornography industry. As evidenced in the many cases included within this casebook, efforts to expand protections for children in response to the ever-advancing capabilities of the Internet to create and disseminate material that involves the sexual exploitation of children, efforts to protect children have expanded into the adult pornography industry. One measure implemented to combat child pornography is the record-keeping, labeling, and inspection requirements of the Child Protection and Obscenity Enforcement Act, *see* 18 U.S.C. §§ 2257 & 2257A, which is discussed in the following case. These provisions require producers of sexually explicit media, of all genres, to maintain records regarding the location and content of all sexually explicit material (primarily, the age of the participating models) and to submit to inspections of their private business premises (and sometimes at producers' private residences if that is where they maintain the relevant records) "at all reasonable times." *Id.* at §§ 2257(c) & 2257A(c). Although the opinion included here is significantly excerpted, note how the court deals with the global accessibility of the Internet, as well as society's alarming growing interest in sexually explicit material involving children. In light of the ever-increasing technological advancements of the Internet, what are the limits of government restriction in combating child pornography?

Free Speech Coalition, Inc. v. Holder

United States District Court, Eastern District of Pennsylvania, 2013
957 F. Supp. 2d 564

BAYLSON, District Judge.

The extent to which the adult porn industry utilizes young-looking performers is the central fact issue in the trial of this case. The attraction of males to younger women is not a new story. Mozart focused on this theme in several of his operas. In *The Magic Flute*, Papageno, the lonely bird-catcher, wonders how he is ever going to meet someone who will become his wife. When a woman dressed as an old hag expresses some interest in him, in a raspy, elderly voice, Papageno expresses revulsion; but when this woman later sheds her outer garments, revealing a very youthful and pretty soprano, they fall in love and prance off to the famous tunes of "Pap, Pap ... Pap, Pap ... Pap, Pap, Pap ..." Mozart used the same theme in *Don Giovanni*, where the nobleman seduces a naïve young lady, Zerlina, and in the *Marriage of Figaro*, where the Count is attracted to the young chamber-maid, Susannah. In literature, Faust was enamored of Margaret; Dante celebrated the youthful Francesca Da Rimini; and Hawthorne created Hester Prynne, heroine of *The Scarlet Letter*. But we need not go back several hundred years for these metaphors. In *Lolita*, Vladmir Nabakov used the same theme to great notoriety, but also to great acclaim. His hero, Humbert Humbert's opening line, "the fire in my loins," set the tone for his enchantment with a nymphet.

Plaintiffs are a group of adult pornography producers, photographers, artists, and educators, who devote substantial time and energies to the creation of erotic and sexually explicit works. They seek a declaratory judgment and an injunction against the enforcement of 18 U.S.C. § 2257 and 2257A ("the Statutes") and their corresponding regulations, which impose recordkeeping, labeling, and inspection requirements on producers of sexually explicit media. Plaintiffs contend the Statutes and their corresponding regulations run afoul of the First and Fourth Amendment because they burden an excessive amount of speech and allow for unreasonable, warrantless inspections....

Eugene Mopsik, the Executive Director of the American Society of Media Photographers ("ASMP"), an organizational plaintiff, testified for Plaintiffs about the burdens that Sections 2257 and 2257A impose on commercial photographers. Mopsik explained that because of the rise of digital media, photographers are no longer constrained "by what they can carry" and instead have the ability to produce thousands of images at a single photo shoot. However, the understanding in the industry is that Section 2257 requires that records be maintained for—and statements about the location of the records be affixed to—every photograph of sexually explicit content taken at a shoot. This is a significant burden. While photographers commonly store information such as whether a photograph is copyrighted in the photograph's "metadata," Mopsik explained, the regulations require that Section 2257 statements be prominently affixed to the exterior of the photograph itself. Mopsik had no idea how a photographer could comply with that particular requirement....

Additionally, Mopsik testified that it is common practice in the commercial photography industry to require that models sign "model releases," authorizing the photographer to license the images taken and to make use of them thereafter. ASMP encourages its members to use model releases. To ensure that the model release is a valid contract, photographers commonly check the model's identification to ensure he or she is at least 18 years old. This testimony by Mopsik suggested that Sections 2257 and 2257A do not make photographers do anything they weren't already doing to ensure their models are adults—they only impose additional, unnecessary record-keeping burdens on photographers....

Barbara Alper also testified for Plaintiffs. She is a commercial photographer who has documented sexual subcultures throughout the world.... Alpre testified to several ways the Statutes suppress her artistic endeavors. First, they have "seriously affected" her ability to photograph couples in intimate settings, because private citizens do not wish to make their identifications available for government inspection.... Additionally, the Statutes are preventing Alper from pursuing a documentary project on Fire Island, New York, where she would photograph members of an adult, gay community engaging in anonymous sex. Section 2257 is an obstacle to this project because the intended subject matter—anonymous sex—is fundamentally at odds with the collection of photo identification of the subjects....

The next category of witnesses to testify for Plaintiffs was individuals who work as sexologists, sex educators and journalists.... Carlin Ross and Betty Dodson are also sex educators ... who produce educational films about sex and maintain a website ... dedicated to sexuality and genitalia. The website offers a weekly podcast about sexual topics ... and for paid subscribers, a "genital art gallery." ... Several individuals who work in or with the commercial pornography industry also testified for Plaintiffs.... [Discussion of the § 2257 burdens faced by these individuals is omitted here]....

Jeffery Douglas, Chairman of the Board of the Free Speech Coalition ("FSC"), also testified for Plaintiffs. FSC is the lead Plaintiff in this case. It is a trade association that represents businesses and individuals who produce adult-oriented materials, often containing actual and/or simulated sexually explicit content.... FSC's members include large-scale producers of commercial pornography, such as Vivid Video, Wicked Pictures, K Beech, and Dark Side.... Since 1988, Douglas has worked as an attorney in the adult entertainment industry, advising clients about Section 2257. Accordingly, he has significant personal knowledge about the compliance issues associated with 2257.... Douglas testified that the Statutes impose onerous burdens on secondary producers of sexually explicit products—distributors have to collect information from primary producers; they have cross-reference the appearances of any model in a work they sell across all other appearances by that model in other works they sell; and they have to hire "screeners" at their warehouses to make sure the labels on the products they receive from primary producers are in the correct location. Douglas also testified that the 20 hour/week requirement is difficult for primary producers to comply with, because they are often in the field on photo shoots. The ability to use a third-party custodian is not a panacea, because if the custodian makes a mistake, the producer is still criminally liable.... Further, Douglas explained that before 2257, "it was universal" for producers in the adult entertainment industry to use model releases and to have "some statement of age" in the release.... Regardless of the Statutes, "no sane producer would knowingly use a minor" because there are criminal sanctions involved, the materials have to be recalled and destroyed, and the model release would be invalid.... Accordingly, similar to Mopsik, Douglas suggested Section 2257 is not forcing primary producers in the pornography business to do anything they wouldn't already do—that is, ensure their subjects are at least 18 years old—but is merely imposing unnecessary costs on producers....

[Omitted here is the court's description of the creation of the inspection program and the dynamics of a typical inspection, as well as the selection process for the producers that were subject to inspection. Testimony evidenced that standard inspections were considerably less time-consuming and less intrusive than those that would normally take place pursuant to a search warrant in an investigation involving business records.]

Reviewing the evidence presented at trial, the Court reaches the following factual findings as to the First and Fourth Amendment issues in the case. These findings supplement those stated on the record at the conclusion of testimony on Friday, June 7, 2013....

1. *Credibility of Plaintiffs' Testimony:* The majority of Plaintiffs ... are "niche" players in the adult entertainment industry with unique and often creative approaches to sexually explicit conduct. These individuals testified, credibly, that it is their sincere belief that the use of sexually explicit material is a valued artistic endeavor and also serves valued educational motives. At the same time, the overwhelming nature of Plaintiffs' involvement in the adult pornography industry is commercial—virtually every witness for Plaintiffs was involved in some form of sale or distribution for income of sexually explicit depictions. Additionally, what these individuals find meaningful at a personal level can often be purchased or used by consumers in different ways. Once the work is distributed to third parties, it may serve other, less noble purposes....

3. *Pervasiveness of Youthful-Looking Performers in Pornography in General:* Youthful-looking performers are ubiquitous in the adult entertainment industry and there is a significant market for pornographic materials depicting such individuals. Some of the most popular categories of commercial pornography, such as "teen porn," "college porn" and "twinks" (gay teen porn), are popular precisely because they depict women and men who appear to be 18, 19 or 20 years old, or younger.

The word "teen" has particular draw to consumers of pornography—one of Plaintiff's experts, Dr. Linz, very significantly related there is nearly *double* the amount of material on the internet tagged as "teen porn" (136 million hits) as compared to the amount of material tagged as "porn, 18 year old" (78 million hits). Plaintiff Marie Levine admitted that employing youthful-looking performers brings financial benefits to producers of sexually explicit depictions and that she derives revenue from providing links to sites which portray such performers.... Moreover, the youthful-looking performer is pervasive across pornography genres. As Dr. Dines' testimony demonstrated and as the "screenshots" that the government introduced as exhibits make clear, such performers appear in "MILF" porn and granny porn, even though the latter genres theoretically focus on showing older-looking adults....

4. *Inclusion of Youthful-Looking Performers in Plaintiffs' Work:* There is no evidence that any Plaintiff is an exclusive producer of sexually explicit depictions of "clearly mature" adults. Rather, on cross-examination by the government during which Plaintiffs were shown images of their own work, every Plaintiff-producer who testified admitted he or she has used models ages 18–24 years old. So despite Plaintiffs' professed interest in not employing women or men aged 17 or younger, the evidence is irrefutable that Plaintiffs are interested in using youthful-looking performers.... [footnote omitted]....

5. *"Chilling Effects" of Statutes on Plaintiffs' Speech:* After all of Plaintiffs' testimony, there is evidence of only two artistic endeavors that have been made practically impossible by the Statutes, because those endeavors require the subjects of the art to have the opportunity to remain anonymous. First, Dodson and Ross's "genital art gallery" has been effectively shut down by Sections 2257 and 2257A, because average individuals are not willing to upload pictures of their genitals to the internet if they have to reveal their identities. Second, Barbara Alper's photo-journalism project on Fire Island has been blocked by Sections

2257 and 2257A, because her intended subject matter is anonymous sex.... [footnote omitted].

Granted, Plaintiffs also testified about expressive endeavors they wish to pursue that are now more challenging or more costly because of the Statutes. However, unlike the genital art gallery and the Fire Island photo project, these endeavors have not necessarily been made impossible because of the Statutes. For instance, Carol Queen stated one reason her Center hasn't live-streamed a "masturbate-a-thon" since 2010 is that the Center is worried about its ability to maintain 2257 paperwork. David Levingston testified that he avoids taking images that could be construed as "simulated" sexual activity, because he does not want to comply with Section 2257A. Thomas Hymes avoids posting images that would require him to comply with Section 2257. And David Steinberg testified that it would be very difficult for him to publish a U.S. edition of Quipido magazine, because he would have to obtain 2257 statements for European models. While all of this testimony demonstrates an arguable "chilling" effect the Statutes are having on Plaintiffs — by making certain expression more costly or burdensome to produce — it did not demonstrate that such forms of expression were being blocked altogether.... [footnote omitted]....

8. *Requirement of Verifying Performers' Ages by Checking Photo Identification:* Most Plaintiffs stated they have no desire to depict individuals under 18 in their works and would continue to request identification from models without Sections 2257 and 2257A, to ensure they were over age 18 and that their model releases were thus valid. But some Plaintiffs suggested that without 2257, they would not necessarily request IDs from every model — only from those they suspected to be under age 18.... (Barbara Alper stated she had not verified the ages of the individuals in her S & M club photographs because she had no reason to suspect they were underage); ... (Carlin Ross stated she did not check IDs for individuals who used to upload to the gallery, but rather inferred their age based on their submissions and essays).

The Court finds the requirement to request and maintain copies of performers' photo identifications is not uniquely onerous or burdensome on producers, but is consistent with other record-keeping requirements mandated by federal, state and local governments. For instance, the federal government requires that every U.S. employer fill out and maintain a record of an "I-9 Form" for each employee, which verifies the identity and employment authorization for that individual. In filling out the I-9, the employer must examine the employee's identity documents. Other federal laws require that employers make and keep records of their employees' wages, hours and conditions of employment, as well as of their premises' occupational safety, and to permit inspectors from the Department of Labor to inspect these records on demand. *See* 29 U.S.C. §§ 211(a)–(c) (records required by Fair Labor Standards Act); 29 U.S.C § 657(c) (records required regarding occupational safety). Manufacturers of foods, drugs, and consumer products have to maintain certain records and permit inspectors to access them to ensure compliance with federal safety standards. 21 U.S.C. §§ 350(c), 373–374 (manufacturers of foods and drugs); 15 U.S.C. § 2065 (manufacturers of consumer products). Federal, state and local governments all require that employers maintain records of their revenues and expenses for tax-filing purposes....

After close consideration of the evidence presented at trial and admitted into the trial record, the Court concludes the government has shown by a preponderance of evidence that the Statutes do not burden substantially more of Plaintiffs' speech than is necessary to further the government's interest in combatting child pornography.... First, the government demonstrated effectively that no one Plaintiff is an exclusive producer of sexually explicit images of "clearly mature adults." The Third Circuit hypothesized that if certain Plaintiffs did meet this description, the Statutes might be overbroad as applied to them.[14] *Free Speech*, 667 F.3d at 537 (holding that "if one of the Plaintiffs employs performers that no reasonable person could conclude were minors," such as for "'an illustrated sex manual for the elderly,'" the Statutes might be unconstitutional as-applied to that Plaintiff (citing *Am. Library Ass'n v. Reno*, 33 F.3d 78, 90 (D.C.Cir.1994)); *Connection Distrib. Co. v. Holder*, 557 F.3d 321, 336 (6th Cir.2009) (en banc) (holding the law might be unconstitutional as applied to a magazine that "confined itself to self-evidently mature models [and] also did not permit the depiction of isolated body parts"); *Am. Library Ass'n*, 33 F.3d at 90 ("We agree with appellees' suggestion that certain applications of the record-keeping requirements may well exceed constitutional bounds, an illustrated sex manual for the elderly being an obvious example."). But no Plaintiff's depictions are confined to clearly mature adults. Rather, as reviewed above, every Plaintiff conceded on cross-examination that its commercially-distributed depictions include youthful-looking performers. No Plaintiff even identified a genre of its works—such as a collection of images or movies—confined to depicting clearly mature adults. And no Plaintiff testified that his or her works going forwards would be confined to such a population of performers....

To be narrowly tailored, the fit between a regulation's effect and its stated objective must be "reasonable, not perfect." *United States v. Marzzarella*, 614 F.3d 85, 98 (3d Cir.2010). Here, the fit between the Statutes' effect on Plaintiffs and its goal of combatting child pornography is reasonable because every Plaintiff that produces sexually explicit depictions uses a considerable number of youthful-looking performers and derives commercial revenue from these depictions, and the burden associated with record-keeping is a justifiable cost of doing business. Ms. Wilson, of the Sinclair Institute, testified that Sinclair spends approximately $75,000 a year on Section 2257 compliance.... This is not an unreasonable sum for the world's "largest producer" of adult sex education media, which makes millions of dollars in revenues from sexually explicit materials every year.... (relating that Sinclair made $53 million in revenues from its sexually explicit videos from 2005–2009)). Even for Plaintiffs who are smaller, more niche players in the adult entertainment industry, there is no evidence that the costs of recordkeeping are disproportionate considering the revenues they derive from such activities. Barbara Nitke conceded the costs of complying with the Statutes are "different" from, but not necessarily greater than, the costs associated with filing her taxes with the IRS....

[T]he Court finds the requirement to inspect and maintain records of performers' identifications is comparable to and consistent with other federal, state and local record-keeping requirements incumbent on employers.... [such as] (record-keeping requirements that pertain to employees' work eligibility, to wages, hours, conditions of employment, to occupational safety, to product safety, and to employers' revenues and expenses). The additional burdens associated with cross-referencing and with affixing labels to depictions are not so great so as to change that conclusion. Many Plaintiffs who complained of significant burdens under the Statutes appear to be misunderstanding the regulatory provisions, using outdated record-keeping systems, or declining to take advantage of the ability to use third-party custodians.[15]

---

14. Note, this was the *only* means by which the Third Circuit contemplated Plaintiffs might prevail in proving a lack of narrow tailoring in their as-applied challenge. *Free Speech Coal.*, 677 F.3d at 519.

15. For instance, several photographers complained of the need to maintain Section 2257 records for every image captured on a camera or printed as a proof. But the regulations do not appear to require a label be affixed until a photograph is made publicly available. See 28 C.F.R. § 75.8(a)–(f). Barbara Nitke testified to maintaining a cumbersome system of paper records, including a paper

Moreover, the government demonstrated the universality of the record-keeping requirement is justified as applied to Plaintiffs because any alternative rule would introduce subjectivity into the regulatory scheme and lessen its effectiveness. *See Ward*, 491 U .S. at 799 ("[T]he requirement of narrow tailoring is satisfied 'so long as the … regulation promotes a substantial government interest that would be achieved less effectively absent the regulation.'" (internal citation omitted)). For instance, if Plaintiffs had to maintain records only for persons who appear to be 25 years old or under, this would leave Plaintiffs to rely on their own judgment in determining whose identifications to check. Not only would the efficacy of the Statutes be reduced—as Plaintiffs would surely make *some* errors in estimating performers' ages—but as Agent Lawrence testified, anything less than a universal requirement would invite disputes between Plaintiffs and law enforcement and complicate the inspections process.… *See Free Speech Coal.*, 677 F.3d at 535 (recognizing the Statutes "combat child pornography" by "eliminat[ing] subjective disputes with producers over whether the producer should have verified the age of a particular performer"); *Connection Distrib. Co.*, 557 F.3d at 329–330 (finding the Statutes to be narrowly tailored because they create "a compliance system … [without] subjective disputes with producers over whether a model's apparent age should have triggered an age-verification check"). In the past, courts have upheld prophylactic measures under narrow-tailoring review precisely because a more targeted measure, such as a 25-year old identification check, would introduce uncertainty and enforcement difficulties. *Hill v. Colorado*, 530 U.S. 703, 729, 120 S.Ct. 2480, 147 L.Ed.2d 597 (2000) ("[T]he statute's prophylactic aspect is justified by the great difficulty of protecting, say, a pregnant woman from physical harassment with legal rules that focus exclusively on the individual impact of each instance of behavior, demanding in each case an accurate characterization (as harassing or not harassing) of each individual movement within the 8-foot boundary. Such individualized characterization of each individual movement is often difficult to make accurately. A bright-line prophylactic rule may be the best way to provide protection, and, at the same time, by offering clear guidance and avoiding subjectivity, to protect speech itself."); *Fed. Election Comm'n v. Nat'l Right to Work Comm.*, 459 U.S. 197, 209, 103 S.Ct. 552, 74 L.Ed.2d 364 (1982) (holding, in the context of a statute regulating campaign contributions by corporations and labor unions, that the Court will not "second guess a legislative determination as to the need for prophylactic measures" given the compelling interest of preventing corruption).

Second, the Statutes are narrowly-tailored as to Plaintiffs not only because Plaintiffs employ considerable numbers of young-looking performers in their works but also because no Plaintiff has demonstrated he or she is a producer of purely private, sexually explicit communications. As the government correctly points out, no Plaintiff referred to the Statutes' burden on his or her private communications in the Amended Complaint when pleading his or her as-applied challenge.… But even putting the pleadings to the side, no Plaintiff demonstrated at trial that he or she produces sexually explicit depictions for purely private purposes or maintains records for such private depictions. While Barbara Alper testified that she has taken explicit photographs of herself and her husband, she conceded she sold

---

cross-referencing document, which she needs to rearrange every time she updates her website.… She was apparently unaware that the Statutes allow for electronic record-keeping. 28 C.F.R. § 75.2(f) ("Records required to be maintained under this part may be kept either in hard copy or digital form.…"). Carol Queen, Thomas Hymes and David Levingston stated they do not have the capacity to personally maintain any sort of records system, but they ignore the possibility for using a third-party custodian. *Id.* § 75.4. And as explained above, Nitke and Alper appear to misunderstand the regulations' requirements regarding compilations of work.…

some of these photographs for publication in a Norwegian magazine.... In sum, there is no evidence in the record of any burden that the Statutes impose on Plaintiffs whatsoever, with respect to the Statutes' application to purely private sexual depictions.

Finally, the Court recognizes there is evidence of two specific projects contemplated by Plaintiffs that will, admittedly, be barred by the Statutes. These are Dodson and Ross' genital art gallery and Barbara Alper's Fire Island project. But the Court concludes this is a reasonable cost given Congress' underlying objective of eliminating child pornography. Plaintiffs Nitke and Alper testified to not being able to publish printed compilations of their works because those books would include pre-1995 and post-1995 images together, and Nitke and Alper only have records for the latter. But as explained, that is a misunderstanding of the Statutes and regulations.... Plaintiff Steinberg testified that to print a U.S. edition of Quipido Magazine, he would have to require foreign photographers to comply with U.S. laws and provide him with Section 2257 documentation. This might be a nuisance, but it is not an infringement of his First Amendment rights....

After close consideration of the evidence adduced at trial, the Court finds Plaintiffs have failed to demonstrate facial overbreadth with respect to the Statutes' application to depictions of clearly mature adults. First and most importantly, Plaintiffs presented no evidence at trial demonstrating there even exist bona fide, compartmentalized genres of commercial pornography dedicated to depicting mature adults, exclusively. The sub-genres of pornography that purport to focus on mature-looking adults—such as MILF porn and granny porn—also include significant numbers of young-looking performers. Dr. Dines testified that based on her analysis of the MILF pornography category on "pornhub," the predominant image was *not* of two clearly mature adults engaging in sexual activity with one another but rather, of young men or young women engaging in sexual activities with older women.... During discovery, Plaintiffs provided the government a list of websites they claimed supported their overbreadth claim in that they focused on clearly mature individuals. But as the government demonstrated through taking screenshots of these websites and moving them into evidence, these websites show an abundance of young-looking performers.... (screenshot from "porno tube—grannies" website, showing young-looking females); ... (screenshots from "youporn—mature sex porn tubes" website, showing young-looking performers); ... (screenshots from "redtube—granny sex videos" website, showing youthful-looking women); ... (screenshot from "spankwireMilf porn tube" website, showing a youthful-looking male).... .

Second, the scope of the Statutes' "plainly legitimate sweep" is vast. Using Dr. Dines' estimate that approximately one-third of commercial pornography on the internet depicts "teens"—which she cautions is under-inclusive, because it only captures pornography tagged with the keyword "teen" or an allied term, while other pornography could and likely does include young-looking performers as well—that is a vast amount of depictions that falls under the Statutes' plainly legitimate sweep. Even Dr. Linz's (methodologically weak) estimate that ten percent of commercial pornography depicts teens yields a considerable number of depictions Congress was properly trying to regulate. Meanwhile, expert witness Janis Wolak related that approximately two-thirds of persons arrested for possessing child pornography were in possession of images of teenagers between the ages of 13 and 17 years. Wolak's testimony demonstrates that child pornographers have an appetite for viewing the very population Congress was seeking to protect in enacting the Statutes, thus underscoring the compelling interest behind the Statutes' plainly legitimate sweep....[16]

---

16. The Court also notes that these percentage figures, estimating the proportion of commercial pornography that depicts teens, offer an incomplete picture of the Statutes' plainly legitimate sweep.

Finally, for the reasons discussed above, the Statutes' prophylactic nature is justified because even though they may reach depictions of mature adults, any more targeted record-keeping requirement, i.e., a record-keeping requirement applying only to individuals who appear to be age 25 or younger, would introduce subjectivity, uncertainty and immeasurable enforcement difficulties into the regulatory scheme. Dr. Biro demonstrated—and nearly all Plaintiffs conceded—that a person's age cannot be determined by visual inspection alone. The general age range of confusion is 15 to 24 years old, but even individuals younger and older can be mistaken for adults or minors, respectively. This is especially true when persons apply make-up and dress to try to appear older or younger. Congress' judgment that a universal record-keeping requirement was necessary to effectuate its interest of combatting child pornography was reasonable. Although some depictions that do not implicate the government's interest, because they depict only mature individuals, will be burdened, Congress was justified in concluding that any effort to unburden that speech by narrowing the record-keeping requirement could undermine the Statutes' efficacy altogether, unleashing producers to make subjective age determinations and leaving law enforcement with no reliable means of policing these decisions. *See Am. Library Ass'n*, 33 F.3d at 90 ("The Government must be allowed to paint with a reasonably broad brush if it is to cover depictions of all performers who might conceivably have been minors at the time they were photographed or videotaped.... The Act ... burdens only that protected speech necessary to advance the Government's interest in preventing child pornography.... [I]t is essential to Congress's design that the Act impose its recordkeeping requirements on all performers who appear in sexually explicit materials.").

Without a strong and robust regime for policing the ages of performers, there would be incentives on both sides of the equation to use minors as performers in sexually explicit depictions. On the employer-side, the record accumulated in this case shows there is a high commercial value associated with the young-looking performer. On the employee side, there are undoubtedly minors who do not contemplate becoming doctors, lawyers or hedge fund zillionaires, and would be attracted to the financial benefits available in the adult pornography industry. The burden must be on the producer to verify that all performers and subjects in its depictions are of age. Congress's determination that the most effective way of imposing that obligation on producers—and of ensuring their compliance—was through a universal record-keeping law, was reasonable. Moreover, as explained above, the labors and costs associated with complying with Sections 2257 and 2257A are not of a different degree or order of magnitude than the labors and costs associated with other record-keeping requirements incumbent on employers under federal, state and local law.[17] ...

Congress's goal in enacting the Statutes was to protect the sizable population of minors in the United States who, without age-verification and record-keeping requirements, could become subjects in sexually explicit depictions and thus victims of child pornography. The U.S. Census Bureau shows that as of 2010, there are 22 million adults ages 15–19 in the United States.... Assuming two-fifths of that group is adults ages 18 and 19, that yields approximately 13 million minors ages 15–17. These are all individuals who could be used as performers in sexually explicit depictions were the Statutes not in place, and who are thus protected by the Statutes' operation.

17. Furthermore, the possibility of doctoring or manipulating digital depictions is another factor justifying the universal age-keeping requirement in the Statutes. Given contemporary technologies in film and in photography, a producer could easily hire a minor under age 18 and dress up the image to make the performer appear older. Alternatively, the producer could create a depiction that shows the performer's body parts, without including his or her face or head. If the record-keeping requirement applied only to performers who appeared to be a particular age, say age 25, federal inspectors could be misled from even perceiving the need to verify the ages of performers in such doctored images.

The question of whether the Statutes are overbroad in their burdening of purely private, noncommercial communications is more difficult, given the high protection afforded such communications under the First Amendment and the Fifth and Fourteenth Amendments' Due Process Clauses. That said, the Court concludes Plaintiffs have failed to prove substantial overbreadth with respect to the Statutes' application to private communications for two reasons—first, they have failed to show there exists a substantial amount of private communications that even fall under the Statutes' scope; second, they have failed to show an actual burden or chilling of such communications caused by the Statutes, such that the "strong medicine" of facial invalidation is justified.

As an initial matter, the Court begins by noting that it is controlled by the Third Circuit's holding, in its remand decision, that the word "producer" in Sections 2257 and 2257A extends to individuals who produce sexually explicit depictions even for purely private, noncommercial purposes. *Free Speech Coal.*, 677 F.3d at 538–39. On appeal, the government argued otherwise—it contended "producer" means only individuals or entities that generate sexually explicit depictions intended "for sale or trade." *See* Brief of Appellee, *Free Speech Coal., Inc. v. Attorney Gen. of the U.S*, 677 F.3d 519 (2012) (No. 10-4085), 2011 WL 1760472 at *49–55. While the government defined "intended for sale or trade" to include pornography posted for free to a publicly-accessible website, such as an adult social networking site, or distributed for free through internet file-sharing," it defined the term to exclude images "not posted on the Internet, but kept for the producer's or a couple's own personal, private use." *Id.* at *50–51. The former images "becom[e] a potential commodity" once they are uploaded because they are then capable of being traded and circulated to "an indeterminate number of people," the government explained, and were therefore intended by Congress to be encompassed by the record-keeping requirements. *Id.* The latter images, which were "create[d] and maintain[ed]" by adult couples for their personal use at home," could not become commoditized and were not intended to be encompassed. *Id.* Thus, the government's position was that depictions exchanged solely between private parties, without commercial exchange and without the possibility for commoditization, are exempt. To support its limiting construction of the Statutes, the government cited the statutory text, which refers to "sexual performers," "place[s] of business," and other terms that connote sale or trade, the preamble to the 2008 regulations, which states the Statutes are "limited to pornography intended for sale or trade," *see* 73 Fed.Reg. 77,432, 77,456 (Dec. 18, 2008); and the history of enforcement, which for twenty years, did not include any enforcement effort vis-à-vis a private individual producing sexually explicit depictions purely for his or her own use....

The Third Circuit rejected the government's limiting construction, holding "limiting constructions are not available where they require 'rewriting, not just reinterpretation' of the statute." *Free Speech Coal.*, 677 F.3d at 539 (internal citation omitted). It found "the plain language of the Statutes makes clear that they apply broadly to all producers of actual or simulated sexually explicit depictions regardless of whether those depictions were created for the purpose of sale or trade," because nowhere in the Statutes is the word "producer" defined as limited to a maker of depictions intended for sale or trade. *Id.* The court also reasoned that the "plain text of the Statutes setting forth their broad scope must

---

Law enforcement's ability to police the production of child pornography would be undermined. Sections 2257 and 2257A avoid this pitfall by imposing a record-keeping requirement as to every performer.

trump any conflicting statement contained within the preamble to the regulations," *id.*, as well as any promises of prosecutorial discretion, *id.* at n. 15.

Based on the factual record now developed, if this Court could analyze the issue on a clean slate, it would endorse the view presented by the government on appeal that depictions made for purely private, noncommercial uses are not—and never were intended to be—captured by the Statutes. The government consistently has rejected any interpretation of the Statutes that would cover such depictions. Agents Lawrence and Joyner, the individuals who established and operated the enforcement program at the FBI during the only years it was in existence, testified there never was any government interest in enforcing the record-keeping requirements vis-à-vis persons producing images for private use. Moreover, the methods of communicating sexually explicit depictions between private persons have been made possible by technologies that did not exist at the time the Statutes were passed and arguably, could not have been contemplated by Congress. Further, the government's proposed construction of "producer," as being limited to one who makes an image intended for sale or trade, would accomplish the goals expressed by Congress—it would enable the government to impose record-keeping requirements on large-scale industry players, such as pornography film producers and photographers, as well as on niche players and even private individuals who choose to upload their depictions to the internet for public viewing.... That said, this Court cannot interpret Sections 2257 and 2257A on a blank slate. It is bound by the Third Circuit's determination that "producer" reaches private persons—be they husbands-and-wives, persons in dating relationships, or strangers exchanging information to potentially date one another—who produce and share sexually explicit depictions with each other for private, noncommercial purposes.

Still, the Court declines to find Plaintiffs have succeeded in their burden of proving facial overbreadth as a result of the Statutes' applications to private depictions. First, Plaintiffs have not proven there is a considerable quantity (or any quantity) of sexually explicit depictions, exchanged privately and not for sale or trade, that fails under the Statutes' scope. Drs. Drouin and Zimmerman testified for Plaintiffs about the prevalence of sext messaging, but they could not provide information on the quantity of images being exchanged that contain "sexually explicit conduct" as defined by the Statutes—i.e., that contain depictions of intercourse, masturbation, bestiality, sadistic or masochistic abuse, or "lascivious exhibitions" of genitals or pubic areas. *See* 18 U.S.C. § 2257(h)(1); 18 U.S.C. § 2256(2)(A). The studies Drouin and Zimmerman conducted and relied upon to arrive at their estimates about sexting had not defined "sexually explicit" images in a uniform way, and only one of these studies differentiated among the types of context depicted at all. Thus, neither expert could determine how many sext messages being exchanged between private persons actually fall within the Statutes' scope. The frequency of sext messaging is irrelevant for Plaintiffs' overbreadth challenge, however, if every sext message were to contain images of breasts, cleavage and nudity that fall short of "lascivious" exhibitions of genitals. Plaintiffs' additional evidence about technologies through which adult couples exchange sexually explicit content—e.g., "instaporn" and "snapchat"—similarly suffers from this shortcoming....[18] ...

---

18. Plaintiffs have also submitted evidence about technologies that enable couples to witness each other engaging in sexual activities in real time, such as Facetime and Skype.... Again, there is no specification in the record about the frequency of use of these technologies to depict content—such as masturbation—that would fall under the Statutes' scope, as opposed to depict content—such as cleavage—that would not. Thus, this evidence does not have considerable probative value for Plaintiffs'

The need for a plaintiff to demonstrate an actual chilling or burdening of speech—based on a realistic threat of the statute's application as to that speech—is particularly true in the context of child-pornography legislation. In *United States v. Williams*, the Supreme Court rejected plaintiffs' argument that a statute criminalizing the pandering and solicitation of child pornography was facially overbroad because it could hypothetically apply to an individual who turns child pornography over to the police. The Court held this objection was a "fanciful hypothetical[ ]." *Williams*, 553 U.S. at 301. It was aware of "no [such] prosecution" and could "hardly say, therefore, that there is a 'realistic danger' that [the law] will deter such activity." *Id.* at 302. In *Connection*, the Sixth Circuit assumed—as the Third Circuit did here—that Sections 2257 and 2257A apply to private communications. But it rejected a facial overbreadth claim precisely because there was no evidence of any actual chilling to date, nor any likely to occur in the future. *See Connection Distrib. Co.*, 557 F.3d at 339–40 ("[I]t is hard to understand who is being hurt by resisting the plaintiffs' call to invalidate the statute on its face. The middle-aged couple is not likely to be chilled by the statute. Over twenty years and numerous administrations, the statute has never been enforced in this setting, and the Attorney General has publicly taken the position that he will not enforce the statute in this setting."). The Eleventh Circuit reached a similar result in a case concerning a child pornography law, where the defendant raised the hypothetical of the law's application to an adult couple making a home video. *United States v. Dean*, 635 F.3d 1200, 1206 (11th Cir.2011) ("At oral argument, Dean suggesting the following as an example of overbreadth: home-made videotapes of sexual intercourse produced by a consenting adult couple, when at least one of the participants was so youthful in appearance to 'appear to be' a minor.... Dean has not carried his burden to establish that, even if all such home-videos were protected, but subject to criminalization, prohibition of these videos would demonstrate substantial overbreadth in an absolute sense or relative to the statute's legitimate sweep.").

Here, as in *Connection*, Plaintiffs have presented no evidence of any private communications that are actually being chilled by the Statutes. No Plaintiff witness stated he or she produces sexually explicit depictions for purely private purposes, or that he or she was being deterred from producing such depictions because of the record-keeping requirement. No Plaintiff witness, including Plaintiffs' experts, testified that in the general population at large, sexting or other methods of privately exchanging sexual depictions are being curbed by the Statutes. To the contrary, several witnesses for Plaintiffs stated they do not think private persons even know about the Statutes' existence or have any sense they are technically (under the Third Circuit's construction) required to comply with them when they send each other sexually explicit content.... (testimony of Carol Queen, stating "I don't believe that the average American knows that this law exists"). Meanwhile, Agents Joyner and Lawrence reiterated the position taken by the government in this litigation and in other cases that it has no interest in enforcing the Statutes as to purely private communications and that it would have no conceivable way of even doing this—because it would have no knowledge of those private communications in the first place....

The utterly depraved nature of child pornography is so revolting to a civilized society that there are no comparisons. It is absolutely devoid of merit or justification. The revulsion of Congress to the practice must be respected by judges; the dangers of its possession and

---

overbreadth claim. Moreover, it is unclear that the use of these technologies by private individuals would trigger Sections 2257 and 2257A even under the Third Circuit's construction, because real-time activities being viewed over electronic channels, but not recorded or captured in any permanent format, may not fall under the definition of a "depiction."

circulation must be treated with the utmost sensitivity. A court should tread most carefully in considering facial challenges to anti-child pornography laws. A judge should invalidate such a law only if there is a "realistic danger that the statute [ ] will significantly compromise recognized First Amendment protections," *Taxpayers for Vincent*, 466 U.S. at 801, due to the "likely frequency of conceivably impermissible applications," *Gibson*, 355 F.3d at 226. There is no such showing in this case. *See generally New York v. Ferber*, 458 U.S. 747, 756, 102 S.Ct. 3348, 73 L.Ed.2d 1113 (1982) ("[L]aws directed at the dissemination of child pornography run the risk of suppressing protected expression by allowing the hand of the censor to become unduly heavy.... [H]owever, we are persuaded that the States are entitled to greater leeway in the regulation of pornographic depictions of children."); *United States v. Malloy*, 568 F.3d 166, 175 (4th Cir.2009) ("Because of the surpassing importance of the government's interest in safeguarding the physical and psychological wellbeing of children, the government has greater leeway to regulate child pornography that it does other areas.")....

Under the factual record developed at trial, the equitable remedy of an injunction is not warranted at this time. The evidence shows the government has not conducted a Section 2257 inspection since 2007. Rather, the FBI dismantled the inspections program in early 2008, and there has been no intent or effort to revive it. It is moribund. As a result, Plaintiffs do not face a realistic threat of "irreparable harm" — due to an inspection — at any point in the foreseeable future. A judge must take a deep breath before enjoining the nation's top law enforcement officer from doing something that the Department of Justice has shown no interest in doing for the last six years. Under these circumstances, the Court believes it would be an abuse of discretion to enter an injunction against the Attorney General.... The Court is mindful that were the FBI to revive the Section 2257 inspections program, and were the DOJ to decline to update the regulations so as to require advance notice at inspections of residences, a producer could bring a lawsuit requesting an injunction at that time.... Except for Plaintiffs' claim that the regulations violate the Fourth Amendment as applied to inspections of records kept at bona fide residences, all other issues are decided in favor of the government, and a final judgment will be entered.

Notes

The Court in *Ashcroft v. Free Speech Coalition* delineates a distinction between child pornography and other genres of pornography that appear to depict children but do not involve actual children who are being directly harmed. The *Holder* decision bridges the gap between the adult pornography and the child pornography industries, within constitutional limits. In May 2015, the United States Court of Appeals for the Third Circuit affirmed that the statutes did not burden substantially more of the producers' speech than was necessary and was not facially overbroad with respect to depictions of clearly mature adults in sexually explicit images created for private use. However, as applied, the warrantless inspections violated the Fourth Amendment. The court remanded the case to the District Court for consideration of the court's Fourth Amendment analysis. *See Free Speech Coalition, Inc. v. Attorney General United States*, 787 F.3d 142 (3d Cir. 2015). For additional commentary on the scope of government protection within the pornography industry, see Carissa Byrne Hessick, *The Limits of Child Pornography*, 89 Ind. L.J. 1437 (2014); Kiernan Dowling, *A Call to Rewrite America's Child Pornography Test: The Dost Factor Test*, 24 Seton Hall J. Sports & Ent. L. 151 (2014); Rosalind E. Bell, *Reconciling the PROTECT Act with the First Amendment*, 87 N.Y.U. L. Rev. 1878 (2012).

B. Defining Child Pornography

United States v. Ward

Eighth Circuit, 2012

686 F.3d 879

LOKEN, Circuit Judge.

A warrant search of Terry Lee Ward's recreational vehicle and his computer yielded a video of Ward positioning W.D., a twelve-year-old girl, while he secretly filmed the front of her nude body, and CDs containing thousands of images of child pornography. After Ward was convicted in Arkansas state court of raping W.D.'s eleven-year-old sister, federal prosecutors charged him with single counts of sexual exploitation of a minor, W.D., and possession of child pornography. *See* 18 U.S.C. §§ 2251(a) and 2252(a)(4)(B). A jury convicted him of both counts, but we reversed after concluding he was denied his Sixth Amendment right to be present at trial. *United States v. Ward*, 598 F.3d 1054, 1060 (8th Cir.2010). On remand, a jury again convicted Ward of both counts. The district court ... [footnote omitted] imposed concurrent sentences of 360 and 120 months in prison, the statutory maximum on each count, consecutive to the unserved portion of his state court sentence of life without parole. Ward appeals his conviction for sexual exploitation of a minor, arguing the evidence was insufficient because the video was not a visual depiction of sexually explicit conduct....

Ward argues the district court erred in denying his motion for judgment of acquittal on the sexual exploitation charge. As relevant here, the statute prohibits employing, using, persuading, or coercing a minor to engage in "sexually explicit conduct for the purpose of producing any visual depiction of such conduct" using materials shipped in interstate commerce. 18 U.S.C. § 2251(a). In this case, the conviction turned on whether, in secretly filming W.D. nude before and after she took a shower, Ward used or persuaded the young girl to take part in producing a visual depiction of sexually explicit conduct. "Sexually explicit conduct" is defined as including the "lascivious exhibition of the genitals or pubic area of any person." 18 U.S.C. § 2256(2)(A)(v). In deciding this issue, the district court instructed the jury to consider non-exclusive factors commonly referred to as the "*Dost* factors":

> Whether a visual depiction of the genitals or pubic area constitutes a lascivious exhibition requires a consideration of the overall content of the material. You may consider such factors as: (1) whether the focal point of the picture is on the minor's genitals or pubic area; (2) whether the setting of the picture is sexually suggestive, that is, in a place or pose generally associated with sexual activity; (3) whether the minor is depicted in an unnatural pose or in inappropriate attire, considering the age of the minor; (4) whether the minor is fully or partially clothed, or nude; (5) whether the picture suggests sexual coyness or a willingness to engage in sexual activity; (6) whether the picture is intended or designed to elicit a sexual response in the viewer; (7) whether the picture portrays the minor as a sexual object; and (8) the caption(s) on the picture(s).... A picture need not involve all of the factors to constitute a lascivious exhibition of the genitals or pubic area.

See United States v. Dost, 636 F.Supp. 828, 832 (S.D.Cal.1986), *aff'd sub nom. United States v. Wiegand*, 812 F.2d 1239 (9th Cir.), *cert. denied*, 484 U.S. 856, 108 S.Ct. 164, 98 L.Ed.2d 118 (1987). We and other circuits have approved use of these factors. *See, e.g., United States v. Wallenfang*, 568 F.3d 649, 657 (8th Cir.2009); *United States v. Rivera*, 546 F.3d

245, 253 (2d Cir.2008) ("the *Dost* factors impose useful discipline on the jury's deliberations"). They have been incorporated into Eighth Circuit Model Criminal Jury Instruction 6.18.2251(a).

As counsel for Ward conceded at oral argument, when the phrase "lascivious exhibition of the genitals or pubic area" has been properly defined for the jury, "the question whether the materials depict lascivious exhibition of the genitals, an element of the crime, is for the finder of fact." *United States v. Rayl*, 270 F.3d 709, 714–15 (8th Cir.2001) (quotation omitted); *accord United States v. Frabizio*, 459 F.3d 80, 85 (1st Cir.2006) ("lascivious" is a "commonsensical term"). Thus, as we explained in upholding a child sexual exploitation verdict in *United States v. Johnson*, 639 F.3d 433, 437–38 (8th Cir.2011), our standard of review is exceedingly deferential:

> In reviewing a district court's grant of a motion for a judgment of acquittal, this court reviews the sufficiency of the evidence *de novo*, viewing evidence in the light most favorable to the government, resolving conflicts in the government's favor, and accepting all reasonable inferences that support the verdict. The standard of review is very strict, and we will reverse a conviction only if we conclude that no reasonable jury could have found the accused guilty beyond a reasonable doubt. (Quotations and citations omitted.)

Summarizing the evidence at trial most favorably to the jury's verdict, investigators discovered the video inside a locked safe in Ward's vehicle, where they also found his expansive collection of child pornography. The video was admitted at trial and is part of the record on appeal. To film the video, Ward positioned a camera under a table at one end of his RV focused on the hallway, with bunk beds visible to the right and the entrance to a shower on the left. Viewers see Ward move a floor fan obstructing the camera's view and hear him tell one child to stay behind a sheet covering the bottom bunk. Ward then retrieves W.D. from the top bunk and helps her undress in the hallway, get into and out of the shower, dry, and dress. Throughout, Ward positions W.D. himself or directs her to orient herself so that the camera repeatedly captures the front of her nude body.

W.D., now nineteen, testified at trial that she knew Ward through an old friend and visited his RV on three weekends in August 2004, where she and other children watched movies and sat on bunk beds playing video games. She recalled taking the shower. She said she did not know Ward was filming her and did not see the film until after its seizure. She testified, "I was going to take a shower and he just started following me there, pretty much, and turning me around. I didn't know why, but I went to get in the shower." When the prosecutor asked W.D. who decided what direction she would face in the hallway, she answered, "He was moving me like in what directions he wanted me to go." Asked if anything else happened after the video was taken, W.D. answered, "he tried to kiss me and that's it." Defense counsel asked W.D. two questions on cross-examination:

> Defense counsel: "it looks like he didn't try to touch you inappropriately or anything like that on the video?"
>
> W.D.: "Well, the way he was turning me around."
>
> Defense counsel: "He turned you around, but it didn't appear that he was touching you inappropriately or anything like that; is that correct?"
>
> W.D.: "Touching my sides is not appropriate."

On appeal, Ward argues the evidence was insufficient as a matter of law because the video depicts "mere nudity" that does not satisfy the element of lasciviousness. As the plain language of § 2256(2)(A)(v) makes clear, "there must be an 'exhibition' of the genital area and this exhibition must be 'lascivious.'" *United States v. Horn*, 187 F.3d 781, 789 (8th Cir.1999). Ward is correct "that more than mere nudity is required before an image can qualify as lascivious within the meaning of the statute." *Johnson*, 639 F.3d at 439, quoting *United States v. Kemmerling*, 285 F.3d 644, 645–46 (8th Cir.), cert. denied, 537 U.S. 860, 123 S.Ct. 237, 154 L.Ed.2d 99 (2002). Emphasizing certain of the *Dost* factors, Ward argues the video depicted W.D.'s "entire body, without a focal point on the child's genitalia or pubic area," neither the setting nor the pose was "generally associated with sexual activity," and "the depiction does not suggest sexual coyness or a willingness to engage in sexual activity."

We acknowledge this is a factually close case because a video of a twelve-year-old child undressing to take a shower, unaware she is being secretly filmed by a pedophile, is unlike the images of overt sexual activity typically encountered in prosecutions involving commercial child pornography. But the focus of § 2251(a) is the sexual exploitation of children. W.D. was exploited, and her response to defense counsel's cross examination made clear to the jury that she considered it sexual exploitation: "Touching my sides is not appropriate." The critical question is, did Ward's video depict a lascivious exhibition? "The 'lascivious exhibition' is not the work of the child, whose innocence is not in question, but of the producer or editor of the video." *Horn*, 187 F.3d at 790; *see Johnson*, 639 F.3d at 440 ("even images of children acting innocently can be considered lascivious if they are intended to be sexual"); *Wiegand*, 812 F.2d at 1244.

We conclude a reasonable jury could find that the exploitation of W.D. included using her to engage in sexually explicit conduct. Although the video may look to many viewers like a series of sexually unfocused pictures of a nude youngster, Ward positioned W.D., using verbal commands and touching her body, so that the secret camera repeatedly filmed her pubic area. "When a photographer selects and positions his subjects, it is quite a different matter from the peeking of a voyeur upon an unaware subject pursuing activities unrelated to sex." *United States v. Steen*, 634 F.3d 822, 828 (5th Cir.2011). Ward's manipulation of W.D. to film her pubic area told the jury he viewed the child as a sexual object. Then, after secretly filming her before and after she took a shower, Ward tried to kiss her. In weighing this evidence, the jury could reasonably consider extrinsic evidence, such as Ward's extensive child pornography collection, to determine "whether the images were intended to elicit a sexual response in the viewer." *Johnson*, 639 F.3d at 441. As in *Rivera*, 546 F.3d at 250, "A reasonable jury could therefore find that [Ward] composed the images in order to elicit a sexual response in a viewer—himself." *Compare Horn*, 187 F.3d at 789–90 (videotapes at beach and jungle gym with freeze framing of children's genitals); *United States v. Larkin*, 629 F.3d 177, 183–84 (3d Cir.2010).

After viewing the video, we conclude the jury reasonably found that the images Ward produced satisfied the statutory standard—visual depictions of sexually explicit conduct. The jury could reasonably reject Ward's "mere nudity" defense because his manipulation of the naked W.D. so as to secretly film her genitals "cannot reasonably be compared to innocent family photos, clinical depictions, or works of art." *Johnson*, 639 F.3d at 439....

The judgment of the district court is affirmed....

Note

In the context of photographic exploitation, the depiction of the child in the photograph becomes significant, and more specific federal statutes, such as 18 U.S.C. § 2256, which defines sexually explicit conduct as including exhibitions of a "lascivious" nature, are applicable. In assessing the lascivious nature of the exhibition of the child in *Ward*, the court relies on the "*Dost*" factors, derived from *United States v. Dost*, 636 F. Supp. 828, 832 (S.D. Cal. 1986), *aff'd sub nom. United States v. Weigand*, 812 F.2d 1239 (9th Cir.), *cert. denied*, 484 U.S. 856, 108 S. Ct. 164 (1987). For a more comprehensive application of the "*Dost*" factors in defining lascivious exhibitions constituting sexually explicit conduct, see *United States v. Goodale*, 831 F. Supp.2d 804 (D. Vt. 2011) (defendant's secret video recording of 17-year-old stepdaughter in the bathroom while she disrobed to shower and use the toilet constituted lascivious exhibition of her genitals or pubic area, amounting to sexually explicit conduct relevant to child pornography).

C. Production of Child Pornography

1. Interstate Commerce Requirement

a. Intent

United States v. Lebowitz

Eleventh Circuit, 2012

676 F.3d 1000

PER CURIAM: ...

When K.S. was 15 years old, he registered for a MySpace account. For MySpace profiles to be viewable by the public, the user must attest to being over the age of 21. K.S. desired such a profile, so he falsely claimed he was 21 years old on the registration form. K.S. then created an on-line profile that suggested his age was either 17 or 18 years old. On October 25, 2006, Lebowitz, whose MySpace profile identified himself as a 47-year-old doctor, sent a message to K.S. via his MySpace account, saying: "that's a great pic of you hitting the [base]ball. [G]ot any more pics of you playing?" Lebowitz provided K.S. with his contact information, and the two engaged in on-line chats and exchanged e-mails. The chats were sexual in nature, and Lebowitz sent K.S. nude photographs of himself. In one of these initial chats, K.S. told Lebowitz he was 15 years old.... After communicating with Lebowitz for a day, K.S. informed his mother of the chats and messages. K.S.'s mother obtained Lebowitz's phone number from one of his e-mails, phoned him, and threatened to kill him if he did not stop contacting her son. Lebowitz then sent K.S. a chat message asking him if anything was wrong. K.S's mother contacted law enforcement.

On October 27, 2006, K.S. and his mother met with Investigator Beth Suber of the Coweta County Sheriff's Office. At Investigator Suber's suggestion, K.S.'s mother agreed to allow K.S. to continue corresponding with Lebowitz in order to determine Lebowitz's intentions. Investigator Suber instructed K.S. to make his true age clear to Lebowitz during on-line conversations. During one on-line chat, K.S. told Lebowitz: "i [sic] would drive up there but im [sic] only 15 and odnt [sic] have a car." Lebowitz replied: "coming to get you is not a problem." ... Lebowitz and K.S. also conversed by phone. Investigator Suber recorded the phone calls. In the last phone call, K.S. and Lebowitz arranged to meet at K.S.'s home the following day. K.S. again mentioned he was only 15 years old. Lebowitz responded in a surprised tone, "I thought you were 17." K.S. again said he was 15. After a pause, Lebowitz responded, "you know, I've never met someone who's underage." Lebowitz claimed he did not want any trouble, and asked K.S. when he would have his next birthday. After hearing that K.S. would not be 16 years old for another 6 months, Lebowitz said he "started" when he was 14, and that they would only "do stuff that feels right" because "friendship is more important than getting off." Lebowitz told K.S. he liked "athletic guys," that he had "been looking for a good friend here that [he] could kinda mess around with," and that K.S. was "definitely that kind of guy." Lebowitz again asked K.S. if it was safe to meet because he did not "want to get arrested or anything." After K.S. reassured him, Lebowitz reminded K.S. to bring his baseball uniform because Lebowitz found it "really hot." Lebowitz also told K.S. that he thought men were better than women at giving other men oral sexual stimulation, and that going out with younger guys was "an adventure."

On November 2, 2006, Lebowitz arrived at K.S.'s home. Investigator Suber arrested Lebowitz and searched his vehicle. In the front seat she found a backpack that contained condoms and lubricants. She also found two sleeping bags and two towels. Investigator Suber then obtained a warrant to search Lebowitz's residence. Upon searching the residence, she seized a Sony notebook computer, an iPod, a HP Pavillion computer with camera, a printout of a phone number "look-up," a piece of paper with the victim's name and address, pieces of paper with various screen names and emails, CD-R's, a Sony CPU, a green file with various MySpace printouts of screen names and email addresses, VHS tapes, bottles of Astro-glide, and various types of condoms. A VHS tape labeled "XXX" contained video of Lebowitz engaged in sexual acts with teenage males.

Agents were able to identify A.G. and C.R. as the males on the VHS tape engaged in sexual activity with Lebowitz. Agents also discovered still images from the videos of A.G. and C.R. on Lebowitz's computer, stored in a manner indicating that the images had been distributed over the internet. A.G. and the defendant began a sexual relationship when A.G. was 16 years old. However, A.G. provided conflicting statements regarding whether he was under the age of 18 at the time the video was made. C.R. began engaging in sexual relations with Lebowitz when C.R. was 15 years old. Lebowitz and C.R. engaged in sexual acts on at least ten occasions. All but the sexual encounter on the videotape occurred in Lebowitz's car. When C.R. was 16 years old, Lebowitz asked C.R. to make a videotape of their sex acts. C.R. agreed. C.R. met Lebowitz at their normal rendezvous location. Lebowitz had brought a tripod and camera, but told C.R. there was not enough space in the car to make the video. Lebowitz crawled through C.R.'s bedroom window, Lebowitz set up the video equipment in C.R.'s bedroom, and Lebowitz recorded their sexual acts....

On June 12, 2007, a federal grand jury charged Lebowitz with two counts of producing child pornography, in violation of 18 U.S.C. §2251(a) and (e).... Lebowitz challenges the constitutionality of 18 U.S.C. §2251(a),[4] contending that the statute conflicts with the age of consent in Georgia and therefore fails to provide sufficient notice that his conduct was illegal.[5] ...

Section 2251(a) required the Government prove beyond a reasonable doubt that one purpose of the sexually explicit conduct was to produce a visual depiction. 18 U.S.C. §2251(a). The Government did not have to prove that Lebowitz was single-minded in

---

4. 18 U.S.C. §2251(a) provides that "[a]ny person who employs, uses, persuades, induces, entices, or coerces any minor to engage in, ... any sexually explicit conduct for the purpose of producing any visual depiction of such conduct ... shall be punished as provided under subsection (e), ... if such visual depiction has actually been ... transmitted using any means or facility of interstate ... commerce...." 18 U.S.C. §2256(1) defines a minor as "any person under the age of eighteen years."

5. Lebowitz also argues that because the age of consent in Georgia is 16, *Lawrence v. Texas*, 539 U.S. 558, 123 S.Ct. 2472, 156 L.Ed.2d 508 (2003), protects his conduct. *Lawrence* concerned private conduct between consenting adults. *Id.* at 578, 123 S.Ct. at 2484. Even if *Lawrence* protected the sexual conduct depicted on the video tape, the jury found beyond a reasonable doubt that the depictions created by Lebowitz traveled across state lines by means of computer. Thus, the depictions of Lebowitz's private conduct became publicly traded contraband. *Lawrence* is therefore immaterial to our as-applied due process analysis.

his purpose. *See Ortiz-Graulau*, 526 F.3d at 19; *cf. United States v. Sirois*, 87 F.3d 34, 39 (2d Cir.1996) ("The criminal law applies to everyone, not just the single-minded. And a person who transports children across state lines both to engage in sexual intercourse with them and to photograph that activity is no less a child pornographer simply because he is also a pedophile.")

Lebowitz claims the recording was only incidental to his sexual encounter with C.R. The evidence belies his argument. C.R. testified that he and Lebowitz discussed videotaping a sexual encounter prior to the recording. Lebowitz brought the camera and a tripod, carried them through C.R.'s bedroom window, and set up the equipment. The sexual encounter occurred in C.R.'s bedroom only because there was not room for the recording equipment in Lebowitz's car. Such purposeful conduct cannot be described as incidental. *See Ortiz-Graulau*, 526 F.3d at 19 ("This is not a case of a security camera mechanically picking up a random act."); *Webster's Third New Int'l Dictionary* 1142 (3d ed.1976) (defining "incidental" as "occurring merely by chance or without intention or calculation"). Whether some other sexual encounter would have occurred even without recording equipment is irrelevant. A reasonable jury could conclude Lebowitz violated 18 U.S.C. § 2251(a)....

Lebowitz argues that the district court failed to adequately instruct the jury as to the elements of § 2251(a). Lebowitz's requested instruction would have required the jury to find beyond a reasonable doubt that "the making of the visual depiction of sexually explicit conduct was a dominant motive for Defendant's actions toward ... C.R...., and was not merely incidental to their interactions." Instead, the district court's instruction tracked the statutory language, requiring the jury to find beyond a reasonable doubt that Lebowitz "employed, used, persuaded, induced, enticed or coerced the minor to engage in sexually explicit conduct for the purpose of producing a visual depiction of such conduct."

In support of his "dominant motive" requirement, Lebowitz cites *Mortensen v. United States*, 322 U.S. 369, 64 S.Ct. 1037, 88 L.Ed. 1331 (1944), and *Forrest v. United States*, 363 F.2d 348 (5th Cir.1966). Both are Mann Act cases involving crimes other than the production of child pornography. Even if Mann Act precedent applies to 18 U.S.C. § 2251(a), refusal to give the requested instruction would not have been error. "This court has long declined to extend the doctrine of *Mortensen* beyond its facts." *Forrest*, 363 F.2d at 350. Instead, we have held that dual purposes are sufficient for a conviction, and we "need not concern ourselves" with whether the illegal purpose was dominant over other purposes. *Id.* at 352. Our model Mann Act jury instructions reflect this holding.... [citation omitted]. Thus, the requested "dominant motive" language was substantively incorrect, and the district court correctly refused to give the instruction.

As for the "merely incidental" language, Lebowitz has not demonstrated that the failure to include this language substantially impaired his ability to present an effective defense. Lebowitz argued repeatedly to the jury that the video recording of C.R. was incidental to their consensual relationship. Lebowitz could make this argument because incidental acts are, by definition, the opposite of purposeful ones. *Webster's Third New Int'l Dictionary* 1142, 1847 (3d ed.1976) (defining "incidental" as "occurring merely by chance or without intention or calculation" and "purposeful" as "guided by a definite aim"). Omission of the requested "merely incidental" language did not impair Lebowitz's ability to present an effective defense, and the district court did not abuse its discretion....

For the reasons stated above, we reject Lebowitz's challenges to his convictions.... The judgment of the district court is affirmed.

AFFIRMED.

Notes

The defendant in *Lebowitz* is convicted under 18 U.S.C. § 2251(a), which prohibits using a minor with the intent that the minor engage in any sexually explicit conduct for the purpose of producing a visual depiction of such conduct and later transmitting it over the internet. *See also U.S. v. Morales-de Jesus*, 372 F.3d 6 (1st Cir. (P.R.) 2004) (defendant actively concealing fact of videotaping from 13-year-old girl, instructing girl's positioning relative to camera, instructing on what to say during taping, using remote control to operate camera's zoom feature, and videotaping multiple encounters, on one occasion returning to car to retrieve video equipment after bringing girl to motel room, was sufficient evidence to find defendant acted "for the purpose" of videotaping sexual conduct). Transmitting photographs by means of the Internet is tantamount to moving photographs across state lines and, thus, constitutes transportation in "interstate commerce," for purposes of the federal child pornography statute. *See U.S. v. Runyan*, 290 F.3d 223 (5th Cir. 2002). Even when the visual depictions are not transmitted over the Internet but, rather, are produced for private viewing and possession in the privacy of one's own home, the child pornography provisions under § 2251(a) may be constitutionally applied, whereas intrastate production of child pornography, taken in aggregation with others engaged in similar activities, substantially affects interstate commerce, and, therefore, criminalizing such activity is necessary to close a loophole that undermines Congress' ability to regulate interstate child pornography. *See U.S. v. Blum*, 534 F.3d 608 (7th Cir. 2008); *U.S. v. Poulin*, 588 F. Supp. 2d 58 (D. Me. 2008). In fact, the statute is applicable even when the defendant is unsuccessful in his or her attempt to actually produce a visual depiction of sexually explicit conduct with a minor. *See U.S. v. Buculei*, 262 F.3d 322 (4th Cir. 2001). "Use" of a minor for purposes of § 2251 may include merely taking sexually explicit photographs of the minor, *see U.S. v. Vanhorn*, 740 F.3d 1166 (8th Cir. 2014); *U.S. v. Sirous*, 87 F.3d 34 (2d Cir. 1996), even if the minor is sleeping, *see U.S. v. Finley*, 726 F.3d 483 (3d Cir. 2013), or even if the minor is married or legally emancipated, *see U.S. v. Stringer*, 739 F.3d 391 (8th Cir. 2014). The statute even applies if the minor is only fictitious. *See U.S. v. Lee*, 603 F.3d 904 (11th Cir. 2010). *See also U.S. v. Puglisi*, 458 Fed. Appx. 31 (2d Cir. 2012) (defendant's explicit text messages to victim attempting to persuade her to touch herself held sufficient to find defendant used, employed, persuaded, induced, enticed, or coerced minor to take part in sexually explicit conduct for purpose of producing visual depiction of that conduct).

b. Use of Materials That Have Traveled in Interstate Commerce

United States v. Foley

Seventh Circuit, 2014
740 F.3d 1079

HAMILTON, Circuit Judge....

After his trial and guilty verdict, Foley filed a motion for acquittal pursuant to Federal Rule of Criminal Procedure 29 challenging the sufficiency of the evidence on the production counts. To convict Foley, the government was required to prove that Foley used "material that had been mailed, shipped, or transported in or affecting interstate or foreign commerce" to produce images of child pornography. 18 U.S.C. § 2251(a). At trial, the government introduced two computer hard drives containing pornographic images and videos. One hard drive had been manufactured in Thailand and the other in China. Both were seized from computers in Foley's apartment during the execution of a search warrant.

The FBI and police had obtained the search warrant after Foley mailed a DVD containing child pornography to a television reporter in an apparent attempt to frame his landlord on possession charges. Foley also met with a private investigator, made allegations against his landlord, and handed over a laptop computer that his landlord supposedly had left behind at Foley's barber shop. A file on the laptop contained several videos and hundreds of still images of child pornography. The government presented testimony that Foley had in fact purchased the computer shortly before turning it over to the investigator. An FBI forensic investigator found that the images on the DVD that Foley sent to the reporter and the images on the hard drive of the laptop Foley turned over to the investigator were similar to the images found on Foley's computers after the execution of the search. Foley appears in at least one of the videos. He can be seen touching a minor's genitals and adjusting the angle of the camera. (To differentiate this victim from another minor who testified against Foley, we will refer to the unfortunate subject of Foley's videography as "Minor Male A.") Minor Male A testified at trial and corroborated the photographed and videotaped incidents.

The production of child pornography is a federal crime under 18 U.S.C. §2251(a). A person commits this crime if, in relevant part, he "employs, uses, persuades, induces, entices or coerces any minor to engage in ... any sexually explicit conduct for the purpose of producing any visual depiction of such conduct." The statute also contains a commerce element. That element requires the government to show either that the images traveled in, or that the defendant knew the images would travel in, interstate or foreign commerce, or that any material used to produce the images traveled in interstate or foreign commerce. *Id.* Here, the government attempted to prove its case under the third route by proving that the visual depictions of Minor Male A engaging in sexual conduct were "produced ... using materials that [had] been mailed, shipped, or transported in or affecting interstate or foreign commerce." *Id.* The government argues that the "materials" Foley used were the Thai- and Chinese-manufactured hard drives.

There is no doubt that the hard drives were manufactured in other countries and thus that they had traveled in foreign commerce. Foley argues, however, that the hard drives were insufficient to meet the prosecution's burden of proof on the commerce element of the production charges because he had not "produced" the images using the hard drives. His theory is that he produced the images using only a camera and that later transfers of the images to the hard drives were not part of the production process. Foley insists that the government was required to prove that the camera he used to create the pornographic images of Minor Male A had traveled in foreign or interstate commerce. Because the government had not offered evidence concerning the unknown camera, he moved for acquittal. The district court denied his motion, and Foley appeals. . . .

For purposes of child pornography crimes, "producing" is defined in 18 U.S.C. §2256(3) as "producing, directing, manufacturing, issuing, publishing, or advertising." Although the statutory definition serves as a guidepost, it does not fully resolve the question before us. Foley argues that "producing" should be interpreted narrowly, limited to the exact moment in time when the visual depiction of the child is first captured on film or digital medium. Under Foley's interpretation, the government could satisfy the commerce element only by proving that the means of that capture—the camera—had traveled in interstate or foreign commerce.

We view the issue as whether a jury could find that storage of a visual image for later retrieval is part of the process of "producing" [sic] under the statutory definition. The answer is yes. Our decision in *United States v. Angle*, 234 F.3d 326, 340–41 (7th Cir.2000), is not controlling but is instructive. Defendant Angle challenged his conviction for possession of child pornography based on the sufficiency of the government's evidence on the commerce element. The government had introduced as evidence the computer diskettes and zip disks onto which Angle had copied pornographic images. The diskettes had been manufactured out of state and then transported in interstate commerce. Angle argued for a narrow interpretation of the word "producing" under which the diskettes, as storage devices onto which he had copied the pornographic images, were insufficient proof that the images had been "produced" using the diskettes. We disagreed. We found that Angle's interpretation would "essentially render[ ] meaningless the statutory definition of 'producing'" and that copying images can be part of the production process. *Id.* at 341. Images may be "produced" when pieces of computer equipment, "including computer diskettes, are used to copy the depictions onto the diskettes that have traveled in interstate commerce." *Angle*, 234 F.3d at 341; see also *United States v. Anderson*, 280 F.3d 1121, 1125 (7th Cir.2002) (rejecting defendant's challenge to the sufficiency of his indictment for child pornography possession where indictment alleged defendant's internationally-manufactured hard drives "contained" images instead of "produced" images; "computerized images are produced when computer equipment is used to copy or download the images").

Though *Angle* was a case of child pornography possession and not production, the commerce elements of the possession and production statutes are nearly identical. Compare 18 U.S.C. § 2251(a) (commerce element for production) ("produced or transmitted using materials that have been mailed, shipped, or transported in or affecting interstate or foreign commerce"), with commerce elements in 18 U.S.C. § 2252(a)(4)(B) (possession) ("produced using materials which have been mailed or so shipped or transported") and 18 U.S.C. § 2252A(a)(5)(B) (possession) ("produced using materials that have been mailed, or shipped or transported in or affecting interstate or foreign commerce"). For purposes of the commerce element and the meaning of "production," we do not see any meaningful distinction between the diskettes that Angle used to copy and store his images and the hard drives that Foley used to copy and store his. Though Foley was free to argue otherwise, a jury certainly could have found that Foley's hard drives were materials used in the production process sufficient to satisfy the commerce element.

Other circuits that have grappled with the meaning of "production" in the federal child pornography statutes have reached similar conclusions. In a child pornography production case in the First Circuit, the defendant argued that the government was required to identify the precise moment at which "production" occurred—at image capture, recording, or storage—and then was required to prove whether the particular device involved at the moment of production had moved in interstate or foreign commerce. *United States v. Poulin*, 631 F.3d 17, 22–23 (1st Cir.2011). Searches had uncovered the defendant's cameras and the DVDs he had recorded, but not the means of transfer between the camera and the DVDs. It was this link that the defendant seemed to believe was crucial to "production."

In rejecting the defendant's argument, the court explained, "Congress intended a broad ban on the production of child pornography and aimed to prohibit the varied means by which an individual might actively create it." *Id.* at 23. The court found that Congress did not mean to enact a hyper-technical definition of the term "producing" and that the term should be interpreted broadly. *Id.* at 22. It was unnecessary for the government either to prove precisely when "production" occurred or to produce at trial the equipment the defendant had used at that moment. The court found that a reasonable fact-finder could have found that the internationally-manufactured media equipment produced at trial were used to "produce" the images.

Likewise, in *United States v. Schene*, 543 F.3d 627, 639 (10th Cir.2008), the Tenth Circuit found that the commerce element was established for a child pornography possession charge where the defendant "produced" the pornographic images by copying or downloading them onto a hard drive that had been manufactured in foreign commerce.[1] The Eighth and Ninth Circuits also have upheld child pornography convictions under a more expansive interpretation of "production." See, *e.g.*, *United States v. Fadl*, 498 F.3d 862, 866–67 (8th Cir.2007) (rejecting defendant's argument that production conviction required proof that he took directorial role or intended commercial distribution of images; Congress intended a nontechnical definition of "producing" and sought to include activities not generally considered to fall within the typical meaning of the term); *United States v. Lacy*, 119 F.3d 742, 750 (9th Cir.1997) (proof that defendant's computer hard drive, monitor, and storage disks had traveled in commerce was sufficient to prove commerce element of possession charge; rejecting defendant's argument that images were "produced" before they were copied or downloaded onto his computer).

Foley cites an Eighth Circuit case, *United States v. Mugan*, 441 F.3d 622, 625–26 (8th Cir.2006), to support his argument that a storage device can be part of the "production" process only when the device is part of the camera that captured the image, such as a camera's memory card or memory stick. The *Mugan* court clearly did not go that far, however. Mugan brought both facial and as-applied challenges to Congress's power to criminalize child pornography, contending there was an insufficient nexus between the local production of child pornography and interstate commerce. The Eighth Circuit rejected Mugan's constitutional challenge and affirmed his conviction for child pornography production based on the government's showing that he used a camera with a memory card that had moved in interstate commerce. *Id.* at 630. The court's finding that Mugan's camera with its memory card was *sufficient* evidence to satisfy the commerce element was not, as Foley contends, a finding that the camera was *necessary*. The court did not hold or imply, for example, that hard drives or other image storage devices, standing alone, would not be sufficient evidence from which a jury could tie the production of the images to interstate or foreign commerce. *Mugan*, therefore, is in line with the precedents discussed above and does not help Foley.

Nor do we share Foley's concern that allowing a jury to apply the word "produced" broadly will result in a conflation of child pornography production crimes and possession crimes. To prove child pornography production, the government must prove that the defendant employed, used, persuaded, induced, enticed, or coerced a minor to engage in sexually explicit conduct for the purpose of producing any visual depiction of such conduct. 18 U.S.C. §2251(a). (Of course, the government must also prove the commerce element of the crime, here that the "visual depiction was produced ... using materials ... transported in or affecting interstate or foreign commerce.") The crimes of child pornography *possession* also include commerce elements that use the word "produced." 18 U.S.C. §2252(a)(4)(B) ("produced using materials which have been mailed or so shipped or transported"); 18 U.S.C. §2252A(a)(5)(B) ("produced using materials that have been mailed, or shipped or transported in or affecting interstate or foreign commerce").

---

1. An earlier ruling of the Tenth Circuit, *United States v. Wilson*, 182 F.3d 737, 743 (10th Cir.1999), called into question "whether a computer graphics file is produced or created prior to being recorded on a particular storage media, or whether, instead, it only comes into being at or after the point it is recorded on the storage media." Because the court was not satisfied that the government had proved that the computer diskette on which the defendant's images were recorded could satisfy the commerce requirement for production, it reversed the defendant's conviction. In *Schene*, however, the Tenth Circuit explicitly found that this question had been answered and that the visual depictions were "produced" when they were copied or downloaded onto the defendant's hard drive. 543 F.3d at 638–39.

We are hard pressed to understand how a prosecution for child pornography possession could be elevated to a prosecution for production based on the commerce element alone. Even if the government can prove that a person in possession of child pornography copied, downloaded, or stored images sufficient to satisfy the commerce element under an expansive interpretation of "produced," the possessor's act of copying, downloading or storing would not amount to proof that the possessor "employed, used, persuaded, induced, enticed, or coerced any minor to engage in … sexually explicit conduct," as required for a production charge. We see little risk of prosecutorial overreach by this theory.

Congress intended a broad definition of "producing" when it defined it as "producing, directing, manufacturing, issuing, publishing, or advertising" a visual depiction. 18 U.S.C. § 2256(3). To "issue" or "publish" a visual depiction, for example, a defendant would need to copy or store the visual depiction. The defendant's chosen storage devices — here, Foley's hard drives — could be considered by a jury as material used in "production" sufficient to satisfy the commerce element, assuming sufficient proof that the storage device at issue traveled in interstate or foreign commerce. A narrower construction, particularly one that would limit "production" to only the moment an image is captured by a camera, is problematic for the simple reason that it is not compatible with Congress's definition of production. How does someone "direct" or "advertise" using a camera? A narrower construction would also enable a producer of child pornography to immunize himself from prosecution for production by copying the digital files to a new storage medium and then simply dropping his camera in the nearest lake. That cannot be what Congress intended. And our conclusion is bolstered by Congress's definition of "visual depiction," which clearly contemplates the digital storage of the images post-creation. 18 U.S.C. § 2256(5) ("visual depiction" includes "data *stored* on computer disk or by electronic means which is capable of conversion into a visual image") (emphasis added). A jury could find that the means of copying or storage — the diskettes in *Angle* and the hard drives here — are part of the production process, and are material that could satisfy the government's burden to prove the commerce element. Accordingly, we affirm the district court's denial of Foley's motion for acquittal on the production charges.

The district court's judgment is AFFIRMED.

United States v. Jeronimo-Bautista

Tenth Circuit, 2005
425 F.3d 1266

SEYMOUR , Circuit Judge. . . .

On January 29, 2004, Mr. Jeronimo-Bautista and two other men, while in the company of a thirteen year-old girl, entered a vacant residence in Magna, Utah. At some point the girl became unconscious, possibly after ingesting an intoxicating substance. After she lost consciousness, the three men removed her clothing, sexually assaulted her, and took photographs of their actions. The camera used to take the photographs was not manufactured in the state of Utah. . . . One of the men took the film to a one-hour photo lab for processing. In the course of developing the film, staff at the lab noticed images that appeared to depict the sexual assault of a minor female. The manager of the lab called the police, who viewed the photographs and then initiated an investigation resulting in the arrest and indictment of Mr. Jeronimo-Bautista. As noted by the district court, it was undisputed that Mr. Jeronimo-Bautista was a citizen of Mexico and resided in the State of Utah. *Jeronimo-Bautista*, 319 F.Supp.2d at 1274. The victim was born in Utah and was not transported across state lines in connection with the acts charged in the indictment. *Id.* Moreover, "[t]he photos were never disseminated, were not stored or transmitted electronically via the Internet, the United States Postal Service, nor by any other method across state lines or internationally. There is no indication that [Mr. Jeronimo-Bautista] had any intention of so transmitting or storing the images." *Id.*

The indictment charged that Mr. Jeronimo-Bautista, along with the two other men ... [footnote omitted]

> did knowingly employ, use, persuade, induce, entice, and coerce a minor ... to engage in sexually explicit conduct for the purpose of producing visual depictions of such conduct, which visual depictions were produced using materials that have been mailed, shipped, and transported in interstate and foreign commerce, and did aid and abet each other therein,

[citation to Record omitted], thereby violating §2251(a) (production of child pornography) ... [footnote omitted] and 18 U.S.C. §2 (aiding and abetting). Mr. Jeronimo-Bautista moved to dismiss the indictment on the ground that the district court did not have subject matter jurisdiction over the acts charged against him, contending §2251(a) violated the Commerce Clause as applied to him. The district court agreed, concluding that Mr. Jeronimo-Bautista's charged activity "was not of a type demonstrated to be *substantially* connected or related to interstate commerce." *Jeronimo-Bautista*, 319 F.Supp.2d at 1282. This case is now before us on the government's appeal....

We review "challenges to the constitutionality of a statute *de novo.*" *United States v. Dorris*, 236 F.3d 582, 584 (10th Cir.2000). The United States Constitution grants to Congress the "Power to ... regulate Commerce ... among the several States." U.S. Const. art I, §8, cl. 3. As relevant here, "Congress' commerce authority includes the power to regulate those activities having a substantial relation to interstate commerce, *i.e.,* those activities that substantially affect interstate commerce." *United States v. Lopez*, 514 U.S. 549, 558–59, 115 S.Ct. 1624, 131 L.Ed.2d 626 (1995) (internal citations omitted). Hence we must determine whether Mr. Jeronimo-Bautista's local production of pornographic images of a child substantially affects interstate commerce.

In addressing Mr. Jeronimo-Bautista's as applied challenge to the statute, the district court noted the four factors delineated by the Supreme Court in *United States v. Morrison*, 529 U.S. 598, 120 S.Ct. 1740, 146 L.Ed.2d 658 (2000), and in *Lopez* "for consideration in addressing the constitutionality of a statute based upon Commerce Clause authority." *Jeronimo-Bautista*, 319 F.Supp.2d at 1278. The court accurately described those factors as (1) whether the prohibited activity is commercial or economic in nature; (2) whether the statute's reach was limited by an express jurisdictional element; (3) whether Congress made findings about the effects of the prohibited conduct on interstate commerce; and (4), whether there exists a link between the prohibited conduct and the effect on interstate commerce. *Id.*

Working its way through the *Lopez/Morrison* factors, the district court first rejected the argument that Mr. Jeronimo-Bautista's activity was economic in nature and, in doing so, rejected the assertion that Mr. Jeronimo-Bautista's intrastate activities could, in the aggregate, affect interstate commerce. *Id.* Second, the court determined §2251(a)'s express jurisdictional element failed "to place any meaningful restrictions on federal jurisdiction and fail[ed] to establish the link between the violation and interstate commerce." *Id.* at 1280. Third, the court was not convinced the existence of Congressional findings regarding the child pornography industry was "sufficient, by itself, to sustain the constitutionality of Commerce Clause legislation as applied to the facts of this case." *Id.* (internal quotation omitted). Finally, referring back to its determination that Mr. Jeronimo-Bautista's activity could not be deemed economic in nature, the court also rejected the use of an aggregation theory to support the argument that there existed something more than only a tenuous link between Mr. Jeronimo-Bautista's prohibited activity and interstate commerce. *Id.* at 1281. The court dismissed the indictment against Mr. Jeronimo-Bautista on the grounds that as applied to the specific facts of his case, § 2251(a) violated the Commerce Clause.... Pending this appeal, the Supreme Court decided *Gonzales v. Raich*, 545U.S. 1, 125 S.Ct. 2195, 162 L.Ed.2d 1 (2005), in which it rejected an as applied challenge to the Controlled Substances Act (CSA), 21 U.S.C. § 801 *et seq.*, and held that Congress could regulate the purely local production, possession, and use of marijuana for personal medical purposes. *Raich*, 125 S.Ct. at 2215. As we discuss in more detail below, the Court's reasoning in *Raich*, coupled with the standard four factor *Lopez/Morrison* analysis, supports our conclusion that the district court erred in concluding § 2251(a) violates the Commerce Clause as applied to Mr. Jeronimo-Bautista.

We begin by examining the findings accompanying the comprehensive scheme developed by Congress to eliminate the production, possession, and dissemination of child pornography. When Congress first passed the Protection of Children Against Sexual Exploitation Act of 1977, it noted "that child pornography ... [has] become [a] highly organized, multimillion dollar industr[y] that operate[s] on a nationwide scale ... [and that] the sale and distribution of such pornographic materials are carried on to a substantial extent through the mails and other instrumentalities of interstate and foreign commerce." S.Rep. No. 95-438, at 5 (1977), *reprinted in* 1978 U.S.C.C.A.N. 40, 42–43.3 Findings supporting the 1977 Act also noted that

> [s]ince the production, distribution and sale of child pornography is often a clandestine operation, it is extremely difficult to determine its full extent. At present, however, a wide variety of child pornography is available in most areas of the country. Moreover, because of the vast potential profits involved, it would appear that this sordid enterprise is growing at a rapid rate.

Id. at 43.

Amendments to the Act in 1984 eliminated the requirement that "the production, receipt, transportation, or distribution of child pornography be for a 'pecuniary profit.'" *United States v. Morales-de Jesus*, 372 F.3d 6, 11 (1st Cir.2004). The purpose of this amendment was to eliminate an enforcement gap in the statute: "Many of the individuals who distribute materials covered [by the statute] do so by gift or exchange without any commercial motive and thus remain outside the coverage of this provision." H.R.Rep. No. 98-536, at 2 (1983), *reprinted in* 1984 U.S.C.C.A.N. 492, 493; *see also* H.R.Rep. No. 99-910, at 4 (1986), *reprinted in* 1986 U.S.C.C.A.N. 5952, 5954 (1984 amendments sought to "eliminate the requirement that interstate distribution be for the purpose of sale; experience revealed that much if not most child pornography material is distributed through an underground network of pedophiles who exchange the material on a non-commercial basis, thus no sale is involved"). Likewise, in 1984, in support of § 2251, Congress echoed its findings supporting the original 1977 legislation, stating in part that "child pornography has developed into a highly organized, multi-million-dollar industry which operates on a nationwide scale." H.R. 3635, 98th Cong. (2nd Sess.1984); *see also* H.J. Res. 738, 99th Cong., 100 Stat. 1783 (1986) ("child exploitation has become a multi-million dollar industry, infiltrated and operated by elements of organized crime, and by a nationwide network of individuals openly advertising their desire to exploit children").

In 1996, Congress further amended the Act regarding the electronic creation of child pornography. *See Morales-de Jesus*, 372 F.3d at 11. The findings supporting those amendments noted that "the existence of ... child pornographic images ... inflames the desires of child molesters, pedophiles, and child pornographers who prey on children, thereby increasing the creation and distribution of child pornography...." S.Rep. No. 104-358, at 2 (1996), *available at* 1996 WL 506545. Congress also stated that "prohibiting the possession and viewing of child pornography will encourage the possessors of such material to rid themselves of or destroy the material, thereby helping to protect the victims of child pornography and to eliminate the market for the sexual exploitative use of children...." *Id.* at 3. Finally, in a 1998 amendment to the Act, a jurisdictional element was added to cover child pornography created "using materials that have been mailed, shipped, or transported in interstate or foreign commerce by any means." § 2251(a). This addition reflected Congress' concern "about federal law enforcement's current inability to prosecute 'a number of cases where the defendant produced the child pornography but did not intend to transport the images in interstate commerce.'" *Morales-de Jesus*, 372 F.3d at 12 (quoting H.R.Rep. No. 105-557, at 27 (1998), *reprinted in* 1998 U.S.C.C.A.N. 678, 695).

In reviewing this history, we acknowledge that Congress may not have engaged in specific fact finding regarding how the intrastate production of child pornography substantially affects the larger interstate pornography market. But the Supreme Court noted in *Raich*, 125 S.Ct. at 2208, that it has "never required Congress to make particularized findings in order to legislate." Moreover, we agree with our colleagues on the First Circuit that Congress' explicit findings regarding the "extensive national market in child pornography and the need to diminish that national market" support the contention that "prohibiting the production of child pornography at the local level" helps to further the Congressional goal. *Morales-de Jesus*, 372 F.3d at 12; *see also United States v. Adams*, 343 F.3d 1024, 1031–32 (9th Cir.2003) (outlining legislative history of child pornography statutes in rejection of Commerce Clause challenge); *United States v. Holston*, 343 F.3d 83, 85–86 (2d Cir.2003) (same); *United States v. Buculei*, 262 F.3d 322, 329 (4th Cir.2001) (same); *United States v. Kallestad*, 236 F.3d 225, 229 (5th Cir.2000) (same); *United States v. Rodia*, 194 F.3d 465, 474–75 (3d Cir.1999) (same).

The decision in *Raich* also supports the conclusion that Mr. Jeronimo-Bautista's production of the images in this case is economic in nature. "Economics refers to the production, distribution, and consumption of commodities." *Raich*, 125 S.Ct. at 2211 (internal quotations omitted). The Court held that the Controlled Substances Act "is a statute that regulates the production, distribution, and consumption of commodities for which there is an established, and lucrative, interstate market. Prohibiting the intrastate possession or manufacture of an article of commerce is a rational (and commonly utilized) means of regulating commerce in that product." *Id.* The same reasoning is applicable to the intrastate production of child pornography. Like the CSA, the child pornography statutes regulate the "production, distribution, and consumption of commodities for which there is an established, and lucrative, interstate market." *Id.* Congress' prohibition against the intrastate possession or manufacture of child pornography "is a rational (and commonly utilized) means of regulating commerce in that product." *Id.*; *see also Morales-de Jesus*, 372 F.3d at 12 (Congress' initial finding in 1977 that child pornography is a "'multimillion dollar industry that operates on a nationwide scale' emphasizes that the underlying activity regulated by the child pornography statutes—the production, distribution, and possession of child pornography—is commercial activity...."); *Holston*, 343 F.3d at 88 (finding activity covered by § 2251 economic in nature); *Buculei*, 262 F.3d at 329 (same); *Kallestad*, 236 F.3d at 228 (same regarding § 2252); *Rodia*, 194 F.3d at 480–81 (same).

In holding that a sufficient link existed between the local production and use of marijuana and its effect on interstate commerce, the Court in *Raich* relied extensively on *Wickard v. Filburn*, 317 U.S. 111, 63 S.Ct. 82, 87 L.Ed. 122 (1942). In *Wickard*, the Court upheld the Agriculture Adjustment Act of 1938, 52 Stat. 31, which permitted congressional regulation of a farmer's wholly intrastate production and consumption of wheat on his farm. *Id.* at 127–29, 63 S.Ct. 82. *Wickard* "establishes that Congress can regulate purely intrastate activity that is not itself 'commercial,' in that it is not produced for sale, if it concludes that failure to regulate that class of activity would undercut the regulation of the interstate market in that commodity." *Raich*, 125 S.Ct. at 2006. The Court noted that

> [i]n *Wickard*, we had no difficulty concluding that Congress had a rational basis for believing that, when viewed in the aggregate, leaving home-consumed wheat outside the regulatory scheme would have a substantial influence on price and market conditions. Here too, Congress had a rational basis for concluding that leaving home-consumed marijuana outside federal control would similarly affect price and market conditions.

Id. at 2207. It viewed its task as not to determine "whether respondents' activities, taken in the aggregate, substantially affect interstate commerce *in fact*, but only whether a 'rational basis' exists for so concluding." *Id.* at 2208 (quoting *Lopez*, 514 U.S. at 557, 115 S.Ct. 1624) (emphasis added).

Dismissing arguments that regulation of locally cultivated and possessed marijuana was beyond the "outer limits" of Congress' Commerce Clause authority, *id.* at 2212, the Court observed:

> [o]ne need not have a degree in economics to understand why a nationwide exemption for the vast quantity of marijuana (or other drugs) locally cultivated for personal use (which presumably would include use by friends, neighbors, and family members) may have a substantial impact on the interstate market for this extraordinarily popular substance. The congressional judgment that an exemption for such a significant segment of the total market would undermine the orderly enforcement of the entire regulatory scheme is entitled to a strong presumption of validity. Indeed, that judgment is not only rational, but "visible to the naked eye," *Lopez*, 514 U.S. at 563, 115 S.Ct. 1624, 131 L.Ed.2d 626, under any commonsense appraisal of the probable consequences of such an open-ended exemption.

Id. Finally, noting the "findings in the CSA and the undisputed magnitude of the commercial market for marijuana, [the] decisions in *Wickard v. Filburn* and the later cases endorsing its reasoning," the Court concluded Congress could regulate the "intrastate, noncommercial cultivation, possession and use of marijuana." *Id.* at 2215.

This reasoning applies to the child pornography statute at issue here. Under the aggregation theory espoused in *Wickard* and in *Raich*, the intrastate production of child pornography could, in the aggregate, have a substantial effect on the interstate market for such materials. In *Raich*, the respondents were "cultivating, for home consumption, a fungible commodity for which there [was] an established, albeit illegal, interstate market." *Id.* at 2206. Child pornography is equally fungible and there is no question an established market exists for its sale and exchange. The Court in *Raich* reasoned that where there is a high demand in the interstate market for a product, the exemption from regulation of materials produced intrastate "tends to frustrate the federal interest in eliminating commercial transactions in the interstate market in their entirety." *Id.* at 2207. For the same reasons, § 2251(a) "is squarely within Congress' commerce power because production of the commodity meant for home consumption, be it wheat…, marijuana [or child pornography], has a substantial effect on supply and demand in the national market for the commodity." *Id.* at 2207.…

Mr. Jeronimo-Bautista is challenging the statute's constitutionality as applied to him. The Court in *Raich* held the plaintiffs' as applied challenges to the CSA failed because the Court had

> no difficulty concluding that Congress acted rationally in determining that [the intrastate, noncommercial, cultivation, possession, and use of marijuana for personal medical uses], whether viewed individually or in the aggregate, [did not] compel[ ] an exemption from the CSA; rather, th[is] subdivided class of activities … was an essential part of the larger regulatory scheme.

Id. at 2211. So too in Mr. Jeronimo-Bautista's case. Congress' decision to deem illegal Mr. Jeronimo-Bautista's local production of child pornography represents a rational determination that such local activities constitute an essential part of the interstate market for child pornography that is well within Congress' power to regulate.

Concluding that § 2251(a), as applied to Mr. Jeronimo-Bautista, is a legitimate exercise of Congress' regulatory powers under the Commerce Clause,[5] we REVERSE the district court and REMAND for further proceedings.

Notes

The defendant in *Foley* was guilty of producing child pornography because he used two computer hard drives to transfer from a camera a visual depiction of sexually explicit conduct of a minor, and those computer hard drives were manufactured outside the United States and, thus, traveled in interstate commerce. For similar holdings in which materials that traveled in interstate commerce were used for the production of child pornography, see *United States v. Wallace*, 713 F.3d 422 (8th Cir. (Ark.) 2013) (videotape on which defendant recorded himself molesting underage female was assembled in China and then shipped to California before arriving in Arkansas); *United States v. McCloud*, 590 F.3d 560 (8th Cir. (Mo.) 2009) (memory card used by defendant was manufactured in Taiwan and shipped to the United States via Korea, and South Carolina plant manufactured paper used by defendant to print photographs of child pornography in Missouri). Several courts have held that § 2251(a) does not require that the defendant have knowledge of the interstate nature of the materials used to produce the depictions.

---

5. In so doing, we join a number of circuits, who, prior to the Supreme Court's decision in *Gonzales v. Raich*, 545 U.S. 1, 125 S.Ct. 2195, 162 L.Ed.2d 1 (2005), rejected, under varying theories, as applied and facial challenges to the child pornography possession and production statutes. *See United States v. Morales-de Jesus*, 372 F.3d 6 (1st Cir.2004) (rejecting facial and as applied challenges to § 2251(a)); *United States v. Adams*, 343 F.3d 1024 (9th Cir.2003) (rejecting facial challenge to § 2252(a)(4)(B)); *United States v. Holston*, 343 F.3d 83 (2d Cir.2003) (rejecting facial and as applied challenges to § 2251(a)); *United States v. Buculei*, 262 F.3d 322 (4th Cir.2001) (rejecting as applied challenge to § 2251(a)); *United States v. Hampton*, 260 F.3d 832 (8th Cir.2001) (rejecting facial challenge to § 2251(a) and § 2252(a)(4)(B)); *United States v. Galo*, 239 F.3d 572 (3d Cir.2001) (rejecting facial and as applied challenge to § 2251(a) and § 2252(a)(4)(B)); *United States v. Kallestad*, 236 F.3d 225 (5th Cir.2000) (rejecting facial challenge to § 2252(a)); *United States v. Angle*, 234 F.3d 326 (7th Cir.2000) (rejecting facial challenge to § 2252(a)(4)(B)). Recently, in *United States v. Riccardi*, 405 F.3d 852 (10th Cir.2005), our circuit rejected an as applied challenge to § 2252(a)(4)(B). *But see United States v. Smith*, 402 F.3d 1303 (11th Cir.) (finding § 2251(a) and § 2252(a)(5)(B) unconstitutional as applied), *vacated and remanded by* 545 U.S. 1125, 125 S.Ct. 2938, 162 L.Ed.2d 863 (2005); *United States v. McCoy*, 323 F.3d 1114 (9th Cir.2003) (same as to § 2252(a)(4)(B)); *United States v. Corp*, 236 F.3d 325 (6th Cir.2001) (same).

See, e.g., United States v. Sheldon, 755 F.3d 1047 (9th Cir. 2014) (government need not prove defendant's knowledge that recorder used to produce videos in Montana was manufactured in China); *United States v. Terrell,* 700 F.3d 755, 759 (5th Cir. 2012) (knowledge must be proven only as to the first jurisdictional basis under § 2251(a) — that a depiction is produced with the intent that it travel in interstate commerce — because each jurisdictional clause within the provision is distinct); *United States v. Smith,* 459 F.3d 1276, 1289 (11th Cir. 2006) ("The text of the statute simply does not provide a basis to conclude that knowledge of the jurisdictional nexus is plainly required.").

The *Jeronimo-Bautista* case demonstrates the scope of Congress's power to regulate child pornography under the commerce clause in cases in which the production of child pornography is entirely intrastate, or in which the defendant produces child pornography for his or her personal use within the home. For a similar holding, see *United States v. Olson,* 317 Fed. Appx. 534 (7th Cir. 2013) (no commerce clause violation despite defendant's claim that only alleged movement in interstate commerce was traveling of blank media, and only subsequent, entirely intrastate activity converted them to pornography, rendering media unlawful). *See also United States v. Sullivan,* 2014 WL 2199316 (9th Cir. 2014); *United States v. Parton,* 2014 WL 1689199 (11th Cir. 2014) (Congress has power to regulate purely intrastate activity, whether economic or not, that it deems to have the capability, in the aggregate, of frustrating the broader regulation of interstate economic activity); *United States v. Rose,* 714 F.3d 362 (6th Cir. 2013) (statute applied to defendant who produced child pornography for noncommercial reasons in his home); *United States v. Culver,* 598 F.3d 740 (11th Cir. 2010) (magnetic tape, which was manufactured in Japan and was component of finished 8mm videotape assembled in Alabama, constituted "materials" within meaning of statute; defendant could not have made visual depictions at issue without the magnetic tape); *United States v. Maxwell,* 446 F.3d 1210 (11th Cir. 2006) ("*Maxwell II*") (Child Pornography Prevention Act (CPPA) provisions criminalizing the production and possession of child pornography applies to the intrastate possession of child pornography, regardless of whether it had traveled in interstate commerce); *United States v. Holston,* 343 F.3d 83, 90 (2d Cir. 2003) ("materials-in-commerce" test applies to child pornography produced intrastate and intended solely for home, personal use).

c. Visual Depictions That Travel in Interstate Commerce

United States v. Smith

Ninth Circuit, 1986
795 F.2d 841

WIGGINS, Circuit Judge: ...

In 1984, Smith took photographs of three teenage girls in various stages of nudity, for the purpose, he asserts, of starting a catalog of lingerie and beauty products for teenage girls. Smith claims the photographs were not to be shown to anyone but himself and the girls themselves, and the government introduced no evidence at trial to contradict this assertion.... Smith mailed the undeveloped, unprocessed film to a photo company in Maryland through a standard "film mailer." The company services only private (as opposed to commercial) photographers. After developing the film, the company contacted U.S. postal inspectors. The postal inspectors examined the photographs, consulted a pediatrician, interviewed Smith and two of the children in the photographs, and then filed an affidavit for a warrant to search Smith's residence. A magistrate issued the warrant, and [a] search ... [ensued].

Smith was charged with three counts of inducing or coercing a minor to engage in sexually explicit conduct (specifically sadistic and masochistic abuse) for the purpose of producing visual depictions of such conduct (18 U.S.C. § 2251(a) (1984 Supp.)) ... [and] three counts of mailing such visual depictions (18 U.S.C. § 2252(a) (1984 Supp.)).... A jury convicted Smith on [both] counts.... Smith contends that there was insufficient evidence to allow a reasonable jury to conclude that he intended to distribute the pictures to others, rather than merely use them himself. The government does not dispute this, but argues that proof of intent to distribute is unnecessary under sections 2251 and 2252.[2] Therefore, although Smith frames his argument in terms of sufficiency of evidence, the real issue turns on interpretation of the statutes, which is a question of law reviewable *de novo*. *See United States v. Wilson*, 720 F.2d 608, 609 n. 2 (9th Cir.1983), *cert. denied*, 465 U.S. 1034, 104 S.Ct. 1304, 79 L.Ed.2d 703 (1984).

The language of sections 2251 and 2252 is clear and unambiguous. The plain language of the sections simply makes illegal the inducement of children into sexual conduct for the purpose of creating visual depictions of that conduct (section 2251) and the mailing of such visual depictions (section 2252). Neither section requires that the defendant's ultimate goal be distribution of the visual depiction.... Earlier versions of sections 2251 and 2252 both required that the prohibited visual depictions be "for the purpose of sale or distribution for sale," *see* 18 U.S.C. §§ 2251, 2252 (1982) (amended), but the 1984 amendments eliminated that language, as Smith concedes. Smith nevertheless argues that the 1984 amendments were intended only to close a potential loophole for distributors who exchanged, lent, or gave away material, rather than selling it. It was not intended, Smith argues, to eliminate the distinction between distributors and mere producers for personal use. He urges us to consider a number of passages in the legislative history that strongly suggest the amendment was designed to allow prosecution of *noncommercial* distributors....

The legislative history in the present case does not outweigh the plain language of the statute. Although the committee reports and the floor debate strongly suggest that Congress deleted the language "for the purpose of sale or distribution for sale" to eliminate the existing loophole for the nonprofit distributor, *see, e.g.*, H. Rep. No. 536, 98th Cong., 2d Sess., *reprinted in* 1984 U.S.Code Cong. & Ad.News 492, the available materials do not explicitly demonstrate that Congress intended to exempt nondistributing producers and users from the scope of the amended statute. The legislators simply seem not to have considered such producers and users at all.... This possible lack of consideration falls short of overcoming the plain language of the statute. In the absence of a clear indication that Congress did not mean what it said, we must abide by the terms of the statute as written,

---

2. The statutes provide in relevant part:
   § 2251
   (a) Any person who employs, uses, persuades, induces, entices, or coerces any minor to engage in, or who has a minor assist any other person to engage in, any sexually explicit conduct for the purpose of producing any visual depiction of such conduct, shall be punished as provided in subsection (c), if such person knows or has reason to know that such visual depiction will be ... mailed, or if such visual depiction has actually been ... mailed.
   § 2252
   (a) Any person who—
       (1) knowingly ... mails any visual depiction, if—
       (A) the producing of such visual depiction involves the use of a minor engaging in sexually explicit conduct; and
       (B) such visual depiction is of such conduct,
   shall be punished as provided in subsection (b) of this section.

which cover Smith's behavior. Smith's assertion that the government must prove that he intended to distribute the visual depictions therefore fails....

Smith also argues that unprocessed, undeveloped film does not constitute a "visual depiction" within the terms of the statute. He argues that substantial, complicated, and costly developing must be done before any visually perceptible image is created, and that as a result his mailing of the unprocessed film did not violate the child pornography statute.... As a preliminary matter, we note that even if Smith's argument is correct, the lack of an accomplished "visual depiction" would affect only Smith's convictions under section 2252(a) (actual transportation of visual depictions). Section 2251(a) does not require the *actual* production of a visual depiction, merely the enticement of minors "*for the purpose of producing*" a visual depiction of sexually explicit conduct. Whether the film involved here had actually reached the point of "visual depiction" or not, Smith's use of the girls was clearly "for the purpose of producing" such visual depictions. That Smith took the pictures and mailed the undeveloped film for processing and printing is sufficient proof of that purpose to allow a jury to find a violation of section 2251(a).

Turning to the merits of Smith's argument, we note that "visual depiction" is not defined in the statute.[3] Smith relies on common sense and dictionary definitions for his assertion that unprocessed film is not covered. He correctly notes that color film must undergo an elaborate developing process before any image can be perceived by the human eye.... Nevertheless, we conclude that the exclusion of unprocessed film from the statute's coverage would impede the child pornography laws by protecting a necessary intermediate step in the sexual exploitation of children. The interpretation urged by Smith would allow unrestricted interstate commerce in child pornography so long as the pornography was still in the form of undeveloped film. Such a loophole is inconsistent with congressional intent; the undeveloped state of the film does not eliminate the harm to the child victims in the film's production or the incentive to produce created by the film's trafficking. We therefore hold that undeveloped film constitutes a "visual depiction" as that term is used in 18 U.S.C. §2252(a).[4] ...

---

3. The former definition of "visual depiction" ("any film, photograph, negative, slide, book, magazine, or other visual or print medium") was deleted and not replaced by the 1984 amendments. The government cites legislative history to the effect that the deletion was merely intended to eliminate written (i.e., nonvisual) material from the reach of the statute. Prohibition of such written material raised first amendment questions, *see New York v. Ferber*, 458 U.S. 747, 764–65, 102 S.Ct. 3348, 3358–59, 73 L.Ed.2d 1113 (1982), and was not considered necessary for the protection of the children Congress identified as the victims of the child pornography industry.

In view of our conclusion below based on the broader, affirmative intent of Congress, however, we need not rely on this narrower, "negative" legislative history to characterize undeveloped film as a "visual depiction" within section 2255.

4. Although Smith did not specifically raise the issue of due process, we feel that our conclusion here compels us to address the issue.

As a matter of due process, "[n]o one may be required at peril of life, liberty or property to speculate as to the meaning of penal statutes. All are entitled to be informed as to what the State commands or forbids." *Lanzetta v. New Jersey*, 306 U.S. 451, 453, 59 S.Ct. 618, 619, 83 L.Ed. 888 (1939), *quoted in Hynes v. Mayor of Oradell*, 425 U.S. 610, 620, 96 S.Ct. 1755, 1760, 48 L.Ed.2d 243 (1976). A statute must fail for vagueness if persons "of common intelligence must necessarily guess at its meaning." *Connally v. General Construction Co.*, 269 U.S. 385, 391, 46 S.Ct. 126, 127, 70 L.Ed. 322 (1926), *quoted in Hynes*, 425 U.S. at 620, 96 S.Ct. at 1760. We must therefore consider whether a statute forbidding the mailing of "visual depictions" of sexually explicit conduct by minors gave Smith fair notice that the mailing of undeveloped film of such activities was thereby prohibited.

We conclude that fair notice was given. The statute clearly forbids the condition precedent of the undeveloped film, the actual inducement of minors into the sexually explicit conduct to be photographed. *See* 18 U.S.C. §2251. The statute likewise prohibits the mailing of negatives and prints,

AFFIRMED.

Notes

In *Smith*, the court held that undeveloped film containing child pornography is a sufficient visual depiction such that the government may regulate it within interstate commerce. Likewise, in *United States v. Sturm*, 672 F.3d 891 (10th Cir. 2012), the court defined "visual depiction" in the context of the requirement that the depiction travel in interstate commerce. In *Sturm*, the defendants reproduced child pornography using a peer-to-peer file sharing program and were charged with receiving, possessing, and distributing child pornography under 18 U.S.C. § 2252A, which includes the same interstate commerce requirements as for production under § 2251(a). In *Sturm*, the court held that for purposes of the visual depiction traveling in interstate commerce, it is not necessary that the specific digital image found on the defendant's computer travel in interstate commerce; instead, only the substantive content of the image depicting a minor engaged in sexually explicit conduct must travel in interstate commerce.

2. Production by a Parent, Guardian, or Custodian

Hoggard v. Arkansas

Eighth Circuit, 2001

254 F.3d 744

RICHARD S. ARNOLD, Circuit Judge.

Roy Adrin Hoggard has been convicted by a jury on eight counts of permitting minor children to engage in sexually explicit conduct for the purpose of producing a visual depiction, in violation of 18 U.S.C. § 2251(b) and 18 U.S.C. § 2. The District Court ... [footnote omitted] sentenced Mr. Hoggard to thirty years in prison (360 months), with supervised release to follow for three years. Mr. Hoggard appeals, urging two points.

First, the District Court denied the defendant's motion to suppress evidence obtained during a search of his car. It is undisputed that the car was lawfully stopped for speeding. The officer who made the stop asked the defendant if he could look in the car. The defendant said that he could, and asked if the officer would like to start with the trunk. The defendant then opened the trunk. A small safe was seen inside. The officer asked if he could look inside the safe, and the defendant said yes. The defendant himself then opened the safe and lifted up the lid. At that point, he said, "wait a minute," "there's some pictures of my wife inside the safe." In reply, the officer said, "I'm not looking for any pictures, I'm just looking for contraband." The defendant then said, "Okay," and the officer opened the safe and examined its contents. Among them were photographs depicting children in sexually explicit poses, including a woman, who turned out to be Mr. Hoggard's wife, engaging in various sex acts with two small children, who were the Hoggards' children. On the basis of these and other photographs, the defendant was convicted of the violation described above.

Was the search of the safe lawful? We think the answer is yes. The defendant gave his consent, but he claims he did not do so knowingly and voluntarily. The officer misled the defendant, it is argued, by assuring him that pictures were not among the items to

---

the logical consequence of mailing undeveloped film to a processor. *See* 18 U.S.C. § 2252. In light of this, we conclude that no person "of common intelligence" would need to "guess" that the intermediate step, the actual mailing of the undeveloped film, was also prohibited. No one fairly reading the statute could reasonably conclude that the statute permitted Smith's acts.

be searched for. We disagree with this argument. At the time, no doubt, the officer had in mind guns or drugs, not photographs. But, when photographs that could informally, at least, be described as "contraband" were discovered, we do not think that the officer was bound to ignore them. The defendant well knew what was inside the safe. He knew what he was doing when he gave his consent, and no coercion was involved. Perhaps the defendant did believe that he would be safe from any censure on account of the photographs, but this erroneous belief, even if based upon an arguable interpretation of the officer's words, is not, in our view, a sufficient reason to render the defendant's consent either involuntary or unknowing.

An argument is also presented with respect to the constitutionality of the federal statute under which defendant was convicted. The statute, as amended in 1998, provides in pertinent part:

> Any parent or ... person having custody or control of a minor who knowingly permits such minor to engage in ... sexually explicit conduct for the purpose of producing any visual depiction of such conduct shall be punished as provided under subsection (d) of this section ... if that visual depiction was produced using materials that have been ... transported in interstate ... commerce....

18 U.S.C. § 2251(b). The statute contains an explicit jurisdictional nexus. It is not simply permitting minor children to engage in sexually explicit conduct for the purpose of producing a visual depiction that is prohibited. The government must also show that the picture was produced using materials (here, film and a camera) that had been transported in interstate commerce. It is undisputed that the defendant took the pictures in question.

This jurisdictional nexus is sufficient to place the statute beyond constitutional attack, and this Court has so held in a very similar case, *United States v. Bausch*, 140 F.3d 739 (8th Cir.1998), *cert. denied*, 525 U.S. 1072, 119 S.Ct. 806, 142 L.Ed.2d 667 (1999), involving 18 U.S.C. § 2252A(a)(4)(B), which makes it a crime knowingly to possess with the intent to sell any child pornography that was produced using materials that had been shipped in interstate commerce. The defendant cites *United States v. Morrison*, 529 U.S. 598, 120 S.Ct. 1740, 146 L.Ed.2d 658 (2000), and *United States v. Lopez*, 514 U.S. 549, 115 S.Ct. 1624, 131 L.Ed.2d 626 (1995), in both of which cases the Supreme Court invalidated statutes as falling outside the authority conferred upon Congress by the Commerce Clause. In neither of those cases, however, did the statute involved contain an express jurisdictional element, requiring the government to prove, in each case, a concrete connection with interstate commerce. This panel is bound by the reasoning of *Bausch*, and we therefore must reject the defendant's Commerce Clause challenge.

For these reasons, the judgment of the District Court is affirmed.

Notes

The constitutionality of 18 U.S.C. § 2251(b) also has been challenged on the basis that it falls outside the scope of Congress' powers under the commerce clause, specifically after the United States Supreme Court's decisions in *United States v. Morrison*, 529 U.S. 598, 120 S. Ct. 1740 (2000) (Court struck down provisions under the Violence Against Women Act that had only an attenuated link to interstate commerce) and *United States v. Lopez*, 514 U.S. 549, 115 S. Ct. 1624 (1995) (Court struck down Gun-Free School Zone Act because Congress exceeded Commerce Clause power). *See, e.g., United States v. Densberger*, 285 Fed. Appx. 926 (3d Cir. 2008) (father, who engaged in and recorded sexual acts involving three sons, challenged constitutionality of 2251(b)). However, post-*Morrison* courts have held that intrastate possession of child pornography may substantially affect interstate commerce. *See United States v. Galo*, 239 F.3d 572, 576 (3d Cir. 2001). The United States Supreme Court's landmark decision in *Gonzales v. Raich*, 545 U.S. 1, 17, 125 S. Ct. 2195 (2005) (federal government may regulate growing or marijuana for home consumption because of likelihood intrastate activity could affect interstate commerce) has given effect to this perspective in cases involving the production of child pornography. *See also United States v. Cramer*, 213 Fed. Appx. 138 (3d Cir. 2007) (government need not prove that parent knew that depiction would be transported in interstate or foreign commerce or mailed, or that depiction was actually transported or mailed); *United States v. Brown*, 327 Fed. Appx. 526 (6th Cir. 2006) (defendant took photographs and videos of twin step-granddaughters; court found sufficient interstate nexus and denied as-applied challenge); *United States v. Andrews*, 383 F.3d 374 (6th Cir. 2004) (where defendant produced child pornography by forcing twelve-year-old niece and seven-year-old step-daughter to take nude pictures of their own genital areas with a "pen camera," and defendant loaded pictures from camera onto computer, but there was no evidence that pictures were uploaded to the Internet, court found jurisdictional nexus between defendant's intrastate child pornography activities and interstate commerce).

Title 18 U.S.C. §2251(b) governs the production of child pornography by a parent, guardian, or custodian. However, when a parent, guardian, or custodian sells or buys a child, or transfers custody of a child, knowing that, as a consequence of that sale or transfer of custody, the child will be portrayed in child pornography or other depiction, 18 U.S.C. §2251A is applicable. The following case illustrates the application of §2251A.

United States v. Buculei

Fourth Circuit, 2001
262 F.3d 322

KING, Circuit Judge:

Catalin Buculei appeals his convictions and sentence in the District of Maryland under 18 U.S.C. §2251(a)[1] and §18 U.S.C. §2251A(b)(2).[2] These convictions arose from Buculei's activities surrounding three automobile trips he made between New York and Maryland in early 1999, with the intention of engaging in sexual activity with a minor, and to carry out his attempt to create in Maryland a visual depiction of a minor engaged in sexually explicit conduct....

In December of 1998, Buculei, who was then thirty-eight years of age and living in New York City, began chatting on the Internet with a thirteen-year-old girl named Megan, who lived in Maryland. Megan, who was having trouble with her family and at school, apparently turned to Buculei for support and friendship. Soon thereafter, the pair began conversing on the telephone, and they made plans to meet on January 18, 1999, near

---

1. Section 2251(a) provides, in pertinent part, that:
   Any person who employs, uses, persuades, induces, entices, or coerces any minor to engage in ... any sexually explicit conduct for the purpose of producing any visual depiction of such conduct, shall be punished as provided under subsection (d), if such person knows or has reason to know that such visual depiction will be transported in interstate or foreign commerce or mailed[.]

2. Section 2251A(b)(2) provides, in pertinent part, as follows:
   (b) Whoever purchases or otherwise obtains custody or control of a minor ...
   (2) with intent to promote ...
   (A) the engaging in of sexually explicit conduct by such minor for the purpose of producing any visual depiction of such conduct ...
   shall be punished by imprisonment for not less than 20 years[.]

Megan's home. On that date, Buculei drove from New York to Maryland, rented a room at a motel, and waited approximately two hours for Megan to arrive at the agreed-upon rendezvous point. Megan, however, chose not to go through with the encounter. Buculei then remained in Maryland, and he unsuccessfully attempted the next day to telephone Megan at her middle school. He thereupon returned to New York.

Undeterred by Megan's failure to show up for the first meeting, Buculei made new arrangements to see her. He returned to Maryland and attempted to meet her just four days later, January 22, 1999, which was also Megan's fourteenth birthday. Megan, however, was grounded, and she was not allowed by her parents to leave her home or use the Internet or telephone. Buculei was nonetheless determined to see her again. He sent an e-mail to one of Megan's friends to confirm his plans, and on this occasion his efforts proved successful. Megan sneaked out of her home at 2:00 a.m. on January 23, 1999, meeting Buculei at the end of her street. He gave her a rose and a hug, and she got into his automobile, believing they would "[j]ust drive around." ... Buculei, however, had other intentions. He drove Megan to a Red Roof Inn in Aberdeen, Maryland, about thirty to forty-five minutes from her home. Buculei registered in the motel, obtained some sodas and snacks, and took Megan to his room. The pair briefly watched television while they ate. When they finished eating, Buculei gave Megan a clear drink that he had retrieved from his vehicle. At trial, Megan testified that the drink tasted "different," and it made her feel "[d]izzy and tired." ... Buculei then removed a video camera from his backpack and put it on a table in the motel room, with the camera's lens facing the bed on which he and Megan lay. He told Megan that, notwithstanding the red light that was illuminated on the front of the video camera, the camera was not working. Buculei and Megan then began to kiss each other, and eventually Buculei removed all of Megan's clothes, as well as his own. He then touched and put his mouth on her breasts and vagina, placed his penis in her mouth, and ultimately engaged in vaginal intercourse with Megan.

Following the sexual encounter at the motel, Buculei drove Megan back to the street on which she lived, and she exited his vehicle. She "fell a few times" before making it home, however, because she was still dizzy.... Megan was back in bed at home before her father awoke at 6:00 a.m., and she did not tell her parents anything about Buculei or the events of the early morning hours.

During the following week, Buculei telephoned Megan several times, continuously expressing his desire to return to Maryland to visit her. Megan, however, advised Buculei that she did not want him to return. In any event, he came back to Maryland from New York less than two weeks later, on February 5, 1999, meeting Megan soon after she was dropped off by her school bus. Megan again got into Buculei's automobile, and he drove her back to the Red Roof Inn. This time Megan refused to go into the motel with Buculei, so he returned her to her home. Although Megan believed that Buculei would then be departing for New York, he instead appeared later that night at a roller skating rink she regularly attended. Megan became frightened, and she advised her friend's mother about her situation with Buculei. Later that evening the authorities were called and Megan was interviewed.

Early the next morning, February 6, 1999, the police arrived at Buculei's motel room. Buculei answered the door and consented to searches of his motel room and his automobile. The searches uncovered, among other items, a video camera loaded with a fully rewound videotape suitable for recording, a Polaroid camera, several condoms, lubricants, an unopened bottle of a ready-made Long Island Iced Tea alcoholic drink,[3] and a bottle of

---

3. The ingredients of the Long Island Iced Tea included rum, vodka, gin, tequila, and triple sec.

Viagra. Later that day, Buculei gave a taped statement to the authorities. He claimed he had not met Megan prior to the previous day, insisting that he had rebuffed her upon learning her real age. Buculei was then detained while a search warrant was obtained for his residence in New York.... On February 9, 1999, the FBI searched Buculei's New York apartment. The search uncovered numerous images of child pornography, correspondence between Buculei and several young girls, and the videotape of his January 23, 1999 encounter with Megan at the Red Roof Inn located in Aberdeen. The videotape does not contain footage of any sexually explicit conduct, however, apparently because Buculei had failed to fully rewind the tape when he commenced recording. Instead, only the last ten minutes of the videotape contain footage of the January 23 encounter, and the video reaches its end immediately before Buculei removed Megan's bra.

Buculei was thereafter indicted in the District of Maryland for five separate violations of federal law. In Counts One, Four, and Five of the indictment, Buculei was charged with violating 18 U.S.C. § 2423(b) (traveling in interstate commerce with the intent to engage in a sexual act with a person under the age of eighteen). These three counts represented each of Buculei's three automobile trips between New York and Maryland in early 1999. In Count Two, Buculei was charged with a violation of 18 U.S.C. § 2251(a), i.e., that he knowingly employed, used, persuaded, induced, and enticed Megan, a minor, to engage in "sexually explicit conduct for the purposes of producing a visual depiction of such conduct," knowing that "such visual depiction would be transported in interstate commerce." *See supra*, note 1. In Count Three, Buculei was charged with violating 18 U.S.C. § 2251A(b)(2), i.e., that he knowingly obtained "custody or control" of a minor, that is, Megan, with the "intent to promote the engaging in of sexually explicit conduct by such minor for the purpose of producing a visual depiction of such conduct[.]" *See supra*, note 2.

Buculei entered a plea of not guilty to the charges, and he was tried by a jury on the indictment. At the close of the Government's case-in-chief, and again at the close of all the evidence, Buculei moved for judgment of acquittal on all counts under Rule 29 of the Federal Rules of Criminal Procedure, which the district court denied. Buculei was then convicted by the jury on all five counts, and he was sentenced to the maximum possible imprisonment on Counts One, Two, Four, and Five.[4] He was sentenced to the statutory minimum of 240 months' imprisonment on Count Three, with all five sentences to run concurrently....

We ... consider Buculei's claims of error with respect to his prosecution under 18 U.S.C. § 2251A(b)(2), as embodied in Count Three of the indictment. Buculei makes two assertions in support of his theory that his conviction on Count Three must be vacated. First, he contends that the statute, entitled "Selling or buying of children," encompasses only the "custody or control" of children that is of the "same degree of control as that exercised by a parent or guardian." ... Second, Buculei insists that, even if the statutory provisions reach his conduct, the doctrine of fair notice and the rule of lenity require that a judgment of acquittal be granted on his Count Three conviction. The Government counters that, notwithstanding the statute's title, the plain language contained in § 2251A(b) clearly encompasses and prohibits Buculei's conduct....

First of all, Buculei strenuously asserts that the title of § 2251A(b), as well as its legislative history and overall structure, compel our conclusion that it only contemplates parental control, or some similar degree of control as that exercised by a parent. In this regard, it is important to recognize that "the title of a statute cannot limit the plain meaning of the text. For interpretive purposes, [the title] is of use only when it sheds light on some

---

4. On Counts One, Four, and Five, Buculei was sentenced to 24 months' imprisonment. On Count Two, Buculei was sentenced to 168 months' imprisonment.

ambiguous word or phrase." ... [citations omitted]. Indeed, the terms contained in the title of § 2251A(b)—buying and selling—do not exclusively define the statute's reach: its provisions also apply to "[w]hoever purchases *or otherwise obtains* custody or control of a minor[.]" Furthermore, the statutory term "custody or control" is clearly defined in 18 U.S.C. § 2256(7) as "includ[ing] temporary supervision over or responsibility for a minor whether legally or illegally obtained[.]" Thus, it cannot be successfully asserted by Buculei that the title of § 2251A somehow limits its reach, and we reject his argument in that regard....

Under § 2251(a), a person is prohibited from "employ[ing], us[ing], persuad[ing], induc[ing], or coerc[ing] any minor to engage in ... sexually explicit conduct for the purpose of producing [a] visual depiction of such conduct[.]" On the other hand, the "control" element of § 2251A(b) (on which Count Three is predicated) involves something more than mere persuasion, inducement, or coercion.[9] The jury—which viewed the limited videotape which Buculei made of his encounter with Megan at the Red Roof Inn—was entitled to conclude, as it did, that Buculei's conduct fully satisfied this element of the charged offense.[10] Put simply, Buculei has not demonstrated anything that would compel us to override the plain language of § 2251A(b)....

Buculei next contends that the doctrine of fair notice and the rule of lenity require that his conviction on Count Three be vacated. However, Buculei's ability to "articulat[e] a narrower construction [of § 2251A(b)(2)] ... does not by itself make the rule of lenity applicable." ... [citations omitted]. We need not "determine the precise contours" of the statute if Buculei's conduct is reasonably encompassed by the statute's provisions.... [citation omitted].... Moreover, it is irrelevant that Buculei's prosecution under this statute is "a novel construction," or that it is the first time the Government has proceeded under this theory. *See United States v. Knox*, 32 F.3d 733, 751 n. 15 (3d Cir.1994) ("[T]he rule of lenity is not dependent whatsoever on whether there have been successful

---

9. Buculei insists on appeal that he "was convicted based solely on his psychological coercion of Megan into making child pornography." ... We need not decide whether psychological control would be sufficient under the statute, since Buculei's assertion is belied by the evidence and the charge to the jury. The district court—upon the joint request of the parties and without objection—instructed the jury:

> Control, as used here, means the power to manage, command, direct or restrain another person. In this case, the government contends that Mr. Buculei obtained control over Megan C. by, among other things, taking her to a motel and giving her an intoxicating drink.
> The government must prove beyond a reasonable doubt that the defendant obtained control over Megan C. by the use of the intoxicating drink and other means in order to find him guilty of the charge in Count Three.
> Even if you find that the defendant did give Megan C. an intoxicating beverage, you must consider whether he obtained control over her as I have defined that term.

We see no error in the jury instruction, which fairly encompasses the plain language of the statute, and which is consistent with both the legislative history of § 2251A and its overall structure and purpose. Buculei was not convicted of coercing Megan; instead, the jury reasonably found that, based on the entirety of the evidence, Buculei exercised the required statutory "control" over Megan.

10. We are similarly unconvinced by Buculei's argument that, if we accept the Government's reading of the statute, all child pornographers would be subject to prosecution under § 2251A(b), since "very few, if any, children would willingly participate in sexual activity in order to make child pornography." It occurs to us that children may well be enticed into production of child pornography, as is often the case, *see, e.g.,* Cong. Rec. S13326-01; 1988 WL 176238 (Sept. 17, 1988) (Reader's Digest article in legislative history of § 2251A which details the many ways child pornographers lure their unsuspecting victims), or they might be forced into such sexually explicit activity against their will— by someone exerting custody or control of them. This latter example is the more egregious crime that Congress criminalized in § 2251A(b).

prosecutions under the statute at issue.... [Otherwise] the government [would never] be able to successfully proceed under a theory different from that which has yielded convictions in the past."). In short, Buculei's conduct with respect to Megan clearly falls within the plain language of § 2251A(b)(2).... [citation omitted]. That Congress may not have foreseen a situation where a stranger from New York could exercise "control" over a fourteen-year-old girl from Maryland, with such control not derived (legally or illegally) from the parent or guardian, simply does not affect our conclusion. If the statute unambiguously reaches the defendant's conduct, as it does here, our inquiry is complete.... [citation omitted]. Thus, we must affirm Buculei's conviction on Count Three, the violation of 18 U.S.C. § 2251A(b).... [footnote omitted].

Pursuant to the foregoing, we affirm the convictions and sentence of Buculei as rendered and imposed in the district court.

AFFIRMED

MICHAEL, Circuit Judge, concurring in part and dissenting in part:

I concur in all but part III of the majority opinion. I disagree, however, that there is sufficient evidence to support a finding that Buculei obtained "custody or control" over Megan C. as required by 18 U.S.C. § 2251A(b). The "custody or control" requirement of § 2251A means that a defendant must exert a significant degree of authority over the minor. In all events, § 2251A must be interpreted as outlawing conduct that is more serious than the lesser-included offense of § 2251(a), which makes it unlawful to employ, use, persuade, induce, entice, or coerce a minor for the purpose of producing child pornography. While Buculei certainly persuaded, induced, and enticed Megan, he never possessed authority over her that amounted to "custody or control." Accordingly, I respectfully dissent from the majority's affirmance of Buculei's conviction on the one count brought under § 2251A(b).

There are two primary offenses dealing with the use of minors in producing child pornography. The baseline offense is § 2251(a), which prohibits the "employ[ment], use[ ], persua[sion], induce[ment], entice[ment], or coerc[ion]" of a minor for the purpose of producing child pornography. Section 2251A, on the other hand, deals with more serious conduct (and carries substantially stiffer penalties) than does § 2251(a).* Titled the "Selling or buying of children," § 2251A has two parts. Section 2251A(a) prohibits a parent, legal guardian, or other person having "custody or control" of a minor from selling or transferring custody or control of the minor for the purpose of producing child pornography. Section 2251A(b), in turn, prohibits any person from buying or obtaining "custody or control" of a minor for the purpose of producing child pornography.

To have "custody or control," the defendant must exert a significant degree of authority over the minor. The plain meaning of the words "custody" and "control" compels this conclusion. The word "control" is defined in the dictionary as the "*power* or *authority* to guide or manage." *Webster's New International Dictionary* 496 (3d ed.1993) (emphasis added). Likewise, "custody" is defined as the "act or duty of *guarding* and preserving." *Id.* at 559 (emphasis added). The statutory definition likewise confirms that the minor must be under the defendant's authority: "custody or control" includes "temporary supervision over or responsibility for a minor whether legally or illegally obtained." *Id.* § 2256(7).

In addition to the plain language of § 2251A and the statutory definition, other factors confirm that it takes a significant degree of authority to have "custody or control" of a minor. First, § 2251A must be interpreted in light of the lesser-included offense of § 2251(a).

---

* Absent special circumstances, § 2251(a) carries a minimum sentence of 10 years and a maximum of 20. Section 2251A carries a minimum of 20 years and a maximum of life.

Again, § 2251(a) prohibits the "employ[ment], use[ ], persua[sion], induce[ment], entice[ment], or coerc[ion]" of a minor for the purpose of producing child pornography. To avoid making § 2251A redundant, "custody or control" must be interpreted to involve something more authoritative than employment, use, persuasion, inducement, enticement, or coercion. *See, e.g., Freytag v. Comm'r*, 501 U.S. 868, 877, 111 S.Ct. 2631, 115 L.Ed.2d 764 (1991) (stating that courts should avoid interpreting one statute in a way that makes another statute redundant). If "custody or control" is equated with a significant degree of authority, § 2251A and § 2251(a) stand apart from each other and cover separate crimes. Otherwise, they do not. Second, the words surrounding "custody or control" in § 2251A(a) suggest that a significant degree of authority is required. *See, e.g., Babbitt v. Sweet Home Chapter of Cmtys. for a Great Or.*, 515 U.S. 687, 695, 115 S.Ct. 2407, 132 L.Ed.2d 597 (1995) ("[A] word is known by the company it keeps."). The section prohibits a "parent," "legal guardian," or "other person having custody or control" of a minor from selling or handing over the minor for use in child pornography. By placing a person with "custody or control" in the same class as a "parent" and "legal guardian," Congress surely meant that a person with custody or control will have significant authority and power over the minor. Third, the statute's title sheds light on the meaning of "custody or control." *See, e.g., Castillo v. United States*, 530 U.S. 120, 125, 120 S.Ct. 2090, 147 L.Ed.2d 94 (2000) (using the statute's title as part of the Court's statutory interpretation analysis). Section 2251A is titled the "Selling or buying of children." This suggests that the section targets defendants who have significant power over their victims, specifically, the power to sell or buy them. Fourth, the structure of section 2251A reveals what is required for custody or control. Here, I repeat that section 2251A(a) prohibits a parent, legal guardian, or any other person having "custody or control" of a minor from selling or transferring custody or control of the minor for the purpose of producing child pornography. This means that a person with "custody or control" of a minor will have enough power and authority over the minor to sell her or transfer custody or control of her to a third person. Section 2251A(b), the basis for the third count against Buculei, prohibits a person from buying or otherwise obtaining custody or control of a minor for the purpose of producing child pornography. Once a person, like Buculei, buys or obtains custody or control of a minor, he would surely be obtaining power and authority equal to that necessary for custody or control under § 2251A(a), that is, sufficient power and authority over the minor to resell her or re-transfer custody or control. As I will explain, the evidence does not establish that Buculei had that sort of power and authority over Megan. This is the case, notwithstanding the strict standard of review: "The verdict of [the] jury must be sustained if there is substantial evidence, taking the view most favorable to the Government, to support it." *Glasser v. United States*, 315 U.S. 60, 80, 62 S.Ct. 457, 86 L.Ed. 680 (1942).

The majority concludes that the effect of the "clear" drink gave Buculei custody or control over Megan. I disagree. At the motel Megan drank less than one-half cup of a clear drink which made her feel "dizzy and tired." Megan's testimony, however, reveals that the drink did not significantly impair her judgment or her ability to function. She remained quite lucid, even reminding Buculei several times that it was getting late and that she had to be home by 6:00 a.m. Megan was able to recount the entire night's experience with Buculei in vivid detail. She remembered many particulars that were incidental. For example, she recalled that she was wearing two shirts, but not a belt; that Buculei got undressed all at once; that the motel room had two beds, a table and chair, and paper cups; that the room had a sink area that was separate from the bathroom; and that the television was turned on. Megan did not testify that the drink had any effect on her other than making her dizzy and tired. For example, she did not say that the drink made her act differently, that it was in any way a factor in bringing about the events that unfolded, or that it impaired her ability to reason. In short, Megan's testimony reveals that the drink had the limited effect of making her somewhat dizzy and tired. Because the drink had such a limited effect, it did not give Buculei custody or control over Megan.

The evidence strongly supports a finding that Buculei persuaded, induced, and enticed Megan to have sex with him for the purpose of producing child pornography in violation of § 2251(a), as charged in count two. The evidence, however, does not show that Buculei had "custody or control" of Megan. I would therefore vacate Buculei's conviction on count three and remand for resentencing on the remaining four counts.

3. Extraterritorial Production

United States v. Kapordelis

Eleventh Circuit, 2009
569 F.3d 1291

HOOD, District Judge:

At the time of his arrest in 2004, Defendant-Appellant Gregory C. Kapordelis ("Defendant" or "Kapordelis") was an anesthesiologist who practiced medicine and had a home in Gainesville, Georgia. His sexual exploits with underage boys, however, took him far from Gainesville, across state lines and around the world. Evidence of his globe-spanning exploits, including the sexually explicit photographs of boys that Defendant made as souvenirs during his travels, and Kapordelis's large collection of child pornography collected from other sources ultimately led to Defendant's indictment and conviction for producing, receiving, and possessing child pornography in violation of 18 U.S.C. §§ 2251(a), 2252A(a)(2)(A), and 2252A(a)(5)(B). Defendant appeals his conviction and his 420-month sentence....

In June 2001, Kapordelis traveled to Greece with his cousin, who was then eleven-years-old. While in Greece, Defendant exposed and took photographs of the boy's genitalia and anus.... [footnote omitted].... In January 2002, Kapordelis met Lawrence Walker when the then fourteen-year-old had surgery and was treated by Defendant. Kapordelis later hired Walker to do chores on the weekends, and, in May of 2002, Kapordelis invited Walker on a trip to Kapordelis's condominium in Kure Beach, North Carolina. The night before they flew to North Carolina from Atlanta, Georgia, Kapordelis and Walker spent the night in a hotel near the airport, and Kapordelis made Walker several mixed drinks containing alcohol. Walker had no recollection of what happened after he started drinking, including anyone taking pictures of him standing in front of a mirror even though such pictures were later shown to him by Kapordelis. During this trip, as the boy lay nonresponsive on a bed, Defendant exposed the boy's genitalia and photographed them with a Sony Cybershot camera manufactured outside the State of Georgia.... [footnote omitted].... In July 2002, Kapordelis and Walker traveled together again, this time to Myrtle Beach, South Carolina, where they shared a room in a condominium occupied by Defendant's friend. During their stay, Defendant again exposed and photographed the boy's genitalia, although Walker did not remember anyone taking his photograph.... [footnote omitted]. The sexually explicit photographs of Walker were found on a computer seized from Defendant's home in Georgia.... In 2004, Kapordelis traveled to St. Petersburg, Russia. During his stay abroad, in late March 2004, the Immigration and Customs Enforcement ("ICE") office in Atlanta was informed by the ICE attaché in Moscow that three minors had complained to Russian authorities that they were molested by Kapordelis and that he took digital videos and pictures of his victims. According to reports from Russian law enforcement, several of the juvenile victims claimed that Defendant had given them pills that made them drowsy or unconscious.

Relying on this information, on April 12, 2004, an ICE agent sought a criminal complaint and express warrant, charging Defendant with traveling in foreign commerce for the purpose of having sex with a minor in violation of 18 U.S.C. § 2423, i.e., "sex tourism." That same day, Defendant returned to the United States. Alerted to the investigation into Defendant's activities but not yet armed with an arrest warrant, ICE agents at New York's John F. Kennedy International airport approached Defendant upon his arrival and asked to speak with him. During that interview, they received word from ICE–Atlanta that the magistrate judge had signed the complaint and issued the warrant. At that time, the New York ICE agents took Defendant into custody, seizing a laptop computer, several digital cameras, and an external hard drive from him which were transferred to ICE Agent Cory E. Brant in Atlanta.

Meanwhile, Agent Brant had also prepared and submitted applications for search warrants for Defendant's home and place of work, seeking court authority to look for evidence of sex tourism and child pornography in both locations, including on computers and other digital storage devices. The affidavit, used to obtain both warrants, was based exclusively on information from two reports from the ICE–Moscow office, interviews with Defendant's two co-workers, notes from telephone conversations with the ICE attaché, and various database checks as to utility service and addresses. On the evening of April 12, 2004, a federal magistrate judge signed both warrants.

During the search of Defendant's home, agents seized (1) a Hewlett-Packard desktop computer from the master bedroom, (2) a Sony Vaio laptop computer with a broken screen from inside a locked closet in the master bathroom, (3) a box imprinted with the name "Rohypnol," on the master bedroom floor, (4) a box that contained Versed, and (5) a Sony Vaio desktop computer in the living room.[5] Forensic examination of one of the desktop computers showed that it contained thousands of images and videos of child pornography downloaded by Defendant.... [footnote omitted]. On the laptop computer with a broken screen, a forensic examiner found a second, larger cache of child pornography, including sexually explicit images of Defendant's eleven-year-old cousin and the fourteen-year-old former patient.... [footnote omitted]. Additionally, the laptop computer seized from Defendant at the airport in New York was found to contain pornographic images of children.... [footnote omitted].

Defendant was initially indicted in May 2004 on two counts of engaging in sex tourism in violation of 18 U.S.C. § 2423(c). As additional evidence was gathered and pre-trial motions were litigated, several superseding indictments were issued. In each instance, Defendant pleaded not guilty. The Fourth Superseding Indictment, in place at the time of trial, charged Defendant with (1) producing child pornography photographs, in violation of 18 U.S.C. § 2251(a), on or about June 28, 2001 ("Count 1"); (2) producing child pornography photographs, in violation of § 2251(a), on or about May 18, 2002 ("Count 2"); (3) producing child pornography photographs, in violation of § 2251(a), on or about July 2, 2002 ("Count 3"); (4) producing a child pornography video, in violation of § 2251(a), on or about December 12, 2001 ("Count 4"); (5) receiving child

---

5. Randell Alexander, a pediatrician, testified at trial that Versed is a relaxant that, depending on the dose, can either make a person sleepy or unconscious. Rohypnol, which commonly is called a date rape drug, causes people to become semi-conscious and not to remember what happened while they are under the influence of the drug. Alexander testified that it is not appropriate to have either Versed or Rohypnol in an individual's home, as they have no home use.

pornography, in violation of 18 U.S.C. §2252A(a)(2)(A), on a Hewlett-Packard desktop computer between March 2002 and April 2004 ("Count 5"); (6) receiving child pornography, in violation of §2252A(a)(2)(A), on a Sony Vaio laptop computer between April and December 2002 ("Count 6"); and (7) possessing child pornography, in violation of §2252A(a)(5)(B), on April 12, 2004 ("Count 7")....

Defendant's trial began on May 7, 2007. In addition to evidence of his travels with his young cousin and Walker, recounted briefly above, the prosecution presented evidence of the contents of Defendant's computer harddrives. James Fottrell, assistant to the chief for computer forensics and investigations in the Department of Justice's Criminal Division's Child Exploitation and Obscenity Section, testified that he found approximately 1,400 images and over 100 videos that he classified as child pornography on the desktop computer found in Kapordelis's home. Fottrell found over 9,000 images and 300 videos that he classified as child pornography on the laptop found in the locked closet of Kapordelis's bedroom, which he believed was last used in February 2003, as well as internet searches for the age of consent laws in Croatia, Peru, Singapore, and Spain. Fottrell also found 180 images of child pornography on the laptop computer seized from Kapordelis at the airport in New York.

On all three computers seized from Defendant, Fottrell found a text file in which Kapordelis appears to memorialize some of his travels to Prague and wrote about his experience with an 18-year-old named Patrick and how he hoped to meet a 17-year-old boy named Lucas the following night. In another text file, Kapordelis described how he spent three days in Prague with a 16-year-old boy named Peter having oral and anal sex. In yet another text file, Kapordelis wrote more introspectively about his sexual interest in boys: "Why am I attracted to young guys? Why does my relationship have to be a controlling one? Why is it difficult for me to enjoy a young guy sexually unless I am in total control?"

Over Defendant's objection, the United States also presented evidence regarding Defendant's periodic travel to Prague, Czech Republic, to engage the services of young male prostitutes.... [footnote omitted]. Christopher Williams testified that Kapordelis told Williams that the reason that Kapordelis went to Prague was to have sex with young men, and the first time that Williams visited Kapordelis in Prague, Kapordelis brought 2 young men, who were 17 or 18 years old, back to the hotel room, where Williams saw Kapordelis give them money. On Williams's second trip to Prague, Kapordelis took Williams to a mall, where Kapordelis liked to find young men, and to a bar, where people went to pick up young male prostitutes. At the bar, Williams observed Kapordelis appear to negotiate with a pimp for a "kid," whom Kapordelis took back to Kapordelis's apartment. Kapordelis later informed Williams that the person was 14 years old.

Lester Andrews testified that Kapordelis had stated that he was interested in, and fantasized about, young boys. Kapordelis told Andrews that he liked having sex with young boys in Prague, where it was legal, and, when Andrews visited Kapordelis in Prague, he took Andrews to the same bar where Kapordelis had taken Williams. Andrews observed Kapordelis putting large sums of money in front of a boy until the boy agreed to leave with him.[10]

---

10. These trysts were not Kapordelis's only connection to the Czech Republic. Eva Racanska, an obstetrician in the Czech Republic, who was by all accounts in St. Petersburg with Kapordelis just prior to his April 2004 arrest, testified that she brought Kapordelis one package of Rohypnol from the Czech Republic, where it is a legally prescribed drug, during one of her trips to the United States. Apparently, Racanska knew Kapordelis well and identified Kapordelis's hand as the one pulling down his young cousin's pants in one of the sexually explicit photographs found on Kapordelis's computer.

Additionally, Deno Contos, Kapordelis's second cousin, testified that, at the age of sixteen, he moved in with Kapordelis. Kapordelis was then in medical school and provided Contos with alcohol and pills. Contos eventually discovered a video of Kapordelis having sex with him although he had no memory of the video being made. The video cassette bore a sticker that stated, in Kapordelis's handwriting, to destroy it if he died. Contos observed five or six other videos that had the same instruction to destroy if Kapordelis died. Contos moved back home when Kapordelis graduated from medical school, although, as Contos was nearing his eighteenth birthday, he moved back in with Kapordelis, who resumed drugging and molesting him. Contos also testified that, years later, in April 2004, he received a frantic telephone call from Kapordelis, who gave Contos the security codes that would permit him to enter Defendant's home and a locked bedroom closet. Kapordelis asked Contos to destroy Kapordelis's homemade videos. Contos refused to destroy them, but agreed to hide them. Contos did not tell anyone about the videotape of himself until Kapordelis was arrested, some 20 years after he discovered it.

Defendant's three week trial concluded on May 24, 2007, when a jury found him guilty on Counts 1–3 and 5–7. Kapordelis was acquitted of the allegations in Count 4.... During a two-day sentencing hearing, the district court heard and considered testimony from some of Kapordelis's friends and family, who testified variously that Defendant was a man of character who would help anyone; supportive; trustworthy with children; the architect of a fine anesthesia practice; a pillar of his family, who went beyond what a normal family member does to make others feel loved and comforted; a loving, good person who did many good deeds for his family and others throughout the world; a great example who provided encouragement; charitable; generous with his time and money; someone who shared his life with everyone and took every opportunity with the witness' children to teach them something; and was someone who would benefit society in the future.

The district court also heard testimony from Fottrell and Kapordelis's brother-in-law concerning used computers provided by Kapordelis to family members which contained images of child pornography. Fottrell testified that, on one of these old computers, he found a total of 33 hours worth of pornographic videos, and each video contained approximately 24 frames per second. Fottrell also identified, on another old computer given to Contos, child pornography news group activity associated with Microsoft's Outlook Express and a user identity, the "authentication identity," which was password protected.[11] Fottrell was also able to determine that 8,000 of the files on Kapordelis's computers were gathered by news groups and uploaded at a very high rate per second.

Kapordelis was hardly penitent during the sentencing proceeding. During his allocution, he accused the United States of falsely accusing him of molesting children in Russia and maintained that the Assistant U.S. Attorneys ("AUSAs") who prosecuted the case were liars. He called the prosecution arrogant and complained that the AUSA had taken on the persona of a dictator, comparing the AUSA to Hitler. While Kapordelis apologized

---

11. News groups allow people to communicate over the internet, and once a person signs up for a news group, articles and images related to the subject matter of the group are sent to the person's computer. Under the authentication identity, Fottrell found subscriptions to the following news groups: (1) alt.binaries.pictures boys; (2) alt.binaries.pictures boys bondage; (3) alt.binaries.pictures. erotica child male; (4) alt.binaries.pictures.erotica teen male anal; (5) alt.binaries.pictures.erotica teen male masturbation; (6) alt.binaries.pictures.sunshine boys; (7) alt.binaries.pictures.youth wrestling; (8) alt.binaries.pictures asparagus; (9) alt.fan.John; (10) alt.fan.prettyboy; and (11) alt.svenshouse. Fottrell testified that, in his experience investigating child pornography, asparagus was a euphemism for a boy's penis.

to anyone affected by his actions, he stressed that he was not referring to sexual molestation victims, as he insisted that he had never sexually molested anyone.... Finally, on September 18, 2007, the district court sentenced Defendant to a total term of 420 months: 240 months for each production count, to run concurrently; 180 months for each receipt count, to run concurrently with each other but consecutively to the production counts; and 120 months for the possession count, to run concurrently with the receipt counts....

Defendant was charged in Counts 1 and 3 of the Fourth Superseding Indictment with violating 18 U.S.C. § 2251(a). As effective from October 30, 1998, to April 29, 2003, 18 U.S.C. § 2251(a) provided that:

> Any person who employs, uses, persuades, induces, entices, or coerces any minor to engage in, ... or who transports any minor in interstate or foreign commerce ... with the intent that such minor engage in, any sexually explicit conduct for the purpose of producing any visual depiction of such conduct, shall be punished as provided under subsection (d), if such person knows or has reason to know that such visual depiction will be transported in interstate or foreign commerce or mailed, if that visual depiction was produced using materials that have been mailed, shipped, or transported in interstate or foreign commerce by any means, including by computer, or if such visual depiction has actually been transported in interstate or foreign commerce or mailed.

Count 1 of the Fourth Superseding Indictment alleged that:

> On or about June 28, 2001, the defendant, GREGORY C. KAPORDELIS, did use a person under the age of eighteen to engage in sexually explicit conduct, specifically, the lascivious exhibition of the genitals and the pubic area of said minor, for the purpose of producing visual depictions of such conduct, specifically digital photographs, such visual depictions have been transported from Greece to Georgia, specifically, the Northern District of Georgia, all in violation of Title 18, United States Code, Section 2251(a).

Count 3 alleged that:

> On or about July 5, 2002, the defendant, GREGORY C. KAPORDELIS, did use a person under the age of eighteen to engage in sexually explicit conduct, specifically, the lascivious exhibition of the genitals and the pubic area of said minor, for the purpose of producing visual depictions of such conduct, specifically digital photographs, by means of a Sony camera, said camera having been mailed, transported and shipped in interstate and foreign commerce, and said visual depictions having been transported from South Carolina to Georgia, specifically, the Northern District of Georgia, all in violation of Title 18, United States Code, Section 2251(a).

Defendant argues that the district court erred when it denied his motion to dismiss Count 1 because 18 U.S.C. § 2251 does not authorize prosecution of conduct by an American national that occurred wholly in a foreign country. He next argues that the district court should have dismissed Counts 1 and 3 because venue in the Northern District of Georgia was improper as the conduct specifically outlawed by 18 U.S.C. § 2251(a), the "use" of a minor in and the production of images of sexually explicit conduct, was alleged to have occurred in either Greece or South Carolina.[12]

---

12. Defendant also argues that the district court erred when it declined to dismiss Counts 1 and 3 as neither alleged that he produced the image with the intent that it be transported across any border to the Northern District of Georgia or, in the case of the image produced in Greece, even to the United States. This argument deserves little attention as the behavior prohibited by § 2251(a) is punishable

Denials of motions to dismiss concerning questions of law are reviewed *de novo*. *United States v. Gupta*, 463 F.3d 1182, 1191 (11th Cir.2006). Having considered the law and the arguments, we affirm the decision of the district court for the reasons which follow.... Defendant argues that 18 U.S.C. § 2251(a) does not authorize prosecution for prohibited acts by an American national that occur in a foreign country, such as Greece, and the application of § 2251(a) in the case of Count 1 constitutes an improper extraterritorial application of the law.[13] Having carefully considered the statute itself, however, we are of the opinion that Congress intended for 18 U.S.C. § 2251(a), as in effect at the time of Kapordelis' conduct, to apply regardless of whether the violation occurred on American soil or abroad, so long as the behavior has a sufficient nexus with this country. In this case, Kapordelis transported his pictures from Greece into the United States. That is clearly sufficient.

Section 2251(a) does not explicitly prohibit conduct outside of the United States, but neither is its application limited to instances where the wrongdoer commits the entire violation within the territory of the United States.[14] Rather, the statute is part of a comprehensive statutory scheme to eradicate sexual exploitation of children, *see* 18 U.S.C. §§ 2241–2257, in which Congress has outlawed the transportation, mailing, and receipt of child pornography. *See United States v. Thomas*, 893 F.2d 1066, 1069 (9th Cir.1990). "Punishing the creation of child pornography outside the United States that is actually, is intended to be, or may reasonably be expected to be transported in interstate or foreign commerce is an important enforcement tool." *Id.* Thus, we conclude that Congress intended to reach extraterritorial acts, such as those of Kapordelis, that otherwise satisfy the statutory elements of 18 U.S.C. § 2251(a) if they were produced using equipment that had traveled into or out of the United States, if the visual depictions were imported or transmitted into the United States, or if the defendant believed or had reason to believe that they

---

"if such person knows or has reason to know that such visual depiction will be transported in interstate or foreign commerce or mailed," "if such visual depiction has actually been transported in interstate or foreign commerce or mailed," or "if that visual depiction was produced using materials that have been mailed, shipped, or transported in interstate or foreign commerce by any means, including by computer." Counts 1 and 3 clearly allege that the images were actually transported from Greece to Georgia and from South Carolina to Georgia, respectively. Further, Count 3 alleges that the depictions were created using a camera which had been mailed, shipped, or transported in interstate commerce. Accordingly, the conduct alleged in Counts 1 and 3 of the Fourth Superseding Indictment would constitute a violation of § 2251(a), and the district court did not err when it declined to dismiss Counts 1 and 3 on these grounds.

13. Defendant does not argue that Congress was without power to enact 18 U.S.C. § 2251(a) or that the application of § 2251(a) would violate due process. *See United States v. Pinto-Mejia*, 720 F.2d 248, 259 (2d Cir.1983) (Congress may apply its penal statutes to extraterritorial acts unless application would violate due process). Thus, whether 18 U.S.C. § 2251(a) applies to Kapordelis's acts abroad is a question of statutory interpretation for this Court. *See Blackmer v. United States*, 284 U.S. 421, 437, 52 S.Ct. 252, 76 L.Ed. 375 (1932); *United States v. Plummer*, 221 F.3d 1298, 1304 (11th Cir.2000) ("Whether Congress has in fact exercised [its authority to create law with extraterritorial application] ... is a matter of statutory construction.").

14. Defendant also argues that the 2003 enactment of the PROTECT ACT, including that portion codified at 18 U.S.C. § 2251(c), demonstrates that § 2251(a) did not reach and that Congress did not intend it to reach extraterritorial sexually explicit conduct with children prior to its passage. While § 2251(c) addresses the act of using a child outside the United States for the purpose of producing images of child pornography which the defendant intends to or does transport to the United States, the passage of that statute did not retroactively restrict the scope of the application of the preexisting portion of the statute, § 2251(a). *See Radzanower v. Touche Ross & Co.*, 426 U.S. 148, 154, 96 S.Ct. 1989, 48 L.Ed.2d 540 (1976) (implied repeals of one statute through enactment of another are not favored) (citations omitted).

would be. The district court did not err when it denied Defendant's motion to dismiss Count 1 on these grounds, and its decision shall be affirmed....

Defendant next contends that the district court should have dismissed Counts 1 and 3 because the alleged "use" of a minor in and the production of images of sexually explicit conduct, the actions specifically outlawed by 18 U.S.C. § 2251(a), occurred in either Greece or South Carolina, not in the Northern District of Georgia. He argues that the indictment alleges only that he possessed sexually explicit images of a minor in Georgia, which conduct, by itself, is not prohibited by § 2251(a). As such, he theorizes that venue in the Northern District of Georgia was inappropriate and that the district court erred when it declined to dismiss those counts of the Fourth Superseding Indictment for inappropriate venue. We disagree.

No doubt, a criminal defendant has a right to have his case adjudicated in the appropriate venue, i.e., in the state and district where the crime or crimes with which he has been charged were committed. U.S. Const. art. III, § 2, cl. 3 (the "Trial of all Crimes ... shall be held in the State where the said Crimes shall have been committed"); U.S. Const. amend. VI (trial of criminal defendants shall be "by an impartial jury of the State and district wherein the crime shall have been committed"); *see also* FED. R.CRIM. P. 18 ("prosecution shall be had in a district in which the offense was committed"). "'[T]he *locus delicti* must be determined from the nature of the crime alleged and the location of the act or acts constituting it.'" *United States v. Cabrales*, 524 U.S. 1, 6, 118 S.Ct. 1772, 141 L.Ed.2d 1 (1998) (quoting *United States v. Anderson*, 328 U.S. 699, 703, 66 S.Ct. 1213, 90 L.Ed. 1529 (1946)). Where a crime "involv[es] the use of the mails, transportation in interstate or foreign commerce, or the importation of an object or person into the United States," the offense is a "continuing crime," i.e., one which begins in one district and is completed in another. 18 U.S.C. § 3237(a); *United States v. Rodriguez-Moreno*, 526 U.S. 275, 279–81, 119 S.Ct. 1239, 143 L.Ed.2d 388 (1999). In such instances, venue is proper in any district in which the offense was started, continued, or completed. *Id.*

Section 2251(a) includes among its required elements ... (1) that the defendant must know or have reason to know that "such visual depiction will be transported in interstate or foreign commerce or mailed," (2) that the "visual depiction was produced using materials that have been mailed, shipped, or transported in interstate or foreign commerce," or (3) that the "visual depiction has actually been transported in interstate or foreign commerce or mailed." Count 1 alleges that the digital photographs were transported from Greece to Georgia and Count 3 alleges that the digital photographs were transported from South Carolina to Georgia and created using a camera that had been "mailed, transported and shipped in interstate and foreign commerce."

While neither the transportation of an image allegedly produced in violation of § 2251(a) from another jurisdiction nor the possession of such an image in the Northern District of Georgia changes the location of the "use" or "production" elements from Greece or South Carolina, as Defendant argues, § 2251(a) ties the punishment for the "use" of a minor in and "production" of visual depictions of sexually explicit conduct to the transport of the visual depictions or the means of producing those visual depictions in interstate or foreign commerce. Thus, under 18 U.S.C. § 3237, the violation of § 2251(a) as alleged in Counts 1 and 3 is a "continuing offense." Venue in the Northern District of Georgia into which the images (and the camera, in the case of Count 3) moved, was appropriate, and the decision of the district court shall be affirmed....

For all of the reasons stated above, Kapordelis's conviction and the decisions of and the sentence by the district court are AFFIRMED.

Notes

Title 18 U.S.C. § 2251(a) and § 2251(c) both apply to acts committed outside the United States. *See also* 18 U.S.C. § 2260 (Production of sexually explicit depictions of a minor for importation into the United States); *United States v. McVicker*, 979 F. Supp. 2d 1154, 1172–73 (Or. Dist. 2013) (defendant produced and transported child pornography while living abroad). However, § 2251(a) does not necessarily require knowledge of the interstate nature of the materials used to produce the sexually explicit depiction. Conversely, § 2251(c) requires the defendant to *intend* that the depictions be transported to the United States or that he or she actually transport the depictions. Thus, § 2251(c) may be used when the application of § 2251(a) might conflict with other jurisdictional principles of international law. *See id.* at 1173–74. *See also United States v. Harvey*, 2 F.3d 1318 (3d Cir. 1993) (extraterritorial provision applied where defendant sexually exploited children abroad, photographed conduct, and possessed photographs in United States); *United States v. Thomas*, 893 F.2d 1066 (9th Cir. 1990) (American national could be convicted of violating child pornography statutes, regardless of whether acts on which conviction was based were committed in United States).

4. *Notice or Advertisement for Child Pornography*

United States v. Rowe

Second Circuit, 2005
414 F.3d 271

FEINBERG, Circuit Judge.

Larry G. Rowe appeals from a judgment of conviction of the United States District Court for the Southern District of New York (Brieant, J.) entered after a jury found him guilty of advertising to receive, exchange or distribute child pornography in violation of 18 U.S.C. § 2251(c) (now designated § 2251(d)).[1] ...

At approximately one o'clock in the morning on April 5, 2002, Shlomo Koenig, a detective on the Computer Crime Task Forces of both the Rockland County Sheriff's Department and the United States Secret Service, connected to the internet and entered a chat room titled "preteen00." ... [footnote omitted]. The detective testified at Rowe's trial

---

1. At the time of Rowe's conduct, 18 U.S.C. § 2251(c) provided in relevant part:
   (1) Any person who, in a circumstance described in paragraph (2), knowingly makes, prints, or publishes, or causes to be made, printed, or published, any notice or advertisement seeking or offering—
     (A) to receive, exchange, buy, produce, display, distribute, or reproduce, any visual depiction, if the production of such visual depiction involves the use of a minor engaging in sexually explicit conduct and such visual depiction is of such conduct ... shall be punished as provided under subsection (d).
   (2) The circumstance referred to in paragraph (1) is that—
     (A) such person knows or has reason to know that such notice or advertisement will be transported in interstate or foreign commerce by any means including by computer or mailed; or
     (B) such notice or advertisement is transported in interstate or foreign commerce by any means including by computer or mailed.
18 U.S.C. § 2251(c) (2000). This language is now located in 18 U.S.C. § 2251(d), in which subsection (1) has been amended to state that violators "shall be punished as provided under subsection (e) [the penalty provision originally in subsection (d)]." Prosecutorial Remedies and Tools Against the Exploitation of Children Today Act of 2003 ("PROTECT Act"), Pub.L. No. 108-21, 117 Stat. 650 (2003).

that the "preteen00" chat room was "a room which I've known from prior [experience] where there is trading of child porn." The detective also testified that the name of the room "is used basically in the pedophile community." Once in the chat room, the detective came across a posting that read: "[v2.3b] Fserve Trigger: *!tun* Ratio 1:1 Offering: *Pre boys/girl pics*. Read the rules. [1 of 2 slots in use]" (emphasis in original). This text had been posted by a person with the screen name "Tunlvd," a name later determined to belong to Rowe.

According to the government's undisputed explanation, "[v2.3b]" indicated that the software program Rowe used was Panzer version 2.3b. "Fserve Trigger: *! tun* " indicated that "!tun" was the password needed to access the file server containing the images on Rowe's computer. "Ratio 1:1" indicated that users wishing to download images from Rowe's computer had to upload an equivalent number of images to his computer. "Offering: *Pre boys/girl pics* "indicated that the images available on Rowe's computer were pictures of pre-teen boys and girls. "Read the rules" indicated that a user wishing to download images had first to read the rules of use. Finally, "[1 of 2 slots in use]" indicated that two users could access Rowe's computer at the same time, and that one user was doing so when Detective Koenig viewed the posting.

When the detective typed the "trigger," he was linked to Rowe's computer. Once connected, he was presented with Rowe's rules of use, which provided:

> By entering this fserve you are agreeing that you are not a law officer or affiliated with the law in any way and do not hold this fserve nor owner there of accountable for anything you upload or download. if u do i guess i'm just screwed:/ If you do not agree to the above LEAVE NOW!
> (now for the rules)
> Rules are
> up only Pre (10−) no clothes no pube hair
> if your pic won't up
> i prolly have it already
> im still sorting so there maybe stuff i havent pulled yet

After reading these rules, Detective Koenig reviewed and copied a text list of the images available for download from Rowe's computer. That list named files such as "dadfucking12yearold.jpg," "10yo_preteen_raped.jpg" and "incest kiddy rape.jpg." When the detective attempted to download an image without also uploading one, as the rules required, he was disconnected from Rowe's computer.

After verifying that the posting in the "preteen00" chat room linked to Rowe's computer and that "Tunlvd" was Rowe, in June 2002 Secret Service agents executed a search warrant at Rowe's home. Among the items seized was a computer hard drive found to contain approximately 12,000 child-pornographic images and videos. As the agents were searching Rowe's home, he spoke with one of them and, after being informed of his right to remain silent, admitted that his screen name was "Tunlvd," that he was likely in the "preteen00" chat room at one o'clock in the morning on April 5, 2002, that he knew it was illegal to download or upload child-pornographic images and that he had downloaded approximately 6,000 such images and had uploaded an equivalent number from his computer to other users.... The following day, June 20, 2002, the government filed a one-count criminal complaint in the Southern District of New York charging Rowe with violating 18 U.S.C. § 2251(c). In February 2003, a federal grand jury sitting in the Southern District of New York returned a single-count indictment charging Rowe with violating § 2251(c)....

Rowe was tried before a jury in November 2003. When the government rested its case, Rowe moved for judgment as a matter of law on the argument that the "preteen00" chatroom posting identified in the indictment "does not make a reference to child pornography.... [T]he charged conduct is only whether or not that specific [posting] amounts to a specific solicitation for exchange of child pornography, and the defendant asserts that it does not." The district judge denied the motion, finding that the "government's evidence can't be viewed in isolation.... [The posting] invites the reader to amplify the statement ... by reference to [Rowe's] rules, which ... are adequate, in the Court's views, to indicate that there is an intention [to] offer or receive only pre-age 10 with no clothes and no pubic hair." The district judge concluded that "these exhibits are adequate to charge validly and prove the offense of the indictment...." The district judge also refused to direct acquittal on the argument that the posting did not travel through interstate commerce.

The defense put its case on and Rowe eventually took the stand, claiming that his posting in the "preteen00" chat room was not an advertisement to exchange child pornography, but a link intended for someone with the screen name "BabyK" to use to gain access to Rowe's computer. According to Rowe, "BabyK" was a woman who claimed to be the "Katie" from a website called "Katie's-World." ... [footnote omitted]. Rowe testified that he "was totally infatuated and head-over-heels in love with ['BabyK'] within — within three days" of meeting her in the "preteen00" chat room. Rowe further testified that "BabyK" told him "that she had been raped by four men," and that "she sent [Rowe] the pictures paralleling what had happened to her" so that Rowe could understand her. Rowe implied that the child-pornographic images found on his computer had been uploaded by "BabyK," to whom he had given "complete, total access to [his] machine." The posting placed in the "preteen00" chat room was merely, Rowe claimed, a convenient means of assuring "BabyK" access to Rowe's computer: "the message that — [the Secret Service agents] referred to it as an advertisement. It was a message between me and ['BabyK']. And I never in any way ever considered it an advertisement." Rowe did not explain why, if this was the case, his posting was "Offering: *Pre boys/girl pics* " (emphasis in original), why a reader of the posting should "Read the Rules" or why there was "1 of 2 slots in use."

The jury found Rowe guilty. At sentencing, the district judge and Rowe's attorney both expressed the belief that Rowe's crime carried a mandatory minimum of 10 years in prison. The district judge voiced his displeasure with this, stating that "statutory minimums generally create a problem" and that "this may be a classic case where the issue of proportionality is presented." The judge sentenced Rowe to 10 years in prison followed by three years of supervised release. The judge also ordered Rowe to undergo sex-offender treatment and forbade him from having any deliberate contact with any child under 17 years of age without the permission of a probation officer.... On appeal, Rowe argues principally that his posting was not a "notice or advertisement" within the meaning of §2251(c)....

Rowe argues that his posting "does not meet the definition of an advertisement prohibited [by 18] U.S.C. §2251(c)," and that his conviction must therefore be reversed. The government apparently asserts that this is an argument regarding the sufficiency of the evidence, and thus urges a deferential standard of review. We believe Rowe's argument is more accurately characterized as a purely legal question of statutory interpretation, and we therefore review the district judge's ruling de novo. *See, e.g., Field v. United States*, 381 F.3d 109, 111 (2d Cir.2004).

Rowe placed his posting — "[v2.3b] Fserve Trigger: *!tun* Ratio 1:1 Offering: *Pre boys/girl pics*. Read the Rules. [1 of 2 slots in use]" (emphasis in original) — in the "preteen00" chat room. The government maintains that "this chatroom was devoted to the exchange of child pornography images," and that typical postings included "anybody with baby sex pics for trade?" and "young teen amateur movie ... cum, gag, teen gangbang, non-nude, and more...." Rowe does not dispute the government's characterization, and effectively concedes it by arguing that "the context of the chat room ... [and] the presence of other explicit advertisements for child pornography in the chat room [do not] make the [posting] an advertisement prohibited by [18] U.S.C. §2251(c)." Rowe contends, as he did unsuccessfully below, that "nothing in [his posting] ... indicates that pornography is involved of any kind...." His posting in the chat room, Rowe asserts, "is only an advertisement offering pictures of 'preboys/girl.'"

Contrary to what Rowe would have us hold, "only" offering pictures of children in a "preteen00" chat room peppered with queries such as "anybody with baby sex pics for trade?" is sufficient to constitute a "notice or advertisement" within the meaning of §2251(c). As the government aptly characterizes it, "Rowe's decision to place into this forum his notice that he was 'Offering: Preboys/girl pics' could have had only a single purpose—to advise others that he had child pornography available for trade."

Rowe insists that his posting is beyond the scope of §2251(c) because it "does not by its very terms indicate it is seeking or offering materials of a pornographic nature." Rowe cites no authority to support this proposition, which is belied by §2251(c)'s plain language, case law and common sense. Section 2251(c) makes it a crime to "knowingly make [ ], print[ ], or publish[ ] ... any notice or advertisement seeking or offering ... any visual depiction, if the production of such visual depiction involves the use of a minor engaging in sexually explicit conduct and such visual depiction is of such conduct." 18 U.S.C. §2251(c)(1)(A). As a recent district court decision in this Circuit correctly observed, "there is no requirement that an advertisement must specifically state that it offers or seeks a visual depiction to violate §2251(c)(1)(A).... '[N]o particular magic words or phrases need to be included.'" *United States v. Pabon-Cruz*, 255 F.Supp.2d 200, 218 (S.D.N.Y.2003) (quoting jury charge), aff'd in relevant part, 391 F.3d 86 (2d Cir.2004).

The question here is thus whether Rowe knowingly offered or sought images depicting minors engaged in sexually explicit conduct. There is no doubt that he did. Section 2251(c) is not so narrow that it captures only those who state, "I have child-pornographic images for trade." We agree with the government that if that were the case, then "all a distributor of child pornograph[y] need do to avoid §2251(c) is use a modicum of sub[t]lety in describing the images sought or offered." We further agree that "Congress did not intend its bar on advertising for child pornography to be so easily evaded." We therefore affirm the district judge's ruling that Rowe's chat-room posting was a "notice or advertisement" within the meaning of §2251(c)....

As for the "conduct constituting the offense," §2251(c) makes it a crime to "knowingly make[ ], print[ ], or publish[ ], or cause[ ] to be made, printed, or published, any notice or advertisement seeking or offering [child pornography]." 18 U.S.C. §2251(c)(1)(A). The statute requires that violators knew or had reason to know that their notice or advertisement would be "transported in interstate or foreign commerce by any means including by computer or mailed," *id.* §2251(c)(2)(A), or simply that the notice or advertisement was in fact so transported. *Id.* §2251(c)(2)(B). Section 2251(c)'s "conduct constituting the offense" is thus the publication of an offer, expected to be or actually communicated across state lines, to provide, receive or exchange child pornography. We hold ... that Rowe's posting in the "preteen00" chat room was an offer to exchange child pornography, and there is no dispute that the offer was transported in interstate commerce by computer....

We affirm the district judge's rulings that Rowe posted an "advertisement or notice" within the meaning of 18 U.S.C. §2251(c).... We therefore affirm Rowe's conviction, but vacate his sentence in light of *Pabon-Cruz* and remand for resentencing.

Notes

As described in *Rowe*, when distributors of child pornography advertise in chat rooms, they describes the content to be shared by using language viewable by other users of the chat room and post instructions on how to access the distributor's server and download the content. No further communication between the distributor and recipient is required. Likewise, in *United States v. Sewell*, 513 F.3d 820 (8th Cir. 2008), the court held that the defendant's use of a peer-to-peer file-sharing program, called Kazaa, by placing files containing child pornography in a shared folder, and using descriptive text, was an "offer" to distribute child pornography. The court held that the peer-to-peer access in *Sewell* was indistinguishable from the exchange conducted in Internet chat rooms applicable in *Rowe*. The court held that "[t]he difference between the two methods is one of efficiency, not substance; the distributor is making an unambiguous offer in both situations."

D. Receipt of Child Pornography

United States v. Watzman

Seventh Circuit, 2007
486 F.3d 1004

SYKES, Circuit Judge....

In early 2003 a federal investigation based in New Jersey uncovered a company called "Regpay" located in Minsk, Belarus, that operated numerous fee-based websites containing pornographic images of children. By purchasing memberships to these sites, federal agents were able to view the websites' content and confirm that they advertised and included child pornography. In June 2003 investigators seized the company's customer database, which consisted of the names, mailing and e-mail addresses, and credit card numbers of the customers who bought access to any of its websites, as well as the dates of purchase and the names of the websites. One such customer was Marc Watzman, a Chicago resident who had paid for access to eight of the company's web-sites, including sites named "www .lolitacastle.com" and "www.undergroundlolitastudio.com." ... In April 2003 Watzman began transacting with "Pedoshop," a "child pornography production organization" based in Russia. Through e-mail, Pedoshop offered Watzman access to its "very big child porno collection," and shortly thereafter Watzman placed an order. Between April and October he ordered 89 video clips that contained child pornography. Watzman paid $9700 to Pedoshop for the videos.

Based on information Watzman had supplied in registering for the websites, investigators tracked him to a post office box in Chicago and from there obtained his home address and driver's license records. Through visual surveillance, investigators confirmed that Watzman, a 37-year-old pediatrician, lived in a garden apartment at 1454 North Wieland Street in Chicago. On October 22, 2003, officers from the Chicago Police Department, cooperating with federal agents, went to Watzman's apartment and told him they were following up on a burglary he had reported two years earlier. Watzman allowed the officers to enter his apartment, where they noticed a desktop computer connected to an active cable modem, as well as a laptop computer.

On October 24, 2003, federal agents applied for a warrant to search Watzman's apartment and seize evidence of his receipt and possession of child pornography, including credit card records; documents confirming his ownership of the post office box used to obtain membership to pornographic websites; computer hardware and software; and any sexually explicit images of children, including videos, photographs, and digital images. The warrant application was supported by a 23-page affidavit by Ronald Wolflick, a special agent from the Bureau of Immigration and Customs Enforcement and supervisor of the Cyber-Crimes Investigations Group in Chicago. Among the information included in the affidavit were four paragraphs in which Wolflick described the contact between Watzman and Chicago police officers two days earlier. The magistrate judge issued the warrant, and a search was conducted the following day. Among the items seized were Watzman's desktop and laptop computers, which held thousands of digital images depicting child pornography, and a number of DVDs with similar content, some encrypted and requiring extensive decoding.

Watzman was ultimately charged with one count of possessing child pornography, nine counts of receiving it, and one count of money laundering. Among various pretrial motions he filed was a motion to quash the search warrant and suppress all evidence seized during its execution on October 25. He principally argued that the ruse engaged in by the Chicago police officers to gain consent to enter his home on October 22 invalidated the search warrant. Watzman contended the ruse was unlawful and any information gleaned during the officers' visit—in particular, the knowledge that he had two computers inside his home—was tainted. Absent this information, he argued, there was no reason to believe contraband would be found in the apartment and thus no basis for the warrant. The district court held that the October 22 consent search was invalid, but declined to suppress the evidence obtained on October 25 pursuant to the warrant. The court reasoned that "the remaining averments in the affidavit of Agent Wolflick provide probable cause for the issuance of the warrant."

Watzman also filed a motion to require the government to prove, as an element of receiving child pornography, that he intended to traffic in child pornography. Otherwise, he argued, no meaningful distinction could be made between "receiving" and "possessing" child pornography and therefore the statute was unconstitutionally vague. The district court denied the motion. Watzman then entered into a plea agreement with the government, pleading guilty to one count of possessing and nine counts of receiving child pornography and reserving his right to challenge the district court's rulings on his suppression motion and his motion challenging the receipt statute. The district court imposed concurrent sentences of five years' imprisonment on each count, the minimum penalty under the statute and below the advisory guidelines range of 78 to 97 months....

Watzman ... challenges the district court's rejection of his argument that the statute criminalizing the receipt of child pornography is unconstitutionally vague "because it does not define 'receipt' or distinguish it from the offense of mere possession." Watzman contends that "without any evidence of trafficking and distributing," "receipt" cannot be distinguished from "possession" and, therefore, the statute "enables arbitrary and discriminatory prosecution." A criminal statute is unconstitutionally vague if it does not define the criminal offense with enough specificity to provide people of ordinary intelligence with notice of what is prohibited or if it fails to provide explicit standards to prevent arbitrary and discriminatory enforcement. *See Kolender v. Lawson*, 461 U.S. 352, 357, 103 S.Ct. 1855, 75 L.Ed.2d 903 (1983); *United States v. Lim*, 444 F.3d 910, 915 (7th Cir.2006). The statute in question makes it a crime for a person to "knowingly receive[ ] or distribute[ ] ... child pornography that has been mailed, or shipped or transported in interstate or foreign commerce by any means, including by computer." 18 U.S.C. § 2252A(a)(2). In contrast, the subsection of § 2252A concerning simple possession targets any individual who "knowingly possesses any book, magazine, periodical, film, videotape, computer disk, or any other material that contains an image of child pornography that has been mailed, or shipped or transported in interstate or foreign commerce by any means, including by computer." § 2252A(a)(5)(B).

Watzman has not established that § 2252A(a)(2) fails either the "notice" or the "arbitrary enforcement" tests for unconstitutional vagueness. We have previously rejected the argument that "the distinction between receipt and possession of child pornography is meaningless, because anyone in possession of child pornography must have received it at some time." *United States v. Myers*, 355 F.3d 1040, 1042–43 (7th Cir.2004). We noted in *Myers* that to be convicted of receiving, the defendant must have known the material he was receiving depicted minors engaged in sexually explicit conduct. *See id.* at 1042 (citing *United States v. X-Citement Video, Inc.*, 513 U.S. 64, 78, 115 S.Ct. 464, 130 L.Ed.2d 372 (1994)). Accordingly, a person who receives child pornography by accident (for example, if he sought adult pornography but was sent child pornography instead) is not guilty of knowingly receiving it, though he is guilty of possessing it if he retains it. *Myers*, 355 F.3d at 1042; *see United States v. Malik*, 385 F.3d 758, 759 (7th Cir.2004) (positing that a person who created an image or found it in trash could "possess" child pornography without ever receiving it). We stated that receiving materials that have been shipped in interstate commerce is conduct more closely linked to the market for child pornography and so "possession and receipt are not the same conduct and threaten distinct harms." *Myers*, 355 F.3d at 1042–43; *see United States v. Barevich*, 445 F.3d 956, 959 (7th Cir.2006) (explaining that "[t]ransporting and receiving child pornography increases market demand"). This is so without an element of "intent to traffic."

Although *Myers* did not address a vagueness challenge, the opinion squarely rejected the premise of Watzman's constitutional argument — that receipt and possession are substantially the same offense. By distinguishing receipt from possession, the two subsections of the statute are sufficiently clear about what conduct each prohibits. In addition, it cannot be said that the receiving child pornography statute relies on the discretion of those who enforce it to define its terms. We have recognized that all receivers are possessors but not all possessors are receivers, and so the matter of which crime to charge is not simply a product of the prosecutor's whims, as Watzman suggests. Watzman's conduct violated multiple statutes, but this is unremarkable, *see Malik*, 385 F.3d at 760, and has no bearing on whether the statute is unconstitutionally vague.

Finally, Watzman contends that receiving child pornography exclusively for his own private use is not the type of conduct at which the statute is aimed. We have previously rejected the argument that there is some sort of "personal use" exception to this statute. *See United States v. Ellison*, 113 F.3d 77, 81 (7th Cir.1997) ("[E]ven the receipt of the prohibited materials for personal use, without more, keeps producers and distributors of this filth in business.").

Affirmed.

United States v. Ramos

Second Circuit, 2012
685 F.3d 120

CHIN, Circuit Judge: ...

In 1990, Ramos was convicted in state court in Saratoga Springs, New York, of sexually abusing two sisters, ages ten and thirteen. After serving approximately fourteen years in prison, he applied in February 2003 for release on parole. In his application, he agreed to certain conditions of supervision, including permitting his parole officer to visit and search his residence and person, replying "promptly, fully and truthfully" to any inquiries from his parole officer, and "fully" complying with any instructions from his parole officer. He also agreed to refrain from "possess[ing], seek [ing] access to or remain[ing] near any pornographic materials." The application was granted, and Ramos was released from custody to the supervision of the New York State Division of Parole in May 2003.

On March 5, 2008, Ramos's parole officer told him that two new conditions—polygraph testing and GPS monitoring—were being added to his conditions of supervision because of changes in the procedures for sex offenders on parole. Ramos complained to his parole officer that the addition of the conditions "violated his rights." Ramos spoke with his parole officer several more times after March 5, 2008, and eventually agreed to participate in the polygraph examination, despite his initial reservations....

On April 4, 2008, Ramos went to the Probation Office for a polygraph test. He first signed several forms. In one, he agreed that "failure to answer questions regarding my conformance to parole ... conditions, in the discretion of the Parole Office and Polygraph Examiner, may be deemed as a failure to participate in a meaningful way and be submitted ... as a parole ... violation." In another, he stated: "I will participate in the Division of Parole's polygraph program as directed by my P.O. I understand this will include periodic polygraph sessions.... I will answer all questions fully and truthfully as well as comply w/ any directives given to me by the polygraph examiner." In yet a third he acknowledged that:

5. Failure to fully cooperate and participate in any aspect of the polygraph examination session, including refusal to answer questions during the examination, may be grounds for violations of my parole.

6. Answers to questions during the polygraph examination session may be used in determining appropriate sanctions to be implemented by the Division of Parole, including a parole violation hearing. Additionally, admissions to criminal behavior will result in referral to appropriate law enforcement authorities for investigation and possible prosecution.

7. Any admission to criminal behavior during the polygraph session may be used against me in a court of law.

[Citation omitted] (emphases omitted)....

In an interview before the test was administered, Ramos told the polygraph examiner that he had viewed both pornography and child pornography on his computer via the internet, "at least somewhere between twelve and eighteen times since his release to parole supervision." Ramos took the test, and the results were inconclusive. Afterwards, Ramos signed an "Admissions Form" in which he confirmed that he had viewed pornography and child pornography "on at least 12 to 18 different occasions," on the internet in his home. Ramos's parole officer immediately imposed a new condition of parole forbidding Ramos from owning or operating a computer and using the internet....

After Ramos left, the parole officer reported Ramos's admissions to U.S. Immigration and Customs Enforcement ("ICE") agents. The same day, April 4, 2008, two ICE agents went to Ramos's residence, a trailer home. They found him outside the trailer. They introduced themselves and said that they had information there might be child pornography on his computer. Ramos agreed to talk to them inside. The agents did not place Ramos under arrest, nor did they handcuff him. They asked him questions, and he admitted that he had a computer in his residence, he used the computer to access the Internet, he had searched for and viewed child pornography on the computer, and thus they would probably find child pornography on the computer.

At some point during the interview, the agents read Ramos his *Miranda* rights.[1] He signed two consent forms, one to a search of his residence and one to a search of his computer equipment. He refused to sign a third document. The agents then conducted a search and seized a desktop computer. As a forensic examination would later reveal, Ramos had used the computer to visit child pornography websites and view images of child pornography. One of the hard drives had deleted "cookie" files from websites with names indicative of sexual interest in minors. There were two deleted web pages with images that were not recoverable, but that bore the names "Lolita Photos" and "9–12yr Pics." The hard drive had been used to conduct a Google search using words such as "twink," which suggested a search for child pornography. One of the hard drives contained software called "Smart Protector Pro" that enabled a user to delete his browser history. There were some 140 images of child pornography in deleted space; the file names indicated these had been temporary internet files that had been deleted.

On November 20, 2008, a grand jury in the Northern District of New York indicted Ramos for knowingly receiving and possessing child pornography. The next day, ICE agents and two parole officers returned to Ramos's residence to arrest him. Again, he was outside the trailer. The officers asked him to step inside so that they could talk to him, and he agreed. Inside, the officers advised Ramos he was being arrested and handcuffed him. The parole officers conducted a sweep of the trailer to determine whether anyone else was present and to look for evidence of any parole violation. They saw computer equipment lying in plain view and discovered beneath the sheet of Ramos's bed a laptop computer that was halfway open. The parole officers opened the laptop, clicked on an icon, and found images of what appeared to be child pornography. The officers seized the laptop and obtained a warrant to search it further.... The laptop was manufactured in Korea and its hard drive was manufactured in Thailand. The hard drive had on it computer software called "Microsoft Picture It," which permitted a user to alter images. The laptop contained images modified to appear as if children were engaged in sexually explicit acts. The original, unaltered images of two young girls, panties, and a penis — which had been used to create the altered image — were also found on the computer....

On March 13, 2009, a grand jury in the Northern District of New York returned a superseding indictment against Ramos charging him with two counts of receiving child pornography, in violation of 18 U.S.C. §§ 2252A(a)(2)(A) and 2256(8)(A), and two counts of possession of child pornography, in violation of 18 U.S.C. §§ 2252A(a)(5)(B), 2256(8)(A), and 2256(8)(C). The two sets of possession and receipt charges referred, respectively, to the two computers seized on April 4 and November 21, 2008.... In September 2009, Ramos moved to suppress his statements to parole officers and the evidence seized during the searches resulting from his statements. The district court denied the motions from the bench on April 5, 2010, following an evidentiary hearing....

Ramos proceeded to trial *pro se*, with advisory counsel. Following a three-day trial, the jury convicted Ramos on three counts of receiving and possessing child pornography.[3] ...

_____

1. At the suppression hearing, Ramos denied receiving *Miranda* warnings at his home on April 4, 2008, although he testified that he was shown a piece of paper that "could have been" *Miranda* warnings. The district court found, however, that Ramos was not in custody and that, in any event, *Miranda* warnings were given to him.

3. One of the counts was dismissed at the government's request at the start of the trial. Ramos was convicted on Count 1, which charged receipt of child pornography in connection with the computer seized on April 4, 2008, in violation of 18 U.S.C. §§ 2252A(a)(2)(A) and 2256(8)(A); Count

Ramos was sentenced on November 23, 2010. Because Ramos had previously been convicted of sexually abusing children, he was subject to a mandatory minimum sentence of imprisonment of fifteen years. *See* 18 U.S.C. § 2252A(b)(1). The district court sentenced Ramos to the statutory minimum: a term of 180 months' imprisonment on each of the three counts, to be served concurrently.... This appeal followed....

Two sufficiency issues are presented: first, whether viewing images in temporary internet files constitutes receipt or possession of child pornography, and, second, whether using computer equipment manufactured abroad to create "morphed" images of child pornography meets the interstate or foreign commerce element of the crimes of conviction.... Ramos argues, with respect to the computer seized on April 4, 2008, that the evidence failed to prove that he knowingly received or possessed images from the internet because the evidence showed only that he viewed images in temporary internet or "cache" files (without saving them) and that the mere viewing of child pornography stored in temporary internet files was insufficient to sustain a conviction under the statute as it then existed.

Ramos was charged with receipt of child pornography in violation of 18 U.S.C. § 2252A(a)(2)(A) and possession of child pornography in violation of 18 U.S.C. § 2252A(a)(5)(B). At the time Ramos committed the acts in question, the statute provided in pertinent part:

> (a) Any person who —
>
> (2) knowingly receives ... (A) any child pornography that has been mailed, or shipped or transported in interstate or foreign commerce by any means, including by computer, ...
>
> [or]
>
> (5) ... (B) knowingly possesses any book, magazine, periodical, film, videotape, computer disk, or any other material that contains an image of child pornography that has been mailed, or shipped or transported in interstate or foreign commerce by any means, including by computer, or that was produced using materials that have been mailed, or shipped or transported in interstate or foreign commerce by any means, including by computer, ...
>
> [commits a crime].

18 U.S.C. § 2252A(a)(2)(A), (5)(B) (effective July 27, 2006 to October 7, 2008).[7]

The statute does not define receipt or possession, and courts have given these terms their plain meaning. *See, e.g., United States v. Pruitt*, 638 F.3d 763, 766 (11th Cir.2011) (per curiam) ("The ordinary meaning of 'receive' is 'to knowingly accept'; 'to take possession

---

2, which charged possession of child pornography, in connection with the computer seized on April 4, 2008, in violation of 18 U.S.C. §§ 2252A(a)(5)(B) and 2256(8)(A); and Count 4 (redesignated Count 3 at trial), which charged possession of child pornography, in connection with the laptop computer seized on November 21, 2008, in violation of 18 U.S.C. §§ 2252A(a)(5)(B), 2256(8)(A), and 2256(8)(C).

7. On October 8, 2008 — after the seizure of Ramos's desktop computer on April 4, 2008, but before the seizure of Ramos's laptop on November 21, 2008 — Congress amended § 2252A(a)(5)(B) to add the words "or knowingly accesses with intent to view," to make clear that accessing child pornography to view it was proscribed. *See* Enhancing the Effective Child Pornography Prosecution Act of 2007, Pub. L. No. 110-358, § 203(b), 122 Stat. 4001, 4003 (2008). A Senate report explained that the amendment "fills a gap in existing law that has led some courts to overturn convictions of possessors of child pornography. It amends the child pornography possession offense to clarify that it also covers knowingly accessing child pornography on the Internet with the intent to view child pornography." S.Rep. No. 110-332, at 5 (2008), *available at* 2008 WL 1885750 (2008).

or delivery of; or 'to take in through the mind or senses.'" (quoting *Webster's Third New International Dictionary: Unabridged* 1894 (1993)), *cert. denied*, ___ U.S. ___, 132 S.Ct. 113, 181 L.Ed.2d 38 (2011)); *United States v. Romm*, 455 F.3d 990, 998–1000 (9th Cir.2006) ("'Possession' is '[t]he fact of having or holding property in one's power; the exercise of dominion over property.'" (quoting *Black's Law Dictionary* 1183 (7th ed. 1999)) (alteration in original)); *United States v. Tucker*, 305 F.3d 1193, 1204 (10th Cir.2002) ("Possession is defined as 'the holding or having something (material or immaterial) as one's own, or in one's control.'" (quoting *Oxford English Dictionary* (2d ed. 1989))).

This Court has not yet decided whether viewing images stored in temporary internet files is sufficient to establish knowing receipt or possession of child pornography. *See United States v. Falso*, 544 F.3d 110, 121 n. 13 (2d Cir.2008); *United States v. Martin*, 426 F.3d 68, 77 (2d Cir.2005) (whether "viewing" child pornography on internet is legal is "an open question"). Other Circuits, however, have upheld child pornography receipt and possession convictions where a defendant viewed child pornography stored in temporary internet files on a computer. *See, e.g., Pruitt*, 638 F.3d at 766–67 ("A person 'knowingly receives' child pornography under 18 U.S.C. §2252A(a)(2) when he intentionally views, acquires, or accepts child pornography on a computer from an outside source," whether or not he "acts to save the images to a hard drive, to edit them, or otherwise to exert more control over them."); *United States v. Kain*, 589 F.3d 945, 948–50 (8th Cir.2009) ("The presence of child pornography in temporary internet and orphan files on a computer's hard drive is *evidence*[, although not conclusive,] of prior possession of that pornography...."); *Romm*, 455 F.3d at 998, 1002 (concluding that knowingly taking possession of files in internet cache, by accessing and manipulating them, constituted knowing receipt of those files); *United States v. Bass*, 411 F.3d 1198, 1201–02 (10th Cir.2005) (affirming conviction for knowing possession where child pornography files viewed on internet were automatically saved to hard drive). *But see United States v. Flyer*, 633 F.3d 911, 918–20 (9th Cir.2011) (vacating conviction for possession under §2252(a)(4)(B) and (b)(2) where images were located in "unallocated space" for deleted data on defendant's computer's hard drive and government presented no evidence that defendant could or did access files).

In the circumstances here, we hold that the evidence was sufficient to prove that Ramos was guilty of knowingly receiving and possessing child pornography under the statute as it was worded in April 2008, even assuming he viewed the images in question only in temporary internet files and did not save them onto his hard drive.... First, giving the words their plain meaning, Ramos clearly "receive[d]" and "possesse[d]" the images, even though they were only in his temporary internet files. As the evidence showed below, Ramos had some control over the images even without saving them — he could view them on his screen, he could leave them on his screen for as long as he kept his computer on, he could copy and attach them to an email and send them to someone, he could print them, and he could (with the right software) move the images from a cached file to other files and then view or manipulate them off-line. *See Romm*, 455 F.3d at 998 (relying on witness's testimony as to what could be done with cached files); *Tucker*, 305 F.3d at 1204–05 (relying on witness's testimony as to what could be done with cached files). Hence, as the evidence showed below, an individual who views images on the internet accepts them onto his computer, and he can still exercise dominion and control over them, even though they are in cache files. In other words, he receives and possesses them.

Second, here there was ample evidence that Ramos intentionally searched for images of child pornography, found them, and knowingly accepted them onto his computer, albeit temporarily. The browsing history on his desktop computer showed that Ramos intentionally searched for child pornography on the internet. *See, e.g., Pruitt*, 638 F.3d at 767 (upholding defendant's conviction where "investigators found a record of internet searches using terms related to child pornography ... and a record of visits to websites with a child-pornography connection"); *Kain*, 589 F.3d at 949–50 (finding sufficient evidence for knowing possession where defendant's browsing history showed repeated accessing of child pornography websites). In fact, he viewed some 140 images of child pornography, which were stored on the computer in temporary internet files. He knew that these images would be found on his computer, as he told the ICE agents that they would probably find child pornography there. Further, he had also attempted to delete the temporary internet files and browsing history from his computer. *See Bass*, 411 F.3d at 1202 ("[T]he jury here reasonably could have inferred that Bass knew child pornography was automatically saved to his mother's computer based on evidence that Bass attempted to remove the images.").... Accordingly, we conclude that there was sufficient evidence from which a rational trier of fact could have found that Ramos knowingly received and possessed child pornography on the computer seized on April 4, 2008....

We have considered Ramos's remaining arguments [regarding morphed images of child pornography] and conclude that they are without merit.[11] For the foregoing reasons, the judgment of the district court is AFFIRMED.

E. Possession of Child Pornography

State v. Ritchie

Supreme Court of Oregon, 2011
349 Or. 572, 248 P.3d 405

GILLETTE, J. pro tempore.

This case is a companion to *State v. Barger*, 349 Or. 553, 247 P.3d 309 (2011) (decided this date). Like the defendant in *Barger*, defendant was convicted of multiple (in defendant's case, 20) counts of Encouraging Child Abuse in the Second Degree, ORS 163.686, based on the presence of sexually explicit digital images of children on the hard drives of his computers. Defendant appealed, arguing, among other things, that the state had failed

---

11. Our decision in *United States v. Hotaling* precludes Ramos's argument that the application of 18 U.S.C. §§ 2252A and 2256 to morphed pornography violates the First Amendment. *United States v. Hotaling*, 634 F.3d 725, 728–30 (2d Cir.2011) (holding that child pornography created by digitally altering images of real children is not protected expressive speech under the First Amendment), *cert. denied*, ___ U.S. ___, 132 S.Ct. 843, 181 L.Ed.2d 548 (2011); *see United States v. Stevens*, ___ U.S. ___, 130 S.Ct. 1577, 1586, 176 L.Ed.2d 435 (2010) (noting that child pornography is a category of speech "fully outside the protection of the First Amendment" (citing *New York v. Ferber*, 458 U.S. 747, 763, 102 S.Ct. 3348, 73 L.Ed.2d 1113 (1982))); *United States v. Bach*, 400 F.3d 622, 632 (8th Cir.2005) (holding that creation of a "lasting record" of an "identifiable minor child, seemingly engaged in sexually explicit activity," would victimize child and thus was properly considered child pornography). Likewise, we reject Ramos's Eighth Amendment challenge to his sentence. The district court acted well within its discretion in imposing the statutory mandatory minimum of 180 months' imprisonment, a sentence that was well below the Guidelines range of 324–405 months, and that was reasonable under all the circumstances. *See United States v. Rivera*, 546 F.3d 245, 254–55 (2d Cir.2008); *United States v. MacEwan*, 445 F.3d 237, 248–50 (3d Cir.2006); *see also United States v. Yousef*, 327 F.3d 56, 163 (2d Cir.2003) ("[L]engthy prison sentences ... do not violate the Eighth Amendment's prohibition against cruel and unusual punishment when based on proper application of the Sentencing Guidelines or statutorily mandated ... terms.").

to prove that he "possesse[d] or control[led]" any of the images within the meaning of the Encouraging Child Abuse statute,[1] and that it also had failed to prove venue with respect to some of the charges. The Court of Appeals rejected defendant's argument with respect to the "possess [ion] or control[ ]" element of the charges, but agreed that the state had failed to prove venue with respect to 10 of the counts — Counts 11 through 20. The court therefore reversed defendant's convictions on Counts 11 through 20 and otherwise affirmed. *State v. Ritchie*, 228 Or.App. 412, 423, 208 P.3d 981 (2009). Defendant and the state both petitioned for review by this court and we allowed both petitions....

In September 2004, while defendant was working as a music teacher in an elementary school in Clackamas County, officers from the Clackamas County Sheriff's Department went to the school to interview him about a report involving a former student. In the course of the interview, defendant consented to a forensic examination of both his laptop computer, which he had with him at the school, and his desktop computer, which he kept in his home. Defendant turned over his laptop to the officers on the spot and gave the officers permission to enter his home and take the desktop computer.... [footnote omitted].

A police computer specialist, White, examined the desktop computer and discovered 600 pornographic images, most of which were of children, in unallocated space[4] on the computer's hard drive. White repeated the procedure with the laptop and found about 500 pornographic images, again primarily of children, in unallocated space in that computer's hard drive. Virtually all of the images that White discovered were accessible only by means of special data recovery software that forensics experts like White used, but that was not commonly used by ordinary computer users.... The state subsequently charged defendant in Clackamas County Circuit Court with 20 counts of Encouraging Child Sexual Abuse in the Second Degree by "possess[ing] and control[ling] a photograph of sexually explicit conduct involving a child." Counts 1 through 10 were based on 10 sexually explicit digital images of young boys that had been recovered from unallocated space on the desktop computer's hard drive, and Counts 11 through 20 were based on 10 similar digital images that had been recovered from unallocated space on the laptop's hard drive.

Defendant waived his right to a jury trial and the case was tried to the court. The state's primary witness was White. White described his examination of defendant's laptop and desktop computers and his discovery of the images that formed the basis of the charges in "unallocated space" in the computers' hard drives. He explained that "unallocated" space "is basically clusters on the hard drive that may or may not have information written to them. If there's information written there, it is * * * a file that was deleted." White then described the process by which deleted files are retained in unallocated space — that, when a "file"[5] is created, the operating system "allocates" the file to a certain location in the

---

1. The relevant part of ORS 163.686 provides:

"(1) A person commits the crime of encouraging child sexual abuse in the second degree if the person:

"(a)(A)(i) Knowingly possesses or controls any photograph, motion picture, videotape or other visual recording of sexually explicit conduct involving a child for the purpose of arousing or satisfying the sexual desires of the person or another person; [and]
" * * * * *

"(B) Knows or is aware of and consciously disregards the fact that creation of the visual recording of sexually explicit conduct involved child abuse[.]"

4. The meaning of the term "unallocated space" is described below, 349 Or. at 577, 248 P.3d at 407.

5. White's testimony was in terms of "files," and we therefore report it that way. But the testimony was, in a sense, abstract: The state's theory of the case was (and has continued throughout to be) that defendant "possessed or controlled" the 20 digital images in question *by displaying them on his computer*

hard drive, that a master file table keeps track of that location, and that, when a file is deleted, the data in the file remains in the physical location that originally was allocated, but the master file table is altered to indicate that that location now is "unallocated," *i.e.*, available to be overwritten by new files. Finally, White explained that, although files in unallocated space generally are not available to a user through ordinary means, they can be recovered with special forensic software like the software that he had used.

White then went on to describe some of the characteristics of the images that he had discovered on the two hard drives, and how he was able to tell that certain of the images had been sent to defendant's computer by another user while others may have come to the computer from ordinary Internet sites. At some point, the parties announced that they would stipulate that four of the images—those associated with Counts 1, 2, 3, and 4—had been sent to defendant's desktop computer in a "zipped folder"[6] through an Internet chat room by another chat room user, "rasputinlives978," and that, when the folder reached defendant's desktop computer, the folder was unzipped in some manner, so that the images within were available for viewing. The parties were not willing to stipulate as to whether the unzipping was an intentional act by defendant or an automatic function of the chat room program. White could not determine whether anyone had ever used defendant's desktop computer to view the images in that folder. (That was important because, as noted elsewhere, the state's theory of the case was that defendant had possessed or controlled the digital images in Counts 1 through 4 by displaying them on a computer screen.)

White then testified to some additional matters that were relevant to the parties' "chat room" stipulation. He testified that the folder at issue was sent to defendant's desktop computer at 9:24 p.m. on July 7, 2002, and was deleted by midnight of the same day. He also testified that, to receive a zipped folder offered by another Internet chat room user, a computer user generally must affirmatively *accept* the folder or file. White also produced data collected from defendant's desktop showing that, in September 2002, defendant's laptop had received a file entitled "youngyoungboys.mpg" by instant messaging in an apparent swap for another file entitled "13suckbrother.jpg." Finally, White produced fragments of online "chat" found in unallocated space on defendant's desktop computer, which suggested that defendant had solicited and received child pornography from other chat room users. In one of those fragments, someone using one of defendant's acknowledged screen names appeared to be responding favorably to material that a user had shared with him ("I'm taking off my clothes for this one"). In another fragment, a person using one of defendant's screen names appeared to be inquiring about how to obtain videos ("u have videos?") that had been mentioned.

The parties also announced that they had entered into a stipulation concerning the digital images taken from the desktop computer that corresponded to Counts 5 through 10 and the images taken from the laptop computer that corresponded to Counts 11 through 20. Specifically, they stipulated that all those digital images were the product of "web browsing," *i.e.*, searching the Internet. White also provided technological background

---

screen, not by having one or more "files" of the images in his computers. A case in which the state asserted that defendant illegally possessed or controlled forbidden digital images by having files of them on his computer that he could potentially access would raise different interpretive problems under ORS 163.686 than those that we address today.

6. A "zipped" file or folder is one that contains data that has been compressed using a mathematical algorithm. The "zipping" process renders the material in the file unreadable until the file is "unzipped" by the recipient. The value of a zipped file or folder is that it can be transmitted from one computer to another more quickly.

evidence that was relevant to that stipulation. He explained how files accessed through web browsing might end up in unallocated space: that, when a computer user accesses a web page, the browser creates a copy of the page and stores it in a temporary Internet file cache; that the next time the user calls up the same web page, the browser pulls up the copy from the temporary Internet file cache, rather than accessing and downloading the same information from the web page; that files held in the temporary Internet file cache may be deleted from the cache in a number of ways, some of which occur automatically and some of which require intentional action by a computer user; and that files that are deleted from the temporary Internet file cache remain in unallocated space unless and until they are overwritten by a new file.

In his testimony, White acknowledged that there was no way of knowing, with respect to any of the files associated with Counts 5 through 20, whether the files had been deleted from the temporary Internet file cache intentionally or by some automatic process. He suggested, however, that the temporary Internet file cache appeared to have been emptied or cleaned more thoroughly and more often than would have occurred by purely automatic processes.

Because of the limitations of his forensic software, White was not able to provide further detail about when and from what website the images associated with Counts 11 through 20 (which had been found on defendant's laptop) had been accessed. He was able, however, to provide a more detailed analysis of the six image files associated with Counts 5 through 10, which had been discovered in unallocated space on defendant's desktop computer. White testified that, insofar as his forensic software enabled him to see at least some dates, file names, and path histories associated with those images, he could determine that all six of the images came from a "photo album" on a single website, that they initially had appeared on the desktop computer's screen as a series of "thumbnail" images,[7] that they had been accessed under one of defendant's user names on December 8, 2002, and that the user had "clicked" on the thumbnail images to enlarge them, but had not printed, saved, or taken other actions concerning them.

After White completed his testimony, defendant moved for a judgment of acquittal on all counts, arguing that there was no evidence that he had knowingly "possessed or controlled" the images at issue within the meaning of ORS 163.686(1)(a)(A)(i). Defendant also moved for a judgment of acquittal on Counts 11 through 20, *i.e.*, the counts associated with images found on defendant's laptop, on the ground that the evidence would not support, beyond a reasonable doubt, a finding that those crimes had been committed in Clackamas County. The trial court denied defendant's motions and, after hearing the remaining evidence, found defendant guilty on all 20 counts.

On defendant's appeal, the Court of Appeals affirmed in part and reversed in part. The court opined that, for purposes of ORS 163.686(1)(a)(A)(i), a person "controls" a visual recording when the person "discovers the presence of that recording on the Internet and causes that recording to appear on a specific computer monitor." 228 Or.App. at 419, 208 P.3d 981. The court concluded that there was sufficient evidence in the record to demonstrate that defendant exercised control in that sense over the images associated with Counts 1 through 10, and affirmed the trial court's findings of guilt with respect to those counts. *Id.* at 419–20, 208 P.3d 981.... As noted, both the state and defendant petitioned for review, and we allowed both petitions. As it turns out, however, we need not address the Court of

---

7. "Thumbnail" images are small images that usually are presented in groups. Larger versions of the thumbnails may be obtained by clicking on the thumbnail images.

Appeals holding respecting venue, and we express no opinion concerning it. We turn directly to questions about defendant's "possess[ion] or control [ ]" of the images in question.

As noted, the Court of Appeals held that defendant "controlled" the visual recordings of child sexual abuse that were discovered on his desktop computer, within the meaning of ORS 163.686(1)(a)(A)(i), by "discover[ing] the presence of [such] recording[s] on the Internet and caus[ing them] to appear on a specific computer monitor." 228 Or.App. at 419, 208 P.3d 981.[8] Defendant contends that, contrary to the Court of Appeals' logic, one cannot "knowingly control" an Internet image in that manner, because the act of "discovering" the image and "causing [it] to appear" are simultaneous. Defendant argues that the Court of Appeals is applying the statutory concept of "possess[ion] or control[ ]" to the mere *viewing* of child pornography on the Internet, and that the legislature did not intend, when it enacted ORS 163.686, to criminalize mere viewing of such images.

The state responds that a rational trier of fact could conclude from the evidence that defendant "possessed or controlled" each of the images associated with the 20 charges. The state argues that, when a person opens a web page and displays images on that page on his or her own computer screen, the person possesses or controls the images that appear on his screen in the course of such browsing in a variety of senses—he *physically* possesses them insofar as he can move the computer screen and control the way the images are displayed; he *constructively* possesses them insofar as he has the latent *ability* to save, forward, or otherwise manipulate them; and he *actually* controls them by bringing them to his computer screen in the first instance. The state argues, in a nearly identical vein that, when a person accepts a zipped folder sent to him or her through a chat room and, by inference, displays the images contained therein on his or her computer, he or she "possesses or controls" the images in the same three senses—by physically controlling the way they are displayed, by having a latent ability to manipulate them, and by accepting and, thus, actually controlling the transfer.[9]

In *State v. Barger*, 349 Or. 553, 247 P.3d 309 (decided this date), we addressed the same explanations for why a user "possesses or controls" any image accessed in the course of web browsing. In *Barger*, the defendant was charged with "knowingly possess[ing] or control[ling]" eight images of child sexual abuse that were discovered in his computer's temporary Internet file cache. The evidence indicated that the images were the product of the defendant's web browsing, but there was no evidence that he had printed, saved, forwarded, or in any other way done anything beyond accessing the images (and, by inference, looking at them). The case thus posed the following question: "Can a computer user be found to have knowingly 'possess[ed] or control[led]' digital images of child sexual abuse, within the meaning of ORS 163.686(1)(a)(A)(i), based solely on evidence showing that, at some time in the past, he intentionally accessed those digital images using his

---

8. The full text of ORS 163.686(1)(a)(A)(i) is set out above, 349 Or. at 575 n. 1, 248 P.3d at 406 n. 1.

9. Before this court, the state observes generally that the crime of Encouraging Child Sexual Abuse under ORS 163.686(1)(a)(A)(i) also can be proved by showing that the defendant understands that files containing sexually explicit images continue to be stored in temporary Internet files or in unallocated space in his or her computer. The state at the same time expressly states that it is not pursuing that "storage" theory on review in this case—in spite of the fact that the trial court alluded to that theory when it denied defendant's motion for a judgment of acquittal. We assume that the state is not pursuing that theory here because there is no evidence in the record to support it: The images that are associated with all of the charges were discovered in unallocated space on defendant's computers and there was no evidence presented that suggested that defendant knew or had reason to believe that the digital images might be retained there (although there was evidence that defendant knew or suspected that the digital images might be retained in the temporary Internet file cache).

computer's Internet browser and—by reasonable inference—looked at them?" *Barger*, 349 Or. at 558, 247 P.3d 309.

This court ultimately answered that question in the negative. We concluded that the theories of possession and control that the state had offered, which are identical to the ones that the state asserts here, were either illogical in and of themselves or inconsistent with what, in our judgment, the legislature intended by the statutory phrase "possesses or controls." *Id.*, 349 Or. at 562–66, 247 P.3d 309. We particularly derived our conclusions about the intended meaning of the phrase "possesses or controls" from contextual evidence showing that the legislature did not intend to criminalize the mere viewing of child pornography.[10] We also were persuaded by certain cases—notably *State v. Casey*, 346 Or. 54, 203 P.3d 202 (2009), *State v. Daniels*, 348 Or. 513, 234 P.3d 976 (2010), and *State v. Weller*, 263 Or. 132, 501 P.2d 794 (1972)—that discussed common-law notions of physical and constructive possession and the relevant statutory definition of the term "possess," which incorporates those common-law notions. Because those cases indicate that a person's constructive possession of a thing (*i.e.*, his or her dominion or control over it) cannot be established merely by showing that the person has a practical *ability* to manipulate or direct the item, we concluded that something more than a latent ability to save, e-mail, or otherwise manipulate a digital image that appears on a computer user's screen is required to "possess[ ] or control[ ]" the image within the meaning of ORS 163.686(1)(a)(A)(i). *Barger*, 349 Or at 562–66, 247 P.3d 309.

Barger appears to control our disposition of the present case. It rejects the state's central idea—that, to the extent that a digitalized image is displayed on a computer screen and, presumably, is viewed by the computer's user, the computer user "possesses or controls" the image.... That is not to say that the facts in the present case are identical in every way to the facts in *Barger*. For example, in *Barger*, there was no evidence that the defendant had taken any intentional action with respect to the images at issue after they appeared on his computer screen; the only inference that could be drawn from the evidence was that the defendant had at some point viewed the images. In the present case, however,

---

10. The dissent contends that *Barger* is incorrect insofar as it treats the act of accessing and "viewing" digitalized images drawn from the web as similar to an act of viewing art in a museum. The dissent argues, in that regard, that images displayed on a computer screen are portable (because a person who has called up an image from a website can move the image from one place to another by moving his or her computer) and controllable (as, for example, when a person replays a specific part of an online video, or skips over uninteresting parts) in a way that art in a museum is not. That argument is unpersuasive for two reasons: First, it depends on the proposition that a mere unexercised ability to move or otherwise physically manipulate something is sufficient to establish possession or control—a proposition that we rejected in *Barger*, 349 Or. at 565, 247 P.3d 309. Second, it ignores the fact that our holding in *Barger* was premised on the absence of any evidence that the defendant there had done anything other than call the images up to his computer screen. If there had been evidence that defendant had, for example, gone back and looked at particular scenes in a video, etc., or that he had passed around his computer screen while an image of child pornography was displayed on the screen, we would have faced a different interpretive task.

The dissent also finds significance in the facts that images accessed through web browsing involve an actual transfer of data from a website *to a person's computer* and the automatic saving in a temporary Internet file of a copy of the data *on the person's computer*. The dissent suggests that that fact makes an analogy to ordinary viewing (as of pictures in a museum) inapt, because the image in fact exists, in digital form, in the user's computer. But what the dissent fails to acknowledge is that, from the user's point of view, the experience of viewing images on the web is *not* different from viewing images in a museum: The ordinary computer user speaks of visiting or "going to" websites, and has no sense that web images are "in" the user's own computer until the user affirmatively saves them. The computer user's vision of what is happening when he or she is web browsing is relevant, of course, because the statute criminalizes "*knowing* possession and control" of child pornography.

there is evidence indicating that defendant enlarged the two images involved in Counts 8 and 9 after he initially accessed the website where they were displayed, and there also is evidence that might support an inference that defendant attempted to remove all traces of the images from his computer's hard drive. Moreover, while the images in *Barger* all had been obtained through web browsing, it appears that certain of the images in the present case came to defendant's computer from a different source. Those images—which are associated with Counts 1 through 4—apparently were transferred to defendant's desktop computer through an instant messaging service by another user of the messaging service.

But the state chose not to make a separate issue out of those factual differences. In the proceedings below and before this court, it has never suggested that Counts 1 through 4, or Counts 8 and 9, should be analyzed any differently than the other counts. With regard to all 20 counts, the state's position has been no different than its position in *Barger*— that defendant "possess[ed] or control[led]" the image at issue as long as the image appeared on his computer screen, because he could change the location where the image was displayed, because he had the capacity to save, forward, and manipulate it, and because he controlled it, in the first instance, by taking affirmative steps to bring it to his screen.[11] We rejected those arguments in *Barger* and, applying *Barger*, we reject them here as well. We conclude, in short, that the evidence presented at trial, with respect to all 20 counts, was insufficient to support a finding of possession or control under any theory of possession or control that the state has urged in this proceeding.

The decision of the Court of Appeals is affirmed in part and reversed in part. The judgment of the circuit court is reversed, and the case is remanded to the circuit court with instructions to enter a judgment of acquittal.

DE MUNIZ, C.J., concurred and filed an opinion.

KISTLER, J., dissented and filed an opinion, in which LINDER, J., joined....

[Concurring opinion omitted].

KISTLER, J., dissenting.

Today, the majority holds that a person who goes onto the Internet, purposefully searches out pictures of child pornography, and displays those pictures on a computer for as long as he or she wishes does not possess or control the pictures. Not only are the factual and legal premises on which the majority's opinion rests suspect, but the majority's decision fails to recognize that today's iPhone is yesterday's photograph. There is no difference between a person who uses his iPhone to pull an image of child pornography off the Internet and then passes that image, displayed on his iPhone, around for his friends to see and a person who passes a photograph of the same image to his friends. Both persons possess or control the image. The fact that the person has not saved the image to his iPhone does not mean that the person does not possess or control it. The majority errs in holding otherwise....

The state charged defendant with 20 counts of encouraging child sexual abuse in the second degree, based on 10 of the 500 images of child pornography found on his laptop

---

11. In fact, it appears that the state's primary concern in the trial court was with convincing the court that it was possible to infer from other evidence that defendant had *actually opened and viewed* the images associated with Counts 1 through 4, which had been sent to defendant in a zipped folder through an Internet chat room. The state had to persuade the trial court that such an inference was permissible in order to prevail on those counts under the theory of possession and control that it was advancing.

and on 10 of the 450 images of child pornography found on his home computer. *See* ORS 163.686(1)(a)(A)(i).[2] To prove those charges, the state needed to establish that defendant (1) knowingly (2) possessed or controlled (3) a visual recording of sexually explicit conduct involving a child (4) for the purpose of arousing or satisfying his or someone else's sexual desires and (5) that defendant knew, or was aware of and consciously disregarded the fact, that the creation of the visual recording involved child abuse. *Id.* In this case, there is no dispute that the trial court, sitting as the trier of fact, reasonably could find that each of the 20 images found on defendant's computers was a visual recording of sexually explicit conduct involving children; that defendant knew that fact; that, if he possessed or controlled the images, he did so for the purpose of arousing or satisfying his own sexual desires; and that he knew that the creation of each visual recording involved child abuse. Given the volume and content of the images that the police found on defendant's computers, defendant would be hard pressed to argue otherwise.

The majority concludes, however, that the evidence was not sufficient to permit a reasonable trier of fact to find one element of the offense—that defendant "possesse[d] or control[led]" the pictures of child pornography that he had sought out on the Internet. According to the majority, all that the evidence permitted the trial court to find was that defendant "viewed" child pornography, and that, the majority reasons, is no crime. At bottom, the majority's opinion rests on the proposition that going onto the Internet and pulling up pictures of child pornography is no different from visiting a museum and viewing the paintings displayed there. In both situations, the majority reasons, the person views but does not possess or control the pictures.

I have no disagreement with the general proposition that a person does not possess or control every image that he or she sees. Nor do I disagree with the specific example that the majority uses—that a person who goes to a museum and views a painting does not possess or control the painting. The majority errs, however, in assuming that a computer user stands in the same position as a visitor to a museum. This case arises on defendant's motion for a judgment of acquittal, and the question is whether the trier of fact reasonably could have inferred that defendant possessed or controlled the images that he sought out on the Internet and displayed on his computer screen.

On that point, the trier of fact reasonably could have found that, when a person uses a computer to display an image from an Internet website, the data is transferred from the website to the person's computer. The person's computer automatically saves a copy of the data from the website to a temporary Internet file on the computer, and the computer displays on the computer screen a graphic image of that data (whether text or a picture). Put in lay terms, the person's computer copies the data from the website and uses that data to re-create on the person's computer screen the image that exists (or existed) separately as data on the website's server.[3]

---

2. ORS 163.686(1) provides, in part:

"A person commits the crime of encouraging child sexual abuse in the second degree if the person:

"(a)(A)(i) Knowingly possesses or controls any photograph, motion picture, videotape or other visual recording of sexually explicit conduct involving a child for the purpose of arousing or satisfying the sexual desires of the person or another person * * *

" * * * and

"(B) Knows or is aware of and consciously disregards the fact that creation of the visual recording of sexually explicit conduct involved child abuse[.]"

3. The state's expert did not explain whether, when a computer user first accesses the Internet, the image displayed on the screen reflects data stored in the computer's temporary memory or whether the image reflects the data saved to a temporary Internet file on the computer's hard drive. For the

A computer user is not passively viewing a picture as a museum patron does, or so the trier of fact could find.[4] Rather, a computer user is free to search out and select the images that he or she wishes to display on the computer screen. The computer copies the data from the website and, using that copied data, recreates the image from the website on the user's screen, giving a computer user the ability to keep that image on the screen as long as he or she wishes. And, when the computer displaying the image is portable, as an iPhone, iPad, or Droid is, then the user can take that displayed image with him or her, move the image from one place to another, and show it to others in different locations, all without ever saving the image to the user's hard drive.[5]

In the same vein, if a computer user watches a child pornography video on the Internet, as one would watch a video on YouTube, the computer user can start the video, stop it, go back and look at a particularly interesting scene a second time, move forward through some activity that does not interest the user, or replay the video completely. It is difficult to see how the majority could say that the user does not "control" an Internet video, even though the data that allows the user to manipulate the video is maintained on the user's computer in the same way as the data that gave rise to the pictures that defendant viewed in this case. Nor is it any answer to say that this case involves Internet photographs, not Internet videos. There is no difference in principle between an Internet video and Internet photographs. Control exists in both instances. It is simply more evident with a video.

Admittedly, the images from the Internet that are displayed on a computer screen (whether a photograph or a video) are not permanent, but we have never suggested that permanence is necessary to establish either possession or control. *See State v. Fries*, 344 Or. 541, 546–47, 185 P.3d 453 (2008) (observing that only momentary or fleeting contacts may be insufficient as a matter of law to establish control); *cf. State v. Hall*, 269 Or. 63, 65–66, 68, 523 P.2d 556 (1974) (a person who temporarily sat on a bag of marijuana when the police entered a room possessed the marijuana). It also may be true that a computer user does not have exclusive possession or control over images (whether photographs or movies) taken from the Internet. But, again, the court has never held that possession or control must be exclusive; rather, it has recognized that two persons may possess property jointly. *See State v. Downing*, 185 Or. 689, 698, 205 P.2d 141 (1949) (jury reasonably could infer that the defendant and his accomplice jointly possessed a stolen watch). And the fact that one person who jointly possesses property has the power to dispose of the property completely (as when a person with joint possession of a bank

---

purposes of this case, the difference is irrelevant. In both circumstances, the image displayed on the computer screen exists as a result of data maintained in the computer separately from the data available on the Internet.

4. Possession involves the question of a person's relation to an object, which ordinarily is determined both by legal definitions of property and societal conventions. *See State v. Casey*, 346 Or. 54, 61, 203 P.3d 202 (2009) (considering the usual relationship between a homeowner and a guest in determining whether the homeowner constructively possessed property that the guest temporarily left in the house). In a museum, not only does the museum have exclusive possession of the objects displayed there, but a visitor to a museum typically is governed by a set of rules that strictly limit the visitor's ability to do anything other than passively view the objects on display. Put differently, the analogy on which the majority's opinion rests is not an apt one.

5. The portability of an iPhone, iPad, or Droid simply illustrates the control that a computer user possesses over an Internet image displayed on a computer screen. The control arises from the fact, which the trier of fact could have inferred from this record, that the data generating the image is copied to and resides independently in the user's computer. Maintaining an image on the screen, as in the example, does not evidence a greater degree of control than exists when a person calls the image to the screen in the first place. In both situations, the image remains on the screen until the person chooses to navigate away from the web page.

account spends all the money) does not mean that both persons did not have joint possession of the property while it existed....

Even if, as the majority reasons, the evidence was insufficient to permit the trier of fact to find that defendant knew why he could control the images he accessed, it was more than sufficient for a reasonable trier of fact to find that defendant could and did exercise control over those images. The level of control over the Internet images that defendant displayed on his computer screen made his relationship to those images markedly different from that of a person who goes, say, to the Brancacci Chapel so that he can view (from a distance) Masaccio's frescos. Put differently, the factual premise on which the majority's opinion rests—that defendant's relationship to the images on his computer was the same as that of a museum patron to the paintings displayed there—is not the only inference that the trier of fact reasonably could have drawn....

The remaining question is whether a reasonable trier of fact could find that defendant possessed or controlled 10 of the approximately 450 images of child pornography recovered from his home computer and 10 of the approximately 500 images of child pornography recovered from his laptop. The 10 images from defendant's home computer divide into three types: (1) four images received in a zip file; (2) four thumbnail images; and (3) two thumbnail images that defendant selected and enlarged.

Regarding the four zip file images, the trial court reasonably could find that another person sent defendant a zip file containing images of child pornography, that defendant received the file on his home computer, that he was aware that the zip file contained child pornography, and that he accepted the zip file. Given that evidence, I would hold that, in accepting the zip file, defendant exercised possession or control of both the file and its contents. In that respect, defendant's receipt of the zip file was no different from a person who receives a package in the mail knowing its contents. That evidence was sufficient for a reasonable trier of fact to find that defendant possessed both the file and its contents.[7]

The four images contained on a thumbnail page present a more difficult issue, but not because of any question whether defendant possessed or controlled those images. Typically, a thumbnail page displays several rows of small pictures or thumbnails. The page functions much like a menu in a restaurant. It displays a series of offerings, only some of which a user may wish to select. If a user wants to see a larger image of a particular thumbnail, he or she can click on the thumbnail and cause a larger image to appear on the computer screen. For the reasons discussed above, I would hold that, when a computer user displays a thumbnail page on the computer, he or she possesses or controls all the images or thumbnails on the page.

To be sure, there may be factual questions regarding the computer user's state of mind: A user may not act knowingly regarding every thumbnail that appears on a web page. And, if a user does not select and enlarge a particular thumbnail, then it may be that the user did not possess or control that thumbnail "for the purpose of arousing or satisfying the [user's or someone else's] sexual desires * * *[.]" *See* ORS 163.686(1)(a)(A)(i) (requiring proof of that state of mind). But those are questions for the trier of fact regarding defendant's state of mind. They have no bearing on whether a reasonable trier of fact could find that defendant "possesse[d] or control [led]" the thumbnail images that he

---

7. To be sure, the state's expert was not able to say whether defendant purposefully opened the zip file or whether defendant's software did so automatically. The state's expert was also not able to say whether, assuming that the file contained 70 images of child pornography, defendant would have in fact looked at all of them. But both those factual issues are immaterial to whether defendant possessed or controlled the file once he received it.

displayed on the computer screen. As to that issue, I would hold that the evidence was sufficient to go to the trier of fact.

Regarding the remaining two images from defendant's home computer, the evidence would permit a reasonable trier of fact to find that defendant selected two of the thumbnails so that he could see a larger image. For the reasons explained above, I would hold that defendant's ability to manipulate and maintain those images on his computer screen constituted "control" within the meaning of ORS 163.686. *Cf. State v. Blake*, 348 Or. 95, 102, 228 P.3d 560 (2010) (explaining that "[t]he ability to manipulate a bank account using a computer is sufficient to constitute 'dominion and control * * *.'").

The 10 images found on defendant's laptop present two issues. The first is whether a reasonable trier of fact could find that defendant possessed or controlled them. All 10 pictures were images that defendant purposefully retrieved from the Internet, or so a reasonable trier of fact could find, and I would hold for the reasons explained above that defendant possessed or controlled those images....

Accordingly, I would affirm all defendant's convictions and respectfully dissent from the majority's contrary holding.

LINDER, J., joins in this dissenting opinion.

United States v. Haymond

Tenth Cir., 2012

672 F.3d 948

SEYMOUR, Circuit Judge....

On October 1, 2007, FBI Special Agent Rich Whisman conducted an undercover online investigation searching for individuals involved with child pornography. He did so using LimeWire, a peer-to-peer file sharing program that allows users to trade computer files over the Internet.[1] When a user launches LimeWire and inputs a search term, the program seeks to match the term in the names of files that other users have designated for sharing. LimeWire then returns a list of available files containing that term, which the user may select and download.

Agent Whisman launched LimeWire and typed in "8yo," an acronym for "8 year old" which is associated with child pornography. His search returned a list of files on LimeWire containing "8yo" in the filename, along with the location of users sharing those files. One of the users sharing responsive files was located in Tulsa, Oklahoma. Using LimeWire's "browse host" function, Agent Whisman reviewed the filenames of all of the files available to download from that user. He observed about seventy files, most of which had filenames suggesting child pornography. He downloaded sixty-two files, each of which he viewed and believed contained child pornography.... The user's internet protocol ("IP") address was subsequently traced to a residential address in Tulsa, Oklahoma, where Mr. Haymond lived with his mother.[2] At the time, Mr. Haymond was eighteen years old, studying computer programing and video game and web design at a nearby community college.

---

1. LimeWire permits sharing of various sorts of computer files, including videos, pictures, and music. It is not limited to pornography. *See, e.g., Arista Records LLC v. Lime Group LLC*, 784 F.Supp.2d 398, 410–11 (S.D.N.Y.2011) (discussing use of LimeWire to download music).

2. "An IP address is a unique number identifying the location of an end-user's computer. When an end-user logs onto an internet service provider, they are assigned a unique IP number that will be used for that entire session. Only one computer can use a particular IP address at any specific date

Based largely on results of his LimeWire investigation, Agent Whisman sought a warrant to search Mr. Haymond's residence. He applied for and obtained that warrant on January 16, 2008. It authorized agents and officers to seize and search Mr. Haymond's computer, other digital media, computer passwords, computer security devices, and other items for evidence of child pornography.... Agent Whisman and other FBI agents executed the search warrant on January 23, 2008. They were accompanied by Scott Gibson, an officer with the Tulsa Police Department, and Buddy Carter, an FBI forensic investigator, whose role was to locate and examine the computers and other digital media. Mr. Carter went to Mr. Haymond's bedroom, where he found a computer. They seized the computer's hard drive, along with other items, and took it to the FBI laboratory for forensic examination.... During the January 23 search, Mr. Haymond consented to an interview. Agent Whisman conducted the interview, during which Mr. Haymond made written and oral admissions about his involvement with online child pornography.... Mr. Haymond was subsequently indicted for knowing possession and attempted possession of child pornography in violation of 18 U.S.C. § 2252(a)(4)(B) and (b)(2). The government based its case at trial on seven images found during the post-seizure forensic search of Mr. Haymond's computer.... [Footnote omitted].... Before trial, Mr. Haymond filed a motion to suppress evidence and statements obtained during the search of his home, and the related forensic search of his computer, on the ground that the underlying search warrant was issued without probable cause. The district court denied the motion after holding a hearing.

At trial, Agent Whisman testified about Mr. Haymond's admissions during and after the January 23 interview.[4] He said that Mr. Haymond admitted he was addicted to child pornography and had been accessing it since 2006 using peer-to-peer file sharing programs.[5] In particular, Mr. Haymond admitted to searching for child pornography and downloading it from such programs, most recently from LimeWire. Although Mr. Haymond initially recounted instances in which he had downloaded child pornography inadvertently when trying to download music from LimeWire, he also admitted to doing so purposefully, providing Agent Whisman with examples of search terms he used specifically to obtain child pornography.[6] ... Agent Whisman further testified that Mr. Haymond admitted to a pattern of searching for, downloading, and then deleting child pornography from his computer. Mr. Haymond explained that, "to remove the temptation," every time after he would download and view child pornography he would delete the images or "wipe" them by reformatting his hard drive and reinstalling the operating system.... Agent Whisman testified that Mr. Haymond told him this process happened frequently and that he had most recently downloaded and deleted child pornography the day before, on January 22.[7]

Consistent with his oral admissions, Mr. Haymond also wrote out and signed a statement during the January 23 interview indicating he had been downloading child pornography

---

and time." *United States v. Renigar*, 613 F.3d 990, 992 n. 2 (10th Cir.2010) (quoting *United States v. Henderson*, 595 F.3d 1198, 1199 n. 1 (10th Cir.2010)) (internal quotation marks omitted).

4. In his brief, Mr. Haymond notes that he and Agent Whisman "agreed on virtually nothing that was said" during the interview.... Given our standard of review, ... we credit Agent Whisman's account. The jury was entitled to believe Agent Whisman's testimony over Mr. Haymond's.

5. Officer Gibson, who was present at the January 23 interview, similarly testified Mr. Haymond admitted that he downloaded child pornography from LimeWire, that he was addicted to it, and that he would delete the files after downloading them.

6. Examples of search terms Mr. Haymond used to locate and download child pornography included: "hard core gay," "rbv," "pthc," "star kiss," and "r@ygold."

7. It is not clear from the trial testimony whether Mr. Haymond's oral admission concerned manual deletion of particular files, "wiping" his computer by reformatting and reinstalling a new operating system, or both.

once or twice every month or two, and that after downloading the files, he would clean the registry, reformat his computer's hard drive, and reinstall his Windows operating system.... Agent Whisman also testified that before the agents left Mr. Haymond's home, Mr. Haymond admitted the seized computer was his and that he "was responsible for any child pornography found on his computer." ... Later that afternoon, Mr. Haymond phoned Agent Whisman and asked what type of forensic software the FBI would use to analyze his computer, a question Agent Whisman declined to answer. Before hanging up, Mr. Haymond said he "knew that [the] computer examiner would find stuff on his hard drive and that he had not wiped it, as he said, the day before." ...

Mr. Carter, the FBI forensic investigator, testified he examined Mr. Haymond's computer using Forensic Toolkit ("FTK"), a specialized software program. FTK recovered a total of 60,000 graphics and video files from the computer's hard drive, including its unallocated space.[8] Using FTK, Mr. Carter compiled the files into a viewable format. After viewing all of the files, he and Agent Whisman found about seventy files they believed contained child pornography.[9] Among those seventy or so files were the seven images that formed the basis of Mr. Haymond's conviction. Mr. Carter also testified the hard drive on which the charged images were found had been manufactured in Korea. The hard drive and the charged images were admitted and published to the jury. Forensic analysis indicated the charged images somehow had been deleted and lacked metadata.[10] It revealed little else. In particular, there was no forensic evidence to show the origin of the images or how they had been deleted — that is, whether by the user or by the computer's automated processes with no prompting at all from the user....

At the close of the government's case and again at the close of trial, Mr. Haymond moved for judgment of acquittal on grounds of insufficient evidence. *See* Fed.R.Crim.P. 29. The district court denied both motions. The jury returned a verdict of guilty. The district court sentenced Mr. Haymond to thirty-eight months in prison and ten years of supervised release.... On appeal, Mr. Haymond contends the evidence at trial was insufficient to support his conviction. He also argues the district court erred in denying his motion to suppress and by permitting Dr. Passmore to testify as an expert....

Mr. Haymond was convicted of one count of possessing child pornography in violation of 18 U.S.C. § 2252(a)(4)(B). At the time, the statute provided for punishment of any person who

> knowingly possesses ... any visual depiction that has been mailed, or has been shipped or transported in interstate or foreign commerce, or which was produced using materials which have been mailed or so shipped or transported, by any means including by computer, if—
>
> (i) the producing of such visual depiction involves the use of a minor engaging in sexually explicit conduct; and
>
> (ii) such visual depiction is of such conduct....

---

8. The "unallocated space" of a computer's hard drive consists of files which do not have a formal file structure and can include deleted files. It is "where deleted data is stored before it is then overwritten with new data." *United States v. Otero*, 563 F.3d 1127, 1131 (10th Cir.2009).

9. Although Mr. Carter and Agent Whisman testified there were between seventy and seventy-eight images of child pornography on Mr. Haymond's computer, at sentencing the probation office indicated that only nine images could be confirmed as depicting minors.

10. Metadata, which is commonly described as "data about data," is defined as "[s]econdary data that organize, manage, and facilitate the use and understanding of primary data." *Black's Law Dictionary* 1080 (9th ed.2009).

18 U.S.C. §2252(a)(4)(B) (2006).[14] ...

Mr. Haymond first claims the evidence was insufficient to establish he "knowingly possessed" child pornography. He argues the government failed to establish this element of the offense because it presented no evidence he knew of or had the ability to access and control the charged images.... As an initial matter, Mr. Haymond points out that possession of child pornography is an image-specific crime. *See United States v. Dobbs*, 629 F.3d 1199, 1204 (10th Cir.2011); *see also United States v. X-Citement Video, Inc.*, 513 U.S. 64, 78, 115 S.Ct. 464, 130 L.Ed.2d 372 (1994). The district court recognized this when it instructed the jury that the government was required to prove its case as to the specific "charged images," noting that Mr. Haymond was "not on trial for ... any image not contained in Government's Exhibits 8–14." ... To convict Mr. Haymond under 18 U.S.C. §2252(a)(4)(B), the government was required to prove he knowingly possessed at least one of the seven charged images listed on the verdict form.

It also is true that "possession" requires, at a minimum, that a defendant have the ability to access and control the images. Although the statute does not define "possession," we have previously defined it as " 'the holding or having something ... as one's own, or in one's control.' " *United States v. Tucker*, 305 F.3d 1193, 1204 (10th Cir.2002) (quoting *Oxford English Dictionary* (2d ed.1989)). As in other contexts, possession of child pornography may be actual or constructive. *Id.* With respect to the former, the district court instructed: "A person who knowingly has direct physical control over an object or thing, at a given time, is then in actual possession of it." ... As for constructive possession, it instructed: "A person who, although not in actual possession, knowingly has the power at a given time to exercise dominion or control over an object, either directly or through another person or persons, is then in constructive possession of it." *Id.* These instructions accord with our case law, *see, e.g., Tucker*, 305 F.3d at 1204, and are undisputed on appeal.

Additionally, for possession of child pornography to be "knowing," a defendant must know the charged images exist. As we have explained in the analogous context of knowing receipt of child pornography, "defendants cannot be convicted for having the ability to control something that they do not even know exists." *Dobbs*, 629 F.3d at 1207. In other words, the defendant's control or ability to control "need[s] to relate to images that the defendant knew existed; otherwise, the defendant's conduct with respect to the images could not be deemed to be *knowing.*" *Id.* To convict Mr. Haymond, the government was required to prove he knew of and also controlled (or at least had the ability to access and control) the particular images that formed the basis of the conviction.

Mr. Haymond argues the government failed to meet this burden because it presented no evidence that he knew these specific images were on his computer or that he had the ability to access them once they were in the unallocated space of his computer. Relying primarily on our decision in *Dobbs*, 629 F.3d 1199, he suggests the charged images were inadvertently downloaded to his computer from internet web pages. He argues we must reverse his conviction because, as in *Dobbs*, there was no forensic evidence to indicate he ever saw, clicked on, enlarged, or otherwise accessed or controlled the specific images charged.... *Dobbs* was decided in an analogous context—a conviction for knowing receipt of child pornography in violation of 18 U.S.C. §2252(a)(2). In that case, unlike this one,

---

14. The statute has since been amended. *See* Enhancing the Effective Prosecution of Child Pornography Act of 2007, Pub.L. No. 110-358, §203(a)(2), 122 Stat. 4003 (2008) (criminalizing "knowingly accessing" child pornography with intent to view). We review Mr. Haymond's challenge to the sufficiency of the evidence challenge under the statute as it existed at the time of the charged offense.

the conviction was based on images found in the cache of the defendant's computer. *See id.* at 1201. There was no serious dispute in *Dobbs* that the charged images originated from web pages or that they had been downloaded to Dobbs' computer through his browser's automatic caching function. *See id.* at 1201–04. As the government's forensic specialist in *Dobbs* explained, "[W]hen a person visits a website, the web browser automatically downloads the images of the web page to the computer's cache ... regardless of whether [the images] are displayed on the computer's monitor." *Id.* at 1201. Thus, "a user does not necessarily have to see an image for it to be captured by the computer's automatic-caching function." *Id.*

Although there was ample evidence in *Dobbs* to indicate the defendant had "received" the images from the internet, we reversed the conviction because there was insufficient evidence to establish he did so "knowingly." *Id.* at 1204. We emphasized that "the government presented no evidence [the defendant] had accessed the files stored in his computer's cache, including the two images at issue. And, more tellingly, there was no evidence that he even knew about his computer's automatic caching function." *Id.* We also noted that, as to the two charged images, "there was no evidence presented to the jury that [the defendant] even saw them, much less had the ability to exercise control over them by, for example, clicking on them or enlarging them." *Id.* Without such evidence, we concluded, no reasonable jury could have found the defendant knew the charged images existed on his computer or had the ability to access and control them, either when he visited the originating web pages or later, after the images had been saved to his computer's cache. *Id.* at 1204–05.

Mr. Haymond's reliance on *Dobbs* is unavailing, however. In this case, unlike in *Dobbs*, there was ample evidence from which a reasonable jury could infer Mr. Haymond knew the charged images were on his computer because he searched for and then downloaded them from LimeWire. Here, Mr. Haymond admitted to frequently searching for and downloading child pornography from LimeWire. Mr. Carter testified he found the LimeWire program on Mr. Haymond's computer. The government also introduced three images of child pornography that Agent Whisman found in Mr. Haymond's shared LimeWire folder, which the district court permitted the jury to consider as "proof of ... [the] absence of mistake," Fed.R.Evid. 404(b), a ruling that is not challenged on appeal. The jury was not required to credit Mr. Haymond's assertions that he inadvertently downloaded child pornography from LimeWire while attempting to obtain music, particularly when he had admitted he was addicted to child pornography and used LimeWire to search for and download it. It was thus permissible for the jury to infer that Mr. Haymond used LimeWire exclusively to search for and download child pornography.[15] Viewing the evidence in the light most favorable to the verdict, we conclude it was sufficient to permit a rational jury to find beyond a reasonable doubt that Mr. Haymond knew the charged images were on his computer once he deliberately selected and downloaded them from LimeWire.

For similar reasons, we conclude the evidence was sufficient to establish Mr. Haymond exercised actual control over the charged images. Unlike the defendant in *Dobbs*, who sought out child pornography on internet websites, Mr. Haymond admitted to seeking out and downloading child pornography through peer-to-peer programs, including LimeWire. As the defense's own forensic specialists testified, downloading from LimeWire does not occur automatically. It requires the user to highlight the names of the file or files

---

15. Although Mr. Haymond correctly points out that his expert testified the charged images were thumbnails which came from web pages and could not have come from LimeWire, Agent Whisman testified for the government that it was not possible to determine whether the images were thumbnails.

he wishes to download and then to press "enter." In contrast to the caching process at issue in *Dobbs*, which occurs automatically, this type of volitional downloading entails "control" sufficient to establish actual possession. Accordingly, the evidence here was sufficient to permit a reasonable jury to conclude beyond a reasonable doubt that Mr. Haymond "knowingly possessed" the charged images.[16] ...

Mr. Haymond also contends the evidence was insufficient to establish he knew the charged images depicted minors engaged in sexually explicit conduct. We are not persuaded.... Mr. Haymond is correct that the "knowledge" requirement of the statute requires more than establishing he knowingly possessed the charged images. In *X-Citement Video, Inc.*, 513 U.S. at 78, 115 S.Ct. 464, the Supreme Court held that "the term 'knowingly' in [18 U.S.C.] § 2252 extends both to the sexually explicit nature of the material and to the age of the performers." Although that case involved a conviction for knowing transportation, receipt, and distribution of child pornography under 18 U.S.C. § 2252(a)(1) and (a)(2), its holding is not limited to offenses specified in those particular sub-sections of the statute. Relevant here, the *mens rea* requirement of *X-Citement Video, Inc.* applies with equal force in the context of "knowing possession" of child pornography under § 2252(a)(4)(B). *See United States v. Alfaro-Moncada*, 607 F.3d 720, 733 (11th Cir.2010) (applying *X-Citement Video, Inc.* in context of "knowing possession"); *United States v. Lacy*, 119 F.3d 742, 747 (9th Cir.1997) (same).... Thus, to convict Mr. Haymond, the government was required to prove he knew that the specific images he was convicted of possessing depicted minors engaged in sexually explicit conduct. Mr. Haymond suggests the government failed to meet this burden because it presented no evidence he knew anything about the content of the charged images. But a showing of *mens rea* "may and often is inferred from circumstantial evidence...." *United States v. Borg*, 501 F.2d 1341, 1343 (10th Cir.1974); *see also United States v. Pires*, 642 F.3d 1, 8–9 (1st Cir.2011) (recognizing principle in context of "knowledge" requirement of 18 U.S.C. § 2252). As we have already held, the jury was presented with sufficient evidence from which to conclude Mr. Haymond used search terms associated with child pornography to find and then download the charged images from LimeWire. In our view, this is determinative. As the Court of Appeals for the First Circuit has explained, evidence that a defendant "deliberately used search terms associated with child pornography ... when trolling on LimeWire ... can support a finding that he knew that the images retrieved contained child pornography." *Pires*, 642 F.3d at 9. We readily conclude that the evidence establishing Mr. Haymond used search terms related to child pornography to obtain the charged images was sufficient to prove beyond a reasonable doubt he knew those images contained child pornography....

Agent Jackson testified that he investigated the origin of the original photos which constituted the substantive content of the seven charged images found on Mr. Haymond's computer. He explained these seven photos were part of the "Brad and Bry" series of photographs and were originally taken in Spring Hill, Florida. By presenting evidence that these photos originated in Florida and that the visual depictions were ultimately found

---

16. Because we conclude there was sufficient evidence to establish Mr. Haymond knowingly possessed the images by downloading them, we need not decide whether he constructively or actually possessed the charged images after they were deleted and resided in his computer's unallocated space. As a result, *United States v. Flyer*, 633 F.3d 911 (9th Cir.2011), which held the defendant could not "knowingly possess" child pornography once it had reached his computer's unallocated space, is inapposite. Nor do we decide whether, as the government claims, Mr. Haymond's admissions were sufficient to prove he exercised control over those particular images by deleting them. *Cf. United States v. Bass*, 411 F.3d 1198, 1201–02 (10th Cir.2005).

on Mr. Haymond's computer in Oklahoma, the government provided sufficient evidence to show the visual depictions had been "mailed, or ... shipped or transported in interstate or foreign commerce." 18 U.S.C. §2252(a)(4)(B); *see Sturm*, 672 F.3d at 897.... ▾

For the reasons stated above, we AFFIRM.

F. Distribution of Child Pornography

United States v. Caparotta

United States District Court, Eastern District of New York, 2012
890 F. Supp. 2d 200

MATSUMOTO, District Judge: ...

The facts surrounding the government's investigation of defendant and his arrest do not appear to be disputed by the defendant. According to the government and the complaint filed in this case..., on August 15, 2011, a Special Agent (the "Agent") of the Federal Bureau of Investigation ("FBI") working in an undercover capacity signed into a publicly available peer-to-peer file-sharing program (a "P2P program") via an internet-connected computer at an FBI office in Florida.... P2P programs, which are used largely for sharing of digital music, images, and video, are "so called because users' computers communicate directly with each other, not through central servers." *MGM Studios Inc. v. Grokster, Ltd.*, 545 U.S. 913, 919–20, 125 S.Ct. 2764, 162 L.Ed.2d 781 (2005).[2] Generally, a P2P program user can search for files made available by all other users, browse all the files made available by a particular user, and download desired files. See *United States v. Chiaradio*, 684 F.3d 265, 271 (1st Cir.2012) (describing LimeWire). A P2P program user can make his files accessible for browsing and downloading by other users by placing such files into a designated folder (the "shared folder") that will automatically share its contents with the network. *Id.*

After logging on to the P2P program, the Agent conducted a search for child pornography and received a response from an Internet Protocol address ("IP address") associated with a computer later determined to be located at defendant's residence (the "Computer").... Because the Computer had been configured to permit browsing and downloading of its shared folder by other users of the P2P program, the Agent was able to connect with the Computer and obtain a list of the files in its shared folder.... After determining that several files in the shared folder had filenames consistent with child pornography, the Agent downloaded nine image files and one video file from the Computer's shared folder, all of which appeared to be child pornography.[3] ...

On October 27, 2011, the government executed a search warrant for defendant's residence — the location of the Computer — during which the defendant was present, and the defendant admitted to downloading child pornography for fifteen years, including via a P2P program called "Bearshare." ... The defendant was also presented with a list of 105 files available for download from his shared folder, and the defendant confirmed that he believed he downloaded those files from Bearshare and that the majority of the files

---

2. Common examples of P2P programs include GigaTribe, LimeWire, KaZaA, BearShare, and Gnutella.

3. Typically, when a user of a P2P program tries to download a file, "the program seeks out all the users who are sharing the same file and downloads different pieces of that file from multiple locations in order to optimize download speed." *Chiaradio*, 684 F.3d at 271. Here, however, the Agent was utilizing a version of a P2P program that was enhanced to limit downloads from a single source, such as the defendant's computer....

contained child pornography.... The defendant was arrested on November 10, 2011, and a Superseding Indictment returned on April 12, 2012 charged him with (1) ten counts of Distribution of Child Pornography in violation of 18 U.S.C. §2252(a)(2), presumably for the ten files downloaded by the Agent[4] (2) six counts of Receipt of Child Pornography in violation of 18 U.S.C. §2252(a)(2), and (3) one count of Possession of Child Pornography in violation of 18 U.S.C. §2252(a)(4)(B).... [5]

Defendant argues that he cannot be charged with "distribution" of child pornography because the Agent downloaded the files at issue from the shared folder on defendant's computer without the defendant's knowledge of or active participation in the download.[6] ... In opposition, the government notes that, although the Second Circuit has not addressed the meaning of "distributes" in Section 2252(a)(2), other Circuit courts "have held that having pornographic material in a file-sharing server constitutes distribution." ...) The question before the court is thus purely a legal one: whether a defendant who places and maintains electronic files containing child pornography in a shared folder accessible to others via a P2P program on the internet can be charged with "distributing" child pornography under Section 2252(a)(2), where a third party downloads those files without the defendant's active participation or knowledge.[7] ...

Section 2252(a)(2) authorizes the punishment of:

> Any person who knowingly receives, or distributes, any visual depiction using any means or facility of interstate or foreign commerce ... by any means including by computer ... if (A) the producing of such visual depiction involves the use of a minor engaging in sexually explicit conduct; and (B) such visual depiction is of such conduct.

18 U.S.C. §2252(a)(2). Because the statute does not contain a definition of "distributes," the court considers the ordinary, common meaning of "distribute," which, *inter alia*, includes "[t]o apportion; to divide among several," "[t]o deliver," and "[t]o spread out; to disperse." Black's Law Dictionary (9th ed.2009); *United States v. Lorge*, 166 F.3d 516, 518 (2d Cir.1999) (interpreting "distribution" under United States Sentencing Guidelines Manual §2G2.2(b)(2) [now §2G2.2(b)(3)] and considering Webster's Third New International Dictionary (unabridged 1981) "defining 'distribution' as, *inter alia*, 'a

---

4. The first count for distribution involves a video file and the remaining nine counts involve image files, the same composition of files downloaded by the Agent....

5. Although the defendant moves to dismiss the distribution charges in connection with his motion to inspect the grand jury minutes, which, as discussed *infra*, is denied, the court finds that it is necessary to address dismissal of the distribution charges prior to defendant proceeding to a guilty plea or trial in light of the uncertainty in this Circuit regarding the definition of "distributes" in Section 2252(a)(2). See *Bousley v. United States*, 523 U.S. 614, 618, 118 S.Ct. 1604, 140 L.Ed.2d 828 (1998) ("We have long held that a plea does not qualify as intelligent unless a criminal defendant first receives 'real notice of the true nature of the charge against him, the first and most universally recognized requirement of due process.'" (quoting *Smith v. O'Grady*, 312 U.S. 329, 334, 61 S.Ct. 572, 85 L.Ed. 859 (1941))); ... ("The question then becomes what definition will this Court be using should this case proceed to trial. Due process requires that defendant should know prior to commencing trial what he is being charged with....")).....

6. There is no dispute that the files at issue constituted a "visual depiction" that was produced "involv[ing] the use of a minor engaging in sexually explicit conduct." 18 U.S.C. §2252(a)(2)(A)–(B). For simplicity's sake, the court will refer to the files at issue as child pornography.

7. The defendant does not dispute that "distribution includes sending pornography to civilians as well as undercover agents." ... Therefore, the fact that the Agent—rather than a civilian—downloaded the child pornography files has no bearing on this issue. *See Chiaradio*, 684 F.3d at 282 ("The fact that distribution was effected to an undercover law enforcement officer does not mitigate the fact that distribution occurred.").

spreading out or scattering over an area or throughout a space' "); *see also Chiaradio*, 684 F.3d at 281–82 ("The word 'distribution' is not defined in [Section 2252(a)(2)] itself, but the plain meaning of distribution is '[t]he act or process of apportioning or giving out.' " (citing Black's Law Dictionary 543 (9th ed.2009))); 3 L. Sand *et al.*, Modern Federal Jury Instructions — Criminal, ¶ 62.02, Instr. 62-15 (stating that "distribute" under Section 2252(a)(2) "means to disseminate or transfer possession to another person."); *cf.* 21 U.S.C. § 802(11) (stating that " 'distribute' means to deliver" for purposes of drug offenses).

Considering the plain meaning of "distribute," the court finds that defendant's placing of child pornography files in a shared folder accessible to others via a P2P program on the internet constitutes "distribution" under Section 2252(a)(2) to persons to share and download. By placing the child pornography files in his shared folder, the defendant distributed those files to any person using the same P2P program, thereby "spreading," "scattering," "disseminating," "delivering," or "transferring possession" of those files to any individual, including the Agent, that downloaded those files. The fact that the defendant did not transfer the files to a *specific* person or that the Agent had to download the files from the defendant's shared folder before possessing or viewing them does not change the nature of defendant's placing of the files into the shared folder from one of distribution to something else.

Moreover, the fact that the Agent could download the files without the defendant's knowledge or active participation is irrelevant because, by actively placing the child pornography files into his shared folder, the defendant deliberately distributed to all users of the P2P program access to those files and forfeited control over who could download them. Indeed, the use of a shared folder on a P2P program is more effective at "distributing" child pornography files than more traditional electronic methods such as email, chat rooms, or a direct private transfer — which require the distributor to actively initiate and monitor the transfer of files — because the same files can be distributed to multiple individuals using the P2P program by the click of a button and without the distributor's participation. *See United States v. Sewell*, 513 F.3d 820, 822 (8th Cir.2008) (distinguishing between distribution of child pornography in a chat room and on a P2P program)....

As defendant concedes, although the Second Circuit has not addressed this issue, other Circuit courts, including the First, Eight, Tenth, and Eleventh Circuits, that have addressed distribution under Section 2252(a)(2) have adopted the view that placing child pornography on a P2P program accessible to other users constitutes "distribution." *See Chiaradio*, 684 F.3d at 282 (upholding conviction for distribution under analogous facts on the basis that "[w]hen an individual consciously makes files available for others to take and those files are in fact taken, distribution has occurred. The fact that the defendant did not actively elect to transmit those files is irrelevant."); *United States v. Dayton*, No. 09-5022, 2012 WL 2369328, at *3, 2012 U.S.App. LEXIS 13283, at *9–10 (10th Cir. June 25, 2012) (unpublished) (upholding jury instruction stating "if a person knowingly makes images available on a peer-to-peer file sharing network ... this is considered 'distribution' of the images. In other words, the Government may meet its burden of proof on this element by showing that Defendant knowingly allowed others access to his [P2P program] shared folder.") (citing *United States v. Shaffer*, 472 F.3d 1219, 1223 (10th Cir.2007)); *United States v. Collins*, 642 F.3d 654, 656–57 (8th Cir.2011) (upholding conviction for attempted distribution where defendant had child pornography saved under his screen name on a P2P program); *United States v. DeGennaro*, 309 Fed.Appx. 350, 351–52 (11th Cir.2009) (upholding conviction for distribution where officer patrolling a P2P program downloaded at least six files containing child pornography from an IP address traced to an account owned by defendant); *see also Sewell*, 513 F.3d at 822 (finding that placing child pornography images in a shared folder on a P2P program constitutes an offer to distribute under 18 U.S.C. §2251(d)(1)(A)).[8]

Moreover, although not explicitly addressing "distribution" under Section 2252(a)(2), the Third, Sixth, and Seventh Circuits have strongly suggested that they would adopt a similar view. *See United States v. Schade*, 318 Fed.Appx. 91, 94–95 (3d Cir.2009) (non-precedential) ("It would be eminently reasonable for the jury to have concluded that [defendant] aided and abetted the transportation of a visual depiction of a minor engaged in sexual activity [under Section 2252(a)(1)] by making the child pornography file available in the 'My Downloads' folder for any part of it to be downloaded, resulting in the utilization of that file by another user of [the P2P program] seeking to download the complete video."); *United States v. Darway*, 255 Fed.Appx. 68, 71 (6th Cir.2007) (noting that "[s]everal courts have held that maintaining files in an accessible public folder constitutes distribution"); *United States v. Carani*, 492 F.3d 867, 876 (7th Cir.2007) (agreeing with *Shaffer* and stating that "[t]he notion that [defendant] could knowingly make his child pornography available for others to access and download without this qualifying as 'distribution' does not square with the plain meaning of the word."). Importantly, no Circuit court has found the opposite—that the placement of files in a shared folder accessible via a P2P program does not as a matter of law constitute "distribution" under Section 2252(a)(2).[9]

The Tenth Circuit's decision in *Shaffer*, which appears to be the most cited case with respect to this issue, is particularly analogous to the facts of this case. In *Shaffer*, like here, the defendant argued that he could not, as a matter of law, "distribute" child pornography under 18 U.S.C. §2252A(a)(2)—an analogous statute[10]—when he stored files containing child pornography in a shared folder on his computer accessible to other users of a P2P program, including a law enforcement agent that downloaded those files. 472 F.3d at 1220–22. After recognizing that the statute contained no definition of "distribute" and considering dictionary definitions of "distribute," the court upheld defendant's conviction for distribution, analogizing a P2P file-sharing network to a self-service gas station:

---

8. *See also United States v. Lavota*, No. SA-11-CR-84-U.S. Dist. LEXIS 142882, at *3 (W.D.Tex. Dec. 12, 2011) (finding guilty of distribution where defendant used a P2P program to make pornography images available to other users and a law enforcement downloaded an image from the defendant's computer); *United States v. Abraham*, No. 05-344, 2006 WL 3052702, at *8, 2006 U.S. Dist. LEXIS 81006, at *22 (W.D.Pa. Oct. 19, 2006) ("find[ing] that the defendant distributed a visual depiction when as a result of the defendant's installation of an internet peer-to-peer video file sharing program on his computer, a Pennsylvania state trooper was able to download the child pornography from the defendant's computer to the trooper's computer."); 3 L. Sand et al., Modern Federal Jury Instructions—Criminal, ¶62.02, Instr. 62-15, Comment ("[K]eeping depictions in a peer-to-peer file sharing program application where it is available for downloading to other subscribers of the application is a 'distribution' when another person does in fact download the depiction.").

9. Additionally, several Circuit courts have concluded that the use of a P2P program by a defendant under circumstances similar to those here is a sufficient basis to impose a sentencing enhancement for "distribution" of child pornography under United States Sentencing Guidelines Manual §2G2.2(b)(3), which defines "distribution" as "any act, including possession with intent to distribute, production, advertisement, and transportation, related to the transfer of material involving the sexual exploitation of a minor.... includ[ing] posting material involving the sexual exploitation of a minor on a website for public viewing...." *See, e.g., United States v. Layton*, 564 F.3d 330, 335 (4th Cir.2009) ("We concur with the Seventh, Eighth, and Eleventh Circuits and hold that use of a peer-to-peer file-sharing program constitutes 'distribution' for the purposes of U.S.S.G. §2G2.2(b)(3)(F)."); *see also Darway*, 255 Fed.Appx. at 71; *Carani*, 492 F.3d at 876; *United States v. Mathenia*, 409 F.3d 1289, 1290 (11th Cir.2005).

10. "[T]here is no material difference between the distribution component of §2252A(a)(2) and that element of [defendant's] statute of conviction—§2252(a)(2)." *See Dayton*, 2012 WL 2369328, at *3 n. 3, 2012 U.S.App. LEXIS 13283, at *10–11 n. 3.

We have little difficulty in concluding that Mr. Shaffer distributed child pornography in the sense of having 'delivered,' 'transferred,' 'dispersed,' or 'dispensed' it to others. He may not have actively pushed pornography on [P2P program] users, but he freely allowed them access to his computerized stash of images and videos and openly invited them to take, or download, those items. It is something akin to the owner of a self-serve gas station. The owner may not be present at the station, and there may be no attendant present at all. And neither the owner nor his or her agents may ever pump gas. But the owner has a roadside sign letting all passersby know that, if they choose, they can stop and fill their cars for themselves, paying at the pump by credit card. Just because the operation is self-serve, or in Mr. Shaffer's parlance, passive, we do not doubt for a moment that the gas station owner is in the business of 'distributing,' 'delivering,' 'transferring' or 'dispersing' gasoline; the *raison d'etre* of owning a gas station is to do just that. So, too, a reasonable jury could find that Mr. Shaffer welcomed people to his computer and was quite happy to let them take child pornography from it.

Id. at 1223–24. Based on this reasoning and the decisions of the other Circuit courts discussed above, the court rejects defendant's argument that his conduct here cannot, as a matter of law, constitute distribution under Section 2252(a)(2)....

Defendant's [arguments] also fail when viewed in light of the statute's requirement that a defendant "*knowingly* ... distribute[ ]" child pornography. 18 U.S.C. § 2252(a)(2) (emphasis added). Without additional facts demonstrating an intent to "knowingly" distribute child pornography, a defendant could not be found guilty of distribution.... [H]ere, as discussed in *Chiaradio*, *Shaffer*, and several of the other Circuit cases cited above, a reasonable jury could infer that the defendant "knowingly" distributed child pornography files by placing them in a shared folder designed to permit searching and downloading of those files by all users of a P2P program. Defendant is certainly free to argue to a jury that he did not have the requisite knowledge because he was not computer savvy and did not know that other users had access to his shared folder, because the particular P2P program he was using automatically placed files he downloaded into his shared folder, or for some other reason. This does not change the fact, however, that the placement of child pornography in a shared folder on a P2P program can constitute "distribution" for purposes of Section 2252(a)(2).

Finally, defendant urges this court to adopt Judge Jack Weinstein's conclusion in *United States v. C.R.*, 792 F.Supp.2d 343 (E.D.N.Y.2011) — the only case defendant cites in support of his position — that Section 2252(a)(2) "require[s] both 1) an active intention to give or transfer a specific visual depiction to another person and 2) active participation in the actual delivery." *Id.* at 355; *see id.* at 486 ("Proof of distribution requires action by the defendant. Material elements include: 1) an intent of the defendant to have some person receive a child pornography image; and 2) the transmission by the defendant of the image to a person."). In *C.R.*, Judge Weinstein accepted a guilty plea to a distribution charge under similar circumstances, where a law enforcement agent downloaded a child pornography file from the defendant's shared folder via a P2P program when the defendant was not home, and the defendant testified that he did not intend for anyone to download the file. *Id.* at 352, 354. Judge Weinstein's interpretation of "distribute" was relevant to his ultimate finding that the five-year mandatory minimum term of imprisonment for distribution was cruel and unusual punishment under the Eighth Amendment when applied to the defendant — a "developmentally immature young adult." *Id.* at 506–11. This decision has been appealed by the government and is pending before the Second Circuit. [For the subsequent history of this case, see notes following *United States v. C.R., supra* Chapter Three, Section I (Internet Parameters: Accessibility and Anonymity).]

Judge Weinstein arrived at his interpretation of "distribute" in Section 2252(a)(2) "[a]fter examining the statute and dictionary definitions" of the term and without discussing any case law. *Id.* at 355. Specifically, he explained that "[d]ictionary definitions establish that 'to distribute' is 'an active not a passive verb,'" and that "distribute" has "two subdivisions": "One, he intends to distribute, he designs, intends; and two, he actually succeeds in distributing a communication, namely the visual depiction; there must be a communicator, namely the defendant [ ] and a communicant, somebody who actually received it." *Id.* at 353 (internal quotation marks omitted). This court does not disagree that distribution under Section 2252(a)(2) requires an intention to give or transfer child pornography to at least one other person, but does not decide if another person must actually download or obtain the child pornography from the defendant, as defendant here concedes that an agent obtained child pornography from his computer.

The first requirement—the intent element—is explicitly included in the statute by the inclusion of the adverb "knowingly," which modifies "distributes." *See* 18 U.S.C. § 2252(a)(2). Where this court most respectfully disagrees with Judge Weinstein is the second requirement as to what constitutes a successful distribution. Judge Weinstein requires a defendant's "active participation in the actual delivery" of a child pornography file to another person that goes beyond placing the file in a shared folder on a P2P program, *C.R.,* 792 F.Supp.2d at 355, which would preclude a finding of distribution where, like here, a third party downloaded the file from the defendant's shared folder without defendant's active participation or knowledge. In contrast, this court finds that, where a defendant places child pornography in a shared folder via a P2P program, a distribution has occurred.

Judge Weinstein's incorporation of an additional requirement into the statute— active participation by the defendant in the actual delivery of child pornography to another person—is not supported by a plain reading of Section 2252(a)(2), which does not contain any requirement that a defendant intend to distribute child pornography to a *specific* person or *actively* participate in the distribution. The statute only requires that a defendant "knowingly ... distributes" the child pornography. 18 U.S.C. § 2252(a)(2). Indeed, it would be an anomalous result under the plain meaning of the statute if a defendant cannot be found to have distributed child pornography even where a defendant knowingly made child pornography files available for sharing and downloading and those files are then downloaded. This court's interpretation of "distribute" is consistent with other Circuit and district court decisions, keeps pace with recent technology that has enormously increased the ways that child pornography can be created, accessed, and distributed, and is consistent with Section 2252's "broad and general purpose of facilitating the prosecution of individuals who are involved with child pornography." *United States v. Mohrbacher,* 182 F.3d 1041, 1049 & n. 10 (9th Cir.1999); *see also* Adam Walsh Child Protection and Safety Act of 2006, Pub.L. No. 109-248, § 501, 120 Stat. 587, 623 (2006) ("The advent of the Internet has greatly increased the ease of transporting, distributing, receiving, and advertising child pornography in interstate commerce.").

For the reasons discussed above, in light of the plain meaning of the word "distributes" in the text of the statute and the overwhelming authority from other Circuit courts, the court finds that a defendant who places files containing child pornography in a shared folder accessible to others via a P2P program on the internet can be charged with "distribution" under Section 2252(a)(2). Accordingly, defendant's motion to dismiss the distribution counts of the Superseding Indictment is denied....

For the reasons set forth above, the court denies defendant's motion to ... dismiss the charges for distribution of child pornography....

SO ORDERED.

Chapter Four

Commercial Exploitation of Children

I. The Commercial Market for Children

A CHILD FOR SALE
On Account of High Cost of Living
AGE ....4 Years
PARENTAGE ....Legitimate
HEALTH ....Excellent
DISPOSITION ....Charming
For further information, date and terms of sale, WATCH NEWSPAPERS.

The advertisement depicted above appeared in the *Reading Eagle* on October 29, 1920. It is a faux advertisement that was used to promote the 1920 silent film *A Child for Sale*. In the film, Charles Stoddard is a poor artist living in Greenwich Village, with a wife and two children. When his wife dies and he is left destitute, he is forced to sell one of his children to a rich, childless woman. Stoddard soon comes to his senses and changes his mind, but the movie builds off of his desperate decision to sell his child. There was no Hollywood script, however, for a 26-year-old Texas mother, Brittany Hill, who, in 2012, listed her child for sale in an online classified advertisement. Her advertisement provided:

> Adoption family needed:
>
> Im [sic] in search of an [sic] great family for my son. He is four months old and he is african American [sic] and Hispanic [sic]. I can no longer care for him the way he needs to be. We are living in a womens [sic] shelter now. Im [sic] working with an adoption agency so there is an adoption fee they have set up. I believe its [sic] $6,500. Thank you and god bless[.]

Meg Neal, *Dallas mom accused of trying to sell baby for $4,000 in classified ad*, N.Y. Daily News, June 23, 2012. A potential buyer of the baby contacted police, who found the baby alone in his crib in Hill's apartment. Police arrested Hill when she returned home, and the boy was placed with Child Protective Services. In this case, Hill was advertising for her child to be cared for through adoption. However, the greater market for children lies in the child pornography and sex trafficking industries. Title 18 U.S.C. § 2251A, discussed in Chapter Three, Section II.C.2 (Production by a Parent, Guardian or Custodian), *supra*, criminalizes buying or selling a child for purposes of child pornography, and 18 U.S.C. § 2422(a) governs buying or selling a child for purposes of prostitution. *See* Chapter Four, Section II.B (Prostitution), *infra*. The right to advertise for certain activities within the child pornography and child prostitution markets, which have become, primarily, online markets—and the government's ability to regulate these markets through its advertising—is the issue addressed in the case that follows the excerpt included below.

Congresswoman Ann Wagner, 2nd District of Missouri
Human Trafficking & Online Prostitution Advertising
http://wagner.house.gov/Human%20Trafficking%20%26%20
Online%20Prostitution%20Advertising

The Internet has dramatically changed the human trafficking landscape in the United States. Over the last ten years, prostitution has slowly but persistently migrated to an online marketplace. Online classified services, such as Backpage.com, are the vehicles for advertising the victims of the child sex trade to the world. Pimps and traffickers blatantly advertise their victim's sexual services with provocative photographs and unsubtle messages complete with per hour pricing. The traffickers pay online classified websites like Backpage.com to display their messages and these websites accordingly reap enormous profits at the expense of the victims of sex trafficking.... Revenue from U.S. online prostitution advertising totaled $45 million in 2013, surpassing a benchmark set when Craigslist abandoned its adult services section in September 2010.... Most of the $45 million generated—82.3%—has been generated by Backpage.com, a general classifieds site that has succeeded Craigslist as the nation's leading publisher of online prostitution advertising.

Id.

Backpage.com, LLC v. Hoffman
United States District Court, District of New Jersey, 2013
2013 WL 4502097

DENNIS M. CAVANAUGH, District Judge....

Backpage.com operates the second largest online classified ad service available nationwide. Backpage.com hosts millions of users' posts each month in numerous categories (e.g., buy/sell/trade, automotive, rentals, real estate, jobs, forums, dating, adult and services) and subcategories. In 2010, when Craigslist.org eliminated its adult services section entirely, adult ads migrated to other Craigslist categories and other websites, notably Backpage.com.... Backpage.com states that it works to prevent misuse of its website, providing in its Terms of Use that users may not offer illegal services and prohibiting content that in any way relates to child exploitation. The site also uses both automatic and manual filtration methods to sort through ads, claiming that over the course of a month Backpage.com blocks over 750,000 inappropriate posts.

The Internet Archive, unlike Backpage.com, is not a host for third party postings. The Internet Archive is a 501(c)(3) non-profit that was founded to build an Internet library.

It offers permanent access for researchers, historians, scholars, people with disabilities, and the general public to historical collections that exist in digital format. The vast majority of the material in the Internet Archive's collection is material authored by third parties. In an effort to create an archive of the Internet, the Internet Archive regularly gathers "snapshots" of content on the Internet through its "crawling" and indexing processes. It currently maintains over 300 billion web pages archived from 1996 to (nearly) the present from websites around the world, including archives of third-party content posted to web sites like Backpage.com and Craigslist.org....

In January 2012, Washington state legislators introduced a bill to address "advertising commercial sexual abuse of a minor." After being enacted by the Washington legislature and signed into law by Washington's governor, the law was set to go into effect on June 7, 2012. *See* Wash. Rev.Code Ann. § 9.68A.104 (2012).... On June 4, 2012, Backpage.com filed suit in the U.S. District Court for the Western District of Washington, seeking a temporary restraining order ("TRO"), preliminary and permanent injunctive relief, and a declaration that the new law was unconstitutional and violated the Communications Decency Act of 1996, 47 U.S.C. § 230 ("CDA"). The Court granted Backpage.com's request for a TRO the next day. After full briefing and argument, on July 27, 2012, the Court entered a preliminary injunction, enjoining enforcement of the law on all six of the grounds asserted by Backpage.com and the Internet Archive (which joined as a co-plaintiff)—the same challenges raised here. *See Backpage.com, LLC v. McKenna*, 881 F.Supp. 1262 (W.D.Wash.2012).... Thereafter, the defendants in *McKenna* (the Washington AG and the county prosecutors) conceded they would not continue to defend the law, and on December 10, 2012, stipulated to a final judgment permanently enjoining its enforcement and awarding Backpage.com attorneys' fees. The Washington AG also agreed to work with the state legislature to repeal the Washington statute, and the legislature has since enacted a measure to repeal the law effective July 28, 2013.

In May 2012, the two houses of the Tennessee general assembly respectively passed similar legislation creating the felony crime of "advertising commercial sex with a minor." The legislation closely tracked the first draft of the Washington law. The governor signed the legislation on May 21, 2012, making it a felony to "knowingly sell[ ] or offer[ ] to sell an advertisement that would appear to a reasonable person to be for the purpose of engaging in what would be a commercial sex act ... with a minor." *See* Term.Code Ann. § 39-13-315. The Tennessee law was scheduled to take effect July 1, 2012.

On June 27, 2012, Backpage.com brought suit to enjoin the law in the U.S. District Court of the Middle District of Tennessee. The defendants (the Tennessee AG and the district attorneys for each of the state's 31 judicial districts) stipulated they would not enforce the Tennessee law pending resolution of Backpage.com's challenges. After extended briefing and a hearing, the court entered a preliminary injunction on January 3, 2013. Like *McKenna*, the Tennessee federal court issued a thorough opinion, invalidating the Tennessee statute on all the grounds urged by Backpage.com. *See Backpage.com, LLC v. Cooper*, No. 3:12-cv-00654, 2013 WL 1558785 (M.D.Tenn. Jan.3, 2013). The Court wrote:

> The Constitution tells us that—when freedom of speech hangs in the balance—
> the state may not use a butcher knife on a problem that requires a scalpel to fix.
> Nor may a state enforce a law that flatly conflicts with federal law. Yet, this appears
> to be what the Tennessee legislature has done in passing the law at issue.

Cooper, 2013 WL 1558785 at *1. As in Washington, the defendants in *Cooper* declined to further defend the Tennessee law after the court's preliminary injunction order. On March 19, 2013, the court granted Backpage.com's unopposed motion to convert the preliminary injunction into a permanent injunction and entered final judgment invalidating the Tennessee law. . . .

S. 2239, entitled the "Human Trafficking Prevention, Protection, and Treatment Act," was introduced in the New Jersey Senate on October 4, 2012. The same bill was introduced a week later in the Assembly, designated A. 3352. The bill included a section creating the offense of "advertising commercial sexual abuse of a minor." The Senate passed A. 3352 on March 18, 2013, and the bill passed in the Assembly three days later. Governor Christie signed the bill on May 6, 2013. The first degree advertising crime created by the Act is codified at N.J.S.A. §2C:13-10.

The Act's legislative history states that it "is modeled after a recently enacted Washington state law," as well a Connecticut bill "that created criminal offenses related to advertising commercial sexual abuse of a minor." As passed and signed into law by the Governor, the material provisions of the Act for purposes of this motion are:

> b. A person commits the offense of advertising commercial sexual abuse of a minor if:
>
>> (1) the person knowingly publishes, disseminates, or displays, or causes directly or indirectly, to be published, disseminated, or displayed, any advertisement for a commercial sex act, which is to take place in this State and which includes the depiction of a minor; or
>>
>> (2) the person knowingly purchases advertising in this State for a commercial sex act which includes the depiction of a minor
>
> c. A person who commits the offense of advertising commercial sexual abuse of a minor as established in subsection b. of this section is guilty of a crime of the first degree. Notwithstanding the provisions of N.J.S.2C:43-3, the fine imposed for an offense under this section shall be a fine of at least $25,000 . . .
>
> e. For the purposes of this section:
>
> "Advertisement for a commercial sex act" means any advertisement or offer in electronic or print media, including the Internet, which includes either an explicit or implicit offer for a commercial sex act to occur in this State.
>
> "Commercial sex act" means any act of sexual contact or sexual penetration, as defined in N.J.S.2C:14-1, or any prohibited sexual act, as defined in N.J.S.2C:24-4, for which something of value is given or received by any person.
>
> "Depiction" means any photograph or material containing a photograph or reproduction of a photograph.
>
> "Minor" means a person who is under 18 years of age.
>
> "Photograph" means a print, negative, slide, digital image, motion picture, or videotape, and includes anything tangible or intangible produced by photographing.
>
> f. It shall not be a defense to a violation of this section that the defendant:
>
>> (1) did not know the age of the minor depicted in the advertisement; or
>>
>> (2) claims to know the age of the person depicted, unless there is appropriate proof of age obtained and produced in accordance with subsections g. and h. of this section
>
> g. It shall be a defense to a violation of this section that the defendant made a reasonable, bona fide attempt to ascertain the true age of the minor depicted in

the advertisement by requiring, prior to publication, dissemination, or display of the advertisement, production of a driver's license, marriage license, birth certificate, or other governmental or educational identification card or paper of the minor depicted in the advertisement and did not rely solely on oral or written representations of the minor's age, or the apparent age of the minor as depicted. The defendant shall prove the defense established in this subsection by a preponderance of the evidence.

h. The defendant shall maintain and, upon request, produce a record of the identification used to verify the age of the person depicted in the advertisement.

N.J.S.A. § 2C:13-10.

The Act thus makes the act of publishing, disseminating or displaying an offending online post "directly or indirectly" a "crime of the first degree. The penalties for the advertising offense are imprisonment for 10–20 years, N.J.S.A. §§ 2C:43-1, 2C:43-6, a minimum $25,000 fine, N.J.S.A. § 2C:13-10(c); P.L.2013, c. 51 § 3(d)(1) (amending N.J.S.A. § 2C:13-8), and the requirement that a convicted defendant must register as a sex offender, P.L.2013, c. 51 prior § 12(b)(2), amending N.J.S.A. § 2C:7-2....

Plaintiff Backpage.com filed a Verified Complaint to Declare Invalid and Enjoin Enforcement of N.J.S.A. § 2C:13-10, along with a supporting Motion for a Temporary Restraining Order and Preliminary Injunction on June 26, 2013.... [citations to Record omitted]. Plaintiff Internet Archive filed the same motions on the same day.... Defendant filed an Opposition Brief to Plaintiffs' Motions on July 19, 2013.... On June 28, 2013, a hearing was held before this Court, where a temporary injunction was issued prior to a full hearing to be held on August 9, 2013. All parties were heard on August 9, 2013, and the Court issued its ruling from the bench, reserving further discussion for this Opinion....

Plaintiffs Backpage.com and the Internet Archive bring this action to preliminary and permanently enjoin Section 12(b)(1) of N.J. Stat. Ann. 2C:13-10 ("the Act"). Federal courts in Tennessee and Washington have entered permanent injunctions prohibiting those states from enforcing statutes that are identical to the Act in all material respects. In both cases, the Courts held that the statutes were unconstitutional and unenforceable on the same grounds that Plaintiffs advance here. *See McKenna*, 881 F.Supp.2d 1262 (W.D.Wash.2012); *Cooper*, 2013 WL 1558785 (M.D.Tenn. Jan.3, 2013).

In determining whether a preliminary injunction should be granted, a district court must consider four factors:

(1) Whether the movant has shown a reasonable probability of success on the merits;

(2) Whether the movant will be irreparably injured by denial of the relief;

(3) Whether granting preliminary relief will result in even greater harm to the nonmoving party; and

(4) Whether granting preliminary relief will be in the public interest.

Gerardi v. Pelullo, 16 F.3d 1363, 1373 (3d Cir.1994)....

Plaintiffs first argue that the Act is both expressly preempted and conflict preempted by Section 230 of the [Communications Decency Act] CDA. Plaintiffs allege the Act violates their rights under 47 U.S.C. § 230(e)(3) because enforcement of the new law would treat Plaintiffs, providers of an interactive computer service, as the publisher or speaker of information provided by another information content provider. Defendants argue that the Act is not preempted by the CDA because the CDA does not preempt state criminal laws and that the Act is consistent with "federal criminal laws regarding the sexual exploitation of children." ... Essentially, Defendants urge this Court to find fault in the reasoning of both the *McKenna* Court and the *Cooper* Court and decline to follow their holdings.... The Court is not persuaded by Defendants arguments and finds that it is likely that Plaintiffs would prevail on the merits of their preemption claim.

There are three circumstances in which Congress has the power to preempt state law. First, Congress may expressly preempt inconsistent state laws. *Arizona v. United States*, ___ U.S. ___, ___–___, 132 S.Ct. 2492, 2500–01, 183 L.Ed.2d 351 (2012) ("There is no doubt that Congress may withdraw specified powers from the States by enacting a statute containing an express preemption provision."). Second, "the States are precluded from regulating conduct in a field that Congress, acting within its proper authority, has determined must be regulated by its exclusive governance." *Id.* (citing *Gade v. National Solid Wastes Management Ass'n*, 505 U.S. 88, 115, 112 S.Ct. 2374, 120 L.Ed.2d 73 (1992). Third, under the doctrine of conflict preemption, state laws are preempted when they conflict with federal law. *Crosby v. Nat'l Foreign Trade Council*, 530 U.S. 363, 372, 120 S.Ct. 2288, 147 L.Ed.2d 352 (2000). "This includes cases where compliance with both federal and state regulations is a physical impossibility and those instances where the challenged state law stands as an obstacle to the accomplishment and execution of the full purposes and objectives of Congress." *Arizona v. U.S.*, 132 S.Ct. at 2501 (internal quotations and citations omitted).

Here, Plaintiffs are likely to succeed on their claim that the Act is preempted both because it is likely expressly preempted and because it likely conflicts with federal law. Under Section 230, "[n]o provider or user of an interactive computer service shall be treated as the publisher or speaker of any information provided by another information content provider." 47 U.S.C. § 230(c)(1). It goes on to state that "no liability may be imposed under any State or local law that is inconsistent with" Section 230. *Id.* § 230(e)(3). Finally, Section 230 states that providers may not be held liable for "any action voluntarily taken in good faith to restrict access to or availability" of material that is "obscene, lewd, lascivious, filthy, excessively violent, harassing, or otherwise objectionable." *Id.* § 230(c)(2).

In enacting the CDA, "Congress decided not to treat providers of interactive computer services like other information providers such as newspapers, magazines or television and radio stations, all of which may be held liable for publishing or distributing obscene or defamatory material written or prepared by others." *Batzel v. Smith*, 333 F.3d 1018, 1026 (9th Cir.2003) (internal citation omitted). Congress enacted Section 230 to achieve two goals. First, "Congress wanted to encourage the unfettered and unregulated development of free speech on the Internet, and to promote the development of e-commerce." *Id.* at 1027. Second, Congress wanted to "encourage interactive computer services and users of such services to self-police the Internet for obscenity and other offensive material." *Id.* at 1028.

The Act in question is likely inconsistent with and therefore expressly preempted by Section 230 as Section 230 prohibits "treat[ing]" a "provider or user of an interactive computer service" as the "publisher or speaker of any information provided by another information content provider." 47 U.S.C. § 230. Both Backpage and Internet Archive are providers of an interactive computer service within the meaning of CDA Section 230. *See* 47 U.S.C. § 230(f)(2) (defining an interactive computer service as "any information service, system, or access software provider that provides or enables computer access by multiple users to a computer server, including specifically a service or system that provides access to the Internet and such systems operated or services offered by libraries or educational institutions.). Section 12(b)(1) of the Act runs afoul of Section 230 by imposing liability on Plaintiffs for information created by third parties—namely ads for commercial sex acts depicting minors—so long as it "knows" that it is publishing, disseminating, displaying, or causing to be published, disseminated, or displayed such information. *See Almeida v. Amazon.com, Inc.*, 456 F.3d 1316, 1321 (11th Cir.2006) (quoting *Zeran v. Am. Online Inc.*, 129 F.3d 327, 330 (4th Cir.1997) ("The majority of federal circuits have interpreted [Section 230] to establish broad federal immunity to any cause of action that would make service providers liable for information originating with a third-party user of the service.") (internal citations omitted); *Barnes v. Yahoo!, Inc.*, 570 F.3d 1096, 1101–02 (9th Cir.2009) ("[W]hat matters is not the name of the cause of action ... [but] whether [it] inherently requires the court to treat the defendant as the 'publisher or speaker' of content provided by another.").... Additionally, the Act is inconsistent with Section 230 of the CDA because it criminalizes the "knowing" publication, dissemination, or display of specified content. As Judge Martinez found in *McKenna*, "in doing so, it creates an incentive for online service providers *not* to monitor the content that passes through its channels. This was precisely the situation that the CDA was enacted to remedy." *McKenna*, 881 F.Supp.2d at 1273 (internal citations omitted).

Even if the language of Section 230 did not expressly preempt the Act, the Act likely conflicts with the CDA because "the challenged state law stands as an obstacle to the accomplishment and execution of the full purposes and objectives of Congress." *Arizona v. U.S.*, 132 S.Ct. at 2501.... While a state can bar unprotected speech, it cannot do so without a scienter requirement. *See, e.g., Smith v. California*, 361 U.S. 147, 153, 80 S.Ct. 215, 4 L.Ed.2d 205 (1959) (holding that a state obscenity statute could not constitutionally eliminate altogether a scienter requirement, and that, in order to be constitutionally applied to a book distributor, it must be shown that he had "knowledge of the contents of the book"). "[I]n order to prevent chilling expression protected by the First Amendment, statutes criminalizing obscenity must require proof of scienter." *U.S. v. Cochran*, 17 F.3d 56, 59 (3d Cir.1994).

The relevant language from the Act provides: "a person commits the offense of advertising commercial sexual abuse of a minor if: the person knowingly publishes, disseminates or displays, or causes directly or indirectly, to be published, disseminates or displayed any ad for a commercial sex act." Plaintiffs argue:

> a prosecutor need not show that a defendant did anything "knowingly" so long as she can establish that the defendant "cause[d] indirectly" third party content "to be published, disseminated or displayed." The Act does not require proof that a defendant knew (or even had reason to believe) that a person depicted in a posting was a minor—it expressly provides that this is *not* a defense. If a user posts content on a website containing a "depiction of a minor" and an "implicit offer" of sex for "something of value," every online service connected in any way to dissemination of that content is subject to criminal liability, whether its conduct was intentional or accidental, knowing or unknowing.

[Citation to Record omitted]. Defendant urges the Court to read the "knowing" culpability requirement into both clauses of the statute, relying on N.J. Stat. Ann. § 2C:2-2(c)(1), which provides that the "[p]rescribed culpability requirement applies to all material elements. When the law defining an offense prescribes the kind of culpability that is sufficient for the commission of an offense, without distinguishing among the material elements thereof, such provision shall apply to all the material elements of the offense, unless a contrary purpose plainly appears."

The Court disagrees with Defendant's reading of the language and agrees with both the *McKenna* and *Cooper* Courts' thorough analysis. A natural reading of the statute indicates that the adverb "knowingly" modifies the verbs that immediately follow it— here, "publishes, disseminates or displays"—and the attached clause creates liability, without the knowledge element being satisfied, if anyone "causes directly or indirectly, to be published, disseminated, or displayed" those same prohibited advertisements. As Judge Nixon stated: "context supports this reading. The subsequent affirmative defense provision confirms that no actual knowledge of the persons' age is necessary, stating that 'it is not a defen[se] that the defendant did not know the age of the minor depicted." *Cooper*, 2013 WL 155875 at *17....

Plaintiffs next argue the Act is invalid because it is a content based restriction that is not narrowly tailored to serve the State's asserted interests and it is not the least restrictive alternative available to address the State's interests. Defendants argue that the Act does not regulate speech protected by the First Amendment because it only prohibits the advertisement of an illegal transaction. Furthermore, Defendants argue that the Act is content neutral and thus only subject to intermediate scrutiny.

A restriction on speech is content-based if it is not "justified without reference to the content of the regulated speech." *Clark v. Cmty. for Creative Non-Violence*, 468 U.S. 288, 293, 104 S.Ct. 3065, 82 L.Ed.2d 221 (1984). In other words, a content-based restriction "focuses only on the content of the speech and the direct impact that speech has on its listeners," *Boos v. Barry*, 485 U.S. 312, 321, 108 S.Ct. 1157, 99 L.Ed.2d 333 (1988), or is "designed or intended to suppress or restrict the expression of specific speakers," *United States v. Playboy Entm't Grp.*, Inc., 529 U.S. 803, 812, 120 S.Ct. 1878, 146 L.Ed.2d 865 (2000).... "Content-based prohibitions, enforced by severe criminal penalties, have the constant potential to be a repressive force in the lives and thoughts of a free people." *Ashcroft v. Am. Civil Liberties Union*, 542 U.S. 656, 660, 124 S.Ct. 2783, 159 L.Ed.2d 690, (2004). "To guard against that threat the Constitution demands that content-based restrictions on speech be presumed invalid and that the Government bear the burden of showing their constitutionality." *Id.* (internal citations omitted). Content-based restrictions on speech receive the highest scrutiny by the courts, and "[i]t is rare that a regulation restricting speech because of its content will ever be permissible." *Playboy Entm't Grp.*, Inc., 529 U.S. at 818. A content-based limitation on speech will be upheld only where the state demonstrates that the limitation "is necessary to serve a compelling state interest and that it is narrowly drawn to achieve that end." *Perry Educ. Ass'n v. Perry Local Educators' Ass'n*, 460 U.S. 37, 45, 103 S.Ct. 948, 74 L.Ed.2d 794 (1983).

This Court finds that the language of the Act in question is a clear cut example of a content based restriction on speech. The statute imposes liability "for advertisements solely on the basis that they contain certain proscribed content: what appears to be the promotion of a sexual act with minors for something of value." *Cooper*, 2013 WL 1558785 at *24.... Additionally, the Act does not need meet strict scrutiny, such that it is narrowly tailored to promote a compelling government interest. *Sable Commc'ns of Cal. Inc. v. FCC*, 492 U.S. 115, 126, 109 S.Ct. 2829, 106 L.Ed.2d 93 (1989). It is the Government's burden to demonstrate that the statute is constitutional. *Ashcroft v. ACLU*, 542 U.S. at 666. Here, the Court finds that Defendants will likely fail to meet their burden, as they have failed to show that the statute is the least speech-restrictive solution to combat child sex trafficking in New Jersey....

Plaintiffs also argue the statute is both over broad as it criminalizes fully protected speech and unduly vague as it imposes severe criminal liability without providing reasonable notice of which speech is prohibited.... With regards to overbreadth, the Constitution "gives significant protection from overbroad laws that chill speech within the First Amendment's vast and privileged sphere." *Ashcroft v. Free Speech Coalition*, 535 U.S. 234, 244, 122 S.Ct. 1389, 152 L.Ed.2d 403 (2002).... Plaintiffs argue that the Act is overbroad in four ways. First, it is overbroad in terms of the parties subject to liability. Plaintiffs allege that the Act could hold multiple parties liable for just one third party post, pursuant to the "indirectly" causing language of the Act. Prosecutors could potentially "charge the website where [the ad] appeared; all search engines that identify the site in response to queries; any blogs, forums social networking sites, or individuals' emails that link to the website; and even ISPs that provide the services for users to access the Internet." ... Next, Plaintiffs argue that the law is overbroad because of the enormous volume of Internet content it burdens, arguing that any dating site, social networking cite or forum for communication could risk prosecution if it does not police or eliminate user postings.... Third, Plaintiffs claim the definition of "commercial sex act," i.e., a sexual act "for which something of value is given or received by any person" is overbroad as it is not limited to an economic exchange. The *McKenna* Court addressed this argument:

> Assuming that the undefined term "something of value" means anything that can be traded on a free market—including a bottle of wine, a nice dinner, or a promise to do the dishes—[the Washington statute]'s definition of "commercial sex act" encompasses vast swaths of legal, consensual, non-commercial sexual acidity.

Finally, Plaintiffs argue that the Act's requirement that online services obtain and retain identification from users posting content—the only defense available under the law—is also vastly overbroad. Plaintiffs claim "the identification requirement is practically impossible and disregards the realities of the Internet." ... Further, "the Act's vague and expansive dictates, which impose unclear burdens on indirect actors, will likely lead to overbroad self-censorship in order to avoid potential criminal liability." ...

Defendant argues that the statute is neither overbroad nor unduly vague because the Act regulates illegal advertisements and thus are not protected by the First Amendment. Specifically, Defendant argues that the Act is not overbroad because "it requires that an actor knowingly engage in the prohibited conduct and it only regulates an illegal activity." ... As shown above, a plain reading of the statutory language shows no "knowingly" culpability requirement for one who directly or indirectly causes the ad to be displayed or disseminated. Thus the Court is not convinced by Defendants' argument regarding overbreadth.... Similarly, the Court is not persuaded by Defendant's argument as to vagueness, as Defendant relies on the same strained reading of the "knowingly" culpability element into all parts of the statute. Defendant argues that neither is the Act unconstitutionally vague "because the 'knowingly' scienter requirement provides sufficient clarity to inform a person of ordinary intelligence of what conduct is prohibited under the Act, and provides sufficient guidance for a fact finder to determine whether an actor has violated its provisions." ... The Court disagrees.

As explained in *McKenna*, 881 F.Supp.2d at 1278–80, and *Cooper*, 2013 WL 1558785, at *21–24, the Act is likely to be found to be unconstitutionally vague. Among the terms the New Jersey legislature has neglected to define are "indirect[ ]," "direct[ ]," "implicit," and "offer." Additionally the Act's definition of "advertisement for a commercial sex act," including any "implicit offer" of sex for "something of value," is also likely impermissibly vague. Describing criminal conduct as anything that is "implicit" is inherently vague, because it means "[n]ot directly expressed [and] existing [only] inferentially" and "fails to clearly mark the boundary between what is permissible and impermissible." *Vt. Right to Life Comm., Inc. v. Sorrell*, 221 F.3d 376, 387–88 (2d Cir.2000) (invalidating state law on political ads that "implicitly" advocate success or defeat of candidate).

Plaintiffs present a number of situations that could be construed as an "implicit offer" of sex for "something of value:"

> If a woman posts on a dating website describing her sexual interests and that she is looking for a "generous man," would that constitute an "implicit offer" under

the law? If a masseuse offers customers "complete satisfaction" or an escort intending nothing more than companionship promises "a night you'll never forget," would those be "implicit offers" contrary to the law? And again, presumably all consensual sex reflects an exchange of "something of value" between the participants, even if no money changes hands.

[Citation to Record omitted]. This central definition of the Act fails to give a person of ordinary intelligence notice of what the law prohibits. "[S]tandards of permissible statutory vagueness are strict in the area of free expression.... Because First Amendment freedoms need breathing space to survive, government may regulate in the area only with narrow specificity." *NAACP v. Button*, 371 U.S. 415, 433, 83 S.Ct. 328, 9 L.Ed.2d 405 (1963). Thus, laws regulating speech are void for vagueness when they are so ambiguous that a reasonable person cannot tell what expression is forbidden and what is allowed. *See, e.g., Smith v. Goguen*, 415 U.S. 566, 569, 94 S.Ct. 1242, 39 L.Ed.2d 605 (1974) (invalidating state law that prohibited treating a flag "contemptuously"); *Baggett v. Bullitt*, 377 U.S. 360, 362, 84 S.Ct. 1316, 12 L.Ed.2d 377 (1964) (loyalty oath preventing "subversive person" from being employed in state was void for vagueness); *Houston v. Hill*, 482 U.S. 451, 107 S.Ct. 2502, 96 L.Ed.2d 398 (1987) (striking down city ordinance that made it unlawful to interrupt police officers in the performance of their duties because the law "effectively grants the police the discretion to make arrests selectively on the basis of the content of the speech").... Thus this Court again agrees with the *McKenna* and *Cooper* Courts in finding that Plaintiffs are likely to succeed in showing that such terms render the statute unconstitutionally vague....

Plaintiffs allege the Act violates the Commerce Clause because it attempts to regulate commercial transactions that take place wholly outside the State of New Jersey, and because it seeks to apply New Jersey law in a manner that constitutes an unreasonable and undue burden on interstate commerce that is excessive in relation to any local benefit conferred on the State of New Jersey and is likely to subject parties to inconsistent state regulations.... The Commerce clause provides: "The Congress shall have Power ... To regulate Commerce ... among the several States...." U.S. Const., Art. 1, § 8, cl. 3. The Supreme Court has long recognized that this affirmative grant of authority to Congress also encompasses an implicit or "dormant" limitation on the authority of the States to enact legislation affecting interstate commerce. *See, e.g., Healy v. Beer Institute, et al.*, 491 U.S. 324, 326, and n. 1, 109 S.Ct. 2491, 105 L.Ed.2d 275 (1989), *Hughes v. Oklahoma*, 441 U.S. 322, 326, and n. 2, 99 S.Ct. 1727, 60 L.Ed.2d 250 (1979); *HP, Hood & Sons, Inc. v. DuMond*, 336 U.S. 525, 534–35, 69 S.Ct. 657, 93 L.Ed. 865 (1949).

A state cannot regulate conduct that takes place exclusively outside the state. *Healy*, 491 U.S. at 336, 109 S.Ct. 2491, 105 L.Ed.2d 275. Where a state statute only has incidental effects on interstate commerce, the statute will be upheld "[w]here the statute regulates even-handedly to effectuate a legitimate local public interest," where "its effects on interstate commerce are only incidental," and where the burden imposed on interstate commerce is not "clearly excessive in relation to the putative local benefits." *Pike v. Bruce Church, Inc.*, 397 U.S. 137, 142, 90 S.Ct. 844, 25 L.Ed.2d 174 (1970).

Here, while an ad may make an offer for a sex act to occur in New Jersey, it is entirely possible that the advertisement or the sex act itself in fact takes place out of state. Thus the Act seeks to regulate conduct that occurs wholly outside the state of New Jersey. Additionally, the out of state burden will be significant. As stated in *McKenna*,

> To escape liability, online service providers that post content that *might* be construed as containing "implicit" offers for sex (including aggregators like 1A, social networking sites like Facebook.com, and dating sites like Match.com) will

> be required to collect government-issued identification, lest one of these offers relates to conduct occurring in Washington. Such a screening process would constitute a significant and costly change to the business operations of these corporations that have little to no connection with the State of Washington. Such a burden would be exponentially exacerbated if every state were permitted to legislate its own requirements. In contrast, Washington's interest in prosecuting wrongdoers is undermined by the practical obstacles to exercising jurisdiction over defendants whose criminal acts take place outside the state.

McKenna, 881 F.Supp.2d at 1285 (W.D.Wash.2012). This Court agrees. "Because the internet does not recognize geographic boundaries, it is difficult, if not impossible, for a state to regulate internet activities without project[ing] its legislation into other States." *Am. Booksellers Found. v. Dean*, 342 F.3d 96, 103 (2d Cir.2003). The Act is likely in violation of the dormant commerce clause, and thus cannot stand....

Having shown a likelihood of success on the merits, Plaintiffs have also adequately satisfied the remaining elements for securing a preliminary injunction: (2) Whether the movant will be irreparably injured by denial of the relief; (3) Whether granting preliminary relief will result in even greater harm to the nonmoving party; and (4) Whether granting preliminary relief will be in the public interest. *Gerardi*, 16 F.3d at 1373.... First, "[t]he loss of First Amendment freedoms for even minimal periods of time, unquestionably constitutes irreparable injury." *Elrod v. Burns*, 427 U.S. 347, 373, 96 S.Ct. 2673, 49 L.Ed.2d 547 (1976). Absent injunctive relief, Plaintiffs may face serious criminal liability.... Second, the balance of equities weighs in Plaintiffs' favor. "No prosecutions have yet been undertaken under the law, so none will be disrupted if the injunction stands." *Ashcroft v. ACLU*, 542 U.S. at 671. While the injunction is upheld, New Jersey can enforce other laws banning prostitution and the exploitation of minors.... Third, an injunction is in the public interest. This is because, "[w]here a prosecution is a likely possibility, yet only an affirmative defense is available, speakers may self-censor rather than risk the perils of trial. There is a potential for extraordinary harm and a serious chill upon protected speech." *Id.* at 670–71. The Court acknowledges the great public interest in preventing and prosecuting human trafficking and child prostitution, but also understands the great necessity of upholding Constitutional protections....

For the above reasons, the Court finds that a preliminary injunction is appropriate to enjoin the enactment of N.J. Stat. Ann..§ 2C:13-10(b)(1). An appropriate Order follows this Opinion.

II. Commercial Sexual Exploitation

The commercial exploitation of children may involve a variety of exploitative behavior described throughout this casebook, including various forms of physical and non-physical interaction, *see* Chapter Two (Parameters of Exploitation), and certain aspects of child pornography, *see* Chapter Three (Internet Sexual Exploitation of Children). Some states specifically define "commercial sexual exploitation," *see, e.g.,* KAN. STAT. ANN. § 21-6422 (defining commercial sexual exploitation of a child), but generally, commercial sexual exploitation includes any transaction involving anything of value exchanged for, or involving, the procurement of children for sex. *See* National Center for Missing & Exploited Children, *Commercial Sexual Exploitation of Children: A Fact Sheet*, available at http://www.missingkids.com/en_US/documents/CCSE_Fact_Sheet.pdf (last accessed Apr. 6,

2015). This generally consists of pornography, sex tourism, sex trafficking, and prostitution. Specific issues related to child pornography are addressed in Chapter Three (Internet Sexual Exploitation of Children), *supra*. Sex tourism is discussed generally, below, but the specific issue of prosecution for sex tourism is addressed in Chapter One, Section I.B.5.b (Exploiters as Travelers, Foreign Travel), *supra*. Issues involving sex trafficking and prostitution are also addressed below.

A. Child Sex Tourism

Child sex tourism involves travel—typically to foreign locations—to engage in sexual activity, particularly with child prostitutes. Child sex tourism is a multi-billion dollar industry involving millions of children world-wide. Travel to foreign countries for such purposes is often motivated by lower costs for sexual services, anonymity within a new environment, and more lenient attitudes toward prostitution and, thereby, greater access to child prostitution. However, when sexual activity in a foreign country involves child prostitution, non-consensual sex, or child sex trafficking, the exploiter may become subject to criminal liability within the United States. The case of *United States v. Pendleton*, 658 F.3d 299 (3rd Cir. 2011), *see* Chapter One, Section I.B.5.b (Exploiter as Traveler, Foreign Travel) addresses this issue. In *Pendleton*, the court held that the provision of the Prosecutorial Remedies and Other Tools to End the Exploitation of Children Today Act of 2003 (PROTECT ACT) that criminalizes international child sex tourism is a valid exercise of Congress's Foreign Commerce power. Thus, the "travel" provisions of the Act, namely those in 18 U.S.C. § 2423, are applicable, even in the noncommercial context.

For further discussion on the topic of sex tourism and proposals to address the issue, see William J. Newman, Ben W. Holt, John S. Rabun, Gary Phillips and Charles L. Scott, *Child Sex Tourism: Extending the Borders of Sexual Offender Legislation*, 34 INTL. J.L. & PSYCH. 116 (2011); John A. Hall, *Sex Offenders and Child Sex Tourism: the Case for Passport Revocation*, 18 VA. J. SOC. POLICY & L. 153 (2011); Mark Orndorf, *The Secret World of Child Sex Tourism: Evidentiary and Procedural Hurdles of the PROTECT Act*, 28 PENN. ST. INTL. L. REV. 789 (2010); Kelly M. Cotter, *Combating Child Sex Tourism in Southeast Asia*, 37 DENV. J. INTL. L. & POLICY 493 (2009); Kalen Fredette, *International Legislative Efforts to Combat Child Sex Tourism: Evaluating the Council of Europe Convention on Commercial Child Sexual Exploitation*, 32 B.C. INTL. & COMP. L. REV. 1 (2009); Maureen Atwell, *Combating American Child Sex Tourism in Cambodia under the 2003 U.S. Protect Act*, 26 WIS. INTL. L.J. 163 (2008); Sara Dillon, *What Human Rights Law Obscures: Global Sex Trafficking and the Demand for Children*, 17 UCLA WOMEN'S L.J. 121 (2008); Kyle Cutts, *A Modicum of Recovery: How Child Sex Tourism Constitutes Slavery under the Alien Tort Claims Act*, 58 CASE. W. RES. L. REV. 277 (2007); Naomi L. Svensson, *Extraterritorial Accountability: An Assessment of the Effectiveness of Child Sex Tourism Laws*, 28 LOY. L.A. INTL. & COMP. L. REV. 641 (2006).

B. Child Sex Trafficking

The "travel" provisions of the PROTECT Act (18 U.S.C. § 2423) are applicable to exploiters who travel to foreign jurisdictions and engage in sexual activity with children. When such crimes occur within the United States and involve the trafficking of children for purposes of sexual acts, for which anything of value is exchanged, the provisions of the Trafficking Victims Protection Act of 2000 (TVPA) are applicable. The TVPA was enacted in 2000 and was reauthorized in 2003, 2006, 2008 (when it was renamed the

William Wilberforce Trafficking Victims Protection Reauthorization Act), and again in 2013. For the key provisions of each of the versions of the Act, see Polaris Project, *Trafficking Victims' Protection Act (TVPA)—Fact Sheet*, available at http://www.rescue.org/sites/default/files/resource-file/trafficking%20victims%20protection%20act%20fact%20sheet_0.pdf (last accessed May 6, 2015). The Act is a comprehensive federal statute designed to address specific issues involving human trafficking: prevention, protection, and prosecution. The Act focuses on prevention through the creation of State Department Office to Monitor and Combat Trafficking, which assesses various countries' efforts to combat trafficking, generally, and imposes sanctions on countries that fall below minimum prevention standards. *See* Polaris Project, *2014 State Ratings on Human Trafficking Laws*, available at http://www.polarisproject.org/what-we-do/policy-advocacy/national-policy/state-ratings-on-human-trafficking-laws (last accessed May 6, 2015). The Act's protection component offers assistance to qualified foreign nationals who are victims of trafficking; these include participation in the Federal Witness Protection Program and other educational, health, and social service programs. Additionally, the Act offers the T-Visa, which grants temporary citizenship to qualified victims of trafficking. Lastly, the Act makes human trafficking, including child sex trafficking, a federal crime, *see* 18 U.S.C. § 1589, and mandates that restitution be paid to victims, *see* 18 U.S.C. § 1593. The restitution aspects of the Act are addressed more fully in Chapter 7, Section II.C (Civil Liability, Victim Restitution), *infra*.

Under the TVPA, trafficking is defined as "the recruitment, harboring, transportation, provision, or obtaining of a person for the purpose of a commercial sex act." 22 U.S.C. § 7102(10). A "commercial sex act" is defined as "any sex act on account of which anything of value is given to or received by any person." *Id*. at § 7102(4). Children who are involved in sex trafficking are deemed victims of "severe forms of trafficking in persons" when the commercial sex act involved "is induced by force, fraud, or coercion, or in which the person induced to perform such act has not attained 18 years of age...." *Id*. at 7102(9)(A). The cases that follow demonstrate the application of these provisions for the prosecution of child sex trafficking within the United States. Note specifically in the *Brooks* decision that the charges against the defendants involve both the "travel" provisions of the PROTECT ACT and the trafficking provision of the TVPA.

United States v. Brooks

Ninth Circuit, 2010
610 F.3d 1186

CANBY, Circuit Judge: ...

In late April 2006, sixteen-year-old N.K. and fifteen-year-old R.O. ran away from a residential treatment center in Scottsdale, Arizona. For a brief time, the girls stayed at a hotel with one of R.O.'s friends, who gave them methamphetamine, N.K.'s first experience with the drug. Eventually, the girls left the hotel and met Brooks and Fields, as well as another man known only as "Lee." The girls told the men that they had nowhere to go, and the men brought the girls to a different hotel room that Brooks had rented.... That night, after Fields had left, the girls told Brooks and Lee that they had run away from a juvenile detention center. The men laughed and made jokes about N.K. and R.O. being juvenile delinquents and suggested that the girls go to San Diego to work for Fields as prostitutes. The next day, Fields told R.O. that he was a pimp and asked her to work for him. When R.O. asked Fields what N.K. would do, Fields responded that R.O. could ask N.K. to come, too. During these initial conversations, R.O. told both Brooks and Fields that she and N.K. were minors.

The next day, Brooks and Fields introduced the girls to Julia Fonteneaux, a prostitute who described herself as Fields's "main chick." After Fonteneaux explained certain details about prostitution to the girls, Brooks and Fields drove R.O. and N.K. to the bus station, where the men bought the girls bus tickets to San Diego, assigning them false names.... The morning after the girls arrived in San Diego, Brooks, Fields, and Fonteneaux met the girls at the apartment of an associate of Fields, where R.O. and N.K. had slept. Fields took R.O. shopping for sexually provocative clothing and shoes, and then both men brought the girls and Fonteneaux to a motel. At Fields's direction, Fonteneaux posted prostitution ads on craigslist.com for N.K., R.O., and herself, and explained to the girls how to handle customers. Over the next two days, R.O. engaged in two or three acts of prostitution at the hotel. N.K., however, who still was disoriented by the drugs she had taken in Arizona, did not engage in any such acts.

Three days later, Brooks, Fields, Fonteneaux, and the girls traveled back to Phoenix in a rented Ford Freestyle. All of the females were dressed in provocative clothing, and R.O. and Fonteneaux understood the trip's purpose to be prostitution. Upon arriving in Phoenix, the men dropped R.O. and Fonteneaux off near the corner of 51st Avenue and McDowell Road, an area of Phoenix known for prostitution. R.O. engaged in two or three acts of prostitution, but later that night she was taken into custody by the Phoenix police after an officer who observed her on the street determined that she was underage.

After Brooks and Fields left R.O. and Fonteneaux, Brooks rented two rooms for the group at nearby hotels. Fonteneaux called Fields later that night to tell him that R.O. had been picked up by the police. The next day, Fields left N.K. at a bus station with her and R.O.'s belongings, but otherwise penniless.... After being taken into custody, R.O. recounted to the police the previous days' events and described the men involved and their rental vehicle. The following evening, using the information provided by R.O., police officers stopped Brooks and Fields in the Ford Freestyle and held them in custody for several hours. The officers also searched the Ford Freestyle at the local police precinct, discovering receipts for motel rooms and car rental and other incriminating evidence.

A federal grand jury returned a superseding indictment against Brooks, Fields, and Fonteneaux, charging each of them with two counts of child sex trafficking, 18 U.S.C. §§ 1591(a) & 2, and two counts of interstate transportation of minors for purposes of prostitution, 18 U.S.C. §§ 2423(a), (e) & 2. Fonteneaux pleaded guilty and received a reduced sentence in exchange for her testimony against Brooks and Fields.... Prior to trial, Brooks and Fields moved to suppress evidence seized from the Ford Freestyle, as well as the fruits of that evidence, arguing that their detention on the night of April 29, 2006, as well as the accompanying search of their vehicle violated the Fourth Amendment. They also moved to dismiss Counts 3 and 4 of the indictment as multiplicitous of Counts 1 and 2. The district court denied both motions. At trial, the district court also overruled Defendants' objections to the introduction of the expert testimony of Phoenix Police Department Detective Christi Hein on the relationship between pimps and prostitutes and the business of prostitution.

A jury found Brooks and Fields guilty on all counts. The district court subsequently denied Defendants' renewed motions for judgment of acquittal. Brooks was sentenced to 97 months in prison for each count, to run concurrently. Fields was sentenced to 198 months in prison for each count, also to run concurrently.... Brooks and Fields both appeal the district court's admission of Detective Hein's expert testimony. We review the district court's decision to admit expert testimony for abuse of discretion, *United States v. Morales*, 108 F.3d 1031, 1035 (9th Cir.1997) (en banc), and find no abuse of discretion here.

First, Detective Hein's training and experience qualified her as an expert on the business of prostitution and the relationships between pimps and prostitutes. *See United States v. Freeman*, 498 F.3d 893, 900 n. 1 (9th Cir.2007). Detective Hein had worked as a police officer for approximately eight years, including two and a half years with the Phoenix vice enforcement unit. She had conducted approximately twenty to twenty-five full-scale child prostitution investigations, completed approximately fifty extended interviews with pimps and prostitutes, and frequently worked undercover, posing as a street prostitute and posting prostitution ads online. Detective Hein had attended several specialized trainings on child prostitution and had lectured on the subject of child prostitution. The fact that Detective Hein lacked an advanced degree, supervisory experience, previous experience as an expert witness, or relevant publications did not render her unfit to provide expert testimony. *See United States v. Smith*, 520 F.3d 1097, 1105 (9th Cir.2008) ("No specific credentials or qualifications are mentioned [by Federal Rule of Evidence 702].").

Detective Hein's testimony was relevant to matters at issue in this case. "By and large, the relationship between prostitutes and pimps is not the subject of common knowledge." *Taylor*, 239 F.3d at 998. Detective Hein's testimony helped place other witnesses' testimony into context and provided the jury a means to assess their credibility. For example, Detective Hein's testimony concerning the role of the "bottom girl"—a pimp's most senior prostitute, who often trains new prostitutes and collects their earnings until they can be trusted—potentially helped the jury evaluate Fonteneaux's testimony that she was acting at Fields's direction, not on her own accord. Similarly, Detective Hein's testimony that pimps often isolate new prostitutes from familiar areas provided context for evaluating Appellants' intentions in initially transporting the girls from Phoenix to San Diego.... [W]e conclude that the district court did not abuse its discretion in admitting the expert testimony....

Brooks and Fields next contend that the district court erred in denying their motions for judgments of acquittal. We review a motion for judgment of acquittal de novo, "viewing the evidence against the appellants in the light most favorable to the government to determine whether any rational trier of fact could have found the essential elements of the crime beyond a reasonable doubt." *United States v. Williams*, 547 F.3d 1187, 1195 n. 6 (9th Cir.2008). We conclude that the evidence was sufficient to sustain all of the convictions....

Counts 1 and 2 of the superseding indictment charged Appellants with child sex trafficking of R.O. and N.K., respectively, in violation of 18 U.S.C. §§ 1591(a) and 2. Brooks challenges the sufficiency of the evidence as to both Count 1 and Count 2, while Fields challenges only Count 2, concerning N.K.... Fields's challenge to Count 2 is limited to the sufficiency of the evidence that he knew N.K. was a minor. *See* 18 U.S.C. § 1591(a) (punishing sex trafficking of children where the defendant "[knew] ... that the [victim] ha[d] not attained the age of 18 years"). This claim is unpersuasive. R.O. testified that both she and N.K. told Fields that they were underage. Further, the jury had the opportunity to consider N.K.'s appearance during her testimony, at which time she was eighteen. This evidence is sufficient to sustain Fields's conviction as to Count 2.

Brooks's challenges to Counts 1 and 2 also fail. As in Fields's case, a rational jury could have found beyond a reasonable doubt that Brooks knew that R.O. and N.K. were under eighteen. R.O. testified that she told Brooks and Lee that she and N.K. were underage and had run away from a juvenile detention center, causing the men to joke about how the girls would get them into trouble. And, as in the case of N.K., the jury had an opportunity to evaluate R.O.'s appearance and demeanor while testifying, at which time she was seventeen.... There also was sufficient evidence to prove that Brooks satisfied the *actus reus* requirement of § 1591(a). While Brooks argues that there was no evidence that he persuaded or enticed either R.O. or N.K. to become involved in prostitution, § 1591 also imposes liability on anyone who "recruits, … harbors, transports, provides, or obtains by any means" a minor for purposes of prostitution. 18 U.S.C. § 1591(a)(1). Here, a rational jury could find beyond a reasonable doubt that Brooks knowingly transported, as well as harbored, the girls. The jury could infer from N.K.'s and R.O.'s testimony that Brooks assisted Fields in purchasing bus tickets for N.K. and R.O. to travel to San Diego. R.O. and Fonteneaux also testified that Brooks personally transported the girls all or part of the way from San Diego to Phoenix. Furthermore, physical evidence introduced at trial, including hotel receipts, was sufficient to prove that Brooks harbored the girls in rented hotel rooms.

A rational jury also could find beyond a reasonable doubt that Brooks acted "knowing … that [R.O. and N.K.] … [would] be caused to engage in a commercial sex act," 18 U.S.C. § 1591(a). R.O. testified that, on the night the girls met the men in Phoenix, Brooks and Lee discussed with R.O. and N.K. the possibility of the girls going to San Diego to work as prostitutes. Then, the next day, Brooks assisted Fields in buying bus tickets so that the girls could travel to San Diego. Later, when Brooks transported the group from San Diego back to Phoenix, both girls were dressed in provocative clothing. And upon arriving back in Phoenix, Brooks left R.O. at 51st Avenue and McDowell Road, an area known for prostitution, and brought N.K. to a hotel, suggesting that the men had plans for her to be caused to engage in prostitution in the future.[4] Therefore, we reject Brooks's sufficiency-of-the-evidence challenge to Counts 1 and 2....

Counts 3 and 4 of the superseding indictment charged Appellants with interstate transportation of minors for purposes of prostitution, in violation of 18 U.S.C. §§ 2423(a) and 2. Brooks challenges the sufficiency of the evidence as to both Count 3 and Count 4, concerning R.O. and N.K., respectively, while Fields challenges only Count 4. These appeals concern just one element of § 2423(a): intent that the minor engage in prostitution. *See* 18 U.S.C. § 2423(a) (criminalizing the knowing transportation of a person under the age of eighteen "with intent that the individual engage in prostitution").

Appellants' contentions have no merit. Fields's acts were sufficient to prove that he intended not just R.O., but also N.K., to engage in prostitution when he transported them to and from San Diego. Fields bought both girls bus tickets to San Diego under false names, bought both girls provocative shoes upon their arrival, and directed Fonteneaux to post prostitution ads for both girls on craigslist.com and to instruct both girls on receiving customers. Further, when the group, at Fields's direction, returned to Phoenix, both girls were dressed in "working clothes," indicating his intent that both R.O. and N.K. be caused to engage in prostitution. Thus, we uphold Fields's conviction as to Count 4.

Although it is a closer case, we also conclude that the evidence, when viewed in the light most favorable to the prosecution, was sufficient for a rational jury to conclude that

---

4. N.K. was not in fact caused to engage in prostitution. The jury, however, could infer that N.K. did not engage in such acts simply because she still was very affected by the drugs she took in Phoenix. Further, as we recently explained in another § 1591(a) appeal,

> [w]hen an act of Congress requires knowledge of a future action, it does not require knowledge in the sense of certainty as to a future act. What the statute requires is that the defendant know in the sense of being aware of an established modus operandi that will in the future coerce a prostitute to engage in prostitution.

United States v. Todd, 584 F.3d 788, 792 (9th Cir.2009). This standard is satisfied here even though N.K. did not ultimately engage in any acts of prostitution.

Brooks, too, acted with the intent that the girls engage in prostitution. R.O. testified that Brooks, with Lee, first talked to the girls about working for Fields as prostitutes in San Diego. Fonteneaux also testified that, while Brooks did not appear to be paid by Fields for his assistance, he benefitted from the association by not having to pay for his food or lodging. These perquisites were funded by money Fields brought in from prostitution, which a rational jury could infer that Brooks knew. These facts, together with Brooks's involvement in transporting the group and securing hotel rooms for them, were sufficient for a rational juror to conclude that Brooks intended that the girls engage in prostitution. Accordingly, Brooks's challenges to Counts 3 and 4 fail. . . .

For the foregoing reasons, we affirm Brooks's and Fields's convictions. . . .

Notes

Note in *Brooks* that under the sex trafficking provision, 18 U.S.C. § 1591, the statute includes a knowledge requirement "that the person has not attained the age of 18 years and will be caused to engage in a commercial sex act. . . ." However, this does not require the state to prove that the defendant actually possessed knowledge of the victim's age, but only that the defendant recklessly disregarded the victim's age. *See United States v. Mozie*, 752 F.3d 1271 (11th Cir. (Fla.) 2014); *United States v. Vanderhorst*, 2 F. Supp. 3d 792 (D.S.C. 2014). Where a defendant has the opportunity to observe the victim and assess his or her age, 18 U.S.C. § 1591(c) provides for strict liability with respect to knowledge of the victim's age. *See* 18 U.S.C. § 1591(c) ("In a prosecution under subsection (a)(1) in which the defendant had a reasonable opportunity to observe the person so recruited, enticed, harbored, transported, provided, obtained or maintained, the Government need not prove that the defendant knew that the person had not attained the age of 18 years."); *United States v. Robinson*, 702 F.3d 22 (2d Cir. 2012). Compare this with the requirements of the "travel" provision, 18 U.S.C. § 2423, which does not require an actual minor or knowledge of the victim's age, but only that the defendant intended the minor to engage in prostitution. 18 U.S.C. § 2423(a) ("A person who knowingly transports an individual who has not attained the age of 18 years in interstate or foreign commerce . . . with intent that the individual engage in prostitution, or in any sexual activity for which any person can be charged with a criminal offense, shall be fined. . . .); *United States v. Washington*, 743 F.3d 938 (4th Cir. 2014). Accordingly, a charge for a criminal offense under 18 U.S.C. § 1591 could satisfy this requirement under 18 U.S.C. § 2423. This issue is discussed in the *Townsend* decision, which follows the *Jungers/Bonestroo* decision below. However, § 2423(g) provides that "[i]n a prosecution . . . based on illicit sexual conduct. . . , it is a defense, which the defendant must establish by a preponderance of the evidence, that the defendant reasonably believed that the person with whom the defendant engaged in the commercial sex act had attained the age of 18 years.").

Furthermore, under 18 U.S.C. 1591(a)(1), the trafficker need not intend or desire to further the trafficking scheme when he or she "recruits, entices, harbors, transports, provides, obtains, or maintains by any means a person;. . . ." *See United States v. Estrada-Tepal*, 2014 WL 4828866 (E.D.N.Y. 2014) (noting that scope of statute "could hypothetically criminalize the conduct of a mother who feeds, clothes and drives around her daughter with knowledge that her daughter is or will be a victim to a sex trafficking scheme, but without any intent or desire to further the trafficking scheme."). In *Brooks*, however, the court determined that the defendants clearly intended for the victims to engage in prostitution and, thereby, committed the predicate acts of commercial sex trafficking under § 1591. In the following case, consider whether the scope of the trafficking provisions extend not only to those, like the defendants in *Brooks*, who procure and traffic children for commercial sexual exploitation, but to those who attempt to purchase and participate in the sexual activities with the children.

United States v. Jungers and Bonestroo

Eighth Circuit, 2013
702 F.3d 1066

RILEY, Chief Judge.

Separate juries convicted Daron Lee Jungers and Ronald Bonestroo (collectively, defendants) of attempted sex trafficking of a minor, in violation of the Trafficking Victim Protection Act of 2000 (TVPA).[1] The district court in each case granted each defendant's motion for judgment of acquittal under Fed.R.Crim.P. 29. The government appeals. Having jurisdiction under 18 U.S.C. § 3731, we reverse. *See United States v. Boesen*, 491 F.3d 852, 855 (8th Cir.2007)....

In February 2011, state and federal law enforcement officers working undercover in Sioux Falls, South Dakota, placed several online advertisements in an effort to apprehend individuals seeking to obtain children for sex. Officers pretended to be a man offering his girlfriend's underage daughters for sex while his girlfriend was out of town.... Jungers and Bonestroo each responded to the advertisements. After several e-mails discussing details about the girls, their ages, and the rates for sex, and after receiving an age-regressed photograph of adult female officers, Jungers indicated he wanted an eleven-year old girl for an hour so she could perform oral sex on him. Jungers then traveled from Sioux City, Iowa, to the house in Sioux Falls that law enforcement officers were using for the undercover operation. Jungers confirmed he would pay to receive oral sex from the eleven-year-old girl, but indicated he was uncomfortable doing so at the house and would prefer to take the girl with him instead. Police arrested Jungers when he entered the house.... Bonestroo also agreed to meet an undercover agent at the house after several e-mails and recorded telephone conversations about the girls and the rates for sex with them. After receiving an age-regressed photograph, Bonestroo agreed to pay $200 to have sex with the fourteen-year-old twin girls for an hour. When Bonestroo arrived at the house, he asked if the twins were there and showed the undercover officer the money he brought to complete the transaction. Officers arrested Bonestroo shortly thereafter.

Jungers and Bonestroo were each charged with attempted commercial sex trafficking, in violation of 18 U.S.C. §§ 1591 and 1594(a). At their respective trials, neither Jungers nor Bonestroo presented any evidence in defense. Rather than challenge the facts, both argued they were merely consumers or purchasers of commercial sex acts, not "sex traffickers" of children. The defendants each timely moved for judgment of acquittal pursuant to Fed.R.Crim.P. 29(a) on that basis. The district court in each case took the motions under advisement. Jungers's and Bonestroo's respective juries found them guilty.... On December 5, 2011, the district court in Jungers's case acquitted Jungers and discharged him from confinement, finding the "evidence presented at trial [was] legally insufficient to support a conviction for sex trafficking under § 1591." The district court reasoned "the purpose of § 1591 is to punish sex traffickers and that Congress did not intend to expand the field of those prosecuted under that statute to those who purchase sex made available by traffickers." ... On January 4, 2012, the district court in Bonestroo's case likewise acquitted Bonestroo of his conviction under §§ 1591 and 1594(a) because of insufficient

---

1. 18 U.S.C. §§ 1591 and 1594(a). See Pub. L. No. 106-386, Div. A, 114 Stat. 1464 (2000).

evidence and discharged him from confinement. The district court concluded "[a]lthough a bare reading of at least one of these three verbs [recruits, entices, and obtains] may support a determination that § 1591 was meant to encompass purchasers of sex acts from minors, the entire language and design of the statute as a whole indicates that it is meant to punish those who are the providers or pimps of children, not the purchasers or the johns." The government appeals both orders, arguing "[t]here is no 'customer exception' to 18 U.S.C. § 1591." ...

Section 1591 prohibits knowingly recruiting, enticing, harboring, transporting, providing, obtaining or maintaining "a minor, knowing the minor would be caused to engage in commercial sex acts."[2] *United States v. Elbert*, 561 F.3d 771, 777 (8th Cir.2009). Section 1594(a) makes an attempted violation of § 1591 a federal crime.... Since Congress enacted § 1591 on October 28, 2000, as part of the TVPA, the lion's share of prosecutions under § 1591 have involved offenders who have played some part in supplying commercial sex acts. *See, e.g., United States v. Chappell*, 665 F.3d 1012, 1014 (8th Cir.2012); *United States v. Palmer*, 643 F.3d 1060, 1063 (8th Cir.2011). In *United States v. Cooke*, 675 F.3d 1153, 1155 (8th Cir.2012), we affirmed the conviction of an attempted purchaser under § 1591, but did not consider the issue raised in this appeal. *Accord United States v. Strevell*, 185 Fed.Appx. 841, 844–46 (11th Cir.2006) (unpublished per curiam) (affirming conviction of attempted purchaser of sex from a minor in violation of §§ 1591 and 1594).... The district court and the parties in these consolidated appeals agree § 1591 is unambiguous. The sole issue raised on appeal is whether "[t]he plain and unambiguous provisions of 18 U.S.C. § 1591 apply to both suppliers and consumers of commercial sex acts." We conclude they do....

Under the heading "Sex trafficking of children or by force, fraud, or coercion," § 1591(a) provides

Whoever knowingly—

(1) in or affecting interstate or foreign commerce, or within the special maritime and territorial jurisdiction of the United States, recruits, entices, harbors, transports, provides, obtains, or maintains by any means a person; or

(2) benefits, financially or by receiving anything of value, from participation in a venture which has engaged in an act described in violation of paragraph (1),

knowing, or in reckless disregard of the fact, that means of force, threats of force, fraud, coercion described in subsection (e)(2), or any combination of such means will be used to cause the person to engage in a commercial sex act, or that the person has not attained the age of 18 years and will be caused to engage in a commercial sex act, shall be punished as provided in subsection (b).

Nothing in the text of § 1591 expressly limits its provisions to suppliers or suggests Congress intended categorically to exclude purchasers or consumers (johns) of commercial sex acts whose conduct otherwise violates § 1591. To the contrary, the expansive language of § 1591 "criminalizes a broad spectrum" of conduct relating to the sex trafficking of children. *Jongewaard*, 567 F.3d at 340 (rejecting the assertion that 18 U.S.C. § 875(c) only prohibited a subcategory of criminal conduct as contrary to the statutory text).

By its terms, § 1591(a)(1) applies to "[w]hoever knowingly ... recruits, entices, harbors, transports, provides, obtains, or maintains [a child] by any means." "These words do not

---

2. "The term 'commercial sex act' means any sex act, on account of which anything of value is given to or received by any person." 18 U.S.C. § 1591(e)(3).

lend themselves to restrictive interpretation." *United States v. Culbert*, 435 U.S. 371, 373, 98 S.Ct. 1112, 55 L.Ed.2d 349 (1978) (interpreting the Hobbs Act, 18 U.S.C. § 1951). The terms "whoever" and "any" are expansive. *See, e.g., Freeman v. Quicken Loans, Inc.*, 566 U.S. ___, ___, 132 S.Ct. 2034, 2042, 182 L.Ed.2d 955 (2012) (explaining the term "any" "has an 'expansive meaning,'" that "can broaden to the maximum, but never change in the least, the clear meaning of the phrase selected by Congress") (quoting *Dep't of Hous. & Urban Dev. v. Rucker*, 535 U.S. 125, 131, 122 S.Ct. 1230, 152 L.Ed.2d 258 (2002)); *United States v. Gonzales*, 520 U.S. 1, 5, 117 S.Ct. 1032, 137 L.Ed.2d 132 (1997) ("Read naturally, the word 'any' has an expansive meaning, that is, 'one or some indiscriminately of whatever kind.'") (quoting *Webster's Third New International Dictionary* 97 (1976)); *United States v. Lucien*, 347 F.3d 45, 51 (2d Cir.2003) (rejecting a defendant's proposed construction of a statute that limited punishment for healthcare fraud to healthcare professionals because the statute applied to "whoever" committed such fraud and the common meaning of "whoever" was "whatever person, any person at all, no matter who") (quoting *Webster's Third New International Dictionary* 2611 (1981)) (internal quotation marks omitted); *United States v. Khatib*, 706 F.2d 213, 218 (7th Cir.1983) (rejecting a defendant's proposed status limitation on the term "whoever" in 7 U.S.C. § 2024(b)(1) because the statutory language was not restrictive). Neither term implicitly limits the application of § 1591(a)(1) to suppliers nor exempts purchasers from prosecution under the statute.[3]

The detailed list of proscribed activities in § 1591(a)(1) likewise does not contain any restrictive or limiting language, beyond requiring the acts fall within Congress's power to regulate commerce. Section 1591(a)(1) makes no distinction between suppliers or purchasers of commercial sex acts with children — it prohibits acts of trafficking regardless of the identity or status of the trafficker.... Despite the absence of restrictive language, the defendants repeatedly assert § 1591(a)(1) is aimed exclusively at organized sex-trafficking rings or ventures that profit from the illicit sex trade. While § 1591 undoubtedly targets such organizations, the language in § 1591 indicates Congress also targeted individual acts of trafficking. To violate § 1591(a)(2), a trafficker must benefit "financially or by receiving anything of value from participation" in a trafficking "venture" — defined as "any group of two or more individuals associated in fact," § 1591(e)(5). Section 1591(a)(1) is not subject to those same limitations.

The defendants maintain this appeal turns on the meaning of the term "obtains." Section 1591 does not define the term "obtains" or any of the other verbs listed. "When a word is not defined by statute, we normally construe it in accord with its ordinary or natural meaning." *Smith v. United States*, 508 U.S. 223, 228, 113 S.Ct. 2050, 124 L.Ed.2d 138 (1993). The defendants acknowledge "obtains," by itself, is "an incredibly broad" verb, devoid of any inherent limitation on the actor or his object. *See United States v. Ramos-Arenas*, 596 F.3d 783, 787 (10th Cir.2010) (defining obtains to include "attaining or acquiring a thing of value in any way," without limiting who ultimately receives it) (quoting *Black's Law Dictionary* 1078 (6th ed. 1990) ("To get hold of by effort; to get possession of; to procure; to acquire, in any way.")). Another dictionary defines obtain to mean "[t]o come into the possession of; to procure; to get, acquire, or secure." *Oxford English Dictionary* Online (September 2012) http://oed.com/view/Entry/130002 (November 2, 2012). The ordinary and natural meaning of "obtains" and the other terms Congress selected in drafting § 1591 are broad enough to encompass the actions of both suppliers and purchasers of commercial sex acts....

---

3. Jungers's brief acknowledges, "Neither Jungers nor the district court has ever contended that the term 'whoever' in [§ 1591(a)], standing on its own, would not include individuals such as Jungers."

The defendants acknowledge the breadth of the statutory language and the absence of any explicit limitation to suppliers, but argue applying § 1591 to purchasers is inconsistent with the purpose, placement, structure, and context of the statute as a whole and renders parts of the TVPA superfluous or meaningless. Specifically, the defendants assert the language of § 1591, read in context, indicates Congress intended to prohibit the potential "chronological" steps a child sex-trafficking organization must take to gain control over child victims and prepare them to engage in commercial sex acts in the future, but stopped short of criminalizing the conduct of the purchasers of such acts. According to the defendants, the definitions of "sex trafficking" and the phrase "will be caused" indicate § 1591 only applies to "predicate conduct" committed by suppliers of commercial sex acts.

Notwithstanding the defendants' argument to the contrary, the TVPA definition of "sex trafficking"—broadly defined as "the recruitment, harboring, transportation, provision, or obtaining of a person *for the purpose of a commercial sex act*"—readily includes the actions of a purchaser whose sole purpose is obtaining a child for sex. 22 U.S.C. § 7102(9) (emphasis added). "'Traffic,' like 'trade,' includes both 'the business of buying and selling for money' and 'the business of exchanging commodities by barter.'" *United States v. Horn*, 187 F.3d 781, 791 (8th Cir.1999) (quoting *May v. Sloan*, 101 U.S. 231, 237, 25 L.Ed. 797 (1879), and citing *Webster's Third New International Dictionary* at 2422 (1986) ("traffic" is "the activity of exchanging commodities by bartering or buying and selling")).... The defendants' interpretation of "trafficking," as restricted to supply only, is too narrow. Bonestroo asserts "[t]he plain meaning of the word 'trafficking' in a commercial sequence does not include the end user." In support, Bonestroo claims "a drug user is not ever described as a 'trafficker.'" To the contrary, in clarifying what constitutes a predicate drug-trafficking offense under 18 U.S.C. § 924(c), Congress defined trafficking to include simple drug possession, which may encompass end users—the consumers. *See* 18 U.S.C. § 924(c)(2); *see also United States v. Knox*, 950 F.2d 516, 518 (8th Cir.1991). The term "trafficking" does not inherently exempt purchasers.

While the defendants are correct that § 1591 does not criminalize engaging in a commercial sex act with a minor, it does not necessarily follow that the statute only applies to suppliers. The defendants fail to explain why a purchaser who entices, transports, or obtains a child "for the purpose of a commercial sex act" cannot be guilty of both sex trafficking under § 1591 and subsequently engaging in the commercial sex act prohibited by another applicable statute. That the defendants can describe hypothetical circumstances under which a purchaser could engage in a commercial sex act without first enticing, transporting, or obtaining a child does not persuade us that § 1591 categorically excludes a purchaser whose conduct otherwise violates the statute by enticing, transporting or obtaining the minor.

The defendants' argument that the disjunctive string of verbs in § 1591(a)(1) limits the ordinarily broad term "obtains" so sharply that it reveals a latent exemption for purchasers and demonstrates § 1591 could not possibly apply to them is based on their mistaken belief that a purchaser cannot commit any of the other "predicate conduct" § 1591 prohibits. We agree with the government that "[t]he fact the district court read the seven verbs listed in § 1591 to describe predicate acts does not mean that a customer or purchaser cannot engage in at least some of the prohibited conduct." ...

We also reject the defendants' arguments that Congress could not have intended that § 1591 apply to purchasers because (1) applying § 1591 to purchasers somehow renders other parts of the TVPA meaningless, and (2) other statutes already prohibit engaging in sex with minors. *See, e.g.,* 18 U.S.C. § 2241(c) (aggravated sexual assault); 18 U.S.C. § 2422(b) (coercion and enticement); and 18 U.S.C. § 2423(b) (transportation of minors). To begin, we do not conclude § 1591 criminalizes the act of engaging in a commercial sex act with a minor. Rather, we conclude a purchaser may be convicted for committing an act prohibited by § 1591 without ever engaging in a sex act.[7] ...

The defendants' assertion that their potential culpability under other statutes indicates Congress intended categorically to exclude purchasers from § 1591 also falls short. In enacting § 1591, Congress found

> Existing legislation and law enforcement in the United States and other countries are inadequate to deter trafficking and bring traffickers to justice, failing to reflect the gravity of the offenses involved. No comprehensive law exists in the United States that penalizes the range of offenses involved in the trafficking scheme. Instead, even the most brutal instances of trafficking in the sex industry are often punished under laws that also apply to lesser offenses, so that traffickers typically escape deserved punishment.

22 U.S.C. § 7101(b)(14). Applying § 1591 to purchasers of commercial sex acts who violate the statute despite their exposure to punishment for related crimes is entirely consistent with Congress's concerted efforts "to combat trafficking in persons" and "ensure just and effective punishment of traffickers." *Id.* at 7101(a)....

In short, "Congress knows how to craft an exception [or impose a status requirement] when it intends one." *See Jonah R. v. Carmona*, 446 F.3d 1000, 1007 (9th Cir.2006). It has not done so in § 1591.... The unambiguous text of § 1591 makes no distinction between suppliers and purchasers of commercial sex acts with children, and the defendants have failed to persuade us Congress intended a supplier-only limitation or a purchaser exception in § 1591 that Congress never stated. We hold § 1591 applies to a purchaser of commercial sex acts who violates the statute's terms.[8]

The question remains whether the defendants' conduct violates §§ 1591 and 1594(a). Having thoroughly reviewed the record in each case, we conclude Jungers's and Bonestroo's respective juries reasonably found each of them guilty beyond a reasonable doubt of attempting to engage in child sex trafficking, in violation of §§ 1591 and 1594(a).... The uncontested evidence adduced at Jungers's trial, viewed "in the light most favorable to the government" along with all "reasonable inferences that support the verdict," *Ward*, 686 F.3d at 882 (quoting *Johnson*, 639 F.3d at 437–38) (internal quotation marks omitted), showed Jungers attempted to obtain an eleven-year-old girl for an hour so she could perform oral sex on him. When he arrived at the designated house, Jungers told the undercover officer he wanted to take the girl somewhere else for sex because he was uncomfortable with having sex at the house. Jungers's attempt to gain exclusive possession, custody, and control of the underage girl knowing she would be caused to engage in a commercial sex act amply supports Jungers's conviction for attempted sex trafficking.

Bonestroo presents a closer case. Bonestroo concedes the term "obtain" is "incredibly broad" and can mean acquiring, controlling, or possessing something "for a short period of time," but asserts there is no evidence he attempted to obtain or possess a minor because he was only attempting to pay for sex. We disagree.... Bonestroo arranged with undercover officers to acquire custody and control of what he believed to be fourteen-year-old twin girls without anyone else present for an hour. In negotiating the transaction, Bonestroo

---

7. Indeed, the Ninth Circuit has held that a jury can find a violation of § 1591(a) even if the minor never engages in a commercial sex act. *See United States v. Brooks*, 610 F.3d 1186, 1197 n. 4 (9th Cir.2010); *United States v. Todd*, 627 F.3d 329, 333–34 (9th Cir.2010).

8. "Because the statutory language is clear," we need not reach the defendants' arguments based on "legislative history, or the rule of lenity." *Boyle v. United States*, 556 U.S. 938, 950, 129 S.Ct. 2237, 173 L.Ed.2d 1265 (2009).

asked "How much for the twins." Bonestroo then agreed to pay $200 to get the girls alone with him in a room so he could do anything he wanted to them short of visible physical abuse. The jury reasonably found Bonestroo attempted to obtain the girls as that term is used in §§ 1591 and 1594(a)....

We reverse the judgment of acquittal entered by the district court for each defendant, and we remand the cases with instructions for the district court in each case to reinstate the jury verdict and proceed with sentencing.

United States v. Townsend

Eleventh Circuit, 2013
521 Fed. Appx. 904

PER CURIAM:

Tyrone Townsend was convicted in a jury trial of five counts related to trafficking two women—C.B. and L.F.: (1) trafficking C.B. in violation of 18 U.S.C. § 1591(a); (2) trafficking L.F. in violation of 18 U.S.C. § 1591(a); (3) knowingly transporting C.B. and L.F. in interstate commerce with the intent that they engage in prostitution in violation of 18 U.S.C. § 2421; [and] (4) knowingly inducing, enticing and coercing L.F. to travel in interstate commerce with the intent that she engage in prostitution in violation of 18 U.S.C. § 2422(a).... He was sentenced to 320 months imprisonment and 10 years supervised release....

> 18 U.S.C. § 1591(a) imposes criminal liability on [w]hoever knowingly ... in or affecting interstate or foreign commerce ... recruits, entices, harbors, transports, provides, obtains, or maintains by any means a person ... knowing, or in reckless disregard of the fact, that means of force, threats of force, fraud, coercion..., or any combination of such means will be used to cause the person to engage in a commercial sex act....

Townsend first argues that Congress did not intend for § 1591(a) to apply to willingly-recruited prostitutes, since the legislative history of the Trafficking Victims Protection Act focuses on international sex slavery and women disproportionally affected by poverty and lack of economic opportunity in their home countries. The statutory language is broader than this purpose. By its plain terms, § 1591(a) criminalizes trafficking in "person[s]," not just in slaves or women from other countries. "The first rule in statutory construction is to determine whether the language at issue has a plain and unambiguous meaning with regard to the particular dispute. If the statute's meaning is plain and unambiguous, there is no need for further inquiry." *United States v. Tobin*, 676 F.3d 1264, 1274 (11th Cir.2012) (quoting *United States v. Fisher*, 289 F.3d 1329, 1337–38 (11th Cir.2002))....

Townsend next argues that both C.B. and L.F. "recounted a relationship with Townsend that was voluntary and from which they always had opportunity to leave." Though some evidence supported that argument, C.B. and L.F. testified to the contrary. C.B. testified that although she voluntarily became a prostitute for Townsend, she remained with him out of fear after he beat and raped her. Although she left Townsend once, she testified that she went back to him partly because she was afraid that he would find her.... L.F. testified that she sought employment as a prostitute for Townsend after seeing a help wanted advertisement he posted, but a few days after she met him, he hit her, took away her passport, phone, and other personal belongings, and told her that she would have to engage in prostitution to get her belongings back. Townsend also raped her, made her perform anilingus on him, and made her have sex with C.B. while he watched. L.F. testified that she felt she could not run away because he had her belongings. She testified that he had threatened her, and that she thought he would hit her again if she did not find customers.

Townsend also argues that there was insufficient evidence to show that he raped and hit C.B. and L.F. in order to make them engage in commercial sex acts. But C.B. testified that when he was raping her, he told her that he was doing so because she was not bringing in enough prostitution money. She also said that his raping, beating, and threatening her made her engage in more commercial sex acts. L.F. testified that Townsend threatened her, that she did not feel she was able to leave him because he took her belongings, and that she engaged in prostitution when she did not want to because of Townsend's behavior towards her. Whether to believe C.B. and L.F. was up to the jury. We are required to resolve credibility questions favorably to the verdict....

Townsend also argues that because C.B. and L.F. were recruited willingly, there is insufficient evidence to show that he knew at the time he recruited them that he would use force, threats of force, or fraud to get them to engage in commercial sex acts. The jury could infer from his prior use of force that he intended, and therefore knew, that he would use it to make them engage in commercial sex. *See United States v. Todd*, 627 F.3d 329, 333–34 (9th Cir.2010). Additionally, the jury could reasonably conclude from the evidence that Townsend was using force and threats of force to make C.B. and L.F. engage in commercial sex when he was harboring and maintaining them after their initial recruitment. There was therefore sufficient evidence to find Townsend guilty of counts 1 and 2....

Townsend argues that there was insufficient evidence to convict him of violating 18 U.S.C. § 2422(a) by knowingly inducing, enticing, or coercing L.F. to travel in interstate commerce with the intent that she engage in prostitution. L.F. testified that she voluntarily traveled to Virginia in order to become Townsend's prostitute. However, she testified that he took her to Florida so that she could engage in commercial sex acts, and that she traveled with him because she was afraid that if she refused he would hit her and keep her passport and other belongings. Her testimony was sufficient for a jury to convict Townsend of violating § 2422(a)....

Townsend argues that count 3 (violating § 2421 by knowingly transporting C.B. and L.F. in interstate commerce with the intent that they engage in prostitution), is subsumed within counts 1 and 2 (trafficking C.B. and L.F. in violation of § 1591(a)), and count 4 (violating § 2422(a) by knowingly inducing, enticing, and coercing C.B. and L.F. to travel in interstate commerce with the intent that they engage in prostitution). Both Townsend and the government agree that the test in *Blockburger v. United States*, 284 U.S. 299, 52 S.Ct. 180, 76 L.Ed. 306 (1932) applies, and that there is no double jeopardy so long as each offense requires proof of an element that the other does not. *United States v. Hassoun*, 476 F.3d 1181, 1186 (11th Cir.2007).... Counts 3 and 4 have different elements. Count 3 requires knowing transportation, whereas count 4 requires that the defendant have knowingly induced, enticed, or coerced a person to travel. *See Wagner v. United States*, 171 F.2d 354, 364 (5th Cir.1948); *United States v. Williams*, 291 F.3d 1180, 1187 (9th Cir.2002), overruled on other grounds by *United States v. Gonzales*, 506 F.3d 940 (9th Cir.2007) (en banc). Thus count 3 is not a lesser included offense of count 4.

Counts 1 and 2 (sex trafficking) require that the defendant know or recklessly disregard the fact that means of force, threats of force, fraud, coercion or a combination of the above will be used to cause a person to engage in commercial sex acts. 18 U.S.C. § 1591(a). Count 3 (transportation) does not require knowledge or disregard of the fact that force, fraud, or coercion may be used. 18 U.S.C. § 2421. Count 3 is not a lesser-included offense of the sex trafficking counts because count 3 requires intent that the victim engage in prostitution or other illegal sex acts, whereas the trafficking counts require only knowledge or reckless disregard of the fact that a victim will be caused to engage in commercial sex. "Thus, for example, if a sex trafficker arranged for a ... victim to be transported to a pimp in another state, the trafficker might *know* that the victim would be caused to engage in a commercial sex act without actually having any specific intent that the victim do so. In that case, the sex trafficker could be convicted of violating § 1591(a), but not [the transport offense]." *United States v. Brooks*, 610 F.3d 1186, 1195 (9th Cir.2010). Count 3 (transporting) is not a lesser-included offense of counts 1 and 2 (sex trafficking), and Townsend was not subjected to double jeopardy. *See Blockburger*, 284 U.S. at 304, 52 S.Ct. 180. [I]t was not error to charge Townsend with counts 1 through 4....

Townsend argues that unlawful restraint of a victim is intrinsic to counts 1 and 2, his § 1591(a) sex trafficking offenses. However, § 1591(a) requires knowledge or reckless disregard of the fact that "means of force, threats of force, fraud, coercion ... or any combination of such means will be used...." 18 U.S.C. § 1591(a). Because the sex trafficking offenses could be accomplished without force, by means such as threats, fraud, and withholding L.F.'s passport, physical restraint was not necessarily intrinsic and an element of the offense itself.

In light of the foregoing, we affirm.

AFFIRMED.

Notes

Sex trafficking is a borderless crime having domestic, international, and global consequences. The Optional Protocol to the United Nations Convention on the Rights of the Child on the Sale of Children, Child Prostitution, and Child Pornography, available at http://www.ohchr.org/Documents/ProfessionalInterest/crc-sale.pdf (2002), is one of several international treaties to combat the problem. Other protocols that address human trafficking with international influence include The Protocol to Prevent, Suppress and Punish Trafficking in Persons, Especially Women and Children, The Convention on the Elimination of All Forms of Discrimination against Women, and The United Nations Convention Against Transnational Organized Crime. *See* Pinghua Sun & Yan Xie, *Human Trafficking and Sex Slavery in the Modern World*, 7 ALBANY GOV'T L. REV. 91, 102–06 (2014) (calling for joint efforts on an international, national, and local level). The Victims of Trafficking and Violence Protection Act of 2000 ("Victims Protection Act" or VPA) (22 U.S.C. 7101 to 7112), now the Trafficking Victims Protection Reauthorization Act of 2013 (TVPRA), is the most significant effort by the United States to contribute to the international efforts to combat sex trafficking. For discussion of the VPA, see Cheryl Nelson Butler, *Kids for Sale: Does America Recognize its Own Sexually Exploited Minors as Victims of Human Trafficking?*, 44 SETON HALL L. REV. 833 (2014); Cheryl Nelson Butler, *Making the Grade: The U.S. TIP Report & the Fight Against Domestic Child Sex Trafficking*, 67 SMU L. REV. 341 (2014); Susan Tiefenbrun, *The Saga of Susannah: A U.S. Remedy for Sex Trafficking in Women: The Victims of Trafficking and Violence Protection Act of 2000*, 2002 UTAH L. REV. 107 (2002). *See also* THE WHITE HOUSE, COORDINATION, COLLABORATION, CAPACITY: FEDERAL STRATEGIC PLAN ON SERVICE FOR VICTIMS OF HUMAN TRAFFICKING IN THE UNITED STATES 2013–2017 (2013), available at http://www.ovc.gov/pubs/FederalHuman TraffickingStrategicPlan.pdf.

Within the United States, the federal laws addressing interstate and foreign travel involving sexual exploitation of minors play a critical role in the effectiveness of international protocols combating the problem of sex trafficking. Likewise, there are a variety of state law approaches to combat the sex trafficking industry. For discussion of various state efforts, see Stephanie Silvano, *Fighting A Losing Battle to Win the War: Can States Combat Domestic Minor Sex Trafficking Despite CDA Preemption*, 83 FORDHAM L. REV. 375 (2014); Nicole Tutrani, *Open for the Wrong Kind of Business: An Analysis of Virginia's Legislative Approach to Combating Commercial Sexual Exploitation*, 26 REGENT UNIV. L. REV. 487 (2013–2014); Melissa Dess, *Walking the Freedom Trail: An Analysis of the Massachusetts Human Trafficking Statute and Its Potential to Combat Child Sex Trafficking*, 33 B.C. J.L. & SOC. JUST. 147 (2013); Tessa L. Dysart, *The Protected Innocence Initiative: Building Protective State Law Regimes for America's Sex-Trafficked Children*, 44 COLUM. HUM. RIGHTS L. REV. 619 (2013); Elizabeth LaMura, *Sex Trafficking of Minors in the United States: State Legislative Response Models*, 33 CHILDREN'S LEGAL RIGHTS J. 301 (2013) (discussing federal, state, and non-profit organization frameworks); Leslie Klaassen, *Breaking the Victimization Cycle: Domestic Minor Trafficking in Kansas*, 52 WASHBURN L.J. 581 (2013) (discussing history of Kansas's human trafficking statutes); Amy Muslim, Melissa Labriola, and Michael Rempel, *The Commercial Sexual Exploitation of Children in New York City*, 218 PLI/CRIM 393 (2009); but these vary and often conflict with federal law and other state law approaches, specifically with respect to state "safe harbor" laws and the issue of the capacity of a minor to consent to prostitution. *See* Butler, *supra*, at 844. *See, e.g., In re B.W.*, 313 S.W.3d 818 (Tex. 2010) (rejecting prosecution of thirteen-year-old prostitute despite state prostitution laws). In 2013, the National Conference of Commissioners on Uniform State Laws completed the Uniform Act on Prevention of and Remedies for Human Trafficking, which seeks to increase punishment for exploiters and protect minor victims of prostitution. The Uniform Act also has an education and public awareness component. In 2014, fourteen states introduced Bills to adopt the Uniform Act. In addition, many individual states adopt laws govern specific aspects of the prostitution industry involving minors. The material that follows discusses some of the criminal aspects of child prostitution at the federal and the state levels.

C. Prostitution

Cheryl Nelson Butler

Kids for Sale: Does America Recognize its Own Sexually Exploited
Minors as Victims of Human Trafficking?

44 SETON HALL L. REV. 833 (2014)

In the United States, ... prostitution is a major lucrative enterprise in which pimps make millions of dollars in profits.... The most profitable legal paradigm involves "pimps"—adults who use psychological methods to target minors because they are "easier to manipulate, work harder to earn money and are more marketable." ... The minors may reach quotas of as much as $400 a day and then turn over all of the money to the adult.... The majority of these child prostitution cases in the United States involve native, as opposed to foreign, youth.... According to the United States Senate, 200,000 to 300,000 domestic minors are at risk of exploitation by America's commercial sex industry.... Moreover, the average age in which minors are trafficked for commercial sex is between twelve and fourteen years old.... Children as young as five years old have been sold for sex, some even by their own parents.... In attempts to escape sexual abuse in their homes, many kids run away from home only to be lured into the commercial sex industry.... They become at risk for all forms of sex trafficking, including pornography, stripping, modeling, and prostitution.... If arrested or detained for prostitution, they face criminal prosecution or adjudication as juvenile delinquents....

Id. at 835 (footnotes omitted).

Notes

Recall that federal law prohibits any parent, guardian, or custodian from buying or selling a child for the purpose of the child engaging in child pornography. *See* 18 U.S.C. § 2251A (Selling or Buying of Children). Likewise, state law may also prohibit a parent, guardian, or custodian from transferring custody of a child with knowledge that the child will engage in prostitution. *See, e.g.,* FLA. STAT. ANN. § 796.035 (Selling or Buying of Minors into Prostitution; penalties). Federal and state laws governing the prostitution of minors cover a broad scope of specific crimes. *See, e.g.,* 18 U.S.C. § 2422(a) (Coercion and enticement); CAL. PENAL CODE §§ 261.9 (Solicitation to engage in prostitution with a person under age 18; additional penalties), 266 (Inveiglement or enticement of unmarried female under 18 for purposes of prostitution, etc....), 266h (Pimping and pimping a minor; punishment), 266i (Pandering and pandering with a minor; punishment), 267 (Abduction; person under 18 for purpose of prostitution; punishment), 309 (Admitting or keeping minors in house of prostitution); COL. REV. STAT. ANN. §§ 18-7-402 (Soliciting for Child Prostitution), 18-7-403 (Pandering of a child), 18-7-403.5 (Procurement of a child), 18-7-404 (Keeping a place of child prostitution); 18-7-405.5 (Inducement of child prostitution), 18-7-406 (Patronizing a prostituted child); CONN. GEN. STAT. ANN. § 53a-86 (Promoting prostitution in the first degree: Class B felony); FLA. STAT. ANN. § 796.03 (Procuring person under age of 18 for prostitution); GA. CODE ANN. § 16-6-13 (Punishment for keeping a place of prostitution, pimping or pandering); 720 ILL. COMP. STAT. §§ 5/11-14.4 (Promoting juvenile prostitution), 5/11-18.1 (Patronizing a minor engaged in prostitution); NEV. REV. STAT. §§ 201.300 (Pandering: Definition; penalties; exception), 201.360 (Placing person in house of prostitution; penalties); 21 OKL. STAT. §§ 1029 (Engaging in prostitution, etc.—Soliciting or procuring—Residing or being in place for prohibited purpose—Aiding, abetting or participating—Child prostitution—Presumption of coercion), 1040.13a (Facilitating, encouraging, offering or soliciting sexual conduct or engaging in sexual communication with a minor or person believed to be a minor). The material that follows addresses several aspects of child prostitution.

1. Coercion and Enticement

United States v. Rashkovski

Ninth Circuit, 2002
301 F.3d 1133

WARDLAW, Circuit Judge....

In March 1999, during an investigation of prostitution rings run through Long Beach hotels, police sergeant Paul LeBaron noticed a small ad in the *L.A. Weekly*'s Adult Classified section reading "European Paradise Birds: Find your paradise." Rashkovski and Kozlova answered the ad's phone line and offered to send a "girl" to LeBaron for $250 per hour.... A few hours later, Elena Zimina showed up at LeBaron's Hilton hotel room. She massaged his back and gestured towards his groin, asking in broken English if he wanted "a kiss." Police officers burst into the room and arrested Zimina for prostitution.... Zimina would later testify that she had been a prostitute for several months before her arrest, having traveled from Russia to the United States in December 1998 to work as an "escort" girl. Rashkovski and Kozlova had helped her cross illegally into the United States via Mexico, rented her an apartment in Los Angeles, and explained that she would be working as a prostitute, charging $200 per hour, of which she could keep $30. When Zimina had refused, Rashkovski and Kozlova had screamed vulgarities at her and threatened to have her put in jail for illegal immigration. Unable to speak English or travel without their permission, Zimina was trapped in their employ until April 1999, when she escaped with the help of a friend.

To recruit more Russian women, Rashkovski and Kozlova flew to Moscow in June 1999 and held meetings to promote the limitless job opportunities in the dynamic field of prostitution in the United States. To the attendees at one of the meetings, which included Vlada Toulousheva and Evgenia Tsimbal, Rashkovski explained that although it was unlikely he could get visas for all of the women, he would make their travel arrangements and pay for the plane tickets. The women would repay him with the money they made in his "established prostitution business"—$60 per hour of the $200 they would charge.... Seizing upon the plan as the way to escape their precarious circumstances in Russia, Toulousheva and Tsimbal flew into Mexico with three other women in August 1999. Rashkovski met them at the Grand Hotel in Tijuana and prepped them for a late night border crossing, instructing them to dress as though they had been at a discotheque, to appear drunk, and to answer "Yes, U.S." to any questions asked by border officials.... Shortly after midnight on August 9, Rashkovski, Toulousheva, and Tsimbal attempted to drive into the United States in Rashkovski's car. When both women claimed American citizenship but could not speak any English, immigration agents grew suspicious and detained Rashkovski.

A federal grand jury indicted Rashkovski and Kozlova for conspiracy to bring in illegal aliens for commercial gain, 8 U.S.C. § 1324(a)(2)(B)(ii); importation of aliens for immoral purposes, 8 U.S.C. § 1328; persuading, inducing, or enticing foreign travel for the purposes of prostitution, 18 U.S.C. § 2422(a); and aiding and abetting, 18 U.S.C. § 2.... Following trial, the jury found Rashkovski and Kozlova guilty of all counts. The court sentenced Rashkovski to concurrent terms totaling 60 months. Kozlova did not appear for sentencing and remains a fugitive....

Two counts of the indictment relating to Toulousheva and Tsimbal charged Rashkovski with violating 18 U.S.C. § 2422(a), which states:

> Whoever knowingly persuades, induces, entices, or coerces any individual to travel in interstate or foreign commerce, ... to engage in prostitution, or in any sexual activity for which any person can be charged with a criminal offense, or attempts to do so, shall be fined under this title or imprisoned not more than 10 years, or both.

Rashkovski argues that insufficient evidence supported his convictions under these two counts because: (1) he did not persuade, induce, entice, or coerce Toulousheva and Tsimbal to travel because they willingly traveled to the United States; and (2) they had no real intention of being prostitutes.... At trial, both women testified that they attended the recruiting meetings voluntarily. Tsimbal sought to leave "criminal Moscow" behind, while Toulousheva viewed America "as a country where you can feel safe." Both testified that, while they viewed Rashkovski's scheme as a prime opportunity to flee Russia for the United States, they did not plan to work as prostitutes once they arrived in the country.... In light of this testimony, Rashkovski first contends that because the women desired of their own accord to travel internationally, he could not have persuaded, induced, enticed, or coerced them to do so, as required under § 2422(a). Upon examination of the relevant language, we conclude that Rashkovski's argument is at odds with the plain meaning of the statute....

None of the statutory language requires Rashkovski to have created out of whole cloth the women's desire to go to the United States; it merely requires that he have convinced or influenced Toulousheva and Tsimbal to actually undergo the journey, or made the possibility more appealing. Thus, it is not significant that Toulousheva and Tsimbal had preexisting wishes to leave Russia for the United States, especially considering that they never acted upon those desires until Rashkovski made it attainable.... The testimony showed that Rashkovski offered to make and pay for the necessary travel arrangements to allow Tsimbal and Toulousheva to go to the United States. That the women accepted Rashkovski's offer and thereafter traveled with his assistance is sufficient evidence from which a rational jury could conclude that Rashkovski persuaded, induced, or enticed them to travel. *See United States v. Pelton*, 578 F.2d 701, 713 (8th Cir.1978) (concluding that defendant had induced a woman to travel by making her travel arrangements, even though the woman had been willing to travel to work as a prostitute). "When an offer to travel interstate for purposes of prostitution elicits a positive response from a woman to whom it is made, it constitutes a requisite inducement under the statute." *Id.*

Rashkovski next contends that he could not have induced or enticed the women to travel "to engage in prostitution" under §2422(a) because Toulousheva and Tsimbal both declared on the stand that they had no intention of working as prostitutes once they reached the United States. However, it is the defendant's intent that forms the basis for his criminal liability, not the victims'. The question under §2422(a) is whether Rashkovski persuaded or enticed the women to travel intending them to engage in prostitution. This is evident from *Simpson v. United States*, 245 F. 278, 279 (9th Cir.1917), in which the defendant was charged with violating section 3 of the Mann Act, 36 Stat. 825, now codified at 18 U.S.C. §2422. *See* Act of June 24, 1948, ch. 645, 62 Stat. 683, 812 (revising and codifying the Mann Act). There, we affirmed the sufficiency of the indictment, which "charged that *the defendant's purpose* [for inducing travel] was to have the woman 'manage a house of prostitution.'" *Simpson*, 245 F. at 279 (emphasis added) (holding that the indictment set forth "the offense in the language of the statute ... with sufficient particularity"). Under §2422(a), the relevant intent remains the defendant's. *United States v. Drury*, 582 F.2d 1181, 1184 (8th Cir.1978) ("To have committed a Mann Act violation, appellant must have knowingly persuaded the women to travel across state lines with the intention that they engage in prostitution."). Whether Toulousheva and Tsimbal themselves intended to engage in prostitution is thus immaterial to Rashkovski's criminal culpability.

Evidence that Rashkovski recruited Russian women for his prostitution business, coupled with Elena Zimina's testimony that Rashkovski had forced her into prostitution after bringing her into the country, sufficiently demonstrated that he intended to prostitute Toulousheva and Tsimbal when he persuaded, induced, or enticed them to travel. Because both of Rashkovski's arguments fail, we conclude that sufficient evidence supported his convictions under §2422(a)....

Rashkovski's conviction and sentence are therefore

AFFIRMED.

2. Pandering

People v. Dixon

Court of Appeal, Third District, California, 2011
119 Cal. Rptr. 3d 901, 191 Cal. App. 4th 1154

SCOTLAND, J....

A jury convicted Todd Robert Dixon of pandering. (Pen.Code, §266i, subd. (a)(2); further section references are to this code). As was charged here, a person who "[b]y promises, threats, violence, or by any device or scheme causes, induces, persuades or encourages another person to become a prostitute" is guilty of pandering. (§ 266i, subd. (a)(2).) ... Defendant's conviction was based on a text message he sent to 17-year-old L.N. that read, "'U with me, 1 night, $200 or more.'" On appeal, defendant contends there was insufficient evidence to support his conviction because "a person who seeks sex for *himself*, and uses the money as an inducement, is not a panderer." ...

Defendant was a family friend of L.N. In December 2007, when defendant was 39 or 40 years old, L.N. received a call from him on her cell phone. L.N. was 17 years old. Defendant asked if L.N. was alone because he wanted to discuss something private and personal. He then asked what she was doing for New Year's Eve. L.N. replied that she was babysitting her younger brother. Defendant asked whether she wanted to make a quick, easy $200. She responded, "[i]t depends," and asked if he wanted her to babysit his children. Defendant said that was possible but then started joking about the $200. Defendant ended the call by saying he would call back when it was "legit." ... Fifteen minutes later, L.N. received a text message from defendant that read, "'U with me, 1 night, $200 or more.'" One and a half to two hours later, L.N. received another text message that read, "[W]hat do you say?" L.N. concluded that defendant was not talking about babysitting and instead was wanting to be alone with her for "sexual intercourse or something like that."

L.N. went home and showed the text messages to her parents. The next day, L.N. and her stepfather went to the police department.... [Using L.N.'s cell phone, a detective texted the defendant and arranged an alleged meeting between L.N. and the defendant]. About 10:00 p.m. the same day, as defendant left room 206 carrying a beer, police stationed at the motel nabbed him. On his person, officers found a cell phone and $226. In the room, officers found beer and a toiletry kit containing "anal lube." In his truck, they found a rubber sex toy, a photo of a penis, 26 DVDs with legal adult pornography, and a portable DVD player....

The sufficiency of evidence argument raised here is one of law. Does pandering require "simply offering money to someone in exchange for sex," as the People argue, or does it require more, namely, causing someone to become a prostitute to satisfy the desires of *another* person, as defendant argues? ... The statute on pandering is silent on this issue.... In relevant part, it states that a person who "[b]y promises, threats, violence, or by any device or scheme causes, induces, persuades or encourages another person to become a prostitute" is guilty of pandering. (§ 266i, subd. (a)(2).)

The instruction on pandering is similarly silent. As was given here, it requires that (1) "The defendant used promises or any device or scheme to encourage L.N. to become a prostitute"; (2) "The defendant intended to influence L.N. to be a prostitute"; and (3) "L.N. was over the age of 16 at the time the defendant acted." It defines prostitute as "a person who engages in sexual intercourse or any lewd act with another person in exchange for money." ... However, case law from California's Supreme Court informs the issue. [*People v. Roderigas* (1874) 49 Cal. 9, 11 (hereafter *Roderigas*)]. Roderigas was charged with violating section 266, which punishes "every person who, by any false pretenses, false representation, or other fraudulent means, procures any female to have illicit carnal connection with any man." The indictment alleged that he "procure[d] [a 16-year-old] female to have illicit carnal connection with himself...." (*Roderigas, supra,* at pp. 9–10.) Roderigas argued the statute did not apply to him. The Supreme Court agreed, explaining:

"To 'procure a female to have illicit carnal connection with any man,' is the offense of a procurer or procuress-of a pander." (*Roderigas, supra,* 49 Cal. at p. 11.) The "recognized meaning" of procure "refers to the act of a person 'who procures the gratification of the passion of lewdness for another.' This is its distinctive signification, as uniformly understood and applied." (*Ibid.*) In so recognizing, *Roderigas* specifically rejected the People's argument that, because "a seducer is a person who prevails upon a female ... to have illicit carnal connection with himself, he is thereby brought within the mere words of the statute, and so made liable to the punishment it inflicts." (*Ibid.*) The Supreme Court stated, "this view cannot be maintained by any rule of fair interpretation." (*Ibid.*) Roderigas "cannot ... be considered to have been both procurer and seducer at the same time, and in one and the same instance, without utterly confounding distinctions and definitions well established, and universally recognized." (*Ibid.*)[1]

The California Supreme Court's analysis of the meaning of "pander" is well reasoned and persuasive, and we follow it here. (See *Dyer v. Superior Court* (1997) 56 Cal.App.4th 61, 67, 65 Cal.Rptr.2d 85 ["dictum of the Supreme Court ...'"carries persuasive weight and should be followed where it demonstrates a thorough analysis of the issue or reflects compelling logic"""].) The ordinary meaning of "pander" is to provide gratification for the desires of *others.* (Webster's 3d New Intern. Dict. (1993) p. 1629.) As to the sexual desires of others, "pandering" means the business of recruiting a prostitute, finding a place of business for a prostitute, or soliciting customers for a prostitute. (Black's Law Dict. (7th ed.1999) p. 1135; see *United States v. Williams* (2008) 553 U.S. 285, 308, fn. 1, 128 S.Ct. 1830, 1847, fn. 1, 170 L.Ed.2d 650, 672, fn. 1.) ... Defendant does not meet the definition of a panderer. He sought to have sex with L.N. and offered her money to persuade her to do so. There is no evidence that he intended to have her become a prostitute for others.

Although the Supreme Court's decision in *Roderigas, supra,* 49 Cal. 9, is discussed at length by defendant, the People ignore the case completely and cite *Mathews, supra,* 119 Cal.App.3d 309, 173 Cal.Rptr. 820, only in a footnote of their brief, stating nothing more than that the case "did not even involve an offer of payment for sex nor did it involve ... section 266i." Instead, the People rely on a number of cases they contend stand for the proposition that pandering is "simply offering money to someone in exchange for sex." But those cases do not stand for that proposition. (See e.g., *People v. Mathis* (1985) 173 Cal.App.3d 1251, 1255–1256, 219 Cal.Rptr. 693 [sufficient evidence of pandering, but reversal was required because the jury was incorrectly instructed that procuring could include merely assisting somebody to become a prostitute]; *People v. Patton* (1976) 63 Cal.App.3d 211, 215, 218, 133 Cal.Rptr. 533 [no defense to pandering that the woman whom the defendant solicited to work as a prostitute had already been one]; ... *People v. Bradshaw* (1973) 31 Cal.App.3d 421, 425–426, 107 Cal.Rptr. 256 [no defense to pandering that a defendant believed the woman he solicited to enter a house of prostitution under his supervision was already a prostitute who simply wanted "a new managerial arrangement"]; *People v. Lax* (1971) 20 Cal.App.3d 481, 483–487, 97 Cal.Rptr. 722 [pandering applied to a defendant who asked a woman to become a prostitute, promising her new clothes and an apartment]; *People v. Frey* (1964) 228 Cal.App.2d 33, 40, 50, 39 Cal.Rptr. 49 [pandering applied to a defendant who encouraged a prostitute to live in his hotel and received a share of her earnings].)

---

1. *Mathews v. Superior Court of Butte County* (1981) 119 Cal.App.3d 309, 173 Cal.Rptr. 820 (hereafter *Mathews*), applied *Roderigas* and issued a writ of prohibition preventing further proceedings against Mathews under section 266. (*Mathews, supra,* at p. 312, 173 Cal.Rptr. 820.) Mathews had snuck into a woman's bedroom pretending to be her lover and fondled her. The People charged him with violating section 266. This court held the charges "cannot stand. [Mathew's] conduct, reprehensible though it was, did not violate section 266. If there is a statutory oversight in this area of the penal law, the Legislature may address it." (*Ibid.*)

Unlike the cases the People cite, the evidence here established that defendant offered L.N. money to have sex only *with him*. As we have explained, under the rationale of *Roderigas, supra*, 49 Cal. at page 11, defendant's actions do not make him a panderer....

The judgment is reversed.

We concur: ROBIE, Acting P.J., and BUTZ, J.

California v. Freeman

Supreme Court of the United States, 1989
488 U.S. 1311, 109 S. Ct. 854

Justice O'CONNOR, Circuit Justice.

The State of California requests that, as Circuit Justice, I stay the enforcement of the judgment of the Supreme Court of California pursuant to 28 U.S.C. §2101(f) pending the disposition of a petition for certiorari ... to review that judgment. Because I think it unlikely that four Justices would vote to grant certiorari, see *Hicks v. Feiock*, 479 U.S. 1305, 1306, 107 S.Ct. 259, 93 L.Ed.2d 237 (1986) (O'CONNOR, J., in chambers), I deny the application for issuance of a stay.

In its petition for certiorari, California seeks review of the State Supreme Court's judgment reversing the conviction of respondent Freeman for pandering under Cal.Penal Code Ann. §266i (West 1988). 46 Cal.3d 419, 250 Cal.Rptr. 598, 758 P.2d 1128 (1988). Freeman is a producer and director of pornographic films who hired and paid adults to perform sexual acts before his film cameras. In 1983, Freeman was arrested and charged with five counts of pandering based on the hiring of five such performers. He was not charged with violation of any of California's obscenity laws. Freeman was tried before a jury and convicted on all five counts of pandering; the State Court of Appeal affirmed the judgment of conviction. 198 Cal.App.3d 292, 233 Cal.Rptr. 510 (1987).

On discretionary review, the California Supreme Court first considered the relevant statutory language of the State Penal Code. In relevant part, §266i of the Penal Code provides that a person is guilty of felonious pandering if that person "procure[s] another person for the purpose of prostitution...." Prostitution, in turn, is defined in §647(b) of the Penal Code as "any lewd act between persons for money or other consideration." Finally, "'for a "lewd" or "dissolute" act to constitute "prostitution," the genitals, buttocks, or female breast, of either the prostitute or the customer must come in contact with some part of the body of the other for the purpose of *sexual arousal or gratification of the customer or of the prostitute*.'" 46 Cal.3d, at 424, 250 Cal.Rptr., at 600, 758 P.2d, at 1130 (emphasis in original), quoting *People v. Hill*, 103 Cal.App.3d 525, 534–535, 163 Cal.Rptr. 99, 105 (1980).

Interpreting these definitions of terms relevant to the state pandering statute, the State Supreme Court held that "in order to constitute prostitution, the money or other consideration must be paid *for the purpose of sexual arousal or gratification*." 46 Cal.3d, at 424, 250 Cal.Rptr., at 600, 758 P.2d, at 1131 (emphasis in original). Applying this principle to Freeman, the court characterized the payments made to the performers as "acting fees" and held that "there is no evidence that [Freeman] paid the acting fees for the purposes of sexual arousal or gratification, his own or the actors." *Id.*, at 424–425, 250 Cal.Rptr., at 600, 758 P.2d, at 1131. Thus, the court held, "[Freeman] did not engage in either the requisite conduct nor did he have the requisite mens rea or purpose to establish procurement for purposes of prostitution." *Ibid.* In the succeeding section of its opinion, the California Supreme Court went on to observe that "even if [Freeman's] conduct could somehow be found to come within the definition of 'prostitution' literally, the application of the pandering statute to the hiring of actors to perform in the production of a nonobscene motion picture would impinge unconstitutionally upon First Amendment values." *Ibid.*

California, in its petition for certiorari, would have us review this First Amendment holding of the State Supreme Court. I recognize that the State has a strong interest in controlling prostitution within its jurisdiction and, at some point, it must certainly be true that otherwise illegal conduct is not made legal by being filmed. I do not, however, think it likely that four Justices would vote to grant the petition because in my view this Court lacks jurisdiction to hear the petition. It appears "clear from the face of the [California Supreme Court's] opinion," *Michigan v. Long*, 463 U.S. 1032, 1041, 103 S.Ct. 3469, 3476, 77 L.Ed.2d 1201 (1983), that its analysis of the pandering provision of the State Penal Code constitutes an adequate and independent state ground of decision. Interpretations of state law by a State's highest court are, of course, binding upon this Court. *O'Brien v. Skinner*, 414 U.S. 524, 531, 94 S.Ct. 740, 743, 38 L.Ed.2d 702 (1974); *Murdock v. City of Memphis*, 20 Wall. 590, 22 L.Ed. 429 (1875). Here, the California Supreme Court has decided that Freeman's hiring and paying of performers for pornographic films does not constitute pandering under § 266i of the California Penal Code. That is an adequate ground for reversing Freeman's conviction....

There is language early in the California Supreme Court's discussion section observing that "the prosecution of [Freeman] under the pandering statute must be viewed as a somewhat transparent attempt at an 'end run' around the First Amendment and the state obscenity laws. Landmark decisions of this court and the United States Supreme Court compel us to reject such an effort." 46 Cal.3d, at 423, 250 Cal.Rptr., at 599, 758 P.2d, at 1130. Nevertheless, in light of the subsequent clear holding based exclusively on the state pandering statute, as well as the State Supreme Court's doubts in its discussion of the First Amendment whether "[Freeman's] conduct could *somehow* be found to come within the definition of 'prostitution' literally," *id.*, at 425, 250 Cal.Rptr., at 600, 758 P.2d, at 1131 (emphasis added), I conclude that the state court's statutory holding is independent from its discussion of the First Amendment and was not driven by that discussion. Because the decision of the California Supreme Court rests on an adequate and independent state ground, the State of California's application for a stay of enforcement of the judgment of the California Supreme Court is denied.

So ordered.

3. Pimping

Allen v. Stratton

United States District Court of California, 2006
428 F. Supp. 2d 1064

SCHIAVELLI, District Judge....

On July 3, 2000, in Los Angeles County Superior Court case no. PA035272, a jury convicted petitioner Troy Allen, aka Troy Bernard Allen, of two counts of pimping in violation of California Penal Code ("P.C.") § 266h(a), and in a bifurcated proceeding, the trial court found petitioner had suffered four prior convictions for "serious" or "violent" felonies within the meaning of P.C. §§ 667(b)–(i) and 1170.12(a)–(d) and four prior convictions for which he served a term of imprisonment but did not remain free of custody for five years thereafter within the meaning of P.C. § 667.5(b).... [2] Petitioner was sentenced under the Three Strikes law to the total term of 54 years to life in state prison.... Petitioner appealed his convictions and sentence to the California Court of Appeal, which affirmed the judgment in an unpublished opinion filed October 4, 2001....

In affirming the trial court's judgment, the California Court of Appeal made the following findings of fact regarding the circumstances underlying petitioner's convictions: ... [footnote omitted] Police Officers Trevin Grant and Pedro Barba stopped petitioner for a traffic violation while he was driving a pickup truck. This was in the City of San Fernando, on January 13, 2000. The officers spoke with petitioner for a few minutes, ascertained that he was from Sacramento, searched the vehicle with his consent, and released him without a citation.... Ten minutes later, the same officers stopped Tyona Dodson and Shannan Bryant on a part of San Fernando Road frequented by prostitutes and known as "the track." The officers stopped Dodson and Bryant on suspicion of prostitution, at the request of an undercover officer. Officer Grant questioned the women, learned that they were from Sacramento, and suspected that they might have a connection with petitioner. When Officer Grant mentioned petitioner's name to the women, Bryant admitted knowing him. Dodson and Bryant were taken to the police station and questioned further but were not arrested.... Petitioner's account of these stops differed in several respects. He testified that Officer Grant made the connection between him and the women only because Officer Grant had seen a photograph of Bryant when he searched the truck, which was owned by Bryant. He also testified that the search was without consent.

Police learned from Dodson and Bryant that each worked for petitioner as a prostitute for the first time during a trip to Las Vegas in November 1999, which was arranged and paid for by petitioner. During that trip, both gave part of their prostitution income to petitioner. Petitioner instructed them how much to charge for various sex acts and how to determine if clients were police.... Dodson and Bryant worked as prostitutes for petitioner during three other trips to Los Angeles, two in December 1999 and one in January 2000. On each occasion they gave part of their prostitution income to petitioner. During both December trips, petitioner stayed with them in a motel and paid for the room. In the course of all three trips, the women paid petitioner more of their prostitution income than he returned to them in money and goods. Dodson and Bryant also prostituted for petitioner in San Francisco and possibly San Diego.... Petitioner was arrested January 14, 2000, the day after the traffic stop. Petitioner denied having anything more than an "inclination" that Dodson and Bryant were prostitutes, and denied explaining to them any of the rules of prostitution, including how to determine if clients were police. He denied ever taking any money from Dodson. He admitted that he took $400 from Bryant during their Las Vegas trip, but said he did so to hold it for her at her request....

In the habeas corpus petition, petitioner raises the following claims for relief:

> Ground One — P.C. § 266h(a) is facially overbroad ... ; Ground Four — Petitioner's conviction under P.C. § 266h(a) violates petitioner's equal protection rights because it imposes more severe punishment than other similar prostitution statutes ... ; Ground Five — Petitioner's conviction under P.C. § 266h(a) violates petitioner's rights to due process and notice because the operative information did not accurately reflect the charges against him ... ;

---

2. In addition to the pimping counts, petitioner was also charged with six counts of pandering in violation of P.C. § 266i(a); however, the jury was unable to reach unanimous verdicts on those counts.... Although the jury deadlocked 9–3 in favor of conviction, the prosecution chose not to retry petitioner on the pandering counts....

The California statute under which petitioner was convicted of pimping, P.C. § 266h(a), provides:

> any person who, knowing another person is a prostitute, lives or derives support or maintenance in whole or in part from the earnings or proceeds of the person's prostitution, or from money loaned or advanced to or charged against that person by any keeper or manager or inmate of a house or other place where prostitution is practiced or allowed ... is guilty of pimping, a felony....

P.C. § 266h(a). In Ground One, petitioner claims Section 266h(a) is unconstitutionally overbroad on its face.[6] Specifically, petitioner contends P.C. § 266h(a) is overbroad because it defines a pimp to be any individual who derives any financial benefit, no matter how slight, from a person they know to be a prostitute, and such individuals include children, psychologists, and the like.... In Ground Four, petitioner claims Section 266h(a) violates the equal protection clause because it authorizes greater punishment than other criminal statutes covering prostitution-related activities. Specifically, petitioner contends he was denied equal protection of the law because pimping is a felony under Section 266h(a), whereas other crimes related to prostitution, such as keeping a house of ill-fame (P.C. § 315), keeping a disorderly house (P.C. § 316), and prevailing upon another to visit a place of prostitution (P.C. § 318), are misdemeanors....

To determine whether Section 266h(a) is unconstitutionally overbroad, this Court's "first task" is to consider "whether the enactment reaches a substantial amount of constitutionally protected conduct." *Hill*, 482 U.S. at 458–59, 107 S.Ct. at 2508 (citations omitted); *Turney*, 400 F.3d at 1200–01. "If it does not, then the overbreadth challenge must fail." *Village of Hoffman Estates v. Flipside, Hoffman Estates, Inc.*, 455 U.S. 489, 494, 102 S.Ct. 1186, 1191, 71 L.Ed.2d 362 (1982); *Hotel & Motel Ass'n of Oakland v. City of Oakland*, 344 F.3d 959, 971 (9th Cir.2003), *cert. denied*, 542 U.S. 904, 124 S.Ct. 2839, 159 L.Ed.2d 268 (2004). "Criminal statutes must be scrutinized with particular care," and "those that make unlawful a substantial amount of constitutionally protected conduct may be held facially invalid even if they also have legitimate application." *Hill*, 482 U.S. at 459, 107 S.Ct. at 2508 (citations omitted). However, "[r]arely, if ever, will an overbreadth challenge succeed against a law or regulation that is not specifically addressed to speech or to conduct necessarily associated with speech (such as picketing or demonstrating)." *Hicks*, 539 U.S. at 124, 123 S.Ct. at 2199; *see also Broadrick*, 413 U.S. at 615, 93 S.Ct. at 2917–18 ("[F]acial overbreadth adjudication is an exception to our traditional rules of practice and ... its function, a limited one at the outset, attenuates as the otherwise unprotected behavior that it forbids the State to sanction moves from 'pure speech' toward conduct...."). Petitioner "bears the burden of demonstrating, 'from the text of [the statute] and from actual fact,' that substantial overbreadth exists." *Hicks*, 539 U.S. at 122, 123 S.Ct. at 2198; *Gospel Missions of Am. v. City of Los Angeles*, 419 F.3d 1042, 1050 (9th Cir.2005).

Penal Code Section 266h is "designed 'to discourage prostitution by discouraging persons other than the prostitute from augmenting and expanding a prostitute's operation or increasing the available supply of prostitutes.'" *People v. Gibson*, 90 Cal.App.4th 371, 387, 108 Cal.Rptr.2d 809 (2001) (citations omitted); *People v. McNulty*, 202 Cal.App.3d 624, 632, 249 Cal.Rptr. 22 (1988). In this regard, Section 266h(a) regulates conduct, i.e.,

---

6. Petitioner's reply or traverse raises various other attacks on P.C. § 266h(a) not raised in the petition, such as vagueness, cruel and unusual punishment, and infringement on the prostitutes' right of intimate association. However, the Court will not consider these claims since "[a] Traverse is not the proper pleading to raise additional grounds for relief." *Cacoperdo v. Demosthenes*, 37 F.3d 504, 507 (9th Cir.1994), *cert. denied*, 514 U.S. 1026, 115 S.Ct. 1378, 131 L.Ed.2d 232 (1995).

supporting or maintaining oneself from the proceeds of another's prostitution, not speech or conduct necessarily associated with speech, *cf. Williams v. Superior Court*, 30 Cal.App.3d 8, 11, 106 Cal.Rptr. 89 (1973) (Prostitution "does not involve First Amendment [ ]or any other constitutionally protected rights."), and petitioner has not met his burden of demonstrating substantial overbreadth exists. *Hicks*, 539 U.S. at 123–24, 123 S.Ct. at 2199; *New York v. Ferber*, 458 U.S. 747, 773–74, 102 S.Ct. 3348, 3363, 73 L.Ed.2d 1113 (1982).[7] ...

Here, California has determined that the crime of pimping requires a more serious penalty than the related crime of prostitution, *People v. Smith*, 44 Cal.2d 77, 80, 279 P.2d 33 (1955); *Williams*, 30 Cal.App.3d at 14, 106 Cal.Rptr. 89; *see also People v. Pangelina*, 117 Cal.App.3d 414, 422, 172 Cal.Rptr. 661 (1981) (California courts "have recognized an affirmative legislative intent to punish prostitutes less severely than those arrested for pimping...."), since "prostitutes are criminally exploited by [pimps]." *Pangelina*, 117 Cal.App.3d at 422, 172 Cal.Rptr. 661. Thus, Section 266h(a) "'discourag[es] persons other than the prostitute from augmenting and expanding a prostitute's operation or increasing the available supply of prostitutes[,]'" *Gibson*, 90 Cal.App.4th at 387, 108 Cal.Rptr.2d 809 (citations omitted); *McNulty*, 202 Cal.App.3d at 632, 249 Cal.Rptr. 22, and punishes more severely those who corrupt others. *People v. Jeffers*, 188 Cal.App.3d 840, 856, 233 Cal.Rptr. 692 (1987); *People v. Jaimez*, 184 Cal.App.3d 146, 150, 228 Cal.Rptr. 852 (1986).

Since there is a legitimate governmental purpose related to punishing pimping as a felony, petitioner has not met his burden of showing an equal protection violation. *Robinson*, 66 F.3d at 251; *United States v. Harding*, 971 F.2d 410, 412–14 (9th Cir.1992), *cert. denied*, 506 U.S. 1070, 113 S.Ct. 1025, 122 L.Ed.2d 170 (1993); *see also Heller v. Doe*, 509 U.S. 312, 320–21, 113 S.Ct. 2637, 2643, 125 L.Ed.2d 257 (1993) ("A statute is presumed constitutional, and '[t]he burden is on the one attacking the legislative arrangement to negative every conceivable basis which might support it,' whether or not the basis has a foundation in the record." (citations omitted))…. For these reasons, the California Supreme Court's denials of Grounds One and Four was neither contrary to, nor an unreasonable application of, clearly established federal law....

4. *Procurement*

People v. Santos

Court of Appeal, Third District, California, 2011
2011 WL 1816946

NICHOLSON, J.

A jury found defendant Deonte Santos guilty on six counts of lewd conduct with a child under 14 (Pen.Code, §288, subd. (a)), ... [footnote omitted] and three counts of procuring a child to engage in a lewd act (§266j). Sentenced to 24 years in state prison,

---

7. Moreover, a natural reading of Section 266h does not support its application to a child who derives his support from his mother's prostitution, *see* P.C. §4 (Penal Code "provisions are to be construed according to the fair import of their terms, with a view to effect its objects and to promote justice."); *People v. Flores*, 51 Cal.App.4th 1199, 1204, 59 Cal.Rptr.2d 637 (1996) ("We must give penal statutes a reasonable and common sense construction."), or to an individual, such as a psychologist, for example, who provides a legitimate professional service to a prostitute. In such circumstances, even if paid with proceeds earned from prostitution, the psychologist derives his support from his own performance of services, and not directly from the prostitute's earnings. *Cf. People v. Reitzke*, 21 Cal.App. 740, 742, 132 P. 1063 (1913) (legitimate defense to pimping is that the prostitute's "money was not given for the defendant's support, but was advanced to him to enable him to engage in some legitimate business....").

defendant appeals his conviction. Defendant contends his convictions for procuring a child to engage in lewd acts are barred by section 656....

In October 2007, defendant was convicted in federal court of the use of an interstate facility to entice a minor to engage in sexual conduct or prostitution (18 U.S.C. §2422(b)) and sex trafficking of children by force, fraud, or coercion (18 U.S.C. §1591). For his crimes, defendant was sentenced to 12 years six months in federal prison.... Defendant was subsequently charged in Sacramento County Superior Court with six counts of committing a lewd and lascivious act on a minor under the age of 14 (§288, subd. (a)), and three counts of procuring a minor for the purpose of a lewd and lascivious act (§266j). Defendant pled not guilty.... Defendant then moved to dismiss the three counts of child procurement (§266j), arguing that the acts for which he was convicted in federal court under Title 18 United States Code section 1591, were the same for which he was now being tried in state court under section 266j. Thus, he argued, the prosecutor was barred under section 656 from charging him with the crime of child procurement. The trial court denied defendant's motion, finding the federal crime of child trafficking (18 U.S.C. §1591) included "a commercial element" not found in the state crime of child procurement (§266j).... Defendant appeals....

Defendant contends the trial court erred in denying his motion to dismiss. Specifically, defendant argues that although the acts constituting the state crime of child procurement are not sufficient to prove the federal crime of child trafficking, they are necessary to do so. Accordingly, he contends, prosecution of the state crimes was barred under section 656. Defendant is wrong.

"The double jeopardy clause of the Fifth Amendment to the United States Constitution does not preclude multiple convictions in different sovereign jurisdictions for the same criminal act. (*Heath v. Alabama* (1985) 474 U.S. 82, 93 [88 L.Ed.2d 387, 397].) However, a state can provide greater double jeopardy protection than is afforded by the federal Constitution. (*People v. Comingore* (1977) 20 Cal.3d 142, 145....) California has done so by statute.... Section 656 states: 'Whenever on the trial of an accused person it appears that upon a criminal prosecution under the laws of the United States, or of another state or territory of the United States based upon the act or omission in respect to which he or she is on trial, he or she has been acquitted or convicted, it is a sufficient defense.'" (*People v. Bellacosa* (2007) 147 Cal.App.4th 868, 873.)

"Decisional authorities demonstrate that in considering whether a California prosecution is barred by a prior conviction or acquittal in another jurisdiction, courts look solely to the physical acts that are necessary for conviction in each jurisdiction. If proof of the same physical act or acts is required in each jurisdiction, then the California prosecution is barred. If, however, the offenses require proof of different physical acts, then the California prosecution is not barred even though some of the elements of the offenses may overlap." (*People v. Bellacosa, supra,* 147 Cal.App.4th p. 874.) ... Thus, "if [a] federal conviction was premised upon a separate act not necessary to obtain [a] California conviction, then defendant[ ][was] not serially convicted for the same wrongful conduct." (*People v. Brown* (1988) 204 Cal.App.3d 1444, 1450.)

Defendant concedes that, unlike the state crime of child procurement, to convict him of sex trafficking, the federal prosecutor was required to prove: (1) defendant's conduct affected interstate commerce; (2) a child was provided for a commercial sex act; and (3) defendant received something "of value" in exchange for the child's sex act.[2] Defendant

2. Title 18 United States Code section 1591 provides in relevant part: "Whoever knowingly—[¶] (1) in or affecting interstate or foreign commerce, or within the special maritime and territorial

nevertheless contends these additional elements are "of no moment," because they are either jurisdictional or do not constitute physical conduct. Defendant provides no legal authority for his assertion. In any event, defendant is wrong.

At least one of the additional elements required to convict defendant of the federal crime is a physical act: defendant had to provide the child for a "commercial sex act." (18 U.S.C. § 1591(a).) A commercial sex act is defined as "any sex act, on account of which anything of value is given to or received by any person." (18 U.S.C. § 1591(e)(3).) Receiving something of value is a physical act, one the prosecution is not required to prove to convict defendant of the state crime, child procurement. (*Compare* 18 U.S.C. § 1591 *with* Pen.Code, § 266j.) Accordingly, even assuming defendant's convictions for child procurement arose from the same sex acts as those which formed the basis for his federal convictions for sex trafficking, section 656 does not bar defendant's prosecution or conviction on the crime of child procurement.[3] ...

The judgment is affirmed.

We concur: BLEASE, Acting P.J., and ROBIE, J.

---

jurisdiction of the United States, recruits, entices, harbors, transports, provides, obtains, or maintains by any means a person; or [¶] (2) benefits, financially or by receiving anything of value, from participation in a venture which has engaged in an act described in violation of paragraph (1), knowing, or in reckless disregard of the fact, that means of force, threats of force, fraud, coercion described in subsection (e)(2), or any combination of such means will be used to cause the person to engage in a commercial sex act, or that the person has not attained the age of 18 years and will be caused to engage in a commercial sex act, shall be punished as provided in subsection (b)."

Section 266j provides in relevant part: "Any person who intentionally gives, transports, provides, or makes available, or who offers to give, transport, provide, or make available to another person, a child under the age of 16 for the purpose of any lewd or lascivious act as defined in Section 288, or who causes, induces, or persuades a child under the age of 16 to engage in such an act with another person, is guilty of a felony...."

3. The People argue it is not evident from the record that defendant's convictions arose from the same sex acts even though the same victim was the complaining witness in both cases.

Chapter Five

Reporting Child Sexual Exploitation

I. Reporting Requirements

A. Who is Required to Report?

All United States jurisdictions statutorily provide for the reporting of suspected child abuse or neglect. For a comprehensive list of state reporting statutes, see Child Welfare Information Gateway, *Mandatory Reporters of Child Abuse and Neglect*, available at https://www.childwelfare.gov/pubpdfs/manda.pdf (current through Nov. 2013). In eighteen states (Delaware, Florida, Idaho, Indiana, Kentucky, Maryland, Mississippi, Nebraska, New Hampshire, New Jersey, New Mexico, North Carolina, Oklahoma, Rhode Island, Tennessee, Texas, Utah, and Wyoming), any person who suspects child abuse or neglect is required to report. Almost all states identify specific persons or professionals who are required to report. Only New Jersey and Wyoming do not enumerate specific professional groups as mandated reporters but rather simply require all persons to report. *See* N.J. Stat. Ann. § 9:6-8.10 ("Any person having reasonable cause to believe that a child has been subjected to child abuse or acts of child abuse shall report the same immediately ..."); Wyo. Stat. Ann. § 14-3-205 ("Any person who knows or has reasonable cause to believe or suspect that a child has been abused or neglected or who observes any child being subjected to conditions or circumstances that would reasonably result in abuse or neglect, shall immediately report ..."). In all other United States jurisdictions, it is considered "permissive" for any person to report. The material that follows addresses some of the categories of persons and professionals who commonly come in contact with children but for whom the application of mandatory reporting requirements is often unclear.

1. Parents and Guardians

State v. Williquette

Supreme Court of Wisconsin, 1986
129 Wis. 2d 239, 385 N.W.2d 145

STEINMETZ, Justice.

The issue in the case is whether a parent who allegedly knew her husband had repeatedly abused her two children both physically and sexually, but who took no action to stop the abuse and instead left the children in the father's sole physical custody for hours at a time, can be tried for the direct commission of the crime of child abuse under sec. 940.201, Stats.[1] ...

In a criminal complaint issued on November 15, 1983, Terri Williquette, the defendant, was charged with two counts of child abuse, contrary to sec. 940.201, Stats. Count one was based on the defendant's alleged failure to take any action to prevent her husband, Bert Williquette, from repeatedly "sexually abusing, beating, and otherwise mistreating" her seven year old son, B.W. Count two was based on the defendant's alleged failure to take any action to prevent her husband from committing similar acts against the defendant's eight year old daughter, C.P.... The complaint was based on information supplied by Sergeant Bies of the Door county sheriff's department. The sergeant obtained his information from conversations with the children, B.W. and C.P., Dr. Ferrin Holmes, Bert Williquette and the defendant, as well as from his review of a conversation B.W. had had with a social worker.

According to the complaint, B.W. stated that on November 10, 1983, he had been beaten with a metal stick on his right foot, ankle and left thigh by his father, Bert Williquette. B.W. also stated he had been beaten by his father on many occasions in the past and that all the bruises visible on his body were the result of being beaten with a metal stick.... The complaint further stated that B.W. reported being forced by his father to stand on one foot and one hand in an unbalanced position. In that position, his father would strike him. B.W. also indicated that on several occasions Bert Williquette had stuck his "bug" up B.W.'s "butt" and in his mouth. B.W. pointed to the penis on an anatomically correct drawing of an unclothed boy when asked what "bug" meant.... B.W. stated that he had told his mother on many occasions that he had been beaten with the metal stick by Bert Williquette, but the defendant never did anything about it. He also reported telling his mother about the incident on November 10, 1983, when he had been struck on the foot with the metal stick. At that time, his mother told him "not to worry about it."

According to the complaint, Dr. Ferrin Holmes, a pediatrician at the Door County Medical Center, examined B.W. on November 11, 1983, and observed numerous bruises on the child's feet, upper and lower legs, lower and upper back, left arm and the side of his chest. Dr. Holmes stated that, in his professional opinion, B.W. had been beaten on at least four separate occasions in the fairly recent past, and that the beatings were inflicted with a metal stick or instrument.... The complaint also describes a conversation that Sergeant Bies had with C.P., defendant's daughter, on November 14, 1983. C.P. stated that Bert Williquette regularly beat her and her brother at their home in Door county, on occasion using a metal stick with a hook on its end. C.P. stated that Bert Williquette would beat her and B.W. so hard that the children would wet their pants. He allegedly would also make the children balance on one hand and one leg, and then he would take the hook end of the metal stick and trip them, causing them to fall down. C.P. told Sergeant Bies that some time after Halloween in 1983, Bert Williquette hit her on the top of the head with the metal stick so hard that she bled. Sergeant Bies examined the area of C.P.'s head where she claimed Bert Williquette had struck her, and he could still feel a lump there. C.P. indicated that she had told the defendant about the incident, and that the defendant had given her an ice pack for her head.... C.P. also stated that in the summer

---

1. Sec. 940.201, Stats., provides as follows:

"940.201 Abuse of children. Whoever tortures a child or subjects a child to cruel maltreatment, including, but not limited, to severe bruising, lacerations, fractured bones, burns, internal injuries or any injury constituting great bodily harm under s. 939.22(14) is guilty of a Class E felony. In this section, 'child' means a person under 16 years of age."

of 1983, when she went swimming in her bathing suit, Bert Williquette would put lotion from a yellow bottle on his "wienie" and would then put his "wienie" in her and B.W.'s "butts." C.P. also pointed to the penis on an anatomically correct drawing of an unclothed boy when asked what she meant by "wienie." C.P. further indicated that on occasion "white stuff" would come out of Bert Williquette's "wiener" when he stuck it in the children's mouths, and when this happened, Williquette would make them swallow the "white stuff." If they refused to do so, Bert Williquette would hit them.

Both B.W. and C.P. also indicated that Bert Williquette would frequently take either a spoon or a cup, go inside the toilet bowl to remove some "poopy," and make the children eat it. If they refused to swallow it, Bert Williquette would strike them.... C.P. said that she had told the defendant about all of the sexual abuse incidents involving her and B.W. but that her mother did not do anything about it. She also indicated to a social worker that she had told her mother on many occasions about the times she and B.W. were beaten by Bert Williquette. Her mother allegedly told C.P. that she would do something about it, but she never did.

A joint preliminary hearing subsequently was held to consider the charges against the defendant and Bert Williquette. B.W., C.P., Dr. Holmes, Sergeant Bies and Allyn Buehler of the Door county sheriff's department testified at the preliminary.... C.P. was either unable or unwilling to answer many of the questions that the district attorney asked her at the preliminary. However, on cross-examination by the defendant's attorney, C.P. testified that she had told the defendant about her dad "putting his wiener up [my] butt" before her dad was put in jail, and that she told her mother about this "many times" a long time ago.... Sergeant Bies testified that C.P. had told him that she informed her mother about "everything" including the abuse inflicted by her father every time it happened. Despite telling her mother, the incidents of abuse allegedly continued.... B.W. testified that he had told the defendant lots of times that his daddy made him eat "poop" and that his mother said "she would tell daddy but she didn't." B.W. also testified he had told his mother "lots" about his father beating him with the metal stick. On cross-examination by his father's attorney, B.W. said he had told no one but his mother about getting hit with the metal stick. On cross-examination by his mother's attorney, B.W. stated that the defendant was never around when his father abused him. She allegedly was at work.... At the close of the testimony, the trial court ordered the defendant bound over on the two counts of child abuse in violation of sec. 940.201, Stats.

On June 6, 1984, the defendant filed a motion to dismiss the information. She claimed that she could not be charged with child abuse because she did not directly commit the abusive conduct. The circuit court granted the motion to dismiss. The court concluded that sec. 940.201, Stats., applies only to the intentional acts of a defendant who directly abuses a child. Accordingly, the mother's alleged failure to take any action to prevent her husband from abusing the children was not covered by the statute.... The state appealed the circuit court's decision to dismiss the charges against the defendant. The state agreed that the defendant did not actively participate in the sexual abuse or beating of her children. However, the state argued that the evidence at the preliminary hearing showed that the children had told the defendant on numerous occasions about the abuse and that she failed to take any action to prevent C.P. and B.W. from being subjected to further beatings and molestation. In fact, the defendant allegedly continued to leave the children in her husband's sole physical custody while she was at work. The state contended that the defendant's acts subjected the children to abuse within the meaning of sec. 940.201, Stats.... The court of appeals reversed the trial court's order of dismissal. The court of appeals reasoned that the defendant could have been bound over for aiding and abetting her husband's abuse of the children, even though the state had not proceeded on this theory. *State v. Williquette*, 125 Wis.2d 86, 90–91, 370 N.W.2d 282 (Ct.App.1985). The court of appeals agreed with the trial court, however, that the defendant could not be tried for directly committing child abuse based on her alleged failure to protect her children....

The parties disagree as to whether sec. 940.201, Stats., requires a person to directly inflict child abuse in order to violate the statute. The defendant contends that the legislature intended the statute to apply only to persons who directly abuse children. She maintains that the statute does not impose a duty on her to protect her own children from abuse. The state, however, argues that the statute is susceptible to an interpretation which includes persons having a special relationship to children who expose them to abuse. The state relies on the statutory language "subjects a child to cruel maltreatment." The state urges the court to construe this language to cover situations in which a parent knowingly exposes a child to abuse by placing the child in a situation where abuse has occurred and is likely to recur....

We conclude that the ordinary and accepted meaning of "subjects" does not limit the application of sec. 940.201, Stats., only to persons who actively participate in abusing children. The common meaning of "subjects" is broader than directly inflicting abuse on children. It covers situations in which a person with a duty toward a child exposes the child to a foreseeable risk of abuse.... Our interpretation of the scope of sec. 940.201, Stats., is consistent with the purpose of the statute. The statute operates to protect children from the consequences of conduct, without regard for any culpable mens rea on the part of the persons causing the consequences. In *State v. Danforth*, 129 Wis.2d 187, 385 N.W.2d 125 (1986), this court expressly held that child abuse does not require criminal intent. This holding is consistent with *State v. Killory*, 73 Wis.2d 400, 413, 243 N.W.2d 475 (1976), in which the court held that the crime of child abuse does not require malice. Thus, child abuse consists of subjecting a child to conduct which is "abhorrent to the sensitivities of the general public." *Id.* at 407, 243 N.W.2d 475. This is an objective standard rather than a subjective one. Applying this objective standard of liability, we conclude that a person's conduct may subject a child to cruel maltreatment when the person exposes a child to a foreseeable risk of abhorrent conduct.

A person exposes a child to abuse when he or she causes the child to come within the influence of a foreseeable risk of cruel maltreatment. Causation in this context means that a person's conduct is a substantial factor in exposing the child to risk, and there may be more than one substantial causative factor in any given case. *See Hart v. State*, 75 Wis.2d 371, 397, 249 N.W.2d 810 (1977). In this case, Bert Williquette's conduct obviously was a direct cause of the abuse his children suffered. However, the defendant's alleged conduct, as the mother of the children, also was a contributing cause of risk to the children. She allegedly knew that the father abused the children in her absence, but she continued to leave the children and to entrust them to his exclusive care, and she allegedly did nothing else to prevent the abuse, such as notifying proper authorities or providing alternative child care in her absence. We conclude that the defendant's conduct, as alleged, constituted a substantial factor which increased the risk of further abuse.

The defendant disputes that an omission to act may constitute a crime. Although the court disagrees with this argument, we specifically note that the alleged conduct in this case involves more than an omission to act. The defendant regularly left the children in the father's exclusive care and control despite allegedly knowing that he abused the children in her absence. We consider leaving the children in these circumstances to be overt conduct. Therefore, even assuming that an overt act is necessary for the commission of a crime, the allegations support the charges in this case.

The court, however, also expressly rejects the defendant's claim that an act of commission, rather than omission, is a necessary element of a crime. The essence of criminal conduct is the requirement of a wrongful "act." LaFave and Scott, Criminal Law, sec. 25 at 177 (West 1972). This element, however, is satisfied by overt acts, as well as omissions to act where there is a legal duty to act. LaFave and Scott, Criminal Law sec. 26 at 182, states the general rule applicable to omissions:

> "Some statutory crimes are specifically defined in terms of omission to act. With other common law and statutory crimes which are defined in terms of conduct producing a specified result, a person may be criminally liable when his omission to act produces that result, but only if (1) he has, under the circumstances, a legal duty to act, and (2) he can physically perform the act. The trend of the law has been toward enlarging the scope of duty to act."

The comments to this section then state the traditional rule that a person generally has no duty to rescue or protect an endangered person unless a special relationship exists between the persons which imposes a legal duty to protect:

> "For criminal liability to be based upon a failure to act it must first be found that there is a duty to act—a legal duty and not simply a moral duty. As we have seen, some criminal statutes themselves impose the legal duty to act, as with the tax statute and the hit-and-run statute. With other crimes the duty must be found outside the definition of the crime itself—perhaps in another statute, or in the common law, or in a contract.

> "Generally one has no legal duty to aid another person in peril, even when that aid can be rendered without danger or inconvenience to himself. He need not shout a warning to a blind man headed for a precipice or to an absent-minded one walking into a gunpowder room with a lighted candle in hand. He need not pull a neighbor's baby out of a pool of water or rescue an unconscious person stretched across the railroad tracks, though the baby is drowning or the whistle of an approaching train is heard in the distance. A doctor is not legally bound to answer a desperate call from the frantic parents of a sick child, at least if it is not one of his regular patients. A moral duty to take affirmative action is not enough to impose a legal duty to do so. But there are situations which do give rise to a duty to act:

> "(1) *Duty based upon relationship.* The common law imposes affirmative duties upon persons standing in certain personal relationships to other persons—upon parents to aid their small children, upon husbands to aid their wives, upon ship captains to aid their crews, upon masters to aid their servants. Thus a parent may be guilty of criminal homicide for failure to call a doctor for his sick child, a mother for failure to prevent the fatal beating of her baby by her lover, a husband for failure to aid his imperiled wife, a ship captain for failure to pick up a seaman or passenger fallen overboard, and an employer for failure to aid his endangered employee. Action may be required to thwart the threatened perils of nature (*e.g.*, to combat sickness, to ward off starvation or the elements); or it may be required to protect against threatened acts by third persons." LaFave and Scott, Criminal Law at 183–84. (Footnotes omitted.)

The requirement of a legal duty to act is a policy limitation which prevents most omissions from being considered the proximate cause of a prohibited consequence. In a technical sense, a person's omission, *i.e.*, whether the person fails to protect, warn or rescue, may be a substantial factor in exposing another person to harm. The concept of causation, however, is not solely a question of mechanical connection between events, but also a question of policy. A particular legal cause must be one of which the law will take cognizance. *See State v. Serebin*, 119 Wis.2d 837, 849, 350 N.W.2d 65 (1984). The rule that persons do not have a general duty to protect represents a public policy choice to limit criminal liability.... The requirement of an overt act, therefore, is not inherently necessary for criminal liability. Criminal liability depends on conduct which is a substantial factor in producing consequences. Omissions are as capable of producing consequences as overt acts. Thus, the common law rule that there is no general duty to protect limits criminal liability where it would otherwise exist. The special relationship exception to the "no duty to act" rule represents a choice to retain liability for some omissions, which are considered morally unacceptable....

We next address the scope of the "legal duty" exception to the rule regarding criminal liability for omissions. Like most jurisdictions, Wisconsin generally does not require a person to protect others from hazardous situations. *De Bauche v. Knott*, 69 Wis.2d 119, 122–23, 230 N.W.2d 158 (1975). When a special relationship exists between persons, however, social policy may impose a duty to protect. The relationship between a parent and a child exemplifies a special relationship where the duty to protect is imposed. We stated the rule applicable to the parent and child relationship in *Cole v. Sears, Roebuck & Co.*, 47 Wis.2d 629, 634, 177 N.W.2d 866 (1970):

> " 'It is the right and duty of parents under the law of nature as well as the common law and the statutes of many states to protect their children, to care for them in sickness and in health, and to do whatever may be necessary for their care, maintenance, and preservation, including medical attendance, if necessary. An omission to do this is a public wrong which the state, under its police powers, may prevent. The child has the right to call upon the parent for the discharge of this duty, and public policy for the good of society will not permit or allow the parent to divest himself irrevocably of his obligations in this regard or to abandon them at his mere will or pleasure....' 39 Am.Jur., *Parent and Child*, p. 669, sec. 46."

From the above discussion, we conclude that a parent who fails to take any action to stop instances of child abuse can be prosecuted as a principal for exposing the child to the abuse, contrary to sec. 940.201, Stats. Consistent with the common law rule, however, we do not hold that all persons, regardless of their relationship or lack of relationship to an abused child, violate the child abuse statute by failing to take remedial action to protect the child. Finally, when liability under sec. 940.201, depends on a breach of the parent's duty to protect, the parent must knowingly act in disregard of the facts giving rise to a duty to act. LaFave and Scott, Criminal Law, sec. 26 at 187. The "knowingly" requirement is necessary for a breach of the parent's duty to protect; it is not imposed as an element of sec. 940.201....

The defendant next argues that the legislature did not intend sec. 940.201, Stats., to apply to a parent's failure to protect her children because a parent does not even have a duty to report child abuse. Section 48.981(2),[5] requires specified professionals to report

---

5. Sec. 48.981(2), Stats., provides as follows:

"(2) PERSONS REQUIRED TO REPORT CASES OF SUSPECTED CHILD ABUSE OR NEGLECT. A physician, coroner, medical examiner, nurse, dentist, chiropractor, optometrist, other medical or mental health professional, social or public assistance worker, school teacher, administrator or counselor, child care worker in a day care center or child caring institution, day care provider, alcohol or other drug abuse counselor, member of the treatment staff employed by or working under contract with a board established under s. 46.23, 51.42 or 51.437, physical therapist, occupational therapist, speech therapist, emergency medical technician–advanced (paramedic), ambulance attendant or police or law enforcement officer having reasonable cause to suspect that a child seen in the course

cases of suspected child abuse or neglect. Parents are not enumerated as having such a statutory duty.... We are unpersuaded that the child abuse reporting statute was intended to relieve parents of their common law duty to protect their children. We construe the statute as creating duties for persons who otherwise had no obligation to protect children because they do not have a recognized special relationship with the child. The creation of duties where none previously existed, however, cannot be construed to relieve parents of their common law duty to their children. Also, the fact that the reporting statute only imposes a duty to report abuse does not mean that a parent's duty is similarly limited. A broader parental duty is indicated by sec. 48.02(12), Stats., which defines "legal custody" to include the duty to protect a child. Thus, we conclude that the reporting statute does not affect our analysis of a parent's criminal liability for failing to protect a child.

The enactment of sec. 940.34, Stats.,[6] subsequent to the commencement of this prosecution also does not indicate that the defendant was previously immune from criminal liability for her conduct. Section 940.34 is a "Good Samaritan" law which imposes criminal liability on "[a]ny person who knows that a crime is being committed and that a victim is exposed to bodily harm" but fails to summon help or provide assistance to the victim. The new statute does not deny the prior existence of a parent's duty to protect. We acknowledge that a parent now could be charged under either statute. Section 939.65, however, provides that if an act forms the basis for a crime punishable under more than one statutory provision, then the state can prosecute under any or all such provisions.

Finally, we reject the defendant's claim that sec. 940.201, Stats., is unconstitutionally vague if it is construed to apply to a parent's knowing failure to protect a child from abuse. In *Killory*, 73 Wis.2d at 407, 243 N.W.2d 475, we defined "cruel maltreatment" to refer to acts which are "abhorrent to the sensitivities of the general public," and we held that this standard is sufficiently definite to give notice of what is prohibited. Our holding in this case is that a parent who knowingly exposes a child to the risk of such abhorrent conduct violates the statute. This construction of sec. 940.201 gives the defendant notice that she has an affirmative duty to protect her children from a foreseeable risk of cruel maltreatment. The statute is not unconstitutionally vague.

We conclude that the defendant's alleged conduct is within the prohibitions of sec. 940.201, Stats. The statute prohibits persons from exposing or subjecting a child to a foreseeable risk of cruel maltreatment. The evidence at the defendant's preliminary hearing

---

of professional duties has been abused or neglected or having reason to believe that a child seen in the course of professional duties has been threatened with an injury and that abuse of the child will occur shall report as provided in sub. (3). Any other person including an attorney having reason to suspect that a child has been abused or neglected or reason to believe that a child has been threatened with an injury and that abuse of the child will occur may make such a report. No person making a report under this subsection may be discharged from employment for so doing."

6. Sec. 940.34, Stats., provides as follows:

"940.34 Duty to aid endangered crime victim. (1) Whoever violates sub. (2) is guilty of a Class C misdemeanor.

"(2) Any person who knows that a crime is being committed and that a victim is exposed to bodily harm shall summon law enforcement officers or other assistance or shall provide assistance to the victim. A person need not comply with this subsection if any of the following apply:

"(a) Compliance would place him or her in danger.

"(b) Compliance would interfere with duties the person owes to others.

"(c) Assistance is being summoned or provided by others.

"(3) If a person renders emergency care for a victim, s. 895.48 applies. Any person who provides other reasonable assistance under this section is immune from civil liability for his or her acts or omissions in providing the assistance. This immunity does not apply if the person receives or expects to receive compensation for providing the assistance."

indicates that she left her children in the exclusive care of her husband despite allegedly knowing that he regularly abused the children in her absence. She allegedly did nothing to protect the children from such abuse, including at least reporting the husband's conduct to proper authorities. This evidence is sufficient to find probable cause that the defendant exposed the children to the risk of continuing and further abuse, thereby requiring that she be bound over for trial.

The decision of the court of appeals is affirmed....

HEFFERNAN, Chief Justice (dissenting).

The majority of the court has decided that the neglectful conduct of the defendant is to be proscribed by the criminal law. Such action by a legislature may well be commendable, but by a court condemnable. I dissent....

This, however, is a criminal case, not an occasion for an emotional cathartic nor for this court's exercise of righteous indignation. The question for a court is whether the legislature has made criminal the action with which Terri Williquette has been charged. The question is not whether a court, were it sitting as a legislature, would have proscribed the conduct. Most egregiously, although it points to no legislative intent contemporaneous with the passage of the law that would make Terri Williquette's conduct a felony, the majority finds that the statute means that conduct which occurred almost three years ago is now to be definitively declared criminal. In the absence of some indicia supporting that interpretation stemming from the time of the law's passage, the best that can be said of the law which the majority now promulgates, assuming it is otherwise appropriate, is that it is unconstitutional as *ex post facto*....

Thus, if one is to accept the position of the state, and I for one would not, that the legislation is ambiguous, the ambiguity is resolved by the clear demonstration that what the drafters intended was that the principal actor be criminally liable even though there was no subjective intent to torture or maltreat. The record is devoid of any material that implies a legislative intent that any person was to be held liable as a principal in a felony action for allowing a child to remain, or to be placed, in a situation where he or she might be abused.... To conclude that such was the intent of the legislature is to attribute to it— and to its staff—a complete lack of drafting expertise and the ordinary usages of the English language. Other jurisdictions have stated specifically in their child abuse statutes that a person not the principal actor or abuser could be liable as the principal when a child was knowingly placed in a circumstance where abuse could occur.[2] I believe that were that the intent of the Wisconsin legislature, the statutory language demonstrates it did not have the ability to make that intent clear. I, however, do not consider that implied

---

2. *See, e.g.*, Colorado Statutes, sec. 18-6-401(1) ("A person commits child abuse if he causes an injury to a child's life or health or permits a child to be unreasonably placed in a situation which poses a threat of injury to the child's life or health."), Florida Statutes (1985), sec. 827.04(1) ("Whoever, willfully or by culpable negligence, deprives a child of, or allows a child to be deprived of, necessary food, clothing, shelter, or medical treatment, or who, knowingly or by culpable negligence, permits physical or mental injury to the child, and in so doing causes great bodily harm, permanent disability, or permanent disfigurement to such child, shall be guilty of a felony of the third degree ..."); Nevada Statutes (1983–84), sec. 200.508 ("1, Any adult person who willfully causes or permits a child who is less than 18 years of age to suffer unjustifiable physical pain or mental suffering as a result of abuse or neglect or who willfully causes or permits a child to be placed in a situation where the child may suffer physical pain or mental suffering as the result of abuse or neglect is guilty of ... ; 2.... ; 3. As used in this section, 'permit' means permission that a reasonable person would not grant and which amounts to a neglect of responsibility attending the care, custody and control of a minor child.")

conclusion an appropriate one for this court to reach. We denigrate the legislature or, alternatively, we, as a court, are invading an area of the law—the proscription of criminal conduct—which is wholly statutory and is beyond the reach of a court's common law or inherent powers. Clearly, the majority's strained interpretation is an invasion of the legislative prerogative.

The majority correctly asserts the criminal conduct can be predicated upon the failure to act when action is required by law. The problem is that nothing in the statutes remotely suggests that a parent has the legislatively prescribed legal duty to act in the instant circumstances or that the omission of the alleged duty will result in criminal sanctions. Certainly, I agree with the majority who, after reciting the catalog of horrors perpetrated upon these children, asserts, citing *Cole v. Sears, Roebuck & Co.*, 47 Wis.2d 629, 634, 177 N.W.2d 866 (1970):

> "An omission to do this [care for and protect children] is a public wrong which the state, under its police powers, may prevent." ...

The problem with this position is that it begs the question. Of course, the state has the police powers which may be exercised for that very purpose. The omission can be categorized as a public wrong which the legislature *may* prevent. But the police power is a power of the legislature. It is not an independent power conferred upon courts. Courts may validate a legislature's conduct by recognizing the legislature's police power, but courts cannot supply that exercise of power where there is no evidence that the legislature so intended to act.... We return to the fundamental defect in the position of the state. There is no evidence that the legislature intended to exercise its police power in the manner urged here. I reiterate, if it desired to do so, the appropriate statutory language was not beyond the capabilities of the legislature....

This statute is not sufficiently definite to give reasonable notice to a parent that the failure to act falls within the prohibited conduct of the statute. Clearly, the state and the majority of this court arrive at their conclusion only by straining reason to its outer limits. The majority opinion speaks for itself in demonstrating that the court has "guessed" at the meaning of the statute. It is apparent that none of the participants in this unfortunate episode, nor the prosecution and the court, could have looked at the statute and have said with any degree of confidence that Terri Williquette's conduct would constitute the felonious act of torturing a child or submitting it to cruel maltreatment. The only thing clearly revealed by a perusal of the statute is vagueness in its application to the present facts.... We have correctly, I believe, concluded that there need be no intent to torture, no intent to maltreat. (*See, State v. Danforth*, 129 Wis.2d 187, 385 N.W.2d 125 (1986).) Hence, the statute comes perilously close to a strict liability statute. I have no quarrel with such an application of the law provided the child abuse statute is applied only in those cases where the legislature has given clear notice of its applicability. To insist on less sanctions the denial of due process....

Notes

In the eighteen jurisdictions that require all persons to report suspected child abuse, parents are included within that requirement. In only five states are parents or guardians specifically included as mandatory reporters. *See* Ariz. Rev. Stat. § 13-3620 (including "parents, stepparents, or guardians"); 325 Ill. Comp. Stat. § 5/4 (homemakers); 22 Me. Rev. Stat. § 4011-A (any person assuming care or custody of the child); Mo. Rev. Stat. § 210.115 ("other person with responsibility for the care of children"); Wash. Rev. Code § 26.44.030 ("any adult with whom a child resides"). Foster parents are specifically included as mandatory reporters in eight states. *See* Ark. Code Ann. § 12-18-402; Cal. Penal Code § 11165.7 (foster parents, group home personnel, and personnel of residential care facilities); Conn. Gen. Stat. §§ 17a-101 & 53a-65 (licensed foster parents); 325 Ill. Comp. Stat. § 5/4 (foster parents or child care workers); La. Children's Code Ann. art 603(15) (foster home parents); Mass. Gen. Laws ch. 119, § 21 (foster parents); Nev. Rev. Stat. § 432B.220 (persons licensed to conduct foster homes); S.C. Ann. Code § 63-7-310 (foster parents). Although other state statutes may not expressly include parents as mandatory reporters, parents may be required to report under a common law duty to protect a child from known abuse by another parent, such as the court determined in *Williquette. See also Schmitz v. Aston*, 197 Ariz. 264, 3 P.3d 1184 (App. Div. 1 2000) (parents have a legal duty to report sexual abuse of a child in their care or custody); *Hite v. Brown*, 100 Ohio App.3d 606, 654 N.E.2d 452 (1995) (mother had duty to report father's alleged sexual abuse of daughter notwithstanding that statute did not include parent or guardian as person required to report knowledge or suspicion of child abuse). For discussion of the common law duty of parents to report, see Angelita Martinez, *Parents as Mandatory Reporters of Child Abuse and Neglect: Establishing an Explicit Duty to Protect*, 51 Wayne L. Rev. 467 (2005); Andrea Saltzman, *Protection for the Child or the Parent? The Conflict Between the Federal Drug and Alcohol Abuse Confidentiality Requirements and the State Child Abuse and Neglect Reporting Laws*, 1985 Ill. U. L.J. 181 (1985).

2. School Authorities

Turner v. Nelson

Supreme Court of Kentucky, 2011
342 S.W.3d 866

Opinion of the Court by Justice SCOTT....

In November 2005, five-year-olds F.B. and C.Y. were female kindergarten students in Dianne Turner's class at Southern Elementary School, a Fayette County public school. Turner had been teaching at Southern since 1990 and had been a kindergarten teacher for ten years before that. She had an exemplary record and had never been reprimanded or disciplined in any way.

On November 18, F.B. described an incident involving C.Y. to her mother, Nelson, who then reported the matter to Turner. The incident had allegedly occurred two days prior. Based upon Nelson's phone conversation with Turner that F.B. had complained that C.Y. had been "up her butt"[2] — and her own knowledge that F.B. often wore low cut jeans with her underwear showing in the back — Turner interpreted the events described to have been a playful "wedgie." ... Despite her belief that the incident was just a childish prank, Turner separated F.B.'s and C.Y.'s seats in the classroom, forbid them from being together in or out of the classroom during school, and discussed with C.Y. that "touching other people on the bottom" is inappropriate. She also informed her teaching assistant of the alleged incident and of her plan to keep the children apart.... Three days later, F.B. told Turner after lunch that C.Y. had been "up [her] butt" again in the classroom during reading class. When then questioned by Turner, C.Y. admitted she had touched F.B., describing it as a "game we play at home." Turner then put her assistant in charge of the classroom and took C.Y. to find the principal, Ms. Collins, or a counselor. Neither

---

2. Nelson disagrees with this description; she claims she told Turner that F.B. said C.Y. had "put her finger up my butt."

were available that afternoon. No other reports of inappropriate touching were ever made to Turner.[3]

Later that evening, F.B. told her mother's sister, Bridget, that C.Y. had touched her genitals. Rather than contact Turner again, on November 22, Nelson spoke with Principal Collins. Collins indicated she was unaware of the previous incidents and subsequently had both children report to her office for a conference. During the conference, Collins learned that C.Y. had "accidentally hit F.B. in between the legs but that there was not an intentional reaching over and touching of F.B. on her vagina." Both girls described to Collins a game in which one would pull the waistband on the other's underwear or pants and yell "up your butt!" Moreover, both girls told her there was no anal violation, stating "that did not happen." Following the conference, Collins called Nelson and told her that she had gathered some facts and would continue her investigation.... At some point later that evening, F.B. told Nelson that C.Y. had pushed her into a table, rubbed and pinched her nipples, and touched her anus and vagina. Nelson then went to the school the next day and informed Collins and law enforcement (who were already there on another matter) of the incident and took F.B. to an emergency room for a medical examination.[4]

Nelson brought suit against Turner in 2006, alleging, among other causes of action not pertinent here, that she failed (1) to exercise ordinary care to supervise the children in her classroom and, (2) to report to enforcement officials the alleged sexual assault perpetrated by C.Y. as required by KRS 620.030.... On March 1, 2007, after discovery, the Fayette Circuit Court entered summary judgment in favor of Turner, concluding that Turner was entitled to "qualified official immunity" because her action—determining whether the facts constituted abuse—was discretionary in nature. The Court of Appeals, however, reversed and remanded the matter back to the trial court with directions to reconsider the mandatory abuse reporting obligation of KRS 620.030 or to provide further analysis as to how the determination of abuse was a discretionary act in light of the statute's mandatory reporting requirement.... On remand, the trial court set out in detail its reasoning for finding Turner's actions discretionary and again found "qualified official immunity" applicable. On further review, the Court of Appeals reversed and held that Turner was not entitled to "qualified official immunity" because the reporting requirement of KRS 620.030 is mandatory and therefore ministerial, obviating any application of "qualified official immunity." This Court then granted Turner's motion for discretionary review....

Turner argues that the mandatory reporting obligation of KRS 620.030(1) does not apply in this case. In support, she points to KRS 600.020(1), which generally addresses abuse by persons in a custodial or supervisory capacity. As a result, Turner contends that she did not violate KRS 620.030(1) because the complaint alleged commission of the act by a child, rather than by a person in a "supervisory or custodial capacity" as required, and further, even under Appellee's view of KRS 620.030, there has to be knowledge of an abuse or reasonable cause to believe it actually occurred before the reporting requirements

---

3. In her deposition, Turner testified that "[i]f I understand that a child is truly sexually abusing another student, then I'm going to call Crimes Against Children."

4. The medical record noted "no obvious laceration" and that "there did appear to be some small irritation of the vagina, with no definite tear, blood seen [and] no discharge." According to Appellant's expert, Dr. David Shraberg, this irritation and a bruise were "possibly consistent with F.B.'s report of ... sexual play and roughhousing." However, he also noted a history of urinary tract infections which "can cause vaginal irritation as well." As to any other complaints, he noted F.B. "appears to have no medical complaints. Insofar as emotional complaints, she did well not only at [the] Academy, but is doing well in the first grade. She does appear to be a rather somewhat 'chatty child.'"

of KRS 620.030(1) could apply; which there was not. We agree, but address the contentions separately.[5]

KRS 620.030(1) mandates that "[a]ny person who knows or has reasonable cause to believe that a child is *dependent, neglected, or abused* shall immediately cause an oral or written report to be made...." (Emphasis added).[6] ... In *Commonwealth v. Allen*, 980 S.W.2d 278, 279 (Ky.1998), this Court deemed the language of KRS 620.030(1) to be "clear and unambiguous." *Id.* at 281. However, Allen involved a teacher's report under KRS 620.030(1) that another teacher had engaged in sexual contact with two sixth-grade students. Here, we are called upon to interpret the mandatory reporting obligations of KRS 620.030(1) where the alleged perpetrator was a five-year-old classmate.... In so doing, we must be mindful of the commands of KRS 446.080(4), which states:

> All words and phrases shall be construed according to the common and approved usage of language, but technical words and phrases, and such others as may have acquired a peculiar and appropriate meaning in the law, shall be construed according to such meaning.

In this regard, KRS 620.030(1) specifically refers to "a child [that] is dependent, neglected, or abused." It falls under KRS Chapter 620, which is entitled "Dependency, Neglect, and Abuse." And, KRS 600.020, which contains the definitions for KRS Chapters 600 to 645, defines an "[a]bused or neglected child" in subsection (1), in pertinent part, as:

> (1) "Abused or neglected child" means a child whose health or welfare is harmed or threatened with harm when his parent, guardian, or other person exercising custodial control or supervision of the child:
>
> (a) Inflicts or allows to be inflicted upon the child physical or emotional injury as defined in this section by other than accidental means;
>
> (b) Creates or allows to be created a risk of physical or emotional injury as defined in this section to the child by other than accidental means;
>
> ....
>
> (e) Commits or allows to be committed an act of sexual abuse, sexual exploitation, or prostitution upon the child;
>
> (f) Creates or allows to be created a risk that an act of sexual abuse, sexual exploitation, or prostitution will be committed upon the child;
>
> ....

KRS 600.020(1). KRS 600.020(19) defines a "[d]ependent child."

For reasons that KRS 620.030(1) premises its application on "a child [who] is dependent, neglected, or abused," we cannot escape the determination, given the definitive and particular wording used, that these are technical words which "have acquired a peculiar and appropriate meaning in the law." KRS 446.080(4). Moreover, given the textual

---

5. Turner also contends that KRS 620.030 does not provide for a private cause of action. Because we have resolved this matter on other grounds, we do not address this specific issue.

6. KRS 620.050(1) provides, in pertinent part:

Anyone acting upon reasonable cause in the making of a report or acting under KRS 620.030 ... in good faith shall have immunity from any liability, civil or criminal, that might otherwise be incurred or imposed.... However, any person who knowingly makes a false report and does so with malice shall be guilty of a Class A misdemeanor.

We surmise that KRS 620.050(1)'s reference to "the making of a report *or acting* under KRS 620.030" at a minimum contemplates and protects one in an initial investigation of the matter.

symmetry, we can find nothing in the context of KRS 620.030 which countermands the application of KRS 600.020(1).... Thus, under the plain language of KRS 600.020(1), the definition of an abused child is *limited* to a scenario in which his or her "parent, guardian, or other person exercising custodial control or supervision" inflicted or committed abuse, allowed abuse to be inflicted or committed, or created or allowed to be created a risk of abuse. As a result, the *mandatory* reporting requirement of KRS 620.030(1) does not apply when a child inappropriately touches another child *unless* a parent, guardian, or other person exercising custodial control or supervision allows such inappropriate touching to be committed or creates or allows such a risk of abuse.

Here, the allegations concern improper touching by a five-year-old girl of another five-year-old girl, not a parent, guardian, or other person exercising custodial control or supervision, as was the case in *Allen.*... In this case, Turner knew that C.Y. touched F.B. based upon her conversation with the children and Nelson. As a result, she separated their classroom seating and forbid them from being together during school hours. She even advised her classroom assistant of this. Thus one, in this circumstance, could not conclude that she allowed the touching or created or allowed the risk to be created. This is not to say that a report could not have been made in this instance, *see* KRS 620.030(1) and KRS 620.040(3), only that it was not mandated by KRS 620.030(1) for the reasons enunciated.

Thus, the mandatory reporting obligation of KRS 620.030(1) did not apply to Turner in this case, as the facts alleged did not constitute a mandatorily reportable "abuse" as envisioned by the legislature. Thus, there was no "genuine issue of material fact for trial." *Steelvest*, 807 S.W.2d at 482....

Finally, while Nelson may find a clear reading of the statute unpalatable because she believes it does not adequately protect abused children,[7] a policy disagreement cannot be cast as an absurd or unreasonable result as a means to ignore the plain meaning of a statute....

KRS 620.030(2) places additional duties upon teachers, and reads in pertinent part:

> Any person, including ... a ... *teacher* ... who knows or has reasonable cause to believe that a child is dependent, neglected, or abused, *regardless of whether the person believed to have caused the dependency, neglect, or abuse is a parent, guardian, person* exercising custodial control or supervision, or another person, or who has attended such child as a part of his or her professional duties *shall, if requested,* in addition to the report required in subsection (1) of this section, file with the local law enforcement agency or the Department of Kentucky State Police or the Commonwealth's or county attorney, the cabinet or its designated representative within forty-eight (48) hours of the original report a written report ...

---

7. We believe the statute adequately protects abused children while affording discretion to teachers such as Turner. For instance, a teacher confronted with inappropriate touching by one child upon another must contemplate a variety of concerns including, but not limited to, the developmental age of each child. And by reporting such an incident to law enforcement officials, without some investigation and analysis, a teacher risks automatically destabilizing the children involved and the classroom as a whole; alternative solutions, if appropriate, after an initial investigation, such as separating the children and explaining why certain touching is inappropriate, will often be preferable to immediate draconian sanctions with all their attendant consequences if the situation was, in fact, misinterpreted. If the belief of any violation remains, the teacher may — and should — report it. Such a scenario is explicitly recognized by KRS 620.030(1) to the effect "[i]f the cabinet receives a report of abuse or neglect allegedly committed by a person other than a parent, guardian, or person exercising custodial control or supervision, the cabinet shall refer the matter to the Commonwealth's attorney or the county attorney...."

(Emphasis added).

Nelson argues that the breadth of KRS 620.030 is demonstrated by subsection (2), which states that mandatory reporting is triggered for teachers "regardless of whether" the abuse was committed by a parent or guardian. According to Nelson, a clear reading of the statute shows that the legislature was trying to provide the broadest, most comprehensive protection available for children. However, Nelson ignores that this reporting requirement applies only "if requested." No such request was made to Turner by anyone. Moreover, the wording "in addition to the report required in subsection (1) of this section" cannot be read to expand the obligatory expanse of KRS 620.030(1); it merely recognizes the secondary report, if requested, is in addition to any report *required* by subsection (1)....

It is imperative that teachers maintain the discretion to teach, supervise, and appropriately discipline children in the classroom. To do this, they must have appropriate leeway to do so, to investigate complaints by parents, or others, as to the conduct of their students, to form conclusions (based on facts not always known) as to what actually happened, and ultimately to determine an appropriate course of action, which may, at times, involve reporting the conduct of a child to the appropriate authorities. In fact, protection of the discretionary powers of our public officials and employees, exercised in good faith, is the very foundation of our doctrine of "qualified official immunity." ... Although we consider Turner's conduct in this case to be discretionary, we recognize the apparent incongruity with our precedent regarding a supervisory duty in the public school setting, as "we have held that a claim of negligent supervision may go to a ministerial act or function in the public school setting." *Id.* at 244. However, *Yanero v. Davis*, 65 S.W.3d 510 (Ky.2001) and *Williams* [*v. Kentucky Department of Education*], 113 S.W.3d 145 [(Ky. 2003)] — the cases relied upon in enunciating the public school distinction — have quite different facts from those before us. *Id.*

In *Yanero*, this Court deemed "enforcement of a known rule requiring that student athletes wear batting helmets during baseball batting practice" to be ministerial. 65 S.W.3d at 522. Unlike the teacher's decision-making in this case, a helmet requirement constitutes "an essentially objective and binary directive." *Haney* [*v. Monsky*], 311 S.W.3d [235,] ... 242 [(Ky. 2010)] (*discussing Yanero*, 65 S.W.3d 510). As a result, "[t]here is no substantial compliance with such an order and it cannot be a matter of degree: its enforcement was absolute, certain, and imperative, involving merely execution of a specific act arising from fixed and designated facts." *Id.* (citation omitted) (internal quotation omitted). You do it or you don't — and unlike here, there is no factual determination required for its application.

Admittedly, we have also "rejected the notion that the *failure* of teachers ... to supervise their students in the face of known and recognized misbehavior was a discretionary act." *Id.* at 244 (*discussing Williams*, 113 S.W.3d at 150). This decision stemmed from the requirement in KRS 161.180(1) that teachers must "hold pupils to strict account for their conduct on school premises, on the way to and from school, and on school sponsored trips and activities." *Id.* The dispute in this case, though, concerns the *means* of supervision rather than a *failure* to supervise students who were drinking and driving to and from a school-sponsored function as occurred in *Williams*.... Moreover, even had we agreed with Appellee's position that KRS 620.030 mandated reports covering children touching or abusing each other and was thus actionable under KRS 446.070,[11] qualified official im-

---

11. KRS 446.070 provides that "[a] person injured by the violation of any statute may recover from the offender such damages as he sustained by reason of the violation, although a penalty or

munity would still be applicable as the trial court aptly noted. KRS 620.030(1) only directs reporting by a "person who knows or has reasonable cause to believe that a child is ... abused." Thus, where there is no actual knowledge of the event, there must be an objective determination that a reasonable belief existed. *Rowan County v. Sloas*, 201 S.W.3d 469, 482 (Ky.2006) ("We make this ... inquiry in light of the information that the defendant official possessed at the time of the incident in question ... and cognizant of the fact that public officials generally are not hermetic, ivory-tower scribes versed in the vagaries of ... law.") (*quoting Kegler v. City of Livonia*, 173 F.3d 429 (6th Cir.1999)); *see also Jefferson County Fiscal Court v. Peerce*, 132 S.W.3d 824, 834 (Ky.2004). Thus, as the learned trial judge noted in her second summary judgment following remand:

> In conducting such an analysis, it is necessary to first review KRS 620.030.... Subsection 1 of this statute states, "[a]ny person *who knows or has reasonable cause to believe* that a child is ... abused shall immediately cause an oral or written report to be made to ..." (the appropriate authorities then listed).
>
> It is clear from this language that the mandatory reporting requirement applies only when a person "knows" or has "reasonable cause to believe" that a child has been abused. The statute clearly does not require the reporting of every allegation of sexual abuse or the reporting of a mere suspicion. The legislature could have required reporting on a mere allegation or statement, but the standard is clearly higher. As stated by the *Kentucky Supreme Court in Beckham v. Board of Education of Jefferson County*, 873 S.W.2d 575, 577 (Ky.1994).
>
>> As with any case involving statutory interpretation, our duty is to ascertain and give effect to the intent of the General Assembly. We are not at liberty to add or subtract from the legislative enactment nor discover mean[ing] not reasonably ascertainable from the language used.
>
> There is no claim in this case that Turner witnessed F.B. being abused or had any personal knowledge that F.B. was abused. Her only information about the event alleged came from what she was told by two five-year[-]old children. There appear to be no other witnesses to the alleged events. These circumstances required Turner to make a judgment about what may have happened and respond appropriately. It is noted that the principal also interviewed these two children and concluded the incidents were accidents and did not report the matter to any other authorities.
>
> Since Turner did not have actual or personal knowledge of the events alleged, the only other basis upon which she was required to make a report would be the development of a "reasonable cause to believe" that one of the children had been abused. Making such a determination clearly involves the exercise of discretion. It is similar to a judicial decision that there is or is not probable cause to support an asserted proposition. The very purpose of the doctrine of qualified official immunity is to protect government officials exercising discretion from second-guessing of their good faith decisions made in difficult situations such as this. The essence of reaching a determination as to whether reasonable cause exists would require discretion. This requires that Turner make reasonable inquiry into the facts, weighing the credibility of each child and then using her judgment and

---

forfeiture is imposed for such violation." A first offense violation of 620.030(1) is a Class B misdemeanor.

experience of a teacher of kindergarten level students, to reach a decision as to whether there was reasonable cause to believe that sexual abuse had occurred.

As the trial court recognized, this typifies a "legally uncertain environment." *Yanero*, 65 S.W.3d at 522 ("[Q]ualified official immunity ... affords protection from damages liability for good faith judgment calls made in a legally uncertain environment.").... Because Turner's actions were discretionary in this case and because she was entitled to qualified official immunity, she could not be held liable for the tort of negligent supervision or the statutory action under KRS 446.070....

For the foregoing reasons, the decision of the Court of Appeals is hereby reversed and the summary judgment of the trial court is reinstated.

All sitting. All concur.

Notes

In every American jurisdiction, teachers or other school authorities are mandated reporters of child abuse. However, in *Turner*, the mandatory reporting statute does not apply because of the limited definition of who qualifies as an "abused" child for purposes of reporting. Under the applicable Kentucky statute, an "abused" child that prompts mandatory reporting must be abused by his or her parent, guardian, or custodian, which was not the case in *Turner*. *See also Collum v. Charlotte-Mecklenburg Bd. of Educ.*, 614 F. Supp. 2d 598 (2008) (school district's law enforcement division had no statutory duty to report school employee's sexual abuse of student and, therefore, was not liable for negligent infliction of emotional distress under exception to public duty doctrine because officer was not present on day-to-day basis and had no direct relationship with students); *People v. Beardsley*, 263 Mich. App. 408, 688 N.W.2d 304 (2004) (in case involving sexual contact between two school children, reporting was not mandated because suspected perpetrator was not parent, legal guardian, teacher, or other person responsible for child's health and welfare). The court in *Turner*, however, recognized that teachers may be required to report when they are requested to do so. In *Turner*, the defendant was not requested to report, nor did she allow for the abuse to occur. Thus, she was not *required* to report.

The *Turner* case demonstrates the difficulty faced by school authorities who are required to exercise discretion in determining whether they must report. *See Crenshaw v. Columbus City School Bd. of Educ.*, 2008-Ohio-1424, 2008 WL 802708 (Ohio App. 10 Dist., Franklin 2008) (report by student's father of sexual assault against student did not relieve school principal of statutory duty to report to appropriate authorities); *Doe v. Dimovski*, 270 Ill. Dec. 618, 336 Ill. App.3d 292, 783 N.E.2d 193 (2003) (once school officials suspect or should suspect child may be sexually abused, they are divested of any discretion and are required to report).

Note that the *Turner* case offers an example of how a teacher's duty is defined by the limited scope of persons to whom the duty to report is owed. A reporter's duty was likewise limited in *Ward v. Greene*, 267 Conn. 539, 839 A.2d 1259 (2004), in which the Supreme Court of Connecticut held that a private child-care placement agency that failed to report suspected abuse by a day care operator did not owe a statutory duty to the mother of a child who was later killed by the same day care operator. The court noted that Connecticut's reporting statutory scheme focused the duty to report on individuals who were already abused or neglected and should have been the subject of a mandated report, rather than those who were subsequently abused by the same perpetrator. *See also Owens v. Garfield*, 784 P.2d 1187 (Utah 1989) (Utah's mandatory reporting statute did not impose duty upon state or county agency to warn parents of potential abuse by day-care worker or to prevent future abuse by worker; Utah's statute placed a duty upon state and county "to protect children *who are identified to them* as suspected victims of child abuse."). However, consider if the duty to report is different in the following case.

Yates v. Mansfield Board of Education

Supreme Court of Ohio, 2004
102 Ohio St. 3d 205, 808 N.E.2d 861, 2004-Ohio-2491

Alice Robie Resnick, J....

In a 2002 affidavit, Amanda, formerly a ninth-grade student at the Cline Avenue campus of Mansfield Senior High School, said that during the 1996–1997 school year, she informed certain school officials, including principal Michael Joseph Dick, that on three separate occasions, "Donald Coots, a coach and teacher at the school, made inappropriate contact with [her] of a sexual nature. He touched [her] with his hands and penis but [they] did not have sex. Mr. Coots also made sexually explicit comments to [her]." ... Dick conducted his own investigation of these allegations and concluded that Amanda was lying. Amanda claims that she was expelled from school for harassing a staff member. No action was taken against Coots, and the alleged abuse was never reported to the police or to a children services agency.

Three years later, on February 5, 2000, Coots engaged in sexual activity with another ninth-grade student at Mansfield High, Ashley, who at that time was 15 years of age. After returning from a boys' basketball game in Findlay at which Ashley helped to record team statistics, and while Ashley waited at the school for her mother to arrive, Coots and Ashley went into the upstairs equipment room where they kissed. Coots pushed Ashley's head down and unzipped his pants, at which time Ashley performed fellatio on Coots.... Early the following week (February 5, 2000, was a Saturday), a friend in whom Ashley had confided over the weekend informed the school counselor about what had transpired between Coots and Ashley. When confronted by the principal, Coots and Ashley admitted to the incident. The police and Ashley's parents were immediately notified, and Coots was forced to resign his employment. Ultimately, Coots was convicted of sexual battery, a third-degree felony.

Appellants brought this action both individually and as parents and legal guardians of their daughter, Ashley, against Coots and appellee. As relevant here, appellants allege that they and Ashley were injured as a proximate result of appellee's failure to report the sexual abuse alleged in 1996–1997 in violation of R.C. 2151.421 and that appellee was negligent in retaining Coots on the teaching staff at Mansfield Senior High School after his earlier alleged sexual encounters without supervising, monitoring, or otherwise protecting against his contacts with female schoolchildren.... Appellee moved for summary judgment on grounds of sovereign immunity as granted to political subdivisions under R.C. 2744.02(A)(1). Appellants opposed the motion on the basis of the exceptions to immunity set forth in R.C. 2744.02(B)(4) and (5). The trial court granted appellee's motion for summary judgment, finding that "the Board is entitled to sovereign immunity because neither of the exceptions cited by the plaintiffs appl[ies]" and ordered that the case proceed against Coots only. Appellants then dismissed their claims against Coots pursuant to Civ.R. 41(A)(1).... In a split decision, the court of appeals affirmed the judgment of the trial court with regard to both exceptions to sovereign immunity. As to former R.C. 2744.02(B)(5), which provides that "a political subdivision is liable for injury * * * when liability is expressly imposed upon the political subdivision by a section of the Revised Code * * *," Am.Sub.H.B. No. 215, 147 Ohio Laws, Part I, 909, 1150, the majority found that R.C. 2151.421 does not impose liability under the present circumstances.[1] According to the court of appeals, "R.C. 2151.421 creates a duty only to a specific child," meaning that the board's failure to report the alleged abuse of Amanda could have resulted in liability for injury only to her, not to subsequent victims. Thus, even though Ashley was sexually abused by the teacher who had molested Amanda, the court of appeals held that the board's "failure to report the prior incident of sexual misconduct between Coots and Amanda did not qualify as an exception to immunity under R.C. 2744.02(B)(5)." ... In *Yates v. Mansfield Bd. of Edn.*, 99 Ohio St.3d 48, 2003-Ohio-2461, 788 N.E.2d 1062, we accepted the discretionary appeal in this cause, reversed the judgment of the court of appeals with regard to the applicability of R.C. 2744.02(B)(4), and ordered that briefing proceed on ... the applicability of R.C. 2744.02(B)(5). The cause is now before this court....

R.C. 2151.421 provides:

"(A)(1)(a) No person described in division (A)(1)(b) of this section who is acting in an official or professional capacity and knows or suspects that a child under eighteen years of age * * * has suffered or faces a threat of suffering any physical or mental wound, injury, disability, or condition of a nature that reasonably indicates abuse or neglect of the child, shall fail to immediately report that knowledge or suspicion to the * * * public children services agency or a municipal or county peace officer in the county in which the child resides or in which the abuse or neglect is occurring or has occurred...."(b) Division (A)(1)(a) of this section applies to any person who is [a] * * * school teacher; school employee; school authority * * *."

In *Campbell* [*v. Burton*, 92 Ohio St.3d 336, 750 N.E.2d 539 (2001)], we were asked to decide whether R.C. 2151.421 expressly imposes liability on political subdivisions and their employees for purposes of the immunity exception in R.C. 2744.02(B)(5). In that case, the parents of Amber Campbell, an eighth-grade student at Baker Junior High, brought suit on behalf of their daughter claiming that the Board of Education of Fairborn City Schools and certain school employees had violated R.C. 2151.421 when they failed to report Amber's allegations that she was sexually abused by a family friend. In determining that the defendants were not entitled to immunity as respectively granted to political subdivisions and their employees under R.C. 2744.02(A)(1) and 2744.03(A)(6), we held: ... "1. Within the meaning of R.C. 2744.02(B)(5)[,] * * * R.C. 2151.421 expressly imposes liability for failure to perform the duty to report known or suspected child abuse...."2. Pursuant to R.C. 2744.02(B)(5), a political subdivision may be held liable for failure to perform a duty expressly imposed by R.C. 2151.421." *Campbell*, 92 Ohio St.3d 336, 750 N.E.2d 539, paragraphs one and two of the syllabus.

In reaching these holdings, we explained: ... "In *Brodie v. Summit Cty. Children Serv. Bd.* (1990), 51 Ohio St.3d 112, 119, 554 N.E.2d 1301, 1308, we found that the General Assembly enacted R.C. 2151.421 to safeguard children from abuse. In many instances, only the state and its political subdivisions can protect children from abuse. *Id.* Additionally, we found that children services agencies must protect children from abuse and eliminate the source of any such abuse. *Id.* Thus, it is clear that the concern of the General Assembly in enacting R.C. 2151.421 was not political subdivisions or their employees, but the protection of children from abuse and neglect.... "The General Assembly enacted R.C. 2151.421 to provide special protection to children from abuse and neglect. In order to

---

1. R.C. 2744.02(B)(5) now reads, "when civil liability is expressly imposed * * *." 2002 Am.Sub.S.B. No. 106.

achieve this goal, the General Assembly had to encourage those with special relationships with children, such as doctors and teachers, to report known or suspected child abuse. R.C. 2151.99 imposes a criminal penalty for failure to report. Furthermore, the General Assembly encouraged reporting by providing immunity from both civil and criminal liability to the persons whose duty it is to report. R.C. 2151.421(G)(1) [now R.C. 2151.421(G)(1)(a)]. Thus, the General Assembly clearly encouraged reporting and specifically discouraged the failure to report by imposing a criminal penalty pursuant to R.C. 2151.99." Id. at 341–342, 750 N.E.2d 539.

It is also clear that the General Assembly enacted R.C. 2151.421 as a mechanism for identifying and protecting abused and neglected children at the earliest possible time. In so doing, the General Assembly did not intend to withhold protection until such time as a child is actually injured. To the contrary, R.C. 2151.421(A)(1)(a) requires designated persons to "*immediately* report" their "knowledge *or suspicion*" that a child "has suffered *or faces a threat of suffering*" any injury indicative of abuse or neglect. Thus, the General Assembly clearly intended to reach potential victims of child abuse, as well as children who have already suffered abuse, in hopes that these children might be protected before they suffer any actual injury or damage.... Moreover, while the board correctly points out that the primary purpose of reporting is to facilitate the protection of abused and neglected children rather than to punish those who maltreat them, it is clear that the General Assembly considered identification and/or prosecution of the perpetrator to be a necessary and appropriate adjunct in providing such protection, especially in the institutional setting. Thus, R.C. 2151.421(F)(1) and (2) provide that children services agencies shall investigate each report of known or suspected child abuse in cooperation with law enforcement to determine, among other things, "the cause of the injuries * * * and the person or persons responsible" and "make any recommendations to the county prosecuting attorney or city director of law that it considers necessary to protect *any children* that are brought to its attention." (Emphasis added.) In addition, R.C. 2151.421(M) provides that in cases involving allegations of institutional abuse, the agency must give special notice to the appropriate officer or authority of the out-of-home care entity regarding "the person named as the alleged perpetrator in the report."

Nevertheless, the court of appeals found that because R.C. 2151.421(A)(1)(a) uses the singular term "child," and because R.C. 2151.421(C) requires the disclosure of personal information with regard to an identified abused child, the General Assembly intended to protect only the one particular child who is alleged to be abused, regardless of the circumstances. By virtue of this finding, the court of appeals confined our holdings in *Campbell* to the situation in which it is alleged that a school board's failure to report the sexual abuse of a minor student resulted in the continued or further abuse *of the same student.* The court was then able to distinguish *Campbell* from this case, since appellants are claiming that the board's failure to report the sexual abuse of a particular minor student resulted not in the further abuse of that student, but ultimately in the sexual abuse *of a different student.*

In reaching these conclusions, the court of appeals relied heavily on *Curran v. Walsh Jesuit High School* (1995), 99 Ohio App.3d 696, 651 N.E.2d 1028, in which the Ninth District Court of Appeals reached the same result, although not on grounds of sovereign immunity. In *Walsh*, two minor students at Walsh Jesuit High School, Mark Cabaniss and Michael Curran, were allegedly abused by the same teacher. Curran brought suit against the school and the Detroit Province Society of Jesus, alleging in part that defendants were negligent in failing to report the prior sexual abuse of Cabaniss in violation of R.C. 2151.421. The court of appeals held that Curran had no standing to bring a claim under

R.C. 2151.421 based on the school's failure to report the abuse of a different student, reasoning as follows: ... "We believe that R.C. 2151.421 imposes a duty which is owed solely to the minor child of whom reports have been received concerning abuse or neglect. Compare *Neuenschwander v. Wayne Cty. Children Serv. Bd.* (1994), 92 Ohio App.3d 767, 637 N.E.2d 102. In so holding, we find instructive the Supreme Court of Ohio's statement in *Brodie* that R.C. 2151.421 is 'intended to protect a specific child who is reported as abused or neglected.' *Brodie* [*v. Summit Cty. Children Serv. Bd.*, 51 Ohio St.3d] at 119, 554 N.E.2d at 1308. Accordingly, any reporting duty imposed upon Walsh officials under R.C. 2151.421 would be owed to Cabaniss rather than to Curran. Therefore, absent a duty running to Curran, it was not error for the trial court to grant the defendants summary judgment on the claims alleging negligence *per se* under R.C. 2151.421." *Curran*, 99 Ohio App.3d at 700, 651 N.E.2d 1028.

Although couched in the amorphous language of legal duty and sovereign immunity, these holdings effectively provide that a school official who responds to an allegation that a teacher sexually assaulted a minor student by arrogating to himself the authority to dispense with the statutory reporting requirements and preempt an investigation by children services — and then grants the alleged perpetrator continued and unfettered access to the children committed to his care and control — may nevertheless escape liability when the same teacher sexually abuses another minor student at the same school. Under these holdings, liability astoundingly pivots on whether the offending teacher is considerate enough of the school's reporting position to avoid molesting the same child twice. Thus, if we carry these holdings to their logical extreme, the school could decide to retain the services of a teacher who sexually abuses one minor student after another ad infinitum, could then fail to report its knowledge of each successive incident, and yet incur no liability under R.C. 2151.421 so long as the abusing teacher happens not to abuse the same child more than once.

We find this result to be entirely inconsistent with the beneficent purpose of the statute. By focusing on the referent "child" in R.C. 2151.421(A)(1)(a) and a few snippets from our opinion in *Brodie*, these courts have managed to extirpate the relational underpinnings of mandatory reporting. Because abused and neglected children lack the ability to ameliorate their own plight, R.C. 2151.421 imposes mandatory reporting duties on "those with special relationships with children, such as doctors and teachers." *Campbell*, supra, 92 Ohio St.3d at 342, 750 N.E.2d 539. See, also, R.C. 2151.421(A)(1)(b). These persons, when acting in their official or professional capacity, hold unique positions in our society. They are not only the most likely and qualified persons to encounter and identify abused and neglected children, but they are often directly responsible for the care, custody, or control of these children in one form or another. See Annotation, supra, 73 A.L.R.4th at 829; Besharov, supra, 23 Vill.L.Rev. at 466–468; Ramsey & Lawler, The Battered Child Syndrome (1974), 1 Pepperdine L.Rev. 372, 381. Those persons who do not have regular contact with children and who lack the necessary training or skill to detect the symptoms of child abuse are permitted, but not required, to report their knowledge or suspicions concerning abuse or neglect. See R.C. 2151.421(B). It is inconsistent with this design to hold that the statutory reporting duty runs solely to the identified abused child in the situation where the reporter to whom that child's control and protection has been entrusted also has direct control over the alleged perpetrator, other potential victims, and the environment in which they are brought together.

Nor does our decision in *Brodie* require or countenance such a result. *Brodie* involved a claim for damages on behalf of Tara Cook, a minor child who ended up in a coma after the Summit County Children Services Board allegedly failed to properly investigate reports that she was being abused at home by her natural father and a female cohabitant. The children services board and its agents moved for dismissal of the claim under several theories of defense, including the public-duty rule. As relevant here, we held: ... "A children services board and its agents have a duty to investigate and report their findings as required by R.C. 2151.421 when a specific child is identified as abused or neglected, and the public duty doctrine may not be raised as a defense for agency failure to comply with such statutory requirements." *Brodie*, 51 Ohio St.3d 112, 554 N.E.2d 1301, paragraph two of the syllabus.[2] ... In holding the public-duty rule inapplicable, we found that "the action required by the statute is not directed at or designed to protect the public at large, but intended to protect a specific child who is reported as abused or neglected." Id. at 119, 554 N.E.2d 1301. We also stated that the statute's "mandate is to take affirmative action on behalf of a specifically identified individual" in order to "prevent further child abuse or neglect in specific, individual cases." Id.

Assuming that the investigative duties of a children services board can be analogized to the initial reporting duties of a person described in R.C. 2151.421(A)(1)(b), our decision in *Brodie* simply does not address the situation where the identified abused child is acted upon in an environment that places other children in danger of being injured by the same perpetrator. Since the child who was reported abused in *Brodie* was also the person claiming injury, there was no occasion to consider any special circumstances involving other children. But it would be perfectly consistent to find that while the statute is not directed at or intended to protect the public at large, it is intended to protect classes of children in certain situations. For example, one would have to interpret *Brodie* quite myopically in order to surmise that our decision would have been any different if the person claiming injury in that case had been a sibling of Tara Cook living in the same household.... In fact, this was precisely the situation that confronted the Supreme Court of South Carolina in *Jensen v. Anderson Cty. Dept. of Social Serv.* (1991), 304 S.C. 195, 403 S.E.2d 615. In that case, an action was brought to recover for the wrongful death of a three-year-old child, Michael Clark, alleging that the Anderson County Department of Social Services and its agents had failed to properly investigate a report of child abuse involving Michael's brother, Shane Clark, pursuant to that state's Child Protection Act, S.C.Code Ann. 20-7-480 et seq. In determining that Michael had a viable cause of action under the Act, the court of appeals in that case employed a "special duty" test that had been formulated as an exception to the public-duty rule. Applying this test, the court of appeals concluded that Michael was plainly a member of the class of persons the statute was designed to protect. In particular, the court of appeals found that since "Shane Clark had visible physical injuries which pointed to child beating * * *, [the agency] could foresee that serious injury was likely to come to the Clark children if there were no intervention to

---

2. *Brodie*, 51 Ohio St.3d 112, 554 N.E.2d 1301, arose out of events that occurred during that twilight period in the early 1980s when the doctrine of municipal immunity had been judicially abolished, R.C. Chapter 2744, 141 Ohio Laws, Part I, 1699, 1743, was not yet effective, and the public-duty rule was clearly viable. Since then, we have held that while political subdivisions may be held liable for failure to comply with the reporting requirements of R.C. 2151.421, they are immune from liability for failure to comply with the investigative requirements of R.C. 2151.421. See *Butler v. Jordan* (2001), 92 Ohio St.3d 354, 750 N.E.2d 554; *Marshall v. Montgomery Cty. Children Serv. Bd.* (2001), 92 Ohio St.3d 348, 750 N.E.2d 549. The court has also abolished the public-duty rule with regard to actions against the state brought pursuant to R.C. Chapter 2743, the Court of Claims Act. See *Wallace v. Ohio Dept. of Commerce, Div. of State Fire Marshal*, 96 Ohio St.3d 266, 2002-Ohio-4210, 773 N.E.2d 1018. At present, the public-duty rule remains viable as applied to actions brought against political subdivisions pursuant to R.C. Chapter 2744. Id. at 281, 2002-Ohio-4210, 773 N.E.2d 1018, fn. 13.

protect them." Id. at 200, 403 S.E.2d 615, citing *Jensen v. South Carolina Dept. of Social Serv.* (S.C.App.1988), 297 S.C. 323, 331, 377 S.E.2d 102.

The agency challenged the special-duty test on the ground that it fails to consider legislative intent or ascertain the existence of a special relationship. The South Carolina Supreme Court disagreed, finding instead that "the special duty analysis is in itself an attempt to determine legislative intent" and that "the finding of a special relationship or special circumstances is implicit in the [test]." Id. at 201–202, 403 S.E.2d 615. The court then went on to explain: ... "[T]he purpose of the child abuse statutes is to provide protection for children from being abused. The statutes mandate investigation and intervention to remove endangered children when abuse has been reported. Therefore, the specific class is identifiable before the fact. When the abuse was reported in this case, a relationship was established between the Clark children and DSS." Id. at 202–203, 403 S.E.2d 615.

A similar analysis is reflected in the Eight Appellate District's decision in *Hite v. Brown* (1995), 100 Ohio App.3d 606, 654 N.E.2d 452. In that case, Sandra Hite's two daughters were allegedly molested by their maternal grandfather, Frank Brown. They brought suit against a psychologist, Robert Rogers, among others, claiming that Rogers had violated R.C. 2151.421 when he failed to report a prior allegation made by Hite's niece that she had been molested by Brown.... In considering whether Rogers's violation of the statute constituted negligence per se, the court found that although R.C. 2151.421 sets forth a specific duty to report known or suspected child abuse, the plaintiffs had not proved themselves to be within the class of persons the statute was designed to protect. In so finding, the court quoted from *Brodie* to the effect that the statutory mandate is to take affirmative action on behalf of a specifically identified child. However, unlike the court in *Curran*, supra, the court in *Hite* did not conclude its analysis at this point. Instead, the court went on to explain, "None of the plaintiffs received treatment or counseling from the psychologist. It follows that they have failed to establish that the psychologist * * * breached any duty owed to them." *Hite*, 100 Ohio App.3d at 617, 654 N.E.2d 452. In other words, in the absence of a special relationship between the psychologist and any of the plaintiffs, the psychologist owed them no duty to report the niece's allegations.

Finally, in *Perry v. S.N.* (Tex.1998), 973 S.W.2d 301, the parents of children designated B.N. and K.N. alleged that certain defendants saw the owner of a day care center bring a number of children out of the center into his adjoining home and sexually abuse them. The record did not indicate, however, whether B.N. and K.N. were among those children. Plaintiffs claimed that these defendants were negligent per se because they had failed to report the abuse pursuant to Tex.Fam.Code 261.109(a), which requires any person who "has cause to believe that a child's physical or mental health or welfare has been or may be adversely affected by abuse" to file a report with an investigative agency.... As relevant here, the Supreme Court of Texas found that "B.N. and K.N. are within the class of persons whom the child abuse reporting statute was meant to protect, and they suffered the kind of injury that the Legislature intended the statute to prevent." Id. at 305. In so finding, the court noted: ... "A few courts in other jurisdictions have interpreted mandatory reporting statutes as intended to protect only the specific child the defendant suspects is being abused, not other potential victims of the same abuser. See *Curran v. Walsh Jesuit High School*, 99 Ohio App.3d 696, 651 N.E.2d 1028, 1030–31 (1995); *Marcelletti v. Bathani*, 198 Mich.App. 655, 500 N.W.2d 124, 127 (1993). It is unclear from the pleadings whether B.N. and K.N. were among the children whom defendants saw being abused. But whether or not *Curran* and *Marcelletti*'s analysis applies to the Texas reporting statute, B.N. and K.N. are within the protected class on the facts of this case. According to the pleadings, defendants saw Daniel Keller take some of the children enrolled in the day care center out of the center into an adjoining room of the Kellers' home and sexually abuse them. This gave defendants 'cause to believe' that the 'physical or mental health or welfare' of all the children attending the day care center—'not only the particular children they saw being abused on that occasion—'may be adversely affected by abuse or neglect.'" Id. at 306, fn. 5, quoting Tex.Fam.Code 261.109(a).

The court of appeals and the board have attempted to distinguish *Perry* on the basis of some obvious language differences between the Texas statute and R.C. 2151.421. In particular, they point out that the Texas statute imposes a mandatory reporting duty on *any person* who has cause to believe that a child's physical or mental health *may be adversely affected* by abuse or neglect. Despite these dissimilarities in the two statutes, we find *Perry* instructive to the extent that it relates to the issue of whether potential victims of the same abuser can be included within the protected class under a statute that imposes a mandatory duty to report the abuse of "a child." ... For purposes of this inquiry, the two statutes are sufficiently similar to merit a comparison, since the Texas statute also begins with a reference to "a child's" physical or mental health.[3]

The proposition that emerges from all of the foregoing is rather simple and straightforward. The question of who is entitled to protection under R.C. 2151.421 in any given case depends on the circumstances and the relationships of the parties. In the typical case, the statute's mandatory reporting provisions will operate to protect only the specific child who is identified as abused because that child alone is in direct danger of further injury. But when the circumstances clearly indicate that there exists a danger of harm to another child from the same source and the reporter has an official or professional relationship with the other child, the statute does not withhold protection until such time as that child's personal security and bodily integrity are actually violated.

Schoolteachers, school officials, and school authorities have a special responsibility to protect those children committed to their care and control. School officials and school authorities, in particular, have special relationships with their teachers and direct control of the environment in which their teachers and students interact. When these persons are informed that one of their schoolchildren has been sexually abused by one of their teachers, they should readily appreciate that all of their schoolchildren are in danger. In no other context would we give even a second thought to the proposition that a school board has an obligation to deal with an instrumentality of harm to one of its students at school for the benefit of all of its students. It is irrational to suggest that the General Assembly intended to protect only the one specific minor student who is actually abused under these circumstances, and we will not interpret the statute so restrictively as to achieve an irrational result.

Accordingly, we hold that pursuant to former R.C. 2744.02(B)(5), a board of education may be held liable when its failure to report the sexual abuse of a minor student by a

---

3. However, the fact that the Texas statute imposes mandatory reporting requirements on all persons as opposed to R.C. 2151.421, which imposes such requirements only on certain officials and professionals having special relationships with children, does serve to distinguish the ultimate holding in *Perry*. The court in *Perry* ultimately concluded that it was inappropriate to adopt Tex.Fam.Code 261.109(a) as establishing a duty and standard of conduct in tort because it would impose liability "on a broad class of individuals whose relationship to the abuse was extremely indirect." *Perry*, 973 S.W.2d at 309. In so holding, the court specifically noted, "The Texas Family Code contains a separate mandatory reporting provision, *not relevant here*, specifically directed to members of certain professions. See Tex. Fam.Code § 261.101(b)." (Emphasis added.) Id. at 308, fn. 6.

teacher in violation of R.C. 2151.421 proximately results in the sexual abuse of another minor student by the same teacher.... Based on all of the foregoing, the judgment of the court of appeals is reversed, and the cause is remanded to the trial court for further proceedings consistent with this opinion.

Judgment reversed and cause remanded.

FRANCIS E. SWEENEY, SR., PFEIFER and O'CONNOR, JJ., concur.

O'DONNELL, J., concurs separately.

MOYER, C.J., and LUNDBERG STRATTON, J., dissent....

Notes

As held by the court in *Yates*, the question of who is entitled to protection under the child abuse reporting statute in a given case may depend on the circumstances of the case and the relationship of the parties. Typically, mandatory reporting statutes operate to protect the specific child that is identified as an abused child. However, as demonstrated in *Yates*, when there is the potential for harm to another child by the same perpetrator, and the reporter has a special relationship with that child, the duty to protect that child may be equally applicable. *See also Doe ex rel. Brown v. Pontotoe County School Dist.*, 957 So. 2d 410 (2007) (statute governing school district's liability for breach of statutory duty to report is more specific than general reporting statute). For further discussion of school officials' duty to report, see Karen J. Krogman, *Protecting Our Children: Reforming Statutory Provisions to Address Reporting, Investigating, and Disclosing Sexual Abuse in Public Schools*, 2011 MICH. ST. L. REV. 1606 (2011); Jason P. Nance and Philip T.K. Daniel, *Protecting Students from Abuse: Public School District Liability for Student Sexual Abuse Under State Child Abuse Reporting Laws*, 36 J.L. & EDUC. 33 (2007); Kevin S. Mahoney, *School Personnel & Mandated Reporting of Child Maltreatment*, 24 J.L. & ED. 227 (1995).

3. Other Professionals

Doe v. Doe (On Remand)

Court of Appeals of Michigan, 2010
289 Mich. App. 211, 809 N.W.2d 163

TALBOT, J....

This case involved the transport by ambulance of a minor female by two emergency medical technicians (EMTs) to a psychiatric facility following her attempted suicide and stabilization at a general hospital. The driver of the ambulance was Timothy O'Connell. The other EMT involved in the transport was Matt DeFillippo, who traveled in the rear of the ambulance with the minor and sexually molested her. The question on remand is whether O'Connell breached a statutory duty, given his suspicions that DeFillippo was engaged in improper and illicit physical contact with the minor, to report the incident of abuse in accordance with MCL 722.623. Although O'Connell did contact his supervisor while en route to seek instruction because of his suspicions and concerns regarding his partner's behavior, resulting in a police investigation and charges brought against DeFillippo, plaintiff contends that defendants also had a duty to report the abuse in accordance with the strictures of the Child Protection Law (CPL), MCL 722.621 *et seq.*...

The language of MCL 722.623 is clear and unambiguous in mandating that EMTs report child abuse to Children's Protective Services. Specifically, MCL 722.623(1) provides, in relevant part:

An *individual is required to report* under this act as follows:

(a) A physician, dentist, physician's assistant, registered dental hygienist, medical examiner, nurse, *person licensed to provide emergency medical care*, audiologist, psychologist, marriage and family therapist, licensed professional counselor, social worker, licensed master's social worker, licensed bachelor's social worker, registered social service technician, social service technician, a person employed in a professional capacity in any office of the friend of the court, school administrator, school counselor or teacher, law enforcement officer, member of the clergy, or regulated child care provider *who has reasonable cause to suspect child abuse or neglect shall make immediately, by telephone or otherwise, an oral report, or cause an oral report to be made, of the suspected child abuse or neglect to the department.* Within 72 hours after making the oral report, the reporting person shall file a written report as required in this act. [Emphasis added.]

While a reporting mandate appears to exist under the language of MCL 722.623, this requirement is limited by MCL 722.622, which provides definitions for some terms "[a]s used in this act[.]"

The term "child abuse" is defined in MCL 722.622(f) as

harm or threatened harm to a child's health or welfare that occurs through nonaccidental physical or mental injury, sexual abuse, sexual exploitation, or maltreatment, by a parent, a legal guardian, or any *other person responsible for the child's health or welfare* or by a teacher, a teacher's aide, or a member of the clergy. [Emphasis added.]

In turn, a "person responsible for the child's health or welfare" is defined in MCL 722.622(u) as encompassing

a parent, legal guardian, person 18 years of age or older who resides for any length of time in the same home in which the child resides, or, except when used in [MCL 722.627(2)(e) or MCL 722.628(8)], *nonparent adult*; or an owner, operator, volunteer, or employee of 1 or more of the following:

(*i*) A licensed or registered child care organization.

(*ii*) A licensed or unlicensed adult foster care family home or adult foster care small group home.... [Emphasis added.]

A "nonparent adult" is defined in MCL 722.622(t) to mean

a person who is 18 years of age or older and who, regardless of the person's domicile, meets *all of the following criteria* in relation to a child:

(*i*) Has substantial and regular contact with the child.

(*ii*) Has a close personal relationship with the child's parent or with a person responsible for the child's health or welfare.

(*iii*) Is not the child's parent or a person otherwise related to the child by blood or affinity to the third degree. [Emphasis added.]

Consequently, the statutory definitions specifically limit the reporting requirements of MCL 722.623 in accordance with the meanings attributed to the terms "child abuse," "person responsible for the child's health or welfare," and "nonparent adult." On the basis of these restrictive definitions, MCL 722.623(1)(a) mandates reporting of suspected child abuse to Children's Protective Services by the enumerated professional disciplines only if the perpetrator of the abuse has a very specific relationship with the minor child. Specifically, MCL 722.623(1)(a) requires reporting of suspected child abuse only if the perpetrator is the parent, legal guardian, teacher, teacher's aide, clergyman, "or any other person responsible for the child's health or welfare," including a "nonparent adult," as those terms are defined by MCL 722.622(u) and (t). In other words, the imposition of a duty to report suspected child abuse to Children's Protective Services is based, not on the occurrence of such abuse, but on the type of relationship the alleged perpetrator has with the minor child. While such an outcome would seem to be contrary to the normal usage or understanding of such phrases and to the mandatory nature of MCL 722.623(1)(a), the statutory definitions encompassing the term "child abuse" preclude the imposition of a reporting requirement on defendants under the factual circumstances of this case.

To explain this apparent discrepancy, we examine both the stated purpose of the CPL and a previous decision by another panel of this Court. The CPL indicates its purpose as comprising:

> An act to require the reporting of child abuse and neglect *by certain persons*; to permit the reporting of child abuse and neglect by all persons; *to provide for the protection of children who are abused or neglected*; to authorize limited detainment in protective custody; to authorize medical examinations.... [Title of 1975 PA 238 (emphasis added).]

In *People v. Beardsley*, 263 Mich.App. 408, 413–414, 688 N.W.2d 304 (2004), a different panel of this Court reconciled the purpose of the act with its definitional limitations, stating, in relevant part:

> This Court must give effect to the interpretation that accomplishes the statute's purpose. The preamble to the CPL states that the purpose of the CPL is, in part, "to require the reporting of child abuse and neglect by certain persons." The statute's definition of "child abuse," which identifies parents and others responsible for a child's health and welfare, reflects the statute's purpose of protecting children in situations where abuse and neglect frequently go unreported, i.e., when perpetrated by family members or others with control over the child. Hence, reports are required to be made to the FIA rather than to the police, which would be the appropriate agency to contact in the case of sexual abuse involving a person without any familial contacts or other authority over the child. Typically, parents, teachers, and others who are responsible for the health and welfare of a child will be the first to report instances of child abuse by unrelated third parties. This act is designed to protect children when the persons who normally do the reporting are actually the persons responsible for the abuse, and thus unlikely to report it. [Citation omitted.]

By way of this ruling, we wish to emphasize that the absence of a statutory duty under MCL 722.623(1)(a) to report this wrongdoing to Children's Protective Services does not affect the propriety or alleviate the moral obligation of contacting law enforcement personnel to seek an investigation of such reprehensible criminal conduct.[2] ... Thus, on the basis of the limiting language of the statutory definitions, we reverse the trial court's

---

2. We note that in the present case a report was made to the police and charges were filed against defendant DeFillippo. DeFillippo pleaded guilty with regard to a charge of third-degree criminal sexual conduct before this action was filed.

denial of defendants' motion for summary disposition regarding the failure to report the suspected abuse in accordance with MCL 722.623(1)(a).

Reversed.

Notes

A majority of states include specific categories of professionals that are mandated reporters. In *Turner*, these included teachers, and in *Doe*, these included emergency medical technicians (EMTs), although in both cases, the duty to report was limited by other statutory definitions. In some states, mandatory reporters include attorneys (including court-appointed advocates) and other law enforcement professionals, *see, e.g.*, Ark. Code Ann. §§ 12-18-402 (judges, law enforcement officials, peace officers, prosecuting attorneys, court-appointed special advocate program staff members or volunteers, and attorneys ad litem); Miss. Code Ann. § 43-21-353 (attorneys or law enforcement officers); N.Y. Soc. Serv. Law § 413 (peace officers, police officers, district attorneys or assistant district attorneys, investigators employed in the office of a district attorney, or other law enforcement officials); Ohio Rev. Code Ann. § 2151.421 (attorneys); S.C. Code Ann. § 63-7-310 (judges). Many states include clergy, *see, e.g.*, Ala. Code § 26-14-3 (members of the clergy); Ark. Code Ann. § 12-18-402 (clergy members, which include ministers, priests, rabbis, accredited Christian Science practitioners, or other similar functionary of a religious organization); Cal. Penal Code § 11165.7 (clergy members and custodians of records of clergy members); N.D. Cent. Code § 50-25.1-03 (religious practitioners of the healing arts; members of the clergy); Ohio Rev. Code Ann. § 2151.421 (persons, other than clerics, rendering spiritual treatment through prayer in accordance with the tenets of a well-recognized religion); Wisc. Stat. § 48.981 (members of the clergy or a religious order, including brothers, ministers, monks, nuns, priests, rabbis, or sisters). The duty to report for attorneys and clergy may also be limited by respective privileges. *See* Chapter Five, Section II.A (Privileged Communications), *infra*.

Many states include other professional categories that are likely to have access to children or information associated with child abuse, including: (1) Athletic coaches and staff, *see, e.g.*, Cal. Penal Code § 11165.7 (athletic coaches, including, but not limited to, assistant coaches or graduate assistants involved in coaching at public or private postsecondary institutions, and athletic administrators, or athletic directors employed by any public or private schools); Colo. Rev. Stat. § 19-3-304 (directors, coaches, assistant coaches, or athletic program personnel employed by private sports organizations or programs); Iowa Code §§ 232.69 & 728.14 (school employees, certified paraeducators, coaches, or instructors employed by community colleges); Or. Rev. Stat. §§ 419B.005 & 419B.010 (coaches, assistant coaches, or trainers of athletes, if compensated and if the athlete is a child); (2) Commercial film or photographic processors, *see, e.g*, Alaska Stat. §§ 47.17.020 & 47.17.023 (persons who process or produce visual or printed matter, either privately or commercially); Cal. Penal Code § 11165.7 (commercial film and photographic print or image processors; computer technicians); Ga. Code Ann. §§ 19-7-5 & 16-12-100 (persons who process or produce visual or printed matter); Mo. Rev. Stat. §§ 210.115, 352.400 & 568.110 (commercial film and photographic print processors; computer providers, installers, or repair persons; or Internet service providers); and (3) Animal Control Officers, *see, e.g.*, Cal. Penal Code § 11165.7 (animal control or Humane Society officers); Colo. Rev. Stat. § 19-3-304 (officers and agents of the State Bureau of Animal Protection and animal control officers); D.C. Code § 4-1321.02 (law enforcement officers or humane officers of any agency charged with the enforcement of animal cruelty laws); 325 Ill. Comp. Stat. § 5/4 & 720 Ill. Comp. Stat. § 5/11-20.2 (animal control officers or Department of Agriculture Bureau of Animal Health and Welfare field investigators); VA. CODE ANN. § 63.2-1509 (animal control officers). The following case involves another category of professional that may be mandated to report—police officers.

Pinto v. City of Visalia

Court of Appeal, Fifth District, California, 2006
43 Cal. Rptr. 3d 613

GOMES, J....

In March 2001, the City of Visalia Police Department (VPD) hired Pinto as a police officer. On March 27, 2003, the VPD, through its Assistant Chief of Police Robert Williams, gave Pinto written notice that VPD intended to terminate his employment effective April 30, 2003. The notice specified four causes for the dismissal: (1) in December 2002/January 2003, he was "informed about a sexual relationship between a minor and an adult and failed to report it"; (2) in November 2002, he was "advised of a sexual assault between an adult suspect and minor victim and failed to report it"; (3) in January 2003, he "lied during the course of a criminal investigation"; and (4) in December 2002/January 2003, he "encouraged an involved party to lie during the course of the investigation." The letter listed seven policies of the Visalia Police Department Manual (VPDM) and two sections of the Visalia City Personnel Policy Guidelines which were claimed to have been violated, and notified Pinto of the opportunity to respond to the allegations. As pertinent here, one of these policies was VPDM section 330.3, which provides: "All employees of this department are responsible for the proper reporting of child abuse. Any employee who encounters any child whom he or she reasonably suspects has been the victim of child abuse, shall immediately take appropriate action and prepare a crime report pursuant to Penal Code Section 11166."... Pinto submitted a response to the notice of intent to terminate his employment, which addressed the charges and requested Williams reconsider the termination decision or consider alternate forms of discipline. VPD Chief of Police Jerry L. Barker reviewed Williams's recommendation of termination, Pinto's response, and the documents from the internal affairs investigation, and concurred termination was appropriate. On April 25, 2003, Barker sent Pinto a notice of termination of employment, which informed Pinto he was being terminated effective April 30, 2003, for the same four reasons set forth in Williams's letter....

Pinto requested an administrative hearing, which was held in January 2004. Documentary evidence was introduced consisting of the internal affairs investigation file, Pinto's employment records, and relevant sections of the VPDM, and testimony received from Pinto, VPD Detective Steven Shear, VPD Lieutenant Michelle Figueroa, Williams, and Barker.... The evidence disclosed the following facts. In September 2002, Pinto was taking a break in a gourmet coffee shop while in uniform and on-duty. A woman approached him and identified herself as the stepmother of 20-year-old Justin Helt. The woman told Pinto Helt was having problems with an ex-boyfriend and needed some advice, and asked Pinto if he could talk to Helt. Pinto gave her his business card, which had his work cell phone and office phone numbers on it. About an hour later, Helt called Pinto on his work cell phone. Helt told Pinto he had recently broken up with 16-year-old C. F., who he had been dating, that he felt C. was stalking and harassing him, and asked what he could do. Pinto told Helt he could take a police report for stalking or harassment, and told him how to get a restraining order. Helt declined to do anything, stating he would deal with it and call Pinto back if the problem continued....

Later that afternoon, Helt called Pinto again to ask a few more questions. During this conversation, Helt and Pinto agreed to meet socially at the coffee shop when Pinto was off duty to "hang out." While at the coffee shop that night around 9:00 p.m., Pinto saw a male come up behind Helt, put his hand over Helt's eyes, and say "guess who." Helt got up from the table and went around the corner to talk to this person. When their conversation ended, C. sat down a few tables away, then left the coffee shop. Helt came back to Pinto's table and told Pinto the person was his ex-boyfriend, C. Pinto was not introduced to C. and did not speak to him.... A couple weeks later, Pinto was on the internet in a gay chat room when a person who identified himself as an 18-year-old male from Tulare started talking to him there. Later in the conversation, the person sent Pinto a picture of himself, which Pinto recognized as C. Pinto told C. he knew both his identity and that he was not 18. From their internet exchange, Pinto believed C. was upset and depressed about his relationship with Helt and life as a gay person. Pinto tried to encourage C. by telling him that although he is gay, he has a career as a police officer. Pinto agreed to pick C. up at his home in Tulare and take him to the coffee shop for coffee, believing he might be able to help mentor him, as Pinto was an explorer advisor for the VPD explorer post and, having been a gay teenager, may have shared some of C.'s experiences and feelings.... At the meeting with C., Pinto became very uncomfortable with C.'s behavior, as it became apparent to Pinto that C. was not despondent and was openly making sexual advances towards him in an attempt to make Helt jealous. C. wanted to "hook up" with Pinto, which means he wanted to have sex with him. Pinto ended the meeting and drove C. back to his home. Pinto gave C. his personal cell phone number so C. could call him if he needed advice. Over the next four to six weeks, Pinto spoke on the phone with C. several times. In those calls, C. asked Pinto about Helt, but also told Pinto about other people he was meeting over the internet. Although C. asked Pinto if he wanted to hang out again, Pinto did not meet with C. again because C. "wanted one thing that night," and Pinto was not going to subject himself to that kind of behavior again....

In late October or early November 2002, Pinto had a one-time sexual "encounter" with an adult man named Aaron Rodriguez. In mid to late November or early December 2002, while he was at home and off-duty, Pinto received a telephone call from C. on his personal cell phone, asking him for general advice. C. asked Pinto if he knew a guy named Aaron. Pinto said he didn't think so. C. told Pinto he had talked online to Aaron, who was about 25 years old, and they agreed to meet for sex. C. told Aaron he was 18 years old. C. said Aaron picked him up at his house and took him to Aaron's house. By the time they got there, C. decided maybe he didn't want to have sex, but he never told Aaron no. C. said Aaron "pressured him to finish" and offered him drugs. After having sex, C. went home. A couple days later, C. learned from others on the internet that Aaron was HIV positive, and told Pinto he was worried about his health. Pinto told C. that: (1) he needed to tell his mother; (2) he needed to get tested for HIV; and (3) he needed to report the incident to the Tulare Police Department, and offered to drive him there so he could make a report. C. declined Pinto's offer and said he wanted to talk to his mother. This was the last conversation Pinto had with C.... At the time of this conversation, Pinto had not made the connection that the "Aaron" C. was referring to was the Aaron Rodriguez Pinto had an encounter with, and Pinto did not believe the alleged sex act had taken place within the jurisdiction of the city of Visalia, as C. appeared to refer to the city of Tulare. Pinto did not report C.'s claims because he had no idea where the incident occurred, he received the information while off duty and was not engaged in any law enforcement activity at the time, and he believed he was not giving advice within the course and scope of his employment. Pinto acknowledged he would have been obligated to file a report had he received the information while on duty. Pinto believed C. contacted him as a civilian, not as an officer, because C. didn't directly ask him to make a report for him and instead asked him what he should do.... C. eventually filed a police report with the Tulare Police Department on December 20, 2002. A few days later, Pinto learned from his roommate, Dan Martin, of a scenario a Tulare Police Department report writing instructor related to Martin's police academy class, which involved a gay male adult and gay male juvenile who met on an internet chat room and agreed to have sex. The adult believed the juvenile to be an adult, based on repeated assurances of his age, and fully believed the one-time sexual encounter was consensual and between adults. Pinto realized from the scenario that this was referring to the case of C. and Aaron, and told Martin that.

Sometime in late December 2002 or early January 2003, Pinto spoke with Helt on his personal cell phone while off-duty. Helt told Pinto he learned from C. that Helt's and Pinto's names were mentioned in the police report, in which C. was accusing Aaron of a sexual act. Pinto asked what he was worried about. Helt admitted that he and C. not only dated, they were also involved in a sexual relationship. This was the first time Pinto learned Helt and C. were having sex and the first time he learned his own name was mentioned in the police report, although he did not know in what context.... The police report was eventually transferred to VPD as it was within VPD's jurisdiction. On January 10, 2003, VPD Detective Steve Shear interviewed Pinto as part of the criminal investigation. Shear advised Pinto he was being interviewed because his name had been brought up both as a witness and suspect in a criminal investigation, but he did not tell Pinto what the investigation was about. Shear told Pinto he wasn't in custody and didn't have to speak to him, but Pinto agreed to do so. Pinto told Shear he believed the investigation had something to do with C. "hooking up" with people on the internet. Shear asked Pinto why he thought that. Pinto responded that C. "is a troubled little boy" and he was introduced to him through Helt after C. and Helt broke up. Pinto admitted he had talked to C. online a couple times, C. was always asking Pinto for advice, which he gave him, and C. called him in regards to his situation with Aaron.... Shear questioned Pinto about how he met Helt and C., and what C. told him about Aaron. Pinto told Shear he knew Helt and C. had a sexual relationship when C. was 16....

After the interview, Pinto was placed on paid administrative leave. As a result of the criminal investigation, an internal affairs investigation was initiated in February 2003 and completed in March 2003. VPD Lieutenant Michelle Figueroa was in charge of the investigation and found several violations of VPD policy including: (1) Pinto failed to report the sexual activity between Aaron and C., and Helt and C., which he was required to do because he learned the information in his capacity as a police officer and he knew he was a police officer 24 hours per day, 7 days per week; ... Figueroa forwarded her findings to her supervisor, Lieutenant Wheeler, for his review, who in turn forwarded them to Assistant Chief of Police Bob Williams.... Figueroa did not consult any legal opinions when determining whether Pinto was required to report the sexual relationships between C., Aaron and Helt. In her opinion, Pinto was a police officer 24 hours per day, 7 days per week, even though no VPD policy states this; neither does any VPD policy state that officers are required to report child abuse when they learn the information while off-duty. Figueroa further explained that because Pinto himself believed he was a police officer 24 hours per day, 7 days per week, he was on duty and therefore obligated to report the sexual relationships. In her report, Figueroa stated that when she interviewed Pinto, she asked him if he would submit to a voice stress analysis test to clear up some inconsistencies if C. would also do so. Pinto said no. Figueroa denied, however, that Pinto's refusal was a factor in her determinations. Figueroa testified that although Pinto was under criminal investigation during the internal affairs investigation, by the time of the administrative hearing, there were no criminal charges pending against him.[2] ...

Assistant Chief Williams reviewed the internal affairs investigation and requested that Lieutenant Wheeler present the case to senior staff, which included those with the rank of lieutenant and above, as well as two civilians. The group unanimously recommended termination. Williams also concluded termination was appropriate.... In Williams's opinion, the nature of a police officer's job is 24 hours per day, 7 days per week, and a police officer is subject to the mandated reporting requirements regardless of whether the officer is on or off duty. Williams believed Pinto was acting as a police officer and was on duty when he gave advice to both C. and Helt, as the advice drew from his training and experience.... In Williams's opinion, a police officer is on duty whenever he learns about something that must be reported, although he admitted this expectation is not spelled out in VPD policy.... Chief Barker testified he believed Pinto's conduct was unbecoming to VPD because he made a series of poor judgments and put VPD in a position of liability by his relationship with C. Barker believed when a police officer takes an oath of office he's an officer 24 hours per day and is held to a higher standard....

On March 14, 2004, the arbitrator issued a proposed decision in which he made findings of fact and concluded the evidence was sufficient to sustain Pinto's termination for the ... allegations, namely that Pinto failed to report the sexual relationships between C., Helt, and Aaron.... The arbitrator further found that the acts of misconduct which the evidence sustained violated the VPDM sections and Visalia Personnel Policy Guidelines enumerated in the notice of termination of employment. He made findings of fact in substance as follows: (1) VPDM section 330, which mandates all VPD employees to report instances of child abuse, does not limit the employee's reporting responsibilities to only times when the employee obtains the information while on duty; (2) nevertheless, Pinto was in performance of his duties when he obtained the information regarding the sexual relationships between C., Aaron and Helt, as the people who contacted him viewed him as an officer, sought his advice based on his status as an officer, and Pinto's advice was based on his knowledge and training as an officer; (3) the fact that Pinto learned Helt and C. were in a dating relationship required him to file a police report; (4) Pinto's awareness of the sexual relationship between C. and Aaron required him to file a police report; [and] (5) Shear's question about Pinto's relationship with Aaron was a legitimate question for police investigation business.... On April 14, 2004, City Manager Steven M. Salomon issued a final administrative decision upholding the arbitrator's proposed decision, and terminated Pinto from his employment effective April 30, 2003....

Pinto filed a petition for writ of mandate in superior court, in which he asserted the City abused its discretion as follows: (1) Pinto complied with VPDM section 330.3 in that he acted pursuant to Penal Code section 11166; (2) the City and VPD have no specific policies regarding mandated reporting requirements while off duty; (3) the City relied on unwritten or unknown policies, violating Pinto's due process rights; and (4) in terminating Pinto. The petition requested a writ issue directing the City to set aside the decision and restore Pinto to employment or, in the alternative, remand the matter to Salomon with directions to set aside the decision and impose a penalty less than termination.... Following oral argument on the petition, the trial court issued a written order granting the writ and remanding the matter to the City to impose a penalty less than ter-

---

2. Figueroa noted in her internal affairs report that Pinto had been criminally charged with two counts of sodomy with a minor and three counts of oral copulation with a minor. A jury later acquitted Pinto of these charges.

mination. With respect to the arbitrator's findings that Pinto was required to report the relationships between C., Helt and Aaron, the trial court found: (1) VPDM section 330.3 required Pinto to be either on duty or have received the information in his professional capacity before he was obligated to make a report; (2) there was no evidence that Pinto knew the relationship between C. and Helt was a sexual one; and (3) while Pinto knew of the sexual relationship between C. and Aaron, he was not on-duty or acting in his professional capacity when he obtained the information, as Helt, C. and Pinto were social friends.... Therefore, making its own independent judgment, the court finds the preponderance of the evidence does not support the finding of the arbitrator or the City for the first two allegations.... The City filed a motion to set aside and vacate the trial court's order, which asserted, in pertinent part, the court's order was incorrect, erroneous and not consistent with the facts as ... the trial court's conclusion that Pinto did not obtain the information about the relationship between Aaron and C. in his professional capacity was contrary to VPD's stated policy.... Following oral argument, the trial court denied the motion....

The City first challenges the trial court's finding that Pinto did not engage in misconduct when he failed to report the relationship between C. and Aaron.[3] The City argues (1) the trial court erroneously interpreted the City's personnel policy regarding mandated reporting as requiring an employee to report suspected child abuse only if the employee receives the information while on duty or within the employee's professional capacity, and (2) even if the trial court construed the policy correctly, substantial evidence does not support the trial court's decision that Pinto was not acting in his professional capacity when he received the information....

VPDM section 330.3 provides: "All employees of this department are responsible for the proper reporting of child abuse. Any employee who encounters any child whom he or she reasonably suspects has been the victim of child abuse, shall immediately take appropriate action and prepare a crime report pursuant to Penal Code § 11166." Subdivision (a) of Penal Code section 11166 provides in pertinent part: "... , a mandated reporter shall make a report to an agency specified in [Penal Code] Section 11165.9 whenever the mandated reporter, in his or her professional capacity or within the scope of his or her employment, has knowledge of or observes a child whom the mandated reporter knows or reasonably suspects has been the victim of child abuse or neglect...."[4] A mandated reporter includes a peace officer. (Pen.Code, § 11165.7, subd. (a)(19).)

The City argued below that VPDM section 330.3 is broader than Penal Code section 11166, in that it requires all employees to report all known and reasonably suspected incidents of child abuse, not just abuse an employee becomes aware of while in the scope of employment or acting within his or her professional capacity. The trial court, however, rejected that interpretation, finding instead that VPDM section 330.3 incorporates the restrictions of Penal Code section 11166, namely that a mandated reporter is only required to report suspected child abuse when the information is obtained in the employee's professional capacity or within the scope of employment, and therefore Pinto only could

---

3. The City does not challenge the trial court's finding that the evidence was insufficient to support the arbitrator's finding that Pinto was informed of a sexual relationship between C. and Helt yet failed to report it.

4. The agencies specified in Penal Code section 11165.9 include "any police department or sheriff's department...."

have violated section 330.3 if he failed to report suspected abuse he learned about either while on duty or within his professional capacity....

The trial court found that Pinto did not violate VPDM section 330.3 when he failed to report the relationship between C. and Aaron because he did not obtain the information either while on duty or in his professional capacity. In so finding, the trial court rejected the arbitrator's determination that because Helt's stepmother contacted Pinto in his official capacity, C.'s later contact was also in Pinto's official capacity. Instead, the trial court found that Pinto did not obtain the information in his professional capacity because Helt and Pinto, both adults, had become social friends; Pinto met C. on the internet and recognized his photograph as being the person he met with Helt; and Pinto took the call in which C. reported his relationship with Aaron while off-duty on his private cell phone two to three months after Helt's stepmother contacted Pinto. The trial court reasoned that this passage of time, coupled with the fact that C. and Pinto had become social friends, showed that Pinto did not obtain the information in his professional capacity.... The City argues these findings are not supported by substantial evidence. Specifically, the City asserts that because Pinto gave C. advice when C. called to discuss his relationship with Aaron, Pinto necessarily was acting in his professional capacity as a law enforcement officer because his responses were based on his police officer training, experience and knowledge. Essentially, the City is contending that when a mandated reporter receives information of suspected child abuse in a personal capacity, but then gives advice based on his or her professional training, the reporter is now acting in his or her professional capacity and therefore is required to comply with Penal Code section 11166.

We do not agree the mere giving of advice means that Pinto received the information about C. and Aaron within his professional capacity. To hold otherwise would mean a mandated reporter who gives advice on an informal basis would be exposed to liability for failure to report suspected child abuse regardless of the circumstances in which the information was obtained. We note that Penal Code section 11166 imposes the obligation to report suspected child abuse on a "mandated reporter" who is acting in either a "professional capacity" or within the scope of employment. (Pen.Code, § 11166, subd. (a).) The apparent reason for including both limitations is that mandated reporters include occupations in which the individual is either an employee, such as teachers, instructional aides, administrators and peace officers, or a professional who renders professional services, such as a physician, psychiatrist, or psychologist, who is not necessarily an employee. (Pen.Code, § 11165.7, subd. (a).) In situations where the mandated reporter renders professional services, the obligation to report is imposed when the mandated reporter obtains the information while rendering such services. (See, e.g., *Krikorian v. Barry* (1987) 196 Cal.App.3d 1211, 1223, 242 Cal.Rptr. 312 ["... in most cases, mandatory child abuse reporting will be preceded by the rendering of professional services by the party making the report...."].)

Here, substantial evidence supports the trial court's finding that Pinto did not receive the information from C. about his relationship with Aaron either within the scope of employment or while rendering professional services. Pinto was not working as a police officer when C. called him and he gave C. advice, as he was off duty and at home when he received C.'s phone call; Pinto did not assume the duties of a police officer during the conversation; and C. and Pinto had a social relationship. That Pinto may have drawn on his training and experience as a police officer when giving C. advice does not mean he was rendering professional services, as Pinto was not working as a police officer at the time. Contrary to the City's assertion, Pinto did not receive the information in his capacity as a police officer, and therefore the fact he gave advice does not transform the conversation with C. into the rendering of professional services.... In sum, the trial court's finding that Pinto did not receive the information about suspected child abuse either in the scope of his employment or in a professional capacity is supported by substantial evidence. Accordingly, the City's claim that Pinto committed misconduct in failing to report that information fails....

The judgment is affirmed and the matter is remanded to the trial court for its determination of the amount of an award to respondent for attorney fees on appeal. Respondent is awarded his costs on appeal.

WE CONCUR: HARRIS, Acting P.J., and CORNELL, J.

Notes

Police and law enforcement officials are included as mandated reporters in most states. However, in the *Pinto* decision, the mandate to report did not apply because the defendant was not on duty or acting in his official capacity as a police officer when he receive the information about the sexual abuse of the child or gave advice. *See also Kassey S. v. City of Turlock*, 212 Cal. App. 4th 1276, 151 Cal. Rptr. 3d 714 (2013) (police included as mandated reporters, but police officer not required to report his own abuse of child). For a detailed discussion of reporting provisions that apply the phrase, "acting in his or her professional capacity," and the relevance of such phrases, see *State v. Strauch*, 2015 WL 1005021 (Sup. Ct. N.M., Mar. 9, 2015) (social worker acting in private capacity still mandated reporter). Note that when mandated reporters fail to make appropriate reports, they may be subject to criminal and civil liability. These issues are addressed below.

B. Liability for Failure to Report

1. Criminal Liability

State v. Grover

Supreme Court of Minnesota, 1989

437 N.W.2d 60

COYNE, Justice.

Defendant Curtis Lowell Grover is the principal of an elementary school. The State charged him with two counts of the misdemeanor offense of failing to report child abuse, Minn.Stat. § 626.556, subd. 6 (1986).... Early in 1987 the Cottage Grove Police Department learned that the Washington County Social Services Department had received two separate complaints of possible sexual abuse of students by a teacher at an elementary school. During the course of their investigation the police obtained the facts on which this two-count misdemeanor prosecution is based. Specifically, they learned that sometime in the spring of 1986 a mother had spoken with defendant about the teacher in question having pinched her son on the buttocks on two occasions, and that in late 1986 another mother had spoken with defendant about the same teacher having squeezed the buttocks of her 11-year-old son sometime that fall.

During their investigation the police also obtained the facts underlying two *Spreigl* notices which the State has filed informing the defendant of the State's intent to present evidence, pursuant to Minn.R.Evid. 404(b), of two other alleged violations of the reporting act by defendant. One notice relates to defendant's failure to report that in February 1984 a mother had complained that the teacher in question had choked her son in class, leaving marks on the boy's neck. The other *Spreigl* notice relates to defendant's failure to report that in September 1984 a mother had complained that the teacher had patted her daughter on the buttocks as she was leaving the classroom and that the teacher had almost choked her son in the boy's bathroom.

Since 1975 Minnesota has had a child abuse reporting law enacted in response to the requirements of the Federal Child Abuse Prevention and Treatment Act of 1974, 42 U.S.C.A. §§ 5101–07, and regulations promulgated pursuant thereto, 45 CFR §§ 1340.1–.15 (1987). *See State v. Andring*, 342 N.W.2d 128, 131 (Minn.1984). Federal assistance for child abuse programs is conditioned on adoption by the state of a child abuse and neglect law providing for the reporting of "*known and suspected* instances of child abuse and neglect." 42 U.S.C.A. § 5103(b)(2)(B) (emphasis supplied). *See also* 45 CFR § 1340.14 (1987)....

The operative portion of [Minn.Stat. § 626.556 (1986)] mandates the reporting of abuse:

A professional * * * who is engaged in the practice of * * * education * * * who knows or has reason to believe a child is being neglected or physically or sexually abused shall immediately report the information to the local welfare agency, police department or the county sheriff * * * *

Minn.Stat. § 626.556, subd. 3(a) (1986). Section 626.556, subd. 2(a) defines "sexual abuse" to include the subjection of a child to any act which constitutes a violation of the criminal sexual conduct statutes, *see* Minn.Stat. §§ 609.342–.345, and any act involving a minor which constitutes a violation of the prostitution laws, *see* Minn.Stat. §§ 609.321–.324, or the laws relating to the use of minors in a sexual performance, *see* Minn.Stat. § 617.246. Section 626.556, subd. 2(d) defines "physical abuse" to include any physical injury inflicted on the child "other than by accidental means" or any physical injury "that cannot reasonably be explained by the child's history of injuries." Section 626.556, subd. 2(c) defines "neglect" to include failure to supply the child with necessary food, clothing, shelter or medical care or failure to protect the child from conditions imminently and seriously endangering the child's health. The act, at subdivision 4, provides a reporter with immunity from any liability that otherwise might result from his making a report if he makes the report in good faith (*i.e.*, not maliciously). The penalty provision, subdivision 6, is the provision with which we are primarily concerned:

A person mandated by this section to report who knows or has reason to believe that a child is neglected or physically or sexually abused, as defined in subdivision 2, and fails to report is guilty of a misdemeanor....

Defendant argues that "reason to believe" and "physically or sexually abused" are all terms which are uncertain or susceptible of arbitrary enforcement. The argument ignores, we think, both the context in which the terms appear and our obligation to uphold the constitutionality of a statute by construing it narrowly. *E.g.*, *Welfare of S.L.J.*, 263 N.W.2d at 419 (constitutionality of disorderly conduct statute overly broad and vague as written upheld by construing it narrowly to refer only to "fighting words"); *State v. Hipp*, 298 Minn. 81, 87, 213 N.W.2d 610, 614 (1973) (construction of unlawful assembly statute narrowed to protect its constitutionality).... Minnesota's criminal code provides that "'know' requires only that the actor believes that the specified fact exists." Minn.Stat. § 609.02, subd. 9(2) (1986). Thus, it is apparent that violation of the child abuse reporting statute entails either one of two levels of culpability: A mandated reporter who knows or believes that a child is being or has been abused but fails to report it exhibits the callousness associated with the knowing commission of a criminal act. On the other hand, neither knowing violation nor conscious disregard of substantial risk are requisite to a violation of the reporting act. A mandated reporter who has reason to know or believe that a child is being or has been abused but fails to recognize it also violates the statute though the actor's culpability is merely negligent rather than purposeful, knowing or reckless. *See* Model Penal Code § 2.02 (1985). *See also*, Robinson & Grall, *Element Analysis in Defining Criminal Liability: The Model Penal Code and Beyond*, 35 Stan.L.Rev. 681, 694 (1983)....

That the term "know or has reason to believe" has acquired a meaning in Minnesota involving reasonably definite standards seems apparent from the use of a variant of the term in Minn.Stat. § 609.53, subd. 1 (1986), which makes it a crime to receive, possess, transfer, buy or conceal stolen property, "knowing or having reason to know the property was stolen or obtained by robbery." Although the constitutionality of Minn.Stat. § 609.53 (1986) has not been challenged on grounds of vagueness or overbreadth, the constitutionality of similar language in other statutes concerning the receipt of stolen property has been upheld, apparently uniformly. *See State v. Emmons*, 57 Ohio App.2d 173, 174, 386 N.E.2d 838, 839–40 (1978); *Newton v. State*, 271 Ark. 427, 431, 609 S.W.2d 328, 330–31 (1980); *People v. Holloway*, 193 Colo. 450, 453, 568 P.2d 29, 31 (1977); *State v. Bandt*, 219 Kan. 816, 820, 549 P.2d 936, 940 (1976); *State v. Chaisson*, 123 N.H. 17, 26, 458 A.2d 95, 100 (1983). If the phrase know or have reason to know or believe is clear, definite, plain and unambiguous enough to provide a standard by which we expect Fagin and his ilk to govern their conduct, it seems sufficiently clear and definite to provide a standard for the governance of the conduct of an educator or other professional.

The United States Supreme Court, too, has upheld statutes making negligent or unreasonable conduct criminal against void-for-vagueness challenges. For example, in *Nash v. United States*, 229 U.S. 373, 377, 33 S.Ct. 780, 781, 57 L.Ed. 1232 (1913), Justice Oliver Wendell Holmes responded to the contention that the criminal provisions against unreasonable restraint of trade contained in the Sherman Act were unconstitutionally vague with these words:

> [T]he law is full of instances where a man's fate depends on his estimating rightly, that is, as the jury subsequently estimates it, some matter of degree. If his judgment is wrong, not only may he incur a fine or a short imprisonment, as here; he may incur the penalty of death.

To the same effect, *see United States v. Ragen*, 314 U.S. 513, 62 S.Ct. 374, 86 L.Ed. 383 (1942). Applying a statute making it a crime for a corporation to knowingly deduct from gross income amounts that are in excess of "reasonable" compensation for any services rendered by the recipients, the court there stated, "The mere fact that a penal statute is so framed as to require a jury upon occasion to determine a question of reasonableness is not sufficient to make it too vague to afford a practical guide to permissible conduct." *Id.* at 523, 62 S.Ct. at 378....

Similarly, we have no difficulty in concluding that the statute in question is not unconstitutionally overbroad in the sense of sweeping too broadly, reaching a significant amount of constitutionally protected activity. *See State v. Krawsky*, 426 N.W.2d 875, 877–78 (Minn.1988) (upholding against overbreadth and vagueness challenge statute making it a misdemeanor to interfere with a police officer in the performance of his duties). Specifically, we find no merit to the argument that requiring compliance with the statute might somehow interfere with the mandatory reporter's right of free speech by compelling him to espouse a viewpoint with which he may not wish to be associated. The mandatory reporting requirement of the child abuse statute compels no "expression" in the sense reflected in *Wooley v. Maynard*, 430 U.S. 705, 715, 97 S.Ct. 1428, 1435, 51 L.Ed.2d 752 (1977), in which it was held that the first amendment prohibits laws that require an individual "to be an instrument for fostering public adherence to an ideological point of view he finds unacceptable." The statute does not compel the dissemination of an "ideological point of view," but only mandates the reporting of information—a requirement not altogether dissimilar from that imposed by the Internal Revenue Code. Moreover, a professional is free to include in a report that although the report is mandated because the reporter has "reason to believe" that a child has been abused, the reporter does not hold a personal belief that the child has been physically or sexually abused. *Cf. PruneYard Shopping Center v. Robins*, 447 U.S. 74, 87, 100 S.Ct. 2035, 2044, 64 L.Ed.2d 741 (1980).

In summary, the issue is not whether this court agrees with the legislature's chosen solution to the admittedly difficult problem of encouraging the reporting of child abuse. Although commentators are in disagreement about the wisdom of the legislature's criminally punishing negligent conduct of this sort, the legislature is clearly free to do so. *Cf. Liparota v. United States*, 471 U.S. 419, 105 S.Ct. 2084, 85 L.Ed.2d 434 (1985) (while interpreting a statute as requiring a showing of knowledge, the Court made it clear that the Congress or a legislature is generally free to spell out the mental state required for a criminal offense). Here the legislature undoubtedly concluded that attaching misdemeanor criminal liability to the negligent failure to file a mandated report was necessary to provide a strong enough motive to comply with the mandatory reporting provisions of the statute. *See* Model Penal Code, §2.02, Comment ¶4 (1985). In any event, the cases support our conclusion that the statute adopted by the legislature and interpreted by us is not unconstitutionally vague or overbroad. Accordingly, the district court erred in dismissing the prosecution on this basis and the case must be remanded to the district court for further proceedings.

Needless to say, we have not by our decision intended to express any opinion concerning the culpability or nonculpability of this defendant. Whether or not to commence a prosecution for violation of the statute was a discretionary decision for the prosecutor in the first instance. The ultimate determination whether the defendant committed the misdemeanor offense of criminal negligence in failing to file reports is a matter for the jury, subject of course to the defendant's right of appeal in the event of conviction.

REVERSED AND REMANDED.

KEITH, J., took no part in the consideration or decision of this case.

Notes

The applicable statute in *Grover* includes, as mandated reporters, those who know or have reason to suspect that abuse or neglect has occurred. In finding that this provision is not unconstitutionally vague, the court held that criminal liability for failure to report may be imposed not only for purposefully, knowingly, or recklessly failing to report, but for negligently failing to report as well. The court recognizes the dilemma of applying criminal liability to the subjective discretion of the reporter, but holds that it is not unconstitutional for state legislatures to do so to encourage reporting. In the following case, note how the culpability of the reporter is determined not by the failure to recognize the mandate to report, but by the failure to report in a timely manner.

Smith v. State of Indiana

Supreme Court of Indiana, 2014

8 N.E.3d 668

DAVID, Justice....

G.G. was a sixteen-year-old student at Muncie Central High School. G.G. had previously been found to be a child in need of services and made a ward of the Madison County office of the Indiana Department of Child Services [(DCS)]. She resided, by court order, at the Youth Opportunity Center [(YOC)] in Muncie. The YOC served as G.G.'s custodial parent and provided care, room, and board to G.G. pursuant to a contract with DCS.

Between 12:20 and 12:25 p.m. on November 9, 2010, a fellow student brought G.G. to the office of Kathy McCord, the assistant principal at Muncie Central. G.G. told McCord that she had been raped (during lunch) by a fellow student, S.M., in a bathroom at the school. McCord immediately went to the office of Christopher Smith, then the principal at Muncie Central, and told him of the rape allegation.... Smith and McCord returned to McCord's office, where G.G. repeated the allegation. Smith contacted Trudy Anderson, the school nurse, at approximately 12:40, and also Jackie Samuels, the associate principal, informing them of the allegation and asking them to come to McCord's office. Anderson went into McCord's office to sit with G.G., and Smith, Samuels, and McCord went to Smith's office. Smith directed McCord to review the school's security footage to identify the whereabouts of the two students—a process that took McCord about an hour. Anderson sat with G.G. until McCord returned, and at some point during that time G.G. was directed to provide a handwritten statement of her allegation, which she did.

At the time, there were between three and five commissioned and sworn police officers on school grounds, serving as security officers. Samuels asked Smith if she should contact one of those officers, call the YOC, or find S.M. Smith directed her to call the YOC. Samuels spoke on the phone with Crystal Dunigan, a staff member at the YOC responsible for G.G.'s cottage, and informed her of the alleged rape. Dunigan asked Samuels to call back, because Dunigan needed to talk to other individuals at the YOC.... Sometime between 12:45 and 1:00, Smith called the administration for the Muncie Community School District and spoke to the director of secondary education, Joann McCowan. Smith was trying to reach Tim Heller, the assistant superintendent. Smith relayed G.G.'s allegation to McCowan, and said his question for Heller was whether a security officer should be present if S.M. was questioned. McCowan reached the district's director of human resources, Lon Sloan, who told her that Smith should have another administrator present, but did not need a security officer as they were not sure if it was a criminal matter or not. Both McCowan and Sloan were headed to Muncie Central later that afternoon for job interviews.... Samuels called Dunigan a second time, shortly before 1:00. Dunigan explained that the YOC would send a driver to take G.G. to the emergency room. The two also discussed G.G.'s credibility, including an incident earlier that year in which Anderson believed G.G. had faked a seizure, and an attendance issue in which G.G. lied about where she had been. After the conversation concluded, Samuels told Smith that the YOC was coming to take G.G. to the emergency room.[1] ... Smith then directed Samuels, at about 1:25, to go get S.M.—who had spent the intervening time finishing lunch and then attending a science class—and bring him to Smith's office. Smith asked the Muncie Central athletic director, Thomas Jarvis, to be a witness while he questioned S.M. Jarvis asked Smith if this should be a police matter instead, but Smith said that it was still a school matter.... Smith questioned S.M. about the allegation, but S.M. denied raping G.G. He was not asked to provide a written statement. The questioning last between fifteen and twenty minutes, and S.M. was then allowed to return to his class and—at the end of the school day—eventually went home.... After S.M. left, Smith asked Jarvis to search S.M.'s and G.G.'s lockers. S.M. indicated during the questioning that he and G.G.

---

1. The YOC driver, Tameka Ross, arrived at a little before 2:00. Ross and G.G. arrived at Ball Memorial Hospital in Muncie at around 2:30. Within about an hour, the hospital's staff contacted the police to report the possible sexual assault, and officers arrived at the hospital just before 4:00.

had exchanged several notes, but that he had thrown them away; but Jarvis and Smith believed the letters would still be in the students' lockers. Jarvis contacted one of the school's security officers, Officer Mike Edwards of the Muncie Police, and asked him for assistance in the search. Jarvis did not, however, tell Officer Edwards that there had actually been an allegation of a rape occurring on school grounds—nor did anyone else at the school.

After completing the search, Officer Edwards continued his normal duties until 3:30, when he left the school for the day. Later that afternoon, Officer Edwards's supervisor with the police department informed him of the rape, and that it had occurred at Muncie Central. Officer Edwards immediately went to Ball Memorial. He served as the lead investigator briefly, before another officer—Detective George Hopper—assumed that function two days later.... Meanwhile, back at Muncie Central, Samuels, Smith, Sloan, and McCowan proceeded to conduct interviews with candidates for an open administrator position. The interviews lasted until after 4:00.... At the conclusion of the second interview, Sloan realized that Heller and the superintendent for the district, Dr. Eric King, still had not yet been notified of the alleged rape. With Sloan and McCowan in the room, Smith then called Heller. Smith explained to Heller that G.G. had reported that she had been raped, and that she was then at the hospital. Heller told Smith to contact DCS.... A little after 4:30, Sloan placed a call to the Indiana Child Abuse Hotline, operated by DCS. Smith then explained the circumstances of G.G.'s allegations to the hotline operator, who indicated that because S.M. was also sixteen, "this would be something I believe that we would probably refer to law enforcement," and that "this looks like something we are going to screen out on our end," but she would forward the report to her supervisors.... [citation to Record omitted]. Smith told the operator that he would contact law enforcement.... Smith then tried several times to contact the YOC to check on G.G., before finally getting ahold of Ross at the hospital, sometime between 4:30 and 4:50. The rape kit had not yet been completed at that time, and Smith asked Ross if the YOC intended to report the allegation, or if Muncie Central should do it. Ross replied that she assumed Muncie Central should make the report, as the rape occurred at the school.... Sloan then called the district's chief of security and operations, Brian Lipscomb, and asked—hypothetically—what Lipscomb's response would be if a student were sexually assaulted at school. Lipscomb responded that he would call the police. Sloan then informed Lipscomb of G.G.'s allegations, and that she was now at Ball Memorial. Lipscomb immediately went to the hospital, where he met with Officer Edwards, and Smith arrived there at about 5:30. Smith remained until about 6:10 and then left for a school board meeting, because he was recognizing several coaches and the volleyball team at the meeting. Lipscomb remained for about another thirty minutes—until G.G. was taken back to the YOC. At no point did Smith, Muncie Central, or the district ever directly contact the Muncie Police Department to report the rape.

On November 11, Detective Hopper began his investigation into the alleged rape. Six days into the investigation, S.M. admitted to raping G.G., and he was arrested and later pleaded guilty.[2] At a point, however, the investigation shifted focus to Smith; why he did not contact the police at all—or DCS sooner—after G.G. informed him of the rape, and why district officials were then claiming G.G. had recanted, been vague in her accusation, or somehow changed her story over the course of the day. Smith told police

---

2. The precise charge(s) S.M. faced, the charge(s) to which he pleaded guilty, and his sentence are not available from the record. We can assume he was charged as an adult, though, because our juvenile courts do not have jurisdiction over a sixteen-year-old alleged to have committed rape. *See* Ind.Code § 31-30-1-4(a)(4)(2008).

he assumed that notifying the YOC and getting G.G. to the hospital would take care of the police notification.

The State eventually charged Smith with failure [to] report G.G.'s allegation to DCS or local law enforcement, a class B misdemeanor under Indiana's statutory scheme requiring school officials to report instances of child abuse.... [footnote omitted]. Ind.Code § 31-33-22-1(a) (2008). Smith filed a motion to dismiss the charges, claiming the State had inappropriately combined the reporting requirements of two statutes, and also arguing that the reporting statute was void for vagueness. The trial court denied Smith's motion and affirmed the constitutionality of the criminal provision, but amended the charging information to cure Smith's claim that the information inappropriately combined two statutory provisions.... [footnote omitted]. Smith was convicted following a bench trial, sentenced to 120 days in jail, all suspended to probation, ordered to serve one hundred hours of community service, and also ordered to pay a fine of one hundred dollars along with court and probation costs.... Smith appealed, claiming the evidence was insufficient to sustain his conviction and also reiterating his claim that the criminal statute was unconstitutionally vague. In a split opinion, the Court of Appeals reversed and vacated Smith's conviction. *Smith v. State*, 982 N.E.2d 348, 363 (Ind.Ct.App.2013).

Without needing to reach the question of the statute's constitutionality, the majority concluded that the State failed to present sufficient evidence that Smith had reason to believe G.G. had been a victim of child abuse as required by the reporting statute, because neither he nor his fellow administrators believed that a student-on-student rape was child abuse as defined by the Indiana Code, and it also interpreted the statutory scheme to permit a reasonable investigation made in good faith. *Id.* at 362–63. Judge Vaidik dissented, believing that the majority's interpretation of the reporting requirements to first allow a reasonable investigation undermined the purpose behind the statutory scheme and might operate to discourage, rather than encourage, the reporting of child abuse. *Id.* at 363–66 (Vaidik, J., dissenting).... We granted transfer, thereby vacating the Court of Appeals opinion. *Smith v. State*, 987 N.E.2d 70 (Ind.2013)....

Indiana Code article 31-33 contains a statutory structure to govern the reporting and investigation of child abuse and neglect. The structure's purpose is to:

(1) encourage effective reporting of suspected or known incidents of child abuse or neglect;

(2) provide effective child services to quickly investigate reports of child abuse or neglect;

(3) provide protection for an abused or a neglected child from further abuse or neglect;

(4) provide rehabilitative services for an abused or a neglected child and the child's parent, guardian, or custodian; and

(5) establish a centralized statewide child abuse registry and an automated child protection system.

Ind.Code § 31-33-1-1 (2008). In furtherance of those aims, the statutes in this article provide that "an individual who has reason to believe that a child is a victim of child abuse or neglect shall make a report as required by this article." Ind.Code § 31-33-5-1 (2008). If the individual is "a member of the staff of a medical or other public or private institution, school, facility, or agency, the individual shall immediately notify the individual in charge." Ind.Code § 31-33-5-2(a) (2008). That "individual in charge ... shall report or cause a report to be made." Ind.Code § 31-33-5-2(b). The report must be made "immediately ...

to: (1) the department [DCS]; or (2) the local law enforcement agency." Ind.Code § 31-33-5-4 (2008).

An individual has "reason to believe" a child is a victim of child abuse or neglect when the individual is presented with "evidence that, if presented to individuals of similar background and training, would cause the individuals to believe that a child was abused or neglected." Ind.Code § 31-9-2-101 (2008). And at the time of the incident here, a "victim of child abuse or neglect" was defined in relevant part as "a child described in: (1) IC 31-34-1-1 through IC 31-34-1-5." Ind.Code § 31-9-2-133(a) (2008).[5] ...

The statutes presume that a person making such a report is acting in good faith, and immunize such good-faith conduct from civil or criminal liability. Ind.Code §§ 31-33-6-1, -3 (2008). But failure to comply with section 31-33-5-1 is a class B misdemeanor. Ind.Code § 31-33-22-1(a).... [footnote omitted].... Therefore, in order for the State to successfully convict Smith of the class B misdemeanor offense of failure to report child abuse or neglect, it was required to prove beyond a reasonable doubt that Smith:

(1) had reason to believe;

(2) that G.G. was a victim of child abuse or neglect as

(a) a victim of rape

(b) who needed care, treatment, or rehabilitation that she was not receiving and that was unlikely to be provided or accepted without the coercive intervention of the court; and

(3) Smith knowingly;

(4) failed to immediately make a report to

(a) DCS or

(b) a local law enforcement agency....

Smith argues that the word "immediately" in Indiana Code § 31-33-5-4 is unconstitutionally vague as it was applied to his reporting duty under section 31-33-5-1. We disagree.... Smith made this same argument in his motion to dismiss, and the trial court also rejected it. Citing to an ordinary dictionary, Judge Cannon defined "immediately" as being "in an immediate manner; specifically, a) without intervening agency or cause; directly; b) without delay; at once; instantly." ... [citation to Record omitted] (citing Webster's New World Dictionary of the American Language, College Edition (1968)).) He therefore found the word to be one commonly understood by ordinary individuals, that "rather straightforwardly and fairly informs a reasonably intelligent person when suspected child abuse must be reported." ... We agree with Judge Cannon's assessment.

Because Smith's claim hinges upon how ordinary people understand statutory language, we will also look to ordinary dictionaries for assistance. And those dictionaries tell us that "immediately" means without any intermediate intervention or appreciable delay.... [footnote omitted]. In other words, when considered within the context of Indiana's reporting statutes, the use of the word "immediately" in Indiana Code § 31-33-5-4 conveys a required strong sense of urgency in action and primacy of purpose in fulfilling the duty to report. *See Anonymous Hosp. v. A.K.*, 920 N.E.2d 704, 707 (Ind.Ct.App.2010) (use of phrase "shall immediately" in reporting statute "makes clear that time is of the essence in such a situation"); *cf. Barber v. State*, 863 N.E.2d 1199, 1206 (Ind.Ct.App.2007) (evidence

---

5. Similarly, "child abuse or neglect," for purposes article 31–33, referred to "a child who is alleged to be a child in need of services as described in IC 31-34-1-1 through IC 31-34-1-5." Ind.Code § 31-9-2-14(a) (2008).

sufficient to show defendant failed to stop immediately after accident when defendant slowed on interstate, observed accident, and turned off at next exit) ... *Jenkins v. State*, 596 N.E.2d 283, 283–84 (Ind.Ct.App.1992) (affirming conviction for driving-related offenses after defendant caused accident and "did not stop immediately after the accident, but just 'kept going' for approximately one block").

We think this ordinary view of the term comports with the General Assembly's intent in enacting the reporting statutes—to encourage effective reporting of potential child abuse or neglect, to facilitate quick investigation of allegations by the proper authorities, and to protect the victims—and is not beyond the rational understanding of a reasonably intelligent person. Such a person would read this statute and clearly understand that his or her highest priority must be to report—or facilitate the report of—the known or suspected child abuse or neglect.[10]

So we reject Smith's implication that the statute must be vague without some explicit time limitation or boundary defining immediately. But alternatively, he argues that the statute could be narrowly construed to incorporate such a boundary—and specifically, he asks for the boundary of "immediately" to be up to twenty-four hours later. He analogizes his reporting requirement to the time frame found in Indiana Code § 31-33-8-1(b) (2008), which provided that when DCS received a report that a child may be a victim of child abuse, it was to initiate an investigation "immediately, but not later than twenty-four (24) hours after receipt of the report." ... There are several problems with this approach. For one thing, it would hardly serve the purpose of the reporting statutes to permit—under every circumstance—school administrators to effectively sit on a report of potential (or even confirmed) child abuse for a full day before reporting it to the authorities. As perhaps the most dangerous resulting hypothetical, this would mean that a child could arrive to school with a black eye, that the child could tell a school official it came from his or her parent, and that the school could then send that child home at the end of the day—back to the abuser's "care"—and not make a report until the following morning. Additionally, this would mean that the DCS investigation might not begin for yet *another* day, meaning that a full forty-eight hours might pass from a school official noticing a child was being beaten at home to when the State could bring its full protective powers to bear.... There is no rational way to permit such a universally broad view of the reporting statutes, given that they exist to quickly and effectively begin the process of investigating incidents of child abuse and removing those victims from their harmful surroundings. Put simply, the statutory scheme contemplates that individuals like teachers, school administrators, and hospital workers are often the first ones to become aware of serious problems in a child's life. The State therefore entrusts those people to be the first lines of defense with respect to our most vulnerable citizens, and it likewise imparts on them a sterner obligation of intervention.... For another thing, the General Assembly itself has rejected Smith's all-encompassing approach for the very statute he uses as authority. The current version of section 31-33-8-1 provides multiple outer limits for DCS, each reflecting different factual circumstances, but all under the broader heading of "immediately." For example, when the report alleges that a child may be a victim of child abuse, "the assessment shall be initiated immediately, but not later than twenty-four (24) hours after receipt of the report," Ind.Code § 31-33-8-1(e) (Supp.2013), but when it is believed that "a child is in imminent danger of serious bodily harm," the assessment shall be initiated "immediately, but not later than one (1) hour, after receiving the report." Ind.Code § 31-33-8-1(d)

---

10. For the same reasons, we do not believe this word's inclusion in the statute renders it subject to arbitrary enforcement.

(Supp.2013). We will not construe a statute in a manner so clearly contrary to the General Assembly's view on the subject....

Under the facts of this case, no reasonable person of ordinary intelligence would have difficulty determining whether or not Smith acted with a sense of urgency or primacy of purpose when his report came after a four-hour delay that included doing intermediary tasks such as conducting a personal interrogation of the alleged rapist, ordering the search of the involved students' lockers for evidence corroborating the alleged rapist's defense, *declining* to contact the police when asked (even though there were multiple officers in the building), and—most notably—conducting two hours' worth of unrelated and purely administrative job interviews. Nor do we think this case indicates that the statute was arbitrarily enforced by the police when the perpetrator of a sex crime was allowed to remain in the general student population and eventually returned home, and the scene of the assault was unsecured and left open for other students to use—all things resulting directly from the delay, which threatened to contaminate (or destroy) evidence of the crime, and all things which were imminently avoidable by the more prompt involvement of law enforcement. We therefore reject Smith's claim that Indiana Code § 31-33-5-4 is unconstitutionally vague as it was applied to him....

Smith argues that of the five individuals of similar background and training who testified—Sloan, McCowan, Samuels, Jarvis, and McCord—none believed (at the time) that an allegation of a sixteen-year-old student raping another sixteen-year-old student constituted child abuse.[11] Smith concedes that Heller testified that he was aware of the need to immediately report the allegation, but argues that Heller was not an "individual of similar background and training" because Heller, Smith says, apparently had a much broader and lengthier level of experience in education and school administration.[12] ... Smith also points to a number of exhibits admitted into evidence at his trial—administrative guidelines and manuals promulgated by the school district and, in one instance, edited and approved by DCS and the Delaware County Prosecutor's office—either not defining child abuse or defining child abuse as a sexual act between an adult and a child.... [footnote omitted]. Thus, he says, to the extent the statutory definition of "reason to believe" encompasses "training," the evidence shows that he was trained to know that he had a duty to report child abuse, but not trained to believe G.G.'s allegation would have been child abuse.... [footnote omitted].

Clearly Smith, Sloan, Samuels, Jarvis, McCowan and McCord were all wrong in their belief that G.G.'s allegation of rape by another minor could not constitute child abuse—

---

11. Sloan testified that he did not think the allegation constituted child abuse, and when he called the DCS hotline the operator asked if he was calling to report an instance of child abuse. Sloan said "[w]ell, I'm not sure, but, that is why I called is to let you tell me." ... McCowan testified that "I didn't see it as child abuse," ... and Samuels testified that "I didn't think of it as child abuse. I thought of it more as a crime." ... McCord and Jarvis both knew the allegation was of a student sexually assaulting another student, but when asked if they thought that might be child abuse, they both testified "No." ...

12. Heller testified that when he was finally notified of the rape allegation, he told Smith to immediately call DCS because he knew Smith had a duty to report the allegation, and he knew this because "I had a superintendent friend in another state where I worked that didn't report child abuse that day, wanted to take another day, wanted to make an investigation himself. Sheriff come picked him up and took him to jail." ..."I knew that you needed to, uh, take the responsibility and get help." ...

At several points in his brief, Smith tries to highlight that neither the police nor the DCS hotline operator initially treated a minor-on-minor rape allegation as potential child abuse either. But if Heller's testimony cannot, for the sake of argument, be relevant to whether an "individual of similar background and training" to Smith had reason to believe this sort of allegation constituted child abuse, the views of a police officer and a DCS hotline operator are even less relevant.

likewise, the training pamphlet available at the school was incorrect.... [footnote omitted]. As the statutory scheme we outlined above makes clear, rape is one of the predicate sex crimes that supports a CHINS determination and therefore, in turn, would constitute an instance of child abuse. *See* Ind.Code §§ 31-9-2-133(a), 31-34-1-3(a), 35-42-4-1(a). And the crime of rape has no limitation or qualification with respect to the ages of either the victim or the perpetrator. *See* Ind.Code § 35-42-4-1. A sixteen-year-old perpetrator commits the same crime as a forty-year-old perpetrator, so the minor victim of the sixteen-year-old would be a victim of child abuse just the same as the victim of the forty-year-old. Smith does not contest his mistake of law.

The real issue in his claim is whether (or how) his error—shared as it was by the training pamphlet and his peers—impacts his culpability for the offense. Does the required "reason to believe" refer to the defendant's awareness that the committed conduct satisfies the statutory definition of child abuse? Or does the phrase refer to the defendant's "reason to believe" that the conduct alleged actually occurred as a factual matter? ... The State argues for the latter perspective. Because rape, as a matter of law, is a predicate offense to child abuse with no age qualification, the State interprets the statutory reporting scheme to mean that "Smith had a duty to immediately report that G.G. may be a rape victim when he knew information which would cause 'individuals of similar background and training ... to believe that' G.G. had been raped." ... The State views the statute's reference to training and background as gauging "the duty to report according to the training and background of the individual with knowledge of the facts," with the baseline standard being "a person of ordinary background and training." ... And the statute operates to excuse such an ordinary person from liability "merely on proof that he or she had observed signs or symptoms that could only have caused a trained expert to reasonably believe that abuse or neglect had occurred." ... "On the other hand, a trained emergency-room physician, or psychologist, might have such knowledge," and in that example assessment of what others with similar backgrounds and training might think would be relevant to such a defendant's criminal liability.... Under this approach, the State argues, the element refers to Smith's knowledge of *factual* information, events, and circumstances, and how he—or other school administrators—would view those facts, and it is irrelevant whether he was operating under an incorrect *legal* assessment of the scope of the child abuse definition: ignorantia juris non excusat.

On one hand, Smith's claim has merit in that a person would only "knowingly" fail to report child abuse or neglect when they actually knew that the conduct constituted child abuse or neglect under the statutory scheme. And the State's position would then criminalize ignorance—that is, if a defendant in good faith did not know that the conduct complained of constituted child abuse or neglect (perhaps a question of negligent behavior on the part of the defendant), they would be subjected to criminal liability. In some cases, Smith's position might be proper.[16] ... In light of the purpose of the reporting statutes, however, we think the State's view is correct. As we mentioned above, the General Assembly has

---

16. For example, under certain (particularly federal) regulatory schemes with punitive consequences for non-compliance, there is some argument for requiring the strictest of "knowing" mens reas—that the defendant both affirmatively knew that the conduct was prohibited/required, and that the defendant acted intentionally regardless—as a way to avoid over-exposing the ordinary citizen to criminal liability under an increasingly large and obtuse body of criminal statutes. *See, e.g., U.S. v. Wilson*, 159 F.3d 280, 293–96 (7th Cir.1998) (Posner, C.J., dissenting). In such cases, as Chief Judge Posner wrote, "the law is not a deterrent. It is a trap." *Id.* at 295.

But Smith's is not one of those cases. Instead, this more readily falls into Chief Judge Posner's other category of offenses, where more stringent liability is permissible: that category where "the defendant is warned to steer well clear of the core of the offense ... or to take the utmost care ... *or to familiarize himself with the laws relating to his business.*" *Id.* at 296 (emphasis added).

expressly charged particular individuals—like Smith—with a significant responsibility: to serve as the first responders to incidents of child abuse and neglect, and to act swiftly to ensure the child is protected from further harm. In furtherance of this responsibility, it has imposed a particular duty, with particular consequences for failure in that duty. Smith does not challenge the existence or propriety of that duty—only whether he can be punished for not knowing its scope.... But if Smith's mistaken interpretation of the law were a defense to his criminal liability, it would remove all incentives from any such professionals to understand the scope of that statutory duty. And it would, in effect, vitiate the duty entirely. The statutes are aimed at "encourag[ing] effective reporting of suspected or known incidents of child abuse or neglect ... provid[ing] effective child services to quickly investigate reports of child abuse or neglect ... [and] provid[ing] protection for an abused or a neglected child from further abuse or neglect," Ind.Code § 31-33-1-1(1)–(3), but Smith would have us announce today that the obligations—and penalties—imposed to further those purposes can be avoided by accidental, or even willful, avoidance of learning what falls under the statutory scheme.... [footnote omitted].

The primary goal of statutory interpretation is to give effect to the General Assembly's intent, *Nicoson v. State*, 938 N.E.2d 660, 663 (Ind.2010), not to undermine it. And to say this approach would chill reporting of child abuse or neglect in Indiana would grossly understate its impact. It would tacitly encourage administrators and other professionals to simply not read the statutes in full because, to sum up Smith's defense: if you just don't learn what child abuse is, you'll never get in trouble for not reporting it. It would reward systemic ignorance in entire school districts and corporations, to the obvious detriment of the very children the statutes are supposed to be protecting. And it would turn the high school principal's decision-making process, when faced with a traumatized child, into a Bar exam question.... And in fact, we think the statutory scheme contemplates just the opposite of Smith's argument: it is designed, if anything, to err on the side of *over* reporting suspected child abuse or neglect. To that end, the statutes presume a report is made in good faith and immunize from civil or criminal liability the person who makes such a report. Ind.Code §§ 31-33-6-1, -3. The statutes do not, however, presume that a *failure* to file a report was done in good faith, or immunize from liability those persons who, even in good faith, believe that a report is not necessary.... In other words, the General Assembly has protected those who report and are mistaken, not those who are mistaken (or intentionally ignorant) and do not report. Our decision today may increase the number of individuals who fall into the former category, but if we did as Smith suggests we would certainly risk increasing the number of individuals in the latter. One outcome comports with the General Assembly's stated intent; the other most certainly does not.

Having resolved this, we reach the question of whether the evidence was sufficient to show that Smith had reason to believe G.G. was the victim of child abuse by virtue of her rape allegation.... [footnote omitted]. And in this regard the record shows that a fellow student brought G.G. to McCord's office, where G.G. told Smith—and every subsequent administrator brought into the room—that she had been raped. G.G. was "humped over, drawn inward, hands, she kept her hands, her face in her hands. Not really making eye contact with [McCord]. Just talking," and she was crying.... She also clearly articulated her attacker's identity, the circumstances, the time she was attacked, and the location of the attack.

It is apparent that Smith had some doubts as to G.G.'s veracity, but it is equally apparent that Smith took the allegation seriously enough to summon the school nurse and direct Samuels to contact the YOC, call the senior administrators in the district to ask for guidance, begin his own personal interrogation of the perpetrator, and direct the search of student lockers. And when reviewing a sufficiency of the evidence claim, we view "[t]he evidence—even if conflicting—and all reasonable inferences drawn from it ... in a light most favorable to the conviction." *Bailey*, 979 N.E.2d at 135. And doing so here leads us to conclude that there was sufficient and substantial evidence of probative value to support the fact-finder's determination that Smith had reason to believe that the factual circumstances alleged by G.G. actually occurred—that she was the victim of a rape....

As we explained, the definition of "victim of child abuse or neglect" at the time of Smith's trial required more than just a reason to believe the predicate offense occurred. The State must also have shown that Smith had reason to believe "the child need[ed] care, treatment, or rehabilitation that: (A) the child [was] not receiving; and (B) [was] unlikely to be provided or accepted without the coercive intervention of the court." Ind.Code § 31-34-1-3(a). This is, as Smith says, because "the General Assembly ha[d] simply adopted the CHINS categories as the definition of child abuse or neglect." ...

At the outset, though we acknowledge that the General Assembly adopted the CHINS statutes in crafting its definition of child abuse, we doubt that its intent in doing so was to require school and hospital officials to make accurate assessments of whether a particular child needed particular care, treatment, or rehabilitation that he or she was not receiving and that could only be provided through court intervention. Under the reporting statutes, this assessment is to be completed by DCS, through its local offices, following the receipt of a report of suspected child abuse or neglect from medical or school personnel. *See* Ind.Code § 31-33-8-1 (2008). Similarly, the filing of a CHINS petition—seeking treatment, care, or rehabilitation through coercive intervention of a court—is a DCS (or prosecutor) responsibility, *see* Ind.Code § 31-34-9-1 (2008), and the scope of any resulting care, treatment, or rehabilitation is a determination the statutes entrust to the presiding juvenile court judge, *see* Ind.Code § 31-34-19-10 (2008).

This aspect of the statutory CHINS definition involves a determination made after deliberate, in-depth, and specialized inquiry and assessment. We cannot imagine it being something that the General Assembly expected a school principal to perform "immediately." We think, and the recent statutory amendments to sections 31-9-2-14 and 31-9-2-133 of the Indiana Code reflect, that the General Assembly intended instead for individuals like Smith to identify—and report—the factual circumstances indicating that the child abuse or neglect was occurring. And by this we mean the "symptoms" of child abuse or neglect, as it were: the marks of physical trauma, signs of malnourishment, or changes in personality or interaction that might be the first visual indications of the underlying "disease" of an abusive environment or neglectful parents....

The reporting statutes required Smith to make his immediate report to DCS or a law enforcement agency. Ind.Code § 31-33-5-4. Smith argues the evidence was insufficient to show that he failed in this obligation because the YOC, which he directed Samuels to contact immediately after hearing G.G.'s allegation, is an agent of DCS (both at the state and county levels), and pursuant to that agency relationship "notification to the YOC is the legal equivalent of notification to DCS. Therefore, DCS was timely given notice of the reported assault, and no liability for failure to report exists." ... First, the statutes explicitly designate two agencies to which the report must be made: DCS or law enforcement. And unlike the YOC, both are neutral and detached entities tasked with investigating and assessing allegations of child abuse and neglect. If we permitted a private entity—into whose care a child is placed in lieu of parents—to also serve as an agent for DCS for purposes of the reporting statutes, we would leave vulnerable to abuse or neglect those children placed with those entities because school officials could simply report the abuse to the abuser and be done with the matter. For example, if G.G. arrived at school with fresh bruises, and a teacher reported those bruises to Smith believing they were signs of child abuse occurring at the YOC, under Smith's rationale he could simply call the YOC and everything would be okay. Moreover, assuming such a third-party agency would then contact DCS to initiate an investigation and assessment, Smith's agency theory adds yet another layer of bureaucracy to what is supposed to be an "immediate" report. Clearly this would support neither the statutes' purposes of encouraging effective reporting, quick investigation, and protecting children, nor the General Assembly's intent in enacting the statutes.... His phone call to the YOC could not, and did not, satisfy his responsibility under the reporting statute, and therefore his argument that "the undisputed evidence was that [Smith] caused a report to be made to the agent of DCS within 25 minutes, and DCS received actual notice from its agent within approximately 40 minutes, both of which time frames should be deemed sufficiently immediate as a matter of law," must fail....

Finally we reach the ultimate question in this case: was Smith's eventual report to DCS—his phone call to the DCS hotline made about four hours after he became aware of G.G.'s rape allegation—sufficiently immediate as to relieve him of criminal liability? He argues that the statutes governing DCS's investigation requirements provide a twenty-four-hour deadline, that the YOC's master contract also provided a twenty-four-hour deadline, and that DCS trained educators that they had twenty-four hours to report abuse. He also asserts that "[s]chool policy was to collect information before reporting matters to the authorities ... and certainly the statute permits a citizen some time to assess and reflect before he reports, without penalty of being labeled a criminal and having his job and license in peril." ... [We reject[ ] Smith's argument....]

We also reject his claim that the school policy permitted him to conduct the level of investigation that he now says justifies his delay in reporting, even assuming his school's policy could trump the statutory requirement and common understanding of the word "immediately" as we provided above. Though McCowan testified that when a report was made, "they are going to ask specific questions about the student's age, the address, where it occurred," and therefore "you have to collect some information," ... this is not evidence that the school's policy of collecting information included interrogating the perpetrator, conducting a search of the victim's and perpetrator's lockers, and seizing notes found in those lockers. McCowan was referring to making sure that the administrator had certain biographical information available to provide to DCS or the police before reporting the child abuse or neglect (all of which Smith already had); but what Smith did was conduct a criminal investigation. And conducting an investigation is expressly forbidden in the training materials that Smith failed to read.... And we also reject his belief that the reporting statutes permit a citizen to delay reporting in order to "assess and reflect" before facing criminal liability and professional censure. In fact, the statutes do the opposite— they *require* immediate reporting of suspected child abuse or neglect, and in furtherance of that aim immunize from criminal and civil liability those who immediately report conduct that turns out after later assessment and reflection *by DCS or law enforcement* to have been innocent.... And while we ... respect ... the gravity of a charge of sexual misconduct, our statutory structure has protections in place to ameliorate the implications of a false report and deter intentional false reporting. The Indiana Code criminalizes the intentional communication of a known false report of child abuse or neglect, and also provides a private right of action for the victim of such an act. *See* Ind.Code § 31-33-22-3 (Supp.2013). Additionally, when a report is investigated and found to be unsubstantiated, any interested person may petition DCS to expunge information related to that assessment. Ind.Code § 31-33-27-3(b) (Supp.2013). And in any event, DCS is required to expunge child abuse or neglect information no later than the twenty-fourth birthday of the youngest child named in the assessment, if the report is unsubstantiated. Ind.Code § 31-33-27-3(a)....

Also, as we discuss above, it is not the school administrator's responsibility to investigate. That responsibility is firmly placed with DCS and law enforcement. The school administrator, under our statutes, is the "trip-wire" that triggers the investigation and assessment, not the one who undertakes the investigation and assessment. And on that point, we have already determined that Smith had reason to believe G.G. was the victim of child abuse without his needing to conduct any further inquiry.... As Smith himself says, "it is left to the trier of fact to determine whether under the circumstances of the case the report was made fast enough in keeping with the purpose of the statute."... And under the definition of "immediately" that we believe most people of ordinary intelligence would employ in such a case—and the one employed by the finder of fact here—the length of the delay is not the only thing that matters. What also matters is the urgency with which the person files the report, the primacy of the action, and the absence of an unrelated and intervening cause for delay....

In sum, it appears from the record as though when time was of the essence, Smith dawdled, delayed, and did seemingly everything he could to *not* contact DCS or the police. It is therefore a reasonable inference to draw, from this evidence, that Smith knowingly failed to "immediately" report the child abuse as he was obligated to do by statute.... It is apparent that Christopher Smith failed in his duty to help protect one of his trusted charges. Whether this failure was out of ignorance, a desire to protect the reputation of the perpetrator, or perhaps a wish to keep his school from receiving negative publicity on his watch is not clear. But none of those possible reasons are excuses under the Indiana Code's statutory provisions compelling him to report instances of child abuse or neglect or face criminal liability. We therefore affirm Smith's conviction and sentence.

MASSA and RUSH, JJ., concur.

RUCKER, J., dissents with separate opinion in which DICKSON, C.J., concurs....

Notes

In the *Smith* decision, in which a student had been raped by another student, a school official was held criminally liable for not "immediately" reporting the crime, as was required by statute; the principal waited four hours before making the report. *See also Rodriguez v. State*, 47 S.W.3d 86 (Tex. App.–Houst. 2001) (two month delay in reporting too long to avoid criminal liability). Criminal liability may be incurred by any person required to report, including a parent. *See State v. Harrod*, 81 S.W.3d 904 (Tex. App.– Dallas 2002) (parent not immune from criminal liability for not reporting sexual abuse of daughters by their father). For further discussion of criminal charges imposed for failure to report child abuse in a case that involved physical abuse but which the court held equally applicable to failure to report sexual offenses, see *White v. State*, 50 S.W.3d 31 (Tex. App.–Waco 2001) (mother charged with five counts of failure to report abuse of child by father).

The majority of states impose criminal penalties on mandated reporters who fail to report suspected child abuse. *See* Child Welfare Information Gateway, *Penalties for Failure to Report and False Reporting of Child Abuse and Neglect*, available at https:// www.childwelfare.gov/pubPDFs/report.pdf (current through Nov. 2013). For the applicable federal statute, see 18 U.S.C. § 2258 (person who "fails to make a timely report ... shall be fined ... or imprisoned not more than 1 year or both). Although in most states, failure to report is classified as a misdemeanor, in some states, it is a felony offense. *See, e.g.*,

FLA. STAT. ANN. § 39.205(1)–(4) (classified as felony, with penalties of imprisonment not to exceed five years and a fine of five-thousand dollars); *see also* ARIZ. REV. STAT. § 13-3620(O) (failure to report is felony "reportable offense"). Some states impose harsher penalties for failure to report sexual offenses. *See, e.g.,* LA. REV. STAT. § 14:403(A)(1) (any person "required to report the sexual abuse of a child … [who] knowingly and willfully fails to so report shall be fined not more than three thousand dollars, imprisoned, with or without hard labor, for not more than three years, or both"). Many states impose similar criminal penalties for false reporting. *See, e.g.,* ARK CODE ANN. § 12-18-203 (misdemeanor, upgraded to felony for second offense); IND. CODE § 31-33-22-3(a)–(b) (felony for second offense). Five states — California, Maine, Montana, Minnesota, and Nebraska — impose no criminal penalties for false reporting.

In addition to criminal liability, a reporter may be civilly liable for any damages caused by the failure to report. There are several states that statutorily impose civil liability. *See* ARK. CODE § 12-18-206 (2014); COLO. REV. STAT. § 19-3-304 (4) (2015); IOWA CODE § 232.75(2) (2015); MICH. COMP. LAWS § 722.633(1) (2015); MONT. CODE ANN. § 41-3-207 (2014); N.Y. SOC. SERV. LAW § 420 (2015) ; R.I. GEN. LAWS § 40-11-6.1 (2014). In *Smith*, the court recognized a statutory private right of action for victims of known false reporting. The cases that follow address the issue of an implied civil cause of action for failure to report.

2. Civil Liability

Beggs v. State, Dept. Of Social & Health Servs.

Supreme Court of Washington, 2011
171 Wash. 2d 69, 247 P.3d 421

SANDERS, J.… [footnote omitted].

Tyler DeLeon died on his seventh birthday of dehydration and starvation — a result of neglect and abuse by his adoptive mother, Carole DeLeon, despite investigations of the DeLeon home by Child Protective Services (CPS). Tyler's adoptive siblings and the personal representative of his estate brought wrongful death and survival actions against the Department of Social and Health Services (DSHS), individual employees of DSHS, Dr. David Fregeau (Tyler's primary care physician), Rockwood Clinic (Dr. Fregeau's employer), and Dr. Sandra Bremner-Dexter (Tyler's psychiatrist). Petitioners also sued Dr. Fregeau, Rockwood Clinic, and Dr. Bremner-Dexter for medical malpractice and failure to report suspected child abuse.… Rockwood Clinic and the doctors filed two motions for partial summary judgment in the superior court, seeking dismissal of the wrongful death and survival actions and dismissal of the action for failure to report suspected child abuse. The superior court granted the motions. Division Three of the Court of Appeals granted discretionary review of both partial summary judgment orders and certified the case to this court.…

Between 1997 and 2002, DSHS placed Tyler DeLeon and six other children in Carole DeLeon's home as foster children.… [footnote omitted]. The State later assisted Carole DeLeon's adoption of Tyler DeLeon and three other children. There were 23 CPS referrals alleging physical and/or sexual abuse and neglect in the home, at least 3 of which involved injuries to Tyler. In June 1999, Tyler fractured his femur and had bruises all over his body. In July 1999, Tyler's two front teeth were knocked out. In April 2004, Tyler arrived at school with bruises on his cheeks and nose and a 1.5 inch mark on his side, a result of being kicked down the stairs. During his time in Carole DeLeon's home, Tyler's weight dropped from the 50th percentile to the 5th percentile for his age. He weighed 28 pounds when he died on his seventh birthday, January 13, 2005.

Carole DeLeon received more than $220,000 from the State between October 1997 and April 2005 to support the children placed in her home. DSHS paid more than $50,000 in foster care support and adoption support for Tyler. At the time of his death, DSHS was paying Carole DeLeon $717 per month for Tyler's care pursuant to an adoption support agreement signed by Carole DeLeon and the State in August 2003.... After Tyler's death, DSHS removed the other children from the DeLeon home and stopped all support payments. Without the payments Carole DeLeon could not make ends meet, as demonstrated by a home mortgage refinancing application she filed 10 months after Tyler's death and 7 months after the other children were removed from the home. Carole DeLeon later claimed she took the children into her home as a way to finance her house.

Tyler DeLeon died leaving no last will and testament; his surviving heirs are his siblings.[2] Breean Beggs is the personal representative of Tyler's estate and guardian ad litem for five of the siblings.[3] Beggs filed wrongful death and survival actions against DSHS, employees of DSHS,[4] Rockwood Clinic, Dr. Fregeau, and Dr. Bremner-Dexter. Beggs claimed Dr. Fregeau knew of Tyler's dramatic weight loss and the numerous reports to CPS regarding Tyler.[5] Beggs claimed Dr. Fregeau was also aware of the severe weight loss of the other children in the DeLeon home. Beggs claimed Dr. Bremner-Dexter knew of Tyler's weight loss, stunted growth and behavioral problems, and the CPS referrals regarding Tyler.... Rockwood Clinic and the doctors (the doctors) filed two motions for partial summary judgment. First, the doctors moved to dismiss Beggs' wrongful death and survival actions on the ground Tyler's siblings were not "dependent" on him as required by the wrongful death and survival action statutes. Second, the doctors moved to dismiss any civil action implied by RCW 26.44.030 (the mandatory reporting statute), claiming chapter 7.70 RCW (the medical malpractice statute) precluded the claim. The superior court granted the motions for partial summary judgment.[6] Beggs sought discretionary review of both superior court orders. Division Three of the Court of Appeals granted review and certified the case to this court. This court accepted certification....

The issue of whether RCW 26.44.030, the mandatory child abuse reporting statute, implies a cause of action against a professional named in the statute who fails to report suspected abuse is a matter of first impression.[7] ... The Court of Appeals has held RCW

---

2. Under the slayer statute, Carole DeLeon, Tyler's adoptive mother, cannot receive any property or benefit from his death because she caused his death. RCW 11.84.020. She is deemed to have predeceased him. RCW 11.84.030.

3. Another minor sibling, represented by a different guardian ad litem, and an adult sibling are also petitioners. For the sake of brevity we refer to the petitioners by Beggs' name only.

4. The State and its employees settled with the petitioners and are no longer parties to this action.

5. In her complaint, Beggs alleged Dr. Fregeau received a letter from a CPS adoption social worker expressing concern about Tyler's condition and a written request from Tyler's school nurse to verify whether there were restrictions on Tyler's fluid intake.... Beggs also alleged Dr. Fregeau was a member of a child protection team that investigated reports of abuse in the DeLeon home in 2004....

6. Beggs also brought medical malpractice claims against Dr. Fregeau, Rockwood Clinic, and Dr. Bremner-Dexter that were not dismissed by the superior court's orders granting partial summary judgment.

7. This court has held RCW 26.44.050, the section requiring law enforcement or DSHS to investigate a report of suspected abuse, implied a civil remedy for a parent who was negligently investigated. *Tyner v. Dep't of Soc. & Health Servs.*, 141 Wash.2d 68, 80, 1 P.3d 1148 (2000). We held the statute's declaration of purpose showed the legislature contemplated parents' interests, and "by recognizing the deep importance of the parent/child relationship, the Legislature intends a remedy for both the parent and the child if that interest is invaded." *Id.*

26.44.030 implies a civil remedy against a mandatory reporter who fails to report suspected abuse. *Jane Doe v. Corp. of the President of the Church of Jesus Christ of Latter-Day Saints*, 141 Wash.App. 407, 423, 167 P.3d 1193 (2007). Citing this court's decision in *Tyner v. Department of Social & Health Services*, 141 Wash.2d 68, 1 P.3d 1148 (2000), the court stated, "If the legislature intended a remedy for parent victims of negligent child abuse investigations, it is reasonable to imply an intended remedy for child victims of sexual abuse when those required to report the abuse fail to do so." 141 Wash.App. at 422, 167 P.3d 1193.[8] "[I]mposing civil consequences for failure to report motivates mandatory reporters to take action to protect victims of childhood sexual abuse." *Id.* Before deciding whether health care providers are exempt from a cause of action arising under RCW 26.44.030, we first must determine whether such an action exists.[9] ...

RCW 26.44.030 requires the named professionals, including health care practitioners, with "reasonable cause to believe that a child has suffered abuse or neglect" to report the suspected abuse to DSHS or the proper law enforcement agency. RCW 26.44.030(1)(a). The statutory definition of "practitioner" includes "a person licensed by this state to practice ... medicine and surgery or to provide other health services." RCW 26.44.020(16). A mandatory reporter named in RCW 26.44.030 who knowingly fails to report suspected child abuse "shall be guilty of a gross misdemeanor." RCW 26.44.080. The statute does not explicitly provide a civil remedy for a child who suffers further injury against a mandatory reporter who failed to report suspected abuse.

In *Bennett v. Hardy*, 113 Wash.2d 912, 920–21, 784 P.2d 1258 (1990), this court explained when a cause of action will be implied from a statute:

> Borrowing from the test used by federal courts in determining whether to imply a cause of action, we must resolve the following issues: first, whether the plaintiff is within the class for whose "especial" benefit the statute was enacted; second, whether the legislative intent, explicitly or implicitly, supports creating or denying a remedy; and third, whether implying a remedy is consistent with the underlying purpose of the legislation.

Under this test, RCW 26.44.030 implies a cause of action against a mandatory reporter who fails to report suspected abuse.

First, victims of child abuse are certainly within the class for whose "especial" benefit the legislature enacted the reporting statute, as this court has acknowledged. *State v. Warner*, 125 Wash.2d 876, 891, 889 P.2d 479 (1995) ("The reporting statute is designed to secure prompt protection and/or treatment for the victims of child abuse. The class of persons it is designed to protect is the victims, not the abusers.").... Second, the statute implicitly supports a civil remedy. This court "'can assume that the legislature is aware of the doctrine of implied statutory causes of action,'" even where the statute is silent as

---

8. Though *Doe* involved allegations of sexual abuse, the statute makes no distinction in the reporting requirements for suspected sexual or physical abuse. *See* RCW 26.44.020(1) (defining "abuse or neglect").

9. The majority of jurisdictions deciding this issue have found no implied cause of action in state reporting statutes. *See, e.g., Cuyler v. United States*, 362 F.3d 949 (7th Cir.2004) (applying Illinois law); *Becker v. Mayo Found.*, 737 N.W.2d 200 (Minn.2007). *See generally* Danny R. Veilleux, Annotation, *Validity, Construction, and Application of State Statute Requiring Doctor or Other Person To Report Child Abuse*, 73 A.L.R.4th 782 (1989). However, at least two states have found implied causes of action in reporting statutes. *See Ham v. Hosp. of Morristown, Inc.*, 917 F.Supp. 531 (E.D.Tenn.1995) (finding an implied cause of action in the Tennessee reporting statute); *Landeros v. Flood*, 17 Cal.3d 399, 551 P.2d 389, 131 Cal.Rptr. 69 (1976) (holding a violation of the statute's mandate to report may constitute negligence per se).

to civil remedies. *Bennett*, 113 Wash.2d at 919, 784 P.2d 1258 (quoting *McNeal v. Allen*, 95 Wash.2d 265, 277, 621 P.2d 1285 (1980) (Brachtenbach, J., dissenting)). Chapter 26.44 RCW provides immunity from civil liability to "[a] person who, in good faith and without gross negligence, cooperates in an investigation arising as a result of a report made pursuant to this chapter." RCW 26.44.060(5). "A grant of immunity from liability clearly implies that civil liability can exist in the first place." *Doe*, 141 Wash.App. at 422–23, 167 P.3d 1193. RCW 26.44.030 imposes a duty to report suspected child abuse on the named professionals. The statutory scheme supports an implied cause of action for a failure to fulfill that duty.... Finally, an implied cause of action is consistent with the underlying purpose of the statute. RCW 26.44.010, the statute's declaration of purpose, states, "It is the intent of the legislature that ... protective services shall be made available in an effort to prevent further abuses, and to safeguard the general welfare of such children." Further, when the legislature amended the reporting statute in 1985, it declared, "Governmental authorities must give the prevention, treatment, and punishment of child abuse the highest priority, and all instances of child abuse must be reported to the proper authorities...." Laws of 1985, ch. 259, § 1.[10] Implying a civil remedy as a means of enforcing the mandatory reporting duty is consistent with this intent....

The doctors argue any civil remedy implied by RCW 26.44.030 does not apply to health care providers because the legislature created a separate liability scheme for negligent health care in chapter 7.70 RCW, the medical malpractice statute. RCW 7.70.010 provides, "The state of Washington, exercising its police and sovereign power, hereby modifies ... certain substantive and procedural aspects of all civil actions and causes of action, whether based on tort, contract, or otherwise, for damages for injury occurring as a result of health care." Chapter 7.70 RCW provides the exclusive remedy for damages for injuries resulting from health care. *Branom v. State*, 94 Wash.App. 964, 969, 974 P.2d 335 (1999). It also determines whether an injury is actionable. *Id.*; *see* RCW 7.70.030.... Chapter 7.70 RCW does not define "health care." The Court of Appeals has defined the term to mean "'the process in which [the physician] was utilizing the skills which he had been taught in examining, diagnosing, treating or caring for the plaintiff as his patient.'" *Estate of Sly v. Linville*, 75 Wash.App. 431, 439, 878 P.2d 1241 (1994) (quoting *Tighe v. Ginsberg*, 146 A.D.2d 268, 540 N.Y.S.2d 99, 100–01 (1989)). This is consistent with a common dictionary definition. *Berger v. Sonneland*, 144 Wash.2d 91, 109, 26 P.3d 257 (2001) (quoting The American Heritage Dictionary 833 (3d ed.1992)).... The doctors argue their reporting duty could arise only when providing Tyler health care because they acted in the course of their employment and in the context of a doctor-patient relationship. However, everything within a doctor-patient relationship is not necessarily health care. *See Linville*, 75 Wash.App. at 438, 440, 878 P.2d 1241 (holding misrepresentations by a doctor about another doctor's previous care of the patient, though "made during the course of the physician/patient relationship," did not "automatically render them 'health care'"); *see also Bundrick v. Stewart*, 128 Wash.App.11, 17, 114 P.3d 1204 (2005) (finding chapter

---

10. The doctors argue the legislature's enactment of the medical malpractice statute in 1976, five years after it adopted the reporting statute, demonstrates an intent to subsume within the malpractice liability scheme any civil remedy for a failure to report suspected abuse. But the legislature has frequently amended the reporting statute, including the 1985 amendment in which it declared the State should give the prevention of child abuse "the highest priority." Laws of 1985, ch. 259, § 1. The legislature made that declaration with full knowledge of the medical malpractice statute. *See Thurston County v. Gorton*, 85 Wash.2d 133, 138, 530 P.2d 309 (1975) ("The legislature is presumed to enact laws with full knowledge of existing laws."). The legislature did not carve out an exception for medical practitioners who fail to report abuse.

7.70 RCW does not supersede the common law cause of action for medical battery for an injury "arising from health care to which the plaintiff gave *no* consent").

A doctor's duty under RCW 26.44.030(1)(a) to report suspected child abuse does not necessarily arise while the doctor is providing health care. The statute imposes the duty on medical practitioners and other health care providers, but also on school and child care personnel, juvenile probation officers, law enforcement officers, pharmacists, and social service counselors. These professionals do not have to provide health care to form a "reasonable cause to believe that a child has suffered abuse or neglect." *See* RCW 26.44.030(1)(a). The mandatory reporters do not have skills or special knowledge in common; rather, the commonality among the class of mandatory reporters is primary and frequent contact with children who might be at risk of abuse. A teacher can form a "reasonable cause to believe" a child has been abused without providing health care. Similarly, a doctor, acting in the course of his professional employment, can also form a "reasonable cause to believe" a child has been abused without employing the special skills in "examining, diagnosing, treating or caring" required to provide health care. *See Linville*, 75 Wash.App. at 439, 878 P.2d 1241.

The reporting statute supports a distinction between a doctor's "reasonable cause to believe" abuse has occurred and a doctor's expert opinion based on examination, diagnosis, treatment, or care. A report based on a "reasonable cause to believe" formed by a doctor or any other professional named in RCW 26.44.030(1)(a) triggers an investigation by DSHS. In contrast, a report based on a doctor's "expert medical opinion" triggers dependency proceedings under RCW 26.44.030(8) unless another doctor contradicts the report. RCW 26.44.030(1)(a) requires a lower threshold of suspicion, a threshold that can be met without utilizing the special skills required to provide health care. Chapter 7.70 RCW does not preclude Beggs' claim against the doctors under RCW 26.44.030(1)(a).... [B]ecause a claim for failure to report suspected child abuse could be brought only as a survival action under RCW 4.20.046 (the general survival action statute) or RCW 4.20.060 (the special survival action statute), we affirm in result the superior court's partial summary judgment order dismissing Beggs' failure-to-report claim. We remand to the superior court for further proceedings on Beggs' remaining claims.

WE CONCUR: BARBARA A. MADSEN, Chief Justice, CHARLES W. JOHNSON, TOM CHAMBERS, SUSAN OWENS, MARY E. FAIRHURST, JAMES M. JOHNSON, and DEBRA L. STEPHENS, Justices.

ALEXANDER, J. (concurring/dissenting).

Although I agree with the majority's conclusion that Tyler DeLeon's siblings are not qualified beneficiaries, I disagree with its holdings that (1) a cause of action against health care providers is implied by RCW 26.44.030, and (2) a medical doctor's duty to report suspected child abuse is not health care. I, therefore, dissent in part for the reasons set forth below....

Pursuant to RCW 26.44.030(1)(a), any "practitioner" who has "reasonable cause to believe that a child has suffered abuse or neglect" shall report the suspected abuse to the Department of Social and Health Services or the proper law enforcement agency. A person licensed by the State of Washington to practice medicine is deemed a " 'practitioner.' " RCW 26.44.020(16). A practitioner who knowingly fails to report suspected child abuse "shall be guilty of a gross misdemeanor." RCW 26.44.080.... The majority concedes that the aforementioned statutes do not explicitly provide a civil remedy against a practitioner who fails to report suspected abuse. It, nevertheless, holds that a civil remedy is implied "as a[n additional] means of enforcing the mandatory reporting duty." 247 P.3d 425–26. This conclusion, it seems to me, flies entirely in the face of what the plain language of the mandatory child abuse reporting statute indicates the legislature intended. I say that because just as we may assume that the legislature is aware of the doctrine of implied statutory causes of action, we can assume that it knows how to explicitly provide a civil cause of action. It declined to do that and, instead, chose to make it a crime to fail to report child abuse.

The result I would have us reach is entirely consistent with our decision in *Tyner v. Department of Social and Health Services*, 141 Wash.2d 68, 1 P.3d 1148 (2000), a case in which we did imply a tort remedy in favor of parents and against the State for negligent investigation of allegations of child abuse. Our decision there turned to a great extent on the fact that the statute was silent as to a remedy. As I have indicated, that is not the case here.... I would, therefore, follow the lead of the majority of jurisdictions in this nation that have found no implied cause of action in state child abuse reporting statutes. *See* 247 P.3d at 424 n. 9....

As the majority observes, the exclusive remedy for damages for injuries resulting from health care is under the provisions of chapter 7.70 RCW. Thus, if the physician's obligation to report suspected child abuse is in the category of health care, the civil remedy the majority says is implied by RCW 26.44.030 is not available to plaintiffs like those in this case. Although "health care" is not defined in chapter 7.70 RCW, the Court of Appeals has appropriately defined "health care" as "'the process in which [the physician] was utilizing the skills which he had been taught in examining, diagnosing, treating or caring for the plaintiff as his patient.'" *Estate of Sly v. Linville*, 75 Wash.App. 431, 439, 878 P.2d 1241 (1994) (quoting *Tighe v. Ginsberg*, 146 A.D.2d 268, 540 N.Y.S.2d 99, 101 (1989)). This definition of "health care," as the majority acknowledges, is consistent with the dictionary definition. It seems obvious that a physician, or any person in the healing arts, is not caring for a patient if the physician fails to carry out his or her statutory obligation to report suspected child abuse to proper authorities. Indeed, I am of the view that even absent a reporting requirement like that which is set forth in RCW 26.44.030, a caring and honorable physician should report suspected child abuse. I say that because from time immemorial the physician's obligation has been to heal the sick and injured. For a physician to remain silent in the face of his or her opinion that a child patient will continue to suffer abuse if the child's home environment remains unchanged undermines the physician's traditional role to heal those who seek help.[1]

Arbaugh v. Board of Educ., County of Pendleton

Supreme Court of Appeals of West Virginia, 2003
214 W. Va. 677, 591 S.E.2d 235

ALBRIGHT, Justice: ...

On July 7, 2001, Tony Dean Arbaugh, Jr. (hereinafter referred to as "Mr. Arbaugh") filed suit in the United States District Court for the Northern District of West Virginia, with one count in his complaint alleging a private cause of action against several education and social service defendants for failure to report suspected abuse pursuant to West Virginia

---

1. Physicians have traditionally observed an oath that is based on the teachings of the Greek physician Hippocrates. A modern version of the so-called Hippocratic oath, penned in 1964 by Dr. Louis Lasagna, a former dean of the School of Medicine at Tufts University, indicates that a physician will apply "all measures [that] are required" for the benefit of the sick. *The Hippocratic Oath: Modern Version*, PBS, http://www.pbs.org/wgbh/nova/doctors/oath_modern.html (last visited Feb. 10, 2011) (alteration in original).

Code § 49-6A-2 (sometimes hereinafter referred to as "reporting statute").[1] The defendants moved to dismiss this count of the complaint, alleging that West Virginia has never recognized a private cause of action for such reporting failure. The dismissal motion was among the preliminary matters assigned to a federal magistrate. After briefing and a hearing on the issues related to the motion to dismiss, the magistrate entered an order on May 9, 2002, in which he found that pursuant to West Virginia Code § 55-7-9 and this Court's decision in *Hurley v. Allied Chemical Corporation*, 164 W.Va. 268, 262 S.E.2d 757 (1980), a private cause of action is implied for violations of West Virginia Code § 49-6A-2. Defendants filed objections and requested review by the district court judge. By order entered April 8, 2003, the district court certified the question to this Court. We agreed to accept the certified question on May 21, 2003....

The question of law, as certified by the United States District Court for the Northern District of West Virginia, reads as follows:

> Whether W.Va.Code § 49-6A-2 creates a private civil cause of action, in addition to the criminal penalties imposed by the statute, for failure to report suspected sexual abuse where an individual is alleged to have had reasonable cause to suspect that a child is being sexually abused and has failed to report suspected abuse.

As related earlier, the federal magistrate to whom this question was referred answered the question in the affirmative based on the provisions of West Virginia Code §§ 49-6A-2 and 55-7-9 and application of this Court's decision in *Hurley*.

The case before the federal court involves a situation where a teacher sexually abused several of his male students over a period of time.[2] Mr. Arbaugh maintains that he was sexually molested by the abuser for a span of four years and is entitled to recover compensatory and punitive damages for the suffering caused by the defendants' failure to act and report. The defendants to this action allegedly had some level of knowledge of incidents of abuse of students by the teacher but never reported their suspicions of child abuse to the authorities as required by the reporting statute. None of the defendants were criminally charged for failure to report. W.Va.Code § 49-6A-8 (1984). While the facts are hotly contested and not completely developed before the federal court, it is clear from the representations made to this Court that Mr. Arbaugh believes civil liability should attach whenever the requirements of the reporting statute are violated regardless of whether the non-reporting teacher had knowledge of any offensive act being committed against the individual student bringing suit.

In deciding whether West Virginia Code § 49-6A-2, relating to mandatory reporting of suspected child abuse and neglect, gives rise to an initial direct cause of action against a person who has failed to report by any child who is subsequently abused by the person who should have been reported, we first recognize that West Virginia Code § 55-7-9 (1923) (Repl. Vol. 2000) generally permits the recovery of damages stemming from a violation of a statute. This statute provides in its entirety that:

---

1. In addition to the teacher who allegedly abused the plaintiff, the defendants against whom this claim was charged include: the Pendleton County Board of Education; a former superintendent of schools and principal at the school where the abuse occurred; a former principal, two teachers and a coach at the school where the abuse occurred; the West Virginia Department of Health and Human Resources and one of its employees; and the West Virginia Children's Home Society and one of its employees. Our general reference herein to the defendants excludes the teacher who committed the abusive acts.

2. The former teacher pled guilty to twenty counts of sexual assault in the third degree and four counts of delivery of a controlled substance and is now incarcerated at the Mount Olive Correctional Facility.

> Any person injured by the violation of any statute may recover from the
> offender such damages as he may sustain by reason of the violation, although a
> penalty or forfeiture for such violation be thereby imposed, unless the same be
> expressly mentioned to be in lieu of such damages.

Id. "Building on this statutory provision, we have consistently held that a violation of a
statute is prima facie evidence of negligence, providing that such violation is the proximate
cause of injury. *See, e.g., Powell v. Mitchell*, 120 W.Va. 9, 196 S.E. 153 (1938); *Porterfield
v. Sudduth*, 117 W.Va. 231, 185 S.E. 209 (1936)." *Yourtee v. Hubbard*, 196 W.Va. 683, 687,
474 S.E.2d 613, 617 (1996) (footnote omitted). *See also* Syl. Pt. 1, *Anderson v. Moulder*,
183 W.Va. 77, 394 S.E.2d 61 (1990) ("Violation of a statute is *prima facie* evidence of negligence. In order to be actionable, such violation must be the proximate cause of the
plaintiff's injury."). Consequently, a violation of a statute could give rise to a common
law negligence action. We went on to say in *Yourtee* that "[w]henever a violation of a
statute is the centerpiece of a theory of liability, the question arises whether the statute
creates an implied private cause of action." 196 W.Va. at 688, 474 S.E.2d at 618. Whether
a private cause of action exists based on a violation of a statute is determined by applying
the four-part test set forth in *Hurley v. Allied Chemical Corporation*, 164 W.Va. 268, 262
S.E.2d 757 (1980). Syllabus point one of *Hurley* states:

> The following is the appropriate test to determine when a State statute gives
> rise by implication to a private cause of action: (1) the plaintiff must be a member
> of the class for whose benefit the statute was enacted; (2) consideration must be
> given to legislative intent, express or implied, to determine whether a private
> cause of action was intended; (3) an analysis must be made of whether a private
> cause of action is consistent with the underlying purposes of the legislative
> scheme; and (4) such private cause of action must not intrude into an area
> delegated exclusively to the federal government.

Id. at 268, 262 S.E.2d at 758.

Applying the *Hurley* test to the case before us, we first must ascertain whether Mr.
Arbaugh is within the class of persons that the statute was meant to benefit. The Legislature
expressed the following purpose for enacting the child abuse reporting article of the Code,
wherein the obligation to report is established:

> It is the purpose of this article, through the complete reporting of child abuse
> and neglect, to protect the best interests of the child, to offer protective services
> in order to prevent any further harm to the child or any other children living in
> the home, to stabilize the home environment, to preserve family life whenever
> possible and to encourage cooperation among the states in dealing with the
> problems of child abuse and neglect.

W.Va.Code § 49-6A-1 (1977). Assuming the facts presented as true, Mr. Arbaugh is unquestionably a member of the class for whose benefit the reporting statute was enacted,
inasmuch as he was a child attending a school where alleged incidents of sexual abuse
were occurring. We can also readily dispose of the fourth element of the *Hurley* test, since
we find that a private cause of action would not intrude into an area delegated exclusively
to the federal government.

The application of the second and third components of the *Hurley* test require a more
detailed examination of the relevant statutes to determine whether the Legislature, by
enacting the reporting statute, intended to protect a private interest through a private
cause of action. According to the second *Hurley* factor, we must decide whether there is
any implication that the Legislature intended to create a private cause of action by enacting

West Virginia Code § 49-6A-2, despite the fact that the statute does not expressly provide for a private cause of action or otherwise reference civil liability.[3] West Virginia Code § 49-6A-2 reads as follows:

> When any medical, dental or mental health professional, christian science practitioner, religious healer, school teacher or other school personnel, social service worker, child care or foster care worker, emergency medical services personnel, peace officer or law-enforcement official, member of the clergy, circuit court judge, family law master, employee of the division of juvenile services or magistrate has reasonable cause to suspect that a child is neglected or abused or observes the child being subjected to conditions that are likely to result in abuse or neglect, such person shall immediately, and not more than forty-eight hours after suspecting this abuse, report the circumstances or cause a report to be made to the state department of human services: Provided, That in any case where the reporter believes that the child suffered serious physical abuse or sexual abuse or sexual assault, the reporter shall also immediately report, or cause a report to be made, to the division of public safety and any law-enforcement agency having jurisdiction to investigate the complaint: Provided, however, That any person required to report under this article who is a member of the staff of a public or private institution, school, facility or agency shall immediately notify the person in charge of such institution, school, facility or agency, or a designated agent thereof, who shall report or cause a report to be made. However, nothing in this article is intended to prevent individuals from reporting on their own behalf.
>
> In addition to those persons and officials specifically required to report situations involving suspected abuse or neglect of children, any other person may make a report if such person has reasonable cause to suspect that a child has been abused or neglected in a home or institution or observes the child being subjected to conditions or circumstances that would reasonably result in abuse or neglect.

The Legislature has expressly provided that failure to report as required is a criminal misdemeanor offense. *See* W.Va. West Virginia Code § 49-6A-8 (1984).[4]

The importance of reporting is definitely stressed in the statute by not only the provisions which establish that reporting is mandatory for individuals in certain professions and occupations, but also in the provisions which prescribe a limited time frame within which the mandated reports are to be made and impose criminal liability for failing to report. These measures clearly encourage early intervention to further the clear overall legislative goal of protecting vulnerable children from abusive situations. The statutory reporting requirement itself is triggered when the persons designated in the statute have "reasonable

---

3. Child abuse reporting statutes in some states expressly create a private cause of action. These states include Arkansas, Colorado, Iowa, Michigan, Montana, New York and Rhode Island.

4. West Virginia Code § 49-6A-8 states:

   Any person, official or institution required by this article to report a case involving a child known or suspected to be abused or neglected, or required by section five [§ 49-6A-5] of this article to forward a copy of a report of serious injury, who knowingly fails to do so or knowingly prevents another person acting reasonably from doing so, shall be guilty of a misdemeanor, and, upon conviction thereof, shall be confined in the county jail not more than ten days or fined not more than one hundred dollars, or both.

cause to suspect" or "observe[ ] *the child* being subjected to conditions that are likely to result in abuse or neglect." W.Va.Code § 49-6A-2 (emphasis added). The plain meaning of the statute[5] is that the mandatory duty to report extends only to the child who is the object of suspected abuse. Nonetheless, we hesitate to extend a private cause of action by implication to any child injured by a non-reported abuser against the person responsible for reporting since substantial questions of causation are raised and the failure to report "would not in the direct sense be a proximate cause of the injury to the child." *Borne by Borne v. Northwest Allen County School Corp.*, 532 N.E.2d 1196, 1203 (Ind.App.1989). The problems with causation are further complicated when one considers that the statute conditions the reporting requirement on the exercise of judgment of an individual reporter who may become aware of a possible case of child abuse only through rumors, innuendo or second-hand reports. The diverse backgrounds, professions and occupations represented in the statutorily defined class of persons required to report make it all the more difficult to define what conduct is required in various conceivable situations. Under such nebulous circumstances, we are unwilling to recognize a new and broad field of tort liability without express legislative designation of a private cause of action. *Accord Marquay v. Eno*, 139 N.H. 708, 662 A.2d 272, 278 (1995) ("Where, as here, civil liability for a statutory violation would represent an abrupt and sweeping departure from the general common law rule of nonliability, we would expect that if the legislature ... intended to impose civil liability it would expressly so provide."); *Freehauf v. School Board of Seminole County*, 623 So.2d 761 (Fla.App., 5th Dist.1993). Application of the final factor in *Hurley* lends further support for finding that a private cause of action is not implicated.

Pursuant to the third *Hurley* criterion, we must determine whether a private cause of action is consistent with the underlying purpose not just of the reporting statute but the entire legislative scheme of which the reporting statute is a part. The reporting statute is one of ten sections in article six-A, chapter forty-nine of the West Virginia Code, entitled "Reports of Children Suspected to be Abused or Neglected." A review of all of the provisions of the article reveals that the primary objective of the enactment is to protect children who are subjected to abuse and neglect by establishing county-based child protective services offices whose purposes are to quickly investigate incidents of suspected abuse reported by those required to report under the article and to take all necessary measures to protect such children from further abuse and neglect, including providing individualized services to affected children and their families. In addition to the reporting and criminal liability provisions we have thus far discussed, the article also contains provisions regarding civil and criminal immunity for those who make a report and abrogation of the rule of privileged communications in certain instances. When the provisions of the article are considered as a whole, we do not see that a private cause of action would meaningfully further the purposes of the article so as to find that such was intended by the Legislature.

Accordingly we conclude that West Virginia Code § 49-6A-2 does not give rise to an implied private civil cause of action, in addition to criminal penalties imposed by the statute, for failure to report suspected child abuse where an individual with a duty to report under the statute is alleged to have had reasonable cause to suspect that a child is being abused and has failed to report suspected abuse. The same conclusion has been

---

5. We note that when the meaning of a statute is clear, it is the duty of the courts to respect legislative intent by applying the statute as written. *See* Syl. pt. 5, *State v. General Daniel Morgan Post No. 548, V.F.W.*, 144 W.Va. 137, 107 S.E.2d 353 (1959).

reached by a decided majority of states which have applied factors comparable to those in *Hurley* when considering whether a private cause of action was implied through mandatory reporting statutes similar to ours. *See Freehauf v. School Board of Seminole County*, 623 So.2d 761 (Fla.App., 5th Dist.1993); *Cechman v. Travis*, 202 Ga.App. 255, 414 S.E.2d 282 (1991); *Borne by Borne v. Northwest Allen County School Corp.*, 532 N.E.2d 1196 (Ind.App.1989); *Kansas State Bank & Trust Co., v. Specialized Transp. Services, Inc.*, 249 Kan. 348, 819 P.2d 587 (1991); *Bradley v. Ray*, 904 S.W.2d 302, (Mo.App.1995); *Marquay v. Eno*, 139 N.H. 708, 662 A.2d 272 (1995); *see also Isely v. Capuchin Province*, 880 F.Supp. 1138 (D.Mich.1995) (applying Wisconsin's reporting statute); Danny R. Veilleux, *Validity, Construction, and Application of State Statute Requiring Doctor or Other Person to Report Child Abuse*, 73 A.L.R.4th 782, 819 (1989).[6]

In so holding, we have not ignored Mr. Arbaugh's plea to carve out a private cause of action for more egregious situations, such as where an eye-witness has failed to report. Despite the underlying merit to this request, we are bound to refrain from making such policy determinations since " '[i]t is not the province of the courts to make or supervise legislation, and a statute may not, under the guise of interpretation, be modified, revised, amended, distorted, remodeled, or rewritten[.]' " *State v. Richards*, 206 W.Va. 573, 577, 526 S.E.2d 539, 543 (1999), quoting *State v. General Daniel Morgan Post No. 548, V.F.W.*, 144 W.Va. 137, 145, 107 S.E.2d 353, 358 (1959) (citation omitted). We note that children harmed by such egregious circumstances are not without remedy, where in an otherwise proper case a cause of action may be brought based on negligence with the failure to report admissible as evidence in that context.

For the reasons herein stated, we answer the certified question in the negative....

Notes

In *Beggs*, the court implied a civil cause of action on behalf of a child based on a doctor's failure to report suspected child abuse. The court found a special relationship existed between the doctor and the subject child such that a civil cause of action may be implied. *See also Radke v. Freeborn*, 694 N.W.2d 788 (Minn. 2005) (court implying civil right of action against Department of Human Services investigator upon finding special relationship imposing duty owed to subject child beyond that owed to general public). Whether liability is imposed statutorily or impliedly, a civil remedy for failure to report suspected child abuse does not impose liability for harm suffered by individuals other than the child who is the subject of the failed report. *See Lurene F. v. Olsson*, 190 Misc.2d 642, 740 N.Y.S.2d 797 (2002). Civil liability may be imposed vicariously as well. *See Wieder v. San Diego Unified School District*, 2011 WL 6372878 (Ct. App. 4th 1 Cal. 2011) (school district vicariously liable for teacher's negligent failure to report sexual abuse of student); *Lee v. Detroit Medical Center*, 775 N.W.2d 326, 285 Mich. App. 51 (2009) (hospital and medical center that employed physicians who allegedly breached statutory duty to report suspected child abuse held vicariously liable for physicians' breach). In *Arbaugh*, although the court held that a civil cause of action may be implied for failure to report suspected child abuse, liability was held not to extend to the defendant, to whom the investigator did not owe a special duty because he was not the subject of the failed report.

---

6. In the only case we have found decided by a state court which allowed a suit on this basis, the cause of action was limited to situations where proof could establish that the person who did not report did so intentionally. *Landeros v. Flood*, 17 Cal.3d 399, 131 Cal.Rptr. 69, 551 P.2d 389 (1976).

C. Immunity

1. Generally

Stecks v. Young

Court of Appeal, Fourth District, Division 1, California, 1995
38 Cal. App. 4th 365, 45 Cal. Rptr. 2d 475

HALLER, Associate Justice.

David and Nancy Stecks brought an action for libel per se, slander per se, and intentional infliction of emotional distress against psychologist Candace Young. The action concerned an oral and a written report Young made to the Child Protective Services regarding the Steckses and others in which she accused these individuals of child abuse and participation in cult activities. The reports were based upon information Young received from her patient, the Steckses' allegedly schizophrenic adult daughter.... Young demurred, contending she was entitled to absolute immunity pursuant to Penal Code ... [footnote omitted] section 11172, subdivision (a). The trial court agreed and sustained the demurrer with leave to amend. After the Steckses filed a first amended complaint, Young filed a second demurrer, again asserting absolute immunity. The court sustained the demurrer without leave to amend and then entered judgment in Young's favor.... On appeal, the Steckses maintain the immunity is inapplicable because (1) Young did not harbor a reasonable suspicion of abuse when she submitted the reports, (2) Young reported issues irrelevant to the prevention of child abuse, and (3) Young conveyed her reports in an untimely manner. Following the thoughtful and well-reasoned reported decisions that previously have interpreted the broadly written Child Abuse and Neglect Reporting Act (§ 11164 et seq.), we affirm the judgment. (*Auto Equity Sales, Inc. v. Superior Court* (1962) 57 Cal.2d 450, 20 Cal.Rptr. 321, 369 P.2d 937.) ...

Young is a licensed marriage, family, and child counselor with a doctorate in clinical psychology. She is a member of the Ritual Abuse Task Force for the San Diego County Commission on Children and Youth. In September 1988, she began treating the Steckses' 29-year-old daughter (hereafter "patient"), who had been diagnosed as schizophrenic and suffering from multiple personality disorder. While in psychotherapy sessions, patient reported that her mother and father had sexually molested her when she was a child, practiced satanic worship, abused alcohol and marijuana, and participated in human and animal sacrifice and brainwashing.... During treatment, patient also told Young she was concerned about the welfare and safety of her niece and nephew, particularly her niece whom she thought might be a victim of sexual molestation by patient's brother-in-law. In April 1990, patient, but not Young, informed Child Protective Services of her concerns. In September 1991, patient informed Young that she had information suggesting her nephew was scheduled to be sacrificed at a cult ritual celebration of the Fall Equinox. Patient again implicated the children's father in the planned cult ritual.

After patient told Young of the anticipated ritualistic sacrifice, Young spoke directly with Wells Gardner of Child Protective Services. On October 16, 1991, Young, at Gardner's request, sent a letter to Gardner in which she conveyed her concerns regarding the children and why she thought patient should be believed. Before sending the letter, Young had never met or communicated with the Steckses, the children, or the children's parents, relying instead solely upon information patient provided. The letter was seen and read by Gardner, others associated with Child Protective Services, medical practitioners and individuals within the criminal justice system.... The letter, which according to the Steckses does not "suggest" they posed any danger to their grandchildren, included serious accusations about the Steckses' relationship with patient when she was a child, their involvement in cult activities, and Young's assessment that neither of the Steckses would be a proper caretaker for their grandchildren. The Steckses contend the letter and all oral representations concerning them were false and that Young made these statements with "a complete absence of reasonable suspicion" they were true. Further, they allege Young's actions have harmed their good reputations and caused them damages, including mental and physical distress.[3] ...

For more than 30 years, California has used mandatory reporting obligations as a way to identify and protect child abuse victims. In 1963, the Legislature passed former Penal Code section 11161.5, its first attempt at imposing upon physicians and surgeons the obligation to report suspected child abuse. Although this initial version and later ones carried the risk of criminal sanctions for noncompliance, the state Department of Justice estimated in November 1978 that only about 10 percent of all cases of child abuse were being reported. (*Krikorian v. Barry* (1987) 196 Cal.App.3d 1211, 1216–1217, 242 Cal.Rptr. 312.) ... Faced with this reality and a growing population of abused children, in 1980 the Legislature enacted the Child Abuse Reporting Law (§ 11165 et seq.), a comprehensive scheme of reporting requirements "aimed at increasing the likelihood that child abuse victims are identified." (*James W. v. Superior Court* (1993) 17 Cal.App.4th 246, 254, 21 Cal.Rptr.2d 169, citing *Ferraro v. Chadwick* (1990) 221 Cal.App.3d 86, 90, 270 Cal.Rptr. 379.) The Legislature subsequently renamed the law the Child Abuse and Neglect Reporting Act (Act) (§ 11164). (Stats.1987, ch. 1444, § 1.5, p. 5369.) ... Against this background, we examine the relevant provisions of the Act:

Section 11166, subdivision (a) identifies mandated reporters, including health practitioners,[4] and defines the circumstances under which these individuals must report. This provision affirmatively "requires persons in positions where abuse is likely to be detected to report promptly all suspected and known instances of child abuse to authorities for follow-up investigation." (*Ferraro v. Chadwick, supra,* 221 Cal.App.3d at p. 90, 270 Cal.Rptr. 379.) Suspected abuse includes circumstances where "it is objectively reasonable for a person to entertain a suspicion, based upon facts that could cause a reasonable person in a like position, drawing when appropriate on his or her training and experience, to suspect child abuse." (§ 11166, subd. (a).) The incident must be reported "as soon as practically possible by telephone," followed by a written report "within 36 hours of receiving the information...." (*Ibid.*) Failure to comply is punishable as a misdemeanor. (§ 11172, subd. (e).) ... Section 11167, subdivision (b) authorizes communications with child abuse protective agencies and provides that "[i]nformation relevant to the incident of child abuse may also be given to an investigator from a child protective agency who is investigating the known or suspected case of child abuse." ... Section 11172, subdivision (a) establishes immunity. It "cloaks mandated reporters with immunity from civil and criminal liability for making any report 'required or authorized' by the Act." (*Ferraro v. Chadwick, supra,*

---

3. From the record, it is clear that Child Protective Services conducted some level of investigation concerning the Steckses' grandchildren, but the record is silent as to what form the investigation took. Although the parties do not reference the filing of a dependency petition or any criminal proceedings, the Steckses did inform the trial court at oral argument on January 22, 1993, that "these two children ... have long since been returned to their parents."

4. Young, a licensed marriage, family, and child counselor, is a health practitioner within the meaning of section 11165.8.

221 Cal.App.3d at pp. 90–91, 270 Cal.Rptr. 379.)[5] Subdivision (c) of section 11172 entitles mandated reporters who incur legal fees defending a legal action brought despite the immunity, to recover their legal fees from the state Board of Control.

The Steckses contend that Young's entitlement to immunity depends upon a factual determination of whether she harbored a reasonable suspicion of abuse when she reported to Child Protective Services. While the Steckses concede that as a health practitioner Young must comply with the Act's mandatory reporting provisions, they argue her immunity is not absolute. From their perspective, they have the right to prove ... the accusations contained in the first amended complaint because the Act does not protect Young from preparing negligent or knowingly false reports.... As respondent argues convincingly, however, the Steckses' position is contrary to existing precedent and is inconsistent with the Act's fundamental premise — reporting protects children. It also disregards those factors which eventually led the Legislature to include absolute immunity within the Act: (1) professionals will be reluctant to report if they face liability for inaccurate reports, and (2) it is inconsistent to expose professionals to civil liability for failing to report[6] and then expose them to liability where their reports prove false. As the Legislature recognized, accurate reports of abuse do not lead to civil lawsuits. Only those which cannot be confirmed, are unfounded, or, worse yet, are intentionally false, do. Faced with a choice between absolute immunity, which would promote reporting but preclude redress to those harmed by false accusations, and conditional immunity, which would limit reporting but allow redress, the Legislature, through various amendments, ultimately selected absolute immunity. (*Storch v. Silverman* (1986) 186 Cal.App.3d 671, 679–681, 231 Cal.Rptr. 27.)

The appellate courts of this state, including our own court, have previously evaluated the Act's immunity provision and, in each case, soundly rejected the argument that immunity does not attach unless "reasonable suspicion" existed. As succinctly stated by the Court of Appeal in *Storch*, which conducted a comprehensive analysis of (1) the statutory language, (2) the legislative purposes, and (3) the historical background of the statutory immunities:

> "Plaintiffs' interpretation, however, renders the immunity statute virtually meaningless. There is no need for immunity when there can be no liability, as in the case of reports that are true or based upon objectively reasonable suspicion.... The issue of the reasonableness of the reporter's suspicions would potentially exist in every reported case.

> "The legislative scheme is designed to encourage the reporting of child abuse to the greatest extent possible to prevent further abuse. Reporters are required to report child abuse promptly and they are subject to criminal prosecution if they fail to report as required. Accordingly, absolute immunity from liability for all reports is consistent with that scheme." (*Storch v. Silverman, supra,* 186 Cal.App.3d at pp. 678–679, 231 Cal.Rptr. 27, fn. omitted; accord *Krikorian v. Barry, supra,* 196 Cal.App.3d at p. 1223, 242 Cal.Rptr. 312; *Thomas v. Chadwick* (1990) 224 Cal.App.3d 813, 819–820, 274 Cal.Rptr. 128; *Ferraro v. Chadwick, supra,* 221 Cal.App.3d at pp. 90–92, 270 Cal.Rptr. 379; see also *James W. v. Superior Court, supra,* 17 Cal.App.4th 246, 21 Cal.Rptr.2d 169 [where we declined

---

5. This statute also affords immunity to nonmandated reporters who report known or suspected child abuse, "unless it can be proven that a false report was made and the [nonmandated reporter] knew that the report was false or was made with reckless disregard of the truth or falsity of the report...." (§ 11172, subd. (a).)

6. See *Landeros v. Flood* (1976) 17 Cal.3d 399, 131 Cal.Rptr. 69, 551 P.2d 389.

to apply immunity to the post reporting activities of a psychologist and foster parents, and reaffirmed that mandated reporters are entitled to absolute immunity even if their reports are negligently prepared or intentionally false].) ...

Without exception, our appellate courts have concluded that immunity is a key ingredient in maintaining the Act's integrity and thus have rejected efforts aimed at narrowing its protection. While we recognize that unfounded reports can lead to serious, sometimes devastating consequences, and we have great sympathy for those who are wrongfully accused, as we noted in *Thomas v. Chadwick, supra*, "[i]n this war on child abuse the Legislature selected absolute immunity as part of its arsenal. This value choice is clearly within the province of the Legislature. We cannot defuse this chosen weapon on the ground that its effect is sometimes ill when its general purpose is good." (*Thomas v. Chadwick, supra*, 224 Cal.App.3d at p. 827, 274 Cal.Rptr. 128.) ... Having reaffirmed prior holdings affording absolute immunity to those individuals the Act designates as mandated reporters, we express our concern that factually this case presses the outer limits of immunity. Typically, mandated reporters base their reports upon personal interviews with or observations of the alleged victim or abuser or upon information derived from other professionals treating or investigating the alleged abuse. By contrast, here the mandated reporter allegedly trusted the accusations of a purportedly schizophrenic patient, who had no personal knowledge that the children were being abused, and conveyed those accusations to the authorities.

In circumstances where the mandated reporter is not drawing upon personal professional assessments of the victim or abuser or is not relying upon other trained professionals who have made such assessments, we submit that the application of absolute immunity warrants further reflection by the Legislature. Where such reports turn out to be false, the Legislature may deem it appropriate to apply qualified immunity and to permit recovery where the wrongfully accused person can establish that the report was known to be false or made in reckless disregard of the truth. However, absent a change in the statute, the trial court properly sustained the demurrer without leave to amend....

Affirmed.

HUFFMAN, Acting P.J., and NARES, J., concur.

Notes

In *Stecks*, absolute immunity is afforded to mandated reporters. Thus, reporters may not be held liable for reports made that are deemed unfounded or that are negligently made. Because absolute immunity applies, the court need not consider the reasonableness of the reporter's decision to report. If absolute immunity is not afforded, qualified immunity may be afforded in cases in which the reporter must exercise discretion to determine if the facts presented to the reporter are sufficient to lead to a reasonable suspicion that child abuse has occurred. For discussion of the difference between general immunity and qualified immunity, see *Wojcik ex rel. Wojcikmv. Town of N. Smithfield*, 874 F. Supp. 508, 521 (D.C. R.I. 1995). *See also Wilkinson ex rel Wilkinson v. Russell*, 182 F.3d 89 (2d Cir, 1999) (discussing social worker's qualified immunity in case involving social worker's substantiation of allegations by mother of sexual abuse of child by father). A reporter is entitled to qualified immunity when it is objectively reasonable to believe that his or her acts do not violate clearly established protected rights and that he or she is acting within the scope of their authority under constitutional, statutory, or common law bounds. *See id.* Thus, qualified immunity is afforded in cases in which the reporter, acting with discretion, makes a report with a good faith reasonable suspicion that child abuse has occurred. *See, e.g., Anonymous Hospital v. A.K.*, 920 N.E.2d 704 (App. 2010) (hospital did not act in bad faith and, therefore, had immunity after making a report of possible child abuse when 11-month-old's urine sample was tested and showed presence of sperm). *But see Chabak v. Monroy*, 154 Cal. App. 4th 1502, 65 Cal. Rptr. 3d 641 (5th Dist. 2007) (17-year old's false report of sexual abuse by therapist was given absolute immunity; qualified immunity and exception to privilege provided in reporting act, permitting recovery of damages, only applies to reports of third parties, not of victims).

2. *Reasonable Suspicion*

Diana G-D ex Rel. Ann D. v. Bedford Central School District

Supreme Court of New York, 2011
33 Misc. 3d 970, 932 N.Y.S.2d 316

WILLIAM J. GIACOMO, J.

In 2005 Diana G-D started 3rd grade at the Bedford Elementary School in Bedford, New York. At that time, she lived in a home with her mother, Ann D., her 2[-]year-old step-brother E. and her step-father defendant Cesar Joel Sagastume Morales.[2] At the beginning of third grade Diana G-D was quiet and shy as observed by her teachers. Her teachers attributed this uncertainty in school to her transition from her native culture and language to the English language and environment at school. As the school year progressed, her teachers noted positive changes in her developing language skills and overall self confidence.... At a regular parent teacher conference in the Fall of 2005, Ann D. met with two of Diana G-D's third grade teachers. Ann D. allegedly asked the teachers if Diana G-D was behaving properly at school. The teachers told her that Diana G-D was a very well behaved child. Ann D. claims that she told the teachers during this conference that at times Diana G-D seemed sad at home and would often misbehave. The teachers told her that was not how Diana G-D behaved at school.

During the first week of December 2005, Mrs. D., the mother of another third-grader at the Bedford Elementary School, came to school to speak with the principal defendant Victoria Graboski. Ms. Graboski was not there so Mrs. D. spoke with acting principal Regina Smith. Mrs. D. told Ms. Smith that her daughter had overheard a conversation at a slumber party concerning Diana G-D. Mrs. D. told Ms. Smith that her daughter told her that several other third graders discussed a conversation Diana G-D had with another third grader on the school playground during recess. Mrs. D. told Ms. Smith that apparently during the conversation on the school playground, Diana G-D told a friend that she was having sex "with her father." ... The next day, Ms. Graboski called Mrs. D. to speak with her directly. Ms. Graboski then spoke to Diana G-D's teachers about her and learned from them that Diana G-D appeared to be a happy child who was developing and growing as a third grader. She was told that Diana G-D had not demonstrated any problems in the classroom. Ms. Graboski then asked Diana G-D's teachers to speak privately with Diana G-D to learn if she had been at the slumber party the prior weekend and to ascertain how she was feeling and doing at home.... Thereafter, Diana G-D's teachers met with her in a school conference room and had a casual conversation with her. Diana G-D told her teachers that she had not been at the slumber party. The teachers then asked her how she was feeling and if everything was well at home. Diana G-D seemed happy and she said that everything was fine at home. The teachers did not ask Diana G-D about the

---

2. Although Ann D. was not married to Cesar Joel Sagastume Morales, Diana G-D considered E. her step-brother and Sagastume Morales her step-father.

conversation which allegedly took place on the playground. Diana G-D's teachers reported their discussion with Diana G-D to Ms. Graboski and the school took no further action.

On August 17, 2006, Ann D. came home from shopping and found the cell phone of her boyfriend Cesar Joel Sagastume Morales on the couch. Ann D. was jealous because Sagastume Morales had other girlfriends so she decided to look at his cell phone. According to Ann D., Sagastume Morales's cell phone contained pictures of Diana G-D which Ann D. believed were inappropriate. When Ann D. asked Diana G-D about the pictures, Diana G-D allegedly told her that Sagastume Morales had been "touching" her in an inappropriate way. When Ann D. confronted Sagastume Morales, he immediately left the house.... Ann D. called the police and turned the cell phone over to them. Sagastume Morales fled to Guatemala. After several years, Sagastume Morales was arrested in Guatemala and extradited to New York. He eventually plead guilty to sexual misconduct against a child and was sentenced to 8 years in prison. He is currently serving his sentence in the Coxsackie Correctional Facility in Ulster County.

Diana G-D and Ann D. commenced this action in the Spring of 2007. They allege that Diana G-D was sexually abused in her home, from December 2005 to August 2006, by Cesar Joel Sagastume Morales. They also allege that the School District, Victoria Graboski (former principal of Bedford Hills Elementary School) and defendant Kelly Cieslinski-Schleuter (former school psychologist for Bedford Hills Elementary School) were negligent in failing to report the suspected abuse as required by Social Services Law § 413....

The School District now moves for summary judgment dismissing the complaint.... In support of its motion, the School District argues that at no time during the 2005/2006 school year did either Diana G-D or Ann D. report to the school that Diana G-D was being sexually abused. The School District notes that at her deposition, Diana G-D testified that she never told her mother about what Sagastume Morales was doing with her. Diana G-D testified that she was afraid to report the sexual touching because Sagastume Morales told her he would kill Ann D. if she revealed the touching. Diana G-D also testified that she never told her teachers about the sexual activity. Diana G-D did, however, tell several of her third grade friends about the sexual activity with Sagastume Morales. However, Diana G-D told her friends not to tell anyone.

The School District also relies on the deposition testimony of plaintiff Ann D. At her deposition, Ann D. testified that she did not learn of the sexual abuse until August 17, 2006. It was at that time that she also learned that Diana G-D had told her friends about the sexual abuse. Ann D. also testified that Diana G-D never told her that her teachers spoke to her and asked Diana G-D if something was making her sad and whether anything was happening at home.... The School District notes that Ann D. never discussed with the school Sagastume Morales's role in the family while Diana G-D was in third grade and she never contacted any parents of Diana G-D's friends regarding Sagastume Morales's behavior. She testified that when Diana G-D was unhappy and not eating while in third grade, she took her to a pediatrician at the Open Door Clinic in Mount Kisco. According to Ann D., the doctor examined Diana G-D and told Ann D. that everything was fine.

The School District also relies on the deposition testimony of Mrs. D. At her deposition, Mrs. D. testified that when she went to the school to discuss what her daughter had overheard at the slumber party, she did not know if the story was true. Mrs. D. did not call the police or Diana G-D's mother because she was not sure that the matter was "real". At her deposition, school employee Regina Smith testified that she found Mrs. D.'s story about the conversation during the slumber party confusing and did not know if it was credible.... The School District also relies on the deposition testimony of Victoria Graboski.

Ms. Graboski testified that after discussing the matter with Regina Smith and Mrs. D., she spoke with school psychologist Kelly Cieslinski. Ms. Graboski told Ms. Cieslinski that this information was received "fourth hand." She also told Ms. Cieslinski that Diana G-D had not demonstrated any problems in the classroom. Ms. Graboski testified that in dealing with these allegations, she was also concerned that prejudice against Hispanic families might have "factored into" the allegations of sexual misconduct.... Ms. Graboski also testified that she asked Diana G-D's teachers to talk to Diana G-D about the slumber party and to ask her if everything was okay at home. The teachers reported back to her that Diana G-D had not been at the slumber party and that she told them that everything was fine at home....

The School District argues that plaintiffs' complaint must be dismissed because pursuant to Social Services Law § 413, it had no duty to report the allegation of suspected child abuse of Diana G-D.

> Social Services Law § 413. Persons and officials required to report cases of suspected child abuse or maltreatment, provides in relevant part:
>
> 1. (a) The following persons and officials are required to report or cause a report to be made in accordance with this title when they have reasonable cause to suspect that a child coming before them in their professional or official capacity is an abused or maltreated child, or when they have reasonable cause to suspect that a child is an abused or maltreated child where the parent, guardian, custodian or other person legally responsible for such child comes before them in their professional or official capacity and states from personal knowledge facts, conditions or circumstances which, if correct, would render the child an abused or maltreated child: ...

The School District asserts that pursuant to Social Services Law § 413 there are two circumstances where a "designated person" such as a school employee, is required to report allegations of suspected child abuse. The first arises when the designated person has "reasonable cause" to suspect that a "child coming before them" is abused. The second arises when the designated person has reasonable cause to suspect a child is abused when the person coming before them and reporting the abuse is a parent or guardian or person in charge of the minor.... The School District argues that the facts of this case cannot trigger the first circumstance for reporting because Diana G-D was not "a child coming before" it as defined by statute. Furthermore, during the period in question the behavior and appearance of Diana G-D, while at school gave it no reason to suspect she was being abused. With respect to the second trigger for mandatory reporting, the School argues that the person providing the report of alleged sexual abuse was Mrs. D., who was not a parent, guardian or person in charge of Diana G-D. Therefore, according to the School District, neither trigger for mandatory reporting is present in this case. Accordingly, it cannot be held liable for failure to report the alleged abuse.

The School District also argues that even if it had a duty to report and failed to report the alleged abuse in this case, it can only be held liable, pursuant to Social Services Law § 420, if it "knowingly and willfully" failed to report the alleged abuse. Further, even if the School District knowingly and willfully failed to report the alleged abuse, it is only liable for damages proximately caused by its failure to report the abuse.... The School District notes that it did not ignore the allegations made by Mrs. D. Rather, it immediately investigated the complaint by discussing the allegations with Diana G-D's teachers and requesting that they meet with her and ask Diana G-D if she was okay and if there was anything wrong at home. When Diana G-D replied that she was fine and nothing was wrong at home, the School District argues that it complied with its statutory obligation with regard to this "third hand" report of abuse.... Finally, the School District argues that there is no evidence that any failure to report the alleged abuse of Diana G-D was the proximate cause of her injuries since there is no proof regarding when the alleged abuse took place....

Defendant Kelly Cieslinski also moves for summary judgment. In support of her motion, Ms. Cieslinski argues that pursuant to Social Services Law § 413, she is not required to report third-hand allegations of abuse from the mother of another third grader. Ms. Cieslinski argues that pursuant to Social Services Law § 413(a)(1) a school employee is required to report abuse when they have reasonable cause to suspect that a "child coming before them" has been abused or "where the parent, guardian, custodian or other person legally responsible for such child comes before them in their professional or official capacity and states from personal knowledge facts, conditions, or circumstances which, if correct, would render the child an abused or maltreated child ..." ... According to Ms. Cieslinski, she never spoke to Diana G-D. Therefore, Diana G-D was not "a child coming before" her. Further, Ms. Cieslinski notes that the only report of abuse was from Mrs. D., who is not the parent, guardian, custodian or person legally responsible for Diana G-D. There is no dispute that Mrs. D. did not have personal knowledge of any of the information she supplied to the school.... Ms. Cieslinski argues further, that even if she had a duty to report what Mrs. D. had told Regina Smith and Ms. Graboski, she can only be held liable for any damages the failure to report caused, under Social Services Law § 420(2), if she knowingly and willfully failed to make the appropriate report. However, there is no evidence that she knowingly and willfully failed to report any alleged abuse of Diana G-D. As Ms. Cieslinski previously argued, Diana G-D did not come before her and the report of the alleged abuse did not come from one of the enumerated people with personal knowledge as set forth in Social Service Law § 413. Accordingly, Ms. Cieslinski seeks summary judgment dismissing the complaint against her....

Ms. Graboski also moves for summary judgment dismissing the complaint and all cross claims asserted against her. In support of her motion, Ms. Graboski argues that she did not breach her statutory duty to report suspected child abuse under Social Services Law §§ 413, 420. Further, any failure to report suspected child abuse was not knowingly or willful as required pursuant to Social Services Law § 420. Finally, Ms. Graboski argues that she had no common law duty to report any suspected child abuse....

Plaintiffs argue in opposition that defendants were mandated to report any and all allegations of suspected sexual abuse because Diana G-D was "a child coming before" it. Plaintiffs acknowledge that there are two triggers for mandatory reporting.[3] The first is when a designated reporter has reasonable cause to believe that a child coming before it is being abused. Plaintiffs argue that Diana G-D, as a third grade student of the School District, unquestionably came before teachers, administrators and other school personnel daily. Therefore, Diana G-D came before several of the enumerated designated persons set forth in Social Service Law § 413. In addition, plaintiffs claim that since Ann D. informed the school of her concern regarding her daughter's behavior at home and Mrs. D. told administrators of the overheard conversation, the defendants had reasonable cause to suspect that Diana G-D as "a child coming before it" who was being abused.... In

---

3. The plaintiffs acknowledge that the second trigger for mandatory reporting i.e. when the abuse is reported by a parent, guardian or a person in charge of the minor with personal knowledge of the abuse, is not applicable in this case. There is no dispute that Ms. D. is not a person legally responsible for Diana G-D.

support of their position, plaintiffs submit the affidavit of Dr. Helen Abramowicz, a consulting psychiatrist, who avers that the concerns expressed by Ann D. at the parent teacher conference coupled with Mrs. D.'s report constitute "reasonable cause" to suspect that Diana G-D was being abused.

Plaintiffs also argue that the defendants' failure to report the alleged abuse was knowingly and willful. In support of this argument, plaintiffs note that the reason why Ms. Graboski did not report the alleged abuse of Diana G-D was that there was discord between American and Latino families, especially in the third grade class where there was a disproportionate number of Latino families. Plaintiffs claim that at her deposition, Ms. Graboski testified that in view of this discord she was concerned about the veracity of a story told by white children at a slumber party about a Latino girl who was not at the slumber party. Plaintiffs claim that this testimony establishes that there is a question of fact regarding whether the failure to report the alleged abuse was knowingly and willful.... With respect to the issue of proximate cause, plaintiffs argue that defendants have not produced evidence to establish that their inaction was not the proximate cause of plaintiffs' injuries....

The defendants' first argument is that Diana G-D was not a "child coming before" them. Defendants argue that the meaning of the phrase "coming before" should not be given an overly broad meaning. Rather, they contend that the phrase contemplates a physical action on the part of the child, i.e., the child physically appears or acts in a manner which suggests abuse or the child herself reports the abuse to a mandatory reporter. Defendants argue that Diana G-D did not "come before" them reporting abuse at home; nor did Diana G-D appear to be physically abused.... Additionally, defendants argue that they had no reason to suspect Diana G-D was being abused because, even if she was "a child coming before" them, she appeared happy, well behaved and was progressing nicely at school. According to defendants, she was not acting in a manner which gave them any indication that she was being sexually abused. She was not acting out in a sexually inappropriate way and she was not saying things to teachers which would indicate sexual abuse. Thus, they assert that they had no duty to report any alleged abuse, especially considering the report came from Mrs. D., a third-party source who had no personal knowledge of any sexual abuse. Finally, when defendants inquired directly of Diana G-D whether anything was happening at home, Diana G-D stated that everything was fine.

Plaintiffs disagree. First, they argue that as a student of the School District Diana G-D was clearly a "child coming before" the defendants. Further, they argue that in view of Ann D.'s concerns about Diana G-D's behavior at home and with Mrs. D.'s report of statements her daughter overheard when other children were discussing statements allegedly made by Diana G-D about sex with her father, there was "reasonable cause" to suspect abuse....

A review of this legislative history discloses that it is clear the intent of Social Services Law § 413 et seq. is to encourage the reporting of suspected child abuse. However, it is also clear that there was a concern about the filing of unfounded reports as well as a concern regarding an overbroad interpretation of the term "reasonable cause" as set forth in the statute....

Although this Court could not find a case which specifically defines "a child coming before" and "reasonable cause" under the statute, ... [B]ased upon this Court's analysis..., it finds that a "child coming before" a designated reporter must reveal facts which provide a designated reporter with reasonable cause to suspect abuse to trigger the reporting requirement of the statute. The School District's argument that Diana G-D was not a "child coming before" it is without merit. Diana G-D is clearly a student of the School District

and, therefore, is a child who comes before it in the same way the infant patient of a pediatrician comes before that physician during a routine medical examination. However,
the act of a child "coming before" a designated mandatory reporter is only the first prong
of a two prong test as set forth in the statute. Not only must the child come before a
mandatory reporter, the child must also provide the mandatory reporter with "reasonable
cause" to suspect abuse.... Here, however, while Diana G-D was a "child coming before"
the defendants she did not provide them with facts which gave them reasonable cause to
suspect that she was being abused. Notably, none of the school employees witnessed any
acts of the alleged abuse, saw any physical injury to Diana G-D, or observed any behavioral
issues from Diana G-D which would have given any of them "reasonable cause" to suspect
abuse or maltreatment at home. Further, when questioned by her teachers, Diana G-D
appeared happy and denied that there were any issues at home.... [footnote omitted].

This is in direct contrast to the two young girls in *Isabelle V. v. City of New York*, 150
A.D.2d 312, 541 N.Y.S.2d 809 [1st Dept. 1989] in which the Appellate Division reversed
the motion court's decision and granted defendant Hospital's motion to dismiss the
complaint based upon the immunity conferred upon it by Social Services § 419. In *Isabelle
V.*, the plaintiff brought her 3[-]year-old daughter to defendant hospital for examination.
The child had a sore throat and vaginal discharge. When plaintiff stated that her daughter's
7[-]year-old cousin who lived in the same household had a similar discharge, she was
told to bring both children in for examination the next day. During the examination of
the 7[-]year-old, the child seemed very frightened and a Spanish interpreter was summoned.
Although the child's answers to questions about sexual abuse by someone in the household
were negative, the interpreter believed that the child was not being truthful and that she
was "afraid of something". A physical examination of the seven year old revealed that she,
too, had a vaginal discharge. Throat and vaginal cultures were taken from both children
and sent to a laboratory for testing for venereal disease. Ultimately the report suspecting
abuse was determined to be unfounded. While the procedural posture of *Isabelle V.* differs
from this case, it is clear that Isabelle V. and her cousin were children "coming before"
the defendant hospital. Additionally, the girls' medical condition as well as the older girl's
appearance of being "afraid of something" provided the defendant with "reasonable cause"
to suspect abuse.

In this case, it is important to note that during the parent-teacher conference, Ann D.
expressed concern about Diana G-D's behavior in school based upon what she claimed
was Diana G-D's behavior at home. However, it is undisputed that Diana G-D appeared
happy and was well behaved in school. Therefore, it is not clear what the School District
was supposed to do about Ann D.'s concern. Furthermore, Ann D. did not raise any
concern to the school at the parent-teacher conference regarding whether Diana G-D was
being sexually abused at home.... Accordingly, based upon the foregoing, the Court finds
that defendants did not have "reasonable cause" to believe that Diana G-D was being
abused. Notably, Diana G-D herself did not provide any reasonable cause to suspect she
was being abused. Defendants could not rely on the third-hand hearsay statements of
Mrs. D. or the general concern of Ann D. regarding Diana G-D's behavior at home to
support "reasonable cause" to believe she was being abused.[5] Thus, in this case defendants
had no duty to report suspected child abuse, pursuant to Social Services Law § 413.

---

5. The Court notes that had defendants made a report of suspected child abuse which was
subsequently determined to be unfounded, they would have been granted qualified immunity pursuant
to Social Services Law § 419, provided there was reasonable cause to suspect that the child might have
been abused and where the defendants had acted in good faith in making the report. Notably, in order
to lose this immunity a plaintiff must establish that the reporter's acts were "willful misconduct or

Nevertheless, even if this Court found that defendants failed to report the alleged abuse, there is simply no evidence that defendants' failure to make such a report was knowingly and willful (*see* Social Services Law § 420; *see also Estate of Pesante v. County of Seneca*, 1 A.D.3d 915, 768 N.Y.S.2d 69 [4th Dept. 2003]; *Estate of Pesante ex rel. Pesante v. Geneva Medical Group, LLP*, 2002 WL 398517 [Sup. Ct. Seneca Cty. 2002]; *Zimmerman ex rel. Zimmerman v. U.S.*, 171 F.Supp.2d 281 [S.D.N.Y. 2001]; *cf. Lara ex rel. Lara v. City of New York*, 187 Misc.2d 882, 726 N.Y.S.2d 217 [Sup. Ct. N.Y. Cty. 2001]).[6] ... First, it is clear that based upon the hearsay statements of Mrs. D. and the concern of Ann D. regarding Diana G-D's behavior at home, defendants took quick action. Ms. Graboski immediately commenced an investigation by gathering information about Diana G-D from her teachers. She then had two of Diana G-D's teachers talk to Diana G-D.[7] The teachers questioned Diana G-D regarding whether she was at the slumber party and then asked her if there were any problems at home.[8] At that time, Diana G-D, who appeared happy, indicated that she was not at the slumber party and that things at home were fine. Therefore, at this time, all defendants knew was that Diana G-D appeared fine and denied any problems at home. They had no knowledge of sexual abuse since they could and should not rely on third hand hearsay statements as the sole basis for suspecting abuse.[9] Thus, as a matter of law the Court finds that defendants did not knowingly and willfully fail to report suspected child abuse.

Based upon the foregoing, the School District's motion for summary judgment is GRANTED, Kelly Cieslinski's motion for summary judgment is GRANTED, and Victoria Graboski's motion for summary judgment is GRANTED.

Notes

The mandate to report in *Diana G-D* is limited by the statutorily required circumstances under which a reporter must report; the reporter must have reasonable cause to suspect

---

gross negligence." In contrast, pursuant to Social Service Law § 420, civil liability is imposed if the reporter knowingly and willfully failed to report suspected child abuse. Reading these two statutes, together, it is clear to this Court that the legislature intended to allow the exercise of good faith professional judgment in reporting or not reporting alleged suspected child abuse, (*see Estate of Pesante ex rel. Pesante v. Geneva Medical Group*, LLP, 2002 WL 398517 [Sup. Ct. Seneca Cty. 2002] [Defendant physicians who did not report alleged suspected abuse, simply used their professional judgment in a reasonable manner, based on what they knew at the time.]; *cf. Alex LL. v. Department of Social Services of Albany County*, 60 A.D.3d 199, 872 N.Y.S.2d 569 [3rd Dept. 2009] lv. denied 12 N.Y.3d 710, 2009 WL 1260181 [2009] [The Court found that two Social Services workers professional judgment was appropriate in view of the decisions they made during a custody proceeding.]). If this were not the case, a mandatory reporter would be expected to automatically report any statements made to it. This type of knee-jerk or automatic reporting was clearly a concern of the Legislature when it enacted Social Service Laws § 413 et seq.

6. The Court notes that both plaintiffs' complaint and bill of particulars allege that defendants negligently failed to report the abuse of Diana G-D. There is no cause of action for negligent reporting pursuant to Social Services Law § 420. (*See Zimmerman ex rel. Zimmerman v. U.S.*, 171 F.Supp.2d 281 [S.D.N.Y. 2001]).

7. The Court makes no determination regarding whether the two teachers who, at Ms. Graboski's request, had a discussion with Diana G-D were the appropriate School District personnel to investigate whether the statements reported by Mrs. D. were true.

8. Contrary to plaintiffs' contentions, whether defendants should have investigated further is not an issue which need be considered. Rather, the issue is based upon the information defendants had at the time they questioned Diana G-D did they knowingly and willfully fail to report suspected child abuse. (*See Mosher-Simons v. County of Allegany*, 1997 WL 662512 [W.D.N.Y. 1997]).

9. As discussed herein, a main concern of the agencies reviewing the statute was that unfounded reports could be filed where there was no abuse.

that: (1) a child coming before him or her is abused; or (2) the child is abused and the parent, guardian or custodian comes before him or her and offers evidence that the child is abused. *See also Hargrove v. District of Columbia*, 5 A.3d 632 (2010) (where parents reported to school authorities that daughter was sexually abused by another student at school, school did not have reasonable suspicion that parent or guardian abused, which is what was required to trigger mandatory report). Because neither prompt for mandatory reporting produced reasonable suspicion of the child as abused, the teacher was not required to report. Compare the circumstances in *Diana G-D* with the circumstances in the following case. Are the circumstances in the *Hughes* case any different, such that the teacher should be held liable for not reporting?

Hughes v. Stanley County School Board

Supreme Court of South Dakota, 1999
1999 S.D. 65, 594 N.W.2d 346

GILBERTSON, Justice ...

This is an appeal from a judgment and order of the circuit court, Sixth Judicial Circuit, affirming a decision of the Stanley County School Board (School Board) terminating the contract of Mary Hughes (Hughes) as a school counselor. We reverse and remand, with instructions....

Hughes was employed as an elementary school guidance counselor for the Stanley County School District between 1990 and 1997. During her employment, her earlier evaluations were predominately positive. The only concerns expressed in the evaluations dealt with promptness and class preparation. However, in 1996, Hughes was commended for improving on both. She had always been recommended for re-employment by the school administration.... In the fall of 1994, M.B., a third grade student, approached Hughes. In her capacity as a guidance counselor, Hughes had worked with M.B. on a number of occasions. M.B. related to Hughes that M.B.'s father, G.B., walked around the house after his showers without a towel. Hughes told M.B. to speak with her mother, F.B., to ask her father to cover up. During a second conversation, M.B. reported her father had touched her in the area of her breast during a playful wrestling match. Hughes described M.B. at the time as having no breast development, but just becoming aware of some of the issues regarding her sexuality. Hughes gave M.B. the same advice as before, to talk to her mother. In a third conversation, M.B. said she had walked in on her father masturbating. Hughes told M.B. to speak to her mother to get her father to be more discreet.... The fourth and final conversation occurred in May 1995. M.B. reported her father had asked her to touch his penis. Hughes again gave M.B. the same advice. Hughes testified later she doubted the claims of M.B. because of her history and experience counseling the child. M.B. had a tendency to fabricate or exaggerate the facts. On at least one prior occasion M.B. had spoken untruthfully and Hughes required her to apologize before the class.... Throughout this series of conversations, Hughes was aware the School Board had a policy requiring teachers to report suspected child abuse to the school administration. She was also aware of the school policy forbidding teachers to contact the parents to determine the cause of the suspected abuse.

After this last conversation, however, Hughes sought advice from the high school counselor on how she should proceed. He agreed with Hughes' assessment of the situation, that M.B. was fabricating the touching incident. Both the high school counselor and Hughes agreed, speaking with the parents was the proper course of action. Hughes spoke with F.B. and G.B. separately to discuss the allegations their daughter had made. Both parents informed Hughes the first three allegations were essentially true and G.B. had taken steps to avoid any reoccurrence in the future. Both parents insisted the last allegation, regarding the request for M.B. to touch G.B.'s penis, was untrue.... Hughes continued to monitor the situation by checking with M.B. on a daily basis. M.B. never related any further incidents with her father. M.B. did tell Hughes that her father was now "wearing a robe and there were no other sexual incidents *ever after that.*"

In July 1996, the Stanley County Sheriff's Office began to investigate an alleged sexual assault by G.B. against a neighbor child. As part of the investigation, Hughes was questioned about her conversations with M.B. Hughes related this to the school superintendent, Jerry Kleinsasser (Kleinsasser), who told her to talk to the school principal, Denise Gebur (Gebur), when Gebur returned from vacation. In August 1996, Hughes submitted a written report to Gebur regarding M.B.'s allegations. G.B. ultimately pled guilty to the sexual assault charge arising out of the incident with the neighbor child.... On September 3, 1996, Hughes was provided a "Plan of Assistance" by Gebur, designed to provide support, guidance and supervision as a result of the concerns generated from the M.B. incident. However, on September 27, 1996, she was served with a "Notice of Intent to Terminate Employment Relationship." This notice, signed by the superintendent of schools, alleged that she had:

> [V]iolated the written policy of Stanley County School District No. 57-1 as set forth at page 5 in the teacher handbook given to you for the 1994–95 school year under the heading 'Child Abuse/Neglect,'[1] and violated state law concerning the reporting of suspected child abuse, including but not limited to, SDCL 26-8A-3 and SDCL 26-8A-2(8) in the fall of 1994, which failure to report has been recently discovered by the administration and the State of South Dakota.[2]

---

1. This policy provides:

"Because of their regular contact with school-age children, school employees are in an excellent position to identify abuse or neglected children. To comply with state law, it is the policy of the Stanley County School District that any teacher or other school employee who suspects that a child under 18 years of age has been neglected or physically abused (including sexual or emotional abuse) shall report orally or in writing to the principal or superintendent who shall then immediately report to the states attorney, Department of Social Services, county sheriff, or city police. The principal or superintendent shall inform the school employee initiating the action within 24 hours in writing that the report has been made. The employee shall make the report directly to the proper authorities if the principal or superintendent fails to do so.

Reports of child abuse/neglect should include the following information: name, address and age of child; name and address of parent or caretaker; nature and extent of injuries or description of neglect; and any other information that might help establish the cause of injuries or condition.

School employees shall not contact the child's family or any other persons to determine the cause of the suspected abuse or neglect. It is not the responsibility of the school employees to prove that the child has been abused or neglected, or to determine whether the child is in need of protection. It is only their responsibility to report his/her suspicions of abuse or neglect. Anyone who participates in making a report in accordance with the law and in good faith is immune from any civil or criminal liability that may otherwise arise from the reporting or from any resulting judicial proceeding even if the suspicion is proved to be unfounded."

2. At the time of the initial conversation between M.B. and Hughes, Hughes was beginning her fourth year as a Stanley County School District employee. The actual contract between the School District and Hughes for the 1994–95 school year (the contract the School Board claims was breached) is not in the court file and was not introduced as an exhibit by either party. However, a copy of the 1996–97 school year contract is provided in the record. This contract does contain certain language incorporating the rules of the school district into the contract, but whether this exact language was contained in the 1994–95 contract while assumed, cannot be ascertained for certain. The incorporating provision in the 1996-7 contract states:

Initially, she was suspended with pay until a hearing was to be held on the matter. Prior to having been served with the termination notice, Hughes was criminally charged with Failure to Report Child Abuse or Neglected Child under SDCL 26-8A-3[3] by the Stanley County State's Attorney. According to the testimony of Principal Gebur, the fact Hughes had been criminally charged after the "Plan of Assistance" was provided, led to her termination notice.... At the conclusion of Hughes' criminal case, the jury split 11–1 for acquittal resulting in a mistrial. Thereafter, the Stanley County State's Attorney dismissed all charges related to this incident. By the time the criminal trial was held, the School Board had suspended Hughes without pay pending the administrative hearing and hired a replacement.

On February 13, 1997, the School Board held a hearing on the "Notice to Terminate."[4] Prior to the hearing, Hughes sought to question the members of the School Board about possible bias. Upon advice of its attorney, the School Board denied Hughes that opportunity. It appears from the record Hughes was concerned about several matters with respect to School Board members: (1) two members of the School Board had children previously counseled by Hughes, resulting in a disagreement with the parents; (2) Hughes felt some members may bring to the deliberations outside information not presented at the hearing; (3) one School Board member was an employee of the South Dakota Department of Social Services, which was involved to some extent in the investigation of this matter; and (4) Hughes believed the School Board members had pre-determined the result of the case. After the hearing, the School Board voted to issue its "Notice of Termination of Employment Relationship," concluding Hughes had "breached [her] contract of employment." The appeal to the circuit court followed.

Before the circuit court, Hughes called the School Board's chairperson, the Superintendent of Schools, Jerry Parkinson (her former supervisor in Court Services) and herself as witnesses. The School Board called no additional witnesses, but introduced several exhibits, including correspondence between the lawyers concerning the scheduling of the hearings, the circuit court order regarding the preliminary injunction, Hughes' employee evaluations from December 1993 to April 1996 and the transcript of the preliminary hearing before the magistrate judge on the criminal charge.... At the conclusion of the trial, the circuit court judge affirmed the decision of the School Board. Thereafter, findings of fact and conclusions of law were entered. This appeal followed....

Hughes was terminated by the Stanley County School Board for two purported violations of school policy: (1) failing to report child abuse; and (2) initiating direct contact with the parents of the child making the child abuse report. Based on our review of the record there is no evidentiary basis to support the School Board's finding on the first purported violation and therefore, we reverse on that point. The second violation is not only proven, it is admitted by Hughes.... As Hughes was governed by school policy, the following was her contractual obligation in this type of situation:

The teacher agrees to perform the duties assigned by the district in accordance with the rules governing teachers adopted by the district, and in accordance with the provisions of the school laws of the State of South Dakota.

3. SDCL 26-8A-3 makes is a Class 1 misdemeanor for any school counselor (among others) who has reasonable cause to believe a child under eighteen has been abused or neglected, to fail to report such information to the authorities designated in the statute.

4. Three hearings or proceedings make up the appeal record. There is a transcript of the criminal preliminary hearing that was received as an exhibit in the termination proceeding. There is a transcript of the termination hearing before the Stanley County School Board. Finally, there is a transcript of the proceeding before the trial court on appeal from the decision of the School Board to terminate.

Because of their regular contact with school-age children, school employees are in an excellent position to *identify* abused or neglected children. To comply with state law, it is the policy of the Stanley County School District that any teacher or other school employee who *suspects* that a child under 18 years of age has been neglected or physically abused (including sexual or emotional abuse) shall report orally or in writing to the principal or superintendent who shall then immediately report to the states attorney, Department of Social Services, county sheriff, or city police[.]

* * *

School employees shall not contact the child's family or any other persons to determine the cause of the suspected abuse or neglect. It is not the responsibility of the school employees to prove that the child has been abused or neglected, or to determine whether the child is in need of protection. *It is only their responsibility to report his/her suspicions of abuse or neglect....*

(Emphasis added).

A review of this policy establishes reporting is subjective to the teacher when that individual teacher "identifies" or "suspects" or "suspicions" abuse.[5] Hughes' subjective opinion was authored by her in a statement given to the Stanley County State's Attorney.... After detailing the incidents reported by M.B., Hughes reasoned:

Normally, this would have sent off red flags in my head, and I would have called Social Services immediately. The reason I did not, is [M.B.] has a real problem with the truth. Students and teachers were always talking about her need to exaggerate and to create a crisis. I, likewise, had caught her in untruths and exaggerations. I made her apologize to all the group members for lying on more than one occasion.... [M.B.] also has an insatiable need for attention, and my reaction was that she might be sensationalizing the situation so I would spend more time with her.... Throughout the years I have probably spent more counseling time with this one student than any other, because she demands it and revels in it. Teachers would verify this.

Neither the School Board nor the circuit court made any findings on a lack of credibility by Hughes. The entire record shows her to be an honest, forthright person. Thus, there is no evidentiary basis to support termination based on the subjective standard found in the language of the school policy.... Instead, the School Board and the circuit court seem to focus on the objective standard ordained by the state statute. At trial, the School Board chairperson testified: "[i]t is my opinion that a reasonable person would have suspected abuse, yes." SDCL 26-8A-3 states in part:

Any ... teacher, school counselor, school official ... who have *reasonable cause to suspect* that a child under the age of eighteen has been abused or neglected as defined in § 26-8A-2 shall report that information in accordance with §§ 26-8A-6, 26-8A-7 and 26-8A-8.... Any person who knows or *has reason to suspect* that a child has been abused or neglected as defined in § 26-8A-2 may report that information as provided in § 26-8A-8.

(Emphasis added). The contract between Hughes and the School District stated in part that Hughes was required to act "in accordance with the provisions of the school laws of

---

5. This is unusual given the objective nature of the reporting requirements under state law (SDCL 26-8A-3) but nevertheless the school policy clearly adopted a subjective requirement. It is a questionable policy as the School Board is subject to state law and cannot modify the requirements of the statute.

the State of South Dakota." Under SDCL 13-43-15 a teacher may be terminated for cause for "violation of contract." Thus, under this contract, a violation of an applicable statute is also a violation of the teaching contract, which could result in dismissal.

Reasonable cause is the same as 'probable cause.' *State v. James*, 286 N.W.2d 534, 536 (S.D.1979); *Klingler v. United States*, 409 F.2d 299, 303 (8th Cir.1969); *State v. Harris*, 295 Minn. 38, 202 N.W.2d 878, 881 (1972); *State v. Vermilya*, 395 N.W.2d 151, 152 (N.D.1986). As such, under SDCL 26-8A-3, reasonable cause exists "where the facts and circumstances within the [school counselor's] knowledge, and of which [she has] reasonably trustworthy information, are sufficient in themselves to warrant a belief by a [woman] of reasonable caution that a crime has been or is being committed." *State v. Stuck*, 434 N.W.2d 43, 51 (S.D.1988).... Reasonable cause is based on all relevant facts of the case. *State v. Baysinger*, 470 N.W.2d 840, 845–6 (S.D.1991). In an application of the reasonable cause standard to Hughes, one must view the credibility of Hughes (see above), M.B., the child making the report and her identified perpetrator, her father G.B. The credibility of M.B. as ascertained by Hughes has been detailed above. Hughes also had substantial previous experience in dealing with children. Prior to her employment as a guidance counselor, she worked as a child protection worker for the State of South Dakota, Department of Social Services for four years; in therapeutic foster care at the Pierre Indian Learning Center for two and one-half years; and as a Court Services' Officer for one year. At the time of the circuit court trial and for many years before that, she was a member of the Child Protection Team for Stanley County.

In addition, M.B.'s mother testified at the preliminary hearing that when informed by Hughes of M.B.'s sex abuse allegation, mother confronted her husband, G.B. and believed his explanation over the allegations of her daughter. Mother was not convinced M.B. was telling the truth until much later.... During this time, the Stanley County School District employed G.B. as a custodian. Hughes knew him. He was also known to Tony Glass, Stanley County School principal who saw G.B. on a daily basis. Glass testified he never saw anything in G.B.'s behavior suggesting an indecent disposition toward children and girls in particular.... Up to this time, there never were suspicions aroused in anyone who knew M.B. well. No one ever took her accusations seriously or found G.B.'s conduct towards her cause for concern about sexual abuse. His acts only became known later as a collateral consequence of the successful investigation and prosecution of G.B. for sexual assault of a neighbor child.

Nevertheless, this is not a matter of weighing the evidence for and against Hughes to determine if she acted with "reasonable cause" in failing to report M.B.'s allegations. If there was evidence to support the School Board's conclusion she did not act with "reasonable cause," it cannot be found in the appeal record. An empty record cannot be the basis to uphold a board decision even considering deference to the board's good faith determination. *Jager*, 444 N.W.2d at 26.... The law does not require Hughes act with the Wisdom of Solomon, the deductive skills of Sherlock Holmes or possess 20–20 hindsight; only that she act reasonably. Reasonable cause or probable cause is not determined with the "benefit of hindsight," it is determined solely by those factors present at the time Hughes was making the determination whether she needed to report the incidents detailed to her by M.B.[6] *See Baysinger*, 470 N.W.2d at 845–6. (In reviewing reasonable cause, "[w]e do not

---

6. At the time Hughes was attempting to deal with M.B.'s allegations and whether to report them, Hughes did discuss what to do about it with the high school counselor. Hughes was not indifferent to the reports but was clearly uncertain on how to proceed due to M.B.'s history of untruths. There was no attempt to terminate the other counselor because according to the School Board chairperson, the other counselor "did not have direct contact with [M.B.]." With the full benefit of hindsight and all facts now being known, Hughes' course of action was an error in judgment but, based on the

approach the facts separately but rather we view the action of the [person] on the basis of the cumulative effect of such facts in the totality of the circumstances.").

If the Legislature had deemed it appropriate to require all such reports by children to teachers and school counselors be reported to the school administration, it could have easily done so.[7] The Legislature chose a middle ground by adopting the reasonable cause standard. In doing so it opted to balance competing public interests. Sexual abuse of children is abhorrent and is perpetrated against those in society who are the least capable of protecting themselves. On the other hand, false reports exist and unfounded accusations can destroy marriages, families and careers of the accused. A distinguished teaching career may also be on the line for improper failure to report. Involuntary termination not only involves disgrace and humiliation, but it may mean the end of the professional career. *See Appeal of Schramm*, 414 N.W.2d 31, 35 (S.D.1987).

For the above reasons, we find the circuit court erred in upholding the School Board's determination that Hughes' act of not reporting child abuse was in violation of her contract. We reverse the decision of the circuit court which affirmed the School Board on this issue as it is arbitrary, capricious and an abuse of discretion as there is no evidence to support it.

There remains the second accusation of a violation of school policy, which was also relied upon by the School Board as a basis for termination, that being the improper direct contact initiated by Hughes with the parents of M.B. Here the evidentiary basis is far different than the first and in fact is admitted by Hughes. It is unknown if the School Board would have terminated Hughes solely for the violation of going to the parents as it never had to face that determination.

We reverse and remand for further proceedings consistent with this opinion.

AMUNDSON, Justice, concurs.

NEILES, Circuit Judge, concurs in part and concurs in result in part.

SABERS, Justice, concurs in result without a writing.

KONENKAMP, Justices, concurs in part and dissents in part.

NEILES, Circuit Judge, sitting for MILLER, Chief Justice, disqualified....

Ramsey v. Yavapai Family Advocacy Center

Court of Appeals of Arizona, 2010
225 Ariz. 132, 235 P.3d 285

OROZCO, Judge....

Ramsey and his ex-wife, A.S, were married in Idaho in 1997. Ramsey and A.S. had one child (Child). During their subsequent divorce, A.S. reported to Idaho authorities

---

record in this case, falls short of becoming a basis for termination based on either the Board's subjective standard or the statutory "reasonable cause" objective standard.

7. This is the position taken by a witness for the Department of Social Services who testified at the preliminary hearing. However, it is clearly at variance with the reasonable cause standard set forth by the Legislature in SDCL 26-8A-3.

Q: You mean on every possible allegation that comes in, that is the way you would do it, you would report it to Social Services, or somebody?
A: I guess I would, yes.
Q: No matter what the child might say?
A: I would.

that she suspected Ramsey was sexually abusing Child. On February 6, 2003, Child was examined by a doctor who found A.S.'s suspicions of sexual abuse to be unsupported.

Soon after the examination, Ramsey, A.S. and Child moved from Idaho to Arizona. On September 9, 2003, A.S. took Child to Cornerstone Family Counseling (Cornerstone) to receive counseling from Sheets. At the first session, A.S. reported to Sheets that she believed Child had been sexually molested by Ramsey. After the first session, Sheets concluded that because of A.S.'s reports and Child's behavior, she "had concerns that some type of abuse may be happening."[2] On September 22, 2003, during Child's third session, Child told Sheets "that her daddy touched her" inappropriately.[3] The same day, Sheets reported to Child Protective Services (CPS) that she believed Ramsey had sexually abused Child.... Based on Sheets's allegations, Clyde Bentley (Bentley), a Yavapai County Sheriff's Detective, initiated a criminal investigation. Interviews and a physical examination of Child took place at [Yavapai Family Advocacy Center] YFAC. YFAC is a facility in which members of law enforcement, county attorneys and CPS assist in the investigation of child abuse, domestic assault, vulnerable adult abuse and other instances of family violence.

Ness, a sexual assault nurse examiner, performed a medical forensic evaluation of Child at YFAC.[4] Ness contracted with the Yavapai County Attorney's Office to perform the evaluation. At no time was Ness employed by YFAC. Ness reported that during the evaluation, Child stated that "her dad" had touched her inappropriately. As part of the examination, Ness took colposcopic photos of Child. Ness's evaluation of Child led her to conclude that there was definitive evidence of sexual abuse. She forwarded her report to Bentley.... Bentley requested a second opinion from Denton, the nursing supervisor at Yavapai Regional Medical Center.[5] Denton reviewed the colposcopic photos taken by Ness and concluded that Child had more than likely suffered from a long history of sexual abuse "since just after her birth." Based on the photos, Denton agreed with Ness's conclusions.... Bentley testified before a grand jury regarding Denton's conclusions. After hearing his testimony, the grand jury indicted Ramsey on multiple criminal charges relating to sexual conduct with a minor. However, the State later voluntarily dismissed the case without prejudice. The prosecutor stated that the "Yavapai County Attorney's Office concluded that the chances of conviction were not high enough to warrant continued prosecution of the case."

Ramsey argues that part of the State's decision to dismiss the charges against him was based on a subsequent evaluation of Child performed by the State's expert, Dr. Kathryn C. (Dr. C.). Dr. C. examined Child on October 1, 2004, more than a year after Ness's original examination. Dr. C. found "no signs of acute or healed injury." Nevertheless, Dr. C. concluded that "[t]his does not preclude the possibility of sexual abuse, as many sexually abusive acts are not associated with physical injury."[6]

---

2. Ramsey argues that Sheets was not licensed to provide therapy for sexual abuse; however, at the time Sheets provided the therapy, there was no licensing requirement in Arizona. In April 2004, Sheets stated she had a bachelor's degree in elementary education, a master's degree in educational counseling and seven years' experience in the mental health field.

3. To protect the privacy of Child, we will not discuss the details of the findings of the therapists and doctors.

4. YFAC and its staff did not participate in Child's examination or any of her interviews. YFAC only provided a location for others to evaluate and interview Child.

5. Denton was not employed by YFAC. Denton contracted with the Yavapai County Attorney's Office to review Ness's report.

6. Dr. C.'s testimony was given at trial in a separate criminal case, *State v. Pacheco*, Yavapai County, No. CR 82003-0474. During the trial in that matter, Dr. C. provided the above mentioned testimony regarding her conclusions on Ramsey's criminal case.

Following the State's dismissal of the charges, Ramsey filed a civil action against each appellee, alleging: (1) negligence and/or gross negligence; (2) malicious prosecution; (3) abuse of process; (4) false light invasion of privacy; (5) wrongful intrusion upon private affairs; (6) false arrest and imprisonment; (7) intentional infliction of emotional distress; (8) aiding and abetting tortious conduct; (9) defamation and defamation per se; and (10) loss of consortium. Each appellee moved for summary judgment.... On August 28, 2008, the trial court entered summary judgment: (1) in favor of Ness on all claims based on the immunity provided by Arizona Revised Statutes (A.R.S.) section 13-3620.J (2010);[7] (2) in favor of Denton on all claims based on the immunity provided by A.R.S. § 13-3620.J; (3) in favor of YFAC because Ramsey failed to produce evidence that would support any claim against YFAC; and (4) in favor of Sheets on claims relating to her reporting or participation in the criminal investigation based on A.R.S. § 13-3620.J. On October 23, 2008, the trial court granted summary judgment in favor of Sheets on all remaining claims, finding no evidence of malice and determining Sheets owed no duty of care to Ramsey as a non-patient parent in counseling Child.

Ramsey filed a timely notice of appeal and we have jurisdiction pursuant to A.R.S. §§ 12-120.21.A.1 and -2101.B (2003).... The majority of Ramsey's arguments focus on Arizona's mandatory reporting statute, A.R.S. § 13-3620. Section 13-3620.A provides:

> Any person who reasonably believes that a minor is or has been the victim of physical injury, abuse, Child abuse, a reportable offense or neglect that appears to have been inflicted on the minor by other than accidental means or that is not explained by the available medical history as being accidental in nature ... shall immediately report or cause reports to be made of this information to a peace officer or to child protective services in the department of economic security, except if the report concerns a person who does not have care, custody or control of the minor, the report shall be made to a peace officer only.... For purposes of this subsection, "person" means:
>
> 1. Any physician, physician's assistant, optometrist, dentist, osteopath, chiropractor, podiatrist, behavioral health professional, nurse, psychologist, counselor or social worker who develops the reasonable belief in the course of treating a patient.

Under the statute, individuals identified in A.R.S. § 13-3620.A.1 have a mandatory duty to report abuse when they reasonably believe a minor is being or has been abused. Individuals not falling within this definition may report suspected abuse pursuant to A.R.S. § 13-3620.F:

> Any person other than one required to report or cause reports to be made under subsection A of this section who reasonably believes that a minor is or has been a victim of abuse, child abuse, physical injury, a reportable offense or neglect may report the information to a peace officer or to child protective services in the department of economic security, except if the report concerns a person who does not have care, custody or control of the minor, the report shall be made to a peace officer only.

Under certain circumstances, A.R.S. § 13-3620.J provides immunity from civil and criminal liability for those who report abuse:

> A person who furnishes a report, information or records required or authorized under this section, or a person who participates in a judicial or administrative

---

7. Unless otherwise specified, we cite to the current version of the applicable statutes because no revisions material to this opinion have since occurred.

proceeding or investigation resulting from a report, information or records required or authorized under this section, is immune from any civil or criminal liability by reason of that action unless the person acted with malice or unless the person has been charged with or is suspected of abusing or neglecting the child or children in question.

Because an individual who acts with "malice" may still be civilly liable, A.R.S. § 13-3620.J only provides *qualified immunity*. *L.A.R. v. Ludwig*, 170 Ariz. 24, 28, 821 P.2d 291, 295 (App.1991)....

Ramsey argues the trial court erroneously granted summary judgment in favor of Sheets, Ness, and Denton because a genuine issue of material fact existed as to whether these defendants "reasonably believed" Child had been abused. Pursuant to A.R.S. § 13-3620.A and F, a person making a report of suspected child abuse is protected from liability only if he or she "reasonably believe[ ]" abuse has occurred. However, this "reasonably believes" requirement is not imposed on individuals receiving qualified immunity based on their "participat[ion] in a judicial or administrative proceeding or investigation resulting from a report." A.R.S. § 13-3620.J.

The undisputed evidence offered on summary judgment was that, as the trial court found, Ness and Denton only participated in the investigation following Sheets's initial report and did not themselves make "reports" within the meaning of the statute. Ramsey does not argue on appeal that we should treat Ness or Denton as anything other than participants in an ongoing investigation. Accordingly, the "reasonably believes" requirement imposed upon mandatory and permissive reporters is not applicable to Ness or Denton. Nevertheless, as the initial reporter of the alleged abuse, Sheets enjoys qualified immunity under the statute only if she "reasonably believe[d]" abuse had occurred.[9]

We have previously articulated that "reasonable grounds" is "a low standard." *Ludwig*, 170 Ariz. at 27, 821 P.2d at 294 (interpreting the provisions of A.R.S. § 13-3620.A and B then in effect).[10] In *Ludwig*, we concluded the trial court did not err in finding a counselor had "reasonable grounds" to report child sexual abuse. *Id.* at 26–27, 821 P.2d at 293–94. We based our decision on the public policy consideration "of encouraging people to report child abuse." *Id.* at 27, 821 P.2d at 294. Based on the facts in *Ludwig*, we cannot say the trial court erred in granting summary judgment in favor of Sheets. In *Ludwig*, the trial court found a counselor had "reasonable grounds" to believe a child had been sexually abused by her father based simply on a statement from the child's mother. *Id.* at 26, 821 P.2d at 293. In this case, Sheets relied on much more than simply A.S.'s statement that she believed Child had been sexually abused. During Child's third session, Child told Sheets "that her daddy touched her" inappropriately. As a result, we conclude there was no genuine issue of material fact as to whether Sheets "reasonably believe[d]" abuse had occurred.

---

9. We do not consider whether Sheets was a mandatory or permissive reporter under A.R.S. § 13-3620.A or F because the issue was not briefed. *See Polanco v. Indus. Comm'n of Ariz.*, 214 Ariz. 489, 491 n. 2, ¶ 6, 154 P.3d 391, 393 n. 2 (App.2007) (failure to develop and support argument waives issue on appeal); *see also* ARCAP 13(a) 6 (an argument in an opening brief "shall contain ... citations to the authorities, statutes and parts of the record relied on"). Furthermore, our determination of whether a genuine issue of material fact existed as to whether Sheets "reasonably believe[d]" Child had been abused would not be affected by whether Sheets is either a permissive or a mandatory reporter.

10. Section 13-3620.A and B were amended in 2003, replacing "reasonable grounds to believe" with "reasonably believes." 2003 Ariz. Sess. Laws, ch. 222, § 2 (1st Reg. Sess.).

On appeal, Ramsey argues that Sheets did not meet the "reasonably believes" requirement because "[t]he only evidence she ever had to base her opinion on was the evidence that she implanted in the child's head through improper therapeutic methods." Ramsey, however, makes this argument without citing to any evidence in the record, and we find nothing in the record that would support it. Alternatively, Ramsey contends Sheets did not meet the "reasonably believes" standard because she lacked credentials, such as licensure, and engaged in improper therapeutic techniques. As Sheets stated in her affidavit, at the time she made her report, "no licensing, certification, or particularized education was required to be a counselor in Arizona." Ramsey does not dispute this fact. Moreover, even if we accepted Ramsey's assertions that Sheets lacked qualifications and used improper therapeutic techniques, Ramsey presented no evidence that Sheets did not "reasonably believe[ ]" Child had been sexually abused. We hold that the trial court did not err in concluding Ramsey had failed to present evidence sufficient to create a genuine issue of material fact about whether Sheets "reasonably believe[d]" Child had been sexually abused....

Ramsey argues the trial court erroneously granted summary judgment in favor of Sheets, Ness, and Denton because a genuine issue of material fact existed as to whether these defendants "acted with malice" in reporting and investigating the child sexual abuse allegations. Pursuant to A.R.S. § 13-3620.J, a person is entitled to immunity so long as his or her participation in either reporting or investigating child sexual abuse was done without "malice." This form of qualified immunity can only be overcome by a showing of "malice." *Id.* We presume that a person acting pursuant to A.R.S. § 13-3620 acted in good faith and with proper motives. *Ludwig,* 170 Ariz. at 28, 821 P.2d at 295. In this case, Ramsey has the burden to prove "malice."

Pursuant to A.R.S. § 1-215.20 (Supp.2009), "[m]alice ... import[s] a wish to vex, annoy or injure another person, or an intent to do a wrongful act, established either by proof or presumption of law." Ramsey has presented no evidence that Sheets, Ness, or Denton were motivated by any malice toward him. Rather, Ramsey argues that each of these defendants acted with malice because they intended to do the actions alleged and that their actions ultimately proved to be "wrong and harmful."[11] We find no support for this interpretation of "malice." ... Ramsey cites to *Fears v. State,* in which the Arizona Supreme Court held in 1928 that "intent to do a wrongful act" is considered "merely malice in law or that which is inferred from the intentional doing of a wrongful act." 33 Ariz. 432, 436, 265 P. 600, 601 (1928). We interpret this definition to imply that the actor must have intended to do something that he or she knew to be wrong. Ramsey failed on summary judgment to offer any evidence that Sheets, Ness, or Denton acted with malice in that they intended to do something they knew to be wrong. Accordingly, the trial court did not err in granting Sheets, Ness, and Denton summary judgment based on the qualified immunity provided by A.R.S. § 13-3620.J.[12] ...

Ramsey alleges that in counseling and treating Child, Sheets destroyed his parental relationship with Child, and argues on appeal that the trial court erred in finding Sheets owed him no duty of care.[14] To maintain a negligence action against Sheets, Ramsey must

---

11. Ramsey's use of "wrong and harmful" refers to his allegation that Defendants' actions were premised on egregious errors and caused the harm he has suffered.

12. Because we affirm the trial court's grant of summary judgment in favor of Ness, we need not consider Ness's statute of limitations argument.

14. Because this claim arises out of the alleged negligent counseling and treatment of Child, qualified immunity under A.R.S. § 13-3620.J does not apply. *See Ludwig,* 170 Ariz. at 28–29, 821 P.2d at 295–96. Qualified immunity under A.R.S. § 13-3620.J applies only to causes of action arising from

first establish that Sheets owed him a duty of care. *Gipson v. Kasey*, 214 Ariz. 141, 143, ¶ 11, 150 P.3d 228, 230 (2007). The existence of duty is a threshold question and absent some duty, "defendants may not be held accountable for damages they carelessly cause, no matter how unreasonable their conduct." *Id.* at 143–44, ¶ 11, 150 P.3d at 230–31.

Ramsey has not cited any Arizona case imposing a duty upon a counselor or therapist owed to an accused sexual abuser; instead, Ramsey suggests that we adopt the reasoning of other jurisdictions. *Montoya v. Bebensee*, 761 P.2d 285, 289 (Colo.App.1988) (holding that "a mental health care provider owes a duty to any person, who is the subject of any public report or other adverse recommendation by that provider, to use due care in formulating any opinion upon which such a report or recommendation is based"); *Sawyer v. Midelfort*, 227 Wis.2d 124, 595 N.W.2d 423, 431 (1999) (recognizing a duty owed by therapists to non-patients only as it applies to "the harm that arises from accusations of sexual assault"). However, we are not bound by the decisions of other states. *State ex rel. Ariz. Dep't of Revenue v. Talley Indus., Inc.*, 182 Ariz. 17, 22, 893 P.2d 17, 22 (App.1994).

Furthermore, our research of this issue, like the trial court's, indicates that a majority of other jurisdictions that have addressed the issue have held a counselor or a therapist owes no duty of care to an alleged sexual abuser. *Trear v. Sills*, 69 Cal.App.4th 1341, 82 Cal.Rptr.2d 281, 288 (1999) (reasoning that a therapist acting in good faith is placed "in an untenable position if a duty is imposed upon him or her toward the patient's possible abuser"); *Doe v. McKay*, 183 Ill.2d 272, 233 Ill.Dec. 310, 700 N.E.2d 1018, 1023–24 (1998) (relying on the rule that "the defendant therapist owed a duty of care to her patient only, and not to nonpatient third parties"); *Flanders v. Cooper*, 706 A.2d 589, 591–92 (Me.1998) (refusing to recognize a duty after reasoning that otherwise, a health care professional "who suspected that a patient had been the victim of sexual abuse and who wanted to explore that possibility in treatment would have to consider the potential exposure to legal action by a third party who committed the abuse").

In *Althaus ex rel. Althaus v. Cohen*, 562 Pa. 547, 756 A.2d 1166, 1170–71 (2000), the Supreme Court of Pennsylvania identified the following factors in refusing to recognize a duty owed to a patient's alleged abuser:

> The foundation for any successful psychiatric treatment is trust by the patient and confidentiality in communications with the provider. In treating patients who have been subjected to sexual abuse, the therapist must be able to rely upon professional confidentiality to facilitate candid discussion. Imposing an additional duty of care upon the therapist to an alleged abuser, parent or otherwise, would certainly alter this important therapeutic relationship. Initially, such an additional duty may cause mental health professionals to avoid providing treatment in sexual abuse cases. Also, victims of sexual abuse may be reluctant to seek treatment if confidentiality of communications is not guaranteed. Finally, such a duty would necessarily change the very nature of the therapeutic treatment in that the therapist would have to constantly evaluate conflicting duties of care to determine the appropriate manner in which treatment should proceed. Tort law considerations should not interfere with a therapist's job in this manner, particularly in the area of the psychological treatment of victims of sexual abuse. Accordingly, this factor weighs heavily against imposing a duty of care beyond that owed to a patient.

The Supreme Court of Connecticut reached a similar conclusion:

---

reporting and investigating child sexual abuse, not counseling and treatment of an alleged abuse victim.

We conclude that imposing a duty on mental health professionals pursuant to the plaintiff's theory of liability in the present case would carry with it the impermissible risk of discouraging such professionals in the future from performing sexual abuse evaluations of children altogether, out of a fear of liability to the very persons whose conduct they may implicate. Such a result would necessarily run contrary to the state's policy of encouraging the reporting and investigation of suspected child abuse because effective evaluation and diagnosis of children is a necessary component of discovering the abuse in the first instance. In addition, imposing such a duty creates too high a risk that, in close cases, mental health professionals would conclude that no sexual abuse had occurred because they feared potential liability to the suspected abusers, rather than because of their professional judgment that, in all likelihood, no abuse had occurred. Because "[r]ules of law have an impact on the manner in which society conducts its affairs" we conclude that the sounder judicial ruling is to hold that no such duty exists.

Zamstein v. Marvasti, 240 Conn. 549, 692 A.2d 781, 787 (1997) (internal citations omitted).

We have weighed the many policy considerations discussed in *Althaus, Zamstein,* and other cases. We agree with the trial court that the recognition of a duty of care in this case is substantially outweighed by those considerations, including, as the trial court noted, "the importance of the availability of treatment for victims of sexual abuse and of allowing and encouraging therapists to evaluate and treat them without fear of potential liability to suspected abusers." Accordingly, we hold that in treating an alleged victim of abuse, a health care professional owes no duty of care to an alleged third-party abuser....

Ramsey argues alternatively that even if we decide therapists "owe no duty to third parties, that protection should not extend to Sheets, because Sheets was not a therapist." Ramsey cites no legal or factual basis for this argument. He states only that Sheets "was a fraud, lacking licensure, education, credentials, experience or knowledge in proper therapeutic methods." Ramsey, however, does not dispute that at the time Sheets was counseling Child, "no licensing, certification, or particularized education was required to be a counselor in Arizona." Additionally, Sheets was practicing as a counselor, a position for which she had education, training, and experience. Based on our previous analysis, ... we hold that in the circumstances presented, a counselor such as Sheets owes no duty to a third-party alleged abuser. Accordingly, the trial court did not err in finding Sheets owed no duty to Ramsey in counseling Child....

For the reasons previously stated, we affirm the trial court's grant of summary judgment in favor of Defendants.

CONCURRING: DIANE M. JOHNSEN, and JON W. THOMPSON, Judges.

Notes

In *Diana G-D* and *Hughes*, the reporters were not liable for not reporting because neither reporter was found to have established the appropriate reasonable suspicion that the child was abused. In *Ramsey*, the reasonable belief required of mandatory and permissive reporters was held inapplicable to two of the defendant nurse examiners because they were not the initial reporters; they were merely participants in the investigation resulting from the report. To be afforded immunity, the actual reporter must have established a "reasonable belief" that abuse had occurred. Because the plaintiff could not establish that the reporter lacked a reasonable belief that abuse had occurred, nor that the reporter acted with malice, the reporter was granted immunity for making the report.

Immunity may be awarded even though there is insufficient basis to support a reasonable suspicion of child abuse, such as when a reporter makes a report with a good faith belief that child abuse has occurred. Consider this scenario in the following cases.

3. Good Faith

O'Heron v. Blaney

Supreme Court of Georgia, 2003
276 Ga. 871, 583 S.E.2d 834

FLETCHER, Chief Justice.

We granted certiorari in this case to address the scope of the immunity defense for doctors who report suspected child abuse. Dr. Thomas Blaney and Jean Blaney sued Dr. Sara O'Heron and her employer, The Emory Clinic, after O'Heron made a report regarding suspected abuse by Thomas Blaney of his granddaughters. The trial court granted O'Heron summary judgment based on the immunity provided in OCGA § 19-7-5(f). The Court of Appeals reversed.[1] Because the Court of Appeals failed to recognize that the statute provides immunity for those who have reasonable cause to make a report and for those who make a report in good faith, we reverse.

The Blaneys's daughter-in-law had first raised questions about possible abuse of her two small daughters after the children had spent the weekend with the Blaneys, their paternal grandparents, in Fayette County. The children's mother contacted a doctor, a social worker, and the Department of Family and Children Services in Columbia County, where she, her husband, and the children resided, regarding her observations and suspicions. Columbia County DFACS reported the allegations of abuse to the Fayette County DFACS. The mother also directly contacted the Fayette County Sheriff's department, which advised her to take the children to O'Heron for an examination. O'Heron examined the children and discussed the situation with the mother. A detective with Fayette County was also present for the examination. Following her examination, O'Heron made a verbal report of suspected abuse to the detective, which she supplemented with a written report four days later. The Blaneys were arrested and indicted for various offenses including child molestation, sodomy, incest, and contributing to the deprivation of a minor. Sometime later, a new assistant district attorney was assigned to the case and presented it to a second grand jury, which issued a "no bill." The Fayette County District Attorney's office subsequently nolle prossed the charges under the initial indictment. Then the Blaneys sued O'Heron and Emory for malicious prosecution, professional malpractice and ordinary negligence.

Nearly 40 years ago, the legislature enacted Georgia's first law requiring the mandatory reporting of child abuse by physicians.[2] That first law contained an immunity provision providing that physicians who in good faith make a report of child abuse shall be immune from civil liability.[3] In numerous amendments to this law, the legislature has consistently expanded the reporting required and the immunity granted. The legislature has imposed

---

1. *Blaney v. O'Heron*, 256 Ga.App. 612, 568 S.E.2d 774 (2002).

2. 1965 Ga. Laws 588, originally codified as Ga.Code Ann. § 74-111 (Harrison). The enactment of child abuse reporting statutes was a response to a 1962 article in the Journal of the American Medical Association that first identified child abuse as a medical condition and to a model statute proposed by the Children's Bureau of the Department of Health, Education and Welfare. See Caroline T. Trost, *Chilling Child Abuse Reporting: Rethinking the CAPTA Amendments*, 51 Vand. L.Rev. 183, 192 (1998).

3. 1965 Ga. Laws 588.

the obligation to report on a wider variety of persons,[4] made reports easier to make and prove,[5] expanded the definition of abuse,[6] expanded immunity,[7] and imposed criminal penalties for the willful failure to make a report.[8] The legislature's conclusion that reporting is essential to protecting innocent children from abuse is abundantly clear. Furthermore, the legislature has specified that this law "shall be liberally construed so as to carry out the purposes thereof."[9] It is within this context that we must construe the requirements of OCGA § 19-7-5.

Subsection (c)(1) provides that specified persons, including physicians, "having reasonable cause to believe that a child has been abused shall report or cause reports of that abuse to be made as provided in this Code section." The report must include any information that "might be helpful in establishing the cause of the injuries and the identity of the perpetrator." Under OCGA § 19-7-5(f) any person who participates in the making of a report is immune from civil or criminal liability that would otherwise be incurred, "provided such participation ... is made in good faith." This immunity also extends to the reporter's participation in any judicial or other proceeding resulting from the report.[10]

Reading these provisions together, we conclude that immunity may attach in two ways, either by showing that "reasonable cause" exists or by showing "good faith." Once a reporter has reasonable cause to suspect child abuse has occurred, she must report it or face criminal penalties. The trigger for the duty to report is "reasonable cause to believe,"[11] which requires an objective analysis. The relevant question is whether the information available at the time would lead a reasonable person in the position of the reporter to suspect abuse.[12] Once reasonable cause has been established under this standard, a reporter complying with the statutory mandate to make a report is, by definition, operating in good faith. Therefore, if the objective analysis supports the reporter's conclusion that child abuse has occurred, then immunity attaches and there is no need to further examine the reporter's good faith.[13]

On the other hand, if under an objective analysis, the information would not lead a reasonable person to suspect child abuse, the reporter may still have immunity if she made the report in good faith. Although we have not previously examined the meaning of good faith under this immunity provision, we held in *Anderson v. Little & Davenport Funeral Home* that good faith under another immunity statute is a subjective standard: "'a state of mind indicating honesty and lawfulness of purpose; belief that one's conduct is not unconscionable or that known circumstances do not require further investigation.'"[14] In *Anderson*, we were construing the predecessor to OCGA § 31-11-8, which protects licensed ambulance services from civil liability arising out of the provision of emergency care. A subjective standard is even more appropriate under the child abuse reporting statute because it, unlike OCGA § 31-11-8, imposes criminal penalties. Thus, the relevant

---

4. See 1968 Ga. Laws 1196, 1973 Ga. Laws 309, 1974 Ga. Laws 438, 1977 Ga. Laws 242.

5. See 1974 Ga. Laws 438 (eliminating requirement of medical exam being made prior to report); 1980 Ga. Laws 921 (allowing photographs to be taken).

6. See, e.g., 1981 Ga. Laws 1034.

7. 1974 Ga. Laws 438 (providing immunity for voluntary reporters).

8. 1977 Ga. Laws 242.

9. OCGA § 19-7-5(a).

10. OCGA § 19-7-5(f).

11. OCGA § 19-7-5(c)(1).

12. 1976 Op. Att'y Gen. 76-131(V).

13. See *Warner v. Mitts*, 211 Mich.App. 557, 536 N.W.2d 564, 566 (1995).

14. 242 Ga. 751, 753, 251 S.E.2d 250 (1978).

question is whether the reporter honestly believed she had a duty to report.[15] A reporter acting in good faith will be immune even if she is negligent or exercises bad judgment.[16]

Having determined the proper legal analysis, we examine the summary judgment record de novo and in the light most favorable to the non-moving party.[17] O'Heron's affidavit in support of the motion for summary judgment details her examination and interviews with each child, in which the children used anatomically descriptive dolls to demonstrate how Thomas Blaney touched their vaginal and anal areas using his hands, mouth, tongue, and penis. No evidence contradicts the testimony of O'Heron and the Fayette County detective that the children made specific allegations of sexual contact by their grandfather. Furthermore, the medical director of the Child Protection Program at Egleston Children's Hospital, with whom the Fayette County district attorney consulted, concluded that the sexually explicit nature of these allegations by such young children raised a concern about the possibility of abuse. We conclude that, as a matter of law, the children's allegations are sufficient to cause a reasonable person to suspect that child abuse has occurred. Therefore, the trial court correctly entered summary judgment for O'Heron and Emory.

The court of appeals confused the two separate aspects of immunity under the statute, superimposing a requirement of reasonableness on the good faith standard. Under the court of appeals standard, even if a reporter has reasonable cause to believe that child abuse has occurred, a jury question could still exist on the issue of bad faith. This interpretation chills the reporting requirement and fails to honor the legislative goal of protecting children by encouraging the reporting of suspected child abuse. It furthermore would require a mandatory reporter to make a detailed investigation before making a report. Such an investigation is contrary to the statutory scheme that places the job of investigation on child welfare authorities and the criminal justice system.[18]

Judgment reversed.

All the Justices concur, except SEARS, P.J., BENHAM and CARLEY, JJ., who dissent.

CARLEY, Justice, dissenting.

I believe that the Court incorrectly analyzes the immunity provided to reporters of child abuse by OCGA § 19-7-5, and then fails to consider evidence which makes summary judgment entirely inappropriate in this case.... The majority correctly holds that immunity from liability for reporting child abuse "may attach in two ways, either by showing that 'reasonable cause' exists or by showing 'good faith[,]'" and that, once reasonable cause is established under an objective analysis, a reporter of child abuse "is, by definition, operating in good faith."... See *Warner v. Mitts*, 211 Mich.App. 557, 536 N.W.2d 564, 566 (1995) (cited in footnote 13 of the majority opinion). However, a reading of subsections (c)(1) and (f) of OCGA § 19-7-5 together, as the majority purports to do, cannot lead to the conclusion that a purely subjective standard applies to the determination of "good faith" and that the only question relevant to that determination "is whether the reporter honestly believed she had a duty to report."... If that were true, then the majority's holding that

15. See also *Rite Aid Corp. v. Hagley*, 374 Md. 665, 681, 824 A.2d 107, 117 (2003) (good faith is subjective under immunity provisions of child abuse reporting statutes); *S.G. v. City of Monroe*, 843 So.2d 657, 664 (La.App. 2d Cir.2003) (same); *Purdy v. Fleming*, 655 N.W.2d 424, 432–433 (S.D.2002); *Garvis v. Scholten*, 492 N.W.2d 402, 403 (Iowa 1992) (same).

16. *Michaels v. Gordon*, 211 Ga.App. 470, 473, 439 S.E.2d 722 (1993).

17. *Youngblood v. Gwinnett Rockdale Newton Community Service Bd.*, 273 Ga. 715, 717–718(4), 545 S.E.2d 875 (2001).

18. OCGA § 19-7-5(a), (e).

reasonable cause necessarily implies good faith would clearly be wrong, because it is certainly possible for a reporter of child abuse to have an objectively reasonable cause to make the report and, at the same time, have a subjective, honest belief that abuse has not occurred.

As *Warner* itself states, "'good faith' pertains to the existence of a reasonable suspicion...." *Warner v. Mitts,* supra at 566. In examining statutory provisions which are substantially identical to OCGA § 19-7-5(c)(1) and (f), a Washington appellate court pointed out that, although "good faith" is not defined, "the reporting statute is framed in terms of reasonableness. The duty to report arises when there is 'reasonable cause to believe' that abuse has occurred...." *Dunning v. Paccerelli,* 63 Wash.App. 232, 818 P.2d 34, 38 (1991). Because "good faith" must necessarily take into account the "reasonable cause" supporting the report, "good faith" cannot be judged by a wholly subjective standard.

When the Court of Appeals referred to the concepts of good faith and reasonable inquiry in other contexts, it was not "superimposing a requirement of reasonableness on the good faith standard." ... The interplay between reasonableness and good faith arises from the statute itself. In construing OCGA § 19-7-5, the Court of Appeals was simply drawing a valid analogy to the duty of reasonable inquiry imposed in another good faith statute. *Blaney v. O'Heron,* 256 Ga.App. 612, 614–615, 568 S.E.2d 774 (2002). Under the analogous statute, the simple assertion of a subjective, honest belief cannot establish good faith. *Kendrick v. Funderburk,* 230 Ga.App. 860, 864(3), 498 S.E.2d 147 (1998); *Kluge v. Renn,* 226 Ga.App. 898, 903(4), 487 S.E.2d 391 (1997). Making a similar analogy, the court in *Dunning v. Paccerelli,* supra at 38, pointed out that, in "actions brought under 42 U.S.C. § 1983, which also measures official conduct by a standard of reasonableness, the courts have refused to employ a totally subjective standard when applying the good faith test for immunity...." ... Therefore, I believe that, in order to have immunity under subsection (f) of OCGA § 19-7-5, the reporter of child abuse is required to "act with a reasonable good faith intent, judged in light of all the circumstances then present...." *Dunning v. Paccerelli,* supra at 38. However, the majority, in its zeal to encourage the reporting of suspected child abuse, has instead encouraged groundless reporting by extending the statutory immunity to all those who subjectively claim to honestly believe that child abuse has occurred, even if the basis for such belief is objectively unreasonable.

The majority concludes that, as a matter of law, the children's allegations are sufficient to cause a reasonable person to suspect that child abuse occurred. For this holding, it relies on the testimony of Dr. O'Heron and that of the Fayette County detective that the children made specific allegations of sexual contact by their grandfather. However, the detective was not even present for the interview of one of the children and never stated that she heard any particular statement regarding sexual abuse from either girl. The majority further relies on the letter of an expert to the assistant district attorney stating that the children's allegations raised a concern about the possibility of abuse. Even assuming that this letter was not inadmissible hearsay, it was rebutted by deposition testimony of a leading child abuse expert that Dr. O'Heron's interview of such young children could not be relied upon, was dangerous medicine, and was a breach of the standard of care. Although such negligence or bad judgment on the part of Dr. O'Heron may not prove the lack of her good faith under a subjective standard, it clearly is some evidence from which a trier of fact could find that she did not have *reasonable* cause to believe that the children's grandfather had abused them.... There is considerable evidence, including the deposition of Appellees' expert, that the findings in Dr. O'Heron's examination did not support her conclusion that the condition of one of the children was abnormal, much less that sexual abuse had occurred on a particular weekend nearly a month before. Furthermore, the Court of Appeals accurately held that the evidence which it extensively reviewed "as to O'Heron's subsequent testimony and prior actions raises material issues of motive, intent, honesty and 'moral obliquity.'" *Blaney v. O'Heron*, supra at 620, 568 S.E.2d 774. Therefore, there was not only evidence that Dr. O'Heron lacked reasonable cause to believe that the children's grandfather sexually abused them, but also that, judged in light of all the circumstances at the time, she did not act with a reasonable good faith intent.

Where, as here, the party responding to a motion for summary judgment "produces or points to any specific evidence, even slight, in the record giving rise to a triable issue of material fact, then summary judgment must be denied by the trial court...." *Five Star Steel Constr. v. Klockner Namasco Corp.*, 240 Ga.App. 736, 738(1)(a), 524 S.E.2d 783 (1999). Thus, I believe that the trial court erroneously granted summary judgment. Accordingly, I dissent to this Court's reversal of the judgment of the Court of Appeals.... I am authorized to state that Presiding Justice SEARS and Justice BENHAM join in this dissent.

Notes

Justice Carley, dissenting in *O'Heron*, asserted that reasonable suspicion does not imply "good faith" because there could be circumstances in which a reporter is presented with an objective reasonable cause to make a report but, at the same time, maintains a subjective belief that abuse has not occurred. Likewise, a reporter could have malicious motives in reporting but still have an objective reasonable belief that abuse has occurred. *See Brown v. Radar*, 299 Ga. App. 606, 683 S.E.2d 16 (2009) (landlord acting with animus against tenant when making report of child abuse still granted immunity because objective basis for the report still based on reasonable suspicion). However, provided the reporter has a reasonable suspicion that child abuse has occurred when he or she reports, then good faith reporting may be presumed. *See, e.g., Howe v. Andereck*, 882 So. 2d 240 (Miss. Ct. App. 2004) (presumption of good faith is to absolve mandatory reporters from having to present evidence that demonstrates they acted in good faith). A plaintiff then may produce affirmative evidence to overcome a presumption of good faith. *See, e.g., Estiverna v. Esernio-Jenssen*, 581 F. Supp.2d 335 (E.D. N.Y. 2008) (bad faith shown on part of physician by allegations that physician knew report was false or recklessly disregarded the truth, that report was not supported by medical evidence, that reporter's medical colleague disagreed with diagnosis, and physician's behavior was part of common practice). To overcome a presumption of good faith, a plaintiff must show more than mere negligence by the reporter. *Doe v. Winny*, 327 Ill. App.3d 668, 261 Ill. Dec. 852, 764 N.E.2d 143, 154 (2002). *See also Michaels v. Gordon*, 211 Ga. App. 470, 439 S.E.2d 722, 725 91993) ("Bad faith" is more than simply bad judgment or negligence; it implies a dishonest purpose or moral deviance).

Rite Aid Corp. v. Hagley

Court of Appeals of Maryland, 2003
374 Md. 665, 824 A.2d 107

BELL, Chief Judge....

Dexter Hagley ("Mr. Hagley") and his former wife, Lystra Martin ("Ms. Martin") are the parents of Kerwyn Hagley (collectively, "respondents"). On March 23, 1999, Mr. Hagley took an undeveloped roll of film to the Rite Aid store ("Rite Aid") in the Alameda Shopping Center in Baltimore City for processing, as he had done on "many" previous occasions. Opting to have the film printed by the store's one-hour developing and printing process, he completed the required form and left the film with the store manager, Robert Rosiak ("Mr. Rosiak"), one of the petitioners, who developed the film.

Sixteen photographs were printed from the roll of film. Four of them depicted Mr. Hagley and a young boy, later determined to be his then eight-year old son, in a bathtub. The Court of Special Appeals described these four photographs, in its unreported opinion, as follows:

> "Mr. Hagley was wearing shorts; Kerwyn was naked. The first of those photographs show Mr. Hagley sitting in the tub of soapy water, with Kerwyn sitting on his lap. Mr. Hagley's left arm was around the upper part of the boy's body, with his left hand on Kerwyn's right shoulder. Kerwyn's left hand was in his lap, and his father's right hand was on or over the boy's left hand. Both were laughing. The second photograph shows Mr. Hagley sitting in the tub, with his left hand hidden behind Kerwyn's thigh. The boy was standing with his back to the camera, looking over his shoulder toward the camera. Both were laughing. The third photograph shows Mr. Hagley sitting in the tub, looking up at Kerwyn, who was standing facing the camera. The fourth photograph shows Mr. Hagley and Kerwyn sitting in the tub, at the tap end, looking toward the camera."

Mr. Rosiak was troubled by the photographs of Mr. Hagley and the child because, in at least one of the photographs, Mr. Hagley's hand appeared to be "cupping" the child's genitals.[1] Finding them ambiguous, he was not certain how to interpret them.

When Mr. Hagley returned to the store to pick up the processed film (i.e. photographs and negatives), Mr. Rosiak refused to give him the photographs. Mr. Hagley asked why, and Mr. Rosiak answered: "I'm seeing some things in those pictures, and I don't think I can give them to you." Despite Mr. Hagley's request that he do so, Mr. Rosiak refused to show Mr. Hagley the photographs or explain their objectionable content. When pressed further for an explanation, he stated "I'm seeing signs of child pornography, pedophile [sic] and improper touching of a minor." That comment, Mr. Hagley alleges, was made loudly and in the presence of other Rite Aid customers. Mr. Hagley advised Mr. Rosiak that the child depicted in the photographs was his eight-year old son, Kerwyn, and that the photographs were taken by the child's mother, Ms. Martin. Mr. Hagley subsequently brought Ms. Martin to the store to verify that statement.

Apparently unsatisfied with Mr. Hagley's explanation and still unsure of how to resolve the matter, Mr. Rosiak requested that Mr. Hagley return to the store at 1:00 p.m., at which time a supervisor would have an answer. He then consulted Rite Aid headquarters, and was instructed to report the matter to law enforcement and turn the photographs over to them. Mr. Rosiak complied with that instruction by contacting the Baltimore City Police. Upon returning to the store a few minutes before the appointed hour, Mr. Hagley observed Mr. Rosiak having a conversation with a group of people. As described by the intermediate appellate court (emphasis added),

> "When Mr. Hagley returned to the store several minutes before 1:00 p.m., he observed Mr. Rosiak *showing the photographs* to three other people and discussing

---

1. For clarification we note that the Court of Special Appeals, in its unreported opinion, indicated that Mr. Rosiak testified that two of the photographs, in his opinion, appeared to show Mr. Hagley "cupping the child's genitals." The petitioners state in their brief, however, citing to Mr. Rosiak's affidavit, that "in one of the pictures" Mr. Rosiak believed that Mr. Hagley's hand was cupping the child's genitals. Our review of Mr. Rosiak's deposition testimony discloses that Mr. Rosiak testified that the "pictures ... seemingly [showed Mr. Hagley] playing with this child's genitals."

the pictures with them. Mr. Hagley recognized those three people: one was an employee of Rite Aid, whom he knew only as "Chris" (assistant manager Carrissa Esposito); the second was a mall security guard he knew as Mr. Byrd; and the third was another mall security guard whose name he did not know. Mr. Rosiak was asking their opinion of the photographs, but each of them declined to venture an opinion. When Mr. Rosiak and the others saw Mr. Hagley, who was about twelve feet away, the conversation stopped."[2]

Shortly after the group that Mr. Rosiak had been talking to dispersed and there had been a brief conversation between Mr. Hagley and Mr. Rosiak, three uniformed Baltimore City Police Officers arrived at the Rite Aid store. They were met by Mr. Rosiak who escorted two of the officers into his office. Mr. Hagley remained in the store with the third officer. After meeting with Mr. Rosiak and examining the photographs, the officers questioned Mr. Hagley briefly. Being, like Mr. Rosiak, uncertain as to whether the photographs depicted child abuse, the officers called a detective with the child abuse unit of the criminal investigation division to examine some "questionable photographs of a young child." ... The detective came to the Rite Aid Store. After reviewing the photographs and questioning a few people, he determined that the child in the photographs was Mr. Hagley's son, but that the photographs were "questionable." Believing, therefore, that further inquiry was warranted, he thus took possession of the photographs, later, submitting them to the evidence control unit, and caused Kerwyn to be taken into the custody of Child Protective Services in order to be interviewed at the Baltimore Child Abuse Center. In addition, the detective sought the opinion of the Baltimore City State's Attorney Office as to whether the content of the photographs warranted the filing of criminal charges.

Mr. Hagley was transported to the police station for questioning by one of the police officers. According to the detective, he was never placed under arrest and, in fact, was free to leave at any time. According to Mr. Hagley, although he was told by the police officers that he could leave, subject to later being picked up at home and taken to the police station, the detective told him that he had to come downtown to answer questions at the police station. He indicated further that he was not told he was free to leave the police station until approximately 7:00 p.m., when, after questioning and investigation, the State's Attorney's Office had determined that no criminal charges were warranted. Thereafter, Mr. Hagley, was driven back to the Alameda Shopping Center to retrieve his car.[3] ...

---

2. Although the petitioners repeated this recitation of the facts in their Petition for Writ of Certiorari and endorsed it, they now maintain that the Court of Special Appeals misstated the facts. They submit that, in his deposition testimony, Mr. Hagley identified only one of the persons to whom Mr. Rosiak was talking, the security guard, Mr. Byrd and that he stated that he *only* overheard the group discussing the decision to be made about the photographs; Mr. Hagley was unable to say whether he had seen Mr. Rosiak actually show the photograph to Mr. Byrd. Mr. Rosiak, the petitioners point out, denied, in his deposition testimony, that he showed the photographs to Mr. Byrd; however, he acknowledged showing them to Ms. Esposito before calling the police. At oral argument in this Court, the respondents conceded that there was no evidence in the record to support the Court of Special Appeal's assertion that Mr. Rosiak showed the photographs to Mr. Byrd or to any other non-Rite Aid employee. It thus appears that the petitioners' factual recitation is correct.

3. Mr. Hagley attempted to pick up his son from Child Protective Services, but was informed that he had to attend a hearing in two days. Because the State had chosen not to pursue criminal charges the entire matter was dropped and no custody hearing was scheduled, or held. Nevertheless, due to an administrative error or failure of communication, Child Protective Services was not informed of the State's Attorney's decision to drop the matter in a timely manner. As a result, Kerwyn was kept at a foster home for two nights before ultimately being reunited with his parents.

The respondents filed a complaint against Mr. Rosiak and Rite Aid Corporation (collectively "the petitioners"), alleging various causes of action arising out of the events, involving the photographs, occurring on May 23, 1999. Their Second Amended Complaint contained eleven counts: Count I, breach of privacy; Count II, false imprisonment; Count III, malicious prosecution; Count IV-A, Negligence; Count IV-B, Negligence of Defendant Rosiak (with Defendant Rite Aid liable under the rule of respondeat superior); Count IV-C, Breach of contractual duty; Count V, Defamation of Character; Count VI, Unreasonable Invasion Upon Seclusion/Breach of Privacy; Count VII, Breach of Privacy/Unreasonable Publicity Given to Private Life; Count VIII, Breach of Privacy/Publicity Unreasonably Placing Person in a False Light; Count IX, untitled, asserting, as next friend for Kerwyn Hagley, Ms. Martin's claim for the alleged injury sustained by Kerwyn as a result of his detention in a foster home against his will. The petitioners answered the complaint and, subsequently, filed a motion for summary judgment, premised on the statutory immunity prescribed by CJ § 5-620 and FL § 5-708. The Circuit Court for Baltimore City, concluding that the "report of suspected child abuse was made in good faith" and, therefore, that there was no genuine dispute of material fact because the petitioners were immune from "*all* civil liability based on Md.Code Ann., Cts & Jud. Proc. § 5-620 and Md.Code Ann., Fam. Law § 5-708," (emphasis added), granted summary judgment.

On direct appeal to the Court of Special Appeals, the respondents challenged the propriety of the trial court's grant of summary judgment in favor of the petitioners. They cited as error, the trial court's conclusion that there was no evidence to rebut the petitioners' assertion that Mr. Rosiak acted in good faith. The intermediate appellate court acknowledged that questions of "good faith 'almost always' present an issue of fact for trial; therefore, 'generally summary judgment is inappropriate where motive or intent is at issue since inferences must be resolved against the moving party.'" Nonetheless, the court determined that, because there was no evidence that contradicted Mr. Rosiak's assertion that his report to law enforcement was made in good faith, *certain* of the claims in the case *sub judice* were appropriately resolved on summary judgment. As to that, the court held:

> "because there is no evidentiary basis for any inference that Rosiak did not act in good faith in reporting to the police his conclusions that the photographs depicted child pornography or child abuse or both, and in delivering the photographs to the police, he, and therefore his employer, were entitled to immunity provided by CJ § 5-620. Consequently, the circuit court did not err in granting summary judgment in favor of [appellants] on Counts II (false imprisonment), III (malicious prosecution), IV-A and IV-B (negligence), IV (breach of contractual duty); and IX (the claims of Kerwyn Hagley and his mother), because all of the alleged wrongs and resulting harms and damages asserted in those counts directly resulted from those acts of Rosiak that were protected by the immunity afforded by CJ § 5-620."

The Court of Special Appeals determined, however, that "[t]he remaining counts, I, VI, VII, and VIII, asserting causes of action for various forms of breach or invasion of privacy, and Count V, asserting a cause of action for defamation, are based, in part, on conduct by Mr. Rosiak that is not protected by the immunity conferred by CJ § 5-620 and FL § 5-708." It explained that the conduct shielded by CJ § 5-620 and FL § 5-708 is the reporting of child abuse or neglect or the participation in an investigation or resulting judicial proceeding. Then, noting that the respondents alleged that Mr. Rosiak slandered Mr. Hagley in the presence of other Rite Aid customers and that he displayed the photographs to persons other than police officers, the intermediate appellate court concluded that neither of these acts was related to Mr. Rosiak's obligation to report suspected child abuse. Consequently, holding that the conduct supporting the allegations of defamation and invasion of privacy exceeded the qualified immunity of the statutes, it vacated the judgment as to those counts and remanded the case to the trial court for further proceedings.... Both parties sought review of the rulings of the Court of Special Appeals, the petitioners filing a petition for writ of certiorari and the respondents, a cross-petition. We granted both petitions. *Rite Aid v. Hagley*, 371 Md. 68, 806 A.2d 679 (2002).[4] ...

To address and combat the problem of child abuse and neglect, the Maryland General Assembly, by Acts of 1987, ch. 635, §2, enacted legislation, *see* Md.Code (1984, 1999 Repl.Vol., 2002 Supp.) §§5-701–5-714 of the Family Law Article, *inter alia*, mandating the reporting of suspected child abuse or neglect to the appropriate authorities and "giving immunity to any individual who reports, in good faith, a suspected incident of abuse or neglect." *See*, §5-702, stating the legislative policy of subtitle 7 of title 5 of the Family Law Article.[5] The policy underlying the reporting requirement imposed, and the immunity given, "is to protect children who have been the subject of abuse or neglect." *See Bentley v. Carroll*, 355 Md. 312, 324, 734 A.2d 697, 704 (1999) (stating that the purpose of the reporting requirements is "to redress previous abuse and to prevent future incidence thereof"). Thus, Md.Code (1984, 1999 Repl.Vol., 2002 Supp.), §5-704 of the Family Law Article imposes a duty on health practitioners, police officers, educators or human service workers, to report suspected child abuse or neglect encountered in their professional capacity to the local department, appropriate law enforcement agency or the appropriate institution head,[6] and Md.Code (1984, 1999 Repl.Vol., 2002 Supp.), §5-705 of the Family

---

4. Although, we have granted the cross-petition and it is proper to refer to Mr. Hagley, Kerwyn Hagley and Ms. Martin as the cross-petitioners, for the sake of convenience and clarity, we shall refer, throughout the entirety of this opinion, to Mr. Hagley, Kerwyn Hagley and Ms. Martin as the respondents. Likewise, we shall refer, throughout the entirety of this opinion, to Rite Aid and Mr. Rosiak as the petitioners.

5. Md. Code (1984, 1999 Repl.Vol., 2002 Supp.) §5-702 of the Family Law Article provides:
"The purpose of this subtitle is to protect children who have been the subject of abuse or neglect by:
"(1) mandating the reporting of any suspected abuse or neglect;
"(2) giving immunity to any individual who reports, in good faith, a suspected incident of abuse or neglect;
"(3) requiring prompt investigation of each reported suspected incident of abuse or neglect;
"(4) causing immediate, cooperative efforts by the responsible agencies on behalf of children who have been the subject of reports of abuse or neglect; and
"(5) requiring each local department to give the appropriate service in the best interest of the abused or neglected child."

6. Md.Code (1984, 1999 Repl.Vol., 2002 Supp.) §5-702 of the Family Law Article provides:
"(a) In general.—Notwithstanding any other provision of law, including any law on privileged communications, each health practitioner, police officer, educator, or human service worker, acting in a professional capacity:
"(1) (i) who has reason to believe that a child has been subjected to abuse, shall notify the local department or the appropriate law enforcement agency; or
"(ii) who has reason to believe that a child has been subjected to neglect, shall notify the local department; and
"(2) if acting as a staff member of a hospital, public health agency, child care institution, juvenile detention center, school, or similar institution, shall immediately notify and give all information required by this section to the head of the institution or the designee of the head."

Law Article imposes a similar obligation on persons, other than a health practitioner, police officer, educator or human services worker.[7]

The Legislature understood that the purpose of mandating reporting of child abuse and neglect would be undermined if a person making a good faith report pursuant to FL § 5-704 or § 5-705, that later proved to be false, were to be subjected to civil liability. Consistent with what every state in the nation was doing, see *Harris v. City of Montgomery*, 435 So.2d 1207, 1213 (Ala.1983); *Elmore v. Van Horn*, 844 P.2d 1078, 1082 (Wy.1992); Child Abuse and Neglect State Statutes Series, U.S. Dept. of Health and Human Services, Compendium of Laws: Reporting Laws: Immunity for Reporters (2002), and with national policy, *see* 42 U.S.C.A. § 5106a (b)(2) (2002), the Legislature intended to encourage the good faith reporting of suspected child abuse to authorities without the fear of civil and criminal liability for reports later determined to be unfounded. *Bentley*, 355 Md. at 323, 734 A.2d at 703 ("The evident purpose behind the statute's grant of immunity to good faith reporters is to instigate the exercise of the duty to report"); *See, Gross v. Haight*, 496 So.2d 1225, 1228 (La.App.1986) ("It would be most unfortunate if the threat of defamation claims should cast a chilling effect upon the willingness of persons to report suspected cases, where reasonable cause for suspicion exists."); *Liedtke v. Carrington*, 145 Ohio App.3d 396, 763 N.E.2d 213, 216 (2001) ("It is clear that the legislature believed that the societal benefits of preventing child abuse outweigh the individual harm that might arise from the filing of a false report."); *Van Horn*, 844 P.2d at 1084 ("We are obligated to honor the determination of the Legislature that protection of one innocent segment of society warrants occasional injury to another. The mute powerless victims of child abuse have long suffered at the hands of their tormentors. Society's protective voice, the legislature has found, has been silenced by the fear of retaliation. The protection of the young victim, the legislature has determined, requires that uncompensated injury occasionally result to an adult.")(quoting *Thomas v. Chadwick*, 224 Cal.App.3d 813, 827, 274 Cal.Rptr. 128, 138 (1990)). Consequently, at the same time that it mandated reporting, the General Assembly granted statutory immunity from civil and criminal liability to "[a]ny person *who in good faith* makes or participates in making a report of abuse or neglect under § 5-704 or 5-705 of the Family Law Article or participates in an investigation or a resulting judicial proceeding." Md.Code (1974, 2002 Repl.Vol.), § 5-620 of the Courts & Judicial Proceedings Article (emphasis added). *See also* Md.Code (1984, 1999 Repl.Vol.), § 5-708 of the Family Law Article, which provides: "[a]ny person who makes or participates in making a report of abuse or neglect under § 5-704 or § 5-705 of this subtitle or participates in an investigation or a resulting judicial proceeding shall have the immunity described under § 5-620 of the Courts and Judicial Proceedings Article from civil liability or criminal penalty." ...

Although critically important to its application in a given factual situation, the statutes do not define "good faith." Under well settled rules of statutory construction, however, its meaning can be discerned. The term should be given its plain and ordinary meaning....

---

7. Md.Code (1984, 1999 Repl.Vol., 2002 Supp.), § 5-705 of the Family Law Article provides:
"(a) In general. —
  "(1) Except as provided in paragraphs (2) and (3) of this subsection, notwithstanding any other provision of law, including a law on privileged communications, a person other than a health practitioner, police officer, or educator or human service worker who has reason to believe that a child has been subjected to abuse or neglect shall:
    "(i) if the person has reason to believe the child has been subjected to abuse, notify the local department or the appropriate law enforcement agency; or
    "(ii) if the person has reason to believe the child has been subjected to neglect, notify the local department."

[citations omitted]. Using that rule as a guide, the Court of Special Appeals has interpreted the "good faith" requirement of FL § 5-708. *See, Catterton v. Coale*, 84 Md.App. 337, 579 A.2d 781 (1990). It reasoned:

> "Good-faith" is an intangible and abstract quality that encompasses, among other things, an honest belief, the absence of malice and the absence of design to defraud or to seek an unconscionable advantage. Black's Law Dictionary 623 (5th ed.1979). To further illuminate the definition of "good-faith," we have found it most instructive to compare the definition of "bad-faith." "Bad-faith" is the opposite of good faith; it is not simply bad judgment or negligence, but implies a dishonest purpose or some moral obliquity and a conscious doing of wrong. *Vickers v. Motte*, 109 Ga.App. 615, 137 S.E.2d 77, 80 (1964) (citing *Spiegel v. Beacon Participations*, 297 Mass. 398, 8 N.E.2d 895, 907 (1937)). Though an indefinite term, "bad-faith" differs from the negative idea of negligence in that it contemplates a state of mind affirmatively operating with a furtive design. *New Amsterdam Cas. Co. v. Nat'l, etc., Banking Co.*, 117 N.J.Eq. 264, 175 A. 609, 616 (Ch.1934), aff'd, 119 N.J.Eq. 540, 182 A. 824 (N.J.Err. & App.1936). Thus, we would infer that the definition of "good-faith" under § 5-708 means with an honest intention."

Id. at 342, 579 A.2d at 783. We agree. Under that definition, to be entitled to the statutory immunity, a person must act with an honest intention (i.e. in good faith), not simply negligently, in making or participating in the making of a report of abuse or neglect under § 5-704 or 5-705 of the Family Law Article or when participating in an investigation or resulting judicial proceeding....

This definition of "good faith" is consistent with that employed by other courts that have interpreted the term in this context. In *B.W. v. Meade County*, 534 N.W.2d 595, 598 (S.D.1995), the Supreme Court of South Dakota, interpreting "good faith," as used in a statute similar to Maryland's,[9] defined it as follows:

> "Within the bounds of our statute, negligence and lack of good faith are not equivalent. Simply put, if good faith immunity can be overcome by establishing negligence, then good faith immunity is a meaningless concept as one would have to be free from negligence, and thus not liable in any event, to also avail one's self of the doctrine of good faith immunity. Acting in good faith denotes performing honestly, with proper motive, even if negligently. *See* BLACK'S LAW DICTIONARY 693 (6th ed.1993); SDCL 55-7-3; *Isaac v. State Farm Mut. Auto. Ins. Co.*, 522 N.W.2d 752 (S.D.1994). The standard for determining good faith is a defendant's honest belief in the suitability of the actions taken. *Mackintosh v. Carter*, 451 N.W.2d 285 (S.D.1990). Thus it is immaterial whether a person is negligent in arriving at a certain belief or in taking a particular action. As there was no genuine issue of material fact to dispute good faith, summary judgment was appropriate." ...

---

9. SDCL 26-8A-14, in effect at the time, provided, in pertinent part:
   "Any person or party participating in good faith in the making of a report ... pursuant to §§ 26-8A-3 to 26-8A-8, inclusive, or pursuant to any other provisions of this chapter, is immune from any liability, civil or criminal, that might otherwise be incurred or imposed ... Immunity also extends in the same manner ... to public officials or employees involved in the investigation and treatment of child abuse or neglect...."

The Court of Special Appeals correctly noted that questions involving determinations of good faith which involve intent and motive "ordinarily" are not resolvable on a motion for summary judgment. *See, Gross, supra*, 332 Md. at 256, 630 A.2d at 1160, citing, *Poller v. Columbia Broadcasting System, Inc.*, 368 U.S. 464, 473, 82 S.Ct. 486, 491, 7 L.Ed.2d 458, 464 (1962). *See, also DiGrazia v. County Executive*, 288 Md. 437, 445, 418 A.2d 1191, 1196 (1980). The Court of Special Appeals has also held that summary judgment was inappropriate in a case involving defamation, false imprisonment, malicious prosecution and abuse of process. *Laws v. Thompson*, 78 Md.App. 665, 669–687, 554 A.2d 1264, 1266–1275 (1989). And in *Coale, supra*, the intermediate appellate court determined that it was error to dismiss, on the basis of FL § 5-708's statutory immunity, the appellant's negligence and malicious prosecution actions against a social worker, who conducted an investigation resulting in the appellant's prosecution for child abuse, when the question of her good faith remained in issue. 84 Md.App. at 343, 579 A.2d at 783....

In the case *sub judice*, the trial court resolved all inferences from the record against the petitioners, as the moving party, and concluded that there was no genuine dispute of material fact, warranting trial. The Court of Special Appeals agreed with respect to the counts other than the defamation count and the breach or invasion of privacy counts.... The respondents do not agree. They submit that they have offered evidence to rebut the petitioners' claim of good faith reporting. In an attempt to ascribe, and justify, a sinister motive to Mr. Rosiak's actions in reporting the contents of the photographs, the respondents have fashioned a number of general allegations, hypothetical scenarios and alternative courses of action that Mr. Rosiak could, and they contend, should, have taken before reporting suspected child abuse based on the photographs. None of these allegations address directly the state of mind of Mr. Rosiak with respect to the content of the photographs. The respondents do not attempt to allege that Mr. Rosiak knew, or had reason to know, that the photographs did not depict child abuse and made a report of suspected child abuse in spite of that knowledge. Nor do they contend that Mr. Rosiak misstated or mischaracterized what he saw on the photographs, either to the police or to anyone else, or that he made untruthful or reckless remarks with regard to their content.... The respondents note, instead, that Mr. Rosiak did not strictly abide by a Rite Aid internal-company memorandum which outlined the procedure for dealing with sexually explicit photographs.[10] In addition, the respondents complain that Mr. Rosiak did not discuss the matter with Mr. Hagley in private, before deciding what to do, although he did discuss the photographs privately with the police officers. The respondents also characterize as evidence of bad faith, Mr. Rosiak's exclusion of Mr. Hagley from the private discussion he had with the police. The respondents contend that if Mr. Rosiak were truly interested in protecting a possible victim of child abuse, he would not have left Mr. Hagley, the potential abuser, alone in the store while making the report to the police, where Mr. Hagley was free to "possibly escape the scene.".... And the fact that Mr. Rosiak, although viewing it as odd, did not inform the police that Mr. Hagley had brought the child's mother to the store to resolve the misunderstanding is further indication, they argue, of the his lack of good faith. Finally, the respondents argue that Mr. Rosiak's bad faith can be inferred because he set Mr. Hagley up to be arrested by instructing him to return to the store at 1:00 p.m. and having the police arrive virtually simultaneously. Collectively, these acts, the respondents

---

10. The internal-company memorandum instructs Rite Aid employees to destroy photographs deemed "sexually explicit." The memorandum further states that Rite Aid employees shall not "keep, reprint or show another individual any photograph processed at a Rite Aid lab, which is deemed sexually explicit."

maintain, could lead a reasonable juror to infer that Mr. Rosiak was not interested in disclosing all sides of the story to the police or that he harbored an ill motive toward Mr. Hagley, and, consequently, was not acting in good faith.

We, however, are at a loss to discern how any of these facts, whether considered singly or collectively, could lead to an inference that Mr. Rosiak lacked good faith in reporting suspected child abuse. As the Court of Special Appeals pointed out:

> "Those assertions do not ... give rise to any reasonable inference that Rosiak did not honestly believe that the photographs were suggestive of child pornography or child abuse. He did not know Hagley; there was no suggestion of any fact that might even suggest a motive, other than a belief that the photographs depicted a form of child abuse, for Rosiak to call the police. Rosiak's conduct toward Hagley after he saw the photographs might suggest feeling of anger, disgust, or perhaps revulsion, but such emotions can only be explained as reactions to what Rosiak believed that the photographs depicted." ...

What the respondents' general allegations do indicate is that there were other alternatives available to Mr. Rosiak for handling the situation and that, perhaps, it could have, and probably, should have been handled better. But the availability of other alternatives, and the possibility, even probability, that the situation might have, or should have, been handled more effectively and sensitively, while perhaps suggesting negligence, does not equate to bad faith or a lack of good faith. And, as we have seen, negligence is not sufficient to negate good faith. *See Coale, supra*, 84 Md.App. at 342, 579 A.2d at 783. What steps Mr. Rosiak could have taken is not determinative; what actions Mr. Rosiak did, in fact, take is the determinative question.... Whether Mr. Rosiak strictly followed the Rite Aid policy in dealing with the photographs cannot rebut his claim of good faith in reporting his suspicion that the photographs depicted child abuse. Mr. Rosiak certainly could have timed his call to the police differently; however, that he did not does nothing to establish that he did not act in good faith in making the report of suspected child abuse.

Furthermore, Mr. Rosiak's discussion of the photographs with the police officers in a private office casts no light whatsoever on his motive in reporting what he believed to be suspected child abuse. The fact that Mr. Rosiak maintained a private office in the store is only relevant to show that he had an alternative forum for discussing the matter with Mr. Hagley and, thus, could have avoided the allegedly defamatory speech. The maintenance of a private office is not relevant, however, to show that Mr. Rosiak did not act in good faith or whether the allegedly defamatory speech is immune from suit under the statutes. Moreover, although Mr. Rosiak may have thought it was odd for Mr. Hagley to return with the child's mother to explain the photographs, his failure to disclose that fact to the police, again, is not suggestive of a lack of good faith. Mr. Rosiak was certainly under no duty to convey the suspected child abusers' explanation of the photographs to the authorities. *See, Hall v. Van's Photo, Inc.*, 595 So.2d 1368, 1370 (Ala.1992)("we conclude that [the reporter] did not have a duty under the Child Abuse Reporting Act to include [the suspect's] explanation in the report"). The immunity statutes do not require a reporter of suspected child abuse to verify every detail of the suspected conduct or perfectly recount all that he or she is told in order to be found to have acted in good faith when making the report. The statutes simply require that the reporter make a report in good faith. Thereafter, law enforcement or the appropriate department of social services personnel are charged with investigating the facts surrounding that report.

For the respondents to oppose the summary judgment motion successfully, they must have made a showing, supported by particular facts sufficient to allow a fact finder to conclude that Mr. Rosiak lacked good faith in making the report of suspected child abuse. They might have done so by producing specific facts showing that Mr. Rosiak knew, or had reason to know, that the photographs did not depict a form of child abuse and, in total disregard of that knowledge, filed a report anyway. What the respondents have produced are general allegations, that simply show that all of Mr. Rosiak's actions in making the report can be second guessed. Legitimizing this sort of Monday-morning quarterbacking would render the immunity conferred by CJ § 5-620 and FL § 5-708 essentially useless. The Court of Special Appeals correctly affirmed the trial court's grant of summary judgment as to Count II, false imprisonment; Count III, malicious prosecution; Count IV-A, Negligence; Count IV-B, Negligence of Defendant Rosiak (with Defendant Rite Aid liable under the rule of respondeat superior); Count IV-C, Breach of contractual duty; and Count IX (relating to the claim by Kerwyn Hagley and Ms. Martin for Kerywn's detainment by social services)....

Notwithstanding its application to the different counts alleged, all of the conduct by Mr. Rosiak in this case was, as the petitioners point out, closely related both in terms of time and subject matter. Thus, what Mr. Rosiak did and the conversations he had with Mr. Hagley all occurred within the space of a few hours, in the Rite Aid store and was concerned with the course of action he should pursue as a result of the contents of some photographs he had developed for Mr. Hagley. What Mr. Rosiak said to Mr. Hagley about what he saw in the photographs had no independent relevance; it was only because of the decision Mr. Rosiak was required to make with respect to reporting suspected child abuse, that the explanation was made. That it was made in the presence of others does not change this basic fact. Neither can the conferring with others concerning the decision to be made separate that fact from the basic issue, whether what Mr. Rosiak observed in the photographs was suspected child abuse, which Mr. Rosiak was legally required to report....

We agree with the petitioners that the Court of Special Appeals has interpreted the child abuse reporting statutes too narrowly. First, the statutes cover more than making a report. They recognize that individuals, other than the reporter, may play a role in the making of the report, although they may not themselves make it. In addition, the statutes cover investigations and resulting judicial proceedings. As the Court of Special Appeals interprets those statutes, a reporter, admittedly acting in good faith in making a report of suspected child abuse, may nevertheless be held liable civilly if, during the course of deciding whether to make a report, he or she mentions the nature of the concern he or she has and happens to do so, perhaps negligently, in the presence of someone other than a police officer, or seeks the advice of someone other than a police officer to assist in the decision making. Thus, the intermediate appellate court does not seem to take into account the breadth of the statutes or give effect to any of the conduct warranting immunity, except reporting. Such an interpretation and result, fly in the face of the purpose of the statutes and undermine the statutes' effectiveness; reports of suspected child abuse, in the case of ambiguous conduct, as in this case, either will not be filed or, if they are, they will be filed without the careful consideration allegations based on ambiguous conduct deserve to, and should, receive.

We hold that the Court of Special Appeals erred in reversing the judgment of the trial court with respect to the counts alleging various forms of breach or invasion of privacy and defamation.... Judgment of the Court of Special Appeals affirmed in part and reversed in part. Case remanded to that court with directions to affirm the judgment of the Circuit Court for Baltimore City. Costs in this court and in the Court of Special Appeals to be paid by the respondents.

II. Privileges and Defenses

A. Privileged Communications

1. *Marital Privilege*

State v. Anderson

Supreme Court of Iowa, 2001
636 N.W.2d 26

CADY, Justice....

The circumstances leading to this criminal prosecution date back to the summer of 1998. At that time, Mark Anderson lived in Keota, Iowa, with his wife and two children. Anderson was a life-long resident of Keota and farmed with his father on the family farm located four miles north of the town. Anderson grew corn and beans on the farm, and raised hogs. He was also a girls' softball and basketball coach for the Keota Community School District. He was thirty-seven years old.... In July of 1998, Anderson hired a fifteen-year-old girl, whom we identify as J.D., to help work on the farm. J.D. had just completed the eighth grade and was a schoolmate of Anderson's children. Anderson had known J.D.'s parents for many years. J.D. and her parents also lived in Keota. J.D.'s parents eventually made J.D. quit her employment with Anderson after they began to feel uncomfortable with the amount of time the two were spending together.... A year later, on September 14, 1999, the principal of the Keota high school notified J.D.'s parents of a report he received that Anderson had engaged in inappropriate contact with J.D. during the summer and fall of 1998. The parents then confronted J.D., who admitted to the report.

On September 15, 1999, J.D. and her mother met with a deputy county sheriff. J.D. gave a detailed statement disclosing four separate occasions in which she engaged in sexual intercourse with Anderson during the summer and fall of 1998. A criminal complaint was then filed on the same date, and the county attorney filed two trial informations against Anderson for sexual abuse in the third degree under Iowa Code section 709.4(2)(c)(4) (1997), commonly known as statutory rape.... On September 17, 1999, the school principal also called J.D. into his office at the school, and asked her to fill out a written report or complaint of abuse of a student by a school employee. The principal did this as a designated abuse investigator for the school district, and J.D. complied with the request. She was subsequently interviewed by the child protective service agency in Cedar Rapids. During the interview, J.D. again described the incidents of sexual intercourse with Anderson.

The trial information was later amended to charge Anderson with two counts of sexual abuse in the third degree, based solely on the commission of a sex act with a minor and the disparity in the age of the participants. Trial commenced on May 2, 2000.... J.D. testified at trial that Anderson first made sexual advances towards her on the evening of July 4, 1998. This occasion was followed by another incident of more aggressive sexual advances a few days later after J.D. had accompanied Anderson to his camper parked at Lake Darling. She then described four occasions in which she engaged in sexual intercourse with Anderson. She testified she had sexual intercourse with Anderson on two occasions in the camper, once in the bedroom of Anderson's home, and once in a schoolroom of the elementary school in Keota. J.D. was able to describe the interior of the camper and bedroom in detail, and described Anderson as having a hairy chest.

The State also called Anderson's ex-wife as a witness at trial. She testified that their seventeen-year marriage ended in divorce on December 20, 1999, four months prior to the trial. She described the interior of the camper and the bedroom, as well as Anderson's body, consistent with the description given by J.D. She also testified to various conversations she had with Anderson about his relationship with J.D., including concerns she expressed to him during the summer of 1998 about the amount of time he was spending with J.D. She also testified to a private conversation she had with Anderson following his arrest in which she asked him why he "let himself get into that situation." In response, Anderson told her "You're right. I should have listened to you before." ... Anderson testified at trial and acknowledged J.D. visited the camper with him, and accompanied him on numerous occasions to various places during the time period she worked for him. However, he denied engaging in any sexual intercourse with her or that any inappropriate behavior occurred. Anderson also acknowledged the comment made to his ex-wife, but testified he was talking about his poor judgment in allowing himself to be placed in the position of being accused of the crime. Anderson also called several witnesses at trial who testified they never observed any inappropriate conduct between Anderson and J.D., including a witness who observed them in the camper on one occasion.... The jury found Anderson guilty of both counts of sexual abuse in the third degree. Anderson was subsequently sentenced to two concurrent ten-year terms of incarceration. He appeals.

Anderson ... claims the district court erred in allowing his former wife to testify about their privileged marital communications.... One recognized privilege involves confidential marital communications. Since medieval times, the law recognized a wife could not testify against her husband. *See Trammel v. United States*, 445 U.S. 40, 43–44, 100 S.Ct. 906, 909, 63 L.Ed.2d 186, 190 (1980). Although this ancient doctrine has been abrogated in Iowa, as well as in nearly all other jurisdictions, our laws still recognize a companion privilege that prohibits the disclosure of testimony concerning a spousal communication made during the marriage. *See* 1 Kenneth S. Broun et al., *McCormick on Evidence* § 78, at 292–94 (John William Strong ed., 4th ed. 1992); 7 Adams & Weeg, *Iowa Practice* § 503.1, at 297.[1] Like its ancient counterpart, this privilege largely exists to promote marital harmony and stability.[2] *See Stein v. Bowman*, 13 Pet. 209, 38 U.S. 209, 223, 10 L.Ed. 129, 136 (1839); *Sexton v. Sexton*, 129 Iowa 487, 489, 105 N.W. 314, 315 (1905); 7 Adams & Weeg, *Iowa Practice* § 503.1, at 297. Marriage has long been considered to be the traditional

---

1. The rule of spousal disqualification can be traced to 1628 when Lord Coke wrote "it hath beene resolved by the Justices that a wife cannot be produced either against or for her husband." *Trammel*, 445 U.S. at 43–44, 100 S.Ct. at 909, 63 L.Ed.2d at 190 (quoting 1 E. Coke, *A Commentarie upon Littleton* 6b (1628)). Iowa repealed the competency statute, formerly Iowa Code section 622.7, in 1983. *See* 1983 Iowa Acts ch. 37, § 6 (codified at Iowa Code § 726.4 (1983)); *see also* 7 Adams & Weeg, *Iowa Practice* § 503.1, at 297 n.3. The statutory privilege against the disclosure of marital communications dates back to 1851. 7 Adams & Weeg, *Iowa Practice* § 503.1, at 297 n.1 (citing Iowa Code § 2392 (1851)).

2. Other reasons support the existence of the marital privilege. *See* 7 Adams & Weeg, *Iowa Practice* § 503.1, at 297 n.4. One additional reason is to respect human privacy, especially in the context of the marital relationship. *Id.* (citing 2 Louisell & Mueller, *Federal Evidence* § 219, at 637–38 (1978)). Another reason is that "it is unseemly, even offensive to many, to use the power of the state to force revelation of marital confidences." *Id.* (quoting 2 Louisell & Mueller, *Federal Evidence* § 219, at 637–38 (1978)). Additionally, "this protected privacy, and the confidence between spouses which it encourages, are utterly essential to the complete fulfillment of marriage." *Id.* The privilege "provides support for the institution of marriage itself—a proposition which is sound even if it be conceded that spouses do not consciously rely upon the privilege in confiding in one another." *Id.*

foundation of the family, and subject to legal protection.... The privilege for marital communications is recognized in Iowa by statute. Iowa Code section 622.9 provides:

> Neither husband nor wife can be examined in any case as to any communication made by the one to the other while married, nor shall they, after the marriage relation ceases, be permitted to reveal in testimony any such communication made while the marriage subsisted.

The privilege, however, is not absolute. Both common law and legislative exceptions have surfaced under circumstances where the purpose for the privilege is diminished or lost. *See State v. Klindt*, 389 N.W.2d 670, 675–76 (Iowa 1986). We adopted a common law exception to the marital privilege in prosecutions for crimes committed by one spouse against the other.[3] *Id.* at 676. Moreover, our legislature crafted another exception to the marital privilege concerning evidence of injuries to children in a civil or a criminal proceeding that resulted from or related to a report of suspected child abuse.[4] Iowa Code § 232.74. It provides:

> Sections 622.9 and 622.10 and any other statute or rule of evidence which excludes or makes privileged the testimony of a husband or wife against the other or the testimony of a health practitioner or mental health professional as to confidential communications, do not apply to evidence regarding a child's injuries or the cause of the injuries in any judicial proceeding, civil or criminal, resulting from a report pursuant to this chapter or relating to the subject matter of such a report.

Id.

We have previously indicated this statute reveals our legislature's intention to abrogate the spousal privilege in most cases involving crimes against children under eighteen years of age. *State v. Cahill*, 186 N.W.2d 587, 589 (Iowa 1971). However, we have not yet considered the contours of those cases that may fall outside the child abuse exception. We first turn to the history and language of the statute to make this determination.... The statutory exception to the marital privilege was first enacted in 1965. *See* 1965 Iowa Acts ch. 217, § 8 (codified at Iowa Code § 235A.8 (1966)). It has been amended on two occasions since that time, but the substantive provisions have remained unchanged. *See* 1987 Iowa Acts ch. 153, § 6 (codified at Iowa Code § 232.74 (1989)) (added mental health professionals); 1983 Iowa Acts ch. 37, § 1 (codified at Iowa Code § 232.74 (1985)) (deleted reference to section 622.7). The statute establishes three central components to the exception to the marital privilege. First, the statutory exception applies "to evidence

---

3. Many other jurisdictions, including federal courts, have established an exception to the marital privilege where a spouse commits an offense against the other spouse. *See Wyatt v. United States*, 362 U.S. 525, 526–27, 80 S.Ct. 901, 902–03, 4 L.Ed.2d 931, 933 (1960); 25 Charles Alan Wright & Kenneth W. Graham, Jr., *Federal Practice and Procedure* § 5592, at 748 (1989) (it is generally agreed that assault, battery, and other types of corporal violence are within the exception).

4. In *State v. Countryman*, we specifically recognized child abuse and crimes against a spouse as the two exceptions to the marital communications privilege. *See State v. Countryman*, 572 N.W.2d 553, 561 (Iowa 1997). We created the latter exception, while the child abuse exception is strictly statutory. Additionally, section 726.4 recognizes what could be considered a third exception to the privilege. This section provides: "In all prosecutions under section 726.3, 726.5 or 726.6, the husband or wife is a competent witness for the [S]tate and may testify to relevant acts or communications between them." Iowa Code § 726.4. The excepted sections deal with neglect or abandonment of a dependent person, nonsupport, and child endangerment, and are closely related to the child abuse exception.

regarding a child's injuries or the cause of the injuries...." Iowa Code § 232.74. Second, the evidence must be presented in any civil or criminal "judicial proceeding." *Id.* Finally, the civil or criminal proceeding must "result[ ] from a report pursuant to this chapter or relat[e] to the subject matter of such a report." *Id.*; *see State v. Johnson*, 318 N.W.2d 417, 439 (Iowa 1982) ("When a report is made and a judicial proceeding either results from the report or relates to the subject matter of the report, section 232.74 prevents the application of any statutory or common-law marital privilege to the child's injuries or the cause of them.").

This case does not implicate the first two requirements. An alleged admission of statutory rape constitutes evidence of an injury to a child-victim or the cause of injury, and the evidence in dispute in this case was presented in a criminal trial. We focus our attention on the third requirement. The exception to the marital privilege not only requires a report to be made, but further requires the report to be made "pursuant to this chapter" or relate to the subject matter of such a report. Iowa Code § 232.74. Clearly, the scope of the exception is defined by the reporting provisions under the governing chapter of the Code. *See Johnson*, 318 N.W.2d at 439 (section 232.74 is found in the division of the Juvenile Justice Act "relating to child abuse reporting, investigat[ion], and rehabilitat[ion]").... Anderson argues the statutory exception does not apply to this case because the criminal charges brought against him by the State do not constitute child abuse and were not subject to the child abuse reporting provisions of chapter 232. The State argues the exception applies because the reporting provisions of the law are broad enough to include all crimes against children, and, notwithstanding, the criminal charges brought against Anderson were within the statutory reporting requirements of a mandatory reporter. The State asserts the report made by the school principal in this case satisfied the third requirement of the statutory exception....

Although chapter 232 generally limits its reporting requirements to child abuse, mandatory reporters are also now given additional reporting requirements under section 232.69 that were not present when the reporting requirements and the exception to the marital privilege were first enacted. Section 232.69(1) was recently amended to require mandatory reporters to report sexual offenses against a child who is under twelve years of age involving abuse, incest, and exploitation, as well as prostitution, which would otherwise constitute child abuse except "the abuse resulted from the acts or omissions of a person other than a person responsible for the care of the child." *Id.* § 232.69(1). Additionally, a mandatory reporter may report such sexual offenses against a child who is twelve years of age or older when the abuse occurred by a non-care provider. *Id.* Thus, even though a sexual offense committed as a result of the acts of a person other than the person responsible for the care of the child falls outside the definition of child abuse for reporting purposes, our legislature made it reportable by designated mandatory reporters. Yet, the reporting provisions relating to permissive reporters continue to be limited to cases of child abuse. *See id.* § 232.70(7).

Thus, unlike the original reporting provisions, chapter 232 has extended the reporting scheme for mandatory reporters to include some cases of non-child abuse, but has continued to limit the reporting provisions for permissive reporters to child abuse. The important consequence of this distinction comes into play when the reporting requirements are applied to the exception to the marital privilege. If we apply the literal language of section 232.74 to the present reporting scheme under section 232.69, it would mean that the exception to the privilege would apply to cases involving sex offenses against children not constituting child abuse, such as the crime of statutory rape, depending upon who filed the report. If the report was made by a mandatory reporter, the exception would apply. If it was made by a permissive reporter, the exception would not apply. This is the interpretation sought by the State in this case. It correctly points out that the school principal was a mandatory reporter, and claims that the report of the sexual offense made by the principal constituted a report under chapter 232.[6] ...

We understand why our legislature would want to expand the reporting requirements in the area of sexual offenses against children. The policy and purpose of reporting requirements is to protect children from abuse as much as possible. Iowa Code § 232.67 (1997). Furthermore, it is even understandable why our legislature would want to extend the marital privilege exception to include proceedings involving sexual offenses against children that fall outside the definition of child abuse.[7] However, we cannot conceive of any rationale for making the expanded exception hinge solely upon the mandatory or permissive nature of the report. Such a distinction has no relationship to abrogating or limiting the marital privilege. The considerations involved in protecting the welfare of children by expanding the reporting and investigation of abuse to children are not necessarily the same as the prosecution of abuse to children. If our legislature had intended to expand the exception to the marital privilege by expanding the reporting requirements, it would not have done so by limiting the expansion to mandatory reporters.... We think our legislature only intended the exception to the marital privilege under section 232.74 to apply to cases resulting from reports of child abuse despite the new provisions of the Code that both permit and compel mandatory reporters to report sexual offenses against children that do not constitute child abuse. This conclusion is not only supported by the illogical distinction created by a literal application of the language of section 232.74 to the reporting requirements of section 232.69, but it is consistent with other principles of statutory construction....

We also recognize that the fundamental purpose of maintaining the marital privilege is served in cases involving injuries to children as a result of a non-care provider with much greater strength than in cases involving a care provider. Like the exception for crimes by one spouse against the other, child abuse inflicted by a spouse upon a child of the family undermines the very relationship the privilege seeks to maintain. *United States v. Allery*, 526 F.2d 1362, 1366 (8th Cir.1975). It is an offense against the family harmony and, at the same time, a wrong against the other spouse. *Id.* These consequences gave rise to the creation of the recognized exceptions to the privilege. On the other hand, the

---

6. There was no evidence produced at trial to show the school principal actually made a report to the Department of Human Services (DHS). However, the record reflects that a deputy sheriff took J.D. to Child Protective Services for an examination and interview. Although we are not required to decide the question, this evidence may constitute an oral report to the DHS under section 232.70.

7. Although the justification for abrogating the marital privilege in cases involving family members does not apply with the same force to cases not involving the same family, there are other reasons for abrogating the marital privilege in child abuse cases that would apply whether or not the abuse occurred within the family. The policy which helps justify the marital privilege relates not only to the sanctity of the relationship and nature of the communications between spouses, but also considers whether the injury that would inure to the marital relationship by permitting disclosure is greater than the benefit that would result from the judicial pursuit of the truth. *See* 8 Wigmore, *Evidence* § 2285, at 527. Thus, an exception to the marital privilege in cases of child abuse can be justified by the general need for evidence to assist in the prosecution of such cases. *United States v. Allery*, 526 F.2d 1362, 1366 (8th Cir.1975). The marital privilege is criticized because it impedes justice by excluding even reliable evidence. *See id.* Our legislature certainly could consider this delicate balancing process in extending the exception to some cases of child sexual offenses not involving family members or care providers.

marital relationship is not directly undermined by acts of a spouse directed to a child outside the marriage relationship.

We further recognize that a limitation on the exception to the marital privilege to cases that fall within the statutory definition of child abuse is compatible to the approach followed in most jurisdictions that have enacted a child abuse exception to the marital privilege. The three federal circuits that have adopted the child abuse exception to the marital privilege did so only in cases where the victim of the offense was a child of one of the spouses, or was at least a child within the household. *See United States v. Bahe*, 128 F.3d 1440, 1446 (10th Cir.1997); *United States v. White*, 974 F.2d 1135, 1138 (9th Cir.1992); *Allery*, 526 F.2d at 1367. Furthermore, most states that have adopted the child abuse exception to the marital privilege appear to have narrowly applied the exception to crimes against children of either spouse or children under their care. *See Commonwealth v. Boarman*, 610 S.W.2d 922, 925 (Ky.Ct.App.1980) (marital privilege not applicable to the prosecution of a man for sexual abuse of adopted daughter); *Adams v. State*, 563 S.W.2d 804, 809 (Tenn.Crim.App.1978) (marital privilege does not apply to acts of violence by a defendant upon the children of either spouse or upon minor children in the custody or dominion or control of either spouse); *State v. Widdison*, 4 P.3d 100, 111–12 (Utah Ct.App.2000) (exception to marital privilege applies to injuries by husband to a child residing in home of either spouse); *State v. Sanders*, 66 Wash.App. 878, 883–84, 833 P.2d 452, 455–56 (1992) (under state statute, the marital privilege does not apply to crimes committed by a husband or wife against any child of whom the husband or wife is a parent or guardian). *But see Ludwig v. State*, 931 S.W.2d 239, 244 (Tex.Crim.App.1996) (interpreting rule to extend exception to marital privilege to any crime against any child).

Finally, the statutory history of section 232.74 reveals our legislature could not have intended to expand the child abuse exception to the marital privilege when it expanded the reporting requirements for mandatory reporters to include two specific incidences of injuries to children not involving child abuse. This interpretation could not reflect the intention of our legislature because it creates the absurd result of making the designated status of the reporter determine the admissibility of privileged communications at trial. Instead, we think the original intent of our legislature to limit the scope of the exception to the marital privilege to cases involving the acts or omissions of a care provider continues to apply today, and the expanded requirements for mandatory reporters were only intended to provide greater protection to children through the reporting and investigation of abuse. Thus, we conclude the exception to the marital privilege under section 232.74 is limited to cases of child abuse that result from acts or omissions of a care provider. It does not apply to injuries to children that result from acts or omissions by a non-care provider.

The State also asserts the statutory exception to the marital privilege should be read to apply to any reports of injuries to children. We have said on prior occasions that our legislature intended a "report" to be broadly defined. *State v. Spaulding*, 313 N.W.2d 878, 880 (Iowa 1981); *Cahill*, 186 N.W.2d at 589. Yet, this broad definition essentially means all child abuse that leads to a judicial proceeding will necessarily be preceded by a report under chapter 232, or at least relate to the subject matter of the report. *See Johnson*, 318 N.W.2d at 439 ("[a]lthough the [criminal] proceedings did not *result from* the report, they clearly relate to the subject matter of the report"). It means the legislature did not intend the reporting requirements to be technical, and that most reports of child abuse will constitute a report under the chapter. However, the broad meaning of "report" cannot be extended beyond the meaning intended by our legislature.... The State's position would require us to read the "report pursuant to this chapter" language out of the statute. We avoid interpreting a statute to render any part of it superfluous. *State v. Graves*, 491

N.W.2d 780, 782 (Iowa 1992). Instead, each part of the statute is presumed to have a purpose. *Id.* We cannot interpret section 232.74 to include reports that are not a part of the reporting provisions of section 232.69. Our legislature intended to qualify "reports" to refer to reports of child abuse....

The State further argues that any error in admitting evidence in violation of the marital privilege did not affect the outcome of the trial. We recognize not all trial error requires a reviewing court to reverse the judgment of the district court. Instead, under the harmless error rule, reversal is not required if the State can establish the error did not cause prejudice to the defendant. *State v. Griffin*, 576 N.W.2d 594, 597 (Iowa 1998). The inquiry turns to whether the guilty verdict was unattributable to the error. *See State v. Leutfaimany*, 585 N.W.2d 200, 206 (Iowa 1998). In making this determination, we consider the probative force of the evidence considered by the jury against the evidence erroneously admitted. *Id.*

The State asserts the evidence of guilt was strong enough to support a verdict of guilty without the evidence of the implied admission of guilt by Anderson. Furthermore, the State maintains that Anderson offered an explanation in response to the evidence of an admission that would support a finding that the evidence did not constitute an admission. We agree the child-victim in this case offered detailed evidence of the crime, which was corroborated by Anderson's former wife. Anderson was also alone with the child on numerous occasions and the child did not accuse Anderson until she was confronted by her parents and authorities almost a year later.... Nevertheless, there was no physical evidence offered at trial and no eye witness testimony to the crime. Instead, the verdict was essentially a product of the credibility of the defendant and the victim. Anderson offered evidence to rebut the testimony offered by the State. Under these circumstances, we cannot conclude beyond a reasonable doubt the guilty verdict was unattributable to the evidence admitted in violation of the marital privilege. In a case of this nature, an admission of guilt could have very well been the decisive piece of evidence that tipped the scale in favor of guilt. Moreover, Anderson's explanation for the implied admission was not so strong that it would have eliminated any impact on the jury.

We are obligated under our governing principles of law to reverse the conviction. The admission of the evidence of the marital communications was prejudicial to Anderson in this case.... We conclude the trial court erred in admitting evidence of marital communications. We find the error was prejudicial. Consequently, we are obligated to reverse the judgment and sentence of the district court and remand the case for a new trial.

REVERSED AND REMANDED FOR A NEW TRIAL.

Notes

The holding in the *Anderson* decision limits the exception to the marital privilege to cases involving the mandatory reporting of "child abuse," as defined by statute, but not the voluntary reporting of other sexual offenses against children that are deemed non-"child abuse." *But see Mullins v. Commonwealth*, 956 S.W.2d 210 (Ky. 1997) (reporting statute's abrogation of marital privilege enhances judicial truth-finding function); *United States v. Allery*, 526 F.2d 1362 (8th Cir. 1975) (expanding marital exception to include crimes committed against the child of either spouse). Note that the scope of the marital privilege and the limitations of statutory reporting requirements are state specific but are strictly construed. *See also Kroh v. Kroh*, 152 N.C. App. 347, 567 S.E.2d 760 (2002) (privilege otherwise afforded to wife regarding husband's alleged molestation of sons negated by bad faith in reporting); *Quiring v. Quiring*, 130 Idaho 560, 944 P.2d 695 (1997) (agreement between husband and wife in which wife agreed to refrain from mandated reporting of husband's sexual improprieties with child in exchange for property interest held unenforceable). For commentary regarding the expansion of the child abuse exception to the marital privilege, see Naomi Harlin Goodno, *Protecting "Any Child": The Use of the Confidential-Marital-Communications Privilege in Child Molestation Cases*, 59 U. Kan. L. Rev. 1 (2011); Emily C. Aldridge, *To Catch a Predator or to Save His Marriage: Advocating for an Expansive Child Abuse Exception to the Marital privileges in Federal Courts*, 78 Fordham L. Rev. 1761 (2010); Damian P. Richard, *Expanding the "Child of Either" Exception to the Husband-Wife Privilege under the New M.R.E. 504(D)*, 60 Air Force L. Rev. 155 (2007); Kimberly Ann Connor, *A Critique of the Marital Privileges: An Examination of the Marital Privileges in the United States Military through the State and Federal Approaches to the Marital Privileges*, 36 Val. U. L. Rev. 119 (2001).

2. Clergy Privilege

State v. Patterson

Court of Appeals of Utah, 2013
213 UT. App. 11, 294 P.3d 662

DAVIS, Judge:

Scott Kirby Patterson appeals his convictions of two counts of aggravated sex abuse of a child and two counts of lewdness involving a child. *See generally* Utah Code Ann. § 76-5-404.1(4) (LexisNexis 2012); *id.* § 76-9-702.5.[1] ... Patterson's convictions arose out of a ten-month period beginning in February 2008, during which he abused his step-daughter (Child), while married to Child's mother (Mother).... [footnote omitted]. Child disclosed the abuse to Mother on the first night that it happened. Mother confronted Patterson in front of Child that night, and he denied the allegations. Mother also asked Child whether she was "really sure" about her accusations and told Child, "[I]f [Patterson]'s done this ... [we] will be fine, we'll go get us an apartment. We're going to move out. We'll be okay, you know, it doesn't matter...." Child, the next morning, decided that she "didn't want to move" because she "liked where [they] were and ... liked [Patterson]" and that she "just didn't want to change [her] life just like that," so she decided to tell Mother to "forget about it" and to "put it behind," and that "it might have been a dream," even though Child knew that "it wasn't a dream." ... Shortly after Christmas that year, Mother confronted Patterson again after realizing that both Child's and Patterson's behavior had changed over the last few months and that the changes had started after Child accused Patterson of abuse in February. On December 27, 2008, Patterson admitted to Mother that he had molested Child twice. Mother immediately planned to move out of the house and filed for divorce on December 29, and in the process she called an ecclesiastical leader from her church (Bishop) to explain the situation and ask for his help. On February 9, 2009, Patterson was charged with two counts of aggravated sexual abuse of a child and two counts of lewdness involving a child.

Patterson also reached out to Bishop for help, meeting him at his office several months after Mother moved out. Patterson later described his meeting with Bishop as "confidential clergy-penitent communication" that involved "discussions about confession in the church." Nonetheless, after Patterson was charged, he offered Bishop's name as a character reference

---

1. Where recent amendments to the Utah Code do not affect our analysis, we cite the most recent version of the code for the reader's convenience.

to the medical professional (Doctor) retained by his trial counsel to prepare a psychosexual evaluation of Patterson; the evaluation was to be used in plea negotiations and, if necessary, during sentencing. The psychosexual evaluation contains Bishop's statement to Doctor that Patterson "told [him] how sorry he was for what he has done." Because of this statement in the psychosexual evaluation, the State, during a recess in the middle of the trial and before Patterson had testified, indicated to Patterson's trial counsel that the State would use Patterson's communication with Bishop to impeach Patterson's testimony denying the abuse. Patterson decided to heed his trial counsel's advice and not testify, even though both he and his trial counsel later testified that they were prepared for him to take the stand.[3]

At trial, the defense posed the theory that Child's allegations were fabricated and used as leverage by a "very vindictive" Mother during her and Patterson's divorce. Throughout the trial, testimony was elicited from both Mother and Child that suggested Patterson was an angry person, who could be frightening at times. Mother's testimony also described some of the details of their divorce and indicated that Patterson got most of the assets because she did not "want to deal with him anymore." Defense counsel used these comments to support the theory that Child is a liar and that Mother convinced Child to fabricate the charges out of bitterness and to gain leverage in the divorce. One of the detectives (Detective) present during Child's interview at the Children's Justice Center (CJC) also testified at trial. Detective's testimony addressed the consistency between Child's trial testimony and her CJC interview.... Patterson was convicted of all four charges and appealed....

We address several issues on appeal. First, Patterson argues that his attorneys were ineffective for advising him not to testify in light of the State's threat to use Bishop's statements to impeach him when the clergy-penitent privilege would have prohibited admission of Bishop's comments. "In ruling on an ineffective assistance claim following a Rule 23B hearing, we defer to the trial court's findings of fact, but review its legal conclusions for correctness." *State v. Bredehoft*, 966 P.2d 285, 289 (Utah Ct.App.1998) (citation and internal quotation marks omitted).... Patterson argues that he "was denied effective assistance of counsel when [his trial attorneys] failed to advise him of the clergy-penitent privilege and did not assert it at trial," thereby leading Patterson to decide against testifying despite his earlier plan to testify.[4] ... This ineffectiveness argument rests on the applicability of the

---

3. Patterson was represented by two attorneys at trial and brings ineffectiveness claims against them both. Additionally, the trial record does not indicate one way or another whether Patterson intended to testify. In a hearing before the trial court following a remand from this court pursuant to rule 23B of the Utah Rules of Appellate Procedure, Patterson and both of his trial attorneys testified that Patterson was prepared to testify at trial and would have denied the abuse.

4. Patterson also argues that the prosecutor committed misconduct by threatening to use privileged communications with Bishop to impeach Patterson if he decided to testify when the clergy-penitent privilege would have likely prohibited the State from doing so. Patterson suggests that the issue was preserved during the rule 23B hearing. However, rule 23B hearings are not the proper forum to preserve such claims; they provide one thing—"a procedural solution to the dilemma created by an inadequate record of trial counsel's ineffectiveness" where ineffective assistance of trial counsel is a claim on appeal. *See State v. Johnston*, 2000 UT App. 290, ¶ 7, 13 P.3d 175 (per curiam); *see also* Utah R.App. P. 23B(a) ("A party to an appeal in a criminal case may move the court to remand the case to the trial court for entry of findings of fact, necessary for the appellate court's determination of a claim of ineffective assistance of counsel."); *Johnston*, 2000 UT App. 290, ¶ 7, 13 P.3d 175 ("The purpose of Rule 23B is for appellate counsel to put on evidence he or she now has, not to amass evidence that might help prove an ineffectiveness of counsel claim. It allows supplementation of the record, in limited circumstances, with nonspeculative facts not fully appearing in the record that would support the claimed deficient performance and the resulting prejudice."). Because this issue was not preserved,

clergy-penitent privilege and whether Patterson waived it by permitting Doctor to contact Bishop. The clergy-penitent privilege is established by rule 503 of the Utah Rules of Evidence,[5] which states,

> A person has a privilege to refuse to disclose, and to prevent another from disclosing, any confidential communication: (1) made to a cleric in the cleric's religious capacity; and (2) necessary and proper to enable the cleric to discharge the function of the cleric's office according to the usual course of practice or discipline.

> Utah R. Evid. 503(b); *see also id.* R. 503(a) (defining "cleric" as "a minister, priest, rabbi, or other similar functionary of a religious organization or an individual reasonably believed to be so by the person consulting that individual," and defining "confidential communication" as "a communication: (A) made privately; and (B) not intended for further disclosure except to other persons in furtherance of the purpose of the communication"); *id.* R. 503(c) (including among the people who can claim the privilege "the person who made the confidential communication" and "the person who was the cleric at the time of the communication on behalf of the communicant"). The privilege protects both penitential and nonpenitential communications. *See Scott v. Hammock*, 870 P.2d 947, 950 & n. 2 (Utah 1994) (interpreting the privilege as it appeared in former Utah Code section 78-24-8, which is virtually identical to the current Utah Code section 78B-1-137); *see also* Utah. R. Evid. 503 & advisory committee's note (explaining that the rule aims "to extend the privilege beyond doctrinally required confessions" and be "broadly applicable to all confidential communications with a cleric").

The parties do not dispute that Patterson's communications with Bishop are covered by the privilege. Rather, the parties dispute whether the privilege was waived. The trial court's rule 23B findings indicate that Patterson waived the privilege when he permitted Doctor to contact Bishop and when a synopsis of Bishop's comments to Doctor that included the statement, "[H]e told me how sorry he was for what he has done," was provided to the prosecution. Specifically, the trial court stated that Patterson, "as holder of the communications to clergy privilege, failed to take reasonable precautions against inadvertent disclosure of his communications with Bishop." ... Waiver of a privilege occurs when the "person who holds a privilege ... (1) voluntarily discloses or consents to the disclosure of any significant part of the matter or communication, or (2) fails to take rea-

---

and Patterson has not demonstrated plain error, Patterson waived this argument. *See State v. King*, 2010 UT App. 396, ¶ 27, 248 P.3d 984 ("[A defendant]'s failure to object to improper remarks waives his prosecutorial misconduct claim unless the remarks reach the level of plain error, meaning that an error exists [that] should have been obvious to the trial court and that the error was harmful." (second alteration in original) (citations and internal quotation marks omitted)).

5. Patterson relies on Utah Code section 78B-1-137 as establishing the clergy-penitent privilege, as well as rule 503. *See* Utah Code Ann. § 78B-1-137(3) (LexisNexis 2012) ("A member of the clergy or priest cannot, without the consent of the person making the confession, be examined as to any confession made to either of them in their professional character in the course of discipline enjoined by the church to which they belong."). Although rule 503 was based on "the basic concept of" section 78B-1-137, it was intended to "expand[ ]" that concept, *see* Utah R. Evid. 503 advisory committee's note, and in accordance with that intent, rule 503 renders "ineffectual" section 78B-1-137, *see id.* R. 501 advisory committee's note. Thus, we rely on rule 503 and other applicable rules of evidence for our analysis. *See generally Debry v. Goates*, 2000 UT App. 58, ¶ 24 n. 2, 999 P.2d 582 ("The Utah Rules of Evidence expressly supersede statutory privileges.... Statutory privileges not in conflict are retained, but when inconsistencies arise, the rules control." (citations omitted)).

sonable precautions against inadvertent disclosure." Utah R. Evid. 510(a).[6] Additionally, "it is not necessary under Rule [510] to show that a [privilege holder] intended to waive the privilege but only that she intended to make the disclosure." *Doe v. Maret*, 1999 UT 74, ¶ 19, 984 P.2d 980, *overruled on other grounds by Munson v. Chamberlain*, 2007 UT 91, 173 P.3d 848.

Here, both Patterson and Bishop held the privilege, *see* Utah R. Evid. 503(c)(1), (4), and both "fail[ed] to take reasonable precautions against inadvertent disclosure," *see id.* R. 510(a)(2). The psychosexual evaluation provided to the prosecution paraphrases Bishop as stating,

> We ha[d Patterson] and his wife teaching a primary class for 6–8 months and I was never aware of any inappropriate sexual behavior ... no incidents. The first I found out anything was when he came and told me about this.... He told me he was in a lot of different leadership positions in the past.... I've never known him to be misleading and has always been upfront ... he told me how sorry he was for what he has done ... all that I know of it is isolated just to this....

(Emphasis omitted) (omissions in original). The implication of Bishop's statement is that Patterson confessed to the charges. Bishop was contacted by Doctor to opine on Patterson's ability to safely be around children, and the first part of Bishop's statement to Doctor does that without implicating a confidential communication. Though Bishop may not have intended to imply that Patterson had confessed, his comments transcribed in the psychosexual evaluation indicate that Bishop "fail[ed] to take reasonable precautions against inadvertent disclosure." *See id.* Likewise, even if Doctor's communication with Bishop did not waive the privilege in and of itself, the fact that Patterson reviewed the psychosexual evaluation with Doctor and trial counsel before permitting the evaluation to be disclosed to the State essentially amounts to his "consent[ing] to the disclosure of a[ ] significant part of the ... [privileged] communication," *see id.* R. 510(a)(1), with that "significant part" being the implication of his having confessed to Bishop. Accordingly, because Patterson and Bishop waived the privilege, trial counsel's performance was not deficient for failing to raise the privilege in deciding on how to advise Patterson regarding his decision to testify.

Although trial counsel could have also taken steps after the disclosure to try to preserve some confidentiality, *cf. Gold Standard, Inc. v. American Barrick Res. Corp.*, 805 P.2d 164, 172 (Utah 1990) (holding that a party's more than three-month delay in filing a motion for a protective order regarding materials that the party seemingly knowingly disclosed, but later claimed to be confidential attorney work product, "constitute[ed] an independent waiver of whatever right [of confidentiality the party] may have been able to assert"), Patterson has failed to convince us that such a step had a reasonable probability of success, especially in light of Patterson's purposeful, rather than inadvertent, disclosure of the psychosexual evaluation to the State. *See Terry v. Bacon*, 2011 UT App. 432, ¶ 19, 269 P.3d 188 (recognizing that principles of fairness dictate that a party "not be permitted to use the [attorney-client] privilege as a sword ... [and] a shield"); *see also Strickland v. Washington*, 466 U.S. 668, 694, 104 S.Ct. 2052, 80 L.Ed.2d 674 (1984) ("The defendant

---

6. Rule 507 of the Utah Rules of Evidence governed waiver of privileges at the time of the rule 23B hearing but was subsequently renumbered as rule 510. Because this amendment to the rule was purely stylistic, we cite the most current version of the rule. *See* Utah R. Evid. 510 advisory committee's note.

must show that there is a reasonable probability that, but for counsel's unprofessional errors, the result of the proceeding would have been different.")....

Trial counsel was not ineffective for failing to assert the clergy-penitent privilege because Patterson waived that privilege when he approved the disclosure of the psychosexual report to the State....

Judge JAMES Z. DAVIS authored this Opinion, in which Judges J. FREDERIC VOROS JR. and MICHELE M. CHRISTIANSEN concurred.

Notes

Like other privileges applicable to confidential communications, the clergy privilege, or its abrogation, is determined by state statute. Approximately 27 states include members of the clergy within their enumerated list of mandatory reporters. *See, e.g.,* ARK. CODE § 12-18-402 (including clergy members, which include ministers, priests, rabbis, accredited Christian Science practitioners, or other similar functionary of a religious organization); CAL. PENAL CODE § 11165.7 (including clergy members and custodians of records of clergy members); 22 ME. REV. CODE § 4011-A (clergy members); MINN. STAT. § 626.556, Subd. 3 (member of the clergy who received the information while engaged in ministerial duties); OHIO REV. CODE § 2151.421 (persons, other than clerics, rendering spiritual treatment through prayer in accordance with the tenets of a well-recognized religion). However, the clergy privilege under the reporting laws is not absolute and may be limited in cases involving child abuse or neglect, or may be abrogated altogether. *See, e.g.,* N.H. REV. STAT. § 169-C:32 (clergy privilege shall not apply to child abuse and neglect proceedings and shall not constitute grounds for failure to report); N.C. GEN. STAT. § 7B-310 (no privilege, other than attorney-client, shall be grounds for failing to report, or excluding from evidence, abuse or neglect of a juvenile, even if such knowledge or suspicion is acquired in an official professional capacity); 10 OKL. STAT. § 1-2-101 (no privilege shall relieve any person from the requirement of reporting); R.I. Gen. Laws § 40-11-11 (privileged communication, except between attorney and client, is abrogated in situations involving known or suspected child abuse or neglect); TEX. FAM. CODE ANN. § 261.101 (requirement to report applies, without exception, to otherwise privileged communications, including a member of the clergy); W.V. CODE ANN. § 49-6A-2 & -7 (any member of the clergy with reasonable cause to suspect child abuse or neglect shall immediately, and not more than 48 hours after suspecting such abuse, report the circumstances to authorities, and privilege of communication is abrogated). *See also State v. Workman,* 2011 WL 6210667 (Tenn. Crim. App. 2011) (exception to clergy privilege); *Bordman v. State,* 56 S.W.3d 63 (App. 14 Dist. 2001) (defendant confessed to clergy that he sexually assaulted his three children; statutory exception to privilege applied).

For some of the numerous commentaries on the application, abrogation, and scope of the clergy privilege, see Jude O. Ezeanokwasa, *The Priest-Penitent Privilege Revisited: A Reply to the Statutes of Abrogation,* 9 INTERCULTURAL HUM. RIGHTS L. REV. 41 (2014); Robert F. Cochran, Jr., *Church Freedom and Accountability in Sexual Exploitation Cases: The Possibility of Both Through Limited Strict Liability,* 21 J. CONTEMP. LEG. ISSUES 427 (2013); Paul Winters, *Whom Must the Clergy Protect? The Interests of At-Risk Children in Conflict with Clergy-Penitent Privilege,* 62 DEPAUL L. REV. 187 (2012); Christopher C. Lund, *In Defense of the Ministerial Exception,* 90 N.C. L. REV. 1 (2012); Kari Mercer Dalton, *The Priest-Penitent Privilege v. Child Abuse Reporting Statutes: How to Avoid the Conflict and Serve Society,* 18 WIDENER L. REV. 1 (2012); Samuel G. Brooks, *Confession and Mandatory Child Abuse Reporting: A New Take on the Constitutionality of Abrogating the Priest-Penitent Privilege,* 24 BYU J. PUB. L. 117 (2009); *See* Julie M. Arnold, *"Divine"*

Justice and the Lack of Secular Intervention: Abrogating the Clergy-Communicant Privilege in Mandatory Reporting Statutes to Combat Child Sexual Abuse, 42 VAL. U. L. REV. 849 (2008); Rena Durrant, *Where There's Smoke, There's Fire (and Brimstone): Is It Time to Abandon the Clergy-Penitent Privilege?*, 39 LOY. L.A. L. REV. 1339 (2006); Ashley Jackson, *The Collision of Mandatory Reporting Statutes and the Priest-Penitent Privilege*, 74 UMKC L. REV. 1057 (2006); Andrew A. Beerworth, *Treating Spiritual and Legal Counselors Differently: Mandatory Reporting Laws and the Limitations of Current Free Exercise Doctrine*, 10 ROGER WILLIAMS U. L. REV. 73 (2004); Christopher R. Pudelski, *The Constitutional Fate of Mandatory Reporting Statutes and the Clergy-Communicant Privilege in a Post-Smith World*, 98 NW. U. L. REV. 703 (2004); R. Michael Cassidy, *Sharing Sacred Secrets: Is It (Past) Time For a Dangerous Person Exception to the Clergy-Penitent Privilege?*, 44 WM. & MARY L. REV. 1627 (2003); Norman Abrams, 2003 Symposium: *The Impact of Clergy Sexual Misconduct Litigation on Religious Liberty, Addressing the Tension Between the Clergy-Communicant Privilege and the Duty to Report Child Abuse in State Statutes*, 44 B.C. L. REV. 1127 (2003); Shawn P. Bailey, *How Secrets Are kept: Viewing the Current Clergy-Penitent Privilege Through a Comparison with the Attorney-Client Privilege*, 2002 BYU L. REV. 489 (2002); J. Thomas Kirkman and Elizabeth R. Thompson, *God May Know All, But the Rest of Us Don't—Mandated Clergy Reporting of Child Abuse*, 87 MASS. L. REV. 155 (2003); Shannon M. O'Malley, *At All Costs: Mandatory Child Abuse Reporting Statutes and the Clergy-Communicant Privilege*, 21 REV. OF LITIG. 701 (2002); Lennard K. Whittaker, *The Priest-Penitent Privilege: Its Constitutionality and Doctrine*, 13 REGENT U. L. REV. 145 (2001); Raymond C. O'Brien and Michael T. Flannery, *The Pending Gauntlet to Free Exercise: Mandating That Clergy Report Child Abuse*, 25 LOY. L.A. L. REV. 1 (1991).

3. *Physician Privilege*

Marks v. Tenbrunsel

Supreme Court of Alabama, 2005
910 So. 2d 1255

LYONS, Justice....

Marks contacted Alabama Psychological Services Center, LLC, to obtain psychological treatment. Marks met with Dr. Thomas W. Tenbrunsel, a psychologist employed by Alabama Psychological Services, at its offices. According to Marks, Dr. Tenbrunsel assured him that anything Marks disclosed during their meeting would remain confidential. Marks then admitted to fondling the genitals of two females under the age of 12. Marks claims that "[a]fter consulting with a colleague, Dr. Tenbrunsel announced to Marks that he would not honor [the confidentiality agreement]." ... Marks alleges in his complaint that Dr. Lois H. Pope was the colleague with whom Dr. Tenbrunsel consulted. Marks further alleges that Dr. Tenbrunsel informed him that "a report [of the suspected child abuse] would be made to Child Protective Services at the Madison County Department of Human Resources."

Marks sued Dr. Tenbrunsel, Dr. Pope, and Alabama Psychological Services, alleging malpractice, misrepresentation of material facts, fraud, and fraudulent deceit. According to Marks, the defendants' actions caused Marks to be prosecuted for his admitted sexual misconduct. He also alleged other damage, including mental anguish, health problems, and monetary loss.... Dr. Tenbrunsel, Dr. Pope, and Alabama Psychological Services moved for a judgment of dismissal pursuant to Rule 12(b)(6), Ala. R. Civ. P., on the basis that Marks had failed to state a claim upon which relief could be granted. The trial court granted that motion, and this appeal followed....

The defendants argue that they are immune from civil liability arising from their reporting of suspected child abuse. Section 26-14-9, Ala.Code 1975, grants immunity to certain persons, firms, corporations, and officials who report child abuse to the appropriate authorities. Included in those granted immunity by that section are persons and entities that are *required*, pursuant to § 26-14-3, Ala.Code 1975, to report suspected child abuse. Section 26-14-3 states:

> "(a) All hospitals, clinics, sanitariums, doctors, physicians, surgeons, medical examiners, coroners, dentists, osteopaths, optometrists, chiropractors, podiatrists, nurses, school teachers and officials, peace officers, law enforcement officials, pharmacists, social workers, day care workers or employees, mental health professionals, members of the clergy as defined in Rule 505 of the Alabama Rules of Evidence, or any other person *called upon to render aid or medical assistance to any child*, when the child is known or suspected to be a victim of child abuse or neglect, shall be required to report, or cause a report to be made of the same, orally, either by telephone or direct communication immediately, followed by a written report, to a duly constituted authority."

(Emphasis added.) Marks argues that the defendants in this case were not "called upon to render aid or medical assistance to any child" within the meaning of § 26-14-3 and therefore are not entitled to the immunity afforded by § 26-14-9.

Section 26-14-3, however, is not the only Code section that authorizes the reporting of suspected child abuse. Section 26-14-4, Ala.Code 1975, provides: "In addition to those persons, firms, corporations, and officials *required* by Section 26-14-3 to report child abuse and neglect, any person *may* make such a report if such person has reasonable cause to suspect that a child is being abused or neglected." (Emphasis added.) In the instant case, because Marks admitted the abuse to Dr. Tenbrunsel, the defendants had reasonable cause to suspect that a child was being abused. Therefore, while Dr. Tenbrunsel and Dr. Pope were not *required* by § 26-14-3 to report the abuse, they were *permitted* to do so under § 26-14-4.

In *Hall v. Van's Photo, Inc.*, 595 So.2d 1368 (Ala.1992), a case ignored by Marks, the plaintiffs sued a photography shop after its vice president notified the FBI that the plaintiffs had the photo shop develop nude pictures of their three-year-old son. This Court held that the photo shop had reasonable cause to make the report pursuant to the permissive reporting provision of § 26-14-4. The Court also applied § 26-14-9, as that section provided at the time *Hall* was decided, and affirmed the trial court's summary judgment for the photo shop based on the immunity provided by § 26-14-9. At the time *Hall* was decided, § 26-14-9 read:

> "'Any person, firm, corporation or official participating in the making of a report or the removal of a child pursuant to this chapter, or participating in a judicial proceeding resulting therefrom, shall, in so doing, be immune from any liability, civil or criminal, that might otherwise be incurred or imposed.'"

595 So.2d at 1370. The plaintiffs in *Hall* argued that there existed a genuine issue of material fact as to whether the photo shop had promised to keep the photographs confidential. This Court rejected that argument and held that the photo shop was entitled to immunity under § 26-14-9. Therefore, even if we assume that Marks could prove a promise of confidentiality or some other similar understanding between him and Dr. Tenbrunsel, Marks would have no remedy in damages for a breach of that promise if the defendants are afforded immunity under § 26-14-9.

The Legislature amended § 26-14-9 in 1998. That section now provides:

"Any person, firm, corporation or official, including members of a multidisciplinary child protection team, quality assurance team, child death review team, or other authorized case review team or panel, by whatever designation, *participating in the making of a good faith report in an investigation or case review authorized under this chapter* [Chapter 14] or other law or department practice or in the removal of a child pursuant to this chapter, or participating in a judicial proceeding resulting therefrom, shall, in so doing, be immune from any liability, civil or criminal, that might otherwise be incurred or imposed."

(Emphasis added.) We conclude that the initial reporting of suspected child abuse to the appropriate authorities is part of the investigation contemplated by Chapter 14, Ala.Code 1975. Therefore, a person who makes such a report or causes such a report to be made is to be considered a person who "participat[es] in the making of a good faith report in an investigation or case review authorized under [Chapter 14]," and is therefore entitled to the benefit of the immunity granted by § 26-14-9, as amended. See Preamble to Act No. 98-371, Ala. Acts 1998 ("An Act, To amend Section [ ] ... 26-14-9 ... to provide immunity from liability for investigations and actions to members of multidisciplinary child protection and other case review teams *and* for good faith reporting of suspected child abuse or neglect."). Construing § 26-14-9 to limit the availability of immunity from liability to only those persons reporting suspected child abuse after an investigation has already begun would deprive persons of the incentive to make an initial report of child abuse, thereby drastically frustrating the legislative purpose in enacting Chapter 14.[1] See *Ex parte Meeks*, 682 So.2d 423, 428 (Ala.1996) ("'A construction [of a statute] resulting in absurd consequences as well as unreasonableness will be avoided.'" (quoting Norman J. Singer, *Sutherland Statutory Construction* § 45.11, p. 61 (5th ed. 1993))).

The immunity from liability provided by § 26-14-9 for reporting suspected child abuse applies only to one who makes such a report in good faith. The year before the Legislature adopted the "good faith" requirement, this Court, in *Evans v. Waddell*, 689 So.2d 23 (Ala.1997), construing the predecessor to § 26-14-9, held that defendants who had allegedly induced others to make *false reports* of child abuse were protected by absolute statutory immunity from liability for those reports. In the next session of the Legislature, § 26-14-9 was amended to add the requirement that the report of suspected child abuse be made in "good faith" as a prerequisite to immunity from liability. See Act No. 98-371, Ala. Acts 1998....

Under the permissive reporting provision of § 26-14-4, the existence of reasonable cause triggers the authority to make a report. We hold that if a person has "reasonable cause to suspect that a child is being abused or neglected," then that person acts in "good faith" within the meaning of § 26-14-9 when making a report authorized under § 26-14-4.[2] Because Marks admitted to the abuse of the two children, Dr. Pope and Dr. Tenbrunsel

---

1. Section 26-14-2, entitled "Purpose of chapter," provides as follows:
   "In order to protect children whose health and welfare may be adversely affected through abuse and neglect, the legislature hereby provides for the reporting of such cases to the appropriate authorities. It is the intent of the legislature that, as a result of such efforts, and through the cooperation of state, county, local agencies and divisions of government, protective services shall be made available in an effort to prevent further abuses and neglect, to safeguard and enforce the general welfare of such children, and to encourage cooperation among the states in dealing with the problems of child abuse."

2. The question whether a person who makes a report of suspected child abuse pursuant to § 26-14-4 without reasonable cause to suspect that a child is being abused or neglected ever acts in good faith is not now before us.

had reasonable cause to suspect that children were being abused.[3] Therefore, we conclude that Dr. Tenbrunsel and Dr. Pope were acting in good faith within the meaning of § 26-14-9 when they determined that a report should be made....

Marks relies substantially on the psychotherapist-patient privilege, which he says trumps the immunity granted by § 26-14-9. The psychotherapist-patient privilege is stated in Rule 503, Ala. R. Evid.:

> "(b) General Rule of Privilege. A patient has a privilege to refuse to disclose and to prevent any other person from disclosing confidential communications, made for the purposes of diagnosis or treatment of the patient's mental or emotional condition, including alcohol or drug addiction, among the patient, the patient's psychotherapist, and persons who are participating in the diagnosis or treatment under the direction of the psychotherapist, including members of the patient's family."

The Advisory Committee's Notes to Rule 503, Ala. R. Evid., refer to § 34-26-2, Ala.Code 1975, stating: "Alabama statutory law has long recognized a psychologist-client privilege. Ala.Code 1975, § 34-26-2." Section 34-26-2 provides that confidential communications between psychologists, psychiatrists, psychological technicians, and their clients are privileged to the same extent as communications between an attorney and his or her clients.

Section 26-14-9, the immunity provision of the child-abuse reporting statutes, was originally enacted in 1965, two years after the Legislature first codified the psychotherapist-patient privilege in § 34-26-2. Ten years after that, the Legislature enacted § 26-14-4, the permissive reporting provision. In *Blue Cross & Blue Shield of Alabama v. Hodurski*, 899 So.2d 949 (Ala.2004), we acknowledged the restatement of the doctrine of implied repeal:

> "Repeal by implication is not favored. It is only when two laws are so repugnant to or in conflict with each other that it must be presumed that the Legislature intended that the latter should repeal the former...."

> "Implied repeal is essentially a question of determining the legislative intent as expressed in the statutes. When the provisions of two statutes are directly repugnant and cannot be reconciled, it must be presumed that the legislature intended an implied repeal, and the later statute prevails as the last expression of the legislative will."

Blue Cross & Blue Shield, 899 So.2d at 959–60 (quoting *Fletcher v. Tuscaloosa Fed. Sav. & Loan Ass'n*, 294 Ala. 173, 177, 314 So.2d 51, 55 (1975), quoting in turn *State v. Bay Towing & Dredging Co.*, 265 Ala. 282, 289, 90 So.2d 743, 749 (1956)).

The last expression of legislative will is § 26-14-9, which confers immunity to persons who make good-faith reports of child abuse pursuant to Chapter 14. Section 26-14-4, which provides for permissive reporting of suspected child abuse, applies to "any person" making such a report. This latter act, § 26-14-9, impliedly repeals anything to the contrary in the earlier enacted § 34-26-2, which recognizes a psychotherapist-patient privilege. The rule that implied repeal is disfavored when the earlier act is specific and the subsequent

---

3. It is not necessary to decide in this case whether only a *confession* to child abuse supports a finding of "reasonable cause to suspect that a child is being abused or neglected" under § 26-14-4.

act is general does not apply here.[4] Chapter 14, entitled "Reporting of Child Abuse or Neglect," is not a general or broad act that cannot impliedly repeal an earlier specific act.[5]

Other jurisdictions have held that the psychotherapist-patient privilege must yield to child-abuse reporting laws. In *Fewell v. Besner*, 444 Pa.Super. 559, 568, 664 A.2d 577, 581 (1995), the Superior Court of Pennsylvania stated:

> "Thus, the psychotherapist-patient privilege and the confidentiality provisions of the [Mental Health Procedures Act] must yield to the immunity provision of the [Child Protective Services Law]. *Cf., People v. John B.*, 192 Cal.App.3d 1073, 237 Cal.Rptr. 659 (1987) (holding that psychotherapist-patient privilege is not absolute and must yield to the reporting requirements outlined in California's Child Abuse Reporting Act); *State ex rel. D.M. v. Hoester*, ... 681 S.W.2d 449 (1984) (holding that child abuse reporting statute vitiated physician-patient privilege and psychiatrist could be compelled to reveal alleged sexual abuser's medical records in a civil action for damages); *People v. Gearhart*, 148 Misc.2d 249, 560 N.Y.S.2d 247 (1990) (holding that the overriding purpose of child abuse reporting statutes is to protect children and the physician-patient privilege cannot be asserted when there is a conflict with child abuse reporting requirements)." ...

...

Dr. Tenbrunsel and Dr. Pope are immune, under to § 26-14-9, from any civil or criminal liability resulting from their good-faith report of suspicions of child abuse. Marks can prove no facts alleged in his complaint that would remove Dr. Tenbrunsel or Dr. Pope from the purview of § 26-14-9, and dismissal was therefore proper. Because Alabama Psychological Services' alleged liability is based on the liability of the individual doctors, it too was entitled to a dismissal. While Marks presents interesting policy arguments dealing with the incentive of sex offenders to seek treatment and the importance of protecting confidential communications in general, these arguments should be directed to the Legislature, not to this Court....

MOTION TO STRIKE RESPONSE GRANTED; AFFIRMED.

NABERS, C.J., and STUART, SMITH, and BOLIN, JJ., concur.

SEE, HARWOOD, and WOODALL, JJ., concur in the result in part and dissent in part.

PARKER, J., dissents.

SEE, Justice (concurring in the result in part and dissenting in part).

I concur with the main opinion insofar as it affirms the trial court's dismissal of David Marks's claims against Dr. Lois H. Pope. However, because I disagree with the main opinion's conclusion that the psychotherapist-patient privilege has been overruled implicitly by § 26-14-9, Ala.Code 1975, which provides immunity for reporters of suspected child abuse, I respectfully dissent as to the affirmance of the dismissal as to Dr. Thomas Tenbrunsel. I also note that because the psychotherapist-patient privilege provides that communications between psychotherapists and their patients are to be afforded the same

---

4. We noted in *Blue Cross & Blue Shield*, supra, that " "'the policy against implied repeals has peculiar and special force when the conflicting provisions, which are thought to work a repeal, are contained in a special or specific act and a later general or broad act." '"(quoting *Connor v. State in re Boutwell*, 275 Ala. 230, 234, 153 So.2d 787, 791 (1963), quoting in turn 50 Am. Jur Statutes § 561).

5. Justice See's dissenting opinion would eliminate the repugnancy here by introducing a judicial exception to the sweep of the later act.

level of protection as those provided by law for communications between an attorney and his or her client, this case is important not only for what it holds, but also for its precedential effect on the scope of the attorney-client privilege.[6] ...

Marks's principal argument on appeal is that the immunity provided to health-care professionals who report child abuse under § 26-14-9, Ala.Code 1975, does not preempt the psychotherapist-patient privilege. Marks argues that his communication with Dr. Tenbrunsel during Marks's treatment is confidential and that Dr. Tenbrunsel breached the psychotherapist-patient privilege when he disclosed information that Marks revealed during his treatment by reporting the suspected child abuse to the Department of Human Resources.... Section 34-26-2, Ala.Code 1975, as most recently amended effective October 1, 1997, provides:

> "For the purpose of this chapter, the confidential relations and communications between licensed psychologists, licensed psychiatrists, or licensed psychologist technicians and their clients are placed upon the same basis as those provided by law between attorney and client, and nothing in this chapter shall be construed to require any such privileged communications to be disclosed."

"The psychotherapist-patient privilege in Alabama is patterned after, and given the same level of protection as, the privilege protecting the confidentiality of lawyer-client communications." *Ex parte Etherton*, 773 So.2d 431, 435 (Ala.2000). Attorneys must " 'maintain inviolate the confidence and at every peril to themselves ... preserve the secrets of their clients.' This we take to be equated to the privilege of psychiatrists and psychologists." *Ex parte Day*, 378 So.2d 1159, 1162 (Ala.1979).

"Accordingly, like the attorney-client privilege on which it is modeled, the psychotherapist-patient privilege is personal to the patient, and only the patient may waive it." *Ex parte United Serv. Stations, Inc.*, 628 So.2d 501, 505 (Ala.1993); *Watson v. State*, 504 So.2d 339 (Ala.Crim.App.1986). "The privilege provides a patient the right to refuse to disclose, and to prevent others from disclosing, confidential communications between the patient and psychotherapist made for the purposes of diagnosis or treatment of the patient's mental condition...." 628 So.2d at 503. In order to waive the privilege, the patient must state a clear intent not to rely upon the privilege. 628 So.2d at 505.

Those who report child abuse should be immune from liability for doing so. However, it is also true that communications between a psychotherapist and his or her patient are afforded the same protection as those between an attorney and his client. § 34-26-2.[10] There are important public policies at issue in situations where the information on which the child-abuse report was based was obtained by a person acting in his or her capacity as the psychotherapist or the attorney for the person who made the disclosure. Discouraging

---

6. Section 34-26-2, Ala.Code 1975, provides:

"For the purpose of this chapter, the confidential relations and communications between licensed psychologists, licensed psychiatrists, or licensed psychological technicians and their clients are placed upon the same basis as those provided by law between attorney and client, and nothing in this chapter shall be construed to require any such privileged communication to be disclosed."

10. *See Ex parte Rudder*, 507 So.2d 411, 416 (Ala.1987). The purpose of the attorney-client privilege, upon which the psychotherapist-patient privilege is modeled, is to "encourage full and frank communication between attorneys and their clients and thereby promote broader public interests in the observance of the law and administration of justice." *Upjohn Co. v. United States*, 449 U.S. 383, 389, 101 S.Ct. 677, 66 L.Ed.2d 584 (1981)(holding that communications by corporate employees to counsel made in order to secure advice were protected); see *also Jay v. Sears Roebuck & Co.*, 340 So.2d 456 (Ala.Civ.App.1976).

patients from going to or trusting a psychotherapist will frustrate society's efforts to correct aberrant behavior. The public policy on which the psychotherapist-patient privilege is based is not easily outweighed by competing interests. *Ex parte United Serv. Stations*, 628 So.2d at 504.[11] ...

The main opinion holds that the immunity statute, § 26-14-9, Ala.Code 1975, repeals by implication the privilege statute, § 34-26-2, with respect to the disclosure of information that falls within the sweep of the immunity statute.[12] Repeal by implication is not a favored rule of statutory construction. *See Fletcher v. Tuscaloosa Fed. Sav. & Loan Ass'n*, 294 Ala. 173, 176–77, 314 So.2d 51 (1975). For the immunity statute to impliedly repeal a portion of the psychotherapist-patient privilege statute, the two laws must be so repugnant to or in conflict with one another that it must be presumed the Legislature intended that the latter repeal the former. 294 Ala. at 176, 314 So.2d at 51.

> "'Implied repeal is essentially a question of determining the legislative intent as expressed in the statutes. When the provisions of two statutes are directly repugnant and cannot be reconciled, it must be presumed that the legislature intended an implied repeal, and the later statute prevails as the last expression of legislative will.'"

294 Ala. at 177, 314 So.2d at 51 (quoting *State v. Bay Towing & Dredging Co.*, 265 Ala. 282, 289, 90 So.2d 743, 749 (1956)).

Dr. Tenbrunsel was not required by § 26-14-3, Ala.Code 1975, to report Marks's conduct. Marks does not dispute that Dr. Tenbrunsel would have been entitled to immunity if he had been required to disclose his actions under § 26-14-3. That section requires psychotherapists who are "called upon to render aid or medical assistance to any child" to report child abuse. Marks agrees that health-care professionals are granted immunity when they act pursuant to the mandate of § 26-14-3. However, while § 26-14-3 imposes a mandatory duty, § 26-14-9 — the Code section at issue in this case — also provides immunity for permissive reporting under § 26-14-4. Section 26-14-9, as most recently amended effective April 22, 1998, states:

> "Any person, firm, corporation, or official, including members of a multidisciplinary child protection team, quality assurance team, child death review team, or other authorized case review team or panel, by whatever designation, participating in the making of a good faith report in an investigation or case review authorized under this chapter or other law or department practice or in the removal of a child pursuant to this chapter, or participating in a judicial proceeding resulting therefrom, shall, in so doing, be immune from any liability, civil or criminal, that might otherwise be incurred or imposed."

The psychotherapist-patient privilege applies to statements made by a patient during the course of the patient's psychological treatment. On the other hand, the immunity statute applies to "any person, firm, corporation, or official ... participating in the making of a good faith report in an investigation or case review authorized under this chapter or

---

11. *But see Rudder*, 507 So.2d at 417 ("[The] psychiatrist-patient privilege may not in all cases be an impenetrable shield."); *see also Harbin v. Harbin*, 495 So.2d 72 (Ala.1986)(recognizing an exception to the privilege in child-custody cases where the mental state of one of the parents is at issue); *Free v. State*, 455 So.2d 137 (Ala.Crim.App.1984)(stating that the privilege is unavailable where a criminal defendant raises an insanity defense).

12. The impact of the immunity statute on the attorney-client privilege, which is the model upon which the psychotherapist-patient privilege is based, is not before us; however, the implications are obvious.

other law or department practice...." § 26-14-9, Ala.Code 1975. The privilege statute is intended to protect patients who seek psychotherapy; the immunity statute is intended to protect those persons who in good faith report child abuse during the course of "an investigation or case review authorized under this chapter or other law or department practice." These two laws are not so repugnant to or in such conflict with one another that it must be presumed that the Legislature intended the latter to repeal the former. The psychotherapist-patient privilege has a substantial field of operation notwithstanding the immunity statute. *See generally Blue Cross & Blue Shield of Alabama v. Hodurski*, 899 So.2d 949, 962 (Ala.2004)(Stuart, J., dissenting). The psychotherapist-patient privilege applies to those communications made by a patient to a psychotherapist during the course of that patient's therapy. In other situations, anyone who reports child abuse under § 26-14-4 is shielded with immunity when he or she does so. The two provisions "can be ascribed mutually exclusive fields of operation thereby avoiding any repeal by implication." *See Fletcher*, 294 Ala. at 177, 314 So.2d at 55.

I therefore respectfully dissent from that portion of the main opinion that affirms the dismissal as to Dr. Tenbrunsel....

Notes

The majority opinion in *Marks* recognized the important policies at stake in applying mandated reporting requirements—the need to encourage reporting of suspected abuse versus the need to protect privacy and disclosure within the therapeutic setting. The court in *Marks* held that the immunity provision under the reporting requirement repealed the privilege that was otherwise afforded within the therapist-patient relationship and, thus, favored immunity for reporting. However, the dissenting opinion argued that the grant of immunity for mandated reporting need not impliedly dismantle the confidentiality of the physician-patient privilege in cases of permissive reporting. *See also State ex rel. Juvenile Dept. of Multnomah County v. Spencer*, 198 Or. App. 599, 108 P.3d 1189 (2005) (legislature's exemption of psychotherapist from reporting requirements of patient's disclosure about engaging in possible child abuse is not irreconcilable with legislature's abrogation of the privilege for those same communications in a child abuse prosecution); *State v. Hyder*, 159 Wash. App. 234, 244 P.3d 454 (2011) (mandatory requirement to report child abuse rendered inapplicable the therapist-client privilege; legislature attached greater importance to prosecution of perpetrators than to counseling and treatment of persons whose emotional problems caused them to inflict such abuse); *U.S. v. Peneaux*, 432 F.3d 882 (2005) (physician's testimony regarding child's identification of abuser was relevant to treatment of the child and so could be disclosed under reporting requirement); *In re J.F.*, 109 Wash. App. 718, 37 P.3d 1227 (2001) (mandatory reporting requirements based on reasonable cause to suspect child abuse trumps the counselor-patient privilege).

The application of the physician- or therapist-patient privilege, and the abrogation of such privileges, may depend on each individual state's statutory scheme and the scope of each state's inclusion of medical physicians and therapists within the category of mandated reporters. *See, e.g.* ARK. CODE § 12-18-402 (including, among other professionals, physicians and mental health professionals); CAL. PENAL CODE § 11165.7 (including physicians, surgeons, psychiatrists, psychologists, dentists, residents, interns, podiatrists, chiropractors, licensed nurses, dental hygienists, optometrists, marriage and family therapists, or social workers); FLA. STAT. § 39.201 (physicians and other health or mental health professionals); IND. CODE ANN. § 31-33-5-2 (any staff member of a medical or other public or private institution, school, facility, or agency); MD. FAMILY LAW CODE § 5-704 (health practitioners); N.M. STAT. ANN. § 32A-4-3 (physicians, residents, interns, or social workers). The physician-patient privilege is the most common privilege to be denied. All states either affirm or abrogate the physician-patient privilege within their reporting requirements. Only Connecticut, Mississippi and New Jersey do not. For comments about a health professional's confidentiality privilege as it relates to the obligation to report child abuse, see Stephanie Conti, 2011 Special Issue: Collaborative Practice Student Note, *Lawyers and Mental Health Professionals Working Together: Reconciling the Duties of Confidentiality and Mandatory Child Abuse Reporting*, 49 FAM. CT. REV. 388 (2011); Alexis Anderson, Paul R. Tremblay and Lynn Barenberg, *Professional Ethics in Interdisciplinary Collaboratives: Zeal, Paternalism and Mandated Reporting*, 13 CLIN. L. REV. 659 (2007); Ben Matthews, Kerryann Walsh and Jennifer A. Fraser, *Mandatory Reporting by Nurses of Child Abuse and Neglect*, 13 J. L. & MED. 505 (2006); Mitch Maio, *When Two Rights Make a Wrong: How Utah's Mandatory Reporting and Rape Crisis Counselor Confidentiality Statutes Combine to Hurt Mature Minors*, 8 J.L. & FAM. STUDIES 265 (2006); Theodore R. LeBlang, *Reporting Child Abuse and Neglect: Good Faith Immunity For Health Care Providers*, 92 ILL. B.J. 356 (2004); Curt Richardson, *Physician/Hospital Liability for Negligently Reporting Child Abuse*, 23 J LEG. MED. 131 (2002).

In *Marks*, the majority and dissenting opinions both recognized the scope of the therapist privilege in relation to the attorney-client privilege. Like the therapist privilege, the attorney-client privilege is often determined by the application of state statutes. The following section discusses the attorney privilege more fully.

4. *Attorney Privilege*

Elijah W. v. Superior Court

Court of Appeal, Second District, Division 7, California, 2013
216 Cal. App. 4th 140, 156 Cal. Rptr. 3d 592

PERLUSS, P.J.

A lawyer is obligated to preserve the confidentiality of client information. (Bus. & Prof.Code, § 6068, subd. (e)(1); Rules Prof. Conduct, rule 3-100(A); see Evid.Code, §§ 954, 955.) As a narrow exception to this duty, a lawyer may, but is not required to, reveal confidential information relating to the representation of a client to the extent the lawyer reasonable believes the disclosure is necessary to prevent a criminal act likely to result in death or substantial bodily harm. (Bus. & Prof.Code, § 6068, subd. (e)(2); Rules Prof. Conduct, rule 3-100(B); see Evid.Code, § 956.5.) An expert engaged to assist the lawyer in his representation of a client is similarly obligated to maintain the confidentiality of client communications obtained in the course of accomplishing the purpose for which the lawyer was consulted. (Evid.Code, §§ 912, subd. (d), 952; see also Cal. Law Revision Com. com., 29B pt. 3A West's Ann. Evid.Code (2009 ed.) foll. § 952, p. 307.)

Under the Child Abuse and Neglect Reporting Act (CANRA) (Pen.Code, § 11164 et seq.) psychiatrists, psychologists, clinical social workers and other mental health professionals are "mandated reporters" (Pen.Code, § 11165.7, subd. (a)(21)) and, as such, have an affirmative duty to report suspected child abuse or neglect to a child protective agency or other appropriate authority. (Pen.Code, § 11165.9.) Failure to report suspected abuse is a misdemeanor. (Pen.Code, § 11166, subd. (c).) The duty to report is not excused or barred by the psychotherapist-patient privilege of Evidence Code section 1014. (Pen.Code, § 11171.2, subd. (b); *People v. Stritzinger* (1983) 34 Cal.3d 505, 512, 194 Cal.Rptr. 431, 668 P.2d 738; see Evid.Code, § 1027.) Lawyers, however, are not mandated reporters.

Faced with these two divergent legislative schemes, what is the obligation of a psychologist retained or appointed as an expert to assist a lawyer representing a juvenile accused of committing a crime who learns the client is either the perpetrator or has been the victim of child abuse? Must the therapist comply with the affirmative duty to report imposed by CANRA? Or does the obligation of the lawyer and the lawyer's team to maintain the confidentiality of client information, together with the lawyer-client privilege, prevail over the mandated reporter law? Do those obligations also trump a psychotherapist's duty under *Tarasoff v. Regents of California* (1976) 17 Cal.3d 425, 131 Cal.Rptr. 14, 551 P.2d 334 (*Tarasoff*) to protect reasonably identifiable victims from a patient's threatened violent behavior?

These vexing questions, without a clear answer under California law, were raised in the juvenile court proceedings now before us. To assist in the preparation of his defense to a wardship petition, Elijah W. sought the appointment of Dr. Catherine Scarf, a psychologist who had indicated she would respect the lawyer-client privilege and defense counsel's duty of confidentiality and would not report client information concerning child abuse/neglect or a so-called *Tarasoff* threat to authorities. The juvenile court denied the motion, ruling Elijah's defense team was limited to members of the court's juvenile competency to stand trial (JCST) panel, notwithstanding that panel members had informed Elijah's counsel they would report to authorities any information of child abuse/neglect or *Tarasoff* threats.... The court erred in limiting Elijah's choice of expert assistance in this manner. In the absence of clear legislative guidance, we decline to read into CANRA a reporting requirement that contravenes established law on confidentiality and privilege governing defense experts and potentially jeopardizes a criminal defendant's right to a fair trial. Accordingly, we grant his petition for a writ of mandate and direct the court to vacate its order denying the motion to appoint Dr. Scarf as a defense expert and to issue a new order granting the motion....

On December 28, 2011 the People filed a two count wardship petition under Welfare and Institutions Code section 602 alleging Elijah, then 10 years old and in the fourth grade, had committed arson (Pen.Code, §§ 451, subd. (c) [willfully setting fire to a structure], 452, subd. (c) [recklessly burning a structure]). A deputy public defender was appointed to represent Elijah.... On March 6, 2012 Elijah, through counsel, moved pursuant to Evidence Code sections 730 and 952 for the appointment of Dr. Scarf as an expert "to assist counsel in conducting reasonably necessary psychological evaluations, assessments and other activities related to the presentation of the case." In particular, Elijah's counsel stated, "Given his age and our minimal communication, I have serious concerns regarding whether he can fully understand these proceedings and cooperate rationally with counsel. Counsel is aware of the high rate of developmental immaturity with younger juveniles in court and it would be ineffective assistance of counsel if counsel did not appoint an expert to evaluate how Elijah['s] age impacts his ability to comprehend the proceedings and participate in his defense."

Elijah explained the selection of Dr. Scarf, who was on the Los Angeles Superior Court's approved panel of psychiatrists and psychologists but not the JCST panel, was based on her assurance she would report any information concerning child abuse and/or neglect or *Tarasoff* threats obtained during her assessment of Elijah only to Elijah's counsel. "Dr. Scarf indicated that it is her position that her duty as a mandated reporter is satisfied by reporting this information to the attorney given her appointment as a forensic expert appointed under the attorney-client privilege. Further, Dr. Scarf stated that the [American Psychological Association] guidelines are consistent with her position." In contrast, the members of the JCST panel, when interviewed by an attorney in the public defender's office, said they would report to law enforcement or child welfare authorities any information regarding child abuse and/or neglect or *Tarasoff* threats despite the fact they were appointed to assist Elijah's counsel and their work would otherwise be protected from disclosure by the lawyer-client privilege. Elijah argued appointment of a defense expert who would not protect the confidentiality of lawyer-client privileged information violated his constitutional right to the effective assistance of counsel....

Welfare and Institutions Code section 709, subdivision (a), provides, "During the pendency of any juvenile proceeding, the minor's counsel or the court may express a doubt as to the minor's competency.... If the court finds substantial evidence raises a doubt as to the minor's competency, the proceedings shall be suspended." Section 709, subdivision (b), in turn, provides, "Upon suspension of proceedings, the court shall order that the question of the minor's competence be determined at a hearing. The court shall appoint an expert to evaluate whether the minor suffers from a mental disorder, developmental disability, developmental immaturity, or other condition and, if so, whether the condition or conditions impair the minor's competency. The expert shall have expertise in child and adolescent development, and training in the forensic evaluation of juveniles, and shall be familiar with competency standards and accepted criteria used in evaluating competence...."

To implement Welfare and Institutions Code section 709, which was enacted in 2010, the Los Angeles Superior Court has adopted a protocol setting forth basic procedures to be followed and establishing a panel of qualified psychiatrists and psychologists to conduct all juvenile competency assessments: "If the court suspends proceedings, or grants minor's request for a CST [(competency to stand trial)] evaluation, it shall appoint an expert from the Juvenile Competency to Stand Trial Panel (JCST Panel) under Evidence Code § 730 to perform a CST evaluation. The JCST Panel shall consist of experts in child and adolescent development, who have training in the forensic evaluation of juveniles, and are familiar with the competency standards and accepted criteria used in evaluating competence.... The Juvenile Court shall maintain a list of approved JCST Panel evaluators and appointments will be made from that list on a rotating basis." (Amended Competency To Stand Trial Protocol, dated January 9, 2012 (Protocol).)[1] ... The Protocol allows for a minor's defense counsel to obtain an assessment and not disclose it unless a doubt is declared as to the minor's competency. In addition, the Protocol provides no statements, admissions or confessions made by, or incriminating information obtained from, a minor in the course of a JCST evaluation shall be admitted into evidence or used against the minor in any juvenile, criminal or civil proceedings....

The juvenile court denied Elijah's motion.[2] In its statement of decision the court initially dismissed Elijah's confidentiality concern as "merely academic," explaining, "In the hundreds of [Evidence Code section] 730 appointments that this court has granted, and in the thousands that have been granted by the juvenile and adult courts, this issue has never been raised. Nor, has there ever been a case brought to the court's attention where a minor has divulged child abuse or made a threat to commit a crime during a competency evaluation and the statement was later introduced in court or even prompted a report. The likelihood of this occurrence is remote because the focus of a competency evaluation is the functional ability of a minor to understand the court process."

Substantively, the court rejected Elijah's argument that any psychiatrist or psychologist appointed to assist in his defense could properly refuse to disclose to a child protection

---

1. The Protocol is in the form of a seven-page memorandum from Michael Nash, Presiding Judge of the Los Angeles Juvenile Court, to all juvenile delinquency court judicial officers and all interested parties, entities and agencies. It covers a variety of topics relating to the proper treatment of competency issues in juvenile court in addition to the procedures for a competency-to-stand-trial evaluation.

2. Apparently because Elijah's motion was expressly limited to the appointment of Dr. Scarf, the motion for appointment of an expert was denied. The court did not appoint a member of the JCST panel to conduct an evaluation of Elijah under the Protocol.

agency or other appropriate authority information concerning suspected child abuse or neglect: "[T]he notion that the mandated reporting duty would be satisfied by reporting potential abuse only to the minor's attorney would frustrate the purpose of the mandated reporting law for the simple reason that the minor's attorney is not a mandated reporter."[3] The court explained the Protocol makes competency-to-stand-trial determinations in juvenile court more efficient and concluded limiting the appointment of an expert to members of the JCST panel does not impermissibly interfere with the lawyer-client privilege or impair the right to effective assistance of counsel.[4]

The precise purpose for which Elijah's counsel sought appointment of Dr. Scarf is unclear. On the one hand, the motion clearly requested an expert generally to assist in the presentation of the defense case by conducting reasonably necessary psychological evaluations and assessments. On the other hand, counsel specifically expressed concern about Elijah's ability to comprehend the proceedings and participate in his defense — that is, his competency. To the extent Elijah was not requesting a competency-to-stand-trial evaluation, the Protocol would not be implicated. Given the potential significance of that threshold issue, it would have been better practice for his lawyer to have more clearly expressed her reasons for requesting the appointment and for the court, in the absence of such clarification, to have inquired....

Several interrelated doctrines ensure that a defendant in a criminal case or a minor subject to a juvenile wardship petition has the right not only to counsel but also to necessary ancillary defense services and that communications with both counsel and any experts engaged to assist counsel will remain protected from disclosure.[5] First, " '[t]he right to counsel guaranteed by both the federal and state Constitutions includes, and indeed presumes, the right to effective counsel [citations], and thus also includes the right to reasonably necessary defense services.' " (*People v. Blair* (2005) 36 Cal.4th 686, 732, 31 Cal.Rptr.3d 485, 115 P.3d 1145, quoting *Corenevsky v. Superior Court* (1984) 36 Cal.3d 307, 319–320, 204 Cal.Rptr. 165, 682 P.2d 360; see *Torres v. Municipal Court* (1975) 50 Cal.App.3d 778, 785, 123 Cal.Rptr. 553 ["there can be no question that equal protection demands that in a proper factual situation a court must appoint an expert that is needed to assist an indigent defendant in his defense"].)

Second, with certain limited exceptions the Evidence Code provides a client has a privilege to refuse to disclose, and to prevent another from disclosing, a confidential communication the client has had with his or her lawyer if the privilege is claimed by someone statutorily authorized to do so. (Evid.Code, § 954.) In addition to this statutory privilege, an attorney owes to his or her client an ethical duty of confidentiality as outlined in Business and Professions section 6068, subdivision (e)(1): "It is the duty of an attorney to do all of the following: ... To maintain inviolate the confidence, and at every peril to himself or herself to preserve the secrets of his or her client." ... [footnote omitted]. (See also Rules Prof.

---

3. The court also noted Evidence Code section 956.5 permits attorneys to disclose otherwise confidential information when it may prevent a criminal act that is likely to result in the death of, or substantial bodily harm to, an individual.

4. By its terms, Welfare and Institutions Code section 709 applies only after a court has suspended proceedings following an expression of doubt as to a minor's competency by the court or the minor's counsel. The Protocol is broader, applying whenever minor's counsel requests a competency-to-stand-trial evaluation; as discussed, in that circumstance counsel may choose not to disclose the evaluation unless a doubt is thereafter expressed.

5. A minor's right to due process in juvenile delinquency proceeds [sic] includes the right to the effective assistance of counsel. (*In re Gault* (1967) 387 U.S. 1, 36–37, 87 S.Ct. 1428, 18 L.Ed.2d 527; *Kent v. United States* (1966) 383 U.S. 541, 554, 86 S.Ct. 1045, 16 L.Ed.2d 84; *In re Harris* (1967) 67 Cal.2d 876, 878–879, 64 Cal.Rptr. 319, 434 P.2d 615.)

Conduct, rule 3–100(A) [a member shall not reveal confidential information relating to the representation without the informed consent of the client].) This duty of confidentiality is broader than the lawyer-client privilege and protects virtually everything the lawyer knows about the client's matter regardless of the source of the information. (See *Dietz v. Meisenheimer & Herron* (2009) 177 Cal.App.4th 771, 787, 99 Cal.Rptr.3d 464; *Goldstein v. Lees* (1975) 46 Cal.App.3d 614, 621, fn. 5, 120 Cal.Rptr. 253; see generally Rest.3d Law Governing Lawyers, § 59, p. 455 ["[c]onfidential client information consists of information relating to representation of a client, other than information that is generally known"]; ABA Model Code Prof. Responsibility, rule 1.6(a) [lawyer is obligated to keep client information confidential].)

Taken together, these fundamental principles mandate that defense counsel's right to appointment of necessary experts, including medical or mental health experts, also includes the right to have communications made to the experts remain confidential to the same extent as communications directly between client and lawyer: "'[W]hen communication by a client to his attorney regarding his physical or mental condition requires the assistance of a physician to interpret the client's condition to the attorney, the client may submit to an examination by the physician without fear that the latter will be compelled to reveal the information disclosed.'" (*People v. Lines* (1975) 13 Cal.3d 500, 510, 119 Cal.Rptr. 225, 531 P.2d 793; accord, *People v. Roldan* (2005) 35 Cal.4th 646, 724, 27 Cal.Rptr.3d 360, 110 P.3d 289, disapproved on another ground in *People v. Doolin* (2009) 45 Cal.4th 390, 421, fn. 22, 87 Cal.Rptr.3d 209, 198 P.3d 11 ["'The attorney-client privilege is "a privilege to refuse to disclose, and to prevent another from disclosing, a confidential communication between client and lawyer." ... That privilege encompasses confidential communications between a client and experts retained by the defense.'"]; *Torres v. Municipal Court, supra*, 50 Cal.App.3d at p. 784, 123 Cal.Rptr. 553.)

This principle is codified in Evidence Code section 952, which defines confidential communications between client and lawyer and expressly provides confidentiality is not destroyed by disclosure of those communications to third persons "to whom disclosure is reasonably necessary for ... the accomplishment of the purpose for which the lawyer is consulted...." The 1965 Law Revision Commission comments to this section explain, "[C]onfidential communications also include those made to third parties—such as the lawyer's secretary, a physician, or similar expert—for the purpose of transmitting such information to the lawyer because they are 'reasonably necessary for the transmission of the information.'"[7] ... The Commission added, "A lawyer at times may desire to have a client reveal information to an expert consultant in order that the lawyer may adequately advise his client. The inclusion of the words 'for the accomplishment of the purpose for which the lawyer is consulted' assures that these communications, too, are within the scope of the privilege." ...

Communications between a psychotherapist and a patient are generally confidential. (Evid.Code, § 1014.) ... [footnote omitted]. Specifically, when a psychotherapist is appointed by the court in a criminal proceeding at the request of defense counsel "in order to provide the lawyer with information needed so that he or she may advise the defendant whether to enter or withdraw a plea based on insanity or to present a defense based on his or her mental or emotional condition," the psychotherapist-patient privilege applies to communications between the defendant and the court-appointed psychotherapist. (Evid.Code, § 1017, subd. (a); see Cal. Law Revision Com. com., 29B pt. 3A West's Ann.

---

7. "While not binding, the Commission's official comments reflect the intent of the Legislature in enacting the Evidence Code and are entitled to substantial weight in construing it." (*HLC Properties, Ltd. v. Superior Court* (2005) 35 Cal.4th 54, 62, 24 Cal.Rptr.3d 199, 105 P.3d 560.)

Evid.Code (2009 ed.) foll. § 1017, p. 34 ["it is essential that the privilege apply where the psychotherapist is appointed by order of the court to provide the defendant's lawyer with the information needed ... to present a defense ..."].) There is no privilege, however, if the psychotherapist is appointed by the court to examine the patient for any other purpose than to assist the defense. (Evid.Code, § 1017, subd. (a).)

As discussed, when a psychotherapist is appointed pursuant to Evidence Code section 730 to assist defense counsel, he or she is obligated to maintain the confidentiality of the client's communications not only by the psychotherapist-patient privilege but also by the lawyer-client privilege. (*People v. Roldan, supra*, 35 Cal.4th at p. 724, 27 Cal.Rptr.3d 360, 110 P.3d 289; *People v. Lines, supra*, 13 Cal.3d at p. 510, 119 Cal.Rptr. 225, 531 P.2d 793.) Moreover as expressly noted by the Law Revision Commission in its comments, "[T]he attorney-client privilege may provide protection in some cases where an exception to the psychotherapist-patient privilege is applicable." (Cal. Law Revision Com. com., 29B pt. 3A West's Ann. Evid.Code (2009 ed.) foll. § 1017, p. 34.) ...

For nearly 50 years California has used mandatory reporting obligations to identify and protect child abuse victims. Under the predecessor to CANRA, former Penal Code section 11161.5, only physicians, surgeons and dentists were required to report instances of known or suspected child abuse to law enforcement officials; and only physical abuse had to be reported. (Stats. 965, ch. 1171, § 2, p. 2971.) Over time both the definition of "mandated reporter" and the type of abuse that must be reported have expanded to implement the belief that "reporting suspected child abuse is fundamental to protecting children." (*Stecks v. Young* (1995) 38 Cal.App.4th 365, 371, 45 Cal.Rptr.2d 475.)

Today, all doctors, psychiatrist, psychologist, clinical social workers and other mental health professionals are included in the nearly four dozen separate categories of mandated reporters identified in CANRA. (Pen.Code, § 11165.7, subd. (a)(1)–(44).)[9] Reports must be made of physical abuse (defined as the infliction of physical injury by other than accidental means); sexual abuse (including both sexual assault and sexual exploitation); neglect either general or severe); willful cruelty or unjustifiable punishment; and unlawful corporal punishment or injury. (Pen.Code, §§ 11165.1, 11165.2, 11165.3, 11165.4 & 11165.5.) The duty to report is triggered when, based on knowledge or observation, the mandated reporter knows or reasonably suspects child abuse or neglect. (See Pen.Code, § 11166, subd. (a).)

The mandated reporter must immediately or as soon as practicably possible make a telephone report of known or suspected child abuse or neglect to any police or sheriff's department, county probation department (if designated by the county to receive such reports) or county welfare department (Pen.Code, §§ 11165.9, 11166, subd. (a)) and follow up with a written report within 36 hours. (Pen.Code, § 11166, subd. (a).) A report by a mandated reporter is confidential, and a mandated reporter is immune from both criminal and civil liability for any report required or authorized by CANRA. (Pen.Code, §§ 11167, subd. (d), 11167.5, 11172, subd. (a).)[10] If a mandated reporter fails to make a report, he or she is subject to misdemeanor penalties. (Pen.Code, § 11166, subd. (c).)

---

9. Penal Code section 11165.7, subdivision (a)(21), provides a "mandated reporter" includes "[a] physician and surgeon, psychiatrist, psychologist, dentist, resident, intern, podiatrist, chiropractor, licensed nurse, dental hygienist, optometrist, marriage and family therapist, clinical social worker, professional clinical counselor, or any other person who is currently licensed under Division 2 (commencing with Section 500) of the Business and Professions Code," which governs "healing arts."

10. Discretionary reporters have only limited immunity: A discretionary reporter is immune from liability unless it can be proved he or she knowingly made a false report or made a false report with reckless disregard for its truth or falsity. (Pen.Code, § 11172, subd. (a).)

CANRA expressly excepts information regarding suspected child abuse or neglect from the psychotherapist-patient privilege: "Neither the physician-patient privilege nor the psychotherapist-patient privilege applies to information reported pursuant to this article in any court proceeding or administrative hearing." (Pen.Code, § 11171.2, subd. (b).) ... Unlike physicians, psychologists and other mental health providers, attorneys are not mandated reporters under CANRA.[11] And there is no provision similar to Penal Code section 11171.2, subdivision (b), that abrogates the lawyer-client privilege for information regarding suspected child abuse or neglect....

The final strand in this intricate tapestry is the psychotherapists' duty to protect potential victims of their dangerous patients recognized in *Tarasoff, supra,* 17 Cal.3d 425, 131 Cal.Rptr. 14, 551 P.2d 334. In *Tarasoff* a patient had confided to his psychotherapist his intent to kill an unnamed but readily identifiable young woman upon her return from South America. The therapist notified police and requested the patient's involuntary commitment for observation in a mental hospital. The police released the patient after they were satisfied he appeared rational and promised to stay away from the woman. The patient killed the woman. Her parents sued the therapist for wrongful death for failure to warn them or their daughter about the danger his patient presented. (*Id.* at pp. 432–433, 131 Cal.Rptr. 14, 551 P.2d 334.) The Supreme Court recognized the general common law rule that there is no duty to protect others from the criminal conduct of third parties, but explained an exception to this rule exists in cases in which the defendant stands in some special relationship to either the person whose conduct needs to be controlled or the foreseeable victim of that conduct. (*Id.* at p. 435, 131 Cal.Rptr. 14, 551 P.2d 334.) The Court rejected the therapist's contention he owed no duty to the victim because she was not his patient and held, "once a therapist does in fact determine, or under applicable professional standards reasonably should have determined, that a patient poses a serious danger of violence to others, he bears a duty to exercise reasonable care to protect the foreseeable victim of that danger." (*Id.* at pp. 431, 439, 131 Cal.Rptr. 14, 551 P.2d 334.)[12]

Acknowledging the public importance of safeguarding the confidential character of psychotherapeutic communications, the Court explained the Legislature had already balanced the importance of effective treatment of mental illness and protecting the privacy rights of patients, on the one hand, and the public interest in safety from violent assault, on the other hand, in Evidence Code section 1024, which creates a specific and limited exception to the psychotherapist-patient privilege: "There is no privilege ... if the psychotherapist has reasonable cause to believe that the patient is in such mental or emotional condition as to be dangerous to himself or to the person or property of another and that disclosure of the communication is necessary to prevent the threatened danger." "We conclude that the public policy favoring protection of the confidential character of patient-

---

11. In contrast to California, several states have expressly included attorneys as mandated child abuse reporters. (See, e.g., Nev.Rev.Stat.Ann.(2012) § 432B.220, subd. (4)(i) [report must be made by "[a]n attorney, unless the attorney has acquired the knowledge of the abuse or neglect from a client who is or may be accused of the abuse or neglect"]; Ohio Rev.Code Ann. § 2151.421, subd. (A)(1)–(3) (2013) [although an attorney is not required to make a report based on information received in a privileged communication with a client, the client is deemed to have waived the privilege if he or she is under 18 years old and the attorney has reasonable cause to believe the client has suffered or faces a threat of suffering child abuse or neglect]; see generally Mosteller, *Child Abuse Reporting Laws and Attorney-Client Confidences: The Reality and the Specter of Lawyer as Informant* (1992) 42 Duke L.J. 203.)

12. Civil Code section 43.92 later limited a therapist's liability for failing to protect from a patient's threatened violent behavior to situations in which "the patient has communicated to the psychotherapist a serious threat of physical violence against a reasonable identifiable victim or victims."

psychotherapist communications must yield to the extent to which disclosure is essential to avert danger to others." (*Tarasoff, supra,* 17 Cal.3d at pp. 440–442, 131 Cal.Rptr. 14, 551 P.2d 334.)

Nonetheless, the *Tarasoff* Court emphasized a psychotherapist's determination a patient poses a serious danger of violence to others does not automatically translate into an obligation to notify either the potential victim or law enforcement authorities. Rather, the psychotherapist's duty is to exercise due care: "[I]n each instance the adequacy of the therapist's conduct must be measured against the traditional negligence standard of the rendition of reasonable care under the circumstances." (*Tarasoff, supra,* 17 Cal.3d at p. 439, 131 Cal.Rptr. 14, 551 P.2d 334; see also *id.* at p. 431, 131 Cal.Rptr. 14, 551 P.2d 334 ["[t]he discharge of this duty may require the therapist to take one or more of various steps, depending on the nature of the case"].) ...

As the foregoing summary demonstrates, if reasonably necessary to assist his counsel in preparing and presenting a defense to the wardship petition, Elijah has a constitutional right to the appointment of a qualified expert, including a psychotherapist, to be part of his defense team and a corollary right to speak in confidence to that expert—a right that is further protected by both his counsel's duty to preserve the confidentiality of client information and the lawyer-client privilege as broadly defined in the Evidence Code. To a very limited extent the Legislature appears to have recognized this principle in Penal Code section 1165.7, subdivision (a)(18), which defines "mandated reporter" to include district attorney investigators and local child support agency caseworkers but relieves them of any reporting obligations when assisting an attorney appointed to represent a minor in dependency proceedings. Yet nothing else in CANRA or its legislative history[13] suggests the Legislature considered, let alone attempted to reconcile, the inconsistent obligations confronting a psychologist or psychiatrist appointed to assist defense counsel in a criminal proceeding: CANRA mandates reports of child abuse or neglect from these mental health professions and expressly waives the psychotherapist-patient privilege, yet omits attorneys from the ranks of mandated reporters and leaves intact the lawyer-client privilege, which extends to psychotherapists when acting as forensic consultants for the defense team.[14] ...

To interpret CANRA to apply to a psychotherapist assisting defense counsel runs afoul of both these principles. The mandatory disclosure of client confidences by a member of the defense to report suspected child abuse or neglect has, at the very least, serious implications for a criminal defendant's constitutional right to the effective assistance of counsel. (See *People v. Roldan, supra,* 35 Cal.4th at p. 724, 27 Cal.Rptr.3d 360, 110 P.3d 289; *Torres v. Municipal Court, supra,* 50 Cal.App.3d at p. 784, 123 Cal.Rptr. 553.) We need not, and do not, decide whether such mandatory reporting, if coupled with

---

13. The parties presented no arguments based on the legislative history of CANRA. Our own review of the former version of Penal Code section 11165 et seq. adopted in 1980 (Stats. 1980, ch. 1071, pp. 3421–3422), the 1987 legislation enacting the current version (Stats. 1987, ch. 1459, p. 5517), and subsequent amendments did not find any discussion of the impact of mandatory reporting on the role of an expert assisting defense counsel in a criminal case.

14. Psychotherapists themselves are divided on the issue, as this case demonstrates. Dr. Scarf believes her responsibilities as a member of the defense team to maintain a client's confidences trumps the statutory reporting duty. The mental health professionals on the JCST panel do not. The professional literature on the topic reveals this split is widespread. (See, e.g., Dixon et al., *Attorney-Client Privilege versus Mandatory Reporting by Psychologists: Dilemma, Conflict, and Solution* (2006) 6 J. Forensic Psych. Practice 69; Connell et al., *Expert Opinion: Does Mandatory Reporting Trump Attorney-Client Opinion?* (2004) 24 Amer. Psych.-Law Soc. News 10; Note, *Lawyers and Mental Health Professionals Working Together: Reconciling the Duties of Confidentiality and Mandatory Child Abuse Reporting* (2011) 39 Fam. Ct. Rev. 388.)

appropriate procedural safeguards, could survive constitutional challenge. Rather, it is our task, if possible, to construe CANRA to avoid this issue. In addition, reporting information obtained from the client while assisting defense counsel plainly violates the lawyer-client privilege as now defined; there is no express statutory exception permitting such a breach of client confidences in CANRA or the Evidence Code. Without clearer legislative direction, we decline to read into CANRA's silence on these points a reporting requirement that contravenes the established law of confidentiality and privilege governing defense experts and potentially jeopardizes a criminal defendant's right to a fair trial.

We reach essentially the same conclusion with respect to the potential disclosure of *Tarasoff* threats. First, it is by no means clear a psychologist engaged to assist counsel as part of a defense team, rather than performing professional services with his or her patient in a therapeutic setting, has a duty to report a threat of serious danger to a known victim. As discussed, the *Tarasoff* Court emphasized the duty it recognized was an exception to the fundamental rule precluding liability for failing to protect others from the criminal conduct of third parties and was predicated on the "special relation that arises between a patient and his doctor or psychotherapist." (*Tarasoff, supra,* 17 Cal.3d at pp. 434, 436, 131 Cal.Rptr. 14, 551 P.2d 334.) The Court employed the seven-factor balancing test it had articulated in *Rowland v. Christian* (1968) 69 Cal.2d 108, 113, 70 Cal.Rptr. 97, 443 P.2d 561, to determine, as a matter of public policy, it was appropriate to extend the protection of negligence law to the victim and her family under the circumstances presented (see *Tarasoff,* at p. 434, 131 Cal.Rptr. 14, 551 P.2d 334), specifically noting that one of the defendant doctors had treated the patient, a second had supervised that treatment and the other two were involved in his examination and commitment. (*Id.* at p. 436, fn. 6, 131 Cal.Rptr. 14, 551 P.2d 334.) The relationship of a forensic psychologist engaged by counsel to the defendant-client is necessarily different from that of the treating psychologists considered in *Tarasoff.* Whether balancing the *Rowland* factors—particularly those relating to the "moral blame" of the expert and the consequences to the community of imposing liability (that is, its chill on lawyer-expert-client communications)—would result in recognizing a duty in this situation is an unresolved question.

Second, even if the defense-expert psychotherapist does have a duty in these circumstances, the discharge of that duty does not necessarily require disclosure of otherwise confidential communications. Rather, under *Tarasoff* the psychotherapist is obligated to use reasonable care under the circumstances. (*Tarasoff, supra,* 17 Cal.3d at pp. 431, 439, 131 Cal.Rptr. 14, 551 P.2d 334.) Dr. Scarf's declaration in support of Elijah's motion indicates, at least inferentially, she believes notifying the deputy public defender representing Elijah would constitute due care, satisfying any obligation she may have to an identifiable potential victim of a *Tarasoff* threat. Such notification would, in turn, trigger the attorney's responsibilities under Business and Professions Code section 6068, subdivision (e)(2), and rule 3-100(C) of the Rules of Professional Conduct to consider whether to reveal confidential information because she believes it necessary to prevent a criminal act likely to result in the death of, or great bodily harm to, an individual.[15]

---

15. Business and Professions Code section 6068, subdivision (e)(2), effective July 1, 2004 (Stats.2003, ch. 765, §§ 1, 4, pp. 5746, 5749), provides, notwithstanding the duty set forth in subdivision (e)(1) to maintain inviolate the confidences of a client, "an attorney may, but is not required to, reveal confidential information relating to the representation of a client to the extent that the attorney reasonably believes the disclosure is necessary to prevent a criminal act that the attorney reasonably believes is likely to result in death of, or substantial bodily harm to, an individual."

In adopting this narrow exception to the duty of confidentiality and making a parallel amendment to Evidence Code section 956.5 creating an exception to the evidentiary privilege, the Legislature

That may indeed be sufficient. What constitutes negligence (or a breach of the duty of due care) in this context, as in most other cases of alleged negligence, depends on all the circumstances of an individual case. (See *Tarasoff, supra*, 17 Cal.3d at p. 439, 131 Cal.Rptr. 14, 551 P.2d 334; see generally *Cabral v. Ralphs Grocery Co.* (2011) 51 Cal.4th 764, 777, 122 Cal.Rptr.3d 313, 248 P.3d 1170 ["[t]he reasonable care required by negligence law depends on all the circumstances"].) We cannot evaluate in advance whether Dr. Scarf's intended notification of Elijah's attorney will insulate her from liability in any particular situation, assuming she owes a *Tarasoff*-type duty to a potential victim in the first place. But her position is certainly reasonable, and her willingness to safeguard the confidentiality of Elijah's communications at the risk of personal liability should not have been discounted by the juvenile court.

In sum, until the Legislature instructs differently, communications from Elijah to a psychotherapist appointed to assist in his defense should remain confidential: He was entitled to the assistance of an expert who would respect the lawyer-client privilege and defense counsel's duty of confidentiality and would not report client information concerning child abuse/neglect or a so-called *Tarasoff* threat to authorities. Because the members of the JCST panel would not agree to this fundamental principle, it was an abuse of discretion to deny Elijah's motion to appoint non-panel member Dr. Scarf....

The petition is granted. Let a peremptory writ of mandate issue directing respondent juvenile court to vacate its order of March 6, 2012 denying Elijah's motion for the appointment of Dr. Scarf and to enter a new order granting the motion.

We concur:

WOODS, J.

ZELON, J.

Notes

Approximately twelve states include attorneys or other legal professionals as mandated reporters of child abuse. *See* Ark. Code § 12-18-402 (including judges, law enforcement officials, peace officers, and prosecuting attorneys); Cal. Penal Code § 11165.7 (District Attorney investigators and inspectors); Fla. Stat. § 39.201 (law enforcement officers or judges); Me. Comp. Laws § 722.623 (persons employed in a professional capacity in any office of the friend of the court); Miss. Code § 43-21-353 (attorneys or law enforcement officers); Nev. Rev. Stat. § 432B.220 (attorneys, with exceptions provided); N.M. Stat. § 32A-4-3 (law enforcement officers or judges); N.Y. Soc. Serv. Law § 413 (peace officers, police officers, district attorneys or assistant district attorneys, investigators employed in the office of a district attorney, or other law enforcement officials); Ohio Rev. Code § 2151.421 (attorneys); Ore. Rev. Stat. §§ 419B.005 & 419B.010 (attorneys or court-appointed special advocates); S.C. Code § 63-7-310 (judges); Tenn. Code §§ 37-1-403 &

directed the creation of an advisory task force to study and make recommendations for a rule of professional conduct to implement this provision. (Stats. 2003, ch. 765, § 3, p. 5748.) As a result, effective July 1, 2004, rule 3-100(C) of the Rules of Professional Conduct provides, "Before revealing confidential information to prevent a criminal act as provided in [Business and Professions Code section 6068, subdivision (e)(2), and rule 3-100(B) of the Rules of Professional Conduct], a member shall, if reasonable under the circumstances: [¶] (1) make a good faith effort to persuade the client: (i) not to commit or to continue the criminal act or (ii) to pursue a course of conduct that will prevent the threatened death or substantial bodily harm; or do both (i) and (ii); and [¶] (2) inform the client, at an appropriate time, of the member's ability or decision to reveal information as provided in paragraph (B)."

-605 (judges or law enforcement officers). Nevertheless, the attorney-client privilege is the most commonly affirmed privilege. Rule 1.6(b) of the American Bar Association Model Rules of Professional Conduct provides that "A lawyer may reveal information relating to the representation of a client to the extent the lawyer reasonably believes necessary: (1) to prevent reasonably certain death or substantial bodily harm; [or] (6) to comply with other law or a court order...." The Rule *is permissive*, but many states have modified the Rule to make disclosure mandatory, and many state ethics panels have allowed a lawyer's disclosure of child abuse. *See, e.g.*, Indianapolis Bar Ass'n Legal Ethics Comm., Op. 1-1986 (1986).

B. Due Process

Roe v. Planned Parenthood Southwest Ohio Region

Supreme Court of Ohio, 2009
122 Ohio St. 3d 399, 912 N.E.2d 61

LUNDBERG STRATTON, J....

The Roes filed this action against Planned Parenthood Southwest Ohio Region and others (collectively, "Planned Parenthood") alleging that Planned Parenthood illegally performed an abortion on their 14-year-old daughter, Jane. The Roes alleged that Planned Parenthood failed to notify them or to secure their consent in advance of the procedure and failed to obtain Jane's informed consent to the procedure in violation of R.C. 2919.121, 2919.12, and 2317.56. The Roes also alleged that Planned Parenthood breached its duty to report suspected child abuse of Jane in violation of former R.C. 2151.421. The plaintiffs sought compensatory and punitive damages and injunctive relief.

In the fall of 2003, when Jane was 13 and in the eighth grade, she began a sexual relationship with her 21-year-old soccer coach, John Haller. In March 2004, Jane discovered that she was pregnant and told Haller. Haller convinced Jane to have an abortion. He called Planned Parenthood and attempted to schedule an abortion for her. Planned Parenthood told Haller that he could not schedule the procedure and that Jane would have to make the appointment. After this conversation, Haller told Jane to schedule it, and he also instructed her that if asked to provide a parent's telephone number, she should give Planned Parenthood his cell phone number in lieu of her father's phone number.... Jane called Planned Parenthood and told an employee that she was 14 years old and that her parents could not accompany her. She asked whether her "stepbrother" could come with her. The employee asked whether Jane's parents knew about her pregnancy. Jane lied and told the employee that one or both of her parents knew. In fact, neither knew. Jane gave the employee her father's correct name and address, but she lied twice more, telling the employee that her father did not have a home phone number and then giving Haller's cell phone number as her father's phone number.... Planned Parenthood scheduled the abortion for March 30, 2004. The employee told Jane that someone would have to stop at Planned Parenthood to pick up an information packet but that Jane did not have to personally retrieve the packet. Sometime before the procedure, Haller picked up the information packet for Jane.

The Roes alleged that they do not know whether Planned Parenthood called or attempted to call the cell phone that belonged to Haller or, if it did, whether Planned Parenthood ever spoke to Haller. Planned Parenthood, on the other hand, presented evidence at a hearing that Jane had admitted that Planned Parenthood had called Haller's cell phone number and that Haller had pretended to be Jane's father and had authorized the procedure.... Planned Parenthood also produced the parental-notification form filled out by the doctor who performed the procedure. The form indicated that the doctor had telephonically notified parent John Roe that Jane Roe was scheduled for an abortion at Planned Parenthood "no sooner than 24 hours from the time" the notice was given.

Haller drove Jane to the clinic on the day of the procedure. When they arrived, a Planned Parenthood employee requested identification. Jane presented her school-identification card, and Haller provided his Ohio driver's license. They submitted the forms that Jane had filled out to an employee, who noted that Jane Roe's "brother John— [was] here today." Haller paid with a credit card.... Before the procedure, Jane signed a form that set forth the nature and purpose of, and the medical risks associated with, the procedure. One form she signed stated that Planned Parenthood had met its statutory obligation to obtain the patient's informed consent. The Roes alleged that even if Jane had been fully informed, her age and emotional state precluded her from comprehending and understanding the risks associated with the procedure. The Roes also alleged that Jane's consent had not been given in a knowing, voluntary, or intelligent manner and that it had been procured under duress and coercion.

Haller ended the relationship soon afterward. After the breakup, a teacher overheard an argument between Jane and Haller's sister, a classmate of Jane's, about Haller and his relationship with Jane, including references to Jane's sexual relationship with Haller. The teacher reported the suspected sexual abuse to the police. After a criminal investigation, Haller was convicted of seven counts of sexual battery. A criminal investigation was also conducted into Planned Parenthood's culpability, but the Hamilton County prosecutor did not prosecute Planned Parenthood for any statutory violation.

After the Roes filed their lawsuit, they sought discovery from Planned Parenthood, including any reports of abuse made pursuant to R.C. 2151.421 and the medical records of nonparty minors who had been patients at Planned Parenthood during a ten-year period. Planned Parenthood produced Jane's medical records but refused to provide the confidential records of nonparties on the basis of the physician-patient privilege.... The plaintiffs moved to compel discovery. Planned Parenthood moved for a protective order to prevent disclosure. The trial court followed *Richards v. Kerlakian*, 162 Ohio App.3d 823, 2005-Ohio-4414, 835 N.E.2d 768, ¶ 5, which cited *Biddle* [*v. Warren Gen. Hosp.*, 86 Ohio St.3d 395, 715 N.E.2d 518 (1999)], for the proposition that confidential information may be discoverable to further a countervailing interest that outweighs the nonparty patient's interest in confidentiality.

The trial court concluded that the Roes had a "tremendous interest" in the requested documents and that their need for the information outweighed the nonparty patients' interest in maintaining the confidentiality of their records. The court ordered all patient-identifying information redacted from the records produced. The court granted the plaintiffs' motion to compel and overruled the defendants' motion for a protective order. The court did not specifically analyze the claims for punitive damages.... The court of appeals reversed. *Roe v. Planned Parenthood Southwest Ohio Region*, 173 Ohio App.3d 414, 2007-Ohio-4318, 878 N.E.2d 1061. The appellate court, citing both *Biddle* and *Richards* for the proposition that "only where the privileged information is necessary to further or protect a countervailing interest is disclosure proper," concluded that the confidential abuse reports and medical records of nonparties were not necessary to the Roes' case and, even if tenuously necessary, the potential invasion of the privacy rights of the nonparties outweighed the probative value of the records to this case. *Id.* at ¶ 34, 42–44. The court concluded that R.C. 2151.421, which imposes the duty to report abuse, does not provide for punitive damages. Thus, the Roes' claim for punitive damages based on this statute had no merit. *Id.* at ¶ 37....

The Roes have alleged that Planned Parenthood breached its duties under R.C. 2919.12 and 2919.121 by failing to notify them of the intent to perform an abortion on Jane and failing to obtain their consent to perform the procedure. R.C. 2919.12 prohibits any person from performing an abortion upon a pregnant, unmarried woman under age 18 without giving at least 24 hours' actual notice in person or by telephone to the woman's parents or obtaining a parent's written consent. R.C. 2919.121 prohibits a person from performing an abortion upon a pregnant minor without the written consent of the minor and one parent.[1] Both statutes provide that one who violates this statute may be liable for compensatory and punitive damages.... The Roes also alleged that Planned Parenthood performed the procedure on Jane without first obtaining her informed consent in violation of R.C. 2317.56. The statute requires that at least 24 hours prior to the procedure, a physician meet with the pregnant woman in person and that published materials about the procedure be given to her. It also requires that she give written consent to the procedure. A person who fails to comply may be liable in compensatory and punitive damages.

The Roes further alleged that Planned Parenthood had reason to suspect that Jane was sexually involved with an adult, but that it did not report the relationship, in violation of R.C. 2151.421. They alleged that as matter of policy and/or pattern and practice, Planned Parenthood does not report known or suspected child abuse with respect to the minors to whom it provides medical services.... The Roes asked the court to enjoin Planned Parenthood from further statutory violations and to require it to comply with the law, and they have asked for compensatory and punitive damages.[2] ... The Roes sought statistical data from Planned Parenthood about the number of abortions performed and the number of reports of suspected or known sexual abuse made over a ten-year period. They also sought the abuse reports made pursuant to R.C. 2151.421 and the redacted medical records of minors who were patients at Planned Parenthood but who are not parties to the action.

The Roes do not dispute that they are seeking confidential, privileged information of third parties, but claim that redaction removes the confidential status. They admit that the statistics are published and available from other sources.[3] This dispute centers solely upon the Roes' request for the abuse reports and medical records of third persons who are not parties. See former R.C. 2151.421(H)(1) (confidentiality of child-abuse reports) and R.C. 2317.02(B)(1) ("A physician or a dentist [shall not testify] concerning a communication made to the physician or dentist by a patient in that relation or the physician's or dentist's advice to a patient, except as otherwise provided * * *").

Civ.R. 26(B)(1) permits discovery "regarding any matter, *not privileged*, which is relevant to the subject matter involved in the pending action." (Emphasis added.) The information sought need not be admissible at trial if it appears reasonably calculated to lead to the discovery of admissible evidence. *Id.* The Roes contend that the documents they seek are

---

1. R.C. 2919.121 was enacted in 1998. 147 Ohio Laws, Part II, 3868, 3875. Shortly afterward, a lawsuit was filed in federal court that challenged its constitutionality. The court issued an order that enjoined the state and county from enforcing the new statute while the case was pending. *Cincinnati Women's Serv., Inc. v. Taft* (S.D.Ohio 2005), 466 F.Supp.2d 934, 937. Since then, the Sixth Circuit has upheld the provision that required 24-hour informed consent, but severed the provision that limited a minor to filing one petition for a judicial bypass of parental consent per pregnancy. *Cincinnati Women's Serv., Inc. v. Taft* (C.A.6, 2006), 468 F.3d 361.

2. The Roes voluntarily dismissed their causes of action for conspiracy and intentional infliction of emotional distress.

3. According to the Roes, Planned Parenthood publishes statistical data on the number of abortions performed and the number of abuse reports made in annual reports and disseminates the information to the Ohio Department of Health and Planned Parenthood Federation of America.

relevant and necessary to their claims and are otherwise unavailable.... Civ.R. 26 clearly excludes privileged information from the general rule of discovery. Thus, even assuming that the information the Roes seek is relevant and may lead to the discovery of admissible evidence, they must establish an exception to the privilege in order to discover this information; relevancy itself is not sufficient for purposes of discovery under Civ.R. 26 when matters are privileged. The Roes rely on *Biddle v. Warren Gen. Hosp.*, 86 Ohio St.3d 395, 715 N.E.2d 518, as authority to discover the medical records of nonparties if a plaintiff's need for the records outweighs the nonparties' interest in protecting the confidential nature of the records....

The Roes' first proposition of law asserts that a plaintiff is entitled to seek punitive damages for a defendant's systematic and intentional breach of the duty to report suspected abuse under R.C. 2151.421. The Roes have requested the abuse reports from Planned Parenthood to establish their claim for punitive damages.... R.C. 2151.421 places a duty on persons with special relationships to minors to report suspected or known abuse or neglect. In December 2008, the General Assembly enacted H.B. 280, which amended R.C. 2151.421, adding division (M) and supplementing division (H), both of which may affect the outcome of this case if applied retroactively. R.C. 2151.421(M) provides that a person may be liable for compensatory and exemplary damages for violating the reporting requirements, and a person who brings a civil action pursuant to division (M) may use reports of other incidents of known or suspected abuse or neglect, with identifying information redacted, in that civil action. R.C. 2151.421(H)(1) was supplemented to allow the use of confidential abuse reports made under that division in a civil action brought pursuant to section (M)....

In this case, the General Assembly expressly provided that the amendments were intended to apply retroactively to civil actions pending on the effective date of the act, April 7, 2009. H.B. 280, Section 4. Thus, they meet the threshold inquiry of retroactivity. We next consider whether the amendments are substantive or remedial. We have held that substantive law "impairs vested rights, affects an accrued substantive right, or imposes new or additional burdens, duties, obligations, or liabilities as to a past transaction." *Bielat*, 87 Ohio St.3d at 354, 721 N.E.2d 28. Procedural or remedial law prescribes methods of enforcement of rights or obtaining redress. *French v. Dwiggins* (1984), 9 Ohio St.3d 32, 34, 9 OBR 123, 458 N.E.2d 827....

The newly enacted division (M) adds a punitive measure of damages that did not previously exist. It does not merely clarify and confirm that a plaintiff had available both compensatory and exemplary damages for a common-law violation of the statute as the Roes contend. Instead, such a change is akin to a statutory penalty, which is substantive. *Osai v. A D Furniture Co.* (1981), 68 Ohio St.2d 99, 100, 22 O.O.3d 328, 428 N.E.2d 857. Thus, we hold that R.C. 2151.421(M) affects a substantive right, and its retroactive application would violate due process.

Former R.C. 2151.421(H)(1) provided that except in limited situations that do not apply here, reports of child abuse made pursuant to R.C. 2151.421 are confidential. H.B. 280 created an exception to nondisclosure by allowing the use of abuse reports in a civil action brought pursuant to R.C. 2151.421(M), provided that any identifying information about the child who is the subject of the report is redacted. Because division (M) may not be retroactively applied in this case, it follows that the Roes may not rely on the discovery provisions of (H)(1), because they apply only to civil actions brought pursuant to division (M). Therefore, we must apply the version of R.C. 2151.421 in effect when the Roes' cause of action arose to determine whether a plaintiff is entitled to seek punitive damages for a defendant's failure to report suspected abuse....

Former R.C. 2151.421 made no reference to any civil damages for a violation of the statute. The Roes contend that the absence of any mention of damages does not preclude the availability of punitive damages. They argue that this court's interpretation of the word "liability" in *Campbell v. Burton* (2001), 92 Ohio St.3d 336, 341–342, 750 N.E.2d 539, to include civil and criminal liability, coupled with the interpretation of "damages" in *Rice v. CertainTeed Corp.* (1999), 84 Ohio St.3d 417, 419–420, 704 N.E.2d 1217, as including both compensatory and punitive damages, entitles them to seek all legally recognized relief. They also contend that courts have permitted plaintiffs to seek both compensatory and punitive damages under Section 1983, Title 42, U.S.Code, although punitive damages are not specified in that statute....

R.C. 2151.421(H)(1) provides for "the use of reports of other incidents of known or suspected abuse or neglect in a civil action or proceedings brought pursuant to division (M) of this section." There is no exception for discovery in other types of civil actions. Because we have determined that division (M) may not be retroactively applied, the Roes do not have a civil action pursuant to division (M), and they may not rely on amended (H)(1) to discover and use reports of other incidents of abuse in this action.... Thus, we look to former R.C. 2151.421(H), which makes no exception for discovery of abuse reports for this kind of civil action. In addition, to the extent that the abuse reports contain information obtained within the physician-patient relationship, that information is privileged from disclosure. This case does not fit within the exception to the physician-patient privilege involving "a child's injuries, abuse, or neglect * * * in any judicial proceeding resulting from a report submitted pursuant to this section." R.C. 2151.421(G)(1)(b). Because this case does not arise from a report submitted about Jane, R.C. 2151.421(G)(1)(b) does not apply. Consequently, these abuse reports are confidential pursuant to former R.C. 2151.421(H) and are not discoverable in this case....

The Roes also seek medical records of nonparties. In general, medical records are confidential and not subject to disclosure. *Hageman v. Southwest Gen. Health Ctr.*, 119 Ohio St.3d 185, 2008-Ohio-3343, 893 N.E.2d 153, ¶ 9. The Roes rely on *Biddle*, 86 Ohio St.3d 395, 715 N.E.2d 518, as authority for discovery of the confidential medical records of nonparties because "disclosure is necessary to protect or further a countervailing interest that outweighs the patient's interest in confidentiality." ...

Biddle was a tort case in which we addressed *liability* for unauthorized disclosure and stressed the utmost importance of the patient's right to confidentiality of medical communications. *Id.*, 86 Ohio St.3d 395, 715 N.E.2d 518, paragraph one of the syllabus. *Biddle* did not involve *discovery* of documents, but rather the *improper release* of documents. Nevertheless, apparently litigants have used *Biddle* to seek nonparty confidential medical information, and courts in several types of tort cases have interpreted *Biddle* as creating a right to obtain nonparty confidential medical information. See *Fair v. St. Elizabeth Med. Ctr.* (2000), 136 Ohio App.3d 522, 527, 737 N.E.2d 106; *Richards v. Kerlakian*, 162 Ohio App.3d 823, 2005-Ohio-4414, 835 N.E.2d 768, ¶ 5; *Alcorn v. Franciscan Hosp. Mt. Airy Campus*, Hamilton App. No. C-060061, 2006-Ohio-5896, 2006 WL 3231208, ¶ 17; *Cepeda v. Lutheran Hosp.*, Cuyahoga App. No. 90031, 2008-Ohio-2348, 2008 WL 2058588, ¶ 15.... However, paragraph two of the syllabus in *Biddle* addressed the *defenses* to the tort of unauthorized disclosure of confidential medical information—i.e., the circumstances under which a physician or hospital may release confidential medical records in the absence of a waiver without incurring tort liability. *Biddle* did not create a litigant's right to discover the confidential medical records of nonparties in a private lawsuit. Any such exception to the physician-patient privilege is a matter for the General Assembly to address. See *Jackson v. Greger*, 110 Ohio St.3d 488, 2006-Ohio-4968, 854 N.E.2d 487, ¶ 13 ("this court

* * * has consistently rejected the adoption of judicially created waivers, exceptions, and limitations for testimonial privilege statutes").

The Roes also argue that the trial court ordered all patient-identifying information redacted, so the anonymity of the patients will be retained, and the confidential and privileged nature of the documents will be removed. Redaction of personal information, however, does not divest the privileged status of confidential records. Redaction is merely a tool that a court may use to safeguard the personal, identifying information within confidential records that have become subject to disclosure either by waiver or by an exception. See R.C. 2317.02(B)(1)(d).... Here, the Roes seek confidential information of third parties that is privileged from disclosure. R.C. 2151.421(H)(1) and 2317.02. Because *Biddle* applies as a defense to the tort of unauthorized disclosures of confidential medical information, we hold that *Biddle* does not authorize the Roes to discover the confidential medical records of nonparties from Planned Parenthood....

The confidential abuse reports and medical records at issue are privileged from disclosure per R.C. 2317.02 and former 2151.421(H)(1). Redaction of personal, identifying information does not remove the privileged status of the records. Therefore, the reports and medical records are not subject to discovery pursuant to Civ.R. 26(B)(1).... *Biddle*, followed by *Hageman*, 119 Ohio St.3d 185, 2008-Ohio-3343, 893 N.E.2d 153, addressed *improper disclosure* without prior authorization and *emphasized* a patient's right to the privacy of medical information. *Id.* at ¶ 17. *Biddle* addressed the privilege to disclose confidential medical information in the context of a defense to the tort of unauthorized disclosure. *Biddle* does not create the right to discover the confidential medical records of nonparties in a private lawsuit.

The Roes still may pursue their private claims for damages against Planned Parenthood for statutory violations: whether Planned Parenthood performed an unlawful abortion on Jane under R.C. 2919.12 and 2919.121, which authorize an award of punitive damages, whether Jane's consent was proper under R.C. 2317.56, which authorizes an award of punitive damages, and whether it had a duty to report suspected abuse of Jane under former R.C. 2151.421. The Roes are entitled to discover Jane's own medical records. They may pursue discovery of other matters, *not privileged*, that are relevant and reasonably calculated to lead to the discovery of admissible evidence. Therefore, for the foregoing reasons, we affirm the judgment of the court of appeals.

Judgment affirmed.

MOYER, C.J., and LANZINGER and CUPP, JJ., concur.

PFEIFER, J., concurs separately.

O'DONNELL, JJ., concurs in part and dissents in part....

DONOVAN, J., dissenting.

I respectfully dissent. I would reverse the judgment of the court of appeals, thus reinstating the trial court's order compelling discovery ... since the Roes, in my view, are entitled to the discovery initially ordered by the trial court under pre-existing, as well as current, law. The Roes should be entitled to redress a pre-existing actionable wrong....

Lost in all this debate is the fact that the confidentiality of patient records is for the protection of the patient, not the physician. (And in this case, we are talking exclusively about children, those under the age of 18 who may be the victims of sexual exploitation.) The defendants should not be permitted to frustrate a civil suit questioning their professional conduct (or lack thereof) by asserting the physician-patient privilege.

On this record, both a private and public interest justified compelling discovery. The Roes, as parents of Jane, a 14-year-old child, have the right to pursue multiple claims for injury and breach of multiple statutory duties. An individual plaintiff or plaintiffs should be permitted the opportunity to discover records that may demonstrate a pattern of ignoring and/or turning a blind eye to child abuse. Such redacted records may indeed bear a direct relation to the issue of whether Planned Parenthood's conduct was reprehensible, thus warranting punitive damages. Should the Roes' lawsuit reveal or expose such a pattern, the public derives a benefit simultaneously by learning of, and demanding accountability for, medical providers who fail to protect vulnerable children from sexual predators.

The appellate court expressed concern that this case may present a situation wherein a jury may decide to punish Planned Parenthood for harm caused to nonparties. See *Philip Morris USA v. Williams* (2007), 549 U.S. 346, 127 S.Ct. 1057, 166 L.Ed.2d 940. This concern clearly places the cart before the horse. We are now addressing only discovery, not admissibility.... Nevertheless, harm to nonparties may be considered by jurors for the limited purpose of helping them decide whether Planned Parenthood showed a conscious disregard for the rights and safety of other persons that had a great probability of causing substantial harm. The majority in *Philip Morris* recognized that "[e]vidence of actual harm to nonparties can help to show that the conduct that harmed the plaintiff also posed a substantial risk * * * to the general public, and so was particularly reprehensible * * *." *Philip Morris*, 549 U.S. at 355, 127 S.Ct. 1057, 166 L.Ed.2d 940. A recognized and principal goal of punitive damages is to deter future reprehensible conduct.

This difference was not overlooked by Justice Stevens, who expressed befuddlement at the distinction drawn by the majority in *Philip Morris* between punishing a defendant based on harm to nonparties (not allowed) and considering the scope of wrongdoing in determining the reprehensibility. *Philip Morris*, 549 U.S. at 359, 127 S.Ct. 1057, 166 L.Ed.2d 940 (Stevens, J., dissenting). Repeated breaches of the duty to report (or a complete failure to report sexual abuse) under R.C. 2151.421 would be admissible under Ohio Evid.R. 404(B) to demonstrate "proof of motive, opportunity, intent, preparation, plan, knowledge, identity, or absence of mistake or accident." This is a simple recognition that "conduct that risks harm to many is likely more reprehensible than conduct that risks harm to only a few." Id. at 357....

Additionally, the majority concludes that because there was no common-law duty to report child abuse, the statute that created the duty, having not explicitly authorized damages for its breach, cannot allow for punitive damages. I believe that first, this conclusion completely overlooks the legislative intent in creating the statute and its amendments, to wit: the protection of vulnerable, victimized women and children. The legislative intent is clearly to prevent further injury, crime, and exploitation.... The majority opinion overlooks basic principles and characteristics of tort law. It is a basic principle of torts that "liability is based upon the relation of persons with others." Prosser & Keeton, Law of Torts (5th Ed.1984) 5. "Torts consists of the breach of duties fixed and imposed upon the parties by the law itself." Id. "The tort-feasor usually is held liable for acting * * * in a way that departs from a reasonable standard of care." Id. at 6. "[T]he law of torts is concerned * * * with acts which are unreasonable, or socially harmful, from the point of view of the community as a whole." Id. at 7. The Roes assert a violation of duty owed to them and their minor child, Jane, and the duty arises by both operation of law and the defendant's relationship to Jane.

Planned Parenthood argues, and the majority holds, that there is no right to punitive damages under R.C. 2151.421 because punitive damages were not expressly provided for in R.C. 2151.99, and the amended sections are unconstitutional. Yet whoever violates R.C. 2151.421(A) is guilty of a misdemeanor of the fourth degree. When the claimed wrong partakes of a criminal nature, the wrongdoer should be brought to justice in a civil suit. Punitive damages do not rest on some abstract concept of justice, but upon sound public policy, which in this instance seeks to promote the safety and health of children and encourage reporting of abuse. We must take into account the importance of the underlying public policy jeopardized by a mandatory reporter's failure to report. As Justice Stevens noted in his dissent in *Philip Morris*, "There is little difference between the justification for a criminal sanction, such as a fine or a term of imprisonment, and an award of punitive damages." Id. at 359, 127 S.Ct. 1057, 166 L.Ed.2d 940 (Stevens, J., dissenting).

It cannot be overlooked that the Roes have also alleged malice and wanton disregard for their rights and those of their minor child, Jane. In cases in which malice is shown, the right to punitive damages is a rule so deeply rooted in Ohio law that this court should not be permitted to carve out an exception thereto governing claims brought under former R.C. 2151.421. Punitive damages have always been two sides of the same coin, one of which is punitive, criminal, and public, and the other of which is in substance private and civil. Criminal statutes should serve as guideposts for the imposition of civil tort duties.

Further, sections R.C. 2151.421(G) and the former (H) support a finding that a civil remedy for punitive damages is available. These sections, by recognizing a civil immunity for "whistleblowers"—i.e., reporters under the statute—do by implication recognize a right to civil redress, including punitive damages against those mandatory reporters who fail to report known or suspected abuse. This reading of the statute recognizes that each section should be construed in connection with every other part or section to promote a harmonious whole. The ultimate inquiry is to ascertain the legislative intent. Here, that intent is to encourage reporting, provide civil immunity for those who make a false report in good faith, and also hold liable those who fail in their duty to protect children such as Jane who are victims of sexual predators. In my view, this intent was clear even before H.B. 280. We should presume that the General Assembly did not intend the absurd results from the operation of the statute reached by the majority, which in effect shields nonreporters.

Jane is certainly a member of the class that the statute is designed to protect. The underlying purpose of the statute is to afford her the full panoply of civil damages when a breach is established. A medical provider, regardless of the area in which the individual physician specializes, obviously has a fiduciary relationship with his or her patient warranting compliance with the standard of care required of all physicians in the medical community at large. Although the majority concludes that there was no common-law duty to report child abuse, there has *always* been a common-law duty to report serious crime. Child abuse, sexual battery, and rape are serious crimes.

The majority opinion rendered today does more to protect the adult defendants (i.e., Planned Parenthood) than sexually abused children. The opinion likewise undermines parents' rights to protect their minor children and to guide their medical treatment. The trial court properly exercised its discretion and granted discovery to the Roes so that they might pursue their claims. Mandatory reporting must be encouraged, expected, and demanded. The Roes should not be effectively denied the opportunity to seek remedies the law affords them. R.C. 1.47(C) provides: "In enacting a statute, it is presumed that: * * * A just and reasonable result is intended." The result today is neither just nor reasonable.

Notes

For other cases addressing due process claims and issues of family privacy involving access to abortion records, see *Alpha Medical Clinic v. Anderson*, 280 Kan. 903, 128 P.3d

364 (2006) (involving question of mandamus jurisdiction of State Supreme Court); *Cincinnati Women's Services, Inc. v. Taft*, 466 F. Supp. 2d 934 (S.D. Ohio 2005) (Ohio statute on judicial bypass for minor to obtain abortion without parental consent adequately ensures confidentiality without exemption from requirements for reporting child abuse). Note that some courts determine, albeit in contexts other than abortion and sexual exploitation, that redaction of personal information may be sufficient to overcome privacy concerns. *See, e.g., Snibbe v. Superior Court*, 224 Cal. App. 4th 184, 168 Cal. Rptr. 3d 548 (2014).

C. Statute of Limitations

Lebo v. State

Court of Appeals of Indiana, 2012
977 N.E.2d 1031

BRADFORD, Judge.

Having convicted former LaPorte High School junior varsity volleyball coach Robert Ashcraft of multiple sex crimes against a minor student athlete, the State of Indiana charged Marybeth Lebo, the school's varsity volleyball coach, with failure to report child abuse or neglect. Lebo appeals the trial court's denial of her motion to dismiss these charges, arguing they are barred by the statute of limitations and lack sufficient specificity. We conclude that failure to report is a continuing offense to which the statute of limitations does not apply and, alternatively, that Lebo's alleged instruction that her volleyball players not discuss Ashcraft's conduct with their parents was sufficient to invoke the concealment exception to the statute of limitations. We also conclude that the charging informations, together with testimony from the probable cause hearing, allege sufficiently specific facts from which Lebo can prepare her defense. Therefore, we affirm....

At all times in question, Lebo was employed as the varsity volleyball coach at LaPorte High School. In this capacity, Lebo supervised Robert Ashcraft, who was employed as the school's junior varsity volleyball coach. K.T., a minor student, began playing volleyball at LaPorte High School on or about August 1, 2007. At that time, K.T. was fifteen years of age, turning sixteen on June 21, 2008.... Ashcraft resigned from his employment with the LaPorte Community School Corporation on October 28, 2008. Around November 21, 2008, the LaPorte City Police Department began investigating allegations of a sexual relationship between Ashcraft and K.T. On December 17, 2009, Ashcraft was arrested and charged with felony sexual misconduct with a minor and felony child seduction. In January of 2010, the Indiana State Police ("ISP") began investigating whether the administration and staff of the LaPorte Community School Corporation, including Lebo, were aware of the relationship between Ashcraft and K.T. and failed to report it to an appropriate authority. The investigation entailed reviewing materials from Ashcraft's criminal case and over 100,000 emails from the LaPorte Community School Corporation, as well as conducting additional interviews with student volleyball players and their parents. The ISP submitted its completed investigation report to the LaPorte County Prosecutor's Office on October 23, 2010.

In July of 2011, a jury convicted Ashcraft of multiple counts of felony sexual misconduct with a minor and felony child seduction. A probable cause hearing regarding potential charges against Lebo was held on September 6, 2011. At the hearing, ISP Detective Michael Robinson testified that the investigation into Lebo revealed that several different parents talked to Lebo about Ashcraft's inappropriate conduct with K.T., describing their relationship as being "almost like they were boyfriend and girlfriend." ... [Citations to record omitted]. Detective Robinson added that "[Lebo] received several reports, all regarding ... Coach Ashcraft, who was forty-two, forty-three years of age, and this player who was fifteen, sixteen years of age during the course of this time period...." ... And at numerous times it wasn't just the coach and some other player or the coach and this other player, it kept coming back to the same player...." ... It specifically even mentioned in [Ashcraft's] personnel file a couple of times, [K.T.'s] name." ...

According to Detective Robinson's testimony, the investigation also revealed that Lebo "documented in Mr. Ashcraft's personnel file [that Lebo] witnessed a couple of instances" of "inappropriate contact" between Ashcraft and K.T.... Specifically, at a volleyball tournament in Crown Point, Lebo observed that "Ashcraft was leaning up against between the legs of the victim [while] watching a movie or something. In her words, [Lebo] was very uncomfortable with that [and] made the girls get up right away and start doing something else." ... Another instance occurred during a bus ride; Lebo noticed that "Ashcraft had put his arm around [K.T.] and was like sharing some food, yogurt, holding the cup for her, just stuff that made [Lebo] feel it was very inappropriate." ... Lebo further documented that "she was in fear of losing her job because of this ... Ashcraft and [K.T.] situation." ...

Detective Robinson also testified that the investigation found no indication that Lebo reported Ashcraft's conduct to any authority at LaPorte High School, the Laporte Community School Corporation, the local or state police department, or the Department of Child Services. Lebo did, however, instruct her student volleyball players "not to tell anybody what was going on. [D]on't tell your parents. Don't tell anybody." ... Lebo also helped prepare Ashcraft's resignation letter, which does not reference Lebo's notes in Ashcraft's personnel file regarding his inappropriate conduct with K.T. The letter states only that there was "some type of coaching problem." ...

On September 6, 2011, the State charged Lebo with two counts of failure to report child abuse or neglect, both Class B misdemeanors. Count I alleged a violation of Indiana Code section 31-33-5-1 as follows:

> Detective Michael Robinson being duly sworn upon his oath says that: in the County of LaPorte, State of Indiana, on or between August 1, 2007 and October 28, 2008, Marybeth Lebo had reason to believe that minor child K.T. was a victim of child abuse or neglect and failed to report such child abuse or neglect to law enforcement or the department of child services and such offense was concealed by the failure to make such report for the duration of the charges and by instructing her players during the 2007 and 2008 season not to discuss team matters or rumors with anyone, and further that the State did not have evidence sufficient to file charges until an investigative report was received after October 22, 2010, and could not have discovered sufficient evidence through due diligence.

[Citation to record omitted]. Count II alleged a violation of Indiana Code section 31-33-5-2 as follows:

> Detective Michael Robinson being duly sworn upon his oath says that: in the county of LaPorte, state of Indiana, on or between August 1, 2007 and October 28, 2008, Marybeth Lebo while employed as a teacher and a coach for LaPorte High School had reason to believe that minor child K.T. was a victim of child abuse or neglect and failed to report such child abuse or neglect to the individual in charge of the school or the individual's designated agent and such offense was concealed by the failure to make such report for the duration of the charges and by instructing her players during the 2007 and 2008 season not to discuss team

matters or rumors with anyone, and further that the State did not have evidence sufficient to file charges until an investigative report was received after October 22, 2010, and could not have discovered sufficient evidence through due diligence.

[Citation to record omitted].

On September 29, 2011, Lebo filed a written motion to dismiss the charges against her, alleging that the charging informations were filed beyond the statute of limitations. At a hearing on this motion, Lebo orally claimed that the informations should also be dismissed because the facts stated did not constitute an offense and because the offenses were not alleged with sufficient specificity. On February 7, 2012, the trial court denied Lebo's motion on all asserted grounds. This court granted Lebo's motion for interlocutory appeal on April 13, 2012....

Lebo argues that the trial court abused its discretion in denying Lebo's motion to dismiss because the State's charges are barred by the statute of limitations. Indiana Code section 35-41-4-2(a)(2) requires the State to commence prosecution of a misdemeanor offense within two years after its commission. "[This] protect[s] defendants from the prejudice that a delay in prosecution could bring, such as fading memories and stale evidence." *Sloan v. State*, 947 N.E.2d 917, 920 (Ind.2011) (citing *Kifer v. State*, 740 N.E.2d 586, 587 (Ind.Ct.App.2000)). "[It] also 'strike[s] a balance between an individual's interest in repose and the State's interest in having sufficient time to investigate and build its case.'" *Id.* (quoting *Heitman v. State*, 627 N.E.2d 1307, 1309 (Ind.Ct.App.1994)). "'[A]n information alleging a time outside the statute of limitations which does not allege facts sufficient to constitute an exception to the statute is subject to a motion to dismiss.'" *Reeves v. State*, 938 N.E.2d 10, 16 (Ind.Ct.App.2010), *trans. denied* (quoting *Greichunos v. State*, 457 N.E.2d 615, 617 (Ind.Ct.App.1983)).

Lebo claims that, because she is charged with failing to report child abuse or neglect between August 1, 2007, and October 28, 2008, the two-year statute of limitations expired no later than October 28, 2010, well before the State filed its charging informations on September 6, 2011. The State claims that its charges were timely filed because the statute of limitations was tolled by virtue of concealment and, alternatively, because the crime of failure to report is a continuing offense...." Indiana Code section 35-41-4-2(h)(2) ... tolls a statute of limitations if 'the accused person conceals evidence of the offense, and evidence sufficient to charge the person with that offense is unknown to the prosecuting authority and could not have been discovered by that authority by exercise of due diligence[.]'" *Sloan*, 947 N.E.2d at 920. "[W]hen the State relies on this exception, it must plead the circumstances of the concealment exception in the information so that the 'defendant is apprised of the facts upon which the State intends to rely and may be prepared to meet that proof at trial.'" *Reeves*, 938 N.E.2d at 17 (quoting *Willner v. State* 602 N.E.2d 507, 509 (Ind.1992)).

In its charging informations, the State alleges that Lebo's offenses were "concealed by ... [Lebo] instructing her players during the 2007 and 2008 seasons not to discuss team matters or rumors with anyone." ... The State further alleges that it "did not have evidence sufficient to file charges until an investigative report was received after October 22, 2010, and [it] could not have discovered sufficient evidence through due diligence." ... Lebo contends that these allegations are not sufficiently specific to allow Lebo to prepare a concealment defense. We, however, agree with the trial court; the allegations of concealment are sufficient to bring the charging informations into compliance with the statute of limitations.... The charging informations explicitly allege that Lebo concealed her failure to report, include facts constituting the act of concealment upon which that allegation is based, and provide a general timeframe in which the alleged concealment occurred. Further, these allegations are supported by Detective Robinson's testimony at the probable cause hearing. In addition to testifying that Lebo instructed her players not to discuss the Ashcraft and K.T. situation with others, Detective Robinson testified that the ISP did not begin to suspect Lebo's failure to report until January 2010, the month after Ashcraft's arrest. Moreover, Detective Robinson testified that the LaPorte County Prosecutor's Office could not have discovered sufficient evidence to charge Lebo with failure to report until it received the ISP's investigation report on October 23, 2010. The trial court did not abuse its discretion in determining that concealment tolled the statute of limitations.

Lebo also contends that the facts alleged in the charging informations do not constitute concealment and that the State failed to exercise the due diligence necessary to invoke the concealment exception to toll the statute of limitations. On this issue, we again agree with the trial court. "'Concealment is a fact-intensive issue.'"... *See Willner*, 602 N.E.2d at 509. Because questions of fact are not properly raised on a motion to dismiss, *Delagrange*, 951 N.E.2d at 594–95, we cannot conclude that the trial court abused its discretion in denying Lebo's motion on this basis....

As an alternative, the State argues that the crime of failure to report is a continuing offense, and therefore, the statute of limitations did not begin to run until the LaPorte County Prosecutor's Office received the ISP's investigation report on October 23, 2010. The doctrine of continuing offenses holds, "Where there is a continuing duty to do some act, the statute of limitations does not apply where some portion of the offense is within the period of limitations." *DeHart v. State*, 471 N.E.2d 312, 315 (Ind.Ct.App.1984). In other words, "The offense continues as long as the duty persists[ ] and there is a failure to perform that duty." *Wright v. Superior Court*, 15 Cal.4th 521, 525, 63 Cal.Rptr.2d 322, 936 P.2d 101 (1997). An offense should not be deemed continuing "unless the explicit language of the substantive criminal statute compels such a conclusion, or the nature of the crime involved is such that [the legislature] must assuredly have intended that it be treated as a continuing one." *Toussie v. United States*, 397 U.S. 112, 115, 90 S.Ct. 858, 25 L.Ed.2d 156 (1970).... We conclude that Indiana's failure to report child abuse or neglect statute contemplates the crime as a continuing offense. Although the statute does not utilize the terms "continuing" or "continuous," it includes the following provision to that effect: "This chapter does not relieve an individual of the obligation to report on the individual's own behalf, unless a report has already been made to the best of the individual's belief." Ind.Code § 31-33-5-3. An individual who has not been "relieved" of his duty to report must be considered to have a continuing duty to do so. To conclude otherwise effectively limits the duty to report to the day on which a "reason to believe" arises. Such a conclusion would frustrate the statute's asserted purpose to "provide protection for an abused or a neglected child from *further* abuse or neglect." Ind.Code § 31-33-1-1 (emphasis added). To permit an individual with a duty to report to avoid prosecution for failure to report because that individual's failure was not discovered within 730 days does nothing to protect a child who may still be the victim of abuse on day 731 or beyond.... Lebo contends that, because that statute requires a person with a duty to report to "*immediately* make an oral report...." Ind.Code § 31-33-5-4 (emphasis added), the offense cannot be considered continuing. But although "the violation is *complete* at the first instance the elements are met[, i]t is nevertheless not *completed* as long as the obligation remains unfulfilled. 'The crime achieves no finality until such time.'" *Wright*, 15 Cal.4th at 526, 63 Cal.Rptr.2d 322, 936 P.2d 101 (quoting *U.S. v. Cores*, 356 U.S. 405, 409, 78 S.Ct. 875, 2 L.Ed.2d 873 (1958)). Lebo's contention merely recognizes one part of this duality....

We add that Lebo's claims in support of her sufficient specificity argument are without merit. First, Lebo's claim that her alleged observations do not give rise to a "reason to believe" presents a question of fact to be resolved at trial and is not properly raised on a motion to dismiss. *Delagrange*, 951 N.E.2d at 594–95. Second, Lebo's claim that the time frame alleged fails to identify whether K.T. was fifteen or sixteen at the time of Lebo's observations is misplaced. The failure to report statute does not require that an individual have actual knowledge of child abuse or neglect. Rather, a duty to report is imposed on an individual who merely has "reason to believe" a child is the victim of such a crime. Ind.Code §§ 31-33-5-1, 31-33-5-2 (2011). *See* Ind.Code § 31-33-1-1(1) (stating one of the purposes of a duty to report is "to encourage effective reporting of *suspected* or known incidents of child abuse or neglect" (emphasis added)). Therefore, the conduct allegedly observed by Lebo need not satisfy the elements of sexual misconduct with a minor, Ind.Code § 35-42-4-9 (requiring a victim less than sixteen years of age), or those of child seduction, Ind.Code § 35-42-4-7 (requiring a victim at least sixteen years of age).

The judgment of the trial court is affirmed.

ROBB, C.J., concurs.

BAKER, J., concurs in part and dissents in part with opinion. . . .

Chapter Six

Evidence of Sexual Exploitation

I. Probable Cause

Thomas K. Clancy

Digital Child Pornography and the Fourth Amendment

49 Judges J. 26 (2010)

The advent of digital evidence is having a profound impact on Fourth Amendment principles and analysis. Yet to be resolved by the courts is the fundamental question whether locations where digital evidence may be found, ranging from desk top computers, cell phones, to countless other digital devices, are subject to special rules or whether traditional search and seizure rules suffice.... [footnotes omitted].... The alcohol prohibition era had a significant influence on Fourth Amendment analysis in the 1920s and 1930s. The drug wars of the last 50 years have also impacted the structure of search and seizure jurisprudence. Now, during the digital age, governmental investigations designed to locate child pornography are having a similar influence....

The concept of probable cause — a familiar but fluid standard for a court to apply ... [footnote omitted] — has created some unique difficulties in the computer context.... To establish probable cause to search, many courts look for additional information — beyond membership in a child pornography site — that substantiates the person's sexual interest in children or in child pornography.... That additional information has included such factors as evidence of actual downloading ... — as opposed to mere viewing, ... automatic transmissions as part of the site's services, ... use of suggestive names, ... expert information on the retention habits of child pornography collectors ... (which often serves to dispel allegations of staleness ... and identifies the house as the place where the materials were viewed), and prior convictions involving sex offenses involving children or child pornography....

Courts are increasingly confronting the problems associated with adapting Fourth Amendment principles to modern technology. Supreme Court jurisprudence, developed to regulate traditional search and seizure practices, presents conceptual problems when applied to the world of cyber-space and electronically stored evidence. Some authorities are reluctant to accept — or outright reject — analogies to physical world searches and seizures.... [H]owever ... there is nothing "special" in the nature of computer searches that differentiate them in any principled way from other document and container searches....

Id. at 26–29.

A. Specificity

Burnett v. State

District Court of Appeal of Florida, 2003
848 So. 2d 1170

CASANUEVA, Judge....

This case began when the father of two boys, ages nine and twelve, contacted a Polk County Sheriff's Office detective with his concern that Mr. Burnett had engaged in inappropriate behavior with his children. The father related his suspicion that Mr. Burnett videotaped his children while they were not wearing any clothing. In a subsequent interview the children told the detective that Mr. Burnett had asked them to remove their clothes and wrap themselves in clear plastic wrap so that he could videotape a temporary tattoo on their buttocks. Additionally, he asked them to place clear plastic wrap on the toilet, then to use the toilet and deliver the plastic wrap to him, and to place quarters in their rectums and shake them out. The children denied that any videotaping actually occurred.

Armed with this information, detectives then contacted Mr. Burnett, who drove to a sheriff's office substation for an interview. There he advised the deputies that he had videotaped the boys but that he had either discarded or recorded over the tape. Upon discovering that Mr. Burnett rented a bedroom from his parents at their residence, the detectives obtained his consent to search his room. Among the targets of their search were the video camera and any videotape of the boys. During the search, Mr. Burnett showed the deputies the camera, demonstrated how it worked, but stated that the tape was not in the camera. Noticing that the camera had no power, a deputy plugged it in, hit the play mode, and watched a videotape that matched the father's allegations. Both the video camera and tape were seized as evidence and the room was searched. Nothing else was seized.

The following day one of the detectives applied for a warrant to search the entire residence. Among the matters set out in the affidavit were the following:

> (1) Your affiant is a duly appointed law enforcement official employed by the Polk County Sheriff's Office. Your affiant is currently a detective assigned to the Bureau of Criminal Investigations in the Sexual Abuse And Family Exploitation Unit. Your affiant has been employed for over three years at the Polk County Sheriff's Office. I have been assigned to the S.A.F.E. Unit for approximately one year. My duties are to investigate any activity involving sex crimes, child abuse, and family exploitation in Polk County, Florida. Your affiant has received specialized training in investigating sex crimes, specifically the Institute of Police Technology and Management course focusing on sexually exploited children and juvenile victims of sexual abuse. This affiant attended the Polk County conference on Sexual Abuse that specialized in recognizing victims of sexual abuse and interviewing them. Your affiant has received specialized training in child injury and death investigations as well as a course on interview and interrogations and search warrant preparations. Your affiant has conducted over two hundred investigations involving crimes against children and has made over thirty arrests

as a direct result of these investigations. Your affiant has previously either written or assisted in the execution of four search warrants....

(7) Based on my expertise and training, people involved in child pornography (as in this case video taping a juvenile's genitals and buttocks) commonly are involved with receiving or transmitting like images of children engaged in sexual performances on their computer. It is not unusual for a suspect to retain images on their computer even when they are under suspicion of committing crimes against children. Furthermore, the majority of people utilizing computers are unable to erase these images from their hard drive. These images can be retrieved during forensic analysis even after an attempt has been made to erase the images. Consequently, I believe there are images related to children involved in sexual performances and/or child pornography as defined in F.S.S. 827.071 still contained on the computer located at the place to be searched. Your affiant also believes due to the suspect's untruthful statements on whether he kept pornographic images on tape (which I viewed), it is believed other child pornographic images may be stored on numerous video tapes located in the suspect's bedroom, the place to be searched.

Based upon this affidavit a judge issued the warrant, and deputies seized Mr. Burnett's computer and numerous diskettes. Mr. Burnett's motion to suppress based upon lack of probable cause in the warrant was denied.

Among the evidence introduced at trial was the testimony of a computer forensics expert, Mr. Gates, who testified that, upon his technical examination using specialized software, the seized diskettes revealed that they at one time had held images, but all of the pictures had been deleted or erased. Mr. Gates's examination could not ascertain when or by whom the images had been deleted. Furthermore, Mr. Gates recovered no images—deleted or otherwise—from the hard drive of Mr. Burnett's computer. However, Mr. Burnett possessed a computer diskette for a program called Paint Shop Pro that can be used to view and manipulate images, and Mr. Gates discovered that someone at some unspecified time had used this program to view at least two pornographic images on Mr. Burnett's computer.... To counter this circumstantial evidence that he possessed child pornography, Mr. Burnett adduced testimony from a friend who was present when Mr. Burnett received a package through an e-Bay auction containing diskettes that he had not specifically ordered. Mr. Burnett's theory of innocence was that he did not know what was on the diskettes when they arrived, that he had never viewed the images on them, and that someone else could have deleted the images before the diskettes ever came into his possession. Similarly, Mr. Burnett attacked the charges stemming from the images viewed through the Paint Shop Pro program on the ground that there was no evidence demonstrating that he actually viewed or manipulated the recovered images.

Although we have misgivings about the sufficiency of the evidence to sustain the possession of child pornography charges, we do not need to reach that issue. On this appeal we reverse the finding that the detectives had probable cause to search for and to seize Mr. Burnett's computer and the diskettes. Consequently, we reverse the convictions on 136 counts of possession of child pornography that flowed from the illegal seizure of those items....

The Fourth Amendment to the United States Constitution recognizes the right of the people to be protected from the government's unreasonable searches and seizures and mandates that no search warrant shall issue "but upon probable cause, supported by oath or affirmation...." U.S. Const. amend. IV. The Constitution of the State of Florida similarly protects against unreasonable searches and seizures by the government: "No warrant shall be issued except upon probable cause, supported by affidavit...." Art. I, § 12, Fla. Const. To further these constitutional imperatives, our legislature has decreed:

> No warrant shall be issued for the search of any private dwelling under any of the conditions hereinabove mentioned except on sworn proof by affidavit of some creditable witness that he or she has reason to believe that one of said conditions exists, which affidavit shall set forth the facts on which such reason for belief is based.

§ 933.18(10), Fla. Stat. (1999). In implementing these constitutional mandates,

> [t]he task of the issuing magistrate is simply to make a practical, common-sense decision whether given all the circumstances set forth in the affidavit before him, including the veracity and basis of knowledge of persons supplying hearsay information, there is a fair probability that contraband or evidence of a crime will be found in a particular place.

Illinois v. Gates, 462 U.S. 213, 238, 103 S.Ct. 2317, 76 L.Ed.2d 527 (1983). Thus, the affidavit in the warrant application must satisfy two elements: first, that a particular person has committed a crime — the commission element, and, second, that evidence relevant to the probable criminality is likely located at the place to be searched — the nexus element. *United States v. Vigeant*, 176 F.3d 565, 569 (1st Cir.1999). As stated in *Gates*, wholly conclusory statements fail to meet the probable cause requirement; the reviewing magistrate cannot abdicate his or her duty and become a mere ratifier of the bare conclusions of others. *Gates*, 462 U.S. at 238, 103 S.Ct. 2317. And, pursuant to *Gates*, as the reviewing court we are required to ensure that a substantial basis existed to support the magistrate's probable cause determination. *Id.* at 238–39, 103 S.Ct. 2317.

Our initial analytical focus will be upon the nexus element of the warrant application. We must measure the affidavit's averments to determine whether evidence relevant to Mr. Burnett's probable criminality — possession of child pornography — was likely located at the place to be searched, that is, his bedroom. Because the affidavit failed to set forth crime-specific facts regarding Mr. Burnett's probable possession of child pornography and the likelihood that it would be found on the computer and diskettes in his bedroom, we conclude that the warrant application failed. *See King v. State*, 779 So.2d 385, 386 (Fla. 2d DCA 2000) (holding that the probable cause statement was totally devoid of any facts leading to the conclusion that probable cause existed to believe that stolen property would be found at the places to be searched).

Although the affidavit in this case properly stated that the seized videotape substantiated the allegations of Mr. Burnett's lewd or lascivious conduct with children, the videotape corroborated only those initial charges and nothing more. The affidavit recited the deputy's observation that videos and magazines were stacked about the bedroom, yet it failed to affirm that the title or cover of any video or magazine suggested it contained child pornography. This is despite the fact that the detective and other law enforcement personnel had already consensually searched the very bedroom in question — a fact also omitted from disclosure to the magistrate.... Furthermore, the general information set forth in paragraphs one and seven of the affidavit manifested no factual foundation for the magistrate's conclusion that probable cause existed in this case. The initial complaint was that Mr. Burnett made a lewd videotape of two young boys, but nothing was elicited suggesting that the father believed Mr. Burnett used his computer to transmit or store images of child pornography. The affidavit contained no specific facts linking Mr. Burnett to this particular criminal conduct; it failed to describe a factual link between the video camera and the functioning capability of the home computer so that images could be transferred. The affidavit also omitted any factual averment that the computer was linked to the internet or that the video camera was compatible with the computer so that images could be downloaded, transferred, or transmitted.

Rather, in this case the affiant averred in only general terms that she had conducted over two hundred investigations involving crimes against children, resulting in over thirty arrests, but she recited no specific experiences in child pornography matters or arrests she had made for this particular crime. Essentially, the affiant failed to describe any personal experience with child pornography from which her conclusions concerning Mr. Burnett were derived. Instead, the affidavit included language such as "[b]ased on my expertise," "commonly are involved," and "it is not unusual." To determine probable cause, the magistrate is required to evaluate whether the case-specific facts yield a legal conclusion that probable cause exists. Here, the affiant's education and experience in matters of child pornography were not set out, nor did the affiant indicate the degree of commonality that is alleged to exist. Although it may not be unusual for suspects such as Mr. Burnett to retain child pornography images, the question is—factually—to what degree that propensity could be attributed to him.

The magistrate's duty is to examine the affidavit for facts and fact-based conclusions. An affidavit is not limited to the affiant's personal knowledge; in some instances information from confidential informants or scientific evidence can be presented. In the same vein, information from experts in the field, such as child pornography, may be made available to the magistrate for consideration, whether it be by scientific studies, statistical analysis, or the like. *See United States v. Ventresca*, 380 U.S. 102, 108, 85 S.Ct. 741, 13 L.Ed.2d 684 (1965) (holding that "hearsay may be the basis for issuance of the warrant 'so long as there … [is] a substantial basis for crediting the hearsay'" (citing *Jones v. United States*, 362 U.S. 257, 272, 80 S.Ct. 725, 4 L.Ed.2d 697 (1960), *overruled on other grounds, United States v. Salvucci*, 448 U.S. 83, 100 S.Ct. 2547, 65 L.Ed.2d 619 (1980))); *see also United States v. Isgut*, No. 95-6199 CR Lenard, 1996 WL 775064 (S.D.Fla. Jul. 23, 1996) (voiding a search warrant for lack of probable cause based on staleness but criticizing the affiant's failure to include specific information about the training he had received and the source of his information concerning "five characteristics of those who are considered 'collectors of child pornography'"). Unfortunately, no scientific information or expert opinion evidence was included in this affidavit for the magistrate's consideration.

In paragraph seven, the affiant described her belief in the generalized behavior of other persons who receive or transmit images of children and who are unable to erase the contents of their computers. From this generalized information, which contained no link to criminal conduct by Mr. Burnett, the officer concluded that Mr. Burnett's computer contained pornographic images. Probable cause analysis focuses not on the evidence that is found as a result of the search but on facts known at the moment of seizure. *See State v. Bond*, 341 So.2d 218, 218 (Fla. 2d DCA 1976) ("Probable cause for issuance of a search warrant is determined solely with reference to facts stated in the warrant and supporting affidavit."). Here, the conclusion that images remained on Mr. Burnett's computer was not supported by the factual allegations of the affidavit. The fact that Mr. Burnett might have lied about or misrepresented the existence of the video of the children established, in this instance, only his questionable veracity; it did not substantiate his commission of another criminal offense. In contrast, in *Schmitt v. State*, 590 So.2d 404, 411 (Fla.1991), in which the supreme court sustained the probable cause determination in a warrant issued to search the defendant's home for evidence of the defendant's knowing possession of child pornography, § 827.071(5), Fla. Stat. (1987), the affidavit revealed that the defendant "made nudity a central and almost obsessive object of his attention" and that "this overall focus of Schmitt's conduct tended to show a lewd intent and thus created a substantial basis for believing that the search would fairly probably yield evidence" that the defendant had violated the laws prohibiting possession of child pornography. The *Schmitt* affidavit alleged that the defendant had taken numerous nude photographs of his daughter over a four-year period beginning when the child was eight years old; that the father had taken photographs of a nude adult female in the presence of the child; that the father had videotaped the daughter and a friend "stripping down to their panties" and "swimming in the nude"; and that the father kept photographs, film, cameras, a television, and a videocassette recorder in the place to be searched. *Schmitt*, 590 So.2d at 408. In Mr. Burnett's case, however, no details in the affidavit supported a conclusion that Mr. Burnett possessed pornographic videotapes, photographs, or computer images other than the single tape that the authorities already possessed. Any conclusion that his room contained other evidence of his possession of pornographic materials was based on mere suspicion.

Years ago, the Supreme Court examined another affiant's statement that he had "cause to suspect and [did] believe" that liquor illegally brought into the United States was located on certain premises. *Nathanson v. United States*, 290 U.S. 41, 44, 54 S.Ct. 11, 78 L.Ed. 159 (1933). That wholly conclusory statement was rejected as a foundation for probable cause. Similarly, we must reject the wholly conclusory statements made here.... We recognize that normally the averments of an experienced officer are accorded some weight. To be given that deference, however, the officer's conclusions must be grounded upon some particular evidence. As stated in *Churney v. State*, 348 So.2d 395, 397 (Fla. 3d DCA 1977), "an affidavit in support of a search warrant for a private dwelling must show probable cause on its face.... Probable cause for issuance of a search warrant cannot be based on mere suspicion, but rather must be based on facts known to exist." The affidavit and search warrant in this case cannot withstand scrutiny under the test of case law, section 933.18(10), or the Florida or federal constitutions.

Because we have resolved this case on the sufficiency of the affidavit, it is not necessary to address the equally difficult question of whether possession of a computer diskette that contained deleted images of child pornography retrievable only through efforts of a computer forensics expert is sufficient evidence to sustain a conviction for possession of child pornography.

Affirmed in part, reversed in part, and remanded for resentencing.

ALTENBERND, C.J., and WHATLEY, J., Concur.

Notes

In *Illinois v. Gates*, 103 S. Ct. 2317, 462 U.S. 213 (1983), cited by the court in *Burnett*, the United States Supreme Court set out the constitutional imperative for finding probable cause: as a threshold matter, the Fourth Amendment requires "a fair probability that evidence of a crime will be found...." *See also United States v. Smith*, 510 F.3d 641, 652 (6th Cir. 2007) (referring to this as the "totality of the circumstances"). The Court has elaborated on this imperative by holding that probable cause does not require the calculation of exact percentages, but may be determined based on the totality of the circumstances. *See Maryland v. Pringle*, 540 U.S. 366, 371 (2003) ("The probable-cause standard is incapable of precise definition or quantification into percentages because it deals with probabilities...."). As stated in *Burnett*, this requires that the affidavit of probable cause demonstrate, with specificity, that: (1) a crime was committed; and (2) evidence relevant to that crime is likely to be located at the place to be searched. In *Burnett*, the court determined that the video tapes were sufficiently relevant to Burnett's lewd and lascivious conduct with his children, but they were not sufficient to support a likelihood that Burnett possessed child pornography on diskettes on his computer. There were no specific averments that created a nexus between video tapes depicting lewd conduct and computer diskettes containing child pornography. And without such specificity, there was no probable cause to search his computer. *See, e.g., State v. Nuss*, 781 N.W.2d 60 (Neb. 2010) (no probable cause where terms "child pornography" or "sexually explicit conduct" are specifically defined, but affidavit's description of pictures sought to be obtained lacked such specificity and were merely conclusory); *see also United States v. Genin*, 594 F. Supp. 2d 412 (S.D.N.Y. 2009) (affidavit describing videos in defendant's possession merely as "child pornography" was insufficient). *But see United States v. Stults*, 575 F.3d 834, 838 (8th Cir. 2009) (affidavit including descriptive names of files found on defendant's file-sharing software, such as "Photo by Carl—pedoincest 13yr girl f****d by daddy," held sufficient for probable cause); *United States v. Lowe*, 516 F.3d 580, 586 (7th Cir. 2008) ("issuing court does not need to look at the images described in an affidavit in order to determine whether there is probable cause to believe that they constitute child pornography. A detailed verbal description is sufficient."); *United States v. Chrobak*, 289 F.3d 1043, 1045 (8th Cir. 2002) (sufficient probable cause where description of images defendant sent to web site as depicting "sexually explicit conduct involving children under the age of 16" was almost identical to language of federal "possession" statute under which defendant was charged).

In assessing the sufficiency of affidavits supporting probable cause, courts often consider the totality of the circumstances. It is not always clear, however, what circumstances establish a sufficient nexus between alleged facts and the likelihood of uncovering additional evidence. For example, it is not always clear that allegations of sexual misconduct or exploitation at a defendant's *place of work* provide probable cause to search for child pornography at a defendant's *residence*. *See Dougherty v. Covina*, 654 F.3d 892, 900 (9th Cir. 2011). Rather, the issue may depend on other circumstances that tie together the two crimes. The following cases address the sufficiency of various circumstances that arguably provide a sufficient nexus to satisfy probable cause to search for, obtain, and admit evidence of sexual exploitation.

B. Sufficient Nexus

1. Sexual Offenses

Dougherty v. City of Covina

Ninth Circuit, 2011
654 F.3d 892

N.R. SMITH, Circuit Judge: ...

On October 12, 2006, Officer Robert Bobkiewicz, of the City of Covina Police Department, and four other police officers (three from the City of Covina and one from the City of Glendora) searched Appellant Bruce Dougherty's ... [footnote omitted] home pursuant to a warrant issued by a magistrate on October 11, 2006 ... [footnote omitted]. The search warrant authorized the officers to search for child pornography on Dougherty's computer and electronic media.... To obtain the search warrant, Officer Bobkiewicz submitted an affidavit reciting that he was involved in the investigation of Dougherty's inappropriate touching of one of his sixth grade students at Royal Oak Elementary School. The student reported that Dougherty had lifted her up in front of the class after she told him that she had won a cross-country meet. She reported that Dougherty's hands were touching her breasts when he lifted her up to a level where he could look at her buttocks. The student told Bobkiewicz that she had seen Dougherty look up the skirts and down the tops of other girls in the class. In interviews, other students confirmed the lifting incident to Bobkiewicz and also reported that Dougherty looked up the skirts and down the shirts of girls in the class. Officer Bobkiewicz also discussed the investigation with the Assistant Superintendent for the School District, Gloria Cortez. Cortez told Officer Bobkiewicz that she had conducted an investigation after the incident with the student described above. Her investigation turned up multiple reports of Dougherty touching girls' backs and appearing to search for bra straps with his hands (this information was corroborated by the former vice-principal at Royal Oak). Cortez's investigation also turned up a 2003 report of a student, who said that Dougherty pulled her shirt down to her waist while they were alone in the classroom. The investigation of that incident was not pursued, after it was determined the student made inconsistent statements. The mother of the student in that incident, however, later believed she made a mistake not believing her daughter. When police contacted that student (then in high school) to discuss the previous allegation, she recounted that Dougherty touched her bare breast and told her she was "a special girl."

In the affidavit, Officer Bobkiewicz also recounts that he had fourteen years of experience on the police force and had worked as a School Resource Officer. He had over 100 hours of training involving juvenile and sex crimes, had conducted hundreds of investigations related to sexual assaults and juveniles, and was the designated "Sex Crimes/Juvenile Detective" for the police department. The affidavit concludes with Officer Bobkiewicz stating that "based upon my training and experience ... I know subjects involved in this type of criminal behavior have in their possession child pornography...." The affidavit then requests the ability to seize Dougherty's computer, cameras, and electronic media and have them searched for child pornography. A magistrate signed the warrant on October 11, 2006.

When officers arrived at Dougherty's house, he allowed the officers to enter and search. However, when Dougherty asked to see a warrant, Officer Bobkiewicz stated that he had forgotten it at the police station. During the search, the officers entered and moved about the house with their guns drawn. They awakened Dougherty's adult son, Jonathan, at gun point and gave him the option of leaving the house or sitting on the couch in the living room during the search. Jonathan chose to remain on the couch. The officers seized computers and "related items" from Dougherty's home. The computers and other items were not returned until December 27, 2007. No charges were filed against Dougherty.

After the search of Dougherty's house, Dougherty sued Officer Bobkiewicz, the City of Covina, and Kim Raney, the Chief of Police, for violating his constitutional rights.... [footnote omitted]. Dougherty claimed ... the City and the officers violated his and his son's Fourth Amendment right to be free from unreasonable search and seizure.... The district court dismissed Dougherty's complaint with prejudice on August 4, 2009. The court reviewed the complaint, the search warrant, and the affidavit. The court found the warrant was supported by probable cause, and that the detention of Dougherty and his son was reasonable. The district court further held Bobkiewicz was entitled to qualified immunity....

"Sufficient information must be presented to the magistrate to allow that official to determine probable cause; his action cannot be a mere ratification of the bare conclusions of others." *Illinois v. Gates*, 462 U.S. 213, 239, 103 S.Ct. 2317, 76 L.Ed.2d 527 (1983). When an affidavit moves "beyond the 'bare bones,'" however, a "totality of the circumstances test" is employed. *Id.* at 238–39, 103 S.Ct. 2317. Under the totality of the circumstances test, a neutral magistrate must "make a practical, common-sense decision whether, given all the circumstances set forth in the affidavit before him, including the 'veracity' and 'basis of knowledge' of persons supplying hearsay information, there is a fair probability that contraband or evidence of a crime will be found in a particular place." *Id.* at 238, 103 S.Ct. 2317. The magistrate is free to draw "reasonable inferences ... from the material supplied to him by applicants for a warrant." *Id.* at 240, 103 S.Ct. 2317.... The "standards for determining probable cause for a search warrant" apply to a search for child pornography on a computer. *United States v. Kelley*, 482 F.3d 1047, 1050 (9th Cir.2007). Neither "certainty nor a preponderance of the evidence is required," but rather a "fair probability" that the evidence will be found. *Id.* The magistrate's determination of probable cause "should be paid great deference." *Id.* (internal citation and quotation marks omitted). " 'Although in a particular case it may not be easy to determine when an affidavit demonstrates the existence of probable cause, resolution of doubtful or marginal cases in this area should largely be determined by the preference to be accorded to warrants.' " *Id.* at 1050–51 (quoting *Gates*, 462 U.S. at 237 n. 10, 103 S.Ct. 2317) (alteration omitted).

Although there does not need to be direct evidence of solicitation of child pornography to create probable cause, *Kelley*, 482 F.3d at 1051–52, the reviewing court must make certain there was a "substantial basis" for the finding, *United States v. Weber*, 923 F.2d 1338, 1343 (9th Cir.1990) (citing *Gates*, 462 U.S. at 238, 103 S.Ct. 2317). In *Weber*, we held that probable cause did not exist to search a house for child pornography when an affidavit recited only that a suspect had two years previously received a catalog of child pornography and had ordered four images of possible child pornography.[5] *Id.* at 1345. The affidavit in *Weber* included a statement from a police detective stating that he knew "the habits of 'child molesters,' 'pedophiles,' and 'child pornography collectors' and that from his knowledge of these classes of persons he could expect certain things to be at their houses, from diaries to sexual aids to photo developing equipment." *Id.* The affidavit did not, however, have a "whit of evidence" that Weber was a child molester, and it did not describe how many magazines or photographs it would take to qualify as a "collector." *Id.* We noted that "[i]t goes without saying that the government could not search Weber's house for evidence to prove Weber was a collector merely by alleging he was a collector." *Id.* We distinguished the probable cause demonstrated in the affidavit in *Weber* from the affidavit in *United States v. Rabe*, 848 F.2d 994 (9th Cir.1988). We noted that, in *Rabe*, there was direct evidence that the defendant had child pornography in his home. *Id.* We also noted that the expert in *Rabe* specifically concluded that the defendant was a pedophile, and the expert and magistrate knew that the defendant admitted to owning child pornography and desired to take nude photos of children before the warrant was issued. *Weber*, 923 F.2d at 1345–46 (citing *Rabe*, 848 F.2d at 995–96).

If probable cause did not exist in *Weber*, it cannot exist here. In *Weber*, the affidavit included at least some direct evidence of the defendant's possible possession of child pornography, including a two-year-old delivery of a catalog containing child pornography, an order from a fake catalog with image names suggesting child pornography, and general information regarding collectors, pedophiles, and molesters. *Weber*, 923 F.2d at 1345. Here, by contrast, the affidavit includes only a three-year-old allegation of attempted molestation by one student and current allegations of inappropriate touching of and looking at students.

The affidavit contains no facts tying the acts of Dougherty as a possible child molester to his possession of child pornography. The affidavit provides no evidence of receipt of

---

5. Probable cause did exist to search for the four images that Weber actually ordered from a fake catalog sent by the government. *Weber*, 923 F.2d at 1346.

child pornography. No expert "specifically concludes" Dougherty is a pedophile. In the affidavit, Officer Bobkiewicz states only that "[b]ased upon [his] training and experience ... subjects in this type of criminal behavior have in their possession child pornography...." The affidavit provides no indication that Dougherty was interested in viewing images of naked children or of children performing sex acts. There is no evidence of conversations with students about sex acts, discussions with children about pictures or video, or other possible indications of interest in child pornography. Officer Bobkiewicz either did not search Dougherty's work computer or email account for indications of pedophilia or child pornography, or did so and did not find any. Indeed, the affidavit does not even verify that Dougherty owned a computer or the other targets of the search or had internet service or another means of receiving child pornography at his home.

Other circuits have split on the question of whether evidence of child molestation, alone, creates probable cause for a search warrant for child pornography. The Second Circuit has stated that a "crime allegedly involv[ing] the sexual abuse of a minor, [does] not relate to child pornography.... That the law criminalizes both child pornography and the sexual abuse (or endangerment) of children cannot be enough."[6] *United States v. Falso*, 544 F.3d 110, 123 (2d Cir.2008). The Sixth Circuit agrees that, when probable cause is established "for one crime (child molestation) but [the warrant is] designed and requested [to] search for evidence of an entirely different crime (child pornography)," it is "beyond dispute that the warrant [i]s defective." *United States v. Hodson*, 543 F.3d 286, 292 (6th Cir.2008). In fact, in *Hodson*, the evidence was much more related to viewing children in sex acts and to computers than the evidence in the affidavit here. There, in an internet chatroom, Hodson "confided that he ... favored young boys, liked looking at his nine-and eleven-year-old sons naked, and had even had sex with his seven-year-old nephew. [Hodson] also expressed his desire to perform oral sex on the presumptive twelve-year-old boy ... and his willingness to travel ... to do so." *Id.* at 287. Nonetheless, the Sixth Circuit firmly held that the warrant was "so lacking in indicia of probable cause that" not even the good-faith exception to unlawfully executed warrants could apply. *Id.* at 292–93.... The Eighth Circuit, however, has rejected the reasoning of *Falso* and *Hodson*, stating "[t]here is an intuitive relationship between acts such as child molestation or enticement and possession of child pornography." *United States v. Colbert*, 605 F.3d 573, 578 (8th Cir.2010). The affidavit in *Colbert*, however, did include evidence that the accused had enticed a child to come to his apartment. *Id.* at 577.

Ultimately, the question of probable cause is "not readily, or even usefully, reduced to a neat set of legal rules." *Gates*, 462 U.S. at 232, 103 S.Ct. 2317. Thus, while the "totality of circumstances" could, in some instances, allow us to find probable cause to search for child pornography, Officer Bobkiewicz's conclusory statement tying this "subject," alleged to have molested two children and looked inappropriately at others, to "having in [his] possession child pornography" is insufficient to create probable cause here....

AFFIRMED.

BREWSTER, Judge, concurring in the judgment:

I conclude the search warrant was supported by probable cause. *United States v. Gourde*, 440 F.3d 1065 (9th Cir.2006) (en banc). I accord more deference to the independent

---

6. The Second Circuit also noted, however, that "nothing in the affidavit draws a correlation between a person's propensity to commit both types of crimes." *Falso*, 544 F.3d at 123. The *Falso* court did not consider whether a conclusory statement tying persons involved with sexual abuse of a minor to possession of child pornography would suffice to create probable cause in absence of more direct evidence or a more detailed explanation of why such a connection exists.

judgment of the magistrate judge and to the experience and training of the investigating officer. Based upon Officer Bobkiewicz's specific training and experience in the field of sex crimes against children, the facts presented led him to conclude that an individual who molests children probably possesses child pornography. I agree with the Eighth Circuit's analysis in *United States v. Colbert*, 605 F.3d 573, 578 (8th Cir.2010), that it is a common sense leap that an adult male, who teaches sixth graders, engaged in this type of inappropriate conduct would likely possess child pornography. *Accord United States v. Byrd*, 31 F.3d 1329, 1340 (5th Cir.1994); *United States v. Houston*, 754 F.Supp.2d 1059, 1062–64 & n. 1 (D.S.D.2010); *see also Osborne v. Ohio*, 495 U.S. 103, 111 n. 7, 110 S.Ct. 1691, 109 L.Ed.2d 98 (1990). Dougherty's pattern of affirmative misconduct with several sixth grade students is closely related to an interest in looking at sexual images of minors. The facts suggested to Officer Bobkiewicz, a highly trained and experienced "Sex Crimes/ Juvenile Detective," that a potential child predator has moved along the continuum of looking and into the realm of touching. Dougherty's active misconduct distinguishes his case from the cases involving defendants who may have passively received unsolicited child pornography. *E.g., United States v. Kelley*, 482 F.3d 1047, 1051 (9th Cir.2007); *United States v. Weber*, 923 F.2d 1338, 1345 (9th Cir.1990). More importantly, the magistrate judge reviewed the affidavit and signed the search warrant. The magistrate judge's determination "should be paid great deference." *Gourde*, 440 F.3d at 1069 (quoting *Illinois v. Gates*, 462 U.S. 213, 236, 103 S.Ct. 2317, 76 L.Ed.2d 527 (1983)).

Although I disagree with the probable cause analysis, I concur that the police officers are entitled to qualified immunity. Accordingly, my position would not alter the outcome of this case.

Notes

The court in *Dougherty* recognized the circuit split on the question of whether reasonable suspicion of sexual offenses are sufficient to create probable cause to search for possession of child pornography. *Compare United States v. Colbert*, 605 F.3d 573 (8th Cir. 2010) (finding sufficient probable cause) with *United States v. Doyle*, 650 F.3d 460, 472 (4th Cir. 2011), *United States v. Falso*, 544 F.3d 110, 122 (2d Cir. 2008), and *United States v. Hodson*, 543 F.3d 286, 289 (6th Cir. 2008) (finding insufficient probable cause). The *Dougherty* court adopted neither position and, instead, adopted an ad hoc approach to determine the totality of the circumstances. Which is the most prudent approach? In cases in which acts of sexual exploitation are sufficient—separately or in conjunction with other facts— to create probable cause to expand a search to areas that may contain evidence of possession of child pornography, some courts automatically include within the scope of that search the defendant's home and personal computers. *See United States v. Clark*, 668 F.3d 934 (7th Cir. 2012) (sexual assault that occurred at brother's home was sufficient to characterize defendant as a collector of child pornography, and once this threshold is satisfied, probable cause exists to extend the search to defendant's home and personal computers).

2. Possession

United States v. Terry

Sixth Circuit, 2008
522 F.3d 645

BOGGS, Chief Judge....

The facts of this case are undisputed. In the early morning hours of October 14, 2004, Internet service provider AOL (formerly known as America Online) intercepted two e-mail messages containing a known child pornography image. These messages were sent from the e-mail address "skippie4u@aol.com" to an unknown recipient (or recipients) at 2:35 a.m. and again at 2:36 a.m. The following day, AOL forwarded the image, along with the screen name, e-mail address, and zip code of the user, to the National Center for Missing and Exploited Children (NCMEC), which in turn forwarded the information to Immigration and Customs Enforcement (ICE) officers. Upon issuance of a summons, AOL provided ICE more information on the "skippie4u" screen name, which revealed that "skippie4u" was one of three screen names assigned to a master AOL account registered to Roy Terry, who lived at 10 Township Avenue in Cincinnati, Ohio. Defendant Brent Terry (Roy's son) was the registered user of the "skippie4u" screen name. ICE confirmed through the Postal Service that both Roy and Brent Terry received mail at 10 Township Avenue.

Based on this information, ICE obtained a search warrant for the Township Avenue address and executed it on March 21, 2005. The record does not reveal what, if anything, was searched and/or seized from the Township Avenue residence. It appears, however, that ICE was most interested in Brent Terry, not his father, because the e-mail account used to send the image was registered specifically to the younger Terry. During the search, ICE reported that Roy Terry

> was interviewed at which time he stated that he has an Internet account through America Online (AOL), which is utilized, by himself, Brenda TERRY and Brent TERRY. Roy TERRY stated that Brent TERRY lives at 16 Walnut St. Cincinnati, OH and has access to the aforementioned AOL account from that address. Roy TERRY also stated that Brent TERRY has a computer that he uses at that address to access the account. Furthermore, Roy TERRY informed [ICE] that Brent TERRY utilizes the screen name Skippie 4U when accessing the aforementioned AOL account from his address 16 Walnut St. Cincinnati, OH.

[Citation to record omitted] (capitalization in original). Roy also told ICE that Brent had lived at the Walnut Street address, which he rented from Roy, for approximately one and a half years. Thus, he was living in the Walnut Street residence at the time his e-mail account was used to send the illegal image.

ICE then obtained the search warrant for 16 Walnut Street that is the subject of this appeal. That warrant was executed on the same day, and agents recovered a laptop computer, three hard drives, and various external media from the residence, which were found to contain a total of 123 images and eight videos of minors engaged in sexually explicit conduct. Terry later moved to suppress this evidence, which motion the district court denied. Thereafter Terry entered a conditional guilty plea pursuant to Federal Rule of Criminal Procedure 11(a)(2) and appealed the denial of his suppression motion to this court....

Terry asserts that there was an insufficient nexus to connect the intercepted child pornography image to his home computer, arguing that the AOL e-mail account used to send the illicit image could have been accessed from any computer with an Internet connection. We certainly agree that to establish probable cause to support a search warrant, there must be some nexus between the illegal activity suspected and the property to be searched. *See United States v. McPhearson*, 469 F.3d 518 (6th Cir.2006) (mere fact that man arrested for non-drug offense had drugs on his person did not establish the requisite nexus to search his home for drugs); *United States v. Carpenter*, 360 F.3d 591, 594 (6th Cir.2004) (en banc) (fact that marijuana was found growing near a residence, by itself, "f[e]ll short of establishing the required nexus between the ... residence and evidence of marijuana manufacturing"). We do not agree, however, that such a nexus was lacking in this case.

The government's affidavit established that (1) the AOL e-mail account belonging to the "skippie4u" screen name sent two e-mail messages at approximately 2:30 a.m. containing a known child pornography image; (2) Brent Terry was the registered user of the "skippie4u" screen name; (3) Brent Terry lived at 16 Walnut Street at the time the e-mail messages were sent; and (4) Brent Terry had a computer at that address through which he accessed the "skippie4u" e-mail account used to send the messages. It requires no great leap of logic to conclude that the computer in Terry's home was probably used to send the intercepted messages. Given that the probable cause standard deals with "the factual and practical considerations of everyday life on which reasonable and prudent men, not legal technicians, act," *Gates*, 462 U.S. at 231, 103 S.Ct. 2317 (quoting *Brinegar v. United States*, 338 U.S. 160, 175, 69 S.Ct. 1302, 93 L.Ed. 1879 (1949)), the district court did not err in concluding that "as a matter of plain common sense, if ... a pornographic image has originated or emanated from a particular individual's email account, it logically follows that the image is likely to be found on that individual's computer or on storage media associated with the computer." ... There are other possibilities, of course—a hacker illicitly using Terry's e-mail account, for example—but probable cause does not require "near certainty," only a "fair probability." *See United States v. Martin*, 289 F.3d 392, 400 (6th Cir.2002) ("Although innocent explanations for some or all of these facts may exist, this possibility does not render the ... determination of probable cause invalid.").[1]

In a similar case, this court upheld probable cause to search a home where the defendant had purchased subscriptions to known child pornography websites, but where it was unknown precisely which computer he had used to access those sites. *See United States v. Wagers*, 452 F.3d 534 (6th Cir.2006). In *Wagers*, the defendant used a business-based checking card to subscribe to two websites that made available both legal and illegal pornography. He argued that since "his subscriptions were connected only to his business office, not to his home," there was "nothing ... [to] connect[ ] the residence to the alleged child pornography offenses." *Id.* at 539. We rejected this "feeble" argument, observing that the affidavit "aver[red] that an [Internet Protocol (IP)] address assigned by Insight [Communications] ... was used to purchase both memberships" and that the defendant "used Insight at his home but not his office...." *Ibid.* Logically, we concluded that the defendant's "home would be well within the ambit of a properly issued search warrant." *Ibid.* We further noted that "[e]ven if the home were only one of two locations—home and office—served by Insight, there would be sufficient evidence to support probable cause." *Ibid.*

Terry attempts to distinguish *Wagers* on the ground that, unlike in *Wagers*, there was no IP information either to tie his computer to the e-mail messages, or even to limit the possible number of computers that could have been used to send the message. But the *Wagers* opinion did not hold that IP information was an indispensable prerequisite to obtaining a search warrant in a case involving Internet-based child pornography, only that such information contributed to the totality of the probable-cause determination. Indeed, *Wagers* favorably cited several cases that arguably involved even less evidence of probable cause than is presented here. *See id.* at 540, 543 (citing *United States v. Gourde*,

---

1. Though not central to our analysis on this point, the fact that the images were sent at approximately 2:30 in the morning further reduces the likelihood that a computer other than the one in Terry's home was used.

440 F.3d 1065 (9th Cir.2006) (en banc); *United States v. Martin*, 426 F.3d 68 (2d Cir.2005); and *United States v. Froman*, 355 F.3d 882 (5th Cir.2004)). All of the cited cases involved defendants who subscribed to websites that were advertised as child pornography sites but contained both legal and illegal material, and in which the government's affidavit supporting a search warrant never stated whether the individuals had actually downloaded any of the *illicit* materials. Nevertheless, the courts universally found that the probable cause threshold had been satisfied because the defendants had purchased *access* to child pornography. In this case, although there was no evidence that Terry belonged to such a website, there was evidence that Terry had actually *possessed* (as opposed to merely having had access to) child pornography. While any IP or other information that could have more specifically tied Terry's home computer to the e-mail messages would certainly have been welcome, we are satisfied that the use of Terry's personal email account in the wee hours of the morning, combined with information that Terry used his home computer to access that account, established at least a "fair probability" that the computer used to send the messages was, in fact, the one in Terry's home. Ergo, there was at least a fair probability that the illicit image (or similar images) would be found there.[2]

We are somewhat troubled by the fact that the *content* of the incriminating e-mail messages was apparently not preserved.[3] It is thus impossible to know the context in which the image was sent; Terry argues that he may have merely been replying to some unsolicited child pornography spam to request that no further such images be sent to him. Although this is theoretically possible,[4] it is not enough for Terry simply to speculate about hypothetical "false-positive" scenarios. He presented no evidence at the suppression hearing about the actual occurrence of such "spam-rejection" transmission of child porn, either in his case or in society generally. Since a probable cause finding does not require a preponderance of the evidence, in order to undermine the magistrate's finding, the likelihood of an innocent explanation must (at the very least) be *greater* than the likelihood of a guilty one. For example, this court has indicated that—given studies demonstrating that a sizable percentage of United States currency in circulation is tainted with a detectable level of cocaine residue—a canine alert to currency, standing alone, will likely not establish probable cause in a forfeiture action. *United States v. $5,000.00 in U.S. Currency*, 40 F.3d 846, 849–50 (6th Cir.1994).[5] In the context of automobiles, however, the rate of false positives is significantly lower, and an alert from a trained, reliable canine will alone

---

2. We do not believe that the passage of five months between the sending of the intercepted e-mail messages and the execution of the warrant changes the probable cause calculus much, if at all. Images typically persist in some form on a computer hard drive even after the images have been deleted and, as ICE stated in its affidavit, such evidence can often be recovered by forensic examiners. *See United States v. Lacy*, 119 F.3d 742, 746 (9th Cir.1997) (holding that the nature of the crime "provided good reason to believe the computerized visual depictions downloaded by Lacy would be present in his apartment when the search was conducted ten months later") (internal quotation omitted).

3. The record does not reveal whether this failure was the fault of AOL, the NCMEC, or ICE.

4. Whether an image that is received via an e-mail message is also included in an outgoing reply would depend on various factors, including the e-mail client settings, whether the image was included within the body of the incoming message or as an attachment, the operation of any filtering software, etc.

5. More recent case law has called this assumption into question. *See United States v. Funds in Amount of Thirty Thousand Six Hundred Seventy Dollars*, 403 F.3d 448, 459 (7th Cir.2005) (skeptically approaching the "currency contamination theory" and citing newer research indicating that "it is likely that trained cocaine detection dogs will alert to currency only if it has been exposed to large amounts of illicit cocaine within the very recent past").

establish probable cause to search the vehicle. *United States v. Diaz*, 25 F.3d 392, 393–94, 396 (6th Cir.1994). Although we recognize that the government ultimately has the burden of demonstrating probable cause, absent *any* evidence that innocent persons frequently receive and reply to unsolicited child pornography spam (and in a way that would produce the computer traces in this case), this court cannot say that the magistrate judge arbitrarily exercised his discretion in issuing a search warrant for Terry's home....

For the foregoing reasons, we AFFIRM the judgment of the district court.

United States v. McArthur

Eighth Circuit, 2009
573 F.3d 608

SHEPHERD, Circuit Judge....

On April 1, 2006, Officer Trent Koppel of the Des Peres Police Department was on patrol at the West County Mall in Des Peres, Missouri, when mall security reported that an older, white male was masturbating inside his vehicle in the mall parking lot. Officer Koppel responded immediately, located the vehicle, and activated her emergency lights. The driver attempted to navigate around the cars in front of him but was unsuccessful. Officer Koppel approached the blocked-in vehicle and ordered the driver to turn off the engine and exit the vehicle. Officer Koppel observed that the driver's penis was exposed. The driver exited the vehicle and handed Officer Koppel his driver's license, which identified the driver as Roderick McArthur. Officer Koppel placed McArthur under arrest for public indecency and transported him to the Des Peres Police Department for booking.

Officers inventoried McArthur's personal property and found in his wallet a laminated photograph of a nude, male child who is looking at and touching an erect, adult penis that is superimposed on the child's body. Officer Koppel advised McArthur of his *Miranda* rights, ... [footnote omitted] which McArthur waived. McArthur stated that he has always had an overactive libido and sometimes could not control his urges. He claimed that he met someone online who agreed to meet him at the West County Mall. When that person did not arrive, McArthur stated that he drove around the parking lot, became aroused, and began to masturbate. In a written statement, McArthur admitted exposing himself in the vehicle and apologized for his "very inappropriate behavior." McArthur posted bond and was released on the same day as his arrest.

Officer Koppel contacted Detective Juan Gomez, then a nine-year veteran of the St. Louis County Police Department with extensive training and experience investigating child pornography offenses, and provided Detective Gomez with information regarding McArthur's arrest. Detective Gomez confirmed McArthur's home address by conducting a utilities check. Detective Gomez also discovered that McArthur was convicted in 1986 for sodomy involving a minor and in 2004 for sexual misconduct and that McArthur had failed to register as a sex offender. Another St. Louis County officer, Sergeant Adam Kavanaugh, procured the nude photograph found in McArthur's wallet from the Des Peres Police Department. Sergeant Kavanaugh showed the photograph to Detective John Schmidt, a forensic analyst in the Computer Fraud Unit. Detective Schmidt stated that the photograph had been modified using computer software.

On April 4, 2006, Detective Gomez applied for a search warrant for McArthur's residence and any digital data devices found therein for evidence of possession of child pornography. Detective Gomez presented an affidavit in support of the application to the Honorable Brenda Stith Loftin, Associate Circuit Judge for the St. Louis County Circuit Court. The affidavit described the property to be searched with particularity, listed Detective Gomez's experience with "subjects known to possess and sell obscene material," detailed the events surrounding McArthur's public indecency arrest (including the discovery of the computer-altered photograph), and stated that "McArthur has been arrested for multiple sex offenses in St. Louis County, Missouri[,] in the past twenty years but has failed to register as a sex offender as required by law."

Judge Loftin authorized the search warrant at 6:30 p.m. on April 4, 2006. Officers executed the warrant later that evening and seized several digital data devices from McArthur's residence, including a computer. Detective Gomez then arrested McArthur, who was present during the search, for failing to register as a sex offender and escorted him to the St. Louis County Police Department. Detective Gomez interviewed McArthur, who again waived his *Miranda* rights. When asked about the photograph found in his wallet when he was arrested in Des Peres, McArthur claimed that his nephew had given the photograph to him 15 to 20 years earlier and that he had placed it in his wallet and forgotten about it. Detective Gomez asked McArthur for consent to search his computer and the other devices. After repeatedly and emphatically denying that there was child pornography on any of his equipment, McArthur consented, in writing, to the search.

Detective Gomez took the seized items to the Regional Computer Crime Education and Enforcement Group ("RCCEEG") to be examined by Detective Leonard Stimmel, a forensic computer analyst. During a brief examination of the computer, Detective Stimmel discovered several images of children involved in sex acts or displaying their genitals in a sexual manner. Even though McArthur had already consented in writing to the search of his computer, out of an abundance of caution, Detective Gomez presented another application and affidavit in support of a search warrant for the computer. In addition to reiterating all of the information contained in the first affidavit, the new affidavit detailed the seizure of the computer and the results of Detective Stimmel's brief search of its contents. The Honorable Dale W. Hood, Associate Circuit Judge for the St. Louis County Circuit Court, found probable cause and signed the search warrant for McArthur's computer.

Detective Kenneth Nix, a computer forensic examiner and the operations supervisor of the RCCEEG, thoroughly examined the hard drive from McArthur's computer. Detective Nix located multiple images in the hard drive's unallocated space[4] that depicted children displaying their genitals and engaging in masturbation, oral sex, and vaginal sex with adults. Also in the unallocated space, Detective Nix found myriad child pornography web pages that the user had visited directly. Detective Nix's examination showed that someone had reinstalled the computer's operating system on April 2, 2006—the day after the Des Peres Police Department released McArthur following his public indecency arrest and two days before the St. Louis County Police Department executed the search warrant for McArthur's home and seized his computer. Detective Nix testified at trial that computers normally come with an operating system already installed and that, when someone reinstalls the operating system, all of the computer's data is moved into unallocated space on the hard drive. Finally, Detective Nix reviewed disks that McArthur's expert witness, Gregory Chatten, claimed to be back-up disks of some of the data on McArthur's computer

---

4. Detective Nix testified that "allocated space" is space on a computer that is usable. When a user deletes a file, it is not erased completely from the computer. Instead, the deleted file is moved to "unallocated space," which is where Detective Nix located child pornography on McArthur's computer.

over a three-year period prior to its seizure. One of the disks contained authentication codes for several websites, including sites that contained child pornography.

Chatten confirmed that images of child pornography were located in the unallocated space on McArthur's hard drive. He also confirmed that reinstalling McArthur's operating system would have moved all of the computer's data into unallocated space. Chatten testified that he could not discern the source of the images. However, he agreed that the user had directly visited some of the child pornography websites found in unallocated space. Chatten further testified that one of McArthur's purported back-up disks was actually created on October 5, 2007, the same day the disks were mailed to McArthur's attorney and more than a year after police seized McArthur's computer. Chatten agreed that it was possible that a person could have copied an actual back-up disk made in 2005 to this new disk and then deleted files that the person did not wish Chatten to see. Chatten testified that he could not determine whether any files had been deleted from the purported back-up disk that was actually created on October 5, 2007.

On appeal, McArthur argues that the district court erred in adopting the [magistrate judge's Report and Recommendation] recommending denial of his motion to suppress because there was not probable cause to believe that there was evidence of child pornography in his home. Thus, McArthur contends, all of the fruits of that initial search, including the cursory examination of the computer and the images discovered as a result of McArthur's subsequent written consent, should have been suppressed. McArthur further argues that the district court erred in denying his motion for judgment of acquittal because the mere presence of child pornography images and websites stored in the computer's unallocated space is insufficient to prove that McArthur *knowingly* possessed child pornography....

McArthur does not challenge any factual determinations made below. He argues that the affidavit Detective Gomez filed in support of the application for the initial search warrant for McArthur's residence "contained insufficient indicia of probable cause to believe that McArthur possessed child pornography, in his home or on his computer." ... [citation to pleadings omitted]. Specifically, McArthur asserts that "the only averment even remotely connected to child pornography was a single laminated photograph in McArthur's wallet...." ... Thus, according to McArthur, "the inference that [he] kept child pornography in his home or on his computer was specious" and insufficient to support probable cause.... We disagree.

The affidavit chronicled the circumstances surrounding McArthur's public-indecency arrest for masturbating in his car in a mall parking lot three days earlier. Most significantly, the affidavit noted that, at the time of his arrest, McArthur possessed a laminated photograph of a nude child that had been modified using computer software. This revelation, standing alone, strongly indicated that child pornography would be found on McArthur's computer. Furthermore, the affidavit revealed that McArthur had been convicted for multiple, prior sex offenses but had failed to register as a sex offender and that Detective Gomez had experience dealing with subjects known to possess and sell obscene material. Finally, other courts have recognized—and Detective Gomez testified at the suppression hearing—that

> [t]he observation that images of child pornography are likely to be hoarded by persons interested in those materials in the privacy of their homes is supported by common sense and the cases. Since the materials are illegal to distribute and possess, initial collection is difficult. Having succeeded in obtaining images, collectors are unlikely to [ ] destroy them. Because of their illegality and the im-primatur of severe social stigma such images carry, collectors will want to secret them in secure places, like a private residence.

United States v. Riccardi, 405 F.3d 852, 861 (10th Cir.2005) (*quoting United States v. Lamb*, 945 F.Supp. 441, 460 (N.D.N.Y.1996)).

Considering the "totality of the circumstances" and examining the affidavit using a "common sense" approach, *Grant*, 490 F.3d at 631–32, we find that "the evidence as a whole provide[d] a substantial basis for finding probable cause to support the issuance of the search warrant" for McArthur's residence because "the affidavit supporting the search warrant set[ ] forth facts sufficient to create a fair probability that evidence of [possession of child pornography would] be found," *Terry*, 305 F.3d at 822. Therefore, the district court did not err when it denied McArthur's motion to suppress.... [footnote omitted]....

Accordingly, we affirm the judgment of the district court.

Notes

In *Terry*, the defendant used his e-mail account on a computer at his parent's home to access web sites from which he downloaded and possessed images of child pornography. In *McArthur*, the defendant possessed in his wallet a computer-generated photograph of a child engaged in lewd conduct, which police found upon arresting the defendant in a mall parking lot. In *Terry* and *McArthur*, the question for the courts was whether there was a sufficient nexis between each defendant's *mere possession* of child pornography *outside of the home* and a search of the defendant's computer *inside the home*. To find a sufficient nexus, the courts took a common sense approach and considered the totality of the circumstances to conclude that the mere possession of child pornography was sufficiently related to the defendants' computers such that there was a likelihood that evidence of child pornography would be found on the computers in their homes. *See also United States v. Lapsins*, 570 F.3d 758 (6th Cir. 2009) (evidence sufficient to connect crime outside the home to likelihood of child pornography inside the home). In light of the accessibility and global application of modern computer technology upon which the child pornography industry has so expansively relied, there is scarcely an item of data or information, or a resource for transmitting such data and information, that is not in some way associated with computer use. And if courts presumptively associate computer access outside the home with computer access inside the home, is there ever a circumstance in which any access or possession of sexually explicit images of children does not "open the door" to the search of one's home? What if the defendant in *McArthur* did not own a computer at his home but had daily access to a computer at his place of employment — would there exist probable cause to search the defendant's computer at work? What if, in *McArthur*, the image contained in the defendant's wallet had not been manipulated by computer enhancement but, instead, the photograph was taken with a disposable camera — would there still be a sufficient nexus to satisfy probable cause to search the defendant's home? What circumstance might the court consider to find such cause?

In the categories and cases that follow, consider what other activities and circumstances are deemed sufficient to produce probable cause to search the defendant's home or personal computers and seize evidence of child pornography that is found there. What role does computer access and modern technology play in satisfying Fourth Amendment standards for searching and seizing evidence of child sexual exploitation?

3. Group Membership

United States v. Gourde

Ninth Circuit, 2006
440 F.3d 1065

McKEOWN, Circuit Judge:

The term "Lolita" conjures up images ranging from the literary depiction of the adolescent seduced by her stepfather in Vladimir Nabokov's novel[1] to erotic displays of young girls and child pornography. This case requires us to consider probable cause to search a computer for child pornography in the context of an Internet website, known as "Lolitagurls.com," that admittedly displayed child pornography.... Micah Gourde appeals from the district court's denial of his motion to suppress more than 100 images of child pornography seized from his home computer. Gourde claims that the affidavit in support of the search lacked sufficient indicia of probable cause because it contained no evidence that Gourde actually downloaded or possessed child pornography. We disagree. Based on the totality of the circumstances, the magistrate judge who issued the warrant made a "practical, common-sense decision" that there was a "fair probability" that child pornography would be found on Gourde's computer. *Illinois v. Gates*, 462 U.S. 213, 238, 103 S.Ct. 2317, 76 L.Ed.2d 527 (1983).[2] The Fourth Amendment requires no more....

In May 2002, the FBI requested a warrant to search the residence of Micah Gourde for the purpose of seizing computer equipment and other materials containing evidence that he "probably caused the uploading, downloading and transmission of child pornography over the Internet" in violation of 18 U.S.C. §§ 2252 and 2252A, which criminalize the possession, receipt and transmission of child pornography. The following facts come from Special Agent David Moriguchi's affidavit in support of the search warrant. *See United States v. Anderson*, 453 F.2d 174, 175 (9th Cir.1971) ("[A]ll data necessary to show probable cause for the issuance of a search warrant must be contained within the four corners of a written affidavit given under oath.").

In August 2001, an undercover FBI agent discovered a website called "Lolitagurls.com." The first page of the site contained images of nude and partially-dressed girls, some prepubescent, along with this text:

> Lolitagurls.com offers hard to find pics! With weekly updates and high quality pix inside, you can[']t go wrong if you like young girls! Lolitas.Full size High Quality Pictures inside Join Now — instant access here THIS SITE updated weekly WITH NEW LOLITA PICS This site is in full compliance with United States Code Title 18 Part I Chapter 110 Section 2256.

The first page directed the user to a second page with more images of nude girls, some prepubescent, including three images displaying the genital areas of minors, and a caption reading "Lolitas age 12–17." The second page contained this text:

> Welcome to Lolitagurls. Over one thousand pictures of girls age 12–17! Naked lolita girls with weekly updates! What you will find here at Lolitagurls.com is a

---

1. Vladimir Nabokov, Lolita (1955).

2. We need not reach the issue of good faith under *United States v. Leon*, 468 U.S. 897, 104 S.Ct. 3405, 82 L.Ed.2d 677 (1984), because we hold there was probable cause to issue a search warrant.

complete collection of young girl pics. BONUS: You can get movies/mpegs at our partners site after you join if you wish.

The second page also had testimonials from website members, such as "This lolita site has everything with young girls!" and "I've never seen in my life the pics of so cute pre-teen girls." This page offered the viewer three ways to see other pages on the website: (1) take a free tour of the site, (2) become a new member of the site, or (3) log in as a returning member.

As part of his investigation, the undercover agent joined the website and was a member from August to December 2001. The membership fee was $19.95 per month, deducted automatically from the member's credit card. Lancelot Security handled credit card processing and access control for Lolitagurls.com. Members received unlimited access to the website and were "allowed … to download images directly from the website." Browsing the entire website, whose "primary feature was the images section," the undercover agent captured "hundreds of images" that "included adult pornography, child pornography, and child erotica." These images included the lascivious display of the breasts and genitalia of girls under the age of eighteen.… The FBI eventually identified the owner and operator of Lolitagurls.com and, in January 2002, executed a search warrant. Among the seized items was his computer, which contained child pornography images that had been posted to the Lolitagurls.com website. The owner "admitted … that 'Lolitagurls.com' was a child pornography website he operated as a source of income."

In response to a follow-up subpoena, Lancelot Security provided the FBI with information on Lolitagurls.com's subscribers. Lancelot's records listed Gourde as a member and provided his home address, date of birth, email address, and the fact that he had been a subscriber from November 2001 until January 2002. Gourde never cancelled his membership—the FBI shut down the site at the end of January, while he was still a member.

The affidavit contained extensive background information on computers and the characteristics of child pornography collectors. One section set out legal and computer terms relevant to understanding how downloading and possessing child pornography would violate 18 U.S.C. § 2252. Citing FBI computer experts, the affidavit explained that if a computer had ever received or downloaded illegal images, the images would remain on the computer for an extended period. That is, even if the user sent the images to "recycle" and then deleted the files in the recycling bin, the files were not actually erased but were kept in the computer's "slack space" until randomly overwritten, making even deleted files retrievable by computer forensic experts. Any evidence of a violation of 18 U.S.C. § 2252 would almost certainly remain on a computer long after the file had been viewed or downloaded and even after it had been deleted.

The affidavit also described the use of computers for child pornography activities. Based on his experience and that of other FBI experts, Moriguchi wrote that "[p]aid subscription websites are a forum through which persons with similar interests can view and download images in relative privacy." He described how collectors and distributors of child pornography use the free email and online storage services of Internet portals such as Yahoo! and Hotmail, among others, to operate anonymously because these websites require little identifying information. Communications through these portals result in both the intentional and unintentional storage of digital information, and a "user's Internet activities generally leave traces or 'footprints' in the web cache.…" Drawing on the expertise of the FBI Behavioral Analysis Unit, the affidavit listed certain "traits and characteristics … generally found to exist and be true in … individuals who collect child pornography." According to the affidavit, the majority of collectors are sexually attracted to children, "collect sexually explicit materials" including digital images for their own sexual gratification, also collect child erotica (images that are not themselves child pornography but still fuel their sexual fantasies involving children), "rarely, if ever, dispose of their sexually explicit materials," and "seek out like-minded individuals, either in person or on the Internet."

The affidavit concluded by identifying facts about Gourde that made it fairly probable that he was a child pornography collector and maintained a collection of child pornography and related evidence: (1) Gourde "took steps to affirmatively join" the website; (2) the website "advertised pictures of young girls"; (3) the website offered images of young girls engaged in sexually explicit conduct; (4) Gourde remained a member for over two months, although he could have cancelled at any time; (5) Gourde had access to hundreds of images, including historical postings to the website; and (6) any time Gourde visited the website, he had to have seen images of "naked prepubescent females with a caption that described them as twelve to seventeen-year-old girls." ... On the strength of Moriguchi's affidavit, the magistrate judge issued a warrant to search Gourde's residence and computers. The FBI searched Gourde's house and seized his computer, which contained over 100 images of child pornography and erotica.

Gourde filed a motion to suppress the images found on his computer. At the suppression hearing, the district court heard testimony from two FBI agents, including Moriguchi. The district court restricted its ruling to "the face of the affidavit," and denied Gourde's motion to suppress. The district court determined that the recitations in the affidavit supported a fair probability that evidence of a crime would be found on Gourde's computer. The judge applied a "common sense approach" to conclude that evidence of a subscription to even a "mixed" site — one that offered both legal adult pornography and illegal child pornography — provided the necessary "fair probability" to "look further." ... Shortly after, Gourde pleaded guilty to one count of possession of visual depictions of minors engaged in sexually explicit conduct in violation of 18 U.S.C. §§ 2252(a)(4)(B), 2252(b)(2) and 2256. In the plea agreement, he admitted to having "hundreds" of such images on his computer. Gourde conditioned his guilty plea on his right to appeal the district court's denial of his motion to suppress....

Our starting point is the Fourth Amendment, which prohibits "unreasonable searches and seizures," and its Warrants Clause, which requires that "no warrants shall issue, but upon probable cause, supported by Oath or affirmation, and particularly describing the place to be searched and the persons or things to be seized." U.S. Const. amend. IV. The contours of probable cause were laid out by the Supreme Court in its 1983 landmark decision, *Illinois v. Gates*, 462 U.S. 213, 103 S.Ct. 2317, 76 L.Ed.2d 527. In contrast to the more exacting, technical approach to probable cause in cases before *Gates, see id.* at 230, 103 S.Ct. 2317 n. 6, *Gates* itself marked a return to the "totality of the circumstances" test and emphasized that probable cause means "fair probability," not certainty or even a preponderance of the evidence. *Id.* at 246, 103 S.Ct. 2317. In short, a magistrate judge is only required to answer the "commonsense, practical question whether there is 'probable cause' to believe that contraband or evidence is located in a particular place" before issuing a search warrant. *Id.* at 230, 103 S.Ct. 2317.

The Supreme Court also used *Gates* as a vehicle to elaborate on our role as a reviewing court. We are not in a position to flyspeck the affidavit through de novo review. *Id.* at 236, 103 S.Ct. 2317 ("[A]fter-the-fact scrutiny by courts of the sufficiency of the affidavit should not take the form of *de novo* review"). Rather, the magistrate judge's determination "should be paid great deference." *Id.* (quoting *Spinelli v. United States*, 393 U.S. 410, 419, 89 S.Ct. 584, 21 L.Ed.2d 637 (1969)). This deferential approach is the antithesis of a "grudging or negative attitude" toward search warrants and "a hypertechnical rather than a commonsense" analysis. *United States v. Ventresca*, 380 U.S. 102, 108–09, 85 S.Ct. 741, 13 L.Ed.2d 684 (1965); *accord United States v. Seybold*, 726 F.2d 502, 505 (9th Cir.1983) (holding that our limited scope to review simply means determining whether the magistrate had a substantial basis for concluding there was a fair probability that evidence would be found).... We conclude that the affidavit contained sufficient facts to support the magistrate judge's finding that there was a "fair probability" that Gourde's computer contained evidence that he violated 18 U.S.C. §§ 2252 or 2252A.[3]

Turning first to the website itself, the evidence is unequivocal that Lolitagurls.com was a child pornography site whose primary content was in the form of images. Indeed, the owner admitted that it "was a child pornography website that he operated as a source of income." The owner's confession to the FBI established that Lolitagurls.com actually contained illegal content, the possession, receipt or transfer of which would be a violation of 18 U.S.C. § 2252. Thus, the magistrate judge had no reason to question whether the images described constituted child pornography because the owner himself acknowledged he purveyed illegal images. This fact alone renders futile Gourde's piecemeal attempts to chip away at the affidavit by identifying shortcomings in the description of images — i.e., that the FBI failed to describe images meeting the definition of child pornography, that the agent had no basis for determining how old the girls were, and that the website also contained legal content (i.e., adult pornography and child erotica). In the face of the owner's admission that he was operating a child pornography website, the prophylactic disclaimer that "[t]his site is in full compliance with United States Code, Title 18 Part I Chapter 110 Section 2256" is mere window dressing that absolves the owner or users of nothing.

The affidavit then moves from one certainty, that child pornography was on the website, to another — that Gourde had access and wanted access to these illegal images. Gourde subscribed to Lolitagurls.com for over two months, from November 2001 to January 2002. As a paying member, Gourde had unlimited access to hundreds of illegal images. He clearly had the means to receive and possess images in violation of 18 U.S.C. § 2252. But more importantly, Gourde's status as a member manifested his intention and desire to obtain illegal images.... Membership is both a small step and a giant leap. To become a member requires what are at first glance little, easy steps. It was easy for Gourde to submit his home address, email address and credit card data, and he consented to have $19.95 deducted from his credit card every month. But these steps, however easy, only could have been intentional and were not insignificant. Gourde could not have become a member by accident or by a mere click of a button.[4] This reality is perhaps easier to see by comparing Gourde to other archetypical visitors to the site. Gourde was not an accidental browser, such as a student who came across the site after "Googling" the term "Lolita" while researching the Internet for a term paper on Nabokov's book. Nor was Gourde someone who took advantage of the free tour but, after viewing the site, balked at taking

---

3. In briefing and argument, the parties focused on whether the affidavit supported a finding of probable cause that Gourde violated 18 U.S.C. § 2252(a)(4)(B), knowing possession of child pornography, presumably because Gourde pleaded guilty to this provision. Significantly, the warrant authorized the FBI to look for evidence that Gourde had violated *any part* of §§ 2252 or 2252A. These provisions criminalize not only possession, but they also criminalize knowing shipment of illegal images, § 2252(a)(1), receipt or distribution, § 2252(a)(2), sale, § 2252(a)(3), or attempt or conspiracy to commit any of these acts, § 2252(b)(1).

4. *Cf. United States v. Froman*, 355 F.3d 882, 885 (5th Cir.2004) (observing that membership in the Candyman eGroup, a forum dedicated to child pornography, was free and as simple as "clicking the subscribe link on the main web page"). In *Froman*, the Fifth Circuit concluded that there was probable cause to believe that members of the eGroup possessed child pornography. *Id.* at 890–91.

the active steps necessary to become a member and gain unlimited access to images of child pornography. Gourde is different still from a person who actually mustered the money and nerve to become a member but, the next morning, suffered buyer's remorse or a belated fear of prosecution and cancelled his subscription. Instead, Gourde became a member and never looked back—his membership ended because the FBI shut down the site. The affidavit left little doubt that Gourde had paid to obtain unlimited access to images of child pornography knowingly and willingly, and not involuntary, unwittingly, or even passively. With evidence from Lancelot Security, the FBI linked the email user— "gilbert_95@yahoo.com," a known subscriber to Lolitagurls.com—to Gourde and to his home address in Castle Rock, Washington.

Having paid for multi-month access to a child pornography site, Gourde was also stuck with the near certainty that his computer would contain evidence of a crime had he received or downloaded images in violation of § 2252. Thanks to the long memory of computers, any evidence of a crime was almost certainly still on his computer, even if he had tried to delete the images. FBI computer experts, cited in the affidavit, stated that "even if ... graphic image files [ ] have been deleted ... these files can easily be restored." In other words, his computer would contain at least the digital footprint of the images. It was unlikely that evidence of a crime would have been stale or missing, as less than four months had elapsed between the closing of the Lolitagurls.com website and the execution of the search warrant. *See United States v. Lacy*, 119 F.3d 742, 746 (9th Cir.1997) (holding that the nature of the crime involving child pornography, as set forth in the affidavit, "provided 'good reason[ ]' to believe the computerized visual depictions downloaded by Lacy would be present in his apartment when the search was conducted ten months later").

Given this triad of solid facts—the site had illegal images, Gourde intended to have and wanted access to these images, and these images were almost certainly retrievable from his computer if he had ever received or downloaded them—the only inference the magistrate judge needed to make to find probable cause was that there was a "fair probability" Gourde had, in fact, received or downloaded images. *Gates* supports the principle that a probable cause determination may be based in part on reasonable inferences. *See* 462 U.S. at 240, 103 S.Ct. 2317 (noting that a magistrate judge may "draw such reasonable inferences as he will from the material supplied to him by applicants for a warrant").

Here, the reasonable inference that Gourde had received or downloaded images easily meets the "fair probability" test. It neither strains logic nor defies common sense to conclude, based on the totality of these circumstances, that someone who paid for access for two months to a website that actually purveyed child pornography probably had viewed or downloaded such images onto his computer. *See Gates*, 462 U.S. at 246, 103 S.Ct. 2317. Together these facts form the basis of the totality-of-the-circumstances analysis that informs the probable cause determination. Employing the principles of *Gates*— practicality, common sense, a fluid and nontechnical conception of probable cause, and deference to the magistrate's determination—we conclude that the search warrant was supported by probable cause....

The details provided on the use of computers by child pornographers and the collector profile strengthen this inference and help "provide[ ] context" for the "fair probability" that Gourde received or downloaded images. *See United States v. Hay*, 231 F.3d 630, 636 (9th Cir.2000) (reasoning that the collector profile "form[ed] the basis upon which the magistrate judge could plausibly conclude that those files were still on the premises"). The FBI agent concluded that Gourde fit the collector profile because he joined a paid subscription website dedicated to child pornography, where "persons with similar interests can view and download images in relative privacy." Most collectors "are persons who have a sexual attraction to children," and Gourde's membership was a manifestation of that attraction. Collectors act like "pack rats" because they have difficulty obtaining images of child pornography. As such, they are inclined to download and keep such images for a long period of time, and they "rarely, if ever, dispose of their sexually explicit materials." This profile tracks the collector profiles that supported a finding of probable cause in other cases in this circuit and others. *See, e.g., Lacy*, 119 F.3d at 746 ("[T]he affiant explained that collectors and distributors of child pornography value their sexually explicit materials highly, 'rarely if ever' dispose of such material, and store it 'for long periods' in a secure place, typically in their homes."); [*United States v. Martin, 426 F.3d 68, 75 (2d Cir. 2005)*]....

Gourde seeks to sidestep the "fair probability" standard and elevate probable cause to a test of near certainty. In the face of the clear teaching of *Gates*, Gourde argues that probable cause was lacking because the government could have determined with certainty whether he had actually downloaded illegal images. According to Gourde, the FBI could have found any records of his downloads from Lolitagurls.com from the owner's computer, which the FBI seized before conducting the search of Gourde's residence. Gourde posits that absent such concrete evidence, the profile data and other facts are insufficient to support a warrant....

We conclude where the dissents begin. Given the current environment of increasing government surveillance and the long memories of computers, we must not let the nature of the alleged crime, child pornography, skew our analysis or make us "lax" in our duty to guard the privacy protected by the Fourth Amendment. We are acutely aware that the digital universe poses particular challenges with respect to the Fourth Amendment. But the result in this case, which hews to Supreme Court precedent, is hardly a step down the path of laxity and into the arms of Big Brother. The district court did not err in its denial of Gourde's motion to suppress the more than 100 images on his computer containing child pornography.

AFFIRMED as to the conviction; REMANDED to the three-judge panel to consider Gourde's request for a limited remand under *United States v. Ameline*, 409 F.3d 1073 (9th Cir.2005) (en banc).

REINHARDT, Circuit Judge, dissenting:

In this age of increasing government surveillance, lawful and unlawful, and of the retention of all our deeds and thoughts on computers long after we may believe they have been removed, it is important that courts not grow lax in their duty to protect our right to privacy and that they remain vigilant against efforts to weaken our Fourth Amendment protections. It is easy for courts to lose sight of these objectives when the government seeks to obtain evidence of child pornography or narcotics violations. Here, I believe, our court is making an unfortunate error. Let me be clear—no one is suggesting "fly-specking" this case. What is needed instead is a sensitivity to constitutional principles.

The government purports to apply the "totality of the circumstances" test when assessing whether there was a "fair probability" that Gourde possessed illegal images on his computer at the time the warrant was issued. In reaching its conclusion that a fair probability did exist, the majority ignores a critical circumstance: At the time the government sought the warrant, it possessed direct evidence that established whether Gourde in fact had or had not downloaded illegal images to his computer (and thus had them in his possession), yet the government chose not to avail itself of that information. It offered no excuse for its failure to do so, despite the critical nature of the evidence it possessed. The government's actions might fairly be said, at the least, to have constituted "conscious avoidance." ...

Had the government not had the critical, indeed dispositive, evidence in its possession, the evidence that is set forth in the affidavit *might* have been sufficient to support a finding of probable cause.[1] However, when the government's failure to examine the critical evidence is considered along with the limited information proffered in the affidavit, it cannot be said that, all things considered, there was a "fair probability" that evidence that Gourde violated 18 U.S.C. §§ 2252 or 2252A would be found on his computer.[2] ...

The majority improperly brushes aside the importance of the government's ability to determine whether Gourde had downloaded or received illegal images. It argues that it did not need to prove that Gourde definitely downloaded or received illegal images in order to show that there was a "fair probability" that he possessed such images on his computer.... That is certainly true—but it is not the issue in the present case. In concluding that the government's ability to determine Gourde's download history is immaterial to the probable cause analysis, the majority confuses two different types of information: evidence that the government could have obtained but that it did not possess at the time it applied for a warrant, and evidence that the government had in its possession at the time it applied for the warrant but did not utilize—evidence that would have answered the question whether there was probable cause. This case involves the latter type. Although the government certainly need not provide definitive proof that an individual downloaded or otherwise received illegal images on his computer to establish probable cause, when it has critical evidence in its possession but decides to avoid becoming aware of the content, it creates a "circumstance" which casts substantial doubt on the probability that the individual does in fact possess illegal images.

When this circumstance is properly weighed along with the others relied upon by the majority, it can no longer be said that the record before the magistrate judge showed a "fair probability" that Gourde downloaded or otherwise received illegal images. The record makes three things clear: First, Gourde paid for a membership in a website that contained

---

1. I have some doubts about the question but I need not decide it here.

2. On this basis, Gourde had a valid *Franks* claim, in that material omissions from the affidavit led the magistrate to issue a warrant for which there was no probable cause. *See Franks v. Delaware*, 438 U.S. 154, 156, 98 S.Ct. 2674, 57 L.Ed.2d 667 (1978). Under *Franks*, if a criminal defendant establishes by a preponderance of the evidence that an officer recklessly omitted material information from the affidavit, and if the affidavit considered with the omitted evidence is insufficient to establish probable cause, then the "warrant must be voided and the fruits of the search excluded to the same extent as if probable cause was lacking." *Id.* Here, the affidavit omitted material information which, if considered along with the material in the affidavit, would have required a finding of a lack of probable cause.

The majority argues that it is irrelevant that the government failed to examine the critical evidence it had in its possession, claiming that "the benchmark is not what the FBI 'could have' done. An affidavit may support probable cause even if the government fails to obtain potentially dispositive information." ... The majority misses the point. In the cases the majority relies upon to support its argument, the potentially dispositive evidence was *not in the government's possession* at the time it applied for the search warrant. In that circumstance, the courts held, the government is not required to go beyond the facts in its possession and obtain additional evidence through further investigation. *See United States v. Miller*, 753 F.2d 1475, 1479–81 (9th Cir.1985); *United States v. Ozar*, 50 F.3d 1440, 1446 (8th Cir.1995); *United States v. Dale*, 991 F.2d 819, 844 (D.C.Cir.1993). Here, however, the government *already had acquired the dispositive facts*, but failed to avail itself of them or to mention in the affidavit that, as a result of having seized the computer of the owner and operator of Lolitagurls.com, it possessed the records of what images, if any, had been sent to Gourde through the website. Nothing in the cases cited by the majority even suggests that the government's failure to disclose that it possessed but did not examine dispositive evidence before it sought a warrant is anything other than a material omission relevant to the magistrate's determination of probable cause.

both legal and illegal images in unknown proportions (i.e., a "mixed" website).[3] Second, the government had the ability to determine—without any significant expenditure of time or effort—from the evidence it possessed whether Gourde had ever downloaded any images from Lolitagurls.com and, if so, whether *any* of those images were illegal.[4] Third, the affidavit that the government offered in support of the warrant provided no evidence that Gourde had ever downloaded any images, legal or illegal, from the website. The "totality of the[se] circumstances" gives rise to one of two conclusions. At best, the "totality of the circumstances" indicates that the government engaged in "conscious avoidance" and deliberately chose not to avail itself of the information in its possession that would have established whether Gourde downloaded or possessed illegal images before seeking the warrant. At worst, the "totality of the circumstances" suggests that the government did access that information and found that Gourde had not downloaded any illegal images, but sought the warrant anyway.[5] Neither "logic" nor "common sense"— to use the guideposts the majority identifies as central to the "totality-of-the-circumstances analysis," ... —provides an answer to the government's irregular behavior. In the absence of some explanation of its failure to provide the magistrate with the evidence in its possession, I do not believe that it can properly establish probable cause.

Perhaps if no evidence as to whether an individual had in fact downloaded or otherwise received illegal images was in the government's possession, membership in a "mixed" website alone would be sufficient to establish a "fair probability" that the individual possessed such images on his computer. Perhaps not. That case is not before us. Here, the government admitted that, at the time it applied for the warrant, it possessed evidence that could have determined conclusively whether Gourde had downloaded or received illegal images as a result of his membership in the "mixed" website. Yet, it failed to provide the court with this dispositive evidence. Regrettably, the majority ignores this critical fact. In doing so, it fails to consider the "totality of the circumstances." Accordingly, I respectfully dissent.

KLEINFELD, Circuit Judge, dissenting:

I respectfully dissent. The careful decision by the panel[1] was correct and should be left alone. There was no probable cause because there was no evidence that Gourde had downloaded any child pornography....

The importance of this case is considerable because, for most people, their computers are their most private spaces. People commonly talk about the bedroom as a very private space, yet when they have parties, all the guests—including perfect strangers—are invited to toss their coats on the bed. But if one of those guests is caught exploring the host's computer, that will be his last invitation.... There are just too many secrets on people's

---

3. Although the majority labels the website a "child pornography site," it was in fact "mixed"— that is, it contained both legal images (such as adult pornography) as well as illegal ones.

4. The majority argues that "[w]hether the FBI could or would have found such data ... is not clear from the record." ... However, the majority's claim ignores strong evidence to the contrary in the record. During the suppression hearing, Special Agent David Moriguchi, who applied for the warrant to search Gourde's home and computer, testified that *four months* before the FBI sought the Gourde search warrant, the FBI had seized the computer of the owner and operator of Lolitagurls.com, and that the seized computer contained the information about what images, if any, had been sent to Gourde through the website.

5. We must consider the circumstances as they existed at the time the warrant was sought by the government, not what we know to be the circumstances after the search. At the time the warrant was issued, these were the two possible conclusions that could have been drawn from the government's failure to include in the affidavit the information contained in the seized computer.

1. *United States v. Gourde*, 382 F.3d 1003 (9th Cir. 2004).

computers, most legal, some embarrassing, and some potentially tragic in their implications, for loose liberality in allowing search warrants. Emails and history links may show that someone is ordering medication for a disease being kept secret even from family members. Or they may show that someone's child is being counseled by parents for a serious problem that is none of anyone else's business. Or a married mother of three may be carrying on a steamy email correspondence with an old high school boyfriend. Or an otherwise respectable, middle-aged gentleman may be looking at dirty pictures. Just as a conscientious public official may be hounded out of office because a party guest found a homosexual magazine when she went to the bathroom at his house, people's lives may be ruined because of legal but embarrassing materials found on their computers. And, in all but the largest metropolitan areas, it really does not matter whether any formal charges ensue — if the police or other visitors find the material, it will be all over town and hinted at in the newspaper within a few days.

Nor are secrets the only problem. Warrants ordinarily direct seizure, not just search, and computers are often shared by family members. Seizure of a shared family computer may, though unrelated to the law enforcement purpose, effectively confiscate a professor's book, a student's almost completed Ph.D. thesis, or a business's accounts payable and receivable. People cannot get their legitimate work done if their computer is at the police station because of someone else's suspected child pornography downloads. Sex with children is so disgusting to most of us that we may be too liberal in allowing searches when the government investigates child pornography cases. The privacy of people's computers is too important to let it be eroded by sexual disgust.... The question an issuing magistrate should ask of a search warrant is fairly stated by the majority: considering the "totality of the circumstances," is there a "fair probability" that what is being looked for will be found at the location to be searched?[2] This is a common sense, practical question that the magistrate is supposed to ask before issuing a search warrant.[3]

The answer has to come from the statute defining the crimes at issue and the search warrant application. Common sense questions for the issuing magistrate to ask are "what are the police looking for?" and "why do they think they will find evidence of it there?" The application for the search warrant says that the FBI wanted to search Gourde's home for "evidence of possession, receipt and transmission of child pornography" in violation of 18 U.S.C. §§ 2252 and 2252A. So the "what are you looking for?" question is answered precisely and satisfactorily.

The serious, unavoidable next question that an issuing magistrate is obligated to ask is "why do you think there is a fair probability of finding such evidence on Gourde's computer?" Here is where the affidavit fails to make out the case. It establishes only that a website, "Lolitagurls.com," had criminal child pornography on it — along with much legally permissible material — and that Gourde had paid $19.95 to subscribe to it. That is not enough, as a common sense matter, because: (1) Gourde might have been using the website to look at the legal rather than the illegal material, and (2) even if Gourde subscribed just because he liked to look at illegal child pornography, common sense suggests that he also liked to stay out of jail, so he would look but avoid possessing....

On the other hand, there were indications that supported the inference that some or most subscribers would want the site for access to legal pornography: the promotional language said "This site is in full compliance with United States Code Title 18 Part I Chapter 110 Section 2256"; the reference to pictures of "naked lolita girls" was in a different

---

2. *Illinois v. Gates*, 462 U.S. 213, 230, 103 S.Ct. 2317, 76 L.Ed.2d 527 (1983).
3. *Id.* at 231, 103 S.Ct. 2317.

sentence from "girls age 12–17"; the price, $19.95 a month, was not extraordinarily high as one might expect of contraband; much of the material on the site (the affidavit does not say whether it is a small portion, a large portion, or almost all) was what the FBI agent's affidavit said was legal pornography, consisting of "adult pornography ... and child erotica." Thus a person might well subscribe to the site to look at and download legal material. The subscriber might well think—knowing the proclivity of merchants for puffing their goods and of the ability of models to make themselves look younger than they are—that he would have the pleasure of looking at the sort of pornography that appealed to him without the legal risk of looking at anything that involved violation of federal law.

Nevertheless, for purposes of argument, let us assume that the subscriber would think that the assurance of lawfulness and all the legal material were mere window dressing. Let us further assume that as a matter of common sense, subscription to Lolitagurls.com suffices in the "totality of circumstances" to establish that there is a "fair probability"[5] that a subscriber has a perverted interest in looking at criminal child pornography. Though satisfied from the affidavit that Gourde probably had this perverted sexual desire, an issuing magistrate should still have rejected the warrant because it still did not establish a "fair probability" that evidence of a child pornography crime would be found on Gourde's computer.... The reason he could not be assumed to possess child pornography is that possession of child pornography is a very serious crime and the affidavit did not say he had downloaded any. He could use the site to look at child pornography without downloading it, a reasonable assumption in the absence of evidence that he had downloaded images. Common sense suggests that everyone, pervert or not, has the desire to stay out of jail. The ordinary desire to stay out of jail is a factor that must be considered in the totality of circumstances. It would be irrational to assume that an individual is indifferent between subjecting himself to criminal sanctions and avoiding them, when he can attain his object while avoiding them. To commit the crime for which the warrant sought evidence, one has to do something more than look: he must ship, produce, or at the least knowingly possess. The two child pornography statutes at issue do not say that *viewing* child pornography is a crime. Congress could perhaps make it a crime to pay to view such images, but it did not....

A careful issuing magistrate would have to ask himself the question, "why should I believe Gourde has such images, that is, that he is a collector?" And the common sense answer would have to be, particularly in the absence of evidence of downloads, "Not unless he is a fool, since he can look without criminal risk, and would likely be deterred from collecting by the heavy sanctions applied to it." Part of the "totality of circumstances" is the legal environment in which the individual lives. Common sense suggests that a lot of people would do a lot of things that they might like to do—going 90 on an empty freeway, paying less taxes than are owed, crossing an intersection on a red light when there is no traffic, downloading pirated music on the internet—were it not for the legal trouble they would generate for themselves by doing them.

Ordinarily the criminal law takes seriously the effectiveness of deterrence. A sentencing court is commanded by Congress to assure that the sentence "afford adequate deterrence to criminal conduct."[12] All of the people are not deterred all of the time, but most people are deterred most of the time. Not everybody is deterred from buying $250,000 cars by

---

5. *Gates*, 462 U.S. at 236, 103 S.Ct. 2317.
12. 18 U.S.C. §3553(a)(2)(B).

the high prices either, but most people are, so it would not be reasonable to assume that a multimillionaire car lover probably has a Ferrari. Applying common sense to the totality of circumstances, the issuing magistrate would have to suppose that while Gourde might well have a perverted sexual interest in little girls, he would also have the normal desire to stay out of prison. He could satisfy both desires by looking but not possessing. If he had a fast internet connection, he could look online about as fast as he could look at images on his hard drive. Considering the legal risk if he downloaded images, it would take something more, such as a statement in the affidavit that the smut purveyor's computer showed that Gourde's computer had received downloads, to establish probable cause that Gourde collected the images. Why would he collect images on his hard drive when, as a subscriber, he could look whenever he wanted without the legal risk? The affidavit provides experienced judgment (though not scientific in the sense that *Daubert*[13] and *Kumho Tire*[14] require) that collectors horde their collectibles, but no probable cause to suggest that Gourde was a collector. . . .

The majority concludes that the affidavit made out probable cause by assuming that anyone who subscribes to an internet site with both legal and illegal material must collect illegal material from the site. This assumption stacks inference upon inference until the conclusion is too weak to support the invasion of privacy entailed by a search warrant. "[W]ith each succeeding inference, the last reached is less and less likely to be true."[19] The privacy of a person with a sexual perversion that might make him a danger to our children seems by itself an unlikely candidate for concern. But the overwhelming importance of the privacy of people's computers makes it essential to assure that — even in this ugly corner of human perversion — probable cause seriously interpreted remain a prerequisite for search warrants.

Therefore, I respectfully dissent.

Notes

The court in *Gourde* finds it to be common sense that someone who pays for a membership in an online group that contains child pornography would be likely to possess child pornography on their computer. Judge Kleinfeld's dissent suggests that just because the site contains child pornography does not mean that members necessarily view it, and even if a member views it, this does not necessarily mean that he or she downloaded it and now possesses it. However, other courts have held similarly as the court in *Gourde* and determined that the common characteristics shared by child pornographers are sufficient for the court to find probable cause to search the group member's computer. *See United States v. Martin*, 426 F.3d 68, 75 (2d Cir. 2005) ("It is common sense that an individual who joins such a site would more than likely download and possess such material."); *United States v. Froman*, 355 F.3d 882, 890–91 (5th Cir. 2004) ("[I]t is common sense that a person who voluntarily joins [such] a group . . . , remains a member of the group for approximately a month without cancelling his subscription, and uses screen names that reflect his interest in child pornography, would download such pornography from the website and have it in his possession."). In *Martin*, which involved several porno- graphic websites — "Candyman," "girls12–16," and "shangri_la," the affidavit contained

---

13. *Daubert v. Merrell Dow Pharmaceuticals, Inc.*, 509 U.S. 579, 113 S.Ct. 2786, 125 L.Ed.2d 469 (1993).

14. *Kumho Tire Co., Ltd. v. Carmichael*, 526 U.S. 137, 119 S.Ct. 1167, 143 L.Ed.2d 238 (1999).

19. *United States v. Weber*, 923 F.2d 1338, 1345 (9th Cir.1990).

"an extensive background discussion of the modus operandi of those who use computers for collecting and distributing child pornography, including their reliance on e-groups, e-mail, bulletin boards, file transfers, and online storage." *Martin*, 426 F.3d at 75. It also detailed "the characteristics and proclivities of child-pornography collectors, specifically how they tend to collect such material, store it, and rarely destroy or discard it." *Id.* This information demonstrated a "fair probability" and established probable cause. *Id.* at 76. *See also United States v. Riccardi*, 405 F.3d 852, 860–61 (10th Cir. 2005) (holding that affidavit's statement that "possessors of child pornography often obtain and retain images of child pornography on their computers," supported probable cause); *United States v. Chrobak*, 289 F.3d 1043, 1046 (8th Cir. 2002) (holding that affidavit supported probable cause, in part, based on "professional experience that child pornographers generally retain their pornography for extended periods"). For commentary about the relevance of group membership in establishing probable cause, see Megan Westenberg, *Establishing the Nexus: The Definitive Relationship Between Child Molestation and Possession of Child Pornography as the Sole Basis for Probable Cause*, 81 Cinn. L. Rev. 337 (2013).

5. File Identification

United States v. Miknevich

Third Circuit, 2011
638 F.3d 178

NYGAARD, Circuit Judge....

We are asked to determine whether an affidavit prepared by a law enforcement officer provided a substantial basis for a Pennsylvania district justice's finding of probable cause to issue a search warrant. Appellant Stephen Miknevich was arrested and charged with possession of child pornography. These charges arose after police executed a search warrant at his home and seized his computer. His computer was later found to contain numerous images of child pornography. After the search and seizure of the computer, Miknevich gave oral and written admissions of guilt to the arresting officers.... Miknevich then filed a motion to suppress in the District Court, arguing that the warrant was issued without probable cause. The District Court denied the motion, finding that the accompanying affidavit contained an adequate description of child pornography so as to support a probable cause determination and, even had it not, the *Leon* good faith exception applied. *See United States v. Leon*, 468 U.S. 897, 104 S.Ct. 3405, 82 L.Ed.2d 677 (1984). Miknevich entered a conditional plea of guilty, reserving the right to challenge the District Court's probable cause determination on appeal. He filed a notice of appeal raising this issue and also challenging his sentence. We will affirm....

Because the contents of the affidavit are at issue, we will quote from it directly as follows:

> On 8/16/2007 at Approx. 1559 hr EDT, Delaware State Police Cpt. R. Scott Garland was conducting an investigation into the use of P2P file sharing networks in the distribution of child pornography images and movies in violation of Pennsylvania Crime Code Section 631(C), (D), Sexual Abuse of Children (Possession and dissemination of Child Pornography). While conducting this investigation, an off-the-shelf publically available gnutella client was used. At this time, the network was queried for files indexed by a term I know to be related to child pornography. The network returned to Det. Garland's computer a list of files associated with this term. The list contained details about these files including the file name, file type, file size, SHA1 value for the file and a number of users

on the network with the file or portions of the file available for download by other gnutella network users.

Det. Garland reviewed the list of files and observed a file named, "!!Novo Ptsc-Alyo(6yo) & Ali(7yo) Ptsc-littlenorwegian angels stroke their erect clits-nudist child," with an SHA1 value of RGQCV2AC6XD3JE5KULOBAJWQTVBBXXHC. Det. Garland knows this file with this SHA1 value to be child pornography. The movie is described as children, under the age of eighteen years old engaged in sexual acts and/or poses. Det. Garland then attempted to download this movie form (sic) those sharing it on the network.

Shortly after Det. Garland indicated to download the movie, the network returned a list of users with their IP address, who had the file or portions of the file available to download from it. Det. Garland reviewed this list and observed a user with the IP address of 75.75.148.179. The software was set to locate computers sharing images of child pornography. Det. Garland was presented with an IP address of 75.75.148.179 and captured this IP address by performing a "Netstat capture" on 8/16/2007 @ 1559 hrs. EDT.

Lt. Peifer viewed the video file based on the SHA1 value and based on my training and experience the children appear to be under the age of 18 years old.

On 9/17/2007, Lt. Peifer prepared a Court Order in the Court of Common Pleas in Delaware County [Pennsylvania] directing Comcast Cable Communications to supply subscriber information on the person assigned to IP address 75.75.148.179 on 8/06/2007 @ 1559 hrs ESDT. This order was submitted to Delaware County Common Please (sic) Court Judge Frank T. Hazel.

On 9/21/2007 at approx. 1616 hrs Lt. Peifer received a response from Comcast Cable Communications in reference to the court order sent.

Comcast indicated that the IP address 75.75.148.179 on 8/16/2007 @1559 hrs EDT was in use by the following subscriber in the name of:

Steven Miknevich, 72 Pincecrest Ave., Lft, Dallas, Pa. 18612 PH# 570-760-7643.

Based on this information, Pennsylvania State Trooper Michael Gownley averred to a Pennsylvania district justice that computer images depicting children less than eighteen years of age engaged in sexual conduct were located at Miknevich's residence and that those depictions were evidence of a crime involving the sexual abuse of children. Gownley obtained a warrant and seized Miknevich's computer.... Miknevich argues that the warrant is infirm because the Pennsylvania district justice premised his probable cause determination on the file name and its related electronic identification SHA1 value[1], not on his or the investigating officers' viewing of the file's contents. Further, he maintains that the only officer who did view the file did not say that he saw child pornography and that the district justice only inferred as much. According to Miknevich, speculation cannot be the basis upon which a probable cause determination is made....

Miknevich argues that the affidavit of probable cause was deficient because it did not contain enough information to give the Pennsylvania district justice a substantial basis to conclude that there was a fair probability that contraband or evidence of criminal

---

1. A SHA1 (or SHA-1) value is a mathematical algorithm that stands for Secured Hash Algorithim used to compute a condensed representation of a message or data file. Thus it can act like a fingerprint. *See, e.g., Lexmark Intern., Inc. v. Static Control Components, Inc.,* 387 F.3d 522, 530 (6th Cir.2004).

activity would be found on his computer. He points to several alleged defects: the affidavit does not indicate that any investigating officer actually downloaded the suspect video file; the affidavit does not indicate that anyone ever actually viewed the suspect file; and the affidavit contains no description of the suspected images or actions in these files.... We credit Miknevich's criticism of the affidavit as far as it goes. The affidavit was, in parts, inartfully drafted. This stems, no doubt, from the fact that the affiant took no direct part in the investigation, and instead related the work of other law enforcement officials— Det. Garland and Lt. Peifer. Although the District Court relied on the fact that the affidavit did not state that Garland never viewed the contents of the file, the opposite is equally true—the affidavit does not specifically state that he did. Garland conducted a search for suspected child pornography using a term he knew to be related to that crime. But Garland does not indicate what that term was. His search generated a list of files associated with this term, but Garland does not provide the district justice with a detailed description of what those files depict. After reviewing the list, one file with a particular SHA1 value was noticed. Garland "knew this file and this SHA1 value to be child pornography." The detective, however, does not indicate how he knew this information.

It is not unreasonable for us to assume that Garland never actually viewed the images or videos. The affidavit relates that he "attempted" to download the file contents, which, we could conclude, means he was unsuccessful and never actually viewed the contents of the files in question. Further, Garland indicates that "[t]he movie is described as children, under the age of eighteen years old engaged in sexual acts and/or poses." Here, Garland relies on what could be a second-hand description of the file's contents—not his own viewing of the contents. That, however, does not make the affidavit infirm.... Garland forwarded his search results to Lt. Peifer of the Delaware County Pennsylvania Internet Crimes Against Children Task Force. The Government maintains that Peifer did indeed view the file's contents. Here again, the affidavit is imprecise, relating that Peifer "viewed the video file based on the SHA1 value and based on [his] training and experience the children appear to be under the age of 18 years old." The statement that he viewed the file "based on its SHA1 value" is confusing. It could indicate that Peifer merely viewed the file as part of the listing generated by the search. Assuming, however, that Peifer did view the contents of the file, he nonetheless failed to describe any of the images contained therein with any detail. He avers, based on his training and experience, that the children "appear to be" under the age of eighteen. Additionally, although the affidavit does state that Peifer is "familiar with Peer-to-Peer file sharing," it does not relate the extent of Peifer's experience and training.

Thus, our review of the affidavit leaves a clear impression: the state magistrate was presented with an affidavit that provided no factual details regarding the substance of the images in question. Although either the actual production of the images, or a sufficiently detailed description of them, satisfies the Fourth Amendment's probable cause requirement, an insufficiently detailed or conclusory description cannot. *See New York v. P.J. Video*, 475 U.S. 868, 874, 106 S.Ct. 1610, 89 L.Ed.2d 871 (1986). We believe, however, that even given the infirmities we highlighted, the affidavit still contained information sufficient to permit a finding of probable cause by the magistrate.... It is clear that a magistrate can determine probable cause without seeing the images and/or viewing the contents of an illicit computer file. The Supreme Court has stated that:

> [W]e have never held that a magistrate must personally view allegedly obscene films prior to issuing a warrant authorizing their seizure. On the contrary, we think that a reasonably specific affidavit detailing the content of a film generally provides an adequate basis for the magistrate to determine whether there is

probable cause to believe that the film is obscene, and whether a warrant authorizing the seizure of the film should issue.

P.J. Video, 475 U.S. at 874, 106 S.Ct. 1610. We therefore reject any suggestion that a magistrate must review the contents of the actual files in question, or that a search warrant must include copies of the images giving rise to the request for a warrant.[5] Although magistrates do not have to view these files, the question more pertinent here is whether the investigating officers must do so.

It can be problematic, to say the least, when a warrant application leaves one questioning whether anyone viewed the contents of the file in question. Nothing in the opinion we announce today should be taken as a rejection or relaxation of what we believe continues to be the best procedure for law enforcement officials to follow. It remains the better practice for an applicant seeking a warrant based on images of alleged child pornography to append the images or to provide a description of the images sufficient to enable the magistrate to determine independently whether probable cause exists. *See, e.g., United States v. LaFortune*, 520 F.3d 50, 56 (1st Cir.2008). Here, however, the magistrate could have drawn a reasonable inference of the file's contents based on its highly descriptive name and SHA1 value....

Determining the existence (or lack) of probable cause involves making a "practical, common-sense decision" as to whether, given the totality of facts, a "fair probability" exists that contraband will be found in a particular place. *Gates*, 462 U.S. at 238, 103 S.Ct. 2317. Probable cause can be inferred by "considering the type of crime, the nature of the items sought, the suspect's opportunity for concealment and normal inferences about where a criminal might hide the fruits of his crime." *United States v. Hodge*, 246 F.3d 301, 305 (3d Cir.2001) (*citing United States v. Jones*, 994 F.2d 1051 (3d Cir.1993)) (internal quotation marks omitted). Indeed, we have specifically instructed that an affidavit filed in support of an application for a search warrant is to be read in its entirety, with the focus on what the affidavit includes, not what is missing. *See Williams*, 124 F.3d at 420; *Jones*, 994 F.2d at 1056.

The affidavit here provided the magistrate with sufficient information to make an independent assessment of probable cause. The title of the computer file at issue contained highly graphic references to specific sexual acts involving children. The file name refers to the ages of the children ("6yo" and "7yo") and to graphic sexual activities ("little norwegian angels stroke their erect clits"). This description indicates minors engaged in sexually explicit conduct. The unmistakable inference arising from this highly descriptive file name is that the file's contents include material pertaining to the sexual exploitation

---

5. Although a magistrate is not required to do so, at least one jurist has urged his colleagues to view such files. Judge John Adams of the United States District Court for the Northern District of Ohio recently wrote a passionate opinion (albeit on sentencing), imploring reviewing courts to "personally examine the images at issue and not simply rely on a written description of their contents. There are some images that are haunting and they cannot be unseen. However, any uneasiness felt by the individual reviewing the images pales in comparison to the harm caused by the image being created in the first place." *United States v. Cunningham*, 680 F.Supp.2d 844, 854 (N.D.Ohio 2010); *see also United States v. Fiorella*, 602 F.Supp.2d 1057, 1075 n. 8 (N.D.Iowa 2009) ("It is easier to overlook the horrors of child pornography when, as is often the case, the material at issue is not presented to the sentencing judge. For purposes of efficiency and minimization of re-victimization of the children depicted, the government and the defendant will often (and rightly so) enter into stipulations about the number and nature of the photographs at issue. But the horrors of child pornography are real even if those who sit in judgment do not have occasion to view them.").

of children. Given the name of the file in question and its graphic reference to specific sexual acts involving young children, and given the file's SHA1 value, this inference is a strong one and established probable cause.

We recognize that file names are not always a definitive indication of actual file content and, therefore, only after downloading and viewing a particular file can one know with certainty whether the content of the file is consistent with its designated name. However, "[c]ertainty has no part in a probable cause analysis." *United States v. Frechette*, 583 F.3d 374, 380 (6th Cir.2009); *see also Vosburgh*, 602 F.3d at 527; *United States v. Urban*, 404 F.3d 754, 774 (3d Cir.2005) (quoting *Tehfe*, 722 F.2d at 1117–18). On the contrary, "probable cause requires only a probability or substantial chance of criminal activity, not an actual showing of such activity." *Gates*, 462 U.S. at 244 n. 13, 103 S.Ct. 2317. We acknowledge that in some circumstances a computer file name may not provide meaningful insight into its contents, especially where the file name contains a term or name that is commonplace or otherwise capable of different interpretations. However, it does not necessarily follow that file names can never be regarded as a logical indication of the file's contents. A file's name may certainly be explicit and detailed enough so as to permit a reasonable inference of what the file is likely to depict. The unmistakable inference which arises from the file name here is that its contents include material pertaining to the sexual exploitation of children.

Further, the affidavit relates that Garland knew the file in question contained child pornography because he recognized the file's SHA1 value, RGQCV2AC6XD3JE5KU-LOBAJWQTVBBXXHC, as one indicating child pornography. This too is relevant to probable cause. The affidavit explains the significance of the SHA1 value as a 'digital fingerprint' and avers that the investigating officers were familiar with the SHA1 value associated with the file on Miknevich's computer. We conclude that the affidavit seeking the search warrant contained sufficient facts to support a finding that there was a fair probability that Miknevich possessed child pornography and that there was evidence of such possession at the location described in the affidavit. The District Court's order upholding the search warrant will be affirmed....

Because we find that the affidavit presented to the district justice was sufficient to provide a "substantial basis" for finding a fair probability that evidence would be located on Miknevich's computer, we need not reach the issue of good faith reliance on a warrant pursuant to *Leon.* Therefore, and for the reasons set forth above, we will affirm the District Court's decision....

The District Court's judgment of conviction and sentence will be affirmed.

Notes

In *Miknevich*, the court found sufficient probable cause, despite the fact that the affidavit contained no specific details about the images to be searched and the fact that the investigator did not actually view the images that prompted the search. Rather, the personal identifying information was sufficient to support probable cause that the defendant possessed child pornography on his computer. *See also U.S. v. Cartier*, 543 F.3d 442 (2d Cir. 2008) (defendant's use of hash values of known child pornography files in peer-to-peer file-sharing network gave sufficient probable cause to search defendant's home, even though no person had seen actual files or images of child pornography on defendant's computer prior to execution of search warrant). For a case holding that the use of hash tag values derived from a defendant's computer to compare to known images of child pornography constitutes a Fourth Amendment search, see *U.S. v. Crist*, 2008 WL 4682806 (M.D. Pa. 2008).

5. *Staleness*

United States v. Vosburgh

Third Circuit, 2010
602 F.3d 512

SMITH, Circuit Judge....

At the center of this case is an underground Internet message board known as Ranchi. Ranchi allows users to post links to images and videos of child pornography.[1] Ranchi is not simply an open forum in which some posts happen to be related to child pornography; child pornography is Ranchi's *raison d'etre*. It describes itself as a place to "share all kinds of material especially for all the kiddy lovers around the world. This material can range from non-nude cuties to hard core baby material." Ranchi allows its users access to a wide range of pornographic pictures and videos, including hard core videos of infants and other children engaging in sexual acts with each other and with adults. Ranchi explicitly warns that the pornographic materials posted to the board are illegal.

Ranchi does not itself host child pornography; instead, it directs users to where it can be found elsewhere on the Internet. For obvious reasons, chiefly among them a desire to evade law enforcement, Ranchi operates in the far recesses of cyberspace. It is accessible through the use of any one of three "gateway" websites that exist at any given time. Each gateway consists of a web page that contains nothing but a hyperlink to the actual Ranchi message board. The gateway sites change approximately every three months, but regardless of their location, they always point to the most recent location of the Ranchi board, which itself moves around the Internet on a weekly basis. It is highly unlikely that an innocent user of the Internet would stumble across Ranchi through an unfortunate Google search. Because Ranchi moves so frequently and has cumbersome URLs, it is most often, if not always, accessed by way of the gateway sites. Interested persons often learn of Ranchi, and where to find the gateways, through postings on other child pornography websites.

A user seeking to access a link to child pornography posted on Ranchi cannot do so with a simple click of the mouse. It requires several steps. URLs as posted by Ranchi users typically begin with the prefix "hxxp," rather than the customary "http," to make it less likely that the links will be detected by search engines. Therefore, a user interested in that link must copy it from the board, paste it into the address bar of a web browser, and then change "hxxp" to "http" so that the address will be recognized by the browser. Only then can the file be accessed and downloaded. Even after downloading, files cannot be viewed immediately. They first must be decrypted, in part through use of a password.

In July 2006, FBI Special Agent Wade Luders learned of Ranchi's existence from a suspect apprehended in an investigation of a different child pornography board. That suspect authorized Luders to use his Ranchi handle, "Bongzilla," to go undercover on the board. On October 25, 2006, Luders posted six links to what purported to be child pornography. One of those links directed users to a video located at the following address: hxxp://uploader.sytes.net/12/05/4yo_suck.rar.html. Along with this link, Luders posted the following description:

> [H]ere is one of my favs—4yo hc with dad (toddler, some oral, some anal)—supercute! Haven't seen her on the board before—if anyone has anymore, PLEASE POST.

---

1. We will state the facts relevant to Ranchi in the present tense, as they are presented that way in the record. It is unknown whether Ranchi is operative today.

In the parlance of Ranchi, "yo" stood for "year old" and "hc" stood for "hard core."[2] Luders quickly realized that because he had mistakenly failed to encrypt the file, it was unlikely to attract attention. He then re-posted the "4yo_suck" link and posted instructions for decrypting the file. He also promised to post the necessary password, but never did.

The "4yo_suck" link (hereinafter the "Link") was, in short, a trap. It did not direct the user to actual child pornography. It was a dummy link which led only to Agent Luders's secure FBI computer. The "video" downloaded by way of the Link generated only gibberish on the recipient's computer screen. Meanwhile, Agent Luders's computer generated a log file containing the Internet Protocol addresses ("IP addresses")[3] of every user who attempted to access the Link, and the date and time of each attempt. Among those who attempted to access the Link was a user at the IP address 69.136.100.151. That individual attempted to download the Link three times in a two-minute period between 11:46 and 11:48 p.m. EST on October 25, 2006. Luders traced this IP address to Comcast Cable Communications. In response to a subpoena, Comcast informed the government that "the individual utilizing the IP address 69.136.100.151 on October 25, 2006 at [the relevant times] did so using an account subscribed to by Rod Vosburgh, residing at 37 State Rd., Apt. B4" in Media, Pennsylvania. Luders forwarded this information to FBI Special Agent David Desy in Philadelphia....

Agent Desy took steps to confirm that Vosburgh lived at the address identified by Comcast, and that he lived there alone. A January 17, 2007, search of Pennsylvania Bureau of Motor Vehicle records confirmed that Vosburgh resided at 37 State Road, Apartment B4 in Media, and a Choicepoint query conducted the same day revealed the same information. On January 31, 2007, through query of the U.S. Postal Service, Agent Desy learned that Vosburgh was the only person receiving mail at the apartment in question. In addition, Agent Desy twice conducted surveillance of the apartments at 37 State Road, and both times observed a vehicle in the parking lot matching the description of the one owned by Vosburgh.... On February 23, 2007, Agent Desy applied for a warrant to search Vosburgh's apartment. The affidavit in support of that application described how computers and the Internet have facilitated the spread of child pornography. It explained what IP addresses are, and how "[l]aw enforcement entities, in conjunction with Internet Service Providers, have the ability to identify a user's IP address to a specific household or residence." It also described certain characteristics and habits of persons interested in child pornography. It noted that "[c]hild pornography collectors almost always maintain and possess their material in the privacy and security of their homes, or some other secure location such as their vehicle(s), where it is readily available," and that collectors tend to hoard their materials:

> Because the collection reveals the otherwise private sexual desires and intent of the collector and represents his most cherished sexual fantasies, the collector rarely, if ever, disposes of the collection. The collection may be culled and refined over time, but the size of the collection tends to increase.

The affidavit also noted that even if a collector deletes illegal materials from his computer's hard drive, law enforcement can often retrieve those files using forensic tools. Next, the affidavit described the nature of Ranchi, with graphic descriptions of some of the illegal

---

2. "Hard core" generally denotes depictions of children engaged in actual sexual activity.

3. An IP address is a number assigned to each device that is connected to the Internet. Although most devices do not have their own, permanent ("static") addresses, in general an IP address for a device connected to the Internet is unique in the sense that no two devices have the same IP address at the same time.

pornographic materials that agents had found posted to the site. It then summarized Agent Luders's posting of the Link, how his computer logged the IP addresses of users who attempted to access the Link, and why it was unlikely that anyone who attempted to download the video promised by the Link would have done so by accident.[4] Finally, the affidavit laid out the facts specific to Vosburgh. It noted that an individual using the IP address 69.136.100.151 attempted to access the Link three times on the night of October 25, 2006. It recounted how Agent Desy traced that IP address back to Vosburgh's apartment, and the subsequent steps Agent Desy took to confirm that Vosburgh actually lived there. It also described in detail the property to be searched and the items to be searched and seized. Those items included "[a]ny and all items which may be used to visually depict child pornography, store information pertaining to the sexual interest in child pornography, or to distribute, possess, or receive child pornography, … including … computer hardware[.]"

Magistrate Judge Felipe Restrepo issued a search warrant on February 23, 2007, approximately four months after Vosburgh's apparent attempts to access the Link. That warrant was executed on February 27, 2007. Before they arrived at his apartment, officers learned that Vosburgh lawfully owned more than a dozen guns. Concerned for their safety, officers attempted to lure Vosburgh out of his apartment with a ruse. They knocked on his door, identified themselves as police, and told him that they wanted to talk to him because his car had been vandalized. Vosburgh did not answer the door, but from the apartment came a sound of "metal on metal" that sounded like the racking of a gun. Alarmed, officers remained outside of the apartment and attempted to persuade Vosburgh to open the door. They knocked at least three times, with the knocks getting louder each time. They also called Vosburgh's telephone several times and left messages asking him to come out of the apartment. Approximately 27 minutes after officers first knocked, Vosburgh opened the door. He told officers that he did not answer sooner because he had been in the bathroom.

Inside Vosburgh's apartment, police found pieces of smashed thumb drives, one of which was floating in the toilet. They also found a hammer and a pair of scissors outside of the bathroom door.[5] They found a screwdriver next to a computer tower in the kitchen. The computer's panel had been forcibly removed and its internal hard drive was missing. Part of an internal drive was found in a trash bag in the kitchen, and the remains of that same hard drive were found on a bookshelf in the living room. The destroyed internal hard drive was compatible with the tower in the kitchen.

In an interview with Agent Desy, Vosburgh acknowledged that he lived alone in the apartment and that he owned a computer. He denied intentionally breaking or destroying the computer's internal hard drive; he claimed that he had discarded it two or three weeks earlier because it was corrupted. He told officers that he owned an external hard drive that contained adult pornography, and a thumb drive that contained work documents and more adult pornography. Officers collected the internal hard drive and the pieces of the

---

4. As explained above, any attempt to access the Link would have been preceded by the following steps: (1) knowing where to find and then accessing a gateway site; (2) clicking on the URL from that gateway to Ranchi; (3) finding a hyperlink on the Ranchi board; (4) copying and pasting that link into a new window on his web browser; (5) changing the letters "hxxp" in the URL as posted to "http"; and (6) downloading the file.

5. One of the officers present that day testified that when he walked into the apartment and saw the hammer, it became "obvious" to him that the "metal on metal" sound that officers feared was the racking of a handgun was actually the sound of a hammer smashing the metal on the thumb drive. Vosburgh claimed that the metallic sound was the sound of him unloading his guns "so there would not be any trouble."

thumb drive, but the FBI's computer forensics experts were unable to recover anything from either. They also took the external hard drive, which was intact and later examined by FBI forensics expert Justin Price.[6] ... The external hard drive contained a folder with hundreds of pictures of what the government calls "child erotica."[7] Many of these were pictures of a young Asian girl known as Loli-chan who has gained some notoriety by posting suggestive photos of herself on the Internet.[8] It also contained a folder called "jap 111." This folder contained twenty pictures of adult women in .jpeg format[9] and a file called thumbs.db which itself contained 68 'thumbnail' images. Two of those images were of child pornography. One depicted a naked prepubescent girl in the computer room of a house, with one leg propped up unnaturally to expose her genitalia. This image became Government Exhibit 14 at trial, and we will refer to it as such. The second depicted four naked young girls, sitting on a couch with their legs spread to expose their genitalia. This became Government Exhibit 15.... Notably, these two images did not exist as full-sized, independent picture files (such as .jpeg files) in the jap111 folder when the government seized the hard drive. Nor were full-sized .jpegs of those images recovered anywhere else on the external hard drive. Rather, they existed only as miniatures within the thumbs.db file in the jap111 folder. Because the nature of thumbs.db is critical to resolution of the issues raised in this appeal, it is necessary to recount the record evidence concerning this file.

On ordinary computers running Windows operating systems, picture files are often stored in folders. When a folder is opened, the user has several options for displaying the pictures contained therein. One option is the "thumbnail" view. When the user selects the thumbnail view, a miniature version of each picture in the folder is displayed. Each of those miniatures is called a "thumbnail." The user can click on the thumbnail to open it and view a full-sized version of the picture. When the user selects the thumbnail viewing option, the Windows operating system automatically creates a hidden system file called "thumbs.db" within that folder. The user need not instruct Windows to do so; it happens automatically as part of the process of viewing the contents of the folder in thumbnail view. Thumbs.db is not a collection of many image files; it is a single file, which can be thought of as a visual catalog of all the image files contained in the folder. It contains a

---

6. The external hard drive was inadvertently left in Vosburgh's apartment on February 27. When Agent Desy learned that it remained in Vosburgh's apartment, he sought a "piggyback" search warrant to return to Vosburgh's apartment. His application incorporated by reference the affidavit used to obtain the February 27 warrant. After Magistrate Judge Thomas Rueter issued this warrant on March 1, agents returned to Vosburgh's apartment and seized the external hard drive.

7. The government distinguishes child pornography from child erotica by defining the latter as material that depicts "young girls as sexual objects or in a sexually suggestive way," but is not "sufficiently lascivious to meet the legal definition of sexually explicit conduct" under 18 U.S.C. §2256. *See also United States v. Gourde*, 440 F.3d 1065, 1068 (9th Cir.2006) (en banc) (citing FBI affidavit describing child erotica as "images that are not themselves child pornography but still fuel ... sexual fantasies involving children").

8. The government described Loli-chan as follows:

Loli-chan is the name given to a 13-year old girl who posts pictures of herself on imageboards and enjoys hearing from her older male fans. In these images, 'Loli-chan' is, for example, licking a lollipop; in a bathroom wearing a robe and making a kissing expression; in a swimsuit at a pool; at the shower, starting to undress from her swimsuit; in a Mini-Mouse outfit; in a school uniform sitting on the floor barefoot; and sitting clothed on a toilet. In many of these images, the girl is holding signs that read "I'm thirteen," "Google your own porn," "kock swurve is gay," [and various other vulgar, non-sensical phrases].

9. "JPEG" stands for Joint Photographic Experts Group and refers to "a commonly used method for compressing and storing electronic photographic images. JPEG files are usually saved with the '.jpg' extension appended to the computer file name and indicate the file contains a photograph or graphical image." *United States v. Andrus*, 483 F.3d 711, 714 n. 2 (10th Cir.2007).

miniature, degraded version of every image in the folder that has been converted into a thumbnail pursuant to the use of the thumbnail view.... The thumbs.db file is stored within the folder whose content it reflects, along with the picture files themselves. But the ordinary user cannot view the contents of thumbs.db. Indeed, the ordinary user does not even know that thumbs.db is there. At trial, the government's expert Justin Price confirmed that opening the thumbs.db file to view its contents requires special software, and that there was no evidence that Vosburgh possessed such software or was otherwise capable of viewing the contents of the thumbs.db file in the jap111 folder.

The significance of the presence of Exhibits 14 and 15 in the thumbs.db file on Vosburgh's external hard drive was one of the central factual issues at trial. The government contended that the existence of Exhibits 14 and 15 in the thumbs.db file was evidence that corresponding full-sized picture files once existed on Vosburgh's hard drive in the jap111 folder. According to the government, Vosburgh knowingly possessed such pictures but then deleted them at some point before the search of his apartment on February 27; this explained why the hard drive contained thumbs.db versions of Exhibits 14 and 15, but not full-sized .jpeg versions of those same images. We will refer to this theory throughout our opinion as the government's "prior possession" theory.... Vosburgh vigorously contested the prior possession theory. He contended at trial, and now contends on appeal, that he conclusively disproved the theory with an in-court demonstration by his expert, Dr. Rebecca Mercuri. He also offered several alternative explanations for the presence of Exhibits 14 and 15 in the jap111 thumbs.db file....

Mercuri was Vosburgh's forensic computer expert, and her testimony formed the bulk of Vosburgh's defense. Mercuri had conducted her own forensic examination of the external hard drive. In her pre-trial expert report, she concluded that "there is absolutely no evidence that the [images in Exhibits 14 and 15] ... ever existed as individual .jpeg files at any time on [Vosburgh's] hard drive." At trial, she likewise fiercely disputed the prior possession theory. According to Mercuri, the fact that a thumbs.db file containing Exhibits 14 and 15 appeared in the jap111 folder was *not* proof that full-sized .jpegs of Exhibits 14 and 15 once existed on the hard drive. To underscore that point, Mercuri conducted a live, in-court demonstration using two computers. Mercuri created a folder with four .jpegs depicting natural scenery: Pond, Blue Hill, Sunset, and Winter. She opened the folder and selected the thumbnail view, thus creating within that folder a thumbs.db file containing all four images. She then deleted Blue Hills and Winter from the folder, leaving only the Pond and Sunset .jpegs. Next, she copied the entire folder onto a second computer. When she opened that folder on the second computer, it contained only the Pond and Sunset .jpegs, but it also contained the thumbs.db file created on the first computer. Using special software to view the contents of thumbs.db on the second computer, she showed that this thumbs.db file contained four thumbnails, one corresponding to each of the .jpegs that originally existed in the folder. The point of her demonstration, Mercuri said, was to show that "you can have a thumbs.db file that contains thumbnails in it that you never had the original pictures of." ... Consistent with her demonstration, Mercuri offered her own theory about how the thumbs.db file containing the pornographic images could have gotten onto Vosburgh's hard drive without the corresponding .jpegs for those pictures doing the same. According to Mercuri, Vosburgh could have gotten the thumbs.db images but not the corresponding originals if he had downloaded the jap111 folder *after* the thumbs.db file was created in that folder but also after the full-sized versions of Exhibits 14 and 15 had been deleted.

With respect to Count II, Mercuri offered several theories as to how Vosburgh's IP address could appear to have attempted to access the Link without Vosburgh himself knowingly doing so. Mercuri speculated that an unknown user could have "spoofed" Vosburgh's IP address, or that Vosburgh's computer could have been infected with malicious software that turned it into a "zombie."[11] She admitted, however, that she had no evidence that such mischief had actually occurred....

The government pressed the prior possession theory throughout its closing argument. For example, the prosecutor told the jury:

> [Vosburgh] viewed [the pictures] on February 22nd. That is what the forensics showed. He viewed them on February 22nd. He went to his view options.... he chose view. In order to choose view, it has to be there and he viewed them. And when he viewed them, it automatically created a thumbnail. And he did this on February 22, 2007. And in order to do this, you have to have the original photos. You have to have the original photos in jap111 before they could be viewed in thumbnail.

In response, Vosburgh emphasized Mercuri's testimony that the existence of Exhibits 14 and 15 in the thumbs.db file did not prove that Vosburgh ever knowingly possessed the full-sized originals on his hard drive. He also reiterated his spoofing and zombie theories for why someone using his IP address appeared to have accessed the Link.

The jury found Vosburgh guilty on Counts I and II [Count I charged that Vosburgh "knowingly possessed one external hard drive that contained visual depictions of child pornography, in violation of 18 U.S.C. § 2252(a)(4)(B), "on or about February 27, 2007...," related to his possession of the hard drive containing the images that became Exhibits 14 and 15, and Count II charged Vosburgh with attempted possession of child pornography in violation of 18 U.S.C. § 2252(b)(2), in connection with Vosburgh's attempts to access the Link].... Vosburgh was sentenced to 15 months of imprisonment and three years of supervised release.... Vosburgh filed a post-trial motion for judgment of acquittal, or in the alternative, for a new trial. He claimed that there was insufficient evidence to convict him on Counts I and II. He also claimed, for the first time, that a new trial should be held because there was a constructive amendment of his indictment and/or a variance between the indictment and the evidence at trial. The District Court denied Vosburgh's motion without opinion.... Vosburgh then filed a timely notice of appeal....

Agent Desy's affidavit explained that on October 25, 2006, someone using a computer with an IP address of 69.136.100.151 attempted to download a video that purported to be hardcore child pornography. It further explained that on the day in question, the relevant IP address was assigned to a Comcast account registered to Vosburgh's apartment. It also asserted that child pornography collectors tend to hoard their materials and "rarely, if ever" dispose of them. We must decide whether these averments provided a "substantial basis" for the magistrate's conclusion that there was a "fair probability that contraband or evidence of a crime [would] be found" in Vosburgh's apartment at the time of the search. *Gates*, 462 U.S. at 238, 103 S.Ct. 2317....

---

11. Mercuri testified that "spoofing is a way of making it appear as though the IP address is from one user when in fact it is coming from another." She explained that "people are instructed if they are going to download illicit materials, ... not to use their own IP address, they have to use some other IP address." She further testified that a computer becomes a "zombie" when it is remotely and surreptitiously hijacked by another user and used to do things that the owner does not know that it is doing. Hackers may use computers that have been turned into zombies to send spam emails, or as a place to store files they do not want to store on their own computers. The malicious programs used to perform these activities can be planted on the computer through websites, through email, or even through an idle Internet connection.

This Court has not squarely addressed the issue, but several Courts of Appeals have held that evidence that the user of a computer employing a particular IP address possessed or transmitted child pornography can support a search warrant for the physical premises linked to that IP address. *See, e.g., United States v. Perez*, 484 F.3d 735 (5th Cir.2007).[13] In *Perez*, a woman contacted law enforcement after she received an unsolicited email containing child pornography from a Yahoo! email address. Yahoo! identified the user who sent the offensive email, and from its records identified that user's IP address. The FBI determined that the IP address belonged to a Time Warner customer, and subpoenaed the identity and address of that customer from Time Warner. A search of that address uncovered child pornography. *Id.* at 738. On appeal, the defendant argued that the images should have been suppressed because the "mere association between an IP address and a physical address is insufficient to establish probable cause." *Id.* at 739. The Fifth Circuit disagreed, concluding that the IP address provided "a substantial basis to conclude that evidence of criminal activity" would be found at the defendant's home, even if it did not *conclusively* link the pornography to the residence. *Id.* at 740. The court noted that although it was technically possible that the offending emails "originated outside of the residence to which the IP address was assigned, it remained *likely* that the source of the transmissions was inside that residence." *Id.* (emphasis added).

We agree with the reasoning in *Perez*. As many courts have recognized, IP addresses are fairly "unique" identifiers.[14] *See, e.g., United States v. Forrester*, 512 F.3d 500, 510 n. 5 (9th Cir.2008) (stating that "every computer or server connected to the Internet has a unique IP address"); *Perrine*, 518 F.3d at 1199 n. 2 (noting that an IP address "is unique to a specific computer"); *Peterson v. Nat'l Telecomm. & Inform. Admin.*, 478 F.3d 626, 629 (4th Cir.2007) (explaining that "[e]ach computer connected to the Internet is assigned a unique numerical [IP] address"); *White Buffalo Ventures, LLC v. Univ. of Texas at Austin*, 420 F.3d 366, 370 n. 6 (5th Cir.2005) (describing an IP address as "a unique 32-bit numeric address" that essentially "identifies a single computer"). The unique nature of the IP address assigned to Vosburgh on October 25 made his attempts to access the Link fairly traceable to his Comcast account and the physical address to which that account was registered.

Attempted possession of child pornography is a federal crime. *See* 18 U.S.C. §2252(b)(2). Therefore, the attempts to access the Link by someone using Vosburgh's IP address were undoubtedly criminal activity. Considering the "totality of the circumstances" outlined in Agent Desy's affidavit, *Gates*, 462 U .S. at 238, 103 S.Ct. 2317, we think it was fairly

---

13. *See also United States v. Stults*, 575 F.3d 834, 843–44 (8th Cir.2009) (holding that probable cause supported warrant where officers used IP address to identify possessor of child pornography on a file-sharing network); *United States v. Perrine*, 518 F.3d 1196, 1205–06 (10th Cir.2008) (upholding probable cause where pornographic images were traced to defendant's residence using IP address); *United States v. Wagers*, 452 F.3d 534, 539 (6th Cir.2006) (upholding probable cause where suspect was identified as a member of child pornography websites through an IP address assigned to his residence); *United States v. Hay*, 231 F.3d 630, 635–36 (9th Cir.2000) (finding a substantial basis for magistrate's probable cause determination where images of child pornography were traced to defendant using an IP address).

14. We say "fairly" unique because there undoubtedly exists the possibility of mischief and mistake with IP addresses. For example, the trial evidence showed that proxy servers can be used to mask IP addresses, and that knowledgeable users can "spoof" the IP addresses of others. In this case, we are confident that Vosburgh's IP address was a fairly reliable identifier of his computer for probable cause purposes, in light of the total lack of record evidence that he was the victim of any mischief. In those cases where officers know or ought to know, for whatever reason, that an IP address does not accurately represent the identity of a user or the source of a transmission, the value of that IP address for probable cause purposes may be greatly diminished, if not reduced to zero.

probable that "instrumentalities or evidence" of that criminal activity—such as computers and computer equipment—would be found in Vosburgh's apartment.[15] *See United States v. Urban*, 404 F.3d 754, 774 (3d Cir.2005) (quoting *United States v. Tehfe*, 722 F.2d 1114, 1117–18 (3d Cir.1983)); *see also Agnellino v. New Jersey*, 493 F.2d 714, 727 (3d Cir.1974) (stating that the standard for probable cause "clearly is something less than 'certainty' or 'evidence of guilt beyond a reasonable doubt'"); *Perez*, 484 F.3d at 740 (recognizing that "[p]robable cause does not require proof beyond a reasonable doubt").

Vosburgh argues that even if the IP address established some connection to the physical location of his apartment, the four-month gap between the warrant application and the attempts to access the Link described in Agent Desy's affidavit rendered the information in the affidavit stale. The "[a]ge of the information supporting a warrant application is a factor in determining probable cause." *United States v. Harvey*, 2 F.3d 1318, 1322 (3d Cir.1993). "If too old, the information is stale, and probable cause may no longer exist." *Zimmerman*, 277 F.3d at 434. "Age alone," however, "is not determinative. *Id*. To analyze a claim of staleness, we must do more than simply count the number of the days between the date of the alleged criminal activity and the date of the warrant. We must also consider "the nature of the crime and the type of evidence" involved. *Id*.

This is not the first time we have had occasion to consider staleness *vel non* in the context of child pornography. *See, e.g., United States v. Shields*, 458 F.3d 269, 279 n. 7 (3d Cir.2006); *Harvey*, 2 F.3d at 1322–23 (rejecting defendant's staleness claim). In *Shields*, FBI agents infiltrated two online groups explicitly dedicated to the exchange of child pornography. Eventually, both groups were shut down and the agents obtained records of group members' email addresses. *Shields*, 458 F.3d at 272. They traced one of those addresses back to Shields. Nine months after the groups were shut down, agents obtained a search warrant for Shields's home, where they found hundreds of images of child pornography. *Id*. at 273. On appeal, we rejected Shields's probable cause challenge. Shields did not argue staleness, but we raised the issue *sua sponte* and concluded that the information in the affidavit was not stale, despite the nine-month gap between the warrant application and any possible participation by Shields in the child pornography groups. *Id*. at 279 n. 7.

We reiterate that staleness is not a matter of mechanically counting days. *Zimmerman*, 277 F.3d at 434. Nevertheless, our conclusion in *Shields* that a nine-month gap did not render the information stale counsels in favor of the same result here, given the similar "nature of the crime[s]" involved, *id*., and the fact that the gap here was only four months. We therefore hold that the information in Agent Desy's affidavit was not stale. As the affidavit explained, and as we have long recognized, persons with an interest in child pornography tend to hoard their materials and retain them for a long time. *See, e.g., Shields*, 458 F.3d at 279 n. 7 (noting that "collectors of child pornography often store their material and rarely discard it"); *Harvey*, 2 F.3d at 1322–23 (rejecting staleness claim in part due to recognition that "pedophiles rarely, if ever, dispose of sexually explicit material"). Child pornography is illegal, and therefore difficult and risky to obtain. Presumably, once a child pornography collector gets his hands on such material he will not be quick to

---

15. The search warrant authorized agents to search for and seize much more than computer equipment. It allowed them to seize all originals, copies, and negatives of any visual depictions of minors engaging in sexually explicit conduct; "[a]ny and all documents ... pertaining to" the possession of child pornography; and diaries, notebooks, records, and notes reflecting contact with minors. Vosburgh does not challenge the scope of the warrant.

discard it. *Zimmerman*, 277 F.3d at 434. Vosburgh argues that this "hoarding" principle had no place in Agent Desy's affidavit (and should not inform this Court's staleness analysis) because the affidavit established no basis for concluding that Vosburgh was a child pornography collector. We disagree. The affidavit described repeated, deliberate attempts to access the Link—which, as the affidavit explained, was advertised as hard core child pornography and posted to an underground website explicitly and exclusively dedicated to such pornography—originating from an apartment in which Vosburgh lived by himself. Under these facts, we cannot say that it was unreasonable for officers to infer that the person responsible for those attempts *already* possessed some quantity of child pornography. *See United States v. Wagers*, 452 F.3d 534, 540 (6th Cir.2006) (noting that "evidence that a person has visited or subscribed to websites containing child pornography supports the conclusion that he has likely downloaded, kept, and otherwise possessed the material." (citing *United States v. Martin*, 426 F.3d 68, 77 (2d Cir.2005), and *United States v. Froman*, 355 F.3d 882, 890–91 (5th Cir.2004))).[16]

We do not hold, of course, that information concerning child pornography crimes can never grow stale. We observe only that information concerning crimes has a relatively long shelf life. It has not been, and should not be, quickly deemed stale. *See, e.g., Shields*, 458 F.3d at 279 n. 7. *See also United States v. Paull*, 551 F.3d 516, 522 (6th Cir.2009) (noting that "the same time limitations that have been applied to more fleeting crimes do not control the staleness inquiry for child pornography"). This is especially true where, as here, the crime in question is accomplished through the use of a computer. As the Ninth Circuit observed in one child pornography case, computers have "long memor[ies]." *United States v. Gourde*, 440 F.3d 1065, 1071 (9th Cir.2006) (en banc); *see also United States v. Frechette*, 583 F.3d 374, 379 (6th Cir.2009) ("Digital images of child pornography can be easily duplicated and ... even if they are sold or traded.... have an infinite life span."). Images stored on computers can be retained almost indefinitely, and forensic examiners can often uncover evidence of possession or attempted possession long after the crime has been completed. *See, e.g., Gourde*, 440 F.3d at 1071 (crediting statement in affidavit that FBI computer experts can resurrect files from a hard drive even after they have been deleted). The staleness inquiry requires us to consider the "type of evidence" at issue, *Zimmerman*, 277 F.3d at 434, and we think it obvious that the type of evidence agents sought from Vosburgh's apartment—computers and/or computer equipment— is not the type of evidence that rapidly dissipates or degrades. Nor is it the type of property that is usually quickly or continuously discarded. *Cf. United States v. Ritter*, 416 F.3d 256, 270–71 (3d Cir.2005) (Smith, J., concurring in the judgment) (discussing the relevance to staleness of the nature of the evidence and how quickly it might reasonably be expected to be discarded). Therefore, the passage of weeks or months here is less important than it might be in a case involving more fungible or ephemeral evidence, such as small quantities of drugs or stolen music. *See id.*

The magistrate's task was to make a practical, commonsense decision as to whether there was a fair probability that evidence of criminal activity—including possession or even attempted possession of child pornography—would be found in Vosburgh's apartment four months after he attempted to access the Link. On the facts before us, and in light of

---

16. *Cf. Shields*, 458 F.3d at 278 (finding it fairly probable that the defendant would be found in possession of child pornography, because he had "voluntarily registered for two e-groups that were devoted principally to sharing and collecting child pornography," using an email address that strongly suggested an interest in such pornography).

our precedents, we agree that the magistrate had a substantial basis for concluding that there was. Our decision fits comfortably within the body of case law concerning staleness in the context of child pornography. *See, e.g., United States v. Morales-Aldahondo*, 524 F.3d 115, 119 (1st Cir.2008) (rejecting defendant's argument that three-year gap between date of download and warrant application rendered information stale, in light of testimony from the "government's knowledgeable witness" that child pornography collectors "do not quickly dispose of their cache"); *United States v. Irving*, 452 F.3d 110, 125 (2d Cir.2006) (holding that twenty-two month old information in affidavit in support of warrant to search for child pornography was not stale); *United States v. Lemon*, 590 F.3d 612, 615–16 (8th Cir.2010) (upholding probable cause determination despite eighteen-month gap between the warrant application and the incident described in the affidavit that suggested possession of child pornography); *United States v. Lacy*, 119 F.3d 742, 745 (9th Cir.1997) (rejecting staleness claim in child pornography case involving ten-month gap); *United States v. Terry*, 522 F.3d 645, 650 n. 2 (6th Cir.2008) (upholding probable cause in child pornography case involving a five-month gap).

Vosburgh claims that *Zimmerman*, in which we held that a search warrant for pornography lacked probable cause, supports his argument that the information in Agent Desy's affidavit was stale. In *Zimmerman*, police obtained a warrant to search the defendant's home for adult and child pornography, and found several images of the latter.[17] 277 F.3d at 429. The warrant application contained no information suggesting that Zimmerman possessed child pornography in his home, and only one piece of information suggesting that adult pornography would be found at the home: a report that six to ten months earlier, a video clip of adult pornography was shown to minors there. *Id.* We concluded that there was no probable cause to search for child pornography, because there was no information suggesting that there was ever child pornography in the home. Indeed, the government conceded as much. *Id.* at 432. We further held that there was no probable cause to search for adult pornography either, because the only piece of information suggesting that pornography could be found at the home—the report about the video clip that was shown to minors—was stale. *Id.* at 433–34.

We cannot agree that *Zimmerman* controls this case. Initially, we note that the four-month gap at issue here is shorter than the six-month gap at issue in *Zimmerman*. Recognizing that staleness is about more than simply counting days, however, we note another important distinguishing fact. In *Zimmerman*, we acknowledged that child pornography collectors hoard and protect their materials closely, but we also noted that there was no information whatsoever in the affidavit to suggest that Zimmerman was a child pornography collector. The affidavit only asserted that Zimmerman had viewed adult pornography in his home. Therefore, the hoarding presumption applicable to child pornography collectors was inapposite, and nowhere did the affidavit address "whether *adult* pornography is typically retained" in the same manner as child pornography. *Id.* at 435 (emphasis added). Largely for that reason, we held that the six-month delay rendered the affidavit's information stale. The case before us is different. As we have explained, there was ample information to suggest that Vosburgh could be a collector of child pornography. Therefore, unlike in *Zimmerman*, the probable cause analysis here must account

---

17. Officers undertook the search for adult pornography pursuant to allegations that Zimmerman was criminally liable under Pennsylvania law for sexually abusing children and corrupting a minor. *Zimmerman*, 277 F.3d at 431.

for the accepted fact that child pornography collectors tend to hoard their materials for long periods of time.[18] *See Shields*, 458 F.3d at 279 n. 7; *Harvey*, 2 F.3d at 1322–23.

In summary, we hold that the search warrant was supported by probable cause. The IP address connected to a criminal attempt to access child pornography was fairly traceable to Vosburgh's apartment, and the information in the warrant application describing that attempt was not stale. Accordingly, the District Court did not err by denying Vosburgh's motion to suppress....

The judgment of conviction will be affirmed.

BARRY, Circuit Judge, Concurring.

It is not disputed that when it applied for the search warrant, the government had no idea, much less evidence, that Vosburgh had ever possessed child pornography. All it knew was that during a two-minute period of time on one day in Vosburgh's life, he attempted to access the Link, and was unsuccessful. That's it. Paltry as that was, I agree with my colleagues that it was nonetheless "fairly probable" that evidence of that attempt would be found in Vosburgh's apartment, that the information in the warrant application describing that attempt was not stale, and that Vosburgh's motion to suppress was properly denied.

I write, however, to note my disappointment that, given how little the government knew about Vosburgh, it somehow believed it appropriate to spend the first fifteen pages of the eighteen-page affidavit supporting the warrant application with what it conceded was "boilerplate"—boilerplate which anything but subtly suggested that Vosburgh, whose name was never mentioned, was someone the government had no reason to believe that he was—a "collector" of child pornography, a child pornographer, and perhaps even a pedophile. Moreover, the boilerplate went into considerable detail describing, for example, the "collection" of the "collector" as revealing his "private sexual desires and intent" and representing his "most cherished sexual fantasies involving children," and into graphic detail describing the numerous ways in which those fantasies can be turned into reality, including the sexual gratification a collector may derive from actual physical contact with children.... The only purpose of those many pages of boilerplate was, at least in my view, to assure that the warrant issued, which assuredly it did. Indeed, the affidavit apparently convinced my colleagues that, although there was not even an allegation that Vosburgh ever possessed child pornography, there was reason to believe he was nonetheless a "collector" or, at least, he "could be." ... I have nothing against boilerplate *per se*. But I am deeply concerned when information and innuendo as serious as that seen here is used so inappropriately. Surely the government wants to win, but it must never forget its obligation to win fairly.

---

18. There is another distinction between this case and *Zimmerman* which, although not directly relevant to staleness, demonstrates why the probable cause showing here was stronger than the showing in *Zimmerman*. In *Zimmerman*, we emphasized that there was no information suggesting that the defendant had ever possessed child pornography in his home. 277 F.3d at 432. Furthermore, there was no indication that even the single pornographic video clip referenced in the warrant application was ever located at the defendant's home. There was no indication that Zimmerman had ever downloaded the clip; it could just as easily have been "located in cyberspace." *Id.* at 435. In other words, nothing in the warrant application established any nexus between the pornography and the residence to be searched. Here, by contrast, the warrant application described Vosburgh's multiple attempts to download the Link, and explained why, based on Comcast's records, there was reason to believe those attempts originated from Vosburgh's apartment.

C. Good Faith Exception

United States v. Falso

Second Circuit, 2008
544 F.3d 110

SOTOMAYOR, Circuit Judge.

Defendant-appellant David J. Falso ("Falso") appeals from the June 6, 2006 judgment of the United States District Court for the Northern District of New York (McAvoy, J.). Falso was convicted, upon his conditional guilty plea to a 242-count indictment, of crimes relating to child pornography and traveling with the intent to engage in illicit sexual conduct with minors. Prior to Falso's guilty plea, the district court denied his motion to suppress evidence seized from his home on the grounds that probable cause for the search existed and that, in any event, the "good-faith" exception to the exclusionary rule applied.[1]

The threshold issue presented on appeal is whether a substantial basis for the district court's finding of probable cause exists where the law enforcement affidavit supporting the search warrant alleged that Falso "appears" to have "gained or attempted to gain" access to a website that distributed child pornography and had been convicted eighteen years earlier of a misdemeanor based on sexual abuse of a minor. In a divided opinion in *United States v. Martin*, 426 F.3d 68 (2d Cir.2005), this Court held that probable cause to search the defendant's home existed, largely based on his membership to a website whose principal purpose was sharing of child pornography (hereafter, a "child-pornography website"). *Id.* at 75–76. In *United States v. Coreas*, 419 F.3d 151 (2d Cir.2005), a different panel expressed its belief that *Martin* "was wrongly decided," but adhered to *Martin's* holding because the cases were indistinguishable and *Martin* was binding precedent. *Id.* at 159 (2d Cir.2005).

Falso's case tests the limits of these precedents, insofar as it presents the following distinguishing factor: Falso was not alleged to be a member or subscriber to a child-pornography website; it was alleged only that Falso "*appeared*" to "*have gained or* attempted to gain" access to a site that contained approximately eleven images of child pornography. Absent any allegation that Falso in fact accessed the website at issue, the question is whether Falso's eighteen-year old conviction involving the sexual abuse of a minor (or some other factor) provides a sufficient basis to believe that evidence of child pornography crimes would be found in Falso's home. A majority of this panel (Jacobs, C.J. & Sotomayor, J.) holds that probable cause was lacking. A differently aligned majority of this panel (Sotomayor & Livingston, JJ.), however, holds that the good-faith exception to the exclusionary rule applies. *See United States v. Leon*, 468 U.S. 897, 923–25, 104 S.Ct. 3405, 82 L.Ed.2d 677 (1984). Thus, notwithstanding the absence of probable cause to sustain issuance of the search warrant, a majority of this panel affirms the district court's denial of Falso's motion to suppress the physical evidence seized from his home.[2] ...

On or about June 1, 2005, the Federal Bureau of Investigation ("FBI") submitted an application for a warrant to search for and seize evidence of child pornography in Fals-

---

1. In this opinion we address only Falso's challenges to the district court's denial of his motion to suppress physical evidence seized from his home pursuant to the search warrant. We address and reject Falso's remaining claims in a companion summary order.

2. Sometimes we have eschewed analyzing probable cause when we rely on the good faith exception, *see, e.g., United States v. Jasorka*, 153 F.3d 58, 60–61 (2d Cir.1998), but here we elect to decide both issues, *Leon*, 468 U.S. at 925, 104 S.Ct. 3405 ("[N]othing will prevent reviewing courts from deciding the [Fourth Amendment] question before turning to the good-faith issue.").

o's home. The application was supported by, *inter alia*, a twenty-six page affidavit by FBI Agent James Lyons ("Agent Lyons"). Among other things, the affidavit provided information about (1) the use of computers and the internet to view and collect child pornography; (2) the characteristics of child-pornography collectors; and (3) the investigation that implicated Falso.... Of the affidavit's generalized information, Agent Lyons explained that individuals who exploit children, including collectors of child pornography, commonly use computers to: communicate with like-minded individuals, store their child pornography collections, and locate, view, download, collect and organize images of child pornography found on the internet. The affidavit further explained that collectors and distributors of child pornography sometime use online resources to retrieve and store child pornography, including services offered by internet portals such as Yahoo! Inc. ("Yahoo"). The affidavit also contained information gathered by a member of the FBI's Behavioral Analysis Unit, including his observations that "[t]he majority of individuals who collect child pornography are persons who have a sexual attraction to children," and that those who collect images of child pornography generally store their collections at home.

Specific to the investigation of Falso, the affidavit explained that the FBI obtained the Internet Protocol address of a website, www.cpfreedom.com, which contained approximately eleven images of child pornography, and which advertised additional child pornography at an internet address that was hidden until a membership was purchased. The affidavit further stated that an undercover FBI agent paid $99 for a one-month membership and received an e-mail from CP Freedom Group, which provided the internet address, login number, and password for its membership website, www.cp-members.com. The affidavit then explained that an FBI forensic examination of "the website hosting www.cpfreedom.com" revealed "several possible subscribers along with e-mail addresses and other information." According to the affidavit, the FBI subpoenaed subscriber information for these e-mail addresses, which included cousy1731@yahoo.com. Records obtained from Yahoo revealed that Falso had an active Yahoo account, with a login name of "cousy1731" and the Yahoo e-mail address referenced above. The affidavit also stated that the residential address associated with Falso's Yahoo account had active internet service during the period immediately preceding the warrant request. The affidavit further stated that, based upon the FBI investigation and the forensic examination, "it appear[ed]" that Falso "either gained access or attempted to gain access to the [non-member] website www.cpfreedom.com."

The affidavit also revealed that on February 18, 1987 — approximately eighteen years earlier — Falso was arrested by the New York State Police for sexually abusing a seven-year old girl and was charged with Sexual Abuse and Endangering the Welfare of a Child. According to the affidavit, the police report relating to this incident stated that Falso placed his hands inside the girl's underwear and digitally penetrated her, and acknowledged to police that he may need counseling for latent problems. The affidavit also stated that, on or about September 21, 1987, Falso pled guilty to Acting in a Manner Injurious to a Child Less than Sixteen, a misdemeanor for which Falso received a sentence of three years probation.[3] ... Based on the foregoing, Agent Lyons opined that "there [was] probable cause to believe that the individual utilizing the Yahoo ID 'cousy1731' [i.e. Falso] ... is a

---

3. In actuality, the conviction records introduced in connection with the pretrial motions clarify that Falso pled guilty to the misdemeanor of Endangering the Welfare of a Child under New York Penal Law § 260.10-1 by knowingly acting in a manner likely to be injurious to the physical, mental or moral welfare of a child under the age of seventeen. The district court took notice of this fact when adjudicating Falso's suppression motion.

collector of child pornography." Judge McAvoy agreed and issued a search warrant on June 1, 2005, permitting the FBI to search Falso's home for, *inter alia*, evidence of child-pornography related crimes....

Five law enforcement officers, including Agent Lyons, executed the search warrant at Falso's home on June 8, 2005. The officers seized Falso's computer and a box containing child pornography in Falso's bedroom. Agent Lyons and another officer also interviewed Falso for approximately ninety minutes during the search. Agent Lyons's report from the interview stated that Falso admitted to, among other things, obtaining child pornography from the internet; engaging in sexual activity with females in other countries whom he believed to be between the ages of sixteen and eighteen; and having been convicted for sexually abusing a seven-year old girl. Falso was placed under arrest at the conclusion of the search. A later search of Falso's computer revealed additional images of child pornography.... Falso was indicted on June 16, 2005 for traveling with the intent to engage in illicit sexual conduct with minors in violation of 18 U.S.C. §§ 2423(b), (f) & 2246 (Counts 1–2); production of child pornography in violation of 18 U.S.C. § 2251(a) (Counts 3–10); receiving child pornography via the internet in violation of 18 U.S.C. §§ 2252A(a)(2)(A), (B) & 2256 (Counts 11–233); transporting and shipping child pornography in violation of 18 U.S.C. §§ 2252A(a)(1) & 2256 (Counts 234–241); and possession of child pornography in violation of 18 U.S.C. § 2252A(a)(5)(B) (Count 242). The indictment also alleged that Falso had a prior conviction relating to the sexual exploitation of children, and sexual abuse involving a minor, which invoked the penalty provisions of 18 U.S.C. §§ 2252A(b)(1), (b)(2) and 2251.

Falso subsequently moved to suppress the evidence seized from his home and computer on the ground that probable cause for the search was lacking. Specifically, Falso claimed that the presence of his e-mail address on the cpfreedom.com website was an insufficient basis for probable cause in the absence of any allegations in the affidavit that Falso was a member or subscriber to the website, or that the overriding purpose of the website was the trading of child pornography.... Falso also sought a *Franks* hearing,[4] claiming that certain of the information in the affidavit was designed to mislead the court into believing that Falso was actually a member of or subscriber to the cpfreedom website, and that the government misleadingly failed to disclose that Falso's e-mail address could have appeared on the cpfreedom.com website for innocent reasons, such as being part of a spam mailing list. In support, Falso submitted an affidavit from a data forensics expert, Robert DeCicco ("DeCicco"). That affidavit explained that "there is a difference between visiting a website, and become [sic] a member and/or subscriber to the site"; the latter normally "involves the assignment of a password and user name conditioned on the payment of a fee or the provision of specific personal information." DeCicco's affidavit further explained that internet service providers [such as Yahoo] do not maintain records identifying the websites visited by their customers and, thus, a review of service provider records "would not disclose whether a customer was a subscriber or member of a particular website." Moreover, his affidavit stated that "[i]t is common practice for websites to obtain lists of e-mail addresses from other sources ... and to send unsolicited e-mail to such addresses." Thus, DeCicco concluded, "the fact that [Falso's] e-mail address appeared on the [cpfreedom.com] website does not mean that he contacted or attempted to contact that site."

---

4. *See Franks v. Delaware*, 438 U.S. 154, 98 S.Ct. 2674, 57 L.Ed.2d 667 (1978) (holding that, under certain limited circumstances, a defendant is entitled under the Fourth Amendment to attack collaterally the veracity of a warrant affidavit in the context of challenging the existence of probable cause).

On February 24, 2006, the district court issued an oral ruling denying Falso's motions, holding that: (1) Falso was not entitled to a *Franks* hearing; (2) probable cause for the search existed; and (3) even if there was an insufficient basis for probable cause, suppression of the evidence was not warranted because the good-faith exception to the exclusionary rule applied.... After the district court denied Falso's motions, he pled guilty to all 242 counts in the indictment. Falso specifically reserved the right to appeal from the district court's denial of his motions to suppress. Falso also objected to the district court's use of his prior state conviction for Endangering the Welfare of a Child as a basis for enhancing the statutory minimum and maximum penalties. On June 2, 2006, the district court sentenced Falso principally to 30 years' imprisonment....

This Court must afford "great deference" to the district court's probable cause determination. *Gates*, 462 U.S. at 236, 103 S.Ct. 2317 (internal quotation marks omitted). Our "duty" on review, therefore, "is simply to ensure that the [district court] had a substantial basis for ... concluding that probable cause existed." *Id.* at 238, 103 S.Ct. 2317 (internal marks omitted). Nevertheless, under this standard, we "may properly conclude that ... [a] warrant was invalid because the [district court's] probable-cause determination reflected an improper analysis of the totality of circumstances." *Leon*, 468 U.S. at 915, 104 S.Ct. 3405 (citing *Gates*, 462 U.S. at 238–39, 103 S.Ct. 2317)....

Falso's case stands apart from those preceding it insofar as he was not alleged to have actually accessed or subscribed to any child-pornography website. Rather, Agent Lyons's affidavit alleged only that Falso was perhaps one of several hundred possible subscribers to the cpfreedom.com website, who *appeared* either to have gained or attempted to gain access to the site.... Agent Lyons's inconclusive statements about whether Falso even accessed the cpfreedom.com website, coupled with the absence of details about the features and nature of the non-member site, falls short of establishing probable cause. The question, then, is whether other allegations in the affidavit, considered as a whole, provide a basis to support the district court's finding of probable cause.... The most obvious other factor that might support a finding of probable cause is Falso's eighteen-year-old misdemeanor conviction for Endangering the Welfare of a Child. The district court found Falso's conviction "[i]mportant [ ]" and "highly relevant" to the probable cause calculus in light of the affidavit's representation that "the majority of individuals who collect child pornography are persons who have a sexual attraction to [children]." But this reasoning falls victim to logic.

"It is an inferential fallacy of ancient standing to conclude that, because members of group A" (those who collect child pornography) "are likely to be members of group B" (those attracted to children), "then group B is entirely, or even largely composed of, members of group A." *See Martin*, 426 F.3d at 82 (Pooler, J., dissenting) (pointing out the fallacy in a different context).[14] Although offenses relating to child pornography and sexual abuse of minors both involve the exploitation of children, that does not compel, or even suggest, the correlation drawn by the district court.[15] Perhaps it is true that all or most people who are attracted to minors collect child pornography. But that association is nowhere stated or supported in the affidavit. *See Gates*, 462 U.S. at 238, 103 S.Ct. 2317 (probable cause assessments are to be made from "all the circumstances set forth in the

---

14. In *Martin*, Judge Pooler criticized the majority's inference that because collectors of child pornography are likely to be subscribers of e-groups, that the inverse also is true: namely, that subscribers are likely to collect child pornography. *Id.* at 82.

15. By analogy, it may be said that "most people who sell drugs do drugs." That is not to say, however, that "most people who do drugs sell drugs."

affidavit"); *Gourde*, 440 F.3d at 1067 ("All data necessary to show probable cause for the issuance of a search warrant must be contained within the four corners of a written affidavit given under oath" (internal marks and citation omitted)). While the district court undoubtedly had the safety of the public in mind, an individual's Fourth Amendment right cannot be vitiated based on fallacious inferences drawn from facts not supported by the affidavit.

Nor is the district court's reasoning saved by the affidavit's general statement, relied upon by the government at oral argument, that "computers are utilized by individuals who exploit children (which includes collectors of child pornography) to ... locate, view, download, collect and organize images of child pornography found through the internet."[16] There simply is nothing in this statement indicating that it is more (or less) likely that Falso's computer might contain images of child pornography. That is, the affidavit's sweeping representation that computers are used by those who exploit children to, *inter alia*, view and download child pornography, would be equally true if 1% or 100% of those who exploit children used computers to do those things.... Furthermore, we agree with Falso that even if his prior conviction were relevant to the analysis, it should have only been marginally relevant because the conviction was stale. This Court has explained that "[t]wo critical factors in determining whether facts supporting a search warrant are stale are 'the age of those facts and the nature of the conduct alleged to have violated the law.'" *United States v. Ortiz*, 143 F.3d 728, 732 (2d Cir.1998) (quoting *United States v. Martino*, 664 F.2d 860, 867 (2d Cir.1981)). Here, both factors combine to undermine the probity of Falso's prior conviction.

First, the sheer length of time that had elapsed renders Falso's prior sex crime only marginally relevant, if at all. Certainly there are cases where it may be appropriate for a district court to consider a dated sex crime; for example, where there is evidence of ongoing impropriety, because in such cases the prior offense would tend to be less aberrational. *See, e.g., United States v. Irving*, 452 F.3d 110, 124–25 (2d Cir.2006) (finding no error in the district court's consideration of defendant's twenty-year-old conviction for attempted sexual abuse of a minor when denying defendant's motion to suppress, where there was evidence of two-year-old letters written by defendant discussing the exploitation of children, evidence that he sexually abused boys in Mexico five years earlier, and the statement of a friend that had used his computer to receive child pornography). But no such evidence was provided in this case to bridge the temporal gap between Falso's eighteen-year old sex offense and the suspected child-pornography offense.

Second, although Falso's crime allegedly involved the sexual abuse of a minor,[17] it did not relate to child pornography. *Cf. Wagers*, 452 F.3d at 537, 541 (finding no error in the district court's reliance on defendant's seven-year-old conviction of possession of child pornography in upholding search warrant directed at same illegal activity). That the law criminalizes both child pornography and the sexual abuse (or endangerment) of children cannot be enough. They are separate offenses and, as explained above, nothing in the affidavit draws a correlation between a person's propensity to commit both types of crimes.[18] ...

---

16. The district court itself does not appear to have relied on this passage; correctly so, for the reasons explained in the text.

17. Falso pled guilty to the offense of Endangering the Welfare of a Child, which criminalizes acts that do not necessarily involve sexual contact with minors. The police report and information, however, allege that Falso digitally penetrated a young girl.

18. Our decision in *United States v. Brand*, 467 F.3d 179, 198 (2d Cir.2006), is not to the contrary. In *Brand*, we affirmed the district court's evidentiary ruling permitting the government, in its prosecution

Absent any allegation that Falso accessed the cpfreedom.com website, and with little or no weight attaching to his prior conviction, the question remains whether other allegations in the affidavit, considered as a whole, support a finding of probable cause. Generalized allegations about: (1) the propensity of collectors of child pornography to intentionally maintain illegal images; (2) law enforcement's ability to retrieve such images from a computer; and (3) the ability to view child pornography on the cpfreedom.com website, fail to establish the requisite nexus of illegal activity to Falso. Although Falso might hoard images of child pornography if he viewed and downloaded them, there is no allegation in the affidavit that he was in a position, or was otherwise inclined, to do so....

In the end, the district court's finding of probable cause in Falso's case required it to make at least two significant additional inferential leaps not required in *Martin* and like cases. First, in Falso's case there is no allegation that he in fact gained access to the cpfreedom.com website, much less that he was a member or subscriber of any child-pornography site. Second, there are no allegations to support an inference that the sole or principal purpose of the cpfreedom.com website was the viewing and sharing of child pornography, much less that images of child pornography were downloadable from the site. Thus, it is only after making the inferences that (1) Falso in fact accessed a website[19] (2) whose principal purpose was the viewing and sharing of child pornography, that the district court could draw the ultimate inference, upheld in *Martin*, that those who become members of a child-pornography website are likely to collect such images. Putting aside the dangers of *Martin*'s ultimate inference, *see Martin*, 426 F.3d at 81–83 (Pooler, J., dissenting); *Coreas*, 419 F.3d at 156–58, the dangers of coupling it with the inferences drawn in Falso's case are exponential.

---

of a defendant for traveling in interstate commerce for the purpose of engaging in illicit sexual contact with a minor, to present the jury with images of child pornography found on the defendant's computer. We explained that the defendant's collection of child pornography indicated an "abnormal sexual attraction to children," and thus was relevant to the offense for which the defendant stood trial, which involved the same abnormalcy. *See id.* at 198 ("The 'similarity or some connection' requirement [for purposes of establishing relevance under the Federal Rules of Evidence] is satisfied in the instant case because a direct connection exists between child pornography and pedophilia."). We drew our conclusion, in part, from the Child Pornography Prevention Act of 1996, in which "Congress found that 'child pornography is often used by pedophiles and child sexual abusers to stimulate and whet their own sexual appetites, and as a model for sexual acting out with children,'" *id.* at 198 (quoting Pub.L. No. 104-208, § 121, 110 Stat. 3009, 3009–26 (1996)), and from congressional testimony of the FBI, which noted "'a strong correlation between child pornography offenders and molesters of children' and that the 'correlation between collection of child pornography and actual child abuse is too real and too grave to ignore,'" *id.* at 198 n. 17 (quoting Enhancing *Child Protection Laws After the April 16, 2002 Supreme Court Decision, Ashcroft v. Free Speech Coalition: Hearing Before the Subcomm. on Crime, Terrorism, and Homeland Security of the H. Comm. on the Judiciary*, 107th Cong. (2002) (statement of Michael J. Heimbach, Crimes Against Children Unit, Criminal Investigative Division, FBI)). It is worthy of observation, however, that the correlation in *Brand* that the government relied upon was that the defendant, a known collector of child pornography, was predisposed or intended to commit the charged offense involving an intended sexual act against a minor. That is precisely the inverse of the correlation relied upon by the district court in Falso's case: that a person convicted of a crime involving the sexual abuse of a minor would likely collect child pornography. But, as explained above, the latter correlation is not supported by the affidavit itself and thus cannot support a probable-cause finding. Moreover, the test of whether evidence is "relevant" for purposes of admission under the rules of evidence is a more flexible standard than whether evidence of a past crime gives rise to an inference of probable cause that a different crime has been committed. *Cf. Brand*, 467 F.3d at 197 (discussing relevancy standard).

19. [That] Falso may have attempted, but failed, to gain access to the cpfreedom.com site requires a separate, but related, inference: that Falso nevertheless obtained child pornography from other unidentified sources.

We are not insensitive to "the need for law enforcement to have a certain amount of latitude in conducting criminal investigations." *Martin*, 426 F.3d at 76. But, as we explained in *Coreas*, requiring the government to gather "evidence *particularized* to the target of the search" before the warrant application is made "will simply focus law enforcement efforts on those who can reasonably be suspected of possessing child pornography." *Id.* at 158 (emphasis added).[20] If this proves to be a hindrance, it is one the Fourth Amendment demands.... Accordingly, we find no substantial basis for probable cause and reverse the district court's conclusion in this regard....

Our determination that the district court erred in finding probable cause does not end the analysis of whether the evidence seized from Falso's home should be suppressed. In *United States v. Leon*, the Supreme Court held that the exclusionary rule barring illegally obtained evidence from the courtroom does not apply to evidence seized "in objectively reasonable reliance on" a warrant issued by a detached and neutral magistrate judge, even where the warrant is subsequently deemed invalid. 468 U.S. 897, 922, 104 S.Ct. 3405, 82 L.Ed.2d 677 (1984). The Court reasoned that, "even assuming that the [exclusionary] rule effectively deters some police misconduct and provides incentives for the law enforcement profession as a whole to conduct itself in accord with the Fourth Amendment, it cannot be expected, and should not be applied, to deter objectively reasonable law enforcement activity." *Id.* at 918–19, 104 S.Ct. 3405.

Consistent with this rationale, there are four circumstances in which the good-faith exception does not apply: "(1) where the issuing [judge] has been knowingly misled; (2) where the issuing [judge] wholly abandoned his or her judicial role; (3) where the application is so lacking in indicia of probable cause as to render reliance upon it unreasonable; and (4) where the warrant is so facially deficient [such as by failing to particularize the place to be searched or the things to be seized] that reliance upon it is unreasonable." *United States v. Moore*, 968 F.2d 216, 222 (2d Cir.1992) (citing *Leon*, 468 U.S. at 922–23, 104 S.Ct. 3405); *accord United States v. Cancelmo*, 64 F.3d 804, 807 (2d Cir.1995). In such circumstances, reliance on the legal judgment of the issuing judge would not be objectively reasonable. *See Leon*, 468 U.S. at 923, 104 S.Ct. 3405. Here, Falso claims that the good-faith exception does not apply on the first and third of these grounds; specifically, that the district court's finding of probable cause was based on knowingly or recklessly misleading statements in Agent Lyons's affidavit, and the affidavit otherwise was "so lacking in indicia of probable cause" as to render reliance upon it unreasonable. Falso also seeks to avoid application of the good-faith exception on the ground that district court improperly denied a *Franks* hearing to challenge the veracity of Agent Lyons's affidavit. A majority of this panel disagrees....

Generally, the way a defendant demonstrates that statements in an affidavit intentionally or recklessly misled a district court is through a *Franks* hearing. In *Franks v. Delaware*, 438 U.S. 154, 98 S.Ct. 2674, 57 L.Ed.2d 667 (1978), the Supreme Court held that although a presumption of validity attaches to a law enforcement affidavit, in certain circumstances a defendant is entitled to a hearing to test the veracity of the affiant's statements. *Id.* at 171, 98 S.Ct. 2674. Specifically, the Court held that the Fourth Amendment entitles a defendant to a hearing if he or she makes a "substantial preliminary showing" that a deliberate falsehood or statement made with reckless disregard for the truth was included in the

---

20. As we admonished in *Coreas*, the "[g]overnment could easily have obtained more information" about Falso. *See Coreas*, 419 F.3d at 158. Among other things, it could have monitored the traffic of the cpfreedom.com website and ascertained whether Falso (and others) actually downloaded pornography from the site. *See id.*

warrant affidavit and the statement was necessary to the judge's finding of probable cause. *Id.* at 155–56, 170–71, 98 S.Ct. 2674; *see also United States v. Salameh*, 152 F.3d 88, 113 (2d Cir.1998). To avoid fishing expeditions into affidavits that are otherwise presumed truthful, the Court in *Leon* held that to mandate an evidentiary hearing:

> [T]he challenger's attack must be more than conclusory and must be supported by more than a mere desire to cross-examine. There must be allegations of deliberate falsehood or of reckless disregard for the truth, and those allegations must be accompanied by an offer of proof. They should point out specifically the portion of the warrant affidavit that is claimed to be false; and they should be accompanied by a statement of supporting reasons. Affidavits or sworn or otherwise reliable statements of witnesses should be furnished, or their absence satisfactorily explained. Allegations of negligence or innocent mistake are insufficient.

Id. at 171, 104 S.Ct. 3405.

In this case, the district court denied Falso's request for a *Franks* hearing because it concluded that there were no false or recklessly misleading statements in the affidavit. We find no error in the district court's denial of a *Franks* hearing, nor in its conclusion that the statements at issue were not false or misleading.[21] ... Falso claims that the following paragraph from Agent Lyons's affidavit was designed to, and did, mislead the district court:

> In or about July 2004, Special Agent Todd Gentry reviewed the comp[l]eted forensic examination of the website hosting www.cpfreedom.com. The forensic examination revealed several hundred possible subscribers along with e-mail addresses and other information. In or about July 2004, subpoenas were served on appropriate ISP's for each e-mail address identified on the www.cpfreedom.com website. In or about September 2004, all subpoena requests were returned to the FBI. Pursuant to a review of the subpoenaed records [from internet service providers], the following subscriber information (among others) was associated with the www.cpfreedom.com website: David J. Falso, 20 Peaceful Drive, Cortland, New York, Yahoo User ID: cousy1731@yahoo.com. Based upon investigation and examination conducted by Special Agent Todd Gentry and others, it appears that a person with [Falso's] e-mail address either gained access or attempted to gain access to the website www.cpfreedom.com Special Agent Gentry's investigation and review of forensic examination revealed the material associated with the www.cpfreedom.com website is hardcore child pornography....

Falso maintains this passage is misleading because it suggests (1) that the FBI's investigation revealed something more than the existence of Falso's e-mail address on the website; and/or (2) that Falso had actually subscribed to the cpfreedom.com website. As an initial matter, we agree that the passage suggests that the FBI's investigation revealed something more than Falso's e-mail address on the site. But the passage is not misleading

---

21. In *United States v. One Parcel of Property Located at 15 Black Ledge*, 897 F.2d 97 (2d Cir.1990), we reviewed the denial of a *Franks* hearing in a forfeiture case for clear error to the extent that denial rested on factual findings. *Id.* at 100. We did not explain why that was the appropriate standard, however, and we note the existence of a circuit court split on the issue. *Compare United States. v. Reiner*, 500 F.3d 10, 14 (1st Cir.2007) (reviewing denial of *Franks* hearing for clear error); *United States v. Stewart*, 306 F.3d 295, 304 (6th Cir.2002) (same); *United States v. Buchanan*, 985 F.2d 1372, 1378 (8th Cir.1993) (same); *United States v. Skinner*, 972 F.2d 171, 177 (7th Cir.1992) (same), *with United States v. Gonzalez, Inc.*, 412 F.3d 1102, 1110 (9th Cir.2005) (applying *de novo* standard); *United States v. Martin*, 332 F.3d 827, 833 (5th Cir.2003) (same). To the extent the issue remains open in our circuit, we need not decide whether the clear error or *de novo* standard applies because, under either standard, we find no error in the district court's denial of a *Franks* hearing.

because the investigation had in fact revealed additional information. In particular, the immediately preceding paragraph in the affidavit explains that an FBI agent, acting in an undercover capacity, signed up for a one-month membership through the cpfreedom.com website and received an email from the CP Freedom Group containing the membership information. Thus, as the district court explained, the FBI's investigation revealed not only that Falso's e-mail address was on the website, but also that the website's administrators communicated with its members through e-mail. If additional information — not mentioned in the affidavit — led the FBI to the qualified conclusion that "*it appear[ed]*" that Falso *either* "gained access or *attempted to gain access*" to the cpfreedom website, it is hard to understand how the district court could have been misled for purposes of the good-faith exception.[22]

We are no more persuaded by Falso's claim that the affidavit misleadingly suggests that he was, in fact, a subscriber to the cpfreedom.com website. The purported confusion arises from Agent Lyons's use of the word "subscriber" in the affidavit to refer to two types of subscribers: those of the cpfreedom.com website and those of internet service providers such as Yahoo. Considered in context, however, one possible — if not most plausible — reading of the final three sentences of the above-quoted passage is the one adopted by the district court: namely, that the "subscriber information" referred to is for Yahoo, not the cpfreedom.com website.[23] Even if there were any suggestion (intentional or otherwise) in the passage quoted above that Falso was in fact a subscriber to the cpfreedom.com website, it was qualified (if not clarified) in the penultimate sentence, which states that "it appears" Falso either "gained access or attempted to gain access" to the site.

In addition to the foregoing alleged misstatements, Falso argues that the affidavit contained material omissions. Specifically, Falso claims that because the government did not disclose incriminating evidence to the contrary, "it is reasonable to assume" that: (1) the government identified all subscribers and that Falso was not one; (2) the government determined that Falso had not contacted the website; and (3) Falso's e-mail address was found in a computer file indicative of spam. Falso, however, has made no offer of proof that the allegedly omitted "facts" exist. *See Franks*, 438 U.S. at 171, 98 S.Ct. 2674 (stating that defendant seeking a *Franks* hearing must support his allegations with an "offer of proof" and lodge an attack that is "more than a mere desire to cross-examine"). It is for this reason that *United States v. Reilly*, 76 F.3d 1271 (2d Cir.1996), upon which Falso relies, is distinguishable. In *Reilly*, this Court held that the good-faith exception did not apply where the affiant knew certain facts that would undermine probable cause yet failed to provide these facts to the magistrate judge. *Id.* at 1280 ("For the good faith exception to apply, the police must reasonably believe that the warrant was based on a valid application

---

22. At oral argument, the government revealed additional information that was not reflected in the affidavit: namely, that Falso's e-mail address on the site appeared with a password and username associated with it. Although the government's revelation at oral argument cannot support its probable cause claim, *cf. Whiteley v. Warden, Wyo. State Penitentiary*, 401 U.S. 560, 565 n. 8, 91 S.Ct. 1031, 28 L.Ed.2d 306 (1971) ("[A]n otherwise insufficient affidavit cannot be rehabilitated by testimony concerning information possessed by the affiant when he sought the warrant but not disclosed to the issuing magistrate [judge]."), it does tend to support the officers' good-faith reliance on the warrant.

23. That the district court reasonably read the term "subscriber" as referring to a Yahoo subscriber is supported by an earlier portion of the affidavit describing the use of computers by persons who collect child pornography. In that section, Agent Lyons notes that collectors of child pornography use services offered by companies, "such as Yahoo!," which include online storage accounts. It then states that a "subscriber assigned to a free online storage account" can set one up with little identifying information, and goes on to use the term "subscriber" or "subscribing" seven more times, in each case clearly referring to Yahoo or similar Internet services.

of the law to the known facts. In the instant matter, the officers failed to give these facts to the magistrate [judge].".). By contrast, here there is no evidence—just conjecture— that the government failed to disclose additional information in its possession that might tend to exculpate Falso or otherwise negate the existence of probable cause.

Moreover, even assuming that any of the statements in the affidavit misled the district court, Falso has not met his burden of demonstrating that Agent Lyons made the alleged misrepresentations and that he omitted material information knowingly or recklessly. We thus reject Falso's challenge to the good-faith exception on the ground that he has failed to make even a preliminary showing that the district court was knowingly or recklessly misled by any statements or omissions in Agent Lyons's affidavit.... Falso's alternative claim, that the affidavit was "so lacking in indicia of probable cause as to render reliance upon it unreasonable,"[24] *see Moore*, 968 F.2d at 222, fares no better. Once the district court ruled on the legal sufficiency of the facts alleged in the affidavit, the officers were justified in executing the warrant. *Cancelmo*, 64 F.3d at 809 ("[W]e decline to hold that the agents acted unreasonably in accepting the magistrate judge's legal conclusion that probable cause existed.").

Even if there may have been an innocent explanation for the presence of Falso's e-mail address on the cpfreedom.com website, that does not undermine the officers' good-faith reliance on the warrant. As this Court explained in *Fama*: "The fact that an innocent explanation may be consistent with the facts alleged ... does not negate probable cause. Neither should it preclude a good faith belief in probable cause." 758 F.2d at 838 (citations omitted)....

In short, the error in this case, as found by a majority of the panel, was committed by the district court in issuing the warrant, not by the officers who executed it. *See Cancelmo*, 64 F.3d at 807. Accordingly, we uphold the district court's application of the good-faith exception to deny Falso's suppression motion.... For the foregoing reasons, we hold that the district court's finding of probable cause was not supported by a substantial basis. However, because the district court properly applied the good-faith exception in denying Falso's suppression motion, and for the additional reasons discussed in our accompanying summary order, we AFFIRM the judgment....

II. Expert Testimony

A. Child Sexual Abuse Accommodation Syndrome

Roland C. Summit, M.D.
The Child Abuse Accommodation Syndrome
7 CHILD ABUSE & NEGLECT 177 (1983)

Clinical study of large numbers of children and their parents in proven cases of sexual abuse provides emphatic contradictions to traditional views. What emerges is a typical behavior pattern or syndrome of mutually dependent variables which allows for immediate

---

24. This is a very difficult threshold to meet, as evidenced by the many decisions of this Court rejecting objections to the good-faith exception on this basis. *See, e.g., United States v. Jasorka*, 153 F.3d 58, 60–61 (2d Cir.1998); *United States v. Cancelmo*, 64 F.3d 804, 807–08 (2d Cir.1995); *Moore*, 968 F.2d at 222–23 (2d Cir.1992); *United States v. Fama*, 758 F.2d 834, 837–38 (2d Cir.1985).

survival of the child within the family but which tends to isolate the child from eventual acceptance, credibility or empathy within the larger society. The mythology and protective denial surrounding sexual abuse can be seen as a natural consequence both of the stereotypic coping mechanisms of the child victim and the need of almost all adults to insulate themselves from the painful realities of childhood victimization.

The accommodation process intrinsic to the world of child sexual abuse inspires prejudice and rejection in any adult who chooses to remain aloof from the helplessness and pain of the child's dilemma or who expects that a child should behave in accordance with adult concepts of self-determinism and autonomous, rational choices. Without a clear understanding of the accommodation syndrome, clinical specialists tend to reinforce the comforting belief that children are only rarely legitimate victims of unilateral sexual abuse and that among the few complaints that surface, most can be dismissed as fantasy, confusion, or a displacement of the child's own wish for power and seductive conquest....

The syndrome includes five categories, two of which are preconditions to the occurrence of sexual abuse. The remaining three categories are sequential contingencies which take on increasing variability and complexity. While it can be shown that each category reflects a compelling reality for the victim, each category represents also a contradiction to the most common assumptions of adults. The five categories of the syndrome are:

1. Secrecy
2. Helplessness
3. Entrapment and accommodation
4. Delayed, conflicted and unconvincing disclosure
5. Retraction ...

It is sad to hear children attacked by attorneys and discredited by juries because they claimed to be molested yet admitted they had made no protest nor outcry. The point to emphasize here is not so much the miscarriage of justice as the continuing assault on the child. If the child's testimony is rejected in court, there is more likely to be a rejection by the mother and other relatives who may be eager to restore trust in the accused adult and to brand the child as malicious. Clinical experience and expert testimony can provide advocacy for the child. Children are easily ashamed and intimidated both by their helplessness and by their inability to communicate their feelings to uncomprehending adults. They need an adult clinical advocate to translate the child's world into an adult acceptable language....

It is worth restating that all these accommodation mechanisms—domestic martyrdom, splitting of reality, altered consciousness, hysterical phenomena, delinquency, sociopathy, projection of rage, even self-mutilation—are part of the survival skills of the child. They can be overcome only if the child can be led to trust in a secure environment which can provide consistent, *noncontingent* acceptance and caring. In the meantime, anyone working therapeutically with the child (or the grown[-]up, still shattered victim) may be tested and provoked to prove that trust is impossible, ... [footnote omitted] and that the only secure reality is negative expectations and self-hate. It is all too easy for the would be therapist to join the parents and all of adult society in rejecting such a child, looking at the results of abuse to assume that such an "impossible wretch" must have asked for and deserved whatever punishment had occurred, if indeed the whole problem is not a hysterical or vengeful fantasy....

Unless specifically trained and sensitized, average adults, including mothers, relatives, teachers, counselors, doctors, psychotherapists, investigators, prosecutors, defense attorneys, judges and jurors, cannot believe that a normal, truthful child would tolerate incest without immediately reporting or that an apparently normal father could be capable of repeated, unchallenged sexual molestation of his own daughter. The child of any age faces an unbelieving audience when she complains of ongoing sexual abuse. The troubled, angry adolescent risks not only disbelief, but scapegoating, humiliation and punishment as well....

Whether the child is delinquent, hypersexual, counter sexual, suicidal, hysterical, psychotic, or perfectly well adjusted, and whether the child is angry, evasive or serene, the immediate affect and the adjustment pattern of the child will be interpreted by adults to invalidate the child's complaint....

It should be obvious that, left unchallenged, the sexual abuse accommodation syndrome tends to reinforce both the victimization of children and societal complacency and indifference to the dimensions of that victimization. It should be obvious to clinicians that the power to challenge and to interrupt the accommodation process carries an unprecedented potential for primary prevention of emotional pain and disability, including an interruption in the intergenerational chain of child abuse.... What is not so obvious is that mental health specialists may be more skeptical of reports of sexual abuse and more hesitant to involve themselves as advocates for children than many professionals with less specific training....

The sexual abuse accommodation syndrome is derived from the collective experience of dozens of sexual abuse treatment centers in dealing with thousands of reports or complaints of adult victimization of young children. In the vast majority of these cases the identified adult claimed total innocence or admitted only to trivial, well-meaning attempts at "sex education," wrestling, or affectionate closeness. After a time in treatment the men almost invariably conceded that the child had told the truth. Of the children who were found to have misrepresented their complaints, most had sought to *understate* the frequency or duration of sexual experiences, even when reports were made in anger and in apparent retaliation against violence or humiliation. Very few children, no more than two or three per *thousand,* have ever been found to exaggerate or to invent claims of sexual molestation ... [footnote omitted]. It has become a maxim among child sexual abuse in-tervention counselors and investigators that children never fabricate the kinds of explicit sexual manipulations they divulge in complaints or interrogations ... [footnote omitted].

The clinician with an understanding of the child sexual abuse accommodation syndrome offers the child a right to parity with adults in the struggle for credibility and advocacy. Neither the victim, the offender, the family, the next generation of children in that family, nor the wellbeing of society as a whole can benefit from continuing secrecy and denial of ongoing sexual abuse. The offender who protects an uneasy position of power over the silent victims will not release his control unless he is confronted by an outside power sufficient to demand and to supervise a total cessation of sexual harassment ... [footnotes omitted]....

The child sexual abuse accommodation syndrome provides a common language for the several viewpoints of the intervention team and a more recognizable map to the last frontier in child abuse.

People v. Spicola

Court of Appeals of New York, 2011
16 N.Y.3d 441, 947 N.E.2d 620

READ, J.

On November 16, 2006, defendant Michael Spicola was charged in a 10-count indictment with six counts of first-degree sodomy (Penal Law § 130.50[3]), three counts of first-degree sexual abuse (Penal Law § 130.65), and one count of endangering the welfare of a child (Penal Law § 260.10) stemming from three occasions when he was accused of engaging in reciprocal oral to genital contact with a young boy. These sexual encounters were alleged to have occurred between March 1, 1999 and April 30, 1999, a 61-day period when the boy was a six-year-old first grader; June 15, 2000 and August 31, 2000, a 77-day period during which the boy turned from seven to eight years old; and September 1, 2000 to November 30, 2000, a 91-day period when the boy was an eight-year-old third grader.

At defendant's subsequent jury trial, the boy's mother, a single parent, explained that defendant, her cousin, had been "involved in [her] life" after she moved back to western New York, where she grew up; he helped her out with chores, and occasionally watched her young son. The boy was friendly with defendant's daughter and youngest stepson, who were just a few years older than he was; he visited defendant's residence and slept over in 1999 and 2000 a "[f]ew times a year," including during spring break in 1999. Defendant took the boy to sporting events, and was his soccer coach during 2004.

The mother first sensed that "something wasn't right" in early 2006, when defendant, who had a college degree in advanced accounting and was self-employed as a tax preparer, stopped by her house to drop off her tax return. Defendant approached her son and started to tickle him, which the mother did not consider to be anything other than ordinary horseplay; however, she thought her son's reactions were "weird." First, he "went ... chest down on the ground ... and tightened up and then ... walked away" from defendant and retreated to the couch next to the chair in which she was seated. When defendant sat down beside the boy and rubbed his back, he responded by curling up into "the fetal position ... and leaned away from" defendant.

At some point the week after this episode, the mother cautioned her son that if "anybody ever touche[d][him] wrong [he] need[ed] to tell," and reassured him that she would not care who it was, even if one of several male relatives whom she named, including defendant. The boy indicated that he had never experienced such a thing, saying "[N]o mom, it's fine." He testified that he answered in this way because he "didn't know if [he] could go to the police or not" and "thought [he] would get in trouble," and defendant "was close to the family and [he] just thought something really bad would happen" if he revealed that defendant had touched him inappropriately. But after the boy saw a video about on-line sexual predators, shown in his eighth-grade technology class in early April 2006, he realized that what defendant had done to him "was wrong," and "felt like [he] should tell someone." He resolved to confide in his mother, but still hesitated. Then, as he was showering before going to school on May 15, 2006, the day after Mother's Day, he felt as though he "couldn't hold it in anymore," and he "just ran and told" his mother that "Mike had touched [him] many different ways."

The boy made this disclosure at the age of 13, seven years after the first and almost six years after the last instance of alleged molestation. Upon hearing her son's account, the mother immediately called her own mother, who was at work at the time, and the boy's father, asking them to come to her house urgently. She testified that her son sat on the living room couch and cried for a long time after he divulged his secret, and that he was "withdrawn, sad, scared" as the day wore on, and for many months thereafter. The boy's grandmother and father recalled finding him crying when they arrived; they described the mother as angry and distraught. The mother contacted the police, and a detective from the Erie County Sheriff's Department called her back later that day. The following day, she took the boy to the Child Advocacy Center (CAC) in Buffalo, where he was interviewed by a prosecutor and examined by a nurse-practitioner, who recommended counseling.

On the witness stand, the boy recounted the sexual abuse as having taken place while defendant played "knee hockey" alone with him, in the nude, in the living room of defendant's home, generally in the afternoon. In this game, the players got down on their knees and tried to shoot a ball into designated goals, using miniature hockey sticks. On cross-examination, defense counsel pressed two considerations in particular: that the boy had taken a long time to report these events; and that he had continued to associate with defendant in the meantime. Thus, defense counsel asked questions causing the boy to acknowledge that for six or seven years he neglected to alert his mother, his grandmother, his friends, his teachers or any doctor who examined him; and that he visited defendant's house after the last alleged sexual encounter, saw defendant several times a week during soccer season in 2004, when defendant coached his team, and accompanied him on outings to stock car races and professional hockey games when he was 12 or 13 years old. Defense counsel also elicited an admission that the boy had not mentioned one vivid detail of his story to the grand jury.

Defendant testified on his own behalf. He stated that the boy first slept over at his residence during Christmas vacation in 1999, not the spring of 1999, and that he next slept over, accompanied by a friend, during Christmas vacation in 2000 and the Martin Luther King holiday weekend in 2001. Defendant asserted that he was never at any time alone in his house with the boy because there were always other family members around while the boy was there. Further, the boy "beg[ged]" to stay overnight after a family reunion in the summer of 2001 because "a week or two before [he] bought [his] kids a trampoline and [the boy] was having a lot of fun playing on the trampoline." According to defendant, the next time the boy slept over was after accompanying him and his youngest stepson to a stock car race over Memorial Day weekend of 2004; and he stayed over again, with another boy after again going to a stock car race with defendant, this time in late September 2004. Defendant testified that he took the boy to professional hockey games in November 2005 and March 2006.... In defendant's telling, "knee hockey" was a game "invented" by his three stepsons, which the children played in the living room of his house. He sometimes joined in, "[j]ust to have fun with [his] kids," and the boy played with them when he visited. Defendant flatly denied ever having played "knee hockey" alone with the boy; he flatly denied the charges in the indictment.

On cross-examination, the prosecutor brought out that defendant had omitted his several-year stint as a full-time school bus driver from the lengthy work history he gave during direct examination. Defendant admitted that he was given a directive by the school superintendent in January 2002, and resigned from his post in May 2003 by mutual agreement with the union and the school district, although he denied ignoring the directive.[1] He called the boy "a normal kid" with whom he had enjoyed good relations; he likewise indicated that he had always gotten along well with the boy's mother. Although defendant suggested that he might have "some ideas" about why the boy would lie, he never shared these ideas with the jury. He admitted tickling and wrestling with the boy on occasion. Defendant denied having told the detective with whom he spoke by telephone on May 20, 2006 that he may have accidentally touched the boy in an intimate area, but noted that "whenever someone is wrestling you can accidentally touch someone's private parts."

The jury convicted defendant on all counts. On August 9, 2007, the trial judge sentenced him to concurrent determinate terms of 12 years for first-degree sodomy; seven years for

---

1. Defense counsel obtained a *Sandoval* ruling proscribing inquiry into the "parent concern" prompting the directive.

first-degree sexual abuse; and one year for endangering the welfare of a child. Defendant appealed on numerous grounds, including that the trial judge erred when he permitted testimony from a nurse-practitioner who examined the boy and expert testimony from a clinical social worker relating to child sexual abuse accommodation syndrome (CSAAS). On April 24, 2009, the Appellate Division affirmed (61 A.D.3d 1434, 877 N.Y.S.2d 591 [4th Dept 2009]). A Judge of this Court granted defendant permission to appeal (14 N.Y.3d 805, 899 N.Y.S.2d 139, 925 N.E.2d 943 [2010]), and we now affirm....

Defense counsel sought to preclude the testimony of the pediatric nurse-practitioner who examined the boy the day after he confided in his mother. He advanced several arguments: first, that the nurse "would not be in any position to give an opinion that the young man was molested or abused"; second, she found no physical evidence of sexual abuse; and third,

> "she would be asked about a history that she received from [the boy], and by allowing that testimony that would be improper bolstering. It's not outcry because it's 6 or 7 years later. Even though they are statements made to a nurse they wouldn't have any relevance to any diagnosis because she doesn't make any diagnosis.

> "So ... to allow her to testify and to tell the jury about the history she received and any of her alleged findings would be unfairly prejudicial."

When the trial judge asked the prosecutor why the nurse was being called, she gave several reasons. First, she pointed out that a nurse-practitioner is, unlike a registered nurse, competent and authorized to make a medical diagnosis; she cited CPLR 4518 (business records); she asserted that jurors may question the lack of physical evidence in a sexual abuse case, and the nurse could explain that this circumstance was not inconsistent with the boy's account, which was especially important "when there [are] references by the defense ... there is no medical evidence." ... The prosecutor also told the judge that she expected the nurse "to describe her actual observations both in terms of physical findings, ... the lack of objective evidence [of sexual abuse], but also her observations of the child's demeanor ... [which] would relate to his credibility to rebut a potential defense of fabrication here." Finally, she argued that the delay in reporting did "not in any way make [the nurse's] subjective history or the patient's objective history irrelevant," as the nurse would still have to ask the same questions and perform the same examination "whether it's 1 month or 6 years" after the alleged sexual abuse occurred.

The judge agreed that "the issue" was whether the boy's statements were germane to his treatment, and asked what the boy told the nurse. The prosecutor responded that he had "describe[d] basically the oral contact." The judge then said, "I presume it's not a detailed account?" The prosecutor answered affirmatively, and told the judge that she had warned the nurse to stay away from identifying the perpetrator, or where or how many times the alleged sexual abuse occurred. The judge asked if she planned to offer the medical record into evidence. The prosecutor responded that she would rely solely on the nurse's testimony "because there [were] so many things ... that would be improper [she] would have to redact the whole record." The judge ruled that the nurse could testify....

The nurse, who had extensive and specialized training and experience examining child victims of sexual and physical abuse, was asked to perform a medical examination of the boy on May 16, 2006 at the CAC, where she was employed. The boy was at the CAC that day for an "MD, multiple disciplinary interview." She testified that she would first take a child's medical history and then perform a "top to bottom physical exam." In terms of taking a medical history, she would ask a child why he or she was at the CAC, and would inquire about the child's health because she "need[ed] to understand if there [were] any concerns or problems going on … [and] what [the child's] developmental ability [was]." She stated that it would be necessary for her to take a subjective history from a patient even where suspected sexual abuse occurred a number of years earlier because she "need[ed] to know [of] any problems, any lesions, any sores, any concerns." When asked if that was why she took a subjective history of the boy, she answered, "Yes, it is."

The prosecutor reminded the witness that she could not "discuss … details other than what was specifically told to [her] that was relevant to [her] diagnosis and treatment"; and then asked what the boy said about what had happened to him. She answered that the boy indicated that "he had been touched inappropriately," and "gestured to his groin that it had been put in his [sic] mouth and he was asked to put somebody else's into his mouth." She testified that the boy was "embarrassed, [with] downcast eyes, flushed face" when he gave her this information.… The prosecutor next posed questions to the nurse about the physical examination that she performed on the boy. The nurse described the first part as a general examination akin to a regular physical; she testified that the boy's heart rate was elevated, which indicated to her that he was "nervous." The last part of the examination focused on the genital and rectal area. Because of what he told her about "what had happened to him," she "was looking to make sure that the exam would have been normal, that there were no lesions or sores, discharges." The prosecutor next asked the nurse if the absence of lesions was in any way "inconsistent with what [the boy] had told [her] about what had happened." She replied that it was not "[b]ecause we generally would not see or many times … do not see medical evidence from children who have been touched inappropriately."

The nurse added that she "spent quite awhile talking with" the boy, who was concerned that "people would know that this happened to him." Additionally, "he had some body changes as he was growing up and he was very uncomfortable with that, so [she] spent a long time talking about body change, hormones, normal growth, normal things that happen to your body." The nurse was asked how she could spot the boy's discomfort, and she replied, "He had downcast eyes. He was flushed, heart rate was up." She "reassured [the boy] that he hadn't done anything wrong and that his body was normal."

On cross-examination, the nurse acknowledged that she had no way of knowing whether the history of sexual abuse that the boy related to her was true or false; and that it would not be unusual for a 13-year-old boy to exhibit signs of nervousness when talking to a stranger about "private matters." Further, defense counsel brought out that she knew what physical signs or symptoms to look for that "could be consistent with abuse," and that she "found no physical evidence to support the history that [the boy] even had been touched inappropriately." … This cross-examination caused the prosecutor to return on redirect examination to ground that she had already covered: whether it was "at all unusual" that the nurse did not detect "any lesions or actual physical injury." The nurse replied that it was not unusual. On re-cross-examination, defense counsel countered, asking "And the fact that you found nothing is just as consistent with this child never having been abused or never having been molested, right?" The nurse responded "That is correct, sir." …

The nurse's testimony rounded out the narrative of the immediate aftermath of the boy's disclosure to his mother and, more importantly, addressed the negative inference that jurors might draw from the absence of medical evidence of abuse.[3] The jury learned essentially three things: that a very thorough medical examination turned up no evidence

---

3. In his closing argument, defense counsel commented that although the nurse testified that she "found nothing, but that is consistent with this type of case[;][i]t's also consistent with the claim never happened."

of sexual abuse, that the boy told the nurse roughly what he told his mother the day before, and that he struck the nurse as nervous and uncomfortable. The first two pieces of information were not harmful to defendant. And assuming the jury believed that the nurse accurately perceived the boy's state of mind, there were, as defense counsel pointed out, any number of different explanations for his demeanor, none conclusively bearing on credibility. After all, he might have appeared nervous whether telling the truth or lying....

The day jury selection was scheduled to begin, defense counsel argued a motion in limine, seeking to preclude certain evidence, including "the alleged expert testimony of an undisclosed prosecution witness on the topic of" CSAAS.[4] In the motion papers, defense counsel mentioned that the prosecution, at a pretrial conference on March 2, 2006, "stated that it anticipate[d] calling an expert witness on the topic of" CSAAS "to address the delayed reporting of the alleged incident"; and that defense counsel, in turn, "anticipated that this prosecution expert [would] testify about CSAAS, a term initially coined by Dr. Roland Summit" to describe a pattern of "secrecy, helplessness, entrapment [and] accommodation, delayed disclosure, and recantation as common characteristics in children who report sexual abuse" (internal quotation marks omitted; *see* Roland C. Summit, *The Child Sexual Abuse Accommodation Syndrome*, 7 Child Abuse & Neglect 177 [1983]; *see also* Roland C. Summit, *Abuse of the Child Sexual Abuse Accommodation Syndrome*, 1 J. Child Sexual Abuse 153 [1992] [emphasizing that CSAAS was not a diagnostic tool—i.e., the fact that a child exhibits one or more aspects of CSAAS does not tend to prove that sexual abuse occurred]).

Defense counsel argued that "[d]elayed disclosure may be indicative of abuse and it might not"; therefore, CSAAS "cannot establish or state that sexual abuse did in fact occur in this case." Further, he complained that

> "[t]o present a prosecution expert to testify that any way a child responds to sexual abuse and later reports the alleged abuse is consistent with the way other children have been observed to have reacted only suggests that any story told by any child should be believed. There is no way for the defense to refute such testimony since it cannot cross-examine that testimony without the expert having the ability to speak to the facts of the case the testimony relates to. Under the guise of objective assistance, the expert is a prosecution advocate by binding him or herself in ignorance of the facts of the case. This sends a message that the jury should consider that no matter the specific facts of this case, the child's report has been made in a manner consistent with how some other sexually abused children reported in the past."

Finally, defense counsel quoted a lengthy excerpt from an article reviewing the disclosure patterns of children with validated histories of sexual abuse. In the excerpt, the authors criticized courts for permitting CSAAS testimony without "carefully scrutiniz[ing]" its scientific basis, and opined that, under the testimonial standard established by *Daubert v. Merrell Dow Pharmaceuticals, Inc.*, 509 U.S. 579, 113 S.Ct. 2786, 125 L.Ed.2d 469 (1993),

> "the only component of the CSAAS that has empirical support is that delay of abuse disclosure is very common. However, the probative value of expert testimony on delayed disclosure, whether for evidentiary or rehabilitative reasons, is un-

---

4. Defense counsel also sought to preclude the prosecution from introducing in its case-in-chief statements alleged to have been made by defendant to the detective in the May 20, 2006 telephone conversation; and asked for a *Sandoval* ruling precluding the questioning of defendant, if he took the stand, "about a matter concerning a student at the North Collins Central Elementary School" (*see supra* ... n. 1).

determined; some evidence suggests that knowledge about delay of disclosure is within the ken of the jury, perhaps therefore obviating the need for expert evidence on the issue of delay ...

"[T]here is no convincing evidence that CSAAS testimony on denial or recantation provides relevant or reliable assistance to the fact finder to assess allegations" (Kamala London et al., *Disclosure of Child Sexual Abuse: What Does the Research Tell Us About the Ways that Children Tell?*, 11 Psychol. Pub. Pol'y & L. 194, 220 [2005]).

Defense counsel took the position that, in light of the quoted excerpt, there did not "appear to be either acceptance within the scientific community that CSAAS identifies and describes behavioral characteristics commonly found in victims of child sexual abuse or that such behavioral characteristics require the use of an expert to assist the jury." ...

The prosecutor asked the expert if he was familiar "with the scientific research" in the field; specifically, CSAAS. The expert answered that he was. He identified CSAAS as originating with Dr. Summit's work in 1983, and listed its five categories — secrecy; helplessness; entrapment and accommodation; delayed, conflicted or unconvincing disclosure; and retraction or recantation. The prosecutor asked if the syndrome was "a diagnosis in any way," and the expert responded "No, it was never intended to be." ... The expert testified that CSAAS was generally accepted as valid within the relevant scientific community of his specialty, and that many follow-on studies, "some focusing on how children disclose," had been undertaken since 1983.[5] The prosecutor asked the expert if "the concepts of the syndrome show contradictions to widely held beliefs and views about behaviors of child sexual abuse victims." He replied "Yes" and that "[f]or one ... adults think that kids are going to immediately say when something happened to them." He was asked if the presence of any one of the five kinds of behavior "mean[s] in and of itself that the child was abused," to which he again warned that CSAAS "was never intended to be used in that manner." He was then asked if the "absence of any one of those categories or behaviors necessarily mean[s] that [a] child was not abused," to which he similarly responded "Again, it was not intended. It's intended [to] get you to think, to include ideas." ...

Defendant maintains that the trial judge improperly admitted the expert's testimony regarding CSAAS because it bolstered the boy's credibility to prove that the abuse, in fact, occurred. This is not the first time we have dealt with this type of bolstering argument, or a close variation of it. In *People v. Keindl*, 68 N.Y.2d 410, 509 N.Y.S.2d 790, 502 N.E.2d 577 (1986), the defendant was convicted of 26 counts of sodomy, sexual abuse and endangering the welfare of his stepchildren. He contended that the trial court erred in admitting the testimony of a psychiatrist, "presented to explain how children who have been repeatedly sexually abused by their stepfather[ ] [were] likely to suffer psychologically," because such testimony would go to the "ultimate question" of the defendant's guilt of endangering the welfare of a child, which was "within the province of the jury to decide and [was] not a subject matter beyond the ken of the ordinary juror" (*id.* at 422, 509 N.Y.S.2d 790, 502 N.E.2d 577).

We disagreed, concluding that

"[f]or the Trial Judge to have ruled that the range of psychological reactions of child victims who suffer from sexual abuse at the hands of their stepparents is

---

5. The expert mentioned the 2005 study by London and colleagues, referenced by defense counsel in his motion in limine, and a subsequent revision of it (*see* London et al., *Disclosure of Child Sexual Abuse: A Review of the Contemporary Empirical Literature*, in Child Sexual Abuse: Disclosure, Delay and Denial, at 11 [Margaret-Ellen Pipe et al. eds. 2007] [hereafter, London 2007]).

not a subject within the ken of the typical juror, and therefore may be addressed by expert testimony, cannot be said to be an abuse of discretion as a matter of law" (*id.*).

In *Keindl*, the defendant (as was the case here) had attempted to discredit the children by evidence that they had not promptly complained of the crimes (*see People v. Taylor*, 75 N.Y.2d 277, 288, 552 N.Y.S.2d 883, 552 N.E.2d 131 [1990]).…

Here, there was no way for defendant to achieve an acquittal if the jury believed the boy because there was no way that the boy might have been honestly mistaken about defendant's conduct; put another way, for defendant to succeed at trial, the jurors had to conclude that the boy was likely deliberately lying. And so from the beginning, defendant attacked the boy's credibility, principally on the basis that he neglected to report the alleged abuse promptly and continued to associate with defendant after the abuse was claimed to have taken place. Defense counsel in his opening statement emphasized the boy's lengthy silence, the six or seven years when he said nothing "to his mother, to his father, to his grandmother … to a teacher at school, to a counselor at school … to any friend." He followed up by describing the several occasions after the fall of 2000 and before May of 2006 when the boy visited defendant's house or went on outings with him. Defense counsel's cross-examination of the boy similarly zeroed in on the delay in reporting and the boy's continued association with defendant after the alleged molestations.[8]

In this context, the trial judge did not abuse his discretion when he allowed the expert to testify about CSAAS to rehabilitate the boy's credibility. The expert stressed that CSAAS was not a diagnosis; rather, it describes a range of behaviors observed in cases of validated child sexual abuse, some of which seem counterintuitive to a layperson. He confirmed that the presence or absence of any particular behavior was not substantive evidence that sexual abuse had, or had not, occurred. He made it clear that he knew nothing about the facts of the case before taking the witness stand; that he was not venturing an opinion as to whether sexual abuse took place in this case; that it was up to the jury to decide whether

---

8. To complete the circle, defense counsel in his closing argument detailed several so-called "unanswered questions," including "[W]hy would that young man go back and return to [defendant's house] time after time if what he says happened happened?" and "[W]hy was there such a long delay, … some 6 or 7 years before the young man said anything?" He asked for, and received, the following instruction from the trial judge related to the boy's delay in reporting:

"There is another consideration that I want to mention to you. *That's a word about [the boy's] failure to promptly complain. Obviously, that's been raised throughout this proceeding.* The defendant contends that the failure of [the boy] to complain to family members, school personnel or law enforcement until approximately 6 or 7 years following the events of March '99 through November of 2000 should be considered by you in assessing the credibility of [the boy]. With reference to the time when [the boy] first complained to his mother … it is for you, the jury, to determine whether or not such complaint was made within a reasonable time or was in fact unreasonably delayed. Either circumstance may be considered by you as a jury as bearing upon the credibility of the complainant. Your evaluation of [the] time in which the complaint was made must be considered in light of all of the surrounding circumstances, particularly including, but not limited to, the opportunity of the complainant to make the complaint. Among other factors that you may wish to consider would be the complainant's age, past experiences, mental state, fear for his own safety or the safety of others in the household or the lack of such fear. You may also wish to consider the circumstances that motivated the complainant and any and all other circumstances which you may find operated to trigger a delayed disclosure. Whatever weight is to be given to the circumstances is entirely in your hands" (emphasis added; see C.J.I.2d[N.Y.] Prompt Outcry).

At defense counsel's request, the trial judge also gave the standard expert witness charge (*see* C.J.I.2d[N.Y.] Expert Witness). He added that "Basically, … opinions of expert witnesses are subject to the same rules and tests concerning reliability as the testimony of any other witness."

the boy was being truthful. In short, defendant staked his defense on the proposition that the boy's behavior, as demonstrated by the evidence, was inconsistent with having been molested; the legitimate purpose of the expert's testimony was to counter this inference. And in the end, the jury obviously believed the boy and disbelieved defendant, who never offered the jurors a motive for the boy to fabricate a report of sexual abuse....

As the discussion of our decisions in *Keindl*, [*Matter of*] *Nicole V.*, [71 N.Y,2d 112, 524 N.Y.S.2d 19, 518 N.E.2d 914 (1987),] *Taylor*[9] and [*People v.*] *Carroll*[, 95 N.Y.2d 375, 718 N.Y.S.2d 10, 740 N.E.2d 1084 (2000),] shows, we have "long held" evidence of psychological syndromes affecting certain crime victims to be admissible for the purpose of explaining behavior that might be puzzling to a jury (*see Carroll*, 95 N.Y.2d at 387, 718 N.Y.S.2d 10, 740 N.E.2d 1084). Indeed, the majority of states "permit expert testimony to explain delayed reporting, recantation, and inconsistency," as well as "to explain why some abused children are angry, why some children want to live with the person who abused them, why a victim might appear 'emotionally flat' following sexual assault, why a child might run away from home, and for other purposes" (*see* 1 Myers on Evidence § 6.24, at 416–422 [collecting cases and noting that Kentucky, Pennsylvania and Tennessee are the only apparent exceptions]).

Defendant complains that the expert's testimony was not adequately constrained because certain of the hypothetical questions too closely mirrored the boy's circumstances and therefore improperly bolstered or vouched for his credibility so as to prove that the charged crimes occurred. To the extent defendant now complains of specific questions, his argument is not preserved because the questions were not objected to at trial. As a whole, the expert's testimony certainly supported the boy's credibility by supplying explanations other than fabrication for his post-molestation behavior. It was offered, after all, for purposes of just such rehabilitation. But as already discussed, the expert did not express an opinion on the boy's credibility. Early on in his testimony he disavowed any intention of giving an opinion about whether the boy was a victim of sexual abuse. And the jurors could not have become confused on this score since it was made plain to them that the expert could not, in fact, even possess an opinion about the boy's credibility: he had never talked to the boy and was ignorant of the particulars of his allegations; he did not know, for example, that the boy waited six or seven years to claim sexual abuse (the subject of one of the complained-of hypothetical questions) until defense counsel informed him of this on cross-examination. We note that in *Taylor*, the expert, who similarly had not interviewed the complainant before the trial and was not therefore testifying about her behavior as such, offered testimony about conduct that closely resembled the facts of that case....

Defendant also attacks the scientific reliability of CSAAS, citing the Second Circuit's decision in *Gersten v. Senkowski*, 426 F.3d 588 (2d Cir.2005). Referring to an expert's affidavit in support of the petitioner's federal petition for a writ of habeas corpus, the court declared in *Gersten* that "[i]t would appear" that CSAAS "lacked any scientific validity for the purpose for which the prosecution utilized it: as a generalized explanation of children's reactions to sexual abuse, including delayed disclosure" (*id.* at 611). While we have no way of knowing whether the record in *Gersten* justified the Second Circuit's conclusions about CSAAS, the record here does not support a similar result.

---

9. In *Nicole V.* we called CSAAS "a recognized diagnosis" (71 N.Y.2d at 120, 524 N.Y.S.2d 19, 518 N.E.2d 914); and in *Taylor*, we repeated this passage from *Nicole V.*, 75 N.Y.2d at 288, 552 N.Y.S.2d 883, 552 N.E.2d 131. As our opinion in *Taylor* establishes, though, CSAAS is *not* a diagnosis in the sense that the presence of a CSAAS behavior proves child sexual abuse (*see* 1 Myers on Evidence in Child Domestic and Elder Abuse Cases § 6.20, at 408–411 [successor edition to Evidence in Child Abuse and Neglect Cases (3d ed. 1997)] [2005] [hereafter, Myers on Evidence] [explaining the difference between diagnostic and nondiagnostic syndromes]).

Defense counsel in this case disputed the scientific reliability of CSAAS in the motion in limine, quoting from a review written by London and colleagues, critics of CSAAS; however, the quoted passage does not question the empirical basis for delayed reporting (*see supra* at 454–455; *see also* Thomas D. Lyon, *Scientific Support for Expert Testimony on Child Sexual Abuse Accommodation*, in Critical Issues in Child Sexual Abuse: Historical, Legal, and Psychological Perspectives, at 107, 108 [2002] ["Observational research demonstrates that a substantial proportion of abused children either delay reporting or fail to report their abuse"]; John E.B. Myers, *Expert Testimony in Child Sexual Abuse Litigation: Consensus and Confusion*, 14 U.C. Davis J. Juv. L. & Pol'y 1, 44 [2010] ["Psychological research demonstrates that delayed reporting is common among sexually abused children"]).[10] Rather, London and colleagues have reservations about the prevalence of denial and recantation, aspects of CSAAS not at issue in this case (*see* London 2007 at 12–13 ["[A]lthough a substantial proportion of children delay reporting or altogether fail to report incidents of child sexual abuse (the secrecy stage), there is little evidence to suggest that denials, recantations, and redisclosures are typical when the abused children are directly asked about abuse during forensic interviews"])....

Accordingly, the order of the Appellate Division should be affirmed.

Chief Judge LIPPMAN (dissenting).

This trial concerned events occurring between seven and eight years earlier, as to which no physical evidence could be produced. Defendant did not admit to any unlawful conduct; nor was there any other direct evidence linking him to the crimes. The case, therefore, was essentially a credibility contest between complainant and defendant. The prosecutor thereupon took several steps to improperly and prejudicially bolster the credibility of complainant, as a result of which defendant was deprived of a fair trial. Accordingly, I would reverse and remit to County Court for a new trial....

I agree with the majority that those portions of the nurse-practitioner's testimony that were relevant to diagnosis and treatment were properly admitted. For example, testimony concerning complainant's account of what had happened to him, the extent of the ensuing physical examination, the absence of any lesions or other visible signs of sexual abuse on complainant's body and the significance of such absence were all properly admitted as relevant to diagnosis and treatment (*see People v. Ortega*, 15 N.Y.3d 610, 617, 917 N.Y.S.2d 1, 942 N.E.2d 210 [2010]).... The same cannot be said about the nurse-practitioner's testimony concerning complainant's demeanor during the examination. The nurse-practitioner testified that when complainant related what had happened to him, "[h]e was embarrassed, downcast eyes, flushed face." She indicated that she had recorded these details "[b]ecause they were definitely significant when I saw them. He was embarrassed." The nurse-practitioner further testified that complainant's elevated heart rate during the examination indicated to her that "[h]e was nervous."... Complainant's embarrassment or nervousness attending the examination had no medical significance whatsoever. The majority's purported justification for the elicitation of this testimony—that it was relevant to whether some type of counseling or therapy would be required ... —is pure invention. To the contrary, the prosecution was perfectly blunt about why the testimony as to com-

---

10. And while London and colleagues assert that CSAAS does not in the main comport with *Daubert* (*see supra* ...), this does not necessarily mean, even if true, that CSAAS is not generally accepted as reliable in the relevant scientific community (*see e.g.* London 2007 at 12 ["The CSAA (child sexual abuse accommodation) model has been endorsed by many clinicians and scholars and has been the basis of clinical and forensic judgments ... Summit's (1983) paper ... was rated by professionals as one of the most influential papers in the field of child sexual abuse"]).

plainant's demeanor was being offered: it was for credibility purposes. The nurse-practitioner's testimony on this point was not relevant to diagnosis and treatment and its admission on that basis was error....

Moreover, the error was egregiously compounded by the scope of the expert testimony on child sexual abuse accommodation syndrome (CSAAS). Prior to trial, defense counsel sought to preclude the CSAAS expert's testimony for two reasons. Counsel argued, first, that the subject matter of the expert's testimony — that children often delay reporting abuse — was not outside the ken of the average juror. In addition, counsel asserted that the expert's testimony would be "overwhelmingly prejudicial and unfair" because the jury would inevitably draw the conclusion that complainant had been abused because he fit within the pattern of behavior recognized by CSAAS. The request was denied and the prosecutor proceeded to ask the expert, in hypothetical terms, about virtually every detail in the case.

Several aspects of complainant's testimony were later raised with the CSAAS expert. Specifically, during his direct testimony, complainant detailed his sexual abuse by a family member — his mother's second cousin. Complainant also related two incidents where he and his young friends had touched each other's penises, which complainant explained was, at least in part, because he was repeating behavior that had been done to him by defendant. Complainant further testified that what ultimately convinced him to tell his mother about the sexual abuse was a video about catching on-line predators that he had watched with his eighth grade computer tech class. Additionally, on cross-examination, complainant testified that his memory had improved as the years passed. Complainant also testified that he was not afraid to return to defendant's house after the alleged abuse, but rather that he wanted to go to the house and had fun when he was there.

The expert testified after the jury had heard complainant's version of events. In response to the prosecution's questions, the expert testified that abuse by a stranger was rare; a child was more likely to be abused by a person he knows and the child's feelings of helplessness would be enhanced if the abuser were a trusted adult who was close to the child's mother. The expert also testified that he had seen children become hyper-sexualized and use sexuality as a coping mechanism. In response to a question about a child's willingness to return to the scene of the abuse, the expert testified that the child could convince himself that the abuse would not happen again and that the child could be willing to spend time with the abuser because he would want to repeat any positive experiences he had with that person. The expert also testified that boys were "far more likely to delay" reporting sexual abuse and that any period of delay was likely to be far longer than for girls — specifically, that a delay of six or seven years would not be unusual. The expert also responded in the affirmative to the prosecutor's query as to whether "an educational component about the awareness of sexual abuse [could] be a triggering event" for the disclosure of abuse. Finally, the expert testified that a child's memory could actually improve and that more details could come to mind after the child disclosed the abuse.[*]

"[E]xpert opinion is proper when it would help to clarify an issue calling for professional or technical knowledge, possessed by the expert and beyond the ken of the typical juror" (*People v. Taylor*, 75 N.Y.2d 277, 288, 552 N.Y.S.2d 883, 552 N.E.2d 131 [1990] [citation omitted]). However, where "the sole reason for questioning the 'expert' witness is to bolster the testimony of [the complainant] by explaining that his version of the events is

---

[*] On cross and redirect, the expert even managed to inform the jury that in his experience of 154 cases, he had seen only four instances of false allegations, three of them in the context of divorce battles.

more believable than the defendant's, the 'expert's' testimony is equivalent to an opinion that the defendant is guilty, and the receipt of such testimony may not be condoned" (*People v. Ciaccio*, 47 N.Y.2d 431, 439, 418 N.Y.S.2d 371, 391 N.E.2d 1347 [1979]). Although we have recognized that CSAAS can be used for the purpose of explaining behavior by a complainant that might appear unusual to the average juror—such as why a child might not immediately report sexual abuse—we have contrasted the permissible use of such testimony with testimony that opines that complainant's "behavior [was] consistent with such abuse" (*People v. Carroll*, 95 N.Y.2d 375, 387, 718 N.Y.S.2d 10, 740 N.E.2d 1084 [2000]; *see also People v. Mercado*, 188 A.D.2d 941, 942, 592 N.Y.S.2d 75 [3d Dept.1992] [expert's testimony "constitute[d] an impermissible comparison of the complainants' behavior with that commonly associated with victims of these crimes"]).

Even though the expert did not expressly render an opinion as to whether or not complainant was a victim of sexual abuse, the expert's confirmation of nearly every detail of the case and of complainant's behavior as consistent with that of a victim of sexual abuse was the functional equivalent of rendering an opinion as to complainant's truthfulness (*see Ciaccio*, 47 N.Y.2d at 439, 418 N.Y.S.2d 371, 391 N.E.2d 1347). The expert's testimony had the effect of improperly bolstering complainant's testimony and, in the context of this case, was extremely prejudicial.... As noted above, this was a case where the credibility of the parties was the key issue facing the jury. Each of the errors, in bolstering complainant's testimony with the nurse-practitioner's perception of his demeanor and the CSAAS expert's validation of his behavior as consistent with that of a victim of sexual abuse, and certainly their cumulative effect, deprived defendant of a fair trial.

Judges GRAFFEO, SMITH and PIGOTT concur with Judge READ; Chief Judge LIPPMAN dissents and votes to reverse in a separate opinion in which Judges CIPARICK and JONES concur.

Order affirmed.

Notes

The court in *Spicola* makes note that Kentucky, Pennsylvania, and Tennessee are exceptions to the majority rule permitting expert testimony to explain the spectrum of victim behaviors following sexual assault, which juries might not fully understand. For the cases in those states relevant to this notation, see *Sanderson v. Commonwealth*, 291 S.W.3d 610, 614 (Ky. 2009); *Commonwealth v. Dunkle*, 529 Pa. 168, 183, 602 A.2d 830 (1992); *State v. Bolin*, 922 S.W.2d 870, 873–74 (Tenn.1996). These decisions "prohibit even generalized expert testimony about behaviors of child sexual assault victims, considering it to be a scientifically unfounded incursion into the jury's role of determining the credibility of witnesses." *State v. Favoccia*, 306 Conn. 770, 51 A.3d 1002 (Conn. 2012). For a comprehensive analysis of various jurisdictional approaches to the admission of such expert testimony, see *Favoccia*, 51 A.3d at 1002 (finding that the appellate court abused its discretion in admitting testimony about the complainant's behaviors being consistent with behaviors generally characteristic of sexual assault victims). For scholarly commentary on the issue of child sexual abuse accommodation syndrome, see Margaret H. Shiu, *Unwarranted Skepticism: The Federal Courts' Treatment of Child Sexual Abuse Accommodation Syndrome*, 18 S. CAL. INTERDISC. L.J. 651 (2009); Cara Gitlin, *Expert Testimony on Child Sexual Abuse Accommodation Syndrome: How Proper Screening Should Severely Limit Its Admission*, 26 QLR 497 (2008); Donna A. Gaffney, *PTSD, RTS, and Child Abuse Accommodation Syndrome: Therapeutic Tools or Fact-Finding Aids*, 24 PACE L. REV. 271 (2003); Cindy Kanusher, *PTSD, RTS, and Child Abuse Accommodation Syndrome: Therapeutic Tools or Fact-Finding Aids*, 24 PACE L. REV. 293 (2003); Michael

D. Stanger, *Throwing the Baby Out With the Bathwater: Why Child Sexual Abuse Accommodation Syndrome Should Be Allowed As A Rehabilitative Tool In the Florida Courts*, 55 U. MIAMI L. REV. 561 (2001); Rosemary L. Flint, *Child Sexual Abuse Accommodation Syndrome: Admissibility Requirements*, 23 AM. J. CRIM. L. 171 (1995); Gail Ezra Cary, *Evidence — Expert Testimony — the Admissibility of Child Sexual Abuse Accommodation Syndrome in Child Sexual Abuse Prosecutions. State v. J.Q., 617 A.2d 1196 (N.J. 1993)*, 26 RUTGERS L.J. 251 (1994); Hillary Moody, *Child Abuse — Expert Opinion Evidence Premised on Child Sexual Abuse Accommodation Syndrome ("CSAAS") Is Scientifically Reliable to Explain Delayed Reporting By the Abused Child But Is Unreliable to Prove Actual Occurrence of Sexual Abuse*, 32 U. LOUIS. J. FAM. L. 147 (1994); Michele Meyer McCarthy, *Admissibility of Expert Testimony on Child Sexual Abuse Accommodation Syndrome in Kentucky*, 81 KY. L.J. 727 (1992/1993); Chandra Lorraine Holmes, *Child Sexual Abuse Accommodation Syndrome: Curing the Effects of a Misdiagnosis in the Law of Evidence*, 25 TULSA L.J. 143 (1989); Patrick Larson, *The Admissibility of Expert Testimony on Child Sexual Abuse Accommodation Syndrome As Indicia of Abuse: Aiding the Prosecution in Meeting Its Burden of Proof*, 16 OHIO N.U. L. REV. 81 (1989); Comment, *The Admissibility of "Child Sexual Abuse Accommodation Syndrome" in California Criminal Courts*, 17 PACIFIC L.J. 1361 (1986).

B. Propensity

People v. Watkins

Supreme Court of Michigan, 2012
491 Mich. 450, 818 N.W.2d 296

ZAHRA, J.

These consolidated cases involve MCL 768.27a(1), which provides in relevant part that "in a criminal case in which the defendant is accused of committing a listed offense against a minor, evidence that the defendant committed another listed offense against a minor is admissible and may be considered for its bearing on any matter to which it is relevant." ... [footnote omitted].... MRE 404(b), ... bars the admission of other-acts evidence for the purpose of showing a defendant's propensity to commit similar acts.... MRE 403 ... provides that a court may exclude relevant evidence if the danger of unfair prejudice, among other considerations, outweighs the evidence's probative value.... [footnote omitted]. In applying the balancing test in MRE 403 to evidence admissible under MCL 768.27a, ... courts must weigh the propensity inference in favor of the evidence's probative value rather than its prejudicial effect....

In Docket No. 142031, defendant, Lincoln Anderson Watkins, appeals by leave granted the judgment of the Court of Appeals affirming his convictions and sentences. Watkins was charged with five counts of first-degree criminal sexual conduct (CSC-I)[3] and one count of second-degree criminal sexual conduct (CSC-II)[4] for allegedly molesting a 12-year-old girl.... The Court of Appeals summarized the allegations of sexual abuse that the prosecution presented at the pretrial stage:

> The victim in the instant case was a 12-year-old girl whose family lived next door to defendant and whose father was defendant's business partner. The victim had known defendant and his wife since she was two years old and regarded de-

---

3. MCL 750.520b(1)(a) (involving a person under the age of 13).
4. MCL 750.520c(1)(a) (involving a person under the age of 13).

fendant as a father figure. The victim babysat defendant's youngest child. In May 2006, defendant showed her a picture of his penis being inserted into a vagina. The next day, while she was playing video games with defendant's daughter in his bedroom, he touched her breasts. The day after that incident the victim was again babysitting at defendant's house when defendant sent his daughter into another room, unbuttoned the victim's pants, and told her to pull them down and get on his bed. She stood up and pulled down her pants, and when she bent over, defendant inserted his penis into her vagina from behind repeatedly until he ejaculated. She and defendant engaged in intercourse again in his bedroom the following day while she was babysitting his daughter. The victim claimed that she and defendant engaged in intercourse yet another time in defendant's bedroom and one time in his living room. The victim alleged that, about two weeks later, defendant asked her if she wanted to have sex, but she declined because she was menstruating. The victim claimed that defendant nevertheless instructed her to stand up and lift her skirt, and, when she complied, he inserted his penis into her vagina. The victim asserted that she worried that defendant might force her to have sexual intercourse in the future, so she told her mother that she had been having a sexual relationship with defendant.[5]

Before trial, the prosecution filed a motion to introduce evidence of other acts to establish a common plan or scheme, as permitted under MRE 404(b).[6] In particular, the prosecution sought to have a witness, EW, testify that Watkins had also engaged in vaginal-penile penetration with her.[7] Like the victim in the instant action, EW was a minor at the time, and she had a close relationship with Watkins's wife. The trial court granted the motion over Watkins's objection. The following is a summary of EW's testimony offered at defendant's first trial:

> At the first trial, [EW] testified that defendant's wife is her first cousin and that she [EW] met defendant when she was 14 years old. [EW] loved defendant like a brother and often babysat for defendant's children. On one occasion when she was 15 years old, she visited defendant and his wife for the weekend and helped them with their infant. While alone with [EW], defendant commented on her sexual attractiveness, took her hand, and began leading her up the stairs to his bedroom on the second floor. [EW] was reluctant to go upstairs, so defendant pulled down her pants and inserted his penis into her vagina while they were still in the hallway. After eventually moving to defendant's bedroom, they continued having intercourse until defendant ejaculated. [EW] stated that the episode began a two-year sexual relationship, during which they had sexual encounters about 15 different times at defendant's home, her mother's home, and in empty houses where defendant was painting. [EW] explained that defendant

---

5. *People v. Watkins*, 277 Mich.App. 358, 360, 745 N.W.2d 149 (2007).

6. MRE 404(b)(1) provides:

Evidence of other crimes, wrongs, or acts is not admissible to prove the character of a person in order to show action in conformity therewith. It may, however, be admissible for other purposes, such as proof of motive, opportunity, intent, preparation, scheme, plan, or system in doing an act, knowledge, identity, or absence of mistake or accident when the same is material, whether such other crimes, wrongs, or acts are contemporaneous with, or prior or subsequent to the conduct at issue in the case.

7. The prosecution also sought to have a second witness testify regarding other-acts evidence. That testimony is not at issue in this appeal.

included her in his family; they went to an amusement park together, went out to eat together, and watched movies together.[8]

Following the close of trial, the jury commenced deliberations but was unable to reach a verdict. Consequently, the trial court declared a mistrial.... [Following a series of procedural rulings related to "other-acts" evidence as sufficient to show a common plan or scheme, the case resulted in several mistrials and remands and eventually proceeded to trial for a third time.]

At the third trial, the victim, then 15 years old, testified that she had known Watkins all her life, having lived next door to him and having occasionally baby-sat one of his children. She also stated that she was good friends with Watkins's wife, whom she considered her godmother. She considered Watkins her boyfriend. According to the victim, when she was 12 years old, Watkins approached her at a Memorial Day gathering and showed her sexually explicit images that were on his cell phone. She claimed that Watkins touched her breasts the next time she baby-sat and penetrated her vaginally the day after that. This conduct allegedly occurred consensually for the next couple of weeks. Sometime thereafter, when the victim arrived to baby-sit, she declined Watkins's request to engage in sexual activity because she was menstruating. She testified that Watkins's insistence disturbed her and she thought he might rape her. She told her mother what had happened. Although the victim did not want to get Watkins in trouble, she agreed to speak with the police.

The trial court allowed EW to testify regarding other-acts evidence under MCL 768.27a. According to EW, about 10 years earlier, when she was 15 years old, she had often baby-sat Watkins's oldest child. She testified that, during one visit, Watkins led her upstairs by the hand. He allegedly began kissing her, and their interactions culminated in sexual penetration. According to EW, their sexual relationship lasted a couple of years.... Watkins did not take the stand or call any witnesses. Defense counsel argued that the witnesses lacked credibility because their statements were inconsistent and uncorroborated. Ultimately, the jury returned a verdict finding Watkins guilty of four counts of CSC-I and one count of CSC-II, but not guilty of the remaining count of CSC-I.

Watkins raised several arguments on appeal ... [but] [t]he Court of Appeals affirmed in an unpublished opinion per curiam.[14] ...

> The evidence that defendant had assaulted another minor ... was relevant because it tended to show that it was more probable than not that the victim was telling the truth. The similarity of the relationships (E.W. was defendant's wife's cousin while the victim thought of his wife as a godmother) and defendant's modus operandi (taking advantage of minors who had a close relationship with his wife and were present in his home to baby sit) also made the likelihood of defendant's behavior toward the victim more probable. Moreover, the probative value of the evidence was not substantially outweighed by the danger of unfair prejudice. Whether the victim was telling the truth had significant probative value in deciding whether defendant should be convicted of the crimes for which he was charged. Further, defense counsel was able to effectively cross-examine E.W. regarding the fact that she thought of defendant as her boyfriend and maintained contact with him after their relationship ended, even expressing a desire

---

8. *Watkins*, 277 Mich.App. at 361, 745 N.W.2d 149.

14. *People v. Watkins*, unpublished opinion per curiam of the Court of Appeals, issued October 5, 2010 (Docket No. 291841), 2010 WL 3893812.

to have his child. Finally, the court instructed the jury on how to properly use the other acts evidence [.][18]

Thus, the Court of Appeals concluded that the testimony was relevant and not more prejudicial than probative and that any error by the trial court was harmless.[19] ...

In Docket No. 142751, the prosecution appeals by leave granted the judgment of the Court of Appeals affirming the trial court's opinion and order granting the motion in limine filed by defendant, Richard Kenneth Pullen. Pullen was charged with two counts of CSC-II[26] and one count of aggravated indecent exposure[27] for acts allegedly committed against his then 12-year-old granddaughter. At the preliminary examination, the victim testified that Pullen had touched her breasts with his hands under her clothes multiple times and that the touching started when she was five or six years old. She also claimed that Pullen touched her "crotch" under her clothes on a weekly basis. With regard to Pullen's alleged indecent exposure, the victim testified that, when she was 11 or 12 years old, she saw Pullen touching his penis in the next room while on the computer and, at the time, Pullen knew she could see him masturbating.

Before trial, the prosecution filed a notice of intent to introduce under MCL 768.27a other acts of sexual misconduct against a minor. Specifically, the prosecution sought to introduce a 1989 police report containing allegations that Pullen had sexually abused his then 16-year-old daughter. In the report, Pullen's daughter alleged multiple instances of digital penetration in which he "checked if [she] was still a virgin." In addition, the report contained allegations that defendant had frequently touched his daughter's breasts, buttocks, and genital area while wrestling and massaging her back, had repeatedly walked in on her while she was undressed, and had arranged to expose himself to her when he was bathing. Although Pullen had apparently admitted engaging in some of the conduct alleged in the report, including the digital penetration, criminal charges were never filed.

In response to the notice of intent to introduce the 1989 police report, Pullen filed a motion in limine to bar the evidence as unduly prejudicial. The trial court granted Pullen's motion and excluded the evidence. After concluding that it "must perform the balancing test set forth in MRE 403 before admitting evidence under MCL 768.27a," the trial court ruled that the 1989 police report failed to survive that balancing:

> [I]t is the opinion of this Court that the prejudicial impact of the evidence proffered by the People substantially outweighs the probative value because it involves more serious facts than those in the case at bar. [Pullen] is charged with having sexual contact with his granddaughter, as well as exposing himself to his granddaughter. The police report from 1989 sets forth facts of a long pattern of sexual abuse by [Pullen] against his daughter, including multiple digital penetrations.... According to the police report, [Pullen] admitted to police that he had perpetrated these acts upon his daughter. Should this evidence be presented to the jury, it is highly probable that the jury would not be able to separate the two cases and would likely decide the case based on emotional impact rather than logical reasons. Thus, this evidence does not survive the balancing test of MRE 403 and is not admissible.

> The Court also finds that it would be fundamentally unfair and a violation of due process to force [Pullen] to defend accusations from over 20 years ago for

---

18. *Id.*
19. *Id.* at 6.
26. MCL 750.520c(1)(a) (involving a person under the age of 13).
27. MCL 750.335a(2)(b).

which charges were never filed. [Pullen] is in an untenable position to try to disprove more serious and greatly dated charges. It is unlikely that he would be able to do so, and to require him to do so would be manifestly unjust.

Following the ruling, the trial court agreed to stay the trial court proceedings to allow the prosecution to pursue an appeal. The Court of Appeals granted the prosecution's interlocutory application for leave to appeal and affirmed the trial court's ruling in an unpublished opinion per curiam.[28] It concluded that MRE 403 applies to evidence admissible under MCL 768.27a and held that the trial court did not abuse its discretion by excluding the evidence:

> Even given the fact that the evidence is relevant because the past conduct also involves a family member, it is highly likely that the jury would convict defendant solely based on his past conduct out of inflamed passion, anger or shock. In addition, because the prior conduct did not result in a conviction or even in the filing of charges, the trial court correctly observed that the necessary presentation of this evidence concerning the earlier alleged conduct would not only overshadow the question of defendant's guilt that is directly at issue in the instant case, it would be virtually impossible for defendant to defend himself against the earlier unproven allegations.[29]

The prosecution applied for leave to appeal in this Court. We granted leave, instructing the parties to address

> (1) whether the omission of any reference to MRE 403 in MCL 768.27a (as compared to MCL 768.27b(1)), while mandating that evidence of other offenses "is admissible and may be considered for its bearing on any matter to which it is relevant," would violate a defendant's due process right to a fair trial and (2) whether the Court should rule that evidence of other offenses described in MCL 768.27a is admissible only if it is not otherwise excluded under MRE 403.[30] ...

In this case, we have little trouble concluding that MCL 768.27a and MRE 404(b) irreconcilably conflict. MRE 404(b)(1) provides:

> Evidence of other crimes, wrongs, or acts is not admissible to prove the character of a person in order to show action in conformity therewith. It may, however, be admissible for other purposes, such as proof of motive, opportunity, intent, preparation, scheme, plan, or system in doing an act, knowledge, identity, or absence of mistake or accident when the same is material, whether such other crimes, wrongs, or acts are contemporaneous with, or prior or subsequent to the conduct at issue in the case.

Thus, MRE 404(b) requires the exclusion of other acts evidence if its only relevance is to show the defendant's character or propensity to commit the charged offense.[41] "Underlying the rule is the fear that a jury will convict the defendant inferentially on the basis of his bad character rather than because he is guilty beyond a reasonable doubt of the crime charged."[42] Preventing the jury from drawing this inference recognizes the risk that propensity evidence might " 'weigh too much with the jury and ... so overpersuade them

---

28. *People v. Pullen*, unpublished opinion per curiam of the Court of Appeals, issued February 15, 2011 (Docket No. 298138), 2011 WL 520837.

29. *Id.* at 4.

30. *People v. Pullen*, 489 Mich. 864, 795 N.W.2d 147 (2011).

41. *People v. Knox*, 469 Mich. 502, 510, 674 N.W.2d 366 (2004).

42. *People v. Crawford*, 458 Mich. 376, 384, 582 N.W.2d 785 (1998).

as to prejudge one with a bad general record and deny him a fair opportunity to defend against a particular charge.' "[43]

By contrast, MCL 768.27a provides:

(1) Notwithstanding [MCL 768.27],[44] in a criminal case in which the defendant is accused of committing a listed offense against a minor, evidence that the defendant committed another listed offense against a minor is admissible and may be considered for its bearing on any matter to which it is relevant. If the prosecuting attorney intends to offer evidence under this section, the prosecuting attorney shall disclose the evidence to the defendant at least 15 days before the scheduled date of trial or at a later time as allowed by the court for good cause shown, including the statements of witnesses or a summary of the substance of any testimony that is expected to be offered.

(2) As used in this section:

(a) "Listed offense" means that term as defined in section 2 of the sex offenders registration act, 1994 PA 295, MCL 28.722.

(b) "Minor" means an individual less than 18 years of age.

Of significance here is the statutory language allowing the admission of evidence that defendant committed another listed offense "for its bearing on any matter to which it is relevant." Evidence is relevant if it has "any tendency to make the existence of any fact that is of consequence to the determination of the action more probable or less probable than it would be without the evidence."[45] Because a defendant's propensity to commit a crime makes it more probable that he committed the charged offense, MCL 768.27a permits the admission of evidence that MRE 404(b) precludes.

As the Court of Appeals has explained, "our cases have never suggested that a defendant's criminal history and propensity for committing a particular type of crime is irrelevant to a similar charge."[46] Quite the opposite, this Court has long recognized that a defendant's character and propensity to commit the charged offense is highly relevant because "an individual with a substantial criminal history is more likely to have committed a crime than is an individual free of past criminal activity."[47] Indeed, "it is because of the human instinct to focus exclusively on the relevance of such evidence that the judiciary has traditionally limited its presentation to juries."[48] Thus, the language in MCL 768.27a allowing admission of another listed offense "for its bearing on any matter to which it is relevant" permits the use of evidence to show a defendant's character and propensity to commit the charged crime, precisely that which MRE 404(b) precludes.

---

43. *Old Chief v. United States*, 519 U.S. 172, 181, 117 S.Ct. 644, 136 L.Ed.2d 574 (1997), quoting *Michelson v. United States*, 335 U.S. 469, 476, 69 S.Ct. 213, 93 L.Ed. 168 (1948).

44. MCL 768.27 provides:

In any criminal case where the defendant's motive, intent, the absence of, mistake or accident on his part, or the defendant's scheme, plan or system in doing an act, is material, any like acts or other acts of the defendant which may tend to show his motive, intent, the absence of, mistake or accident on his part, or the defendant's scheme, plan or system in doing the act, in question, may be proved, whether they are contemporaneous with or prior or subsequent thereto; notwithstanding that such proof may show or tend to show the commission of another or prior or subsequent crime by the defendant.

The statute essentially parallels MRE 404(b).

45. MRE 401.

46. *People v. Pattison*, 276 Mich.App. 613, 620, 741 N.W.2d 558 (2007).

47. *People v. Allen*, 429 Mich. 558, 566, 420 N.W.2d 499 (1988).

48. *Pattison*, 276 Mich.App. at 620, 741 N.W.2d 558.

That the Legislature envisioned and intended the statute to supersede MRE 404(b) is unmistakable given the statute's prefatory phrase "[n]otwithstanding [MCL 768.27]." MCL 768.27 codified what later essentially became the substance of MRE 404(b). Both MCL 768.27 and MRE 404(b) limit the admissibility of other-acts evidence to consideration for noncharacter purposes, such as to show a defendant's motive, intent, or common plan or scheme. "Notwithstanding" is defined as "in spite of" or "without being opposed or prevented by[.]"[49] Parsed out, MCL 768.27a can be rephrased as follows: In spite of the statute limiting the admissibility of other-acts evidence to consideration for noncharacter purposes, other-acts evidence in a case charging the defendant with sexual misconduct against a minor is admissible and may be considered for its bearing on any matter to which it is relevant. Thus, the statute establishes an exception to MRE 404(b) in cases involving a charge of sexual misconduct against a minor.

Although an issue of first impression for this Court, federal courts have concluded that FRE 414,[50] the federal counterpart of MCL 768.27a, conflicts with FRE 404(b).[51] One court explained, "[FRE 414] allows the prosecution to use evidence of a defendant's prior acts for the purpose of demonstrating to the jury that the defendant had a disposition of character, or propensity, to commit child molestation."[52] As another federal court succinctly stated, "[p]ropensity evidence is precisely what [FRE] 414 permits."[53] The Michigan Court of Appeals has similarly reasoned:

> When a defendant is charged with a sexual offense against a minor, MCL 768.27a allows prosecutors to introduce evidence of a defendant's uncharged sexual offenses against minors without having to justify their admissibility under MRE 404(b). In many cases, it allows evidence that previously would have been inadmissible, because it allows what may have been categorized as propensity evidence to be admitted in this limited context.[54]

We reach the same conclusion. Because we cannot read MCL 768.27a and MRE 404(b) in harmony, the question becomes which decree prevails — that of the Legislature or that of the judiciary.... A rule of evidence will prevail over a conflicting statute only if the statute unconstitutionally infringes on this Court's authority under Const. 1963, art. 6, §5 to "establish, modify, amend and simplify the practice and procedure in all courts of this state." In accordance with separation-of-powers principles, this Court's authority in

---

49. *Random House Webster's College Dictionary* (2001).

50. In pertinent part, FRE 414, regarding similar crimes in child-molestation cases, provides: "In a criminal case in which a defendant is accused of child molestation, the court may admit evidence that the defendant committed any other child molestation. The evidence may be considered on any matter to which it is relevant." FRE 414(a).

51. FRE 404(b)(1) provides: "Evidence of a crime, wrong, or other act is not admissible to prove a person's character in order to show that on a particular occasion the person acted in accordance with the character."

52. *United States v. Castillo*, 140 F.3d 874, 879 (C.A.10, 1998). Our discussion of federal cases is limited to the initial question whether MCL 768.27a conflicts with MRE 404(b). Turning to federal cases addressing whether FRE 414 and FRE 404(b) conflict is useful given that MCL 768.27a and MRE 404(b) were clearly drawn from their federal counterparts. See note to MRE 404. 402 Mich. xcvi. The constitutional question whether MCL 768.27a violates separation-of-powers principles, however, is unique to Michigan law. It is necessary to address the issue only because Michigan's Constitution vests in the Supreme Court the exclusive authority regarding rules of practice and procedure. Const. 1963, art. 6, §5. In the federal system, "Congress has power to prescribe what evidence is to be received in the courts of the United States." *Tot v. United States*, 319 U.S. 463, 467, 63 S.Ct. 1241, 87 L.Ed. 1519 (1943). See 28 USC 2071 *et seq.*

53. *United States v. Bentley*, 561 F.3d 803, 815 n. 7 (C.A.8, 2009).

54. *Pattison*, 276 Mich.App. at 618–619, 741 N.W.2d 558.

matters of practice and procedure is exclusive and therefore beyond the Legislature's power to exercise.[55] This exclusive authority, however, extends only to rules of practice and procedure, as "this Court is not authorized to enact court rules that establish, abrogate, or modify the substantive law."[56] Accordingly, our task is to determine whether MCL 768.27a is an impermissible rule governing the practice and procedure of the courts or a valid enactment of substantive law.

McDougall v. Schanz addressed whether MCL 600.2169, a statute requiring that expert witnesses offered in medical malpractice actions possess certain medical practice or teaching experience, violated the Court's exclusive authority regarding rules of practice and procedure.[57] We harbored no doubt in *McDougall* that MCL 600.2169 acts as a rule of evidence, given that its application determines the admissibility of expert testimony in medical malpractice cases.[58] MCL 768.27a similarly determines the admissibility of evidence that the defendant committed an offense against a minor in a case charging the defendant with the commission of a separate offense against a minor. Therefore, MCL 768.27a is also a rule of evidence.

But our analysis does not end upon reaching this conclusion. In *McDougall*, we rejected the mechanical approach of characterizing all rules of evidence as procedural.[59] Instead, we established a sensible approach to separate procedural rules of evidence on the one hand from substantive rules of evidence on the other:

> [A] statutory rule of evidence violates Const. 1963, art. 6, §5 only when "'no clear legislative policy reflecting considerations other than judicial dispatch of litigation can be identified....'" Therefore, "[i]f a particular court rule contravenes a legislatively declared principle of public policy, having as its basis something other than court administration ... the [court] rule should yield." We agree ... that "[m]ost rules of evidence have been made by courts. Now and then the legislature has, as a result of policy consideration [sic] over and beyond matters involving the orderly dispatch of judicial business, enacted rules of evidence. The distinction previously pointed out between policy considerations involving the orderly dispatch of judicial business on the one hand and policy considerations involving something more than that on the other hand is the distinction that must be carried through into the evidence field."[60]

Thus, statutory rules of evidence that reflect policy considerations limited to "the orderly dispatch of judicial business," i.e., court administration, are procedural and violate Const. 1963, art. 6, §5. But statutory rules of evidence that reflect policy considerations "over and beyond matters involving the orderly dispatch of judicial business" are substantive, and in the case of a conflict with a court rule, the legislative enactment prevails. As noted in *McDougall*, procedural rules of evidence involving the orderly dispatch of judicial business are "'those rules of evidence designed to allow the adjudicatory process to function

---

55. See *McDougall*, 461 Mich. at 27, 597 N.W.2d 148; *Pattison*, 276 Mich.App. at 619, 741 N.W.2d 558.

56. *McDougall*, 461 Mich. at 27, 597 N.W.2d 148; see also *Shannon v. Ottawa Circuit Judge*, 245 Mich. 220, 223, 222 N.W. 168 (1928) ("'A rule of court cannot enlarge or restrict jurisdiction, or abrogate or modify the substantive law.'") (citation omitted).

57. *McDougall*, 461 Mich. at 18, 597 N.W.2d 148. The Court determined that MCL 600.2169 conflicted with MRE 702, which permits the admission of expert testimony on the basis of "knowledge, skill, experience, training, or education." "Anyone qualified by virtue of the MRE 702 criteria of skill, training, or education could nonetheless be excluded under the statute's strict practice or teaching requirements." *McDougall*, 461 Mich. at 25, 597 N.W.2d 148.

58. *Id.* at 27–28, 597 N.W.2d 148.

59. *Id.* at 29, 597 N.W.2d 148.

60. *Id.* at 30–31, 597 N.W.2d 148 (citations omitted).

effectively.... Examples are rules of evidence designed to let the jury have evidence free from the risks of irrelevancy, confusion and fraud.'"[61] *McDougall* identified the line separating statutory rules of evidence that are constitutional from those that impermissibly venture into the area of practice and procedure over which this Court has exclusive authority.

Applying *McDougall*, we conclude that MCL 768.27a is a valid enactment of substantive law to which MRE 404(b) must yield. The statute is based on policy considerations over and beyond the orderly dispatch of judicial business. We note several policy reasons that support the Legislature's decision to allow other-acts evidence in cases involving sexual misconduct against minors. As the United States Supreme Court has observed, "[w]hen convicted sex offenders [including child molesters] reenter society, they are much more likely than any other type of offender to be rearrested for a new rape or sexual assault."[62] Evidence of guilt in child molestation cases is typically hard to come by because in most cases the only witness is the victim, whose testimony may not be available, helpful, or deemed credible because of his or her age. It may also be difficult for a jury to believe that a defendant is capable of engaging in such egregious behavior with a child. Consistent with our analysis is the fact that federal courts considering the validity of FRE 414 have identified similar policy considerations underlying the rule that are over and beyond the orderly dispatch of judicial business. Those considerations include "[p]romoting the effective prosecution of sex offenses," "the reliance of sex offense cases on difficult credibility determinations," and "the 'exceptionally probative' value of a defendant's sexual interest in children."[63] In our judgment, MCL 768.27a was not "'designed to allow the adjudicatory process to function effectively....'"[64] Rather, it reflects a substantive legislative determination that juries should be privy to a defendant's behavioral history in cases charging the defendant with sexual misconduct against a minor.

In sum, the reasons for enacting MCL 768.27a were not to further the orderly dispatch of judicial business, but to address a substantive concern about the protection of children and the prosecution of persons who perpetrate certain enumerated crimes against children and are more likely than others to reoffend. Accordingly, we hold that MCL 768.27a does not run afoul of Const. 1963, art. 6, §5, and in cases in which the statute applies, it supersedes MRE 404(b).[65]

---

61. *Id.* at 31 n. 15, 597 N.W.2d 148, quoting 3 Honigman & Hawkins, Michigan Court Rules Annotated (2d ed), p 403. Although we refrain from deciding cases not before us, it is not hard to see that MRE 402 and 403 are rules of the procedural variety. Likewise, it appears beyond debate that matters of discovery embody purely procedural considerations. See *United States v. Nobles*, 422 U.S. 225, 241, 95 S.Ct. 2160, 45 L.Ed.2d 141 (1975) (rejecting the Sixth Amendment claim of a defendant who failed to comply with the trial court's discovery order because "the Sixth Amendment does not confer the right to present testimony free from the legitimate demands of the adversarial system").

62. *McKune v. Lile*, 536 U.S. 24, 33, 122 S.Ct. 2017, 153 L.Ed.2d 47 (2002).

63. *United States v. Mound*, 149 F.3d 799, 801 (C.A.8, 1998) (citation omitted). Although the defendant in *Mound* challenged the validity of FRE 413, as opposed to FRE 414, the court indicated that its analysis applied equally to FRE 414. *Mound*, 149 F.3d at 800 n. 2. We also note that the court mentioned these policy considerations in the context of an equal-protection analysis to support the conclusion that FRE 413 survived rational-basis review. *Id.* at 801. As noted previously, the separation-of-powers concern at issue in this case does not arise in the federal system.

64. *McDougall*, 461 Mich. at 31 n. 15, 597 N.W.2d 148, quoting 3 Honigman & Hawkins, p 403. By enacting MCL 768.27a, the Legislature merely deemed other acts of sexual misconduct against a minor substantively admissible, avoiding intrusion into the court's province over the procedural aspects of the evidence's admissibility such as relevancy, risk of prejudice, and adherence to proper discovery practices. See ... this opinion (holding that MCL 768.27a remains subject to MRE 403).

65. The dissent criticizes our analysis as brief and oversimplified. To the extent that our analysis is to the point, by no means do we view drawing the line between procedural and substantive rules of evidence as an easy endeavor. Nor do we take lightly the task of line-drawing in this case. Like the

The dissent would instead hold that MCL 768.27a is unconstitutional. The dissent first takes the position that MCL 768.27a should fail the *McDougall* test because the statute primarily concerns the judicial dispatch of litigation, which the dissent says is true of all rules that have the "effect" of "telling [courts] what evidence juries can hear."[66] This is a misapplication of *McDougall*. If it were true that all rules that operate to tell courts what evidence is admissible concerned the judicial dispatch of litigation, then all rules of evidence would be procedural. But *McDougall* specifically rejected the approach of mechanically characterizing all rules of evidence as procedural. Therefore, the dissent's position is inconsistent with a proper reading of *McDougall*.

Alternatively, the dissent would refine or discard the *McDougall* test. The dissent's proposed test would treat the legislative policy concerns surrounding a statute's enactment as irrelevant to whether an evidentiary rule is substantive or procedural.[67] According to the dissent, the only inquiry should be whether the *function* of the statute "is to tell the courts what evidence they may admit in a court proceeding...."[68] This approach would also mechanically characterize all rules of evidence as procedural because, as a purely *functional* matter (if we truly disregard every underlying policy concern), all evidentiary rules tell the courts what evidence is admissible.[69] Thus, although the dissent criticizes the majority's application of the *McDougall* test as vastly underinclusive in defining which evidentiary rules qualify as procedural, the dissent's alternative approaches are vastly overinclusive in defining the same.

The dissent cites the rules of privilege as an example of an area of substantive rulemaking. But rules relating to privilege still serve the exclusive *function* of telling the courts what evidence is admissible at trial and, therefore, would be procedural under the dissent's test. Privilege rules function to dictate the admissibility of communications made between parties in certain relationships; accordingly, privilege rules tell the courts what evidence is admissible at trial.[70] ... The dissent asserts that privileges and other substantive rules of evidence "do far more than dictate what evidence is admissible in a court proceeding; they directly affect people's out-of-court behavior."[71] We do not disagree that privileges

---

Court in *McDougall*, we too "appreciate the difficulty that attends the drawing of the line between 'practice and procedure' and substantive law." *McDougall*, 461 Mich. at 36, 597 N.W.2d 148.

66. *Post* at 322, 324 (emphasis omitted).

67. *Post* at 322–23 (stating that the "laudatory nature" of the policy concerns identified in the majority opinion "is irrelevant for purposes of this Court's analysis of the issue involved in this case" because "[t]he Legislature's public policy considerations in enacting a statute can neither dictate nor disguise whether the statute enacted to address those considerations is a proper exercise of legislative authority").

68. *Post* at 325.

69. The dissent emphasizes the placement of MCL 768.27a in the Code of Criminal *Procedure*. Reliance on labels is a reflexive practice that the United States Supreme Court and the courts of this state have admonished against. See, e.g., *Henneford v. Silas Mason Co., Inc*, 300 U.S. 577, 586, 57 S.Ct. 524, 81 L.Ed. 814 (1937) ("Catch words and labels ... are subject to the dangers that lurk in metaphors and symbols, and must be watched with circumspection lest they put us off our guard."); *People v. Evans*, 491 Mich. 1, 810 N.W.2d 535 (2012) (applying the Supreme Court's holding that a trial court's label of "acquittal" for a given ruling does not determine whether an acquittal actually occurred for double-jeopardy purposes); *Klein v. Kik*, 264 Mich.App. 682, 686, 692 N.W.2d 854 (2005) (reasoning that a party's label for its cause of action is not dispositive of the actual nature of the claim).

70. We disagree with the dissent's characterization of privilege rules as having only "an incidental effect on the admissibility of evidence in a court proceeding." *Post* at 326. For example, Michigan's marital privilege statute, MCL 600.2162(1), provides: "In a civil action or administrative proceeding, a husband shall not be examined as a witness for or against his wife without her consent or a wife for or against her husband without his consent...." The statute pertains precisely to the admissibility of a spouse's testimony in court.

71. *Post* at 325.

influence out-of-court behavior by "promot[ing] free and open expression in certain relationships with the confidence that what is communicated will not be revealed in a court proceeding."[72] What the dissent fails to appreciate, however, is that the goal of promoting free expression and confidence in certain relationships is nothing more than a policy concern advanced by the Legislature, which runs directly counter to the dissent's position that legislative policy concerns are irrelevant. It is neither proper nor sensible to conclude that court rules should yield to statutes that are grounded in some policy concerns (e.g., a concern for promoting free expression and confidence in certain relationships) but not others (e.g., a concern for protecting children and addressing the high recidivism rates of child molesters). Thus, we question the wisdom of drawing a distinction that is based on whether an evidentiary rule directly influences people's out-of-court behavior.... We reiterate our belief that the sensible divide is between rules involving considerations limited to the orderly dispatch of judicial business, which are procedural, and rules involving considerations over and beyond the orderly dispatch of judicial business, which are substantive. This position recognizes the powers and limitations of both the judicial and the legislative rulemaking authority....

Having determined that MCL 768.27a is a valid enactment of substantive law, the question remains whether evidence admissible under the statute may nonetheless be excluded under MRE 403. For the reasons that follow, we hold that evidence admissible pursuant to MCL 768.27a may nonetheless be excluded under MRE 403 if "its probative value is substantially outweighed by the danger of unfair prejudice, confusion of the issues, or misleading the jury, or by considerations of undue delay, waste of time, or needless presentation of cumulative evidence." ... The argument against applying MRE 403 to evidence admissible under MCL 768.27a comes not from the text of either MRE 403 or MCL 768.27a, but from the text of MCL 768.27b, which pertains to other-acts evidence in domestic violence cases. MCL 768.27b provides that "evidence of the defendant's commission of other acts of domestic violence is admissible for any purpose for which it is relevant, *if it is not otherwise excluded under Michigan rule of evidence 403.*"[76] It is this emphasized portion of the statute that has generated disagreement surrounding whether MRE 403 applies to MCL 768.27a.

Unlike MCL 768.27b, MCL 768.27a does not explicitly mention MRE 403: "Notwithstanding [MCL 768.27], ... evidence that the defendant committed another listed offense against a minor is admissible and may be considered for its bearing on any matter to which it is relevant." Accordingly, it is argued that if the Legislature expressly made other-acts evidence under MCL 768.27b subject to MRE 403 in cases of domestic violence, then the failure to mention MRE 403 in MCL 768.27a indicates that the Legislature did not intend MRE 403 to apply with regard to other-acts evidence in cases involving sexual misconduct against minors. We reject the invitation to draw this inference.... Significantly, the Legislature did not draft these statutes simultaneously. MCL 768.27a was enacted by 2005 PA 135, which became effective January 1, 2006, whereas MCL 768.27b was enacted by 2006 PA 78, which became effective March 24, 2006. The Legislature's "silence" from which it is urged we draw an inference occurred in the earlier enactment. It is one thing to infer legislative intent through silence in a simultaneous or subsequent enactment, but quite another to infer legislative intent through silence in an earlier enactment, which is only "silent" by virtue of the subsequent enactment.

---

72. Baughman, *The emperor's old clothes: A prosecutor's reply to Mr. Leitman concerning exclusion of evidence for statutory violations,* 1999 L. R. Mich. St. U. Det. C. L. 701, 716.

76. Emphasis added.

We are also mindful of "consider[ing] whether [the statute and rule of evidence] can be construed so as not to conflict,"[77] and "[w]e do not lightly presume that the Legislature intended a conflict...."[78] Unlike the irreconcilable conflict between MCL 768.27a and MRE 404(b), there is nothing inherent in the statute that prevents the application of MRE 403. And because MCL 768.27a makes no specific mention of MRE 403, we choose not to presume that the Legislature intended that MRE 403 not apply to other-acts evidence admissible under the statute. The Legislature could have expressly exempted evidence admissible under MCL 768.27a from analysis under MRE 403, but it did not.

Furthermore, as the United States Supreme Court has observed,

"not every silence is pregnant." In some cases, Congress intends silence to rule out a particular statutory application, while in others Congress' silence signifies merely an expectation that nothing more need be said in order to effectuate the relevant legislative objective. An inference drawn from congressional silence certainly cannot be credited when it is contrary to all other textual and contextual evidence of congressional intent.[79]

In closely examining the statutes, all other textual and contextual evidence of the Legislature's intent runs contrary to inferring that MRE 403 does not apply to evidence admissible under MCL 768.27a.... In sum, the "silence" in MCL 768.27a arose only by virtue of the subsequent enactment of MCL 768.27b, MCL 768.27a can be read in harmony with MRE 403, and we must give effect to the permissive term "may" and the phrase "[n]otwithstanding [MCL 768.27]" that are present in MCL 768.27a but absent from MCL 768.27b. For all these reasons, we hold that MRE 403 applies to evidence admissible under MCL 768.27a.[82] ...

Our conclusion that other-acts evidence admissible under MCL 768.27a remains subject to MRE 403 gives rise to the question of proper application. As with any balancing test, MRE 403 involves two sides of a scale — a probative side and a prejudicial side. Propensity evidence is prejudicial by nature, and it is precisely the danger of prejudice that underlies the ban on propensity evidence in MRE 404(b). Yet were a court to apply MRE 403 in such a way that other-acts evidence in cases involving sexual misconduct against a minor was considered on the prejudicial side of the scale, this would gut the intended effect of MCL 768.27a, which is to allow juries to consider evidence of other acts the defendant committed to show the defendant's character and propensity to commit the charged crime. To weigh the propensity inference derived from other-acts evidence in cases involving sexual misconduct against a minor on the prejudicial side of the balancing test would be to resurrect MRE 404(b), which the Legislature rejected in MCL 768.27a.... Accordingly, when applying MRE 403 to evidence admissible under MCL 768.27a, courts must weigh the propensity inference in favor of the evidence's probative value rather than its prejudicial effect. That is, other-acts evidence admissible under MCL 768.27a may not be excluded under MRE 403 as overly prejudicial merely because it allows a jury to draw a propensity inference. In reaching this conclusion, we join several federal courts that have addressed this issue with respect to FRE 414 and 403.[83]

---

77. *McDougall*, 461 Mich. at 24, 597 N.W.2d 148.

78. *Dobben*, 440 Mich. at 697 n. 22, 488 N.W.2d 726.

79. *Burns v. United States*, 501 U.S. 129, 136, 111 S.Ct. 2182, 115 L.Ed.2d 123 (1991), quoting *Illinois Dep't of Pub. Aid v. Schweiker*, 707 F.2d 273, 277 (C.A.7, 1983).

82. Given this conclusion, we need not address whether, if evidence admissible under MCL 768.27a were *not* subject to MRE 403, the statute would violate a defendant's due-process right to a fair trial or interfere with the judicial power to ensure that a criminal defendant receives a fair trial.

83. See, e.g., *United States v. Loughry*, 660 F.3d 965, 970 (C.A.7, 2011) ("[A]lthough evidence cannot be excluded under [FRE] 403 simply because it tends to show that the defendant has a propensity

This does not mean, however, that other-acts evidence admissible under MCL 768.27a may never be excluded under MRE 403 as overly prejudicial. There are several considerations that may lead a court to exclude such evidence. These considerations include (1) the dissimilarity between the other acts and the charged crime, (2) the temporal proximity of the other acts to the charged crime, (3) the infrequency of the other acts, (4) the presence of intervening acts, (5) the lack of reliability of the evidence supporting the occurrence of the other acts, and (6) the lack of need for evidence beyond the complainant's and the defendant's testimony.[84] This list of considerations is meant to be illustrative rather than exhaustive.... Several of these considerations are challenged in this appeal. Regarding the decision whether to exclude evidence admissible under MCL 768.27a when applying MRE 403, it is argued that courts should not be permitted to consider how long ago the other act occurred, its dissimilarity to the charged offense, or the fact that the defendant was never convicted of the other act. We disagree.

Although MCL 768.27b expressly imposes a 10-year limitation on the admissibility of other-acts evidence in domestic violence cases, whereas MCL 768.27a provides no such limitation, there is simply no legal basis for concluding that the lack of a temporal limitation in MCL 768.27a somehow means that the length of time since the other act of sexual misconduct against a minor occurred cannot be considered when weighing prejudice under MRE 403. Just as the statute's failure to refer to MRE 403 did not bar the court rule's application, the failure to temporally limit the admissibility of other-acts evidence does not preclude a court from considering under MRE 403 how long ago the other act occurred.

The argument that the dissimilarity of the other-acts evidence and the charged offense should not be considered under MRE 403 similarly fails. Although MCL 768.27a, by its terms, applies to all listed offenses, there is no indication that the Legislature intended to suggest that all listed offenses are sufficiently similar to each other that the dissimilarity between them and the charged offense could never be weighed in favor of concluding that the other-acts evidence presents the danger of unfair prejudice under MRE 403.

Finally, it is argued that, because MCL 768.27a applies to more than conduct that resulted in a conviction, whether the evidence of the other act resulted in a conviction is irrelevant under MRE 403. We disagree. That MCL 768.27a *permits* the introduction of other-acts evidence that did not result in a conviction does not mean that evidence that did not result in a conviction *must* be admitted or that a court may not consider whether charges were filed or a conviction rendered when weighing the evidence under MRE 403.[85]

The foregoing considerations may be used by trial courts to determine whether the probative value of evidence admissible under MCL 768.27a — which includes the propensity inference derived from the other-acts evidence — is nonetheless outweighed by the danger

---

to commit a sex offense, [FRE] 403 continues to rigorously apply to [FRE] 414 evidence."); *United States v. Benais*, 460 F.3d 1059, 1063 (C.A.8, 2006) ("[FRE] 403 must be applied in this context in a manner that permits [FRE] 413 and 414 to have their intended effect, namely, to permit the jury to consider a defendant's prior bad acts in the area of sexual abuse or child molestation for the purpose of showing propensity."); *United States v. Gabe*, 237 F.3d 954, 960 (C.A.8, 2001) ("[Other-acts evidence] tends to prove [a defendant's] propensity to molest young children.... Because propensity evidence is admissible under [FRE] 414, this is not *unfair* prejudice."); *United States v. Larson*, 112 F.3d 600, 604–605 (C.A.2, 1997) (stating that evidence admissible under FRE 414 is presumed relevant and probative).

84. See *United States v. LeMay*, 260 F.3d 1018, 1032 (C.A.9, 2001); *United States v. Guardia*, 135 F.3d 1326, 1331 (C.A.10, 1998).

85. At relevant times, a conviction was not required for many types of other-acts evidence to qualify as a listed offense, but a conviction was required for an act of indecent exposure to be admissible under MCL 768.27a. See MCL 28.722(e)(iii) as added by 2005 PA 301....

of unfair prejudice. Trial courts should apply this balancing to each separate piece of evidence offered under MCL 768.27a. In addition, trial courts retain their discretion under MRE 403 to determine how many separate pieces of other-acts evidence may be admitted before the probative value of such evidence is outweighed by the danger of "confusion of the issues, or misleading the jury, or by considerations of undue delay, waste of time, or needless presentation of cumulative evidence."[86] This determination can only be made in the context of the entire trial, considering all the other-acts evidence offered under MCL 768.27a as well as the evidence as a whole. There is no bright-line rule for how many "other acts" may be admitted before the scale tips in favor of exclusion. Rather, ensuring that the probative value of other-acts evidence is not outweighed by the danger of "confusion of the issues, or misleading the jury, or by considerations of undue delay, waste of time, or needless presentation of cumulative evidence" is a responsibility left to the trial court's discretion.

A final tool available for trial courts when admitting other-acts evidence under MCL 768.27a is CJI2d 20.28a, the standard instruction on evidence of other acts of child sexual abuse:

> (1) The prosecution has introduced evidence of claimed acts of sexual misconduct by the defendant with [a minor / minors] for which [he / she] is not on trial.

> (2) Before you may consider such alleged acts as evidence against the defendant, you must first find that the defendant actually committed those acts.

> (3) If you find that the defendant did commit those acts, you may consider them in deciding if the defendant committed the [offense / offenses] for which [he / she] is now on trial.

> (4) You must not convict the defendant here solely because you think [he / she] is guilty of other bad conduct. The evidence must convince you beyond a reasonable doubt that the defendant committed the alleged crime, or you must find [him / her] not guilty.

In cases in which a trial court determines that MRE 403 does not prevent the admission of other-acts evidence under MCL 768.27a, this instruction is available to ensure that the jury properly employs that evidence....

In Docket No. 142031, at Watkins's third and final trial, the trial court permitted EW to testify regarding other acts of alleged criminal sexual conduct and their surrounding circumstances. On appeal, the Court of Appeals properly confirmed its earlier holding that MCL 768.27a conflicts with MRE 404(b) and that the statute prevails over the rule of evidence.[87] It also properly held that evidence admissible under MCL 768.27a remains subject to MRE 403.[88] Further, we agree with the Court of Appeals' conclusion that the trial court's failure to apply MRE 403 was harmless. In addition to being probative because of the propensity inference, the other-acts evidence also supported the victim's credibility, presented circumstances similar to those underlying the charged offense, and established Watkins's modus operandi. And although the trial court failed to determine which aspects of EW's testimony met the requirements of MCL 768.27a, we agree with the Court of Appeals that the only incident for which EW provided specific details met the statute's

---

86. MRE 403.
87. *Watkins*, unpub. op. at 4.
88. *Id.* at 5.

requirements and, therefore, any error in admitting all of EW's testimony "was not inconsistent with substantial justice."[89] Finally, in accordance with CJI2d 20.28a, the jury was instructed on how to properly use the other-acts evidence. Accordingly, we affirm in *Watkins*. . . .

In Docket No. 142751, the trial court granted Pullen's motion in limine, excluding a 1989 police report containing allegations that Pullen had sexually abused his daughter more than 20 years ago. Although the trial court properly concluded that evidence admissible under MCL 768.27a remains subject to MRE 403, it abused its discretion by misapplying MRE 403.

First, the trial court failed to weigh the propensity inference in favor of the evidence's probative value. Nowhere in its analysis did the trial court mention that the other-acts evidence was probative of Pullen's character or propensity to commit the charged offense. Instead, the court stated that, "[s]hould this evidence be presented to the jury, it is highly probable that the jury would not be able to separate the two cases and would likely decide the case based on emotional impact rather than logical reasons." The Court of Appeals affirmed, characterizing this flawed reasoning as having "provided a reasoned basis" for the trial court's decision.[90]

Second, the trial court failed to weigh in favor of the evidence's probative value the extent to which the other-acts evidence supported the victim's credibility and rebutted the defense's attack thereof.[91] Pullen admitted that his trial strategy was to attack the victim's credibility, and the other-acts evidence was highly probative for rebuttal purposes and tended to support the victim's credibility.[92]

Third, the trial court failed to review separately under MRE 403 each act alleged in the 1989 report and instead lumped all of the evidence together. The trial court apparently believed that the egregiousness of some of the other-acts evidence—e.g., the allegation made by Pullen's daughter that he "checked if [she] was still a virgin"—justified excluding all the other-acts evidence as overly prejudicial. The various acts revealed in the 1989

---

89. *Id.* at 8.

90. *Pullen*, unpub. op. at 4.

91. The dissent disagrees, but offers no authority or rationale for doing so.

92. We acknowledge the holdings in *People v. Sabin (After Remand)*, 463 Mich. 43, 71, 614 N.W.2d 888 (2000), and *People v. Jones*, 417 Mich. 285, 289–290, 335 N.W.2d 465 (1983), both of which precluded the introduction of evidence of sexual acts between the defendant and persons other than the complainant to bolster the complainant's credibility. This case is distinguishable because it involved the admissibility of other-acts evidence under MCL 768.27a. In *Sabin*, for example, the reason for disallowing the admission of other-acts evidence under MRE 404(b) to bolster the complainant's credibility was that the resulting inference essentially involved propensity. As explained in *People v. Oliphant*, 399 Mich. 472, 517, 250 N.W.2d 443 (1976):

> Other allegations of rape do tend to make the complainant's story more believable, not because we know more about her or Oliphant's tendency to tell the truth, but because such evidence gives us reason to believe that he is the kind of man who would commit the charged offense. That, however, is precisely the purpose for which this evidence may not be admitted.

Stated differently, the danger in admitting other-acts evidence to bolster the complainant's credibility is that it essentially invites the jury to draw a propensity inference. As we concluded in ... this opinion, however, MCL 768.27a specifically *permits* the use of other-acts evidence to show a defendant's propensity to commit the charged crime. Because propensity evidence tends to make the complainant's story more believable, it would not make sense to conclude that evidence admissible to show the defendant's propensity to commit the charged offense is inadmissible to bolster the complainant's credibility. The defendant's propensity and the complainant's credibility are two sides of the same coin.

report included digital penetration, unwelcome and inappropriate touching, and indecent exposure. The trial court should have considered each act separately.[93]

Finally, the evidence of indecent exposure at issue here did not qualify as a listed offense under MCL 768.27a at times relevant to the instant case and, therefore, its admissibility should have been analyzed under MRE 404(b). The offense of aggravated indecent exposure is set forth at MCL 750.335a.[94] Currently, § 2 of the Sex Offenders Registration Act (SORA), MCL 28.721 *et seq.*, defines "listed offense" as including "[a] violation of [MCL 750.335a(2)(b)] ... if a victim is a minor."[95] At times relevant to this case, however, § 2 of SORA defined "listed offense" to mean "[a] violation of [MCL 750.335a(2)(b)] ... *if that individual was previously convicted of violating [MCL 750.335a]*."[96] Pullen was never convicted of violating MCL 750.335a for exposing himself to his daughter more than 20 years ago, as alleged in the 1989 police report. Indeed, criminal charges were never filed. Because the evidence was not a listed offense under SORA and hence not admissible as a listed offense under MCL 768.27a, the trial court should have analyzed its admissibility under MRE 404(b).[97] Accordingly, we vacate the judgments of the lower courts in *Pullen* and remand the case to the trial court for further proceedings consistent with this opinion....

---

93. Support for this conclusion exists in the language of MRE 403, which provides that "evidence may be excluded if *its* probative value is substantially outweighed by the ... *needless presentation of cumulative evidence*." (Emphasis added.) The rule thus contemplates the evaluation of an individual piece of evidence and how it compares to the other evidence sought to be admitted. This is not, as the dissent believes, a mere difference in judicial opinion. The dissent fails to cite any authority to support the proposition that the trial court did not err by lumping the other-acts evidence together for purposes of applying MRE 403. Rather than offer support for its own position, the dissent criticizes our analysis as selectively quoting MRE 403 by omitting all the language preceding "needless presentation of cumulative evidence," as if we have not considered the statute as a whole. Not so. Although, as the dissent observes, the "needless presentation of cumulative evidence" is but one basis for finding evidence excludable under MRE 403, the dissent does not explain how a trial court can consider this basis if it assesses the evidence when it is lumped together. The lumping of evidence leads to an all-or-nothing determination of admissibility; it does not leave room to determine a cumulative breaking point. Thus, unlike the dissent's position, our reading of MRE 403 adheres to the interpretive canon that "[c]ourts must give effect to every word, phrase, and clause in a statute and avoid an interpretation that renders nugatory or surplusage any part of a statute." *People v. Couzens*, 480 Mich. 240, 249, 747 N.W.2d 849 (2008) (citation and quotation marks omitted).

94. MCL 750.335a provides:

(1) A person shall not knowingly make any open or indecent exposure of his or her person or of the person of another.

(2) A person who violates subsection (1) is guilty of a crime, as follows:

(a) Except as provided in subdivision (b) or (c), the person is guilty of a misdemeanor punishable by imprisonment for not more than 1 year, or a fine of not more than $1,000.00, or both.

(b) If the person was fondling his or her genitals, pubic area, buttocks, or, if the person is female, breasts, while violating subsection (1), the person is guilty of a misdemeanor punishable by imprisonment for not more than 2 years or a fine of not more than $2,000.00, or both.

(c) If the person was at the time of the violation a sexually delinquent person, the violation is punishable by imprisonment for an indeterminate term, the minimum of which is 1 day and the maximum of which is life.

95. MCL 28.722(k) and (s)(ii). This amended version of § 2 of SORA became effective July 1, 2011. See enacting § 2 of 2011 PA 17.

96. MCL 28.722(e)(iii), as added by 2005 PA 301 (emphasis added). This amended version of § 2 of SORA became effective February 1, 2006.

97. By "fail[ing] to see how the trial court can apply MRE 403 to [the indecent exposure] evidence differently if it is admitted under MRE 404(b) rather than MCL 768.27a," ... that MRE 403 applies differently to evidence admissible under MCL 768.27a. The difference is that courts must weigh the propensity inference in favor of the evidence's probative value. Nonetheless, the dissent is correct in pointing out that because MRE 404(b) does not allow other-acts evidence to be admitted to show propensity, the evidence of indecent exposure may well be *less* probative under MRE 404(b) than

In conclusion, we hold that MCL 768.27a irreconcilably conflicts with MRE 404(b) and that the statute prevails over the court rule. We also hold that evidence admissible under MCL 768.27a remains subject to MRE 403, but that courts must weigh the propensity inference in favor of the evidence's probative value rather than its prejudicial effect. For the foregoing reasons, we affirm the Court of Appeals' judgment in *Watkins*, Docket No. 142031, vacate the judgments of the lower courts in *Pullen*, Docket No. 142751, and remand the latter case to the trial court for further proceedings consistent with this opinion.

YOUNG, C.J., and MARKMAN and MARY BETH KELLY, JJ., concurred with ZAHRA, J.

Dissenting Opinion by MARILYN KELLY, J … [is omitted].

CAVANAGH and HATHAWAY, JJ., concurred with Marilyn Kelly, J.

Hamm v. State

Supreme Court of Arkansas, 2006
365 Ark. 647, 232 S.W.3d 463

BETTY C. DICKEY, Justice.

Appellant Phillip Hamm was convicted of the rape of M.C., a minor, by a jury in the Faulkner County Circuit Court. The Arkansas Court of Appeals reversed the decision of the trial court and remanded for a new trial, ruling that the testimony of a witness for the State had been improperly admitted under the "pedophile exception" to Ark. R. Evid. 404(b). See *Hamm v. State*, 91 Ark.App. 177, 209 S.W.3d414 (2005). We granted the State's petition for review pursuant to Ark. Sup. Ct. R. 2–4 (2005). We find no error and affirm the decision of the circuit court.

Although his only child is an adult living in another state, Phillip Hamm often worked with children at his church, serving at times as a Sunday school teacher and as an adult supervisor at church functions. Through that association he met the victim, M.C., a nine-year-old girl, and often invited her, her brother, and other children to his home. At times M.C.'s mother asked Hamm to babysit for her. He entertained M.C. while she was at his home by providing various recreational activities, including video games, television, movies, four-wheeler rides, and fishing. In March, 2002, two girls, N.C. and M.C., who had been frequent guests in the appellant's home, reported that he had initiated sexual contact with them during their visits. Both girls gave interviews to a state police investigator detailing their experiences with Hamm.

---

under MCL 768.27a. However, this does not mean that "there is no basis for concluding that the trial court's MRE 403 balancing would come out differently." … In this case, the inquiry of outcome-determinative error is complicated by the fact that the trial court improperly lumped all the evidence together for purposes of applying MRE 403. Just because the trial court applied MRE 403 to exclude *all* evidence contained in the 1989 police report that it believed was admissible under MCL 768.27a does not mean that it would have applied MRE 403 to exclude the evidence of indecent exposure had it properly considered its admissibility *separately* under MRE 404(b). This is the same reason for our reservations regarding the trial court's second basis for excluding the 1989 police report in its entirety, which was that "it would be fundamentally unfair and a violation of due process to force [Pullen] to defend accusations from over 20 years ago for which charges were never filed." Although every piece of evidence contained in the report would be equally prejudicial on this basis if admitted, not every piece of evidence contained in the report would be equally probative if admitted. Given the varying probative values of the evidence contained in the report, in our view, the dissent's preference to affirm the judgments below would involve too much speculation.

The appellant was originally charged with one count of sexual assault for each girl. The cases were severed, and following a second interview in which M.C. made allegations of digital vaginal penetration by Hamm, this charge was amended to rape. A Faulkner County Circuit Court jury acquitted the appellant in a trial for the sexual assault of N.C. At his subsequent trial for the rape of M.C., N.C. was allowed to testify about her experiences with the appellant. Another witness, Robbie Sullivan, testified that she had observed the appellant at a church function lying on his back on an air mattress, holding a little girl astraddle his pelvic area. Both witnesses' statements were admitted pursuant to the "pedophile exception" to Ark. R. Evid. 404(b). The appellant was convicted of rape and sentenced to seventeen years in the Arkansas Department of Corrections.... When we grant a petition for review, we treat the appeal as if it were originally filed in this court. Thus, we review the circuit court's judgment, not that of the court of appeals. *Elser v. State*, 353 Ark. 143, 114 S.W.3d 168 (2003)....

The appellant asserts that the trial court's admission of the testimony of N.C. was an abuse of its discretion because appellant's conduct towards N.C. was of a non-sexual nature, in contrast to his conduct with M.C. The cases cited by the State, such as *Smallwood v. State*, 326 Ark. 813, 935 S.W.2d 530 (1996), stand for the acknowledged proposition that once a defendant refers to a subject during direct examination, he opens the door for the prosecution to bring up the matter during cross-examination.... Here the trial judge originally granted appellant's motion in limine and excluded N.C.'s testimony, despite the pedophile exception. After Hamm stated during direct examination that he "never had and never would touch a female inappropriately," the trial judge reconsidered his ruling disallowing N.C.'s testimony, and granted the State's motion to allow her testimony for purposes of rebuttal. Since N.C.'s testimony would ordinarily be inadmissible under Rule 404(b), the decisive question is whether it was within the trial court's discretion to admit N.C.'s testimony under the pedophile exception to that rule.

Rule 404(b) states:

> Evidence of other crimes, wrongs, or acts is not admissible to prove the character of a person in order to show that he acted in conformity therewith. It may, however, be admissible for other purposes, such as proof of motive, opportunity, intent, preparation, plan, knowledge, identity or absence of mistake or accident.

The admission or rejection of evidence under Rule 404(b) is left to the sound discretion of the trial court and will not be disturbed absent a manifest abuse of discretion. *Hernandez v. State*, 331 Ark. 301, 962 S.W.2d 756 (1998). The list of exceptions set out in the rule is exemplary and not exhaustive. *White v. State*, 290 Ark. 130, 717 S.W.2d 784 (1986). Testimony is admissible pursuant to Rule 404(b) if it is independently relevant to the main issue, relevant in the sense of tending to prove some material point rather than merely to prove that the defendant is a criminal or a bad person. *Mosley v. State*, 325 Ark. 469, 929 S.W.2d 693 (1996).

This court has recognized a "pedophile exception" to Rule 404(b), which allows evidence of similar acts with the same or other children when it is helpful in showing a proclivity for a specific act with a person or class of persons with whom the defendant has an intimate relationship. *Berger v. State*, 343 Ark. 413, 36 S.W.3d 286 (2001). The rationale for recognizing the exception is that such evidence helps to prove the depraved instinct of the accused. *Id.* The basis of the pedophile exception to Rule 404(b) is our acceptance of the notion that evidence of sexual acts with children may be shown, as that evidence demonstrates a particular proclivity or instinct. *Hernandez*, 331 Ark. 301, 962 S.W.2d 756 (1998). For the pedophile exception to apply, we require that there be a sufficient degree of similarity between the evidence to be introduced and the sexual conduct of the defendant. *See id.; Berger*, 343 Ark. 413, 36 S.W.3d 286. We also require that there be an "intimate relationship" between the perpetrator and the victim of the prior act. *Hernandez*, 331 Ark. at 308, 962 S.W.2d at 760; *Berger*, 343 Ark. at 421, 36 S.W.3d at 291. Some of our earlier cases seemed to hold that for the pedophile exception to apply, the perpetrator and victim must reside in the same household. *See Free v. State*, 293 Ark. 65, 732 S.W.2d 452 (1987). Other cases dealing with the pedophile exception either did not mention the household element, such as *Thompson v. State*, 322 Ark. 586, 910 S.W.2d 694 (1995), or applied the exception to situations where the perpetrator did not live with the victim, as in *Greenlee v. State*, 318 Ark. 191, 884 S.W.2d 947 (1994). In *Berger*, 343 Ark. 413, 36 S.W.3d 286, we explicitly rejected a requirement that the perpetrator and the victim must live in the same household, and in so doing we adopted the reasoning of the court of appeals in *Brewer v. State*, 68 Ark.App. 216, 6 S.W.3d 124 (1999), which was that the pedophile exception was applicable if the victim was under the authority of the perpetrator or in his care. *Berger*, 343 Ark. at 420, 36 S.W.3d at 290.

The appellant avers that N.C.'s testimony was inadmissible because it involved conduct of a non-sexual nature, pointing out that he only inserted his hand about an inch down N.C.'s pants. However, N.C.'s testimony was that the appellant put his hand inside her pants and rubbed her "butt" using an up and down motion, that she got an awkward feeling in her stomach, and that at some point she objected, whereupon the appellant stopped. N.C. testified that the appellant had her sit on him while she played games on his computer, and that she slept overnight at times on the same couch with the appellant, while his wife slept in their bedroom. N.C. also reported that she would "snuggle" with Hamm, that he told her that he loved her, that she was beautiful, and that she was his "little girlfriend."

In N.C.'s case, the appellant rubbed her buttocks beneath her clothing, while with M.C., he engaged in more extensive sexual activity, culminating in digital vaginal penetration. The similarities include: both children were female; both were nine years old when the abuse began; both met the appellant at church; both were under his supervision at church; both were frequently invited to his home; both were at times sitting on Hamm when the abuse occurred; both reported abuse while home alone with him; and, he was not related to either of them. Because of the numerous similarities between the two cases, we conclude that it was not a manifest abuse of discretion for the trial judge to admit N.C.'s testimony under the pedophile exception to Rule 404(b).

The appellant asserts that the trial court abused its discretion by not allowing him to introduce evidence of his exoneration in his trial for the sexual assault of N.C.

When the appellant asked to admit his judgment of acquittal, the trial court said:

> If I allow the evidence of the other trial to come in, then that is going to leave both parties to argue what the jury meant by that which I don't think either one of you can do that because you don't know what the jury meant. They may have felt like what she said happened but what happened wasn't a criminal act. They may not have believed what she said, they may have believed we don't know. The verdict in that case can cut both ways in this trial. It can be good for the defendant or it can be bad for the defendant for them to know.

We agree with the State that acquittal does not necessarily mean that the events described in N.C.'s testimony did not occur, a distinction which might be lost on some jurors. An acquittal does not equate with a finding of innocence or a finding that the complaining witness's testimony was false, but rather an acquittal means simply that the jury was not convinced beyond a reasonable doubt that the charges were true. *Hughes v. State*, 347 Ark. 696, 66 S.W.3d 645 (2002). Given these considerations, and the possibility of prejudice to both sides which a mention of the previous trial could have entailed, we cannot conclude that the trial court's exclusion of this evidence was a manifest abuse of discretion....

The evidence which the State sought to admit under the pedophile exception to Rule 404(b) is the testimony of Robbie Sullivan, a witness who observed the appellant at a church lock-in and became concerned about his conduct. She observed the appellant lying on his back with an unidentified little girl straddling his pelvic area ... [the specific testimony is omitted]. There are similarities between the appellant's actions toward the victim and his actions toward the little girl at church. Both incidents involved female children. The victim was nine years old when the alleged abuse occurred, and the church incident involved a "little girl" of unspecified age. M.C. testified that Hamm had her sit on his lap, and Robbie Sullivan testified that Hamm held the little girl astraddle his pelvic area in an inappropriate manner. The appellant was acquainted with both children through his supervisory duties at his church.

In her interview with the state police investigator, the victim said that the appellant often encouraged children from the church to visit him at his home. There he entertained them in various ways, such as video games and fishing, four-wheeling, and other outdoor activities. The State argues that these recreational activities served to lure children into his home, to keep them coming back, and were thus used by the appellant to develop their friendship and trust, culminating in incidents of sexual abuse. Similarly, the appellant came to the church lock-in, which was an activity for children. He brought his air mattress, a magnet for children who had brought their sleeping bags. There he held the little girl on the mattress in an inappropriate position, straddling his pelvic area.

The appellant asserts that what occurred at the lock-in between the appellant and the little girl was non-sexual conduct. As the State points out, the conduct in question could constitute the sexual act of "frottage." Frottage is defined as: "The act of rubbing against the body of another person ... to attain sexual gratification." *The American Heritage Dictionary of the English Language* (4th Ed.2000). What Robbie Sullivan saw could be interpreted as a rubbing against the body of another to attain sexual gratification, and thus it could be defined as frottage, which is a sexual act. We agree with the dissent to the denial of petition for rehearing in the Court of Appeals, "There is nothing innocent about an adult male lying on his back and having a young girl straddle him, even when they are fully clothed, so that their pelvic regions are in contact." *Hamm v. State*, 91 Ark.App. 177, 209 S.W.3d 414 (2005) (dissenting opinion to denial of rehearing).

The contact between the appellant and the little girl described by Robbie Sullivan involved a fifty-year-old man who was a Sunday school teacher and a church worker. It occurred at a lock-in, a church function where there were sure to be children, but at which no children of the appellant's were in attendance. There he held a little girl of unspecified age in an inappropriate manner, straddling his pelvic area.... In comparing his relationships with these two girls, the appellant initially contacted M.C. and the unidentified little girl through his association with the church. Both girls were approximately of the same age, one was nine years old and the other was a "little girl." The initial contacts occurred at church, viewed by the children and their parents as a safe place where there were safe adults. As a supervisor of children at the church function, the appellant stood in a fiduciary relationship to the little girls, vested with a presumption of trust and confidence by virtue of that association. The appellant babys[a]t M.C. and was often the sole adult responsible for her care, and he was also acting in a supervisory capacity when he encountered the little girl at the lock-in. The appellant was an adult who was there to supervise the children, thus he stood in a position of authority or control *vis-a-vis* the unidentified little girl. The appellant also touched the vaginal areas of M.C. and the little girl. M.C. testified that Hamm touched her vaginal area in the manner already described, and Robbie Sullivan testified that the little girl was being "held" and that Hamm "had" the little girl straddling his pelvic area in an inappropriate way.

While there are differences between the contact that the appellant had with M.C. and the contact he had with the unidentified "little girl," in cases such as *Hernandez*, 331 Ark. 301, 962 S.W.2d 756, and *Flanery v. State*, 362 Ark. 311, 208 S.W.3d 187 (2005), we have recognized that the sexual acts admitted pursuant to the pedophile exception need not be identical to the abuse suffered by the present victim. In *Hernandez* we said, "[T]he pedophile exception seems especially applicable in view of the evidence that Mr. Hernandez was attracted to the physical characteristics of young girls." *Hernandez*, 331 Ark. at 308, 962 S.W.2d at 760. Hamm's conduct in frequently inviting young girls to his home while he was there alone, and his conduct at the lock-in, first in the incident on the air mattress, then sitting beside the little girls watching them, at least, until Robbie Sullivan fell asleep, is also evidence that the appellant was attracted to the physical characteristics of young girls. This evidence, considered in conjunction with Hamm's actions toward the girls, likewise makes the pedophile exception applicable in this case. Based on the facts of this case and the extant case law, we cannot conclude that the trial court manifestly abused its discretion in holding that the act described by Robbie Sullivan was relevant to show that the appellant was possessed of a depraved sexual instinct and had a proclivity for molesting young girls.

If evidence of past behavior is not admissible under the pedophile exception, it is still admissible if it is independently relevant to prove motive, intent, preparation, or plan. Robbie Sullivan's testimony is relevant to show the appellant's plan to meet children at church, to invite them back to his home, to keep them returning by offering them treats and entertainment, then to proceed to molest them. In the cases of M.C. and N.C., the appellant first contacted the girls at church, then invited them to visit his house, where he molested them. With the little girl described in Robbie Sullivan's testimony, the contact at the lock-in could reasonably be seen as a prelude to the same pattern as existed in the prior two cases, i.e., meeting a young girl at church, a presumably safe environment, generating a close friendship with her, inviting her into his home, and then molesting her. When the appellant attended the lock-in, he brought a full-size air mattress, something that would presumably be attractive to children. Subsequent to the contact with the "little girl" described by Robbie Sullivan, and even after the boys and girls were separated, he contrived to place himself near the little girls throughout the night. Thus the testimony was relevant to show preparation or plan on the part of the defendant. For the foregoing reasons, we conclude that the trial court did not abuse its wide discretion in evidentiary matters by admitting the testimony of Robbie Sullivan....

Affirmed.... [the dissenting opinion of Chief Justice Hannah, with which Justice Glaze joins, is omitted].

Notes

For discussion of the pedophile exception to Ark. R. Evid. 404(b), see Kassandra M. Bentley, *Lost or Just Bewildered?: The Exceptions to Rule 404(b), the Pedophile Exception in Hamm v. State, and the Perversion of the Independent Relevance Standard in Davis v. State*, 59 ARK. L. REV. 917 (2007). For other commentary, see Basyle J. Tchividjian, *Predators and Propensity: The Proper Approach for Determining the Admissibility of Prior Bad Acts Evidence in Child Sexual Abuse Prosecutions*, 39 AM. J. CRIM. L. 327 (2012); Joletta Friesen,

How Similar Is Similar?: Confusing the Similarity Standard for the Admission of Prior Crimes Evidence Under the Plan Exception in Child Molestation Cases, 44 Washburn L.J. 157 (2004); Russell L. Jones, *"If It Ain't Broke, Don't Fix It!" An Unnecessary Tampering With A Well Established Rule: Louisiana Code of Evidence Article 412.2 Admits Criminal Propensity Evidence*, 48 Loy. L. Rev. 17 (2002); Clara Gimenez, *Vermont Rule of Evidence 404(b) Admissibility of Prior Bad Acts in the "Context" of Child Molestation Cases*, 27 Vt. L. Rev. 217 (2002); Christie I. Floyd, *Admissibility of Prior Acts Evidence in Sexual Assault and Child Molestation Cases in Kentucky: A Proposed Solution That Recognizes Cultural Context*, 38 Brandeis L.J. 133 (1999/2000); Joseph A. Aluise, *Evidence of Prior Sexual Misconduct in Sexual Assault and Child Molestation Proceedings: Did Congress Err in Passing Federal Rules of Evidence 413, 414, and 415?*, 14 J.L. & Pol. 152 (1998); Sara S. Beale, *Prior Similar Acts in Prosecutions for Rape and Child Sex Abuse*, 4 Crim. L. Forum 307 (1993); Chris Hutton, *Commentary: Prior Bad Acts Evidence in Cases of Sexual Contact With A Child*, 34 S.D. L. Rev. 604 (1989); *Corroboration or Propensity? An Empty Distinction in the Admissibility of Similar Fact Evidence. Heuring v. State*, 513 So. 2d 122 (Fla.), 18 Stetson L. Rev. 171 (1988).

C. "Grooming"

Recall from Chapter Two the excerpt by Kenneth Lanning discussing the process of "grooming," which typically is employed by sex offenders to gain access to, and control over, child victims. *See supra*, Chapter Two, Section I.D (Sexual Abuse through Physical Conduct, "Grooming"). The *Morris* decision in Chapter Two demonstrates the exploitative dynamic of grooming behavior and its effect on the relationship between the offender and the child victim, as well as those who must respond to the offenses. Recall that, in *Morris*, the court accepted the inquiry about grooming behaviors as a "soft" science and admitted the testimony of the State's expert regarding the typical grooming pattern of child molesters, finding that "the legitimacy of 'grooming' as a subject of expert testimony has been established sufficiently to be judicially noticed." *Morris*, 361 S.W.3d at 669. The following excerpt in *State v. Transfiguracion*, however, confronts the issue of the admissibility of expert testimony about the grooming dynamic and the responsive behaviors of child victims associated with it.

State v. Transfiguracion
Supreme Court of Hawai'i, 2013
2013 WL 1285112

RECKTENWALD, C.J., NAKAYAMA, and McKENNA, JJ., with ACOBA, J., dissenting, with whom POLLACK, J., joins....

[In 2010, the defendant, Faustino Transfiguracion, was convicted of two counts of Continuing Sexual Assault Against a Minor Under the Age of Fourteen and three counts of Sexual Assault in the Third Degree against a minor under age fourteen. At trial, the Circuit Court admitted the testimony of Dr. Alex Bivens, who testified about external statistics and case studies evaluating the behavior of minor complainants related to child sexual exploitation, specifically with respect to "the existence of myths and public misconceptions related to a child's response to sexual abuse," — i.e., grooming. *State v. Transfiguracion*, 128 Haw. 476, 290 P.3d 546, *1 (2012). The court held that

> even if the circuit court were to credit Transfiguracion's unsubstantiated assertion
> that the news and entertainment media depict child sex abuse and delayed reporting

on a regular basis, it does not necessarily follow that there has been any change in the public's understanding of the psychological effects of childhood sexual abuse. Likewise, a juror's exposure to childhood sexual abuse (whether through personal or secondhand experience) does not necessarily imply that a juror would not be aided by expert testimony that speaks to the psychological effects of such experiences. Supporting the point that there was no obvious error, courts routinely permit expert testimony on the subjects covered by Dr. Bivens, implicitly finding that the issues remain outside the common understanding of a lay jury.

Id. at *2. Thus, the court admitted Dr. Biven's grooming testimony.

Transfiguracion appealed, claiming that the court erred by admitting the testimony because it improperly bolstered the complainants' credibility and profiled Transfiguracion as a child molester. However, the Hawai'i Intermediate Court of Appeals affirmed the Circuit Court's Final Judgment and Sentence. Transfiguracion then filed an Application for Writ of Certiorari to the Intermediate Court of Appeals, which the Supreme Court of Hawai'i rejected in this decision. The following excerpt is the dissenting opinion by Justices Acoba and Pollack from the Supreme Court's rejection of Transficuracion's Writ of Certiorari.]

The Application for Writ of Certiorari filed on February 11, 2013 by Petitioner/ Defendant-Appellant Faustino Transfiguracion is hereby rejected.

Dissent by ACOBA, J., with whom POLLACK, J., Joins.

Respectfully, in rejecting certiorari, the majority denies consideration on the degree of impact that a multitude of statistics has on the presumption of innocence, the standard of proof beyond a reasonable doubt, and the assessment of credibility by the factfinder. On its face, this case presents a significant issue regarding the use of statistics that has been reviewed in other jurisdictions and has yet to be addressed by this court,[1] and thus leaves the ICA [Intermediate Court of Appeals] and the trial courts bereft of authoritative guidance. Inasmuch as we are the court of last resort under the Hawai'i constitution, this court should grant certiorari because of the prior rulings and to fulfill our educative role. Accordingly, I disagree with rejection of the application for certiorari. In my view, certiorari should be granted for the reasons that follow, as factors that our courts may consider in this area....

This case involves allegations by five separate witnesses, "K.C.," "J.H.," "C.C.," "E.C.," and "D.C." (collectively, complaining witnesses) of varying degrees of sexual abuse by Pe-

---

1. Neither *State v. Machado*, 109 Hawai'i 424, 127 P.3d 84 (App .2005) nor *State v. Maelega*, 80 Hawai'i 172, 907 P.2d 758 (1995) address the circumstances presented by the instant case. In *Machado*, the ICA held that it was not error to admit testimony that "ninety-five percent of domestic violence is male to female." 109 Hawai'i at 431, 127 P.3d at 91. However, the ICA also acknowledged that "if error there was, under the foregoing circumstances it was harmless beyond a reasonable doubt," because *inter alia*, the defendant was convicted of a misdemeanor and not the felony charged. *Id.* at 435, 127 P.3d at 95. Moreover, the use of statistics in the instant case was far more extensive.

In *Maelega*, testimony regarding the typical actions of domestic batterers was admitted to rebut the defendant's Extreme Mental or Emotional Disturbance (EMED) defense. 80 Hawai'i at 182, 907 P.2d at 768. In other words, the defendant in that case did not dispute that he committed the act in question, but argued that he was entitled to a mitigating defense due to his mental state. It may be permissible to introduce evidence regarding typical actions of batterers when the only issue is the defendant's mental state. *See State v. Stafford*, 957 P.2d 47 (Or.App.1998) (discussed *infra*). However, in the instant case, the mental state of Petitioner/Defendant-Appellant Faustino Transfiguracion (Petitioner) was not at issue because *Petitioner denied ever abusing the complaining witnesses*. Hence, *Maelega* is inapposite. In sum, neither case justifies the rejection of certiorari in this case.

titioner. At trial, Respondent/Plaintiff-Appellee State of Hawai'i (Respondent) elicited testimony from each witness that he or she was abused by Petitioner. Respondent also presented testimony from Dr. Alex Bivens (Dr. Bivens), who apparently testified for Respondent as an expert[2] in the field of child sexual abuse....

K.C. explained that Leonida, her aunt, occasionally babysat her when she was younger. Petitioner was Leonida's husband at the time and present when K.C. went to Leonida's house. When K.C. was "probably six," and while Leonida was in the shower, Petitioner took off his pants and told K.C. to play with his penis. Petitioner "kept telling [her] it's all right" and "it's not bad." Petitioner then took K.C.'s hand and placed it on his penis....

J.H. was eighteen at the time of trial. She recounted that when she had been at her Aunt Leonida's house, Petitioner touched her "legs, arms" and "vagina and breasts" from outside her clothing. Petitioner also touched her vagina over her clothing "more than three times." She did not remember how many times he touched her breasts. J.H. explained that "most of the times" Petitioner touched her, he would "sweet-talk" her by "mak[ing] promises" to "take [her] to the park" or "Fun Factory." He would also "tell [her] he loved [her]." She had seen Petitioner put his hands in C.C.'s pants, but could not remember seeing this occur more than once....

Petitioner was never charged with any crime regarding M.H. M.H.'s testimony was introduced to prove an alleged prior bad act of Petitioner. However, M.H. was fourteen at the time of trial. She explained that C.C. was a year older than she was. When she was five or six and C.C. was six or seven, she saw Petitioner grab C.C. by the waist and put his hand down C.C.'s pants. She stated that C.C. cried but that she could not remember what happened after that.

Following this testimony, Respondent requested that the court issue a limiting instruction because it was "going to go into [Petitioner] touching [M.H.]." Respondent requested the court to instruct the jury that the evidence may only be used for "motive, intent, opportunity, and lack of mistake." Respondent stated that the testimony demonstrated motive or opportunity because "it's another child who says there was the opportunity for [Petitioner] to touch them without anyone seeing it." The court allowed the testimony to show motive or opportunity.

M.H. then testified that when she was "between four to six," she was at C.C.'s house in the living room along with J.H., K.C., and C.C. M.H. stated that Petitioner told her to sit on his lap, and started rubbing her legs and back. She did not remember Petitioner telling her anything while he was rubbing her legs. She stated that she felt Petitioner's penis and it was "hard." ...

Lourdes Hartmann (Lourdes) was the mother of J.H. and M.H., and the sister of Leonida. Lourdes recounted that when J.H. was between the ages of five and seven, her sister Leonida took care of J.H., picked her up from school, and took J.H. to her house. She explained that Petitioner lived with Leonida at the time....

C.C. testified that when he was "like eight" he was at Leonida's house and alone in the living room with Petitioner. C.C. stated that while he was sitting on the couch, Petitioner "pretend[ed] that he was hugging [C.C.]," and then reached "down [C.C.'s] pants." Petitioner "almost" touched his penis, but C.C. "push[ed] him away." This occurred "once or twice a month" when he was eight.... C.C. also related that Petitioner would touch his penis

---

2. Dr. Bivens was not explicitly qualified as an expert or qualified to render an expert opinion in a specialized area.

through his clothes "whenever [Leonida] wasn't ... watching." This occurred "more than two [times]," but "less than five." He then recounted that "more than once," Petitioner reached his hand down C.C.'s pants and "just barely" touched "the top of his penis." Petitioner also touched him in C.C.'s own house in June of 2008, during a family gathering. C.C. was in the living room with Petitioner and walked past him when Petitioner grabbed C.C. and touched his penis over his clothes....

E.C. testified that at some point prior to October, 2008, he was in Petitioner's truck with his brother and Petitioner. E.C. related that Petitioner was tickling him and then touched his penis over his clothes for less than three seconds. E.C. then told Petitioner to stop twice and after the second time, Petitioner stopped.... On recross-examination, E.C. testified that he had a "little bit" of a memory of the event and then stated that he "didn't really" have a memory of the event. On further redirect examination, E.C. testified that he knew Petitioner touched him because "he remember[ed]," but when asked again if he remembered, E.C. stated that he did not. He believed that Petitioner touched him in the truck because Petitioner "did it to the other people." ...

D.C. testified that when he was six, he would go to his Aunt Leonida's house. He stated that when he was at Leonida's house, he was sitting on the couch and Petitioner touched his "balls" "like two times." Petitioner tickled D.C.'s feet before he touched him....

Dr. Bivens provided extensive testimony regarding his credentials as an expert in the field of child sexual abuse. Defense counsel also conducted voir dire examination of Dr. Bivens and read from Dr. Bivens' CV. Dr. Bivens explained that he had not seen any information about this specific case, but that his intention was "to provide information about what the general science says about child sexual abuse." ... First, Dr. Bivens discussed the phenomenon of "delayed disclosure," where victims of child sexual abuse do not report the abuse until well after the abuse occurred. He explained that in child sexual abuse cases, "the delay of disclosures is the rule, not the exception." According to Dr. Bivens, the reasons that victims gave for delaying their disclosures were embarrassment, not wanting to hurt anyone, wanting to protect the abuser, and the fear of not being believed.... Dr. Bivens explained that "the closer the relationship" between the victim and the abuser, "the longer ... for the child to disclose." Dr. Bivens explained that "it was also common for children who had delayed disclosure to require a trigger." He stated that the most common trigger for disclosures was "an anger-inducing event," and that under one study "about a quarter of the [disclosures] reported fell into that category."

Dr. Bivens also addressed the phenomenon of incomplete disclosures. He explained that in one study, children initially only reported "half the severity [of acts] and half of the number of acts that were actually committed," so that "when children tell us, they probably aren't telling us the whole story at once." Regarding children's memory, Dr. Bivens explained that due to a phenomenon he termed "tunnel memory," children "are pretty good at explaining the actual incident," but "not quite as good" at remembering peripheral details about the event.

Dr. Bivens then answered several questions from Respondent regarding the characteristics of child molesters:

Q. Are there any studies concerning whether children are more likely to be abused by strangers or someone they know?

A. So all of the studies that I've talked about today were identifying people who have been molested, have revealed a very consistent finding. Perhaps one of the most consistent findings in the field of child sexual abuse is that *eighty-five percent of children or people who report being abused report that they had a preexisting re-*

lationship with their molester that was not based on sex, a preexisting, often trusting relationship.

Q. I'd like to talk a little bit about the abuse process itself. Any studies on where abuse occurs, where sexual abuse occurs?

A. Yes. *There was a study of over a hundred child molesters, and it found that incest[3] molesters molested in their home and they endorsed doing so a hundred percent of the time. Non-incest molesters reported molesting in their own home about half the time and in the child's home about half the time.* Doesn't mean the molestation wasn't taking place elsewhere, but it was endorsed by all of them that typically the child's home and their own home were the most common places.

Q. Are there any studies on whether or not persons molest in front of others?

A. Well, *there is one study that gave a questionnaire to over a hundred convicted child molesters who were assured that answering these questions wouldn't get them into any additional trouble.* And all the molesters did was fill out whether or not they endorsed this item or not. *But a sizable percentage, over forty percent, of the child molesters said that they had molested with another child present who was not involved in the molestation.* And about a quarter of them said that they molested in front of a non-participating adult who did not know about the abuse. . . .

Q. Did they provide reasons for abusing children while others were present?

A. The reasons cited by the convicted child molesters were a sense of mastery and control, you know, having that sense of power over the child, and sexual compulsivity, just not being able to resist doing so. And twelve percent admitted to molesting a child while they were in the same bed as a non-participating adult.

Q. I'd like to turn to how abusers gain the trust of children. Is there literature on how, basically how abuse occurs?

A. Yes. And there's even a measure to determine what methods are used most frequently by child molesters.

Q. And what is that?

A. *So it's something like the gaining-trust scale, or something like that.*

Q. And what did they do to gain trust?

A. *Well, treating them nicely, developing a loving relationship, touching them non-sexually, doing them favors, telling them they're special, these kinds of things.*[4]

Q. *Are there any studies that discuss whether or not a[n] average child molester is likely to have one or multiple victims?* . . .

A. *So multiple victims are the rule, and not the exception.* So the average number of victims per molester ranges from study to study between three to over eleven.

(Emphases added.) . . .

Petitioner denied the allegations of all of the complaining witnesses. He testified that when the complaining witnesses were watched by Leonida, there were times when the children were alone with him. He also acknowledged tickling the children, but denied touching their private parts. . . .

---

3. "Incest" is defined as "*sexual relations between family members or close relatives.*" *Black's Law Dictionary* 829 (9th ed.2009) (emphasis added).

4. The parties' briefs and cases from other jurisdictions refer to this as the "grooming" process.

In Respondent's closing argument, Respondent made several references to Dr. Bivens' testimony. First, Respondent contended that Dr. Bivens' testimony regarding the relationship of the victim and the abuser was relevant to explain delayed disclosure:

> Relationship to the abuser. Again, the reason that Dr. Bivens—that his testimony is relevant is because it contradicts all of the stereotypes that we hold. The stereotypes that we hold are that children don't know the people who abuse them. And the bottom line is that the child who knows the abuser is more likely never to disclose, ever, and to delay disclosure. And the bottom line is that the child who knows the abuser is more likely never to disclose, ever, and to delay disclosure.

Respondent also contended that the evidence at trial was consistent with Dr. Bivens' testimony regarding incomplete disclosures and child memory. Respondent then reminded the jury of Dr. Bivens' statements about a relationship of trust between children and abusers:

> Relationship of trust. *100 percent of incest offenders and a majority of other pedophile offenders were assaulted in their own homes. Again, [this] dispels the myth that persons are out there waiting to snatch kids.* The kids walk into their homes. Things like being baby-sat by a trusted uncle. 44 percent also chose the child's home. You know, once you've abused a child in their own home, where, where would that child go to be safe?
>
> *A majority molested with another child present ...* : 23.9 percent molested with a noncollaborating adult present. Again, at first it's hard to wrap your head around how that could happen, until you realize that motivations can be a lot of different things. Motivations can be increased excitement, sense of mastery, power over children, compulsion.

(Emphases added.) ...

In his Application, Petitioner asked, first, whether the court and the ICA erred by allowing the testimony of Dr. Bivens, and second, whether the court and the ICA erred by allowing M.H.'s testimony as to a prior bad act.... Regarding Petitioner's first question, Dr. Bivens' testimony can be divided into two categories. First, Dr. Bivens presented testimony regarding the reactions of child victims to sexual abuse. Dr. Bivens explained that abuse victims are likely to delay disclosure, that initial disclosure is likely to be incomplete, and that child witnesses may struggle to remember the peripheral details of events. Such testimony is admissible under this court's holding in *State v. Batangan*, 71 Haw. 552, 799 P.2d 48 (1990).... Second, however, Dr. Bivens also testified regarding the actions said to be commonly performed by the so-called typical sexual abuser and the typical characteristics of a sexual abuser, i.e. "profile evidence," as exhibited in the "abuse process" and "grooming process" discussed *infra*....

With respect to profile evidence, jurisdictions have considered some statistical evidence inherently prejudicial because of the possibility that jurors will *misinterpret* the statistical evidence offered. Some courts apparently reject "profile evidence," on this basis.[5] Courts have often held that profile evidence is "inherently prejudicial" because "of the potential [it has] for including innocent citizens as profiled [criminals]." *United States v. Beltran-Rios*, 878 F.2d 1208, 1210 (1989). Profile evidence "guide[s] the jury to the conclusion that a defendant is guilty because he fit[s] a particular profile," even though the profile

---

5. "Profile evidence" generally "describes sets of observable behavioral patterns," which can be used "as a tool to identify crime suspects." Christopher B. Mueller and Laird C. Kirkpatrick, *Evidence*, § 7.22 (4th ed.2009). "Profile evidence" is distinct from "syndrome" evidence, which generally involves a defendant's "psychological characteristics." *Id.*

itself "may be consistent with both innocent and guilty behavior." *People v. Robbie*, 92 Cal.App. 4th 1075, 1086–87 (2001).... In other words, testimony that a certain characteristic is commonly possessed by a certain type of criminal may suggest to the jury that an individual with that characteristic is guilty. However, such testimony *actually has no probative value* for that purpose, because it says nothing about how many innocent individuals also possess that characteristic.[6] Therefore, juries could use such testimony to draw the "unwarranted" inference that the defendant was more likely to be guilty because he possessed that characteristic. *State v. Hansen*, 743 P.2d 157, 176 (Or.1987)....

Petitioner's objection that Dr. Bivens' use of statistics had the effect of bolstering the complaining witnesses' testimony raises similar concerns. Here, potential prejudice would arise because the expert's testimony could "guide the jury to a conclusion" that the complaining witnesses were telling the truth by demonstrating that the details in their testimony matched the details in a typical child abuse case, even though fabricated testimony also may include such details. *See State v. Petrich*, 683 P.2d 173, 180 (Wash.1984) (rejecting testimony that in "eighty-five to ninety percent of our cases, the child is molested by someone they already know," because it "invite[d] the jury to conclude that a defendant" was "statistically more likely to have committed the crime"); *see also Hall v. State*, 692 S.W.2d 769, 773 (Ark.App.1985) (rejecting evidence that "in 75 [percent] to 80 [percent] of such cases the perpetrator is known to the children involved," and "50 [percent] of child sexual abuse cases occur in either the home of the child or the perpetrator" as tending "to focus the attention of the jury upon whether the evidence against the defendant matched the evidence in the usual case involving the sexual abuse of a young child."); *Stephens v. State*, 774 P.2d 60, 64 (Wyo.1989) (noting that a "doctor advised the jury that statistically eighty to eighty-five percent of child sexual abuse is committed by a relative close to the child," and that it was "difficult [ ] to understand how statistical information would assist a trier of fact in reaching a determination as to guilt in an individual case.")....

With respect to "the abuse process," Dr. Bivens testified that "between thirteen and a half and seventeen percent of female adolescents and adults and maybe two and a half to six percent of adults and adolescent males will say they were sexually abused," that "eighty-five percent of children or people who report being abused report that they had a preexisting relationship with the molester," that "multiple victims were the rule, not the exception," that "100 percent of incest molesters do so in their own homes," and that "40 percent of molesters had done so with children present and that 25 percent had done so in front of a non-participating adult." Respondent urged that such testimony was relevant to "eliminate [ ] the [jurors'] preconceived notions" concerning child sexual abuse....

Several cases from other jurisdictions appear to support Petitioner's contention that Dr. Bivens' testimony regarding the abuse process was unduly prejudicial. In *Robbie*, the California Court of Appeals rejected expert testimony that demonstrated that a witness' recollection of a defendant's actions during a rape was consistent with conduct which is commonly reported in rape cases. In that case, the complainant's testimony established that the defendant had often acted friendly towards her during the alleged rape. 92 Cal.App.

---

6. For example, it has been noted that "carrying little or no luggage" is a common characteristic of a drug courier. *See, e.g., United States v. Elmore*, 595 F.2d 1036, 1039 n. 3. However, even assuming, *arguendo*, that statistical evidence could be admitted to prove guilt in a criminal case, this evidence would have no probative value on the issue of a particular individual's guilt. The proper statistical evidence would be evidence of *how many people who carry little or no luggage are drug couriers*. Hypothetically, it may be true that 80% of drug couriers carry little or no luggage, but that only 3% of travelers with little or no luggage are drug couriers. Hence, informing the jury that 80% of drug couriers carry little or no luggage is seriously misleading.

4th at 1078. The State called an expert who, although not acquainted with the facts in the specific case, testified in response to hypothetical questions that the specific allegations of the complainant were "common" and that the behavior pattern described "was the most common type of behavior pattern" in cases with sex offenders. *Id.* at 1083.... As in this case, in *Robbie*, the State justified the use of the expert testimony as necessary to "disabuse the jury of common misperceptions about the conduct of a rapist." *Id.* at 1082 (internal quotation marks omitted). The California court noted that in a prior California case, the court had allowed testimony of an expert to disabuse a stereotype about the typical child molester by explaining that "there is no profile of a 'typical' child molester." *Id.* at 1086. However, in *Robbie*, the State went further by "replacing the brutal rapist archetype with another image: *an offender whose behavioral pattern exactly matched the defendant's.*" *Id.* at 1087 (emphasis added). Thus, the California court concluded that "the effect of [the expert's] testimony was not to help the jury objectively evaluate the prosecution evidence," but to "guide the jury to the conclusion that [the] defendant was guilty." *Id.*... Similarly, in *Petrich*, as a part of a statement explaining the extent of delayed reporting, the State's expert testified that in "'eighty-five to ninety percent of our cases, the child is molested by someone they already know.'" 683 P.2d at 180. That court held that the "potential for prejudice [was] significant compared to [the evidence's] minimal probative value, because it "invite[d] the jury to conclude that because of defendant's particular relationship to the victim, he is statistically more likely to have committed the crime." *Id.* Finally, in *Hall v. State*, the court rejected expert testimony because "much of the expert's testimony highlighted details [about the usual sexual abuse case] that were *parallel to the details in the case at hand.*" 692 S.W.2d at 316 (emphasis added)....

Under the analysis suggested by Professor McCord, which compares the necessity of admitting expert testimony to the "understandability" of the statistical evidence, *see* [David] McCord, *Expert Psychological Testimony* [*About Child Complainants In Sexual Abuse Prosecutions: A Foray Into the Admissibility of Novel Psychological Evidence*, 77 J. Crim. L. & Criminology 1,] at 32–33 [(1986)], it appears that Dr. Bivens' testimony regarding the abuse process was erroneously admitted. First, the necessity of introducing such testimony was low when compared to the necessity of introducing expert testimony to explain delayed disclosure or recantation. This court has approved the use of evidence about the "usual" response of a victim in rape cases to explain delayed disclosure or recantation. *See, e.g., Batangan*, 71 Haw. at 557, 799 P.2d at 52, *see also State v. Clark*, 83 Hawai'i 289, 299, 926 P.2d 194, 204 (1996) (allowing expert testimony stating that "victims of domestic violence commonly recant their allegations against their abuser"). In such cases, testimony about whether a scenario was "common" was necessary because without such testimony it was impossible for the jury to accurately assess the witnesses.... In the instant case, however, Respondent sought to admit the testimony regarding the abuse process to "rebut the myth that a sexual abuser tends to be someone who goes to the playground and snatches a kid." As said in *Batangan*, unless it was explained to the jury that delayed reporting and recantation were normal, "such behavior would be attributed to inaccuracy and prevarication," and the jury would likely conclude that the witness' testimony was fabricated. 71 Haw. at 557, 799 P.2d at 52. Unlike in the area of delayed reporting or recantation, such testimony will not necessarily be required to rebut the circumstances posited by Respondent or similar alleged stereotypes.

It is not evident that contemporary jurors continue to possess the stereotypes attributed to them by Respondent. *See United States v. Raymond*, 700 F.Supp.2d 142, 151 (D.Me.2010) ("A jury in 2010 does not need expert testimony to help it understand that not every child abuser is a dirty old man in a wrinkled raincoat who snatches children off the street as they wait for the school bus."); *but see United States v. Romero*, 189 F.3d 576, 584 (7th Cir.1999) (holding that testimony regarding the typical characteristics of sex abusers was "critical in dispelling from the jurors' minds [a] widely held stereotype"). Finally, it may have been possible to rebut the common stereotype Respondent attributed to the jurors without introducing evidence suggesting that the testimony of the complaining witnesses matched the "typical" sexual assault. *See Robbie*, 92 Cal.App. 4th at 1086–87. Thus, Dr. Bivens' testimony regarding the abuse process did not possess the same probative value as his testimony regarding delayed disclosure.

In contrast to the minimal probative value of Dr. Bivens testimony, as discussed *supra*, the potential for prejudice arising from the introduction of evidence regarding the abuse process was high. First, the abundance of statistics presented to the jury which suggested that the testimony of the complaining witnesses matched the "typical" sexual assault and that Petitioner possessed the characteristics of a "typical" sexual offender could have "overwhelmed" the jury and led it to convict on a statistical basis.... This is inconsistent with the concept of proof beyond a reasonable doubt. Second, the statistics may have improperly bolstered the credibility of the complaining witnesses. The jury may have compared the extensive statistics provided regarding the typical perpetrator of sexual abuse and the typical sexual abuse event, and after comparing the statistics to the testimony of the complaining witnesses, used the statistics to conclude that it was likely that the complaining witnesses were telling the truth. However, ... the statistics cited by Dr. Bivens provided no basis for that conclusion. *See Hansen*, 743 P.2d at 176; *see also Hall v. State*, 692 S.W.2d at 773 (holding that testimony that "highlighted details that were parallel to the case at hand" were "prejudicial and distractive"). Therefore, the statistics regarding a "typical" sexual abuse case would have inappropriately bolstered the complaining witnesses' credibility.

The ICA held that Dr. Bivens could not have bolstered the credibility of the complaining witnesses because he "had no knowledge about the facts of the case" and "was only there to give a general overview of the scientific literature on sexual abuse of children." *Transfiguracion*, 2012 WL 5897413 at *2. Dr. Bivens may not have been aware of the facts of the case, but Respondent was. By the nature of the questions asked, studies or statistics may be lined up with the testimony of the complaining witnesses.... [S]uch testimony would lead the jury to improperly conclude that the complaining witnesses were more likely to be telling the truth based on the statistics concerning perpetrators that was provided by Dr. Bivens.... In sum, due to the low probative value of the evidence regarding the abuse process and the significant prejudicial potential of such evidence, substantial concern would arise that the admission of such evidence was erroneous....

With respect to the "grooming process," Dr. Bivens testified that abusers often gain the trust of victims by "developing a loving relationship, touching them non-sexually, doing them favors, telling them they're special." Unlike the evidence regarding the abuse process, Respondent did not contend that this evidence was necessary to rebut a common stereotype. Instead, Respondent argued that the testimony regarding grooming (1) "help[ed][to] explain delayed reporting," and (2) was relevant to show Petitioner's intent. (Citing *State v. Stafford*, 957 P.2d 47 (Or.App.1998).) ...

As to (1), the Oregon Supreme Court's decision in *Hansen* is instructive. In *Hansen*, a detective testified as an expert that "it was normal for child victims of sexual assault to deny that the abuse occurred because they felt guilty and embarrassed and, where they had an emotional tie to the abuser, because they wished to protect the abuser." 743 P.2d at 159. The detective also testified regarding certain "methods an offender will use to get close to the victim." *Id.* He stated that "there is usually a lot of gift giving, a lot of affection, praising, rewards, anything to make the individual more comfortable ... they often establish some emotional dependency." *Id.* at 160.... In evaluating the admissibility of the detective's testimony, the Oregon Supreme Court separated the detective's general testimony that children would not disclose when they had an emotional tie to the abuser from his testimony about the techniques used to gain trust. The Oregon court noted that in Oregon, it was permissible to allow testimony to explain "superficially bizarre behavior" of child sex abuse victims, such as a victims "initial denial." *Id.* (citing *State v. Middleton*, 657 P.2d 1215 (Or.1983)). The Oregon court ruled that, therefore, the detective's testimony that sexually abused children are reluctant to admit the abuse because they were emotionally dependent on the abuser was admissible. *Id.*... However, *Hansen* found the testimony regarding "the specific techniques used by some child abusers" to be "irrelevant to the effect the dependence has on the child's willingness to implicate the abuser." *Id.* at 161. This was because "[i]t is the emotional dependence, *and not the specific acts that produce it*, that helps to explain the child's behavior." *Id.* at 161 (emphasis added).

The distinction drawn by the Oregon Supreme Court in *Hansen* applies to Dr. Bivens' testimony. At one point, Dr. Bivens explained one reason children would delay disclosure would be to protect the abuser. He further explained that "children who have a close relationship with the abuser were almost four times more likely to delay their disclosure beyond a month." Under the distinction drawn by *Hansen*, such testimony serves to explain the delayed disclosure and may have been admissible. *Hansen*, 743 P.2d at 159; *see also Batangan*, 71 Haw. at 556–58, 799 P.2d at 51–52.

However, Dr. Bivens also testified that abusers use tactics such as "treating them nicely, developing a loving relationship, touching them non-sexually, doing them favors, [and] telling them they're special" to gain trust. As explained by *Hansen*, the close relationship, "and not the specific acts that produce it," explain why the child would delay disclosure. *Hansen*, 743 P.2d at 160. Therefore, Dr. Bivens' testimony about the specific tactics of sex offenders was irrelevant to explain why the complaining witnesses in this case delayed disclosure. Therefore, that portion of Dr. Bivens' testimony should have been ruled inadmissible. *Hansen*, 743 P.2d at 160; *cf. Petrich*, 683 P.2d at 180 (holding that testimony that in "eighty-five to ninety percent of our cases, the child is molested by someone they already know" was inadmissible even though it was "made in the context of explaining the extent of delayed reporting in certain types of cases").

Respondent's argument that Dr. Bivens' testimony regarding tactics used to gain trust explained why delayed disclosure occurs misstates Dr. Bivens' testimony. According to Respondent, "Dr. Bivens explained that given the innocent nature of starting behavior, children often did not realize that the succeeding behavior was wrong until they had participated in it to the extent that they would feel guilty in reporting it." ... Respondent's assertion contains no citation to any portion of Dr. Bivens' testimony. Respondent's questioning of Dr. Bivens demonstrates that his testimony about tactics used to gain trust was separate from his discussion about delayed disclosure. After explaining that a close relationship often leads to delayed disclosure, Dr. Bivens then discussed incomplete disclosure, child memory, the location where abuse occurs, and whether abuse occurs with others present, *before* turning to "how abusers gain the trust of children."[7] *Nothing*

---

7. Dr. Bivens testified on this issue as follows:
   Q. *I'd like to turn to how abusers gain the trust of children.* Is there literature on how, basically how abuse occurs?
   A. Yes. And there's even a measure to determine what methods are used most frequently by child molesters.
   Q. And what is that?
   A. So it's something like the gaining-trust scale, or something like that.

indicated that Dr. Bivens connected the methods used to gain trust to delayed disclosure. Contrary to Respondent's position, Dr. Bivens did *not* testify that children delay disclosure because they are confused by the abusers' methods. . . .

As to (2), Respondent and the ICA both cited *State v. Stafford*, 957 P.2d 47 (Or.App.1998), and *Hernandez v. State*, 973 S.W.2d 787 (Tex.App.1998), as holding that testimony about the grooming process can be used to show intent. Both cases are distinguishable. . . . In *Stafford*, the defendant was not charged with sexual assault, but with attempted sexual assault. *Id.* at 48. Testimony by the complainant established that on several occasions, the defendant had placed his hand on the complainant's thigh for approximately five seconds on multiple occasions. *Id.* at 48. The defendant's position was that "his behavior had been misinterpreted by the children and was not related to any sexual gratification." *Id.* To rebut the defendant's argument, the state sought to introduce evidence that the defendant's actions constituted "grooming" and therefore *the act itself* constituted attempted sexual abuse. *Id.* . . . The Oregon Appellate Court distinguished *Stafford* from *Hansen* by explaining that "in *Hansen*, the relevance of the detective's testimony depended on whether the evidence about grooming could explain the student's initial denial of sexual relations with the defendant." *Id.* at 52. In contrast, in *Stafford*, "the evidence about grooming is the gravamen of the charges against defendant" because "[d]efendant's position that his conduct was not intended as grooming behavior puts his intent directly in issue." *Id.* Therefore, the grooming evidence made it "more probable that defendant's motivation for his conduct was for his own eventual sexual gratification." *Id.* . . . Unlike in *Stafford*, in the instant case, Petitioner is not charged with attempted sexual assault, and there is no issue of whether or not his behavior prior to allegedly abusing the complaining witnesses was intended sexually. Instead, as in *Hansen*, "the relevance of the detective's testimony depended on whether the evidence about grooming could explain the student's initial denial of sexual relations with [Petitioner]." *Id.* Thus, *Stafford* is inapplicable.

Respondent and the ICA also cite *Hernandez*. In *Hernandez*, although the Texas court did refer to an expert's testimony on "grooming," there is no indication that the admissibility of the expert's testimony was at issue in the case. *See id.* at 790. Furthermore, the extent of the Texas court's analysis of the expert's testimony was the conclusory assertion that "taken with the expert's testimony on grooming behavior, the boy's testimony tends to make it more likely that Hernandez assaulted the victim." *Id.* Thus, *Hernandez* does not provide a persuasive rationale for admitting the testimony of Dr. Bivens. . . . Accordingly, Respondent offers no reason to suggest that Dr. Bivens' testimony about methods used to gain victims' trust was relevant to a fact at issue in the case. *Hansen*, 743 P.2d at 161. Hence, Dr. Bivens' testimony regarding grooming was irrelevant. . . .

Additionally, evidence regarding the grooming process likely prejudiced Petitioner. Petitioner points to J.H.'s testimony that Petitioner would offer "to take her to Fun Factory" or "tell her that he loved her," as examples of acts that the jury could have examined and "concluded that [Petitioner] must also be a sex offender" on the basis of Dr. Bivens' testimony that "touching [the children] non-sexually," and "telling them they're special," were among the "methods used most frequently by child molesters." Dr. Bivens' testimony therefore suggested that, based on the methods used by Petitioner, there was a "high probability" that Petitioner was a child molester. Testimony that such actions were used "most

---

Q. And what did they do to gain trust?
A. *Well, treating them nicely, developing a loving relationship, touching them non-sexually, doing them favors, telling them they're special, these kinds of things.*
(Emphases added.)

frequently" could have "overwhelmed the jury" and led the jury to convict on the basis of probabilistic evidence. *Cf.* McCord, *Expert Psychological Testimony* at 55–56 (arguing that testimony that an action is "rare" is likely to have "overbearing impressiveness.").

Moreover, … expert testimony that certain actions match the actions of the "typical" sexual abuser can be misleading and may serve to impermissibly bolster the credibility of the complaining witnesses. The jury may use such testimony to infer that it is more likely that the complaining witnesses are telling the truth, even though testimony about the "typical" sexual assault is actually irrelevant for that purpose. In the instant case, Dr. Bivens' testimony could have led the jury to draw the unwarranted inference that the complaining witnesses were likely telling the truth because their testimony about Petitioner's behavior matched the "typical behavior of a child molester." Consequently, even if Dr. Bivens testimony regarding the grooming process was relevant, its probity was outweighed by the danger that statistical evidence would overwhelm the jury and that the jury would improperly use the testimony as evidence that the complaining witnesses testified truthfully.…

There is a likelihood the court erred in allowing Dr. Bivens to testify regarding the characteristics of typical sexual abusers and the typical actions of sexual abusers. Given the record, it cannot be said that these errors were harmless beyond a reasonable doubt. In that regard, this court has held that "where there is a wealth of overwhelming and compelling evidence tending to show the defendant guilty beyond a reasonable doubt, errors in the admission or exclusion of evidence are deemed harmless." *State v. Veikoso*, 126 Hawai'i 267, 277, 270 P.3d 997, 1007 (2011) (internal quotation marks and brackets omitted). In the instant case, it cannot be said that the evidence was overwhelming.[8] As to each count, there was no physical evidence supporting the testimony of the complaining witnesses. The case amounted to a credibility determination regarding the complaining witnesses and Petitioner. Additionally, the erroneously admitted testimony of Dr. Bivens undermined the presumption of innocence, the standard of proof beyond a reasonable doubt, and bolstered the complaining witnesses' credibility. Hence, it cannot be said that the errors were harmless.

III. Child Victim Testimony

A. Right to Confrontation

State v. Arnold

Supreme Court of Ohio, 2010
126 Ohio St. 3d 290, 933 N.E.2d 775

O'CONNOR, J.

Appellant, Michael Arnold, appeals his conviction for raping his four-year-old daughter, M.A. Arnold argues that statements that M.A. made to social worker Kerri Marshall at the Center for Child and Family Advocacy at Nationwide Children's Hospital ("CCFA") were admitted contrary to his rights under the Confrontation Clause of the Sixth Amendment to the United States Constitution and Section 10, Article I of the Ohio Constitution. The court of appeals affirmed Arnold's conviction, holding that Marshall did

---

8. Even including M.H.'s testimony, the evidence was not overwhelming.…

not act as an agent of the police when she questioned M.A. and that M.A.'s statements during the interview were nontestimonial....

In December 2005, Arnold and Wendy Otto lived together in Hilliard, Ohio, with their two young children. Otto testified that upon awakening one night, she discovered that Arnold and their four-year-old daughter, M.A., were locked in a bedroom. Otto demanded that Arnold unlock the door, and when he did, she observed that his boxer shorts were halfway off. Otto also observed that M.A.'s underwear was around her ankles. She suspected sexual abuse, demanded that Arnold leave the premises, and called 9-1-1. Arnold left immediately. By the time paramedics arrived, many police officers were present. M.A. told firefighter-paramedic Charles Fritz that she had been touched in her private area.... Paramedics took Otto and M.A. to Nationwide Children's Hospital, where evidence for a rape kit was collected. While at the hospital, Otto was advised to take M.A. to the CCFA the next day. The record is unclear whether this advice came from the police, paramedics, hospital personnel, or some other source. At some point that night, M.A. was released.

The next morning, Otto took M.A. to the CCFA. The CCFA is part of Children's Hospital and is located across the street from the main hospital. At the CCFA, Marshall, a Nationwide Children's Hospital employee, interviewed M.A. M.A.'s responses to Marshall's questions indicated that she had been sexually abused. This interview is at the heart of Arnold's Confrontation Clause claim.... The interview yielded a variety of relevant information. For example, M.A. stated that Arnold's "pee-pee" went inside her "pee-pee" and that Arnold's mouth touched her "pee-pee." These statements were necessary for M.A.'s medical evaluation and treatment. But M.A. also answered questions that related to the ongoing investigation. For example, in response to Marshall's questions, M.A. stated that Arnold closed and locked the bedroom door before raping her and that Arnold removed her underwear.... After the interview with Marshall, M.A. was physically examined by a pediatric nurse practitioner, Gail Horner, a hospital employee who worked in the CCFA. Horner found two abrasions to M.A.'s hymen, which she concluded had been caused by acute trauma, likely from penetration, within the previous 24 to 72 hours. Horner testified that the abrasions were "diagnostic" of sexual abuse.

Based on this and other information, including Otto's testimony, Arnold was indicted on two counts of rape in violation of R.C. 2907.02. The first count charged rape by vaginal intercourse; the second charged rape by cunnilingus.... At trial, the court determined that M.A. was unavailable to testify. After watching the DVD recording of M.A.'s interview with Marshall, the court determined that the statements had been made for the purpose of medical diagnosis and were admissible hearsay under Evid.R. 803(4). The court also determined that the statements were not barred by the Confrontation Clause. Accordingly, the DVD was played for the jury.... The jury found Arnold guilty of rape by vaginal intercourse, but not guilty of rape by cunnilingus. R.C. 2907.02. Arnold was sentenced to life in prison.

On appeal, the Tenth District affirmed Arnold's conviction. *State v. Arnold*, Franklin App. No. 07AP-789, 2008-Ohio-3471, 2008 WL 2698885. We accepted Arnold's discretionary appeal to determine whether, in a criminal prosecution, the out-of-court statements made by a child to an interviewer employed by a child-advocacy center violates the right to confront witnesses provided by the Sixth Amendment to the United States Constitution and Section 10, Article I of the Ohio Constitution. *State v. Arnold*, 120 Ohio St.3d 1452, 2008-Ohio-6813, 898 N.E.2d 967....

In *Crawford* [*v. Washington*, 541 U.S. 36, 42, 124 S.Ct. 1354 (2004)], the Supreme Court of the United States considered whether the introduction of a hearsay statement admissible under state law violated a defendant's Sixth Amendment right to confront the witnesses against him. The court held that out-of-court statements violate the Sixth Amendment when they are testimonial and the defendant has had no opportunity to cross-examine the declarant. 541 U.S. at 68, 124 S.Ct. 1354, 158 L.Ed.2d 177. See also *State v. Siler*, 116 Ohio St.3d 39, 2007-Ohio-5637, 876 N.E.2d 534, ¶ 21–26. The court did not comprehensively define "testimonial" but stated that the core class of testimonial statements includes statements "'that were made under circumstances which would lead an objective witness reasonably to believe that the statement would be available for use at a later trial.'" *Crawford*, 541 U.S. at 52, 124 S.Ct. 1354, 158 L.Ed.2d 177, quoting Brief of Amicus Curiae National Association of Criminal Defense Lawyers 3. Accord *State v. Stahl*, 111 Ohio St.3d 186, 2006-Ohio-5482, 855 N.E.2d 834, paragraph one of the syllabus. The court emphasized that the objective-witness test was but one of many possible ways to determine whether a statement is testimonial, and it expressly stated, "We leave for another day any effort to spell out a comprehensive definition of 'testimonial.'" *Crawford*, 541 U.S. at 68, 124 S.Ct. 1354, 158 L.Ed.2d 177.

Two years later, in *Davis v. Washington* (2006), 547 U.S. 813, 821, 126 S.Ct. 2266, 165 L.Ed.2d 224, the court considered whether a caller's responses to a dispatcher's interrogation during a 9-1-1 telephone conversation were testimonial when the caller failed to appear to testify at trial. The court stated (1) that the statements described the events as they were happening, as opposed to explaining events that had happened in the past, (2) that any reasonable listener would conclude that the statements were made in the face of an ongoing emergency, (3) that the interrogation was objectively necessary to resolve the ongoing emergency, and (4) that the interrogation was informal because it was conducted over the phone and the answers were provided frantically while in an unsafe environment. Id. at 827. The court concluded that the circumstances surrounding the interrogation "objectively indicate [that] its primary purpose was to enable police assistance to meet an ongoing emergency. [The caller] simply was not acting as a *witness*; she was not *testifying*." (Emphasis sic.) Id. at 828. Accordingly, the court concluded that the caller's hearsay statements were not testimonial and, therefore, that they were not barred by the Sixth Amendment. Id. at 829.

In *Davis*, the court also considered a second case in which a domestic-violence complainant did not appear at trial. Id. at 819–820. The police officer who interviewed the victim at the scene of the incident and who witnessed her complete and sign an affidavit concerning the abuse testified at trial in order to authenticate the affidavit. Id. at 820. The court determined (1) that the interrogation sought to determine what had happened, not what was happening, (2) that there was no ongoing emergency, (3) that the interrogation was not needed to resolve an emergency, and (4) that the interrogation was "formal enough" that it was conducted in a room separate from the complainant's husband. Id. at 830. The court concluded that "[i]t is entirely clear from the circumstances that the interrogation was part of an investigation into possibly criminal past conduct— as, indeed, the testifying officer expressly acknowledged." Id. at 829. Accordingly, the court concluded that the hearsay evidence was testimonial and, therefore, that it was barred by the Sixth Amendment. Id. at 834.... The court held that "[s]tatements are non-testimonial when made in the course of police interrogation under circumstances objectively indicating that the primary purpose of the interrogation is to enable police assistance to meet an ongoing emergency. They are testimonial when the circumstances objectively indicate that there is no such ongoing emergency, and that the primary purpose of the interrogation is to establish or prove past events potentially relevant to later criminal prosecution." Id. at 822. Accord *Siler*, 116 Ohio St.3d 39, 2007-Ohio-5637, 876 N.E.2d 534, paragraph one of the syllabus....

In *Stahl*, this court considered whether hearsay statements by a rape victim to a nurse practitioner during a medical examination at a hospital DOVE[1] unit were admissible when the victim was not available to testify at trial. *Stahl*, 111 Ohio St.3d 186, 2006-Ohio-5482, 855 N.E.2d 834, at ¶ 1. The defendant argued that the statements violated his Sixth Amendment right to confront witnesses. Id. at ¶ 1, 9. This court distinguished *Davis*, stating: "They involve statements made to law-enforcement officers, while the statement at issue here covers one made to a medical professional at a medical facility for the *primary* purpose of receiving proper medical treatment and not investigating past events related to criminal prosecution." (Emphasis sic.) Id. at ¶ 25. We concluded that the primary purpose of the examination was to receive medical treatment, not to investigate past events, applied the objective-witness test outlined in *Crawford*, and held that the challenged statements were nontestimonial. Id. at ¶ 47, 48.

In *State v. Muttart*, 116 Ohio St.3d 5, 2007-Ohio-5267, 875 N.E.2d 944, a child victim of sexual abuse was interviewed by a social worker at a child-advocacy center. Id., ¶ 14–15. As in the case before us now, the social worker interviewed the child before she was examined by a doctor. Id., ¶ 15. During the interview, the child disclosed to the social worker that her father had put his penis in her mouth and had " 'put his pee-pee in her pee-pee.' " Id., ¶ 16. The child also disclosed that similar conduct had happened " 'a whole bunch of times.' " Id. We held that the child's statements were nontestimonial because "[s]tatements made to medical personnel for purposes of diagnosis or treatment are not inadmissible under *Crawford*." Id., ¶ 63. This is true because statements for medical diagnosis and treatment "are not even remotely related to the evils that the Confrontation Clause was designed to avoid." Id.

In *Siler*, we considered whether statements made by a child to a sheriff's deputy in the course of a police interrogation were testimonial. *Siler*, 116 Ohio St.3d 39, 2007-Ohio-5637, 876 N.E.2d 534, at ¶ 2. We concluded that "the statements made to the deputy sheriff were testimonial because the circumstances objectively indicate that no ongoing emergency existed and that the primary purpose of the police interrogation was to establish past events potentially relevant to a later criminal prosecution." Id. We held that courts in Ohio should apply the primary-purpose test set forth in *Davis* to determine "whether a child declarant's statement made in the course of police interrogation is testimonial or nontestimonial." Id. at paragraph one of the syllabus, citing *Davis*, 547 U.S. at 821–822, 126 S.Ct. 2266, 165 L.Ed.2d 224....

We recognize that a number of ... decisions held that statements by child-sexual-abuse victims at child-advocacy centers or their functional equivalent are testimonial and, therefore, inadmissible pursuant to the Confrontation Clause and *Crawford* when the defendant has no opportunity to cross-examine the victim at trial. See, e.g., *State v. Contreras* (Fla.2008), 979 So.2d 896; *State v. Hooper* (2007), 145 Idaho 139, 176 P.3d 911; *In re Rolandis G.* (2008), 232 Ill.2d 13, 327 Ill.Dec. 479, 902 N.E.2d 600; *State v. Bentley* (Iowa 2007), 739 N.W.2d 296; *State v. Henderson* (2007), 284 Kan. 267, 160 P.3d 776; *State v. Snowden* (2005), 385 Md. 64, 867 A.2d 314; *State v. Justus* (Mo.2006), 205 S.W.3d 872; *State v. Blue*, 2006 ND 134, 717 N.W.2d 558. But in each of these cases, the interviews were conducted solely for forensic purposes. The situation we are presented with in this case is distinct from those considered in the above-cited cases. Here we are asked to determine whether statements that contain distinct forensic and medical diagnostic in-

---

1. "DOVE" stands for "Developing Options for Violent Emergencies." *Stahl*, 111 Ohio St.3d 186, 2006-Ohio-5482, 855 N.E.2d 834, at ¶ 2. The unit specializes in health-care services for victims of sexual assault and domestic disturbances. Id.

formation and were made to a social worker during one interview implicate the Confrontation Clause. For example, in *Contreras*, the Florida Supreme Court held that a statement taken by the coordinator of a "child protection team" ("CPT") was testimonial. Id. at 905. The interview was conducted and videotaped at a shelter for victims of domestic violence, and a police officer was connected electronically to the CPT coordinator in order to suggest questions. Id. There was no evidence that the child received medical treatment based on the interview. The court held that "the primary, if not the sole, purpose of the CPT interview was to investigate whether the crime of child sexual abuse had occurred, and to establish facts potentially relevant to a later criminal prosecution." Id.

Similarly, the Illinois Supreme Court excluded statements made in a forensic interview when there was "absolutely no indication that * * * [the] interview * * * was conducted, to a substantial degree, for treatment rather than investigative purposes." *In re Rolandis G.*, 232 Ill.2d at 33, 327 Ill.Dec. 479, 902 N.E.2d 600. In that case, after stating that an older child forced him to perform fellatio, a six-year-old was taken to a child-advocacy center and was interviewed by a child advocate. Id. at 19. The interview was video recorded and observed by a detective through a one-way mirror. Id. As with *Contreras*, there was no indication that the child received a medical evaluation or treatment based on the interview. The Illinois Supreme Court concluded that "the interview took place at the behest of the police so that a more detailed account of the alleged sexual abuse could be obtained by a trained interviewer and memorialized on videotape" and held that the child's statements were testimonial. Id. at 32.

In *Hooper*, the Idaho Supreme Court excluded statements in a video-recorded forensic interview taken at a Sexual Trauma Abuse Response Center ("STAR"). 145 Idaho at 141, 176 P.3d 911. In that case, a child was taken to the STAR center after her mother discovered the child and her father locked in the bathroom and suspected sexual abuse. Id. at 140. Upon arrival at the STAR center, the child met with a doctor and the doctor conducted a sexual-abuse examination. Id. at 141. After the medical examination, a forensic interviewer conducted a video-recorded interview with the child, which a detective observed via a closed-circuit system. Id. Because the interview occurred after the child met with and was examined by the physician, the subsequent interview served a forensic, not a medical or treatment-oriented, purpose.

In the same vein, the Kansas Supreme Court held that a child's statements during an interview conducted by a detective and a social worker, both members of the Exploited and Missing Children Unit, were testimonial. *Henderson*, 284 Kan. at 294, 160 P.3d 776. In *Henderson*, a mother took her three-year-old daughter to a medical clinic after noticing discharge from the child's vagina and after the child complained that her "potty place" hurt. Id. at 269. Test results revealed that the child had gonorrhea. Id. After learning about the test results, the detective and social worker interviewed the child, who disclosed that her mother's boyfriend had "touched her 'potty in a bad way.'" Id. at 270. This interview was video and audio recorded. Id. Again, there is no indication that the child received additional medical treatment based on the interview.

These cases that stand for the proposition that the admission of statements obtained during interviews at CACs or their functional equivalents result in violations of the Confrontation Clause when the declarant is unavailable at trial arise from scenarios in which the statements at issue were solely for forensic purposes, rather than for ameliorative or therapeutic ones.... In the latter category, our sister courts hold that statements made by child-sexual-abuse victims for the purpose of medical diagnosis and treatment are not testimonial and, therefore, do not implicate the Confrontation Clause even if they are used subsequently by the state in a prosecution. *Seely v. State* (2008), 373 Ark. 141, 282

S.W.3d 778 (holding that a child's statements about abuse to a social worker at a children's hospital before the child was examined by a doctor were nontestimonial); *State v. Arroyo* (2007), 284 Conn. 597, 935 A.2d 975 (holding that statements made to a social worker were nontestimonial because the primary purpose of the interview was to provide medical assistance to the child); *State v. Krasky* (Minn.2007), 736 N.W.2d 636 (holding that a child's statements to a nurse alleging sexual abuse were nontestimonial because the nurse's primary purpose was to assess and protect the child's health and welfare); *State v. Spencer*, 339 Mont. 227, 2007 MT 245, 169 P.3d 384 (holding that statements to a counselor regarding sexual abuse were nontestimonial); *People v. Vigil* (Colo.2006), 127 P.3d 916 (holding that responses to questions by a doctor as part of a sexual-assault examination were nontestimonial); *Commonwealth v. DeOliveira* (2006), 447 Mass. 56, 849 N.E.2d 218 (holding that statements to a physician were made for the purposes of medical evaluation and treatment and were not testimonial); *Hobgood v. State* (Miss.2006), 926 So.2d 847 (holding that a child's description of sexual abuse to his doctor was not given for the purpose of prosecuting the accused and was not testimonial); *State v. Vaught* (2004), 268 Neb. 316, 682 N.W.2d 284 (holding that a child's statements to an emergency-room physician identifying the perpetrator of sexual assault were nontestimonial).

With this background in mind, we turn to whether M.A.'s statements to Marshall were testimonial.... Pursuant to *Stahl, Muttart,* and *Siler,* to determine whether M.A.'s statements to Marshall were testimonial, we must identify the primary purpose of the statements. Statements made for the purpose of medical diagnosis and treatment are nontestimonial. *Muttart*, 116 Ohio St.3d 5, 2007-Ohio-5267, 875 N.E.2d 944, ¶ 63. However, statements made to agents of the police for the primary purpose of forensic investigation are testimonial. *Siler*, 116 Ohio St.3d 39, 2007-Ohio-5637, 876 N.E.2d 534, at ¶ 2....

The objective of a child-advocacy center like the CCFA is neither exclusively medical diagnosis and treatment nor solely forensic investigation. "'The purpose of a Children's Advocacy Center is to provide a comprehensive, culturally competent, multidisciplinary response to allegations of child abuse in a dedicated, child friendly setting.'" Nancy Chandler, Children's Advocacy Centers: Making a Difference One Child at a Time (2006), 28 Hamline J.Pub.L. & Policy 315, quoting National Children's Alliance, Accreditation Guidelines for Children's Advocacy Centers (2004) 5.... "Prior to the development of the Children's Advocacy Center model, 'traditional child abuse investigations often subject[ed] the child to multiple interviews.'" Id. at 332, quoting Lisa Snell, Child Advocacy Centers: One Stop on the Road to Performance-Based Child Protection (June 2003) 1. A child-advocacy center's "'number one goal'" is to reduce trauma to a child-abuse victim by coordinating the interview to include professionals from multiple agencies, which, in turn, can reduce the number of interviews needed and improve the quality of the investigation, the diagnosis, and the recommendation for treatment. Id. at 323. Additionally, "'[t]hey help children avoid the trauma of repeating their story at various stops along the legal and judicial path.'" Id. These interdisciplinary teams often include law-enforcement professionals, prosecutors, medical and mental-health personnel, and child advocates. Id. at 324.

At the CCFA, Marshall, a social worker employed by Nationwide Children's Hospital, interviews children who are suspected victims of physical or sexual abuse. The purpose of the interview is to gather as much information as possible. The interview is both recorded on a DVD and transmitted to another room via closed-circuit television. Typically, a nurse practitioner or doctor, a children's services caseworker, and a law-enforcement representative watch the interview from a separate room. Marshall does not inform the child that the team members are watching the interview, but does tell him or her that he or she will be examined by a doctor or nurse after the interview.

After Marshall interviews the child, she meets with the doctor or nurse practitioner who will perform the medical examination to review the child's statements. The nurse or doctor conducts the appropriate medical examination based on the child's statements during the interview. The nurse or doctor relies on information obtained during Marshall's interview to determine what examination and tests are needed. For example, information regarding the identity of the perpetrator, the age of the perpetrator, the type of abuse alleged, and the time frame of the abuse allows the doctor or nurse to determine whether to test the child for sexually transmitted infections....

Child-advocacy centers are unique. Multidisciplinary teams cooperate so that the child is interviewed only once and will not have to retell the story multiple times. Most members of the team retain their autonomy. Neither police officers nor medical personnel become agents of the other. However, to ensure that the child victim goes through only one interview, the interviewer must elicit as much information from the child as possible in a single interview and must gather the information needed by each team member. Thus, the interview serves dual purposes: (1) to gather forensic information to investigate and potentially prosecute a defendant for the offense and (2) to elicit information necessary for medical diagnosis and treatment of the victim. The interviewer acts as an agent of each member of the multidisciplinary team....

Certainly, some of the statements that M.A. made to Marshall primarily served a forensic or investigative purpose. Those statements include M.A.'s assertion that Arnold shut and locked the bedroom door before raping her; her descriptions of where her mother and brother were while she was in the bedroom with Arnold, of Arnold's boxer shorts, of him removing them, and of what Arnold's "pee-pee" looked like; and her statement that Arnold removed her underwear. These statements likely were not necessary for medical diagnosis or treatment. Rather, they related primarily to the state's investigation. Marshall effectively acted as an agent of the police for the purpose of obtaining these statements.

Because Marshall acted as an agent of the police in obtaining these statements, pursuant to *Davis* and *Siler*, we must employ the primary-purpose test to determine whether the primary purpose of the interrogation was " 'to enable police assistance to meet an ongoing emergency.' " *Siler*, 116 Ohio St.3d 39, 2007-Ohio-5637, 876 N.E.2d 534, at paragraph one of the syllabus, quoting *Davis*, 547 U.S. at 822, 126 S.Ct. 2266, 165 L.Ed.2d 224. We hold that it was not. First, the statements involved a description of past events. The alleged abuse occurred the previous evening, and the questioning specifically attempted to obtain a description of the abuse. Second, a reasonable observer would not perceive an ongoing emergency at the time of questioning. The patient had been discharged from the hospital the previous evening. At oral argument, counsel conceded that no medical emergency existed at the time of Marshall's interview. Third, the questioning was not objectively necessary to resolve an emergency because there was no ongoing emergency. Finally, the interview was rather formal, more akin to the videotaped, planned interview of *Crawford* than to the frantic 9-1-1 call or the sequestered but spur-of-the-moment interview recounted in *Davis*.

The primary purpose of that portion of the interview was not to meet an ongoing emergency but, rather, to further the state's forensic investigation. Thus, these statements were testimonial in nature and their admission without a prior opportunity for cross-examination is prohibited by the Confrontation Clause. *Crawford*, 541 U.S. at 68, 124 S.Ct. 1354, 158 L.Ed.2d 177.... Although the statements obtained during Marshall's interview of M.A. that related primarily to the state's forensic investigation are testimonial and thus inadmissible pursuant to *Crawford*, other statements provided information that was necessary to diagnose and medically treat M.A. The history obtained during the interview is important for the doctor or nurse practitioner to make an accurate diagnosis and to determine what evaluation and treatment are necessary. For example, the nurse practitioner conducts a "head to toe" examination of all children, but only examines the genital area of patients who disclose sexual abuse. That portion of the exam is to identify any trauma or injury sustained during the alleged abuse.... M.A.'s statements that described the acts that Arnold performed, including that Arnold touched her "pee-pee," that Arnold's "pee-pee" went inside her "pee-pee," that Arnold's "pee-pee" touched her "butt," that Arnold's hand touched her "pee-pee," and that Arnold's mouth touched her "pee-pee," were thus necessary for the proper medical diagnosis and treatment of M.A.

In his dissent, Justice Pfeifer states that he is troubled by our conclusion that these statements were medically necessary because M.A. had been examined at the hospital on the night of the rape. However, although M.A. was taken to the hospital on the night of the rape, the record establishes only that a rape-kit examination was performed, not that she was examined for medical diagnosis or treated. M.A. was referred to the CCFA for further medical examination and treatment. Justice Pfeifer also contends that the nurse practitioner who examined M.A. after the interview would have asked all medically relevant questions during the examination. This is not true. The history obtained during Marshall's interview was necessary for the nurse practitioner to make an accurate diagnosis and to determine what treatment was necessary. Horner, the nurse practitioner who examined M.A., testified that the "forensic interview guides my exam in that it lets me know whether or not I need to test the child for sexually transmitted infection. For instance, if a child says that a penis touched their vagina, it means to me that I need to test to make sure that child didn't get a sexually transmitted infection." ... In eliciting these medically necessary statements, Marshall acted as an agent of the nurse practitioner who examined M.A., not of the investigating police officers. Because Marshall did not act as an agent of the police in obtaining these statements, they are not inadmissible pursuant to *Davis*. *Stahl*, 111 Ohio St.3d 186, 2006-Ohio-5482, 855 N.E.2d 834, at ¶ 25, 36.

Statements made for medical diagnosis and treatment are nontestimonial. *Muttart*, 116 Ohio St.3d 5, 2007-Ohio-5267, 875 N.E.2d 944, ¶ 63. There is no basis in the law for concluding that Marshall's dual capacity renders statements made by M.A. for the purpose of medical diagnosis and treatment inadmissible pursuant to the Confrontation Clause. Indeed, in *Davis*, the United States Supreme Court acknowledged that the same interview or interrogation might produce both testimonial and nontestimonial statements. *Davis*, 547 U.S. at 828–829, 126 S.Ct. 2266, 165 L.Ed.2d 224. As the court stated in *Davis*, "This presents no great problem." Id. at 829. "[T]rial courts will recognize the point at which, for Sixth Amendment purposes, statements in response to interrogations become testimonial. Through *in limine* procedure, they should redact or exclude the portions of any statement that have become testimonial, as they do, for example, with unduly prejudicial portions of otherwise admissible evidence." Id.

Both dissents criticize our reliance on *Davis* in support of our conclusion that although M.A.'s forensic statements to Marshall were testimonial, her statements for the purpose of medical diagnosis and treatment were properly admitted. First, Justice Pfeifer argues that pursuant to *Davis*, when evidence includes testimonial and nontestimonial statements, the testimonial statements must be redacted or excluded to avoid violating the defendant's right to confront witnesses against him. We agree that M.A.'s testimonial statements should have been excluded, and we remand the case to the court of appeals to determine whether the admission of M.A.'s testimonial statements was harmless error. Next, both dissents argue that our reliance on *Davis* is erroneous because we examine the statements on a question-by-question basis and the testimonial and nontestimonial statements were interspersed, rather than being obtained in separate and distinct portions of the interview. Justice Pfeifer argues that this will make it difficult to distinguish the statements that should be redacted from those that may be properly admitted. However, our guiding consideration is the purpose for which the statements are made, not the order in which they are obtained. Finally, he notes that unlike in *Davis*, there was no ongoing emergency in this case and, therefore, there was no occasion for the questioning in this case to evolve from nontestimonial to testimonial. Our decision is not based on the evolution of M.A.'s statements, but on the fact that the statements were made for different purposes. The fact that *Davis* involved an evolution from nontestimonial to testimonial statements does not preclude its application in instances in which an interview simultaneously serves dual purposes.... Further, the fact that police officers watched the interview and that it was recorded does not change the fact that the statements were necessary for M.A.'s medical diagnosis and treatment. Similarly, the fact that information gathered for medical purposes is subsequently used by the state does not change the fact that the statements were made for medical diagnosis and treatment. *Muttart*, 116 Ohio St.3d 5, 2007-Ohio-5267, 875 N.E.2d 944, ¶ 62. M.A.'s statements that were necessary for medical diagnosis and treatment were nontestimonial and were properly admitted without violating Arnold's Confrontation Clause rights....

When Marshall interviewed M.A. at the CCFA, she occupied dual capacities: she was both a forensic interviewer collecting information for use by the police and a medical interviewer eliciting information necessary for diagnosis and treatment. We hold that statements made to interviewers at child-advocacy centers that are made for medical diagnosis and treatment are nontestimonial and are admissible without offending the Confrontation Clause. Thus, we affirm the judgment of the court of appeals to the extent that M.A.'s statements to Marshall for the purpose of medical treatment and diagnosis were properly admitted. We further hold that statements made to interviewers at child-advocacy centers that serve primarily a forensic or investigative purpose are testimonial and are inadmissible pursuant to the Confrontation Clause when the declarant is unavailable for cross-examination at trial. We agree with Arnold that the trial court erred in admitting the forensic statements made by M.A. to Marshall and reverse the court of appeal's judgment insofar as it held that these forensic statements were admissible. However, because the court of appeals did not consider whether the admission of M.A.'s forensic statement to Marshall was harmless, see *State v. Conway*, 108 Ohio St.3d 214, 2006-Ohio-791, 842 N.E.2d 996, we remand the case to the court of appeals to consider this issue.

Judgment affirmed in part and reversed in part, and cause remanded.

LUNDBERG STRATTON, LANZINGER, and CUPP, JJ., concur.

PFEIFER and O'DONNELL, JJ., dissent.

BROWN, C.J., not participating....

[Pfeifer and O'Donnell, JJ., dissenting opinions are omitted].

Notes

For commentary regarding confrontation and capacity issues, see Thomas D. Lyon and Stacia N. Stolzenberg, *Children's Memory for Conversations About Sexual Abuse: Legal and Psychological Implications*, 19 ROGER WILLIAMS U. L. REV. 411 (2014); Deborah Paruch, *Silencing the Victims in Child Sexual Abuse Prosecutions: the Confrontation Clause and Children's Hearsay Statements Before and After Michigan v. Bryant*, 28 TOURO L. REV. 85 (2012); Thomas D. Lyon and Julia A. Dente, *Child Witnesses and the Confrontation Clause*, 102 J. CRIM. L. & CRIMINOLOGY 1181 (2012); Laurie Shanks, *Evaluating Children's Competency to Testify: Developing A Rational Method to Assesss A Young Child's Capacity to Offer Reliable Testimony In Cases Alleging Child Sex Abuse*, 58 Clev. St. L. Rev. 575 (2010); Kimberly Y. Chin, *"Minute and Separate": Considering the Admissibility of Videotaped Forensic Interviews in Child Sexual Abuse Cases After Crawford and Davis*, 30 B.C. Third World L.J. 67 (2010); John J. Gochnour, *The First Complaint: An Approach to the Admission of Child-Hearsay Statements Under the Alaska Rules of Evidence*, 27 Alaska L. Rev. 71 (2010); Note, *Presuming Innocence: Expanding the Confrontation Clause Analysis to Protect Children and Defendants in Child Sexual Abuse Prosecutions*, 93 Minn. L. Rev. 1090 (2009). For discussion of the use of therapy dogs to accompany children when testifying in sexual abuse cases, see Abigayle L. Grimm, *An Examination of Why Permitting Therapy Dogs to Assist Child-Victims When Testifying During Criminal Trials Should Not Be Permitted*, 16 J. Gend., Race & Just. 263 (2013).

B. Repressed Memory

State v. Burke ex Rel. County of La Paz

Court of Appeals of Arizona, 2012
2012 WL 1470103

SWANN, Judge.

In January 2010, Defendant was convicted of three counts of sexual conduct with a minor under the age of twelve and one count of aggravated assault; those convictions were subsequently overturned by this court in 1 CA-CR 10-0504, 2011 WL 3805914 (Aug. 25, 2011), because the trial court improperly allowed the entirety of the interviews with the victim to be played for the jury. At Defendant's first trial in January 2010, Defendant introduced expert testimony from Dr. Phillip Esplin. Dr. Esplin is a licensed psychologist who specializes in forensic psychology and more specifically in interview techniques for and investigation of child sex crimes.

On December 5, 2011, and again on January 6, 2012, the state requested disclosure of information and documentation to establish the reliability of Dr. Esplin's opinions and expected testimony at a second trial under Ariz. R.Crim. Proc. 15.2. Defendant never provided the documentation. On January 5, 2012, Defendant responded to the state's motion ... [footnote omitted] to exclude Dr. Esplin's testimony and the state's request for an evidentiary hearing under *Daubert v. Merrell Dow Pharmaceuticals, Inc.*, 509 U.S. 579 (1993). In the response, Defendant outlined the criteria set forth in *United States v. Amaral*, 488 F.2d 1148 (9th Cir.1973), and *State v. Chapple*, 135 Ariz. 281, 660 P.2d 1208 (1983), and explained without documentation or external citation that Dr. Esplin's testimony satisfied the admissibility criteria. Defendant argued that credibility of witnesses was a matter for the jury and that "challenges to Dr. Esplin's factual basis or the sufficiency of his methodology are issues for cross-examination and not a basis for exclusion." Defendant made no attempt to explain the admissibility of Dr. Esplin's testimony under the substantially revised Arizona Rule of Evidence 702 now in effect. The state replied, highlighting this omission and Defendant's failure to provide the basis for Dr. Esplin's opinions, and arguing that Dr. Esplin's testimony is inadmissible under Rule 702.... The court examined the transcript of Dr. Esplin's testimony from the first trial and pointed out a series of questions and answers that would not be allowed for the second trial because they impinged on the jury's role in determining credibility. The court ultimately ruled that Dr. Esplin would be able to testify as an expert and that his testimony could include testimony about "false memory."

The state brought this petition for special action, arguing that the trial court erred by ruling *in limine* to allow Dr. Esplin to testify about "False Memory Syndrome" without properly considering or finding any of the Rule 702 factors prior to the ruling. Accordingly, the state requests that this court exclude Dr. Esplin's testimony about "False Memory Syndrome" or, in the alternative, remand and require Defendant to disclose the basis for Dr. Esplin's testimony so the trial court can make an "adequate admissibility determination."...

Because we agree that this is an issue of first impression and statewide importance, and that no other remedy is available to the state, we exercise our discretion to accept jurisdiction.... [citations omitted].... The current Arizona Rule of Evidence 702, effective January 1, 2012, adopts Federal Rule of Evidence 702 and states:

> A witness who is qualified as an expert by knowledge, skill, experience, training, or education may testify in the form of an opinion or otherwise if:
>
> (a) the expert's scientific, technical, or other specialized knowledge will help the trier of fact to understand the evidence or to determine a fact in issue;
>
> (b) the testimony is based on sufficient facts or data;
>
> (c) the testimony is the product of reliable principles and methods; and
>
> (d) the expert has reliably applied the principles and methods to the facts of the case.

The new language of Rule 702 marks a notable departure from Arizona's former test for the admissibility of expert testimony that was detailed in *Logerquist v. McVey*, 196 Ariz. 470, 1 P.3d 113 (2000).[2] The comment to the new Arizona Rule 702 notes that the change from *Logerquist* and the former Rule 702 "recognizes that trial courts should serve as gatekeepers in assuring that proposed expert testimony is reliable and thus helpful to the jury's determination of facts at issue."

Because no Arizona case law exists to provide guidance to trial courts considering admissibility of expert testimony under the new Rule 702, we look to the decisions of federal courts applying *Daubert* and Federal Rule 702. In *Kumho Tire Co., Ltd. v. Carmichaei*, 526 U.S. 137 (1999)—the third case in the *Daubert* trilogy that resulted in the current Federal Rule 702—the Supreme Court noted that when considering the admissibility of expert testimony, the trial judge has the discretion "both to avoid unnecessary 'reliability' proceedings in ordinary cases where the reliability of an expert's methods is properly taken for granted, and to require appropriate proceedings in the less usual or more complex cases where cause for questioning the expert's reliability arises." *Id.* at 152. Accordingly, because it is within the trial court's discretion to hold a hearing to determine the reliability of expert testimony, the lack of a hearing constitutes an abuse of that discretion when the evidentiary record is insufficient to allow the court to make a proper reliability determination under Rule 702. *Padillas v. Stork–Gamco, Inc.*, 186 F.3d 412, 418 (3d Cir.1999).

Here, the court did not conduct a hearing in accordance with Rule 702 or *Daubert* before the first trial. Indeed, given the lax standards of *Logerquist* and the version of Rule 702 then in effect, there would have been no reason to do so. But under the new rule, it is difficult to discern how the trial court could have conducted the requisite analysis without the benefit of a hearing or, at a minimum, review of the requested disclosures regarding the basis of Dr. Esplin's testimony. Though the trial court did review the testimony from the first trial, and may have some personal recollection of the general

---

2. *Logerquist* prescribed a very low threshold for the admissibility of scientific evidence, rooted in the test outlined in *Frye v. United States*, 293 F. 1013 (D.C.Cir.1923)—the same test rejected by the federal courts in *Daubert* and the subsequent amendment to Federal Rule 702.

methodologies used by Dr. Esplin, the court has been provided no offer of proof regarding False Memory Syndrome.[3]

The trial court pointed to *Steward v. State*, 652 N.E.2d 490 (Ind.1995), to justify admitting Dr. Esplin's proposed testimony under a *Daubert*[-]style test. In *Steward*, the Indiana court explained in dicta that "once a child's credibility is called into question, proper expert testimony *may* be appropriate" to explain "unexpected behavior patterns seemingly inconsistent with the claim of abuse." *Id.* at 499 (emphasis added). The Indiana court continued that "a trial court may consider permitting [such] expert testimony, *if [it is] based upon reliable scientific principles.*" *Id.* (emphasis added). Even under the authority upon which the trial court relied, therefore, a reliability determination is necessarily a precursor to admissibility. The record here shows that no such determination was made.

As for the court's reliance on *State v. Speers*, 209 Ariz. 125, 98 P.3d 560 (App.2005), that too is ultimately misplaced. The most obvious distinguishing characteristic between *Speers* and the present case is that *Speers* relied on *Logerquist*—a case without continuing force as a matter of Arizona law. *Id.* at 129, ¶ 14, 98 P.3d at 564. Though it is true that we recognized *Frye*'s inapplicability to expert testimony that was not about "scientific principles advanced by others," there still was no discussion of how the proposed testimony in *Speers* satisfied the elements of *Daubert* (or any rule substantially equivalent to the new Rule 702) in a manner that justifies admission under current law. *Id.* at 130, ¶¶ 18–19, 98 P.3d at 565. An additional and equally important factual difference is that in *Speers* we made explicit reference to "material provided to the trial court in support of the expert testimony." *Id.* at 130, ¶ 15, 98 P.3d at 565. Not only is no such material in the record of this case, such material is exactly what the state requested and Defendant failed to provide.

Accordingly, we hold that the evidentiary record available to the court here was insufficient to permit it to make a legally adequate determination that Dr. Esplin's testimony was admissible. The trial court therefore abused its discretion by failing to perform its gatekeeping role as required by Rule 702....

We accept jurisdiction of this special action and grant relief. We remand this case to the trial court for an evidentiary hearing or for the consideration of written evidence (after disclosure) and argument regarding the manner in which Dr. Esplin's testimony squares with the requirements of Rule 702.

CONCURRING: MICHAEL J. BROWN, and JON W. THOMPSON, Judges.

Notes

The court in *Burke* referenced *Logerquist v. McVey*, 196 Ariz. 470, 1 P.3d 113 (2000), which, until 2010 in Arizona, had allowed for a much less stringent admission policy with respect to expert testimony on repressed memory. For commentary on the issue of repressed memory and the *Logerquist* decision specifically, see Crane McClennen, *Frye, Daubert, and Logerquist: Is Arizona Moving Ahead or Going in Circles?*, 34 ARIZ. ST. L.J. 571 (2002); Lori A. Van Daele, *Logerquist v. McVey: Frye, Daubert, or "Non-Scientific" Expert Testimony?*, 42 JURIMETRICS 85 (2001); D.H. Kaye, *Choice and Boundary Problems in Logerquist, Hummert,*

---

3. The trial court noted that this court did not "say anything about either party's expert testimony at the last trial" in the appeal from the resulting convictions. We note that not only was the propriety of the expert testimony not an issue in the former appeal, the current version of Rule 702 was not in effect—our silence on the issue therefore lends nothing to the trial court's ruling or Defendant's position.

and Kumho Tire, 33 ARIZ. ST. L.J. 41 (2001); David L. Faigman, *Embracing the Darkness: Logerquist v. McVey and the Doctrine of Ignorance of Science Is An Excuse*, 33 ARIZ. ST. L.J. 87 (2001); Edward J. Imwinkelried, *Logerquist v. McVey: the Majority's Flawed Procedural Assumptions*, 33 ARIZ. ST. L.J. 122 (2001); Tomika N. Stevens, *The Admissibility of Expert Testimony on Repressed Memories of Childhood Sexual Abuse in Logerquist v. McVey: Reliability Takes A Backseat to Relevancy*, 46 VILL. L. REV. 385 (2001). In 2010, however, Arizona began a legislative movement to revise its decade-long *Frye/Logerquist* approach and amend its Rule 702 to adopt the *Daubert* perspective on the admissibility of expert opinion. In 2012, the version of Rule 702 described in *Burke* became effective, thereby forcing trial courts to serve as gatekeepers for all expert testimony. Under the amended *"Daubert"* standard, an expert must explain his or her methodology and demonstrate in some objectively verifiable way that he or she has chosen a reliable method and followed it. This may have a greater effect on the reliability of scientific-based testimony and less effect on experience-based expert opinion and, therefore, despite a seemingly stricter standard, may not preclude general testimony by experts on issues related to child sexual abuse behaviors. For example, in *State v. Salazar-Mercado*, 234 Ariz. 590, 325 P.3d 996 (2014), the court held that Arizona's amended Rule 702 and *Daubert* did not bar a forensic expert's "cold" testimony about Child Sexual Abuse Accommodation Syndrome, based purely on the expert's professional experience, without considering the specific facts of the subject case. However, an experience-based expert must still be prepared to discuss applicable methodologies and how his or her experience leads to a reliable opinion.

For other commentary on the issue of repressed memory, see Joshua Lushnat, *Sexual Abuse Memory Repression: The Questionable Injustice of Demeyer*, 13 J. L. SOCIETY 529 (2012); John Daly Cooney, *Determining When to Start the Clock: The "Capable of Ascertainment" Standard and Repressed Memory Sexual Abuse Cases*, 72 MO. L. REV. 633 (2007); Peter E. Smith, *The Massachusetts Discovery Rule and Its Application to Non-perpetrators in "Repressed Memory" Child Sexual Abuse Cases*, 30 NEW ENG. J. ON CRIM & CIV. CONFINEMENT 179 (2004); Elizabeth A. Wilson, *Child Sexual Abuse, the Delayed Discovery Rule, and the Problem of Finding Justice for Adult-Survivors of Child Abuse*, 12 UCLA WOMEN'S L.J. 145 (2003); Caia Johnson, *Traumatic Amnesia in the New Millennium: A New Approach to the Exhumed Memories of Childhood Sexual Abuse*, 21 HAMLINE J. PUB. L. & POLICY 387 (2000).

Chapter Seven

Criminal and Civil Liability

I. Criminal Liability

A. Statute of Limitations

Stogner v. California

United States Supreme Court, 2003
539 U.S. 607, 123 S. Ct. 2446

Justice BREYER delivered the opinion of the Court.

California has brought a criminal prosecution after expiration of the time periods set forth in previously applicable statutes of limitations. California has done so under the authority of a new law that (1) permits resurrection of otherwise time-barred criminal prosecutions, and (2) was itself enacted *after* pre-existing limitations periods had expired.... In 1993, California enacted a new criminal statute of limitations governing sex-related child abuse crimes. The new statute permits prosecution for those crimes where "[t]he limitation period specified in [prior statutes of limitations] has expired"—provided that (1) a victim has reported an allegation of abuse to the police, (2) "there is independent evidence that clearly and convincingly corroborates the victim's allegation," and (3) the prosecution is begun within one year of the victim's report. 1993 Cal. Stats. ch. 390, § 1 (codified as amended at Cal.Penal Code Ann. § 803(g) (West Supp.2003)). A related provision, added to the statute in 1996, makes clear that a prosecution satisfying these three conditions "shall revive any cause of action barred by [prior statutes of limitations]." 1996 Cal. Stats. ch. 130, § 1 (codified at Cal.Penal Code Ann. § 803(g)(3)(A) (West Supp.2003)). The statute thus authorizes prosecution for criminal acts committed many years beforehand—and where the original limitations period has expired—as long as prosecution begins within a year of a victim's first complaint to the police.

In 1998, a California grand jury indicted Marion Stogner, the petitioner, charging him with sex-related child abuse committed decades earlier—between 1955 and 1973. Without the new statute allowing revival of the State's cause of action, California could not have prosecuted Stogner. The statute of limitations governing prosecutions at the time the crimes were allegedly committed had set forth a 3-year limitations period. And that period had run 22 years or more before the present prosecution was brought.... Stogner moved for the complaint's dismissal. He argued that the Federal Constitution's *Ex Post Facto* Clause, Art. I, § 10, cl. 1, forbids revival of a previously time-barred prosecution. The trial court agreed that such a revival is unconstitutional. But the California Court of

Appeal reversed, citing a recent, contrary decision by the California Supreme Court, *People v. Frazer*, 21 Cal.4th 737, 88 Cal.Rptr.2d 312, 982 P.2d 180 (1999), cert. denied, 529 U.S. 1108, 120 S.Ct. 1960, 146 L.Ed.2d 792 (2000). Stogner then moved to dismiss his indictment, arguing that his prosecution is unconstitutional under both the *Ex Post Facto* Clause and the Due Process Clause, Amdt. 14, § 1. The trial court denied Stogner's motion, and the Court of Appeal upheld that denial. *Stogner v. Superior Court*, 93 Cal.App.4th 1229, 114 Cal.Rptr.2d 37 (2001). We granted certiorari to consider Stogner's constitutional claims. 537 U.S. 1043, 123 S.Ct. 658, 154 L.Ed.2d 514 (2002)....

First, the new statute threatens the kinds of harm that, in this Court's view, the *Ex Post Facto* Clause seeks to avoid. Long ago Justice Chase pointed out that the Clause protects liberty by preventing governments from enacting statutes with "manifestly *unjust and oppressive*" retroactive effects. *Calder v. Bull*, 3 Dall. 386, 391, 1 L.Ed. 648 (1798). Judge Learned Hand later wrote that extending a limitations period after the State has assured "a man that he has become safe from its pursuit ... seems to most of us unfair and dishonest." *Falter v. United States*, 23 F.2d 420, 426 (C.A.2), cert. denied, 277 U.S. 590, 48 S.Ct. 528, 72 L.Ed. 1003 (1928). In such a case, the government has refused "to play by its own rules," *Carmell v. Texas*, 529 U.S. 513, 533, 120 S.Ct. 1620, 146 L.Ed.2d 577 (2000). It has deprived the defendant of the "fair warning," *Weaver v. Graham*, 450 U.S. 24, 28, 101 S.Ct. 960, 67 L.Ed.2d 17 (1981), that might have led him to preserve exculpatory evidence. F. Wharton, Criminal Pleading and Practice § 316, p. 210 (8th ed. 1880) ("The statute [of limitations] is ... an amnesty, declaring that after a certain time ... the offender shall be at liberty to return to his country ... and ... may cease to preserve the proofs of his innocence"). And a Constitution that permits such an extension, by allowing legislatures to pick and choose when to act retroactively, risks both "arbitrary and potentially vindictive legislation," and erosion of the separation of powers, *Weaver, supra*, at 29, and n. 10, 101 S.Ct. 960. See *Fletcher v. Peck*, 6 Cranch 87, 137–138, 3 L.Ed. 162 (1810) (viewing the *Ex Post Facto* Clause as a protection against "violent acts which might grow out of the feelings of the moment").

Second, the kind of statute at issue falls literally within the categorical descriptions of *ex post facto* laws set forth by Justice Chase more than 200 years ago in *Calder v. Bull, supra*— a categorization that this Court has recognized as providing an authoritative account of the scope of the *Ex Post Facto* Clause. *Collins v. Youngblood*, 497 U.S. 37, 46, 110 S.Ct. 2715, 111 L.Ed.2d 30 (1990); *Carmell, supra*, at 539, 120 S.Ct. 1620. Drawing substantially on Richard Wooddeson's 18th-century commentary on the nature of *ex post facto* laws and past parliamentary abuses, Chase divided *ex post facto* laws into categories that he described in two alternative ways. See 529 U.S., at 522–524, and n. 9, 120 S.Ct. 1620. He wrote:

> "I will state what laws I consider *ex post facto* laws, within the words and the intent of the prohibition. 1st. Every law that makes an action done before the passing of the law, and which was innocent when done, criminal; and punishes such action. *2d. Every law that aggravates a crime, or makes it greater than it was, when committed.* 3d. Every law that changes the punishment, and inflicts a greater punishment, than the law annexed to the crime, when committed. *4th. Every law that alters the legal rules of evidence, and receives less, or different, testimony, than the law required at the time of the commission of the offence, in order to convict the offender.* All these, and similar laws, are manifestly unjust and oppressive." *Calder, supra*, at 390–391, 1 L.Ed. 648 (emphasis altered from original)....

The second category—including any "law that *aggravates a crime*, or makes it greater than it was, when committed," *id.*, at 390, 1 L.Ed. 648—describes California's statute as long as those words are understood as Justice Chase understood them—*i.e.*, as referring to a statute that "inflict[s] *punishments*, where the party was not, by law, liable to *any punishment*," *id.*, at 389, 1 L.Ed. 648. See also 2 R. Wooddeson, A Systematical View of the Laws of England 638 (1792) (hereinafter Wooddeson, Systematical View) (discussing the *ex post facto* status of a law that affects punishment by "making therein some innovation, *or creating some forfeiture or disability, not incurred in the ordinary course of law*" (emphasis added)). After (but not before) the original statute of limitations had expired, a party such as Stogner was not "liable to any punishment." California's new statute therefore "aggravated" Stogner's alleged crime, or made it "greater than it was, when committed," in the sense that, and to the extent that, it "inflicted punishment" for past criminal conduct that (when the new law was enacted) did not trigger any such liability. See also H. Black, American Constitutional Law §266, p. 700 (4th ed.1927) (hereinafter Black, American Constitutional Law) ("[A]n act condoned by the expiration of the statute of limitations is no longer a punishable offense"). It is consequently not surprising that New Jersey's highest court long ago recognized that Chase's alternative description of second category laws "*exactly describes* the operation" of the kind of statute at issue here. *Moore v. State*, 43 N.J.L. 203, 217, 1881 WL 8329 (1881) (emphasis added). See also H. Black, Constitutional Prohibitions Against Legislation Impairing the Obligation of Contracts, and Against Retroactive and Ex Post Facto Laws §235, p. 298 (1887) (hereinafter Black, Constitutional Prohibitions) ("Such a statute" "certainly makes that a punishable offense which was previously a condoned and obliterated offense").... So to understand the second category (as applying where a new law inflicts a punishment upon a person not then subject to that punishment, to any degree) explains why and how that category differs from both the first category (making criminal noncriminal behavior) and the third category (aggravating the punishment). And this understanding is consistent, in relevant part, with Chase's second category examples—examples specifically provided to illustrate Chase's *alternative* description of laws "'inflict[ing] *punishments*, where the party was not, by *law*, liable to *any punishment*,'" *Calder*, 3 Dall., at 389, 1 L.Ed. 648....

In finding that California's law falls within the literal terms of Justice Chase's second category, we do not deny that it may fall within another category as well. Justice Chase's fourth category, for example, includes any "law that alters the *legal* rules of *evidence*, and receives less, or different, testimony, than the law required at the time of the commission of the offence, *in order to convict the offender*." *Calder, supra*, at 390, 1 L.Ed. 648. This Court has described that category as including laws that diminish "the quantum of evidence required to convict." *Carmell, supra*, at 532, 120 S.Ct. 1620.

Significantly, a statute of limitations reflects a legislative judgment that, after a certain time, no quantum of evidence is sufficient to convict. See *United States v. Marion*, 404 U.S. 307, 322, 92 S.Ct. 455, 30 L.Ed.2d 468 (1971). And that judgment typically rests, in large part, upon evidentiary concerns—for example, concern that the passage of time has eroded memories or made witnesses or other evidence unavailable. *United States v. Kubrick*, 444 U.S. 111, 117, 100 S.Ct. 352, 62 L.Ed.2d 259 (1979); 4 W. LaFave, J. Israel, & N. King, Criminal Procedure §18.5(a), p. 718 (1999); Wharton, Criminal Pleading and Practice §316, at 210. Indeed, this Court once described statutes of limitations as creating "a presumption which renders proof unnecessary." *Wood v. Carpenter*, 101 U.S. 135, 139, 25 L.Ed. 807 (1879).... Consequently, to resurrect a prosecution after the relevant statute of limitations has expired is to eliminate a currently existing conclusive presumption forbidding prosecution, and thereby to permit conviction on a quantum of evidence where that quantum, at the time the new law is enacted, would have been legally insufficient. And, in that sense, the new law would "violate" previous evidence-related legal rules by authorizing the courts to " receiv[e] evidence ... which the courts of justice would not [previously have] admit[ted]'" as sufficient proof of a crime, *supra*, at 2450. Cf. *Collins*, 497 U.S., at 46, 110 S.Ct. 2715 ("Subtle *ex post facto* violations are no more permissible than overt ones"); *Cummings v. Missouri*, 4 Wall. 277, 329, 18 L.Ed. 356 (1867) (The *Ex Post Facto* Clause "cannot be evaded by the form in which the power of the State is exerted"). Nonetheless, given Justice Chase's description of the second category, we need not explore the fourth category, or other categories, further.

Third, likely for the reasons just stated, numerous legislators, courts, and commentators have long believed it well settled that the *Ex Post Facto* Clause forbids resurrection of a time-barred prosecution. Such sentiments appear already to have been widespread when the Reconstruction Congress of 1867 — the Congress that drafted the Fourteenth Amendment — rejected a bill that would have revived time-barred prosecutions for treason that various Congressmen wanted brought against Jefferson Davis and "his coconspirators," Cong. Globe, 39th Cong., 2d Sess., 279 (1866–1867) (comments of Rep. Lawrence). Radical Republicans such as Roscoe Conkling and Thaddeus Stevens, no friends of the South, opposed the bill because, in their minds, it proposed an "*ex post facto* law," *id.*, at 68 (comments of Rep. Conkling), and threatened an injustice tantamount to "judicial murder," *id.*, at 69 (comments of Rep. Stevens). In this instance, Congress ultimately passed a law extending *unexpired* limitations periods, ch. 236, 15 Stat. 183 — a tailored approach to extending limitations periods that has also been taken in modern statutes, *e.g.*, 18 U.S.C. § 3293 (notes on effective date of 1990 amendment and effect of 1989 amendment); Cal.Penal Code Ann. § 805.5 (West Supp.2003).

Further, Congressmen such as Conkling were not the only ones who believed that laws reviving time-barred prosecutions are *ex post facto*. That view was echoed in roughly contemporaneous opinions by State Supreme Courts. *E.g., State v. Sneed*, 25 Tex. Supp. 66, 67, 1860 WL 5750 (1860); *Moore*, 43 N.J.L., at 216–217. Cf. *State v. Keith*, 63 N.C. 140, 145, 1869 WL 1378 (1869) (A State's repeal of an amnesty was "substantially an *ex post facto* law"). Courts, with apparent unanimity until California's decision in *Frazer*, have continued to state such views, and, when necessary, so to hold. *E.g., People ex rel. Reibman v. Warden*, 242 A.D. 282, 285, 275 N.Y.S. 59, 62 (1934); *United States v. Fraidin*, 63 F.Supp. 271, 276 (D.Md.1945); *People v. Shedd*, 702 P.2d 267, 268 (Colo.1985) (en banc) (*per curiam*); *State v. Hodgson*, 108 Wash.2d 662, 667–669, 740 P.2d 848, 851–852 (1987) (en banc), cert. denied *sub nom. Fied v. Washington*, 485 U.S. 938, 108 S.Ct. 1117, 99 L.Ed.2d 277 (1988); *Commonwealth v. Rocheleau*, 404 Mass. 129, 130–131, 533 N.E.2d 1333, 1334 (1989); *State v. Nunn*, 244 Kan. 207, 218, 768 P.2d 268, 277–278 (1989); *State v. O'Neill*, 118 Idaho 244, 247, 796 P.2d 121, 124 (1990); *State v. Hirsch*, 245 Neb. 31, 39–40, 511 N.W.2d 69, 76 (1994); *State v. Schultzen*, 522 N.W.2d 833, 835 (Iowa 1994); *State v. Comeau*, 142 N.H. 84, 88, 697 A.2d 497, 500 (1997) (citing *State v. Hamel*, 138 N.H. 392, 395–396, 643 A.2d 953, 955–956 (1994)); *Santiago v. Commonwealth*, 428 Mass. 39, 42, 697 N.E.2d 979, 981, cert. denied, 525 U.S. 1003, 119 S.Ct. 514, 142 L.Ed.2d 426 (1998). Cf. *Thompson v. State*, 54 Miss. 740, 743 (1877) (stating, without specifying further grounds, that a new law could not take away a vested statute-of-limitations defense); *State v. Cookman*, 127 Or.App. 283, 289, 873 P.2d 335, 338 (1994) (holding that a law resurrecting a time-barred criminal case "violates the Due Process Clause"), aff'd on state-law grounds, 324 Or. 19, 920 P.2d 1086 (1996); *Commonwealth v. Guimento*, 341 Pa.Super. 95, 97–98, 491 A.2d 166, 167–168 (1985) (enforcing a state ban on *ex post facto* laws apparently equivalent to the federal prohibition); *People v. Chesebro*, 185 Mich.App. 412, 416, 463 N.W.2d 134, 135–136 (1990) (reciting "the general rule" that, "'where a complete defense has arisen under [a statute of limitations], it cannot be taken away by a subsequent repeal thereof'").

Even where courts have upheld extensions of *unexpired* statutes of limitations (extensions that our holding today does not affect ... , they have consistently distinguished situations where limitations periods have *expired*. Further, they have often done so by saying that extension of existing limitations periods is not *ex post facto* "provided," "so long as," "because," or "if" the prior limitations periods have not expired — a manner of speaking that suggests a presumption that revival of time-barred criminal cases is *not* allowed. *E.g., United States v. Madia*, 955 F.2d 538, 540 (C.A.8 1992) ("'provided'"); *United States v. Richardson*, 512 F.2d 105, 106 (C.A.3 1975) ("provided"); *People v. Anderson*, 53 Ill.2d 437, 440, 292 N.E.2d 364, 366 (1973) ("so long as"); *United States v. Haug*, 21 F.R.D. 22, 25 (N.D.Ohio 1957) ("so long as"), aff'd, 274 F.2d 885 (C.A.6 1960), cert. denied, 365 U.S. 811, 81 S.Ct. 688, 5 L.Ed.2d 691 (1961); *United States v. Kurzenknabe*, 136 F.Supp. 17, 23 (D.N.J.1955) ("so long as"); *State v. Duffy*, 300 Mont. 381, 390, 6 P.3d 453, 460 (2000) ("because"); *State v. Davenport*, 536 N.W.2d 686, 688 (N.D.1995) ("because"); *Andrews v. State*, 392 So.2d 270, 271 (Fla.App.1980) ("if"), review denied, 399 So.2d 1145 (Fla.1981). See, *e.g., Shedd, supra*, at 268 (citing *Richardson, supra*, and *Andrews, supra*, as directly supporting a conclusion that a law reviving time-barred offenses is *ex post facto*). Cf. *Commonwealth v. Duffy*, 96 Pa. 506, 514, 1880 WL 13543 (1881) ("[I]n any case where a right to acquittal has not been absolutely acquired by the completion of the period of limitation, that period is subject to enlargement or repeal without being obnoxious to the constitutional prohibition against *ex post facto* laws")....

This Court itself has not previously spoken decisively on this matter. On the one hand, it has clearly stated that the Fifth Amendment's privilege against self-incrimination does not apply after the relevant limitations period has expired. *Brown v. Walker*, 161 U.S. 591, 597–598, 16 S.Ct. 644, 40 L.Ed. 819 (1896). And that rule may suggest that the expiration of a statute of limitations is irrevocable, for otherwise the passage of time would not have eliminated fear of prosecution.... Instead, we believe that the outcome of this case is determined by the nature of the harms that California's law creates, by the fact that the law falls within Justice Chase's second category as Chase understood that category, and by a long line of authority holding that a law of this type violates the *Ex Post Facto* Clause....

[W]e agree that the State's interest in prosecuting child abuse cases is an important one. But there is also a predominating constitutional interest in forbidding the State to revive a long-forbidden prosecution. And to hold that such a law is *ex post facto* does not prevent the State from extending time limits for the prosecution of future offenses, or for prosecutions not yet time barred.... In sum, California's law subjects an individual such as Stogner to prosecution long after the State has, in effect, granted an amnesty, telling him that he is "at liberty to return to his country ... and that from henceforth he may cease to preserve the proofs of his innocence," Wharton, Criminal Pleading and Practice § 316, at 210. See also *Moore*, 43 N.J.L., at 223–224. It retroactively withdraws a complete defense to prosecution after it has already attached, and it does so in a manner that allows the State to withdraw this defense at will and with respect to individuals already identified.... "Unfair" seems to us a fair characterization.

The statute before us is unfairly retroactive as applied to Stogner. A long line of judicial authority supports characterization of this law as *ex post facto*. For the reasons stated, we believe the law falls within Justice Chase's second category of *ex post facto* laws. We conclude that a law enacted after expiration of a previously applicable limitations period violates the *Ex Post Facto* Clause when it is applied to revive a previously time-barred prosecution. The California court's judgment to the contrary is

Reversed.

Justice KENNEDY, with whom THE CHIEF JUSTICE, Justice SCALIA, and Justice THOMAS join, dissenting.

California has enacted a retroactive extension of statutes of limitations for serious sexual offenses committed against minors. Cal.Penal Code Ann. § 803(g) (West Supp.2003). The new period includes cases where the limitations period has expired before the effective date of the legislation. To invalidate the statute in the latter circumstance, the Court tries to force it into the second category of *Calder v. Bull*, 3 Dall. 386, 1 L.Ed. 648 (1798), which prohibits a retroactive law "'that *aggravates a crime*, or makes it *greater* than it was, when committed.'"... (quoting *Calder, supra*, at 390, 1 L.Ed. 648 (emphasis in original)). These words, in my view, do not permit the Court's holding, but indeed foreclose it. A law which does not alter the definition of the crime but only revives prosecution does not make the crime "greater than it was, when committed." Until today, a plea in bar has not been thought to form any part of the definition of the offense....

The majority seems to suggest that retroactive extension of expired limitations periods is "'arbitrary and potentially vindictive legislation,'"... but does not attempt to support this accusation. And it could not do so. The California statute can be explained as motivated by legitimate concerns about the continuing suffering endured by the victims of childhood abuse.... The California Legislature noted that "young victims often delay reporting sexual abuse because they are easily manipulated by offenders in positions of authority and trust, and because children have difficulty remembering the crime or facing the trauma it can cause." *People v. Frazer*, 21 Cal.4th 737, 744, 88 Cal.Rptr.2d 312, 982 P.2d 180, 183–184 (1999). The concern is amply supported by empirical studies. See, *e.g.*, Summit, Abuse of the Child Sexual Abuse Accommodation Syndrome, in 1 J. of Child Sexual Abuse 153, 156–163 (1992); Lyon, Scientific Support for Expert Testimony on Child Sexual Abuse Accommodation, in Critical Issues in Child Sexual Abuse 107, 114–120 (J. Conte ed.2002).

The problem the legislature sought to address is illustrated well by this case. Petitioner's older daughter testified she did not report the abuse because she was afraid of her father and did not believe anyone would help her. After she left petitioner's home, she tried to forget the abuse. Petitioner's younger daughter did not report the abuse because she was scared. He tried to convince her it was a normal way of life. Even after she moved out of petitioner's house, she was afraid to speak for fear she would not be believed. She tried to pretend she had a normal childhood. It was only her realization that the father continued to abuse other children in the family that led her to disclose the abuse, in order to protect them.

The Court tries to counter by saying the California statute is "'unfair and dishonest'" because it violated the State's initial assurance to the offender that "'he has become safe from its pursuit'" and deprived him of "the 'fair warning.'"... The fallacy of this rationale is apparent when we recall that the Court is careful to leave in place the uniform decisions by state and federal courts to uphold retroactive extension of unexpired statutes of limitations against an *ex post facto* challenge.... There are two rationales to explain the proposed dichotomy between unexpired and expired statutes, and neither works. The first rationale must be the assumption that if an expired statute is extended, the crime becomes more serious, thereby violating category two; but if an unexpired statute is extended, the crime does not increase in seriousness. There is no basis in logic, in our cases, or in the legal literature to support this distinction. Both extensions signal, with equal force, the policy to prosecute offenders.

This leaves the second rationale, which must be that an extension of the expired statute destroys a reliance interest. We should consider whether it is warranted to presume that criminals keep calendars so they can mark the day to discard their records or to place a gloating phone call to the victim. The first expectation is minor and likely imaginary; the second is not, but there is no conceivable reason the law should honor it. And either expectation assumes, of course, the very result the Court reaches; for if the law were otherwise, there would be no legitimate expectation. The reliance exists, if at all, because of the circular reason that the Court today says so; it does not exist as part of our traditions or social understanding.

In contrast to the designation of the crime, which carries a certain measure of social opprobrium and presupposes a certain punishment, the statute of limitations has little or no deterrent effect. See Note, Retroactive Application of Legislatively Enlarged Statutes of Limitations for Child Abuse: Time's No Bar to Revival, 22 Ind. L.Rev. 989, 1014 (1989) ("The statute of limitations has no measurable impact on allegedly criminal behavior, neither encouraging nor deterring such conduct"); Note, Ex Post Facto Limitations on Legislative Power, 73 Mich. L.Rev. 1491, 1513 (1975) ("[W]hile many defendants rely on substantive definitions of proscribed conduct, few rely on many of the numerous laws regulating the enforcement processes"). The Court does not claim a sex offender would desist if he knew he would be liable to prosecution when his offenses were disclosed.

The law's approach to the analogous problem of reliance by wrongdoers in the civil sphere is instructive. We have held that expired statutes of limitations can be repealed to revive a civil action. See, *e.g.*, *Chase Securities Corp.*, 325 U.S., at 314, 65 S.Ct. 1137; *Plaut v. Spendthrift Farm, Inc.*, 514 U.S. 211, 229, 115 S.Ct. 1447, 131 L.Ed.2d 328 (1995). These holdings were made in the areas of contracts and investments where reliance does exist and does matter. We allow the civil wrong to be vindicated nonetheless. If we do so in the civil sphere where reliance is real, we should do so in the criminal sphere where it is, for the most part, a fictional construct.

When a child molester commits his offense, he is well aware the harm will plague the victim for a lifetime. See Briere & Runtz, Post Sexual Abuse Trauma: Data and Implications for Clinical Practice, 2 J. of Interpersonal Violence 367, 374–376 (1987); 1 J. Myers, Evidence in Child Abuse and Neglect Cases § 4.2, pp. 221–223 (2d ed.1992); Browne & Finkelhor, Initial and Long-Term Effects: A Review of the Research, in A Sourcebook on Child Sexual Abuse 143, 150–164 (D. Finkelhor et al. eds.1986). The victims whose interests § 803(g) takes into consideration have been subjected to sexual abuse within the confines of their own homes and by people they trusted and relied upon for protection. A familial figure of authority can use a confidential relation to conceal a crime. The violation of this trust inflicts deep and lasting hurt. Its only poor remedy is that the law will show its compassion and concern when the victim at last can find the strength, and know the necessity, to come forward. When the criminal has taken distinct advantage of the tender years and perilous position of a fearful victim, it is the victim's lasting hurt, not the perpetrator's fictional reliance, that the law should count the higher. The victims whose cause is now before the Court have at last overcome shame and the desire to repress these painful memories. They have reported the crimes so that the violators are brought to justice and harm to others is prevented. The Court now tells the victims their decision to come forward is in vain.

The gravity of the crime was known, and is being measured, by its wrongfulness when committed. It is a common policy for States to suspend statutes of limitations for civil harms against minors, in order to "protec[t] minors during the period when they are unable to protect themselves." 2 C. Corman, Limitation of Actions § 10.2.1, p. 104 (1991). Some States toll the limitations periods for minors even where a guardian is appointed, see *id.*, at 105–106, and even when the tolling conflicts with statutes of repose, *id.*, at

108. The difference between suspension and reactivation is so slight that it is fictional for the Court to say, in the given context, the new policy somehow alters the magnitude of the crime. The wrong was made clear by the law at the time of the crime's commission. The criminal actor knew it, even reveled in it. It is the commission of the then-unlawful act that the State now seeks to punish. The gravity of the crime is left unchanged by altering a statute of limitations of which the actor was likely not at all aware.

The California statute does not fit any of the remaining *Calder* categories: It does not criminalize conduct which was innocent when done; it allows the prosecutor to seek the same punishment as the law authorized at the time the offense was committed and no more; and it does not alter the government's burden to establish the elements of the crime. Any concern about stale evidence can be addressed by the judge and the jury, and by the requirement of proof beyond reasonable doubt. Section 803(g), moreover, contains an additional safeguard: It conditions prosecution on a presentation of independent evidence that corroborates the victim's allegations by clear and convincing evidence. Cal.Penal Code Ann. §§ 803(g)(1), (2)(B) (West Supp.2003). These protections, as well as the general protection against oppressive prosecutions offered by the Due Process Clause, should assuage the majority's fear ... that the statute will have California overrun by vindictive prosecutions resting on unreliable recovered memories. See *United States v. Lovasco*, 431 U.S. 783, 789, 97 S.Ct. 2044, 52 L.Ed.2d 752 (1977).... The statute does not violate petitioner's rights under the Due Process Clause. We have held, in the civil context, that expired statutes of limitations do not implicate fundamental rights under the Clause. See, *e.g., Chase Securities Corp., supra*, at 314, 65 S.Ct. 1137. For reasons already explained, ... there is no reason to reach a different conclusion here.

The Court's stretching of *Calder's* second category contradicts the historical understanding of that category, departs from established precedent, and misapprehends the purposes of the *Ex Post Facto* Clause. The Court also disregards the interests of those victims of child abuse who have found the courage to face their abusers and bring them to justice. The Court's opinion harms not only our *ex post facto* jurisprudence but also these and future victims of child abuse, and so compels my respectful dissent.

Notes

There is a distinction between criminal proceedings and civil proceedings with respect to any applicable statute of limitations. A limitations period for a criminal proceeding governs the time within which a prosecutor may bring criminal charges against an offender after the time of injury. A limitations period for a civil proceeding governs the time period within which victims may raise a claim to recover damages for their injuries. Civil statutes of limitations will be discussed more specifically in Chapter Seven, Section II.A (Civil Liability, Statute of Limitations), *infra*. The applicable criminal or civil statute of limitations for any sex offense against a child is state-specific. Within each state, the limitation period also may vary among offenses. For federal sex offenses, the applicable statute of limitations is determined by federal statute. For a comprehensive comparison of the various, state criminal and civil statutes of limitations and the current status of state legislative reform in this area, see Professor Marci A. Hamilton's analysis at www.sol-reform.com (last viewed Apr. 7, 2015). There are a variety of comparative resources available on the Internet. For a comparison of state criminal statutes of limitations, see, *e.g.,* National District Attorneys Association, *Statutes of Limitation for Prosecution of Offenses Against Children*, available at http://www.ndaa.org/pdf/Statute%20of%20Limitations%20for%20Prosecution%20of%20 Offenses%20Against%20Children%202012.pdf (Aug. 2012); *Statutes of Limitations for Sexual Assault: A State-by-State Comparison*, available at http://victimsofcrime.org/docs/

DNA%20Resource%20Center/sol-for-sexual-assault-check-chart---final---copy.pdf?sfvrsn=2 (last viewed Apr. 7, 2015).

Because of the advancing social science research offering continued insight on child sexual abuse responsive behaviors and evidence of Child Sexual Abuse Accommodation Syndrome, many states are reforming their approach to statutes of limitations with respect to child sexual abuse. *See* Marci A. Hamilton, *The Time Has Come for a Restatement of Child Sex Abuse*, 79 Brooklyn L. Rev. 397 (2014) (calling for a "re-statement" of child sex abuse laws). The growing trend is toward increasing or eliminating the limitations period for crimes related to sexual abuse of children. In the *Stogner* decision, the United States Supreme Court finds unconstitutional, under the *Ex Post Facto* Clause, state efforts to retroactively apply the criminal statutory limitation period. For discussion of *Stogner* as applied to the extension of *unexpired* statute of limitations periods, see Judge Joan Comparet-Cassani, *Extending the Statute of Limitations in Child Molestation Cases Does Not Violate the Ex Post Facto Clause of Stogner*, 5 Whittier J. Child. & Fam. Advoc. 303 (2005–2006). The application of limitation periods may be further complicated by laws that allow for the tolling of prescribed periods, under certain circumstances. In a majority of states, the applicable statute of limitations for crimes involving a minor is tolled until the child reaches the age of majority, which usually is 18.

Despite the trending expansive approach toward criminal prosecution for crimes involving the sexual abuse of children, consider the limitations on sentencing employed by the courts in the following decisions.

B. Sentencing

1. Adults

Kennedy v. Louisiana

United States Supreme Court, 2008
554 U.S. 407, 128 S. Ct. 2641

Justice KENNEDY delivered the opinion of the Court.

The National Government and, beyond it, the separate States are bound by the proscriptive mandates of the Eighth Amendment to the Constitution of the United States, and all persons within those respective jurisdictions may invoke its protection. See Amdts. 8 and 14, § 1; *Robinson v. California*, 370 U.S. 660, 82 S.Ct. 1417, 8 L.Ed.2d 758 (1962). Patrick Kennedy, the petitioner here, seeks to set aside his death sentence under the Eighth Amendment. He was charged by the respondent, the State of Louisiana, with the aggravated rape of his then-8-year-old stepdaughter. After a jury trial petitioner was convicted and sentenced to death under a state statute authorizing capital punishment for the rape of a child under 12 years of age. See La. Stat. Ann. § 14:42 (West 1997 and Supp.1998). This case presents the question whether the Constitution bars respondent from imposing the death penalty for the rape of a child where the crime did not result, and was not intended to result, in death of the victim. We hold the Eighth Amendment prohibits the death penalty for this offense. The Louisiana statute is unconstitutional....

Petitioner's crime was one that cannot be recounted in these pages in a way sufficient to capture in full the hurt and horror inflicted on his victim or to convey the revulsion society, and the jury that represents it, sought to express by sentencing petitioner to death. At 9:18 a.m. on March 2, 1998, petitioner called 911 to report that his stepdaughter, referred to here as L.H., had been raped. He told the 911 operator that L.H. had been in the garage while he readied his son for school. Upon hearing loud screaming, petitioner said, he ran outside and found L.H. in the side yard. Two neighborhood boys, petitioner told the operator, had dragged L.H. from the garage to the yard, pushed her down, and raped her. Petitioner claimed he saw one of the boys riding away on a blue 10-speed bicycle.

When police arrived at petitioner's home between 9:20 and 9:30 a.m., they found L.H. on her bed, wearing a T-shirt and wrapped in a bloody blanket. She was bleeding profusely from the vaginal area. Petitioner told police he had carried her from the yard to the bathtub and then to the bed. Consistent with this explanation, police found a thin line of blood drops in the garage on the way to the house and then up the stairs. Once in the bedroom, petitioner had used a basin of water and a cloth to wipe blood from the victim. This later prevented medical personnel from collecting a reliable DNA sample.... L.H. was transported to the Children's Hospital. An expert in pediatric forensic medicine testified that L.H.'s injuries were the most severe he had seen from a sexual assault in his four years of practice. A laceration to the left wall of the vagina had separated her cervix from the back of her vagina, causing her rectum to protrude into the vaginal structure. Her entire perineum was torn from the posterior fourchette to the anus. The injuries required emergency surgery.

At the scene of the crime, at the hospital, and in the first weeks that followed, both L.H. and petitioner maintained in their accounts to investigators that L.H. had been raped by two neighborhood boys. One of L.H.'s doctors testified at trial that L.H. told all hospital personnel the same version of the rape, although she reportedly told one family member that petitioner raped her. L.H. was interviewed several days after the rape by a psychologist. The interview was videotaped, lasted three hours over two days, and was introduced into evidence at trial. On the tape one can see that L.H. had difficulty discussing the subject of the rape. She spoke haltingly and with long pauses and frequent movement. Early in the interview, L.H. expressed reservations about the questions being asked:

> "I'm going to tell the same story. They just want me to change it.... They want me to say my Dad did it.... I don't want to say it.... I tell them the same, same story."...

She told the psychologist that she had been playing in the garage when a boy came over and asked her about Girl Scout cookies she was selling; and that the boy "pulled [her by the legs to] the backyard,"... [citations to record omitted], where he placed his hand over her mouth, "pulled down [her] shorts,"... and raped her, ...

Eight days after the crime, and despite L.H.'s insistence that petitioner was not the offender, petitioner was arrested for the rape. The State's investigation had drawn the accuracy of petitioner and L.H.'s story into question. Though the defense at trial proffered alternative explanations, the case for the prosecution, credited by the jury, was based upon the following evidence: An inspection of the side yard immediately after the assault was inconsistent with a rape having occurred there, the grass having been found mostly undisturbed but for a small patch of coagulated blood. Petitioner said that one of the perpetrators fled the crime scene on a blue 10-speed bicycle but gave inconsistent descriptions of the bicycle's features, such as its handlebars. Investigators found a bicycle matching petitioner and L.H.'s description in tall grass behind a nearby apartment, and petitioner identified it as the bicycle one of the perpetrators was riding. Yet its tires were flat, it did not have gears, and it was covered in spider webs. In addition police found blood on the underside of L.H.'s mattress. This convinced them the rape took place in her bedroom, not outside the house.... Police also found that petitioner made four telephone calls on the morning of the rape. Sometime before 6:15 a.m., petitioner called his employer and left a message that he was unavailable to work that day. Petitioner called back between 6:30 and 7:30 a.m. to ask a colleague how to get blood out of a white carpet because his daughter had "'just become a young lady.'" ... At 7:37 a.m., petitioner called B & B Carpet Cleaning and requested urgent assistance in removing bloodstains from a carpet. Petitioner did not call 911 until about an hour and a half later....

The State charged petitioner with aggravated rape of a child under La. Stat. Ann. § 14:42 (West 1997 and Supp.1998) and sought the death penalty.... The trial began in August 2003. L.H. was then 13 years old. She testified that she "'woke up one morning and Patrick was on top of [her].'" She remembered petitioner bringing her "'[a] cup of orange juice and pills chopped up in it'" after the rape and overhearing him on the telephone saying she had become a "'young lady.'" ... 957 So.2d 757, 767, 769, 770. L.H. acknowledged that she had accused two neighborhood boys but testified petitioner told her to say this and that it was untrue. *Id.*, at 769.... The jury having found petitioner guilty of aggravated rape, the penalty phase ensued. The State presented the testimony of S.L., who is the cousin and goddaughter of petitioner's ex-wife. S.L. testified that petitioner sexually abused her three times when she was eight years old and that the last time involved sexual intercourse. *Id.*, at 772. She did not tell anyone until two years later and did not pursue legal action.

The jury unanimously determined that petitioner should be sentenced to death. The Supreme Court of Louisiana affirmed. See *id.*, at 779–789, 793; see also *State v. Wilson*, 96-1392, 96-2076 (La.12/13/96), 685 So.2d 1063 (upholding the constitutionality of the death penalty for child rape). The court rejected petitioner's reliance on *Coker v. Georgia*, 433 U.S. 584, 97 S.Ct. 2861, 53 L.Ed.2d 982 (1977), noting that, while *Coker* bars the use of the death penalty as punishment for the rape of an adult woman, it left open the question which, if any, other nonhomicide crimes can be punished by death consistent with the Eighth Amendment. Because "'children are a class that need special protection,'" the state court reasoned, the rape of a child is unique in terms of the harm it inflicts upon the victim and our society. 957 So.2d, at 781.

The court acknowledged that petitioner would be the first person executed for committing child rape since La. Stat. Ann. § 14:42 was amended in 1995 and that Louisiana is in the minority of jurisdictions that authorize the death penalty for the crime of child rape. But following the approach of *Roper v. Simmons*, 543 U.S. 551, 125 S.Ct. 1183, 161 L.Ed.2d 1 (2005), and *Atkins v. Virginia*, 536 U.S. 304, 122 S.Ct. 2242, 153 L.Ed.2d 335 (2002), it found significant not the "numerical counting of which [S]tates ... stand for or against a particular capital prosecution," but "the direction of change." 957 So.2d, at 783 (emphasis deleted). Since 1993, the court explained, four more States—Oklahoma, South Carolina, Montana, and Georgia—had capitalized the crime of child rape, and at least eight States had authorized capital punishment for other nonhomicide crimes. By its count, 14 of the then-38 States permitting capital punishment, plus the Federal Government, allowed the death penalty for nonhomicide crimes and 5 allowed the death penalty for the crime of child rape. See *id.*, at 785–786.

The state court next asked whether "child rapists rank among the worst offenders." *Id.*, at 788. It noted the severity of the crime; that the execution of child rapists would serve the goals of deterrence and retribution; and that, unlike in *Atkins* and *Roper*, there were no characteristics of petitioner that tended to mitigate his moral culpability. 957 So.2d, at 788–789. It concluded: "[S]hort of first-degree murder, we can think of no other nonhomicide crime more deserving [of capital punishment]." *Id.*, at 789.... On this reasoning the Supreme Court of Louisiana rejected petitioner's argument that the death penalty for the rape of a child under 12 years is disproportionate and upheld the constitutionality of the statute. Chief Justice Calogero dissented. *Coker, supra,* and *Eberheart v. Georgia*, 433 U.S. 917, 97 S.Ct. 2994, 53 L.Ed.2d 1104 (1977), in his view, "set out a bright-line and easily administered rule" that the Eighth Amendment precludes capital punishment for any offense that does not involve the death of the victim. 957 So.2d, at 794.... We granted certiorari. See 552 U.S. 1087, 128 S.Ct. 829, 169 L.Ed.2d 625 (2008)....

The Eighth Amendment, applicable to the States through the Fourteenth Amendment, provides that "[e]xcessive bail shall not be required, nor excessive fines imposed, nor cruel and unusual punishments inflicted." The Amendment proscribes "all excessive punishments, as well as cruel and unusual punishments that may or may not be excessive." *Atkins*, 536 U.S., at 311, n. 7, 122 S.Ct. 2242. The Court explained in *Atkins, id.*, at 311, 122 S.Ct. 2242, and *Roper, supra*, at 560, 125 S.Ct. 1183, that the Eighth Amendment's protection against excessive or cruel and unusual punishments flows from the basic "precept of justice that punishment for [a] crime should be graduated and proportioned to [the] offense." *Weems v. United States*, 217 U.S. 349, 367, 30 S.Ct. 544, 54 L.Ed. 793 (1910). Whether this requirement has been fulfilled is determined not by the standards that prevailed when the Eighth Amendment was adopted in 1791 but by the norms that "currently prevail." *Atkins, supra*, at 311, 122 S.Ct. 2242. The Amendment "draw[s] its meaning from the evolving standards of decency that mark the progress of a maturing society." *Trop v. Dulles*, 356 U.S. 86, 101, 78 S.Ct. 590, 2 L.Ed.2d 630 (1958) (plurality opinion). This is because "[t]he standard of extreme cruelty is not merely descriptive, but necessarily embodies a moral judgment. The standard itself remains the same, but its applicability must change as the basic mores of society change." *Furman v. Georgia*, 408 U.S. 238, 382, 92 S.Ct. 2726, 33 L.Ed.2d 346 (1972) (Burger, C. J., dissenting).

Evolving standards of decency must embrace and express respect for the dignity of the person, and the punishment of criminals must conform to that rule. See *Trop, supra*, at 100, 78 S.Ct. 590 (plurality opinion). As we shall discuss, punishment is justified under one or more of three principal rationales: rehabilitation, deterrence, and retribution. See *Harmelin v. Michigan*, 501 U.S. 957, 999, 111 S.Ct. 2680, 115 L.Ed.2d 836 (1991) (KENNEDY, J., concurring in part and concurring in judgment); ... It is the last of these, retribution, that most often can contradict the law's own ends. This is of particular concern when the Court interprets the meaning of the Eighth Amendment in capital cases. When the law punishes by death, it risks its own sudden descent into brutality, transgressing the constitutional commitment to decency and restraint.

For these reasons we have explained that capital punishment must "be limited to those offenders who commit 'a narrow category of the most serious crimes' and whose extreme culpability makes them 'the most deserving of execution.'" *Roper, supra*, at 568, 125 S.Ct. 1183 (quoting *Atkins, supra*, at 319, 122 S.Ct. 2242). Though the death penalty is not invariably unconstitutional, see *Gregg v. Georgia*, 428 U.S. 153, 96 S.Ct. 2909, 49 L.Ed.2d 859 (1976), the Court insists upon confining the instances in which the punishment can be imposed.... Applying this principle, we held in *Roper* and *Atkins* that the execution of juveniles and mentally retarded persons are punishments violative of the Eighth Amendment because the offender had a diminished personal responsibility for the crime. See *Roper, supra*, at 571–573, 125 S.Ct. 1183; *Atkins, supra*, at 318, 320, 122 S.Ct. 2242. The Court further has held that the death penalty can be disproportionate to the crime itself where the crime did not result, or was not intended to result, in death of the victim. In *Coker*, 433 U.S. 584, 97 S.Ct. 2861, 53 L.Ed.2d 982, for instance, the Court held it would be unconstitutional to execute an offender who had raped an adult woman. See also *Eberheart, supra* (holding unconstitutional in light of *Coker* a sentence of death for the kidnaping and rape of an adult woman). And in *Enmund v. Florida*, 458 U.S. 782, 102 S.Ct. 3368, 73 L.Ed.2d 1140 (1982), the Court overturned the capital sentence of a defendant who aided and abetted a robbery during which a murder was committed but did not himself kill, attempt to kill, or intend that a killing would take place. On the other hand, in *Tison v. Arizona*, 481 U.S. 137, 107 S.Ct. 1676, 95 L.Ed.2d 127 (1987), the Court allowed the defendants' death sentences to stand where they did not themselves kill the victims but their involvement in the events leading up to the murders was active, recklessly indifferent, and substantial.

In these cases the Court has been guided by "objective indicia of society's standards, as expressed in legislative enactments and state practice with respect to executions." *Roper*, 543 U.S., at 563, 125 S.Ct. 1183; see also *Coker, supra*, at 593–597, 97 S.Ct. 2861 (plurality opinion) (finding that both legislatures and juries had firmly rejected the penalty of death for the rape of an adult woman); *Enmund*, 458 U.S., at 788, 102 S.Ct. 3368 (looking to "historical development of the punishment at issue, legislative judgments, international opinion, and the sentencing decisions juries have made"). The inquiry does not end there, however. Consensus is not dispositive. Whether the death penalty is disproportionate to the crime committed depends as well upon the standards elaborated by controlling precedents and by the Court's own understanding and interpretation of the Eighth Amendment's text, history, meaning, and purpose. See *id.*, at 797–801, 102 S.Ct. 3368; *Gregg, supra*, at 182–183, 96 S.Ct. 2909 (joint opinion of Stewart, Powell, and STEVENS, JJ.); *Coker, supra*, at 597–600, 97 S.Ct. 2861 (plurality opinion).... Based both on consensus and our own independent judgment, our holding is that a death sentence for one who raped but did not kill a child, and who did not intend to assist another in killing the child, is unconstitutional under the Eighth and Fourteenth Amendments....

Louisiana reintroduced the death penalty for rape of a child in 1995. See § 14:42 (West Supp.1996). Under the current statute, any anal, vaginal, or oral intercourse with a child under the age of 13 constitutes aggravated rape and is punishable by death. See La. Stat. Ann. § 14:42 (West Supp.2007). Mistake of age is not a defense, so the statute imposes strict liability in this regard. Five States have since followed Louisiana's lead: Georgia, see Ga.Code Ann. § 16-6-1 (2007) (enacted 1999); Montana, see Mont.Code Ann. § 45-5-503 (2007) (enacted 1997); Oklahoma, see Okla. Stat., Tit. 10, § 7115(K) (West 2007 Supp.) (enacted 2006); South Carolina, see S.C.Code Ann. § 16-3-655(C)(1) (Supp.2007) (enacted 2006); and Texas, see Tex. Penal Code Ann. § 12.42(c)(3) (West Supp.2007) (enacted 2007); see also § 22.021(a). Four of these States' statutes are more narrow than Louisiana's in that only offenders with a previous rape conviction are death eligible. See Mont.Code Ann. § 45-5-503(3)(c); Okla. Stat., Tit. 10, § 7115(K); S.C.Code Ann. § 16-3-655(C)(1); Tex. Penal Code Ann. § 12.42(c)(3). Georgia's statute makes child rape a capital offense only when aggravating circumstances are present, including but not limited to a prior conviction. See Ga.Code Ann. § 17-10-30 (Supp.2007).... By contrast, 44 States have not made child rape a capital offense. As for federal law, Congress in the Federal Death Penalty Act of 1994 expanded the number of federal crimes for which the death penalty is a permissible sentence, including certain nonhomicide offenses; but it did not do the same for child rape or abuse. See 108 Stat.1972 (codified as amended in scattered sections of 18 U.S.C.). Under 18 U.S.C. § 2245, an offender is death eligible only when the sexual abuse or exploitation results in the victim's death.

Petitioner claims the death penalty for child rape is not authorized in Georgia, pointing to a 1979 decision in which the Supreme Court of Georgia stated that "[s]tatutory rape is not a capital crime in Georgia." *Presnell v. State*, 243 Ga. 131, 132–133, 252 S.E.2d 625, 626 (1979). But it appears *Presnell* was referring to the separate crime of statutory rape, which is not a capital offense in Georgia, see Ga.Code Ann. § 26-2018 (1969); § 16-6-3 (2007). The State's current capital rape statute, by contrast, is explicit that the rape of "[a] female who is less than ten years of age" is punishable "by death." §§ 16-6-1(a)(2), (b). Based on a recent statement by the Supreme Court of Georgia it must be assumed that this law is still in force: "Neither the United States Supreme Court, nor this Court, has yet addressed whether the death penalty is unconstitutionally disproportionate for the crime of raping a child." *State v. Velazquez*, 283 Ga. 206, 208, 657 S.E.2d 838, 840 (2008).

Respondent would include Florida among those States that permit the death penalty for child rape. The state statute does authorize, by its terms, the death penalty for "sexual battery upon ... a person less than 12 years of age." Fla. Stat. §794.011(2) (2007); see also §921.141(5) (2007). In 1981, however, the Supreme Court of Florida held the death penalty for child sexual assault to be unconstitutional. See *Buford, supra*. It acknowledged that *Coker* addressed only the constitutionality of the death penalty for rape of an adult woman, 403 So.2d, at 950, but held that "[t]he reasoning of the justices in *Coker* ... compels [the conclusion] that a sentence of death is grossly disproportionate and excessive punishment for the crime of sexual assault and is therefore forbidden by the Eighth Amendment as cruel and unusual punishment," *id.*, at 951. Respondent points out that the state statute has not since been amended. Pursuant to Fla. Stat. §775.082(2) (2007), however, Florida state courts have understood *Buford* to bind their sentencing discretion in child rape cases. See, *e.g., Gibson v. State*, 721 So.2d 363, 367, and n. 2 (Fla.App.1998) (deeming it irrelevant that "the Florida Legislature never changed the wording of the sexual battery statute"); *Cooper v. State*, 453 So.2d 67 (Fla.App.1984) ("After *Buford*, death was no longer a possible penalty in Florida for sexual battery"); see also Fla. Stat. §775.082(2) ("In the event the death penalty in a capital felony is held to be unconstitutional by the Florida Supreme Court ... the court having jurisdiction over a person previously sentenced to death for a capital felony ... shall sentence such person to life imprisonment")....

The evidence of a national consensus with respect to the death penalty for child rapists, as with respect to juveniles, mentally retarded offenders, and vicarious felony murderers, shows divided opinion but, on balance, an opinion against it. Thirty-seven jurisdictions—36 States plus the Federal Government—have the death penalty. As mentioned above, only six of those jurisdictions authorize the death penalty for rape of a child. Though our review of national consensus is not confined to tallying the number of States with applicable death penalty legislation, it is of significance that, in 45 jurisdictions, petitioner could not be executed for child rape of any kind. That number surpasses the 30 States in *Atkins* and *Roper* and the 42 States in *Enmund* that prohibited the death penalty under the circumstances those cases considered....

Respondent insists that the six States where child rape is a capital offense, along with the States that have proposed but not yet enacted applicable death penalty legislation, reflect a consistent direction of change in support of the death penalty for child rape. Consistent change might counterbalance an otherwise weak demonstration of consensus. See *Atkins*, 536 U.S., at 315, 122 S.Ct. 2242 ("It is not so much the number of these States that is significant, but the consistency of the direction of change"); *Roper*, 543 U.S., at 565, 125 S.Ct. 1183 ("Impressive in *Atkins* was the rate of abolition of the death penalty for the mentally retarded"). But whatever the significance of consistent change where it is cited to show emerging support for expanding the scope of the death penalty, no showing of consistent change has been made in this case.

Respondent and its *amici* identify five States where, in their view, legislation authorizing capital punishment for child rape is pending. See Brief for Missouri Governor Matt Blunt et al. as *Amici Curiae* 2, 14. It is not our practice, nor is it sound, to find contemporary norms based upon state legislation that has been proposed but not yet enacted. There are compelling reasons not to do so here. Since the briefs were submitted by the parties, legislation in two of the five States has failed. See, *e.g.*, S. 195, 66th Gen. Assembly, 2d Reg. Sess. (Colo.2008) (rejected by Senate Appropriations Committee on Apr. 11, 2008); S. 2596, 2008 Leg., Reg. Sess. (Miss.2008) (rejected by House Committee on Mar. 18, 2008). In Tennessee, the House bills were rejected almost a year ago, and the Senate bills appear to have died in committee. See H.R. 601, 105th Gen. Assembly, 1st Reg. Sess. (2007) (taken off Subcommittee Calendar on Apr. 4, 2007); H.R. 662, *ibid.* (failed for lack of second on Mar. 21, 2007); H.R. 1099, *ibid.* (taken off notice for Judiciary Committee calendar on May 16, 2007); S. 22, *ibid.* (referred to General Subcommittee of Senate Finance, Ways, and Means Committee on June 11, 2007); S. 157, *ibid.* (referred to Senate Judiciary Committee on Feb. 7, 2007; action deferred until Jan. 2008); S. 841, *ibid.* (referred to General Subcommittee of Senate Judiciary Committee on Mar. 27, 2007). In Alabama, the recent legislation is similar to a bill that failed in 2007. Compare H.R. 456, 2008 Leg., Reg. Sess. (2008), with H.R. 335, 2007 Leg., Reg. Sess. (2007). And in Missouri, the 2008 legislative session has ended, tabling the pending legislation. See Mo. Const., Art. III, §20(a).

Aside from pending legislation, it is true that in the last 13 years there has been change toward making child rape a capital offense. This is evidenced by six new death penalty statutes, three enacted in the last two years. But this showing is not as significant as the data in *Atkins*, where 18 States between 1986 and 2001 had enacted legislation prohibiting the execution of mentally retarded persons. See *Atkins, supra*, at 313–315, 122 S.Ct. 2242. Respondent argues the instant case is like *Roper* because, there, only five States had shifted their positions between 1989 and 2005, one less State than here. See *Roper, supra*, at 565, 125 S.Ct. 1183. But in *Roper*, we emphasized that, though the pace of abolition was not as great as in *Atkins*, it was counterbalanced by the total number of States that had recognized the impropriety of executing juvenile offenders. See 543 U.S., at 566–567, 125 S.Ct. 1183. When we decided *Stanford v. Kentucky*, 492 U.S. 361, 109 S.Ct. 2969, 106 L.Ed.2d 306 (1989), 12 death penalty States already prohibited the execution of any juvenile under 18, and 15 prohibited the execution of any juvenile under 17. See *Roper, supra*, at 566–567, 125 S.Ct. 1183 ("If anything, this shows that the impropriety of executing juveniles between 16 and 18 years of age gained wide recognition earlier"). Here, the total number of States to have made child rape a capital offense after *Furman* is six. This is not an indication of a trend or change in direction comparable to the one supported by data in *Roper*. The evidence here bears a closer resemblance to the evidence of state activity in *Enmund*, where we found a national consensus against the death penalty for vicarious felony murder despite eight jurisdictions having authorized the practice. See 458 U.S., at 789, 792, 102 S.Ct. 3368....

There are measures of consensus other than legislation. Statistics about the number of executions may inform the consideration whether capital punishment for the crime of child rape is regarded as unacceptable in our society. See, *e.g., id.*, at 794–795, 102 S.Ct. 3368; *Roper, supra*, at 564–565, 125 S.Ct. 1183; *Atkins, supra*, at 316, 122 S.Ct. 2242; cf. *Coker*, 433 U.S., at 596–597, 97 S.Ct. 2861 (plurality opinion). These statistics confirm our determination from our review of state statutes that there is a social consensus against the death penalty for the crime of child rape.... Nine States—Florida, Georgia, Louisiana, Mississippi, Montana, Oklahoma, South Carolina, Tennessee, and Texas—have permitted capital punishment for adult or child rape for some length of time between the Court's 1972 decision in *Furman* and today. See ... *Coker, supra*, at 595, 97 S.Ct. 2861 (plurality opinion). Yet no individual has been executed for the rape of an adult or child since 1964, and no execution for any other nonhomicide offense has been conducted since 1963. See Historical Statistics of the United States, at 5-262 to 5-263 (Table Ec343-357). Cf. *Thompson v. Oklahoma*, 487 U.S. 815, 852–853, 108 S.Ct. 2687, 101 L.Ed.2d 702 (1988) (O'Connor, J., concurring in judgment) (that "four decades have gone by since the last execution of a defendant who was younger than 16 at the time of the offense ... support[s] the inference of a national consensus opposing the death penalty for 15-year-olds").... Louisiana is the only State since 1964 that has sentenced an individual to death for the crime of child rape; and petitioner and Richard Davis, who was convicted and sentenced to death for the aggravated rape of a 5-year-old child by a Louisiana jury in December 2007, see *State v. Davis*, Case No. 262,971 (1st Jud. Dist., Caddo Parish, La.) ... are the only two individuals now on death row in the United States for a nonhomicide offense.

After reviewing the authorities informed by contemporary norms, including the history of the death penalty for this and other nonhomicide crimes, current state statutes and new enactments, and the number of executions since 1964, we conclude there is a national consensus against capital punishment for the crime of child rape....

As we have said in other Eighth Amendment cases, objective evidence of contemporary values as it relates to punishment for child rape is entitled to great weight, but it does not end our inquiry. "[T]he Constitution contemplates that in the end our own judgment will be brought to bear on the question of the acceptability of the death penalty under the Eighth Amendment." *Coker, supra*, at 597, 97 S.Ct. 2861 (plurality opinion); see also *Roper, supra*, at 563, 125 S.Ct. 1183; *Enmund, supra*, at 797, 102 S.Ct. 3368 ("[I]t is for us ultimately to judge whether the Eighth Amendment permits imposition of the death penalty"). We turn, then, to the resolution of the question before us, which is informed by our precedents and our own understanding of the Constitution and the rights it secures.

It must be acknowledged that there are moral grounds to question a rule barring capital punishment for a crime against an individual that did not result in death. These facts illustrate the point. Here the victim's fright, the sense of betrayal, and the nature of her injuries caused more prolonged physical and mental suffering than, say, a sudden killing by an unseen assassin. The attack was not just on her but on her childhood. For this reason, we should be most reluctant to rely upon the language of the plurality in *Coker*, which posited that, for the victim of rape, "life may not be nearly so happy as it was," but it is not beyond repair. 433 U.S., at 598, 97 S.Ct. 2861. Rape has a permanent psychological, emotional, and sometimes physical impact on the child. See C. Bagley & K. King, Child Sexual Abuse: The Search for Healing 2–24, 111–112 (1990); Finkelhor & Browne, Assessing the Long-Term Impact of Child Sexual Abuse: A Review and Conceptualization, in Handbook on Sexual Abuse of Children 55–60 (L. Walker ed.1988). We cannot dismiss the years of long anguish that must be endured by the victim of child rape.

It does not follow, though, that capital punishment is a proportionate penalty for the crime. The constitutional prohibition against excessive or cruel and unusual punishments mandates that the State's power to punish "be exercised within the limits of civilized standards." *Trop*, 356 U.S., at 99, 100, 78 S.Ct. 590 (plurality opinion). Evolving standards of decency that mark the progress of a maturing society counsel us to be most hesitant before interpreting the Eighth Amendment to allow the extension of the death penalty, a hesitation that has special force where no life was taken in the commission of the crime. It is an established principle that decency, in its essence, presumes respect for the individual and thus moderation or restraint in the application of capital punishment. See *id.*, at 100, 78 S.Ct. 590....

Consistent with evolving standards of decency and the teachings of our precedents we conclude that, in determining whether the death penalty is excessive, there is a distinction between intentional first-degree murder on the one hand and nonhomicide crimes against individual persons, even including child rape, on the other. The latter crimes may be devastating in their harm, as here, but "in terms of moral depravity and of the injury to the person and to the public," *Coker*, 433 U.S., at 598, 97 S.Ct. 2861 (plurality opinion), they cannot be compared to murder in their "severity and irrevocability." *Ibid.*

In reaching our conclusion we find significant the number of executions that would be allowed under respondent's approach. The crime of child rape, considering its reported incidents, occurs more often than first-degree murder. Approximately 5,702 incidents of vaginal, anal, or oral rape of a child under the age of 12 were reported nationwide in 2005; this is almost twice the total incidents of intentional murder for victims of all ages (3,405) reported during the same period. See Inter-University Consortium for Political and Social Research, National Incident-Based Reporting System, 2005, Study No. 4720, online at http://www.icpsr.umich.edu (as visited June 12, 2008, and available in Clerk of Court's case file). Although we have no reliable statistics on convictions for child rape, we can surmise that, each year, there are hundreds, or more, of these convictions just in jurisdictions that permit capital punishment. Cf. Brief for Louisiana Association of Criminal Defense Lawyers et al. as *Amici Curiae* 1–2, and n. 2 (noting that there are now at least 70 capital rape indictments pending in Louisiana and estimating the actual number to be over 100). As a result of existing rules, see generally *Godfrey*, 446 U.S., at 428–433, 100 S.Ct. 1759 (plurality opinion), only 2.2% of convicted first-degree murderers are sentenced to death, see Blume, Eisenberg, & Wells, Explaining Death Row's Population and Racial Composition, 1 J. of Empirical Legal Studies 165, 171 (2004). But under respondent's approach, the 36 States that permit the death penalty could sentence to death all persons convicted of raping a child less than 12 years of age. This could not be reconciled with our evolving standards of decency and the necessity to constrain the use of the death penalty.

It might be said that narrowing aggravators could be used in this context, as with murder offenses, to ensure the death penalty's restrained application. We find it difficult to identify standards that would guide the decisionmaker so the penalty is reserved for the most severe cases of child rape and yet not imposed in an arbitrary way. Even were we to forbid, say, the execution of first-time child rapists, … or require as an aggravating factor a finding that the perpetrator's instant rape offense involved multiple victims, the jury still must balance, in its discretion, those aggravating factors against mitigating circumstances. In this context, which involves a crime that in many cases will overwhelm a decent person's judgment, we have no confidence that the imposition of the death penalty would not be so arbitrary as to be "freakis[h]," *Furman*, 408 U.S., at 310, 92 S.Ct. 2726 (Stewart, J., concurring). We cannot sanction this result when the harm to the victim, though grave, cannot be quantified in the same way as death of the victim.

It is not a solution simply to apply to this context the aggravating factors developed for capital murder. The Court has said that a State may carry out its obligation to ensure individualized sentencing in capital murder cases by adopting sentencing processes that rely upon the jury to exercise wide discretion so long as there are narrowing factors that have some "'common-sense core of meaning … that criminal juries should be capable of understanding.'" *Tuilaepa*, 512 U.S., at 975, 114 S.Ct. 2630 (quoting *Jurek v. Texas*, 428 U.S. 262, 279, 96 S.Ct. 2950, 49 L.Ed.2d 929 (1976) (White, J., concurring in judgment)). The Court, accordingly, has upheld the constitutionality of aggravating factors ranging from whether the defendant was a "'cold-blooded, pitiless slayer,'" *Arave v. Creech*, 507 U.S. 463, 471–474, 113 S.Ct. 1534, 123 L.Ed.2d 188 (1993), to whether the "'perpetrator inflict[ed] mental anguish or physical abuse before the victim's death,'" *Walton*, 497 U.S., at 654, 110 S.Ct. 3047, to whether the defendant "'would commit criminal acts of violence that would constitute a continuing threat to society,' " *Jurek, supra*, at 269–270, 274–276, 96 S.Ct. 2950 (joint opinion of Stewart, Powell, and STEVENS, JJ.). All of these standards have the potential to result in some inconsistency of application.... As noted above, the resulting imprecision and the tension between evaluating the individual circumstances and consistency of treatment have been tolerated where the victim dies. It should not be introduced into our justice system, though, where death has not occurred.

Our concerns are all the more pronounced where, as here, the death penalty for this crime has been most infrequent.... We have developed a foundational jurisprudence in the case of capital murder to guide the States and juries in imposing the death penalty. Starting with *Gregg*, 428 U.S. 153, 96 S.Ct. 2909, 49 L.Ed.2d 859, we have spent more than 32 years articulating limiting factors that channel the jury's discretion to avoid the death penalty's arbitrary imposition in the case of capital murder. Though that practice remains sound, beginning the same process for crimes for which no one has been executed in more than 40 years would require experimentation in an area where a failed experiment would result in the execution of individuals undeserving of the death penalty. Evolving standards of decency are difficult to reconcile with a regime that seeks to expand the death penalty to an area where standards to confine its use are indefinite and obscure.... The goal of retribution, which reflects society's and the victim's interests in seeing that the offender is repaid for the hurt he caused, see *Atkins*, 536 U.S., at 319, 122 S.Ct. 2242; *Furman, supra*, at 308, 92 S.Ct. 2726 (Stewart, J., concurring), does not justify the harshness of the death penalty here. In measuring retribution, as well as other objectives of criminal law, it is appropriate to distinguish between a particularly depraved murder that merits death as a form of retribution and the crime of child rape. See ... *Coker, supra*, at 597–598, 97 S.Ct. 2861 (plurality opinion).

There is an additional reason for our conclusion that imposing the death penalty for child rape would not further retributive purposes. In considering whether retribution is served, among other factors we have looked to whether capital punishment "has the potential ... to allow the community as a whole, including the surviving family and friends of the victim, to affirm its own judgment that the culpability of the prisoner is so serious that the ultimate penalty must be sought and imposed." *Panetti v. Quarterman*, 551 U.S. 930, 958, 127 S.Ct. 2842, 2847, 168 L.Ed.2d 662 (2007). In considering the death penalty for nonhomicide offenses this inquiry necessarily also must include the question whether the death penalty balances the wrong to the victim. Cf. *Roper*, 543 U.S., at 571, 125 S.Ct. 1183.

It is not at all evident that the child rape victim's hurt is lessened when the law permits the death of the perpetrator. Capital cases require a long-term commitment by those who testify for the prosecution, especially when guilt and sentencing determinations are in multiple proceedings. In cases like this the key testimony is not just from the family but from the victim herself. During formative years of her adolescence, made all the more daunting for having to come to terms with the brutality of her experience, L.H. was required to discuss the case at length with law enforcement personnel. In a public trial she was required to recount once more all the details of the crime to a jury as the State pursued the death of her stepfather. Cf. G. Goodman et al., Testifying in Criminal Court: Emotional Effects on Child Sexual Assault Victims 50, 62, 72 (1992); Brief for National Association of Social Workers et al. as *Amici Curiae* 17–21. And in the end the State made L.H. a central figure in its decision to seek the death penalty, telling the jury in closing statements: "[L.H.] is asking you, asking you to set up a time and place when he dies." Tr. 121 (Aug. 26, 2003).... Society's desire to inflict the death penalty for child rape by enlisting the child victim to assist it over the course of years in asking for capital punishment forces a moral choice on the child, who is not of mature age to make that choice. The way the death penalty here involves the child victim in its enforcement can compromise a decent legal system; and this is but a subset of fundamental difficulties capital punishment can cause in the administration and enforcement of laws proscribing child rape.

There are, moreover, serious systemic concerns in prosecuting the crime of child rape that are relevant to the constitutionality of making it a capital offense. The problem of unreliable, induced, and even imagined child testimony means there is a "special risk of wrongful execution" in some child rape cases. *Atkins, supra,* at 321, 122 S.Ct. 2242. See also Brief for National Association of Criminal Defense Lawyers et al. as *Amici Curiae* 5– 17. This undermines, at least to some degree, the meaningful contribution of the death penalty to legitimate goals of punishment. Studies conclude that children are highly susceptible to suggestive questioning techniques like repetition, guided imagery, and selective reinforcement. See Ceci & Friedman, The Suggestibility of Children: Scientific Research and Legal Implications, 86 Cornell L.Rev. 33, 47 (2000) (there is "strong evidence that children, especially young children, are suggestible to a significant degree — even on abuse-related questions"); Gross, Jacoby, Matheson, Montgomery, & Patil, Exonerations in the United States 1989 Through 2003, 95 J.Crim. L. & C. 523, 539 (2005) (discussing allegations of abuse at the Little Rascals Day Care Center); see also Quas, Davis, Goodman, & Myers, Repeated Questions, Deception, and Children's True and False Reports of Body Touch, 12 Child Maltreatment 60, 61–66 (2007) (finding that 4- to 7-year-olds "were able to maintain [a] lie about body touch fairly effectively when asked repeated, direct questions during a mock forensic interview").

Similar criticisms pertain to other cases involving child witnesses; but child rape cases present heightened concerns because the central narrative and account of the crime often comes from the child herself. She and the accused are, in most instances, the only ones present when the crime was committed. See *Pennsylvania v. Ritchie*, 480 U.S. 39, 60, 107 S.Ct. 989, 94 L.Ed.2d 40 (1987). Cf. Goodman, *supra*, at 118. And the question in a capital case is not just the fact of the crime, including, say, proof of rape as distinct from abuse short of rape, but details bearing upon brutality in its commission. These matters are subject to fabrication or exaggeration, or both. See Ceci & Friedman, *supra*; Quas, *supra*. Although capital punishment does bring retribution, and the legislature here has chosen to use it for this end, its judgment must be weighed, in deciding the constitutional question, against the special risks of unreliable testimony with respect to this crime.

With respect to deterrence, if the death penalty adds to the risk of nonreporting, that, too, diminishes the penalty's objectives. Underreporting is a common problem with respect to child sexual abuse. See Hanson, Resnick, Saunders, Kilpatrick, & Best, Factors Related to the Reporting of Childhood Rape, 23 Child Abuse & Neglect 559, 564 (1999) (finding that about 88% of female rape victims under the age of 18 did not disclose their abuse to authorities); Smith et al., Delay in Disclosure of Childhood Rape: Results From A National Survey, 24 Child Abuse & Neglect 273, 278–279 (2000) (finding that 72% of women raped as children disclosed their abuse to someone, but that only 12% of the victims reported the rape to authorities). Although we know little about what differentiates those who report from those who do not report, see Hanson, *supra*, at 561, one of the most commonly cited reasons for nondisclosure is fear of negative consequences for the perpetrator, a concern that has special force where the abuser is a family member, see Goodman-Brown, Edelstein, Goodman, Jones, & Gordon, Why Children Tell: A Model of Children's Disclosure of Sexual Abuse, 27 Child Abuse & Neglect 525, 527–528 (2003); Smith, *supra*, at 283–284 (finding that, where there was a relationship between perpetrator and victim, the victim was likely to keep the abuse a secret for a longer period of time, perhaps because of a "greater sense of loyalty or emotional bond"); Hanson, *supra*, at 565–566, and Table 3 (finding that a "significantly greater proportion of reported than nonreported cases involved a stranger"); see also *Ritchie, supra*, at 60. The experience of the *amici* who work with child victims indicates that, when the punishment is death, both the victim and the victim's family members may be more likely to shield the perpetrator from discovery, thus increasing underreporting. See Brief for National Association of Social Workers et al. as *Amici Curiae* 11–13. As a result, punishment by death may not result in more deterrence or more effective enforcement.

In addition, by in effect making the punishment for child rape and murder equivalent, a State that punishes child rape by death may remove a strong incentive for the rapist not to kill the victim. Assuming the offender behaves in a rational way, as one must to justify the penalty on grounds of deterrence, the penalty in some respects gives less protection, not more, to the victim, who is often the sole witness to the crime. See Rayburn, Better Dead Than R(ap)ed?: The Patriarchal Rhetoric Driving Capital Rape Statutes, 78 St. John's L.Rev. 1119, 1159–1160 (2004). It might be argued that, even if the death penalty results in a marginal increase in the incentive to kill, this is counterbalanced by a marginally increased deterrent to commit the crime at all. Whatever balance the legislature strikes, however, uncertainty on the point makes the argument for the penalty less compelling than for homicide crimes.

Each of these propositions, standing alone, might not establish the unconstitutionality of the death penalty for the crime of child rape. Taken in sum, however, they demonstrate the serious negative consequences of making child rape a capital offense. These considerations lead us to conclude, in our independent judgment, that the death penalty is not a proportional punishment for the rape of a child....

Our determination that there is a consensus against the death penalty for child rape raises the question whether the Court's own institutional position and its holding will have the effect of blocking further or later consensus in favor of the penalty from developing. The Court, it will be argued, by the act of addressing the constitutionality of the death penalty, intrudes upon the consensus-making process. By imposing a negative restraint, the argument runs, the Court makes it more difficult for consensus to change or emerge. The Court, according to the criticism, itself becomes enmeshed in the process, part judge and part the maker of that which it judges.

These concerns overlook the meaning and full substance of the established proposition that the Eighth Amendment is defined by "the evolving standards of decency that mark the progress of a maturing society." *Trop*, 356 U.S., at 101, 78 S.Ct. 590 (plurality opinion). Confirmed by repeated, consistent rulings of this Court, this principle requires that use of the death penalty be restrained. The rule of evolving standards of decency with specific marks on the way to full progress and mature judgment means that resort to the penalty must be reserved for the worst of crimes and limited in its instances of application. In most cases justice is not better served by terminating the life of the perpetrator rather than confining him and preserving the possibility that he and the system will find ways to allow him to understand the enormity of his offense. Difficulties in administering the penalty to ensure against its arbitrary and capricious application require adherence to a rule reserving its use, at this stage of evolving standards and in cases of crimes against individuals, for crimes that take the life of the victim.

The judgment of the Supreme Court of Louisiana upholding the capital sentence is reversed. This case is remanded for further proceedings not inconsistent with this opinion.

It is so ordered.

Justice ALITO, with whom THE CHIEF JUSTICE, Justice SCALIA, and Justice THOMAS join, dissenting.

The Court today holds that the Eighth Amendment categorically prohibits the imposition of the death penalty for the crime of raping a child. This is so, according to the Court, no matter how young the child, no matter how many times the child is raped, no matter how many children the perpetrator rapes, no matter how sadistic the crime, no matter how much physical or psychological trauma is inflicted, and no matter how heinous the perpetrator's prior criminal record may be. The Court provides two reasons for this sweeping conclusion: First, the Court claims to have identified "a national consensus" that the death penalty is never acceptable for the rape of a child; second, the Court concludes, based on its "independent judgment," that imposing the death penalty for child rape is inconsistent with "'the evolving standards of decency that mark the progress of a maturing society.'" ... Because neither of these justifications is sound, I respectfully dissent. ...

For the past three decades, interpretations [of *Coker*] have posed a very high hurdle for state legislatures considering the passage of new laws permitting the death penalty for the rape of a child. The enactment and implementation of any new state death penalty statute—and particularly a new type of statute such as one that specifically targets the rape of young children—imposes many costs. There is the burden of drafting an innovative law that must take into account this Court's exceedingly complex Eighth Amendment jurisprudence. Securing passage of controversial legislation may interfere in a variety of ways with the enactment of other bills on the legislative agenda. Once the statute is enacted, there is the burden of training and coordinating the efforts of those who must implement the new law. Capital prosecutions are qualitatively more difficult than noncapital prosecutions and impose special emotional burdens on all involved. When a capital sentence is imposed under the new law, there is the burden of keeping the prisoner on death row and the lengthy and costly project of defending the constitutionality of the statute on appeal and in collateral proceedings. And if the law is eventually overturned, there is the burden of new proceedings on remand. Moreover, conscientious state lawmakers, whatever their personal views about the morality of imposing the death penalty for child rape, may defer to this Court's dicta, either because they respect our authority and expertise in interpreting the Constitution or merely because they do not relish the prospect of being held to have violated the Constitution and contravened prevailing "standards of decency." ...

Seeking to counter the significance of the new capital child-rape laws enacted during the past two years, the Court points out that in recent months efforts to enact similar laws in five other States have stalled. ... These developments, however, all took place after our decision to grant certiorari in this case, see 552 U.S. 1087, 128 S.Ct. 829, 169 L.Ed.2d 625 (2008), which gave state legislators reason to delay the enactment of new legislation until the constitutionality of such laws was clarified. And there is no evidence of which I am aware that these legislative initiatives failed because the proposed laws were viewed as inconsistent with our society's standards of decency. ... On the contrary, the available evidence suggests otherwise. For example, in Colorado, the Senate Appropriations Committee in April voted 6 to 4 against Senate Bill 195, reportedly because it "would have cost about $616,000 next year for trials, appeals, public defenders, and prison costs." Associated Press, Lawmakers Reject Death Penalty for Child Sex Abusers, Denver Post, Apr. 11, 2008. Likewise, in Tennessee, the capital child-rape bill was withdrawn in committee "because of the high associated costs." The bill's sponsor stated that "'[b]ecause of the state's budget situation, we thought to withdraw that bill. ... We'll revisit it next year to see if we can reduce the cost of the fiscal note.'" Green, Small Victory in Big Fight for Tougher Sex Abuse Laws, The Leaf-Chronicle, May 8, 2008, p. 1A. Thus, the failure to enact capital child-rape laws cannot be viewed as evidence of a moral consensus against such punishment....

Aside from its misleading tally of current state laws, the Court points to two additional "objective indicia" of a "national consensus,"... but these arguments are patent makeweights. The Court notes that Congress has not enacted a law permitting a federal district court to impose the death penalty for the rape of a child, ... but due to the territorial limits of the relevant federal statutes, very few rape cases, not to mention child-rape cases, are prosecuted in federal court. See 18 U.S.C. §§ 2241, 2242 (2000 ed. and Supp. V); United States Sentencing Commission, Report to Congress: Analysis of Penalties for Federal Rape Cases, p. 10, Table 1. Congress' failure to enact a death penalty statute for this tiny set of cases is hardly evidence of Congress' assessment of our society's values.[6]

Finally, the Court argues that statistics about the number of executions in rape cases support its perception of a "national consensus," but here too the statistics do not support the Court's position. The Court notes that the last execution for the rape of a child occurred in 1964, ... but the Court fails to mention that litigation regarding the constitutionality of the death penalty brought executions to a halt across the board in the late 1960's. In 1965 and 1966, there were a total of eight executions for all offenses, and from 1968 until 1977, the year when *Coker* was decided, there were no executions for any crimes.[7] The Court also fails to mention that in Louisiana, since the state law was amended in 1995 to make child rape a capital offense, prosecutors have asked juries to return death verdicts in four cases. See *State v. Dickerson*, 01-1287 (La.App.6/26/02), 822 So.2d 849; *State v. Leblanc*, 00-1322 (La.App.5/31/01), 788 So.2d 1255; 957 So.2d 757; *State v. Davis*, Case No. 262,971 (1st Jud. Dist., Caddo Parish, La.) (cited in Brief for Respondent 42, and n. 38). In two of those cases, Louisiana juries imposed the death penalty. See 957 So.2d 757; *Davis, supra*. This 50% record is hardly evidence that juries share the Court's view that the death penalty for the rape of a young child is unacceptable under even the most aggravated circumstances.[8]...

In light of the points discussed above, I believe that the "objective indicia" of our society's "evolving standards of decency" can be fairly summarized as follows. Neither Congress nor juries have done anything that can plausibly be interpreted as evidencing the "national consensus" that the Court perceives. State legislatures, for more than 30 years, have operated under the ominous shadow of the *Coker* dicta and thus have not been free to express their own understanding of our society's standards of decency. And in the months following our grant of certiorari in this case, state legislatures have had an additional reason to pause. Yet despite the inhibiting legal atmosphere that has prevailed since 1977, six States have recently enacted new, targeted child-rape laws.... I do not

---

6. Moreover, as noted in the petition for rehearing, the Uniform Code of Military Justice permits such a sentence. See 10 U.S.C. § 856 (2000 ed.); Manual for Courts-Martial, United States, Part II, Ch. X, Rule 1004(c)(9), p. II–31 (2008); *id.*, Part IV, Art. 120, p. IV–78 ¶ 45.f(1).

7. Department of Justice, Bureau of Justice Statistics, online at http://www.ojp.usdoj.gov/bjs/glance/tables/exetab.htm; see also Death Penalty Information Center, Executions in the U.S. 1608–2002: The ESPY File Executions by Date (2007), online at http://www.deathpenaltyinfo.org/ESPYyear.pdf.

8. Of course, the other five capital child-rape statutes are too recent for any individual to have been sentenced to death under them.

suggest that six new state laws necessarily establish a "national consensus" or even that they are sure evidence of an ineluctable trend. In terms of the Court's metaphor of moral evolution, these enactments might have turned out to be an evolutionary dead end. But they might also have been the beginning of a strong new evolutionary line. We will never know, because the Court today snuffs out the line in its incipient stage.... The Court is willing to block the potential emergence of a national consensus in favor of permitting the death penalty for child rape because, in the end, what matters is the Court's "own judgment" regarding "the acceptability of the death penalty." ... (internal quotation marks omitted). Although the Court has much to say on this issue, most of the Court's discussion is not pertinent to the Eighth Amendment question at hand. And once all of the Court's irrelevant arguments are put aside, it is apparent that the Court has provided no coherent explanation for today's decision....

The Court's final—and, it appears, principal—justification for its holding is that murder, the only crime for which defendants have been executed since this Court's 1976 death penalty decisions,[9] is unique in its moral depravity and in the severity of the injury that it inflicts on the victim and the public.... But the Court makes little attempt to defend these conclusions.... With respect to the question of moral depravity, is it really true that every person who is convicted of capital murder and sentenced to death is more morally depraved than every child rapist? Consider the following two cases. In the first, a defendant robs a convenience store and watches as his accomplice shoots the store owner. The defendant acts recklessly, but was not the triggerman and did not intend the killing. See, *e.g., Tison v. Arizona,* 481 U.S. 137, 107 S.Ct. 1676, 95 L.Ed.2d 127 (1987). In the second case, a previously convicted child rapist kidnaps, repeatedly rapes, and tortures multiple child victims. Is it clear that the first defendant is more morally depraved than the second?

The Court's decision here stands in stark contrast to *Atkins* and *Roper,* in which the Court concluded that characteristics of the affected defendants—mental retardation in *Atkins* and youth in *Roper*—diminished their culpability. See *Atkins,* 536 U.S., at 305, 122 S.Ct. 2242; *Roper,* 543 U.S., at 571, 125 S.Ct. 1183. Nor is this case comparable to *Enmund v. Florida,* 458 U.S. 782, 102 S.Ct. 3368, 73 L.Ed.2d 1140 (1982), in which the Court held that the Eighth Amendment prohibits the death penalty where the defendant participated in a robbery during which a murder was committed but did not personally intend for lethal force to be used. I have no doubt that, under the prevailing standards of our society, robbery, the crime that the petitioner in *Enmund* intended to commit, does not evidence the same degree of moral depravity as the brutal rape of a young child. Indeed, I have little doubt that, in the eyes of ordinary Americans, the very worst child rapists—predators who seek out and inflict serious physical and emotional injury on defenseless young children—are the epitome of moral depravity.

With respect to the question of the harm caused by the rape of a child in relation to the harm caused by murder, it is certainly true that the loss of human life represents a unique harm, but that does not explain why other grievous harms are insufficient to permit a death sentence. And the Court does not take the position that no harm other than the loss of life is sufficient. The Court takes pains to limit its holding to "crimes

---

9. *Gregg v. Georgia,* 428 U.S. 153, 96 S.Ct. 2909, 49 L.Ed.2d 859; *Proffitt v. Florida,* 428 U.S. 242, 96 S.Ct. 2960, 49 L.Ed.2d 913; *Jurek v. Texas,* 428 U.S. 262, 96 S.Ct. 2950, 49 L.Ed.2d 929; *Woodson v. North Carolina,* 428 U.S. 280, 96 S.Ct. 2978, 49 L.Ed.2d 944; *Roberts v. Louisiana,* 428 U.S. 325, 96 S.Ct. 3001, 49 L.Ed.2d 974.

against individual persons" and to exclude "offenses against the State," a category that the Court stretches—without explanation—to include "drug kingpin activity." ... But the Court makes no effort to explain why the harm caused by such crimes is necessarily greater than the harm caused by the rape of young children. This is puzzling in light of the Court's acknowledgment that "[r]ape has a permanent psychological, emotional, and sometimes physical impact on the child." ... As the Court aptly recognizes, "[w]e cannot dismiss the years of long anguish that must be endured by the victim of child rape." *Ibid.*

The rape of any victim inflicts great injury, and "[s]ome victims are so grievously injured physically or psychologically that life is beyond repair." *Coker*, 433 U.S., at 603, 97 S.Ct. 2861 (opinion of Powell, J.). "The immaturity and vulnerability of a child, both physically and psychologically, adds a devastating dimension to rape that is not present when an adult is raped." Meister, Murdering Innocence: The Constitutionality of Capital Child Rape Statutes, 45 Ariz. L.Rev. 197, 208–209 (2003). See also *State v. Wilson*, 96-1392, p. 6 (La.12/13/96), 685 So.2d 1063, 1067; Broughton, "On Horror's Head Horrors Accumulate": A Reflective Comment on Capital Child Rape Legislation, 39 Duquesne L.Rev. 1, 38 (2000). Long-term studies show that sexual abuse is "grossly intrusive in the lives of children and is harmful to their normal psychological, emotional, and sexual development in ways which no just or humane society can tolerate." C. Bagley & K. King, Child Sexual Abuse: The Search for Healing 2 (1990).

It has been estimated that as many as 40% of 7- to 13-year-old sexual assault victims are considered "seriously disturbed." A. Lurigio, M. Jones, & B. Smith, Child Sexual Abuse: Its Causes, Consequences, and Implications for Probation Practice, 59 Fed. Probation 69, 70 (Sept.1995). Psychological problems include sudden school failure, unprovoked crying, dissociation, depression, insomnia, sleep disturbances, nightmares, feelings of guilt and inferiority, and self-destructive behavior, including an increased incidence of suicide. Meister, *supra*, at 209; Broughton, *supra*, at 38; Glazer, Child Rapists Beware! The Death Penalty and Louisiana's Amended Aggravated Rape Statute, 25 Am. J.Crim. L. 79, 88 (1997).

The deep problems that afflict child-rape victims often become society's problems as well. Commentators have noted correlations between childhood sexual abuse and later problems such as substance abuse, dangerous sexual behaviors or dysfunction, inability to relate to others on an interpersonal level, and psychiatric illness. Broughton, *supra*, at 38; Glazer, *supra*, at 89; Handbook on Sexual Abuse of Children 7 (L. Walker ed.1988). Victims of child rape are nearly 5 times more likely than nonvictims to be arrested for sex crimes and nearly 30 times more likely to be arrested for prostitution. *Ibid.*... The harm that is caused to the victims and to society at large by the worst child rapists is grave. It is the judgment of the Louisiana lawmakers and those in an increasing number of other States that these harms justify the death penalty. The Court provides no cogent explanation why this legislative judgment should be overridden. Conclusory references to "decency," "moderation," "restraint," "full progress," and "moral judgment" are not enough....

In summary, the Court holds that the Eighth Amendment categorically rules out the death penalty in even the most extreme cases of child rape even though: (1) This holding is not supported by the original meaning of the Eighth Amendment; (2) neither *Coker* nor any other prior precedent commands this result; (3) there are no reliable "objective indicia" of a "national consensus" in support of the Court's position; (4) sustaining the constitutionality of the state law before us would not "extend" or "expand" the death penalty; (5) this Court has previously rejected the proposition that the Eighth Amendment is a one-way ratchet that prohibits legislatures from adopting new capital punishment statutes to meet new problems; (6) the worst child rapists exhibit the epitome of moral depravity; and (7) child rape inflicts grievous injury on victims and on society in general.

The party attacking the constitutionality of a state statute bears the "heavy burden" of establishing that the law is unconstitutional. *Gregg*, 428 U.S., at 175, 96 S.Ct. 2909 (joint opinion of Stewart, Powell, and STEVENS, JJ.). That burden has not been discharged here, and I would therefore affirm the decision of the Louisiana Supreme Court.

United States v. Youngs

Second Circuit, 2012
687 F.3d 56

DRONEY, Circuit Judge:

Defendant Mark Allen Youngs ("Youngs") appeals from his judgment of conviction. On August 27, 2008, Youngs waived indictment and pleaded guilty in the U.S. District Court for the Western District of New York to a two-count Superseding Information that charged him with producing child pornography in violation of 18 U.S.C. § 2251(a) ("Count One"); and possessing child pornography in violation of 18 U.S.C. § 2252A(a)(5)(B), (b)(2) ("Count Two")....

Youngs pleaded guilty pursuant to a plea agreement that set forth the possible sentences for each count of the child pornography offenses in the Information: Count One carried a mandatory minimum sentence of 15 years' imprisonment and a possible maximum sentence of 30 years' imprisonment, a fine of $250,000, a mandatory special assessment, and a term of supervised release of up to life; and Count Two carried a maximum sentence of 10 years' imprisonment, a fine of $250,000, a mandatory special assessment, and a term of supervised release of up to life.... At his plea hearing, the district court reviewed in detail the plea agreement with Youngs and the various rights set forth in Rule 11. As a part of this review, the court described the minimum and maximum sentences of imprisonment, the supervised release term that Youngs faced, the forfeiture of his computer equipment, and his obligations under the Sex Offender Registration and Notification Act[1] following his release from incarceration. Youngs responded that he understood all of these consequences. He waived his right to indictment and pleaded guilty to both Counts of the Information. The court accepted his plea.... On October 15, 2010, the court sentenced Youngs to concurrent sentences of imprisonment for 240 months on Count One and 120 months on Count Two, and 40 years of supervised release with numerous conditions. The court also imposed the special assessment for each count....

On appeal, Youngs disputes the validity of his guilty plea because the district court did not inform Youngs that by pleading guilty, he faced the possibility of civil commitment under the Adam Walsh Child Protection and Safety Act of 2006 (the "Act") following the completion of his incarceration. *See* 18 U.S.C. § 4248(a) (2006).... The Act permits the Attorney General or the Director of the Bureau of Prisons ("BOP") to certify an individual in the custody of the BOP approaching the end of his period of incarceration as a "sexually dangerous person." *Id.* The inmate is provided a hearing in the district court, and his release from incarceration is stayed. *Id.* If, at the hearing, the Government demonstrates

---

1. This act requires a sex offender to register with each jurisdiction in which he resides, is employed, or is a student, and it requires states to impose a criminal penalty upon any sex offender who fails to register. 42 U.S.C. § 16913.

by clear and convincing evidence that the inmate is "sexually dangerous," the inmate is committed to further custody until the court determines that he is no longer sexually dangerous. *Id.* § 4248(d)–(e). A "sexually dangerous person" is defined as a person who (1) "has engaged or attempted to engage in sexually violent conduct or child molestation" and (2) "is sexually dangerous to others" in that he "suffers from a serious mental illness, abnormality, or disorder as a result of which he would have serious difficulty in refraining from sexually violent conduct or child molestation if released." *Id.* § 4247(a)(5)–(6)....

"It is a settled principle of federal constitutional law that a guilty plea violates due process and is therefore invalid if not entered voluntarily and intelligently." *Wilson v. McGinnis*, 413 F.3d 196, 199 (2d Cir.2005) (citing *Brady v. United States*, 397 U.S. 742, 748, 90 S.Ct. 1463, 25 L.Ed.2d 747 (1970); *Boykin v. Alabama*, 395 U.S. 238, 242–43, 89 S.Ct. 1709, 23 L.Ed.2d 274 (1969)). A district court may not accept a guilty plea "without an affirmative showing that it was intelligent and voluntary." *Boykin*, 395 U.S. at 242, 89 S.Ct. 1709. Rule 11 sets forth certain requirements of the district court's plea allocution to assist the court with "making the constitutionally required determination that a defendant's guilty plea is truly voluntary." *McCarthy v. United States*, 394 U.S. 459, 465, 89 S.Ct. 1166, 22 L.Ed.2d 418 (1969). To abide by Rule 11, the district court must advise the defendant of the right to plead not guilty, the rights waived by pleading guilty, and other specific consequences of pleading guilty, such as the maximum penalties he faces, "including imprisonment, fine, and term of supervised release." Fed.R.Crim.P. 11(b)(1); *Zhang v. United States*, 506 F.3d 162, 168 (2d Cir.2007) ("Rule 11 sets forth requirements for a plea allocution and is designed to ensure that a defendant's plea of guilty is a voluntary and intelligent choice...." (internal quotation marks omitted)).

However, any "variance from the requirements of [Rule 11] is harmless error if it does not affect substantial rights." Fed.R.Crim.P. 11(h). Rule 11 violations that are not objected to at the time of the plea are subject to plain error review under Rule 52(b) of the Federal Rules of Criminal Procedure. *United States v. Vonn*, 535 U.S. 55, 62–63, 122 S.Ct. 1043, 152 L.Ed.2d 90 (2002). Plain error review requires a defendant to demonstrate that "(1) there was error, (2) the error was plain, (3) the error prejudicially affected his substantial rights, and (4) the error seriously affected the fairness, integrity or public reputation of judicial proceedings." *United States v. Flaharty*, 295 F.3d 182, 195 (2d Cir.2002) (internal quotation marks and brackets omitted). To be plain, an error of the district court must be "obviously wrong in light of existing law." *United States v. Pipola*, 83 F.3d 556, 561 (2d Cir.1996). Additionally, to show that a Rule 11 violation was plain error, the defendant must demonstrate "that there is 'a reasonable probability that, but for the error, he would not have entered the plea.'" *United States v. Vaval*, 404 F.3d 144, 151 (2d Cir.2005) (quoting *United States v. Dominguez Benitez*, 542 U.S. 74, 83, 124 S.Ct. 2333, 159 L.Ed.2d 157 (2004)).... The Government asserts that Youngs did not timely object during his plea proceeding, and therefore this Court should review his claim under the plain error standard. Youngs does not disagree, and issues not argued in the briefs are considered waived. *See Norton v. Sam's Club*, 145 F.3d 114, 117 (2d Cir.1998). Moreover, regardless of the standard of review, we hold that the district court did not err by accepting Youngs's guilty plea without advising him of the civil commitment implications of the Act.

The United States Supreme Court has concluded that a defendant can make an intelligent and voluntary guilty plea satisfying due process if he is "fully aware of the *direct* consequences" of a guilty plea. *Brady*, 397 U.S. at 755, 90 S.Ct. 1463 (emphasis added) (adopting the language of the Fifth Circuit in *Shelton v. United States*, 246 F.2d 571, 572 n. 2 (5th Cir.1957) (en banc), *rev'd on other grounds*, 356 U.S. 26, 78 S.Ct. 563, 2 L.Ed.2d 579 (1958)). However, "[c]ertain possible consequences of a guilty plea are 'collateral' rather than direct and need not be explained to the defendant in order to ensure that the plea is voluntary." *United States v. U.S. Currency in the Amount of $228,536.00*, 895 F.2d 908, 915 (2d Cir.1990) (listing examples of collateral consequences, such as parole revocation, the likelihood of an unfavorable military discharge, and the potential for civil commitment proceedings). Thus, district courts need not inform a defendant of collateral consequences during the plea colloquy. *See United States v. Salerno*, 66 F.3d 544, 550–51 (2d Cir.1995) (holding that an enhancement in a future sentence based on the present conviction is a collateral consequence and need not be advised of by the district court in its plea colloquy). The requirements of Rule 11 are consistent with the principle that due process only requires courts to advise of direct consequences. *Michel v. United States*, 507 F.2d 461, 465 (2d Cir.1974) ("Rule 11 does not affect the long-standing rule in this as well as other circuits that the trial judge when accepting a plea of guilty is not bound to inquire whether a defendant is aware of the collateral effects of his plea.").

This Court has described direct consequences as those that have a "definite, immediate and largely automatic effect on the range of the defendant's punishment," and any other consequence is merely collateral. *Wilson*, 413 F.3d at 199 (internal quotation marks omitted); *see also Salerno*, 66 F.3d at 551 (affirming a conviction because an increased penalty for a future drug offense, while a "foreseeable possibility," is not "definite, immediate, and largely automatic" and therefore did not void the original guilty plea (internal quotation marks omitted)); *U.S. Currency*, 895 F.2d at 916 ("[C]ivil forfeiture is not a direct consequence of a guilty plea because it does not represent a definite, immediate and largely automatic effect on the range of the defendant's punishment." (internal quotation marks omitted)).

Civil commitment under the Act is not "definite, immediate, and largely automatic." *See U.S. Currency*, 895 F.2d at 916. Youngs will not face possible confinement under the Act until the end of his period of incarceration. Once he reaches that time, civil commitment is uncertain; the Government would first have to choose to certify Youngs for civil commitment and then would have to prove by clear and convincing evidence that Youngs is, *at that time*, a sexually dangerous person. To do so, it will have to demonstrate both a predicate act of sexual violence or child molestation as well as an illness, abnormality or disorder that makes him dangerous to others. The evidence available to support Youngs's conviction on Count One likely satisfies the first element, but the future satisfaction of the second element is far from certain at this time.[2] Because the possibility of civil commitment will only arise at the end of Youngs's twenty-year prison sentence and then will occur only if the Government meets its high burden under the Act, civil commitment is not definite, immediate, and automatic, and is therefore not a "direct" consequence of a guilty plea as defined by this Court. Other circuits have come to the same conclusion regarding similar civil commitment statutes. *Steele v. Murphy*, 365 F.3d 14, 17 (1st Cir.2004)

---

2. As described above, Youngs was convicted of both the possession and production of child pornography. At the time of his guilty plea, Youngs reserved his right to challenge a five-level increase in his total offense level for engaging in a pattern of activity involving the sexual abuse or exploitation of a minor pursuant to Section 2G2.2(b)(5) of the United States Sentencing Guidelines. At sentencing, the district court indicated that there was evidence to support one instance of sexual abuse of a minor, but declined to apply the enhancement because one instance did not constitute a pattern of activity. We highlight these facts not to comment on the likelihood of the Government succeeding in a future civil commitment proceeding, but rather to emphasize that many factual and legal issues would have to be resolved before a court decides to civilly commit Youngs.

(holding that potential civil commitment under a state statute was a "collateral consequence of pleading guilty"); *George v. Black*, 732 F.2d 108, 110–11 (8th Cir.1984) (holding that the possibility that a sex offender could face civil commitment under a state statute was a collateral consequence because "civil commitment does not flow automatically from the plea"). Because civil commitment is a collateral consequence, the district court was not required to advise of the possibility of civil commitment before accepting Youngs's plea....

Youngs, however, urges this Court to ignore what he terms the "formalist distinction between direct and collateral consequences." He relies upon the United States Supreme Court's holding in *Padilla v. Kentucky* that a defense attorney's incorrect advice to his client about the risk of deportation constituted ineffective assistance of counsel in violation of the Sixth Amendment and the language in the opinion that indicates that the direct/collateral distinction may not be apt in the Sixth Amendment context. ___ U.S. ___, 130 S.Ct. 1473, 1481–82, 176 L.Ed.2d 284 (2010).

In *Padilla*, the Kentucky Supreme Court had rejected below the defendant's ineffective assistance of counsel claim based on his lawyer's advice that he was unlikely to be deported as a result of his guilty plea for a state drug charge. *Id.* at 1478, 1481. The U.S. Supreme Court reversed, finding that the severity of deportation as a consequence of a guilty plea, as well as the changes in federal immigration law that have made deportation "virtually inevitable" for many offenses, require that counsel give accurate advice on deportation to noncitizens prior to a guilty plea proceeding involving those offenses. *Id.* at 1478. In the context of the Sixth Amendment right-to-counsel analysis, the Court found deportation "uniquely difficult to classify as either a direct or collateral consequence," *id.* at 1482, because noncitizens convicted of certain crimes faced almost certain deportation and deportation is an "integral part" of the penalty for those crimes, *id.* at 1480. Noting that it had "never applied a distinction between direct and collateral consequences" to define reasonable assistance of counsel in the Sixth Amendment context, the Court determined that the distinction was "ill-suited" for evaluating the effectiveness of counsel in advising of deportation, and held that "advice regarding deportation is not categorically removed from the ambit of the Sixth Amendment right to counsel." *Id.* at 1481–82.

While Youngs refers to *Padilla* as representing a "trend away from the distinction between direct and collateral consequences," ... [citations to record omitted], *Padilla*'s holding was limited to the requirement of counsel to advise of deportation pursuant to their Sixth Amendment responsibilities. These Sixth Amendment responsibilities of counsel to advise of the advantages and disadvantages of a guilty plea are greater than the responsibilities of a court under the Fifth Amendment. *See Libretti v. United States*, 516 U.S. 29, 50–51, 116 S.Ct. 356, 133 L.Ed.2d 271 (1995) (holding that counsel, not the court, bears the responsibility of advising a defendant of the consequences of a guilty plea, apart from the "small class of rights" enumerated in Rule 11). Thus, the *Padilla* Court's unwillingness to apply the direct/collateral distinction in the Sixth Amendment context does not demonstrate the Court's intention to do away with that distinction entirely in the Fifth Amendment context. *See United States v. Delgado-Ramos*, 635 F.3d 1237, 1240 (9th Cir.2011) (noting that in *Padilla* the Court "had no occasion to consider the scope of a district court's obligation" under due process or Rule 11, or "the continued viability of the distinction between direct and collateral consequences in the due process context"); *see also United States v. Nicholson*, 676 F.3d 376, 381 n. 3 (4th Cir.2012) (noting that the Court in *Padilla* did not address district courts' Rule 11 obligations).

While the Court in *Padilla* did not discard the direct/collateral distinction for due process, we recognize that *Padilla* may create some uncertainty as to the usefulness of categorizing *certain* consequences as either "direct" or "collateral" in the Fifth Amendment context.[3] We nonetheless conclude that advising of the possibility of civil commitment under the Act does not fall within the scope of a district court's due process obligations because the concerns expressed by the Supreme Court in *Padilla* as to deportation in the context of adequate counsel under the Sixth Amendment do not apply to such a remote and uncertain consequence as civil commitment.[4]

In deeming deportation a "virtually inevitable" result of a noncitizen's conviction for certain offenses, the Supreme Court pointed out in *Padilla* that the only way for such defendants to avoid deportation is the "possible exercise of limited remnants of equitable discretion vested in the Attorney General to cancel removal for noncitizens convicted of particular classes of offenses." *Padilla*, 130 S.Ct. at 1478, 1480. Because deportation under these circumstances is nearly automatic, the Court concluded that deportation must be reviewed by counsel. *Id.* at 1482–83. As discussed above, however, future civil commitment under the Act is not nearly as certain. The Act provides discretion to the Government in choosing whom to certify for possible civil commitment. Unlike deportation, the district court ultimately determines whether a defendant is civilly committed. While the qualifying misconduct here is likely a predicate to consideration for civil commitment, once the Government decides to certify an inmate — Youngs or anyone else — for civil commitment, the Government will still have to establish by clear and convincing evidence that the inmate suffers from a condition that will make him sexually dangerous to others.[5] Thus, the likelihood of Youngs's civil commitment is uncertain, both at the time of his plea and at the completion of his period of incarceration.

We conclude, therefore, that the district court had no obligation to advise Youngs of the possibility of civil commitment prior to accepting his guilty plea.[6] ... The district court was not required to advise Youngs of the possibility of civil commitment under the Act before accepting his guilty plea. Therefore, we hold that Youngs's plea was knowing and voluntary and AFFIRM his conviction.

---

3. For example, the Advisory Committee on Criminal Rules has proposed an amendment to Rule 11 to include a "generic warning" of deportation risks in the plea colloquy, and this proposed amendment has been published for public comment. Report of the Advisory Committee on Criminal Rules at 2, 3 (Dec. 8, 2010).

4. Although the Eleventh Circuit recently extended *Padilla*'s reasoning to affirmative misrepresentations by counsel regarding civil commitment, its holding was also limited to the Sixth Amendment context. *See Bauder v. Dep't of Corr.*, 619 F.3d 1272, 1275 (11th Cir.2010) (per curiam). Moreover, that court reinforced the notion that civil commitment is a collateral consequence by using "collateral" in its discussion of *Padilla*: "Even if one could argue that the law was unclear, the Supreme Court has noted that when the law is unclear a criminal defense attorney must advise his client that the 'pending criminal charges may carry a risk of adverse [collateral] consequences.'" *Bauder*, 619 F.3d at 1275 (quoting *Padilla*, 130 S.Ct. at 1483) (alteration in *Bauder*)....

5. While no formal statistical analysis has been done of the Act's civil commitment provisions, the Court of Appeals for the Fourth Circuit noted recently that although approximately 130 individuals have been certified for civil commitment since the Act was enacted, nearly two dozen of the certifications were subsequently dismissed by the Government because it determined that the individual did not meet the requirements of the Act. *United States v. Timms*, 664 F.3d 436, 440 n. 3 & 452 (4th Cir.2012).

6. With this conclusion, we do not mean to discourage district courts from alerting defendants to the possibility of civil commitment during the plea allocation. To the contrary, we think district judges might well want to include the risks of potential post-sentence long-term civil commitment when allocuting defendants who plead guilty to offenses subjecting them to that risk. While such a warning is not required, it is a potential consequence that could affect defendants' assessment of the costs and benefits of a guilty plea, and alerting defendants to it on the record could forestall later claims by defendants that they were misadvised by counsel concerning the relative costs and benefits of the plea.

2. Minors

People v. Samantha R.

Criminal Court, City of New York, Kings County, New York, 2011
33 Misc. 3d 1235, 941 N.Y.S.2d 540

JOHN T. HECHT, J.

The defendant is a 16-year old with no criminal history who is charged with the offense of loitering for the purpose of prostitution. The charge is a non-criminal violation punishable by no more than fifteen days jail. When she appeared before me in the arraignment part she was also the subject of a warrant that had issued out of Family Court.

> The accusatory instrument pertinently alleges that Police Officer Albert Q. Dodson:

> observed the defendant remain in or wander about a public place for twenty minutes, during which defendant repeatedly beckoned to passers-by and stopped two passers-by, engaging in conversation with said passers-by; stop only male passers-by and defendant did not beckon to or converse with female passers-by who passed by during the same period ... ; standing in the middle of the road while beckoning to motorists. ...

[D]efendant stated, in substance, "I was coming from a party with my cousin."

At defendant's arraignment, I addressed *sua sponte* whether I should dismiss this prosecution both as an exercise of my interests-of-justice power and in light of the recently enacted Safe Harbour for Exploited Children Act (the "Safe Harbour Act") (as added by L 2008, ch 569 [eff Apr. 1, 2010]), which I read to express the intent of the Legislature that 16- and 17-year-olds who are charged with prostitution offenses should be referred to Family Court rather than prosecuted criminally. The People requested an opportunity to address my proposed dismissal in writing, even though I noted that the legislative sponsors of the Safe Harbour Act believed that the mere pendency of criminal charges against these children was itself harmful:

> [A]rresting, prosecuting and incarcerating victimized youth serves to retraumatize them and to increase their feelings of low self-esteem. This only makes the process of recovery more difficult. Appropriate services for sexually exploited youth do not exist in the juvenile justice system and both federal and international law recognize that sexually exploited youth are the victims of crime and should be treated as such. Therefore, *sexually exploited youth should not be prosecuted under the Penal Law for acts of prostitution.* Instead services should be created to meet the needs of these youth outside of the justice system. Sexually exploited youth deserve the protection and services of the family court through processes in place for persons in need of supervision, including diversion, crisis intervention, counseling, and emergency and long term housing services.

(Sponsor's Mem, Bill Jacket, Safe Harbour Act, L 2008, ch 569 [emphasis supplied]).

Ultimately, I afforded the People and the defense an opportunity to respond to the proposed dismissal, not only in fairness to the People (*see People v. Clayton*, 41 A.D.2d 204, 208, 342 N.Y.S.2d 106 [2nd Dep't 1973]), but also to assure that any decision I made would be based on a consideration of all appropriate arguments. ... Now, on a record that includes a submission by the People, I conclude that this prosecution should be dismissed in the interests of justice. ... A court may dismiss a prosecution on its own motion (*see*

CPL 170.40[2]; *People v. Wingard*, 33 N.Y.2d 192 [1973]). My review of the factors relevant to such a dismissal is informed by recent legislative enactments that reveal an understanding that the victim of a prostitution offense may be the prostitute herself. In fact, if the prostitute or, as here, alleged would-be prostitute, is 16- or 17-years-old, the Legislature defines her as a "sexually exploited child" who may obtain child welfare services for sexually exploited children (*see* Social Services Law 447-a [1][b]; [d]; 447-b).

The Legislature passed the Safe Harbour Act, among other things, to make the Family Court's services available to sexually exploited children up to the age of 18. It amended the definition of a "person in need of supervision" ("PINS"), with regard to whom a Family Court proceeding may be originated, to include a child under 18 charged with prostitution (*see* Family Ct Act 712[a]) or loitering for the purpose of prostitution (*see* Family Ct Act 712[a]; Social Services Law 447-a [1][d]).[1] As a Family Court judge has observed, the Safe Harbour Act "expresses a preference that children who have been sexually exploited be spared criminal prosecution ... in favor of receiving rehabilitative services." (*Matter of Bobby P.*, 28 Misc.3d 959, 969, 907 N.Y.S.2d 540 [Fam Ct Queens County 2010]; *see also* Sobie, Practice Commentaries, McKinney's Cons Laws of NY, Family Ct Act 732 ["The intent is to immunize most children who have committed sexual offenses from criminal prosecution..., substituting PINS adjudication and services."]).

The Safe Harbour Act came into effect against the backdrop of the federal Victims of Trafficking and Violence Protection Act of 2000 (22 U.S.C. § 7101 *et seq.*, as added by Pub L 106-386, 114 U.S. Stat 1464), which defined the crimes of forced labor and sex trafficking, provided support for trafficking victims, and established a system for monitoring worldwide anti-trafficking efforts (*see* Hon. Betty Weinberg Ellerin, *Introduction*, Lawyers Manual on Human Trafficking ("Lawyers Manual"), Supreme Court of the State of New York, Appellate Division, First Department and the New York State Judicial Committee on Women in the Courts, xx [2011]). Under federal law, if a 16- or 17-year-old has been induced to be a prostitute, she is considered to be a victim of a "severe form[ ] of trafficking in persons" (*see* Victims of Trafficking and Violence Protection Act of 2000, § 103[8] [22 USC 7102[8][a]]). In 2000, Congress also provided avenues of immigration relief for children under 18 who are victims of a severe form of trafficking, i.e., prostitution, through "T" and "U" visas (*see* Slocum, *Immigration Remedies for Victims of Human Trafficking*, Lawyers Manual, at 209, 215).

The Safe Harbour Act added to the protections put in place by New York's Anti-Human Trafficking Act of 2006 (as added by L 2007, ch 74, sec 2 [eff Nov. 1, 2007]), which created the new offense of sex trafficking (*see* Penal Law 230.34). In passing this act, New York joined 29 states and the federal government in an effort not only "to prosecute the traffickers" but also to "provide[ ] these unique victims with the social services they need to break the ties with their traffickers and the opportunity to live healthy and productive lives" (*see* Letter from Mayor Michael R. Bloomberg, June 4, 2007, at 22, Bill Jacket, L 2007, ch 74; *see also* Letter from Michael E. Bongiorno, President, District Attorneys Association of the State of New York, May 31, 2007, at 24, Bill Jacket, L 2007, ch 74 [Act "addresses the abhorrent act of human trafficking by going after the traffickers and aiding their victims"]).

---

1. Although sections 712[a] and 732[b] of the Family Court Act appear to require the consent of the 16- or 17-year-old in order for a loitering allegation to form the basis of a PINS petition, section 732 [a][i] of the Act does not and it applies to loitering by referencing Social Services Law 447-a [1][d]. (*See* Sobie, Practice Commentaries, McKinney's Cons Laws of NY, Family Ct Act 732 [Section 732[a] "paints with a far broader brush than" Section 712[a]].)

More recently, the Criminal Procedure Law was amended to provide that a victim of sex trafficking may seek vacatur of judgments of conviction for loitering (the charge here) and prostitution (*see* CPL 440.10[i] [eff Aug.13, 2010]). As a result, courts have vacated convictions of individuals who had engaged in prostitution as a result of their having been trafficking victims (*see People v. Gonzalez*, 32 Misc.3d 831, 927 N.Y.S.2d 567 [Crim Ct, N.Y. County 2011]; *People v. G.M.*, 32 Misc.3d 274, 922 N.Y.S.2d 761 [Crim Ct, Queens County 2011]), including at least one who was first convicted of prostitution when she was 17, and who had been prostituted from as young as 13 (*see People v. Jane Doe*, ___ Misc.3d ___, 2011 N.Y. Slip op 21411, 2011 WL 5865295 [Sup Ct, Bronx County 2011]).

In connection with the passage of the Safe Harbour Act, many graphic details of the situation of, and consequences to, the children involved in child prostitution came into public focus. For example, a report prepared for the New York State Office of Children and Family Services determined that, in this state, the overwhelming majority of children who were identified as having been subjected to commercial sexual exploitation, including prostitution, had prior child-welfare involvement through child abuse and neglect investigations and/or foster care placement. In New York City, almost half had been adjudicated PINS, and over half had a prior juvenile justice placement. Demographically, they were identified predominantly as female (85%), black (67%), and 16- or 17-years-old (59%) (*see* Gragg, Petta, Bernstein, Eisen and Quinn, *New York Prevalence Study of Commercially Sexually Exploited Children, Final Report*, at 42, 86 [NYS Office of Children and Family Services, Apr. 18, 2007 ("OCFS Report")].

The OCFS Report estimated that the commercial sexual exploitation of children affects 2,500 children in New York State each year, although it suggested that many more such children are "hidden" because they are runaways or homeless or, out of shame or embarrassment, do not disclose their sexual exploitation. Many of these children have been the victims of sexual and other physical abuse; many suffer from learning disabilities and limitations; many engage in what has been called "survival sex." They are at risk for HIV infection, post-traumatic stress disorder and other forms of mental illness and violence (*id.* at 3–5, 8, 25).

The Safe Harbour Act did not amend the Penal Law and provide a defense of infancy to a 16- or 17-year-old charged with a prostitution offense.[2] Yet a Penal Law prosecution of such an individual, whom the Legislature elsewhere defines as a "sexually exploited child," whom the legislative materials reviewed above depict as vulnerable and likely already known to Family Court, and who may qualify as a "victim" under both federal and state

---

2. I note that Social Services Law 447-b [2] provides that "[a]ll of the services created under this title may, to the extent possible provided by law, be available to all sexually exploited children whether they are accessed voluntarily, [or] as a condition of an adjournment in contemplation of dismissal issued in criminal court...." Although this reference to criminal court might be read as contemplating that sexually exploited children will continue to be prosecuted for prostitution offenses, I read this language otherwise. It emphasizes that the intent of the Safe Harbour Act is to make social services available to all sexually exploited children, including those who may have matters, of whatever nature, pending in criminal court. In other words, this section of the Social Services Law, which pertains to the availability of social services to exploited children, says nothing about jurisdiction. To the extent that the Safe Harbour Act does address jurisdiction, as discussed above, it expands Family Court's PINS jurisdiction in preference to that of criminal court for sexually exploited children charged with prostitution offenses.

anti-trafficking laws and therefore for vacatur of any conviction here, is inconsistent with the ameliorative intent of the Safe Harbour Act and other statutes cited.[3]

Further, as the Chief Judge of this State has recently pointed out, New York is out of step with virtually every other jurisdiction in this country (48 states and the District of Columbia) with regard to the age of criminal responsibility (*see* Chief Judge Jonathan Lippman, *Remarks to Citizens Crime Commission of New York City* [Sept. 1, 2011], available at http:// www.nycourts.gov/ip/sentencing/CJLippmansRemarksCitizensCrime Commission September21201.pdf). He has queried whether 16- and 17-year-olds charged with non-violent offenses should continue to be prosecuted in criminal court rather than have their alleged offenses adjudicated in Family Court:

> Do we really want these teenagers to be processed in an adult criminal justice system focused on punishment and incarceration? ... where rehabilitative options are limited ... where they may be jailed ... where they may be victimized ... and where they may be burdened with a criminal record that bars them from future employment and educational opportunities?
>
> Or do we as a state want these young people to go through a family court system that is equipped to intervene meaningfully in their lives, before their troubles escalate into more serious criminality, and without exposing them to a criminal record? ... a system that is focused on rehabilitation and getting children back on the right track, that offers supervision, mental health treatment, remedial education and other services and programs ... a system where judges are obligated by law to act in the "best interests" of the children who come before them—a mandate that does not exist in criminal court.

Id....

The factors set forth in CPL 170.40 clearly demonstrate to me that the prosecution of this defendant would constitute injustice.... First, the seriousness and circumstances of the offense alleged here are as minimally serious as can be. The charged offense, Penal Law 240.37, is a violation, which is not even a "crime" under the Penal Law's classification scheme (*see* Penal Law 10.00[3]; [4]). The circumstances of the offense are likewise minimally serious: the defendant is alleged to have engaged in the proscribed conduct— loitering in the middle of the street—for a total of twenty minutes and to have stopped two passers-by to engage them in "conversation."

Second, the extent of harm caused by the offense is likewise minimal. Although I recognize, as Judge Richard Weinberg of Midtown Community Court reasoned when he denied a motion similar to the present (*see People v. Lewis*, 2010NY03560, NYLJ, decided July 12, 2011, at *1 [Crim Ct, N.Y. County, Weinberg, J.]), that prostitution may negatively impact all participants as well as the neighborhoods where it occurs, the harm of the

---

3. Another inconsistency that arises from prosecuting a 16-year-old child, such as defendant here, lies within the Penal Law itself, which provides that a 16-year-old cannot legally consent to engage in sexual intercourse (*see* Penal Law 130.05[3]), and is a rape victim if she engages in intercourse with someone who is 21 or older (*see* Penal Law 130.25[2]; 130.40[2]); yet at the same time she is a criminal if she consents to have intercourse for money. The Penal Law's provisions in this regard can more easily be reconciled if a 16-year-old were considered to be incapable of consenting to intercourse, whether or not money is involved, for if she is incapable of consenting to intercourse, that incapacity does not change because she also agrees to accept money. While I do not need to resolve this inconsistency, I note that it demonstrates another legislative indication that, for certain purposes at least, the Penal Law does not treat 16-year-olds as adults.

violation charged here is minimal. More importantly, I am persuaded that the harm to defendant's own physical and mental welfare from the alleged conduct is greater than any other societal harm that I can see in this particular case.

Third, I will assume that evidence of guilt is strong. Further, I am aware of no misconduct in the investigation, arrest and prosecution of defendant. To the contrary, the District Attorney is prosecuting this case with a focus on rehabilitative, rather than punitive, concerns. But even so, the absence of these factors does not dissuade me from my conclusion that dismissal is appropriate.

Fourth, the history, character and condition of defendant as revealed in this record are a 16-year-old who has no prior involvement with the criminal justice system, who has lived her entire life with her grandmother in New York City, who has completed the 11th grade, and who attends school.

Fifth, I find that there would be little purpose in imposing a sentence on defendant and that the effect of any sentence would do more harm than good.... The sentencing options in Criminal Court are limited. The likely sentence in a case such as this would not involve jail. Even if the sentence were a conditional discharge with required attendance at a counseling program, I see no purpose in imposing such a sentence when the options available in Family Court, as suggested by the Chief Judge, are likely superior because of the statutory mandate of considering the child's "best interests."... On the other hand, the effect of a conviction in this case would be seriously and inappropriately detrimental to the defendant. If convicted and sentenced, she would have a record, albeit for a non-criminal offense. Such a record — unlike that for a conviction of virtually any other violation — would not be subject to sealing pursuant to the general sealing statute (*see* CPL 160.55 [1]). And, as a result of another legal anomaly that arises from the definition of "youth" in the Criminal Procedure Law (*see* CPL 720.10[1] [a "youth" is a person 16- to 18-years-old charged with a "crime"]), a conviction of this offense would not be subject to replacement by a youthful offender adjudication and sealing under the youthful offender law (*see People v. Caruso*, 92 Misc.2d 559, 400 N.Y.S.2d 686 [Onandaga County Ct 1977]). By contrast, any other adolescent with no prior record would be entitled to have her first *misdemeanor* conviction replaced by a youthful offender finding (*see* CPL 720.20[1][b] [court must find eligible youth to be a youthful offender upon her first conviction in criminal court]) — even though a misdemeanor is a more serious offense than the one charged here. Indeed, an adolescent convicted of a felony may be eligible to have her first felony conviction replaced by a youthful offender adjudication (*see* CPL 720.20[1][a]), leaving that adolescent with no public record of conviction. In sum, defendant here may have a life-long record of conviction of a stigmatizing offense (unless it were subsequently vacated pursuant to CPL 440.10[i] or some other provision of law),[5] when other adolescents whose cases were resolved in more unfavorable circumstances (*i.e.*, conviction of a misdemeanor or felony) or adults similarly situated (*i.e.*, convicted of a violation other than Penal Law 240.37) would not suffer that same detriment.

Sixth, I do not believe that dismissal will impact the safety or welfare of the community. Although prostitution may have negative collateral effects on the community, attributing such effects to the alleged conduct of this particular defendant would surely be an exag-

---

5. *See* Letter from Danielle Grant, Girls Educational and Mentoring Services, July 3, 2008, at 82, Bill Jacket, Safe Harbour Act, L 2008, ch 569 [their "records have been tarnished, so that now as adults they can't do the basic things, like getting a real job and anything else that requires background checks"].

geration.... I further surmise that the District Attorney may find that maintaining a prosecution against an alleged teen prostitute might give law enforcement a tool with which to fight trafficking. Yet I doubt whether any public interest in this regard cannot equally be achieved if this case were handled in Family rather than Criminal Court. That is, the venue of the adjudication should not preclude a District Attorney from investigating the allegation that a teenager has been prostituted. More importantly, I would find it hard to justify refusing to dismiss the case against a teenager only so that prosecutors might prove that she is the victim of the crime with which she is charged (*cf.* Penal Law 230.36 ["In a prosecution for sex trafficking, a person from whose prostitution activity another person is alleged to have advanced or ... profited ... shall not be deemed to be an accomplice"]).

Seventh, I believe that the public's confidence in the criminal justice system will be enhanced by a dismissal here. The criminal justice system is not always the best venue for addressing societal problems. Here, the alleged offense—which is not a crime—involves someone who, according to the Penal Law, is barely an adult, if even that (see n. 3 *supra*), and who, according to the Social Services Law, is a "sexually exploited child." In these circumstances, the purposes of the Penal Law, which include providing "an appropriate public response to particular offenses" (*see* Penal Law 1.05[5]), favor an exercise of the criminal justice system's mercy-dispensing power to dismiss this prosecution. I believe that as a result of a dismissal here, the public will be confident that our laws are not inflexible or unduly harsh and that they do not operate in isolation of a growing awareness that, in the appropriate case, the lessened culpability of a 16-year-old vis-á-vis an adult, as well as the recognition that she is exploited if not also victimized, may require that the allegations against her be addressed outside criminal court.

For these reasons, this matter is dismissed. Sealing is stayed 30 days to allow the People an opportunity to seek Family Court adjudication of this matter and to appeal.... The foregoing constitutes the decision and order of the court.

C. Sentencing Factors

1. Sentencing Guidelines

Kaleb Noblett

Caging Uncertainty: Responsible Reform of Federal
Child Pornography Sentencing Guidelines

42 N. Ky. L. Rev. 65, 68–69 (2015)

The U.S. Sentencing Guidelines Manual contains chapters and sections, each one relating to specific violations of U.S. Code provisions.... The offense is assigned a "base offense level," which serves as the numerical starting point for the offense.... The practitioners—typically a probation officer, the prosecution, and defense—then apply the facts of the case to any number of "specific offense characteristics".... Each specific offense characteristic includes a number that, if applicable, is added to the base offense level.... Mitigating factors may also be included in a specific guideline, in which case a set number is subtracted from the total.... An offender's criminal history is figured, and he is assigned a category (I–VI) that generally corresponds to the depth of the offender's prior record.... Finally, the total number derived from combining the base level, specific offense characteristics, and any mitigating factors is found on a chart that includes columns for each category of criminal history.... The defendant thus lands in a range of months that corresponds to his number.... There are also separate considerations that may result in an upward or downward variance or "departure." ...

United States v. Blinkinsop

Ninth Circuit, 2010
606 F.3d 1110

GOODWIN, Senior Circuit Judge:

Paul Blinkinsop, who pled guilty to one count of receiving child pornography in violation of 18 U.S.C. § 2252A(a)(2), appeals his sentence as to his 97-month imprisonment and three special conditions of his 5-year supervised release. We affirm in part, vacate in part, and order a limited remand for resentencing....

In 2008, the Wyoming Internet Crimes Against Children Task Force determined that a computer registered to Blinkinsop contained images of child pornography available to other users on an Internet shared program, LimeWire File Share.[1] This information was reported to the Air Force Office of Special Investigations, which, with Immigration and Customs Agents, interviewed Blinkinsop, an Air Force Staff Sergeant, stationed at Malmstron Air Force Base in Great Falls, Montana. During the interview, Blinkinsop admitted that he viewed child pornography over the Internet via his computer and that he used search terms, such as "teenage" and "school girl." ... When Blinkinsop refused consent to search his computer, investigators obtained a search warrant and seized his computer and external storage equipment from his residence. A forensic analysis of Blinkinsop's equipment revealed more than 600 images of child pornography created from 2002–2008, including 42 videos and 99 still pictures, with some of the children younger than 12 years old. Videos on Blinkinsop's computer included depictions of prepubescent girls being penetrated in anal and vaginal intercourse, bondage, and urination.

Blinkinsop was indicted in Count I for Receipt of Child Pornography, in violation of 18 U.S.C. § 2252A(a)(2), and, in Count II, for Possession of Child Pornography, in violation of 18 U.S.C. § 2252A(a)(5)(B); the indictment included a forfeiture allegation under 18 U.S.C. § 2252A(a)(3) for Blinkinsop's computer and data-storage equipment. At his change-of-plea hearing, Blinkinsop admitted that he sought and downloaded child pornography from the Internet. He pled guilty to receiving child pornography and admitted the forfeiture allegation. In accordance with Blinkinsop's plea agreement, the government dismissed Count II for possessing child pornography.

The probation office calculated Blinkinsop's advisory Sentencing Guidelines range at 97 to 121 months of imprisonment and his supervised release term of 5 years to life under 18 U.S.C. § 3583(k). The district judge considered the 18 U.S.C. § 3553(a) factors and weighed the serious nature of Blinkinsop's crime against his personal record, military service, and lack of criminal history before imposing the low-end, 97-month imprisonment term with 5 years of supervised release. In addition, the judge imposed thirteen special conditions of supervised release without explanation. Although the judge asked counsel if they had any statements that they wanted placed on the record "as to why sentence as stated should not be the judgment entered," neither counsel objected to the sentence, and Blinkinsop thanked the judge for it.... On appeal, Blinkinsop challenges his imprisonment term as being unreasonable, because the district judge allegedly failed to take into account

---

1. "LimeWire is a peer-to-peer file sharing application that connects users who wish to share data files with one another." *United States v. Lewis*, 554 F.3d 208, 211 (1st Cir.2009).

fully his background, potential for rehabilitation, and low recidivism risk. He also argues that his supervised-release special conditions, relating to his proximity to children, possession of a camera phone, and ban on his access to the Internet are unreasonable and overbroad....

We review a district judge's sentence for abuse of discretion. *Gall v. United States*, 552 U.S. 38, 51, 128 S.Ct. 586, 169 L.Ed.2d 445 (2007). This two-part analysis requires determining: (1) whether there was procedural error in formulating the sentence, and (2) whether the sentence is substantively reasonable. *Id.* "[W]hen the judge's discretionary decision accords with the Commission's view of the appropriate application of § 3553(a) in the mine run of cases, it is probable that the sentence is reasonable." *Rita v. United States*, 551 U.S. 338, 351, 127 S.Ct. 2456, 168 L.Ed.2d 203 (2007); *see United States v. Carty*, 520 F.3d 984, 994 (9th Cir.2008) (en banc) (adopting this standard in our circuit). Since "'[t]he sentencing judge has access to, and greater familiarity with, the individual case and the individual defendant before him than the Commission or the appeals court,'" our determination that "a 'different sentence [i]s appropriate is insufficient to justify reversal of the district court.'" *United States v. Carter*, 560 F.3d 1107, 1120 (9th Cir.) (quoting *Gall*, 552 U.S. at 51, 128 S.Ct. 586), *cert. denied*, ___ U.S. ___, 130 S.Ct. 273, 175 L.Ed.2d 184 (2009)....

Because Blinkinsop did not object to his imprisonment term at sentencing, the district judge's sentencing procedure is reviewed for plain error.[2] *United States v. Sylvester Norman Knows His Gun, III*, 438 F.3d 913, 918 (9th Cir.2006). Proper sentencing procedure requires that, before imposing sentence, the district judge: (1) correctly calculate the Sentencing Guidelines range; (2) treat the Guidelines as advisory; (3) consider the 18 U.S.C. § 3553(a) factors;[3] (4) choose a sentence that is not based on clearly erroneous facts; (5) adequately explain the sentence; and (6) not presume that the Guidelines range is reasonable. *Carty*, 520 F.3d at 991–93; *see Gall*, 552 U.S. at 49–50, 128 S.Ct. 586. Adequate explanation not only derives from the judge's pronouncement of the sentence, but "may also be inferred from the PSR [presentence investigation report] or the record as a whole." *Carty*, 520 F.3d at 992.

At sentencing, the district judge recounted the calculation of Blinkinsop's sentence under the Sentencing Guidelines, including the adjustments that he had made.[4] Blinkinsop's

---

2. Plain error is (1) an error that (2) is plain, (3) affects substantial rights, and (4) seriously affects the fairness, integrity or public reputation of judicial proceedings. *United States v. Olano*, 507 U.S. 725, 732, 113 S.Ct. 1770, 123 L.Ed.2d 508 (1993) (citations, quotation marks, and alterations omitted).

3. These factors include: (1) the nature and circumstances of the offense and the history and characteristics of the defendant; (2) the need for the sentence imposed to reflect the seriousness of the offense, to promote respect for the law, and to provide just punishment, afford adequate deterrence to criminal conduct, to protect the public from further crimes by the defendant, and to provide the defendant with needed educational or vocational training, medical care, or other correctional treatment in the most effective manner; (3) the kinds of sentences available; (4) the Sentencing Guidelines; (5) policy statements issued by the Sentencing Commission; (6) the need to avoid unwarranted sentencing disparities; and (7) the need to provide restitution to any victims of the offense. 18 U.S.C. § 3553(a) (citations and quotation marks omitted).

4. The sentencing judge accepted the findings of fact in Blinkinsop's PSR, since there were no objections, and his plea agreement. The judge also accepted the probation office's calculation of Blinkinsop's Guidelines sentence, which was a total offense level of 30. This included a "two-level increase for the depiction of prepubescent minors in the material [U.S.S.G. § 2G2.2(b)(2)]; an additional four-level increase for the depiction of sadistic and masochistic conduct depicted in the material [U.S.S.G. § 2G2.2(b)(4)]; an additional two-level increase for the use of a computer [U.S.S.G. § 2G2.2(b)(6)]; and a five-level increase for the number of images being in excess of 600 [U.S.S.G. § 2G2.2(b)(7)]." Sentencing Transcript at 4–5. Blinkinsop's sentence included the following downward

total offense level of 30 and his criminal history of I, the lowest level, yielded an advisory Sentencing Guidelines range of 97 to 121 months of imprisonment. The judge explained to Blinkinsop that the Sentencing Guidelines range was "advisory" and "not binding upon the court," but that it did "serve as a kind of starting point or an initial benchmark ... for determination of an appropriate sentence." ... The judge also addressed the § 3553(a) factors.[5] ... Thereafter, the district judge sentenced Blinkinsop to an imprisonment term of 97 months and 5 years of supervised release.

Blinkinsop concedes that the sentencing judge correctly calculated his Guidelines range. He has not alleged that the judge relied on erroneous facts. The judge treated the Guidelines as advisory, and he considered the § 3553(a) factors, including the nature and circumstances of the crime in conjunction with Blinkinsop's military service and family support. In addition to the sentencing judge's explanation of Blinkinsop's sentence, his PSR advises that no factors were identified under § 3553(a) that would warrant sentencing Blinkinsop outside the advisory Guidelines range. The sentencing judge did not plainly err in carefully calculating Blinkinsop's imprisonment term at the lowest end of the Guidelines range....

Substantive reasonableness of a sentence, reviewed for abuse of discretion, is applicable in all sentencing decisions and is not affected by failure to object. *United States v. Autery*, 555 F.3d 864, 871 (9th Cir.2009). Having determined that Blinkinsop's sentence was procedurally proper, we consider in our substantive-reasonableness review the "totality of the circumstances" and recognize that "[t]he sentencing judge is in a superior position to find facts and judge their import under § 3553(a) in the individual case." *Gall*, 552 U.S. at 51, 128 S.Ct. 586 (citation and internal quotation marks omitted). We "'assume that district judges know the law and understand their obligation to consider all of the § 3553(a) factors, not just the Guidelines.'" *Autery*, 555 F.3d at 873 (quoting *Carty*, 520 F.3d at 992).

This court previously has confronted the arguments relating to substantive reasonableness raised by Blinkinsop on appeal. In *Carty*, the defendant, convicted of sexually abusing

---

adjustments: two-levels, because Blinkinsop's conduct was limited to receipt of materials concerning the sexual exploitation of minors rather than distribution, U.S.S.G. § 2G2.2(b)(1); two-levels for acceptance of responsibility, U.S.S.G. § 3E1.1(a); and one level for timely notification of his plea, on motion of the government.

5. Concerning the § 3553(a) factors, the sentencing judge explained:

Those [§ 3553(a)] factors are to be weighed and considered in your case, and indeed, they have been. And they include not only the kinds of sentences legally available, which we have spoken to, but the nature and the circumstances of these offenses—or the offense; your history and characteristics. And we are going to say more about that.

But *I also have an obligation to impose a sentence that reflects the seriousness of this criminal conduct; that will promote respect for the law and afford an adequate deterrent not only to you, but to others who might elect to engage in this kind of conduct.*

I have an obligation to fix a sentence that provides appropriate and just punishment; that will serve to incapacitate you, to the extent that is necessary, ... and appropriate to protect the public.

I am going to make provision in the sentence by way of recommendation that you be afforded an opportunity for residential sex offender treatment while in custody.... I am satisfied those are good programs. And they provide help to those who will participate in them....

I also have an obligation in making this determination to avoid unwarranted sentencing disparities within the federal criminal justice system. And in the process, to be mindful of decisions from the United State[s] Supreme Court.... [a]nd Ninth Circuit decisions.... All of those factors are to be considered, and, indeed, have been considered in your case.

[Citations to record omitted] (emphasis added).

his young niece, argued that the Guidelines sentence was "much greater than necessary" to achieve the goals of § 3553(a). 520 F.3d at 990. Like Blinkinsop's PSR, Carty's PSR advised that there was "no information concerning the offense or the offender which would warrant a departure from the sentencing guidelines." *Id.* The court imposed a Guidelines sentence, which this court held was substantively reasonable. *Id.* at 996. We determined that, when a district judge imposes a sentence within the Guidelines range, "it is probable that the sentence is reasonable," because the judge's application of the § 3553(a) factors accords with the Sentencing Commission's independent application of those factors in the "'mine run of cases.'" *Id.* at 994 (quoting *Rita*, 551 U.S. at 351, 127 S.Ct. 2456); *see Carter*, 560 F.3d at 1120 (determining that the Guidelines sentence, reflecting a defendant's criminal history and applying the § 3553(a) factors, was substantively reasonable and recognizing our deference to the sentencing judge).

When a district judge has considered the § 3553(a) factors and the totality of the circumstances supports the sentence, we have held that the sentence is substantively reasonable and that "[w]e may not reverse just because we think a different sentence is appropriate," particularly when a convicted defendant reargues his leniency plea from district court. *United States v. Overton*, 573 F.3d 679, 700 (9th Cir.) (citation and internal quotation marks omitted) (receipt-of-child-pornography case, where sentence was at the high end of the Guidelines range and the district judge considered the § 3553(a) factors as well as the needs for treatment and protection of the public), *cert. denied*, ___ U.S. ___, 130 S.Ct. 480, 175 L.Ed.2d 321 (2009).

In this case, Blinkinsop admittedly obtained in excess of 600 images, including 42 videos, showing prepubescent children engaged in sadistic and masochistic sexual acts by using specific search terms over the Internet. These facts contradict Blinkinsop's contention that he was merely a "passive collector of [child] pornography" and "a marginal player in the overall child pornography business." ... The images he collected were downloaded from the Internet, then moved and saved in electronic storage equipment. Blinkinsop incurred specific sentencing enhancements because his child pornography images involved the use of a computer and more than 600 images. U.S.S.G. §§ 2G2.2(b)(6), (b)(7). Blinkinsop has not challenged the application of these enhancements....

After reviewing the legislative history of 18 U.S.C. § 2252, we held that "the primary 'victims' that Congress sought to protect by enacting § 2252 were ... the children involved in the production of pornography." *United States v. Boos*, 127 F.3d 1207, 1211 (9th Cir.1997).[7] Photographs and films showing juveniles engaged in sexual activity "'is intrinsically related to the sexual abuse of children,'" because this documentation is "'a permanent record of the children's participation and the harm to the child is exacerbated by their circulation.'" *Id.* (quoting *New York v. Ferber*, 458 U.S. 747, 759, 102 S.Ct. 3348, 73 L.Ed.2d 1113 (1982)); *see Ashcroft v. Free Speech Coalition*, 535 U.S. 234, 244, 122 S.Ct. 1389, 152 L.Ed.2d 403 (2002) ("The sexual abuse of a child is a most serious crime and an act repugnant to the moral instincts of a decent people."). The children involved in pictorial and cinematic pornography additionally endure ongoing harm because their

---

7. *See United States v. Daniels*, 541 F.3d 915, 924 (9th Cir.2008) (recognizing that "merely possessing [or receiving] child pornography is not a victimless crime," because "it fuels the demand for the creation and distribution of child pornography," and evidence shows "the harm that children suffer when they are used in the creation of child pornography[,] ... when that pornography is distributed to others"), *cert. denied*, ___ U.S. ___, 129 S.Ct. 1600, 173 L.Ed.2d 687 (2009).

images have been preserved in a permanent medium.[8] Criminalizing possession and receipt of child pornography gives an incentive to such individuals to destroy these materials to alleviate continuing harm to the children exploited. *See Osborne v. Ohio*, 495 U.S. 103, 111, 110 S.Ct. 1691, 109 L.Ed.2d 98 (1990) ("The State's ban on possession and viewing encourages the possessors of [child pornography] to destroy them.").

The district judge considered the § 3553(a) factors and the totality of circumstances supporting Blinkinsop's sentence. Blinkinsop's arguments omit the recognition that the children depicted in the pornography that he received, viewed, stored, and transmitted are the real victims of his crime and that time is required for the sex-offender treatment during incarceration that Blinkinsop needs for his child-pornography addiction. In addition to being procedurally correct, Blinkinsop's imprisonment term, the lowest under the Sentencing Guidelines, is substantively reasonable, because it is well supported by the record and the governing law....

Blinkinsop concedes that he did not object at sentencing to the special conditions of his supervised release that he challenges on appeal. Therefore, our review is limited to plain error. *United States v. Rearden*, 349 F.3d 608, 618 (9th Cir.2003); *see United States v. Sullivan*, 451 F.3d 884, 894 (D.C.Cir.2006) ("Standing mute [after a sentence has been pronounced] is not an option, not if a litigant wishes to avoid a plain error standard of review on appeal."). Under 18 U.S.C. § 3583(d), a district judge has discretion to order special conditions of supervised release that are "reasonably related to the factors" in 18 U.S.C. § 3553(a).[9] *Rearden*, 349 F.3d at 618. Because the sentencing judge has all the evidence and impressions of a defendant's credibility, we accord wide latitude to the judge's imposition of supervised-release conditions, *United States v. Daniels*, 541 F.3d 915, 924 (9th Cir.2008), *cert. denied*, ___ U.S. ___, 129 S.Ct. 1600, 173 L.Ed.2d 687 (2009), "including restrictions that infringe on fundamental rights," *United States v. Bee*, 162 F.3d 1232, 1234 (9th Cir.1998). Special conditions are permissible, provided that "they are reasonably related to the goal[s] of deterrence, protection of the public, or rehabilitation of the offender, and involve no greater deprivation of liberty than is reasonably necessary for the purposes of supervised release." *Rearden*, 349 F.3d at 618 (citation and internal quotation marks omitted); *see*

---

8. The Supreme Court has recognized that

> [b]ecause the child's actions are reduced to a recording, the pornography may haunt him in future years, long after the original misdeed took place. A child who has posed for a camera must go through life knowing that the recording is circulating within the mass distribution system for child pornography.

Ferber, 458 U.S. at 759 n. 10, 102 S.Ct. 3348 (citation and quotation marks omitted).

9. In pertinent part, § 3553(a) provides:

> (a) **Factors to be considered in imposing a sentence.** — The court shall impose a sentence sufficient, but not greater than necessary, to comply with the purposes set forth in paragraph (2) of this subsection. The court, in determining the particular sentence to be imposed, shall consider —
> (1) the nature and circumstances of the offense and the history and characteristics of the defendant;
> (2) the need for the sentence imposed —
> (A) to reflect the seriousness of the offense, to promote respect for the law, and to provide just punishment for the offense;
> (B) to afford adequate deterrence to criminal conduct;
> (C) to protect the public from further crimes of the defendant; and
> (D) to provide the defendant with needed educational or vocational training, medical care, or other correctional treatment in the most effective manner[.]

18 U.S.C. § 3553(a).

United States v. T.M., 330 F.3d 1235, 1240 (9th Cir.2003) ("The conditions imposed run afoul of the supervised release statute because there is no reasonable relationship between them and either deterrence, public protection or rehabilitation."). Blinkinsop has the burden of showing that the special conditions that he appeals "involve[ ] a greater deprivation of liberty than is reasonably required to achieve deterrence, public protection, and offender rehabilitation." *United States v. Jeremiah*, 493 F.3d 1042, 1047 (9th Cir.2007)....

Relevant to this case is the statutory mandate that conviction under § 2252A requires supervised release for a "term of years *not less than 5*, or life." 18 U.S.C. § 3583(k) (emphasis added); *see* U.S.S.G. § 5D1.2(b)(2) (providing that "the length of the term of supervised release shall not be less than the minimum term of years specified for the offense ... and may be up to life, if the offense is a sex offense"). Therefore, Blinkinsop was sentenced to the mandatory minimum term of supervised release during which his conditions apply, special and otherwise, as opposed to life.[10] He challenges three special conditions of his supervised release: staying away from places frequented by children (Special Condition 4), possessing a camera phone (Special Condition 7), and banning his possession of a computer capable of accessing the Internet (Special Condition 13)....

Special Condition 4 provides: "Defendant shall not go to or loiter near school yards, parks, play grounds, arcades, or other paces primarily used by children under the age of 18." ... Blinkinsop argues that prohibiting him from going to or loitering near any school or place primarily used by children under 18 is overbroad. This court has upheld a more restrictive condition prohibiting a defendant, convicted of a child-pornography crime, *for life* from "frequent [ing], or loiter[ing], *within 100 feet* of school yards, parks, public swimming pools, playgrounds, youth centers, video arcade facilities, or other places primarily used by persons under the age of 18" or living "within direct view" of any of these areas. *Daniels*, 541 F.3d at 928 (alterations and emphases added); *see Rearden*, 349 F.3d at 620 (affirming special condition prohibiting defendant convicted of a child-pornography crime from "frequenting or loitering *within one hundred feet* of schoolyards, parks, public swimming pools, playgrounds, youth centers, video arcade facilities, or other places primarily used by children under the age of eighteen" (emphasis added)); *see also United States v. Brogdon*, 503 F.3d 555, 558 (6th Cir.2007) (affirming supervised-release conditions prohibiting defendant convicted of a child-pornography crime from "engag[ing] in *any* direct or indirect contact with *any* child under the age of eighteen," requiring that he "not loiter near schoolyards, playgrounds, swimming pools, arcades, theaters, or other places frequented by children," that "he not date any woman who has children under the age of eighteen in her custody," that "his place of residence not be located close to any childhood parks, schools, playgrounds, public pools or *any other location frequented by children*," and that his "probation officer may impose a curfew if it is deemed necessary" (alteration and emphases added)).

Like Blinkinsop, Daniels had no prior record of sex-crime convictions; he was convicted of receiving child pornography and had downloaded hundreds of images of child pornography from the Internet, including many "sadomasochistic images of prepubescent children and over 600 images depicting identified victims of child sexual abuse." *Daniels*, 541 F.3d at 927 (internal quotation marks omitted). Our court concluded that there was no error in prohibiting his access to children, because the "sheer volume" of Daniel's child-pornography collection suggested that he "at least had a sexual interest in children

---

10. Blinkinsop's counsel noted at sentencing that "the law provides for a lifetime of supervised release." ...

and that preventing his loitering around or living near areas where children frequent was reasonably related to his offense of conviction and to the goals of rehabilitating Daniels and protecting the public from his potential sexual interest in children." *Id.* at 928. In addition, Special Condition 9, which Blinkinsop did not appeal, states that, if required, he must "register as a sex offender" under the Adam Walsh Sex Offender Registration and Notification Act of 2006 ("SORNA"), 42 U.S.C. §§ 16901–16981, which registration would result in more stringent restrictions.[11] ... During pretrial supervision, Blinkinsop was subject to SORNA conditions, including electronic monitoring.

Although the sentencing judge did not explain his reasoning in imposing Special Condition 4, the record shows Blinkinsop's continued sexual interest in children, including images of sadistic and masochistic acts performed on prepubescent children. *See United States v. Betts*, 511 F.3d 872, 876 (9th Cir.2007) ("Circuit law establishes that a sentencing judge is not required to articulate on the record at sentencing the reasons for imposing each condition of supervised release, where we can determine from the record whether the court abused its discretion." (footnote, citation, and internal quotation marks omitted)). After analyzing Blinkinsop's child-pornography propensities and background, the probation officer recommended this special condition in the PSR, and the district judge adopted it. *See Daniels*, 541 F.3d at 921 (recognizing that "issues [including addictive behaviors] underlying sex offenses are typically deeply ingrained and require life long management" (internal quotation marks omitted)). Because Special Condition 4 addresses Blinkinsop's conduct, promotes his rehabilitation, and protects the public, it generally does not appear overbroad in achieving these results. *See Bee*, 162 F.3d at 1236 (recognizing that "even very broad conditions are reasonable if they are intended to promote the probationer's rehabilitation and to protect the public").

Blinkinsop has failed to show that Special Condition 4, a standard prohibition in child-pornography cases, is a greater deprivation on his liberty than required to achieve deterrence, public protection, and rehabilitation, as a general matter. *See Daniels*, 541 F.3d at 928. He has argued specifically on appeal, however, that this condition of his supervised release is overbroad in that it prevents him from attending school events in which his own children are participants. *Cf. United States v. Kerr*, 472 F.3d 517, 523 (8th Cir.2006) (noting that, "because [a convicted possessor and distributor of child pornography, prohibited access on supervised release to children] is childless, he is not restricted from contacting his own children"). Although the sentencing judge recognized that Blinkinsop "has two young children," he did not address this aspect of Special Condition 4 at the sentencing proceeding, and the record otherwise gives us no indication that Blinkinsop's being able to attend school events involving his children was considered in formulating this supervised-release special condition.... We note with approval that such a special condition can be tailored so that some access to a defendant, convicted of a child-pornography crime, may be allowed by requiring written permission from the probation officer, after consulting with treatment provider(s), to attend school events at which the offender's children are involved. *See, e.g., United States v. Stults*, 575 F.3d 834, 850 (8th Cir.2009) (finding reasonable special supervised-release conditions for defendant, convicted of possessing child pornography, that prohibited him from "having contact or residing with children under the age of 18,

---

11. With SORNA, Congress established a national registration system for sex offenders. 42 U.S.C. § 16901. *See United States v. Utesch*, 596 F.3d 302, 306–07 (6th Cir.2010) (discussing requirements and application of SORNA).

including his own children, unless approved in advance and in writing by the probation officer in consultation with the treatment providers," and "accessing or coming within 500 feet of schools, school yards, parks, arcades, playgrounds, amusement parks, or other places used primarily by children under the age of 18 *unless approved in advance and in writing by the probation officer*" (emphases added)), *cert. denied,* ___ U.S. ___, 130 S.Ct. 1309, 175 L.Ed.2d 1093 (2010).

The probation officer, who has regular contact with a sex offender on supervised release, in consultation with treatment provider(s), is in the best position to determine the appropriate contact with minors for a released defendant convicted of a child-pornography crime, even with the defendant's children. In fashioning an appropriate supervised-release special condition concerning contact with minors, even with the children of a defendant convicted of a child-pornography crime, the sentencing judge considers the triple goals of supervised release of rehabilitation, deterrence, and public protection — and children are members of the public, who must be protected. *See id.* at 850. While these supervised-release goals remain constant, the release progress of individual convicted, child-pornography defendants and the circumstances of each case will vary, which places the probation officer, rather than the sentencing judge, in a position to monitor a special condition of release involving access to children by a released convicted defendant of a child-pornography crime. *See Kerr,* 472 F.3d at 523 (concluding that there was no plain error because the sentencing judge "considered the possibility of revisiting these conditions [supervised-release restrictions as to contact with children] at a later date"). School events that involve Blinkinsop's children also will include other minors, and a probation officer monitoring Blinkinsop's progress on supervised release will know when it is appropriate for him to attend various school events where these minors are present.[12]

Therefore, we vacate supervised-release Special Condition 4 for the district judge to reconsider on limited remand. Recognizing that the district judge must protect the public, including other children, the judge specifically should address Blinkinsop's argument concerning attending school events involving his children and determine if Special Condition 4 should be tailored to provide for this contingency as well as to have written permission of his probation officer prior to each such attendance.[13] Notably, the special conditions of Blinkinsop's supervised release are for only 5 years and not for the rest of his life. We leave to the district judge on remand the factual determination concerning whether Special Condition 4, regarding Blinkinsop's proximity to places frequented by children during his 5-year term of supervised release, is overbroad in view of his conviction for receiving a considerable amount of child pornography yet desiring to attend school events involving

---

12. In reconsidering Special Condition 4, regarding Blinkinsop's argument that it prevents him from attending school events involving his children, the district judge should consider the applicability of this special condition, in view of Blinkinsop's 8-year imprisonment term and the fact that his children were 8 and 5, when his PSR was prepared in 2009. Other relevant factors include the custodial circumstances of Blinkinsop's children and their geographic location. We do not preclude the district judge's maintaining Special Condition 4, if the judge decides that it is necessary for the shortest statutory time for supervised release, 5 years as opposed to life, for a defendant convicted of a child-pornography crime. We do suggest that the written permission of Blinkinsop's probation officer, after consultation with *any* treatment providers, is an appropriate monitoring of Blinkinsop's progress on supervised release relative to Special Condition 4.

13. We note that Special Conditions 3 and 5, relating respectively to residing or being "in the company of any child under the age of 18" or socializing "with anybody who has children under the age of 18," require prior approval or "permission of the probation office." ...

his children and whether it can be revised to accommodate Blinkinsop, while complying with the goals of supervised release....

Special Condition 7 provides: "Defendant shall not possess camera phones or electronic devices that could be used for covert photography." ... In opposing Special Condition 7, Blinkinsop argues that this condition is "over broad, vague, and unjustified," because "photography played no role in his offense," and there is no need to prohibit him from "using or possessing this new technology." ... Conditions of supervised release are not required to be "related to the offense of conviction"; instead, they *can anticipate* crimes that a defendant convicted of a child-pornography crime might commit in the future. *Wise*, 391 F.3d at 1031. The Eighth Circuit has held that a supervised-release restriction on "use of photographic equipment, including cameras," did not deprive the defendant convicted of a child-pornography crime "of a greater liberty interest than is reasonably necessary" under plain-error review. *United States v. Ristine*, 335 F.3d 692, 696 (8th Cir.2003).[14] "Although there was no evidence in the record that Ristine photographed any minors, he possessed thousands of photos of underage women," making it "reasonable to believe that Ristine likely would photograph underage women and would exchange those photographs with other Internet users." *Id.; see United States v. Paul*, 274 F.3d 155, 170, 171 (5th Cir.2001) (affirming supervised-release condition restricting "access to photographic and audio/video equipment [ ]as necessary to protect the public," which prevented the convicted defendant, who pled guilty to possessing "photographs of naked children, including some children that were identified as being local neighborhood children" from his "hobbies" of "photography and repairing cameras" as "necessary to protect the public and to prevent [the convicted defendant] from committing future criminal conduct").

The large number of images stored on Blinkinsop's computer and storage equipment make it reasonable to anticipate that, even if he has not engaged in covert photography yet, he might do so in the future. Condition 7 does not impose any significant deprivation on Blinkinsop's liberty; it requires only that he not possess a camera phone or other device for covert photography. He may have a cell phone, as long as it does not have a camera module, and he can have a camera, as long as it is readily identifiable as a camera. The minor incursion on Blinkinsop's liberty by this condition is not greater than is reasonably necessary to protect the public and to promote Blinkinsop's rehabilitation. The district judge did not plainly err by imposing Special Condition 7 during Blinkinsop's 5-year, supervised-release term....

Special Condition 13 provides: "Defendant shall not possess or use any computer or other electronic device which can provide access to the Internet." ... Blinkinsop's challenge to this special-condition prohibition is reviewed for plain error, since Blinkinsop did not object at sentencing, *Jeremiah*, 493 F.3d at 1046. As the government concedes, banning Blinkinsop's Internet usage contravenes *United States v. Riley*, 576 F.3d 1046, 1050 (9th Cir.2009). Therefore, Special Condition 13 must be amended or deleted on limited remand....

As we have explained, we AFFIRM in part Blinkinsop's sentence as to his term of imprisonment and supervised-release Special Condition 7. We VACATE Blinkinsop's sentence

---

14. More inclusive and restrictive than Blinkinsop's Special Condition 7 was the special condition in *Ristine*, which prohibited that defendant, convicted of a child-pornography crime, "from owning or operating *any* photographic equipment including, but not limited to, cameras, digital cameras, video-taping recorder, camcorders, computers, scanners, and printers." 335 F.3d at 695 (emphasis added).

as to supervised-release Special Conditions 4 and 13 and order a LIMITED REMAND for reconsideration consistent with this opinion.

AFFIRMED in part; VACATED and REMANDED in part.

Notes

Sentences like that considered in *Blinkinsop* are determined by applying the Federal Sentencing Guidelines. For comprehensive access to the Guidelines Manual and other relevant resources, see United States Sentencing Commission, *2015 USSC Guidelines Manual*, available at http://www.ussc.gov/sites/default/files/pdf/guidelines-manual/2015/sentencing_table.pdf (effective Nov. 1, 2015) (last accessed Nov. 15, 2015). Included below is the 2015 Sentencing Table, which constructs the available sentence ranges for various levels of offenses under the Guidelines. Each individual offense is designated a base offense level on the vertical scale of seriousness—the more serious the crime, the higher the starting base level offense. Additionally, each offense may also include various adjustments, such as specific offense characteristics (for example, the use of a weapon during an offense), adjustment variables (perhaps based on the characteristics of the victim, the role of the offender in the offense, or the acceptance of responsibility for the offense), all of which can increase or decrease the base offense level. As demonstrated on the Table, the guidelines take into account the seriousness of the offense (indicated vertically by 43 levels of offense seriousness) and the criminal history of the offender (indicated horizontally by six categories of criminal history). Together, these establish a range of possible sentences (indicated within the body of the Table by respective ranges of months of imprisonment). For example, in *Blinkinsop*, the court calculated a total offense level of 30 and a criminal history of I, which yielded an advisory sentence range of 97 to 121 months. *See* Sentencing Table, *infra*. Pursuant to *United States v. Booker*, 543 U.S. 220, 264, 125 S.Ct. 738 (2005), "district courts, while not bound to apply the Guidelines, must consult those Guidelines and take them into account when sentencing," subject to review of presumptive reasonableness. *See Rita v. United States*, 551 U.S. 338, 127 S. Ct. 2456 (2007).

For a history of the United States Sentencing Guidelines, see United States Sentencing Commission, *Report to the Congress: Federal Child Pornography Offenses*, available at http://www.ussc.gov/news/congressional-testimony-and-reports/sex-offense-topics/report-congress-federal-child-pornography-offenses (Dec. 2012). For other commentary on the subject of sentencing in child pornography cases and with respect to the specific variables that affect sentencing in this area, see Dana Brudvig, *Today's Tool for Interpreting Yesterday's Conviction: Understanding the Mandatory Statutory Sentence Enhancement in Federal Child Pornography Cases*, 2015 WISC. L. REV. 153 (2015); Kaleb Noblett, *Caging Uncertainty: Responsible Reform of Federal Child Pornography Sentencing Guidelines*, 42 KY. L. REV. 65 (2015); D. Patrick Huyett, *The Potential Power of Federal Child Pornography Sentencing Disparities*, 86 TEMPLE L. REV. 629 (2014); Melissa Hamilton, *Sentencing Adjudication: Lessons From Child Pornography Policy Nullification*, 30 GA. ST. U. L. REV. 375 (2014); John T. Hughes, *Reacting to the Judicial Revolt: Applying Innovations in Narcotics Sentencing to Federal Non-Production Child Pornography Cases*, 47 COLUMBIA J.L. & SOC. PROB. 31 (2013); Kathryn A. Kimball, *Losing Our Soul: Judicial Discretion in Sentencing Child Pornography Offenders*, 63 FLA. L. REV. 1515 (2011); Melissa Hamilton, *The Efficacy of Severe Child Pornography Sentencing: Empirical Validity or Political Rhetoric?*, 22 STANFORD L. & POLICY REV. 545 (2011); Thomas M. Hardiman and Richard L. Heppner, Jr., *Policy Disagreements with the United States Sentencing Guidelines: A Welcome Expansion of Judicial Discretion or the Beginning of the End of the Sentencing Guidelines?*, 50 DUQUESNE L. REV.

5 (2012). In the cases that follow, note how other variables affect the application of the applicable guideline ranges.

SENTENCING TABLE
(in months of imprisonment)

Offense Level	Criminal History Category (Criminal History Points)					
	I (0 or 1)	II (2 or 3)	III (4, 5, 6)	IV (7, 8, 9)	V (10, 11, 12)	VI (13 or more)
1	0-6	0-6	0-6	0-6	0-6	0-6
2	0-6	0-6	0-6	0-6	0-6	1-7
3	0-6	0-6	0-6	0-6	2-8	3-9
4	0-6	0-6	0-6	2-8	4-10	6-12
5	0-6	0-6	1-7	4-10	6-12	9-15
6	0-6	1-7	2-8	6-12	9-15	12-18
7	0-6	2-8	4-10	8-14	12-18	15-21
8	0-6	4-10	6-12	10-16	15-21	18-24
9	4-10	6-12	8-14	12-18	18-24	21-27
10	6-12	8-14	10-16	15-21	21-27	24-30
11	8-14	10-16	12-18	18-24	24-30	27-33
12	10-16	12-18	15-21	21-27	27-33	30-37
13	12-18	15-21	18-24	24-30	30-37	33-41
14	15-21	18-24	21-27	27-33	33-41	37-46
15	18-24	21-27	24-30	30-37	37-46	41-51
16	21-27	24-30	27-33	33-41	41-51	46-57
17	24-30	27-33	30-37	37-46	46-57	51-63
18	27-33	30-37	33-41	41-51	51-63	57-71
19	30-37	33-41	37-46	46-57	57-71	63-78
20	33-41	37-46	41-51	51-63	63-78	70-87
21	37-46	41-51	46-57	57-71	70-87	77-96
22	41-51	46-57	51-63	63-78	77-96	84-105
23	46-57	51-63	57-71	70-87	84-105	92-115
24	51-63	57-71	63-78	77-96	92-115	100-125
25	57-71	63-78	70-87	84-105	100-125	110-137
26	63-78	70-87	78-97	92-115	110-137	120-150
27	70-87	78-97	87-108	100-125	120-150	130-162
28	78-97	87-108	97-121	110-137	130-162	140-175
29	87-108	97-121	108-135	121-151	140-175	151-188
30	97-121	108-135	121-151	135-168	151-188	168-210
31	108-135	121-151	135-168	151-188	168-210	188-235
32	121-151	135-168	151-188	168-210	188-235	210-262
33	135-168	151-188	168-210	188-235	210-262	235-293
34	151-188	168-210	188-235	210-262	235-293	262-327
35	168-210	188-235	210-262	235-293	262-327	292-365
36	188-235	210-262	235-293	262-327	292-365	324-405
37	210-262	235-293	262-327	292-365	324-405	360-life
38	235-293	262-327	292-365	324-405	360-life	360-life
39	262-327	292-365	324-405	360-life	360-life	360-life
40	292-365	324-405	360-life	360-life	360-life	360-life
41	324-405	360-life	360-life	360-life	360-life	360-life
42	360-life	360-life	360-life	360-life	360-life	360-life
43	life	life	life	life	life	life

Zone A (Offense Levels 1–8)
Zone B (Offense Levels 9–11)
Zone C (Offense Levels 11–13)
Zone D (Offense Levels 13–43)

Kaleb Noblett

*Caging Uncertainty: Responsible Reform of Federal
Child Pornography Sentencing Guidelines*

42 N. Ky. L. Rev. 65, 67 (2015)

The Guidelines were put in place to resolve a lack of uniformity in federal sentencing resulting from the broad discretion left to district court judges.... [footnotes omitted]. The [Sentencing Reform Act of 1984 (SRA)] also noted a concern that serious criminals were not always receiving due punishment.... The [United States Sentencing Commission ("USSC")] was charged with following the basic standards promulgated in 18 USC § 3553(a); namely, the Guidelines were to consider certain characteristics of the offense, including:

> [T]he nature and degree of harm caused by the offense, the community view of the gravity of the offense, the public concern generated by the offense, the deterrent effect a particular sentence may have on the commission of the offense by others, and the current incidence of the offense in the community and in the Nation as a whole....

The USSC must also provide for consideration of the particular offender's criminal history and personal background, while maintaining the assurance of equal application of the law.... Congress retained control of the final text of the Guidelines, but the USSC was given broad discretion—its findings were quite persuasive....

Under the SRA, federal judges were originally bound to the range configured for the offense by application of the Guidelines.... However, a series of Supreme Court decisions, capped by the Court's 2005 opinion in *United States v. Booker,* rendered the Guidelines merely advisory.... While *Booker* may have emasculated the Guidelines, it was not a death blow.... The Guidelines are still a part of everyday federal practice and a major player in sentencing hearings.... But, in fraud offenses and child pornography crimes, judges are relying less and less on the Guidelines....

2. Proportionality

United States v. Reingold

Second Circuit, 2013
731 F.3d 204
(Appeal of *United States v. C.R., supra,* Chapter Three)

REENA RAGGI, Circuit Judge:

Corey Reingold pleaded guilty in the United States District Court for the Eastern District of New York (Jack B. Weinstein, *Judge*) to one count of distributing child pornography. *See* 18 U.S.C. § 2252(a)(2). The United States now appeals from that part of the June 21, 2011 judgment of conviction [that] sentenced Reingold to 30 months' incarceration. The government contends that the district court erred in refusing to impose the minimum five-year prison term mandated by 18 U.S.C. § 2252(b)(1) on the ground that applying such a punishment to this immature 19-year-old defendant would violate the Cruel and Unusual Punishment Clause. *See* U.S. Const. amend. VIII. The government further disputes the district court's Sentencing Guidelines calculations. The district court explained its sentencing decisions both on the record and in a 401-page opinion accompanied by 55 pages of appendices. *See United States v. C.R.,* 792 F.Supp.2d 343

(E.D.N.Y.2011).[2] Having carefully reviewed that opinion, the applicable law, and the record as a whole, we conclude that the district court erred in both respects identified by the government. We therefore remand the case to the district court with directions that it vacate the sentence and resentence the defendant consistent with this opinion....

On November 16, 2008, an agent of the Federal Bureau of Investigation ("FBI"), investigating child pornography in an undercover capacity, accessed a computer program called "GigaTribe," which allows users to download material onto their computers and then to place some in folders designated for sharing with others. For GigaTribe users to access each other's designated sharing folders, they must be on the same "closed network of buddies," which is accomplished by invitation. *Id.* at 352 (internal quotation marks omitted) (citing *United States v. Ladeau*, No. 09-CR-40021-FDS, 2010 WL 1427523, at *1 (D.Mass. Apr. 7, 2010) (describing operation of GigaTribe)).

When the undercover agent accessed GigaTribe on November 16, he observed child pornography in the mini-profile of a person with the username "Boysuck0416." The agent also noted that this user's full profile contained the terms "Boy Love KDV PJK BCP," which the agent identified as child pornography search terms. The agent invited the user to share files, and after the user agreed, the agent downloaded ten videos and one still image of child pornography from the user's designated share folder. *See United States v. Ladeau*, 2010 WL 1427523, at *1 ("A user can also join the networks of other GigaTribe users, but only with the permission of the user who created the network."). He then proceeded to trace the user's Internet Protocol address to a residence at 3-14 Beach 147th Street in Queens, New York, which turned out to be the home of Jamie and Brian McLeod, the mother and stepfather of defendant Corey Reingold.

On January 15, 2009, FBI agents executed a search warrant at the McLeod home and seized two computers used exclusively by Reingold, each of which contained child pornography. Reingold, who was present at the time of the search, admitted that he was "Boysuck0416"; that he had opened a GigaTribe account in November 2008 and used it and another file sharing program, LimeWire, to download "a ton" of child pornography onto the seized computers; and that he had shared child pornography files in designated folders with between 10 and 20 other GigaTribe users. Pre-Sentence Report ("PSR") ¶ 9; *see United States v. C.R.*, 792 F.Supp.2d at 353. Subsequent forensic analysis would confirm that the seized Reingold computer linked to GigaTribe contained more than 100 video files and at least 208 digital images of child pornography, while the seized computer linked to LimeWire contained 10 videos of child pornography....

---

2. In its opinion, as well as in various filings, the district court referred to Reingold by his initials "C.R." We note that, at the same time, Reingold was identified by his full name in certain documents that remain electronically available from the files of the Eastern District of New York.

We identify no basis in law for shielding the identity of an adult criminal defendant. *Cf.* Fed.R.Crim.P. 49.1 (providing privacy protections in limited circumstances). No different conclusion obtains from *United States v. Amodeo*, 71 F.3d 1044 (2d Cir.1995), cited by Reingold. At issue in that case was the propriety of unsealing an investigative report that, among other things, would have identified confidential informants in an ongoing criminal investigation and circulated anonymous and unverified accusations of doubtful veracity against uncharged persons. *See id.* at 1047–48. By contrast, as the named adult defendant in a criminal case in which he has been adjudicated guilty, Reingold has no expectation of privacy in his identity. *See id.* at 1048 (noting public's presumptive right of access to information pertaining to judicial adjudications); *cf. id.* at 1050–51 (recognizing that privacy interests of "innocent third parties" may warrant exception to presumption of public access). We therefore refer to Reingold by his name on our docket and in this opinion. Nevertheless, because the district court's published opinion is reported as *United States v. C.R.*, we cite it as such.

As part of initial plea negotiations with federal prosecutors, Reingold agreed to take a polygraph examination with the understanding that he would be allowed to plead guilty to simple possession of child pornography, *see* 18 U.S.C. § 2252(a)(4)(B),[3] if he could truthfully state that he had not had any sexual contact with minors. Even before the polygraph examination, however, Reingold admitted to federal authorities that he had engaged his minor half-sister in sexual activities on three occasions over a course of three years. Specifically, Reingold stated that (1) when he was 15 and his sister eight, he had the child manually stimulate his penis; (2) when Reingold was 16 and his sister nine, he again had the girl manually stimulate his penis while he rubbed his hand over her vagina through her underwear; and (3) when Reingold was 18 and his sister 11, he had the girl manually stimulate his penis while he rubbed her vagina both over and beneath her underwear. Reingold subsequently admitted that during this third sexual encounter, he also coached the child to perform oral sex on him and, in turn, performed oral sex on her.[4] ...

On March 18, 2009, Reingold was indicted by a grand jury sitting in the Eastern District of New York on four counts of distributing child pornography based on the GigaTribe "sharing" of four specified video files to the undercover agent on November 17, 2008, *see* 18 U.S.C. § 2252(a)(2), (b)(1); and one count of possessing child pornography, *see id.* § 2252(a)(4)(B), (b)(2). On September 16, 2009, Reingold pleaded guilty before a magistrate judge to the first distribution count.... Before formally accepting Reingold's guilty plea and in anticipation of sentencing, the district court conducted hearings between September 2009 and May 2011 where it heard from "a dozen expert witnesses in the fields of child sexual abuse; online child pornography; risk assessment; treatment of sex offenders; and neuropsychology and adolescent brain development." *United States v. C.R.*, 792 F.Supp.2d at 349. Together with prosecutors, defense counsel, and two of his law clerks, the district judge also traveled to Massachusetts and personally toured FMC Devens, the Bureau of Prisons facility that offers inmates sex offender treatment. *See id.* at 520–24.

On May 10, 2011, the initial sentencing date, the district court declined to accept Reingold's guilty plea before the magistrate judge, questioning whether the undercover agent's retrieval of child pornography from Reingold's designated shared folder on GigaTribe was enough to make the defendant guilty of distribution under 18 U.S.C. § 2252(a)(2). Although the government and defense counsel both urged acceptance of the plea,[5] the district court adjourned the case to May 16, 2011, to allow it to consider the matter further.... On May 16, 2011, the district court accepted Reingold's guilty plea. On the record, it explained that its acceptance was "based on the allocution and all other information now known to me." ... In its published opinion filed the same day, however, the district court expressed continued reservations as to whether the defendant had

---

3. A violation of 18 U.S.C. § 2252(a)(4)(B) carries no mandatory minimum penalty but is punishable by a prison term of "not more than 10 years." 18 U.S.C. § 2252(b)(2).

4. Reingold further admitted that, at times when he was either 18 or 19, he had engaged three friends who were minors in sexual activity: (1) a 15-year-old boy whose penis Reingold had stimulated to the point of ejaculation; (2) a 15-year-old girl with whom Reingold had performed mutual genital stimulation and oral sex; and (3) a 16-year-old girl whose vagina Reingold had touched through her sweat pants. Because the government focuses on Reingold's sexual activity with his sister rather than these other encounters in making certain arguments on appeal, we do not discuss this additional conduct further.

5. Defense counsel submitted that a guilty plea to a distribution count carrying a five-year minimum was in Reingold's interest because the government was considering superseding the indictment to add an advertising charge carrying a 15-year mandatory minimum sentence. *See* 18 U.S.C. § 2251(d)(2), (e).

adequately admitted knowing and intentional distribution of child pornography as proscribed by 18 U.S.C. § 2252(a)(2). *See United States v. C.R.*, 792 F.Supp.2d at 353–55 (construing statute to require proof of both "active intent[ ]" to transfer child pornography to another person and "active participation" in delivery of such pornography).[6] In the end, however, the district court accepted the guilty plea, explaining that the statute's distribution element might be construed to reach Reingold's conduct; that "a jury could reasonably find that [Reingold] was not truthful when he testified that he did not intend to distribute his files to another individual"; that a court can accept a guilty plea even when a defendant maintains his innocence, "as long as there is a strong factual basis for the plea"; and that the record showed Reingold to have thoroughly considered his decision to plead guilty with the support of close relatives and able counsel, and to have demonstrated a wish to accept responsibility for his conduct. *Id.* at 356–57 (citing *North Carolina v. Alford*, 400 U.S. 25, 37–38, 91 S.Ct. 160, 27 L.Ed.2d 162 (1970)).[7] ...

In its PSR to the district court, the Probation Department advised that Reingold's crime of conviction was subject to a mandatory minimum prison sentence of five years pursuant to 18 U.S.C. § 2252(b)(1). Further, based on Sentencing Guidelines calculations yielding a total offense level of 35 and a criminal history category of I, the PSR reported that Reingold's recommended sentencing range was 168 to 210 months' imprisonment.[8] ... The district court viewed the case quite differently. Rejecting the Probation Department's application of various enhancements to Reingold's Guidelines calculation, the district court concluded that the applicable Sentencing Guidelines range in Reingold's case was 63 to 78 months' imprisonment.[9] The district court further determined that Reingold should not be sentenced even within that reduced Guidelines range because such a term of imprisonment was greater than necessary to achieve the objectives of 18 U.S.C. § 3553(a). Insofar as Congress had statutorily mandated a prison sentence of at least five years for any defendant guilty of distributing child pornography, the district court concluded that

---

6. In hearings conducted by the district court, Reingold stated that his goal in participating in the GigaTribe website was "to receive child pornography." *United States v. C.R.*, 792 F.Supp.2d at 354. Nevertheless, "in achieving that goal he knew that he had to make his child pornography files available to others." *Id.*

7. Because no party challenges the sufficiency of Reingold's plea allocution or of these findings by the district court in support of its decision to accept the plea, we deem any challenge to the plea itself forfeited and do not discuss it further in this opinion.

8. The Probation Department arrived at offense level 35 by starting with a base offense level of 22, *see* U.S.S.G. § 2G2.2(a)(2), to which it added two points for the presence of pre-pubescent images, *see id.* § 2G2.2(b)(2); two points for distribution in a manner not otherwise described in the Guidelines, *see id.* § 2G2.2(b)(3)(F); five points for a pattern of abuse, based on Reingold's molestation of his half-sister, *see id.* § 2G2.2(b)(5); two points for use of a computer, *see id.* § 2G2.2(b)(6); and five points for possession of 600 or more images of child pornography, *see id.* § 2G2.2(b)(7)(D); after which it subtracted three points for timely acceptance of responsibility, *see id.* § 3E1.1.

9. The district court agreed that Reingold's base offense level was 22, that enhancements were warranted for the presence of pre-pubescent images and for the possession of 600 or more images of child pornography, and that a reduction was warranted for timely acceptance of responsibility. *See United States v. C.R.*, 792 F.Supp.2d at 511–12. But it declined to impose any distribution enhancement, concluding that Reingold's "actions did not constitut[e] distribution under the statute." *Id.* at 511. The district court also rejected application of the pattern of abuse enhancement because two of the incidents with Reingold's half-sister had occurred while Reingold was a minor, *see id.*, and the trio of activities "were aberrant acts separated by long periods, in large measure, due to the failure of proper parental supervision," ... Finally, the district court concluded that application of the computer-use enhancement would "result[ ] in double counting and is not sufficiently particularized to the facts of the case." *United States v. C.R.*, 792 F.Supp.2d at 512. Accordingly, the district court calculated Reingold's total offense level at 26, which with a criminal history category of I, yielded an advisory Guidelines imprisonment range of 63 to 78 months.

such a sentence would constitute cruel and unusual punishment in Reingold's case given his particular immaturity and the relative passivity of his crime. *See United States v. C.R.*, 792 F.Supp.2d at 509–10. Accordingly, the district court sentenced Reingold to 30 months' imprisonment, five years' supervised release, and a $100 special assessment. It recommended that Reingold serve his term in the FMC Devens Sex Offender Treatment Program and allowed him to self-surrender.[10] ...

The government argues that the district court was legally obligated to sentence Reingold to the minimum five-year prison term mandated by 18 U.S.C. § 2252(b)(1) for any distribution of child pornography. It submits that the district court erred as a matter of law in holding that the application of that mandated minimum sentence to Reingold would violate the Eighth Amendment. We review de novo a district court's "[c]onclusions of law, including those involving constitutional questions," *United States v. Fell*, 531 F.3d 197, 209 (2d Cir.2008), and here conclude that the district court erred in holding the mandatory minimum sentence unconstitutional.... The Eighth Amendment states that "[e]xcessive bail shall not be required, nor excessive fines imposed, nor cruel and unusual punishments inflicted." U.S. Const. amend. VIII. In identifying cruel and unusual punishments, the Supreme Court has not limited itself to "historical conceptions" of impermissible sanctions, *Graham v. Florida*, 560 U.S. 48, 130 S.Ct. 2011, 2021, 176 L.Ed.2d 825 (2010), but has looked to " 'the evolving standards of decency that mark the progress of a maturing society,'" *Kennedy v. Louisiana*, 554 U.S. 407, 419, 128 S.Ct. 2641, 171 L.Ed.2d 525 (2008) (quoting *Trop v. Dulles*, 356 U.S. 86, 101, 78 S.Ct. 590, 2 L.Ed.2d 630 (1958) (plurality opinion)). A punishment will be deemed "cruel and unusual" not only when it is "inherently barbaric," but also when it is "disproportionate to the crime." *Graham v. Florida*, 130 S.Ct. at 2021; *see Harmelin v. Michigan*, 501 U.S. 957, 997–98, 111 S.Ct. 2680, 115 L.Ed.2d 836 (1991) (Kennedy, J., concurring in part and concurring in the judgment) (tracing history of proportionality principle).[11] ...

This appeal focuses on the proportionality aspect of Eighth Amendment jurisprudence. The Supreme Court first interpreted the Eighth Amendment to prohibit " 'greatly disproportioned'" sentences in *Weems v. United States*, 217 U.S. 349, 371, 30 S.Ct. 544, 54 L.Ed. 793 (1910) (quoting *O'Neil v. Vermont*, 144 U.S. 323, 340, 12 S.Ct. 693, 36 L.Ed. 450 (1892) (Field, J., dissenting)). Since then, the Court has emphasized that constitutional proportionality is a "narrow" principle in that it "does not require strict proportionality," and it "forbids only extreme sentences that are 'grossly disproportionate' to the crime." *Harmelin v. Michigan*, 501 U.S. at 997, 1001, 111 S.Ct. 2680 (Kennedy, J., concurring) (quoting *Solem v. Helm*, 463 U.S. 277, 288, 103 S.Ct. 3001, 77 L.Ed.2d 637 (1983)); *accord Graham v. Florida*, 130 S.Ct. at 2021.

A number of principles inform this narrow view of the constitutional mandate of proportionality: (1) the "substantial deference" generally owed by reviewing courts "to the broad authority that legislatures necessarily possess in determining the types and limits

---

10. The government argues that self-surrender was precluded by 18 U.S.C. § 3143(c)(1). Because Reingold did surrender and is now imprisoned, the point is moot, which the government concedes, and we do not discuss it further on this appeal.

11. In *Graham*, the Supreme Court recognized Justice Kennedy's concurring opinion in *Harmelin*. joined in by Justices O'Connor and Souter, as "controlling" in its discussion of constitutional proportionality. *Graham v. Florida*, 130 S.Ct. at 2022; *see also Marks v. United States*, 430 U.S. 188, 193, 97 S.Ct. 990, 51 L.Ed.2d 260 (1977) ("When a fragmented court decides a case and no single rationale explaining the result enjoys the assent of five Justices, the holding of the Court may be viewed as that position taken by those members who concurred in the judgments on the narrowest grounds." (internal quotation marks omitted)).

of punishments for crimes"; (2) a recognition that the Eighth Amendment does not mandate "any one penological theory" and that "competing theories of mandatory and discretionary sentencing have been in varying degrees of ascendancy or decline since the beginning of the Republic"; (3) respect for the "marked divergences both in underlying theories of sentencing and in the length of prescribed prison terms" that "are the inevitable, often beneficial, result of the federal structure"; and (4) prudential understanding that proportionality review "should be informed by objective factors to the maximum possible extent," that the "most prominent objective factor is the type of punishment imposed," and that while the Supreme Court has frequently referenced "the objective line between capital punishment and imprisonment for a term of years," it has itself acknowledged a "lack [of] clear objective standards to distinguish between sentences for different terms of years." *Harmelin v. Michigan*, 501 U.S. at 998–1001, 111 S.Ct. 2680 (Kennedy, J., concurring) (internal quotation marks omitted)....

The Supreme Court's proportionality cases fall into two classifications. "The first involves challenges to the length of term-of-years sentences given all the circumstances in a *particular case*." *Graham v. Florida*, 130 S.Ct. at 2021 (emphasis added). In making a case-particular assessment of proportionality, the Court has employed a two-step analysis, first "comparing the gravity of the offense and the severity of the sentence." *Id.* at 2022. Given the principles already discussed, the Court has observed that it will be "'the rare case in which this threshold comparison ... leads to an inference of gross disproportionality.'" *Id.* (quoting *Harmelin v. Michigan*, 501 U.S. at 1005, 111 S.Ct. 2680 (Kennedy, J., concurring) (first alteration in *Graham* omitted)). Should such an inference arise, however, the second step of the analysis requires a court to "compare the defendant's sentence with the sentences received by other offenders in the same jurisdiction and with the sentences imposed for the same crime in other jurisdictions." *Id.* Only "[i]f this comparative analysis 'validate[s] an initial judgment that [the] sentence is grossly disproportionate'" will the sentence be deemed "cruel and unusual." *Id.* (quoting *Harmelin v. Michigan*, 501 U.S. at 1005, 111 S.Ct. 2680 (Kennedy, J., concurring) (alterations in original)).

In this case-particular review, the Supreme Court has thus far identified a term-of-years sentence as grossly disproportionate on only one occasion. In *Solem v. Helm*, a South Dakota court sentenced a defendant with a prior record of six non-violent felony convictions to a non-mandatory term of life imprisonment without parole for passing a bad check in the amount of $100. *See* 463 U.S. at 279, 281–82, 103 S.Ct. 3001. The Supreme Court drew a threshold inference of gross disproportionality from the fact that the crime of conviction was "one of the most passive felonies a person could commit," involving "neither violence nor threat of violence to any person," *id.* at 296, 103 S.Ct. 3001 (internal quotation marks omitted), while the punishment was "the most severe" non-capital sentence "that the State could have imposed on any criminal for any crime," *id.* at 297, 103 S.Ct. 3001. That inference of disproportionality was then validated by the fact that "Helm was treated more severely than he would have been in any other State." *Id.* at 300, 103 S.Ct. 3001.

Since *Solem*, the Supreme Court has consistently rejected proportionality challenges to prison sentences in particular cases. In *Harmelin v. Michigan*, the Court upheld a statutorily mandated term of life imprisonment without parole in the Michigan case of a recidivist defendant convicted of possessing 672 grams of cocaine. *See* 501 U.S. at 1009, 111 S.Ct. 2680 (Kennedy, J., concurring). Declining to draw a threshold inference of gross disproportionality, Justice Kennedy observed that Harmelin's crime was distinguishable from the "relatively minor, nonviolent crime at issue in *Solem*," because the "[p]ossession, use, and distribution of illegal drugs represent one of the greatest problems affecting the health and welfare of our population." *Id.* at 1002, 111 S.Ct. 2680 (internal quotation marks omitted) (recognizing range of criminal activity associated with drug possession). In such circumstances, "the Michigan Legislature could with reason conclude that the threat posed to the individual and society by possession of this large an amount of cocaine — in terms of violence, crime, and social displacement — is momentous enough to warrant the deterrence and retribution of a life sentence without parole." *Id.* at 1003, 111 S.Ct. 2680.

Thereafter, in *Ewing v. California*, 538 U.S. 11, 123 S.Ct. 1179, 155 L.Ed.2d 108 (2003), the Supreme Court rejected a proportionality challenge to a prison sentence of 25 years to life imposed pursuant to California's Three Strikes Law on a recidivist felon convicted of stealing $1,200 worth of golf clubs, *see id.* at 16–18, 123 S.Ct. 1179 (plurality) (referencing Cal.Penal Code Ann. § 667(e)(2)(A)). Declining to draw an inference of gross disproportionality, the Court plurality reasoned that defendant's grand theft felony was not one of the most passive crimes a person could commit, that the California legislature "made a judgment that protecting the public safety requires incapacitating criminals who have already been convicted of at least one serious or violent crime[, and that n]othing in the Eighth Amendment prohibits California from making that choice." *Id.* at 25, 28, 123 S.Ct. 1179; *see Lockyer v. Andrade*, 538 U.S. 63, 77, 123 S.Ct. 1166, 155 L.Ed.2d 144 (2003) (rejecting prisoner's Eighth Amendment habeas challenge to sentence of 25 years to life under California's Three Strikes law for stealing approximately $150 worth of videotapes).

As these cases make plain, at the same time that the Eighth Amendment prohibits grossly disproportionate sentences, it is rare that a sentence falling within a legislatively prescribed term of years will be deemed grossly disproportionate. *See Harmelin v. Michigan*, 501 U.S. at 1001, 111 S.Ct. 2680 (Kennedy, J., concurring) (noting that "outside the context of capital punishment, *successful* challenges to the proportionality of particular sentences are exceedingly rare" (alterations and internal quotation marks omitted; emphasis in original)); *accord United States v. Polk*, 546 F.3d 74, 76 (1st Cir.2008) (observing that "instances of gross disproportionality" are "hen's-teeth rare")....

"The second classification of [proportionality] cases has used categorical rules to define Eighth Amendment standards." *Graham v. Florida*, 130 S.Ct. at 2022. Until *Graham*, such categorical pronouncements were made with respect to a single punishment — the death penalty — and fell into "two subsets, one considering the nature of the offense" for which death was ordered, "the other considering the characteristics of the offender" sentenced to death. *Id.* Thus, the Supreme Court has categorically prohibited death sentences for "nonhomicide crimes against individuals," *id.*, such as rape, *see Kennedy v. Louisiana*, 554 U.S. at 413, 128 S.Ct. 2641, or felony murder where the defendant participated in the felony but did not kill or intend to kill anyone, *see Enmund v. Florida*, 458 U.S. 782, 801, 102 S.Ct. 3368, 73 L.Ed.2d 1140 (1982). The Court has also categorically prohibited death sentences for juvenile defendants, *see Roper v. Simmons*, 543 U.S. 551, 578, 125 S.Ct. 1183, 161 L.Ed.2d 1 (2005), and persons who are mentally retarded, *see Atkins v. Virginia*, 536 U.S. 304, 321, 122 S.Ct. 2242, 153 L.Ed.2d 335 (2002).

In identifying types of crimes or types of defendants for whom capital punishment is categorically disproportionate, the Supreme Court has prescribed a two-step analysis. It "first considers objective indicia of society's standards, as expressed in legislative enactments and state practice to determine whether there is a national consensus against the sentencing practice at issue." *Graham v. Florida*, 130 S.Ct. at 2022 (internal quotation marks omitted). But because "[c]ommunity consensus, while entitled to great weight, is not itself determinative of whether a punishment is cruel and unusual," it then proceeds to a second step. *Id.* at 2026 (internal quotation marks omitted). "[G]uided by the standards elaborated by controlling precedents and by the Court's own understanding and interpretation of the Eighth Amendment's text, history, meaning, and purpose, the Court must determine in the exercise of its own independent judgment whether the punishment in question violates the Constitution." *Id.* at 2022 (internal quotation marks omitted). In this inquiry, a court properly considers "the culpability of the [class of] offenders at issue in light of their crimes and characteristics, along with the severity of the punishment in question." *Id.* at 2026. It "also considers whether the challenged sentencing practice serves legitimate penological goals." *Id.*

In *Graham v. Florida*, the Supreme Court for the first time applied this analysis to pronounce a categorical rule for a non-capital sentencing practice: the imposition of life imprisonment without parole on juvenile offenders for nonhomicide crimes. The Court concluded that just as the Eighth Amendment categorically prohibits capital punishment for juvenile offenders, so too does it categorically prohibit life without parole for those same offenders when they stand convicted of nonhomicide crimes. *See* 130 S.Ct. at 2030. In reaching this conclusion, the Court identified a kinship between sentences of death and of life imprisonment without parole that warranted certain categorical rules to ensure proportionality. *See id.* at 2027, 2033 (observing that although "[t]he State does not execute the offender sentenced to life without parole," "Graham's sentence guarantees he will die in prison"). Nevertheless, the Court did not construe the Eighth Amendment to require that juvenile defendants be released at some time during their natural life. *See id.* at 2030 ("A State is not required to guarantee eventual freedom to a juvenile offender convicted of a nonhomicide crime."). It required only that juveniles be given "some meaningful opportunity to obtain release based on demonstrated maturity and rehabilitation." *Id.*

Last term, the Court pronounced another categorical rule for a sentence of life without parole, barring its mandatory application to juvenile offenders convicted of homicide crimes. *See Miller v. Alabama*, ___ U.S. ___, 132 S.Ct. 2455, 183 L.Ed.2d 407 (2012). Here, the Supreme Court identified no categorical constitutional requirement that juveniles sentenced to life imprisonment for murder be afforded some opportunity for release. It ruled only that life without parole for such juvenile offenders could not be mandatory and had to reflect an individualized sentencing determination. *See id.* at 2460.... In reaching this conclusion, the Court not only reiterated the analogy *Graham* drew between a death sentence and life without parole, but also clarified that the kinship between these two harshest possible sentences explained *Graham*'s pronouncement of a categorical rule "in a way unprecedented for a term of imprisonment." *Id.* at 2466. Relying on that kinship, and on precedent categorically barring both capital punishment for juveniles and mandatory capital punishment for adults, *Miller* held that the Eighth Amendment's "principle of proportionality" categorically prohibited mandatory life without parole for juveniles. *Id.* at 2475. Thus, "a judge or jury must have the opportunity to consider mitigating circumstances before imposing the harshest possible penalty for juveniles." *Id.*....

The district court appears to have construed *Graham* to invite categorical rule analysis of any term-of-years sentence, including the mandatory five-year sentence at issue here. *See United States v. C.R.*, 792 F.Supp.2d at 507. This misconstrues *Graham*.... First, as *Miller* recognized, *Graham*'s "unprecedented" imposition of a categorical ban outside the context of capital sentencing derives from the Court's recognition that life without parole for juveniles was "akin to the death penalty." *Miller v. Alabama*, 132 S.Ct. at 2466. Nothing in *Graham* or *Miller* suggests that a five-year prison term is the sort of inherently harsh sentence that—like the death penalty or its deferred equivalent, life imprisonment without parole—requires categorical rules to ensure constitutional proportionality as applied to particular felony crimes or classes of defendants. Certainly, a five-year sentence does not deprive a defendant of all hope of release, the only categorical limitation the Supreme Court thought constitutionally necessary for mandatory life sentences imposed on juvenile defendants imprisoned for nonhomicide crimes. *See Graham v. Florida*, 130 S.Ct. at 2030. Much less does a five-year sentence equate to one of "the law's most serious punishments" so as to raise the constitutional concerns identified in *Miller v. Alabama* about the mandatory application of life without parole to all juveniles. 132 S.Ct. at 2467, 2471; *see also Harmelin v. Michigan*, 501 U.S. at 995, 111 S.Ct. 2680 ("[A] sentence which is not otherwise cruel and unusual" does not "become[ ] so simply because it is mandatory." (internal quotation marks omitted)). Accordingly, a mandatory minimum five-year sentence is not the sort of sentencing practice that the Supreme Court has ever signaled requires categorical rules to ensure constitutional proportionality.

Second, insofar as the district court purported to identify a consensus against five-year prison terms for juveniles convicted of child pornography crimes, we are by no means persuaded by its analysis. We need not discuss the point, however, because any such consensus is not relevant here. Reingold was already 19 when he committed the crime of conviction. In short, he was an adult, not a juvenile. The district court tries to blur the distinction between juvenile and adult offenders by finding that, "at the time of the crime," Reingold was "a developmentally immature young adult." *United States v. C.R.*, 792 F.Supp.2d at 506.[12] Even if we accept this assessment, however, it hardly supports categorical rule analysis in this case. Nowhere does the record reveal any consensus about how immature adults should be sentenced for child pornography crimes. Moreover, immaturity, unlike age, is a subjective criterion, ill suited to the pronouncement of categorical rules. *See generally Harmelin v. Michigan*, 501 U.S. at 1000, 111 S.Ct. 2680 (Kennedy, J., concurring) (emphasizing that proportionality review "should be informed by objective factors to the maximum possible extent" (internal quotation marks omitted)). The Supreme Court recognized as much when, in "[d]rawing the line at 18 years of age" for death eligibility in *Roper v. Simmons*, it acknowledged that "[t]he qualities that distinguish juveniles from adults do not disappear when an individual turns 18." 543 U.S. at 574, 125 S.Ct. 1183. Nevertheless, "a line must be drawn" to pronounce a categorical rule, and because "[t]he age of 18 is the point where society draws the line for many purposes between childhood and adulthood," the Court used that age to distinguish the class of offenders that categorically could not be sentenced to death from others to whom no such categorical prohibition would apply. *Id.* This is not to suggest that an adult defendant's immaturity is irrelevant to sentencing. To the contrary, that circumstance is appropriately considered by a judge in making a case-specific choice of sentence within a statutorily prescribed range. *See generally* 18 U.S.C. §§ 3553(a), 3661. We here conclude only that the district court could not substitute the defendant's relative immaturity for the actual age of minority in applying categorical-rule analysis to the mandated five-year minimum sentence at issue.

Third, the district court did not, in any event, employ *Graham*'s analytic approach to pronounce a categorical rule. Rather, it employed such analysis to find a five-year minimum sentence "disproportionate to the offense" of conviction "*as applied to this defendant.*" *United States v. C.R.*, 792 F.Supp.2d at 510 (emphasis added and internal quotation marks omitted). The Supreme Court's proportionality jurisprudence does not support such a substitution of *Graham*'s categorical-rule approach for *Harmelin*'s particular-case approach

---

12. Reingold's "immaturity" did not have its origins in any organic brain damage or cognitive limitations. To the contrary, at least one doctor who interviewed Reingold found that his "level of intellectual functioning is in the high-average range." *United States v. C.R.*, 792 F.Supp.2d at 412 (internal quotation marks omitted).

to assess the proportionality of an otherwise permissible term-of-years sentence as applied to a particular case. As the Court explained in *Graham*, where the proportionality of a term-of-years sentence is challenged as applied to a particular defendant convicted for a specific crime, the proper analytic approach is that employed in *Harmelin* and *Ewing*, which requires "a threshold comparison between the severity of the penalty and the gravity of the crime." *Graham v. Florida*, 130 S.Ct. at 2023. It is where a "type of sentence" is challenged "as it applies to an entire class of offenders who have committed a range of crimes" that such "a threshold comparison ... does not advance the analysis" and "the categorical approach" is properly employed. *Id.* at 2022–23. Thus, in *Graham*, a categorical approach was required to assess a proportionality challenge to a sentence of life imprisonment without parole as applied to the class of persons under the age of 18 convicted of a range of nonhomicide crimes. By contrast, here, a mandatory minimum sentence of five years is challenged as applied to Reingold because of his particular immaturity and the circumstances under which he distributed child pornography. That proportionality inquiry is properly conducted by reference to *Harmelin*'s case-specific rather than *Graham*'s categorical-rule analysis....

In reviewing the proportionality of a challenged sentence as applied to a particular case, a court must first consider whether the "gravity of the offense and the severity of the sentence" give rise to an "inference of gross disproportionality." *Graham v. Florida*, 130 S.Ct. at 2022 (internal quotation marks omitted). The district court failed to make this comparative assessment. We do so here and conclude that the comparison supports no inference of gross disproportionality in applying the minimum five-year sentence mandated by 18 U.S.C. §2252(b)(1) to Reingold....

Starting with the gravity of the offense at issue, there can be no question that the dissemination of child pornography is a serious crime that causes real injury to particularly vulnerable victims. As Congress, courts, and scholars all recognize, child pornography crimes at their core demand the sexual exploitation and abuse of children. Not only are children seriously harmed — physically, emotionally, and mentally — in the process of producing such pornography, but that harm is then exacerbated by the circulation, often for years after the fact, of a graphic record of the child's exploitation and abuse. *See New York v. Ferber*, 458 U.S. 747, 757–59 & nn.9–10, 102 S.Ct. 3348, 73 L.Ed.2d 1113 (1982) (citing congressional and scholarly reports, and court cases).... The circumstances of this case do not mitigate the general severity of such criminal conduct.[14] The pornography that is the subject of Reingold's distribution count of conviction is a video depicting a female child, approximately eight years old, unclothed, as an adult male penetrates her mouth with his erect penis and then places his mouth on her vagina. It is not necessary for us to detail similar depictions of the sexual exploitation of children in the materials that Reingold designated for sharing with — *i.e.*, distribution to — other GigaTribe users, to confirm the seriousness of the criminal conduct at issue.

Nor can any mitigation be located in the fact that Reingold's crimes were facilitated by a recent "digital revolution" that has "enormously increased the ways that child pornography can be created, accessed, and distributed." *United States v. C.R.*, 792 F.Supp.2d at 367. The ease with which a person can access and distribute child pornography from his home — often with no more effort than a few clicks on a computer — may make it easier for perpetrators to delude themselves that their conduct is not deviant or harmful. But

---

14. It is necessary to discuss these case-specific circumstances to explain why the district court's characterization of them as mitigating is not persuasive and, therefore, does not permit a conclusion favorable to Reingold at the first step of proportionality analysis.

technological advances that facilitate child pornography crimes no more mitigate the real harm caused by these crimes than do technological advances making it easier to perpetrate fraud, traffic drugs, or even engage in acts of terrorism—all at a distance from victims—mitigate those crimes. If anything, the noted digital revolution may actually aggravate child pornography crimes insofar as an expanding market for child pornography fuels greater demand for perverse sexual depictions of children, making it more difficult for authorities to prevent their sexual exploitation and abuse. *See generally United States v. Lewis*, 605 F.3d 395, 403 (6th Cir.2010) (noting that distribution through computers "is particularly harmful because it can reach an almost limitless audience" (internal quotation marks omitted) (citing H.R.Rep. No. 104-90, at 3–4 (1995), *reprinted in* 1995 U.S.C.C.A.N. 759, 760–61)). But precisely because the prevention of such exploitation and abuse is "a government objective of surpassing importance," *New York v. Ferber*, 458 U.S. at 757, 102 S.Ct. 3348; *see id.* at 756–57, 102 S.Ct. 3348 ("It is evident beyond the need for elaboration that a State's interest in safeguarding the physical and psychological well-being of a minor is compelling." (internal quotation marks omitted)), we cannot view the distribution of child pornography, however accomplished, as anything but a serious crime that threatens real, and frequently violent, harm to vulnerable victims, *cf. Harmelin v. Michigan*, 501 U.S. at 1002–03, 111 S.Ct. 2680 (Kennedy, J., concurring) (observing that characterization of drug possession with intent to distribute as "nonviolent and victimless" crime "is false to the point of absurdity" given "pernicious effects" of drug use).

No different conclusion is warranted because Reingold professed a principal interest in receiving rather than distributing child pornography. *See United States v. C.R.*, 792 F.Supp.2d at 354. Reingold acknowledged that when he joined GigaTribe he knew that in order to secure child pornography from others, he would have to share child pornography with them in return. In short, Reingold understood from the start that, in this barter-like market, distribution was integral to receipt. To the extent such arrangements only expand the market in which child pornography is disseminated, Reingold's interest in augmenting his own collection of child pornography does not render his distribution of such pornography any less serious a crime.

Nor is Reingold's crime mitigated by the fact that, once he established his GigaTribe share folder, users on the same "closed network of buddies," *id.* at 352 (internal quotation marks omitted), could access its content without further action by Reingold. Reingold was obliged in the first instance to create a share folder and had to designate materials to be included therein. The materials he elected to share were child pornography, and among the child pornography he designated for sharing was the described video depicting the sexual exploitation of an eight-year-old girl. From the totality of affirmative actions that Reingold took to allow others to gain access to his share file, we cannot conclude that his was among the "most passive" felony crimes. *Solem v. Helm*, 463 U.S. at 296, 103 S.Ct. 3001 (internal quotation marks omitted). Nor, for reasons already discussed, can we conclude that the distribution of child pornography is a victimless crime or one posing no threat of violence or physical harm. *Cf. id.* (noting that passing bad check posed no threat of violence); *Harmelin v. Michigan*, 501 U.S. at 1002, 111 S.Ct. 2680 (Kennedy, J., concurring) (declining to view drug possession with intent to distribute as "nonviolent and victimless" crime).

Such a conclusion seems particularly unwarranted here, where Reingold admitted that in addition to viewing and distributing child pornography, he repeatedly engaged his prepubescent sister in sexual activity. Indeed, his last reported sexual interaction with the child, when he was 18 and she was 11, was disturbingly similar to the conduct depicted on the video that is the subject of the distribution count of conviction. The district court concluded that Reingold's sexual conduct with his sister was mitigated by the lack of adequate parental supervision, Reingold's minority during the first two encounters, and his continued immaturity as an adult. *See United States v. C.R.*, 792 F.Supp.2d at 511; ... Even if correct, such excuses cannot transform the admitted three encounters into something benign, or deny their scarring effect on the girl. Much less do these excuses mitigate the exacerbating harm caused to children by Reingold's distribution of pornography in which they are depicted....

As has long been recognized, "it is difficult, if not impossible to halt" the sexual exploitation and abuse of minors by pursuing only the producers of child pornography. *New York v. Ferber*, 458 U.S. at 759–60, 102 S.Ct. 3348. Thus, the Supreme Court has acknowledged that "[t]he most expeditious if not the only practical method of law enforcement may be to dry up the market for this material by imposing *severe criminal penalties*" on all persons in the distribution chain. *Id.* at 760, 102 S.Ct. 3348 (emphasis added). With precisely this objective in mind, *see* H.R. Conf. Rep. 108-66, at *28 (2003), *reprinted in* 2003 U.S.C.C.A.N. 683 (quoting *New York v. Ferber*, 458 U.S. at 760, 102 S.Ct. 3348), Congress, in 2003, established a graduated sentencing regime for crimes involving child pornography, with any knowing receipt or distribution of child pornography transmitted in interstate or foreign commerce punishable by a prison term of "not less than five years and not more than 20 years" in prison. 18 U.S.C. §2252(b)(1).[15] The question on this appeal is not whether we would ourselves have made that precise policy decision if charged with legislative responsibility. In our judicial capacity, we conclude simply that no inference of "gross disproportionality" can be drawn from Congress's enactment of a five-year minimum sentence for as serious a felony crime as the distribution of child pornography. *See Harmelin v. Michigan*, 501 U.S. at 999, 111 S.Ct. 2680 (Kennedy, J., concurring) (emphasizing "substantial deference" that reviewing courts owe legislature's "broad authority ... in determining the types and limits of punishments for crimes" (internal quotation marks omitted)).

In making that determination, we need not look beyond the depicted sexual exploitation of an eight-year old on the distributed video to conclude that the crime of conviction here is a more serious offense than the golf club and videotape thefts in *Ewing* and *Lockyer*, for which the Supreme Court upheld prison sentences of 25 years to life. To be sure, those sentences were informed by the defendants' prior criminal records. Nevertheless, a large number of federal felony crimes carry the possibility of five-year prison terms for first time offenders.[16] In such circumstances, we can hardly infer gross disproportionality from

---

15. Pursuant to this graduated scheme, simple possession of child pornography carries no mandatory minimum sentence and a possible maximum of "not more than 10 years." 18 U.S.C. §2252(b)(2). Meanwhile, the production of child pornography in interstate commerce or the publication of an "advertisement seeking or offering ... to receive, exchange, buy, produce, display, distribute, or reproduce" such child pornography is punishable by a prison term of "not less than 15 years nor more than 30 years." *Id.* §2251(d), (e). The penalties for each of these proscribed activities are increased for defendants with prior child pornography convictions. *See id.* §§2251(e), 2252(b)(2)-(2).

16. *See, e.g.,* 18 U.S.C. §81 (providing for sentence up to 25 years for arson); *id.* §115(b)(1)(B)(ii)–(iv) (providing for sentence up to 10 years for physical assault on federal official, with possible higher sentences depending on degree of injury); *id.* §201 (providing for sentence up to 15 years for bribery); *id.* §371 (providing for sentence up to five years for conspiracy); *id.* §471 (providing for sentence up to 20 years for forgery of United States securities); *id.* §545 (providing for sentence up to 20 years for smuggling); *id.* §659 (providing for sentence up to 10 years for theft of goods in interstate commerce); *id.* §892 (providing for sentence up to 20 years for making an extortionate extension of credit); *id.* §924(c)(1) (providing for mandatory consecutive sentence of five years for carrying firearm during crime of violence or drug trafficking, with possible enhancements for how gun was used, type of firearm, and criminal record); *id.* §1001 (providing for sentence up to five years for making false statement to federal official); *id.* §1341 (providing for sentence up to 20 years for mail fraud); *id.*

Congress's decision to apply such a punishment to a felony crime presenting the serious harms associated with the distribution of child pornography.

No different conclusion is warranted because Congress mandated a minimum five-year sentence rather than leaving the possibility of such a punishment to the discretion of the sentencing judge. As the Supreme Court observed in *Harmelin v. Michigan*, the legislature's "'power to define criminal punishments without giving the courts any sentencing discretion'" is "beyond question." 501 U.S. at 1006, 111 S.Ct. 2680 (Kennedy, J., concurring) (quoting *Chapman v. United States*, 500 U.S. 453, 467, 111 S.Ct. 1919, 114 L.Ed.2d 524 (1991)); *see id.* at 999, 111 S.Ct. 2680 (recognizing that "competing theories of mandatory and discretionary sentencing have been in varying degrees of ascendancy or decline since the beginning of the Republic"). Precisely because statutorily mandated sentences represent not the judgment of a single judge but "the collective wisdom of the ... Legislature and, as a consequence, the ... citizenry," in *Harmelin* the Court accorded great deference to a state legislature's policy decision to mandate life sentences for persons who possessed more than 650 grams (approximately a pound and a half) of cocaine. *Id.* at 1006, 111 S.Ct. 2680. Indeed, the Court there noted that it had "never invalidated a penalty mandated by a legislature based only on the length of sentence, and, especially with a crime as severe as [drug possession], we should do so only in the most extreme circumstance." *Id.*

This case does not present that extreme circumstance. The crime here at issue is as harmful as that in *Harmelin*, while the challenged five-year minimum is far less "severe and unforgiving" than the life sentence upheld in that case. *Id.* at 1008, 111 S.Ct. 2680. Indeed, here Congress did not mandate a single sentence for all persons who distribute child pornography, nor set a maximum sentence that was the harshest term of incarceration permitted by law. *See generally Miller v. Alabama*, 132 S.Ct. at 2467–68. Rather, it provided a sentencing range of "not less than 5 years and not more than 20 years" for the distribution of child pornography. 18 U.S.C. § 2252(b)(1). To the extent every sentence is a function of both the crime committed and the character of the defendant who committed it, Congress decided only that the distribution of child pornography was a sufficiently serious crime as to require at least a five-year sentence even for the most sympathetic defendant. But having set this floor, Congress then left it entirely to district courts to assess the particulars of the crime and the character of the defendant to determine whether some other sentence, between the five-year minimum and twenty-year maximum, might be warranted to serve the interests of justice. In this respect it afforded more "mechanisms for consideration of individual circumstances" in child pornography distribution cases than were available for drug trafficking in *Harmelin*. *Harmelin v. Michigan*, 501 U.S. at 1008, 111 S.Ct. 2680 (Kennedy, J., concurring); *see id.* (noting that "[p]rosecutorial discretion before sentence and executive or legislative clemency afterwards provide means for the State to avert or correct unjust sentences").

Nor does Reingold's immaturity give rise to an inference of gross disproportionality. An adult defendant's immaturity may mitigate his moral culpability, but it does not reduce the harmful effects of his crime, which, as we have explained, are properly viewed as quite serious in cases of distribution of child pornography. Indeed, where the sentence at issue for such a serious crime is a minimum prison term of five years, the punishment is not so severe as to permit us to infer gross disproportionality from Congress's decision to mandate its imposition on all adult defendants, without regard to their relative maturity.

---

§ 1542 (providing for sentence up to 10 years for passport fraud); *id.* § 1621 (providing for sentence up to five years for perjury); *id.* § 1956 (providing for sentence up to 20 years for money laundering).

See generally Miller v. Alabama, 132 S.Ct. at 2460 (prohibiting mandatory life imprisonment without parole only for juvenile, not adult, offenders); *United States v. Merchant*, No. 12-12957, 2013 WL 461218, at *1 (11th Cir. Feb. 7, 2013) (rejecting argument that 25-year-old defendant's lack of sophistication, limited life experience, and amenability to treatment rendered 17.5-year sentence for distribution of large quantity of child pornography grossly disproportionate); *cf United States v. Moore*, 643 F.3d 451, 454 (6th Cir.2011) (rejecting claim that imposition of 15-year mandatory minimum sentence on four-time felon convicted of carrying firearm was grossly disproportionate in light of defendant's diminished mental capacity). We nevertheless reiterate the point we made earlier: the district court may, of course, take the defendant's immaturity into account in deciding where within the prescribed statutory range to sentence Reingold. *See* 18 U.S.C. §§ 3553(a), 3661; *see also United States v. Moore*, 643 F.3d at 455 (noting district court's consideration of defendant's reduced mental capacity in imposing sentence at very bottom of Guidelines range); *United States v. Stern*, 590 F.Supp.2d 945, 953 (N.D.Ohio 2008) (concluding that fact that defendant began downloading child pornography at 14 "weigh[ed] heavily in favor of a deviation [from Guidelines range] under § 3553(a)"); *cf. United States v. Wachowiak*, 412 F.Supp.2d 958, 964 (E.D.Wis.2006) (imposing 70-month sentence on defendant subject to mandatory minimum sentence of five years with applicable Guidelines range of 121 to 151 months' imprisonment in light of various mitigating factors). But it cannot rely on Reingold's relative immaturity to hold a five-year minimum sentence for the distribution of child pornography to be cruel and unusual punishment....

In sum, the application of a mandatory five-year sentence to the distribution crime of conviction in this particular case does not give rise to an inference of gross disproportionality suggestive of cruel and unusual punishment. Thus, we need not engage in any sentencing comparison to determine, as we do here, that the district court erred in concluding that the Eighth Amendment barred the application of a five-year mandatory minimum sentence in this case. Accordingly, we remand the case for the district court to vacate its original sentence and to resentence Reingold consistent with the statutory mandate....

The United States submits that the district court erred in failing to apply certain Sentencing Guidelines enhancements to the calculation of Reingold's applicable Guidelines range. Specifically, it contends that enhancements were warranted for (1) Reingold's engagement in a pattern of sexual abuse or exploitation of a minor, *see* U.S.S.G. § 2G2.2(b)(5); (2) the use of a computer to commit the crime of conviction, *see id.* § 2G2.2(b)(6); and (3) the distribution of child pornography, *see id.* § 2G2.2(b)(3)(F). Reingold responds that the district court correctly declined to apply these enhancements, but asserts that, if there was error, it was necessarily harmless because "the record is abundantly clear that Judge Weinstein would have imposed the same sentence regardless of the recommended guideline range."...

Our identification of a Guidelines calculation error as "harmless" allows us to uphold an otherwise valid sentence and to avoid vacatur and remand where it is clear that the district court would impose the same sentence in any event. *See United States v. Jass*, 569 F.3d 47, 68 (2d Cir.2009). In this case, however, we cannot avoid remand and resentencing because we have identified a non-Guidelines sentencing error, *i.e.*, the district court's refusal to impose a mandatory five-year minimum sentence based on an erroneous Eighth Amendment determination. Thus, on remand, the district court will not be able to impose the same sentence. We recognize that the district court may well choose on remand to impose a non-Guidelines sentence. Nevertheless, "we have indicated that a correct Guidelines calculation must normally precede [such a] decision." *United States v. Rodriguez*, 587 F.3d 573, 584 (2d Cir.2009). Accordingly, we proceed to consider the government's Guidelines calculation challenge.... In doing so, we interpret relevant Guidelines provisions *de novo*, but we defer to the district court's findings of facts pertinent to the Guidelines absent clear error. *See United States v. Broxmeyer*, 699 F.3d 265, 281 (2d Cir.2012)....

Guideline § 2G2.2, which applies to defendants convicted of child pornography crimes pursuant to 18 U.S.C. § 2252, provides for a five-level enhancement in offense level "[i]f the defendant engaged in a pattern of activity involving the sexual abuse or exploitation of a minor." U.S.S.G. § 2G2.2(b)(5). This Guideline attempts to assess both a defendant's risk of recidivism and the potential harm to others that such recidivism could present. *See United States v. Laraneta*, 700 F.3d 983, 987 (7th Cir.2012) (observing that, with respect to § 2G2.2(b)(5), defendant's "[o]ther acts of sexual predation ... have predictive significance with regard to the likelihood of recidivism, ... [a] relevant consideration in deciding how long a defendant should be incapacitated (by being imprisoned) from committing further crimes"). The Probation Department initially recommended, and the government urged, that this five-level enhancement be applied to Reingold based on his admitted three sexual contacts with his half-sister. The district court disagreed, finding § 2G2.2(b)(5) inapplicable because Reingold was a minor when the first two contacts with his sister occurred. Further, it observed that the acts were attributable largely to a lack of "proper parental supervision," and were so lacking in temporal proximity as to appear "aberrant." ... These circumstances do not, in fact, make § 2G2.2(b)(5) inapplicable here.

The "pattern of activity involving the sexual abuse or exploitation of a minor" required to warrant a § 2G2.2(b)(5) enhancement is specifically defined in the Guideline's application notes to mean "any combination of two or more separate instances of the sexual abuse or sexual exploitation of a minor by the defendant, whether or not the abuse or exploitation (A) occurred during the course of the offense; (B) involved the same minor; or (C) resulted in a conviction for such conduct." U.S.S.G. § 2G2.2 cmt. n.1. The same application note defines "sexual abuse or exploitation" to mean

> (A) conduct described in 18 U.S.C. § 2241, § 2242, § 2243, § 2251(a)–(c), § 2251(d)(1)(B), § 2251A, § 2260(b), § 2421, § 2422, or § 2423; (B) an offense under state law, that would have been an offense under any such section if the offense had occurred within the special maritime or territorial jurisdiction of the United States; or (C) an attempt or conspiracy to commit any of the offenses under subdivisions (A) or (B).

Id. The note also specifically excludes from the definition of "sexual abuse or exploitation" the "possession, accessing with intent to view, receipt, or trafficking in material relating to the sexual abuse or exploitation of a minor." *Id.*

Read together, these definitions signal that § 2G2.2(b)(5) is narrow in one respect and expansive in another. The specifically referenced federal statutes cabin the conduct that qualifies as "sexual abuse or exploitation" for purposes of a § 2G2.2(b)(5) enhancement. At the same time, the expansive word "any" in the phrase "*any* combination of two or more separate instances of the sexual abuse or sexual exploitation of a minor by the defendant" signals that any conduct described within one of the specified statutes is properly considered in making a § 2G2.2(b)(5) assessment and that nothing more than two separate instances of such conduct is required to demonstrate the requisite pattern....

We further conclude that the district court erred in excluding from § 2G2.2(b)(5) consideration of Reingold's first two sexual contacts with his half-sister on the ground that defendant was then himself a minor. This court has not previously had occasion to consider whether acts of sexual abuse or exploitation of a minor by a minor can support a § 2G2.2(b)(5) enhancement. We have however, considered that question in similar circumstances and held that they can. *See United States v. Phillips*, 431 F.3d 86, 90–93 (2d Cir.2005).

In *Phillips*, a defendant convicted of sexually exploiting a minor in violation of 18 U.S.C. § 2251(a) and (b) argued that the "§ 4B1.5(b) enhancement for a pattern of prohibited sexual behavior does not apply to unadjudicated conduct perpetrated by an adolescent because neither the Guidelines nor the Application Notes explicitly say that it does." *Id.* at 90. In rejecting this argument, we noted that one of the statutes defining conduct supporting the enhancement, 18 U.S.C. § 2243,[18] does not "limit[ ] its coverage to violators over the age of eighteen," thus making "sexual abuse of a minor by a minor ... prohibited conduct constituting an offense under federal law." *Id.* at 91. We further observed that, by contrast to other Guidelines, which condition enhancements on whether relevant offenses were adult convictions, § 4B1.5(b) contained no comparable language "placing constraints on the use of a conviction based on the defendant's age." *Id.* at 93; *see* U.S.S.G. §§ 4A1.1, 4B1.1. Accordingly, we concluded that, under § 4B1.5(b), "the district court [was] permitted to take into account sexually exploitive conduct that occurred when the defendant was himself a juvenile." *United States v. Phillips*, 431 F.3d at 93.

The same reasoning applies to § 2G2.2(b)(5). Among the statutes whose conduct describes the sexual abuse or exploitation of a minor relevant to this Guideline is 18 U.S.C. § 2241(c), which makes it a crime knowingly to engage "in a sexual act with another person who has not attained the age of 12" within the jurisdiction of the United States. Like § 2243, § 2241(c) does not limit its coverage to offenders over the age of 18. Nor does any language in § 2G2.2(b)(5) or its application notes require consideration of a defendant's age at the time of past instances of sexual abuse or exploitation. In the absence of such language, and consistent with our decision in *Phillips*, we here conclude that sexual abuse or exploitation of a minor undertaken by a defendant who was a juvenile at the time of the incident is properly considered in applying the § 2G2.2(b)(5) pattern enhancement. The two of our sister circuits to have considered this question have reached the same conclusion. *See United States v. Woodard*, 694 F.3d at 953 [8th Cir.]; *United States v. Olfano*, 503 F.3d at 243 [3d Cir.].

We therefore conclude that the district court erred in relying on Reingold's minority, lack of temporal proximity, and inadequate supervision as grounds not to consider his contacts with his sister as a basis for a § 2G2.2(b)(5) enhancement in this case. In rejecting these grounds for decision, we do not, however, conclude that Reingold warrants a § 2G2.2(b)(5) enhancement. That depends on whether his sexual contacts with his sister qualify as "sexual abuse or exploitation," a factual finding that the district court never made.... As we have already observed, "sexual abuse or exploitation," as used in § 2G2.2(b)(5), means only such conduct as is described in certain criminal statutes. The definition of a "sexual act" for purposes of § 2241(c), which appears to be the relevant statute here, derives from 18 U.S.C. § 2246(2)(D), which defines the phrase to mean, *inter alia*, "the intentional touching, not through the clothing, of the genitalia of another person who has not attained the age of 16 years with an intent to abuse, humiliate, harass, degrade, or arouse or gratify the sexual desire of any person." ... Of Reingold's three sexual contacts with his sister, the last—when he was 18 and she was 11—appears plainly to qualify. Reingold admitted that on that occasion, he had his sister "manually stimulate

---

18. 18 U.S.C. § 2243 makes it a felony for any person:
    in the special maritime and territorial jurisdiction of the United States or in a Federal prison, ... knowingly [to] engage[ ] in a sexual act with another person who—
    (1) has attained the age of 12 years but has not attained the age of 16 years; and
    (2) is at least four years younger than the person so engaging; or attempts to do so....
    Id. § 2243(a).

his penis, while he rubbed her breasts and manually stimulated her vagina, both over and under her panties," ... and "coached her on how to perform oral sex on him" and performed oral sex on her, ... The siblings' first encounter might also qualify in that Reingold admitted that on that first occasion, when he was 15 and his sister eight, he had her sister manually stimulate his penis while he touched the girl's "privates, under her clothing." *Id.*...

Guideline § 2G2.2(b)(6) provides for a two-level enhancement "[i]f the offense involved the use of a computer." The district court declined to apply the enhancement in this case, finding it to constitute impermissible "double counting." *United States v. C.R.*, 792 F.Supp.2d at 512. That conclusion was unwarranted in light of *United States v. Johnson*, 221 F.3d 83, 99 (2d Cir.2000), in which we specifically rejected a double-counting challenge to the application of a § 2G2.2(b)(6) enhancement. As *Johnson* observed, the use of a computer is not essential to the act of distributing child pornography. A person "can traffic in child pornography without using a computer much like one could commit a robbery without the use of a gun." *Id.* (internal quotation marks omitted). Thus, the enhancement does not result in double counting because it does not "increase a defendant's sentence to reflect the kind of harm that has already been fully accounted for" by the base offense level. *United States v. Volpe*, 224 F.3d 72, 76 (2d Cir.2000) (internal quotation marks omitted).... This conclusion is reinforced by our earlier observation that the digital revolution, which may be responsible for more child pornography crimes' being committed by computer, has aggravated rather than mitigated the harms associated with such crime.... By making it easier to retrieve and distribute child pornography, computers have expanded the market for child pornography, which in turn fuels a greater demand for a product that can only be produced by abusing and exploiting children. *See generally United States v. Lewis*, 605 F.3d at 403. Moreover, once child pornography is circulated by computer, it becomes almost impossible to remove or destroy. In such circumstances, it was hardly unreasonable, much less double counting, for the Sentencing Commission to conclude that the base offense level applicable to all distributors of child pornography—even those who share items non-electronically—should be enhanced for persons who commit the crime by using a computer....

To assist sentencing judges in distinguishing among such varied crimes and assessing their severity in particular cases, § 2G2.2 draws various distinctions. To begin, the Guideline draws a gross distinction between crimes of conviction implicating only simple possession of child pornography[21] and all other covered crimes, assigning a base offense level of 18 to the former, *see* U.S.S.G. § 2G2.2(a)(1), and a base offense level of 22 to the latter, *see id.* § 2G2.2(a)(2). Within the latter set—which includes the receipt, solicitation, transportation, and advertisement of child pornography, as well as its sale or distribution—the Guideline provides for the base offense level to be reduced two levels in cases where "the defendant's conduct was limited to the receipt or solicitation" of child pornography, *and* "the defendant did not intend to traffic, or distribute, in such material." *Id.* § 2G2.2(b)(1). At the same time, however, the Guideline provides for an enhancement to the base offense level for offenses that involved the distribution of child pornography. *See id.* § 2G2.2(b)(3). Specifically, it dictates a two-level enhancement whenever an offense involved distribution, *see id.* § 2G2.2(b)(3)(F), with the possibility of greater enhancements if the distribution was for pecuniary or other tangible gain, *see id.* § 2G2.2(b)(3)(A)–(B), or to a minor, *see id.* § 2G2.2(b)(3)(C)–(E).

---

21. This first set also includes production and distribution crimes involving adapted or modified depictions of a minor. *See* 18 U.S.C. § 2252A(a)(7).

This structure cannot be understood to address the harm associated with the distribution of child pornography in a base offense level of 22 that applies equally to a variety of offenses, some involving distribution and others not. Rather, § 2G2.2 is structured so that the range of harms associated with distribution can be addressed through various enhancements. Indeed, that conclusion has been so obvious to those of our sister circuits to have considered the question that they have employed little discussion to reject double counting challenges to the application of a § 2G2.2(b)(3)(F) enhancement to defendants convicted of distribution offenses. *See United States v. Chiaradio*, 684 F.3d 265, 283 (1st Cir.2012) (identifying "absolutely no basis" for inferring that distribution enhancement did not apply to defendant convicted of distribution crime); *United States v. Frakes*, 402 Fed.Appx. 332, 335–36 (10th Cir.2010) ("Rather than forbidding double-counting, § 2G2.2 expressly *allows* a two-level enhancement for distribution," such that a minimum two-point enhancement "will always apply" to defendants convicted of distribution offenses (emphasis in original)).... We agree that a minimum two-level enhancement for distribution applies to the calculation of Reingold's Guidelines, and we conclude that the district court erred as a matter of law in holding that such an enhancement constituted impermissible double counting.... Thus, on remand, the district court should recalculate Reingold's Guidelines before resentencing, applying enhancements under U.S.S.G. § 2G2.2(b)(3)(F), (b)(5), and (b)(6), as warranted consistent with this opinion. While the district court is required correctly to calculate and fairly to consider the Guidelines, *see* 18 U.S.C. § 3553(a)(4), nothing in this opinion is intended to limit the district court's discretion to consider a non-Guidelines sentence pursuant to *United States v. Booker*, 543 U.S. 220, 245, 125 S.Ct. 738, 160 L.Ed.2d 621 (2005)....

To summarize, we conclude as follows:

1. The application of the five-year minimum sentence mandated by 18 U.S.C. § 2252(b)(1) is not so grossly disproportionate to the crime of distributing child pornography as to be precluded in this case by the Cruel and Unusual Punishment Clause of the Eighth Amendment. Accordingly, in exercising its sentencing discretion in this case, the district court cannot impose a lesser prison sentence than the statutorily mandated minimum.

2. In calculating a defendant's Sentencing Guidelines range for distributing child pornography:

a. A pattern enhancement pursuant to U.S.S.G. § 2G2.2(b)(5) applies to a defendant who commits *any* two acts fitting the Guidelines definition of "sexual abuse or exploitation of a minor," without regard to the temporal proximity of those acts, the defendant's own minority at the time of such acts, or mitigating circumstances. Such circumstances may inform a district court's exercise of discretion in selecting a within-Guidelines sentence or in imposing a non-Guidelines sentence, but they do not permit the court to refrain from applying an otherwise warranted § 2G2.2(b)(5) enhancement to the calculation of a defendant's Guidelines range.

b. Because a computer is not essential to the crime of distributing child pornography, the computer-use enhancement provided in U.S.S.G. § 2G2.2(b)(6) does not constitute impermissible double counting simply because an ever larger number of child pornography distribution crimes are committed with computers.

c. Because neither the statute of conviction, 18 U.S.C. § 2252(a)(2), nor the applicable Guideline, § 2G2.2, is limited to distribution crimes, the distribution enhancement provided in § 2G2.2(b)(3)(F) does not constitute impermissible double counting.

Accordingly, we remand this case to the district court with direction that it vacate Reingold's sentence and resentence him consistent with this opinion, specifically recalculating his Sentencing Guidelines range as indicated herein, and adhering to the statutorily mandated minimum sentence of five years' imprisonment.

Judge SACK concurs in a separate opinion.

SACK, Circuit Judge, concurring [opinion is omitted]....

Notes

Like the court in *Reingold*, several courts have concluded that imposition of the five-year mandatory minimum sentence in similar cases does not give rise to an inference of gross disproportionality manifesting cruel and unusual treatment. For example, in *United States v. Ramos*, 685 F.3d 120 (2d Cir.2012), the defendant was convicted of receiving and possessing child pornography and faced a 15-year minimum sentence; in rejecting an Eighth Amendment challenge to the higher minimum, the court noted that "'[l]engthy prison sentences ... do not violate the Eighth Amendment's prohibition against cruel and unusual punishment when based on proper application of the Sentencing Guidelines or statutorily mandated ... terms,'" *id.* at 134 n. 11 (quoting *United States v. Yousef*, 327 F.3d 56, 163 (2d Cir. 2003)). For other cases in which the court has rejected Eighth Amendment challenges to mandatory minimum sentences in child pornography or exploitation cases, see *United States v. Hart*, 635 F.3d 850, 859 (6th Cir. 2011) (upholding 15-year mandatory minimum under 18 U.S.C. § 2251 for persuading minor to engage in sexually explicit conduct for purpose of producing visual depictions, and noting same ruling with respect to 10-year mandatory minimum for enticing minor into sexual relations in violation of 18 U.S.C. §§ 2422(b) and 2251); *United States v. Nagel*, 559 F.3d 756, 762 (7th Cir. 2009) (holding 10-year mandatory minimum sentence under 18 U.S.C. § 2422(b) not grossly disproportionate to crime of attempting to entice minor to engage in criminal sexual act); *United States v. Malloy*, 568 F.3d 166, 180 & n. 14 (4th Cir. 2009) (upholding 15-year mandatory minimum sentence under 18 U.S.C. § 2251); *United States v. Gross*, 437 F.3d 691, 695 (7th Cir. 2006) (15-year mandatory minimum sentence under 18 U.S.C. § 2252A(b)(1) for distribution of child pornography was not grossly disproportionate to crime in light of seriousness of crime and defendant's prior record); *United States v. MacEwan*, 445 F.3d 237, 250 (3d Cir. 2006) (rejecting gross disproportionality challenge to 15-year minimum sentence mandated by 18 U.S.C. § 2252(a)(2)(B), (b)(1) for repeat offender convicted of receipt of child pornography); *United States v. Dwinells*, 508 F.3d 63, 69 (1st Cir. 2007) (rejecting Eighth Amendment challenge to mandatory minimum sentence for attempting to persuade, induce, entice, or coerce minor to engage in criminal sexual activity in violation of 18 U.S.C. § 2242(b), resting on legislative function to prescribe "penological determinations"). For arguments against mandatory minimum sentencing, see Mary Price, *Mill(er)ing Mandatory Minimums: What Federal Lawmakers Should Take From Miller v. Alabama*, 78 Mo. L. Rev. 1147, 1153 (2013) (commenting on Judge Weinstein's ruling and calling for reform of mandatory minimum sentencing). For the subsequent history to *Reingold*, see Chapter Three, Section I (Internet Parameters: Accessibility and Anonymity), *United States v. C.R.*, Notes, *supra*.

United States v. Goldberg

Seventh Circuit, 2007
491 F.3d 668

POSNER, Circuit Judge.

The government appeals from the imposition of a sentence of one day in prison, time served, for a violation of the Child Pornography Prevention Act of 1996. The specific section of the Act that the defendant violated, 18 U.S.C. §2252A(a)(5)(B), authorizes, so far as bears on this case, the imposition of a maximum prison sentence of 10 years on anyone who "knowingly possesses any book, magazine, periodical, film, videotape, computer disk, or any other material that contains an image of child pornography that has been mailed, or shipped or transported in interstate or foreign commerce by any means, including by computer." For the defendant's particular offense, the federal guidelines sentence range was at least 63 to 78 months—"at least" because, as noted at the end of this opinion, it appears to have been miscalculated in the defendant's favor.... The judge imposed a nominal prison sentence, though her preference was to impose no prison sentence at all, because without imposing a prison sentence she could not have imposed supervised release. The statute that authorizes supervised release, 18 U.S.C. §3583(a), states that "the court, in imposing a sentence to a term of imprisonment for a felony or a misdemeanor, may include as a part of the sentence a requirement that the defendant be placed on a term of supervised release after imprisonment." The Sentencing Commission understands supervised release to presuppose a prison sentence. See U.S.S.G. ch. 7, pt. A, §2(b); see also *United States v. Sanchez-Estrada*, 62 F.3d 981, 994 (7th Cir.1995).

The defendant, who is now 23 years old, is the son of a prosperous couple in the wealthy Chicago suburb of Highland Park. He downloaded file-sharing software that gave him access to a web site called "# 100% PreTeenGirlPics." Over a period of some 18 months, he downloaded hundreds of pornographic photographic images, some depicting children as young as 2 or 3 being vaginally penetrated by adult males. He offered these images to other subscribers to the web site to induce them to send similar images in return. He masturbated while viewing the pornographic images. He has a history of drug abuse. His lawyers describe him as a "normal young adult."

The district judge justified the remarkably light sentence that she gave the defendant as follows:

> It's a very, very difficult case, but I have concluded that I'm going to begin with a lengthy period of supervision rather than a period of incarceration, with the idea that it's going to be very intensive, and if there is a problem, Mr. Goldberg is going to go away for a very long time.
>
> But the way I look at this case, ... I think that if I sent Mr. Goldberg away for 63 months or anything close to it with the hope that he gets sex offender treatment in prison, we're pretty much guaranteeing his life will be ruined. And I think there's some possibility here that his life can go in a different way, and I'd like to try that, but I'm very worried, because what's gone on here is very, very difficult for me to deal with. I mean, these pictures, I can't even bear to look at them they're so horrible. And what spiraling downward does to you so that you can stand looking at pictures like that I don't know, but it's spiraling pretty far downward.
>
> The guidelines allow me to place Mr. Goldberg, and I'm going to ... I don't know what our current word is ... deviate from the guidelines under 3553, and I'm going to impose a period ... as I said, the supervised release can be any years up to life. I'm going to impose a ten-year period of supervised release.
>
> It's more supervised release than I have ever imposed before, but I really think that given the psychiatric reports and given what transpired here, that the period of supervision has to be long enough to ensure that if Mr. Goldberg turns his life in a different direction he does it for a long time.
>
> I also want to make sure that if there is further ... any evidence of further problem, that the Court retains a handle over Mr. Goldberg for a long time.

Now, during that period of supervision, I really need a little help in figuring out . . . and I have been trying to get the lawyers to give it to me, but I don't know that I've gotten it yet. Maybe it depends on what kind of financial commitment people are able to make, I don't know, but I need to have close supervision in both the drug area and in the therapy area to make sure that we're not having a problem here. And I know that . . . I think Ms. Cohen is the one who suggested some kind of periodic polygraph examinations, and I think that should be an important part of this. . . .

I think I better now talk about why under Section 3553 I deviated from the guidelines. My reason in this case is less . . . well, it's this: It's considering the history and characteristics of the defendant I think that there's a substantial likelihood . . . and also considering the psychiatric reports, that this offense was committed out of boredom and stupidity and not because Mr. Goldberg has a real problem with the kind of deviance that these cases usually suggest. I believe that if that is correct, and if he is sent to prison for a lengthy period, anything of any consequence at all, I think it's going to ruin his life in many ways.

I think that sex offender treatment within the Bureau of Prisons is going to expose him to people who are dangerous to him. I think any substantial period of incarceration is going to ensure that he's not able to take advantage of his education and get a good job, and I think all of this will reinforce whatever negative things he's done in the past rather than pushing him in a positive direction.

I recognize that the viewing of child pornography over the Internet destroys the lives of young children, but I also recognize that the life that I'm concerned with here, the life that I can affect, is Mr. Goldberg's life, and I don't want to destroy his life in the hope that maybe in some very indirect way it's going to help somebody else's life. I don't think it is. And I would like, if I can, to support him in putting his life on a positive direction rather than in destroying it.

The reason for the long period of supervision and the close supervision that I believe I've required is to make sure that if he indeed represents a threat, and if I'm wrong in my assessment of what went on here, that we are able to catch it before any damage is done.

This is kind of an odd balancing of factors under 3553, but I think I do have the discretion in an unusual case like this one to choose not to incarcerate and to choose close supervision to see what transpires over the next few years.

[Emphasis added].

There is also a brief "statement of reasons" appended to the original judgment that the judge entered. But it is omitted from the amended judgment (entered because the original judgment was discovered to contain clerical errors) and is not in the appellate record, although the defendant's counsel quotes from it in his brief and the clerk of the district court has found a copy for us. In the oral statement, which we just quoted, the grounds on which the judge justified the sentence were that the defendant was not a real deviant because he had committed the crime out of "boredom and stupidity," that it would ruin his life to be imprisoned because he would be exposed to "people who are dangerous to him," and that his life, rather than the lives of the small children who had been raped in order to enable the creation of sadistic child pornography to assist the defendant in masturbating, was the only "life that I can affect." The written statement of reasons is similar. In it the judge attributes the defendant's pornographic activity to boredom resulting from his being confined at home as a result of being convicted of a drug offense and states that he "has normal sexual interests and is not a pedophile, internet or otherwise." She states that "no one argues that any actual children are at risk from any conduct of [the defendant] (other than the harm to children who are used to make images used on the internet)," but she assigns no weight to that harm — the harm to the children — consistent with her oral statement that the only life she can affect by her sentence is the defendant's. The written statement assigns weight to the fact that if the defendant is sent to prison, "his education will be interrupted."

These grounds, and the passages we quoted in which they appear, do not comply with the requirement that the sentencing judge conscientiously consider the factors set forth in 18 U.S.C. § 3553(a) to guide sentencing. Those factors, so far as pertain to this case, are

> (1) the nature and circumstances of the offense and the history and characteristics of the defendant;

> (2) the need for the sentence imposed —

>> (A) to reflect the seriousness of the offense, to promote respect for the law, and to provide just punishment for the offense;

>> (B) to afford adequate deterrence to criminal conduct;

>> (C) to protect the public from further crimes of the defendant; and ...

> (6) the need to avoid unwarranted sentence disparities among defendants with similar records who have been found guilty of similar conduct.

A prison sentence of one day for a crime that Congress and the American public consider grave, in circumstances that enhance the gravity (we refer to the character of some of the images), committed by a convicted drug offender, does not give due weight to the "nature and circumstances of the offense" and the "history and characteristics of the defendant." It does not "reflect the seriousness of the offense," "promote respect for the law," or "provide just punishment for the offense." It does not "afford adequate deterrence to criminal conduct." And it creates an unwarranted sentence disparity, since similarly situated defendants are punished with substantial prison sentences. See, e.g., *United States v. Lange*, 445 F.3d 983 (7th Cir.2006); *United States v. Grigg*, 442 F.3d 560 (7th Cir.2006); *United States v. Baker*, 445 F.3d 987 (7th Cir.2006); *United States v. Perez*, 484 F.3d 735 (5th Cir.2007); *United States v. Nikonova*, 480 F.3d 371 (5th Cir.2007); *United States v. Rolfsema*, 468 F.3d 75 (1st Cir.2006); *United States v. Branson*, 463 F.3d 1110 (10th Cir.2006). *United States v. Grinbergs*, 470 F.3d 758 (8th Cir.2006), reversed a sentence of a year and a day (a sentence 366 times longer than the sentence imposed by the district judge in this case) imposed on a defendant who had pleaded guilty to one count of possessing child pornography and faced a guidelines sentence of 46 to 57 months in prison, lower than our defendant's guidelines sentencing range.

It is true as the defendant points out that the statute under which he was convicted contains no mandatory minimum. But it does not follow that Congress envisaged no prison time for violators. The absence of a mandatory minimum sentence may signify no more than that the legislature did not want to take the time to try to determine what the minimum sentence should be or did not think it could anticipate unusual cases in which a light sentence might be appropriate. We can imagine a case, involving the downloading of a handful of images none showing any prepubescent child or depicting any sexual activity, yet still constituting child pornography (the statute defines "child" as any minor and "pornography" as including besides actual sexual activity "lascivious exhibition of the genitals or pubic area," 18 U.S.C. §§ 2256(1), (2)(A)(v)), in which a permissible sentence might be light. The hundreds of images in this case include as we have noted images of prepubescent children being penetrated by adults.

The district judge was influenced by the erroneous belief that a sentence affects only the life of the criminal and not the lives of his victims. Young children were raped in order to enable the production of the pornography that the defendant both downloaded and uploaded—both consumed himself and disseminated to others. The greater the customer demand for child pornography, the more that will be produced. E.g., *Osborne v. Ohio*, 495 U.S. 103, 109–11, 110 S.Ct. 1691, 109 L.Ed.2d 98 (1990); *United States v. Barevich*, 445 F.3d 956, 959 (7th Cir.2006); *United States v. Richardson*, 238 F.3d 837, 839 (7th Cir.2001); *United States v. Angle*, 234 F.3d 326, 337–38 (7th Cir.2000). Sentences influence behavior, or so at least Congress thought when in 18 U.S.C. § 3553(a) it made deterrence a statutory sentencing factor. The logic of deterrence suggests that the lighter the punishment for downloading and uploading child pornography, the greater the customer demand for it and so the more will be produced.

Why the fact that the defendant committed the offense out of "boredom and stupidity," if it were a fact, should be thought a mitigating factor escapes us and was not explained by the judge. Anyway it is not a fact; the defendant obtained sexual gratification from the pornographic images that he so sedulously collected. It is also inconsistent with the 10-year term of supervised release that the judge imposed, which includes conditions that require the defendant's participation in programs for the psychological treatment of sex offenders.

The judge's suggestion that the defendant does not have "a real problem" could be interpreted to mean that she disparages Congress's decision to criminalize the consumption and distribution of child pornography, perhaps because she thinks that only people who actually molest children, rather than watching them being molested, have "a real problem." This interpretation is reinforced by her statement elsewhere in the transcript of the sentencing hearing that the defendant's crime was just "a kind of mischief." This characterization cannot be reconciled with the judge's having fully credited (as she said she did) the report of a psychologist who stated that the defendant has been using pornography for more than a decade, that he "believed he was smart enough not to get caught and if he were caught he believed he would not have any consequences," that he has "little knowledge, understanding or empathy for the little girls depicted in the images," that "he began using pornography when he was 12–13 and continues to fantasize about the same age girls he looked at then," that he has "persistent sexual interest in adolescent males and females," that he is a "pedophile," that he "has admitted to other deviant behaviors, namely voyeurism, scatological phone calls and the stealing of a 14 year old girl's panties," that he has "sociopathic traits," that "he doesn't think of the consequences of his behavior," that "he has had two convictions within two years," and that "he has little respect for the law or social conventions."

The district judge's assertion "that sex offender treatment within the Bureau of Prisons is going to expose [the defendant] to people who are dangerous to him" is ill informed. Sex-offender treatment in federal prisons is voluntary. Statement of Andres E. Hernandez, Director of the Sex Offender Treatment Program Federal Correctional Institution Butner, N.C., Concerning "Sexual Exploitation of Children Over the Internet: The Face of a Child Predator and Other Issues," Before the H. Subcomm. on Oversight and Investigations of the H. Comm. on Energy and Commerce, 152 Cong. Rec. D1035-01, D1038 (Sept. 26, 2006), http://projectsafechildhood.gov/HernandezTestimonyCongress.pdf, p. 2 (visited June 1, 2007). And "the vast majority" of sex offenders in the program are individuals convicted of "Possession, Receipt, Distribution, and Transportation of Child Pornography," like the defendant. *Id.* at 3. The judge gave no explanation for why she thought a prison sentence would be more ruinous for the defendant than for any other imprisoned criminal other than her mistaken belief that he would be thrown in with violent sexual offenders.

The judge's balancing of the section 3553(a) sentencing factors was indeed "odd," as she acknowledged, but, more to the point, it was unreasonable. *United States v. Roberson*, 474 F.3d 432, 435 (7th Cir.2007); *United States v. Repking*, 467 F.3d 1091, 1094 (7th Cir.2006) (per curiam); *United States v. Walker*, 447 F.3d 999, 1007 (7th Cir.2006). When the guidelines, drafted by a respected public body with access to the best knowledge and practices of penology, recommend that a defendant be sentenced to a number of years in prison, a sentence involving no (or, as in this case, nominal) imprisonment can be justified only by a careful, impartial weighing of the statutory sentencing factors. It may not be based on idiosyncratic penological views (such as that the severity of criminal punishment has no significance for the victims of crime, but only for the criminals), disagreement with congressional policy, or weighting criminals' interests more heavily than those of victims and potential victims. See, e.g., *United States v. Grinbergs, supra*, 470 F.3d at 759; *United States v. Davis*, 458 F.3d 491, 498–500 (6th Cir.2006); *United States v. Martin*, 455 F.3d 1227, 1239–42 (11th Cir.2006); *United States v. Crisp*, 454 F.3d 1285 (11th Cir.2006); *United States v. Robinson*, 454 F.3d 839 (8th Cir.2006); *United States v. Cage*, 451 F.3d 585, 595–96 (10th Cir.2006). The judge neglected considerations of deterrence and desert, which dominate the federal criminal code, in favor of undue emphasis on rehabilitation, and seemed even to think that any prison sentence, however short, is inconsistent with rehabilitation. That is not the theory of either the criminal code or the Sentencing Reform Act, which actually downplays the significance of rehabilitation as a penological goal by rejecting imprisonment as a means of promoting it. 28 U.S.C. § 994(k); *Mistretta v. United States*, 488 U.S. 361, 367, 109 S.Ct. 647, 102 L.Ed.2d 714 (1989); *Kerr v. Puckett*, 138 F.3d 321, 324 (7th Cir.1998).

Finally, the guidelines sentencing range appears to have been miscalculated. The district judge did not make the upward adjustment required by U.S.S.G. § 2G2.2(b)(3) for sadistic images, even though at the sentencing hearing the government pointed out that some of the images on the defendant's computer involved "bondage of these young children" and "sadistic and masochistic sexual activity with these children," as well as girls "as young as two and three years old being vaginally penetrated with an adult male penis."

We do not rule that a sentence below a properly calculated guidelines range would have been improper in this case. The guidelines are merely advisory, and the statutory sentencing factors (a laundry list of incommensurables which guides consideration but does not dictate the sentence or even the sentencing range) leave plenty of discretion to the sentencing judge. But that discretion was abused in this case, and the judgment is therefore reversed and the case remanded for resentencing.

Notes

In *Goldberg*, Judge Posner did not hold that the sentence may not fall below the sentence guideline range, but only that the sentence imposed — one day of incarceration — was unreasonable in light of the sentence factors enumerated in 18 U.S.C. § 3553(a). Likewise, in *United States v. Robinson*, 669 F.3d 767 (6th Cir. 2012) ("*Robinson I*"), in which the defendant possessed more than seven thousand images of child pornography — many of which included acts as horrific as those described in *Goldberg* — and was sentenced to one day of incarceration and five years of supervised release, the United States Court of Appeals for the Sixth Circuit held the sentence to be unreasonable and remanded the case for resentencing. On remand, the district court again sentenced the defendant to one day of incarceration, with credit for time served, but imposed a longer period of supervised release and additional conditions of release. *Id.* On appeal for the second time, the court vacated the sentence as unreasonable and remanded the case to be assigned to a new judge for resentencing. *United States v. Robinson*, 778 F.3d 515 (6th Cir. 2015) (*"Robinson II"*). *See also United States v. Bistline*, 720 F.3d 631, 632 (6th Cir. 2013) (despite reversal by the appellate court, district court twice imposed one-day sentence of confinement for possession arguably less culpable than that in *Robinson* and *Goldberg*). In all of these cases, the courts considered the seriousness of the offenses, the need for deterrence, and unwarranted sentence disparities, in mandating a more proportional sentence.

3. Special Circumstances

United States v. Olhovsky

Third Circuit, 2009
562 F.3d 530

McKEE, Circuit Judge....

Nicolau Olhovsky was born with several birth defects, including a concave chest (pectus excavatum). When he was eight months old, he underwent heart surgery in an attempt to correct defects in his heart and aorta, and he underwent a second operation at age 14 to correct his concave chest.... [1] ... Olhovsky's parents divorced when he was seven years old. Following the divorce, he and his sister lived with their mother until his arrest in this case. His mother has been permanently disabled as a result of an automobile accident in 1997.... It is uncontested that Olhovsky was awkward and isolated as a child. He was bullied and teased at school because of his slight build and physical limitations. As a result, he spent much of his time alone in his room with a computer. It is also uncontested that he was so depressed and suicidal at times that he was admitted to a psychiatric facility in 2004, and that he cut himself with a knife at one point.

The events underlying his prosecution for child pornography began in August of 2004 when an undercover law enforcement officer who was investigating internet child pornography logged onto an Internet Relay Chat ("IRC") channel labeled: "# 100% PRE-TEENGIRLSEXPICS." While monitoring that web site, agents learned that Olhovsky was among those using it to trade child pornography. In December of 2004, shortly after Olhovsky turned eighteen, agents searched the home that Olhovsky shared with his mother and sister. During the course of that search, the agents seized Olhovsky's computer and hard drive. Subsequent examination of that hard drive disclosed over 600 images of child pornography, including photographs of prepubescent girls engaging in sexual activity with adult men.... Olhovsky admitted that the hard drive was his and that he collected and traded child pornography through the IRC. He also told the agents that he began viewing and collecting child pornography when he was about fifteen. Olhovsky further admitted setting up a file server and posting an advertisement offering to trade pornographic materials.

Olhovsky was subsequently arrested pursuant to a criminal complaint charging possession of child pornography based on the results of the aforementioned search and statements Olhovsky had made during the course of the search. Thereafter, Olhovsky waived his right to indictment, and pled guilty to possession of child pornography, in violation of 18 U.S.C. § 2252A(a)(5)(B).... Prior to sentencing, Olhovsky participated in mental health counseling arranged by Probation and Pretrial Services. During the almost two years that passed while Olhovsky was awaiting sentencing, he continued in counseling and therapy, including regular meetings with Dr. Howard Silverman, a psychologist spe-

---

1. Given Olhovsky's unique circumstances and their relevance to his challenge to the reasonableness of his sentence, we will set forth his personal characteristics in detail.

cializing in the treatment of sex offenders. Dr. Silverman's psychological services were provided pursuant to his vendor contract with Pretrial Services.

In August 2006, after he had been treating Olhovsky for over a year, and well before Olhovsky was to be sentenced, Dr. Silverman learned that Olhovsky faced up to ten years in prison pursuant to his guilty plea. That prompted Dr. Silverman to write a letter to Pretrial Services expressing his concerns about Olhovsky's potential incarceration. He sent copies of the letter to defense counsel, the prosecutor and the court. In his letter, Dr. Silverman explained: "despite ... having worked with many Federal Pre-Trial clients in the past, this is the first letter of its kind that I have ever composed." ... In that letter, Dr. Silverman stated:[2]

> When Mr. Olhovsky first consulted with me, he was eighteen years of age. He will only be twenty years of age this coming September 14. However, despite his chronological age as an adult, I have always worked with him with the view of his being a notably immature adolescent who is, perhaps, a juvenile sexual offender but should not be viewed as an adult offender. It is important to make note of the fact that there are significant differences between adult and juvenile sexual abusers. Patterns of sexual interest and arousal are developing and not yet fixed in adolescents. Situational and opportunity factors appear more typical in juvenile sexual offenses, rather than the fixed internal cognitive factors often found in adult offenders. Adolescents have less developed sexual knowledge. Protective factors are especially important when dealing with youngsters. In addition, recidivism rates are notably lower with adolescents.

> I would also like to comment upon the motivational aspects that I believe impacted upon Mr. Olhovsky. Some of these motivators include, in his case, loneliness (as an inappropriate and ineffective means of connecting and engaging with others), naïve experimentation (in which [Olhovsky] is likely to not have been fully aware of the antisocial nature of his actions but was motivated primarily to learn about sex and sex-related matters), to gratify sexual needs (which he believed he was incapable of doing with age-appropriate peers) and as one way in which he could establish social competence or mastery due to the interpersonal difficulties he had experienced throughout much of his life.

> Upon presenting to me initially, [Olhovsky] indicated an, overall, unhappy childhood marked by not having enough friends, school problems, and a history of being severely bullied and teased. He was extremely fearful of experiencing further teasing, humiliation, and social rejection. Most of his time was spent alone in which he could escape the very sad reality of his life by going into a world of fantasy available to him on the Internet.

> Mr. Olhovsky acknowledged a number of behavioral problems in which he included "odd behavior" because he did not see himself as mature as a typical eighteen year old. He also indicated phobic avoidance of people due to the negative experiences he had had.

> Emotionally, Mr. Olhovsky indicated not one positive emotion but a long list of negative ones including feeling depressed, anxious, guilty, regretful, hopeless, helpless, lonely and tense. His main fears included "being alone my whole life" and "not being able to support myself."

---

2. Because this letter is central to the issues raised on appeal, we take the liberty of quoting it at length.

Mr. Olhovsky described himself as a useless, unattractive, ugly, stupid and lazy individual who also was unable to make decisions, had memory problems and concentration difficulties.

Interpersonally, he reported having few, if any, friends and not being able to maintain relationships. [Olhovsky] reported no significant emotional/romantic relationships and he had no sexual relationships with others. The primary focus of his sexuality had been via the computer. He maintained, however, that his primary sexual fantasies were of age-appropriate females where mutuality was a part of the experience.

I am also very concerned about Mr. Olhovsky's being able to deal with incarceration due to the physical limitations he has. Not only is he very slightly built (and, quite frankly, incapable of physically protecting himself), but he has a history of open-heart surgery and has physical limitations. Not being a medical doctor, I will not, however, comment further about his medical condition.

I would also like to comment upon my view of the progress that Mr. Olhovsky has made since being in treatment. While he seems to have little, if any, guidance from his mother (who reportedly is quite physically ill herself with a number of emotional problems), or his father (divorced from his mother and with whom he has limited contact), or any substantial support from any other family member he has, with the assistance of Federal Pre-Trial officers and myself, shown signs of growth both inter- and intra-personally. However, Mr. Olhovsky is at the beginning stages of that growth. Rather than being a nineteen (soon to be twenty) year old, he, actually, more impresses me as being a fourteen or fifteen year old who is stumbling toward adulthood. However, he is moving in the right direction. His self-image is improving, his interactional skills are improving, his assertiveness has increased, his communication skills are improving, he has taken risks regarding being with others which has included going down the Jersey Shore and going to concerts, and he continuously expresses the desire for further social contact with age-appropriate peers.

Mr. Olhovsky still makes certain mistakes such as those which resulted in his being currently unemployed. However, these are mistakes not of maliciousness but, rather, immaturity.

While I cannot represent to you that Mr. Olhovsky will never behave inappropriately in the future (none of us can predict the future with certainty), I do hope that Mr. Olhovsky can be viewed much more as a juvenile rather than adult sexual offender. I do not view him as being a fixated pedophile or incapable or lacking desire in being with age-appropriate consenting females. He has made progress both interpersonally and intrapersonally. If incarcerated, however, whatever progress that he has made will likely be for naught and, if anything, he will just regress terribly. Additionally, as I noted earlier, I do fear for his physical safety.

I hope the above information is of value to you in having a better understanding of my work with Mr. Olhovsky....

[Citations to record omitted].

   In the course of preparing for sentencing, Olhovsky's counsel spoke with Dr. Silverman after obtaining a court order authorizing limited disclosure of Olhovsky's treatment records.... Defense counsel claimed that Dr. Silverman was initially "amenable" to appearing as a witness at Olhovsky's sentencing.... [footnote omitted]. Although it is not entirely clear what happened next, upon learning of Dr. Silverman's intent to testify, it appears that Pretrial Services took the position that Dr. Silverman's vendor contract precluded him from appearing voluntarily on behalf of Olhovsky at sentencing.... [footnote omitted]. It is clear that Pretrial Services "asserted that Dr. Silverman's testimony in this case, because it is expected to be favorable to Mr. Olhovsky, would make him a partisan, and that it is improper to have a 'contract court employee' be turned into a partisan in the matter." ... [footnote omitted]. Accordingly, Pretrial Services contacted the district court and expressed its opposition to having Dr. Silverman testify at sentencing....

Upon learning of Pretrial Services' position, defense counsel moved to subpoena Dr. Silverman to testify at Olhovsky's sentencing. The court offered the following explanation for denying the motion:

> I have concluded, based upon two factors, that I am not going to permit Dr. Silverman to testify in this matter. One is because it would appear to me that there's an effort, indeed, to have him testify in some manner as an expert, in short, to give a prognosis and opinion about Mr. Olhovsky's future potential risk and so on....

[Citations to record omitted].

Defense counsel indicated at this point that Dr. Silverman had already stated his own willingness to testify, and the subpoena was only requested because of the opposition from Pretrial Services. The court responded: "[g]iven this unique situation which is *sui generis*, if he personally wishes to testify, he can testify, and Pretrial Services and I will work it out between us.... Dr. Silverman did not appear at the sentencing as it appears that nothing could be "worked out" regarding his testimony. Moreover, it is not at all clear what the court intended to do, or what it expected defense counsel to do to "work out" an arrangement whereby Dr. Silverman would appear at sentencing. Defense counsel did send one last letter to Dr. Silverman after her request for a subpoena was denied. In that letter, she explained that the court had refused a subpoena and she made the following final plea for Dr. Silverman's assistance:

> Notwithstanding the contract between Discovery House and Pretrial Services, I am writing to ask you to voluntarily testify for Mr. Olhovsky. I am sure that you are in a difficult position vis-a-vis Pretrial Services, and I understand that voluntarily testifying on Mr. Olhovsky's behalf may jeopardize the contract between Discovery House and Pretrial and/or Probation. Quite candidly, [a representative of the Pretrial Services Office] has indicated to me that she cannot guarantee that your choice to testify would not jeopardize your contract with either Probation or Pretrial Services.

[Citations to record omitted]. This letter went unanswered....

Prior to sentencing, Pretrial Services prepared a Presentence Report ("PSR"), pursuant to Fed.R.Crim.P. 32(d). That PSR includes the following reference to a letter from Olhovsky discussing his understanding of his own behavior:

> When I was a teenager, I usually spent a lot of time on my computer, and I got a lot of emails from people on line. I got an email from someone that had a picture of a child in a sexual pose. I was in high school and I was around 15 or 16 years old. At first, I did not really think about it, but I just kept receiving more and more pictures. I got interested in the pictures out of curiosity. I wasn't really thinking about how children were being abused. I was very lonely and did not spend a lot of time with friends. At school, I was pretty much an outcast,

with people making fun of me all the time for no reason. I spent all my time at home and on the computer. I just gradually got more and more curious about the pictures. I downloaded some software to make an IRC or "internet relay chat" that let other people upload and download pictures, too.

I wasn't thinking about a child being abused when I was swapping pictures. I guess I wasn't thinking of it as that "real." I felt sort of detached from the whole thing. Since I was arrested, I have made a turn around—I totally "get it" that it was wrong and I am really sorry about what I did. Dr. Silverman has helped me see why it was so wrong and I feel really bad about the little kids in those pictures. I am embarrassed about what I did. Before this whole thing happened, I wasn't very good at putting myself in other people's shoes. But I can understand that what I do effects other people much better now. I am very, very, sorry.

[Citations to record omitted].

Defense counsel also submitted a letter brief in advance of sentencing and attached several supportive letters from family and friends, as well as a copy of Dr. Silverman's letter to Pretrial Services and expert reports from two other mental health professionals. Defense counsel emphasized that psychologists who had seen Olhovsky agreed that he was an "immature, adolescent" at the time of his offenses.[6] The letter brief also emphasized the progress Olhovsky had made since being in treatment: he had a job, was attending classes at community college, and was spending more time socializing with his peers....

While acknowledging that most clinical assessment tools have been designed for actual child molesters rather than passive viewers of pornography, Dr. Witt nevertheless attempted to assess Olhovsky's risk for future sex offenses:

To at least obtain an estimate of his current and recent functioning, I am scoring Mr. Olhovsky on the SONAR, which focuses entirely on this area. On the SONAR, Mr. Olhovsky received a score of −1 point, placing him in this instrument's low risk range (three points or less). On the stable dynamic risk factors, he receives no points. He is in a sexually and emotionally intimate romantic relationship [with an 18-year-old]; he does not associate with negative social influences; he does not presently espouse attitudes that support or condone sex offending; during the past six months, both his general and his sexual self-regulation have been good. On the acute dynamic risk factors, he has one point subtracted for no longer accessing or downloading child pornography on the Internet.

Overall, a score in this instrument's low risk range is found roughly nine times as frequently among nonrecidivists as among recidivists in the standardization sample upon which this instrument was developed.

[Citations to record omitted].

Finally, Dr. Witt opined that (1) Olhovsky's offense was not "a reflection of a broadly antisocial personality and lifestyle"; (2) "the weight of the evidence [shows] that at the present time, [Olhovsky] does not have a pedophilic sexual interest pattern"; and (3) that Olhovsky, "whatever his initial motivations were for viewing such a vast quantity of child pornography (and at the time, those motivations might well have been a sexual interest pattern focused on minors), appears to presently have a sexual interest pattern focused on adults."... Dr. Witt agreed that "social anxiety may have led to Mr. Olhovsky's use of

---

6. In fact, the majority of Olhovsky's offense behavior (downloading and trading pictures) occurred while he was under the age of 18. He was arrested only a few months after his 18th birthday.

child pornography." ... Dr. Witt concluded that "clinically, taking all factors into account, Mr. Olhovsky presents as within the limits of risk appropriate for outpatient management." ...

In response, the government submitted a three-page expert report prepared by John S. O'Brien II, M.D., J.D., in which Dr. O'Brien offered his "opinion regarding Mr. Olhovsky's diagnosis and potential dangerousness as a sex offender in the future." ... Dr. O'Brien reviewed "a printout regarding the items found on Mr. Olhovsky's computer, including his posting in the internet relay chat room pertaining to child pornography; report of psychological evaluation of Nic[ ]olau Olhovsky, completed by Philip H. Witt, PhD on January 19, 2007; and report of forensic evaluation of Nic[ ]olau Olhovsky, completed by Kirk Heilbrun, PhD on January 6, 2006." ... However, it appears that Dr. O'Brien never spoke to Olhovsky's treating psychologist, Dr. Silverman, or reviewed his treatment notes, nor did he ever meet or interview Olhovsky or his mother.

Dr. O'Brien noted his "serious concerns regarding Mr. Olhovsky's prediliction for child pornography and propensity for future involvement in either procuring, distributing, and/or collecting child pornographic materials." ... The report concludes:

> Based upon my review of the records I remain unconvinced that Mr. Olhovsky no longer has a pedophilic sexual excitation pattern, or even a pedophilic sexual excitation preference. It is my opinion that he warrants a more intensive degree of psychosexual disorder evaluation and a longer period of observation as a condition of his sentence in order to more effectively, appropriately, and thoroughly evaluate his potential psychosexual disorder, determine whether his alleged "gradual transition in his sexual excitation pattern" is more than just a fleeting byproduct of the serious circumstances which currently confront him and the extent to which he does, in fact, pose a future risk to the community as a predatory sexual offender.

[Citations to record omitted]....

At the sentencing hearing, the district court heard testimony from both Dr. Heilbrun and Dr. Witt. Dr. Silverman did not appear, nor did he submit any additional materials to the court. The district court calculated Olhovsky's total offense level pursuant to the advisory United States Sentencing Commission Guidelines as 33.[7] That offense level, combined with his lack of any criminal history, resulted in a Guideline range of 135 to 168 months imprisonment. However, Olhovsky was subject to a statutory maximum sentence of 10 years pursuant to 18 U.S.C. § 2252A(a)(5)(B).[8] Accordingly, the Guideline recommendation was 120 months. Nevertheless, the court imposed a sentence of six years imprisonment and offered the following explanation:

> The guidelines [ ] have been issued [ ] for a reason. Sex child pornography has become more and more recognized as a serious threat to society. It's compounded by the anonymity in which individuals can access child pornography on the Internet and feel insulated. Every one of those downloads represents sexual

---

7. We need not discuss the Guideline calculations in detail because Olhovsky does not challenge the offense level or criminal history category as calculated by the district court.

8. 18 U.S.C. § 2252A(a)(5)(B), establishes a maximum sentence of 10 years imprisonment for any person who: "knowingly possesses, or ... accesses with intent to view, any ... computer disk, or any other material that contains an image of child pornography that has been ... transported using any ... facility of interstate or foreign commerce ... any means, including by computer, ..." unless the person has a prior conviction for such conduct, in which case a sentence of imprisonment of "not less than 10 nor more than 20 years" is mandated. 18 U.S.C. § 2252A(b)(2).

abuse. The pictures which were handed up to the Court essentially represent in some manner or other the rape of little children, and every individual who seeks to access this material on the Internet has aided and abetted in that activity....

Every one of these postings [on the Internet] can only be regarded as a request by Mr. Olhovsky for someone to produce material or obtain material for him that met this description.... This is not a victimless crime....

So, I'm presented quite frankly with a situation in which Mr. Olhovsky, as the government has indicated, engaged in just extraordinarily extensive conduct in this area. Is he young? He's young. He's young and as the psychologists have admitted, they don't know what he's going to do. He certainly has indicated pedophile proclivities in the past and they can't tell me whether or not he will be a pedophile in the future.

[A]t a minimum this Court has an obligation to make sure that it imposes a sentence which indeed conforms with the provisions of Section 3553 and that includes the need of the sentence imposed to reflect the seriousness of the offense, to promote the law and to provide just punishment and to afford adequate deterrence to criminal conduct, and the problem is this is an incredibly difficult offense to catch and people have to understand that if you are caught, simply because you think you're doing this in the privacy of your own home and that somehow this is not affecting victims, you're wrong. You are affecting victims. You are hurting little children. [ ]

There is only, as far as I'm concerned, one significant mitigating factor in Mr. Olhovsky's favor, his youth. He might stand some chance but, you know something, he also could turn around and become again a predator — a pedophile monster, and this Court is not prepared to impose any sentence which, one, denigrates the significance of the conduct which Mr. Olhovsky has done, suggest that this does not warrant substantial, indeed, potentially draconian punishment and, three, make sure that if he gets treatment, that it's in an environment where indeed it can be ensured that treatment is under close custody, so [ ] the Court rejects [the defense] arguments for probation. The Court rejects your argument that being treated in a custodial psychiatric facility in the prison system will not help Mr. Olhovsky.

As far as the Court is concerned, it is the best hope that this society has for Mr. Olhovsky given how it *appears that prior efforts have largely failed*. I understand [the defense is] presenting arguments that the past few years have been successful in some manner or other but, quite frankly, the Court is unpersuaded that that is an overwhelming predictor of success; that at a minimum, both incarceration and custodial treatment are required.

[Citations to record omitted] (emphasis added).

It is not at all clear what (if any) basis the court had for making the italicized statement. We have discussed the only evidence of treatment that appears on this record, and nothing suggests that "prior efforts have largely failed." In fact, the entire record is to the contrary. The only mental health professionals who actually interviewed, tested or treated Olhovsky concluded that he was quite responsive to treatment. Indeed, not even the government's expert concludes that Olhovsky's treatment has "failed." Rather, Dr. O'Brien concluded that additional observation and therapy was required to determine if Olhovsky's positive response to treatment "is more than just a fleeting byproduct of the serious circumstances which currently confront him and the extent to which he does, in fact, pose a future risk to the community as a predatory sexual offender." ... We are similarly troubled by the court's perplexing characterization of defense counsel as arguing that "the past few years have been successful in some manner or other...." That characterization of the evidence before the court is both inaccurate and unfair. It suggests vagaries and generalites (i.e. "successful in some manner or other"), and ignores the very specific evidence of Olhovsky's positive response to treatment. That response includes: his newfound ability to have an age-appropriate intimate relationship, his employment history and college attendance and the growth in social interaction it both reflects and requires, and his expressions of remorse and the concomitant realization of the harmful nature of his conduct. Although the latter could certainly be feigned in hopes of a more lenient sentence, no one who examined Olhovsky (including the government's own expert) suggested that his positive progress while in treatment, the specific steps he has taken were anything other than an honest reflection of who he was becoming or his introspection and remorse.[9]

At the conclusion of the hearing, the district court sentenced Olhovsky to six years incarceration followed by three years of supervised release, with various special conditions. This appeal followed.... [10] ... We review the sentence that was imposed to determine if it was reasonable. *See Cooper*, 437 F.3d at 329–30. In doing so, we are guided by the requirement that sentencing courts give "meaningful consideration" to all of the sentencing factors in 18 U.S.C. § 3553(a). *Id.* at 329. Moreover, "the record must show a true, considered exercise of discretion on the part of a district court, including a recognition of, and response to, the parties' non-frivolous arguments." *United States v. Jackson*, 467 F.3d 834, 841 (3d Cir.2006).

District courts must engage in the following three step process when determining an appropriate sentence:

(1) Courts must continue to calculate a defendant's Guidelines sentence precisely as they would have before *Booker*.[15]

(2) In doing so, they must formally rule on the motions of both parties and state on the record whether they are granting a departure....

(3) Finally, they are to exercise their discretion by considering the relevant § 3553(a)[16] factors in setting the sentence they impose regardless whether it varies from the sentence calculated under the Guidelines.

---

9. As noted, Dr. Silverman described him as a developmental "fourteen or fifteen year old who is stumbling toward adulthood"; but nothing suggests he has done anything but respond positively to treatment.

10. The district court had subject matter jurisdiction pursuant to 18 U.S.C. § 3231. We have jurisdiction under 28 U.S.C. § 1291 and 18 U.S.C. § 3742(a).

15. *United States v. Booker*, 543 U.S. 220, 125 S.Ct. 738, 160 L.Ed.2d 621 (2005)[.]

16. The factors set forth in 18 U.S.C. § 3553(a) are:

(1) the nature and circumstances of the offense and the history and characteristics of the defendant;

(2) the need for the sentence imposed — (A) to reflect the seriousness of the offense, to promote respect for the law, and to provide just punishment for the offense; (B) to afford adequate deterrence to criminal conduct; (C) to protect the public from further crimes of the defendant; and (D) to provide the defendant with needed educational or vocational training, medical care, or other correctional treatment in the most effective manner;

(3) the kinds of sentences available;

(4) the kinds of sentence and the sentencing range established for — (A) the applicable category of offense committed by the applicable category of defendant as set forth in the guidelines ... ;

(5) any pertinent policy statement ... issued by the Sentencing Commission ... [that] is in effect on the date the defendant is sentenced.

(6) the need to avoid unwarranted sentence disparities among defendants with similar records

United States v. Gunter, 462 F.3d 237, 247 (3d Cir.2006) (citations omitted). Olhovsky claims that the district court erred at the third step of this process by failing adequately to consider all of the § 3553(a) factors and instead unduly emphasized the need to punish, deter and protect society.... We have explained that sentencing courts must give "meaningful consideration" to *all* of the statutory factors in 18 U.S.C. § 3553(a). *Cooper*, 437 F.3d at 329. It is not enough for a sentencing court to "recit[e] the § 3553(a) factors, say[ ] that counsel's arguments have been considered, and then declar[e] a sentence." *Jackson*, 467 F.3d at 842. Such a "rote statement" will "not suffice if at sentencing either the defendant or the prosecution properly raises 'a ground of recognized legal merit (provided it has a factual basis)' and the court fails to address it." *Cooper*, 437 F.3d at 329 (citation omitted).

Here, it is not at all apparent that the court actually considered the lengthy, very specific and highly positive reports of any of the three defense experts. Rather, the court focused on incapacitation, deterrence and punishment to the exclusion of other sentencing factors. The court's suggestion that Olhovsky "could turn around and become again a predator — a pedophile monster," and its statement that a sentence must not "denigrate, the significance of the conduct ... [or suggest that Olhovsky] does not warrant substantial, indeed, potentially draconian punishment ..." can not be interpreted in any other way.

While sentencing courts need not discuss each of the § 3553(a) factors "if the record makes clear the court took the factors into account in sentencing," *Cooper*, 437 F.3d at 329, where, as here, the record strongly suggests that some of the statutorily prescribed sentencing factors were ignored, we can not conclude that the resulting sentence was reasonable. Section 3553(a) clearly states that a court must impose a sentence that is "sufficient *but not greater than necessary*, to comply with the purposes of [sentencing]" (emphasis added). This requirement is often referred to as "the parsimony provision," and the Supreme Court has referred to it as the "overarching instruction" of 18 U.S.C. § 3553(a). *See Kimbrough v. United States*, 552 U.S. 85, 128 S.Ct. 558, 563, 169 L.Ed.2d 481 (2007). It has particular relevance to our inquiry here.

The court imposed a custodial sentence that was less than suggested by the Guidelines but still sufficiently lengthy to satisfy the court's conclusion that a "substantial, indeed, potentially draconian" punishment was required. The result is a sentence that appears inconsistent with all of the psychological testimony with the *possible* exception of the expert who testified for the government, Dr. O'Brien. However, Dr. O'Brien's testimony does not negate our conclusion that the district court failed to adequately consider a less retributive or incapacitative sentence for several reasons.

As noted above, Dr. O'Brien's letter expressed his opinion that more evaluation and observation was required in order to determine whether Olhovsky's behavior "is more than just a fleeting byproduct of the serious circumstances and the extent to which he does, in fact, pose a future risk to the community as a predatory sexual offender." Thus, not even Dr. O'Brien's letter supports a conclusion that a "pedophile monster" lurks inside of Olhovsky. However, even if we assume that the concerns expressed in Dr. O'Brien's letter support a sentence of six years imprisonment, we could still not conclude that the court gave adequate consideration to all of the sentencing factors.

As we explained above, Dr. O'Brien's three-page report was based primarily on the nature of the images on computer rather than any interaction with Olhovsky. O'Brien did not interview Olhovsky or speak to his mother. He did not even bother to speak to

---

who have been found guilty of similar conduct; and
    (7) the need to provide restitution to any victims of the offense.

the behavioral therapist who had been treating Olhovsky for nearly two years or review that therapist's treatment notes. On the other hand, Dr. Heilbrun and Dr. Witt interviewed Olhovsky as well as his mother before authoring their reports, and Dr. Witt administered psychological tests specifically designed to assess recidivism risks.... Moreover, even if the court could somehow conclude that Dr. O'Brien's cautions outweighed the more therapeutically focused recommendations of Drs. Silverman, Heilbrun and Witt, the court never explained why it rejected Dr. Silverman's assessment of the likelihood of recidivism.[17] In fact, as noted earlier, in the face of very specific positive reports of Olhovsky's response to therapy, the court stated that Olhovsky had not been responsive to therapy. The only thing on this record that even tangentially supports that statement is Dr. O'Brien's report. We have already explained why that is simply not adequate to ignore the demand of parsimony that is the "overarching instruction" of the congressionally mandated sentencing factors. However, there is even more reason to doubt the reasonableness of sentencing Olhovsky to six years in prison.

In the area of disabilities law, we recognize "[t]he treating physician doctrine — a doctrine long accepted by this court." *Mason v. Shalala*, 994 F.2d 1058, 1067 (3d Cir.1993). Pursuant to that doctrine, "a court considering a claim for disability benefits must give greater weight to the findings of a treating physician than to the findings of a physician who has examined the claimant only once or not at all." *Id.; see also Morales v. Apfel*, 225 F.3d 310, 317 (3d Cir.2000) ("Where ... the opinion of a treating physician conflicts with that of a non-treating, non-examining physician, the ALJ may choose whom to credit but cannot reject evidence for no reason or for the wrong reason.") (citation omitted). No less consideration should govern when one's liberty is at stake than when disability benefits hang in the balance.

We have similar concerns over the court's approach to 18 U.S.C. §3553(a)(2)(D). That provision requires that the court consider the need for any sentence to "provide the defendant with needed educational or vocational training, medical care, or other correctional treatment in the most effective manner." Although the district court did mention the obvious need for continued treatment, the court noted only that "if he gets treatment" it should be "in an environment where ... it can be ensured that [ ] treatment is under close custody." There is no indication that the district court considered Dr. Silverman's opinion that "[i]f incarcerated ... he will just regress terribly." Yet, Dr. Silverman's fears about the effect of a lengthy term of imprisonment were sufficient to motivate him to write a letter to the sentencing court; something he had never done before. The court certainly did not have to accept Dr. Silverman's concerns and refrain from incarcerating Olhovsky, but the record must reflect the reason for believing that treatment in prison would "provide ... correctional treatment in the most effective manner" despite Dr. Silverman's opinion to the contrary.... Moreover, it is exceedingly difficult to review this sentencing transcript without becoming convinced that the district court was so appalled by the offense that it lost sight of the offender. The fact that the record does not reflect the required consideration of "the history and characteristics of the defendant," 18 U.S.C. §3553(a)(1), is particularly troubling given the professional opinions of the psychologists who treated or interviewed him. Our concern that the court lost sight of the offender is only slightly mitigated by the below Guideline sentence that the court imposed.

---

17. Dr. Silverman's letter stated that "recidivism rates are notably lower in adolescents" and that "[s]ituational and opportunity factors" play a larger role in adolescent offenses as opposed to "fixed internal cognitive factors" that motivate adult offenders. The applicability of these generalized observations to Olhovsky is supported by the results of testing administered by Dr. Witt, which placed Olhovsky in the "low risk" category for repeat offenses.

We do not suggest that the court acted unreasonably merely because it rejected defense counsel's request for probation or that the court's concern about this category of offense is misplaced. Offenses involving the sexual exploitation of children foster a market that destroys lives. Therefore, the court was correct in refusing to view Olhovsky's "passive" behavior as a victimless crime. Nevertheless, 18 U.S.C. § 3553(a) applies to all offenders, and Congress requires that courts sentence the *individual offender*. Although the offender's conduct is part of the sentencing equation, it is not the totality of it, and this record does not establish the reasonableness of focusing on the offense at the expense of the individual offender.

As we mentioned earlier, this sentence was below the advisory Guideline range and that range had been lowered to comply with the statutory maximum sentence. However, that does not obviate the necessity of our inquiry into the reasonableness of this sentence. "Regardless of whether the sentence imposed is inside or outside the Guidelines range, [we] must review the sentence under an abuse-of-discretion standard. [We] must first ensure that the district court committed no significant procedural error, such as ... failing to consider [each of] the § 3553(a) factors ..." *Gall v. United States*, 552 U.S. 38, 128 S.Ct. 586, 597, 169 L.Ed.2d 445 (2007). For reasons we have already explained, we conclude that the district court did commit a procedural error in imposing this sentence. However, we also conclude that, notwithstanding the Guideline range, the sentence was not substantively reasonable.[18] ... We are, of course, acutely aware of the limitations placed on an appellate court reviewing the district court's sentence. The issue is not whether we would have imposed the same sentence, or even a similar sentence. Rather, the issue is whether the sentence is reasonable in light of this record and the sentencing factors. The suggested Guideline range does not define the parameters of that inquiry. *See Cooper*, 437 F.3d at 332.

Here, the district court imposed a substantial prison term while explaining that it could not predict the future (*i.e.* Olhovsky's likelihood of recidivism) with any certainty and that prior treatment efforts had failed. We have already explained how the latter statement is simply incorrect. The former explanation is of little assistance because no court can ever be absolutely certain that a defendant will not reoffend. Moreover, that rationale would justify an incapacitative sentence for any defendant regardless of criminal history or the success of any therapy because the possibility of recidivism can never be reduced to zero.[19] ... Moreover, these expressions by the sentencing court reinforce our concern that the court was so offended by the nature of Olhovsky's conduct that it sentenced the offense at the expense of determining an appropriate sentence for the offender:

> It has been uniform and constant in the federal judicial tradition for the sentencing judge to consider every convicted person as an individual and every case as a unique study in the human failings that sometimes mitigate, sometimes magnify, the crime and the punishment to ensue.

Gall, 128 S.Ct. at 597. Our concern is reinforced by the court's omission of any consideration for Olhovsky's subnormal social development. Drs. Silverman, Witt and Heilbrun all referred to Olhovsky's developmental problems. Indeed, Dr. Silverman stressed that Olhovsky had been quite slow to mature and that he was therefore immature even given his chronological age. Yet, it does not appear that the court considered that

---

18. *See Gall v. United States*, 552 U.S. 38, 128 S.Ct. 586, 597, 169 L.Ed.2d 445 (2007) (appellate review for procedural error such as "failing to consider the 3553(a) factors" should precede review for substantive reasonableness).

19. Regrettably, the probability of anyone committing a crime can never be reduced to zero.

testimony in sentencing Olhovsky to six years in prison, nor did the court explain why it was rejecting concerns about the impact of a lengthy prison sentence on Olhovsky's chances for continuing healthy social adjustment. In *Gall*, the Court noted the significance of considering immaturity at sentencing. 128 S.Ct. at 601. The Court specifically mentioned that the district court there had stressed Gall's relative immaturity at the time of the offense and had referenced the Court's opinion in *Roper v. Simmons*, 543 U.S. 551, 569, 125 S.Ct. 1183, 161 L.Ed.2d 1 (2005). In *Roper*, the Court had quoted a study that concluded "lack of maturity and an underdeveloped sense of responsibility are qualities that often result in impetuous and ill-considered actions." *Id.* (internal quotation marks omitted). *Gall* quoted the reasoning of the district court that:

> Immaturity at the time of the offense conduct is not an inconsequential consideration ... [T]he recent [National Institute of Health] report confirms that there is no bold line demarcating at what age a person reaches full maturity. While age does not excuse behavior, a sentencing court should account for age when inquiring into the conduct of a defendant.

Id. Given Dr. Silverman's letter and concerns that Olhovsky's lack of emotional maturity directly contributed to this offense, the sentencing court should have either explained the extent to which, if any, Olhovsky's immaturity factored into its sentence of six years imprisonment, or explained why it was irrelevant. While the district court did mention Olhovsky's "youth" as a mitigating factor, it is clear that was a reference to Olhovsky's chronological age. Olhovsky was 18 when he was arrested and 20 when sentenced. As noted earlier, Dr. Silverman viewed Olhovsky as a 14 or 15 year old juvenile.

We realize that it could be argued that the court did consider Olhovsky's immaturity and relied in part on that to impose a sentence that was substantially below the Guideline range. However, nothing on this record supports that claim, and any such argument fails to explain why the sentencing court did not address the therapist's concern about the effect of a long prison term on Olhovsky, or his developmental immaturity. Nor is our concern for the substantive reasonableness of the sentence mitigated by the argument that serious crimes like this must necessarily be punished with substantial prison terms in order to preserve respect for the law. In affirming the sentence that the government appealed in *Gall*, the Supreme Court noted that the district court had there observed that "a sentence of imprisonment may work to promote not respect, but derision, of the law if the law is viewed as merely a means to dispense harsh punishment without taking into account the real conduct and circumstances involved in sentencing." 128 S.Ct. at 599.... That statement has particular significance here. As noted above, the district court did not offer any explanation for accepting the government's three-page expert report and ignoring the substantial evidence derived from the contrary expert opinions of the psychologists who actually interviewed Olhovsky and his mother, or the opinion of his treating psychologist. Instead, the sentencing judge spoke extensively about the insidious nature of child pornography, the difficulty of catching offenders, and the need for "substantial, indeed, potentially draconian punishment." ...

The hideous nature of an offender's conduct must not drive us to forget that it is not *severe* punishment that promotes respect for the law, it is *appropriate* punishment. Although there are clearly times when anything less than severe punishment undermines respect for the law, it is just as certain that unduly severe punishment can negatively affect the public's attitude toward the law and toward the criminal justice system. It is no doubt partly for that reason that jurists have referred to the responsibility of sentencing as "daunting." *See United States v. Grober*, 595 F.Supp.2d 382, 383 (D.N.J.2008) (quoting then Chief Judge Becker in *United States v. Faulks*, 201 F.3d 208, 209 (3d Cir.2000)). The power and responsibility of a sentencing court is indeed, nothing short of "daunting." It requires a careful balancing of societal and individual needs, and an ability to determine a sentence based on dispassionate analysis of those often competing concerns.

It has often been stated that possession and distribution of child pornography are very serious crimes that have a terrible impact on real victims. *See United States v. Goff*, 501 F.3d 250, 258 n. 13 & 259 (3d Cir.2007) (noting "evidence of Congress's intent that offenses involving child pornography be treated severely" as well as the impact on children who are "exploited, molested and raped" to support the demand of the industry). No one could sincerely disagree with that statement, and the seriousness of the crimes is reflected in the penalties that Congress has prescribed as well as in the Guidelines that have been promulgated by the Sentencing Commission. However, revulsion over these crimes can not blind us as jurists to the individual circumstances of the offenders who commit them. *Id.* at 260 ("Child pornography is so odious, so obviously at odds with common decency, that there is a real risk that offenders will be subjected to indiscriminate punishment based solely on the repugnance of the crime and in disregard of other Congressionally mandated sentencing considerations.") ... As we have emphasized, the "overarching principle" of parsimony that Congress included in § 3553 directs the courts to impose a sentence "sufficient, but not greater than necessary, to comply with the purposes set forth in [this section]." 18 U.S.C. § 3553(a).

A district court has a duty to evaluate the quality of mitigating evidence presented to it. Yet, here, the district court concluded that "draconian" punishment was warranted with only minimal consideration of substantial evidence to the contrary. The Supreme Court has recently stated:

> The appropriateness of brevity or length, conciseness or detail, when to write, what to say, depends upon circumstances.... In the [sentencing] context, a statement of reasons is important. The sentencing judge should set forth enough to satisfy the appellate court that he has considered the parties' arguments and has a reasoned basis for exercising his own legal decisionmaking authority.... Where the defendant or prosecutor presents nonfrivolous reasons for imposing a different sentence, however, the judge will normally go further and explain why he has rejected those arguments.

Rita v. United States, 551 U.S. 338, 127 S.Ct. 2456, 2468, 168 L.Ed.2d 203 (2007). There was clearly nothing frivolous about defense counsel's argument that Olhovsky was not a typical offender nor counsel's suggestion that his crime did not fall within the minerun of cases the Guidelines are intended to address. The court responded by stating: "[t]he guidelines [ ] have been issued [ ] for a reason ...", and that strongly suggests that the court did not give adequate consideration to the extent to which Olhovsky fit within the "heartland" of offenders.[20]

As we have explained, that is but one example of the procedural errors committed by the district court. In *United States v. Levinson*, 543 F.3d 190, 195 (3d Cir.2008), we explained that "procedural problems may lead to substantive problems, so there are times when a discussion of procedural error will necessarily raise questions about the substantive reasonableness of a sentence." This is clearly such a case. Given the factual and procedural

---

20. *Cf. United States v. Iannone*, 184 F.3d 214, 226 (3d Cir.1999) (explaining that the Guidelines are designed for the "heartland" of cases and that "[i]n the unusual case ... the court may consider a departure from the Guidelines sentence").

error here, it was substantively unreasonable to sentence Olhovsky to six years imprisonment. On remand, the district court will impose a reasonable sentence based upon all of the § 3553(a) factors, including the "overarching" principle of parsimony....

[B]ecause the court's failure to consider Olhovsky's individual circumstances pursuant to 18 U.S.C. § 3553(a) resulted in an unreasonable sentence, we will vacate the sentence and remand for further proceedings consistent with this opinion.

United States v. Kemmish

Ninth Circuit, 1990
120 F.3d 937

LEAVY, Senior Circuit Judge: ...

On June 29, 1994, U.S. Customs agents arrested James Leroy Kemmish at the San Diego International Airport after he attempted to smuggle into the United States child pornography videotapes and more than $16,000 in unreported American currency. An examination of Kemmish's luggage revealed mailing lists, advertisements, and notices for Overseas Male ("OSM"), a Mexico City-based producer of child pornography. Armed with a search warrant, law enforcement officers went to Kemmish's residence the following day. There they found sophisticated video reproduction equipment and several hundred blank videotapes; 204 master videotapes and 332 non-master videotapes, all depicting child pornography; photograph albums and slides containing child pornography; large quantities of OSM advertisements; and mailing supplies.

On November 2, 1995, a federal grand jury handed down a six-count second superseding indictment, charging Kemmish with failing to report transportation of currency in violation of 31 U.S.C. §§ 5316, 5322(a) and 5324(b)(1) (Count I); making a false statement in violation of 18 U.S.C. § 1001 (Count II); advertising to distribute child pornography in violation of 18 U.S.C. §§ 2251(c)(1)(A) and 2251(c)(2)(A) (Count III); transporting child pornography in violation of 18 U.S.C. § 2252(a)(1) (Count IV); reproducing child pornography for distribution in violation of 18 U.S.C. § 2252(a)(2) (Count V); and possessing with the intent to sell child pornography in violation of 18 U.S.C. § 2252(a)(3)(B) (Count VI).

Following the district court's rulings on various preliminary matters, including Kemmish's motions to dismiss the indictment and suppress the evidence, Kemmish pleaded guilty to all six counts of the indictment and consented to forfeiture of his goods pursuant to the terms of a written plea agreement. Although the probation office recommended, and the government acquiesced in, a mid-range sentence of 295 months' imprisonment, the district court departed downward and imposed a sentence of only 63 months. The government has timely appealed from the sentence, and Kemmish has timely cross-appealed from the denial of his motion to suppress....

The government ... argues that the district court erred by failing to enhance Kemmish's sentence because his conduct as a major distributor of child pornography amounted to a pattern of sexual exploitation of minors. Although the question is one of first impression in this Circuit, we conclude that Kemmish's extensive activities as a trafficker in child pornography do not constitute a pattern of sexual exploitation of minors within the meaning of the relevant law.

Section 2251 of Title 18 generally governs the offense of sexual exploitation of minors.[2] The relevant subsection of that statute reads as follows:

(c)(1) Any person who ... knowingly makes, prints, or publishes, or causes to be made, printed, or published, any notice or advertisement seeking or offering—

(A) to ... distribute, or reproduce, any visual depiction ... involv[ing] the use of a minor engaging in sexually explicit conduct and such visual depiction is of such conduct[,] ...

shall be punished as provided under subsection (d).

18 U.S.C. § 2251(c)(1)(A) (in relevant part).

The Guidelines provide that, "If the defendant engaged in a pattern of activity involving the sexual abuse or exploitation of a minor, increase [his base offense] by 5 levels." U.S.S.G. § 2G2.2(b)(4). "'Pattern of activity involving the sexual abuse or exploitation of a minor,' for the purposes of subsection (b)(4), means any combination of two or more separate instances of the sexual abuse or the sexual exploitation of a minor, whether involving the same or different victims." U.S.S.G. § 2G2.2, comment. (n.4).... The few reported decisions involving 18 U.S.C. § 2251(c) and U.S.S.G. § 2G2.2(b)(4) have unanimously interpreted the latter as being inapplicable to traffickers in child pornography who are not directly involved in the actual sexual abuse or exploitation of minors. *See, e.g., United States v. Ketcham*, 80 F.3d 789, 794 (3d Cir.1996); *United States v. Barton*, 76 F.3d 499, 503 (2d Cir.1996); *United States v. Chapman*, 60 F.3d 894, 898 (1st Cir.1995). *Cf. United States v. Surratt*, 87 F.3d 814, 819–20 (6th Cir.1996). As the Third Circuit recently noted,

The terms "sexual abuse" and "exploitation" as those terms are used in U.S.S.G. § 2G2.2(b)(4) are terms of art. "Sexual abuse" refers to the conduct covered by U.S.S.G. §§ 2A3.1, 2A3.2, 2A3.3, and 2A3.4. "Sexual exploitation of a minor" refers to conduct covered by U.S.S.G. § 2G2.1.

Sections 2A3.1, 2A3.2, 2A3.3, and 2A3.4 of the Guidelines set out the offense levels for the various forms of "sexual abuse" proscribed in §§ 2241 ("Aggravated sexual abuse"), 2242 ("Sexual abuse"), 2243 ("Sexual abuse of a minor or ward"), and 2244 ("Abusive sexual contact") of Title 18 of the United States Code. These offenses make it criminal for anyone to engage in sexual activity with another under stipulated circumstances or to cause or permit another to engage in sexual activity under stipulated circumstances.

Section 2G2.1 of the Guidelines sets out the offense level for the various forms of "Sexually Exploiting a Minor" proscribed in subsections 2251(a) (employing, inducing, coercing or transporting, etc., a minor "with the intent that such minor engage in any sexually explicit conduct for the purpose of producing any visual depiction of such conduct"), § 2251(b) (as a parent, guardian or person having custody of a minor, permitting the minor to engage in sexually explicit conduct

---

2. Section 2251 is divided into four subsections, (a) through (d). Subsection (a) applies to "[a]ny person" who arranges for a minor to engage in "sexually explicit conduct for the purpose of producing any visual depiction of such conduct," provided the person knows or reasonably should know that the visual depiction has been or will be transported in interstate commerce or through the mails. 18 U.S.C. § 2251(a). Subsection (b) applies to parents, legal guardians, or others "having custody or control of a minor who knowingly permit[ ]" such conduct involving the minor while the latter is under their care or control. 18 U.S.C. § 2251(b). Subsection (c), discussed above, involves those who traffic in child pornography. Subsection (d) sets forth the range of punishments for violations of section 2251(a)–(c).

for the purpose of producing a visual depiction), and §2251(c)(1)(B) (seeking or offering by advertisement participation in any act of sexually explicit conduct with a minor for the purpose of producing a visual depiction) of Title 18 of the United States Code. These offenses make it criminal to engage in stipulated activities in connection with the *production* of materials containing visual depictions of sexually explicit conduct involving a minor....

None of these Guidelines refer to the possession, transportation, trafficking, receipt, reproduction, or distribution of child pornography as "sexual abuse" or "exploitation of a minor." ... Thus, a defendant who possesses, transports, reproduces, or distributes child pornography does not sexually exploit a minor even though the materials possessed, transported, reproduced, or distributed "involve" such sexual exploitation by the producer.

United States v. Ketcham, 80 F.3d at 794 (emphasis in original).

On November 1, 1996, the Sentencing Commission adopted the above reasoning by amending Application Note 1 to U.S.S.G. §2G2.2(b)(4). That Note now reads, in relevant part, "'Sexual abuse or exploitation' does not include trafficking in material relating to the sexual abuse or exploitation of a minor." *See* U.S.S.G. §2G2.2(b)(4), comment. n. 1 (Nov.1996) (Appendix C, amendment 537).... In the absence of any showing of a more direct involvement on Kemmish's part in the sexual abuse or exploitation of minors, we conclude that the 5-level sentence enhancement provided by U.S.S.G. §2G2.2(b)(4) does not apply to Kemmish's trafficking in child pornography.... The district court's denial of Kemmish's motion to suppress is AFFIRMED. The sentence imposed is VACATED and the case REMANDED for resentencing.

FERGUSON, Circuit Judge, concurring in part and dissenting in part:

I concur in the majority opinion except with regard to ... "Pattern of Sexual Exploitation." I disagree with the majority's analysis of that issue because as the sole U.S. distributor of OSM's pornography and a businessman in close contact with the pornography producer, Kemmish's role was crucial to the ongoing success and viability of the business. As such, he was certainly "engaged in a pattern of activity involving the sexual abuse or exploitation of" minors, and therefore deserved the five-level enhancement under U.S.S.G. §2G2.2(b)(4). The facts of this case are far more egregious than the typical child pornography trafficking or distribution case and therefore the district court should have considered departing from the usual conception of "distributor" in analyzing the applicability of the guideline. *See* 1995 U.S.S.G. ch. 1 pt. A intro. comment. 4(b)....

The majority correctly points out that the Sentencing Commission Commentary supports the conclusion that the §2G2.2(b)(4) five-level enhancement should not be applied to traffickers and distributors who were not physically involved in the production of child pornography. U.S.S.G. §2G2.2(b)(4), comment. n. 1 (Nov.1996) (Appendix C, amendment 537). However, the Sentencing Commission Guidelines' note did not contemplate the situation, such as this one, where a trafficker or distributor is necessary and central to the viability of a child pornography business and therefore the creation of pornography involving the physical abuse and exploitation of children. Because Kemmish was clearly "engaged in a pattern of activity involving the sexual abuse or exploitation of a minor," he should have been given the increase under §2G2.2(b)(4)....

The Commission adopted this departure policy because it recognized the difficulty in prescribing "a single set of sentencing guidelines to encompass the vast range of human conduct potentially relevant to a sentencing decision." *Id.* The differences between a trafficker of child pornography who sends several photographs to a fellow pedophile and the sole distributor of a child pornography video line whose video tapes and equipment have reproductive capabilities with a retail value of over two million dollars are just the sort of differences contemplated by the Commission's departure policy. Although this case does not involve departure from a guideline, but rather interpretation of a guideline, the principles underlying the Commission's departure policy also apply here. These principles support interpreting the guideline as allowing for a five-level enhancement in atypical cases where an individual distributor is necessary to a business which engages in the sexual abuse and exploitation of hundreds of children.[1] In essence, Kemmish was *not* a mere distributor. Rather, his involvement was extensive enough — he did everything but photograph the children — that he is better characterized as a producer of child pornography. Therefore, the commentary accompanying § 2G2.2 should not prevent the district court from imposing the five-level enhancement for Kemmish's pattern of activity involving the sexual abuse and exploitation of the child victims of OSM's pornography business. I would remand the case for resentencing to allow the district court to apply a five-level enhancement under § 2G2.2(b)(4).

4. Enhancements

United States v. Garcia

Tenth Circuit, 2005
411 F.3d 1173

McCONNELL, Circuit Judge.

Martin Garcia pleaded guilty to charges of interstate transportation of child pornography, in violation of 18 U.S.C. §§ 2252A(a)(1) and (b)(1). Pursuant to the then-mandatory Federal Sentencing Guidelines, the district court applied the cross-reference found at U.S.S.G. § 2G2.2(c)(1) and, after applying two sentence enhancements and one sentence reduction, determined that Mr. Garcia's final base offense level was 30. The district court sentenced Mr. Garcia to 97 months' imprisonment, the low end of the applicable range. Mr. Garcia raises three arguments on appeal: (1) the district court erred in applying the cross-reference; (2) the district court erred in refusing to grant a downward departure in sentencing for government misconduct; and (3) his sentence is unconstitutional in light of *United States v. Booker*, 543 U.S. 220, 125 S.Ct. 738, 160 L.Ed.2d 621 (2005)....

On July 17, 2003, Special Agent Robert Leazenby of the Wyoming Division of Criminal Investigation ("DCI") entered an internet chat room entitled "PRETEEN POSTINGS & TRADING." Agent Leazenby engaged in internet chat via Yahoo Instant Messenger, using the undercover identity of "ibalissasmom." Mr. Garcia, located in Texas, sent an instant message to "ibalissasmom," initiating a private conversation. Agent Leazenby portrayed "ibalissasmom" as a 35 year-old mother with two daughters. When Mr. Garcia learned that the daughters' ages were 7 and 12, he replied "mmmmmmmmmm perfect ages." ... [citations to record omitted]. During the course of the conversation, Mr. Garcia expressed interest in becoming sexually active with minor girls, and stated a particular preference for girls ages 11–15. Mr. Garcia also stated that he wished he "could meet someone who was willing to share." ... From the context of their conversation, it is evident that Mr. Garcia meant that he was seeking to sexually abuse minor children with the consent of the parent.

---

1. We review this decision by the district court *de novo*, rather than for an abuse of discretion, because the district court decided that the guideline did not include distribution as exploitation as a matter of law. *See U.S. v. Robinson*, 94 F.3d 1325, 1327 (9th Cir.1996) (we review interpretation of the Sentencing Guidelines *de novo*).

The next day, Mr. Garcia again initiated an internet chat with "ibalissasmom." Mr. Garcia asked "ibalissasmom" to send him pictures of herself and her girls. When asked what kind of pictures he wanted, Mr. Garcia replied "nasty would be great but id settle for sexy or whatever you want to send." … "Ibalissasmom" claimed not to have digital pictures that could be sent via the internet. "Ibalissasmom" also stated that she did not "have the nasty ones, [but] would need to photo them." … Mr. Garcia then made the following offer: "ill send u [polaroid film] if u will take some nasty [pictures] for me." … Mr. Garcia then described explicit sexual acts that he wanted the mother and both daughters to perform for the camera. Agent Leazenby gave Mr. Garcia the address of a post office box in Cheyenne, Wyoming, to which he should send the film. Unbeknownst to Mr. Garcia, the post office box belonged to DCI. Mr. Garcia sent Polaroid film that day and it arrived in the DCI post office box on July 23, 2003.

On July 25, 2003, "ibalissasmom" sent an e-mail to Mr. Garcia asking him again to describe what he wanted in the pictures. Mr. Garcia replied via e-mail and suggested specific sexual acts involving the mother and both daughters. On August 3, 2003, Agent Leazenby initiated an internet chat with Mr. Garcia for purposes of obtaining a photograph of him in order to confirm his identity before arresting him. Agent Leazenby, still undercover, asked "do you have a pic for me?" … Mr. Garcia said, "sure what u wanna see?" … Agent Leazenby replied, "I meant of you, but what do you suggest?" … Mr. Garcia then suggested that he send photos depicting minors engaged in sexual conduct with adults, and he sent two photos…. One of the pictures depicted an adult male ejaculating on the face of an adolescent female. With respect to this picture, Mr. Garcia said, "heres one that I imagine is me with ur oldest." …

Based on the foregoing, Mr. Garcia was charged with interstate distribution of child pornography in violation of 18 U.S.C. §§ 2252A(a)(1) and (b)(1). Mr. Garcia pleaded guilty and in the plea agreement acknowledged that he had been advised of U.S.S.G. § 1B1.3 regarding the use of relevant conduct in establishing his sentence. For the crime to which Mr. Garcia pleaded guilty, the base offense level for purposes of sentencing is normally 17, as provided in U.S.S.G. § 2G2.2 (2003). However, the district court determined that the cross-reference at § 2G2.2(c)(1) should apply. This cross-reference states that "[i]f the offense involved causing, transporting, permitting, or offering or seeking by notice or advertisement, a minor to engage in sexually explicit conduct for the purpose of producing a visual depiction of such conduct, apply § 2G2.1." U.S.S.G. 2G2.2(c)(1).

Applying this cross-reference, Mr. Garcia's original base offense level was 27. The district court then applied a four-level enhancement pursuant to § 2G2.1(b)(1) because the offense involved a victim who had not attained the age of twelve, a two-level enhancement pursuant to § 2G2.1(b)(3) because the crime involved the use of a computer, and a three-level reduction pursuant to § 3E1.1(a) and (b) for acceptance of responsibility. Mr. Garcia's final base offense level was therefore 30 and, coupled with a Criminal History Category "I", his sentencing range was 97–121 months. The district court sentenced him to 97 months….

Mr. Garcia argues that the district court erred when it applied the cross-reference. "[T]his Court continues to have the same jurisdiction to review Guidelines sentences as it had before the Supreme Court's decision in *Booker*." *United States v. Sierra-Castillo*, 405 F.3d 932, 936 n. 2 (10th Cir.2005). In considering the application of the sentencing guidelines, we review the district court's factual findings for clear error, and its legal determinations de novo. *United States v. Dillon*, 351 F.3d 1315, 1318 (10th Cir.2003). We will "give due deference to the district court's application of the guidelines to the facts." *United States v. Norris*, 319 F.3d 1278, 1284 (10th Cir.2003)….

Mr. Garcia first argues that the offense with which he was charged did not "involve" the behavior listed in the cross-reference. According to Mr. Garcia, his decision to send two pornographic images of children to "ibalissasmom" on August 3rd was in no way related or relevant to his quest to obtain pornographic pictures of the two minor daughters of "ibalissasmom." ... The term "offense," as used in the cross-reference, includes both charged and uncharged relevant conduct. *United States v. Tagore*, 158 F.3d 1124, 1128 (10th Cir.1998); *United States v. Miller*, 166 F.3d 1153, 1155 (11th Cir.1999); U.S.S.G. § 1B1.1 n. 1(H). Relevant uncharged conduct must be proven by a preponderance of the evidence. *United States v. Magallanez*, 408 F.3d 672, 684 (10th Cir.2005). This court has broadly construed the meaning of relevant conduct. *United States v. Asch*, 207 F.3d 1238, 1243 (10th Cir.2000). Relevant conduct consists of "all acts or omissions ... that were part of the same course of conduct or common scheme or plan as the offense of conviction." U.S.S.G. § 1B1.3(a)(2). The commentary to § 1B1.3 explains what constitutes a "common scheme" or "the same course of conduct":

> *Common scheme or plan.* For two or more offenses to constitute part of a common scheme or plan, they must be substantially connected to each other by at least one common factor, such as common victims, common accomplices, common purpose, or similar modus operandi....

> *Same course of conduct.* Offenses that do not qualify as part of a common scheme or plan may nonetheless qualify as part of the same course of conduct if they are sufficiently connected or related to each other as to warrant the conclusion that they are part of a single episode, spree, or ongoing series of offenses....

U.S.S.G. 1B1.3, n. 9(A) and (B).

Mr. Garcia does not dispute that he attempted to persuade "ibalissasmom" to engage in sexual activity with her two daughters and to photograph the event. Rather, he argues that this conduct was not related to his decision to send the child pornography on August 3rd. Specifically, he points to the temporal relationship between the two events, noting that "the images were sent well after, and without any connection to the first set of conversations involving the mailing of the film...." ... Mr. Garcia's argument is not persuasive, for several reasons. The internet chat room in which Mr. Garcia made the acquaintance of "ibalissasmom" was entitled "PRETEEN POSTINGS AND TRADING." "Trading" is defined by Webster's Dictionary as "to make an exchange of one thing for another ... to pass back and forth." Webster's II New Riverside University Dictionary 1223 (1984). "Trading" in this context refers to the exchanging of "preteen" pornographic material. Mr. Garcia repeatedly offered to make exchanges. He offered to send beauty products to "ibalissasmom" in exchange for her "daughters." He offered to send Polaroid film if she would use it to photograph herself and her daughters. When viewed in this "barter" context, Mr. Garcia's decision to send child pornography to "ibalissasmom" is relevant to his quest to obtain child pornography from "ibalissasmom."

The fact that Mr. Garcia did not send the two images until a few days after requesting the Polaroid images does little to bolster his argument. This Court has held that conduct stretching out over a five-year period was not too remote to be considered relevant conduct if those acts were part of the same course of conduct. *United States v. Neighbors*, 23 F.3d 306, 310–11 (10th Cir.1994). Here, a mere eight days had passed from the time that Mr. Garcia requested specific sexual conduct to be photographed and when he sent child pornography to "ibalissasmom." ... On August 3rd, Mr. Garcia continued to await the arrival of the pictures he had "ordered." During the same conversation in which he sent the two child pornography images to "ibalissasmom," he also stated, "can't wait to see ur pics." Mr. Garcia was anxious not only to receive the pictures but to meet in person with "ibalissasmom" and her daughters. He stated, as he sent one of the two pornographic pictures, "heres one that I imagine is me with ur oldest [daughter]." Mr. Garcia's decision to send the digital pornography and his requests for sexual images of "ibalissasmom" and her daughters were united by the same purpose — the eventual sexual abuse of two minor children. This predatory scheme was common throughout the conversations between Mr. Garcia and "ibalissasmom." In every chat between the two, Mr. Garcia expressed an interest in both daughters. His purpose in conversing with "ibalissasmom" is best explained in his own words: "would u really consider sharing urself and your girls with me? ... Really? Then I feel privileged ... [I] want to visit u and the girls every chance I got." ... Mr. Garcia's quest to obtain sexually explicit images of the daughters of "ibalissasmom" was part of a common scheme and common course of conduct that were relevant to his charged conduct. Therefore, the district court judge did not commit error when he considered this relevant conduct in sentencing Mr. Garcia....

Mr. Garcia urges us to adopt a narrow and hyper-technical interpretation of the cross-reference. According to Mr. Garcia, if one is not physically standing behind the camera or involved in a multi-person conspiracy to distribute child pornography, then one is not "producing" child pornography, and thus the cross-reference does not apply. Such an interpretation is contradicted by a plain reading of the cross-reference, the commentary following the guideline, and case law.

The conduct the guideline seeks to punish is not only the actual production of child pornography, but the active solicitation for the production of such images. Where, as here, the images are not actually produced, the cross-reference may still apply so long as the defendant "offer[ed] or [sought] by notice or advertisement, a minor to engage in sexually explicit conduct...." U.S.S.G. 2G2.2(c)(1). There is no doubt that Mr. Garcia sought to have minors engage in sexually explicit conduct. Mr. Garcia asked for "nasty" pictures of "ibalissasmom" and her two daughters. Mr. Garcia offered to send Polaroid film to "ibalissasmom" if she would take "nasty" pictures for him. Mr. Garcia asked for pictures of "ibalissasmom" and her daughters "nude doing things to each other" and described on at least two occasions specific sexual acts of which he wanted close-up photographs.

The commentary following the guideline states that the cross-reference "*is to be construed broadly* to include all instances where the offense involved employing, using, persuading, inducing, enticing, coercing, transporting, permitting, or offering or seeking by notice or advertisement, a minor to engage in sexually explicit conduct for the purpose of producing any visual depiction of such conduct." U.S.S.G. 2G2.2 n. 3 (emphasis added). Neither the guideline nor the commentary states that in cases where actual images are produced, the defendant must be the one who is behind the camera. A defendant's conduct may be one step removed from the actual production and still fall within the ambit of the cross-reference. *United States v. Whitesell*, 314 F.3d 1251, 1255 (11th Cir.2002) (rejecting the defendant's argument that he did not "cause" the production of images when he asked a fifteen year old girl to take pictures of herself and send them to him); *United States v. Anderton*, 136 F.3d 747, 750 n. 2; U.S.S.G. 2G2.2 n. 1. It is clear, based on his explicit statements to "ibalissasmom," that Mr. Garcia was *offering or seeking by notice or advertisement*, a minor to engage in sexual activity....

Mr. Garcia's final argument with respect to the application of the cross-reference is that if the purpose for which a defendant sought to have minors engage in sexual activity is something other than producing a visual depiction of the activity, then the cross-reference may not apply. To support this proposition, he relies on *United States v. Crandon*, 173 F.3d 122 (3rd Cir.1999). In *Crandon*, the court held that a district court must consider the defendant's "state of mind to ensure that the defendant acted for purposes of producing a visual depiction of [sexually explicit] conduct" when determining whether to apply the cross-reference. *Crandon*, 173 F.3d at 130. The *Crandon* court posited that "it is conceivable that [the defendant] did have alternative ... purposes in taking the photographs." *Id.*

Mr. Garcia's argument suffers from the same flaw as his previous argument, namely, that he misconstrues the reason the district court applied the cross-reference. The cross-reference was not, as he alleges, applied for his conduct involving the two photographs he sent on August 3, 2003. Rather, it was applied for his entire course of conduct involving "ibalissasmom" and her two daughters. When the issue is properly re-framed as, "for what purpose did Mr. Garcia seek to have the daughters of "ibalissasmom" engage in sexual activity," then *Crandon* is of no help to Mr. Garcia. The district judge who sentenced Mr. Garcia stated that he would be "engage[d] in flights of fantasy and fiction" if he were to believe that Mr. Garcia's purpose in seeking to have these two girls engage in sexual activity was for anything other than producing visual depictions to satisfy his perverse sexual desires. ... Mr. Garcia's conversations with "ibalissasmom" reveal that his purpose in asking her to engage in sex with her two daughters was to produce child pornography. Mr. Garcia told "ibalissasmom" that it "would be great" if she would take "nasty" pictures of her daughters and send them to him.... Mr. Garcia said, "ill send u some [film] if u will take some nasty [pictures] for me." ... Later, he said, "im excited about seeing u and the girls ... even if it is just on film." ... Combined with numerous other requests for these pictures and explicit descriptions of the sexual activity, this evidence clearly establishes that Mr. Garcia's purpose was to produce visual depictions of sexually explicit conduct involving minors....

Mr. Garcia argues that he should have received a downward departure in his sentence due to government misconduct. Mr. Garcia makes two attacks on the conduct of Agent Leazenby, who posed online as "ibalissasmom." First, he argues that Agent Leazenby enticed him into seeking the sexual exploitation of the daughters of "ibalissasmom," and that such enticement constitutes outrageous government conduct. Second, he argues that Agent Leazenby deliberately structured the operation in such a way as to achieve the highest sentence possible, i.e., that Agent Leazenby's choice to portray one of the daughters as age 7 constitutes sentence manipulation because it leads to the highest enhancement—4 levels. We have not to date recognized a claim of "sentence manipulation" and find no occasion to do so here. *United States v. Lacey*, 86 F.3d 956, 963 (10th Cir.1996); *United States v. Scull*, 321 F.3d 1270, 1276 n. 3 (10th Cir.2003). However "we have addressed the same concept under the appellation of "outrageous" governmental conduct." *Lacey*, 86 F.3d at 963. We will therefore address Mr. Garcia's allegation that Agent Leazenby deliberately set out to achieve the highest sentence possible under the rubric of outrageous government conduct....

"[T]he relevant inquiry" when assessing claims of outrageous government conduct "is whether, considering the totality of the circumstances ... the government's conduct is so shocking, outrageous and intolerable that it offends the 'universal sense of justice.'" *Lacey*, 86 F.3d at 964, quoting *United States v. Mosley*, 965 F.2d 906, 910 (10th Cir.1992), *United States v. Russell*, 411 U.S. 423, 432, 93 S.Ct. 1637, 36 L.Ed.2d 366 (1973). This court has recognized the defense of outrageous government conduct, *United States v. Spivey*, 508 F.2d 146 (10th Cir.1975), but has never rendered a decision upholding such a claim. "The absence of any decision by this court upholding such a claim ... bears testament to its narrow scope." *Lacey*, 86 F.3d at 964. "To succeed on an outrageous conduct defense, the defendant must show either (1) excessive government involvement in the creation of the crime, or (2) significant governmental coercion to induce the crime." *United States v. Pedraza*, 27 F.3d 1515, 1521 (10th Cir.1994)....

With respect to sentencing manipulation, Mr. Garcia argues that it was outrageous for Agent Leazenby to portray one of the daughters of "ibalissasmom" as seven years old since this led to a four-level enhancement for sexual exploitation of a minor less than twelve years old. His argument is not supported by any additional facts to suggest misbehavior on the part of Agent Leazenby and is undermined by his own stated preference for girls ages "11 and up to 15." ... Sexual abuse of an eleven year old would also lead to a four-level enhancement. Mr. Garcia apparently is urging us to adopt a per se rule whereby law enforcement officers are never allowed to structure "bait and hook" operations where the "bait," if taken, leads to the highest level sentence enhancement. We decline to adopt such a rule. "[I]t is not outrageous for the government ... to induce a defendant to repeat, continue, or even expand previous criminal activity." *Pedraza*, 27 F.3d at 1521. "[I]n inducing a defendant to repeat or expand his criminal activity, it is permissible for the government to suggest the illegal activity...." *Id.* Here, Agent Leazenby did not even suggest the activity; Mr. Garcia did. We perceive no misconduct on the part of Agent Leazenby, let alone conduct that is so outrageous that it "offends the universal sense of justice." *Lacey*, 86 F.3d at 964[.] ...

Mr. Garcia argues that his sentence violates his Sixth Amendment right to a trial by jury because the sentencing judge considered facts that were not proven to a jury beyond a reasonable doubt and to which he did not admit. The government concedes that, in light of *United States v. Booker*, 543 U.S. 220, 125 S.Ct. 738, 160 L.Ed.2d 621 (2005) and this Court's recent decision in *United States v. Dazey*, 403 F.3d 1147 (10th Cir.2005), Mr. Garcia's sentence is constitutionally infirm and asks us to grant his motion to vacate his sentence and remand for resentencing.... Based on the foregoing, though we reject Mr. Garcia's arguments regarding the application of the cross-reference and outrageous government conduct, his sentence is VACATED in light of *Booker*. We REMAND to the district court for resentencing consistent with the Supreme Court's decision in *Booker*.

Notes

For commentary on sentence enhancements, see Kaleb Noblett, *Caging Uncertainty: Responsible Reform of Federal Child Pornography Sentencing Guidelines*, 42 N. Ky. L. Rev. 65 (2015); Holly H. Crohel, *Dangerous Discretion: Protecting Children by Amending the Federal Child Pornography Statutes to Enforce Sentencing Enhancements and Prevent Noncustodial Sentences*, 48 S.D. L. Rev. 623 (2011); Nolan Johnson, *Criminal Law—United States v. Chriswell: The Sixth Circuit Holds Sentence Enhancements for Unduly Influencing A Minor to Enage in Sexual Conduct Inapplicable When the "Victim" Is An Undercover Officer*, 36 U. Mem. L. Rev. 1141 (2006); Ashley A. Halfman, *Giving Offenders What They Deserve: Amendments to Federal Sentencing Guidelines Section 2G2.2, Addressing Child Pornography Distribution*, 36 Ga. L. Rev. 219 (2001). *But see U.S. v. Chriswell*, 401 F.3d 459 (6th Cir. 2004) (two level enhancement for unduly influencing a minor to engage in prohibited sexual conduct was not available in cases where victim was an undercover law enforcement officer)—*U.S. v. Faris*, 583 F.3d 756 (11th Cir. (Fla.) 2009) (declined to follow *Chriswell*), superseded by statute as stated in *U.S. v. Jerchower*, 631 F.3d 1181 (11th Cir. (Fla.) 2011).

5. *Abuse of Discretion*

United States v. Autery

Ninth Circuit, 2009
555 F.3d 864

MILAN D. SMITH, JR., Circuit Judge:

Defendant-Appellee Jim Bryan Autery pled guilty to possession of child pornography and entered into a plea bargain that called for the imposition of a forty-one to fifty-one month prison sentence pursuant to the United States Sentencing Guidelines. The district court deviated from the Guidelines and imposed a sentence of five years probation. The government did not object to the sentence when the district court imposed it, but now appeals, arguing that the sentence is substantively unreasonable.... We hold that the appropriate standard of review under the circumstances of this case is abuse of discretion. Reviewing the sentence under that standard, we affirm....

Based on evidence obtained in a U.S. Postal Service and Immigration and Customs Enforcement sting operation, Autery was indicted in September 2006 on two counts of attempted receipt of child pornography, one count of possession of child pornography, and a forfeiture allegation. Following Autery's arrest, federal agents found at least 150 images of child pornography[1] stored in Autery's personal computers.... Autery pled guilty in May 2007 to one count of possession of child pornography, a violation of 18 U.S.C. § 2252A(a)(5)(b), pursuant to a plea agreement. The presentence report (PSR) calculated Autery's offense level to be twenty-two, and his criminal history within Category I, yielding a Guidelines range of between forty-one and fifty-one months incarceration.

Autery was sentenced before United States District Judge Robert E. Jones on October 1, 2007. Both parties and the court accepted the accuracy of the PSR sentencing calculations. The government requested that the court impose a fifty-one month sentence—at the top of the Guidelines range—and the defense urged the court to impose a sentence at the bottom of the Guidelines range. The court did neither; it deviated from the Guidelines and sentenced Autery to no period of incarceration and five years of probation. In doing so, the court explained its decision both from the bench and in a "Statement of Reasons" in a *Judgment in a Criminal Case* order.

At sentencing, the court noted that it was "required to make the determinations under the sentencing guidelines and then after that, look at the guidelines as advisory only." The court then confirmed that pro-forma application of the Guidelines would yield a range of forty-one to fifty-one months incarceration.... The court began its analysis of the appropriate sentence by noting that Autery's was "a very difficult case" because there was "no evidence that [Autery] was purchasing evident child pornography involving real children"[2] (although the court stated that Autery *believed* they were real children). The court also noted that there was no evidence of Autery's ever abusing family members and

---

1. The precise number of images is disputed.

2. The court may have been referring to the images that Autery received in the government sting operation, images which the government stated were not of real children. Count 3 of the indictment, to which Autery pled guilty, alleges that Autery possessed "visual depictions of actual minors." Regardless, the government does not argue that the district court erred in making this finding or in considering it in sentencing.

that he did not "fit the profile of a pedophile." These facts, the court concluded, made Autery "totally different than what ... [the] court has normally experienced with people who are ordering this sort of child pornography."

The court also described what it considered to be Autery's redeeming personal characteristics: no history of substance abuse, no "interpersonal instability," no "sociopathic or criminalistic attitudes," and that he was motivated and intelligent. The court thought it critical that Autery enjoys the continuing support of his family, especially his wife and children.... The court acknowledged that child pornography is "terrible stuff" and that it believed Autery "ordered it knowing that it was wrong and illegal." But the court found that in several ways, Autery's case differed from the "hundreds and hundreds" of other child pornography cases the court had adjudicated.... The court also believed that Autery could not "be accommodated adequately in a federal institution," and that he needed "outpatient psychiatric monitoring and management" instead. Concluding its sentencing justification, the court stated that it decided on a sentence of probation only "after a lot of soul-searching." It further determined that imposing prison time would create "a much more disruptive situation and, actually, could be more damaging than the rehabilitation [regime the court believed would] work." The court also opined in its written "Statement of Reasons" that the sentence "is fully justified in this exceptional case."

The court observed that the five-year probationary sentence "would be subject to some very special conditions of supervision." It also warned Autery, saying, "believe me, if you have any violation [of those conditions], you'll be back before me and receive the maximum penalty allowed by law." Some of the conditions of probation included a prohibition on viewing any pornography whatsoever and on being within 100 feet of places where minors congregate unless approved by his probation officer. Autery was also not permitted to travel outside the State of Oregon without prior approval. He was required to participate in mental health evaluation and counseling, including psychotherapy, and to take any prescription drugs as directed. He was not permitted to possess any firearm, or to use any computer except for work, or, without approval, any other electronic media — such as a personal digital assistant or cellular phone — with Internet capability. In addition, Autery was not permitted to have "direct or indirect" contact with anyone under the age of eighteen, except his own children. Finally, Autery was required to register with the state sex offender registry.

After imposing sentence and discussing the terms of the probation, the court asked the government if it had anything else for the court. The government said it did not, and specifically, it did not object to the sentence or its method of determination. The government now appeals the sentence, challenging it as substantively unreasonable.... Before deciding whether to uphold the district court's sentence, we must first determine the appropriate standard of review under the facts presented. After weighing Supreme Court authority, the views of other circuits, and public policy considerations, we hold that abuse of discretion is the proper standard of review in this case.

The government urges, without providing analysis, that the standard of review here is abuse of discretion. In support, it cites *Gall v. United States*, 552 U.S. 38, 128 S.Ct. 586, 591, 169 L.Ed.2d 445 (2007). Autery, without citing any authority, urges the court to employ a plain error standard.... Neither this circuit nor the Supreme Court has squarely addressed the proper standard of review where the appellant fails to object to the sentence's substantive reasonableness at sentencing. In *Gall*, the Court noted that after *Booker*, appellate review of sentencing decisions is limited to determining whether they are reasonable, *Gall*, 128 S.Ct. at 591, and that the abuse of discretion standard applies to review of all reasonableness sentencing questions. *Id.* at 594. However, the Court did not indicate whether this rule applies even where a party fails to object at sentencing to the substantive reasonableness of the sentence.

In *United States v. Carty*, we stated that the reviewing court "first consider[s] whether the district court committed significant procedural error, then … consider[s] the substantive reasonableness of the sentence." 520 F.3d 984, 993 (9th Cir.2008) (citing *Gall*, 128 S.Ct. at 597). However, *Carty* did not discuss the proper standard of review upon a party's failure to object to either alleged error.… In *United States v. Sylvester Norman Knows His Gun, III*, 438 F.3d 913 (9th Cir.2005) (*Knows His Gun*), we considered a closely related issue that provides a useful starting point for the next step of our analysis. In *Knows His Gun*, we held that a party's failure to object "on the ground that the district court did not sufficiently address and apply the factors listed in § 3553(a)" triggered plain error review.[3] *Id.* at 918; *see also United States v. Waknine*, 543 F.3d 546, 553–54 & n. 4 (9th Cir.2008) (applying *Knows His Gun* and reversing in part where the district court failed to consider any § 3553(a) factors).

Knows His Gun and its progeny illustrate the crucial—but often-overlooked—distinction between procedural error and substantive reasonableness. *See Carty*, 520 F.3d at 993 (citing 18 U.S.C. § 3553(a)). In *Carty*, we held that "[o]n appeal, we first consider whether the district court committed significant procedural error, then we consider the substantive reasonableness of the sentence." *Id.* Elaborating, we explained that

> [i]t would be *procedural* error for a district court to fail to calculate—or to calculate incorrectly—the Guidelines range; to treat the Guidelines as mandatory instead of advisory; to fail to consider the § 3553(a) factors; to choose a sentence based on clearly erroneous facts; or to fail adequately to explain the sentence selected, including any deviation from the Guidelines range.

Id. (emphasis added) (citing *Gall*, 128 S.Ct. at 597). But "[i]n determining *substantive reasonableness*, we are to consider the totality of the circumstances, including the degree of variance for a sentence imposed outside the Guidelines range." *Id.* (emphasis added).

Thus, it is possible for a sentence to pass procedural muster and yet be substantively unreasonable. As a result, *Knows His Gun*'s standard of review rule for whether the district court "sufficiently address[ed] and appl[ied] the factors listed in § 3553(a)" does not apply in a case where the sentencing court carefully considered the statutory factors listed in *Carty*, and the sole issue is substantive reasonableness. That is the situation here, as the government's

---

3. Section 3553(a) of United States Code Title 18 requires the district court to consider the following factors in sentencing (the § 3553(a) factors):
    (1) the nature and circumstances of the offense and the history and characteristics of the defendant;
    (2) the need for the sentence imposed—
        (A) to reflect the seriousness of the offense, to promote respect for the law, and to provide just punishment for the offense;
        (B) to afford adequate deterrence to criminal conduct;
        (C) to protect the public from further crimes of the defendant; and
        (D) to provide the defendant with needed educational or vocational training, medical care, or other correctional treatment in the most effective manner;
    (3) the kinds of sentences available;
    (4) the kinds of sentence and the sentencing range established [and recommended by the Guidelines] … ;
    (5) any pertinent policy statement … issued by the Sentencing Commission … ;
    (6) the need to avoid unwarranted sentence disparities among defendants with similar records who have been found guilty of similar conduct; and
    (7) the need to provide restitution to any victims of the offense.

chief argument on appeal is that the sentence is substantively unreasonable.... ("This sentence represents a departure of 41–51 months or 22 levels from the low end of the applicable Sentencing Guideline range.... This sentence is plainly 'unreasonable' under 18 U.S.C. § 3553(a)."). The government buttresses its argument with references to the § 3553(a) factors and contends that the district court's unreasonable weighing of those factors rendered the resulting sentence unreasonable, but the government alleges neither that the district court failed to address the factors, nor that it committed any other procedural error. Therefore, *Knows His Gun* does not resolve the appropriate standard of review in this case.

While neither the Supreme Court nor this circuit has squarely resolved the standard of review at issue here, a few other circuits have done so. The slight majority of those courts has held that where no objection was made to the sentence at sentencing, the court still reviews for *abuse of discretion* to determine whether the sentence was reasonable. *See, e.g., United States v. Bras*, 483 F.3d 103, 113 (D.C.Cir.2007) (rejecting argument that non-objecting defendant's sentence should be reviewed for plain error because "[r]easonableness ... is the standard of *appellate* review, not an objection that must be raised upon the pronouncement of a sentence") (citation omitted); *United States v. Castro-Juarez*, 425 F.3d 430, 434 (7th Cir.2005) (holding that "review of a sentence for reasonableness is not affected by whether the defendant had the foresight to label his sentence 'unreasonable' before the sentencing hearing adjourned"); *cf. United States v. Lopez–Flores*, 444 F.3d 1218, 1221 (10th Cir.2006) (noting that the Seventh Circuit's *Castro-Juarez*'s standard of review applies to challenges to the reasonableness of a sentence's length, but holding that unchallenged errors in the *method* of sentence determination are still reviewed for plain error). *But see United States v. Peltier*, 505 F.3d 389, 391–92 (5th Cir.2007) (holding that "a defendant's failure to object at sentencing to the reasonableness of his sentence" triggers plain error review).[4]

While instructive and often persuasive, other circuits' decisions do not bind this court; in the absence of controlling authority, our approach should be guided by consideration of the legal and policy rationales underlying the alternatives. *Cf. Biro v. United States*, 24 F.3d 1140, 1142 (9th Cir.1994).... In *Castro-Juarez*, the Seventh Circuit reasoned that "[t]o insist that defendants object at sentencing to preserve appellate review for reasonableness would create a trap for unwary defendants and saddle busy district courts with the burden of sitting through an objection—probably formulaic—in every criminal case." 425 F.3d at 433–34. "Since the district court will already have heard argument and allocution from the parties and weighed the relevant § 3553(a) factors before pronouncing sentence," the court reasoned, "we fail to see how requiring the defendant to then protest the term handed down as unreasonable will further the sentencing process in any meaningful way." *Id.* at 434.

The Fifth Circuit has taken a different approach. In defending the plain error standard, the court in *United States v. Peltier* stressed the longstanding rule that issues are not preserved for appeal unless objected to in the district court.[5] 505 F.3d at 391–92 (calling

---

4. Although each of the authorities establishing the abuse of discretion standard of review involves the *defendant's* failing to object to his sentence, no principled reason exists to apply a different rule where the government similarly fails to object.

5. In *Peltier*, the Fifth Circuit acknowledged that the Seventh Circuit held that a defendant need not object at sentencing to the reasonableness of his sentence to preserve the issue for review, and then stated that various other circuits have taken a contrary view. 505 F.3d at 391. In support of this latter point, the court cited decisions from the Second, Sixth, Tenth, Third, and Ninth Circuits. *Id.* at 391 n. 5. In so doing, however, the *Peltier* court apparently mistook the holdings of some of those cases, conflating substantive reasonableness with the procedural failure to consider the § 3553(a) factors, discussed *supra. See id.* (citing, *e.g., United States v. Villafuerte*, 502 F.3d 204, 208–09 (2d Cir.2007) (holding that failure to object to court's neglecting to consider the § 3553(a) factors (not to substantive reasonableness of sentence) triggers plain error review); *Knows His Gun*, 438 F.3d at 918

the objection rule "one of the most familiar procedural rubrics in the administration of justice") (quoting *United States v. Calverley*, 37 F.3d 160, 162 (5th Cir.1994) (en banc), *abrogated on other grounds*). *Peltier* further states that the objection requirement "serves a critical function by encouraging informed decisionmaking and giving the district court an opportunity to correct errors before they are taken up on appeal." *Id.* at 392.

We find *Castro-Juarez*'s reasoning more persuasive than *Peltier*'s. Peltier notes that a key rationale for requiring formal objection to a potential error is to allow the district court to hear and weigh the parties' positions, thus avoiding or correcting that error. 505 F.3d at 392. This rationale makes sense in many contexts, such as where the court miscalculates the Guidelines sentencing range or neglects to consider an essential statutory factor. But in a substantive reasonableness challenge, the parties have already fully argued the relevant issues (usually both in their briefs and in open court), and the court is already apprised of the parties' positions and what sentences the parties believe are appropriate. In such a case, requiring the parties to restate their views after sentencing would be both redundant and futile, and would not "further the sentencing process in any meaningful way." *Castro-Juarez*, 425 F.3d at 434.... Therefore, for the reasons described in *Castro-Juarez*, we hold that the substantive reasonableness of a sentence—whether objected to or not at sentencing—is reviewed for abuse of discretion. We proceed to review Autery's sentence under that standard....

In the post-*Booker* era, district courts making sentencing decisions must make the Guidelines "the starting point and the initial benchmark" for their decisions. *Gall v. United States*, 552 U.S. 38, 128 S.Ct. 586, 596, 169 L.Ed.2d 445 (2007); *United States v. Carty*, 520 F.3d 984, 992 (9th Cir.2008) (quoting *Gall*). While district courts are not required to impose a sentence within the Guidelines, *Booker*, 543 U.S. at 249–53, 125 S.Ct. 738, they must "give serious consideration to the extent of any departure from the Guidelines," and they must then "explain [the] conclusion that an unusually lenient or an unusually harsh sentence is appropriate in a particular case with sufficient justifications." *Carty*, 520 F.3d at 992 (quoting *Gall*, 128 S.Ct. at 594).

The Supreme Court has emphasized that "extraordinary circumstances" are not a prerequisite to upholding a sentence outside the Guidelines. *Gall*, 128 S.Ct. at 594 (internal quotation marks omitted). Indeed, sentences outside the Guidelines are subject to the same standard—i.e., abuse of discretion—as those within the Guidelines. *Id.* at 596 (noting that "abuse-of-discretion standard of review applies to appellate review of all sentencing decisions—whether inside or outside the Guidelines range"). And where the sentence under review is outside the Guidelines, we may not presume the sentence is unreasonable. *Id.* at 597. We may, however, "take the degree of variance into account and consider the extent of a deviation from the Guidelines." *Id.* at 595.

"While the Guidelines are to be respectfully considered, they are one factor among the § 3553(a) factors that are to be taken into account in arriving at an appropriate sentence." *Carty*, 520 F.3d at 991 (citing *Kimbrough v. United States*, 552 U.S. 85, 128 S.Ct. 558, 570, 169 L.Ed.2d 481 (2007)). "[T]he Guidelines factor [may not] be given more or less weight than any other." *Id.* So while the Guidelines are the "starting point and initial benchmark" and must "be kept in mind throughout the [sentencing] process," *id.*, the Guidelines range constitutes only a touch-stone in the district court's sentencing considerations. *See id.*

(holding that failure to object "on the ground that the district court did not sufficiently address and apply the factors listed in § 3553(a)" triggered plain error review)). Thus, contrary to the *Peltier* court's characterization, the circuits listed above have not all clearly held that unobjected-to sentences challenged for substantive unreasonableness are subject to plain error review.

Thus, in sum, the district court must consider both the seven § 3553(a) factors and the Guidelines when imposing sentence.[6]

Finally, appellate courts must "give due deference to the district court's decision that the § 3553(a) factors, on a whole, justify the extent of the variance."[7] *Gall*, 128 S.Ct. at 597. This deference is required because the sentencing judge "is in a superior position to find facts and judge their import under § 3553(a) in the individual case. The judge sees and hears the evidence, makes credibility determinations, has full knowledge of the facts and gains insights not conveyed by the record." *Id.* "The sentencing judge has access to, and greater familiarity with, the individual case and the individual defendant before him than the Commission or the appeals court." *Id.* at 597–98 (citing *Rita v. United States*, 551 U.S. 338, 127 S.Ct. 2456, 2469, 168 L.Ed.2d 203 (2007)). Moreover, "[d]istrict courts have an institutional advantage over appellate courts in making these sorts of determinations, especially as they see so many more Guidelines sentences than appellate courts do." *Id.* (citing *Koon v. United States*, 518 U.S. 81, 98, 116 S.Ct. 2035, 135 L.Ed.2d 392 (1996)). In arriving at a sentence, a district court need not expressly state how each of the § 3553(a) factors influenced its decision: "[t]he district court need not tick off each of the § 3553(a) factors to show that it has considered them." *Carty*, 520 F.3d at 992. Instead, appellate courts "assume that district judges know the law and understand their obligation to consider all of the § 3553(a) factors, not just the Guidelines." *Id.* (citing *Walton v. Arizona*, 497 U.S. 639, 653, 110 S.Ct. 3047, 111 L.Ed.2d 511 (1990)).

With these principles in mind, we review the district court's sentence to determine whether the court abused its discretion in imposing it. We conclude that it did not.... The government first argues that the district court did not treat the Guidelines range as a "benchmark." The sentencing transcript belies that claim. Before announcing and explaining the basis for the sentence, the district court stated that it was "required to make the determinations under the sentencing guidelines and then after that, look at the guidelines as advisory only." The court referred to the Guidelines range twice again during its sentencing explanation. To the extent the government's argument alleges procedural error rather than substantive unreasonableness, it is reviewed for plain error. *Knows His Gun*, 438 F.3d at 918. Regardless, the government's argument fails under abuse of discretion review, and *a fortiori*, it fails under plain error review....

The government claims that the district court failed to reasonably consider the "nature and circumstances of the offense," as required by 18 U.S.C. § 3553(a)(1). Specifically, the government notes that Autery actively solicited the pornography instead of just possessing it and that the court never mentioned this during the hearing. The record, however, shows that the court did reasonably consider the nature of the offense. While acknowledging that the illicit material was "terrible stuff" and that Autery had "ordered it knowing that it was wrong and illegal," the district court stated that there was "no evidence that [Autery] was

---

6. Section 3553(a)(4) incorporates consideration of the Guidelines by reference, requiring the court to consider "the kinds of sentence and the sentencing range established [and recommended by the Guidelines]."

7. The *Gall* Court repeatedly refers to "variances" from the sentencing range, instead of "departures." *Gall* was decided before *Irizarry v. United States*, 553 U.S. 708, 128 S.Ct. 2198, 2203–04, 171 L.Ed.2d 28 (2008), in which the Court clarified that the two terms continue to have legally distinctive meanings post-*Booker*. Moreover, as a concurring Sixth Circuit judge noted recently in *United States v. Smith*, "the word 'variance,'... has been used both precisely and imprecisely post-*Booker* to refer to certain departures from the advisory guideline range. When used precisely, the term 'variance' refers to departures based on § 3553(a) factors rather than departures under § 5, Part K, of the guidelines." 474 F.3d 888, 896 n. 3 (6th Cir.2007) (Gibbons, J., concurring).

purchasing evident child pornography involving real children." Moreover, there was a dispute over whether Autery solicited customized material (thus contributing directly to child exploitation), and that act was not an element of the offense to which Autery pled guilty. Certainly, the district court *could* have expressly considered this fact in fashioning an appropriate sentence. *See Rita*, 127 S.Ct. at 2465–66 (noting that "[t]his Court's Sixth Amendment cases do not automatically forbid a sentencing court to take account of factual matters not determined by a jury and to increase the sentence in consequence"). However, especially given the uncertainty of the evidence on this issue, the district court did not abuse its discretion by declining to further consider the disputed evidence in imposing sentence....

The government next contends that the district court misjudged "the history and characteristics of the defendant," 18 U.S.C. § 3553(a)(1), in determining the sentence. The government specifically alleges it was error to consider Autery's lack of a criminal history, because that characteristic is already part of the Guidelines criminal history calculation. This argument overlooks the fact that a defendant with a minor criminal history can still fall within Criminal History Level I. *See U.S. Sentencing Guidelines Manual* § 4A1.1 & Ch. 5, Pt. A (2007). Therefore, because Autery's Criminal History Level I did not fully account for his complete lack of criminal history, considering it as a mitigating factor was not redundant or improper. *See United States v. Rowan*, 530 F.3d 379, 381 (5th Cir.2008) (holding probation reasonable for defendant convicted of possessing hundreds of hardcore child pornography images where defendant had no criminal history).

The government also notes that Autery was a former reserve police officer and claims this fact should have been considered an aggravating factor, because Autery should have known the law and its consequences. The notion that a defendant's status as a former law enforcement officer justifies a *per se* sentence enhancement is dubious. Indeed, one could reasonably argue that a defendant's law enforcement service could, in certain circumstances, constitute a *mitigating* factor in sentencing because a former law enforcement officer has shown at some point in his past that he can lead an honorable and responsible life. Defense counsel frequently use similar arguments before sentencing courts in order to highlight a defendant's best qualities. Because the issue can cut either way, the district court's failure to treat such service as an aggravating factor was not an abuse of discretion.

In addition, the government takes exception to the district court's commenting on Autery's various positive characteristics, such as his having no history of substance abuse, no "interpersonal instability" nor "sociopathic or criminalistic attitudes," his motivation and intelligence, and that he has the support of his wife and children. But the government offers little support for why these attributes, which undoubtedly constitute "history and characteristics of the defendant," *see* 18 U.S.C. § 3553(a)(1), are inappropriate considerations. The government cites *United States v. Thompson*, 315 F.3d 1071 (9th Cir.2002), for the proposition that, in departing downward, a district court should not rely on a defendant's lack of history of committing sexual abuse. To the extent *Thompson's ratio decidendi* survives *Booker* (which we do not here decide), *Thompson* does not help the government. While the district court mentioned that Autery had no history of committing sexual abuse, the court also relied on the various other attributes listed above. Each of those attributes, in the reasonable judgment of the court, increases the likelihood that Autery can again become a productive, non-threatening member of free society, thus making more severe punishment less appropriate than if Autery lacked those characteristics.

Our dissenting colleague objects to our reliance on the district court's characterization of Autery as not "fit[ting] the profile of a pedophile." He argues that the district court erred in making this finding because neither the PSR nor the district court itself described the elements of such a "profile" or why it was relevant to sentencing. However, § 3553(a)(1) merely directs the court to consider "the history and characteristics of the defendant." Nothing in this section requires the district court to base its application of the factor on the PSR, scientific studies, or anything other than the court's experience and judgment. *See* 18 U.S.C. § 3553(a)(1). The section also does not require the district court to provide an elaborate foundation for its determination. *See id.* Here, the district court found, relying on its extensive experience and, in particular, the experience of handling "hundreds and hundreds" of other child pornography cases, that Autery did not "fit the profile of a pedophile." Under the district court's reasoned judgment, this "characteristic" of the defendant (like, *inter alia*, his lack of "interpersonal instability" and his motivation and intelligence) is unusual for someone in Autery's position. Indeed, the court found Autery "totally different than what ... [the] court has normally experienced with people who are ordering this sort of child pornography." Thus, the court impliedly found that the other people he had sentenced for "ordering this sort of pornography" posed a greater threat to society than does Autery. As a result, this consideration is valid under § 3553(a)(1), and it was a reasonable basis for concluding that Autery's sentence should be lower than other defendants who do fit that profile. Accordingly, we cannot say that the court's judgment on this issue was an abuse of discretion, and, while it is clear that our dissenting colleague would have ruled otherwise had he been sitting as the sentencing judge, we do not believe he has shown that the district court here abused its discretion on this factor either....

The government next suggests that the sentence does not, under 18 U.S.C. § 3553(a)(2)(A), adequately "reflect the seriousness of the offense, ... promote respect for the law, [or] provide just punishment for the offense." Reasonable minds can differ as to whether a five-year probation provides "just" punishment, but the district court clearly, and we believe, reasonably, weighed this factor in imposing sentence. First, the sentencing transcript reveals that the district court was desirous of doing what was "just" in this case. Furthermore, in its "Statement of Reasons," the court observed that the statute provides for a term of probation of between one and five years, and stated that it "impose[d] the maximum term of probation because of the seriousness of the offense, to promote respect for the law, [and] to provide just punishment for the offense." Finally, Autery's sentence was not just a term of probation: (i) Autery was required to register as a sex offender, a punishment of lifelong significance (which can cause the listed person to become so socially ostracized that he has difficulty living in many communities); (ii) he is barred from viewing any pornography whatsoever; (iii) he is barred from being within 100 feet of places where minors congregate unless approved by his probation officer; (iv) he is not permitted to travel outside the State of Oregon without prior approval; (v) he is required to participate in mental health evaluation and counseling, including psychotherapy, and to take any prescription drugs as directed; (vi) he is not permitted to possess any firearm; (vii) he is barred from using any computer except for work, or, without approval, any other electronic media—such as a personal digital assistant or cellular phone—with Internet capability; and (viii) he is not permitted to have "direct or indirect" contact with anyone under the age of eighteen, except his own children. Although our colleague may disagree with the district court's decision on this factor, none of the government's arguments persuades us that the way the district court considered the "seriousness of the offense, respect for the law, and just punishment" was an abuse of discretion....

The government also argues that the sentence in this case does not reflect "the need for the sentence imposed ... to afford adequate deterrence to criminal conduct," in accordance with 18 U.S.C. § 3553(a)(2)(B). For the same reasons that the sentence passes muster under 18 U.S.C. § 3553(a)(2)(A), the district court's sentence is also not an abuse of discretion under this provision. Moreover, as a further deterrent, the district court threatened that if Autery violated any of the conditions of his probation, he would "be back before me and receive the maximum penalty allowed by law." It is said that there is nothing like being sentenced to hang in the morning to focus a man's thoughts, and it is improbable that the district court's stern warning will be an ineffective deterrent in this case....

The government next contends that the sentence imposed failed to "protect the public from further crimes of the defendant," pursuant to 18 U.S.C. § 3553(a)(2)(C). As the district court stressed, however, Autery's probation comes with many strings attached, which are detailed [*supra*] (Seriousness of the Offense, Respect for the Law, and Just Punishment), and the threat of maximum punishment if any condition of probation is violated, detailed [*supra*] (Adequate Deterrence). Moreover, as stated, Autery must register as a sex offender, a designation that carries both societal stigma and numerous practical restrictions designed to protect children. Under the circumstances, it was not an abuse of discretion to conclude that—compared with a prison sentence of forty-one to fifty-one months—a sixty-month probationary period combined with all the referenced restrictions will adequately protect the public....

The government also takes issue with the district court's alleged failure to impose a sentence reflecting "the need to avoid unwarranted sentence disparities among defendants with similar records who have been found guilty of similar conduct" under 18 U.S.C. § 3553(a)(6). The record shows, however, that the district court's sentence depended heavily on Autery's *dis*similarity with others convicted of the same offense. According to the district court, Autery did not "fit the profile of a pedophile." He is in many ways, the court found, qualitatively different from the "hundreds and hundreds" of others the court had encountered who had engaged in similar behavior. If this is true—and we have no basis reflected in the record to conclude otherwise—then it was not an abuse of discretion to impose a sentence that is dissimilar from the sentence that those other defendants received....

Finally, the government argues that the district court erred when it improperly made rehabilitation one of the bases for the probation sentence. Section 3553(a)(2)(D) speaks to "the need for the sentence imposed ... to provide the defendant with needed educational or vocational training, medical care, or other correctional treatment in the most effective manner." The government argues that Autery could have been ordered to undergo treatment in prison. The district court *could* have handed down such an order, but what the court did order was based on its knowledge of the case and what it believed were Autery's "exceptional" circumstances. Instead, the district court commented that, in its judgement, incarceration would *undermine* Autery's rehabilitation.... (court stating that incarceration would likely create "a much more disruptive situation and, actually, could be more damaging than the rehabilitation that [it] contemplate[d] will work"). As a result, the court ordered Autery to undergo mental health counseling and to submit to any prescription medication or other treatment deemed appropriate. Thus, rehabilitation was one of the factors most carefully considered by the district court in arriving at its sentence, and its conclusion that Autery's prospects for rehabilitation are greater out of prison than in is not unreasonable....

In sum, the district court—based on its unique familiarity with the defendant, the case's circumstances, and numerous other cases like it—considered the required factors and imposed a sentence that was not substantively unreasonable. That sentence was not necessarily what this court would have imposed. But under our controlling precedent, that determination alone is insufficient for reversal: "[w]e may not reverse just because we think a different sentence is appropriate." *Carty*, 520 F.3d at 993.... Our dissenting colleague believes that our review is overly deferential to the district court and that we are affirming simply because we find no procedural error.[8] ... ("[R]eview for abuse of discretion should be more than simply policing the district courts for proper procedure."). We respectfully disagree. Under *Gall* and *Carty*, we must consider both the procedural and substantive reasonableness of the sentence. *Gall*, 128 S.Ct. at 597; *Carty*, 520 F.3d at 993. In this opinion, we have carefully reviewed each criterion used by the district court in making its sentencing decision, compared those criteria against the record and the requirements of governing law requiring "sufficient justifications" for the sentence, *Carty*, 520 F.3d at 992 (quoting *Gall*, 128 S.Ct. at 594), and we have found no abuse of discretion....

We readily concede that in this post-*Booker* era lower courts may occasionally feel a little like Hansel and Gretel, looking for the now-missing breadcrumbs that would lead us back to clarity in sentencing. However, *it is clear* that in determining the substantive reasonableness of a sentence, we are to "consider the totality of the circumstances" *id.* at 993, and that we are to give "due deference to the district court's decision that the § 3553(a) factors, on a whole, justify the extent of the variance" because the sentencing judge "is in a superior position to find facts and judge their import under § 3553(a) in the individual case. The judge sees and hears the evidence, makes credibility determinations, has full knowledge of the facts and gains insights not conveyed by the record." *See Gall*, 128 S.Ct. at 594. This we have done. The Supreme Court's instructions about the deference due to the district court because of its unique perspective is even more compelling in a highly unusual case, which the district court found this case to be, stating that it was "exceptional" and unlike the "hundreds and hundreds" of others that had come before it. Accordingly, we affirm....

We hold that abuse of discretion is the proper standard of review where a party challenges a sentence's substantive reasonableness on appeal but did not object to the sentence's reasonableness before the district court. We further hold that the district court did not abuse that discretion in sentencing Autery to five years probation with conditions.

AFFIRMED.

TASHIMA, Circuit Judge, dissenting: ...

In this case, the district court sentenced a defendant, who showed little indication of being anything other than a run-of-the-mill child pornographer, to probation, rather than to the 41–51 months' imprisonment that the Sentencing Guidelines indicated and which the parties agreed was appropriate—a departure of at least 14 levels. Because the district court's reasoning in arriving at this sentence leaves me with a "definite and firm conviction that the district court committed a clear error of judgment," *United States v. Whitehead*, 532 F.3d 991, 996 (9th Cir.2008) (Bybee, J., dissenting), I believe that the sentence was an abuse of discretion.

It is understandable that the majority would adopt a highly deferential standard of reviewing the substantive reasonableness of the district court's decision, given that the Supreme Court's opinion in *Gall* focused primarily on what an appellate court may *not* do. It may not overturn an out-of-Guidelines sentence merely because it "might reasonably have concluded that a different sentence was appropriate." 128 S.Ct. at 597. Nor may it require district courts to follow rigid mathematical formulas or demonstrate that extraordinary circumstances exist in order to justify a sentence outside the Guidelines. *Id.* at 595. Missing from the majority opinion in *Gall*, however, is any discussion of the

---

8. The dissent refers to Autery as a "child pornographer." This term is misleading, as a "pornographer" is defined as "one that *produces* pornography." *Webster's Third New International Dictionary* 1767 (2002) (emphasis added). Without minimizing the seriousness of child pornography possession, we note that Autery was not charged with or convicted of producing pornography.

circumstances under which a court of appeals may reverse a district court's sentence as substantively unreasonable. It is possible to read *Gall* as limiting the role of the court of appeals to ensuring that district courts follow the proper procedures in determining sentences, and that appears to be the trend of our case law. So long as the district court does not commit any procedural errors, the court of appeals should almost always defer to the district court's familiarity with the case and greater experience in sentencing. *See Whitehead*, 532 F.3d at 993.... I do not believe, however, that the Court in *Gall* intended to require such extreme deference from courts of appeals. The Court explicitly stated that "the familiar abuse-of-discretion standard of review now applies to appellate review of sentencing decisions." *Gall*, 128 S.Ct. at 594. As Justice Alito noted in his dissent in *Gall*, "Appellate review for abuse of discretion is not an empty formality. A decision calling for the exercise of judicial discretion 'hardly means that it is unfettered by meaningful standards or shielded from thorough appellate review.'" *Id.* at 607 (Alito, J., dissenting) (quoting *Albemarle Paper Co. v. Moody*, 422 U.S. 405, 416, 95 S.Ct. 2362, 45 L.Ed.2d 280 (1975))....

The ordinariness of Autery as a defendant, and the inappropriateness of the district court's imposition of a probationary sentence, is particularly pronounced in comparison with the circumstances of the defendant in *Gall*. Brian Gall participated in a conspiracy to sell ecstasy while attending college in Iowa. 128 S.Ct. at 591–92. He voluntarily withdrew from the conspiracy after seven months and moved to Arizona, where he lived as a law-abiding citizen. *Id.* at 592. When his role in the drug ring was discovered by law enforcement, he confessed his involvement and cooperated fully with the authorities. *Id.* While he was in Iowa on bail during the time his case was pending, he started his own construction business. *Id.* Reasonable minds might differ as to the proper sentence for Gall, but he provided strong evidence that he had self-rehabilitated and was no longer a threat to commit more crimes. There were clear reasons to support the district court's decision that Gall differed from other defendants convicted of similar crimes and that probation was more appropriate than a within-Guidelines sentence of 30–37 months.

Here, the district court followed the proper procedures, but the sentence it reached, unlike in *Gall*, is simply not supported by the record. A meaningful abuse-of-discretion review can overturn a sentence in a case like this and maintain some sense of uniformity in sentencing while still allowing district courts to sentence defendants such as Gall to sentences substantially lower than suggested by the Guidelines.... Because I am firmly convinced that the district court committed a clear error in judgment in sentencing Autery, I would vacate the sentence as unreasonable and remand the case to the district court for resentencing.

6. Conditions Imposed in Sentencing

a. Limitations on Computer Use

United States v. Thielemann

Third Circuit, 2009

575 F.3d 265

GARTH, Circuit Judge:

The defendant, Paul Thielemann, was indicted and pleaded guilty to one count of receiving child pornography. He was sentenced to the statutory maximum of 240 months of imprisonment, plus 10 years of supervised release subject to a number of conditions, including two Special Conditions of Supervision.... Thielemann appeals his prison sentence because the District Court considered non-charged relevant conduct in fashioning his sentence. Thielemann also challenges the two Special Conditions of Supervised Release imposed by the District Court. These conditions restricted Thielemann's computer use and his viewing of sexually explicit material....

On January 19, 2007, Thielemann transmitted child pornography to another internet user through his America Online e-mail. America Online detected the transmission and reported it to the Delaware State Police ("DSP"), who executed a search warrant and seized Thielemann's computer on February 23, 2007. The DSP found several hundred pornographic images of children, as well as computerized logs of online "chats" with Christopher Phillips ("Phillips"),[1] an internet user with whom Thielemann had a sexual relationship.[2] ... The transcripts of the online "chats" revealed, among other things, that after boasting about a number of alleged sexual encounters with minors, Thielemann encouraged Phillips to have sex with an eight-year-old victim — a female child whom Phillips could control ("the victim").... Thielemann then sent Phillips a picture of a toddler performing a sexual act on an adult male and claimed the picture depicted him (Thielemann) and a minor over whom Thielemann had control. Thielemann offered to "walk [Phillips] through" these sex acts with the victim.... Later, Thielemann offered Phillips $20 to turn on his web cam and place the victim on Phillips's lap so the victim would see Thielemann's exposed penis. Phillips complied. Thielemann then offered Phillips $100 to rub the victim's genitals and lift up her skirt, which Phillips did. The "chat" transcript implies that Phillips also exposed himself to the victim. Thielemann then asked Phillips to masturbate with the victim on his lap, but it is unclear if Phillips did so.... These saved "chat" files on Thielemann's computer led the police to Phillips, who denied exposing himself to the victim or touching her inappropriately.[3] Thielemann later claimed he did not know the child was on the web cam.

On June 26, 2007, a Grand Jury convened in the United States District Court for the District of Delaware and returned an eighteen-count indictment against Thielemann charging him with the following: Counts One and Two, production of child pornography and conspiracy to produce child pornography in violation of 18 U.S.C. §2251(a) & (e); Counts Three through Six, receipt of child pornography in violation of 18 U.S.C. §2252A(a)(2) & (b)(1); Counts Seven through Eleven, distribution of child pornography in violation of 18 U.S.C. §2252A(a)(1) & (b)(1); Count Twelve, possession of child pornography in violation of 18 U.S.C. §2252A(a)(5)(B) & (b)(2); Counts Thirteen through Seventeen, receipt/distribution of obscenity depicting children in violation of 18 U.S.C. §§1466A(a)(2)(A) & (B), and 2252A(b)(1); and Count Eighteen, possession of obscenity depicting children in violation of 18 U.S.C. §§1466A(b)(2)(A) & (B), and 2252A(b)(2). The offense conduct charged in this indictment occurred between June 16, 2006, and February 23, 2007.[4]

Prior to trial, the Government disclosed copies of the "chat" logs to Thielemann. However, on October 12, 2007, Thielemann moved to compel production of a copy of his computer's entire hard drive. The Government refused to produce it, citing 18 U.S.C. §3509(m)(2)(A), which provides:

> Notwithstanding Rule 16 of the Federal Rules of Criminal Procedure, a court shall deny, in any criminal proceeding, any request by the defendant to copy,

---

1. Phillips is a co-defendant who eventually pleaded guilty to distribution of child pornography in violation of 18 U.S.C. §2252A(a)(1) & (b)(1). He received a 240-month sentence.

2. We reproduce, *infra*, a segment of a "chat" between Thielemann and Phillips on June 11, 2006, as an example of the "chats" that took place between these two men. ["Chats" are omitted here.]

3. The victim contradicted Phillips's statement: "During the initial interview, when asked if she ever had to touch a male penis, the 8 year old girl [identified Phillips]." ...

4. Thielemann had also engaged in explicit chats with other men during which he discussed having sexual relations with children, and sent and received child pornography. A number of Thielemann's associates were separately indicted and pleaded guilty to various similar charges.

photograph, duplicate, or otherwise reproduce any property or material that constitutes child pornography..., so long as the Government makes the property or material reasonably available to the defendant.

The Government told Thielemann he would have sufficient access to the computer files.... [footnote omitted].

On January 18, 2008, Thielemann pleaded guilty to a one-count Information charging him with receipt of child pornography (18 U.S.C. §2252A(a)(2) & (b)(1)). In the Memorandum of Plea Agreement, Thielemann admitted that he engaged in "chats" with Phillips, and that during a "chat," Phillips "had on his lap a minor, visible to the defendant, and at the defendant's encouragement and inducement [Phillips] did simulate masturbation of the minor, and did pose the minor in order to effect the lascivious exhibition of the minor's pubic area." ... Thielemann accordingly suspended his motions to compel production of evidence....

District courts may impose special conditions of supervised release, but such conditions must be "reasonably related to the factors set forth in [§3553(a)]" and must "involve[ ] no greater deprivation of liberty than is reasonably necessary" to deter future crime, protect the public, and rehabilitate the defendant. 18 U.S.C. §3583(d)(1)–(2); *Voelker*, 489 F.3d at 144 (requiring some evidence of a tangible relationship between the terms of supervised release and the offense or the history of the defendant).... On appeal, Thielemann claims that two special conditions (restricting his access to computers and sexually explicit material) were imposed in error. However, Thielemann registered no objection to these conditions in the District Court. We accordingly review for plain error.... We hold that the District Court did not err when it required Thielemann to comply with these conditions....

District courts generally must make factual findings to justify special terms of supervised release. *Voelker*, 489 F.3d at 144. If a court does not explain its reasons, "we may nevertheless affirm the condition if we can 'ascertain any viable basis for the ... restriction in the record before the District Court ... on our own.'" *Id.* (citation omitted).... While the District Court did not specifically explain its rationale in barring Thielemann from sexually explicit materials, the record clearly shows that the District Court's purpose was to rehabilitate Thielemann, to protect children, and to deter future criminal activity.

We have held that "District Court[s] could, perfectly consonant with the Constitution, restrict [a defendant's] access to sexually oriented materials" if, like any other restriction, the term had a clear nexus to the goals of supervised release. *United States v. Loy*, 237 F.3d 251, 267 (3d Cir.2001). However, "there are First Amendment implications for a ban that extends to explicit material involving adults."[13] *Voelker*, 489 F.3d at 151. When a ban restricts access to material protected by the First Amendment,[14] courts must balance the §3553(a) considerations "against the serious First Amendment concerns endemic in such a restriction." *Id.*[15] It is evident that the District Court's restriction in this case would

---

13. A ban on sexually explicit material involving children is, of course, reasonable, but unnecessary considering child pornography is already illegal "and the statutorily mandated conditions of supervised release require [defendants] to comply with" child pornography laws. *United States v. Voelker*, 489 F.3d 139, 151 (3d Cir.2007).

14. Protected materials include "nonobscene, sexually explicit materials involving persons over the age of 17." *United States v. X-Citement Video, Inc.*, 513 U.S. 64, 72, 115 S.Ct. 464, 130 L.Ed.2d 372 (1994).

15. We recognize that a term of supervised release restricting access to adult sexually oriented materials must be "narrowly tailored," *i.e.*, that the restriction must result in a benefit to public safety. *United States v. Loy*, 237 F.3d 251, 266 (3d Cir.2001).

protect children from the predatory conduct of Thielemann and thus could contribute to Thielemann's rehabilitation. Accordingly, the purposes served by the Special Condition far outweigh any Constitutional concerns raised in *Loy* and *Voelker*.

In *Loy*, we rejected a condition which prohibited Loy from possessing pornography. Loy had pleaded guilty to receipt of child pornography. His terms of supervised release included a provision prohibiting him from possessing "all forms of pornography, including legal adult pornography." *Loy*, 237 F.3d at 253. We noted that restrictions on sexual materials were generally permissible because "almost any restriction upon sexually explicit material may well aid in rehabilitation and protection of the public. Only in the exceptional case, where a ban could apply to any art form that employs nudity, will a defendant's exercise of First Amendment rights be unconstitutionally circumscribed or chilled." *Id.* at 266.... However, after discussing the mercurial meaning of the term "pornography," we held that the provision was (1) overly broad and violated the First Amendment because it "might apply to a wide swath of work ranging from serious art to ubiquitous advertising," and that it was (2) unconstitutionally vague because "its breadth is unclear." *Id.* at 267.... Nonetheless, we suggested that "the Constitution would not forbid a more tightly defined restriction on legal, adult pornography, perhaps one that ... borrowed applicable language from the federal statutory definition of child pornography located at 18 U.S.C. §2256(8)." *Id.* Several years later, the District Court in *Voelker* took heed of our suggestion and handed down just such a reformulated restriction relying on 18 U.S.C. §2256(2).

In *Voelker*, among other holdings, we overturned a lifetime ban on Voelker's access to sexually explicit material. Voelker had pleaded guilty to possession of child pornography after he was caught briefly exposing his three-year-old daughter's buttocks over web cam, and later admitted to downloading pornographic images of children. *United States v. Voelker*, 489 F.3d 139, 142 (3d Cir.2007). The District Court imposed a lifelong term of supervised release which, *inter alia*, prohibited Voelker from possessing "any materials ... depicting and/or describing sexually explicit conduct as defined at Title 18, United States Code, Section 2256(2)." *Id.* at 143 (And, see the definition of "sexually explicit conduct" at note 8, *supra*).[16] Voelker argued that the condition violated the First Amendment and involved a "greater deprivation of liberty than is reasonably necessary to deter future criminal conduct and protect the public." *Id.* at 150.... We held in *Voelker* that a nexus between the restriction and the goals of supervised release was absent. *Id.* In particular, we explained that "nothing on th[e] record suggests that sexually explicit material involving *only adults* contributed in any way to Voelker's offense, nor is there any reason to believe that viewing such material would cause Voelker to reoffend." *Id.* at 151 (emphasis added).

We do not read our precedents as foreclosing the use of conditions banning access to *sexually explicit* adult materials, particularly when children are victims and are victimized sexually by adults as a means to gratify adult desires. Rather, *Loy* stood for the proposition that a blanket ban on "all forms of pornography" may be constitutionally infirm, but that more limited provisions "borrow[ing] applicable language from the federal statutory definition of child pornography," *Loy*, 237 F.3d at 267, are permissible. Whatever may be the parameters of "pornography," *see id.* at 263–65, the present record transcends the characterization of mere pornography. Here, the record reveals explicit child exploitation and victimization by Thielemann in order to satisfy his sexual appetite for adult men.

---

16. The "sexually explicit" materials condition in *Voelker* is nearly identical to the analogous Special Condition at issue in this appeal.

Unlike in *Voelker*, there is overwhelming evidence in this record to conclude that Thielemann's exposure to sexual material, albeit involving only adults, will contribute to future offenses by Thielemann. The report of Thielemann's own forensic psychiatrist, Carla Rodgers, M.D., reiterates Thielemann's commingling of adult and child sexual conduct. The report indicates that Thielemann "used [pornographic images of children] in order to seduce heterosexual males into allowing him to perform fellatio on them." ... While Dr. Rodgers concluded that Thielemann's primary interest was in men, and that he was "not at risk of child molestation," the report clearly demonstrates Thielemann's sexual predilections.[17] ... Moreover, the "chats" unambiguously reveal that Thielemann's sexual experiences with adults and adult pornography were inextricably linked to his sexual interest in children. Thielemann made no secret of the fact that his desire arose from adult men who are aroused and sexually excited by children. Said Thielemann: "I used [children] to get what I wanted. I wanted to see men turned on to their peak so they could come and do stuff to me." ... Indeed, every one of Thielemann's adult sexual interactions with Phillips involved children....

As we held in *Loy*, 237 F.3d at 266, "almost any restriction upon sexually explicit material may well aid in rehabilitation and protection of the public." Here, a reading of the "chats" reveals that restricting Thielemann's access to adult sexually explicit material will undoubtedly aid in rehabilitation and protection of the public.... Given Thielemann's sexual desire for *adult* men who abuse children, banning Thielemann from adult sexually explicit material would be an additional deterrent to Thielemann's sexual arousal and sexual excitement, as it would preclude him from including children in his future sexual experiences.[19] Otherwise, exposure to adult sexually explicit material might very well lead Thielemann to encourage his male associates either to initiate or to continue their abuse of children....

We hold that there is a significant nexus between restricting Thielemann from access to adult "sexually explicit" material and the goals of supervised release, and that the restriction here is not overbroad or vague considering the content of the instant record. As such, First Amendment implications are not involved. The balancing protocol required by *Voelker* tilts heavily in favor of protection of the public and children when we consider this record of "inciting to child abuse." We are fully satisfied that the very unusual situation presented in this case thoroughly predominates over the First Amendment concerns raised in *Loy*. Accordingly, the District Court committed no error, let alone plain error, in requiring Thielemann's compliance with this Special Condition of Supervised Release. *See United States v. Voelker*, 489 F.3d 139, 143 n. 1 (3d Cir.2007); *United States v. Olano*, 507 U.S. 725, 113 S.Ct. 1770, 123 L.Ed.2d 508 (1993)....

The District Court's rationale for imposing the computer restriction is self-evident. Even a cursory reading of the record (and the reproduced sample of the June 11, 2006 "chat," ["chat" omitted here]) and the evidence acknowledged by Thielemann when he pleaded guilty, reveal that the offenses in this case evolved from the use of a computer

---

17. The children subjected to Thielemann's sexual predilection may not, in the opinion of Thielemann's psychiatrist, be directly physically harmed by Thielemann, but Dr. Rodgers, at no time, expressed herself about the psychological trauma experienced by these abused children. Can anyone doubt that an eight-year-old victim, abused by Phillips under the direction of Thielemann, will be psychologically scarred at present and during her later years?

19. Indeed, it is clear that the restriction on "sexually explicit" materials would encompass the activities Thielemann engaged in with Phillips, including explicit web "chats," transmission of homemade pornography, and real-time sexual interactions over web cam.

and the internet. The District Court clearly and properly imposed the computer condition to deter future crimes via the internet and to protect children.... The issue is whether this restriction was reasonably related to the § 3553(a) factors and "involve[d] no greater deprivation of liberty than is reasonably necessary" to meet those goals. 18 U.S.C. § 3583(d)(1)–(2). An analysis of two of our prior cases is instructive in this regard.

In *United States v. Crandon*, 173 F.3d 122 (3d Cir.1999), the defendant met a teenager on the internet and traveled across state lines to take photos of their sexual encounter. Crandon pleaded guilty to receipt of child pornography and the District Court imposed a three-year ban prohibiting him from using any "computer network, bulletin board, Internet, or exchange format involving computers" without permission from the Probation Office. *Id.* at 125. We upheld the provision because Crandon used the internet to exploit a child, and the restriction would deter him from future crimes and protect the public.

As noted above, in *Voelker*, the defendant challenged a lifelong ban on using computers and the internet consequent to a guilty plea to receipt of child pornography. We held that the restriction was not narrowly tailored because it was lifelong, contained no exceptions, and ignored the "ubiquitous presence of the internet." 489 F.3d at 144–46. The terms of Thielemann's supervised release are more analogous to those we upheld in *Crandon*. *See also United States v. Paul*, 274 F.3d 155, 167–70 (5th Cir.2001).... Admittedly, "[c]omputers and Internet access have become virtually indispensable in the modern world." *Voelker*, 489 F.3d at 148 n. 8 (citation and quotation marks omitted). However, Thielemann can own or use a *personal* computer as long as it is not connected to the internet; thus he is allowed to use word processing programs and other benign software. Further, he may seek permission from the Probation Office to use the internet during the term of his ten-year restriction, which is a far cry from the unyielding lifetime restriction in *Voelker*.

The parameters of the computer restriction in this case are far less troubling than those in *Voelker*. Moreover, the restriction is not disproportionate when viewed in the context of Thielemann's conduct. Thielemann did more than simply trade child pornography; he utilized internet communication technologies to facilitate, entice, and encourage the real-time molestation of a child.... The restriction on computer and internet use therefore shares a nexus to the goals of deterrence and protection of the public, and does not involve a greater deprivation of liberty than is necessary in this case. There was no plain error....

For the reasons stated above, we affirm Thielemann's sentence and the two challenged Special Conditions of Supervised Release.

Notes

Prohibiting sex offenders from accessing pornography as a part of sentence condition is common for federal and state courts. *See, e.g., United States v. Locke*, 482 F.3d 764 (5th Cir. 2007) (upholding federal district court's special probation condition prohibiting defendant, who possessed child pornography, from having access to the Internet and from viewing, possessing, or obtaining pornography in any form); *State v. Murphy*, No. CR9688132 (Conn. Super. Ct. Jan. 23, 2007), 2007 WL 354870 (defendant violated probation conditions by possessing pornography while a sex offender); *Farrell v. Burke*, 449 F.3d 470 (2d Cir. 2006) (upholding special condition prohibiting defendant, who paid four 13- to 16-year-old boys to engage in sex with him, from possessing pornographic material); *People v. Huber*, 139 P.3d 628 (Colo. 2006) (holding that defendant, who was charged with sexual assault on a child by one in a position of trust and indecent exposure, violated conditions of judgment by possessing pornographic images); *Fernandez v. State*, No. A-8484, (Alaska Ct. App. Mar. 31, 2004), 2004 WL 719553 (affirming lower court's imposition of probation condition that barred appellant, who pleaded guilty to two counts of first-degree sexual abuse of a minor, from possessing adult pornography).

As demonstrated in the *Thielemann* decision, a proper sentence restriction requires a sufficient nexus between the restriction imposed and the defendant's conduct. The *Thielemann* court found a sufficient nexus between a restriction on computer access to adult sexually explicit material and the defendant's receipt of child pornography. *See also Kasischke v. State*, 991 So. 2d 803 (Fla. 2008). In *Kasischke v. State*, the defendant pled guilty to three counts of lewd or lascivious battery and exhibition on a child under age 16 after paying a 15-year-old boy to allow him to perform oral sex on the boy and masturbating in the boy's presence. *Kasischke*, 991 So. 2d at 805, 806. As part of his sentence condition, Kasischke was prohibited from "viewing, owning, or possessing any obscene, pornographic, or sexually stimulating visual or auditory material, including telephone, electronic media, computer programs, or computer services that are relevant to the offender's deviant behavior patterns." *Id.* at 806. After his release from prison, a search of the defendant's home revealed allegedly pornographic material; his community control was revoked and he was again incarcerated. The issue for the court in *Kasischke* was whether the scope of the statutory prohibition covered *all* pornographic material or only material relevant to the defendant's "particular deviant behavior pattern." In finding the statute ambiguous and applying the rule of lenity, the court held that the statute must be interpreted to require *any* prohibited material to be relevant to the defendant's particular deviant behavior pattern. However, other courts have held that a sufficient nexus is lacking when the defendant did not use the Internet to actively contact a child and solicit sexual contact. *See, e.g., United States v. Miller*, 594 F.3d 172 (3d Cir. 2010) (distinguishing *Thielemann*). *But see United States v. Borders*, 489 Fed. Appx. 858, 864 (6th Cir. 2012) (declining to follow *Miller* and summarizing circuit split on issue of whether Internet bans, subject to approval by probation officer, may "impose a greater deprivation of liberty than is reasonably necessary to deter illegal conduct and protect the public.") (internal quotation marks omitted).

Notwithstanding the requirement for a sufficient nexus, some courts "condition a sex offender's ability to live in the community on total abstinence from sexual materials as well as the Internet and other computerized/telephonic equipment that facilitate one's access to prohibited materials." *Id.* at 808, n.5. *See, e.g., United States v. Ristine*, 335 F.3d 692, 694 (8th Cir. 2003) (upholding special conditions prohibiting the defendant from "owning or possessing 'any pornographic materials,'" and from having Internet service at his house); *United States v. Taylor*, 338 F.3d 1280, 1285 (11th Cir. 2003) (upholding a special condition of probation prohibiting the defendant from "using or possessing a computer with Internet access"); *State v. Ehli*, 681 N.W.2d 808, 810 (N.D. 2004) (upholding a condition prohibiting the defendant from using the Internet); *People v. Harrisson*, 134 Cal. App. 4th 637, 36 Cal. Rptr. 3d 264, 266, 271 (2005) (upholding a condition prohibiting use of the Internet "in any way whatsoever").

b. Satellite-Based Monitoring

State v. Dykes

Supreme Court of South Carolina, 2013
403 S.C. 499, 744 S.E.2d 505

Justice KITTREDGE.

Jennifer Dykes appeals the circuit court's order requiring that she be subject to satellite monitoring for the rest of her life pursuant to sections 23-3-540(C) and (H) of the South

Carolina Code of Laws (Supp.2011).... Section 23-3-540 represents a codification of what is commonly referred to as Jessica's Law. Many states have some version of this law, which was enacted in memory of Jessica Lunsford, a nine-year-old girl who was raped and murdered by a convicted sex offender in Florida. Across the country, these laws heightened criminal sentences and post-release monitoring of child sex offenders. The specific issue presented in this case concerns the mandate for lifetime global positioning satellite monitoring with no judicial review. The complete absence of judicial review under South Carolina's legislative scheme is more stringent than the statutory scheme of other jurisdictions. A common approach among other states is either to require a predicate finding of probability to re-offend or to provide a judicial review process, which allows for, upon a proper showing, a court order releasing the offender from the satellite monitoring requirements. *See generally*, N.C. Gen.Stat. Ann. § 14-208.43 (West 2010) (providing a termination procedure one year after the imposition of the satellite based monitoring or a risk assessment for certain offenders). While we hold that the statute's initial mandatory imposition of satellite monitoring is constitutional, the lifetime requirement without judicial review is unconstitutional....

Dykes, when twenty-six years old, was indicted for lewd act on a minor in violation of Section 16-15-140 of the South Carolina Code (2006) as a result of her sexual relationship with a fourteen-year-old female. Dykes pled guilty to lewd act on a minor and was sentenced to fifteen years' imprisonment, suspended upon the service of three years and five years' probation.[1] ... Upon her release, Dykes was notified verbally and in writing that pursuant to section 23-3-540(C) she would be placed on satellite monitoring if she were to violate the terms of her probation. Shortly thereafter, Dykes violated her probation in multiple respects.[2] Dykes did not contest any of these violations, though she did offer testimony in mitigation.

The State recommended a two-year partial revocation of Dykes' probation and mandatory lifetime satellite monitoring. S.C.Code Ann. section 23-3-540(A) mandates that when an individual has been convicted of engaging in or attempting criminal sexual conduct with a minor in the first degree (CSC-First) or lewd act on a minor, the court must order that person placed on satellite monitoring. Likewise, if a person has been convicted of such offenses before the effective date of the statute and violates a term of her probation, parole, or supervision program, she must also be placed on satellite monitoring. *See* S.C.Code Ann. § 23-3-540(C). The individual must remain on monitoring for as long as she is to remain on the sex offender registry, which is for life. S.C.Code Ann. § 23-3-540(H); *see also* S.C.Code Ann. § 23-3-460 (requiring biannual registration for life).[3] Significantly, the lifetime monitoring requirement for one convicted of CSC-First or lewd act on a minor is not subject to any judicial review process. *See* S.C.Code Ann. § 23-3-540(H) (prohibiting judicial review of the lifetime monitoring for CSC-First and lewd act on a minor).... In contrast, if a person is convicted of committing or attempting any offense which requires registration as a sex offender *other than* CSC-First or lewd act on a minor, the court has discretion with respect to whether the individual

---

1. Because her offense predated the satellite monitoring statute, she was not subject to monitoring at the time of her plea.

2. Five citations and arrest warrants were issued to her for various probation violations: a citation pertaining to her relationship with a convicted felon whom Dykes met while incarcerated and with whom she was then residing; an arrest warrant for Dykes' continued relationship with that individual; a citation for drinking an alcoholic beverage; a citation for being terminated from sex offender counseling after she cancelled or rescheduled too many appointments; and an arrest warrant for failing to maintain an approved residence and changing her address without the knowledge or consent of her probation agent.

3. Once activated, the monitor can pinpoint the individual's location to within fifteen meters.

should be placed on satellite monitoring. *See* S.C.Code Ann. § 23-3-540(B), (D), (G)(1).[4] In addition, after ten years, an individual who has committed the above-stated crimes may petition the court to have the monitoring removed upon a showing that she has complied with the monitoring requirements and there is no longer a need to continue monitoring her. If the court denies her petition, she may petition again every five years.[5] S.C.Code Ann. § 23-3-540(H)....

At her probation revocation hearing, Dykes objected to the constitutionality of mandatory lifetime monitoring. In support of her arguments, Dykes presented expert testimony that she poses a low risk of reoffending and that one's risk of reoffending cannot be determined solely by the offense committed. The State offered no evidence, relying instead on the mandatory, nondiscretionary requirement of the statute.... The circuit court found Dykes to be in willful violation of her probation and that she had notice of the potential for satellite monitoring. The court denied Dykes' constitutional challenges and found it was statutorily mandated to impose satellite monitoring without making any findings as to Dykes' likelihood of reoffending. The court also revoked Dykes' probation for two years, but it ordered that her probation be terminated upon release. This appeal followed....

Dykes asserts she has a fundamental right to be "let alone." We disagree. The United States Supreme Court has cautioned restraint in the recognition of rights deemed to be fundamental in a constitutional sense. *See Washington v. Glucksberg*, 521 U.S. 702, 117 S.Ct. 2258, 138 L.Ed.2d 772 (1997) (noting the Supreme Court's reluctance to expand the concept of substantive due process). Indeed, courts must "exercise the utmost care whenever we are asked to break new ground in this field, lest the liberty protected by the Due Process Clause be subtly transformed into the policy preferences of [members of the judiciary]." *Id.* at 720, 117 S.Ct. 2258. The Due Process Clause protects only "those fundamental rights and liberties which are, objectively, 'deeply rooted in this Nation's history and tradition.'" *Id.* at 720–21, 117 S.Ct. 2258 (internal citations omitted). We reject the suggestion that a convicted child sex offender has a fundamental right to be "let alone" that is "deeply rooted in this Nation's history and tradition."

Our rejection of Dykes' fundamental right argument flows in part from the premise that satellite monitoring is predominantly civil. *See Smith v. Doe*, 538 U.S. 84, 123 S.Ct. 1140, 155 L.Ed.2d 164 (2003) (noting that whether a statute is criminal or civil primarily is a question of statutory construction). Where, as here, the legislature deems a statutory scheme civil, "only the clearest proof" will transform a civil regulatory scheme into that which imposes a criminal penalty. *Id.* at 92, 123 S.Ct. 1140 (quoting *Hudson v. United States*, 522 U.S. 93, 100, 118 S.Ct. 488, 139 L.Ed.2d 450 (1997)) (internal quotations omitted).

---

4. The offenses include: criminal sexual conduct with a minor in the second degree; engaging a child for sexual performance; producing, directing, or promoting sexual performance by a child; assaults with intent to commit criminal sexual conduct involving a minor; violation of the laws concerning obscenity, material harmful to minors, child exploitation, and child prostitution; kidnapping of a person under the age of eighteen unless the defendant is a parent; and trafficking in persons under the age of eighteen if the offense includes a completed or attempted criminal sexual offense. S.C.Code Ann. § 23-3-540(G)(1).

5. As long as the individual is being monitored, she must comply with all the terms set by the State, report damage to the device, pay for the costs of the monitoring (unless she can show financial hardship), and not remove or tamper with the device; failure to follow these rules may result in criminal penalties. S.C.Code Ann. §§ 23-3-540(I) to (L).

Notwithstanding the absence of a fundamental right, we do find that lifetime imposition of satellite monitoring implicates a protected liberty interest to be free from permanent, unwarranted governmental interference. We agree with other jurisdictions that have held the requirement of satellite monitoring places significant restraints on offenders that amount to a liberty interest. *See Commonwealth v. Cory*, 454 Mass. 559, 911 N.E.2d 187, 196 (2009) (finding satellite monitoring burdens an offender's liberty interest in two ways, by "its permanent, physical attachment to the offender, and by its continuous surveillance of the offender's activities"); *United States v. Smedley*, 611 F.Supp.2d 971, 975 (E.D.Mo.2009) (holding that imposing home detention with electronic monitoring as condition of release impinged on liberty interest); *United States v. Merritt*, 612 F.Supp.2d 1074, 1079 (D.Neb.2009) (stating that "[a] curfew with electronic monitoring restricts the defendant's ability to move about at will and implicates a liberty interest protected under the Due Process Clause"); *State v. Stines*, 200 N.C.App. 193, 683 S.E.2d 411 (2009) (holding that requiring enrollment in satellite-based monitoring program deprives an offender of a significant liberty interest). Therefore, having served her sentence, Dykes' mandatory enrollment in the satellite monitoring program invokes minimal due process protection.

Thus, courts must "ensure[ ] that legislation which deprives a person of a life, liberty, or property right have, at a minimum, a rational basis, and not be arbitrary...." In *re Treatment and Care of Luckabaugh*, 351 S.C. 122, 139–40, 568 S.E.2d 338, 346 (2002); *see also Nebbia v. N.Y.*, 291 U.S. 502, 525, 54 S.Ct. 505, 78 L.Ed. 940 (1934) ("[T]he guarant[ee] of due process, as has often been held, demands only that the law shall not be unreasonable, arbitrary, or capricious...."); *Hamilton v. Bd. of Trs. of Oconee Cnty. Sch. Dist.*, 282 S.C. 519, 319 S.E.2d 717 (Ct.App.1984) (holding that, to comport with due process, the legislation must have a rational basis for the deprivation and may not be "so inadequate that the judiciary will characterize it as arbitrary")....

The General Assembly has expressly outlined the purpose of the state's sex offender registration and electronic monitoring provisions:

> The intent of this article is to promote the state's fundamental right to provide for the public health, welfare, and safety of its citizens [by] ... provid[ing] law enforcement with the tools needed in investigating criminal offenses. Statistics show that sex offenders often pose a high risk of reoffending. Additionally, law enforcement's efforts to protect communities, conduct investigations, and apprehend offenders who commit sex offenses are impaired by the lack of information about these convicted offenders who live within the law enforcement agency's jurisdiction.

S.C.Code Ann. § 23-3-400 (2007). This Court has examined this language and held "it is clear the General Assembly did not intend to punish sex offenders, but instead intended to protect the public from those sex offenders who may re-offend and to aid law enforcement in solving sex crimes." *State v. Walls*, 348 S.C. 26, 31, 558 S.E.2d 524, 526 (2002). Thus, a likelihood of re-offending lies at the core of South Carolina's civil statutory scheme.

In light of the General Assembly's stated purpose of protecting the public from sex offenders and aiding law enforcement, we find that the initial mandatory imposition of satellite monitoring for certain child-sex crimes satisfies the rational relationship test. Accordingly, we find constitutional the baseline requirement of section 23-3-540(C) that individuals convicted of CSC-First or lewd act on a minor mandatorily submit to electronic monitoring upon their release from incarceration or violation of their probation or parole.

Although we find the initial mandatory imposition of satellite monitoring under section 23-3-540(C) constitutional, we believe the final sentence of section 23-3-540(H) is unconstitutional, for it precludes judicial review for persons convicted of CSC-First or lewd act on a minor.[6] The complete absence of any opportunity for judicial review to assess a risk of re-offending, which is beyond the norm of Jessica's law, is arbitrary and cannot be deemed rationally related to the legislature's stated purpose of protecting the public from those with a high risk of re-offending. *See Luckabaugh,* 351 S.C. at 139–40, 568 S.E.2d at 346 (finding due process ensures that a statute which deprives a person of a liberty interest has "at a minimum, a rational basis, and may not be arbitrary"); *see also Lyng v. Int'l Union,* 485 U.S. 360, 375, 108 S.Ct. 1184, 99 L.Ed.2d 380 (1988) (Marshall, J., dissenting) (noting that although allegedly arbitrary legislation invokes the least intrusive rational basis test, that standard of review "is not a toothless one") (quoting *Mathews v. De Castro,* 429 U.S. 181, 185, 97 S.Ct. 431, 50 L.Ed.2d 389 (1976)); *Addington v. Texas,* 441 U.S. 418, 427, 99 S.Ct. 1804, 60 L.Ed.2d 323 (1979) (noting that although Texas has legitimate interest to protect the community from those that are mentally ill, Texas "has no interest in confining individuals involuntarily if they are not mentally ill or if they do not pose some danger to themselves or others").[7] Thus, we hold it is unconstitutional to impose lifetime satellite monitoring with no opportunity for judicial review, as is the case with CSC-First or lewd act pursuant to section 23-3-540(H).

The finding of unconstitutionality with respect to the non-reviewable lifetime monitoring requirement in section 23-3-540(H) does not require that we invalidate the remainder of the statute. This is so because of the legislature's inclusion of a severability clause. *See* 2006 Act No. 346 § 8 (stating that if a court were to find any portion of the statute unconstitutional, that holding does not affect the rest of the statute and the General Assembly would have passed it without that ineffective part). The only provision invalidated by today's decision is the portion of section 23-3-540(H) that prohibits only those convicted of CSC-First and lewd act on a minor from petitioning for judicial relief from the satellite monitoring.... [footnote omitted].

Consequently, Dykes and others similarly situated must comply with the monitoring requirement mandated by section 23-3-540(C). However, persons convicted of CSC-First and lewd act on a minor are entitled to avail themselves of the section 23-3-540(H) judicial review process as outlined for the balance of the offenses enumerated in section 23-3-540(G). We affirm the circuit court as modified.

AFFIRMED AS MODIFIED.

TOAL, C.J., concurs. PLEICONES, J., concurring in result only.

---

6. "A person may not petition the court if the person is required to register pursuant to this article for committing criminal sexual conduct with a minor in the first degree, pursuant to Section 16-3-655(A)(1), or committing or attempting a lewd act upon a child under sixteen, pursuant to Section 16-15-140."

7. This finding of arbitrariness is additionally supported by the South Carolina Constitution, which, unlike the United States Constitution, has an express privacy provision. *See* S.C. Const. art. I, § 10 ("The right of the people to be secure in their persons, houses, papers, and effects against unreasonable searches and seizures and unreasonable invasions of privacy shall not be violated...."). Our constitution's privacy provision informs the analysis of whether a state law is arbitrary and lends additional support to the conclusion that section 23-3-540(H)'s preclusion of judicial review for those offenders mandated to satellite monitoring under section 23-3-540(C) is unconstitutional. *Cf. State v. Weaver,* 374 S.C. 313, 649 S.E.2d 479 (2007) (holding that by articulating a specific prohibition against unreasonable invasions of privacy, the people of South Carolina have indicated a higher level of privacy protection than the federal Constitution).

HEARN, J., dissenting in a separate opinion in which BEATTY, J., concurs.

Justice HEARN.

Respectfully, I dissent. Because I believe Dykes' status as a sex offender does not diminish her entitlement to certain fundamental rights, I would hold section 23-3-540(C) is unconstitutional because it is not narrowly tailored. I express no opinion on the constitutionality of section 23-3-540(H) because that subsection was never challenged and is thus not before us.... [footnote omitted]. Dykes' argument is, and always has been, that subsection (C) of 23-3-540—the provision requiring lifetime satellite monitoring for persons who violate a term of probation and were convicted of committing criminal sexual conduct with a minor in the first degree or committing or attempting a lewd act upon a child under sixteen—violates her substantive due process rights by imposing monitoring without any showing of her likelihood to reoffend. By invalidating a statutory provision not challenged, the majority ignores those settled principles of error preservation and appellate jurisprudence, and awards Dykes a consolation prize she has never requested and arguably has no standing to accept....

In articulating the precise right that section 23-3-540(C) infringes, Dykes frames it as the right "to be let alone." However, in determining whether the right at stake is fundamental, we must first make "a 'careful description' of the asserted liberty right or interest [to] avoid[ ] overgeneralization in the historical inquiry." *Hawkins*, 195 F.3d at 747. I profoundly disagree with the majority's characterization of the right at issue as the right of "a convicted sex offender" to be "let alone." Formulating the right by couching it in terms of a specific class of persons fails to appreciate the extent of the right at stake and instead focuses on the the State's asserted justification for infringing upon that right. The Constitution does not recognize separate rights for different classes of citizens and instead guarantees rights to all American citizens. Furthermore, determining whether a law violates an individual's substantive due process rights is a two-pronged analysis that first requires a determination as to whether a fundamental right has been implicated, and if so, whether the State has a compelling interest to justify the infringement. Injecting the State's interest—here, Dykes' status as a convicted sex offender—into the articulation of the right at stake conflates the analysis and dooms from the outset any possibility of finding the alleged right fundamental. While a person's status as a sex offender may affect whether the State can infringe upon her fundamental rights in certain ways, that factor should be considered in the second part of the analysis. Therefore, when viewed in light of the facts of this case and the authorities relied upon by Dykes, I believe the narrow right on which she relies is the right to be free from the permanent, continuous tracking of her movements....

Recognizing the growing threat of technological advances on individual liberty, Justice Douglas warned almost fifty years ago that "[t]he dangers posed by wiretapping and electronic surveillance strike at the very heart of the democratic philosophy." *Osborn v. United States*, 385 U.S. 323, 352, 87 S.Ct. 429, 17 L.Ed.2d 394 (1966) (Douglas, J., dissenting). Even then, the scope of the government's ability to enter an individual's private life was troubling, and it has only increased with the advent of GPS monitoring. I therefore believe an examination of the general impact of the satellite monitoring scheme is helpful in understanding how the articulated right is here infringed and the extent to which Dykes' liberty is impacted. Recently, the Supreme Court had the opportunity to consider a similar issue in *United States v. Jones*, ___ U.S. ___, 132 S.Ct. 945, 181 L.Ed.2d 911 (2012), albeit in a different context. At issue in *Jones* was whether the government's surreptitious placement of a GPS tracking device on Jones's car without a warrant was an unreasonable search in violation of the Fourth Amendment to the United States Constitution. *Id.* at 947. The majority held it was because the attachment of the monitor to the car was a physical trespass on personal property for the purpose of obtaining information. *Id.* at 949.

In his concurring opinion, Justice Alito tackled the thornier question of whether this satellite monitoring violated an individual's reasonable expectation of privacy. Justice Alito observed that recent technological advancements have placed vast swaths of information in the public realm, a development which "will continue to shape the average person's expectations about the privacy of his or her daily movements."[11] *Id.* at 963 (Alito, J., concurring). With that in mind, he concluded monitoring one's movements on a public street for a relatively short period of time would not violate an individual's reasonable expectations of privacy. *Id.* at 964 (citing *United States v. Knotts*, 460 U.S. 276, 281–82, 103 S.Ct. 1081, 75 L.Ed.2d 55 (1983)). When that monitoring becomes long-term, however, the nature of the invasion changes:

> But the use of longer term GPS monitoring in investigations of most offenses impinges on expectations of privacy. For such offenses, society's expectation has been that law enforcement agents and others would not—and indeed, in the main, simply could not—secretly monitor and catalogue every single movement of an individual's car for a very long period.

Id. Applying this principle to the four-week monitoring at issue in *Jones*, Justice Alito concluded, "We need not identify with precision the point at which the tracking of th[e] vehicle became a search, for the line was surely crossed before the 4-week mark." *Id.*

Justice Sotomayor similarly noted we live in an age so inundated with technology that we may unwittingly "reveal a great deal of information about [our]selves to third parties in the course of carrying out mundane tasks." *Id.* at 957 (Sotomayor, J., concurring). In that vein, she agreed with Justice Alito's concerns about the intrusiveness of satellite monitoring: "GPS monitoring generates a precise, comprehensive record of a person's public movements that reflects a wealth of detail about her familial, political, professional, religious, and sexual associations."[12] *Id.* at 955. Thus, satellite monitoring invites the State into the subject's world twenty-four hours per day, seven days per week, and it provides the State with a precise view of her intimate habits, whether she is in public or not. If we are not careful about and cognizant of this fact, "the Government's unrestrained power to assemble data that reveal private aspects of identity is susceptible to abuse" and "may 'alter the relationship between citizen and government in a way that is inimical to democratic society.'" *Id.* at 956 (quoting *United States v. Cuevas-Perez*, 640 F.3d 272, 285 (7th Cir.2011) (Flaum, J., concurring)).

Although decided under the rubric of the Fourth Amendment, *Jones* is nevertheless instructive here. As Justice Alito and Justice Sotomayor incisively observed, the very concept of what we as citizens view as private is called into question by technology which facilitates unprecedented oversight of our lives. More importantly, at issue in this case is not just the tracking of individuals for a period of time while they are being investigated

---

11. In *Jones*, the monitor placed on the underside of Jones's car constantly tracked the car's movements over a four-week period without his knowledge. 132 S.Ct. at 947. The majority's contention to the contrary, Justice Alito noted there is no eighteenth century analogue to this type of investigation, because that "would have required either a gigantic coach, a very tiny constable, or both—not to mention a constable with incredible fortitude and patience." *Id.* at 958 (Alito, J., concurring).

12. Justice Alito's concurrence was joined by three other members of the Court, Justice Ginsburg, Justice Breyer, and Justice Kagan. After noting she shared the same concerns as Justice Alito, Justice Sotomayor wrote that "[r]esolution of these difficult questions ... is unnecessary" at this time because the majority's trespass theory was dispositive of the case. *Jones*, 132 S.Ct. at 957 (Sotomayor, J., concurring).

for a specific crime — as with a Fourth Amendment search — but the statutorily mandated monitoring of certain individuals for as long as they live with no ability to have it removed. *See Osborn*, 385 U.S. at 343, 87 S.Ct. 429 (Douglas, J., dissenting) ("These examples ... demonstrate an alarming trend whereby the privacy and dignity of our citizens is being whittled away by sometimes imperceptible steps. Taken individually, each step may be of little consequence. But when viewed as a whole, there begins to emerge a society quite unlike any we have seen — a society in which government may intrude into the secret regions of man's life at will."); *United States v. Pineda-Moreno*, 617 F.3d 1120, 1124 (9th Cir.2010) (Kozinski, J., dissenting from the denial of rehearing en banc) ("By holding that this kind of surveillance doesn't impair an individual's reasonable expectation of privacy, the panel hands the government the power to track the movements of every one of us, every day of our lives.").

I therefore conclude that the right of an individual to be free from the government's permanent, continuous tracking of her movements is easily encompassed by the larger protection of liberty and personal privacy accorded by the Constitution. As our history of protestations on government intrusion from Blackstone to *Jones* illustrates, our Constitution was designed to guarantee a certain freedom from government interference in the day-to-day order of our lives which lies at the heart of a free society. Accordingly, I believe neither liberty nor justice would exist if the government could, without sufficient justification, constantly monitor the precise location of an individual twenty-four hours a day until she dies. In my opinion, safeguarding against this Orwellian nightmare[13] falls squarely within the ambit of fundamental precepts embraced by the drafters of the Constitution. I would therefore hold that Dykes has a fundamental right to be free from the permanent, continuous tracking of her movements which the State may only infringe upon where it demonstrates the statute at issue is narrowly tailored to serve a compelling interest....

It is beyond question that "[s]ex offenders are a serious threat in this Nation." *McKune v. Lile*, 536 U.S. 24, 32, 122 S.Ct. 2017, 153 L.Ed.2d 47 (2002). In fact, "the victims of sexual assault are most often juveniles," and "[w]hen convicted sex offenders reenter society, they are much more likely than any other type of offender to be rearrested for a new rape or sexual assault." *Id.* at 32–33, 122 S.Ct. 2017. Thus, the General Assembly noted "[s]tatistics show that sex offenders often pose a high risk of re-offending," S.C.Code Ann. § 23-3-400 (2007), prompting it to enact provisions "to protect the public from those sex offenders who may re-offend," *State v. Walls*, 348 S.C. 26, 31, 558 S.E.2d 524, 526 (2002). Accordingly, I recognize Dykes' status as a convicted sex offender is relevant to the analysis. However, any infringement which is substantially justified by the possibility that an individual may reoffend — without any actual consideration of her likelihood to reoffend — belies a conclusion that the statute is narrowly tailored. Monitoring sex offenders who pose a low risk of reoffending for the rest of their lives is not "sufficiently weighty" such that the subject's liberty interest in being free from government monitoring must be "subordinated to the greater needs of society." *Salerno*, 481 U.S. at 750–51, 107 S.Ct. 2095.

I therefore find that requiring Dykes to submit to satellite monitoring for the rest of her life without an assessment of her risk of reoffending violates her substantive due process rights. To paraphrase Blackstone, section 23-3-540(C)'s application to Dykes has

---

13. George Orwell's novel 1984 increasingly appears less of a dystopian fantasy and more a cautionary tale:

> There was of course no way of knowing whether you were being watched at any given moment. How often, or on what system, the Thought Police plugged in on any individual wire was guesswork. It was even conceivable that they watched everybody all the time.

George Orwell, 1984 6 (1949).

the potential to decrease her natural liberty without any attendant increase in overall civil liberty. Accordingly, I would hold that subsection (C) of 23-3-540 is unconstitutional and must be stricken from the statute.

BEATTY, J., concurs.

Notes

In *Dykes*, the court found that convicted sex offenders do not have a fundamental right to be "let alone," but that a "lifetime imposition of satellite monitoring implicates a protected liberty interest to be free from permanent, unwarranted governmental interference." *State v. Dykes*, 403 S.C. 499, 744 S.E.2d 505, 509 (2013). Therefore, mandatory enrollment in the satellite monitoring program invoked minimal due process protection. *Id.* The court found the state's purpose of protecting the public from sex offenders and to aid law enforcement as sufficient basis for the initial mandatory imposition of satellite monitoring for certain offenders upon their release from incarceration or violation of their parole. *Id.* at 510. However, the court held unconstitutional the portion of the statute that precluded any judicial review of the offender's risk of re-offending, thereby relegating the offender to non-reviewable lifetime monitoring. *Id.* For other cases involving the issue of satellite monitoring of sex offenders in other contexts, see *People v. Younger*, 2015 Ill. App. (1st) 130540-U (Sept. 21, 2015) (distinguishing *Dykes* as inapplicable to application of relevant provision of Illinois mandatory electronic monitoring statute, which was not imposed for life, without the possibility of review); *United States v. Polouizzi*, 697 F. Supp. 2d 381 (E.D.N.Y. 2010); *Commonwealth v. Cory*, 911 N.E.2d 187 (Mass. 2009) (involving *ex post facto* application of monitoring statute); *United States v. Smedley*, 611 F. Supp. 2d 971 (E.D. Mo. 2009); *State v. Stines*, 683 S.E.2d 411 (N.C. Ct. App. 2009) (regarding notice requirement of hearing to determine enrollment in program); *United States v. Torres*, 566 F. Supp. 2d 591 (W.D. Tex. 2008) (involving electronic monitoring of defendant during pretrial release). In the following case, the issue of satellite monitoring is analyzed in the context of the Fourth Amendment right to be free from unreasonable searches and seizures.

Grady v. North Carolina

Supreme Court of the United States, 2015
575 U.S. ___, 135 S. Ct. 1368

PER CURIAM.

Petitioner Torrey Dale Grady was convicted in North Carolina trial courts of a second degree sexual offense in 1997 and of taking indecent liberties with a child in 2006. After serving his sentence for the latter crime, Grady was ordered to appear in New Hanover County Superior Court for a hearing to determine whether he should be subjected to satellite-based monitoring (SBM) as a recidivist sex offender. See N.C. Gen.Stat. Ann. §§ 14-208.40(a)(1), 14-208.40B (2013). Grady did not dispute that his prior convictions rendered him a recidivist under the relevant North Carolina statutes. He argued, however, that the monitoring program—under which he would be forced to wear tracking devices at all times—would violate his Fourth Amendment right to be free from unreasonable searches and seizures. Unpersuaded, the trial court ordered Grady to enroll in the program and be monitored for the rest of his life.... [citation to Record omitted].

Grady renewed his Fourth Amendment challenge on appeal, relying on this Court's decision in *United States v. Jones*, 565 U.S. ___, 132 S.Ct. 945, 181 L.Ed.2d 911 (2012).

In that case, this Court held that police officers had engaged in a "search" within the meaning of the Fourth Amendment when they installed and monitored a Global Positioning System (GPS) tracking device on a suspect's car. The North Carolina Court of Appeals rejected Grady's argument, concluding that it was foreclosed by one of its earlier decisions.... In that decision, coincidentally named *State v. Jones*, the court had said:

> "Defendant essentially argues that if affixing a GPS to an individual's vehicle constitutes a search of the individual, then the arguably more intrusive act of affixing an ankle bracelet to an individual must constitute a search of the individual as well. We disagree. The context presented in the instant case—which involves a civil SBM proceeding—is readily distinguishable from that presented in [*United States v.*] *Jones*, where the Court considered the propriety of a search in the context of a motion to suppress evidence. We conclude, therefore, that the specific holding in [*United States v.*] *Jones* does not control in the case *sub judice*." ___ N.C.App. ___, ___, 750 S.E.2d 883, 886 (2013).

The court in Grady's case held itself bound by this reasoning and accordingly rejected his Fourth Amendment challenge.... The North Carolina Supreme Court in turn summarily dismissed Grady's appeal and denied his petition for discretionary review. 367 N.C. 523, 762 S.E.2d 460 (2014). Grady now asks us to reverse these decisions.* ... The only explanation provided below for the rejection of Grady's challenge is the quoted passage from *State v. Jones*. And the only theory we discern in that passage is that the State's system of nonconsensual satellite-based monitoring does not entail a search within the meaning of the Fourth Amendment. That theory is inconsistent with this Court's precedents.

In *United States v. Jones*, we held that "the Government's installation of a GPS device on a target's vehicle, and its use of that device to monitor the vehicle's movements, constitutes a 'search.'" 565 U.S., at ___, 132 S.Ct., at 949 (footnote omitted). We stressed the importance of the fact that the Government had "physically occupied private property for the purpose of obtaining information." *Id.*, at ___, 132 S.Ct., at 949. Under such circumstances, it was not necessary to inquire about the target's expectation of privacy in his vehicle's movements in order to determine if a Fourth Amendment search had occurred. "Where, as here, the Government obtains information by physically intruding on a constitutionally protected area, such a search has undoubtedly occurred." *Id.*, at ___, n. 3, 132 S.Ct., at 950, n. 3.

We reaffirmed this principle in *Florida v. Jardines*, 569 U.S. ___, ___–___, 133 S.Ct. 1409, 1413–1414, 185 L.Ed.2d 495 (2013), where we held that having a drug-sniffing dog nose around a suspect's front porch was a search, because police had "gathered ... information by physically entering and occupying the [curtilage of the house] to engage in conduct not explicitly or implicitly permitted by the homeowner." See also *id.*, at ___, 133 S.Ct., at 1417 (a search occurs "when the government gains evidence by physically intruding on constitutionally protected areas"). In light of these decisions, it follows that a State also conducts a search when it attaches a device to a person's body, without consent, for the purpose of tracking that individual's movements.

In concluding otherwise, the North Carolina Court of Appeals apparently placed decisive weight on the fact that the State's monitoring program is civil in nature. See *Jones*, ___

---

* Grady aims his petition at the decisions of both North Carolina appellate courts.... Because we treat the North Carolina Supreme Court's dismissal of an appeal for lack of a substantial constitutional question as a decision on the merits, it is that court's judgment, rather than the judgment of the Court of Appeals, that is subject to our review under 28 U.S.C. § 1257(a). See *R.J. Reynolds Tobacco Co. v. Durham County*, 479 U.S. 130, 138–139, 107 S.Ct. 499, 93 L.Ed.2d 449 (1986).

N.C.App., at ___, 750 S.E.2d, at 886 ("the instant case ... involves a civil SBM proceeding"). "It is well settled," however, "that the Fourth Amendment's protection extends beyond the sphere of criminal investigations," *Ontario v. Quon*, 560 U.S. 746, 755, 130 S.Ct. 2619, 177 L.Ed.2d 216 (2010), and the government's purpose in collecting information does not control whether the method of collection constitutes a search. A building inspector who enters a home simply to ensure compliance with civil safety regulations has undoubtedly conducted a search under the Fourth Amendment. See *Camara v. Municipal Court of City and County of San Francisco*, 387 U.S. 523, 534, 87 S.Ct. 1727, 18 L.Ed.2d 930 (1967) (housing inspections are "administrative searches" that must comply with the Fourth Amendment).

In its brief in opposition to certiorari, the State faults Grady for failing to introduce "evidence about the State's implementation of the SBM program or what information, if any, it currently obtains through the monitoring process." ... Without evidence that it is acting to obtain information, the State argues, "there is no basis upon which this Court can determine whether North Carolina conducts a 'search' of an offender enrolled in its SBM program." *Ibid.* (citing *Jones*, 565 U.S., at ___, n. 5, 132 S.Ct., at 951, n. 5 (noting that a government intrusion is not a search unless "done to obtain information")). In other words, the State argues that we cannot be sure its program for satellite-based *monitoring* of sex offenders collects any information. If the very name of the program does not suffice to rebut this contention, the text of the statute surely does:

> "The satellite-based monitoring program shall use a system that provides all of the following:
>
> "(1) Time-correlated and continuous tracking of the geographic location of the subject....
>
> "(2) Reporting of subject's violations of prescriptive and proscriptive schedule or location requirements." N.C. Gen.Stat. Ann. § 14-208.40(c).

The State's program is plainly designed to obtain information. And since it does so by physically intruding on a subject's body, it effects a Fourth Amendment search.

That conclusion, however, does not decide the ultimate question of the program's constitutionality. The Fourth Amendment prohibits only *unreasonable* searches. The reasonableness of a search depends on the totality of the circumstances, including the nature and purpose of the search and the extent to which the search intrudes upon reasonable privacy expectations. See, *e.g.*, *Samson v. California*, 547 U.S. 843, 126 S.Ct. 2193, 165 L.Ed.2d 250 (2006) (suspicionless search of parolee was reasonable); *Vernonia School Dist. 47J v. Acton*, 515 U.S. 646, 115 S.Ct. 2386, 132 L.Ed.2d 564 (1995) (random drug testing of student athletes was reasonable). The North Carolina courts did not examine whether the State's monitoring program is reasonable—when properly viewed as a search—and we will not do so in the first instance.

The petition for certiorari is granted, the judgment of the Supreme Court of North Carolina is vacated, and the case is remanded for further proceedings not inconsistent with this opinion.

It is so ordered.

Notes

In *Grady*, the United States Supreme Court held that the government's use of satellite-based monitoring (SBM) systems to track sex offenders constitutes a Fourth Amendment search. The holding did not decide the constitutionality of the SBM program, however, since the Fourth Amendment prohibits only *unreasonable* searches, and the North Carolina courts had not examined the reasonableness of the applicable SBM program. For commentary on the use of GPS tracking statutes as applied to sex offenders, see Eric M. Dante, *Tracking the Constitution — The Proliferation and Legality of Sex-Offender GPS-Tracking Statutes*, 42 SETON HALL L. REV. 1169 (2012); Marisa L. Mortensen, *GPS Monitoring: An Ingenious Solution to the Threat Pedophiles Pose to California's Children*, 27 J. JUV. L. 17 (2006). For discussion of probation conditions imposed on youthful offenders, see Richard Sanders, *Imposing Mandatory Sex Offender Probation Conditions on Youthful Offenders*, FLA. BAR J., at 21 (Apr. 2014). For a discussion of zoning restrictions as a means of addressing residency restrictions for sex offenders, see Asmara Tekle-Johnson, *In the Zone: Sex Offenders and the Ten-Percent Solutions*, 94 IOWA L. REV. 607 (2009).

c. *Sex Offender Registration and Notification Act ("SORNA")*

18 U.S.C. § 2250(a) (Failure to Register)

(a) In general.—Whoever—

> (1) is required to register under the Sex Offender Registration and Notification Act;

> (2)(A) is a sex offender as defined for the purposes of the Sex Offender Registration and Notification Act by reason of a conviction under Federal law (including the Uniform Code of Military Justice), the law of the District of Columbia, Indian tribal law, or the law of any territory or possession of the United States; or

>> (B) travels in interstate or foreign commerce, or enters or leaves, or resides in, Indian country; and

> (3) knowingly fails to register or update a registration as required by the Sex Offender Registration and Notification Act;

> shall be fined under this title or imprisoned not more than 10 years, or both.

(b) Affirmative defense.—In a prosecution for a violation under subsection (a), it is an affirmative defense that—

> (1) uncontrollable circumstances prevented the individual from complying;

> (2) the individual did not contribute to the creation of such circumstances in reckless disregard of the requirement to comply; and

> (3) the individual complied as soon as such circumstances ceased to exist.

(c) Crime of violence.—

> (1) In general.—An individual described in subsection (a) who commits a crime of violence under Federal law (including the Uniform Code of Military Justice), the law of the District of Columbia, Indian tribal law, or the law of any territory or possession of the United States shall be imprisoned for not less than 5 years and not more than 30 years.

> (2) Additional punishment.—The punishment provided in paragraph (1) shall be in addition and consecutive to the punishment provided for the violation described in subsection (a).

U.S.S.G. 2A3.5 (Failure to Register as a Sex Offender)

(a) Base Offense Level (Apply the greatest):

> (1) 16, if the defendant was required to register as a Tier III offender;

(2) 14, if the defendant was required to register as a Tier II offender; or

(3) 12, if the defendant was required to register as a Tier I offender.

(b) Specific Offense Characteristics

(1) (Apply the greatest):

If, while in a failure to register status, the defendant committed—

(A) a sex offense against someone other than a minor, increase by 6 levels;

(B) a felony offense against a minor not otherwise covered by subdivision (C), increase by 6 levels; or

(C) a sex offense against a minor, increase by 8 levels.

(2) If the defendant voluntarily (A) corrected the failure to register; or (B) attempted to register but was prevented from registering by uncontrollable circumstances and the defendant did not contribute to the creation of those circumstances, decrease by 3 levels.

United States v. Kebodeaux

United States Supreme Court, 2013
___ U.S. ___, 133 S. Ct. 2496

Justice BREYER delivered the opinion of the Court.

In 1999 a special court-martial convicted Anthony Kebodeaux, a member of the United States Air Force, of a sex offense. It imposed a sentence of three months' imprisonment and a bad conduct discharge. In 2006, several years after Kebodeaux had served his sentence and been discharged, Congress enacted the Sex Offender Registration and Notification Act (SORNA), 120 Stat. 590, 42 U.S.C. § 16901 *et seq.*, a federal statute that requires those convicted of federal sex offenses to register in the States where they live, study, and work. § 16913(a); 18 U.S.C. § 2250(a). And, by regulation, the Federal Government made clear that SORNA's registration requirements apply to federal sex offenders who, when SORNA became law, had already completed their sentences. 42 U.S.C. § 16913(d) (Attorney General's authority to issue regulations); 28 CFR § 72.3 (2012) (regulation specifying application to pre-SORNA offenders).

We here must decide whether the Constitution's Necessary and Proper Clause grants Congress the power to enact SORNA's registration requirements and apply them to a federal offender who had completed his sentence prior to the time of SORNA's enactment. For purposes of answering this question, we assume that Congress has complied with the Constitution's *Ex Post Facto* and Due Process Clauses. See *Smith v. Doe*, 538 U.S. 84, 105–106, 123 S.Ct. 1140, 155 L.Ed.2d 164 (2003) (upholding a similar Alaska statute against *ex post facto* challenge); ... [Citations to record omitted]. We conclude that the Necessary and Proper Clause grants Congress adequate power to enact SORNA and to apply it here....

As we have just said, in 1999 a special court-martial convicted Kebodeaux, then a member of the Air Force, of a federal sex offense. He served his 3-month sentence; the Air Force released him with a bad conduct discharge. And then he moved to Texas. In 2004 Kebodeaux registered as a sex offender with Texas state authorities.... In 2006 Congress enacted SORNA. In 2007 Kebodeaux moved within Texas from San Antonio to El Paso, updating his sex offender registration.... But later that year he returned to San Antonio without making the legally required sex-offender registration changes.... And the Federal Government, acting under SORNA, prosecuted Kebodeaux for this last-mentioned SORNA registration failure.... A Federal District Court convicted Kebodeaux of having violated SORNA. See 687 F.3d 232, 234 (C.A.5 2012) (en banc). On appeal a panel of the United States Court of Appeals for the Fifth Circuit initially upheld the conviction. 647 F.3d 137 (2011) (*per curiam*). But the Circuit then heard the appeal en banc and, by a vote of 10 to 6, reversed. 687 F.3d, at 234. The court stated that, by the time Congress enacted SORNA, Kebodeaux had "fully served" his sex-offense sentence; he was "no longer in federal custody, in the military, under any sort of supervised release or parole, or in any other special relationship with the federal government." *Ibid.*

The court recognized that, even before SORNA, federal law required certain federal sex offenders to register. *Id.*, at 235, n. 4. See Jacob Wetterling Crimes Against Children and Sexually Violent Offender Registration Act, § 170101, 108 Stat. 2038–2042. But it believed that the pre-SORNA federal registration requirements did not apply to Kebodeaux. 687 F.3d, at 235, n. 4. Hence, in the Circuit's view, Kebodeaux had been "*unconditionally* let ... free." *Id.*, at 234. And, that being so, the Federal Government lacked the power under Article I's Necessary and Proper Clause to regulate through registration Kebodeaux's intrastate movements. *Id.*, at 234–235. In particular, the court said that after "the federal government has *unconditionally* let a person free ... the fact that he once committed a crime is not a jurisdictional basis for subsequent regulation and possible criminal prosecution." *Ibid.*

The Solicitor General sought certiorari. And, in light of the fact that a Federal Court of Appeals has held a federal statute unconstitutional, we granted the petition. See, *e.g.*, *United States v. Morrison*, 529 U.S. 598, 605, 120 S.Ct. 1740, 146 L.Ed.2d 658 (2000); *United States v. Edge Broadcasting Co.*, 509 U.S. 418, 425, 113 S.Ct. 2696, 125 L.Ed.2d 345 (1993).... We do not agree with the Circuit's conclusion. And, in explaining our reasons, we need not go much further than the Circuit's critical assumption that Kebodeaux's release was "unconditional," *i.e.*, that after Kebodeaux's release, he was not in "any ... special relationship with the federal government." 687 F.3d, at 234. To the contrary, the Solicitor General, tracing through a complex set of statutory cross-references, has pointed out that at the time of his offense and conviction Kebodeaux was subject to the federal Wetterling Act, an Act that imposed upon him registration requirements very similar to those that SORNA later mandated....

Congress enacted the Wetterling Act in 1994 and updated it several times prior to Kebodeaux's offense. Like SORNA, it used the federal spending power to encourage States to adopt sex offender registration laws. 42 U.S.C. § 14071(i) (2000 ed.); *Smith, supra*, at 89–90, 123 S.Ct. 1140. Like SORNA, it applied to those who committed federal sex crimes. § 14071(b)(7)(A). And like SORNA, it imposed federal penalties upon federal sex offenders who failed to register in the States in which they lived, worked, and studied. §§ 14072(i)(3)–(4).... In particular, § 14072(i)(3) imposed federal criminal penalties upon any "person who is ... described in section 4042(c)(4) of title 18, and knowingly fails to register in any State in which the person resides." The cross-referenced § 4042(c)(4) said that a "person is described in this paragraph if the person was convicted of" certain enumerated offenses or "[a]ny other offense designated by the Attorney General as a sexual offense for purposes of this subsection." 18 U.S.C. § 4042(c)(4). In 1998 the Attorney General "delegated this authority [to designate sex offenses] to the Director of the Bureau of Prisons." Dept. of Justice, Bureau of Prisons, Designation of Offenses Subject to Sex Offender Release Notification, 63 Fed.Reg. 69386. And that same year the Director of the Bureau of Prisons "designate[d]" the offense of which Kebodeaux was convicted, namely the military offense of "carnal knowledge" as set forth in Article 120(B) of the Code of

Military Justice. *Id.*, at 69387[.] See 28 CFR §571.72(b)(2) (1999). A full reading of these documents makes clear that, contrary to Kebodeaux's contention, the relevant penalty applied to crimes committed by military personnel.

Moreover, a different Wetterling Act section imposed federal criminal penalties upon any "person who is ... sentenced by a court martial for conduct in a category specified by the Secretary of Defense under section 115(a)(8)(C) of title I of Public Law 105-119, and knowingly fails to register in any State in which the person resides." 42 U.S.C. §14072(i)(4) (2000 ed.). The cross-referenced section, §115(a)(8)(C), said that the "Secretary of Defense shall specify categories of conduct punishable under the Uniform Code of Military Justice which encompass a range of conduct comparable to that described in [certain provisions of the Violent Crime Control and Law Enforcement Act of 1994], and such other conduct as the Secretary deems appropriate." 1998 Appropriations Act, §115(a)(8)(C)(i), 111 Stat. 2466. See note following 10 U.S.C. §951 (2000 ed.). The Secretary had delegated certain types of authority, such as this last mentioned "deem[ing]" authority, to an Assistant Secretary of Defense. DoD Directive 5124.5, p. 4 (Oct. 31, 1994). And in December 1998 an Assistant Secretary, acting pursuant to this authority, published a list of military crimes that included the crime of which Kebodeaux was convicted, namely Article 120(B) of the Uniform Code of Military Justice.... The provision added that "[c]onvictions ... shall trigger requirements to notify state and local law enforcement agencies and to provide information to inmates concerning sex offender registration requirements." ... And, the provision says (contrary to Kebodeaux's reading, ...), that it shall "take effect immediately." It contains no expiration date....

We are not aware of any plausible counterargument to the obvious conclusion, namely that as of the time of Kebodeaux's offense, conviction and release from federal custody, these Wetterling Act provisions applied to Kebodeaux and imposed upon him registration requirements very similar to those that SORNA later imposed. Contrary to what the Court of Appeals may have believed, the fact that the federal law's requirements in part involved compliance with state-law requirements made them no less requirements of federal law. See generally *United States v. Sharpnack*, 355 U.S. 286, 293–294, 78 S.Ct. 291, 2 L.Ed.2d 282 (1958) (Congress has the power to adopt as federal law the laws of a State and to apply them in federal enclaves); *Gibbons v. Ogden*, 9 Wheat. 1, 207–208, 6 L.Ed. 23 (1824) ("Although Congress cannot enable a State to legislate, Congress may adopt the provisions of a State on any subject.... The act [adopts state systems for regulation of pilots] and gives [them] the same validity as if its provisions had been specially made by Congress")…. Both the Court of Appeals and Kebodeaux come close to conceding that if, as of the time of Kebodeaux's offense, he was subject to a federal registration requirement, then the Necessary and Proper Clause authorized Congress to modify the requirement as in SORNA and to apply the modified requirement to Kebodeaux. See 687 F.3d, at 234–235, and n. 4; ... And we believe they would be right to make this concession.

No one here claims that the Wetterling Act, as applied to military sex offenders like Kebodeaux, falls outside the scope of the Necessary and Proper Clause. And it is difficult to see how anyone could persuasively do so. The Constitution explicitly grants Congress the power to "make Rules for the ... Regulation of the land and naval Forces." Art. I, §8, cl. 14. And, in the Necessary and Proper Clause itself, it grants Congress the power to "make all Laws which shall be necessary and proper for carrying into Execution the foregoing Powers" and "all other Powers" that the Constitution vests "in the Government of the United States, or in any Department or Officer thereof." *Id.*, cl. 18.

The scope of the Necessary and Proper Clause is broad. In words that have come to define that scope Chief Justice Marshall long ago wrote:

"Let the end be legitimate, let it be within the scope of the constitution, and all means which are appropriate, which are plainly adapted to that end, which are not prohibited, but consist with the letter and spirit of the constitution, are constitutional." McCulloch v. Maryland, 4 Wheat. 316, 421, 4 L.Ed. 579 (1819).

As we have come to understand these words and the provision they explain, they "leav[e] to Congress a large discretion as to the means that may be employed in executing a given power." *Lottery Case*, 188 U.S. 321, 355, 23 S.Ct. 321, 47 L.Ed. 492 (1903). See *Morrison*, 529 U.S., at 607, 120 S.Ct. 1740. The Clause allows Congress to "adopt any means, appearing to it most eligible and appropriate, which are adapted to the end to be accomplished and consistent with the letter and spirit of the Constitution." *James Everard's Breweries v. Day*, 265 U.S. 545, 559, 44 S.Ct. 628, 68 L.Ed. 1174 (1924).

The Constitution, for example, makes few explicit references to federal criminal law, but the Necessary and Proper Clause nonetheless authorizes Congress, in the implementation of other explicit powers, to create federal crimes, to confine offenders to prison, to hire guards and other prison personnel, to provide prisoners with medical care and educational training, to ensure the safety of those who may come into contact with prisoners, to ensure the public's safety through systems of parole and supervised release, and, where a federal prisoner's mental condition so requires, to confine that prisoner civilly after the expiration of his or her term of imprisonment. See *United States v. Comstock*, 560 U.S. 126, 136–137, 130 S.Ct. 1949, 176 L.Ed.2d 878 (2010).... Here, under the authority granted to it by the Military Regulation and Necessary and Proper Clauses, Congress could promulgate the Uniform Code of Military Justice. It could specify that the sex offense of which Kebodeaux was convicted was a military crime under that Code. It could punish that crime through imprisonment and by placing conditions upon Kebodeaux's release. And it could make the civil registration requirement at issue here a consequence of Kebodeaux's offense and conviction. This civil requirement, while not a specific condition of Kebodeaux's release, was in place at the time Kebodeaux committed his offense, and was a consequence of his violation of federal law.

And Congress' decision to impose such a civil requirement that would apply upon the release of an offender like Kebodeaux is eminently reasonable. Congress could reasonably conclude that registration requirements applied to federal sex offenders after their release can help protect the public from those federal sex offenders and alleviate public safety concerns. See *Smith*, 538 U.S., at 102–103, 123 S.Ct. 1140 (sex offender registration has "a legitimate nonpunitive purpose of 'public safety, which is advanced by alerting the public to the risk of sex offenders in their community'"). There is evidence that recidivism rates among sex offenders are higher than the average for other types of criminals. See Dept. of Justice, Bureau of Justice Statistics, P. Langan, E. Schmitt, & M. Durose, Recidivism of Sex Offenders Released in 1994, p. 1 (Nov. 2003) (reporting that compared to non-sex offenders, released sex offenders were four times more likely to be rearrested for a sex crime, and that within the first three years following release 5.3% of released sex offenders were rearrested for a sex crime). There is also conflicting evidence on the point. Cf. R. Tewsbury, W. Jennings, & K. Zgoba, Final Report on Sex Offenders: Recidivism and Collateral Consequences (Sept. 2011) (concluding that sex offenders have relatively low rates of recidivism, and that registration requirements have limited observable benefits regarding recidivism). But the Clause gives Congress the power to weigh the evidence and to reach a rational conclusion, for example, that safety needs justify postrelease registration rules. See *Lambert v. Yellowley*, 272 U.S. 581, 594–595, 47 S.Ct. 210, 71 L.Ed. 422 (1926) (upholding congressional statute limiting the amount of spirituous liquor that may be prescribed by a physician, and noting that Congress' "finding [regarding the appropriate amount], in the presence of the well-known diverging opinions of physicians, cannot be regarded as arbitrary or without a reasonable basis"). See also *Gonzales v. Raich*, 545 U.S. 1, 22, 125 S.Ct. 2195, 162 L.Ed.2d 1 (2005) ("In assessing the scope of Congress' authority under the Commerce Clause, we stress that the task before us is a modest one. We need not determine whether respondents' activities, taken in the aggregate, substantially affect interstate commerce in fact, but only whether a 'rational basis' exists for so concluding"). See also H.R.Rep. No. 109-218, pt. 1, pp. 22, 23 (2005) (House Report) (citing statistics compiled by the Justice Department as support for SORNA's sex offender registration regime).

At the same time, "it is entirely reasonable for Congress to have assigned the Federal Government a special role in ensuring compliance with SORNA's registration requirements by federal sex offenders—persons who typically would have spent time under federal criminal supervision." *Carr v. United States*, 560 U.S. 438, ___, 130 S.Ct. 2229, 176 L.Ed.2d 1152 (2010). The Federal Government has long kept track of former federal prisoners through probation, parole, and supervised release in part to prevent further crimes thereby protecting the public against the risk of recidivism. See Parole Act, 36 Stat. 819; Probation Act, ch. 521, 43 Stat. 1259; Sentencing Reform Act of 1984, ch. II, 98 Stat. 1987. See also 1 N. Cohen, The Law of Probation and Parole §§ 7:3, 7:4 (2d ed. 1999) (principal purposes of postrelease conditions are to rehabilitate the convict, thus preventing him from recidivating, and to protect the public). Neither, as of 1994, was registration particularly novel, for by then States had implemented similar requirements for close to half a century. See W. Logan, Knowledge as Power: Criminal Registration and Community Notification Laws in America 30–31 (2009). Moreover, the Wetterling Act took state interests into account by, for the most part, requiring released federal offenders to register in accordance with state law. At the same time, the Wetterling Act's requirements were reasonably narrow and precise, tying time limits to the type of sex offense, incorporating state-law details, and relating penalties for violations to the sex crime initially at issue. See 42 U.S.C. § 14071(b) (2000 ed.).

The upshot is that here Congress did not apply SORNA to an individual who had, prior to SORNA's enactment, been "unconditionally released," *i.e.*, a person who was not in "any ... special relationship with the federal government," but rather to an individual already subject to federal registration requirements that were themselves a valid exercise of federal power under the Military Regulation and Necessary and Proper Clauses.... SORNA, enacted after Kebodeaux's release, somewhat modified the applicable registration requirements. In general, SORNA provided more detailed definitions of sex offenses, described in greater detail the nature of the information registrants must provide, and imposed somewhat different limits upon the length of time that registration must continue and the frequency with which offenders must update their registration. 42 U.S.C. §§ 16911, 16913–16916 (2006 ed. and Supp. V). But the statute, like the Wetterling Act, used Spending Clause grants to encourage States to adopt its uniform definitions and requirements. It did not insist that the States do so. See §§ 16925(a), (d) (2006 ed.) ("The provisions of this subchapter that are cast as directions to jurisdictions or their officials constitute, in relation to States, only conditions required to avoid the reduction of Federal funding under this section").

As applied to an individual already subject to the Wetterling Act like Kebodeaux, SORNA makes few changes. In particular, SORNA modified the time limitations for a sex offender who moves to update his registration to within three business days of the move from both seven days before and seven days after the move, as required by the Texas law enforced under the Wetterling Act.... SORNA also increased the federal penalty for a federal offender's registration violation to a maximum of 10 years from a maximum of 1 year for a first offense. Compare 18 U.S.C. §2250(a) with 42 U.S.C. §14072(i) (2000 ed.). Kebodeaux was sentenced to one year and one day of imprisonment. For purposes of federal law, SORNA *reduced* the duration of Kebodeaux's registration requirement to 25 years from the lifetime requirement imposed by Texas law, ... and *reduced* the frequency with which Kebodeaux must update his registration to every six months from every 90 days as imposed by Texas law, ... And as far as we can tell, while SORNA punishes violations of its requirements (instead of violations of state law), the Federal Government has prosecuted a sex offender for violating SORNA only when that offender also violated state-registration requirements.

SORNA's general changes were designed to make more uniform what had remained "a patchwork of federal and 50 individual state registration systems," *Reynolds v. United States*, 565 U.S. ___, ___, 132 S.Ct. 975, 978, 181 L.Ed.2d 935 (2012), with "loopholes and deficiencies" that had resulted in an estimated 100,000 sex offenders becoming "missing" or "lost," House Report 20, 26. See S.Rep. No. 109-369, pp. 16–17 (2006). See also *Jinks v. Richland County*, 538 U.S. 456, 462–463, 123 S.Ct. 1667, 155 L.Ed.2d 631 (2003) (holding that a statute is authorized by the Necessary and Proper Clause when it "provides an alternative to [otherwise] unsatisfactory options" that are "obviously inefficient"). SORNA's more specific changes reflect Congress' determination that the statute, changed in respect to frequency, penalties, and other details, will keep track of more offenders and will encourage States themselves to adopt its uniform standards. No one here claims that these changes are unreasonable or that Congress could not reasonably have found them "necessary and proper" means for furthering its pre-existing registration ends.

We conclude that the SORNA changes as applied to Kebodeaux fall within the scope Congress' authority under the Military Regulation and Necessary and Proper Clauses. The Fifth Circuit's judgment to the contrary is reversed, and the case is remanded for further proceedings consistent with this opinion.

It is so ordered....

Notes

The implementation of sex offender registration laws has both criminal and civil relevance. Recall that SORNA was discussed in Chapter One with respect to society's perception of the sex offender as criminal or patient. *See Smith v. Doe, supra* Chapter One, at Section II.B. *See also Connecticut Department of Public Safety v. Doe*, 538 U.S. 1 (2003). The application of registration laws as criminal or civil regulations has raised much constitutional debate. *See, e.g.*, Catherine L. Carpenter and Amy E. Beverlin, *The Evolution of Unconstitutionality in Sex Offender Registration Laws*, 63 Hastings L.J. 1071 (2012); Corey Rayburn Yung, *One of These Laws Is Not Like the Others: Why the Federal Sex Offender Registration and Notification Act Raises New Constitutional Questions*, 46 Harv. J. Legis. 369 (2009).

II. Civil Liability

A. Statute of Limitations

Sheehan v. Oblates of St. Francis de Sales

Supreme Court of Delaware, 2011
15 A.3d 1247

STEELE, Chief Justice:

James E. Sheehan filed a personal injury action under 10 *Del. C.* §8145, the Child Victim's Act, against several institutional defendants, including the Oblates of St. Francis de Sales and Salesianum School, for the alleged sexual abuse he suffered in 1962 by Father Francis Norris, a teacher at Salesianum. The Child Victim's Act (CVA), enacted in 2007, abolished the civil statute of limitations for claims of childhood sexual abuse and created a two year window to allow victims of childhood sexual abuse to bring civil suits that the statute of limitations previously barred. After a jury trial, the jury found the Oblates, but not Salesianum, negligent under Section 8145. However, the jury did not find that the Oblates' negligence had proximately caused Sheehan's injuries.... Sheehan asserts that the trial judge committed numerous reversible errors....

James E. Sheehan attended Salesianum School during 1961–1964. While Sheehan was a student at Salesianum, Father Francis Norris, a priest of the Oblates of St. Francis de Sales, was assigned to a teaching position at Salesianum. Sheehan alleges that one night in April 1962, during the spring of his sophomore year, Norris offered him a ride home after a basketball game and Norris forced him to engage in sexual masturbation in the car. Sheehan never reported the incident to the Oblates or to Salesianum. However, Sheehan testified that decades before he had any motive to lie, he told his family members about the sexual abuse.

Eyewitness testimony, as well as the Oblates' own business records, demonstrated that the Oblates had prior notice that Norris was an alcoholic and had attempted suicide, and that the Oblates' own doctors urged his immediate psychiatric hospitalization. Sheehan's expert witness testified that in the 1960's priest records used code words to refer to sexual abuse of a child. These code words included "health problems," "depression," "nervous breakdown," and "alcoholism." The expert also testified that alcoholism was not considered a scandal at the time because it was so prevalent in the religious communities of priests. Norris' personnel file was filled with the words "health problems," "depression," and "alcoholism." Shortly before his transfer to Salesianum, his file noted that it was preferable to remove him from his then current locality (New York) and out of direct contact with his present community.... Norris died on March 24, 1985, and the Oblates remained unaware of Sheehan's allegations until Section 8145 became law in July 2007.

In 2007, after a Boston Globe investigation revealed a pattern of sexual abuse against minors by Catholic priests, the Delaware Legislature enacted Section 8145, to repeal the statute of limitations in civil suits relating to child sex abuse.... [footnote omitted]. The CVA provided a two year window, during which time prior victims of abuse would be permitted to file civil actions previously barred by the then applicable statute of limitations. The statute also revived claims against institutional defendants who employed or controlled alleged abusers, for claims arising from "gross negligence."

Sheehan filed his complaint against Oblates of St. Francis de Sales, Oblates of St. Francis de Sales, Inc., and Salesianum School, Inc., on November 30, 2007. A seven day jury trial began on November 16, 2009. Sheehan contended at trial that the Oblates were aware of the "red flags" yet failed to keep Norris away from children as required by the educational standard of care in Delaware schools in the 1950s and 1960s.... Before trial, but after completion of discovery, the Oblates had moved for summary judgment on numerous grounds. On October 27, 2009, the Superior Court issued an opinion holding, *inter alia*, that Section 8145 did not revive intentional torts.... [footnote omitted]. The court denied the Oblates' remaining motions for summary judgment, including motions challenging the constitutionality of Section 8145.... [footnote omitted].... The Oblates also filed a pretrial motion *in limine* to strike the testimony of Sheehan's general causation expert, Diane Mandt Langberg, Ph.D. On November 9, 2009, the trial judge issued an order granting the motion and precluding Langberg from testifying for lack of relevance.... [footnote omitted]. The Oblates also moved *in limine* to exclude the testimony of Sheehan's corroborative witnesses who Norris also allegedly abused. The trial judge denied the motion and permitted the witnesses to testify where the alleged abuse of a corroborative witness occurred during the same time Sheehan was abused.

At the prayer conference on November 20, 2009, each party submitted a proposed special verdict form for the trial judge's consideration. The trial judge rejected Sheehan's version, which contained the standard of "a proximate cause," in favor of a special verdict form with the language of "the proximate cause." Sheehan did not object to the language of the special verdict form at trial. The trial judge further ruled that the 1962 Delaware Criminal Code governed the types of sexual acts which Sheehan needed to prove under the CVA rather than the current version of the criminal code.... [footnote omitted].... Following a seven day trial, the jury returned a verdict form that found the Oblates negligent, but not Salesianum. The form further indicated that the jury found that Sheehan had failed to prove that the Oblates' negligence proximately caused his injuries. Consequently, a verdict was entered for the defendant.... On appeal, Sheehan alleges the trial judge erred and abused [its] discretion by (i) excluding his general causation expert, (ii) using a special verdict form that referred to "the" proximate cause rather than "a" proximate cause, (iii) that the CVA did not revive intentional torts and (iv) incorrectly applying the 1962 criminal code rather than the current Delaware criminal code. The Oblates have cross appealed, contending that the CVA is unconstitutional either facially or if not facially, as applied. They also contend on cross appeal that the trial judge erred by admitting the testimony of Norris' other alleged victims, because that testimony was unfairly prejudicial and constituted improper character evidence....

10 *Del. C.* § 8145(a) states that "[a] civil cause of action for sexual abuse of a minor shall be based upon sexual acts that would constitute a criminal offense under the Delaware Code." The trial judge found that the plain language of the CVA did not address which version of the Delaware Code to apply. The trial judge "determined applying anything other than the code in existence at the time of the alleged abuse would be a violation of due process." ... [footnote omitted]. The judge so concluded because the CVA requires that a claim must be premised upon the commission of a sexual crime.... [footnote omitted.] A sexual crime is a predicate element to a civil claim against an institutional defendant for grossly negligently failing to protect a plaintiff from sexual criminal acts of its employee or agent.... [footnote omitted.] Moreover, fundamental due process dictates

that the scope of liability imposed by a retroactive law cannot substantially change the scope of liability existing at the time of the alleged abuse.[43]

If the current Delaware criminal code were found applicable, the sexual acts alleged in this case could fall within the definition of a criminal offense that did not exist at the time of the alleged abuse. The result would be to create a cause of action where none existed in 1962. The current Code criminalizes multiple sexual acts that were not criminalized in 1962.[44] Under the 1962 Code, the only crime that related to the facts in the record here was lewdly playing with a child under 16 years.[45] . . . We agree that the CVA's reference to the Criminal Code does not transform this civil statute into a criminal one to which *ex post facto* analysis applies. The Act is and continues to be a civil statute of limitations affecting matters of procedure and remedy.[46] However, an essential predicate to civil claims prosecuted under the CVA is a sexual act that would constitute a criminal offense. If an act was not a crime in 1962, we cannot hold the defendants to reasonably have been on notice of a duty to prevent the now criminalized act from occurring. To hold an institutional defendant liable today for failing to protect a plaintiff from conduct that was not criminal at the time of the conduct violates all notions of fairness by failing to put the defendant on notice that a failure to act could incur civil or criminal liability. . . . For the above reasons, we hold that the trial judge correctly held that the Criminal Code to be applied to claims under the CVA is the Code that was in existence when the alleged abuse occurred. . . .

Historically, the due process clause of the Delaware constitution[50] has substantially the same meaning as the due process clause contained in its federal counterpart. . . . [footnote omitted]. The expression "due process of law, as it appears in the Constitution of the United States, and the expression 'law of the land' as used in the Delaware Constitution, have generally been held to have the same meaning." . . . [footnote omitted]. . . . The Oblates argue that the expiration of a statute of limitations for a civil action is a fundamental vested right, and once the time has lapsed, a defendant has a vested right in knowing that no person or entity can bring a claim against him. We do not agree. Delaware constitutional due process is coextensive with federal due process. . . . [footnote omitted]. Federal precedent has long held that unless the expiration of a statute of limitation creates a prescriptive property right, such as title in adverse possession, the legislature can revive a cause of action after the statute of limitation has expired.[55] In 1945, the United States Supreme

---

43. *See Landgraf v. USI Film Prods.*, 511 U.S. 244, 265, 114 S.Ct. 1483, 128 L.Ed.2d 229 (1994) (explaining the principle that the legal effect of conduct should ordinarily be assessed under the law that existed when the conduct took place—has timeless and universal appeal); *Doe I v. Boy Scouts of America*, 148 Idaho 427, 224 P.3d 494, 498 (2009) (holding a statute governing tort actions in child abuse cases could not be retroactively applied to expand liability for perpetration of acts where liability did not previously exist).

44. For example: sexual harassment, incest, unlawful sexual contact, sexual extortion, continuous sexual abuse of a child, sexual exploitation of a child, and sexual solicitation of a child. *See e.g.*, 11 Del. C. Part I, Chapter 5, Subchapter II, Subpart D: Sexual Offenses.

45. *See* 11 *Del. C.* § 822 (1953): Lewdly playing with a child under 16 years.
> Whoever lewdly and lasciviously plays or toys with a child under the age of 16 years may
> be fined not more than $500 or imprisoned not more than 3 years, or both.

46. *See, e.g.*, *Cheswold Volunteer Fire Co. v. Lambertson Constr. Co.*, 489 A.2d 413, 421 (Del.1984) (explaining that "the running of a statute of limitations will nullify a party's remedy" and that a "statute of limitations is . . . a procedural mechanism").

50. Del. Const. art. I, § 9 ("All courts shall be open; and every man for an injury done him in his reputation, person, movable or immovable possessions, shall have a remedy by the due course of law, and justice administered according to the very right of the cause and the law of the land, without sale, denial, or unreasonable delay or expense. Suits may be brought against the State, according to such regulations as shall be made by law.").

55. [*Campbell*] *v. Holt*, 115 U.S. 620, 627–28, 6 S.Ct. 209, 29 L.Ed. 483 (1885).

Court concluded that revival of a personal cause of action, that did not involve the creation of title, does not offend the Federal Constitution.[56] Explicitly rejecting the fundamental right argument, the Court held that:

> Statutes of limitation find their justification in necessity and convenience rather than in logic ... They are by definition arbitrary, and their operation does not discriminate between the just and the unjust claim, or the avoidable and unavoidable delay ... Their shelter has never been regarded as ... a 'fundamental right'... the history of pleas of limitation shows them to be good only by legislative grace and to be subject to a relatively large degree of legislative control.[57]

As a matter of constitutional law, statutes of limitation go to matters of remedy, not destruction of fundamental rights.[58] Under Delaware law, the CVA can be applied retroactively because it affects matters of procedure and remedies, not substantive or vested rights.... [footnote omitted]. Accordingly, the General Assembly "has the power to determine a statute of limitations and such a determination does not violate [Article 1, Section 9] if it is reasonable." ... [footnote omitted]. Furthermore, we do not sit as an überlegislature to eviscerate proper legislative enactments. It is beyond the province of courts to question the policy or wisdom of an otherwise valid law. Rather, we must take and apply the law as we find it, leaving any desirable changes to the General Assembly.... [footnote omitted].

To prevail on an as applied due process challenge, a defendant must show not only the loss of the witness and/or evidence but also that that loss prejudiced him.... [footnote omitted]. The complaining party must specifically identify witnesses or documents lost during delay properly attributable to the plaintiff.... [footnote omitted]. Furthermore, the proof must be definite and not speculative. An assertion that a missing witness might have been useful does not show the actual prejudice required.... [footnote omitted].... The Oblates claim that the CVA violates due process as applied to them, because there is no direct evidence that the defendants had notice or knowledge of the risk of abuse that Norris posed. According to the Oblates, this lack of "notice" violates due process, and therefore, it is unjust for them to defend against a claim for gross negligence based on actions that occurred over 40 years ago.

Here, the Oblates fail to demonstrate special hardships, oppressive effects or actual prejudice because there is abundant evidence — including the Oblates' own records demonstrating prior knowledge of Norris' sexual abuse of children and his many other problems — that the Oblates may have violated the educational standard of care for Delaware schools. Additionally, the Oblates were not unduly prejudiced by Norris' death and his inability to testify, because the question to be decided was whether the Oblates and Salesianum had knowledge of Norris' history as an abuser and failed to act in response. A review of the record evidence shows that there was sufficient circumstantial evidence to support the jury verdict.... [footnote omitted]. Indeed, the evidence is taken directly from the defendants' own still existing internal records. Furthermore, several of Norris' coworkers are still alive and testified at trial. Therefore, we find the CVA does not violate due process as applied to the Oblates.... The judgment of the Superior Court is REVERSED and the action is REMANDED for proceedings consistent with this Opinion.

---

56. *Chase Sec. Corp. v. Donaldson*, 325 U.S. 304, 316, 65 S.Ct. 1137, 89 L.Ed. 1628 (1945).
57. *Id.* at 314, 65 S.Ct. 1137.
58. *Id.*

Notes

Recall that in *Stogner v. California, supra,* Chapter Seven, Section I.A, the Court held as unconstitutional, under the *Ex Post Facto* Clause, state efforts to retroactively apply the *criminal* statutory limitation period. However, in *Sheehan,* within the *civil* context, the Supreme Court of Delaware upheld Delaware's statutory repeal of the limitations period on child sex-related abuse and its implementation of a two-year window for victims to file civil claims on actions that were previously barred under the formerly applicable statute of limitations.

The civil statutes of limitations for specific causes of action are state-specific. For a comprehensive comparison of various state approaches to civil statute of limitations periods, see Professor Marci A. Hamilton's analysis at www.sol-reform.com (last viewed Apr. 7, 2015). When sexual crimes involve minor victims, the majority of states "toll" the statute of limitations for a specific period of time—usually until the child victim turns 18 or other designated age of majority. *See, e.g.,* Alaska Stat. § 09.10.140(a) (2014) (2–3 year limitation tolled until child turns 18); Ark. Code Ann. § 16-56-116 (2014) (action may be brought within 3 years of turning 21 years of age); Mo. Rev. Stat. § 537.046(2) (2014) (action may be brought within the later of 10 years of turning 21 or 3 years of discovering injuries resulting from childhood sexual abuse); N.M. Stat. Ann. § 37-1-30(A)(1) (2014) (action allowed until victim turns 24 or within 3 years from discovery of injuries, which ever is later); Wisc. Stat. Ann. § 893.587 (2015) (action must be commenced before victim reaches 35 years of age). Once the window closes, however, the claims are not revived. *See Miller v. Subiaco Academy,* 386 F. Supp. 2d 1025 (W.D. Ark. 2005) (cause of action statutorily tolled until three years after former student reached age of majority, then time-barred by terms of statute).

As indicated in the state statutes cited above, states may also apply a "discovery rule," whereby, rather than running from the date of an actual injury, the limitation period begins to run from the date of "accrual," which, in the context of child sexual abuse, usually does not occur until the victim discovers his or her injuries. And some states have opted to abolish their civil statute of limitations. For example, Utah employed a 4-year statute of limitations, tolled until the child attains the age of 18, *see* Utah Code Ann. § 78B-2-308(2)(a)-(5) (2014), but 2015 Utah Laws H.B. 277 (West's No. 49) (approved Mar. 2015), abolished the civil statute of limitations in child sexual abuse cases. For the most current information on state statute of limitation reform, go to www.sol-reform.com. There are a variety of other comparative resources available on the Internet that address all aspects of state civil statutes of limitations. *See, e.g.,* National Conference of State Legislatures, *State Civil Statutes of Limitations in Child Sexual Abuse Cases,* available at http://www.ncsl.org/research/human-services/state-civil-statutes-of-limitations-in-child-sexua.aspx (last visited Apr. 15, 2015); National District Attorneys Association, *Statutes of Limitation for Civil Action for Offenses Against Children Compilation,* available at http://www.ndaa.org/pdf/Statutes%20of%20Limitations%20for%20Civil%20Actions%20for%20Offenses%20Against%20Children%20(2013%20Update).pdf (last updated May 2013); Rape, Abuse & Incest National Network, *Statutes of Limitations,* available at https://apps.rainn.org/CrimeDef/landing-page-statutes.cfm (last visited Apr. 16, 2015).

B. Civil Commitment

Kansas v. Crane

United States Supreme Court, 2002
534 U.S. 407, 122 S. Ct. 867

Justice BREYER delivered the opinion of the Court.

This case concerns the constitutional requirements substantively limiting the civil commitment of a dangerous sexual offender — a matter that this Court considered in *Kansas v. Hendricks*, 521 U.S. 346, 117 S.Ct. 2072, 138 L.Ed.2d 501 (1997). The State of Kansas argues that the Kansas Supreme Court has interpreted our decision in *Hendricks* in an overly restrictive manner. We agree and vacate the Kansas court's judgment....

In *Hendricks*, this Court upheld the Kansas Sexually Violent Predator Act, Kan. Stat. Ann. § 59-29a01 *et seq.* (1994), against constitutional challenge. 521 U.S., at 371, 117 S.Ct. 2072. In doing so, the Court characterized the confinement at issue as civil, not criminal, confinement. *Id.*, at 369, 117 S.Ct. 2072. And it held that the statutory criterion for confinement embodied in the statute's words "mental abnormality or personality disorder" satisfied "'substantive' due process requirements." *Id.*, at 356, 360, 117 S.Ct. 2072.... In reaching its conclusion, the Court's opinion pointed out that "States have in certain narrow circumstances provided for the forcible civil detainment of people who are unable to control their behavior and who thereby pose a danger to the public health and safety." *Id.*, at 357, 117 S.Ct. 2072. It said that "[w]e have consistently upheld such involuntary commitment statutes" when (1) "the confinement takes place pursuant to proper procedures and evidentiary standards," (2) there is a finding of "dangerousness either to one's self or to others," and (3) proof of dangerousness is "coupled ... with the proof of some additional factor, such as a 'mental illness' or 'mental abnormality.'" *Id.*, at 357–358, 117 S.Ct. 2072. It noted that the Kansas "Act unambiguously requires a finding of dangerousness either to one's self or to others," *id.*, at 357, 117 S.Ct. 2072, and then "links that finding to the existence of a 'mental abnormality' or 'personality disorder' that makes it difficult, if not impossible, for the person to control his dangerous behavior," *id.*, at 358, 117 S.Ct. 2072 (citing Kan. Stat. Ann. § 59-29a02(b) (1994)). And the Court ultimately determined that the statute's "requirement of a 'mental abnormality' or 'personality disorder' is consistent with the requirements of ... other statutes that we have upheld in that it narrows the class of persons eligible for confinement to those who are unable to control their dangerousness." 521 U.S., at 358, 117 S.Ct. 2072.

The Court went on to respond to Hendricks' claim that earlier cases had required a finding, not of "mental abnormality" or "personality disorder," but of "mental illness." *Id.*, at 358–359, 117 S.Ct. 2072. In doing so, the Court pointed out that we "have traditionally left to legislators the task of defining [such] terms." *Id.*, at 359, 117 S.Ct. 2072. It then held that, to "the extent that the civil commitment statutes we have considered set forth criteria relating to an individual's inability to control his dangerousness, the Kansas Act sets forth comparable criteria." *Id.*, at 360, 117 S.Ct. 2072. It added that Hendricks' own condition "doubtless satisfies those criteria," for (1) he suffers from pedophilia, (2) "the psychiatric profession itself classifies" that condition "as a serious mental disorder," and (3) Hendricks conceded that he cannot "'control the urge'" to molest children. And it concluded that this "admitted lack of volitional control, coupled with a prediction of future dangerousness, adequately distinguishes Hendricks from other dangerous persons who are perhaps more properly dealt with exclusively through criminal proceedings." *Ibid.*...

In the present case the State of Kansas asks us to review the Kansas Supreme Court's application of *Hendricks*. The State here seeks the civil commitment of Michael Crane, a previously convicted sexual offender who, according to at least one of the State's psychiatric witnesses, suffers from both exhibitionism and antisocial personality disorder. *In re Crane*, 269 Kan. 578, 580–581, 7 P.3d 285, 287 (2000); cf. also American Psychiatric Association, Diagnostic and Statistical Manual of Mental Disorders 569 (rev. 4th ed. 2000) (DSM-IV) (detailing exhibitionism), 701–706 (detailing antisocial personality disorder). After a jury trial, the Kansas District Court ordered Crane's civil commitment. 269 Kan., at 579–584, 7 P.3d, at 286–288. But the Kansas Supreme Court reversed. *Id.*, at 586, 7 P.3d, at 290. In that court's view, the Federal Constitution as interpreted in *Hendricks* insists upon "a finding that the defendant cannot control his dangerous behavior" — even if (as provided by Kansas law) problems of "emotional capacity" and not "volitional capacity" prove the "source of bad behavior" warranting commitment. 269 Kan., at 586, 7 P.3d, at 290; see also Kan. Stat. Ann. § 59-29a02(b) (2000 Cum.Supp.) (defining "[m]ental abnormality" as a condition that affects an individual's emotional *or* volitional capacity). And the trial court had made no such finding.

Kansas now argues that the Kansas Supreme Court wrongly read *Hendricks* as requiring the State *always* to prove that a dangerous individual is *completely* unable to control his behavior. That reading, says Kansas, is far too rigid.... We agree with Kansas insofar as it argues that *Hendricks* set forth no requirement of *total* or *complete* lack of control. *Hendricks* referred to the Kansas Act as requiring a "mental abnormality" or "personality disorder" that makes it "*difficult,* if not impossible, for the [dangerous] person to control his dangerous behavior." 521 U.S., at 358, 117 S.Ct. 2072 (emphasis added). The word "difficult" indicates that the lack of control to which this Court referred was not absolute. Indeed, as different *amici* on opposite sides of this case agree, an absolutist approach is unworkable. Brief for Association for the Treatment of Sexual Abusers as *Amicus Curiae* 3; cf. Brief for American Psychiatric Association et al. as *Amici Curiae* 10; cf. also American Psychiatric Association, Statement on the Insanity Defense 11 (1982), reprinted in G. Melton, J. Petrila, N. Poythress, & C. Slobogin, Psychological Evaluations for the Courts 200 (2d ed. 1997) ("'The line between an irresistible impulse and an impulse not resisted is probably no sharper than that between twilight and dusk'"). Moreover, most severely ill people — even those commonly termed "psychopaths" — retain some ability to control their behavior. See Morse, Culpability and Control, 142 U. Pa. L.Rev. 1587, 1634–1635 (1994); cf. Winick, Sex Offender Law in the 1990s: A Therapeutic Jurisprudence Analysis, 4 Psychol. Pub. Pol'y & L. 505, 520–525 (1998). Insistence upon absolute lack of control would risk barring the civil commitment of highly dangerous persons suffering severe mental abnormalities.

We do not agree with the State, however, insofar as it seeks to claim that the Constitution permits commitment of the type of dangerous sexual offender considered in *Hendricks* without *any* lack-of-control determination.... *Hendricks* underscored the constitutional importance of distinguishing a dangerous sexual offender subject to civil commitment "from other dangerous persons who are perhaps more properly dealt with exclusively through criminal proceedings." 521 U.S., at 360, 117 S.Ct. 2072. That distinction is necessary lest "civil commitment" become a "mechanism for retribution or general deterrence" — functions properly those of criminal law, not civil commitment. *Id.*, at 372–373, 117 S.Ct. 2072 (KENNEDY, J., concurring); cf. also Moran, The Epidemiology of Antisocial Personality Disorder, 34 Social Psychiatry & Psychiatric Epidemiology 231, 234 (1999) (noting that 40%–60% of the male prison population is diagnosable with antisocial personality disorder). The presence of what the "psychiatric profession itself classifie[d] ... as a serious mental disorder" helped to make that distinction in *Hendricks*.

And a critical distinguishing feature of that "serious ... disorder" there consisted of a special and serious lack of ability to control behavior.

In recognizing that fact, we did not give to the phrase "lack of control" a particularly narrow or technical meaning. And we recognize that in cases where lack of control is at issue, "inability to control behavior" will not be demonstrable with mathematical precision. It is enough to say that there must be proof of serious difficulty in controlling behavior. And this, when viewed in light of such features of the case as the nature of the psychiatric diagnosis, and the severity of the mental abnormality itself, must be sufficient to distinguish the dangerous sexual offender whose serious mental illness, abnormality, or disorder subjects him to civil commitment from the dangerous but typical recidivist convicted in an ordinary criminal case. 521 U.S., at 357–358, 117 S.Ct. 2072; see also *Foucha v. Louisiana*, 504 U.S. 71, 82–83, 112 S.Ct. 1780, 118 L.Ed.2d 437 (1992) (rejecting an approach to civil commitment that would permit the indefinite confinement "of any convicted criminal" after completion of a prison term).

We recognize that *Hendricks* as so read provides a less precise constitutional standard than would those more definite rules for which the parties have argued. But the Constitution's safeguards of human liberty in the area of mental illness and the law are not always best enforced through precise bright-line rules. For one thing, the States retain considerable leeway in defining the mental abnormalities and personality disorders that make an individual eligible for commitment. *Hendricks*, 521 U.S., at 359, 117 S.Ct. 2072; *id.*, at 374–375, 117 S.Ct. 2072 (BREYER, J., dissenting). For another, the science of psychiatry, which informs but does not control ultimate legal determinations, is an ever-advancing science, whose distinctions do not seek precisely to mirror those of the law. See *id.*, at 359, 117 S.Ct. 2072. See also, *e.g.*, *Ake v. Oklahoma*, 470 U.S. 68, 81, 105 S.Ct. 1087, 84 L.Ed.2d 53 (1985) (psychiatry not "an exact science"); DSM-IV xxx ("concept of mental disorder ... lacks a consistent operational definition"); *id.*, at xxxii–xxxiii (noting the "imperfect fit between the questions of ultimate concern to the law and the information contained in [the DSM's] clinical diagnosis"). Consequently, we have sought to provide constitutional guidance in this area by proceeding deliberately and contextually, elaborating generally stated constitutional standards and objectives as specific circumstances require. *Hendricks* embodied that approach....

The State also questions how often a volitional problem lies at the heart of a dangerous sexual offender's serious mental abnormality or disorder. It points out that the Kansas Supreme Court characterized its state statute as permitting commitment of dangerous sexual offenders who (1) suffered from a mental abnormality properly characterized by an "emotional" impairment and (2) suffered no "volitional" impairment. 269 Kan., at 583, 7 P.3d, at 289. It adds that, in the Kansas court's view, *Hendricks* absolutely forbids the commitment of any such person. 269 Kan., at 585–586, 7 P.3d, at 290. And the State argues that it was wrong to read *Hendricks* in this way....

We agree that *Hendricks* limited its discussion to volitional disabilities. And that fact is not surprising. The case involved an individual suffering from pedophilia—a mental abnormality that critically involves what a lay person might describe as a lack of control. DSM-IV 571–572 (listing as a diagnostic criterion for pedophilia that an individual have acted on, or been affected by, "sexual urges" toward children). Hendricks himself stated that he could not "'control the urge'" to molest children. 521 U.S., at 360, 117 S.Ct. 2072. In addition, our cases suggest that civil commitment of dangerous sexual offenders will normally involve individuals who find it particularly difficult to control their behavior—in the general sense described above. Cf. *Seling v. Young*, 531 U.S. 250, 256, 121 S.Ct. 727, 148 L.Ed.2d 734 (2001); cf. also Abel & Rouleau, Male Sex Offenders, in Handbook of Outpatient Treatment of Adults: Nonpsychotic Mental Disorders 271 (M. Thase, B. Edelstein, & M. Hersen eds.1990) (sex offenders' "compulsive, repetitive, driven behavior … appears to fit the criteria of an emotional or psychiatric illness"). And it is often appropriate to say of such individuals, in ordinary English, that they are "unable to control their dangerousness." *Hendricks, supra*, at 358, 117 S.Ct. 2072.

Regardless, *Hendricks* must be read in context. The Court did not draw a clear distinction between the purely "emotional" sexually related mental abnormality and the "volitional." Here, as in other areas of psychiatry, there may be "considerable overlap between a … defective understanding or appreciation and … [an] ability to control … behavior." American Psychiatric Association Statement on the Insanity Defense, 140 Am. J. Psychiatry 681, 685 (1983) (discussing "psychotic" individuals). Nor, when considering civil commitment, have we ordinarily distinguished for constitutional purposes among volitional, emotional, and cognitive impairments. See, *e.g., Jones v. United States*, 463 U.S. 354, 103 S.Ct. 3043, 77 L.Ed.2d 694 (1983); *Addington v. Texas*, 441 U.S. 418, 99 S.Ct. 1804, 60 L.Ed.2d 323 (1979). The Court in *Hendricks* had no occasion to consider whether confinement based solely on "emotional" abnormality would be constitutional, and we likewise have no occasion to do so in the present case.…

For these reasons, the judgment of the Kansas Supreme Court is vacated, and the case is remanded for further proceedings not inconsistent with this opinion.

It is so ordered.

Justice SCALIA, with whom Justice THOMAS joins, dissenting.

Today the Court holds that the Kansas Sexually Violent Predator Act (SVPA) cannot, consistent with so-called substantive due process, be applied as written. It does so even though, less than five years ago, we upheld the very same statute against the very same contention in an appeal by the very same petitioner (the State of Kansas) from the judgment of the very same court. Not only is the new law that the Court announces today wrong, but the Court's manner of promulgating it—snatching back from the State of Kansas a victory so recently awarded—cheapens the currency of our judgments. I would reverse, rather than vacate, the judgment of the Kansas Supreme Court.…

Respondent was convicted of lewd and lascivious behavior and pleaded guilty to aggravated sexual battery for two incidents that took place on the same day in 1993. In the first, respondent exposed himself to a tanning salon attendant. In the second, 30 minutes later, respondent entered a video store, waited until he was the only customer present, and then exposed himself to the clerk. Not stopping there, he grabbed the clerk by the neck, demanded she perform oral sex on him, and threatened to rape her, before running out of the store. Following respondent's plea to aggravated sexual battery, the State filed a petition in State District Court to have respondent evaluated and adjudicated a sexual predator under the SVPA. That Act permits the civil detention of a person convicted of any of several enumerated sexual offenses, if it is proven beyond a reasonable doubt that he suffers from a "mental abnormality"—a disorder affecting his "emotional or volitional capacity which predisposes the person to commit sexually violent offenses" —or a "personality disorder," either of "which makes the person likely to engage in repeat acts of sexual violence." Kan. Stat. Ann. §§ 59-29a02(a), (b) (2000 Cum.Supp.).

Several psychologists examined respondent and determined he suffers from exhibitionism and antisocial personality disorder. Though exhibitionism alone would not support classification as a sexual predator, a psychologist concluded that the two in combination did place respondent's condition within the range of disorders covered by the SVPA, "cit[ing] the increasing frequency of incidents involving [respondent], increasing intensity of the incidents, [respondent's] increasing disregard for the rights of others, and his increasing daring and aggressiveness." *In re Crane*, 269 Kan. 578, 579, 7 P.3d 285, 287 (2000). Another psychologist testified that respondent's behavior was marked by "impulsivity or failure to plan ahead," indicating his unlawfulness "was a combination of willful and uncontrollable behavior," *id.*, at 584–585, 7 P.3d, at 290. The State's experts agreed, however, that "'[r]espondent's mental disorder does not impair his volitional control to the degree he cannot control his dangerous behavior.'" *Id.*, at 581, 7 P.3d, at 288.

Respondent moved for summary judgment, arguing that for his detention to comport with substantive due process the State was required to prove not merely what the statute requires—that by reason of his mental disorder he is "likely to engage in repeat acts of sexual violence"—but also that he is unable to control his violent behavior. The trial court denied this motion, and instructed the jury pursuant to the terms of the statute. *Id.*, at 581, 7 P.3d, at 287–288. The jury found, beyond a reasonable doubt, that respondent was a sexual predator as defined by the SVPA. The Kansas Supreme Court reversed, holding the SVPA unconstitutional as applied to someone, like respondent, who has only an emotional or personality disorder within the meaning of the Act, rather than a volitional impairment. For such a person, it held, the State must show not merely a likelihood that the defendant would engage in repeat acts of sexual violence, but also an inability to control violent behavior. It based this holding solely on our decision in *Kansas v. Hendricks*, 521 U.S. 346, 117 S.Ct. 2072, 138 L.Ed.2d 501 (1997)....

Hendricks also involved the SVPA, and, as in this case, the Kansas Supreme Court had found that the SVPA swept too broadly. On the basis of considerable evidence showing that Hendricks suffered from pedophilia, the jury had found, beyond a reasonable doubt, that Hendricks met the statutory standard for commitment. See *id.*, at 355, 117 S.Ct. 2072; *In re Hendricks*, 259 Kan. 246, 247, 912 P.2d 129, 130 (1996). This standard (to repeat) was that he suffered from a "mental abnormality"—a disorder affecting his "emotional or volitional capacity which predisposes [him] to commit sexually violent offenses"—or a "personality disorder," either of which "makes [him] likely to engage in repeat acts of sexual violence." Kan. Stat. Ann. §§ 59-29a02(a), (b) (2000 Cum.Supp.). The trial court, after determining as a matter of state law that pedophilia was a "mental abnormality" within the meaning of the Act, ordered Hendricks committed. See 521 U.S., at 355–356, 117 S.Ct. 2072. The Kansas Supreme Court held the jury finding to be constitutionally inadequate. "Absent ... a finding [of mental illness]," it said, "the Act does not satisfy ... constitutional standard[s]," 259 Kan., at 261, 912 P.2d, at 138. (Mental illness, as it had been defined by Kansas law, required a showing that the detainee "[i]s suffering from a severe mental disorder"; "lacks capacity to make an informed decision concerning treatment"; and "is likely to cause harm to self or others." Kan. Stat. Ann. § 59-2902(h) (1994).) We granted the State of Kansas's petition for certiorari.

The first words of our opinion dealing with the merits of the case were as follows: "Kansas argues that the Act's definition of 'mental abnormality' satisfies 'substantive' due process requirements. We agree." *Hendricks*, 521 U.S., at 356, 117 S.Ct. 2072. And the *reason* it found substantive due process satisfied was clearly stated:

> "The Kansas Act is plainly of a kind with these other civil commitment statutes [that we have approved]: It requires a finding of future dangerousness [viz., that the person committed is 'likely to engage in repeat acts of sexual violence'], and then links that finding to the existence of a 'mental abnormality' or 'personality disorder' *that makes it difficult, if not impossible, for the person to control his dangerous behavior.* Kan. Stat. Ann. § 59-29a02(b) (1994)." *Id.*, at 358, 117 S.Ct. 2072 (emphasis added).

It is the italicized language in the foregoing excerpt that today's majority relies upon as establishing the requirement of a separate *finding* of inability to control behavior....

That is simply not a permissible reading of the passage, for several reasons. First, because the authority cited for the statement—in the immediately following reference to the Kansas Statutes Annotated—is the section of the SVPA that defines "mental abnormality," *which contains no requirement of inability to control.*[1] What the opinion was obviously saying was that the SVPA's required finding of a *causal connection* between the likelihood of repeat acts of sexual violence and the existence of a "mental abnormality" or "personality disorder" *necessarily* establishes "difficulty if not impossibility" in controlling behavior. This is clearly confirmed by the very next sentence of the opinion, which reads as follows:

> "The precommitment requirement of a 'mental abnormality' or 'personality disorder' is consistent with the requirements of ... other statutes that we have upheld in that it narrows the class of persons eligible for confinement to those who are unable to control their dangerousness." 521 U.S., at 358, 117 S.Ct. 2072.

It could not be clearer that, in the Court's estimation, the very existence of a mental abnormality or personality disorder *that causes* a likelihood of repeat sexual violence in itself *establishes* the requisite "difficulty if not impossibility" of control. Moreover, the passage in question cannot possibly be read as today's majority would read it because nowhere did the jury verdict of commitment that we reinstated in *Hendricks* contain a separate finding of "difficulty, if not impossibility, to control behavior." That finding must (as I have said) have been embraced within the finding of mental abnormality *causing* future dangerousness. And finally, the notion that the Constitution requires in every case a finding of "difficulty if not impossibility" of control does not fit comfortably with the broader holding of *Hendricks*, which was that "we have never required state legislatures to adopt any particular nomenclature in drafting civil commitment statutes. Rather, we have traditionally left to legislators the task of defining terms of a medical nature that have legal significance." *Id.*, at 359, 117 S.Ct. 2072.

The Court relies upon the fact that "*Hendricks* underscored the constitutional importance of distinguishing a dangerous sexual offender subject to civil commitment 'from other dangerous persons who are perhaps more properly dealt with exclusively through criminal proceedings.'" ... But the SVPA as written—without benefit of a supplemental control finding—already achieves that objective. It conditions civil commitment not upon a mere finding that the sex offender is likely to reoffend, but only upon the additional finding (beyond a reasonable doubt) that the *cause* of the likelihood of recidivism is a "mental abnormality or personality disorder." Kan. Stat. Ann. §59-29a02(a) (2000 Cum.Supp.). Ordinary recidivists *choose* to reoffend and are therefore amenable to deterrence through the criminal law; those subject to civil commitment under the SVPA, because their mental illness is an affliction and not a choice, are unlikely to be deterred. We specifically pointed this out in *Hendricks*. "Those persons committed under the Act," we said, "are, by definition, suffering from a 'mental abnormality' or a 'personality disorder' that prevents them from exercising adequate control over their behavior. Such persons are therefore unlikely to be deterred by the threat of confinement." 521 U.S., at 362–363, 117 S.Ct. 2072....

Not content with holding that the SVPA cannot be applied as written because it does not require a separate "lack-of-control determination," ... the Court also reopens a question

---

1. As quoted earlier in the *Hendricks* opinion, see 521 U.S., at 352, 117 S.Ct. 2072, §59-29a02(b) defines "mental abnormality" as a "congenital or acquired condition affecting the emotional or volitional capacity which predisposes the person to commit sexually violent offenses in a degree constituting such person a menace to the health and safety of others."

closed by *Hendricks*: whether the SVPA also cannot be applied as written because it allows for the commitment of people who have mental illnesses other than volitional impairments. "*Hendricks*," the Court says, "had no occasion to consider" this question....

But how could the Court possibly have avoided it? The jury whose commitment we affirmed in *Hendricks* had not been asked to find a volitional impairment, but had been charged in the language of the statute, which quite clearly covers nonvolitional impairments. And the fact that it did so had not escaped our attention. To the contrary, our *Hendricks* opinion explicitly and repeatedly recognized that the SVPA reaches individuals with personality disorders, 521 U.S., at 352, 353, 357, 358, 117 S.Ct. 2072, and quoted the Act's definition of mental abnormality (§ 59-29a02(b)), which makes plain that it embraces both emotional and volitional impairments, *id.*, at 352, 117 S.Ct. 2072. It is true that we repeatedly referred to Hendricks's "volitional" problems—because that was evidently the sort of mental abnormality that he had. But we nowhere accorded any legal significance to that fact—as we could not have done, since it was not a fact that the jury had been asked to determine. We held, without any qualification, "that the Kansas Sexually Violent Predator Act comports with [substantive] due process requirements," *id.*, at 371, 117 S.Ct. 2072, because its "precommitment requirement of a 'mental abnormality' or 'personality disorder' is consistent with the requirements of ... other statutes that we have upheld in that it narrows the class of persons eligible for confinement to those who are unable to control their dangerousness," *id.*, at 358, 117 S.Ct. 2072.

The Court appears to argue that, because *Hendricks* involved a defendant who indeed *had* a volitional impairment (even though we made nothing of that fact), its narrowest holding covers only *that* application of the SVPA, and our statement that the SVPA in its entirety was constitutional can be ignored.... This cannot be correct. The narrowest holding of *Hendricks* affirmed the constitutionality of commitment on the basis of the jury charge given in that case (to wit, the language of the SVPA); and since that charge did not require a finding of volitional impairment, neither does the Constitution.

I cannot resist observing that the distinctive status of volitional impairment which the Court mangles *Hendricks* to preserve would not even be worth preserving by more legitimate means. There is good reason why, as the Court accurately says, "when considering civil commitment ... we [have not] ordinarily distinguished for constitutional purposes among volitional, emotional, and cognitive impairments," ... We have not done so because it makes no sense. It is obvious that a person may be able to exercise volition and yet be unfit to turn loose upon society. The man who has a will of steel, but who delusionally believes that every woman he meets is inviting crude sexual advances, is surely a dangerous sexual predator....

I not only disagree with the Court's gutting of our holding in *Hendricks*; I also doubt the desirability, and indeed even the coherence, of the new constitutional test which (on the basis of no analysis except a misreading of *Hendricks*) it substitutes. Under our holding in *Hendricks*, a jury in an SVPA commitment case would be required to find, beyond a reasonable doubt, (1) that the person previously convicted of one of the enumerated sexual offenses is suffering from a mental abnormality or personality disorder, and (2) that this condition renders him likely to commit future acts of sexual violence. Both of these findings are coherent, and (with the assistance of expert testimony) well within the capacity of a normal jury. Today's opinion says that the Constitution requires the addition of a third finding: (3) that the subject suffers from an inability to control behavior—not utter inability, ... and not even inability in a particular constant degree, but rather inability in a degree that will vary "in light of such features of the case as the nature of the psychiatric diagnosis, and the severity of the mental abnormality itself," ...

This formulation of the new requirement certainly displays an elegant subtlety of mind. Unfortunately, it gives trial courts, in future cases under the many commitment statutes similar to Kansas's SVPA, *not a clue* as to how they are supposed to charge the jury! Indeed, it does not even provide a clue to the trial court, on remand, *in this very case*. What is the judge to ask the jury to find? It is fine and good to talk about the desirability of our "proceeding deliberately and contextually, elaborating generally stated constitutional standards and objectives as specific circumstances require," ... but one would think that this plan would at least produce the "elaboration" of what the jury charge should be in the "specific circumstances" of the present case. "[P]roceeding deliberately" is not synonymous with not proceeding at all.

I suspect that the reason the Court avoids any elaboration is that elaboration which passes the laugh test is impossible. How is one to frame for a jury the degree of "inability to control" which, in the particular case, "the nature of the psychiatric diagnosis, and the severity of the mental abnormality" require? Will it be a percentage ("Ladies and gentlemen of the jury, you may commit Mr. Crane under the SVPA only if you find, beyond a reasonable doubt, that he is 42% unable to control his penchant for sexual violence")? Or a frequency ratio ("Ladies and gentlemen of the jury, you may commit Mr. Crane under the SVPA only if you find, beyond a reasonable doubt, that he is unable to control his penchant for sexual violence 3 times out of 10")? Or merely an adverb ("Ladies and gentlemen of the jury, you may commit Mr. Crane under the SVPA only if you find, beyond a reasonable doubt, that he is appreciably—or moderately, or substantially, or almost totally—unable to control his penchant for sexual violence")? None of these seems to me satisfactory.... But if it is indeed possible to "elaborate" upon the Court's novel test, surely the Court has an obligation to do so in the "specific circumstances" of the present case, so that the trial court will know what is expected of it on remand. It is irresponsible to leave the law in such a state of utter indeterminacy....

Today's holding would make bad law in any circumstances. In the circumstances under which it is pronounced, however, it both distorts our law and degrades our authority. The State of Kansas, unable to apply its legislature's sexual predator legislation as written because of the Kansas Supreme Court's erroneous view of the Federal Constitution, sought and received certiorari in *Hendricks*, and achieved a reversal, in an opinion holding that "the Kansas Sexually Violent Predator Act comports with [substantive] due process requirements," 521 U.S., at 371, 117 S.Ct. 2072. The Kansas Supreme Court still did not like the law and prevented its operation, on substantive due process grounds, once again. The State of Kansas again sought certiorari, asking nothing more than reaffirmation of our 5-year-old opinion —only to be told that what we said then we now unsay. There is an obvious lesson here for state supreme courts that do not agree with our jurisprudence: ignoring it is worth a try.

A jury determined beyond a reasonable doubt that respondent suffers from antisocial personality disorder combined with exhibitionism, and that this is either a mental abnormality or a personality disorder making it likely he will commit repeat acts of sexual violence. That is all the SVPA requires, and all the Constitution demands. Since we have already held precisely that in another case (which, by a remarkable feat of jurisprudential jujitsu the Court relies upon as the only authority for its decision), I would reverse the judgment below.

Notes

Kansas v. Hendricks (1997) and *Kansas v. Crane* (2002) are the foundation of the development of federal civil commitment law. In *Hendricks*, the Court upheld, as a civil remedy, a Kansas law authorizing the commitment of sex offenders who suffered from a mental abnormality, including mental illness or personality disorder, presented as likely to engage in future acts of dangerous sexual offenses. *Hendricks*, 521 U.S. at 363. In *Crane*, the Court focused on the volitional requirements and the offender's lack of ability to control his or her behavior as qualification for commitment, thus distinguishing the commitable offender from the dangerous recidivist. *Crane*, 534 U.S. at 413. The *Crane* Court required only "serious difficulty in controlling behavior," as opposed to a "*total* or *complete* lack of control." *Id.* at 411. While the *Hendricks* standard of future dangerousness remains the constitutional requirement, the assessment of volition distinction considered in *Crane* is also a viable application within the 20 states that have implemented civil commitment statutes as of 2014.

In 2006, Congress passed the Adam Walsh Child Protection and Safety Act (AWA), 42 U.S.C. § 16911 et seq. (2006), which became the most comprehensive sex offender law to date, through its enhanced penalties for specific sex crimes, creation of new sex offenses, and its implementation of a national sex offender registry database. The AWA also implemented a standard for the civil commitment of federal sex offenders. The AWA standard does not include a consideration of the likelihood for future dangerousness, as in *Hendricks*. Instead, the qualification for commitment under the AWA is sexual dangerousness. 18 U.S.C. § 4248 (Civil commitment of a sexually dangerous person). The AWA defines a "sexually dangerous person" as "a person who has engaged or attempted to engage in sexually violent conduct or child molestation and who is sexually dangerous to others." 18 U.S.C. § 4147(a)(5) (2014). The term "sexually dangerous to others" "means that the person suffers from a serious mental illness, abnormality, or disorder as a result of which he would have serious difficulty in refraining from sexually violent conduct or child molestation if released." *Id.* at (a)(6). However, the AWA does not define "serious mental illness," "abnormality," "disorder," or "sexually violent conduct" and presents other shortcomings, such as allowance for indefinite commitment. *See* John Fabian, *The Adam Walsh Child Protection and Safety Act: Legal and Psychological Aspects of the New Civil Commitment Law for Federal Sex Offenders*, 60 CLEV. ST. L. REV. 307, 310–16 (2012) (describing the AWA and comparing the AWA and specific state civil commitment standards). The constitutionality of the Act is addressed in *United States v. Comstock*, 551 F.3d 274, 276 (4th Cir. 2009) (holding that Congress lacked authority to implement § 4248), *rev'd and remanded*, 560 U.S. 126, 130, 130 S.Ct. 1949, 176 L.Ed.2d 878 (2010) (reversing on issue of Congressional authority but remanding for due process consideration); 627 F.3d 513, 515 (4th Cir. 2010) (subsequently holding that § 4248 satisfies due process clause), *cert. denied*, ___ U.S. ___, 131 S. Ct. 3026 (2011).

In adopting state civil commitment standards, the AWA and some states opt for the volitional impairment standard described in *Crane*, *see, e.g.*, N.Y. MENTAL HYG. § 10.03(e) (McKinney 2015) ("'Dangerous sex offender requiring confinement' means a person who is a detained sex offender suffering from a mental abnormality involving such a strong predisposition to commit sex offenses, and such an inability to control behavior, that the person is likely to be a danger to others and to commit sex offenses if not confined to a secure treatment facility."), while others require a mere showing of likely future dangerousness, akin to the *Hendricks* standard, *see, e.g.*, WASH. REV. CODE § 71.09.020(18) ("'Sexually violent predator' means any person who has been convicted of or charged with a crime of sexual violence and who suffers from a mental abnormality or personality disorder which makes the person likely to engage in predatory acts of sexual violence if not confined in a secure facility."). States vary in their approaches. For a comparison of state civil commitment statutes, see National District Attorneys Association, *Civil Commitment of Sex Offenders*, available at http://www.ndaa.org/pdf/Sex%20Offender%20 Civil%20Commitment-April%202012.pdf (last updated Apr. 2012). *See also* National Conference of State Legislatures, *Sex Offender Enactments Database*, available at http://

www.ncsl.org/research/civil-and-criminal-justice/sex-offender-enactments-database.aspx (last updated Dec. 2014) (including current legislative updates since 2008).

For commentary on the widely debated topic of civil commitment policies for sex offenders, see Rebecca M. Ullian, *United States v. Youngs: The Intersection of Guilty Pleas, Procedural Due Process, and Indefinite Civil Commitment of Sexually Dangerous Persons*, 40 NEW ENG. J. ON CRIM. & CIV. CONFINEMENT 555 (2014); Jefferson C. Knighton, Daniel C. Murrie, Marcus T. Boccaccini, and Darrel B. Turner, *How Likely Is "Likely To Reoffend" in Sex Offender Civil Commitment Trials?*, 38 L. & HUM. BEHAV. 293 (2014); Alexander J. Blenkinsopp, *Dangerousness and the Civil-Criminal Distinction: Another Reason to Rethink the Indefinite Detention of Sex Offenders*, 45 CONN. L. REV. 9 (2013); John Fabian, *The Adam Walsh Child Protection and Safety Act: Legal and Psychological Aspects of the New Civil Commitment Law for Federal Sex Offenders*, 60 CLEV. ST. L. REV. 307, 310–16 (2012) (describing the AWA and comparing the AWA and specific state civil commitment standards); Ryan K. Melcher, *There Ain't No End for the "Wicked": Implications of and Recommendations for § 4248 of the Adam Walsh Act After United States v. Comstock*, 97 IOWA L. REV. 629 (2012); Tamara Rice Lave, *Throwing Away the Key: Has the Adam Walsh Act Lowered the Threshold for Sexually Violent Predator Commitments Too Far?*, 14 U. PA. J. CONST. L. 391 (2011).

The following cases apply the civil commitment standards of the Adam Walsh Child Protection and Safety Act to inmates deemed to be sexually dangerous persons who warranted commitment. Consider how the standard applies and the sufficiency of the evidence in each case. What is the basis for the different outcomes in the cases?

United States v. Cooke

Fourth Circuit, 2014
565 Fed. Appx. 193

PER CURIAM:

On this appeal, Randle Porter Cooke challenges his designation as a sexually dangerous person and consequent civil commitment under the Adam Walsh Child Protection and Safety Act of 2006, 18 U.S.C. § 4248.... Cooke has been convicted and imprisoned three times as a result of sexual contact with minors. In 1981, Cooke was charged with aggravated sexual assault for fondling a boy under the age of 13. He pleaded guilty to an attempted felony, for which he received a suspended two-year sentence.... In 1991, Cooke was convicted in Texas state court of sexual assault of a child and indecency with a child. The first of these charges related to his performing oral sex on and touching the genitals of a fourteen-year-old boy. The second related to his touching the genitals of another boy under the age of 17. He was sentenced to 10 years' imprisonment and was released in November of 2000.

The events leading to Cooke's most recent incarceration began seven months later. In May of 2001, he met a twelve-year-old boy in a bookstore. Cooke told the boy and the boy's mother that he was a "big brother" who mentored young people. Cooke began communicating with the boy by email and was allowed to take him on an outing. He drove the boy to a cemetery and, en route, Cooke attempted to hypnotize the boy and placed his hand on the boy's penis. At the cemetery, Cooke gave the boy marijuana and asked him to engage in oral sex. The boy declined.... Cooke took the boy home, but continued to try to contact him until October of 2001. To avoid detection by the boy's parents, Cooke asked the boy to refer to him as though he were a 15-year-old boy named "Josh," and wrote the boy letters under that name. Cooke also contacted one of the boy's schoolmates online, again posing as a boy named "Josh," in an attempt to set up a meeting.

In October of 2001, Federal Bureau of Investigation agents interviewed Cooke. He told the officers that he was initially sexually attracted to the boy and had hoped to have a sexual relationship. He claimed, however, to have since regained control over his sexual urges. Cooke permitted the FBI to search his computer where investigators found more than 100 photographs of teenaged males between the ages of 11 and 20 engaged in sexual conduct and one photograph of a 9-year-old boy posed provocatively with his underwear exposed.... As a result, Cooke was charged with and pleaded guilty to one count of possession of child pornography in violation of 18 U.S.C. § 2252(a)(4)(B) and two counts of receipt of child pornography in violation of 18 U.S.C. § 2252(a)(2). He was sentenced to 87 months' imprisonment and three years' supervised release.

Prior to Cooke's 2010 release date, the Attorney General filed a certification in the Eastern District of North Carolina that Cooke is a sexually dangerous person.[1] This filing automatically stayed Cooke's release from prison and initiated commitment proceedings.... During those proceedings, an evidentiary hearing was held before a magistrate judge to determine Cooke's status as a sexually dangerous person. Cooke and two experts testified on his behalf and three experts testified for the government.... The government also introduced instances of Cooke's misconduct in prison. For example, Cooke sought to have himself placed in protective custody by presenting prison officials with what purported to be a threatening note. It was later discovered that Cooke had written the note himself. On another occasion, Cooke developed a relationship with a 22-year-old fellow inmate, with whom he tried to secure private time in the prison chapel. This inmate was a mental health patient with his own history of sexual offenses. Discussing his fondness for this inmate, Cooke confided in a prison official that he liked "young, troubled boys."

Cooke was transferred to FCI Butner where he sought to participate in the the Sex Offender Treatment Program, but was initially denied access because his release date was too distant. When he became eligible for the program, however, Cooke declined to participate because statements made in the program could be used against him in proceedings such as this. Cooke testified that he would gladly participate in treatment, but his plans for doing so were vague. Cooke's only specific post-release plan to avoid relapse was to live at the same assisted living facility as his mother. His plan indicated his desire to live peacefully, have long-postponed surgery, seek therapy, and generally avoid returning to his former habits. It did not indicate the development of any special knowledge or skills to help him avoid situations or stimuli that might lead him to reoffend. To the contrary, the government introduced correspondence between Cooke and another convicted sex offender exchanged in late 2011 and early 2012.

Two forensic psychologists, Dr. Gary Zinik and Dr. Lela Demby, testified as expert witnesses for the government on direct. Dr. Zinik diagnosed Cooke with "Paraphilia NOS, Hebephilia, attracted to Adolescent Males, Nonexclusive Type,"[2] "Cannabis Dependence by history, in remission in a controlled environment," "Narcotics Dependence (pain medication), in remission in a controlled environment," and "Personality Disorder NOS, with

---

1. Though Cooke was convicted of the underlying offenses in the Western District of Tennessee, he was in custody within the Eastern District of North Carolina at the time the certification was filed. The Adam Walsh Act provides that the certification is to be filed, and commitment proceedings conducted, in the district within which the respondent is incarcerated, not the district in which he was convicted. 18 U.S.C. § 4248(a).

2. "NOS" is an abbreviation for "not otherwise specified."

Antisocial and Narcissistic Features." ... Dr. Zinik concluded that there was a "high level" of risk that Cooke would reoffend, despite the fact that Cooke is paralyzed from the waist down and is often catheterized. Dr. Zinik noted that Cooke was similarly impaired at the time of most of his previous offenses.

Dr. Zinik observed that Cooke's "predatory" advances towards a vulnerable fellow inmate belies Cooke's claims that he has changed his behavior.... Cooke's "vague, evasive" responses to questions about his past offenses suggest that Cooke does not really "get" his condition and that he "*thinks* and *talks* like an untreated sex offender." ... Dr. Zinik concluded that "Mr. Cooke is still at least a medium-high to high risk for sexual reoffense" and that he remains "physically capable of molesting young boys in the same fashion as he has in the past if he were motivated to do so." ...

Dr. Demby similarly concluded that "it is highly likely that Mr. Cooke will continue to sexually reoffend." ... She diagnosed Cooke with "Paraphilia Not Otherwise Specified," "Narcotic Dependence in a Controlled Environment (by history)," and "Personality Disorder Not Otherwise Specified with borderline Traits." ... She further opined that Cooke's physical condition would not impede him from reoffending, noting as Dr. Zinik did, that Cooke has offended repeatedly in his current condition. In fact, Dr. Demby observed that "[Cooke's] disability appears to serve as part of his ability to get parents and victims to trust him." ... Also like Dr. Zinik, Dr. Demby concluded that Cooke "demonstrates extreme minimization and denial of his offenses, as well as attitudes that support his sex offenses. Both of these factors exacerbate his risk of reoffense." ...

Dr. Joseph Plaud, a psychiatric expert, testified on Cooke's behalf. Dr. Plaud testified that Cooke's evident attraction to young pubescent boys did not constitute a diagnosable mental illness. He also criticized the predictive models used by Dr. Zinik and Dr. Demby, contending that there is no model that could reliably determine Cooke's risk of reoffending given his physical condition.... Dr. Moira Artigues also testified on Cooke's behalf, recounting his painful and debilitating conditions and opining that these conditions had worsened while he was in custody. Although these impairments reduced the risk that Cooke would reoffend, Dr. Artigues did not testify that Cooke presented a "low risk" of reoffense. She did not physically examine Cooke and did not have the opportunity to review all of Cooke's most recent medical records. Her testimony was largely based on Cooke's own statements and the other expert reports.... Finally, Dr. Roscoe Ramsey, Cooke's treating physician at FCI Butner, testified for the government on rebuttal. Dr. Ramsey testified that Cooke's physical condition had not deteriorated during his last three years of detention.

The magistrate judge recommended that "the court enter an order finding by clear and convincing evidence that respondent is a sexually dangerous person within the meaning of 18 U.S.C. § 4247(a)(5) and committing him to the custody and care of the Attorney General pursuant to 18 U.S.C. § 4248(d)." ... On de novo review, the district court agreed....

18 U.S.C. § 4248 provides for the civil commitment of individuals in the custody of the Federal Bureau of Prisons following the expiration of their prison sentences if the government can prove, by clear and convincing evidence, that they are "sexually dangerous." To establish this, the government must show that an individual "has engaged or attempted to engage in sexually violent conduct or child molestation," 18 U.S.C. § 4247(a)(5); that he "suffers from a serious mental illness, abnormality, or disorder," 18 U.S.C. § 4247(a)(6); and that, as a result, he "would have serious difficulty in refraining from sexually violent conduct or child molestation if released." *Id. See also United States v. Hall*, 664 F.3d 456, 458 (4th

Cir.2012). Cooke concedes the first prong. He maintains, however, that the government failed to prove, and the district court erred in finding, that he satisfies the latter two.[3]

The district court's determinations that Cooke presently suffers from a serious mental illness and that he "would have serious difficulty in refraining from sexually violent conduct or child molestation if released" are factual determinations, which we review for clear error. *See United States v. Wooden*, 693 F.3d 440, 451 (4th Cir.2012); *Hall*, 664 F.3d at 462.... We turn first to the district court's finding that Cooke presently "suffers from a serious mental illness, abnormality, or disorder." 18 U.S.C. §4247(a)(6). We find the district court's conclusion amply supported by the record developed at the evidentiary hearing.

Of the three experts who testified about whether Cooke suffers from a serious mental disorder, two concluded that he did: Dr. Zinik and Dr. Demby diagnosed him with both Personality disorder and Paraphilia NOS, which they characterized as serious, relating to his inability to refrain from sexual contact with pubescent boys. Dr. Plaud disagreed with these diagnoses, but primarily on the basis that the paraphilia with which Dr. Zinik and Dr. Demby diagnosed Cooke—hebephilia—was not a diagnosable mental disorder and was not included in the current version of the Diagnostic and Statistical Manual of Mental Disorders ("DSM").

At most, however, this indicates a conflict in the experts' testimony, the district court's resolution of which we are "especially reluctant to set aside." *Hall*, 664 F.3d at 462 (quoting *Hendricks v. Central Reserve Life Ins. Co.*, 39 F.3d 507, 513 (4th Cir.1994)). In the absence of any other indication that Dr. Plaud's testimony should have been credited over Dr. Zinik's and Dr. Demby's, we decline to do so.... In a similar context, we have also cautioned against overreliance on the availability of a formal label:

> [O]ne will search §4247(a)(6) in vain for any language purporting to confine the universe of qualifying mental impairments within clinical or pedagogical parameters. The statute could have been drafted to comport with clinical norms, but inasmuch as Congress chose not to do so, it has been left to the courts to develop the meaning of "serious mental illness, abnormality, or disorder" as a legal term of art.

United States v. Caporale, 701 F.3d 128, 136 (4th Cir.2012). Our discussion of Dr. Plaud's views in *Caporale* is equally applicable here: while "Dr. Plaud's testimony cast some doubt that hebephilia may [qualify as Paraphilia NOS as listed in the DSM] ... the scope of 'illness, abnormality, or disorder' in §4247(a)(6) is certainly broad enough to include hebephilia, by its own or any other name." *Id.* at 137. Here, the district court properly focused not on labels, but on whether Cooke's condition—whatever it may be called, and whether or not it could form the basis of a formal psychiatric diagnosis—substantially impairs his ability to function normally in society. It concluded that Cooke's impairment was clear, as manifested in his "long periods of incarceration, feelings of shame and humiliation, and distressed familial relationships." ... Nothing in the record persuades us that this conclusion was erroneous.

Cooke contends that, whatever serious mental illness he may have suffered from in the past, he does not presently suffer from one as required by 18 U.S.C. §4247(a)(6). But there was ample evidence to suggest that Cooke's condition persists. While Cooke testified that he no longer experiences the urge to have sexual contact with pubescent males, there was substantial evidence in the record to suggest otherwise. Both Dr. Zinik and Dr. Demby

---

3. Cooke also argues that the Adam Walsh Act violates his right to equal protection under the Fifth Amendment because it treats Bureau of Prisons detainees differently from all other federal detainees. He acknowledges, however, that we have already considered and rejected this argument, *see United States v. Timms*, 664 F.3d 436, 449 (4th Cir.2012), and we do not consider it further.

both spoke directly to this point, testifying that Cooke remains in the grip of his illness. The district court noted that hebephilia is a persistent condition as evidenced both by expert testimony and Cooke's own history of repeated reoffense. Cooke's failure to undergo treatment, and his continued communication with another sex offender, similarly undermine Cooke's contention that he has taken control of his own behavior through self help....

Cooke also objects to the district court's conclusion that he "would have serious difficulty in refraining from sexually violent conduct or child molestation if released." 18 U.S.C. § 4247(a)(6). This inquiry focuses on "the extent to which the inmate is controlled by the illness." *Wooden*, 693 F.3d at 460. On this prong as well, the district court's conclusion is adequately supported by the evidence.... The district court properly observed that Cooke has a long history of child molestation that, in itself, demonstrates occasions on which Cooke was controlled by his illness, and with tragic results. "When the question is whether an inmate ... will have serious difficulty refraining from re-offending if released, consideration of the nature of his prior crimes provides a critical part of the answer." *Wooden*, 693 F.3d at 458. While Cooke was evidently able to control his behavior during his most recent time in prison, the same could be said of his prior incarceration in Texas state prison after which Cooke reoffended within months. Moreover, as the district court observed, Cooke had no access to pubescent males while he was incarcerated. It is therefore difficult to say with certainty whether Cooke was able to control his own behavior, or whether the prison environment controlled it for him. In this context, we cannot conclude that the district court erred in considering Cooke's interactions with a "young, troubled" fellow inmate, even if there was nothing inherently inappropriate about their relationship.

Cooke's own testimony also indicated to the district court that he was not prepared to accept responsibility for his past actions. The district court observed that Cooke's responses to questions typically minimized his own responsibility, suggesting that he "fails to appreciate the seriousness of his hebephilia and the extent to which it controls his offending." ... Such a judgment about a witness's demeanor on the stand is another textbook example of a determination to which we owe particular deference. *See United States v. McGee*, 736 F.3d 263, 270 (4th Cir.2013). Dr. Zinik and Dr. Demby corroborated this observation.

The district court discussed Cooke's relapse-prevention plan as well. The district court noted Dr. Zinik's testimony that such a plan could be valuable in "identifying triggers of sexual offending and effective prevention measures to serve as a resource for both respondent and his support group." ... Measured against this standard, Cooke's plan—which consists of nothing more than his intended living arrangements and the generalized aspiration to seek treatment and avoid reoffense—falls well short. This suggested to the district court, not unreasonably, that "respondent does not appear to comprehend the risk of reoffense he faces in the community upon release, as opposed to in BOP [Bureau of Prisons] custody where he has no access to pubescent males." ... The district court drew a similar inference from the fact that Cooke has not participated in the sex offender treatment program available at FCI Butner since it became available to him. Cooke maintains that he had good grounds for not doing so, and that may be. An Adam Walsh Act detainee is not obliged to participate in such a program to secure his release. But treatment programs teach skills to help an individual avoid reoffending, and the failure to obtain or develop such a skill set is a relevant consideration in determining the likelihood of a relapse.[4]

---

4. Cooke maintains that he has managed to teach these skills to himself. As we discuss above, however, the district court had ample grounds to disbelieve this testimony, given the contrary testimony of the government's expert witnesses and its own assessment of Cooke's credibility on the stand.

Finally, in view of the fact that every one of Cooke's offenses were committed while he was paralyzed from the waist down and confined to a wheelchair, the district court reasonably concluded that Cooke's many physical impairments did not substantially reduce his risk of reoffense. Even Dr. Artigues testified that Cooke's physical impairments merely reduce that risk; she did not say to what extent.... For the foregoing reasons, the district court's order committing Cooke to the custody of the Attorney General is ... *AFFIRMED.*

DAVIS, Senior Circuit Judge, concurring in the judgment:

This is a close case. Ultimately, I vote to affirm because evidence of Cooke's recent history and his own testimony meaningfully contribute to the satisfaction of the Government's burden to establish by clear and convincing evidence that he still suffers from a volitional impairment that makes his likelihood of reoffending higher than that of the typical recidivist....

It is important that an appellate court's reasoning take care not to shift the burden to an offender to show that he will not offend again; over-reliance on an offender's pre-incarceration history poses that risk. For example, the majority concedes that it is "difficult to say with certainty whether Cooke was able to control his own behavior, or whether the prison environment controlled it for him." ... But the point of the Walsh Act inquiry is to put in place a standard that the Government must meet with a relatively precise degree of certainty, i.e., a certainty tested by the exacting clear and convincing evidentiary standard. Similarly, the majority approvingly cites the district court's observation "that Cooke has a long history of child molestation that, in itself, demonstrates occasions on which Cooke was controlled by his illness, and with tragic results." ... But our case law forsakes this myopic focus on the past, instead highlighting that *recent* behavior is also a particularly probative data point in these cases....

Despite my concerns about the majority's approach, I agree with its ultimate conclusion because ... Cooke's recent history strongly suggests that he suffers from a current volitional impairment. Most importantly, the district court's assessment of Cooke's testimony revealed that he was simply not a credible witness: (1) his plans for obtaining treatment were not credible; (2) his claimed willingness to take responsibility for his prior conduct was not credible; and (3) his purported understanding of the nature of his illness was not credible. At least one expert testified that his behavior was demonstrative of an untreated sex offender. These credibility determinations, combined with the lack of a concrete post-release treatment plan and the record evidence that his interest in young and troubled boys had endured, were — in the light of the totality of the factual record — sufficient for the district court find that Cooke currently suffers from a volitional impairment and would likely reoffend if not committed for treatment. The district court was amply justified in rejecting Cooke's assertion (only implied, to be sure) that if he were to reoffend upon release, it would be because he *chose* to reoffend and not because he lacked the volitional control needed to avoid doing so....

United States v. Antone

Fourth Circuit, 2014
742 F.3d 151

DAVIS, Circuit Judge: ...

Byron Neil Antone, now forty-one years old, was born in and raised on the Tohono O'odham Indian Reservation in south central Arizona.... [footnote omitted]. Until age nine or ten, Antone was raised by his mother; after that point, he resided with his grandmother and his godmother.... Antone's mother and grandmother were heavy drinkers and Antone was often neglected and verbally and physically abused as a child. At seven years old, Antone was on several occasions sexually abused by his aunt, who was a teenager at the time. By the time he was fifteen years old, he had had sexual intercourse with at least two adult women, one of whom was twenty-six.... Antone had serious behavioral issues as a child, which led to school expulsions and stints in juvenile detention. He dropped out of high school in ninth grade. He did not maintain steady employment thereafter, although he was employed seasonally as a firefighter with the United States Forestry Service and had attended specialized training classes in that field.

In 1991, when Antone was nineteen years old, he was arrested and charged with sexual misconduct with a minor, sexual abuse, and contributing to the delinquency of a minor. The arrest related to two sexual acts with a sixteen-year-old who was Antone's girlfriend at the time. The first sexual act was consensual, but the second was forcible rape. Antone pled guilty to the sexual abuse charge in the Judicial Court of the Tohono O'odham Nation ("tribal court") and served about six months in jail.... In 1997, tribal authorities charged Antone with threatening and disorderly conduct. He admitted to rubbing the buttocks of his cousin, then twenty-one years old, while she was sleeping on the couch. He was sentenced to 60 days in tribal jail.... From 1998 to 1999, Antone was charged by tribal authorities for several acts of sexual misconduct, which resulted in a consolidated plea agreement and tribal judgment entered on March 16, 1999. The consolidated tribal judgment related to four victims and spanned incidents from 1992 through 1997:

1) Forcible rape of a fourteen or fifteen-year-old in 1992 or 1993.

2) Touching of the crotch area of an eleven-year-old in 1996.

3) Sexual assault of C.R., a woman of unknown age, in June 1997. During this incident, Antone tried to force C.R. to have sex with him, and when she refused, he threw her on the bed, held her hands down, touched her breasts, and touched her crotch area. C.R. was able to escape by jumping out of her bedroom window.

4) Forcible rape of R.J., age twenty-five, in November 1997. During this incident, R.J. awoke to find Antone on top of her. He then forced her to have sex for five to fifteen minutes.

Antone pled guilty to charges related to these four incidents in the consolidated plea agreement. He was sentenced to 3,600 days in jail by the tribal court.... Almost all of the incidents described above, and certainly the June and November 1997 incidents, took place when Antone was either intoxicated from alcohol and/or high on cocaine. Indeed, Antone has a serious history of substance abuse. When he was arrested in February 1998, he was drinking 3 to 5 quarts of beer a day on average, and up to 11 quarts on some days. He was also abusing a number of drugs, including marijuana, LSD, and crack cocaine. As a result, Antone has little to no recollection of these incidents.

In November 1999, Antone was sentenced in the United States District Court for the District of Arizona on a sexual assault charge. The particular charge related to Antone's assault against C.R. in June 1997, which was also a subject of his consolidated tribal judgment. In addition, Antone admitted in the federal plea agreement to sexual misconduct as to all the incidents covered in the tribal court convictions.... According to the testimony of Antone's attorney at the time, which the magistrate judge fully credited, the federal criminal charge was actually initiated by Antone and his attorney. "The reason was to enable [Antone] to be transferred to federal custody and thereby have access to sex offense treatment at FCI–Butner, which [the attorney] believed would be designed specifically for Native Americans." ... The federal district court in Arizona sentenced Antone to 114 months of incarceration, with credit for time served, and 60 months of supervised release. The plea agreement reflected Antone's request to receive sex offender treatment in federal custody, and the district court included a recommendation in its judgment that Antone participate in the residential drug treatment and sex offender treatment programs....

In accordance with the federal judgment and commitment order, Antone was incarcerated in the federal Bureau of Prisons system from November 1999 through February 23, 2007, when the Government initiated the instant proceeding four days before his expected release. Since then, Antone has resided in FCI–Butner, a medium security correctional institution in North Carolina, awaiting his civil commitment hearing and its resolution. As a result, Antone has been in continuous federal custody for the past fourteen years, or since he was twenty-seven years old.... During the entire period of his federal custody, Antone has not been shown to have consumed alcohol or drugs. Antone's prison record contains no sanctions or nonsanctioned incidents related to alcohol or drugs, and he testified that he has been sober for fourteen years. The Bureau of Prisons regularly administers Breathalyzer tests on inmates in recognition of the fact that it is possible to make and obtain contraband alcohol within the prison. Antone has never tested positive on those tests.... Antone has attended Alcoholics Anonymous and Narcotics Anonymous on his own initiative. He attended meetings during the first year and a half of his prison term and restarted about a year before his commitment hearing. He also completed a Drug Education Program and a non-residential substance abuse program.

Antone's behavioral problems while in prison have been minimal. He has been sanctioned for four incidents, twice for fighting without serious injury and twice for minor rule violations; the last of these sanctions occurred in 2004.[2] He obtained his GED in 2001. In addition, he has maintained employment as an orderly in his housing unit. His work performance therein was characterized as "superior." ... Antone regularly seeks out advice and counseling from his prison's counselors and treatment specialists. In particular, he has asked his counselors how to communicate with his son, with whom he corresponds by mail, and for advice on anger management. Antone has taken classes in art, beading, meditation, and guitar. He teaches other inmates how to play the guitar.

As for sexual conduct, Antone's record indicates that he has "not engaged in sexual misconduct during his extended incarceration." ... At the time of the evidentiary hearing, however, he had not attended sex offender therapy or treatment. Antone and his former attorney testified that he had made several requests for treatment at the early side of his incarceration period, but it was apparently not then available to him because "his release date was so far in the future." ... [footnote omitted]. When it became available in September 2008, after the Government filed its § 4248(a) petition, Antone did not participate in the treatment. He indicated that he did not do so because he knew that statements made during treatment "could be used against him" in the commitment proceeding....

On February 23, 2007, four days before Antone's expected release date, the Government filed a certification, pursuant to 18 U.S.C. § 4248(a), of Antone as a sexually dangerous person.... In June 2010, Antone filed a motion for a hearing on the merits of the certification, and the district court referred the matter to a magistrate judge for an evidentiary hearing and report and recommendation.... The magistrate judge held an evidentiary hearing over the course of three days in October 2011.... On April 30, 2012,

---

2. The Bureau of Prisons records also refer to three events that did not result in disciplinary sanction. They primarily stem from the attempted delivery of the magazine Maxim to Antone, and the presence in Antone's cell of a number of pictures, cut out from magazines, of scantily-clad adult women.

the magistrate judge issued his M & R [Memorandum and Recommendation], in which he recommended that Antone not be found a sexually dangerous person.... On September 20, 2012, the district court issued its order and judgment on the instant certification. Although it accepted all of the magistrate judge's credibility determinations and findings of historical fact, it rejected the M & R's ultimate recommendation of a finding of not sexually dangerous. It found that the combination of Antone's serious mental illnesses — namely antisocial personality disorder and polysubstance dependence — would cause him to have serious difficulty in refraining from sexually violent conduct if released. It therefore committed Antone to the custody of the United States Attorney General as a sexually dangerous person. The instant appeal followed....

The Government seeks the commitment of Antone pursuant to 18 U.S.C. § 4248, which was enacted as part of the Adam Walsh Child Safety and Protection Act of 2006. Under § 4248, the Government may seek the civil commitment of certain individuals in the custody of the Federal Bureau of Prisons who are determined to be "sexually dangerous person[s]." 18 U.S.C. § 4248(d). The commitment process is initiated when the Attorney General or his designee files a certification attesting that an individual is sexually dangerous as defined by the Walsh Act, after which the respondent is entitled to an evidentiary hearing. "If, after the hearing, the court finds by clear and convincing evidence that the person is a sexually dangerous person, the court shall commit the person to the custody of the Attorney General." *Id.*

To demonstrate that an individual should be civilly committed under § 4248, the Government must prove, by clear and convincing evidence, that each one of the following criteria has been satisfied: (1) the individual has previously "engaged or attempted to engage in sexually violent conduct or child molestation" (the "prior conduct" element), 18 U.S.C. § 4247(a)(5); (2) the individual currently "suffers from a serious mental illness, abnormality, or disorder" (the "serious illness" element), *id.* § 4247(a)(6); and (3) as a result of such a condition, the individual "would have serious difficulty in refraining from sexually violent conduct or child molestation if released" (the "serious difficulty" or "volitional impairment" element), *id. See also* [*United States v.*] *Comstock*, 560 U.S. [126] at 130, 130 S.Ct. 1949 [(2010)]; *United States v. Springer*, 715 F.3d 535, 538 (4th Cir.2013). Antone has conceded that the Government has met its burden with regard to the prior conduct element as well as the finding of a serious mental illness. He disputes, however, the district court's conclusion as to the third element, that the Government has demonstrated a sufficient likelihood that Antone will re-offend....

The standard set forth for civil commitment under § 4248 is clear and convincing evidence. This so-called "intermediate" standard is mandated not only by the plain language of the statute, 18 U.S.C. § 4248(d), but by constitutional due process constraints, as well. *See Addington v. Texas*, 441 U.S. 418, 427, 99 S.Ct. 1804, 60 L.Ed.2d 323 (1979) (observing that the clear and convincing evidence standard is required in civil commitment proceedings because "[t]he individual's interest in the outcome of a civil commitment proceeding is of such [great] weight and gravity")....

In applying the first two commitment criteria under the Walsh Act, the question is whether the Government has established with clear and convincing evidence that the respondent acted or acts in a certain manner. The third element, however, is more complicated, in that it requires the court to issue a predictive judgment: has the Government met its burden by presenting clear and convincing evidence that, in the uncertain future, the respondent will have "serious difficulty in refraining from sexually violent conduct or child molestation"? 18 U.S.C. § 4247(a)(6).... We are mindful that the Supreme Court has explained that such an inquiry "will not be demonstrable with mathematical precision."

Kansas v. Crane, 534 U.S. 407, 413, 122 S.Ct. 867, 151 L.Ed.2d 856 (2002). Instead, in order to find that the third criterion is satisfied, the court must look for

> proof of serious difficulty in controlling behavior. And this, when viewed in light of such features of the case as the nature of the psychiatric diagnosis, and the severity of the mental abnormality itself, must be sufficient to distinguish the dangerous sexual offender whose serious mental illness, abnormality, or disorder subjects him to civil commitment from the dangerous but typical recidivist convicted in an ordinary criminal case.

Id. In other words, the Government must demonstrate that the serious illness, as it has manifested in the particular respondent, has so significantly diminished his volitional capacity such that he is distinguishable from the ordinary "dangerous but typical recidivist." *Id.*; *see also* [*United States v.*] *Wooden*, 693 F.3d [440] at 460 [4th Cir. 2012)] (framing the third criterion as "the extent to which the inmate is controlled by the illness")....

We now assess the instant record with this exacting standard in mind. As to the third criterion, we find that the aggregate of historical, direct, and circumstantial evidence contained therein may be best described (as the magistrate judge seemed to regard it) as in equipose, or, at most, as rising to a level of preponderance in favor of commitment. But this is simply not enough to satisfy the statutory burden of clear and convincing evidence.... [citations omitted]. We thus have no hesitation in finding a fatal evidentiary insufficiency in the Government's presentation....

The majority of the evidentiary record consists of reports and testimony presented at the three-day hearing in front of the magistrate judge. At the hearing, the Government presented testimony from Antone himself, and expert witnesses Dr. Amy Phenix, Ph.D. and Manuel E. Gutierrez, Psy.D. Antone then presented the testimony of Clement Gallop, a treatment specialist in the commitment and treatment program at FCI–Butner; Andre Taylor, a counselor at FCI–Butner; Anne Schauder, a United States Probation Officer from Arizona; and an expert witness, licensed psychologist Roy G. Daum, Psy.D. The magistrate judge found all of the witnesses credible, with a single exception related to Antone's account of certain past crimes.... Because the sole issue on appeal is whether there was sufficient evidence of Antone's future volitional impairment, we summarize the evidence only as it pertains to that issue....

The Government first called respondent Antone. Antone testified that he was unable to recall the majority of his sexual assaults because he was either drunk or high at the time of the incidents. He then testified about his upbringing, substance abuse, and progress while in prison. He stated that he would always be an alcoholic and there would always be a risk that he would drink again, but that he knew to stay away from high risk places and people. He also stated that while in prison he had learned how to talk to others about his problems and to "release [his] feelings in a positive way." ...

Subsequently, Antone presented the lay testimony of Clement Gallop and Andre Taylor. Gallop is employed as a treatment specialist in the commitment and treatment program at FCI–Butner and Taylor is a counselor at FCI–Butner. Gallop testified that he is approached by Antone on a weekly basis, and that they have discussed issues related to Antone's son and anger management in general. Taylor testified that Antone has never tested positive or been observed to have imbibed alcohol or used drugs, even though such substances are available in prison and Taylor had disciplined others for alcohol-related issues. Both Gallop and Taylor had positive impressions of their interactions with Antone.... Antone also presented the testimony of Allan Duprey and Anne Schauder. Duprey, who was Antone's attorney on the federal criminal charges, testified that the federal charges were initiated at his urging so that Antone could have access to sex offense treatment designed specifically for Native Americans. Duprey also testified that he had inquired about the availability of sex offender treatment, but was told by the Bureau of Prisons that Antone would not receive treatment until the last five years of his ten-year sentence. Schauder is a United States Probation Officer in the District of Arizona. She explained the support and supervision that her district provides to sex offenders, including the utilization of halfway houses, sex offender treatment, and polygraph tests.... [footnote omitted].

The Government also presented the testimony of two expert witnesses, Dr. Amy Phenix and Dr. Manuel Gutierrez, who were admitted as experts in the field of forensic psychology without objection. Both Government experts testified that Antone met the criteria for civil commitment as a sexually dangerous person. Their conclusions were based on their review of Antone's written records. Dr. Gutierrez was unable to conduct an interview of Antone, and the portion of Dr. Phenix's report that related to an interview she conducted with Antone was excluded by the magistrate judge and the Government does not challenge that order.

Dr. Phenix diagnosed Antone with paraphilia not otherwise specified, nonconsent ("paraphilia NOS, nonconsent");[5] alcohol dependence;[6] and antisocial personality disorder ("APD");[7] and she testified that as a result, he would have serious difficulty refraining from sexually violent conduct. She opined that the primary cause of Antone's volitional impairment was his paraphilia NOS, nonconsent, mental illness. Dr. Phenix found that Antone's paraphilia NOS, nonconsent, caused him to deviate from ordinary sexual impulses and behaviors, and then his alcohol dependence would serve as a disinhibitor and his antisocial personality disorder would reinforce his paraphilic impulses. When specifically questioned by the court, Dr. Phenix added that, even if the paraphilia diagnosis was disregarded, she would still "believe that [Antone] will go on to commit criminal sexual behavior." ...

Dr. Phenix's conclusion on the volitional impairment prong was based on (1) the pattern and duration of Antone's offending; (2) his commission of additional offenses after his 1991 sexual abuse conviction; (3) an actuarial assessment of risk based on static risk factors; (4) the presence of dynamic risk factors; and (5) the absence of protective factors. Dr. Phenix explained at the hearing that her first methodology was to "look at the pattern and duration of his offending to see how well his behavioral controls were when he was in the community." ... She focused on certain undisputed historical factors, emphasizing the repeated nature and aggression of Antone's assaults and that he continued to commit assaults even after his first arrest in 1991.[8] ... Dr. Phenix viewed Antone's behavior while incarcerated only as a secondary consideration. When questioned on why

---

5. Paraphilia is defined as "recurrent, intense sexually arousing fantasies, urges and behaviors" involving, in the context of the "nonconsent" specifier, sexual arousal "by the nonconsenting aspect of nonconsensual sexual encounters." ...

6. Alcohol/substance dependence is defined as a "maladaptive pattern of substance use, leading to clinically significant impairment or distress[.]" ... There is no dispute that Antone suffers from substance dependence.

7. Antisocial personality disorder is defined as "an enduring pattern of inner experience and behavior that deviates markedly from the expectations of the individual's culture, is pervasive and inflexible, has an onset in adolescence or early adulthood, is stable over time, and leads to distress or impairment." ... At the appellate level, Antone does not challenge the diagnosis of antisocial personality disorder.

8. With respect to her actuarial analysis, Dr. Phenix utilized several predictive models, in which she inputted a number of "static," mostly historical facts, including the number of prior sex offenses; whether the offender was single at the time of offending; and whether any victims were related to the offender.

she relied almost exclusively on pre-incarceration conduct, Dr. Phenix responded that "I think the best measure of his volition is prior to being in a prison where you have such strict structure and rules for your behavior[.]" ... The magistrate judge also heard similar testimony from Government witness Dr. Gutierrez. Dr. Gutierrez's diagnoses matched those of Dr. Phenix — paraphilia NOS, nonconsent; polysubstance (including alcohol) dependence; and antisocial personality disorder — and also included an additional diagnosis of paraphilia NOS, hebephilia. He concluded that a combination of all of the above-listed illnesses, or alternatively a sole diagnosis of APD, would "cumulative[ly]" cause Antone to have serious difficulty refraining from sexually violent conduct....

Antone subsequently presented the testimony of his expert witness, Dr. Roy Daum, who was admitted as an expert in the field of forensic psychology over the Government's objection. After conducting a forensic evaluation of Antone in February 2011, Dr. Daum diagnosed Antone with polysubstance dependence; frotteurism; and borderline personality disorder.[9] He agreed with the Government's experts that Antone met the first and second criteria of § 4248 confinement. He disagreed, however, that Antone had demonstrated that he would have serious difficulty refraining from sexually violent conduct if released.... Dr. Daum reasoned that Antone's offense conduct had not been rooted in sexual deviance, but rather stemmed from a lack of interpersonal skills and a serious substance abuse. Dr. Daum's conclusion considered as a central part of his analysis certain "dynamic" factors observed during Antone's incarceration, including the absence of evidence of any use of drugs or alcohol or any engagement in antisocial activities; the absence of records showing that Antone had a general sexual preoccupation; Antone's positive management records; and evidence of his completion of several self-help programs, learning of vocational skills, and seeking counseling while incarcerated. Of the difference between his opinion and that of Dr. Phenix and Dr. Gutierrez, he remarked the following:

> I believe there are many factors that you look at as far as a civil commitment is concerned. Certainly you have heard the last two days of a lot of discussion about actuarials. One of the things that is really missing is the dynamic factors of how that person is now [as compared to his former] acts. Static, meaning it's all said and done and it's easy to score, ... but the dynamic factors allow for the growth of a person to change or it allows for the person not to change.

[Citation to Record omitted]. Finally, Dr. Daum opined that outpatient treatment of Antone during supervised release could adequately address his sex offense and substance abuse problems....

On April 30, 2012, the magistrate judge issued a comprehensive M & R recommending that the district court reject the Government's certification of Antone as a sexually dangerous person. The magistrate judge concluded that the Government had met its burden with

---

9. Notably, Dr. Daum did not diagnose Antone with any form of paraphilia NOS, be it nonconsent (when an individual is aroused by nonconsent) or hebephilia (when an individual is aroused by pubescent individuals). He explained that after interviewing Antone for five hours, he had not seen any evidence or admission by Antone — for example, an interest in deviant sexual fantasies or a physical arousal to certain images — that would suggest that Antone was aroused by forced sex. Dr. Daum also referred to a psychophysiological evaluation taken in 1999 in anticipation of Antone's federal sentencing. Although the report did not make a formal diagnosis, it observed that "[i]t is possible that [Antone's] sexually aggressive and sexually deviant behavior patterns are the result of emotional and psychological disturbance, rather than persistent deviant sexual arousal or attraction[.]" ...

As will be discussed *infra*, both the magistrate judge and the district court adopted Dr. Daum's conclusion that Antone did not suffer from any form of paraphilia.

regard to the first element, in that Antone had previously engaged in sexually violent conduct. The magistrate judge also accepted the Government's contention that Antone suffered from certain serious mental illnesses within the scope of § 4247(a)(6). Specifically, the magistrate judge found evidence of polysubstance dependence, but it rejected the rest of the Government experts' diagnoses, most notably paraphilia NOS, nonconsent and antisocial personality disorder. It also rejected Dr. Daum's diagnoses of frotteurism and borderline personality disorder.... The magistrate judge ultimately concluded, however, that the Government had not presented sufficient evidence to demonstrate that Antone's polysubstance dependence would result in a serious difficulty refraining from sexually violent conduct. The magistrate judge emphasized that the Government's position on volitional impairment was "based on [a theory of] multiple diagnoses," but it had decided that the Government had not met its burden on any of those diagnoses except polysubstance dependence. As a result, the magistrate judge was not persuaded by the Government's presentation as to Antone's volitional impairment. It cited, for example, to Dr. Gutierrez's understanding that "just a substance diagnosis alone could not essentially stand by itself for civil commitment." ...

The magistrate judge afforded near determinative weight to Antone's conduct "over the last 13 or so years," during his time in federal prison. It noted that Antone had not been shown to have consumed alcohol or drugs or to have engaged in sexual misconduct during his extended incarceration. It also pointed to his attendance in Alcoholics Anonymous and his eagerness to seek out counseling for anger management.... The magistrate judge recognized that Antone's achievements while incarcerated came about in a controlled environment where access to his vices was limited. Nevertheless, its review of the evidence—including the testimony of Dr. Daum, who had stressed the utility of dynamic factors in Antone's case-led it to conclude that over the past thirteen years, Antone "has achieved a level of sexual self-regulation" and "a measure of self-control" that significantly undercut the Government's position that he would have serious difficulty refraining if released.... It observed that certain evidence relied upon by the Government's expert witnesses, such as the nature, pattern, and duration of offense conduct, "is not as reliable an indicator of his behavior if released ... because of, among other reasons, the extended intervening period in which there was no manifestation of such conduct." ...

The magistrate judge also considered as "significant[ ]" the fact that Antone would be subject to "an extended term of supervised release." ... It noted that he would spend his first year of supervised release in a halfway house and that throughout his term, he would be subject to supervision and participation in substance abuse and sex offender treatment programs, periodic drug tests, and prohibitions against contact with children.... In light of the "paucity" of evidence that Antone would have serious difficulty refraining from sexually violent conduct if released, the magistrate judge concluded that the Government had failed to meet its burden of establishing, by clear and convincing evidence, that Antone was a sexually dangerous person under § 4248....

On September 24, 2012, the district court issued an order rejecting the magistrate judge's ultimate recommendation and civilly committing Antone. It accepted the M & R's findings of historical fact and witness credibility, and noted that it reviewed de novo those aspects of the M & R that were objected to by the parties.... In applying the three-prong test, the district court first accepted the magistrate judge's conclusion that the Government had established that Antone had engaged in sexually violent conduct. It also agreed with the majority of the magistrate judge's recommendations as to the diagnoses of Antone's mental illnesses. Notably, the district court found that Antone suffered from polysubstance dependence and that he did not suffer from paraphilia NOS, nonconsent. In disagreement with the magistrate judge, however, the district court found sufficient evidence of a diagnosis of antisocial personality disorder and held that these two diagnoses, as manifested in Antone, qualified as serious mental illnesses.

The district court then found that the Government had satisfied the volitional impairment requirement of §4248. In doing so, its primary focus appeared to be Antone's admitted alcoholism. It stated:

> Respondent admits that he is and will always be an alcoholic. To his credit, respondent has participated in substance abuse treatment and evidently has refrained from using alcohol and drugs while incarcerated.... [However,] the risk that respondent will relapse into abusing alcohol and other substances would be much higher in the community.

[Citation to Record omitted]. It continued, "[t]he court is convinced that if respondent uses alcohol he will have serious difficulty stopping himself from sexually attacking persons he finds desirable, despite their nonconsent." ...

The district court looked to the combination of Antone's substance dependence and APD diagnoses to predict that his past history of sexual attacks would continue once released. "This volitional impairment has resulted in a consistent pattern of numerous violent sexual attacks in the past, and the court finds that the impairment will persist if respondent is released." ... The court also relied on Dr. Phenix's testimony that her conclusion on the volitional impairment prong would not change without the paraphilia NOS, nonconsent diagnosis.

Finally, the court expressed concern that it would not be able to require Antone to undergo sex offender treatment. All parties—including Dr. Daum as well as Antone himself—agreed that Antone would benefit from sex offender treatment. According to the district court, however, under a recent Ninth Circuit case, *United States v. Turner*, a §4248 detainee's term of supervised release is not tolled while he remains in custody awaiting a commitment hearing. 689 F.3d 1117, 1121 (9th Cir.2012). Assuming Antone's period of supervised release actually had begun when he was due to be released from the Bureau of Prisons, supervision would have ended on February 27, 2012, but he was still civilly committed at that point. The district court thus predicted that without a tolling mechanism, Antone would not be subject to any term of supervised release under Ninth Circuit law. It also rejected as "irrelevant" the testimony of the probation officer from Arizona based on similar reasoning.... Accordingly, the district court rejected the magistrate judge's ultimate recommendation, instead finding that the Government had established that Antone was a sexually dangerous person within the meaning of 18 U.S.C. §4247(a)(5) and (6)....

We may ... reverse if, upon reviewing the district court's ultimate mixed findings, we are "left with the definite and firm conviction that a mistake has been committed." ... That is precisely what is at stake here: our review of the lower court opinion leads us to conclude that the district court's inadequate consideration of certain "substantial evidence"—namely Antone's behavior in the past fourteen years or so—constitutes reversible error. And our subsequent analysis of the evidentiary record leaves us with a definite and firm conviction that Antone's commitment should be reversed.

That Antone has "responded very well" to incarceration is not in dispute.... Antone has not tested positive for any substances while in prison, and he testified that he has been sober during his extended incarceration. Antone's conduct as it relates to sexual deviance is equally commendable. Not only has he not engaged in any actual sexual misconduct or hostility toward women, but, just as importantly, his record is devoid of any indication that he has even desired to manifest such misconduct.... Instead, Antone has presented significant testimony to the contrary. Two employees from the correctional facility testified on Antone's behalf, and the magistrate judge found credible their assurances that their interactions with Antone have been consistently positive and that he has demonstrated self-awareness and control on a regular basis. He has for the most part avoided conflicts with superiors or fellow inmates. Antone has completed his GED, as well as other professional programs, and he readily seeks out the prison's mental health resources. He has expressed remorse for his past acts.

Yet the district court's discussion of Antone's behavior while incarcerated is negligible at best. It failed to discuss the opinions of Gallop or Taylor, the only witnesses who have had consistent contact with Antone since his incarceration. It considered the testimony of Antone only to the extent that he admitted that he will always be an alcoholic.... [footnote omitted]. And it failed to mention the nearly ten-year period in which Antone has had zero disciplinary infractions and the nearly fifteen-year period in which Antone has had no sex-related incidents.... In fact, in the "serious difficulty" section of its opinion, the district court's analysis of Antone's conduct while incarcerated is limited to a single sentence acknowledging his "evident[ ]" abstinence from alcohol.... [footnote omitted]. Relying again on Antone's past history of "numerous violent sexual attacks," it concluded that his volitional impairment would persist if released.

Since upholding the constitutionality of the Walsh Act in 2010, we have disposed of more than a handful of § 4248 appeals involving the volitional impairment prong, but none of them involved a respondent who had demonstrated such positive behavior during the extended period of his incarceration.... Here, Antone's behavior during the past fourteen years—indeed, during a period of time that spans the majority of his adult life—reveals no acts that conceivably come close to the sort of malfeasance present in our aforementioned precedent.[12] On these facts, there is not much more that he could have done to demonstrate that he is in control of his volitional faculties and that such control is likely to persist after his release. The district court should have been aware of the uniqueness of Antone's factual record. As such, it was imperative for the court to comprehensively address why it believed Antone's recent behavior was overshadowed by his past acts. It failed to do so.

In *Wooden*, we recently confronted a situation in which we believed that the district court had failed to consider relevant and substantial evidence of a respondent's volitional impairment. 693 F.3d at 458–62. There, the district court had rejected the petition for civil commitment, finding that the Government had failed to demonstrate clear and convincing evidence that the respondent would have serious difficulty refraining from reoffending. Our review of the evidentiary record led us to hold otherwise. Because the district court relied on a flawed expert opinion and ignored or otherwise failed to account for a "substantial body of contradictory evidence," we found reversible error. *Id.* at 461.... Here, as in *Wooden*, we have again been "left with the definite and firm conviction that

---

12. The district court made reference to the fact that Antone had not attended sex offender treatment. Antone had, however, repeatedly sought this treatment at the beginning of his incarceration to no avail. It is true that he was eventually offered sex offender treatment sometime in September 2008, but this choice was effectively no choice at all. At that point, the Government was proceeding with its efforts to civilly commit Antone, and any treatment received would be at the cost of providing the Government with additional fodder to use against him in those proceedings.

The district court also noted that Antone's institutional conduct "has not been without incident."... It cited to his two sanctions for fighting, both of which occurred before 2004, and the presence of "inappropriate materials" in his cell. We reject the notion that the prison's confiscation of the magazine Maxim can rise to the level of malfeasance discussed above.

a mistake has been committed." *Id.* The "core" of Antone's case was his decade-long process of rehabilitation. Antone called three separate witnesses to support his position that, as a result of his efforts to obtain treatment, he had improved his ability to control his impulses. The district court's one-sentence dismissal of Antone's case in chief does not sufficiently address the valid and important evidence contained therein.

We hasten to note that it was not clearly erroneous for the district court to place significant weight on Antone's pre-incarceration acts and behavior in reaching its predictive finding. A respondent's criminal record "may well be a historical factor, but it is by no means a stale or irrelevant one. When the question is whether an inmate ... will have serious difficulty refraining from re-offending if released, consideration of the nature of his prior crimes provides a critical part of the answer." *Wooden*, 693 F.3d at 458. Rather, the deficiency here lies primarily in the Government's failure to muster, and the district court's failure to hold the Government to its obligation to muster, sufficient evidence of an *ongoing volitional impairment* in this case. The mixed finding that ensues is "against the clear weight of the evidence considered as a whole" and constitutes reversible error.

As both the magistrate judge and Dr. Daum recognized, in analyzing whether a respondent will have serious difficulty refraining from re-offending, one must look to his past *and* his present condition. Here, Antone has presented significant indicators that he presently "has problems, takes responsibility for them, and seeks help for them," and his pre-incarceration malfeasance cannot be the sole relevant factor of consideration.... We certainly do not fault the Government, as whatever evidence it had, it presented, but that evidence largely (and certainly equally) serves to bolster Antone's asserted rehabilitation and his subsequent capacity for volitional control....

Dr. Phenix's evaluation of Antone suffers from the same flaw as the conclusion ultimately put forth by the district court. The expert report submitted by Dr. Phenix focuses almost exclusively on events that occurred prior to 1997; indeed, she admitted as much during her testimony. Dr. Phenix explained that her decision to focus on pre-incarcerative acts stemmed from her belief that actions taken while in the outside world are more accurate predictors of future behavior upon release. That is, of course, her choice, but as it relates to our review of the evidentiary record, it will not carry the day. The district court should have at the very least explained why it found Dr. Phenix's unadorned conclusion more persuasive than that of Dr. Daum, who specifically critiqued the former's technique because it did not allow for a respondent's subsequent growth. We find that Dr. Phenix's conclusion on volitional impairment is insufficient to satisfy the Government's heightened clear and convincing evidence burden. *Cf. Wooden*, 693 F.3d at 457 (finding that the "many deficiencies" in an expert's testimony "leave us firmly and definitely convinced that the district court's factual findings were mistaken.")....

Nor can we, on the merits of the matter, find that the Government presented clear and convincing evidence that Antone will have serious difficulty refraining from re-offending if released. The Supreme Court has stated that the serious difficulty element is intended to distinguish the "dangerous sexual offender" from the "dangerous but typical recidivist convicted in an ordinary criminal case who, having been convicted and punished for one crime, proceeds through his own free choice to commit another." *Kansas v. Crane*, 534 U.S. at 413, 122 S.Ct. 867. Here, then, the Government must demonstrate that Antone's particular manifestation of his mental illnesses are so severe and controlling as to deprive him of his liberty for an indeterminate future.... That is not the case. Clear and convincing evidence equips a factfinder with "a firm belief or conviction, without hesitancy," of the truth of the matter asserted, and, on the record before us, we possess no such conviction about the grip strength of Antone's mental illness on his behavior.

Springer, 715 F.3d at 538. We have already cited the substantial evidence in the record indicating that Antone has developed a level of general and social self-regulation; indeed, on these facts, we are hard-pressed to suggest much else that he could possibly do to undercut the notion that he would have serious difficulty in restraining from re-offending. What's more, Antone's civil commitment is based on two mental disorders that are undisputedly prevalent in the nationwide prison population.[15] *See, e.g., Kansas v. Crane*, 534 U.S. at 412, 122 S.Ct. 867; *see also* Jack Vognsen & Amy Phenix, *Antisocial Personality Disorder is Not Enough: A Reply to Sreeivasan, Weinburger, and Garrick*, 32 J. Am. Acad. Psychiatry Law 440, 442 (2004) (J.A. 1035–37) (noting that 50 to 70 percent of the ordinary prison population suffers from antisocial personality disorder); ... [citation omitted]. We conclude that, under the clear and convincing evidence standard, the Government has failed to distinguish Antone's alleged volitional impairment from that of a "dangerous but typical recidivist." *Kansas v. Crane*, 534 U.S. at 413, 122 S.Ct. 867....

At oral argument before us, counsel for Antone reported that Antone is currently attending sex offender therapy.[17] One can only be encouraged by Antone's commitment to self-improvement, rehabilitation, and recidivism prevention.... For the reasons set forth, we conclude that the appellate record does not support the district court's determination that Antone would have serious difficulty refraining from sexually violent conduct if released. It may be that we would affirm the judgment were the Government's burden one of a mere preponderance, but it is not and we do not. The Government has not established *by clear and convincing evidence* that the facts and circumstances of this case establish that Antone is a sexually dangerous individual subject to commitment under § 4248. Accordingly, we reverse the judgment of the district court and remand the matter to the district court with instructions to dismiss the petition....

Notes

In *Cooke*, the court found sufficient evidence to determine that the defendant suffered from a current and persistent mental illness and that he would have serious difficulty in refraining from sexually violent conduct if released. In *Antone*, the court held that the government failed to establish that the defendant was a sexually violent person. In *Antone*, the court assessed the defendant's volitional impairment in the context of his recent history and did not simply assign determinative weight to the existence of his prior offenses. *See also United States v. Heyer*, 740 F.3d 284, 287–89, 294–95 (4th Cir. 2014) (noting respondent's admission of "ongoing sexual interest in children," including showing child pornography to a teenage boy while on probation); *United States v. Bolander*, 722 F.3d 199, 204 (4th Cir. 2013) (affirming commitment of respondent who stole pornographic

---

15. In *Kansas v. Crane*, the Supreme Court recognized the "constitutional importance of distinguishing a dangerous sexual offender subject to civil commitment from other dangerous persons who are perhaps more properly dealt with exclusively through criminal proceedings." 534 U.S. at 412, 122 S.Ct. 867. In fact, in making this precise point, the Court cited to the wide prevalence of antisocial personality disorder among inmates—one of the two mental illnesses at issue in the instant case.

In his brief, Antone has contended that the language in *Crane* supports his position that it is unconstitutional to commit individuals under § 4248 who do not suffer from a paraphilia. Because we hold that, on the evidentiary record before us, Antone has not been shown to be a sexually dangerous person, we do not reach this question.

17. We note that Antone has been attending sex offender therapy in spite of its potential impact on future civil commitment hearings. *See generally* Jeslyn A. Miller, Comment, *Sex Offender Civil Commitment: The Treatment Paradox*, 98 Cal. L.Rev. 2093, 2115 (2010) (explaining that "[e]verything that an offender confesses during these multiple stages of treatment—including sexual fantasies, uncharged offenses, and gruesome details regarding sexual offenses—is discoverable.").

materials from the treatment lab while incarcerated and collected child pornography while on supervised release); *United States v. Wooden*, 693 F.3d 440, 445 (4th Cir. 2012) (respondent wrote letter to one of his previous victims, demonstrating serious volitional impairment issues). *But see United States v. Hall*, 664 F.3d 456, 464 (4th Cir. 2012) (respondent demonstrated ongoing interest in collecting pictures and drawings of children and adolescents while in custody and reported that he often masturbated to memories of his child victims, but due to his abstention from offenses during his twenty-eight months of release, court held defendant to be not sexually dangerous under § 4248); *United States v. Francis*, 686 F.3d 265, 271 (4th Cir. 2012) (considering respondent's perceived hostility towards women and his noncompliance with supervised release, but affirming denial of government's commitment petition).

C. Victim Restitution

Paroline v. United States

Supreme Court of the United States, 2014
___ U.S. ___, 134 S. Ct. 1710

Justice KENNEDY delivered the opinion of the Court.

This case presents the question of how to determine the amount of restitution a possessor of child pornography must pay to the victim whose childhood abuse appears in the pornographic materials possessed. The relevant statutory provisions are set forth at 18 U.S.C. § 2259. Enacted as a component of the Violence Against Women Act of 1994, § 2259 requires district courts to award restitution for certain federal criminal offenses, including child-pornography possession.... Petitioner Doyle Randall Paroline pleaded guilty to such an offense. He admitted to possessing between 150 and 300 images of child pornography, which included two that depicted the sexual exploitation of a young girl, now a young woman, who goes by the pseudonym "Amy" for this litigation. The question is what causal relationship must be established between the defendant's conduct and a victim's losses for purposes of determining the right to, and the amount of, restitution under § 2259....

Three decades ago, this Court observed that "the exploitive use of children in the production of pornography has become a serious national problem." *New York v. Ferber*, 458 U.S. 747, 749, 102 S.Ct. 3348, 73 L.Ed.2d 1113 (1982). The demand for child pornography harms children in part because it drives production, which involves child abuse. The harms caused by child pornography, however, are still more extensive because child pornography is "a permanent record" of the depicted child's abuse, and "the harm to the child is exacerbated by [its] circulation." *Id.*, at 759, 102 S.Ct. 3348. Because child pornography is now traded with ease on the Internet, "the number of still images and videos memorializing the sexual assault and other sexual exploitation of children, many very young in age, has grown exponentially." United States Sentencing Comm'n, P. Saris et al., Federal Child Pornography Offenses 3 (2012) (hereinafter Sentencing Comm'n Report).

One person whose story illustrates the devastating harm caused by child pornography is the respondent victim in this case. When she was eight and nine years old, she was sexually abused by her uncle in order to produce child pornography. Her uncle was prosecuted, required to pay about $6,000 in restitution, and sentenced to a lengthy prison term. The victim underwent an initial course of therapy beginning in 1998 and continuing into 1999. By the end of this period, her therapist's notes reported that she was "'back to normal' "; her involvement in dance and other age-appropriate activities, and the support of her family, justified an optimistic assessment. . . . [Citations to Record omitted]. Her functioning appeared to decline in her teenage years, however; and a major blow to her recovery came when, at the age of 17, she learned that images of her abuse were being trafficked on the Internet. . . . The digital images were available nationwide and no doubt worldwide. Though the exact scale of the trade in her images is unknown, the possessors to date easily number in the thousands. The knowledge that her images were circulated far and wide renewed the victim's trauma and made it difficult for her to recover from her abuse. As she explained in a victim impact statement submitted to the District Court in this case:

> "Every day of my life I live in constant fear that someone will see my pictures and recognize me and that I will be humiliated all over again. It hurts me to know someone is looking at them—at me—when I was just a little girl being abused for the camera. I did not choose to be there, but now I am there forever in pictures that people are using to do sick things. I want it all erased. I want it all stopped. But I am powerless to stop it just like I was powerless to stop my uncle. . . . My life and my feelings are worse now because the crime has never really stopped and will never really stop. . . . It's like I am being abused over and over and over again." . . .

The victim says in her statement that her fear and trauma make it difficult for her to trust others or to feel that she has control over what happens to her. . . .

The full extent of this victim's suffering is hard to grasp. Her abuser took away her childhood, her self-conception of her innocence, and her freedom from the kind of nightmares and memories that most others will never know. These crimes were compounded by the distribution of images of her abuser's horrific acts, which meant the wrongs inflicted upon her were in effect repeated; for she knew her humiliation and hurt were and would be renewed into the future as an ever-increasing number of wrongdoers witnessed the crimes committed against her.

Petitioner Paroline is one of the individuals who possessed this victim's images. In 2009, he pleaded guilty in federal court to one count of possession of material involving the sexual exploitation of children in violation of 18 U.S.C. § 2252. 672 F.Supp.2d 781, 783 (E.D.Tex.2009). Paroline admitted to knowing possession of between 150 and 300 images of child pornography, two of which depicted the respondent victim. *Ibid.* The victim sought restitution under § 2259, asking for close to $3.4 million, consisting of nearly $3 million in lost income and about $500,000 in future treatment and counseling costs. . . . She also sought attorney's fees and costs. 672 F.Supp.2d, at 783. The parties submitted competing expert reports. They stipulated that the victim did not know who Paroline was and that none of her claimed losses flowed from any specific knowledge about him or his offense conduct. *Id.*, at 792, and n. 11; . . .

After briefing and hearings, the District Court declined to award restitution. 672 F.Supp.2d, at 793. The District Court observed that "everyone involved with child pornography—from the abusers and producers to the end-users and possessors—contribute[s] to [the victim's] ongoing harm." *Id.*, at 792. But it concluded that the Government had the burden of proving the amount of the victim's losses "directly produced by Paroline that would not have occurred without his possession of her images." *Id.*, at 791. The District Court found that, under this standard, the Government had failed to meet its burden of proving what losses, if any, were proximately caused by Paroline's offense. It thus held that "an award of restitution is not appropriate in this case." *Id.*, at 793.

The victim sought a writ of mandamus, asking the United States Court of Appeals for the Fifth Circuit to direct the District Court to order Paroline to pay restitution in the amount requested. *In re Amy*, 591 F.3d 792, 793 (2009). The Court of Appeals denied relief. *Id.*, at 795. The victim sought rehearing. Her rehearing request was granted, as was her petition for a writ of mandamus. *In re Amy Unknown*, 636 F.3d 190, 201 (2011).

The Fifth Circuit reheard the case en banc along with another case, in which the defendant, Michael Wright, had raised similar issues in appealing an order of restitution under § 2259, see *United States v. Wright*, 639 F.3d 679, 681 (2011) (*per curiam*). As relevant, the Court of Appeals set out to determine the level of proof required to award restitution to victims in cases like this. It held that § 2259 did not limit restitution to losses proximately caused by the defendant, and each defendant who possessed the victim's images should be made liable for the victim's entire losses from the trade in her images, even though other offenders played a role in causing those losses. *In re Amy Unknown*, 701 F.3d 749, 772–774 (2012) (en banc).... Paroline sought review here. Certiorari was granted to resolve a conflict in the Courts of Appeals over the proper causation inquiry for purposes of determining the entitlement to and amount of restitution under § 2259. 570 U.S. ___, 133 S.Ct. 2886, 186 L.Ed.2d 932 (2013). For the reasons set forth, the decision of the Court of Appeals is vacated....

Title 18 U.S.C. § 2259(a) provides that a district court "shall order restitution for any offense" under Chapter 110 of Title 18, which covers a number of offenses involving the sexual exploitation of children and child pornography in particular. Paroline was convicted of knowingly possessing child pornography under § 2252, a Chapter 110 offense.... Section 2259 states a broad restitutionary purpose: It requires district courts to order defendants "to pay the victim ... the full amount of the victim's losses as determined by the court," § 2259(b)(1), and expressly states that "[t]he issuance of a restitution order under this section is mandatory," § 2259(b)(4)(A). Section 2259(b)(2) provides that "[a]n order of restitution under this section shall be issued and enforced in accordance with section 3664," which in turn provides in relevant part that "[t]he burden of demonstrating the amount of the loss sustained by a victim as a result of the offense shall be on the attorney for the Government," § 3664(e).

The threshold question the Court faces is whether § 2259 limits restitution to those losses proximately caused by the defendant's offense conduct. The Fifth Circuit held that it does not, contrary to the holdings of other Courts of Appeals to have addressed the question. Compare, *e.g.*, 701 F.3d, at 752 (no general proximate-cause requirement applies under § 2259), with *United States v. Rogers*, 714 F.3d 82, 89 (C.A.1 2013) (general proximate-cause requirement applies under § 2259); *United States v. Benoit*, 713 F.3d 1, 20 (C.A.10 2013) (same); *United States v. Fast*, 709 F.3d 712, 721–722 (C.A.8 2013) (same); *United States v. Laraneta*, 700 F.3d 983, 989–990 (C.A.7 2012) (same); *United States v. Burgess*, 684 F.3d 445, 456–457 (C.A.4 2012) (same); *United States v. Evers*, 669 F.3d 645, 659 (C.A.6 2012) (same); *United States v. Aumais*, 656 F.3d 147, 153 (C.A.2 2011) (same); *United States v. Kennedy*, 643 F.3d 1251, 1261 (C.A.9 2011) (same); *United States v. Monzel*, 641 F.3d 528, 535 (C.A.D.C.2011) (same); *United States v. McDaniel*, 631 F.3d 1204, 1208–1209 (C.A.11 2011) (same).

As a general matter, to say one event proximately caused another is a way of making two separate but related assertions. First, it means the former event caused the latter. This is known as actual cause or cause in fact. The concept of actual cause "is not a metaphysical one but an ordinary, matter-of-fact inquiry into the existence ... of a causal relation as laypeople would view it." 4 F. Harper, F. James, & O. Gray, Torts § 20.2, p. 100 (3d ed. 2007).

Every event has many causes, however, see *ibid.*, and only some of them are proximate, as the law uses that term. So to say that one event was a proximate cause of another means that it was not just any cause, but one with a sufficient connection to the result. The idea of proximate cause, as distinct from actual cause or cause in fact, defies easy summary. It is "a flexible concept," *Bridge v. Phoenix Bond & Indemnity Co.*, 553 U.S. 639, 654, 128 S.Ct. 2131, 170 L.Ed.2d 1012 (2008), that generally "refers to the basic requirement that ... there must be 'some direct relation between the injury asserted and the injurious conduct alleged,'" *CSX Transp., Inc. v. McBride*, 564 U.S. ___, ___, 131 S.Ct. 2630, 2645, 180 L.Ed.2d 637 (2011) (ROBERTS, C.J., dissenting) (quoting *Holmes v. Securities Investor Protection Corporation*, 503 U.S. 258, 268, 112 S.Ct. 1311, 117 L.Ed.2d 532 (1992)). The concept of proximate causation is applicable in both criminal and tort law, and the analysis is parallel in many instances. 1 W. LaFave, Substantive Criminal Law §6.4(c), p. 471 (2d ed. 2003) (hereinafter LaFave). Proximate cause is often explicated in terms of foreseeability or the scope of the risk created by the predicate conduct. See, *e.g.*, *ibid.*; 1 Restatement (Third) of Torts: Liability for Physical and Emotional Harm §29, p. 493 (2005) (hereinafter Restatement). A requirement of proximate cause thus serves, *inter alia*, to preclude liability in situations where the causal link between conduct and result is so attenuated that the consequence is more aptly described as mere fortuity. *Exxon Co., U.S.A. v. Sofec, Inc.*, 517 U.S. 830, 838–839, 116 S.Ct. 1813, 135 L.Ed.2d 113 (1996).

All parties agree §2259 imposes some causation requirement. The statute defines a victim as "the individual harmed as a result of a commission of a crime under this chapter." §2259(c). The words "as a result of" plainly suggest causation. See *Pacific Operators Offshore, LLP v. Valladolid*, 565 U.S. ___, ___, 132 S.Ct. 680, 690–691, 181 L.Ed.2d 675 (2012); see also *Burrage v. United States*, 571 U.S. ___, ___, 134 S.Ct. 881, 886–887, 187 L.Ed.2d 715 (2014). And a straightforward reading of §2259(c) indicates that the term "a crime" refers to the offense of conviction. Cf. *Hughey v. United States*, 495 U.S. 411, 416, 110 S.Ct. 1979, 109 L.Ed.2d 408 (1990). So if the defendant's offense conduct did not cause harm to an individual, that individual is by definition not a "victim" entitled to restitution under §2259.

As noted above, §2259 requires a court to order restitution for "the full amount of the victim's losses," §2259(b)(1), which the statute defines to include "any costs incurred by the victim" for six enumerated categories of expense, §2259(b)(3). The reference to "costs incurred by the victim" is most naturally understood as costs stemming from the source that qualifies an individual as a "victim" in the first place—namely, ones arising "as a result of" the offense. Thus, as is typically the case with criminal restitution, §2259 is intended to compensate victims for losses caused by the offense of conviction. See *id.*, at 416, 110 S.Ct. 1979. This is an important point, for it means the central concern of the causal inquiry must be the conduct of the particular defendant from whom restitution is sought.

But there is a further question whether restitution under §2259 is limited to losses proximately caused by the offense. As noted, a requirement of proximate cause is more restrictive than a requirement of factual cause alone. Even if §2259 made no express reference to proximate causation, the Court might well hold that a showing of proximate cause was required. Proximate cause is a standard aspect of causation in criminal law and the law of torts. See 1 LaFave §6.4(a), at 464–466; W. Keeton, D. Dobbs, R. Keeton, & D. Owen, Prosser and Keeton on Law of Torts §41, p. 263 (5th ed. 1984) (hereinafter Prosser and Keeton). Given proximate cause's traditional role in causation analysis, this Court has more than once found a proximate-cause requirement built into a statute that did not expressly impose one. See *Holmes, supra*, at 265–268, 112 S.Ct. 1311; *Associated Gen. Contractors of Cal., Inc. v. Carpenters*, 459 U.S. 519, 529–536, 103 S.Ct. 897, 74

L.Ed.2d 723 (1983); see also *CSX Transp., Inc., supra*, at ___, 131 S.Ct., at 2646 (ROBERTS, C.J., dissenting) ("We have applied the standard requirement of proximate cause to actions under federal statutes where the text did not expressly provide for it"); *Lexmark Int'l, Inc. v. Static Control Components, Inc., ante*, at 13–14.... Here, however, the interpretive task is easier, for the requirement of proximate cause is in the statute's text. The statute enumerates six categories of covered losses. §2259(b)(3). These include certain medical services, §2259(b)(3)(A); physical and occupational therapy, §2259(b)(3)(B); transportation, temporary housing, and child care, §2259(b)(3)(C); lost income, §2259(b)(3)(D); attorney's fees and costs, §2259(b)(3)(E); and a final catchall category for "any other losses suffered by the victim as a proximate result of the offense," §2259(b)(3)(F).

The victim argues that because the "proximate result" language appears only in the final, catchall category of losses set forth at §2259(b)(3)(F), the statute has no proximate-cause requirement for losses falling within the prior enumerated categories. She justifies this reading of §2259(b) in part on the grammatical rule of the last antecedent, "according to which a limiting clause or phrase ... should ordinarily be read as modifying only the noun or phrase that it immediately follows." *Barnhart v. Thomas*, 540 U.S. 20, 26, 124 S.Ct. 376, 157 L.Ed.2d 333 (2003). But that rule is "not an absolute and can assuredly be overcome by other indicia of meaning." *Ibid.* The Court has not applied it in a mechanical way where it would require accepting "unlikely premises." *United States v. Hayes*, 555 U.S. 415, 425, 129 S.Ct. 1079, 172 L.Ed.2d 816 (2009).

Other canons of statutory construction, moreover, work against the reading the victim suggests. "When several words are followed by a clause which is applicable as much to the first and other words as to the last, the natural construction of the language demands that the clause be read as applicable to all." *Porto Rico Railway, Light & Power Co. v. Mor*, 253 U.S. 345, 348, 40 S.Ct. 516, 64 L.Ed. 944 (1920). Furthermore, "[i]t is ... a familiar canon of statutory construction that [catchall] clauses are to be read as bringing within a statute categories similar in type to those specifically enumerated." *Federal Maritime Comm'n v. Seatrain Lines, Inc.*, 411 U.S. 726, 734, 93 S.Ct. 1773, 36 L.Ed.2d 620 (1973). Here, §2259(b)(3)(F) defines a broad, final category of "other losses suffered ... as a proximate result of the offense." That category is most naturally understood as a summary of the type of losses covered—*i.e.*, losses suffered as a proximate result of the offense.

The victim says that if Congress had wanted to limit the losses recoverable under §2259 to those proximately caused by the offense, it could have written the statute the same way it wrote §2327, which provides for restitution to victims of telemarketing fraud. Section 2327, which is written and structured much like §2259, simply defines the term "full amount of the victim's losses" as "all losses suffered by the victim as a proximate result of the offense." §2327(b)(3). In essence the victim argues that the first five categories of losses enumerated in §2259(b)(3) would be superfluous if all were governed by a proximate-cause requirement. That, however, is unpersuasive. The first five categories provide guidance to district courts as to the specific types of losses Congress thought would often be the proximate result of a Chapter 110 offense and could as a general matter be included in an award of restitution.

Reading the statute to impose a general proximate-cause limitation accords with common sense. As noted above, proximate cause forecloses liability in situations where the causal link between conduct and result is so attenuated that the so-called consequence is more akin to mere fortuity. For example, suppose the traumatized victim of a Chapter 110 offender needed therapy and had a car accident on the way to her therapist's office. The resulting medical costs, in a literal sense, would be a factual result of the offense. But it would be strange indeed to make a defendant pay restitution for these costs. The victim herself concedes Congress did not intend costs like these to be recoverable under § 2259.... But she claims that it is unnecessary to "read ... into" § 2259 a proximate-cause limitation in order to exclude costs of that sort. *Ibid.* She says the statute "contextually and inferentially require[s] a nexus for why" the losses were sustained—*i.e.*, a sufficient connection to child pornography....

The victim may be right that the concept of proximate cause is not necessary to impose sensible limitations on restitution for remote consequences. But one very effective way, and perhaps the most obvious way, of excluding costs like those arising from the hypothetical car accident described above would be to incorporate a proximate-cause limitation into the statute. Congress did so, and for reasons given above the proximate-cause requirement applies to all the losses described in § 2259. Restitution is therefore proper under § 2259 only to the extent the defendant's offense proximately caused a victim's losses....

There remains the difficult question of how to apply the statute's causation requirements in this case. The problem stems from the somewhat atypical causal process underlying the losses the victim claims here. It is perhaps simple enough for the victim to prove the aggregate losses, including the costs of psychiatric treatment and lost income, that stem from the ongoing traffic in her images as a whole. (Complications may arise in disaggregating losses sustained as a result of the initial physical abuse, but those questions may be set aside for present purposes.) These losses may be called, for convenience's sake, a victim's "general losses." The difficulty is in determining the "full amount" of those general losses, if any, that are the proximate result of the offense conduct of a particular defendant who is one of thousands who have possessed and will in the future possess the victim's images but who has no other connection to the victim.

In determining the amount of general losses a defendant must pay under § 2259 the ultimate question is how much of these losses were the "proximate result," § 2259(b)(3)(F), of that individual's offense. But the most difficult aspect of this inquiry concerns the threshold requirement of causation in fact. To be sure, the requirement of proximate causation, as distinct from mere causation in fact, would prevent holding any possessor liable for losses caused in only a remote sense. But the victim's costs of treatment and lost income resulting from the trauma of knowing that images of her abuse are being viewed over and over are direct and foreseeable results of child-pornography crimes, including possession, assuming the prerequisite of factual causation is satisfied. The primary problem, then, is the proper standard of causation in fact....

The traditional way to prove that one event was a factual cause of another is to show that the latter would not have occurred "but for" the former. This approach is a familiar part of our legal tradition, see 1 LaFave § 6.4(b), at 467–468; Prosser and Keeton § 41, at 266, and no party disputes that a showing of but-for causation would satisfy § 2259's factual-causation requirement. Sometimes that showing could be made with little difficulty. For example, but-for causation could be shown with ease in many cases involving producers of child pornography, see § 2251(a); parents who permit their children to be used for child-pornography production, see § 2251(b); individuals who sell children for such purposes, see § 2251A; or the initial distributor of the pornographic images of a child, see § 2252.

In this case, however, a showing of but-for causation cannot be made. The District Court found that the Government failed to prove specific losses caused by Paroline in a but-for sense and recognized that it would be "incredibly difficult" to do so in a case like this. 672 F.Supp.2d, at 791–793. That finding has a solid foundation in the record, and it is all but unchallenged in this Court.... From the victim's perspective, Paroline was just one of thousands of anonymous possessors. To be sure, the victim's precise degree of trauma likely bears a relation to the total number of offenders; it would probably be less if only 10 rather than thousands had seen her images. But it is not possible to prove that her losses would be less (and by how much) but for one possessor's individual role in the large, loosely connected network through which her images circulate.... Even without Paroline's offense, thousands would have viewed and would in the future view the victim's images, so it cannot be shown that her trauma and attendant losses would have been any different but for Paroline's offense. That is especially so given the parties' stipulation that the victim had no knowledge of Paroline....

Recognizing that losses cannot be substantiated under a but-for approach where the defendant is an anonymous possessor of images in wide circulation on the Internet, the victim and the Government urge the Court to read § 2259 to require a less restrictive causation standard, at least in this and similar child-pornography cases. They are correct to note that courts have departed from the but-for standard where circumstances warrant, especially where the combined conduct of multiple wrongdoers produces a bad outcome. See *Burrage*, 571 U.S., at ___, 134 S.Ct., at 890 (acknowledging "the undoubted reality that courts have not *always* required strict but-for causality, even where criminal liability is at issue").

The victim and the Government look to the literature on criminal and tort law for alternatives to the but-for test. The Court has noted that the "most common" exception to the but-for causation requirement is applied where "multiple sufficient causes independently ... produce a result," *ibid.*; see also 1 LaFave § 6.4(b), at 467–469; 1 Restatement § 27, at 376. This exception is an ill fit here, as all parties seem to recognize. Paroline's possession of two images of the victim was surely not sufficient to cause her entire losses from the ongoing trade in her images. Nor is there a practical way to isolate some subset of the victim's general losses that Paroline's conduct alone would have been sufficient to cause....

Understandably, the victim and the Government thus concentrate on a handful of less demanding causation tests endorsed by authorities on tort law. One prominent treatise suggests that "[w]hen the conduct of two or more actors is so related to an event that their combined conduct, viewed as a whole, is a but-for cause of the event, and application of the but-for rule to them individually would absolve all of them, the conduct of each is a cause in fact of the event." Prosser and Keeton § 41, at 268. The Restatement adopts a similar exception for "[m]ultiple sufficient causal sets." 1 Restatement § 27, Comment f, at 380–381. This is where a wrongdoer's conduct, though alone "insufficient ... to cause the plaintiff's harm," is, "when combined with conduct by other persons," "more than sufficient to cause the harm." *Ibid.* The Restatement offers as an example a case in which three people independently but simultaneously lean on a car, creating enough combined force to roll it off a cliff. *Ibid.* Even if each exerted too little force to move the car, and the force exerted by any two was sufficient to the move the car, each individual is a factual cause of the car's destruction. *Ibid.* The Government argues that these authorities "provide ample support for an 'aggregate' causation theory," ... and that such a theory would best effectuate congressional intent in cases like this, ... The victim says much the same....

These alternative causal tests are a kind of legal fiction or construct. If the conduct of a wrongdoer is neither necessary nor sufficient to produce an outcome, that conduct cannot in a strict sense be said to have caused the outcome. Nonetheless, tort law teaches that alternative and less demanding causal standards are necessary in certain circumstances to vindicate the law's purposes. It would be anomalous to turn away a person harmed by the combined acts of many wrongdoers simply because none of those wrongdoers alone caused the harm. And it would be nonsensical to adopt a rule whereby individuals hurt by the combined wrongful acts of many (and thus in many instances hurt more badly than otherwise) would have no redress, whereas individuals hurt by the acts of one person alone would have a remedy. Those are the principles that underlie the various aggregate causation tests the victim and the Government cite, and they are sound principles.

These alternative causal standards, though salutary when applied in a judicious manner, also can be taken too far. That is illustrated by the victim's suggested approach to applying § 2259 in cases like this. The victim says that under the strict logic of these alternative causal tests, each possessor of her images is a part of a causal set sufficient to produce her ongoing trauma, so each possessor should be treated as a cause in fact of all the trauma and all the attendant losses incurred as a result of the entire ongoing traffic in her images.... And she argues that if this premise is accepted the further requirement of proximate causation poses no barrier, for she seeks restitution only for those losses that are the direct and foreseeable result of child-pornography offenses. Because the statute requires restitution for the "full amount of the victim's losses," including "any ... losses suffered by the victim as a proximate result of the offense," § 2259(b), she argues that restitution is required for the entire aggregately caused amount.

The striking outcome of this reasoning—that each possessor of the victim's images would bear the consequences of the acts of the many thousands who possessed those images—illustrates why the Court has been reluctant to adopt aggregate causation logic in an incautious manner, especially in interpreting criminal statutes where there is no language expressly suggesting Congress intended that approach. See *Burrage*, 571 U.S., at ___, 134 S.Ct., at 890–891. Even if one were to refer just to the law of torts, it would be a major step to say there is a sufficient causal link between the injury and the wrong so that all the victim's general losses were "suffered ... as a proximate result of [Paroline's] offense," § 2259(b)(3)(F).

And there is special reason not to do so in the context of criminal restitution. Aside from the manifest procedural differences between criminal sentencing and civil tort lawsuits, restitution serves purposes that differ from (though they overlap with) the purposes of tort law. See, *e.g.*, *Kelly v. Robinson*, 479 U.S. 36, 49, n. 10, 107 S.Ct. 353, 93 L.Ed.2d 216 (1986) (noting that restitution is, *inter alia*, "an effective rehabilitative penalty"). Legal fictions developed in the law of torts cannot be imported into criminal restitution and applied to their utmost limits without due consideration of these differences.

Contrary to the victim's suggestion, this is not akin to a case in which a "gang of ruffians" collectively beats a person, or in which a woman is "gang raped by five men on one night or by five men on five sequential nights." ... First, this case does not involve a set of wrongdoers acting in concert, see Prosser and Keeton § 52, at 346 (discussing full liability for a joint enterprise); for Paroline had no contact with the overwhelming majority of the offenders for whose actions the victim would hold him accountable. Second, adopting the victim's approach would make an individual possessor liable for the combined consequences of the acts of not just 2, 5, or even 100 independently acting offenders; but instead, a number that may reach into the tens of thousands....

It is unclear whether it could ever be sensible to embrace the fiction that this victim's entire losses were the "proximate result," § 2259(b)(3)(F), of a single possessor's offense. Paroline's contribution to the causal process underlying the victim's losses was very minor, both compared to the combined acts of all other relevant offenders, and in comparison to the contributions of other individual offenders, particularly distributors (who may have caused hundreds or thousands of further viewings) and the initial producer of the child pornography. See 1 Restatement § 36, and Comment a, at 597–598 (recognizing a rule excluding from liability individuals whose contribution to a causal set that factually caused the outcome "pales by comparison to the other contributions to that causal set"). But see *id.*, § 27, Reporters' Note, Comment *i*, at 395 ("The conclusion that none of" two dozen small contributions to a sufficient causal set was a cause of the outcome "is obviously untenable"). Congress gave no indication that it intended its statute to be applied in the expansive manner the victim suggests, a manner contrary to the bedrock principle that restitution should reflect the consequences of the defendant's own conduct, see *Hughey*, 495 U.S., at 416, 110 S.Ct. 1979, not the conduct of thousands of geographically and temporally distant offenders acting independently, and with whom the defendant had no contact.

The victim argues that holding each possessor liable for her entire losses would be fair and practical, in part because offenders may seek contribution from one another.... If that were so, it might mitigate to some degree the concerns her approach presents. But there is scant authority for her contention that offenders convicted in different proceedings in different jurisdictions and ordered to pay restitution to the same victim may seek contribution from one another. There is no general federal right to contribution. *Northwest Airlines, Inc. v. Transport Workers*, 451 U.S. 77, 96–97, 101 S.Ct. 1571, 67 L.Ed.2d 750 (1981). Nor does the victim point to any clear statutory basis for a right to contribution in these circumstances. She thus suggests that this Court should imply a cause of action.... But that is a rare step in any circumstance. See, *e.g.*, *Stoneridge Investment Partners, LLC v. Scientific-Atlanta, Inc.*, 552 U.S. 148, 164–165, 128 S.Ct. 761, 169 L.Ed.2d 627 (2008); *Musick, Peeler & Garrett v. Employers Ins. of Wausau*, 508 U.S. 286, 291, 113 S.Ct. 2085, 124 L.Ed.2d 194 (1993) (noting that this Court's precedents "teach that the creation of new rights ought to be left to legislatures, not courts"). And it would do little to address the practical problems offenders would face in seeking contribution in any event, ... problems with which the victim fails to grapple.

The reality is that the victim's suggested approach would amount to holding each possessor of her images liable for the conduct of thousands of other independently acting possessors and distributors, with no legal or practical avenue for seeking contribution. That approach is so severe it might raise questions under the Excessive Fines Clause of the Eighth Amendment. To be sure, this Court has said that "the Excessive Fines Clause was intended to limit only those fines directly imposed by, and payable to, the government." *Browning-Ferris Industries of Vt., Inc. v. Kelco Disposal, Inc.*, 492 U.S. 257, 268, 109 S.Ct. 2909, 106 L.Ed.2d 219 (1989). But while restitution under § 2259 is paid to a victim, it is imposed by the Government "at the culmination of a criminal proceeding and requires conviction of an underlying" crime, *United States v. Bajakajian*, 524 U.S. 321, 328, 118 S.Ct. 2028, 141 L.Ed.2d 314 (1998). Thus, despite the differences between restitution and a traditional fine, restitution still implicates "the prosecutorial powers of government," *Browning-Ferris*, *supra*, at 275, 109 S.Ct. 2909. The primary goal of restitution is remedial or compensatory, cf. *Bajakajian*, *supra*, at 329, 118 S.Ct. 2028, but it also serves punitive purposes, see *Pasquantino v. United States*, 544 U.S. 349, 365, 125 S.Ct. 1766, 161 L.Ed.2d 619 (2005) ("The purpose of awarding restitution" under 18 U.S.C. § 3663A "is ... to mete out appropriate criminal punishment"); *Kelly*, 479 U.S., at 49, n. 10, 107 S.Ct. 353. That may be "sufficient to bring [it] within the purview of the Excessive Fines Clause," *Bajakajian*, *supra*, at 329, n. 4, 118 S.Ct. 2028. And there is a real question whether holding a single possessor liable for millions of dollars in losses collectively caused by thousands of independent actors might be excessive and disproportionate in these circumstances. These concerns offer further reason not to interpret the statute the way the victim suggests....

The contention that the victim's entire losses from the ongoing trade in her images were "suffered ... as a proximate result" of Paroline's offense for purposes of § 2259 must be rejected. But that does not mean the broader principles underlying the aggregate causation theories the Government and the victim cite are irrelevant to determining the proper outcome in cases like this. The cause of the victim's general losses is the trade in her images. And Paroline is a part of that cause, for he is one of those who viewed her images. While it is not possible to identify a discrete, readily definable incremental loss he caused, it is indisputable that he was a part of the overall phenomenon that caused her general losses. Just as it undermines the purposes of tort law to turn away plaintiffs harmed by several wrongdoers, it would undermine the remedial and penological purposes of § 2259 to turn away victims in cases like this.

With respect to the statute's remedial purpose, there can be no question that it would produce anomalous results to say that no restitution is appropriate in these circumstances. It is common ground that the victim suffers continuing and grievous harm as a result of her knowledge that a large, indeterminate number of individuals have viewed and will in the future view images of the sexual abuse she endured.... Harms of this sort are a major reason why child pornography is outlawed. See *Ferber*, 458 U.S., at 759, 102 S.Ct. 3348. The unlawful conduct of everyone who reproduces, distributes, or possesses the images of the victim's abuse—including Paroline—plays a part in sustaining and aggravating this tragedy. And there can be no doubt Congress wanted victims to receive restitution for harms like this. The law makes restitution "mandatory," § 2259(b)(4), for child-pornography offenses under Chapter 110, language that indicates Congress' clear intent that victims of child pornography be compensated by the perpetrators who contributed to their anguish. It would undermine this intent to apply the statute in a way that would render it a dead letter in child-pornography prosecutions of this type.

Denying restitution in cases like this would also be at odds with the penological purposes of § 2259's mandatory restitution scheme. In a sense, every viewing of child pornography is a repetition of the victim's abuse. One reason to make restitution mandatory for crimes like this is to impress upon offenders that their conduct produces concrete and devastating harms for real, identifiable victims. See *Kelly, supra*, at 49, n. 10, 107 S.Ct. 353 ("Restitution is an effective rehabilitative penalty because it forces the defendant to confront, in concrete terms, the harm his actions have caused"). It would be inconsistent with this purpose to apply the statute in a way that leaves offenders with the mistaken impression that child-pornography possession (at least where the images are in wide circulation) is a victimless crime.

If the statute by its terms required a showing of strict but-for causation, these purposes would be beside the point. But the text of the statute is not so limited. Although Congress limited restitution to losses that are the "proximate result" of the defendant's offense, such unelaborated causal language by no means requires but-for causation by its terms. See *Burrage*, 571 U.S., at ___, 134 S.Ct., at 888 (courts need not read phrases like "results from" to require but-for causality where there is "textual or contextual" reason to conclude otherwise).... In this special context, where it can be shown both that a defendant possessed a victim's images and that a victim has outstanding losses caused by the continuing traffic in those images but where it is impossible to trace a particular amount of those losses to the individual defendant by recourse to a more traditional causal inquiry, a court applying § 2259 should order restitution in an amount that comports with the defendant's relative role in the causal process that underlies the victim's general losses. The amount would not be severe in a case like this, given the nature of the causal connection between the conduct of a possessor like Paroline and the entirety of the victim's general losses from the trade in her images, which are the product of the acts of thousands of offenders. It would not, however, be a token or nominal amount. The required restitution would be a reasonable and circumscribed award imposed in recognition of the indisputable role of the offender in the causal process underlying the victim's losses and suited to the relative size of that causal role. This would serve the twin goals of helping the victim achieve eventual restitution for all her child-pornography losses and impressing upon offenders the fact that child-pornography crimes, even simple possession, affect real victims.

There remains the question of how district courts should go about determining the proper amount of restitution. At a general level of abstraction, a court must assess as best it can from available evidence the significance of the individual defendant's conduct in light of the broader causal process that produced the victim's losses. This cannot be a precise mathematical inquiry and involves the use of discretion and sound judgment. But that is neither unusual nor novel, either in the wider context of criminal sentencing or in the more specific domain of restitution. It is well recognized that district courts by necessity "exercise ... discretion in fashioning a restitution order." § 3664(a). Indeed, a district court is expressly authorized to conduct a similar inquiry where multiple defendants who have "contributed to the loss of a victim" appear before it. § 3664(h). In that case it may "apportion liability among the defendants to reflect the level of contribution to the victim's loss ... of each defendant." *Ibid.* Assessing an individual defendant's role in the causal process behind a child-pornography victim's losses does not involve a substantially different or greater exercise of discretion.

There are a variety of factors district courts might consider in determining a proper amount of restitution, and it is neither necessary nor appropriate to prescribe a precise algorithm for determining the proper restitution amount at this point in the law's development. Doing so would unduly constrain the decisionmakers closest to the facts of any given case. But district courts might, as a starting point, determine the amount of the victim's losses caused by the continuing traffic in the victim's images (excluding, of course, any remote losses like the hypothetical car accident described above ...), then set an award of restitution in consideration of factors that bear on the relative causal significance of the defendant's conduct in producing those losses. These could include the number of past criminal defendants found to have contributed to the victim's general losses; reasonable predictions of the number of future offenders likely to be caught and convicted for crimes contributing to the victim's general losses; any available and reasonably reliable estimate of the broader number of offenders involved (most of whom will, of course, never be caught or convicted); whether the defendant reproduced or distributed images of the victim; whether the defendant had any connection to the initial production of the images; how many images of the victim the defendant possessed; and other facts relevant to the defendant's relative causal role.... These factors need not be converted into a rigid formula, especially if doing so would result in trivial restitution orders. They should rather serve as rough guideposts for determining an amount that fits the offense. The resulting amount fixed by the court would be deemed the amount of the victim's general losses that were the "proximate result of the offense" for purposes of § 2259, and thus the "full amount" of such losses that should be awarded. The court could then set an appropriate payment schedule in consideration of the defendant's financial means. See § 3664(f)(2).

The victim says this approach is untenable because her losses are "indivisible" in the sense that term is used by tort law, *i.e.*, that there is no "reasonable basis for the factfinder to determine ... the amount of damages separately caused by" any one offender's conduct. Restatement (Third) of Torts: Apportionment of Liability § 26, p. 320 (1999). The premise of her argument is that because it is in a sense a fiction to say Paroline caused $1,000 in losses, $10,000 in losses, or any other lesser amount, it is necessary to embrace the much greater fiction that Paroline caused all the victim's losses from the ongoing trade in her images. But that is a non sequitur. The Court is required to define a causal standard that effects the statute's purposes, not to apply tort-law concepts in a mechanical way in the criminal restitution context. Even if the victim's losses are fully "indivisible" in this sense (which is debatable), treating Paroline as a proximate cause of all the victim's losses — especially in the absence of a workable system of contribution — stretches the fiction of aggregate causation to its breaking point. Treating him as a cause of a smaller amount of the victim's general losses, taking account of his role in the overall causal process behind those losses, effects the statute's purposes; avoids the nonsensical result of turning away victims emptyhanded; and does so without sacrificing the need for proportionality in sentencing.

The victim also argues that this approach would consign her to "piecemeal" restitution and leave her to face "decades of litigation that might never lead to full recovery," ... which "would convert Congress's promise to child pornography victims into an empty gesture," ... But Congress has not promised victims full and swift restitution at all costs. To be sure, the statute states a strong restitutionary purpose; but that purpose cannot be twisted into a license to hold a defendant liable for an amount drastically out of proportion to his own individual causal relation to the victim's losses. ... Furthermore, an approach of this sort better effects the need to impress upon defendants that their acts are not irrelevant or victimless. As the Government observes, ... it would undermine this important purpose of criminal restitution if the victim simply collected her full losses from a handful of wealthy possessors and left the remainder to pay nothing because she had already fully collected. Of course the victim should someday collect restitution for all her child-pornography losses, but it makes sense to spread payment among a larger number of offenders in amounts more closely in proportion to their respective causal roles and their own circumstances so that more are made aware, through the concrete mechanism of restitution, of the impact of child-pornography possession on victims. ...

This approach is not without its difficulties. Restitution orders should represent "an application of law," not "a decisionmaker's caprice," *Philip Morris USA v. Williams*, 549 U.S. 346, 352, 127 S.Ct. 1057, 166 L.Ed.2d 940 (2007) (internal quotation marks omitted), and the approach articulated above involves discretion and estimation. But courts can only do their best to apply the statute as written in a workable manner, faithful to the competing principles at stake: that victims should be compensated and that defendants should be held to account for the impact of their conduct on those victims, but also that defendants should be made liable for the consequences and gravity of their own conduct, not the conduct of others. District courts routinely exercise wide discretion both in sentencing as a general matter and more specifically in fashioning restitution orders. There is no reason to believe they cannot apply the causal standard defined above in a reasonable manner without further detailed guidance at this stage in the law's elaboration. Based on its experience in prior cases of this kind, the Government — which, as noted above, ... bears the burden of proving the amount of the victim's losses, § 3664(e) — could also inform district courts of restitution sought and ordered in other cases. ...

The Fifth Circuit's interpretation of the requirements of § 2259 was incorrect. The District Court likewise erred in requiring a strict showing of but-for causation. The judgment of the Court of Appeals is vacated, and the case is remanded for further proceedings consistent with this opinion.

It is so ordered.

Chief Justice ROBERTS, with whom Justice SCALIA and Justice THOMAS join, dissenting.

I certainly agree with the Court that Amy deserves restitution, and that Congress—by making restitution mandatory for victims of child pornography—meant that she have it. Unfortunately, the restitution statute that Congress wrote for child pornography offenses makes it impossible to award that relief to Amy in this case. Instead of tailoring the statute to the unique harms caused by child pornography, Congress borrowed a generic restitution standard that makes restitution contingent on the Government's ability to prove, "by the preponderance of the evidence," "the amount of the loss sustained by a victim as a result of" the defendant's crime. 18 U.S.C. §3664(e). When it comes to Paroline's crime—possession of two of Amy's images—it is not possible to do anything more than pick an arbitrary number for that "amount." And arbitrary is not good enough for the criminal law.

The Court attempts to design a more coherent restitution system, focusing on "the defendant's relative role in the causal process that underlies the victim's general losses." ... But this inquiry, sensible as it may be, is not the one Congress adopted. After undertaking the inquiry that Congress *did* require, the District Court in this case concluded that the Government could not meet its statutory burden of proof. Before this Court, the Government all but concedes the point.... I must regretfully dissent....

Congress has authorized restitution only for "the amount of the loss sustained by a victim as a result of the offense." §3664(e). We have interpreted virtually identical language, in the predecessor statute to section 3664, to require "restitution to be tied to the loss caused *by the offense of conviction.*" *Hughey v. United States*, 495 U.S. 411, 418, 110 S.Ct. 1979, 109 L.Ed.2d 408 (1990) (citing 18 U.S.C. §3580(a) (1982 ed.); emphasis added). That is, restitution may not be imposed for losses caused by any other crime or any other defendant.[1]

Justice SOTOMAYOR's dissent dismisses section 3664(e), which is Congress's direct answer to the very question presented by this case, namely, how to resolve a "dispute as to the proper amount ... of restitution." Justice SOTOMAYOR thinks the answer to that question begins and ends with the statement in section 2259(b)(1) that the defendant must pay "the full amount of the victim's losses." ... But losses from what? The answer is found in the rest of that sentence: "the full amount of the victim's losses *as determined by the court pursuant to paragraph 2.*" §2259(b)(1) (emphasis added). "[P]aragraph 2," of course, instructs that "[a]n order of restitution under this section shall be issued and enforced in accordance with section 3664 in the same manner as an order under section 3663A." §2259(b)(2). And it is section 3664 that provides the statute's burden of proof and specifies that the defendant pay for those losses sustained "as a result of *the* offense"— that is, his offense. §3664(e).... The offense of conviction here was Paroline's possession of two of Amy's images. No one suggests Paroline's crime actually caused Amy to suffer millions of dollars in losses, so the statute does not allow a court to award millions of dollars in restitution. Determining what amount the statute does allow—the amount of Amy's losses that Paroline's offense caused—is the real difficulty of this case....

Regrettably, Congress provided no mechanism for answering that question. If actual causation is to be determined using the traditional, but-for standard, then the Court acknowledges that "a showing of but-for causation cannot be made" in this case.... Amy

---

1. In a case "where the loss is the product of the combined conduct of multiple offenders," ... (SOTOMAYOR, J., dissenting), section 3664(h) provides that a court may "make each defendant liable for payment of the full amount of restitution or may apportion liability among the defendants to reflect the level of contribution to the victim's loss and economic circumstances of each defendant." As the Court notes, however, this provision applies only when multiple defendants are sentenced in the same proceeding, or charged under the same indictment....

would have incurred all of her lost wages and counseling costs even if Paroline had not viewed her images. The Government and Amy respond by offering an "aggregate" causation theory borrowed from tort law. But even if we apply this "legal fiction," ... and assume, for purposes of argument, that Paroline's crime contributed something to Amy's total losses, that suffices only to establish causation in fact. It is not sufficient to award restitution under the statute, which requires a further determination of the *amount* that Paroline must pay. He must pay "the full amount of the victim's losses," yes, but "as determined by" section 3664—that is, the full amount of the losses *he* caused. The Government has the burden to establish that *amount*, and no one has suggested a plausible means for the Government to carry that burden.[2]

The problem stems from the nature of Amy's injury. As explained, section 3664 is a general statute designed to provide restitution for more common crimes, such as fraud and assault. The section 3664(e) standard will work just fine for most crime victims, because it will usually not be difficult to identify the harm caused by the defendant's offense. The dispute will usually just be over the amount of the victim's loss—for example, the value of lost assets or the cost of a night in the hospital.... Amy has a qualitatively different injury. Her loss, while undoubtedly genuine, is a result of the collective actions of a huge number of people—beginning with her uncle who abused her and put her images on the Internet, to the distributors who make those images more widely available, to the possessors such as Paroline who view her images. The harm to Amy was produced over time, gradually, by tens of thousands of persons acting independently from one another.[3] She suffers in particular from her knowledge that her images are being viewed online by an unknown number of people, and from her fear that any person she meets might recognize her from having witnessed her abuse.... But Amy does not know who Paroline is.... Nothing in the record comes close to establishing that Amy would have suffered less if Paroline had not possessed her images, let alone how much less.... Amy's injury is indivisible, which means that Paroline's particular share of her losses is unknowable. And yet it is proof of Paroline's particular share that the statute requires.

By simply importing the generic restitution statute without accounting for the diffuse harm suffered by victims of child pornography, Congress set up a restitution system sure to fail in cases like this one. Perhaps a case with different facts, say, a single distributor and only a handful of possessors, would be susceptible of the proof the statute requires. But when tens of thousands of copies (or more) of Amy's images have changed hands all across the world for more than a decade, a demand for the Government to prove "the amount of the loss sustained by a victim as a result of *the* offense"—the offense before the court in any particular case—is a demand for the impossible. §3664(e) (emphasis added). When Congress conditioned restitution on the Government's meeting that burden of proof, it effectively precluded restitution in most cases involving possession or distribution of child pornography....

The District Court in Paroline's case found that the Government could not meet its statutory burden of proof. The Government does not really contest that holding here; it instead asks to be held to a less demanding standard. Having litigated this issue for years

---

2. The correct amount is not the one favored by Justice SOTOMAYOR's dissent, which would hold Paroline liable for losses that he certainly *did not* cause, without any right to seek contribution from others who harmed Amy.

3. The gang assaults discussed by Justice SOTOMAYOR, ... are not a fair analogy. The gang members in those cases acted together, with a common plan, each one aiding and abetting the others in inflicting harm. But Paroline has never met or interacted with any, or virtually any, of the other persons who contributed to Amy's injury, and his possession offense did not aid or abet anyone.

now in virtually every Circuit, the best the Government has come up with is to tell courts awarding restitution to look at what other courts have done. But that is not a workable guide, not least because courts have taken vastly different approaches to materially indistinguishable cases. According to the Government's lodging in this case, District Courts awarding less than Amy's full losses have imposed restitution orders varying from $50 to $530,000.[4] ... How is a court supposed to use those figures as any sort of guidance? Pick the median figure? The mean? Something else? ...

The majority's proposal is to have a district court "assess as best it can from available evidence the significance of the individual defendant's conduct in light of the broader causal process that produced the victim's losses." ... Even if that were a plausible way to design a restitution system for Amy's complex injury, there is no way around the fact that it is not the system that Congress created. The statute requires restitution to be based exclusively on *the losses that resulted from the defendant's crime*—not on the defendant's relative culpability. The majority's plan to situate Paroline along a spectrum of offenders who have contributed to Amy's harm will not assist a district court in calculating *the amount* of Amy's losses—the amount of her lost wages and counseling costs—that was caused by Paroline's crime (or that of any other defendant).

The Court is correct, of course, that awarding Amy no restitution would be contrary to Congress's remedial and penological purposes.... But we have previously refused to allow "policy considerations"—including an "expansive declaration of purpose," and the need to "compensate victims for the full losses they suffered"—to deter us from reading virtually identical statutory language to require proof of the harm caused solely by the defendant's particular offense. *Hughey*, 495 U.S., at 420–421, 110 S.Ct. 1979.... Moreover, even the Court's "relative role in the causal process" approach to the statute ... is unlikely to make Amy whole. To the extent that district courts do form a sort of consensus on how much to award, experience shows that the amount in any particular case will be quite small—the significant majority of defendants have been ordered to pay Amy $5,000 or less.... This means that Amy will be stuck litigating for years to come. The Court acknowledges that Amy may end up with "piecemeal" restitution, yet responds simply that "Congress has not promised victims full and swift restitution at all costs." ...

Amy will fare no better if district courts consider the other factors suggested by the majority, including the number of defendants convicted of possessing Amy's images, a rough estimate of those likely to be convicted in the future, and an even rougher estimate of the total number of persons involved in her harm.... In the first place, only the last figure is relevant, because Paroline's relative significance can logically be measured only in light of everyone who contributed to Amy's injury—not just those who have been, or will be, caught and convicted. Even worse, to the extent it is possible to project the total number of persons who have viewed Amy's images, that number is tragically large, which means that restitution awards tied to it will lead to a pitiful recovery in every case.... [Citation to Record omitted] (estimating Paroline's "'market share'" of Amy's harm at 1/71,000, or $47). The majority says that courts should not impose "trivial restitution orders," ... but it is hard to see how a court fairly assessing this defendant's relative contribution could do anything else.

Nor can confidence in judicial discretion save the statute from arbitrary application.... It is true that district courts exercise substantial discretion in awarding restitution and imposing sentences in general. But they do not do so by mere instinct. Courts are instead

---

4. Amy's uncle—the initial source of *all* of her injuries—was ordered to pay $6,325 in restitution, which only underscores how arbitrary the statute is when applied to most child pornography offenses.

guided by statutory standards: in the restitution context, a fair determination of the losses caused by the individual defendant under section 3664(e); in sentencing more generally, the detailed factors in section 3553(a). A contrary approach—one that asks district judges to impose restitution or other criminal punishment guided solely by their own intuitions regarding comparative fault—would undermine the requirement that every criminal defendant receive due process of law....

The Court's decision today means that Amy will not go home with nothing. But it would be a mistake for that salutary outcome to lead readers to conclude that Amy has prevailed or that Congress has done justice for victims of child pornography. The statute as written allows no recovery; we ought to say so, and give Congress a chance to fix it.

I respectfully dissent.

Justice SOTOMAYOR, dissenting.

This Court has long recognized the grave "physiological, emotional, and mental" injuries suffered by victims of child pornography. *New York v. Ferber*, 458 U.S. 747, 758, 102 S.Ct. 3348, 73 L.Ed.2d 1113 (1982). The traffic in images depicting a child's sexual abuse, we have observed, "'poses an even greater threat to the child victim than does sexual abuse or prostitution'" because the victim must "'go through life knowing that the recording is circulating within the mass distribution system for child pornography.'" *Id.*, at 759, n. 10, 102 S.Ct. 3348. As we emphasized in a later case, the images cause "continuing harm by haunting the chil[d] in years to come." *Osborne v. Ohio*, 495 U.S. 103, 111, 110 S.Ct. 1691, 109 L.Ed.2d 98 (1990).

Congress enacted 18 U.S.C. § 2259 against this backdrop. The statute imposes a "mandatory" duty on courts to order restitution to victims of federal offenses involving the sexual abuse of children, including the possession of child pornography. § 2259(b)(4). And it commands that for any such offense, a court "shall direct the defendant to pay the victim ... the full amount of the victim's losses." § 2259(b)(1).... The Court interprets this statute to require restitution in a "circumscribed" amount less than the "entirety of the victim's ... losses," a total it instructs courts to estimate based on the defendant's "relative role" in the victim's harm.... That amount, the Court holds, should be neither "nominal" nor "severe." *Ibid.*

I appreciate the Court's effort to achieve what it perceives to be a just result. It declines to require restitution for a victim's full losses, a result that might seem incongruent to an individual possessor's partial role in a harm in which countless others have participated. And it rejects the position advanced by Paroline and the dissenting opinion of THE CHIEF JUSTICE, which would result in no restitution in cases like this for the perverse reason that a child has been victimized by too many.... The Court's approach, however, cannot be reconciled with the law that Congress enacted. Congress mandated restitution for the "full amount of the victim's losses," § 2259(b)(1), and did so within the framework of settled tort law principles that treat defendants like Paroline jointly and severally liable for the indivisible consequences of their intentional, concerted conduct. And to the extent an award for the full amount of a victim's losses may lead to fears of unfair treatment for particular defendants, Congress provided a mechanism to accommodate those concerns: Courts are to order "partial payments" on a periodic schedule if the defendant's financial circumstances or other "interest [s] of justice" so require. §§ 3664(f)(3), 3572(d)(1). I would accordingly affirm the Fifth Circuit's holding that the District Court "must enter a restitution order reflecting the 'full amount of [Amy's] losses,'" *In re Amy Unknown*, 701 F.3d 749, 774 (2012), and instruct the court to consider a periodic payment schedule on remand....

Starting with the text, § 2259 declares that a court "shall order restitution for any offense under this chapter." The possession of child pornography, § 2252, is an offense under the relevant chapter, and the term "shall" creates "an obligation impervious to judicial discretion," *Lexecon Inc. v. Milberg Weiss Bershad Hynes & Lerach*, 523 U.S. 26, 35, 118 S.Ct. 956, 140 L.Ed.2d 62 (1998). So the text could not be clearer: A court must order restitution against a person convicted of possessing child pornography. Section 2259(b)(4) underscores this directive by declaring that "[t]he issuance of a restitution order under this section is mandatory." And the statute's title—"mandatory restitution"—reinforces it further still....

When Congress passed § 2259 in 1994, it was common knowledge that child pornography victims suffer harm at the hands of numerous offenders who possess their images in common, whether in print, film, or electronic form. See, *e.g.*, Shouvlin, Preventing the Sexual Exploitation of Children: A Model Act, 17 Wake Forest L.Rev. 535, 544 (1981) (describing the "enormous number of magazines" and "hundreds of films" produced each year depicting the sexual abuse of children, which were circulated to untold numbers of offenders through a "well-organized distribution system [that] ensures that even the small towns have access to [the] material"); Doyle, FBI Probing Child Porn on Computers, San Francisco Chronicle, Dec. 5, 1991, p. A23 (describing complaint that "child pornographic photographs" were circulating via the "America On-Line computer service"). Congress was also acutely aware of the severe injuries that victims of child pornography suffer at the hands of criminals who possess and view the recorded images of their sexual abuse. Congress found, for example, that the "continued existence" and circulation of child pornography images "causes the child victims of sexual abuse continuing harm by haunting those children in future years." Child Pornography Prevention Act of 1996, § 121, 110 Stat. 3009-26, Congressional Findings (2), notes following 18 U.S.C. § 2251 (hereinafter § 2251 Findings). It is inconceivable that Congress would have imposed a mandatory restitution obligation on the possessors who contribute to these "continuing harm[s]," *ibid.*, only to direct courts to apply a but-for cause requirement that would prevent victims from actually obtaining any recovery.

There is, of course, an alternative standard for determining cause-in-fact that would be consistent with the text of § 2259 and the context in which it was enacted: aggregate causation.... And under this standard, "'[w]hen the conduct of two or more actors is so related to an event that their combined conduct, viewed as a whole, is a but-for cause of the event, and application of the but-for rule to them individually would absolve all of them, the conduct of each is a cause in fact of the event.'" ... [1] Paroline and his fellow offenders plainly qualify as factual causes under this approach because Amy's losses would not have occurred but for their combined conduct, and because applying the but-for rule would excuse them all.

There is every reason to think Congress intended § 2259 to incorporate aggregate causation. Whereas a but-for requirement would set § 2259's "mandatory" restitution command on a collision course with itself, the aggregate causation standard follows directly from the statute. Section 2259 is unequivocal; it offers no safety-in-numbers exception

---

1. The Fifth Circuit recognized this standard more than 60 years ago when it observed that "'[a]ccording to the great weight of authority where the concurrent or successive acts or omissions of two or more persons, although acting independently of each other, are in combination, the direct or proximate cause of a single injury,'" any of them may be held liable "'even though his act alone might not have caused the entire injury, or the same damage might have resulted from the act of the other tort-feasor[s].'" *Phillips Petroleum Co. v. Hardee*, 189 F.2d 205, 212 (1951) (quoting 38 Am.Jur. Negligence § 257, p. 946 (1941)).

for defendants who possess images of a child's abuse in common with other offenders. And the aggregate causation standard exists to avoid exactly that kind of exception. See Prosser and Keeton § 41, at 268–269 (aggregate causation applies where multiple defendants "bea[r] a like relationship" to a victim's injury, and where "[e]ach seeks to escape liability for a reason that, if recognized, would likewise protect each other defendant in the group, thus leaving the [victim] without a remedy in the face of the fact that had none of them acted improperly the [victim] would not have suffered the harm"); Restatement (Third) of Torts: Liability for Physical and Emotional Harm § 27, Comment *f*, p. 380 (2005) (similar).... At bottom, Congress did not intend § 2259 to create a safe harbor for those who inflict upon their victims the proverbial death by a thousand cuts. Given the very nature of the child pornography market — in which a large class of offenders contribute jointly to their victims' harm by trading in their images — a but-for causation requirement would swallow § 2259's "mandatory" restitution command, leaving victims with little hope of recovery. That is all the "textual [and] contextual" reason necessary to conclude that Congress incorporated aggregate causation into § 2259. *Burrage*, 571 U.S., at ___, 134 S.Ct., at 888–889....

As the majority recognizes, Congress did not draft § 2259 in a vacuum; it did so in the context of settled tort law traditions.... Section 2259 functions as a tort statute, one designed to ensure that victims will recover compensatory damages in an efficient manner concurrent with criminal proceedings. See Restatement of Torts § 901, p. 537 (1939) (the purposes of tort law include "to give compensation, indemnity, or restitution for harms" and "to punish wrongdoers"); *Dolan v. United States*, 560 U.S. 605, 612, 130 S.Ct. 2533, 177 L.Ed.2d 108 (2010) (the "substantive purpose" of the related Mandatory Victims Restitution Act of 1996, § 3664, is "to ensure that victims of a crime receive full restitution"). And the nature of the child pornography industry and the indivisible quality of the injuries suffered by its victims make this a paradigmatic situation in which traditional tort law principles would require joint and several liability. By requiring restitution for the "full amount of the victim's losses," § 2259(b)(1), Congress did not depart from these principles; it embraced them.

First, the injuries caused by child pornography possessors are impossible to apportion in any practical sense. It cannot be said, for example, that Paroline's offense alone required Amy to attend five additional minutes of therapy, or that it caused some discrete portion of her lost income. The majority overlooks this fact, ordering courts to surmise some "circumscribed" amount of loss based on a list of factors.... Section 2259's full restitution requirement dispenses with this guesswork, however, and in doing so it harmonizes with the settled tort law tradition concerning indivisible injuries. As this Court explained this rule in *Edmonds v. Compagnie Generale Transatlantique*, 443 U.S. 256, 99 S.Ct. 2753, 61 L.Ed.2d 521 (1979), unless a plaintiff's "injury is divisible and the causation of each part can be separately assigned to each tortfeasor," the rule is that a "tortfeasor is not relieved of liability for the entire harm he caused just because another's negligence was also a factor in effecting the injury." *Id.*, at 260, n. 8, 99 S.Ct. 2753; see also Prosser and Keeton § 52, at 347 (joint and several liability applies to injuries that "are obviously incapable of any reasonable or practical division"); *Feneff v. Boston & Maine R. Co.*, 196 Mass. 575, 580, 82 N.E. 705, 707 (1907) (similar).

Second, Congress adopted § 2259 against the backdrop of the rule governing concerted action by joint tortfeasors, which specifies that "[w]here two or more [tortfeasors] act in concert, it is well settled ... that each will be liable for the entire result." Prosser and Keeton § 52, at 346. The degree of concerted action required by the rule is not inordinate; "if one person acts to produce injury with full knowledge that others are acting in a similar manner and that his conduct will contribute to produce a single harm, a joint tort has been consummated even when there is no prearranged plan." 1 F. Harper, F. James, & O. Gray, The Law of Torts § 10.1, p. 699 (1st ed. 1956) (hereinafter 1 Harper and James); see also, *e.g., Troop v. Dew*, 150 Ark. 560, 565, 234 S.W. 992, 994 (1921) (defendants jointly liable for uncoordinated acts where they were "working to a common purpose").

Child pornography possessors are jointly liable under this standard, for they act in concert as part of a global network of possessors, distributors, and producers who pursue the common purpose of trafficking in images of child sexual abuse. As Congress itself recognized, "possessors of such material" are an integral part of the "market for the sexual exploitative use of children." § 2251 Finding (12). Moreover, although possessors like Paroline may not be familiar with every last participant in the market for child sexual abuse images, there is little doubt that they act with knowledge of the inevitable harms caused by their combined conduct. Paroline himself admitted to possessing between 150 and 300 images of minors engaged in sexually explicit conduct, which he downloaded from other offenders on the Internet. See 672 F.Supp.2d 781, 783.... By communally browsing and downloading Internet child pornography, offenders like Paroline "fuel the process" that allows the industry to flourish. O'Connell, Paedophiles Networking on the Internet, in Child Abuse on the Internet: Ending the Silence 77 (C. Arnaldo ed. 2001). Indeed, one expert describes Internet child pornography networks as "an example of a complex criminal conspiracy," *ibid.* — the quintessential concerted action to which joint and several liability attaches.

Lastly, § 2259's full restitution requirement conforms to what Congress would have understood to be the uniform rule governing joint and several liability for intentional torts. Under that rule, "[e]ach person who commits a tort that requires intent is jointly and severally liable for any indivisible injury legally caused by the tortious conduct." Restatement (Third) of Torts: Apportionment of Liability § 12, p. 110 (2007). There is little doubt that the possession of images of a child being sexually abused would amount to an intentional invasion of privacy tort — and an extreme one at that. See Restatement (Second) of Torts § 652B, p. 378 (1976) ("One who intentionally intrudes, physically or otherwise, upon [another's] private affairs or concerns, is subject to liability ... if the intrusion would be highly offensive to a reasonable person").[4]

Section 2259's imposition of joint and several liability makes particular sense when viewed in light of this intentional tort rule. For at the end of the day, the question of how to allocate losses among defendants is really a choice between placing the risk of loss on the defendants (since one who is caught first may be required to pay more than his fair share) or the victim (since an apportionment regime would risk preventing her from obtaining full recovery). Whatever the merits of placing the risk of loss on a victim in the context of a negligence-based offense, Congress evidently struck the balance quite differently in this context, placing the risk on the morally culpable possessors of child pornography and not their innocent child victims....

Notwithstanding § 2259's text and the longstanding tort law traditions that support it, the majority adopts an apportionment approach based on its concern that joint and

---

4. Possession of child pornography under § 2252 constitutes an intentional tort notwithstanding that the offense requires a *mens rea* of knowledge. See § 2252(a)(3)(B) (punishing one who "knowingly sells or possesses" child pornography). One is "said to act knowingly if he is aware ' "that [a] result is practically certain to follow from his conduct." ' " *United States v. Bailey*, 444 U.S. 394, 404, 100 S.Ct. 624, 62 L.Ed.2d 575 (1980). That definition is, if anything, more exacting than the kind of "intent" required for an intentional tort under the Restatement, which defines "intent" to include situations where an actor "believes that ... consequences are substantially certain to result from [his act]." Restatement (Second) of Torts § 8A, p. 15 (1965).

several liability might lead to unfairness as applied to individual defendants.... The majority finds this approach necessary because § 2259 does not provide individual defendants with the ability to seek contribution from other offenders.... I agree that the statute does not create a cause of action for contribution, but unlike the majority I do not think the absence of contribution suggests that Congress intended the phrase "full amount of the victim's losses" to mean something less than that. For instead of expending judicial resources on disputes between intentional tortfeasors, Congress crafted a different mechanism for preventing inequitable treatment of individual defendants—the use of periodic payment schedules.

Section 2259(b)(2) directs that "[a]n order of restitution under this section shall be issued and enforced in accordance with section 3664." Section 3664(f)(1)(A) in turn reiterates § 2259's command that courts "shall order restitution to each victim in the full amount of each victim's losses." But § 3664 goes on to distinguish between the *amount* of restitution ordered and the *schedule* on which payments are to be made. Thus, § 3664(f)(2) states that a court "shall ... specify in the restitution order ... the schedule according to whic[h] the restitution is to be paid," and § 3664(f)(3)(A) provides that "[a] restitution order may direct the defendant to make a single, lump sum payment" or "partial payments at specified intervals." Critically, in choosing between lump-sum and partial payments, courts "shall" consider "the financial resources and other assets of the defendant," along with "any financial obligations of the defendant, including obligations to dependents." §§ 3664(f)(2)(A), (C).

Applying these factors to set an appropriate payment schedule in light of any individual child pornography possessor's financial circumstances would not be difficult; indeed, there is already a robust body of case law clarifying how payment schedules are to be set under § 3664(f). For example, Courts of Appeals have uniformly found it an abuse of discretion to require defendants to make immediate lump-sum payments for the full amount of a restitution award when they do not have the ability to do so. In such cases, Congress has instead required courts to impose periodic payment schedules. See, *e.g.*, *United States v. McGlothlin*, 249 F.3d 783, 784 (C.A.8 2001) (reversing lump-sum payment order where defendant "had no ability to pay the restitution immediately," and requiring District Court to set a periodic payment schedule); *United States v. Myers*, 198 F.3d 160, 168–169 (C.A.5 1999) (same). The existing body of law also provides guidance as to proper payment schedules. Compare, *e.g.*, *United States v. Calbat*, 266 F.3d 358, 366 (C.A.5 2001) (annual payment of $41,000 an abuse of discretion where defendant had a net worth of $6,400 and yearly income of $39,000), with *United States v. Harris*, 60 F.Supp.2d 169, 180 (S.D.N.Y.1999) (setting payment schedule for the greater of $35 per month or 10% of defendant's gross income).

Section 3664's provision for partial periodic payments thus alleviates any concerns of unfairness for the vast number of child pornography defendants who have modest financial resources. A more difficult challenge is presented, however, by the case of a wealthy defendant who would be able to satisfy a large restitution judgment in an immediate lump-sum payment. But the statute is fully capable of ensuring just results for these defendants, too. For in addition to an offender's financial circumstances, § 3664 permits courts to consider other factors "in the interest of justice" when deciding whether to impose a payment schedule. See § 3664(f)(2) (district court shall specify payment schedule "pursuant to section 3572"); § 3572(d)(1) (restitution order shall be payable in periodic installments if "in the interest of justice").

Accordingly, in the context of a restitution order against a wealthy child pornography possessor, it would likely be in the interest of justice for a district court to set a payment schedule requiring the defendant to pay restitution in amounts equal to the periodic losses that the district court finds will actually be "incurred by the victim," § 2259(b)(3), in the given timeframe. In this case, for example, Amy's expert estimates that she will suffer approximately $3.4 million in losses from medical costs and lost income over the next 60 years of her life, or approximately $56,000 per year. If that estimate is deemed accurate, a court would enter a restitution order against a wealthy defendant for the full $3.4 million amount of Amy's losses, and could make it payable on an annual schedule of $56,000 per year. Doing so would serve the interest of justice because the periodic payment schedule would allow the individual wealthy defendant's ultimate burden to be substantially offset by payments made by other offenders,[5] while the entry of the full restitution award would provide certainty to Amy that she will be made whole for her losses....

Although I ultimately reach a different conclusion as to the proper interpretation of the statutory scheme, I do appreciate the caution with which the Court has announced its approach. For example, the Court expressly rejects the possibility of district courts entering restitution orders for "token or nominal amount[s]." ... That point is important because, if taken out of context, aspects of the Court's opinion might be construed otherwise. For instance, the Court states that in estimating a restitution amount, a district court may consider "the broader number of offenders involved (most of whom will, of course, never be caught or convicted)." ... If that factor is given too much weight, it could lead to exactly the type of trivial restitution awards the Court disclaims. Amy's counsel has noted, for instance, that in light of the large number of persons who possess her images, a truly proportional approach to restitution would lead to an award of just $47 against any individual defendant.... Congress obviously did not intend that outcome, and the Court wisely refuses to permit it.[6]

In the end, of course, it is Congress that will have the final say. If Congress wishes to recodify its full restitution command, it can do so in language perhaps even more clear than § 2259's "mandatory" directive to order restitution for the "full amount of the victim's losses." Congress might amend the statute, for example, to include the term "aggregate causation." Alternatively, to avoid the uncertainty in the Court's apportionment approach, Congress might wish to enact fixed minimum restitution amounts. See, e.g., § 2255 (statutorily imposed $150,000 minimum civil remedy). In the meanwhile, it is my hope that the Court's approach will not unduly undermine the ability of victims like Amy to recover for — and from — the unfathomable harms they have sustained.

---

5. As the facts of this case show, the offset would be significant. Between June 2009 and December 11, 2013, Amy obtained restitution awards from 182 persons, 161 of whom were ordered to pay an amount between $1,000 and $530,000.... If these offenders (and new offenders caught each month) were instead ordered to pay the full amount of restitution in periodic amounts according to their financial means, a wealthy defendant's annual obligation would terminate long before he would be required to pay anything close to the full $3.4 million. For once a victim receives the full amount of restitution, all outstanding obligations expire because § 2259 does not displace the settled joint and several liability rule forbidding double recovery. See Restatement (Second) of Torts § 885(3) (1979), see also, e.g., United States v. Nucci, 364 F.3d 419, 423 (C.A.2 2004).

6. The Court mentions that Amy received roughly $6,000 from her uncle, the person responsible for abusing her as a child.... Care must be taken in considering the amount of the award against Amy's uncle, however, ... because as Amy's expert explained, Amy was "back to normal" by the end of her treatment for the initial offense.... It was chiefly after discovering, eight years later, that images of her sexual abuse had spread on the Internet that Amy suffered additional losses due to the realization that possessors like Paroline were viewing them and that "the sexual abuse of her has never really ended." ...

Notes

"Amy" and "Vicky" are the child victims in two of the world's most prevalent and widely-distributed child pornography series. "Amy" is the subject of the *Paroline* case. For a case involving "Vicky," see *United States v. Kearney*, 672 F.3d 81 (1st Cir. 2012). In *Paroline*, the United States Supreme Court limited recovery to particular harms proximately caused by the individual defendant's offenses and recognized the inadequacy of § 2259 for providing appropriate recovery for victims. This case, and other cases confronting similar shortcomings, prompted a popular public response, *see, e.g.*, Emily Bazelon, *Money Is No Cure: The Price of a Stolen Childhood*, N.Y. Times Mag., Jan.27, 2013, at MM22; John Schwartz, *Child Pornography, and an Issue of Restitution*, N.Y. Times, Feb. 3, 2010, at A19, and a plethora of legal commentary on the subject. *See, e.g.*, Mary Margaret Giannini, *Continuous Contamination: How Traditional Criminal Restitution Principles and § 2259 Undermine Cleaning up the Toxic Waste of Child Pornography Possession*, 40 New Eng. J. on Crim. & Civ. Confinement 21 (2014); Paul G. Cassell, James R. Marsh, and Jeremy M. Christiansen, *The Case for Full Restitution for Child Pornography Victims*, 82 Geo. Wash. L. Rev. 61 (2013); Cortney E. Lollar, *Child Pornography and the Restitution Revolution*, 103 J. Crim. L. & Criminology 343 (2013); Michelle Minarcik, *The Proper Remedy for Possession of Child Pornography: Shifting from Restitution to a Victims Compensation Program*, 57 N.Y.L. Sch. L. Rev. 941 (2012/2013); Jennifer A.L. Sheldon-Sherman, *Rethinking Restitution in Cases of Child Pornography Possession*, 17 Lewis & Clark L. Rev. 215 (2013); Amber Pruitt, *An Argument for Child Pornography Victim Restitution in the Ninth Circuit: United States v. Kennedy*, 43 Golden Gate U. L. Rev. 105 (2013); Dianne Weiskittle, *Proximate Cause, Joint and Several Liability, and Child Pornography Possession: Determining and Calculating Restitution Awards Under 18 U.S.C. § 2259*, 38 U. Dayton L. Rev. 275 (2013); Mary Margaret Giannini, *Slow Acid Drips and Evidentiary Nightmares: Smoothing Out the Rough Justice of Child Pornography Restitution With a Presumed Damages Theory*, 49 Am. Crim. L. Rev. 1723 (2012); Melanie Reid and Curtis L. Collier, *When Does Restitution Become Retribution?*, 64 Okla. L. Rev. 653 (2012); Tyler Morris, *Perverted Justice: Why Courts Are Ruling Against Restitution in Child Pornography Possession Cases, and How a Victim Compensation Fund Can Fix the Broken Restitution Framework*, 57 Vill. L. Rev. 391 (2012); Dennis F. DiBari, *Restoring Restitution: the Role of Proximate Causation in Child Pornography Possession Cases Where Restitution Is Sought*, 33 Cardozo L. Rev. 297 (2011); Bradley P. Reiss, *Restitution Devolution?*, 85 St. John's L. Rev. 1621 (2011); Adam D. Lewis, *Dollars and Sense: Restitution Orders for Possession of Child Pornography Under 18 U.S.C. § 2259*, 37 New. Eng. J. on Crim. & Civ. Confinement 413 (2011); Katherine M. Giblin, *Click, Download, Causation: A Call for Uniformity and Fairness in Awarding Restitution to Those Victimized by Possessors of Child Pornography*, 60 Cath. U. L. Rev. 1109 (2011); Robert William Jacques, *Amy and Vicky's Cause: Perils of the Federal Restitution Framework for Child Pornography Victims*, 45 Ga. L. Rev. 1167 (2011); Dina McLeod, *Section 2259 Restitution Claims and Child Pornography Possession*, 109 Mich. L. Rev. 1327 (2011); Michael A. Kaplan, *Mandatory Restitution: Ensuring That Possessors of Child Pornography Pay for Their Crimes*, 61 Syracuse L. Rev. 531 (2011); Ashleigh B. Boe, *Putting A Price on Child Porn: Requiring Defendants Who Possess Child Pornography Images to Pay Restitution to Child Pornography Victims*, 86 N.D. L. Rev. 205 (2010). In response, Utah Senator Orrin G. Hatch introduced the Amy and Vicky Child Pornography Victim Restitution Improvement Act of 2015, 2015 FD S.B. 295, 114th Cong. (2015–2016), which expands the definition of the "full amount of the victim's losses" to consider the total harm to the victims, sets out guidelines for determining specific minimum restitution amounts for victims, requires joint and several liability involving multiple defendants to spread the restitution cost among defendants, and sets forth timely contribution claim procedures. The Bill has garnered overwhelming support in the Senate and was introduced in the House in February 2015. *See United States v. Baslan*, 2015 WL 1258158 (E.D.N.Y., Mar. 17, 2015) (factoring the "Amy and Vicky CPVRIA" in determining proper amount of restitution from child pornography defendants).

Chapter Eight

Institutional Exploitation of Children

I. Basis of Liability

Although a significant percentage of sexual exploitation of children occurs in the home or by family members, sexual abuse also occurs at the hands of institutional authorities who hold fiduciary positions over children, such as teachers, religious leaders, and community organization leaders, whose access to children is gained, and exploitative behavior is perpetrated, through one's respective position within the institution. Criminally, such abuse may be prosecuted according to applicable federal and state abuse or exploitation laws. Some states may prescribe heightened penalties for sexual abuse of an institutional nature. Pennsylvania, for example, increases the penalty for specifically-defined sexual assault crimes perpetrated by

> a person who is an employee or agent of the Department of Corrections or a county correctional authority, youth development center, youth forestry camp, State or county juvenile detention facility, other licensed residential facility serving children and youth, or mental health or mental retardation facility or institution ... when that person engages in sexual intercourse, deviate sexual intercourse or indecent contact with an inmate, detainee, patient or resident.

18 Pa. Cons. Stat. Ann. §3124.2(a) (categorizing such a crime as a felony of the third degree, specifically applicable to schools and child care centers). However, civil relief for such institutional abuse is not specifically statutorily defined. Instead, civil actions generally are derived through satisfaction of standard common law tort claims applied not just to the individual offender, but to authorities within the institution who fail to act to protect children, and to the institution as well. The cases that follow address several such civil claims.

A. Common Law Torts

1. Generally

John Doe CS v. Capuchin Franciscan Friars

United States District Court, Eastern District, Missouri, 2007
520 F. Supp. 2d 1124

THOMAS C. MUMMERT, III, United States Magistrate Judge.

This matter ... [footnote omitted] is before the Court ... [footnote omitted] on the motion of defendant, The Capuchin Franciscan Friars, doing business as, the Capuchin Franciscan Friars Province of Mid-America, St. Patrick Friary ("Defendants"), to dismiss all but one of the counts in the complaint filed by John Doe CS ("Plaintiff").... [Citations to record omitted].... Defendants are a world-wide Roman Catholic religious order of priests and conduct business in Missouri.... They and their agents and employees select and assign clergy, supervise clergy activities, exercise authority over members of their Order, and maintain "the well-being of its members attending schools and parishes which are owned and/or operated" by Defendants.... One such employee and member was, at all times relevant, Father Thaddeus Posey.... Father Posey taught at Cardinal Ritter Preparatory High School in St. Louis, Missouri ("Cardinal Ritter").... When serving in this capacity, Father Posey sexually abused Defendants' minor parishioners.... One such parishioner was Plaintiff, a student at Cardinal Ritter from approximately late 1982 through early 1984.... At the time of the sexual abuse, Father Posey "falsely represented to Plaintiff that Fr. Posey was providing spiritual counseling, comfort, mentor [sic], and advice to Plaintiff." ... Father Posey and Defendants portrayed themselves to Plaintiff as counselors and instructors on spiritual, moral, and ethical matters; consequently, Defendants had domination and influence over Plaintiff.... "Plaintiff trusted and relied upon Defendant[s] to nurture and protect him while he was in Defendants' care and custody." ... Moreover, "[t]he power imbalance between Defendant[s] and Plaintiff increased the boy's vulnerability to Fr. Posey." ...

"At all times material[,] [Father] Posey was under the direct supervision, employ and control of Defendant[s][,]" as was Cardinal Ritter.... He was hired, supervised, trained, and paid by Defendants.... He acted upon the authority of Defendants, at their request, or with their permission.... His conduct at issue "was undertaken while in the course and scope of his employment with Defendant[s]." ... Defendants also "ratified the wrongful conduct ... by failing to report it to law enforcement authorities, prospective parishioners, current parishioners, their families, victims, and the public." ...

In Count I of his complaint, titled "Child Sexual Abuse and/or Battery," Plaintiff alleges that Father Posey was acting in the course and scope of his employment with Defendants when he sexually abused Plaintiff and that Defendants ratified this abuse and aided and abetted Father Posey in committing the abuse, in concealing the abuse, and in avoiding a criminal investigation....

In Count II, titled "Breach of Fiduciary Duty," Plaintiff alleges that Defendants held a position of empowerment over Plaintiff and held Cardinal Ritter out to be a safe and secure institution and themselves and Father Posey to be shepherds and leaders of the Roman Catholic Church.... "This empowerment prevented the then minor Plaintiff from effectively protecting himself and Defendant[s] thus entered into a fiduciary relationship with Plaintiff." ... As a result of this fiduciary relationship, Defendants had certain duties to Plaintiff, including a duty of disclosure, and breached these duties by, inter alia, using his "dependency and innocence as a child to prevent him from recognizing that the abuse was wrongful" and by "[k]eeping a known pedophile in the presence of children," such as Plaintiff ...

Plaintiff alleges in Count III, titled "Fiduciary Fraud and Conspiracy to Commit Fiduciary Fraud," that the earlier-described fiduciary relationship between Defendants and Plaintiff and the duty of disclosure owed by Defendants to Plaintiff was breached when Defendants used "Plaintiff's dependency and innocence as a child to prevent him from recognizing that the abuse was wrongful." ... Defendants enforced the secrecy about the sexual abuse "and/or" taught Plaintiff that the abuse "was normal or necessary to the relationship." ... The existence of past, present, or future sexual misconduct by Father Posey and Defendants's other agents was a consideration in Plaintiff's and his family's decision on whether he should attend Cardinal Ritter.... Defendants knowingly failed to disclose Father Posey's sexual misconduct.... "... Defendant[s] and the Roman Catholic Archdiocese of St Louis and the Archbishop of the Archdiocese of St Louis, in conceit with one another, and with the intent to conceal and defraud, conspired and came to a meeting of the minds whereby they would misrepresent, conceal, or fail to disclose information relating to the sexual misconduct of Defendant[s]' agents. By so concealing, Defendant[s] committed at least one act in furtherance of the conspiracy." ...

In Count IV, titled "Fraud and Conspiracy to Commit Fraud," Plaintiff alleges that Defendants knew, or should have known, of the sexual misconduct of their agents, including Father Posey, and concealed or failed to disclose such information to Plaintiff.... The threat of sexual misconduct was a material factor in Plaintiff's and his family's decision whether he was to attend Cardinal Ritter.... As in Count III, Defendants conspired with the Archdiocese and the Archbishop....

In Count V, titled "Intentional Infliction of Emotional Distress," Plaintiff also alleges that Defendants intentionally failed to supervise, remove, or sanction Father Posey after learning of his previous sexual abuse to other children, and continued to place Father Posey in a position of authority over children.... Although they knew Father Posey was unsuitable for his position, they failed to review and monitor his performance, to confront him, and to sanction him about "known irregularities in his employment," e.g., taking young children on trips and to his home.... This "extreme and outrageous" conduct caused Plaintiff severe emotional distress....

Plaintiff alleges in Count VI, titled "Negligence," that Defendants knew or should have known of Father Posey's dangerous sexual propensities, and despite such knowledge, failed to protect Plaintiff....

In Count VII, titled "Vicarious Liability (Respondeat Superior)," Plaintiff alleges that Defendants consented to, or knowingly permitted, Father Posey to exercise authority on their behalf; that Father Posey was under their direct supervision, employ, and control; and that his alleged conduct was undertaken when in the course and scope of his employment with Defendants....

In Count VIII, titled "Negligent Supervision, Retention, and Failure to Warn," Plaintiff alleges that Defendants knew, or should have known, of Father Posey's dangerous sexual propensities toward minors and (a) negligently retained and/or failed to supervise him, (b) did not use reasonable care in investigating Father Posey, and (c) failed to provide adequate warning to Plaintiff....

Defendants move to dismiss Counts I through II and V through VIII for failure to state a claim, *see* Fed.R.Civ.P. 12(b)(6), and Counts III and IV for failure to plead fraud with the requisite particularity, *see* Fed.R.Civ.P. 9(b). Plaintiff opposes the motion.... In considering a motion to dismiss pursuant to Rule 12(b)(6), this Court must "tak[e] all well pleaded factual allegations as true and draw[ ] all reasonable inferences in favor of [Plaintiff]." *Katun Corp. v. Clarke*, 484 F.3d 972, 975 (8th Cir.2007). "'A motion to dismiss should be granted only if it appears beyond doubt that the plaintiff can prove no set of facts to warrant a grant of relief.'" *Id.* (quoting *Knieriem v. Group Health Plan, Inc.*, 434 F.3d 1058, 1060 (8th Cir.2006)). *Accord Kforce, Inc. v. Surrex Solutions Corp.*, 436 F.3d 981, 983 (8th Cir.2006). "'However, the complaint must contain sufficient facts, as opposed to mere conclusions, to satisfy the legal requirements of the claim to avoid dismissal.'" *Levy v.Ohl*, 477 F.3d 988, 991 (8th Cir.2007) (quoting *DuBois v. Ford Motor Credit Co.*, 276 F.3d 1019, 1022 (8th Cir.2002)). *See also Great Plains Trust Co. v. Union Pacific R.R. Co.*, 492 F.3d 986, 995 (8th Cir.2007) (noting that court must assume factual allegations are true, but need not accept conclusory legal allegations as true). In diversity cases, the Court interprets the law of the forum state, i.e., Missouri, to determine whether the elements of the offenses have been pled. *Moses.com Securities, Inc. v. Comprehensive Software Sys., Inc.*, 406 F.3d 1052, 1062 (8th Cir.2005).

In addition to citing Rule 12(b)(6) in support of their request that certain counts be dismissed, Defendants cite Rule 9(b) in support of their request that Counts III and IV be dismissed. Rule 9(b) requires that "the circumstances constituting fraud ... be stated with particularity." Fed.R.Civ.P. 9(b) (alteration added). Consequently, "the complaint must plead such facts as the time, place, and content of the defendant's false representations, as well as the details of the defendant's fraudulent acts, including when the acts occurred, who engaged in them, and what was obtained as a result." *United States ex rel. Joshi v. St. Luke's Hosp., Inc.*, 441 F.3d 552, 556 (8th Cir.2006). "Put another way, the complaint must identify the 'who, what, where, when, and how' of the alleged fraud." *Id.* (quoting *United States ex rel. Costner v. URS Consultants, Inc.*, 317 F.3d 883, 888 (8th Cir.2003)).

Count I: Sexual Abuse and Battery. The factual allegations on which this count is based are that Father Posey sexually abused Plaintiff when acting within the course and scope of his employment with Defendants and that Defendants ratified this abuse and aided and abetted Father Posey in committing the abuse, in concealing the abuse, and in avoiding a criminal investigation....

In *H.R.B. v. J.L.G.*, 913 S.W.2d 92, 97 (Mo.Ct.App.1995), the court discussed the requirement of respondeat superior that the act of an agent be done in the furtherance of the principal's business, holding that an act satisfies this requirement "if it is done by virtue of the employment and in furtherance of the business or interest of the employer, regardless of the time, or motive of the conduct." *Id.* (citing *P.S. v. Psychiatric Coverage, Ltd.*, 887 S.W.2d 622, 624 (Mo.Ct.App.1994)). "'If the act is fairly and naturally incident to the employer's business, although mistakenly or ill advisedly done, and did not arise wholly from some external, independent or personal motive, it is done while engaged in the employer's business.'" *Id.* (quoting *P.S.*, 887 S.W.2d at 624). The sexual misconduct of a priest against a student is not intended to further the employer's business, but rather results from "'purely private and personal desires.'" *Id.* (quoting *P.S.*, 887 S.W.2d at 624). *See also Newyear*, 155 F.3d at 1044–45 (noting that under Missouri case law, "a priest does not act in the furtherance of the business or interests of his employer when he engages in sexual misconduct with parishioners"); *Gibson v. Brewer*, 952 S.W.2d 239, 246 (Mo.1997) (en banc) (rejecting attempt by parents of minor who was sexually abused by Catholic priest to hold Catholic Diocese liable under theory that priest was acting with[in] the scope of employment, and holding that "intentional sexual misconduct by a priest and intentional infliction of emotional distress are not within the scope of employment of a priest and are in fact forbidden"); *Gray v. Ward*, 950 S.W.2d 232, 234 (Mo.1997) (en banc) (holding that intentional sexual activity by a priest does not "fall within the scope of employment of a priest, and the Diocese cannot be held liable under an agency theory").

The foundation for Plaintiffs claims against Defendants are his allegations that Father Posey sexually abused him when he was a student at Cardinal Ritter. This misconduct clearly reflects "purely private and personal desires" and not Defendants' business or interests. Plaintiff also alleges that Defendants ratified the alleged sexual abuse by Father Posey.... "Ratification in agency is an adoption or confirmation by one person of an act [such as entering into a contract] performed *on his behalf* by another without authority...." *Springfield Land and Dev. Co. v. Bass*, 48 S.W.3d 620, 628 (Mo.Ct.App.2001) (quoting 2A *C.J.S. Agency*, §63 (1972)) (alteration in original) (emphasis added). "[R]atification occurs when person A confirms or adopts the conduct of person B, who acted on behalf of person A in absence of person A's authority." *Murphy v. Jackson Nat'l Life Ins. Co.*, 83 S.W.3d 663, 668 (Mo.Ct.App.2002) (alteration added). Additionally, it is essential that person A have knowledge of all the material facts when charged with accepting the acts of person B. *Id.* "Thus, knowledge is an essential element of ratification." *Id....* Plaintiff's attempt to hold Defendants liable under a ratification theory must fail because there is no allegation that the sexual misconduct of Father Posey was performed on their behalf. As noted above, that misconduct was not done to further Defendants' business or interests, nor is there any other alleged reason why the misconduct would benefit Defendants. Count I will be dismissed.

Counts II and III: Breach of Fiduciary Duty and Fiduciary Fraud. Both Counts II and III are based upon an alleged fiduciary relationship between Defendants and Plaintiff.... " 'Breach of fiduciary duty is a claim arising in tort....' " *State Res. Corp. v. Lawyer's Title Ins. Corp.*, 224 S.W.3d 39, 48 (Mo.Ct.App.2007) (quoting *Preferred Physician's Mut. Mgmt. Group v. Preferred Physician's Mut. Risk Retention*, 918 S.W.2d 805, 810 (Mo.Ct.App.1996)) (alteration in original). In a breach of fiduciary duty claim, "the proponent must establish that a fiduciary duty existed between it and the defending party; that the defending party breached the duty; and that the breach caused the proponent to suffer harm." *Id. Accord Grewell v. State Farm Mut. Auto. Ins. Co.*, 162 S.W.3d 503, 508 (Mo.Ct.App.2005).

The Missouri Court of Appeals has expressly declined to "recognize breach-of-fiduciary-duty actions against clergy for sexual misconduct." *H.R.B.*, 913 S.W.2d at 98. The conduct at issue in that case was also sexual abuse of a minor student by a priest who taught at a school run by the church. Claims of breach of fiduciary duty against the church and the archbishop, who directly supervised and controlled the church, were dismissed because allowing such actions "places courts on the slippery slope and is an unnecessary venture, since existing laws ... provide adequate protection for society's interests." *Id.* (interim quotations omitted) (alteration in original). Other available causes of action "(i.e., intentional infliction of emotional distress, childhood sexual abuse), ... do not require the trial court to determine whether defendant breached his trusted, confidential relationship with the plaintiff or whether the archbishop and the church breached their fiduciary duties towards their parishioners, including plaintiff, and abused their position of trust and confidence[,] as alleged[.]" *Id.* at 99 (internal quotations omitted) (last alteration added).

The court in *H.R.B.* noted that the question whether religious organizations can be held liable for breach of fiduciary duty based on allegations of a clergy member's sexual misconduct had not been addressed before by Missouri courts. 913 S.W.2d at 98. The Court can find no decision, nor do the parties cite to one, of the Missouri Supreme Court on this issue. " 'When a state's highest court has not decided an issue, it is up to this [C]ourt to predict how the state's highest court would resolve the issue.' " *Allstate Ins. Co.*

v. Blount, 491 F.3d 903, 908 (8th Cir.2007) (quoting *Minn. Supply Co. v. Raymond Corp.*, 472 F.3d 524, 534 (8th Cir.2006)) (alteration added). "'Decisions of intermediate state appellate courts are persuasive authority that [the Court] follow[s] when they are the best evidence of what state law is.'" *Id.* (alterations added).... The appellate court's holding in *H.R.B.*, *supra*, is "the best evidence" of what Missouri law is. Additionally, the holding is consistent with the well-established requirement under Missouri law that one element of a fiduciary relationship is that "things of value such as land, monies, a business, or other things of value which are the property of the subservient party, must be possessed or managed by the dominant party." *Roth v. Equitable Life Assur. Soc.*, 210 S.W.3d 253, 260 (Mo.App.2006); *A.G. Edwards & Sons v. Drew*, 978 S.W.2d 386, 394 (Mo.Ct.App.1998); *Matlock v. Matlock*, 815 S.W.2d 110, 115 (Mo.Ct.App.1991). *See also Shervin v. Huntleigh Securities Corp.*, 85 S.W.3d 737, 741 (Mo.Ct.App.2002) ("The question in determining whether a fiduciary relationship ... exists is whether or not trust is reposed with respect *to property or business affairs* of the other.") (alteration and emphasis added). Assuming, without deciding, that the allegations of sexual abuse are true, the harm caused by that abuse is tragic but is not to the category of things necessary to establish a fiduciary relationship.... The Court finds, therefore, that the holding of *H.R.B.* precluding a claim for breach of fiduciary duty under the circumstances alleged here is dispositive of Counts II and III. These Counts will be dismissed.

Count IV: Fraud. Plaintiff alleges in Count IV that Defendants knew or should have known of Father Posey's sexual misconduct, and that of other of their agents, but failed to disclose such and that the threat of such misconduct was a material factor in his and his family's selection of a school for him to attend. Plaintiff further alleges that Defendants conspired with the Archdiocese and the Archbishop to conceal the misconduct and to defraud Plaintiff. As noted above, when alleging fraud, a plaintiff "must identity the who, what, where, when, and how of the alleged fraud." *Joshi*, 441 F.3d at 556 (interim quotations omitted).

Under Missouri law, the elements of a submissible case of fraud are:

> "1) a false, material representation; 2) the speaker's knowledge of its falsity or his/her ignorance of the truth; 3) the speaker's intent that his/her representation should be acted upon by the hearer in the manner reasonably contemplated; 4) the hearer's ignorance of the falsity of the representation; 5) the hearer's reliance on the representation being true; 6) the hearer's right to rely thereon; and 7) the hearer's consequent and proximately-caused injuries."

BMK Corp. v. Clayton Corp., 226 S.W.3d 179, 193 (Mo.Ct.App.2007) (quoting *Murray v. Crank*, 945 S.W.2d 28, 31 (Mo.Ct.App.1997)). The failure to establish any one of these elements is fatal. *Paul v. Farmland Indus., Inc.*, 37 F.3d 1274, 1277 (8th Cir.1994).

Plaintiff does not allege that Defendants represented that there was no sexual misconduct at Cardinal Ritter; rather, he pleads that the fraud was in not disclosing the misconduct that did indeed exist. Fraudulent nondisclosure is not recognized in Missouri as a separate tort *Hess v. Chase Manhattan Bank*, 220 S.W.3d 758, 765 (Mo.2007) (en banc). "Instead, ... a party's silence in the face of a legal duty to speak replaces the first element: the existence of a representation." *Id.* (alteration added). There is a duty to speak "when there is a relation of trust and confidence between the parties or when one of the parties has superior knowledge or information not within the fair and reasonable reach of the other parry." *Bohac v. Walsh*, 223 S.W.3d 858, 864 (Mo.Ct.App.2007).... Plaintiff has alleged that Defendants (who) committed fraud by not disclosing the sexual misconduct of their agents, including Father Posey (what and how), when he and his family were deciding whether he should attend Cardinal Ritter (when and where). These allegations satisfy Rule 9(b)'s criteria for alleging fraud.... Plaintiff's allegations of a conspiracy do not fare as well. These allegations include only the who and are fatally vague as to the what, how, when, and where. The conspiracy allegations will be dismissed.

Count V: Intentional Infliction of Emotional Distress. Based on allegations that Defendants intentionally and recklessly failed to supervise Father Posey after learning of his sexual misconduct and instead retained him without review, monitoring, or sanctions, Plaintiff seeks recovery in Count V for the intentional infliction of severe emotional distress.... "To recover for intentional infliction of emotional distress, [a plaintiff] must show (1) the defendant's conduct was extreme and outrageous; (2) the defendant acted intentionally or recklessly; and (3) the defendant's conduct caused extreme emotional distress resulting in bodily harm." *Cent Mo. Elec. Co-op. v. Balke*, 119 S.W.3d 627, 636 (Mo.Ct.App.2003) (citing *Thomas v. Special Olympics Missouri. Inc.*, 31 S.W.3d 442, 446 (Mo.Ct.App.2000)) (alteration added).

Citing *K.G. v. R.T.R.*, 918 S.W.2d 795 (Mo.1996) (en banc), Defendants move to dismiss Count V on the grounds that Plaintiff's emotional distress is premised on, or based upon, another tort. In that case, a daughter argued that she stated a claim for the intentional infliction of emotional distress against her father for sexual abuse that allegedly occurred when she was a child. Noting that subjecting a child to sexual contact was "unquestionably extreme and outrageous conduct," the court held that a claim for intentional infliction of emotional distress would "not lie where the alleged conduct is intended to invade other legally protected interests of the plaintiff or intended to cause bodily harm." *Id.* at 799. The court further noted that "where one's conduct amounts to the commission of one of the traditional torts, such as battery, and the conduct was not intended only to cause extreme emotional distress to the victim, the tort of intentional emotional distress will not lie...." *Id.* (alteration added). Although the alleged conduct of Father Posey might be a battery, and thus not allowable of a claim against him for intentional emotional distress, *see id.* at 800, the claim at issue is against Defendants and is not only for the sexual abuse. Rather, it is for retaining Father Posey in a position where he had access to students regardless of the knowledge that he abused students and without taking any action to prevent him for doing so again. A separate emotional distress claim may "be supported by pleading some additional wanton and outrageous act [.]" *Nazeri v. Missouri Valley Coll.*, 860 S.W.2d 303, 316 (Mo.1993) (en banc) (alteration added). Plaintiffs allegations in Count V state a claim.

Count VI: Negligence. Plaintiff alleges in Count VI that Defendants knew, or should have known, that Father Posey had a history of sexually exploiting minors in his care and failed to act on this information. Defendants move to dismiss this Count on the basis of the First Amendment and of the Missouri Supreme Court's ruling in *Gibson, supra*.... Holding that "[r]eligious organizations are not immune from civil liability for the acts of their clergy," the court in *Gibson* explored the limits of that liability. 952 S.W.2d at 246 (alteration added). "If neutral principles of law can be applied without determining questions of religious doctrine, polity, and practice, then a court may impose liability." *Id.* (alteration added). However, "[q]uestions of hiring, ordaining, and retaining clergy ... necessarily involve interpretation of religious doctrine, policy, and administration." *Id.* at 246–47 (alterations added). This "excessive entanglement between church and state has the effect of inhibiting religion, in violation of the First Amendment." *Id.* at 247.

The First Amendment holding in *Gibson* would appear to bar Plaintiffs claims in Count V. The parties disagree, however, on whether this Court is bound by that holding. The question whether a federal court is bound by a state court's interpretation of the United

States Constitution has been resolved for sometime. "*Except* in matters governed by the Federal Constitution or by acts of Congress, the law to be applied in any case is the law of the state." *Erie RR. Co. v. Tompkins*, 304 U.S. 64, 78, 58 S.Ct. 817, 82 L.Ed. 1188 (1938) (emphasis added). If there is a federal constitutional issue, a federal court "[has] the duty to make [its] independent inquiry and determination." *Aftanase v. Econ. Baler Co.*, 343 F.2d 187, 192 (8th Cir.1965) (alterations added).... [footnote omitted]. A state court's interpretation of the United States Constitution is "of weight," but is "not binding upon a Federal Court." *Id.* at 193.

The First Amendment to the Federal Constitution provides, in relevant part, that "Congress shall make no law respecting an establishment of religion, or prohibiting the free exercise thereof...." U.S. Const., amend. 1. These two prohibitions are referred to as the Establishment Clause and the Free Exercise Clause. *See Engel v. Vitale*, 370 U.S. 421, 430, 82 S.Ct. 1261, 8 L.Ed.2d 601 (1962).... "The Establishment Clause ... does not depend upon any showing of direct governmental compulsion and is violated by the enactment of laws which establish an official religion whether those laws operate directly to coerce individuals or not." *Id.* (alteration added). State action does not violate the Establishment Clause if it: "(1) has a secular ... purpose, (2) neither advances nor inhibits religion in its principal or primary effect, and (3) does not foster an excessive government entanglement with religion." *United States v. Corum*, 362 F.3d 489, 495 (8th Cir.2004) (citing *Lemon v. Kurtzman*, 403 U.S. 602, 612–13, 91 S.Ct. 2105, 29 L.Ed.2d 745 (1971)). *Accord Clayton by Clayton v. Place*, 884 F.2d 376, 379 (8th Cir.1999) (applying test to public school district rule prohibiting dancing).

Count V is a negligence claim and does not single out or specifically protect any religion. "[T]he objective of the 'secular legislative purpose' requirement is to 'prevent the relevant government decision maker ... from abandoning neutrality and acting with the intent of promoting a particular point of view in religious matters.'" *Corum*, 362 F.3d at 496 (quoting *Corp. of Presiding Bishop of the Church of Jesus Christ of the Latter-Day Saints v. Amos*, 483 U.S. 327, 335, 107 S.Ct. 2862, 97 L.Ed.2d 273 (1987)) (alterations added). Plaintiff's allegations are that an employer and school owner and operator, i.e., Defendants, continued to employ a teacher, i.e., Father Posey, after knowing he sexually abused their student. Civil liability based on these allegations are secular in nature. For the action to advance or inhibit religion, "'it must be fair to say that the government itself has advanced religion through its own activities and influences.'" *Id.* at 496 (quoting *Amos*, 483 U.S. at 337, 107 S.Ct. 2862). This cannot be said in this case. Nor can it be said that this action fosters an excessive entanglement with religion. "[C]ertain practices that affect religion in some manner, or carry a religious connotation, are permissible in some phases of our governmental operation." *Bogen v. Doty*, 598 F.2d 1110, 1113 (8th Cir.1979). And, "where there is some peripheral effect or entanglement, it does appear to be a matter of degree." *Id.* Plaintiff's negligence claim affects Defendants, but has, at best, only a peripheral effect on religion. The claim does not violate the Establishment Clause....

Plaintiff alleges in Count V that Defendants knew, or should have known, of Father Posey's propensities and failed to take action to protect their students from his misdeeds. "[T]he Free Exercise Clause protects religious relationships ... primarily by preventing the judicial resolution of ecclesiastical disputes turning on matters of religious doctrine or practice." *Sanders v. Casa View Baptist Church*, 134 F.3d 331, 335–36 (5th Cir.1998) (alterations added). However, "[t]he First Amendment does not categorically insulate religious relationships from judicial scrutiny, for to do so would necessarily extend constitutional protection to the secular components of these relationships." *Id.* at 336 (alteration added). To hold otherwise would "impermissibly place a religious leader in a preferred position in our society." *Id.* Accordingly, the court held that the First Amendment did not bar claims against a minister who allegedly engaged in sexual relationships with plaintiffs when providing them marital counseling. *Id.* at 336. *See also Bollard v. Cal. Province of the Society of Jesus*, 196 F.3d 940, 947 (9th Cir.1999) (Free Exercise Clause did not preclude action by novice alleging that he was sexually harassed while training to be a priest; order did not offer religious justification for harassment, but did condemn it as inconsistent with its beliefs); *Martinelli v. Bridgeport Roman Catholic Diocesan Corp.*, 196 F.3d 409 (2nd Cir.1999) (Free Exercise Clause did not preclude tort action between diocese and child parishioner alleging he was sexually abused by priest). *But see Scharon v. St. Luke's Episcopal Presbyterian Hosps.*, 929 F.2d 360, 363 (8th Cir.1991) (Free Exercise Clause did bar employment discrimination claims of chaplain allegedly terminated for violating several canonical laws; although chaplain claimed that defendants' contention that religious issues were basis for her termination was a mere pretext for unlawful discrimination, the resolution of those claims would require court to determine the meaning of religious doctrine and canonical law).

There is no allegation (or defense at this point in the case) that ecclesiastical and canon law is relevant to this case. The factual issues raised in Count V appear to be secular in nature and do require this Court to not resolve or inquire into any religious doctrines of Defendants. *See Drevlow v. Lutheran Church, Missouri Synod*, 991 F.2d 468, 471 (8th Cir.1993) (reversing district court's dismissal of an ordained minister's action for libel, negligence, and intentional interference with his employment on grounds that, although the First Amendment proscribes a secular court's "intervention into many employment decisions made by religious organizations *based on* religious doctrine or beliefs," there was no indication that the resolution of the action would involve an impermissible inquiry into the church's bylaws or religious beliefs) (emphasis added).... For the foregoing reasons, Count V will not be dismissed.

Count VII: Vicarious Liability (Respondeat Superior). In this Count, Plaintiff alleges that Defendants consented to, or knowingly permitted, Father Posey to exercise authority on their behalf, that he was under their direct supervision, employ, and control, and that his alleged conduct was undertaken when in the course and scope of his employment with Defendants. These allegations are insufficient to state a claim for the reasons set forth above in the discussion on Count I.

Count VIII: Negligent Supervision, Retention, and Failure to Warn. The allegations in this Count are sufficient to state a claim for the reasons set forth above in the discussion on Count VI....

Plaintiffs allegations in Count I, II, III, and VII and his conspiracy allegations in Count IV do not state a claim and are DISMISSED. Plaintiff's allegations in Counts V, VI, and VIII and his fraud allegations in Count IV do state a claim and will not be dismissed. Accordingly,

IT IS HEREBY ORDERED that Defendants' motion to dismiss is GRANTED in part and DENIED in part as set forth above....

IT IS FURTHER ORDERED that Plaintiffs motion for a hearing on the motion to dismiss is DENIED....

Notes

In *Capuchin Franciscan Friars*, the court addressed many of the tort claims commonly raised, in the context of institutional abuse, against persons within the institution who did not actually commit the abuse against the child, but who knew or should have known about the risk of abuse and failed to act to prevent the abuse. For discussion of the decline of constitutional protections prohibiting such tort claims, see Scott C. Idleman, *Tort Liability, Religious Entities, and the Decline of Constitutional Protection*, 75 IND. L.J. 219 (2000); *see also*, Robert F. Cochran, Jr., *Church Freedom and Accountability in Sexual Exploitation Cases: The Possibility of Both Through Limited Strict Liability*, 21 J. CONTEMP. LEG. ISSUES 427, 440–47 (2013) (discussing tension between church discretion and accountability and calling for limited strict liability as balance). As we will see, *infra*, particularly in cases involving institutional abuse within religious organizations, many authorities are held liable for acting affirmatively to conceal the abuse. However, the following cases address more specifically two common tort claims raised against institutional authorities—vicarious liability, under which an institution or institutional authority is held liable for the harms caused by its employee who causes harm within the scope of his or her employment, and direct negligence for the hiring, retaining, or failure to supervise an employee who causes harm. In each case, note the claims that are raised and the standards that must be met to satisfy the *prima facie* elements of each cause of action.

2. *Vicarious Liability (Respondeat Superior)*

Jane Doe 130 v. Archdiocese of Portland in Oregon

United States District Court, Oregon, 2010
717 F. Supp. 2d 1120

MOSMAN, District Judge [adopting as his own the Findings and Recommendations of PAPAK, Magistrate Judge]:

Fictitiously-named plaintiff Jane Doe 130 ("Jane") filed this action against defendants The Archdiocese of Portland in Oregon (the "Archdiocese"), The Roman Catholic Archbishop of Portland in Oregon (the "Archbishop" and, collectively with the Archdiocese, the "archdiocesan defendants"), and Father J.V.H. on February 14, 2008. On November 26, 2008, Farley, Piazza & Associates were appointed as Jane's guardian *ad litem*. Jane alleges defendants' vicarious liability for sexual battery of a child prior to July 6, 2004,[1] sexual battery of a child following July 6, 2004, intentional infliction of emotional distress prior to July 6, 2004, and intentional infliction of emotional distress following July 6, 2004, on a theory of *respondeat superior*, and direct liability for negligence and for misrepresentation. This court has jurisdiction over Jane's action pursuant to 28 U.S.C. § 1334(b), based on the relatedness of these proceedings to a case arising under Title 11 of the United States Code.[2] ...

Jane is a minor female born in 1991. Between August of 1993 and June of 1999, J.V.H. was a seminarian at Mt. Angel Seminary in Oregon, an educational institution within the authority of the archdiocesan defendants. Between June 1999 and 2007, Fr. J.V.H. was a Catholic priest directly employed by the Archdiocese Defendants. Jane alleges that Fr. J.V.H. provided pastoral and educational services to her in his capacity as a priest,[3] in

---

1. Claims arising prior to July 6, 2004, are to be paid out of the future claims fund, and are subject to the cap on the total amount to be paid toward such claims *see infra*, whereas claims arising on or after July 6, 2004, constitute administrative claims against the archdiocesan defendants outside the scope of the future claims fund.

2. Specifically, this action is subject to the future claims fund under the Third Amended and Restated Joint Plan of Reorganization confirmed in *In re Roman Catholic Archbishop of Portland*, 04-37154, which, in relevant part, sets a $20 million cap on the total funds available to pay all claims made against the Archdiocese through 2023.

3. Although the parties have asserted in other contexts that J.V.H. is Jane's paternal uncle, Jane's blood relationship to J.V.H. is not alleged in the complaint.

the course of which he acted within the course and scope of his employment or agency in performing duties for and on behalf of the archdiocesan defendants.... Jane testified in deposition that J.V.H. first began touching her sexually when she was approximately 6 or 7 years old, in or around 1997. At that time, Jane lived in Virginia, and J.V.H. was a seminary student in Mt. Angel, Oregon. The initial sexual touching took place in Virginia, in Jane's grandmother's home.

J.V.H. was ordained as a priest of the Archdiocese of Portland in June 1999. Jane moved to Portland, Oregon, in 2004, when she was approximately 14. It appears that Fr. J.V.H. continued abusing Jane from approximately 1997 through some time in 2004, after Jane's family moved to Oregon.... Neither Jane nor her parents have ever been members of a parish to which Fr. J.V.H. was assigned. The Archdiocese has not received any complaints of sexual misconduct by Fr. J.V.H. other than in connection with this action....

Jane alleges that:

> For the purpose of furthering his duties as a priest, Fr. J.V.H. sought and gained the trust, admiration, and obedience of the Plaintiff in this case. Plaintiff was also conditioned by her church, school and family to respect and obey priests, including Fr. J.V.H..As a result, Plaintiff was conditioned to trust Fr. J.V.H., to comply with Fr. J.V.H.'s direction, and to respect Fr. J.V.H. as a person of authority in spiritual, moral and ethical matters....

Jane further alleges that Fr. J.V.H., "while acting within the course and scope of his employment and agency, and using the authority and position of trust as a priest for the Archdiocese Defendants — through the Grooming process — induced and directed Plaintiff to engage in sexual contact with Fr. J.V.H. both prior to and after July 6, 2004." She alleges that this sexual abuse continued for approximately six years, from a time when she was approximately eight years old to a time when she was approximately 14.... In connection with Jane's claims against the archdiocesan defendants for sexual battery of a child and for intentional infliction of emotional distress, alleged on a theory of *respondeat superior*, Jane alleges that "Fr. J.V.H. used the Grooming process to accomplish his sexual battery of Plaintiff," and that "Fr. J.V.H. used the Grooming process to intentionally inflict severe emotional distress by his acts of sexual molestation of the Plaintiff." ... In connection with Jane's claim against the archdiocesan defendants for negligence, alleged on a theory of direct liability, Jane alleges as follows. First, she alleges that the archdiocesan defendants owed her a special duty of care:

> As a young girl entrusted to the care and influence of the Catholic Church and Fr. J.V.H., an agent and employee of Archdiocese Defendants, Plaintiff has a special relationship with Defendants. This special relationship created a requirement that Archdiocese Defendants act with care to ensure Plaintiff's safety while interacting with Archdiocese Defendants' agents and employees.

Second, she alleges that the archdiocesan defendants had notice that Fr. J.V.H. posed a threat to children by not later than August 1993:

> By approximately August of 1993, prior to final acceptance of Fr. J.V.H. as a priest, Archdiocese Defendants became aware that Fr. J.V.H. posed an emotional, physical or sexual danger to those in his care and influence. Specifically, Archdiocese Defendant had knowledge of the following facts:
>
> > A. Archdiocese Defendants knew that Fr. J.V.H. had left the Holy Cross Fathers, and knew or should have known that a part of the reason for his leaving was the resistance Fr. J.V.H. received from the Holy Cross Fathers in response to his quest towards becoming a priest, ...

B. Archdiocese Defendants knew from Fr. J.V.H.'s screening psychological examinations that evaluators had concerns about whether he was being truthful and accurate with them in relation to his sexuality. . . .

C. Archdiocese Defendants knew from Fr. J.V.H.'s screening psychological examinations that Fr. J.V.H. had reported to evaluators that he was concerned that psychological testing might indicate he was a child molester. . . .

D. Archdiocese Defendants knew from Fr. J.V.H.'s psychological examinations that evaluators recommended that the Archdiocese Defendants' formation team closely monitor him regarding sexual matters.

Prior to the last of the abuse suffered by Plaintiff, Archdiocese Defendants knew or should have known that Fr. J.V.H. was repeatedly ineffective in his assignments for reasons centering around lack of energy or initiative. This knowledge might have been unremarkable in isolation, but taken in conjunction with the factors listed in subparagraphs A–D, above, should have indicated to Archdiocese Defendants that Fr. J.V.H. was emotionally unwell, that his celibacy was at risk, and that children in his care might be unsafe.

Third, she alleges that the archdiocesan defendants were actionably negligent in the following ways:

A. Failing to investigate or otherwise follow up on findings in Fr. J.V.H.'s psychological examinations that indicated that evaluators had concerns about the accuracy of Fr. J.V.H.'s reporting regarding his sexuality. . . .

B. Failing to investigate or otherwise follow up on findings in Fr. J.V.H.'s psychological examinations that indicated that Fr. J.V.H. had concerns that the results of the examinations would indicate that he was a child molester. . . .

C. Failing to supervise, monitor, or otherwise follow the recommendation of professional psychologists that Fr. J.V.H. be watched closely, including failing to watch, supervise and monitor Fr. J.V.H. closely throughout his formation, particularly in relation to his interactions with minors. . . .

D. Failing to either remove Fr. J.V.H. from ministry or to restrict or monitor his interactions with those under his care and influence.

Fourth, she alleges that:

Archdiocese Defendants' failure to investigate, monitor, supervise, restrict, or remove Fr. J.V.H. during his formation and ministry, despite having received notice of his danger to those under his care and influence, created a foreseeable risk of harm to the safety of those in his care and influence, including Plaintiff in this case. Plaintiff's interest in being free from sexual and physical abuse is an interest of a kind that the law protects against negligent invasion. Archdiocese Defendants' failure to investigate, monitor, supervise, restrict, or remove Fr. J.V.H. once Archdiocese Defendants knew of his danger to those under his care and influence was unreasonable in light of the risk posed to children in his charge. Archdiocese Defendants' failure to investigate, monitor, supervise, or remove Fr. J.V.H. was a cause of the abuse and molestation suffered by Plaintiff. . . . Finally, as a child who was sexually and physically assaulted, Plaintiff was within the class of persons and Plaintiff's injury was within the general type of potential incidents and injuries that made Archdiocese Defendants' conduct negligent.

In connection with her claim of entitlement to punitive damages, Jane alleges as follows:

In their negligence toward the rights and safety of Plaintiff, Archdiocese Defendants acted with malice or a reckless and outrageous indifference to a highly unreasonable risk of harm and with a conscious indifference to the health, safety and welfare of Plaintiff. Plaintiff is therefore entitled to punitive damages against Archdiocese Defendants in the amount of $10,000,000.00....

I recommend that ... the court take judicial notice of the following facts for the purpose of determining the archdiocesan defendants' motion to dismiss:

(1) The Archdiocese is a Roman Catholic, non-profit organization that operates as a corporation sole....

(2) In 1983, a former priest of the Archdiocese, Thomas B. Laughlin, was criminally convicted of sexual abuse....

(3) In October 2000, Archbishop John G. Vlazny issued a public apology that acknowledged and apologized for sexual abuse that priests in the Archdiocese had committed against children....

(4) On July 6, 2004, the Archdiocese filed for Chapter 11 bankruptcy....

(5) Following the Archdiocese's bankruptcy filing, it was reported in news media that the filing was prompted by the costs of legal actions against the Archdiocese for alleged sexual abuse by Archdiocesan priests.

(6) News reports of allegations of sexual abuse by Archdiocesan priests issued prior to the Archdiocese's bankruptcy filing....

The archdiocesan defendants move to dismiss Jane's claims against them for sexual battery of a child and for intentional infliction of emotional distress on the grounds that Jane has not met her burden to plead the elements of *respondeat superior liability*. The archdiocesan defendants likewise move to dismiss Jane's claim against them for negligence, on the ground that Jane has not met her burden to plead that the archdiocesan defendants owed her any particular duty of care, and on the alternative ground that the archdiocesan defendants enjoy First Amendment protections that foreclose Jane's claims. The archdiocesan defendants also move to dismiss Jane's claim for punitive damages.... According to Oregon law:

Under the doctrine of *respondeat superior*, an employer is liable for an employee's torts when the employee acts within the scope of employment. Negligence or other tortious conduct by the employer is not required....

Three requirements must be met to conclude that an employee was acting within the scope of employment. These requirements traditionally have been stated as: (1) whether the act occurred substantially within the time and space limits authorized by the employment; (2) whether the employee was motivated, at least partially, by a purpose to serve the employer; and (3) whether the act is of a kind which the employee was hired to perform.

Chesterman v. Barmon, 305 Or. 439, 442, 753 P.2d 404 (1988) (citations omitted).

The *Chesterman* court specified, however, that where there is a "'time-lag' between the act allegedly producing the harm and the resulting harm," it is inappropriate to analyze the applicability of the *respondeat superior* doctrine "as of the time that the injury occurred." *Id.* at 444, 753 P.2d 404. Under that circumstance, the court ruled, "[t]he focus should be on the act on which vicarious liability is based and not on when the act results in *injury*." *Id.* (emphasis original). Applying that principle, the court found that an employer could be vicariously liable for its employee's acts where the employee ingested a hallucinogenic drug allegedly for the purpose of maintaining focus at work and then later, outside the workplace and outside the scope of his employment—but still under the influence of the drug and, allegedly, in consequence of the drug's effects—entered a woman's home and sexually assaulted her. *See id.* at 443–444, 753 P.2d 404.

Eleven years later, in a case (like the one now before the court) involving sexual assault allegedly committed by an employee of the Archdiocese, the Oregon Supreme Court had occasion to clarify the *Chesterman* ruling. Noting that "an employee's intentional tort rarely, if ever, will have been authorized expressly by the employer," the court in *Fearing v. Bucher*, 328 Or. 367, 977 P.2d 1163 (1999), acknowledged that the employee's "sexual assaults ... clearly were outside the scope of his employment," but held that "the [vicarious liability] inquiry does not end there." *Fearing v. Bucher*, 328 Or. 367, 374, 374 n. 4, 977 P.2d 1163 (1999). Instead, the court held, "[t]he Archdiocese still could be found vicariously liable, if acts that were within [the employee]'s scope of employment *resulted* in the acts which led to injury to plaintiff." *Id.* (citation, internal quotation marks omitted; emphasis supplied). That is, "where ... the employer's vicarious liability arises out of the employee's commission of an intentional tort, [the court] must consider whether ... allegations contained in the ... complaint state ultimate facts sufficient to establish that acts that were within [the employee]'s scope of employment resulted in the acts that caused injury to plaintiff." *Id.* .... The *Fearing* court recited the material allegations of the plaintiff's complaint as follows:

> The complaint alleges that [the employee priest] used his position as youth pastor, spiritual guide, confessor, and priest to plaintiff and his family to gain their trust and confidence, and thereby to gain the permission of plaintiff's family to spend large periods of time alone with plaintiff. By virtue of that relationship, [the employee] gained the opportunity to be alone with plaintiff, to touch him physically, and then to assault him sexually. The complaint further alleges that those activities were committed in connection with [the employee]'s employment as youth pastor and priest, that they were committed within the time and space limitations of [the employee]'s employment, that they were committed out of a desire, at least partially and initially, to fulfill [the employee]'s employment duties as youth pastor and priest, and that they generally were of a kind and nature that was required to perform as youth pastor and priest.

Id. Based on these allegations, the *Fearing* court reasoned that "a jury could infer that the sexual assaults were the culmination of a progressive series of actions that began with and continued to involve [the employee]'s performance of [his] ordinary and authorized duties." *Id.* at 375, 977 P.2d 1163.

> Viewing the complaint in that light, the jury also could infer that, in cultivating a relationship with plaintiff and his family, [the employee], at least initially, was motivated by a desire to fulfill his ... duties and that, over time, his motives became mixed. We conclude that the ... complaint contains allegations sufficient to satisfy all three *Chesterman* requirements for establishing that employee conduct was within the scope of employment.

Id. The *Fearing* court expressly rejected the Archdiocese's argument that the allegations of the complaint amounted only to legal conclusions or mere restatements of the *Chesterman* factors themselves. *Id.* at 375 n. 5, 977 P.2d 1163. The court reasoned that:

> An ultimate fact is a fact from which legal conclusions are drawn. A conclusion of law, by contrast, is merely a judgment about a particular set of circumstances and assumes facts that may or may not have been pleaded.... Allegations of when particular conduct occurred, of the motivation behind that conduct, and of the

employment-related nature of that conduct all are assertions of fact, which can be proved or disproved.

Id. (citations omitted).

The *Fearing* court further expressly rejected the argument that, because the alleged sexual abuse could not reasonably have furthered any interest of the employer, it could not have been within the scope of the employee's duties, reasoning that:

> in the intentional tort context, it usually is inappropriate for the court to base its decision regarding the adequacy of the complaint on whether the complaint contains allegations that the intentional tort *itself* was committed in furtherance of any interest of the employer or was of the same kind of activities that the employee was hired to perform. Such circumstances rarely will occur and are not, in any event, necessary to vicarious liability. Rather, the focus properly is directed at whether the complaint contains sufficient allegations of [the employee]'s conduct that was within the scope of his employment that arguably resulted in the acts that caused plaintiff's injury.

Id. at 375–376, 977 P.2d 1163 (emphasis original).

The *Fearing* court specifically distinguished the facts before it from those where the circumstances of employment merely created an opportunity for an intentional tort to be committed, indicating that mere *opportunity* was not sufficient to support a finding of vicarious liability:

> Here, plaintiff alleges that [the employee] "used and manipulated his fiduciary position, respect and authority as youth pastor and priest" to befriend plaintiff and his family, gain their trust, spend large periods of time alone with plaintiff, physically touch plaintiff and, ultimately, to gain the opportunity to commit the sexual assaults upon him. A jury reasonably could infer that [the employee]'s performance of his pastoral duties with respect to plaintiff and his family were a necessary precursor to the sexual abuse and that the assaults thus were a direct outgrowth of and were engendered by conduct that was within the scope of [the employee]'s employment.

Id. at 377, 977 P.2d 1163 (citation omitted).

Finally, the *Fearing* court also affirmed the well-established proposition that "[w]hether an employee has acted within the scope of employment at any given time generally is a question for the trier of fact, except in cases where only one reasonable conclusion may be drawn from the facts pled." *Id.* at 374, 977 P.2d 1163.

Shortly after the *Fearing* opinion issued, in *Lourim v. Swensen*, 328 Or. 380, 977 P.2d 1157 (1999), a case involving sexual assault upon a minor Boy Scout by a Boy Scout troop leader, the Oregon Supreme Court relied upon the same reasoning employed in *Fearing* to conclude that an extended course of employment-related cultivation of the trust of a minor and his family could give rise to vicarious employer liability.... [A]pplying the principles articulated in *Fearing*, the court concluded that "a jury reasonably could infer that the sexual assaults were merely the culmination of a progressive series of actions that involved the ordinary and authorized duties of a Boy Scout leader." *Id.* at 396, 977 P.2d 1163. The court further concluded that:

> a jury could infer that, in cultivating a relationship with plaintiff and his family, [the employee defendant], at least initially, was motivated by a desire to fulfill his duties as troop leader and that, over time, his motives became mixed. A jury also reasonably could infer that [the employee defendant]'s performance of his

duties as troop leader with respect to plaintiff and his family was a necessary precursor to the sexual abuse and that the assaults were a direct outgrowth of and were engendered by conduct that was within the scope of [the employee defendant]'s employment. Finally, a jury could infer that [the employee defendant]'s contact with plaintiff was the direct result of the relationship sponsored and encouraged by the Boy Scouts, which invested [the employee defendant] with authority to decide how to supervise minor boys under his care. Based on the foregoing, we conclude, as we did in *Fearing*, that the amended complaint contains allegations sufficient to satisfy all three *Chesterman* requirements.

Id. at 386–387, 977 P.2d 1157.

Similarly, in *Bray v. American Prop. Mgmt. Corp.*, 164 Or.App. 134, 988 P.2d 933 (1999), the Oregon Court of Appeals applied the *Fearing/Lourim* standard to find an employer vicariously liable for its employee's actions when an employee fatally stabbed a third party in the workplace. The third party habitually parked a delivery van in the defendant's parking garage without permission, and the defendant instructed its employee parking attendant to prevent the third party from continuing to do so; the defendant neither authorized nor prohibited the use of force in carrying out its instruction. *See Bray*, 164 Or.App. at 136–137, 988 P.2d 933. When the attendant informed the third party that he could no longer park in the garage, a scuffle ensued which culminated in the attendant killing the third party with a knife. *See id.* at 137, 988 P.2d 933. The court concluded that:

> as in *Fearing* and *Lourim*, the jury could find that *the stabbing was merely the culmination of a progressive series of actions that involved [the attendant's] ordinary and authorized duties.* That is, reasonable jurors could find that the stabbing was the product of the escalating antagonism between [the attendant] and [the third party] centering on [the third party]'s obstruction of access to the parking garage and use of that garage.... Moreover, reasonable jurors could find that *"[the employer]'s directive to [the attendant] not to permit [the third party] to park in the garage was a necessary precursor to the stabbing and that the stabbing was a direct outgrowth and was engendered by conduct that was within the scope of [the attendant's] employment,"* viz., [the attendant]'s telling [the third party] that he could not park in the garage.

Bray, 164 Or.App. at 140–141, 988 P.2d 933 (emphasis supplied; citations, internal quotation marks, and modifications omitted). The court expressly observed that, under "*Fearing* and *Lourim*, direct causation, not 'reasonable foreseeability'..., *is the sine qua non of respondeat superior* liability." *Id.* at 141, 988 P.2d 933.

Three years later, in *Minnis v. Oregon Mutual Ins. Co.*, 334 Or. 191, 48 P.3d 137 (2002), the Oregon Supreme Court found that no vicarious liability attached in connection with a managerial employee's sexual assault of an employee under his supervision. The managerial employee allegedly both sexually harassed the supervised employee in the workplace and sexually assaulted her outside the workplace, specifically in his own apartment, *See Minnis*, 334 Or. at 197, 48 P.3d 137. The *Minnis* court held that because the *Minnis* plaintiff had testified that the workplace conduct and the sexual assault were "episodes in a series," rather than that the sexual harassment "*resulted in or caused*" the sexual assault, "the *Chesterman* 'time-lag' standard" was inapplicable, and the respondeat superior test was to be applied solely to the conduct taking place at the managerial employee's apartment. *Id.* at 202, 48 P.3d 137 (emphasis original) .... Because this conduct was not within the manager's employment duties, the court found that the employer was not vicariously liable under *Chesterman. See id.* at 203–204, 48 P.3d 137. The *Minnis* court expressly distinguished *Fearing* and *Lourim* on the ground that the tortfeasor's workplace conduct had not been alleged to be a necessary precursor or otherwise a cause of the subsequent sexual assault. *See id.* at 204–206, 48 P.3d 137.

The Oregon Court of Appeals recently applied the *Fearing/Lourim* standard once again to allegations of sexual assault by priest employees of the Archdiocese. In *Schmidt v. Archdiocese of Portland*, 218 Or.App. 661, 180 P.3d 160 (Or.Ct.App.2008), Father F., one of two priests alleged to have molested the plaintiff during his minority, was present when the plaintiff, then aged seven or eight, fell while rollerskating and skinned his knees. *Schmidt*, 218 Or.App. at 665, 180 P.3d 160. Fr. F. helped the boy to his feet, took him into a church basement on the pretext of examining his scraped knees, and there sodomized him. *See id.* The plaintiff had never met his abuser before the incident occurred. *See id.* at 667, 694, 180 P.3d 160.... In analyzing whether the priest's employers could be found vicariously liable for their agent's sexual assault, the *Schmidt* court affirmed the *Fearing* court's holding that:

> in the intentional tort context, the relevant question is not whether the intentional tort itself was committed in furtherance of any interest of the employer or involved the kind of activity that the employee was hired to perform [but] [r]ather ... whether there is evidence of acts that were within the scope of employment that, in turn, *resulted in* the acts that caused the plaintiff's injury.

Id. at 690, 180 P.3d 160 (emphasis supplied). Applying that analysis, the court found, first, that the record contained no evidence that Fr. F. had, as had the priest in *Fearing*, cultivated a relationship of trust with his victim before assaulting him. *See id.* at 694, 180 P.3d 160. Next, "[a]s an alternative to cultivation of a trust relationship as a basis for imposing vicarious liability," the court analyzed the priest's conduct immediately preceding the assault to determine whether the record contained "evidence of conduct by [Fr. F.] that was motivated, at least in part, by a purpose to serve the archdiocese; that was of a kind that [Fr. F.] was hired to perform; and that resulted in the acts causing plaintiff's injury" *Id.* The court found that the record contained no evidence from which a jury could conclude either that the priest had been motivated to serve his employer by picking up the fallen child and taking him into a church basement or that helping fallen children was among his authorized employment duties. *See id.* at 695–696, 180 P.3d 160. The court expressly found evidence that Roman Catholic priests were expected to care for their parishioners insufficient to establish a particular employment duty to do so. *See id.* ("[a]bstract doctrine regarding the status of priests within the Catholic Church sheds no light on the question whether the particular actions at issue here were employment duties imposed on [this priest], in his capacity as a parish priest of St. Mary's Church, by the archdiocese"). Similarly, the court expressly found "evidence relating to the respect and obedience that parishioners are trained to show to priests"—including plaintiff's own affidavit that he believed from Catholic teaching that he had no choice but to obey a priest's commands—irrelevant to the question whether Fr. F. was carrying out authorized employment duties when he took the boy into the church basement. *Id.* at 696, 180 P.3d 160. Based on these findings, the court affirmed summary judgment in favor of the employer defendants. *See id.*

Here, it is clear that Jane has alleged that Fr. J.V.H. engaged in conduct referred to as "grooming" her within the course and scope of his employment duties, and that such grooming resulted in the abuse she suffered.[4] For purposes of the archdiocesan defendants'

---

4. At oral argument, Jane's counsel expressly disavowed the "grooming" theory of *respondeat superior* liability alleged in Jane's second amended complaint and argued instead that, as in *Bray, supra*, the abuse Jane suffered was "the culmination of a progressive series of actions that involved [Fr. J.V.H.'s] ordinary and authorized duties." *Bray*, 164 Or.App. at 140, 988 P.2d 933. In offering this

motion to dismiss, these allegations must be accepted as true. However, Jane has further alleged that J.V.H, began abusing her before he became a priest, and therefore that the abuse she suffered began before J.V.H. could have owed the archdiocesan defendants any employment duties. At a minimum, therefore, the sexual abuse Jane suffered before J.V.H. was ordained and before he became an employee of the Archdiocese could not have resulted from grooming that occurred within the course and scope of Fr. J.V.H.'s employment duties, and cannot give rise to *respondeat superior* liability. Indeed, Jane's allegations raise serious concerns as to whether Jane will be able to establish that *any* of the abuse she suffered was a consequence of actions Fr. J.V.H. took in furtherance of his employment duties. These concerns, however, are properly addressed by motion for summary judgment or at trial rather than at this stage of these proceedings.

Despite these concerns, for purposes of the archdiocesan defendants' motion to dismiss I construe the allegations of the complaint in the light most favorable to Jane and therefore acknowledge the logical possibility that at or around the time of Fr. J.V.H.'s ordination the abuse would not have continued but for the alleged employment-related grooming. On this construal of Jane's allegations, Jane's allegations state claims for sexual battery of a child and for intentional infliction of emotional distress, and meet the *Fearing/Lourim* standard for establishing an employer's vicarious liability. That is, she has alleged that Fr. J.V.H. engaged in conduct of a kind he was (allegedly) hired to perform, that in engaging in this conduct he was motivated, at least in part, to serve his employer, and that the conduct took place within the time and space limits authorized by his employment, *see Chesterman*, 305 Or. at 442, 753 P.2d 404, and that this conduct later resulted in the abuse she suffered at his hands, *see Fearing*, 328 Or. at 375–376, 977 P.2d 1163. In consequence, I conclude that Jane has met her burden at the pleading stage of these proceedings[5] to state the archdiocesan defendants' vicarious liability for Fr. J.V.H.'s tortious conduct.[6] The archdiocesan defendants' motion to dismiss should therefore be denied as to Jane's *respondeat superior* claims[.] ...

Jane alleges that all defendants—apparently including Fr. J.V.H. as well as the archdiocesan defendants—were negligent in failing "to investigate, monitor, supervise, restrict, or remove Fr. J.V.H. during his formation and ministry" despite having allegedly become aware of "potential warning signs" that he might be dangerous to those entrusted to his care or influence. Jane alleges that the "potential warning signs" the archdiocesan defendants had reason to be aware of created a foreseeable risk of danger to persons entrusted to Fr. J.V.H.'s care or influence.... To state a claim for negligence under Oregon

---

argument, counsel gave short shrift to the conceded fact that the bulk of the putative progressive series of actions took place before Fr. J.V.H. became an employee of the archdiocesan defendants. Nevertheless, the merits of the archdiocesan defendants' motion to dismiss must be measured against the allegations of Jane's pleading rather than against the argument offered by her counsel, so I disregard counsel's disavowal of Jane's allegations.

5. I acknowledge that Jane's allegations in this action are close to formulaic, in that they recite the *Chesterman* factors for *respondeat superior* liability with only minimal factual support, and are less well developed than the pleadings in *Fearing* or *Lourim*. Nevertheless, in *Fearing* the Oregon Supreme Court found allegations of ultimate facts similar to those alleged here to be sufficient to survive a motion to dismiss for failure to state a claim, and I therefore so find here.

6. The archdiocesan defendants advance the argument that *respondeat superior* liability is not cognizable as to the tort of intentional infliction of emotional distress where it is not an employee's job duty to intentionally inflict emotional distress. This argument does not modify my conclusion that Jane has pled the elements of *respondeat superior* liability as to both the sexual battery claim and the intentional infliction claim, The intentional act alleged to have inflicted severe emotional distress is the sex abuse Jane suffered at Fr. J.V.H.'s hands, and that abuse is alleged to have resulted from acts taken within the course and scope of Fr. J.V.H.'s employment.

common law, a plaintiff must show that the defendant owed the plaintiff a duty, that the duty was breached, and that the breach caused the plaintiff harm. *See, e.g., Fazzolari v. Portland School Dist.*, 303 Or. 1, 14–17, 734 P.2d 1326 (1987). In the absence of a specific duty created, defined, or limited by a specified status, relationship or standard of conduct, a defendant may be liable for negligence if the defendant's conduct "unreasonably created a foreseeable risk to a protected interest of the kind of harm that befell the plaintiff." *Cowan v. Nortdyke*, 232 Or.App. 384, 384, 222 P.3d 1093 (Or.Ct.App.2009). The archdiocesan defendants argue that a claim for negligent supervision of a priest is simply not cognizable against a church authority under First Amendment principles requiring civil courts to defer to ecclesiastic authority in deciding matters related to religious dogma, and in the alternative that Jane has failed to plead ultimate facts that, if proven, would establish the existence of a special relationship between them and Jane of a kind that would create a duty of care and/or any foreseeable risk to Jane of the harm she actually suffered, and in the further alternative that Jane has failed to plead ultimate facts that, if proven, would establish that Jane's injuries were caused by the archdiocesan defendants' alleged breach of a duty of care.

As to the archdiocesan defendants' Constitutional argument, the First Amendment "requires that civil courts defer to the resolution of issues of religious doctrine or polity by the highest court of a hierarchical church organization." *Jones v. Wolf*, 443 U.S. 595, 602, 99 S.Ct. 3020, 61 L.Ed.2d 775 (1979) (citations omitted). Based on this consideration, "[i]n the absence of fraud, collusion, or arbitrariness, the decisions of the proper church tribunals on matters purely ecclesiastical, although affecting civil rights, are accepted in litigation before the secular courts as conclusive, because the parties in interest made them so by contract or otherwise." *Presbyterian Church in United States v. Mary Elizabeth Blue Hull Mem'l Presbyterian Church*, 393 U.S. 440, 447, 89 S.Ct. 601, 21 L.Ed.2d 658 (1969). Courts therefore must apply neutral principles of law in deciding disputes involving ecclesiastical issues. *See id.* at 449, 89 S.Ct. 601. Here, no ecclesiastical issues are raised by Jane's claim; the same neutral principles of law would apply whether the alleged abuser were a priest or a groundskeeper, and the factors considered in determining whether a man may be ordained as a priest do not arise. The First Amendment therefore cannot bar Jane's negligence claim.

As to whether Jane has adequately pled a special relationship between herself and the archdiocesan defendants of a kind that would create a cognizable duty of care, Jane alleges and argues that "[a]s a young girl entrusted to the care and influence of the Catholic Church and Fr. J.V.H., an agent and employee of Archdiocese Defendants," she had "a special relationship with Defendants." However, under Oregon law:

> The common thread among [such] special relationships—that is, those warranting a heightened duty of care—is that "the party who owes the duty has a special responsibility toward the other party":
>
>> This is so because the party who is owed the duty effectively has authorized the party who owes the duty to exercise independent judgment in the former party's behalf and in the former party's interests. In doing so, the party who is owed the duty is placed in a position of reliance upon the party who owes the duty; that is, because the former has given responsibility and control over the situation at issue to the latter, the former has a right to rely upon the latter to achieve a desired outcome or resolution.

Shin v. Sunriver Preparatory Sch., Inc., 199 Or.App. 352, 367, 111 P.3d 762 (Or.Ct.App.2005) (emphasis original), *quoting Conway v. Pacific Univ.*, 324 Or. 231, 239–240, 924 P.2d 818

(1995). Under this standard, it is clear that the kind of "special relationship" Jane pled is not of a kind that gives rise to a heightened duty of care. Jane does not allege that she was a parishioner of any church of the Archdiocese. Neither Jane nor her family authorized the Archbishop or the Archdiocese to exercise independent judgment in Jane's interests or gave the archdiocesan defendants responsibility for or control over Jane's welfare. That is, although Jane's allegations contain the phrase "special relationship," no ultimate facts are pled that suggest the existence of the kind of relationship that could give rise to a duty of care. I therefore conclude that defendants are correct to the extent they argue that Jane has not adequately pled the existence of a duty of care owed by the archdiocesan defendants to Jane.

As to whether Jane has pled facts giving rise to a foreseeable risk to a protected interest of the kind of harm she suffered, Jane has alleged that the archdiocesan defendants had knowledge of specific facts that a reasonable person would have construed as creating a risk that children entrusted to Fr. J.V.H.'s care might be unsafe. However, for purposes of the foreseeability analysis, the issue is not solely one of the archdiocesan defendants' knowledge, but whether, in light of that knowledge, the archdiocesan defendants' *conduct* created a foreseeable risk to a protected interest of the kind of harm Jane suffered. Assuming without deciding that a reasonable person possessed of the knowledge Jane imputes to the archdiocesan defendants would have understood that children would be unsafe with Fr. J.V.H., it would clearly have constituted actionable negligence had the archdiocesan defendants permitted Fr. J.V.H. to conduct a youth ministry, formally entrusted children to his care, or otherwise authorized him to minister to children unsupervised. Here, however, there is no allegation that the archdiocesan defendants did any of these things. Instead, the question for the court is whether the archdiocesan defendants' alleged failures to investigate or follow up on potentially troubling findings from J.V.H.'s psychological examinations, to monitor or supervise Fr. J.V.H.'s interactions with minors, to restrict Fr. J.V.H.'s interactions with children, and/or to remove Fr. J.V.H. from the ministry created an unreasonable risk of harm.

Jane has expressly alleged that the abuse she suffered resulted from "grooming" conduct that Fr. J.V.H. engaged in within the course and scope of his employment duties. Assuming the truth of Jane's allegations, some of the abuse she suffered at Fr. J.V.H.'s hands therefore would not have occurred but for J.V.H.'s status as an ordained priest of the Roman Catholic church. That is, assuming the truth of Jane's allegations, some of the abuse would not have taken place but for the archdiocesan defendants' failure to investigate, monitor, restrict, and/or defrock Fr. J.V.H. Moreover, in light of the authority and status enjoyed by Roman Catholic priests within the Roman Catholic community, a finder of fact could reasonably conclude that failure to investigate, monitor, restrict, and/or defrock a Roman Catholic priest whose record and behavior suggested a potential sex abuse risk created a foreseeable, unreasonable risk to children entrusted to his care or permitted to come into unsupervised contact with him.... Because the record does not foreclose the possibility that the archdiocesan defendants' conduct could give rise to liability for negligence, motion to dismiss should be denied as to Jane's negligence claim....

Jane has met her burden to plead an evidentiary basis for her prayer for punitive damages at this stage of these proceedings. Because a reasonable finder of fact could conclude on the basis of the Jane's allegations that the archdiocesan defendants' conduct met the appropriate standard for award of punitive damages, the motion to dismiss should be denied as to Jane's punitive damages request.... For the reasons set forth above, I recommend that ... the archdiocesan defendants' motion ... for judicial notice be granted in part and denied in part as discussed above....

Notes

As a general rule, employers are liable for torts committed by their employees "in the course and scope of their employment." But the applicability of vicarious liability in cases of sexual abuse is far from a uniform principle, whereas courts are disinclined to find that an employee is hired to sexually offend as part of one's employment duties. Thus, courts have varied in identifying the acts that fall within the scope of one's employment, with the more restrictive approach limiting liability to those acts that are motivated by service to the employer, and the more flexible approach focusing on acts that are reasonably foreseeable or predictable. For an excellent discussion of the issue of vicarious liability involving institutional child sexual abuse and exploitation and the various standards that apply, see Martha Chamallas, *Vicarious Liability in Torts: The Sex Exception*, 48 Val. U. L. Rev. 133 (2013) (describing confusion in applicability of vicarious liability standards and drawing distinction between sexual and non-sexual cases applying vicarious liability); *see also* Phillip Morgan, *Revising Vicarious Liability: A Commercial Perspective*, Lloyd's Mar. & Com. L.Q. 175 (2012); Catherine E. Sweetser, *Providing Effective Remedies to Victims of Abuse by Peace-keeping Personnel*, 83 N.Y.U. L. Rev. 1643 (2008). For foreign commentary addressing other approaches toward the applicability of vicarious liability in cases of sexual abuse outside of the United States, see M.H. Ogilvie, *Are Members of the Clergy Without the Law? Hart v. Roman Catholic Episcopal Corporation of the Diocese of Kingston*, 39 Queen's L.J. 441 (2014) (discussing Canadian approach to vicarious liability jurisdiction); David Neild, *Vicarious Liability and the Employment Rationale*, 44 Vict. U. Wellington L. Rev. 707 (2013) (comparing approaches in England and New Zealand). In the case of *Jane Doe*, however, although the court left the ultimate question to the trier of facts, the court determined that it is at least possible that a jury could find that the sexual abuse of the child—particularly through the process of 'grooming," *see* Chapter Two, Section I.D ("Grooming")—fell within the course and scope of the defendant's duties.

Despite the limited application of vicarious liability to employers for the intentional sexual exploitation of a child by an employee, more difficult still is satisfying the prima facie elements of a cause of action against an institution for negligently hiring, retaining, or supervising an employee.

3. Negligent Hiring, Retaining, or Supervising

Krystal G. v. Roman Catholic Diocese of Brooklyn

Supreme Court, Kings County, New York, 2011
34 Misc. 3d 531, 933 N.Y.S.2d 515

KAREN B. ROTHENBERG, J.

Defendant Joseph Agostino (Agostino), former pastor at defendant St. John the Baptist Roman Catholic Church (Church) in Brooklyn, moves, pursuant to CPLR 3211(a)(7) and/or CPLR 3212, to dismiss the claims against him. Plaintiffs, Krystal G., an infant, and Vivian and Juan G., her parents, proceeding on their child's and their own behalf, have sued Agostino and others ... [footnote omitted] for negligently hiring, retaining and supervising defendant Augusto Cortez (Cortez), the former assistant pastor, who allegedly sexually assaulted Krystal G....

Plaintiffs' amended complaint alleges that defendant Cortez sexually assaulted and abused the infant plaintiff at defendant St. John the Baptist School (School) on May 28, 2008, when she was 12 years old, by touching, holding and fondling her breast. Plaintiffs also claim that defendant Agostino, for whom Cortez worked, negligently hired, retained and/or supervised Cortez.... Agostino served as Church pastor from September 2000 through May 2009 and is still employed by defendant Eastern Province of the Congregation of the Mission of St. Vincent De Paul (Eastern Province). Agostino, as Church pastor, bore responsibility for the daily operation and governance of defendant St. John the Baptist Parish (Parish). Additionally, Agostino allegedly exerted influence over defendant School, which was located across the street from the Church where the sexual abuse purportedly occurred.

Defendant Congregation in or around September 2003 made Cortez assistant Church pastor. Cortez frequented defendant School and resided in defendant Church's Local Community House (Community House), located on the same block as defendant Church and defendant School. Agostino served as the "Local Superior" at the Community House, from 2007 through the time of the alleged abuse, and had oversight responsibilities over Cortez and other Community House residents.

The affidavit of Juan G., infant plaintiff's father, avers that both defendant School's principal and assistant principal will confirm that Agostino authorized Cortez's presence at the School, even though school administrators objected to Cortez's presence. In particular, the principal and assistant principal, according to Mr. G., were concerned about Cortez's contact with the School children and the fact that he was summoning children out of class to perform chores unrelated to school work. Accordingly, the School's administrators undertook to remove Cortez from School premises. However, Agostino, allegedly overruled the administrators' decision and validated Cortez's continuing presence at the school. Plaintiffs commenced this action on December 11, 2009 and filed an amended summons and amended complaint on January 27, 2010.... [footnote omitted]. The amended complaint alleges, in essence, causes of action for: (1) sexual assault and battery, infliction of emotional distress and violation of the Penal Law against defendant Cortez; (2) negligent hiring, retention and supervision of defendant Cortez against all other defendants; (3) failure by defendants to properly train, supervise, instruct and manage Agostino so that he would properly supervise Cortez; and (4) loss of companionship and services of the infant plaintiff to each of her parents.

Plaintiffs served discovery demands on September 9, 2010, but defendant Cortez and the Vincentian defendants have asserted privilege and have refused to comply with those demands. The Vincentian defendants proposed, on September 29, 2010, that all parties execute a protective order which was written by the Vincentian defendants' counsel. Plaintiffs have refused to sign the protective order, resulting in this motion and cross motions.... Essentially, plaintiffs claim that Agostino negligently supervised and/or hired and retained Cortez because Agostino either knew or should have known, through "direct information, records, discipline, conversations, behavior, mannerisms, speech, and [Cortez's] other conduct" that Cortez posed a sexual threat to the School children ... [citations to record omitted].... Agostino seeks dismissal as against him, pursuant to either CPLR 3211(a)(7) or 3212. First, Agostino argues that plaintiffs cannot satisfy the elements of negligent supervision because (a) he is not Cortez's employer; (b) he denied knowledge of Cortez's propensity, if any, for sexual abuse, and (c) Cortez's alleged abuse did not occur on his employer's premises. Also, Agostino argues that any negligence attributed to him is automatically "imputed to [Agostino's] employer, under the doctrine of *respondeat superior*, thereby alleviating any direct cause of action against [him]," because he did not commit an "independent tortious act" outside the scope of his employment....

A claimant states a cause of action for negligent hiring and retention by adequately alleging that the "employer knew or should have known of the employee's propensity for the conduct which caused the injury" (*Bumpus v. New York City Tr. Auth.*, 47 A.D.3d 653, 654, 851 N.Y.S.2d 591 [2008] [internal quotation marks and citation omitted]; *see also Jackson v. New York Univ. Downtown Hosp.*, 69 A.D.3d 801, 801–02, 893 N.Y.S.2d 235 [2010]; *Kenneth R. v. Roman Catholic Diocese of Brooklyn*, 229 A.D.2d 159, 161, 654 N.Y.S.2d 791 [1997], *cert. denied* 522 U.S. 967, 118 S.Ct. 413, 139 L.Ed.2d 316 [1997], *lv. dismissed* 91 N.Y.2d 848, 667 N.Y.S.2d 683, 690 N.E.2d 492 [1997] [Appellate Division, Second Department modified Kings County Supreme Court's decision and granted motion to dismiss plaintiff's claim that the Roman Catholic Diocese of Brooklyn was negligent in hiring and failing to establish proper guidelines and procedures for screening and investigating priests since there is "no common-law duty to institute specific procedures for hiring employees unless the employer knows of facts that would lead a reasonably prudent person to investigate the prospective employee"] [*Id.* at 163, 654 N.Y.S.2d 791]). Even assuming arguendo that Agostino was Cortez's employer, plaintiffs allege no factual scenario allowing an inference that Agostino should have known that Cortez would present a sexual threat to the students at the School at the time Cortez was assigned to the Church. Therefore, Agostino had no common law duty to initiate an investigation absent facts that would have put Agostino on notice of Cortez's propensity to engage in the claimed behavior.... However, Agostino's duty to investigate Cortez's background for the protection of the School's children would have arisen once facts existed which Agostino either knew or should have known about concerning Cortez's unlawful sexual propensities. Consequently, *Kenneth R.*'s proscription against an employer's initial duty to institute specific procedures for investigating employees does not apply regarding Cortez's continued employment. Therefore, plaintiff has adequately plead its negligent retention claim against Agostino.... Stating a claim for negligent supervision, likewise requires that the supervisor must have "kn[own] or should have known of the employee's propensity for the conduct which caused the injury" (*Kenneth R.*, 229 A.D.2d at 161, 654 N.Y.S.2d 791). Defendant Agostino cites a case from the Southern District of New York to urge that three elements are necessary to state a cause of action for negligent supervision: (1) that the tortfeasor and defendant were in an employer-employee relationship; (2) that the employer knew or should have known of the employee's propensity to commit the act(s) which caused the injury before the injury's occurrence; and (3) that the tort occurred on the employer's premises or with the employer's chattels (*Bouchard v. New York Archdiocese*, 719 F.Supp.2d 255, 261 [S.D.N.Y. 2010] citing *Ehrens v. Lutheran Church*, 385 F.3d 232, 235 [2d Cir.2004]).

However, an employer-employee relationship is not required under New York case law (*see e.g. Connell v. Hayden*, 83 A.D.2d 30, 50, 443 N.Y.S.2d 383 [1981]). The court concluded in *Connell*, that a co-employee could be liable for the torts of a co-employee: "(1) where one [co-employee] is charged with negligent supervision of the other or (2) where neither is a supervisor but both combined to cause plaintiff's injury" (*Id.* at 50, 443 N.Y.S.2d 383). New York's common law follows the Restatement [Second] of Agency, which expressly states that an agent may be liable for another agent's torts if he negligently supervised the other agent (Restatement [Second] of Agency § 358).... Here, Agostino's own affidavit states that he "was responsible for the spiritual and material well being of the community at St. John the Baptist parish, including oversight of its governance" and "was responsible for day-to-day operations of the Church".... It necessarily follows, drawing all favorable inferences for plaintiffs, that these oversight responsibilities included supervision of his assistant pastor, Augusto Cortez. Therefore, a sufficient relationship exists between defendant Agostino, as supervisor, and Cortez, as Agostino's subordinate, to sustain a cause of action for negligent supervision under New York law.

Prevailing on a negligent supervision claim, though, requires a claimant prove that the defendant knew or should have known about his subordinate's propensity for the conduct that caused the plaintiff's injury (*see e.g. Mirand v. City of New York*, 84 N.Y.2d 44, 49, 614 N.Y.S.2d 372, 637 N.E.2d 263 [1994]; *Jackson v. New York Univ. Downtown Hosp.*, 69 A.D.3d at 801, 893 N.Y.S.2d 235; *Bumpus*, 47 A.D.3d at 654, 851 N.Y.S.2d 591; *Peter T. v. Children's Vil., Inc.*, 30 A.D.3d 582, 586, 819 N.Y.S.2d 44 [2006]; *Kenneth R.*, 229 A.D.2d at 161, 654 N.Y.S.2d 791). No statutory requirement exists that negligent supervision claims be plead with specificity (*Id.* at 162, 654 N.Y.S.2d 791) but "bare legal conclusions and/or factual claims flatly contradicted by documentary evidence should be dismissed pursuant to CPLR 3211(a)(7)" (*id.* [internal quotation marks and citation omitted]).…

Here, plaintiffs allege that the School's administrators sought to forbid Cortez from coming onto the School's premises because of their concern about Cortez's excessive physical contact with the School's children, and that Agostino overrode the School administrator's wishes. The court takes these allegations as true, because defendants have not conclusively proved otherwise,[3] and views them, as required, in the light most favorable to plaintiff (*Samiento v. World Yacht Inc.*, 10 N.Y.3d at 79, 854 N.Y.S.2d 83, 883 N.E.2d 990; *Branham v. Loews Orpheum Cinemas, Inc.*, 8 N.Y.3d 931, 932, 834 N.Y.S.2d 503, 866 N.E.2d 448 [2007]). Consequently, the facts alleged in the plaintiff's complaint, as supplemented by Juan G.'s affidavit, may be reasonably construed to demonstrate that Agostino knew or should have known of Cortez's propensity to commit the sexual abuse that plaintiffs allege occurred.

Finally, Agostino's argument that New York law requires that a negligent supervision claim involves tortious conduct committed with the defendant's chattels or on the defendant's property is unpersuasive. *D'Amico v. Christie*, 71 N.Y.2d 76, 524 N.Y.S.2d 1, 518 N.E.2d 896 [1987], cited by Agostino, concerns the specialized duty to control and supervise intoxicated persons, rather than the more general negligent supervision claim at issue in the present case. There, the Court of Appeals refused to extend a landowner's duty to supervise subordinates to alcohol providers and their inebriates in light of the Dram Shop Act (General Obligations Law § 11-101).[4] This case does not involve a third-party's duty to supervise inebriants, and *D'Amico* does not control the present case, and it is thus unnecessary for plaintiffs to allege that Cortez's tort was committed on his employer's premises or with his employer's chattels.[5]

In summary, a sufficient relationship exists between Cortez and Agostino to create Agostino's duty to supervise Cortez, and plaintiffs' amended complaint and supporting papers adequately allege that Agostino knew or should have known of Cortez's propensity to engage in the alleged tortious conduct. Consequently, plaintiff has a cause of action sounding in negligent supervision and negligent retention.… In addition, Agostino argues

---

3. Agostino's bald allegation in his affidavit that he was "unaware of any history of or prior propensity for sexual misconduct as has been alleged against Augusto Cortez" and "neither knew nor should have known of Augusto Cortez's propensity for the conduct which caused the alleged injury," clearly does not qualify as documentary evidence that would conclusively refute facts alleged by plaintiff.…

4. The Dram Shop Act limits liability for injuries caused by inebriates to those that unlawfully sell alcohol, rather than imposing a general duty on all providers of alcohol to reasonably supervise inebriates (*see e.g. D'Amico*, 71 N.Y.2d at 86–87, 524 N.Y.S.2d 1, 518 N.E.2d 896).

5. Plaintiffs, in any event, likely satisfy *D'Amico*, if it were applicable, because the alleged tortious acts were committed on the School's premises, and it is reasonable to assume, based on the pleadings and supporting papers, that Cortez's employer also owned the School.

for dismissal on the operation of the respondeat superior doctrine. However, the doctrine does not ordinarily operate to extinguish the principal tortfeasor's liability because the tortious conduct fell within the scope of the principal tortfeasor's employment. Rather, respondeat superior allows a claimant, at his or her *option*, to recover from a person or entity that is vicariously liable for the acts of the principal tortfeasor. It does not *automatically* impute liability from [an] employee to his employer. Therefore, the mere fact that Cortez might have been acting within the scope of his employment does not, contrary to Agostino's contention, "alleviat[e] any direct cause of action" against Agostino.

The Appellate Division, Second Department in *Segal v. St. John's Univ.*, 69 A.D.3d 702, 703, 893 N.Y.S.2d 221 [2010] held that "[g]enerally, when a plaintiff seeks to recover damages against an employer based on an employee's actions committed within the scope of his or her employment, the employer is liable under the doctrine of respondeat superior, not negligent hiring or supervision" (*Segal v. St. John's Univ.*, 69 A.D.3d at 703, 893 N.Y.S.2d 221). This policy underlying this rule seeks to remove the potential for an employer to be doubly liable for an employee's single tortious act. However, *Segal* does not control in this case. Agostino is not Cortez's employer, and *Segal* applies only to negligent hiring, retention and supervision claims *against employers*. Thus, it is inconsequential if Agostino was acting within the scope of his employment when he supervised Cortez because plaintiffs here are suing Agostino—a supervisor, not an employer—for negligent supervision. Second, even assuming Agostino was Cortez's employer, Cortez—an *employee*—was acting *outside* of the scope of *his* employment when he allegedly sexually abused the infant plaintiff.

Agostino further incorrectly relies on several decisions for the proposition that an employee cannot be held liable for torts committed within the scope of his or her employment absent an "independent tortious act." The Appellate Division, Second Department provided a summary of this area of the law in *Courageous Syndicate v. People-to-People Sports Comm.*, 141 A.D.2d 599, 600, 529 N.Y.S.2d 520 [1988] by relying on the Court of Appeals decision in *Murtha v. Yonkers Child Care Assn.*, 45 N.Y.2d 913, 915, 411 N.Y.S.2d 219, 383 N.E.2d 865 [1978]:

> "Generally, a director of a corporation is not personally liable to one who has contracted with a corporation on the theory of inducing a breach of contract, merely due to the fact that, while acting for the corporation, he has made decisions and taken steps that resulted in the corporation's promise being broken ... Moreover, [a] corporate officer who is charged with inducing the breach of a contract between the corporation and a third party is immune from liability if it appears that he is acting in good faith ... [and did not commit] independent torts or predatory acts directed at another ... The complaint must allege that the officers' or directors' acts were taken outside the scope of their employment or that they personally profited from their acts" (internal quotation marks and citation omitted).

(*See also Burger v. Brookhaven Med. Arts Bldg.*, 131 A.D.2d 622, 623, 516 N.Y.S.2d 705 [1987]; *Citicorp Retail Servs. v. Wellington Mercantile Servs.*, 90 A.D.2d 532, 532, 455 N.Y.S.2d 98 [1982]; *Buckley v. 112 Cent. Park S., Inc.*, 285 App.Div. 331 at 334, 136 N.Y.S.2d 233).

Here, breach of contract is neither alleged nor apparent from the pleadings. Therefore, even assuming Agostino did not commit an "independent tortious act," the argument that Agostino's liability is automatically impugned to his employers under *Murtha* must be rejected. In any event, the Appellate Division, Second Department unequivocally held in *Bellinzoni v. Seland*, 128 A.D.2d 580, 580–581, 512 N.Y.S.2d 846 [1987], that a corporate officer or agent may be found liable for negligently supervising a third party that was responsible for the plaintiff's injury, even if that corporate officer was acting in his or her official capacity. Thus, even if Agostino is a corporate agent or officer acting within the scope of his employment, he may still be liable to plaintiff.... Plaintiffs' amended complaint, together with Juan G.'s affidavit, sufficiently allege a cause of action sounding in negligent retention and supervision under CPLR 3211(a)(7), and Agostino's arguments that his potential liability is automatically impugned to his employer are without merit. Therefore, the motion to dismiss under 3211(a)(7) is denied with respect to plaintiffs' claims of negligent retention and supervision....

Accordingly it is:

ORDERED that defendant Agostino's motion to dismiss is granted as to plaintiffs' negligent hiring claim, only; and it is further

ORDERED that defendant Agostino's motion to dismiss is denied as to plaintiffs' negligent supervision and retention claims; and it is further

ORDERED that the branch of defendant Agostino's motion for summary judgment is denied.... This constitutes the decision and order of this court.

B. Defenses

As described in *Krystal*, the basis for institutional liability for the sexual exploitation of children by individual employees is based on common causes of action in tort that might otherwise apply to individual actors. In addition, the institutional aspect of these cases often introduces other theories of liability, like *respondeat superior* as a form of vicarious liability, and negligence in supervising, investigating, hiring, or removing liable employees. Throughout this casebook, we have illustrated common defenses to such individual claims by demonstrating facts that satisfy—or fail to satisfy—the *prima facie* elements of various criminal and civil claims, as well as more specific defenses, like the various statutes of limitations, which are applicable in both the criminal and civil context. *See* Chapter 7, Section I.A (criminal statute of limitations) and II.A (civil statute of limitations), *supra*. Likewise, these common forms of defenses are applicable to cases involving institutional abuse and exploitation of children as well. *See, e.g., R. v. R.*, 37 A.D.3d 577, 829 N.Y.S.2d 659 (A.D.2d 2007) (granting motion to dismiss complaint for negligence and vicarious liability against Roman Catholic Diocese of Brooklyn and other individual defendants, as a matter of law). *See also Kestel v. Kurzak*, 803 N.W.2d 870 (Iowa App. 2011); *Doe v. Archdiocese of Cincinnati*, 109 Ohio St. 3d 491, 849 N.E.2d 268 (2006) (applying statute of limitations to deny claims against individual and institutional defendants). The following case offers an example of the application of the statute of limitations to causes of action raised against institutional authorities.

1. *Statute of Limitations*

Doe v. Roman Catholic Bishops of Sacramento

Court of Appeal, Third District, California, 2010
189 Cal. App. 4th 1423, 117 Cal. Rptr. 3d 597

NICHOLSON, Acting P.J.

Two priests employed by defendant Roman Catholic Bishop of Sacramento (the Diocese) molested two young sons of plaintiff Jane Doe and other children about 20 or more years ago. The two priests fled the country—one in 1989, after pleading guilty to child molestation charges unrelated to Doe's sons, and the other in 1991, after being accused by another family of child molestation.... In 2008, Doe sued the Diocese, alleging that she suffered damages as a result of the priests' molestation of her sons. She asserted causes of action for fraud and negligence.[1] However, the trial court sustained the Diocese's demurrer to the complaint because, among other reasons, Doe's action was barred by the statute of limitations.

Doe appeals. On the issue of the statute of limitations, she contends that the trial court erred in sustaining the demurrer because, under the discovery rule, her causes of action against the Diocese did not accrue until 2007, when her sons told her about the molestations. We conclude that Doe had a duty of inquiry, under the circumstances as alleged in her complaint, when the priests fled the country. Therefore, her causes of action, even assuming without deciding that they have substantive merit, accrued almost 20 years ago and are now barred by the statute of limitations.... Accordingly, we affirm....

In 1989, Doe went to work for the Diocese and, at the time of filing of the complaint, had been an employee of the Diocese for nearly 20 years. She is a devout Catholic who was taught to admire, trust, revere, respect, and obey the church's clergy. She is an uneducated Mexican immigrant and single mother of 10 children, divorced from a man to whom she was married when she was 15 years old.... Jose Luis Urbina and Gerardo Beltran were priests in Doe's parish, which is part of the Diocese. Beltran was also her employer. Both priests gave Doe spiritual and secular counseling. Urbina had counseled Doe to divorce her husband and had driven her to the attorney's office to file for divorce. Urbina and Beltran visited Doe's home regularly and functioned as surrogate fathers to Doe's children.... The complaint does not state when Doe and her children began associating with the Diocese, but it mentions that, in 1984, Doe was counseled by Urbina to divorce her husband.

The Diocese knew or should have known that Urbina and Beltran were pedophiles and child molesters. However, the Diocese did not tell any of the parishioners at Doe's parish. Instead of disclosing this information to the parishioners, the Diocese, by holding Urbina and Beltran out as respected priests, "affirmatively represented" to the parishioners that Urbina and Beltran had no history of child molestation and were not a danger to children. Doe believed and relied on these "misrepresentations." ... Two of Doe's sons were molested by Urbina and Beltran. Because of the Diocese's "misrepresentations," Doe gave Urbina and Beltran unsupervised access to her sons. (The complaint does not say when the molestations occurred.)

In June 1989, Urbina pled guilty to molesting another minor parishioner, but he fled the country before sentencing. The majority of the parishioners believed he was falsely accused.... In late 1991, Beltran also fled the country after being accused of child molestation. The "overwhelming majority" of parishioners believed that Beltran's accusers were lying. Doe "could not believe that her priests would commit such horrific acts." ... The Diocese never informed Doe that the accusations against Urbina and Beltran were credible. Instead, the Diocese "remained silent in order to foster the mistaken idealization of [Urbina and Beltran] by the parishioners and allow it to go uncorrected and to crystallize, thereby perpetuating the shame of sex abuse victims and ensuring their silence." ... The complaint alleged: "Had [Doe] known what [the Diocese] knew — that the priests supposedly caring for her and her family and providing secular counseling were in fact pedophiles and a danger to her children — her sons would not have been molested and

---

1. Doe's sons have their own action against the Diocese.

she would not have suffered her injuries alleged herein." . . . Doe discovered the abuse of her sons in April 2007 when they told her they had been molested by Urbina and Beltran. She later learned that Urbina and Beltran had, in fact, molested other children before molesting her sons.

The complaint alleged four causes of action: (1) fraud, (2) fraudulent concealment or intentional nondisclosure, (3) negligence, and (4) negligent retention or supervision and failure to warn. . . . The injuries to Doe were alleged as follows:

> "[Doe] lost the services of her sons and her relationships with her sons were adversely affected as a result of [the Diocese's] conduct. [Doe's] children suffered individual and relationship problems as a result of [the Diocese's] conduct. As a parent who was responsible for any needs of her children while they were minors, including but not limited to legal, psychiatric or academic, [Doe] was a foreseeable victim of the [Diocese's] failure to manage the priests' conduct and to warn parents of their crimes. Further, [Doe] was unable to get timely psychiatric care for her children, which resulted in serious irreparable psychological damages to her sons, which continue to exist. . . ."[Doe] has suffered psychological and emotional injury and harm caused by [the Diocese] and [its] conduct, including long-term psychological injuries, which have developed and occurred, and will in the future continue to develop and occur in [Doe], all to [Doe's] general damages in a sum to be proven. . . . "[Doe] has suffered physical, mental and emotional health problems as a result of which she has had to employ, and will in the future continue to have to employ, medical and mental health professionals for diagnosis and treatment and has incurred and will in the future continue to incur expenses therefore, in a sum as yet unascertained." . . .

The Diocese demurred to Doe's complaint. The demurrer stated two grounds, generally, for demurring as to all four causes of action—each cause of action (1) was barred by the statute of limitations and (2) failed to state facts sufficient to constitute a cause of action. In addition, as to each of the two fraud-related causes of action, the Diocese asserted that the cause of action was (1) uncertain and (2) not pled with specificity. . . . After a hearing, the trial court sustained the demurrer without leave to amend. The court ruled that: (1) all causes of action are time-barred, and the discovery rule did not delay accrual of the causes of action because, when Urbina and Beltran fled the country because of molestation of children, Doe had a duty of inquiry concerning whether her sons had been molested; (2) Doe cannot recover emotional and psychological damages from injuries to other persons because she was not present and aware of the molestations when they happened; (3) assignment of priests to specific parishes is not an "affirmative representation" that they are not child molesters; and (4) the complaint failed to plead fraud with sufficient specificity. . . . Having sustained the Diocese's demurrer without leave to amend, the trial court entered judgment in favor of the Diocese. . . .

Doe asserts her action is not barred by the statute of limitations. We conclude that Doe's action is barred because her reliance on the discovery rule to delay accrual of the causes of action is misplaced. Given our conclusion that the action is barred by the statute of limitations, we need not address the other bases upon which the trial court relied in sustaining the demurrer without leave to amend. . . .

The limitations period for a fraud cause of action is three years from accrual. (Code Civ. Proc., § 338, subd. (d).) However, "[t]he cause of action in that case is not to be deemed to have accrued until the discovery, by the aggrieved party, of the facts constituting the fraud or mistake." (*Ibid.*) This discovery element has been interpreted to mean "the discovery by the aggrieved party of the fraud or facts that would lead a reasonably prudent person to *suspect* fraud. (*Miller v. Bechtel Corp.* (1983) 33 Cal.3d 868, 875 [191 Cal.Rptr. 619, 663 P.2d 177].)" (*Debro v. Los Angeles Raiders* (2001) 92 Cal.App.4th 940, 950, 112 Cal.Rptr.2d 329, original italics.) ... At the time of the alleged injuries, more than 20 years ago, the limitations period for a negligence cause of action was one year from accrual. In 2002, the limitations period for negligence was changed to two years from accrual.[2] (*Fox v. Ethicon Endo-Surgery, Inc.* (2005) 35 Cal.4th 797, 809 and fn. 3, 27 Cal.Rptr.3d 661, 110 P.3d 914 (*Fox*).) As with a fraud cause of action, the discovery rule also applies to delay accrual of a negligence cause of action. (*Id.* at pp. 808–809, 27 Cal.Rptr.3d 661, 110 P.3d 914.) ... "In order to rely on the discovery rule for delayed accrual of a cause of action, '[a] plaintiff whose complaint shows on its face that his claim would be barred without the benefit of the discovery rule must specifically plead facts to show (1) the time and manner of discovery *and* (2) the inability to have made earlier discovery despite reasonable diligence.' ... In assessing the sufficiency of the allegations of delayed discovery, the court places the burden on the plaintiff to 'show diligence'; 'conclusory allegations will not withstand demurrer.' ..." (*Fox, supra,* 35 Cal.4th at p. 808, 27 Cal.Rptr.3d 661, 110 P.3d 914, original italics.) ...

"'Statute of limitations' is the collective term applied to acts or parts of acts that prescribe the periods beyond which a plaintiff may not bring a cause of action.... There are several policies underlying such statutes. One purpose is to give defendants reasonable repose, thereby protecting parties from 'defending stale claims, where factual obscurity through the loss of time, memory or supporting documentation may present unfair handicaps.'... A statute of limitations also stimulates plaintiffs to pursue their claims diligently.... A countervailing factor, of course, is the policy favoring disposition of cases on the merits rather than on procedural grounds...."A plaintiff must bring a claim within the limitations period after accrual of the cause of action. (Code Civ. Proc., § 312 ['Civil actions, without exception, can only be commenced within the periods prescribed in this title, after the cause of action shall have accrued']....) In other words, statutes of limitation do not begin to run until a cause of action accrues...." (*Fox, supra,* 35 Cal.4th at p. 806, 27 Cal.Rptr.3d 661, 110 P.3d 914.) ..."Generally speaking, a cause of action accrues at 'the time when the cause of action is complete with all of its elements.'... An important exception to the general rule of accrual is the 'discovery rule,' which postpones accrual of a cause of action until the plaintiff discovers, or has reason to discover, the cause of action....

"A plaintiff has reason to discover a cause of action when he or she 'has reason at least to suspect a factual basis for its elements.'... Under the discovery rule, suspicion of one or more of the elements of a cause of action, coupled with knowledge of any remaining elements, will generally trigger the statute of limitations period.... [The Supreme Court] explained that by discussing the discovery rule in terms of a plaintiff's suspicion of 'elements' of a cause of action, it was referring to the 'generic' elements of wrongdoing, causation, and harm.... In so using the term 'elements,' [the Supreme Court does] not take a hypertechnical approach to the application of the discovery rule. Rather than examining whether the plaintiffs suspect facts supporting each specific legal element of a particular cause of action, we look to whether the plaintiffs have reason to at least suspect that a type of wrongdoing has injured them." (*Fox, supra,* 35 Cal.4th at pp. 806–807, 27 Cal.Rptr.3d 661, 110 P.3d 914.) ... "The discovery rule only delays accrual until the plaintiff

---

2. The parties make no argument concerning whether the one-year or two-year limitations period applies in this case. We need not decide the issue because, even if the applicable period is two years from accrual, that period expired long before Doe filed her complaint.

has, or should have, inquiry notice of the cause of action. The discovery rule does not encourage dilatory tactics because plaintiffs are charged with presumptive knowledge of an injury if they have ‘ “ “ ‘information of circumstances to put [them] *on inquiry*’ ” ’ ” or if they have “ “ ‘*the opportunity to obtain knowledge* from sources open to [their] investigation.’ ” ’ … In other words, plaintiffs are required to conduct a reasonable investigation after becoming aware of an injury, and are charged with knowledge of the information that would have been revealed by such an investigation.” (*Fox, supra,* 35 Cal.4th at pp. 807–808, 27 Cal.Rptr.3d 661, 110 P.3d 914, fn. omitted, original italics.) …

Doe filed her complaint many years after her sons were molested. Recognizing this, Doe contends that her fraud causes of action are timely because she did not learn of the molestations until April 2007. She further contends that she was not on inquiry notice before she gained actual knowledge of the molestations.… Doe bases her delayed discovery argument on the fact that she did not know about the molestation of her sons until within three years of the filing of her complaint. However, the circumstances of nearly 20 years ago, known to Doe, prompted a duty to investigate whether her sons had been molested. Doe knew that Urbina and Beltran had considerable unsupervised access to her sons. Thereafter, Urbina fled the country in 1989, having pled guilty to child molestation charges. Beltran fled the country in 1991, accused of child molestation. After her sons’ molestations, they suffered individual and relationship problems, including with Doe, and she lost their “services.” These facts, which appear on the face of the complaint, taken together, constituted “ “ “ ‘information of circumstances’ ” ’ ” sufficient to “ “ “ ‘put [Doe] on inquiry.’ ” ’ ” (*Fox, supra,* 35 Cal.4th at pp. 807–808, 27 Cal.Rptr.3d 661, 110 P.3d 914, italics omitted.) Doe was “required to conduct a reasonable investigation after becoming aware of an injury” and therefore was “charged with knowledge of the information that would have been revealed by such an investigation.” (*Id.* at p. 808, 27 Cal.Rptr.3d 661, 110 P.3d 914.)

Doe makes several arguments against the conclusion that she was put on inquiry nearly 20 years before she filed the complaint. She claims (1) her sons may not have told her of the molestations if she asked, (2) the Diocese misrepresented the facts to her, (3) she did not discover the molestation of her sons until April 2007, and (4) the complaint does not establish that she knew that Urbina and Beltran fled the country because of their molestation of children. Each claim fails to persuade us that she was not put on inquiry nearly 20 years earlier.… Doe claims that she should be excused from having investigated nearly 20 years ago because an investigation may not have revealed the abuse. In support of this, she claims generally that there are “volumes of literature on child sexual abuse” suggesting that “mortification, self-blame, fear, guilt, shame or a combination of these and other emotions common to victims of sexual abuse—not to mention the influence of cultural taboos, especially in the Mexican-American community—would lead the boys to tell their mother that nothing had happened.” This claim misconstrues the duty to investigate. Doe was not under a duty to discover, merely to investigate diligently. If she had diligently investigated nearly 20 years ago, she would have satisfied her duty to investigate, regardless of whether other forces, such as her sons’ emotional state, may or may not have prevented her from gaining actual knowledge of the molestation. If she had diligently investigated, she could now show that diligent investigation did not reveal the molestation, rather than simply speculating that might be so. Because she did not diligently investigate—she did not investigate at all—she cannot now rebut the presumptive knowledge she had nearly 20 years ago of the abuse. (See *Fox, supra,* 35 Cal.4th at pp. 807–808, 27 Cal.Rptr.3d 661, 110 P.3d 914.) …

Furthermore, neither the Diocese’s alleged misrepresentations nor Doe’s actual ignorance of the molestations relieved Doe of the duty to investigate. Misrepresentations are a part of every fraud cause of action; nonetheless, the duty to investigate arises if the circumstances indicate that the defendant's representations may have been false. (*Vai v. Bank of America* (1961) 56 Cal.2d 329, 343, 15 Cal.Rptr. 71, 364 P.2d 247.) Here, Doe alleges that the Diocese represented that Urbina and Beltran were not child molesters. The circumstances, however, cast serious doubt on those representations, to the extent that Doe cannot now simply allege that the Diocese misrepresented the facts. "'[D]iscovery is different from knowledge, [so] that where a party defrauded has received information of facts which should put him upon inquiry, and the inquiry if made would disclose the fraud, he will be charged with a discovery as of the time the inquiry would have given him knowledge.' ..." (*Ibid.*) Even taking as true the allegations that the Diocese misrepresented the facts and that Doe did not know about the molestations until April 2007, Doe had a duty to investigate nearly 20 years before she filed the complaint. At that point, the fraud causes of action accrued.

Equally unavailing is Doe's assertion the complaint does not establish she knew that Urbina and Beltran fled the country because of their molestation of children. On appeal, Doe argues that "[t]he complaint does not allege that she knew [at the time the priests fled] of the molestation charges against the priests." It is true that the complaint does not plead that she knew why the priests fled, but the only reasonable interpretation of the complaint as a whole is that she knew. (See *Fox, supra,* 35 Cal.4th at p. 810, 27 Cal.Rptr.3d 661, 110 P.3d 914 [we give complaint reasonable interpretation].) ... Doe alleged that she was associated with the Diocese for more than 20 years. She was employed by the Diocese for nearly 20 years, in the parish where Urbina and Beltran were employed. Urbina was her counselor, and Beltran was her counselor and employer. Urbina pled guilty to child molestation charges, then fled the country. Beltran fled under accusation of child molestation. Both priests had unsupervised access to Doe's sons. The majority of parishioners believed that the priests were falsely accused. This attitude was "widespread" in the parish. The complaint alleged that "[Doe] could not believe that her priests would commit such horrific acts." She shared the belief that the priests were falsely accused.... No reasonable person could conclude from these alleged facts that Doe did not know, nearly 20 years ago, why Urbina and Beltran fled the country. She was closely associated with the parish and, especially, the specific priests. The reason for the priests' flight was well known. She, herself, did not believe the accusations. Therefore, her argument that she did not know why Urbina and Beltran fled fails.

Doe has not carried her burden to establish, through adequate pleading, that the fraud causes of action did not accrue nearly 20 years ago. She has failed to show diligence in investigating her claims; therefore, she has not rebutted the presumption that she knew of the cause of her injuries when it occurred. (*Fox, supra,* 35 Cal.4th at pp. 807–808, 27 Cal.Rptr.3d 661, 110 P.3d 914.) The trial court did not err in sustaining the demurrer as to those causes of action....

Concerning her negligence causes of action, Doe repeats her assertion that the discovery rule delayed accrual of her causes of action until she actually knew that her sons had been molested. This assertion is without merit for the reasons already discussed.... Doe additionally asserts, however, that "the Diocese was negligent toward *her,* and her claims are controlled by when *she, herself, became aware* that her rights and interests had been harmed—*i.e.* when she learned for the first time that her sons had been molested." (Original italics.) For this proposition, Doe offers no authority. The point is therefore forfeited. (*Badie v. Bank of America* (1998) 67 Cal.App.4th 779, 784–785, 79 Cal.Rptr.2d 273 [appellant forfeits any point not supported by reasoned argument and citations to authority].) In any event, the actions giving rise to Doe's negligence causes of action occurred about two decades ago. As discussed above, she is charged with presumptive knowledge of the injury when it occurred and has failed to rebut the presumption by application of the discovery rule. (*Fox, supra,* 35 Cal.4th at pp. 807–808, 27 Cal.Rptr.3d 661, 110 P.3d 914.) ...

The judgment is affirmed. The Diocese is awarded its costs on appeal. (Cal. Rules of Court, rule 8.278(a).)

We concur: ROBIE and CANTIL-SAKAUYE, JJ.

2. Public Policy

Hornback v. Archdiocese of Milwaukee

Supreme Court of Wisconsin, 2008
2008 WI 98, 313 Wis. 2d 294, 752 N.W.2d 862

LOUIS B. BUTLER, JR., J.

Kenneth W. Hornback, Dennis L. Bolton, Ronald W. Kuhl, David W. Schaeffer and Glenn M. Bonn (the plaintiffs) seek review of a court of appeals decision[1] that affirmed the circuit court's dismissal of the plaintiffs' complaint against the Archdiocese of Milwaukee (the Archdiocese) and the Diocese[2] of Madison (the Diocese), along with their insurance companies....

On October 3, 2005, the plaintiffs filed a complaint against the Archdiocese of Milwaukee, the Diocese of Madison, and their insurance companies. In the complaint, each of the plaintiffs alleges being a child victim of sexual abuse at some point between the years of 1968 and 1973 at the hands of Gary Kazmarek, who was a teacher at the Catholic school the plaintiffs attended in Louisville, Kentucky, Our Mother of Sorrows. The complaint describes an ongoing pattern of sexual abuse of children by Kazmarek over the years. The plaintiffs allege that prior to 1964, he had engaged in inappropriate sexual conduct while at a Catholic seminary; that between 1964 and 1966, he abused more than two dozen children while a teacher at St. John de Nepomuc School in the Milwaukee Archdiocese; that he subsequently admitted to sexually abusing up to ten more children at St. Bernard School in the Madison Diocese; and that the pattern of sexual abuse continued while he was a teacher at Our Mother of Sorrows for approximately five years, beginning in 1967.

The complaint alleges that the Diocese "knew or should have known of Kazmarek's propensity for sexually abusing children and, despite this knowledge, did not refer Kazmarek to the police or take any other action to prevent Kazmarek from continuing his pattern of sexually abusing children." The complaint further alleges that the failure of the Diocese to refer Kazmarek to the police and/or to take "other action to prevent Kazmarek's continuation of his pattern of sexually abusing children"[4] constitutes negligence, and that

---

1. *Hornback v. Archdiocese of Milwaukee,* No.2006AP291, 298 Wis.2d 248, 726 N.W.2d 357, unpublished slip op. (Wis.Ct.App. Nov. 28, 2006).

2. Although the plaintiffs alternatively refer to the Diocese of Madison as an "Archdiocese," their caption correctly identifies it as the "Madison Diocese," which is also the title most frequently used by the parties in this case, and the title we will use. The correct title of the Diocese of Madison is not at issue and has no substantive bearing on our decision.

4. At oral argument to this court, the plaintiffs specified that such negligence in failing to take other action specifically included a negligent failure to warn unforeseeable third parties—including "other dioceses within the United States, the parochial school systems ... or the parents of unforeseeable victims"—of Kazmarek's propensity for sexual abuse.

the Diocese's negligent conduct was a substantial factor in causing Kazmarek's sexual abuse of and resulting injuries to the plaintiffs. The complaint adds that discovery of Kazmarek's sexual abuse of children in Wisconsin and of the Diocese's negligent conduct did not occur until October 2002.

The Archdiocese filed a motion to dismiss parallel claims against it on October 21, 2005, arguing that the plaintiffs' claims were barred by the statute of limitations. In the alternative, the Archdiocese argued that public policy considerations regarding the delay in bringing this case preclude the liability for the plaintiffs' claims, maintaining that such public policy concerns "strongly militate against permitting 32 year old claims based on alleged assaults, where most other witnesses and relevant evidence are dead." On October 27, 2005, the Diocese also filed a motion to dismiss, adopting the Archdiocese's memorandum in support of dismissal.... The plaintiffs responded that the motions to dismiss should be denied because the plaintiffs' claims were not barred by the statute of limitations and because public policy favors litigation of the issues presented in the case rather than encouraging the concealment of information by employers about sexual abusers in their midst.

The circuit court held a motion hearing on December 19, 2005. In a ruling based on statute of limitations grounds, the court granted the defendants' motions to dismiss, and an order dismissing the case was filed on January 4, 2006.... The plaintiffs appealed, and on November 28, 2006, the court of appeals affirmed the circuit court's order, also confining its discussion to the statute of limitations issue. *Hornback v. Archdiocese of Milwaukee*, No.2006AP291, 298 Wis.2d 248, 726 N.W.2d 357, unpublished slip op. (Wis.Ct.App. Nov. 28, 2006). Review was granted on October 11, 2007....

In Wisconsin, the sufficiency of a negligence claim depends on whether a complaint alleges facts adequately establishing the following four required elements: "(1) the existence of a duty of care on the part of the defendant, (2) a breach of that duty of care, (3) a causal connection between the defendant's breach of the duty of care and the plaintiff's injury, and (4) actual loss or damage resulting from the injury." *Gritzner*, 235 Wis.2d 781, ¶ 19, 611 N.W.2d 906 (citing *Miller v. Wal-Mart Stores, Inc.*, 219 Wis.2d 250, 260, 580 N.W.2d 233 (1998); *Rockweit v. Senecal*, 197 Wis.2d 409, 418, 541 N.W.2d 742 (1995)). The first two elements, duty and breach, are often presented to juries in the form of a question about whether the defendant was negligent, with the causation and damages questions asked separately. *See Nichols v. Progressive N. Ins. Co.*, 2008 WI 20, ¶ 12, 308 Wis.2d 17, 746 N.W.2d 220 (citing Wis JI—Civil 1005 (2006))....

As we summarized the law in *Nichols*, we said that although "liability has been limited in a negligence case based on the absence of a duty, liability in the vast majority of negligence cases in Wisconsin is guided, when determining whether to limit liability, by consideration of public policy factors, as *Gritzner* [lead opinion] and *Rockweit* demonstrate." *Id.*, ¶ 47.... Negligence and liability are two distinct concepts. *See Hoida*, 291 Wis.2d 283, ¶ 25, 717 N.W.2d 17. Even if the elements of negligence are established or assumed in a case, liability is not guaranteed, but may still be restricted by Wisconsin courts on the basis of judicially recognized policy factors. *Id.*, ¶ 24 (citing *Smaxwell v. Bayard*, 2004 WI 101, ¶ 39, 274 Wis.2d 278, 682 N.W.2d 923). Even though we can consider the public policy factors to preclude liability, such an analysis generally first requires a determination of whether the elements of negligence have been sufficiently alleged, or at least an assumption that negligence exists. *See Nichols*, 308 Wis.2d 17, ¶¶ 18, 19, 746 N.W.2d 220.... In this case, we proceed to first examine the claims under a standard motion to dismiss inquiry focusing on the elements of the claim alleged. For the reasons below, we conclude that the plaintiffs have not set forth a claim against the Diocese upon which relief may be granted because the plaintiff has not alleged that the defendant has failed to exercise ordinary care under the circumstances of the case; the failure to warn alleged by the plaintiffs does not constitute negligence in the instant case. We then separately examine whether, even assuming negligence had been sufficiently claimed, public policy factors would nonetheless preclude liability....

As a starting point of a negligence analysis, we recognize in Wisconsin that everyone has a duty to act with reasonable and ordinary care under the circumstances. *See Hoida*, 291 Wis.2d 283, ¶ 30, 717 N.W.2d 17. This "first element, a duty of care, is established under Wisconsin law whenever it was foreseeable to the defendant that his or her act or omission to act might cause harm to some other person." *Gritzner*, 235 Wis.2d 781, ¶ 20, 611 N.W.2d 906 (citations omitted).... The more specific component of a standard negligence inquiry involves whether there has been a breach of that ordinary care under the circumstances of the case. As we explained in *Hoida*, "what is comprised within ordinary care may depend on ... whether the alleged tortfeasor assumed a special role in regard to the injured party." *Hoida*, 291 Wis.2d 283, ¶ 32, 717 N.W.2d 17. In *Gritzner*, we recognized that the specific type of negligence alleged, a negligent failure to warn, "depending on the circumstances, may be a breach of the duty of ordinary care." *See Gritzner*, 235 Wis.2d 781, ¶ 76, 611 N.W.2d 906 (Abrahamson, C.J., concurring).... Thus, in the vast majority of cases, whether a defendant has acted negligently "'is not examined in terms of whether or not there is a duty to do a specific act, but rather whether the conduct satisfied the duty placed upon individuals to exercise that degree of care as would be exercised by a reasonable person under the circumstances.'" *Nichols*, 308 Wis.2d 17, ¶ 45, 746 N.W.2d 220. *See also Schuster v. Altenberg*, 144 Wis.2d 223, 238 n. 3, 424 N.W.2d 159 (1988) (citations omitted):

> Under Wisconsin's broad definition of duty, we need not engage in analytical gymnastics to arrive at our result by first noting that at common law, a person owes no duty to control the conduct of another person or warn of such conduct, and then finding exception to that general rule where the defendant stands in a special relationship to either the person whose conduct needs to be controlled or in a relationship to the foreseeable victim of the conduct.

In this case, the plaintiffs' complaint alleges that the elements constituting negligence include the facts that the Diocese "knew or should have known of Kazmarek's propensity for sexually abusing children and, despite this knowledge, did not refer Kazmarek to the police or take any other action to prevent Kazmarek from continuing his pattern of sexually abusing children." ... The plaintiffs' description of the "other action" the Diocese failed to take, thereby constituting negligence, has varied. In their brief to this court, the plaintiffs alleged that the Diocese:

> (1) knew or should have known of the dangerous propensities of Kazmarek, (2) attempted to conceal the sexual assaults from authorities, (3) represented to parents that Kazmarek would be sent for treatment, [and] (4) represented to parents [that] Kazmarek would never have contact with children again, yet despite this knowledge and these representations, failed to report Kazmarek to authorities, send him for treatment, or take any other action consistent with their duty of care.

However, during oral arguments, the plaintiffs acknowledged that it had been the Milwaukee Archdiocese only that had, as the complaint claims, made representations that Kazmarek would be sent for treatment, and that he would never have contact with children again. The plaintiffs asserted at oral argument that it made no difference to their negligence claim that only the Archdiocese had made an affirmative promise, because the specific breach of duty claim they allege in this case emanated from the knowledge that both the Diocese and Archdiocese had of Kazmarek's propensity. The plaintiffs then reframed their negligence claim, clarifying that the complaint's reference to a failure to take "other action" is, more specifically, a failure to warn unforeseeable third parties—including "other dioceses within the United States, the parochial school systems ... or the parents" of unforeseeable victims—of Kazmarek's propensity for sexual abuse.... Viewing the complaint in conjunction with the plaintiffs' clarification of their arguments during oral argument, we conclude that the plaintiffs' negligence claim is premised on an alleged failure to warn unforeseeable third parties, including any potential future employers of Kazmarek at dioceses and parochial school systems everywhere in the country, as well as parents of unforeseeable victims.[6]

Incorporating the arguments made in the Archdiocese's brief to this court, the Diocese argues that common law tort rules do not impose a duty on employers to seek out and disclose information to an employee's subsequent employers or the public at large concerning a former employee's history of misconduct or antisocial behavior. The Diocese argues that under the law of "negligent referral or duty to warn," unless an employer gives a favorable reference to a subsequent employer or third party about the former employee while withholding negative information, there is no breach of duty established by the employer's failure to seek out subsequent employers and alert them to prior negative history of the former employee.

Although acknowledging that this has not been expressly adopted in Wisconsin case law, the Diocese cites as an analogous case *Mackenzie v. Miller Brewing Co.*, 2000 WI App 48, 234 Wis.2d 1, 608 N.W.2d 331, in which the court of appeals declined to recognize a duty of employers to disclose to employees possible negative corporate events and developments. The Diocese suggests that in Wisconsin, we should follow the rationale of a California negligent referral case, *Randi W. v. Muroc Joint Unified School District*, 14 Cal.4th 1066, 60 Cal.Rptr.2d 263, 929 P.2d 582, 591–93 (1997), and recognize that absent a positive job reference, mere knowledge of an employee's negative personal history is not enough to create a duty of notification to subsequent employers. As such, in this case, there should be no such duty imposed on the defendants, argues the Diocese, considering how far removed the plaintiffs are from the relationships between Kazmarek and the Diocese of Madison. The Diocese emphasizes that it never spoke to the Archdiocese of Louisville about Kazmarek, that the plaintiffs never allege such communication occurred, and that there is therefore no negligence under these circumstances.

The plaintiffs respond that this case fits squarely within the duty of ordinary care all persons owe one another, and should be guided by passages from two specific Wisconsin precedents addressing negligent failure to warn, *Gritzner*, 235 Wis.2d 781, ¶¶ 23, 43, 611 N.W.2d 906, and *Schuster*, 144 Wis.2d at 235, 424 N.W.2d 159. The plaintiffs argue that because the Diocese in this case knew Kazmarek abused up to ten children at one of its schools, it should have deduced Kazmarek's continued danger to other children; and that its failure to warn constituted negligence.... A proper analysis of this issue is framed in terms of the ordinary care all persons owe one another under the circumstances, as opposed to a particular "duty to warn." However, we also recognize that in some cases,

---

6. During oral argument, upon conceding that it was the Archdiocese of Milwaukee only and not the Diocese of Madison that made affirmative promises to report Kazmarek to the police and keep him from children, and upon reframing the claimed breach of duty as a failure to warn dioceses, schools and parents, the plaintiffs also appeared to drop their claim that the failure to report Kazmarek to the police also constituted negligence.

the failure to warn may be a breach of duty of ordinary care. *Gritzner*, 235 Wis.2d 781, ¶ 76, 611 N.W.2d 906 (Abrahamson, C.J., concurring).

We conclude that the third party failure to warn claims recognized in this state do not encompass the type of failure to warn claimed by the plaintiffs. We do not decide today whether to adopt the negligent referral approach of *Randi W.* We emphasize that even if we did recognize such negligent referral claims, the general rule under *Randi W.* is that employers who actively provide recommendations of employees "should not be held accountable to third persons for failing to disclose negative information regarding a former employee...." *Randi W.*, 60 Cal.Rptr.2d 263, 929 P.2d at 584 (emphasis added). *Randi W.* provides only a narrow exception allowing that tort liability for fraud or negligent misrepresentation may be created "if, as alleged here, the recommendation letter amounts to an *affirmative misrepresentation* presenting a foreseeable and substantial risk of physical harm to a third person." *Id.*[7] (Emphasis in original.) ...

In this case, no affirmative misrepresentation of the type recognized under a negligent referral analysis has been alleged, let alone any type of communication about Kazmarek from the Diocese of Madison to the Archdiocese of Louisville. The Diocese's mere knowledge of Kazmarek's past sexual abuse, or a presumed knowledge of a continued sexual propensity for abuse, is not enough to establish negligence. Reasonable and ordinary care does not require the Diocese to notify all potential subsequent employers within dioceses and parochial school systems across the country, along with all parents of future unforeseeable victims. Requiring such notification under these circumstances would create a vast obligation dramatically exceeding any approach to failure to warn recognized either in this state or in other jurisdictions....

More importantly, in this case, the specific victims were unforeseeable. Foreseeability of specific victims becomes relevant when an affirmative obligation is argued, such as the obligation to warn. *See Hoida*, 291 Wis.2d 283, ¶¶ 32, 34, 717 N.W.2d 17. Moreover, the Diocese did not assume a special role in regard to the injured parties.... Thus, the rationale in *Gritzner* for recognizing a potential negligence failure to warn claim does not extend to this case in part because there is no direct contact of any sort alleged between the plaintiffs and defendants in this case....

On the one hand, the plaintiffs in this case had virtually no relationship with the Diocese. There are significant gaps temporally and geographically, with the plaintiffs separated from the Diocese by several state lines and their abuse separated from Kazmarek's employment with the Diocese by a number of years, and the complaint never indicated that their paths crossed at all prior to the plaintiffs filing this action. Thus, the relationship between the parties in this case is quite attenuated.... There is no state in which employers are recognized as being negligent for failing to seek out, find, and warn future employers of sexually dangerous former employees. Even those states that have recognized a negligent referral doctrine do not impose liability when a referral letter is sent by a past employer to a future employer of such an employee unless actual misrepresentations are made in

---

7. In *Randi W.*, an employer alleged to have knowingly concealed material facts about a past employee's sexual misconduct with students wrote a letter of reference for the employee that "allegedly extolled Gadams's [the employee's] 'genuine concern' for and 'outstanding rapport' with students, knowing that Gadams had engaged in inappropriate physical contact with them. [The former employer] declared in the letter that he 'wouldn't hesitate to recommend Mr. Gadams for any position!'" *Randi W. v. Muroc Joint Unified Sch. Dist.*, 14 Cal.4th 1066, 60 Cal.Rptr.2d 263, 929 P.2d 582, 592–93 (1997).

such a letter. *See Randi W.*, 60 Cal.Rptr.2d 263, 929 P.2d at 584.... Thus, we conclude that the plaintiffs' complaint fails to allege negligence (duty of care and breach thereof) sufficiently to survive a motion to dismiss. Although the plaintiffs allege that the Diocese knew that Kazmarek had a propensity for sexual abuse, what is more pertinent is what the plaintiffs did not allege. They did not allege that the Diocese knew that Kazmarek was in Kentucky, still teaching children, or working for the Archdiocese in Louisville. They did not allege any knowledge that the children at the Mother of Sorrow School in Louisville were in any danger. They did not allege that the Archdiocese of Louisville asked the Diocese for a reference, that the Diocese made a reference recommending Kazmarek, or that the Diocese had any communication whatsoever with the Archdiocese of Louisville regarding Kazmarek.

The plaintiffs also fail to provide legal authority supporting their arguments. They argue that the duty of ordinary care in this case encompasses a specific obligation to warn all parochial schools and dioceses in this country, as well as future parents of unforeseeable victims, but have cited no cases in which the failure to warn third parties has been described in such sweeping terms.... Consequently, the plaintiffs have not stated a claim for negligence. They have not alleged that the defendant fell below the standard of care under the circumstances. We decline to rule that under the general duty of ordinary care recognized in Wisconsin, an employer may be found negligent for failing to warn unforeseen third parties of a dangerous former employee. Such a ruling would extend an employer's obligation to warn indefinitely into the future to a sweeping category of persons, thereby requiring employers to warn nearly all potential future employers or victims, as the plaintiffs in this case argue....

We next address the public policy concerns generated by this case. In Wisconsin, we recognize six public policy grounds upon which this court may deny liability even in the face of proven or assumed negligence:

> (1) "the injury is too remote from the negligence"; (2) the recovery is " 'wholly out of proportion to the culpability of the negligent tort-feasor' "; (3) the harm caused is highly extraordinary given the negligent act; (4) recovery "would place too unreasonable a burden" on the negligent tort-feasor; (5) recovery would be "too likely to open the way to fraudulent claims"; and (6) recovery would enter into " 'a field that has no sensible or just stopping point.' "

Hoida, 291 Wis.2d 283, ¶41, 717 N.W.2d 17. This court may refuse to impose liability on the basis of any of these factors without full resolution of a cause of action by trial. *Stephenson v. Universal Metrics, Inc.*, 2002 WI 30, ¶¶42–43, 251 Wis.2d 171, 641 N.W.2d 158....

Even assuming the complaint in this case stated a claim for negligence, the plaintiffs' claims would nonetheless be precluded because allowing recovery would be the beginning of a descent down a slippery slope with no sensible or just stopping point. A decision to the contrary would create precedent suggesting that employers have an obligation to search out and disclose to all potential subsequent employers, which could include in an employment context every school in the country or beyond, all matters concerning an ex-employee's history. In *Gritzner*, this court contrasted its decision to remand the case for further fact-finding with a decision in another case to deny liability on public policy grounds, *Kelli T-G v. Charland*, 198 Wis.2d 123, 542 N.W.2d 175 (Ct.App.1995).[9] The

---

9. In *Gritzner*, this court also emphasized that the reason for remanding for fact-finding rather than deciding that case on public policy grounds was because we knew

difference, a majority of this court explained in *Gritzner*, is that in *Kelli T-G*, there was not the same kind of special relationship as there was between the defendant in *Gritzner* and the children who had been entrusted into his care. *Gritzner*, 235 Wis.2d 781, ¶ 77 n. 2, 86, 611 N.W.2d 906 (Abrahamson, C.J., concurring).

This case is more akin to *Kelli T-G* than to *Gritzner*. *Kelli T-G* was a case involving negligence claims brought by the guardian ad litem of a child who had been sexually abused and the child's mother. *Kelli T-G*, 198 Wis.2d at 125–26, 542 N.W.2d 175. The mother argued that the one of the defendants, who was formerly married to the perpetrator at the time, had failed to warn the mother that her ex-husband was a pedophile who posed a danger to the child. *Id.* In that case, the defendant testified in deposition that even though she was concerned at the time and felt that she had an obligation to warn the child's mother about her ex-husband's pedophile offenses, she did not follow up with the mother after initially giving the mother her phone number. *See id.* at 127–28, 542 N.W.2d 175.

The court of appeals concluded in that case that liability was precluded by the judicially recognized public policy ground that "allowance of recovery would enter a field that has no sensible or just stopping point." *Id.* at 130, 542 N.W.2d 175 (citation omitted). Specifying its concerns in that case, the court explained that the plaintiffs' failure to warn arguments left unresolved such questions as whether an obligation to warn depended on specific types of knowledge about a person's proclivity to pedophilia, how the obligation would vary if the defendant were a mental health or criminal justice professional, whether an obligation to warn exists regardless of whether a believed pedophile had been charged but never criminally convicted, whether a person could be liable for issuing a warning about someone who was not actually a pedophile, and to whom warnings must be given beyond the parties. *Id.* at 130–32, 542 N.W.2d 175.

Such questions remain unanswered in this case as well. It appears that the plaintiffs here would require that every individual with knowledge about a former employee potentially posing a danger to unforeseen future victims must warn thousands of individuals and organizations across the country, from dioceses to parochial school systems to even a broad and undefined category of parents of unforeseen future victims. The plaintiffs offer no parameters or guidance about how to make such a warning requirement feasible. Feasibility notwithstanding, there are other serious policy concerns which we share with the *Kelli T-G* court. The court of appeals in *Kelli T-G* explained:

> Tragically, sexual abuse has brought devastating consequences to countless children and their families. Sadly, our society has discovered that many pedophiles elude the control of the criminal justice system. Many seem unchanged despite psychotherapeutic intervention and the rehabilitation efforts of corrections, probation, and parole. As pedophiles sexually abuse children again and again, some state legislatures, in a desperate effort to locate new methods to stop the

---

> very little of the circumstances and facts of this case. We do not know, for example, about Michael's prior "inappropriate sexual acts" with female children, or how many victims were involved. We do not know whether Michael was adjudged a delinquent. We do not know whether Michael's previous inappropriate sexual act or acts were the subject of any juvenile court proceedings.

Gritzner, 235 Wis.2d 781, ¶ 81, 611 N.W.2d 906 (Abrahamson, C.J., concurring) (citations omitted). Such is not the case here.

assaults, debate whether to enact "neighborhood notification" laws to warn citizens of paroled child molesters living in their communities. Thus, legislatures debate the appropriate scope of *government's* duty to warn and they struggle to define sensible starting and stopping points. For government, the struggle is extremely difficult as a matter of public policy. For an individual citizen, the struggle is extremely difficult as a matter of morality, and virtually impossible as a matter of law.

Kelli T-G, 198 Wis.2d at 131–32, 542 N.W.2d 175 (emphasis in original). We agree.

We emphasize that this court finds abhorrent any type of facilitation of sexual abuse by third parties. It is critical that sexual abuse victims receive full justice through our criminal and civil laws to the extent legally possible. In this case, the plaintiffs are not being denied compensation for their alleged injuries at the hands of Kazmarek. To the contrary, the record in this case contains undisputed information that prior to filing this lawsuit, the plaintiffs had already received compensation for a settlement received in a lawsuit directly against Kazmarek and the Louisville Archdiocese.

Furthermore, unlike the allegation against the Milwaukee Archdiocese, there was no similar allegation that the Madison Diocese made affirmative statements to parents in Wisconsin about steps it would take to try to prevent future abuse by Kazmarek. Without concluding one way or another what effect the statements made by the Milwaukee Archdiocese would make on our determination of their liability,[11] we conclude that as to the Diocese, the plaintiffs ask us to grant liability on the basis of nothing more than a breach of duty created by the Diocese's knowledge of Kazmarek's propensity for sexual abuse combined with the Diocese's failure to warn a broad group of potential future employers of Kazmarek and parents of unforeseen victims about Kazmarek.

The primary public policy problem with recognizing the claim as presented by the plaintiffs is that there is no sensible stopping point to recognizing negligence claims for such an open-ended and ill-defined sweeping claim. Recognizing the plaintiffs' claim against the Diocese in this case could result in requiring all employers to warn all unforeseen potential future employers of any number of problems related to any number of past employees. It could further result in all parents who become aware that their child was sexually abused then facing potential liability for not warning every other parent who might also have children at risk of being in contact with the perpetrator.... There must be limits. We draw one here....

We further conclude that the plaintiffs have not alleged an actionable claim for negligence against the Diocese of Madison under which relief could be granted under Wisconsin negligence law. The type of failure to warn claim recognized under Wisconsin law does not extend as far as the plaintiffs argue. We finally conclude that even if a viable negligence claim had been made, recovery against the Diocese would be precluded on the public policy ground that allowing recovery would send this court down a slippery slope with no sensible or just stopping point. We therefore affirm the decision of the court of appeals, on different grounds.

The decision of the court of appeals is affirmed....

---

11. This court is equally divided on whether to affirm or reverse the decision of the court of appeals dismissing the plaintiffs' complaint against the Archdiocese of Milwaukee. Consequently, we affirm the court of appeals' decision to affirm the circuit court's dismissal of the plaintiffs' claims against the Archdiocese of Milwaukee, without further analysis of that issue.

3. Charitable Immunity

Stephen J. Riccardulli, Michael D. Dillon, and Amy S. Beard

Tort Liability of Religious Organizations

http://www.americanbar.org/newsletter/publications/law_trends_news_
practice_area_e_newsletter_home/litigation_runquist.html (2009)

As a general rule, churches and other religious institutions are not immune from tort liability in the modern world. For many years, the courts recognized a "charitable immunity" for certain religious and/or charitable institutions, but there is little left of such an immunity today. This follows the idea that injured parties be compensated for injuries caused by others, regardless of the intent of the actor.... [footnote omitted]. For the most part, courts will address wrongs caused by religious organizations in much the same manner as they would any other public or private entity....

Charitable immunity originated in England in 1846, and was adopted in the United States in 1876.... [footnote omitted]. The theories advanced for charitable immunity were varied. A "trust fund" theory held, in essence, that the monies possessed by charities were actually monies held "in trust" by the charity for distribution to others; and, as such, were not available to tort plaintiffs because the donor's intent would be frustrated, and the operation or existence of the charity compromised.... [footnote omitted]. Some jurisdictions recognized an "implied waiver" theory, which held that the beneficiary of a charity impliedly waived his right to sue the same charity for the negligence of its personnel, and assumed the risks of accepting the "benefits" of the aid provided.... [footnote omitted].... Another reason advanced for charitable immunity was that the rule of respondeat superior, whereby a master is liable for the torts of his servants acting within the scope of their employment, did not apply to charities because they derived no gain or benefit of their own for services rendered.... [footnote omitted]. Still another rationale was a vague "public policy" argument advocating immunity for charities, but typically adopting one of the other theories as validation for its application.

Charitable and religious organizations were granted immunity from tort liability by most jurisdictions in the United States until 1942, when it was abolished in the District of Columbia in the landmark case of *President and Dirs. of Georgetown College v. Hughes*, 130 F.2d 810 (D.C. Cir. 1942). A large number of states now follow that decision or have otherwise qualified the scope of their charitable immunity law.... [footnote omitted]. The change in the law may be attributed to changes in society. By the middle of the 20th century, charity had become "big business" and an exception to the general rule that "liability follows responsibility" no longer made sense.... [footnote omitted]. Nevertheless ... some jurisdictions still acknowledge some degree of charitable immunity.[9] Those

---

9. For example, in New Jersey, the Charitable Immunity Act protects any "nonprofit corporation, society or association organized exclusively for religious, charitable or educational purposes" from tort liability arising from negligence. N.J. Stat. Ann. 2A:53A-7 (West 2006); *see also Schultz v. Roman Catholic Archdiocese*, 472 A.2d 531 (N.J. 1984) (dismissing negligent hiring claims based on charitable immunity). Although still law, the N.J. Legislature proposed legislation that would abolish the charitable immunity with respect to claims related to sexual assault or other crimes of a sexual nature. *See* S. 487, 212 Leg., 2006 Sess. (N.J. 2006).

that still observe a level of charitable immunity may observe the immunity for religious organizations, but not for charitable hospitals; or may abolish the immunity to the extent that the charity is covered by liability insurance, or to the extent that the judgment can be satisfied by funds other than those held "in trust" by the charity. Because of the remaining vestiges of immunity in certain states, any analysis of a tort claim against a religious institution should begin with an examination of the existence of whether there is still any charitable immunity within the relevant jurisdiction.

Picher v. Roman Catholic Bishop of Portland

Supreme Judicial Court of Maine, 2009
2009 Me. 67, 974 A.2d 286

SILVER, J.

William Picher appeals from a judgment of the Superior Court (Kennebec County, *Marden, J.*) granting a summary judgment to the Roman Catholic Bishop of Portland on its affirmative defense of charitable immunity. Picher argues that we should abrogate the doctrine of charitable immunity for acts of negligence associated with the sexual abuse of a minor, and that we should not extend the doctrine to intentional torts. We hold that the doctrine should not be abrogated as to Picher's negligence claims because we see no basis for permitting charitable immunity as a defense to some types of negligence claims but not others. However, we also decline to interpret the relevant statute, 14 M.R.S. § 158 (2008),[1] to extend the reach of charitable immunity to intentional torts. We therefore vacate the judgment as to the intentional tort claim of fraudulent concealment but affirm the judgment as to the remaining claims....

Picher brought this suit against a former priest, Raymond Melville, and the Bishop, based on sexual abuse of Picher by Melville when Picher was a minor in the late 1980s. Picher asserted claims against Melville for negligence, sexual assault and battery, invasion of privacy, intentional infliction of emotional distress, clergy malpractice, and breach of fiduciary duty. Melville defaulted. Picher asserts claims against the Bishop for negligent supervision, breach of fiduciary duty, canonical agency, and fraudulent concealment of facts.... Picher alleges that the Bishop was on notice that Melville had abused a child before he was ordained as a priest and before he was assigned to the parish where the abuse of Picher occurred. Picher further alleges that the Bishop failed to report Melville to law enforcement officials and concealed Melville's propensities from parishioners and the public. The Bishop denies these allegations.

The Bishop is a corporation sole.[2] *See Fortin v. Roman Catholic Bishop of Portland*, 2005 ME 57, ¶ 3 & n. 1, 871 A.2d 1208, 1212. It operates as a non-profit organization and

---

1. Title 14 M.R.S. § 158 (2008) states:
A charitable organization shall be considered to have waived its immunity from liability for negligence or any other tort during the period a policy of insurance is effective covering the liability of the charitable organization for negligence or any other tort. Each policy issued to a charitable organization shall contain a provision to the effect that the insurer shall be estopped from asserting, as a defense to any claim covered by said policy, that such organization is immune from liability on the ground that it is a charitable organization. The amount of damages in any such case shall not exceed the limits of coverage specified in the policy, and the courts shall abate any verdict in any such action to the extent that it exceeds such policy limit.

2. The Bishop was formed as a corporation sole pursuant to P. & S.L. 1887, ch. 151, which states:
Sect. 1. The present Roman Catholic Bishop of the Diocese of Portland, and his successors

owns, maintains, and operates multiple churches, schools, and other properties. It has no capital stock and no provision for making dividends or profits, and it derives most of its revenues from charitable sources, although parochial school tuition and fees are not considered one of its charitable sources of revenue.... From July 1, 1986, to July 1, 1988, during the period when the alleged acts occurred, the Bishop was insured by Lloyd's of London pursuant to two consecutive policies, each of which contained an endorsement entitled "Sexual Misconduct Exclusion." This endorsement provides that "[s]exual or physical abuse or molestation of any person by the Assured, any employee of the Assured or any volunteer worker does not constitute personal injury within the terms of this policy and as such any claim arising, directly or indirectly, from the aforementioned is excluded."

The Bishop moved for summary judgment based on its affirmative defense of charitable immunity. The court granted the Bishop's motion, holding that the Bishop qualifies as a charitable organization and has not waived its charitable immunity pursuant to 14 M.R.S. § 158 because it has no insurance coverage for the claims made by Picher. The court also held that the doctrine of charitable immunity covers both intentional and negligent torts. After a damages hearing, a final judgment was entered against Melville in the amount of $4,227,875. Picher appealed the grant of a summary judgment in favor of the Bishop.... Picher does not explicitly argue that charitable immunity should be abrogated for all acts of negligence, but he does contend that it should be abrogated for acts of negligence in cases, such as this, involving the sexual abuse of a minor. The policy rationale supporting charitable immunity is the protection of charitable funds. *See Jensen v. Me. Eye & Ear Infirmary*, 107 Me. 408, 410–11, 78 A. 898, 899 (1910). Although the rationale itself may be challenged as outdated, as we discuss below, we would need persuasive grounds to hold that charitable funds should be protected against certain types of negligence claims but not others. Without any such grounds, we decline Picher's invitation and do not address the issue further.

Picher has, however, directly challenged the application of charitable immunity to all intentional torts, an issue we have not previously had occasion to consider. Our decision not to extend the doctrine to intentional torts is based on three aspects of its history: (1) charitable immunity is discredited and has been abandoned in the majority of jurisdictions; (2) the Legislature did not intend to expand the scope of the common law doctrine of charitable immunity when it enacted section 158; and (3) we have previously held that we would maintain, but not expand, the doctrine, and we would leave it to the Legislature to decide whether to abolish it. We address each of these in turn....

This Court introduced charitable immunity as a judicial doctrine almost one hundred years ago and adopted it as an affirmative defense available to non-profit organizations to bar negligence claims. *Jensen*, 107 Me. at 410–11, 78 A. at 899. In *Mendall v. Pleasant Mountain Ski Development, Inc.*, 159 Me. 285, 290, 191 A.2d 633, 636 (1963), we acknowledged, for historical purposes, the two policy justifications for charitable immunity that had been advanced in *Jensen*. These were "(1) that funds donated for charitable

---

in office, be and is hereby created a body politic and a corporation sole, under the name and style of the Roman Catholic Bishop of Portland, and by that name the said bishop and his successors in office, shall be known and shall hereafter have succession, with all the powers, rights and privileges prescribed, and subject to all the liabilities imposed by the general statutes of the state.

Sect. 2. The said corporation shall be empowered to receive, take and hold by sale, gift, lease, devise or otherwise, real and personal estate of every description for charitable, educational, burial, religious and church purposes, and to manage and dispose of the same by any form of legal conveyance or transfer according to the discipline and government of the Roman Catholic church, with full power and authority to borrow money and to convey by mortgage deed.

purposes are held in trust to be used exclusively for those purposes, and (2) that to permit the invasion of these funds to satisfy tort claims would destroy the sources of charitable support upon which the enterprise depends." *Id.* We upheld charitable immunity in *Mendall*, not because we concluded that these policy reasons were sound, but rather because non-profit organizations had relied upon charitable immunity for so long that abrogation of the doctrine would be far-reaching and should be undertaken by the Legislature. *Id.* ...

A review of the history of charitable immunity and its widespread rejection in other jurisdictions confirms that it remains a doctrine in general disrepute. Charitable immunity had a precarious start in this country after it had been tried and rejected in Great Britain. It was first adopted in the United States in *McDonald v. Massachusetts General Hospital*, 120 Mass. 432 (1876). The court relied on a line of English cases, originating in 1846 from *The Feoffes of Heriot's Hospital v. Ross*, (1846) 8 Eng. Rep. 1508 (H.L.). *See* Restatement (Second) of Torts § 895E cmt. b (1979) (discussing the history of charitable immunity). However, even before *McDonald* was decided, this line of cases had already been repudiated. *See id.* (citing *Mersey Docks v. Gibbs*, (1866) 11 Eng. Rep. 1500 (H.L.)). Eventually, however, most states recognized the doctrine. Restatement § 895E cmt. b.; *see also Flagiello v. Pa. Hosp.*, 417 Pa. 486, 208 A.2d 193, 200 (1965) (discussing the growth of the charitable immunity doctrine in the United States).

Despite its widespread adoption in the late nineteenth century and the first half of the twentieth century, charitable immunity began to erode quickly by the 1960s. Ira C. Lupu & Robert W. Tuttle, *Sexual Misconduct and Ecclesiastical Immunity*, 2004 BYU L.Rev. 1789, 1797–99 (2004). The Pennsylvania Supreme Court noted that the doctrine of charitable immunity "was built on a foundation of sand." *Flagiello*, 208 A.2d at 200 (citing *President & Dirs. of Georgetown Coll. v. Hughes*, 130 F.2d 810 (D.C.Cir.1942)). By 1984, "virtually all states with decisions on the subject at all ha[d] rejected the complete immunity of charities" with only two or three states having retained "full immunity in the absence of legislation to the contrary." W. Page Keeton et al., *Prosser & Keeton on the Law of Torts* § 133, at 1070 (W. Page Keeton ed., 5th ed.1984).

With respect to our neighboring states, charitable immunity has either never been adopted or has long been abolished. New Hampshire and Vermont have never adopted the doctrine. *Welch v. Frisbie Mem'l Hosp.*, 90 N.H. 337, 9 A.2d 761, 763–64 (1939); *Foster v. Roman Catholic Diocese of Vt.*, 116 Vt. 124, 70 A.2d 230, 237 (1950). In 1961, the Rhode Island Supreme Court upheld a statute establishing charitable immunity for hospitals, but it stated that "[t]he question of whether such immunity as a matter of public policy is sound or otherwise may be open to debate," and it left the debate to the legislature. *Fournier v. Miriam Hosp.*, 93 R.I. 299, 175 A.2d 298, 302 (1961). Seven years later, the legislature repealed the statute, *Carroccio v. Roger Williams Hosp.*, 104 R.I. 617, 247 A.2d 903, 904 n. 1 (1968), and thus abolished the last remaining application of charitable immunity in that state, *see Fournier*, 175 A.2d at 300–02 (noting that charitable immunity had been abolished judicially, except where the legislature had provided immunity to charitable hospitals). Connecticut abolished charitable immunity by statute in 1967. *See* Conn. Gen.Stat. Ann. § 52-557d (2005).

In 1971, after the Massachusetts Supreme Judicial Court threatened to abolish charitable immunity, the state legislature took note and abolished it, but limited the liability of charitable institutions to $20,000 for torts committed in the course of carrying out the charitable purpose. *English v. New England Med. Ctr., Inc.*, 405 Mass. 423, 541 N.E.2d 329, 331 (1989). An intentional tort, such as the one being alleged in this case, would likely fall outside of Massachusetts' statutory immunity, as it would not be considered to have been committed in the course of carrying out the charitable purpose. *See id.* In addition, even when Massachusetts first brought the doctrine of charitable immunity to America (before later abolishing it), the state's highest court implied that an exception existed for charities that did not hire their employees with due care. *McDonald*, 120 Mass. at 436 ("[I]f due care has been used by [the charity] in the selection of [its] inferior agents ... it cannot be made responsible.").

A review of the remaining jurisdictions shows that only a minority of them still recognize charitable immunity, and no state has applied the doctrine to intentional torts. According to the Restatement (Second) of Torts § 895E, Reporter's Notes (1982),[3] twenty-eight states, in addition to those mentioned above, and the District of Columbia have abolished the doctrine of charitable immunity by either supporting or adopting section 895E, which provides: "One engaged in a charitable, educational, religious or benevolent enterprise or activity is not for that reason immune from tort liability."[4] Restatement (Second) of Torts § 895E (1979). Ohio, Louisiana, and Nebraska have also abrogated the common law doctrine of charitable immunity. *Albritton v. Neighborhood Ctrs. Ass'n for Child Dev.*, 12 Ohio St.3d 210, 466 N.E.2d 867, 871 (1984); *Jackson v. Doe*, 296 So.2d 323, 323 (La.1974) (citing *Garlington v. Kingsley*, 289 So.2d 88, 93 (La.1974)); *Myers v. Drozda*, 180 Neb. 183, 141 N.W.2d 852, 854 (1966).

South Carolina initially recognized the doctrine of charitable immunity, but, in 1973, the South Carolina Supreme Court explicitly declined to extend it to intentional torts. In *Jeffcoat v. Caine*, the court noted the absence of a public policy rationale for extending charitable immunity to intentional torts, stating,

> Regardless of the public policy support, if there now be such, for a rule exempting a charity from liability for simple negligence, we know of no public policy, and none has been suggested, which would require the exemption of the charity from liability for an *intentional tort*; and we refuse to so extend the charitable immunity doctrine. 261 S.C. 75, 198 S.E.2d 258, 260 (1973) (emphasis added). South Carolina has since abolished the doctrine of charitable immunity as to all torts, although it limits the amount of damages one can recover from a charitable institution. *Bergstrom v. Palmetto Health Alliance*, 358 S.C. 388, 596 S.E.2d 42, 46 (2004).

New Jersey still recognizes charitable immunity, but does not grant immunity for intentional torts. *Hardwicke v. Am. Boychoir Sch.*, 902 A.2d 900, 917 (2006). In New Jersey, charitable immunity is provided by statute, immunizing charities from liability for negligence. *Id.* at 915. In *Hardwicke*, the New Jersey Supreme Court held that the state statute granting charitable immunity did not grant immunity for intentional torts. *Id.* at 917. Therefore, notwithstanding the New Jersey Legislature's codification of charitable immunity, the court declined to interpret the statute to provide immunity for intentional torts. *Id.*

Of the remaining states that retain some form of charitable immunity, no state has explicitly applied the doctrine to intentional torts. Virginia recognizes charitable immunity, but provides an exception for the negligent hiring of an employee who commits an

---

3. The 1982 publication of the appendix to the Restatement (Second) of Torts included a list of jurisdictions in support of section 895E. Restatement (Second) of Torts § 895E, Reporter's Notes (1982). Because later publications of the appendix to the Restatement do not include this information, we cite to the 1982 publication for this purpose only.

4. Those jurisdictions include: Alaska, Arizona, California, Delaware, District of Columbia, Florida, Idaho, Illinois, Indiana, Iowa, Kansas, Kentucky, Michigan, Minnesota, Mississippi, Missouri, Montana, Nevada, New York, North Carolina, North Dakota, Oklahoma, Oregon, Pennsylvania, Texas, Utah, Washington, West Virginia, and Wisconsin. Restatement § 895E, Reporter's Notes.

intentional tort. *J. v. Victory Tabernacle Baptist Church*, 236 Va. 206, 372 S.E.2d 391, 394 (1988). In *Victory Tabernacle Baptist Church*, a church hired an employee recently convicted of aggravated sexual assault of a minor. *Id.* at 392. As was the case here, the employee had duties that put him in contact with children. *Id.* The Virginia Supreme Court held that "the independent tort of negligent hiring operates as an exception to the charitable immunity of religious institutions." *Id.* at 394.

Alabama has not directly addressed whether charitable institutions should be liable for intentional torts, but the Alabama Supreme Court has otherwise limited the doctrine of charitable immunity, and in dicta implied that charities could be liable for the failure to use ordinary care in the selection of employees. *See Tucker v. Mobile Infirmary Ass'n*, 191 Ala. 572, 68 So. 4, 11 (1915). In addition, an Alabama statute granting immunity to the unpaid directors and officers of non-profit organizations does so only when individuals have not acted with willful or wanton misconduct. Ala.Code § 10-11-3 (Michie, LEXIS through 2009 Reg. Sess.).

In Maryland and Wyoming, the highest courts have not addressed whether the doctrine applies to intentional torts, but both have created intentional tort exceptions to other doctrines of immunity. *Lusby v. Lusby*, 283 Md. 334, 390 A.2d 77, 89 (1978) (noting that there is no interspousal immunity for intentional torts); *Mills v. Reynolds*, 837 P.2d 48, 55 (Wyo.1992) (holding that immunity for co-employees in workers' compensation cases does not apply to intentional tortfeasors). Arkansas and Colorado retain some form of charitable immunity, *see Low v. Insurance Co. of North America*, 364 Ark. 427, 220 S.W.3d 670, 674–80 (2005); *Hemenway v. Presbyterian Hospital Ass'n*, 161 Colo. 42, 419 P.2d 312, 313 (1966), but have never expressly applied it to intentional torts. The highest courts in Georgia and Tennessee have not addressed charitable immunity for intentional torts, but charitable immunity in both states only protects the property of charitable trusts. *Morehouse Coll. v. Russell*, 219 Ga. 717, 135 S.E.2d 432, 434 (1964); *Baptist Mem'l Hosp. v. Couillens*, 176 Tenn. 300, 140 S.W.2d 1088, 1091 (1940). Therefore, charitable institutions in those jurisdictions could potentially be liable for any tort, as long as the judgment is applied to non-charitable trust property. In Georgia, however, charitable trust funds can be used to satisfy a judgment against a charity that has failed to use ordinary care in the selection of its employees. *Morehouse Coll.*, 135 S.E.2d at 434.... Hawaii and South Dakota appear not to have addressed the doctrine of charitable immunity. Finally, New Mexico has not addressed the existence of charitable immunity. *See, e.g., Los Alamos Med. Ctr. v. Coe*, 58 N.M. 686, 275 P.2d 175, 181 (1954) (reserving the issue of the existence of charitable immunity)....

In 1965, the Legislature enacted 14 M.R.S. § 158, which limits the extent of the charitable immunity defense available to a non-profit organization that is covered by liability insurance. *See* P.L.1965, ch. 383. The Bishop argues that 14 M.R.S. § 158 should be interpreted to apply charitable immunity to intentional torts. This interpretation would require a determination that the Legislature intended to modify the common law because, at the time section 158 was enacted in 1965, the doctrine of charitable immunity had been applied to negligence actions, *see Mendall*, 159 Me. at 286–90, 191 A.2d at 634–36; *Jensen*, 107 Me. at 410–11, 78 A. at 899, but we had not had occasion to consider whether to apply the doctrine to intentional torts. When the Legislature modifies the common law by statute, it must do so with clear and unambiguous language:

> [W]e have long embraced the well-established rule of statutory construction that the common law is not to be changed by doubtful implication, be overturned except by clear and unambiguous language, and that a statute in derogation of it will not effect a change thereof beyond that clearly indicated either by express terms or by necessary implication.

Batchelder v. Realty Res. Hospitality, LLC, 2007 ME 17, ¶ 23, 914 A.2d 1116, 1124 (quotation marks omitted).

Section 158 does not clearly and unambiguously express legislative intent to expand the scope of the common law doctrine of charitable immunity. Section 158 states: "A charitable organization shall be considered to have waived its immunity from liability for negligence or any other tort during the period a policy of insurance is effective...." This language is ambiguous; the words "or any other tort," plausibly suggest that section 158 was meant to expand the applicability of charitable immunity beyond its historical bounds, to cover any tort, including intentional torts. The other interpretation is that the statute has only one purpose, which is to deny charitable immunity, to the extent it would otherwise be available under the charitable immunity doctrine, when the non-profit organization is covered by insurance....

Charitable immunity remains a judicial doctrine, subject to our interpretation, notwithstanding that the Legislature created an exception to the doctrine with the enactment of section 158. *Child v. Cent. Me. Med. Ctr.,* 575 A.2d 318, 319 (Me.1990); *Thompson,* 483 A.2d at 707 & n. 3. In *Thompson,* we noted that "[t]he doctrine of charitable immunity is a creation of our common law. Except for one significant restriction imposed by statute, its applicability in Maine is controlled entirely by the precedents of this Court." 483 A.2d at 707 (footnotes omitted). It is therefore appropriate for this Court to continue to determine the scope of charitable immunity.... We have previously held that we would maintain, but neither expand nor eliminate, the doctrine of charitable immunity. We noted in *Rhoda* that the adoption of section 158 provides a basis "for our continued adherence to the charitable immunity doctrine." 226 A.2d at 532. Although we have maintained the doctrine to date, we have declined either to expand it beyond its traditional bounds or to contract it. *Child,* 575 A.2d at 319–20; *Thompson,* 483 A.2d at 708; *Rhoda,* 226 A.2d at 532–33....

For three reasons, we do not recognize the defense of charitable immunity in claims involving intentional torts. First, applying charitable immunity to intentional torts would set Maine so far outside the mainstream that it would put this State in a class by itself. We do not believe it advisable to expand so profoundly a doctrine that has generally been acknowledged as bankrupt. Second, nothing in the legislative history of section 158 indicates any legislative intent to so interpret the doctrine of charitable immunity. Third, there are no convincing policy reasons to apply charitable immunity to intentional torts. We therefore hold that charitable immunity is not available as a defense to intentional torts.

We now consider whether Picher has stated a cause of action against the Bishop, as a corporation sole, for fraudulent concealment. The elements of a claim of fraudulent concealment are: (1) a failure to disclose; (2) a material fact; (3) where a legal or equitable duty to disclose exists; (4) with the intention of inducing another to act or to refrain from acting in reliance on the non-disclosure; and (5) which is in fact relied upon to the aggrieved party's detriment. *See Letellier v. Small,* 400 A.2d 371, 376 (Me.1979) (stating the elements of fraud); *Morrow v. Moore,* 98 Me. 373, 57 A. 81 (1903) (holding that the withholding of information does not amount to fraudulent concealment absent a duty to disclose), *overruled on other grounds by Rulon-Miller v. Carhart,* 544 A.2d 340, 342 (Me.1988); *Marcotte v. Allen,* 91 Me. 74, 77, 39 A. 346, 347 (1897) (holding that silence may be fraudulent). Picher alleges that the Bishop had actual or constructive knowledge that Melville sexually assaulted minors, breached its duty to disclose that knowledge, and affirmatively concealed the knowledge with the intent to mislead Picher and his family. Picher and his family relied on the Bishop to Picher's detriment. Picher has stated a claim for fraudulent concealment.

The Bishop argues that it is entitled to a summary judgment on vicarious liability because the alleged actions in furtherance of fraudulent concealment were, as a matter of law, outside of the scope of employment. Vicarious liability on the fraudulent concealment claim is distinct from vicarious liability for Melville's sexual misconduct. Vicarious liability for fraudulent concealment is a claim of liability based on the actions of an agent or agents of the Bishop, other than Melville, for fraudulently concealing from Picher the propensity of Melville to commit sexual misconduct. The Bishop, however, sought summary judgment based solely on its charitable immunity defense. The Bishop did not make any argument about vicarious liability before the Superior Court and consequently did not preserve this issue for appeal. *See Foster v. Oral Surgery Assocs., P.A.*, 2008 ME 21, ¶ 22, 940 A.2d 1102, 1107. We therefore decline to decide this issue.... However, because vicarious liability will be at issue on the fraudulent concealment claim on remand, we provide updated guidance on the applicable law. We have previously turned to the Restatement (Second) of Agency §§ 219, 228 (1958) for guidance on issues pertaining to employer vicarious liability. *Mahar v. StoneWood Transp.*, 2003 ME 63, ¶¶ 13–14, 19–21, 823 A.2d 540, 544, 545–46; *McLain v. Training & Dev. Corp.*, 572 A.2d 494, 497–98 (Me.1990). The Restatement (Third) of Agency has since been published and states:

> (1) An employer is subject to vicarious liability for a tort committed by its employee acting within the scope of employment.

> (2) An employee acts within the scope of employment when performing work assigned by the employer or engaging in a course of conduct subject to the employer's control. An employee's act is not within the scope of employment when it occurs within an independent course of conduct not intended by the employee to serve any purpose of the employer.

> (3) For purposes of this section,

>> (a) an employee is an agent whose principal controls or has the right to control the manner and means of the agent's performance of work, and

>> (b) the fact that work is performed gratuitously does not relieve a principal of liability.

Restatement (Third) of Agency § 7.07 (2006).... [footnote omitted]. The Restatement (Third) of Agency § 7.08 (2006) may also be relevant, as this section is the counterpart to the Restatement (Second) of Agency § 219(2)(d) (1958) and also addresses vicarious liability in the employment context. We express no opinion as to the applicability of either section 7.07 or section 7.08 of the Restatement (Third) of Agency to the facts of this case, except to say that on remand, the court may look to these sections to provide the appropriate framework for analyzing the vicarious liability issues raised in this case....

Having addressed Picher's intentional tort claim, we turn to his negligence claims. Because we reject Picher's argument that charitable immunity should be abrogated as a defense as to some types of negligence claims but not others, we must address two additional issues relevant to the Bishop's assertion of this defense: (1) whether the Bishop, as a corporation sole and a non-profit institution, is entitled to assert charitable immunity, and (2) whether the Bishop waived immunity through the purchase of insurance.... Principles of tort law and charitable immunity apply to the Bishop as they do to any corporation. The Bishop, as a corporation sole, is "[a] series of successive persons holding an office; a continuous legal personality that is attributed to successive holders of certain monarchical or ecclesiastical positions, such as kings, bishops, rectors, vicars, and the like." Black's Law Dictionary 366 (8th ed.2004). "This continuous personality is viewed, by legal fiction, as having the qualities of a corporation." *Id.* In accordance with the private and special law pursuant to which the Bishop was established as a corporation sole, it is to be treated as a corporation under Maine law, "with all the powers, rights and privileges prescribed, and subject to all the liabilities imposed by the general statutes of the state." P. & S.L. 1887, ch. 151, §1. Thus, the defense of charitable immunity applies no differently to a corporation sole than to other types of organizations.

A party seeking charitable immunity bears the burden of establishing both that it is entitled to charitable immunity and that it has not waived immunity. *Coulombe v. Salvation Army*, 2002 ME 25, ¶¶ 10, 13, 790 A.2d 593, 595–96. The Bishop meets the requirements for non-profit status. We have held that an organization is entitled to charitable immunity if it "has no capital stock and no provision for making dividends or profits and ... derive [s] its funds mainly from public and private charity, ... hold[ing] them in trust for the object of the institution." *Id.* ¶ 10, 790 A.2d at 595 (quotation marks omitted). The parties do not dispute that the Bishop meets these requirements.... The parties dispute whether the Bishop has waived charitable immunity, pursuant to 14 M.R.S. §158, through the purchase of insurance. We have held that a charitable organization with insurance coverage is deemed to have waived its tort immunity to the extent of its insurance coverage. *Thompson*, 483 A.2d at 707 n. 3. We have previously noted that the Legislature modified charitable immunity "to the extent of permitting recovery of damages to an amount not exceeding the limits of insurance coverage which the charity might be carrying at the time of the negligent or tortious act." *Rhoda*, 226 A.2d at 531....

We have not previously had occasion to consider whether an exclusion similar to that in this case could bar a claim of negligent supervision. In *Sarah G.*, we did not reach the issue because the plaintiffs conceded that if the conduct at issue constituted abuse pursuant to the insurance policy, the sexual misconduct exclusion at issue in that case would bar a negligence claim. *Id.* ¶ 9, 866 A.2d at 838. In other jurisdictions, courts have interpreted sexual misconduct exclusions and other types of misconduct exclusions to preclude coverage for negligent hiring and supervision claims. *See, e.g., Gulf Underwriters Ins. Co. v. KSI Servs., Inc.*, 233 Fed.Appx. 239, 241–42 (4th Cir.2007) (holding that negligent supervision claim was barred due to exclusion for dishonest or criminal acts); *All Am. Ins. Co. v. Burns*, 971 F.2d 438 (10th Cir.1992) (holding that claims for negligent failure to investigate and negligent failure to discharge were barred due to sexual misconduct exclusion); *Am. Commerce Ins. Co. v. Porto*, 811 A.2d 1185 (R.I.2002) (holding that negligent supervision claim was barred due to sexual misconduct exclusion). As a matter of law, Picher's claims against the Bishop are excluded from coverage, and therefore the Bishop has not waived charitable immunity.

The entry is: ... Judgment affirmed as to all claims against the Bishop except fraudulent concealment. Judgment vacated as to the claim of fraudulent concealment. Remanded for further action consistent with this opinion.

ALEXANDER, J., with whom CLIFFORD, J., joins, dissenting....

The Court's opinion, holding that charitable immunity protection may be avoided simply by pleading some intentional act or failure to act, effectively ends charitable immunity in Maine. I respectfully dissent from the Court's opinion. The articulate policy arguments expressed by the Court should be addressed to the Legislature to support legislative action to amend the law that, without ambiguity, protects charities from suit "for negligence or any other tort." 14 M.R.S. §158 (2008)....

Today's opinion has great significance beyond this case. The existence of charitable immunity and the protection it creates is important to the planning and continued existence of many community-based organizations including local granges, arts organizations, fraternal groups, youth programs, churches, and some schools and health care providers. As we held in *Jensen*, such protection is important because funds donated for charitable purposes are held in trust to be used exclusively for those purposes and, without charitable immunity, resources could be sacrificed "to feed the hungry maw of litigation, and charitable institutions of all kinds would ultimately cease or become greatly impaired in their usefulness." *Id.* at 411, 78 A. at 899.... Just seven years ago, we confirmed our holding in *Jensen*, observing that, "to permit the invasion of these funds to satisfy tort claims would destroy the sources of charitable support upon which the enterprise depends." *Coulombe*, 2002 ME 25, ¶ 10, 790 A.2d at 596 (quotation marks omitted); *accord Mendall*, 159 Me. at 290, 191 A.2d at 636....

Legislative enactment of broad-based charitable immunity, now more than forty years in the past, allows many poorly funded organizations to provide important community services using facilities such as grange halls, art museums, Little League ball fields, or houses of worship. These organizations serve their communities without facing the Hobson's choice of shutting down because they cannot afford the cost of insurance or remaining open to face the risk of lawsuits which, even if successfully defended, may cost more than the organization can afford.... Today the Court sweeps away the protection enacted by the Legislature. In so doing, the Court invades the province of the Legislature in an area where, in *Rhoda* and *Mendall*, we acknowledged that the Legislature had primary authority to act to adopt, reject, expand, or modify the doctrine of charitable immunity. *Rhoda*, 226 A.2d at 532–33; *Mendall*, 159 Me. at 290, 191 A.2d at 636. In *Mendall*, addressing a proposal to abolish charitable immunity, we stated words that ring true today: "[S]uch ... a far reaching change in policy should be initiated in the Legislature and receive careful legislative consideration." 159 Me. at 290, 191 A.2d at 636.

To justify its invasion of the Legislature's province to amend 14 M.R.S. § 158, the Court appears to conduct a referendum of actions by other state supreme courts to conclude that since those courts appear to be cutting back on charitable immunity, we should follow suit. The Court's referendum, however, lacks citations to other state statutes similar to section 158.[6] It is that statute, and our obligation to respect it until amended by the Legislature, that necessarily separates Maine from other states in our approach to charitable immunity....

A claim of fraud, fraudulent misrepresentation, or fraudulent concealment is a tort like any other, although one that must be proved by clear and convincing evidence. *See Rand v. Bath Iron Works Corp.*, 2003 ME 122, ¶ 9, 832 A.2d 771, 773. It is a tort easily pled, but difficult to prove. Nothing in legislation or our prior precedents creates a charitable immunity exception to blow open the courthouse door for those who employ the tactic of adding a fraud or intentional inaction claim to a negligence claim to force charities to defend against tort actions and confront all of the attendant costs and risks to the trust resources that we have stated must be protected from such actions.

---

6. The Court's opinion also may overstate the extent to which charitable immunity has been limited in other states. It correctly quotes Prosser's observation that "virtually all states" have "rejected the complete immunity of charities," and that only two or three states have retained "full immunity in the absence of legislation to the contrary." W. Page Keeton et al., *Prosser and Keeton on the Law of Torts* § 133 at 1070 (W. Page Keeton ed., 5th ed.1984). But the Court's authority for these observations, Prosser, qualifies those broad observations, noting that some states, like Maine, "permit a recovery against a charity's non-trust fund assets—usually insurance—but not otherwise," and that in some states "immunity has been retained or reinstituted by statute, but only for certain particular cases," *id.*, including protection for religious institutions, *id.* at 1070 n. 15. The Court also counts Massachusetts among the states to have abolished charitable immunity. But with today's costs of litigation, Massachusetts' "abolition" of immunity that imposes a $20,000 limit on damages seems more like a qualified acceptance of charitable immunity than an abolition of it.

Forty-six years ago, in *Mendall*, we stated that changes in the doctrine of charitable immunity have far-reaching policy implications that should be initiated in the Legislature and receive careful legislative consideration. 159 Me. at 290, 191 A.2d at 636. That is as true today as it was then. The Court should leave amendment or abolition of the doctrine of charitable immunity and section 158 to the Maine Legislature. I would affirm the judgment of the Superior Court.

SAUFLEY, C.J., with whom LEVY, J., joins, concurring.... [Opinion is omitted].

Notes

The court in *Picher* held that the Bishop may not claim charitable immunity as a defense to the intentional tort of fraudulent concealment, but that it is sufficient to bar negligence claims based on the sexual abuse of a child. For a comparison of the application of the doctrine of charitable immunity in *Picher* and in other jurisdictions, see Matthew Cobb, *A Strange Distinction: Charitable Immunity and Clergy Sexual Abuse in Picher v. Roman Catholic Bishop of Portland*, 62 Me. L. Rev. 703 (2010) (arguing for an exception to the charitable immunity defense for negligent supervision based on public policy reasons). *See also* Robert F. Cochran, Jr., *Church Freedom and Accountability in Sexual Exploitation Cases: The Possibility of Both Through Limited Strict Liability*, 21 J. Contemp. Leg. Issues 427 (2013) (favoring religious autonomy but asserting limited strict liability in cases of clergy sexual exploitation). New Jersey is one of the few jurisdictions that continues to recognize the applicability of charitable immunity as a defense. *See Davis v. Devereux Found.*, 37 A.3d 469 (N.J. 2012) (narrowly construing the New Jersey Charitable Immunity Act and holding charity liable for negligent hiring and supervision). *See also* Samantha Kluxen LaBarbera, *Secrecy and Settlements: Is the New Jersey Charitable Immunity Act Justified in Light of the Clergy Sexual Abuse Crisis?*, 50 Vill. L. Rev. 261 (2005); Rev. Raymond C. O'Brien, *Clergy, Sex and the American Way*, 31 Pepp. L. Rev. 363, 447 (2004); Catherine Pierce Wells, *Churches, Charities, and Corrective Justice: Making Churches Pay for the Sins of Their Clergy*, 44 B.C. L. Rev. 1201 (2003).

4. Religious Constitutional Claims

a. Free Exercise

Kenneth R. v. Roman Catholic Diocese of Brooklyn

Supreme Court, Appellate Division, Second Department, New York, 1997
229 A.D.2d 159, 654 N.Y.S.2d 791

GOLDSTEIN, Justice....

At issue here is whether the plaintiffs have stated causes of action against the appellant Roman Catholic Diocese of Brooklyn sounding in negligent hiring, negligent retention, and negligent supervision. We find that their allegations with respect to negligent retention and negligent supervision are sufficient to withstand the appellant's cross motion to dismiss the complaint pursuant to CPLR 3211(a)(7), but that they do not have a cause of action to recover damages for negligent hiring.

The plaintiffs' amended complaint alleges that, "on or about or between July 13, 1983, and August 31, 1989", the appellant's codefendant, Enrique Diaz Jimenez, an ordained Roman Catholic priest, sexually abused the infant plaintiffs. Enrique Diaz Jimenez pleaded guilty to sexual abuse in the third degree based upon this conduct. However, as noted by the Supreme Court, that conduct did not fall within the scope of his employment and therefore the appellant is not vicariously liable for his conduct under the theory of respondeat superior (see, *Cornell v. State of New York*, 46 N.Y.2d 1032, 416 N.Y.S.2d 542, 389 N.E.2d 1064; *Mercer v. State of New York*, 125 A.D.2d 376, 509 N.Y.S.2d 103). Consequently, the Supreme Court granted those branches of the appellant's cross motion which were to dismiss the first and second causes of action insofar as asserted against it. The Supreme Court also dismissed the plaintiffs' third cause of action sounding in clergy malpractice, and their tenth cause of action alleging that the appellant created a "climate and custom" of indifference to sexual abuse. Those rulings are not before us on this appeal....

The plaintiffs' amended complaint alleges that the appellant "had prior knowledge or should have known that the defendant Jimenez was a sexual deviant" and therefore was negligent in hiring, supervising, and retaining him. The plaintiffs further contend that the appellant failed to "establish proper guidelines and procedures", failed to "properly screen and hire applicants to the priesthood", and "failed to have Defendant Jimenez examined psychiatrically and/or psychologically to determine his fitness for serving in the capacity as a Roman Catholic priest".

Certain undisputed facts emerge from the documentary evidence in the record. The codefendant Jimenez was ordained a Roman Catholic priest in 1977, in Venezuela. He came to the Roman Catholic Diocese of Brooklyn in 1983, with a letter of reference from the Archbishop of Merida, Venezuela, and was assigned to work in St. Leo's Church.... Ordination to the priesthood confers a religious, not legal status, and may be characterized as a "quintessentially religious" matter (*Serbian Eastern Orthodox Diocese v. Milivojevich*, 426 U.S. 696, 720, 96 S.Ct. 2372, 2385, 49 L.Ed.2d 151). Imposing liability for conferring that status would create serious concerns of excessive entanglement in religious affairs, in violation of the First Amendment of the United States Constitution (see, *Pritzlaff v. Archdiocese of Milwaukee*, 194 Wis.2d 302, 327, 533 N.W.2d 780, 790, cert. denied 516 U.S. 1116, 116 S.Ct. 920, 133 L.Ed.2d 849; see also, *Rayburn v. General Conference of Seventh-day Adventists*, 772 F.2d 1164, cert. denied 478 U.S. 1020, 106 S.Ct. 3333, 92 L.Ed.2d 739; *Downs v. Roman Catholic Archbishop of Baltimore*, 111 Md.App. 616, 683 A.2d 808).

However, the question of whether liability could ever be imposed for ordination to the priesthood need not be determined here since the only entity of the Roman Catholic Church sued by the plaintiffs is the appellant Roman Catholic Diocese of Brooklyn which the amended complaint alleges "is a corporation duly licensed to do business in the State of New York". Thus, pursuant to the allegations in the amended complaint, the appellant is a separate entity (see generally, *Heenan v. Roman Catholic Diocese of Rockville Centre*, 158 A.D.2d 587, 551 N.Y.S.2d 555). The plaintiffs assert no facts from which one could infer that the appellant was responsible for Jimenez's status as a Roman Catholic priest, since he was ordained in Venezuela by officials of the diocese there. Accordingly, the fifth and eighth causes of action, alleging that the appellant failed to screen or determine Jimenez's fitness for the priesthood, must be dismissed.

With respect to negligent hiring, the documentary evidence in the record establishes that the appellant did not and could not have known of Jimenez's propensities when he arrived here from Venezuela with a letter of reference. The plaintiffs allege that the appellant should have initiated some investigations of Jimenez before hiring him to work in a church under its control. The question of whether there is such a common-law duty is a question of law for the courts (see, *D'Amico v. Christie*, 71 N.Y.2d 76, 524 N.Y.S.2d 1, 518 N.E.2d 896; *Eiseman v. State of New York*, 70 N.Y.2d 175, 190, 518 N.Y.S.2d 608, 511 N.E.2d 1128).... There is no common-law duty to institute specific procedures for hiring employees unless the employer knows of facts that would lead a reasonably prudent person to investigate the prospective employee (see, *Ford v. Gildin*, 200 A.D.2d 224, 226–227, 613 N.Y.S.2d 139; *Stevens v. Lankard*, 31 A.D.2d 602, 297 N.Y.S.2d 686, affd. 25 N.Y.2d 640, 306 N.Y.S.2d 257, 254 N.E.2d 339; *Amendolara v. Macy's N.Y.*, 19 A.D.2d 702, 241 N.Y.S.2d 39; cf., *Rhames v. Supermarkets Gen. Corp.*, 230 A.D.2d 780, 646 N.Y.S.2d 622). Since Jimenez came to the appellant with a letter of reference from his Archbishop, which gave the appellant no reason to believe there was any problem, the appellant cannot be charged with negligence for failing to investigate further (see, *Lopez v. William J. Burns Int. Detective Agency*, 48 A.D.2d 645, 368 N.Y.S.2d 221; *Roman Catholic Bishop of San Diego v. Superior Ct.*, 42 Cal.App.4th 1556, 50 Cal.Rptr.2d 399; *Kennedy v. Roman Catholic Diocese of Burlington, Vermont, Inc.*, 921 F.Supp. 231).* Accordingly, the plaintiffs' sixth cause of action, alleging "failure to establish proper guidelines and procedures", and the plaintiffs' seventh cause of action, alleging that the appellant "was negligent in hiring Jimenez", must be dismissed.

In their bill of particulars, the plaintiffs allege that the appellant acquired actual or constructive notice of the codefendant Jimenez's propensity to sexually abuse children from "statements made by the infant plaintiffs to priests at St. Leo's Church and Our Lady of Sorrows Church", and from the codefendant Jimenez himself. Allegations in a "bill of particulars are to be taken into account in considering the sufficiency of the challenged causes of action" (*Moore v. Johnson*, 147 A.D.2d 621, 538 N.Y.S.2d 28; see, *Nader v. General Motors Corp.*, 25 N.Y.2d 560, 565, 307 N.Y.S.2d 647, 255 N.E.2d 765). If, as the plaintiffs allege in their bill of particulars, the infant plaintiffs and/or Jimenez himself made statements to other priests at St. Leo's Church or Our Lady of Sorrows Church giving them notice of Jimenez's conduct, the plaintiffs may have causes of action sounding in negligent retention and negligent supervision. Pursuant to prevailing case law, as a general rule, imposition of such liability would not violate constitutional and statutory guarantees of free exercise of religion and separation of church and State.

It is well settled that generally, "a law that is neutral and of general applicability need not be justified by a compelling governmental interest even if the law has the incidental effect of burdening a particular religious practice" (*Church of Lukumi Babalu Aye v. City of Hialeah*, 508 U.S. 520, 531, 113 S.Ct. 2217, 2226, 124 L.Ed.2d 472; see, *Employment Division, Dept. of Human Resources of Ore. v. Smith*, 494 U.S. 872, 110 S.Ct. 1595, 108 L.Ed.2d 876). Some cases have indicated that the First Amendment to the United States Constitution may be asserted as a defense if the defendant's conduct that caused the plaintiff's injury finds its basis in religious beliefs and practices (see, *Wisconsin v. Yoder*, 406 U.S. 205, 215–216, 92 S.Ct. 1526, 1533–1534, 32 L.Ed.2d 15; *Konkle v. Henson*, 672 N.E.2d 450 [Ind App]; *Destefano v. Grabrian*, 763 P.2d 275, 283 [Colo]). Here, however, there is no indication that requiring increased supervision of Jimenez or the termination of his employment by the appellant based upon Jimenez's conduct would violate any religious doctrine or inhibit any religious practice (see, *Jimmy Swaggart Ministries v. Board of Equalization of Cal.*, 493 U.S. 378, 110 S.Ct. 688, 107 L.Ed.2d 796; *L.L.N. v. Clauder*, 203 Wis.2d 570, 552 N.W.2d 879).

The enactment of the Religious Freedom Restoration Act of 1993 (42 U.S.C. § 2000bb, et seq.) does not alter this analysis. That statute provides that if a law of general applicability

---

* The plaintiffs allege in their bill of particulars that certain unspecified "studies" have been published "showing the existence of ongoing problems in the priesthood relating to sexual activity with children thereby raising a duty to inquire". However, imposing a special duty to inquire as to backgrounds of priests as a class has no legal basis, and carries with it discriminatory overtones against individuals merely because they have been ordained to the priesthood (see generally, *McDaniel v. Paty*, 435 U.S. 618, 98 S.Ct. 1322, 55 L.Ed.2d 593).

substantially burdens the exercise of religion, such application must be in furtherance of a compelling state interest and must constitute "the least restrictive means of furthering that compelling governmental interest" (42 U.S.C. § 2000bb-1[b][2]). However, that statute only applies if the free exercise of religion is " 'substantially' burdened" (*Geisinsky v. Village of Kings Point*, 226 A.D.2d 340, 341, 640 N.Y.S.2d 212) because the activities in question are motivated by religious beliefs (see, *Mack v. O'Leary*, 7th Cir., 80 F.3d 1175, 1178; *Bryant v. Gomez*, 9th Cir., 46 F.3d 948, 949; *Matter of Salahuddin v. Coughlin*, 222 A.D.2d 950, 636 N.Y.S.2d 145, cert. denied 519 U.S. 937, 117 S.Ct. 317, 136 L.Ed.2d 232). As previously noted, there is no indication that the level of supervision exercised over Jimenez, or his retention in the appellant's employ, was dictated by any religious doctrine. Indeed, it appears from the record that Jimenez's employment relationship with the appellant was ultimately terminated, and his requests for additional employment were denied (cf., *Schmidt v. Bishop*, 779 F.Supp. 321, 331).

Moreover, while the First Amendment to the United States Constitution prohibits regulation of religious beliefs, conduct by a religious entity "remains subject to regulation for the protection of society" (*Cantwell v. State of Connecticut*, 310 U.S. 296, 304, 60 S.Ct. 900, 903, 84 L.Ed. 1213; see, *Employment Division Dept. of Human Resources of Oregon v. Smith*, 494 U.S. 872, 110 S.Ct. 1595, *supra*; *Destefano v. Grabrian*, 763 P.2d 275, 283, *supra*). The First Amendment does not grant religious organizations absolute immunity from tort liability (see, *Konkle v. Henson*, 672 N.E.2d 450, 456, *supra*; *Moses v. Diocese of Colorado*, 863 P.2d 310, 319). Therefore, religious entities must be held accountable for their actions, "even if that conduct is carried out as part of the church's religious practices" (*Meroni v. Holy Spirit Assn. for Unification of World Christianity*, 119 A.D.2d 200, 203, 506 N.Y.S.2d 174). Religious entities have some duty to prevent injuries inflicted by persons in their employ whom they have reason to believe will engage in injurious conduct (see, *Konkle v. Henson, supra*, at 456; *L.L.N. v. Clauder*, 203 Wis.2d 570, 552 N.W.2d 879, *supra*; *Erickson v. Christenson*, 99 Or.App. 104, 109, 781 P.2d 383, 386–387; *Gallas v. Greek Orthodox Archdiocese of N & S Am.*, 154 Misc.2d 494, 499–500, 587 N.Y.S.2d 82; *Jones v. Trane*, 153 Misc.2d 822, 830–831, 591 N.Y.S.2d 927, *supra*).... Therefore, the plaintiffs' fourth and ninth causes of action, sounding in negligent supervision and retention, and the eleventh cause of action, asserting a derivative claim, are sufficient to withstand a motion to dismiss the complaint pursuant to CPLR 3211....

ORDERED that the order is modified, on the law, by deleting the provisions thereof which denied those branches of the appellant's cross motion which were to dismiss the fifth, sixth, seventh, and eighth causes of action, and substituting therefor provisions granting those branches of the cross motion; as so modified, the order is affirmed insofar as appealed from, without costs or disbursements.

MILLER, J.P., and JOY, and ALTMAN, JJ., concur.

b. Establishment Clause

Turner v. Roman Catholic Diocese of Burlington, Vermont

Supreme Court of Vermont, 2009
186 Vt. 396, 987 A.2d 960

DOOLEY, J....

Father Alfred Willis, a Roman Catholic priest, sexually assaulted plaintiff in June 1977 in a motel room in Albany, New York, following the ordination of plaintiff's brother as a Roman Catholic priest. Plaintiff was sixteen years old at the time. That same summer,

Willis attempted to assault plaintiff again at plaintiff's parents' home in Derby, Vermont. At the time of these events, Willis was assigned to a parish under defendant's authority.... In 2004, plaintiff filed suit against defendant, alleging that the diocese negligently hired, trained, supervised and retained Willis.[1] The case first went to trial in June 2007, but ended in a mistrial, with the court imposing a monetary sanction on defendant for causing the mistrial. At the second trial in December 2007, the jury found that defendant negligently supervised Willis and caused him damages of $15,000, but that plaintiff sued over six years after he knew of the molestation, the resulting harm, and defendant's responsibility for such conduct. Although the jury's finding on when plaintiff had the requisite knowledge would normally have meant that the suit was barred by the statute of limitations, the trial judge concluded that the finding lacked evidentiary support and ruled that the jury verdict on liability and damages would stand. Both defendant and plaintiff appeal....

[W]e address defendant's arguments involving the First Amendment to the Federal Constitution.... With respect to the First Amendment, defendant argues that the suit against it violates its rights under the Free Exercise and Establishment Clauses, and the religious autonomy doctrine under these clauses.... In May 2007, before the first trial in this case, defendant moved for summary judgment, or in the alternative, a judgment as a matter of law under Vermont Rule of Civil Procedure 50. It argued, among other claims, that any imposition of liability on defendant would violate both the Free Exercise and the Establishment Clauses of the First Amendment to the Federal Constitution.[4] The motion was accompanied by a statement of undisputed facts containing the basic facts of this case. Although plaintiff filed a statement of disputed facts in response, he did not respond directly to the motion for summary judgment or to defendant's First Amendment claims. The court did not decide the summary judgment motion either before the first trial or before the second trial. At the close of plaintiff's case in the second trial, defense counsel argued that liability would violate the First Amendment, stating: "this is an unnecessary complication and involvement of the courts with the church's First Amendment rights."[5] The court responded that it was "just using neutral principles of civil law [so] there's no improper First Amendment entanglement with religion." This is the only ruling on the merits of defendant's argument. Defendant failed to renew the motion post-trial as required by Rule 50(b). Inexplicably, after the jury charge was delivered, defendant objected to the jury instruction on liability as a " violation of the First Amendment." The court did not modify the instruction after the objection, ruling the objection had nothing to do with the charge language.

---

1. The text represents the state of the case when submitted to the jury. Plaintiff originally also sued Willis, but plaintiff settled with Willis and dropped him from the case before it went to the jury. Plaintiff also alleged that the diocese was liable on a theory of respondeat superior. This theory was abandoned in light of this Court's decision in *Doe v. Newbury Bible Church*, 2007 VT 72, 182 Vt. 174, 933 A.2d 196. Plaintiff also had other theories that never went to the jury.

4. As we express in other parts of this opinion, we are frustrated by the failure of the parties to include key documents in the printed case, to specify what rulings are on appeal, and to explain how the appeal arguments have been preserved. In this instance, the motion for summary judgment is not in either printed case, nor are the objections to the jury instructions or the motion for judgment as a matter of law. Defendant has not specified what ruling we are reviewing, and has failed to describe how it has preserved its arguments.

5. The statement was made as part of defendant's motion for judgment as a matter of law, which argued that plaintiff had failed to establish a "legally sufficient evidentiary basis for a reasonable jury" to find that it had been negligent and was therefore liable. V.R.C.P. 50(a)(1). The court ruled against defendant, thus allowing the case to go to the jury. Defendant has not appealed that ruling.

The only decision we can review, if we can call it that, is the decision not to grant the motion for summary judgment. We review an appeal from a trial court's denial of summary judgment de novo. *Concord General Mut. Ins. Co. v. Woods*, 2003 VT 33, ¶ 5, 175 Vt. 212, 824 A.2d 572. Summary judgment should be granted only where there are no genuine issues of material fact and any party is entitled to judgment as a matter of law. *Id.*; V.R.C.P. 56(c). In this case, while there are extensive disputes over the facts, none of these disputes are particularly relevant to this issue. Defendant has argued the issue based on the allegations and theories of liability in plaintiff's complaint. Thus, as the claim is presented to us, our review is functionally equivalent of that for denial of a motion to dismiss for failure to state a claim on which relief can be granted under Vermont Rule of Civil Procedure 12(b)(6). See *Powers v. Office of Child Support*, 173 Vt. 390, 395, 795 A.2d 1259, 1263 (2002) (Rule 12(b)(6) motion should not be granted "unless it is beyond doubt that there exist no facts or circumstances that would entitle [plaintiff] to relief").

We set out the record and standard of review to emphasize what is not before us. In its memorandum of law to the superior court, and to a lesser extent in its brief to this Court, defendant has set forth doctrine from religious sources, including the Bible, to explain why applying tort standards would burden the free exercise of its religion. We are not inclined to enter a dispute over religious doctrine based on arguments of lawyers. To the extent these sources are relevant, they must be offered by traditional methods of proof.... Defendant argues that allowing plaintiff to pursue a negligent hiring claim against it would violate the Free Exercise Clause because in order to assess the reasonableness of defendant's decision to ordain Willis, the court has to pass judgment on an ecclesiastical decision. Defendant further argues that allowing plaintiff to pursue a negligent supervision claim transgresses both the Free Exercise and Establishment Clauses and the religious autonomy doctrine because the supervision of clergy is inextricably rooted in religious doctrine and belief....

The Free Exercise Clause guarantees the freedom to hold religious beliefs and the freedom to act in accordance with those beliefs. *Id.* However, the freedom to act in accordance with religious beliefs is not absolute. *Id.* at 303–04 ("Conduct remains subject to regulation for the protection of society."). To be protected under the Free Exercise Clause, the conduct that the state seeks to regulate must be "rooted in religious belief." *Wisconsin v. Yoder*, 406 U.S. 205, 215, 92 S.Ct. 1526, 32 L.Ed.2d 15 (1972). Laws that are neutral and of general applicability do not violate the Free Exercise Clause. *Church of Lukumi Babalu Aye, Inc. v. City of Hialeah*, 508 U.S. 520, 531, 113 S.Ct. 2217, 124 L.Ed.2d 472 (1993) ("[A] law that is neutral and of general applicability need not be justified by a compelling governmental interest even if the law has the incidental effect of burdening a particular religious practice."); *Employment Div., Dep't of Human Res. of Or. v. Smith*, 494 U.S. 872, 878–82, 110 S.Ct. 1595, 108 L.Ed.2d 876 (1990) (stating that, unless the state attempts to regulate religious beliefs, the communication of religious beliefs, or the raising of one's children in those beliefs, the Free Exercise Clause does not bar neutral, generally applicable laws).[6]

---

6. To counter the Free Exercise Clause standard announced in *Smith*, Congress enacted the Religious Freedom Restoration Act of 1993 (RFRA), Pub.L. No. 103-141, 107 Stat. 1488 (codified at 5 U.S.C. § 504, 42 U.S.C. §§ 1988, 2000bb to 2000bb-4). Congress's stated purpose in enacting the RFRA was "to restore the compelling interest test as set forth in *Sherbert v. Verner* and *Wisconsin v. Yoder* and to guarantee its application in all cases where free exercise of religion is substantially burdened." 42 U.S.C. § 2000bb(b)(1) (citations omitted). Four years after the enactment of RFRA, the Supreme Court invalidated the RFRA as applied to the states. *City of Boerne v. Flores*, 521 U.S. 507, 529, 536, 117 S.Ct. 2157, 138 L.Ed.2d 624 (1997) (noting that under the Fourteenth Amendment the federal

We reject defendant's Free Exercise Clause argument. Defendant does not argue that the common law of negligence is something other than a neutral law of general applicability or that it is directed specifically towards a religious belief or practice of defendant. Nor has defendant identified a specific doctrine or practice that will be burdened if plaintiff's suit goes forward. We do not believe defendant's generalized assertion that requiring it to hire and supervise priests in a nonnegligent manner would constitute undue interference in church governance.... Defendant has further argued that *Kedroff v. St. Nicholas Cathedral of Russian Orthodox Church in North America*, 344 U.S. 94, 116, 73 S.Ct. 143, 97 L.Ed. 120 (1952), and *Serbian Eastern Orthodox Diocese v. Milivojevich*, 426 U.S. 696, 96 S.Ct. 2372, 49 L.Ed.2d 151 (1976), prohibit secular courts from ruling upon matters of clergy selection. We decline to interpret either case as requiring such a broad construction of its holding. Requiring defendant to comply with a generally applicable secular law by non-negligently hiring and supervising priests is not the equivalent of the state statute in *Kedroff* that transferred the control of certain churches from one central governing hierarchy to another. 344 U.S. at 107, 73 S.Ct. 143 (holding that a state statute that determined a dispute over the control of Russian Orthodox churches in New York was unconstitutional because the statute prohibited the free exercise of religion). Nor does the resolution of the case before us require applying church doctrine as in *Serbian E. Orthodox Diocese*, 426 U.S. at 708–09, 96 S.Ct. 2372 (holding that the Free Exercise Clause prohibits civil interference in the allocation of hierarchical authority within a church as directed by the church's governing documents).... In reaching this decision, we are following many precedents from other courts which reached the same conclusion in similar circumstances. See *Martinelli v. Bridgeport Roman Catholic Diocesan Corp.*, 196 F.3d 409, 431–32 (2d Cir.1999); *Doe v. Norwich Roman Catholic Diocesan Corp.*, 268 F.Supp.2d 139, 144–46 (D.Conn.2003); *Moses v. Diocese of Colorado*, 863 P.2d 310, 320–21 (Colo.1993); *Malicki v. Doe*, 814 So.2d 347, 360–63 (Fla.2002) (collecting cases); *Fortin v. Roman Catholic Bishop of Portland*, 2005 ME 57, ¶¶ 49–54, 871 A.2d 1208; *Roman Catholic Diocese of Jackson v. Morrison*, 905 So.2d 1213 (Miss.2005) (en banc) (collecting cases in Appendix A). While there are others that reach the opposite conclusion, we do not find these persuasive.

We turn now to the Establishment Clause, which prohibits government action that tends to endorse, favor, or in some manner promote religion. See *Zelman v. Simmons-Harris*, 536 U.S. 639, 648–49, 122 S.Ct. 2460, 153 L.Ed.2d 604 (2002). In *Lemon v. Kurtzman*, 403 U.S. 602, 612–13, 91 S.Ct. 2105, 29 L.Ed.2d 745 (1971), the Supreme Court announced a three-prong Establishment Clause test: (1) governmental action must have a secular purpose; (2) its primary effect must not enhance or inhibit religion; and (3) the action must not foster an excessive government entanglement with religion. In evaluating whether a law that is religiously neutral on its face violates the Establishment Clause, we must inquire if the law has either the purpose or principal effect of advancing or inhibiting religion. *Zelman*, 536 U.S. at 648–49, 122 S.Ct. 2460. Whether there is excessive government entanglement with religion is a factor to consider in evaluating whether the principal effect of the governmental action is to advance or inhibit religion. *Agostini v. Felton*, 521 U.S. 203, 232, 117 S.Ct. 1997, 138 L.Ed.2d 391 (1997); see also *Zelman*, 536 U.S. at 648–49, 122 S.Ct. 2460; *id.* at 668, 122 S.Ct. 2460 (O'Connor, J.,

government did not have the power to substantively alter constitutional rights). Therefore, the standard articulated by the Supreme Court in *Smith* remains the relevant standard for evaluating whether plaintiff's negligence claims violate the Free Exercise Clause. See *Office of Child Support, ex. rel. Stanzione v. Stanzione*, 2006 VT 98, ¶10 n. 1, 180 Vt. 629, 910 A.2d 882 (mem.) (stating that *Hunt v. Hunt*, 162 Vt. 423, 648 A.2d 843 (1994), decided during the RFRA's brief application to the states, was inapposite to the extent the decision depended upon the stringent RFRA test).

concurring); *Mitchell v. Helms*, 530 U.S. 793, 807, 120 S.Ct. 2530, 147 L.Ed.2d 660 (2000) (plurality opinion). Not all "entanglements" are constitutionally proscribed. *Chittenden v. Waterbury Ctr. Cmty. Church, Inc.*, 168 Vt. 478, 487, 726 A.2d 20, 26 (1998). Excessive entanglement between church and state may occur when governmental regulation necessitates an examination of religious doctrine or results in a close surveillance of religious institutions. *Hernandez v. Comm'r*, 490 U.S. 680, 696–97, 109 S.Ct. 2136, 104 L.Ed.2d 766 (1989); see also *Lemon*, 403 U.S. at 615, 91 S.Ct. 2105 (instructing that an excessive entanglement inquiry should "examine the character and purposes of the institutions that are benefitted, the nature of the aid that the State provides, and the resulting relationship between the government and the religious authority").

Defendant does not contend that a judicial inquiry into the negligent supervision claim serves any purpose other than a secular purpose, or that such an inquiry has as its primary effect the endorsement or inhibition of religion. Rather, defendant argues that there is excessive entanglement because the "supervision of clergy is inextricably rooted in religious belief" and that such an inquiry would require an examination of the religious doctrine of the Catholic Church. There is no excessive entanglement because the negligence claim is not measured against canon law, but rather against secular legal standards. To prevail, plaintiff had to prove that he was owed a duty, the duty was breached, and he suffered damages that were caused by the breach. Common law, not ecclesiastical principles, establishes the scope of that duty. The duty owed by defendant to protect minors from sexual abuse is not different from the duty owed by other institutions to which the common law applies. We find that there was no excessive entanglement, and thus, no violation of the Establishment Clause. Again, we note that many other courts have reached the same result in similar circumstances. See *Martinelli*, 196 F.3d at 431; *Doe*, 268 F.Supp.2d at 145–46; *Smith v. O'Connell*, 986 F.Supp. 73, 80–82 (D.R.I.1997); *Malicki*, 814 So.2d at 363–64; *Konkle v. Henson*, 672 N.E.2d 450, 454–56 (Ind.Ct.App.1996); *Roman Catholic Diocese of Jackson*, 905 So.2d at 1229–30.

Finally, defendant argues that plaintiff's suit violates the religious autonomy doctrine,[7] as recognized by the U.S. Supreme Court in *Watson v. Jones*, 80 U.S. (13 Wall.) 679, 20 L.Ed. 666 (1871). In *Watson*, the Court declined jurisdiction over a property dispute between two factions within a church that had already been adjudicated by the highest Presbyterian church authorities, stating:

> Each [church] has a body of constitutional and ecclesiastical law of its own, to be found in their written organic laws, their books of discipline, in their collections of precedents, in their usage and customs, which as to each constitute a system of ecclesiastical law and religious faith that tasks the ablest minds to become familiar with. It is not to be supposed that the judges of the civil courts can be as competent in the ecclesiastical law and religious faith of all these bodies as the ablest men in each are in reference to their own.

Id. at 729. The Court later characterized this doctrine as a constitutional imperative. *Kedroff*, 344 U.S. at 116, 73 S.Ct. 143. This doctrine bars courts from becoming too closely involved in the internal, ecclesiastical matters of religious institutions. See *Serbian E. Orthodox Diocese*, 426 U.S. at 708–09, 96 S.Ct. 2372; *Presbyterian Church v. Mary Elizabeth*

---

7. This doctrine has been called by various names, such as the "church autonomy" or "ecclesiastical abstention" doctrine. See *Roman Catholic Diocese of Jackson*, 905 So.2d at 1235. Further, the analysis of this doctrine often is intertwined with a discussion of the Establishment Clause or the Free Exercise Clause. See, e.g., *Bryce v. Episcopal Church in Diocese of Colo.*, 289 F.3d 648, 655–56 (10th Cir.2002); *Malicki*, 814 So.2d at 363–64.

Blue Hull Mem'l Presbyterian Church, 393 U.S. 440, 449–50, 89 S.Ct. 601, 21 L.Ed.2d 658 (1969). Sitting alone as a circuit justice, Justice Rehnquist later addressed the attempted application of the religious autonomy doctrine to secular disputes involving a church, as opposed to internal, ecclesiastical disputes, stating:

> There are constitutional limitations on the extent to which a civil court may inquire into and determine matters of ecclesiastical cognizance and polity in adjudicating intrachurch disputes. But this Court never has suggested that those constraints similarly apply outside the context of such intraorganization disputes. Thus *Serbian Eastern Orthodox Diocese* and the other cases cited by applicant are not in point. Those cases are premised on a perceived danger that in resolving intrachurch disputes the State will become entangled in essentially religious controversies or intervene on behalf of groups espousing particular doctrinal beliefs. Such considerations are not applicable to purely secular disputes between third parties and a particular defendant, albeit a religious affiliated organization, in which fraud, breach of contract, and statutory violations are alleged. As the Court stated in another context: "Nothing we have said is intended even remotely to imply that, under the cloak of religion, persons may, with impunity, commit frauds upon the public."

General Council on Fin. & Admin. v. Cal. Super. Ct., 439 U.S. 1369, 1372–73, 99 S.Ct. 35, 58 L.Ed.2d 63 (1978) (citations omitted). The threshold inquiry is whether the underlying dispute is a secular one, capable of review by a secular court, or an ecclesiastical one about "discipline, faith, internal organization, or ecclesiastical rule, custom or law." *Bell v. Presbyterian Church (U.S.A.)*, 126 F.3d 328, 331 (4th Cir.1997) (quoting *Serbian E. Orthodox Diocese*, 426 U.S. at 713, 96 S.ct. 2372)[.]

Consistent with *General Council*, we do not read the religious autonomy doctrine to require a blanket protection of a church from any and all accountability in secular courts. This case is not an intrachurch dispute; the claim was not brought under church law, nor did it seek to enforce the duties of defendant according to religious beliefs. This case was litigated to a jury verdict without, appropriately, inquiry into the validity of religious doctrine. See *Serbian E. Orthodox Diocese*, 426 U.S. at 709, 96 S.Ct. 2372 (noting that courts that probe too deeply into the allocation of power within a hierarchical church violate the First Amendment in much the same manner as civil determination of religious doctrine). Further, defendant did not invoke any religious doctrine in defense of its actions, nor does it claim that the reason it failed to act in a non-negligent manner was because of a religious belief or practice. See, e.g., *Bryce*, 289 F.3d at 657. In these circumstances, the religious autonomy doctrine does not shield a church from accountability for its negligent actions. See *Martinelli*, 196 F.3d at 431–32; *Nielsen v. Archdiocese of Denver*, 413 F.Supp.2d 1181, 1184–85 (D.Colo.2006); *Malicki*, 814 So.2d at 363–64; *Roman Catholic Diocese of Jackson*, 905 So.2d at 1235–37.... For the above reasons, we reject defendant's First Amendment arguments. In doing so, we find persuasive and follow the majority of decisions that have addressed similar arguments....

5. *Foreign Sovereign Immunity*

Doe v. Holy See

Ninth Circuit, 2009

557 F.3d 1066

[*cert. denied* 2010; sub. hist.: 2011 WL 1541275 (D. Or. 2011)]

PER CURIAM:

We consider whether, on the allegations made in the Plaintiff's complaint in this case, the Holy See is entitled to immunity from suit under the Foreign Sovereign Immunities Act ("FSIA"), 28 U.S.C. §§ 1330, 1602–1611.... John V. Doe brought suit in the United States District Court for the District of Oregon against the Holy See, the Archdiocese of Portland, Oregon ("Archdiocese"), the Catholic Bishop of Chicago ("Chicago Bishop"), and the Order of the Friar Servants ("Order"), alleging that when he was fifteen or sixteen years old he was sexually abused by Father Ronan, a priest in the Archdiocese and a member of the Order. Doe alleged various causes of action against the Holy See: (1) for vicarious liability based on the actions of the Holy See's instrumentalities, the Archdiocese, the Chicago Bishop, and the Order; (2) for respondeat superior liability based on the actions of the Holy See's employee, Ronan; and (3) for direct liability for the Holy See's own negligent retention and supervision of Ronan and its negligent failure to warn Doe of Ronan's dangerous proclivities. The Holy See contended in the district court that all of Doe's causes of action against it must be dismissed because, as a foreign sovereign, it is immune from suit in U.S. courts. The district court disagreed, holding that it has jurisdiction over all but one of Doe's claims under the FSIA's tortious act exception to sovereign immunity. The Holy See appeals....

In his amended complaint, filed April 1, 2004, Doe describes as follows Father Andrew Ronan's alleged sexual abuse of young boys: In 1955 or 1956, while employed as a parish priest in the Archdiocese of Armagh, Ireland, Father Ronan molested a minor and admitted to doing so. Ronan was later removed from Our Lady of Benburb and placed in the employ of the Chicago Bishop, at St. Philip's High School. At St. Philip's, Ronan molested at least three male students. Confronted with allegations of abuse, Ronan admitted to molesting the boys. The Chicago Bishop, "acting in accordance with the policies, practices, and procedures" of the Holy See, did not discipline or remove Ronan from his post.[1]

In approximately 1965, when Doe was 15 or 16 years old, the Holy See and the Order of the Friar Servants, of which Ronan was a member, "placed" Ronan in a parish priest position at St. Albert's Church in Portland, Oregon. Doe met Ronan at St. Albert's and came to know Ronan "as his priest, counselor and spiritual adviser." Doe was a devout Roman Catholic, and for him "Ronan was a person of great influence and persuasion as a holy man and authority figure." Using his position of trust and authority, Ronan "engaged in harmful sexual contact upon" Doe on repeated occasions. The sexual contact occurred "in several places including the monastery and surrounding areas."

Based on these facts, Doe alleged causes of action against the Holy See, its "instrumentalities or agents" ("Does 1–10"), the Archdiocese, the Chicago Bishop, and the Order, all of whom it alleged were employers of Ronan. According to the amended complaint:

> Defendant Holy See is the ecclesiastical, governmental, and administrative capital of the Roman Catholic Church. Defendant Holy See is the composite of the au-

---

1. These are, of course, only allegations, but we are required to take them as true for the purposes of this appeal. *See infra*, Part III.A.

thority, jurisdiction, and sovereignty vested in the Pope and his delegated advisors to direct the world-wide Roman Catholic Church. Defendant Holy See has unqualified power over the Catholic Church including each and every individual and section of the [C]hurch. Defendant Holy See directs, supervises, supports, promotes[,] and engages in providing religious and pastoral guidance, education[,] and counseling services to Roman Catholics world-wide in exchange for all or a portion of the revenues derived from its members for these services. The Holy See engages in these activities through its agents, cardinals, bishops[,] and clergy, including religious order priests, brothers[,] and sisters, who engage in pastoral work under the authority of its bishop[s]. The Holy See is supported through the contributions of the faithful[,] which are received through donations from the dioceses around the world, including those in the United States. Defendant Holy See promotes and safeguards the morals and standards of conduct of the clergy of the [C]atholic [C]hurch. Defendant Holy See does this by and through its agents and instrumentalities, including the Congregation for the Clergy and the Congregation for Religious both delegated by the Pope and acting on his behalf. It creates, divides[,] and re-aligns dioceses, archdioceses[,] and ecclesiastical provinces. It also gives final approval to the creation, division[,] or suppression of provinces of religious orders.... It creates, appoints, assigns and re-assigns bishops [and] superiors of religious orders, and through the bishops and superiors of religious orders [it] has the power to directly assign and remove individual clergy. All bishops, clergy, and priests, including religious order priests, vow to show respect and obedience to the Pope and their bishop. Defendant Holy See also examines and is responsible for the work and discipline and all those things which concern bishops, superiors of religious orders, priests[,] and deacons of the religious clergy. In furtherance of this duty, Defendant Holy See requires bishops to file a report, on a regular basis, outlining the status of, and any problems with, clergy. Defendant Holy See promulgates and enforces the laws and regulations regarding the education, training[,] and standards of conduct and discipline for its members and those who serve in the governmental, administrative, judicial, educational[,] and pastoral workings of the Catholic [C]hurch world-wide. Defendant Holy See is also directly responsible for removing superiors of religious orders, bishops, archbishops[,] and cardinals from service and/or making them ineligible for positions of leadership in the various divisions and offices of the Catholic [C]hurch.

The Archdiocese, according to the amend[ed] complaint, is a corporation incorporated under the laws of the state of Oregon and is therefore a citizen of that state. It "provided pastoral services to [Doe] and his immediate family through its parishes." The Chicago Bishop is incorporated under the laws of the state of Illinois and is a citizen of that state. Finally, the Order is "a citizen of the state of Illinois," but it operates worldwide. It is under the "ultimate authority of" the Holy See.

Doe alleged that the Archdiocese and the Order were vicariously liable for Ronan's abuse of Doe, and that the Chicago Bishop and the Order were negligent in failing to warn the Archdiocese and Doe of Ronan's propensities. Doe also alleged that the Holy See was vicariously liable for Ronan's abuse of Doe and for the negligent actions of the Archdiocese, the Order, and the Chicago Bishop, and that the Holy See was itself negligent in its retention and supervision of Ronan and in failing to warn of his propensities....

The Holy See moved to dismiss the complaint in its entirety for lack of subject-matter jurisdiction, arguing that as a foreign sovereign, it is presumptively immune from suit under the FSIA, and that neither the "tortious act" exception to sovereign immunity, 28 U.S.C. § 1605(a)(5), nor the "commercial activity" exception to sovereign immunity, 28 U.S.C. § 1605(a)(2), applies. The district court held that the commercial activity exception does not apply to permit the exercise of jurisdiction over Doe's claims; the court did not view the Holy See's activities as commercial because "the true essence of the complaint ... clearly sound[s] in tort." *Doe v. Holy See*, 434 F.Supp.2d 925, 942 (D.Or.2006). In contrast, the district court held that the tortious act exception does apply, permitting it to exercise jurisdiction over all Doe's claims except for the fraud claim. *Id.* at 957. The district court therefore granted the Holy See's motion to dismiss as to the fraud claim, but it denied the motion as to all of Doe's other claims.... The Holy See appeals the district court's decision that the tortious act exception applies. Doe cross-appeals the district court's dismissal of his fraud claim, contending that the commercial activity exception permits federal court jurisdiction over that cause of action....

For much of our nation's history, from at least 1812 until 1952, "the United States generally granted foreign sovereigns complete immunity from suit in the courts of this country." *Verlinden B.V. v. Cent. Bank of Nigeria*, 461 U.S. 480, 486, 103 S.Ct. 1962, 76 L.Ed.2d 81 (1983) (citing *The Schooner Exchange v. M'Faddon*, 7 Cranch 116, 3 L.Ed. 287 (1812)). In 1952, however, the State Department adopted a more "restrictive" theory of foreign sovereign immunity, under which sovereign "immunity is confined to suits involving the foreign sovereign's public acts." *Id.* at 487, 103 S.Ct. 1962. Applying this restrictive approach, questions of foreign sovereign immunity arising in U.S. courts were decided on a case-by-case basis, often with the assistance of letters from the State Department containing "suggestions of immunity." *Id.*... In 1976, to "clarify the governing standards" and to insulate the issue of sovereign immunity from the impact of "case-by-case diplomatic pressures," Congress enacted the FSIA, 28 U.S.C. §§ 1330, 1602–1611. *Verlinden*, 461 U.S. at 488, 103 S.Ct. 1962. The FSIA contains "a comprehensive set of legal standards governing claims of immunity in every civil action against a foreign state or its political subdivisions, agencies, or instrumentalities." *Id.* at 488, 103 S.Ct. 1962. It is this set of legal standards with which we deal today.

Under the FSIA, a foreign state is "immune from the jurisdiction of the courts of the United States and of the States" unless one of the statute's enumerated exceptions applies. 28 U.S.C. § 1604. A foreign state "includes a political subdivision of a foreign state or an agency or instrumentality of a foreign state." *Id.* § 1603(a). An "agency or instrumentality of a foreign state" is defined in turn as any entity:

(1) which is a separate legal person, corporate or otherwise, and

(2) which is an organ of a foreign state or political subdivision thereof, ... and

(3) which is neither a citizen of a State of the United States ... nor created under the laws of any third country.

Id. § 1603(b).

Section 1605[2] contains "[g]eneral exceptions to the jurisdictional immunity of a foreign state," providing in relevant part that:

(a) A foreign state shall not be immune from the jurisdiction of courts of the United States or of the States in any case—

...

---

2. All statutory citations are to Title 28 of the United States Code unless otherwise indicated.

(2) in which the action is based upon a commercial activity carried on in the United States by the foreign state; or upon an act performed in the United States in connection with a commercial activity of the foreign state elsewhere; or upon an act outside the territory of the United States in connection with a commercial activity of the foreign state elsewhere and that act causes a direct effect in the United States;

...

(5) not otherwise encompassed in paragraph (2) above, in which money damages are sought against a foreign state for personal injury or death, or damage to or loss of property, occurring in the United States and caused by the tortious act of that foreign state or of any official or employee of that foreign state while acting within the scope of his office or employment; except this paragraph shall not apply to—

(A) any claim based upon the exercise or performance or the failure to exercise or perform a discretionary function regardless of whether the discretion be abused, or

(B) any claim arising out of malicious prosecution, abuse of process, libel, slander, misrepresentation, deceit, or interference with contract rights ...

The statute further defines the elements of the commercial activity exception: A "'commercial activity' means either a regular course of commercial conduct or a particular commercial transaction or act. The commercial character of an activity shall be determined by reference to the nature of the course of conduct or particular transaction or act, rather than by reference to its purpose." *Id.* § 1603(d). A "'commercial activity carried on in the United States by a foreign state' means commercial activity carried on by such state and having substantial contact with the United States." *Id.* § 1603(e).... The statute does not set out any substantive rules of liability, but instead provides that, "[a]s to any claim for relief with respect to which a foreign state is not entitled to immunity under" the statute, "the foreign state shall be liable in the same manner and to the same extent as a private individual under like circumstances." *Id.* § 1606....

The Holy See has brought a facial attack on the subject matter jurisdiction of the district court under Rule 12(b)(1). We therefore "assume [plaintiff's] [factual] allegations to be true and draw all reasonable inferences in his favor." *Wolfe v. Strankman*, 392 F.3d 358, 362 (9th Cir.2004); *see also McNatt v. Apfel*, 201 F.3d 1084, 1087 (9th Cir.2000) (holding that we "favorably view[ ] the facts alleged to support jurisdiction"). We do not, however, accept the "truth of *legal* conclusions merely because they are cast in the form of factual allegations." *Warren v. Fox Family Worldwide, Inc.*, 328 F.3d 1136, 1139 (9th Cir.2003) (emphasis added; internal quotations omitted) (quoting *W. Mining Council v. Watt*, 643 F.2d 618, 624 (9th Cir.1981))....

Doe cross-appeals and argues that his claims come within the FSIA's commercial activity exception to sovereign immunity, § 1605(a)(2). The Holy See contends that we do not have jurisdiction over Doe's cross-appeal because it is not "inextricably intertwined" with the collaterally appealable issue of whether the Holy See is immune from suit. *See Burlington N. & Santa Fe Ry. Co. v. Vaughn*, 509 F.3d 1085, 1093–94 (9th Cir.2007) (in a case involving a collaterally appealable order, denying a tribe sovereign immunity, but holding that the court could not reach other issues raised on appeal because they were not "inextricably intertwined" with the collaterally appealable issue). According to the Holy See, we do not have jurisdiction to consider Doe's argument that his claims come within the commercial activity exception. We agree.... Here, the tort causes of action are not inextricably intertwined with Doe's other claims. Thus, that concept is not sufficient to allow Doe to appeal the district court's grant of immunity as far as that exception is concerned.[3] ... Thus, we will not consider issues regarding the district court's grant of immunity under the commercial exception to the FSIA....

Before turning to the question of which, if any, of the FSIA's exceptions to immunity apply, we must determine which of the acts alleged in the complaint may legitimately be attributed to the Holy See for purposes of establishing jurisdiction. Doe's complaint alleges tortious acts by the Archdiocese, the Order, and the Bishop, all alleged to be corporations created by the Holy See. The Holy See argues that we may not consider these alleged acts by the Archdiocese, the Order, and the Bishop when determining whether jurisdiction exists over the Holy See, because Doe has not alleged facts that would overcome the presumption of separate juridical status such that the acts of the latter could be attributed to the former.[6] For the reasons explained below, given the allegations that Doe has pleaded, we agree with the Holy See. In addition, however, the complaint alleges a number of actions performed by the Holy See itself, such as "creat[ing]" dioceses and archdioceses, "giv[ing] final approval to the creation, division or suppression of provinces of religious orders," "employ[ing]" Ronan, and "plac[ing]" Ronan in the Archdiocese in Portland, Oregon. We conclude below that these acts do establish jurisdiction over the Holy See for the claims to which the acts are relevant....

In arguing that the actions of the corporations are not attributable to Holy See for purposes of determining jurisdiction, the Holy See relies on *First Nat. City Bank v. Banco Para el Comercio Exterior de Cuba ("Bancec"),* 462 U.S. 611, 103 S.Ct. 2591, 77 L.Ed.2d 46 (1983). In *Bancec,* the Supreme Court considered whether an instrumentality created by a foreign state could be held liable for the actions of the foreign state itself, a question the reverse of ours. Bancec was "the Cuban Government's exclusive agent in foreign trade," and the "government supplied all of [Bancec]'s capital and owned all of its stock." *Id.* at 614, 103 S.Ct. 2591. Soon after Bancec sought to collect on a letter of credit that had been issued in its favor by Citibank, the Cuban government seized and nationalized all of Citibank's assets in Cuba. *Id.* So, when Bancec filed an action in U.S. federal court to

---

3. We are aware of the fact that § 1605(a)(5), identifying the tortious act exception, is applicable to cases "not otherwise encompassed in paragraph (2) [the commercial activity exception] above." This language does not mean that, in interpreting the tortious act exception in (a)(5), we must always first consider whether the commercial activity exception in (a)(2) applies. Courts have not proceeded in that fashion. *See, e.g., Argentine Republic v. Amerada Hess Shipping Corp.,* 488 U.S. 428, 439–43, 109 S.Ct. 683, 102 L.Ed.2d 818 (1989); *Blaxland v. Commonwealth Dir. of Public Prosecutions,* 323 F.3d 1198, 1203–04 (9th Cir.2003); *Risk v. Halvorsen,* 936 F.2d 393, 395–96 (9th Cir.1991). Indeed, in *Joseph,* 830 F.2d at 1025, we explicitly stated that because we could decide the question presented under subsection (a)(5), there was no need to consider subsection (a)(2) at all. Other courts have reached the same result. *See, e.g., Robinson v. Gov't of Malay.,* 269 F.3d 133, 145–47 (2d Cir.2001); *Cabiri v. Gov't of Republic of Ghana,* 165 F.3d 193, 199–201 (2d Cir.1999); *Frolova v. Union of Soviet Socialist Republics,* 761 F.2d 370, 379 (7th Cir.1985); *Asociacion de Reclamantes v. United Mexican States,* 735 F.2d 1517, 1524–25 (D.C.Cir.1984); *Persinger v. Islamic Republic of Iran,* 729 F.2d 835, 838–39 (D.C.Cir.1984).

6. We note that the question we address here is distinct from the question whether the Archdiocese, the Chicago Bishop, and the Order are themselves immune from suit under the FSIA. An "agency or instrumentality" of a foreign state, as defined by the FSIA, is immune from suit because it is itself a "foreign state" within the meaning of the Act. § 1603(a), (b). On the allegation of the complaint, however, the Archdiocese, the Chicago Bishop, and the Order are not "agencies or instrumentalities" of a foreign state within the meaning of the FSIA, because they are all citizens of the United States. *See* § 1603(b) (an agency or instrumentality of a foreign state means, among other things, an entity "which is neither a citizen of a State of the United States ... nor created under the laws of any third country"). They are therefore not immune from suit.

recover on the letter of credit, Citibank counterclaimed, seeking a setoff for the value of its expropriated Cuban branches. *Id.* at 614–15, 103 S.Ct. 2591. In the meantime, Bancec was dissolved, and Bancec filed a stipulation "stating that ... its claim had been transferred to the Ministry of Foreign Trade" of Cuba. *Id.* at 615–16, 103 S.Ct. 2591.... Jurisdiction in *Bancec* existed under FSIA's counterclaim provision, 28 U.S.C. § 1607(c).[7] *Id.* at 620–21, 103 S.Ct. 2591. Because jurisdiction was not at issue, the question for the Supreme Court was one of liability: whether Bancec could be held liable for the act of expropriation committed by the Cuban government. *Id.* at 617, 103 S.Ct. 2591.

The Supreme Court began by noting that, although Bancec was an "agency or instrumentality" of Cuba within the meaning of FSIA § 1603(b), this status was relevant only to jurisdiction; it did not control the question of Bancec's liability for Cuba's actions. The FSIA "was not intended to affect the substantive law determining the liability of a foreign state or instrumentality." *Id.* at 620, 103 S.Ct. 2591. Instead, liability was to be assessed according to corporate law principles "common to both international law and federal common law." *Id.* at 623, 103 S.Ct. 2591. Surveying international and federal law on the status of corporations, the Supreme Court recognized a presumption of "separate juridical [status]" for the instrumentalities of foreign states. *Id.* at 624, 624–28, 103 S.Ct. 2591.... That presumption can be overcome, the Court explained, in two instances: when "a corporate entity is so extensively controlled by its owner that a relationship of principal and agent is created," or when recognizing the separate status of a corporation "would work fraud or injustice." *Id.* at 629, 103 S.Ct. 2591. The Court then held the latter standard dispositive of Bancec's case: The Cuban government could not have sued in its own name in a U.S. court "without waiving its sovereign immunity and answering for [its] seizure of Citibank's assets." *Id.* at 633, 103 S.Ct. 2591. Instead, Cuba had transferred its assets to separate entities, and Bancec then sought to avoid liability for the seizure. "[T]he Cuban government ... [and] not any third parties that may have relied on Bancec's separate juridical identity" would be the real beneficiary if Bancec was not held liable for the Cuban government's actions. *Id.* at 631–32, 103 S.Ct. 2591. Given this circumstance, the Court concluded that to "adhere blindly to the corporate form" would work such an "injustice" that the presumption of separate juridical status had been overcome. *Id.* at 632, 103 S.Ct. 2591. Holding Bancec liable for the Cuban government's actions, the Court held that Citibank was entitled to offset the value of its seized assets from the amount it owed to Bancec. *Id.* at 634, 103 S.Ct. 2591.

The Supreme Court in *Bancec* did not have the opportunity to consider whether the actions of a *corporation* may be attributed to the *sovereign*— the reverse of the *Bancec* scenario — for purposes of determining whether jurisdiction over that sovereign exists. This Circuit has not previously addressed that question either.... [footnote omitted]. At least two other circuits, however, faced with such a scenario, have applied *Bancec*'s substantive corporate law principles in determining whether jurisdiction exists under the FSIA....

Bancec provides a workable standard for deciding this question. Applying *Bancec*'s presumption in favor of separate juridical status for foreign state instrumentalities at the jurisdiction phase, not just at the liability phase, is consistent with the FSIA's broad policy goals. In *Bancec*, the Court discussed at length the comity considerations at play when entertaining suits against foreign government instrumentalities in U.S. courts. 462 U.S. at 626, 103 S.Ct. 2591; *see also Republic of Austria v. Altmann*, 541 U.S. 677, 688, 124

---

7. "In any action brought by a foreign state [or its agency or instrumentality] ... in a court of the United States or of a State, the foreign state shall not be accorded immunity with respect to any counterclaim ... to the extent that the counterclaim does not seek relief exceeding in amount or differing in kind from that sought by the foreign state." 28 U.S.C. § 1607(c).

S.Ct. 2240, 159 L.Ed.2d 1 (2004). As at the merits phase, failing to recognize the presumption of separate juridical status at the jurisdictional phase could "result in substantial uncertainty over whether an instrumentality's assets would be diverted to satisfy a claim against the sovereign," and might frustrate "the efforts of sovereign nations to structure their governmental activities in a manner deemed necessary to promote economic development and efficient administration." *Bancec*, 462 U.S. at 626, 103 S.Ct. 2591. Applying *Bancec*'s presumption—as well as the standard for overcoming that presumption—at the outset of a suit as well as at the merits phase makes good sense.... With these considerations in mind, we conclude that it is appropriate to use the *Bancec* standard to determine whether Doe's allegations are sufficient to permit jurisdiction over the Holy See based on acts committed by its affiliated domestic corporations....

Applying the rule of Bancec to the allegations in Doe's complaint, we conclude that Doe has not alleged sufficient facts to overcome the "presumption of separate juridical status," for reasons similar to those dispositive in the converse situation in *Flatow v. Islamic Republic of Iran*, 308 F.3d 1065 (9th Cir.2002). In *Flatow*, we applied *Bancec* to the relationship between the Iranian government and the Bank Saderat Iran ("BSI"). BSI was created by the Iranian government and fully owned by it. *Id.* at 1072–73. Its actions were regulated by Iran's General Assembly of Banks and High Council of Banks, which reviewed BSI's annual statements and "perform[ed] broad policymaking functions." *Id.* at 1073. *Flatow* held these facts insufficient to overcome the presumption of separate juridical status, because the government's "involvement [did not] rise to a [sufficiently] high [ ] level," and in particular, did not involve "day-to-day" control. *Id.* (citing *McKesson Corp. v. Islamic Republic of Iran*, 52 F.3d 346, 351–52 (D.C.Cir.1995)) (holding the presumption of separateness overcome where Iran controlled routine business decisions, such as declaring and paying dividends and honoring contracts).

Doe's complaint does not allege day-to-day, routine involvement of the Holy See in the affairs of the Archdiocese, the Order, and the Bishop. Instead, it alleges that the Holy See "creates, divides[,] and re-aligns dioceses, archdioceses and ecclesiastical provinces" and "gives final approval to the creation, division or suppression of provinces of religious orders." Doe also alleges that the Holy See "promulgates and enforces the laws and regulations regarding the education, training[,] and standards of conduct and discipline for its members and those who serve in the governmental, administrative, judicial, educational[,] and pastoral workings of the Catholic [C]hurch world-wide." These factual allegations— that the Holy See participated in creating the corporations and continues to promulgate laws and regulations that apply to them—are quite similar to the facts in *Flatow*, and are, as in *Flatow*, insufficient to overcome the presumption of separate juridical status.

Doe does directly allege in his complaint that the corporations are "agents" of the Holy See. In this context, however, the term "agent" is not self-explanatory. "Agent" can have more than one legal meaning: the standard for determining that a natural person is the agent of another differs from the standard for attribution of the actions of a corporation to another entity. *See, e.g., Rough & Ready Lumber Co. v. Blue Sky Forest Products*, 105 Or.App. 227, 231, 804 P.2d 498 (1991) (an agency relationship between two natural persons "results from the manifestation of consent by one person to another that the other shall act on his behalf and subject to his control, and consent by the other so to act.") (quoting Restatement (Second) of Agency § 1 (1958)). The *Bancec* standard is in fact most similar to the "alter ego" or "piercing the corporate veil" standards applied in many state courts to determine whether the actions of a corporation are attributable to its owners. *See, e.g., Amfac Foods, Inc. v. Int'l Sys. & Controls Corp.*, 294 Or. 94, 107–08, 654 P.2d 1092 (1982) (holding that to demonstrate alter ego status, plaintiff must show control of the subsidiary and that "the plaintiff's inability to collect from the corporation resulted from some form of improper conduct" on part of parent corporation). Even reading the complaint generously to Doe, as we must, we cannot infer from the use of the word "agent" that Doe is alleging the type of day-to-day control that *Bancec* and *Flatow* require to overcome the presumption of separate juridical status.

The district court apparently found jurisdiction proper by relying on the second, equitable prong of *Bancec*, noting that "foreign states cannot avoid their obligations to third parties by engaging in abuses of the corporate form." *Doe*, 434 F.Supp.2d at 936. But Doe has not alleged that the Holy See has inappropriately used the separate status of the corporations to its own benefit, as in *Bancec*, or that the Holy See created the corporations for the purpose of evading liability for its own wrongs. Rather, in ruling for Doe on this point, the district court seemed to be influenced by the complaint's allegations of wrongful acts perpetrated directly by the Holy See. *See Doe*, 434 F.Supp.2d at 937. The existence of such *direct* wrongful acts cannot determine whether the distinct wrongful acts of the affiliated *corporations* should also be attributed to the Holy See.

Doe's vicarious liability claim for the actions of the Archdiocese, Chicago Bishop, and Order is based entirely on an allegation that the actions of the domestic corporations are attributable to the Holy See. Doe has therefore not alleged sufficient facts to demonstrate that any exception to sovereign immunity applies to that cause of action. We therefore conclude that the district court lacked jurisdiction over the Holy See for the tortious acts allegedly committed by the Archdiocese, the Chicago Bishop, and the Order....

As to Doe's other causes of action, the Holy See contends that Doe has failed to allege any facts in support of his claims based on the actions of the Holy See itself, rather than of its domestic corporations. We do not agree. Doe has made several allegations regarding actions taken by the Holy See itself—namely, its negligent retention and supervision of Ronan and its failure to warn Doe of Ronan's dangerousness. Doe has also alleged respondeat superior liability against the Holy See for Ronan's actions as an alleged employee of the Holy See. We turn now to those allegations, considering whether they are sufficient to support jurisdiction over the Holy See....

The district court held that all of Doe's claims, except the one for fraud, come within the exception to immunity for a "tortious act or omission of [a] foreign state or of any official or employee of that foreign state while acting within the scope of his or her employment." § 1605(a)(2); *Doe*, 434 F.Supp.2d at 950. We agree in part.... Doe's respondeat superior claim based on Ronan's actions comes within the tortious act exception. Doe has clearly alleged that Ronan was an employee of the Holy See, acting within the scope of his employment, when he molested Doe. We conclude, however, that Doe's claims against the Holy See for negligent retention and supervision and failure to warn cannot be brought under the tort exception because they are barred by the FSIA's exclusion for discretionary functions, § 1605(a)(5)(A)....

In his complaint, Doe alleges that the Holy See "employed priests, including one Father Andrew Ronan" and that Ronan was under the "direct supervision and control" of the Holy See. The Holy See was further "responsible for the work and discipline [of] ... priests." According to the complaint, the Holy See on at least one occasion was responsible for controlling where Ronan performed his functions: the Holy See "placed Ronan in [the] Archdiocese at St. Albert's Church in Portland, Oregon." ... The Holy See maintains that Doe has not alleged sufficient facts to demonstrate that Ronan was an "employee" of the Holy See for purposes of the tortious act exception, because the word "employee" is a legal conclusion we are not required to accept as true. We are highly skeptical of the notion that, under notice pleading, use of the word "employee" in a complaint is insufficient to establish an allegation of an employment relationship. True, in addition to being a word used in everyday speech, "employee" does have a common law legal definition. *See, e.g., Schaff v. Ray's Land & Sea Food Co.*, 334 Or. 94, 45 P.3d 936, 939 (2002) (defining "employee" for purposes of Oregon law). But then, of course, so do the words "person," "corporation," "citizen," and "molest," also used in this complaint—and, undoubtedly, in many other complaints filed each year in federal courts—without further definition. Were we to require that every such word used in a complaint be broken down into its constituent factual predicates, we would undermine the purpose of notice pleading— that is, "to focus litigation on the merits of a claim" rather than on procedural requirements. *Galbraith v. County of Santa Clara*, 307 F.3d 1119, 1125 (9th Cir.2002). Thus, while we do not accept Doe's legal conclusions as true, we also do not engage in "a hypertechnical reading of the complaint inconsistent with the generous notice pleading standard." *Mendoza v. Zirkle Fruit Co.*, 301 F.3d 1163, 1168 (9th Cir.2002). Although there is undoubtedly a line beyond which the legal definition of a commonly used term is so complex or contentious that failure to allege each element of the definition would prevent a defendant from understanding the factual basis for the claim, use of the word "employee" falls well short of that line....

More complicated under Oregon law is the question of whether Ronan's actions were "within the scope of employment" as the FSIA requires. In *Joseph*, we indicated that the "'scope of employment' provision of the tortious activity exception essentially requires a finding that the doctrine of respondeat superior applies to the tortious acts of individuals." 830 F.2d at 1025. "This determination is governed by state law." *Id.; see also Randolph*, 97 F.3d at 327.... As it happens, the Oregon Supreme Court has directly addressed whether a church can be liable under respondeat superior for the actions of a priest who sexually assaults a parishioner. In *Fearing v. Bucher*, 328 Or. 367, 977 P.2d 1163 (1999), the plaintiff alleged that he had been sexually molested by a Catholic priest who "used his position as youth pastor, spiritual guide, confessor, and priest to plaintiff and his family to gain their trust and confidence" and "[b]y virtue of that relationship ... gained the opportunity to be alone with plaintiff" and sexually assault him. *Id.* at 1166. *Fearing* began its analysis from the proposition that, in a respondeat superior action, an employer can be liable for intentional as well as unintentional torts of an employee if committed "within the scope of employment." *Id.* Generally, under Oregon law, "three requirements must be met to demonstrate that an employee was acting within the course and scope of employment":

(1) the act must have occurred substantially within the time and space limits authorized by the employment;

(2) the employee must have been motivated, at least partially, by a purpose to serve the employer; and

(3) the act must have been of a kind which the employee was hired to perform.

Id. at 1166.

Applying these three factors, *Fearing* stated that the priest's "alleged sexual assaults on plaintiff clearly were outside the scope of his employment" under the traditional test, but held that the "inquiry does not end there." *Id.* at 1166. Instead, the court went on to ask whether "acts that *were* within [the priest's] scope of employment resulted in the acts which led to injury to [the] plaintiff." *Id.* (emphasis added; internal quotation marks and citation omitted). The court concluded that because a jury could infer from the facts alleged that "performance of ... pastoral duties with respect to plaintiff and his family were a necessary precursor to the sexual abuse and that the assaults thus were a direct outgrowth of and were engendered by conduct that was within the scope of ... employment," *id.* at 1168, the complaint satisfied "all three ... requirements for establishing that employee conduct was within the scope of employment." *Id.* at 1167.

The Oregon Supreme Court has since clarified that *Fearing* created a "scope of employment" test specifically applicable to intentional torts. *Minnis v. Oregon Mut. Ins. Co.*, 334 Or. 191, 48 P.3d 137 (Or.2002), observed that, in *Fearing*, there was no question that the first requirement of "the within the scope of employment" test was met, because the abuse occurred "within the time and space limits" of the priest's employment. 48 P.3d at 144–45. But because *Fearing* involved an intentional tort, it was inappropriate to focus on whether the tort itself was committed in furtherance of the employer's objectives or was an act of the kind the employee was hired to perform:

> Rather, for the purpose of determining whether a complaint meets the second and third ... requirements..., the focus properly is directed at whether the complaint contains sufficient allegations of employee's conduct that was within the scope of his employment, that is, conduct that the employee was hired to perform, that arguably resulted in the acts that caused plaintiff's injury.

Id. at 144–45 (internal quotation marks, alterations, and citations omitted). *Minnis* thus makes clear that, rather than holding that sexual abuse is not within the scope of employment, *Fearing* created an alternative test with respect to the second and third factors of the "within the scope of employment" standard, applicable when a plaintiff has alleged an intentional tort: An intentional tort is within the scope of employment, and can support respondeat superior liability for the employer, if conduct that was within the scope of employment was "a necessary precursor to the" intentional tort and the intentional tort was "a direct outgrowth of ... conduct that was within the scope of ... employment." *Fearing*, 977 P.2d at 1163.

Doe's allegations meet this standard. Doe has asserted that he "came to know Ronan as his priest, counselor and spiritual adviser," and that Ronan used his "position of authority" to "engage in harmful sexual contact upon" Doe in "several places including the monastery and surrounding areas in Portland, Oregon." His allegations are thus very similar to those in *Fearing*, 977 P.2d at 1166.... Under Oregon law, then, Doe has clearly alleged sufficient facts to show that his claim is based on an injury caused by an "employee" of the foreign state while acting "within the scope of his ... employment," as required to come within the FSIA's tortious act exception. § 1605(a)(5). The Holy See is therefore not immune from Doe's respondeat superior claim.... [[footnote omitted].

According to Doe's complaint, the Holy See "negligently retained Ronan and failed to warn those coming into contact with him," even though it knew or should have known that Ronan had a history of sexually abusing children. The Holy See also "failed to provide reasonable supervision of Ronan." Whether or not this alleged negligence otherwise comes within the language of the FSIA's tortious act exception—a question we do not decide—these causes of action may not go forward under that section because they are barred by the exclusion for "discretionary functions." The district court thus erred in exercising jurisdiction over these claims.... The discretionary function exclusion shields foreign sovereigns from tort claims "based upon the exercise or performance or the failure to exercise or perform a discretionary function regardless of whether the discretion be abused." § 1605(5)(A). The language of the discretionary function exclusion closely parallels the language of a similar exclusion in the Federal Tort Claims Act ("FTCA"), so we look to case law on the FTCA when interpreting the FSIA's discretionary function exclusion. *See* 28 U.S.C. § 2680(a); *Joseph*, 830 F.2d at 1026. Extrapolating from FTCA case law, the

Holy See is protected by the discretionary function exclusion if the challenged action meets two criteria: (1) it is "discretionary in nature" or "involve[s] an element of judgment or choice" and (2) "the judgment is of the kind that the discretionary function exception was designed to shield." *United States v. Gaubert*, 499 U.S. 315, 322, 111 S.Ct. 1267, 113 L.Ed.2d 335 (1991) (internal quotation marks and citation omitted); *see also Soldano v. United States*, 453 F.3d 1140, 1145 (9th Cir.2006) (clarifying that judgments "of the kind that the discretionary function exception was designed to shield" are "governmental actions and decisions based on considerations of public policy.") (internal quotation marks and citations omitted).

As to the first *Gaubert* criterion, Doe refers vaguely in his complaint to the Holy See's "policies, practices, and procedures" of not firing priests for, and not warning others about, their abusive acts. He also refers in his brief to a "policy promulgated by the Holy See to cover up incidents of child abuse," which he argues removed "an[y] element of judgment or choice" from the Holy See's actions "to the extent that Appellants were acting pursuant to" it. Yet nowhere does Doe allege the existence of a policy that is *"specific* and *mandatory"* on the Holy See. *Kennewick Irrigation Dist. v. United States*, 880 F.2d 1018, 1026 (9th Cir.1989) (emphasis in original). He does not state the terms of this alleged policy, or describe any documents, promulgations, or orders embodying it. Nor does the complaint in any other way allege that the Holy See's decisions to retain Doe and not warn about his proclivities involved no element of judgment, choice, or discretion. While the burden of proving the *Gaubert* factors ultimately falls on the sovereign entity asserting the discretionary function exception, "a plaintiff must advance a claim that is facially outside the discretionary function exception in order to survive a motion to dismiss." *Prescott v. United States*, 973 F.2d 696, 702 & n. 4 (9th Cir.1992) (citing *Carlyle v. U.S. Dep't of the Army*, 674 F.2d 554, 556 (6th Cir.1982) ("Only after a plaintiff has successfully invoked jurisdiction by a pleading that facially alleges matters not excepted by [the FTCA] does the burden fall on the government to prove the applicability of a specific provision of [the FTCA].")). Doe has not pled any actions that fall facially outside the discretionary function exception.

As to the second *Gaubert* criterion, the decision of whether and how to retain and supervise an employee, as well as whether to warn about his dangerous proclivities, are the type of discretionary judgments that the exclusion was designed to protect. We have held the hiring, supervision, and training of employees to be discretionary acts. *See Nurse v. United States*, 226 F.3d 996, 1001 (9th Cir.2000) (holding that plaintiff's claims of "negligent and reckless employment, supervision and training of" employees "fall squarely within the discretionary function exception"); *see also Burkhart v. Washington Metro. Area Transit Auth.*, 112 F.3d 1207, 1217 (D.C.Cir.1997) (holding that "decisions concerning the hiring, training, and super[vision]" of employees are discretionary). Moreover, failure to warn about an individual's dangerousness is discretionary.[10] *See Sigman v. United States*, 217 F.3d 785, 797 (9th Cir.2000) (failure to warn individuals on Air Force Base about po-

---

10. Even were it not the case that the "failure to warn" claim is barred by the discretionary function exclusion, it would be barred by the "misrepresentation" exclusion. Like the discretionary function exclusion, the misrepresentation exclusion in the FSIA, § 1605(a)(5)(B), has been interpreted in light of the misrepresentation exclusion in the FTCA, § 2680(h). *See de Sanchez v. Banco Central de Nicaragua*, 770 F.2d 1385, 1398 (5th Cir.1985). The misrepresentation exclusion covers both acts of affirmative misrepresentation and failure to warn. *See City and County of San Francisco v. United States*, 615 F.2d 498, 505 (9th Cir.1980) (holding that "a negligent failure to inform, without more, is misrepresentation within the meaning of" the misrepresentation exclusion). In particular, we have held that government officials' failure to warn about an individual's dangerousness, which ultimately led to sexual abuse of a minor, comes within the misrepresentation exclusion. *See Lawrence v. United States*, 340 F.3d 952, 958 (9th Cir.2003).

tentially dangerous serviceman was a discretionary function, because it "brought into play sensitive and competing policy considerations of protecting safety while preserving resources and preventing unwarranted alarm"); *Weissich v. United States*, 4 F.3d 810, 814–15 (9th Cir.1993) (failure of probation officers to warn a prosecutor that probationer was a threat to him was a discretionary decision).

The Holy See's failure to present any evidence that its actions were actually based on policy considerations is not relevant to whether the discretionary function exception applies. A foreign state's decision "need not *actually* be grounded in policy considerations so long as it is, by its nature [,] *susceptible* to a policy analysis." *See Kelly v. United States*, 241 F.3d 755, 764 n. 5 (9th Cir.2001) (second emphasis added). A policy analysis is one that implements "political, social, and economic judgments." *Berkovitz v. United States*, 486 U.S. 531, 539, 108 S.Ct. 1954, 100 L.Ed.2d 531 (1988) (internal quotation marks and citations omitted). In the case of Father Ronan's alleged abuse, the Holy See might have decided to retain him and not to warn his parishioners because it felt that to do otherwise would have harmed the Church's reputation locally, or because it felt that pastoral stability was sufficiently important for the parishioners' well-being, or because low ordination rates or staffing shortages made it necessary to keep Ronan on. That such social, economic, or political policy considerations could have influenced the decision renders it the kind of judgment that the discretionary function exception was designed to shield.... In sum, the tortious act exception does not provide jurisdiction over Doe's negligent hiring, supervision, and failure to warn claims because they are barred by the discretionary function exclusion.... [footnote omitted]. We therefore cannot affirm the district court's judgment on this ground....

In conclusion, we observe once again that the Holy See has brought a facial attack on the allegations of subject-matter jurisdiction in the complaint. It remains to be seen whether Doe can prove his allegations. While the Holy See was certainly entitled to bring a facial attack on the complaint, such an approach is not without risk, for it "call[s] upon [us] to decide far-reaching ... questions" of some importance "on a nonexistent factual record, even where ... discovery" might "reveal the plaintiff's claims to be factually baseless." *Kwai Fun Wong v. United States*, 373 F.3d 952, 957 (9th Cir.2004). After careful consideration, we have reached the conclusion that most of Doe's causes of action are not covered by the tort exception and overturn the district court's denial of immunity as to those. However, because it would be improper to consider the commercial activity exception, we express no opinion regarding that exception.

For the foregoing reasons, in appeal No. 06-35563 the decision of the district court is AFFIRMED in part, REVERSED in part, and REMANDED. The cross-appeal (No. 06-35587) is DISMISSED. Each party shall bear their own costs.

BERZON, Circuit Judge, dissenting in part:

I agree with the majority that Doe's negligence claims against the Holy See, as currently pleaded, cannot proceed under the tortious act exception to the Foreign Sovereign Immunities Act ("FSIA"). Unlike the majority, however, I would affirm the district court's holding that the FSIA does not give the Holy See immunity from Doe's claims of negligent retention, supervision, and failure to warn. As explained below, we have jurisdiction to affirm the district court on any grounds that were raised below and supported by the record, and our case law compels the conclusion that Doe's negligence claims come within the FSIA's commercial activity exception....

So, if we conclude that the tortious act exception is insufficient to support jurisdiction over any of Doe's non-fraud claims, we may look to the commercial activity exception as an alternative ground on which to affirm the district court. Contrary to the majority's assertion, by doing so we would not be exercising jurisdiction over Doe's cross-appeal, in which Doe raises a commercial activity exception argument that would permit the exercise of jurisdiction over his fraud claim. Rather, we would be determining whether the record supports *affirmance* of the district court's order as to Doe's non-fraud claims, which is the subject of the Holy See's appeal. Put another way, Doe's cross-appeal asks us to "'enlarge' the rights [he] obtained under the district court judgment," *Rivero*, 316 F.3d at 862, so the majority is quite right that we may not consider his arguments regarding the fraud claim. But Doe needed no cross-appeal to respond to the Holy See's appeal; Doe could — and did — respond by asking us simply to preserve the result that the district court reached, either by following the district court's reasoning or by a different rationale. Our case law clearly permits us to do so.... The majority concludes otherwise, maintaining that deciding the commercial activity issues involves review of a *grant* of immunity.... But that is simply not so. The district court did decide that the commercial activity exception does not apply, but — except for the fraud cause of action — it did not grant immunity on that basis, as it concluded that there was another basis for denying immunity. So the majority is just wrong when it states, repeatedly, that our reaching the commercial activity exception would entail reviewing a *grant* of immunity.

Moreover, I see no prudential reasons whatever for refusing to exercise our jurisdiction. The application of the commercial activity exception was fully litigated below, the district court decided the question, and the issue has been fully briefed and argued here. *See McClure v. Life Ins. Co. of N. Am.*, 84 F.3d 1129, 1133 (9th Cir.1996) (holding that we can decline on appeal to affirm a summary judgment on grounds not relied on by the district court if the record is inadequate or the grounds not purely legal); *Badea v. Cox*, 931 F.2d 573, 575 n. 2 (9th Cir.1991) (declining to affirm the district court on an alternative basis "as a prudential matter," because the issue had not been briefed by the government, and raised a question of first impression in this Circuit) (internal quotation marks omitted).... Given my view of the jurisdictional posture of the case, I would reach the merits of the commercial activity question and hold that, although the district court erred in applying the tortious act exception to preserve federal jurisdiction over Doe's non-fraud negligence claims, the district court's result should be affirmed on the alternative rationale that the commercial activity exception applies.... [footnote omitted].

As the majority explains, Doe's complaint sufficiently alleged an employment relationship between Ronan and the Holy See under Oregon law.... For the reasons explained in greater detail below, I would hold that that relationship constitutes "commercial activity" for purposes of the FSIA.... Ronan was employed not as a member of the Vatican's diplomatic, civil service, or military personnel, the employment of whom we have held to be a quintessentially sovereign activity under the FSIA, but in a non-sovereign — here, religious — capacity. *See Holden v. Canadian Consulate*, 92 F.3d 918, 921 (9th Cir.1996). Further, Doe's negligence claims are "based upon" the employment relationship between Ronan and the Holy See, as the FSIA requires. 28 U.S.C. § 1605(a)(2). Doe's negligent retention, supervision, and failure to warn causes of action against the Holy See therefore fall within FSIA's commercial activity exception, and the district court has jurisdiction to decide them....

The FSIA is often described as having codified the "restrictive" theory of sovereign immunity. *See, e.g.*, H.R.Rep. No. 94-1487, 7 (1976), U.S.Code Cong. & Admin.News 6604; *Verlinden B.V. v. Cent. Bank of Nigeria*, 461 U.S. 480, 487, 103 S.Ct. 1962, 76 L.Ed.2d 81 (1983). Under the restrictive theory, "a state is immune from the jurisdiction of foreign courts as to its sovereign or public acts (*jure imperii*), but not as to those that are private or commercial in character (*jure gestionis*)." *Saudi Arabia v. Nelson*, 507 U.S. 349, 359–60, 113 S.Ct. 1471, 123 L.Ed.2d 47 (1993). The Supreme Court has explained that a foreign state engages in "commercial" activities when it "do[es] not exercise powers peculiar to sovereigns," but rather "exercise[s] only those powers that can be exercised by private citizens." *Republic of Argentina v. Weltover*, 504 U.S. 607, 614, 112 S.Ct. 2160, 119 L.Ed.2d 394 (1992) (alteration in original) (internal quotation marks omitted). Clarifying the statute's requirement that courts look not at the "purpose" of a foreign state's actions but rather at the "nature" of its actions, 28 U.S.C. § 1603(e), *Weltover* explained that "the question is not whether the foreign government is acting with a profit motive or instead with the aim of fulfilling uniquely sovereign objectives," but whether the government's actions "are the *type* of actions by which a private party engages in" commerce. 504 U.S. at 614, 112 S.Ct. 2160. The reason *why* the sovereign engages in that activity—its purpose or motive—is immaterial.

What is more, no profit need be made, or need even be possible, for the activity to qualify as "commercial." In *Weltover*, Argentina's issuance of bonds to refinance its debt was held to be "commercial activity," even though the consideration Argentina received for them was "in no way commensurate with [their] value." *Id.* at 616, 112 S.Ct. 2160 (alteration in original). That fact, the Court held, "ma[de] no difference," because "[e]ngaging in a commercial act does not require the receipt of fair value, or even compliance with the common-law requirements of consideration." *Id.* Applying this understanding, courts have found that non-profit organizations can engage in commercial activity. *See, e.g., Malewicz v. City of Amsterdam*, 362 F.Supp.2d 298, 314 (D.D.C.2005) (holding that the loan of artwork by a Dutch non-profit museum to non-profit museums in the United States constitutes commercial activity, because exchanging artwork is an activity in which private individuals can engage, sometimes for profit).

In sum, a foreign state engages in commercial activity when it engages in acts that any private citizen has the power to undertake, regardless of the state's motive or the possibility of making a profit therefrom. Applying the *Weltover* definition of "commercial activity," this Circuit has repeatedly held that an employment relationship between a foreign sovereign and its employee constitutes commercial activity, so long as the employee is not a civil service, diplomatic, or military employee. In *Holden v. Canadian Consulate*, 92 F.3d 918 (9th Cir.1996), for example, a former "Commercial Officer" in the "Trade and Investment Section" of the Canadian Consulate in San Francisco brought an action alleging that the Canadian government illegally discriminated against her on the basis of sex and age. *Id.* at 919–20. Examining the FSIA's legislative history, we noted that the House Report listed "the employment of diplomatic, civil service, or military personnel ... by the Foreign state in the United States" as examples of acts that are "public or governmental and not commercial in nature." *Id.* at 921 (quoting H.R.Rep. No. 94-1487, at 16, U.S.Code Cong. & Admin.News at 6615). In contrast, the "employment or engagement of [such other employees as] laborers, clerical staff or public relations or marketing agents would be ... included within the definition of commercial activity." *Id.* (quoting H.R.Rep. No. 94-1487, at 16, U.S.Code Cong. & Admin.News at 6615). Based on this legislative history, we held that employment "of diplomatic, civil service or military personnel is governmental and the employment of other personnel is commercial." *Id.* ...

I recognize that the Holy See's dual role as not only a sovereign government but also the head of a worldwide church gives this case a peculiar complexion. But that sense of oddity comes about because the Holy See is a sovereign of a very unusual kind. Both in physical size and number of inhabitants, the land it governs is tiny. Its role as a traditional, sovereign government entity is correspondingly small, when compared to its role in running an extremely large international religious organization.... The fact that the Holy See is unique among sovereigns in this respect does not, however, necessitate deviating from the rules we normally follow in construing and applying the FSIA. The operation of a huge international religious institution is a large task, and one of great importance to many people. But it is not an activity that may be undertaken only by *sovereign* states, which is the focus of the FSIA's commercial activity exception. Indeed, in most cases it is non-governmental entities, not governments, that operate international religious institutions, the Mormon Church and the Greek Orthodox Church being two prominent examples. The FSIA's purpose is not to insulate religious institutions from suit; it juxtaposes commercial activities not to *religious* activities, but to *governmental* activities. The Holy See differs from other foreign states in the *nature* of the non-sovereign activities it carries out and, in all likelihood, in the ratio of its non-sovereign activities to its sovereign activities. But it is like other sovereigns in the respect essential here: It engages in a range of non-sovereign activities in the United States, and the FSIA's commercial activity exception lifts the shield of immunity from such non-sovereign activities.

The district court nonetheless expressed discomfort with characterizing the Holy See's employment of Ronan as "commercial" activity for FSIA purposes, observing that the Holy See's employment of clergy is "widely viewed as the antithesis of commerciality." *Doe*, 434 F.Supp.2d at 941. Commerciality and religiosity are, indeed, often viewed as antithetical categories. But, as I have explained, the FSIA's "commercial activity" phrase, as it has been interpreted in the case law, is a term of art, not reliant on common usage, which reflects the special concerns of a sovereign immunity statute. The district court's discomfort notwithstanding, under well-established FSIA principles and our own binding case law the employment relationship that existed between Ronan and the Holy See does constitute "commercial activity of a foreign state." ...

Under the FSIA's commercial activity exception, it is not enough for the plaintiff to show that the defendant engaged in something that qualifies as a commercial activity under the *Weltover* test. The plaintiff must also show that his cause of action is related to that commercial activity in one of three ways, depending upon the geographical location where the activity occurred. 28 U.S.C. § 1605(a)(2). In Clause 1 of § 1605(a)(2), the FSIA requires that if the foreign state's commercial activity is carried on inside the United States, the plaintiff's cause of action must be "based upon" that activity itself. Alternatively, if the commercial activity is not carried on inside the United States, the plaintiff's cause of action must be "[based] upon" an act performed inside the United States in connection with the commercial activity elsewhere, *id.* [Clause 2], or else "[based] upon" an act performed outside the United States in connection with commercial activity elsewhere that causes a "direct effect" in the United States. *Id.* [Clause 3]. Doe asserts that his claims may go forward under either Clause 1 or Clause 3 of the commercial activity exception....

Applying this standard, I would hold that Doe's negligence claims were "based upon" the Holy See's employment of Ronan within the meaning of the statute. The existence of that employment relationship is a necessary element of at least the negligent retention and supervision claims. *See Chesterman v. Barmon*, 82 Or.App. 1, 4, 727 P.2d 130 (1986) (in assessing whether plaintiff had sufficiently alleged a negligent retention claim, requiring that the individual who caused the harm be an "employee" of defendant). *See also* Restatement (Second) of Torts § 317 ("A master is under a duty to exercise reasonable care so to control his servant.") ... [footnote omitted]; *accord DiPietro v. Lighthouse Ministries*, 159 Ohio App.3d 766, 772, 825 N.E.2d 630 (2005) (holding that "[i]n order to prevail on a claim of negligent retention, plaintiff must establish ... the existence of an employment relationship") (internal quotation marks and citation omitted)....

For the foregoing reasons, I would affirm the district court's judgment, holding that the FSIA's commercial activity exception permits it to exercise jurisdiction over Doe's non-fraud negligence claims.

FERNANDEZ, Circuit Judge, concurring:

I agree that we cannot consider the commercial exception to the Foreign Sovereign Immunities Act, 28 USC § 1605(a)(2). But, Judge Berzon does not and has, therefore, gone on to opine that all (or virtually all) activities by churches are actually commercial activity. While I recognize that her opinion cannot be precedential and that a response from me cannot be either, I am loath to leave her disquisition standing alone. Thus, I cannot (or at least will not) refrain from offering my own view on the rather oxymoronic proposition that church functions are commercial.

As I see it, Doe's claim that church functions are simply commercial transactions because parishioners do give donations to the church bespeaks the veriest cynicism about religion and a church's position within religion.... [footnote omitted]. Could a church spread the word of God without some funds? Would that it could, but the need for support does not mean that the holy activity is commercial. Is the Mass the marketing of a form of edifying entertainment? Is hearing confessions and giving religious advice — an age-old function of churches — really no more than a commercial activity similar to psychological counseling? Is the sacrament of Holy Eucharist the marketing of bread and wine or is the sacrament of Extreme Unction the marketing of oil? I think not. Normal legal usage and common sense recoil from those possibilities. *See United States v. Lamont*, 330 F.3d 1249, 1254–55 (9th Cir.2003).... Nor does the statute or the case law suggest that the Holy See's religious activities must be commercial. The FSIA tells us that "[a] 'commercial activity' means either a regular course of commercial conduct or a particular commercial transaction or act." 28 U.S.C. § 1603(d). That does not help much, but it also does not say that every possibly private activity is commercial. It says only that commercial behavior is commercial activity. As the Supreme Court has, somewhat more helpfully, stated:

> [W]e conclude that when a foreign government acts, not as a regulator of a market, but in the manner of private player within it, the foreign sovereign's actions are "commercial" within the meaning of the FSIA. Moreover, because the Act provides that the commercial character of an act is to be determined by reference to its "nature" rather than its "purpose"..., the question is not whether the foreign government is acting with a profit motive or instead with the aim of fulfilling uniquely sovereign objectives. Rather, the issue is whether the particular actions that the foreign state performs ... are the *type* of actions by which a private party engages in "trade and traffic or commerce[.]"

Republic of Arg. v. Weltover, Inc., 504 U.S. 607, 614, 112 S.Ct. 2160, 2166, 119 L.Ed.2d 394 (1992) (citations omitted). Some have focused on the "private player" language, but what is truly significant is the emphasis on the market and on "trade and traffic or commerce." *Id.*

I fail to see how engaging in providing religious counseling is "trade and traffic or commerce." *Id.* Nor, by the way, can a mere private actor give priestly counseling or consolation to a believer. This does not require a focus on purpose; it goes to the very nature of the religious activity itself. Similarly, we have noted that: "[t]he commercial activity exception applies only where the sovereign acts 'in the market in the manner of a private player.'" *Holden v. Canadian Consulate*, 92 F.3d 918, 920 (9th Cir.1996). Again, Holy See has not acted in the market at all. It has simply supplied religious counseling to a church communicant, a service that this unique sovereign entity is designed for.... [footnote omitted].

I think that the problem this case seems to present lies in the fact that Holy See is an unusual type of foreign sovereign. Most governments do, indeed, exist to afford their citizens a degree of physical protection and guidance, so that they may thrive in this world. Holy See is more focused on the next world, and that makes a universe of difference. Because of that, Holy See's sovereign activities are not simply the passage of mortal laws and the enforcement of those. They, basically, encompass the furnishing of the kinds of services that only Holy See can give: its own kind of religious help, guidance and counseling. It may do more than most sovereigns do, but it is not engaged in the market or in commerce.... [footnote omitted].... In short, Holy See may not be your typical sovereign, but neither is it your typical merchant. Does that lead to some kind of impasse? Of course not. It leads back to the statute itself. Holy See is a foreign state and the commercial activity exception does not strip its immunity from it. Something else may do so, but not that exception.... [footnote omitted]. We hierophants of the law are adept at redefining ordinary concepts, but it is no more appropriate to declare that religious services are commercial activities than it would be to declare that ponies are small birds.... [footnote omitted].... Therefore, if we had jurisdiction I would not apply the commercial activity exception to this case.

Notes

In *Doe v. Holy See*, the Ninth Circuit Court held that the plaintiff had sufficiently alleged that Andrew Ronin was an employee of the defendant, the Holy See, acting within the scope of his employment and, therefore, the tortuous activity exception to sovereign immunity afforded the court jurisdiction over plaintiff's vicarious liability claims against the Holy See. *Doe v. Holy See*, 557 F.3d 1066, 1081–83 (9th Cir. 2009). *See also O'Bryan v. Holy See*, 556 F.3d 361 (6th Cir. 2009) (applying similar exclusions under Foreign Sovereign Immunities Act in case involving abuse by Roman Catholic priest occurring in the 1920s). However, because the court found that the plaintiff did not sufficiently allege that the Holy See exerted day-to-day, routine control over the Archdiocese and other institutional defendants, there was no jurisdiction for vicarious liability claims against the Holy See for the conduct of the Archdiocese and other defendants. Further, the court held that the tortuous act exception did not apply to Doe's negligent hiring, supervision, and failure to warn claims, which the court held barred by the discretionary function exclusion and, thus, dismissed the vicarious liability and negligence claims based on the conduct of the Archdiocese and other defendants. In 2010, the Holy See filed a second motion to dismiss, challenging the factual basis for the court's jurisdiction under the Foreign Sovereign Immunities Act—i.e., that Ronin was an employee of the Holy See—which led to further discovery requests, to which the Holy See objected. The court subsequently allowed limited discovery on the issue of the extent to which the Holy See exercised control over Ronin's activities. *See Doe v. Holy See*, 2011 WL 1541275 (April 21, 2011).

For commentary on the applicability of sovereign immunity in cases involving sexual abuse, see James Fantau, *Rethinking the Sovereign Status of the Holy See: Towards a Greater Equality of States and Greater Protection of Citizens in United States Courts*, 19 Cardozo J. Intl & Comp. L. 487 (2011); Benjamin David Landry, *The Church Abuse Scandal: Prosecuting the Pope Before the International Criminal Court*, 12 Chi. J. Intl. L. 341 (2011); Jacob William Neu, *"Workers of God": The Holy See's Liability for Clerical Sexual Abuse*, 63 Vand. L. Rev. 1507 (2010); Edan Burkett, *Victory for Clergy Sexual Abuse Victims: The Ninth Circuit Strips the Holy See of Foreign Sovereign Immunity in Doe v. Holy See*, 2010 BYU L. Rev. 35 (2010); Lucian C. Martinez, Jr., *Sovereign Impunity: Does the Foreign Sovereign Immunities Act Bar Lawsuits Against the Holy See in Clerical Sexual Abuse Cases?*, 44 Tex. Intl. L.J. 123 (2008).

II. Insurance Coverage

A. Generally

Cincinnati Insurance Co. v. Oblates of St. Francis De Sales, Inc.

Court of Appeals of Ohio, Sixth District, 2010
2010 WL 3610451

HANDWORK, J.

This case is before the court on appeal from the judgment of the Lucas County Court of Common Pleas, filed on April 28, 2009, ... [footnote omitted] which granted summary judgment in favor of appellee, Cincinnati Insurance Company ("CIC"), against appellant, the Archdiocese of Oklahoma City ("Archdiocese"), and denied the Archdiocese's motion for summary judgment.... On July 7, 2000, CIC filed a complaint seeking declaratory judgment regarding its obligations to defend or indemnify the Oblates of St. Francis de Sales, Inc. ("Oblates") pursuant to two commercial umbrella liability insurance policies the Oblates had with CIC from January 1, 1994, through January 1, 1997, and from January 1, 1997, through January 1, 2000.[2] The issue of coverage arose as a result of a claim filed by a minor victim and his parents ("the claimants"), who alleged that the victim had been sexually abused by James Francis Rapp, a priest of the Oblates and employee of the Archdiocese, between approximately 1993 and 1997, while Rapp was assigned by the Oblates to serve as pastor of Assumption Parish in Duncan, Oklahoma ("Assumption"). The complainants asserted that the Oblates negligently failed to supervise Rapp and disclose Rapp's history of pedophilia to the parish members.

Because the Oblates' primary insurer, the Transcontinental and Continental Insurance Companies ("CNA"),[3] and CIC both denied coverage, the Archdiocese lent the Oblates $5,000,000 to settle with the claimants. On or about May 5, 2003, CNA paid $1,000,000 in coverage as full settlement of its single occurrence limit of liability. CNA's payment extinguished the Oblates primary insurance coverage, thereby allowing the Oblates to pursue coverage from CIC pursuant to its excess umbrella coverage.... In 2004, the Oblates assigned its rights under its insurance policies to the Archdiocese. The Oblates were dismissed from this action and CIC and the Archdiocese filed cross-motions for summary judgment. In determining CIC's declaratory judgment action, the trial court held that CIC had no duty to indemnify the Archdiocese with respect to the settlement amount paid to the claimants because the Oblates conduct was expected, and therefore not an occurrence pursuant to the policy, and the policy excluded coverage for "claims arising out of the sexual or physical abuse or molestation of any person." ...

The Archdiocese argues in its first assignment of error that the trial court erred in finding that the Oblates' negligence was not an "occurrence" under CIC's policy. Specifically, the Archdiocese argues that the Oblates' hiring of Rapp, lack of supervision, and failure to warn the parishioners at Assumption regarding Rapp's history of ephebophiliac behavior were merely negligent acts and that the Oblates did not "expect" or "intend" Rapp to molest more boys. As such, the Archdiocese argues that the Oblates' negligent actions, which allowed Rapp to have access to his victim, were "occurrences" under CIC's policy

---

2. CIC's policies each had a $4,000,000 per occurrence and $4,000,000 aggregate limit of liability.

3. CNA's limit of liability was $1,000,000 for each occurrence, with a $2,000,000 general aggregate limit.

and coverage should be provided.... CIC's policy states that it will pay "on behalf of the Insured the ultimate net loss for occurrences during the policy period in excess of the underlying insurance * * *." An "occurrence" is defined by the policy as "an accident, or a happening or event, or a continuous or repeated exposure to conditions which occurs during the policy period which unexpectedly or unintentionally results in personal injury * * *."

"In order to avoid coverage on the basis of an exclusion for expected or intentional injuries, the insurer must demonstrate that the injury itself was expected or intended." *Physicians Ins. Co. of Ohio v. Swanson* (1991), 58 Ohio St.3d 189, 569 N.E.2d 906, syllabus. For example, an intentional injury exclusion "'will not apply if the insured intentionally does an act, but has no intent to commit harm, even if the act involves the foreseeable consequences of great harm or even amounts to gross or culpable negligence.'" *Id.* citing *Allstate Ins. Co. v. Steinemer* (C.A.11, 1984), 723 F.2d 873, 875. Likewise, "'the resulting injury which ensues from the volitional act of an insured is still an "accident" within the meaning of an insurance policy if the insured does not specifically intend to cause the resulting harm or *is not substantially certain that such harm will occur.*'" (Emphasis added.) *Id.* citing *Quincy Mut. Fire Ins. Co. v. Abernathy* (1984), 393 Mass. 81, 84, 469 N.E.2d 797, 799.... Thus, in order for the Archdiocese to be indemnified for the damages it paid to the claimants, the happenings or events that caused the claimants' injuries must have been caused by continuous or repeated exposure to conditions which were not *expected* or *intended* by the Oblates to cause such injuries. The trial court held that the Oblates "expected," i.e. knew that Rapp was substantially certain to molest more boys if Rapp was allowed to remain in contact with adolescent boys without appropriate supervision. Because the injuries suffered by the claimants were expected by the Oblates, the trial court found that the Oblates' actions were not "occurrences" and, therefore, were not covered by CIC's policy.

According to Rapp's personnel file and evidence submitted to the trial court, Rapp was accused in 1969 of sexual misconduct toward male students while teaching at a boy's high school in Salt Lake City, Utah. Rapp admitted to these accusations and underwent psychiatric evaluation. Thereafter, Rapp took an extended leave of absence from the Oblates in the 1970's. In 1978, he returned to the Oblates and again was assigned to teach boys at high schools in New York and Michigan. In 1984, he was accused of sexually molesting a 15-year-old male student in Michigan. Again, Rapp admitted to the allegations and underwent additional psychiatric counseling.... On October 17, 1986, St. Luke's Institute ("St.Luke's") evaluated Rapp and informed the Oblates that Rapp's history of sexual contact with youngsters spanned slightly less than 20 years, with the most recent contact being six months prior to St. Luke's evaluation. The evaluation stated, "It is clear from Father Rapp's history that his ephebophiliac behavior extends over many years with a number of contacts * * *. Given the severity of his problem, it is unlikely that any progress could be made other than in an intensive comprehensive setting. These sexual disorders are apparently not curable but manageable, much the way alcoholism is an [incurable] but manageable condition. * * * In any case, it is important that Father Rapp not be in the presence of youth without another responsible adult there." Thereafter, in October 1986, Rapp was sent to the House of Affirmation ("Affirmation") in Montara, California for in-patient therapy.

Upon the closing of Affirmation in June 1987, Rapp concluded his inpatient therapy and was assigned to a church in Illinois. While Rapp's treatment at Affirmation was considered "very successful," and it was thought that Rapp should be able "to function well in pastoral ministry," the director of Affirmation noted that "[a]s was always the case, some sort of ongoing counseling was certainly recommended." ... There was no allegation of sexual misconduct in Illinois, but, in 1990, Rapp was reassigned to Assumption. The assignment was made without any warning to the church regarding Rapp's extended history of repeated ephebophiliac behavior, the fact that his condition was incurable, but manageable, that he needed to maintain ongoing counseling for his sexual deviance, or that it was important that he not be in the presence of youth without another responsible adult there. Assumption had no restrictions in place for Rapp and no counseling was undertaken.

On March 30, 1994, the Oblates received notice that Rapp was accused of molesting a Michigan boy in 1984. The Oblates' Provincial in 1994 examined Rapp's personnel file, which contained information concerning his past misconduct and misgivings people had about him; however, because the allegations brought forth in 1994 concerned incidents prior to Rapp's in-patient therapy in 1986, the Provincial did not inform the Archdiocese or the other Oblate pastors at Assumption regarding Rapp's history or diagnosis.... On April 17, 1994, the Oblates notified the Archdiocese of the Michigan allegations against Rapp. The Archdiocese responded that since it had never been informed of Rapp's ephebophiliac predation, it had "not supervised his ministry or provided him with any special guidance" for "three years." For Rapp to continue at Assumption, the Archdiocese stated, in part, that Rapp's personnel file and evaluations from St. Luke's and Affirmation needed to be produced. The Oblates' Provincial requested that Rapp seek counseling; however, there is no record of any counseling occurring. Nevertheless, Rapp remained at Assumption until his arrest in 1999.

The Archdiocese argues that no harm was intended. We note, however, that an insured's denial of an intention to harm anyone is "only relevant where the intentional act at issue is not substantially certain to result in injury." *Gearing v. Nationwide Ins. Co.* (1996), 76 Ohio St.3d 34, 39, 665 N.E.2d 1115. Based upon the Oblates' knowledge of Rapp's history and his need for supervision and ongoing treatment, the Oblates decision to give Rapp unfettered access to Assumption's parishioners, without warning, was substantially certain to result in additional incidents of sexual molestation of boys. Accordingly, we find that the Oblates' actions did not cause accidental injury to Rapp's victim. Rather, the injury to Rapp's victim was expected, i.e., substantially certain to occur, and, therefore, the Oblates' actions were not "occurrences" pursuant to CIC's policy.[4]

We recognize that in *Doe v. Shaffer* (2000), 90 Ohio St.3d 388, 393, 738 N.E.2d 1243, the Ohio Supreme Court held that allegations of negligent hiring related to sexual molestation could constitute a policy "occurrence," and therefore afford coverage. Relying on *Silverball Amusement, Inc. v. Utah Home Fire Ins. Co.* (W.D.Ark.1994), 842 F.Supp. 1151, 1158, affirmed (C.A.8, 1994), 33 F.3d 1476, the Ohio Supreme Court in *Shaffer* held that a ruling that the Diocese expected or intended the injuries sustained by a mentally retarded man who was molested while in a residential facility operated by a religious order of the Roman Catholic Church, known as the Little Brothers of the Good Shepherd, would be "a tortured interpretation of the facts" and "an inherently illogical interpretation." We, however, find that, unlike the facts in this case, the facts in *Shaffer* and *Silverball* do not demonstrate that the molester in either case had any history of sexual abuse or that the respective

---

4. Accord *Diocese of Winona v. Interstate Fire & Cas. Co.* (C.A.8, 1996), 89 F.3d 1386, 1394, where court found that knowledge of priest's sexual abuse of boys, failed treatment attempts, and lack of warning or supervision when priest transferred to new church demonstrated "overwhelming evidence that the Diocese knew or should have known that [the priest's] continued sexual abuse was highly likely to reoccur."

employers knew of the molesters' potential propensities toward sexual abuse. As such, we find that these cases are distinguishable on their facts.... Additionally, based on the facts presented in this case, we find that a conclusion that the Oblates were substantially certain that Rapp would continue to sexually assault boys in his care, if he was unsupervised and not undergoing continued therapy for his incurable condition, is not a tortured interpretation of the facts or inherently illogical. As such, we find that the actions of the Oblates were not "occurrences" pursuant to CIC's policy and, therefore, the Archdiocese is not entitled to indemnification from CIC for the damages paid to the claimants. Accordingly, the Archdiocese's first assignment of error is found not well-taken.

The Archdiocese argues in its second assignment of error that the trial court erred in finding that coverage for negligence claims is excluded by the "abuse to persons in the insured's care" exclusion of CIC's policy. Based upon the authority of *Safeco Ins. Co. of Am. v. White*, 122 Ohio St.3d 562, 913 N.E.2d 426, 2009-Ohio-3718, paragraph two of the syllabus, we find the Archdiocese's second assignment of error well-taken. However, based upon our ruling with respect to the first assignment of error, we nevertheless find that CIC is entitled to judgment as a matter of law.

The Archdiocese argues in its third assignment of error that the trial court erred by denying the Archdiocese's motion for summary judgment. Again, however, based upon our ruling with respect to the first assignment of error, we find that CIC was entitled to judgment as a matter of law and that the trial court correctly denied the Archdiocese's motion. The Archdiocese's third assignment of error is therefore found not well-taken.... On consideration whereof, the court finds substantial justice has been done the party complaining and the judgment of the Lucas County Court of Common Pleas is affirmed. The Archdiocese is ordered to pay the costs of this appeal pursuant to App. R. 24.

JUDGMENT AFFIRMED....

PETER M. HANDWORK, MARK L. PIETRYKOWSKI, and KEILA D. COSME, JJ., Concur.

Notes

James F. Rapp, who is incarcerated in Oklahoma, was eligible for discharge from prison in 2016. However, in 2013, two men came forward and reported new allegations of sexual abuse by Rapp. An investigation revealed several more victims. On January 12, 2015, Rapp was charged with three counts of first-degree criminal sexual conduct and 10 counts of second-degree criminal sexual conduct for other crimes he allegedly committed at Lumen Christi High School, in Michigan, from 1980 to 1986. *See* Attorney General Press Release, *Schuette Charges Former Michigan Priest in 1980s Sexual Abuse Cases*, available at http://www.michigan.gov/ag/0,4534,7-164-46849_47203-345115-,00.html (last accessed Apr. 22, 2015); Theresa Ghiloni, *Former Jackson Lumen Christi High School priest charged with criminal sexual conduct 30 years after alleged abuse*, available at http://blog.mlive.com/citpat/news_impact/print.html?entry=/2015/01/former_jackson_lumen_christi_h.html (last accessed Apr. 22, 2015).

The *Oblates of St. Francis De Sales* case involved whether the abuse that was sought to be covered qualified under the applicable policy coverage as an "accident" or an "expected or intended" occurrence. Based on the defendant's history, the court found that the abuse was to be expected and denied coverage. Other courts find an irrebuttable presumption that sexual molestation implies intent and, therefore, such intentional torts may not be covered. *See Erie Insurance Exchange v. Claypoole*, 449 Pa. Super. 142, 673 A.2d 348 (1996) (liability insurer had no duty to defend or indemnify school bus driver or owners against allegations of sexual molestation by driver). The question of whether such an exclusion might extend to the negligent acts of institutional supervisors is a matter of policy language and state law. For a comprehensive survey of state insurance coverage in sexual misconduct cases, see American Re-Insurance Company, *Coverage and Liability Issues in Sexual Misconduct Claims*, available at www.amre.com (last accessed Apr. 25, 2015); see also American Bar Association Section of Litigation, *Insurance Coverage for Sexual Misconduct Claims*, available at www.americanbar.org (last accessed Apr. 25, 2015). For commentary on the issue of insurance coverage, see Peter Nash Swisher and Richard C. Mason, *Liability Insurance Coverage for Clergy Sexual Abuse Claims*, 17 Conn. Ins. L.J. 355 (2011) (analyzing legal theories supporting and rejecting liability insurance coverage claims involving institutional sexual abuse); Alana Bartley, *The Liability Insurance Regulation of Religious Institutions After the Catholic Church Sexual Abuse Scandal*, 16 Conn. Ins. L.J. 505 (2010) (discussing history and changes in industry regulations).

With increased financial liability imposed on institutional authorities, the issue of insurance coverage becomes increasingly important. For example, a basic tenet of insurance coverage law is that if one cause of action in a complaint is covered under a specific insurance policy, then the insurance company must cover the defense for the entire complaint. *See* Michael Conley and Meghan Finnerty, *Abuse and Molestation Claims: Insurance Issues for Policyholders*, Legal Intelligencer, Dec. 5, 2011. In light of the variety of causes of action that typically are raised in institutional sexual exploitation cases, as is demonstrated in the *Oblates of St. Francis De Sales* case, the issue arises as to whether insurance companies will exclude sexual molestation from general policy coverage, or whether specific policies, at higher premiums, will be available. Even if such claims are included, coverage may be limited by the number of occurrences that are claimed. *See General Accident Insurance Company of America v. Allen*, 547 Pa. 693, 692 A.2d 1089 (1997) (in case involving sexual abuse of three children, with one occurrence per child, court held that first occurrence prompted failure to prevent abuse for purposes of coverage). Also, when one complaint names numerous institutional defendants, all of whom require representation, the limits of the applicable policy coverage often become exhausted. Again, allocation of policy coverage resources is defined by policy language and applicable state law.

In the following two cases involving insurance coverage resulting from the sexual abuse perpetrated by Jerry Sandusky in the Penn State University scandal, consider how insurance issues come to bear and by what basis the court determines the insurer's liability to offer coverage.

B. Public Policy

Federal Insurance Company v. Sandusky

United States District Court, Middle District of Pennsylvania, 2012
2012 WL 1988971

YVETTE KANE, Chief Judge.

Plaintiff Federal Insurance Company brought this civil action seeking a declaration of its obligations under an insurance policy issued to The Second Mile, a non-profit organization.... [Citations to record omitted]. Currently pending before the Court is Plaintiff's motion for judgment on the pleadings.... In its motion, Plaintiff asks the Court to strike as against public policy any obligations it may owe to provide indemnity or defense costs to one Gerald A. Sandusky, an officer or agent of The Second Mile. The Court heard argument on the motion on May 22, 2012. The motion is now ripe, and for the reasons that follow, the Court will grant the motion in part and deny the motion in part....

On March 22, 2011, Federal contracted to insure The Second Mile and all of its directors and officers for the period of April 1, 2011, to April 1, 2012, on a "claims made" basis for both Directors & Officers Liability and Entity Liability Coverage Section ("D & O") and Employment Practices Liability Coverage Section ("EPL").... The D & O section provides that Federal shall indemnify any "Loss" which an Insured Person becomes obligated to pay for a wrongful act committed, attempted, or allegedly committed by an Insured Person. The EPL section provides that Federal shall pay "Loss on account of any Third Party Claim," which includes amounts that an insured becomes obligated to pay for civil proceedings arising from "sexual harassment, including unwelcome sexual advances, requests for sexual favors or other conduct of a sexual nature against a Third Party." Under both the D & O and EPL coverage, Federal has included within the definition of "Loss" the costs of defending civil actions and criminal prosecutions. The policy liability section of the policy includes a $1,000,000 liability limit for all claims under all liability sections of the policy for each policy year, exclusive of defense costs. The parties agree that Defendant Sandusky, who has served in various roles for The Second Mile, facially meets the definition of an "Insured Person" under both the D & O and EPL sections of the insurance policy....

On November 5, 2011, Pennsylvania's Thirty-Third Statewide Investigating Grand Jury returned a report regarding an investigation of Defendant Sandusky. The Grand Jury report identified eight minor male children whom Defendant Sandusky allegedly sexually abused. As a result of the Grand Jury report, Defendant Sandusky has been charged with forty criminal counts, including but not limited to counts for involuntary deviate sexual intercourse, aggravated indecent assault, unlawful contact with a minor, endangering the welfare of a child, and corruption of minors. Subsequently, the Grand Jury found that Defendant Sandusky engaged in unlawful acts with two additional male minors, and Defendant Sandusky was charged with twelve additional criminal counts of sexual abuse. Defendant Sandusky denies the criminal allegations against him and maintains his innocence.... Defendant Sandusky has also been named as a defendant in a civil action filed in the Court of Common Pleas of Philadelphia, *John Doe A v. The Second Mile, Gerald Sandusky, and The Pennsylvania State University*. In the civil action, John Doe A alleges that Defendant Sandusky sexually abused him over one hundred times and that he molested multiple other victims. Defendant Sandusky denies the allegations of the civil complaint.

On December 16, 2011, Defendant Sandusky informed Plaintiff that he is seeking coverage under the insurance policy for loss related to the civil complaint and the criminal charges under both the D & O and EPL sections of the policy.... In response, on December 23, 2011, Plaintiff informed Defendant Sandusky that it would provide him with a defense in the civil and criminal matters, with a reservation of all rights available at law to deny coverage.... Thereafter, Federal advanced $125,000 to Sandusky's criminal defense attorney, subject to its reservation of rights.... On December 23, 2011, Federal brought this declaratory judgment action seeking a declaration that it is not required to provide insurance coverage to Defendant Sandusky with respect to the criminal charges and civil complaint against him. Federal alleges that no coverage is owed to Sandusky under the contract because Sandusky was not acting in an insured capacity as an employee or executive of The Second Mile, if and when he committed the alleged criminal acts, and because the exclusions contained in the D & O policy—for bodily injury and emotional distress, willful statutory violations, and sexual harassment of persons that are not insured—limit or exclude coverage. No discovery has occurred that would enable the Court to resolve these coverage issues. However, Federal suggests that the Court should decide

Sandusky's rights under the insurance policy at this early stage, without the benefit of a factual record. Federal urges the Court to set aside the outstanding issues regarding coverage and decide Sandusky's right to coverage purely on public policy grounds.

Plaintiff argues that were The Second Mile's insurance policy ultimately interpreted to cover losses stemming from the allegations of sexual abuse and molestation of minors, the insurance policy would be void as against Pennsylvania's public policy. Therefore, Plaintiff argues that it should not be required to defend or indemnify against damages arising out of these claims against Defendant Sandusky. Defendant Sandusky opposes Plaintiff's motion....

The unique posture of the case requires the Court, at this juncture, to adopt Sandusky's assertions, which he argues entitle him to the insurance coverage that The Second Mile bargained for. It is against this backdrop that Federal asks this Court for a declaration that, notwithstanding Sandusky's version of the events, public policy in Pennsylvania, as established by its highest court, would bar recovery under the insurance policy in any event. To address the question, the Court necessarily looks to the Pennsylvania courts.... "The law has a long history of recognizing the general rule that certain contracts, though properly entered into in all other respects, will not be enforced fully, if found to be contrary to public policy." 15 Corbin on Contracts § 79.1 (rev. ed.2003) (collecting cases). However, "the power of courts to formulate pronouncements of public policy is sharply restricted; otherwise they would become judicial legislatures rather than instrumentalities for the interpretation of law." *Mamlin v. Genoe*, 340 Pa. 320, 17 A.2d 407, 409 (Pa.1941). In *Mamlin*, the Supreme Court of Pennsylvania explained the circumstances in which courts may invalidate contracts on the basis of public policy:

> The right of a court to declare what is or is not in accord with public policy does not extend to specific economic or social problems which are controversial in nature and capable of solution only as the result of a study of various factors and conditions. It is only when a given policy is so obviously for or against the public health, safety, morals or welfare that there is a virtual unanimity of opinion in regard to it, that a court may constitute itself the voice of the community in so declaring. There must be a positive, well-defined, universal public sentiment, deeply integrated in the customs and beliefs of the people and in their conviction of what is just and right and in the interests of the public weal.

Id. The court went on to explain that "[o]nly in the clearest of cases ... may a court make an alleged public policy the basis of judicial decision." *Id.*

Sexual abuse and molestation of children are "so obviously ... against the public health, safety, morals or welfare that there is a virtual unanimity of opinion in regard to it." *See Mamlin*, 17 A.2d at 409. Accordingly, Pennsylvania's legislature and judiciary have repeatedly expressed a strong public policy of protecting children from abuse and molestation. Pennsylvania's legislature has enacted several criminal laws against abuse, endangerment, corruption, and sexual contact with minors. *See, e.g.*, 18 Pa. Cons.Stat. §§ 3123(b) (involuntary sexual deviate intercourse with a child), 3125 (aggravated indecent assault of a child), 4304 (endangering welfare of children), 6301(a)(1) (corruption of minors). Additionally, the legislature has enacted laws to encourage reporting of suspected child abuse and to require registration of convicted sex offenders. *See, e.g.*, 23 Pa. Cons.Stat. §§ 6301–6385 (Child Protective Services Law); 42 Pa. Cons.Stat. §§ 9791–9799 (Megan's Law). Pennsylvania courts have also expressed their strong disapproval of sexual contact between an adult and a child by adopting the inferred intent rule for liability insurance cases involving the sexual abuse of a child by an insured adult. *See Aetna Cas. & Sur. Co. v. Roe*,

437 Pa.Super. 414, 650 A.2d 94, 102 (Pa.Super.Ct.1994) (citing *Wiley v. State Farm Fire & Cas. Co.*, 995 F.2d 457, 464 (3d Cir.1993) (concluding that the "harm to children in sexual molestation cases is inherent in the very act of sexual assault committed on a child, regardless of the motivation for or nature of such assault, and that the resulting injuries are, as a matter of law, intentional")).

The Pennsylvania Supreme Court has further held that public policy bars enforcement of insurance contracts that indemnify insured persons for damages arising from certain reprehensible conduct, stressing that "it would be against public policy of this Commonwealth to permit a carrier to offer insurance for damages assessed as a result of evil or illegal conduct." *Mut. Benefit Ins. Co. v. Haver*, 555 Pa. 534, 725 A.2d 743, 747 (Pa.1999) (stating in dicta that it would violate Pennsylvania's public policy to indemnify a pharmacist who repeatedly distributed drugs to individuals without prescriptions). The Pennsylvania Supreme Court has also held that public policy prohibits insurance coverage for damages arising from a "situation where an insured commits a criminal act, with respect to a Schedule I controlled substance." *Minn. Fire & Cas. Co. v. Greenfield*, 579 Pa. 333, 855 A.2d 854, 866 (Pa.2004). Significantly, in a case with facts analogous to the instant matter, the United States District Court for the Eastern District of Pennsylvania held that the defined and dominant public policy of Pennsylvania bars "insuring against damages resulting from sexual contacts between a public school teacher and his student." *Teti v. Huron Ins. Co.*, 914 F.Supp. 1132, 1141 (E.D.Pa.1996). The court examined legislative enactments and judicial decisions that support the proposition that "a teacher's sexual molestation of a student could not possibly be deemed an acceptable practice." *Id.* at 1142 (quoting *Stoneking v. Bradford Area Sch. Dist.*, 882 F.2d 720, 727 (3d Cir.1989)).

Pennsylvania's judicial and legislative pronouncements with respect to child abuse and molestation constitute a "positive, well-defined, universal public sentiment, deeply integrated in the customs and beliefs of the people and in their conviction of what is just and right and in the interests of the public weal" that bars the enforcement of a contract that would indemnify the perpetrator of intentional sexual molestation of a minor for damages arising from that conduct. *See Mamlin*, 17 A.2d at 409. Such a contract would allow an insured to shift the consequences of intentional, reprehensible conduct to an insurance company, thereby abdicating personal responsibility. It is entirely clear, and this Court holds, that the public policy of Pennsylvania as announced by its courts prohibits the reimbursement of Sandusky for any damage award that he may ultimately be found to owe arising from the allegations that he molested and sexually abused children.... What is not so clear, and must not be prejudged, is whether the same public policy bars coverage for The Second Mile for a judgment issued against that organization or any other principal of that organization in favor of a Sandusky victim. This question is not now before the Court and is specifically reserved. The Court's ruling does nothing to disadvantage the potential claim of any alleged victim of Sandusky as against The Second Mile or any other person not named here. The Court writes only to address the legal duty owed to Sandusky.... Likewise, the Pennsylvania courts have not squarely addressed the remaining and most pressing issue before the Court: whether in light of the strong public policy against allowing a perpetrator to insure against the consequences of his own intentional wrongdoing, Federal's duty to provide Sandusky with a defense to a civil action or a criminal indictment is likewise unenforceable as against public policy because of the nature of the conduct alleged. On this issue, the Court writes upon a blank slate. The parties have cited no case and the Court's own research has discovered no case in which the Pennsylvania courts have evaluated any EPL or D & O policy that specifically provides coverage for defense costs, let alone one involving the most infamous of crimes.[1]

As a general matter, in a civil suit, the duty to defend an insured arises only where the complaint contains allegations that are potentially covered by the insurance policy. *See Am. & Foreign Ins. Co. v. Jerry's Sport Ctr., Inc.*, 606 Pa. 584, 2 A.3d 526, 541 (Pa.2010) ("An insurer is obligated to defend its insured if the factual allegations of the complaint on its face encompass an injury that is actually or potentially within the scope of the policy."). Typical liability policies provide that the insurer has the right and duty to defend any suit seeking damages to which the insurance policy applies. *See, e.g., Casper v. Am. Guar. & Liab. Ins. Co.*, 408 Pa. 426, 184 A.2d 247 (Pa.1962) (holding that insurance company had no duty to defend where damages alleged in complaint were not potentially within the scope of the insurance policy and where the insurance policy provided for a duty to defend only against any suit alleging damages covered by the policy). However, where, as here, an insurance policy specifically includes defense costs as covered loss, separate and apart from damages, the mechanical process of determining whether there could be coverage for damages in order to determine whether there is a duty to defend cannot be applied. Furthermore, the general rule is not instructive where the policy provides for payment of criminal defense costs, and a judgment against a criminal defendant results in criminal penalties rather than liability for damages.

Although D & O policies that provide for defense costs in criminal cases are rare, it is possible to imagine valid public interest considerations that would favor the issuance of these policies. For example, it might be argued that such a policy enhances the ability of a non-profit organization to recruit volunteers and executives who might otherwise decline to serve because of the fear of vexatious lawsuits or even criminal prosecutions.[2] It might also be argued that the presumption of innocence that remains a bedrock principle of our Constitution makes insurance to cover defense costs in the public interest. These considerations may inform the Court in predicting how the highest court of Pennsylvania would decide this matter, but they are not presented here for the Court's consideration.... [footnote omitted].

Because discovery has not commenced, the Court is also without facts specific to this case that may bear on the Court's public policy determination and may dictate the breadth of any rule that the Court may craft. Was it Sandusky himself who procured this policy? Did he do so knowing that criminal charges were imminent? ... [footnote omitted]. Many other factual considerations may inform the Court's understanding of whether the contractual obligation of Federal to provide for defense costs is enforceable in whole or part, or entirely contrary to public policy and void ab initio.... Without the benefit of a

---

1. The Court notes that the insurance policies issued to The Second Mile have the approval of the Pennsylvania Department of Insurance, which is charged with oversight of insurance matters generally, and is empowered to deny certain types of coverage that are *ipso facto* against the public interest. *See* 40 P.S. § 477b ("It shall be unlawful for any insurance company ... doing business in this Commonwealth, to issue, sell or dispose of any ... contracts of insurance ... until the forms of the same have been submitted to and formally approved by the Insurance Commissioner...."); *INA Life Ins. Co. v. Com., Ins. Dep't*, 374 A.2d 670 (Pa.Commw.Ct.1977) (affirming the Department of Insurance's rejection of a proposed insurance rider on public policy grounds).

2. *See* Sean J. Griffith, *Uncovering a Gatekeeper: Why the SEC Should Mandate Disclosure of Details Concerning Directors' and Officers' Liability Insurance Policies*, 154 U. Pa. L.Rev. 1147, 1171 (2006) (noting that insurance policies that protect executives from potential personal liabilities may have an impact on the ability of some organizations to attract qualified individuals to serve as executives and officers).

factual record, it is not entirely clear that Pennsylvania's public policy would prohibit enforcement of the insurance policy to the extent that it provides Sandusky with defense costs. Accordingly, the Court must defer issuance of a ruling on the public policy question as it relates to Federal's obligation to provide for Sandusky's legal costs to defend the civil action and criminal prosecution. *See Mamlin*, 17 A.2d at 409 ("Only in the clearest of cases ... may a court make an alleged public policy the basis of judicial decision.")....

For the foregoing reasons, the Court will grant Plaintiff's motion for judgment on the pleadings in part and will deny Plaintiff's motion in part. The Court will grant Plaintiff's motion to the extent that it seeks a declaration that Pennsylvania's public policy would not permit enforcement of the insurance policy that Plaintiff issued to The Second Mile to the extent that it provides for indemnification to Sandusky for civil liability for damages arising out of Defendant Sandusky's alleged molestation and sexual abuse of children. The Court must defer the question of whether any obligation Federal owes to Sandusky to provide a legal defense to the civil claims or criminal prosecution are void as against public policy in Pennsylvania....

Federal Insurance Company v. Sandusky

United States District Court, Middle District of Pennsylvania, 2013
2013 WL 785269

YVETTE KANE, Chief Judge.

[In *Federal Ins. Co. v. Sandusky*, 2012 WL 1988971], [w]hile it was clear that indemnification would violate public policy, this Court declined to decide the issue of whether insurance coverage for the legal costs of defending such allegations would also violate public policy. The Court did not consider the question of whether the insurance policy at issue actually covered Defendant Sandusky's defense costs, as Federal's motion for judgment on the pleadings related solely to its argument that any coverage should be voided as against public policy.... Now, in its motion for summary judgment, Plaintiff seeks a declaration that it has no duty to provide any coverage to Defendant under the insurance policy because: (1) the criminal and civil lawsuits arising out of Defendant Sandusky's wrongful acts were not committed in Sandusky's "insured capacity;" (2) the doctrine of collateral estoppel precludes Defendant from denying the facts underlying his criminal conviction; and (3) Defendant's conduct is uninsurable as contrary to Pennsylvania's public policy.... In response, Defendant argues that Plaintiff's motion for summary judgment is premature, and requests an opportunity to conduct discovery....

First, Plaintiff argues that there is no coverage under the insurance policy, including no duty to defend Defendant Sandusky, because Sandusky was not acting in his insured capacity as an executive or employee of The Second Mile when he engaged in the wrongdoing now the subject of civil and criminal actions.... Therefore, in order to determine whether Plaintiff must provide coverage for the criminal and civil actions against Defendant Sandusky, the Court must compare the allegations of the complaints with the language of the insurance policy. First, in the D & O section, coverage for "Wrongful Acts" is limited to certain wrongful acts committed or attempted by an insured person in his or her "Insured Capacity," meaning "the position or capacity of an Insured Person that causes him or her to meet the definition of Insured Person set forth in the applicable Coverage Section." ... "Insured Person" is defined in the D & O section as "any natural person who was, now is or shall become an Executive or Employee of [The Second Mile]." ... Under the EPL section, coverage for wrongful acts against a third party is limited to acts committed or attempted "by an Insured Person in his or her capacity as such." ... In that section, "Insured Person" is defined broadly to include any employee, volunteer, director, officer, trustee, committee member, or independent contractor "but only while acting in his or her capacity as such." ...

While Defendant summarily argues that the language defining "Insured Capacity" is ambiguous, Defendant does not offer any support for such an argument.[2] The Court finds the policy language regarding "Insured Capacity" to be unambiguous in limiting coverage to those acts conducted by an Insured Person acting in his or her capacity as such. Capacity is not defined in the policy, but its ordinary meaning is the "role in which one performs an act." *Black's Law Dictionary* 235 (9th ed.2009). Here, Plaintiff does not dispute that Defendant, as a former executive or employee of The Second Mile, facially meets the definition of an "Insured Person" under the D & O and EPL sections.... In order to determine whether the actions that form the basis of the claims against Defendant were performed in his capacity or role as an executive or employee of The Second Mile, the Court must refer only to the precise civil and criminal allegations made against Defendant. *See Baumhammers*, 938 A.2d at 290 (holding that the determination of whether a claim is covered by an insurance policy is determined by comparing the four corners of the policy to the four corners of the underlying complaint).

The report of the Thirty-Third Statewide Investigating Grand Jury describes Sandusky as the founder and primary fundraiser for The Second Mile, an organization whose stated mission is "to help children who need additional support and would benefit from positive human interaction." ... The Grand Jury report details Defendant's acts of sexually abusing eight victims, many of whom he met through The Second Mile. The abuses detailed in the report occurred at various locations, including Defendant Sandusky's home, a high school, Defendant's car, Penn State football locker rooms, the Penn State campus, and hotel rooms. A second Grand Jury report, issued separately, details Defendant Sandusky's sexual abuse of a ninth and tenth victim.... The report indicates that Defendant met these two victims through The Second Mile; however, the sexual assaults described in the report occurred in the basement of Defendant Sandusky's home, at a hotel, in Defendant's car, and on the Penn State campus.

The complaint in *John Doe A v. The Second Mile, Gerald Sandusky, and The Pennsylvania State University*, describes Sandusky as "the founder of, and principal in" The Second Mile, and its primary fundraiser.... The complaint alleges that Defendant met Doe while he was a participant in programs sponsored by The Second Mile, and that Defendant sexually abused Doe over one hundred times.... According to the complaint, these abuses occurred in the facilities of Penn State, including the football locker room, within Philadelphia County, at out-of-state facilities connected with a Penn State bowl game,

---

2. Contract ambiguity is an "intellectual uncertainty; ... the condition of admitting of two or more meanings, of being understood in more than one way, or referring to two or more things at the same time." *Int'l Union, UAW v. Mack Trucks, Inc.*, 917 F.2d 107, 111 (3d Cir.1990) (quoting *Mellon Bank N.A. v. Aetna Bus. Credit*, 619 F.2d 1001, 1011 (3d Cir.1980)). In determining whether a term is ambiguous, the Third Circuit has warned courts that "[t]he language of the policy may not be tortured ... to create ambiguities where none exist." *St. Paul Fire & Marine Ins. Co. v. Lewis*, 935 F.2d 1428, 1431 (3d Cir.1991) (quoting *Pacific Indem. Co. v. Linn*, 766 F.2d 754, 761 (3d Cir.1985)). The language defining "Insured Capacity" is not ambiguous because it is not subject to multiple interpretations. In the absence of ambiguity, the Court looks to the "plain and ordinary meaning" of the contract language. *See Penn. Mfrs. Ass'n Ins. Co. v. Aetna Cas. & Sur. Ins. Co.*, 426 Pa. 453, 233 A.2d 548, 551 (Pa.1967).

and at the Sandusky home. The complaint alleges that Sandusky "molested multiple victims through his activities with Second Mile and Penn State, dating back to the 1970's," and that some of the sexual abuse occurred "during the course of activities of Second Mile." ... From a comparison of these allegations to the four corners of the insurance policy, it is clear that Defendant Sandusky was not acting in his capacity as an employee or executive of The Second Mile in sexually abusing and molesting the victims named in the criminal and civil cases brought against him, and the Court so finds. While the plain language of the insurance policy dictates this conclusion, the Court will briefly discuss the cases cited by the parties in support of their respective positions.

In support of its argument that Defendant was not acting in his insured capacity, Plaintiff refers to a number of cases analyzing whether employees' acts were committed within the scope of their employment.... First, Plaintiff refers to *Plavi v. Nemacolin Voluntary Fire Department*, 151 Pa.Cmwlth. 587, 618 A.2d 1054 (Pa.Commw.Ct.1992), in which the Pennsylvania Commonwealth Court found that a firefighter's act of molesting a minor "was so outrageous, so criminal, and so incapable of anticipation by his employer that it must be held, as a matter of law, to have exceeded the scope of his employment." *Id.* at 1055. The *Plavi* court referred to the following test used for determining the scope of employment for the purpose of governmental immunity:

> Conduct of an employee is within the scope of employment if it is of a kind and nature that the employee is employed to perform; it occurs substantially within the authorized time and space limits; it is actuated, at least in part, by a purpose to serve the employer; and if force is intentionally used by the employee against another, it is not unexpected by the employer.

Id. (quoting *Natt v. Labar*, 117 Pa.Cmwlth. 207, 543 A.2d 223, 225 (Pa.Commw.Ct .1988)). While this test refers to a distinct legal issue involving governmental immunity, the Court finds the test to be instructive to the analogous determination of whether Defendant acted in his capacity as an employee or executive of The Second Mile.

Plaintiff also relies on *Sanchez by Rivera v. Montanez*, 165 Pa.Cmwlth. 381, 645 A.2d 383 (Pa.Commw.Ct.1994), in which the Commonwealth Court relied on *Plavi* in holding that an employee's actions of molesting a child "were conducted for personal reasons only and were utterly outrageous in manner," such that the acts were outside the scope of his employment at a day care center. *Id.* at 391, 645 A.2d 383. In holding that the employee's conduct was not within the scope of his employment and that the employer was not vicariously liable, the Commonwealth Court reasoned that when "an assault is committed for personal reasons or in an outrageous manner, it is not actuated by an intent of performing the business of the employer and is not done within the scope of employment." *Id.* (quoting *Fitzgerald v. McCutcheon*, 270 Pa.Super. 102, 410 A.2d 1270, 1272 (Pa.Super.Ct.1979))....

Applying the facts set forth in the criminal and civil claims against Defendant Sandusky to the language of the insurance policy leads to the clear conclusion that Defendant Sandusky's offenses against children — whether proven or merely alleged — were not conducted in his capacity as an employee or executive of The Second Mile. While the *John Doe A* complaint references sexual molestation "during the course of activities of Second Mile," the acts of sexual abuse and molestation detailed in both the civil complaint and the Grand Jury report cannot be said to have been in Sandusky's capacity as an executive or employee of The Second Mile. Defendant did not engage in this wrongful conduct in furtherance of his duties for The Second Mile. The fact that Sandusky met his victims through The Second Mile — or even sexually abused victims "during the course of activities of Second Mile"—does not change the fact that his sexual abuse of children was personal in nature, and performed in his individual capacity. While the legal issues in the cases cited by both parties are distinct from the issues now before the Court, application of these persuasive sources of authority serves only to strengthen the Court's determination that there is no coverage for Defendant Sandusky's offenses against children. Like the conduct at issue in *Pavi* and *Sanchez*, there is nothing in the record in this case to support the notion that Defendant's sexual abuse of minors was actuated by a purpose to serve The Second Mile....

Defendant also argues that Plaintiff's "insured capacity" argument renders the insurance policy's provision of criminal defense costs through a final and non-appealable judgment illusory, because no criminal conduct is within the scope of any legitimate job description.... This Court need not reach the question of whether some conduct, although criminal, may be performed by an insured person in furtherance of his or her duties to an insured entity, and thus entitled to coverage under the criminal defense provision. In this case, because Defendant Sandusky's conduct was clearly personal in nature and not in furtherance of his duties for The Second Mile, he is owed no criminal defense under the policy.... The Court will grant Plaintiff's motion for summary judgment to the extent that Plaintiff seeks a declaration that the claims against Defendant Sandusky are not covered by the insurance policy because the acts alleged therein cannot be said to have been in Defendant Sandusky's capacity as an employee or executive of The Second Mile....

Next, Plaintiff argues that Defendant is collaterally estopped from denying the conduct underlying his criminal conviction, and thus any duty that it may have owed to Defendant has extinguished.... Plaintiff argues that the criminal conviction makes the continued provision of defense costs in his criminal case uninsurable as a violation of Pennsylvania's public policy.... Because the Court has determined that there is no coverage for the criminal and civil claims against Defendant Sandusky, ... the Court need not reach the question of whether coverage should be disallowed on public policy grounds....

Even if Defendant's inquiries are resolved in his favor, permitting discovery will not alter the Court's conclusion that the Federal policy does not cover the acts in question. Sandusky makes no argument that disputed facts—if resolved in his favor—would support a finding that his acts served his employer's purpose rather than his own. Instead, Sandusky argues that the discovery he requests might support his theory that Federal intended to provide coverage for claims related to sexual abuse and molestation. While this may be true, such extrinsic evidence of Plaintiff's intent is not admissible when the language of the policy at issue is clear and unambiguous.... [T]he Court finds that the language of the insurance policy that Plaintiff issued to The Second Mile clearly and unambiguously limits coverage to those acts done by an "Insured Person" in his or her capacity as such. In an unambiguous, written contract, the intent of the parties is to be ascertained by the document itself, without inquiry into extrinsic evidence. *Ins. Adjustment Bureau, Inc. v. Allstate Ins. Co.*, 588 Pa. 470, 905 A.2d 462, 468 (Pa.2006). Therefore, extrinsic information relevant to Plaintiff's intent is not material and cannot alter this Court's determination that the insurance policy does not provide coverage here. Accordingly, the Court will deny Defendant's Rule 56(d) request for more discovery....

For the reasons set forth above, the Court will grant Plaintiff's summary judgment motion. Upon review of the criminal and civil complaints lodged against Defendant Sandusky, the Court is satisfied that the conduct at issue did not arise in Sandusky's capacity as an employee or executive of The Second Mile; therefore, the conduct at issue is beyond the scope of the insurance policy's coverage. Accordingly, the Court will declare that Plaintiff has no obligation to provide any coverage to Defendant related to the criminal case brought against him or to the *John Doe A* complaint. Because the insurance policy at issue does not provide coverage for Sandusky, the Court declines to expand its previous analysis of public policy to determine the discrete question of whether a D & O policy that provides coverage for legal costs associated with allegations related to infamous crimes violates the public policy of Pennsylvania as a matter of law. Moreover, because the information that Defendant seeks to discover is not material to the Court's determination, the Court will deny Defendant's Rule 56(d) request to conduct discovery....

III. Financial Considerations

A. Assessing Damages

Doe v. United States
Seventh Circuit, 1992
976 F.2d 1071

FLAUM, Circuit Judge....

We begin with an abbreviated overview of the facts. [The plaintiff children, although not related, are referred to as "Alexis Doe" and "John Doe."] At about 8:15 a.m. on September 24, 1984, Alexis' mother took Alexis, then three years old, to the [Scott Air Force Base Day Care Center ("Center")]. She retrieved her daughter shortly after 3:00 p.m., and during the car ride home Alexis told her mother that an unidentified "purple man" had poked her "gina"—Alexis' word for vagina—with a "scrape." On October 19, 1984, after reading an article in the Scott Air Force Base newsletter discussing allegations of sexual abuse at the Center, John's mother asked three-year-old John whether anyone at the Center had touched him in a "bad way." John responded in the affirmative, and said that a man had touched his penis and a woman had touched his "bombosity"—John's word for buttocks.

After unsuccessfully seeking administrative relief, the parents of Alexis and John ultimately filed suit in district court on behalf of themselves and their children. The complaints, premised on the [Federal Tort Claims Act (FTCA), 28 U.S.C. § 1346(b)], sought damages of $8 million for medical expenses and emotional injuries to the parents and to their children. The district court consolidated the cases, and initially granted summary judgment to the government on the ground that the claim asserted was one "arising out of assault [or] battery," 28 U.S.C. §§ 1346(b), 2680(h), and therefore was not cognizable under the FTCA. We reversed, holding that the claims arose out of a breach of an affirmative duty to the victims even if the persons committing the alleged assaults were government employees, and remanded the case for trial. *Doe v. United States*, 838 F.2d 220, 225 (7th Cir.1988). The district court then dismissed the parents' claims for their own emotional injuries, but allowed them to remain as plaintiffs to pursue recovery for their children's medical expenses and emotional injuries.... On cross-appeal, the plaintiffs maintain first, that the court improperly dismissed the parental claims for emotional distress, and second, that the damage awards are inadequate. We affirm....

At trial, Alexis' mother testified that she had picked up her daughter at the Center shortly after 3:00 p.m. on September 25, 1984. During the car ride home, Mrs. Doe asked Alexis about her friends and if she wanted to visit the Center again. According to Mrs. Doe, Alexis replied that she had made friends, but asked her mother not to take her back to the Center any more. She further told her mother "that the teacher was very nice to her and that she put water [on] what she called her gina." Mrs. Doe stated:

> A: I felt pretty shocked and so I asked her what happened to her gina, why did she need it to feel better, and she said that the purple man had poked it with a … scrape and that it hurt and so that the white teacher made it feel better by putting water on it.
>
> Q: What was said next?
>
> A: I asked her what, I guess I just tried to figure out what all that meant, and asked her if they had touched her, and she said that yes, you know, yes they had, that they had poked her vagina and that the man said that he was sorry he hurt her, and [I] asked her what else happened and she said that the man had pulled his pants up and down, pulled them down and then pulled them up and then pulled them down, and then the mommy teacher … opened up her blouse and she said that she showed her titties to the man, and the man peed on both of them, and she had asked me to not take her there any more and she said I called you and called you, mommy, and you wouldn't come.

[Citation to record omitted]. Upon reaching their home, Mrs. Doe examined Alexis but discovered no visible physical signs of abuse. She then called her husband, a pediatrician at the Base, and told him the story. He told her to come to the Base hospital, which she did, where Alexis was examined by Dr. Donald Dicheson, the Base's chief pediatrician. Like Mrs. Doe, he discovered no signs of physical abuse.…

The Does subsequently reported the incident to the police. At the station, Alexis and her parents met with a Sergeant Lofties, and Alexis again stated that a purple man had poked her vagina with a scrape. When asked where the scrape was, Alexis said "it fell off in the car," which, according to Mrs. Doe, was "a new thing she had not told me." … Mrs. Doe testified that she and Lofties then took Alexis to a snack shop and then back to the Center; Lofties went inside, and, during his absence, Alexis made further statements regarding the alleged incident.

> I think she was still eating her sandwich or I was trying to get to her [sic] eat the sandwich, and she had said that earlier the purple man had put his penis in her mouth and peed in her mouth and made her throw up her sandwich.

[Citation to Record omitted]. When bathing Alexis on the evening of the incident, Mrs. Doe, a registered nurse, noticed that "she had a little pin prick or needle prick mark in her toe" which appeared to be "an injection site, where you put the needle and there is just a little dot of blood on it." … In response to her mother's query about the marks, Alexis "said she was screaming and crying and making too much noise when these people had her, and so they gave her a shot and they said that if she was crying any more, they were going to give her another shot." …

The next day, Mrs. Doe took Alexis to the local rape crisis center, where Alexis was interviewed in a play room while Mrs. Doe watched through a one-way mirror. Mrs. Doe stated that her daughter removed the clothing from the dolls and pushed the naked dolls together on their genital areas.… According to Mrs. Doe, Alexis had never witnessed adults having any kind of sexual relations.

Mrs. Doe then testified that at some point over the next few days, Alexis mentioned that a boy named Joey had been present, and revealed additional details.

> I remember her saying that these people gave her a bath after they had squashed her in between them and she couldn't breathe and the man rubbed his penis on

her stomach and that they gave her a bath afterwards, they took her clothes off and folded them and gave her a bath, and the purple man told her that if she said anything, he would bite her....

[Citation to Record omitted]. According to Mrs. Doe, Alexis then told her "that the purple man touched the lady's titties, and they did ballet. The mommy teacher did ballet on the purple man, and that the lady said that when she got to be a woman or grown up that she could do ballet on the man, too."... At some point, Alexis also told her mother that while "the purple man and the teacher were in the other room doing bad things," Alexis "was in the kitchen, and the dog was making her food."... Alexis told her mother on another occasion that the dog drove her in a police car to a safe place....

John's mother testified that upon reading about allegations of child abuse at the Center in the base newsletter in October 1984, she asked John whether anybody had ever touched him or done something bad to him at the nursery (the family's term for the Center):

[A]nd he said yes, they did, and I guess I was in shock that he said yes, so I just remember that I tried to stay calm, and I asked him, I guess I remember, I said, what happened John, and he went on—actually, I said who touched you, and he said a man, and he said a lady. I asked him where they had touched him and John at the time pointed to his penis and to his bottom, and I asked him if the man had a name, and he said yes, I said what was the man's name. He said the man's name was John. I asked him if the lady had a name, and he said no, he just referred to her as a lady.

[Citation to Record omitted]. According to Mrs. Doe, John became "very angry and very uncomfortable," and asked her "why did you take me there?"... Mrs. Doe stated that she decided "not to push John" about the matter until her husband, who was out of town, returned, although in the interim she occasionally raised the issue. In response to questions about the lady's identity, John would say he did not remember, and when asked about the man's name, John "would become very angry and [say] I told you Mom, the man's name is John."... Mrs. Doe testified that John would then tell her that he did not want to discuss the matter any further.

Mr. Doe testified that he waited several days after returning from his trip to see whether John would initiate a discussion of the incident. When he failed to do so, Mr. Doe asked his son whether anything ever happened to him at the nursery. According to Mr. Doe, "without any interruption [John] began a detailed description of what had happened to him."... Mr. Doe said that John "could not tell me where it had happened exactly, what room or anything like that, but he said that a man had touched him on his weenie, his term for penis," and further, "that a woman had touched him on his bombosity, which was his term for his bottom or his buttocks."... Mr. Doe asked if the man had a name, and his son responded, "yes, John," and when asked if the woman had a name, John replied no. When asked what they were wearing, John told his father that the man wasn't wearing any clothes, and that "the lady had red legs."... Mr. Doe stated that John offered this information in response to very general questions about the Center, and that he "didn't initiate the conversation in the context of 'something bad happened to you, didn't it, John.'"...

The Does testified that John later supplemented his story, stating that the "bad people" at the nursery had a snake, which "they put [on] my hand and it bit me."... John also drew oval shapes on a piece of paper, and told his father that there were bags used in a game whereby "the man would jump in and out of the bag and then the kids would jump in and out of he [sic] bag"... According to Mrs. Doe, after the incident John began to draw pictures "of things with straight lines" and cages, and to talk about being burned. And at one time, at one point he had said the people told me that this is what would happen if I talked, and he drew a picture of a figure and then he scribbled it out with an orange marker and he said this is the fire and this is what would happen to me if I ever told anybody.

[Citation to Record omitted]. Mrs. Doe testified that John drew pictures of two people, and later referred to another little boy, "Tonya," stating "that they did this to Tonya, Tonya was a nice little boy, but they did this to Tonya too." ...

On cross-appeal, the parents contend that the district court improperly dismissed the state common-law counts, premised upon the tort of seduction, for their own emotional injuries suffered as a result of the molestations of their children. Under the FTCA, the United States is, as a general matter, liable in tort "in the same manner and to the same extent as a private individual under like circumstances." 28 U.S.C. § 2674. The plaintiffs contend that Illinois law—the substantive law applicable here—recognizes this cause of action. The district court disagreed and dismissed the claim. We likewise conclude that Illinois courts would no longer recognize a cause of action for the tort of seduction.

In pressing this claim, the plaintiffs rely exclusively on nineteenth- and early twentieth-century cases. Of course, the mere fact that a case is old does not mean it is no longer good law, *see Marbury v. Madison*, 5 U.S. (1 Cranch) 137, 2 L.Ed. 60 (1803); here, however, we believe the cases the plaintiffs rely upon are both inapposite and rest upon outmoded premises no longer accepted by Illinois courts. As the government points out, the plaintiffs allege that their children were abused as a result of the government's neglect; they do not claim, and the court did not find, that a government agent had perpetrated the abuse. None of the cases relied upon by the plaintiffs allow recovery from a defendant on the ground that a "seduction" was *negligently permitted* to occur and, therefore, are inapplicable here. Moreover, as the district court observed, the seduction cases rest upon a conception of the parent-child relationship, and specifically, the father-daughter relation, as one of master and servant. *See, e.g., Ball v. Bruce*, 21 Ill. 161, 163 (1859) ("If plaintiff was the master and [his daughter] was the servant, and in consequence of her seduction he was deprived of her services, why may he not recover as any other master for the seduction of his servant."); *see also Hobson v. Fullerton*, 4 Ill.App. 282, 284 (1879) (requiring proof of master-servant relationship to recover on seduction theory). This outdated conception clearly is untenable today. *See, e.g. Bullard v. Barnes*, 102 Ill.2d 505, 82 Ill.Dec. 448, 453–54, 468 N.E.2d 1228, 1233–34 (1984) (contrasting nineteenth-century view, "when children were valued largely for their capacity to contribute to the family income," with modern view that "the chief value of children to their parents is the intangible benefits they provide in the form of comfort, counsel and society").

Finally, as the government observes, the type of damages for which the parents here seek recovery are sufficiently analogous to damages alleged for emotional injuries in other scenarios in which Illinois courts have rejected recovery, *see, e.g., Rickey v. Chicago Transit Auth.*, 98 Ill.2d 546, 75 Ill.Dec. 211, 215, 457 N.E.2d 1, 5 (1983) (party must satisfy "zone-of-physical-danger" test, which requires proximity to accident in which direct victim was physically injured and high risk to plaintiff of physical impact, to recover damages for emotional distress); *Dralle v. Ruder*, 124 Ill.2d 61, 124 Ill.Dec. 389, 392–94, 529 N.E.2d 209, 212–14 (1988) (no recovery to parents for loss of their society resulting from nonfatal injury to child), to conclude that recovery would be rejected here as well. As a general matter under Illinois law, "before a plaintiff can recover for negligently caused emotional distress, he must have, himself, been endangered by the negligence, and he must have suffered physical injury or illness as a result of the emotional distress caused by the defendant's negligence." *Siemieniec v. Lutheran General Hosp.*, 117 Ill.2d 230, 111 Ill.Dec.

302, 318, 512 N.E.2d 691, 707 (1987). The plaintiffs here do not satisfy these prerequisites. The district court properly dismissed the parents' claims for recovery grounded on the common-law tort of seduction....

The parents' primary contention on cross-appeal is that the district court's damages awards of $25,000 to each child were inadequate. Under the FTCA, damages determinations are governed under the clearly erroneous standard, and the nature and measure of damages are assessed according to state law. *Jastremski v. United States*, 737 F.2d 666, 672 (7th Cir.1984). We cannot overturn the district court's damage award unless its factual basis is clearly erroneous. *Wheel Masters, Inc. v. Jiffy Metal Prods. Co.*, 955 F.2d 1126, 1131 (7th Cir.1992); *Wolkenhauer v. Smith*, 822 F.2d 711, 715 (7th Cir.1987); *Adams Apple Distr. Co. v. Papeleras Reunidas, S.A.*, 773 F.2d 925, 930 (7th Cir.1985). Our task is limited to inquiring whether the trial court abused its discretion; it is not to consider whether we personally would have made the same award. *DeSantis v. Parker Feeders, Inc.*, 547 F.2d 357, 365 (7th Cir.1976); *see also Wolkenhauer*, 822 F.2d at 715.

The plaintiffs assign numerous errors to the district court's damages findings. The first involves the court's reference to the anatomical dolls used during the course of the investigations. In assessing damages, the district judge observed that the children's current psychological problems, which we discuss below, may not have been caused by the abuse, but "could well have been caused by something else, for example, the use of anatomically correct dolls by the Air Force and Illinois state investigator, Dr. Gerwell, or the people at [the] Rape Crisis Center where the Air Force referred the Does." ...

The plaintiffs are correct (as the government concedes) that under Illinois law, "a person injured through another's negligence can recover from the original tortfeasor not only for the original injury but for any aggravation of the injury caused by a physician's malpractice, assuming that there was no want of ordinary care in the selection of the physician." *Gertz v. Campbell*, 55 Ill.2d 84, 302 N.E.2d 40, 43 (1973). According to the plaintiffs, since the government is the original tortfeasor, and the sexual abuse constitutes the original injury, the government also is liable for any enhanced traumatization caused by the government investigators' use of anatomically correct dolls in diagnosing and treating the children's abuse. While this may be correct as a purely legal matter, as a factual matter the district court did not, contrary to the plaintiffs' contention, explicitly find that the use of the dolls had resulted in emotional damages to the children. The plaintiffs' contention therefore fails.

The plaintiffs also contend that the court erred in "failing to consider elements of damage in the same manner a jury would have." Underlying this contention is the following statement by the district court:

> I can recognize the parents feel that these children have been severely traumatized and damaged. If I were in your position, I would feel the same way. If this were my child and my grandchild, I would have the same feelings that you have. I can't indulge the luxury of approaching the case from that standpoint.

[Citation to Record omitted]. According to the plaintiffs, the judge erred because he "should be able to let his own emotions be a guide" in assessing damages. To buttress their claim, the plaintiffs provide capsule summaries of six sexual abuse cases yielding larger verdicts than the one rendered here. But aside from the superficial similarity of subject matter, these cases offer little in the way of useful comparison. That a six-year-old Texas boy suffering from chronic post-traumatic stress syndrome recovered $237,000 plus attorney fees following sexual abuse by a bus driver, *see Spann v. Tyler Indep. School Dist.*, No. TY 6 213 CA (E.D.Tex. Mar. 25, 1988), does little to illuminate the propriety or impropriety of the damages verdict here. We believe that the judge's statements were merely expressions of sympathy to the parents, and agree with the government that the court here simply recognized that a factfinder — be it judge or jury — must base its damages determination on the evidence and the appropriate legal standards, rather than adopt the perspective of the aggrieved party.

Finally, emphasizing the preponderance of the evidence standard, the plaintiffs dispute the court's finding that the plaintiffs had failed to adequately prove future or permanent emotional damages to either John or Alexis. In reviewing the damages ruling in this regard, it is helpful first to review the court's ruling on liability, for this determination affects its damages assessment. In its oral ruling that the plaintiffs had proved by a pre-ponderance of the evidence that some sort of abuse had occurred, the court emphasized:

> I do think that these children were molested in some term of that word, they were molested in some way. I do not think that there was any — well, obviously from the evidence, there was no objective evidence of any physical injury, but there doesn't have to be. The slightest touch would have breached the duty, and would have resulted in an actionable situation.

[Citation to Record omitted]. As the government correctly observes, it is this conclusion that lays the foundation for the court's assessment of damages. We turn now to the awards in regard to each child.

Shortly after the molestation occurred, John began suffering extremely severe nightmares, known as "night terrors." He also began to engage in violent behavior, and became obsessed with violent themes in his play — ranging from an insistence on carrying knives, guns, and swords, to an obsession with sharks, viewing the movie "JAWS" some 100 times over a span of a few months. After the frequency of his night terrors alarmed his parents, John spent two and one-half years in therapy with a clinical psychologist, George Kinsey. According to the plaintiffs, "John Doe is a troubled child." This may well, unfortunately, be all too true; but to recover damages the plaintiffs must establish to the factfinder both a nexus between John's emotional damages and the molestation, and that the damages are permanent or certain to recur in the future.

Under Illinois law, the plaintiff has the burden of establishing that damages were sustained, and of providing the court with a reasonable basis for computing those damages. *Adams Apple*, 773 F.2d at 930; *Schoeneweis v. Herrin*, 110 Ill.App.3d 800, 66 Ill.Dec. 513, 519, 443 N.E.2d 36, 42 (1982). "Damages may not be awarded on the basis of conjecture or speculation; if the plaintiff establishes that he is entitled to damages but fails to provide a proper basis with which to determine those damages, he may be awarded only nominal damages." *Adams Apple*, 773 F.2d at 930; *Schoeneweis*, 66 Ill.Dec. at 519, 443 N.E.2d at 42. Damages are legally recoverable under Illinois law if they can be proved to a degree of reasonable certainty. *Chicago Title & Trust Co. v. Walsh*, 34 Ill.App.3d 458, 340 N.E.2d 106 (1975); *Cummings v. Chicago Transit Auth.*, 86 Ill.App.3d 914, 42 Ill.Dec. 159, 164, 408 N.E.2d 737, 742 (1980).

Here, the district court found no evidence to relate causally to either John's preoccupation with violence or his night terrors to his abuse while under the Center's care, and no evidence to show that John will need future medical or psychological treatment. Further, the court credited Dr. Gerwell's testimony that little, if any, damage, emotional or otherwise, should result from the incident, and found no evidence of any permanent or future damages. We find that the court did not abuse its discretion in determining that John's future or permanent damages were not established to a degree of reasonable certainty.

It is true, for example, that children often experience anxiety attacks soon after abuse has occurred, which may manifest itself through increased fear and nightmares. *Hagen*, *supra*, at 359.... But this does not translate into a causal relationship between John's abuse and his nightmares. *See* [Citation to Record omitted] (although quite often children have nightmares subsequent to sexual abuse, "that's not the only reason why, of course."). Indeed, although Kinsey noted that John's nightmares and fixation with monsters is "consistent" with a history of sexual abuse, he declined to find a causal relationship:

> Again, you know, the fact that John had night terrors and had marked changes in mood and difficulty with frustration and so forth. There can be a lot of contributing factors to that; having had a trauma in his life could be one of those factors ... could be. There's no way for me to know for sure.

[Citation to Record omitted]. The plaintiffs also maintain that the district court improperly concluded that John had not been grossly traumatized by the event because he did not immediately report the incident to his parents and appeared bored during his interview with Dr. Gerwell. Whether or not the court's observations on these points were correct as a factual matter, however, its assessment of damages did not flow from these comments. Rather, the court emphasized that the plaintiffs had not established any *causation* between John's emotional problems and the abuse....

Moreover, although the plaintiffs point out that John required extensive therapy to treat the night terrors, the court awarded damages to cover these costs. The damages the court declined to award were for alleged future damages. Although the plaintiffs focus on John's preoccupation with violence and his night terrors, they do not provide the necessary link between these behaviors and the abuse. The range of emotional problems suffered by John, coming as they did on the heels of the abuse, leads one to conclude intuitively that they are linked to one another; but, as noted, damages awards may not be based on mere intuition or speculation alone, and the trial court did not abuse its discretion in finding that a causal relationship was insufficiently established.

With regard to Alexis, Mrs. Doe testified that for an approximately two-week period following the abuse, Alexis became depressed, very quiet, and withdrawn.... According to Mrs. Doe, during the next couple months Alexis "masturbated a lot with her dolls on her bed, she would take all their clothes off and be like a third person with two dolls.... She would rub her vagina where the dolls [sic] vagina would be, and there was [sic] always three of them." ... Mrs. Doe further testified that Alexis played as a "participant" with the dolls for approximately three years, and that although Alexis no longer "get[s] on the dolls any more and participate[s], ... her dolls do have intercourse, she takes their clothes off and Barbie and Ken also have intercourse." ... Mrs. Doe also testified that Alexis exhibits an aversion to any show of affection between her mother and father. "[S]he complains a lot when my husband and I do, show each other simple affection, a hello kiss from work, she comes up and tells us to just stop that, that's nasty and that's dirty, which is very different from other children." ... According to Mrs. Doe, Alexis gets angry when she sees such kissing, ... and her father testified that since the incident Alexis is "deathly afraid of anyone vomiting." ... Mrs. Doe stated that she had no plans to seek additional therapy for Alexis in the future, "unless I can see that things just aren't going right with her and she needs that. I fear making this an issue for her to identify really strongly with," ... but indicated that she had not ruled out therapy if it is needed in the future....

As with John, the district court determined that the plaintiffs had not established the necessary link between the abuse and Alexis' behavior. The following statement by the district court regarding Alexis' preoccupation with sexual matters is illustrative:

> Why do we assume that it's a result of this incident? Now it may well be, I am not saying it isn't. I am just saying that it's your burden to prove, just as it was

> your burden to prove that this happened, it's your burden to prove that her reaction to displays of affection between her parents is causally related to this incident. You have to prove that. I can't assume that.

[Citation to Record omitted]. The plaintiffs contend that, under this reasoning, a plaintiff never could recover for emotional injuries, which by their very nature lack tangible physical evidence. In our view, however, the district court did not apply such a restrictive approach. Several times during the plaintiffs' closing argument, the court indicated that the plaintiffs had failed to provide a sufficient link, even if that link was only in the way of circumstantial evidence. The court did not require tangible, physical evidence but only a causal link, which it did not find. *See, e.g.,* [Citation to Record omitted] ("What I do expect ... is some expert opinion that will tie these two things together, and there isn't. There is absolutely no evidence, *not even circumstantial*, because we can think of all kinds of things that would cause—the same way with the nightmares with John, is there a child that hasn't had nightmares, and for various reasons, for many reasons, but there is nothing to tie the nightmares to this.") (emphasis added); ... ("I think that a psychiatrist or a qualified psychologist with experience and background in these things could have opined something for us.").

The plaintiffs also argue that the abuse negatively affected Alexis' family environment—for example, Alexis' parents find themselves engaging in overprotective behavior—and that the resulting damages are recoverable under Illinois law. Although Dr. Gerwell did testify that the negative repercussions could be magnified by the children's environment and the way it is influenced by the abuse, ... the court did not abuse its discretion in refusing to render an increased damages award on this basis.

The district court's statements indicate that, had the plaintiffs more clearly established some sort of link between the children's behavior and the abuse, the damages awards would have been greater. The evidence provided by the plaintiffs did not establish that future damages were reasonably certain to occur, or even that the existing behavioral problems were more probably than not a result of the sexual abuse. Dr. Gerwell, for example, stated that in a single incident scenario, such as that which occurred with Alexis and John, standard criteria "would dictate that there would be minimal long term recall, if any, or any long term effects...." ... Gerwell noted that he had yet to deal with a case in which the individual independently recalls sexual abuse before approximately age five or six, and further stated that "it would be conjecture" to say that Alexis' current conduct is necessarily related to the prior abuse. "It may sound logical to make that leap, but in our field, we have found quite clearly that all kinds of other things can precipitate behaviors." ... ; *see also* [citation to Record omitted] ("it becomes very very cloudy as to what is causing behaviors") (Gerwell); [citation to Record omitted] ("In my opinion I would say it is extremely unlikely" that the abuse might or could have caused the reactions exhibited by Alexis) (Gerwell). The plaintiffs offered no credible testimony to counter Gerwell's statements.

Again, we emphasize the narrow scope of our review. We are limited to reviewing the district court's determinations under an abuse of discretion standard. As the government correctly observed in its brief, the district court did not credit every detail of the children's stories; it concluded only that the plaintiffs had proved, by a preponderance of the evidence, that the children had been subjected to some form of improper touching while under the Center's care. In assessing damages, the court determined that the plaintiffs had failed to establish the necessary causal link between that touching and the alleged resulting psychological harm. The effect of childhood sexual abuse varies with the individual, Hagen, *supra*, at 359, and while clinical studies suggest that sexually victimized children share recurrent emotional and psychological characteristics that manifest in later adult life, *id.*, general statistics do not establish causation in a specific case.

Perhaps in the future, experts will develop new methods for assessing damages in cases involving unique emotional traumas, such as those resulting from child sexual abuse. On the liability end, courts and legislatures have increasingly permitted the tolling of the statute of limitations for adult survivors of child sexual abuse. *See generally* Hagen, *supra.* Perhaps similarly novel approaches—akin to those developed in other contexts, *see, e.g.,* Marcus L. Plant, *Periodic Payment of Damages for Personal Injury,* 44 La.L.Rev. 1327 (1984) (analyzing use of installment payment of judgments in products liability and medical malpractice cases)—likewise will emerge on the damages front. But that is an issue for another day, and another forum. *Cf. id.* at 1333 (although occasionally employed solely by judicial decision, incorporation of periodic payment plans in judgments involves such a substantial departure from common-law practices that it requires statutory authorization). On the facts and law before us, we find that, although a reasonable factfinder might reach a different conclusion, the district court did not abuse its discretion in setting the children's damages awards.

Affirmed.

Notes

Assessing compensable damages for victims of child sexual abuse is based on reasonableness under common tort principles. The *Doe* decision offers an example of the courts' assessment of reasonableness and the limits of applicable considerations. The broader issue, of course, is the courts' ability to fully assess the direct damages that result from child sexual abuse and exploitation, as well as the indirect costs that extend far beyond the act of abuse, long into the child's future, with concomitant emotional effects on families and financial costs to society. The national estimated annual cost of child abuse and neglect is as high as $124 billion. *See* Xiangming Fanga, Derek S. Brown, Curtis S. Florence, and James A. Mercy, *The Economic Burden of Child Maltreatment in the United States and Implications for Prevention,* 36 CHILD ABUSE & NEGLECT 156 (Feb. 2012); *see also* Prevent Child Abuse America, Richard J. Gelles and Staci Perlman, *Estimated Annual Cost of Child Abuse and Neglect,* Economic Impact Study (2007), available at www.preventchildabusenc.org/assets/preventchildabusenc/files/cms/100/1299.pdf (last accessed Apr. 25, 2015) (estimating annual costs at $80.3 billion).

B. Punitive Damages

Hutchison ex Rel. Hutchison v. Luddy

Superior Court of Pennsylvania, 2006
2006 Pa. Super. 59, 896 A.2d 1260

OPINION BY FORD ELLIOTT, J.: ...

On second remand from our supreme court, we are asked to decide a single issue: whether the evidence presented in this case supported the jury's award of punitive damages against the Diocesan parties.... This case has traveled a long and tortured path through our appellate courts since it arrived on our dockets in July of 1994. Prior to its arrival here, the case, which began with the filing of a complaint in 1987, resulted in an order, affirmed on appeal, to unseal the Diocesan records containing information regarding instances of priest pedophilia in the Diocese.[1] The case then proceeded through years of

---

1. The psychiatric community refers to the conduct at issue in this case, involving sexual attraction to minors, adolescents, and children under the age of consent, as ephebophilia; and sexual attraction

depositions and discovery and finally reached a jury for an 11-week trial in January 1994....
"The heart of the controversy is the alleged sexual molestation of appellee Michael
Hutchison, ("Michael") a minor male with limited mental competency, by Father Francis
Luddy, a Catholic priest." *Hutchison v. Luddy*, 763 A.2d 826, 829 (Pa.Super.2000) (*"Hutchison
III"*). Michael's mother Mary Hutchison brought an action against Father Luddy and also
against the Diocesan parties: St. Therese's Catholic Church ("St. Therese's"), Bishop James
Hogan ("Bishop Hogan"), and the Diocese of Altoona-Johnstown ("the Diocese"). On
April 19, 1994, the jury returned its verdict, finding in favor of Michael and against all
defendants. The jury awarded $519,000 in compensatory damages, assigning 36% to
Father Luddy, 53% to Bishop Hogan and/or the Diocese, and 11% to St. Therese's. In
addition, the jury awarded $50,000 in punitive damages against Father Luddy and $1
million in punitive damages against the remaining defendants, collectively "the Diocesan
parties."

Following the denial of both Father Luddy's and the Diocesan parties' motions for
post-trial relief, each filed an appeal to this court. Father Luddy's appeal was subsequently
dismissed. The Diocesan parties raised ten issues in their appeal; however, a panel of this
court addressed only the first of those issues: "Whether the trial court erred in allowing
Michael to proceed under the theory set forth in Restatement (Second) of Torts §317 for
negligent hiring, supervision, and retention of Luddy by appellants." *Hutchison v. Luddy*,
453 Pa.Super. 420, 683 A.2d 1254, 1255 (1996) (*"Hutchison I"*).... [footnote omitted]....
Writing for the majority in *Hutchison I*, the Honorable John Brosky concluded the Diocesan
parties could not be liable pursuant to §317, and the Honorable Patrick J. Tamilia concurred
in the result, thereby entering judgment notwithstanding the verdict ("jnov") in favor of
all of the Diocesan parties. *Hutchison I*, 683 A.2d at 1256. This author dissented, agreeing
that jnov should have been granted as to the punitive damages claim but disagreeing that
Michael had failed to present evidence to support a §317 liability claim. *Hutchison I*, 683
A.2d at 1256–1261 (Ford Elliott, J., dissenting). This author questioned, however, whether
the trial court properly admitted evidence of a pattern or practice of the Diocese in its
handling of other claims of pedophilic conduct involving other priests. *Id.* at 1261–1262....
Our supreme court granted allocatur and vacated this court's order, holding that the jury
properly found the Diocesan parties liable pursuant to §317, negligent supervision.
Hutchison v. Luddy, 560 Pa. 51, 67, 742 A.2d 1052, 1060 (1999) (plurality) (*"Hutchison
II"*). The *Hutchison II* court found St. Therese's was not liable, however, because Father
Luddy had left St. Therese's prior to the incidents that survived the statute of limitations.
Id. at 61, 742 A.2d at 1057.

Having concluded that the jury's verdicts against the Diocesan parties were legally sus-
tainable, our supreme court remanded for this court to consider the issues those parties
raised but that this court did not decide in *Hutchison I*. *Hutchison II, supra* at 70, 742
A.2d at 1062. Thus, in *Hutchison III, supra*, the same panel that decided *Hutchison I*
addressed the Diocesan parties' remaining nine issues. Particularly germane herein was
the panel's conclusion that evidence of the Diocesan parties' awareness and handling of
other instances of pedophilia involving other priests was properly admitted as it was highly
probative as to the question of the Diocese's notice or knowledge to sustain a §317 claim.
Hutchison III, 763 A.2d at 842. *See id.* at 839–841 (setting forth the facts surrounding the
Diocesan parties' knowledge regarding other priests). *See also id.* at 841 (holding that
Father Luddy's history of pedophilia and other problems, which he acknowledged, was

---

to prepubertal children as pedophilia.... [Citations to record omitted]. For ease of discussion, however,
we refer to the instances of sexual attraction and molestation at issue in this case as pedophilia.

properly admitted to assess his credibility as he continued to deny he molested Michael). As the *Hutchison III* court opined:

> The crucial issue with respect to Appellants' liability is their knowledge when confronted with signs that Luddy was engaging in improper conduct. Liability could attach to Appellants only if the jury determined that they 'knew or should have known' that they should exercise control over Luddy. Whether Luddy was the first known priest-pedophile with whom Appellants had experience is clearly relevant to a determination of whether they 'should have known' about his improper conduct at some point prior to Michael's unfortunate experiences. Clearly an individual or organization which has been exposed to and has had some experience in dealing with a particular situation may better be able to recognize a subsequent, similar situation.

Id. at 845.

With regard to the jury's punitive damages award, however, the *Hutchison III* panel concluded that: (a) because the only remaining cause of action upon which the jury could properly award damages was negligent supervision pursuant to §317; and (b) because punitive damages cannot be awarded for misconduct that constitutes only ordinary negligence; therefore, (c) a negligent supervision claim cannot support a claim for punitive damages. *Hutchison III*, 763 A.2d at 837, citing *Mullen v. Topper's Salon and Health Spa, Inc.*, 99 F.Supp.2d 553 (E.D.Pa.2000).[3] ... Once again, our supreme court granted allocatur limited to the narrow issue whether this court "properly determined that a negligent supervision claim sounding under §317 can never support an award of punitive damages." *Hutchison v. Luddy*, 582 Pa. 114, 120, 870 A.2d 766, 769 (2005) ("*Hutchison IV*"). After reviewing cases in which a claim grounded in negligence supported a punitive damages award, the supreme court concluded that an action bottomed in §317 can sustain an award of punitive damages, providing that the plaintiff can show "the conduct of the defendant[s] went well beyond negligence and in to the realm of the outrageous." *Id.* at 124, 870 A.2d at 772. As Justice Castille, writing for a unanimous court, recognized, however:

> It may be that, as a practical matter, it proves more *difficult* to sustain a claim for punitive damages against the 'master' in the negligent supervision context than it might be with other negligence-based torts, given that the more direct harm (which, as here, may well involve an intentional tort) will usually have been inflicted directly by the 'servant.' But, that is a matter for proof that attends the particular case; there is no general proscription in law against pursuing punitive damages in the Section 317 context, where the facts so warrant.

Id. at 126, 870 A.2d at 773 (emphasis in *Hutchison IV*)....

---

3. In *Hutchison I*, this author, writing in dissent, stated that the evidence concerning the Diocesan parties' reactions to instances of pedophilia indicated they were at worst inept and grossly negligent. *Hutchison I*, 683 A.2d at 1261 (Ford Elliott, J., dissenting). At that time, this author did not agree that evidence of the Diocese's response to instances of pedophilia involving other priests should have gone to the jury. *Id.* at 1261–1262. However, because the majority concluded jnov was appropriate as to the entire jury verdict, including punitive damages, this author chose not to engage in an extensive analysis of that evidence or that issue at that time. *Id.*

In *Hutchison III*, this author again noted her disagreement with allowing evidence of the Diocesan pattern or practice of dealing with other complaints of pedophilia involving other priests to go to the jury. *Hutchison III*, 763 A.2d at 853. The majority's analysis on that point is now, however, the law of the case, as our supreme court denied the Diocesan parties' petition for allowance of appeal from the *Hutchison III* court's affirmance of the trial court's order. *Hutchi[]son v. Luddy*, 567 Pa. 743, 788 A.2d 377 (2001).

Pursuant to *Hutchison IV*, "'Punitive damages may be awarded for conduct that is outrageous, because of the defendant's evil motive or his reckless indifference to the rights of others.'" *Hutchison IV, supra* at 121, 870 A.2d at 770, quoting *Feld v. Merriam*, 506 Pa. 383, 395, 485 A.2d 742, 747 (1984), quoting Restatement (Second) of Torts § 908(2) (1979) (other citation omitted). Further, "[P]unitive damages are penal in nature and are proper only in cases where the defendant's actions are so outrageous as to demonstrate willful, wanton or reckless conduct." *Id.* (citations omitted). Because punitive damages are intended to punish the tortfeasor for outrageous conduct and to deter him and others like him from similar conduct in the future, "'[t]he state of mind of the actor is vital. The act, or the failure to act, must be intentional, reckless or malicious.'" *Id.* at 121–122, 870 A.2d at 770–771, quoting *Feld, supra* at 396, 485 A.2d at 748; citing *Martin v. Johns-Manville Corp.*, 508 Pa. 154, 171 n. 12, 494 A.2d 1088, 1097 n. 12 (1985) (plurality opinion).... [footnote omitted].

As the *Hutchison IV* court further observed, when the *Martin* court considered the requisite state of mind necessary to constitute reckless indifference, the court adopted only the first type of reckless conduct set forth in § 500 of the Restatement, "Reckless Disregard of Safety Defined":

> 'The actor's conduct is in reckless disregard of the safety of another if he does an act or intentionally fails to do an act which it is his duty to the other to do, *knowing or having reason to know* of facts which would lead a reasonable man to realize, not only that his conduct creates an unreasonable risk of physical harm to another, but also that such risk is substantially greater than that which is necessary to make his conduct negligent.'

Id., quoting Restatement (Second) of Torts § 500 (emphasis added). Pursuant to this test, the actor must not only know or have reason to know of facts that create a high degree of risk, but must deliberately proceed to act in conscious disregard of, or indifference to, that risk. *Id.*, citing *Martin, supra* at 171, 494 A.2d at 1097 (other citation omitted).... The state of mind of the actor in Pennsylvania therefore requires a higher degree of culpability than the alternative state of mind set forth in § 500, necessitating only that while the actor is or should be aware of the facts, the actor does not realize or appreciate the high degree of risk involved, even though a reasonable person in his position would do so. In this regard, our supreme court reasoned:

> 'The only purpose of punitive damages is to deter outrageous conduct. It is impossible to deter a person from taking risky action if he is not conscious of the risk. Thus, in *Feld v. Merriam*, 506 Pa. 383, 485 A.2d 742 (1984), we addressed the issue of when punitive damages are warranted and stressed that, in determining whether certain conduct is outrageous, "[t]he state of mind of the actor is vital. The act, or the failure to act, must be intentional, reckless or malicious." Similarly, the Restatement explains that "reckless indifference to the rights of others and conscious action in *deliberate* disregard of them ... may provide the necessary state of mind to justify punitive damages." [Section 500] Comment b (emphasis in *Hutchison IV*). Therefore, an appreciation of the risk is a necessary element of the mental state required for the imposition of such damages.'

Id. at 123–124, 870 A.2d at 771–772, quoting *Martin, supra* at 171 n. 12, 494 A.2d at 1097 n. 12.

As the *Hutchison IV* court therefore opined:

> Thus, in Pennsylvania, a punitive damages claim must be supported by evidence sufficient to establish that (1) a defendant had a subjective appreciation of the

risk of harm to which the plaintiff was exposed and that (2) he acted, or failed to act, as the case may be, in conscious disregard of that risk.

Id. at 124, 870 A.2d at 772, citing *Martin, supra* at 171–172, 494 A.2d at 1097–1098.

Also of particular importance to our analysis herein is the recognition in Pennsylvania that "'While the commission of an act charged cannot be proved by showing the commission of a like act at a different time, an exception to this rule exists where knowledge or intent is a material fact to be proved.'" *Hutchison III*, 763 A.2d at 842, quoting *General Equipment Manufacturers v. Westfield Ins. Co.* ("*General Equipment*"), 430 Pa.Super. 526, 635 A.2d 173, 185 (1993), *appeal denied*, 537 Pa. 663, 644 A.2d 1200 (1994) (citations omitted in *Hutchison III*). *Accord Jones v. Faust*, 852 A.2d 1201, 1205 (Pa.Super.2004.) *See also Keiter v. Miller*, 170 A. 364, 365 (Pa.Super.1934) (providing that the cases excepted from the general rule that the commission of the act charged cannot be proved by showing a like act to have been committed by the same person are those in which "the knowledge or intent of the party was a material fact to be proved, and on which the evidence, apparently collateral, had a direct bearing[ ]"), citing 1 Greenleaf on Evidence, § 53; Stephen's Digest of the Law of Evidence, art. 11.... As the *General Equipment* court continued, "Under such circumstances, evidence of similar acts or transactions is admissible when relevant to prove an issue in the case." *General Equipment*, 635 A.2d at 185 (citations omitted). Continuing, the *General Equipment* court recognized, "Accordingly, evidence of a course of conduct or dealing followed by a person may be admitted to prove that he acted in accordance with it on a given occasion, provided such a course of conduct or dealing is shown to have been continuous and systematic." *Id.*, citing *Pennsylvania Company v. Philadelphia Electric Co.*, 331 Pa. 125, 200 A. 18 (1938); *White v. Rosenthal*, 173 Pa. 175, 33 A. 1027 (1896).

We have already referred to evidence of the Diocesan parties' pattern or practice in handling complaints of priest pedophilia, set forth in *Hutchison III*, 763 A.2d at 839–841.... [footnote omitted]. Although the *Hutchison III* panel did not reach the issue whether the evidence supported a finding of intent with regard to a punitive damages claim, the panel found the evidence admissible for the purpose of showing whether the Diocesan parties knew or should have known of Luddy's pedophilic behavior for purposes of § 317 liability based upon the parties' familiarity with such incidents, which should have put the parties on notice so they could respond more appropriately to the Luddy situation. *Id.* at 838–839.

Because our supreme court requires us to determine whether the evidence admitted at trial also supports a claim for punitive damages, we set forth additional evidence with which the jury was presented regarding the Diocesan parties' conduct, keeping in mind the evidence must be sufficient to establish that "(1) a defendant had a subjective appreciation of the risk of harm to which the plaintiff was exposed and that (2) he acted, or failed to act, as the case may be, in conscious disregard of that risk." *Hutchison IV, supra* at 124, 870 A.2d at 772, citing *Martin, supra* at 171–172, 494 A.2d at 1097–1098. Pursuant to this test, the actor must "'know[ ] or ha[ve] reason to know ... of facts which create a high degree of risk..., and deliberately proceed[] to act, or fail to act, in conscious disregard of, or indifference to, that risk[.]'" *Id.* at 122–123, 870 A.2d at 771, quoting *Martin, supra* at 171, 494 A.2d at 1097 (other citation omitted).

We address first the evidence indicating the Diocesan parties subjectively knew or had reason to know of facts creating a high degree of risk to the children and families of the Diocese. With regard to the general subject of pedophilia, Bishop Hogan, who had a degree in Canon Law, acknowledged that [Canon] Law required him to investigate claims of child sexual molestation, being "very much concerned with the person against whom the complaint is filed, ... but at the same time proceed[ing] with all due regard for the welfare of the person that the complaint touches." ... [footnote omitted]. Bishop Hogan also testified that under Canon Law, a priest having any contact with the genitalia of a child is considered very serious....

Dr. Frank Valcour, a psychiatrist and one of the Diocesan parties' experts, testified that prior to 1980, pedophilia was considered an antisocial act, a wrongful act, a moral lapse, a bad thing to do, and in most jurisdictions, a crime.... Monsignor Saylor, who was subpoenaed to testify after trial commenced based on information plaintiffs' counsel received during trial, testified he reported an instance of pedophilia to Bishop Hogan in 1975, at which time Bishop Hogan directed the Monsignor to arrange for out-patient psychiatric care for the priest.... Based on Monsignor Saylor's testimony, Dr. Fred Berlin, another of the Diocesan experts, acknowledged Bishop Hogan apparently knew by 1975 that, at least in that instance, a priest who was sexually involved with a child required a minimum of out-patient psychiatric intervention.... Bishop Hogan also knew by 1979 that sexual molestation is bad for a child, especially if the priest is the molester.... In addition, the jury heard evidence that other Diocesan parties, including Monsignors Kiniry, Saylor, Madden, and Kline, knew molesting a child was morally and/or legally wrong.... The jury also had before it evidence in the form of letters parents of some of the abused boys wrote to Bishop Hogan, asking him to transfer or otherwise remove the offending priest because their children and families were being harmed by the priest's continuing presence in the parish.

In order to put these letters, which go to the Diocesan parties' subjective appreciation of the risk of harm, in context, we will first set forth the evidence the jury heard, as set forth in *Hutchison III*, regarding each incident. For the sake of clarity, we will then address the second prong of a punitive damages claim, evidence of acting, or failing to act, in conscious disregard of the risk, as it pertains to each incident. We start with the second priest the *Hutchison III* panel discussed, Father G.[7]

> There was a second priest about whom Bishop Hogan received complaints of unpriestly behavior beginning in 1972. In March of 1984, Bishop Hogan received two letters from parishioners, but, rather than contacting the parishioners, he contacted the priest. The priest admitted to sexual involvement with children but stated that nothing sloppy had occurred with the boys. Bishop Hogan gave the second priest a good dressing down. Bishop Hogan took no further action until the Pennsylvania State Police became involved. Bishop Hogan wrote a letter to the second priest and directed him to keep his big mouth shut with regard to his having sexually molested the boys. Bishop Hogan sent this second priest away from the parish for professional help.

Hutchison III, 763 A.2d at 840.

Father G. received "a good dressing down" but nothing more after Bishop Hogan received a letter from one boy and from the mother of another boy Father G. had molested in or around 1982. After describing the circumstances involving Father G.'s attempted molestation, the boy wrote:

> I pushed his hand away and I couldn't believe this was happening. I was really shocked when he tried it again. He tried it three or four more times. I then drew my fist back, but I couldn't hit him. I told him to quit.... He said he was sorry

---

7. Although the names of the priests and the children were used at trial and are therefore part of the public record, both this court and our supreme court have avoided using the names in published opinions; therefore, we will continue this practice.

and admitted to me that he had made sexual contact with boys that he had working for him in the past. He also told me he had other instances with other guys. I think the man needs help with his problem because I know of . . . at least one person besides me that Father [G.] has tried this with. I have talked with his mother and she said he is also very upset and hurt. I think something has to be done before someone else gets hurt real bad. . . . I hope something can be done.

[Citations to record omitted]. Bishop Hogan did not respond to this letter although the boy gave his address, and did not contact Father G. for an explanation.

With regard to the second boy, the boy's mother wrote to Bishop Hogan in 1984, describing an incident that occurred two years earlier, in which Father G. made sexual advances toward her son, who was working at the church mowing the lawn and painting. One evening when the boy's parents went to pick him up, they found him over a mile away from the church, having fled in terror when Father G. told the boy he would wait until later to renew his advances. The mother called Father G. that night and confronted him. Father G. did not deny any of it, asking only for forgiveness and saying he "would try to control his homosexual tendencies that he had for some time." . . .

Because her son did not want Father G. to lose his priesthood or harm him in any way, the mother waited two years to write to the Bishop. During the two-year period, the mother saw her son change from a quiet, trusting person to someone who no longer trusted people or cared about anything, especially himself. Despite her son's belief it would be his fault if Father G. were disciplined in any way, the mother wrote to the Bishop out of fear Father G. would hurt another boy and his family the way her son and family had been hurt. . . . Bishop Hogan testified he did not contact either of the boys or the mother. . . . After the state police got involved, Bishop Hogan agreed to send Father G. to Orchard Lake, a seminary for boys of Polish extraction Father G. attended as a youth, for a one-month sabbatical, during which he received psychiatric treatment. . . . At the end of the month, Bishop Hogan assigned Father G. as a pastor at two parishes, where he would have no supervision, and did not notify anyone at these parishes regarding Father G.'s admitted history. . . . Upon receiving renewed complaints concerning Father G. after he was reassigned, Bishop Hogan wrote to him in December 1985 but did nothing further. Father G. was still a priest in the Diocese when Bishop Hogan retired in 1987. . . .

Turning to the third priest the *Hutchison III* panel discussed, Father K., the panel observed:

There was also a third priest in the Diocese about whom Hogan received notification of pedophilic activity in 1982. Bishop Hogan confronted the priest and attributed the matter to an isolated falling apart. The third priest admitted to having engaged in a number of sexual acts over a period in excess of a year with a fifteen-year-old boy.[8] The only allegation made by the boy that the priest denied to Bishop Hogan was that he engaged in sodomy. Bishop Hogan took the priest's word that he could correct the problem, and he took no action toward him except to check on him at his parish seven to eight times in the following five years.

Hutchison III, 763 A.2d at 840–841.

---

8. The acts to which Father K. admitted, which took place over a period of one year, included fondling the boy's exposed genitals and having the boy fondle his exposed genitals; showing the boy X-rated movies and encouraging him to drink alcohol, and "making dirty remarks with respect to passing girls." . . .

Bishop Hogan received two letters from the parents of the boy Father K. molested. After receiving a letter from the Bishop in which he outlined his discussion with Father K., the boy's father wrote to Bishop Hogan on October 8, 1982, indicating that his son no longer wished to be an altar boy and that the family was no longer comfortable receiving Holy Communion from Father K. or having Father K. hear confession. The boy's father therefore asked the Bishop to transfer Father K. to another parish.... The boy's father indicated, however, the family would be willing to live by the Bishop's decision.... Almost one year later, on September 22, 1983, the boy's mother wrote to Bishop Hogan when she discovered Father K. was not among the priests who were to be reassigned to another parish during the ensuing year. According to the boy's mother, her son had been diagnosed with migraine headaches during the preceding year, which the experts attributed to stress as the boy was so young, and which the mother attributed to the stress of the boy's having repeatedly to encounter Father K. The mother therefore pointedly asked Bishop Hogan to remove Father K. from the parish.... Bishop Hogan neither contacted the family nor transferred Father K., who was still the pastor at the same church four years later, when Bishop Hogan retired....

The jury also heard evidence regarding another priest, Father C., whose pedophilic activities first came to Bishop Hogan's attention in 1979. The *Hutchison III* panel discussed Father C. in its opinion:

> Upon receiving the first complaint about a priest in 1979, Bishop Hogan confronted the priest with the allegation. The priest denied the allegation that he had rubbed his penis on a ten-year-old boy's feet. Bishop Hogan did not consider the allegation to be pedophilic behavior, and he transferred the priest to another church.

Hutchison III, 763 A.2d at 840. Bishop Hogan testified that the parents who accused Father C. of the incident outlined *supra* indicated there were three boys whom Father C. would invite to the rectory when the pastor was away.... Bishop Hogan also testified Father C. admitted the boys slept over at the rectory and he hypnotized them.... Excerpts from Bishop Hogan's letter to Father C. regarding this incident follow:

> Painful as the situation is, we must safeguard your own good name, protect the priestly reputation and prevent scandal from touching the church—even if unjust....

> At the moment I seek one to take your place, as I do a fitting place for you— after you have had a few days of needed rest.

[Citations to record omitted].

As the *Hutchison III* panel observed:

> Seven years later, in 1986, Bishop Hogan began receiving additional similar complaints about that same priest from his pastor, Monsignor Kiniry, who stated that both he and the parish school's principal had been receiving complaints for over six months. This priest was sent for treatment, but remained an active priest in the Diocese until Hogan retired in 1987.

Hutchison III, 763 A.2d at 840. In response to these additional complaints, Bishop Hogan wrote to Father C. on January 17, 1986, and, after outlining the steps the Diocese and Father C. were to take, stated, "Permit me to note that failure to comply with these directives may very likely result in legal action against you and almost certainly in litigation involving the Diocese (its bishop) and its assets." ... After counseling, Father C. was transferred to a convent but continued to bring children to his sleeping quarters. Upon learning of his activities from the sisters at the convent, Bishop Hogan again wrote to Father C. on January 13, 1987, stating in pertinent part:

> I deem it prudent to send along a little precautionary suggestion. Especially when the attorneys are struggling energetically but concernedly with our legal realities. We're not yet out of the woods—and they beg for the cooperation of all involved.
>
> The problem? The [B.] family is nervous of your frequent visits. The [T.] girl considers herself harassed. Anonymous letters add to her annoyance and suspicion. The Johnstown young lady ... has made known ... her familiarity with our story....
>
> My suggestion? *For the time being, cool any and all association with youth.* You already know of the storm raised by the irate mother in Johnstown. Let's get the case settled first. Don't jeopardize it. For it could yet cause you and the Diocese a bit of heartache.

[Citations to record omitted] (emphasis added).

On March 19, 1987, while Father C. was still at the convent, Bishop Hogan sent him another letter upon learning Father C. had not stopped his "youth involvement":

> I experienced a greater degree of genuine worry over the matter of youth involvement. Especially when trips to ... transport, the loaning of car to, the bringing of one or more [to] the convent for overnight—even in your room. You see [the sisters] know of my contrary stipulation—apparently you told them of it.
>
> ... If this youth involvement is discoverable, and how can it not be, there is extreme danger of courtroom disaster....
>
> [Lest] you think that I try to level a sand castle with battleship rifles, allow me to cite this: last week I learned that the Johnstown family, armed with professional reports, will seek damages. If a conference fails to resolve the issue, it will go into a court action—publicity and all. *No wonder I asked you to lie low,* or that I fear further compromising of the case and jeopardizing of the Diocese.
>
> *If there is to be any youth association for the time being—i.e. until the case is settled,* I shall want to know. For you will be immediately removed from your assignment. As long as you have a diocesan assignment, the responsibility is diocesan. *Apart, off on your own, so to speak, it is yours.* Moreover, there is to be no permitting of any youthful people to visit the convent for any reason.
>
> Father [C.], I am not happy with such bluntness. But I cannot afford not to be. Danger flags are up, for you, for me (*for 1979 may well not be out of the picture*), for the Diocese.

Id. at 100–101 (emphasis added).... Despite Bishop Hogan's testimony that he knew by 1986 Father C. lied to him in 1979 and was a pedophile, these letters fail to mention any concern for the eight children Father C. was known to have molested by 1986, instead expressing concern with Father C.'s continuing molestation only if it occurred while Father C. had a Diocesan assignment....

Bishop Hogan acknowledged receiving a letter from Monsignor Kiniry in which Monsignor Kiniry admitted he knew Father C. was molesting children as early as July of 1985 but did not bring the matter to Bishop Hogan's attention for six months.... The Bishop also testified that the Diocese offered no help or counseling to the boys beyond that which Monsignor Kiniry initiated on his own, if any, did not advise the parishioners whose children came into contact with Father C. to avoid him, and through the pastor, actually took up a collection to help Father C. with his "nervous problem." ...

Probably the single most damaging evidence the jury heard came in the form of excerpts from Bishop Hogan's 1988 deposition, taken prior to the court order unsealing the Diocesan "secret archives." Bishop Hogan testified that, until the Hutchison/Luddy incident was brought to his attention in 1987, none of the situations brought to his attention during his tenure as Bishop involved pedophilia.... Specifically, in response to appellees' counsel's questioning regarding instances other than alcoholism that were serious enough to require Bishop Hogan's intervention, the Bishop testified, "In general terms I will say none of them involved pedophilia." ... As the Bishop testified in 1988, "Disciplinary measures — were called for in that two or three — I'd have to go back to do some recollecting here — instances that I thought were sufficient gravity to intervene." ... When asked again, "But none of them dealt with pedophilia?" the Bishop responded, "None." ... From the evidence and letters set forth *supra*, the jury knew that Bishop Hogan's 1988 deposition testimony was not true, thereby giving the jury reason to question not only the credibility of the Bishop, but also the credibility of the other Diocesan parties, all of whom reported to the Bishop. *See Berger v. Schetman*, 883 A.2d 631, 640 (Pa.Super.2005) (observing that "'[t]he fact finder is free to believe all, part, or none of the evidence and the Superior Court will not disturb the credibility determinations of the court below'"), quoting *Nicholson v. Johnston*, 855 A.2d 97, 102 (Pa.Super.2004), *appeal denied*, 582 Pa. 665, 868 A.2d 453 (2005).

Turning next to Father Luddy, the *Hutchison III* panel has amply set forth evidence of Father Luddy's behavior with Michael, his brother Mark, and other boys, as well as Bishop Hogan's and the other Diocesan parties' acts or failures to act with regard to that behavior. *Hutchison III*, 763 A.2d at 839–840. We will therefore expand on that evidence only as it relates to the punitive damages claim.... As the *Hutchison III* panel observed, "Luddy was ordained as a priest of the Diocese in 1967 and did not leave until asked in May of 1987, following the allegations concerning this appeal. Hogan was the Bishop of the Diocese from July of 1966 until May 20, 1987, during Luddy's entire tenure." *Id.* at 839.... According to Luddy's testimony, Luddy's first molestation of a minor male occurred when Luddy was an associate pastor at St. Mark's Roman Catholic Church in Altoona, in approximately 1969.... Luddy took the boy, who was 15, to Puerto Rico for eight days and also took the boy on three overnight trips to visit Luddy's sister, during which the boy and Luddy shared a bed at the Holiday Inn.... None of the abuse occurred at the rectory, however.

The second boy, who testified at trial, claimed he and a friend stayed at St. John's rectory one night after a trip to Johnstown with Luddy some time between 1967 and 1969. When the boy awoke, Father Luddy had his mouth on the boy's penis and told the boy he wanted to sodomize him.... The boy woke his friend and fled from the rectory.... The boy testified he told Father Mulvehill, the pastor at St. John's, exactly what had happened, and Father Mulvehill promised the boy his report would be "taken care of." ... Luddy admitted his involvement with the boy but denied he attempted to sodomize him. Luddy also testified he last had contact with that boy in 1970, after he had been transferred to St. John's Cathedral in Johnstown for reasons unrelated to sexual activity. Father Mulvehill denied the boy's allegations....

The third boy Luddy admitted he molested was approximately 14–15 years of age at the time. Luddy gave the boy alcohol and invited him to spend the night at the rectory. The molestation began in 1972 at the Cathedral of the Blessed Sacrament, where Monsignor Thomas Madden was pastor and Father Leonard Inman had a room on the same floor as Luddy. Luddy assumed both Monsignor Madden and Father Inman were in the rectory while he was molesting this boy.... Luddy continued to molest the boy after he was transferred to St. Therese's.

Prior his transfer:

> The evidence showed that Luddy had developed a problem with alcoholism beginning in 1968 and continuing until 1982. Monsignor Madden had observed problems with Luddy's behavior, e.g., tardiness, disappearances from the rectory until the wee hours of the morning, and driving problems involving possible hit and run activity. Monsignor Madden had attributed these problems, which he described as a failure to fulfill obligations, to a Peter Pan syndrome, meaning Luddy was immature. He [testified he] knew nothing of the pedophilic activity specifically. Monsignor Madden wrote to Bishop Hogan concerning Luddy's problems. Bishop Hogan responded by informing Luddy that his behavior was intolerable. Luddy promised to stop drinking and was transferred to St. Therese's.

Hutchison III, 763 A.2d at 839. In his letter to Bishop Hogan, Monsignor Madden also told the Bishop he suspected that a deeper malaise was causing Luddy to turn to alcohol. *Id.*

Monsignor Kline, who was pastor at St. Therese's during Luddy's tenure there, testified, however, that he knew nothing of Monsignor Madden's letter to Bishop Hogan until the trial in this case, although the Bishop told Monsignor Kline that Luddy had some problems having to do with his use of alcohol.... Monsignor Kline also testified that due to his "compassion," he would give a priest who admitted molesting a child a second chance before reporting the molestation to the Bishop, unless the molestation became a habit.... As the *Hutchison III* court also observed, Monsignor Saylor testified he received a report that Luddy's predecessor at St. Therese's, Father T.C., had sexually molested a minor while Monsignor Kline was pastor. In that instance, the child's mother reported the incident, Monsignor Saylor went immediately to the Bishop, and the Bishop instructed Monsignor Saylor to send the priest for psychiatric counseling. *Hutchison III*, 763 A.2d at 839–840.[9] Monsignor Kline testified, however, that he had never been informed of this incident and had no knowledge of Father T.C.'s sexual activity with children prior to being asked about it at trial.... He also testified that he thought Luddy occupied the same rooms Father T.C. occupied while assigned to St. Therese's....

Mark Hutchison, Michael's brother, was the fourth boy whom Luddy admitted molesting, beginning in approximately 1977 when Mark was eleven or twelve years old, and continuing for four years, until 1980. Luddy admitted he molested Mark at least once a week or once every other week at the rectory during the four years, and also molested him on trips to Spain and France, for which Luddy paid.... Mark testified Luddy molested him over 300 times, approximately 200 times of which occurred in St. Therese's Rectory....[10] ... Monsignor Kline was aware that Luddy would take the Hutchison brothers to his rooms at the rectory to watch television, although he testified he thought their mother was with them 90 percent of the time.... Monsignor Kline admitted that he should have known, through his own observations and suspicions, that Luddy was engaged in sexual activity with minor males, based on the frequency of the Hutchison boys' visits to Luddy's private quarters.... In 1980, Mark reported Luddy's abuse to Father Gabriel Zeis, a Franciscan priest who is not with the Diocese; and between 1981 and 1983, Mark informed Father Bernard Gratten, a priest in the Diocese, of his sexual relationship with

---

9. Father T.C. remained a priest in the Diocese until his death approximately three years prior to trial, however....

10. Michael testified Luddy molested him 50 to 75 times in the church rectory.... Michael also testified he saw Monsignor Kline in a downstairs doorway on one occasion when Michael and Luddy were on their way to Luddy's private quarters....

Luddy. Mark testified Father Zeis, who met with Mark and his mother, assured them he would contact Bishop Hogan and that the church could provide help to Luddy....

As the trial court observed in its opinion denying the Diocesan parties' post-trial motions, "Church Defendants argue their evidence and/or interpretation of Plaintiff's evidence as if it was the only evidence and/or interpretation available to the jury."... With regard to Bishop Hogan's and Monsignor Kline's testimony, the trial court observed, "These witnesses simply were not believed by this jury. Nothing could be clearer."... Continuing, the trial court opined that the jury "clearly believed both the diocese (through Monsignor Kline at a minimum) and Bishop Hogan had both notice and knowledge. Further, that they/he avoided their responsibility."...

Viewing the evidence set forth *supra* in the light most favorable to Michael as verdict winner, as we must, we find the record supports the jury's finding the Diocese subjectively appreciated the risk of harm of pedophilia long before Father Luddy molested Michael, yet acted, or failed to act, in conscious disregard of the risk despite knowing or having reason to know priests within the Diocese were molesting its children. In particular, the jury could have properly found outrageous the Diocesan parties' failure to investigate and discipline its priests, including Father Luddy, for acts of molestation occurring as early as 1967, in conscious disregard of the rights of Michael and his family, who placed their trust and unwavering loyalty in the Diocesan parties.

We find the evidence before the jury in this case far more egregious than the facts our supreme court has previously confronted when finding the evidence did not support a punitive damages verdict. Even in *Martin, supra,* in which the defendants were aware asbestos could cause illness among employees at an asbestos manufacturing plant, the defendants did not have knowledge that asbestos insulation installers faced the same risk. *Martin, supra* at 174–175, 494 A.2d at 1099. Of even more significance, the defendants in *Martin* most assuredly did not know that specific insulation installers had developed asbestos-related diseases and did not have pleas from them or their families to stop using asbestos-containing products. Only such a fact pattern could closely parallel the evidence before the jury in this case. As the *Martin* court opined, "On this appeal Martin has not argued that the appellants appreciated the risk of asbestos insulation installers face and, nevertheless, acted or failed to act in flagrant disregard of their safety." *Id.* at 176, 494 A.2d at 1100....

Finally, St. Therese's liability for punitive damages was joint and several with the Diocesan parties' and was predicated on the practice of ignoring complaints and flagrant evidence of priest pedophilia altogether, of transferring priests who admitted molesting children without warning anyone at the new parish, and of failing to offer any help to the numerous victims these priests molested. These were not the practices of St. Therese's; rather, they were the practices of the Diocesan parties, particularly Bishop Hogan and including Monsignor Kline while he was pastor at St. Therese's. During his tenure, both Father T.C. and Father Luddy sexually molested minors for years while Monsignor Kline was under the same roof. Monsignor Kline's abysmal disregard for the safety of the Hutchison brothers and other minors prior to the incidents underlying this case led directly to Luddy's opportunity to molest Michael. As the trial court observed:

> As we have opined throughout and truly believe, affirmative answers to the first eight questions on the verdict slip in our judgment demanded an award of punitive damages. We cannot envision a situation much more outrageous or detrimental to the advancement of a civilized society than what the jury had concluded occurred by their responses to the first eight questions.

[Citation to record omitted]. We therefore find no merit to the Diocesan parties' claim they are entitled to a new trial as to the amount of punitive damages for which they should be held liable.... We affirm the trial court's entry of judgment in favor of Michael in the amount of $1 million in punitive damages. Jurisdiction is relinquished.

Notes

Punitive damages are awarded to punish an offender for intentional or malicious misconduct and to deter similar misconduct in the future. The amount of punitive damages may be limited by state law and is the subject of much debate about tort reform. For a survey of state tort reform laws, see American Tort Reform Association, *Punitive Damages Reform*, available at http://www.atra.org/issues/punitive-damages-reform (last accessed Apr. 25, 2015). In 2012, a jury in Oregon awarded the largest punitive damage award to a single plaintiff in a child abuse case in the United States—$18.5 million—against the Boy Scouts of America, for the sexual abuse of a former scout, Kerry Lewis. *See* Aimee Green, *Portland jury awards $18.5 million in punitive damages in Boy Scout sexual-abuse case*, The Oregonian, Apr. 23, 2010, available at http://www.oregonlive.com/portland/index.ssf/2010/04/jury_awards_millions_in_punati.html (last accessed Apr. 25, 2015). For further discussion about the Boy Scouts, see Chapter 8, Section IV.A (Social Institutions: The Boy Scouts of America), *infra*. Under Oregon law, 60% of that award went to the state's crime victim's compensation fund. Lewis also had been awarded $1 million in compensatory damages.

Significant punitive damages also have been awarded in cases involving the Roman Catholic Church. One of the largest awards—$120 million, $18 of which was punitive—was levied against the Diocese of Dallas, Texas, which was determined to have ignored evidence that one of its priests, Rudolph Kos, was sexually abusing boys and then took steps to cover-up the abuse. *See* Peter Steinfels, *$120 Million Damage Award for Sexual Abuse by Priest*, N.Y. Times, July 25, 1997. The award was divided among 10 plaintiffs and the family of another man, who committed suicide when he was 20 years old. *Id.* For a sampling of damages awarded in sexual abuses cases involving Roman Catholic priests, see *Sexual Abuse Civil Lawsuits That Have Gone to Trial*, available at http://www.bishop-accountability.org/legal/civil_trials.htm (last updated Dec. 6, 2010). *See also Wisniewski v. Diocese of Belleville*, 406 Ill. App.3d 1119, 347 Ill. Dec. 753, 943 N.E.2d 43 (2011) (upholding $2.4 million compensatory and $2.6 million punitive award against diocese for sexual abuse by priest). For further discussion about the sex abuse scandal in the Roman Catholic Church, see Chapter 8, Section IV.B (Religious Institutions: The Roman Catholic Church), *infra*.

C. Protective Discovery Orders

In re Roman Catholic Archbishop of Portland in Oregon

Ninth Circuit, 2011
661 F.3d 417

IKUTA, Circuit Judge:

Documents produced in discovery and filed in the bankruptcy court contained allegations that Fathers M and D, two priests who were not parties to the Portland Archdiocese's bankruptcy case, had sexually abused children. The bankruptcy court held that the discovery documents at issue could be disclosed to the public, because the public's interest in disclosure of these discovery documents outweighed the priests' privacy interests under Rule 26(c) of the Federal Rules of Civil Procedure. It also held that the documents filed in court could be disclosed to the public because they did not contain "scandalous" allegations for purposes of 11 U.S.C. § 107(b). The district court affirmed. We affirm in part and reverse in part....

The Portland Archdiocese was the subject of multiple lawsuits seeking millions of dollars in compensatory and punitive damages for sexual abuse of children by specific clergy members of the Archdiocese. In July 2004, while the tort claimants' lawsuits were pending, the Archdiocese filed for Chapter 11 bankruptcy protection. The bankruptcy case thus became the forum for many of the proceedings relating to the tort claims.[1] The appellees (referred to here as Appellee Claimants) are a small subset of the many tort claimants who were parties to the bankruptcy case.[2]

After the Chapter 11 filing, the bankruptcy court scheduled mediation to give the tort claimants and the Archdiocese an opportunity to settle the tort claims. Before mediation commenced, the tort claimants sought discovery regarding their claims pursuant to Rule 26 of the Federal Rules of Civil Procedure (which is made applicable to bankruptcy proceedings by Federal Rule of Bankruptcy Procedure 7026). In order to prove that the Archdiocese had engaged in a pattern and practice of misconduct, the tort claimants sought discovery regarding, among other things, all reports of sexual abuse by priests within the Archdiocese, not just reports regarding the priests who were the defendants in the tort suits.

The bankruptcy court entered two orders governing premediation discovery, both dated January 14, 2005. The first order directed the Archdiocese to produce the personnel files of 37 accused priests identified by the Archdiocese for the "John Jay Study," a national study of clergy abuse commissioned by the United States Conference of Catholic Bishops, and to make available four officials for deposition. Second, the court entered a stipulated protective order, which had been negotiated between the Archdiocese and the tort claimants. Relevant here, paragraph 7 of the protective order provided as follows:

> In the event that tort claimants wish to remove from the restrictions of this order any document designated as "Confidential" by Debtor pursuant to this order, tort claimants shall provide prior written notice to Debtor's counsel and counsel for the priest whose file is at issue, if any. Counsel shall then have seven (7) days to file a motion with the court seeking an order preventing the disclosure of such document. The document or documents shall remain subject to this order unless the court rules otherwise following the filing of counsel's motion.

The protective order allowed the Archdiocese to designate "any and all documents produced pursuant to the [first discovery] order" as confidential.

Among the documents disclosed pursuant to the bankruptcy court's discovery order were the personnel files of Father M and Father D. The Archdiocese produced these files only because their names were included in the John Jay Study; neither had been sued by the tort claimants. Father M, 72 years old, had left Portland in 2000 or 2001, and Father D, 88 years old, had retired in 1989. Neither was notified about the parties' negotiation of the discovery order, nor that their files had been disclosed. Their personnel files, along with the others, were filed under seal in the bankruptcy case.

---

1. Subject to certain exceptions, "all proceedings that arise during the case are to take place before the bankruptcy court." *Collier on Bankruptcy* ¶ 3.02[2] (16th ed. rev.2011). A bankruptcy court is not, however, authorized to determine the amount of damages awarded in a tort lawsuit; that duty is entrusted only to the district court. *See* 28 U.S.C. § 157(b)(1), (5).

2. There are about two dozen Appellee Claimants out of over 140 tort claimants.

During 2007, the Archdiocese and the tort claimants engaged in negotiations regarding both the damage claims and the scope of disclosure of documents produced in the bankruptcy filing.... In connection with the negotiations to settle the damage claims, the Appellee Claimants filed a memorandum on March 6, 2007, which "summarize[d] the pattern and practice evidence and the punitive damages evidence in support of the estimation" of five unresolved tort claims. The memorandum included, as attachments, the clergy personnel files of 27 priests (including Father M and Father D), plus deposition excerpts and other documents. These documents were filed under seal pursuant to the court's protective order. The tort claimants (including the Appellee Claimants) settled most of the claims against the Archdiocese.

While these settlement talks were underway, the parties also negotiated the scope of release of bankruptcy documents. Counsel for several tort claimants (but not Appellee Claimants) invoked paragraph 7 of the protective order, notifying the Archdiocese of their intent to release some 1,760 pages of material that were produced by the Archdiocese in discovery as well as deposition transcripts. As was their right under the protective order, the Archdiocese and nine individual priests moved the bankruptcy court to prevent the release of the discovery material. The parties entered into a new round of negotiations regarding which sealed documents would be made public. Fathers M and D were not part of these negotiations. On May 24, 2007, counsel for the tort claimants informed the bankruptcy court that the parties had agreed to a resolution. As a result of this agreement, the Archdiocese released over 2,000 documents and posted them to a public website. This resolution did not bind Appellee Claimants.

On September 28, 2007, the bankruptcy court closed the Archdiocese's Chapter 11 case, retaining jurisdiction over any pending adversary proceedings. The conclusion of the Archdiocese's bankruptcy proceedings did not, however, resolve whether there would be public disclosure of documents designated as confidential or filed under seal. As noted above, Appellee Claimants were not bound by the May 24, 2007 mediation agreement, and they filed a motion to unseal the punitive damage estimation memorandum and exhibits filed as part of the successful negotiations to settle the tort claims. Appellee Claimants also notified the Archdiocese that they intended to release all personnel records from the clergy files that were produced in discovery. The Archdiocese opposed the Appellee Claimants' motion to unseal the court documents and also sought an order preventing the disclosure of the discovery documents. A number of priests whose files stood to be released, including Fathers M and D, filed similar motions.

After a hearing in which counsel for Fathers M and D participated, the bankruptcy court ruled in favor of the Appellee Claimants. The court first considered the personnel records produced in discovery. Applying Rule 26(c),[3] the court concluded that the Archdiocese had not demonstrated "good cause" sufficient to overcome the presumption

---

3. Rule 26(c) of the Federal Rules of Civil Procedure provides, in pertinent part:
  (c) Protective Orders.
    (1) In General. A party or any person from whom discovery is sought may move for a protective order in the court where the action is pending—or as an alternative on matters relating to a deposition, in the court for the district where the deposition will be taken. The motion must include a certification that the movant has in good faith conferred or attempted to confer with other affected parties in an effort to resolve the dispute without court action. The court may, for good cause, issue an order to protect a party or person from annoyance, embarrassment, oppression, or undue burden or expense, including one or more of the following:
  (A) forbidding the disclosure or discovery....

of public access to the names of and allegations against the accused clergy, although there was good cause to redact the addresses, social security numbers, financial information, and family information of those priests. This ruling applied with equal force to the personnel files of Fathers M and D. The bankruptcy court also considered the Appellee Claimants' motion to make public certain deposition transcripts and attached exhibits, and held that even if these documents were covered by the protective order, no party had opposed the Appellee Claimants' motion or shown good cause to continue any protection. Accordingly, the court also permitted their release.

Second, the court considered whether 11 U.S.C. § 107[4] precluded the release of attachments to the Appellee Claimants' punitive damage estimation memorandum that had been filed with the court. The priests argued that the personnel files attached to the memorandum contained "scandalous" materials, and thus qualified for the exception to disclosure in § 107(b). The bankruptcy court rejected this argument. It defined the word "scandalous" to mean a document that "improperly casts a derogatory light on someone," and determined that the Appellee Claimants were not using the personnel files for an improper purpose. Therefore, it ordered the release of these files.

Fathers M and D appealed the bankruptcy court's order to the district court. The district court affirmed, and Fathers M and D timely appealed. The bankruptcy court stayed the order pending the outcome of this appeal.... We review the district court's decision on appeal from a bankruptcy court de novo, giving no "deference to the district court's determinations." *In re Mantz*, 343 F.3d 1207, 1211 (9th Cir.2003) (quoting *Batlan v. TransAm. Commercial Fin. Corp.*, 265 F.3d 959, 963 (9th Cir.2001) (internal quotation marks omitted))....

We first consider the bankruptcy court's ruling under Rule 26 of the Federal Rules of Civil Procedure allowing the release of Fathers M and D's personnel files, which were produced during discovery but not filed with the court.... As a general rule, the public is permitted "access to litigation documents and information produced during discovery." *Phillips*, 307 F.3d at 1210; *see also San Jose Mercury News, Inc. v. U.S. Dist. Court*, 187 F.3d 1096, 1103 (9th Cir.1999) ("It is well-established that the fruits of pretrial discovery are, in the absence of a court order to the contrary, presumptively public."). Under Rule 26, however, "[t]he court may, for good cause, issue an order to protect a party or person from annoyance, embarrassment, oppression, or undue burden or expense." Fed.R.Civ.P. 26(c)(1). The party opposing disclosure has the burden of proving "good cause," which requires a showing "that specific prejudice or harm will result" if the protective order is not granted. *Foltz v. State Farm Mut. Auto. Ins. Co.*, 331 F.3d 1122, 1130 (9th Cir.2003).... While courts generally make a finding of good cause before issuing a protective order, a court need not do so where (as here) the parties stipulate to such an order. When the protective order "was a stipulated order and no party ha[s] made a 'good cause' showing," then "the burden of proof ... remain[s] with the party seeking protection." *Phillips*, 307 F.3d at 1211 n. 1. If a party takes steps to release documents subject to a stipulated order, the party opposing disclosure has the burden of establishing that there is good cause to continue the protection of the discovery material.

---

4. 11 U.S.C. § 107 provides, in pertinent part:
   (a) Except as provided in subsections (b) and (c) and subject to section 112, a paper filed in a case under this title and the dockets of a bankruptcy court are public records and open to examination by an entity at reasonable times without charge.
   (b) On request of a party in interest, the bankruptcy court shall, and on the bankruptcy court's own motion, the bankruptcy court may ...
      (2) protect a person with respect to scandalous or defamatory matter contained in a paper filed in a case under this title.

A court considering a motion for a continuation of the protective order must proceed in two steps. First, it must determine whether "particularized harm will result from disclosure of information to the public." *Id.* at 1211. As we have explained, "[b]road allegations of harm, unsubstantiated by specific examples or articulated reasoning, do not satisfy the Rule 26(c) test." *Beckman Indus., Inc. v. Int'l Ins. Co.*, 966 F.2d 470, 476 (9th Cir.1992) (quoting *Cipollone v. Liggett Group, Inc.*, 785 F.2d 1108, 1121 (3rd Cir.1986)) (internal quotation marks omitted). Rather, the person seeking protection from disclosure must "allege specific prejudice or harm." *See id.* Second, if the court concludes that such harm will result from disclosure of the discovery documents, then it must proceed to balance "the public and private interests to decide whether [maintaining] a protective order is necessary." *Phillips*, 307 F.3d at 1211. We have directed courts doing this balancing to consider the factors identified by the Third Circuit in *Glenmede Trust Co. v. Thompson*, 56 F.3d 476, 483 (3d Cir.1995).[5] *See Phillips*, 307 F.3d at 1211.

But even when the factors in this two-part test weigh in favor of protecting the discovery material (i.e., where the court determines that disclosure of information may result in "particularized harm," and the private interest in protecting the discovery material outweighs the public interest in disclosure), a court must still consider whether redacting portions of the discovery material will nevertheless allow disclosure. *Foltz*, 331 F.3d at 1136–37. In *Foltz*, an insurer argued that documents produced in discovery "contained confidential information that would satisfy the 'good cause' standard of Rule 26(c)," *id.* at 1131, such as "confidential financial information, third-party medical records, personnel files, and trade secrets," *id.* at 1136. Based on our review of the record, we concluded that "the limited number of third-party medical and personnel records [could] be redacted easily to protect third-party privacy interests while leaving other meaningful information." *Id.* at 1137.... Accordingly, in determining whether to protect discovery materials from disclosure under Rule 26(c), a court must not only consider whether the party seeking protection has shown particularized harm, and whether the balance of public and private interests weighs in favor, but also keep in mind the possibility of redacting sensitive material....

In light of these principles, we now turn to Fathers M and D's argument that the bankruptcy court erred in rejecting their motion under Rule 26(c) to protect their personnel files from disclosure. The priests raise two different arguments: first, that the bankruptcy court should have presumed that they had good cause to protect their personnel files from disclosure, because they were not sued and had not intervened; and second, even if they were not relieved of the burden of proving good cause, they had carried that burden, and the bankruptcy court erred in concluding otherwise. We address their arguments in turn....

We begin by considering Fathers M and D's request that we develop a new rule governing the disclosure of discovery material containing confidential information about third parties. First, the priests assert that the types of personnel files at issue raise privacy concerns that are appropriately subject to protective orders, particularly with respect to

---

5. Those factors are:
   (1) whether disclosure will violate any privacy interests; (2) whether the information is being sought for a legitimate purpose or for an improper purpose; (3) whether disclosure of the information will cause a party embarrassment; (4) whether confidentiality is being sought over information important to public health and safety; (5) whether the sharing of information among litigants will promote fairness and efficiency; (6) whether a party benefitting from the order of confidentiality is a public entity or official; and (7) whether the case involves issues important to the public.
   Glenmede Trust, 56 F.3d at 483.

third parties. *See Foltz*, 331 F.3d at 1130; *Knoll v. AT & T*, 176 F.3d 359 (6th Cir.1999) (upholding a protective order limiting plaintiffs' access to the personnel files of non-party AT & T employees). Given the likelihood that third parties may not be notified when their confidential information is at risk of being disclosed by a defendant (such as an employer, hospital, or computerized data management company), Fathers M and D propose that we adopt a presumption of good cause to forbid disclosure of third party records, which the party seeking disclosure would have to rebut. According to Fathers M and D, the justification for such a rule is even stronger when modification is sought after a case has settled, by which point only the non-parties whose private information is at risk have a stake in the proceedings.

Although this argument is not without merit, we decline to adopt the priests' proposed rule because it is not consistent with the language of Rule 26(c)(1) or our precedent. As noted above, Rule 26(c) provides that "[t]he court may, for good cause, issue an order to protect a party or person from annoyance, embarrassment, oppression, or undue burden or expense" by, among other things, "forbidding the disclosure" of discovery material. Fed.R.Civ.P. 26(c)(1). We have consistently read this language against the background principle that material produced in pretrial discovery is "presumptively public," *San Jose Mercury News*, 187 F.3d at 1103, and held that this presumption can be rebutted only by a showing of good cause by the one seeking protection, *Phillips*, 307 F.3d at 1210–11 (holding that the party or intervenor "seeking protection bears the burden of showing specific prejudice or harm will result if no protective order is granted"). *See Beckman*, 966 F.2d at 475. Under Rule 26(c)(1), the one seeking protection may be either a "party" or a "person." Fed.R.Civ.P. 26(c)(1). The plain meaning of the word "person" would include third parties who are not part of the litigation. Thus, we cannot logically exclude third parties from our rule that whoever is seeking protection under Rule 26(c) bears the burden of showing good cause.

Our reading is supported by the observation that the drafters of the Federal Rules of Civil Procedure knew how to vary from the general rule that discovery material is presumptively public when they wanted to. Thus, Rule 5.2 provides that "[u]nless the court orders otherwise," and subject to certain exemptions inapplicable to third parties, an "electronic or paper filing with the court" may include only "(1) the last four digits of [a person's] social-security number and taxpayer-identification number; (2) the year of the individual's birth; (3) [a] minor's initials; and (4) the last four digits of the financial-account number." Fed.R.Civ.P. 5.2(a). While Rule 5.2 makes certain types of confidential information presumptively confidential, nothing in Rule 26(c), or any other rule, suggests a similar intent by the drafters to presume confidentiality of all sensitive information about third parties. Thus, we decline to fashion such a rule....

We now turn to Fathers M and D's second argument, that the bankruptcy court erred in concluding that there was not good cause to protect their personnel files from disclosure. As noted above, the good cause analysis proceeds in three steps.... First, a bankruptcy court must consider the evidence of particularized harm resulting from disclosure. The priests submitted the following evidence of the "specific prejudice or harm" that will result if their personnel files are disclosed. Father M stated that no claims were made against him in the bankruptcy proceeding, but if his name "is associated with the Archdiocese bankruptcy proceeding and settlements in any way, people will assume [he] was guilty of wrongdoing." Because of the seriousness of the allegations, and because people will not "move forward and regain their trust" in the priests involved in the matter, Father M concluded that "if my name is released in connection with this case[,] I honestly think my career and life will be ruined."

In a June 2008 declaration, Father D stated that he was currently 85 years old, and had retired in August 1989 due to severe depression. Further, he stated that "[n]o person has ever filed a claim of sexual abuse against me or demanded any settlement from the Archdiocese as a result of something I allegedly did or did not do." And he made clear that as a retiree, he did not want the "public attention and humiliation" that would result from being associated with the Archdiocese child sex abuse settlements. Father D concluded that publication of his name "would ruin my reputation amongst my friends, family and community," and "cause me to lose my residence where, as a retired priest, I can live the remainder of my life." Finally, he stated that "I fear the stress caused from being associated with this matter would be extremely detrimental to my health."

The bankruptcy court here did not directly address whether Fathers M and D had shown a particularized harm resulting from disclosure. We may, however, infer that it implicitly determined that the priests did carry their burden of showing such a harm, because otherwise it would not have proceeded to balance private and public interests. *See Phillips*, 307 F.3d at 1211. In any event, given the priests' declarations regarding the harm they would experience should their names be associated with the Archdiocese bankruptcy and settlement, including public humiliation, loss of career (in the case of Father M), and possible eviction from a retirement home (in the case of Father D), a finding that these priests did not show particularized harm would have been "illogical, implausible, or without support in inferences that may be drawn from the facts in the record." *Hinkson*, 585 F.3d at 1263.

Accordingly, we proceed to the second step, namely, whether the balance of public and private interests weighed in favor of the priests' interest in confidentiality. Here, the bankruptcy court concluded that Fathers M and D's "desire to be protected from scandal does not demonstrate a clearly defined and serious injury outweighing the public interest necessary to establish good cause." The bankruptcy court reasoned that although no claims of misconduct had been filed against the priests in the bankruptcy case, the personnel files established that "there were credible allegations of abuse made." According to the court, allegations against Father M had been brought to the attention of the district attorney, who did not prosecute because the statute of limitations had run. Further, the court noted that allegations had been made against Father M in a newspaper article posted on a public website. Turning to Father D, the court noted that he had admitted misconduct to the Archbishop, and that his name appeared on the exhibit list for the Archbishop's deposition, which had been posted on a public website.

While the bankruptcy court did not expressly identify the public and private interests, we infer that it concluded that the private interest was small, given that Fathers M and D's names had both been publicly disclosed, and that the public interest was large due to the credibility of the allegations of misconduct. The Appellee Claimants provide additional arguments regarding the public interest in disclosure of Fathers M and D's personnel files. Specifically, they argue that the public has an interest in identifying sexual abusers of children, particularly those occupying positions of power and trust; public safety; giving other victims comfort from knowing they are not alone; and exposing church officials' knowledge of the rampant abuse.

Thus, we must now consider whether the bankruptcy court abused its discretion in determining that the balance between public and private interests weighed in favor of disclosure. We first note that the mere allegation of misconduct in the discovery documents filed in this case, without more, does not create a public interest sufficiently large to outweigh the priests' private interests in confidentiality. There has been no judicial determination regarding the truth of the allegations against Fathers M and D, and neither priest has been given an opportunity to put on evidence, provide argument, or otherwise litigate the allegations either in the bankruptcy court or elsewhere. Second, given the nature of the allegations, the private interest in confidentiality is significant, and it is not eviscerated by a small number of public disclosures of a third party's name. Indeed, we recently held that even after accurate confidential information has been disclosed in national newspapers, the subjects of such leaked confidential data retained their interests in preventing further disclosures. *See United States v. Comprehensive Drug Testing, Inc.*, 621 F.3d 1162, 1174 (9th Cir.2010) (en banc) (holding that the court did not abuse its discretion in concluding that "equitable considerations" required sequestration and the return of copies of illegally seized evidence, even though some professional baseball players' positive drug tests had already been reported in the *New York Times* and other newspapers).

The public does, however, have a weighty interest in public safety and in knowing who might sexually abuse children. *See New York v. Ferber*, 458 U.S. 747, 756–63, 102 S.Ct. 3348, 73 L.Ed.2d 1113 (1982) (recognizing the government's compelling interest in "safeguarding the physical and psychological well-being" of children, such as by preventing sexual abuse). Although the bankruptcy court did not mention this reason, we may affirm on any ground supported by the record, even if not relied upon by the bankruptcy court or district court. *See Tanaka v. Univ. of S. Cal.*, 252 F.3d 1059, 1062 (9th Cir.2001). The record reflects that Father M is not retired but continues to work as a priest in his community, where his clerical duties may bring him into contact with children. In light of this evidence, we cannot say the bankruptcy court's conclusion as to Father M is "illogical, implausible, or without support in ... the record." *Hinkson*, 585 F.3d at 1263.... This public safety concern is not applicable to Father D, however. Father D has been retired for many years, and nothing in the record indicates that he continues working in the community. Nor is it clear that the other public interests identified by the Appellee Claimants, namely comforting victims of abuse and exposing church officials, outweigh Fathers D's privacy interests.... But even assuming that they do, we must still consider the third step in the good cause analysis, the question of redaction. Fathers M and D argue that redacting their identifying information, as we did in *Foltz*, would not undermine the interests identified by Appellee Claimants. We agree as to Father D: victims can know that they are not alone, and church officials' complicity in the abuse can be revealed, without disclosing the identity of accused priests. By contrast, the public safety concern discussed above cannot be satisfied if Father M's identifying information is redacted. We therefore hold that the bankruptcy court abused its discretion in declining to redact Father D's identifying information from the personnel files, but we uphold the court's decision as to Father M....

We now turn to Fathers M and D's argument that the bankruptcy court erred in unsealing the punitive damage estimation memorandum and the attached documents concerning Fathers M and D that were filed in bankruptcy court.... [footnote omitted]. The determination as to whether to release documents filed with the court is governed by 11 U.S.C. § 107(a), which establishes a general right of public access to bankruptcy filings. It states broadly that "a paper filed in a case under this title and the dockets of a bankruptcy court are public records." 11 U.S.C. § 107(a). This general rule is subject to exceptions, however, including the one invoked by Fathers M and D here: "On request of a party in interest, the bankruptcy court shall ... protect a person with respect to scandalous or defamatory matter contained in a paper filed in a case under this title." 11 U.S.C. § 107(b)(2).

For its part, the bankruptcy court held that the documents attached to the tort claimants' punitive damage estimation memorandum were not "scandalous" matter for purposes of § 107(b), ... [footnote omitted] and therefore did not constitute an exception to the general right of public access established by § 107(a). Relying on two out-of-circuit cases, *In re Gitto Global Corp.*, 422 F.3d 1 (1st Cir.2005), and *In re Neal*, 461 F.3d 1048 (8th Cir.2006), the court held that materials were "scandalous" if they were likely to cause a reasonable person to alter his or her opinion of the priests, and were either "untrue" or "potentially untrue and irrelevant or included within a bankruptcy filing for an improper end." Fathers M and D argue that the bankruptcy court erred in construing the word "scandalous" in this manner, and thus erred in ruling that the § 107(b) exception was inapplicable to them. We review the bankruptcy court's interpretation of a statute de novo. *In re Cellular 101, Inc.*, 377 F.3d 1092, 1095 (9th Cir.2004)....

Before we address Fathers M and D's argument based on their interpretation of the statutory language of § 107(b), we must address the parties' arguments as to whether the statute supplants the common law right of public access to judicial documents. At common law, there is a "strong presumption in favor of access" to information filed with a court. *Kamakana v. City and Cnty. of Honolulu*, 447 F.3d 1172, 1178 (9th Cir.2006) (quoting *Foltz*, 331 F.3d at 1135) (internal quotation marks omitted). To overcome the presumption, a party seeking to seal a judicial record must demonstrate not just "good cause," but "compelling reasons," *Foltz*, 331 F.3d at 1135–36, or "sufficiently important countervailing interests," *Phillips*, 307 F.3d at 1212. Generally speaking, compelling reasons exist when court records "might have become a vehicle for improper purposes," such as to gratify private spite, promote public scandal, commit libel, or release trade secrets. *Nixon v. Warner Commc'ns, Inc.*, 435 U.S. 589, 598, 98 S.Ct. 1306, 55 L.Ed.2d 570 (1978).

There is, however, a narrow exception to the presumption in favor of access for documents that were (1) subject to a protective order issued by a court pursuant to a finding of good cause, and (2) attached to non-dispositive motions. *Phillips*, 307 F.3d at 1213. In such a case, the burden is on the party seeking disclosure to "present sufficiently compelling reasons why the sealed discovery document should be released."... [footnote omitted]. *Id.* We have not yet ruled on whether discovery documents subject to a *stipulated* protective order and attached to a non-dispositive motion, as in this case, fall within this exception.

We need not address this novel issue, however, because we conclude that this common law right is not applicable here. Although § 107(a) addresses the same public access right as the common law, our comparison of common law principles with the statute leads us to conclude that § 107 displaces the common law right of access in the bankruptcy context. A statutory provision abrogates a well-established common law rule if it "speak [s] directly to the question addressed by the common law," *United States v. Texas*, 507 U.S. 529, 534, 113 S.Ct. 1631, 123 L.Ed.2d 245 (1993) (internal quotation marks omitted), and indicates a statutory purpose not to apply the common law, *see id.* ("[C]ourts may take it as a given that Congress has legislated with an expectation that the [common law] principle will apply except when a statutory purpose to the contrary is evident.") (quoting *Astoria Fed. Sav. & Loan Ass'n v. Solimino*, 501 U.S. 104, 108, 111 S.Ct. 2166, 115 L.Ed.2d 96 (1991) (internal quotation marks omitted)). A "statutory purpose to the contrary is evident" when there is a divergence between the statute's direction and the common law. Thus, for example, in *In re Hanford Nuclear Reservation Litigation*, we held that a statute compensating victims of nuclear incidents and indemnifying contractors was contrary to, and therefore abrogated, the common law "government contractor defense," which exempted contractors from liability for design defects in military equipment only under limited circumstances. 534 F.3d 986, 1000–02 (9th Cir.2008).

We perceive such a divergence between § 107 and the common law. The statute speaks directly to, and diverges from, the common law right of judicial access. First, the common law rule distinguishes between dispositive and non-dispositive motions, while § 107 covers all papers filed in a bankruptcy case. Second, the common law rule gives courts the discretion to create exceptions to the general rule of disclosure to the public. *See, e.g., Times Mirror Co. v. United States*, 873 F.2d 1210, 1218–19 (9th Cir.1989) (extending exceptions to common law right of access to search warrant materials, at least while pre-indictment investigation is ongoing). By contrast, § 107 has only three exceptions: confidential business information, 11 U.S.C. § 107(b)(1), "scandalous or defamatory matter," *id.* § 107(b)(2), and "means of identification," *id.* § 107(c)(1)(A). Third, the common law rule gives courts discretion to determine whether to protect or disclose documents, while § 107 eliminates a court's discretion by making it mandatory for a court to protect documents falling into one of the enumerated exceptions. *See* 11 U.S.C. § 107(b) (specifying that "the bankruptcy court *shall*" provide specified protections on "request of a party in interest" (emphasis added)). Because § 107(b) imposes this mandatory requirement, it eliminates the balancing of public and private interests required by the common law rule if a document is scandalous or defamatory. Under § 107, the strength of the public's interest in a particular judicial record is irrelevant; if the exception pertains, the bankruptcy court must issue a protective order on a motion by the affected person or party.

Because § 107 speaks directly to and conflicts with significant aspects of the common law right of access, we join our sister circuits in holding that § 107 preempts the common law right of access in bankruptcy proceedings. *See Gitto Global*, 422 F.3d at 7–8 ("Because § 107 speaks directly to the question of public access ... it supplants the common law for purposes of determining public access to papers filed in a bankruptcy case."); *In re Neal*, 461 F.3d at 1053. Therefore, we conclude that the bankruptcy court correctly held that § 107 supplanted the common law right of access in bankruptcy proceedings....

In light of this conclusion, we must now determine whether the bankruptcy court was correct in holding that to invoke the "scandalous" exception to public disclosure in § 107(b), the priests had to show "not only that the materials are likely to cause a reasonable person to alter his or her opinion of the person who is the subject of the materials, but also that they contain material that is either untrue, or potentially untrue and either irrelevant or included in the record for improper purposes." Because this rule is based primarily on *Gitto Global* and *Neal*, we begin with those cases.

In *Gitto Global*, a court-appointed examiner submitted, under seal, an investigative report of fraud by the debtor corporation and corporate officers. 422 F.3d at 5. In response, certain officers claimed that the report was defamatory, and invoked § 107(b) in order to keep the report under seal. *Id.* After determining that § 107 abrogated the common law, and did not merely trigger common law analysis of when the public was entitled to public disclosure, *Gitto Global* concluded that it was "left to the courts to determine the specific contours of the exception" for defamatory material. (The parties did not raise the "scandalous" materials exceptions.) *Id.* at 11. In determining these contours, *Gitto Global* developed the following test: "to implicate § 107(b)(2) in the context of *potentially* untrue material, the information would also have to be [(1)] irrelevant [or (2)] included for improper ends." *Id.* at 14.

The *Gitto Global* court derived this test from a number of different sources. It created the "*potentially* untrue" prong by rejecting as unworkable a test adopted by the bankruptcy court below, whereby the party seeking non-disclosure had to prove the allegedly defamatory material was in fact untrue. *Id.* at 11. *Gitto Global* adopted the "irrelevant" prong from bankruptcy court decisions that had considered the relevance and purpose of material in determining whether the § 107(b) exception applies. *Id.* at 12–13 (citing *In re Commodore*

Corp., 70 B.R. 543 (Bankr.N.D.Ind.1987); *In re Cont'l Airlines*, 150 B.R. 334 (D.Del.1993)). Finally, it adopted the "improper ends" prong from another bankruptcy case, *In re Phar-Mor, Inc.*, 191 B.R. 675, 678–80 (Bankr.N.D.Ohio 1995), which in turn had borrowed this test from Rule 12(f) of the Federal Rules of Civil Procedure.[9] As explained in *Gitto Global*, because § 107(b) and Rule 12(f) draw from common historical roots and premises, that is, the protection of parties from the improper use of judicial filings to broadcast scandalous or defamatory material, § 107(b) is applicable only when a filing is made for an improper purpose. 422 F.3d at 11.

Although *Gitto Global* focused only on the "defamatory" exception in § 107(b), *Neal* relied on it in defining the "scandalous" exception. Thus, *Neal* held that to determine whether the exception applies, a court should consider whether "'a reasonable person could alter their [sic] opinion'" of the person moving for non-disclosure, 461 F.3d at 1054 (quoting *In re Phar-Mor*, 191 B.R. at 679), and whether the statements were "filed for an improper purpose, such as to gratify public spite or promote public scandal," *id.* (citing *Nixon*, 435 U.S. at 598, 98 S.Ct. 1306).

We are not persuaded by either case. Because we have concluded that § 107 displaced the common law right of access to judicial records, and agree that a party's invocation of the exception in § 107(b) does not trigger the common law analysis, there is no basis for incorporating common law concepts derived from *Nixon* (as *Neal* did) or the historical roots and premises underlying equity rules (as in *Gitto Global*). Nor is there anything in § 107 or its legislative history suggesting that Congress intended to interpret the word "scandalous" in § 107(b) in the same manner as courts have interpreted "scandalous" in Rule 12(f), or to adopt any special common law or historical interpretation of the word.... [footnote omitted].

Instead of relying on the interpretative aids adopted in *Gitto Global* and *Neal*, we must apply our standard tools of statutory analysis. And "[a]s with any statutory interpretation, we start with the plain meaning of the statute's text." *United States v. Wright*, 625 F.3d 583, 591 (9th Cir.2010) (internal quotation marks omitted). As the Supreme Court has reminded us, "courts must presume that a legislature says in a statute what it means and means in a statute what it says there." *Conn. Nat'l Bank v. Germain*, 503 U.S. 249, 253– 54, 112 S.Ct. 1146, 117 L.Ed.2d 391 (1992). The statute does not define "scandalous," so we turn to its ordinary, dictionary meaning. *See Transwestern Pipeline Co. v. 17.19 Acres of Property Located in Maricopa Cnty.*, 627 F.3d 1268, 1270 (9th Cir.2010). The Oxford English Dictionary defines "scandalous" as, among other things, "bringing discredit on one's class or position" or "grossly disgraceful." Oxford English Dictionary 575 (2d ed.2001). Other dictionaries offer similar definitions. *See, e.g.,* Webster's New World College Dictionary 1279 (4th ed.2005) ("offensive to a sense of decency or shocking to the moral feelings of the community; shameful"). Under ordinary usage, then, matter is "scandalous" if it disgraceful, offensive, shameful and the like. There is no requirement that the material be either "untrue" or "potentially untrue" or that it be irrelevant or included within a court filing for "an improper end." Because the statute is unambiguous, and does not include the glosses provided by *Gitto Global* and *Neal*, our interpretative inquiry is at an end. *See Germain*, 503 U.S. at 254, 112 S.Ct. 1146 ("When the words of a statute are unambiguous, then ... judicial inquiry is complete." (internal quotation marks omitted)). We therefore

---

9. Rule 12(f) provides that "the court may strike from any pleading any ... redundant, immaterial, impertinent, or scandalous matter."

hold that the party seeking non-disclosure must establish only that the matter is scandalous as that word is commonly understood.... Under the common usage of the word, allegations that a priest has sexually abused children are most assuredly "scandalous" because they bring discredit onto the alleged perpetrators. In light of the mandatory language of § 107(b), the bankruptcy court erred in not granting Fathers M and D's motion to strike the punitive damage estimation memorandum and its attachments....

Fathers M and D also invoke Rule 26(c) and § 107(b) in requesting redaction of identifying information contained in the deposition transcripts and exhibits.... [footnote omitted]. Our ruling here applies equally to the deposition transcripts, so that Fathers M and D's identifying information should be redacted from the depositions filed with the bankruptcy court, and Father D's identifying information (but not Father M's) should be redacted from the depositions that were not so filed.... Rule 26(c) and § 107(b), as we have interpreted them, require courts to use care in determining when documents containing sensitive information affecting a person's privacy interests can be made public over that person's objections. A court must implement the procedure for making such a determination even more carefully when the person objecting to the disclosure was not a party to the proceeding and had limited notice (and, thus, little or no ability to negotiate privacy issues or to challenge the damaging information). Although the public's right of access to documents produced in litigation is long established and has been given great weight from the time of the equity courts in England, courts have likewise given serious consideration to privacy interests of those involved.

In sum, we affirm the bankruptcy court's ruling as to the release of discovery documents disclosing Father M's name under Rule 26(c), because the public's serious safety concerns cannot be addressed if Father M's name is redacted. But because the record does not reflect the existence of any similar significant public interest that requires the disclosure of Father D's identifying information, we hold that Father D's identifying information must be redacted from any discovery documents that are released. Finally, because of the mandatory duty to keep scandalous material confidential at the request of a party under § 107(b), we reverse the court's decision to release the punitive damages memorandum and attached documents.... [footnote omitted].

AFFIRMED in part and REVERSED in part.

IV. Notable Institutions

As demonstrated in this Chapter, liability for institutional sexual abuse may be based on either vicarious liability (respondeat superior) — premised on the acts of an employee, or it may derive from the direct negligence of the institutional authority — typically through negligence in hiring, supervising, or retaining an employee who perpetrates abuse within the scope of his or her employment. Over the past several decades, there have been three landmark contexts in which institutional sexual abuse as occurred and through which developments in the law or social awareness of the issue have resulted. These are: (1) social programs, primarily exhibited in the cases involving the Boy Scouts of America; (2) religious institutions, primarily detailed through the scandal involving the Roman Catholic Church; and (3) educational programs, most recently and poignantly involving Penn State and Jerry Sandusky. Each of these institutional contexts have generated a plethora of litigation and media attention, from which society continues to digest preventative lessons and implement expansive change. For commentary on institutional abuse, see Allegra M.

McLeod, *Regulating Sexual Harm: Strangers, Intimates, and Social Institutional Reform*, 102 CAL. L. REV. 1553 (2014); Nancy Levit, *Forward—Institutional Responsibility for Sex and Gender Exploitation*, 17 J. GENDER, RACE & J. 279 (2014); Luke Beck, *Institutional Responses to Child Sex Abuse*, 38 ALT. L.J. 14 (2013). Included below is a brief summary of institutional exploitation that has originated in each of these contexts. In light of the issues already discussed in this Chapter, as well as those discussed throughout this casebook, consider what, if any, common elements exist from which positive change may be implemented to prevent and respond to the sexual exploitation of children within the institutional setting.

A. Social Institutions: The Boy Scouts of America

Since its inception in 1910, with nearly 3 million youth members and over 1 million adult volunteers, the Boy Scouts of America has become one of the largest youth organizations in the world. It is not surprising, then, that the issue of sexual abuse by Scout leaders has become the focus of attention. In addition to high-profile litigation involving the constitutionality of the Boy Scouts' revocation of membership of a member avowing homosexuality, *see Boy Scouts of America v. Dale*, 530, U.S. 640. 120 S. Ct. 2446 (2000) (applying New Jersey's public accommodations law to require Boy Scouts to admit plaintiff violated Boy Scouts' First Amendment right of expressive association), the Boy Scouts of America has faced thousands of allegations of sexual abuse by Scout leaders.

In response to ongoing abuse allegations throughout the 1980s, the Boy Scouts implemented one of the most comprehensive programs to educate about, and prevent against, institutional sexual abuse—the Youth Protection Program, which is a series of policies designed to protect children from the risk of abuse and protect Scout leaders from false allegations of wrong-doing. One of the hallmark policies of the program is the "Two Deep" leadership criterion, mandating that no adult leader can ever be alone with any youth member. *See* U.S. Department of Health and Human Services, Centers for Disease Control and Prevention, National Center for Injury Prevention and Control, Janet Saul and Natalie C. Audage, *Preventing Child Sexual Abuse Within Youth-Serving Organizations: Getting Started on Policies and Procedures* (2007), available at http://www.cdc.gov/violenceprevention/pdf/PreventingChildSexualAbuse-a.pdf (last accessed Apr. 27, 2015). Shortly after the program started, however, in 1991, the Washington Times reported on the history of sex abuse within the Boy Scouts, *see* Patrick Boyle, *Scouting's sex abuse trail leads to 50 states*, WASH. TIMES, May 20, 1991, available at http://www.newsline.umd.edu/Boyle/shonor1.htm (last accessed Apr. 27, 2015), and litigation has continued.

One of the law suits filed in Oregon—*Jack Doe 1 v. Corporation of Presiding Bishop of Church of Jesus Christ of Latter-Day Saints*, 352 Or. 77, 280 P.3d 377 (2012)—resulted in an $18.5 million award—the largest punitive damage award in the United States to an individual plaintiff in a child abuse case. *See* Chapter 8, *supra*. In the *Lewis* case, the court ordered the Boy Scouts of America to release historically confidential files, known as "the perversion files." The perversion files consisted of 20,000 pages of documents that detailed approximately 1,200 cases of abuse between 1965 and 1985, as well as a long history of cover-ups and out-of-court settlements. It also contained a list of "Ineligible Volunteers," which included the files of thousands of men whom the Boy Scouts considered unfit to participate as a volunteer, some of whom nevertheless continued to serve in the organization. *See Boy Scout Ineligible Volunteer Files (Perversion Files) (1965–1985)*, available at http://www.kellyclarkattorney.com/files/ (accessible through this web site, maintained by the attorneys involved in the case). Courts in other suits filed in Texas and Minnesota have ordered the release of over 100,000 pages of additional files that regard abuses occurring since 1985. *See Calif. attorney seeks to use 'perversion' files in Boy Scout sex abuse trial*, available at http://www.chicagotribune.com/news/nationworld/chi-perversion-files-boy-scout-sex-abuse-trial-20150108-story.html (Jan. 8, 2015). The Los Angeles Times has created a database updating the released information, much of which remains sealed by court order. *See Tracking decades of allegations in the boy scouts*, available at http://spreadsheets.latimes.com/boyscouts-cases/ (last updated Jan. 3, 2013).

B. Religious Institutions: The Roman Catholic Church

As with the Boy Scouts of America, a focus on sexual abuse of children by clergy, and others in leadership roles, in the Roman Catholic Church drew particular attention in the 1980s, and litigation surrounding alleged abuse continues to raise legal, social, and religious issues not only for the alleged perpetrators, but for the Catholic hierarchy that often ignored or concealed the abuse. Thousands of cases have been reported and have received world-wide media attention. Many cases have been brought years after the abuse occurred, and this casebook has addressed many of the issues raised by this circumstance.

It is estimated that as much as "6% of Catholic clergy [approximately 4,000 priests] have had some sexual experience with minors." Thomas G. Plante and Courtney Daniels, *The Sexual Abuse Crisis in the Roman Catholic Church: What Psychologists and Counselors Should Know*, 52 PASTORAL PSYCHOL. 381, 383 (2004). This rate is comparable to that of the general adult population. *See* Pat Wingert, *Priests Commit No More Abuse Than Other Males*, NEWSWEEK, Apr. 7, 2010, available at http://www.newsweek.com/priests-commit-no-more-abuse-other-males-70625 (last accessed Apr. 27, 2015).

Although abuse scandals within the Church have arisen in countries all over the world, none have garnered more world-wide attention than that of Father Marcial Maciel Degollado, founder of the Legion of Christ movement in Latin America and high-ranking Catholic official who was removed from active ministry in 2006. Maciel died in the United States in 2008. For Maciel's story, see Jason Berry and Gerald Renner, VOWS OF SILENCE: THE ABUSE OF POWER IN THE PAPACY OF JOHN PAUL II (Free Press, 2004) and a documentary film by Jason Berry: *Vows of Silence*, available at http://www.vowsofsilencefilm.com/ (documenting the story of Maciel). The issue has been most prominent, however, within the United States. In 2002, five Roman Catholic priests in the Boston area (John Geoghan, John Hanlon, Paul Shanley, Robert V. Gale and James Talbot) faced criminal prosecution for sexual abuse; each was convicted and sentenced to prison. A Pulitzer Prize-winning *Boston Globe* series that covered their stories shed new light on the prevalence of the problem throughout the United States. *See* Michael Paulson, *World doesn't share US view of scandal*, BOST. GLOBE, Apr. 8, 2002, at A1, available at http://www.pulitzer.org/archives/6741 (last accessed Apr. 28, 2015). In 2004, the U.S. Conference of Catholic Bishops commissioned the "John Jay Report," which studied over 10,000 allegations against over 4,000 priests accused of sexual abuse between 1950 and 2002. *See* The United States Conference of Catholic Bishops and The John Jay College of Criminal Justice, *The Nature and Scope of Sexual Abuse of Minors by Catholic Priests and Deacons in the United States 1950–2002*, available at http://www.bishop-accountability.org/reports/2004_02_27_JohnJay_revised/2004_02_27_John_Jay_Main_Report_Optimized.pdf (last accessed Apr. 28, 2015). The report only further revealed the systemic nature of the problem throughout the United States. In response to the issues that led to the report, the U.S. Catholic Bishops implemented stronger standards for reporting sexual abuse allegations to civil authorities, among other policy changes addressing the problem. *See* United States Conference of Catholic Bishops, *Charter for the Protection of Children and Young People*, available at http://www.usccb.org/

issues-and-action/child-and-youth-protection/charter.cfm (June 2002). *See* Rev. Raymond C. O'Brien, *Clergy, Sex and the American Way*, 31 Pepp. L. Rev. 363, 407–76 (2004).

As media attention continued and public awareness increased, so too did civil lawsuits resulting in monetary awards for victims. The online archive "BishopAccountability.org" estimates that there have been over 3,000 civil lawsuits filed against the Catholic Church, resulting in over $3 billion in major settlements as of 2012. *See Sexual Abuse by U.S. Catholic Clergy Settlements and Monetary Awards in Civil Suits*, available at http://www.bishop-accountability.org/settlements/ (last accessed Apr. 28, 2015). Many Catholic Archdiocese have filed bankruptcy as a result. *See* Amy Julia Harris, The Center for Investigative Reporting, *Catholic diocese declare bankruptcy on eve of sexual abuse trials*, available at http://www.revealnews.org/article/catholic-dioceses-declare-bankruptcy-on-eve-of-sexual-abuse-trials/ (Feb. 2, 2015) (describing Archdiocese of St. Paul and Minneapolis as most recent of 12 diocese to file bankruptcy as a result of sex abuse litigation).

Although many priests accused of sexual abuse have been convicted or "defrocked" from their religious duties, many of the civil lawsuits that continue are based on the negligent or fraudulent efforts by institutional authorities who ignored or concealed long histories of abuse. The most prominent of such cases involved Bernard Francis Law, Cardinal and Archbishop of Boston, Massachusetts, who resigned in disgrace in 2002 after failing to remove accused priests from their posts and authorizing reassignments to other parishes, where further abuse occurred. *See* Martine Powers, *Pope's visit with Cardinal Law criticized*, Bost. Globe, Mar. 17, 2013. The Boston scandal led to similar scandals in other cities, like Philadelphia, where Monsignor William J. Lynn was prosecuted for similar mishandlings. However, Monsignor Lynn was the first Catholic authority to be prosecuted for endangering the welfare of a child in his authoritative role within the Church. Lynn was convicted of endangering the welfare of a child in 2012. His conviction was overturned on appeal when the appellate court determined that Lynn could not have endangered the welfare of a child when he had no direct supervision of the child, but rather, the sexual abuse of the child was perpetrated by another priest, over whom Lynn had authority. *See Commonwealth of Pennsylvania v. Lynn*, 2013 Pa. Super. 328, 83 A.3d 434 (2013). Below is the Pennsylvania Supreme Court's opinion reviewing that 2013 decision.

Commonwealth of Pennsylvania v. Lynn

Supreme Court of Pennsylvania, 2015
114 A.3d 796

MR. JUSTICE BAER[:]

Following a jury trial on charges that he endangered the welfare of children, William Lynn (Appellee) was convicted and sentenced to a term of three to six years of incarceration. On appeal from his judgment of sentence, he challenged the sufficiency of the evidence to sustain his conviction, contending that he had no direct supervision of the children he was found to have endangered. The Superior Court agreed, and reversed his conviction. On the Commonwealth's appeal, we reverse the Superior Court, concluding that there is no statutory requirement of direct supervision of children. Rather, that which is supervised is the child's welfare. Under the facts presented at trial, Appellee was a person supervising the welfare of many children because, as a high-ranking official in the Archdiocese of Philadelphia, he was specifically responsible for protecting children from sexually abusive priests.

Following eight years of education at St. Charles Borromeo Seminary in Wynnewood, Pennsylvania, Appellee graduated with a Bachelor's degree in Philosophy, and went on to earn two Master's degrees, in Divinity and Education Administration. Appellee was ordained as a priest in the Catholic Church on May 15, 1976. He served as a parish priest for eight years before becoming the Dean of Men at St. Charles Borromeo Seminary in 1984. In January 1991, Appellee was appointed Associate Vicar in the Office of the Vicar for Administration in the Archdiocese of Philadelphia. As Associate Vicar, one of Appellee's responsibilities was to assist Monsignor James Molloy by taking notes when they met with people regarding the sexual abuse of a minor by a member of the clergy, and, consequently, Appellee learned how to interview sexual abuse victims and record their allegations against a priest.... [Citations to Record omitted]. In June 1992, Cardinal Anthony Bevilacqua appointed Appellee Secretary for Clergy for the Archdiocese of Philadelphia, where he served for twelve years, until June 2004.

As Secretary for Clergy, Appellee was responsible for ensuring that parishes were filled with enough priests, resolving disputes among priests, and handling clergy sexual abuse issues.... [footnote omitted]. Building upon the experience he acquired assisting Monsignor Molloy, Appellee learned how to handle the victims of clergy sex abuse and the priests who sexually abused minors, becoming the "point man" in the investigation into such allegations of clergy sexual abuse of minors within the Archdiocese of Philadelphia.... In this regard, it was his role to collect and assess information concerning allegations of sexual abuse against priests in the Archdiocese, discuss the allegations with the accused priests, participate in deciding how to address the allegations, and make recommendations to the Cardinal about the priests against whom allegations were made.

Indeed, by his own account, Appellee was the sole "funnel" of information concerning instances of clergy sex abuse, and it was his office alone that was responsible for not only receiving the allegations and exploring them, but also for passing vital information about abusive priests and their young victims up the chain of command in the Archdiocese.... Although he could only independently remove a priest from a parish if that priest admitted that he had abused someone, ... it was Appellee's responsibility to make recommendations about assignments to the Cardinal, who had the ultimate decision making authority. For example, Appellee could make recommendations to place a priest on administrative leave or restrict a priest's ministry by, for instance, prohibiting contact with the public or with children. In this respect, Appellee characterized protecting children as the most important part of his job, and explained that he worked "for" the children of the Archdiocese.... Upon learning of an abusive priest, Appellee considered his first priority to be the welfare of the victim.... According to Appellee, the purpose of his investigations was, at least in part, to determine whether the offending priest "should be removed from ministry and taken out of the—and children could be taken out of his way." ...

When Appellee first assumed the office of Secretary for Clergy in June 1992, he collected information about "problem priests" on a "need-be basis," whenever he received complaints about them.... In addition, his position authorized him to be one of the few officials within the Archdiocese of Philadelphia with access to the "Secret Archives." The Secret Archives were located on the 12th floor of the Office of Clergy and maintained under lock and key; they contained information about "any kind of major infractions a priest would have," and which only a "very, very limited number of people within the Archdiocese had access to or a key to." ... The Secret Archives were largely in Appellee's control as Secretary for Clergy, and he routinely consulted them to determine if there was already information contained therein relevant to a priest about whom he had received complaints.

In early 1994, after receiving information about a particular priest, Rev. Dux, who was then in active ministry, Appellee consulted the Secret Archives and discovered documentation that this particular priest had engaged in serious sexual misconduct in the past. This discovery caused Appellee to become concerned that there were other priests in active service against whom allegations of abuse had been asserted, and accordingly prompted him to conduct a comprehensive review of the Secret Archives to check for incidents of child sexual abuse among all priests in active ministry within the Archdiocese of Philadelphia.... This review encompassed 323 priests and resulted in a report created by Appellee on February 18, 1994, entitled "Report from the Secretariat for Clergy" (referred hereafter as "February 18, 1994 Report"). This report identified 35 priests in active service with previous complaints of sexual abuse of minors. Appellee placed each of these 35 priests on one of three lists: three priests were identified as "pedophiles;" 12 priests as "Guilty of Sexual Misconduct with Minors;" and 20 were included on a list entitled "Allegations of Sexual Misconduct with Minors with No Conclusive Evidence." ... Regarding the 12 priests that Appellee determined were guilty of sexual misconduct with minors, he considered it his job "to do something about [them]." ...

Reverend Edward V. Avery was the first name on Appellee's list of priests whom he considered to be guilty of sexual misconduct with minors.[3] Appellee was personally familiar with Rev. Avery, who had come to Appellee's attention about a year and a half earlier when he first became Secretary for Clergy, before he performed the comprehensive review of the Secret Archives. Appellee had investigated allegations into Rev. Avery's conduct, and memorialized his understanding of these allegations with notations to Rev. Avery's Secret Archives file indicating "alcoholism and action with same minor three times," and "action occurred more than five years ago." As will be discussed more fully below, the information contained in Rev. Avery's Secret Archives file revealed that he had built a trusting relationship with this minor, R.F., in his church, groomed R.F. with attention outside of the religious context, and, on several occasions, supplied R.F. with alcohol and engaged in inappropriate sexual conduct.

Specifically, Rev. Avery's Secret Archives file contained a letter written by R.F. on March 31, 1992, to Appellee's predecessor as Secretary for Clergy, Monsignor Jagodzinski, regarding his sexual abuse by Rev. Avery in the 1970s when R.F. was an adolescent. R.F. indicated that he wrote the letter out of concern for "other adolescent boys" who may also have been abused by Rev. Avery.... R.F. attached a copy of a letter he had previously written to Rev. Avery in which he recounted the bond that had been formed between them when R.F. was around 11 years old, in the sixth grade, and Rev. Avery was the assistant pastor at St. Philip Neri Parish in East Greenville, and how Rev. Avery's sexual groping of him on multiple occasions had wreaked emotional havoc upon him at a young age.[4] Allegedly because Monsignor Jagodzinski was in the process of ending his term, he had not responded to R.F.'s March 31, 1992 letter.

Once Appellee assumed the position of Secretary for Clergy, he reviewed R.F.'s letter, and, on September 28, 1992, met with him to discuss the allegations contained therein. R.F. provided further details regarding how Rev. Avery had victimized him at a young age. Specifically, when R.F. was an altar boy he helped Rev. Avery serve Mass at St. Philip Neri. He described Rev. Avery as very charismatic, popular with young people, and active with the youth in the parish. Outside of church, Rev. Avery gave R.F. his first beer at age

---

3. Because Appellee's knowledge of Rev. Avery's history of abuse was the basis of the Commonwealth's case against Appellee for endangering the welfare of children, these details are of paramount importance when considering this case.

4. R.F. further explained that he had put off writing the letter for years, because of the shame and fear he felt at confronting his abuse....

12, and took R.F. and other boys from the parish to his home in New Jersey, where he supplied them with alcohol. There was a loft in Rev. Avery's New Jersey home with several beds where the boys would sleep, and Rev. Avery would join the boys in the loft to wrestle with them. According to Appellee's notes of his interview with R.F., during two or three such encounters, Rev. Avery's hand "slipped to [R.F.'s] crotch." ...

According to R.F., Rev. Avery continued this pattern of inviting him to participate in seemingly innocuous activities, and then groping him when vulnerable. By the time R.F. was 15 in 1978, Rev. Avery had been transferred from St. Philip Neri, but maintained contact with R.F. by telephone and invited him to parties where Rev. Avery was the disc jockey; a particular avocation of Rev. Avery's, and, notably, one that brought him into contact with multiple young men. Eventually R.F. began to assist Rev. Avery at parties. At a college party where R.F. helped Rev. Avery disc jockey, Rev. Avery supplied R.F. with alcohol, resulting in him becoming sick a few hours later, vomiting in the bathroom, and passing out in a hallway. Rev. Avery took R.F. back to the rectory where he resided, and encouraged R.F. to sleep in Rev. Avery's bed. When R.F. awoke several hours later, Rev. Avery's hands were inside R.F.'s shorts. In June 1981, when R.F. was 18, Rev. Avery invited him on a ski trip to Vermont. Rev. Avery, R.F., and his brother (J.F.) shared a hotel room. In the night, Rev. Avery joined R.F. in bed, and again molested him after he had fallen asleep, massaging his penis until it became erect and R.F. ejaculated.

The Secret Archives revealed that Rev. Avery had committed these offenses against R.F. after church officials had gone out of their way to accommodate Rev. Avery: when Rev. Avery was assistant pastor at Immaculate Heart of Mary Church in Chester, Pennsylvania, a church official had suggested in a memorandum to the Cardinal that Rev. Avery be appointed to St. Philip Neri to "avoid another breakdown" (the details of which are apparently unknown), which prompted Rev. Avery's gratitude to the church official for accommodating his "euphemistically speaking, predicament." ... Rather than utilizing his transfer to St. Philip Neri as an opportunity to focus on his priestly obligations, however, Rev. Avery had instead engaged in the grooming behavior and sexual molestation of R.F. described above.

After revealing the details of his sexual abuse to Appellee, R.F. sought assurances that Rev. Avery would not be permitted to harm anyone else. Appellee assured R.F. that the Archdiocese's "order of priorities is the victim, the victim's family, the Church, and the priest himself." ... Appellee met with Rev. Avery a week later on October 7, 1992, regarding R.F.'s allegations. Although Rev. Avery initially denied R.F.'s account and expressed shock that R.F. was in counseling for this issue, Rev. Avery confirmed many of the details R.F. had provided, including that he took kids to his house in New Jersey and "would roughhouse with the boys ..." and that he shared a bed with R.F. on the ski trip to Vermont, but stated that if he touched R.F. in the night, it was "accidental." ...

Regarding the incident after the college party in 1978, Rev. Avery claimed he had consumed too much alcohol to remember any details about that night, but admitted that it could be that something happened while he was intoxicated, and he did not remember.... Appellee again spoke with Rev. Avery two days later by phone; Appellee's notes from this conversation do not include a denial, but reflected Rev. Avery's retort that R.F. "has a selective memory." ... Following R.F.'s allegations and Rev. Avery's concession that the abuse could have happened, on October 16, 1992, Appellee informed Cardinal Bevilacqua of R.F.'s account, stated that Rev. Avery "expressed absolute denial," and informed the Cardinal that R.F. did not mention legal action. On November 2, 1992, Appellee informed R.F. that Rev. Avery had denied his allegations. Appellee recommended to Cardinal Bevilacqua that Rev. Avery be sent to an Archdiocese-affiliated mental health treatment facility, the St. John Vianney Center in Downingtown,[5] for a four-day outpatient evaluation beginning November 30, 1992.

The Cardinal accepted the recommendation, and Rev. Avery went to St. John Vianney. As part of the evaluation process for Rev. Avery, Appellee had to complete a referral form intended to detail the background of issues important to Rev. Avery's assessment. Despite this request for details, Appellee did not include any information about Rev. Avery touching R.F. while wrestling, placing his hands inside R.F.'s shorts, massaging R.F.'s penis during the trip to Vermont, and did not mention that Rev. Avery conceded "it could be" that something happened. Rather, Appellee merely indicated there were allegations against Rev. Avery by an adult male about events that occurred when the man was in his teenage years, and focused on the fact that Rev. Avery had supplied alcohol to minors.... Even with such an incomplete picture of Rev. Avery's background, the staff at St. John Vianney recommended inpatient hospitalization, a recommendation which Cardinal Bevilacqua again accepted, and Rev. Avery was admitted for long term treatment on February 18, 1993. Less than three weeks later, on March 11, 1993, Appellee responded to a parishioner who had written about "unfavorable" calls that had been made regarding Rev. Avery by affirmatively misrepresenting that there had "never been anything but compliments heard in this office about Father Avery...." ... About six months after he was admitted to St. John Vianney, Rev. Avery's primary therapist, Wayne Pellegrini, Ph.D., reported to Appellee that Rev. Avery was ashamed and "acknowledged that the incident [with R.F.] must have happened...." ... Additionally, Dr. Pellegrini informed Appellee that "there remains [sic] concerns about the existence of other victims," and, based on Rev. Avery's failure to accept fully his own responsibility, continued treatment was strongly recommended "to prevent further acting out." ...

On September 28, 1993, Appellee received Dr. Pellegrini's treatment plan for Rev. Avery's October 1993 release from St. John Vianney, which provided that Rev. Avery was not diagnosed with a sexual disorder for two reasons: "there is only one report of abuse," and Rev. Avery "had been drinking during those incidents...." ... Nevertheless, Dr. Pellegrini recommended that Rev. Avery continue to receive outpatient treatment and an assignment where he would not be around children:

> The treatment team's recommendations for [Rev. Avery] post discharge ... include: One, continued outpatient treatment. Two, an aftercare integration team, ministry supervision. Three, a ministry excluding adolescents and with a population other than vulnerable minorities [sic] with whom [Rev. Avery] tends to overidentify with [sic]. Four, attendance at a 12-step [Alcoholics Anonymous] meeting for priests.

[Citation to Record omitted].

Despite Rev. Avery's admission to Appellee that "it could be" that what R.F. alleged really happened, his admission to the staff at St. John Vianney that his abuse of R.F. "must have happened," Dr. Pellegrini's concern about the existence of other victims, and the recommendation of the treatment team at St. John Vianney that Rev. Avery be kept away

---

5. The St. John Vianney Center is a mental health treatment facility operated by the Archdiocese; Appellee sat on the Board of Directors there, at the request of Cardinal Bevilacqua. Moreover, according to a detective who investigated clergy sex abuse in the Archdiocese, St. John Vianney was where the Archdiocese routinely sent priests who "had problems dealing, basically, sexually abusing minors, alcohol treatment programs, psychological problems. The center itself was owned and operated by the Archdiocese, and they would send priests with problems to the center to be evaluated." ...

from minors, Appellee's first recommendation for Rev. Avery's postdischarge assignment was as associate pastor at Our Lady of Ransom in Philadelphia, a parish with a grade school.... Appellee made this recommendation, at least in part, because Rev. Avery had not been diagnosed as a pedophile. Appellee later admitted on cross-examination that the lack of a pedophilia diagnosis is a poor indicator of whether an individual will engage in acts of pedophilia....

Cardinal Bevilacqua rejected Appellee's recommendation for Rev. Avery's placement for unknown reasons, suggesting instead that Rev. Avery be placed in a chaplaincy assignment. On November 22, 1993, Appellee recommended an assignment for Rev. Avery as Chaplain at Nazareth Hospital in Philadelphia, which would have provided housing for Rev. Avery on site. Pursuant to Rev. Avery's request, however, and despite Dr. Pellegrini's warning against placing him in a position that would give him access to minors, Appellee petitioned the Cardinal to permit Rev. Avery to live in a nearby rectory at St. Jerome's Church, which had a grade school attached. The Cardinal accepted this recommendation. Rev. Avery's placement was effective December 13, 1993, less than three months before Appellee placed Rev. Avery's name atop his list of "Priests Guilty of Sexual Misconduct with Minors," demonstrating his belief that R.F.'s allegations were credible. Despite his conclusion in this regard, Appellee never shared his belief that Rev. Avery was guilty of sexual misconduct with minors or Rev. Avery's admissions with anyone, while housing him where he had access to grade school children.... With the exception of St. Jerome's pastor, Father Joseph Graham, Appellee did not notify any of the priests who lived in St. Jerome's rectory about any of Rev. Avery's past conduct. Although Appellee informed Father Graham that Rev. Avery was not to be around children, he did not explain this directive, and he also informed Father Graham that he had asked Rev. Avery to offer assistance in the parish. Accordingly, Rev. Avery assisted the parish by celebrating Mass and helping with children's confessions on occasion.... Although Father Graham was allegedly assigned to help monitor Rev. Avery, he later testified that he was unaware of Rev. Avery's aftercare treatment plan, and he did not consider himself Rev. Avery's supervisor.

In the first year following his discharge from St. John Vianney, Rev. Avery met with a psychologist weekly, who notified Appellee on at least two occasions that Rev. Avery's aftercare integration team, which was to include Appellee, Father Graham, another priest, and his outpatient care providers from St. John Vianney, was initially slow to organize and met only sporadically thereafter. In November 1994, Appellee learned from Father Graham that Rev. Avery was again disc jockeying at weddings and parties. In December 1994, during a meeting of Rev. Avery and his aftercare integration team, Appellee instructed him to focus on his chaplaincy and his recovery, and stated that he should not be working as a disc jockey.

In February 1995, Appellee learned from another chaplain at Nazareth Hospital, Father Kerper, that Rev. Avery had disregarded this direction, continued to accept outside commitments, and had arranged for substitutes to cover his work at Nazareth Hospital on 25 of 31 Saturdays because of his disc jockeying priorities, one of which was at a dance at St. Jerome's Parish. Appellee's subsequent testimony revealed his knowledge that this was a grade school dance.... Also around this time, Appellee learned that Rev. Avery's psychologist had agreed, at his request, to decrease the frequency of his sessions.

In September 1995, Appellee received a complaint from Father Kerper about Rev. Avery's activities as a disc jockey, stating that Rev. Avery had booked three events in one weekend and was soliciting new engagements, shirking his chaplaincy responsibilities within the hospital.... Appellee brushed these concerns aside and instructed Father Kerper, who did not know that there were allegations of sexual misconduct against Rev. Avery, to take his concerns about Rev. Avery to his supervisor at Nazareth Hospital instead of the Secretary for Clergy.

In September 1996, Appellee again ignored R.F.'s attempts to ensure that other children were safe from Rev. Avery, choosing not to respond when R.F. requested by email that the diocese vouch for the safety of its children. Nor was there any indication in the Secret Archives or elsewhere that Appellee followed up on R.F.'s concern, or that of the staff at St. John Vianney, inquiring as to whether Rev. Avery was cultivating or, indeed, exploiting new victims from among the children he came into regular contact with at St. Jerome's parish, its grade school, or through the many parties and dances where he served as disc jockey.... Despite Rev. Avery's past transgressions, complaints that he was neglecting his work obligations, and information that he was instead again focusing on disc jockeying, an activity he had utilized in the past to put him in contact with minors, when Rev. Avery requested assistance to advance his career, Appellee was willing to help. In August 1997, Appellee assisted in the preparation of a letter to the National Association of Catholic Chaplains which stated that Rev. Avery was "a priest in good standing" and "has given exemplary service these past four years" as Chaplain at Nazareth Hospital.

On September 5, 1997, Appellee wrote to Cardinal Bevilacqua requesting a letter of recommendation for Rev. Avery to pursue a Doctorate of Ministry in Spirituality from the Lutheran Theological Seminary in Philadelphia. Appellee was permitted to write the letter of recommendation himself, as the Cardinal's delegate, which he did, describing Rev. Avery as a "very sincere, hard working priest. He is honest and trustworthy. He is a man who is in touch with his spiritual life and this becomes evident in his work and service." ... Despite describing Rev. Avery as trustworthy, he told Rev. Avery that "in the future he should play things low-key," and that he should be "more low-key than he has been recently." ... Consistent with Dr. Pellegrini's 1993 warning to Appellee that Rev. Avery failed to accept responsibility for his actions, indicating the potential for "further acting out," ... an April 2, 1998 meeting between Appellee and Rev. Avery left Appellee with the impression (recorded in the Secret Archives) that Rev. Avery was again minimizing his need for treatment and "the allegations against him." During this meeting, Appellee informed Rev. Avery that he would be unable to recommend him to another diocese, because that would require the completion of a form stating that the priest had no allegations against him....

Several months later, in the fall of 1998, D.G., a ten-year-old boy in approximately fifth grade, began training to serve Mass as an altar boy at St. Jerome's. When he became an altar boy shortly thereafter, he served Mass with the priests of St. Jerome's: Father Graham, Father McBride, Father Englehardt, and Rev. Avery. Neither D.G. nor his parents, nor anyone in the parish, knew either that Appellee had determined nearly four years before that Rev. Avery was guilty of sexual misconduct with a minor (R.F.) or his extensive and troubled history as recounted herein.... From around December 1998 through January 1999, Father Englehardt began sexually abusing D.G. after Mass, during what Father Englehardt referred to as "sessions." In early 1999, Rev. Avery encountered D.G. inside the church after school on a Friday afternoon. Rev. Avery pulled D.G. aside, informed the boy that he had heard about his "sessions" with Father Englehardt, and stated that "ours were going to begin soon." ... A week later, after D.G. served weekend Mass with Rev. Avery, he asked D.G. to stay because their "sessions" were about to begin. After everyone else left, Rev. Avery took D.G. to the sacristy, where he made the boy do a "striptease" to music.... While telling the boy "[t]his is what God wants," Rev. Avery fondled D.G.'s penis with his hands, performed oral sex on him, and penetrated the boy's anus with his finger.... Rev. Avery instructed D.G. to perform oral sex on him until he ejaculated on the boy's neck and chest.... About two weeks later, Rev. Avery abused D.G. again in a similar fashion, this time also licking his anus. Rev. Avery told D.G. that he did a good job, God loved him, and they would be seeing each other again soon.... D.G., however, successfully found ways to avoid Rev. Avery and therefore to avoid further abuse by him. Nevertheless, the effect of this abuse was devastating: by the time D.G. was approximately 11 years old, he became withdrawn and began using drugs, which developed into a heroin addiction by age 17.... [6]

In 2002, following the eruption of the child sex abuse scandal in the Archdiocese of Boston, the leaders of the Catholic Church met in Dallas and produced the Dallas Charter for the Protection of Children and Young People of the United States Conference of Catholic Bishops (Dallas Charter), which established protocols for the Catholic Church with regard to child sex abuse. Among other things, the Charter required each diocese to establish an Archdiocesan Review Board (Review Board) to evaluate and act upon allegations of clergy sex abuse and eliminated the possibility of merely restricting a priest's ministry.... [7]

Shortly following the Dallas Charter, on June 20, 2002, R.F.'s brother, J.F., called Appellee and detailed how he too was fondled by Rev. Avery when he was 14 or 15 years old, in the late 1970s. He explained that Rev. Avery had driven a van of several children to his house in New Jersey where he supplied them with alcohol. J.F. stated that Rev. Avery was "jumping on each kid.... tickling me ... felt like he was going to grab me." ... J.F. additionally informed Appellee that Rev. Avery had been seen in the recent weeks of 2002 disc jockeying at parties.

On June 2, 2003, in accord with the procedure established by the Dallas Charter, Appellee initiated a "preliminary investigation" into the accusations made against Rev. Avery "on or about September 28, 1992, which resurfaced on or around June 19, 2002." ... On September 27, 2003, the Review Board found Rev. Avery in violation of the Essential Norms defining sexual abuse of a minor and concluded that he should be removed from active ministry and rectory living, "or any other living situation in which he would have unrestrained access to children now or in the future." ...

On December 5, 2003, Cardinal Justin Rigali, Cardinal Bevilacqua's successor,[8] signed a decree excluding Rev. Avery from ministry, living in any ecclesiastical residence without prior permission, celebrating public Mass, or administering the sacraments. On June 20, 2005, Cardinal Rigali requested that Rev. Avery be laicized,[9] and on January 20, 2006, Pope Benedict XVI granted him dispensation from all priestly obligations. In January 2009, D.G. contacted the Archdiocese to make his allegations against Rev. Avery, leading to criminal charges against, *inter alia*, Appellee, as further described below.

---

6. Rev. Avery's abuse of D.G. was not reported until January 30, 2009, when D.G. was 21 years of age and Appellee was no longer Secretary for Clergy.

7. Although the Dallas Charter marked a turning point for the Catholic Church's response to allegations of clergy sex abuse, canonical law, specifically, Number 8 of the Essential Norms, had always prohibited such abuse as follows:

> When even a single act of sexual abuse by a priest or deacon is admitted or is established after an appropriate process in accord with canon law, the offending priest or deacon will be removed permanently from ecclesiastical ministry, not excluding dismissal from the clerical state, if the case so warrants.

[Citation to Record omitted].

8. Upon Cardinal Bevilacqua's retirement in 2003, he was replaced by Cardinal Rigali. Cardinal Bevilacqua died in 2012.

9. As the trial court explained, laicization is the process which takes from a priest or other cleric the use of his powers, rights, and authority....

Towards of the end of Appellee's tenure as Secretary for Clergy, the Philadelphia District Attorney began to investigate the Archdiocese of Philadelphia for clergy sex abuse. In 2002, a grand jury was empanelled at the request of the District Attorney to investigate the Archdiocese's treatment of allegations of such abuse. On May 24, 2002, the grand jury subpoenaed documents from Appellee pertaining to priests accused of sexual abuse, and Appellee and other Archdiocese officials were summoned to testify repeatedly. In 2005, the grand jury issued a report detailing the sexual abuse of minors in the Archdiocese of Philadelphia. *In RE: County Investigating Grand Jury of September 17, 2003* (2005) (hereafter, the 2005 Grand Jury Report). The report concluded that the statute that criminalized endangering the welfare of a child (EWOC), 18 Pa.C.S. §4304 (1995), as it existed, at that time, was written in a manner that allowed church officials such as Appellee to escape criminal liability. The version of the EWOC statute under consideration by the grand jury and under which Appellee was ultimately charged provided as follows:

(A) OFFENSE DEFINED: A parent, guardian, or other person supervising the welfare of a child under 18 years of age commits an offense if he knowingly endangers the welfare of the child by violating a duty of care, protection or support.

(B) GRADING: An offense under this section constitutes a misdemeanor of the first degree. However, where there is a course of conduct of endangering the welfare of a child, the offense constitutes a felony of the third degree.

18 Pa.C.S. §4304 (1995).

Examining the language of Section 4304(A), the grand jury concluded as follows:

As defined under the law, ... the offense of endangering the welfare is too narrow to support a successful prosecution of the decision-makers who were running the Archdiocese. The statute confines its coverage to parents, guardians, and other persons "supervising the welfare of a child." High level Archdiocesan officials, however, were far removed from any direct contact with children.

See Commonwealth v. Lynn, 83 A.3d 434, 445 n.15 (Pa.Super. 2013).

Based on its construction of Section 4304(A), the grand jury did not recommend any criminal charges, but instead recommended amending the statute with language to expand the reach of the provision to encompass conduct by individuals in an employer or supervising capacity. The Philadelphia District Attorney's Office decided not to bring charges against Appellee. According to Appellee, following this recommendation, legislators, the Philadelphia District Attorney's Office, and others advocated for a change in the law throughout Pennsylvania. In 2006, the legislature obliged, and amended the EWOC statute, effective January 27, 2007, to read:

A parent, guardian, or other person supervising the welfare of a child under 18 years of age, or a person *who employs or supervises such a person*, commits an offense if he knowingly endangers the welfare of a child by violating a duty of care, protection or support.

18 Pa.C.S. §4304(a)(1) (2007) (emphasis added).

Notwithstanding the grand jury's failure to recommend criminal charges and the prior Philadelphia District Attorney's decision not to prosecute based on the belief that the 1995 EWOC statute could not reach the conduct of church officials in a supervisory capacity, the Commonwealth changed course, and in 2011 charged Appellee with two counts of EWOC pursuant to the 1995 version of the statute because the criminal course of conduct in which Appellee was alleged to have engaged occurred from 1992–2004 while he was Secretary for Clergy.[10] In addition, the Commonwealth charged Appellee with two counts of conspiracy to commit EWOC, 18 Pa.C.S. § 903,[11] relating to his supervision of Rev. Avery and another priest, Rev. Brennan. Appellee was initially going to be tried together with both Rev. Avey and Rev. Brennan. Rev. Avery, however, pled guilty to involuntary deviate sexual intercourse and conspiring to endanger the welfare of children on March 22, 2012, after the jury had been selected, but before trial began.[12] The trial, therefore, continued with Appellee and Rev. Brennan.... Appellee sought to quash the charges of EWOC on the basis that he had "no connection whatsoever" to the children whose welfare he was accused of having endangered.... Once this motion was denied, Appellee moved for extraordinary relief in this Court pursuant to 42 Pa.C.S. §§ 726 and 502, arguing that the version of the EWOC statute applicable to him did "not cover Archdiocese managers who did not directly supervise children."... We denied Appellee's petition on February 12, 2012.

Appellee's and Rev. Brennan's jury trial commenced on March 26, 2012. The Commonwealth sought to prove that Appellee had engaged in a pattern of concealment and facilitation of child sexual molestation by abusive priests, conduct which led directly to Rev. Avery's abuse of D.G. The Commonwealth introduced extensive evidence that Appellee's handling of Rev. Avery's case was not an anomaly, but was in accord with his established practice for dealing with sexually abusive priests. The evidence demonstrated that Appellee violated his duty to prevent priests from sexually molesting children in order to protect their reputations in furtherance of his objective to conceal the misconduct and to protect instead the reputation of the Archdiocese.

In addition to the conduct and abuse committed by Rev. Avery, the Commonwealth sought to introduce "other acts evidence" pursuant to Rule 404(b)(2) of the Rules of Evidence,[13] arguing that to understand Appellee's intent, knowledge, motivation, and absence of mistake when handling Rev. Avery's case, it was necessary for the jury to hear how he personally handled other cases involving sexual abuse allegations against priests and the knowledge he acquired from reviewing the Secret Archives. The Commonwealth specifically alleged that evidence in the files of other priests revealed that Appellee routinely failed to act in his supervisory capacity to protect the welfare of children when faced with reports of priests who were raping, molesting, and acting immorally with these children,

---

10. Unless otherwise noted, therefore, all references to EWOC and Section 4304 will be to the 1995 version.

11. Conspiracy is defined as follows:
   (a) Definition of conspiracy.—A person is guilty of conspiracy with another person or persons to commit a crime if with the intent of promoting or facilitating its commission he:
   (1) agrees with such other person or persons that they or one or more of them will engage in conduct which constitutes such crime or an attempt or solicitation to commit such crime; or
   (2) agrees to aid such other person or persons in the planning or commission of such crime or of an attempt or solicitation to commit such crime.
   18 Pa.C.S. § 903(a).

12. *See* 18 Pa.C.S. §§ 3123(a) and 903(c), respectively.

13. Rule 404(b) in relevant part provides as follows:
   (1) Prohibited Uses. Evidence of a crime, wrong, or other act is not admissible to prove a person's character in order to show that on a particular occasion the person acted in accordance with the character.
   (2) Permitted Uses. This evidence may be admissible for another purpose, such as proving motive, opportunity, intent, preparation, plan, knowledge, identity, absence of mistake, or lack of accident. In a criminal case this evidence is admissible only if the probative value of the evidence outweighs its potential for unfair prejudice.
Pa.R.E. 404(b).

repeatedly made transfers to facilities where clergy could continue abusing children when trouble arose, and permitted abusing priests to continue in the ministry while keeping parents and law enforcement ignorant of the peril....

Specifically, the Commonwealth sought to present evidence concerning Appellee's knowledge of abusive behavior by 27 priests in addition to Rev. Avery and his reaction to this knowledge. The trial court permitted the Commonwealth to introduce evidence pertaining to 20 priests pursuant to Rule 404(b)(2), agreeing with the Commonwealth that the evidence would assist the jury in evaluating whether Appellee was aware of the danger presented by priests who had abused children in the past; whether he knowingly disregarded that risk; whether Appellee knowingly put D.G. and other unnamed minors to whom Rev. Avery had access in jeopardy; and whether Appellee intended to permit sexually abusive priests to operate within the Archdiocese without supervision. The trial court has thoroughly recounted the prior bad acts evidence in its opinion. For ease of discussion, what follows is a brief description of the prior bad acts evidence pertaining to several of the abusive priests whom Appellee managed, as demonstrative of the cumulative prior bad acts evidence, which is relevant to our legal analysis of Appellee's role as a supervisor of the welfare of children in his capacity as Secretary for Clergy, and our application of the law to the facts presented at trial.

In particular, the Commonwealth introduced evidence that on July 18, 1991, while Appellee served as Associate Vicar in the Office of the Vicar for Administration assisting Monsignor Molloy in looking into allegations of sexual abuse, Appellee learned that two county detectives were investigating Father Michael Bolesta concerning allegations made by the parents of several teenage boys that Father Bolesta had inappropriately touched the boys on several occasions. The pastor of the church where Father Bolesta was a parochial vicar informed the detectives that he had questioned one of the boys, who stated that Father Bolesta had inappropriately touched him and invited the child to go swimming naked. Additionally, about seven months previously, the parents of another boy complained to the pastor of similar conduct. The pastor sought direction from the Archdiocese, and Appellee's predecessor noted in the Secret Archives file that because charges had not been filed, the parents of these boys would likely drop the matter if the Church acted on it.

On July 20, 1991, Appellee and Monsignor Molloy interviewed one of Father Bolesta's victims and learned not only of the priest's inappropriate conduct and touching, but also the names of nine other possible victims. Appellee assisted the Monsignor in interviewing the families of these boys, and learned that Father Bolesta repeated the same *modus operandi*: inappropriate touching, swimming naked with the boys, groping, and showering together. During interviews with the victims and their families, Appellee repeatedly faced not only the rage, anger, and disgust directed at Father Bolesta, but the concern that the abusing priest should never be around children again. Appellee met with Father Bolesta on August 5, 1991, and he denied the allegations. Appellee, however, shielded Father Bolesta from the families' emotions, instead indicating to him only that the families and the victims were concerned for the priest and appreciated the good work he had done.[14] ... Despite the numerous accusations and consistent details, Appellee accepted Father Bolesta's denials and suggested that he may have just been fatigued: "[Appellee] stated that perhaps even though there was no action committed, perhaps the behavior has to be examined

---

14. Appellee shielded another priest, Father Albert T. Kostelnick, from allegations of sexual abuse entirely by failing to inform the priest that several young girls alleged they had been fondled by him. Following the allegations, the Archdiocese transferred Father Kostelnick to a parish with a grade school.

especially because of the stress and tiredness Father Bolesta said he was experiencing." ...[15] Appellee and the Monsignor asked Father Bolesta to receive counseling and stated that his parishioners would be told that Father Bolesta had other commitments that prevented him from serving at such a busy parish.[16]

Following Father Bolesta's removal from his parish, he was evaluated and diagnosed with an unspecified sexual disorder, and his treatment team recommended that he be enjoined from one-on-one contact with minors and be reevaluated a year later. Several months later, his counselor repeated that he should not be around minors.[17] Following his reevaluation in October 1992, the treatment team stated that he had not shown the improvement they had hoped for; however, because of his cooperation with the treatment plan they saw no need for continued restrictions on his ministry.

When the families who had raised allegations against Father Bolesta learned of his re-assignment, they expressed deep resentment and anger to Rev. Thomas O'Brien, whom the Church had tasked with meeting with them. Although Rev. O'Brien assured the families that the Archdiocese did not intend to cover up Father Bolesta's conduct by reassigning him, he conveyed to Appellee that the Church should be more discreet when reassigning priests against whom allegations of sexual abuse had been made, because it was the Church's publishing of the reassignment that prompted the resurfacing of the families' anger and concern, a suggestion for which Appellee thanked him.... On November 4, 1992, Appellee responded to a parishioner who was concerned that Father Bolesta's reassignment was due to allegations of sexual abuse at his prior position by stating that the parishioner was "not in possession of the proper facts and information."[18] In the February 18, 1994 Report, Father Bolesta was the first name Appellee included under the heading "Allegations of Sexual Misconduct with Minors with No Conclusive Evidence."

Turning to the other acts evidence regarding Father Nicholas Cudemo, there were several incidents alleged in his Secret Archives file prior to Appellee's appointment as Secretary for Clergy: a 1966 allegation that Father Cudemo had been in a three-year sexually abusive

---

15. This was not the only time Appellee suggested explanations for sexual misconduct. On another occasion, when a man came forward with accusations of inappropriate contact with Father Thomas J. Smith when he was 12 years old, Appellee proposed to the accused priest that perhaps the incident occurred in a manner that differed from the accuser's recollection, and that the 12-year-old boy had misconstrued what occurred. When another priest, Father Thomas F. Shea, admitted to sexually abusing an adolescent boy, Appellee suggested to the priest that perhaps the boy had seduced him.

16. Similarly, when another priest, Father Thomas Wisniewski, stood accused of sexually abusing a 15-year-old boy and reported for inpatient mental health treatment, Appellee instructed him to tell his parishioners he was going on vacation.

17. Notwithstanding this recommendation, Cardinal Bevilacqua appointed Father Bolesta as an associate pastor at St. Agatha-St. James in Philadelphia with no restriction on his ministry, effective June 15, 1992.

18. Appellee routinely misled individuals who were concerned about priests with sexual abuse allegations against them. For instance, in May 1993, colleagues of Father David C. Sicoli witnessed disturbing behavior and voiced their concern to Appellee about Father Sicoli developing a consuming and odd relationship with a young teenage boy. Despite allegations dating back to 1977 about Father Sicoli, Appellee responded to his concerned colleagues that Father Sicoli had "no other problems before." ... Shortly thereafter, two pastors met with Appellee to protest against Father Sicoli's continued behavior and threatening to resign if he was not removed. Appellee recommended the transfer of one of the complaining pastors, ... and the other voluntarily left the parish, ...

As to Father Robert Brennan, who had been through treatment at St. John Vianney and transferred to another parish following allegations of sexual misconduct, Appellee informed concerned colleagues that Father Brennan's treatment and transfer were because of "boundary issues," and that there were no allegations of sexual misconduct....

relationship with a teenage girl; a 1969 allegation by an assistant pastor that Father Cudemo had been seen trying to calm a hysterical girl in the high school, who loudly shouted that she loved him; about a month later the same pastor reported that Father Cudemo had taken a different young woman into his room and closed the door; in 1977, a recent high school graduate revealed that her best friend had been involved in a sexually abusive relationship with the Father for a couple of years and may have become pregnant.... On September 25, 1991, Appellee met with three other women, each of whom provided details of sexual abuse by Father Cudemo. Two stated that the abuse began when they were 15 years old, and another indicated it started around age ten. When one of the women asked if there were other allegations of abuse, Monsignor Molloy stated that there had been nothing of that nature, although in fact several months before the September 1991 meeting, another woman had contacted the Archdiocese to state that she and Father Cudemo had been in a sexually abusive relationship for 15 years, beginning when she was 16 years old.

When Appellee confronted Father Cudemo with these accusations, he initially reacted by disclaiming responsibility and stating that individuals were "out to get" him.... When asked about specific details, however, Father Cudemo conceded that "possibly" they were accurate. In October 1991, yet another woman came forward with similar allegations, and, in November 1991, several victims wrote to the Archdiocese to characterize the Church's failure to remove Father Cudemo as "immoral and negligent" and threatened to bring a lawsuit.... Within a week of receiving the letter, Appellee and Monsignor Molloy met with Father Cudemo to ask him to withdraw from the parish. Father Cudemo resisted, and similarly resisted treatment. When he was directed to be hospitalized for evaluation and treatment, he refused. From February 1992 through December 1994, Appellee repeatedly instructed Father Cudemo to comply, to no avail. In February 1994, Appellee placed Father Cudemo's name on the list of "Diagnosed Pedophile" priests, but permitted him to continue to operate in active ministry.

In May 1996, Father Cudemo resigned as pastor at St. Callistus Parish in Philadelphia, and his clinical psychologist, who was not part of the Archdiocese ordered treatment, wrote to Appellee to provide his opinion that Father Cudemo is not a pedophile and was not a danger to anyone. Cardinal Bevilacqua permitted Father Cudemo to retire as a priest in good standing. Notwithstanding his inclusion on a list of pedophile priests, in February 1997, Appellee encouraged Father Cudemo to participate as a retired priest in the Archdiocese of Philadelphia.

In January 2001, a Philadelphia Police Officer called Appellee concerning allegations made against Father Cudemo by a former student at St. Irenaeus School in Philadelphia, who alleged sexual abuse while she was in the fifth through seventh grades. The police officer requested any information Appellee had about allegations arising from Father Cudemo's time at St. Irenaeus. Instead of informing the officer of the extensive allegations of sexual abuse made by multiple other girls as recounted above, or that he considered Father Cudemo to be a pedophile, Appellee stated that there were none.

The Commonwealth also introduced other acts evidence in relation to Father Stanley Gana. In 1991, Appellee began investigating allegations of sexual abuse of a minor boy, R.K., by Father Gana, which was alleged to have occurred over a period of several years, three to four times a week, beginning when R.K. was 13, and eventually involving anal penetration. R.K. informed Appellee in April of 1992 of two other boys who had similar experiences with Father Gana. On May 26, 1992, Appellee met with Father Gana concerning R.K.'s accusations; Father Gana denied them, explaining that perhaps R.K. misunderstood signs of affection. Cardinal Bevilacqua accepted Father Gana's explanations, determining the investigation into R.K.'s accusations to be inconclusive. On February 18, 1994, Appellee placed Father Gana's name on his list of priests alleged to have had sexual misconduct with minors "with no conclusive evidence." ...

In early September 1995, M.B., one of the victims identified by R.K. to Appellee, contacted the Archdiocese and told Appellee that Father Gana had abused him beginning when he was 11 years old in 1978 and continuing beyond high school graduation. He stated the abuse involved anal sex once or twice a week when he was a freshman in high school, and that he was part of a "rotation" of boys with whom Father Gana shared a bed and had sex. M.B. told Appellee that he desired to take out a fullpage advertisement identifying Father Gana as a pedophile and inviting other victims to come forward; Appellee told him that was not possible, as it would infringe on Father Gana's rights.... Appellee confronted Father Gana with M.B.'s allegations on September 5, 1995, and Father Gana denied all allegations of wrongdoing. He did, however, admit that he shared a bed with the boys, but that it was their choice to do so. Appellee suggested Father Gana report to St. John Vianney for a psychological evaluation, which resulted in several diagnoses, including a sexual disorder not otherwise specified. The staff at St. John Vianney recommended further treatment and considered Father Gana to be at risk for further "inappropriate and dangerous behavior." ... Father Gana resigned from his assignment, purportedly for health reasons, less than a week later, and Appellee helped to arrange inpatient treatment for him at a Church-affiliated treatment facility, Southdown, in Ontario.

In February 1996, the director of clinical services at Southdown, Sister Donna Markham, confronted Father Gana about the accusations against him, and he admitted they were all true. Even though the accusations were that he raped multiple boys under the age of 14, Sister Markham declined to diagnose him with pedophilia, stating rather that he was a person who acted under the influence of drugs or alcohol. Less than a month into his four-to-six week inpatient stay, Father Gana checked himself out of Southdown and moved to Florida. Less than ten days later, Sister Lucy Vasquez, the Chancellor of the Diocese of Orlando, Florida, spoke to Rev. Michael T. McCulken, Assistant Director in the Office for Clergy in the Archdiocese of Philadelphia, to report that some of her parishioners had expressed concern "about what might be happening at [Father Gana's] house" in Orlando, where a number of young people from Slovakia were staying....

In early June 1996, M.B. followed up with Appellee, questioning the lack of communication. Although Sister Markham had told Appellee that Father Gana had admitted the truth of the accusations, Appellee informed M.B. that Father Gana continued to deny them but had agreed to a psychological evaluation. By the time Appellee informed M.B. that Father Gana agreed to the evaluation, he had already quit his inpatient treatment and moved to Orlando.

Appellee wrote to Father Gana shortly after speaking with M.B. and expressed concern that he had quit treatment, which, he later explained to a grand jury, was out of concern for possible future victims of abuse. In September and October 1996, Father Gana expressed interest in completing treatment and returning to active ministry, which Appellee said was possible because of the lack of a diagnosis of pedophilia. However, he warned Father Gana of the danger that M.B. would take his accusations to the press. Father Gana returned for treatment at Southdown and admitted to having sexual contact with eight individuals in the 1970s and 1980s, three of whom were adolescents, including R.K. and M.B. Southdown staff informed Appellee that Father Gana claimed to have been chaste for ten years; Appellee recommended to Cardinal Bevilacqua that Father Gana be permitted to return to a limited form of ministry to keep him from the public eye, specifically recommending him as a chaplain to the Carmelite Ministry in Philadelphia. The Cardinal approved Appellee's recommendation. Two Mother Superiors were informed Father Gana would be joining them; they were not, however, informed that he had been accused of sexually abusing minors.... Five years later, Appellee informed Father Gana of a change in Church policy that would no longer permit priests who had sexually abused minors, even absent a declaration of pedophilia, to operate in limited ministry. Father Gana was relieved of his assignment effective February 2002.

Finally, for our purposes, information in the Secret Archives regarding Father Edward DePaoli indicated that he had pled guilty in federal court to receiving child pornography in the mail. While serving one year of probation for this offense, on June 26, 1985, he was admitted to St. John Vianney for an evaluation and treatment, where he was diagnosed with an unspecified sexual disorder. The Archdiocese of Philadelphia arranged for Father DePaoli to transfer to a New Jersey diocese, where he served for nearly three years, until his psychologist reported that he was ready to return to Philadelphia. He resumed active ministry in Philadelphia on July 1, 1991, as an associate pastor at St. John the Baptist Church in Philadelphia. In May 1992, the pastor of St. John the Baptist, Rev. Feeny, found pornographic material in the rectory mail addressed to Father DePaoli. Rev. Feeny reported this to Monsignor Jagodzinski in the Archdiocese, and further informed him of other inappropriate behavior in which Father DePaoli had engaged. In one incident, he had fourth through sixth grade girls dress in "paper cutouts" and act out a story in which he instructed each of them to act sexy and pretend to be enticing; in another incident when children were having Mass, he stated that he would like to see one of the eighth grade girls naked....

On July 7, 1992, Appellee met with Father DePaoli to assist Cardinal Bevilacqua in deciding Father DePaoli's future. At this meeting, Father DePaoli placed blame on other individuals and took no responsibility for his own conduct. Appellee recommended that Father DePaoli be placed on a leave of absence with restricted ministry, be informed that he would not receive another assignment in the Archdiocese of Philadelphia, and be encouraged to seek voluntary laicization. The Cardinal approved these recommendations. In February 1995, however, when Father DePaoli requested permission to celebrate his 25th anniversary of entering the priesthood (the "Silver Jubilee"), Appellee granted permission and provided a letter stating that Father DePaoli was a priest in good standing.

In September 12, 1995, Cardinal Bevilacqua approved a recommendation made by Appellee for Father DePaoli's residential assignment at St. Gabriel Rectory in Montgomery County, which Appellee had chosen because it did not have a grade school. While Father DePaoli resided at St. Gabriel Rectory, Sister Joan Scary, Director of Religious Education at St. Gabriel's, complained on several occasions to the Vicar for Montgomery County, who passed the information along to the Archdiocese, that Father DePaoli was not restricting his ministry as directed and was instead repeatedly celebrating public liturgies, and was receiving suspicious packages in the mail.

In the spring of 1996, the pastor of St. Gabriel's Parish warned Sister Scary to stop making reports regarding Father DePaoli or she "could pack [her] bags" and "get the hell out of here." ... She ignored this warning and repeated her concerns to the Archdiocese, for which she was immediately "fired" from her assignment on May 30, 1996.[19] On July 1, 1996, Appellee summarized the circumstances of Sister Scary's removal as resulting from making unfounded accusations against Father DePaoli, although he acknowledged that Father DePaoli had received a magazine from a division of "Gentleman's Quarterly," which had some "inappropriate content," and was improperly celebrating public Mass in violation of the restriction on his ministry....

---

19. The ramifications of a nun's "firing" are not apparent on the record.

In June 2002, Appellee met with a woman who reported that Father DePaoli had fondled her breasts in 1969–70 when she was 12 years old. Ultimately, following the Dallas Charter, the Archdiocese Review Board concluded that Father DePaoli had to be permanently removed from ministry based on "credible allegations of sexual abuse," which included his federal conviction, possession of pornography while on probation, credible allegations of inappropriate touching in 1969–70, recent possession of inappropriate magazines, and overt violations of his restricted ministry.

After several months of testimony against Appellee, including the above recounted prior bad acts evidence, the Commonwealth rested its case on May 17, 2012, and, at that time, the trial court granted Appellee's motion for judgment of acquittal as to the charge of conspiring with Rev. Brennan. *See* Pa.R.Crim.P. 606(A)(1). Appellee further sought judgment of acquittal for the EWOC charge as well, which the trial court denied. Trial ended June 22, 2012, and the trial court charged the jury to consider whether Appellee was culpable for EWOC either as a principal or as Rev. Avery's accomplice.[20] The jury returned a verdict of guilty with respect EWOC as it related to Rev. Avery (as to D.G. and other unnamed minors), which the trial court graded as a third-degree felony because the jury found a "course of conduct of endangering the welfare of a child[.]" 18 Pa.C.S. § 4304(b).[21] The jury acquitted Appellee of EWOC as it related to Rev. Brennan and of conspiring with Rev. Avery.[22] The trial court sentenced Appellee to a term of three to six years of imprisonment.

In Appellee's statement of errors complained of on appeal, *see* Pa.R.A.P. 1925(b), he asserted, among other things, that the evidence was insufficient as a matter of law because he had no supervisory role over D.G. or the other children of St. Jerome's. The trial court responded in its Rule 1925(a) opinion that the statute did not require that an individual be a supervisor of a child to fall under the EWOC statute's reach. Rather, the person had to be a supervisor of the welfare of a child. The trial court held that the Commonwealth met its burden of proving this element of the offense by showing that Appellee oversaw, managed, or had authority over the well-being of children; specifically, by proving that

---

20. The Crimes Code provides accomplice liability as follows:
　　(a) General rule.—A person is guilty of an offense if it is committed by his own conduct or
　　by the conduct of another person for which he is legally accountable, or both.
　　(b) Conduct of another.—A person is legally accountable for the conduct of
　　another person when:
　　　　(1) acting with the kind of culpability that is sufficient for the commission of the offense,
　　　　he causes an innocent or irresponsible person to engage in such conduct;
　　　　(2) he is made accountable for the conduct of such other person by this title or by the
　　　　law defining the offense; or
　　　　(3) he is an accomplice of such other person in the commission of the offense.
　　(c) Accomplice defined.—A person is an accomplice of another person in the commission
　　of an offense if:
　　　　(1) with the intent of promoting or facilitating the commission of the offense, he:
　　　　(i) solicits such other person to commit it; or
　　　　(ii) aids or agrees or attempts to aid such other person in planning or committing it; or
　　　　(2) his conduct is expressly declared by law to establish his complicity.
　．．．
18 Pa.C.S. § 306(a)–(c).
　　21. It is not known whether the jury considered Appellee guilty of EWOC as a principal or as an accomplice to Rev. Avery.
　　22. The jury failed to reach a verdict on the charges against Rev. Brennan.

Appellee controlled sexually abusive priests, and that it was his responsibility to protect the children of the Archdiocese of Philadelphia from future harm at the hands of these sexually abusive priests.

Appealing his judgment of sentence to the Superior Court, Appellee raised ten issues, two of which challenged the sufficiency of the evidence to sustain his conviction for EWOC. The first concerned his culpability as a principal actor, and the second his culpability as an accomplice. The basis of Appellee's argument as to principal liability was that he was not within the scope of individuals subject to the EWOC statute because he did not directly supervise children. Rather, according to Appellee, he supervised Rev. Avery, who was supervising the children. In support of his argument, Appellee relied on the 2007 amendment to the EWOC statute as a compelling indication that the relevant (1995) version of the statute did not encompass individuals described by the amended language, *i.e.*, those who employ or supervise the class of individuals who were within the preview of the pre-amended version.

Responding to this argument, it was the Commonwealth's position that the plain meaning of the 1995 EWOC statute clearly encompassed the class of persons added by the 2007 amendment, and the amendment merely clarified, rather than changed, the statute's scope of liability. Examining the plain language, the Commonwealth argued that the phrase "the welfare of" would be rendered superfluous by Appellee's interpretation. In this respect, the Commonwealth endorsed the trial court's distinction between actual supervision of children and supervision of the welfare of children as the basis for Appellee's liability for EWOC as a principal.

Considering first whether the evidence was sufficient to sustain Appellee's conviction for EWOC as a principal, the Superior Court examined the statutory language of the EWOC statute and concluded that because Appellee was not a parent or guardian, the issue in this case was the scope or breadth of the phrase "or other person supervising the welfare of a child[.]" Although the Superior Court acknowledged direction from this Court that the EWOC statute was intended "to cover a broad range of conduct in order to safeguard the welfare and security of our children," *Lynn*, 83 A.3d at 449 (citing *Commonwealth v. Mack*, 359 A.2d 770, 772 (Pa. 1976)), it observed that neither it nor this Court had ever affirmed a conviction for EWOC where the accused was not actually engaged in or was responsible for the supervision of an endangered child. *Id.* at 450. Rather, it construed its decision in *Commonwealth v. Halye*, 719 A.2d 763 (Pa.Super. 1998) (*en banc*), to require proof that the defendant was directly supervising the child.

In *Halye*, the defendant was visiting the home of a family member. While the adults were in one part of the home, the children were in their bedroom playing. The defendant excused himself to use the restroom, but went instead into the children's bedroom. When he did not promptly return, the children's mother went to check on him, and discovered the defendant in the closet with her son, his head placed near her son's exposed privates. *Halye*, 719 A.2d at 765. On appeal from the defendant's subsequent conviction for EWOC,[23] the Superior Court reversed, finding "insufficient evidence of [the defendant's] role as a supervisor or guardian of the child to support the [EWOC] conviction." *Id.* Specifically, the Superior Court observed that there was no testimony that the defendant had been asked to supervise the children in any capacity or that such a role was expected of him,

---

23. The defendant in *Halye* was also convicted of involuntary deviate sexual intercourse, indecent assault, and corruption of minors.

and instead characterized him as a mere visitor to the home, where the children's parents were home and supervising them.

The Commonwealth had argued against the applicability of *Halye*, asserting that the Superior Court in that case simply applied the law to the facts presented and overturned the conviction because the defendant was not supervising the children or their welfare in any respect, being just a visitor in the house, in contrast to Appellee, whose responsibility was to protect the welfare of the children of the Archdiocese from sexually abusive priests.... The Superior Court disagreed with the Commonwealth about the persuasive authority of *Halye* for several reasons. First, it interpreted that case as requiring actual supervision of children as an element of EWOC. *Lynn*, 83 A.3d at 452 (citing *Halye*, 719 A.2d at 765 (" ... we conclude that [the Commonwealth] failed in its burden of proving that [the defendant] was in the position of supervising the children at the time of the assault.")). Second, the Superior Court considered that by focusing on Appellee's responsibility to the children of the Archdiocese, the Commonwealth's argument improperly conflated two distinct elements of EWOC: supervision and duty. Third, although the factual circumstances of *Halye* were distinct, the Superior Court therein confronted the same legal issue presented in this case: whether the accused must be a supervisor of a child for culpability to arise under the EWOC statute.

Because the trial court did not consider *Halye*, the Superior Court considered its statutory construction to be faulty, and was further not convinced by the trial court's "parsing of the terms 'the welfare of'" because it "adds ambiguity where none need exist." *Id.* at 453. For EWOC criminal liability to attach, according to the Superior Court, a person who is not a parent or a guardian of the endangered child must be engaged in the supervision, or be responsible for the supervision, of a child. *Id.* In this respect, the Superior Court found most significant the lack of evidence that Appellee had any direct supervision over D.G. or any other child put at risk by Rev. Avery's presence at St. Jerome's, and held that the evidence was therefore not sufficient to support Appellee's conviction for EWOC as a principal actor. *Lynn*, 83 A.3d at 447.

Although the Superior Court concluded that Appellee could not be convicted as a principal for EWOC, it recognized that there was an independent avenue by which the jury could have convicted him because it had been charged to consider Appellee's culpability for EWOC as Rev. Avery's accomplice. The court concluded, however, that Appellee's accomplice liability was not supported by sufficient evidence that Appellee acted with the intent to promote or facilitate the commission of EWOC by Rev. Avery, because Appellee did not know D.G. or know of him, was not sufficiently aware of Rev. Avery's supervision of him or any other child at St. Jerome's, and he had no specific information that Rev. Avery intended to or was preparing to molest D.G. or any other child.... Accordingly, the Superior Court determined the evidence was not sufficient to support the EWOC conviction as either a principal or an accomplice, and reversed the judgment of sentence. We granted the Commonwealth's petition for allowance of appeal....

Generally speaking, under the rule of lenity, penal statutes are to be strictly construed, with ambiguities resolved in favor of the accused. *Commonwealth v. Lassiter*, 722 A.2d 657, 660 (Pa. 1998). In the peculiar context of EWOC, however, we have held that the statute is protective in nature, and must be construed to effectuate its broad purpose of sheltering children from harm. *Mack*, 359 A.2d at 770. Specifically, the purpose of such juvenile statutes is defensive; they are written expansively by the legislature "to cover a broad range of conduct in order to safeguard the welfare and security of our children." *Id.* at 772 (quoting *Commonwealth v. Marlin*, 305 A.2d 14, 18 (Pa. 1973)). In the context of protective juvenile legislation, therefore, we have sanctioned statutes that, rather than itemizing every undesirable type of conduct, criminalize instead the "conduct producing or tending to produce a [c]ertain defined result ..." *Marlin*, 305 A.2d at 18. We have accordingly observed:

> The common sense of the community, as well as the sense of decency, propriety and the morality which most people entertain is sufficient to apply the statute to each particular case, and to individuate what particular conduct is rendered criminal by it.

Id. (quoting *Commonwealth v. Randall*, 133 A.2d 276, 280 (Pa.Super. 1957)). In the face of a challenge to the EWOC statute as being unconstitutionally vague, being cognizant of the protective purpose of such juvenile acts, we held the EWOC criminal statute was not facially unconstitutionally imprecise. *Mack*, 359 A.2d at 772. We considered that the language contained therein, specifically, "endangers the welfare of the child" and "duty of care, protection or support," are not esoteric; rather, we discerned that they are easily understood and given content by the community at large. *Id.* Accordingly, we reasoned that "an individual who contemplates a particular course of conduct will have little difficulty deciding whether his intended act 'endangers the welfare of the child' by his violation of a 'duty of care, protection or support.'" *Id.*[24]

With these principles in mind, we turn to the parties' arguments as to the first issue: whether the evidence was sufficient to prove EWOC where Appellee did not have direct contact with children. Relying on our holding in *Mack*, that the EWOC statute is necessarily drawn broadly to capture conduct that endangers the welfare of a child, and Superior Court precedent explaining that EWOC "involves the endangering of the physical or moral welfare of a child by an act or omission in violation of a legal duty," *Commonwealth v. Taylor*, 471 A.2d 1228, 1230 (Pa.Super. 1984), the Commonwealth focuses on the intent element of the offense. Because the crime of EWOC is a specific intent crime, *Commonwealth v. Cardwell*, 515 A.2d 311, 313 (Pa.Super. 1986), and the intent required is the knowing violation of a duty of care, *id.*, the Superior Court has long interpreted the intent element to require that: (1) the accused is aware of his/her duty to protect the child; (2) the accused is aware that the child is in circumstances that could threaten the child's physical or psychological welfare; and (3) the accused has either failed to act or has taken action so lame or meager that such actions cannot reasonably be expected to protect the child's welfare. *Commonwealth v. Wallace*, 817 A.2d 485, 490–91 (Pa.Super. 2002); *Commonwealth v. Vining*, 744 A.2d 310, 315 (Pa.Super. 1999) (*en banc*); *Commonwealth v. Martir*, 712 A.2d 327, 328–29 (Pa.Super. 1998); *Commonwealth v. Pahel*, 689 A.2d 963, 964 (Pa.Super. 1997); *Commonwealth v. Fewell*, 654 A.2d 1109, 1118 (Pa.Super. 1995)[;] *Commonwealth v. Miller*, 600 A.2d 988, 990 (Pa.Super. 1992); *Commonwealth v. Campbell*, 580 A.2d 868, 870 (Pa.Super. 1990); *Cardwell*, 515 A.2d 311, 315.

Applying the evidence presented to the legal question of whether Appellee knowingly endangered the welfare of a child by violating a duty of care, protection, or support, the Commonwealth argues that it clearly established that it was Appellee's undisputed duty to protect children from sexual predator priests; he was aware that children were in danger of sexual abuse when exposed to such priests; and he failed to take protective action and, indeed, actually exposed children to the danger of being sexually molested.

---

24. Appellee has attempted to limit the persuasiveness of *Mack* by characterizing it as dealing with conduct, not potential defendants, and therefore shedding no light on the meaning of "a person supervising the welfare of a child." The import of *Mack*, however, is that the legislature intended to draw the EWOC statute broadly to give effect to its protective purpose, an intent that guides our interpretation and application of the statute herein.

Addressing the class of individuals to whom the EWOC statute applies, the Commonwealth argues that it has never been in dispute, until this case, that the offense involves endangering the physical or moral welfare of a child by an act or omission in violation of a legal duty; that is, a "person supervising the welfare of a child" means a person who has a duty to provide "care, protection, or support" to a child. *See* 18 Pa.C.S. §4304 (1995); *Taylor*, 471 A.2d at 1230; *Vining*, 744 A.2d at 315 ("[O]ne endangers the welfare of a child if he or she knowingly violates a duty of care, protection or support."); *Commonwealth v. Ogin*, 540 A.2d 549, 553 (Pa.Super. 1988) (*en banc*) (providing that the statute "is a comprehensive provision designed to penalize those who knowingly breach a legal duty to protect the well-being of children who are entrusted to their care."). According to the Commonwealth, a duty of care can be proven through evidence of a supervisory role. *See Commonwealth v. Bryant*, 57 A.3d 191, 198 (Pa.Super. 2012) (recognizing that the duty of care has, on multiple occasions, been extended to those who exercise a supervisory role over children).

According to the Commonwealth, one who acts in a capacity of protecting children, supervises another person who interacts with those children, and is aware that this other person is a threat to the welfare of those children, but does nothing, or, as in this case, takes actions which exacerbate child abuse, violates the EWOC statute. Because supervision is routinely accomplished through others, the Commonwealth argues that the statute is broad enough to cover the conduct of individuals who may not personally encounter the children, such as school principals or day care managers, as long as the other elements of the EWOC statute are met. Under the facts presented, the Commonwealth argues that Appellee endangered the welfare of children, including D.G., by breaching his undisputed duty to prevent priests whom he knew to be a danger to children and who were under his supervision from sexually molesting them; in other words, his supervision of Rev. Avery was the supervision of the welfare of children.

The Commonwealth criticizes the Superior Court opinion for adding a nonstatutory element to the offense of "actual" or "direct" child supervision, noting that the statute says nothing that would exclude supervision of the welfare of a child that is not sufficiently actual or direct. Moreover, the Commonwealth observes that the text of the statute refers to a person supervising "the welfare of a child," not a person supervising "a child."

Turning to the Superior Court's reliance on *Halye*, the Commonwealth argues that this reliance was misplaced. Rather than holding that supervision as used in the EWOC statute must be actual or direct supervision of the child or children, as the Superior Court interpreted *Halye* to do, the Commonwealth views that case much more narrowly. According to the Commonwealth, *Halye* says nothing about whether supervision must be actual or direct, and did not conclude that the defendant therein was supervising too indirectly to be guilty of the offense. Rather, the Commonwealth argues that the *Halye* court found the defendant was not supervising the children at all, having no duty whatsoever to the children, and therefore could not be guilty of having violated that duty. The Commonwealth considers *Halye* to hold merely that the sexual molestation of a child does not prove that the assailant had a duty of care to that child.

Having refuted the Superior Court's statutory construction and reliance on *Halye*, the Commonwealth argues that the Superior Court's decision in the instant case is left unsupported. Reviewing the evidence against Appellee that it introduced at trial, the Commonwealth concludes that it sufficed to demonstrate that Appellee had a duty, as he readily conceded at trial, to protect children from abusive priests under his control; he knew that children who encountered such priests were in danger of sexual assault; and he failed to take action to remove priests from the locations or roles which allowed them to abuse children freely, thereby exposing children to the very danger it was his duty to prevent....

Confronting the legislative amendment of the EWOC statute, effective in 2007, the Commonwealth makes several arguments. First, it argues that the pre-amended version is to be interpreted on the unambiguous language contained therein and that the amendment is irrelevant to this interpretation. Second, the only way in which another version of the law is relevant to statutory interpretation is upon the finding of ambiguity, and consideration is then limited to the former law, not a subsequent amendment. *See* 1 Pa.C.S. § 1921(c) (providing that when there is statutory ambiguity, it may be resolved by consideration of, *inter alia*, the former law); *Commonwealth v. Shaffer*, 734 A.2d 840, 843–44 (Pa. 1999) (providing that a subsequent amendment cannot retroactively define legislative intent in the pre-amendment provision). Third, the Commonwealth argues that to the extent this Court considers this particular change in the law to be relevant, it represented not a change in intent, but a clarification and reinforcement of the existing intent. *See, e.g., Commonwealth v. Corporan*, 613 A.2d 530, 531 (Pa. 1992). Finally, the Commonwealth notes that notwithstanding earlier prosecutorial reluctance to bring criminal charges against church officials, the 2005 Grand Jury Report itself stated that actions of Archdiocesan officials clearly constituted endangerment of the welfare of children, but recommended amending the statute to clarify that a Church official not in contact with a child may nevertheless be supervising the welfare of a child.

Appellee responds to the Commonwealth's arguments by relying on the statutory language, the Superior Court's analysis, and the 2007 amendment to the EWOC statute. Appellee argues, based on the statutory language, that the requirements of "supervising the welfare of a child" and "violating a duty of care" are distinct. As support, Appellee relies primarily on *Commonwealth v. Brown*, 721 A.2d 1105, 1107 (Pa.Super. 1998), where the Superior Court rejected the defendant's argument that he was not supervising the welfare of a child because he had no duty to report the child abuse he witnessed, stating that "person" and "duty" were two elements, not one, *id.* at 1107 & n.3.

Appellee further purports to rely on the plain language of the pre-amended EWOC statute to argue that that because the phrase "a person supervising the welfare of a child" follows the words "parent or guardian," it applies exclusively to individuals who stand in the place of parents. *See, e.g., Commonwealth v. Martir*, 712 A.2d 327, 330 (Pa.Super. 1998) (Beck, J., concurring) (nothing that EWOC is contained in Article D of the Crimes Code, entitled "Offenses Against the Family" as opposed to "Offenses Against the Person"). In this respect, Appellee asserts that appellate courts have only applied the EWOC statute to parents or parental surrogates. *See, e.g., Commonwealth v. Kellam*, 719 A.2d 792, 796 (Pa.Super. 1998) (affirming a conviction for EWOC and stating that the statute applies to babysitters and others who have permanent or temporary custody and control of a child); *Commonwealth v. Brown*, 721 A.2d 1105, n.6 (Pa.Super. 1998) (opining that "[p]roof that such adults were actually supervising a child requires evidence that the adult was involved with the child.").

Additionally, Appellee argues that every EWOC conviction in reported cases has arisen out of the defendant's involvement with a particular child rather than a nonspecific class of possible victims. *See, e.g., Commonwealth v. Smith*, 956 A.2d 1029 (Pa.Super. 2008) (father convicted of EWOC for abusing his own child over whom he had exclusive supervisory control); *Commonwealth v. Trippett*, 932 A.2d 188 (Pa.Super. 2007) (defendant convicted of EWOC for abuse he perpetrated against a child with whom he lived and directly supervised). Considering this case law, Appellee argues that he was not a supervisor of any child under the EWOC statute because he had no direct contact with any children.... Like the Superior Court, Appellee finds *Halye* particularly persuasive. According to Appellee, by focusing on the fact that the defendant in *Halye* had neither been asked to supervise the children nor expected to do so, the Superior Court therein indicated that actual supervision of the child is essential to EWOC liability. Because Appellee neither met D.G. nor knew of him, Appellee argues he, like the defendant in *Halye*, could not be a person supervising D.G.'s welfare.

Turning away from the Superior Court's analysis and to the 2007 amendment of the EWOC statute, and to how it bears on our interpretation of the pre-amendment language, Appellee relies on the Commonwealth's prosecutorial decisions prior to bringing charges against Appellee. Specifically, in 2005, following the Grand Jury Report, the District Attorney's Office indicated in a report that high level Archdiocesan officials were far removed from direct contact with children. The Grand Jury Report and the District Attorney's decision not to prosecute at that time prompted the legislative amendment effective 2007. These circumstances, and the concurrence of legislators who advocated for the amendment, indicate, in Appellee's mind, that there was consensus that his conduct was outside the reach of the EWOC statute. Appellee suggests that the District Attorney's Office cannot now change course, and is bound by its prior decision that it could not hold him accountable for his conduct as a supervisor. In this respect, Appellee argues that the Commonwealth's 2011 decision to charge him under the 1995 version of the EWOC statute belies its present argument that the 2007 statute was merely a clarification of the prior version.[25]

According to Appellee, the 2007 amendment was necessary to expand the reach of the statute to add a class of persons not originally subject to liability: "a person that employs or supervises" an individual who is directly responsible for the welfare of a child. *See Masland v. Bachman*, 374 A.2d 517, 521 (Pa. 1977) ("[A] change in the language of a statute ordinarily indicates a change in legislative intent."). Appellee argues that the new language of the amendment would be rendered superfluous if it has the same meaning as the pre-amended statute. *See Commonwealth v. Dixon*, 53 A.3d 839, 845–46 (Pa.Super. 2012) ("Where certain things are designated in a statute, all omissions should be understood as exclusions," as the "General Assembly [is] more than capable of drafting [the statute to include what it wishes to include].")....

[W]e turn to the language of the 1995 statute, which defines EWOC as follows: "A parent, guardian, or other person supervising the welfare of a child under 18 years of age commits an offense if he knowingly endangers the welfare of the child by violating a duty of care, protection or support." 18 Pa.C.S. §4304 (1995).... [footnote omitted]. In commenting on this statute, the Pennsylvania Joint State Government Commission stated that the offense "involves the endangering of the physical or moral welfare of a child by an act or omission in violation of legal duty even though such legal duty does not itself carry a criminal sanction." *Mack*, 359 A.2d at 771. As Appellee was neither parent nor guardian, the Commonwealth had to prove that he fell within "other person supervising the welfare of a child...."

Although the Commonwealth argues that the statutory element requiring one to be "a parent, guardian or other person supervising the welfare of a child ..." is defined by whether that person has a "duty of care, protection or support," so that the elements of

---

25. Specifically, Appellee argues that a clarification in the law would not implicate *ex post facto* concerns, and the Commonwealth therefore would have been free to pursue charges under the 2007 version notwithstanding that Appellee's criminal conduct took place years before.

supervision and duty are entwined, we find it unnecessary to resolve the merit of this proposition. Appellee's sufficiency challenge was confined to whether he could be criminally liable for "supervising the welfare of a child" in the absence of direct supervision of children. The Commonwealth's issue on appeal is whether the evidence was insufficient to prove EWOC because Appellee did not have direct contact with children.

Therefore, whether Appellee owed a duty of care to the children of St. Jerome's, or to D.G. in particular, is not an issue in this appeal and was not encompassed within our grant of allowance of appeal. Rather, the legal issue we address concerns solely whether the evidence sufficed to prove Appellee's supervision of the welfare of a child. While we recognize that the answer to this question will in most circumstances be informed by exploring the extent of the duty owed to the endangered child, we need not engage in such an exploration herein; nor do we wade into an unnecessary review of the trial court's conclusions regarding other elements of EWOC, including that the Commonwealth's evidence sufficed to prove that Appellee was aware of his duty of care, protection or support, that he violated this duty, or that he knowingly endangered the welfare of a child, because, again, these questions are beyond our grant of allowance of appeal.

Focusing on the supervision element, the statute is plain and unambiguous that it is not the child that Appellee must have been supervising, but the child's welfare, including that of D.G. As the Pennsylvania Joint State Government Commission observed, welfare encompasses the physical or moral welfare of a child. 18 Pa.C.S. §4304 (comment); *Mack*, 359 A.2d at 771. And as the Superior Court observed, "welfare" is defined by the American Heritage Dictionary as "health, happiness, or prosperity; well-being," and by Black's Law Dictionary as "[w]ell-being in any respect; prosperity." *Lynn*, 83 A.2d at 453 (citing American Heritage Dictionary 923 (4th ed. 2001) and Black's Law Dictionary 1625 (8th ed. 1999)). By requiring supervision of the child's welfare rather than of the child, the statute endeavors to safe-guard the emotional, psychological, and physical well-being of children.

Because that which is supervised is the child's physical or moral welfare, the Commonwealth's evidence must demonstrate just that: Appellee was supervising the welfare of a child, here, D.G., as well as other unnamed minors. Indeed, criminal liability does not turn on whether the offender was supervising D.G. or the other children of St. Jerome's, a construction which would render meaningless the precise statutory language encompassing the child's welfare. Moreover, the requirement of supervision is not limited to only certain forms of supervision, such as direct or actual, as the Superior Court held. By its plain terms it encompasses all forms of supervision of a child's welfare. Respectfully, the Superior Court disregarded this plain language when it attempted to modify it with the qualifiers of direct or actual supervision of children. Further, as the Commonwealth correctly argues, supervision is routinely accomplished through subordinates, and is no less supervisory if it does not involve personal encounters with the children. Like Appellee, school principals and managers of day care centers supervise the welfare of the children under their care through their management of others. Depending upon the facts, they could be criminally liable for endangering the welfare of the children under their supervision if they knowingly place sexually abusive employees in such proximity to them as to allow for the abuse of these youth.

Simply put, Appellee did not safeguard the physical and moral welfare of D.G. by placing Rev. Avery, a known child molester, in a position to molest him. For all his legal gyrations, it was precisely this conduct that brought Appellee within the class of individuals subject to criminal liability for EWOC: by his own concession, he supervised the welfare of the children of the Archdiocese, including D.G., and knowingly endangered D.G.'s welfare by placing Rev. Avery in a location and situation that gave him free license to abuse D.G.

Specifically, examining the supervision element against the facts presented, we agree with the Commonwealth that extensive evidence established that Appellee was supervising the welfare of D.G. and other children of the Archdiocese in his capacity as Secretary for Clergy because he was uniquely responsible for safeguarding all of their physical and moral welfare, and he supervised and directed the priests who directly interacted with them. The evidence demonstrates that in his position as Secretary for Clergy, Appellee was the "point man" in the Archdiocese to address allegations of sexual abuse by clergy, spending much of his time in this endeavor. According to Appellee's trial testimony, he considered protecting children, including D.G., to be the most important part of his job, a duty that encompassed investigating reports of sexual misconduct by Archdiocesan priests, including the sexual abuse of children in the Archdiocese, and acting to protect them by determining whether to remove a priest from ministry so "children could be taken out of his way." ... It was Appellee's responsibility "to ensure that no child would be hurt." ...

The Commonwealth's evidence established that despite being responsible for responding to sexual abuse allegations against priests for the purpose of protecting the welfare of D.G. and other children, Appellee mollified victims of sexual abuse by falsely telling them their allegations were being seriously investigated and that the particular priest would never again be assigned around children, despite knowing that the priests under his supervision would merely be reassigned to another parish with no ministry restrictions on contact with children; he informed parishioners that the priests he transferred were moved for health reasons, leaving the welfare of children in jeopardy; he routinely disregarded treatment recommendations for priests; he failed to inform the relocated priest's new supervisor about abuse allegations; he took no action to ensure that the abusive priest was kept away from children at his new assignment; he suppressed complaints and concerns by the colleagues of the priests; all with the knowledge that sexually abusive priests rarely had only one victim and that all of these actions would endanger the welfare of the diocese's children, including D.G. Finally, and even more egregiously, when Appellee was contacted by law enforcement, he misrepresented facts to thwart their investigation of these priests, and their crimes.

Examining his conduct specifically in relation to Rev. Avery and D.G., the evidence established that Appellee endangered D.G.'s welfare by facilitating the living arrangement that gave Rev. Avery access to him, while believing Rev. Avery to be "guilty of sexual misconduct with minors." The information that convinced Appellee that Rev. Avery was "guilty of sexual misconduct with minors" involved the allegations brought by R.F. in 1992 and Rev. Avery's admission that "it could be" that the events described by R.F. occurred under the influence of alcohol.... When Appellee referred Rev. Avery for mental health treatment at St. John Vianney prior to placing him in proximity to D.G., Appellee failed to provide details of the sexual abuse and focused instead of Rev. Avery's propensity to consume alcohol. Despite the warnings of the staff at St. John Vianney that they were concerned about other victims, that Rev. Avery should be placed in an assignment that excluded children, and Rev. Avery's own admission that the conduct R.F. reported "must have happened," Appellee initially recommended that Rev. Avery be made associate pastor at a parish with a grade school. When Cardinal Bevilacqua rejected this recommendation, Appellee found a chaplaincy for him that included housing away from children, but, at Rev. Avery's request, Appellee petitioned Cardinal Bevilacqua to allow Rev. Avery to live instead in the rectory of St. Jerome's Church, a parish with a grade school and where D.G. was to become an altar boy.

Appellee instructed Father Graham that Rev. Avery was not to be around children, but that Rev. Avery was to offer his assistance at the parish, which necessarily brought him into regular contact with children acting as altar boys, including D.G..Although Father Graham was purportedly assigned to help monitor Rev. Avery, he did not understand himself to be Rev. Avery's supervisor. Other priests in the rectory believed Rev. Avery was there because of overwork. Appellee did not warn parishioners of St. Jerome's about Rev. Avery, and informed his former parishioners that his departure was for health reasons.

When Rev. Avery's associate at the hospital reported to Appellee that Rev. Avery's disc jockeying priorities were consuming much of his time, the same grooming behavior in which he had engaged with regard to R.F. prior to sexually abusing him, Appellee disregarded these warning signs. Appellee did nothing even when R.F. expressed shock at seeing Rev. Avery disc jockeying a dance in 1998, and when Appellee became aware that Rev. Avery was minimizing his sexual abuse of R.F. He further instructed Father Kerper, who had reported Rev. Avery's behavior to Appellee, to take his complaints about Rev. Avery to the hospital, not the Archdiocese.

Several months before D.G. began to train to serve Mass at St. Jerome's, and to fall victim to Rev. Avery's deviant proclivities, Dr. Pellegrini expressed concern that Rev. Avery's behavior indicated there was potential "for further acting out," ... and after meeting with Rev. Avery on April 2, 1998, Appellee perceived that Rev. Avery was minimizing his treatment and the allegations against him. Yet he did nothing to prevent Rev. Avery from further "acting out." ... Indeed, it was shortly after Dr. Pellegrini voiced his concern, R.F. expressed shock at seeing Rev. Avery disc jockeying a dance, and Appellee perceived that Rev. Avery was once again minimizing his need for treatment and the sexual abuse — 57 allegations against him, that Rev. Avery sexually abused D.G. In early 1999, after school one afternoon, Rev. Avery pulled D.G. aside and instructed him that their "sessions" were about to begin. A week later, following Mass, Rev. Avery asked the boy to stay behind. Once everyone left, Rev. Avery took D.G. to the sacristy and sexually assaulted him, repeating this behavior again about two weeks later.

The plain reading and common sense of the phrase "supervising the welfare of a child" leaves little doubt that Appellee's actions constituted endangerment of D.G., whose welfare he was responsible for safeguarding. Further, the broad protective purpose of the statute, the common sense of the community, and the sense of decency, propriety, and morality which most people entertain, coalesce and are actualized in our conclusion that Appellee's particular conduct is rendered criminal in accord with the EWOC statute. *See Mack*, 359 A.2d at 772; *Randall*, 133 A.2d at 280. Viewing the evidence in the light most favorable to the Commonwealth as verdict winner, the Commonwealth proved beyond a reasonable doubt that as Secretary for Clergy Appellee's day-to-day responsibilities involved receiving allegations of clergy sexual abuse and reacting to them for the protection of the children of the Archdiocese from harm by sexually abusive priests over whose assignments Appellee exercised significant influence. Appellee endangered the welfare of D.G., whose well-being he supervised, when he placed Rev. Avery in a position to have access to him.

The Superior Court below faulted the trial court in this case for failing to consider *Halye*, which it found to be directly on point and in conflict with the trial court's reasoning that actual/direct supervision of a child is not required for an EWOC conviction under the 1995 version of the statute. *Lynn*, 83 A.3d at 451. *Halye*, however, is factually distinct and not persuasive for the Superior Court's conclusion that supervision has to be direct or actual. The defendant in *Halye* was a mere visitor to the house of the child whose welfare he was convicted of endangering; he had no supervisory authority over anyone. *Halye*, 719 A.2d at 765. The children's parents were home, and were supervising their children's welfare. *Id.* *Halye* signifies nothing with respect to the element of supervision and merely held that one's conduct in molesting a child they happened upon, while serious criminal behavior, is not the conduct the EWOC statute was designed to criminalize. The Superior Court's criticism of the trial court for failing to consider *Halye* was not only uncalled for, but the Superior Court's analysis of the controlling nature of that case was incorrect.

Nor are we persuaded by Appellee's reliance on the 2005 Grand Jury Report reflecting the belief that the 1995 EWOC statute could not reach his conduct, the prior Philadelphia District Attorney's decision not to prosecute due to the same belief, or the subsequent legislative amendment of the penal statute. The decisions of neither the grand jury nor a prior District Attorney prove the meaning of the EWOC statute, which is determined by analyzing the plain language contained therein. What the members of the grand jury or the prior District Attorney believed about the scope of the statute is irrelevant.

So too is the legislature's subsequent amendment of the statute. First, legislative history is not to be consulted where, as here, the statute is explicit. 1 Pa.C.S. § 1921. We have applied the plain language of the relevant, pre-amendment statute to hold that it did not exclude those who supervised the welfare of a child, regardless of whether they directly supervised the child. Appellee cannot avoid the plain language by relying on a subsequent amendment. A subsequent change in language does not retroactively alter the legislative intent that is apparent in the plain language of the prior version of the statute.... Legislative history is generally understood to encompass a retrospective review of the legislative consideration of a statute, not a review of the oxymoronic subsequent legislative history. *See, e.g., Sullivan v. Finkelstein*, 496 U.S. 617, 631 (1990) (Scalia, J., concurring) ("The legislative history of a statute is the history of its consideration and enactment. 'Subsequent legislative history'—which presumably means the postenactment history of a statute's consideration and enactment—is a contradiction in terms."). We cannot discern the legislative intent of the General Assembly that passed the relevant, prior version of the EWOC statute by examining the intent of the General Assembly that amended that statute. *See Axe Science Corp. v. Commonwealth*, 293 A.2d 617, 620 (Pa.Cmwlth. 1972) (" ... to hold that subsequently drafted amendatory legislation ... can somehow demonstrate a legislative intent as to the previously enacted legislation ... would be to hold that legislators in a subsequent legislative session could be permitted to indicate the legislative intent of legislators at a prior legislative session ..."). Further, while the former version of a statute is relevant to discern the legislative intent of a later version when the statutory language is ambiguous, the inverse is not true. *See* 1 Pa.C.S. § 1921(c)(5) (providing that when the words of the statute are not explicit, the General Assembly's intent may be ascertained by considering, among other things, the former law).

Finally, Appellee argues that the EWOC statute has not heretofore been applied to someone like himself, who did not come into contact with the children whose welfare he endangered. We find this argument to be inconsequential and irrelevant. Our analysis of the plain language of the EWOC statute and examination of whether the voluminous facts of record met the supervision element of the offense are not dependent on the factual circumstances that led to convictions in prior cases.

The Superior Court erred in holding that the EWOC statute required evidence of direct supervision of children and overturning Appellee's conviction on that basis. The Commonwealth's evidence sufficed to show that that Appellee was a person supervising the welfare of many children, including D.G. Because we conclude that the Commonwealth's evidence was sufficient to sustain the conviction for EWOC as a principal, we do not address the separate contention that the evidence was insufficient to sustain the EWOC conviction as an accomplice. The Order of the Superior Court is reversed, and the matter is remanded for further proceedings consistent with this opinion.

Former Chief Justice Castille did not participate in the decision of this case.

Mr. Justice Eakin, Madame Justice Todd and Mr. Justice Stevens join the opinion.

Mr. Chief Justice Saylor files a dissenting opinion.

MR. CHIEF JUSTICE SAYLOR[:]

Because I differ with the majority's interpretation of the endangerment statute reposed in Section 4304(a) of the Crimes Code, I respectfully dissent.... Preliminarily, the evidence viewed favorably to the Commonwealth suggests that Appellee is indeed guilty of gross derelictions which caused widespread harm. The only question before the Court, however, is whether the text of the endangerment statute, as it existed in the pre-amendment timeframe, allowed the imposition of criminal culpability upon Appellee. For the reasons which follow, I would find that it did not.

The statute makes it an offense for a "parent, guardian or other person supervising the welfare of a child" to knowingly endanger a child's welfare by violating a duty of care, protection, or support. 18 Pa.C.S. § 4304(a) (1995).... The principal issue in this appeal pertains to the "supervision" element of the pre-amendment offense. The question is whether that element was directed to a person who supervised *other people* who were responsible for supervising a child's welfare, since there is little evidence that Appellee directly supervised the welfare of any child at Saint Jerome's Church or elsewhere....

In the present context, there is, to my mind, substantial doubt that the preamendment statute was intended to apply to individuals such as Appellee. It is true that Appellee was obligated to protect children from sexually-abusive priests. However, I find persuasive the Superior Court's explanation that this amounted to a duty on the part of Appellee, which is to be distinguished from supervision. *See Commonwealth v. Lynn*, 83 A.3d 434, 453 (Pa. Super. 2013). Additionally, the two examples provided by the Legislature— parents and guardians—are in a very different position from Appellee relative to the children under their care. *See generally Commonwealth v. Russo*, 594 Pa. 119, 130, 934 A.2d 1199, 1206 (2007) (noting that under the doctrine of *ejusdem generis*, a general phrase "should be construed in light of the particular words preceding it"). Although these factors may not be determinative of legislative intent, they demonstrate the existence of an ambiguity as to whether the pre-amendment statute was meant to subsume supervisors-of-supervisors such as Appellee. That being the case, I would resolve the ambiguity in Appellee's favor consistent with the foregoing discussion.

Finally, Appellee cannot, in my view, have been validly convicted as an accomplice because the accomplice statute requires an intent to promote or facilitate the offense in question. *See* 18 Pa.C.S. § 306(c).... Although, as observed, Appellee may have been substantially derelict in his obligations, as I read the record there were no facts placed before the jury by which it could reasonably conclude he affirmatively intended that children's welfare be endangered.

Notes

Lynn's testimony at his trial implicated Cardinal Anthony J. Bevilacqua, under whom Lynn served. Bevilacqua is alleged to have ordered aides to destroy files of priests accused of sexual abuse and, as described in the *Lynn* Record, was as complicit as Lynn through his authority over him. However, Bevilacqua died before charges could be brought against him. Like Cardinal Bevilacqua, many priests who abused children die before charges are brought, while others voluntarily leave the priesthood and move on to other cities and professions, although relocation is no bar to prosecution or civil liability for past crimes. For commentary on these issues, see Paul Madrid, *The Liability of Catholic Parishes in America: What Went Wrong and How to Fix It*, 28 REV. LITIG. 707 (2009).

As focus on the scandals within the Catholic Church continue to reveal deeper institutional negligence for the mishandling and, often, concealment, of complaints of clergy misconduct, prosecutors in Minnesota took the nearly unprecedented step of filing criminal charges against the Archdiocese of St. Paul and Minneapolis. The criminal charges that accompany a civil complaint stem from abuse perpetrated by Curtis Wehmeyer, who sexually abused three underage males after providing them with drugs and alcohol, between 2008 and 2010, but for which parishioners voiced concerns since 2001. *See* Mitch Smith, *Catholic Archdiocese in Minnesota Charged Over Sex Abuse by Priest*, N.Y. TIMES, June 5, 2015, available at http://www.nytimes.com/2015/06/06/us/catholic-archdiocese-in-minnesota-charged-over-sex-abuse-by-priest.html (last accessed June 29, 2015). Wehmeyer was defrocked as a priest and sentenced to five years in prison in 2013. *Id.* The six criminal charges filed against the Archdiocese are misdemeanors with a maximum fine of $3,000 each. *Id.* As a result of the charges, Archbishop John C. Nienstedt and Auxiliary Bishop Lee A. Piché resigned from their posts within the Archdiocese. *See* Mitch Smith and Laurie Goodstein, *2 Bishops Resign in Minnesota Over Sexual Abuse Scandal*, N.Y. TIMES, June 15, 2015, available at http://www.nytimes.com/2015/06/15/us/archbishop-nienstedt-and-aide-resign-in-minnesota-over-sex-abuse-scandal.html?_r=0 (last visited June 29, 2015).

The criminal charges against the Archdiocese of St. Paul and Minneapolis were filed shortly after the Supreme Court of Pennsylvania reversed the Superior Court and reinstated William Lynn's conviction. At the time that Lynn's conviction had been overturned by the Pennsylvania Superior Court in 2013, however, the sexual abuse scandal at Penn State University was already grounded in media attention, not only with respect to the case of Jerry Sandusky, who perpetrated the abuse, but for Penn State officials who were complicit in covering it up, and who, like William Lynn, were also charged with endangering the welfare of a child. Consider what effect the Pennsylvania Supreme Court's decision in the *Lynn* case, in April 2015, would have had in the case against Sandusky and the institutional authorities at Penn State.

C. Educational Institutions: Penn State University

The Penn State sex abuse scandal involves former Penn State football coordinator Jerry Sandusky, who sexually abused numerous young boys between 1994 and 2009. Sandusky groomed his victims through "The Second Mile," which was a charity organization for troubled boys that Sandusky founded in 1977. The scandal also involved several Penn State University officials—University President Graham Spanier, senior Vice President Gary Schultz, Athletic Director Tim Curly, and Head Football Coach Joe Paterno—who were alleged to have violated their moral, ethical, and legal obligations to report Sandusky's abuse. A grand jury investigation began in 2008 and continued until 2011. *See Sandusky Grand Jury Presentment*, available at http://www.washingtonpost.com/wp-srv/sports/documents/sandusky-grand-jury-report11052011.html (last accessed Apr. 29, 2015).

In November 2011, Sandusky was arraigned on 48 criminal counts of child sexual abuse but was released on $100,000 bail; Curley, who was fired, and Schultz, who resigned from his position, were charged with one count of felony perjury and one count of failure to report abuse allegations. Paterno announced that he planned to retire after the 2011 football season but, within hours of his announcement, Paterno was fired, effective immediately, along with University President Graham Spanier, who later claimed that he had never been informed of any incident involving Sandusky.

Also in November 2011, Penn State University hired former FBI Director Louis Freeh to conduct an investigation into the school's response to the sexual abuse allegations. *See Report of the Special Investigative Counsel Regarding the Actions of the Pennsylvania State University Related to the Child Sexual Abuse Committed by Gerald A. Sandusky*, available at http://www.nytimes.com/interactive/2012/07/12/sports/ncaafootball/13pennstate-document.html?_r=0 (last accessed Apr. 29, 2015). The report concluded that Spanier, Schultz, Curley, and Paterno knew about allegations of Sandusky's sexual abuse of children as early as 1998 and were complicit in failing to disclose them, which empowered Sandusky to continue sexually abusing children.

In December 2011, Sandusky was arrested and charged with additional charges for involuntary deviate sexual intercourse, unlawful contact with a minor, indecent assault, endangering the welfare of a child, and corruption of a minor; he was released on $250,000 bail and placed under house arrest. Coach Joe Paterno died in January 2012, and Sandusky's trial began in June 2012. For a discussion of the effect of the case on Joe Paterno's legacy, see Brian R. Gallini, *Bringing Down A Legend: How An "Independent" Grand Jury Ended Joe Paterno's Career*, 80 Tenn. L. Rev. 705 (2013). During the trial, one of Sandusky's six adopted children raised allegations of abuse against Sandusky; he later reached a settlement agreement with Sandusky, along with six other victims. On June 22, 2012, Sandusky was found guilty of 45 of the 48 counts against him involving child sexual abuse. On October 9, 2012, Sandusky was sentenced to 30–60 years in prison. In November 2012, criminal charges for endangering the welfare of a child were brought against President Spanier, Vice President Schultz, and Athletic Director Curley. As of April 2015, the cases have not yet been scheduled for trial but are expected to take place by 2016.

Several civil law suits were filed, naming Sandusky, Penn State, The Second Mile, and school officials Spanier, Curley, and Schultz, as liable for the sexual abuse that occurred. In October 2013, Penn State University reached settlement agreements, totaling nearly $60 million, with 26 victims. *See* Ellen M. Bublick, *Who Is Responsible for Child Sexual Abuse? A View from the Penn State Scandal*, 17 J. Gender, Race & J. 297 (2014); John G. Culhane, *Sandusky's Victims: Compensation, Vindication, and Blame*, 22 Widener L.J. 589 (2013). Based on the Freeh Report, the NCAA imposed on the Penn State football program the most severe sanctions ever imposed on an NCAA member school, but many of the sanctions were later rescinded. The case opinion that follows deals with the consequences of those sanctions. President Graham Spanier has filed a civil defamation suit against Louis Freeh over the allegations in the Report. *See Spanier v. Freeh*, 95 A.3d 342 (Pa. Sup. Ct. 2014) (ordering Stay of proceedings until criminal matters are resolved).

Commonwealth v. National Collegiate Athletic Association

United States District Court, Middle District of Pennsylvania, 2013
2013 WL 2450291

YVETTE KANE, Chief Judge....

This case finds its origins in sanctions imposed against the football program at the Pennsylvania State University (Penn State) by the governing body of college sports, the NCAA. Penn State agreed to the sanctions at issue here and waived any legal challenge to the sanctions or the manner in which they were adopted. The Governor of the Commonwealth of Pennsylvania brings this antitrust action on behalf of the natural citizens of Pennsylvania, challenging the sanctions under Section 1 of the Sherman Act as an unlawful agreement to restrain trade and seeks an order enjoining enforcement of the sanctions. Penn State is not a party to this action and takes no position in this litigation....

The challenged sanctions were imposed following a widely publicized child sex abuse scandal that implicated Penn State officials. On November 4, 2011, after an extensive grand jury investigation into horrific allegations that former Penn State assistant football coach Gerald A. Sandusky sexually abused children for over a decade, Sandusky was criminally charged.... That same day, charges were brought against senior Penn State officials alleged to have covered up the Sandusky accusations in an effort to protect the university's football program; these officials included Penn State Athletic Director Timony M. Curley and Penn State Senior Vice-President of Finance and Business Gary C. Schultz.... Shortly thereafter, Defendant NCAA issued a letter to Penn State President Rodney Erickson demanding that the university produce information related to the grand jury indictment to assist the NCAA in its review of Penn State's response to the sexual abuse scandal.... Following the initiation of these criminal charges, the law firm of Freeh, Sporkin & Sullivan LLP was charged with investigating and reporting the failure of Penn State personnel to respond to and report to authorities the sexual abuse of children (Freeh Report)....

On June 22, 2012, after a three-week trial, a jury in the Court of Common Pleas of Centre County found Sandusky guilty of 45 counts of the criminal charges against him.[2] ... Approximately one month later, Freeh, Sporkin & Sullivan LLP issued its findings. The Freeh Report confirmed that senior Penn State officials had collaborated to conceal accusations that Sandusky sexually abused children, and that Penn State leadership had exhibited a "total and consistent disregard ... for the safety of Sandusky's victims" and worked together to conceal Sandusky's crimes for fear of bad publicity and out of sympathy for Sandusky. The Freeh Report described Penn State's culture as including an "excessive focus on athletics" and cited the failure of former President Spanier, former head football coach Joe Paterno, and former Athletic Director Tim Curley to protect children as not only "reveal[ing] numerous individual failings," but also "reveal[ing] weaknesses of the University's culture, governance, administration, compliance policies and procedures for protecting children." ... The university accepted full responsibility for the failure of its administration to protect the victims abused by Sandusky, and began the process of implementing many of the recommendations contained in the Freeh Report....

Following the publication of the Freeh Report, Defendant NCAA initiated sanctions against Penn State. At the direction of NCAA President Dr. Mark Emmert, the NCAA's established disciplinary procedures were bypassed and the matter was directed to the NCAA's Executive Committee and the Division I Board of Directors.... Dr. Emmert, along with the NCAA Executive Committee and Division I Board of Directors, informed Penn State that if it did not accept Defendant's proposed consent decree and sanctions, Defendant would impose the football "death penalty" on the school for a period of four

---

2. On November 1, 2012, the Attorney General of Pennsylvania announced that former Penn State officials Curley and Schultz, and former Penn State President Graham Spanier, had been indicted by a grand jury on charges of perjury, conspiracy, obstruction of justice, and child endangerment in connection with their alleged role in covering up Sandusky's crimes. [At the time of this decision, these] cases ha[d] not yet been brought to trial....

years.[3] ... The proposed consent decree, which accepted as true the findings contained in the Freeh Report, justified the imposition of the proposed sanctions on the basis of Penn State's failure to value and uphold Defendant's principles of institutional integrity, responsible conduct, and individual integrity....

By its terms, the consent decree: (1) required that Penn State pay a $60 million dollar fine into an endowment for sexual abuse education and sexual abuse victims over a period of five years; (2) banned Penn State from football post-season play for a period of four years; (3) reduced the number of football scholarships that Penn State was authorized to offer from 85 to 65 total scholarships per year for a period of four years, and 25 to 15 initial scholarships per year for a period of four years; (4) placed Penn State on probation for four years, necessitating the appointment of an on-campus integrity monitor; (5) vacated Penn State's football wins between 1998 and 2011; (6) waived the NCAA's bylaw restricting transfer of student athletes from Penn State to other colleges; and (7) required that Penn State permit football players to retain their athletic scholarships regardless of whether they continued to play football....

On July 23, 2012, Penn State President Rodney Erickson accepted the terms of the consent decree, and waived any claim to further process or appeal under NCAA rules and any judicial process related to the subject matter of the consent decree.... Though widely debated elsewhere, the wisdom of President Erickson's decision is not a question for this Court, nor is the relative fairness of the sanctions selected by the NCAA to address the university's admitted failings in the Sandusky matter. The complaint limits this Court's review to the question of whether Plaintiff has articulated a violation of federal antitrust law....

Before this Court for resolution is a discrete claim by Governor Tom Corbett on behalf of the Commonwealth of Pennsylvania that NCAA President Dr. Emmert, and the NCAA Executive Committee and Division I Board of Directors, participated in an unlawful antitrust conspiracy designed to destroy Penn State as an athletic competitor and cause a cascading economic fallout throughout Pennsylvania. The Governor's complaint is an impassioned indictment of the sanctions against Penn State. Citing the complete lack of authority by the NCAA President and its Executive Committee and Division I Board of Directors to involve themselves in disciplinary matters, and the unprecedented imposition of sanctions to address actions that did not directly affect student athletes or member competitiveness, the Governor condemns the NCAA's sanctions as "arbitrary and capricious," and personally motivated by a new NCAA President who was out to make a name for himself at Penn State's expense.

As the complaint observes, these allegations were the subject of lively debate in the court of public opinion. They are not the subject of the Governor's claim for relief, and are not before the Court for a review on their merits. The Court emphasizes that the Commonwealth's legal claim in this lawsuit is based only on its allegation that the NCAA is guilty of an antitrust violation. To establish its Section 1 antitrust claim under the Sherman Act, Plaintiff cannot allege just any harm, but must point to harm directed at commercial activity of the type the Sherman Act is designed to address. Further, Plaintiff must establish that Defendant's action affected the kind of antitrust activity over which this Court has jurisdiction....

The NCAA did not respond to the Governor's complaint with an answer, but instead moved to dismiss the complaint under Federal Rule of Civil Procedure 12(b)(6), arguing

---

3. Imposition of the football "death penalty" would have cancelled Penn State's football program for four years.

that the Commonwealth can prove no set of facts that would entitle it to relief. In an all-out blitz, Defendant attacks every aspect of the complaint as bereft of the essential elements of an antitrust claim. First, Defendant objects on the grounds that the singular focus of the Sherman Act is to protect consumers from reduced competition caused by those who would artificially manipulate *commercial* markets. Justifying its imposition of sanctions as within its discretion to protect amateur athletics, Defendant argues that its actions do not merit review under the antitrust laws because it did not seek to regulate commercial activity and Plaintiff does not so allege.

Even assuming that Plaintiffs allegations make out commercial activity, Defendant points out that Plaintiff must still identify the commercial market affected by the alleged wrongdoing and then articulate how the complained-of behavior stifled competition in those markets. Defendant argues that the complaint fails because it does not allege how Plaintiff's identified nationwide markets for post-secondary education, Division I football players, and college football-related memorabilia will be less competitive because of the NCAA's actions against Penn State. Rather, the complaint is driven by the allegation that Penn State as an institution, and all those who rely on its success, will fail to thrive athletically or economically because of the draconian nature of the NCAA sanctions.... Defendant goes on to argue that even were Plaintiff able to articulate a Sherman Act claim (by pleading that the NCAA's actions touch commercial activity and have suppressed competition and injured consumers in the markets for post-secondary education, Division I football players, and college football-related memorabilia), the injuries alleged in the complaint are either remote and not recognizable under antitrust law, or solely impact Penn State, which is not a party to this action. In other words, Defendant asserts that Plaintiff alleges derivative injury, rather than injury suffered from a "competition-reducing" aspect of the allegedly illegal restraint that would qualify it as antitrust injury.... Each of Defendant's arguments is strong enough to render the Governor's action under antitrust law a Hail Mary pass. As the Court explains in some detail below, these arguments are well-founded in the law and require that the Governor's complaint be dismissed....

The threshold question for this Court is whether the alleged NCAA conspiracy to render Penn State's football program less competitive by harshly sanctioning the school constitutes commercial activity under established law, or whether it evades antitrust scrutiny because it is a legitimate enforcement action relating to amateurism and fair play. The Court now turns to the relevant law.... Section 1 of the Sherman Act only applies to conspiracies which restrain "trade or commerce." 15 U.S.C. § 1; *see Klor's, Inc. v. Broadway-Hale Stores, Inc.*, 359 U.S. 207, 213 n. 7, 79 S.Ct. 705, 3 L.Ed.2d 741 (1959). The leading case for the Court is *Smith v. NCAA*, in which the United States Court of Appeals for the Third Circuit held that Defendant's enforcement of its bylaw restricting postgraduate athletic participation did not implicate Section 1 of the Sherman Act. 139 F.3d 180, 185–86 (3d Cir.1998) (rev'd on other grounds). There, a former undergraduate volleyball player applied for a waiver of the NCAA's bylaw prohibiting her from competing at a graduate institution other than the one she competed at as an undergraduate.... [footnote omitted]. *Id.* at 183. The NCAA refused to waive the bylaw, and the player subsequently brought suit, challenging the bylaw as an unreasonable restraint of trade under Section 1 of the Sherman Act. *Id.* at 184.

As a threshold question, the Third Circuit considered whether the challenged action was sufficiently commercial to merit application of the Sherman Act: "[t]he question which we now face ... is whether antitrust laws apply only to the alleged infringer's commercial activities." *Id.* at 185. Reasoning that the bylaw at issue was not related to the NCAA's commercial or business activities, and, recognizing that "the Supreme Court has suggested that antitrust laws are limited in their application to commercial and business endeavors,"[5] the Third Circuit concluded that "the Sherman Act does not apply to the NCAA's promulgation of eligibility requirements." *Id.* at 186. Although *Smith* is limited to eligibility rules, the Third Circuit's reasoning suggests that it would decline to apply the Sherman Act to any NCAA regulation that "primarily seek[s] to ensure fair competition in intercollegiate athletics." *Id.* at 185.... [footnote omitted].

Extending *Smith's* reach beyond eligibility rules, the Eastern District of Pennsylvania held that NCAA bylaws addressing recruiting and accreditation at institutional basketball camps for high school students were non-commercial in nature in *Pocono Invitational Sports Camp, Inc. v. NCAA*, 317 F.Supp.2d 569, 584 (E.D.Pa.2004). Drawing on the evidence presented with the NCAA's motion for summary judgment, the court found that the NCAA had enacted the certification and recruiting requirements at issue in response to college basketball recruiting "becoming a showplace that seemed inconsistent and inappropriate for college athletic recruiters." *Id.* at 583. Accordingly, the court concluded that "when the NCAA promulgated these rules it was acting in a paternalistic capacity to promote amateurism and education. Thus, for the same reasons the Third Circuit found eligibility rules immune from antitrust scrutiny, [the Court] find[s] that these recruiting rules are also immune." *Id.*

In one of the few reported cases involving the application of the "death penalty," players from the University of Arizona sought to enjoin the NCAA's sanctions on both due process grounds and as an antitrust violation. *Justice v. NCAA*, 577 F.Supp. 356, 360 (D.Ariz.1983). The Court denied injunctive relief on both claims. Without addressing the "commercial or non-commercial" nature of the sanction, the court soundly rejected Plaintiff's arguments that the sanctions constituted a Sherman Act violation because it was driven by the NCAA's desire to make the University of Arizona less competitive. *Id.* at 379. Although the court did not analyze whether the regulation was "commercial," the court upheld the sanctions because the regulatory action at issue "pertain[ed] solely to the NCAA's stated goal of preserving amateurism." *Id.* at 380. In other words, there had been "no showing by the plaintiffs that the NCAA, its member institutions, or the Infractions Committee had any purpose to insulate themselves from competition by imposing sanctions on the University of Arizona" for its violations of eligibility and recruiting bylaws. *Id.* at 379. Moreover, the Court noted that "[t]he fact that the sanctions might have an incidental anticompetitive effect on coaches or athletes does not in itself render them unreasonable restraints." *Id.* at 382.

The Court now turns to the parties' arguments on whether Defendant's complained-of conduct falls under the Sherman Act. Defendant urges the Court to find that the consent decree falls squarely within *Smith's* definition of non-commercial activity, and is a lawful exercise of its authority to enforce the standards of amateur play. Defendant emphasizes that the consent decree includes Penn State's admission that it violated Defendant's "basic standards of honesty, ethical conduct, and institutional control that the NCAA and its members deem necessary to preserve the character and integrity of college sports," and argues that these principles are just as focused on the promotion of amateurism and fair play as its rules on recruiting and eligibility, which courts have repeatedly found to be

---

5. In *NCAA v. Board of Regents of the University of Oklahoma*, 468 U.S. 85, 94, 104 S.Ct. 2948, 82 L.Ed.2d 70 (1984), the Supreme Court distinguished between "most of the regulatory controls of the NCAA ... [as] justifiable means of fostering competition among amateur athletic teams," in contrast to the "specific restraints on football telecasts" at issue that violated Section 1. *Id.* at 117, 104 S.Ct. 2948.

non-commercial in nature.... [footnote omitted]. The Court does not agree. Unlike the cases cited by Defendant and discussed by the Court, the factual allegations of conspiracy and state-wide economic fallout at play in this case place the complaint outside previous examples of NCAA enforcement actions related to amateurism and fair play held to be non-commercial.

The Court next turns to Plaintiff, who ambitiously maintains that "[t]he Penn State sanctions fall well on the commercial side of the line." ... In making its argument, Plaintiff urges alternate theories on the Court: first, that the sanctions agreement contains scholarship limits, which have been held to be commercial activity and subject to review under the Sherman Act, and, second, that the sanctions will reduce the Penn State football program's ability to generate revenue for the university.... Plaintiff also argues that the Court must disregard Defendant's purported rationale for imposing the sanctions agreement because Defendant's departure from established enforcement procedures demonstrates that its imposition of the sanctions hides an ulterior motive....

At the outset, the Court will dispense with Plaintiff's two initial arguments. First, the Court finds Plaintiff's argument that scholarship limits constitute commercial activity under the United States Court of Appeals for the Seventh Circuit's opinion in *Agnew v. NCAA* to be unpersuasive. Contrary to the Third Circuit's opinion in *Smith*, which distinguished between non-commercial and commercial activity for the purposes of applying the Sherman Act to Defendant's regulatory activity, the Seventh Circuit held in *Agnew* that the Sherman Act "applies generally" to Defendant's actions. *Agnew v. NCAA*, 683 F.3d 328, 340 (7th Cir.2012). That is not the law in this Circuit, and thus the Court declines to find that the scholarship limits portion of the sanctions agreement is sufficient to render the entire agreement "commercial" on the basis of *Agnew*.

Second, the Court is not persuaded by Plaintiff's alternative argument: that the sanctions agreement is commercial because it will cause Penn State's revenue to decline. There are two fundamental flaws to Plaintiff's approach. First, the Third Circuit rejected this approach in *Smith*, making it clear that any derivative effect of Defendant's regulatory activity is irrelevant to the "commercial nature" inquiry. *See Smith*, 139 F.3d at 185 ("[R]ather than focus on Smith's alleged injuries, we consider the character of the NCAA's activities."). Moreover, as the Court details below, the Governor represents the natural citizens of the Commonwealth as *parens patriae*, not Penn State. Even were Plaintiff able to articulate financial injury to Penn State cognizable under the Sherman Act, the Governor cannot lawfully advance this claim on Penn State's behalf.

Having disposed of Plaintiff's first two points, the Court turns to Plaintiff's more creative argument: that the Court must disregard Defendant's purported non-commercial rationale for imposing sanctions on Penn State because Defendant failed to give the school sufficient due process and had not previously sanctioned any other university for violating its institutional principles outlining honesty and ethical conduct.... In other words, Plaintiff asserts that Defendant's actions are such an aberration that the Court must necessarily find that its proposed rationale is a pretext....

Plaintiff's argument faces two hurdles. First, although Plaintiff makes sweeping allegations that Defendant imposed the sanctions on Penn State for the "purpose of enhancing their own public image at the expense of a competitor," and the NCAA Executive Committee and Division I Board of Directors wanted to "severely cripple a major competitor and irreparably harm the citizens of the Commonwealth," these conclusory allegations, without more, do not permit the Court to draw the *reasonable* inference that Defendant's justification for imposing the sanctions is a pretext. Indeed, Plaintiff offers no facts to support this allegation. *See* [*Bell Atl. Corp. v.*] *Twombly*, 550 U.S. [544] at 556, 127 S.Ct. 1955 [(2007)]. Rather, Plaintiff relies on its contention that Defendant's behavior is so inconsistent with its actions in the past that its rationale for imposing sanctions on Penn State must be a pretext.... This is not enough under *Twombly*.

Not only do Plaintiff's allegations of ulterior motive lack the factual enhancement that would allow the Court to accept them as plausible under the *Twombly* analysis ... [*], the Court is still faced with a more pressing problem: the complaint is fundamentally lacking in allegations that Defendant's alleged ulterior motive hid a commercial purpose.[8] Although Plaintiff alleges that the NCAA sought to improve its own reputation for being soft on discipline by harshly sanctioning Penn State ... and that unidentified members of the Executive Committee and Division I Board of Directors wished to cripple Penn State as an athletic competitor and harm the citizens of the Commonwealth ... the Court finds that these allegations, without any indication that Defendant sought a commercial advantage for itself or sought to regulate commercial activity, are not enough to render Defendant's complained-of conduct commercial. *See Smith*, 139 F.3d at 185.

On review, the Court finds that Plaintiffs argument that the Court can intuit commercial motive from Defendant's actions is deficient under *Twombly*. Moreover, the complaint is devoid of allegations that Defendant sought to regulate commercial activity or obtain any commercial advantage for itself by imposing sanctions on Penn State. *See Smith*, 139 F.3d at 185; *see also Klor's, Inc. v. Broadway-Hale Stores, Inc.*, 359 U.S. 207, 213 n. 7, 79 S.Ct. 705, 3 L.Ed.2d 741 (1959) ("[T]he Act is aimed primarily at combinations having commercial objectives"). Given the benchmark set by *Smith* and its progeny, the Court finds that Plaintiff's allegations do not make out commercial activity subject to the Sherman Act.... Were the Court to find otherwise—that the Sherman Act does apply to Defendant's behavior—Plaintiff must still plow through Defendant's numerous objections to its antitrust claim in order for the complaint to survive. An antitrust plaintiff must plead the following to make out a Section 1 claim: (1) that the defendant was party to a "contract, combination ... or conspiracy," and (2) "that the conspiracy to which the defendant was a party imposed an unreasonable restraint on trade." *Burtch v. Milberg Factors, Inc.*, 662 F.3d 212 (3d Cir.2011) (citation and quotation marks omitted). The Court will look at each element in turn....

The first element—a contract, combination, or conspiracy—requires that a plaintiff allege "some form of concerted action." *Ins. Brokerage*, 618 F.3d at 321. Thus, the plaintiff must allege that the defendants acted with "unity of purpose or a common design and understanding," and "a conscious commitment to a common scheme." *In re Flat Glass Antitrust Litig.*, 385 F.3d 350, 357 (3d Cir.2004) (citation and quotation marks omitted). Without the existence of an agreement reflecting "a meeting of the minds in an unlawful

---

* "[T]o determine the sufficiency of a complaint under *Twombly*..., the Court must do the following: (1) identify the elements a plaintiff must plead to state a claim; (2) identify any conclusory allegations contained in the complaint "not entitled" to the assumption of truth; and (3) determine whether any "well-pleaded factual allegations" contained in the complaint "plausibly give rise to an entitlement for relief." *See Santiago v. Warminster Tp.*, 629 F.3d 121, 130 (3d Cir.2010) (citation and quotation marks omitted)."

Commw. v. NCAA, 2013 WL 2450291 at *4.

8. *See Bassett v. NCAA*, No. 04-425, 2005 WL 3767016, at *3 (E.D.Ky. May 3, 2005) ("Rather than intending to provide the NCAA or any of its member schools with a commercial advantage, enforcement of rules governing recruiting, improper inducements, and academic fraud primarily seek to ensure fair competition") (citation and internal quotation marks omitted).

arrangement," liability under Section 1 is not triggered. *In re Baby Food Antitrust Litig.*, 166 F.3d 112, 117 (3d Cir.1999) (citation and internal quotation marks omitted).

The Court turns to whether Plaintiffs['] allegations of "concerted action" reflect the "conscious commitment to a common scheme" necessary to make out a Section 1 violation. Plaintiff alleges that "[t]he actions by the NCAA, its member institutions, and specifically the institutions represented on the NCAA's executive committee and board of directors, in threatening Penn State with the football "death penalty" and forcing Penn State into accepting the consent decree, constitute concerted action within the meaning of Section 1 of the Sherman Act." ... In support, Plaintiff alleges that "Dr. Emmert took the matter directly to the Executive Committee and Division I Board of Directors" who "chose to seize the opportunity to impose swift and severe sanctions." ... Plaintiff supplies two separate motivations behind this alleged conspiracy: that Defendant was motivated to impose sanctions on Penn State because Defendant wanted to "assert its relevance as a protector of student athletes," and, that unidentified members of Defendant's Executive Committee and the Division I Board of Directors, which were made up of representatives of competitor colleges, wanted to "severely cripple a major competitor and irreparably harm the citizens of the Commonwealth." ...

These allegations fall short of a Section 1 claim, which requires the "existence of an agreement." *Burtch*, 662 F.3d at 221. Putting aside Plaintiff's conclusory allegation that the NCAA's actions "constitute concerted action," the Court cannot find any factual allegations supporting Plaintiff's argument that Defendant engaged in concerted action that would "raise [its] right to relief above the speculative level." *Twombly*, 550 U.S. at 555, 127 S.Ct. 1955. Here, Plaintiff alleges that Dr. Emmert "took the matter" to unidentified members on the Executive Committee and Division I board of directors, who then "seized the opportunity" to impose sanctions on Penn State.... The Court does not find that this allegation, without any supporting factual allegations, rises to the level of "concerted action." Nowhere does Plaintiff allege that Dr. Emmert, and unidentified members of the Division I Board of Directors and Executive Committee, agreed together to punish Penn State in an effort to achieve an unlawful purpose forbidden by the antitrust laws. Returning to *Twombly's* requirement that a plaintiff must plead "factual conduct that allows the court to draw the reasonable inference that the defendant is liable for the misconduct alleged," the Court cannot find any factual allegations supporting Plaintiffs allegation of "concerted action" that might nudge its conspiracy claim into "plausible" territory. *See also Gordon v. Lewistown Hosp.*, 423 F.3d 184, 208 (3d Cir.2005) ("[T]he alleged conspirators [must have] had a conscious commitment to a common scheme designed to achieve an unlawful objective."). Thus, the Court finds that Plaintiff fails to sufficiently plead concerted action....

Even assuming that Plaintiff sufficiently alleged that Defendant engaged in "concerted action," Plaintiff must still defend the challenge to the second element of its claim: that the terms of the consent decree and the manner in which it was imposed constitute an unreasonable restraint on trade. The reasonableness of any restraint on trade is evaluated under one of three standards, depending on the nature of the alleged restraint: (1) rule of reason, (2) quick look, and (3) *per se* illegality.... Plaintiff urges the Court to apply *per se* review, the least rigorous of these standards, which eliminates the need to study the reasonableness of an individual restraint in light of the real market forces at work. *Leegin Creative Leather Prods. v. PSKS, Inc.*, 551 U.S. 877, 886, 127 S.Ct. 2705, 168 L.Ed.2d 623 (2007). Agreements that fall under established *per se* categories of illegality, such as group boycotts and horizontal agreements to fix prices, are "conclusively presumed to unreasonably restrain competition." *Ins. Brokerage*, 618 F.3d at 316 (citation and quotation marks omitted). Under the *per se* standard, the plaintiff need not define a market or allege market power in her complaint, as she would under the rule of reason. *Pace Elec., Inc. v. Canon Computer Sys.*, 213 F.3d 118, 123 (3d Cir.2000).

Plaintiff argues that its complaint justifies application of the *per se* standard because its allegations make out a group boycott: "joint efforts by NCAA members to disadvantage a competitor (Penn State) by directly denying it relationships (full participation in the NCAA) it needs to compete." ... The Court is not persuaded. A group boycott is made out when a plaintiff sufficiently alleges "concerted action with a purpose either to exclude a person or group from the market, or to accomplish some other anti-competitive objective, or both." *See Malley-Duff Assoc., Inc. v. Crown Life Ins. Co.*, 734 F.2d 133, 140 (3d Cir.1984) (citation and quotation marks omitted). Here, as analyzed previously, Plaintiff's allegations fall short of "concerted action." Thus, the Court need not credit Plaintiff's allegations that Defendant and its member institutions' "joint efforts" to disadvantage PSU constitutes a group boycott and thus merits *per se* review.... [footnote omitted].

The Court looks next to quick look review, which may be applied in the exceptional case when an observer with "even a rudimentary understanding of economics" could conclude that the restraint at issue would have an anticompetitive effect on customers and markets. *California Dental Ass'n v. FTC*, 526 U.S. 756, 770, 119 S.Ct. 1604, 143 L.Ed.2d 935 (1999). Examples of restraints justifying quick look review include: an absolute ban on competitive bidding, *Nat'l Soc. of Prof'l Engineers*, 435 U.S. 679, 692, 98 S.Ct. 1355, 55 L.Ed.2d 637 (1978); a horizontal agreement among dentists to withhold a certain service from their customers, *FTC v. Ind. Fed.'n of Dentists*, 476 U.S. 447, 459, 106 S.Ct. 2009, 90 L.Ed.2d 445 (1986); and express output limitations on live telecasts of football games, *NCAA v. Bd. of Regents of the Univ. of Ok.*, 468 U.S. 85, 99–100, 104 S.Ct. 2948, 82 L.Ed.2d 70 (1984). If quick look analysis applies, the Court presumes competitive harm, and the burden is thus placed on the defendant to set forth some competitive justification for the restraint at issue. *Gordon*, 423 F.3d at 210.... Plaintiff's complaint does not outline the exceptional case warranting quick look review, because it does not allege a restraint of the type whose anticompetitive effects are so obvious that even an onlooker with a "rudimentary understanding of economics" could conclude that the sanctions suffered by Penn State would have an "anticompetitive effect on customers and markets." Although Plaintiff alleges that consumers will face anticompetitive effects in the nationwide markets for post-secondary education, Division I football players, and college-football related memorabilia as the probable result of Penn State becoming less competitive as a football program, these speculative allegations do not make out the "obvious" anticompetitive effects that would require quick look analysis.

Having concluded that Plaintiff's complaint demands more than *per se* or quick look review, the Court arrives at the rule of reason.... [footnote omitted]. Under rule of reason analysis, the plaintiff bears the initial burden of demonstrating that the alleged restraint produced an adverse anticompetitive effect within the relevant geographic market. *Gordon*, 423 F.3d at 210. This can be achieved by alleging that the restraint at issue is facially anticompetitive, or, that its enforcement reduced output, raised prices, or reduced quantity. *Id.* If the plaintiff carries this burden, the Court next evaluates whether the alleged anticompetitive effects are justified by any countervailing procompetitive benefits. *Eichorn v. AT & T Corp.*, 248 F.3d 131, 143 (3d Cir.2001).

The Court turns to whether Plaintiff adequately alleges anticompetitive effects in the markets identified in its complaint. Plaintiff outlines three relevant markets allegedly harmed by Defendant's actions: (1) the nationwide market for post-secondary education, which comprises colleges and universities across the United States that offer education at the post-secondary level; (2) the nationwide market for Division I football players, which comprises all NCAA Division I football programs that compete for top football talent emerging from the nation's high schools; and (3) the nationwide market for the sale of college football-related apparel and memorabilia, which comprises the numerous major college athletic programs that compete against each other to build national brands beyond their campus communities ... [.]

Plaintiff argues that it has carried its burden by alleging anticompetitive effects in each of these markets. First, Plaintiff argues that it alleged a "direct effect on output in the market for Division I football players: the temporary reduction in scholarships that Penn State may offer recruits.... Second, Plaintiff argues that it alleged "reduced quality" in the market for post-secondary education, because the complaint alleges that by virtue of denying Penn State football-related revenue, and imposing a $60 million fine, the sanctions are likely to force Penn State to "reduce the availability and/or quality of some of its programs." ... The Court observes that Plaintiff only addressed two of its relevant markets in its brief in opposition: the market for post-secondary education and the market for Division I football players. On review, the Court finds that Plaintiff's allegations fail with respect to both markets under the rule of reason. First, even assuming that Penn State will face difficulty in competing for Division I football players as a result of the sanctions, the antitrust laws are not implicated. The fact that Penn State will offer fewer scholarships over a period of four years does not plausibly support its allegation that the reduction of scholarships at Penn State will result in a market-wide anticompetitive effect, such that the "nation's top scholastic football players" would be unable to obtain a scholarship in the *nationwide* market for Division I football players.

Neither does Plaintiff plausibly allege an anticompetitive effect in the national market for post-secondary education. Plaintiff's argument that Penn State's payment of the $60 million dollar fine, in combination with its diminished football revenue, will likely result in such a significant reduction in the quality of Penn State's programs that competition will be eased in the *nationwide* market for post-secondary education, is simply not plausible. Furthermore, Plaintiff's allegation that the sanctions will result in Penn State raising tuition and reducing its investment in programs and facilities, thereby removing incentive for its competitor schools in the nationwide market to keep tuition low and improve their own facilities, fails for the same reason. Because Plaintiff has not sufficiently alleged anticompetitive effects in the relevant markets identified in its complaint, the Court finds that Plaintiff has failed to carry its burden under the rule of reason. Thus, the Court need not proceed to Defendant's procompetitive justifications....

The Court will now address the parties' final dispute: whether Plaintiff is the proper party to bring this lawsuit under the rules that apply to antitrust actions. The pleadings present three separate points relating to Plaintiff's standing for the Court's review: Plaintiff's authority to bring this action *parens patriae*, the sufficiency of Plaintiff's alleged antitrust injury, and, whether Plaintiff has "antitrust standing." ... The Court begins with whether Plaintiff may bring this action in its *parens patriae* capacity. The doctrine of *parens patriae* standing allows states to bring suit on behalf of their citizens in certain circumstances by asserting an injury to a "quasi-sovereign interest." *Alfred L. Snapp & Son, Inc. v. Puerto Rico, ex rel., Barez*, 458 U.S. 592, 601, 102 S.Ct. 3260, 73 L.Ed.2d 995 (1982). For a state to bring suit in its *parens patriae* capacity in federal court, it must establish that its *parens patriae* interest satisfies both Article III standing and, is a proper basis for suit under the applicable statute.... [footnote omitted]. Article III injury in a suit brought by a state in its *parens patriae* capacity rests on whether the complaint alleges harm to the welfare of that state's citizens, rather than harm to the proprietary interest of the state. Injury to the state's economy or the health and welfare of its citizens, if sufficiently severe and generalized, can give rise to a quasi-sovereign interest in relief justifying an action brought in *parens patriae. See, e.g., Com. of Pa., by Shapp v. Kleppe*, 533 F.2d 668, 674 (D.C.Cir.1976). In this case, Plaintiff alleges that Defendant's behavior has harmed and will continue to harm the natural citizens of Pennsylvania, as well as the Commonwealth's economy. Thus, the Court is satisfied that Plaintiff satisfies Article III's threshold standing requirement.

The Court now turns to the second prong of Plaintiff's *parens patriae* standing: whether the suit is authorized under the applicable statute. It is beyond dispute that federal antitrust law, specifically Section 16 of the Clayton Act,[12] provides statutory authorization for claims brought *parens patriae. Georgia v. Penn. R.R. Co.*, 324 U.S. 439, 447, 65 S.Ct. 716, 89 L.Ed. 1051 (1945); *see also Hawaii v. Standard Oil Co. of Cal.*, 405 U.S. 251, 259, 92 S.Ct. 885, 31 L.Ed.2d 184 (1972). Thus, the Court finds that Plaintiff may seek injunctive relief under Section 16 in its *parens patriae* capacity. However, Plaintiff "must still show that residents on whose behalf it sues have a cause of action" under the antitrust laws, and Plaintiff must adequately allege both an antitrust injury and demonstrate that it has antitrust standing.... [footnote omitted]. The Court will review each requirement.

First, stating a claim under Section 1 of the Sherman Act requires that a plaintiff sufficiently plead an antitrust injury. *See Toledo Mack Sales & Serv. v. Mack Trucks, Inc.*, 530 F.3d 204, 225 (3d Cir.2008). This requirement applies whether a plaintiff is seeking treble damages or injunctive relief; in order to "seek injunctive relief under § 16, a private plaintiff must allege threatened loss or damage of the type the antitrust laws were designed to prevent and that flows from that which makes defendants' acts unlawful." *Cargill, Inc. v. Monfort of Co., Inc.*, 479 U.S. 104, 113, 107 S.Ct. 484, 93 L.Ed.2d 427 (1986) (citing *Brunswick Corp. v. Pueblo Bowl-O-Mat, Inc.*, 429 U.S. 477, 489, 97 S.Ct. 690, 50 L.Ed.2d 701 (1977)). In other words, the alleged injury must be caused by the competition-reducing aspect of the defendant's illegal conduct in order to be considered an "antitrust injury." *W. Penn Allegheny Health System, Inc. v. UPMC*, 627 F.3d 85, 101 (3d Cir.2010). Alleged harms that are causally related to Defendant's complained-of conduct, but are not alleged to have occurred as a result of lessened competition—do not qualify as antitrust injury. *Id.*

Moreover, because antitrust laws aim to protect competition, not competitors, the Court must analyze the antitrust injury from the point of view of the consumer. *Mathews v. Lancaster General Hosp.*, 87 F.3d 624, 641 (3d Cir.1996). Thus, the Court must assess whether the antitrust plaintiff sufficiently alleged that the challenged conduct affected "prices, quantity, or quality of goods and services" in the relevant market, not just his own welfare. *Id.* (citation omitted). It also bears mentioning that "[a]s a general matter, the class of plaintiffs capable of satisfying the antitrust-injury requirement is limited to consumers and competitors in the restrained market," and to "those whose injuries are the means by which the defendants seek to achieve their anticompetitive ends." *W. Penn*, 627 F.3d at 102 (internal citations omitted).

Interrelated with the concept of antitrust injury is the notion of "antitrust standing," which represents the court's evaluation of the relationship between the antitrust plaintiff's alleged injury and the defendant's alleged wrongdoing. *Associated Gen. Contractors of Cal., Inc. v. Cal. State Council of Carpenters*, 459 U.S. 519, 535, 103 S.Ct. 897, 74 L.Ed.2d 723 (1983) ("[T]he question requires us to evaluate the plaintiff's harm, the alleged wrongdoing by the defendants, and the relationship between them."). In other words, antitrust standing captures the requirement that a plaintiff must demonstrate a direct link between the

---

12. Although Plaintiff alleges a violation of Section 1 of the Sherman Act, 15 U.S.C. § 1, its right to injunctive relief arises under Section 16 of the Clayton Act, 15 U.S.C. § 26.

alleged antitrust violation and the antitrust injury, and is thus the proper plaintiff to bring the antitrust action before the court.... [footnote omitted].... Because Plaintiff's complaint must make out an antitrust injury in order to have antitrust standing, the Court will begin with Plaintiff's alleged injury. *See Cargill*, 479 U.S. at 110 n. 5, 107 S.Ct. 484. Plaintiff's complaint alleges the following harm to the Commonwealth: (1) harm to the natural citizens of Pennsylvania who depend on the Penn State football program for their jobs and livelihoods; (2) harm to the state revenue base from diminished Penn State football ticket sales, lessened hospitality revenue on Penn State football weekends, diminished interested in Penn State football apparel and memorabilia sales, expected decline in jobs attributable to a diminished football program, diminished spending by Penn State on capital improvements and supplies, and diminished interest in Penn State-themed events, such as summer football camps; (3) additional harm to the Commonwealth from payment of the $60 million fine, which will necessarily be paid through some combination of tuition hikes and increased appropriations from the Commonwealth's treasury; and (4) harm to Penn State students from the diminished value of the Penn State educational and community experience.... At this juncture, it bears repeating that Plaintiff outlined three relevant markets threatened by Defendant's behavior in its complaint: (1) the nationwide market for post-secondary education; (2) the nationwide market for Division I football players; and (3) the nationwide market for the sale of college football-related apparel and memorabilia....

The Court now turns to whether the harms alleged in Plaintiff's complaint constitute antitrust injury. As explained, an antitrust injury must stem from a "competition-*reducing*" aspect of the defendant's behavior. *See Atl. Richfield Co. v. USA Petroleum Co.*, 495 U.S. 328, 334, 110 S.Ct. 1884, 109 L.Ed.2d 333 (1990). Injuries that are "causally related" to the complained-of behavior, but do not result from any alleged injury to competition in the relevant markets, do not qualify as antitrust injury. *Id.* Thus, Plaintiff would need to allege that the harms threatening the natural citizens of Pennsylvania result from reduced competition in the markets identified in Plaintiff's complaint, not that citizens will suffer if Penn State and its football program alone is weakened as the result of the sanctions. *See W. Penn.*, 627 F.3d at 101.

On review of the complaint, the Court finds that Plaintiff has not cleared this hurdle. At core, Plaintiff's complaint alleges derivative injury to Pennsylvania citizens as the result of Penn State's football program becoming less competitive, not to lessened competition in the relevant markets. *See Bassett v. NCAA*, No. 04-425, 2005 WL 3767016, at *4 (E.D.Ky. May 3, 2005) ("At best, Basset alleged injury to himself as a competitor in the marketplace and not an injury to competition in a relevant market."). Nowhere in Plaintiff's complaint does Plaintiff link any alleged harm to the natural citizens of Pennsylvania to *reduced competition* in the relevant markets for post-secondary education, Division I football players, and college football-related memorabilia identified in Plaintiff's complaint. Without more, Plaintiff's allegations do not make out an antitrust injury. *See Atl. Richfield Co.*, 495 U.S. at 334, 110 S.Ct. 1884 (citations omitted) ("[I]njury, although causally related to an antitrust violation, nevertheless will not qualify as antitrust injury unless it is attributable to an anti-competitive aspect of the practice under scrutiny"). The Court's conclusion that Plaintiff's complaint fails to make out an antitrust injury obviates the need to analyze whether Plaintiff has antitrust standing. *See Cargill*, 479 U.S. at 110 n. 5, 107 S.Ct. 484 ("A showing of antitrust injury is necessary, but not always sufficient, to establish standing")....

The Governor's complaint implicates the extraordinary power of a non-governmental entity to dictate the course of an iconic public institution, and raises serious questions about the indirect economic impact of NCAA sanctions on innocent parties. These are important questions deserving of public debate, but they are not antitrust questions. In another forum the complaint's appeal to equity and common sense may win the day, but in the antitrust world these arguments fail to advance the ball. Plaintiff's complaint fails on all prongs: it fails to allege commercial activity subject to the Sherman Act; it fails to allege that Defendant's activity constituted a violation of Section 1 of the Sherman Act; and, it fails to allege that Plaintiff suffered an antitrust injury. On thorough review, this Court can find no basis in antitrust law for concluding that the harms alleged entitle Plaintiff to relief. Accordingly, the complaint must be dismissed....

AND NOW, on this 6th day of June 2013, IT IS HEREBY ORDERED THAT Defendant's motion to dismiss Plaintiff's complaint ... is GRANTED.

Notes

We began this casebook, in Chapter One, with very personal cases that describe difficult facts involving explicit sexual acts perpetrated against children. As authors, we are loathe to bring this project to its completion with a case that addresses the legal effect of the sexual exploitation of children on the sale of athletic apparel and memorabilia within the college sports industry. But the *NCAA* case included here demonstrates a poignant consideration—one that we hope has permeated the entirety of this casebook—that the scope and breadth of the sexual exploitation of children, and society's response to it, is defined by what the law prescribes as the necessary balance of legal interests between a child (and, perhaps, his or her family), a sexual offender (and, in the institutional context, his or her employer), and the State. Within the context of federal anti-trust law, the *NCAA* decision, on its face, offers scant attention to the consideration of the interests of child victims. However, in implementing the required balance of legal interests, the court nevertheless adopted an expansive view of child protection. For commentary, see Brian L. Porto, *Can the NCAA Enforcement Process Protect Children From Abuse in the Wake of the Sandusky Scandal?*, 22 WIDENER L.J. 555 (2013). This expansive view is also seen in the case of *Commonwealth v. Lynn*, *supra*, and the many legislative developments regarding protection of children that have been discussed throughout this casebook.

Rev. Raymond C. O'Brien

Clergy, Sex and the American Way

31 PEPP. L. REV. 363 (2004)

America is unique among the nations of the world. It is an open society as is evidenced by the media blitz accompanying the revelations of sexual abuse by American priests. News stories concerning sexual abuse, initiated by the *Boston Globe*, ... [footnote omitted] quickly became headlines in most major cities and the preamble of articles in such media stalwarts as *Vanity Fair* ... [footnote omitted] and *The New Yorker*.... [footnote omitted]. Nevertheless, the stories also responded to another facet that makes America unique in spite of what television, movies, and our music may portray: America takes sexual abuse of minors very seriously. Federal and state governments have coordinated efforts to prosecute child neglect, abandonment, and abuse, with increasing attention paid to child sexual abuse. Registration of convicted child sex offenders under Megan's law, so as to alert the public of the presence of offenders, is only one example of those coordinated efforts.... [footnote omitted]. Additionally, there has been increasing vigilance in the prosecution and prevention of abuse in intimate relations between adults under the aegis of domestic violence legislation. Thus, sexual abuse of minors ... in America occurs within the panoply of these aspects of American society, and whatever is decided as the proper remedy for errant [institutional authorities] must take into account the evolving body of secular law directed towards the protection of children and adults in abusive situations. Precisely put, any fair response to the sexual abuse of minors in America ... must take into consideration the fact that America's sophisticated prosecution of sexual abuse is unique among nations and provides a backdrop for the crisis involving sexual abuse by [institutional authorities].

Id. at 367–68.

The clergy sex abuse scandal affecting the Roman Catholic Church [is] a situation that challenges the traditional arrangement of the church-state relationship in America. It occurs in a country that is an open society, catapulted into this reality by a media that ensures that neither the Oval Office nor the Church sacristy is a privileged zone. Because of this openness and the scandal that it chronicled, the Church is exposed to scandal, financial retribution, and a clamor for reform from within and outside of the institution.

Id. at 473–74.

[W]hat will happen with the lay organizations, the vast array of theological issues simmering under the surface, continuing civil and criminal litigation, and the loss of deference among civil leaders ... ? Mark E. Chopko, General Counsel for the United States Conference of Catholic Bishops, writing long before the current sexual abuse of minors scandal occurred, captures a sense of the past and a prediction of the future when he writes:

[L]iability theory is often used as a means through which social change is either encouraged or regulated. To the extent that substantial liabilities can occur to [social and] religious organizations for actions of their members or their ministers, even when they are acting in complete accord with [institutional or] religious doctrine, litigation has a substantial educative effect on the organization. The effect litigation has on the organization is illustrated in both extraordinary and ordinary ways.... [footnote omitted].

Id. at 476 (quoting Mark E. Chopko, *Ascending Liability of Religious Entities for the Actions of Others*, 17 Am. J. Trial Advoc. 289 (1993)).

Index